Thank you for picking up
The 1992 Information Please Sports Alma...

NOW IN ITS THIRD YEAR A...
FAVORITE SPORTS REFERENCE BOOK

"It's fast, it's accurate and it's all there. I find myself going back-back-back-back-back to it all the time."
—Chris Berman, ESPN

"A valuable tool to anyone who needs to know anything about sports. I don't know how I got along without it."
—Jim Lehrer, "The MacNeil/Lehrer Newshour"

"I keep the *IPSA* next to my computer and I'm much more confident using it than I am using my computer."
—Dick Schaap, ABC News

"Tops. Absolutely the best. There's nothing it doesn't have."
—Brent P. Holshouser, Sports Editor, *Petersburg (VA) Progress-Index*

"A commodious compendium."
—Gene Shalit, "The Today Show"

"Fabulous reference book. We would be lost without it!"
—Mike Huss, WGNU, St. Louis

"Remarkable. Will be an invaluable addition to sports libraries for writers and fans."
—Rod Rose, *The Lebanon (IN) Reporter*

"Important sports facts at your fingertips...data is easy to find—the first almanac to put sports in perspective with its Years in Review."
—Mark Drucker, WMMR, Philadelphia

"The finest publication and reference guide for sports aficionados who enjoy stats plus history and can't find the information elsewhere."
—Bob Hohrman, KJJO, Eden Prairie, MN

"A *must* for all sports-minded consumers."
—Samuel P. Levine, *Consumer Dilemma-USA*, Temecula, CA

"An indispensable reference."
—John Heckathorn, *Honolulu (HI) Magazine*

THE 1992
INFORMATION PLEASE®
SPORTS
ALMANAC

Mike Meserole

EDITOR

PRODUCTION SUPERVISOR
Michael Michaud

Research assistance by
Rick Sayers,
Howie Schwab and **Edward R. Pete**

Typesetting by
Publication Services, Inc. of Boston, Mass.

HOUGHTON MIFFLIN COMPANY   BOSTON

The Information Please Sports Almanac

ISSN: 1045-4980

Comments and Suggestions

Comments and suggestions from readers are invited. Because of the many letters received, however, it is not possible to respond personally to every correspondent. Nevertheless, all letters are welcome and each will be carefully considered. **The Information Please Sports Almanac** does not rule on bets or wagers. Address all correspondence to Houghton Mifflin Company, 2 Park Street, Boston, Massachusetts 02108.

Additional copies of **The 1992 Information Please Sports Almanac** may be ordered directly by mail from:
Customer Service Department
Houghton Mifflin Company
Burlington, MA 01803
Phone toll-free (800) 225-3362 for price and shipping information. In Massachusetts, phone (617) 272-1500.

CONTENTS   5

Byron (Whizzer) White, the former All-America halfback at Colorado who won a Rhodes scholarship, two NFL rushing titles, a law degree, and appointment to the U.S. Supreme Court by President Kennedy in 1962, is the judge I think of when it comes to sports. He may sit on the bench now, but back in his senior year of 1937-38, White was all action— playing football in the Orange Bowl and basketball in the NIT final at Madison Square Garden.

Anyway, when news of the year's supreme sports moment arrived on Aug.30, it wasn't White's name that came to mind but that of his former high bench colleague, Lewis Powell. That day, at the World Track & Field Championships in Tokyo, Carl Lewis had gotten off three leaps of 29 feet or more in the long jump, but lost the event for the first time in 10 years when Mike Powell soared two inches past Bob Beamon's "unbreakable" 1968 world record of 29-2½.

Lewis and Powell headline the International Sports chapter of *The 1992 Information Please Sports Almanac* and are included in the new "Big Dozen," a special section on the most notable sports figures of 1990-91, which begins on page 17. The Big Dozen (hey, even the Big Ten can't hold the line at 10 anymore) is one of several new wrinkles in this third edition. Others include the addition of baseball correspondent Peter Gammons, a wartime sports essay by John Underwood, a special 80-page chapter covering all the Summer and Winter Olympic Games held since 1896, and a humorous look at the not-so-dandy achievements of the year in a section called "After Further Review . . ."

Nearly every chapter of the 1992 almanac has been expanded to provide more of the detailed information readers have come to expect from us. In fact, we've added 96 pages for the second year in a row while keeping the price of the book the same. No small amount of credit for both these accomplishments goes to my production coordinator and right hand Michael Michaud and my publisher Steve Lewers of Houghton Mifflin.

My thanks also goes to Charley Monagan, Dawn Longo, Lynn Michaud, the 27 writers whose essays give this book character, everyone at Publication Services, Inc. in Boston, Jill Lazer, Mab Gray, Chris Leonesio, Jim Murphy and the crew at Western Publishing, Nat Andriani, John Kelly, George Dostaler, Mary Vaughn, Bob Magaradi, Harvey Abrams, Harry Carson Frye, Bob Kirlin, Chris Berman, Bob Ley, Tom Hart, Gary Johnson and everybody at the NCAA, and all the communications department and public relations folks at the other end of the phone or fax machine who were nice enough to take the time and provide the needed information when asked.

Finally, another name from the year in sports: Frank Brothers, the trainer of Preakness and Belmont winner Hansel. Seeing him in the winner's circle last spring reminded me of two fellows named George and Raymond Frank, who ran a boys' summer camp in Weld, Maine, where I went as a kid. The Frank Brothers were to camping what Lewis and Powell are to long jumping. This year's almanac is dedicated to their memory.

—Mike Meserole

Wolcott, Conn.
October, 1991

Major League Cities & Teams

At the end of 1991, there were 118 major league sports teams playing or scheduled to play baseball, basketball, football, hockey and indoor soccer in 64 cities in the United States and Canada. Listed below are the cities and the teams that play there. If a team actually plays in a nearby suburb, that town is in parentheses.

Anaheim
AL   California Angels
NFL   Los Angeles Rams

Arlington
AL   Texas Rangers

Atlanta
NL   Braves
NBA   Hawks
NFL   Falcons

Baltimore
AL   Orioles
MSL   Blast

Boston
AL   Red Sox
NBA   Celtics
NFL   N.E.Patriots (Foxboro)
NHL   Bruins

Buffalo
NFL   Bills (Orchard Park)
NHL   Sabres

Calgary
CFL   Stampeders
NHL   Flames

Charlotte
NBA   Hornets

Chicago
AL   White Sox
NL   Cubs
NBA   Bulls
NFL   Bears
NHL   Blackhawks

Cincinnati
NL   Reds
NFL   Bengals

Cleveland
AL   Indians
MSL   Crunch
NBA   Cavaliers (Richfield)
NFL   Browns

Dallas
MSL   Sidekicks
NBA   Mavericks
NHL   Cowboys (Irving)

Denver
NL   Colorado Rockies (1993)
NBA   Nuggets
NFL   Broncos

Detroit
AL   Tigers
NBA   Pistons (Auburn Hills)
NFL   Lions (Pontiac)
NHL   Red Wings

East Rutherford
NBA   New Jersey Nets
NFL   New York Giants
NFL   New York Jets
NHL   New Jersey Devils

Edmonton
CFL   Eskimos
NHL   Oilers

Green Bay
NFL   Packers

Hamilton
CFL   Tiger-Cats

Hartford
NHL   Whalers

Houston
NL   Astros
NBA   Rockets
NFL   Oilers

Indianapolis
NBA   Pacers
NFL   Colts

Kansas City
AL   Royals
NFL   Chiefs

Los Angeles
NL   Dodgers
NBA   Clippers
NBA   Lakers (Inglewood)
NFL   Raiders
NHL   Kings (Inglewood)

Miami
NL   Florida Marlins (1993)
NBA   Heat
NFL   Dolphins

Milwaukee
AL   Brewers
NBA   Bucks

Minneapolis
AL   Minn. Twins
NBA   Minn. Timberwolves
NFL   Minn. Vikings
NHL   Minn. North Stars
        (Bloomington)

Montreal
NL   Expos
NHL   Canadiens

New Orleans
NFL   Saints

New York
AL   Yankees
NL   Mets
NBA   Knicks
NHL   Rangers

Oakland
AL   Athletics
NBA   Golden St. Warriors

Orlando
NBA   Magic

Ottawa
CFL   Rough Riders
NHL   Senators (1992-93)

Philadelphia
NL   Phillies
NBA   76ers
NFL   Eagles
NHL   Flyers

Phoenix
NBA   Suns
NFL   Cardinals (Tempe)

Pittsburgh
NL   Pirates
NFL   Steelers
NHL   Penguins

Portland
NBA   Trail Blazers

Quebec City
NHL   Nordiques

Regina
CFL   Saskatchewan Roughriders

Sacramento
NBA   Kings

St.Louis
MSL   Storm
NL   Cardinals
NHL   Blues

Salt Lake City
NBA   Jazz

San Antonio
NBA   Spurs

San Diego
MSL   Sockers
NL   Padres
NFL   Chargers

San Francisco
NL   Giants
NFL   49ers

San Jose
NHL   Sharks

Seattle
AL   Mariners
NBA   SuperSonics
NFL   Seahawks

Tacoma
MSL   Stars

Tampa
NFL   Buccaneers
NHL   Lightning (1992-93)

Toronto
AL   Blue Jays
CFL   Argonauts
NHL   Maple Leafs

Uniondale
NHL   New York Islanders

Vancouver
CFL   B.C. Lions
NHL   Canucks

Washington
NBA   Bullets (Landover)
NFL   Redskins
NHL   Capitals (Landover)

Wichita
MSL   Wings

Winnipeg
NHL   Jets
CFL   Blue Bombers

UPDATES

Wide World Photos

An upbeat **Magic Johnson** delivers his shocking news.

AIDS Virus Ends Magic Show

Magic Johnson, the all-time NBA assist leader who led the Los Angeles Lakers to five world championships and the league to unprecedented financial success and international popularity, announced on Nov. 7 that he had been infected by the virus that causes AIDS and would retire immediately.

Johnson, 32, dropped his bombshell at a crowded press conference at the Forum Club in Inglewood Calif., saying, "Because of the HIV virus I have attained, I will have to announce my retirement from the Lakers today." He added that he learned only the day before of his infection and spoke of his plans to educate the public about AIDS and the virus that causes it.

The 12-year NBA veteran, a three-time MVP in both the regular season and the playoffs, is by far the most famous athlete to be infected by the AIDS virus.

PRO FOOTBALL

The **Washington Redskins** emerged from the first nine weeks of the NFL season with the league's only unblemished record at 8-0. The Skins came from behind to beat the Super Bowl champion New York Giants, 17-13, after trailing 13-0 at halftime (Oct.27). **Buffalo, Houston** and **New Orleans** were all at 7-1, but the Giants and San Francisco were only 4-4. Indianapolis started off at 0-5, which made **Ron Meyer** the season's first head coaching casualty (Oct.1). He was replaced by assistant **Rick Venturi.**

Miami head coach **Don Shula** won the 300th game of his career (Sept.22) when the Dolphins rallied for 10 points in the fourth quarter to beat Green Bay, 16-13. Chicago Bears' legend George Hallas (325) is the only other member of the NFL's 300-win club.

Wide World Photos

Don Shula
300th career victory in NFL.

Two of the league's premier quarterbacks, **Joe Montana** of the 49ers and **Randall Cunningham** of Philadelphia, were lost for the season. Cunningham suffered ligament damage to his left knee in the Eagles' opening game against Green Bay (Sept.1), while Montana underwent surgery to repair a torn tendon in his right elbow (Oct.9).

COLLEGE FOOTBALL

Preseason favorite **Florida State** was unbeaten in eight games going into November, although the Seminoles had to come from behind to beat LSU, 27-14 (Oct.26) to stay that way. FSU walloped **Michigan,** 51-31 (Sept.28) in Ann Arbor and was scheduled to meet second-ranked **Miami-FL** in Tallahassee (Nov.16) and then No.6 **Florida** in Gainesville (Nov.30).

Michigan and **Notre Dame** were ranked Nos. 4 and 5 after October. The Wolverines beat the Irish for the first time in five years (Sept.14) with a 24-14 victory at home.

Elsewhere, 1990 Heisman Trophy winner **Ty Detmer** of BYU became the NCAA's all-time career passing leader (11,606 yards) early in the season. And San Diego State freshman running back **Marshall Faulk** set an NCAA single-game rushing record, carrying the ball 37 times for 386 yards, as the Aztecs beat Pacific, 55-34.

AP Top 25

(as of Monday, Oct.28, 1991)

Writers' poll, including games through Oct.26, 1991. First place votes in parentheses, followed by record, total votes and ranking in preseason poll.

		Record	Pts	Preseason			Record	Pts	Preseason
1	Florida St.(53)	8-0-0	1492	1	14	Tennessee	4-2-0	693	11
2	Miami-FL (3)	7-0-0	1415	3	15	Colorado	5-2-0	657	13
3	Washington (4)	7-0-0	1412	4	16	Clemson	4-1-1	570	9
4	Michigan	6-1-0	1312	2	17	East Carolina	6-1-0	535	—
5	Notre Dame	7-1-0	1247	6	18	Syracuse	6-2-0	486	25
6	Florida	6-1-0	1210	5	19	N.C.State	6-1-0	401	31
7	Alabama	6-1-0	1058	22	20	Oklahoma	5-2-0	378	10
8	Penn St	7-2-0	1046	7	21	Baylor	6-2-0	287	27
9	Nebraska	6-1-0	1002	15	22	Georgia	6-2-0	251	38
10	California	6-1-0	991	32	23	UCLA	5-2-0	156	24
11	Iowa	6-1-0	910	18	24	Arkansas	5-2-0	140	—
12	Texas A&M	5-1-0	822	21	25	Fresno St	7-0-0	97	—
13	Ohio St	6-1-0	743	23					

AUTO RACING

Michael Andretti won his first Indy-car driving championship in the final CART race of the year (Oct.20), winning the Toyota Monterey (Calif.) Grand Prix at Laguna Seca. The victory was the eighth of the season for Michael, who also won his eighth pole. Father **Mario** placed third in the race, behind defending CART champion **Al Unser Jr.**

The younger Andretti finished the season with a PPG Cup record 234 points, 34 more than runner-up **Bobby Rahal.** Little Al was third with 197 points. Mario Andretti and nephew John placed seventh and eighth in the final standings with 132 and 105 points, while Mario's other son, **Jeff,** was 15th and earned Rookie of the Year honors.

The NASCAR Winston Cup title was unclaimed at the end of October, but defending champion **Dale Earnhardt** had a 157-point advantage over second place **Ricky Rudd** with two races to go. Earnhardt snapped 51-year-old **Harry Gant's** four-race winning streak (Sept.29), winning the Holly Farms 400 while Gant took second.

In Formula One, **Ayrton Senna** of Brazil captured his third world championship in four years (Oct.20), with a second place in the Japanese Grand Prix. Senna clinched the title when his only challenger, England's **Nigel Mansell,** went out on the 10th lap of the 53-lap race.

Although the final decision will not be made until December, on Oct. 9 FISA removed the **United States Grand Prix** from its 1992 schedule. The Phoenix race had not proven to be as popular as expected.

PRO BASKETBALL

Ten NBA players were named (Sept. 21) to the U.S. Olympic basketball team that will compete in Barcelona in 1992. Instantly billed the greatest team ever assembled, coach Chuck Daly's squad will include (in alphabetical order) **Charles Barkley, Larry Bird, Patrick Ewing, Magic Johnson, Michael Jordan, Karl Malone, Chris Mullin, Scottie Pippen, David Robinson, and John Stockton.** Not among the chosen was **Isiah Thomas,** which led Detroit GM **Jack McCloskey** to quit as member of the selection committee. The two remaining spots on the roster will be filled by college players.

Johnson stunned the basketball world by retiring from the NBA (Nov. 7) due to the AIDS virus, but indicated later that he still wanted to participate in the Olympics if he was healthy enough. Team officials agreed to hold his roster spot open.

Meanwhile, the top three picks in the 1991 NBA Draft finally signed contracts within a week of opening night for the 1991-92 regular season (Nov. 1): overall No. 1 **Larry Johnson** with Charlotte (6 years, $19 million); overall No. 2 **Kenny Anderson** with New Jersey (5 years, $14.5 million), and No. 3 **Billy Owens** with Golden State (7 years, $19.6 million) after the Warriors acquired him from Sacramento for Mitch Richmond.

BOXING

What surely would have been the highest-grossing prize fight of all time—with anticipated revenues of $100 million or more—was put on hold (Oct.18) when challenger **Mike Tyson** was forced to pull out of his scheduled Nov. 8 heavyweight title bout with champion **Evander Holyfield** because of an injured rib cage.

Efforts to reschedule the fight for January failed, in part because Caesar's Palace in Las Vegas was unable to come up with a suitable date and because of Holyfield's reluctance to fight outdoors in cold weather, which he perceived as an advantage for Tyson. In light of Tyson's Jan.27, 1992, rape trial in Indianapolis, it is conceivable he will never fight Holyfield—or anyone else—for that matter.

On Oct. 24, Holyfield signed to fight Italy's **Francesco Damiani** at the Omni in Atlanta on Nov. 23.

BUSINESS & MEDIA

After fighting off two straight years of negative publicity over its costly four-year, $1 billion deal with **Major League Baseball, CBS** finally got something for its money during the World Series—big ratings.

Game Seven—the 10-inning, 1-0 thriller between small market foes Minnesota and Atlanta—pulled in an overnight Neilsen rating of 31.5 (Oct.27) from the top 25 markets in the country, making it the second highest-rated TV show of the year (after the Super Bowl). It was also the highest-rated World Series game since the seventh game of the 1987 Series between Minnesota and St.Louis.

Also, the **NHL** and **Sports Channel America** agreed to a one-year extension of their cable-TV contract (Oct. 3). The old, three-year deal which paid the league $17 million a season, expired after the 1990-91 season. The new deal, however, will only fetch the NHL a total of $5.5 million for 1991-92.

DEATHS

Bill Bevens, 75, pitcher with the New York Yankees, who was 40-36 from 1944-47; best known for hurling eight and two-thirds innings of no-hit ball against Brooklyn in Game 4 of the 1947 World Series before Cookie Lavagetto doubled home two runs to win the game for the Dodgers; of cancer; in Salem, Ore., Oct.26.

GOLF

Eighteen-year LPGA veteran **Pat Bradley** won back-to-back tournaments in late September to clinch the 1991 Player of the Year award and, more importantly, gain admittance to the LPGA Hall of Fame. Victories at the Safeco and MBS Classics gave Bradley 30 career tournament wins and automatic entry into the hall. She is the first player to meet the entry requirements since Nancy Lopez in 1987. A player must have 30 official titles including two different major championships to gain entry, or 35 official titles and one major, or 40 official titles and no majors.

On the men's tour, Ryder Cup team member **Chip Beck** joined Al Geiberger as the only golfers to break 60 in a PGA event. Beck entered the record book in the third round of the Las Vegas Invitational (Oct.11), firing 13 birdies and five pars for a 59 at Sunrise Golf Club. Beck didn't win the 90-hole tournament, however, placing third behind **Andrew Magee** and **D.A.Weibring,** who tied at a PGA-record 31-under par. Magee won the title on the second playoff hole.

HOCKEY

The NHL got its 75th regular season underway (Oct.3) after a very busy off-season that included Team Canada's victory over the United States in the **Canada Cup** (see page 306) in September.

Otherwise, several big name players changed uniforms, capped by Edmonton captain **Mark Messier's** trade to the New York Rangers (Oct.4) for center **Bernie Nicholls** and other players; and the New York Islanders' dealing of All-Star center **Pat LaFontaine** to Buffalo in a seven player deal (Oct.26).

Other trades sent former All-Stars **Grant Fuhr** and **Glenn Anderson** from Edmonton to Toronto for **Vincent Damphousse** and two others, and **Stephane Richter** from Montreal to New Jersey for **Kirk Muller.** In the summer's blockbuster compensation ruling, arbitrator Ed Houston directed St.Louis to send defenseman and captain **Scott Stevens** to New Jersey in return for having signed Devils' forward **Brendan Shanahan**. The Blues had given up five first round picks for signing Stevens as a "free" agent in 1990.

Meanwhile, No.1 draft pick **Eric Lindros** returned to Oshawa of the Ontario League rather than skate with the Quebec Nordiques, who lost 9 of their first 12 games of the season. And Pittsburgh named **Scotty Bowman** as interim coach while **Bob Johnson** recovered from brain cancer surgery (Aug.29). Bowman is the all-time winningest NHL coach with 853 career wins, and won five Stanley Cups with Montreal in the 1970s.

New Steroids Focus Is On Life And Death

by Jeffrey Marx

For several years the sports world had accepted the notion that any discussion of steroids and other performance-enhancing drugs would begin with Canadian sprinter Ben Johnson. The 1988 Seoul Olympics—during which Johnson won the 100-meter gold, then tested positive and was stripped of his medal—would serve as a new dimension of time. We would talk about years in sports B.B. (Before Ben) and A.B. (After Ben). When it came to steroid use, the most important statistics, even more crucial than wins and losses,would be getting away with it or getting caught.

In 1991, however, that changed dramatically. The new focus was life and death.

First, on July 8, former NFL star Lyle Alzado was staring at us from the cover of *Sports Illustrated*, sharing his story of drugs and deceit. He was very sick, struggling with inoperable brain cancer, and he blamed the whole mess on massive use of steroids and human growth hormone.

"It wasn't worth it," Alzado told the magazine. "Sure, I played 15 years as a defensive end with the Denver Broncos, Cleveland Browns, and Los Angeles Raiders and twice made All-Pro. But look at me now. I wobble when I walk and sometimes have to hold on to somebody. You have to give me time to answer questions, because I have trouble remembering things. I'm down to 215 pounds, 60 pounds less than I weighed just a few months ago. . ."

"I know there's no written, documented proof that steroids and human growth hormone caused this cancer. But it's one of the reasons you have to look at. You have to. And I think that there are a lot of athletes in danger. So many of them have taken this same human growth hormone, and so many of them are on steroids. Almost everyone I know. They are so intent on being successful that they're not concerned with anything else."

At the same time *Sports Illustrated* was

Wide World Photos

Former All-Pro **Lyle Alzado** says his
steroid use wasn't worth it.

preparing its Alzado story, testimony in a Pennsylvania courtroom was documenting pro wrestling as the steroid infested "sport" it had long been rumored to be. Again, the toughest statements to take centered on health issues. Former champion "Superstar" Billy Graham, 48, testified that steroids had damaged his liver, hips and ankles, leaving him crippled. Dr. George Zahorian III, an osteopath and urological surgeon charged with distributing steroids, admitted that between November, 1989, and March, 1990, he sold the drugs to World Wrestling Federation owner Vince McMahon and to many wrestlers, including one of the most famous, Hulk Hogan.

Then came the disturbing news out of the Pittsburgh Steelers training camp that an offensive lineman, Terry Long, had attempted suicide after finding out he had tested positive for steroids. Long was hospitalized in a psychiatric ward, his mental and physical health in jeopardy. Upon his release, all the talk was optimistic. But again, for the third time in weeks, the new focus for steroid-users—life and death—had been reinforced, and in full view of the public.

By this time, Ben Johnson was back on the track in Europe, having completed a two-year ban. But he was running poorly, only in the 10.4 second range for the 100. Other than his temporary attraction as a sideshow, few people on the track circuit seemed to care that he was back in action.

Jeffrey Marx, a free lance journalist based in Washington, D.C., shared the 1986 Pulitzer Prize for investigative reporting.

TENNIS

U.S. Open champion **Stefan Edberg** won the Australian Indoor in Sydney and Seiko Super Tennis in Tokyo in the fall, but lost to **Boris Becker** in five sets in the final of the Stockholm Open (Oct.27).

Heading into November, Edberg and Becker had clinched two of the eight berths in the second ATP Tour World Championship scheduled for Nov. 12-17 in Frankfurt. **Jim Courier, Ivan Lendl, Michael Stich, Guy Forget** and **Pete Sampras** were also in, while **Sergei Bruguera** and **Karel Novacek** were challenging 1990 champion **Andre Agassi** for the eighth and final spot.

On the WTA tour, **Steffi Graf** won autumn titles in Leipzig, Zurich and Brighton, while **Monica Seles** won the Ladies Indoor in Milan. Seles was also fined $20,000 by the WTA (Oct.23) for playing an exhibition in the Canary Islands rather than the Brighton, England tour stop. Ten other players were also fined, including **Arantxa Sanchez Vicario** and **Helena Sukova**, who were hit for $10,000 each. The season ending Virginia Slims Championships, featuring the 16 highest-rated players, was scheduled for Nov.18-24 at Madison Square Garden.

Late Season Results

AUTO RACING

NASCAR

Date	Event	Winner (Pos.)	Avg.mph	Earnings	Pole	Qual.mph
Sept.29	Tyson Holly Farms 400	Dale Earnhardt (16)	94.113	$69,350	H.Gant	116.871
Oct. 6	Mello Yello 500	Geoff Bodine (6)	138.984	92,200	M.Martin	176.499*
Oct. 20	AC Delco 500	Davey Allison (10)	127.292	66,050	K.Petty	149.461*

*Track record.
Winning Cars: Ford Thunderbird 2 (Allison, Bodine); Chevrolet Lumina (Earnhardt).
Remaining races (2): Pyroil 500 (formerly Checker 500, Nov.3) and Hardee's 500 (formerly Atlanta Journal 500, Nov.17).

CART

Date	Event	Winner (Pos.)	Avg.mph	Earnings	Pole	Qual.mph
Oct. 6	Bosch Spark Plug GP	Arie Luyendyk (11)	131.310	$63,452	R.Mears	178.740
Oct. 20	Toyota Monterey GP	Michael Andretti (1)	103.604*	83,700	Mi.Andretti	110.555*

*Track record
Winning car: Lola-Chevrolet 2 (Mi.Andretti, Luyendyk).
Remaining races: none (season over).

Formula One

Date	Grand Prix	Winner (Pos)	Time	Avg.mph	Pole	Qual.mph
Sept.29	Spain............................	Nigel Mansell (2)	1:38:41.541	116.561	G.Berger	134.839
Oct. 20	Japan	Gerhard Berger (1)	1:32:10.695	125.702	G.Berger	138.515

Winning Constructors: McLaren-Honda (Berger); Williams-Renault (Mansell).
Remaining races (1): Australia (Nov.3).

BOWLING

PBA

Final	Event	Winner	Earnings	Final	Runner-up
Oct. 5	Toyota Classic............................	Danny Wiseman	$27,000	204-200	John Mazza
Oct.16	Japan Cup '91 (Tokyo)	Walter R.Williams Jr.	18,500	211-189	John Mazza

Remaining events (4)—Brunswick World Open (Nov.10-16); Chevy Truck Classic (Nov.18-23); Touring Players Championship (Nov.25-30); Cambridge Mixed Doubles (Dec.5-8).

Seniors

Final	Event	Winner	Earnings	Final	Runner-up
Oct. 3	Woodside Open..........................	Robert Gibbs	$5,000	203-196	John Hricsina
Oct.10	Villages Open............................	John Handegard	5,000	259-254	Teata Semiz

Remaining events—none (season over).

LPBT

Final	Event	Winner	Earnings	Final	Runner-up
Oct. 9	Hammer Eastern Open	Tish Johnson	$9,000	187-174	D.Miller-Mackie
Oct.16	Columbia 300 Delaware Open	Donna Adamek	12,600	195-189	Carol Norman
Oct.23	Brunswick Open	Leanne Barrette	9,000	234-171	Donna Adamek
Oct.30	Hammer Midwest Open	Carol Norman	9,000	195-193	Anne M. Duggan

Remaining events (4): Denver Open (Nov.2-6); Ebonite Fall Classic (Nov.9-13); **Sam's Town Invitational** (Nov.16-23); Cambridge Mixed Doubles (Dec.5-8).

BOXING

Light Heavyweights
Charles Williams gained a 2nd round TKO over Fred Delgado to retain IBF title (Williamson, W.Va., Oct.19).

Middleweights
James Toney knocked out Francisco Dell-Aquila on 4th round to retain IBF title (Monte Carlo, Oct.12).

Junior Featherweights
(Super Bantamweights)
  Raul Perez scored a 12-round split decision ober champion Luis Mendoza to win WBA title (Inglewood Oct. 7).

Bantamweight
Israel Contreras scored a unanimous 12-round decision over champion Luisito Espinosa to win WBA title (Manilla, Oct. 19).

Strawweights
(Minimum)
  Phalan Lukmingkwan scored a unanimous 12-round decision over Andy Tabanas to retain IBF title (Bangkok, Oct.21).

GOLF

PGA Tour

Last Rd	Tournament	Winner	Earnings	Runner-Up
Sep.29	Buick Southern Open	David Peoples (276)	126,000	R.Gamez (275)
Oct. 6	H.E.B. Texas Open	Blaine McCallister (269)*	180,000	G.Hallberg (269)
Oct.13	Las Vegas Invitational	Andrew Magee (329)*	252,000	D.A.Weibring (329)
Oct.19	Disney World/Olds Classic	Mark O'Meara (267)	180,000	D.Peoples (268)
Oct.26	Indep.Insurance Agent Open	Fulton Allem (273)	144,000	3-way tie (274)

*Playoffs (2): **Texas**—McCallister won in 2 holes; **Las Vegas**—Magee won in 2 holes.
Second place ties (3 players or more): 3-WAY—**Insurance** (B.R.Brown, M.Hulbert, T.Kite).
Remaining events (7): PGA Tour Championship (Oct.31-Nov.3); Asahi Four Tours WCOG (Nov.7-10); Kapalua International (Nov.14-17); RMCC Invitational (Nov.21-24); Skins Game (Nov.30-Dec.1); JCPenny Classic (Dec.5-8) and Sazale Classic (Dec.12- 15).

Seniors Tour

Last Rd	Tournament	Winner	Earnings	Runner-Up
Sep.29	Bank One Classic	DeWitt Weaver (207)*	45,000	J.C.Snead (207)
Oct. 6	Vantage Championship	Jim Colbert (205)	202,500	3-way tie (206)
Oct.13	Raley's Gold Rush	George Archer (206)	60,000	S.Hobday (207)
Oct.20	TransAmerica Championship	Charles Coody (204)	75,000	L.Trevino (206)
Oct.27	Security Pacific Classic	John Brodie (200)*	75,000	C.C.Rodriguez & G.Archer (200)

*Playoffs (2): **Bank One**—Weaver won in 2 holes; **Security**—Brodie won on 1st hole.
Second place ties (3 players or more): 3-WAY—**Vantage** (G.Archer, J.Dent, G.Gilbert).
Remaining events (3): DuPont Cup (Nov.15-17); Kaanapali Classic (Dec.6-8) and New York Life Champions (Dec.13-15).

LPGA Tour

Last Rd	Tournament	Winner	Earnings	Runner-Up
Sep.29	MBS Classic	Pat Bradley (277)	$ 52,550	M.Estill (278)
Oct. 6	Daikyo World Championship	Meg Mallon (216)	100,000	D.Mochrie (221)

Remaining events (4): Nichirei International (Nov.1-3); Mazda Japan Classic (Nov.8-10); JCPenny Classic (Dec.5-8) and Itoman Match Play Championship (Dec.12-15).

HOCKEY

1991 Canada Cup

Round Robin Standings

	W	L	T	Pts	GF	GA
Canada	3	0	2	8	21	11
United States	4	1	0	8	19	15
Finland	2	2	1	5	10	13
Sweden	2	3	0	4	13	17
Soviet Union	1	3	1	3	14	14
Czechoslovakia	1	4	0	2	11	18

Semifinals

Date	City	Score
9/11	Hamilton	United States 7, Finland 3
9/12	Toronto	Canada 4, Sweden 0

Finals (Best of 3)

Date	City	Score
9/14	Montreal	Canada 4, United States 1
9/16	Hamilton	Canada 4, United States 2

Leading Scorers
1. Wayne Gretzky, Canada (4-8—12); **2.** Steve Larmer, Canada (6-5—11); **3.** Brett Hull, USA (2-7—9); **4.** Mike Modano, USA (2-7—9); **5.** Mark Messier, Canada (2-6—8).

All-Star Team
Goal—Bill Ranford, Canada; **Defense**—Al MacInnis, Canada and Chris Chelios, USA; **Forwards**—Wayne Gretzky, Canada, Jeremy Roenick, USA and Mats Sundin, Sweden.

Most Valuable Player
Bill Ranford, Canada

THOROUGHBRED RACING

Late 1991 Major Stakes Races

Date	Race	Location	Miles	Winner	Jockey	Purse
Sept.22	Man o'War Stakes	Belmont	1⅜	Solar Splendor	Herb McCauley	$ 240,000
Sept.23	Super Derby XII	La.Downs	1¼	Free Spirit's Joy	Calvin Borel	600,000
Oct. 5	Jockey Club Gold Cup	Belmont	1¼	Festin	Eddie Delahoussaye	510,000
Oct. 6	Arc de Triomphe	Longchamp	1½	Suave Dancer	Cash Asmussen	1,677,900
Oct. 6	Oak Tree Invitational	Santa Anita	1½	Filago	Pat Valenzuela	300,000
Oct. 6	Turf Classic	Belmont	1½	Solar Splendor	Herb McCauley	300,000
Oct. 12	Champagne Stakes	Belmont	1	Tri to Watch	Angel Cordero,Jr.	300,000
Oct. 13	Fla.Stallion S.(Girl Div.)	Calder	1¹⁄₁₆	Miss Jealski	Jose Velez,Jr.	240,000
Oct. 18	Meadowlands Cup	Meadowlands	1⅛	Twilight Agenda	Chris McCarron	300,000
Oct. 19	Budweiser International	Laurel	1¼	Leariva	Edgar Prado	450,000
Oct. 20	Fla.Stallion S.(Real.Div.)	Calder	1¹⁄₁₆	Naked Greed	Jose Velez,Jr.	296,000
Oct. 20	Rothmans International	Woodbine	1½	Sky Classic	Pat Day	624,750
Oct. 26	NYRA Mile Handicap	Aqueduct	1	Rubiano	Jose Santos	300,000

HARNESS RACING

Late 1991 Major Stakes Races

Date	Race	Raceway	Winner	Driver	Value to Winner
Sept. 7	Messenger Stakes	Rosecroft	Die Laughing	Richard Silverman	$237,500
Sept.19	Little Brown Jug	Delaware,OH	Precious Bunny	Jack Moiseyev	228,334
Oct. 4	Kentucky Futurity	The Red Mile	Whiteland Janice	Michel Lachance	67,514

TENNIS

Men's Tour

Finals	Tournament	Winner	Earnings	Loser	Score
Sep.29	Swiss Indoors (Basel)	Jakob Hlasek	$97,200	J.McEnroe	76 60 63
Sep.29	Championship of Sicily	Frederick Fontang	38,800	E.Sanchez	16 63 63
Sep.29	Queensland Open (Brisbane)	Gianluca Pozzi	32,400	A.Krickstein	63 76
Oct. 6	Australian Indoor (Sydney)	Stefan Edberg	122,700	B.Gilbert	62 62 62
Oct. 6	Toulouse Grand Prix	Guy Forget	37,440	A.Mansdorf	62 76
Oct. 6	Athens International	Sergei Bruguera	18,000	J.Arrese	75 63
Oct.12	Riklis Classic (Tel Aviv)	Leonardo LaValle	18,000	C.Van Rensburg	62 36 63
Oct.13	Seiko Super Tennis (Toyko)	Stefan Edberg	122,700	D.Rostagno	63 16 62
Oct.13	Holsen International (Berlin)	Petr Korda	37,440	A.Boetsch	63 64
Oct.20	CA Tennis Trophy (Vienna)	Michael Stich	32,400	J.Siemerink	64 64 64
Oct.20	Lyon Grand Prix	Pete Sampras	65,040	O.Delaitre	61 61
Oct.27	Stockholm Open	Boris Becker	137,450	S.Edberg	36 64 16 62 62

Remaining events (9): Stockholm Open and Philips Open (Oct.21-27); Paris Open and Kolynos Cup (Oct.28-Nov.3); Diet Pepsi Indoor, Bayer Kremlin Cup and Citibank Open (Nov.4-10); ATP Tour World Championship (Nov.11-17); ATP Doubles World Championship (Nov.18-24).

Women's Tour

Finals	Tournament	Winner	Earnings	Loser	Score
Sept.29	Bayonne Open (France)	Manuela Fragniere	$27,000	L.Meskhi	46 63 64
Sept.29	St.Petersburg Cup (USSR)	Larisa Savchenko	18,000	B.Rittner	36 63 64
Oct. 6	Milan Ladies Indoor	Monica Seles	45,000	M.Navratilova	63 36 64
Oct. 6	Volkswagen Grand Prix (Leipzig)	Steffi Graf	45,000	J.Novotna	63 63
Oct. 13	European Indoors (Zurich)	Steffi Graf	70,000	N.Tauziat	64 64
Oct. 20	Porsche Grand Prix (Filderstadt)	Anke Huber	70,000	M.Navratilova	26 62 76
Oct. 27	Midland Bank Champs.(Brighton)	Steffi Graf	70,000	Z.Garrison	57 64 61
Oct. 27	Puerto Rico Open (Dorado)	Julie Halard	27,000	A.Coetzer	75 75

Remaining events (6): Arizona Classic (Oct.28-Nov.3); Va.Slims/California and Va.Slims/Nashville (Nov.4-10); Jell-O Classic and Va.Slims/Philadelphia (Nov.11-17); Va.Slims Championships/New York (Nov.18-24).

Jim Gund/Allsport

Of all the personalities that paraded across the sports pages and TV screens of 1990-91, nobody seemed to have more fun than the baseball fans of Atlanta and Minnesota, who reveled in their heroes' mutual rise from last place to the World Series. Their contribution to the success of the Series and the year cannot be ignored.

THE BIG DOZEN

The Top Personalities

The 12 months covered in the third edition of *The Sports Almanac*—November, 1990, through October, 1991—have yielded a bumper crop of first-rate performances, performers and personalities. So many, in fact, that selecting a conventional Top 10 list of sports figures proved to be impossible. So the editors made the cut at 12.

And not just 12 individuals. In an effort to consider all the highlights of the year, the Big Dozen includes one family of race car drivers and two stadiums full of Tomahawk Choppers and Homer Hanky wavers.

The 1990-91 list is in alphabetical order and further details on each entry can be found in the appropriate chapters elsewhere in the book.

The 1990-91 Big Dozen

The Andrettis	Carl Lewis
Sergei Bubka	Mike Powell
Jimmy Connors	Cal Ripken Jr.
John Daly	Monica Seles
Braves/Twins Fans	Jerry Tarkanian
Michael Jordan	Mike Tyson

Allsport

Sergei Bubka

The greatest pole vaulter in track and field history added to his legendary status by setting eight world records and becoming the first man ever to clear 20 feet. He broke through the 20-foot barrier three times indoors and once outside, reaching a PR of 20-1 at an indoor meet in Grenoble in March.

The 28-year-old Ukrainian topped off a remarkable season by claiming his third world championship in Tokyo, winning on his final jump of 19-6¼.

Dan R. Boyd/CART

The Andrettis

Solidified their standing as auto racing's first family with a CART Driving Championship, a Rookie of the Year award and three places among the Top 8 PPG Cup point leaders.

No. 1 son Michael (right), 28, led the way by winning his first CART title with eight victories and a record 134 points. Father Mario, 51, made the first row at Indy and finished 7th in points (one place ahead of nephew John, 28), and No. 2 son Jeff was the top rookie.

Bob Martin/Allsport

Jimmy Connors

The comeback story of the year. Laid low by foot surgery in late 1989 and another injury to his left wrist in 1990, Jimbo had fallen all the way to No. 936 on the ATP computer before staging his '91 return.

He didn't win any tournaments, but he captured a few hearts at age 39—playing into the later rounds at the French Open and Wimbledon and then stealing the show at the U.S. Open by entering as a wild card and exiting in the semifinals.

Steve Munday/Allsport

John Daly

The out-of-nowhere, one-week-wonder of the year. A No. 9 alternate who was invited to the PGA Championship at the last minute, drove all night to get there, then ended up winning the tournament with four rounds of power golf that took the PGA Tour's breath away.

Daly, 25, a self-taught long ball hitting native of small-town Arkansas, lived out every weekend duffer's fantasy and knew it, saying, "I just came here to play golf and got lucky."

Mike Powell/Allsport

Carl Lewis

Removed any remaining doubt that he is the greatest performer in the annals of track and field competition by his record-breaking showing at the World Championships in Tokyo.

In the space of seven days, the 30-year-old, six-time Olympic gold medalist set a world record of 9.86 seconds in the 100 meters, leaped 29 feet or better three times in the long jump, and anchored the U.S. 400-meter relay team to a world record of 37.50.

Kevin Levine/Allsport

Michael Jordan

NBA MVP and *Forbes* magazine VIP. Most Valuable Player during the regular season and in the playoffs. He led the league in scoring for the fifth straight year and led the Bulls to the NBA title for the first time ever. Averaged 31.5 points a game and made All-Defensive first team for the fourth straight year.

Also the highest-paid team athlete in the world in salary and outside income according to *Forbes*. Jordan reportedly earned $16 million in 1990-91.

Mike Powell/Allsport

Mike Powell

Produced the sports year's single most outstanding achievement when he surpassed Bob Beamon's "unbreakable" world long jump record of 29 feet, 2½ inches by two inches at the World Track and Field Championships in Tokyo.

In the process, the 27-year old Philadelphia native now living in L.A. not only erased Beamon's mark after 22 years and 10 months, but snapped archrival Carl Lewis's 10 year, 65-meet unbeaten streak in the event.

John Swart/Allsport

Cal Ripken Jr.

The AP and *Sporting News* Major League Player of the Year. Enjoyed his finest season as the only shortstop the Baltimore Orioles need. Batted .323, with 210 hits, 34 home runs and 114 batted in. Also led the majors in total bases (368) and extra base hits (85) and made only 11 errors in the field.

He also stretched his consecutive game playing streak to 1,573 and is now within 3½ seasons of Lou Gehrig's iron man record of 2,130.

Tim DeFrisco/Allsport

Jerry Tarkanian

He may not be the most-admired coach in college basketball, but nobody's program attracted more attention—good and bad—than UNLV's in 1990-91.

Tark had the roller coaster ride of the year: surprise reinstatement as defending NCAA champs, unbeaten regular season, upset by Duke in Final Four, four players selected in NBA Draft, three players in a hot tub with a known fixer, more NCAA charges, and, finally, Tark's decision to step down in 1992.

Dan Smith/Allsport

Monica Seles

Sure, she skipped Wimbledon with a mysterious shin injury that was never really explained and wouldn't play for Yugoslavia in the Federation Cup, but the 17-year-old grunt-and-volleyer won practically everything else on the women's tennis circuit.

She began by taking the Virginia Slims Championships in November, 1990, then gathered up three-quarters of the Grand Slam with victories at the Australian, French and U.S. Opens.

Stephen Dunn/Allsport

Mike Tyson

Boxing's troubled soul. He beat Razor Ruddock twice, but couldn't put him away. He signed for a $100 million Nov. 8 title fight with champion Evander Holyfield, then had to pull out with an injured rib cage on Oct. 18. Now he faces a Jan. 27, 1992, rape trial that could put him away for 63 years, if convicted.

Holyfield had the championship belt and George Foreman had the personality in 1991, but Tyson was the heavyweight everyone talked about.

THE YEAR
IN REVIEW

THE YEAR IN REVIEW
By Scott Ostler

Power Outage

It was a year of turmoil and change at the top.
Just ask the Reds in Cincinnati and Moscow.

John Daly and Sergeant Slaughter. How about those two for heads and tails, respectively, on the 1991 commemorative sports coin and video arcade token?

With sincere apologies to Michael Jordan/Howie Spira, to Mike Powell/Mike Tyson, to Monica Seles/Diego Maradona, it was Daly and Slaughter who symbolized the best and worst of an unusual sports year.

Upheaval. Turmoil. Revolution. Shifts in power. Undercurrents and overthrows. Cataclysmic change in the established order.

No, we're not talking about the life expectancy of major league baseball managers. We're talking about the world, the big playing field, where the goal-line stand of the year was made by a few thousand gutsy Soviet citizens at the barricades in Moscow; where Saddam Hussein made the mother of all mistakes taking on Stormin' Norman Schwartzkopf; where South Africa was awarded an expansion franchise in the League of Human Beings.

Against the backdrop of alternately exhilarating and terrifying events, is it any wonder the sports world seemed to wobble a bit on its axis, too? And that sometimes it was hard to separate the realpolitik from the real sports?

Reds collapsed in Moscow and in Cincinnati, both groups deposed by underdogs and bounced into the street on their once-proud keisters. But the ultimate blurring of reality and sport took place on Super Sunday when we tuned in ABC and got football and a war. Side by side. Al Michaels handing off to Peter Jennings.

As America geared up for the Super Bowl, the Allies were attacking Iraq. Debate raged: should the Super Bowl be cancelled out of respect for American soldiers on the front lines? Should the game go on, the better for morale at home and in the Gulf?

Or should we postpone the war, so as not to interfere with the Super Bowl? After all, as Buffalo quarterback Jim Kelly noted sagely, "War is stupid."

It turned out that our hearts and our TVs were big enough to embrace both events. Operation Desert Storm I and Super Bowl XXV shared TV billing on Super Storm Sunday. The ground-pounding Giants won by a narrow margin in Tampa, while in the desert, Saddam elected to receive and got buried on the opening kickoff.

U.S. troops in Saudi Arabia watched the telecast from their bunkers, the odd misguided missile flying overhead. Yet,

---

Scott Ostler is a former columnist for *The National* and the *Los Angeles Times*.

Jeff MacNelly, whose cartoon appears on page 21, is an editorial cartoonist for the *Chicago Tribune*. He has won three Pulitzer Prizes and is the creator of the comic strip "Shoe."

Lee Wardle/SportsFile

A flip of the 1991 commemorative sports coin came to this: heads, PGA golf champion **John Daly** (left); tails, pro wrestling turncoat, **Sgt.Slaughter**.

they seemed safer than the folks who packed Tampa Stadium, where every fan was frisked and scanned with metal detectors, where bomb-sniffing dogs outnumbered ballplayers, where crates of anti-nerve gas syringes were secretly stashed in the bowels of the stadium with the weenie buns and beer kegs.

A patriotic good time was had by all, except Scott Norwood, the Buffalo placekicker whose last-ditch field goal attempt floated wide right, and pro wrestler Sergeant Slaughter. Sarge, a former Worldwide Wrestling Federation good guy, suddenly switched allegiance in the midst of the Gulf Crisis and became an Iraqi sympathizer.

Pro wrestling is a sport only in the sense that cotton candy is a food, and you don't look to pro wrestlers for good taste and positive role-modeling. But the sight of Slaughter trivializing the war, daring his detractors to "form a coalition to stop me," turned more than a few stomachs.

Fortunately, zapping the chowderhead turncoat non-com was as easy as punching the channel changer on the TV remote control, and what awaited us as we spun around the dial were enough heart-warming and inspiring stories to stamp the year with greatness.

And none was warmer than Walter Mitty winning the PGA Championship, fulfilling the ultimate fantasy of every weekend hacker.

Walter's real name is John Daly—age 25, a self-taught PGA tour rookie from Arkansas with a rep for being lo-o-o-ong off the tees and de-e-e-ep into the woods. But for one magic week in August, Daly found the fairways and took our breath away, playing four days of magnificent, power-and-touch golf and winning by three strokes. His secret? When he addressed the ball, Daly didn't remind himself to keep his left arm straight or his hips square. He reminded himself: "Kill."

Daly's miracle at Crooked Stick was in keeping with the theme for 1991: Do it BIG. Drive big, win big, sin big, lose big, accuse big. Just big, baby.

Nolan Ryan pitched big, Cal Ripken Jr. played big, George Foreman ate big, Evander Holyfield earned big, Bruce

Jane Fonda, Ted Turner and **Jimmy Carter** doing the politically incorrect Tomahawk Chop in Atlanta.

McNall spent big, Calumet Farm went broke big, Monica Seles won big, the Quebec Nordiques lost big, Bill Parcells quit big, *The National* folded big, Joe Montana got injured big, Jimmy Connors came back big, and Ernie Harwell said "goodbye" big.

The Minnesota Twins and Atlanta Braves came back big—from last place in 1990 to the World Series in '91. While Twins' fans waved their Homer Hankies, Braves' supporters weighed in with the biggest fan fad of the year—the Tomahawk Chop 'n Chant, which they shamelessly stole from fans of the Florida State Seminoles.

The cuteness of the Chop 'n Chant wore off somewhat when Native American groups pointed out that such behavior was insensitive at best and racist stereotyping at worst. But that was after even the usually politically correct Jane Fonda had been seen "doin' the chop" down in the owner's box with Ted Turner and Jimmy Carter.

You could understand the protesters' anger, of course—they thought they'd packed Chief Noc-a-homa off to his Happy Hunting Ground long ago—but at least the Braves were winning. What about

that last place team in Cleveland that has really been giving Indians a bad name?

Minnesota, however, won the World Series in seven games and there were no protests from organized groups of twins, be they identical, fraternal or Siamese.

The Series also featured a big switcheroo—a nation of baseball fans and players rooting for an umpire. AL ump Steve Palermo was shot in the spine in July while breaking up a mugging in Dallas. He battled back to regain partial use of his legs and threw out the first ball before Game One. His walk to the mound on crutches was one of the year's most emotional moments.

The Twins, incidentally, weren't the only major surprise in Minnesota. The North Stars went into the 1990-91 NHL season floundering financially, artistically and at the box office. But the "No Stars" somehow got themselves into the playoffs, filled the Met Center with rabid fans and made it all the way to the Stanley Cup final before bowing to another Cinderella team—the Pittsburgh Penguins.

Big breakthroughs? In sports medicine, doctors mended injuries to Mark Bavaro and Randall Cunningham by transplanting bones and ligaments from cadavers. It was a glimpse into the future, when every fan can make a real contribution to the home team—in the form of spare parts. Soon tickets may actually cost an arm and leg.

At Wimbledon, tennis fans definitely were alive and kicking. Heavy rains forced officials to reschedule play on the middle Sunday, traditionally a day off. For the first time in tournament history, prim and proper centre court was turned over to the common fans, and the common fans got down. They cheered the warmups, heckled and encouraged the players, chanted, did the wave and broke all Wimbledon records for fun and frolic. True to form, All-England Club officials promised it would not happen again.

Big losers? Bernhard Langer missed a five-foot putt on the final hole that would have kept the Ryder Cup in Europe's golf bag for another two years. Victor Kiam was sued for sexual harassment by *Boston Herald* sportswriter Lisa Olson, then ran out of money and had to cough up the New England Patriots to the NFL (ain't life a "classic bitch," Vic?). And troubled Roy Tarpley was bounced out of the NBA for life for refusing to take a drug test—a DNP that cost him an $8 million contract with Dallas.

College football's bowl system was a flop again, the season ending with Colorado (AP) and Georgia Tech (UPI) sharing the mythical national crown. The NCAA was still resisting a formal playoff, but did propose that any future ties for the No. 1 spot be decided by the paper-scissors-rock method.

And may we have a moment of silence to mourn the death of gravity? How else to explain John Daly's drives, Michael Jordan's flights, Sergei Bubka's 20-foot pole vaults and Mike Powell's 29-foot, 4½-inch long jump?

At the World Track & Field Championships in Tokyo, Powell hooked up with the acknowledged master—teammate Carl Lewis, who hadn't lost a long jump competition in 10 years. Powell took off on his fifth jump, soared with the eagles and came down two inches past Bob Beamon's miracle leap in the 1968 Olympics. The feat devastated Lewis, who has been pounding at Beamon's door for the last decade.

Wide World Photos

Victor Kiam
Sued and sans Patriots.

"It's just one jump," Lewis grumped uncharitably.

Right. And Neil Armstrong's moonwalk was just one step.

One thing seems assured—Nobody will outjump the U.S. Olympic team in '92 at Barcelona. Powell and Lewis will be playing long jump leapfrog, and the U.S. Olympic basketball team will feature a bounding young man named Michael Jordan. The U.S. will also bring to the fray Magic Johnson, Mailman Malone and seven other pro superstars, taking advantage of the newly-liberalized eligibility rules.

The NBA All-Star team approach was a reaction to U.S. college kids failing to win against international competition in recent years. But isn't sending Charles Barkley and Larry Bird in there against Albania something akin to suiting up Schwartzkopf & Co. to take on Iraq?

It will be embarrassing if the USA loses, and embarrassing if it wins. But it won't be as embarrassing as the way the Yankees went down in flames at the Pan American Games in Cuba.

AFP

A Johannesburg policeman buys a morning newspaper from a vendor on July 10, the day after the International Olympic Committee readmitted South Africa after 21 years in athletic exile.

With Fidel Castro opening his country to outsiders for the first time in memory, the accent was on cultural interaction and fellowship among athletes. But the bureaucrats behind the U.S. basketball team decided the athletes' village was too spartan. Twice during the games, the U.S. hoopsters were flown to Miami and put up in an opulent hotel that featured a VCR and a hot tub in every suite.

"If we're spoiled and arrogant, so be it," said Bill Wall, executive director of USA Basketball.

A charming sentiment, the pomposity of which would have been slightly mitigated by a gold medal. Unfortunately, the U.S. lost to Puerto Rico in the semifinals, and American officials went skittering off to order room service and re-order their priorities.

The big Olympic news of the year, however, was not the re-tooling of the U.S. basketball team, but the readmittance of South Africa to the party. South Africa has been banned from the Olympics since 1964 because of its official policy of apartheid, but major political change has brought the country more into line with Olympian ideals of freedom and civil rights.

Ironically, while South Africa was being nudged forward by the pressures and demands of the United States and other countries, the apartheid on U.S. golf courses was alive and unwell. America celebrated the one-year anniversary of the Shoal Creek controversy and found that not much has changed. While Shoal Creek itself had admitted one black member, and so had Augusta National, such membership drives smacked of tokenism. Many clubs simply ignored the fuss. A Chicago newspaper polled 74 private golf clubs and found that 10 had accepted blacks and 26 let women have equal access.

Nine host golf clubs forfeited PGA golf tournaments rather than cave in to the PGA's bland new requirements for membership policies and practices. And when Caldwell Parish Country Club in Columbia, La., hosted a high school tournament, club officials refused to let the one black competitor tee off. The club later fell back on what has become the motto of American Golf in such matters: "It was all a misunderstanding."

Also claiming to be misunderstood was former heavyweight champ Mike Tyson. Pig Iron Mike all but melted down on Sept. 9, when he was indicted on charges of raping an 18-year-old contestant in the Miss Black America Pageant. He took another hit—to the rib cage—training for his Nov. 8 title fight with Evander Holyfield and had to pull out, kissing $20 million or so goodbye. In January, he goes to trial with the next 63 years of his life in the balance.

Tyson wasn't the only athlete in hot water. Three Nevada-Las Vegas basketball players were there, too.

Coach Jerry Tarkanian's Runnin' Rebels, in keeping with our big theme—won big and lost big. On Nov. 30, 1990, UNLV received an early Christmas present from the NCAA when it was allowed to plea-bargain its way back into defending its national title. The NCAA enforcement division turned itself into a Chinese menu—choose one penalty from Column A and one from Column B. Tark chose to let his team defend its championship and serve its tournament ban in 1992.

So the unbeaten Rebs went to the Final Four heavily favored, and fell heavily to Duke in the semifinals.

What could be more embarrassing? This: the *Las Vegas Review Journal* ran photos of three UNLV players bobbing happily in the back-yard hot tub of UNLV booster Richard (the Fixer) Perry, who has twice been convicted of sports bribery (see page 349). In the future, UNLV players will be counseled to use greater discretion. Or snorkels.

Bad as things were at Vegas, at least nobody was saying it was a matter of life and death.

Not so in Chaska, Minn. and Carmel, Ind., where the old bromide about lightning never striking twice was laid to rest when spectators were struck and killed at

St.Louis Post-Dispatch

Roderick Fisher Jr.
Escapes 'kill the ump' attempt.

two of golf's four majors—the U.S. Open and PGA Championship.

Far less chancy and much more sinister were the goings on in East St.Louis, Ill., and Channelview, Texas.

In East St.Louis, a boys' baseball coach named Curtis Fair tried to kill a 16-year-old umpire named Roderick Fisher Jr. With a gun. In broad daylight. Fisher, you see, had called one of Fair's nine-year-old players out at the plate. Fair, who is 31, ran on to the field to argue and Fisher ejected him. Irate, Fair came after the kid with a baseball bat, but was restrained by spectators. He then went home, got a gun, came back to the game and squeezed off a few rounds in Fisher's general direction.

Fortunately, Fair's aim was as wild as his temper and nobody got hurt. Fair ran off and was later taken into custody. Fisher went back to umpiring.

In Channelview, Wanda Webb Holloway, 37, tried to bump off a neighbor in order to assure her 13-year-old daughter of a place on the junior high school cheerleading team. The neighbor's daughter was also trying out for the team and Mrs. Holloway figured that killing the girl's mother would rattle the competition.

Wide World Photos

Wanda Webb Holloway
Ultimate cheerleader mom.

Cited for unnecessary roughness, Mrs. Holloway was found guilty of a murder-for-hire plot and sentenced to 15 years in prison. Sis-boom-bah.

Elsewhere on the crime front, admitted New York gambler Howie Spira was convicted on five counts of extortion, a verdict that cast George Steinbrenner into a strange new role—victim rather than bully. Still, commissioner Fay Vincent refused to reconsider George's lifetime banishment from baseball.

And in the NBA, the original Bad Boys took a fall. As Michael Jordan was leading his Chicago Bulls to a wipeout of the defending champion Detroit Pistons in the Eastern Conference Finals, he delivered the keynote address at the Detroit Pistons funeral.

"They dirty up the game of basketball," Jordan explained. "Sportsmanship should always be a part of sport, but they have taken that away. Now other teams want to play that way because of their success."

It's more likely—since the Bulls won the NBA Finals in five over the Lakers—that other teams will want to play it the Bulls' way, which is to turn your team over to an indestructible superhuman who can leap tall buildings and Bill Laimbeer, score 40 on demand, dance in midair, inspire teammates, play great defense, pack

arenas and dazzle corporate America with his smile and personality.

The NHL had its own version of Air Jordan—Ice Lemieux. Mario, elbowing Wayne Gretzky aside as THE star of the NHL—at least in the playoffs—led Pittsburgh to the Stanley Cup title. Lemieux, like Jordan, was playing his seventh season, and like Jordan he brought a championship to his city for the first time ever in his sport.

Finally, we have Rickey Henderson of the Oakland A's—the AL's 1990 MVP and the man who, on the occasion of breaking Lou Brock's career stolen base record in May, accepted a trophy from Brock and said, "Lou Brock was certainly a great base stealer, but today, I'm the greatest of all time."

Henderson held out in the spring, demanding that his year-old (and outdated) $3.25-million a year contract be renegotiated. "It [a chintzy contract] takes the heart out of you," Rickey lamented. "Say there's a fastball coming. If you're thinking about your contract, you might get hit by that pitch."

He seemed to be saying, "Meet my demands or you'll never see the real Rickey Henderson again." Thus Rickey became the first athlete to hold himself hostage.

Where was Sergeant Slaughter when you really needed him? □

Wide World Photos

Rickey Henderson
"I'm the greatest."

After further review. . .

by Charles Monagan

MAKEOVER OF THE YEAR

In between winning the Australian Open in January and the French in June, 18-year-old Monica Seles changed hairstyles. A few months later, she skipped Wimbledon, pulled out of the Federation Cup after pledging to play for Yugoslavia, was banned from the 1992 Olympics for missing the Fed Cup, and finally was fined $20,000 by the Women's Tennis Assn. for playing an October exhibition in the Canary Islands when she should have been at a WTA event in England. Something's gone to her head—the shampoo, perhaps.

Matrix Essentials, Inc.

Before   **After**

GEEZERS' CORNER

We cheered: George Foreman
            Jimmy Connors
            Nolan Ryan
            Harry Gant

We cringed: Bjorn Borg
            Mark Spitz
            Jim Palmer
            Larry Holmes

Wide World Photos

Borg   **Foreman**

HUMORLESS:

The NFL, for fining Redskin receiver Gary Clark $1,000 and penalizing the team five yards when he high-fived fans in the end zone after a touchdown (The NFL later rescinded its no celebration rule).

BRAINLESS:

Officials at Louisiana's all-white Caldwell Parish Country Club barred black high school player Dondre Green from competing on its golf course in a high school match.

GUTLESS:

Pete Sampras, for claiming to be relieved not to have repeated as U.S. Open tennis champion.

CLUELESS:

Mark Gastineau, who, following his 12-second bout with tomato can Derrick Dukes, told reporters he'd disposed of his opponent with "a left hook that felt really good." In reality, it was a right uppercut that had caused Dukes to faint.

FLAWLESS:

Dennis Martinez, who overcame a big-time problem with alcohol to become the ace of the Expos staff, pitch a perfect game against the Dodgers in July, and lead the NL in earned run average.

FEARLESS:

Rodney McCray, leftfielder for the Vancouver Canadians of the Pacific Coast League, smashed straight through the outfield fence while trying to catch a fly ball.

RUTHLESS:

The New York Yankees, whose leading home run hitter this year was Matt Nokes with 23, and whose most pressing mid-season concern was the length of Don Mattingly's hair.

Charles A. Monagan is the editor of *Connecticut* magazine.

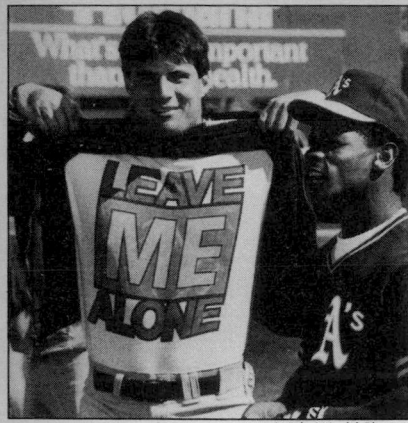

Wide World Photos

BUBBLEHEADS

"This is a piece of history," said sports memorabilia collector Mark Friedland. "It's like the Declaration of Independence coming up for auction." Friedland was hyperventilating over the 1910 Honus Wagner baseball card, for which Wayne Gretzky and Bruce McNall had just paid a staggering $451,000, thus smashing the previous record for the amount of money paid for a card.

Meanwhile, in a not entirely unrelated event, The Topps Co. has decided to take the gum out of its packages of sports cards, claiming it tends to stain the cards and thus reduce their value.

At the same time, the company was quick to cash in on the war in the Persian Gulf with a series of Desert Storm cards.

Southeby's   The Topps Co.

Wagner   **Schwarzkopf**

FLYING

When stopped by the Florida Highway Patrol for doing 104 mph in a 55-mph zone, Jose Canseco explained he was testing a high-octane aviation fuel.

HAPPENING COUPLES

Monica Seles and Donald Trump
Jose Canseco and Madonna
Martina Navratilova and Judy Nelson
Victor Kiam and Lisa Olson
George Steinbrenner and Howard Spira
Lou Piniella and Gary Darling
Fred (if he's making birdies)

ALL-TIME LEADING SCORER

In his new book, *A View from Above*, former seven-time NBA scoring champion Wilt Chamberlain revealed: ". . .don't be shocked to hear that if I had to count my sexual encounters, I would be closing in on 20,000 women. Yes, that's correct, 20,000 women. At my age, that equals out to having sex with 1.2 women a day, every day since I was 15 years old."

While an impressive stat, at 55, Wilt is starting to run of time if he wants to match his career NBA point total of 31,419.

KICK ME

After missing the field goal that could have won the Super Bowl for Buffalo, Scott Norwood endured an off-season of ridicule (Joke: "Norwood *tried to shoot himself—but missed wide right*"), only to miss his first three-point attempt of the new season against Miami—you guessed it, wide right.

SALARY REPORT

The world's highest-paid athletes had a very good year, but if you think they're paid too much, just take a look at a companion list of the highest-paid entertainers.

According to *Forbes*, Evander Holyfield topped the list of athletes as he pocketed a cool $60 million, but Madonna pulled in $63 million and Oprah Winfrey was paid $80 million, while Bill Cosby and New Kids on the Block soared into nine figures, at $113 million and $115 million, respectively.

Did Michael Jordan have a good year? Sure he did—at $16 million, third on the list of athletes. But entertainers earning more included Charles M. Schulz, Siegfried & Roy, Matt Groening and somebody named Xuxa.

INJURY OF THE YEAR

The Sacramento Kings guard Lionel Simmons missed two games during the season due to wrist and forearm tendinitis, the result of playing too much Nintendo Gameboy.

THE CHARLIE FINLEY INNOVATION AWARDS

2nd Runner-Up: To the Liberty Basketball Association, a women's pro league, for devising the "unitard," a form-fitting Spandex uniform so revealing that it was later modified.

1st Runner-Up: To none other than Charlie Finley himself, for proposing a football with concave rather than convex dimples, thus, he said, making it easier to grip, throw and catch.

The Winner: To the World League of American Football (the "Laugh League"), for the helmet cam, which allowed us at home to look for the first time down a linebacker's throat.

USA Network

JOHN 3:16, MEET JOHN LAW

Rockin' Rollen Stewart, the obnoxious guy with the rainbow afro who made a career of sorts by holding up the JOHN 3:16 sign at major sporting events, was sought during the year by police for allegedly setting off explosive devices in various public places.

HE'S SO FINED

Rob Dibble threw at two players and hit a women in the bleachers from 400 feet away, which cost him 7 games in suspensions and undisclosed fines.

Charles Barkley spit at a heckler, slimed an 8-year-old girl by mistake and was docked $10,000 and a game.

John McEnroe cursed out a Wimbledon linesman and was fined $10,000.

THE ROBERT IRSAY SPORTS EXECUTIVE OF THE YEAR AWARDS

2nd Runner-Up: To comedian John Candy, co-owner of the CFL's Toronto Argos and chairman of the league's expansion committee. Now *there's* a committee meeting we'd actually *like* to attend.

1st Runner-Up: To Detroit Tigers President Bo Schembechler, who during the year decided to fire legendary play-by-play announcer Ernie Harwell, to abandon Tiger Stadium for a new ballpark, and, while the Tigers were still in the chase for the division title, to sign with ABC to do college football halftime shows that would have conflicted with any post-season role for the Tigers.

The Winner: To NHL President John Ziegler, who, to honor the 75th anniversary of the league, began the season without a players agreement contract, with expansion teams unable to make expansion fee payments, with a national TV contract more suited to a pro windsurfing league, and with cash-starved franchises trying to cope with out-of-control salary demands.

PRETTY BAD IN PINK

After his University of Hawaii football team lost on the road to both Colorado State and Iowa, coach Bob Wagner said he thought the pink locker rooms might have had something to do with it. He cited studies that have shown pink reduces strength and makes people more passive and less aggressive.

"This is a lot different and more serious than growing the grass higher, if you believe those who have done research in this area," Wagner said.

Wide World Photos

Dibble   **Barkley**   **McEnroe**

QUOTES OF THE YEAR

"I know you're really a transvestite and really like me . . . I'm gonna make you my girlfriend."
—Mike Tyson to Razor Ruddock during a May press conference

"If Jesus were on the field, he'd be pitching inside and breaking up double plays."
—Tim Burke, born-again pitcher

"Get a life, would you?"
—Bengals coach Sam Wyche to reporters after an 0-3 start.

"When you see that big zero up there for wins, it's like somebody put a dead rat in your mouth."
—Colts coach Ron Meyer after an 0-4 start.

"I don't think I should be asked to play when the temperature drops below my age."
—Carlton Fisk, 43, after playing on a 40-degree night in April.

"Where's the National Rifle Association when you really need them?"
—Giants' announcer Ron Fairly, after listening to a trumpeter in Montreal play selections such as "The Happy Wanderer" and "Happy Birthday."

"This number 72 is unbelievable. He's eaten many hamburgers."
—German football fan Holger Hintze, after watching "Refrigerator" Perry play an exhibition game in Berlin.

"I couldn't believe I swam that slow. I didn't feel slow."
—Mark Spitz after his comeback try.

"Don't blame me. Blame the foursome in front of me."
—Lawrence Taylor upon reporting six hours late to the first day of training camp.

"I appreciate their support, but I couldn't believe they ended a sentence with a preposition. How embarrassing."
—Walter Palmer, Jazz rookie forward, commenting on sign held up by fans that said, "Put Walt In."

GOLFER OF THE YEAR

Vice President Dan Quayle, whose golf outing to Augusta, Ga., in April cost taxpayers roughly $27,000 for the use of an Air Force plane, housing and feeding the plane's crew and Quayle's secret service detail. The vice president did manage to get in 36 holes, however.

TROPHY TROUBLE

It was a bad year for championship trophies. The trouble began at the PBA's U.S. Open, when the crystal trophy top simply fell off during the awards presentation and smashed to the floor in full view of fans and a national television audience.

American Bowling Congress

Then, in June, the Stanley Cup wound up at the bottom of Mario Lemieux's swimming pool during a Penguins party at his house in suburban Pittsburgh (this, after spending the previous night on goalie Tom Barrasso's front lawn).

Finally, in September the Canada Cup ended up in the lost and found department of the Westin Harbor Castle hotel in Toronto after no one on the victorious Canadian team remembered to take it home with him.

THREE STEEDS FOR THE AGES

Tony Leonard

Northern Dancer
(1961-91)

Kentucky Derby and Preakness winner; sire of 143 stakes winners.

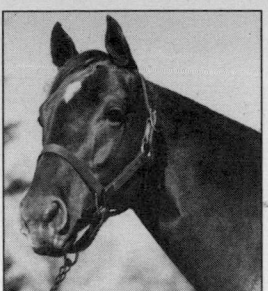

Tony Leonard

Alydar
(1975-91)

Runner-up to Affirmed in all three Triple Crown races; sire of 45 stakes winners.

Cincinnati Enquirer

Schottzie
(1982-91)

Mascot of 1990 World Champion Cincinnati Reds; buried wearing a Reds cap.

SCANDAL WATCH

Charges of cheating rocked the curling world after Canada beat Scotland, 8-5, in the 1991 world championship game. David Smith, of Scotland, accused Canada's Kevin Martin of bringing an illegally-dirty broom into play late in the game. "There was so much garbage on the ice, nobody could throw a decent shot," said Smith.

Players on the Burrton (Kansas) High School girls' basketball team were barred from further play after accepting 3-inch-high teddy bears worth $1 each during a boosters' dinner.

The Hawaii House of Representatives approved a resolution urging that Shoeless Joe Jackson be exonerated from conspiring to fix the 1919 World Series.

WAIVING THE FLAG

The Marriott Corp. tried to fly in the face of a patriotic wave when it ordered its vendors at Dodger Stadium to keep moving and working while the national anthem was played. The workers objected and Marriott, faced with a publicity nightmare, promptly reversed its order.

FRESH WIND OF CAPITALISM DEPT.

Sergei Bubka, the Ukrainian pole vault whiz, broke the indoor and outdoor records a total of eight times in 1991, each time upping the old record by about a quarter-inch—and each time earning a bonus from his shoe contract.

BAD CAREER MOVES

Mats Wilander, rock guitarist.
"All people have a right to enjoy a hobby, but there is a limit—like charging $15 for a show like this."
—Mans Ivarsson of *Expressen*, Sweden's largest newspaper

Mickey Rourke, boxer.
"I don't got no future, really, as a boxer."
—Rourke himself

Pete Rose, actor.
"How ill at ease is Pete? He looks like he just stepped into shoes filled with tobacco juice."
—*Entertainment Weekly*

Wide World Photos

THE VICE OF THE FAN

Sacramento bank robber Claude Jones robbed 24 banks in 10 weeks to finance trips to and tickets for Raiders games. He was caught and sentenced to 10 years.

WORST LOSER

On the 200-meter winners' podium at an ACC indoor meet, Kevin Braunskill of North Carolina hit James Trapp of Clemson in the head with his trophy. Trapp needed stitches and suffered a mild concussion. Trapp earlier had upset Braunskill in the 55-meter dash.

Wide World Photos

EYE ON THE ROYALS

It was another nutty year for the sports-mad Royal Family of England. In January, Princess Diana was photographed wearing a Philadelphia Eagles jacket; in May, her mother-in-law Queen Elizabeth visited an Orioles-Oakland A's game where she hobnobbed with Jose Canseco; in June, Prince William, 8, was beaned by another student's putter (and needed 24 stitches) while golfing during recess at Ludgrove Preparatory School; and in August, an injury-plagued Prince Charles fell from the ranks of the world's top 35 polo players when his rating was lowered by the Hurlington Polo Association.

BEST NEW SPORTS LOGO

The Big Ten, which cleverly incorporated Penn State as its eleventh member.

WORST NEW SPORTS LOGO

The San Francisco 49ers. Reaction to it was so immediate and so bad that it was scrapped before the season began.

BEST MEMORY

John Candelaria, during a 1991 intrasquad game, drilled Juan Samuel with a pitch because Samuel beat him with a home run. In 1983.

FIRED!

It was a bad year to be at the helm. Here is the list of the 26 head coaches and managers who got the boot from Nov. 1, 1990 through Oct. 31, 1991:

NFL
Bud Carson, Browns
Ray Perkins, Buccaneers
Rod Rust, Patriots
Buddy Ryan, Eagles
Ron Meyer, Colts

NBA
Stu Jackson, Knicks
Dick Versace, Pacers
Bill Musselman, Timberwolves
Gene Littles, Hornets

NHL
Bob McCammon, Canucks
John Cunniff, Devils
Bob Murdoch, Jets
Rick Ley, Whalers

Baseball
Nick Leyva, Phillies
Don Zimmer, Cubs
John Wathan, Royals
Frank Robinson, Orioles
Buck Rodgers, Expos
John McNamara, Indians
Doug Rader, Angels
Bud Harrelson, Mets
Stump Merrill, Yankees
Joe Morgan, Red Sox
Tom Trebelhorn, Brewers
Jim Lefebvre, Mariners
Jim Essian, Cubs

Tour veteran **Pat Bradley** won both the MBS Classic and an automatic berth in the LPGA Hall of Fame with her 30th career victory Sept. 29.

1990-1991 CALENDAR

SUN	MON	TUE	WED	THU	FRI	SAT
				1	2	3
4	5	6	7	8	9	10
11	12	13	14	15	16	17
18	19	20	21	22	23	24
25	26	27	28	29	30	

Wide World Photos

Darryl Strawberry
Goes West.

3 Georgia Tech upsets top-ranked Virginia, 41-38, on Scott Sisson's 37-yard field goal with seven seconds left.

4 Douglas Wakiihuri of Kenya wins 21st running of New York City Marathon in 2:12:39. Poland's Wanda Panfil is women's winner at 2:30:45.

5 Cleveland fires second-year head coach Bud Carson after 42-0 loss to Buffalo at home. Browns, now 2-7, name offensive coordinator Jim Shofner to take over.

IAAF suspends world track and field record holders Butch Reynolds (400 meters) and Randy Barnes (shotput) for two years after testing positive for steroid use.

6 Arizona voters jeopardize scheduling of 1993 Super Bowl in Tempe by rejecting Martin Luther King holiday at the polls.

In California, Santa Clara voters turn thumbs down on 1 percent utility tax that would have financed $153 million stadium for S.F.Giants.

7 Illinois basketball placed on three years' probation by NCAA for recruiting and ticket selling violations. Illini also barred from postseason play in 1991.

8 Darryl Strawberry, a free agent, leaves N.Y. Mets after eight seasons to sign five-year, $20.25 million deal with L.A. Dodgers.

Missouri basketball gets two-year probation from NCAA for recruiting violations and academic irregularities. Tigers also barred from 1991 postseason.

11 Major League All-Star team defeats Japanese All-Stars, 5-0, as Chuck Finley and Randy Johnson combine on no-hitter. MLB All-Stars finish tour with 3-4-1 record.

15 Alydar destroyed at Calumet Farm after breaking right hind leg in his stall for second time in one week.

17 No.1 Notre Dame upset, 24-21, by No.18 Penn State on 34-yard Craig Fayak field goal with eight seconds left in South Bend.

18 Sixteen-year-old Monica Seles defeats Gabriela Sabatini in five sets to win Virginia Slims Championships in New York. Meanwhile, in Frankfurt, Germany, **Andre Agassi** upsets No.1 Stefan Edberg in four sets to win inaugural ATP Championships.

Dale Earnhardt clinches fourth NASCAR driving title by finishing third in Atlanta Journal 500. Race is marred by death of Bill Elliott crew member Mike Rich in pit crash.

19 Dexter Manley reinstated by NFL after serving one year of "lifetime" suspension for drug abuse. Veteran defensive end is immediately waived by Washington.

20 Rickey Henderson of Oakland outpolls Detroit slugger Cecil Fielder, 317-286, to win AL Most Valuable Player award and close out baseball's trophy season. Other major prize winners include: Barry Bonds of Pittsburgh (NL MVP), the Pirates' Doug Drabek (NL Cy Young), the A's Bob Welch (AL Cy Young), and rookies Sandy Alomar Jr. of Cleveland (AL) and David Justice of Atlanta (NL).

Roger Clemens suspended for first five games of 1991 and fined $10,000 by AL president Bobby Brown for his ALCS Game 4 run-in with plate umpire Terry Cooney.

23 New Jersey Nets snap NBA-record 34-game road losing streak, beating Phoenix, 116-114.

25 Eighteen-game winning streak of S.F.49ers ends as struggling L.A.Rams (3-7) beat the two-time defending Super Bowl champs, 28-17. Unbeaten N.Y.Giants also lose—31-13 to Philadelphia.

Winnipeg Blue Bombers win CFL Grey Cup for second time in three years, routing Edmonton, 50-11, at B.C.Place in Vancouver.

27 NFL fines New England Patriots and players Zeke Mowatt, Michael Timpson and Roger Perryman a total of $72,500 in Lisa Olson sexual harassment case.

30 NCAA alters penalties against UNLV basketball program. Rebels allowed to defend title in 1991, but are banned from postseason play and live TV in 1991-92.

Sun	Mon	Tue	Wed	Thu	Fri	Sat
						1
2	3	4	5	6	7	8
9	10	11	12	13	14	15
16	17	18	19	20	21	22
23	24	25	26	27	28	29
30	31					

Wide World Photos

Pete Sampras
$2 million payday.

1 Junior quarterback Ty Detmer named winner of Heisman Trophy, but BYU loses final regular season game to Hawaii, 59-28.

U.S. clinches 29th Davis Cup title with four-set doubles win over Australia at the Suncoast Dome in St. Petersburg.

3 Once-beaten S.F.49ers and N.Y.Giants meet in probable NFC Championship preview at Candlestick Park. Niners win, 7-3.

New York Knicks fire second-year head coach Stu Jackson after 7-8 start, replace him with 17-year NBA veteran John MacLeod.

Tampa Bay Buccaneers make fourth-year head coach Ray Perkins walk the plank, name assistant Richard Williamson as interim coach.

6 Baseball meetings in Chicago heat up as San Diego sends OF Joe Carter and 2B Roberto Alomar to Toronto for 1B Fred McGriff and SS Tony Fernandez. The real story of the meetings, however, are the free agent signings as teams spend $150 million in six days on players like George Bell (Cubs), Vince Coleman (Mets), Willie McGee (Giants), Terry Pendleton (Braves) Dave Righetti (Giants), Steve Sax (Yankees), Matt Young (Red Sox) and others.

6 Baseball players union executive board votes to accept $280 million collusion award in largest management-to-players settlement in sports history.

Ottawa and Tampa Bay are surprise choices as NHL awards expansion franchises for 1992-93 season. Both clubs agree to pay entry fee of $50 million.

7 Seattle and Phoenix swap forwards, the Sonics sending Xavier McDaniel to the Suns for Eddie Johnson and two No.1 draft picks.

Agreement reached in organized baseball's troublesome player development contract negotiations. Seven-year deal preserves 87-year relationship between major and minor leagues.

15 L.A.Dodgers sign free agent OF Brett Butler to three-year, $10 million contract, while Boston signs DH Jack Clark for three years and $8.7 million.

16 U.S.Open champ Pete Sampras defeats Brad Gilbert in Munich to win $2 million first prize in finals of inaugural ITF Grand Slam Cup.

Playoff-bound QBs Phil Simms of New York (right foot) and Jim Kelly of Buffalo (left knee) injured in Giants-Bills game won by Bills, 17-13.

20 NCAA charges UNLV basketball program with 29 rules violations stemming from 1986 recruiting of New York high school star Lloyd Daniels.

20 Miami of Florida athletic director Sam Jankovich hired as CEO of New England Patriots by team owner Victor Kiam.

Bo Jackson named to AFC Pro Bowl team, making him first player ever picked to play in both baseball and NFL all-star games.

Indiana Pacers fire third-year coach Dick Versace after 9-16 start, replace him with assistant Bob Hill.

23 Chicago White Sox get OF Tim Raines and two others from Montreal for OF Ivan Calderon and P Barry Jones.

30 Orlando guard Scott Skiles sets NBA single-game assists record with 30 as Magic rout Denver, 155-116.

31 George Allen dies in Rancho Palos Verdes, Calif., at age 72. Former NFL coach won 118 games in 12 years and had just come out of retirement to lead Long Beach State to a 6-5 record in 1990.

NFL regular season comes to a close as New Orleans (8-8) clinches the last playoff berth with a Monday Night win over the L.A.Rams. The expanded (12 teams) playoff field includes Buffalo, Cincinnati, Houston, Kansas City, L.A.Raiders and Miami in the AFC; and Chicago, New Orleans, N.Y. Giants, Philadelphia, San Francisco and Washington in the NFC.

Sun	Mon	Tue	Wed	Thu	Fri	Sat
		1	2	3	4	5
6	7	8	9	10	11	12
13	14	15	16	17	18	19
20	21	22	23	24	25	26
27	28	29	30	31		

UPI/Bettmann

Scott Norwood
Wide right.

1 Colorado (11-1-1) and **Georgia Tech** (11-0-1) stake claims to national championship after No.1 Buffaloes edge Notre Dame, 10-9, in Orange Bowl and No.2 Yellow Jackets rout Nebraska, 45-21, in Citrus.

2 Wire service polls disagree on 1990 national champion: AP names Colorado, but UPI selects Georgia Tech.

3 Hat trick against the N.Y.Islanders enables Wayne Gretzky to join Gordie Howe (801), Marcel Dionne (731) and Phil Esposito (717) as NHL's only 700-goal scorers.

5 Kevin Bradshaw of U.S.International breaks NCAA Division I single game scoring record with 72 points in 186-140 loss to Loyola Marymount.

7 Pete Rose released from Federal Prison Camp in Marion, Ill., after completing five-month sentence for tax violations.
U.S.Supreme Court refuses to hear NFL players appeal of lower court ruling protecting league free-agency restrictions.

8 Baseball writers elect Rod Carew, Gaylord Perry and Ferguson Jenkins to Hall of Fame. Carew is the 22nd player named in first year of eligibility.

Philadelphia owner Norman Braman fires head coach Buddy Ryan two days after the Eagles lose to Washington in first round of NFL playoffs. Ryan was 31-17 over last three years, but 0-3 in postseason. Offensive coordinator Rich Kotite takes over.

9 Dean Smith gains 700th victory of his 30-year career as North Carolina routs Maryland, 105-73. He joins Adolph Rupp (875), Hank Iba (767), Ed Diddle (759), Phog Allen (746) and Ray Meyer (724) as the only Division I coaches to win 700.

11 NCAA Convention ends in Nashville after passing new restrictions on size of coaching staffs, eliminating athletic dorms, reducing training table meals to one a day, cutting scholarships 10 percent, and raising minimum number of Division I sports at Division I schools to seven men's and seven women's (up from six each).

Banished Canadian sprinter Ben Johnson, returning to competition 28 months after testing positive for steriod use at the Seoul Olympics, finishes second to Andre Cason of the U.S. at 50 meters in Hamilton, Ont.

13 Phil Mickelson, the reigning NCAA and U.S.Amateur golf champion, wins PGA Northern Telecom Open in Tucson but has to pass up the $180,000 first prize.

16 United Nations coalition forces, led by the U.S., go to war in the Persian Gulf. Operation Desert Storm begins at 7 p.m. EST with massive Allied air and missle attacks on targets in Iraq and Kuwait. Outbreak of hostilities leads North Carolina and N.C. State to postpone ACC game at Chapel Hill.

19 Toronto forward Vincent Damphousse scores four goals to lead Campbell Conference to 11-5 victory in 42nd NHL All-Star Game at Chicago Stadium.

24 Notre Dame junior flanker and kick returner Raghib (Rocket) Ismail declares for NFL Draft.

25 St.Louis Blues right wing Brett Hull scores twice against Detroit to become third NHL player to score 50 goals in 49 games.

26 Australian Open ends with Boris Becker beating Ivan Lendl for men's championship. Monica Seles defeated Jana Novotna for women's title on Jan.25.

Mario Lemieux returns to NHL action after July 11 back surgery to assist on three goals as Pittsburgh beats Quebec, 6-5.

27 N.Y. Giants win closest Super Bowl ever, beating Buffalo, 20-19, when Bills' kicker Scott Norwood's 47-yard field goal attempt misses wide right with 0:04 left.

28 Pro Football Hall of Fame announces election of five new members: contributor Tex Schramm, running back Earl Campbell, linemen John Hannah and Stan Jones, and the Hall's first pure kicker, Jan Stenerud.

Sun	Mon	Tue	Wed	Thu	Fri	Sat
					1	2
3	4	5	6	7	8	9
10	11	12	13	14	15	16
17	18	19	20	21	22	23
24	25	26	27	28		

3 **AFC rallies** to beat NFC in Pro Bowl, 23-21. Two Jim Kelly TD passes in 4th quarter spark victory.

4 **Hall of Fame** board of directors votes 12-0 to bar any player on the permanently ineligible list. Ruling means Pete Rose cannot be on ballot until reinstated.

5 **Cleveland Browns** sign N.Y.Giants' 38-year-old defensive coordinator Bill Belichick to five-year pact as new head coach.

Big East officially announces plans for eight-team football league beginning in fall. Conference members Boston College, Miami-FL, Pittsburgh and Syracuse will be joined by "associate members" Rutgers, Temple, Virginia Tech and West Virginia.

Minnesota Twins sign free agent pitcher and St.Paul native Jack Morris for one year and $3 million. Morris, 35, won 198 games for Detroit in 14 years.

6 **Diana Golden**, world disabled skiing champion, receives fifth Flo Hyman Award from Women's Sports Foundation.

7 **Basketball Hall of Fame** announces election of coach Bob Knight, players Nate Archibald, Dave Cowens and Harry Gallatin, late NBA commissioner Larry O'Brien and late player union boss Larry Fleisher.

8 **Boston Red Sox** make pitcher Roger Clemens the highest paid player in baseball with four-year contract extension at $5.4 million per year.

9 **Sugar Ray Leonard** retires after one-sided 12-round loss to WBC super welterweight champ Terry Norris in New York.

Horse of the Year Eclipse Award goes to Criminal Type, who won 7 of 11 races and $2.2 million as 5-year-old in 1990.

10 **Number One UNLV** humbles No.2 Arkansas, 112-105 at Fayetteville. Unbeaten Rebels led by as many as 23 points in second half.

East beats West 116-114 in 41st NBA All-Star Game at Charlotte. MVP Charles Barkley of Philadelphia has 17 points and 22 rebounds.

13 **Leroy Burrell** sets world indoor record of 6.48 seconds for 60 meters in Madrid, Spain.

14 **Pittsburgh pitcher** and NL Cy Young Award winner Doug Drabek is awarded record $3.33 million salary in arbitration case.

15 **Milwaukee Bucks** trade All-Star guard Ricky Pierce to Seattle for Dale Ellis.

Detroit Pistons' Chuck Daly named head coach of 1992 U.S. Olympic basketball team, which will include NBA players for first time.

Gary Hubbell

Diana Golden
Flo Hyman honoree.

16 **Tonya Harding** lands triple axel in electrifying free skate to win U.S. Women's Figure Skating title at Minneapolis.

17 **Ernie Irvan** outruns favorite Dale Earnhardt and pole sitter Davey Allison to capture 33rd Daytona 500.

Pittsburgh Pirates "win" arbitration cases with star outfielders Bobby Bonilla and Barry Bonds, paying Bonilla $2.4 million (not $3.5) and Bonds $2.3 million (not $3.3).

18 **Edmonton goalie** Grant Fuhr, whose one-year suspension for drug abuse was lifted on Feb. 4, returns to blank New Jersey, 4-0, in his first NHL game since Mar. 30, 1990.

20 **Ex-Postmaster General** Robert Tisch buys 50 percent of Super Bowl champion N.Y. Giants for reported $75 million.

23 **Ground offensive begins** in Gulf War at 8 p.m. EST. Allied troops enter Kuwait and Iraq.

25 **N.C.State guard** Chris Corchiani collects 13 assists in win over Tennessee, breaks all-time NCAA career assist record of 960.

Toronto Argonauts of Canadian Football League sold for $5 million to L.A.Kings' owner Bruce McNall, Wayne Gretzky, and comedian John Candy.

26 **Veterans' Committee** of Baseball Hall of Fame elects owner/promoter Bill Veeck and 2B Tony Lazzeri. Both are deceased.

27 **President Bush declares** suspension of hostilities in Gulf War and lays out conditions for permanent cease-fire.

Sun	Mon	Tue	Wed	Thu	Fri	Sat
					1	2
3	4	5	6	7	8	9
10	11	12	13	14	15	16
17	18	19	20	21	22	23
24	25	26	27	28	29	30
31						

Wide World Photos

John Smith
Top U.S. amateur.

1 **New York Knicks** fire GM Al Bianchi, name former Utah Jazz executive David Checketts as team president.

3 **Battle of McEnroes** takes place in Volvo/Chicago tennis final with John beating brother Patrick 3-6, 6-2, 6-4.

4 **With 13 games left** in the NHL regular season, New Jersey (28-28-11) fires head coach John Cunniff and names Tom McVie.

Pittsburgh Penguins send high scorer John Cullen and defenseman Zarley Zalapski to Hartford for center Ron Francis and defenseman Ulf Samuelsson in six-player deal.

10 **German men and women** break world indoor 1,600-meter relay records at World Championships in Seville, Spain. World marks also equalled in women's 60-meter dash and broken in men's 5,000-meter walk.

Formula One season opens with Ayrton Senna winning USA Grand Prix in Phoenix. d Prix in Phoenix.

11 **UNLV tops** final AP poll with 30-0 record, aims to become first unbeaten NCAA champion since Indiana in 1976.

Women's tennis computer ranks Monica Seles at No.1, ending Steffi Graf's 3½-year reign at the top.

Three-time world wrestling champion and 1988 gold medalist John Smith wins AAU Sullivan Award as country's top amateur athlete of 1990.

12 **Hall of Fame pitcher** Jim Palmer, 45, ends comeback attempt with Baltimore one day after being rocked by Boston in exhibition game.

15 **Soviet pole vaulter** Sergei Bubka becomes first man to clear 20 feet, raising world record for 13th time at indoor meet in San Sebastian, Spain.

16 **American women** Kristi Yamaguchi, Tonya Harding and Nancy Kerrigan sweep medals at World Figure Skating Championships in Munich. Canada's Kurt Browning won third straight men's title on Mar.14.

18 **Kansas City Royals** release Bo Jackson after club doctors conclude that his Jan.13 football injury damaged cartilage in his left hip socket.

Mike Tyson wins controversial 7th round TKO over Razor Ruddock in Las Vegas when referee Richard Steele stops fight with Ruddock still on his feet.

19 **NFL owners**, meeting in Hawaii, decide to move 1993 Super Bowl out of Phoenix and approve instant replay for another year.

19 **Knight Commission** releases report calling for reform in college sports and urging school presidents to take control of their athletic programs.

22 **Washington judge** orders NFL owners to pay 1,100 present and former NFL players an average of $13,000 each for refusing to let them play Oct. 18, 1987, after union ended 24-day walkout.

23 **World League** of American Football debuts in Frankfurt, Germany with London Monarchs beating the hometown Galaxy, 24-11, before 23,619.

26 **International Tennis** Hall of Fame announces election of Ilie Nastase, Guillermo Vilas and Ashley Cooper.

27 **U.S. Soccer Federation** names Bora Milutinovic as head coach of national team. No stranger to World Cup play, Milutinovic led Mexico to quarterfinals in 1986 and Costa Rica to second round in 1990.

28 **NBA suspends** Philadelphia forward Charles Barkley for one game and fines him $10,000 for spitting at heckler in March 26 game at New Jersey.

30 **UNLV upset** by Duke, 79-77, in semifinals of NCAA tournament at Indianapolis. Rebels end season at 34-1. Kansas beats North Carolina, 79-73, to gain final.

Northern Michigan beats Boston University, 8-7, in triple overtime to win NCAA Division I hockey title.

31 **Tennessee wins** NCAA Women's basketball title for third time in five years, defeating Virginia, 70-67, in overtime.

Sun	Mon	Tue	Wed	Thu	Fri	Sat
	1	2	3	4	5	6
7	8	9	10	11	12	13
14	15	16	17	18	19	20
21	22	23	24	25	26	27
28	29	30				

Wide World Photos

Mike Krzyzewski
Duke finally does it.

1 **Duke wins first** NCAA basketball title after nine trips to Final Four, beating Kansas, 72-65, before Hoosier Dome crowd of 47,100.

2 **Denver Nuggets'** co-owner Bertram Lee is ousted for failing to make his share of $5 million capital call. He and partner Peter Bynoe were NBA's first black owners.

3 **Two weeks after** being released by Kansas City, Bo Jackson signs one-year, $700,000 deal with Chicago White Sox that could earn him $8 million, if he plays for three years.

World record-holding swimmers Janet Evans of Stanford and Melvin Stewart of Tennessee say they will pass up remaining college eligibility to train for 1992 Summer Olympics.

6 **Diego Maradona** is suspended 15 months by FIFA, soccer's international governing body, and the Italian league for cocaine use.

8 **Baseball season opens** without Major League umpires, who will return April 9 after ending two-day walkout over salaries. Roger Clemens, allowed to pitch while he appeals five-day AL suspension, beats Toronto at SkyDome.

Retired jockey Bill Shoemaker, 59, fractures his neck and is paralyzed from the shoulders down after jeep he is driving tumbles 50 feet down highway embankment in suburban Los Angeles.

NFL names Antrak executive Harold Henderson as executive vice president for labor relations, making him the league's highest-ranking black official.

13 **Almost two decades** after winning seven gold medals at Munich, 41-year-old Mark Spitz loses ballyhooed 50-meter butterfly match race by a length and a half to Tom Jager, 26.

14 **Ian Woosnam** outlasts Jose-Maria Olazabal and Tom Watson to win Masters golf on final hole.

15 **Magic Johnson** breaks Oscar Robertson's all-time NBA assist mark of 9,887 in second quarter as Lakers beat Dallas in L.A.

Sacramento Kings set NBA record with 35th straight road defeat, losing to Minnesota, 112-94.

Notre Dame head coach Digger Phelps, 49, announces retirement after 20 seasons with the Irish and career record of 419-200.

Boston Marathon won by Ibrahim Hussein of Kenya in 2:11:06. Poland's Wanda Panfil (2:24:18) is women's winner, while 83-year-old Johnny Kelly runs 60th Boston in 5:42:54.

18 **New Comiskey Park** opens in Chicago as 42,191 watch White Sox get pounded, 16-0, by Detroit.

18 **Utah Jazz guard** John Stockton picks up 11 assists against Seattle to break his own NBA single-season assist record of 1,134.

19 **Evander Holyfield** retains world heavyweight championship, winning unanimous 12-round decision over 257-pound former champion George Foreman at Atlantic City.

20 **Toronto Argonauts** of CFL steal thunder of NFL Draft by signing Notre Dame's Rocket Ismail for guaranteed $18.2 million plus incentives over four years.

21 **Dallas Cowboys** make Miami-FL defensive tackle Russell Maryland first pick of 60th NFL College Draft.

23 **Philadelphia fires** first manager of the year after 4-10 start, replacing third-year pilot Nick Leyva with Jim Fregosi.

Five-time Wimbledon champion Bjorn Borg, 34, loses 6-2, 6-3, to 54th-ranked Jordi Arrese of Spain in first tournament match since retiring eight years ago.

Jockey Pat Day, trainer Mesh Tenney and three horses are elected to Thoroughbred Racing Hall of Fame.

25 **Boston Herald** sportswriter Lisa Olson sues New England Patriots for sexual harassment and civil rights violation.

26 **Buenos Aires police** arrest soccer star Diego Maradona for drug possession.

Sun	Mon	Tue	Wed	Thu	Fri	Sat
				1	2	3	4
5	6	7	8	9	10	11
12	13	14	15	16	17	18
19	20	21	22	23	24	25
26	27	28	29	30	31	

1 **Rickey Henderson** becomes baseball's all-time stolen base leader, swiping No. 939 against N.Y.Yankees to break Lou Brock's record in afternoon game at Oakland.

Nolan Ryan hurls seventh career no-hitter, striking out 16 in 3-0 victory against Toronto in night game at Arlington, Texas. The 44-year-old Ryan now has 304 wins.

4 **Kentucky Derby** won by Strike the Gold with Chris Antley in the saddle. Best Pal is second and Mane Minister third.

NBA coaching veteran John MacLeod, who resigned as coach of N.Y. Knicks on May 2, is introduced as Digger Phelps' successor at Notre Dame.

Sweden captures gold medal in World Hockey Championships, beating the Soviet Union 2-1 in Turko, Finland.

6 **Early morning car crash** in suburban Philadelphia lands Phillies' regulars Lenny Dykstra and Darren Doulton in hospital. Dykstra later charged with drunken driving.

8 **New York jury** finds gambler Howard Spira guilty on five counts of extortion involving former N.Y. Yankees general partner George Steinbrenner and three other charges.

CBS Televlsion chairman Laurence Tisch calls four-year, $1.06 billion baseball contract his network signed in 1988, "a mistake." CBS lost $165 million on baseball in 1990.

10 **The surprising** Minnesota North Stars, who were 27-39-14 during regular season, advance to Stanley Cup final, eliminating defending champion Edmonton in five games.

15 **Two-time Super Bowl** winner Bill Parcells, 49, resigns as head coach of N.Y. Giants after eight years and 85-52-1 record. Assistant Ray Handley takes over.

Queen Elizabeth II attends two innings of A's-Orioles game in Baltimore with President Bush. Oakland wins, 6–3.

18 **Hansel wins Preakness** by seven lengths under jockey Jerry Bailey. Kentucky Derby winner Strike the Gold finishes sixth.

19 **Willy T.Ribbs** makes Indianapolis 500 field on last day of qualifying, becoming first black driver to earn starting berth.

20 **NBA's MVP Award** goes to Michael Jordan of Chicago for second time in four years. Three-time winner Magic Johnson a distant second in voting.

Wide World Photos

Jose Canseco
Home Run King meets Queen.

21 **Chicago Cubs** fire Don Zimmer after 18-19 start, name Joe Altobelli interim manager (Jim Essian gets job May 22).

22 **NFL expansion plans** announced, league will add two new clubs for 1994 season.

Kansas City Royals fire John Wathan after 15-22 start, name Bob Schaefer interim replacement (Hal McRae gets job May 24).

23 **Baltimore Orioles** fire manager Frank Robinson after 13-24 start, name Johnny Oates to replace him.

Philadelphia righthander Tommy Greene throws no-hitter against Expos in Montreal, striking out 10 and walking seven.

25 **Pittsburgh Penguins** rout Minnesota, 8-0, in Game 6 to win first Stanley Cup. Mario Lemieux named Conn Smythe winner as MVP.

26 **Rick Mears outruns** Michael Andretti on last lap to win Indianapolis 500 for record-tying fourth time.

27 **Defending champion** Detroit loses Eastern Conference showdown with Chicago in four straight as Bulls advance to NBA finals for first time.

28 **Federal judge** David Doty, sitting in Minneapolis, clears way for NFL players to sue for free agency by ending league's labor exemption from antitrust law.

31 **Former L.A.Lakers** coach Pat Riley signs five-year, $6 million deal to lead N.Y. Knicks.

Sun	Mon	Tue	Wed	Thu	Fri	Sat
						1
2	3	4	5	6	7	8
9	10	11	12	13	14	15
16	17	18	19	20	21	22
23	24	25	26	27	28	29
30						

Wide World Photos

Payne Stewart
Open champion in overtime.

2 NBA Finals open in Chicago with Magic Johnson and Lakers beating Michael Jordan and Bulls, 93-91.

3 Thomas Hearns wins WBA light heavyweight title, scoring unanimous 12-round decision over champion Virgil Hill.

Montreal Expos fire manager Buck Rodgers after losing 10 of 11 to fall to 20-29. Coach Tom Runnells takes over.

High school lefthander Brien Taylor of Beaufort, N.C., selected by N.Y. Yankees as top pick in baseball amateur draft.

5 Federal judge Royce C. Lamberth rules in Washington, D.C., that NFL's exemption from antitrust laws ended when collective bargaining agreement with players expired in 1987.

NHL hands out annual awards: Brett Hull of St. Louis is MVP, Ed Belfour of Chicago is best goalie and rookie, and Boston's Ray Bourque is best defensman for fourth time.

6 Baseball commissioner Fay Vincent rules that 14 AL clubs will share 22 percent ($41.8 million) of the NL's $190 million expansion money, but must contribute three players each to draft stocking two new NL teams.

7 UNLV coach Jerry Tarkanian announces he will step down as Rebels basketball coach after 1991-92 season.

8 Belmont Stakes won by Preakness winner Hansel by a neck over Kentucky Derby winner Strike the Gold.

Defending champion Monica Seles wins second Grand Slam title of the year, taking French Open title in straight sets over Arantxa Sanchez Vicario.

LSU captures first College World Series title, beating Wichita St., 6-3, in Omaha.

9 First All-American French Open men's final since 1954 won by Jim Courier in five sets over Andre Agassi.

London Monarchs rule WLAF after shutting out Barcelona, 21-0, in first World Bowl before 61,108 at London's Wembley Stadium.

12 Chicago Bulls win first NBA title in five games, beating Lakers, 108-101, in L.A. Michael Jordan unanimous pick for MVP.

13 Lightning kills spectator as 91st U.S. Open golf gets underway at Hazeltine National GC in Chaska, Minn.

The National Sports Daily ceases publication after 16 months and losses of up to $100 million.

14 Sprinter Leroy Burrell beats Carl Lewis in 100 meters, setting world record of 9.90 seconds at U.S. National Championships in New York.

15 IOC awards 1998 Winter Olympic Games to Nagano, Japan. Salt Lake City second in vote.

17 Payne Stewart defeats Scott Simpson by two strokes to win 18-hole playoff for U.S. Open golf title.

19 UNLV coach Jerry Tarkanian blasts NCAA before House subcommittee investigating the college governing body's history of due process.

21 Wimbledon stunned as Monica Seles forfeits shot at Grand Slam by withdrawing three days before start of tournament. Undisclosed injury blamed for pullout.

Hockey Hall of Fame announces election of former N.Y. Islanders Mike Bossy and Denis Potvin. They join coach Scotty Bowman and linesman Neil Armstrong, who were named in March.

22 Quebec Nordiques select 18-year-old Eric Lindros as first pick in NHL draft, despite his warning that he will not sign with them.

26 Charlotte Hornets make college Player of the Year Larry Johnson the first pick in NBA draft.

28 Mike Tyson scores unanimous 12-round decision in rematch with Razor Ruddock at Las Vegas.

Sun	Mon	Tue	Wed	Thu	Fri	Sat
	1	2	3	4	5	6
7	8	9	10	11	12	13
14	15	16	17	18	19	20
21	22	23	24	25	26	27
28	29	30	31			

Wide World Photos

Steffi Graf
Wins third Wimbledon.

1 **Long-awaited rematch** of Carl Lewis and Ben Johnson takes place in Villeneuve D'Ascq, France, but Dennis Mitchell wins 100-meter race with Lewis second and Johnson seventh.

3 **Nine-time champion** Martina Navratilova beaten by 15-year-old Jennifer Capriati 6-4, 7-5 in Wimbledon quarterfinals. Also, John McEnroe fined $10,000 for verbally abusing official on July 1.

5 **National League** awards expansion franchises to Denver and Miami. Colorado Rockies and Florida Marlins each agree to pay $95 million entry fee and will begin play in 1993.

6 **Cleveland Indians** fire John McNamara after 25-52 first half and name coach Mike Hargrove as manager.

7 **Germany sweeps** Wimbledon singles titles, as Michael Stich defeats countryman Boris Becker in three sets. Steffi Graf beat Gabriela Sabatini for women's crown July 6.

AL umpire Steve Palermo listed in fair condition after getting shot in the back trying to break up a robbery in the parking lot of a Dallas restaurant.

9 **South Africa** invited back into Olympic movement by IOC after 21-year exile. Reinstatement comes two weeks after South Africa's parliament repealed its laws of racial segregation (apartheid).

Three-run homer by MVP Cal Ripken of Baltimore leads AL to 4-2 victory over NL in All-Star game at Toronto.

10 **Holyfield-Tyson** title fight set for Nov. 8 in Las Vegas. Heavyweight champ Evander Holyfield will get $30 million and former titleholder Mike Tyson $15 million.

College football bowl alliance formed to improve chances of an annual No.1 vs. No.2 bowl game on New Year's Day. Members include four bowls (Cotton, Fiesta, Orange and Sugar), four conferences (ACC, Big East, Big Eight, SEC and SWC) and Notre Dame.

11 **Calumet Farm** files for bankruptcy.

14 **Meg Mallon captures** second major golf title in three weeks, winning U.S. Women's Open by two strokes. Mallon won the LPGA Championship on June 30.

18 **Rocket Ismail** gains 213 total yards in CFL debut as Toronto trounces Hamilton, 41-18, before 41,178 at SkyDome.

21 **Australian golfer** Ian Baker-Finch shoots final round 66 to win British Open by two strokes at Royal Birkdale.

23 **Cincinnati reliever** Rob Dibble is thrown out of game with Chicago for throwing at baserunner Doug Dascenzo. Ejection comes on first day back from three-game suspension for throwing at batter Eric Yelding of Houston on April 11. He also threw a ball into the stands and hit a female fan on April 28.

26 **Montreal Expos'** Mark Gardner hurls no-luck, nine-inning no-hitter against Dodgers, losing 1-0 in the bottom of the 10th.

Mike Tyson accused of raping a Miss Black America beauty pageant contestant on July 19 in Indianapolis.

28 **Dennis Martinez** of Expos pitches 15th perfect game in major league history, blanking Dodgers 2-0, in L.A.

Miguel Indurain of Spain wins Tour de France by 3:36 over runner-up Gianni Bugno of Italy. Three-time winner Greg LeMond of U.S. finishes seventh, over 13 minutes behind.

Spain upsets United States, 2-1, to win Federation Cup women's tennis title in Nottingham, England.

29 **Final round 65** lifts Jack Nicklaus to four-stroke win over Chi Chi Rodriguez in 18-hole playoff for U.S. Seniors Open title.

31 **NBA salary cap** raised to $12.5 million for 1991-1992 season.

Rob Dibble suspended again, this time for four games, and fined $1,000 for throwing ball into stands on April 28 and accidently hitting female fan.

Sun	Mon	Tue	Wed	Thu	Fri	Sat
				1	2	3
4	5	6	7	8	9	10
11	12	13	14	15	16	17
18	19	20	21	22	23	24
25	26	27	28	29	30	31

Wide World Photos
Buck Rodgers
Unemployed three months.

1 **Troubled Argentine** soccer star Diego Maradona, suspended by FIFA until June of 1992 for drug abuse, announces retirement.

2 **Pan Am Games** begin with opening ceremonies in Havana, Cuba. Over 6,000 athletes from 39 nations will compete in 11th Games.

3 **Giant Victory**, driven by Jack Moiseyev, wins $1.24 million Hambletonian harness race.

Santa Monica Track Club quartet of Mike Marsh, Leroy Burrell, Floyd Heard and Carl Lewis ties 400-meter relay world record of 37.79 seconds in Monaco.

4 **Brazil stuns** U.S. women's basketball team, 87-84, at Pan Am Games. Forty-two game international winning streak snapped.

5 **Paul Brown dies.** Founder of Cleveland Browns and Cincinnati Bengals was 82.

Sergei Bubka clears 20 feet outdoors with 20-foot ¼-inch pole vault at Malmo, Sweden.

7 **Santa Monica** Track Club foursome of Mike Marsh, Leroy Burrell, Dennis Mitchell and Carl Lewis breaks 400-meter relay world record with time of 37.67 in Zurich.

Cincinnati manager Lou Piniella hit with $5 million defamation of character suit by umpires union for saying on Aug. 3 that NL ump Gary Darling "deliberately makes bad calls against the Reds."

8 **Another spectator** killed by lightning at major golf tournament as PGA Championship begins at Crooked Stick GC in Carmel, Ind.

11 **Rookie unknown** John Daly wins PGA Championship by three strokes with 12-under par 276.

White Sox rookie Wilson Alvarez throws no-hitter in second career start, blanks Baltimore, 7-0.

14 **Dave Winfield hits** 400th career home run off Minnesota's David West at Metrodome. Angels' 41-year-old slugger now 23rd on all-time HR list.

16 **ITF bars** Monica Seles from 1992 Olympics for refusing to play for Yugoslavia in Federation Cup.

18 **Pan Am Games** end with USA winning most medals (352), but Cuba beating the U.S. in gold medals 140-130.

20 **Miami quarterback** Dan Marino becomes NFL's highest-paid player, signing five-year contract extension for $25 million.

21 **IAAF doubles** drug abuse suspension period to four years and announces World Track & Field Championships will be held every two years instead of every four.

22 **Hard-line Communist** coup attempt collapses in Soviet Union after three days as population and military resist takeover.

24 **Taiwan routs** San Ramon Valley, Calif., 11-0, to win its 15th Little League World Series.

25 **Carl Lewis regains** world record in 100 meters with run of 9.86 seconds at World Track & Field Championships in Tokyo.

U.S. Amateur golf championship won by 41-year-old Mitch Vogues who beats 21-year-old Manny Zerman, 7 and 6. Vogues is the third oldest player to win title. Defending champion Phil Mickelson beaten in third round.

26 **Bret Saberhagen** of Kansas City hurls season's fifth complete-game no-hitter, beating White Sox at home, 7-0.

California replaces manager Doug Rader with Buck Rodgers, who was fired by Montreal on June 2.

No. 1 draft pick Brien Taylor signed by N.Y. Yankees to record $1.55 million minor league contract.

28 **College football** season opens as Penn State beats Georgia Tech, 34-22, in Kickoff Classic.

29 **Bob Johnson**, coach of the Pittsburgh Penguins and Team USA in upcoming Canada Cup, undergoes emergency surgery to remove cancerous brain tumor.

30 **Mike Powell breaks** Bob Beamon's 23-year-old long jump mark with world record leap of 29-feet, 4½-inches at Track & Field Championships in Tokyo.

Sun	Mon	Tue	Wed	Thu	Fri	Sat
1	2	3	4	5	6	7
8	9	10	11	12	13	14
15	16	17	18	19	20	21
22	23	24	25	26	27	28
29	30					

Wide World Photos

Randall Cunningham
Out for the season.

1 Opening day ligament injury to left knee knocks Philadelphia QB Randall Cunningham out for rest of NFL season.

American 400-meter relay team of Andre Cason, Leroy Burrell, Dennis Mitchell and Carl Lewis sets world record of 37.50 seconds on final day of World Track & Field Championships.

2 Jimmy Connors celebrates 39th birthday by reaching U.S. Open quarterfinals, outlasting 24-year-old Aaron Krickstein in 4 hours and 41 minutes, 3-6, 7-6 (10-8), 1-6, 6-3, 7-6 (7-4).

Bo Jackson returns, goes 0-for-3 with sacrifice fly RBI in debut with Chicago White Sox.

3 U.S. Court of Appeals orders NFL to pay more than $18 million in delinquent payments to players' pension fund.

NHL arbitrator awards St.Louis defenseman and captain Scott Stevens to New Jersey as compensation for Blues' signing of Devils' free agent forward Brendan Shanahan on July 24.

4 Major League Baseball finally recognizes 61 homers by **Roger Maris** as official single season HR record.

6 Whitey Herzog named chief baseball executive of California Angels.

7 Jimmy Connors' improbable march to U.S.Open title stopped in semifinals by Jim Courier, who wins in straight sets.

Monica Seles beats Martina Navratilova 7-6 (7-1), 6-1, to win U.S. Open and three of four 1991 Grand Slam titles.

8 Stefan Edberg wins first U.S.Open, routing Jim Courier, 6-2, 6-4, 6-0.

9 Former heavyweight champion Mike Tyson indicted on rape charges by Marion County (Ind.) grand jury. Trial set for January. Title fight still on for Nov.8 (see Oct.18).

11 Atlanta Braves trio of Kent Mercker, Mark Wohlers and Alejandro Pena hurl first combined no-hitter in NL history. Padres fall, 1-0.

13 U.S. gymnast Kim Zmeskal, 15, becomes first American to win women's all-around title at World Gymnastics Championships in Indianapolis.

14 Michigan snaps four-game losing streak against Notre Dame, beating Irish, 24-14, before 106,138 in Ann Arbor.

San Diego State freshman Marshall Faulk sets NCAA single game rushing record with 386 yards against Pacific.

16 Atlanta outfielder and NL stolen base leader Otis Nixon suspended 60 days for failing drug test.

Team Canada beats Team USA, 4-2, to win Canada Cup finals in two straight games.

18 Robert Helmick resigns under fire as president of U.S. Olympic Committee.

20 Olympic Stadium ordered closed for season in Montreal. Expos will play final nine home games on road. On Sept. 13, a 55-ton concrete beam fell from side of ballpark, forcing four games to be moved to New York and Philadelphia.

21 NBA-dominated 1992 U.S. Olympic basketball team announced. Ten pros, including Michael Jordan, Magic Johnson and Larry Bird on roster.

22 Don Shula gains 300th career coaching victory in NFL as Dolphins beat Green Bay, 16-13, in Miami.

28 Top-ranked Florida State routs No.3 Michigan, 51-31, before 106,145 in Ann Arbor.

U.S. Olympic Committee names William Hybl as interim president.

29 Ryder Cup returns to U.S. as American pros beat Europe, 14½-13½ on final hole.

Pat Bradley wins MBS Classic, gains entry into LPGA Hall of Fame with 30th career victory.

Sun	Mon	Tue	Wed	Thu	Fri	Sat
		1	2	3	4	5
6	7	8	9	10	11	12
13	14	15	16	17	18	19
20	21	22	23	24	25	26
27	28	29	30	31		

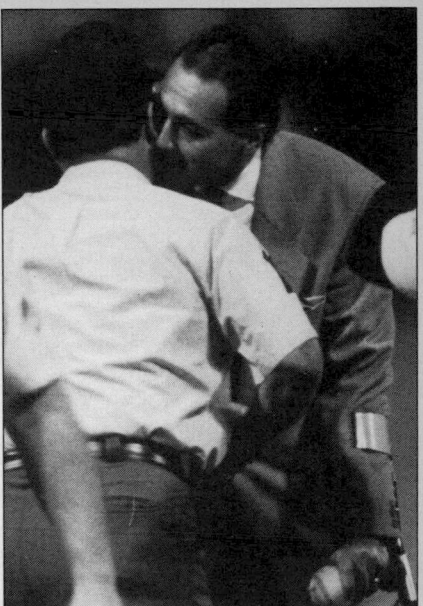

Wide World Photos

Steve Palermo
Emotional return for Series.

1 **Indianapolis Colts** fire 6th year coach Ron Meyer after 0-5 start, name Rick Venturi interim coach.

Scotty Bowman named interim coach of Pittsburgh Penguins while Bob Johnson recovers from brain cancer surgery.

All-time NASCAR driving champion Richard Petty announces he will retire after 1992 season. Petty has 200 career wins and seven Winston Cup titles.

2 **South Africa** granted provisional membership in International Tennis Federation and will play in 1992 Davis Cup.

3 **NHL begins 75th** season with original six teams— Boston, Chicago, Detroit, Montreal, N.Y. Rangers and Toronto—suiting up in replicas of original uniforms.

4 **Mark Messier traded** from Edmonton to N.Y. Rangers for center Bernie Nicholls and two forwards.

5 **Martina Navratilova** breaks Chris Evert's all-time record for match victories, notching No. 1,310 over Mary Joe Fernandez in semifinals of Milan Indoor tennis.

6 **Baseball regular season** ends with Pittsburgh, Atlanta, Toronto and Minnesota qualifying for NL and AL playoffs, and Baltimore playing final game at Memorial Stadium.

9 **Joe Montana undergoes** surgery to repair torn tendon in right elbow, 49ers' QB will miss rest of NFL season.

10 **Fourth manager fired** in four days as Seattle dumps Jim Lefebvre despite team's first winning record ever. He joins Yankees' Stump Merrill (Oct. 7), Red Sox' Joe Morgan (Oct. 8) and Brewers' Tom Trebelhorn (Oct. 9) on unemployment line.

Bo Jackson fails physical, will not play for L.A. Raiders this season.

11 **Golfer Chip Beck** shoots 59 in third round of Las Vegas Invitational, becoming only second player to ever break 60 on PGA Tour.

Chicago White Sox manager Jeff Torborg quits to accept 4-year deal as skipper of N.Y. Mets.

13 **Minnesota Twins** win AL pennant, eliminating Toronto in five games. OF Kirby Puckett named MVP.

N.Y. Rangers Winger Mike Gartner becomes 16th player to score 500 goals in NHL career.

15 **New England owner** Victor Kiam given 30 days to come up with $38 million to buy out minority partner Fran Murray or lose Patriots. NFL will take control of club until then.

16 **Dallas Mavericks** forward Roy Tarpley refuses to take drug test and is banned for life from NBA. He has already been suspended twice for drug abuse.

17 **Atlanta Braves clinch** NL pennant, beating Pittsburgh, 4-0 in Game 7. Pitcher Steve Avery named MVP.

17 **Angel Cordero Jr.** becomes only third jockey to win 7,000 races, riding Don't Cross the Law to victory in 8th race at Belmont.

18 **Holyfield-Tyson fight** postponed after rib cage injury forces Mike Tyson to pull out of scheduled Nov. 8 title bout.

Chicago Cubs fire 1st year manager Jim Essian, who replaced Don Zimmer in May.

19 **AL umpire Steve Palermo,** who was partially paralyzed when shot trying to break up a robbery in July, throws out first ball as World Series gets under way in Minneapolis. Twins win opener, 5-2.

20 **Michael Andretti wins** first Indy-car driving championship with victory in final CART race of season.

Ayrton Senna clinches third Formula One driving title with second place in Japanese Grand Prix.

22 **Holyfield-Tyson fight** called off indefinitely when two camps can't agree on rescheduling fight before start of Mike Tyson's rape trial on Jan. 27.

24 **Evander Holyfield** signs to fight Francesco Damiani of Italy on Nov. 23 in Atlanta. Holyfield will earn about $7 million.

26 **Buffalo Sabres acquire** center Pat LaFontaine from N.Y. Islanders in seven player deal.

27 **Minnesota wins** World Series for second time in five years as MVP Jack Morris blanks Atlanta, 1-0, in Game 7. Pinch hitter Gene Larkin drives in winning run in bottom of 10th at Metrodome.

30 **Top NBA Draft** pick Larry Johnson signs 6-year, $19 million contract with Charlotte Hornets, two days before start of season.

DECEMBER, 1991

6 Baseball Winter Meetings begin in Miami Beach.
7 Army-Navy Game (Philadelphia).
14 Heisman Trophy winner announced (New York).
23 NFL regular season ends.
28 NFL playoffs (2): AFC/NFC wild card games.
29 NFL playoffs (2): AFC/NFC wild card games.

JANUARY

1 Bowl games (8): Cotton (Dallas); Citrus (Orlando); Fiesta (Tempe); Hall of Fame (Tampa); Orange (Miami); Peach (Atlanta); Rose (Pasadena); Sugar (New Orleans).
4 NFL playoffs (2): AFC/NFC semifinal games.
4 U.S. Figure Skating Championships begin (Orlando).
5 NFL playoffs (2): AFC/NFC semifinal games.
7 NCAA Convention begins (Anaheim).
12 NFL playoffs (2): AFC/NFC championship games.
13 Australian Open tennis begins (Melbourne).
14 America's Cup Defender Selection Trials begin (San Diego).
18 NHL Hockey All-Star Game (Philadelphia).
25 America's Cup Challenger Selection Trials begin (San Diego).
26 Super Bowl XXVI (Minneapolis).

FEBRUARY

1 24 Hours at Daytona begins (Daytona Beach).
2 NFL Pro Bowl (Honolulu).
6 National Girls & Women in Sports Day.
8 Winter Olympics begin (Albertville).
9 NBA All-Star Game (Orlando).
16 Daytona 500 (Daytona Beach).
23 Winter Olympics end.
24 U.S. Women's Open bowling begins (Fountain Valley, Calif.).
28 U.S. Mobil Indoor Track Championships (New York).

MARCH

1 U.S. Swimming Olympic Trials begin (Indianapolis).
7 Iditarod Trail Sled Dog race begins (Anchorage to Nome).
11 Lipton International Tennis Championships begin (Key Biscayne, Fla.).
14 NCAA Indoor Track & Field Championships begin (Indianapolis).
15 NCAA Division I Basketball tournament seeds announced.
15 NFL Annual Meeting begins (Phoenix).
18 NCAA Women's Division I Basketball tournament begins.
19 NCAA Men's Division I Basketball tournament begins.
19 NCAA Division I Wrestling tournament begins (Oklahoma City).
22 PBA National bowling begins (Toledo).
24 World Figure Skating Championships begin (Oakland).
26 PGA Players Championship golf begins (Ponte Vedra, Fla.).
26 NCAA Swimming Championships begin (Indianapolis).
26 LPGA Dinah Shore golf begins (Rancho Mirage, Calif.).

APRIL

2 NCAA Division I Hockey Final Four begins (Albany).
4 NCAA Women's Basketball Final Four begins (Los Angeles).
4 NCAA Men's Basketball Final Four begins (Minneapolis).
5 NHL regular season ends.
5 U.S. Men's Open bowling begins (Canandaigua, N.Y.).
6 Baseball Opening Day.
8 NHL Stanley Cup playoffs begin.
9 Masters golf begins (Augusta).
14 World Gymnastics Championships begin (Paris).
19 NBA regular season ends.
20 Boston Marathon.
21 PBA Firestone Tournament of Champions bowling begins (Akron).
23 NBA playoffs begin.
26 NFL Draft begins (New York).
29 ABC Masters bowling begins (Corpus Christi, Texas).

MAY

2 Kentucky Derby (Louisville).
9 America's Cup Final begins (San Diego).
14 LPGA Championship golf begins (Bethesda, Md.).
16 Preakness Stakes (Baltimore).
23 NCAA Lacrosse Final Four begins (Philadelphia).
24 Indianapolis 500.
25 French Open tennis begins (Paris).
30 NCAA College World Series begins (Omaha).

JUNE

3 NCAA Track & Field Championships begin (Austin).
6 Belmont Stakes (Elmont,NY).
10 European Soccer Championship begins (Sweden).
11 U.S. Gymnastics Olympic Trials begin (Baltimore).
12 National Collegiate Rowing Championships begin (Cincinnati).
18 U.S. Open golf begins (Pebble Beach).
19 U.S. Track & Field Olympic Trials begin (New Orleans).
20 NHL Draft (Montreal).
20 24 Hours of Le Mans auto race begins (Le Mans, France).
22 Wimbledon tennis begins.
24 NBA Draft (Portland).

JULY

4 Tour de France cycling race begins (through July 26).
9 U.S. Senior Open golf begins (Bethlehem, Pa.).
14 Baseball All-Star Game (San Diego).
16 British Open golf begins (Muirfield).
23 U.S. Women's Open golf begins (Oakmont, Pa.).
25 Summer Olympics begin (Barcelona).

AUGUST

1 Hambletonian harness race (E.Rutherford).
8 All-American Soap Box Derby (Akron).
9 Summer Olympics end.
10 U.S. Women's Amateur golf begins (Hawthorne Woods, Ill.).
11 Women's Major Fast Pitch softball tournament begins (Redding, Calif.).
13 PGA Championship golf begins (St.Louis).
13 LPGA du Maurier Classic begins (Winnipeg).
25 U.S. Men's Amateur golf begins (Dublin, Ohio).
25 Little League Baseball World Series begins (Williamsport, Pa).
31 U.S. Open tennis begins (Flushing, N.Y.).

SEPTEMBER

6 NFL regular season opens.
11 Men's Major Fast Pitch softball tournament begins (Bloomington, Ill.).

OCTOBER

3 College football: Florida St at Miami-FL.
4 Baseball regular season ends.
7 Baseball AL/NL Championship Series begin.
10 College football: Oklahoma vs Texas (Dallas).
17 World Series begins (in city of NL champion).
31 Breeders' Cup horse racing (Gulfstream).

NOVEMBER

1 New York City Marathon.
16 Virginia Slims Tennis Championships begin (New York).
21 College football: Yale at Harvard; Michigan at Ohio St.; Nebraska at Oklahoma; USC at UCLA.
24 ATP Men's Tennis Championships begin (Frankfurt).
28 College football: Alabama vs Auburn (Birmingham); Notre Dame at USC.
29 CFL Grey Cup (Toronto).

DECEMBER

4 National Finals Rodeo (Las Vegas).
5 College football: SEC Championship Game (Birmingham); Army vs Navy (Philadelphia).
Note: NFL regular season ends Jan.4, 1993 and playoffs begin following week.

Princeton All-America **Hobey Baker** flew with the Lafayette Escadrille in World War I, but most of our sports heroes have not been warriors.

WARTIME SPORTS

War Bond

War and sports are kindred spirits, but the record shows star athletes and combat duty don't usually go together.

War and sport being kindred spirits—a connection that is easy to make but not always easy to take—what could be more natural in a "war year" than to find the two so mutually-inspirational?

Long before dawn's early light on January 28, 1991, American warriors on the Iraqi border forsook sleep and swarmed like moths to the glow of television sets situated at various stations to receive Super Bowl XXV. The chilled, black desert air was rent with the cries of homage to American football as they followed the action, and the course of their bets. "It brings home to here," said one Marine, snugged in a sleeping bag on the front row of a viewing area. He had Buffalo and four. In Tampa, at the same time but in a different time zone (Sunday afternoon, January 27), a Super Bowl crowd of 73,800, awash in red, white and blue, sang lusty backup for Whitney Houston to take the National Anthem to a breathtaking climax. Fans waved tiny American flags and chanted "U-S-A, U-S-A, U-S-A," and any reference to the "war in the Gulf" brought new bursts of approbation. The game itself was a good one as Super Bowls go (Giants 21, Bills 20), but

it played second fiddle to the rampant patriotism.

"This one's for our boys over there," said a middle-aged man in a Giants cap with a yellow ribbon pinned to the bill. He had a flag in one hand and a beer in the other, and tears in his eyes.

Well, why not? Reconciling the joy of sport with the joylessness of war is an old trick, and who is to say it shouldn't be done? Sport energizes as a metaphor for war—teams "battle," linebackers "blitz," quarterbacks throw "bombs"—and war reciprocates. In World War II, American pilots flew into combat wearing big league baseball caps sent them by favorite teams. "Play Ball" was the code name for the allied invasion of North Africa. General Norman Schwarzkopf characterized a crucial battlefield ploy in the rout of Iraq as a "Hail Mary," after the football pass play that calls for receivers to speed *en masse* downfield for a, uh, bomb.

The Gulf War was too small and too short to reconnect all the salient points, but sport and war have always been the best of bedfellows, and if it makes us uneasy to say so, it shouldn't. Much of early sport, after all, was derived from warring. With some contests you could hardly tell the difference—the bloody gladiatorial games, the jousting, the deadly boxing with leather thongs and metal studs. Early settlers in this country found American Indians playing a riotous

Author **John Underwood** is a former reporter and columnist for *The Miami Herald*, and a former senior editor at *Sports Illustrated*.

Gen. **Norman Schwarzkopf**, commander of allied forces in the Persian Gulf, briefing the press Feb. 27, on the "Hail Mary" strategy that helped bring Operation Desert Storm to a successful conclusion.

game that featured large numbers of participants thrashing at a ball (and each other) with curved sticks. Fractures and fatalities were considered part of the action. The game sprawled across the countryside, losing players as it went. The Indians called it "Teiontsesiksaheks," or baggataway. Today, we call it lacrosse.

True athletic ability in what we now think of as "team" sports celebrates the same qualities respected in the warrior: courage, fighting spirit, coolness under fire, fealty to the goals of the group, etc. The historical superstars of war have confirmed that good athletes make the best soldiers. The Duke of Wellington: "The battle of Waterloo was won on the playing fields of Eton." Douglas MacArthur: "Upon the fields of friendly strife are sown the seeds that, upon other fields, on other days, will bear the fruits of victory." Etc., etc. Tap into a war hero and chances are you'll find an athlete. The newly esteemed General Schwarzkopf lettered in three sports at West Point: wrestling, soccer and football (and sang tenor in the chapel choir). WWII Chief of Staff George C. Marshall was an All-Southern tackle at

VMI, Admiral William (Bull) Halsey a Navy fullback, and General George Patton an outstanding pentathlete good enough to finish fifth in the 1912 Olympics. MacArthur, decorated 13 times in World War I for "extreme bravery," was a West Point left fielder and football manager. He never really *stopped* managing his beloved Army teams.

When the Cadets beat Navy to complete an unbeaten national championship season in 1944, MacArthur wired from the Pacific: "We have stopped the war to celebrate. . . ."

But these were soldiers who happened to be athletes. Does the chemistry work when it's the other way 'round—when athletes, in a national emergency, are required to be soldiers? One reason we love sport so much is that it satisfies our competitive instincts. If war is the ultimate competition, it would follow that great athletes should naturally rush to take part.

And some do, with awesome enthusiasm.

On the eve of WWII, Hank Greenberg was among the first 650 men in the country to volunteer for the draft. His was a

Wide World Photos

Sgt. **Hank Greenberg** sits in the rear cockpit of a bomber at MacDill Field, Fla. and tells civilian visitor **Joe DiMaggio** about Army life in February, 1942.

notable sacrifice: a then-enviable $55,000 salary as the Tigers' home run king (and 1940 American League Most Valuable Player) in exchange for $21 a month Army pay. Greenberg's induction was so popular that 5,000 men of the Fifth Division cheered his arrival at Camp Custer, Michigan. He was later honored at an Armistice Day Parade, riding on a gun carrier. He trained as an antitank gunner, and went on maneuvers in Tennessee.

Then, having fulfilled the service commitment of the day, Greenberg was discharged. It was December 5, 1941. The war he rushed to get into hadn't even started yet. Two days later, the Japanese bombed Pearl Harbor. Greenberg reenlisted.

Ty Cobb, Christy Mathewson and George Sisler all volunteered for Chemical Warfare Service (the ''Gas and Flame'' division) in World War I. Bruce Smith of Minnesota, the 1941 Heisman Trophy winner, made it into the Navy as a combat pilot in 1942 by doing the physical fitness test virtually on one leg—to hide the fact that the knee of his other leg was permanently damaged. Barney Ross,

the former lightweight boxing champion, joined the Marines at age 32 and fought at Guadalcanal, where he cut down 20 Japanese soldiers in a fire fight and was awarded the Congressional Medal of Honor. Tom Harmon of Michigan, the 1940 Heisman winner, got the Silver Star flying combat for the Army Air Corps. Three times Harmon was shot down, once in occupied China where he was missing for 32 days. When he returned home to marry movie star—what else?—Elyse Knox, the bride's wedding gown was sewn from the silk of what was said to be one of Harmon's ''bullet-riddled'' parachutes.

But not every great athlete rushes into war at the first opportunity. Two of the most famous draft evaders of the century were not only athletes, but men who made their living fighting. Who were, in fact, terrific at it. And it is at this dogleg left in our perceptions that the sports/war mix gets a little quirky, so stay with us.

Jack Dempsey chose to skip World War I, ostensibly to serve in a defense plant. But among other bonehead moves that marked his life, Dempsey posed for a photograph that showed him ''working'' in a shipyard, bare to the waist and hefting a sledge hammer—in striped dress pants and patent leather shoes. Wrote Grantland Rice: ''If (Dempsey) had been a fighting man, he would have been in khaki when at 22 he had no other responsibility but to protect his own hide.''

Cassius Clay had only recently emerged as Muhammed Ali when he refused induction as a ''conscientious objector'' during the Vietnam war. Like Dempsey, he was vilified in the press. Like Dempsey, he botched the public relations. Among other things, he said, ''I ain't got nothin' against them Viet Cong.''

Both fighters were charged with draft evasion. Dempsey was tried and acquitted in 1920. Ali was found guilty, but never did jail time. His appeal took four years to reach the Supreme Court where, in 1971, the guilty verdict was reversed by an 8-0 vote.

Both fighters eventually made it back into the people's favor, Dempsey as a kind of rough-hewn national heirloom, complete with his own Broadway restaurant where he could be found until his death talking boxing and autographing napkins. People who knew Ali best said that it wasn't the Viet Cong that scared him out of the service, it was the prospect of getting shot by somebody on his own side—his popularity at the time being very much in doubt. Now, of course, he is a beloved symbol of black individuality who draws adoring crowds wherever he goes (ain't got nothing against them crowds).

But the point to make is that draft evasion is quite unnecessary for well-known athletes. A big waste of time.

Because anybody who knows anything about sports heroes and combat duty knows that the two don't usually go together. Joe Louis joined the Army in WWII with every stated intention of seeing combat, but the only fighting he did was in the ring—performing exhibitions for the troops and defending his title twice for Army and Navy relief funds. By the same token, it is highly unlikely that Dempsey and Ali would have ever "gone to war."

The larger point, however, is the more important one: we really wouldn't have wanted them to. Because although we demand that our sports heroes serve (and we foam at the mouth in our columns and statehouse chambers when they balk), we really are not at all eager to have them put in harm's way. We know them too well, and need them too much.

To understand that, and our own curious ambivalence on the subject, we should remember the experience of Ted Williams, who was hooted by the crowds and showered with hate mail in 1942 when he clung to his draft exemption as sole support of his mother to get in one more paycheck with the Boston Red Sox. It was typical of the times. Joe DiMaggio also played in '42, and when he held out for more money that spring, soldiers from Camp Blanding sent him a scornful invitation to join them at $21 a month. Thirty-three GIs signed a letter of protest to a serviceman's magazine when the Cardinals' Terry Moore attended the '43 World Series on a pass from his duty in the Panama Canal Zone. An entire local draft board in North Carolina resigned when its medical examiner rejected a minor league player on the grounds that he had varicose veins. The Williams controversy cooled when he re-registered after the '42 season and was called up by the Navy. He earned his wings and served as

Three-time world boxing champion **Barney Ross**, seen here receiving a sharpshooter's medal at Marine base camp in 1942, later won the Congressional Medal of Honor at Guadalcanal.

a flight instructor until his discharge in '45. But in 1952, at age 34, he was called back in for the Korean War, and not only did it cost him two more seasons from the heart of his career, it almost cost him his life. On one of the last of his 39 combat missions over North Korea, Williams was hit by enemy fire and had to crash-land his flaming jet on a remote airstrip near the 38th parallel. Williams didn't complain at the time, but he was deeply resentful. He thought the whole thing "very unfair," and blamed "the gutless politicians"—then-Senators Robert Taft and John F. Kennedy drew his particular scorn—for not interceding on his behalf.

And he was right. It *was* unfair. But more than that, it was dumb.

Because patriotic breastbeating aside, the truth is that while we would love to see our sports stars came home laden with medals, *we don't expect them to die*. That happens to real soldiers in war, and when it happens to one of our heroes, it's a downer of major proportions. Nile Kinnick of Iowa, the 1939 Heisman trophy winner, rushed to join the Naval Air Corps in '42, and crashed to his death trying to return to his aircraft carrier on a training mission. Big, bold, demoralizing headlines.

Hobey Baker rushed to join the Lafayette Escadrille in 1917 when he thought America was dragging its feet getting into WWI. The consummate athlete-warrior, Baker had made All-America in both hockey (the hockey equivalent of the Heisman is named in his honor) and football (he played without a helmet) at Princeton, but the dogfights over France thrilled him more than anything he had ever done and he won the *Croix de Guerre*. The day the war ended, Baker,

Red Sox star **Ted Williams** had the right stuff in combat too, flying 39 missions as a Marine fighter pilot in the Korean War.

Baseball Hall of Fame

dreading his return to an anti-climactic life on Wall Street, broke a pilot's taboo by going up for "one last flight." That's what it turned out to be. His Spad crashed nose-first into a field 100 yards from the landing strip. Princeton still grieves. Many athletes die in war, of course, but most of them are knights of lesser realms who go without fanfare. The entire starting lineup of the 1942 Montana State football team was killed in WWII, but it wasn't a national headline until the last one died, and even then it was treated more as a novelty. It may sound callous to say it, but it's better that way.

For it is one thing to have Joe DiMaggio slay the enemy with base hits for the camp team, or Joe Louis box exhibitions for "troop morale"—morale is a major factor in war and those are acknowledged morale boosters—it is quite another to read that Joe DiMaggio's legs have been blown off in combat, or that Joe Louis has been returned from the front in a body bag. Imagine the despair if it had been the starting lineup of the Chicago Bears instead of the Montana State team.

So in that ironic way war has of turning things inside out, "provisions" are made to keep that from happening. Strings are pulled, special treatment granted so that sport can help preserve the illusion that our heroes are indestructible.

In World War II, almost 250 active big league baseball players served in the military. Not one was killed. Some stars, indeed, saw action: Harry (The Hat) Walker of the Cardinals won the Bronze Star in Germany. Cecil Travis suffered frozen feet in the Battle of the Bulge. Bob Feller might have pitched his way safely through WWII in Hawaii had he not insisted on serving as an anti-aircraft gunner on the battleship Alabama with the Third Fleet. "I could've sat in Honolulu drinking beer, but the hell with that," Feller said. The Third Fleet saw action at Tarawa, Iwo Jima and the Marshall Islands.

But more often than not, it's more a challenge for the star athlete to get *into* war than out of it. As hard as he tried, Hank Greenberg never made it all the way to the front in WWII. The closest he came was as a base commander in China before being discharged (in time for the 1945 season). In Korea only one

UPI/Bettman

Cleveland Indians' pitcher **Bob Feller** (left) is sworn into the Navy four days after Pearl Harbor by Lt. Commander **Gene Tunney** in Chicago. Tunney is the former world heavyweight champion.

ex-big league player, Bob Neighbors, was killed, but Neighbors passed without notice. He had played only one season (1939), for a total of seven games with the St. Louis Browns. No big leaguers died in Vietnam.

The National Football League hadn't attained the status it now enjoys when 638 of its players served in WWII. Twenty were killed, but the only "name" in the group was Giants lineman Al Blozis. No NFL player was killed in Korea, and only Bob Kalsu of the Bills was killed in Vietnam.

No one knows for sure when special treatment for star athletes became accepted. Bill Tilden was inducted into the Signal Corps in 1917, but was diagnosed with flat feet and sent to a base in Pittsburgh, where he played out WWI under a commanding officer who loved tennis. It may have started there. But there has never been any real criticism of the practice. Indeed, it was encouraged.

Many of the best teams in sport in WWII were put together by wheeling, dealing commanding officers of military bases. The Navy squad at Norfolk was so well stocked Pee Wee Reese couldn't make the starting lineup—he couldn't beat out Phil Rizzuto.

The Great Lakes Naval Training Center near Chicago could have won either major league pennant and the NFL championship with the athletes it accumulated. Feller was there for one baseball season, as were Virgil Trucks, Schoolboy Rowe, Johnny Mize, Billy Herman, Pinky Higgins, Ken Keltner and Gene Woodling. Great Lakes won 48 of 50 games in 1944, and beat 11 of the 12 big league teams it was able to coax into competition. In its last game of the year, Great Lakes embarrassed the Cleveland Indians, 17-4.

Most of the good football players were drafted off college campuses and wound up at bases or colleges with V-12 and A-12 programs and actually competed as "college" teams. They were even included in the polls. In 1943, according to the AP, the second best team in the country after Notre Dame was Iowa Pre-Flight. Great Lakes was sixth, Del Monte Pre-Flight eighth, and March Field 10th. In 1944, 10 of the top 20 were service teams—12, if you include No.1 Army and No.4 Navy. Notre Dame's only loss in 1943 was to Great Lakes. In fact, from 1942-45, the Irish were a mere 1-2-1 against them.

So why go through the charade of drafting top athletes at all? Because if we didn't it would spoil a very real need for them to appear to be part of the war effort—which, of course, they are. In much the same way as Bob Hope has been, or the Andrews Sisters. Besides that, the fans back home need to experience a little "sacrificing," too, and what better way than to be made to cheer the leftovers and the left-behinds?

A certain number of abolitionists always try to sacrifice sport entirely when the guns begin to shoot, apparently out of embarrassment that something so warlike would be allowed when actual war is going on. (They never suggest blackening movie theaters or cancelling the opera, only spectator sport.) President Franklin D. Roosevelt issued his famous "green light" letter to baseball early in WWII, bidding the games go on as a necessary diversion—something for both the front and the homefront to tie to.

As for the quality of play, it was every bit as impaired as it should have been. Manpower shortages made for malfunctioning leagues and patchwork teams. To call them second-rate would be to overrate them. In 1943, the depleted Pittsburgh and Philadelphia franchises of the NFL joined to become the "Phil-Pitt Steagles."

The Steagles, in combined form, were not "twice as good"; they were "doubly bad." In their next incarnation the Steelers allied with the Cardinals in 1944, and were even worse, finishing 0-10.

But, ah, only those who have no appreciation for the unusual, no affection for the bizarre and the absurd, would conclude that the home fans got short shrift. As with the fascination we have for watching a one-legged man dance, sport, if anything, gets more interesting in wartime.

The analogy isn't as much a reach as it sounds. A one-armed man, Pete Gray, played in 77 games for the St. Louis

Browns in 1945. Bert Shepard, a war veteran with an artificial leg, pitched a game for the Senators. Service rejects of all kinds (the color blind, the hard of hearing) made teams. George Case of the Senators, 4-F due to a shoulder problem, ran smack into centerfielder George Binks a number of times chasing flies because Binks couldn't hear him calling for the ball.

Desperate for players, the St. Louis Cardinals took out a help-wanted ad in The Sporting News in 1943. Branch Rickey of the Dodgers sent 20,000 letters to high school coaches, seeking recommendations. Among the fuzzy cheeks Rickey hired were shortstop Tommy Brown, age 16, and three teenagers who made the 1944 Dodger pitching staff: Ralph Branca, Clyde King and Cal McLish. Cincinnati signed 15-year-old Joe Nuxhall, let him pitch one game (two-thirds of an inning, for a 67.50 earned run average), and didn't invite him back until he grew up—in 1952.

The golden oldies were even more fascinating. The 1945 Yankees activated a batting practice pitcher named Paul Schreiber, who hadn't played in a big league game since 1923. Jimmy Foxx, long since finished as a slugger, pitched in nine games for the Phillies. And Paul Waner returned to the Boston Braves as a pinch hitter at age 42. Inserted in the lineup one hot August afternoon, he quickly wore himself out chasing down two triples. When another ball was hit his way, Waner ran for it, stretched out his glove—and collapsed in a heap. The ball came to rest a few feet away, but Waner didn't move. He was exhausted.

Under such pressure do miracles occur. The St. Louis Browns, who were never called anything but "lowly" in all their history (it was like part of their nickname: "The Lowly Browns"), fielded an all-4F infield in 1944—and won their only American League pennant. In '43, Bronko Nagurski came out of a six-year retirement at age 35 to help lead the Bears to the NFL championship, then retired again.

Mainly, however, it was a time to embrace mediocrity, and if came with a sense of humor, all the better. The Cubs' Lou Novikoff, whose stunning inability to field batted balls would have kept him out

Philadelphia A's manager **Connie Mack** (center left) and the Kenosha (Wisc.) Comets before an All American Girls Professional Baseball League game during World War II.

of the majors forever if it hadn't been for WWII, made it to Chicago. The Mad Russian hung on through 1944, singing and playing his harmonica in the clubhouse and doing impressions. Manager Charlie Grimm saw fiscal beauty in the beast: "People are willing to pay good money to see a ball go through Lou's legs." And they did. Proving forever that the American sports fan will support the handicapped, 12 of the 16 major league teams made money those years. A 15-year American League attendance record was broken in 1945.

The colleges, meanwhile, were a beehive of improvisation. College players earmarked for service were switched from school to school, depending on their training requirements. As a result, Wisconsin's Elroy Hirsch and Minnesota's Bill Daley wound up playing football at Michigan. Northwestern's lineup for its '43 game with Minnesota included eight former Minnesota players who had helped the Gophers whip the Wildcats the year before. Alex Agase of Illinois also played for Purdue, and made All-America at both schools.

If war must be blamed for the confusion, so must it be credited with the innovations such conditions inspire. Unlimited substitution in football was born one afternoon during WWII when Fritz Crisler of Michigan, facing a far superior West Point team, kept shoving fresh players into the breach. Basketball initiated goaltending as a foul with the new dominance in the game of players too tall for military service—for example, 6-10 George Mikan of DePaul and the 7-foot Bob Kurland of Oklahoma A&M. Scores soared. Fans applauded.

Night baseball was encouraged in WWII so that factories producing war goods wouldn't have as many workers skipping off during the day. But civil defense officials often called for black-outs at night, and they came without warning, sometimes in the middle of a pitch. Debates raged over who had done what to whom before the lights went out. In one minor league game, when the lights came back on second base was missing. Perhaps the most intriguing phenomenon of all was the birth and short, sweet life of "The All American Girls Professional

Baseball League." Dreamed up by Philip Wrigley, owner of the Cubs, the AAGPBL was a kind of benevolent specter in bare legs. The game was called baseball, but it really wasn't. The balls were bigger, the base paths shorter, the pitches thrown underhanded (until 1948, when after an annual series of rules changes the game did begin to resemble the real thing), and the hitting was anemic. A team could lead the league in batting with a .218 average, and one did.

As Wrigley saw it, the game was secondary to how good the girls looked. Men coached the players, but beauty expert Helena Rubenstein taught them the *real* skills: how to apply lipstick, how to style their hair, how to take off their coats like ladies. Team nicknames pounded home their femininity: the Racine "Belles," the Fort Wayne "Daisies," the Kalamazoo "Lassies." No butch haircuts, no long pants on or off the field. On the field the girls wore short skirts that exposed their legs to the paying customers—and also to the rigors of sliding, which produced some spectacular strawberries.

The girls drew pretty well, and were happy in their work. Why not? They were pulling down $60 to $125 a week, the envy of many men in regular jobs during the war. Dorothy Collins, a pitcher for Fort Wayne who won more than 20 games several times, enjoyed herself so much she played when she was six months pregnant with her first child.

The AAGBL finally de-materialized in 1954, but its impact marches on. A special place in the Hall of Fame was granted in 1988. A movie about it is in progress. Who knows how great its effect has been on the advance of women's sport in America, but clearly a door had been opened, if only to reveal that women with painted lips could also work up a significant sweat.

War does that to sport—opens doors, makes converts, spreads the word. The Civil War is generally credited with fertilizing the interest in baseball in the South. Yankee teams played it there, sometimes as prisoners of war. At Hilton Head, S.C., 40,000 soldiers were said to have watched a game between teams from the 165th New York Volunteer Infantry. The pollination was extended into the Caribbean by the Spanish-American War.

Baseball is now the national pastime in Nicaragua partly because American Marines occupied that country four times in the first half of the century.

The French Army was ordered to learn baseball when American soldiers brought it there in WWI. Canadian forces started a league in England that had more than 100 teams. WWII spread the game into the Pacific, where many of the contests between service teams were integrated. It doesn't take much of a stretch to believe that those good examples of racial melding had a hand in breaking down the color line in the big leagues in 1947.

To say that sport contributes to the healing process after a war is to say the obvious. The one and only "Inter-Allied Games," a kind of military Olympiad, was held in Paris in 1919, in a stadium built for the occasion and named after General Pershing. It brought together 1,500 athletes from 18 nations to compete for two weeks in what was called "the most revealing, most harmonizing, most natural way"—through athletics. In post-WWII Germany, a baseball diamond was cut for play in the grass of the huge stadium at Nuremberg where the Nazi Party had held its rallies before the war.

The one and only "Atom Bowl" football game was played on New Year's Day, 1946, in Nagasaki, Japan, virtually on the spot where the bomb struck in August the year before. The two teams—one quarterbacked by Notre Dame's '43 Heisman winner, Angelo Bertilli—had to play touch instead of tackle because the field was littered with pieces of brick and slithers of steel and glass.

The brief Gulf War, fought solely by the new "professional" all-volunteer military—no draft necessary, no enlistments called for—would seem to have touched sport only lightly. Some reborn abolitionists wanted to cancel Super Bowl XXV because of it, but there was no real danger of that. Sooner or later, however, we will be given evidence to show that sport did more for the war effort than just improve the television opportunities at the front, or the content of our lead general's briefings.

And we'll learn that the war made an imprint on sport, too, in some way or another—most likely for the better.

It always seems to work out that way. □

Minnesota outfielder **Kirby Puckett** reacts to his 11th-inning home run in Game Six, which forced a seventh and deciding game against Atlanta in one of the most thrilling World Series ever.

BASEBALL

BASEBALL
by Peter Gammons

Fall Classic!

In a World Series that will rank with the greatest ever,
Jack Morris and the Twins peak in the seventh game.

It was 3:30 the afternoon of the seventh game, and Twins third baseman Mike Pagliarulo was hitting baseballs off a tee into a screen.

"Didn't they play nine-game series back around the turn of the century?" asked Pagliarulo. Yes.

"Then why can't we?" he said. "I wish this could go on forever."

The 1991 World Series was one that could have lasted forever. But, instead, it went to a seventh game after an American Hero named Kirby Puckett hit an 11th inning homer, and it became history when Jack Morris turned in one of the greatest clutch performances ever as the Twins stole the 1-0 finale and their second world championship in five years.

It was a Series in which four games were decided on the final pitch, which is twice as many as ever before. It set records for extra inning games (3), and five times the final margin was a single run. It featured a third game in which the only players Minnesota manager Tom Kelly didn't use were two starting pitchers. There were two unforgettable home plate collisions, two straight games in which the winning run slid around Twins catcher Brian Harper and even a seventh game

Fred Snodgrass/Bill Buckner goat in Lonnie Smith of the Braves.

Played before a rocking crowd that exchanged Tomahawk Chops and Homer Hankies, the finale was one for the ages. It began when the leadoff hitter Smith shook hands with Harper, whom Smith had flattened in the fourth game. The handshake served as a symbol of the Series' complete lack of acrimony or negativity. In the ninth inning, Braves catcher Greg Olson turned to Harper and said, "Is this what we've waited all our lives for, or what? And, to think, we have the best seat in the house." Then, finally, when pinch hitter Gene Larkin's fly ball fell in the outfield, warrior Jack Morris had won the game of his lifetime for his hometown team (his hometown paper, the *St. Paul Pioneer-Press*, had as its front page headline, "St. Jack").

"This was arguably the greatest World Series ever," said Commissioner Fay Vincent. "And a very important one for baseball." Indeed, 1991 may or may not be greater than 1912 or '24 or '34, or '47 or '75, but it has its place. The '75 series helped boost the game; football had become king thanks to television, and that classic between the Reds and Red Sox, with six or eight Hall of Famers on the field, not only glamorized the game—just months before the Messersmith Decision opened up the free agency gates—but it was the year television really learned

---

Peter Gammons is a columnist for *The Boston Globe* and ESPN's major league baseball analyst.

Lonnie Smith of the Braves (left) was out at home in this Game Four collision with Twins' catcher **Brian Harper**. Their handshake before Game Seven symbolized the Series' lack of acrimony.

baseball. In 1991, baseball was glamorous, perhaps too glamorous—with players averaging more than $900,000 a year apiece. It had become a game whose image was mercenary, and thus a perfect time for two fresh, new teams to battle joyfully right to the 10th inning of the seventh game, proving that no matter what they're making, some players do really give a damn whether they win or lose.

Like 1987, it was a Series in which each team won every game at home. "I lost all four in this Metrodome place with the Cardinals in '87, too," said Braves' third baseman Terry Pendleton. "I never want to play here again unless I'm in a Twins uniform." The Braves started out with a disadvantage because their two best pitchers down the stretch, Steve Avery and John Smoltz, had to work the final two games in Pittsburgh and so they had to open with Charlie Leibrandt and Tom Glavine. Minnesota swept the first two games 5-2 and 3-2, winning the first behind Morris and the second when third baseman Scott Leius homered in the eighth off Glavine.

Back in Atlanta, the Series rose to another level. Game Three was unforgettable, a 12-inning classic that Chili Davis tied in the eighth with a two-run homer off Alejandro Pena. Minnesota used 23 players, and in the 10th, 11th and 12th had the winning run in scoring position. In the top of the 12th, it came down to the bases loaded and two outs against veteran Jim Clancy with pitcher Mark Guthrie batting. Kelly gambled, sending closer Rick Aguilera—a terrific hitter—up for Guthrie. Aguilera hit a line drive to center field and had to go in to pitch. If the game had gone three more innings, Kelly likely would have had to pitch left-fielder Dan Gladden and use Morris in left. In the bottom of the 12th, off-released Jerry Willard's fly ball produced the winning run and the Series had taken on the look of a classic.

The Braves went up three games to two with 3-2 and 14-5 wins, the former when Mark Lemke knocked in David Justice with two out in the bottom of the ninth, the second straight night that the winning run scored with two out.

The Braves' 14-5 blowout in Game Five also starred Justice and Lemke. Justice had a two-run homer and five RBI, while Lemke tripled twice and drove in three. Lemke, a .234 hitter during the regular season, was a sensation in the Series, batting .417.

The Series went back to the Thunderdome with the Braves one game away from their first title since 1957 and Avery and Smoltz in line to pitch.

Puckett, who was 3-for-18, came out for extra hitting at 3:15 the afternoon of the sixth game. "This is my night," he said. "It's time to hoist this team on my back. Watch me."

In the first inning, Puckett tripled to key a two-run rally for an immediate lead off Avery. Then, when Scott Erickson was being hit hard and trying to survive, Puckett made a sensational, leaping catch off the left center field glass atop the fence, which kept the game tied at 2-2 and might have prevented a blowout. Puckett later knocked in another run for a 3-2 lead, then, finally, in the 11th, he greeted Leibrandt—Cox's bizarre choice to relieve Pena—with the home run that took it to seven. "That might have been one of the greatest individual World Series performances ever," said Morris.

It was, Jack, but yours was greater. "Smoltz came out with such incredible stuff that I had to pitch to survive," said Morris. And survive, he did. Morris blew away Pendleton and Ronnie Gant with two on and one out in the fifth. Then in the eighth came the blunder of the Series. With Smith on first and none out, Pendleton hit a shot to left-center. Smith was running on the pitch and did not look up. He never picked up the ball, and as he looked around to find it, he saw Chuck Knoblaugh on his knees, pretending to start a double play. Smith hesitated, stopped, and could get no further than third. Given the break, Morris blew them away, finishing with a forkball that Sid Bream hit into a double play. The Twins then had the bases loaded in the bottom of the eighth and failed to score, and, finally in the 10th, Gladden hustled a double out of a bloop into left center. After a bunt and two intentional walks, Kelly sent up Gene Larkin, who hit a fly ball for the winning run. Morris threw 122 pitches in 10 innings, allowed seven hits

Worst to 1st: How Braves, Twins Did It

Never in baseball history had a team finished in last place one year, then finished first the next. So, naturally, this being 1991, not only did one team, the Minnesota Twins, accomplish this historic feat, but there had to be a sequel. So the Atlanta Braves immediately came out with Worst-to-First II.

In 1990, the Braves were 65-97, which was the worst record not only in the National League West, but in the majors. The Twins finished 74-88, some 29 games behind the Oakland Athletics. "We'd like to say this all went according to plan," said Twins general manager Andy MacPhail. "But our year is a testament to a lot of plans working out the way we hoped.

"We knew we had the foundation for a good team because we had such good young pitching," said Atlanta GM John Schuerholz. "So when we went out and signed some free agents, we were fairly certain that we could reach respectability. But all of a sudden respectability got out of hand and look where we ended up."

Schuerholz had actually been brought in from Kansas City the previous October, five months after Bobby Cox moved downstairs from the general manager's chair to the manager's hot seat during a disappointing season in which the Atlanta fans and media became impatient with Cox's rebuilding. But as Schuerholz pointed out during the season, "rebuilding an organization isn't an instant gratification thing, and Cox laid a foundation that we can build upon for years. Who else could walk into a GM job and be handed a pitching rotation of three potential Cy Young candidates (Tom Glavine, John Smoltz and Steve Avery)?" As modest as Schuerholz may be, Cox found out just how ambitious and industrious his new boss was when Schuerholz acquired pitcher Mike Bielecki and catcher Damon Berryhill from the Cubs with a week left in the season to get an early start on 1992. "When players know that the front office is as competitive as the players, you have an ideal situation," said catcher Greg Olson.

In reality, the success of both the Twins and Braves was the residue of hard work, luck, the traditional farm system approach and free agents. The biggest difference was that the Twins had a foundation that had already won. Just four years before, Minnesota stole the World Series from the Cardinals, and Kirby Puckett, Greg Gagne, Dan Gladden, Kent Hrbek, Randy Bush, Al Newman and Gene Larkin were left over from that team. However, not one pitcher remained from the '87 champs. "That staff was essentially four pitchers," said MacPhail. Bert Blyleven was dealt after 1988, Jeff Reardon and Juan Berenguer left as free agents, and on July 31, 1989, MacPhail made the bold move of trading World Series and Cy Young Award hero Frank Viola to the Mets. "We knew that we were in the strongest division in baseball, that that division was built upon pitching and that we had to rebuild our pitching staff," explained MacPhail. In return, the Twins got Rick Aguilera, whose 42 saves in '91 made him one of the league's three best relievers. They got Kevin Tapani, who was 16-9 and their most consistent starter, as well as lefthander David West.

MacPhail rebuilt his pitching staff with that trade. Then in '91, his farm system and free agency came together. Actually, there was luck involved. Because of the collusion decision, the Twins lost Gary Gaetti and Berenguer to new look free agency in January. MacPhail had tried to sign free agent Mike Boddicker, but when Boddicker went to Kansas City, he signed St. Paul native Jack Morris and Angel DH Chili Davis. His fastball restored, Morris returned home to be the bellwether of the staff, winning 18 games and being the first pitcher ever to start Opening Day, the All-Star Game and the playoff and World Series openers. Out of the farm system came Scott Erickson, who started 14-4 and won 20 games. Presto! the Twins had the best Big Three starters in the league, and Davis hit 29 homers as DH. Not only that, but MacPhail signed Mike Pagliarulo to replace Gaetti and Pags hit .279. He signed vagabond Carl Willis as a minor league free agent, and he filled out the bullpen by going 8-3.

Schuerholz took over the Braves and made an immediate impact. He sought to rebuild the defense, and signed three of the best at their positions—Terry Pendleton (third base), Sid Bream (first) and Rafael Belliard (shortstop). When the season started, he needed a leadoff hitter and stole Otis Nixon away from Montreal. Until he

Atlanta catcher **Greg Olson** jumps into the arms of pitcher **John Smoltz** after the Braves won the NL West.

was suspended in September for failing a drug test, Nixon was leading the majors in steals with 72. Schuerholz needed an experienced closer for the stretch, and right before the August 31 trading deadline turned to the Mets for Alejandro Pena, who simply pitched 15 games, saved 13 and won two.

But it was the organization that Cox had rebuilt from the bottom that was the heart of Atlanta's revival. Glavine won 20 games, Avery 18. They were the orchids of the scouting department, but Cox also drafted and developed such brilliant young prospects as Mark Wohlers, Mike Stanton and Kent Mercker. He had traded for John Smoltz and Charlie Leibrandt. Budding stars David Justice, Ronnie Gant, Brian Hunter and Keith Mitchell all came out of the system, while catcher Greg Olson was a minor league free agent.

"Both the Braves and Twins did great jobs building creatively," said Whitey Herzog, a month after taking over the California Angels. "But the difference between last and first place isn't as great as it used to be."

After all, the '91 Angels were the first last-place team ever to finish at .500, so the difference between the Worst Angels and First Twins was simply fodder for the winter fires.

Wide World Photos

St. Paul native **Jack Morris** came to the Twins as a free agent at the start of the year and ended up as the World Series MVP.

and was the MVP.

Three starts in nine days. Two wins, one no decision. Morris pitched more innings than all the other starters combined and had a 1.17 earned run average. He was Bob Gibson, Sandy Koufax and Smokey Joe Wood all rolled into one. "Maybe it's good it ends here," said Pagliarulo. "But the way we feel, we could play all winter."

The Minnesota-Atlanta match-up came out of two league championship series that developed into the Las Vegas bookies' worst nightmare: the Tomahawk Chop against the Homer Hankies. As the Braves took Pittsburgh in seven games in what will forever be remembered as the series a 21-year old kid named Steve Avery applied for early admission to the

history books and the Twins wiped out the Blue Jays, the bookies prepared for a $10-12 million loss with what were the two longest shots—250-to-1—to make the World Series. Their only consolation was that as Native Americans protested the Atlanta crowds' chops and war chants, Jane Fonda was finally on the wrong side of a right issue.

It wasn't as if the Twins won the ALCS in conventional fashion. They actually lost a game in the Metrodome for the first time in eight post-season home games. Then they went across the border and swept the Blue Jays in three straight with the ever-lovable Kirby Puckett as MVP.

But the 1991 playoff series that will linger in memory was the Braves' thrilling seven game win over Pittsburgh, which may rank just below the 1980 and '86 NLCS playoffs.

The 98-64 Pirates had been the rational, if not sentimental favorites going in, and when Doug Drabek bested 20-game winner Tom Glavine, 5-1, in the opener, it appeared the Bucs might be on their way. But in Game Two, Avery forced the series' first turnaround. In what Pirate manager Jim Leyland called "the best performance I saw all year," Avery fanned nine and allowed six hits before Alejandro Pena closed out the 1-0 victory—Atlanta's first after seven straight post-season losses. The game was won when Pittsburgh's brilliant fielding Steve Buechelle misplayed Mark Lemke's hopper inside the third base bag, one of those hairpin turns that marked the seven games.

The Braves went home and battered 20-game winner John Smiley 10-3, but then the Pirates turned the series back their way with two more dramatic victories. Catcher Mike (Smokey) Lavalliere, 0-for-3 during the season as a pinch hitter, singled for a dramatic 3-2 victory, which in turn was followed by a Pittsburgh 1-0 win that was decided when David Justice stumbled rounding third in the fourth inning and was ruled to have missed the bag, thus erasing the Braves' last chance against Zane Smith.

But then Avery, who just three years before chose the Braves over Stanford when he was the third pick in the nation, did it again. He blew Pittsburgh away for eight innings (extending his personal streak to a record 16⅓ without a run). Then in the ninth, catcher Greg Olson—who grew up outside Minneapolis and was actually let go by the Twins in 1989—hit a double for the only run and Atlanta won a 1-0 masterpiece. The drama lasted right to the last out, as Andy Van Slyke battled Pena for seven pitches with the tying run on base, barely missing hits down each foul line, before Pena froze him with a changeup for the third strike. The next night the Braves smoked Smiley for three runs in the first inning and Smoltz dominated Pittsburgh's lineup with an eight-strikeout, six-hit, 4-0 victory that brought the Braves their first pennant in Atlanta.

"It will be a long time before we see much better pitching than that in any series," said Braves manager Bobby Cox. "I don't think the people in Pittsburgh will ever forget Avery."

Well, maybe they'll just forget baseball in Pittsburgh, period; there were more than 10,000 empty seats for the seventh game.

It was as if the city accepted that it was the end of an era. For the second straight year, Barry Bonds, Andy Van Slyke and Bobby Bonilla (a combined 17-for-75, .200, 1 HR, 3 RBI) failed to hit as the Bucs scored seven runs in their final six games. Over them hung the spectre of Bonilla, Lavalliere and Buechelle leaving for free agency and Leyland being openly discussed as a potential manager for the Chicago White Sox.

The Twins won more easily in the AL's War of the Domes, but they, too, needed drama. Pagliarulo, whose average in 1988 and 1989 had fallen to .216 and .197 and who was so desperate for a job that he attended the winter baseball meetings and hung out in the hotel lobby, capped his marvelous (.279) comeback year by hitting a 10th inning pinch hit homer off rookie Mike Timlin to give the Twins a 3-2 victory in what unquestionably was the fork in the series. In this game, Tom Kelly yanked 10-game winner Scott Erickson with a 1-2 count on Joe Carter and the Twins down 2-1 and brought in a *lefthander*, David West. West then struck out Carter, fanned two more righthanders, and Kelly guided his bullpen through six shutout innings and stole a game Toronto will not soon forget. "Better guts than brains sometimes," said Kelly.

Atlanta's **Steve Avery** shut down Pittsburgh for 16⅓ innings in the NLCS and won MVP honors.

The Minnesota manager is known for his self-deprecating style, but his tireless preparation and superb handling of this pitching staff was a big part of his team's success. The bullpen set a playoff record with 18⅓ innings without allowing an earned run, shutting out the Jays for five innings of the 8-5 fifth game. Altogether, it was not a pleasant series for the Blue Jays, whose manager, Cito Gaston, was in pain with a bad back and whose primary power hitter, Carter, injured his ankle in Game Three and was forced to bravely play on one leg. "We thought this was our year," said GM Pat Gillick.

In the National League, the year, at least the regular season portion of it, came down to a cold and windy October night at Candlestick Park in San Francisco where thousands of Giants fans pumped their arms forward, doing the Tomahawk Chop that had become the romance dance of America's Cinderella Braves. The next afternoon, Oct.5, there was the split screen image of Braves' pitcher Smoltz, on the field in Atlanta, watching a TV monitor as the Giants eliminated the Los Angeles Dodgers on the west coast.

The mice had roared: the Braves had risen from last to first and knocked off the IBM Dodgers.

It was a season in which nearly half the Opening Day managers were gone by the World Series, and the Cubs, who once featured a college of coaches, burned through two skippers. There was a manager a day fired in a three-day stretch in May and a four-day stretch in October, and three of the latter had managed winning teams. Detroit had the American League leaders in home runs and wins, and they were both imports from Japan.

It was the year of streaks, with the Rangers and Twins each hitting the 14-win mark, and another year that Cal Ripken kept on running for another 162 games and posted Player of the Year numbers. It was the year that a new Comiskey Park opened, with Frank Tanana beating the White Sox, and Baltimore's Memorial Stadium closed, with Frank Tanana beating the Orioles.

History was observed: the 50th anniversary of Ted's .406 and Joe D's 56-game streak, the 40th anniversary of Bobby Thomson's homer and the 30th of Roger Maris' 61st. The future was richened with a 19-year old kid from North Carolina named Brien Taylor getting $1.55 million from the Yankees. Jose Canseco was photographed coming out of Madonna's apartment, Bo Jackson threw down his crutches, Darryl Strawberry found The Lord in L.A., Rickey Henderson compared himself to Mike Gallego (then almost duplicated his season), Don Mattingly was benched because he didn't cut his hair, Atlanta's Otis Nixon was banned for drug abuse in the middle of the pennant race, Cincinnati's Nasty Boys trashed National League ballparks like The Doors going through a Marriott suite, and White Sox pitchers Jack McDowell and Wayne Edwards got a boffo review in *Rolling Stone* for the debut

LP of their band, V.I.E.W.

Montreal pitcher and Nicaraguan national hero Dennis Martinez tossed a perfect game and led the NL in ERA for the last place Expos, while one of the nation's great voices, Ernie Harwell, said goodbye to Detroit. In the Year of Desert Storm, a Reds rookie named Steven Foster was going through Canadian customs for the first time, and when asked, "Do you have anything to declare?" he replied, "I'm proud to be an American." Foster was detained.

Topsy-turbulent 1991 was the year that the last really were first, and the first last. The Cincinnati Reds' .457 winning percentage (and fifth place finish) was the worst of any defending world champion ever. And while the Twins and Braves became the first and second teams ever to go all the way from last place to first (see box), they were also a part of the reversal of fortune in which the four teams that finished last in 1990 compiled a better combined record than the four teams that participated in the '90 playoffs. "There's no sense to anything anymore," said Jack Morris, who used free agency to return home to Minnesota and become the leader of a strong Twins staff.

All sense stopped because in 1991, if anyone didn't realize it before, baseball very clearly came down to dollars and cents. Some owners, like Jerry Reinsdorf of the White Sox, stopped pretending to be running a philanthropic institute years ago. But when the shackles of collusion were removed, some clubs started firing money around as if it were plastic. The Cubs spent $27 million on George Bell and pitchers Danny Jackson and Dave Smith; Jackson and Smith were a combined 1-11. The Red Sox invested $8.7 million in Jack Clark and another $11.8 million in Danny Darwin (who was 71-85 as a starter) and Matt Young (39-65 as a starter). Clark hit 28 homers, but Darwin and Young combined for six victories. The Yankees gave $8.6 million to Mike Witt, who didn't win a game. The Brewers—in one of the two smallest markets in either league—paid nearly $17 million to Ted Higuera and Ron Robinson, who between them won . . . twice.

Then, to make matters worse, the players were awarded collusion damages that forced a settlement costing each

Wide World Photos

Nolan Ryan notched his seventh career no-hitter against Toronto on May 1, the same day Oakland's Rickey Henderson passed Lou Brock to become the game's all-time leading base stealer.

team $10 million. In Seattle, Emmis Broadcasting czar Jeff Smulyan found himself in a severe cash bind, and his situation summed up the changing face of baseball: the Mariners had the first winning season in their 15 years, they drew more than two million fans, and yet, because of the lack of corporate and political support (well, they did start a bus service from downtown Seattle to the Kingdome, but it stopped at 7 p.m., roughly gametime), he saw his gross income of $35 million approximately equal the payrolls of Oakland, Boston and Los Angeles. By October, Smulyan was seriously investigating the possibility of moving to St. Petersburg.

While CBS claimed it was losing millions on its national television deal and owners were warned that they would never again come close to the current package—"which we've already spent," says Reinsdorf—there was some relief when in June, Denver and Miami were awarded the National League expansion franchises for 1993. But, because this was the year baseball realized the paper

eighties were over, there was an ugly battle between the two leagues over what percentage of the combined $190 million entry fees the American League would get. Commissioner Fay Vincent settled on 23%, which infuriated AL owners.

"Now that we're seeing average salaries creep towards the $1 million mark—which they could be in 1992—we're seeing a lot of pressure on every level of management," said Toronto Vice-President Pat Gillick. "It puts extraordinary pressure on general managers, and when we hand out millions to players, if those players don't produce, ownership figures it's easier to dismiss a $300,000 manager than eat the contract on a $3 million player.

Only half the current general managers have been in office for two years. But the managerial firings were more graphic demonstrations. Philadelphia's Nick Legva was gone after 13 games, on April 23. Don Zimmer (Cubs), John Wathan (Royals) and Frank Robinson (Orioles) were dismissed on successive days in May. Buck Rodgers, the most popular baseball figure in Montreal, was fired on

Wide World Photos

A largely forgettable season in New York was brightened somewhat by the Mets' **Howard Johnson**, who led the NL in home runs and RBI.

June 3, then rehired by California on August 26 when Doug Rader was axed. But the most astounding stretch came at season's end. Stump Merrill, who guided the Yankees from last to fifth, was fired on Oct. 7. The next day Joe Morgan, who had two division titles and a second place finish in four years, was fired by the Red Sox. The day after that, Tom Trebelhorn, whose Brewers had the best record in the league after Aug. 9, was ushered out. And the day after that Jim LeFebvre, the winningest manager in Mariners history, was rewarded for the club's record number of wins and paying customers by being relieved of his duty.

Owner after owner turned into a George Steinbrenner clone: lose today, fire someone. At the press conference announcing Morgan's firing and the hiring of replacement Butch Hobson, GM Lou Gorman was flanked by owners and owners' representatives, all nattily attired in suits. After ten minutes, club counsel John Donovan told Gorman, "Lou, you have to cut it short. We have a meeting." Morgan was only the most popular coaching figure in Boston since Red Auerbach or Dick Williams. Cut the explanation short. We've got a meeting.

How crazy has it become? The first coach Hobson hired was Don Zimmer, fired by the Tribune Corp., and vilified for years in New England for the Red Sox collapse and loss to the Yankees in 1978.

It was said many years ago that the game succeeds in spite of itself, and 1991 was delightful proof. All four races were stories unto themselves, headlined by the worst-to-first charge of the Braves. At the All-Star break, they were in third place, 9½ games in back of the star-studded mercenaries in Los Angeles. But they began their charge, only to take first place and then lose it again. They endured problems, like Nixon's positive test for cocaine on Sept. 16 that got him suspended for 60 days. Finally the race became a two-team affair and, thanks to TBS, the nation fell in love with players like Steve Avery, Ronnie Gant and Terry Pendleton. Their home-and-home weekends in Atlanta and L.A stole the nation's spotlight. They split those six games, and the Dodgers still led with five days to go. But on the final Tuesday, Atlanta fell behind the Reds and ace Jose Rijo 6-0, rallied and won it in the ninth inning on a David Justice homer off Rob Dibble.

For a week at that point, the Dodgers had been complaining that Cincinnati and Houston weren't playing their hardest against the Braves. L.A. manager Tommy Lasorda criticized Padre third base coach Bruce Kimm for holding a runner up at third with two outs in the ninth of a tie game the Braves eventually won. Then the Dodgers protested on the second-to-last weekend when Houston started rookie Jeff Juden against the Braves. "They became more concerned with the Braves' opponents than their own, and when they'd start their own games on the West Coast knowing the Braves had won, night after night, it got to the Dodgers," said one Dodger official. Sure enough, the Dodgers were buried by the Padres on the final Wednesday to make the race a flat tie. When they went to San Francisco for the final three days as the Braves hosted the Astros in Atlanta, it was obvious the Dodgers were dead. Atlanta won on Friday night, then watched as the Giants scored three in the first off Dodger ace Ramon Martinez. Less than 20 hours after those three runs, it was over. The Braves were NL West champions.

In contrast, the Pittsburgh Pirates were the lone repeater, winning the NL East in machine-like form. Outfielders Bonds and Bonilla each had 100 RBI, and when the Cardinals made one belated run that got the lead down to four games in August, Bonds hit one dramatic two-run homer in the seventh, then another in the 11th against Lee Smith for a 4-3 win that allowed the Bucs to mark St. Louis absent the rest of the season. The Cards made a terrific charge from last to second, but no one in the regular season was any match for the Pirates.

Minnesota made its move from worst to first in the AL West with fewer histrionics than the Braves. They began 3-9, but soon their improved pitching, bolstered by free agent Morris and aided by the development of Tapani and Erickson, made it apparent they were serious contenders. They won 15 games in a row beginning on the first of June, which took them from 5½ games out to a half-game lead. Erickson dominated the league, winning 16 of 17 decisions after losing his first two starts, and when he hurt his arm in early July, Morris and Tapani moved to the forefront and stopper Aguilera was on his way to 42 saves.

The first weekend of August they faced their showdown in Oakland with a two game lead. After losing the opener, they fell behind 6-0 on six Athletics homers the next afternoon. But they rallied to win 8-6, and the next day brought what Oakland manager Tony LaRussa called "the biggest game of the year." In years past, when the A's faced adversity, Dave Stewart always shut the door. Oakland sent out Stewart. The Twins promptly carved him up for three runs before the A's got to the plate, won 6-2 and were on their way to winning the AL West by eight games.

Despite Minnesota's healthy margin, the division remained as advertised: the best and deepest in baseball. The Angels finished last at 81-81, the first time in baseball history that a league or division did not have a team with a losing record.

The AL East was obviously far weaker than its western counterpart, but the race was exciting until the final week. The Red Sox went to Toronto on August 9 in third place, 11½ games behind the Jays. Ev-

Wide World Photos

Baltimore shortstop **Cal Ripken** picked up the MVP award at the All-Star Game in Toronto, posted the best offensive numbers of his career and continued to reel in Lou Gehrig.

eryone figured this Jay team was different. Gillick had gotten rid of Tony Fernandez, Fred McGriff and George Bell and replaced them with Roberto Alomar, Devon White and Carter. He also made a deal with Cleveland for knuckleballer Tom Candiotti. But the Sox swept that four-game series, and on Sept. 22, they were a half game back playing the Yankees in the afternoon while Toronto waited to play a night contest in Oakland. Boston was one strike away from a 6-5 win and first place tie when Yankee Roberto Kelly homered off Jeff Reardon. New York won in extra innings, the relaxed Jays beat the A's with rookie Juan Guzman and the race was essentially over. Fifteen days after being one strike out of first, Morgan was canned and Toronto was in the playoffs.

There were seven no-hitters during the season, including two group efforts with three Baltimore and three Atlanta pitchers. A kid named Wilson Alvarez threw his for the White Sox the day he was recalled from Birmingham; his only other major league start had been for Texas two years before. In fact, with 16 no-hitters in two seasons, the no-hitter became so devalued that the Commissioner's Office gathered the rules committee and decided that hundreds of so-called no-hitters—games that were lost or games in which the opposing team got a hit in extra innings—should be stripped of their status. Which means that when you mention Harvey Haddix's 1959 12-inning perfect game, you must refer to it as Haddix's 12 inning imperfect game.

Despite the Dennis Martinez perfecto against the Dodgers on July 28, the only no-hitter that truly struck the nation's attention came on May 1, when 44-year old Nolan Ryan blew away Toronto's Roberto Alomar for the final out, and got his seventh career no-no. It happened the same day that Rickey Henderson broke Lou Brock's stolen base record of 938 and declared, "and now, I am the greatest." The country's eyes turned to Ryan who, for some perspective, had a second baseman named Sandy Alomar, Sr. behind him for two of his no-hitters with the Angels. "I was so happy for him I wanted to run out and shake his hand," said Roberto Alomar, Sandy's son and Toronto's 23-year old marvel. "But I thought someone might get upset with me. When I was a little boy coming into the clubhouse with the Angels, Nolan Ryan is the player I remember being so nice to me. He'd take me out to the field and flip me the whiffle ball. I hit him better at the age of six than I do at 23."

Some other guys don't age, either. Carlton Fisk, 43, made the AL All-Star team and hit 17 homers with 76 RBI. Ozzie Smith, 36, made eight errors, stole 35 bases and scored 97 runs.

Meanwhile in Baltimore, Ripkin pushed his consecutive game playing streak to 1,573 (he trails Lou Gehrig by 557) while batting .323 with 210 hits, 34 homers, 114 RBI and 368 total bases.

Canseco and Cecil Fielder got into a wild battle for the AL home run lead and finished tied with 44, while the Mets' Howard Johnson gave his club a little final dignity by winning the NL homer title

with 38 in a remarkable season that saw him become the first man in baseball history to have 30 homers, 30 steals, 100 runs, 100 RBI and 30 errors. Atlanta's Pendleton, one of the keys to the Atlanta revival, won the NL batting title at .319 and Texas second baseman Julio Franco led the AL at .341. There were only three 20-game winners: Detroit's other Japanese import, journeyman Bill Gullickson, as well as Erickson and Atlanta's Tommy Glavine.

Bo Jackson was released by the Kansas City Royals in spring training when he showed up on crutches as a result of a serious hip injury suffered in the Los Angeles Raiders' playoff game. Bo was signed by the White Sox on April 3 and returned to a standing ovation on Labor Day, limping and unable to use his lower body while swinging. Bo is business; the night of his return, his agent Richard Woods estimated his off-field annual income to be in the $9 million vicinity with Nike, Pepsi and many other ads. The White Sox owners understand business, too, as their new Comiskey Park attracted a record number of South Side customers, their black-and-silver cap became the third biggest selling hat in the licensing business.

The Baltimore Orioles, meanwhile, tearfully left Memorial Stadium knowing they move into their state-of-the-art Orioles Park at Camden Yards in 1992. The Cleveland Indians may have lost 105 games, but they're hoping to move into a new downtown park in 1994, which will mark the 40th anniversary of their last AL pennant. Not everyone is happy with their ballpark, however. The Montreal Expos, who have had to live with Exhibition Stadium where the roof can't close and the concrete is life-threatening, had their worst nightmare come true in September. Part of the concrete fell away, so the club had to play its last 13 games on the road. That meant that the last place team had to finish the season with a 26 game road trip, and in one stretch played 15 games in 10 different venues requiring five different trips through customs.

And Jose and Madonna? The New York Post headline read, "Material Girl's Bat Boy." "It's all show business," said Canseco. "Publicity doesn't hurt. It's good. This isn't serious, it's fun." □

THE 1992 INFORMATION PLEASE SPORTS ALMANAC

BASEBALL
STATISTICS

THE SEASON IN REVIEW
1991

LEAGUE LEADERS • POSTSEASON

SEC
A

PAGE
71

Final Major League Standings

Division champions (*) are noted. Number of seasons listed after each manager refers to tenure with club through 1991 season.

American League

East Division

	W	L	Pct	GB	Home	Away
*Toronto	91	71	.562	—	46-35	45-36
Boston	84	78	.519	7	43-38	41-40
Detroit	84	78	.519	7	49-32	35-46
Milwaukee	83	79	.512	8	43-37	40-42
New York	71	91	.438	20	39-42	32-49
Baltimore	67	95	.414	24	33-48	34-47
Cleveland	57	105	.352	34	30-52	27-53

1991 Managers: Tor—Cito Gaston (3rd season) went on 33-day medical leave (Aug.26-Sept.27) and was spelled by coach Gene Tenace (19-14); **Bos**—Joe Morgan (4th); **Det**—Sparky Anderson (13th); **Mil**—Tom Trebelhorn (6th); **NY**—Stump Merrill (2nd); **Bal**—replaced Frank Robinson (4th, 13-24) with John Oates (54-71) on May 23; **Cle**—replaced John McNamara (2nd, 25-52) with Mike Hargrove (32-53) on July 6.

1990 Standings: 1. Boston (88-74); 2. Toronto (86-76); 3. Detroit (79-83); 4. Cleveland (77-85); 5. Baltimore (76-85); 6. Milwaukee (74-88); 7. New York (67-95).

West Division

	W	L	Pct	GB	Home	Away
*Minnesota	95	67	.586	—	51-30	44-37
Chicago	87	75	.537	8	46-35	41-40
Texas	85	77	.525	10	46-35	39-42
Oakland	84	78	.519	11	47-34	37-44
Seattle	83	79	.512	12	45-36	38-43
Kansas City	82	80	.506	13	40-41	42-39
California	81	81	.500	14	40-41	41-40

1991 Managers: Min—Tom Kelly (6th season); **Chi**—Jeff Torborg (3rd); **Tex**—Bobby Valentine (7th); **Oak**—Tony LaRussa (6th); **Sea**—Jim Lefebvre (3rd); **KC**—replaced John Wathan (5th, 15-22) with Bob Schaefer (1-0) on May 22, then Hal McRae (66-58) on May 24; **Cal**—replaced Doug Rader (3rd, 61-63) with Buck Rodgers (20-18) on Aug.26.

1990 Standings: 1. Oakland (103-59); 2. Chicago (94-68); 3. Texas (83-79); 4. California (80-82); 5. Seattle (77-85); 6. Kansas City (75-86); 7. Minnesota (74-88).

National League

East Division

	W	L	Pct	GB	Home	Away
*Pittsburgh	98	64	.605	—	52-32	46-32
St.Louis	84	78	.519	14	52-32	32-46
Philadelphia	78	84	.481	20	47-36	31-48
Chicago	77	83	.481	20	46-37	31-46
New York	77	84	.475	20½	40-42	37-42
Montreal	71	90	.441	26½	33-35	38-55

1991 Managers: Pit—Jim Leyland (6th season); **StL**—Joe Torre (2nd); **Phi**—replaced Nick Leyva (3rd, 4-9) with Jim Fregosi (74-75) on Apr.23; **Chi**—replaced Don Zimmer (4th, 18-19) with Joe Altobelli (0-1) on May 21 and Jim Essian (59-63) on May 22; **NY**—replaced Bud Harrelson (2nd, 74-80) with Mike Cubbage (3-4) on Sept.28; **Mon**—replaced Buck Rodgers (7th, 20-29) with Tom Runnells (51-61) on June 3.

1990 Standings: 1. Pittsburgh (95-67); 2. New York (91-71); 3. Montreal (85-77); 4. Philadelphia (77-85) and Chicago (77-85); 6. St.Louis (70-92).

West Division

	W	L	Pct	GB	Home	Away
*Atlanta	94	68	.580	—	48-33	46-35
Los Angeles	93	69	.574	1	54-27	39-42
San Diego	84	78	.519	10	42-39	42-39
San Francisco	75	87	.463	19	43-38	32-49
Cincinnati	74	88	.457	20	39-42	35-46
Houston	65	97	.401	29	37-44	28-53

1991 Managers: Atl—Bobby Cox (2nd season); **LA**—Tom Lasorda (16th); **SD**—Greg Riddoch (2nd); **SF**—Roger Craig (7th); **Cin**—Lou Piniella (2nd); **Hou**—Art Howe (3rd).

1990 Standings: 1.Cincinnati (91-71); 2.Los Angeles (86-76); 3.San Francisco (85-77); 4.Houston (75-87) and San Diego (75-87); 6. Atlanta (65-97).

1991 AP All-Star Team

American and National Leagues combined; voting done by nationwide panel of sportswriters and sportscasters. Holdovers from 1990 All-Star first team in **bold** type; votes inn parentheses.

First Team

C—Mickey Tettleton, Detroit (41 votes); **1B—Cecil Fielder**, Detroit (95½); **2B**—Julio Franco, Texas (104); **SS**—Cal Ripken Jr., Baltimore (166); **3B**—Terry Pendleton, Atlanta (126); **OF— Barry Bonds**, Pittsburgh (117); **OF**—Ken Griffey Jr., Seattle (80); **OF**—Jose Canseco, Oakland (79); **DH—Frank Thomas**, Chicago-AL (49); **RHP**—Roger Clemens, Boston (109); **LHP**—Tom Glavine, Atlanta (149); **RP**—Lee Smith, St-.Louis (127).

Second Team

C—Brian Harper, Minnesota (36 votes); **1B**—Frank Thomas, Chicago-AL (48); **2B**—Ryne Sandberg, Chicago-NL (57); **SS**—Barry Larkin, Cincinnati (9); **3B**—Howard Johnson, N.Y.Mets (36); **OF**—Joe Carter, Toronto (52); **OF**—Bobby Bonilla, Pittsburgh (40); **OF**—Ron Gant, Atlanta (31½) **DH**—Cecil Fielder, Detroit (39); **RHP**—Scott Erickson, Minnesota (43); **LHP**—Jim Abbott, California (11); **RP**—Bryan Harvey, California (26).

AL Regular Season Individual Leaders

Batting
(Minimum of 502 plate appearances.)

	Avg	AB	R	H	HR	RBI
Julio Franco, Tex	.341	589	108	201	15	78
Wade Boggs, Bos	.332	546	93	181	8	51
Willie Randolph, Mil	.327	431	60	141	0	54
Ken Griffey Jr. Sea	.327	548	76	179	22	100
Paul Molitor, Mil	.325	665	133	216	17	75
Cal Ripken, Bal	.323	650	99	210	34	114
Rafael Palmeiro, Tex	.322	631	115	203	26	88
Kirby Puckett, Min	.319	611	92	195	15	89
Frank Thomas, Chi	.318	559	104	178	32	109
Danny Tartabull, KC	.316	484	78	153	31	100
Ruben Sierra, Tex	.307	661	110	203	25	116
Edgar Martinez, Sea	.307	544	98	167	14	52
Steve Sax, NY	.304	652	85	198	10	56
Wally Joyner, Cal	.301	551	79	166	21	96
Mike Greenwell, Bos	.300	544	76	163	9	83

Pitching
(Minimum of 162 innings pitched)

	ERA	W-L	IP	H	SO
Roger Clemens, Bos	2.62	18-10	271.1	219	241
Tom Candiotti, Cle-Tor	2.65	13-13	238.0	202	167
Bill Wegman, Mil	2.84	15-7	193.1	176	89
Jim Abbott, Cal	2.89	18-11	243.0	222	158
Nolan Ryan, Tex	2.91	12-6	173.0	102	203
Mike Moore, Oak	2.96	17-8	210.0	176	153
Kevin Tapani, Min	2.99	16-9	244.0	225	135
Mark Langston, Cal	3.00	19-8	246.1	190	183
Jimmy Key, Tor	3.05	16-12	209.1	207	125
Bret Saberhagen, KC	3.07	13-8	196.1	165	136
Jose Guzman, Tex	3.08	13-7	169.2	152	125
Scott Erickson, Min	3.18	20-8	204.0	189	108
Chris Bosio, Mil	3.25	14-10	204.2	187	117
Jack McDowell, Chi	3.41	17-10	253.2	212	191
Kevin Appier, KC	3.42	13-10	207.2	205	158

Home Runs

Canseco, Oak	44
Fielder, Det	44
C.Ripken, Bal	34
Carter, Tor	33
Thomas, Chi	32
Tartabull, KC	31
Tettleton, Det	31
Davis, Min	29
Belle, Cle	28
Clark, Bos	28
Winfield, Cal	28

Runs Batted In

Fielder, Det	133
Canseco, Oak	122
Sierra, Tex	116
C.Ripken, Bal	114
Thomas, Chi	109
Carter, Tor	108
Gonzalez, Tex	102
Griffey Jr., Sea	100
Tartabull, KC	100
Ventura, Chi	100

Wins

Erickson, Min	20-8
Gullickson, Det	20-9
Langston, Cal	19-8
Finley, Cal	18-9
Clemens, Bos	18-10
J.Abbott, Cal	18-11
Morris, Min	18-12
Moore, Oak	17-8
McDowell, Chi	17-10
Tapani, Min	16-9
Sanderson, NY	16-10
Key, Tor	16-12

Saves

Harvey, Cal	46
Eckersley, Oak	43
Aguilera, Min	42
Reardon, Bos	40
Montgomery, KC	33
Henke, Tor	32
Olson, Bal	31
Je.Russell, Tex	30
Thigpen, Chi	30
Farr, NY	23
D.Ward, Tor	23
Henneman, Det	21

Stolen Bases

	SB	CS
R. Henderson, Oak	58	18
Alomar, Tor	53	11
Raines, Chi	51	15
Polonia, Cal	48	23
Cuyler, Det	41	10
Franco, Tex	36	9
White, Tor	33	10
R.Kelly, NY	32	9
Sax, NY	31	11
Pettis, Tex	29	13

Hits

Molitor, Mil	216
C.Ripken, Bal	210
Palmeiro, Tex	203
Sierra, Tex	203
Franco, Tex	201
Sax, NY	198
Puckett, Min	195
Alomar, Tor	188
Boggs, Bos	181
White, Tor	181

Appearances

D.Ward, Tor	81
Jackson, Sea	72
Olson, Bal	72
Swift, Sea	71
Eichhorn Cal	70
Jeffcoat, Tex	70

Innings

Clemens, Bos	271.1
McDowell, Chi	253.2
Morris, Min	246.2
Langston, Cal	246.1
Tapani, Min	244.0
J.Abbott, Cal	243.0

Games Started

Clemens, Bos	35
Gullickson, Det	35
McDowell, Chi	35
Morris, Min	35
Stewart, Oak	35
Welch, Oak	35

Games Finished

Harvey, Cal	63
Olson, Bal	62
Aguilera, Min	60
Eckersley, Oak	59
Thigpen. Chi	58
Je.Russell, Tex	56

Triples

Johnson, Chi	13
Molitor, Mil	13
Alomar, Tor	11
Devereaux, Bal	10
White, Tor	10

Doubles

Palmeiro, Tex	49
C.Ripken, Bal	46
Sierra, Tex	44
Boggs, Bos	42
Carter, Tor	42
Griffey Jr., Sea	42
Reed, Bos	42

Complete Games

McDowell, Chi	15
Clemens, Bos	13
Morris, Min	10
Navarro, Mil	10
Terrell, Det	8
Five tied with 7	

Shutouts

Clemens, Bos	4
Appier, KC	3
Erickson, Min	3
Holman, Sea	3
McDowell, Chi	3
Ten tied with 2	

Runs

Molitor, Mil	133
Canseco, Oak	115
Palmeiro, Tex	115
Sierra, Tex	110
White, Tor	110

On Base Pct.

Thomas, Chi	.453
Randolph, Mil	.424
Boggs, Bos	.421
Franco, Tex	.408
E.Martinez, Sea	.405

Strikeouts

Clemens, Bos	241
Johnson, Sea	228
Ryan, Tex	203
McDowell, Chi	191
Langston, Cal	183
Finley, Cal	171
Swindell, Cle	169

Walks

Johnson, Sea	152
Moore, Oak	105
Stewart, Oak	105
Finley, Cal	101
Langston, Cal	96
Hough, Chi	94
Morris, Min	92

Total Bases

C.Ripken, Bal	368
Palmeiro, Tex	336
Sierra, Tex	332
Molitor, Mil	325
Carter, Tor	321

Slugging Pct.

Tartabull, KC	.593
C.Ripken, Bal	.566
Canseco, Oak	.556
Thomas, Chi	.553
Palmeiro, Tex	.532

Losses

McCaskill, Cal	10-19
Swindell, Cle	9-16
Nagy, Cle	10-15
Gordon, KC	9-14
Terrell, Det	12-14
Holman, Sea	13-14

HRs Given Up

DeLucia, Sea	31
Langston, Cal	30
Tanana, Det	26
Welch, Oak	25
Anderson, Min	24
Stewart, Oak	24
Wells, Tor	24

Times Walked

Thomas, Chi	138
Tettleton, Det	101
R.Henderson, Oak	98
Clark, Bos	96
Davis, Min	95

Times Struck Out

Deer, Det	175
Canseco, Oak	152
Fielder, Det	151
Fryman, Det	149
White, Tor	135

NL Regular Season Individual Leaders

Batting
(Minimum of 502 plate appearances.)

	Avg	AB	R	H	HR	RBI
Terry Pendleton, Atl	.319	586	94	187	22	86
Hal Morris, Cin	.318	478	72	152	14	59
Tony Gwynn, SD	.317	530	69	168	4	62
Willie McGee, SF	.312	497	67	155	4	43
Felix Jose, St.L	.305	568	69	173	8	77
Barry Larkin, Cin	.302	464	88	140	20	69
Bobby Bonilla, Pit	.302	577	102	174	18	100
Will Clark, SF	.301	565	84	170	29	116
Chris Sabo, Cin	.301	582	91	175	26	88
Ivan Calderon, Mon	.300	470	69	141	19	75
Brett Butler, LA	.296	615	112	182	2	38
Craig Biggio, Hou	.295	546	79	161	4	46
Jeff Bagwell, Hou	.294	554	79	163	15	82
John Kruk, Phi	.294	538	84	158	21	92
Barry Bonds, Pit	.292	510	95	149	25	116

Home Runs
Johnson, NY	38
Williams, SF.	34
Gant, Atl	32
Dawson, Chi	31
McGriff, SD	31
Clark, SF	29
O'Neill, Cin.	28
Strawberry, LA.	28
Mitchell, SF	27
Sabo, Cin	26
Sandberg, Chi	26

Stolen Bases
	SB	CS
Grissom, Mon	76	17
Nixon, Atl	72	21
DeShields, Mon	56	23
Lankford, St.L	44	20
Bonds, Pit	43	13
Butler, LA	38	28
Coleman, NY	37	14
O.Smith, St.L	35	9
Finley, Hou.	34	18
Gant, Atl.	34	15

Triples
Lankford, St.L	15
Gwynn, SD	11
Finley, Hou	10
Gonzalez, Hou	9
Grissom, Mon	9

Runs
Butler, LA.	112
Johnson, NY	108
Sandberg, Chi	104
Bonilla, Pit	102
Gant, Atl	101

Total Bases
Clark, SF	303
Pendleton, Atl	303
Johnson, NY	302
Sabo, Cin	294
Williams, SF	294

Times Walked
Butler, LA.	108
Bonds, Pit	107
McGriff, SD	105
DeShields, Mon.	95
Bonilla, Pit	90

Runs Batted In
Johnson, NY	117
Bonds, Pit	116
Clark, SF	116
McGriff, SD	106
Gant, Atl	105
Dawson, Chi	104
Bonilla, Pit	100
Sandberg, Chi	100
Strawberry, LA	99
Williams, SF	98

Hits
Pendleton, Atl	187
Butler, LA	182
Sabo, Cin	175
Bonilla, Pit	174
Jose, St.L	173
Clark, SF	170
Finley, Hou	170
Sandberg, Chi.	170
Grace, Chi.	169
Gwynn, SD	168
Bell, Pit	164

Doubles
Bonilla, Pit	44
Jose, St.L	40
O'Neill, Cin.	36
Zeile, St.L	36
Gant, Atl	35
Sabo, Cin	35

On Base Pct.
Bonds, Pit	.410
Butler, LA	.401
McGriff, SD.	.396
Bonilla, Pit.	.391
Bagwell, Hou	.387

Slugging Pct.
Clark, SF.	.536
Johnson, NY	.535
Pendleton, Atl	.517
Bonds, Pit	.514
Larkin, Cin	.506

Times Struck Out
DeShields, Mon	151
McGriff, SD.	135
Samuel, LA	133
Williams, SF	128
Strawberry, LA	125

Pitching
(Minimum of 162 innings pitched)

	ERA	W-L	IP	H	SO
Dennis Martinez, Mon	2.39	14-11	222.0	187	123
Jose Rijo, Cin	2.51	15-6	204.1	165	172
Tom Glavine, Atl	2.55	20-11	246.2	201	192
Tim Belcher, LA	2.62	10-9	209.1	189	156
Pete Harnisch, Hou	2.70	12-9	216.2	169	172
Jose DeLeon, St.L	2.71	5-9	162.2	144	118
Mike Morgan, LA	2.78	14-10	236.1	197	140
Randy Tomlin, Pit	2.98	8-7	175.0	170	104
Andy Benes, SD	3.03	15-11	223.0	194	167
Doug Drabek, Pit	3.07	15-14	234.2	245	142
John Smiley, Pit	3.08	20-8	207.2	194	129
Bob Ojeda, LA	3.18	12-9	189.1	181	120
Zane Smith, Pit	3.20	16-10	228.0	234	120
Bob Tewksbury, St.L	3.25	11-12	191.0	206	75
Ramon Martinez, LA	3.27	17-13	220.1	190	150

Wins
Smiley, Pit	20-8
Glavine, Atl	20-11
Avery, Atl	18-8
Martinez, LA	17-13
Smith, Pit	16-10
Mulholland, Phi.	16-13
Rijo, Cin	15-6
Hurst, SD	15-8
Benes, SD	15-11
Maddux, Chi	15-11
Leibrandt, Atl.	15-13
Drabek, Pit	15-14

Saves
L.Smith, St.L	47
Dibble, Cin	31
Franco, NY	30
Williams, Phi	30
Righetti, SF.	24
Lefferts, SD	23
Berenguer, Atl	17
Landrum, Pit	17
Da.Smith, Chi	17
Belinda, Pit	16
Howell, LA	16
Three tied at 15	

Appearances
Jones, Mon	77
Assenmacher, Chi	75
Stanton, Atl	74
Agosto, St.L	72
Burke, Mon-NY	72
Three tied at 71	

Innings
Maddux, Chi	263.0
Glavine, Atl	246.2
Morgan, LA	236.1
Drabek, Pit.	234.2
Cone, NY	232.2
Mulholland, Phi.	232.0

Games Started
Maddux, Chi	37
Browning, Cin	36
Leibrandt, Atl.	36
Smoltz, Atl	36
Four tied at 35	

Games Finished
L.Smith, St.L	61
Williams, Phi	60
Dibble, Cin	57
Righetti, SF.	49
Franco, NY	48

Complete Games
Glavine, Atl	9
De.Martinez, Mon	9
Mulholland, Phi.	8
Maddux, Chi	7
Martinez, LA	6
Smith, Pit	6

Shutouts
De.Martinez, Mon	5
Martinez, LA	4
Black, SF	3
Mulholland, Phi.	3
Smith, Pit	3
Seven tied with 2	

Strikeouts
Cone, NY	241
Maddux, Chi.	198
Glavine, Atl	192
Harnisch, Hou	172
Rijo, Cin	172
Benes, SD	167
Belcher, LA	156
Greene, Phi.	154

Walks
DeJesus, Phi	128
Barnes, Mon	84
Kile, Hou	84
Harnisch, Hou.	83
Myers, Cin.	80
Smoltz, Atl	77
Wilson, SF	77
Two tied at 75	

Losses
Black, SF	12-16
Viola, NY	13-15
Browning, Cin	14-14
Cone, NY	14-14
Drabek, Pit	15-14
Seven tied at 13	

HRs Given Up
Browning, Cin.	32
Armstrong, Cin	25
Black, SF	25
Viola, Oak.	25
Benes, SD	23
Avery, Atl.	21

1991 All-Star Game

62nd Baseball All-Star game. **Date:** July 9 at SkyDome in Toronto; **Managers:** Lou Piniella, Cincinnati (NL) and Tony LaRussa, Oakland (AL); **Most Valuable Player:** shortstop Cal Ripken Jr., Baltimore (AL): 2-for-3, three-run HR in third inning.

National League

	ab	r	h	bi	po	a	e
Tony Gwynn, SD, cf.........	4	1	2	0	6	0	0
l-Brett Butler, LA, pr-cf......	1	0	0	0	0	0	0
Ryne Sandberg, Chi, 2b......	3	0	1	0	2	1	0
e-Juan Samuel, LA, 2b.......	1	0	0	0	2	1	0
Will Clark, SF, 1b..........	2	0	1	0	2	0	0
h-Eddie Murray, LA, 1b......	1	0	0	0	3	0	0
Bobby Bonilla, Pit, dh........	4	0	2	1	0	0	0
Andre Dawson, Chi, rf.......	2	1	1	1	0	0	0
b-Felix Jose, St.L, rf........	2	0	1	0	1	0	0
Ivan Calderon, Mon, lf.......	2	0	1	0	1	0	0
f-Paul O'Neill, Cin, lf........	2	0	0	0	0	0	0
Chris Sabo, Cin, 3b..........	2	0	0	0	1	0	0
g-Howard Johnson, NY, 3b...	2	0	0	0	0	0	0
Benito Santiago, SD, c......	3	0	0	0	4	0	0
m-Craig Biggio, Hou, c......	1	0	0	0	2	0	1
Ozzie Smith, St.L, ss........	1	0	0	0	1	1	0
d-Barry Larkin, Cin, ss.......	1	0	0	0	0	2	0
q-George Bell, Chi, ph.......	1	0	0	0	0	0	0
TOTALS.................	35	2	10	2	24	7*	1

* Pitchers Dibble and Morgan each had one assist.

American League

	ab	r	h	bi	po	a	e
Rickey Henderson, Oak, lf ..	2	1	1	0	0	0	0
a-Joe Carter, Tor, lf........	1	1	1	0	1	0	0
Wade Boggs, Bos, 3b......	2	1	1	0	1	2	0
n-Paul Molitor, 3b.........	0	0	0	0	0	0	0
Cal Ripken, Bal, ss.........	3	1	2	3	2	1	0
o-Ozzie Guillen, Chi, ss....	0	0	0	0	1	0	0
Cecil Fielder, Det, 1b......	3	0	0	0	6	2	0
p-Rafael Palmeiro, Tex, 1b..	0	0	0	0	0	0	0
Danny Tartabull, dh	2	0	0	0	0	0	0
i-Harold Baines, Oak, dh...	1	0	0	1	0	0	0
Dave Henderson, Oak, rf...	2	0	0	0	2	0	0
j-Ruben Sierra, Tex, rf......	2	0	0	0	0	0	0
Ken Griffey Jr, Sea, cf......	3	0	2	0	2	0	0
k-Kirby Puckett, Min, cf....	1	0	0	0	1	0	0
Sandy Alomar, Cle, c......	2	0	0	0	3	0	0
c-Carlton Fisk, Chi, c.......	2	0	1	0	5	0	0
Roberto Alomar, Tor, 2b....	4	0	0	0	2	5	0
TOTALS.................	30	4	8	4	27	12*	0

* Pitcher Eckersley had one assist.

a- replaced R.Henderson in 4th; **b**- replaced Dawson in 4th; **c**- replaced S.Alomar in 5th; **d**- replaced O.Smith in 5th; **e**- replaced Sandberg in 5th; **f**- batted for Calderon in 6th; **g**- batted for Sabo in 6th; **h**- replaced Clark in 6th; **i**- batted for D.Henderson in 6th; **k**- replaced Griffey in 7th; **l**- ran for Gwynn in 7th; **m**- replaced Santiago in 7th; **n**- batted for Boggs in 7th (reached first on catcher interference); **o**- batted for Ripken in 7th; **p**- batted for Fielder in 7th; **q**- batted for Larkin in 9th.

Players not used: AL—batter Julio Franco (Tex.) and pitchers Bryan Harvey (Cal.), Mark Langston (Cal.) and Scott Sanderson (NY) NL—batter John Kruk (Phi.) and pitchers Tom Browning (Cin.) and Lee Smith (St.L.).

	1	2	3	4	5	6	7	8	9		R	H	E
National League.............................	1	0	0	1	0	0	0	0	0	—	2	10	1
American League.............................	0	0	3	0	0	0	1	0	0	—	4	8	0

E—Baggio (interference). **DP**—American (2). **LOB**—National (8), American (8); **2B**—Sandberg, NL. **HR**—Dawson, NL; Ripken, AL. **SB**—Calderon. **S**—Guillen. **SF**—Baines, AL.

NL Pitching	IP	H	R	ER	BB	SO
Tom Glavine, Atl	2.0	1	0	0	1	3
Dennis Martinez, Mon (L) ..	2.0	4	3	3	0	0
Frank Viola, NY	1.0	0	0	0	1	0
Pete Harnisch, Hou	1.0	2	0	0	1	0
John Smiley, Pit.	0.0*	1	1	1	0	0
Rob Dibble, Cin	1.0	0	0	0	1	1
Mike Morgan, LA.	1.0	0	0	0	1	0
TOTALS.................	8.0	8	4	4	3	6

*Smiley pitched to two batters in 7th.

AL Pitching	IP	H	R	ER	BB	SO
Jack Morris, Min............	2.0	4	1	1	0	1
Jimmy Key, Tor (W)........	1.0	1	0	0	0	1
Roger Clemens, Bos........	1.0	1	1	1	0	0
Jack McDowell, Chi	2.0	1	0	0	2	0
Jeff Reardon, Bos..........	0.2	1	0	0	0	0
Rick Aguilera, Min	1.1	2	0	0	0	3
Dennis Eckersley, Oak (S)...	1.0	0	0	0	0	1
TOTALS.................	9.0	10	2	2	2	6

Umpires—Joe Brinkman (AL) plate; John McSherry (NL) 1b; Ken Kaiser (AL) 2b; Jim Quick (NL) 3b; Larry Young (AL) lf; Greg Bonin (NL) rf. **Attendance**—52,383. **Time**—3:04.

Home Attendance

Overall 1991 regular season attendance in Major League Baseball was 56,858,010 in 2076 games for an average per game crowd of 27,388; numbers in parentheses indicate ranking in 1990.

American League
Based on tickets sold.

		Attendance	Gm	Average
1	Toronto (1)............	4,001,526	81	49,402
2	Chicago (8)	2,934,154	80	36,677
3	Oakland (2)...........	2,713,463	81	33,500
4	Boston (3)............	2,562,438	80	32,030
5	Baltimore (5).........	2,552,808	79	32,314
6	California (4)	2,416,236	81	29,830
7	Texas (7).............	2,297,718	79	29,085
8	Minnesota (11)........	2,293,842	81	28,319
9	Kansas City (6).......	2,161,524	80	27,019
10	Seattle (13)...........	2,147,905	81	26,517
11	New York (9)	1,863,731	78	23,894
12	Detroit (12)...........	1,641,661	80	20,521
13	Milwaukee (10)........	1,478,814	79	18,719
14	Cleveland (14).........	1,051,863	79	13,315
	TOTAL	32,117,696	1119	28,702

National League
Based on turnstile count.

		Attendance	Gm	Average
1	Los Angeles (1)	3,348,170	81	41,335
2	St.Louis (3)	2,449,537	82	29,872
3	Cincinnati (4).........	2,372,377	80	29,655
4	Chicago (5)...........	2,314,250	81	28,571
5	New York (2)	2,284,484	79	28,918
6	Atlanta (12)	2,140,217	78	27,439
7	Pittsburgh (6)........	2,065,302	83	24,883
8	Philadelphia (7).......	2,050,012	83	24,699
9	San Diego (9).........	1,804,289	81	22,275
10	San Fran.(8)..........	1,737,479	81	21,450
11	Houston (11)	1,196,152	81	14,767
12	Montreal (10)	978,045	81	14,598
	TOTAL	24,740,314	957	25,852

Note: Montreal had to play its last 14 home games on the road when a concrete section of Olympic Stadium fell off and the park was declared unsafe.

AL Team by Team Statistics

At least 150 at bats or 50 innings pitched during the regular season. Players who played with more than one AL team during the season are listed with their final clubs. Players traded from the NL are listed with AL team only if they have 150 AB or 50 IP. Note that (*) indicates rookie.

Baltimore Orioles

Batting (150 AB)

	Avg	AB	R	H	HR	RBI	SB
Cal Ripken Jr.	.323	650	99	210	34	114	6
David Segui*	.278	212	15	59	2	22	1
Joe Orsulak	.278	486	57	135	5	43	6
Dwight Evans	.270	270	35	73	6	38	2
Chito Martinez*	.269	216	32	58	13	33	1
Randy Milligan	.263	483	57	127	16	70	0
Mike Devereaux	.260	608	82	158	19	59	16
Bob Melvin	.250	228	11	57	1	23	0
Chris Hoiles	.243	341	36	83	11	31	0
Sam Horn	.233	317	45	74	23	61	0
Leo Gomez*	.233	391	40	91	16	45	1
Brady Anderson	.230	256	40	59	2	27	12
Glenn Davis	.227	176	29	40	10	28	4
Billy Ripken	.216	287	24	62	0	14	0
Tim Hulett*	.204	206	29	42	7	18	0
Juan Bell*	.172	209	26	36	1	15	0

Pitching (50 IP)

	ERA	W-L	Gm	IP	BB	SO
Todd Frohwirth	1.87	7-3	51	96.1	29	77
Mike Flanagan	2.38	2-7	64	98.1	25	55
Mike Mussina*	2.87	4-5	12	87.2	21	52
Gregg Olson	3.18	4-6	72	73.2	29	72
Bob Milacki	4.01	10-9	31	184.0	53	108
Mark Williamson	4.48	5-5	65	80.1	35	53
Ben McDonald	4.84	6-8	21	126.1	43	85
Paul Kilgus	5.08	0-2	38	62.0	24	32
Jeff Robinson	5.18	4-9	21	104.1	51	65
Roy Smith	5.60	5-4	17	80.1	24	25
Jeff Ballard	5.60	6-12	26	123.2	28	37
Jose Mesa	5.97	6-11	23	123.2	62	64
Dave Johnson	7.07	4-8	22	84.0	24	38

Saves: Olson (31); Williamson (4); Flanagan and Frohwirth (3); Kilgus and Jim Poole (1). **Complete games:** Milacki (3); Mesa and Mussina (2); McDonald (1). **Shutouts:** Mesa and Milacki (1).

Boston Red Sox

Batting (150 AB)

	Avg	AB	R	H	HR	RBI	SB
Wade Boggs	.332	546	93	181	8	51	1
Mike Greenwell	.300	544	76	163	9	83	15
Carlos Quintana	.295	478	69	141	11	71	1
Jody Reed	.283	618	87	175	5	60	6
Mo Vaughn*	.260	219	21	57	4	32	2
Luis Rivera	.258	414	64	107	8	40	4
Ellis Burks	.251	474	56	119	14	56	6
Jack Clark	.249	481	75	120	28	87	0
Steve Lyons	.241	212	15	51	4	17	10
Tony Pena	.231	464	45	107	5	48	8
Tom Brunansky	.229	459	54	105	16	70	1

Acquired: P Gardiner from Sea.(Apr.1) for P Rob Murphy; P Petry from Atl.(Aug.16) for minor leaguer to be named later. **Claimed:** INF-OF Lyons on waivers from Chisox (Apr.18).

Pitching (50 IP)

	ERA	W-L	Gm	IP	BB	SO
Jeff Gray	2.34	2-3	50	61.2	10	41
Roger Clemens	2.62	18-10	35	271.1	65	241
Jeff Reardon	3.03	1-4	57	59.1	16	44
Joe Hesketh	3.29	12-4	39	153.1	53	104
Tony Fossas	3.47	3-2	64	57.0	28	29
Greg Harris	3.85	11-12	53	173.0	69	127
Kevin Morton*	4.59	6-5	16	86.1	40	45
Dennis Lamp	4.70	6-3	51	92.0	31	57
Dan Petry	4.79	2-3	30	77.0	31	30
Mike Gardiner*	4.85	9-10	22	130.0	47	91
Danny Darwin	5.16	3-6	12	68.0	15	42
Matt Young	5.18	3-7	19	88.2	53	69
Tom Bolton	5.24	8-9	25	110.0	51	64

Saves: Reardon (40); Harris (2); Fosses, Gray and Petry (1). **Complete games:** Clemens (13); Harris and Morton (1). **Shutouts:** Clemens (4).

California Angels

Batting (150 AB)

	Avg	AB	R	H	HR	RBI	SB
Wally Joyner	.301	551	79	166	21	96	2
Luis Polonia	.296	604	92	179	2	50	48
Dave Gallagher	.293	270	32	79	1	30	2
Junior Felix	.283	230	32	65	2	26	7
Dave Winfield	.262	568	75	149	28	86	7
Luis Sojo	.258	364	38	94	3	20	4
Max Venable	.246	187	24	46	3	21	2
Gary Gaetti	.246	586	58	144	18	66	5
Donnie Hill	.239	209	36	50	1	20	1
Dick Schofield	.225	427	44	96	0	31	8
Lance Parrish	.216	402	38	87	19	51	0

Pitching (50 IP)

	ERA	W-L	Gm	IP	BB	SO
Bryan Harvey	1.60	2-4	67	78.2	17	101
Mark Eichhorn	1.98	3-3	70	81.2	13	49
Jim Abbott	2.89	18-11	34	243.0	73	158
Mark Langston	3.00	19-8	34	246.1	96	183
Chuck Finley	3.80	18-9	34	227.1	101	171
Scott Bailes	4.18	1-2	42	51.2	22	41
Kirk McCaskill	4.26	10-19	30	177.2	66	71
Joe Grahe*	4.81	3-7	18	73.0	33	40
Jeff Robinson	5.37	0-3	39	57.0	29	72
Scott Lewis*	6.27	3-5	16	60.1	21	37

Saves: Harvey (46); Robinson (3); Eichhorn (1). **Complete games:** Langston (7); Abbott (5); Finley (4); Grahe and McCaskill (1). **Shutouts:** Finley (2); Abbott (1).

Chicago White Sox

Batting (150 AB)

	Avg	AB	R	H	HR	RBI	SB
Frank Thomas	.318	559	104	178	32	109	1
Robin Ventura	.284	606	92	172	23	100	2
Craig Grebeck	.281	224	37	63	6	31	1
Lance Johnson	.274	588	72	161	0	49	26
Ozzie Guillen	.273	524	52	143	3	49	21
Tim Raines	.268	609	102	163	5	50	51
Dan Pasqua	.259	417	71	108	18	66	0
Mike Huff*	.251	243	42	61	3	25	14
Ron Karkovice	.246	167	25	41	5	22	0
Carlton Fisk	.241	460	42	111	18	74	1
Joey Cora	.241	228	37	55	0	18	11
Scott Fletcher	.206	248	14	51	1	28	0
Sammy Sosa	.203	316	39	64	10	33	13

Claimed: OF Huff on waivers from Cle.(July 15).

Pitching (50 IP)

	ERA	W-L	Gm	IP	BB	SO
Scott Radinsky	2.02	5-5	67	71.1	23	49
Donn Pall	2.41	7-2	51	71.0	20	40
Ken Patterson	2.83	3-0	43	63.2	35	32
Melido Perez	3.12	8-7	49	135.2	52	128
Jack McDowell	3.41	17-10	35	253.2	82	191
Bobby Thigpen	3.49	7-5	67	69.2	38	47
Wilson Alvarez*	3.51	3-2	10	56.1	29	32
Charlie Hough	4.02	9-10	31	199.1	94	107
Greg Hibbard	4.31	11-11	32	194.0	57	71
Alex Hernandez	4.51	9-13	34	191.2	88	145
Ramon Garcia*	5.40	4-4	16	78.1	31	40

Saves: Thigpen (30); Radinsky (8); Patterson and Perez (1). **Complete games:** McDowell (15); Hibbard (5); Hough (4); Alvarez and Fernandez (2). **Shutouts:** MacDowell (3); Alvarez and Hough (1).

Cleveland Indians

Batting (150 AB)

	Avg	AB	R	H	HR	RBI	SB
Alex Cole............	.295	387	58	114	0	21	27
Carlos Baerga........	.288	593	80	171	11	69	3
Carlos Martinez	.284	257	22	73	5	30	3
Albert Belle	.282	461	60	130	28	95	3
Mark Lewis*..........	.264	314	29	83	0	30	2
Mike Aldrete.........	.262	183	22	48	1	19	1
Felix Fermin.........	.262	424	30	111	0	31	5
Glenallen Hill	.258	221	29	57	8	25	6
Mark Whiten*........	.243	407	46	99	9	45	4
Joel Skinner..........	.243	284	23	69	1	24	0
Chris James	.238	437	31	104	5	41	3
Jerry Browne	.228	290	28	66	1	29	2
Sandy Alomar........	.217	184	10	40	0	7	0

Acquired: OF Hill, OF Whiten, and P Boucher from Tor.(June 27) for P Tom Candiotti and OF Turner Ward.

Pitching (50 IP)

	ERA	W-L	Gm	IP	BB	SO
Steve Olin	3.36	3-6	48	56.1	23	38
Jeff Shaw	3.36	0-5	29	72.1	27	31
Greg Swindell	3.48	9-16	33	238.0	31	169
Rod Nichols..........	3.54	2-11	31	137.1	30	76
Charles Nagy*	4.13	10-15	33	211.1	66	109
Dave Otto*	4.23	2-8	18	100.0	27	47
Shawn Hillegas.......	4.34	3-4	51	83.0	46	66
Eric King	4.60	6-11	25	150.2	44	59
Doug Jones..........	5.54	4-8	36	63.1	17	48
Denis Boucher*.......	6.05	1-7	12	58.0	24	29

Saves: Olin (17); Hillegas and Jones (7); Nichols and Shaw (1). **Complete games:** Swindell (7); Nagy (6); Nichols (3); King (2); Otto (1). **Shutouts:** King, Nagy and Nichols (1).

Kansas City Royals

Batting (150 AB)

	Avg	AB	R	H	HR	RBI	SB
Danny Tartabull	.316	484	78	153	31	100	6
Jim Eisenreich	.301	375	47	113	2	47	5
Todd Benzinger.......	.294	293	29	86	2	40	2
Bill Pecota	.286	398	53	114	6	45	16
Gary Thurman	.277	184	24	51	2	13	15
Mike Macfarlane......	.277	267	34	74	13	41	1
Kevin Seitzer	.265	234	28	62	1	25	4
Kurt Stillwell..........	.265	385	44	102	6	51	3
Brian McRae.........	.261	629	86	164	8	64	20
George Brett	.255	505	77	129	10	61	2
Brent Mayne*	.251	231	22	58	3	31	2
Kirk Gibson	.236	462	81	109	16	55	18
Terry Shumpert*	.217	369	45	80	5	34	17
David Howard*........	.216	236	20	51	1	17	3

Acquired: 1B-OF Carmelo Martinez from Pit.(May 4) for P Victor Cole; 1B-OF Benzinger from Cin.(July 11) for 1B-OF Carmelo Martinez.

Pitching (50 IP)

	ERA	W-L	Gm	IP	BB	SO
Mike Magnante*......	2.45	0-1	38	55.0	23	42
Jeff Montgomery......	2.90	4-4	67	90.0	28	77
Bret Saberhagen.....	3.07	13-8	28	196.1	45	136
Kevin Appier	3.42	13-10	34	207.2	61	158
Luis Aquino	3.44	8-4	38	157.0	47	80
Tom Gordon	3.87	9-14	45	158.0	87	167
Mike Boddicker.......	4.08	12-12	30	180.2	59	79
Mark Davis	4.45	6-3	29	62.2	39	47
Storm Davis	4.96	3-9	51	114.1	46	53
Mark Gubicza........	5.68	9-12	26	133.0	42	89

Saves: Montgomery (33); Aquino (3); S.Davis (2); Steve Crawford, Gordon and M.Davis (1). **Complete games:** Saberhagen (7); Appier (6); Aquino, Boddicker, S.Davis and Gordon (1). **Shutouts:** Appier (3); Saberhagen (2); Aquino and S.Davis (1).

Detroit Tigers

Batting (150 AB)

	Avg	AB	R	H	HR	RBI	SB
Skeeter Barnes	.289	159	28	46	5	17	10
Tony Phillips	.284	564	87	160	17	72	10
Lou Whitaker.........	.279	470	94	131	23	78	4
Mickey Tettleton	.263	501	85	132	31	89	3
Lloyd Moseby	.262	260	37	68	6	35	8
Cecil Fielder	.261	624	102	163	44	133	0
Travis Fryman	.259	557	65	144	21	91	12
Milt Cuyler*	.257	475	77	122	3	33	41
Alan Trammell	.248	375	57	93	9	55	11
Dave Bergman	.237	194	23	46	7	29	1
Andy Allanson........	.232	151	10	35	1	16	0
Pete Incaviglia........	.214	337	38	72	11	38	1
Rob Deer.............	.179	448	64	80	25	64	1

Pitching (50 IP)

	ERA	W-L	Gm	IP	BB	SO
Mike Henneman.......	2.88	10-2	60	84.1	34	61
Frank Tanana	3.77	13-12	33	217.1	78	107
Bill Gullickson	3.90	20-9	35	226.1	44	91
Jerry Don Gleaton	4.06	3-2	47	75.1	39	47
Mark Leiter*	4.21	9-7	38	134.2	50	103
Walt Terrell	4.24	12-14	35	218.2	79	80
John Cerutti..........	4.57	3-6	38	88.2	37	29
Paul Gibson	4.59	5-7	68	96.0	48	52
Scott Aldred*	5.18	2-4	11	57.1	30	35
Dan Gakeler*	5.74	1-4	31	73.2	39	43

Saves: Henneman (21); Gibson (8); Cerutti, Gakeler, Gleaton and Jeff Kaiser (2); Leiter (1). **Complete games:** Terrell (8); Gullickson (4); Tanana (3); Aldred, Cerutti and Leiter (1). **Shutouts:** Tanana and Terrell (2).

Milwaukee Brewers

Batting (150 AB)

	Avg	AB	R	H	HR	RBI	SB
Willie Randolph	.327	431	60	141	0	54	4
Paul Molitor..........	.325	665	133	216	17	75	19
Darryl Hamilton	.311	405	64	126	1	57	16
B.J. Surhoff	.289	505	57	146	5	68	5
Jim Gantner	.283	526	63	149	2	47	4
Bill Spiers	.283	414	71	117	8	54	14
Robin Yount	.260	503	66	131	10	77	6
Greg Vaughn.........	.244	542	81	132	27	98	2
Dale Sveum..........	.241	266	33	64	4	43	2
Dante Bichette........	.238	445	53	106	15	59	14
Franklin Stubbs.......	.213	362	48	77	11	38	13
Gary Sheffield........	.194	175	25	34	2	22	5

Pitching (50 IP)

	ERA	W-L	Gm	IP	BB	SO
Doug Henry*.........	1.00	2-1	32	36.0	14	28
Bill Wegman	2.84	15-7	28	193.1	40	89
Chris Bosio	3.25	14-10	32	204.2	58	117
Julio Machado	3.45	3-3	54	88.2	55	98
Mark Lee*	3.86	2-5	62	67.2	31	43
Jaime Navarro	3.92	15-12	34	234.0	73	114
Dan Plesac	4.29	2-7	45	92.1	39	61
Chuck Crim..........	4.63	8-5	66	91.1	25	39
Darren Holmes*......	4.72	1-4	40	76.1	27	59
Don August	5.47	9-8	28	138.1	47	62
Kevin Brown*........	5.51	2-4	15	63.2	34	30

Saves: Doug Henry (15); Edwin Nunez and Plesac (8); Crim, Holmes and Machado (3); Lee (1). **Complete games:** Navarro (10), Wegman (7); Bosio (5); August (1). **Shutouts:** Navarro and Wegman (2); August and Bosio (1).

Minnesota Twins

Batting (150 AB)	Avg	AB	R	H	HR	RBI	SB
Kirby Puckett	.319	611	92	195	15	89	11
Brian Harper	.311	441	54	137	10	69	1
Shane Mack	.310	442	79	137	18	74	13
Randy Bush	.303	165	21	50	6	23	0
Scott Leius*	.286	199	35	57	5	20	5
Gene Larkin	.286	255	34	73	2	19	2
Kent Hrbek	.284	462	72	131	20	89	4
Chuck Knoblauch*	.281	565	78	159	1	50	25
Mike Pagliarulo	.279	365	38	102	6	36	1
Chili Davis	.277	534	84	148	29	93	5
Greg Gagne	.265	408	52	108	8	42	11
Dan Gladden	.247	461	65	114	6	52	15
Al Newman	.191	246	25	47	0	19	4

Pitching (50 IP)	ERA	W-L	Gm	IP	BB	SO
Rick Aguilera	2.35	4-5	63	69.0	30	61
Carl Willis	2.63	8-3	40	89.0	19	53
Kevin Tapani	2.99	16-9	34	244.0	40	135
Scott Erickson	3.18	20-8	32	204.0	71	108
Jack Morris	3.43	18-12	35	246.2	92	163
Terry Leach	3.61	1-2	50	67.1	14	32
Mark Guthrie	4.32	7-5	41	98.0	41	72
Steve Bedrosian	4.42	5-3	56	77.1	35	44
Dave West	4.54	4-4	15	71.1	28	52
Allan Anderson	4.96	5-11	29	134.1	42	51

Saves: Aguilera (40); Bedrosian (6); Guthrie and Willis (2); Gary Wayne (1). **Complete games:** Morris (10); Erickson (5); Tapani (4); Anderson (2). **Shutouts:** Erickson (3); Morris (2); Tapani (1).

Oakland Athletics

Batting (150 AB)	Avg	AB	R	H	HR	RBI	SB
Harold Baines	.295	488	76	144	20	90	0
Dave Henderson	.276	572	86	158	25	85	6
Terry Steinbach	.274	456	50	125	6	67	2
Rickey Henderson	.268	470	105	126	18	57	58
Jose Canseco	.266	572	115	152	44	122	26
Jamie Quirk	.261	203	16	53	1	17	0
Lance Blankenship	.249	185	33	46	3	21	12
Mike Gallego	.247	482	67	119	12	49	6
Mike Bordick*	.238	235	21	56	0	21	3
Willie Wilson	.238	294	38	70	0	28	20
Brook Jacoby	.224	419	28	94	4	44	2
Ernest Riles	.214	281	30	60	5	32	3
Mark McGwire	.201	483	62	97	22	75	2

Acquired: 3B Jacoby from Cle.(July 26) for OF Lee Tinsley and P Apolinar Garcia; P Ron Darling from Mon.(July 31) for two minor league pitchers. **Claimed:** P Andy Hawkins on waivers from NY Yanks (May 18), then released him (Aug.15).

Pitching (50 IP)	ERA	W-L	Gm	IP	BB	SO
Mike Moore	2.96	17-8	33	210.0	105	153
Dennis Eckersley	2.96	5-4	67	76.0	9	87
Ron Darling	4.08	3-7	12	75.0	38	60
Steve Chitren*	4.33	1-4	56	60.1	32	47
Joe Klink	4.35	10-3	62	62.0	21	34
Bob Welch	4.58	12-13	35	220.0	91	101
Curt Young	5.00	4-2	41	68.1	34	27
Dave Stewart	5.18	11-11	35	226.0	105	144
Joe Slusarski*	5.27	5-7	20	109.1	52	60
Andy Hawkins	5.52	4-6	19	89.2	42	45
Eric Show	5.92	1-2	23	51.2	17	20

Saves: Eckersley (43); Chitren (4); Klink (2). **Complete games:** Welch (7); Moore (3); Stewart (2); Hawkins and Slusarski (1). **Shutouts:** Moore, Stewart and Welch (1).

New York Yankees

Batting (150 AB)	Avg	AB	R	H	HR	RBI	SB
Steve Sax	.304	652	85	198	10	56	31
Don Mattingly	.288	587	64	169	9	68	2
Mel Hall	.285	492	67	140	19	80	0
Matt Nokes	.268	456	52	122	24	77	3
Roberto Kelly	.267	486	68	130	20	69	32
Alvero Espinoza	.256	480	51	123	5	33	4
Randy Velarde	.245	184	19	45	1	15	3
Pat Kelly*	.242	298	35	72	3	23	12
Bernie Williams*	.238	320	43	76	3	34	10
Jesse Barfield	.225	284	37	64	17	48	1
Hensley Meulens*	.222	288	37	64	6	29	3
Kevin Maas	.220	500	69	110	23	63	5

Pitching (50 IP)	ERA	W-L	Gm	IP	BB	SO
Steve Farr	2.19	5-5	60	70.0	20	60
John Habyan	2.30	4-2	66	90.0	20	70
Pascual Perez	3.18	2-4	14	73.2	24	41
Greg Cadaret	3.62	8-6	68	121.2	59	105
Lee Guetterman	3.68	3-4	64	88.0	25	35
Scott Sanderson	3.81	16-10	34	208.0	29	130
Scott Kamieniecki*	3.90	4-4	9	55.1	22	34
Eric Plunk	4.76	2-5	43	111.2	62	103
Dave Eiland	5.33	2-5	18	72.2	23	18
Chuck Cary	5.91	1-6	10	53.1	32	34
Jeff Johnson*	5.95	6-11	23	127.0	33	62
Wade Taylor*	6.27	7-12	23	116.1	53	72
Tim Leary	6.49	4-10	28	120.2	57	83

Saves: Farr (23); Guetterman (6); Cadaret and Steve Howe (3); Habyan (2). **Complete games:** Sanderson (2); Leary (1). **Shutouts:** Sanderson (2).

Seattle Mariners

Batting (150 AB)	Avg	AB	R	H	HR	RBI	SB
Ken Griffey Jr	.327	548	76	179	22	100	18
Edgar Martinez	.307	544	98	167	14	52	0
Henry Cotto	.305	177	35	54	6	23	16
Greg Briley	.260	381	39	99	2	26	23
Harold Reynolds	.254	631	95	160	3	57	28
Tracy Jones	.251	175	30	44	3	24	2
Jeff Schaefer	.250	164	19	41	1	11	3
Pete O'Brien	.248	560	58	139	17	88	0
Dave Cochrane	.247	178	16	44	2	22	0
Jay Buhner	.244	406	64	99	27	77	0
Omar Vizquel	.230	426	42	98	1	41	7
Alvin Davis	.221	462	39	102	12	69	0
Scott Bradley	.203	172	10	35	0	11	0
Dave Valle	.194	324	38	63	8	32	0

Pitching (50 IP)	ERA	W-L	Gm	IP	BB	SO
Bill Swift	1.99	1-2	71	90.1	26	48
Mike Jackson	3.25	7-7	72	88.2	34	74
Russ Swan	3.43	6-2	63	78.2	28	33
Bill Krueger	3.60	11-8	35	175.0	60	91
Brian Holman	3.69	13-14	30	195.1	77	108
Erik Hanson	3.81	8-8	27	174.2	56	143
Randy Johnson	3.98	13-10	33	201.1	152	228
Scott Bankhead	4.90	3-6	17	60.2	21	28
Rich DeLucia*	5.09	12-13	32	182.0	78	98

Saves: Swift (17); Jackson (14); Mike Schooler (7); Rob Murphy (4); Calvin Jones and Swan (2); Dave Burba and Gene Harris (1). **Complete games:** Holman (5); Hanson and Johnson (2); Krueger (1). **Shutouts:** Holman (3); Hanson and Johnson (1).

Texas Rangers

Batting (150 AB)

	Avg	AB	R	H	HR	RBI	SB
Julio Franco	.341	589	108	201	15	78	36
Rafael Palmeiro	.322	631	115	203	26	88	4
Ruben Sierra	.307	661	110	203	25	116	16
Brian Downing	.278	407	76	113	17	49	1
Geno Petralli	.271	199	21	54	2	20	2
Kevin Reimer	.269	394	46	106	20	69	0
Steve Buechele	.267	416	58	111	18	66	0
Ivan Rodriguez*	.264	280	24	74	3	27	0
Juan Gonzalez	.264	545	78	144	27	102	4
Mario Diaz	.264	182	24	48	1	22	0
Mike Stanley	.249	181	25	45	3	25	0
Gary Pettis	.216	282	37	61	0	19	29
Jeff Huson	.213	268	36	57	2	26	8
Dean Palmer*	.187	268	38	50	15	37	0

Traded: 3B Buechele to Pit.(Aug.30) for P Kurt Miller and P Hector Fajardo. **Acquired:** P Boyd from Mon.(July 21) for three minor leaguers. **Signed:** DH Downing (Apr.13) after inviting him to training camp.

Pitching (50 IP)

	ERA	W-L	Gm	IP	BB	SO
Nolan Ryan	2.91	12-6	27	173.0	72	203
Jose Guzman	3.08	13-7	25	169.2	84	125
Jeff Russell	3.29	6-4	68	79.1	26	52
Terry Mathews	3.61	4-0	34	57.1	18	51
Kevin Brown	4.40	9-12	33	210.2	90	96
John Barfield	4.54	4-4	28	83.1	22	27
Mike Jeffcoat	4.63	5-3	70	79.2	25	43
Brian Bohanon	4.84	4-3	11	61.1	23	34
Gerald Alexander*	5.24	5-3	30	89.1	48	50
Wayne Rosenthal*	5.25	1-4	36	70.1	36	61
Kenny Rogers	5.42	10-10	63	109.2	61	73
Bobby Witt	6.09	3-7	17	88.2	74	82
Oil Can Boyd	6.68	2-7	12	62.0	17	33

Saves: Russell (30); Rogers (5); Barfield, Goose Gossage, Jeffcoat, Mathews and Rosenthal (1). **Complete games:** Guzman (5); Ryan (2); Bohanon and Witt (1). **Shutouts:** Ryan (2); Guzman and Witt (1).

Toronto Blue Jays

Batting (150 AB)

	Avg	AB	R	H	HR	RBI	SB
Roberto Alomar	.295	637	88	188	9	69	53
Devon White	.282	642	110	181	17	60	33
Ed Sprague*	.275	160	17	44	4	20	0
Joe Carter	.273	638	89	174	33	108	20
Greg Myers	.262	309	25	81	8	36	0
John Olerud	.256	454	64	116	17	68	0
Kelly Gruber	.252	429	58	108	20	65	12
Candy Maldonado	.250	288	37	72	12	48	4
Rance Mulliniks	.250	240	27	60	2	24	0
Pat Borders	.244	291	22	71	5	36	0
Mookie Wilson	.241	241	26	58	2	28	11
Dave Parker	.239	502	47	120	11	59	3
Manuel Lee	.234	445	41	104	0	29	7
Pat Tabler	.216	185	20	40	1	21	0
Cory Snyder	.175	166	14	29	3	17	0

Acquired: P Candiotti and OF Turner Ward from Cle.(June 27) for OF Glenallen Hill, OF Mark Whiten and P Denis Boucher; OF Snyder from Chisox (July 14) for two minor leaguers; OF Maldonado from Mil.(Aug.9) for two minor leaguers. **Claimed:** DH Parker on waivers from Cal.(Sept.14).

Pitching (50 IP)

	ERA	W-L	Gm	IP	BB	SO
Tom Henke	2.32	0-2	49	50.1	11	53
Tom Candiotti	2.65	13-13	34	238.0	73	167
Duane Ward	2.77	7-6	81	107.1	33	132
Bob MacDonald*	2.85	3-3	45	53.2	25	24
Juan Guzman*	2.99	10-3	23	138.2	66	123
Jimmy Key	3.05	16-12	33	209.1	44	125
Mike Timlin*	3.16	11-6	63	108.1	50	85
Dave Stieb	3.17	4-3	9	59.2	23	29
David Wells	3.72	15-10	40	198.1	49	106
Todd Stottlemyre	3.78	15-8	34	219.0	75	116
Jim Acker	5.20	3-5	54	88.1	36	44

Saves: Henke (32); Ward (23); Timlin (3); Acker and Wells (1). **Complete games:** Candiotti (6); Key and Wells (2); Guzman, Stieb and Stottlemyre (1). **Shutouts:** Key (2).

Team Leaders
AL

Batting	Avg	AB	R	H	HR	RBI	SB
Minnesota	.280	5556	776	1557	140	733	107
Milwaukee	.271	5611	799	1523	116	750	106
Texas	.270	5703	829	1539	177	774	102
Boston	.269	5530	731	1486	126	691	59
Kansas City	.264	5584	727	1475	117	689	119
Chicago	.262	5594	758	1464	139	722	134
Toronto	.257	5489	684	1412	133	649	148
New York	.256	5541	674	1418	147	630	109
California	.255	5470	653	1396	115	607	94
Seattle	.255	5494	702	1400	126	665	97
Cleveland	.254	5470	576	1390	79	546	84
Baltimore	.254	5604	686	1421	170	660	50
Oakland	.248	5410	760	1342	159	716	151
Detroit	.247	5547	817	1372	209	778	109

Pitching	ERA	W	Sv	CG	ShO	HR	BB	SO
Toronto	3.50	91	60	10	16	121	523	971
California	3.69	81	50	18	10	141	543	990
Minnesota	3.69	95	53	21	12	139	488	876
Seattle	3.79	83	48	10	13	136	628	1003
Chicago	3.79	87	40	28	8	154	601	923
Kansas City	3.92	82	41	17	12	105	529	1004
Boston	4.01	84	45	15	13	147	530	999
Milwaukee	4.14	83	41	23	11	147	527	859
Cleveland	4.23	57	33	22	8	110	441	862
New York	4.42	71	37	3	11	152	506	936
Texas	4.47	85	41	9	10	151	662	1022
Detroit	4.51	84	38	18	8	148	593	739
Oakland	4.57	84	49	14	10	155	655	892
Baltimore	4.59	67	42	8	8	147	504	868

NL

Batting	Avg	AB	R	H	HR	RBI	SB
Pittsburgh	.263	5449	768	1433	126	725	124
Cincinnati	.258	5501	689	1419	164	654	124
Atlanta	.258	5456	749	1407	141	704	165
St.Louis	.255	5362	651	1366	68	599	202
Chicago	.253	5522	695	1395	159	654	123
Los Angeles	.253	5408	665	1366	108	605	126
San Francisco	.246	5463	649	1345	141	605	95
Montreal	.246	5412	579	1329	95	536	221
Houston	.244	5504	605	1345	79	570	125
San Diego	.244	5408	636	1321	121	591	101
New York	.244	5359	640	1305	117	605	153
Philadelphia	.241	5521	629	1332	111	590	92

Pitching	ERA	W	Sv	CG	ShO	HR	BB	SO
Los Angeles	3.06	93	40	15	14	96	500	1028
Pittsburgh	3.44	98	51	18	11	117	401	919
Atlanta	3.49	94	48	18	7	118	481	969
New York	3.56	77	39	12	11	108	410	1028
San Diego	3.57	84	47	14	11	139	457	921
Montreal	3.64	71	39	12	14	111	584	909
St.Louis	3.69	84	51	9	5	114	454	822
Cincinnati	3.83	74	43	7	11	127	560	997
Philadelphia	3.86	78	35	16	11	111	670	988
Houston	4.00	65	36	7	13	129	651	1033
San Francisco	4.03	75	45	10	10	143	544	905
Chicago	4.03	77	40	12	4	117	542	927

NL Team by Team Statistics

At least 150 at bats or 50 innings pitched during the regular season. Players who played with more than one NL team during the season are listed with their final clubs. Players traded from the AL are listed with NL team only if they have 150 AB or 50 IP. Note that (*) indicates rookie.

Atlanta Braves

Batting (150 AB)	Avg	AB	R	H	HR	RBI	SB
Jeff Treadway	.320	306	41	98	3	32	2
Terry Pendleton	.319	586	94	187	22	86	10
Otis Nixon	.297	401	81	119	0	26	72
David Justice	.275	396	67	109	21	87	8
Lonnie Smith	.275	353	58	97	7	44	9
Jeff Blauser	.259	352	49	91	11	54	5
Sid Bream	.253	265	32	67	11	45	0
Ron Gant	.251	561	101	141	32	105	34
Brian Hunter*	.251	271	32	68	12	50	0
Rafael Belliard	.249	353	36	88	0	27	3
Greg Olson	.241	411	46	99	6	44	1
Mark Lemke	.234	269	36	63	2	23	1
Damon Berryhill	.188	160	13	30	5	14	1

Acquired: P Clancy from Hou.(July 31) for two minor leaguers; P Pena from NY Mets (Aug.29) for P Tony Castillo and a player to be named later; C Berryhill and P Bielecki from Chi.Cubs (Sept.29) for two minor league pitchers.

Pitching (50 IP)	ERA	W-L	Gm	IP	BB	SO
Juan Berenguer	2.24	0-3	49	64.1	20	53
Alejandro Pena	2.40	8-1	59	82.1	22	62
Tom Glavine	2.55	20-11	34	246.2	69	192
Kent Mercker	2.58	5-3	50	73.1	35	62
Mike Stanton*	2.88	5-5	74	78.0	21	54
Steve Avery	3.38	18-8	35	210.1	65	137
Charlie Leibrandt	3.49	15-13	36	229.2	56	128
John Smoltz	3.80	14-13	36	229.2	77	148
Jim Clancy	3.91	3-5	54	89.2	34	50
Mike Bielecki	4.46	13-11	41	173.2	56	75
Rick Mahler	4.50	2-4	23	66.0	28	27

Saves: Berenguer (17); Pena (15); Clancy (8); Stanton (7); Mercker (6); Mark Wohlers (2); Marvin Freeman and Jeff Parrett (1). **Complete games:** Glavine (9); Smoltz (5); Avery (3); Leibrandt (1). **Shutouts:** Avery, Glavine and Leibrandt (1).

Cincinnati Reds

Batting (150 AB)	Avg	AB	R	H	HR	RBI	SB
Hal Morris	.318	478	72	152	14	59	10
Barry Larkin	.302	464	88	140	20	69	24
Chris Sabo	.301	582	91	175	26	88	19
Bill Doran	.280	361	51	101	6	35	5
Jeff Reed	.267	270	20	72	3	31	0
Billy Hatcher	.262	442	45	116	4	41	11
Glenn Braggs	.260	250	36	65	11	39	11
Mariano Duncan	.258	333	46	86	12	40	5
Paul O'Neill	.256	532	71	136	28	91	12
Eric Davis	.235	285	39	67	11	33	14
Carmelo Martinez	.234	154	13	36	6	19	0
Herm Winningham	.225	169	17	38	1	4	4
Luis Quinones	.222	212	15	47	4	20	1
Joe Oliver	.216	269	21	58	11	41	0

Acquired: 1B-OF Carmelo Martinez from KC (July 11) for 1B-OF Benzinger.

Pitching (50 IP)	ERA	W-L	Gm	IP	BB	SO
Jose Rijo	2.51	15-6	30	204.1	55	172
Norm Charlton	2.91	3-5	39	108.1	34	77
Rob Dibble	3.17	3-5	67	82.1	25	124
Kip Gross*	3.47	6-4	29	85.2	40	40
Randy Myers	3.55	6-13	58	132.0	80	108
Ted Power	3.62	5-3	68	87.0	31	51
Chris Hammond*	4.06	7-7	20	99.2	48	50
Tom Browning	4.18	14-14	36	230.1	56	115
Scott Scudder	4.35	6-9	27	101.1	56	51
Jack Armstrong	5.48	7-13	27	139.2	54	93

Saves: Dibble (31); Myers (6); Power (3); Don Carman, Charlton and Scudder (1). **Complete games:** Rijo (3); Armstrong, Browning, Gross and Myers (1). **Shutouts:** Rijo (1).

Chicago Cubs

Batting (150 AB)	Avg	AB	R	H	HR	RBI	SB
Ryne Sandberg	.291	585	104	170	26	100	22
George Bell	.285	558	63	159	25	86	2
Hector Villanueva	.276	192	23	53	13	32	0
Mark Grace	.273	619	87	169	8	58	3
Andre Dawson	.272	563	69	153	31	104	4
Shawon Dunston	.260	492	59	128	12	50	21
Luis Salazar	.258	333	34	86	14	38	0
Chico Walker	.257	374	51	96	6	34	13
Doug Dascenzo	.255	239	40	61	1	18	14
Dwight Smith	.228	167	16	38	3	21	2
Rick Wilkins*	.222	203	21	45	6	22	3
Jerome Walton	.219	270	42	59	5	17	7

Traded: C Damon Berryhill and P Mike Bielecki to Atl.(Sept.29) for two minor league pitchers.

Pitching (50 IP)	ERA	W-L	Gm	IP	BB	SO
Chuck McElroy*	1.95	6-2	71	101.1	57	92
Paul Assenmacher	3.24	7-8	75	102.2	31	117
Greg Maddux	3.35	15-11	37	263.0	66	198
Heath Slocumb*	3.45	2-1	52	62.2	30	34
Les Lancaster	3.52	9-7	64	156.0	49	102
Bob Scanlan*	3.89	7-8	40	111.0	40	44
Rick Sutcliffe	4.10	6-5	19	96.2	45	52
Frank Castillo*	4.35	6-7	18	111.2	33	73
Shawn Boskie	5.23	4-9	28	129.0	52	62
Danny Jackson	6.75	1-5	17	70.2	48	31

Saves: Dave Smith (17); Assenmacher (15); Lancaster and McElroy (3); Scanlon and Slocumb (1). **Complete games:** Maddux (7); Castillo (4); Lancaster (1). **Shutouts:** Maddux (2).

Houston Astros

Batting (150 AB)	Avg	AB	R	H	HR	RBI	SB
Craig Biggio	.295	546	79	161	4	46	19
Jeff Bagwell*	.294	554	79	163	15	82	7
Steve Finley	.285	596	84	170	8	54	34
Casey Candaele	.262	461	44	121	4	50	9
Luis Gonzalez*	.254	473	51	120	13	69	10
Ken Caminiti	.253	574	65	145	13	80	4
Andujar Cedeno*	.243	251	27	61	9	36	4
Eric Yelding	.243	276	19	67	1	20	11
Rafael Ramirez	.236	233	17	55	1	20	3

Pitching (50 IP)	ERA	W-L	Gm	IP	BB	SO
Pete Harnisch	2.70	12-9	33	216.2	83	172
Dwayne Henry	3.19	3-2	52	67.2	39	51
Al Osuna*	3.42	7-6	71	81.2	46	68
Darryl Kile*	3.69	7-11	37	153.2	84	100
Jim Corsi	3.71	0-5	47	77.2	23	53
Curt Schilling	3.81	3-5	56	75.2	39	71
Jimmy Jones	4.39	6-8	26	135.1	51	88
Mark Portugal	4.49	10-12	32	168.1	59	120
Xavier Hernandez	4.71	2-7	32	63.0	32	55
Jim Deshaies	4.98	5-12	28	161.0	72	98
Ryan Bowen*	5.15	6-4	14	71.2	36	49

Saves: Osuna (12); Schilling (8); Mike Capel and Hernandez (3); Henry (2); Bob Mallicoat, Portugal and Dean Wilkins (1). **Complete games:** Harnisch (4); Deshaies, Jones and Portugal (1). **Shutouts:** Harnisch (2); Jones (1).

Los Angeles Dodgers

Batting (150 AB)

	Avg	AB	R	H	HR	RBI	SB
Brett Butler............	.296	615	112	182	2	38	38
Lenny Harris.........	.287	429	59	123	3	38	12
Mike Sharperson.....	.278	216	24	60	2	20	1
Juan Samuel.........	.271	594	74	161	12	58	23
Darryl Strawberry.....	.265	505	86	134	28	99	10
Mike Scioscia	.264	345	39	91	8	40	4
Eddie Murray.........	.260	576	69	150	19	96	10
Kal Daniels	.249	461	54	115	17	73	6
Gary Carter..........	.246	248	22	61	6	26	2
Alfredo Griffin.......	.243	350	27	85	0	27	5
Mitch Webster........	.222	171	21	38	2	19	0
Stan Javier...........	.205	176	21	36	1	11	7

Acquired: OF Webster from Pit.(July 3) for OF Jose Gonzalez; P McDowell from Phi.(Aug.1) for P Mike Hartley and OF Braulio Castillo.

Pitching (50 IP)

	ERA	W-L	Gm	IP	BB	SO
Tim Belcher	2.62	10-9	33	209.1	75	156
Mike Morgan	2.78	14-10	34	236.1	61	140
Roger McDowell	2.93	9-9	71	101.1	48	50
Jim Gott.............	2.96	4-3	55	76.0	32	73
Jay Howell...........	3.18	6-5	44	51.0	11	40
Bob Ojeda	3.18	12-9	31	189.1	70	120
Ramon Martinez	3.27	17-13	33	220.1	69	150
Tim Crews	3.43	2-3	60	76.0	19	53
Orel Hershiser	3.46	7-2	21	112.0	32	73
Kevin Gross	3.58	10-11	46	115.1	50	95

Saves: Howell (16); McDowell (10); Crews (6); Gross (3); Jim Candelaria, Gott and Steve Wilson (2); Morgan (1). **Complete games:** Martinez (6); Morgan (5); Belcher and Ojeda (2); **Shutouts:** Martinez (4); Belcher, Morgan and Ojeda (1).

New York Mets

Batting (150 AB)

	Avg	AB	R	H	HR	RBI	SB
Keith Miller.........	.280	275	41	77	4	23	14
Daryl Boston	.275	255	40	70	4	21	15
Rick Cerone.........	.273	227	18	62	2	16	1
Mackey Sasser........	.272	228	18	62	5	35	0
Gregg Jefferies	.272	486	59	132	9	62	26
Mark Carreon........	.260	254	18	66	4	21	2
Howard Johnson.....	.259	564	108	146	38	117	30
Kevin McReynolds.....	.259	522	65	135	16	74	6
Dave Magadan	.258	418	58	108	4	51	1
Vince Coleman	.255	278	45	71	1	17	37
Kevin Elster	.241	348	33	84	6	36	2
Hubie Brooks	.238	357	48	85	16	50	3
Garry Templeton	.221	276	25	61	3	26	3
Charlie O'Brien	.185	168	16	31	2	14	0

Acquired: SS Templeton from SD (May 31) for 2B Tim Teufel; P Burke from Mon.(July 15) for P Ron Darling and minor leaguer. **Traded:** P Alejandro Pena to Atl.(Aug.29) for P Tony Castillo and a minor leaguer.

Pitching (50 IP)

	ERA	W-L	Gm	IP	BB	SO
Jeff Innis	2.66	0-2	69	84.2	23	47
John Franco	2.93	5-9	52	55.1	18	45
David Cone..........	3.29	14-14	34	232.2	73	241
Tim Burke	3.36	6-7	72	101.2	26	59
Dwight Gooden	3.60	13-7	27	190.0	56	150
Frank Viola	3.97	13-15	35	231.1	54	132
Wally Whitehurst......	4.19	7-12	36	133.1	25	87
Pete Schourek*	4.27	5-4	35	86.1	43	67
Doug Simons*........	5.19	2-3	42	60.2	19	38

Saves: Franco (30); Burke (6); Schourek (2); Simons and Whitehurst (1). **Complete games:** Cone (5); Gooden and Viola (3); Schourek (1). **Shutouts:** Cone (2); Gooden and Schourek (1).

Montreal Expos

Batting (150 AB)

	Avg	AB	R	H	HR	RBI	SB
Ivan Calderon........	.300	470	69	141	19	75	31
Dave Martinez.......	.295	396	47	117	7	42	16
Larry Walker.........	.290	487	59	141	16	64	14
Marquis Grissom.....	.267	558	73	149	6	39	76
Spike Owen	.255	424	39	108	3	26	2
Delino DeShields	.238	563	83	134	10	51	56
Tim Wallach	.225	577	60	130	13	73	2
Andres Galarraga	.219	375	34	82	9	33	5
Gil Reyes	.217	207	11	45	0	13	2
Tom Foley	.208	168	12	35	0	15	2
Mike Fitzgerald	.202	198	17	40	4	28	4

Acquired: P Darling and minor leaguer from NY Mets (July 15) for P Tim Burke. **Traded:** P Boyd to Texas (July 21) for three minor leaguers; P Darling to Oakland (July 31) for two minor leaguers.

Pitching (50 IP)

	ERA	W-L	Gm	IP	BB	SO
Dennis Martinez......	2.39	14-11	31	222.0	62	123
Jeff Fassero*	2.44	2-5	51	55.1	17	42
Barry Jones	3.35	4-9	77	88.2	33	46
Oil Can Boyd	3.52	6-8	19	120.1	40	82
Chris Nabholz........	3.63	8-7	24	153.2	57	99
Mark Gardner........	3.85	9-11	27	168.1	75	107
Bill Sampen..........	4.00	9-5	43	92.1	46	52
Chris Haney*.........	4.04	3-7	16	84.2	43	51
Brian Barnes*	4.22	5-8	28	160.0	84	117
Scott Ruskin	4.24	4-4	64	63.2	30	46
Ron Darling	4.37	5-8	20	119.1	33	69

Saves: Jones (13); Fassero (8); Mel Rojas and Ruskin (6); Steve Frey (1). **Complete games:** Martinez (9); Barnes, Boyd and Nabholz (1). **Shutouts:** Martinez (5); Boyd (1).

Philadelphia Phillies

Batting (150 AB)

	Avg	AB	R	H	HR	RBI	SB
Dave Hollins	.298	151	18	45	6	21	1
Lenny Dykstra	.297	246	48	73	3	12	24
John Kruk	.294	538	84	158	21	92	7
Ricky Jordan	.272	301	38	82	9	49	0
Dickie Thon	.252	539	44	136	9	44	11
Dale Murphy..........	.252	544	66	137	18	81	1
Mickey Morandini*....	.249	325	38	81	1	20	13
Randy Ready	.249	205	32	51	1	20	2
Wally Backman.......	.243	185	20	45	0	15	3
Wes Chamberlain*.....	.240	383	51	92	13	50	9
Charlie Hayes........	.230	460	34	106	12	53	3
Steve Lake...........	.228	158	12	36	1	11	0
Von Hayes...........	.225	284	43	64	0	21	9
Darren Daulton	.196	285	36	56	12	42	5

Acquired: P Hartley and OF Braulio Castillo from LA (Aug.1) for P Roger McDowell.

Pitching (50 IP)

	ERA	W-L	Gm	IP	BB	SO
Mitch Williams........	2.34	12-5	69	88.1	62	84
Wally Ritchie	2.50	1-2	39	50.1	17	26
Tommy Greene........	3.38	13-7	36	207.2	66	154
Jose DeJesus.........	3.42	10-9	31	181.2	128	118
Terry Mulholland	3.61	16-13	34	232.0	49	142
Bruce Ruffin	3.78	4-7	31	119.0	38	85
Joe Boever..........	3.84	3-5	68	98.1	54	89
Mike Hartley	4.21	4-1	58	83.1	47	63
Danny Cox	4.57	4-6	23	102.1	39	46
Jason Grimsley*	4.87	1-7	12	61.0	41	42
Pat Combs	4.90	2-6	14	64.1	43	41

Saves: Williams (30); Hartley (2); DeJesus (1). **Complete games:** Mulholland (8); DeJesus and Greene (3); Combs and Ruffin (1). **Shutouts:** Mulholland (3); Greene (2); Ruffin (1).

Pittsburgh Pirates

Batting (150 AB)

	Avg	AB	R	H	HR	RBI	SB
Bobby Bonilla	.302	577	102	174	18	100	2
Don Slaught	.295	220	19	65	1	29	1
Barry Bonds	.292	510	95	149	25	116	43
Mike LaValliere	.289	336	25	97	3	41	2
Lloyd McClendon	.288	163	24	47	7	24	2
Orlando Merced*	.275	411	83	113	10	50	8
Gary Varsho	.273	187	23	51	4	23	9
Jay Bell	.270	608	96	164	16	67	10
Jose Lind	.265	502	53	133	3	54	7
Andy Van Slyke	.265	491	87	130	17	83	10
Gary Redus	.246	252	45	62	7	24	17
Curtis Wilkerson	.188	191	20	36	2	18	2

Pitching (50 IP)

	ERA	W-L	Gm	IP	BB	SO
Randy Tomlin	2.98	8-7	31	175.0	54	104
Doug Drabek	3.07	15-14	35	234.2	62	142
John Smiley	3.08	20-8	33	207.2	44	129
Bill Landrum	3.18	4-4	61	76.1	19	45
Zane Smith	3.20	16-10	35	228.0	29	120
Stan Belinda	3.45	7-5	60	78.1	35	71
Bob Walk	3.60	9-2	25	115.0	35	67
Vicente Palacios	3.75	6-3	36	81.2	38	64
Bob Patterson	4.11	4-3	54	65.2	15	57
Neal Heaton	4.33	3-3	42	68.2	21	34
Bob Kipper	4.65	2-2	52	60.0	22	38

Saves: Landrum (17); Belinda (16); Rosario Rodriguez (6); Kipper (4); Roger Mason and Palacios (3); Patterson (2). **Complete games:** Smith (6); Drabek (5); Tomlin (4); Smiley (2); Palacios (1). **Shutouts:** Smith (3); Drabek and Tomlin (2); Palacios and Smiley (1).

San Diego Padres

Batting (150 AB)

	Avg	AB	R	H	HR	RBI	SB
Tony Gwynn	.317	530	69	168	4	62	8
Bip Roberts	.281	424	66	119	3	32	26
Fred McGriff	.278	528	84	147	31	106	4
Tony Fernandez	.272	558	81	152	4	38	23
Benito Santiago	.267	580	60	155	17	87	8
Darrin Jackson	.262	359	51	94	21	49	5
Thomas Howard*	.249	281	30	70	4	22	10
Jerald Clark	.228	369	26	84	10	47	2
Tim Teufel	.217	341	41	74	12	44	9
Scott Coolbaugh	.217	180	12	39	2	15	0
Jack Howell	.206	160	24	33	6	16	0

Acquired: 2B Teufel from NY Mets (May 31) for SS Garry Templeton; INF Howell from Cal.(July 30) for OF Shawn Abner.

Pitching (50 IP)

	ERA	W-L	Gm	IP	BB	SO
Greg Harris	2.23	9-5	20	133.0	27	95
Mike Maddux	2.46	7-2	64	98.2	27	57
Andy Benes	3.03	15-11	33	223.0	59	167
Rich Rodriguez	3.26	3-1	64	80.0	44	40
Jose Melendez*	3.27	8-5	31	93.2	24	60
Bruce Hurst	3.29	15-8	31	221.2	59	141
Dennis Rasmussen	3.74	6-13	24	146.2	49	75
Craig Lefferts	3.91	1-6	54	69.0	14	48
Adam Peterson	4.45	3-4	13	54.2	28	37
Ricky Bones*	4.83	4-6	11	54.0	18	31
Ed Whitson	5.03	4-6	13	78.2	17	40

Saves: Lefferts (23); Larry Andersen (13); Maddux (5); Melendez (3); Jeremy Hernandez (2); Wes Gardner (1). **Complete games:** Benes and Hurst (4); Harris (3); Whitson (2); Rasmussen (1). **Shutouts:** Harris (2); Benes and Rasmussen (1).

St. Louis Cardinals

Batting (150 AB)

	Avg	AB	R	H	HR	RBI	SB
Milt Thompson	.307	326	55	100	6	34	16
Felix Jose	.305	568	69	173	8	77	20
Ozzie Smith	.285	550	96	157	3	50	35
Todd Zeile	.280	565	76	158	11	81	17
Pedro Guerrero	.272	427	41	116	8	70	4
Tom Pagnozzi	.264	459	38	121	2	57	9
Ray Lankford*	.251	566	83	142	9	69	44
Geronimo Pena*	.243	185	38	45	5	17	15
Jose Oquendo	.240	366	37	88	1	26	1
Gerald Perry	.240	242	29	58	6	36	15
Rex Hudler	.227	201	21	47	1	15	12
Bernard Gilkey*	.216	268	28	58	5	20	14

Pitching (50 IP)

	ERA	W-L	Gm	IP	BB	SO
Lee Smith	2.34	6-3	67	73.0	13	67
Jose DeLeon	2.71	5-9	28	162.2	61	118
Scott Terry	2.80	4-4	65	80.1	32	52
Bob Tewksbury	3.25	11-12	30	191.0	38	75
Ken Hill	3.57	11-10	30	181.1	67	121
Omar Olivares*	3.71	11-7	28	167.1	61	91
Bryn Smith	3.85	12-9	31	198.2	45	94
Rheal Cormier*	4.12	4-5	11	67.2	8	38
Cris Carpenter	4.23	10-4	59	66.0	20	47
Juan Agosto	4.81	5-3	72	86.0	39	34

Saves: L.Smith (47); Agosto (2); Olivares and Terry (1). **Complete games:** B.Smith and Tewksbury (3); Cormier (2); DeLeon (1). **Shutouts:** none.

San Francisco Giants

Batting (150 AB)

	Avg	AB	R	H	HR	RBI	SB
Willie McGee	.312	497	67	155	4	43	17
Will Clark	.301	565	84	170	29	116	4
Matt Williams	.268	589	72	158	34	98	5
Mike Felder	.264	348	51	92	0	18	21
Robby Thompson	.262	492	74	129	19	48	14
Kevin Mitchell	.256	371	52	95	27	69	2
Dave Anderson	.248	226	24	56	2	13	2
Darren Lewis*	.248	222	41	55	1	15	13
Terry Kennedy	.234	171	12	40	3	13	0
Kevin Bass	.233	361	43	84	10	40	7
Kirt Manwaring	.225	178	16	40	0	19	1
Jose Uribe	.221	231	23	51	1	12	3
Tom Herr	.209	215	23	45	1	21	9
Steve Decker*	.206	233	11	48	5	24	0

Claimed: 2B Herr on waivers from NY Mets (Aug.15), then released him (Oct.6).

Pitching (50 IP)

	ERA	W-L	Gm	IP	BB	SO
Jeff Brantley	2.45	5-2	67	95.1	52	81
Dave Righetti	3.39	2-7	61	71.2	28	51
Trevor Wilson	3.56	13-11	44	202.0	77	139
Bryan Hickerson*	3.60	2-2	17	50.0	17	43
Rod Beck*	3.78	1-1	31	52.1	13	38
Francisco Oliveras	3.86	6-6	55	79.1	22	48
Bud Black	3.99	12-16	34	214.1	71	104
John Burkett	4.18	12-11	36	206.2	60	131
Kelly Downs	4.19	10-4	45	111.2	52	62
Don Robinson	4.38	5-9	34	121.1	50	78
Paul McClellan*	4.56	3-6	13	71.0	25	44

Saves: Righetti (24); Brantley (15); Oliveras (3); Beck, Eric Gunderson and Robinson (1). **Complete games:** Black and Burkett (3); Wilson (2); McClellan and Mike Remlinger (1). **Shutouts:** Black (3); Burkett, Remlinger and Wilson (1).

American League Championship Series
Composite Box Score

Minnesota Twins

Batting (1 AB)	Avg	AB	R	H	HR	RBI
Kirby Puckett, cf	.429	21	4	9	2	6
Chuck Knoblauch, 2b	.350	20	5	7	0	3
Shane Mack, rf	.333	18	4	6	0	3
Mike Pagliarulo, 3b-ph	.333	15	3	5	1	3
Chili Davis, dh	.294	17	3	5	0	2
Brian Harper, c	.278	18	1	5	0	1
Dan Gladden, lf	.261	23	4	6	0	3
Greg Gagne, ss	.235	17	2	4	0	1
Kent Hrbek, 1b	.143	21	0	3	0	3
Paul Sorrento, ph	.000	1	0	0	0	0
Gene Larkin, ph	.000	3	0	0	0	0
Junior Ortiz, c	.000	3	0	0	0	0
Scott Leius, ph-3b	.000	4	0	0	0	0
TOTALS	.276	181	27	50	3	25

Pitching	W-L	ERA	Gm	IP	H	BB	SO
Dave West	1-0	0.00	2	5.2	1	4	4
Carl Willis	0-0	0.00	3	5.1	2	0	3
Rick Aguilera	0-0	0.00	3	3.1	1	0	3
Mark Guthrie	1-0	0.00	2	2.2	0	0	0
Steve Bedrosian	0-0	0.00	2	1.1	3	2	2
Jack Morris	2-0	4.05	2	13.1	17	1	7
Scott Erickson	0-0	4.50	1	4.0	3	5	2
Kevin Tapani	0-1	7.84	2	10.1	16	3	9
TOTALS	4-1	3.33	5	46.0	43	15	30

Saves: Aguilera (3); **WP:** West 2, Morris.

Toronto Blue Jays

Batting (1 AB)	Avg	AB	R	H	HR	RBI
Roberto Alomar, 2b	.474	19	3	9	0	4
Devon White, cf	.364	22	5	8	0	0
Pat Borders, c	.263	19	0	5	0	2
Joe Carter, rf-dh	.263	19	3	5	1	4
Mookie Wilson, pr-dh-lf	.250	8	1	2	0	0
Kelly Gruber, 3b	.238	21	1	5	0	4
John Olerud, 1b	.211	19	1	4	0	3
Manuel Lee, ss	.125	16	3	2	0	0
Rance Mulliniks, dh-ph	.125	8	1	1	0	0
Candy Maldonado, lf-rf	.100	20	1	2	0	1
Rob Ducey, pr-rf	.000	1	0	0	0	0
Pat Tabler, ph	.000	1	0	0	0	0
TOTALS	.249	173	19	43	1	18

Pitching	W-L	ERA	Gm	IP	H	BB	SO
Jim Acker	0-0	0.00	1	0.2	1	0	1
Tom Henke	0-0	0.00	2	2.2	0	1	5
David Wells	0-0	2.35	4	7.2	6	2	9
Jimmy Key	0-0	3.00	1	6.0	5	1	1
Juan Guzman	1-0	3.18	1	5.2	4	4	2
Mike Timlin	0-1	3.18	4	5.2	5	2	5
Duane Ward	0-0	6.23	2	4.1	4	1	6
Tom Candiotti	0-1	8.22	1	7.2	17	2	5
Bob MacDonald	0-0	9.00	1	1.0	1	1	0
Todd Stottlemyre	0-1	9.81	1	3.2	7	1	3
TOTALS	1-4	4.60	5	45.0	50	15	37

Saves: Ward (1); **WP:** Candiotti, Guzman; **HBP:** Stottlemyre (Gagne); **PB:** Borders (2).

Score by Innings

	1	2	3	4	5	6	7	8	9	10	R	H	E
Minnesota	3	3	2	4	1	7	1	4	1	1	27	50	4
Toronto	3	1	5	3	0	4	2	0	1	0	19	43	7

DP: Minnesota 3, Toronto 5; **LOB:** Minnesota 38, Toronto 35; **2B:** Minnesota—Davis 2, Harper 2, Knoblauch 2, Mack, Puckett, Pagliarulo; Toronto—Carter 2, Borders, Maldonado, Olerud, White. **3B:** Minnesota—Mack. **SB:** Minnesota—Gladden 3, Knoblauch 2, Mack 2, Davis; Toronto—Carter. **CS:** Minnesota—Gagne 2, Knoblauch, Mack; Toronto—Carter. **S:** Minnesota—Pagliarulo; Toronto—Alomar 2, Borders. **SF:** Minnesota—Mack, Puckett; Toronto—Carter.

Umpires: Larry Barnett, Mark Johnson, Jim McKean, Mike Reilly, Rocky Roe, Tim Welke.

Game 1
Tuesday, Oct. 8 at Minnesota

	1	2	3	4	5	6	7	8	9	R	H	E
Toronto	0	0	0	1	0	3	0	0	0	4	9	2
Minnesota	2	2	1	0	0	0	0	0	x	5	11	0

Win—Morris, Min.(1-0); **Save**—Aguilera (1); **Loss**—Candiotti, Tor.(0-1).
2B: Toronto—Carter; Minnesota—Harper. **RBI:** Toronto—Gruber 2, Olerud 2; Minnesota—Davis 2, Gagne, Knoblauch, Mack. **SB:** Toronto—Gruber (1); Minnesota—Knoblauch (2), Davis (1), Mack (1).
Attendance—54,766. **Time**—3:17.

Game 2
Wednesday, Oct. 9 at Minnesota

	1	2	3	4	5	6	7	8	9	R	H	E
Toronto	1	0	2	0	0	0	2	0	0	5	9	0
Minnesota	0	0	1	0	0	1	0	0	0	2	5	1

Win—Guzman, Tor.(1-0); **Save**—D.Ward, Tor.(1); **Loss**—Tapani, Min.(0-1).
2B: Toronto—White. **RBI:** Toronto—Carter 2, Gruber 2; Minnesota—Harper. **SB:** Toronto—Alomar (1), White (1); Minnesota—Gladden (1).
Attendance—54,816. **Time**—3:02.

Game 3
Friday, Oct. 11 at Toronto

	1	2	3	4	5	6	7	8	9	10	R	H	E
Minnesota	0	0	0	0	1	1	0	0	0	1	3	7	0
Toronto	2	0	0	0	0	0	0	0	0		2	5	1

Win—Guthrie, Min.(1-0); **Save**—Aguilera, Min.(2); **Loss**—Timlin, Tor.(0-1).
2B: Minnesota—Knoblauch, Puckett; Toronto—Maldonado. **3B:** Minnesota—Mack. **HR:** Minnesota—Pagliarulo (1); Toronto—Carter (1). **RBI:** Minnesota—Hrbek, Pagliarulo, Puckett; Toronto—Carter, Maldonado.
Attendance—51,454. **Time**—3:36.

Game 4
Saturday, Oct. 12 at Toronto

	1	2	3	4	5	6	7	8	9	R	H	E
Minnesota	0	0	0	4	0	2	1	1	1	9	13	1
Toronto	0	1	0	0	0	1	0	0	1	3	11	2

Win—Morris, Min.(2-0); **Loss**—Stottlemyre, Tor.(0-1).
2B: Minnesota—Davis 2, Harper, Pagliarulo; Toronto—Borders, Gruber. **HR:** Minnesota—Puckett (1). **RBI:** Minnesota—Gladden 3, Pagliarulo 2, Puckett, Mack; Toronto—Borders 2, Alomar. **SB:** Minnesota—Gladden (2); Toronto—Alomar (2), White (2).
Attendance—51,526. **Time**—3:15.

Game 5
Sunday, Oct. 13 at Toronto

	1	2	3	4	5	6	7	8	9	R	H	E
Minnesota	1	1	0	0	0	3	0	3	0—	8	14	2
Toronto	0	0	3	2	0	0	0	0	0—	5	9	1

Win—West, Min.(1-0); **Save**—Aguilera, Min.(3); **Loss**—D.Ward, Tor.(0-1).

2B: Minnesota—Knoblauch; Toronto—Carter. **HR:** Minnesota—Puckett (2). **RBI:** Minnesota—Hrbek 2, Knoblauch 2, Puckett 2, Mack; Toronto—Alomar 3, Carter, Olerud.

Attendance—51,425. **Time**—3:29.

Most Valuable Player
Kirby Puckett, Minnesota
Centerfielder

Avg	AB	R	H	2B	3B	HR	RBI
.429	21	4	9	1	0	2	6

National League Championship Series
Composite Box Score

Atlanta Braves

Batting (1 AB)	Avg	AB	R	H	HR	RBI
Brian Hunter, 1b	.333	18	2	6	1	4
Greg Olson, c	.333	24	3	8	1	4
Jeff Treadway, 2b	.333	3	0	1	0	0
Sid Bream, 1b-ph	.300	10	1	3	1	3
Ron Gant, cf	.259	27	4	7	1	3
Tom Glavine, p	.250	4	0	1	0	0
Tommy Gregg, ph	.250	4	0	1	0	0
Lonnie Smith, lf	.250	24	3	6	0	0
Rafael Belliard, ss	.211	19	0	4	0	1
David Justice rf	.200	25	4	5	1	2
Mark Lemke, 2b	.200	20	1	4	0	1
John Smoltz, p	.200	5	0	1	0	0
Terry Pendleton, 3b	.167	30	1	5	0	1
Steve Avery, p	.143	7	0	1	0	0
Charlie Leibrandt, p	.000	1	0	0	0	0
Jeff Blauser, ss-ph	.000	2	0	0	0	0
Jerry Willard, ph	.000	2	0	0	0	0
Keith Mitchell, pr-lf-ph	.000	4	0	0	0	0
TOTALS	.231	229	19	53	5	19

Pitching	W-L	ERA	Gm	IP	H	BB	SO
Steve Avery	2-0	0.00	2	16.1	9	4	17
Alejandro Pena	0-0	0.00	4	4.1	1	0	4
Mark Wohlers	0-0	0.00	3	1.2	3	1	1
Jim Clancy	0-0	0.00	1	0.1	0	0	0
Charlie Leibrandt	0-0	1.35	1	6.2	8	3	6
John Smoltz	2-0	1.76	2	15.1	14	3	15
Mike Stanton	0-0	2.45	8	3.2	4	3	3
Tom Glavine	0-2	3.21	2	14.0	12	6	11
Kent Mercker	0-1	13.50	1	0.2	0	2	0
TOTALS	4-3	1.57	7	63.0	51	22	57

Saves: Pena (3); **WP:** Pena, Stanton.

Pittsburgh Pirates

Batting (1 AB)	Avg	AB	R	H	HR	RBI
Gary Varsho, ph	.500	2	0	1	0	0
Jay Bell, ss	.414	29	2	12	1	1
Mike LaValliere, c-ph	.333	6	0	2	0	1
Bobby Bonilla, rf	.304	23	2	7	0	1
Steve Buechele, 3b	.304	23	2	7	0	0
Don Slaught, c-ph	.235	17	0	4	0	1
Orlando Merced, 1b-ph	.222	9	1	2	1	1
Doug Drabek, p	.200	5	0	1	0	0
Jose Lind, 2b	.160	25	0	4	0	3
Andy Van Slyke, cf	.160	25	3	4	1	2
Gary Redus, 1b	.158	19	1	3	0	0
Barry Bonds, lf	.148	27	1	4	0	0
Roger Mason, p	.000	1	0	0	0	0
Cecil Espy, ph	.000	2	0	0	0	0
Lloyd McClendon, ph-1b	.000	2	0	0	0	0
Randy Tomlin, p	.000	2	0	0	0	0
Bob Walk, p	.000	2	0	0	0	0
Curtis Wilkerson, ph	.000	4	0	0	0	0
Zane Smith, p	.000	5	0	0	0	0
TOTALS	.224	228	12	51	3	11

Pitching	W-L	ERA	Gm	IP	H	BB	SO
Stan Belinda	1-0	0.00	3	5.0	0	3	4
Roger Mason	0-0	0.00	3	4.1	3	1	2
Bob Patterson	0-0	0.00	1	2.0	1	0	3
Doug Drabek	1-1	0.60	2	15.0	10	5	10
Zane Smith	1-1	0.61	2	14.2	15	3	10
Bob Walk	0-0	1.93	3	9.1	5	3	5
Randy Tomlin	0-0	3.00	1	6.0	6	2	1
Bob Kipper	0-0	4.50	1	2.0	2	0	1
Bill Landrum	0-0	9.00	1	1.0	2	2	2
John Smiley	0-2	23.63	2	2.2	8	1	3
Rosario Rodriguez	0-0	27.00	1	1.0	1	2	1
TOTALS	3-4	2.57	7	63.0	53	22	42

Saves: Mason, Walk; **Balk:** Walk; **HBP:** Smiley (L.Smith), Z.Smith (Gant).

Score by Innings

	1	2	3	4	5	6	7	8	9	10	R	H	E
Atlanta	9	1	1	0	1	1	1	3	2	0—	19	53	4
Pittsburgh	2	1	2	1	2	1	1	0	1	1—	12	51	6

DP: Atlanta 6, Pittsburgh 3; **LOB:** Atlanta 51, Pittsburgh 54; **2B:** Atlanta—L.Smith 3, Hunter 2, Gant, Justice, Lemke, Olson, Pendleton; Pittsburgh—Bell 2, Bonilla 2, Buechele 2, Van Slyke 2, Bonds, Drabek. **3B:** Atlanta—Pendleton. **SB:** Atlanta—Gant 7, L.Smith 2, Olson, Smoltz; Pittsburgh—Bonds 3, Redus 2, Van Slyke. **CS:** Atlanta—Hunter, Justice, L.Smith; Pittsburgh—Bonilla. **S:** Atlanta—Belliard 2, Leibrandt, Smoltz, Treadway; Pittsburgh—Bell, Buechele, Merced, Slaught. **SF:** Atlanta—Gant; Pittsburgh—Lind.

Umpires: Bob Davidson, Dana DeMuth, Bruce Froemming, Eric Gregg, Doug Harvey, Frank Pulli.

Game 1
Wednesday, Oct. 9 at Pittsburgh

	1	2	3	4	5	6	7	8	9	R	H	E
Atlanta	0	0	0	0	0	0	0	0	1—	1	5	1
Pittsburgh	1	0	2	0	0	1	0	1	x—	5	8	1

Win—Drabek, Pit.(1-0); **Save**—Walk (1); **Loss**—Glavine, Atl.(0-1).

2B: Pittsburgh—Buechele, Drabek, Van Slyke. **HR:** Atlanta—Justice (1); Pittsburgh—Van Slyke (1). **RBI:** Atlanta—Justice; Pittsburgh—Van Slyke 2, Bonilla, Drabek, Lind. **SB:** Pittsburgh—Redus (1).

Attendance—57,347. **Time**—2:51.

Game 2
Thursday, Oct. 10 at Pittsburgh

	1	2	3	4	5	6	7	8	9	R	H	E
Atlanta	0	0	0	0	0	1	0	0	0—	1	8	0
Pittsburgh	0	0	0	0	0	0	0	0	0—	0	6	0

Win—Avery, Atl.(1-0); **Save**—Pena, Atl.(1); **Loss**—Z.Smith, Pit.(0-1).

2B: Atlanta—Lemke; Pittsburgh—Bonilla. **RBI:** Atlanta—Lemke. **SB:** Atlanta—Gant 3 (3); Pittsburgh—Bonds 2 (2), Redus (2).

Attendance—57,533. **Time**—2:46.

National League Championship Series (Cont.)

Game 3
Saturday, Oct. 12 at Atlanta

	1	2	3	4	5	6	7	8	9	R	H	E
Pittsburgh	1	0	0	1	0	0	1	0	0—	3	10	2
Atlanta	4	1	1	0	0	0	1	3	x—	10	11	0

Win—Smoltz, Atl.(1-0); **Save**—Pena, Atl.(2); **Loss**—Smiley, Pit.(0-1).

2B: Pittsburgh—Bell, Buechele; Atlanta—Hunter, Justice, Pendleton. **HR:** Pittsburgh—Bell, Merced; Atlanta—Bream (1), Gant (1), Olson (1). **RBI:** Pittsburgh—Bell, Lind, Merced; Atlanta—Bream 3, Olson 2, Belliard, Gant, Hunter, Justice, Pendleton. **SB:** Pittsburgh—Bonds (3); Atlanta—Olson (1), Smoltz (1). **Attendance**—50,905. **Time**—3:21.

Game 4
Sunday, Oct. 13 at Atlanta

	1	2	3	4	5	6	7	8	9	10	R	H	E
Pittsburgh	0	1	0	0	1	0	0	0	0	1—	3	11	1
Atlanta	2	0	0	0	0	0	0	0	0	0—	2	7	1

Win—Belinda, Pit.(1-0); **Loss**—Mercker, Atl.(0-1).

2B: Atlanta—L.Smith. **RBI:** Pittsburgh—LaValliere, Slaught; Atlanta—Gant, Olson. **SB:** Pittsburgh—Van Slyke. **Attendance**—51,109. **Time**—3:43.

Game 5
Monday, Oct. 14 at Atlanta

	1	2	3	4	5	6	7	8	9	R	H	E
Pittsburgh	0	0	0	0	1	0	0	0	0—	1	6	2
Atlanta	0	0	0	0	0	0	0	0	0—	0	9	1

Win—Z.Smith, Pit.(1-1); **Save**—Mason, Pit.(1); **Loss**—Glavine, Atl.(0-2).

2B: Pittsburgh—Bell, Bonilla, Van Slyke. **3B:** Atlanta—Pendleton. **RBI:** Pittsburgh—Lind. **SB**—Atlanta—Gant (4), L.Smith (1). **Attendance**—51,109. **Time**—2:51.

Game 6
Wednesday, Oct. 16 at Pittsburgh

	1	2	3	4	5	6	7	8	9	R	H	E
Atlanta	0	0	0	0	0	0	0	0	1—	1	7	0
Pittsburgh	0	0	0	0	0	0	0	0	0—	0	4	0

Win—Avery, Atl.(2-0); **Save**—Pena, Pit.(3); **Loss**—Drabek, Pit.(1-1).

2B: Atlanta—L.Smith 2, Olson. **RBI:** Atlanta—Olson. **SB:** Atlanta—Gant 2 (6). **Attendance**—54,508. **Time**—3:09.

Game 7
Thursday, Oct. 17 at Pittsburgh

	1	2	3	4	5	6	7	8	9	R	H	E
Atlanta	3	0	0	0	1	0	0	0	0—	4	6	1
Pittsburgh	0	0	0	0	0	0	0	0	0—	0	6	0

Win—Smoltz, Atl.(2-0); **Loss**—Smiley, Pit.(0-2).

2B: Atlanta—Hunter; Pittsburgh—Bonds. **HR:** Atlanta—Hunter. **RBI:** Atlanta—Hunter 3, Gant. **SB:** Atlanta—Gant (7). **Attendance**—46,932. **Time**—3:04.

Most Valuable Player
Steve Avery, Atlanta
Pitcher

W-L	ERA	Gm	IP	H	BB	SO
2-0	0.00	2	16.1	9	4	17

World Series
Composite Box Score

Minnesota Twins

Batting (1 AB)	Avg	AB	R	H	HR	RBI
Gene Larkin, ph	.500	4	0	2	0	1
Al Newman, ph-3b-2b-ss	.500	2	0	1	0	1
Brian Harper, c-ph	.381	21	2	8	0	1
Scott Leius, 3b-ph-ss	.357	14	2	5	1	2
Chuck Knoblauch, 2b	.308	26	3	8	0	2
Mike Pagliarulo, ph-3b	.273	11	1	3	1	2
Kirby Puckett, cf	.250	24	4	6	2	4
Randy Bush, ph-rf	.250	4	0	1	0	0
Dan Gladden, lf	.233	30	5	7	0	0
Chili Davis, dh-ph-rf	.222	18	4	4	2	4
Junior Ortiz, c	.200	5	0	1	0	1
Greg Gagne, ss	.167	24	1	4	1	3
Shane Mack, rf	.130	23	0	3	0	1
Kent Hrbek, 1b	.115	26	2	3	1	2
Rick Aguilera, ph-p	.000	1	0	0	0	0
Scott Erickson, p	.000	1	0	0	0	0
Kevin Tapani, p	.000	1	0	0	0	0
Jarvis Brown, rf-ph-cf-pr	.000	2	0	0	0	0
Jack Morris, p	.000	2	0	0	0	0
Paul Sorrento, ph-1b	.000	2	0	0	0	0
TOTALS	.232	241	24	56	8	24

Pitching	W-L	ERA	Gm	IP	H	BB	SO
Jack Morris	2-0	1.17	3	23.0	18	9	15
Rick Aguilera	1-1	1.80	4	5.0	6	1	3
Mark Guthrie	0-0	2.25	4	4.0	3	4	3
Terry Leach	0-0	3.86	2	2.1	2	0	2
Kevin Tapani	1-1	4.50	2	12.0	13	2	7
Scott Erickson	0-0	5.06	2	10.2	10	4	5
Carl Willis	0-0	5.14	4	7.0	6	2	2
Steve Bedrosian	0-0	5.40	3	3.1	0	3	2
Dave West	0-0	—	2	0.2	4	0	0
TOTALS	4-3	3.74	7	67.1	63	26	39

Saves: Aguilera (2); **CG:** Morris; **WP:** Morris 2, Bedrosian, Erickson, Guthrie; **HBP:** Erickson (Smith); **PB:** Harper.

Atlanta Braves

Batting (1 AB)	Avg	AB	R	H	HR	RBI
Mark Lemke, 2b	.417	24	4	10	0	4
Rafael Belliard, ss	.375	16	0	6	0	4
Terry Pendleton, 3b	.367	30	6	11	2	3
Ron Gant, cf	.267	30	3	8	0	4
David Justice rf	.259	27	5	7	2	6
Jeff Treadway, 2b-ph	.250	4	1	1	0	0
Lonnie Smith, ph-lf	.231	26	5	6	3	3
Greg Olson, c	.222	27	3	6	0	1
Brian Hunter, lf-ph-1b	.190	21	2	4	1	3
Jeff Blauser, ph-ss	.167	6	0	1	0	0
Sid Bream, 1b	.125	24	0	3	0	0
Francisco Cabrera, ph-c	.000	1	0	0	0	0
Jim Clancy, p	.000	1	0	0	0	0
Tom Glavine, p	.000	2	0	0	0	0
Keith Mitchell, lf-pr	.000	2	0	0	0	0
John Smoltz, p	.000	3	0	0	0	0
Steve Avery, p	.000	3	0	0	0	0
Tommy Gregg, ph	.000	3	0	0	0	0
Jerry Willard, ph	—	0	0	0	0	1
TOTALS	.253	249	29	63	8	29

Pitching	W-L	ERA	Gm	IP	H	BB	SO
Mike Stanton	1-0	0.00	5	7.1	5	2	7
Mark Wohlers	0-0	0.00	3	1.2	2	1	1
Kent Mercker	0-0	0.00	2	1.0	0	1	1
John Smoltz	0-0	1.26	2	14.1	13	1	11
Tom Glavine	1-1	2.70	2	13.1	8	7	8
Alejandro Pena	0-1	3.38	5	5.1	6	3	7
Steve Avery	0-0	3.46	2	13.0	10	1	8
Jim Clancy	1-0	4.15	3	4.1	3	4	2
Randy St.Claire	0-0	9.00	1	1.0	1	0	0
Charlie Leibrandt	0-2	11.25	2	4.0	8	1	3
TOTALS	3-4	2.89	7	65.1	56	21	48

Saves: none; **CG:** Glavine; **WP:** Pena; **Balk:** Glavine; **HBP:** Smoltz (Hrbek).

Score by Innings

	1	2	3	4	5	6	7	8	9	10	11	12		R	H	E
Atlanta	0	2	1	5	6	3	8	4	1	0	0	1	—	29	63	6
Minnesota	5	1	1	0	4	4	2	4	1	1	0	—		24	56	4

DP: Atlanta 6, Minnesota 5. **LOB:** Atlanta 44, Minnesota 35. **2B:** Atlanta—Pendleton 3, Bream 2, Olson 2, Belliard, Hunter, Lemke; Minnesota—Gladden 2, Harper 2, Gagne, Hrbek, Knoblauch, Mack. **3B:** Atlanta—Lemke 3, Gant; Minnesota—Gladden 2, Newman, Puckett. **SB:** Atlanta—Justice, Gant, Olson, Smith; Minnesota—Knoblauch 4, Gladden 2, Puckett. **CS:** Atlanta—Mitchell; Minnesota—Gladden, Leius, Mack. **S:** Atlanta—Belliard, Smith, Treadway; Minnesota—Puckett. **SF:** Atlanta—Belliard, Hunter, Willard; Minnesota—Puckett.

Umpires: AL—Drew Coble, Don Denkinger, Rick Reed; NL—Ed Montague, Terry Tata, Harry Wendlestedt.

Game 1
Saturday, Oct. 19 at Minnesota

	1	2	3	4	5	6	7	8	9	R	H	E
Atlanta	0	0	0	0	0	1	0	1	0	2	6	1
Minnesota	0	0	1	0	3	1	0	0	x	5	9	1

Win—Morris, Min.(1-0); **Save**—Aguilera, Min.(1); **Loss**—Leibrandt, Atl.(0-1). **2B:** Minnesota—Harper, Hrbek. **HR:** Minnesota—Gagne (1), Hrbek (1). **RBI:** Atlanta—Gant 2; Minnesota—Gagne 3, Hrbek, Knoblauch. **SB:** Minnesota—Knoblauch 2, Gladden.
Attendance—55,108. **Time**—3:00.

Game 2
Sunday, Oct. 20 at Minnesota

	1	2	3	4	5	6	7	8	9	R	H	E
Atlanta	0	1	0	0	1	0	0	0	0	2	8	1
Minnesota	2	0	0	0	0	0	1	x		3	4	1

Win—Tapani, Min.(1-0); **Save**—Aguilera, Min.(2); **Loss**—Glavine, Atl.(0-1).
2B: Atlanta—Bream, Olson. **HR:** Minnesota—Davis (1), Leius (1); **RBI:** Atlanta—Belliard, Hunter; Minnesota—Davis 2, Leius.
Attendance—55,145. **Time**—2:37.

Game 3
Tuesday, Oct. 22 at Atlanta

	1	2	3	4	5	6	7	8	9	10	11	12	R	H	E
Minnesota	1	0	0	0	0	1	2	0	0	0	0	—	4	10	1
Atlanta	0	1	0	1	0	2	0	0	0	0	0	1	5	8	2

Win—Clancy, Atl.(1-0); **Loss**—Aguilera, Min.(0-1).
2B: Atlanta—Bream, Olson. **3B:** Minnesota—Gladden. **HR:** Atlanta—Justice (1), Smith (1); Minnesota—Davis (2), Puckett (1). **RBI:** Atlanta—Belliard, Justice, Lemke, Olson, Smith; Minnesota—Davis 2, Knoblauch, Puckett.
Attendance—50,878. **Time**—4:04.

Game 4
Wednesday, Oct. 23 at Atlanta

	1	2	3	4	5	6	7	8	9	R	H	E
Minnesota	0	1	0	0	0	0	1	0	0	2	7	0
Atlanta	0	0	1	0	0	1	0	1	x	3	8	0

Win—Stanton, Atl.(1-0); **Loss**—Guthrie, Min.(0-1).
2B: Atlanta—Lemke, Pendleton; Minnesota—Harper, Knoblauch. **3B:** Atlanta—Pendleton (1), Smith (2); Minnesota—Pagliarulo (1). **RBI:** Atlanta—Pendleton, Smith, Williard; Minnesota—Pagliarulo 2. **SB:** Atlanta—Gant (1), Smith (1); Minnesota—Knoblauch (4).
Attendance—50,878. **Time**—2:57.

Game 5
Thursday, Oct. 24 at Atlanta

	1	2	3	4	5	6	7	8	9	R	H	E
Minnesota	0	0	0	0	3	0	1	1	—	5	7	1
Atlanta	0	0	4	1	0	6	3	x		14	17	1

Win—Glavine, Atl.(1-1); **Loss**—Tapani, Min.(1-1).
2B: Atlanta—Belliard, Pendleton; Minnesota—Gagne. **3B:** Atlanta—Lemke 2, Gant; Minnesota—Gladden, Newman. **HR:** Atlanta—Hunter (1), Justice (2), Smith (3). **RBI:** Atlanta—Justice 5, Lemke 3, Belliar 2, Hunter 2, Gant, Smith; Minnesota—Harper, Hrbek, Leius, Newman, Ortiz. **SB:** Atlanta—Justice (2), Olson (1).
Attendance—50,878. **Time**—2:59.

Game 6
Saturday, Oct. 26 at Minnesota

	1	2	3	4	5	6	7	8	9	10	11	R	H	E
Atlanta	0	0	0	0	2	0	1	0	0	0	0	3	9	1
Minnesota	2	0	0	1	0	0	0	1	0	0	1	4	9	0

Win—Aguilera, Min.(1-1); **Loss**—Leibrandt, Atl.(0-2).
2B: Minnesota—Mack. **3B:** Minnesota—Puckett; **HR:** Atlanta—Pendleton (2); Minnesota—Puckett (2). **RBI:** Atlanta—Pendleton 2, Gant; Minnesota—Puckett 3, Mack. **SB:** Minnesota—Gladden (2), Puckett (1).
Attendance—55,155. **Time**—3:46.

Game 7
Sunday, Oct. 27 at Minnesota

	1	2	3	4	5	6	7	8	9	10	R	H	E
Atlanta	0	0	0	0	0	0	0	0	0	0	0	7	0
Minnesota	0	0	0	0	0	0	0	0	0	1	1	10	0

Win—Morris, Min.(2-0); **Loss**—Pena, Atl.(0-1).
2B: Atlanta—Hunter, Pendleton; Minnesota—Gladden 2. **RBI:** Minnesota—Larkin.
Attendance—55,118. **Time**—3:23.

Most Valuable Player
Jack Morris, Minnesota
Pitcher

W-L	ERA	Gm	IP	H	BB	SO
2-0	1.17	3	23.0	18	9	15

Major League Amateur Draft

First round selections at the 27th Amateur Draft held on June 3, 1991.

No		Pos	No		Pos
1	NY Yankees ..... Brien Taylor, HS, Beaufort, N.C.	lhp	14	Montreal .... Cliff Floyd, HS, S. Holland, Ill.	1b
2	Atlanta .... Mike Kelly, Arizona St.	of	15	Milwaukee .... Tyrone Hill, HS, Yucaipa, Calif.	lhp
3	Minnesota .... David McCarty, Stanford	1b	16	Toronto .... Shawn Green, HS, Tustin, Calif.	of
4	St.Louis .... Dmitri Young, HS, Oxnard, Calif.	ss	17	California .... Eduardo Perez, Florida St.	1b
5	Milwaukee .... K.Henderson, HS, Ringgold, Ga.	of	18	NY Mets .... Al Shirley, HS, Danville, Va.	of
6	Houston .... John Burke, Florida	rhp	19	Texas .... Benji Gil, HS, Chula Vista, Calif.	ss-of
7	Kansas City .... Joe Vitiello, Alabama	of	20	Cincinnati .... Calvin Reese, HS, Hopkins, S.C.	ss
8	San Diego .... Joey Hamilton, Ga.Southern	rhp	21	St.Louis .... Allen Watson, N.Y. Tech	lhp
9	Baltimore .... Mark Smith, USC	of	22	St.Louis .... Brian Barber, HS, Orlando, Fla.	rhp
10	Philadelphia .... Tyler Green, Wichita St.	rhp	23	Boston.............. Aaron Sele, Washington St.	rhp
11	Seattle........... Shawn Estes, HS, Minden, Nev.	lhp	24	Pittsburgh................ John Farrell, Florida JC	c-of
12	Chi.Cubs........... Doug Glanville, Penn	of	25	Chisox.................... Scott Ruffcorn, Baylor	rhp
13	Cleveland .... Manny Ramirez, HS , New York, NY	of	26	Oakland .... Brent Gates, Minnesota	ss

Colleges
Final 1991 *Baseball America* Top 25

Division I poll released after the NCAA College World Series. records include all postseason games.

		W	L				W	L				W	L
1	LSU	55	18	10	Texas	48	18	18	SW Louisiana	49	20
2	Wichita St	66	13	11	CS-Northridge	44	18	19	Texas A&M	44	23
3	Florida	51	21	12	Oklahoma St	47	20	20	Maine	48	18
4	Clemson	60	10	13	Ohio St	53	13	21	N.C.State	48	20
5	Florida St.	56	15	14	Hawaii	51	18	22	Notre Dame	45	16
6	Creighton	51	22	15	Stanford	39	23	23	California	37	37
7	USC	46	17	16	Miami-FL	46	17	24	Alabama	42	20
8	Long Beach St.	45	22	17	Pepperdine	41	17	25	Southern Miss	42	24
9	Fresno St	42	23								

College World Series

Fourth-seeded LSU defeated Wichita State, 6-3, to win its first NCAA Division I College World Series on June 8 at Rosenblatt Stadium in Omaha. The Tigers, who were the first team since Texas in 1983 to go through the CWS unbeaten, hit .329 with nine home runs and averaged a tournament-record 12 runs a game in four outings.

Results

Game 1— Fresno St. 6 .... Florida St. 3
Game 2— LSU 8 .... Florida 1
Game 3— Creighton 8 .... Clemson 4
Game 4— Wich.St. 8 .... Long Beach St. 5
Game 5— Florida 5 .... Florida St. 0
Game 6— LSU 15 .... Fresno St. 3

Game 7— Long Beach St. 12 .... Clemson 11
Game 8— Wichita St. 3 .... Creighton 2
Game 9— Florida 2 .... Fresno St. 1
Game 10— Creighton 13 .... Long Beach St. 4
Game 11— LSU 19 .... Florida 8
Game 12— Wichita St. 11 .... Creighton 3

Championship Game
Saturday, June 8 at Omaha, Neb.

	1	2	3	4	5	6	7	8	9	R	H	E
LSU	2	2	0	2	0	0	0	0	0—	6	8	0
Wichita St	1	0	0	1	0	0	1	0—		3	5	1

Win—Chad Ogea, LSU (14-5). **Save**—Rick Greene, LSU (14); **Loss**—Tyler Green, Wichita (11-2). **2B:** LSU—Armando Rios. **3B:** LSU—Rich Cordani **HR:** LSU—Rios (4); Wichita—Tommy Tilma (6). **RBI:** LSU—Cordani 3, Rios 2, Pat Garrity; Wichita—Jim Audley, Todd Dreifort, Tilma. **SB:** Wichita—Billy Hall 3 (59), Chris Wimmer (54).
Attendance—16,612. **Time**—2:54.

Most Outstanding Player
Gary Hymel, LSU
Catcher

Avg	AB	R	H	2B	3B	HR	RBI
.500	14	5	7	0	0	4	10

All-Tournament Team

C—Gary Hymel, LSU; **1B**—Johnny Tellechea, LSU; **2B**—Mike McCafferty, Creighton; **SS**—Kevin Polcovich, Florida; **3B**—Jason Giambi, Long Beach St.; **OF**—Jim Audley, Wichita St., Steve Hinton, Creighton, and Lyle Mouton, LSU; **DH**—Mario Linares, Florida; **P**—Chad Ogea, LSU, and Kennie Steenstra, Wichita St.

1991 All-America Team
Selected by *Baseball America*.

First Team

Pos		Class	Hgt	Wgt
C—	Pedro Grifol, Fla.St	Jr.	6-1	196
1B—	David McCarty, Stanford	Jr.	6-5	210
2B—	Steve Rodriguez, Pepperdine	So.	5-9	170
SS—	Brent Gates., Minnesota	Jr.	6-1	180
3B—	Scott Stahoviak, Creighton	Jr.	6-5	205
OF—	Mike Kelly, Arizona St	Jr.	6-4	195
OF—	Mark Smith, USC	Jr.	6-2	195
OF—	Joe Vitiello, Alabama	Jr.	6-3	205
DH—	Mike Daniel, Oklahoma St.	Sr.	6-1	195

Pos		Class	Hgt	Wgt
P—	John Burke, Florida	So.	6-4	200
P—	Craig Clayton, CS-Northridge	Jr.	6-0	180
P—	Bobby Jones, Fresno St	Jr.	6-4	210
P—	Kennie Steenstra, Wichita St	So.	6-5	210
P—	Steve Whitaker, Long Beach St	Jr.	6-6	225

Player of the Year
David McCarty, Stanford, 1B

Avg	AB	R	H	HR	RBI
.420	238	71	100	24	66

THE 1992 INFORMATION PLEASE SPORTS ALMANAC

BASEBALL STATISTICS

THROUGH THE YEARS
1900-1991
WORLD SERIES • ALL-TIMERS

SEC B

PAGE 87

The World Series

The World Series began in 1903 when Pittsburgh of the older National League (founded in 1876) invited Boston of the American League (founded in 1901) to play a best-of-9 game series to determine which of the two league champions was the best. Boston was the surprise winner, 5 games to 3.

The 1904 NL champion New York Giants refused to play Boston the following year, so there was no series. Giants' owner John T. Brush hated AL president Ban Johnson and considered the junior circuit to be a minor league. By the following year, however, Brush and Johnson had smoothed out their differences and the Giants agreed to play Philadelphia in a best-of-7 game series.

Since then the World Series has been best-of-7 format, except from 1919-21 when it returned to best-of-9.

In the chart below, the National League teams are listed in CAPITAL letters. Also, each World Series champion's wins and losses are noted in parentheses after the series score.

Year	Winner	Manager	Series	Loser	Manager
1903	Boston Red Sox	Jimmy Collins	5-3 (LWLLWWWW)	PITTSBURGH	Fred Clarke
1904	No Series				
1905	NY GIANTS	John McGraw	4-1 (WLWWW)	Philadelphia A's	Connie Mack
1906	Chicago White Sox	Fielder Jones	4-2 (WLWLWW)	CHICAGO CUBS	Frank Chance
1907	CHICAGO CUBS	Frank Chance	4-0-1 (TWWWW)	Detroit	Hugh Jennings
1908	CHICAGO CUBS	Frank Chance	4-1 (WWLWW)	Detroit	Hugh Jennings
1909	PITTSBURGH	Fred Clarke	4-3 (WLWLWLW)	Detroit	Hugh Jennings
1910	Philadelphia A's	Connie Mack	4-1 (WWLWW)	CHICAGO CUBS	Frank Chance
1911	Philadelphia A's	Connie Mack	4-2 (LWWWLW)	NY GIANTS	John McGraw
1912	Boston Red Sox	Jake Stahl	4-3-1 (WTLWWLLW)	NY GIANTS	John McGraw
1913	Philadelphia A's	Connie Mack	4-1 (WLWWW)	NY GIANTS	John McGraw
1914	BOSTON BRAVES	George Stallings	4-0	Philadelphia A's	Connie Mack
1915	Boston Red Sox	Bill Carrigan	4-1 (LWWWW)	PHILA.PHILLIES	Pat Moran
1916	Boston Red Sox	Bill Carrigan	4-1 (WWLWW)	BKLN.DODGERS	Wilbert Robinson
1917	Chicago White Sox	Pants Rowland	4-2 (WWLLWW)	NY GIANTS	John McGraw
1918	Boston Red Sox	Ed Barrow	4-2 (WLWWLW)	CHICAGO CUBS	Fred Mitchell
1919	CINCINNATI	Pat Moran	5-3 (WWLWWLLW)	Chicago White Sox	Kid Gleason
1920	Cleveland	Tris Speaker	5-2 (WLLWWWW)	BKLN.DODGERS	Wilbert Robinson
1921	NY GIANTS	John McGraw	5-3 (LLWWWLWWW)	NY Yankees	Miller Huggins
1922	NY GIANTS	John McGraw	4-0-1 (WTWWW)	NY Yankees	Miller Huggins
1923	NY Yankees	Miller Huggins	4-2 (LWLWWW)	NY GIANTS	John McGraw
1924	Washington	Bucky Harris	4-3 (LWLWLWW)	NY GIANTS	John McGraw
1925	PITTSBURGH	Bill McKechnie	4-3 (LWLLWWW)	Washington	Bucky Harris
1926	ST.L.CARDINALS	Rogers Hornsby	4-3 (LWWLLWW)	NY Yankees	Miller Huggins
1927	NY Yankees	Miller Huggins	4-0	PITTSBURGH	Donie Bush
1928	NY Yankees	Miller Huggins	4-0	ST.L.CARDINALS	Bill McKechnie
1929	Philadelphia A's	Connie Mack	4-1 (WWLWW)	CHICAGO CUBS	Joe McCarthy
1930	Philadelphia A's	Connie Mack	4-2 (WWLLWW)	ST.L.CARDINALS	Gabby Street
1931	ST.L.CARDINALS	Gabby Street	4-3 (LWWLWLW)	Philadelphia A's	Connie Mack
1932	NY Yankees	Joe McCarthy	4-0	CHICAGO CUBS	Charlie Grimm
1933	NY GIANTS	Bill Terry	4-1 (WWLWW)	Washington	Joe Cronin
1934	ST.L.CARDINALS	Frankie Frisch	4-3 (WLWLLWW)	Detroit	Mickey Cochrane
1935	Detroit	Mickey Cochrane	4-2 (LWWWLW)	CHICAGO CUBS	Charlie Grimm
1936	NY Yankees	Joe McCarthy	4-2 (LWWWLW)	NY GIANTS	Bill Terry
1937	NY Yankees	Joe McCarthy	4-1 (WWWLW)	NY GIANTS	Bill Terry
1938	NY Yankees	Joe McCarthy	4-0	CHICAGO CUBS	Gabby Hartnett
1939	NY Yankees	Joe McCarthy	4-0	CINCINNATI	Bill McKechnie
1940	CINCINNATI	Bill McKechnie	4-3 (LWLWLWW)	Detroit	Del Baker
1941	NY Yankees	Joe McCarthy	4-1 (WLWWW)	BKLN.DODGERS	Leo Durocher
1942	ST.L.CARDINALS	Billy Southworth	4-1 (LWWWW)	NY Yankees	Joe McCarthy
1943	NY Yankees	Joe McCarthy	4-1 (WLWWW)	ST.L.CARDINALS	Billy Southworth
1944	ST.L.CARDINALS	Billy Southworth	4-2 (LWLWWW)	St.Louis Browns	Luke Sewell
1945	Detroit	Steve O'Neill	4-3 (LWLWWLW)	CHICAGO CUBS	Charlie Grimm

World Series (Cont.)

Year	Winner	Manager	Series	Loser	Manager
1946	ST.L.CARDINALS	Eddie Dyer	4-3 (LWLWLWW)	Boston Red Sox	Joe Cronin
1947	NY Yankees	Bucky Harris	4-3 (WWLLWLW)	BKLN.DODGERS	Burt Shotton
1948	Cleveland	Lou Boudreau	4-2 (LWWWLW)	BOSTON BRAVES	Billy Southworth
1949	NY Yankees	Casey Stengel	4-1 (WLWWW)	BKLN.DODGERS	Burt Shotton
1950	NY Yankees	Casey Stengel	4-0	PHILA.PHILLIES	Eddie Sawyer
1951	NY Yankees	Casey Stengel	4-2 (LWLWWW)	NY GIANTS	Leo Durocher
1952	NY Yankees	Casey Stengel	4-3 (LWLWLWW)	BKLN.DODGERS	Charlie Dressen
1953	NY Yankees	Casey Stengel	4-2 (WWLLWW)	BKLN.DODGERS	Charlie Dressen
1954	NY GIANTS	Leo Durocher	4-0	Cleveland	Al Lopez
1955	BKLN.DODGERS	Walter Alston	4-3 (LLWWWLW)	NY Yankees	Casey Stengel
1956	NY Yankees	Casey Stengel	4-3 (LLWWWLW	BKLN.DODGERS	Walter Alston
1957	MILW.BRAVES	Fred Haney	4-3 (WLLWWLW)	NY Yankees	Casey Stengel
1958	NY Yankees	Casey Stengel	4-3 (LLWLWWW)	MILW.BRAVES	Fred Haney
1959	LA DODGERS	Walter Alston	4-2 (LWWWLW)	Chicago White Sox	Al Lopez
1960	PITTSBURGH	Danny Murtaugh	4-3 (WLLWLWW)	NY Yankees	Casey Stengel
1961	NY Yankees	Ralph Houk	4-1 (WLWWW)	CINCINNATI	Fred Hutchinson
1962	NY Yankees	Ralph Houk	4-3 (WLWLWLW)	SF GIANTS	Alvin Dark
1963	LA DODGERS	Walter Alston	4-0	NY Yankees	Ralph Houk
1964	ST.L.CARDINALS	Johnny Keane	4-3 (WLLWW)	NY Yankees	Yogi Berra
1965	LA DODGERS	Walter Alston	4-3 (LLWWWLW)	Minnesota	Sam Mele
1966	Baltimore	Hank Bauer	4-0	LA DODGERS	Walter Alston
1967	ST.L.CARDINALS	Red Schoendienst	4-3 (WLWWLLW)	Boston Red Sox	Dick Williams
1968	Detroit	Mayo Smith	4-3 (LWLLWWW)	ST.L.CARDINALS	Red Schoendienst
1969	NY METS	Gil Hodges	4-1 (LWWWW)	Baltimore	Earl Weaver
1970	Baltimore	Earl Weaver	4-1 (WWWLW)	CINCINNATI	Sparky Anderson
1971	PITTSBURGH	Danny Murtaugh	4-3 (LLWWWLW)	Baltimore	Earl Weaver
1972	Oakland A's	Dick Williams	4-3 (WWLWLLW)	CINCINNATI	Sparky Anderson
1973	Oakland A's	Dick Williams	4-3 (WLWLLWW)	NY METS	Yogi Berra
1974	Oakland A's	Alvin Dark	4-1 (WLWWW)	LA DODGERS	Walter Alston
1975	CINCINNATI	Sparky Anderson	4-3 (LWWWLWW)	Boston Red Sox	Darrell Johnson
1976	CINCINNATI	Sparky Anderson	4-0	NY Yankees	Billy Martin
1977	NY Yankees	Billy Martin	4-2 (WLWWLW)	LA DODGERS	Tommy Lasorda
1978	NY Yankees	Bob Lemon	4-2 (LLWWWW)	LA DODGERS	Tommy Lasorda
1979	PITTSBURGH	Chuck Tanner	4-3 (LWLLWWW)	Baltimore	Earl Weaver
1980	PHILA.PHILLIES	Dallas Green	4-2 (WWLLWW)	Kansas City	Jim Frey
1981	LA DODGERS	Tommy Lasorda	4-2 (LLWWWW)	NY Yankees	Bob Lemon
1982	ST.L.CARDINALS	Whitey Herzog	4-3 (WLWLLWW)	Milwaukee Brewers	Harvey Kuenn
1983	Baltimore	Joe Altobelli	4-1 (LWWWW)	PHILA.PHILLIES	Paul Owens
1984	Detroit	Sparky Anderson	4-1 (WLWWW)	SAN DIEGO	Dick Williams
1985	Kansas City	Dick Howser	4-3 (LLWLWWW)	ST.L.CARDINALS	Whitey Herzog
1986	NY METS	Davey Johnson	4-3 (LLWWLWW)	Boston Red Sox	John McNamara
1987	Minnesota	Tom Kelly	4-3 (WWLLLWW)	ST.L.CARDINALS	Whitey Herzog
1988	LA DODGERS	Tommy Lasorda	4-1 (WWLWW)	Oakland A's	Tony LaRussa
1989	Oakland A's	Tony LaRussa	4-0	SF GIANTS	Roger Craig
1990	CINCINNATI	Lou Piniella	4-0	Oakland A's	Tony LaRussa
1991	Minnesota	Tom Kelly	4-3 (WWLLLWW)	ATLANTA BRAVES	Bobby Cox

Most Valuable Players

Currently selected by media panel made up of representatives of CBS Sports, CBS Radio, AP, UPI, and World Series official scorers. Presented by *Sport* magazine from 1955-88 and by Major League Baseball since 1989. Winners who did not play for World Series champions are in **bold** type.

Multiple winners: Bob Gibson, Reggie Jackson and Sandy Koufax (2).

Year		Year		Year	
1955	Johnny Podres, Bklyn, P	1970	Brooks Robinson, Bal., 3B	1982	Darrell Porter, St.L., C
1956	Don Larsen, NY, P	1971	Roberto Clemente, Pit., OF	1983	Rick Dempsey, Bal., C
1957	Lew Burdette, Mil., P	1972	Gene Tenace, Oak., C	1984	Alan Trammell, Det., SS
1958	Bob Turley, NY, P	1973	Reggie Jackson, Oak., OF	1985	Bret Saberhagen, KC, P
1959	Larry Sherry, LA, P	1974	Rollie Fingers, Oak., P	1986	Ray Knight, NY, 3B
1960	**Bobby Richardson**, NY, 2B	1975	Pete Rose, Cin., 3B	1987	Frank Viola, Min., P
1961	Whitey Ford, NY, P	1976	Johnny Bench, Cin., C	1988	Orel Hershiser, LA, P
1962	Ralph Terry, NY, P	1977	Reggie Jackson, NY, OF	1989	Dave Stewart, Oak., P
1963	Sandy Koufax, LA, P	1978	Bucky Dent, NY, SS	1990	Jose Rijo, Cin., P
1964	Bob Gibson, St.L., P	1979	Willie Stargell, Pit., 1B	1991	Jack Morris, Min., P
1965	Sandy Koufax, LA, P	1980	Mike Schmidt, Phi., 3B		
1966	Frank Robinson, Bal., OF	1981	Pedro Guerrero, LA, OF;		
1967	Bob Gibson, St.L., P		Ron Cey, LA, 3B;		
1968	Mickey Lolich, Det., P		& Steve Yeager, LA, C		
1969	Donn Clendenon, NY, 1B				

All-Time World Series Leaders
CAREER
World Series leaders through 1991. Years listed indicate number of World Series appearances.

Hitting

Games

	Yrs	Gm
Yogi Berra, NY Yankees	14	75
Mickey Mantle, NY Yankees	12	65
Elston Howard, NY Yankees-Boston	10	54
Hank Bauer, NY Yankees	9	53
Gil McDougald, NY Yankees	8	53

At Bats

	Yrs	AB
Yogi Berra, NY Yankees	14	259
Mickey Mantle, NY Yankees	12	230
Joe DiMaggio, NY Yankees	10	199
Frankie Frisch, NY Giants-St.L Cards	8	197
Gil McDougald, NY Yankees	8	190

Batting Avg. (minimum 50 AB)

	AB	H	Avg
Pepper Martin, St.L Cards	55	23	.418
Lou Brock, St.Louis	87	34	.391
Thurman Munson, NY Yankees	67	25	.373
George Brett, Kansas City	51	19	.373
Hank Aaron, Milw. Braves	55	20	.364

Hits

	AB	H	Avg
Yogi Berra, NY Yankees	259	71	.274
Mickey Mantle, NY Yankees	230	59	.257
Frankie Frisch, NYG-St.L Cards	197	58	.294
Joe DiMaggio, NY Yankees	199	54	.271
Hank Bauer, NY Yankees	188	46	.245
Pee Wee Reese, Brooklyn	169	46	.272

Runs

	Gm	R
Mickey Mantle, NY Yankees	65	42
Yogi Berra, NY Yankees	75	41
Babe Ruth, NY Yankees	41	37
Lou Gehrig, NY Yankees	34	30
Joe DiMaggio, NY Yankees	51	27

Home Runs

	AB	HR
Mickey Mantle, NY Yankees	230	18
Babe Ruth, NY Yankees	129	15
Yogi Berra, NY Yankees	259	12
Duke Snider, Brooklyn-LA	133	11
Lou Gehrig, NY Yankees	119	10
Reggie Jackson, Oakland-NY Yankees	98	10

Runs Batted In

	Gm	RBI
Mickey Mantle, NY Yankees	65	40
Yogi Berra, NY Yankees	75	39
Lou Gehrig, NY Yankees	34	35
Babe Ruth, NY Yankees	41	33
Joe DiMaggio, NY Yankees	51	30

Stolen Bases

	Gm	SB
Lou Brock, St.Louis	21	14
Eddie Collins, Phi.A's-Chisox	34	14
Frank Chance, Chi.Cubs	20	10
Davey Lopes, Los Angeles	23	10
Phil Rizzuto, NY Yankees	52	10

Total Bases

	Gm	TB
Mickey Mantle, NY Yankees	65	123
Yogi Berra, NY Yankees	75	117
Babe Ruth, NY Yankees	41	96
Lou Gehrig, NY Yankees	34	87
Joe DiMaggio, NY Yankees	51	84

Slugging Avg. (50 AB)

	AB	Avg
Reggie Jackson, Oakland-NY Yankees	98	.755
Babe Ruth, NY Yankees	129	.744
Lou Gehrig, NY Yankees	119	.731
Al Simmons, Phi.A's-Cincinnati	73	.658
Lou Brock, St.Louis	87	.655

World Series Appearances

In the 88 years that the World Series has been contested, American League teams have won 51 championships while National League teams have won 37.

The New York Yankees have appeared in the Series on 33 occasions and won a record 22 titles. The Brooklyn-Los Angeles Dodgers are second in appearances with 18. The following teams are ranked by number of appearances through the 1991 World Series; (*) indicates AL teams.

	App	W	L	Pct.	Last Series	Last Title
NY Yankees*	33	22	11	.667	1981	1978
Bklyn/LA Dodgers	18	6	12	.333	1988	1988
NY/SF Giants	16	5	11	.313	1989	1954
St.L.Cardinals	15	9	6	.600	1987	1982
Phi/KC/Oak.A's*	14	9	5	.643	1990	1989
Chicago Cubs	10	2	8	.200	1945	1908
Boston Red Sox*	9	5	4	.556	1986	1918
Cincinnati Reds	9	5	4	.556	1990	1990
Detroit Tigers*	9	4	5	.444	1984	1984
Pittsburgh Pirates	7	5	2	.714	1979	1979
St.L/Bal.Orioles*	7	3	4	.429	1983	1983
Wash/Min.Twins*	6	3	3	.500	1991	1991
Bos/Mil/Atl.Braves	5	2	3	.400	1991	1957
Chi.White Sox*	4	2	2	.500	1959	1917
Phi.Phillies	4	1	3	.250	1983	1980
Cle.Indians*	3	2	1	.667	1954	1948
NY Mets	3	2	1	.667	1986	1986
KC Royals*	2	1	1	.500	1985	1985
Sea/Mil.Brewers*	1	0	1	.000	1982	—
SD Padres	1	0	1	.000	1984	—

Pitching
Games

	Yrs	Gm
Whitey Ford, NY Yankees	11	22
Rollie Fingers, Oakland	3	16
Allie Reynolds, NY Yankees	6	15
Bob Turley, NY Yankees	5	15
Clay Carroll, Cincinnati	3	14

Wins

	Gm	W-L
Whitey Ford, NY Yankees	22	10-8
Bob Gibson, St.Louis	9	7-2
Allie Reynolds, NY Yankees	15	7-2
Red Ruffing, NY Yankees	10	7-2
Lefty Gomez, NY Yankees	7	6-0
Chief Bender, Philadelphia A's	10	6-4
Waite Hoyt, NY Yankees-Phi.A's	12	6-4

All-Time World Series Leaders (Cont.)

Losses

	Gm	W-L
Whitey Ford, NY Yankees	22	10-8
Christy Mathewson, NY Giants	11	5-5
Joe Bush, Phi.A's-Bosox-NY Yankees	9	2-5
Rube Marquard, NY Giants-Brooklyn	11	2-5
Eddie Plank, Philadelphia A's	7	2-5
Schoolboy Rowe, Detroit	8	2-5

Strikeouts

	Gm	IP	SO
Whitey Ford, NY Yankees	22	146	94
Bob Gibson, St.Louis	9	81	92
Allie Reynolds, NY Yankees	15	77	62
Sandy Koufax, Los Angeles	8	57	61
Red Ruffing, NY Yankees	10	86	61

ERA (minimum 25 IP)

	Gm	IP	ERA
Jack Billingham, Cincinnati	7	25	0.36
Harry Brecheen, St.Louis	7	33	0.83
Babe Ruth, Boston Red Sox	3	31	0.87
Sherry Smith, Brooklyn	3	30	0.89
Sandy Koufax, Los Angeles	8	57	0.95

Bases on Balls

	Gm	IP	BB
Whitey Ford, NY Yankees	22	146	34
Allie Reynolds, NY Yankees	15	77	32
Art Nehf, NY Giants-Chi.Cubs	12	79	32
Jim Palmer, Baltimore	9	65	31
Bob Turley, NY Yankees	15	54	29

Innings Pitched

	Gm	IP
Whitey Ford, NY Yankees	22	146
Christy Mathewson, NY Giants	11	102
Red Ruffing, NY Yankees	10	86
Chief Bender, Philadelphia A's	10	85
Waite Hoyt, NY Yankees-Phi.A's	12	84

Complete Games

	GS	CG	W-L
Christy Mathewson, NY Giants	11	10	5-5
Chief Bender, Philadelphia A's	10	9	6-4
Bob Gibson, St.Louis	9	8	7-2
Whitey Ford, NY Yankees	22	7	10-8
Red Ruffing, NY Yankees	10	7	7-2

Saves

	Gm	IP	Sv
Rollie Fingers, Oakland	16	33	6
Allie Reynolds, NY Yankees	15	77	4
Johnny Murphy, NY Yankees	8	16	4
Seven pitchers tied with 3 each.			

Shutouts

	GS	CG	ShO
Christy Mathewson, NY Giants	11	10	4
Three Finger Brown, Phi.A's	7	5	3
Whitey Ford, NY Yankees	22	7	3
Seven pitchers tied with 2 each.			

League Championship Series

Division play came to the major leagues in 1969 when both the American and National Leagues expanded to 12 teams. With an East and West Division in each league, League Championship Series (LCS) became necessary to determine the NL and AL pennant winners. In the charts below, the East Division champions are noted by the letter E and the West Division champions by W. Also, each playoff winner's wins and losses are noted in parentheses after the series score. The LCS changed from best-of-5 to best-of-7 in 1985.

American League

Year	Winner	Manager	Series	Loser	Manager
1969	E- Baltimore	Earl Weaver	3-0	W- Minnesota	Billy Martin
1970	E- Baltimore	Earl Weaver	3-0	W- Minnesota	Bill Rigney
1971	E- Baltimore	Earl Weaver	3-0	W- Oakland	Dick Williams
1972	W- Oakland	Dick Williams	3-2 (WWLLW)	E- Detroit	Billy Martin
1973	W- Oakland	Dick Williams	3-2 (LWWLW)	E- Baltimore	Earl Weaver
1974	W- Oakland	Alvin Dark	3-1 (LWWW)	E- Baltimore	Earl Weaver
1975	E- Boston	Darrell Johnson	3-0	W- Oakland	Alvin Dark
1976	E- New York	Billy Martin	3-2 (WLWLW)	W- Kansas City	Whitey Herzog
1977	E- New York	Billy Martin	3-2 (LWLLW)	W- Kansas City	Whitey Herzog
1978	E- New York	Bob Lemon	3-1 (WLWW)	W- Kansas City	Whitey Herzog
1979	E- Baltimore	Earl Weaver	3-1 (WWLW)	W- California	Jim Fregosi
1980	W- Kansas City	Jim Frey	3-0	E- New York	Dick Howser
1981	E- New York	Bob Lemon	3-0	W- Oakland	Billy Martin
1982	E- Milwaukee	Harvey Kuenn	3-2 (LLWWW)	W- California	Gene Mauch
1983	E- Baltimore	Joe Altobelli	3-1 (LWWW)	W- Chicago	Tony LaRussa
1984	E- Detroit	Sparky Anderson	3-0	W- Kansas City	Dick Howser
1985	W- Kansas City	Dick Howser	4-3 (LLWLWWW)	E- Toronto	Bobby Cox
1986	E- Boston	John McNamara	4-3 (LWLLWWW)	W- California	Gene Mauch
1987	W- Minnesota	Tom Kelly	4-1 (WWLWW)	E- Detroit	Sparky Anderson
1988	W- Oakland	Tony LaRussa	4-0	E- Boston	Joe Morgan
1989	W- Oakland	Tony LaRussa	4-1 (WWLWW)	E- Toronto	Cito Gaston
1990	W- Oakland	Tony LaRussa	4-0	E- Boston	Joe Morgan
1991	W- Minnesota	Tom Kelly	4-1 (WLWWW)	E- Toronto	Cito Gaston

ALCS Most Valuable Players

Year		Year		Year	
1980	Frank White, KC, 2B	1984	Kirk Gibson, Det., OF	1988	Dennis Eckersley, Oak., P
1981	Graig Nettles, NY, 3B	1985	George Brett, KC, 3B	1989	Rickey Henderson, Oak., OF
1982	Fred Lynn, Cal., OF	1986	Marty Barrett, Bos., 2B	1990	Dave Stewart, Oak., P
1983	Mike Boddicker, Bal., P	1987	Gary Gaetti, Min., 3B	1991	Kirby Puckett, Min., OF

National League

Year	Winner	Manager	Series	Loser	Manager
1969	E- New York	Gil Hodges	3-0	W- Atlanta	Lum Harris
1970	W- Cincinnati	Sparky Anderson	3-0	E- Pittsburgh	Danny Murtaugh
1971	E- Pittsburgh	Danny Murtaugh	3-1 (LWWW)	W- San Francisco	Charlie Fox
1972	W- Clncinnati	Sparky Anderson	3-2 (LWLWW)	E- Pittsburgh	Bill Virdon
1973	E- New York	Yogi Berra	3-2 (LWWLW)	W- Cincinnati	Sparky Anderson
1974	W- Los Angeles	Walter Alston	3-1 (WWLW)	E- Pittsburgh	Danny Murtaugh
1975	W- Cincinnati	Sparky Anderson	3-0	E- Pittsburgh	Danny Murtaugh
1976	W- Cincinnati	Sparky Anderson	3-0	E- Philadelphia	Danny Ozark
1977	W- Los Angeles	Tommy Lasorda	3-1 (LWWW)	E- Philadelphia	Danny Ozark
1978	W- Los Angeles	Tommy Lasorda	3-1 (WWLW)	E- Philadelphia	Danny Ozark
1979	E- Pittsburgh	Chuck Tanner	3-0	W- Cincinnati	John McNamara
1980	E- Philadelphia	Dallas Green	3-2 (WLLWW)	W- Houston	Bill Virdon
1981	W- Los Angeles	Tommy Lasorda	3-2 (WLLWW)	E- Montreal	Jim Fanning
1982	E- St. Louis	Whitey Herzog	3-0	W- Atlanta	Joe Torre
1983	E- Philadelphia	Paul Owens	3-1 (WLWW)	W- Los Angeles	Tommy Lasorda
1984	W- San Diego	Dick Williams	3-2 (LLWWW)	E- Chicago	Jim Frey
1985	E- St. Louis	Whitey Herzog	4-2 (LLWWWW)	W- Los Angeles	Tommy Lasorda
1986	E- New York	Davey Johnson	4-2 (LWWLWW)	W- Houston	Hal Lanier
1987	E- St. Louis	Whitey Herzog	4-3 (WLWLLWW)	W- San Francisco	Roger Craig
1988	W- Los Angeles	Tommy Lasorda	4-3 (LWLWWLW)	E- New York	Davey Johnson
1989	W- San Francisco	Roger Craig	4-1 (WLWWW)	E- Chicago	Don Zimmer
1990	W- Cincinnati	Lou Piniella	4-2 (LWWWW)	E- Pittsburgh	Jim Leyland
1991	W-Atlanta	Bobby Cox	4-3 (LWWWLLWW)	E- Pittsburgh	Jim Leyland

NLCS Most Valuable Players

Year			Year			Year		
1977	Dusty Baker, LA, OF		1983	Gary Matthews, Phi., OF		1989	Will Clark, SF, 1B	
1978	Steve Garvey, LA, 1B		1984	Steve Garvey, SD, 1B		1990	Rob Dibble, Cin., P	
1979	Willie Stargell, Pit., 1B		1985	Ozzie Smith, St.L., SS			& Randy Myers, Cin., P	
1980	Manny Trillo, Phi., 2B		1986	Mike Scott, Houston, P		1991	Steve Avery, Atl., P	
1981	Burt Hooton, LA, P		1987	Jeff Leonard, San Fran., OF				
1982	Darrell Porter, St.L., C		1988	Orel Hershiser, LA, P				

Other Playoffs

Seven times from 1946-80, playoffs were necessary to decide league or division championships when two teams tied for first place at the end of the regular season. In the strike year of 1981, there were playoffs between the first and second half-season champions in both leagues.

American League

Year	AL	W	L	Manager	Year	AL East	W	L	Manager
1948	Boston	96	58	Joe McCarthy	1981	(1st Half) N.Y.	34	22	Bob Lemon
	Cleveland	96	58	Lou Boudreau		(2nd Half) Milw.	31	22	Buck Rodgers
	Playoff: (1 game) Cleveland, 8-3 (at Boston)					Playoff: (Best-of-5) New York, 3-2 (WWLLW)			
	AL East	**W**	**L**	**Manager**		**AL West**	**W**	**L**	**Manager**
1978	Boston	99	63	Don Zimmer		(1st Half) Oakland	37	23	Billy Martin
	New York	99	63	Bob Lemon		(2nd Half) Kan.City	30	23	Jim Frey
	Playoff: (1 game) New York, 5-4 (at Boston)					Playoff: (Best-of-5), Oakland, 3-0			

National League

Year	NL	W	L	Manager	Year	NL West	W	L	Manager
1946	Brooklyn	96	58	Leo Durocher	1980	Houston	101	61	Bill Virdon
	St.Louis	96	58	Eddie Dyer		Los Angeles	101	61	Tommy Lasorda
	Playoff: (Best-of-3) St.Louis, 2-0					Playoff: (1 game) Houston, 7-1 (at LA)			
	NL	**W**	**L**	**Manager**		**NL East**	**W**	**L**	**Manager**
1951	Brooklyn	96	58	Charlie Dressen	1981	(1st Half) Phila.	34	21	Dallas Green
	New York	96	58	Leo Durocher		(2nd Half) Montreal	30	23	Jim Fanning
	Playoff: (Best-of-3) New York, 2-1 (WLW)					Playoff: (Best-of-5) Montreal, 3-2 (WWLLW)			
	NL	**W**	**L**	**Manager**		**NL West**	**W**	**L**	**Manager**
1959	Milwaukee	86	68	Fred Haney	1981	(1st Half) Los Ang.	36	21	Tommy Lasorda
	Los Angeles	86	68	Walter Alston		(2nd Half) Houston	33	20	Bill Virdon
	Playoff: (Best-of-3) Los Angeles, 2-0					Playoff: (Best-of-5) Los Angeles, 3-2 (LLWWW)			
	NL	**W**	**L**	**Manager**					
1962	Los Angeles	101	61	Walter Alston					
	San Francisco	101	61	Alvin Dark					
	Playoff: (Best-of-3) San Francisco, 2-1 (WLW)								

Major League Franchise Origins

Here is what the current 26 teams in Major League Baseball have to show for the years they have put in as members of the National League (NL) and American League (AL).

National League

	1st Year	Pennants & World Series	Franchise Stops
Atlanta Braves	1876	5 NL (1914,48,57-58,91) 2 WS (1914,57)	Boston (1876-1952) Milwaukee (1953-65) Atlanta (1966—)
Chicago Cubs	1876	10 NL (1906-08,10,18,29,32,35,38,45) 2 WS (1907-08)	Chicago (1876—)
Cincinnati Reds	1876	9 NL (1919,39-40,61,70,72,75-76,90) 5 WS (1919,40,75-76,90)	Cincinnati (1876-80) Cincinnati (1890—)
Houston Astros	1962	None	Houston (1962—)
Los Angeles Dodgers	1890	18 NL (1916,20,41,47,49,52-53,55-56,59,63, 65-66,74,77-78, 81,88) 6 WS (1955,59,63,65,81,88)	Brooklyn (1890-1957) Los Angeles (1958—)
Montreal Expos	1969	None	Montreal (1969—)
New York Mets	1962	3 NL (1969,73,86) 2 WS (1969,86)	New York (1962—)
Philadelphia Phillies	1880	4 NL (1915,50,80,83) 1 WS (1980)	Philadelphia (1883—)
Pittsburgh Pirates	1887	7 NL (1903,09,25,27,60,71,79) 5 WS (1909,25,60,71,79)	Pittsburgh (1887—)
St.Louis Cardinals	1892	15 NL (1926,28,30-31,34,42-44,46,64, 67-68,82,85,87) 9 WS (1926,31,34,42,44,46,64,67,82)	St.Louis (1892—)
San Diego Padres	1969	1 NL (1984)	San Diego (1969—)
San Francisco Giants	1883	16 NL (1905,11-13,17,21-24,33,36-37,51, 54,62,89) 5 WS (1905,21-22,33,54)	New York (1883–1957) San Francisco (1958—)

American League

	1st Year	Pennants & World Series	Franchise Stops
Baltimore Orioles	1902	7 AL (1944,66,69-71,79,83) 3 WS (1966,70,83)	Milwaukee (1901) St.Louis (1902-53) Baltimore (1954—)
Boston Red Sox	1901	9 AL (1903,12,15-16,18,46,67,75,86) 5 WS (1903,12,15-16,18)	Boston (1901—)
California Angels	1961	None	Los Angeles (1961-65) Anaheim, CA (1966—)
Chicago White Sox	1901	4 AL (1906,17,19,59) 2 WS (1906,17)	Chicago (1901—)
Cleveland Indians	1901	3 AL (1920,48,54) 2 WS (1920,48)	Cleveland (1901—)
Detroit Tigers	1901	9 AL (1907-09,34-35,40,45,68,84) 4 WS (1935,45,68,84)	Detroit (1901—)
Kansas City Royals	1969	2 AL (1980,85) 1 WS (1985)	Kansas City (1969—)
Milwaukee Brewers	1969	1 AL (1982)	Seattle (1969) Milwaukee (1970—)
Minnesota Twins	1901	6 AL (1924-25,33,65,87,91) 3 WS (1924,87,91)	Washington, DC (1901-60) Bloomington, MN (1961-81) Minneapolis (1982—)
New York Yankees	1901	33 AL (1921-23,26-28,32,36-39,41-43,47, 49-53,55-58,60-64,76-78,81) 22 WS (1923,27-28,32,36-39,41,43,47,49-53, 56,58,61-62,77-78)	Baltimore (1901-02) New York (1903—)
Oakland Athletics	1901	14 AL (1905,10-11,13-14,29-31,72-74,88-90) 9 WS (1910-11,13,29-30,72-74,89)	Philadelphia (1901-54) Kansas City (1955-67) Oakland (1968—)
Seattle Mariners	1977	None	Seattle (1977—)
Texas Rangers	1961	None	Washington, DC (1961-71) Arlington, TX (1972—)
Toronto Blue Jays	1977	None	Toronto (1977—)

Annual Batting Leaders (since 1900)
Batting Average
National League

Multiple winners: Honus Wagner (8); Rogers Hornsby and Stan Musial (7); Roberto Clemente, Tony Gwynn and Bill Madlock (4); Pete Rose and Paul Waner (3); Hank Aaron, Richie Ashburn, Jake Daubert, Tommy Davis, Ernie Lombardi, Willie McGee, Lefty O'Doul, Dave Parker and Edd Roush (2).

Year		Avg	Year		Avg	Year		Avg
1900	Honus Wagner, Pit	.381	1932	Lefty O'Doul, Bklyn	.368	1962	Tommy Davis, LA	.346
1901	Jesse Burkett, St.L	.382	1933	Chuck Klein, Phi	.368	1963	Tommy Davis, LA	.326
1902	Ginger Beaumont, Pit	.357	1934	Paul Waner, Pit	.362	1964	Roberto Clemente, Pit	.339
1903	Honus Wagner, Pit	.355	1935	Arkie Vaughan, Pit	.385	1965	Roberto Clemente, Pit	.329
1904	Honus Wagner, Pit	.349	1936	Paul Waner, Pit	.373	1966	Matty Alou, Pit	.342
1905	Cy Seymour, Cin	.377	1937	Joe Medwick, St.L	.374	1967	Roberto Clemente, Pit	.357
1906	Honus Wagner, Pit	.339	1938	Ernie Lombardi, Cin	.342	1968	Pete Rose, Cin	.335
1907	Honus Wagner, Pit	.350	1939	Johnny Mize, St.L	.349	1969	Pete Rose, Cin	.348
1908	Honus Wagner, Pit	.354	1940	Debs Garms, Pit	.355	1970	Rico Carty, Atl	.366
1909	Honus Wagner, Pit	.339	1941	Pete Reiser, Bklyn	.343	1971	Joe Torre, St.L	.363
1910	Sherry Magee, Phi	.331	1942	Ernie Lombardi, Bos	.330	1972	Billy Williams, Chi	.333
1911	Honus Wagner, Pit	.334	1943	Stan Musial, St.L	.357	1973	Pete Rose, Cin	.338
1912	Heinie Zimmerman, Chi	.372	1944	Dixie Walker, Chi	.357	1974	Ralph Garr, Atl	.353
1913	Jake Daubert, Bklyn	.350	1945	Phil Cavarretta, Chi	.355	1975	Bill Madlock, Chi	.354
1914	Jake Daubert, Bklyn	.329	1946	Stan Musial, St.L	.365	1976	Bill Madlock, Chi	.339
1915	Larry Doyle, NY	.320	1947	Harry Walker, St.L-Phi	.363	1977	Dave Parker, Pit	.338
1916	Hal Chase, Cin	.339	1948	Stan Musial, St.L	.376	1978	Dave Parker, Pit	.334
1917	Edd Roush, Cin	.341	1949	Jackie Robinson, Bklyn	.342	1979	Keith Hernandez, St.L	.344
1918	Zack Wheat, Bklyn	.335	1950	Stan Musial, St.L	.346	1980	Bill Buckner, Chi	.324
1919	Edd Roush, Cin	.321	1951	Stan Musial, St.L	.355	1981	Bill Madlock, Pit	.341
1920	Rogers Hornsby, St.L	.370	1952	Stan Musial, St.L	.336	1982	Al Oliver, Mon	.331
1921	Rogers Hornsby, St.L	.397	1953	Carl Furillo, Bklyn	.344	1983	Bill Madlock, Pit	.323
1922	Rogers Hornsby, St.L	.401	1954	Willie Mays, NY	.345	1984	Tony Gwynn, SD	.351
1923	Rogers Hornsby, St.L	.384	1955	Richie Ashburn, Phi	.338	1985	Willie McGee, St.L	.353
1924	Rogers Hornsby, St.L	.424	1956	Hank Aaron, Mil	.328	1986	Tim Raines, Mon	.334
1925	Rogers Hornsby, St.L	.403	1957	Stan Musial, St.L	.351	1987	Tony Gwynn, SD	.370
1926	Bubbles Hargrave, Cin	.353	1958	Richie Ashburn, Phi	.350	1988	Tony Gwynn, SD	.313
1927	Paul Waner, Pit	.380	1959	Hank Aaron, Mil	.355	1989	Tony Gwynn, SD	.336
1928	Rogers Hornsby, Bos	.387	1960	Dick Groat, Pit	.325	1990	Willie McGee, St.L	.335
1929	Lefty O'Doul, Phi	.398	1961	Roberto Clemente, Pit	.351	1991	Terry Pendleton, Atl	.319
1930	Bill Terry, NY	.401						
1931	Chick Hafey, St.L	.349						

American League

Multiple winners: Ty Cobb (12); Rod Carew (7); Ted Williams (6); Wade Boggs (5); Harry Heilmann (4); George Brett, Tony Oliva and Carl Yastrzemski (3); Luke Appling, Joe DiMaggio, Ferris Fain, Jimmie Foxx, Nap Lajoie, Pete Runnels, Al Simmons, George Sisler and Mickey Vernon (2).

Year		Avg	Year		Avg	Year		Avg
1901	Nap Lajoie, Phi	.422	1923	Harry Heilmann, Det	.403	1945	Snuffy Stirnweiss, NY	.309
1902	Ed Delahanty, Wash	.376	1924	Babe Ruth, NY	.378	1946	Mickey Vernon, Wash	.353
1903	Nap Lajoie, Cle	.355	1925	Harry Heilmann, Det	.393	1947	Ted Williams, Bos	.343
1904	Nap Lajoie, Cle	.381	1926	Heine Manush, Det	.378	1948	Ted Williams, Bos	.369
1905	Elmer Flick, Cle	.306	1927	Harry Heilmann, Det	.398	1949	George Kell, Det	.343
1906	George Stone, St.L	.358	1928	Goose Goslin, Wash	.379	1950	Billy Goodman, Bos	.354
1907	Ty Cobb, Det	.350	1929	Lew Fonseca, Cle	.369	1951	Ferris Fain, Phi	.344
1908	Ty Cobb, Det	.324	1930	Al Simmons, Phi	.381	1952	Ferris Fain, Phi	.327
1909	Ty Cobb, Det	.377	1931	Al Simmons, Phi	.390	1953	Mickey Vernon, Wash	.337
1910	Ty Cobb, Det	.385	1932	Dale Alexander, Det-Bos	.367	1954	Bobby Avila, Clev	.341
1911	Ty Cobb, Det	.420	1933	Jimmie Foxx, Phi	.356	1955	Al Kaline, Det	.340
1912	Ty Cobb, Det	.410	1934	Lou Gehrig, NY	.363	1956	Mickey Mantle, NY	.353
1913	Ty Cobb, Det	.390	1935	Buddy Myer, Wash	.349	1957	Ted Williams, Bos	.388
1914	Ty Cobb, Det	.368	1936	Luke Appling, Chi	.388	1958	Ted Williams, Bos	.328
1915	Ty Cobb, Det	.369	1937	Charlie Gehringer, Det	.371	1959	Harvey Kuenn, Det	.353
1916	Tris Speaker, Cle	.386	1938	Jimmie Foxx, Bos	.349	1960	Pete Runnels, Bos	.320
1917	Ty Cobb, Det	.383	1939	Joe DiMaggio, NY	.381	1961	Norm Cash, Det	.361
1918	Ty Cobb, Det	.382	1940	Joe DiMaggio, NY	.352	1962	Pete Runnels, Bos	.326
1919	Ty Cobb, Det	.384	1941	Ted Williams, Bos	.406	1963	Carl Yastrzemski, Bos	.321
1920	George Sisler, St.L	.407	1942	Ted Williams, Bos	.356	1964	Tony Oliva, Min	.323
1921	Harry Heilmann, Det	.394	1943	Luke Appling, Chi	.328	1965	Tony Oliva, Min	.321
1922	George Sisler, St.L	.420	1944	Lou Boudreau, Clev	.327	1966	Frank Robinson, Bal	.316

Batting Average (Cont.)

Year		Avg	Year		Avg	Year		Avg
1967	Carl Yastrzemski, Bos	.326	1976	George Brett, KC	.333	1985	Wade Boggs, Bos.	.368
1968	Carl Yastrzemski, Bos	.301	1977	Rod Carew, Min.	.388	1986	Wade Boggs, Bos.	.357
1969	Rod Carew, Min.	.332	1978	Rod Carew, Min.	.333	1987	Wade Boggs, Bos.	.363
			1979	Fred Lynn, Bos	.333	1988	Wade Boggs, Bos.	.366
1970	Alex Johnson, Cal	.329				1989	Kirby Puckett, Min	.339
1971	Tony Oliva, Min	.337	1980	George Brett, KC	.390			
1972	Rod Carew, Min.	.318	1981	Carney Lansford, Bos	.336	1990	George Brett, KC	.329
1973	Rod Carew, Min.	.350	1982	Willie Wilson, KC	.332	1991	Julio Franco, Tex	.341
1974	Rod Carew, Min.	.364	1983	Wade Boggs, Bos.	.361			
1975	Rod Carew, Min.	.359	1984	Don Mattingly, NY	.343			

Home Runs
National League

Multiple winners: Mike Schmidt (8); Ralph Kiner (7); Gavvy Cravath and Mel Ott (6); Hank Aaron, Chuck Klein, Willie Mays, Johnny Mize, Cy Williams and Hack Wilson (4); Willie McCovey (3); Ernie Banks, Johnny Bench, George Foster, Rogers Hornsby, Tim Jordan, Dave Kingman, Eddie Mathews, Dale Murphy, Bill Nicholson, Dave Robertson, Wildfire Schulte and Willie Stargell (2).

Year		Avg	Year		HR	Year		HR
1900	Herman Long, Bos	12	1930	Hack Wilson, Chi	56	1959	Eddie Mathews, Mil.	46
1901	Sam Crawford, Cin.	16	1931	Chuck Klein, Phi	31	1960	Ernie Banks, Chi	41
1902	Tommy Leach, Pit	6	1932	Chuck Klein, Phi	38	1961	Orlando Cepeda, SF	46
1903	Jimmy Sheckard, Bklyn	9		& Mel Ott, NY	38	1962	Willie Mays, SF	49
1904	Harry Lumley, Bklyn	9	1933	Chuck Klein, Phi	28	1963	Hank Aaron, Mil	44
1905	Fred Odwell, Cin	9	1934	Rip Collins, St.L	35		& Willie McCovey, SF	44
1906	Tim Jordan, Bklyn	12		& Mel Ott, NY	35	1964	Willie Mays, SF	47
1907	Dave Brain, Bos.	10	1935	Wally Berger, Bos	34	1965	Willie Mays, SF	52
1908	Tim Jordan, Bklyn	12	1936	Mel Ott, NY	33	1966	Hank Aaron, Atl	44
1909	Red Murray, NY	7	1937	Joe Medwick, St.L	31	1967	Hank Aaron, Atl	39
1910	Fred Beck, Bos.	10		& Mel Ott, NY	31	1968	Willie McCovey, SF	36
	& Wildfire Schulte, Chi	10	1938	Mel Ott, NY	36	1969	Willie McCovey, SF	45
1911	Wildfire Schulte, Chi	21	1939	Johnny Mize, St.L.	28			
1912	Heinie Zimmerman, Chi.	14	1940	Johnny Mize, St.L.	43	1970	Johnny Bench, Cin	45
1913	Gavvy Cravath, Phi	19	1941	Dolf Camilli, Bklyn	34	1971	Willie Stargell, Pit.	48
1914	Gavvy Cravath, Phi	19	1942	Mel Ott, NY	30	1972	Johnny Bench, Cin	40
1915	Gavvy Cravath, Phi	24	1943	Bill Nicholson, Chi.	29	1973	Willie Stargell, Pit.	44
1916	& Cy Williams, Chi	12	1944	Bill Nicholson, Chi.	33	1974	Mike Schmidt, Phi	36
	Dave Robertson, NY	12	1945	Tommy Holmes, Bos.	28	1975	Mike Schmidt, Phi	38
1917	Gavvy Cravath, Phi.	12	1946	Ralph Kiner, Pit	23	1976	Mike Schmidt, Phi	38
	& Dave Robertson, NY	12	1947	Ralph Kiner, Pit	51	1977	George Foster, Cin	52
1918	Gavvy Cravath, Phi.	8		& Johnny Mize, NY	51	1978	George Foster, Cin	40
1919	Gavvy Cravath, Phi	12	1948	Ralph Kiner, Pit	40	1979	Dave Kingman, Chi	48
				& Johnny Mize, NY	40	1980	Mike Schmidt, Phi	48
1920	Cy Williams, Phi.	15	1949	Ralph Kiner, Pit	54	1981	Mike Schmidt, Phi	31
1921	George Kelly, NY	23	1950	Ralph Kiner, Pit	47	1982	Dave Kingman, NY.	37
1922	Rogers Hornsby, St.L.	42	1951	Ralph Kiner, Pit	42	1983	Mike Schmidt, Phi	40
1923	Cy Williams, Phi.	41	1952	Ralph Kiner, Pit	37	1984	Dale Murphy, Atl	36
1924	Jack Fournier, Bklyn	27		& Hank Sauer, Chi	37		& Mike Schmidt, Phi	36
1925	Rogers Hornsby, St.L.	39	1953	Eddie Mathews, Mil.	47	1985	Dale Murphy, Atl	37
1926	Hack Wilson, Chi	21	1954	Ted Kluszewski, Cin.	49	1986	Mike Schmidt, Chi.	37
1927	Cy Williams, Phi.	30	1955	Willie Mays, NY.	51	1987	Andre Dawson, Chi.	49
	& Hack Wilson, Chi.	30	1956	Duke Snider, Bklyn	43	1988	Darryl Strawberry, NY.	39
1928	Jim Bottomley, St.L	31	1957	Hank Aaron, Mil	44	1989	Kevin Mitchell, SF.	47
	& Hack Wilson, Chi.	31	1958	Ernie Banks, Chi	47	1990	Ryne Sandberg, Chi	40
1929	Chuck Klein, Phi	43				1991	Howard Johnson, NY.	38

American League

Multiple winners: Babe Ruth (12); Harmon Killebrew (6); Home Run Baker, Harry Davis, Jimmie Foxx, Hank Greenberg, Reggie Jackson, Mickey Mantle and Ted Williams (4); Lou Gehrig and Jim Rice (3); Dick Allen, Tony Armas, Jose Canseco, Joe DiMaggio, Larry Doby, Cecil Fielder, Frank Howard, Wally Pipp, Al Rosen and Gorman Thomas (2).

Year		HR	Year		HR	Year		HR
1901	Nap Lajoie, Phi	14	1908	Sam Crawford, Det	7	1914	Home Run Baker, Phi	9
1902	Socks Seybold, Phi.	16	1909	Ty Cobb, Det	9	1915	Braggo Roth, Chi-Cle	7
1903	Buck Freeman, Bos	13	1910	Jake Stahl, Bos	10	1916	Wally Pipp, NY	12
1904	Harry Davis, Phi.	10	1911	Home Run Baker, Phi	11	1917	Wally Pipp, NY.	9
1905	Harry Davis, Phi.	8	1912	Home Run Baker, Phi	10	1918	Babe Ruth, Bos	11
1906	Harry Davis, Phi	12		& Tris Speaker, Bos.	10		& Tilly Walker, Phi.	11
1907	Harry Davis, Phi.	8	1913	Home Run Baker, Phi	12	1919	Babe Ruth, Bos	29

Year	HR	Year	HR	Year	HR
1920	Babe Ruth, NY 54	1946	Hank Greenberg, Det 44	1972	Dick Allen, Chi 37
1921	Babe Ruth, NY 59	1947	Ted Williams, Bos 32	1973	Reggie Jackson, Oak 32
1922	Ken Williams, St.L 39	1948	Joe DiMaggio, NY 39	1974	Dick Allen, Chi 32
1923	Babe Ruth, NY 41	1949	Ted Williams, Bos 43	1975	Reggie Jackson, Oak 36
1924	Babe Ruth, NY 46	1950	Al Rosen, Cle 37		& George Scott, Mil 36
1925	Bob Meusel, NY 33	1951	Gus Zernial, Chi-Phi 33	1976	Graig Nettles, NY 32
1926	Babe Ruth, NY 47	1952	Larry Doby, Cle 32	1977	Jim Rice, Bos 39
1927	Babe Ruth, NY 60	1953	Al Rosen, Cle 43	1978	Jim Rice, Bos 46
1928	Babe Ruth, NY 54	1954	Larry Doby, Cle 32	1979	Gorman Thomas, Mil 45
1929	Babe Ruth, NY 46	1955	Mickey Mantle, NY 37	1980	Reggie Jackson, NY 41
1930	Babe Ruth, NY 49	1956	Mickey Mantle, NY 52		& Ben Ogilvie, Mil 41
1931	Lou Gehrig, NY 46	1957	Roy Sievers, Wash 42	1981	Tony Armas, Bos 22
	& Babe Ruth, NY 46	1958	Mickey Mantle, NY 42		Dwight Evans, Bos 22
1932	Jimmie Foxx, Phi 58	1959	Rocky Colavito, Cle 42		Bobby Grich, Cal 22
1933	Jimmie Foxx, Phi 48		& Harmon Killebrew, Wash 42		& Eddie Murray, Bal 22
1934	Lou Gehrig, NY 49	1960	Mickey Mantle, NY 40	1982	Reggie Jackson, Cal 39
1935	Jimmie Foxx, Phi 36	1961	Roger Maris, NY 61		& Gorman Thomas, Mil 39
	& Hank Greenberg, Det 36	1962	Harmon Killebrew, Min 48	1983	Jim Rice, Bos 39
1936	Lou Gehrig, NY 49	1963	Harmon Killebrew, Min 45	1984	Tony Armas, Bos 43
1937	Joe DiMaggio, NY 46	1964	Harmon Killebrew, Min 49	1985	Darrell Evans, Det 40
1938	Hank Greenberg, Det 58	1965	Tony Conigliaro, Bos 32	1986	Jesse Barfield, Tor 40
1939	Jimmie Foxx, Bos 35	1966	Frank Robinson, Bal 49	1987	Mark McGwire, Oak 49
1940	Hank Greenberg, Det 41	1967	Harmon Killebrew, Min 44	1988	Jose Canseco, Oak 42
1941	Ted Williams, Bos 37		& Carl Yastrzemski, Bos 44	1989	Fred McGriff, Tor 36
1942	Ted Williams, Bos 36	1968	Frank Howard, Wash 44	1990	Cecil Fielder, Det 51
1943	Rudy York, Det 34	1969	Harmon Killebrew, Min 49	1991	Jose Canseco, Oak 44
1944	Nick Etten, NY 22	1970	Frank Howard, Wash 44		& Cecil Fielder, Det 44
1945	Vern Stephens, St.L 24	1971	Bill Melton, Chi 33		

Runs Batted In
National League

Multiple winners: Hank Aaron, Rogers Hornsby, Sherry Magee, Mike Schmidt and Honus Wagner (4); Johnny Bench, George Foster, Joe Medwick, Johnny Mize and Heinie Zimmerman (3); Ernie Banks, Jim Bottomley, Orlando Cepeda, Gavvy Cravath, George Kelly, Chuck Klein, Willie McCovey, Dale Murphy, Stan Musial, Bill Nicholson and Hack Wilson (2).

Year	RBI	Year	RBI	Year	RBI
1900	Elmer Flick, Phi 110	1930	Hack Wilson, Chi 190	1962	Tommy Davis, LA 153
1901	Honus Wagner, Pit 126	1931	Chuck Klein, Phi 121	1963	Hank Aaron, Mil 130
1902	Honus Wagner, Pit 91	1932	Don Hurst, Phi 143	1964	Ken Boyer, St.L 119
1903	Sam Mertes, NY 104	1933	Chuck Klein, Phi 120	1965	Deron Johnson, Cin 130
1904	Bill Dahlen, NY 80	1934	Mel Ott, NY 135	1966	Hank Aaron, Atl 127
1905	Cy Seymour, Cin 121	1935	Wally Berger, Bos 130	1967	Orlando Cepeda, St.L 111
1906	Jim Nealon, Pit 83	1936	Joe Medwick, St.L 138	1968	Willie McCovey, SF 105
	& Harry Steinfeldt, Chi 83	1937	Joe Medwick, St.L 154	1969	Willie McCovey, SF 126
1907	Sherry Magee, Phi 85	1938	Joe Medwick, St.L 122	1970	Johnny Bench, Cin 148
1908	Honus Wagner, Pit 109	1939	Frank McCormick, Cin 128	1971	Joe Torre, St.L 137
1909	Honus Wagner, Pit 100	1940	Johnny Mize, St.L 137	1972	Johnny Bench, Cin 125
1910	Sherry Magee, Phi 123	1941	Dolph Camilli, Bklyn 120	1973	Willie Stargell, Pit 119
1911	Wildfire Schulte, Chi 121	1942	Johnny Mize, NY 110	1974	Johnny Bench, Cin 129
1912	Heinie Zimmerman, Chi 99	1943	Bill Nicholson, Chi 128	1975	Greg Luzinski, Phi 120
1913	Gavvy Cravath, Phi 128	1944	Bill Nicholson, Chi 122	1976	George Foster, Cin 121
1914	Sherry Magee, Phi 103	1945	Dixie Walker, Bklyn 124	1977	George Foster, Cin 149
1915	Gavvy Cravath, Phi 115	1946	Enos Slaughter, St.L 130	1978	George Foster, Cin 120
1916	Heinie Zimmerman, Chi-NY 99	1947	Johnny Mize, NY 138	1979	Dave Winfield, SD 118
1917	Heinie Zimmerman, NY 102	1948	Stan Musial, St.L 131	1980	Mike Schmidt, Phi 121
1918	Sherry Magee, Cin 76	1949	Ralph Kiner, Pit 127	1981	Mike Schmidt, Phi 91
1919	Hy Myers, Bklyn 73	1950	Del Ennis, Phi 126	1982	Dale Murphy, Atl 109
1920	Rogers Hornsby, St.L 94	1951	Monty Irvin, NY 121		& Al Oliver, Mon 109
	& George Kelly, NY 94	1952	Hank Sauer, Chi 121	1983	Dale Murphy, Atl 121
1921	Rogers Hornsby, St.L 126	1953	Roy Campanella, Bklyn 142	1984	Gary Carter, Mon 106
1922	Rogers Hornsby, St.L 152	1954	Ted Kluszewski, Cin 141		& Mike Schmidt, Phi 106
1923	Irish Meusel, NY 125	1955	Duke Snider, Bklyn 136	1985	Dave Parker, Cin 125
1924	George Kelly, NY 136	1956	Stan Musial, St.L 109	1986	Mike Schmidt, Phi 119
1925	Rogers Hornsby, St.L 143	1957	Hank Aaron, Mil 132	1987	Andre Dawson, Chi 137
1926	Jim Bottomley, St.L 120	1958	Ernie Banks, Chi 129	1988	Will Clark, SF 109
1927	Paul Waner, Pit 131	1959	Ernie Banks, Chi 143	1989	Kevin Mitchell, SF 125
1928	Jim Bottomley, St.L 136	1960	Hank Aaron, Mil 126	1990	Matt Williams, SF 122
1929	Hack Wilson, Chi 159	1961	Orlando Cepeda, SF 142	1991	Howard Johnson, NY 117

Runs Batted In (Cont.)
American League

Multiple winners: Babe Ruth (6); Lou Gehrig (5); Ty Cobb and Hank Greenberg (4); Sam Crawford, Jimmie Foxx, Jackie Jensen, Harmon Killebrew, Vern Stephens and Ted Williams (3); Home Run Baker, Cecil Cooper, Harry Davis, Joe DiMaggio, Cecil Fielder, Buck Freeman, Nap Lajoie, Roger Maris, Jim Rice, Al Rosen, and Bobby Veach (2).

Year		RBI	Year		RBI	Year		RBI
1901	Nap Lajoie, Phi	125	1932	Jimmie Foxx, Phi	169	1961	Roger Maris, NY	142
1902	Buck Freeman, Bos	121	1933	Jimmie Foxx, Phi	163	1962	Harmon Killebrew, Min	126
1903	Buck Freeman, Bos	104	1934	Lou Gehrig, NY	165	1963	Dick Stuart, Bos	118
1904	Nap Lajoie, Cle	102	1935	Hank Greenberg, Det	170	1964	Brooks Robinson, Bal	118
1905	Harry Davis, Phi	83	1936	Hal Trosky, Cle	162	1965	Rocky Colavito, Cle	108
1906	Harry Davis, Phi	96	1937	Hank Greenberg, Det	183	1966	Frank Robinson, Bal	122
1907	Ty Cobb, Det	116	1938	Jimmie Foxx, Bos	175	1967	Carl Yastrzemski, Bos	121
1908	Ty Cobb, Det	108	1939	Ted Williams, Bos	145	1968	Ken Harrelson, Bos	109
1909	Ty Cobb, Det	107	1940	Hank Greenberg, Det	150	1969	Harmon Killebrew, Min	140
1910	Sam Crawford, Det	120	1941	Joe DiMaggio, NY	125	1970	Frank Howard, Wash	126
1911	Ty Cobb, Det	144	1942	Ted Williams, Bos	137	1971	Harmon Killebrew, Min	119
1912	Home Run Baker, Phi	133	1943	Rudy York, Det	118	1972	Dick Allen, Chi	113
1913	Home Run Baker, Phi	126	1944	Vern Stephens, St.L	109	1973	Reggie Jackson, Oak	117
1914	Sam Crawford, Det	104	1945	Nick Etten, NY	111	1974	Jeff Burroughs, Tex	118
1915	Sam Crawford, Det	112	1946	Hank Greenberg, Det	127	1975	George Scott, Mil	109
1916	Del Pratt, St.L	103	1947	Ted Williams, Bos	114	1976	Lee May, Bal	109
1917	Bobby Veach, Det	103	1948	Joe DiMaggio, NY	155	1977	Larry Hisle, Min	119
1918	Bobby Veach, Det	78	1949	Ted Williams, Bos	159	1978	Jim Rice, Bos	139
1919	Babe Ruth, Bos	114		& Vern Stephens, Bos	159	1979	Don Baylor, Cal	139
1920	Babe Ruth, NY	137	1950	Walt Dropo, Bos	144	1980	Cecil Cooper, Mil	122
1921	Babe Ruth, NY	171		& Vern Stephens, Bos	144	1981	Eddie Murray, Bal	78
1922	Ken Williams, St.L	155	1951	Gus Zernial, Chi-Phi	129	1982	Hal McRae, KC	133
1923	Babe Ruth, NY	131	1952	Al Rosen, Cle	105	1983	Cecil Cooper, Mil	126
1924	Goose Goslin, Wash	129	1953	Al Rosen, Cle	145		& Jim Rice, Bos	126
1925	Bob Meusel, NY	138	1954	Larry Doby, Cle	126	1984	Tony Armas, Bos	123
1926	Babe Ruth, NY	145	1955	Ray Boone, Det	116	1985	Don Mattingly, NY	145
1927	Lou Gehrig, NY	175		& Jackie Jensen, Bos	116	1986	Joe Carter, Cle	121
1928	Lou Gehrig, NY	142	1956	Mickey Mantle, NY	130	1987	George Bell, Tor	134
	& Babe Ruth, NY	142	1957	Roy Sievers, Wash	114	1988	Jose Canseco, Oak	124
1929	Al Simmons, Phi	157	1958	Jackie Jensen, Bos	122	1989	Ruben Sierra, Tex	119
1930	Lou Gehrig, NY	174	1959	Jackie Jensen, Bos	112	1990	Cecil Fielder, Det	132
1931	Lou Gehrig, NY	184	1960	Roger Maris, NY	112	1991	Cecil Fielder, Det	133

Stolen Bases
National League

Multiple winners: Max Carey (10); Lou Brock (8); Vince Coleman and Maury Wills (6); Honus Wagner (5); Bob Brescher, Kiki Cuyler, Willie Mays and Tim Raines (4); Bill Bruton, Frankie Frisch and Pepper Martin (3); George Burns, Frank Chance, Augie Galan, Stan Hack, Sam Jethroe, Davey Lopes, Omar Moreno, Pete Reiser and Jackie Robinson (2).

Year		SB	Year		SB	Year		SB
1900	Patsy Donovan, St.L	45	1920	Max Carey, Pit	52	1941	Danny Murtaugh, Phi	18
	& George Van Haltren, NY	45	1921	Frankie Frisch, NY	49	1942	Pete Reiser, Bklyn	20
1901	Honus Wagner, Pit	49	1922	Max Carey, Pit	51	1943	Arky Vaughan, Bklyn	20
1902	Honus Wagner, Pit	42	1923	Max Carey, Pit	51	1944	Johnny Barrett, Pit	28
1903	Frank Chance, Chi	67	1924	Max Carey, Pit	49	1945	Red Schoendienst, St.L	26
	& Jimmy Sheckard, Bklyn	67	1925	Max Carey, Pit	46	1946	Pete Reiser, Bklyn	34
1904	Honus Wagner, Pit	53	1926	Kiki Cuyler, Pit	35	1947	Jackie Robinson, Bklyn	29
1905	Art Devlin, NY	59	1927	Frankie Frisch, St.L	48	1948	Richie Ashburn, Phi	32
	& Billy Maloney, Chi	59	1928	Kiki Cuyler, Chi	37	1949	Jackie Robinson, Bklyn	37
1906	Frank Chance, Chi	57	1929	Kiki Cuyler, Chi	43	1950	Sam Jethroe, Bos	35
1907	Honus Wagner, Pit	61	1930	Kiki Cuyler, Chi	37	1951	Sam Jethroe, Bos	35
1908	Honus Wagner, Pit	53	1931	Frankie Frisch, St.L	28	1952	Pee Wee Reese, Bklyn	30
1909	Bob Bescher, Cin	54	1932	Chuck Klein, Phi	20	1953	Bill Bruton, Mil	26
1910	Bob Bescher, Cin	70	1933	Pepper Martin, St.L	26	1954	Bill Bruton, Mil	34
1911	Bob Bescher, Cin	81	1934	Pepper Martin, St.L	23	1955	Bill Bruton, Mil	35
1912	Bob Bescher, Cin	67	1935	Augie Galan, Chi	22	1956	Willie Mays, NY	40
1913	Max Carey, Pit	61	1936	Pepper Martin, St.L	23	1957	Willie Mays, NY	38
1914	George Burns, NY	62	1937	Augie Galan, Chi	23	1958	Willie Mays, SF	31
1915	Max Carey, Pit	36	1938	Stan Hack, Chi	16	1959	Willie Mays, SF	27
1916	Max Carey, Pit	63	1939	Stan Hack, Chi	17	1960	Maury Wills, LA	50
1917	Max Carey, Pit	46		& Lee Handley, Pit	17	1961	Maury Wills, LA	35
1918	Max Carey, Pit	58	1940	Lonny Frey, Cin	22	1962	Maury Wills, LA	104
1919	George Burns, NY	40						

Year		SB	Year		SB	Year		SB
1963	Maury Wills, LA	40	1973	Lou Brock, St.L	70	1983	Tim Raines, Mon	90
1964	Maury Wills, LA	53	1974	Lou Brock, St.L	118	1984	Tim Raines, Mon	75
1965	Maury Wills, LA	94	1975	Davey Lopes, LA	77	1985	Vince Coleman, St.L	110
1966	Lou Brock, St.L	74	1976	Davey Lopes, LA	63	1986	Vince Coleman, St.L	107
1967	Lou Brock, St.L	52	1977	Frank Tavares, Pit	70	1987	Vince Coleman, St.L	109
1968	Lou Brock, St.L	62	1978	Omar Moreno, Pit	71	1988	Vince Coleman, St.L	81
1969	Lou Brock, St.L	53	1979	Omar Moreno, Pit	77	1989	Vince Coleman, St.L	66
1970	Bobby Tolan, Cin	57	1980	Ron LeFlore, Mon	97	1990	Vince Coleman, St.L	77
1971	Lou Brock, St.L	64	1981	Tim Raines, Mon	71	1991	Marquis Grissom, Mon	76
1972	Lou Brock, St.L	63	1982	Tim Raines, Mon	78			

American League

Multiple winners: Rickey Henderson (11); Luis Aparicio (9); Bert Campaneris, George Case and Ty Cobb (6); Ben Chapman, Eddie Collins and George Sisler (4); Bob Dillinger, Minnie Minoso and Bill Werber (3); Elmer Flick, Tommy Harper, Clyde Milan, Johnny Mostil, Bill North and Snuffy Stirnweiss (2).

Year		SB	Year		SB	Year		SB
1901	Frank Isbell, Chi	52	1932	Ben Chapman, NY	38	1963	Luis Aparicio, Bal	40
1902	Topsy Hartsel, Phi	47	1933	Ben Chapman, NY	27	1964	Luis Aparicio, Bal	57
1903	Harry Bay, Cle	45	1934	Bill Werber, Bos	40	1965	Bert Campaneris, KC	51
1904	Elmer Flick, Cle	42	1935	Bill Werber, Bos	29	1966	Bert Campaneris, KC	52
1905	Danny Hoffman, Phi	46	1936	Lyn Lary, St.L	37	1967	Bert Campaneris, KC	55
1906	John Anderson, Wash	39	1937	Ben Chapman, Wash-Bos	35	1968	Bert Campaneris, Oak	62
	& Elmer Flick, Cle	39		& Bill Werber, Phi	35	1969	Tommy Harper, Sea	73
1907	Ty Cobb, Det	49	1938	Frank Crosetti, NY	27			
1908	Patsy Dougherty, Chi	47	1939	George Case, Wash	51	1970	Bert Campaneris, Oak	42
1909	Ty Cobb, Det	76				1971	Amos Otis, KC	52
			1940	George Case, Wash	35	1972	Bert Campaneris, Oak	52
1910	Eddie Collins, Phi	81	1941	George Case, Wash	33	1973	Tommy Harper, Bos	54
1911	Ty Cobb, Det	83	1942	George Case, Wash	44	1974	Bill North, Oak	54
1912	Clyde Milan, Wash	88	1943	George Case, Wash	61	1975	Mickey Rivers, CA	70
1913	Clyde Milan, Wash	75	1944	Snuffy Stirnweiss, NY	55	1976	Bill North, Oak	75
1914	Fritz Maisel, NY	74	1945	Snuffy Stirnweiss, NY	33	1977	Freddie Patek, KC	53
1915	Ty Cobb, Det	96	1946	George Case, Cle	28	1978	Ron LeFlore, Det	68
1916	Ty Cobb, Det	68	1947	Bob Dillinger, St.L	34	1979	Willie Wilson, KC	83
1917	Ty Cobb, Det	55	1948	Bob Dillinger, St.L	28			
1918	George Sisler, St.L	45	1949	Bob Dillinger, St.L	20	1980	Rickey Henderson, Oak	100
1919	Eddie Collins, Chi	33				1981	Rickey Henderson, Oak	56
			1950	Dom DiMaggio, Bos	15	1982	Rickey Henderson, Oak	130
1920	Sam Rice, Wash	63	1951	Minnie Minoso, Cle-Chi	31	1983	Rickey Henderson, Oak	108
1921	George Sisler, St.L	35	1952	Minnie Minoso, Chi	22	1984	Rickey Henderson, Oak	66
1922	George Sisler, St.L	51	1953	Minnie Minoso, Chi	25	1985	Rickey Henderson, NY	80
1923	Eddie Collins, Chi	47	1954	Jackie Jensen, Bos	22	1986	Rickey Henderson, NY	87
1924	Eddie Collins, Chi	42	1955	Jim Rivera, Chi	25	1987	Harold Reynolds, Sea	60
1925	Johnny Mostil, Chi	43	1956	Luis Aparicio, Chi	21	1988	Rickey Henderson, NY	93
1926	Johnny Mostil, Chi	35	1957	Luis Aparicio, Chi	28	1989	R.Henderson, NY-Oak	77
1927	George Sisler, St.L	27	1958	Luis Aparicio, Chi	29			
1928	Buddy Myer, Bos	30	1959	Luis Aparicio, Chi	56	1990	Rickey Henderson, Oak	65
1929	Charlie Gehringer, Det	28				1991	Rickey Henderson, Oak	58
1930	Marty McManus, Det	23	1960	Luis Aparicio, Chi	51			
1931	Ben Chapman, NY	61	1961	Luis Aparicio, Chi	53			
			1962	Luis Aparicio, Chi	31			

Batting Triple Crown Winners

Players who led either league in Batting Average, Home Runs and Runs Batted In over a single season.

National League

	Year	Avg	HR	RBI
Paul Hines, Providence	1878	.358	4	50
Hugh Duffy, Boston	1894	.438	18	145
Heinie Zimmerman, Chicago	1912	.372	14	103
Rogers Hornsby, St.Louis	1922	.401	42	152
Rogers Hornsby, St.Louis	1925	.403	39	143
Chuck Klein, Philadelphia	1933	.368	28	120
Joe Medwick, St.Louis	1937	.374	31*	154

*Tied for league lead in HRs with Mel Ott, NY.

American League

	Year	Avg	HR	RBI
Nap Lajoie, Philadelphia	1901	.422	14	125
Ty Cobb, Detroit	1909	.377	9	115
Jimmie Foxx, Philadelphia	1933	.356	48	163
Lou Gehrig, New York	1934	.363	49	165
Ted Williams, Boston	1942	.356	36	137
Ted Williams, Boston	1947	.343	32	114
Mickey Mantle, New York	1956	.353	52	130
Frank Robinson, Baltimore	1966	.316	49	122
Carl Yastrzemski, Boston	1967	.326	44*	121

*Tied for league lead in HRs with Harmon Killebrew, Min.

Annual Pitching Leaders (since 1900)
Winning Percentage
At least 15 wins, except in strike year of 1981 when minimum was 10.

National League
Multiple winners: Ed Reulbach and Tom Seaver (3); Larry Benton, Harry Brecheen, Jack Chesbro, Paul Derringer, Freddie Fitzsimmons, Carl Hubbell, Sandy Koufax, Bill Lee, Christy Mathewson, Don Newcombe and Preacher Roe (2).

Year		W-L	Pct	Year		W-L	Pct
1900	Joe McGinnity, Brooklyn	28-8	.778	1947	Larry Jansen, New York	21-5	.808
1901	Jack Chesbro, Pittsburgh	21-10	.677	1948	Harry Brecheen, St. Louis	20-7	.741
1902	Jack Chesbro, Pittsburgh	28-6	.824	1949	Preacher Roe, Brooklyn	15-6	.714
1903	Sam Leever, Pittsburgh	25-7	.781	1950	Sal Maglie, New York	18-4	.818
1904	Joe McGinnity, New York	35-8	.814	1951	Preacher Roe, Brooklyn	22-3	.880
1905	Sam Leever, Pittsburgh	20-5	.800	1952	Hoyt Wilhelm, New York	15-3	.833
1906	Ed Reulbach, Chicago	19-4	.826	1953	Carl Erskine, Brooklyn	20-6	.769
1907	Ed Reulbach, Chicago	17-4	.810	1954	Johnny Antonelli, New York	21-7	.750
1908	Ed Reulbach, Chicago	24-7	.774	1955	Don Newcombe, Brooklyn	20-5	.800
1909	Howie Camnitz, Pittsburgh	25-6	.806	1956	Don Newcombe, Brooklyn	27-7	.794
	& Christy Mathewson, New York	25-6	.806	1957	Bob Buhl, Milwaukee	18-7	.720
1910	King Cole, Chicago	20-4	.833	1958	Warren Spahn, Milwaukee	22-11	.667
1911	Rube Marquard, New York	24-7	.774		& Lew Burdette, Milwaukee	20-10	.667
1912	Claude Hendrix, Pittsburgh	24-9	.727	1959	Roy Face, Pittsburgh	18-1	.947
1913	Bert Humphries, Chicago	16-4	.800	1960	Ernie Broglio, St. Louis	21-9	.700
1914	Bill James, Boston	26-7	.788	1961	Johnny Podres, Los Angeles	18-5	.783
1915	Grover Alexander, Phila.	31-10	.756	1962	Bob Purkey, Cincinnati	23-5	.821
1916	Tom Hughes, Boston	16-3	.842	1963	Ron Perranoski, Los Angeles	16-3	.842
1917	Ferdie Schupp, New York	21-7	.750	1964	Sandy Koufax, Los Angeles	19-5	.792
1918	Claude Hendrix, Chicago	20-7	.741	1965	Sandy Koufax, Los Angeles	26-8	.765
1919	Dutch Ruether, Cincinnati	19-6	.760	1966	Juan Marichal, San Francisco	25-6	.806
1920	Burleigh Grimes, Brooklyn	23-11	.676	1967	Dick Hughes, St. Louis	16-6	.727
1921	Bill Doak, St.Louis	15-6	.714	1968	Steve Blass, Pittsburgh	18-6	.750
1922	Pete Donohue, Cincinnati	18-9	.667	1969	Tom Seaver, New York	25-7	.781
1923	Dolf Luque, Cincinnati	27-8	.771	1970	Bob Gibson, St. Louis	23-7	.767
1924	Emil Yde, Pittsburgh	16-3	.842	1971	Don Gullett, Cincinnati	16-6	.727
1925	Bill Sherdel, St.Louis	15-6	.714	1972	Gary Nolan, Cincinnati	15-5	.750
1926	Ray Kremer, Pittsburgh	20-6	.769	1973	Tommy John, Los Angeles	16-7	.696
1927	Larry Benton, Boston-NY	17-7	.708	1974	Andy Messersmith, Los Angeles	20-6	.769
1928	Larry Benton, New York	25-9	.735	1975	Don Gullett, Cincinnati	15-4	.789
1929	Charlie Root, Chicago	19-6	.760	1976	Steve Carlton, Philadelphia	20-7	.741
1930	Freddie Fitzsimmons, NY	19-7	.731	1977	John Candelaria, Pittsburgh	20-5	.800
1931	Paul Derringer, St.Louis	18-8	.692	1978	Gaylord Perry, San Diego	21-6	.778
1932	Lon Warneke, Chicago	22-6	.786	1979	Tom Seaver, Cincinnati	16-6	.727
1933	Ben Cantwell, Boston	20-10	.667	1980	Jim Bibby, Pittsburgh	19-6	.760
1934	Dizzy Dean, St.Louis	30-7	.811	1981	Tom Seaver, Cincinnati	14-2	.875
1935	Bill Lee, Chicago	20-6	.769	1982	Phil Niekro, Atlanta	17-4	.810
1936	Carl Hubbell, New York	26-6	.813	1983	John Denny, Philadelphia	19-6	.760
1937	Carl Hubbell, New York	22-8	.733	1984	Rick Sutcliffe, Chicago	16-1	.941
1938	Bill Lee, Chicago	22-9	.710	1985	Orel Hershiser, Los Angeles	19-3	.864
1939	Paul Derringer, Cincinnati	25-7	.781	1986	Bob Ojeda, New York	18-5	.783
1940	Freddie Fitzsimmons, Bklyn	16-2	.889	1987	Dwight Gooden, New York	15-7	.682
1941	Elmer Riddle, Cincinnati	19-4	.826	1988	David Cone, New York	20-3	.870
1942	Larry French, Brooklyn	15-4	.789	1989	Mike Bielecki, Chicago	18-7	.720
1943	Mort Cooper, St. Louis	21-8	.724	1990	Doug Drabek, Pittsburgh	22-6	.786
1944	Ted Wilks, St. Louis	17-4	.810	1991	John Smiley, Pittsburgh	20-8	.714
1945	Harry Brecheen, St. Louis	15-4	.789		& Jose Rijo, Cincinnati	15-6	.714
1946	Murray Dickson, St. Louis	15-6	.714				

Note: In 1984, Sutcliffe was also 4-5 with Cle.(AL) for a combined record of 20-6 (.769).

American League
Multiple winners: Lefty Grove (5); Chief Bender and Whitey Ford (3); Johnny Allen, Eddie Cicotte, Roger Clemens, Mike Cuellar, Lefty Gomez, Catfish Hunter, Walter Johnson, Jim Palmer, Pete Vuckovich and Smokey Joe Wood (2).

Year		W-L	Pct	Year		W-L	Pct
1901	Clark Griffith, Chicago	24-7	.774	1908	Ed Walsh, Chicago	40-15	.727
1902	Bill Bernhard, Phila-Cleve.	18-5	.783	1909	George Mullin, Detroit	29-8	.784
1903	Cy Young, Boston	28-9	.757	1910	Chief Bender, Philadelphia	23-5	.821
1904	Jack Chesbro, New York	41-12	.774	1911	Chief Bender, Philadelphia	17-5	.773
1905	Andy Coakley, Philadelphia	20-7	.741	1912	Smokey Joe Wood, Boston	34-5	.872
1906	Eddie Plank, Philadelphia	19-6	.760	1913	Walter Johnson, Washington	36-7	.837
1907	Wild Bill Donovan, Detroit	25-4	.862				

Year		W-L	Pct	Year		W-L	Pct
1914	Chief Bender, Philadelphia	17-3	.850	1954	Sandy Consuegra, Chicago	16-3	.842
1915	Smokey Joe Wood, Boston	15-5	.750	1955	Tommy Byrne, New York	16-5	.762
1916	Eddie Cicotte, Chicago	15-7	.682	1956	Whitey Ford, New York	19-6	.760
1917	Reb Russell, Chicago	15-5	.750	1957	Dick Donovan, Chicago	16-6	.727
1918	Sad Sam Jones, Boston	16-5	.762		& Tom Sturdivant, New York	16-6	.727
1919	Eddie Cicotte, Chicago	29-7	.806	1958	Bob Turley, New York	21-7	.750
				1959	Bob Shaw, Chicago	18-6	.750
1920	Jim Bagby, Cleveland	31-12	.721				
1921	Carl Mays, New York	27-9	.750	1960	Jim Perry, Cleveland	18-10	.643
1922	Joe Bush, New York	26-7	.788	1961	Whitey Ford, New York	25-4	.862
1923	Herb Pennock, New York	19-6	.760	1962	Ray Herbert, Chicago	20-9	.690
1924	Walter Johnson, Washington	23-7	.767	1963	Whitey Ford, New York	24-7	.774
1925	Stan Coveleski, Washington	20-5	.800	1964	Wally Bunker, Baltimore	19-5	.792
1926	George Uhle, Cleveland	27-11	.711	1965	Mudcat Grant, Minnesota	21-7	.750
1927	Waite Hoyt, New York	22-7	.759	1966	Sonny Siebert, Cleveland	16-8	.667
1928	General Crowder, St. Louis	21-5	.808	1967	Joe Horlen, Chicago	19-7	.731
1929	Lefty Grove, Philadelphia	20-6	.769	1968	Denny McLain, Detroit	31-6	.838
				1969	Jim Palmer, Baltimore	16-4	.800
1930	Lefty Grove, Philadelphia	28-5	.848				
1931	Lefty Grove, Philadelphia	31-4	.886	1970	Mike Cuellar, Baltimore	24-8	.750
1932	Johnny Allen, New York	17-4	.810	1971	Dave McNally, Baltimore	21-5	.808
1933	Lefty Grove, Philadelphia	24-8	.750	1972	Catfish Hunter, Oakland	21-7	.750
1934	Lefty Gomez, New York	26-5	.839	1973	Catfish Hunter, Oakland	21-5	.808
1935	Eldon Auker, Detroit	18-7	.720	1974	Mike Cuellar, Baltimore	22-10	.688
1936	Monte Pearson, New York	19-7	.731	1975	Mike Torrez, Baltimore	20-9	.690
1937	Johnny Allen, Cleveland	15-1	.938	1976	Bill Campbell, Minnesota	17-5	.773
1938	Red Ruffing, New York	21-7	.750	1977	Paul Splittorff, Kansas City	16-6	.727
1939	Lefty Grove, Boston	15-4	.789	1978	Ron Guidry, New York	25-3	.893
				1979	Mike Caldwell, Milwaukee	16-6	.727
1940	Schoolboy Rowe, Detroit	16-3	.842				
1941	Lefty Gomez, New York	15-5	.750	1980	Steve Stone, Baltimore	25-7	.781
1942	Ernie Bonham, New York	21-5	.808	1981	Pete Vuckovich, Milwaukee	14-4	.778
1943	Spud Chandler, New York	20-4	.833	1982	Pete Vuckovich, Milwaukee	18-6	.750
1944	Tex Hughson, Boston	18-5	.783		& Jim Palmer, Baltimore	15-3	.750
1945	Hal Newhouser, Detroit	25-9	.735	1983	Rich Dotson, Chicago	22-7	.759
1946	Boo Ferriss, Boston	25-6	.806	1984	Doyle Alexander, Toronto	17-6	.739
1947	Allie Reynolds, New York	19-8	.704	1985	Ron Guidry, New York	22-6	.786
1948	Jack Kramer, Boston	18-5	.783	1986	Roger Clemens, Boston	24-4	.857
1949	Ellis Kinder, Boston	23-6	.793	1987	Roger Clemens, Boston	20-9	.690
				1988	Frank Viola, Minnesota	24-7	.774
1950	Vic Raschi, New York	21-8	.724	1989	Bret Saberhagen, Kansas City	23-6	.793
1951	Bob Feller, Cleveland	22-8	.733				
1952	Bobby Shantz, Philadelphia	24-7	.774	1990	Bob Welch, Oakland	27-6	.818
1953	Ed Lopat, New York	16-4	.800	1991	Scott Erickson, Minnesota	20-8	.714

Earned Run Average

Earned Run Averages were based on at least 10 complete games pitched (1900-50), at least 154 innings pitched (1950-60), and at least 162 innings pitched since 1961 in the AL and 1962 in the NL. In the strike year of 1981, qualifiers had to pitch at least as many innings as the total number of games their team played that season.

National League

Multiple winners: Grover Alexander, Sandy Koufax and Christy Mathewson (5); Carl Hubbell, Tom Seaver, Warren Spahn and Dazzy Vance (3); Bill Doak, Ray Kremer, Dolf Luque, Howie Pollett, Nolan Ryan, Bill Walker and Bucky Walters (2).

Year		ERA	Year		ERA	Year		ERA
1900	Rube Waddell, Pit.	2.37	1917	Grover Alexander, Phi	1.83	1933	Carl Hubbell, NY	1.66
1901	Jesse Tannehill, Pit	2.18	1918	Hippo Vaughn, Chi	1.74	1934	Carl Hubbell, NY	2.30
1902	Jack Taylor, Chi	1.33	1919	Grover Alexander, Chi	1.72	1935	Cy Blanton, Pit	2.59
1903	Sam Leever, Pit.	2.06				1936	Carl Hubbell, NY	2.31
1904	Joe McGinnity, NY	1.61	1920	Grover Alexander, Chi	1.91	1937	Jim Turner, Bos	2.38
1905	Christy Mathewson, NY	1.27	1921	Bill Doak, St.L	2.59	1938	Bill Lee, Chi	2.66
1906	Three Finger Brown, Chi	1.04	1922	Rosy Ryan, NY	3.01	1939	Bucky Walters, Cin	2.29
1907	Jack Pfiester, Chi	1.15	1923	Dolf Luque, Cin	1.93			
1908	Christy Mathewson, NY	1.43	1924	Dazzy Vance, Bklyn	2.16	1940	Bucky Walters, Cin	2.48
1909	Christy Mathewson, NY	1.14	1925	Dolf Luque, Cin	2.63	1941	Elmer Riddle, Cin	2.24
			1926	Ray Kremer, Pit.	2.61	1942	Mort Cooper, St.L	1.77
1910	George McQuillan, Phi	1.60	1927	Ray Kremer, Pit.	2.47	1943	Howie Pollet, St.L	1.75
1911	Christy Mathewson, NY	1.99	1928	Dazzy Vance, Bklyn	2.09	1944	Ed Heusser, Cin	2.38
1912	Jeff Tesreau, NY	1.96	1929	Bill Walker, NY	3.08	1945	Hank Borowy, Chi	2.14
1913	Christy Mathewson, NY	2.06				1946	Howie Pollet, St.L	2.10
1914	Bill Doak, St.L	1.72	1930	Dazzy Vance, Bklyn	2.61	1947	Warren Spahn, Bos	2.33
1915	Grover Alexander, Phi	1.22	1931	Bill Walker, NY	2.26	1948	Harry Brecheen, St.L	2.24
1916	Grover Alexander, Phi	1.55	1932	Lon Warneke, Chi	2.37	1949	Dave Koslo, NY	2.50

Earned Run Average (Cont.)

Year		ERA	Year		ERA	Year		ERA
1950	Jim Hearn, St.L-NY	2.49	1965	Sandy Koufax, LA.	2.04	1979	J.R. Richard, Hou	2.71
1951	Chet Nichols, Bos.	2.88	1966	Sandy Koufax, LA.	1.73	1980	Don Sutton, LA.	2.21
1952	Hoyt Wilhelm, NY	2.43	1967	Phil Niekro, Atl.	1.87	1981	Nolan Ryan, Hou.	1.69
1953	Warren Spahn, Mil	2.10	1968	Bob Gibson, St.L	1.12	1982	Steve Rogers, Mon	2.40
1954	Johnny Antonelli, NY.	2.29	1969	Juan Marichal, SF	2.10	1983	Atlee Hammaker, SF	2.25
1955	Bob Friend, Pit	2.84				1984	Alejandro Pena, LA	2.48
1956	Lew Burdette, Mil	2.71	1970	Tom Seaver, NY.	2.81	1985	Dwight Gooden, NY	1.53
1957	Johnny Podres, Bklyn.	2.66	1971	Tom Seaver, NY.	1.76	1986	Mike Scott, Hou	2.22
1958	Stu Miller, SF.	2.47	1972	Steve Carlton, Phi.	1.98	1987	Nolan Ryan, Hou.	2.76
1959	Sam Jones, SF	2.82	1973	Tom Seaver, NY.	2.08	1988	Joe Magrane, St.L	2.18
			1974	Buzz Capra, Atl	2.28	1989	Scott Garrelts, SF	2.28
1960	Mike McCormick, SF	2.70	1975	Randy Jones, SD	2.24			
1961	Warren Spahn, Mil	3.01	1976	John Denny, St.L	2.52	1990	Danny Darwin, Hou.	2.21
1962	Sandy Koufax, LA.	2.54	1977	John Candelaria, Pit	2.34	1991	Dennis Martinez, Mon	2.39
1963	Sandy Koufax, LA.	1.88	1978	Craig Swan, NY.	2.43			
1964	Sandy Koufax, LA.	1.74						

Note: In 1945, Borowy had a 3.13 ERA in 18 games with New York (AL) for a combined ERA of 2.65.

American League

Multiple winners: Lefty Grove (9); Walter Johnson (5); Roger Clemens (3); Spud Chandler, Stan Coveleski, Red Faber, Whitey Ford, Lefty Gomez, Ron Guidry, Addie Joss, Hal Newhouser, Jim Palmer, Gary Peters, Luis Tiant and Ed Walsh (2).

Year		ERA	Year		ERA	Year		ERA
1901	Cy Young, Bos	1.62	1932	Lefty Grove, Phi	2.84	1963	Gary Peters, Chi.	2.33
1902	Ed Siever, Det.	1.91	1933	Monte Pearson, Cle	2.33	1964	Dean Chance, LA	1.65
1903	Earl Moore, Cle	1.77	1934	Lefty Gomez, NY	2.33	1965	Sam McDowell, Cle	2.18
1904	Addie Joss, Cle.	1.59	1935	Lefty Grove, Bos.	2.70	1966	Gary Peters, Chi.	1.98
1905	Rube Waddell, Phi	1.48	1936	Lefty Grove, Bos.	2.81	1967	Joe Horlen, Chi	2.06
1906	Doc White, Chi.	1.52	1937	Lefty Gomez, NY	2.33	1968	Luis Tiant, Cle.	1.60
1907	Ed Walsh, Chi	1.60	1938	Lefty Grove, Bos.	3.08	1969	Dick Bosman, Wash	2.19
1908	Addie Joss, Cle.	1.16	1939	Lefty Grove, Bos.	2.54			
1909	Harry Krause, Phi.	1.39				1970	Diego Segui, Oak	2.56
			1940	Bob Feller, Cle	2.61	1971	Vida Blue, Oak.	1.82
1910	Ed Walsh, Chi	1.27	1941	Thorton Lee, Chi	2.37	1972	Luis Tiant, Bos	1.91
1911	Vean Gregg, Cle	1.81	1942	Ted Lyons, Chi.	2.10	1973	Jim Palmer, Bal	2.40
1912	Walter Johnson,Wash	1.39	1943	Spud Chandler, NY	1.64	1974	Catfish Hunter, Oak	2.49
1913	Walter Johnson,Wash	1.09	1944	Dizzy Trout, Det	2.12	1975	Jim Palmer, Bal	2.09
1914	Dutch Leonard, Bos.	1.01	1945	Hal Newhouser, Det	1.81	1976	Mark Fidrych, Det	2.34
1915	Smokey Joe Wood,Bos	1.49	1946	Hal Newhouser, Det	1.94	1977	Frank Tanana, Cal	2.54
1916	Babe Ruth, Bos.	1.75	1947	Spud Chandler, NY	2.46	1978	Ron Guidry, NY	1.74
1917	Eddie Cicotte, Chi	1.53	1948	Gene Bearden, Cle	2.43	1979	Ron Guidry, NY	2.78
1918	Walter Johnson,Wash	1.27	1949	Mel Parnell, Bos	2.77			
1919	Walter Johnson,Wash	1.49				1980	Rudy May, NY	2.47
			1950	Early Wynn, Cle	3.20	1981	Steve McCatty, Oak.	2.32
1920	Bob Shawkey, NY	2.45	1951	Saul Rogovin,Det-Chi	2.78	1982	Rick Sutcliffe, Cle	2.96
1921	Red Faber, Chi.	2.48	1952	Allie Reynolds, NY	2.06	1983	Rick Honeycutt, Tex	2.42
1922	Red Faber, Chi.	2.80	1953	Ed Lopat, NY	2.42	1984	Mike Boddicker, Bal	2.79
1923	Stan Coveleski, Cle	2.76	1954	Mike Garcia, Cle	2.64	1985	Dave Stieb, Tor.	2.48
1924	Walter Johnson,Wash	2.72	1955	Billy Pierce, Chi.	1.97	1986	Roger Clemens, Bos	2.48
1925	Stan Coveleski, Wash	2.84	1956	Whitey Ford, NY.	2.47	1987	Jimmy Key, Tor.	2.76
1926	Lefty Grove, Phi	2.51	1957	Bobby Shantz, NY	2.45	1988	Allen Anderson, Min	2.45
1927	Wilcy Moore, NY	2.28	1958	Whitey Ford, NY.	2.01	1989	Bret Saberhagen, KC.	2.16
1928	Garland Braxton,Wash	2.51	1959	Hoyt Wilhelm, Bal	2.19			
1929	Lefty Grove, Phi	2.81				1990	Roger Clemens, Bos	1.93
			1960	Frank Baumann, Chi.	2.67	1991	Roger Clemens, Bos	2.62
1930	Lefty Grove, Phi	2.54	1961	Dick Donovan, Wash.	2.40			
1931	Lefty Grove, Phi	2.06	1962	Hank Aguirre, Det	2.21			

Note: In 1940, Ernie Bonham of NY had a 1.90 ERA and 10 complete games, but appeared in only a total of 12 games and 99 innings.

Strikeouts

National League

Multiple winners: Dazzy Vance (7); Grover Alexander (6); Steve Carlton, Christy Mathewson and Tom Seaver (5); Dizzy Dean, Sandy Koufax and Warren Spahn (4); Don Drysdale, Sam Jones and Johnny Vander Meer (3); David Cone, Dwight Gooden, Bill Hallahan, J.R. Richard, Robin Roberts, Nolan Ryan and Hippo Vaughn (2).

Year		SO	Year		SO	Year		SO
1900	Rube Waddell, Pit	130	1904	Christy Mathewson, NY	212	1908	Christy Mathewson, NY	259
1901	Noodles Hahn, Cinn	239	1905	Christy Mathewson, NY	206	1909	Orval Overall, Chi	205
1902	Vic Willis, Bos.	225	1906	Fred Beebe, Chi-St.L.	171	1910	Earl Moore, Phi	185
1903	Christy Mathewson, NY	267	1907	Christy Mathewson, NY	178	1911	Rube Marquard, NY	237

Year		SO	Year		SO	Year		SO
1912	Grover Alexander, Phi	195	1940	Kirby Higbe, Phi	137	1966	Sandy Koufax, LA	317
1913	Tom Seaton, Phi	168	1941	John Vander Meer,Cin	202	1967	Jim Bunning, Phi	253
1914	Grover Alexander, Phi	214	1942	John Vander Meer,Cin	186	1968	Bob Gibson, St.L	268
1915	Grover Alexander, Phi	241	1943	John Vander Meer,Cin	174	1969	Ferguson Jenkins, Chi	273
1916	Grover Alexander, Phi	167	1944	Bill Voiselle, NY	161	1970	Tom Seaver, NY	283
1917	Grover Alexander, Phi	201	1945	Preacher Roe, Pitt	148	1971	Tom Seaver, NY	289
1918	Hippo Vaughn, Chi.	148	1946	Johnny Schmitz, Chi	135	1972	Steve Carlton, Phi	310
1919	Hippo Vaughn, Chi.	141	1947	Ewell Blackwell, Cin	193	1973	Tom Seaver, NY	251
1920	Grover Alexander, Chi	173	1948	Harry Brecheen, St.L	149	1974	Steve Carlton, Phi	240
1921	Burleigh Grimes, Bklyn	136	1949	Warren Spahn, Bos.	151	1975	Tom Seaver, NY	243
1922	Dazzy Vance, Bklyn	134	1950	Warren Spahn, Bos.	191	1976	Tom Seaver, NY	235
1923	Dazzy Vance, Bklyn	197	1951	Don Newcombe, Bklyn.	164	1977	Phil Niekro, Atl	262
1924	Dazzy Vance, Bklyn	262		& Warren Spahn, Bos.	164	1978	J.R. Richard, Hou	303
1925	Dazzy Vance, Bklyn	221	1952	Warren Spahn, Bos.	183	1979	J.R. Richard, Hou	313
1926	Dazzy Vance, Bklyn	140	1953	Robin Roberts, Phi	198	1980	Steve Carlton, Phi	286
1927	Dazzy Vance, Bklyn	184	1954	Robin Roberts, Phi	185	1981	F. Valenzuela,LA	180
1928	Dazzy Vance, Bklyn	200	1955	Sam Jones, Chi	198	1982	Steve Carlton, Phi	286
1929	Pat Malone, Chi	166	1956	Sam Jones, Chi	176	1983	Steve Carlton, Phi	275
1930	Bill Hallahan, St.L	177	1957	Jack Sanford, Phi	188	1984	Dwight Gooden, NY	276
1931	Bill Hallahan, St.L	159	1958	Sam Jones, St.L	225	1985	Dwight Gooden, NY	268
1932	Dizzy Dean, St.L	191	1959	Don Drydale, LA	242	1986	Mike Scott, Hou	306
1933	Dizzy Dean, St.L	199	1960	Don Drysdale, LA	246	1987	Nolan Ryan, Hou	270
1934	Dizzy Dean, St.L	195	1961	Sandy Koufax, LA	269	1988	Nolan Ryan, Hou	228
1935	Dizzy Dean, St.L	182	1962	Don Drysdale, LA	232	1989	Jose DeLeon, St.L	201
1936	Van Lingle Mungo,Bklyn.	238	1963	Sandy Koufax, LA	306	1990	David Cone, NY	233
1937	Carl Hubbell, NY	159	1964	Bob Veale, Pit	250	1991	David Cone, NY	241
1938	Clay Bryant, Chi	135	1965	Sandy Koufax, LA	382			
1939	Claude Passeau,Phi-Chi.	137						
	& Bucky Walters, Cin	137						

American League

Multiple winners: Walter Johnson (12); Nolan Ryan (9); Bob Feller and Lefty Grove (7); Rube Waddell (6); Sam McDowell (5); Lefty Gomez, Camilo Pascual and Mark Langston (3); Len Barker, Tommy Bridges, Jim Bunning, Roger Clemens, Hal Newhouser, Allie Reynolds, Herb Score, Ed Walsh and Early Wynn (2).

Year		SO	Year		SO	Year		SO
1901	Cy Young, Bos	158	1932	Red Ruffing, NY	190	1962	Camilo Pascual, Min	206
1902	Rube Waddell, Phi.	210	1933	Lefty Gomez, NY	163	1963	Camilo Pascual, Min	202
1903	Rube Waddell, Phi.	302	1934	Lefty Gomez, NY	158	1964	Al Downing, NY	217
1904	Rube Waddell, Phi.	349	1935	Tommy Bridges, Det	163	1965	Sam McDowell, Cle	325
1905	Rube Waddell, Phi.	287	1936	Tommy Bridges, Det	175	1966	Sam McDowell, Cle	225
1906	Rube Waddell, Phi.	196	1937	Lefty Gomez, NY	194	1967	Jim Lonborg, Bos	246
1907	Rube Waddell, Phi.	232	1938	Bob Feller, Cle.	240	1968	Sam McDowell, Cle	283
1908	Ed Walsh, Chi	269	1939	Bob Feller, Cle.	246	1969	Sam McDowell, Cle	279
1909	Frank Smith, Chi	177	1940	Bob Feller, Cle.	261	1970	Sam McDowell, Cle	304
1910	Walter Johnson, Wash	313	1941	Bob Feller, Cle.	260	1971	Mickey Lolich, Det	308
1911	Ed Walsh, Chi	255	1942	Tex Hughson, Bos	113	1972	Nolan Ryan, Cal	329
1912	Walter Johnson, Wash	303		& Bobo Newsom,Wash	113	1973	Nolan Ryan, Cal	383
1913	Walter Johnson, Wash	243	1943	Allie Reynolds, Cle	151	1974	Nolan Ryan, Cal	367
1914	Walter Johnson, Wash	225	1944	Hal Newhouser, Det	187	1975	Frank Tanana, Cal	269
1915	Walter Johnson, Wash	203	1945	Hal Newhouser, Det	212	1976	Nolan Ryan, Cal	327
1916	Walter Johnson, Wash	228	1946	Bob Feller, Cle.	348	1977	Nolan Ryan, Cal	341
1917	Walter Johnson, Wash	188	1947	Bob Feller, Cle.	196	1978	Nolan Ryan, Cal	260
1918	Walter Johnson, Wash	162	1948	Bob Feller, Cle.	164	1979	Nolan Ryan, Cal	223
1919	Walter Johnson, Wash	147	1949	Virgil Trucks, Det	153	1980	Len Barker, Cle	187
1920	Stan Coveleski, Cle	133	1950	Bob Lemon, Cle	170	1981	Len Barker, Cle	127
1921	Walter Johnson, Wash	143	1951	Vic Raschi, NY	164	1982	Floyd Bannister, Sea	209
1922	Urban Shocker, St.L	149	1952	Allie Reynolds, NY	160	1983	Jack Morris, Det	232
1923	Walter Johnson, Wash	130	1953	Billy Pierce Chi	186	1984	Mark Langston, Sea	204
1924	Walter Johnson, Wash	158	1954	Bob Turley, Bal	185	1985	Bert Blyleven,Cle-Min	206
1925	Lefty Grove, Phi	116	1955	Herb Score, Cle.	245	1986	Mark Langston, Sea	245
1926	Lefty Grove, Phi	194	1956	Herb Score, Cle.	263	1987	Mark Langston, Sea	262
1927	Lefty Grove, Phi	174	1957	Early Wynn, Cle.	184	1988	Roger Clemens, Bos	291
1928	Lefty Grove, Phi	183	1958	Early Wynn, Chi	179	1989	Nolan Ryan, Tex	301
1929	Lefty Grove, Phi	170	1959	Jim Bunning, Det.	201	1990	Nolan Ryan, Tex	232
1930	Lefty Grove, Phi	209	1960	Jim Bunning, Det.	201	1991	Roger Clemens, Bos	241
1931	Lefty Grove, Phi	175	1961	Camilo Pascual, Min.	221			

Pitching Triple Crown Winners

Pitchers who led either league in Earned Run Average, Wins and Strikeouts over a single season.

National League

	Year	ERA	W-L	SO
Tommy Bond, Bos	1877	2.11	40-17	170
Hoss Radbourn, Prov	1884	1.38	60-12	441
Tim Keefe, NY	1888	1.74	35-12	333
John Clarkson, Bos.	1889	2.73	49-19	284
Amos Rusie, NY	1894	2.78	36-13	195
Christy Mathewson, NY	1905	1.27	31-8	206
Christy Mathewson, NY	1908	1.43	37-11	259
Grover Alexander, Phi	1915	1.22	31-10	241
Grover Alexander, Phi	1916	1.55	33-12	167
Grover Alexander, Phi	1917	1.86	30-13	201
Hippo Vaugh, Chi	1918	1.74	22-10	148
Grover Alexander, Chi	1920	1.91	27-14	173
Dazzy Vance, Bklyn.	1924	2.16	28-6	262
Bucky Walters, Cin	1939	2.29	27-11	137
Sandy Koufax, LA	1963	1.88	25-5	306
Sandy Koufax, LA	1965	2.04	26-8	382
Sandy Koufax, LA	1966	1.73	27-9	317

	Year	ERA	W-L	SO
Steve Carlton, Phi	1972	1.97	27-10	310
Dwight Gooden, NY	1985	1.53	24-4	268

Ties: in 1894, Rusie tied for league lead in wins with Jouett Meekin, NY (36-10); in 1939, Walters tied for league lead in strikeouts with Claude Passeau, Phi-Chi; in 1963, Koufax tied for the league lead in wins with Juan Marichal, SF.

American League

	Year	ERA	W-L	SO
Cy Young, Bos	1901	1.62	33-10	158
Rube Waddell, Phi	1905	1.48	26-11	287
Walter Johnson, Wash	1913	1.09	36-7	243
Walter Johnson, Wash	1918	1.27	23-13	162
Walter Johnson, Wash	1924	2.72	23-7	158
Lefty Grove, Phi.	1930	2.54	28-5	209
Lefty Grove, Phi.	1931	2.06	31-4	175
Lefty Gomez, NY	1934	2.33	26-5	158
Lefty Gomez, NY	1937	2.33	21-11	194
Hal Newhouser, Det.	1945	1.81	25-9	212

Perfect Games

Fifteen pitchers have thrown perfect games (27 up, 27 down) in major league history.

National League

	Game	Date	Score
Lee Richmond	Wor.vs Cle.	6/12/1880	1-0
Monte Ward	Prov.vs Bos.	6/17/1880	5-0
Harvey Haddix	Pit.at Mil.	5/26/1959	0-1*
Jim Bunning	Phi.at NY	6/21/1964	6-0
Sandy Koufax	LA vs Chi.	9/9/1965	1-0
Tom Browning	Cin.vs LA	9/16/1988	1-0
Dennis Martinez	Mon. at LA	7/28/1991	2-0

*Haddix pitched 12 perfect innings before losing in the 13th. Braves' lead-off batter Felix Mantilla reached on a throwing error by Pirates 3B Don Hook, Eddie Mathews sacrificed Mantilla to 2nd, Hank Aaron was walked intentionally, and Joe Adcock hit a 3-run HR. Adcock, however, passed Aaron on the bases and was only credited with a 1-run double.

American League

	Game	Date	Score
Cy Young	Bos.vs Phi.	5/5/1904	3-0
Adrian Joss	Cle.vs Chi.	10/2/1908	1-0
Ernie Shore	Bos.vs Wash.	6/23/1917	4-0*
Charlie Robertson	Chi.at Det.	4/30/1922	2-0
Catfish Hunter	Oak.vs Min.	5/8/1968	4-0
Len Barker	Cle.vs Tor.	5/15/1981	3-0
Mike Witt	Cal.at Tex.	9/30/1984	1-0

*Babe Ruth started for Boston, walking Senators' lead-off batter Ray Morgan, then was thrown out of game by umpire Brick Owens for arguing the call. Shore came on in relief. Morgan was caught stealing and Shore retired the next 26 batters in a row. While technically not a perfect game—since he didn't start—Shore gets credit anyway.

World Series

Pitcher	Game	Date	Score
Don Larsen	NY vs Bklyn	10/8/1956	2-0

Consecutive Game Streaks

Regular season games through 1991.

Games Played

Active streak in **bold** type.

Gm		Dates of Streak
2130	Lou Gehrig, NY	6/1/25 to 4/30/39
1573	**Cal Ripken Jr**, Bal	5/30/82 to —
1307	Everett Scott, Bos-NY	6/20/16 to 5/5/25
1207	Steve Garvey, LA-SD	9/3/75 to 7/29/83
1117	Billy Williams, Cubs	9/22/63 to 9/2/70
1103	Joe Sewell, Cle	9/13/22 to 4/30/30
895	Stan Musial, St.L	4/15/52 to 8/23/57
829	Eddie Yost, Wash	4/30/49 to 5/11/55
822	Gus Suhr, Pit	9/11/31 to 6/4/37
798	Nellie Fox, Chisox	8/8/55 to 9/3/60
745	Pete Rose, Cin-Phi	9/2/78 to 8/23/83
740	Dale Murphy, Atl	9/26/81 to 7/8/86
730	Richie Ashburn, Phi	6/7/50 to 4/13/55
717	Ernie Banks, Cubs	8/28/56 to 6/22/61
678	Pete Rose, Cin.	9/28/73 to 5/7/78

Hitting

	Gm	Year
Joe DiMaggio, New York (AL)	56	1941
Willie Keeler, Baltimore (NL)	44	1897
Pete Rose, Cincinnati (NL)	44	1978
Bill Dahlen, Chicago (NL)	42	1894
George Sisler, St.Louis (AL)	41	1922
Ty Cobb, Detroit (AL)	40	1911
Paul Molitor, Milwaukee (AL)	39	1987
Tommy Holmes, Boston (NL)	37	1945
Billy Hamilton, Philadelphia (NL)	36	1894
Fred Clarke, Louisville (NL)	35	1895
Ty Cobb, Detroit (AL)	35	1917
Benito Santiago, San Diego (NL)	34	1987
George Sisler, St.Louis (AL)	34	1925
John Stone, Detroit (AL)	34	1930
George McQuinn, St.Louis (AL)	34	1938
Dom DiMaggio, Boston (AL)	34	1949

All-Time Major League Leaders

Through 1991 regular season

CAREER

Players active in 1991 in **bold** type.

Batting

Note that (*) indicates left-handed hitter and (†) indicates switch-hitter. Active player leaders are listed for batting average, hits, HRs and RBI.

Batting Average

		Yrs	AB	H	Avg
1	Ty Cobb*	24	11,429	4191	.367
2	Rogers Hornsby	23	8,137	2930	.358
3	Joe Jackson*	13	4,981	1774	.356
4	Ed Delahanty	16	7,502	2591	.345
5	**Wade Boggs***	10	5,699	1965	.345
6	Ted Williams*	19	7,706	2654	.344
7	Tris Speaker*	22	10,208	3515	.344
8	Billy Hamilton*	14	6,284	2163	.344
9	Willie Keeler*	19	8,585	2947	.343
10	Dan Brouthers*	19	6,711	2296	.342
11	Babe Ruth*	22	8,399	2873	.342
12	Harry Heilmann	17	7,787	2660	.342
13	Pete Browning	13	4,820	1646	.341
14	Bill Terry*	14	6,428	2193	.341
15	George Sisler*	15	8,267	2812	.340
16	Lou Gehrig*	17	8,001	2721	.340
17	Jesse Burkett*	16	8,413	2853	.339
18	Nap Lajoie	21	9,592	3244	.338
19	Riggs Stephenson	14	4,508	1515	.336
20	Al Simmons	20	8,761	2927	.334
21	Paul Waner*	20	9,459	3152	.333
22	Eddie Collins*	25	9,949	3311	.333
23	Stan Musial*	22	10,972	3630	.331
24	Sam Thompson*	14	6,005	1986	.331
25	Heinie Manush*	17	7,653	2524	.330

Hits

		Yrs	AB	H	Avg
1	Pete Rose†	24	14,053	4256	.303
2	Ty Cobb*	24	11,429	4191	.367
3	Hank Aaron	23	12,364	3771	.305
4	Stan Musial*	22	10,972	3630	.331
5	Tris Speaker*	22	10,208	3515	.344
6	Carl Yastrzemski*	23	11,988	3419	.285
7	Honus Wagner	21	10,443	1418	.327
8	Eddie Collins*	25	9,949	3311	.333
9	Willie Mays	22	10,881	3283	.302
10	Nap Lajoie	21	9,592	3244	.338
11	Paul Waner*	20	9,459	3152	.333
12	Rod Carew*	19	9,315	3053	.328
13	Lou Brock*	19	10,332	3023	.293
14	Al Kaline	22	10,116	3007	.297
15	Cap Anson	22	9,108	3000	.329
16	Roberto Clemente	18	9,454	3000	.317
17	Sam Rice*	20	9,269	2987	.322
18	Sam Crawford*	19	9,580	2964	.309
19	Willie Keeler*	19	8,585	2947	.343
20	Frank Robinson	21	10,006	2943	.294
21	Jake Beckley*	20	9,527	2931	.308
22	Rogers Hornsby	23	8,173	2930	.358
23	Al Simmons	20	8,761	2927	.334
24	Zack Wheat	19	9,106	2884	.317
25	Frankie Frisch	19	9,112	2880	.316

Players Active in 1991

		Yrs	AB	Hits	Avg
1	Wade Boggs*	10	5699	1965	.345
2	Tony Gwynn*	10	5181	1699	.328
3	Kirby Puckett	8	5006	1602	.320
4	Don Mattingly*	10	5003	1570	.314
5	Mike Greenwell*	7	2800	870	.311
6	George Brett*	19	9197	2836	.308
7	Pedro Guerrero	14	5246	1586	.302
8	Paul Molitor	14	6911	2086	.302
9	Tim Raines	13	5914	1761	.298
10	Ken Griffey Sr	19	7229	2143	.296

Players Active in 1991

		Yrs	AB	Hits	Avg
1	Robin Yount	18	9997	2878	.288
2	George Brett*	19	9197	2836	.308
3	Dave Parker*	19	9358	2712	.290
4	Dave Winfield	18	9464	2697	.285
5	Eddie Murray†	15	8573	2502	.292
6	Dwight Evans	20	8996	2446	.272
7	Andre Dawson	16	8348	2354	.282
8	Carlton Fisk	22	8515	2303	.270
9	Ken Griffey Sr	19	7229	2143	.296
10	Willie Randolph†	17	7732	2138	.277

Games Played

1	Pete Rose	3562
2	Carl Yastrzemski	3308
3	Hank Aaron	3298
4	Ty Cobb	3034
5	Stan Musial	3026
6	Willie Mays	2992
7	Rusty Staub	2951
8	Brooks Robinson	2896
9	Al Kaline	2834
10	Eddie Collins	2826
11	Reggie Jackson	2820
12	Frank Robinson	2808
13	Tris Speaker	2789
	Honus Wagner	2789
15	Tony Perez	2777
16	Mel Ott	2734
17	Graig Nettles	2700
18	Darrell Evans	2687
19	Rabbit Maranville	2670
20	Joe Morgan	2649

At Bats

1	Pete Rose	14,053
2	Hank Aaron	12,364
3	Carl Yastrzemski	11,988
4	Ty Cobb	11,429
5	Stan Musial	10,972
6	Willie Mays	10,881
7	Brooks Robinson	10,654
8	Honus Wagner	10,441
9	Lou Brock	10,332
10	Luis Aparicio	10,230
11	Tris Speaker	10,208
12	Al Kaline	10,116
13	Rabbit Maranville	10,078
14	Frank Robinson	10,006
15	**Robin Yount**	9,997
16	Eddie Collins	9,949
17	Reggie Jackson	9,864
18	Tony Perez	9,778
19	Rusty Staub	9,720
20	Vada Pinson	9,645

Total Bases

1	Hank Aaron	6856
2	Stan Musial	6134
3	Willie Mays	6066
4	Ty Cobb	5863
5	Babe Ruth	5793
6	Pete Rose	5752
7	Carl Yastrzemski	5539
8	Frank Robinson	5373
9	Tris Speaker	5104
10	Lou Gehrig	5059
11	Mel Ott	5041
12	Jimmie Foxx	4956
13	Ted Williams	4884
14	Honus Wagner	4868
15	Al Kaline	4852
16	Reggie Jackson	4834
17	Rogers Hornsby	4712
18	Ernie Banks	4706
19	Al Simmons	4685
20	Billy Williams	4599

All-Time Major League Leaders (Cont.)

Home Runs

		Yrs	AB	HR	Pct
1	Hank Aaron	23	12,364	755	6.1
2	Babe Ruth*	22	8,399	714	8.5
3	Willie Mays	22	10,881	660	6.1
4	Frank Robinson	21	10,006	586	5.9
5	Harmon Killebrew	22	8,147	573	7.0
6	Reggie Jackson*	21	9,864	563	5.7
7	Mike Schmidt	18	8,352	548	6.6
8	Mickey Mantle†	18	8,102	536	6.6
9	Jimmie Foxx	20	8,134	534	6.6
10	Ted Williams*	19	7,706	521	6.8
	Willie McCovey*	22	8,197	521	6.4
12	Eddie Mathews*	17	8,537	512	6.0
	Ernie Banks	19	9,421	512	5.4
14	Mel Ott*	22	9,456	511	5.4
15	Lou Gehrig*	17	8,001	493	6.2
16	Willie Stargell*	21	7,927	475	6.0
	Stan Musial*	22	10,972	475	4.3
18	Carl Yastrzemski*	23	11,988	452	3.8
19	Dave Kingman	16	6,677	442	6.6
20	Billy Williams*	18	9,350	426	4.6
21	Darrell Evans*	21	8,973	414	4.6
22	Duke Snider*	18	7,161	407	5.7
23	**Dave Winfield**	18	9,464	406	4.3
24	Al Kaline	22	10,116	399	3.9
25	**Eddie Murray†**	15	8,573	398	4.6

Players Active in 1991

		Yrs	AB	HR	Pct
1	Dave Winfield	18	9464	406	4.3
2	Eddie Murray†	15	8573	398	4.6
3	Dale Murphy	16	7856	396	5.0
4	Dwight Evans	20	8996	385	4.3
5	Andre Dawson	16	8348	377	4.5
6	Carlton Fisk	22	8515	372	4.4
7	Dave Parker*	19	9358	339	3.6
8	Jack Clark	17	6590	335	5.1
9	Gary Carter	18	7686	319	4.2
10	Lance Parrish	15	6468	304	4.7
11	George Brett*	19	9197	291	3.2
12	Darryl Strawberry	9	4408	280	6.4
13	Brian Downing	19	7533	265	3.5
14	Cal Ripken Jr.	11	6305	259	4.1
15	Jesse Barfield	11	4664	239	5.1

Runs Batted In

		Yrs	Gm	RBI	P/G
1	Hank Aaron	23	3298	2297	.70
2	Babe Ruth*	22	2503	2211	.88
3	Lou Gehrig*	17	2164	1990	.92
4	Ty Cobb*	24	3034	1961	.65
5	Stan Musial*	22	3026	1951	.64
6	Jimmie Foxx	20	2317	1921	.83
7	Willie Mays	22	2992	1903	.64
8	Mel Ott*	22	2732	1861	.68
9	Carl Yastrzemski*	23	3308	1844	.56
10	Ted Williams*	19	2292	1839	.80
11	Al Simmons	20	2215	1827	.82
12	Frank Robinson	21	2808	1812	.65
13	Honus Wagner	21	2786	1732	.62
14	Cap Anson	22	2276	1715	.75
15	Reggie Jackson*	21	2820	1702	.60
16	Tony Perez	23	2777	1652	.59
17	Ernie Banks	19	2528	1636	.65
18	Goose Goslin*	18	2287	1609	.70
19	**Dave Winfield**	18	2551	1602	.63
20	Nap Lajoie	21	2475	1599	.65
21	Mike Schmidt	18	2404	1595	.66
22	Rogers Hornsby	23	2259	1584	.70
	Harmon Killebrew	22	2435	1584	.65
24	Al Kaline	22	2834	1583	.56
25	Jake Beckley*	20	2386	1575	.66

Players Active in 1991

		Yrs	AB	HR	P/G
1	Dave Winfield	18	2551	1602	.63
2	Dave Parker*	19	2466	1493	.61
3	Eddie Murray†	15	2288	1469	.64
4	George Brett*	19	2410	1459	.61
5	Dwight Evans	20	2606	1384	.53
6	Andre Dawson	16	2167	1335	.62
7	Carlton Fisk	22	2412	1305	.54
8	Robin Yount	18	2579	1278	.50
9	Dale Murphy	16	2136	1252	.59
10	Gary Carter	18	2201	1196	.54
11	Jack Clark	17	1913	1147	.60
12	Brian Downing	19	2237	1034	.46
13	Lance Parrish	15	1775	998	.56
14	Harold Baines	12	1704	990	.58
15	Cal Ripken Jr.	11	1638	942	.58

Runs

1	Ty Cobb	2245
2	Babe Ruth	2174
	Hank Aaron	2174
4	Pete Rose	2165
5	Willie Mays	2062
6	Stan Musial	1949
7	Lou Gehrig	1888
8	Tris Speaker	1881
9	Mel Ott	1859
10	Frank Robinson	1829
11	Eddie Collins	1818
12	Carl Yastrzemski	1816
13	Ted Williams	1798
14	Charlie Gehringer	1774
15	Jimmie Foxx	1751
16	Honus Wagner	1735
17	Willie Keeler	1727
18	Cap Anson	1719
19	Jesse Burkett	1718
20	Billy Hamilton	1692

Extra Base Hits

1	Hank Aaron	1477
2	Stan Musial	1377
3	Babe Ruth	1356
4	Willie Mays	1323
5	Lou Gehrig	1190
6	Frank Robinson	1186
7	Carl Yastrzemski	1157
8	Ty Cobb	1139
9	Tris Speaker	1132
10	Ted Williams	1117
	Jimmie Foxx	1117
12	Reggie Jackson	1075
13	Mel Ott	1071
14	Pete Rose	1041
15	**George Brett**	1019
16	Mike Schmidt	1015
17	Rogers Hornsby	1011
18	Ernie Banks	1009
19	Honus Wagner	996
20	Al Simmons	995

Slugging Average

1	Babe Ruth	.690
2	Ted Williams	.634
3	Lou Gehrig	.632
4	Jimmie Foxx	.609
5	Hank Greenberg	.605
6	Joe DiMaggio	.579
7	Rogers Hornsby	.577
8	Johnny Mize	.562
9	Stan Musial	.559
10	Willie Mays	.557
11	Mickey Mantle	.557
12	Hank Aaron	.555
13	Ralph Kiner	.548
14	Hack Wilson	.545
15	Chuck Klein	.543
16	Duke Snider	.540
17	Frank Robinson	.537
18	Al Simmons	.535
19	Dick Allen	.534
20	Earl Averill	.533

Stolen Bases

1	Rickey Henderson	994
2	Lou Brock	938
3	Billy Hamilton	915
4	Ty Cobb	892
5	Eddie Collins	743
6	Arlie Latham	739
7	Max Carey	738
8	Honus Wagner	720
9	Joe Morgan	689
10	Tim Raines	685
11	Bert Campaneris	649
12	Willie Wilson	632
13	Tom Brown	627
14	George Davis	615
15	Hugh Duffy	583
16	Dummy Hoy	597
17	Vince Coleman	586
	Maury Wills	586
19	George Van Haltren	583
20	Davey Lopes	557

Walks

1	Babe Ruth	2056
2	Ted Williams	2019
3	Joe Morgan	1865
4	Carl Yastrzemski	1845
5	Mickey Mantle	1734
6	Mel Ott	1708
7	Eddie Yost	1614
8	Darrell Evans	1605
9	Stan Musial	1599
10	Pete Rose	1566
11	Harmon Killebrew	1559
12	Lou Gehrig	1508
13	Mike Schmidt	1507
14	Eddie Collins	1503
15	Willie Mays	1463
16	Jimmie Foxx	1452
17	Eddie Mathews	1444
18	Frank Robinson	1420
19	Hank Aaron	1402
20	Dwight Evans	1391

Strikeouts

1	Reggie Jackson	2597
2	Willie Stargell	1936
3	Mike Schmidt	1883
4	Tony Perez	1867
5	Dave Kingman	1816
6	Bobby Bonds	1757
7	Lou Brock	1730
8	Dale Murphy	1720
9	Mickey Mantle	1710
10	Harmon Killebrew	1699
11	Dwight Evans	1697
12	Lee May	1570
13	Dick Allen	1556
14	Willie McCovey	1550
15	Dave Parker	1537
16	Frank Robinson	1532
17	Willie Mays	1526
18	Rick Monday	1513
19	Greg Luzinski	1495
20	Eddie Mathews	1487

Pitching

Note that (*) indicates left-handed pitcher. Active pitcher leaders are listed for wins, strikeouts and saves.

Wins

		Yrs	GS	W	L	Pct
1	Cy Young	22	815	511	313	.620
2	Walter Johnson	21	666	416	279	.599
3	Christy Mathewson	17	551	373	188	.665
	Grover Alexander	20	598	373	208	.642
5	Warren Spahn*	21	665	363	245	.597
6	Kid Nichols	15	561	361	208	.634
	Pud Galvin	14	682	361	308	.540
8	Tim Keefe	14	594	342	225	.603
9	Steve Carlton*	24	709	329	244	.574
10	Eddie Plank*	17	527	327	193	.629
11	John Clarkson	12	518	326	177	.648
12	Don Sutton	23	756	324	256	.559
13	Phil Niekro	24	716	318	274	.537
14	Gaylord Perry	22	690	314	265	.542
	Nolan Ryan	25	733	314	278	.530
16	Old Hoss Radbourn	12	503	311	194	.616
	Tom Seaver	20	647	311	205	.603
18	Mickey Welch	13	549	308	209	.596
19	Lefty Grove*	17	456	300	141	.680
	Early Wynn	23	612	300	244	.551
21	Tommy John*	26	700	288	231	.555
22	Robin Roberts	19	609	286	245	.539
23	Tony Mullane	13	505	285	220	.564
24	Ferguson Jenkins	19	594	284	226	.557
25	Jim Kaat*	25	625	283	237	.544
26	Bert Blyleven	21	661	279	238	.540
27	Red Ruffing	22	536	273	225	.548
28	Burleigh Grimes	19	495	270	212	.560
29	Jim Palmer	19	521	268	152	.638
30	Bob Feller	18	484	266	162	.621

Strikeouts

		Yrs	IP	SO	P/9
1	Nolan Ryan	25	5163.1	5511	9.60
2	Steve Carlton*	24	5217.1	4136	7.13
3	Tom Seaver	20	4782.2	3640	6.85
4	Bert Blyleven	21	4837.1	3631	6.76
5	Don Sutton	23	5282.1	3574	6.09
6	Gaylord Perry	22	5350.1	3534	5.94
7	Walter Johnson	21	5923.2	3509	5.33
8	Phil Niekro	24	5404.1	3342	5.57
9	Ferguson Jenkins	19	4500.2	3192	6.38
10	Bob Gibson	17	3884.1	3117	7.22
11	Jim Bunning	17	3760.1	2855	6.83
12	Mickey Lolich*	16	3638.1	2832	7.01
13	Cy Young	22	7354.2	2800	3.42
14	Warren Spahn*	21	5243.2	2583	4.43
15	Bob Feller	18	3827.0	2581	6.07
16	Frank Tanana*	19	3797.1	2566	6.08
17	Jerry Koosman*	19	3839.1	2556	5.99
18	Tim Keefe	14	5061.1	2527	4.50
19	Christy Mathewson	17	4781.0	2502	4.71
20	Don Drysdale	14	3432.0	2486	6.52
21	Jim Kaat*	25	4530.1	2461	4.89
22	Sam McDowell*	15	2492.1	2453	8.86
23	Luis Tiant	19	3486.1	2416	6.24
24	Sandy Koufax*	12	2324.1	2396	9.28
25	Robin Roberts	19	4688.2	2357	4.52
26	Early Wynn	23	4564.0	2334	4.60
27	Rube Waddell*	13	2961.1	2316	7.04
28	Juan Marichal	16	3507.1	2303	5.91
29	Lefty Grove*	17	3940.2	2266	5.17
30	Eddie Plank*	17	4495.2	2246	4.48

Pitchers Active in 1991

		Yrs	GS	W	L	Pct
1	Nolan Ryan	25	733	314	278	.530
2	Bert Blyleven (injured)	21	661	279	238	.540
3	Frank Tanana*	19	553	220	208	.514
4	Jack Morris	15	443	216	162	.571
5	Rick Reuschel	19	529	214	191	.528
6	Charlie Hough	22	358	195	179	.521
7	Bob Welch	14	406	188	122	.606
8	Dennis Martinez	16	410	177	145	.550
9	John Candelaria*	17	356	175	114	.606
10	Dennis Eckersley	17	361	174	144	.547

Pitchers Active in 1991

		Yrs	IP	SO	P/9
1	Nolan Ryan	25	5163.1	5511	9.60
2	Bert Blyleven (injured)	21	4837.1	3631	6.76
3	Frank Tanana*	19	3797.1	2566	6.08
4	Jack Morris	15	3290.0	2143	5.86
5	Charlie Hough	22	3306.0	2095	5.70
6	Dennis Eckersley	17	2891.1	2025	6.30
7	Rick Reuschel	19	3549.2	2015	5.11
8	Bob Welch	14	2732.1	1815	5.98
9	Fernando Valenzuela*	12	2355.1	1764	6.74
10	Roger Clemens	8	1784.1	1665	8.40

Note: Blyleven underwent shoulder surgery in 1991 and sat out entire season.

All-Time Major League Leaders (Cont.)

Winning Pct.

		Yrs	W-L	Pct
1	**Dwight Gooden**	8	132-53	.714
2	Dave Foutz	11	147-66	.690
3	Whitey Ford*	16	236-106	.690
4	Bob Caruthers	9	218-99	.688
5	**Roger Clemens**	8	134-61	.687
6	Lefty Grove*	17	300-141	.680
7	Vic Raschi	10	132-66	.667
8	Christy Mathewson	17	373-188	.665
9	Larry Corcoran	8	177-90	.663
10	Sam Leever	13	194-101	.658
11	Sal Maglie	10	119-62	.657
12	Sandy Koufax*	12	165-87	.655
13	Johnny Allen	13	142-75	.654
14	Ron Guidry*	14	170-91	.651
15	Lefty Gomez*	14	189-102	.649

Losses

		Yrs	GS	W	L	Pct
1	Cy Young	22	815	511	313	.620
2	Pud Galvin	14	682	361	310	.538
3	Walter Johnson	21	666	416	279	.599
4	**Nolan Ryan**	25	733	314	278	.530
5	Phil Niekro	24	716	318	274	.537
6	Gaylord Perry	22	690	314	265	.542
7	Jack Powell	16	517	245	256	.489
	Don Sutton	23	756	324	256	.559
9	Eppa Rixey*	21	552	266	251	.515
10	Robin Roberts	19	609	286	245	.539
	Warren Spahn*	21	665	363	245	.597
12	Early Wynn	23	612	300	244	.551
	Steve Carlton*	24	709	329	244	.574
14	Bert Blyleven	21	661	279	238	.544
15	Jim Kaat*	25	625	283	237	.544

Games

1	Hoyt Wilhelm	1070
2	Kent Tekulve	1050
3	Lindy McDaniel	987
4	Rollie Fingers	944
5	Gene Garber	931
6	Cy Young	906
7	Sparky Lyle	899
8	Jim Kaat	898
9	**Rich Gossage**	897
10	Don McMahon	874
11	Phil Niekro	864
12	Roy Face	848
13	Tug McGraw	824
14	Walter Johnson	801
15	Gaylord Perry	777

Innings Pitched

1	Cy Young	7354.2
2	Pud Galvin	5941.1
3	Walter Johnson	5923.2
4	Phil Niekro	5404.1
5	Gaylord Perry	5350.1
6	Don Sutton	5282.1
7	Warren Spahn	5243.2
8	Steve Carlton	5217.1
9	Grover Alexander	5189.1
10	**Nolan Ryan**	5163.1
11	Tim Keefe	5061.1
12	Kid Nichols	5057.1
13	**Bert Blyleven**	4837.1
14	Mickey Welch	4802.0
15	Tom Seaver	4782.2

Earned Run Avg.

1	Ed Walsh	1.82
2	Addie Joss	1.88
3	Three Finger Brown	2.06
4	Monte Ward	2.10
5	Christy Mathewson	2.13
6	Rube Waddell	2.16
7	Walter Johnson	2.17
8	Orval Overall	2.24
9	Tommy Bond	2.25
10	Will White	2.28
11	Ed Reulbach	2.28
12	Jim Scott	2.32
13	Eddie Plank	2.34
14	Larry Corcoran	2.36
15	Eddie Cicotte	2.37

Shutouts

1	Walter Johnson	110
2	Grover Alexander	90
3	Christy Mathewson	80
4	Cy Young	76
5	Eddie Plank	69
6	Warren Spahn	63
7	**Nolan Ryan**	61
	Tom Seaver	61
9	Bert Blyleven	60
10	Don Sutton	58
11	Three Finger Brown	57
	Pud Galvin	57
	Ed Walsh	57
14	Bob Gibson	56
15	Steve Carlton	55

Walks Allowed

1	**Nolan Ryan**	2686
2	Steve Carlton	1833
3	Phil Niekro	1809
4	Early Wynn	1775
5	Bob Feller	1764
6	Bobo Newsom	1732
7	Amos Rusie	1704
8	Gus Weyhing	1566
9	Red Ruffing	1541
10	**Charlie Hough**	1476
11	Bump Hadley	1442
12	Warren Spahn	1434
13	Earl Whitehill	1431
14	Tony Mullane	1409
15	Sad Sam Jones	1396

HRs Allowed

1	Robin Roberts	505
2	Ferguson Jenkins	484
3	Phil Niekro	482
4	Don Sutton	472
5	Warren Spahn	434
6	Steve Carlton	414
7	Bert Blyleven	413
8	Gaylord Perry	399
9	**Frank Tanana**	398
10	Jim Kaat	395
11	Tom Seaver	380
12	Catfish Hunter	374
13	Jim Bunning	372
14	Mickey Lolich	347
15	Luis Tiant	346

Saves

1	Rollie Fingers	341	22	Lindy McDaniel	172
2	**Jeff Reardon**	327	23	Stu Miller	154
3	**Lee Smith**	312	24	Don McMahon	153
4	**Rich Gossage**	308	25	Greg Minton	150
5	Bruce Sutter	300	26	**Jay Howell**	149
6	**Dave Righetti**	248	27	Ted Abernathy	148
7	Dan Quisenberry	244	28	Willie Hernandez	147
8	Sparky Lyle	238	29	Dave Giusti	145
9	Hoyt Wilhelm	227	30	Clay Carroll	143
10	Gene Garber	218		Darold Knowles	143
11	**Dave Smith**	216			
12	**John Franco**	211			
13	Roy Face	193			
14	**Dennis Eckersley**	188			
	Mike Marshall	188			
16	**Tom Henke**	186			
17	**Steve Bedrosian**	184			
	Kent Tekulve	184			
19	Tug McGraw	180			
20	Ron Perranoski	179			
21	**Bobby Thigpen**	178			

Relief Pitchers Active in 1991

1	Jeff Reardon	327	6	John Franco	211	11	Jay Howell	149
2	Lee Smith	312	7	Dennis Eckersley	188	12	Roger McDowell	135
3	Rich Gossage	308	8	Tom Henke	186	13	Dan Plesac	132
4	Dave Righetti	248	9	Steve Bedrosian	184	14	Doug Jones	128
5	Dave Smith	216	10	Bobby Thigpen	178	15	Jesse Orosco	121

SINGLE SEASON
Through 1991 regular season.
Batting

Home Runs

		Year	Gm	AB	HR
1	Roger Maris, NY-AL	1961	162	590	61
2	Babe Ruth, NY-AL	1927	151	540	60
3	Babe Ruth, NY-AL	1921	152	540	59
4	Hank Greenberg, Det.	1938	155	556	58
	Jimmie Foxx, Phi-AL	1932	154	585	58
6	Hack Wilson, Chi-NL	1930	155	585	56
7	Babe Ruth, NY-AL	1920	142	458	54
	Mickey Mantle, NY-AL	1961	153	514	54
	Babe Ruth, NY-AL	1928	154	536	54
	Ralph Kiner, Pit	1949	152	549	54
11	Mickey Mantle, NY-AL	1956	150	533	52
	Willie Mays, SF.	1965	157	558	52
	George Foster, Cin	1977	158	615	52
14	Ralph Kiner, Pit	1947	152	565	51
	Cecil Fielder, Det.	1990	159	573	51
	Willie Mays, NY-NL	1955	152	580	51
	Johnny Mize, NY-NL	1947	154	586	51
18	Jimmie Foxx, Bos-AL	1938	149	565	50

Hits

		Year	AB	H	Avg
1	George Sisler, StL-AL	1920	631	257	.407
2	Bill Terry, NY-NL	1930	633	254	.401
	Lefty O'Doul, Phi-NL	1929	638	254	.398
4	Al Simmons, Phi-AL.	1925	658	253	.384
5	Rogers Hornsby, StL-NL	1922	623	250	.401
6	Chuck Klein, Phi-NL	1930	648	250	.386
7	Ty Cobb, Det	1911	591	248	.420
8	George Sisler, StL-AL	1922	586	246	.420
9	Babe Herman, Bklyn.	1930	614	241	.393
	Heinie Manush, StL-AL	1928	638	241	.378
11	Wade Boggs, Bos	1985	653	240	.368
12	Rod Carew, Min	1977	616	239	.388
13	Don Mattingly, NY-AL	1986	677	238	.352
14	Harry Heilmann, Det.	1921	602	237	.394
	Paul Waner, Pit	1927	623	237	.380
	Joe Medwick, StL-NL.	1937	633	237	.374
17	Jack Tobin, StL-AL.	1921	671	236	.352
18	Rogers Hornsby, StL-NL	1921	592	235	.397

Batting Average

From 1900-49

		Year	AB	H	Avg
1	Rogers Hornsby, StL-NL	1924	536	227	.424
2	Nap Lajoie, Phi-AL	1901	543	229	.422
3	George Sisler, StL-AL	1922	586	246	.420
	Ty Cobb, Det	1911	591	248	.420
5	Ty Cobb, Det	1912	533	227	.410
6	Joe Jackson, Cle	1911	571	233	.408
7	George Sisler, StL-AL	1920	631	257	.407
8	Ted Williams, Bos-AL	1941	456	185	.406
9	Rogers Hornsby, StL-NL	1925	504	203	.403
10	Harry Heilmann, Det.	1923	524	211	.403

Since 1950

		Year	AB	H	Avg
1	George Brett, KC	1980	449	175	.390
2	Ted Williams, Bos	1957	420	163	.388
	Rod Carew, Min	1977	616	239	.388
4	Tony Gwynn, SD	1987	589	218	.370
5	Wade Boggs, Bos	1985	653	240	.368
6	Wade Boggs, Bos	1988	584	214	.366
	Rico Carty, Atl	1970	478	175	.366
8	Mickey Mantle, NY-AL	1957	474	173	.365
9	Rod Carew, Min	1974	599	218	.364
10	Joe Torre, St.L	1971	634	230	.363
	Wade Boggs, Bos	1987	551	200	.363

Total Bases

From 1900-49

		Year	TB
1	Babe Ruth, New York-AL	1921	457
2	Rogers Hornsby, St.Louis-NL	1922	450
3	Lou Gehrig, New York-AL	1927	447
4	Chuck Klein, Philadelphia-NL	1930	445
5	Jimmie Foxx, Philadelphia-AL	1932	438
6	Stan Musial, St.Louis-NL	1948	429
7	Hack Wilson, Chicago-NL	1930	423
8	Chuck Klein, Philadelphia-NL	1932	420
9	Lou Gehrig, New York-AL	1930	419
10	Joe DiMaggio, New York-AL	1937	418

Since 1950

		Year	TB
1	Jim Rice, Boston	1978	406
2	Hank Aaron, Milwaukee	1959	400
3	George Foster, Cincinnati	1977	388
	Don Mattingly, New York-AL	1986	388
5	Willie Mays, New York-NL	1955	382
	Willie Mays, San Francisco.	1962	382
	Jim Rice, Boston	1977	382
8	Frank Robinson, Cincinnati	1962	380
9	Ernie Banks, Chicago-NL.	1958	379
10	Duke Snider, Brooklyn	1954	378

Runs Batted In

From 1900-49

		Year	Avg	HR	RBI
1	Hack Wilson, Chi-NL	1930	.356	56	190
2	Lou Gehrig, NY-AL	1931	.341	46	184
3	Hank Greenberg, Det.	1937	.337	40	183
4	Lou Gehrig, NY-AL	1927	.373	47	175
	Jimmie Foxx, Bos-AL	1938	.349	50	175
6	Lou Gehrig, NY-AL	1930	.379	41	174
7	Babe Ruth, NY-AL	1921	.378	59	171
8	Chuck Klein, Phi-NL	1930	.386	40	170
	Hank Greenberg, Det.	1935	.328	36	170
10	Jimmie Foxx, Phi-AL	1932	.364	58	169

Since 1950

		Year	Avg	HR	RBI
1	Tommy Davis, LA-NL	1962	.346	27	153
2	George Foster, Cin	1977	.320	52	149
3	Johnny Bench, Cin	1970	.293	45	148
4	Al Rosen, Cle	1953	.336	43	145
	Don Mattingly, NY-AL	1985	.324	35	145
6	Walt Dropo, Bos-AL	1950	.322	34	144
	Vern Stephens, Bos-AL	1950	.295	30	144
8	Ernie Banks, Chi-NL	1959	.304	45	143
9	Roy Campanella, Bklyn.	1953	.312	41	142
	Orlando Cepeda, SF	1961	.311	46	142
	Roger Maris, NY-AL	1961	.269	61	142

All-Time Major League Leaders (Cont.)

Runs

		Year	Runs
1	Babe Ruth, New York-AL	1921	177
2	Lou Gehrig, New York-AL	1936	167
3	Babe Ruth, New York-AL	1928	163
	Lou Gehrig, New York-AL	1931	163
5	Babe Ruth, New York-AL	1920	158
	Babe Ruth, New York-AL	1927	158
	Chuck Klein, Philadelphia-NL	1930	158
8	Rogers Hornsby, Chicago-NL	1929	156
9	Kiki Cuyler, Chicago-NL	1930	155
10	Lefty O'Doul, Philadelphia-NL	1929	152
	Woody English, Chicago-NL	1930	152
	Al Simmons, Philadelphia-AL	1930	152
	Chuck Klein, Philadelphia-NL	1932	152
14	Babe Ruth, New York-AL	1923	151
	Jimmie Foxx, Philadelphia-AL	1932	151
	Joe DiMaggio, New York-AL	1937	151
17	Babe Ruth, New York-AL	1930	150
	Ted Williams, Boston-AL	1940	150
19	Lou Gehrig, New York-AL	1927	149
	Babe Ruth, New York-AL	1931	149

Bases on Balls

		Year	BB
1	Babe Ruth, New York-AL	1923	170
2	Ted Williams, Boston-AL	1947	162
	Ted Williams, Boston-AL	1949	162
4	Ted Williams, Boston-AL	1946	156
5	Eddie Yost, Washington	1956	151
6	Eddie Joost, Philadelphia-AL	1949	149
7	Babe Ruth, New York-AL	1920	148
	Eddie Stanky, Brooklyn	1945	148
	Jimmy Wynn, Houston	1969	148
10	Jimmy Sheckard, Chicago-NL	1911	147

Extra Base Hits

		Year	EBH
1	Babe Ruth, New York-AL	1921	119
2	Lou Gehrig, New York-AL	1927	117
3	Chuck Klein, Philadelphia-NL	1930	107
5	Chuck Klein, Philadelphia-NL	1932	103
	Hank Greenberg, Detroit	1937	103
	Stan Musial, St.Louis-NL	1948	103
7	Rogers Hornsby, St.Louis-NL	1922	102
8	Lou Gehrig, New York-AL	1930	100
	Jimmie Foxx, Philadelphia-AL	1933	100
	Three tied with 99.		

Slugging Average
From 1900-49

		Year	Avg
1	Babe Ruth, New York-AL	1920	.847
2	Babe Ruth, New York-AL	1921	.846
3	Babe Ruth, New York-AL	1927	.772
4	Lou Gehrig, New York-AL	1927	.765
5	Babe Ruth, New York-AL	1923	.764
6	Rogers Hornsby, St.Louis-NL	1925	.756
7	Jimmie Foxx, Philadelphia-AL	1932	.749
8	Babe Ruth, New York-AL	1924	.739
9	Babe Ruth, New York-AL	1926	.737
10	Ted Williams, Boston-AL	1941	.735

Since 1950

		Year	Avg
1	Ted Williams, Boston-AL	1957	.731
2	Mickey Mantle, New York-AL	1956	.705
3	Mickey Mantle, New York-AL	1961	.687
4	Hank Aaron, Atlanta	1971	.669
5	Willie Mays, New York-NL	1954	.667

Stolen Bases

		Year	SB
1	Rickey Henderson, Oakland	1982	130
2	Lou Brock, St.Louis	1974	118
3	Vince Coleman, St.Louis	1985	110
4	Vince Coleman, St.Louis	1987	109
5	Rickey Henderson, Oakland	1983	108
6	Vince Coleman, St.Louis	1986	107
7	Maury Wills, Los Angeles-NL	1962	104
8	Rickey Henderson, Oakland	1980	100
9	Ron LeFlore, Montreal	1980	97
10	Ty Cobb, Detroit	1915	96
11	Omar Moreno, Pittsburgh	1980	96
12	Maury Wills, Los Angeles	1965	94
13	Rickey Henderson, New York-AL	1988	93
14	Tim Raines, Montreal	1983	90
15	Clyde Milan, Washington	1912	88
16	Rickey Henderson, New York-AL	1986	87
17	Ty Cobb, Detroit	1911	83
	Willie Wilson, Kansas City	1979	83
19	Bob Bescher, Cincinnati	1911	81
	Eddie Collins, Philadelphia-AL	1910	81
	Vince Coleman, St.Louis	1988	81

Strikeouts

		Year	SO
1	Bobby Bonds, San Francisco	1970	189
2	Bobby Bonds, San Francisco	1969	187
3	Rob Deer, Milwaukee	1987	186
4	Pete Incaviglia, Texas	1986	185
5	Cecil Fielder, Detroit	1990	182
6	Mike Schmidt, Philadelphia	1975	180
7	Rob Deer, Milwaukee	1986	179
8	Dave Nicholson, Chicago-AL	1963	175
	Gorman Thomas, Milwaukee	1979	175
	Jose Canseco, Oakland	1986	175
	Rob Deer, Detroit	1991	175

Pinch Hits
Career pinch hits in parentheses.

		Year	PH	
1	Jose Morales, Montreal	1976	25	(123)
2	Dave Philley, Baltimore	1961	24	(93)
	Vic Davalillo, St.Louis	1970	24	(95)
	Rusty Staub, New York-NL	1983	24	(100)
5	Wallace Johnson, Montreal	1988	22	(78)
	Peanuts Lowrey, St.Louis	1953	22	(62)
	Sam Leslie, New York-NL	1932	22	(59)
	Red Schoendienst, St.Louis	1962	22	(56)

Note: The all-time career pinch hit leader is Manny Mota (150), followed by Smoky Burgess (145) and Greg Gross (143).

Four Home Runs in One Game
National League

	Date	H/A	Inn
Bobby Lowe, Boston	5/30/1894	H	9
Ed Delahanty, Philadelphia	7/13/1896	A	9
Chuck Klein, Philadelphia	7/10/1936	A	10
Gil Hodges, Brooklyn	8/31/1950	H	9
Joe Adcock, Milwaukee	7/31/1954	A	9
Willie Mays, San Francisco	4/30/1961	A	9
Mike Schmidt, Philadelphia	4/17/1976	A	10
Bob Horner, Atlanta	7/6/1986	H	9

American League

	Date	H/A	Inn
Lou Gehrig, New York	6/3/1932	A	9
Pat Seerey, Chicago	7/18/1948	A	11
Rocky Colavito, Cleveland	6/10/1959	A	9

Pitching

Wins

From 1900-49

		Year	W	L	Pct
1	Jack Chesbro, NY-AL	1904	41	12	.774
2	Ed Walsh, Chi-AL	1908	40	15	.727
3	Christy Mathewson, NY-NL	1908	37	11	.771
4	Walter Johnson, Wash	1913	36	7	.837
5	Joe McGinnity, NY-NL	1904	35	8	.814
6	Smokey Joe Wood, Bos-AL	1912	34	5	.872
7	Cy Young, Bos-AL	1901	33	10	.767
	Grover Alexander, Phi-NL	1916	33	12	.733
	Christy Mathewson, NY-NL	1904	33	12	.733

Since 1950

		Year	W	L	Pct
1	Denny McLain, Det	1968	31	6	.838
2	Robin Roberts, Phi-NL	1952	28	7	.800
3	Bob Welch, Oak	1990	27	6	.818
4	Don Newcombe, Bklyn	1956	27	7	.794
	Sandy Koufax, LA	1966	27	9	.750
6	Steve Carlton, Phi	1972	27	10	.730
7	Sandy Koufax, LA	1965	26	8	.765
	Juan Marichal, SF	1968	26	9	.743

Note: 11 pitchers tied with 25 wins, including Marichal twice.

Earned Run Average

From 1900-1949

		Year	ShO	ERA
1	Dutch Leonard, Bos-AL	1914	7	1.01
2	Three Finger Brown,	1906	10	1.04
3	Walter Johnson, Wash	1913	11	1.09
4	Bob Gibson, St.L.	1968	13	1.12
5	Christy Mathewson, NY-NL	1909	8	1.14
6	Jack Pfiester, Chi-NL	1907	3	1.15
7	Addie Joss, Cle	1908	9	1.16
8	Carl Lundgren, Chi-NL	1907	7	1.17
9	Grover Alexander, Phi-NL	1915	12	1.22
10	Cy Young, Bos-AL	1908	3	1.26

Since 1950

		Year	ShO	ERA
1	Bob Gibson, St.L.	1968	13	1.12
2	Dwight Gooden, NY-NL	1985	8	1.53
3	Luis Tiant, Cle	1968	9	1.60
4	Dean Chance, LA-AL	1964	11	1.65
5	Nolan Ryan, Cal	1981	3	1.69
6	Sandy Koufax, LA	1966	5	1.73
7	Sandy Koufax, LA	1964	7	1.74
8	Ron Guidry, NY-AL	1978	9	1.74
9	Tom Seaver, NY-NL	1971	4	1.76
10	Sam McDowell, Cle	1968	3	1.81

Winning Pct.

		Year	W-L	Pct
1	Roy Face, Pit	1959	18-1	.947
2	Rick Sutcliffe, Chi-NL*	1984	16-1	.941
3	Johnny Allen, Cle	1937	15-1	.938
4	Ron Guidry, NY-AL	1978	25-3	.893
5	Freddie Fitzsimmons, Bklyn	1940	16-2	.889
6	Lefty Grove, Phi-AL	1931	31-4	.886
7	Bob Stanley, Bos	1978	15-2	.882
8	Preacher Roe, Bklyn	1951	22-3	.880
9	Tom Seaver, Cin	1981	14-2	.875
10	Smokey Joe Wood, Bos-AL	1912	34-5	.872

*Sutcliffe began 1984 with Cleveland and was 4-5 before being traded to the Cubs; his overall winning pct. was .769 (20-6).

Strikeouts

		Year	SO	P/G
1	Nolan Ryan, Cal	1973	383	10.57
2	Sandy Koufax, LA	1965	382	10.24
3	Nolan Ryan, Cal	1974	367	9.92
4	Rube Waddell, Phi-AL	1904	349	8.12
5	Bob Feller, Cle	1946	348	8.45
6	Nolan Ryan, Cal	1977	341	10.26
7	Nolan Ryan, Cal	1972	329	10.43
8	Nolan Ryan, Cal	1976	327	10.36
9	Sam McDowell, Cle	1965	325	10.71
10	Sandy Koufax, LA	1966	317	8.83

Games

		Year	Gm	Sv
1	Mike Marshall, LA	1974	106	21
2	Kent Tekulve, Pit	1979	94	31
3	Mike Marshall, LA	1973	92	31
4	Kent Tekulve, Pit	1978	91	31
5	Wayne Granger, Cin	1969	90	27
	Mike Marshall, Min	1979	90	32
	Kent Tekulve, Phi	1987	90	3

Saves

		Year	Gm	Sv
1	Bobby Thigpen, Chi-AL	1990	77	57
2	Dennis Eckersley, Oak	1990	63	48
3	Lee Smith, St. L	1991	67	47
4	Dave Righetti, NY-AL	1986	74	46
	Bryan Harvey, Cal	1991	67	46

Innings Pitched (since 1920)

		Year	IP	W-L
1	Wilbur Wood, Chi-AL	1972	377	24-17
2	Mickey Lolich, Det	1971	376	25-14
3	Bob Feller, Cle	1946	371	26-15
4	Grover Alexander, Chi-NL	1920	363	27-14
5	Wilbur Wood, Chi-AL	1973	359	24-20

Shutouts

		Year	ShO	ERA
1	Grover Alexander, Phi-NL	1916	16	1.55
2	Jack Coombs, Phi-AL	1910	13	1.30
	Bob Gibson, St.L.	1968	13	1.12
4	Christy Mathewson, NY-NL	1908	12	1.43
	Grover Alexander, Phi-NL	1915	12	1.22

Walks Allowed

		Year	BB	SO
1	Bob Feller, Cle	1938	208	240
2	Nolan Ryan, Cal	1977	204	341
3	Nolan Ryan, Cal	1974	202	367
4	Bob Feller, Cle	1941	194	260
5	Bobo Newsom, St.L-AL	1938	192	226

Home Runs Allowed

		Year	HRs
1	Bert Blyleven, Minnesota	1986	50
2	Robin Roberts, Philadelphia	1956	46
	Bert Blyleven, Minnesota	1987	46
4	Pedro Ramos, Washington	1957	43
5	Denny McLain, Detroit	1966	42

The All-Star Game

Baseball's first All-Star Game was held on July 6, 1933, before 47,595 at Comiskey Park in Chicago. From that year on, the All-Star Game has matched the best players in the American League against the best in the National. From 1959-62, two All-Star Games were played and in 1945, World War II travel restrictions made it necessary to call the All-Star Game off. The NL leads the series, 37-24-1. In the chart below, the American League is listed in **bold** type.

Year	Result	Host (Ballpark)	AL Manager	NL Manager
1933	**American,** 4-2	Chicago (Comiskey Park)	Connie Mack	John McGraw
1934	**American,** 9-7	New York (Polo Grounds)	Joe Cronin	Bill Terry
1935	**American,** 4-1	Cleveland (Cleveland Stadium)	Mickey Cochrane	Frankie Frisch
1936	National, 4-3	Boston (Braves Field)	Joe McCarthy	Charlie Grimm
1937	**American,** 8-3	Washington (Griffith Stadium)	Joe McCarthy	Bill Terry
1938	National, 4-1	Cincinnati (Crosley Field)	Joe McCarthy	Bill Terry
1939	**American,** 3-1	New York (Yankee Stadium)	Joe McCarthy	Gabby Hartnett
1940	National, 4-0	St.Louis (Sportsman's Park)	Joe Cronin	Bill McKechnie
1941	**American,** 7-5	Detroit (Briggs Stadium)	Del Baker	Bill McKechnie
1942	**American,** 3-1	New York (Polo Grounds)	Joe McCarthy	Leo Durocher
1943	**American,** 5-3	Philadelphia (Shibe Park)	Joe McCarthy	Billy Southworth
1944	National, 7-1	Pittsburgh (Forbes Field)	Joe McCarthy	Billy Southworth
1945	No Game			
1946	**American,** 12-0	Boston (Fenway Park)	Steve O'Neill	Charlie Grimm
1947	**American,** 2-1	Chicago (Wrigley Field)	Joe Cronin	Eddie Dyer
1948	**American,** 5-2	St.Louis (Sportsman's Park)	Bucky Harris	Leo Durocher
1949	**American,** 11-7	Brooklyn (Ebbets Field)	Lou Boudreau	Billy Southworth
1950	National, 4-3 (14)	Chicago (Comiskey Park)	Casey Stengel	Burt Shotton
1951	National, 8-3	Detroit (Briggs Stadium)	Casey Stengel	Eddie Sawyer
1952	National, 3-2	Philadelphia (Shibe Park)	Casey Stengel	Leo Durocher
1953	National, 5-1	Cincinnati (Crosley Field)	Casey Stengel	Charlie Dressen
1954	**American,** 11-9	Cleveland (Cleveland Stadium)	Casey Stengel	Walter Alston
1955	National, 6-5 (12)	Milwaukee (County Stadium)	Al Lopez	Leo Durocher
1956	National, 7-3	Washington (Griffith Stadium)	Casey Stengel	Walter Alston
1957	**American,** 6-5	St.Louis (Busch Stadium)	Casey Stengel	Walter Alston
1958	**American,** 4-3	Baltimore (Memorial Stadium)	Casey Stengel	Fred Haney
1959 Game 1	National, 5-4	Pittsburgh (Forbes Field)	Casey Stengel	Fred Haney
Game 2	**American,** 5-3	Los Angeles (Memorial Coliseum)	Casey Stengel	Fred Haney
1960 Game 1	National, 5-3	Kansas City (Municipal Stadium)	Al Lopez	Walter Alston
Game 2	National, 6-0	New York (Yankee Stadium)	Al Lopez	Walter Alston
1961 Game 1	National, 5-4 (10)	San Francisco (Candlestick Park)	Paul Richards	Danny Murtaugh
Game 2	TIE, 1-1 (9,rain)	Boston (Fenway Park)	Paul Richards	Danny Murtaugh
1962 Game 1	National, 3-1	Washington (D.C.Stadium)	Ralph Houk	Fred Hutchinson
Game 2	**American,** 9-4	Chicago (Wrigley Field)	Ralph Houk	Fred Hutchinson
1963	National, 5-3	Cleveland (Cleveland Stadium)	Ralph Houk	Alvin Dark
1964	National, 7-4	New York (Shea Stadium)	Al Lopez	Walter Alston
1965	National, 6-5	Minnesota (Metropolitan Stadium)	Al Lopez	Gene Mauch
1966	National, 2-1 (10)	St.Louis (Busch Memorial Stadium)	Sam Mele	Walter Alston
1967	National, 2-1 (15)	California (Anaheim Stadium)	Hank Bauer	Walter Alston
1968	National, 1-0	Houston (The Astrodome)	Dick Williams	Red Schoendienst
1969	National, 9-3	Washington (RFK Stadium)	Mayo Smith	Red Schoendienst
1970	National, 5-4	Cincinnati (Riverfront Stadium)	Earl Weaver	Gil Hodges
1971	**American,** 6-4	Detroit (Tiger Stadium)	Earl Weaver	Sparky Anderson
1972	National, 4-3	Atlanta (Atlanta Stadium)	Earl Weaver	Danny Murtaugh
1973	National, 7-1	Kansas City (Royals Stadium)	Dick Williams	Sparky Anderson
1974	National, 7-2	Pittsburgh (Three Rivers Stadium)	Dick Williams	Yogi Berra
1975	National, 6-3	Milwaukee (County Stadium)	Alvin Dark	Walter Alston
1976	National, 7-1	Philadelphia (Veterans Stadium)	Darrell Johnson	Sparky Anderson
1977	National, 7-5	New York (Yankee Stadium)	Billy Martin	Sparky Anderson
1978	National, 7-3	San Diego (San Diego Stadium)	Billy Martin	Tommy Lasorda
1979	National, 7-6	Seattle (The Kingdome)	Bob Lemon	Tommy Lasorda
1980	National, 4-2	Los Angeles (Dodger Stadium)	Earl Weaver	Chuck Tanner
1981	National, 5-4	Cleveland (Cleveland Stadium)	Jim Frey	Dallas Green
1982	National, 4-1	Montreal (Olympic Stadium)	Billy Martin	Tommy Lasorda
1983	**American,** 13-3	Chicago (Comiskey Park)	Harvey Kuenn	Whitey Herzog
1984	National, 3-1	San Francisco (Candlestick Park)	Joe Altobelli	Paul Owens
1985	National, 6-1	Minnesota (HHH Metrodome)	Sparky Anderson	Dick Williams
1986	**American,** 3-2	Houston (The Astrodome)	Dick Howser	Whitey Herzog
1987	National, 2-0 (13)	Oakland (Oakland Coliseum)	John McNamara	Davey Johnson
1988	**American,** 2-1	Cincinnati (Riverfront Stadium)	Tom Kelly	Whitey Herzog
1989	**American,** 5-3	California (Anaheim Stadium)	Tony LaRussa	Tommy Lasorda
1990	**American,** 2-0	Chicago (Wrigley Field)	Tony LaRussa	Roger Craig
1991	**American,** 4-2	Toronto (SkyDome)	Tony LaRussa	Lou Piniella

Arch Ward Memorial Award

The All-Star Game MVP award is named after Arch Ward, the Chicago Tribune sports editor who founded the game in 1933. First given at the two All-Star games in 1962, the name of the award was changed to the Commissioner's Trophy in 1970 and back to the Ward Memorial Award in 1985.

Multiple winners: Gary Carter, Steve Garvey and Willie Mays (2).

Year		Year		Year	
1962-a	Maury Wills, LA (NL), SS	1972	Joe Morgan, Cin., 2B	1982	Dave Concepcion, Cin., SS
1962-b	Leon Wagner, LA (AL), OF	1973	Bobby Bonds, SF, OF	1983	Fred Lynn, Cal., OF
1963	Willie Mays, SF, OF	1974	Steve Garvey, LA, 1B	1984	Gary Carter, Mon., C
1964	Johnny Callison, Phi., OF	1975	Bill Madlock, Chi.(NL), 3B	1985	LaMarr Hoyt, SD, P
1965	Juan Marichal, SF, P		& Jon Matlock, NY (NL), P	1986	Roger Clemens, Bos., P
1966	Brooks Robinson, Bal., 3B	1976	George Foster, Cin., OF	1987	Tim Raines, Mon., OF
1967	Tony Perez, Cin., 3B	1977	Don Sutton, LA, P	1988	Terry Steinbach, Oak., C
1968	Willie Mays, SF, OF	1978	Steve Garvey, LA, 1B	1989	Bo Jackson, KC, OF
1969	Willie McCovey, SF, 1B	1979	Dave Parker, Pit, OF		
1970	Carl Yastrzemski, Bos., OF-1B	1980	Ken Griffey, Cin., OF	1990	Julio Franco, Tex., 2B
1971	Frank Robinson, Bal., OF	1981	Gary Carter, Mon., C	1991	Cal Ripken, Bal., SS

All-Time Winningest Managers

Top 20 Major League career victories through the 1991 season. Career, regular season and postseason (playoffs and World Series) records are noted along with AL and NL pennants and World Series titles won. Managers active during 1991 season in **bold** type.

		Career			Regular Season			Postseason			
	Yrs	W	L	Pct	W	L	Pct	W	L	Pct	Titles
Connie Mack	53	**3755**	3967	.486	3731	3948	.486	24	19	.558	9 AL, 5 WS
John McGraw	33	**2810**	1987	.586	2784	1959	.587	26	28	.482	10 NL, 2 WS
Bucky Harris	29	**2168**	2228	.493	2157	2218	.493	11	10	.524	3 AL, 2 WS
Joe McCarthy	24	**2155**	1346	.616	2125	1333	.615	30	13	.698	1 NL, 8 AL, 7 WS
Walter Alston	23	**2063**	1634	.558	2040	1613	.558	23	21	.523	7 NL, 4 WS
Leo Durocher	24	**2015**	1717	.540	2008	1709	.540	7	8	.467	3 NL, 1 WS
Sparky Anderson	22	**1955**	1545	.559	1921	1524	.558	34	21	.618	4 NL, 1 AL, 3 WS
Casey Stengel	25	**1942**	1868	.510	1905	1842	.508	37	26	.587	10 AL, 7 WS
Gene Mauch	26	**1907**	2044	.483	1902	2037	.483	5	7	.417	—None—
Bill McKechnie	25	**1904**	1737	.523	1896	1723	.524	8	14	.364	1 NL, 2 WS
Ralph Houk	20	**1627**	1539	.514	1619	1531	.514	8	8	.500	3 AL, 2 WS
Fred Clarke	19	**1609**	1189	.575	1602	1181	.576	7	8	.467	2 NL, 1 WS
Dick Williams	21	**1592**	1474	.519	1571	1451	.520	21	23	.477	3 AL, 1 NL, 2 WS
Earl Weaver	17	**1506**	1080	.582	1480	1060	.583	26	20	.565	4 AL, 1 WS
Clark Griffith	20	**1491**	1367	.522	1491	1367	.522	0	0	.000	1 AL (1901)
Miller Huggins	17	**1431**	1149	.555	1413	1134	.555	18	15	.545	6 AL, 3 WS
Al Lopez	17	**1412**	1012	.583	1410	1004	.584	2	8	.200	2 AL
Jimmy Dykes	21	**1406**	1541	.477	1406	1541	.477	0	0	.000	—None—
Wilbert Robertson	19	**1402**	1407	.499	1399	1398	.500	3	9	.250	2 NL
Chuck Tanner	19	**1359**	1384	.495	1352	1381	.495	7	3	.700	1 NL, 1 WS

Notes: John McGraw's postseason record also includes two World Series tie games (1912,'22); Miller Huggins postseason record also includes one World Series tie game (1922).

Regular Season Winning Percentage

Minimum of 750 victories.

	Yrs	W	L	Pct	Pen
Joe McCarthy	24	2125	1333	**.614**	9
Charlie Comiskey	12	838	541	**.608**	4
Frank Selee	16	1284	862	**.598**	5
Billy Southworth	13	1044	704	**.597**	4
Frank Chance	11	946	648	**.593**	4
John McGraw	33	2784	1959	**.587**	9
Al Lopez	17	1410	1004	**.584**	2
Earl Weaver	17	1480	1060	**.583**	4
Harry Wright	23	1225	885	**.581**	6
Cap Anson	20	1296	947	**.578**	5
Fred Clarke	19	1602	1181	**.576**	2
Steve O'Neill	14	1040	821	**.559**	1
Walter Alston	23	2040	1613	**.558**	7
Sparky Anderson	22	1921	1524	**.558**	5
Bill Terry	10	823	661	**.555**	3
Miller Huggins	17	1413	1134	**.554**	6
Billy Martin	16	1253	1013	**.553**	2
Charlie Grimm	19	1287	1067	**.547**	3
Hugh Jennings	15	1163	984	**.542**	3
Tony LaRussa	13	1038	883	**.540**	3

World Series Victories

	App	W	L	T	Pct	WS
Casey Stengel	10	**37**	26	0	.587	7
Joe McCarthy	9	**30**	13	0	.698	7
John McGraw	9	**26**	28	2	.482	2
Connie Mack	8	**24**	19	0	.558	5
Walter Alston	7	**20**	20	0	.523	4
Miller Huggins	6	**18**	15	1	.544	3
Sparky Anderson	5	**16**	12	0	.571	3
Tommy Lasorda	4	**12**	11	0	.522	2
Dick Williams	4	**12**	14	0	.462	2
Frank Chance	4	**11**	9	1	.548	2
Bucky Harris	3	**11**	10	0	.524	2
Billy Southworth	4	**11**	11	0	.500	2
Earl Weaver	4	**11**	13	0	.458	1
Whitey Herzog	3	**10**	11	0	.476	1
Bill Carrigan	2	**8**	2	0	.800	2
Danny Murtaugh	2	**8**	6	0	.571	2
Ralph Houk	3	**8**	8	0	.500	2
Bill McKechnie	4	**8**	14	0	.364	2
Tom Kelly	2	**8**	6	0	.571	2

Seven tied with 7 wins each.

All-Time Winningest Managers (Cont.)

Where They Managed

Alston—Brooklyn/Los Angeles NL (1954-76); **Anderson**—Cincinnati NL (1970-78), Detroit AL (1979—); **Clarke**—Louisville NL (1897-99), Pittsburgh NL (1900-15); **Durocher**—Brooklyn NL (1939-46,48), New York NL (1948-55), Chicago NL (1966-72), Houston NL (1972-73); **Dykes**—Chicago AL (1934-46), Philadelphia AL (1951-53), Baltimore AL (1954), Cincinnati NL (1958), Detroit AL (1959-60), Cleveland AL (1960-61); **Griffith**—Chicago AL (1901-02), New York AL (1903-08), Cincinnati NL (1909-11), Washington AL (1912-20); **Harris**—Washington AL (1924-28,35-42,50-54), Detroit AL (1929-33,55-56), Boston AL (1934), Philadelphia NL (1943), New York AL (1947-48); **Houk**—New York AL (1961-63,66-73), Detroit AL (1974-78), Boston AL (1981-84); **Huggins**—St.Louis NL (1913-17), New York AL (1918-29); **Lopez**—Cleveland AL (1951-56), Chicago AL (1957-65,68-69).

Mack—Pittsburgh NL (1894-96), Philadelphia AL (1901-50); **Mauch**—Philadelphia NL (1960-68), Montreal NL (1969-75), Minnesota AL (1976-80), California AL (1981-82,85-87); **McCarthy**—Chicago NL (1926-30), New York AL (1931-46), Boston AL (1948-50); **McGraw**—Baltimore NL (1899), Baltimore AL (1901-02), New York NL (1902-32); **McKechnie**—Newark FL (1915), Pittsburgh NL (1922-26), St.Louis NL (1928-29), Boston NL (1930-37), Cincinnati NL (1938-46); **Robertson**—Baltimore AL (1902), Brooklyn NL (1914-31); **Stengel**—Brooklyn NL (1934-36), Boston NL (1938-43), New York AL (1949-60), New York NL (1962-65); **Tanner**—Chicago AL (1970-75), Oakland AL (1976), Pittsburgh NL (1977-85), Atlanta NL (1986-88); **Weaver**—Baltimore AL (1968-82,85-86); **Williams**—Boston AL (1967-69), Oakland AL (1971-73), California AL (1974-76), Montreal NL (1977-81), San Diego NL (1982-85), Seattle AL (1986-88).

Active Managers Records

Through the 1991 regular season.

National League

	Yrs	W	L	Pct
Tommy Lasorda, LA	16	**1278**	1102	.537
Bobby Cox, Atl.	10	**755**	740	.505
Roger Craig, SF	9	**666**	647	.507
Joe Torre, St.L	10	**651**	761	.461
Jim Fregosi, Phi	8	**504**	550	.478
Jim Leyland, Pit	7	**497**	475	.511
Jeff Torborg, NY	6	**407**	436	.483
Lou Piniella, Cin	5	**389**	352	.525
Art Howe, Hou	3	**226**	260	.465
Greg Riddoch, SD	2	**122**	122	.500
Tom Runnells, Mon	1	**51**	61	.455

Chicago job vacant as of Oct. 31.

American League

	Yrs	W	L	Pct
Sparky Anderson, Det	22	**1921**	1524	.558
Tony LaRussa, Oak	13	**1038**	883	.540
Buck Rodgers, Cal	10	**664**	619	.518
Bobby Valentine, Tex	7	**536**	564	.487
Tom Kelly, Min	6	**437**	396	.525
Cito Gaston, Tor	3	**227***	176	.563
Hal McRae, KC	1	**66**	58	.532
John Oates, Bal	1	**54**	71	.432
Mike Hargrove, Cle	1	**32**	53	.376
Butch Hobson, Bos	0	**0**	0	.000
Bill Plummer, Sea	0	**0**	0	.000
Buck Showalter, NY	0	**0**	0	.000
Phil Garner, Mil	0	**0**	0	.000

Chicago job vacant as of Oct. 31.

*Gaston's total does not include Toronto's 19-14 record while he was on a 33-day medical leave from Aug.26-Sept.27. Coach and interim manager Gene Tenace gets credit for those 33 games.

Annual Awards
Manager of the Year

Given by The Sporting News. One award was presented from 1936-85. Two awards (one for each league) have been presented since 1986. Note than (*) indicates a league pennant (1936-68) or division championship (since 1969).
Multiple winners: Walter Alston, Leo Durocher, Joe McCarthy and Casey Stengel (3); Tony LaRussa, Jim Leyland, Bill McKechnie, Danny Murtaugh, Billy Southworth, Bill Virdon and Earl Weaver (2).

AL and NL Combined

Year		Improvement		Year		Improvement	
1936	Joe McCarthy, NY (AL)	89-60	to 102-51*	1955	Walter Alston, Bklyn	92-62	to 98-55*
1937	Bill McKechnie, Bos.(NL)	71-83	to 79-73	1956	Birdie Tebbetts, Cin	75-79	to 91-63
1938	Joe McCarthy, NY (AL)	102-52*	to 99-53*	1957	Fred Hutchinson, St.L	76-78	to 87-67
1939	Leo Durocher, Bklyn.(NL)	69-80	to 84-69	1958	Casey Stengel, NY (AL)	98-56 *	to 92-62*
				1959	Walter Alston, LA	71-83	to 88-68*
1940	Bill McKechnie, Cin	97-57*	to 100-53*				
1941	Billy Southworth, St.L.(NL)	84-69	to 97-56	1960	Danny Murtaugh, Pit	78-76	to 95-59*
1942	Billy Southworth, St.L.(NL)	97-56	to 106-48*	1961	Ralph Houk, NY (AL)	97-57 *	to 109-53*
1943	Joe McCarthy, NY (AL)	103-51*	to 98-56*	1962	Bill Rigney, LA (AL)	70-91	to 86-76
1944	Luke Sewell, St.L.(AL)	72-80	to 89-65*	1963	Walter Alston, LA	102-63	to 99-63*
1945	Ossie Bluege, Wash	64-90	to 87-67	1964	Johnny Keane, St.L	93-69	to 93-69*
1946	Eddie Dyer, St.L.(NL)	95-59	to 98-58*	1965	Sam Mele, Min	79-83	to 102-60*
1947	Bucky Harris, NY (AL)	87-67	to 97-57*	1966	Hank Bauer, Bal	94-68	to 97-63*
1948	Bill Meyer, Pit	62-92	to 83-71	1967	Dick Williams, Bos	72-90	to 92-70*
1949	Casey Stengel, NY (AL)	94-60	to 97-57*	1968	Mayo Smith, Det	91-71	to 103-59*
				1969	Gil Hodges, NY (NL)	73-89	to 100-62*
1950	Red Rolfe, Det	87-67	to 95-59				
1951	Leo Durocher, NY (NL)	86-68	to 98-59*	1970	Danny Murtaugh, Pit	88-74	to 89-73*
1952	Eddie Stanky, St.L	81-73	to 88-66	1971	Charlie Fox, SF	86-76	to 90-72*
1953	Casey Stengel, NY (AL)	95-59*	to 99-52*	1972	Chuck Tanner, Chi. (AL)	79-83	to 87-67
1954	Leo Durocher, NY (NL)	70-84	to 97-57*	1973	Gene Mauch, Mon	70-86	to 79-83

Year		Improvement		Year		Improvement	
1974	Bill Virdon, NY (AL)	80-82	to 89-73	1980	Bill Virdon, Hou	89-73	to 93-70*
1975	Darrell Johnson, Bos.	84-78	to 95-65*	1981	Billy Martin, Oak	83-79	to 64-45*
1976	Danny Ozark, Phi	86-76	to 101-61*	1982	Whitey Herzog, St.L.	59-43	to 92-70*
1977	Earl Weaver, Bal	88-74	to 97-64	1983	Tony LaRussa, Chi. (AL)	87-75	to 99-63*
1978	George Bamberger, Mil	67-95	to 93-69	1984	Jim Frey, Chi. (NL)	71-91	to 96-75*
1979	Earl Weaver, Bal	90-71	to 102-57*	1985	Bobby Cox, Tor	89-73	to 99-62*

Note: In 1981, both league seasons were reduced to 110 games or less due to a players' strike.

National League

Year		Improvement	
1986	Hal Lanier, Hou	83-79	to 96-66*
1987	Buck Rodgers, Mon	78-83	to 91-71
1988	Tommy Lasorda, LA	73-89	to 94-67*
	& Jim Leyland, Pit	80-82	to 85-75
1989	Don Zimmer, Chi	77-85	to 93-69*
1990	Jim Leyland, Pit	74-88	to 95-67

American League

Year		Improvement	
1986	John McNamara, Bos	81-81	to 95-66*
1987	Sparky Anderson, Det	87-75	to 98-64*
1988	Tony LaRussa, Oak	81-81	to 104-58*
1989	Frank Robinson, Bal	54-107	to 87-75
1990	Jeff Torborg, Chi	69-92	to 94-68

Most Valuable Player

There have been three different Most Valuable Player awards in baseball since 1911—the Chalmers Award (1911-14), presented by the Detroit-based automobile company; the League Award (1922-29), presented by the National and American Leagues; and the Baseball Writers' Award (since 1931), presented by the Baseball Writers' Association of America. Statistics for winning players are provided below. Stats for winning pitchers are listed separately.

Multiple winners: NL—Roy Campanella, Stan Musial and Mike Schmidt (3); Ernie Banks, Johnny Bench, Rogers Hornsby, Carl Hubbell, Willie Mays, Joe Morgan and Dale Murphy. **AL**—Yogi Berra, Joe DiMaggio, Jimmie Foxx and Mickey Mantle (3); Mickey Cochrane, Lou Gehrig, Hank Greenberg, Walter Johnson, Roger Maris, Hal Newhouser and Ted Williams. **NL & AL**—Frank Robinson (2, one in each).

Chalmers Award

Winning pitchers' statistics on next page.

National League

Year		Pos	HR	RBI	Avg
1911	Wildfire Schulte, Chi.	OF	21	121	.300
1912	Larry Doyle, NY	2B	10	90	.330
1913	Jake Daubert, Bklyn	1B	2	52	.350
1914	Johnny Evers, Bos	2B	1	40	.279

American League

Year		Pos	HR	RBI	Avg
1911	Ty Cobb, Det	OF	8	144	.420
1912	Tris Speaker, Bos	OF	10	98	.383
1913	Walter Johnson, Wash.	P	—	—	—
1914	Eddie Collins, Phi	2B	2	85	.344

League Award

Winning pitchers' statistics on next page.

National League

Year		Pos	HR	RBI	Avg
1922	No selection				
1923	No selection				
1924	Dazzy Vance, Bklyn	P	—	—	—
1925	Rogers Hornsby, St.L.	2B-Mgr	29	143	.403
1926	Bob O'Farrell, St.L	C	7	68	.293
1927	Paul Waner, Pit	OF	9	131	.380
1928	Jim Bottomley, St.L	1B	31	136	.325
1929	Rogers Hornsby, Chi	2B	39	149	.380

American League

Year		Pos	HR	RBI	Avg
1922	George Sisler, St.L.	1B	8	105	.420
1923	Babe Ruth, NY	OF	41	131	.393
1924	Walter Johnson, Wash.	P	—	—	—
1925	Roger Peckinpaugh, Wash	SS	4	64	.294
1926	George Burns, Cle	1B	4	114	.358
1927	Lou Gehrig, NY	1B	47	175	.373
1928	Mickey Cochrane, Phi	C	10	57	.293
1929	No selection				

Baseball Writers' Award

Winning pitchers' statistics on next page.

National League

Year		Pos	HR	RBI	Avg
1930	Hack Wilson, Chi	OF	56	190	.356
1931	Frankie Frisch, St.L.	2B	4	82	.311
1932	Chuck Klein, Phi	OF	38	137	.348
1933	Carl Hubbell, NY	P	—	—	—
1934	Dizzy Dean, St.L	P	—	—	—
1935	Gabby Hartnett	C	13	91	.344
1936	Carl Hubbell, NY	P	—	—	—
1937	Joe Medwick, St.L	OF	31	154	.374
1938	Ernie Lombardi, Cin	C	19	95	.342
1939	Bucky Walters, Cin	P	—	—	—
1940	Frank McCormick, Cin	1B	19	127	.309
1941	Dolf Camilli, Bklyn	1B	34	120	.285
1942	Mort Cooper, St.L	P	—	—	—
1943	Stan Musial, St.L	OF	13	81	.357
1944	Marty Marion, St.L	SS	6	63	.267
1945	Phil Cavarretta, Chi	1B	6	97	.355

American League

Year		Pos	HR	RBI	Avg
1930	Joe Cronin, Wash	SS	13	126	.346
1931	Lefty Grove, Phi	P	—	—	—
1932	Jimmie Foxx, Phi	1B	58	169	.364
1933	Jimmie Foxx, Phi	1B	48	163	.356
1934	Mickey Cochrane, Det	C-Mgr	2	76	.320
1935	Hank Greenberg, Det	1B	36	170	.328
1936	Lou Gehrig, NY	1B	49	152	.354
1937	Charlie Gehringer, Det	2B	14	96	.371
1938	Jimmie Foxx, Bos	1B	50	175	.349
1939	Joe DiMaggio, NY	OF	30	126	.381
1940	Hank Greenberg, Det	OF	41	150	.340
1941	Joe DiMaggio, NY	OF	30	125	.357
1942	Joe Gordon, NY	2B	18	103	.322
1943	Spud Chandler, NY	P	—	—	—
1944	Hal Newhouser, Det	P	—	—	—
1945	Hal Newhouser, Det	P	—	—	—

Annual Awards (Cont.)
Most Valuable Player

National League

Year	Pos	HR	RBI	Avg
1946	Stan Musial, St.L 1B-OF	16	103	.365
1947	Bob Elliott, Bos............. 3B	22	113	.317
1948	Stan Musial, St.L............ OF	39	131	.376
1949	Jackie Robinson, Bklyn 2B	16	124	.342
1950	Jim Konstanty, Phi .... P	—	—	—
1951	Roy Campanella, Bklyn C	33	108	.325
1952	Hank Sauer, Chi.............. OF	37	121	.270
1953	Roy Campanella, Bklyn C	41	142	.312
1954	Willie Mays, NY .... OF	41	110	.345
1955	Roy Campanella, Bklyn C	32	107	.318
1956	Don Newcombe, Bklyn .... P	—	—	—
1957	Hank Aaron, Mil............. OF	44	132	.322
1958	Ernie Banks, Chi.............. SS	47	129	.313
1959	Ernie Banks, Chi.............. SS	45	143	.304
1960	Dick Groat, Pit .... SS	2	50	.325
1961	Frank Robinson, Cin.......... OF	37	124	.323
1962	Maury Wills, LA .... SS	6	48	.299
1963	Sandy Koufax, LA............. P	—	—	—
1964	Ken Boyer, St.L.............. 3B	24	119	.295
1965	Willie Mays, SF .... OF	52	112	.317
1966	Roberto Clemente, Pit......... OF	29	119	.317
1967	Orlando Cepeda, St.L. 1B	25	111	.325
1968	Bob Gibson, St.L.............. P	—	—	—
1969	Willie McCovey, SF 1B	45	126	.320
1970	Johnny Bench, Cin C	45	148	.293
1971	Joe Torre, St.L 3B	45	137	.363
1972	Johnny Bench, Cin C	40	125	.270
1973	Pete Rose, Cin............... OF	5	64	.338
1974	Steve Garvey, LA 1B	21	111	.312
1975	Joe Morgan, Cin 2B	17	94	.327
1976	Joe Morgan, Cin 2B	27	111	.320
1977	George Foster, Cin............ OF	52	149	.320
1978	Dave Parker, Pit .... OF	30	117	.334
1979	Keith Hernandez, St.L 1B	11	105	.344
	& Willie Stargell, Pit........... 1B	32	82	.281
1980	Mike Schmidt, Phi 3B	48	121	.286
1981	Mike Schmidt, Phi 3B	31	91	.316
1982	Dale Murphy, Atl .... OF	36	109	.281
1983	Dale Murphy, Atl .... OF	36	121	.302
1984	Ryne Sandberg, Chi 2B	19	84	.314
1985	Willie McGee, St.L .... OF	10	82	.353
1986	Mike Schmidt, Phi 3B	37	119	.290
1987	Andre Dawson, Chi .... OF	49	137	.287
1988	Kirk Gibson, LA.............. OF	25	76	.290
1989	Kevin Mitchell, SF .... OF	47	125	.291
1990	Barry Bonds, Pit............. OF	33	114	.301

American League

Year	Pos	HR	RBI	Avg
1946	Ted Williams, Bos............. OF	38	123	.342
1947	Joe DiMaggio, NY .... OF	20	97	.315
1948	Lou Boudreau, Cle .... SS-Mgr	18	106	.355
1949	Ted Williams, Bos............. OF	43	159	.343
1950	Phil Rizzuto, NY .... SS	7	66	.324
1951	Yogi Berra, NY C	27	88	.294
1952	Bobby Shantz, Phi .... P	—	—	—
1953	Al Rosen, Cle................. 3B	43	145	.336
1954	Yogi Berra, NY C	22	125	.307
1955	Yogi Berra, NY C	27	108	.272
1956	Mickey Mantle, NY .... OF	52	130	.353
1957	Mickey Mantle, NY .... OF	34	94	.365
1958	Jackie Jensen, Bos .... OF	35	122	.286
1959	Nellie Fox, Chi................ 2B	2	70	.306
1960	Roger Maris, NY.............. OF	39	112	.283
1961	Roger Maris, NY.............. OF	61	142	.269
1962	Mickey Mantle, NY .... OF	30	89	.321
1963	Elston Howard, NY............ C	28	85	.287
1964	Brooks Robinson, Bal 3B	28	118	.317
1965	Zoilo Versalles, Min........... SS	19	77	.273
1966	Frank Robinson, Bal........... OF	49	122	.316
1967	Carl Yastrzemski, Bos.......... OF	44	121	.326
1968	Denny McLain, Det .... P	—	—	—
1969	Harmon Killebrew, Min...... 3B-1B	49	140	.276
1970	Boog Powell, Bal 1B	35	114	.297
1971	Vida Blue, Oak............... P	—	—	—
1972	Dick Allen, Chi............... 1B	37	113	.308
1973	Reggie Jackson, Oak .... OF	32	117	.293
1974	Jeff Burroughs, Tex........... OF	25	118	.301
1975	Fred Lynn, Bos .... OF	21	105	.331
1976	Thurman Munson, NY C	17	105	.302
1977	Rod Carew, Min.............. 1B	14	100	.388
1978	Jim Rice, Bos .... OF-DH	46	139	.315
1979	Don Baylor, Cal............ OF-DH	36	139	.296
1980	George Brett, KC............. 3B	24	118	.390
1981	Rollie Fingers, Mil............. P	—	—	—
1982	Robin Yount, Mil.............. SS	29	114	.331
1983	Cal Ripken, Bal............... SS	27	102	.318
1984	Willie Hernandez, Det......... P	—	—	—
1985	Don Mattingly, NY............ 1B	35	145	.324
1986	Roger Clemens, Bos .... P	—	—	—
1987	George Bell, Tor.............. OF	47	134	.308
1988	Jose Canseco, Oak .... OF	42	124	.307
1989	Robin Yount, Mil .... OF	21	103	.318
1990	Rickey Henderson, Oak....... OF	28	61	.325

MVP Pitchers' Statistics

Pitchers have been named Most Valuable Player on 22 occasions, 10 times in the NL and 12 in the AL. Three have been relief pitchers—Jim Konstanty, Rollie Fingers and Willie Hernandez.

National League

Year	Gm	W-L	SV	ERA
1924	Dazzy Vance, Bklyn.........35	28-6	0	2.16
1933	Carl Hubbell, NY...........45	23-12	5	1.66
1934	Dizzy Dean, St.L............50	30-7	7	2.65
1936	Carl Hubbell, NY...........42	26-6	3	2.31
1939	Bucky Walters, Cin 39	27-11	0	2.29
1942	Mort Cooper, St.L 37	22-7	0	1.77
1950	Jim Konstanty, Phi..........74	16-7	22	2.66
1956	Don Newcombe, Bklyn.......38	27-7	0	3.06
1963	Sandy Koufax, LA 40	25-5	0	1.88
1968	Bob Gibson, St.L............34	22-9	0	1.12

American League

Year	Gm	W-L	SV	ERA
1913	Walter Johnson, Wash 47	36-7	2	1.09
1924	Walter Johnson, Wash 38	23-7	0	2.72
1931	Lefty Grove, Phi 41	31-4	5	2.05
1943	Spud Chandler, NY.........30	20-4	0	1.64
1944	Hal Newhouser, Det.........47	29-9	2	2.22
1945	Hal Newhouser, Det.........40	25-9	2	1.81
1952	Bobby Shantz, Phi 33	24-7	0	2.48
1968	Denny McLain, Det 41	31-6	0	1.96
1971	Vida Blue, Oak..............39	24-8	0	1.82
1981	Rollie Fingers, Mil 47	6-3	28	1.04
1984	Willie Hernandez, Det........80	9-3	32	1.92
1986	Roger Clemens, Bos 33	24-4	0	2.48

Cy Young Award

Voted on by the Baseball Writers Association of America. One award was presented from 1956-66, two since 1967. Pitchers who won the MVP and Cy Young awards in the same season are in **bold** type.

Multiple winners: NL—Steve Carlton (4); Sandy Koufax and Tom Seaver (3); Bob Gibson (2). **AL**—Jim Palmer (3); Roger Clemens and Denny McLain (2). **NL & AL**—Gaylord Perry (2, one in each).

NL-AL Combined

Year	National League	Gm	W-L	SV	ERA	Year	American League	Gm	W-L	SV	ERA
1956	**Don Newcombe**, Bklyn	38	27-7	0	3.06	1958	Bob Turley, NY	33	21-7	1	2.97
1957	Warren Spahn, Mil	39	21-11	3	2.69	1959	Early Wynn, Chi	37	22-10	0	3.17
1960	Vernon Law, Pit	35	20-9	0	3.08	1961	Whitey Ford, NY	39	25-4	0	3.21
1962	Don Drysdale, LA	43	25-9	1	2.83	1964	Dean Chance, LA	46	20-9	4	1.65
1963	**Sandy Koufax**, LA	40	25-5	0	1.88						
1965	Sandy Koufax, LA	43	26-8	2	2.04						
1966	Sandy Koufax, LA	41	27-9	0	1.73						

Separate League Awards

	National League						American League				
Year		Gm	W-L	SV	ERA	Year		Gm	W-L	SV	ERA
1967	Mike McCormick, SF	40	22-10	0	2.85	1967	Jim Lonborg, Bos	39	22-9	0	3.16
1968	**Bob Gibson**, St.L	34	22-9	0	1.12	1968	**Denny McLain**, Det	41	31-6	0	1.96
1969	Tom Seaver, NY	36	25-7	0	2.21	1969	Denny McLain, Det	42	24-9	0	2.80
							& Mike Cuellar, Bal	39	23-11	0	2.38
1970	Bob Gibson, St.L	34	23-7	0	3.12	1970	Jim Perry, Min	40	24-12	0	3.03
1971	Ferguson Jenkins, Chi	39	24-13	0	2.77	1971	Vida Blue, Oak	39	24-8	0	1.82
1972	Steve Carlton, Phi	41	27-10	0	1.97	1972	Gaylord Perry, Cle	41	24-16	1	1.92
1973	Tom Seaver, NY	36	19-10	0	2.08	1973	Jim Palmer, Bal	38	22-9	1	2.40
1974	Mike Marshall, LA	106	15-12	21	2.42	1974	Catfish Hunter, Oak	41	25-12	0	2.49
1975	Tom Seaver, NY	36	22-9	0	2.38	1975	Jim Palmer, Bal	39	23-11	1	2.09
1976	Randy Jones, SD	40	22-14	0	2.74	1976	Jim Palmer, Bal	40	22-13	0	2.51
1977	Steve Carlton, Phi	36	23-10	0	2.64	1977	Sparky Lyle, NY	72	13-5	26	2.17
1978	Gaylord Perry, SD	37	21-6	0	2.72	1978	Ron Guidry, NY	35	25-3	0	1.74
1979	Bruce Sutter, Chi	62	6-6	37	2.23	1979	Mike Flanagan, Bal	39	23-9	0	3.08
1980	Steve Carlton, Phi	38	24-9	0	2.34	1980	Steve Stone, Bal	37	25-7	0	3.23
1981	Fernando Valenzuela, LA	25	13-7	0	2.48	1981	**Rollie Fingers**, Mil	47	6-3	28	1.04
1982	Steve Carlton, Phi	38	23-11	0	3.10	1982	Pete Vuckovich, Mil	30	18-6	0	3.34
1983	John Denny, Phi	36	19-6	0	2.37	1983	LaMarr Hoyt, Chi	36	24-10	0	3.66
1984	Rick Sutcliffe, Chi	20 *	16-1	0	2.69	1984	**Willie Hernandez**, Det	80	9-3	32	1.92
1985	Dwight Gooden, NY	35	24-4	0	1.53	1985	Bret Saberhagen, KC	32	20-6	0	2.87
1986	Mike Scott, Hou	37	18-10	0	2.22	1986	**Roger Clemens**, Bos	33	24-4	0	2.48
1987	Steve Bedrosian, Phi	65	5-3	40	2.83	1987	Roger Clemens, Bos	36	20-9	0	2.97
1988	Orel Hershiser, LA	35	23-8	1	2.26	1988	Frank Viola, Min	35	24-7	0	2.64
1989	Mark Davis, SD	70	4-3	44	1.85	1989	Bret Saberhagen, KC	36	23-6	0	2.16
1990	Doug Drabek, Pit	33	22-6	0	2.76	1990	Bob Welch, Oak	35	27-6	0	2.95

*NL games only, Sutcliffe pitched 15 games with Cleveland before being traded to the Cubs.

The Sporting News' MVP Awards

When the major leagues temporarily discontinued their Most Valuable Player awards in 1929 (AL) and 1930 (NL), *The Sporting News* stepped in to present its own league honors—for MVP from 1929-45 and for Player and Pitcher of the Year since 1948. There were no awards given in 1946 and '47.

National League

Multiple winners: Carl Hubbell and Chuck Klein (2).

Year		Pos	Year		Pos	Year		Pos
1929	No selection		1935	Arky Vaughan, Pit	SS	1941	Dolf Camilli, Bklyn	1B
1930	Bill Terry, NY	1B	1936	Carl Hubbell, NY	P	1942	Mort Cooper, St.L	P
1931	Chuck Klein, Phi	OF	1937	Joe Medwick, St.L	OF	1943	Stan Musial, St.L	OF
1932	Chuck Klein, Phi	OF	1938	Ernie Lombardi, Cin	C	1944	Marty Marion, St.L	SS
1933	Carl Hubbell, NY	P	1939	Bucky Walters, Cin	P	1945	Tommy Holmes, Bos	OF
1934	Dizzie Dean, St.L	P	1940	Frank McCormick, Cin	1B			

American League

Multiple winners: Jimmie Foxx and Lou Gehrig (3); Joe DiMaggio and Hank Greenberg (2).

Year		Pos	Year		Pos	Year		Pos
1929	Al Simmons, Phi	OF	1935	Hank Greenberg, Det	1B	1941	Joe DiMaggio, NY	OF
1930	Joe Cronin, Wash	SS	1936	Lou Gehrig, NY	1B	1942	Joe Gordon, NY	2B
1931	Lou Gehrig, NY	1B	1937	Charlie Gehringer, Det	2B	1943	Spud Chandler, NY	P
1932	Jimmie Foxx, Phi	1B	1938	Jimmie Foxx, Bos	1B	1944	Bobby Doerr, Bos	2B
1933	Jimmie Foxx, Phi	1B	1939	Joe DiMaggio, NY	OF	1945	Eddie Mayo, Det	2B
1934	Lou Gehrig, NY	1B	1940	Hank Greenberg, Det	OF			

Annual Awards (Cont.)
The Sporting News' Players of the Year
National League

Multiple winners: Hank Aaron, Ernie Banks, Andre Dawson, George Foster, Willie Mays, Dale Murphy, Stan Musial and Mike Schmidt (2).

Year	Pos	Year	Pos	Year	Pos
1948 Stan Musial, St.L	OF-1B	1963 Hank Aaron, Mil	OF	1978 Dave Parker, Pit	OF
1949 Enos Slaughter, St.L	OF	1964 Ken Boyer, St.L	3B	1979 Keith Hernandez, St.L	1B
1950 Ralph Kiner, Pit	OF	1965 Willie Mays, SF	OF	1980 Mike Schmidt, Phi	3B
1951 Stan Musial, St.L	OF	1966 Roberto Clemente, Pit	OF	1981 Andre Dawson, Mon	OF
1952 Hank Sauer, Chi	OF	1967 Orlando Cepeda, St.L	1B	1982 Dale Murphy, Atl	OF
1953 Roy Campanella, Bklyn	C	1968 Pete Rose, Cin	OF	1983 Dale Murphy, Atl	OF
1954 Willie Mays, NY	OF	1969 Willie McCovey, SF	1B	1984 Ryne Sandberg, Chi	2B
1955 Duke Snider, Bklyn	OF	1970 Johnny Bench, Cin	C	1985 Willie McGee, St.L	OF
1956 Hank Aaron, Mil	OF	1971 Joe Torre, St.L	3B	1986 Mike Schmidt, Phi	3B
1957 Stan Musial, St.L	1B	1972 Billy Williams, Chi	OF	1987 Andre Dawson, Chi	OF
1958 Ernie Banks, Chi	SS	1973 Bobby Bonds, SF	OF	1988 Andy Van Slyke, St.L	OF
1959 Ernie Banks, Chi	SS	1974 Lou Brock, St.L	OF	1989 Kevin Mitchell, SF	OF
1960 Dick Groat, Pit	SS	1975 Joe Morgan, Cin	2B	1990 Barry Bonds, Pit	OF
1961 Frank Robinson, Cin	OF	1976 George Foster, Cin	OF		
1962 Maury Wills, LA	SS	1977 George Foster, Cin	OF		

American League

Multiple winners: Don Mattingly (3); Al Kaline, Harmon Killebrew, Mickey Mantle, Roger Maris, Tony Oliva and Ted Williams (2).

Year	Pos	Year	Pos	Year	Pos
1948 Lou Boudreau, Cle	SS	1963 Al Kaline, Det	OF	1978 Jim Rice, Bos	OF
1949 Ted Williams, Bos	OF	1964 Brooks Robinson, Bal	3B	1979 Don Baylor, Cal	OF-DH
1950 Phil Rizzuto, NY	SS	1965 Tony Oliva, Min	OF	1980 George Brett, KC	3B
1951 Ferris Fain, Phi	1B	1966 Frank Robinson, Bal	OF	1981 Tony Armas, Oak	OF
1952 Luke Easter, Cle	1B	1967 Carl Yastrzemski, Bos	OF	1982 Robin Yount, Mil	SS
1953 Al Rosen, Cle	3B	1968 Ken Harrelson, Bos	OF	1983 Cal Ripken, Bal	SS
1954 Bobby Avila, Cle	3B	1969 Harmon Killebrew, Min	INF	1984 Don Mattingly, NY	1B
1955 Al Kaline, Det	OF	1970 Harmon Killebrew, Min	INF	1985 Don Mattingly, NY	1B
1956 Mickey Mantle, NY	OF	1971 Tony Oliva, Min	OF	1986 Don Mattingly, NY	1B
1957 Ted Williams, Bos	OF	1972 Dick Allen, Chi	1B	1987 George Bell, NY	OF
1958 Jackie Jensen, Bos	OF	1973 Reggie Jackson, Oak	OF	1988 Jose Canseco, Oak	OF
1959 Nellie Fox, Chi	2B	1974 Jeff Burroughs, Tex	OF	1989 Ruben Sierra, Tex	OF
1960 Roger Maris, NY	OF	1975 Fred Lynn, Bos	OF	1990 Cecil Fielder, Det	1B
1961 Roger Maris, NY	OF	1976 Thurman Munson, NY	C		
1962 Mickey Mantle, NY	OF	1977 Rod Carew, Min	1B		

The Sporting News' Pitchers of the Year
National League

Multiple winners: Steve Carlton, Sandy Koufax and Warren Spahn (4); Bob Gibson, Robin Roberts, Tom Seaver and Rick Sutcliffe (2).

Year	Year	Year
1948 Johnny Sain, Bos.	1963 Sandy Koufax, LA	1978 Vida Blue, SF
1949 Howie Pollet, St.L.	1964 Sandy Koufax, LA	1979 Joe Niekro, Hou.
1950 Jim Konstanty, Phi.	1965 Sandy Koufax, LA	1980 Steve Carlton, Phi.
1951 Preacher Roe, Bklyn.	1966 Sandy Koufax, LA	1981 F.Valenzuela, LA
1952 Robin Roberts, Phi.	1967 Mike McCormick, SF	1982 Steve Carlton, Phi.
1953 Warren Spahn, Mil.	1968 Bob Gibson, St.L.	1983 John Denny, Phi.
1954 Johnny Antonelli, NY	1969 Tom Seaver, NY	1984 Rick Sutcliffe, Chi.
1955 Robin Roberts, Phi.	1970 Bob Gibson, St.L.	1985 Dwight Gooden, NY
1956 Don Newcombe, Bklyn.	1971 Ferguson Jenkins, Chi.	1986 Mike Scott, Hou.
1957 Warren Spahn, Mil.	1972 Steve Carlton, Phi.	1987 Rick Sutcliffe, Chi.
1958 Warren Spahn, Mil.	1973 Ron Bryant, SF	1988 Orel Hershiser, LA
1959 Sam Jones, SF	1974 Mike Marshall, LA	1989 Mark Davis, SD
1960 Vernon Law, Pit.	1975 Tom Seaver, NY	1990 Doug Drabek, Pit.
1961 Warren Spahn, Mil.	1976 Randy Jones, SD	
1962 Don Drysdale, LA	1977 Steve Carlton, Phi.	

American League

Multiple winners: Whitey Ford, Bob Lemon and Jim Palmer (3); Denny McLain, Billy Pierce and Bret Saberhagen (2).

Year		Year		Year	
1948	Bob Lemon, Cle.	1963	Whitey Ford, NY	1978	Ron Guidry, NY
1949	Ellis Kinder, Bos.	1964	Dean Chance, LA	1979	Mike Flanagan, Bal.
		1965	Mudcat Grant, Min.		
1950	Bob Leman, Cle.	1966	Jim Kaat, Min.	1980	Steve Stone, Bal.
1951	Bob Feller, Cle.	1967	Jim Lonborg, Bos.	1981	Jack Morris, Det.
1952	Bobby Shantz, Phi.	1968	Denny McLain, Det.	1982	Dave Stieb, Tor.
1953	Bob Porterfield, Wash.	1969	Denny McLain, Det.	1983	LaMarr Hoyt, Chi.
1954	Bob Lemon, Cle.			1984	Willie Hernandez, Det.
1955	Whitey Ford, NY.	1970	Sam McDowell, Cle	1985	Bret Saberhagen, KC
1956	Billy Pierce, Chi.	1971	Vida Blue, Oak.	1986	Roger Clemens, Bos.
1957	Billy Pierce, Chi.	1972	Wilbur Wood, Chi.	1987	Jimmy Key, Tor.
1958	Bob Turley, NY	1973	Jim Palmer, Bal.	1988	Frank Viola, Min.
1959	Early Wynn, Chi.	1974	Catfish Hunter, Oak.	1989	Bret Saberhagen, KC
		1975	Jim Palmer, Bal.		
1960	Chuck Estrada, Bal.	1976	Jim Palmer, Bal.	1990	Bob Welch, Oak.
1961	Whitey Ford, NY	1977	Nolan Ryan, Cal.		
1962	Dick Donavan, Cle.				

Rookie of the Year

Voted on by the Baseball Writers Assn. of America. One award was presented from 1947-48. Two awards (one for each league) have been presented since 1949.

AL and NL Combined

Year		Pos	Year		Pos
1947	Jackie Robinson, Brooklyn	1B	1948	Alvin Dark, Boston, NL	SS

National League

Year		Pos	Year		Pos	Year		Pos
1949	Don Newcombe, Bklyn	P	1963	Pete Rose, Cin	2B	1977	Andre Dawson, Mon	OF
1950	Sam Jethroe, Bos	OF	1964	Richie Allen, Phi	3B	1978	Bob Horner, Atl	3B
1951	Willie Mays, NY.	OF	1965	Jim Lefebvre, LA	2B	1979	Rick Sutcliffe, LA	P
1952	Joe Black, Bklyn	P	1966	Tommy Helms, Cin	3B			
1953	Jim Gilliam, Bklyn	2B	1967	Tom Seaver, NY	P	1980	Steve Howe, LA	P
1954	Wally Moon, St.L.	OF	1968	Johnny Bench, Cin	C	1981	Fernando Valenzuela, LA	P
1955	Bill Virdon, Pit	OF	1969	Ted Sizemore, LA.	2B	1982	Steve Sax, LA	2B
1956	Frank Robinson, Cin.	OF				1983	Darryl Strawberry, NY	OF
1957	Jack Sanford, Phi	P	1970	Carl Morton, Mon	P	1984	Dwight Gooden, NY	P
1958	Orlando Cepeda, St.	1B	1971	Earl Williams, Atl.	C	1985	Vince Coleman, St.L.	OF
1959	Willie McCovey, SF	1B	1972	Jon Matlack, NY.	P	1986	Todd Warrell, St.L	P
			1973	Gary Matthews, SF	OF	1987	Benito Santiago, SD	C
1960	Frank Howard, LA	OF	1974	Bake McBride, St.L	OF	1988	Chris Sabo, Cin	3B
1961	Billy Williams, Chi.	OF	1975	John Montefusco, SF	P	1989	Jerome Walton, Chi	OF
1962	Ken Hubbs, Chi	2B	1976	Butch Metzger, SD	P			
				& Pat Zachry, Cin	P	1990	David Justice, Atl.	OF

American League

Year		Pos	Year		Pos	Year		Pos
1949	Roy Sievers, St.L	OF	1964	Tony Oliva, Min	OF	1979	John Castino, Min	3B
			1965	Curt Blefary, Bal	OF		& Alfredo Griffin, Tor.	SS
1950	Walt Dropo, Bos	1B	1966	Tommie Agee, Chi	OF			
1951	Gil McDougald, NY.	3B	1967	Rod Carew, Min.	2B	1980	Joe Charboneau, Cle	OF-DH
1952	Harry Byrd, Phi	P	1968	Stan Bahnsen, NY	P	1981	Dave Righetti, NY.	P
1953	Harvey Kuenn, Det.	SS	1969	Lou Piniella, KC	OF	1982	Cal Ripken, Bal.	SS-3B
1954	Bob Grim, NY	P				1983	Ron Kittle, Chi	OF
1955	Herb Score, Cle	P	1970	Thurman Munson, NY	C	1984	Alvin Davis, Sea	1B
1956	Luis Aparicio, Chi.	SS	1971	Chris Chambliss, Cle	1B	1985	Ozzie Guillen, Chi	SS
1957	Tony Kubek, NY	INF-OF	1972	Carlton Fisk, Bos.	C	1986	Jose Canseco, Oak	OF
1958	Albie Pearson, Wash	OF	1973	Al Bumbry, Bal	OF	1987	Mark McGwire, Oak	1B
1959	Bob Allison, Wash.	OF	1974	Mike Hargrove, Tex.	1B	1988	Walt Weiss, Oak	SS
			1975	Fred Lynn, Bos	OF	1989	Gregg Olson, Bal.	P
1960	Ron Hansen, Bal	SS	1976	Mark Fidrych, Det.	P			
1961	Don Schwall, Bos.	P	1977	Eddie Murray, Bal.	DH-1B	1990	Sandy Alomar, Cle	C
1962	Tom Tresh, NY.	SS-OF	1978	Lou Whitaker, Det.	2B			
1963	Gary Peters, Chi.	P						

College Baseball
College World Series

The NCAA Division I College World Series has been held in Kalamazoo, Mich. (1947-48), Wichita, Kan. (1949) and Omaha, Neb. (since 1950).

Multiple winners: USC (11); Arizona St. (5); Texas (4); Arizona and Minnesota (3); Cal State Fullerton, California, Miami-FL, Michigan and Stanford (2).

Year	Winner	Coach	Score	Loser	Year	Winner	Coach	Score	Loser
1947	California	Clint Evans	8-7	Yale	1970	USC	Rod Dedeaux	2-1	Fla.St.
1948	USC	Sam Barry	9-2	Yale	1971	USC	Rod Dedeaux	7-2	So.Ill.
1949	Texas	Bibb Falk	10-3	W.Forest	1972	USC	Rod Dedeaux	1-0	Ariz.St.
					1973	USC	Rod Dedeaux	4-3	Ariz.St.
1950	Texas	Bibb Falk	3-0	Wash.St.	1974	USC	Rod Dedeaux	7-3	Miami,FL
1951	Oklahoma	Jack Baer	3-2	Tennessee	1975	Texas	Cliff Gustafson	5-1	S.Carolina
1952	Holy Cross	Jack Barry	8-4	Missouri	1976	Arizona	Jerry Kindall	7-1	E.Michigan
1953	Michigan	Ray Fisher	7-5	Texas	1977	Arizona St.	Jim Brock	2-1	S.Carolina
1954	Missouri	Hi Simmons	4-1	Rollins	1978	USC	Rod Dedeaux	10-3	Ariz.St.
1955	W. Forest	Taylor Sanford	7-6	W.Mich.	1979	CS Fullerton	Augie Garrido	2-1	Arkansas
1956	Minnesota	Dick Siebert	12-1	Arizona					
1957	California	Geo. Wolfman	1-0	Penn St.	1980	Arizona	Jerry Kindall	5-3	Hawaii
1958	USC	Rod Dedeaux	8-7	Missouri	1981	Arizona St.	Jim Brock	7-4	Okla.St.
1959	Oklahoma St.	Toby Greene	5-3	Arizona	1982	Miami,FL	Ron Fraser	9-3	Wichita St.
					1983	Texas	Cliff Gustafson	4-3	Alabama
1960	Minnesota	Dick Siebert	2-1	USC	1984	CS Fullerton	Augie Garrido	3-1	Texas
1961	USC	Rod Dedeaux	1-0	Okla.St.	1985	Miami,FL	Ron Fraser	10-6	Texas
1962	Michigan	Don Lund	5-4	S.Clara	1986	Arizona	Jerry Kindall	10-2	Fla.St.
1963	USC	Rod Dedeaux	5-2	Arizona	1987	Stanford	M.Marquess	9-5	Okla.St.
1964	Minnesota	Dick Siebert	5-1	Missouri	1988	Stanford	M.Marquess	9-4	Ariz.St.
1965	Arizona St.	Bobby Winkles	2-1	Ohio St.	1989	Wichita St.	G.Stephenson	5-3	Texas
1966	Ohio St.	Marty Karow	8-2	Okla.St.					
1967	Arizona St.	Bobby Winkles	11-2	Houston	1990	Georgia	Steve Webber	2-1	Okla.St.
1968	USC	Rod Dedeaux	4-3	So.Ill.	1991	LSU	Skip Bertman	6-3	Wichita St.
1969	Arizona St.	Bobby Winkles	10-1	Tulsa					

Most Outstanding Players

The Most Outstanding Player has been selected every year of the College World Series since 1949. Winners who did not play for the CWS champion are listed in **bold** type. No player has won the award more than once.

Year		Year		Year	
1949	**Charles Teague,** W.Forest	1963	Bud Hollowell, USC	1978	Rod Boxberger, USC
1950	**Ray VanCleef,** Rutgers	1964	**Joe Ferris,** Maine	1979	Tony Hudson, CS-Full.
1951	**Sidney Hatfield,** Tenn.	1965	Sal Bando, Ariz.St.		
1952	James O'Neill, Holy Cross	1966	Steve Arlin, Ohio St.	1980	Terry Francona, Arizona
1953	**J.L. Smith,** Texas	1967	Ron Davini, Ariz.St.	1981	Stan Holmes, Ariz.St.
1954	**Tom Yewcic,** Mich.St.	1968	Bill Seinsoth, USC	1982	Dan Smith, Miami-FL
1955	**Tom Borland,** Okla.St.	1969	John Dolinsek, Ariz.St.	1983	Calvin Schiraldi, Texas
1956	Jerry Thomas, Minn.			1984	John Fishel, CS-Full.
1957	**Cal Emery,** Penn St.	1970	**Gene Ammann,** Fla.St.	1985	Greg Ellena, Miami-FL
1958	Bill Thom, USC	1971	**Jerry Tabb,** Tulsa	1986	Mike Senne, Arizona
1959	Jim Dobson, Okla.St.	1972	Russ McQueen, USC	1987	Paul Carey, Stanford
		1973	**Dave Winfield,** Minn.	1988	Lee Plemel, Stanford
1960	John Erickson, Minn.	1974	George Milke, USC	1989	Greg Brummett, Wich.St.
1961	**Littleton Flower,** Okla.St.	1975	Mickey Reichenbach, Tex.		
1962	**Bob Garibaldi,** S.Clara	1976	Steve Powers, Arizona	1990	Mike Rebhan, Georgia
		1977	Bob Horner, Ariz. St.	1991	Gary Hymel, LSU

Golden Spike Award

First presented in 1978 by the U.S. Baseball Federation, honoring the nation's best amateur player. Alex Fernandez, the 1990 winner, was the first junior college player chosen.

Year		Year		Year	
1978	Bob Horner, Ariz.St, 2b	1983	Dave Madagan, Alabama, 1b	1987	Jim Abbott, Michigan, p
1979	Tim Wallach, CS-Fullerton, 1b	1984	Oddibe McDowell, Ariz.St., of	1988	Robin Ventura, Okla.St., 3b
1980	Terry Francona, Arizona, of	1985	Will Clark, Miss.St., 1b	1989	Ben McDonald, LSU, p
1981	Mike Fuentes, Fla.St., of	1986	Mike Loynd, Fla.St., p	1990	Alex Fernandez, Miami-Dade, p
1982	Augie Schmidt, N.Orleans, ss				

Notre Dame's **Rocket Ismail** in full flight during his last-minute 91-yard touchdown run New Year's Night. The play, however, was called back.

COLLEGE FOOTBALL

Polls Apart

*Colorado and Georgia Tech split Number 1 vote
in one of the most out-of-control seasons ever.*

If some latter day Grantland Rice had saddled up the Four Horsemen for the 1990 college football season, Notre Dame's famed 1924 quartet of Stuhldreher, Miller, Crowley and Layden would have been replaced by Raghib Ismail and three other guys—probably a referee, a conference commissioner and a television executive. Famine, Pestilence, Destruction and Death meet Chaos, Expansion, Litigation and Anarchy.

Chaos. Over the course of the '90 season, six teams were ranked No. 1—seven if you count Notre Dame's two stints at the top. In the end, the wire-service voters still couldn't agree on who the national champion was. The Associated Press writers and broadcasters said it was Colorado with its 11-1-1 record and a 10-9 victory over Notre Dame in the Orange Bowl. UPI's board of coaches disagreed, picking Georgia Tech, the only unbeaten team in Divisionn I-A at 11-0-1.

Colorado played a tougher schedule than Tech, but the Buffaloes' two most important victories were near-defeats and clouded by controversial calls. On Oct. 6, Colorado unwittingly took five downs to score a last-play touchdown to beat Missouri, 33-31. Three months later, the Buffaloes held off Notre Dame

by one point in the Orange Bowl when a clipping penalty in the last minute wiped out an electrifying, 91-yard punt return touchdown run by Ismail.

By Jan. 2 then, there were two national champions—three if you agreed with *The New York Times* computer, which said Miami of Florida was the top team—and no sign of an annual playoff to settle the matter.

Expansion. The Southeastern Conference announced it would become a 12-team league in time for the 1992 season by adding Arkansas and South Carolina to its rolls. The SEC then charged through a loophole in the NCAA bylaws and unveiled a plan to split into two divisions. The purpose: to schedule an unprecedented conference championship game between the two divisional winners and collect a windfall of television money, perhaps as much as $10 million annually.

The SEC had also planned to recruit independent Florida State and further raid the SWC for Texas and Texas A&M, but FSU was wooed and won by the Atlantic Coast Conference, and the two Texas schools decided to sit tight for the immediate future.

Miami, the other big-time independent looking for a home, signed up with the Big East, which quickly shed its basketball-only image and formed a new eight-team football league that would be ready for round-robin play in 1993. (See "College Sports.")

Ivan Maisel is the national college football writer for the *Dallas Morning News* and a columnist for the *The Sporting News*.

Steve Levin/Columbia Daily Tribune

Two-picture sequence indicates that Colorado quarterback **Charles Johnson** is down short of the goal line (left) before extending the ball into the end zone on the controversial "5th down play" at Missouri on Oct. 6.

Litigation. The Federal Trade Commission voted to charge the College Football Association—the 63-member group of Division I-A schools outside the Big 10 and Pac-10—with illegal restraint of trade in the matter of television contracts negotiated by the CFA. Hanging in the balance is the CFA's five-year, $300 million deal with ABC Sports and ESPN scheduled to begin in the fall of 1991. A long court battle awaits.

In addition, the Internal Revenue Service audited the Cotton Bowl and determined that the rights fee paid by sponsor Mobil Oil should be categorized as unrelated business income and therefore taxable at a rate of 34 percent. All bowls, which have joined forces to contest the ruling, maintain they are non-profit organizations that turn the money over to the participating universities. At stake is about $5 million.

Anarchy. Nearly all the bowls and the schools that played in them made their 1990 postseason reservations on the first weekend of November, three weeks prior to the NCAA-mandated date of invitations. As a result, Virginia, unbeaten and ranked No. 1 in the polls as of Nov. 3, secured a spot in the Sugar Bowl and then proceeded to limp to New Orleans by losing three of its final four regular season games. The NCAA, knowing a lost cause when it sees one, abruptly abandoned its policy of policing the bowls. Beginning in '91, the bowls intend to police themselves. Stay tuned.

The Sugar Bowl's miscalculation paled in comparison to the problems suffered by the Fiesta Bowl when Arizona voters rejected a state holiday to honor Martin Luther King. Not only did the NFL quickly make good on its threat to withdraw the 1993 Super Bowl, but top college teams that normally would have begged for a $2.4 million berth in the 1991 Fiesta Bowl suddenly weren't available.

Eventually, Louisville and Alabama agreed to come to Tempe, but there was little interest. Louisville won, 34-7, but the big news came two weeks later, when Sunkist quit as sponsor of the game, citing the December freeze that devastated California orange crops.

Other signs of anarchy could be found in Miami's loutish behavior in the Cotton Bowl, where the Hurricanes blew out Texas by 43 points and rubbed it in with a dancing and taunting exhibition that cost them a bowl record 202 yards in penalties. Miami officials were apologetic, but not the players. "It might be embarrassing to the university and the coaches," said center Darren Handy, "but it's not to the players. We enjoy it. It's like a show." Such showmanship has prompted the NCAA to adopt stronger rules to crack down on unsportsmanlike conduct on the field.

Even one of the year's nicest stories turned sad when coach George Allen died on Dec. 31 at age 72. Allen, one of pro football's greatest coaches, returned to college after a 34-year absence and led a losing Long Beach State program to a 6-5 record. Allen called it his "most gratifying year in coaching."

Fifteen other Division I-A coaching positions turned over during the off-season, highlighted by the departure of Syracuse's Dick MacPherson to the New England Patriots of the NFL and the hiring of former Texas A&M coach Jackie Sherrill by Mississippi State.

On the field, Ismail, Notre Dame's fuel-injected junior flanker, was the most exciting player of the year (see box), but he didn't win the Heisman Trophy. Brigham Young quarterback Ty Detmer did. On Sept. 8, in the cool of a mountain evening in Provo, Utah, Detmer sent the first shock waves through the 1990 season when he passed for 406 yards and three touchdowns in leading the Cougars to a 28-21 victory over top-ranked Miami.

Notre Dame replaced Miami as No. 1, then beat No. 4 Michigan in the opener for both teams on Sept. 15. Trailing the Wolverines by 10 in the fourth quarter, the Irish came back to win, 28-24, behind sophomore quarterback Rick Mirer, who

grew up in Goshen, Ind., just 35 miles east of South Bend.

September ended with 12 teams undefeated and untied. A week later, all hell broke loose. On Oct. 6, the top two teams in the country—Notre Dame and Florida State—lost and Colorado was saved by a fifth down.

Notre Dame was brought low at home by a 1-3 Stanford team that beat the Irish, 36-31, in the game's last minute. Down at the Orange Bowl, Florida State fell behind early (24-0) against Miami and lost, 31-22.

Losing to Miami snapped a 14-game FSU winning streak and kept coach Bobby Bowden from his 200th victory. Although it would take him two more attempts to win it, Bowden added to his considerable stature at season's end. Florida State and Penn State, both having spurned the Fiesta Bowl, agreed to play in the inaugural Blockbuster Bowl for $1.6 million apiece. In a matchup of the nation's two winningest active I-A coaches, Bowden (205 wins) defeated Joe Paterno (229) by a 24-17 score at Joe Robbie Stadium near Miami.

But back to Oct. 6. Nothing else that occurred on that Saturday, or any other Saturday in 1990, compared to the Colorado "fifth-down victory" at Missouri. The Tigers led the 12th-ranked Buffaloes 31-27 when Colorado reached the Mizzou 3-yard line with 31 seconds to play. On first down, Colorado quarterback Charles Johnson threw the ball into the ground to stop the clock. Tailback Eric Bieniemy gained two yards on second down and Colorado called time with 0:18 to play.

During this time-out, the officials working the down markers neglected to flip the "2" to a "3". No one on the field caught the mistake. On the next play, Bieniemy was stopped short of the goal line and on the next, Johnson took the snap and spiked the ball. After four downs, the Buffaloes still had possession inside the 1 with 0:02 to go. Johnson then scored on a quarterback option, although still photos and replays seemed to show that Johnson's shoulders had touched the ground before the ball broke the plane.

In 1940, Cornell returned a 7-3 victory to Dartmouth when it became apparent that the Big Red had scored the deciding

Division I-A's two 200-win coaches, **Joe Paterno** of Penn State (left) and Florida State's **Bobby Bowden**, meet at midfield following the Seminoles' victory over the Nittany Lions in the inaugural Blockbuster Bowl.

touchdown on a fifth down. Fifty years later, Colorado coach Bill McCartney blasted Missouri for the slippery condition of Faurot Field and said, "It was not a fair test for our team. For us to forfeit the game under all these circumstances is absurd."

And the crew that officiated the game? "We are human," said crew chief J.C. Louderback afterward. "We erred and we feel terrible in regards to the circumstances at the end of the game." The Big Eight was equally chagrined, and suspended Louderback and his seven-man crew for one game.

The last word on all of this is that in college the referees' decision is final. A week later, Michigan, which had replaced Notre Dame at No. 1, was upset by Michigan State, 28-27, when pass interference was not called against Spartan cornerback Eddie Brown. Brown tripped Michigan receiver Desmond Howard, preventing Howard from catching a game-winning two-point conversion in the final two minutes. Big Ten supervisor of officials David Parry called Michigan coach Gary Moeller later to apologize for the no-call.

Said Moeller, "You see it on TV every week. The philosophy of officials is 'Don't throw the flag.' It's a shame we have to sit around and accept these things, because somebody's being cheated."

The second half of the season saw Virginia rise to the top of the Division I-A heap by mid-October, then fall at home to Georgia Tech in a battle of ACC unbeatens. Tech rallied in the second half and won, 41-38, on Scott Sisson's 37-yard field goal with seven seconds to play. Virginia Heisman candidate, quarterback Shawn Moore, passed for a school-record 344 yards but was upstaged by another Shawn—the Yellow Jackets' Shawn Jones, who gained 309 yards in total offense, threw for two touchdowns and ran for a third.

The regular season rivalry between Notre Dame and Miami ended on Oct.

20 after 23 games, including 19 in the last 20 years. The sixth-ranked Irish, underdogs at home, defeated the No. 2 Hurricanes, 29-20. Miami turned the ball over four times, but its biggest error came late in the first quarter when kicker Carlos Huerta failed to boot a kickoff beyond the end zone. Instead, the ball landed in the arms of Ismail at the 6-yard-line and the Rocket left a 94-yard vapor trail on his way to the Canes' end zone to tie the score at 10-10. Four Craig Hentrich field goals, a touchdown and a resolute Irish defense took it from there.

The Big Eight title was settled on Nov. 3 in the cold and rain of Lincoln, Neb., where No. 9 Colorado overcame No. 3 Nebraska, 27-12, with 27 unanswered points in the fourth quarter. Buffaloes' tailback Bieniemy, who had fumbled four times earlier in the game, redeemed himself by scoring four touchdowns. Nebraska never recovered—ending the regular season with an embarrassing 45-10 loss to Oklahoma and falling 45-21 to Georgia Tech in the Citrus Bowl.

Once-beaten Notre Dame (7-1) returned to Number One after the games of Nov. 3, followed by Washington (8-1) and unbeaten Houston (8-0). Washington and Houston both lost the next week—the Huskies to struggling UCLA, 25-22, and the Cougars to rejuvenated Texas, 45-24. Houston's defeat ended its shot at becoming the first team on probation to win the national championship since Oklahoma in 1974.

Houston quarterback David Klingler, who was held to just 299 yards passing by Texas, rebounded the following week with 572 yards and an NCAA-record 11 touchdowns in an 84-21 thrashing of Eastern Washington. Not taking any chances against the Division I-AA Eagles, Houston coach John Jenkins didn't lift Klingler until the fourth quarter when the Cougars were up by 63. Klingler went on to set or tie 33 NCAA records (22 more than Detmer), throw for 5,140 yards and 54 touchdowns, and lead the nation in total offense. Like Detmer, Klingler passed on the NFL Draft and returned to Houston for his senior season.

Texas, meanwhile, had signalled its return to the Top 25 on Oct. 13 with a 14-13 upset of fourth-ranked Oklahoma in Dallas. Longhorns' coach David

Rocket Blasts Off, While Ty Hangs Around

On Jan. 24, Raghib Ismail announced that he was giving up his final year of eligibility at Notre Dame and making himself available for the NFL Draft.

Four days later, Red Grange died at age 87.

Ismail may be the Rocket, but Grange was the legendary "Galloping Ghost." A three-time All-America at Illinois from 1923-25, Grange brought instant credibility to the then struggling NFL when he decided to turn pro immediately after his final game as a senior.

The year before, Grange had run for an unheard-of five touchdowns and passed for a sixth against Michigan, moving University of Chicago coach Amos Alonzo Stagg to call it "the most spectacular single-handed performance ever made in a major game."

Ismail's game-breaking abilities inspired the same kind of awe in 1990.

Like Grange, Ismail was college football's most exciting player. His 91-yard punt return for a touchdown in the waning seconds of the Orange Bowl may have been nullified by a clipping penalty, but it solidified the Rocket's reputation.

As a receiver, tailback and kick return specialist for Notre Dame, the 5-10, 175-pound junior gained 1,726 all-purpose yards during the regular season. He scored only six touchdowns, but what touchdowns they were: a 64-yard run, a 52-yard reception, a 94-yard kickoff return, a 76-yard run, a 54-yard reception and a 44-yard run.

Still, Ismail finished a distant second in the Heisman Trophy vote to another junior, Brigham Young quarterback Ty Detmer. The 6-0, 175-pound Detmer had some dazzling statistics of his own—among them, throwing for 5,188 yards and 41 touchdowns. He also made a strong first impression on voters by engineering BYU's opening game upset of No. 1 Miami.

Admittedly, there was some justice in a record-setting BYU quarterback finally winning the Heisman. Before Detmer there had been Marc Wilson, Jim McMahon, Steve Young and Robbie Bosco. Between 1979 and 1985, they finished among the top five vote-getters six times. Besides, Notre Dame has won seven Heismans.

The spoils of the 1990 season went to juniors **Rocket Ismail** (left) and **Ty Detmer**. Detmer, the BYU quarterback, won the Heisman Trophy, but Ismail, the Notre Dame running back, got over $18 million to turn pro.

Detmer had both shoulders separated in a 65-14 loss to Texas A&M in the Holiday Bowl. He underwent surgery soon afterwards, which would have lessened his appeal to NFL scouts had he intended to turn pro. He had been adamant from the start of the season, however, that he would return to school in 1991. "I signed a scholarship to play four years," he said. "And I intend to honor it. The big dollars will still be there. If not, then it's not meant to be."

Detmer passed or carried the ball 635 times in 1990. Ismail, on the other hand, only touched the pigskin around 12 times a game as Notre Dame coach Lou Holtz maximized Ismail's talents by deploying him in a masterful fashion. After serving as a decoy early in the game, Ismail would shift to tailback in the fourth quarter, when defenses would be at their weakest. Many Heisman voters conceded Ismail's explosiveness, but was he a full-time contributor?

All doubts vanished the instant he completed his star-crossed touchdown dash against Colorado. "That punt return was the greatest individual effort I've ever seen," said Holtz, echoing Stagg.

Like Detmer, Ismail maintained through-out the season that he would return to Notre Dame for his senior year. On the eve of the Orange Bowl, though, he publicly voiced doubts in an interview with ESPN. The day after the game, one of Ismail's teammates, nose guard Chris Zorich, came home to Chicago to find his mother had died that morning. Ismail, who is very close to his mother in Wilkes-Barre, Pa., decided to take the money and run.

"It made me realize that things in life don't always happen the way you expect them to," Ismail said. "Chris's mother's passing away was a reality check. If the people I want to do something for aren't there, it would really crush me."

As soon as Ismail declared his intention to turn pro he became the best player available in the NFL Draft. The Dallas Cowboys traded up to sign him, but when draft day arrived April 21, the Rocket bypassed the established NFL to sign a staggering, four-year, $18.2 million contract to play with the Toronto Argonauts of the struggling Canadian Football League.

Clearly, Argos' owner Bruce NcNall hoped that Ismail could do for the CFL what Grange had done for the NFL 70 years before.

McWilliams entered his fourth season with an overall record of 15-19, one bowl appearance and the very real possibility that his team was playing for his job. After splitting the first two games with Penn State and Colorado, however, Texas won nine straight and landed in the Cotton Bowl for the first time in seven years. McWilliams got a five-year extension.

Notre Dame relinquished No. 1 for the second time on Nov. 17, losing at home again—this time to Penn State, 24-21, on a 34-yard field goal by the Nittany Lions' Craig Fayak with eight seconds left. In all, Penn State scored 17 points and held the Irish scoreless in the second half, which Ismail sat out with a thigh muscle strain. He also missed every play save one in the loss to Stanford. That's how important he had become to the Notre Dame offense.

By the end of the regular season, AP and UPI agreed on the top four teams— Colorado, Georgia Tech, Miami and Texas, in that order. No. 2 Georgia Tech made it a two-team race on New Year's Day, beating Nebraska by 23 points in the Citrus Bowl to finish the season undefeated and once tied (the lone imperfection was a 13-13 draw with North Carolina back on Oct. 20 in Chapel Hill).

The season came down to the Orange Bowl. Colorado vs. Notre Dame on New Year's Night. An Irish win and Georgia Tech would be champion. A convincing victory by Colorado, however, and the Buffaloes would win the title that eluded them in 1989.

As a fitting conclusion to this confusing season, Colorado beat Notre Dame by a point, 10-9, and resolved little.

At halftime, Notre Dame had a 6-3 lead and Colorado's starting quarterback Darian Hagan was out of the game with a ruptured tendon in his left knee.

Charles Johnson, a fourth-year junior, replaced Hagan and, following a Notre Dame fumble in the third quarter, drove the Buffaloes 40 yards in eight plays for their only touchdown. Colorado asserted control in the final quarter, but could not score again. The Buffs were forced to punt with the clock ticking inside of 1:10 to play. When the ball came down, there was Ismail.

Rocket made the catch at the Notre Dame nine and headed straight upfield. He appeared to have a lane along the right

Marlene Karas/Atlanta Constitution

Quarterback **Shawn Jones** led unbeaten Georgia Tech to victory over Virginia in Charlottesville and Nebraska in the Citrus Bowl to earn a share of the national championship.

sideline. Colorado safety Tim James tried to cut him off, but Irish defensive back Greg Davis brushed James away and Ismail was gone. Notre Dame 15, Colorado 10.

But there was a flag.

Davis' block had been ruled a clip by the Southwest Conference officials and the TV replay seemed to back them up. The touchdown was called back and Colorado was saved again.

The next day, it was Georgia Tech by one point. AP's 60 voters chose Colorado as the national champion, but UPI's 59 coaches went for Tech, 847 to 846.

Split decision. □

THE 1992 INFORMATION PLEASE SPORTS ALMANAC

COLLEGE FOOTBALL
S T A T I S T I C S

THE SEASON IN REVIEW
1990-1991
TOP 25 • BOWLS • STANDINGS

SEC A

PAGE 127

Final AP Top 25 Poll

Voted on by panel of 60 sportswriters & broadcasters following Jan.1, 1991 bowl games: first place votes in parentheses, records, total points (based on 25 for 1st, 24 for 2nd, etc.) bowl game result, head coach and career record (including bowl games), preseason rank and final regular season rank.

		Final Record	Points	Bowl Game	Head Coach	Aug. 25 Rank	Dec. 3 Rank
1	Colorado (39)	11-1-1	1475	Won Orange	Bill McCartney (9 yrs: 57-46-2)	5	1
2	Georgia Tech (20)	11-0-1	1441	Won Citrus	Bobby Ross (14 yrs: 86-71-2)	34	2
3	Miami-FL (1)	10-2-0	1388	Won Cotton	Dennis Erickson (9 yrs: 71-34-1)	1	4
4	Florida St	10-2-0	1303	Won Blockbuster	Bobby Bowden (25 yrs: 205-74-3)	4	6
5	Washington	10-2-0	1246	Won Rose	Don James (20 yrs: 155-75-3)	20	8
6	Notre Dame	9-3-0	1179	Lost Orange	Lou Holtz (21 yrs: 162-79-5)	2	5
7	Michigan	9-3-0	1025	Won Gator	Gary Moeller (3 yrs: 15-27-3)	6	12
8	Tennessee	9-2-2	993	Won Sugar	Johnny Majors (23 yrs: 159-99-10)	8	10
9	Clemson	10-2-0	950	Won Hall/Fame	Ken Hatfield (12 yrs: 91-51-2)	10	14
10	Houston	10-1-0	940	On probation	John Jenkins (1 yr: 10-1-0)	24	9
11	Penn St.	9-3-0	907	Lost Blockbuster	Joe Paterno (25 yrs: 229-60-3)	21	7
12	Texas	10-2-0	887	Lost Cotton	David McWilliams (5 yrs: 33-24-0)	35	3
13	Florida	9-2-0	863	On probation	Steve Spurrier (4 yrs: 29-15-1)	31	11
14	Louisville	10-1-1	775	Won Fiesta	H.Schnellenberger (11 yrs: 73-49-2)	32	18
15	Texas A&M	9-3-1	627	Won Holiday	R.C.Slocum (2 yrs: 17-7-1)	13	26
16	Michigan St.	8-3-1	610	Won Hancock	George Perles (8 yrs: 54-36-4)	23	22
17	Oklahoma	8-3-0	452	On probation	Gary Gibbs (2 yrs: 15-7-0)	22	20
18	Iowa	8-4-0	370½	Lost Rose	Hayden Fry (29 yrs: 179-139-8)	—	17
19	Auburn	8-3-1	288	Won Peach	Pat Dye (17 yrs: 143-51-4)	3	28
20	USC	8-4-1	266	Lost Hancock	Larry Smith (15 yrs: 101-67-5)	9	21
21	Mississippi	9-3-0	253	Lost Gator	Billy Brewer (17 yrs: 105-80-6)	36	15
22	BYU	10-3-0	246	Lost Holiday	LaVell Edwards (19 yrs: 175-59-1)	16	13
23	Virginia	8-4-0	188	Lost Sugar	George Welsh (18 yrs: 113-90-3)	15	27
24	Nebraska	9-3-0	185	Lost Citrus	Tom Osborne (18 yrs: 177-41-2)	7	19
25	Illinois	8-4-0	146½	Lost Hall/Fame	John Mackovic (6 yrs: 38-31-1)	11	16

Other teams receiving votes: 26. San Jose St.(9-2-1, 138 points, won Raisin); 27. Syracuse (7-4-2, 121 pts, won Aloha); 28. Colorado St.(9-4, 67 pts, won Freedom); 29. Southern Miss (8-4, 48 pts, lost All American); 30. California (7-4-1, 37 pts, won Copper); 31. N.C.State (7-5, 30 pts, won All American); 32. Alabama (7-5, 13 pts, lost Fiesta); 33. Ohio St.(7-4-1, 7 pts, lost Liberty) and Wyoming (9-4, 7 pts, lost Copper); 35. Oregon (8-4, 6 pts, lost Freedom) and UCLA (5-6, 6 pts, no bowl); 37. Air Force (7-5, 5 pts, won Liberty) and Virginia Tech (6-5, 5 pts, no bowl); 39. North Carolina (6-4-1, 4 pts, no bowl); 40. Hawaii (7-5, 2 pts, no bowl).

Bowl Games

Date	Result	Date	Result
12/ 8	California Raisin . . . . S.Jose St.48, C.Mich.24	1/1	Gator . . . . Michigan 35, Ole Miss 3
12/15	Independence . . . . La.Tech 34, Maryland 34	1/1	Hall/Fame . . . . Clemson 30, Illinois 0
12/25	Aloha . . . . Syracuse 28, Arizona 0	1/1	Citrus . . . . Ga.Tech 45, Nebraska 21
12/27	Liberty . . . . Air Force 23, Ohio St.11	1/1	Cotton . . . . Miami-FL 46, Texas 3
12/28	All-American . . . . N.C.State 31, So.Miss.27	1/1	Fiesta . . . . Louisville 34, Alabama 7
12/28	Blockbuster . . . . Florida St.24, Penn St.17	1/1	Rose . . . . Washington 46, Iowa 34
12/29	Peach . . . . Auburn 27, Indiana 23	1/1	Orange . . . . Colorado 10, N.Dame 9
12/29	Holiday . . . . Texas A&M 65, BYU 14	1/1	Sugar . . . . Tennessee 23, Virginia 22
12/29	Freedom Colo.St.32, Ore.St.31		
12/31	John Hancock . . . . Michigan St.17, USC 16		
12/31	Copper . . . . Cal 17, Wyoming 15		

Bowl Payouts for Teams

Rose ($6 million each); Federal Express Orange ($4.2 million); USF&G Sugar ($3.25 million); Mobil Cotton ($3 million);Sunkist Fiesta ($2.5 million); Blockbuster ($1.6 million); Florida Citrus ($1.35 million); Mazda Gator and Sea World Holiday ($1.2 million); Hall of Fame and Liberty ($1 million); Peach ($900,000); John Hancock ($880,000); All American, Eagle Aloha, Domino's Pizza Copper, Anaheim Freedom and Poulan/Weed Eater Independence ($600,000); California Raisin ($275,000).

NCAA Division I-A Final Standings
Overall records include postseason games.

Atlantic Coast Conference

	Conference				Overall			
	W	L	T	PF	PA	W	L	T	PF	PA
*Ga.Tech	6	0	1	217	124	11	0	1	379	186
*Clemson	5	2	0	138	91	10	2	0	333	109
*Virginia	5	2	0	251	107	8	4	0	464	227
*Maryland	4	3	0	142	158	6	5	1	237	284
N.Carolina	3	3	1	124	125	6	4	1	227	186
*N.C.State	3	4	0	90	113	7	5	0	298	189
Duke	1	6	0	137	216	4	7	0	240	295
W.Forest	0	7	0	99	264	3	8	0	247	351

*Bowls (3-1-1): Georgia Tech (won Citrus); Clemson (won Hall of Fame); Virginia (lost Sugar); Maryland (tied Independence); N.C. State (won All American).

Big Eight Conference

	Conference				Overall			
	W	L	T	PF	PA	W	L	T	PF	PA
*Colorado	7	0	0	266	113	11	1	1	399	229
*Nebraska	5	2	0	253	126	9	3	0	434	192
Oklahoma	5	2	0	250	126	8	3	0	401	174
Iowa St	2	4	1	150	216	4	6	1	270	307
Kansas	2	4	1	149	232	3	7	1	213	365
Kansas St	2	5	0	103	232	5	6	0	255	293
Missouri	2	5	0	177	263	4	7	0	278	360
Okla.St	2	5	0	162	202	4	7	0	233	309

Note: Oklahoma on probation, ineligible for postseason play.
*Bowls (1-1): Colorado (won Orange); Nebraska (lost Citrus).

Big Ten Conference

	Conference				Overall			
	W	L	T	PF	PA	W	L	T	PF	PA
*Iowa	6	2	0	264	169	8	4	0	427	288
*Michigan	6	2	0	247	135	9	3	0	389	198
*Mich.St	6	2	0	219	154	8	3	1	312	223
*Illinois	6	2	0	198	145	8	4	0	293	246
*Ohio St	5	2	1	264	142	7	4	1	349	220
Minnesota	5	3	0	175	174	6	5	0	224	281
*Indiana	3	4	1	166	174	6	5	1	329	238
N'western	1	7	0	148	305	2	9	0	210	370
Purdue	1	7	0	111	267	2	9	0	177	337
Wisconsin	0	8	0	79	226	1	10	0	133	285

Tiebreaker: Iowa beat Michigan St.(12-7, Oct.6), Michigan (24-23, Oct.20) and Illinois (54-28, Nov.3).
*Bowls (2-4): Iowa (lost Rose); Michigan (won Gator); Michigan St.(won Hancock); Illinois (lost Hall of Fame); Ohio St.(lost Liberty); Indiana (lost Peach).

Big West Conference

	Conference				Overall			
	W	L	T	PF	PA	W	L	T	PF	PA
*San Jose St	7	0	0	297	116	9	2	1	435	228
Fresno St.	5	1	1	232	123	8	2	1	346	230
Utah St	5	1	1	260	149	5	5	1	287	310
L.Beach St	4	3	0	183	190	6	5	0	249	331
UNLV	3	4	0	147	210	4	7	0	239	324
Pacific	2	5	0	240	253	4	7	0	353	411
N.Mexico St	1	6	0	147	279	1	10	0	200	422
CS-Fullerton	0	7	0	117	303	1	11	0	223	485

*Bowl (1-0): San Jose St.(won California Raisin).

Mid-American Conference

	Conference				Overall			
	W	L	T	PF	PA	W	L	T	PF	PA
*C.Michigan	7	1	0	194	64	8	3	1	283	146
Toledo	7	1	0	208	122	9	2	0	284	178
Ball St	5	3	0	142	94	7	4	0	204	121
W.Michigan	5	3	0	178	160	7	4	0	249	235
Miami-OH	4	3	1	177	144	5	5	1	200	225
Bowl.Green	2	4	2	97	122	3	5	2	138	163
E.Michigan	2	6	0	149	199	2	9	0	179	301
Kent	2	6	0	119	228	2	9	0	177	328
Ohio Univ.	0	7	1	117	248	1	9	1	162	342

Tiebreaker: Central Mich. beat Toledo (13-12, Oct.20).
*Bowl (0-1): Central Mich.(lost California Raisin).

Pacific-10 Conference

	Conference				Overall			
	W	L	T	PF	PA	W	L	T	PF	PA
*Washington	7	1	0	340	99	10	2	0	440	184
*USC	5	2	1	238	191	8	4	1	348	274
*Oregon	4	3	0	129	122	8	4	0	341	221
*California	4	3	1	221	228	7	4	1	325	341
*Arizona	5	4	0	214	257	7	5	0	267	311
Stanford	4	4	0	187	203	5	6	0	263	284
UCLA	4	4	0	231	229	5	6	0	305	332
Arizona St	2	5	0	153	169	4	7	0	272	294
Wash.St.	2	6	0	216	294	3	8	0	286	381
Oregon St	1	6	0	98	235	1	10	0	152	371

*Bowls (2-3): Washington (won Rose); USC (lost Hancock); Oregon (lost Freedom); California (won Copper); Arizona (lost Aloha).

Southeastern Conference

	Conference				Overall			
	W	L	T	PF	PA	W	L	T	PF	PA
Florida	6	1	0	221	116	9	2	0	387	171
*Tennessee	5	1	1	230	106	9	2	1	465	220
*Mississippi	5	2	0	140	119	9	3	0	260	226
*Alabama	5	2	0	159	78	7	5	0	260	161
*Auburn	4	2	1	170	132	8	3	1	283	216
Kentucky	3	4	0	163	214	4	7	0	228	316
LSU	2	5	0	112	168	5	6	0	183	238
Georgia	2	5	0	122	187	4	7	0	185	293
Miss.St.	1	6	0	102	173	5	6	0	207	236
Vanderbilt	1	6	0	140	266	1	10	0	227	457

Note: Florida on probation, ineligible for postseason play.
*Bowls (2-2): Tennessee (won Sugar); Ole Miss (lost Gator); Alabama (lost Fiesta); Auburn (won Peach).

Southwest Conference

	Conference				Overall			
	W	L	T	PF	PA	W	L	T	PF	PA
*Texas	8	0	0	302	126	10	2	0	358	227
Houston	7	1	0	328	228	10	1	0	511	303
*Texas A&M	5	2	1	261	166	9	3	1	465	232
Baylor	5	2	1	199	146	6	4	1	225	202
Rice	3	5	0	182	206	5	6	0	256	258
TCU	3	5	0	238	292	5	6	0	292	353
Texas Tech	3	5	0	268	262	4	7	0	322	356
Arkansas	1	7	0	187	316	3	8	0	263	360
SMU	0	8	0	139	362	1	10	0	197	426

Note: Houston on probation, ineligible for postseason play.
*Bowls (1-1): Texas (lost Cotton); Texas A&M (won Holiday).

Western Athletic Conference

	Conference					Overall			
	W	L	T	PF	PA	W	L	T	PF	PA
*BYU	7	1	0	371	186	10	3	0	524	350
*Colo.St	6	1	0	198	260	9	4	0	372	302
S.Diego St	5	2	0	341	249	6	5	0	459	386
*Wyoming	5	3	0	185	205	9	4	0	327	297
Hawaii	4	4	0	237	181	7	5	0	374	257
*Air Force	3	4	0	163	198	7	5	0	262	283
Utah	2	6	0	153	282	4	7	0	214	342
New Mexico	1	6	0	185	267	2	10	0	279	400
UTEP	1	7	0	147	252	3	8	0	191	342

Bowls (2-2): BYU (lost Holiday); Colo.St.(won Freedom); Wyoming (lost Copper); Air Force (won Liberty).

Major Independents

	W	L	T	PF	PA
*Louisville	10	1	1	345	149
*Florida St	10	2	0	459	206
*Miami-FL	10	2	0	447	184
*Notre Dame	9	3	0	359	259
*Penn St	9	3	0	297	179
*Louisiana Tech	8	3	1	365	219
*Southern Mississippi	8	4	0	220	172
Temple	7	4	0	261	269
*Syracuse	7	4	2	341	213
Army	6	5	0	295	264
Northern Illinois	6	5	0	333	260
South Carolina	6	5	0	282	237
Virginia Tech	6	5	0	245	227
East Carolina	5	6	0	254	267
Navy	5	6	0	209	294
Southwestern Louisiana	5	6	0	197	242
Memphis St	4	6	1	212	233
Boston College	4	7	0	190	288
Tulane	4	7	0	237	253
West Virginia	4	7	0	217	238
Akron	3	7	1	233	263
Pittsburgh	3	7	1	240	293
Rutgers	3	8	0	173	302
Tulsa	3	8	0	183	281
Cincinnati	1	10	0	172	460

Bowls (4-3-1): Louisville (won Fiesta); Fla.St.(won Blockbuster); Miami-FL (won Sugar); Notre Dame (lost Orange); Penn St.(lost Blockbuster); La.Tech (tied Maryland); Southern Miss (lost All American); Syracuse (won Aloha).

Final UPI Top 25 Poll

Voted on by panel of 50 Division I-A head coaches: first place votes in parentheses with total points (based on 15 for 1st, 14 for 2nd, etc.).

	Pts			Pts
1 Ga.Tech (30)	847	14	Michigan St	120
2 Colorado (27)	846	15	Virginia	65
3 Miami-FL (2)	763	16	Iowa	57
4 Florida St	677	17	BYU	41
5 Washington	664		Nebraska	41
6 Notre Dame	548	19	Auburn	39
7 Tennessee	449	20	San Jose St	16
8 Michigan	426	21	Syracuse	12
9 Clemson	420	22	USC	9
10 Penn St	301	23	Mississippi	7
11 Texas	268	24	Illinois	6
12 Louisville	245	25	Virginia Tech	5
13 Texas A&M	204			

Other teams receiving votes (in alphabetical order): Baylor, Louisiana Tech, N.C.State and Ohio St. **Teams on probation** (and ineligible to receive votes): Florida, Houston, Memphis St., Oklahoma and Oklahoma St.

Final NY Times Top 20

Based on an analysis of each team's scores with emphasis on three factors: who won, by what margin, and against what quality opposition. Computer balances lop-sided scores, notes home field advantage and gives late season games more weight than those played earlier in the schedule. The top team is assigned a rating of 1.000, ratings of all other teams reflect their strength relative to strength of No.1 team.

		Rating			Rating
1	Miami-FL	1.000	11	Notre Dame	.859
2	Ga.Tech	.986	12	Louisville	.851
3	Colorado	.969	13	Penn St	.847
4	Washington	.940	14	Tennessee	.846
5	Clemson	.931	15	Oklahoma	.842
6	Florida St	.929	16	Texas A&M	.831
7	Michigan	.921	17	Nebraska	.785
8	Florida	.905	18	BYU	.760
9	Texas	.902	19	Auburn	.755
10	Houston	.862		Michigan St	.755

Records of Top 3 Teams

Games with ranked opponents, according to weekly AP Top 25 polls, are indicated.

Colorado (11-1-1)

Date	Opponent	Result
Aug.26	#8 Tennessee (@ Anaheim)	T, 31-31
Sep. 6	Stanford	W, 21-17
Sep.15	at #21 Illinois	L, 22-23
Sep.22	at #22 Texas	W, 29-22
Sep.29	#12 Washington	W, 20-14
Oct. 6	at Missouri	W, 33-31
Oct.13	Iowa St	W, 28-12
Oct.20	at Kansas	W, 41-10
Oct.27	#22 Oklahoma	W, 32-23
Nov. 3	at #3 Nebraska	W, 27-12
Nov.10	Oklahoma St	W, 41-22
Nov.17	Kansas St	W, 64-3
Jan. 1	#5 Notre Dame (Orange Bowl)	W, 10-9

Georgia Tech (11-0-1)

Date	Opponent	Result
Sep. 8	N.C.State	W, 21-13
Sep.22	Tennessee-Chattanooga	W, 44-9
Sep.29	#25 South Carolina	W, 27-6
Oct. 6	at Maryland	W, 31-3
Oct.13	#15 Clemson	W, 21-19
Oct.20	at North Carolina	T, 13-13
Oct.27	Duke	W, 48-31
Nov. 3	at #1 Virginia	W, 41-38
Nov.10	Virginia Tech	W, 6-3
Nov.17	at Wake Forest	W, 42-7
Dec. 1	at Georgia	W, 40-23
Jan. 1	#19 Nebraska (Citrus Bowl)	W, 45-21

Miami-FL (10-2)

Date	Opponent	Result
Sep. 8	at #16 BYU	L, 21-28
Sep.15	at California	W, 52-24
Sep.29	Iowa	W, 48-21
Oct. 6	#2 Florida St	W, 31-22
Oct.13	Kansas	W, 34-0
Oct.20	at #6 Notre Dame	L, 20-29
Oct.27	at Texas Tech	W, 45-10
Nov. 3	Pittsburgh	W, 45-0
Nov.17	Boston College	W, 42-12
Nov.24	Syracuse	W, 33-7
Dec. 1	at San Diego St	W, 30-28
Jan. 1	#3 Texas (Cotton Bowl)	W, 46-3

Annual Awards

Heisman Trophy Vote

Presented since 1935 by the Downtown Athletic Club of New York and named after former college coach and DAC athletic director John W.Heisman. Voting done by national media and former Heisman winners. Each ballot allows for three names (points based on 3 for 1st, 2 for 2nd and 1 for 3rd).

Top 10 Vote-Getters

	Pos	1st	2nd	3rd	Pts
Ty Detmer, BYU	QB	316	208	118	1482
Rocket Ismail, N.Dame	FL	237	174	118	1177
Eric Bieniemy, Colo	RB	114	153	150	798
Shawn Moore, Virg	QB	46	96	135	465
David Klingler, Hou	QB	7	27	50	125
Herman Moore, Virg	WR	6	14	22	68
Greg Lewis, Wash	RB	4	5	19	41
Darren Lewis, Tex.A&M	RB	0	9	13	31
Craig Erickson, Miami	QB	0	6	19	31
Mike Mayweather, Army	RB	3	4	3	20

Note: Detmer, Ismail, Klingler and H.Moore were juniors. All other players were seniors.

Offensive Players of the Year

Maxwell Award (Top Player) .... Ty Detmer
UPI Player of Year .... Ty Detmer
Walter Camp Award (Top Player)...... Rocket Ismail
Wash.TD Club Camp Award (Top Back)
.... David Klingler
Davey O'Brien Award(Top QB) .... Ty Detmer

Defensive Players of the Year

UPI Lineman of Year...... Russell Maryland, Miami-FL
Outland Trophy (Top Interior Lineman)
.... Russell Maryland
Wash.TD Club Rockne Award (Top Lineman)
.... Chris Zorich, Notre Dame
Lombardi Award (Top Lineman).......... Chris Zorich
Butkus Award (Top LB) .... Alfred Williams, Colo.
Thorpe Award (Top DB) .... Darryl Lewis, Arizona

Coaches of the Year

FWAA Writers .... Bobby Ross, Ga.Tech
AFCA Coaches .... Bobby Ross

Consensus All-America Team

NCAA Division I-A players cited most frequently by the following five selectors: AFCA, AP, FWAA, UPI and Walter Camp Foundation. Holdovers from 1989 All-America team are in **bold** type; (*) indicates unanimous selection.

Offense

	Class	Hgt	Wgt
WR—Rocket Ismail, Notre Dame*	Jr.	5-10	175
WR—Herman Moore, Virginia	Jr.	6-5	197
TE—Chris Smith, BYU*	Sr.	6-4	230
L—Antone Davis, Tennessee*	Sr.	6-4	310
L—**Joe Garten**, Colorado*	Sr.	6-3	280
L—Ed King, Auburn*	Jr.	6-4	284
L—Stacy Long, Clemson	Sr.	6-2	275
C—John Flannery, Syracuse	Sr.	6-4	301
QB—Ty Detmer, BYU	Jr.	6-0	175
RB—Eric Bieniemy, Colorado*	Jr.	5-7	195
RB—Darren Lewis, Texas A&M	Sr.	6-0	220
K—Philip Doyle, Alabama*	Sr.	6-1	190

Defense

	Class	Hgt	Wgt
L—Russell Maryland, Miami-FL*	Sr.	6-2	273
L—**Chris Zorich**, Notre Dame*	Sr.	6-1	266
L—**Moe Gardner**, Illinois	Sr.	6-2	258
L—Davis Rocker, Auburn	Sr.	6-4	264
LB—**Alfred Williams**, Colorado*	Jr.	6-6	236
LB—Michael Stonebreaker, N.Dame*	Sr.	6-1	228
LB—Maurice Crum, Miami-FL	Sr.	6-0	222
B—**Tripp Welborne**, Michigan*	Sr.	6-1	201
B—Darryl Lewis, Arizona*	Sr.	5-9	186
B—Ken Swilling, Ga.Tech*	Jr.	6-3	230
B—**Todd Lyght**, Notre Dame*	Sr.	6-1	184
P—Brian Greenfield, Pitt	Sr.	6-1	210

Underclassmen Selected in 1991 NFL Draft

Twenty-nine players—all juniors except sophomores Todd Marinovich, Jon Vaughn and Chuck Webb—forfeited the remainder of their college eligibility and declared for the NFL Draft in 1991. NFL teams drafted 22 underclassmen, including Notre Dame's Raghib (Rocket) Ismail, who decided the night before the NFL Draft to sign with Toronto of the Canadian Football League.

First Round (4) | **Drafted by**
6 Eric Swann, no college, DE................. Phoenix
10 Herman Moore, Virginia, WR............... Detroit
14 Leonard Russell, Ariz.St., RB .... New England
24 Todd Marinovich, USC, QB.............. LA Raiders
Second Round (2)
29 Ed King, Auburn, G...................... Cleveland
48 Jesse Campbell, N.C.State, DB .... Philadelphia
Third Round (4)
74 David Daniels, Penn St., WR................. Seattle
78 Chris Gardocki, Clemson, PK............... Chicago
80 Robert Wilson, Texas A&M, RB........... Tampa Bay
81 Chuck Webb, Tennessee, RB.............. Green Bay

Fourth Round (6)
86 Dexter Davis, Clemson, DB .... Phoenix
88 Sammy Walker, Texas Tech, DB......... Pittsburgh
92 Randy Baldwin, Mississippi, RB............. Minnesota
97 Curvin Richards, Pitt, RB..................... Dallas
100 Rocket Ismail, Notre Dame, WR .... LA Raiders
109 Rob Carpenter, Syracuse, WR.............. Cincinnati
Fifth Round (3)
112 Jon Vaughn, Michigan, RB .... New England
124 Ben Coates, Livingstone, TE .... New England
126 Reggie Jones, Memphis St., DB.......... New Orleans
Tenth Round (2)
258 Pete Lucas, WI-Stevens Pt., OT .... Atlanta
264 Sean Love, Penn St., G .... Dallas
Twelfth Round (1)
312 Ernie Thompson, Indiana, RB .... LA Rams

Underclassmen Left Undrafted (7)

Chris Blackmon (LB), S.Carolina St.; Dennis Brown (PK), Abilene Christian; Richard Buchanan (WR), Northwestern; Irvin Clark (DL) Florida A&M; Ryan Duve (TE), Utah St.; Jerry Renners (TE), Butler; Rob Turner (WR), Indiana.

NCAA Division I-A Individual Leaders

REGULAR SEASON

Total Offense

		Rushing			Passing		Total Offense				
	Car	Gain	Loss	Net	Att	Yds	Plays	Yds	YdsPP	TDR	YdsPG
David Klingler, Houston	61	245	164	+81	643	5140	704	5221	7.42	55	474.64
Ty Detmer, BYU	73	145	311	−166	562	5188	635	5022	7.91	45	418.50
Troy Kopp, Pacific	57	134	169	−35	428	3311	485	3276	6.75	32	364.00
Dan McGwire, San Diego St.	35	35	204	−169	449	3833	484	3664	7.57	28	333.09
Craig Erickson, Miami-FL	46	146	120	+26	393	3363	439	3389	7.72	25	308.09
Shane Matthews, Florida	72	180	207	−27	378	2952	450	2925	6.50	27	265.91
Ralph Martini, San Jose St.	51	136	141	−5	362	2928	413	2923	7.08	25	265.73
Tommy Maddox, UCLA	90	368	220	+148	327	2682	417	2830	6.79	19	257.27
Shawn Moore, Virginia	94	404	98	+306	241	2262	335	2568	7.67	29	256.80
Mark Barsotti, Fresno St.	61	350	102	+248	346	2534	407	2782	6.84	14	252.91

Games: All played 11, except Detmer (12); Moore (10); Kopp (9).

All-Purpose Running

	Gm	Rush	Rec	PR	KOR	Total Yds	YdsPG
Glyn Milburn, Stanford	11	729	632	267	594	2222	202.00
Sheldon Canley, San Jose St	11	1248	386	5	574	2213	201.18
Chuck Weatherspoon, Houston	11	1097	560	196	185	2038	185.27
Eric Bieniemy, Colorado	11	1628	159	0	31	1818	165.27
Jeff Sydner, Hawaii	12	390	820	483	265	1958	163.17
Greg Lewis, Washington	10	1279	345	0	0	1624	162.40
Russell White, California	11	1000*	127	0	629	1756	159.64
Dwayne Owens, Oregon St	9	364	49	0	1014	1427	158.56
Rocket Ismail, Notre Dame	11	537	702	151	336	1726	156.91
Dion Johnson, East Carolina	9	266	90	167	879	1402	155.78

Passing Efficiency
(Minimum 15 attempts per game)

	Gm	Att	Cmp	Cmp Pct	Int	Int Pct	Yds	Yds/ Att	TD	TD Pct	Rating Points
Shawn Moore, Virginia	10	241	144	59.75	8	3.32	2262	9.39	21	8.71	160.7
Ty Detmer, BYU	12	562	361	64.23	28	4.98	5188	9.23	41	7.30	155.9
Casey Weldon, Florida St	11	182	112	61.54	4	2.20	1600	8.79	12	6.59	152.7
Dan McGwire, San Diego St	11	449	270	60.13	7	1.56	3833	8.54	27	6.01	148.6
David Klingler, Houston	11	643	374	58.16	20	3.11	5140	7.99	54	8.40	146.8
Craig Erickson, Miami-FL	11	393	225	57.25	7	1.78	3363	8.56	22	5.60	144.0
Shane Matthews, Florida	11	378	229	60.58	12	3.17	2952	7.81	23	6.08	139.9
Garrett Gabriel, Hawaii	12	320	165	51.56	16	5.00	2752	8.60	25	7.81	139.6
Troy Kopp, Pacific	9	428	243	56.78	14	3.27	3311	7.74	31	7.24	139.1
Rick Mirer, Notre Dame	11	200	110	55.00	6	3.00	1824	9.12	8	4.00	138.8

Scoring

Non-Kickers

	Gm	TD	Pts	P/Gm
Stacey Robinson, No.Ill	11	19	120*	10.91
Aaron Craver, Fresno St	10	18	108	10.80
Amp Lee, Florida St.	11	18	108	9.82
Darren Lewis, Texas A&M	12	19	114	9.50
Eric Bieniemy, Colorado	11	17	102	9.27

Note: Robinson also had 6 extra points.

Kickers

	Gm	FG	XP	Pts	P/Gm
Roman Anderson, Hou	11	19	58	115	10.45
Andy Trakas, S.Diego St	11	18	53	107	9.73
Carlos Huerta, Miami-FL	11	17	50	101	9.18
Michael Pollak, Texas	11	20	39	99	9.00
Greg Burke, Tenn	12	19	50	107	8.92

Abbreviation Key

Att—Attempted passes; **Avg**—Average; **Car**—Carries; **CPG**—Catches Per Game; **Cmp**—Completions; **Ct**—Catches; **FG**—Field Goals; **FGA**—Field Goal Attempts; **FGPG**—Field Goals Per Game; **Gain**—Yards Gained; **Gm**—Games played; **Int**—Interceptions; **IPG**—Interceptions Per Game; **KOR**—Kickoff Return yards; **Loss**—Yards Lost; **Net**—Net yards gained; **No**—Number; **Pct**—Percentage; **Plays**—Plays from scrimmage; **PR**—Punt Return yards; **Pts**—points; **P/Gm**—Points Per Game; **Rec**—Receiving yards; **Rush**—Rushing yards; **TD**—Touchdowns; **TDR**—Touchdowns Responsible for; **XP**—Extra Points; **Yds**—Yards; **Yds/Att**—Yards per Attempt; **YdsPG**—Yards Per Game.

NCAA Division I-A Individual Leaders (Cont.)

Rushing

	Car	Yds	TD	YdsPG
Gerald Hudson, Okla St	279	1642	10	149.27
Eric Bieniemy, Colo.	288	1628	17	148.00
Darren Lewis, Tex.A&M	291	1691	18	140.92
Greg Lewis, Wash.	229	1279	8	127.90
Tico Duckett, Mich.St.	249	1376	10	125.09
Roger Grant, Utah St	266	1370	8	124.55
Mike Mayweather, Army.	274	1338	10	121.64
Trevor Cobb, Rice	283	1325	10	120.45
Sheldon Canley, S.Jose St	296	1248	12	113.45
Stacey Robinson, No.Ill.	193	1238	19	112.55

Games: All played 11, except D.Lewis (12); G.Lewis (10).

Receiving

	Ct	Yds	TD	CPG
Manny Hazard, Houston	78	946	9	7.80
Bobby Slaughter, La.Tech.	78	994	5	7.09
Eric Morgan, New Mexico	80	1043	6	6.67
Andy Boyce, BYU	79	1241	13	6.58
Patrick Rowe, S.Diego St	71	1392	8	6.45
Frank Wycheck, Maryland	58	509	1	6.44
Dennis Arey, S.Diego St	68	1118	10	6.18
Keenan McCardell, UNLV	68	1046	8	6.18
Ed McCaffrey, Stanford.	61	917	8	6.10
Tracy Good, Houston	67	616	5	6.09

Games: All played 11, except Boyce and Morgan (12); Hazard and McCaffrey (10); Wycheck (9).

Interceptions

	No	Yds	TD	IPG
Jerry Parks, Houston	8	124	1	0.73
Will Lewis, Florida	7	116	0	0.70
Darryl Lewis, Arizona	7	192	2	0.64
Shawn Vincent, Akron	7	191	0	0.64
Ron Carpenter, Miami-OH.	7	164	1	0.64
Darren Perry, Penn St	7	125	1	0.64
Mike Welch, Baylor	7	80	0	0.64
Ozzie Jackson, Akron	7	50	0	0.64

Games: All played 11, except White (10).

Field Goals

	FGA	FG	Pct	FGPG
Philip Doyle, Alabama	29	24	.828	2.18
Clint Gwaltney, N.Carolina	27	21	.778	1.91
Michael Pollak, Texas	26	20	.769	1.82
Chris Gardocki, Clemson.	24	19	.792	1.73
John Kasay, Georgia	24	19	.792	1.73
Roman Anderson, Houston	25	19	.760	1.73
Bob Wright, Temple	25	19	.760	1.73
Jeff Shudak, Iowa St	27	19	.704	1.73
Andy Trakas, S.Diego St	26	18	.692	1.64
Rusty Hanna, Toledo.	29	18	.621	1.64

Games: All played 11.

Punting
(Minimum of 3.6 per game)

	No	Yds	Avg
Cris Shale, Bowling Green	66	3087	46.77
Brian Greenfield, Pittsburgh	50	2280	45.60
Jason Hanson, Washington St	59	2679	45.41
Chris Gardocki, Clemson	53	2350	44.34
Greg Hertzog, West Virginia	62	2697	43.50
Scott McAlister, North Carolina	79	4334	33.46

Punt Returns
(Minimum of 1.2 per game)

	No	Yds	TD	Avg
Dave McCloughan, Colorado	32	524	2	16.38
Beno Bryant, Washington	36	560	3	15.56
Jeff Graham, Ohio St	22	327	2	14.86
Tony James, Miss.St	23	341	2	14.83
Tripp Welborne, Michigan	31	455	0	14.68

Kickoff Returns
(Minimum of 1.2 per game)

	No	Yds	TD	Avg
Dale Carter, Tennessee	17	507	1	29.82
Desmond Howard, Michigan	16	472	1	29.50
Tyrone Hughes, Nebraska	18	523	1	29.06
Ray Washington, N.Mexico St	22	638	1	29.00
Randy Jones, Duke	24	678	2	28.25

NCAA Division I-A Team Leaders

REGULAR SEASON

Scoring Offense

	Gm	Record	Pts	Avg
Houston.	11	10-1-0	511	46.5
BYU	12	10-2-0	510	42.5
San Diego St.	11	6-5-0	459	41.7
Virginia	11	8-3-0	442	40.2
Florida St	11	9-2-0	435	39.5
Nebraska	11	9-2-0	413	37.5
Tennessee	12	8-2-2	442	36.8
Miami-FL.	11	9-2-0	401	36.5
Oklahoma.	11	8-3-0	401	36.5
Washington.	11	9-2-0	394	35.8

Scoring Defense

	Gm	Record	Pts	Avg
Central Michigan	11	8-2-1	98	8.9
Clemson	11	9-2-0	109	9.9
Ball St.	11	7-4-0	121	11.0
Alabama.	11	7-4-0	127	11.5
Southern Mississippi	11	8-3-0	141	12.8
Louisville	11	9-1-1	142	12.9
Nebraska	11	9-2-0	147	13.4
Washington.	11	9-2-0	150	13.6
Penn St.	11	9-2-0	155	14.1
N.C.State.	11	6-5-0	162	14.7

Total Offense

	Gm	Plays	Yds	Avg	TD	YdsPG
Houston.	11	905	6455	7.1	63	586.82
BYU	12	968	6788	7.0	64	565.67
San Diego St	11	927	5798	6.3	57	527.09
Virginia	11	804	5516	6.9	55	501.45
Miami-FL.	11	842	5312	6.3	49	482.91
Texas A&M	12	875	5653	6.5	50	471.08
San Jose St	11	872	5116	5.9	51	465.09
Pacific	11	835	5080	6.1	47	461.82
Fresno St	11	868	5026	5.8	45	456.91
Florida.	11	855	4978	5.8	44	452.55

Note: Touchdowns scored by rushing and passing only.

Total Defense

	Gm	Plays	Yds	Avg	TD	YdsPG
Clemson	11	678	2386	3.5	10	216.9
Ball St.	11	708	2449	3.5	12	222.6
Alabama.	11	711	2523	3.5	11	229.4
Central Michigan	11	681	2559	3.8	8	232.6
Florida	11	708	2834	4.0	17	257.6
Louisville	11	737	2855	3.9	13	259.5
Nebraska	11	724	2898	4.0	16	263.5
Auburn	11	738	3002	4.1	22	272.9
Miami-OH.	11	765	3036	4.0	26	276.0
N.C.State.	11	772	3054	4.0	17	277.6

Note: Opponents' TDs scored by rushing and passing only.

1990 NCAA DIVISION I-AA PLAYOFFS

1ST ROUND Nov. 24	QUARTERS Dec. 1	SEMIFINAL Dec. 8		SEMIFINAL Dec. 8	QUARTERS Dec. 1	1ST ROUND Nov. 24

Mid. Tenn. St. 28
Jackson St. 7
Mid. Tenn. St. 13
Boise St. 20
Northern Iowa 3
Boise St. 20
Boise St. 52

Central Fla. 7
Central Fla. 52
Wm. & Mary 38

Youngstown St. 17
Central Fla. 20
Wm. & Mary 38
Massachusetts 0

NCAA

CHAMPIONSHIP GAME
Ga. Southern 36
Nevada 13
Dec. 15, 1990
Statesboro, GA

Nevada 27
NE Louisiana 14 (3OT)
Nevada 42
Nevada 59 (3OT)

Eastern Ky. 17
Furman 45
Furman 35

Ga. Southern 44
Ga. Southern 28
Idaho 27

Ga. Southern 31
The Citadel 0
SW Mo. St. 35
Idaho 41

Seeded Teams
1. Mid. Tenn. St. 2. Youngstown St. 3. Ga. Southern 4. Nevada

NCAA Division I-AA Final Standings
Overall records include postseason games.

Big Sky Conference

	Conference				Overall			
	W	L	T	PF	PA	W	L	T	PF	PA
*Nevada.........	7	1	0	239	147	13	2	0	497	321
*Idaho...........	6	2	0	289	168	9	4	0	477	342
*Boise St.........	6	2	0	222	131	10	4	0	382	258
Montana........	4	4	0	243	238	7	4	0	372	275
East.Wash.......	3	5	0	213	257	5	6	0	300	360
No.Ariz........	3	5	0	196	344	5	6	0	290	417
Weber St........	3	5	0	233	258	5	6	0	309	307
Montana St.....	3	5	0	223	227	4	7	0	268	304
Idaho St........	1	7	0	188	276	3	8	0	265	359

*Playoffs (6-3): Nevada (3-1, lost Final); Idaho (1-1,lost Quarterfinal); Boise St.(2-1, lost Semifinal).

Gateway Athletic Conference

	Conference				Overall			
	W	L	T	PF	PA	W	L	T	PF	PA
*No.Iowa	5	1	0	170	83	8	4	0	334	209
*SW Mo.St	5	1	0	209	103	9	3	0	413	219
Eastern Ill	3	3	0	95	134	5	6	0	180	219
Illinois St	3	3	0	120	131	5	6	0	198	189
Western Ill.......	3	3	0	118	151	3	8	0	194	314
Indiana St.......	1	5	0	132	163	4	7	0	263	289
Southern Ill	1	5	0	64	143	2	9	0	174	313

Note: No.Iowa beat SW Mo.St. (20-17, Nov.3).
*Playoffs (0-2): SW Mo.St.(0-1,lost 1st Round); No.Iowa (0-1, lost 1st Round).

Ivy League

	Conference				Overall			
	W	L	T	PF	PA	W	L	T	PF	PA
Dartmouth	6	1	0	147	65	7	2	1	211	121
Cornell	6	1	0	180	95	7	3	0	263	212
Yale............	5	2	0	201	132	6	4	0	233	223
Harvard	3	4	0	140	158	5	5	0	199	206
Penn	3	4	0	123	138	3	7	0	155	197
Princeton........	2	5	0	123	157	3	7	0	168	224
Brown..........	2	5	0	129	186	2	8	0	160	299
Columbia........	1	6	0	56	168	1	9	0	115	292

Note: Dartmouth beat Cornell (11-6, Oct.20).
*Playoffs: league does not play postseason games.

Mid-Eastern Athletic Conference

	Conference				Overall			
	W	L	T	PF	PA	W	L	T	PF	PA
Florida A&M.....	6	0	0	209	125	7	4	0	349	289
N.Car.A&T.......	5	1	0	179	83	9	2	0	311	175
Delaware St......	4	2	0	218	154	7	3	0	330	251
Howard	3	3	0	141	141	6	5	0	261	205
S.C.State........	2	4	0	111	113	4	6	0	191	176
Beth-Cook.......	1	5	0	117	181	4	7	0	205	312
Morgan St	0	6	0	42	220	1	10	0	81	412

Playoffs: no teams from league qualified.

Ohio Valley Conference

	Conference				Overall			
	W	L	T	PF	PA	W	L	T	PF	PA
*Eastern Ky.......	5	1	0	191	85	10	2	0	369	200
*Mid.Tenn.St......	5	1	0	211	33	11	2	0	425	128
Tenn.St	3	2	0	115	131	7	4	0	268	261
Morehead St......	3	2	0	137	91	5	6	0	268	223
Tenn.Tech.......	3	3	0	94	131	6	5	0	242	256
Murray St	1	5	0	67	205	2	9	0	95	429
Austin Peay......	0	6	0	73	212	0	11	0	108	339

Note: Eastern Ky. beat Mid.Tenn.St. (10-7, Oct.6).
*Playoffs (1-2): Eastern Ky.(0-1,lost 1st Round); Mid.Tenn.St.(1-1,lost Quarterfinal).

Patriot League

	Conference				Overall			
	W	L	T	PF	PA	W	L	T	PF	PA
Holy Cross	5	0	0	194	45	9	1	1	339	106
Bucknell	3	2	0	139	119	7	4	0	337	278
Colgate..........	3	2	0	108	128	7	4	0	296	248
Lehigh..........	3	2	0	171	88	7	4	0	329	211
Lafayette........	1	4	0	97	143	4	7	0	223	318
Fordham	0	5	0	31	217	1	9	0	127	342

*Playoffs: league does not play postseason games.

NCAA Division I-AA Final Standings (Cont.)

Southern Conference

	Conference					Overall			
	W	L	T	PF	PA	W	L	T	PF	PA
*Furman	6	1	0	227	99	9	4	0	425	237
Appalach.St	5	2	0	135	139	6	5	0	171	266
Tenn-Chatt	4	2	0	119	114	6	5	0	227	243
*The Citadel	4	3	0	139	102	7	5	0	266	223
Marshall	4	3	0	204	116	6	5	0	310	162
W.Carolina	2	5	0	112	199	3	8	0	169	362
VMI	1	5	0	73	191	4	7	0	251	346
E.Tenn.St.	1	6	0	130	179	2	9	0	240	330

*Playoffs (1-2): Furman (1-1,lost Quarterfinal); The Citadel (0-1,lost 1st Round).

Southland Conference

	Conference					Overall			
	W	L	T	PF	PA	W	L	T	PF	PA
NE Louisiana	5	1	0	111	77	7	5	0	208	218
McNeese St	4	2	0	112	104	5	6	0	183	265
SW Texas	3	3	0	131	101	6	5	0	268	220
N'western St.	3	3	0	111	104	5	6	0	203	203
Sam Houston	3	3	0	101	109	4	7	0	163	187
North Texas	2	4	0	108	125	6	5	0	223	211
S.F.Austin	1	5	0	63	117	1	10	0	149	230

*Playoffs (0-1): NE Louisiana (0-1,lost 1st Round).

Southwestern Athletic Conference

	Conference					Overall			
	W	L	T	PF	PA	W	L	T	PF	PA
*Jackson St.	5	1	0	258	143	8	4	0	425	262
Alabama St.	4	2	0	192	82	8	2	1	384	177
Grambling	3	3	0	172	166	8	3	0	364	227
Miss.Valley	3	3	0	148	206	5	6	0	237	327
Southern-BR	2	4	0	106	155	4	7	0	231	277
Tex.Southern	2	4	0	147	200	4	7	0	220	363
Alcorn St	2	4	0	114	185	2	7	0	128	268

*Playoffs (0-1): Jackson St.(0-1,lost 1st Round).

Yankee Conference

	Conference					Overall			
	W	L	T	PF	PA	W	L	T	PF	PA
*UMass	7	1	0	186	106	8	2	1	224	175
New Hamp.	5	3	0	183	136	7	3	1	301	186
Connecticut.	5	3	0	236	202	6	5	0	308	281
Delaware	5	3	0	164	168	6	5	0	216	233
Villanova	5	3	0	143	87	6	5	0	204	161
Boston Univ	4	4	0	177	211	5	6	0	246	273
Rhode Island	2	6	0	151	158	5	6	0	245	193
Maine	2	6	0	138	192	3	8	0	200	281
Richmond	1	7	0	106	224	1	10	0	133	312

*Playoffs (0-1): Massachusetts (0-1,lost 1st Round).

Division I-AA, II and III Awards

Players of the Year

Payton Award (Div.I-AA) .... Walter Dean, RB
Grambling
Hill Trophy (Div.II) .... Chris Simdorn, QB
N.Dakota St.

Coaches of the Year

AFCA (NCAA Div.I-AA) Tim Stowers, Ga.Southern
AFCA (College Div.I) Rocky Hager, N.Dakota St.
AFCA (College Div.II) Ken O'Keefe, Allegheny

I-AA Independents

	W	L	T	PF	PA
*Youngstown St.	11	1	0	340	146
*Georgia Southern	12	3	0	436	272
*William & Mary	10	3	0	467	322
*Central Florida	10	4	0	444	277
Liberty	7	4	0	296	236
Samford	6	4	1	268	233
James Madison	5	6	0	228	191
Nicholls St.	5	6	0	250	246
Arkansas St.	3	7	1	200	313
Western Kentucky	2	8	0	159	234
Towson St	2	9	0	163	336
Northeastern	1	10	0	144	342

*Playoffs (7-3): Youngstown St.(0-1,lost 1st Round); Ga.Southern (4-0, won Final); Wm.& Mary (1-1,lost Quarterfinal); Central Fla.(2-1, lost Semifinal).

NCAA Playoffs
Division II

First Round—Mississippi College 70, Wofford,SC 19; Jacksonville St.,AL 38, North Alabama 14; Indiana,PA 48, Winston-Salem St.,NC 0; Edinboro,PA 38, Virginia Union 14; North Dakota St. 17, Northern Colorado 7; Cal Poly-SLO 14, CS-Northridge 7; Pittsburg St.,KS 59, NE Missouri St. 3; East Texas St. 20, Grand Valley St.,MI 14.

Quarterfinals—Mississippi Col. 14, Jacksonville St. 7; Indiana,PA 14, Edinboro 7; North Dakota St. 47, Cal Poly-SLO 0; Pittsburg St. 60, East Texas St. 28. **Semifinals**—Indiana,PA 27, Mississippi Col. 8; North Dakota St. 39, Pittsburg St. 29.

Championship Game (Dec.8 at Florence, Ala.)—North Dakota St. 51, Indiana,PA 11. Final records—North Dakota St. (14-0), Indiana,PA (12-2).

Division III

First Round—Hofstra,NY 35, Cortland St.,NY 9; Trenton St.,NJ 24, Ithaca,NY 14; Washington & Jefferson,PA 10, Ferrum,VA 7; Lycoming,PA 17, Carnegie Mellon,PA 7; Dayton,OH 24, Augustana,IL 14; Allegheny,PA 26, Mount Union,OH 15; St.Thomas,MN 24, Wisc-Whitewater 23; Central,IA 44, Redlands,CA 14.

Quarterfinals—Hofstra 38, Trenton St. 3; Lycoming 24, Washington & Jefferson 0; Allegheny 31, Dayton 23; Central 33, St.Thomas 32. **Semifinals**—Lycoming 20, Hofstra 10; Allegheny 24, Central 7.

Amos Alonzo Stagg Bowl (Dec.8 at Bradenton, Fla.)—Allegheny 21, Lycoming 14. Final records—Allegheny (13-0-1), Lycoming (12-1).

NAIA Playoffs
Division I

First Round—Mesa St.,CO 37, Western New Mexico 30 (OT); Central Arkansas 26, Northeastern St.,OK 14; Carson-Newman,TN 35, Southwest St.,MN 6; Central St.,OH 48, Fort Hayes St.,KS 10. **Semifinals**—Mesa St. 10, Central Arkansas 9; Central St. 41, Carson-Newman 14.

Championship—Central St. 38, Mesa St. 16. Final records—Central St.(9-1), Mesa St.(9-3).

Division II

First Round—Westminster,PA 19, Tarleton St.,TX 17; Central Washington 24, Pacific Lutheran,WA 6; Peru St.,NE 38, Dickinson St.,ND 34; Baker,KS 56, William Jewell,MO 29. **Semifinals**—Westminster 24, Central Washington 17; Peru St. 9, Baker 3.

Championship—Peru St. 17, Westminster 7. Final records—Peru St.(12-0-1), Westminster (11-2).

COLLEGE FOOTBALL
S T A T I S T I C S

THE 1992 INFORMATION PLEASE SPORTS ALMANAC

SEC **B**

PAGE 135

THROUGH THE YEARS
1883-1991

BOWLS • ALL-TIME LEADERS

National Champions

Over the years, 23 different national selectors have chosen college football's Number One team by way of polls (12), mathematical rating systems (10) and historical research (1). The list below has been culled from six of those groups: the Helms Athletic Foundation (1883–1935), the Dickinson system (1924–40), the Associated Press (since 1936), United Press International (1950–57 as UP, since 1958 as UPI), the Football Writers Association of America (since 1954), and the National Football Foundation and Hall of Fame (since 1959).

Bowl game results were counted in the Helms selections but not in the Dickinson picks. The final AP poll was taken following the bowl games for the first time in 1965. After returning to a pre-bowls final vote in 1966 and '67, the AP poll has been taken following the bowls since 1968. The FWAA has selected its champion after the bowl games since 1955, the NFF since 1971, and UPI since 1974.

In years where more than one champion has been named, the selectors' initials are given.

Multiple champions (1883–1935): Yale (11), Princeton and Harvard (7); Michigan and Penn (4); Cornell, Notre Dame and USC (3); Alabama, Georgia Tech, Illinois, Minnesota and Pittsburgh (2).

Multiple champions (since 1936): Notre Dame (9); Alabama, Ohio St. and Oklahoma (6); USC (5); Minnesota (4); Miami-Fl, Michigan St. and Texas (3); Nebraska, Penn St. and Pittsburgh (2).

Year		Record	Year		Record	Year		Record
1883	Yale	8–0–0	1889	Princeton	10–0–0	1895	Penn	14–0–0
1884	Yale	9–0–0	1890	Harvard	11–0–0	1896	Princeton	10–0–1
1885	Princeton	9–0–0	1891	Yale	13–0–0	1897	Penn	15–0–0
1886	Yale	9–0–1	1892	Yale	13–0–0	1898	Harvard	11–0–0
1887	Yale	9–0–0	1893	Princeton	11–0–0	1899	Harvard	10–0–1
1888	Yale	13–0–0	1894	Yale	16–0–0			

Year		Record	Bowl Game	Head Coach	Outstanding Player
1900	Yale	12–0–0	No bowl	Malcolm McBride	Perry Hale, HB
1901	Michigan	11–0–0	Won Rose	Hurry Up Yost	Willie Heston, HB
1902	Michigan	11–0–0	No bowl	Hurry Up Yost	Willie Heston, HB
1903	Princeton	11–0–0	No bowl	Art Hillebrand	John DeWitt, G
1904	Penn	12–0–0	No bowl	Carl Williams	Andy Smith, HB
1905	Chicago	11–0–0	No bowl	Amos Alonzo Stagg	Walter Eckersall, QB
1906	Princeton	9–0–1	No bowl	Bill Roper	Ed Dillon, HB
1907	Yale	9–0–1	No bowl	Bill Knox	T.A.D. Jones, HB
1908	Penn	11–0–1	No bowl	Sol Metzger	Hunter Scarlett, E
1909	Yale	10–0–0	No bowl	Howard Jones	Ted Coy, FB
1910	Harvard	8–0–1	No bowl	Percy Houghton	Percy Wendell, HB
1911	Princeton	8–0–2	No bowl	Bill Roper	Sanford White, E
1912	Harvard	9–0–0	No bowl	Percy Houghton	Charley Brickley, HB
1913	Harvard	9–0–0	No bowl	Percy Houghton	Eddie Mahan, FB
1914	Army	9–0–0	No bowl	Charley Daly	John McEwan, C
1915	Cornell	9–0–0	No bowl	Al Sharpe	Charley Barrett, HB
1916	Pittsburgh	8–0–0	No bowl	Pop Warner	Bob Peck, C
1917	Georgia Tech	9–0–0	No bowl	John Heisman	George Strupper, HB
1918	Pittsburgh	4–1–0	No bowl	Pop Warner	Tom Davies, HB
1919	Harvard	9–0–1	Won Rose	Bob Fisher	Ed Casey, HB
1920	California	9–0–0	Won Rose	Andy Smith	Brick Muller, E
1921	Cornell	8–0–0	No bowl	Gil Dobie	Eddie Kaw, HB
1922	Cornell	8–0–0	No bowl	Gil Dobie	George Pfann, QB
1923	Illinois	8–0–0	No bowl	Bob Zuppke	Red Grange, HB
1924	Notre Dame	10–0–0	Won Rose	Knute Rockne	"The Four Horsemen"*
1925	Alabama (H)	10–0–0	Won Rose	Wallace Wade	Johnny Mack Brown, HB
	Dartmouth (D)	8–0–0	No bowl	Jesse Hawley	Andy Oberlander, HB
1926	Alabama (H)	9–0–1	Tied Rose	Wallace Wade	Hoyt Winslett, E
	Stanford (D)	10–0–1	Tied Rose	Pop Warner	Ted Shipkey, E

*Notre Dame's **Four Horsemen** were Harry Stuhldreher (QB), Jim Crowley (HB), Don Miller (HB-P) and Elmer Layden (FB).

National Champions (Cont.)

Year		Record	Bowl Game	Head Coach	Outstanding Player
1927	**Illinois**	7-0-1	No bowl	Bob Zuppke	Russ Crane, G
1928	**Georgia Tech** (H)	10-0-0	Won Rose	Bill Alexander	Pete Pund, C
	USC (D)	9-0-1	No bowl	Howard Jones	Lloyd Thomas, HB
1929	**Notre Dame**	9-0-0	No bowl	Knute Rockne	Frank Carideo, QB
1930	**Notre Dame**	10-0-0	No bowl	Knute Rockne	Frank Carideo, QB
1931	**USC**	10-1-0	Won Rose	Howard Jones	Ernie Pinckert, HB
1932	**USC** (H)	10-0-0	Won Rose	Howard Jones	Ernie Smith, T-K
	Michigan (D)	8-0-0	No bowl	Harry Kipke	Harry Newman, QB
1933	**Michigan**	7-0-1	No bowl	Harry Kipke	Frank Wistert, T
1934	**Minnesota**	8-0-0	No bowl	Bernie Bierman	Pug Lund, HB
1935	**Minnesota** (H)	8-0-0	No bowl	Bernie Bierman	Dick Smith, T
	SMU (D)	12-1-0	Lost Rose	Matty Bell	Bobby Wilson, HB
1936	**Minnesota**	7-1-0	No bowl	Bernie Bierman	Ed Widseth, T
1937	**Pittsburgh**	9-0-1	No bowl	Jock Sutherland	Marshall Goldberg, HB
1938	**TCU**	11-0-0	Won Sugar	Dutch Meyer	Davey O'Brien, QB
1939	**Texas A&M**	11-0-0	Won Sugar	Homer Norton	John Kimbrough, FB
1940	**Minnesota**	8-0-0	No Bowl	Bernie Bierman	George Franck, FB
1941	**Minnesota**	8-0-0	No bowl	Bernie Bierman	Bruce Smith, HB
1942	**Ohio St.**	9-1-0	No bowl	Paul Brown	Gene Fekete, FB
1943	**Notre Dame**	9-1-0	No bowl	Frank Leahy	Angelo Bertelli, QB
1944	**Army**	9-0-0	No bowl	Red Blaik	Glenn Davis, HB
1945	**Army**	9-0-0	No bowl	Red Blaik	Doc Blanchard, FB
1946	**Notre Dame**	8-0-1	No bowl	Frank Leahy	Johnny Lujack, QB
1947	**Notre Dame**	9-0-0	No bowl	Frank Leahy	Johnny Lujack, QB
	Michigan†	10-0-0	Won Rose	Fritz Crisler	Bob Chappuis, HB
1948	**Michigan**	9-0-0	No bowl	Bennie Oosterbaan	Dick Rifenburg, E
1949	**Notre Dame**	10-0-0	No bowl	Frank Leahy	Leon Hart, E
1950	**Oklahoma**	10-1-0	Lost Sugar	Bud Wilkinson	Leon Heath, FB
1951	**Tennessee**	10-0-0	Lost Sugar	Bob Neyland	Hank Lauricella, QB
1952	**Michigan St.**	9-0-0	No bowl	Biggie Munn	Don McAuliffe, HB
1953	**Maryland**	10-1-0	Lost Orange	Jim Tatum	Bernie Faloney, QB
1954	**Ohio St.** (AP)	10-0-0	Won Rose	Woody Hayes	Howard Cassady, HB
	UCLA (UP, FW)	9-0-0	No bowl	Red Sanders	Bob Davenport, FB
1955	**Oklahoma**	11-0-0	Won Orange	Bud Wilkinson	Jerry Tubbs, C
1956	**Oklahoma**	10-0-0	No bowl	Bud Wilkinson	Tommy McDonald, HB
1957	**Auburn**	10-0-0	No bowl	Shug Jordan	Jimmy Phillips, E
	Ohio St. (UP, FW)	9-1-0	Won Rose	Woody Hayes	Bob White, FB
1958	**LSU** (AP, UPI)	11-0-0	Won Sugar	Paul Dietzel	Billy Cannon, HB
	Iowa (FW)	8-1-1	Won Rose	Forest Evdshevski	Ranky Duncan, QB
1959	**Syracuse**	11-0-0	Won Cotton	Ben Schwartzwalder	Ernie Davis, HB
1960	**Minnesota** (AP, UPI, NFF)	8-2-0	Lost Rose	Murray Warmath	Tom Brown, G
	Mississippi (FW)	10-0-1	Won Sugar	Johnny Vaught	Jake Gibbs, QB
1961	**Alabama** (AP, UPI, NFF)	11-0-0	Won Sugar	Bear Bryant	Billy Neighbors, T
	Ohio St. (FW)	8-0-1	No bowl	Woody Hayes	Bob Ferguson, HB
1962	**USC**	11-0-0	Won Rose	John McKay	Hal Bedsole, E
1963	**Texas**	11-0-0	Won Cotton	Darrell Royal	Scott Appleton, T
1964	**Alabama** (AP, UPI)	10-1-0	Lost Orange	Bear Bryant	Joe Namath, QB
	Arkansas (FW)	11-0-0	Won Cotton	Frank Broyles	Ronnie Caveness, LB
	Notre Dame (NFF)	9-1-0	No bowl	Ara Parseghian	John Huarte, QB
1965	**Alabama** (AP, FW-tie)	9-1-1	Won Orange	Bear Bryant	Paul Crane, C
	Michigan St. (UPI, NFF, FW-tie)	10-1-0	Lost Rose	Duffy Daugherty	George Webster, LB
1966	**Notre Dame** (AP, UPI, FW, NFF-tie)	9-0-1	No bowl	Ara Parseghian	Jim Lynch, LB
	Michigan St. (NFF-tie)	9-0-1	No bowl	Duffy Daugherty	Bubba Smith, DE
1967	**USC**	10-1-0	Won Rose	John McKay	O.J. Simpson, HB
1968	**Ohio St.**	10-0-0	Won Rose	Woody Hayes	Rex Kern, QB
1969	**Texas**	11-0-0	Won Cotton	Darrell Royal	James Street, QB
1970	**Nebraska** (AP, FW)	11-0-1	Won Orange	Bob Devaney	Jerry Tagge, QB
	Texas (UPI, NFF-tie)	10-1-0	Lost Cotton	Darrell Royal	Steve Worster, RB
	Ohio St. (NFF-tie)	9-1-0	Lost Rose	Woody Hayes	Jim Stillwagon, MG
1971	**Nebraska**	13-0-0	Won Orange	Bob Devaney	Johnny Rodgers, WR
1972	**USC**	12-0-0	Won Rose	John McKay	Charles Young, TE
1973	**Notre Dame** (AP, FW, NFF)	11-0-0	Won Sugar	Ara Parseghian	Mike Townsend, DB
	Alabama (UPI)	11-1-0	Lost Sugar	Bear Bryant	Buddy Brown, OT
1974	**Oklahoma** (AP)	11-0-0	No bowl	Barry Switzer	Joe Washington, RB
	USC (UPI, FW, NFF)	10-1-1	Won Rose	John McKay	Anthony Davis, RB
1975	**Oklahoma**	11-1-0	Won Orange	Barry Switzer	Lee Roy Selmon, DT
1976	**Pittsburgh**	12-0-0	Won Sugar	Johnny Majors	Tony Dorsett, RB
1977	**Notre Dame**	11-1-0	Won Cotton	Dan Devine	Ross Browner, DE

Year		Record	Bowl Game	Head Coach	Outstanding Player
1978	**Alabama** (AP, FW, NFF)	11-1-0	Won Sugar	Bear Bryant	Marty Lyons, DT
	USC (UPI)	12-1-0	Won Rose	John Robinson	Charles White, RB
1979	**Alabama**	12-0-0	Won Sugar	Bear Bryant	Steadman Shealy, QB
1980	**Georgia**	12-0-0	Won Sugar	Vince Dooley	Herschel Walker, RB
1981	**Clemson**	12-0-0	Won Orange	Danny Ford	Jeff Davis, LB
1982	**Penn St.**	11-1-0	Won Sugar	Joe Paterno	Todd Blackledge, QB
1983	**Miami-FL**	11-1-0	Won Orange	H. Schnellenberger	Bernie Kosar, QB
1984	**BYU**	13-0-0	Won Holiday	LaVell Edwards	Robbie Bosco, QB
1985	**Oklahoma**	11-1-0	Won Orange	Barry Switzer	Brian Bosworth, LB
1986	**Penn St.**	12-0-0	Won Fiesta	Joe Paterno	D.J. Dozier, RB
1987	**Miami-FL**	12-0-0	Won Orange	Jimmy Johnson	Steve Walsh, QB
1988	**Notre Dame**	12-0-0	Won Fiesta	Lou Holtz	Tony Rice, QB
1989	**Miami-FL**	11-1-0	Won Sugar	Dennis Erickson	Craig Erickson, QB
1990	**Colorado** (AP, FW, NFF)	11-1-1	Won Orange	Bill McCartney	Eric Bieniemy, RB
	Georgia Tech (UPI)	11-0-1	Won Citrus	Bobby Ross	Shawn Jones, QB

Number 1 vs Number 2

Since the Associated Press writers poll started keeping track of such things in 1936, the No.1 and No.2 ranked teams in the country have met 25 times; 17 during the regular season and eight in bowl games. Since the first showdown in 1943, the No.1 team has beaten the No.2 team 15 times, lost eight and there have been two ties. Notre Dame (3-3-2) has been involved in eight of these games, two more than Oklahoma (1-5).

Each showdown is listed below with the date, the match-up, each team's record going into the game, the final score, the stadium and site.

Date	Match–up		Stadium
Oct. 9	#1 Notre Dame (2-0)	35	Michigan
1943	#2 Michigan (3-0)	12	(Ann Arbor)
Nov. 20	#1 Notre Dame (8-0)	14	Notre Dame
1943	#2 Iowa Pre-Flight (8-0)	13	(South Bend)
Dec. 2	#1 Army (8-0)	23	Municipal
1944	#2 Navy (6-2)	7	(Baltimore)
Nov. 10	#1 Army (6-0)	48	Yankee
1945	#2 Notre Dame (5-0-1)	0	(New York)
Dec. 1	#1 Army (8-0)	32	Municipal
1945	#2 Navy (7-0-1)	13	(Phila.)
Nov. 9	#1 Army (7-0)	0	Yankee
1946	#2 Notre Dame (5-0)	0	(New York)

• • • • •

Jan. 1	#1 USC (10-0)	42	ROSE BOWL
1963	#2 Wisconsin (8-1)	37	(Pasadena)
Oct. 12	#2 Texas (3-0)	28	Cotton Bowl
1963	#1 Oklahoma (2-0)	7	(Dallas)
Jan. 1	#1 Texas (10-0)	28	COTTON BOWL
1964	#2 Navy (9-1)	6	(Dallas)
Nov. 19	#1 Notre Dame (8-0)	10	Spartan
1966	#2 Michigan St. (9-0)	10	(E. Lansing)
Sep. 28	#1 Purdue (1-0)	37	Notre Dame
1968	#2 Notre Dame (1-0)	22	(South Bend)
Jan. 1	#1 Ohio St. (9-0)	27	ROSE BOWL
1969	#2 USC (9-0-1)	16	(Pasadena)
Dec. 6	#1 Texas (9-0)	15	Razorback
1969	#2 Arkansas (9-0)	14	(Fayetteville)

Date	Match–up		Stadium
Nov. 25	#1 Nebraska (10-0)	35	Owen Field
1971	#2 Oklahoma (9-0)	31	(Norman)
Jan. 1	#1 Nebraska (12-0)	38	ORANGE BOWL
1972	#2 Alabama (11-0)	6	(Miami)
Jan. 1	#2 Alabama (10-1)	14	SUGAR BOWL
1979	#1 Penn St. (11-0)	7	(New Orleans)

• • • • •

Sep. 26	#1 USC (2-0)	28	Coliseum
1981	#2 Oklahoma (1-0)	24	(Los Angeles)
Jan. 1	#2 Penn St. (10-1)	27	SUGAR BOWL
1983	#1 Georgia (11-0)	23	(New Orleans)
Oct. 19	#1 Iowa (5-0)	12	Kinnick
1985	#2 Michigan (5-0)	10	(Iowa City)
Sep. 27	#2 Miami, FL (3-0)	28	Orange Bowl
1986	#1 Oklahoma (2-0)	16	(Miami)
Jan. 2	#2 Penn St. (11-0)	14	FIESTA BOWL
1987	#1 Miami, FL (11-0)	10	(Tempe)
Nov. 21	#2 Oklahoma (10-0)	17	Memorial
1987	#1 Nebraska (10-0)	7	(Lincoln)
Jan. 1	#2 Miami, FL (11-0)	20	ORANGE BOWL
1988	#1 Oklahoma (11-0)	14	(Miami)
Nov. 26	#1 Notre Dame (10-0)	27	Coliseum
1988	#2 USC (10-0)	10	(Los Angeles)
Sep. 16	#2 Notre Dame (1-0)	24	Michigan
1989	#1 Michigan (0-0)	19	(Ann Arbor)

The Special Election That Didn't Count

There was one other No. 1 vs No. 2 confrontation, but it came in a special election or re-vote of AP selectors following the 1948 Rose Bowl. Here's what happened:

Unbeaten Notre Dame was declared 1947 national champion by AP on Dec. 8, two days after closing out an undefeated season with a 38-7 rout of then third-ranked USC in Los Angeles. Twenty-four days later, however, unbeaten Michigan, AP's final No. 2 team, clobbered now 8th-ranked USC, 49-0, in the Rose Bowl.

An immediate cry went up for an unprecedented two-team, "Who's No. 1," ballot and AP gave in. Michigan won the election, 226-119, with 12 voters calling it even, but AP ruled that the Dec. 8 final poll won by Notre Dame would be the vote of record.

Associated Press Final Polls

The Associated Press introduced its weekly college football poll of sportswriters (later, sportwriters and broadcasters) in 1936. The final AP poll was released at the end of the regular season until 1965, when bowl results were included for one year. After a two-year return to regular season games only, the final poll has come out after the bowls since 1968. The AP poll has appeared as a Top 20 (1936–61 and 68–88), Top 10 (1962–67) and Top 25 (since 1989).

1936

Final poll released Nov. 30. Top 20 regular season results after that: **Dec.5**—#8 Notre Dame tied USC, 13-13; #17 Tennessee tied Ole Miss, 0-0; #18 Arkansas over Texas, 6-0. **Dec.12**—#16 TCU over #6 Santa Clara, 9-0.

		As of Nov. 30	Head Coach	After Bowls
1	Minnesota	7-1-0	Bernie Bierman	same
2	LSU	9-0-1	Bernie Moore	9-1-1
3	Pittsburgh	7-1-1	Jock Sutherland	8-1-1
4	Alabama	8-0-1	Frank Thomas	same
5	Washington	7-1-1	Jimmy Phelan	7-2-1
6	Santa Clara	7-0-0	Buck Shaw	8-1-0
7	Northwestern	7-1-0	Pappy Waldorf	same
8	Notre Dame	6-2-0	Elmer Layden	6-2-1
9	Nebraska	7-2-0	Dana X.Bible	same
10	Penn	7-1-0	Harvey Harman	same
11	Duke	9-1-0	Wallace Wade	same
12	Yale	7-1-0	Ducky Pond	same
13	Dartmouth	7-1-1	Red Blaik	same
14	Duquesne	7-2-0	John Smith	8-2-0
15	Fordham	5-1-2	Jim Crowley	same
16	TCU	7-2-2	Dutch Meyer	9-2-2
17	Tennessee	6-2-1	Bob Neyland	6-2-2
18	Arkansas	6-3-0	Fred Thomsen	7-3-0
	Navy	6-3-0	Tom Hamilton	same
20	Marquette	7-1-0	Frank Murray	7-2-0

Key Bowl Games

Sugar—#6 Santa Clara over #2 LSU, 21-14; **Rose**—#3 Pitt over #5 Washington, 21-0; **Orange**—#14 Duquesne over Mississippi St., 13-12; **Cotton**—#16 TCU over #20 Marquette, 16-6.

1937

Final poll released Nov.29. Top 20 regular season results after that: **Dec.4**—#18 Rice over SMU, 15-7.

		As of Nov. 29	Head Coach	After Bowls
1	Pittsburgh	9-0-1	Jock Sutherland	same
2	California	9-0-1	Stub Allison	10-0-1
3	Fordham	7-0-1	Jim Crowley	same
4	Alabama	9-0-0	Frank Thomas	9-1-0
5	Minnesota	6-2-0	Bernie Bierman	same
6	Villanova	8-0-1	Clipper Smith	same
7	Dartmouth	7-0-2	Red Blaik	same
8	LSU	9-1-0	Bernie Moore	9-2-0
9	Notre Dame	6-2-1	Elmer Layden	same
	Santa Clara	8-0-0	Buck Shaw	9-0-0
11	Nebraska	6-1-2	Biff Jones	same
12	Yale	6-1-1	Ducky Pond	same
13	Ohio St.	6-2-0	Francis Schmidt	same
14	Holy Cross	8-0-2	Eddie Anderson	same
	Arkansas	6-2-2	Fred Thomsen	same
16	TCU	4-2-2	Dutch Meyer	same
17	Colorado	8-0-0	Bunnie Oakes	8-1-0
18	Rice	4-3-2	Jimmy Kitts	6-3-2
19	North Carolina	7-1-1	Ray Wolf	same
20	Duke	7-2-1	Wallace Wade	same

Key Bowl Games

Rose—#2 Cal over #4 Alabama, 13-0; **Sugar**—#9 Santa Clara over #8 LSU, 6-0; **Cotton**—#18 Rice over #17 Colorado, 28-14; **Orange**—Auburn over Michigan St., 6-0.

1938

Final poll released Dec.5. Top 20 regular season results after that: **Dec.26**—#14 Cal over Georgia Tech, 13-7.

		As of Dec. 5	Head Coach	After Bowls
1	TCU	10-0-0	Dutch Meyer	11-0-0
2	Tennessee	10-0-0	Bob Neyland	11-0-0
3	Duke	9-0-0	Wallace Wade	9-1-0
4	Oklahoma	10-0-0	Tom Stidham	10-1-0
5	Notre Dame	8-1-0	Elmer Layden	same
6	Carnegie Tech	7-1-0	Bill Kern	7-2-0
7	USC	8-2-0	Howard Jones	9-2-0
8	Pittsburgh	8-2-0	Jock Sutherland	same
9	Holy Cross	8-1-0	Eddie Anderson	same
10	Minnesota	6-2-0	Bernie Bierman	same
11	Texas Tech	10-0-0	Pete Cawthon	10-1-0
12	Cornell	5-1-1	Carl Snavely	same
13	Alabama	7-1-1	Frank Thomas	same
14	California	9-1-0	Stub Allison	10-1-0
15	Fordham	6-1-2	Jim Crowley	same
16	Michigan	6-1-1	Fritz Crisler	same
17	Northwestern	4-2-2	Pappy Waldorf	same
18	Villanova	8-0-1	Clipper Smith	same
19	Tulane	7-2-1	Red Dawson	same
20	Dartmouth	7-2-0	Red Blaik	same

Key Bowl Games

Sugar—#1 TCU over #6 Carnegie Tech, 15-7; **Orange**—#2 Tennessee over #4 Oklahoma, 17-0; **Rose**—#7 USC over #3 Duke, 7-3; **Cotton**—St.Mary's over #11 Texas Tech 20-13.

1939

Final poll released Dec.11. Top 20 regular season results after that: None.

		As of Dec. 11	Head Coach	After Bowls
1	Texas A&M	10-0-0	Homer Norton	11-0-0
2	Tennessee	10-0-0	Bob Neyland	10-1-0
3	USC	7-0-2	Howard Jones	8-0-2
4	Cornell	8-0-0	Carl Snavely	same
5	Tulane	8-0-1	Red Dawson	8-1-1
6	Missouri	8-1-0	Don Faurot	8-2-0
7	UCLA	6-0-4	Babe Horrell	same
8	Duke	8-1-0	Wallace Wade	same
9	Iowa	6-1-1	Eddie Anderson	same
10	Duquesne	8-0-1	Buff Donelli	same
11	Boston College	9-1-0	Frank Leahy	9-2-0
12	Clemson	8-1-0	Jess Neely	9-1-0
13	Notre Dame	7-2-0	Elmer Layden	same
14	Santa Clara	5-1-3	Buck Shaw	same
15	Ohio St.	6-2-0	Francis Schmidt	same
16	Georgia Tech	7-2-0	Bill Alexander	8-2-0
17	Fordham	6-2-0	Jim Crowley	same
18	Nebraska	7-1-1	Biff Jones	same
19	Oklahoma	6-2-1	Tom Stidham	same
20	Michigan	6-2-0	Fritz Crisler	same

Key Bowl Games

Sugar—#1 Texas A&M over #5 Tulane, 14-13; **Rose**—#3 USC over #2 Tennessee, 14-0; **Orange**—#16 Georgia Tech over #6 Missouri, 21-7; **Cotton**—#12 Clemson over #11 Boston College, 6-3.

1940

Final poll released Dec.2. Top 20 regular season results after that: **Dec.7**—#16 SMU over Rice, 7-6.

		As of Dec. 2	Head Coach	After Bowls
1	Minnesota	8-0-0	Bernie Bierman	same
2	Stanford	9-0-0	C.Shaughnessy	10-0-0
3	Michigan	7-1-0	Fritz Crisler	same
4	Tennessee	10-0-0	Bob Neyland	10-1-0
5	Boston College	10-0-0	Frank Leahy	11-0-0
6	Texas A&M	8-1-0	Homer Norton	9-1-0
7	Nebraska	8-1-0	Biff Jones	8-2-0
8	Northwestern	6-2-0	Pappy Waldorf	same
9	Mississippi St.	9-0-1	Allyn McKeen	10-0-1
10	Washington	7-2-0	Jimmy Phelan	same
11	Santa Clara	6-1-1	Buck Shaw	same
12	Fordham	7-1-0	Jim Crowley	7-2-0
13	Georgetown	8-1-0	Jack Hagerty	8-2-0
14	Penn	6-1-1	George Munger	same
15	Cornell	6-2-0	Carl Snavely	same
16	SMU	7-1-1	Matty Bell	8-1-1
17	Hardin-Simmons	9-0-0	Abe Woodson	same
18	Duke	7-2-0	Wallace Wade	same
19	Lafayette	9-0-0	Hooks Mylin	same
20	—			

Note: Only 19 teams ranked.

Key Bowl Games

Rose—#2 Stanford over #7 Nebraska, 21-13; **Sugar**—#5 Boston College over #4 Tennessee, 19-13; **Cotton**—#6 Texas A&M over #12 Fordham, 13-12; **Orange**—#9 Mississippi St. over #13 Georgetown, 14-7.

1941

Final poll released Dec.1. Top 20 regular season results after that: **Dec.6**—#4 Texas over Oregon, 71-7; #9 Texas A&M over #19 Washington St., 7-0; #16 Mississippi St. over San Francisco, 26-13.

		As of Dec. 1	Head Coach	After Bowls
1	Minnesota	8-0-0	Bernie Bierman	same
2	Duke	9-0-0	Wallace Wade	9-1-0
3	Notre Dame	8-0-1	Frank Leahy	same
4	Texas	7-1-1	Dana X.Bible	8-1-1
5	Michigan	6-1-1	Fritz Crisler	same
6	Fordham	7-1-0	Jim Crowley	8-1-0
7	Missouri	8-1-0	Don Faurot	8-2-0
8	Duquesne	8-0-0	Buff Donelli	same
9	Texas A&M	8-1-0	Homer Norton	9-2-0
10	Navy	7-1-1	Swede Larson	same
11	Northwestern	5-3-0	Pappy Waldorf	same
12	Oregon St.	7-2-0	Lon Stiner	8-2-0
13	Ohio St.	6-1-1	Paul Brown	same
14	Georgia	8-1-1	Wally Butts	9-1-1
15	Penn	7-1-1	George Munger	same
16	Mississippi St.	7-1-1	Allyn McKeen	8-1-1
17	Mississippi	6-2-1	Harry Mehre	same
18	Tennessee	8-2-0	John Barnhill	same
19	Washington St.	6-3-0	Babe Hollingbery	6-4-0
20	Alabama	8-2-0	Frank Thomas	9-2-0

Note: 1942 Rose Bowl moved to Durham, NC, for one year after outbreak of World War II.

Key Bowl Games

Rose—#12 Oregon St. over #2 Duke, 20-16; **Sugar**—#6 Fordham over #7 Missouri, 2-0; **Cotton**—#20 Alabama over #9 Texas A&M, 29-21; **Orange**—#14 Georgia over TCU, 40-26.

1942

Final poll released Nov.30. Top 20 regular season results after that: **Dec.5**—#6 Notre Dame tied Great Lakes Naval Station, 13-13; #13 UCLA over Idaho, 40-13; #14 William & Mary over Oklahoma, 14-7; #17 Washington St. lost to Texas A&M, 21-0; #18 Mississippi St. over San Francisco, 19-7. **Dec.12**—#13 UCLA over USC, 14-7.

		As of Nov. 30	Head Coach	After Bowls
1	Ohio St.	9-1-0	Paul Brown	same
2	Georgia	10-1-0	Wally Butts	11-1-0
3	Wisconsin	8-1-1	Harry Stuhldreher	same
4	Tulsa	10-0-0	Henry Frnka	10-1-0
5	Georgia Tech	9-1-0	Bill Alexander	9-2-0
6	Notre Dame	7-2-1	Frank Leahy	7-2-2
7	Tennessee	8-1-1	John Barnhill	9-1-1
8	Boston College	8-1-0	Denny Myers	8-2-0
9	Michigan	7-3-0	Fritz Crisler	same
10	Alabama	7-3-0	Frank Thomas	8-3-0
11	Texas	8-2-0	Dana X.Bible	9-2-0
12	Stanford	6-4-0	Marchie Schwartz	same
13	UCLA	5-3-0	Babe Horrell	7-4-0
14	William & Mary	8-1-1	Carl Voyles	9-1-1
15	Santa Clara	7-2-0	Buck Shaw	same
16	Auburn	6-4-1	Jack Meagher	same
17	Washington St.	6-1-2	Babe Hollingbery	6-2-2
18	Mississippi St.	7-2-0	Allyn McKeen	8-2-0
19	Minnesota	5-4-0	George Hauser	same
	Holy Cross	5-4-1	Ank Scanlon	same
	Penn St.	6-1-1	Bob Higgins	same

Key Bowl Games

Rose—#2 Georgia over #13 UCLA, 9-0; **Sugar**—#7 Tennessee over #4 Tulsa, 14-7; **Cotton**—#11 Texas over #5 Georgia Tech, 14-7; **Orange**—#10 Alabama over #8 Boston College, 37-21.

1943

Final poll released Nov.29. Top 20 regular season results after that: **Dec.11**—#10 March Field over #19 Pacific, 19-0.

		As of Nov. 29	Head Coach	After Bowls
1	Notre Dame	9-1-0	Frank Leahy	same
2	Iowa Pre-Flight	9-1-0	Don Faurot	same
3	Michigan	8-1-0	Fritz Crisler	same
4	Navy	8-1-0	Billick Whelchel	same
5	Purdue	9-0-0	Elmer Burnham	same
6	Great Lakes Naval Station	10-2-0	Tony Hinkle	same
7	Duke	8-1-0	Eddie Cameron	same
8	Del Monte Pre-Flight	7-1-0	Bill Kern	same
9	Northwestern	6-2-0	Pappy Waldorf	same
10	March Field	8-1-0	Paul Schissler	9-1-0
11	Army	7-2-1	Red Blaik	same
12	Washington	4-0-0	Ralph Welch	4-1-0
13	Georgia Tech	7-3-0	Bill Alexander	8-3-0
14	Texas	7-1-0	Dana X.Bible	7-1-1
15	Tulsa	6-0-1	Henry Frnka	6-1-1
16	Dartmouth	6-1-0	Earl Brown	same
17	Bainbridge Navy Training School	7-0-0	Joe Maniaci	same
18	Colorado College	7-0-0	Hal White	same
19	Pacific	7-1-0	Amos A.Stagg	7-2-0
20	Penn	6-2-1	George Munger	same

Key Bowl Games

Rose—USC over #12 Washington, 29-0; **Sugar**—#13 Georgia Tech over #15 Tulsa, 20-18; **Cotton**—#14 Texas tied Randolph Field, 7-7; **Orange**—LSU over Texas A&M, 19-14.

Associated Press Final Polls (Cont.)

1944

Final poll released Dec.4. Top 20 regular season results after that: **Dec.10**—#3 Randolph Field over #10 March Field, 20-7; #18 Fort Pierce over Kessler Field, 34-7; Morris Field over #20 Second Air Force, 14-7.

		As of Dec. 4	Head Coach	After Bowls
1	Army	9-0-0	Red Blaik	same
2	Ohio St.	9-0-0	Carroll Widdoes	same
3	Randolph Field	10-0-0	Frank Tritico	12-0-0
4	Navy	6-3-0	Oscar Hagberg	same
5	Bainbridge Navy Training School	10-0-0	Joe Maniaci	same
6	Iowa Pre-Flight	10-1-0	Jack Meagher	same
7	USC	7-0-2	Jeff Cravath	8-0-2
8	Michigan	8-2-0	Fritz Crisler	same
9	Notre Dame	8-2-0	Ed McKeever	same
10	March Field	7-0-2	Paul Schissler	7-1-2
11	Duke	5-4-0	Eddie Cameron	6-4-0
12	Tennessee	7-0-1	John Barnhill	7-1-1
13	Georgia Tech	8-2-0	Bill Alexander	8-3-0
14	Norman Pre-Flight	6-0-0	John Gregg	same
15	Illinois	5-4-1	Ray Eliot	same
16	El Toro Marines	8-1-0	Dick Hanley	same
17	Great Lakes Naval Station	9-2-1	Paul Brown	same
18	Fort Pierce	8-0-0	Hamp Pool	9-0-0
19	St.Mary's Pre-Flight	4-4-0	Jules Sikes	same
20	Second Air Force	10-2-1	Bill Reese	10-4-1

Key Bowl Games

Treasury—#3 Randolph Field over #20 Second Air Force, 13-6; **Rose**—#7 USC over #12 Tennessee, 25-0; **Sugar**—#11 Duke over Alabama, 29-26; **Orange**—Tulsa over #13 Georgia Tech, 26-12; **Cotton**—Oklahoma A&M over TCU, 34-0.

1945

Final poll released Dec.3. Top 20 regular season results after that: None.

		As of Dec. 3	Head Coach	After Bowls
1	Army	9-0-0	Red Blaik	same
2	Alabama	9-0-0	Frank Thomas	10-0-0
3	Navy	7-1-1	Oscar Hagberg	same
4	Indiana	9-0-1	Bo McMillan	same
5	Oklahoma A&M	8-0-0	Jim Lookabaugh	9-0-0
6	Michigan	7-3-0	Fritz Crisler	same
7	St.Mary's-CA	7-1-0	Jimmy Phelan	7-2-0
8	Penn	6-2-0	George Munger	same
9	Notre Dame	7-2-1	Hugh Devore	same
10	Texas	9-1-0	Dana X.Bible	10-1-0
11	USC	7-3-0	Jeff Cravath	7-4-0
12	Ohio St.	7-2-0	Carroll Widdoes	same
13	Duke	6-2-0	Eddie Cameron	same
14	Tennessee	8-1-0	John Barnhill	same
15	LSU	7-2-0	Bernie Moore	same
16	Holy Cross	8-1-0	John DeGrosa	8-2-0
17	Tulsa	8-2-0	Henry Frnka	8-3-0
18	Georgia	8-2-0	Wally Butts	9-2-0
19	Wake Forest	4-3-1	Peahead Walker	5-3-1
20	Columbia	8-1-0	Lou Little	same

Key Bowl Games

Rose—#2 Alabama over #11 USC, 34-14; **Sugar**—#5 Oklahoma A&M over #7 St.Mary's, 33-13; **Cotton**—#10 Texas over Missouri, 40-27; **Orange**—Miami-FL over #16 Holy Cross, 13-6.

1946

Final poll released Dec.2. Top 20 regular season results after that: None.

		As of Dec. 2	Head Coach	After Bowls
1	Notre Dame	8-0-1	Frank Leahy	same
2	Army	9-0-1	Red Blaik	same
3	Georgia	10-0-0	Wally Butts	11-0-0
4	UCLA	10-0-0	Bert LaBrucherie	10-1-0
5	Illinois	7-2-0	Ray Eliot	8-2-0
6	Michigan	6-2-1	Fritz Crisler	same
7	Tennessee	9-1-0	Bob Neyland	9-2-0
8	LSU	9-1-0	Bernie Moore	9-1-1
9	North Carolina	8-1-1	Carl Snavely	8-2-1
10	Rice	8-2-0	Jess Neely	9-2-0
11	Georgia Tech	8-2-0	Bobby Dodd	9-2-0
12	Yale	7-1-1	Howard Odell	same
13	Penn	6-2-0	George Munger	same
14	Oklahoma	7-3-0	Jim Tatum	8-3-0
15	Texas	8-2-0	Dana X.Bible	same
16	Arkansas	6-3-1	John Barnhill	6-3-2
17	Tulsa	9-1-0	J.O.Brothers	same
18	N.C.State	8-2-0	Beattie Feathers	8-3-0
19	Delaware	9-0-0	Bill Murray	10-0-0
20	Indiana	6-3-0	Bo McMillan	same

Key Bowl Games

Sugar—#3 Georgia over #9 N.Carolina, 20-10; **Rose**—#5 Illinois over #4 UCLA, 45-14; **Orange**—#10 Rice over #7 Tennessee, 8-0; **Cotton**—#8 LSU tied #16 Arkansas, 0-0.

1947

Final poll released Dec.8. Top 20 regular season results after that: None.

		As of Dec. 8	Head Coach	After Bowls
1	Notre Dame	9-0-0	Frank Leahy	same
2	Michigan	9-0-0	Fritz Crisler	10-0-0
3	SMU	9-0-1	Matty Bell	9-0-2
4	Penn St.	9-0-0	Bob Higgins	9-0-1
5	Texas	9-1-0	Blair Cherry	10-1-0
6	Alabama	8-2-0	Red Drew	8-3-0
7	Penn	7-0-1	George Munger	same
8	USC	7-1-1	Jeff Cravath	7-2-1
9	North Carolina	8-2-0	Carl Snavely	same
10	Georgia Tech	9-1-0	Bobby Dodd	10-1-0
11	Army	5-2-2	Red Blaik	same
12	Kansas	8-0-2	George Sauer	8-1-2
13	Mississippi	8-2-0	Johnny Vaught	9-2-0
14	William & Mary	9-1-0	Rube McCray	9-2-0
15	California	9-1-0	Pappy Waldorf	same
16	Oklahoma	7-2-1	Bud Wilkinson	same
17	N.C.State	5-3-1	Beattie Feathers	same
18	Rice	6-3-1	Jess Neely	same
19	Duke	4-3-2	Wallace Wade	same
20	Columbia	7-2-0	Lou Little	same

Key Bowl Games

Rose—#2 Michigan over #8 USC, 49-0; **Cotton**—#3 SMU tied #4 Penn St., 13-13; **Sugar**—#5 Texas over #6 Alabama, 27-7; **Orange**—#10 Georgia Tech over #12 Kansas, 20-14.

1948

Final poll released Nov.29. Top 20 regular season results after that: **Dec.3**—#12 Vanderbilt over Miami-FL, 33-6. **Dec.4**—#2 Notre Dame tied USC, 14-14; #11 Clemson over The Citadel, 20-0.

		As of Nov.29	Head Coach	After Bowls
1	Michigan	9-0-0	Bennie Oosterbaan	same
2	Notre Dame	9-0-0	Frank Leahy	9-0-1
3	North Carolina	9-0-1	Carl Snavely	9-1-1
4	California	10-0-0	Pappy Waldorf	10-1-0
5	Oklahoma	9-1-0	Bud Wilkinson	10-1-0
6	Army	8-0-1	Red Blaik	same
7	Northwestern	7-2-0	Bob Voigts	8-2-0
8	Georgia	9-1-0	Wally Butts	9-2-0
9	Oregon	9-1-0	Jim Aiken	9-2-0
10	SMU	8-1-1	Matty Bell	9-1-1
11	Clemson	9-0-0	Frank Howard	11-0-0
12	Vanderbilt	7-2-1	Red Sanders	8-2-1
13	Tulane	9-1-0	Henry Frnka	same
14	Michigan St.	6-2-2	Biggie Munn	same
15	Mississippi	8-1-0	Johnny Vaught	same
16	Minnesota	7-2-0	Bernie Bierman	same
17	William & Mary	6-2-2	Rube McCray	7-2-2
18	Penn St.	7-1-1	Bob Higgins	same
19	Cornell	8-1-0	Lefty James	same
20	Wake Forest	6-3-0	Peahead Walker	6-4-0

Note: Big Nine "no-repeat" rule kept Michigan from Rose Bowl.

Key Bowl Games

Sugar—#5 Oklahoma over #3 North Carolina, 14-6; **Rose**—#7 Northwestern over #4 Cal, 20-14; **Orange**—Texas over #8 Georgia, 41-28; **Cotton**—#10 SMU over #9 Oregon, 21-13.

1949

Final poll released Nov.28. Top 20 regular season results after that: **Dec.2**—#14 Maryland over Miami-FL, 13-0. **Dec.3**—#1 Notre Dame over SMU, 27-20; #10 Pacific over Hawaii, 75-0.

		As of Nov. 28	Head Coach	After Bowls
1	Notre Dame	9-0-0	Frank Leahy	10-0-0
2	Oklahoma	10-0-0	Bud Wilkinson	11-0-0
3	California	10-0-0	Pappy Waldorf	10-1-0
4	Army	9-0-0	Red Blaik	same
5	Rice	9-1-0	Jess Neely	10-1-0
6	Ohio St.	6-1-2	Wes Fesler	7-1-2
7	Michigan	6-2-1	Bennie Oosterbaan	same
8	Minnesota	7-2-0	Bernie Bierman	same
9	LSU	8-2-0	Gaynell Tinsley	8-3-0
10	Pacific	10-0-0	Larry Siemering	11-0-0
11	Kentucky	9-2-0	Bear Bryant	9-3-0
12	Cornell	8-1-0	Lefty James	same
13	Villanova	8-1-0	Jim Leonard	same
14	Maryland	7-1-0	Jim Tatum	9-1-0
15	Santa Clara	7-2-1	Len Casanova	8-2-1
16	North Carolina	7-3-0	Carl Snavely	7-4-0
17	Tennessee	7-2-1	Bob Neyland	same
18	Princeton	6-3-0	Charlie Caldwell	same
19	Michigan St.	6-3-0	Biggie Munn	same
20	Missouri	7-3-0	Don Faurot	7-4-0
	Baylor	8-2-0	Bob Woodruff	same

Key Bowl Games

Sugar—#2 Oklahoma over #9 LSU, 35-0; **Rose**—#6 Ohio St. over #3 Cal, 17-14; **Cotton**—#5 Rice over #16 North Carolina, 27-13; **Orange**—#15 Santa Clara over #11 Kentucky, 21-13.

1950

Final poll released Nov.27. Top 20 regular season results after that: **Nov.30**—#3 Texas over Texas A&M, 17-0. **Dec.1**—#15 Miami-FL over Missouri, 27—9. **Dec.2**—#1 Oklahoma over Okla. A&M, 41-14; Navy over #2 Army, 14-2; #4 Tennessee over Vanderbilt, 43-0; #16 Alabama over Auburn, 34-0; #19 Tulsa over Houston, 28-21; #20 Tulane tied LSU, 14-14. **Dec.9**—#3 Texas over LSU, 21-6.

		As of Nov. 27	Head Coach	After Bowls
1	Oklahoma	9-0-0	Bud Wilkinson	10-1-0
2	Army	8-0-0	Red Blaik	8-1-0
3	Texas	7-1-0	Blair Cherry	9-2-0
4	Tennessee	9-1-0	Bob Neyland	11-1-0
5	California	9-0-1	Pappy Waldorf	9-1-1
6	Princeton	9-0-0	Charlie Caldwell	same
7	Kentucky	10-1-0	Bear Bryant	11-1-0
8	Michigan St.	8-1-0	Biggie Munn	same
9	Michigan	5-3-1	Bennie Oosterbaan	6-3-1
10	Clemson	8-0-1	Frank Howard	9-0-1
11	Washington	8-2-0	Howard Odell	same
12	Wyoming	9-0-0	Bowden Wyatt	10-0-0
13	Illinois	7-2-0	Ray Eliot	same
14	Ohio St.	6-3-0	Wes Fesler	same
15	Miami-FL	8-0-1	Andy Gustafson	9-1-1
16	Alabama	8-2-0	Red Drew	9-2-0
17	Nebraska	6-2-1	Bill Glassford	same
18	Wash.& Lee	8-2-0	George Barclay	8-3-0
19	Tulsa	8-1-1	J.O.Brothers	9-1-1
20	Tulane	6-2-0	Henry Frnka	6-2-1

Key Bowl Games

Sugar—#7 Kentucky over #1 Oklahoma, 13-7; **Cotton**—#4 Tennessee over #3 Texas, 20-14; **Rose**—#9 Michigan over #5 Cal, 14-6; **Orange**—#10 Clemson over #15 Miami-FL, 15-14.

1951

Final poll released Dec.3. Top 20 regular season results after that: None.

		As of Dec. 3	Head Coach	After Bowls
1	Tennessee	10-0-0	Bob Neyland	10-1-0
2	Michigan St.	9-0-0	Biggie Munn	same
3	Maryland	9-0-0	Jim Tatum	10-0-0
4	Illinois	8-0-1	Ray Eliot	9-0-1
5	Georgia Tech	10-0-1	Bobby Dodd	11-0-1
6	Princeton	9-0-0	Charlie Caldwell	same
7	Stanford	9-1-0	Chuck Taylor	9-2-0
8	Wisconsin	7-1-1	Ivy Williamson	same
9	Baylor	8-1-1	George Sauer	8-2-1
10	Oklahoma	8-2-0	Bud Wilkinson	same
11	TCU	6-4-0	Dutch Meyer	6-5-0
12	California	8-2-0	Pappy Waldorf	same
13	Virginia	8-1-0	Art Guepe	same
14	San Francisco	9-0-0	Joe Kuharich	same
15	Kentucky	7-4-0	Bear Bryant	8-4-0
16	Boston University.	6-4-0	Buff Donelli	same
17	UCLA	5-3-1	Red Sanders	same
18	Washington St.	7-3-0	Forest Evashevski	same
19	Holy Cross	8-2-0	Eddie Anderson	same
	Clemson	7-2-0	Frank Howard	7-3-0

Key Bowl Games

Sugar—#3 Maryland over #1 Tennessee, 28-13; **Rose**—#4 Illinois over #7 Stanford, 40-7; **Orange**—#5 Georgia Tech over #9 Baylor, 17-14; **Cotton**—#15 Kentucky over #11 TCU, 20-7.

Associated Press Final Polls (Cont.)

1952

Final poll released Dec.1. Top 20 regular season results after that: **Dec.6**—#15 Florida over #20 Kentucky, 27-20.

		As of Dec. 1	Head Coach	After Bowls
1	Michigan St.	9-0-0	Biggie Munn	same
2	Georgia Tech	11-0-0	Bobby Dodd	12-0-0
3	Notre Dame	7-2-1	Frank Leahy	same
4	Oklahoma	8-1-1	Bud Wilkinson	same
5	USC	9-1-0	Jess Hill	10-1-0
6	UCLA	8-1-0	Red Sanders	same
7	Mississippi	8-0-2	Johnny Vaught	8-1-2
8	Tennessee	8-1-1	Bob Neyland	8-2-1
9	Alabama	9-2-0	Red Drew	10-2-0
10	Texas	8-2-0	Ed Price	9-2-0
11	Wisconsin	6-2-1	Ivy Williamson	6-3-1
12	Tulsa	8-1-1	J.O.Brothers	8-2-1
13	Maryland	7-2-0	Jim Tatum	same
14	Syracuse	7-2-0	Ben Schwartzwalder	7-3-0
15	Florida	6-3-0	Bob Woodruff	8-3-0
16	Duke	8-2-0	Bill Murray	same
17	Ohio St.	6-3-0	Woody Hayes	same
18	Purdue	4-3-2	Stu Holcomb	same
19	Princeton	8-1-0	Charlie Caldwell	same
20	Kentucky	5-3-2	Bear Bryant	5-4-2

Note: Michigan St. would officially join Big Ten in 1953.

Key Bowl Games

Sugar—#2 Georgia Tech over #7 Ole Miss, 24-7; **Rose**—#5 USC over #11 Wisconsin, 7-0; **Cotton**—#10 Texas over #8 Tennessee, 16-0; **Orange**—#9 Alabama over #14 Syracuse, 61-6.

1953

Final poll released Nov.30. Top 20 regular season results after that: **Dec.5**—#2 Notre Dame over SMU, 40-14.

		As of Nov. 30	Head Coach	After Bowls
1	Maryland	10-0-0	Jim Tatum	10-1-0
2	Notre Dame	8-0-1	Frank Leahy	9-0-1
3	Michigan St.	8-1-0	Biggie Munn	9-1-0
4	Oklahoma	8-1-1	Bud Wilkinson	9-1-1
5	UCLA	8-1-0	Red Sanders	8-2-0
6	Rice	8-2-0	Jess Neely	9-2-0
7	Illinois	7-1-1	Ray Eliot	same
8	Georgia Tech	8-2-1	Bobby Dodd	9-2-1
9	Iowa	5-3-1	Forest Evashevski	same
10	West Virginia	8-1-0	Art Lewis	8-2-0
11	Texas	7-3-0	Ed Price	same
12	Texas Tech	10-1-0	DeWitt Weaver	11-1-0
13	Alabama	6-2-3	Red Drew	6-3-3
14	Army	7-1-1	Red Blaik	same
15	Wisconsin	6-2-1	Ivy Williamson	same
16	Kentucky	7-2-1	Bear Bryant	same
17	Auburn	7-2-1	Shug Jordan	7-3-1
18	Duke	7-2-1	Bill Murray	same
19	Stanford	6-3-1	Chuck Taylor	same
20	Michigan	6-3-0	Bennie Oosterbaan	same

Key Bowl Games

Orange—#4 Oklahoma over #1 Maryland, 7-0; **Rose**—#3 Michigan St. over #5 UCLA, 28-20; **Cotton**—#6 Rice over #13 Alabama, 28-6; **Sugar**—#8 Georgia Tech over #10 West Virginia, 42-19.

1954

Final poll released Nov.29. Top 20 regular season results after that: **Dec.4th**—#4 Notre Dame over SMU, 26-14.

		As of Nov. 29	Head Coach	After Bowls
1	Ohio St.	9-0-0	Woody Hayes	10-0-0
2	UCLA	9-0-0	Red Sanders	same
3	Oklahoma	10-0-0	Bud Wilkinson	same
4	Notre Dame	8-1-0	Terry Brennan	9-1-0
5	Navy	7-2-0	Eddie Erdelatz	8-2-0
6	Mississippi	9-1-0	Johnny Vaught	9-2-0
7	Army	7-2-0	Red Blaik	same
8	Maryland	7-2-1	Jim Tatum	same
9	Wisconsin	7-2-0	Ivy Williamson	same
10	Arkansas	8-2-0	Bowden Wyatt	8-3-0
11	Miami-FL	8-1-0	Andy Gustafson	same
12	West Virginia	8-1-0	Art Lewis	same
13	Auburn	7-3-0	Shug Jordan	8-3-0
14	Duke	7-2-1	Bill Murray	8-2-1
15	Michigan	6-3-0	Bennie Oosterbaan	same
16	Virginia Tech	8-0-1	Frank Moseley	same
17	USC	8-3-0	Jess Hill	8-4-0
18	Baylor	7-3-0	George Sauer	7-4-0
19	Rice	7-3-0	Jess Neely	same
20	Penn St.	7-2-0	Rip Engle	same

Note: PCC and Big Seven "no-repeat" rules kept UCLA and Oklahoma from Orange and Rose bowls, respectively.

Key Bowl Games

Rose—#1 Ohio St. over #17 USC, 20-7; **Sugar**—#5 Navy over #6 Ole Miss, 21-0; **Cotton**—Georgia Tech over #10 Arkansas, 14-6; **Orange**—#14 Duke over Nebraska, 34-7.

1955

Final poll released Nov.28. Top 20 regular season results after that: None.

		As of Nov. 28	Head Coach	After Bowls
1	Oklahoma	10-0-0	Bud Wilkinson	11-0-0
2	Michigan St.	8-1-0	Duffy Daugherty	9-1-0
3	Maryland	10-0-0	Jim Tatum	10-1-0
4	UCLA	9-1-0	Red Sanders	9-2-0
5	Ohio St.	7-2-0	Woody Hayes	same
6	TCU	9-1-0	Abe Martin	9-2-0
7	Georgia Tech	8-1-1	Bobby Dodd	9-1-1
8	Auburn	8-1-1	Shug Jordan	8-2-1
9	Notre Dame	8-2-0	Terry Brennan	same
10	Mississippi	9-1-0	Johnny Vaught	10-1-0
11	Pittsburgh	7-3-0	John Michelosen	7-4-0
12	Michigan	7-2-0	Bennie Oosterbaan	same
13	USC	6-4-0	Jess Hill	same
14	Miami-FL	6-3-0	Andy Gustafson	same
15	Miami-OH	9-0-0	Ara Parseghian	same
16	Stanford	6-3-1	Chuck Taylor	same
17	Texas A&M	7-2-1	Bear Bryant	same
18	Navy	6-2-1	Eddie Erdelatz	same
19	West Virginia	8-2-0	Art Lewis	same
20	Army	6-3-0	Red Blaik	same

Note: Big Ten "no-repeat" rule kept Ohio St. from Rose Bowl.

Key Bowl Games

Orange—#1 Oklahoma over #3 Maryland, 20-6; **Rose**—#2 Michigan St. over #4 UCLA, 17-14; **Cotton**—#10 Ole Miss over #6 TCU, 14-13; **Sugar**—#7 Georgia Tech over #11 Pitt, 7-0; **Gator**—Vanderbilt over #8 Auburn, 25-13.

1956

Final poll released Dec.3. Top 20 regular season results after that: **Dec.8**—#13 Pitt over #6 Miami-FL, 14-7.

		As of Dec. 3	Head Coach	After Bowls
1	Oklahoma	10-0-0	Bud Wilkinson	same
2	Tennessee	10-0-0	Bowden Wyatt	10-1-0
3	Iowa	8-1-0	Forest Evashevski	9-1-0
4	Georgia Tech	9-1-0	Bobby Dodd	10-1-0
5	Texas A&M	9-0-1	Bear Bryant	same
6	Miami-FL	8-0-1	Andy Gustafson	8-1-1
7	Michigan	7-2-0	Bennie Oosterbaan	same
8	Syracuse	7-1-0	Ben Schwartzwalder	7-2-0
9	Michigan St.	7-2-0	Duffy Daugherty	same
10	Oregon St.	7-2-1	Tommy Prothro	7-3-1
11	Baylor	8-2-0	Sam Boyd	9-2-0
12	Minnesota	6-1-2	Murray Warmath	same
13	Pittsburgh	6-2-1	John Michelosen	7-3-1
14	TCU	7-3-0	Abe Martin	8-3-0
15	Ohio St.	6-3-0	Woody Hayes	same
16	Navy	6-1-2	Eddie Erdelatz	same
17	G. Washington	7-1-1	Gene Sherman	8-1-1
18	USC	8-2-0	Jess Hill	same
19	Clemson	7-1-2	Frank Howard	7-2-2
20	Colorado	7-2-1	Dallas Ward	8-2-1

Note: Big Seven "no-repeat" rule kept Oklahoma from Orange Bowl and Texas A&M was on probation.

Key Bowl Games

Sugar—#11 Baylor over #2 Tennessee, 13-7; **Rose**—#3 Iowa over #10 Oregon St., 35-19; **Gator**—#4 Georgia Tech over #13 Pitt, 21-14; **Cotton**—#14 TCU over #8 Syracuse, 28-27; **Orange**—#20 Colorado over #19 Clemson, 27-21.

1957

Final poll released Dec.2. Top 20 regular season results after that: **Dec.7th**—#10 Notre Dame over SMU, 54-21.

		As of Dec. 2	Head Coach	After Bowls
1	Auburn	10-0-0	Shug Jordan	same
2	Ohio St.	8-1-0	Woody Hayes	9-1-0
3	Michigan St.	8-1-0	Duffy Daugherty	same
4	Oklahoma	9-1-0	Bud Wilkinson	10-1-0
5	Navy	8-1-1	Eddie Erdelatz	9-1-1
6	Iowa	7-1-1	Forest Evashevski	same
7	Mississippi	8-1-1	Johnny Vaught	9-1-1
8	Rice	7-3-0	Jess Neely	7-4-0
9	Texas A&M	8-2-0	Bear Bryant	8-3-0
10	Notre Dame	6-3-0	Terry Brennan	7-3-0
11	Texas	6-3-1	Darrell Royal	6-4-1
12	Arizona St.	10-0-0	Dan Devine	same
13	Tennessee	7-3-0	Bowden Wyatt	8-3-0
14	Mississippi St.	6-2-1	Wade Walker	same
15	N.C. State	7-1-2	Earle Edwards	same
16	Duke	6-2-2	Bill Murray	6-3-2
17	Florida	6-2-1	Bob Woodruff	same
18	Army	7-2-0	Red Blaik	same
19	Wisconsin	6-3-0	Milt Bruhn	same
20	VMI	9-0-1	John McKenna	same

Note: Auburn on probation, ineligible for bowl game.

Key Bowl Games

Rose—#2 Ohio St. over Oregon, 10-7; **Orange**—#4 Oklahoma over #16 Duke, 48-21; **Cotton**—#5 Navy over #8 Rice, 20-7; **Sugar**—#7 Ole Miss over #11 Texas, 39-7; **Gator**—#13 Tennessee over #9 Texas A&M, 3-0.

1958

Final poll released Dec.1. Top 20 regular season results after that: None.

		As of Dec. 1	Head Coach	After Bowls
1	LSU	10-0-0	Paul Dietzel	11-0-0
2	Iowa	7-1-1	Forest Evashevski	8-1-1
3	Army	8-0-1	Red Blaik	same
4	Auburn	9-0-1	Shug Jordan	same
5	Oklahoma	9-1-0	Bud Wilkinson	10-1-0
6	Air Force	9-0-1	Ben Martin	9-0-2
7	Wisconsin	7-1-1	Milt Bruhn	same
8	Ohio St.	6-1-2	Woody Hayes	same
9	Syracuse	8-1-0	Ben Schwartzwalder	8-2-0
10	TCU	8-2-0	Abe Martin	8-2-1
11	Mississippi	8-2-0	Johnny Vaught	9-2-0
12	Clemson	8-2-0	Frank Howard	8-3-0
13	Purdue	6-1-2	Jack Mollenkopf	same
14	Florida	6-3-1	Bob Woodruff	6-4-1
15	South Carolina	7-3-0	Warren Giese	same
16	California	7-3-0	Pete Elliott	7-4-0
17	Notre Dame	6-4-0	Terry Brennan	same
18	SMU	6-4-0	Bill Meek	same
19	Oklahoma St.	7-3-0	Cliff Speegle	8-3-0
20	Rutgers	8-1-0	John Stiegman	same

Key Bowl Games

Sugar—#1 LSU over #12 Clemson, 7-0; **Rose**—#2 Iowa over #16 Cal, 38-12; **Orange**—#5 Oklahoma over #9 Syracuse, 21-6; **Cotton**—#6 Air Force tied #10 TCU, 0-0.

1959

Final poll released Dec.7. Top 20 regular season results after that: None.

		As of Dec. 7	Head Coach	After Bowls
1	Syracuse	10-0-0	Ben Schwartzwalder	11-0-0
2	Mississippi	9-1-0	Johnny Vaught	10-1-0
3	LSU	9-1-0	Paul Dietzel	9-2-0
4	Texas	9-1-0	Darrell Royal	9-2-0
5	Georgia	9-1-0	Wally Butts	10-1-0
6	Wisconsin	7-2-0	Milt Bruhn	7-3-0
7	TCU	8-2-0	Abe Martin	8-3-0
8	Washington	9-1-0	Jim Owens	10-1-0
9	Arkansas	8-2-0	Frank Broyles	9-2-0
10	Alabama	7-1-2	Bear Bryant	7-2-2
11	Clemson	8-2-0	Frank Howard	9-2-0
12	Penn St.	8-2-0	Rip Engle	9-2-0
13	Illinois	5-3-1	Ray Eliot	same
14	USC	8-2-0	Don Clark	same
15	Oklahoma	7-3-0	Bud Wilkinson	same
16	Wyoming	9-1-0	Bob Devaney	same
17	Notre Dame	5-5-0	Joe Kuharich	same
18	Missouri	6-4-0	Dan Devine	6-5-0
19	Florida	5-4-1	Bob Woodruff	same
20	Pittsburgh	6-4-0	John Michelosen	same

Note: Big Seven "no-repeat" rule kept Oklahoma from Orange Bowl.

Key Bowl Games

Cotton—#1 Syracuse over #4 Texas, 23-14; **Sugar**—#2 Ole Miss over #3 LSU, 21-0; **Orange**—#5 Georgia over #18 Missouri, 14-0; **Rose**—#8 Washington over #6 Wisconsin, 44-8; **Bluebonnet**—#11 Clemson over #7 TCU, 23-7; **Gator**—#9 Arkansas over Georgia Tech, 14-7; **Liberty**—#12 Penn St. over #10 Alabama, 7-0.

Associated Press Final Polls (Cont.)

AP ranked only 10 teams from 1962-67.

1960

Final poll released Nov.28. Top 20 regular season results after that: **Dec.3**—UCLA over #10 Duke, 27-6.

		As of Nov. 28	Head Coach	After Bowls
1	Minnesota	8-1-0	Murray Warmath	8-2-0
2	Mississippi	9-0-1	Johnny Vaught	10-0-1
3	Iowa	8-1-0	Forest Evashevski	same
4	Navy	9-1-0	Wayne Hardin	9-2-0
5	Missouri	9-1-0	Dan Devine	10-1-0
6	Washington	9-1-0	Jim Owens	10-1-0
7	Arkansas	8-2-0	Frank Broyles	8-3-0
8	Ohio St.	7-2-0	Woody Hayes	same
9	Alabama	8-1-1	Bear Bryant	8-1-2
10	Duke	7-2-0	Bill Murray	8-3-0
11	Kansas	7-2-1	Jack Mitchell	same
12	Baylor	8-2-0	John Bridgers	8-3-0
13	Auburn	8-2-0	Shug Jordan	same
14	Yale	9-0-0	Jordan Olivar	same
15	Michigan St.	6-2-1	Duffy Daugherty	same
16	Penn St.	6-3-0	Rip Engle	7-3-0
17	New Mexico St.	10-0-0	Warren Woodson	11-0-0
18	Florida	8-2-0	Ray Graves	9-2-0
19	Syracuse	7-2-0	Ben Schwartzwalder	same
	Purdue	4-4-1	Jack Mollenkopf	same

Key Bowl Games

Rose—#6 Washington over #1 Minnesota, 17-7; **Sugar**—#2 Ole Miss over Rice, 14-6; **Orange**—#5 Missouri over #4 Navy, 21-14; **Cotton**—#10 Duke over #7 Arkansas, 7-6; **Bluebonnet**—#9 Alabama tied Texas, 3-3.

1961

Final poll released Dec.4. Top 20 regular season results after that: None.

		As of Dec. 4	Head Coach	After Bowls
1	Alabama	10-0-0	Bear Bryant	11-0-0
2	Ohio St.	8-0-1	Woody Hayes	same
3	Texas	9-1-0	Darrell Royal	10-1-0
4	LSU	9-1-0	Paul Dietzel	10-1-0
5	Mississippi	9-1-0	Johnny Vaught	9-2-0
6	Minnesota	7-2-0	Murray Warmath	8-2-0
7	Colorado	9-1-0	Sonny Grandelius	9-2-0
8	Michigan St.	7-2-0	Duffy Daugherty	same
9	Arkansas	8-2-0	Frank Broyles	8-3-0
10	Utah St.	9-0-1	John Ralston	9-1-1
11	Missouri	7-2-1	Dan Devine	same
12	Purdue	6-3-0	Jack Mollenkopf	same
13	Georgia Tech	7-3-0	Bobby Dodd	7-4-0
14	Syracuse	7-3-0	Ben Schwartzwalder	8-3-0
15	Rutgers	9-0-0	John Bateman	same
16	UCLA	7-3-0	Bill Barnes	7-4-0
17	Rice	7-3-0	Jess Neely	7-4-0
	Penn St.	7-3-0	Rip Engle	8-3-0
	Arizona	8-1-1	Jim LaRue	same
20	Duke	7-3-0	Bill Murray	same

Note: Ohio St. faculty council turned down Rose Bowl invitation citing concern with OSU's overemphasis on sports.

Key Bowl Games

Sugar—#1 Alabama over #9 Arkansas, 10-3; **Cotton**—#3 Texas over #5 Ole Miss, 12-7; **Orange**—#4 LSU over #7 Colorado, 25-7; **Rose**—#6 Minnesota over #16 UCLA, 21-3; **Gotham**—Baylor over #10 Utah St., 24-9.

1962

Final poll released Dec.3. Top 10 regular season results after that: None.

		As of Dec. 3	Head Coach	After Bowls
1	USC	10-0-0	John McKay	11-0-0
2	Wisconsin	8-1-0	Milt Bruhn	8-2-0
3	Mississippi	9-0-0	Johnny Vaught	10-0-0
4	Texas	9-0-1	Darrell Royal	9-1-1
5	Alabama	9-1-0	Bear Bryant	10-1-0
6	Arkansas	9-1-0	Frank Broyles	9-2-0
7	LSU	8-1-1	Charlie McClendon	9-1-1
8	Oklahoma	8-2-0	Bud Wilkinson	8-3-0
9	Penn St.	9-1-0	Rip Engle	9-2-0
10	Minnesota	6-2-1	Murray Warmath	same

Key Bowl Games

Rose—#1 USC over #2 Wisconsin, 42-37; **Sugar**—#3 Ole Miss over #6 Arkansas, 17-13; **Cotton**—#7 LSU over #4 Texas, 13-0; **Orange**—#5 Alabama over #8 Oklahoma, 17-0; **Gator**—Florida over #9 Penn St., 17-7.

1963

Final poll released Dec.9. Top 10 regular season results after that: **Dec.14**—#8 Alabama over Miami-FL, 17-12.

		As of Dec. 9	Head Coach	After Bowls
1	Texas	10-0-0	Darrell Royal	11-0-0
2	Navy	9-1-0	Wayne Hardin	9-2-0
3	Illinois	7-1-1	Pete Elliott	8-1-1
4	Pittsburgh	9-1-0	John Michelosen	same
5	Auburn	9-1-0	Shug Jordan	9-2-0
6	Nebraska	9-1-0	Bob Devaney	10-1-0
7	Mississippi	7-0-2	Johnny Vaught	7-1-2
8	Alabama	7-2-0	Bear Bryant	9-2-0
9	Michigan St.	6-2-1	Duffy Daugherty	same
10	Oklahoma	8-2-0	Bud Wilkinson	same

Key Bowl Games

Cotton—#1 Texas over #2 Navy, 28-6; **Rose**—#3 Illinois over Washington, 17-7; **Orange**—#6 Nebraska over #5 Auburn, 13-7; **Sugar**—#8 Alabama over #7 Ole Miss, 12-7.

1964

Final poll released Nov.30. Top 10 regular season results after that: **Dec.5th**—Florida over #7 LSU, 20-6.

		As of Nov. 30	Head Coach	After Bowls
1	Alabama	10-0-0	Bear Bryant	10-1-0
2	Arkansas	10-0-0	Frank Broyles	11-0-0
3	Notre Dame	9-1-0	Ara Parseghian	same
4	Michigan	8-1-0	Bump Elliott	9-1-0
5	Texas	9-1-0	Darrell Royal	10-1-0
6	Nebraska	9-1-0	Bob Devaney	9-2-0
7	LSU	7-1-1	Charlie McClendon	8-2-1
8	Oregon St.	8-2-0	Tommy Prothro	8-3-0
9	Ohio St.	7-2-0	Woody Hayes	same
10	USC	7-3-0	John McKay	same

Key Bowl Games

Orange—#5 Texas over #1 Alabama, 21-17; **Cotton**—#2 Arkansas over #6 Nebraska, 10-7; **Rose**—#4 Michigan over #8 Oregon St., 34-7; **Sugar**—#7 LSU over Syracuse, 13-10.

1965

Final poll taken **after** bowl games for the first time.

		After Bowls	Head Coach	Regular Season
1	Alabama	9-1-1	Bear Bryant	8-1-1
2	Michigan St.	10-1-0	Duffy Daugherty	10-0-0
3	Arkansas	10-1-0	Frank Broyles	10-0-0
4	UCLA	8-2-1	Tommy Prothro	7-1-1
5	Nebraska	10-1-0	Bob Devaney	10-0-0
6	Missouri	8-2-1	Dan Devine	7-2-1
7	Tennessee	8-1-2	Doug Dickey	6-1-2
8	LSU	8-3-0	Charlie McClendon	7-3-0
9	Notre Dame	7-2-1	Ara Parseghian	same
10	USC	7-2-1	John McKay	same

Key Bowl Games

Rankings below reflect final regular season poll, released Nov.29. No bowls for then #8 USC or #9 Notre Dame.
Rose—#5 UCLA over #1 Michigan St., 14-12; **Cotton**—LSU over #2 Arkansas, 14-7; **Orange**—#4 Alabama over #3 Nebraska, 39-28; **Sugar**—#6 Missouri over Florida, 20-18; **Bluebonnet**—#7 Tennessee over Tulsa, 27-6; **Gator**—Georgia Tech over #10 Texas Tech, 31-21.

1966

Final poll released Dec.5, returning to pre-bowl status. Top 10 regular season results after that: None.

		As of Dec. 5	Head Coach	After Bowls
1	Notre Dame	9-0-1	Ara Parseghian	same
2	Michigan St.	9-0-1	Duffy Daugherty	same
3	Alabama	10-0-0	Bear Bryant	11-0-0
4	Georgia	9-1-0	Vince Dooley	10-1-0
5	UCLA	9-1-0	Tommy Prothro	same
6	Nebraska	9-1-0	Bob Devaney	9-2-0
7	Purdue	8-2-0	Jack Mollenkopf	9-2-0
8	Georgia Tech	9-1-0	Bobby Dodd	9-2-0
9	Miami-FL	7-2-1	Charlie Tate	8-2-1
10	SMU	8-2-0	Hayden Fry	8-3-0

Key Bowl Games

Sugar—#3 Alabama over #6 Nebraska, 34-7; **Cotton**—#4 Georgia over #10 SMU, 24-9; **Rose**—#7 Purdue over USC, 14-13; **Orange**—Florida over #8 Georgia Tech, 27-12; **Liberty**—#9 Miami-FL over Virginia Tech, 14-7.

1967

Final poll released Nov.27. Top 10 regular season results after that: **Dec.2**—#2 Tennessee over Vanderbilt, 41-14; #3 Oklahoma over Oklahoma St., 38-14; #8 Alabama over Auburn, 7-3.

		As of Nov. 27	Head Coach	After Bowls
1	USC	9-1-0	John McKay	10-1-0
2	Tennessee	8-1-0	Doug Dickey	9-2-0
3	Oklahoma	8-1-0	Chuck Fairbanks	10-1-0
4	Indiana	9-1-0	John Pont	9-2-0
5	Notre Dame	8-2-0	Ara Parseghian	same
6	Wyoming	10-0-0	Lloyd Eaton	10-1-0
7	Oregon St.	7-2-1	Dee Andros	same
8	Alabama	7-1-1	Bear Bryant	8-2-1
9	Purdue	8-2-0	Jack Mollenkopf	same
10	Penn St.	8-2-0	Joe Paterno	8-2-1

Key Bowl Games

Rose—#1 USC over #4 Indiana, 14-3; **Orange**—#3 Oklahoma over #2 Tennessee, 26-24; **Sugar**—LSU over #6 Wyoming, 20-13; **Cotton**—Texas A&M over #8 Alabama, 20-16; **Gator**—#10 Penn St. tied Florida St. 17-17.

1968

Final poll taken after bowl games for first time since close of 1965 season.

		After Bowls	Head Coach	Regular Season
1	Ohio St.	10-0-0	Woody Hayes	9-0-0
2	Penn St.	11-0-0	Joe Paterno	10-0-0
3	Texas	9-1-1	Darrell Royal	8-1-1
4	USC	9-1-1	John McKay	9-0-1
5	Notre Dame	7-2-1	Ara Parseghian	same
6	Arkansas	10-1-0	Frank Broyles	9-1-0
7	Kansas	9-2-0	Pepper Rodgers	9-1-0
8	Georgia	8-1-2	Vince Dooley	8-0-2
9	Missouri	8-3-0	Dan Devine	7-3-0
10	Purdue	8-2-0	Jack Mollenkopf	same
11	Oklahoma	7-4-0	Chuck Fairbanks	7-3-0
12	Michigan	8-2-0	Bump Elliott	same
13	Tennessee	8-2-1	Doug Dickey	8-1-1
14	SMU	8-3-0	Hayden Fry	7-3-0
15	Oregon St.	7-3-0	Dee Andros	same
16	Auburn	7-4-0	Shug Jordan	6-4-0
17	Alabama	8-3-0	Bear Bryant	8-2-0
18	Houston	6-2-2	Bill Yeoman	same
19	LSU	8-3-0	Charlie McClendon	7-3-0
20	Ohio Univ.	10-1-0	Bill Hess	10-0-0

Key Bowl Games

Rankings below reflect final regular season poll, released Dec.2. No bowls for then #7 Notre Dame and #11 Purdue.
Rose—#1 Ohio St. over #2 USC, 27-16; **Orange**—#3 Penn St. over #6 Kansas, 15-14; **Sugar**—#9 Arkansas over #4 Georgia, 16-2; **Cotton**—#5 Texas over #8 Tennessee, 36-13; **Bluebonnet**—#20 SMU over #10 Oklahoma, 28-27; **Gator**—#16 Missouri over #12 Alabama, 35-10.

1969

Final poll taken after bowl games.

		After Bowls	Head Coach	Regular Season
1	Texas	11-0-0	Darrell Royal	10-0-0
2	Penn St.	11-0-0	Joe Paterno	10-0-0
3	USC	10-0-1	John McKay	9-0-1
4	Ohio St.	8-1-0	Woody Hayes	same
5	Notre Dame	8-2-1	Ara Parseghian	8-1-1
6	Missouri	9-2-0	Dan Devine	9-1-0
7	Arkansas	9-2-0	Frank Broyles	9-1-0
8	Mississippi	8-3-0	Johnny Vaught	7-3-0
9	Michigan	8-3-0	Bo Schembechler	8-2-0
10	LSU	9-1-0	Charlie McClendon	same
11	Nebraska	9-2-0	Bob Devaney	8-2-0
12	Houston	9-2-0	Bill Yeoman	8-2-0
13	UCLA	8-1-1	Tommy Prothro	same
14	Florida	9-1-1	Ray Graves	8-1-1
15	Tennessee	9-2-0	Doug Dickey	9-1-0
16	Colorado	8-3-0	Eddie Crowder	7-3-0
17	West Virginia	10-1-0	Jim Carlen	9-1-0
18	Purdue	8-2-0	Jack Mollenkopf	same
19	Stanford	7-2-1	John Ralston	same
20	Auburn	8-3-0	Shug Jordan	8-2-0

Key Bowl Games

Rankings below reflect final regular season poll, released Dec.8. No bowls for then #4 Ohio St., #8 LSU and #10 UCLA.
Cotton—#1 Texas over #9 Notre Dame, 21-17; **Orange**—#2 Penn St. over #6 Missouri, 10-3; **Sugar**—#13 Ole Miss over #3 Arkansas, 27-22; **Rose**—#5 USC over #7 Michigan, 10-3.

Associated Press Final Polls (Cont.)

1970

Final poll taken after bowl games.

		After Bowls	Head Coach	Regular Season
1	Nebraska	11-0-1	Bob Devaney	10-0-1
2	Notre Dame	10-1-0	Ara Parseghian	9-0-1
3	Texas	10-1-0	Darrell Royal	10-0-0
4	Tennessee	11-1-0	Bill Battle	10-1-0
5	Ohio St.	9-1-0	Woody Hayes	9-0-0
6	Arizona St.	11-0-0	Frank Kush	10-0-0
7	LSU	9-3-0	Charlie McClendon	9-2-0
8	Stanford	9-3-0	John Ralston	8-3-0
9	Michigan	9-1-0	Bo Schembechler	same
10	Auburn	9-2-0	Shug Jordan	8-2-0
11	Arkansas	9-2-0	Frank Broyles	same
12	Toledo	12-0-0	Frank Lauterbur	11-0-0
13	Georgia Tech	9-3-0	Bud Carson	8-3-0
14	Dartmouth	9-0-0	Bob Blackman	same
15	USC	6-4-1	John McKay	same
16	Air Force	9-3-0	Ben Martin	9-2-0
17	Tulane	8-4-0	Jim Pittman	7-4-0
18	Penn St.	7-3-0	Joe Paterno	same
19	Houston	8-3-0	Bill Yeoman	same
20	Oklahoma	7-4-1	Chuck Fairbanks	7-4-0
	Mississippi	7-4-0	Johnny Vaught	7-3-0

Key Bowl Games

Rankings below reflect final regular season poll, released Dec.7. No bowls for then #4 Arkansas and #7 Michigan.
Cotton—#6 Notre Dame over #1 Texas, 24-11; **Rose**—#12 Stanford over #2 Ohio St., 27-17; **Orange**—#3 Nebraska over #8 LSU, 17-12; **Sugar**—#5 Tennessee over #11 Air Force, 34-13; **Peach**—#9 Ariz.St. over N.Carolina, 48-26;

1972

Final poll taken after bowl games.

		After Bowls	Head Coach	Regular Season
1	USC	12-0-0	John McKay	11-0-0
2	Oklahoma	11-1-0	Chuck Fairbanks	10-1-0
3	Texas	10-1-0	Darrell Royal	9-1-0
4	Nebraska	9-2-1	Bob Devaney	8-2-1
5	Auburn	10-1-0	Shug Jordan	9-1-0
6	Michigan	10-1-0	Bo Schembechler	same
7	Alabama	10-2-0	Bear Bryant	10-1-0
8	Tennessee	10-2-0	Bill Battle	9-2-0
9	Ohio St.	9-2-0	Woody Hayes	9-1-0
10	Penn St.	10-2-0	Joe Paterno	10-1-0
11	LSU	9-2-1	Charlie McClendon	9-1-1
12	North Carolina	11-1-0	Bill Dooley	10-1-0
13	Arizona St.	10-2-0	Frank Kush	9-2-0
14	Notre Dame	8-3-0	Ara Parseghian	8-2-0
15	UCLA	8-3-0	Pepper Rodgers	same
16	Colorado	8-4-0	Eddie Crowder	8-3-0
17	N.C.State	8-3-1	Lou Holtz	7-3-1
18	Louisville	9-1-0	Lee Corso	same
19	Washington St.	7-4-0	Jim Sweeney	same
20	Georgia Tech	7-4-1	Bill Fulcher	6-4-1

Key Bowl Games

Rankings below reflect final regular season poll, released Dec.4. No bowl for then #8 Michigan.
Rose—#1 USC over #3 Ohio St., 42-17; **Sugar**—#2 Oklahoma over #5 Penn St., 14-0; **Cotton**—#7 Texas over #4 Alabama, 17-13; **Orange**—#9 Nebraska over #12 Notre Dame, 40-6; **Gator**—#6 Auburn over #13 Colorado, 24-3; **Bluebonnet**—#11 Tennessee over #10 LSU, 24-17.

1971

Final poll taken after bowl games.

		After Bowls	Head Coach	Regular Season
1	Nebraska	13-0-0	Bob Devaney	12-0-0
2	Oklahoma	11-1-0	Chuck Fairbanks	10-1-0
3	Colorado	10-2-0	Eddie Crowder	9-2-0
4	Alabama	11-1-0	Bear Bryant	11-0-0
5	Penn St.	11-1-0	Joe Paterno	10-1-0
6	Michigan	11-1-0	Bo Schembechler	11-0-0
7	Georgia	11-1-0	Vince Dooley	10-1-0
8	Arizona St.	11-1-0	Frank Kush	10-1-0
9	Tennessee	10-2-0	Bill Battle	9-2-0
10	Stanford	9-3-0	John Ralston	8-3-0
11	LSU	9-3-0	Charlie McClendon	8-3-0
12	Auburn	9-2-0	Shug Jordan	9-1-0
13	Notre Dame	8-2-0	Ara Parseghian	same
14	Toledo	12-0-0	John Murphy	11-0-0
15	Mississippi	10-2-0	Billy Kinard	9-2-0
16	Arkansas	8-3-1	Frank Broyles	8-2-1
17	Houston	9-3-0	Bill Yeoman	9-2-0
18	Texas	8-3-0	Darrell Royal	8-2-0
19	Washington	8-3-0	Jim Owens	same
20	USC	6-4-1	John McKay	same

Key Bowl Games

Rankings below reflect final regular season poll, released Dec.6.
Orange—#1 Nebraska over #2 Alabama, 38-6; **Sugar**—#3 Oklahoma over #5 Auburn, 40-22; **Rose**—#16 Stanford over #4 Michigan, 13-12; **Gator**—#6 Georgia over N.Carolina, 7-3; **Bluebonnet**—#7 Colorado over #15 Houston, 29-17; **Fiesta**—#8 Ariz. St. over Florida St., 45-38; 14-13; **Cotton**—#10 Penn St. over #12 Texas, 30-6.

1973

Final poll taken after bowl games.

		After Bowls	Head Coach	Regular Season
1	Notre Dame	11-0-0	Ara Parseghian	10-0-0
2	Ohio St.	10-0-1	Woody Hayes	9-0-1
3	Oklahoma	10-0-1	Barry Switzer	same
4	Alabama	11-1-0	Bear Bryant	11-0-0
5	Penn St.	12-0-0	Joe Paterno	11-0-0
6	Michigan	10-0-1	Bo Schembechler	same
7	Nebraska	9-2-1	Tom Osborne	8-2-1
8	USC	9-2-1	John McKay	9-1-1
9	Arizona St.	11-1-0	Frank Kush	10-1-0
	Houston	11-1-0	Bill Yeoman	10-1-0
11	Texas Tech	11-1-0	Jim Carlen	10-1-0
12	UCLA	9-2-0	Pepper Rodgers	same
13	LSU	9-3-0	Charlie McClendon	9-2-0
14	Texas	8-3-0	Darrell Royal	8-2-0
15	Miami-OH	11-0-0	Bill Mallory	10-0-0
16	N.C.State	9-3-0	Lou Holtz	8-3-0
17	Missouri	8-4-0	Al Onofrio	7-4-0
18	Kansas	7-4-1	Don Fambrough	7-3-1
19	Tennessee	8-4-0	Bill Battle	8-3-0
20	Maryland	8-4-0	Jerry Claiborne	8-3-0
	Tulane	9-3-0	Bennie Ellender	9-2-0

Key Bowl Games

Rankings below reflect final regular season poll, released Dec.3. No bowls for then #2 Oklahoma (probation), #5 Michigan and #9 UCLA.
Sugar—#3 Notre Dame over #1 Alabama, 24-23; **Rose**—#4 Ohio St. over #7 USC, 42-21; **Orange**—#6 Penn St. over #13 LSU, 16-9; **Cotton**—#12 Nebraska over #8 Texas, 19-3; **Fiesta**—#10 Ariz.St. over Pitt, 28-7; **Bluebonnet**—#14 Houston over #17 Tulane, 47-7.

1974

Final poll taken after bowl games.

		After Bowls	Head Coach	Regular Season
1	Oklahoma	11-0-0	Barry Switzer	same
2	USC	10-1-1	John McKay	9-1-1
3	Michigan	10-1-0	Bo Schembechler	same
4	Ohio St.	10-2-0	Woody Hayes	10-1-0
5	Alabama	11-1-0	Bear Bryant	11-0-0
6	Notre Dame	10-2-0	Ara Parseghian	9-2-0
7	Penn St.	10-2-0	Joe Paterno	9-2-0
8	Auburn	10-2-0	Shug Jordan	9-2-0
9	Nebraska	9-3-0	Tom Osborne	8-3-0
10	Miami-OH	10-0-1	Dick Crum	9-0-1
11	N.C.State	9-2-1	Lou Holtz	9-2-0
12	Michigan St.	7-3-1	Denny Stolz	same
13	Maryland	8-4-0	Jerry Claiborne	8-3-0
14	Baylor	8-4-0	Grant Teaff	8-3-0
15	Florida	8-4-0	Doug Dickey	8-3-0
16	Texas A&M	8-3-0	Emory Ballard	same
17	Mississippi St.	9-3-0	Bob Tyler	8-3-0
	Texas	8-4-0	Darrell Royal	8-3-0
19	Houston	8-3-1	Bill Yeoman	8-3-0
20	Tennessee	7-3-2	Bill Battle	6-3-2

Key Bowl Games

Rankings below reflect final regular season poll, released Dec.2. No bowls for #1 Oklahoma (probation) and then #4 Michigan.
Orange—#9 Notre Dame over #2 Alabama, 13-11; **Rose**—#5 USC over #3 Ohio St., 18-17; **Gator**— #6 Auburn over #11 Texas, 27-3; **Cotton**—#7 Penn St. over #12 Baylor, 41-20; **Sugar**—#8 Nebraska over #18 Florida, 13-10; **Liberty**—Tennessee over #10 Maryland, 7-3.

1975

Final poll taken after bowl games.

		After Bowls	Head Coach	Regular Season
1	Oklahoma	11-1-0	Barry Switzer	10-1-0
2	Arizona St.	12-0-0	Frank Kush	11-0-0
3	Alabama	11-1-0	Bear Bryant	10-1-0
4	Ohio St.	11-1-0	Woody Hayes	11-0-0
5	UCLA	9-2-1	Dick Vermeil	8-2-1
6	Texas	10-2-0	Darrell Royal	9-2-0
7	Arkansas	10-2-0	Frank Broyles	9-2-0
8	Michigan	8-2-2	Bo Schembechler	8-1-2
9	Nebraska	10-2-0	Tom Osborne	10-1-0
10	Penn St.	9-3-0	Joe Paterno	9-2-0
11	Texas A&M	10-2-0	Emory Bellard	10-1-0
12	Miami-OH	11-1-0	Dick Crum	10-1-0
13	Maryland	9-2-1	Jerry Claiborne	8-2-1
14	California	8-3-0	Mike White	same
15	Pittsburgh	8-4-0	Johnny Majors	7-4-0
16	Colorado	9-3-0	Bill Mallory	9-2-0
17	USC	8-4-0	John McKay	7-4-0
18	Arizona	9-2-0	Jim Young	same
19	Georgia	9-3-0	Vince Dooley	9-2-0
20	West Virginia	9-3-0	Bobby Bowden	8-3-0

Key Bowl Games

Rankings below reflect final regular season poll, released Dec.1. Texas A&M was unbeaten and ranked 2nd in that poll, but lost to #18 Arkansas, 31-6, in its final regular season game on Dec.6.
Rose—#11 UCLA over #1 Ohio St., 23-10; **Liberty**—#17 USC over #2 Texas A&M, 20-0; **Orange**—#3 Oklahoma over #5 Michigan, 14-6; **Sugar**—#4 Alabama over #8 Penn St., 13-6; **Fiesta**—#7 Ariz. St. over #6 Nebraska, 17-14; **Bluebonnet**—#9 Texas over #10 Colorado, 38-21; **Cotton**—#18 Arkansas over #12 Georgia, 31-10.

1976

Final poll taken after bowl games.

		After Bowls	Head Coach	Regular Season
1	Pittsburgh	12-0-0	Johnny Majors	11-0-0
2	USC	11-1-0	John Robinson	10-1-0
3	Michigan	10-2-0	Bo Schembechler	10-1-0
4	Houston	10-2-0	Bill Yeoman	9-2-0
5	Oklahoma	9-2-1	Barry Switzer	8-2-1
6	Ohio St.	9-2-1	Woody Hayes	8-2-1
7	Texas A&M	10-2-0	Emory Bellard	9-2-0
8	Maryland	11-1-0	Jerry Claiborne	11-0-0
9	Nebraska	9-3-1	Tom Osborne	8-3-1
10	Georgia	10-2-0	Vince Dooley	10-1-0
11	Alabama	9-3-0	Bear Bryant	8-3-0
12	Notre Dame	9-3-0	Dan Devine	8-3-0
13	Texas Tech	10-2-0	Steve Sloan	10-1-0
14	Oklahoma St.	9-3-0	Jim Stanley	8-3-0
15	UCLA	9-2-1	Terry Donahue	9-1-1
16	Colorado	8-4-0	Bill Mallory	8-3-0
17	Rutgers	11-0-0	Frank Burns	same
18	Kentucky	8-4-0	Fran Curci	7-4-0
19	Iowa St.	8-3-0	Earle Bruce	same
20	Mississippi St.	9-2-0	Bob Tyler	same

Key Bowl Games

Rankings below reflect final regular season poll, released Nov.29. No bowl for then #20 Miss. St. (probation).
Sugar—#1 Pitt over #5 Georgia, 27-3; **Rose**—#3 USC over #2 Michigan, 14-6; **Cotton**—#6 Houston over #4 Maryland, 30-21; **Liberty**—#16 Alabama over #7 UCLA, 36-6; **Fiesta**—#8 Oklahoma over Wyoming, 41-7; **Bluebonnet**—#13 Nebraska over #9 Texas Tech, 27-24; **Sun**—#10 Texas A&M over Florida, 37-14; **Orange**—#11 Ohio St. over #12 Colorado, 27-10.

1977

Final poll taken after bowl games.

		After Bowls	Head Coach	Regular Season
1	Notre Dame	11-1-0	Dan Devine	10-1-0
2	Alabama	11-1-0	Bear Bryant	10-1-0
3	Arkansas	11-1-0	Lou Holtz	10-1-0
4	Texas	11-1-0	Fred Akers	11-0-0
5	Penn St.	11-1-0	Joe Paterno	10-1-0
6	Kentucky	10-1-0	Fran Curci	same
7	Oklahoma	10-2-0	Barry Switzer	10-1-0
8	Pittsburgh	9-2-1	Jackie Sherrill	8-2-1
9	Michigan	10-2-0	Bo Schembechler	10-1-0
10	Washington	8-4-0	Don James	7-4-0
11	Ohio St.	9-3-0	Woody Hayes	9-2-0
12	Nebraska	9-3-0	Tom Osborne	8-3-0
13	USC	8-4-0	John Robinson	7-4-0
14	Florida St.	10-2-0	Bobby Bowden	9-2-0
15	Stanford	9-3-0	Bill Walsh	8-3-0
16	San Diego St.	10-1-0	Claude Gilbert	same
17	North Carolina	8-3-1	Bill Dooley	8-2-1
18	Arizona St.	9-3-0	Frank Kush	9-2-0
19	Clemson	8-3-1	Charley Pell	8-2-1
20	BYU	9-2-0	LaVell Edwards	same

Key Bowl Games

Rankings below reflect final regular season poll, released Nov.28. No bowl for then #7 Kentucky (probation).
Cotton—#5 Notre Dame over #1 Texas, 38-10; **Orange**—#6 Arkansas over #2 Oklahoma, 31-6; **Sugar**—#3 Alabama over #9 Ohio St., 35-6; **Rose**—#13 Washington over #4 Michigan, 27-20; **Fiesta**—#8 Penn St. over #15 Ariz. St., 42-30; **Gator**—#10 Pitt over #11 Clemson, 34-3.

Associated Press Final Polls (Cont.)

1978

Final poll taken after bowl games.

		After Bowls	Head Coach	Regular Season
1	Alabama	11-1-0	Bear Bryant	10-1-0
2	USC	12-1-0	John Robinson	11-1-0
3	Oklahoma	11-1-0	Barry Switzer	10-1-0
4	Penn St.	11-1-0	Joe Paterno	11-0-0
5	Michigan	10-2-0	Bo Schembechler	10-1-0
6	Clemson	11-1-0	Charley Pell	10-1-0
7	Notre Dame	9-3-0	Dan Devine	8-3-0
8	Nebraska	9-3-0	Tom Osborne	9-2-0
9	Texas	9-3-0	Fred Akers	8-3-0
10	Houston	9-3-0	Bill Yeoman	9-2-0
11	Arkansas	9-2-1	Lou Holtz	9-2-0
12	Michigan St.	8-3-0	Darryl Rogers	same
13	Purdue	9-2-1	Jim Young	8-2-1
14	UCLA	8-3-1	Terry Donahue	8-3-0
15	Missouri	8-4-0	Warren Powers	7-4-0
16	Georgia	9-2-1	Vince Dooley	9-1-1
17	Stanford	8-4-0	Bill Walsh	7-4-0
18	N.C.State	9-3-0	Bo Rein	8-3-0
19	Texas A&M	8-4-0	E.Bellard (4-2) & T.Wilson (4-2)	7-4-0
20	Maryland	9-3-0	Jerry Claiborne	9-2-0

Key Bowl Games

Rankings below reflect final regular season poll, released Dec. 4. No bowl for then #12 Michigan St. (probation).

Sugar—#2 Alabama over #1 Penn St., 14-7; **Rose**—#3 USC over #5 Michigan, 17-10; **Orange**—#4 Oklahoma over #6 Nebraska, 31-24; **Gator**—#7 Clemson over #20 Ohio St., 17-15; **Fiesta**—#8 Arkansas tied #15 UCLA, 10-10; **Cotton**—#10 Notre Dame over #9 Houston, 35-34;

1980

Final poll taken after bowl games.

		After Bowls	Head Coach	Regular Season
1	Georgia	12-0-0	Vince Dooley	11-0-0
2	Pittsburgh	11-1-0	Jackie Sherrill	10-1-0
3	Oklahoma	10-2-0	Barry Switzer	9-2-0
4	Michigan	10-2-0	Bo Schembechler	9-2-0
5	Florida St.	10-2-0	Bobby Bowden	10-1-0
6	Alabama	10-2-0	Bear Bryant	9-2-0
7	Nebraska	10-2-0	Tom Osborne	9-2-0
8	Penn St.	10-2-0	Joe Paterno	9-2-0
9	Notre Dame	9-2-1	Dan Devine	9-1-1
10	North Carolina	11-1-0	Dick Crum	10-1-0
11	USC	8-2-1	John Robinson	same
12	BYU	12-1-0	LaVell Edwards	11-1-0
13	UCLA	9-2-0	Terry Donahue	same
14	Baylor	10-2-0	Grant Teaff	10-1-0
15	Ohio St.	9-3-0	Earle Bruce	9-2-0
16	Washington	9-3-0	Don James	9-2-0
17	Purdue	9-3-0	Jim Young	8-3-0
18	Miami-FL	9-3-0	H.Schnellenberger	8-3-0
19	Mississippi St.	9-3-0	Emory Bellard	9-2-0
20	SMU	8-4-0	Ron Meyer	8-3-0

Key Bowl Games

Rankings below reflect final regular season poll, released Dec.8.

Sugar—#1 Georgia over #7 Notre Dame, 17-10; **Orange**—#4 Oklahoma over #2 Florida St., 18-17; **Gator**—#3 Pitt over #18 S.Carolina, 37-9; **Rose**—#5 Michigan over #16 Washington, 23-6; **Cotton**—#9 Alabama over #6 Baylor, 30-2; **Sun**—#8 Nebraska over #17 Miss. St., 31-17; **Fiesta**—#10 Penn St. over #11 Ohio St., 31-19; **Bluebonnet**—#13 N.Carolina over Texas, 16-7.

1979

Final poll taken after bowl games.

		After Bowls	Head Coach	Regular Season
1	Alabama	12-0-0	Bear Bryant	11-0-0
2	USC	11-0-1	John Robinson	10-0-1
3	Oklahoma	11-1-0	Barry Switzer	10-1-0
4	Ohio St.	11-1-0	Earle Bruce	11-0-0
5	Houston	11-1-0	Bill Yeoman	10-1-0
6	Florida St.	11-1-0	Bobby Bowden	11-0-0
7	Pittsburgh	11-1-0	Jackie Sherrill	10-1-0
8	Arkansas	10-2-0	Lou Holtz	10-1-0
9	Nebraska	10-2-0	Tom Osborne	10-1-0
10	Purdue	10-2-0	Jim Young	9-2-0
11	Washington	9-3-0	Don James	8-3-0
12	Texas	9-3-0	Fred Akers	9-2-0
13	BYU	11-1-0	LaVell Edwards	11-0-0
14	Baylor	8-4-0	Grant Teaff	7-4-0
15	North Carolina	8-3-1	Dick Crum	7-3-1
16	Auburn	8-3-0	Doug Barfield	same
17	Temple	10-2-0	Wayne Hardin	9-2-0
18	Michigan	8-4-0	Bo Schembechler	8-3-0
19	Indiana	8-4-0	Lee Corso	7-4-0
20	Penn St.	8-4-0	Joe Paterno	7-4-0

Key Bowl Games

Rankings below reflect final regular season poll, released Dec.3. No bowl for then #17 Auburn (probation).

Sugar—#2 Alabama over #6 Arkansas, 24-9; **Rose**—#3 USC over #1 Ohio St., 17-16; **Orange**—#5 Oklahoma over #4 Florida St., 24-7; **Sun**—#13 Washington over #11 Texas, 14-7; **Cotton**—#8 Houston over #7 Nebraska, 17-14; **Fiesta**—#10 Pitt over Arizona, 16-10;

1981

Final poll taken after bowl games.

		After Bowls	Head Coach	Regular Season
1	Clemson	12-0-0	Danny Ford	11-0-0
2	Texas	10-1-1	Fred Akers	9-1-1
3	Penn St.	10-2-0	Joe Paterno	9-2-0
4	Pittsburgh	11-1-0	Jackie Sherrill	10-1-0
5	SMU	10-1-0	Ron Meyer	same
6	Georgia	10-2-0	Vince Dooley	10-1-0
7	Alabama	9-2-1	Bear Bryant	9-1-1
8	Miami-FL	9-2-0	H.Schnellenberger	same
9	North Carolina	10-2-0	Dick Crum	9-2-0
10	Washington	10-2-0	Don James	9-2-0
11	Nebraska	9-3-0	Tom Osborne	9-2-0
12	Michigan	9-3-0	Bo Schembechler	8-3-0
13	BYU	11-2-0	LaVell Edwards	10-2-0
14	USC	9-3-0	John Robinson	9-2-0
15	Ohio St.	9-3-0	Earle Bruce	8-3-0
16	Arizona St.	9-2-0	Darryl Rogers	same
17	West Virginia	9-3-0	Don Nehlen	8-3-0
18	Iowa	8-4-0	Hayden Fry	8-3-0
19	Missouri	8-4-0	Warren Powers	7-4-0
20	Oklahoma	7-4-1	Barry Switzer	6-4-1

Key Bowl Games

Rankings below reflect final regular season poll, released Nov.30. No bowl for then #5 SMU (probation), #9 Miami-FL (probation), and #17 Ariz. St. (probation).

Orange—#1 Clemson over #4 Nebraska, 22-15; **Sugar**—#10 Pitt over #2 Georgia, 24-20; **Cotton**—#6 Texas over #3 Alabama, 14-12; **Fiesta**—#7 Penn St. over #8 USC, 26-10; **Gator**—#11 N.Carolina over Arkansas, 31-27; **Rose**—#12 Washington over #13 Iowa, 28-0.

1982

Final poll taken after bowl games.

		After Bowls	Head Coach	Regular Season
1	Penn St.	11-1-0	Joe Paterno	10-1-0
2	SMU	11-0-1	Bobby Collins	10-0-1
3	Nebraska	12-1-0	Tom Osborne	11-1-0
4	Georgia	11-1-0	Vince Dooley	11-0-0
5	UCLA	10-1-1	Terry Donahue	9-1-1
6	Arizona St.	10-2-0	Darryl Rogers	9-2-0
7	Washington	10-2-0	Don James	9-2-0
8	Clemson	9-1-1	Danny Ford	same
9	Arkansas	9-2-1	Lou Holtz	8-2-1
10	Pittsburgh	9-3-0	Foge Fazio	9-2-0
11	LSU	8-3-1	Jerry Stovall	8-2-1
12	Ohio St.	9-3-0	Earle Bruce	8-3-0
13	Florida St.	9-3-0	Bobby Bowden	8-3-0
14	Auburn	9-3-0	Pat Dye	8-3-0
15	USC	8-3-0	John Robinson	same
16	Oklahoma	8-4-0	Barry Switzer	8-3-0
17	Texas	9-3-0	Fred Akers	9-2-0
18	North Carolina	8-4-0	Dick Crum	7-4-0
19	West Virginia	9-3-0	Don Nehlen	9-2-0
20	Maryland	8-4-0	Bobby Ross	8-3-0

Key Bowl Games

Rankings below reflect final regular season poll, released Dec.6. No bowl for then #7 Clemson (probation) and #15 USC (probation).

Sugar—#2 Penn St. over #1 Georgia, 27-23; **Orange**—#3 Nebraska over #13 LSU, 21-20; **Cotton**—#4 SMU over #6 Pitt, 7-3; **Rose**—#5 UCLA over #19 Michigan, 24-14; **Aloha**—#9 Washington over #16 Maryland, 21-20; **Fiesta**—#11 Ariz. St. over #12 Oklahoma, 32-21; **Bluebonnet**—#14 Arkansas over Florida, 28-24.

1983

Final poll taken after bowl games.

		After Bowls	Head Coach	Regular Season
1	Miami-FL	11-1-0	H.Schnellenberger	10-1-0
2	Nebraska	12-1-0	Tom Osborne	12-0-0
3	Auburn	11-1-0	Pat Dye	10-1-0
4	Georgia	10-1-1	Vince Dooley	9-1-1
5	Texas	11-1-0	Fred Akers	11-0-0
6	Florida	9-2-1	Charley Pell	8-2-1
7	BYU	11-1-0	LaVell Edwards	10-1-0
8	Michigan	9-3-0	Bo Schembechler	9-2-0
9	Ohio St.	9-3-0	Earle Bruce	8-3-0
10	Illinois	10-2-0	Mike White	10-1-0
11	Clemson	9-1-1	Danny Ford	same
12	SMU	10-2-0	Bobby Collins	10-1-0
13	Air Force	10-2-0	Ken Hatfield	9-2-0
14	Iowa	9-3-0	Hayden Fry	9-2-0
15	Alabama	8-4-0	Ray Perkins	7-4-0
16	West Virginia	9-3-0	Don Nehlen	8-3-0
17	UCLA	7-4-1	Terry Donahue	6-4-1
18	Pittsburgh	8-3-1	Foge Fazio	8-2-1
19	Boston College	9-3-0	Jack Bicknell	9-2-0
20	East Carolina	8-3-0	Ed Emory	same

Key Bowl Games

Rankings below reflect final regular season poll, released Dec.5. No bowl for then #12 Clemson (probation).

Orange—#5 Miami-FL over #1 Nebraska, 31-30; **Cotton**—#7 Georgia over #2 Texas, 10-9; **Sugar**—#3 Auburn over #8 Michigan, 9-7; **Rose**—UCLA over #4 Illinois, 45-9; **Holiday**—#9 BYU over Missouri, 21-17; **Gator**—#11 Florida over #10 Iowa, 14-6; **Fiesta**—#14 Ohio St. over #15 Pitt, 28-23.

1984

Final poll taken after bowl games.

		After Bowls	Head Coach	Regular Season
1	BYU	13-0-0	LaVell Edwards	12-0-0
2	Washington	11-1-0	Don James	10-1-0
3	Florida	9-1-1	C.Pell (0-1-1) & G.Hall (9-0)	same
4	Nebraska	10-2-0	Tom Osborne	9-2-0
5	Boston College	10-2-0	Jack Bicknell	9-2-0
6	Oklahoma	9-2-1	Barry Switzer	9-1-1
7	Oklahoma St.	10-2-0	Pat Jones	9-2-0
8	SMU	10-2-0	Bobby Collins	9-2-0
9	UCLA	9-3-0	Terry Donahue	8-3-0
10	USC	9-3-0	Ted Tollner	8-3-0
11	South Carolina	10-2-0	Joe Morrison	10-1-0
12	Maryland	9-3-0	Bobby Ross	8-3-0
13	Ohio St.	9-3-0	Earle Bruce	9-2-0
14	Auburn	9-4-0	Pat Dye	8-4-0
15	LSU	8-3-1	Bill Arnsparger	8-2-1
16	Iowa	8-4-1	Hayden Fry	7-4-1
17	Florida St.	7-3-2	Bobby Bowden	7-3-1
18	Miami-FL	8-5-0	Jimmy Johnson	8-4-0
19	Kentucky	9-3-0	Jerry Claiborne	8-3-0
20	Virginia	8-2-2	George Welsh	7-2-2

Key Bowl Games

Rankings below reflect final regular season poll, released Dec.3. No bowl for then #3 Florida (probation).

Holiday—#1 BYU over Michigan, 24-17; **Orange**—#4 Washington over #2 Oklahoma, 28-17; **Sugar**—#5 Nebraska over #11 LSU, 28-10; **Rose**—#18 USC over #6 Ohio St., 20-17; **Gator**—#9 Okla. St. over #7 S. Carolina, 21-14; **Cotton**—#8 BC over Houston, 45-28; **Aloha**—#10 SMU over #17 Notre Dame, 27-20.

1985

Final poll taken after bowl games.

		After Bowls	Head Coach	Regular Season
1	Oklahoma	11-1-0	Barry Switzer	10-1-0
2	Michigan	10-1-1	Bo Schembechler	9-1-1
3	Penn St.	11-1-0	Joe Paterno	11-0-0
4	Tennessee	9-1-2	Johnny Majors	8-1-2
5	Florida	9-1-1	Galen Hall	same
6	Texas A&M	10-2-0	Jackie Sherrill	9-2-0
7	UCLA	9-2-1	Terry Donahue	8-2-1
8	Air Force	12-1-0	Fisher DeBerry	11-1-0
9	Miami-FL	10-2-0	Jimmy Johnson	10-1-0
10	Iowa	10-2-0	Hayden Fry	10-1-0
11	Nebraska	9-3-0	Tom Osborne	9-2-0
12	Arkansas	10-2-0	Ken Hatfield	9-2-0
13	Alabama	9-2-1	Ray Perkins	8-2-1
14	Ohio St.	9-3-0	Earle Bruce	8-3-0
15	Florida St.	9-3-0	Bobby Bowden	8-3-0
16	BYU	11-3-0	LaVell Edwards	11-2-0
17	Baylor	9-3-0	Grant Teaff	8-3-0
18	Maryland	9-3-0	Bobby Ross	8-3-0
19	Georgia Tech	9-2-1	Bill Curry	8-2-1
20	LSU	9-2-1	Bill Arnsparger	9-1-1

Key Bowl Games

Rankings below reflect final regular season poll, released Dec. 9. No bowl for then #6 Florida (probation).

Orange—#3 Oklahoma over #1 Penn St., 25-10; **Sugar**—#8 Tennessee over #2 Miami-FL, 35-7; **Rose**—#13 UCLA over #4 Iowa, 45-28; **Fiesta**—Michigan over #7 Nebraska, 27-23; **Bluebonnet**—#10 Air Force over Texas, 24-16; **Cotton**—#11 Texas A&M over #16 Auburn, 36-16.

Associated Press Final Polls (Cont.)

1986
Final poll taken after bowl games.

		After Bowls	Head Coach	Regular Season
1	Penn St.	12-0-0	Joe Paterno	11-0-0
2	Miami-FL	11-1-0	Jimmy Johnson	11-0-0
3	Oklahoma	11-1-0	Barry Switzer	10-1-0
4	Arizona St.	10-1-1	John Cooper	9-1-1
5	Nebraska	10-2-0	Tom Osborne	9-2-0
6	Auburn	10-2-0	Pat Dye	9-2-0
7	Ohio St.	10-3-0	Earle Bruce	9-3-0
8	Michigan	11-2-0	Bo Schembechler	11-1-0
9	Alabama	10-3-0	Ray Perkins	9-3-0
10	LSU	9-3-0	Bill Arnsparger	9-2-0
11	Arizona	9-3-0	Larry Smith	8-3-0
12	Baylor	9-3-0	Grant Teaff	8-3-0
13	Texas A&M	9-3-0	Jackie Sherrill	9-2-0
14	UCLA	8-3-1	Terry Donahue	7-3-1
15	Arkansas	9-3-0	Ken Hatfield	9-2-0
16	Iowa	9-3-0	Hayden Fry	8-3-0
17	Clemson	8-2-2	Danny Ford	7-2-2
18	Washington	8-3-1	Don James	8-2-1
19	Boston College	9-3-0	Jack Bicknell	8-3-0
20	Virginia Tech	9-2-1	Bill Dooley	8-2-1

Key Bowl Games

Rankings below reflect final regular season poll, released Dec.1.
Fiesta—#2 Penn St. over #1 Miami-FL, 14-10; **Orange**—#3 Oklahoma over #9 Arkansas, 42-8; **Rose**—#7 Ariz. St. over #4 Michigan, 22-15; **Sugar**—#6 Nebraska over #5 LSU, 30-15; **Cotton**—#11 Ohio St. over #8 Texas A&M, 28-12; **Citrus**—#10 Auburn over USC, 16-7; **Sun**—#13 Alabama over #12 Washington, 28-6.

1987
Final poll taken after bowl games.

		After Bowls	Head Coach	Regular Season
1	Miami-FL	12-0-0	Jimmy Johnson	11-0-0
2	Florida St.	11-1-0	Bobby Bowden	10-1-0
3	Oklahoma	11-1-0	Barry Switzer	11-0-0
4	Syracuse	11-0-1	Dick MacPherson	11-0-0
5	LSU	10-1-1	Mike Archer	9-1-1
6	Nebraska	10-2-0	Tom Osborne	10-1-0
7	Auburn	9-1-2	Pat Dye	9-1-1
8	Michigan St.	9-2-1	George Perles	8-2-1
9	UCLA	10-2-0	Terry Donahue	9-2-0
10	Texas A&M	10-2-0	Jackie Sherrill	9-2-0
11	Oklahoma St.	10-2-0	Pat Jones	9-2-0
12	Clemson	10-2-0	Danny Ford	9-2-0
13	Georgia	9-3-0	Vince Dooley	8-3-0
14	Tennessee	10-2-1	Johnny Majors	9-2-1
15	South Carolina	8-4-0	Joe Morrison	8-3-0
16	Iowa	10-3-0	Hayden Fry	9-3-0
17	Notre Dame	8-4-0	Lou Holtz	8-3-0
18	USC	8-4-0	Larry Smith	8-3-0
19	Michigan	8-4-0	Bo Schembechler	7-4-0
20	Arizona St.	7-4-1	John Cooper	6-4-1

Key Bowl Games

Rankings below reflect final regular season poll, released Dec.7.
Orange—#2 Miami-FL over #1 Oklahoma, 20-14; **Fiesta**—#3 Florida St. over #5 Nebraska, 31-28; **Sugar**—#4 Syracuse tied #6 Auburn, 16-16; **Gator**—#7 LSU over #9 S.Carolina, 30-13; **Rose**—#8 Mich. St. over #16 USC, 20-17; **Aloha**—#10 UCLA over Florida, 20-16; **Cotton**—#13 Texas A&M over #12 Notre Dame, 35-10.

1988
Final poll taken after bowl games.

		After Bowls	Head Coach	Regular Season
1	Notre Dame	12-0-0	Lou Holtz	11-0-0
2	Miami-FL	11-1-0	Jimmy Johnson	10-1-0
3	Florida St.	11-1-0	Bobby Bowden	10-1-0
4	Michigan	9-2-1	Bo Schembechler	8-2-1
5	West Virginia	11-1-0	Don Nehlen	11-0-0
6	UCLA	10-2-0	Terry Donahue	9-2-0
7	USC	10-2-0	Larry Smith	10-1-0
8	Auburn	10-2-0	Pat Dye	10-1-0
9	Clemson	10-2-0	Danny Ford	9-2-0
10	Nebraska	11-2-0	Tom Osborne	11-1-0
11	Oklahoma St.	10-2-0	Pat Jones	9-2-0
12	Arkansas	10-2-0	Ken Hatfield	10-1-0
13	Syracuse	10-2-0	Dick MacPherson	9-2-0
14	Oklahoma	9-3-0	Barry Switzer	9-2-0
15	Georgia	9-3-0	Vince Dooley	8-3-0
16	Washington St.	9-3-0	Dennis Erickson	8-3-0
17	Alabama	9-3-0	Bill Curry	8-3-0
18	Houston	9-3-0	Jack Pardee	9-2-0
19	LSU	8-4-0	Mike Archer	8-3-0
20	Indiana	8-3-1	Bill Mallory	7-3-1

Key Bowl Games

Rankings below reflect final regular season poll, released Dec.5.
Fiesta—#1 Notre Dame over #3 West Va., 34-21; **Orange**—#2 Miami-FL over #6 Nebraska, 23-3; **Sugar**—#4 Florida St. over #7 Auburn, 13-7; **Rose**—#11 Michigan over #5 USC, 22-14; **Cotton**—#9 UCLA over #8 Arkansas, 17-3; **Citrus**—#13 Clemson over #10 Oklahoma, 13-6.

All-Time AP Top 20

The composite AP Top 20 from the 1936 season through 1990, based on the final rankings of each year. The final AP poll has been taken after the bowl games in 1965 and since 1969. Team point totals are based on 20 points for all 1st place finishes, 19 for each 2nd, etc.). Also listed are the number of times named national champion by AP, and times ranked in the final Top 10 and Top 20.

		Pts	AP No. 1	Top 10	Top 20
1	Notre Dame	570	8	32	39
2	Oklahoma	549	6	29	39
3	Michigan	501	1	30	39
4	Alabama	482	5	27	36
5	Ohio St.	436	3	21	34
6	USC	397	3	20	34
7	Nebraska	395	2	22	30
8	Texas	393	2	19	30
9	Tennessee	332	1	17	28
10	Penn St.	312	2	17	27
11	UCLA	288	0	14	25
12	LSU	260	1	14	23
13	Arkansas	259	0	13	23
14	Auburn	242	1	12	23
15	Michigan St	238	1	12	19
16	Georgia	221	0	12	18
17	Miami FL	197	3	10	15
18	Pittsburgh	194	2	10	16
19	Georgia Tech	188	0	9	17
	Mississippi	188	0	10	16

1989

Final poll taken after bowl games.

		After Bowls	Head Coach	Regular Season
1	Miami-FL	11-1-0	Dennis Erickson	10-1-0
2	Notre Dame	12-1-0	Lou Holtz	11-1-0
3	Florida St.	10-2-0	Bobby Bowden	9-2-0
4	Colorado	11-1-0	Bill McCartney	11-0-0
5	Tennessee	11-1-0	Johnny Majors	10-1-0
6	Auburn	10-2-0	Pat Dye	9-2-0
7	Michigan	10-2-0	Bo Schembechler	10-1-0
8	USC	9-2-1	Larry Smith	8-2-1
9	Alabama	10-2-0	Bill Curry	10-1-0
10	Illinois	10-2-0	John Mackovic	9-2-0
11	Nebraska	10-2-0	Tom Osborne	10-1-0
12	Clemson	10-2-0	Danny Ford	9-2-0
13	Arkansas	10-2-0	Ken Hatfield	10-1-0
14	Houston	9-2-0	Jack Pardee	same
15	Penn St.	8-3-1	Joe Paterno	7-3-1
16	Michigan St.	8-4-0	George Perles	7-4-0
17	Pittsburgh	8-3-1	M.Gottfried (7-3-1) & P.Hackett (1-0)	7-3-1
18	Virginia	10-3-0	George Welsh	10-2-0
19	Texas Tech	9-3-0	Spike Dykes	8-3-0
20	Texas A&M	8-4-0	R.C.Slocum	8-3-0
21	West Virginia	8-3-1	Don Nehlen	8-2-1
22	BYU	10-3-0	LaVell Edwards	10-2-0
23	Washington	8-4-0	Don James	7-4-0
24	Ohio St.	8-4-0	John Cooper	8-3-0
25	Arizona	8-4-0	Dick Tomey	7-4-0

Key Bowl Games

Rankings below reflect final regular season poll, released Dec.11. No bowl for then #13 Houston (probation).

Orange—#4 Notre Dame over #1 Colorado, 21-6; **Sugar**—#2 Miami-FL over #7 Alabama, 33-25; **Rose**—#12 USC over #3 Michigan, 17-10; **Fiesta**—#5 Florida St. over #6 Nebraska, 41-17; **Cotton**—#8 Tennessee over #10 Arkansas, 31-27; **Hall of Fame**—#9 Auburn over #21 Ohio St., 31-14; **Citrus**—#11 Illinois over #15 Virginia, 31-21.

1990

Final poll taken after bowl games.

		After Bowls	Head Coach	Regular Season
1	Colorado	11-1-1	Bill McCartney	10-1-1
2	Georgia Tech	11-0-1	Bobby Ross	10-0-1
3	Miami-FL	10-2-0	Dennis Erickson	9-2-0
4	Florida St.	10-2-0	Bobby Bowden	9-2-0
5	Washington	10-2-0	Don James	9-2-0
6	Notre Dame	9-3-0	Lou Holtz	9-2-0
7	Michigan	9-3-0	Gary Moeller	8-3-0
8	Tennessee	9-2-2	Johnny Majors	8-2-2
9	Clemson	10-2-0	Ken Hatfield	9-2-0
10	Houston	10-1-0	John Jenkins	same
11	Penn St.	9-3-0	Joe Paterno	9-2-0
12	Texas	10-2-0	David McWilliams	10-1-0
13	Florida	9-2-0	Steve Spurrier	same
14	Louisville	10-1-1	H.Schnellenberger	9-1-1
15	Texas A&M	9-3-1	R.C.Slocum	8-3-1
16	Michigan St.	8-3-1	George Perles	7-3-1
17	Oklahoma	8-3-0	Gary Gibbs	same
18	Iowa	8-4-0	Hayden Fry	8-3-0
19	Auburn	8-3-1	Pat Dye	7-3-1
20	USC	8-4-1	Larry Smith	8-3-1
21	Mississippi	9-3-0	Billy Brewer	9-2-0
22	BYU	10-3-0	LaVell Edwards	10-2-0
23	Virginia	8-4-0	George Welsh	8-3-0
24	Nebraska	9-3-0	Tom Osborne	9-2-0
25	Illinois	8-4-0	John Mackovic	8-3-0

Key Bowl Games

Rankings below reflect final regular season poll, released Dec.3. No bowl for then #11 Houston (probation), #11 Florida (probation) and #20 Oklahoma (probation).

Orange—#1 Colorado over #5 Notre Dame, 10-9; **Citrus**—#2 Ga. Tech over #19 Nebraska, 45-21; **Cotton**—#4 Miami-FL over #3 Texas, 46-3; **Blockbuster**—#6 Florida St. over #3 Penn St., 24-17; **Rose**—#8 Washington over #17 Iowa, 46-34; **Sugar**—#10 Tennessee over Virginia, 23-22; **Gator**—#12 Michigan over #15 Ole Miss, 35-3.

Longest Division I Streaks

Winning Streaks
(Including bowl games)

No		Seasons	Spoiler	Score
47	Oklahoma	1953-57	Notre Dame	7-0
39	Washington	1908-14	Oregon St.	0-0
37	Yale	1890-93	Princeton	6-0
37	Yale	1887-89	Princeton	10-0
35	Toledo	1969-71	Tampa	21-0
34	Penn	1894-96	Lafayette	6-4
31	Oklahoma	1948-50	Kentucky	13-7*
31	Pittsburgh	1914-18	Cleve. Naval	10-9
31	Penn	1896-98	Harvard	10-0
30	Texas	1968-70	Notre Dame	24-11*
29	Michigan	1901-03	Minnesota	6-6
28	Alabama	1978-80	Miss.St.	6-3
28	Oklahoma	1973-75	Kansas	23-3
28	Mich.St.	1950-53	Purdue	6-0
27	Nebraska	1901-04	Colorado	6-0
26	Cornell	1921-24	Williams	14-7
26	Michigan	1903-05	Chicago	2-0
25	BYU	1983-85	UCLA	27-24
25	Michigan	1946-49	Army	21-7
25	Army	1944-46	Notre Dame	0-0
25	USC	1931-33	Oregon St.	0-0

*Note: Kentucky beat Oklahoma in 1951 Sugar Bowl and Notre Dame beat Texas in 1971 Cotton Bowl.

Unbeaten Streaks
(Including bowl games)

No	W-T		Seasons	Spoiler	Score
63	59-4	Washington	1907-17	California	27-0
56	55-1	Michigan	1901-05	Chicago	2-0
50	46-4	California	1920-25	Olympic	15-0
48	47-1	Oklahoma	1953-57	N. Dame	7-0
48	47-1	Yale	1885-89	Princeton	10-0
47	42-5	Yale	1879-85	Princeton	6-5
44	42-2	Yale	1894-96	Princeton	24-6
42	39-3	Yale	1904-08	Harvard	4-0
39	37-2	N. Dame	1946-50	Purdue	28-14
37	36-1	Oklahoma	1972-75	Kansas	23-3
35	34-1	Minnesota	1903-05	Wisconsin	16-12

Losing Streaks

No		Seasons	Victim	Score
44	Columbia	1983-88	Princeton	16-14
34	Northwestern	1979-82	No.Illinois	31-6
28	Virginia	1958-60	Wm.&Mary	21-6*
28	Kansas St.	1945-48	Arkansas St	37-6
27	E.Michigan	1980-82	Kent St.	9-7

*Note: Virginia ended its losing streak in the opening game of the 1961 season.

All-Time Winningest Division I-A Teams

Schools classified as Divison I-A for at least 10 years; through 1990 season (including bowl games).

Top 25 Winning Percentage

		Yrs	Gm	W	L	T	Pct	Bowls App	Bowls Record
1	Notre Dame	102	938	692	206	40	.759	16	10-6-0
2	Michigan	111	981	712	236	33	.743	22	10-12-0
3	Alabama	96	934	658	233	43	.728	43	23-17-3
4	Oklahoma	96	916	636	230	50	.722	29	18-10-1
5	Texas	98	959	671	257	31	.716	34	16-16-2
6	Southern Cal	98	900	613	236	51	.709	34	22-12-0
7	Ohio State	101	941	633	257	51	.700	23	11-12-0
8	Penn State	104	969	646	282	41	.688	27	16-9-2
9	Nebraska	101	967	644	284	39	.686	29	14-15-0
10	Tennessee	94	929	609	268	52	.684	31	17-14-0
11	Central Michigan	90	738	464	242	32	.650	4	3-1-0
12	Army	101	932	573	309	50	.642	3	2-1-0
13	Louisiana State	97	911	561	304	46	.641	28	11-16-1
14	Miami, Ohio	102	863	530	293	40	.637	7	5-2-0
15	Arizona State	78	690	426	240	24	.635	15	9-5-1
16	Washington	101	886	534	303	49	.630	19	11-7-1
17	Georgia	97	940	565	322	53	.629	29	13-13-3
18	Auburn	98	906	537	324	45	.618	23	12-9-2
19	Florida State	44	470	282	172	16	.617	20	11-7-2
20	Michigan State	94	858	507	308	43	.616	10	5-5-0
21	Minnesota	107	924	547	334	43	.615	5	2-3-0
22	Colorado	101	905	532	340	33	.606	15	5-10-0
23	Arkansas	97	917	536	343	38	.605	26	9-14-3
24	UCLA	72	719	414	268	37	.602	17	9-7-1
25	Pittsburgh	101	957	554	361	42	.601	18	8-10-0

Top 50 Victories

		Wins			Wins			Wins
1	Michigan	712	18	Auburn	537	35	Vanderbilt	489
2	Notre Dame	692	19	Arkansas	536	36	Illinois	479
3	Texas	671		Georgia Tech	536		Virginia	479
4	Alabama	658	21	West Virginia	535	38	Kentucky	477
5	Penn St.	646	22	Washington	534	39	Boston College	476
6	Nebraska	644	23	Colorado	532	40	Central Michigan	464
7	Oklahoma	636	24	Miami-OH	530	41	Purdue	462
8	Ohio State	633	25	North Carolina	522	42	Florida	461
9	Southern Cal	613	26	Texas A&M	517	43	Stanford	458
10	Tennessee	609	27	Rutgers	513		Wisconsin	458
11	Army	573	28	Michigan St.	507		Kansas	458
12	Georgia	565		California	507	46	Tulsa	456
13	Louisiana St.	561	30	Clemson	503	47	Utah	453
14	Syracuse	557	31	Missouri	498	48	Baylor	448
15	Pittsburgh	554		Maryland	498	49	Iowa	444
16	Minnesota	547	33	Virginia Tech	497	50	Arizona	439
17	Navy	540	34	Mississippi	494			

Note: Division I-AA schools with over 500 wins through 1990: Yale (760), Harvard (691), Princeton (682), Penn (675), Dartmouth (569), Lafayette (545), Cornell (532), Holy Cross (502).

Bowl Appearances

		App	Overall W	L	T	Big Four W	L	T
1	Alabama	43	23	17	3	17	12	1
2	Southern Cal	34	22	12	0	19	8	0
	Texas	34	16	16	2	12	10	0
4	Tennessee	31	17	14	0	7	9	0
5	Oklahoma	29	18	10	1	15	6	0
	Georgia	29	13	13	3	7	6	0
	Nebraska	29	14	15	0	9	10	0
8	LSU	28	11	16	1	7	10	1
9	Penn St.	27	16	9	2	6	5	1
10	Arkansas	26	9	14	3	4	10	1
11	Georgia Tech	24	16	8	0	9	3	0
	Mississippi	24	13	11	0	6	5	0
13	Auburn	23	12	9	2	2	4	1
	Ohio State	23	11	12	0	7	8	0
15	Michigan	22	10	12	0	6	10	0
16	Florida St	20	11	7	2	1	2	0
17	Missouri	19	8	11	0	2	5	0
	Washington	19	11	7	1	6	5	1
19	Texas A&M	18	11	7	0	5	3	0
	Pittsburgh	18	8	10	0	3	5	0
	Florida	18	8	10	0	1	2	0
	Texas Tech	18	4	13	1	0	1	0

Note: The "Big Four" bowls are the Rose, Orange, Sugar and Cotton. Only Alabama, Georgia, Georgia Tech and Notre Dame have won all four.

Bowl Games
JAN. 1, 1902 — JAN. 1, 1991
Rose Bowl

City: Pasadena, CA; **Stadium:** Rose Bowl; **Capacity:** 104,091; **Playing surface:** grass; **Automatic berths:** Pac-10 champion vs Big 10 champion (since 1947). **First year:** 1902; **Playing sites:** Tournament Park (1902, 1916–22), Rose Bowl (1923–41), Duke Stadium, Durham, NC (1942); Rose Bowl (since 1943).

Multiple wins: USC (19); Michigan (6); Ohio St., Stanford, UCLA and Washington (5); Alabama (4); Illinois and Michigan St. (3); California and Iowa (2).

Year		Year		Year	
1902*	Michigan 49, Stanford 0	1941	Stanford 21, Nebraska 13	1967	Purdue 14, USC 13
1916	Washington St. 14, Brown 0	1942	Oregon St. 20, Duke 16	1968	USC 14, Indiana 3
1917	Oregon 14, Penn 0	1943	Georgia 9, UCLA 0	1969	Ohio St. 27, USC 16
1918	Mare Island 19, Camp Lewis 7	1944	USC 29, Washington 0		
1919	Great Lakes 17, Mare Is. 0	1945	USC 25, Tennessee 0	1970	USC 10, Michigan 3
		1946	Alabama 34, USC 14	1971	Stanford 27, Ohio St. 17
1920	Harvard 7, Oregon 6	1947	Illinois 45, UCLA 14	1972	Stanford 13, Michigan 12
1921	California 28, Ohio St. 0	1948	Michigan 49, USC 0	1973	USC 42, Ohio St. 17
1922	0–0, California vs Wash.& Jeff.	1949	N'western 20, California 14	1974	Ohio St. 42, USC 21
1923	USC 14, Penn St. 0			1975	USC 18, Ohio St. 17
1924	14–14, Navy vs Washington	1950	Ohio St. 17, California 14	1976	UCLA 23, Ohio St. 10
1925	Notre Dame 27, Stanford 10	1951	Michigan 14, California 6	1977	USC 14, Michigan 6
1926	Alabama 20, Washington 19	1952	Illinois 40, Stanford 7	1978	Washington 27, Michigan 20
1927	7–7, Alabama vs Stanford	1953	USC 7, Wisconsin 0	1979	USC 17, Michigan 10
1928	Stanford 7, Pittsburgh 6	1954	Michigan St. 28, UCLA 20		
1929	Ga.Tech 8, California 7	1955	Ohio St. 20, USC 7	1980	USC 17, Ohio St. 16
		1956	Michigan St. 17, UCLA 14	1981	Michigan 23, Washington 6
1930	USC 47, Pittsburgh 14	1957	Iowa 35, Oregon St. 19	1982	Washington 28, Iowa 0
1931	Alabama 24, Wash.St. 0	1958	Ohio St. 10, Oregon 7	1983	UCLA 24, Michigan 14
1932	USC 21, Tulane 12	1959	Iowa 38, California 12	1984	UCLA 45, Illinois 9
1933	USC 35, Pittsburgh 0			1985	USC 20, Ohio St. 17
1934	Columbia 7, Stanford 0	1960	Washington 44, Wisconsin 8	1986	UCLA 45, Iowa 28
1935	Alabama 29, Stanford 13	1961	Washington 17, Minnesota 7	1987	Arizona St. 22, Michigan 15
1936	Stanford 7, SMU 0	1962	Minnesota 21, UCLA 3	1988	Michigan St. 20, USC 17
1937	Pitt 21, Washington 0	1963	USC 42, Wisconsin 37	1989	Michigan 22, USC 14
1938	California 13, Alabama 0	1964	Illinois 17, Washington 7		
1939	USC 7, Duke 3	1965	Michigan 34, Oregon St. 7	1990	USC 17, Michigan 10
1940	USC 14, Tennessee 0	1966	UCLA 14, Michigan St. 12	1991	Washington 46, Iowa 34

*January game since 1902.

Orange Bowl

City: Miami, FL; **Stadium:** Orange Bowl; **Capacity:** 75,500; **Playing surface:** grass; **Automatic berths:** Big 8 champion (1954–64 and 1976–present). **First year:** 1935; **Playing sites:** Orange Bowl (since 1935).

Multiple wins: Oklahoma (11); Nebraska (5); Alabama and Miami-FL (4); Georgia Tech and Penn St. (3); Clemson, Colorado, Georgia, LSU, Notre Dame and Texas (2).

Year		Year		Year	
1935*	Bucknell 26, Miami-FL 0	1954	Oklahoma 7, Maryland 0	1973	Nebraska 40, Notre Dame 6
1936	Catholic U. 20, Mississippi 19	1955	Duke 34, Nebraska 7	1974	Penn St. 16, LSU 9
1937	Duquesne 13, Miss.St. 12	1956	Oklahoma 20, Maryland 6	1975	Notre Dame 13, Alabama 11
1938	Auburn 6, Michigan St. 0	1957	Colorado 27, Clemson 21	1976	Oklahoma 14, Michigan 6
1939	Tennessee 17, Oklahoma 0	1958	Oklahoma 48, Duke 21	1977	Ohio St. 27, Colorado 10
		1959	Oklahoma 21, Syracuse 6	1978	Arkansas 31, Oklahoma 6
1940	Georgia Tech 21, Missouri 7			1979	Oklahoma 31, Nebraska 24
1941	Miss.St. 14, Georgetown 7	1960	Georgia 14, Missouri 0		
1942	Georgia 40, TCU 26	1961	Missouri 21, Navy 14	1980	Oklahoma 24, Florida St. 7
1943	Alabama 37, Boston Col. 21	1962	LSU 25, Colorado 7	1981	Oklahoma 18, Florida St. 17
1944	LSU 19, Texas A&M 14	1963	Alabama 17, Oklahoma 0	1982	Clemson 22, Nebraska 15
1945	Tulsa 26, Georgia Tech 12	1964	Nebraska 13, Auburn 7	1983	Nebraska 21, LSU 20
1946	Miami-FL 13, Holy Cross 6	1965‡	Texas 21, Alabama 17	1984	Miami-FL 31, Nebraska 30
1947	Rice 8, Tennessee 0	1966	Alabama 39, Nebraska 28	1985	Washington 28, Oklahoma 17
1948	Georgia Tech 20, Kansas 14	1967	Florida 27, Georgia Tech 12	1986	Oklahoma 25, Penn St. 10
1949	Texas 41, Georgia 28	1968	Oklahoma 26, Tennessee 24	1987	Oklahoma 42, Arkansas 8
		1969	Penn St. 15, Kansas 14	1988	Miami-FL 20, Oklahoma 14
1950	Santa Clara 21, Kentucky 13			1989	Miami-FL 23, Nebraska 3
1951	Clemson 15, Miami-FL 14	1970	Penn St. 10, Missouri 3		
1952	Georgia Tech 17, Baylor 14	1971	Nebraska 17, LSU 12	1990	Notre Dame, 21, Colorado 6
1953	Alabama 61, Syracuse 6	1972	Nebraska 38, Alabama 6	1991	Colorado 10, Notre Dame 9

*January game since 1937.   ‡Night game since 1965.

Bowl Games (Cont.)

Sugar Bowl

City: New Orleans, LA; **Stadium:** Louisiana Superdome; **Capacity:** 69,548; **Playing surface:** AstroTurf; **Automatic berths:** Southeastern Conference champion (since 1977). **First year:** 1935; **Playing sites:** Tulane Stadium (1935–74), Superdome (since 1974).

Multiple wins: Alabama (7); Mississippi (5); Georgia Tech, Oklahoma and Tennessee (4); LSU and Nebraska (3); Georgia, Pittsburgh, Santa Clara and TCU (2).

Year		Year		Year	
1935*	Tulane 20, Temple 14	1954	Georgia Tech 42, West Va. 19	1972	Oklahoma 14, Penn St. 0
1936	TCU 3, LSU 2	1955	Navy 21, Mississippi 0	1973	Notre Dame 24, Alabama 23
1937	Santa Clara 21, LSU 14	1956	Georgia Tech 7, Pittsburgh 0	1974	Nebraska 13, Florida 10
1938	Santa Clara 6, LSU 0	1957	Baylor 13, Tennessee 7	1975	Alabama 13, Penn St. 6
1939	TCU 15, Carnegie Tech 7	1958	Mississippi 39, Texas 7	1977*	Pittsburgh 27, Georgia 3
		1959	LSU 7, Clemson 0	1978	Alabama 35, Ohio St. 6
1940	Texas A&M 14, Tulane 13			1979	Alabama 14, Penn St. 7
1941	Boston Col. 19, Tennessee 13	1960	Mississippi 21, LSU 0		
1942	Fordham 2, Missouri 0	1961	Mississippi 14, Rice 6	1980	Alabama 24, Arkansas 9
1943	Tennessee 14, Tulsa 7	1962	Alabama 10, Arkansas 3	1981	Georgia 17, Notre Dame 10
1944	Georgia Tech 20, Tulsa 18	1963	Mississippi 17, Arkansas 13	1982	Pittsburgh 24, Georgia 20
1945	Duke 29, Alabama 26	1964	Alabama 12, Mississippi 7	1983	Penn St. 27, Georgia 23
1946	Okla.A&M 33, St.Mary's 13	1965	LSU 13, Syracuse 10	1984	Auburn 9, Michigan 7
1947	Georgia 20, N.Carolina 10	1966	Missouri 20, Florida 18	1985	Nebraska 28, LSU 10
1948	Texas 27, Alabama 7	1967	Alabama 34, Nebraska 7	1986	Tennessee 35, Miami-FL 7
1949	Oklahoma 14, N.Carolina 6	1968	LSU 20, Wyoming 13	1987	Nebraska 30, LSU 15
		1969	Arkansas 16, Georgia 2	1988	16–16, Syracuse vs Auburn
1950	Oklahoma 35, LSU 0			1989	Florida St. 13, Auburn 7
1951	Kentucky 13, Oklahoma 7	1970	Mississippi 27, Arkansas 22		
1952	Maryland 28, Tennessee 13	1971	Tennessee 34, Air Force 13	1990	Miami-FL 33, Alabama 25
1953	Georgia Tech 24, Mississippi 7	1972‡	Oklahoma 40, Auburn 22	1991	Tennessee 23, Virginia 22

*January game from 1935–72 and since 1977.   ‡Game played on Dec. 31 from 1972–75.

Cotton Bowl

City: Dallas, TX; **Stadium:** Cotton Bowl; **Capacity:** 72,032; **Playing surface:** AstroTurf; **Automatic berths:** Southwest Athletic Conference champion (since 1942). **First year:** 1937; **Playing sites:** Fair Park Stadium (1937); Cotton Bowl (since 1938).

Multiple wins: Texas (9); Texas A&M (4); Notre Dame and Rice (3); Alabama, Arkansas, Georgia, Houston, LSU, Penn St., SMU, Tennessee and TCU (2).

Year	Result	Year	Result	Year	Result
1937*	TCU 16, Marquette 6	1956	Mississippi 14, TCU 13	1975	Penn St. 41, Baylor 20
1938	Rice 28, Colorado 14	1957	TCU 28, Syracuse 17	1976	Arkansas 31, Georgia 10
1939	St.Mary's 20, Texas Tech 13	1958	Navy 20, Rice 7	1977	Houston 30, Maryland 21
		1959	0–0, TCU vs Air Force	1978	Notre Dame 38, Texas 10
1940	Clemson 6, Boston Col. 3			1979	Notre Dame 35, Houston 34
1941	Texas A&M 13, Fordham 12	1960	Syracuse 23, Texas 14		
1942	Alabama 29, Texas A&M 21	1961	Duke 7, Arkansas 6	1980	Houston 17, Nebraska 14
1943	Texas 14, Georgia Tech 7	1962	Texas 12, Mississippi 7	1981	Alabama 30, Baylor 2
1944	7–7, Texas vs Randolph Field	1963	LSU 13, Texas 0	1982	Texas 14, Alabama 12
1945	Oklahoma A&M 34, TCU 0	1964	Texas 28, Navy 6	1983	SMU 7, Pittsburgh 3
1946	Texas 40, Missouri 27	1965	Arkansas 10, Nebraska 7	1984	Georgia 10, Texas 9
1947	0–0, Arkansas vs LSU	1966	LSU 14, Arkansas 7	1985	Boston Col. 45, Houston 28
1948	13–13, SMU vs Penn St.	1966‡	Georgia 24, SMU 9	1986	Texas A&M 36, Auburn 16
1949	SMU 21, Oregon 13	1968*	Texas A&M 20, Alabama 16	1987	Ohio St. 28, Texas A&M 12
		1969	Texas 36, Tennessee 13	1988	Texas A&M 35, Notre Dame 10
1950	Rice 27, N.Carolina 13			1989	UCLA 17, Arkansas 3
1951	Tennessee 20, Texas 14	1970	Texas 21, Notre Dame 17		
1952	Kentucky 20, TCU 7	1971	Notre Dame 24, Texas 11	1990	Tennessee 31, Arkansas 27
1953	Texas 16, Tennessee 0	1972	Penn St. 30, Texas 6	1991	Miami-FL 46, Texas 3
1954	Rice 28, Alabama 6	1973	Texas 17, Alabama 13		
1955	Georgia Tech 14, Arkansas 6	1974	Nebraska 19, Texas 3		

*January game from 1937–66 and since 1968.   ‡Game played on Dec. 31, 1966.

National Championship Bowl Alliance Formed

On July 10, the Orange, Sugar and Cotton Bowls officially invited the Fiesta Bowl to join a partnership with the ACC, Big East, Big 8, SEC, SWC and Notre Dame to match the No. 1 and No. 2 teams in a New Year's Day bowl game. See "College Sports" for further details.

Fiesta Bowl

City: Tempe, AZ; **Stadium:** Sun Devil Stadium; **Capacity:** 74,000; **Playing surface:** grass; **Automatic berths:** none. **First year:** 1971; **Playing sites:** Sun Devil Stadium (since 1971).
  Multiple wins: Arizona St. (5); Penn St. (4); Florida St. (2).

Year		Year		Year	
1971*	Arizona St. 45, Florida St. 38	1978	10–10, Arkansas vs UCLA	1986	Michigan 27, Nebraska 23
1972	Arizona St. 49, Missouri 35	1979	Pittsburgh 16, Arizona 10	1987	Penn St. 14, Miami-FL 10
1973	Arizona St. 28, Pittsburgh 7			1988	Florida St. 31, Nebraska 28
1974	Oklahoma St. 16, BYU 6	1980	Penn St. 31, Ohio St. 19	1989	Notre Dame 34, West Va. 21
1975	Arizona St. 17, Nebraska 14	1982‡	Penn St. 26, USC 10		
1976	Oklahoma 41, Wyoming 7	1983	Arizona St. 32, Oklahoma 21	1990	Florida St. 41, Nebraska 17
1977	Penn St. 42, Arizona St. 30	1984	Ohio St. 28, Pittsburgh 23	1991	Louisville 34, Alabama 7
		1985	UCLA 39, Miami-FL 37		

*December game from 1971–80.   ‡January game since 1982.

Gator Bowl

City: Jacksonville, FL; **Stadium:** Gator Bowl; **Capacity:** 82,000; **Playing surface:** grass; **Automatic berths:** none. **First year:** 1946; **Playing sites:** Gator Bowl (since 1946).
  Multiple wins: Florida (5); Auburn and Clemson (4); Florida St. and North Carolina (3); Georgia, Georgia Tech, Maryland, Pittsburgh, Tennessee and Texas Tech (2).

Year		Year		Year	
1946*	W.Forest 26, S.Carolina 14	1961	Penn St. 30, Georgia Tech 15	1977	Pittsburgh 34, Clemson 3
1947	Oklahoma 34, N.C.State 13	1962	Florida 17, Penn St. 7	1978	Clemson 17, Ohio St. 15
1948	20–20, Maryland vs Georgia	1963	N.Carolina 35, Air Force 0	1979	N.Carolina 17, Michigan 15
1949	Clemson 24, Missouri 23	1965*	Florida St. 36, Oklahoma 19	1980	Pittsburgh 37, S.Carolina 9
1950	Maryland 20, Missouri 7	1965‡	Georgia Tech 31, Texas Tech 21	1981	N.Carolina 31, Arkansas 27
1951	Wyoming 20, Wash.& Lee 7	1966	Tennessee 18, Syracuse 12	1982	Florida St. 31, West Va. 12
1952	Miami-FL 14, Clemson 0	1967	17–17, Florida St. vs Penn St.	1983	Florida 14, Iowa 6
1953	Florida 14, Tulsa 13	1968	Missouri 35, Alabama 10	1984	Okla.St. 21, S.Carolina 14
1954	Texas Tech 35, Auburn 13	1969	Florida 14, Tennessee 13	1985	Florida St. 34, Okla.St. 23
1954‡	Auburn 33, Baylor 13			1986	Clemson 27, Stanford 21
1955	Vanderbilt 25, Auburn 13	1971*	Auburn 35, Mississippi 28	1987	LSU 30, S.Carolina 13
1956	Georgia Tech 21, Pittsburgh 14	1971‡	Georgia 7, N.Carolina 3	1989*	Georgia 34, Michigan St. 27
1957	Tennessee 3, Texas A&M 0	1972	Auburn 24, Colorado 3	1989‡	Clemson 27, West Va. 7
1958	Mississippi 7, Florida 3	1973	Texas Tech 28, Tennessee 19		
		1974	Auburn 27, Texas 3	1991*	Michigan 35, Mississippi 3
1960*	Arkansas 14, Georgia Tech 7	1975	Maryland 13, Florida 0		
1960‡	Florida 13, Baylor 12	1976	Notre Dame 20, Penn St. 9		

*January game from 1946–54, 1960, 1965, 1971, 1989 and 1991.
‡December game from 1954–58, 1960–63, 1965–69, 1971–88 and 1989.

Florida Citrus Bowl

City: Orlando, FL; **Stadium:** Florida Citrus Bowl-Orlando; **Capacity:** 52,300; **Playing surface:** grass; **Automatic berths:** none. **First year:** 1947; **Name change:** Tangerine Bowl (1947–82), Florida Citrus Bowl (since 1983); **Playing sites:** Tangerine Bowl (1947–72), Florida Field, Gainesville (1973), Tangerine Bowl (1974–82), Orlando Stadium (1983–85), Florida Citrus Bowl-Orlando (since 1986). The Tangerine Bowl, Orlando Stadium and Citrus Bowl are all the same stadium. No major college teams played in the Tangerine Bowl from 1947–61 or 1963–67.
  Multiple wins: East Texas St., Miami-OH and Toledo (3); Auburn, Catawba, Clemson, East Carolina (2).

Year		Year		Year	
1947*	Catawba 31, Maryville 6	1961	Lamar 21, Middle Tenn. 14	1976	Oklahoma 49, BYU 21
1948	Catawba 7, Marshall 0	1962	Houston 49, Miami-OH 21	1977	Florida St. 40, Texas Tech 17
1949	21–21, Murray St. vs. Sul Ross St.	1963	West.Ky. 27, Coast Guard 0	1978	N.C.State 30, Pittsburgh 17
		1964	E.Carolina 14, Mass. 13	1979	LSU 34, Wake Forest 10
1950	St.Vincent 7, Em.& Henry 6	1965	E.Carolina 31, Maine 0		
1951	M.Harvey 35, Em.& Henry 14	1966	Morgan St. 14, W.Chester 6	1980	Florida 35, Maryland 20
1952	Stetson 35, Arkansas St. 20	1967	Tenn.Martin 25, W.Chester 8	1981	Missouri 19, Southern Miss. 17
1953	E.Texas St. 33, Tenn. Tech 0	1968	Richmond 49, Ohio U. 42	1982	Auburn 33, Boston Col. 26
1954	7–7, E.Texas St. vs Ark.St.	1969	Toledo 56, Davidson 33	1983	Tennessee 30, Maryland 23
1955	Neb.-Omaha 7, Eastern Ky. 6			1984	17–17, Florida St. vs Georgia
1956	6–6, Juniata vs Mo.Valley	1970	Toledo 40, Wm.& Mary 12	1985	Ohio St. 10, BYU 7
1957	W.Texas St. 20, So.Miss. 13	1971	Toledo 28, Richmond 3	1987*	Auburn 16, USC 7
1958	Tenn. St. 10, So.Miss. 9	1972	Tampa 21, Kent St. 18	1988	Clemson 35, Penn St. 10
1958‡	E.Texas St. 26, Mo.Valley 7	1973	Miami-OH 16, Florida 7	1989	Clemson 13, Oklahoma 6
1960*	Mid.Tenn. 21, Presbyterian 12	1974	Miami-OH 21, Georgia 10		
		1975	Miami-OH 20, S.Carolina 7	1990	Illinois 31, Virginia 21
1960‡	Citadel 27, Tenn. Tech 0			1991	Georgia Tech 45, Nebraska 21

*January game from 1947–58, in 1960 and since 1987.   ‡December game from 1958 and 1960–85.

Bowl Games (Cont.)

John Hancock Bowl

City: El Paso, TX; **Stadium:** Sun Bowl; **Capacity:** 52,000; **Playing surface:** AstroTurf; **Automatic berths:** none. **First year:** 1936; **Name changes:** Sun Bowl (1936–86), John Hancock Sun Bowl (1987–88); John Hancock Bowl (since 1989); **Playing sites:** Kidd Field (1936–62), Sun Bowl (since 1963).
Multiple wins: UTEP (5); Alabama and Wyoming (3); Nebraska, New Mexico St., North Carolina, Pittsburgh, Southwestern-Texas, West Texas St. and West Virginia (2).

Year		Year		Year	
1936*	14–14, Hardin-Simmons vs New Mexico St.	1953	Pacific 26, Southern Miss. 7	1972	N.Carolina 32, Tex.Tech 28
1937	Hardin-Simmons 34, Texas Mines 6	1954	Tex.Western 37, Southern Miss. 14	1973	Missouri 34, Auburn 17
		1955	Tex.Western 47, Florida St. 20	1974	Miss.St. 26, N.Carolina 24
1938	West Va. 7, Texas Tech 6	1956	Wyoming 21, Texas Tech 14	1975	Pittsburgh 33, Kansas 19
1939	Utah 26, New Mexico 0	1957	Geo.Wash. 13, Tex.Western 0	1977*	Texas A&M 37, Florida 14
		1958	Louisville 34, Drake 20	1977‡	Stanford 24, LSU 14
1940	0–0, Catholic U. vs Arizona St.	1958*	Wyoming 14, Hard.-Simmons 6	1978	Texas 42, Maryland 0
1941	W.Reserve 26, Ariz.St. 13	1959	New Mex.St. 28, N.Texas 8	1979	Washington 14, Texas 7
1942	Tulsa 6, Texas Tech 0				
1943	Second Air Force 13, Hardin-Simmons 7	1960	New Mex.St. 20, Utah St. 13	1980	Nebraska 31, Miss.St. 17
		1961	Villanova 17, Wichita 9	1981	Oklahoma 40, Houston 14
		1962	West Texas 15, Ohio U. 14	1982	N.Carolina 26, Texas 10
1944	SW Texas 7, New Mexico 0	1963	Oregon 21, SMU 14	1983	Alabama 28, SMU 7
1945	SW Texas 35, U.of Mexico 0	1964	Georgia 7, Gergia Tech 0	1984	Maryland 28, Tennessee 27
1946	New Mexico 34, Denver 24	1965	Texas Western 13, TCU 12	1985	13–13, Georgia vs Arizona
1947	Cincinnati 18, Va.Tech 6	1966	Wyoming 28, Florida St. 20	1986	Alabama 28, Washington 6
1948	Miami-OH 13, Texas Tech 12	1967	UTEP 14, Mississippi 7	1987	Okla.St. 35, West Va. 33
1949	West Va. 21, Texas Mines 12	1968	Auburn 34, Arizona 10	1988	Alabama 29, Army 28
		1969	Nebraska 45, Georgia 6	1989	Pittsburgh 31, Texas A&M 28
1950	Tex.Western 33, Geo'town 20				
1951	West Texas 14, Cincinnati 13	1970	Georgia Tech 17, Texas Tech 9	1990	Michigan St. 17, USC 16
1952	Texas Tech 25, Pacific 14	1971	LSU 33, Iowa St. 15		

*January game from 1936–58 and in 1977.   ‡December game from 1958–75 and since 1977.

Liberty Bowl

City: Memphis, TN; **Stadium:** Liberty Bowl Memorial Stadium; **Capacity:** 63,000; **Playing surface:** grass; **Automatic berths:** The winner of the Commander-in-Chief's Trophy (Army, Navy or Air Force)—if Air Force is also WAC champion, it is obligated to play in the Holiday Bowl, in which case the Liberty Bowl decides between Army and Navy. Representative must have overall record of .500 or better to qualify. **First year:** 1959; **Playing sites:** Philadelphia, PA (Municipal Stadium, 1959–63); Atlantic City, NJ (Convention Hall, 1964); Memphis (since 1965). **Multiple wins:** Mississippi, Penn St. and Tennessee (3); Alabama and N.C. State (2).

Year		Year		Year	
1959*	Penn St. 7, Alabama 0	1970	Tulane 17, Colorado 3	1980	Purdue 28, Missouri 25
		1971	Tennessee 14, Arkansas 13	1981	Ohio St. 31, Navy 28
1960	Penn St. 41, Oregon 12	1972	Georgia Tech 31, Iowa St. 30	1982	Alabama 21, Illinois 15
1961	Syracuse 15, Miami-FL 14	1973	N.C.State 31, Kansas 18	1983	N.Dame 19, Boston Col. 18
1962	Oregon St. 6, Villanova 0	1974	Tennessee 7, Maryland 3	1984	Auburn 21, Arkansas 15
1963	Mississippi St. 16, N.C.State 12	1975	USC 20, Texas A&M 0	1985	Baylor 21, LSU 7
1964	Utah 32, West Virginia 6	1976	Alabama 36, UCLA 6	1986	Tennessee 21, Minnesota 14
1965	Mississippi 13, Auburn 7	1977	Nebraska 21, N.Carolina 17	1987	Georgia 20, Arkansas 17
1966	Miami-FL 14, Va.Tech 7	1978	Missouri 20, LSU 15	1988	Indiana 34, S.Carolina 10
1967	N.C.State 14, Georgia 7	1979	Penn St. 9, Tulane 6	1989	Mississippi 42, Air Force 29
1968	Mississippi 34, Va.Tech 17				
1969	Colorado 47, Alabama 33			1990	Air Force 23, Ohio St. 11

*December game since 1959.

Peach Bowl

City: Atlanta, GA; **Stadium:** Atlanta Fulton County Stadium; **Capacity:** 59,800; **Playing surface:** grass; **Automatic berths:** none. **First year:** 1968; **Playing sites:** Grant Field (1968–70), Atlanta Stadium (since 1971). **Multiple wins:** N.C. State and West Virginia (3).

Year		Year		Year	
1968*	LSU 31, Florida St. 27	1976	Kentucky 21, N.Carolina 0	1984	Virginia 27, Purdue 24
1969	West Va. 14, S.Carolina 3	1977	N.C.State 24, Iowa St. 14	1985	Army 31, Illinois 29
		1978	Purdue 41, Georgia Tech 21	1986	Va.Tech 25, N.C.State 24
1970	Ariz.St. 48, N.Carolina 26	1979	Baylor 24, Clemson 18	1988‡	Tennessee 27, Indiana 22
1971	Mississippi 41, Georgia Tech 18			1988*	N.C.State 28, Iowa 23
1972	N.C.State 49, West Va. 13	1981‡	Miami-FL 20, Va.Tech 10	1989	Syracuse 19, Georgia 18
1973	Georgia 17, Maryland 16	1981*	West Va. 26, Florida 6		
1974	6–6, Vanderbilt vs Texas Tech	1982	Iowa 28, Tennessee 22	1990	Auburn 27, Indiana 23
1975	West Va. 13, N.C.State 10	1983	Florida St. 28, N.Carolina 3		

*December game from 1968–79, 1981–86, and since 1988.   ‡January game in 1981 and 1988.

Independence Bowl

City: Shreveport, LA; **Stadium:** Independence Stadium; **Capacity:** 50,560; **Playing surface:** grass; **Automatic berths:** none. **First year:** 1976; **Playing sites:** Independence Stadium (since 1976).
Multiple wins: Air Force and Southern Miss. (2).

Year		Year		Year	
1976*	McNeese St. 20, Tulsa 16	1981	Texas A&M 33, Okla.St. 16	1986	Mississippi 20, Texas Tech 17
1977	La.Tech 24, Louisville 14	1982	Wisconsin 14, Kansas St. 3	1987	Washington 24, Tulane 12
1978	E.Carolina 35, La.Tech 13	1983	Air Force 9, Mississippi 3	1988	So.Miss 38, UTEP 18
1979	Syracuse 31, McNeese St. 7	1984	Air Force 23, Va.Tech 7	1989	Oregon 27, Tulsa 24
1980	So.Miss 16, McNeese St. 14	1985	Minnesota 20, Clemson 13	1990	34-34, La.Tech vs Maryland

*December game since 1976.

Holiday Bowl

City: San Diego, CA; **Stadium:** San Diego Jack Murphy Stadium; **Capacity:** 60,750; **Playing surface:** grass; **Automatic berths:** Western Athletic Conference champion (except 1985). **First year:** 1978; **Playing sites:** Jack Murphy Stadium (since 1978).
Multiple wins: BYU (4); Iowa (2).

Year		Year		Year	
1978*	Navy 23, BYU 16	1983	BYU 21, Missouri 17	1987	Iowa 20, Wyoming 19
1979	Indiana 38, BYU 37	1984	BYU 24, Michigan 17	1988	Okla.St. 62, Wyoming 14
1980	BYU 46, SMU 45	1985	Arkansas 18, Arizona St. 17	1989	Penn St. 50, BYU 39
1981	BYU 38, Wash.St. 36	1986	Iowa 39, San Diego St. 38	1990	Texas A&M 65, BYU 14
1982	Ohio St. 47, BYU 17				

*December game since 1978.

California Raisin Bowl

City: Fresno, CA; **Stadium:** Bulldog Stadium; **Capacity:** 30,000; **Playing surface:** grass; **Automatic berths:** Mid-American Conference and Big West champions (since 1981). **First year:** 1981; **Playing sites:** Bulldog Stadium (since 1981).
Multiple wins: Fresno St. (4); San Jose St. and Toledo (2).

Year		Year		Year	
1981*	Toledo 27, San Jose St. 25	1985	Fresno St. 51, Bowl.Green 7	1989	Fresno St. 27, Ball St. 6
1982	Fresno St. 29, Bowl.Green 28	1986	San Jose St. 37, Miami-OH 7	1990	San Jose St. 48, C.Michigan 24
1983	Northern Ill. 20, CS-Fullerton 13	1987	E.Michigan 30, S.Jose St. 27		
1984	UNLV 30, Toledo 13	1988	Fresno St. 35, W.Michigan 30		

*December game since 1981.
Note: Toledo ruled winner of 1984 game by forfeit when UNLV was found to have used ineligible players.

Aloha Bowl

City: Honolulu, HI; **Stadium:** Aloha Stadium; **Capacity:** 50,000; **Playing surface:** AstroTurf; **Automatic berths:** none. **First year:** 1982; **Playing sites:** Aloha Stadium (since 1982).

Year		Year		Year	
1982*	Washington 21, Maryland 20	1985	Alabama 24, USC 3	1988	Wash.St. 24, Houston 22
1983	Penn St. 13, Washington 10	1986	Arizona 30, N.Carolina 21	1989	Michigan St. 33, Hawaii 13
1984	SMU 27, Notre Dame 20	1987	UCLA 20, Florida 16	1990	Syracuse 28, Arizona 0

*December game since 1982.

Freedom Bowl

City: Anaheim, CA; **Stadium:** Anaheim Stadium; **Capacity:** 70,500; **Playing surface:** grass; **Automatic berths:** none. **First year:** 1984; **Playing sites:** Anaheim Stadium (since 1984).
Multiple wins: Washington (2).

Year		Year		Year	
1984*	Iowa 55, Texas 17	1987	Arizona St. 33, Air Force 28	1989	Washington 34, Florida 7
1985	Washington 20, Colorado 17	1988	BYU 20, Colorado 17	1990	Colo.St. 32, Oregon St. 31
1986	UCLA 31, BYU 10				

*December game since 1984.

Hall of Fame Bowl

City: Tampa, FL; **Stadium:** Tampa Stadium; **Capacity:** 74,315; **Playing surface:** grass; **Automatic berths:** none. **First year:** 1986; **Playing sites:** Tampa Stadium (since 1986).

Year		Year		Year	
1986*	Boston College 27, Georgia 24	1989	Syracuse 23, LSU 10	1991	Clemson 30, Illinois 0
1988‡	Michigan 28, Alabama 24	1990	Auburn 31, Ohio St. 14		

*December game in 1986.   ‡January game since 1988.

Bowl Games (Cont.)
Copper Bowl

City: Tucson, AZ; **Stadium:** Arizona Stadium; **Capacity:** 57,000; **Playing surface:** grass; **Automatic berths:** none.
First year: 1989; **Playing sites:** Arizona Stadium (since 1989).

Year		Year	
1989*	Arizona 17, N.C.State 10	1990	California 17, Wyoming 15

*December game since 1989.

Blockbuster Bowl

City: Miami; **Stadium:** Joe Robbie Stadium; **Capacity:** 73,000; **Playing surface:** grass; **Automatic berths:** none. **First year:** 1990; **Playing sites:** Joe Robbie Stadium (since 1990).

Year	Result
1990	Florida St. 24, Penn St. 17

Discontinued in the 1990s
All-American Bowl (Birmingham, AL)

Years: 1977–90; **Name change:** Hall of Fame Classic (1977–84), All-American Bowl (1985–90); **Playing sites:** Legion Field.

Year		Year		Year	
1977*	Maryland 17, Minnesota 7	1982	Air Force 36, Vanderbilt 28	1987	Virginia 22, BYU 16
1978	Texas A&M 28, Iowa St. 12	1983	West Va. 20, Kentucky 16	1988	Florida 14, Illinois 10
1979	Missouri 24, S.Carolina 14	1984	Kentucky 20, Wisconsin 19	1989	Texas Tech 49, Duke 21
1980	Arkansas 34, Tulane 15	1985	Georgia Tech 17, Mich.St. 14	1990	N.C.State 31, So.Miss 27
1981	Miss.St. 10, Kansas 0	1986	Florida St. 27, Indiana 13		

*December game every year.

Top 50 Rivalries

Top Division I series records, including games through the 1990 season. Note that the Boston College-Holy Cross series ended after the 1986 season, while Notre Dame and Miami-FL concluded their series in 1990. The series between Miami-FL and Florida was suspended after the 1987 season and formally cancelled in 1991.

	Gm	Series Leader		Gm	Series Leader
Air Force-Army	25	Air Force (13-11-1)	**Kansas-Kansas St.**	88	Kansas (60-23-5)
Air Force-Navy	23	Air Force (15-8-0)	**Kentucky-Tennessee**	86	Tennessee (54-23-9)
Alabama-Auburn	55	Alabama (31-23-1)	**Lafayette-Lehigh**	131	Lafayette (69-52-10)
Alabama-Tennessee	73	Alabama (39-27-7)	**LSU-Tulane**	88	LSU (59-22-7)
Arizona-Arizona St.	64	Arizona (37-26-1)	**Miami-FL-Notre Dame**	23	Notre Dame (15-7-1)
Arkansas-Texas	72	Texas (54-18-0)	**Michigan-Michigan St.**	83	Michigan (54-24-5)
Army-Navy	91	TIED (42-42-7)	**Michigan-Notre Dame**	22	Michigan (13-9-0)
Auburn-Georgia	94	Auburn (45-42-7)	**Michigan-Ohio St.**	87	Michigan (49-33-5)
Baylor-TCU	97	TCU (46-44-7)	**Minnesota-Wisconsin**	100	Minnesota (55-37-8)
Boston Col-Holy Cross	79	BC (48-31-0)	**Mississippi-Miss.St.**	87	Mississippi (51-30-6)
BYU-Utah	66	Utah (40-22-4)	**Nebraska-Oklahoma**	71	Oklahoma (39-29-3)
California-Stanford	93	Stanford (45-37-11)	**N.Carolina-N.C.State.**	80	N.Carolina (52-22-6)
Cincinnati-Miami, OH	95	Miami (51-38-6)	**Notre Dame-Purdue**	62	Notre Dame (39-21-2)
Clemson-S.Carolina	88	Clemson(52-32-4)	**Notre Dame-USC**	62	Notre Dame (35-23-4)
Colorado-Colorado St	66	Colorado (48-16-2)	**Oklahoma-Okla.St.**	85	Oklahoma (67-12-6)
Duke-North Carolina	76	N.Carolina (37-35-4)	**Oklahoma-Texas**	85	Texas (49-32-4)
Florida-Florida St	33	Florida (22-10-1)	**Oregon-Oregon St**	94	Oregon (46-38-10)
Florida-Miami, FL	49	Florida (25-24-0)	**Penn St.-Pittsburg.**	90	Penn St. (45-41-4)
Florida-Georgia	68	Georgia (43-23-2)	**Pittsburgh-West Va**	83	Pitt (54-26-3)
Florida St.-Miami, Fl	34	Miami (20-14-0)	**Princeton-Yale**	113	Yale (63-40-1)
Georgia-Georgia Tech	85	Georgia (45-35-5)	**Richmond-Wm. & Mary**	100	Wm. & Mary (48-47-5)
Harvard-Yale	107	Yale (58-41-8)	**Tennessee-Vanderbilt**	84	Tennessee (53-26-5)
Indiana-Purdue	93	Purdue (57-30-6)	**Texas-Texas A&M**	97	Texas (64-28-5)
Iowa-Iowa St.	38	Iowa (26-12-0)	**UCLA-USC**	60	USC (34-19-7)
Kansas-Missouri	99	Missouri (47-43-9)	**Washington-Wash.St.**	83	Washington (53-24-6)

Major Conference Champions
Big Ten Conference

Originally founded in 1895 as the Intercollegiate Conference of Faculty Representatives, better known as the Western Conference. **Charter members** (7): Chicago, Illinois, Michigan, Minnesota, Northwestern, Purdue and Wisconsin. **Admitted later** (5): Indiana and Iowa in 1899, Ohio St. in 1912, Michigan St. in 1950 (began play in '53) and Penn St. in 1990 (will begin play in 1993). **Withdrew later** (2): Michigan in 1907 (rejoined in 1917), Chicago in 1940. **Note:** Iowa belonged to both the Missouri Valley and Western conferences from 1907–10.
   Unofficially called **Big Ten** from 1912 until Chicago withdrew after 1939 season, then **Big Nine** from 1940 until Michigan St. began conference play in 1953. Formally renamed **Big Ten** in 1984.
   Current playing membership (10): Illinois, Indiana, Iowa, Michigan, Michigan St., Minnesota, Northwestern, Ohio St., Purdue and Wisconsin.

Year		Year		Year		Year	
1896	Wisconsin (2-0-1)	1919	Illinois (6-1)	1945	Indiana (5-0-1)	1972	Ohio St. (8-0)
1897	Wisconsin (3-0)			1946	Illinois (6-1)		& Michigan (7-1)
1898	Michigan (3-0)	1920	Ohio St. (5-0)	1947	Michigan (6-0)	1973	Ohio St. (7-0-1)
1899	Chicago (4-0)	1921	Iowa (5-0)	1948	Michigan (6-0)		& Michigan (7-0-1)
		1922	Iowa (5-0)	1949	Ohio St. (4-1-1)	1974	Ohio St. (7-1)
1900	Iowa (3-0-1)		& Michigan (4-0)		& Michigan (4-1-1)		& Michigan (7-1)
	& Minnesota (3-0-1)	1923	Illinois (5-0)			1975	Ohio St. (8-0)
1901	Michigan (4-0)		& Michigan (4-0)	1950	Michigan (4-1-1)	1976	Michigan (7-1)
	& Wisconsin (2-0)	1924	Chicago (3-0-3)	1951	Illinois (5-0-1)		& Ohio St. (7-1)
1902	Michigan (5-0)	1925	Michigan (5-1)	1952	Wisconsin (4-1-1)	1977	Michigan (7-1)
1903	Michigan (3-0-1),	1926	Michigan (5-0)		& Purdue (4-1-1)		& Ohio St. (7-1)
	Minnesota (3-0-1)		& Northwestern (5-0)	1953	Michigan St. (5-1)	1978	Michigan (7-1)
	& Northwestern (1-0-2)	1927	Illinois (5-0)		& Illinois (5-1)		& Mich.St. (7-1)
1904	Minnesota (3-0)	1928	Illinois (4-1)	1954	Ohio St. (7-0)	1979	Ohio St. (8-0)
	& Michigan (2-0)	1929	Purdue (5-0)	1955	Ohio St. (6-0)		
1905	Chicago (7-0)			1956	Iowa (5-1)	1980	Michigan (8-0)
1906	Wisconsin (3-0),	1930	Michigan (5-0)	1957	Ohio St. (7-0)	1981	Iowa (6-2)
	Minnesota (2-0)		& Northwestern (5-0)	1958	Iowa (5-1)		& Ohio St. (6-2)
	& Michigan (1-0)	1931	Purdue (5-1),	1959	Wisconsin (5-2)	1982	Michigan (8-1)
1907	Chicago (4-0)		Michigan (5-1)			1983	Illinois (9-0)
1908	Chicago (5-0)		& Northwestern (5-1)	1960	Minnesota (5-1)	1984	Ohio St. (7-2)
1909	Minnesota (3-0)	1932	Michigan (6-0)		& Iowa (5-1)	1985	Iowa (7-1)
		1933	Michigan (5-0-1)	1961	Ohio St. (6-0)	1986	Michigan (7-1)
1910	Illinois (4-0)	1934	Minnesota (5-0)	1962	Wisconsin (6-1)		& Ohio St. (7-1)
	& Minnesota (2-0)	1935	Minnesota (5-0)	1963	Illinois (5-1-1)	1987	Michigan St. (7-0-1)
1911	Minnesota (3-0-1)		& Ohio St. (5-0)	1964	Michigan (6-1)	1988	Michigan (7-0-1)
1912	Wisconsin (6-0)	1936	Northwestern (6-0)	1965	Michigan St. (7-0)	1989	Michigan (8-0)
1913	Chicago (7-0)	1937	Minnesota (5-0)	1966	Michigan St. (7-0)		
1914	Illinois (6-0)	1938	Minnesota (4-1)	1967	Indiana (6-1),	1990	Iowa (6-2),
1915	Minnesota (3-0-1)	1939	Ohio St. (5-1)		Purdue (6-1)		Michigan (6-2),
	& Illinois (3-0-2)				& Minnesota (6-1)		Michigan St. (6-2)
1916	Ohio St. (4-0)	1940	Minnesota (6-0)	1968	Ohio St. (7-0)		& Illinois (6-2)
1917	Ohio St. (4-0)	1941	Minnesota (5-0)	1969	Ohio St. (6-1)		
1918	Illinois (4-0),	1942	Ohio St. (5-1)		& Michigan (6-1)		
	Michigan (2-0)	1943	Purdue (6-0)				
	& Purdue (1-0)		& Michigan (6-0)	1970	Ohio St. (7-0)		
		1944	Ohio St. (6-0)	1971	Michigan (8-0)		

Big Eight Conference

Originally founded in 1907 as Missouri Valley Intercollegiate Athletic Assn. **Charter members** (5): Iowa, Kansas, Missouri, Nebraska, and Washington Univ.of St.Louis. **Admitted later** (6): Drake and Iowa St.(then Ames College) in 1908; Kansas St. in 1913, Grinnell in 1919, Oklahoma in 1920 and Oklahoma St.(then Okla.A&M) in 1925. **Withdrew later** (1): Iowa in 1911. **Note:** Iowa belonged to both the MVIAA and Western Conference from 1907–10.
   Big Six founded in 1928 when charter members left MVIAA. **Charter members** (6): Iowa St., Kansas, Kansas St., Missouri, Nebraska and Oklahoma. **Admitted later** (2): Colorado in 1947 (began play in '48), Oklahoma St. in 1957 (began play in '60). Renamed **Big Seven** in 1948 and **Big Eight** in 1958.
   Current playing membership (8): Colorado, Iowa St., Kansas, Kansas St., Missouri, Nebraska, Oklahoma and Oklahoma St.

Year		Year		Year		Year	
1907	Iowa (1-0)	1913	Missouri (4-0)	1922	Nebraska (5-0)	1932	Nebraska (5-0)
	& Nebraska (1-0)		& Nebraska (3-0)	1923	Nebraska (3-0-2)	1933	Nebraska (5-0)
1908	Kansas (4-0)	1914	Nebraska (3-0)	1924	Missouri (5-1)	1934	Kansas St. (5-0)
1909	Missouri (4-0-1)	1915	Nebraska (4-0)	1925	Missouri (5-1)	1935	Nebraska (4-0-1)
		1916	Nebraska (3-1)	1926	Oklahoma A&M (3-0-1)	1936	Nebraska (5-0)
1910	Nebraska (2-0)	1917	Nebraska (2-0)	1927	Missouri (5-1)	1937	Nebraska (3-0-2)
1911	Iowa St. (2-0-1)	1918	Vacant (WW I)	1928	Nebraska (4-0)	1938	Oklahoma (5-0)
	& Nebraska (2-0-1)	1919	Missouri (4-0-1)	1929	Nebraska (3-0-2)	1939	Missouri (5-0)
1912	Iowa St. (2-0)						
	& Nebraska (2-0)	1920	Oklahoma (4-0-1)	1930	Kansas (4-1)	1940	Nebraska (5-0)
		1921	Nebraska (3-0)	1931	Nebraska (5-0)	1941	Missouri (5-0)

Major Conference Champions (Cont.)
Big Eight Conference

Year		Year		Year		Year	
1942	Missouri (4-0-1)	1955	Oklahoma (6-0)	1969	Missouri (6-1)	1979	Oklahoma (7-0)
1943	Oklahoma (5-0)	1956	Oklahoma (6-0)		& Nebraska (6-1)	1980	Oklahoma (7-0)
1944	Oklahoma (4-0-1)	1957	Oklahoma (6-0)	1970	Nebraska (7-0)	1981	Nebraska (7-0)
1945	Missouri (5-0)	1958	Oklahoma (6-0)	1971	Nebraska (7-0)	1982	Nebraska (7-0)
1946	Oklahoma (4-1)	1959	Oklahoma (5-1)	1972	Nebraska (5-1-1)*	1983	Nebraska (7-0)
	& Kansas (4-1)	1960	Missouri (7-0)	1973	Oklahoma (7-0)	1984	Oklahoma (6-1)
1947	Kansas (4-0-1)	1961	Colorado (7-0)	1974	Oklahoma (7-0)		& Nebraska (6-1)
	& Oklahoma (4-0-1)	1962	Oklahoma (7-0)	1975	Nebraska (6-1)	1985	Oklahoma (7-0)
1948	Oklahoma (5-0)	1963	Nebraska (7-0)		& Oklahoma (6-1)	1986	Oklahoma (7-0)
1949	Oklahoma (5-0)	1964	Nebraska (6-1)	1976	Colorado (5-2),	1987	Oklahoma (7-0)
1950	Oklahoma (6-0)	1965	Nebraska (7-0)		Oklahoma (5-2)	1988	Nebraska (7-0)
1951	Oklahoma (6-0)	1966	Nebraska (6-1)		& Oklahoma St. (5-2)	1989	Colorado (7-0)
1952	Oklahoma (5-0-1)	1967	Oklahoma (7-0)	1977	Oklahoma (7-0)	1990	Colorado (7-0)
1953	Oklahoma (6-0)	1968	Kansas (6-1)	1978	Nebraska (6-1)		
1954	Oklahoma (6-0)		& Oklahoma (6-1)		& Oklahoma (6-1)		

*Oklahoma forfeited share of title in 1972.

Southwest Conference

Founded in 1914 as Southwest Athletic Conference. **Charter members** (8): Arkansas, Baylor, Oklahoma, Oklahoma A&M, Rice, Southwestern, Texas, Texas A&M. **Admitted later** (5): SMU in 1918, Phillips in 1920, TCU in 1923, Texas Tech in 1956 (began play in 1960), Houston in 1971 (began play in 1976). **Withdrew later** (5): Southwestern in 1917, Oklahoma in 1920, Phillips in 1921, Oklahoma A&M in 1925, Arkansas in 1990 (will play through 1991 season when leave for SEC).

Current playing membership (9): Arkansas, Baylor, Houston, Rice, SMU, Texas, Texas A&M, TCU and Texas Tech.

Year		Year		Year		Year	
1914	No champion	1937	Rice (4-1-1)	1957	Rice (5-1)	1975	Arkansas (6-1),
1915	Oklahoma (3-0)	1938	TCU (6-0)	1958	TCU (5-1)		Texas (6-1)
1916	No champion	1939	Texas A&M (6-0)	1959	Texas (5-1),		& Texas A&M (6-1)
1917	Texas A&M (2-0)	1940	Texas A&M (5-1)		TCU (5-1)	1976	Houston (7-1)
1918	No champion		& SMU (5-1)		& Arkansas (5-1)		& Texas Tech (7-1)
1919	Texas A&M (4-0)	1941	Texas A&M (5-1)	1960	Arkansas (6-1)	1977	Texas (8-0)
1920	Texas (5-0)	1942	Texas (5-1)	1961	Texas (6-1)	1978	Houston (7-1)
1921	Texas A&M (3-0-2)	1943	Texas (5-0)		& Arkansas (6-1)	1979	Houston (7-1)
1922	Baylor (5-0)	1944	TCU (3-1-1)	1962	Texas (6-0-1)		& Arkansas (7-1)
1923	SMU (5-0)	1945	Texas (5-1)	1963	Texas (7-0)	1980	Baylor (8-0)
1924	Baylor (5-0-1)	1946	Rice (5-1)	1964	Arkansas (7-0)	1981	SMU (7-1)†
1925	Texas A&M (4-1)		& Arkansas (5-1)	1965	Arkansas (7-0)	1982	SMU (7-0-1)
1926	SMU (5-0)	1947	SMU (5-0-1)	1966	SMU (6-1)	1983	Texas (8-0)
1927	Texas A&M (4-0-1)	1948	SMU (5-0-1)	1967	Texas A&M (6-1)	1984	SMU (6-2)
1928	Texas (5-1)	1949	Rice (6-0)	1968	Arkansas (6-1)		& Houston (6-2)
1929	TCU (4-0-1)	1950	Texas (6-0)		& Texas (6-1)	1985	Texas A&M (7-1)
1930	Texas (4-1)	1951	TCU (5-1)	1969	Texas (7-0)	1986	Texas A&M (7-1)
1931	SMU (5-0-1)	1952	Texas (6-0)	1970	Texas (7-0)	1987	Texas A&M (6-1)
1932	TCU (6-0)	1953	Rice (5-1)	1971	Texas (6-1)	1988	Arkansas (7-0)
1933	Arkansas (4-1)*		& Texas (5-1)	1972	Texas (7-0)	1989	Arkansas (7-1)
1934	Rice (5-1)	1954	Arkansas (5-1)	1973	Texas (7-0)	1990	Texas (8-0)
1935	SMU (6-0)	1955	TCU (5-1)	1974	Baylor (6-1)		
1936	Arkansas (5-1)	1956	Texas A&M (6-0)				

*Title vacated.   †On probation, ineligible for championship.

Pacific-10 Conference

Originally founded in 1915 as Pacific Coast Conference. **Charter members** (4): California, Oregon, Ore.St. and Washington. **Admitted later** (6): Wash.St. in 1917, Stanford in 1918, Southern Cal and Idaho in 1922, Montana in 1924, UCLA in 1928. **Withdrew later** (1): Montana in 1950.

The **PCC** dissolved in 1959 and the **AAWU** (Athletic Assn. of Western Universities) was founded. **Charter members** (5): California, Southern Cal, Stanford, UCLA and Washington. **Admitted later** (5): Washington St. in 1962, Oregon and Oregon St. in 1964, Arizona and Arizona St. in 1978. Conference renamed **Pac-8** in 1968 and **Pac-10** in 1978.

Current playing membership (10): Arizona, Arizona St., California, Oregon, Oregon St., Stanford, Southern Cal, UCLA, Washington and Washington St.

Year		Year		Year		Year	
1916	Washington (3-0-1)	1919	Oregon (2-1)	1920	California (3-0)	1923	California (5-0)
1917	Washington St. (3-0)		& Washington (2-1)	1921	California (5-0)	1924	Stanford (3-0-1)
1918	California (3-0)			1922	California (3-0)	1925	Washington (5-0)

Year		Year		Year		Year	
1926	Stanford (4-0)	1940	Stanford (7-0)	1958	California (6-1)	1975	UCLA (6-1)
1927	USC (4-0-1)	1941	Oregon St. (7-2)	1959	Washington (3-1),		& California (6-1)
	& Stanford (4-0-1)	1942	UCLA (6-1)		USC (3-1)	1976	USC (7-0)
1928	USC (4-0-1)	1943	USC (4-0)		& UCLA (3-1)	1977	Washington (6-1)
1929	USC (6-1)	1944	USC (3-0-2)	1960	Washington (4-0)	1978	USC (6-1)
1930	Washington St. (6-0)	1945	USC (5-1)	1961	UCLA (3-1)	1979	USC (6-0-1)
1931	USC (7-0)	1946	UCLA (7-0)	1962	USC (4-0)		
1932	USC (6-0)	1947	USC (6-0)	1963	Washington (4-1)	1980	Washington (6-1)
1933	Oregon (4-1)	1948	California (6-0)	1964	Oregon St. (3-1)	1981	Washington (6-2)
	& Stanford (4-1)		& Oregon (6-0)		& USC (3-1)	1982	UCLA (5-1-1)
1934	Stanford (5-0)	1949	California (7-0)	1965	UCLA (4-0)	1983	UCLA (6-1-1)
1935	California (4-1),	1950	California (5-0-1)	1966	USC (4-1)	1984	USC (7-1)
	Stanford (4-1)	1951	Stanford (6-1)	1967	USC (6-1)	1985	UCLA (6-2)
	& UCLA (4-1)	1952	USC (6-0)	1968	USC (6-0)	1986	Arizona St. (5-1-1)
1936	Washington (6-0-1)	1953	UCLA (6-1)	1969	USC (6-0)	1987	USC (7-1)
1937	California (6-0-1)	1954	UCLA (6-0)	1970	Stanford (6-1)		& UCLA (7-1)
1938	USC (6-1)	1955	UCLA (6-0)	1971	Stanford (6-1)	1988	USC (8-0)
	& California (6-1)	1956	Oregon St. (6-1-1)	1972	USC (7-0)	1989	USC (6-0-1)
1939	USC (5-0-2)	1957	Oregon (6-2)	1973	USC (7-0)		
	& UCLA (5-0-3)		& Oregon St. (6-2)	1974	USC (6-0-1)	1990	Washington (7-1)

Southeastern Conference

Founded in 1933 when charter members all left Southern Conference to form SEC. **Charter members** (13): Alabama, Auburn, Florida, Georgia, Georgia Tech, Kentucky, LSU, Mississippi, Mississippi St., Sewanee, Tennessee, Tulane and Vanderbilt. **Admitted later** (2): Arkansas and South Carolina in 1990 (both will begin play in '92). **Withdrew later** (3): Sewanee in 1940, Georgia Tech in 1964, Tulane in 1966. **Current playing membership** (10): Alabama, Auburn, Florida, Georgia, Kentucky, LSU, Mississippi, Mississippi St., Tennessee and Vanderbilt.

Year		Year		Year		Year	
1933	Alabama (5-0-1)	1948	Georgia (6-0)	1965	Alabama (6-1-1)	1980	Georgia (6-0)
1934	Tulane (8-0)	1949	Tulane (5-1)	1966	Alabama (6-0)	1981	Georgia (6-0)
	& Alabama (7-0)	1950	Kentucky (5-1)		& Georgia (6-0)		& Alabama (6-0)
1935	LSU (5-0)	1951	Georgia Tech (7-0)	1967	Tennessee (6-0)	1982	Georgia (6-0)
1936	LSU (6-0)		& Tennessee (5-0)	1968	Georgia (5-0-1)	1983	Auburn (6-0)
1937	Alabama (6-0)	1952	Georgia Tech (6-0)	1969	Tennessee (5-1)	1984	Florida (5-0-1)*
1938	Tennessee (7-0)	1953	Alabama (4-0-3)	1970	LSU (5-0)	1985	Florida (5-1)†
1939	Tennessee (6-0),	1954	Mississippi (5-1)	1971	Alabama (7-0)		& Tennessee (5-1)
	Georgia Tech (6-0)	1955	Mississippi (5-1)	1972	Alabama (7-1)	1986	LSU (5-1)
	& Tulane (5-0)	1956	Tennessee (6-0)	1973	Alabama (8-0)	1987	Auburn (5-0-1)
1940	Tennessee (5-0)	1957	Auburn (7-0)	1974	Alabama (6-0)	1988	Auburn (6-1)
1941	Mississippi St. (4-0-1)	1958	LSU (6-0)	1975	Alabama (6-0)		& LSU (6-1)
1942	Georgia (6-1)	1959	Georgia (7-0)	1976	Georgia (5-1)	1989	Alabama (6-1),
1943	Georgia Tech (3-0)	1960	Mississippi (5-0-1)		& Kentucky (5-1)		Tennessee (6-1)
1944	Georgia Tech (4-0)	1961	Alabama (7-0)	1977	Alabama (7-0)		& Auburn (6-1)
1945	Alabama (6-0)		& LSU (6-0)		& Kentucky (6-0)	1990	Florida (6-1)†
1946	Georgia (5-0)	1962	Mississippi (6-0)	1978	Alabama (6-0)		
	& Tennessee (5-0)	1963	Mississippi (5-0-1)	1979	Alabama (6-0)		
1947	Mississippi (6-1)	1964	Alabama (8-0)				

*Title vacated   †On probation, ineligible for championship.

Mid-American Conference

Founded in 1946. **Charter members** (6): Butler, Cincinnati, Miami of Ohio, Ohio Univ., Western Mich. and Western Reserve (Miami and W.Mich began play in '48). **Admitted later** (8): Kent State (now Kent) and Toledo in 1951 (Toledo began play in '52), Bowling Green in 1952, Marshall in 1954, Central Mich. and Eastern Mich. in 1972 (CMU began play in '75, EMU in '76), Ball St. and Northern Ill. in 1973 (both began play in '75). **Withdrew later** (5): Butler in 1950, Cincinnati in 1953, Western Reserve in 1955, Marshall in 1969, Northern Ill. in 1986. **Current playing membership** (9): Ball St., Bowling Green, Central Mich., Eastern Mich., Kent, Miami-OH, Toledo and Western Mich.

Year		Year		Year		Year	
1947	Cincinnati (3-1)	1951	Cincinnati (3-0)	1956	Bowling Green (5-0-1)	1960	Ohio Univ. (6-0)
1948	Miami-OH (4-0)	1952	Cincinnati (3-0)	1957	Miami-OH (5-0)	1961	Bowling Green (5-1)
1949	Cincinnati (4-0)	1953	Ohio Univ. (5-0-1)	1958	Miami-OH (5-0)	1962	Bowling Green (5-0-1)
1950	Miami-OH (4-0)	1954	Miami-OH (4-0)	1959	Bowling Green (6-0)	1963	Ohio Univ. (5-1)
		1955	Miami-OH (5-0)			1964	Bowling Green (5-1)

Major Conference Champions (Cont.)
Mid-American Conference

Year		Year		Year		Year	
1965	Bowling Green (5-1) & Miami-OH (5-1)	1970	Toledo (5-0)	1978	Ball St. (8-0)	1986	Miami-OH (6-2)
1966	Miami-OH (5-1) & W Michigan (5-1)	1971	Toledo (5-0)	1979	C.Michigan. (8-0-1)	1987	E.Michigan (7-1)
		1972	Kent St. (4-1)	1980	C.Michigan (7-2)	1988	W.Michigan (7-1)
1967	Toledo (5-1) & Ohio Univ. (5-1)	1973	Miami-OH (5-0)	1981	Toledo (8-1)	1989	Ball St. (6-1-1)
		1974	Miami-OH (5-0)	1982	Bowling Green (7-2)	1990	C.Michigan (7-1) & Toledo (7-1)
1968	Ohio Univ. (6-0)	1975	Miami-OH (6-0)	1983	Northern Ill. (8-1)		
1969	Toledo (5-0)	1976	Ball St. (4-1)	1984	Toledo (7-1-1)		
		1977	Miami-OH (5-0)	1985	Bowling Green (9-0)		

Atlantic Coast Conference

Founded in 1953 when charter members all left Southern Conference to form ACC. **Charter members** (7): Clemson, Duke, Maryland, North Carolina, N.C.State, South Carolina, and Wake Forest. **Admitted later** (3): Virginia in 1953 (began play in '54), Georgia Tech in 1978 (began play in '83), Florida St. in 1990 (will begin play in '92). **Withdrew later** (1): South Carolina in 1971.

Current playing membership (8): Clemson, Duke, Georgia Tech, Maryland, North Carolina, N.C.State, Virginia and Wake Forest.

Year		Year		Year		Year	
1953	Duke (4-0) & Maryland (3-0)	1962	Duke (6-0)	1971	North Carolina (6-0)	1982	Clemson (6-0)
1954	Duke (4-0)	1963	North Carolina (6-1) & N.C.State (6-1)	1972	North Carolina (6-0)	1983	Maryland (5-0)
1955	Maryland (4-0) & Duke (4-0)	1964	N.C.State (5-2)	1973	N.C.State (6-0)	1984	Maryland (5-0)
1956	Clemson (4-0-1)	1965	Clemson (5-2) & N.C.State (5-2)	1974	Maryland (6-0)	1985	Maryland (6-0)
1957	N.C.State (5-0-1)	1966	Clemson (6-1)	1975	Maryland (5-0)	1986	Clemson (5-1-1)
1958	Clemson (5-1)	1967	Clemson (6-0)	1976	Maryland (5-0)	1987	Clemson (6-1)
1959	Clemson (6-1)	1968	N.C.State (6-0)	1977	North Carolina (5-0-1)	1988	Clemson (6-1)
1960	Duke (5-1)	1969	South Carolina (6-0)	1978	Clemson (6-0)	1989	Virginia (6-1) & Duke (6-1)
1961	Duke (5-1)	1970	Wake Forest (5-1)	1979	N.C.State (5-1)	1990	Georgia Tech (6-0-1)
				1980	North Carolina (6-0)		
				1981	Clemson (6-0)		

Western Athletic Conference

Founded in 1962 when charter members left the Skyline and Border Conferences to form the WAC. **Charter members** (6): Arizona (an independent), Arizona St. (from the Border), BYU, New Mexico, Utah and Wyoming (from the Skyline). **Added later** (6): Colorado St. and Texas-El Paso in 1967 (both began play in '68), San Diego St. in 1978, Hawaii in 1979, Air Force in 1980, Fresno St. in 1991 (will begin play in '92). **Withdrew later** (2): Arizona and Arizona St. in 1978.

Current playing membership (9): Air Force, BYU, Colorado St., Hawaii, New Mexico, San Diego St., UTEP, Utah and Wyoming.

Year		Year		Year		Year	
1962	New Mexico (2-1-1)	1969	Arizona St.(6-1)	1976	BYU (6-1) & Wyoming (6-1)	1983	BYU (7-0)
1963	New Mexico (3-1)	1970	Arizona St.(7-0)			1984	BYU (8-0)
1964	Utah (3-1), New Mexico (3-1) & Arizona (3-1)	1971	Arizona St.(7-0)	1977	Arizona St.(6-1) & BYU (6-1)	1985	Air Force (7-1) & BYU (7-1)
		1972	Arizona St.(5-1)	1978	BYU (5-1)	1986	San Diego St.(7-1)
		1973	Arizona St.(6-1) & Arizona (6-1)	1979	BYU (7-0)	1987	Wyoming (8-0)
1965	BYU (4-1)	1974	BYU (6-0-1)	1980	BYU (6-1)	1988	Wyoming (8-0)
1966	Wyoming (5-0)	1975	Arizona St.(7-0)	1981	BYU (7-1)	1989	BYU (8-0)
1967	Wyoming (5-0)			1982	BYU (7-1)	1990	BYU (7-1)
1968	Wyoming (6-1)						

Big West Conference

Originally founded in 1969 as Pacific Coast Athletic Assn. **Charter members** (7): Cal-Santa Barbara, Cal St.-Los Angeles, Fresno St., Long Beach St., Pacific, San Diego St. and San Jose St. **Admitted later** (4): Cal St.-Fullerton in 1974, Utah St. in 1977 (began play in '78), Nevada-Las Vegas in 1982 and New Mexico St. in 1983 (began play in '84). **Withdrew later** (4): UC-Santa Barbara in 1972, CS-Los Angeles in 1974, San Diego St. in 1976, Fresno St. in 1991 (will play through '91 season then leave for WAC). Renamed **Big West** in 1988.

Current playing membership (8): CS-Fullerton, Fresno St., Long Beach St., UNLV, New Mexico St., Pacific, San Jose St. and Utah St.

Year		Year		Year		Year	
1969	San Diego St. (6-0)	1974	San Diego St. (4-0)	1979	Utah St. (5-0)	1985	Fresno St. (7-0)
1970	Long Beach St. (5-1) & San Diego St. (5-1)	1975	San Jose St. (5-0)	1980	Long Beach St. (5-0)	1986	San Jose St. (7-0)
		1976	San Jose St. (4-0)	1981	San Jose St. (5-0)	1987	San Jose St. (7-0)
1971	Long Beach St. (5-1)	1977	Fresno St. (4-0)	1982	Fresno St. (6-0)	1988	Fresno St. (7-0)
1972	San Diego St. (4-0)	1978	San Jose St. (4-1) & Utah St. (4-1)	1983	CS-Fullerton (5-1)	1989	Fresno St. (7-0)
1973	San Diego St. (3-0-1)			1984	CS-Fullerton (6-1)*	1990	San Jose St. (7-0)

*UNLV forfeited title in 1984.

Annual NCAA Division I-A Leaders
Rushing

Individual championship decided on Rushing Yards (1937–69), and on Yards Per Game (since 1970).

Year		Car	Yards
1937	Byron (Whizzer) White, Colorado	181	1121
1938	Len Eshmont, Fordham	132	831
1939	John Polansky, Wake Forest	137	882
1940	Al Ghesquiere, Detroit	146	957
1941	Frank Sinkwich, Georgia	209	1103
1942	Rudy Mobley, Hardin-Simmons	187	1281
1943	Creighton Miller, Notre Dame	151	911
1944	Red Williams, Minnesota	136	911
1945	Bob Fenimore, Oklahoma A&M*	142	1048
1946	Rudy Mobley, Hardin-Simmons	227	1262
1947	Wilton Davis, Hardin-Simmons	193	1173
1948	Fred Wendt, Texas Mines*	184	1570
1949	John Dottley, Ole Miss	208	1312
1950	Wilford White, Arizona St	199	1502
1951	Ollie Matson, San Francisco	245	1566
1952	Howie Waugh, Tulsa	164	1372
1953	J.C.Caroline, Illinois	194	1256
1954	Art Luppino, Arizona	179	1359
1955	Art Luppino, Arizona	209	1313
1956	Jim Crawford, Wyoming	200	1104
1957	Leon Burton, Arizona St	117	1126
1958	Dick Bass, Pacific	205	1361
1959	Pervis Atkins, New Mexico St	130	971
1960	Bob Gaiters, New Mexico St	197	1338
1961	Jim Pilot, New Mexico St	191	1278
1962	Jim Pilot, New Mexico St	208	1247
1963	Dave Casinelli, Memphis St	219	1016
1964	Brian Piccolo, Wake Forest	252	1044

Year		Car	Yards
1965	Mike Garrett, USC	267	1440
1966	Ray McDonald, Idaho	259	1329
1967	O.J.Simpson, USC	266	1415
1968	O.J.Simpson, USC	355	1709
1969	Steve Owens, Oklahoma	358	1523

Years		Car	Yards	P/Gm
1970	Ed Marinaro, Cornell	285	1425	158.3
1971	Ed Marinaro, Cornell	356	1881	209.0
1972	Pete VanValkenburg, BYU	232	1386	138.6
1973	Mark Kellar, Northern Ill.	291	1719	156.3
1974	Louie Giammona, Utah St.	329	1534	153.4
1975	Ricky Bell, USC	357	1875	170.5
1976	Tony Dorsett, Pittsburgh	338	1948	177.1
1977	Earl Campbell, Texas	267	1744	158.5
1978	Billy Sims, Oklahoma	231	1762	160.2
1979	Charles White, USC	293	1803	180.3
1980	George Rogers, S.Carolina	297	1781	161.9
1981	Marcus Allen, USC	403	2342	212.9
1982	Ernest Anderson, Okla.St	353	1877	170.6
1983	Mike Rozier, Nebraska	275	2148	179.0
1984	Keith Byars, Ohio St	313	1655	150.5
1985	Lorenzo White, Mich.St	386	1908	173.5
1986	Paul Palmer, Temple	346	1866	169.6
1987	Ickey Woods, UNLV	259	1658	150.7
1988	Barry Sanders, Okla.St	344	2628	238.9
1989	Anthony Thompson, Ind	358	1793	163.0
1990	Gerald Hudson, Okla.St	279	1642	149.3

*Oklahoma A&M is now Oklahoma St. and Texas Mines is now UTEP.

All-Purpose Running

Championship decided on Running Yards Per Game.

Year		Yards	P/Gm
1937	Byron (Whizzer) White, Colorado	1970	246.3
1938	Parker Hall, Ole Miss	1420	129.1
1939	Tom Harmon, Michigan	1208	151.0
1940	Tom Harmon, Michigan	1312	164.0
1941	Bill Dudley, Virginia	1674	186.0
1942	Records not available		
1943	Stan Koslowski, Holy Cross	1411	176.4
1944	Red Williams, Minnesota	1467	163.0
1945	Bob Fenimore, Oklahoma A&M*	1577	197.1
1946	Rudy Mobley, Hardin-Simmons	1765	176.5
1947	Wilton Davis, Hardin-Simmons	1798	179.8
1948	Lou Kusserow, Columbia	1737	193.0
1949	Johnny Papit, Virginia	1611	179.0
1950	Wilford White, Arizona St	2065	206.5
1951	Ollie Matson, San Francisco	2037	226.3
1952	Billy Vessels, Oklahoma	1512	151.2
1953	J.C.Caroline, Illinois	1470	163.3
1954	Art Luppino, Arizona	2193	219.3
1955	Jim Swink, TCU	1702	170.2
	& Art Luppino, Arizona	1702	170.2
1956	Jack Hill, Utah St.	1691	169.1
1957	Overton Curtis, Utah St	1608	160.8
1958	Dick Bass, Pacific	1878	187.8
1959	Pervis Atkins, New Mexico St	1800	180.0
1960	Pervis Atkins, New Mexico St	1613	161.3
1961	Jim Pilot, New Mexico St	1606	160.6
1962	Gary Wood, Cornell	1395	155.0
1963	Gary Wood, Cornell	1508	167.6

Year		Yards	P/Gm
1964	Donny Anderson, Texas Tech	1710	171.0
1965	Floyd Little, Syracuse	1990	199.0
1966	Frank Quayle, Virginia	1616	161.6
1967	O.J.Simpson, USC	1700	188.9
1968	O.J.Simpson, USC	1966	196.6
1969	Lynn Moore, Army	1795	179.5
1970	Don McCauley, North Carolina	2021	183.7
1971	Ed Marinaro, Cornell	1932	214.7
1972	Howard Stevens, Louisville	2132	213.2
1973	Willard Harrell, Pacific	1777	177.7
1974	Louie Giammona, Utah St	1984	198.4
1975	Louie Giammona, Utah St	2045	185.9
1976	Tony Dorsett, Pittsburgh	2021	183.7
1977	Earl Campbell, Texas	1855	168.6
1978	Charles White, USC	2096	174.7
1979	Charles White, USC	1941	194.1
1980	Marcus Allen, USC	1794	179.4
1981	Marcus Allen, USC	2559	232.6
1982	Carl Monroe, Utah	2036	185.1
1983	Napoleon McCallum, Navy	2385	216.8
1984	Keith Byars, Ohio St	2284	207.6
1985	Napoleon McCallum, Navy	2330	211.8
1986	Paul Palmer, Temple	2633	239.4
1987	Eric Wilkerson, Kent St	2074	188.6
1988	Barry Sanders, Oklahoma St.	3250	295.5
1989	Mike Pringle, CS-Fullerton	2690	244.6
1990	Glyn Milburn, Stanford	2222	202.0

*Oklahoma A&M is now Oklahoma St.

Annual NCAA Division I-A Leaders (Cont.)
Total Offense

Individual championship decided on Total Yards (1937–69), and on Yards Per Game (since 1970).

Year		Plays	Yards
1937	Byron (Whizzer) White, Colorado	224	1596
1938	Davey O'Brien, TCU	291	1847
1939	Kenny Washington, UCLA	259	1370
1940	Johnny Knolla, Creighton	298	1420
1941	Bud Schwenk, Washington-MO	354	1928
1942	Frank Sinkwich, Georgia	341	2187
1943	Bob Hoernschemeyer, Indiana	355	1648
1944	Bob Fenimore, Oklahoma A&M*	241	1758
1945	Bob Fenimore, Oklahoma A&M	203	1641
1946	Travis Bidwell, Auburn	339	1715
1947	Fred Enke, Arizona	329	1941
1948	Stan Heath, Nevada-Reno	233	1992
1949	Johnny Bright, Drake	275	1950
1950	Johnny Bright, Drake	320	2400
1951	Dick Kazmaier, Princeton	272	1827
1952	Ted Marchibroda, Detroit	305	1813
1953	Paul Larson, California	262	1572
1954	George Shaw, Oregon	276	1536
1955	George Welsh, Navy	203	1348
1956	John Brodie, Stanford	295	1642
1957	Bob Newman, Washington St	263	1444
1958	Dick Bass, Pacific	218	1440
1959	Dick Norman, Stanford	319	2018
1960	Bill Kilmer, UCLA	292	1889
1961	Dave Hoppmann, Iowa St	320	1638
1962	Terry Baker, Oregon St	318	2276
1963	George Mira, Miami-FL	394	2318
1964	Jerry Rhome, Tulsa	470	3128

*Oklahoma A&M is now Oklahoma St.

Year		Plays	Yards	
1965	Bill Anderson, Tulsa	580	3343	
1966	Virgil Carter, BYU	388	2545	
1967	Sal Olivas, New Mexico St	368	2184	
1968	Greg Cook Cincinnati	507	3210	
1969	Dennis Shaw, San Diego St	388	3197	

Year		Plays	Yards	P/Gm
1970	Pat Sullivan, Auburn	333	2856	285.6
1971	Gary Huff, Florida St	386	2653	241.2
1972	Don Strock, Va.Tech	480	3170	288.2
1973	Jesse Freitas, S.Diego St	410	2901	263.7
1974	Steve Joachim, Temple	331	2227	222.7
1975	Gene Swick, Toledo	490	2706	246.0
1976	Tommy Kramer, Rice	562	3272	297.5
1977	Doug Williams, Grambling	377	3229	293.5
1978	Mike Ford, SMU	459	2957	268.8
1979	Marc Wilson, BYU	488	3580	325.5
1980	Jim McMahon, BYU	540	4627	385.6
1981	Jim McMahon, BYU	487	3458	345.8
1982	Todd Dillon, L.Beach St	585	3587	326.1
1983	Steve Young, BYU	531	4346	395.1
1984	Robbie Bosco, BYU	543	3932	327.7
1985	Jim Everett, Purdue	518	3589	326.3
1986	Mike Perez, San Jose St	425	2969	329.9
1987	Todd Santos, S.Diego St	562	3688	307.3
1988	Scott Mitchell, Utah	589	4299	390.8
1989	Andre Ware, Houston	628	4661	423.7
1990	David Klingler, Houston	704	5221	474.6

Passing

Individual championship decided on Completions (1937-69), on Completions Per Game (1970–78), and on Passing Efficiency rating points (since 1979).

Year		Cmp	Pct	TD	Yds
1937	Davey O'Brien, TCU	94	.402	—	969
1938	Davey O'Brien, TCU	93	.557	—	1457
1939	Kay Eakin, Arkansas	78	.404	—	962
1940	Billy Sewell, Wash.St	86	.494	—	1023
1941	Bud Schwenk, Wash.-MO	114	.487	—	1457
1942	Ray Evans, Kansas	101	.505	—	1117
1943	Johnny Cook, Georgia	73	.465	—	1007
1944	Paul Rickards, Pittsburgh	84	.472	—	997
1945	Al Dekdebrun, Cornell	90	.464	—	1227
1946	Travis Tidwell, Auburn	79	.500	5	943
1947	Charlie Conerly, Ole Miss	133	.571	18	1367
1948	Stan Heath, Nev-Reno	126	.568	22	2005
1949	Adrian Burk, Baylor	110	.576	14	1428
1950	Don Heinrich, Washington	134	.606	14	1846
1951	Don Klosterman, Loyola-CA	159	.505	9	1843
1952	Don Heinrich, Washington	137	.507	13	1647
1953	Bob Garrett, Stanford	118	.576	17	1637
1954	Paul Larson, California	125	.641	10	1537
1955	George Welsh, Navy	94	.627	8	1319
1956	John Brodie, Stanford	139	.579	12	1633
1957	Ken Ford, H-Simmons	115	.561	14	1254
1958	Buddy Humphrey, Baylor	112	.574	7	1316
1959	Dick Norman, Stanford	152	.578	11	1963
1960	Harold Stephens, H-Simm.	145	.566	3	1254
1961	Chon Gallegos, S.Jose St	117	.594	14	1480
1962	Don Trull, Baylor	125	.546	11	1627
1963	Don Trull, Baylor	174	.565	12	2157
1964	Jerry Rhome, Tulsa	224	.687	32	2870
1965	Bill Anderson, Tulsa	296	.582	30	3464

Year		Cmp	Pct	TD	Yds
1966	John Eckman, Wichita St	195	.426	7	2339
1967	Terry Stone, N.Mexico	160	.476	9	1946
1968	Chuck Hixon, SMU	265	.566	21	3103
1969	John Reaves, Florida	222	.561	24	2896

Year		Cmp	P/Gm	TD	Yds
1970	Sonny Sixkiller, Wash	186	18.6	15	2303
1971	Brian Sipe, S.Diego St	196	17.8	17	2532
1972	Don Strock, Va.Tech	228	20.7	16	3243
1973	Jesse Freitas, S.Diego St	227	20.6	21	2993
1974	Steve Bartkowski, Cal	182	16.5	12	2580
1975	Craig Penrose, S.Diego St	198	18.0	15	2660
1976	Tommy Kramer, Rice	269	24.5	21	3317
1977	Guy Benjamin, Stanford	208	20.8	19	2521
1978	Steve Dils, Stanford	247	22.5	22	2943

Year		Cmp	TD	Yds	Rating
1979	Turk Schonert, Stanford	148	19	1922	163.0
1980	Jim McMahon, BYU	284	47	4571	176.9
1981	Jim McMahon, BYU	272	30	3555	155.0
1982	Tom Ramsey, UCLA	191	21	2824	153.5
1983	Steve Young, BYU	306	33	3902	168.5
1984	Doug Flutie, BC	233	27	3454	152.9
1985	Jim Harbaugh, Michigan	139	18	1913	163.7
1986	V.Testaverde, Miami-FL	175	26	2557	165.8
1987	Don McPherson, Syracuse	129	22	2341	164.3
1988	Timm Rosenbach, Wash.St	199	23	2791	162.0
1989	Ty Detmer, BYU	265	32	4560	175.6
1990	Shawn Moore, Virginia	144	21	2262	160.7

Receiving

Championship decided on Passes Caught (1937–69), and on Catches Per Game (since 1970).

Year		No	TD	Yds
1937	Jim Benton, Arkansas	47	—	754
1938	Sam Boyd Baylor	32	—	537
1939	Ken Kavanaugh, LSU	30	—	467
1940	Eddie Bryant, Virginia	30	—	222
1941	Hank Stanton, Arizona	50	—	820
1942	Bill Rogers, Texas A&M	39	—	432
1943	Neil Armstrong, Okla.A&M*	39	—	317
1944	Reid Moseley, Georgia	32	—	506
1945	Reid Moseley, Georgia	31	—	662
1946	Neil Armstrong, Okla.A&M	32	1	479
1947	Barney Poole, Ole Miss.	52	8	513
1948	Red O'Quinn, Wake Forest	39	7	605
1949	Art Weiner, N.Carolina	52	7	762
1950	Gordon Cooper, Denver	46	8	569
1951	Dewey McConnell, Wyoming	47	9	725
1952	Ed Brown, Fordham	57	6	774
1953	John Carson, Georgia	45	4	663
1954	Jim Hanifan, California	44	7	569
1955	Hank Burnine, Missouri	44	2	594
1956	Art Powell, San Jose St	40	5	583
1957	Stuart Vaughan, Utah	53	5	756
1958	Dave Hibbert, Arizona	61	4	606
1959	Chris Burford, Stanford	61	6	756
1960	Hugh Campbell, Wash.St.	66	10	881
1961	Hugh Campbell, Wash.St.	53	5	723
1962	Vern Burke, Oregon St	69	10	1007
1963	Lawrence Elkins, Baylor	70	8	873
1964	Howard Twilley, Tulsa	95	13	1178

*Oklahoma A&M now Oklahoma St.

Year		No	TD	Yds
1965	Howard Twilley, Tulsa	134	16	1779
1966	Glenn Meltzer, Wichita St	91	4	1115
1967	Bob Goodridge, Vanderbilt	79	6	1114
1968	Ron Sellers, Florida St	86	12	1496
1969	Jerry Hendren, Idaho	95	12	1452

Year		No	P/Gm	TD	Yds
1970	Mike Mikolayunas, Davidson	87	8.7	8	1128
1971	Tom Reynolds, S.Diego St.	67	6.7	7	1070
1972	Tom Forzani, Utah St	85	7.7	8	1169
1973	Jay Miller, BYU	100	9.1	8	1181
1974	Dwight McDonald, S.Diego St	86	7.8	7	1157
1975	Bob Farnham, Brown	56	6.2	2	701
1976	Billy Ryckman, La.Tech	77	7.0	10	1382
1977	Wayne Tolleson, W.Carolina	73	6.6	7	1101
1978	Dave Petzke, Northern Ill	91	8.3	11	1217
1979	Rick Beasley, Appalach.St	74	6.7	12	1205
1980	Dave Young, Purdue	67	6.1	8	917
1981	Pete Harvey, N.Texas St	57	6.3	3	743
1982	Vincent White, Stanford	68	6.8	8	677
1983	Keith Edwards, Vanderbilt	97	8.8	8	909
1984	David Williams, Illinois	101	9.2	8	1278
1985	Rodney Carter, Purdue	98	8.9	4	1099
1986	Mark Templeton, L.Beach St.	99	9.0	2	688
1987	Jason Phillips, Houston	99	9.0	3	875
1988	Jason Phillips, Houston	108	9.8	15	1444
1989	Manny Hazard, Houston	142	12.9	22	1689
1990	Manny Hazard, Houston	78	7.8	9	946

Scoring

Championship decided on Total Points (1937–69), and on Points Per Game (since 1970).

Year		TD	XP	FG	Pts
1937	Byron (Whizzer) White, Colo	16	23	1	122
1938	Parker Hall, Ole Miss	11	7	0	73
1939	Tom Harmon, Michigan	14	15	1	102
1940	Tom Harmon, Michigan	16	18	1	117
1941	Bill Dudley, Virginia	18	23	1	134
1942	Bob Steuber, Missouri	18	13	0	121
1943	Steve Van Buren, LSU	14	14	0	98
1944	Glenn Davis, Army	20	0	0	120
1945	Doc Blanchard, Army	19	1	0	115
1946	Gene Roberts, Tenn-Chatt	18	9	0	117
1947	Lou Gambino, Maryland	16	0	0	96
1948	Fred Wendt, Texas Mines*	20	32	0	152
1949	George Thomas, Oklahoma	19	3	0	117
1950	Bobby Reynolds, Oklahoma	22	25	0	157
1951	Ollie Matson, San Francisco	21	0	0	126
1952	Jackie Parker, Miss.St.	16	24	0	120
1953	Earl Lindley, Utah St.	13	3	0	81
1954	Art Luppino, Arizona	24	22	0	166
1955	Jim Swink, TCU	20	5	0	125
1956	Clendon Thomas, Oklahoma	18	0	0	108
1957	Leon Burton, Ariz.St.	16	0	0	96
1958	Dick Bass, Pacific	18	8	0	116
1959	Pervis Atkins, N.Mexico St.	17	5	0	107
1960	Bob Gaiters, N.Mexico St.	23	7	0	145
1961	Jim Pilot, N.Mexico St.	21	12	0	138
1962	Jim Logan, W.Texas St.	13	32	0	110
1963	Cosmo Iacavazzi, Princeton	14	0	0	84
	& Dave Casinelli, Memphis St.	14	0	0	84
1964	Brian Piccolo, Wake Forest	17	9	0	111

*Texas Mines is now UTEP.

Year		TD	XP	FG	Pts	
1965	Howard Twilley, Tulsa	16	31	0	127	
1966	Ken Hebert, Houston	11	41	2	113	
1967	Leroy Keyes, Purdue	19	0	0	114	
1968	Jim O'Brien, Cincinnati	12	31	13	142	
1969	Steve Owens, Oklahoma	23	0	0	138	

Year		TD	XP	FG	Pts	P/Gm
1970	Brian Bream, Air Force	20	0	0	120	12.0
	& Gary Kosins, Dayton	18	0	0	108	12.0
1971	Ed Marinaro, Cornell	24	4	0	148	16.4
1972	Harold Henson, Ohio St	20	0	0	120	12.0
1973	Jim Jennings, Rutgers	21	2	0	128	11.6
1974	Bill Marek, Wisconsin	19	0	0	114	12.7
1975	Pete Johnson, Ohio St	25	0	0	150	13.6
1976	Tony Dorsett, Pitt	22	2	0	134	12.2
1977	Earl Campbell, Texas	19	0	0	114	10.4
1978	Billy Sims, Oklahoma	20	0	0	120	10.9
1979	Billy Sims, Oklahoma	22	0	0	132	12.0
1980	Sammy Wilder, So.Miss	20	0	0	120	10.9
1981	Marcus Allen, USC	23	0	0	138	12.5
1982	Greg Allen, Fla.St.	21	0	0	126	11.5
1983	Mike Rozier, Nebraska	29	0	0	174	14.5
1984	Keith Byars, Ohio St	24	0	0	144	13.1
1985	Bernard White, B.Green	19	0	0	114	10.4
1986	Steve Bartalo, Colo.St	19	0	0	114	10.4
1987	Paul Hewitt, S.Diego St	24	0	0	144	12.0
1988	Barry Sanders, Okla.St	39	0	0	234	21.3
1989	Anthony Thompson, Ind	25	4	0	154	14.0
1990	Stacey Robinson, No.Ill	19	6	0	120	10.9

All-Time NCAA Division I-A Individual Leaders
CAREER

Through the 1990 regular season. Players with eligibility remaining after the 1990 season in **bold** type. Note that the NCAA does not recognize active players among career Per Game leaders.

Total Offense

Yards Gained	Years	Yards
Doug Flutie, Boston College	1981-84	11,317
Ty Detmer, BYU	1988-90	10,664
Todd Santos, San Diego St	1984-87	10,513
Kevin Sweeney, Fresno St	1983-86	10,252
Brian McClure, Bowling Green	1982-85	9,774

Yards Per Game	Years	Yards	P/Gm
Mike Perez, San Jose St	1986-87	6,182	309.1
Doug Gaynor, L.Beach St	1984-85	6,710	305.0
Tony Eason, Illinois	1981-82	6,589	299.5
Steve Young, BYU	1981-83	8,817	284.4
Doug Flutie, Boston Col	1981-84	11,317	269.5

Rushing

Yards Gained	Years	Yards
Tony Dorsett, Pitt	1973-76	6082
Charles White, USC	1976-79	5598
Herschel Walker, Georgia	1980-82	5259
Archie Griffin, Ohio St	1972-75	5177
Darren Lewis, Texas A&M	1987-90	5012

Yards Per Game	Years	Yards	P/Gm
Ed Marinaro, Cornell	1969-71	4715	174.6
O.J.Simpson, USC	1967-68	3124	164.4
Herschel Walker, Georgia	1980-82	5259	159.4
Tony Dorsett, Pitt	1973-76	6082	141.4
Mike Rozier, Nebraska	1981-83	4780	136.6

All-Purpose Running

Yards Gained	Years	Yards
Napoleon McCallum, Navy	1981-85	7172
Darrin Nelson, Stanford	1977-78,80,81	6885
Terance Mathis, N.Mexico	1985-87,89	6691
Tony Dorsett, Pitt	1973-76	6615
Paul Palmer, Temple	1983-86	6609

Yards Per Game	Years	Yards	P/Gm
Sheldon Canley, S.Jose St	1988-90	5146	205.8
Howard Stevens, L'ville	1971-72	3873	193.7
O.J.Simpson, USC	1967-68	3666	192.9
Ed Marinaro, Cornell	1969-71	4940	183.0
Herschel Walker, Georgia	1980-82	5749	174.2

Passing
(Minimum 500 Completions)

Passing Efficiency	Years	Rating
Jim McMahon, BYU	1977-78,80,81	156.9
Steve Young, BYU	1982,84-86	149.8
Troy Aikman, Okla-UCLA	1984-85,87,88	149.7
Robbie Bosco, BYU	1981-83	149.4
Chuck Hartlieb, Iowa	1985-88	148.9

Yards Gained	Years	Yards
Todd Santos, San Diego St	1984-87	11,425
Ty Detmer, BYU	1988-90	11,000
Kevin Sweeney, Fresno St	1983-86	10,623
Doug Flutie, Boston College	1981-84	10,579
Brian McClure, Bowling Green	1982-85	10,280

Completions	Years	No
Todd Santos, San Diego St	1984-87	910
Brian McClure, Bowling Green	1982-85	900
Ben Bennett, Duke	1980-83	820
John Elway, Stanford	1979-82	774
Jack Trudeau, Illinois	1981,83-85	736

Receiving

Catches	Years	No
Terance Mathis, New Mexico	1985-87,89	263
Mark Templeton, Long Beach St	1983-86	262
Howard Twilley, Tulsa	1963-65	261
David Williams, Illinois	1983-85	245
Marc Zeno, Tulane	1984-87	236

Catches Per Game	Years	No	P/Gm
Manny Hazard, Houston	1989-90	220	10.5
Howard Twilley, Tulsa	1963-65	261	10.0
Jason Phillips, Houston	1987-88	207	9.4
Neal Sweeney, Tulsa	1965-66	134	7.4
David Williams, Illinois	1983-85	245	7.4

Yards Gained	Years	No	Yards
Terance Mathis, N.Mex.	1985-87,89	263	4254
Marc Zeno, Tulane	1984-87	236	3725
Ron Sellers, Florida St	1966-68	212	3598
Elmo Wright, Houston	1968-70	153	3347
Howard Twilley, Tulsa	1963-65	261	3343
Gerald Harp, W.Carolina	1977-80	197	3305

Scoring

KICKERS

Points	Years	FG	XP	Pts
Derek Schmidt, Fla.St	1984-87	73	174	393
Luis Zendejas, Ariz.St	1981-84	78	134	368
Jeff Jaeger, Wash	1983-86	80	118	358
Roman Anderson, Hou	1988-90	60	174	354
John Lee, UCLA	1982-85	79	116	353
Max Zendejas, Arizona	1982-85	77	122	353
Kevin Butler, Georgia	1981-84	77	122	353

Field Goals	Years	No
Jeff Jaeger, Washington	1983-86	80
John Lee, UCLA	1982-85	79
Philip Doyle, Alabama	1987-90	78
Luis Zendejas, Arizona St	1981-84	78
Kevin Butler, Georgia	1981-84	77
Max Zendejas, Arizona	1982-85	77

NON-KICKERS

Points	Years	TD	Xpt	FG	Pts
Anthony Thompson, Ind.	1986-89	65	4	0	394
Tony Dorsett, Pitt	1973-76	59	2	0	356
Glenn Davis, Army	1943-46	59	0	0	354
Art Luppino, Ariz.	1953-56	48	49	0	337
Steve Owens, Okla.	1967-69	56	0	0	336

Points Per Game	Years	Pts	P/Gm
Bob Gaiters, N.Mexico St	1959-60	203	11.9
Ed Marinaro, Cornell	1969-71	318	11.8
Bill Burnett, Arkansas	1968-70	294	11.3
Steve Owens, Oklahoma	1967-69	336	11.2
Eddie Talboom, Wyoming	1948-50	303	10.8

Touchdowns Rushing	Years	No
Steve Owens, Oklahoma	1967-69	56
Tony Dorsett, Pittsburgh	1973-76	55
Anthony Thompson, Indiana	1986-89	54
Ed Marinaro, Cornell	1969-71	50
Mike Rozier, Nebraska	1981-83	50

Touchdowns Passing	Years	No
Ty Detmer, BYU	1988-90	86
Jim McMahon, BYU	1977-78,80-81	84
Joe Adams, Tenn.St	1977-80	81
John Elway, Stanford	1979-82	77
Andre Ware, Houston	1987-89	75

Touchdown Catches	Years	No
Clarkston Hines, Duke	1986-89	38
Terance Mathis, New Mexico	1985-87,89	36
Elmo Wright, Houston	1968-70	34
Howard Twilley, Tulsa	1963-65	32
Manny Hazard, Houston	1989-90	31

Miscellaneous

Interceptions	Years	No
Al Brosky, Illinois	1950-52	29
John Provost, Holy Cross	1972-74	27
Martin Bayless, Bowling Green	1980-83	27
Tom Curtis, Michigan	1967-69	25
Tony Thurman, Boston College	1981-84	25

Punt Return Average*	Years	Avg
Jack Mitchell, Oklahoma	1946-48	23.6
Gene Gibson, Cincinnati	1949-50	20.5
Eddie Macon, Pacific	1949-51	18.9
Jackie Robinson, UCLA	1939-40	18.8
Mike Fuller, Auburn	1972-74	17.7
Bobby Dillon, Texas	1949-51	17.7

*At least 1.2 punt returns per game

Punting Average*	Years	Avg
Reggie Roby, Iowa	1979-82	45.6
Greg Montgomery, Michigan St	1985-87	45.4
Tom Tupa, Ohio St	1984-87	45.2
Barry Helton, Colorado	1984-87	44.9
Ray Guy, Southern Miss	1970-72	44.7

*At least 150 punts kicked

Kickoff Return Average*	Years	Avg
Forrest Hall, San Francisco	1946-47	36.2
Anthony Davis, USC	1972-74	35.1
Overton Curtis, Utah St	1957-58	31.0
Altie Taylor, Utah St	1966-68	29.3
Stan Brown, Purdue	1968-70	28.8

*At least 1.2 kickoff returns per game

SINGLE SEASON

Through the 1990 regular season.

Total Offense

Yards Gained	Year	Gm	Plays	Yards
David Klingler, Houston	1990	11	704	5221
Ty Detmer, BYU	1990	12	635	5022
Andre Ware, Houston	1989	11	628	4661
Jim McMahon, BYU	1980	12	540	4627
Ty Detmer, BYU	1989	12	497	4433

Yards Per Game	Year	Gm	Yards	P/Gm
David Klingler, Houston	1990	11	5221	474.6
Andre Ware, Houston	1989	11	4661	423.7
Ty Detmer, BYU	1990	12	5022	418.5
Steve Young, BYU	1983	11	4346	395.1
Scott Mitchell, Utah	1988	11	4299	390.8

Rushing

Yards Gained	Year	Gm	Car	Yards
Barry Sanders, Okla.St	1988	11	344	2628
Marcus Allen, USC	1981	11	403	2342
Mike Rozier, Nebraska	1983	12	275	2148
Tony Dorsett, Pitt	1976	11	338	1948
Lorenzo White, Mich.St	1985	11	386	1908

Yards Per Game	Year	Gm	Yards	P/Gm
Barry Sanders, Okla.St	1988	11	2628	238.9
Marcus Allen, USC	1981	11	2342	212.9
Ed Marinaro, Cornell	1971	9	1881	209.0
Charles White, USC	1979	10	1803	180.3
Mike Rozier, Nebraska	1983	12	2148	179.0

All-Purpose Running

Yards Gained	Year	Yards
Barry Sanders, Oklahoma St	1988	3250
Paul Palmer, Temple	1986	2633
Marcus Allen, USC	1981	2559
Mike Rozier, Nebraska	1983	2486
Napoleon McCallum, Navy	1983	2385

Yards Per Game	Year	Yards	P/Gm
Barry Sanders, Oklahoma St	1988	3250	295.5
Byron (Whizzer) White, Colo	1937	1970	246.3
Mike Pringle, CS-Fullerton	1989	2690	244.6
Paul Palmer, Temple	1986	2633	239.4
Marcus Allen, USC	1981	2559	232.6

Passing

(Minimum 15 Attempts Per Game)

Passing Efficiency	Year	Rating
Jim McMahon, BYU	1980	176.9
Ty Detmer, BYU	1989	175.6
Jerry Rhome, Tulsa	1964	172.6
Steve Young, BYU	1983	168.5
Vinny Testaverde, Miami-FL	1986	165.8
Brian Dowling, Yale	1968	165.8

Yards Gained	Year	Yards
Ty Detmer, BYU	1990	5188
David Klingler, Houston	1990	5140
Andre Ware, Houston	1989	4699
Jim McMahon, BYU	1980	4571
Ty Detmer, BYU	1989	4560

Completions	Year	Att	No
David Klingler, Houston	1990	643	374
Andre Ware, Houston	1989	578	365
Ty Detmer, BYU	1990	562	361
Robbie Bosco, BYU	1985	511	338
Scott Mitchell, Utah	1988	533	323

Receiving

Catches	Year	Gm	No
Manny Hazard, Houston	1989	11	142
Howard Twilley, Tulsa	1965	10	134
Jason Phillips, Houston	1988	11	108
James Dixon, Houston	1988	11	102
David Williams, Illinois	1984	11	101

Catches Per Game	Year	No	P/Gm
Howard Twilley, Tulsa	1965	134	13.4
Manny Hazard, Houston	1989	142	12.9
Jason Phillips, Houston	1988	108	9.8
Jerry Hendren, Idaho	1969	95	9.5
Howard Twilley, Tulsa	1964	95	9.5

Yards Gained	Year	No	Yards
Howard Twilley, Tulsa	1965	134	1779
Manny Hazard, Houston	1989	142	1689
Chuck Hughes, Texas Western*	1965	80	1519
Henry Ellard, Fresno St	1982	62	1510
Ron Sellers, Florida St	1968	86	1496

*Texas Western is now UTEP.

All-Time NCAA Division I-A Individual Leaders (Cont.)
Scoring

Points	Year	TD	Xpt	FG	Pts
Barry Sanders, Okla.St.	1988	39	0	0	234
Mike Rozier, Nebraska	1983	29	0	0	174
Lydell Mitchell, Penn St.	1971	29	0	0	174
Art Luppino, Arizona	1954	24	22	0	166
Bobby Reynolds, Nebraska	1950	22	25	0	157

Points Per Game	Year	Pts	P/Gm
Barry Sanders, Oklahoma St.	1988	234	21.3
Bobby Reynolds, Nebraska	1950	157	17.4
Art Luppino, Arizona	1954	166	16.6
Ed Marinaro, Cornell	1971	148	16.4
Lydell Mitchell, Penn St.	1971	174	15.8

Touchdowns Rushing	Year	No
Barry Sanders, Oklahoma St.	1988	37
Mike Rozier, Nebraska	1983	29
Ed Marinaro, Cornell	1971	24
Anthony Thompson, Indiana	1988	24
Anthony Thompson, Indiana	1989	24

Touchdowns Passing	Year	No
David Klingler, Houston	1990	54
Jim McMahon, BYU	1980	47
Andre Ware, Houston	1989	46
Ty Detmer, BYU	1990	41
Dennis Shaw, San Diego St	1969	39

Touchdown Catches	Year	No
Manny Hazard, Houston	1989	22
Tom Reynolds, San Diego St	1969	18
Dennis Smith, Utah.	1989	18
Clarkston Hines, Duke	1989	17
Howard Twilley, Tulsa	1965	16
Dan Bitson, Tulsa	1989	16

Field Goals	Year	No
John Lee, UCLA	1984	29
Paul Woodside, West Virginia	1982	28
Luis Zendejas, Arizona St.	1983	28
Fuad Reveiz, Tennessee	1982	27
Three tied at 25		

Miscellaneous

Interceptions	Year	No
Al Worley, Washington.	1968	14
George Shaw, Oregon	1951	13
Seven tied at 12		

Punt Return Average*	Year	Avg
Bill Blackstock, Tennessee	1951	25.9
George Sims, Baylor	1948	25.0
Gene Derricotte, Michigan.	1947	24.8
Erroll Tucker, Utah	1985	24.3
George Hoey, Michigan	1967	24.3

*At least 1.2 returns per game

Punting Average*	Year	Avg
Reggie Roby, Iowa	1981	49.8
Kirk Wilson, UCLA	1956	49.3
Zack Jordan, Colorado	1950	48.2
Ricky Anderson, Vanderbilt	1984	48.2
Marv Bateman, Utah	1971	48.1
Reggie Roby, Iowa	1982	48.1

*Qualifiers for championship

Kickoff Return Average*	Year	Avg
Forrest Hall, San Francisco	1946	38.2
Tony Ball, Tenn-Chattanooga	1977	36.4
Rocket Ismail, Notre Dame	1988	36.1
George Marinkov, N.C. State	1954	35.8
Bob Baker, Cornell	1964	35.1

*At least 1.2 kickoff returns per game

SINGLE GAME

Through the 1990 regular season.

Total Offense

Yards Gained	Opponent	Year	Yds
David Klingler, Houston	Ariz.St.	1990	732
Matt Vogler, TCU	Houston	1990	696
David Klingler, Houston	TCU	1990	625
Scott Mitchell, Utah	Air Force	1988	625
Troy Kopp, Pacific	N.Mex.St.	1990	601

Passing

Yards Gained	Opponent	Year	Yds
David Klingler, Houston	Ariz.St.	1990	716
Matt Vogler, TCU	Houston	1990	690
Scott Mitchell, Utah	Air Force	1988	631
Jeremy Leach, New Mexico	Utah	1989	622
Dave Wilson, Illinois	Ohio St.	1980	621

Completions

	Opponent	Year	No
David Klingler, Houston	SMU	1990	48
Sandy Schwab, Northwestern	Michigan	1982	45
Chuck Hartlieb, Iowa	Indiana	1988	44
Jim McMahon, BYU	Colo.St.	1981	44
Matt Vogler, TCU	Houston	1990	44

Rushing

Yards Gained	Opponent	Year	Yds
Anthony Thompson, Ind	Wisconsin	1989	377
Rueben Mayes, Wash.St.	Oregon	1984	357
Mike Pringle, CS-Fullerton	N.Mex.St	1989	357
Eddie Lee Ivery, Ga.Tech	Air Force	1978	356
Eric Allen, Michigan St.	Purdue	1971	350

Receiving

Catches	Opponent	Year	No
Jay Miller, BYU	New Mexico	1973	22
Rick Eber, Tulsa	Idaho St.	1967	20
Howard Twilley, Tulsa	Colo.St.	1965	19
Ron Fair, Arizona St	Wash.St	1989	19
Manny Hazard, Houston	TCU	1989	19
Manny Hazard, Houston	Texas	1989	19

Yards Gained	Opponent	Year	Yds
Chuck Hughes, UTEP*	N.Texas St.	1965	349
Rick Eber, Tulsa	Idaho St.	1967	322
Harry Wood, Tulsa	Idaho St.	1967	318
Jeff Evans, New Mexico St	So.Ill.	1978	316
Tom Reynolds, San Diego St	Utah St.	1971	290

*UTEP was Texas Western in 1965.

Scoring

Points

	Opponent	Year	Pts
Howard Griffith, Illinois	So.Ill.	1990	48
Jim Brown, Syracuse	Colgate	1956	43
Showboat Boykin, Mississippi	Miss.St.	1951	42
Fred Wendt, UTEP*	N.Mex.St.	1948	42
Dick Bass, Pacific	S.Diego St.	1958	38

*UTEP was Texas Mines in 1948.

Touchdowns Rushing

	Opponent	Year	No
Howard Griffith, Illinois	So.Ill	1990	8
Showboat Boykin, Mississippi	Miss.St.	1951	7

Note: Griffith's TD runs (5-51-7-41-5-18-5-3).

Touchdowns Passing

	Opponent	Year	No
David Klingler, Houston	E.Wash.	1990	11
Dennis Shaw, San Diego St	N.Mex.St.	1969	9

Note: Klingler's TD passes (5-48-29-7-3-7-40-8-7-8-51).

Touchdown Catches

	Opponent	Year	No
Tim Delaney, San Diego St.	N.Mex.St.	1969	6

Note: Delaney TD catches (2-22-34-31-30-9).

Field Goals

	Opponent	Year	No
Dale Klein, Nebraska	Missouri	1985	7
Mike Prindle, W.Michigan	Marshall	1984	7

Note: Klein's FGs (32-22-43-44-29-43-43); Prindle's FGs (32-44-42-23-48-41-27).

Extra Points (Kick)

	Opponent	Year	No
Terry Leiweke, Houston	Tulsa	1968	13

Extra Points (2-Pts)

	Opponent	Year	No
Jim Pilot, N.Mexico St.	H-Simmons	1961	6

Longest Plays (since 1941)

Rushing

	Opponent	Year	Yds
Gale Sayers, Kansas	Nebraska	1963	99
Max Anderson, Ariz.St	Wyoming	1967	99
Ralph Thompson, W.Texas St	Wich.St.	1970	99
Kelsey Finch, Tennessee	Florida	1977	99

Passing

	Opponent	Year	Yds
Fred Owens to Jack Ford, Portland	St.Mary's	1947	99
Bo Burris to Warren McVea, Houston	Wash.St.	1966	99
Colin Clapton to Eddie Jenkins, H.Cross	Boston U.	1970	99
Terry Peel to Robert Ford, Houston	Syracuse	1970	99
Terry Peel to Robert Ford, Houston	S.Diego St.	1972	99
Cris Collinsworth to Derrick Gaffney, Fla	Rice	1977	99
Scott Ankrom to James Maness, TCU	Rice	1984	99

Field Goals

	Opponent	Year	Yds
Steve Little, Arkansas	Texas	1977	67
Russell Erxleben, Texas	Rice	1977	67
Joe Williams, Wichita St	So.Ill.	1978	67

Punts

	Opponent	Year	Yds
Pat Brady, Nevada-Reno	Loyola-CA	1950	99
George O'Brien, Wisconsin	Iowa	1952	98

Punt Returns
100-yd punt returns since 1941: 7 players.

Kickoff Returns
100-yd kickoff returns since 1941: 161 players.

Interception Returns
100-yd interception returns since 1941: 56 players.

Annual Awards
Heisman Trophy

Originally presented in 1935 as the DAC Trophy by the Downtown Athletic Club of New York City to the best college football player east of the Mississippi. In 1936, players across the country were eligible and the award was renamed the Heisman Trophy following the death of former college coach and DAC athletic director John W.Heisman. Players listed in **bold** type helped lead their team to a national championship (according to AP).

Multiple winner: Archie Griffin (1974-75). **Winners in junior year:** Doc Blanchard (1945), Doak Walker (1948), Vic Janowicz (1950), Roger Staubach (1963), Griffin (1974), Billy Sims (1978), Herschel Walker (1982), Barry Sanders (1988), Andre Ware (1989), Ty Detmer (1990).

Year		Year	
1935	Jay Berwanger, Chicago, HB	1954	Alan Ameche, Wisconsin, FB
1936	Larry Kelley, Yale, E	1955	Howard Cassady, Ohio St., HB
1937	Clint Frank, Yale, HB	1956	Paul Hornung, Notre Dame, QB
1938	**Davey O'Brien, TCU, QB**	1957	John David Crow, Texas A&M, HB
1939	Nile Kinnick, Iowa, HB	1958	Pete Dawkins, Army, HB
		1959	Billy Cannon, LSU, HB
1940	Tom Harmon, Michigan, HB		
1941	**Bruce Smith, Minnesota, HB**	1960	Joe Bellino, Navy, HB
1942	Frank Sinkwich, Georgia, TB	1961	Ernie Davis, Syracuse, HB
1943	**Angelo Bertelli, Notre Dame, QB**	1962	Terry Baker, Oregon St., QB
1944	Les Horvath, Ohio St., TB-QB	1963	Roger Staubach, Navy, QB
1945	**Doc Blanchard, Army, FB**	1964	John Huarte, Notre Dame, QB
1946	Glenn Davis, Army, HB	1965	Mike Garrett, USC, HB
1947	**Johnny Lujack, Notre Dame, QB**	1966	Steve Spurrier, Florida, QB
1948	Doak Walker, SMU, HB	1967	Gary Beban, UCLA, QB
1949	**Leon Hart, Notre Dame, E**	1968	O.J.Simpson, USC, HB
		1969	Steve Owens, Oklahoma, HB
1950	Vic Janowicz, Ohio St., HB		
1951	Dick Kazmaier, Princeton, TB	1970	Jim Plunkett, Stanford, QB
1952	Billy Vessels, Oklahoma, HB	1971	Pat Sullivan, Auburn, QB
1953	Johnny Lattner, Notre Dame, HB	1972	Johnny Rodgers, Nebraska, FL

Annual Awards (Cont.)
Heisman Trophy

Year		Year	
1973	John Cappelletti, Penn St., RB	1982	Herschel Walker, Georgia, RB
1974	Archie Griffin, Ohio St., RB	1983	Mike Rozier, Nebraska, RB
1975	Archie Griffin, Ohio St., RB	1984	Doug Flutie, Boston College, QB
1976	**Tony Dorsett, Pittsburgh, RB**	1985	Bo Jackson, Auburn, RB
1977	Earl Campbell, Texas, RB	1986	Vinny Testaverde, Miami-FL, QB
1978	Billy Sims, Oklahoma, RB	1987	Tim Brown, Notre Dame, WR
1979	Charles White, USC, RB	1988	Barry Sanders, Oklahoma St., RB
		1989	Andre Ware, Houston, QB
1980	George Rogers, South Carolina, RB		
1981	Marcus Allen, USC, RB	1990	Ty Detmer, BYU, QB

Maxwell Award

First presented in 1937 by the Maxwell Memorial Football Club of Philadelphia, the award is named after Robert "Tiny" Maxwell, a Philadelphia native who was a standout lineman at the University of Chicago at the turn of the century.

Like the Heisman, the Maxwell is given to the outstanding college player in the nation. Both awards have gone to the same player in the same season 27 times. Those players are preceded by (#). Glenn Davis of Army and Doak Walker of SMU won both but in different years.

Multiple winner: Johnny Lattner (1952-53).

Year		Year		Year	
1937	#Clint Frank, Yale, HB	1955	#Howard Cassady, Ohio St., HB	1973	#John Cappelletti, Penn St., RB
1938	#Davey O'Brien, TCU, QB	1956	Tommy McDonald, Okla., HB	1974	Steve Joachim, Temple, QB
1939	#Nile Kinnick, Iowa, HB	1957	Bob Reifsnyder, Navy, T	1975	#Archie Griffin, Ohio St., RB
		1958	#Pete Dawkins, Army, HB	1976	#Tony Dorsett, Pitt, RB
1940	#Tom Harmon, Michigan, HB	1959	Rich Lucas, Penn St., QB	1977	Ross Browner, Notre Dame, DE
1941	Bill Dudley, Virginia, HB			1978	Chuck Fusina, Penn St., QB
1942	Paul Governali, Columbia, QB	1960	#Joe Bellino, Navy, HB	1979	Charles White, USC, RB
1943	Bob Odell, Penn, HB	1961	Bob Ferguson, Ohio St., HB		
1944	Glenn Davis, Army, HB	1962	#Terry Baker, Oregon St., QB	1980	Hugh Green, Pitt, DE
1945	#Doc Blanchard, Army, FB	1963	#Roger Staubach, Navy, QB	1981	#Marcus Allen, USC, RB
1946	Charley Trippi, Georgia, HB	1964	Glenn Ressler, Penn St., G	1982	#Herschel Walker, Georgia, RB
1947	Doak Walker, SMU, HB	1965	Tommy Nobis, Texas, LB	1983	#Mike Rozier, Nebraska, RB
1948	Chuck Bednarik, Penn, C	1966	Jim Lynch, Notre Dame, LB	1984	#Doug Flutie, Boston Col., QB
1949	#Leon Hart, Notre Dame, E	1967	#Gary Beban, UCLA, QB	1985	Chuck Long, Iowa, QB
		1968	#O.J.Simpson, USC, RB	1986	#V. Testaverde, Miami-FL, QB
1950	Reds Bagnell, Penn, HB	1969	Mike Reid, Penn St., DT	1987	Don McPherson, Syracuse, QB
1951	#Dick Kazmaier, Princeton, TB			1988	#Barry Sanders, Okla.St., RB
1952	Johnny Lattner, Notre Dame, HB	1970	#Jim Plunkett, Stanford, QB	1989	Anthony Thompson, Indiana, RB
1953	#Johnny Lattner, N. Dame, HB	1971	Ed Marinaro, Cornell, RB		
1954	Ron Beagle, Navy, E	1972	Brad VanPelt, Michigan St., DB	1990	#Ty Detmer, BYU, QB

Outland Trophy

First presented in 1946 by the Football Writers Association of America, honoring the the nation's outstanding interior lineman. The award is named after its benefactor, Dr. John H. Outland (Kansas, Class of 1898). Players listed in **bold** type helped lead their team to a national championship (according to AP).

Multiple winner: Dave Rimmington (1981-82). **Winners in junior year:** Ross Browner (1976), Rimmington (1981).

Year		Year		Year	
1946	**George Connor,** Notre Dame, T	1961	Merlin Olsen, Utah St., T	1977	Brad Shearer, Texas, DT
1947	Joe Steffy, Army, G	1962	Bobby Bell, Minnesota, T	1978	Greg Roberts, Oklahoma, G
1948	Bill Fischer, Notre Dame, G	1963	**Scott Appleton,** Texas, T	1979	Jim Richter, N.C.State, C
1949	Ed Bagdon, Michigan St., G	1964	Steve DeLong, Tennessee, T		
		1965	Tommy Nobis, Texas, G	1980	Mark May, Pittsburgh, OT
1950	Bob Gain, Kentucky, T	1966	Loyd Phillips, Arkansas, T	1981	Dave Rimmington, Nebraska, C
1951	Jim Weatherall, Oklahoma, T	1967	**Ron Yary,** USC, T	1982	Dave Rimmington, Nebraska, C
1952	Dick Modzelewski, Maryland, T	1968	Bill Stanfill, Georgia, T	1983	Dean Steinkuhler, Nebraska, G
1953	J.D.Roberts, Oklahoma, G	1969	Mike Reid, Penn St., DT	1984	Bruce Smith, Virginia Tech, DT
1954	Bill Brooks, Arkansas, G			1985	Mike Ruth, Boston College, NG
1955	Calvin Jones, Iowa, G	1970	Jim Stillwagon, Ohio St., MG	1986	Jason Buck, BYU, DT
1956	Jim Parker, Ohio St., G	1971	**Larry Jacobson,** Neb., DT	1987	Chad Hennings, Air Force, DT
1957	Alex Karras, Iowa, T	1972	Rich Glover, Nebraska, MG	1988	Tracy Rocker, Auburn, DT
1958	Zeke Smith, Auburn, G	1973	John Hicks, Ohio St., OT	1989	Mohammed Elewonibi, BYU, G
1959	Mike McGee, Duke, T	1974	Randy White, Maryland, DT		
		1975	**Lee Roy Selmon,** Okla., DT	1990	Russell Maryland, Miami-FL, NT
1960	**Tom Brown,** Minnesota, G	1976	Ross Browner, Notre Dame, DE		

Lombardi Award

First presented in 1970 by the Rotary Club of Houston, honoring the nation's best lineman. The award is named after pro football coach Vince Lombardi, who, as a guard, was a member of the famous "Seven Blocks of Granite" at Fordham in the 1930s. The Lombardi and Outland awards have gone to the same player in the same year eight times. Those players are preceded by (#). Ross Browner of Notre Dame won both, but in different years.

Year		Year		Year	
1970	#Jim Stillwagon, Ohio St., MG	1978	Bruce Clark, Penn St., DT	1985	Tony Casillas, Oklahoma, NG
1971	Walt Patulski, Notre Dame, DE	1979	Brad Budde, USC, G	1986	Cornelius Bennett, Alabama, LB
1972	#Rich Glover, Nebraska, MG	1980	Hugh Green, Pitt, DE	1987	Chris Spielman, Ohio St., LB
1973	#John Hicks, Ohio St., OT	1981	Kenneth Sims, Texas, DT	1988	#Tracy Rocker, Auburn, DT
1974	#Randy White, Maryland, DT	1982	#Dave Rimmington, Neb., C	1989	Percy Snow, Michigan St., LB
1975	#Lee Roy Selmon, Okla., DT	1983	#Dean Steinkuhler, Neb., G	1990	Chris Zorich, Notre Dame, NT
1976	Wilson Whitley, Houston, DT	1984	Tony Degrate, Texas, DT		
1977	Ross Browner, Notre Dame, DE				

O'Brien Quarterback Award

First presented in 1977 as the O'Brien Memorial Trophy, the award went to the outstanding player in the Southwest. In 1981, however, the Davey O'Brien Educational and Charitable Trust of Ft. Worth renamed the prize the O'Brien National Quarterback Award and now honors the nation's best quarterback. The award is named after 1938 Heisman Trophy-winning QB Davey O'Brien of Texas Christian.

Multiple winner: Mike Singletary (1979-80).

Memorial Trophy

Year		Year		Year	
1977	Earl Campbell, Texas, RB	1979	Mike Singletary, Baylor, LB	1980	Mike Singletary, Baylor, LB
1978	Billy Sims, Oklahoma, RB				

Quarterback Award

Year		Year		Year	
1981	Jim McMahon, BYU	1985	Chuck Long, Iowa	1988	Troy Aikman, UCLA
1982	Todd Blackledge, Penn St.	1986	Vinny Testaverde, Miami,FL	1989	Andre Ware, Houston
1983	Steve Young, BYU	1987	Don McPherson, Syracuse	1990	Ty Detmer, BYU
1984	Doug Flutie, Boston College				

Butkus Award

First presented in 1985 by the Downtown Athletic Club of Orlando, Fla., to honor the nation's outstanding linebacker. The award is named after Dick Butkus, two-time consensus All-America at Illinois and six-time All-Pro with the Chicago Bears.

Multiple winner: Brian Bosworth (1985-86).

Year		Year		Year	
1985	Brian Bosworth, Oklahoma	1987	Paul McGowan, Florida St.	1989	Percy Snow, Michigan St.
1986	Brian Bosworth, Oklahoma	1988	Derrick Thomas, Alabama	1990	Alfred Williams, Colorado

Thorpe Award

First presented in 1986 by the Jim Thorpe Athletic Club of Oklahoma City to honor the nation's outstanding defensive back. The award is named after Jim Thorpe—Olympic champion, two-time consensus All-America HB at Carlisle, and pro football pioneer.

Year		Year		Year	
1986	Thomas Everett, Baylor	1988	Deion Sanders, Florida St.	1990	Darryl Lewis, Arizona
1987	Bennie Blades, Miami-FL & Rickey Dixon, Oklahoma	1989	Mike Carrier, USC		

Payton Award

First presented in 1987 by the Sports Network and Division I-AA sports information directors to honor the nation's outstanding Division I-AA player. The award is named after Walter Payton, the NFL's all-time leading rusher who was an All-America RB at Jackson St.

Year		Year		Year	
1987	Kenny Gamble, Colgate, RB	1989	John Friesz, Idaho, QB	1990	Walter Dean, Grambling, RB
1988	Dave Meggett, Towson St., RB				

Hill Trophy

First presented in 1986 by the Harlon Hill Awards Committee in Florence, AL, to honor the nation's outstanding Division II player. The award is named after three-time NFL All-Pro Harlon Hill who played college ball at North Alabama.

Multiple winner: Johnny Bailey (1987-88-89).

Year		Year		Year	
1986	Jeff Bentrim, N.Dakota St., QB	1988	Johnny Bailey, Texas A&I,RB	1990	Chris Simdorn, N.DakotaSt.,QB
1987	Johnny Bailey, Texas A&I,RB	1989	Johnny Bailey, Texas A&I,RB		

All-Time Winningest Division I-A Coaches

Minimum of 10 years in Division I-A through 1990 season. Regular season and bowl games included. Coaches active in 1990 in **bold** type.

Top 25 Winning Percentage

	Yrs	W	L	T	Pct
Knute Rockne	13	105	12	5	.881
Frank Leahy	13	107	13	9	.864
George Woodruff	12	142	25	2	.846
Barry Switzer	16	157	29	4	.837
Percy Haughton	13	96	17	6	.832
Bob Neyland	21	173	31	12	.829
Fielding (Hurry Up) Yost	29	196	36	12	.828
Bud Wilkinson	17	145	29	4	.826
Jock Sutherland	20	144	28	14	.812
Tom Osborne	18	177	41	2	.809
Bob Devaney	16	136	30	7	.806
Frank Thomas	19	141	33	9	.795
Joe Paterno	25	229	60	3	.789
Henry Williams	23	139	34	10	.787
Gil Dobie	33	180	45	15	.781
Bear Bryant	38	323	85	17	.780
Fred Folsom	19	106	28	6	.779
Bo Schembechler	27	234	65	8	.775
Fritz Crisler	18	116	32	9	.768
Charley Moran	18	122	33	12	.766
Wallace Wade	24	171	49	10	.765
Frank Kush	22	176	54	1	.764
Dan McGugin	30	197	55	19	.762
Andy Smith	17	116	32	13	.761
Jim Crowley	13	78	21	10	.761

Top 25 Victories

	Yrs	W	L	T	Pct
Bear Bryant	38	323	85	17	.780
Amos Alonzo Stagg	57	314	199	35	.605
Pop Warner	44	313	106	32	.729
Woody Hayes	33	238	72	10	.759
Bo Schembechler	27	234	65	8	.775
Joe Paterno	25	229	60	3	.789
Jess Neely	40	207	176	19	.539
Bobby Bowden	25	205	74	3	.732
Warren Woodson	31	203	95	14	.673
Vince Dooley	25	201	77	10	.715
Eddie Anderson	39	201	128	15	.606
Dana X. Bible	33	198	72	23	.715
Dan McGugin	30	197	55	19	.762
Fielding (Hurry Up) Yost	29	196	36	12	.828
Howard Jones	29	194	64	21	.733
Johnny Vaught	25	190	61	12	.745
John Heisman	36	185	70	17	.711
Darrell Royal	23	184	60	5	.749
Gil Dobie	33	180	45	15	.781
Carl Snavely	32	180	96	16	.644
Jerry Claiborne	28	179	122	8	.592
Hayden Fry	29	179	139	8	.561
Ben Schwartzwalder	28	178	96	3	.648
Tom Osborne	18	177	41	2	.809
Frank Kush	22	176	54	1	.764
Shug Jordan	25	176	83	6	.675

Note: Eddie Robinson of Division I-AA Grambling (1941-42, 1945-present) is the all-time NCAA leader in coaching wins with a 366-128-15 record and .734 winning pct. over 48 seasons.

Where They Coached

Anderson—Loras (1922-24), DePaul (1925-31), Holy Cross (1933-38), Iowa (1939-42), Holy Cross (1950-64); **Bible**—Mississippi Col.(1913-15), LSU (1916), Texas A&M (1917, 1919-28), Nebraska (1929-36), Texas (1937-46); **Bowden**—Samford (1959-62), West Va.(1970-75), Florida St.(1976-present); **Bryant**—Maryland (1945), Kentucky (1946-53), Texas A&M (1954-57), Alabama (1958-82); **Claiborne**—Va.Tech (1961-70), Maryland (1972-81), Kentucky (1982-89); **Crisler**—Minnesota (1930-31), Princeton (1932-37), Michigan (1938-47); **Crowley**—Michigan St.(1929-32), Fordham (1933-41); **Devaney**—Wyoming (1957-61), Nebraska (1962-72); **Dobie**—N.Dakota St.(1906-07), Washington (1908-16), Navy (1917-19), Cornell (1920-35), Boston Col.(1936-38); **V.Dooley**—Georgia (1964-88).

Folsom—Colorado (1895-99, 1901-02), Dartmouth (1903-06), Colorado (1908-15); **Fry**—SMU (1962-72), North Texas (1973-78), Iowa (1979-present); **Haughton**—Cornell (1899-1900), Harvard (1908-16), Columbia (1923-24); **Hayes**—Denison (1946-48), Miami-OH (1949-50), Ohio St.(1951-78); **Heisman**—Oberlin (1892), Akron (1893), Oberlin (1894), Auburn (1895-99), Clemson (1900-03), Ga.Tech (1904-19), Penn (1920-22), Wash.& Jeff.(1923), Rice (1924-27); **H.Jones**—Syracuse (1908), Yale (1909), Ohio St.(1910), Yale (1913), Iowa (1916-23), Duke (1924), Southern Cal (1925-40); **Jordan**—Auburn (1951-75); **Kush**—Arizona St.(1958-79); **Leahy**—Boston Col.(1939-40), Notre Dame (1941-43, 1946-53); **McGugin**—Vanderbilt (1904-17, 1919-34); **Moran**—Texas A&M (1909-14), Centre (1919-23), Bucknell (1924-26), Catawba (1930-33).

Neely—Rhodes (1924-27), Clemson (1931-39), Rice (1940-66); **Neyland**—Tennessee (1926-34, 1936-40, 1946-52); **Osborne**—Nebraska (1973-present); **Paterno**—Penn St.(1966-present); **Rockne**—Notre Dame (1918-30); **Royal**—Mississippi St.(1954-55), Washington (1956), Texas (1957-76); **Schembechler**—Miami-OH (1963-68), Michigan (1969-89); **Schwartzwalder**—Muhlenberg (1946-48), Syracuse (1949-73); **A.Smith**—Penn (1909-12), Purdue (1913-15), California (1916-25); **Snavely**—Bucknell (1927-33), N.Carolina (1934-35), Cornell (1936-44), N.Carolina (1945-52), Washington-MO (1953-58); **Stagg**—Springfield (1890-91), Chicago (1892-1932), Pacific (1933-46); **Sutherland**—Lafayette (1919-23), Pittsburgh (1924-38); **Switzer**—Oklahoma (1973-88).

Thomas—Chattanooga (1925-28), Alabama (1931-42, 1944-46); **Vaught**—Mississippi (1947-70); **Wade**—Alabama (1923-30), Duke (1931-41, 1946-50); **Warner**—Georgia (1895-96), Cornell (1897-98), Carlisle (1899-1903), Cornell (1904-06), Carlisle (1907-13), Pittsburgh (1915-23), Stanford (1924-32), Temple (1933-38); **Wilkinson**—Oklahoma (1947-63); **Williams**—Army (1891), Minnesota (1900-21), Woodruff—Penn (1892-1901), Illinois (1903), Carlisle (1905); **Woodson**—Cen.Ark.(1935-39), Hardin-Simmons (1941-42, 1946-51), Arizona (1952-56), N.Mexico St.(1958-67), Trinity-TX (1972-73); **Yost**—Ohio Wesleyan (1897), Nebraska (1898), Kansas (1899), Stanford (1900), Michigan (1901-23, 1925-26).

All-Time Bowl Appearances

Active coaches in **bold** type.

	App	Overall W	L	T	Big Four W	L	T
Bear Bryant	29	15	12	2	12	8	0
Joe Paterno	21	13	7	1	6	4	0
Vince Dooley	20	8	10	2	3	5	0
Johnny Vaught	18	10	8	0	6	4	0
Tom Osborne	18	8	10	0	5	6	0
Bo Schembechler	17	5	12	0	2	10	0
Darrell Royal	16	8	7	1	6	6	0
Johnny Majors	15	9	6	0	4	0	0
Lou Holtz	15	7	6	2	2	3	0
LaVell Edwards	15	5	10	0	-	-	-
Bobby Bowden	14	10	3	1	2	2	0
Bobby Dodd	13	9	4	0	6	1	0
Don James	13	9	4	0	4	1	0
Barry Switzer	13	8	5	0	6	3	0
Charlie McClendon	13	7	6	0	4	2	0
Earle Bruce	12	7	5	0	1	2	0
Woody Hayes	12	6	6	0	5	5	0
Shug Jordan	12	5	7	0	0	2	0
Hayden Fry	12	5	7	0	0	4	0

Active Coaches' Victories

Minimum 5 years in Division I-A.

	Yrs	W	L	T	Pct
Joe Paterno, Penn St	25	229	60	3	.789
Bobby Bowden, Fla.St	25	205	74	3	.732
Hayden Fry, Iowa	29	179	139	8	.561
Tom Osborne, Nebraska	18	177	41	2	.809
LaVell Edwards, BYU	19	175	59	1	.747
Lou Holtz, Notre Dame	21	162	79	5	.669
Jim Sweeney, Fresno St	26	159	123	3	.563
Johnny Majors, Tenn.	23	159	99	10	.612
Grant Teaff, Baylor	28	155	142	8	.521
Bill Dooley, W.Forest	24	150	115	5	.565
Don James, Washington	20	155	75	3	.672
Earle Bruce, Colo.St	19	146	75	2	.659
Pat Dye, Auburn	17	143	51	4	.732
Jim Wacker, TCU	20	137	87	3	.610
Don Nehlen, West Va.	20	134	81	6	.620
Bill Mallory, Indiana	21	136	94	3	.590
Terry Donahue, UCLA	15	116	51	8	.686
George Welsh, Virginia	18	113	90	3	.556
Jim Harkema, East.Mich.	18	106	75	5	.583
Jackie Sherrill, Miss.St	13	105	45	2	.697
Billy Brewer, Ole Miss	17	105	80	6	.565

Note: The "Big Four" bowls are the Rose, Orange, Sugar and Cotton. Only three coaches—Bill Alexander, Ga.Tech (1920-44); Bob Neyland, Tenn.(1926-34,36-40,46-52); and Frank Thomas, Ala.(1931-42,44-46)—have taken teams to all four. Alexander and Thomas won three of the Big Four, Neyland two.

AFCA Coach of the Year

First presented in 1935 by the American Football Coaches Association.

Multiple winners: Joe Paterno (4), Bear Bryant (3), John McKay and Darrell Royal (2).

Year	
1935	Pappy Waldorf, Northwestern
1936	Dick Harlow, Harvard
1937	Hooks Mylin, Lafayette
1938	Bill Kern, Carnegie Tech
1939	Eddie Anderson, Iowa
1940	Clark Shaughnessy, Stanford
1941	Frank Leahy, Notre Dame
1942	Bill Alexander, Georgia Tech
1943	Amos Alonzo Stagg, Pacific
1944	Carroll Widdoes, Ohio St.
1945	Bo McMillin, Indiana
1946	Red Blaik, Army
1947	Fritz Crisler, Michigan
1948	Bennie Oosterbaan, Michigan
1949	Bud Wilkinson, Oklahoma
1950	Charlie Caldwell, Princeton
1951	Chuck Taylor, Stanford
1952	Biggie Munn, Michigan St.
1953	Jim Tatum, Maryland
1954	Red Sanders, UCLA
1955	Duffy Daugherty, Michigan St.
1956	Bowden Wyatt, Tennessee
1957	Woody Hayes, Ohio St.
1958	Paul Dietzel, LSU
1959	Ben Schwartzwalder, Syracuse
1960	Murray Warmath, Minnesota
1961	Bear Bryant, Alabama
1962	John McKay, USC
1963	Darrell Royal, Texas
1964	Frank Broyles, Arkansas & Ara Parseghian, Notre Dame
1965	Tommy Prothro, UCLA
1966	Tom Cahill, Army
1967	John Pont, Indiana
1968	Joe Paterno, Penn St.
1969	Bo Schembechler, Michigan
1970	Charlie McClendon, LSU & Darrell Royal, Texas
1971	Bear Bryant, Alabama
1972	John McKay, USC
1973	Bear Bryant, Alabama
1974	Grant Teaff, Baylor
1975	Frank Kush, Arizona St.
1976	Johnny Majors, Pittsburgh
1977	Don James, Washington
1978	Joe Paterno, Penn St.
1979	Earle Bruce, Ohio St.
1980	Vince Dooley, Georgia
1981	Danny Ford, Clemson
1982	Joe Paterno, Penn St.
1983	Ken Hatfield, Air Force
1984	LaVell Edwards, BYU
1985	Fisher DeBerry, Air Force
1986	Joe Paterno, Penn St.
1987	Dick MacPherson, Syracuse
1988	Don Nehlen, West Virginia
1989	Bill McCartney, Colorado
1990	Bobby Ross, Georgia Tech

FWAA Coach of the Year

First presented in 1957 by the Football Writers Association of America. The FWAA and AFCA awards have both gone to the same coach in the same season 24 times. Those double winners are preceded by (#).

Multiple winners: Woody Hayes and Joe Paterno (3); Lou Holtz, Johnny Majors and John McKay (2).

Year	
1957	#Woody Hayes, Ohio St.
1958	#Paul Dietzel, LSU
1959	#Ben Schwartzwalder, Syracuse
1960	#Murray Warmath, Minnesota
1961	Darrell Royal, Texas
1962	#John McKay, USC
1963	#Darrell Royal, Texas
1964	#Ara Parseghian, Notre Dame
1965	Duffy Daugherty, Michigan St.
1966	#Tom Cahill, Army
1967	#John Pont, Indiana
1968	Woody Hayes, Ohio St.
1969	#Bo Schembechler, Michigan
1970	Alex Agase, Northwestern
1971	Bob Devaney, Nebraska
1972	#John McKay, USC
1973	Johnny Majors, Pitt
1974	#Grant Teaff, Baylor
1975	Woody Hayes, Ohio St.
1976	#Johnny Majors, Pitt
1977	Lou Holtz, Arkansas
1978	#Joe Paterno, Penn St.
1979	#Earle Bruce, Ohio St.
1980	#Vince Dooley, Georgia
1981	#Danny Ford, Clemson
1982	#Joe Paterno, Penn St.
1983	Howard Schnellenberger, Miami-FL
1984	#LaVell Edwards, BYU
1985	#Fisher DeBerry, Air Force
1986	#Joe Paterno, Penn St.
1987	#Dick MacPherson, Syracuse
1988	Lou Holtz, Notre Dame
1989	#Bill McCartney, Colorado
1990	#Bobby Ross, Georgia Tech

Divisional Playoffs

The NCAA has decided its Division I-AA champion with a postseason playoff since 1978. Divisions II and III have had playoffs since 1973.

The NAIA has used playoffs since 1956 for Division I and since 1970 for Division II.

NCAA Divisional Champions
Division I-AA

Year	Winner	Score	Loser
1978	Florida A&M	35-28	Massachusetts
1979	Eastern Kentucky	30-7	Lehigh,PA
1980	Boise St., ID	31-29	Eastern Kentucky
1981	Idaho St.	34-23	Eastern Kentucky
1982	Eastern Kentucky	17-14	Delaware
1983	Southern Illinois	43-7	Western Carolina
1984	Montana St.	19-6	Louisiana Tech
1985	Georgia Southern	44-42	Furman, SC
1986	Georgia Southern	48-21	Arkansas St.
1987	NE Louisiana	43-42	Marshall,WV
1988	Furman, SC	17-12	Georgia Southern
1989	Georgia Southern	37-34	S.F.Austin St.
1990	Georgia Southern	36-13	Nevada-Reno

Division II

Year	Winner	Score	Loser
1973	Louisiana Tech	34-0	Western Kentucky
1974	Central Michigan	54-14	Delaware
1975	Northern Michigan	16-14	Western Kentucky
1976	Montana St.	24-13	Akron,OH
1977	Lehigh,PA	33-0	Jacksonville,AL
1978	Eastern Illinois	10-9	Delaware
1979	Delaware	38-21	Youngstown St.,OH
1980	Cal Poly-SLO	21-13	Eastern Illinois
1981	SW Texas St.	42-13	North Dakota St.
1982	SW Texas St.	34-9	UC-Davis
1983	North Dakota St.	41-21	Central St.,OH
1984	Troy St.,AL	18-17	North Dakota St.
1985	North Dakota St.	35-7	North Alabama
1986	North Dakota St.	27-7	South Dakota
1987	Troy St.,AL	31-17	Portland St.,OR
1988	North Dakota St.	35-21	Portland St.,OR
1989	Mississippi Col.	3-0	Jacksonville St.
1990	North Dakota St.	51-11	Indiana, PA

Division III

Year	Winner	Score	Loser
1973	Wittenberg,OH	41-0	Juniata,PA
1974	Central, IA	10-8	Ithaca,NY
1975	Wittenberg,OH	28-0	Ithaca,NY
1976	St.John's,MN	31-28	Towson St.,MD
1977	Widener,PA	39-36	Wabash,IN
1978	Baldwin-Wallace	24-10	Wittenberg,OH
1979	Ithaca,NY	14-10	Wittenberg,OH
1980	Dayton,OH	63-0	Ithaca,NY
1981	Widener,PA	17-10	Dayton,OH
1982	West Georgia	14-0	Augustana,IL
1983	Augustana,IL	21-17	Union,NY
1984	Augustana,IL	21-12	Central,IA
1985	Augustana,IL	20-7	Ithaca,NY
1986	Augustana,IL	31-3	Salisbury St.,MD
1987	Wagner,NY	19-3	Dayton,OH
1988	Ithaca,NY	39-24	Central,IA
1989	Dayton,OH	17-7	Union,NY
1990	Allegheny, PA	21-14	Lycoming, PA

NAIA Divisional Champions
Division I

Year	Winner	Score	Loser
1956	Montana St. & St.Joseph's,IN	0-0	—
1957	Pittsburg St.,KS	27-26	Hillsdale,MI
1958	NE Oklahoma	19-13	Northern Arizona
1959	Texas A&I	20-7	Lenoir-Rhyne,NC
1960	Lenoir-Rhyne,NC	15-14	Humboldt St.,CA
1961	Pittsburg St.,KS	12-7	Linfield,OR
1962	Central St.,OK	28-13	Lenoir-Rhyne,NC
1963	St.John's,MN	33-27	Prairie View,TX
1964	Concordia,MN & Sam Houston,TX	7-7	
1965	St.John's,MN	33-0	Linfield,OR
1966	Waynesburg,PA	42-21	WI-Whitewater
1967	Fairmont St.,WV	28-21	Eastern Wash.
1968	Troy St.,AL	43-35	Texas A&I
1969	Texas A&I	32-7	Concordia,MN
1970	Texas A&I	48-7	Wofford,SC
1971	Livingston,AL	14-12	Arkansas Tech
1972	East Texas St.	21-18	Car-Newman,TN
1973	Abilene Christian	42-14	Elon,NC
1974	Texas A&I	34-23	Henderson St.,AR
1975	Texas A&I	37-0	Salem, WV
1976	Texas A&I	26-0	Central Arkansas
1977	Abilene Christian	24-7	SW Oklahoma
1978	Angelo St.,TX	24-14	Elon,NC
1979	Texas A&I	20-14	Central St.,OK
1980	Elon,NC	17-10	NE Oklahoma
1981	Elon,NC	3-0	Pittsburg St.,KS
1982	Central St.,OK	14-11	Mesa,CO
1983	Carson-Newman,TN	36-28	Mesa,CO
1984	Carson-Newman,TN & Central Arkansas	19-19	—
1985	Hillsdale,MI & Central Arkansas	10-10	—
1986	Carson-Newman,TN	17-0	Cameron,OK
1987	Cameron,OK	30-2	Car-Newman,TN
1988	Carson-Newman,TN	56-21	Adams St.,CO
1989	Carson-Newman,TN	34-20	Emporia St.,KS
1990	Central St., OH	38-16	Mesa, CO

Division II

Year	Winner	Score	Loser
1970	Westminster,PA	21-16	Anderson,IN
1971	Calif.Lutheran	30-14	Westminster,PA
1972	Missouri Southern	21-14	Northwestern,IA
1973	Northwestern,IA	10-3	Clenville St.,WV
1974	Texas Lutheran	42-0	Missouri Valley
1975	Texas Lutheran	34-8	Calif.Lutheran
1976	Westminster,PA	20-13	Redlands,CA
1977	Westminster,PA	27-9	Calif.Lutheran
1978	Concordia,MN	7-0	Findlay,OH
1979	Findlay,OH	51-6	Northwestern,IA
1981	Austin College,TX & Concordia,MN	24-24	—
1982	Linfield,OR	33-15	Wm. Jewell, MO
1983	Northwestern,IA	25-21	Pacific Lutheran
1984	Linfield, OR	33-22	Northwestern,IA
1985	WI-La Crosse	24-7	Pacific Lutheran
1986	Linfield,OR	17-0	Baker,KS
1987	Pacific Lutheran & WI-Stevens Pt.*	16-16	—
1988	Westminster,PA	21-14	WI-La Crosse
1989	Westminster,PA	51-30	WI-La Crosse
1990	Peru St., NE	17-7	Westminster, PA

*Wisconsin-Stevens Point forfeited its entire 1987 schedule due to its use of an ineligible player.

New York coach **Bill Parcells** is carried off the field in Tampa after his Giants beat Buffalo, 10-9, to win their second Super Bowl in five years.

PRO FOOTBALL

War Game

Persian Gulf conflict transforms Tampa Stadium into an armed camp, but Super Bowl XXV was super.

It was four hours that transcended sport. Twelve days into the Persian Gulf War, with U.S. and Allied fighter planes bombing Iraq and a half million American troops in Saudi Arabia waiting for the land battle to come, a tense nation turned to the Super Bowl looking for a badly-needed distraction.

And got it.

In its 25-year run as the country's unofficial winter home of the Fourth of July, the Super Bowl had never given rise to such bellicose and buoyant feelings as were exhibited on Jan. 27. Staged in an armed camp that made Tampa Stadium the safest building this side of Allied headquarters in Riyadh, Super Sunday went from somber to star-spangled to sensational as the New York Giants beat the Buffalo Bills in the first one-point Super Bowl ever, 20-19.

Ironically, as the Allies' high-tech air war was drawing praise for the precision of its ordnance, Super Bowl XXV was decided on a missed field goal attempt. With eight seconds left, the Bills' Scott Norwood kicked a 47-yarder that had the distance but lacked the necessary accuracy and drifted wide right.

The victory was the second Super Bowl title in five years for the Giants and their

second straight playoff win that hinged on a last-second field goal try. The preceding Sunday—there was no week off before the Super Bowl this year—New York beat the defending champion 49ers in San Francsico, 15-13, when Matt Bahr connected from 42 yards out as time expired.

Meanwhile in Buffalo, the Bills were busy stampeding an overmatched Los Angeles Raiders team, 51-3, for the AFC title. A 44-34 winner over Miami in their first playoff game, the Bills headed south as 7-point favorites.

A week later in Tampa, as military helicopters whirled overhead and 2,500 security personnel prowled the stadium grounds, fans with Super Bowl tickets waited on Disney World-like lines and willingly submitted to the scrutiny of hand-held metal detectors and thorough baggage searches. The electronic frisking created 30- to 45-minute backups at most gates, but everybody seemed to accept the inconvenience in light of the very real threat of a terrorist attack.

Once inside, the crowd all but wrapped itself in the American flag. Resounding chants of "U-S-A, U-S-A, U-S-A," last heard with such emotion when the American hockey team upset the Russians at the 1980 Winter Olympics in Lake Placid, rocked the stadium. By the time Whitney Houston belted out the National Anthem and four F-15 fighter jets screamed in for the traditional pre-game fly-by, the crowd

Gary Myers is the national pro football columnist for the New York *Daily News* and a reporter on HBO's "Inside the NFL."

A military helicopter hovers over the press box at Tampa Stadium prior to the start of Super Bowl XXV. With the country at war, extraordinary security measures were taken to protect the crowd of 73,813.

was in such a state of anticipation you'd swear that smart bombs, Scuds and Patriot missiles might actually start bursting in air.

There was little pre-game hype as talk of Buffalo's no-huddle offense and New York's bruising defense took a back seat to the heart-wrenching stories of six players with close relatives in Saudi Arabia, including the father of Bills' linebacker Carlton Bailey and the first cousin of Giants' linebacker Pepper Johnson. There was talk, too, about whether or not the game should be postponed or even canceled. "The war makes the Super Bowl seem pretty insignificant," said Giants' center Bart Oates. "If we lose, we'll still be able to walk or limp off the field. If our troops lose, they're dead."

NFL commissioner Paul Tagliabue consulted with cabinet secretary and former Bills' quarterback Jack Kemp and other Washington officials before deciding to play the game. Quoting President Bush, Tagliabue said, "Life will go on. We're not going to be intimidated by a dictator in the Middle East."

No one knew at the time, of course, that the war would be over a month later

or that Desert Storm commander Norman Schwarzkopf would return home to Tampa in April to a tumultuous welcome at this very same stadium.

The game itself boiled down to a contest between offensive styles—Buffalo's no-huddle against New York's no-hurry. In basketball terms, the Bills wanted to fast break and the Giants were determined to take the air out of the ball. The Giants won out, controlling the ball for a Super Bowl-record 40 minutes and 33 seconds. Down 12-10 at halftime, the NFC champs opened the second half with a 14-play, 75-yard drive that consumed 9:29 and ended with Ottis Anderson taking the ball in from one yard out.

The 34-year-old Anderson, who gained 102 yards in 21 carries, was named the game's Most Valuable Player, but the victory would not have been possible without the season's most improbable hero, quarterback Jeff Hostetler. After seven years on coach Bill Parcells' bench, Hostetler finally got the call on Dec. 15, when starter Phil Simms suffered a severely sprained right foot in a 17-13 regular season loss to Buffalo. Before that

Giants kicker **Matt Bahr** (9) seems unsure, but holder and quarterback **Jeff Hostetler** exults as Bahr's 42-yard field goal beats San Francisco, 15-13, in the last seconds of the NFC title game.

game, Hostetler had completed just 49 of 93 passes since being drafted out of West Virginia in 1984.

But Hoss was ready. After winning the last two games of the regular season, he directed New York to a 31-3 win over Chicago in the Giants' playoff opener, then engineered the two-point victory over Joe Montana and the 49ers in the NFC title game. (It was the second Giants-Niners game at San Francisco's Candlestick Park in seven weeks and evened things for the visitors, who had lost a 7-3 thriller on Dec. 3.) Finally, in the Super Bowl, Hostetler outplayed the Bills' heralded Jim Kelly, going 20 for 32 for 222 yards and a touchdown pass. "I've heard so many guys say that I'd never be able to do it," he said afterward. "Now it's done and nobody can take it away from me."

Three and half months later, Parcells resigned as the Giants' head coach and was replaced by offensive coordinator Ray Handley. Parcells succeeded Ray Perkins in 1983 after two years as an assistant and posted a record of 85-52-2 over

eight seasons. He gave no specific reasons for quitting, saying only that he felt "like it's time" to take a break from coaching and go catch some fish.

"I've given all I have here for 10 years," he said. "Don't confuse this with burnout, I'm not burned out—I just don't feel I could've given all I would have needed to in order to get the job done." After a year or two off, he is expected to resurface with another NFL team, perhaps at Tampa Bay as coach and general manager.

Parcells' defensive coordinator Bill Belichick left the team in January to become the new head coach in Cleveland, where the suddenly hapless Browns had given up a league-leading 462 points.

Three other new head coaches were set to preside over their first training camps in 1991: Richard Williamson in Tampa Bay, Rich Kotite in Philadelphia and Dick MacPherson in New England.

Williamson, who replaced Ray Perkins with three games left in the regular season and went 1-2, got the Bucs' full-time job after ex-49ers coach Bill Walsh turned it down. Kotite was promoted by the Eagles after owner Norman Braman tired of Buddy Ryan following the playoffs. And MacPherson, the 1987 college Coach of the Year at Syracuse, joined former Miami of Florida athletic director (and new Patriots' GM) Sam Jankovich in New England.

The Dallas Cowboys, who went 1-15 in Jimmy Johnson's first year as coach in 1989, were the most improved team of the year. Dallas bettered its record by six games and went 7-9. In fact, with two games remaining in the regular season the Cowboys were 7-7 and needed just one more win to reach the playoffs. But then quarterback Troy Aikman separated his right shoulder against Philadelphia, and the Cowboys, who had traded backup Steve Walsh to New Orleans on Sept. 25, were through.

On the down side, three defending divisional champions—Cleveland, Denver and the Los Angeles Rams—all lost more than twice as many games as they did in 1989 and finished in last or second-to-last place. The Broncos' plunge to 5-11 came after Super Bowl appearances in two of the last three years and marked their first losing season since 1982.

The run-and-shoot offense became an official trend in 1990. It enjoyed its greatest success in Houston, where quarterback Warren Moon passed for 4,689 yards and 33 TDs, including a 527-yard and three-TD effort against Kansas City on Dec. 16. His quarterback rating of 96.8 was second only to that of Buffalo's Kelly, who registered a 101.2 with a 63.3 completion percentage, 24 TD passes and 2,829 yards. Both players were injured late in the season—Kelly sprained his left knee against the Giants on Dec. 15 and Moon broke his right thumb against Cincinnati a week later. Kelly recovered and made the playoffs. Moon didn't and could only watch as the Oilers lost to Cincinnati in the opening round.

Moon, Montana and the Eagles' Randall Cunningham all had outstanding years, but the best quarterback story of the regular season was in Kansas City, where journeyman Steve DeBerg led the Chiefs into the playoffs for only the second time since 1971. DeBerg, who entered his 14th NFL season with 143 touchdown passes and 171 intercep-

tions, pulled himself together and sailed through 1990 with 23 TDs and only 4 INTs. He also fractured the little finger in his left hand against Houston on Dec. 16 and played the rest of the season with a steel rod in his pinky.

Two other pivotal players in Kansas City's rise to prominence were placekicker Nick Lowery, who booted 34 field goals and led the NFL in scoring with 139 points, and linebacker Derrick Thomas, who led the league with 20 sacks, including a record seven in a game against Seattle.

Former Oklahoma State running mates Barry Sanders of Detroit and Thurman Thomas of Buffalo were the league's top running backs. Thomas led the AFC in rushing with 1,297 yards, while Sanders was the overall NFL champion with 1,304.

Eric Dickerson and Bo Jackson didn't carry the ball at all until Oct. 21. Dickerson, suspended six weeks in a contract dispute with Indianapolis, ended up with 677 yards in 11 games and moved to fifth place on the all-time NFL rushing list. Jackson returned to the Raiders' backfield after the baseball season and gained 698 yards in 10 games. Named to the AFC Pro Bowl team in December, Bo became the first athlete ever selected for major league all-star games in both baseball and football.

Jackson never made it to Honolulu, however. In the Raiders' opening playoff game against Cincinnati, he was tackled by Bengals' linebacker Kevin Walker, injured his left hip and was out of the game and the postseason. Although not considered serious at first, by March, Kansas City Royals' doctors said the damage to the hip cartilage was so bad they doubted Bo would ever play baseball or football again. The Royals waived him on March 18, but the Raiders kept him on their roster.

San Francisco wide receiver Jerry Rice became only the fourth player in league history to catch 100 passes in a single season, gaining 1,502 yards and scoring 13 TDs.

The patriotic fervor displayed at the Super Bowl provided a much-needed public relations lift for the NFL. Until then, 1990 had been a P.R. disaster for the league in the wake of the Lisa Olson Affair in New England and the election day defeat of the Martin Luther King holiday proposition in Arizona.

Olson, a reporter covering the Patriots for the *Boston Herald*, was interviewing a player in the Pats' locker room on Sept. 17 when three players—Zeke Mowatt, Robert Perryman and Michael Thompson—came over and harassed her with lewd suggestions. Olson reported the incident to her editor, who told the team's front office. As is their heritage (see box), the Pats did nothing to defuse the situation. Three days later, the media found out about it and the story exploded, generating headlines, sound bites and off-color jokes from coast to coast. Olson, subjected to withering fan abuse in Foxboro, was given some time off by her paper and then reassigned.

The league appointed a special counsel to investigate the matter and in November fined the three players for their behavior and the Pats for their handling of the mess. By April, Olson had left the *Herald* and decided to leave Boston, but sued the Pats for sexual harassment and civil rights violations before she left.

Back on Oct. 2, shortly after the Olson-Pats incident had come to light, Cincinnati coach Sam Wyche injected himself into the issue when he barred *USA Today* reporter Denise Tom from the Bengals' locker room following a loss to Seattle. Tagliabue fined the outspoken coach $27,000 and Wyche responded by ordering a locker room curtain for his blushing behemoths.

Meanwhile in Arizona, 51 percent of those voting on Nov. 6 defeated Initiative 302, which would have made Martin Luther King's birthday (Jan.21) a paid state holiday. The NFL had granted Phoenix the 1993 Super Bowl after being assured that state voters would approve the MLK holiday. The day after the proposition was voted down, Tagliabue took the game back and it was eventually given to Pasadena, which has hosted four previous Super Bowls. Phoenix was promised the 1996 game, if a King holiday is in place by then.

The 1991 NFL Draft will be remembered for the runaway Rocket that landed in Canada. Dallas Cowboys' owner Jerry Jones tried to lasso Notre Dame junior sensation Raghib (Rocket) Ismail, but Ismail ended up dodging the draft. Trading up with New England for the number one pick, the Cowboys lost a pre-draft bidding

Patriots' Fans Can Blame It On The Jets

Back in January of 1969, after losing 10 games for two seasons in a row, Boston Patriots' owner Billy Sullivan was looking for a new head coach. An extensive search had narrowed the field of candidates down to two assistants: Clive Rush of the New York Jets and Chuck Noll of the Baltimore Colts.

What to do? The Jets and Colts were playing in Super Bowl III and Sullivan decided he would hire the guy from the team that won. The rest, as they say, is history. The Jets' monumental 16-7 upset of the Colts may have been the making of the AFL, but it broke the Pats.

Rush was fired in the middle of his second season with a record of 7-16. Noll, meanwhile, was hired by Pittsburgh, where he and the Steelers have won four Super Bowls.

The Patriots are as bizzare a franchise as the NFL has. The 1990 team with its 1-15 record and the Lisa Olson mess fits right in.

► In 1961, over 25,000 fans filled tiny Nickerson Field to overflowing on a rainy Friday night for a game against the Dallas Texans. The Texans trailed by a touchdown but were driving in the final seconds, when a fan in a slouch hat and beige raincoat dashed into the end zone, leaped into the air and knocked down a sure TD pass on the final play. Game over. Nobody knew a spectator made the big play until Dallas coach Hank Stram noticed the Pats' mysterious 12th man in the game films the following week.

► In 1969, Clive Rush, the new head coach, called a press conference to announce the team's new general manager. Grabbing the microphone for his opening remarks, Rush instead let out an agonizing scream and began to twitch before minority owner Dan Marr, Jr. had the presence of mind to run over and pull the faulty microphone plug out of the wall socket. Nearly electrocuted, Rush remarked: "I heard the Boston press was rough, but I never expected this!"

► In 1978, the Pats had clinched the AFC East and were in Miami for the final game of the regular season when coach Chuck Fairbanks announced he was

Wide World Photos

Guess what team Pittsburgh Steelers coach **Chuck Noll** beat on Dec. 17 to reach 200 career wins in the NFL? That's Noll (right) shaking hands with the Patriots' Rod Rust after the game.

leaving after the playoffs for the University of Colorado. The club was stunned. Sullivan fired Fairbanks on the spot and named assistants Ron Erhardt and Hank Bullough co-coaches. The Pats lost by 20, whereupon Sullivan reinstated Fairbanks for the playoffs and the Pats lost by 17 in the first round.

▶ In 1982, a work-release parolee won a snowy Dec. 12 game against Miami when he drove his tractor onto the field late in the fourth quarter and plowed a space for Pats' placekicker John Smith to kick the winning 33-yard field goal in a 3-0 victory.

▶ In 1985, wide receiver Irving Fryar had his thumb sliced in a domestic dispute a week before the AFC championship game. The following season, Fryar was injured in a home game against Buffalo and decided to duck out early. Leaving the ballpark by car, he got into an accident near the team practice field when he missed the turn where the road forked. That prompted the classic line from *Providence Journal* sportswriter Jimmy Donaldson: "First the knife in the kitchen, now the fork in the road."

▶ In 1986, Chuck Sullivan decided to bankroll the Michael Jackson Victory Tour in partnership with boxing promoter Don King. Chuck lost $16 million and couldn't even get a date at Sullivan Stadium, which was named after his father.

"I don't really like it when people say it's been a comedy of errors," Billy's other son, Patrick, said before quitting as general manager on Jan.29. "We've just had a lot of challenges that other teams have not had to face."

Patrick's resignation ended the Sullivan family's association with the Patriots after 31 years. Thanks to brother Chuck's disastrous rock'n roll career, the Sullivans' debt load rose to $35 million by 1988 and Billy was obliged to sell the team to electric shaver magnate Victor Kiam for $85 million.

Kiam has carried on in the bungling Patriot tradition. At the height of the Lisa Olson troubles last September, he screwed up the retiring of John Hannah's uniform number by marching onto the field with Hannah and subjecting the seven-time All-Pro to a thundering chorus of boos that lasted throughout the ceremony.

In January, however, Hannah became the first Patriot ever elected to the Pro Football Hall of Fame. His induction on July 27 received nothing but applause in Canton.

Two-sport All-Star **Bo Jackson** was named to the AFC Pro Bowl team, but this tackle by Cincinnati's **Kevin Walker** in the first round of the playoffs put Bo's football and baseball careers on hold.

contest with Toronto of the Canadian Football League when Argonauts owner Bruce McNall and his partners Wayne Gretzky and actor John Candy agreed to fuel the Rocket with a guaranteed $18.2 million plus incentives over four years.

Ismail will pull down $3.5 million a year to play and another $4 million or so over the life of the contract in endorsement money. The average wage in the eight-team CFL in 1990 was $57,496.

The Los Angeles Raiders, who drafted troubled USC quarterback Todd Marinovich in the first round, claimed Ismail's rights in the fourth with the 100th overall pick. Al Davis traded up with New England to get the pick, meaning the Pats had two shots at the Rocket and passed both times.

Across the bay, the 49ers spent the 1990 season talking of becoming the first team ever to "three-peat" as Super Bowl champions. That dream ended in the NFC championship game, where they were eliminated by the Giants on Bahr's last second field goal. The winning drive

began after New York's Lawrence Taylor recovered a Roger Craig fumble knocked loose by Erik Howard. Nobody knew it at the time, but it was Craig's last carry in a San Francisco uniform. He was left unprotected on the Niners' Plan B list after the season and was signed by the Raiders—as was teammate and free safety Ronnie Lott. San Francisco also lost linebacker Matt Millen to the Redskins.

The NFL introduced its new playoff format in 1990 with three wild cards in each conference. The 16-game season was spread over 17 weeks to create another TV weekend and the off-week between the conference championship games and the Super Bowl was eliminated.

Finally, the NFL launched the World League of American Football in the Spring with three of its 10 teams in Europe and one in Canada. As expected, the WLAF was received with more enthusiasm overseas than in the States and the London Monarchs won the first World Bowl at Wembley. □

THE 1992 SPORTS ALMANAC
INFORMATION PLEASE

PRO FOOTBALL
STATISTICS

THE SEASON IN REVIEW
1990-1991
STANDINGS • PLAYOFFS • DRAFT

SEC **A**

PAGE **183**

Final NFL Standings

Division champions (*) and Wild Card playoff qualifiers (†) are noted. Number of seasons listed after each head coach refers to tenure with club through 1990 season.

American Football Conference

Eastern Division

	W	L	T	PF	PA	vs. Div.	vs. AFC
*Buffalo	13	3	0	428	263	7-1-0	10-2-0
†Miami	12	4	0	336	242	7-1-0	10-2-0
Indianapolis	7	9	0	281	353	3-5-0	5-7-0
NY Jets	6	10	0	295	345	2-6-0	4-10-0
New England	1	15	0	181	446	1-7-0	1-11-0

1990 Head Coaches: Buf—Marv Levy (5th season); **Mia**—Don Shula (21st); **Ind**—Ron Meyer (5th); **NY**—Bruce Coslet (1st); **NE**—Rod Rust (1st).

1989 Standings: 1.Buffalo (9-7); 2.Indianapolis (8-8); 3.Miami (8-8); 4.New England (5-11); 5.NY Jets (4-12).

Central Division

	W	L	T	PF	PA	vs. Div.	vs. AFC
*Cincinnati	9	7	0	360	352	5-1-0	8-4-0
†Houston	9	7	0	405	307	4-2-0	8-4-0
Pittsburgh	9	7	0	292	240	2-4-0	6-6-0
Cleveland	3	13	0	228	462	1-5-0	2-10-0

1990 Head Coaches: Cin—Sam Wyche (7th season); **Hou**—Jack Pardee (1st); **Pit**—Chuck Noll (22nd); **Cle**—replaced Bud Carson (2nd, 2-7) with assistant Jim Shofner (1-6) on Nov.5.

1989 Standings: 1.Cleveland (9-6-1); 2.Houston (9-7); 3.Pittsburgh (9-7); 4.Cincinnati (8-8).

Western Division

	W	L	T	PF	PA	vs. Div.	vs. AFC
*LA Raiders	12	4	0	337	268	6-2-0	9-3-0
†Kansas City	11	5	0	369	257	5-3-0	7-5-0
Seattle	9	7	0	306	286	4-4-0	7-5-0
San Diego	6	10	0	315	281	2-6-0	5-9-0
Denver	5	11	0	331	374	3-5-0	4-8-0

1990 Head Coaches: LA—Art Shell (2nd season); **KC**—Marty Schottenheimer (2nd); **Sea**—Chuck Knox (8th); **SD**—Dan Henning (2nd); **Den**—Dan Reeves (9th season).

1989 Standings: 1.Denver (11-5); 2.Kansas City (8-7-1); 3.LA Raiders (8-8); 4.Seattle (7-9); 5.San Diego (6-10).

National Football Conference

Eastern Division

	W	L	T	PF	PA	vs. Div.	vs. NFC
*NY Giants	13	3	0	335	211	7-1-0	10-2-0
†Philadelphia	10	6	0	396	299	5-3-0	9-3-0
†Washington	10	6	0	381	301	4-4-0	7-5-0
Dallas	7	9	0	244	308	2-6-0	6-8-0
Phoenix	5	11	0	268	396	2-6-0	3-9-0

1990 Head Coaches: NY—Bill Parcells (8th season); **Phi**—Buddy Ryan (5th); **Wash**—Joe Gibbs (10th); **Dal**—Jimmy Johnson (2nd); **Pho**—Joe Bugel (1st).

1989 Standings: 1.NY Giants (12-4); 2.Philadelphia (11-5); 3.Washington (10-6); 4.Phoenix (5-11); 5.Dallas (1-15).

Central Division

	W	L	T	PF	PA	vs. Div.	vs. NFC
*Chicago	11	5	0	348	280	6-2-0	9-3-0
Tampa Bay	6	10	0	264	367	5-3-0	6-8-0
Detroit	6	10	0	373	413	3-5-0	5-7-0
Green Bay	6	10	0	271	347	3-5-0	5-7-0
Minnesota	6	10	0	351	326	3-5-0	4-8-0

1990 Head Coaches: Chi—Mike Ditka (9th season); **TB**—replaced Ray Perkins (4th, 5-8) with assistant Richard Williamson (1-2) on Dec.3; **GB**—Lindy Infante (3rd); **Det**—Wayne Fontes (3rd); **Min**—Jerry Burns (5th).

1989 Standings: 1.Minnesota (10-6); 2.Green Bay (10-6); 3.Detroit (7-9); 4.Chicago (6-10); 5.Tampa Bay (5-11).

Western Division

	W	L	T	PF	PA	vs. Div.	vs. NFC
*San Francisco	14	2	0	353	239	4-2-0	10-2-0
†New Orleans	8	8	0	274	275	4-2-0	6-6-0
LA Rams	5	11	0	345	412	2-4-0	3-9-0
Atlanta	5	11	0	348	365	2-4-0	3-9-0

1990 Head Coaches: SF—George Seifert (2nd season); **NO**—Jim Mora (4th); **LA**—John Robinson (8th); **Atl**—Jerry Glanville (1st).

1989 Standings: 1.San Francisco (14-2); 2.LA Rams (11-5); 3.New Orleans (9-7); 4.Atlanta (3-13).

Tiebreakers

Division champion: AFC CENTRAL—Cincinnati beat Pittsburgh twice and split with Houston, but the Bengals had a better division record than the Oilers. **Wild Card qualifiers:** AFC—Houston, Pittsburgh and Seattle were all 9-7, but the Oilers had a better conference record than either the Steelers or the Seahawks.

Division 2nd place: AFC CENTRAL—Houston had a better division record than Pittsburgh; NFC EASTERN—Philadelphia had a better division record than Washington; NFC CENTRAL—Tampa Bay had a 5-1 record against Detroit, Green Bay and Minnesota.

Division 3rd place: NFC CENTRAL—Detroit and Green Bay had better conference records than Minnesota and the Lions (minus 8) had a better net division points total than the Packers (minus 40); NFC WESTERN—the LA Rams (plus 1) had a better net division points total than Atlanta (minus 31).

NFL Regular Season Individual Leaders

Passing Efficiency
(Minimum of 192 attempts)

AFC	Att	Cmp	Cmp%	Yards	Avg	TD	TD%	Long	Int	Int%	Rating
Jim Kelly, Buf	346	219	63.3	2829	8.18	24	6.9	71	9	2.6	101.2
Warren Moon, Hou	584	362	62.0	4689	8.03	33	5.7	87-td	13	2.2	96.8
Steve DeBerg, KC	444	258	58.1	3444	7.76	23	5.2	90-td	4	0.9	96.3
Jay Schroeder, LA	334	182	54.5	2849	8.53	19	5.7	68-td	9	2.7	90.8
Dan Marino, Mia	531	306	57.6	3563	6.71	21	4.0	69-td	11	2.1	82.6
Bubby Brister, Pit	387	223	57.6	2725	7.04	20	5.2	90	14	3.6	81.6
John Elway, Den	502	294	58.6	3526	7.02	15	3.0	66	14	2.8	78.5
Ken O'Brien, NY	411	226	55.0	2855	6.95	13	3.2	69-td	10	2.4	77.3
Boomer Esiason, Cin	402	224	55.7	3031	7.54	24	6.0	53	22	5.5	77.0
Jeff George, Ind	334	181	54.2	2152	6.44	16	4.8	75	13	3.9	73.8

NFC	Att	Cmp	Cmp%	Yards	Avg	TD	TD%	Long	Int	Int%	Rating
Phil Simms, NY	311	184	59.2	2284	7.34	15	4.8	80-td	4	1.3	92.7
Randall Cunningham, Phi	465	271	58.3	3466	7.45	30	6.5	95-td	13	2.8	91.6
Joe Montana, SF	520	321	61.7	3944	7.58	26	5.0	78-td	16	3.1	89.0
Jim Harbaugh, Chi	312	180	57.7	2178	6.98	10	3.2	80-td	6	1.9	81.9
Rodney Peete, Det	271	142	52.4	1974	7.28	13	4.8	68-td	8	3.0	79.8
Jim Everett, LA	554	307	55.4	3989	7.20	23	4.2	55-td	17	3.1	79.3
Chris Miller, Atl	388	222	57.2	2735	7.05	17	4.4	75-td	14	3.6	78.7
Mark Rypien, Wash	304	166	54.6	2070	6.81	16	5.3	53-td	11	3.6	78.4
Vinny Testaverde, TB	365	203	55.6	2818	7.72	17	4.7	89-td	18	4.9	75.6
Don Majkowski, GB	264	150	56.8	1925	7.29	10	3.8	76-td	12	4.5	73.5

Receiving

AFC	No	Yards	Avg	TD
Haywood Jeffires, Hou	74	1048	14.2	8
Drew Hill, Hou	74	1019	13.8	5
John L.Williams, Sea	73	699	9.6	0
Ernest Givens, Hou	72	979	13.6	9
Andre Reed, Buf	71	945	13.3	8
Albert Bentley, Ind	71	664	9.4	2
Curtis Duncan, Hou	66	785	11.9	1
Stephone Paige, KC	65	1021	15.7	5
Anthony Miller, SD	63	933	14.8	7
Bill Brooks, Ind	62	823	13.3	5

NFC	No	Yards	Avg	TD
Jerry Rice, SF	100	1502	15.0	13
Andre Rison, Atl	82	1208	14.7	10
Keith Byars, Phi	81	819	10.1	3
Henry Ellard, LA	76	1294	17.0	4
Gary Clark, Wash	75	1112	14.8	8
Anthony Carter, Min	70	1008	14.4	8
Art Monk, Wash	68	770	11.3	5
Sterling Sharpe, GB	67	1105	16.5	6
Kelvin Martin, Dal	64	732	11.4	0
Richard Johnson, Det	64	727	11.4	6

Rushing

AFC	Att	Yards	Avg	TD
Thurman Thomas, Buf	271	1297	4.8	11
Marion Butts, SD	265	1225	4.6	8
Bobby Humphrey, Den	288	1202	4.2	7
Barry Word, KC	204	1015	5.0	4
James Brooks, Cin	195	1004	5.1	5
Derrick Fenner, Sea	215	859	4.0	14
Sammie Smith, Mia	226	831	3.7	8
John Stephens, NE	212	808	3.8	2
Christian Okoye, KC	245	805	3.3	7
Merril Hoge, Pit	203	772	3.8	7

NFC	Att	Yards	Avg	TD
Barry Sanders, Det	255	1304	5.1	13
Earnest Byner, Wash	297	1219	4.1	6
Neal Anderson, Chi	260	1078	4.1	10
Randall Cunningham, Phi	118	942	8.0	5
Emmitt Smith, Dal	241	937	3.9	11
Johnny Johnson, Pho	234	926	4.0	5
Cleveland Gary, LA	204	808	4.0	14
Ottis Anderson, NY	225	784	3.5	11
Herschel Walker, Min	184	770	4.2	5
Mike Rozier, Atl	163	717	4.4	3

All-Purpose Running

AFC	Rush	Rec	Ret	Total
Thurman Thomas, Buf	1297	532	0	1829
Eric Metcalf, Cle	248	452	1052	1752
Albert Bentley, Ind	556	664	211	1431
John L.Williams, Sea	714	699	0	1413
Bobby Humphrey, Den	1202	152	0	1354
Marion Butts, SD	1225	117	0	1342
James Brooks, Cin	1004	269	0	1273
Rod Woodson, Pit	0	0	1229	1229
Merril Hoge, Pit	772	342	0	1114
Lorenzo White, Hou	702	368	0	1070
Kevin Mack, Cle	702	360	1	1063
Haywood Jeffires, Hou	0	1048	0	1048
Ernest Givens, Hou	65	979	0	1044
Barry Word, KC	1015	28	10	1043
Stephone Paige, KC	0	1021	0	1021

NFC	Rush	Rec	Ret	Total
Herschel Walker, Min	770	315	966	2051
Barry Sanders, Det	1304	480	0	1784
Neal Anderson, Chi	1078	484	0	1562
Dave Meggett, NY	164	410	959	1533
Jerry Rice, SF	0	1502	0	1502
Earnest Byner, Wash	1219	279	0	1498
Henry Ellard, LA	21	1294	15	1330
Mel Gray, Det	0	0	1300	1300
Deion Sanders, Atl	0	0	1254	1254
Gary Anderson, TB	646	464	123	1233
Andre Rison, Atl	0	1208	10	1218
Johnny Johnson, Pho	926	241	0	1167
Rodney Hampton, NY	455	274	340	1069
Emmitt Smith, Dal	937	228	0	1165
Sterling Sharpe, GB	14	1105	0	1119

Note: Returns (Ret) includes kickoffs, punts, fumbles and interceptions returned.

Scoring

Kickers

AFC	PAT	FG	Long	Pts
Nick Lowery, KC	37/38	34/37	48	139
Scott Norwood, Buf.	50/52	20/29	48	110
David Treadwell, Den	34/36	25/34	49	109
Norm Johnson, Sea	33/34	23/32	51	102
Pat Leahy, NY	32/32	23/26	47	101
Pete Stoyanovich, Mia.	37/37	21/25	53	100
Gary Anderson, Pit	32/32	20/25	48	92
Jim Breech, Cin	41/44	17/21	46	92
Jeff Jaeger, LA.	40/42	15/20	50	85
John Carney, SD	27/28	19/21	43	84

NFC	PAT	FG	Long	Pts
Chip Lohmiller, Wash	41/41	30/40	56	131
Kevin Butler, Chi	36/37	26/37	52	114
Mike Cofer, SF.	39/39	24/36	56	111
Roger Ruzek, Phi	45/48	21/29	53	108
Greg Davis, Atl	40/40	22/23	53	106
Chris Jacke, GB.	28/29	23/30	53	97
Steve Christie, TB.	27/27	23/27	54	96
Morten Andersen, NO	29/29	21/27	52	92
Mike Lansford, LA.	42/43	15/24	46	87
Al Del Greco, Pho	31/31	17/27	50	82

Touchdowns

AFC	TD	Rush	Rec	Ret	Pts
Derrick Fenner, Sea	15	14	1	0	90
Marcus Allen, LA	13	12	1	0	78
Thurman Thomas, Buf	13	11	2	0	78
Lorenzo White, Hou	12	8	4	0	72
Merril Hoge, Pit	10	7	3	0	60
James Brooks, Cin.	9	5	4	0	54
Eddie Brown, Cin.	9	0	9	0	54
Ernest Givins, Hou.	9	0	9	0	54
Sammie Smith, Mia.	9	8	1	0	54
Three tied with 8 each.					

NFC	TD	Rush	Rec	Ret	Pts
Barry Sanders, Det	16	13	3	0	96
Cleveland Gary, LA.	15	14	1	0	90
Neal Anderson, Chi	13	10	3	0	78
Jerry Rice, SF	13	0	13	0	78
Ottis Anderson, NY	11	11	0	0	66
Emmitt Smith, Dal	11	11	0	0	66
Andre Rison, Atl.	10	0	10	0	60
Herschel Walker, Min	9	5	4	0	54
Calvin Williams, Phi.	9	0	9	0	54
Four tied with 8 each.					

Interceptions

AFC	No	Yds	Long	TD
Richard Johnson, Hou	8	100	35	1
Gill Byrd, SD	7	63	24	0
Kevin Ross, KC	5	97	40	0
Erik McMillan, NY	5	92	25	0
Louis Oliver, Mia.	5	87	35	0
Jarvis Williams, Mia	5	82	42-td	1
Rod Woodson, Pit	5	67	34	0

NFC	No	Yds	Long	TD
Mark Carrier, Chi.	10	39	14	0
Wayne Haddix, TB	7	231	65-td	3
Joey Browner, Min	7	103	31	1
Dave Waymer, SF.	7	64	24	0
Martin Mayhew, Wash	7	20	15	0
Everson Walls, NY.	6	80	40	1
Lemuel Stinson, Chi	6	66	30	0

Sacks

AFC	No
Derrick Thomas, Kansas City	20
Bruce Smith, Buffalo	19
Leslie O'Neal, San Diego	13½
Dennis Byrd, New York	13
Jacob Green, Seattle.	12½
Sean Jones, Houston	12½
Greg Townsend, Los Angeles	12½

NFC	No
Charles Haley, San Francisco	16
Reggie White, Philadelphia	15
Kevin Greene, Los Angeles	13
Richard Dent, Chicago	12
Chris Doleman, Minnesota.	11
Pat Swilling, New Orleans	11

Punting

AFC	No	Yards	Long	Avg	In 20
Mike Horan, Den	58	2575	67	44.4	14
Rohn Stark, Ind	71	3048	61	43.4	24
Lee Johnson, Cin.	64	2705	70	42.3	12
Reggie Roby, Mia	72	3022	62	42.0	20
Brian Hansen, NE	90	3752	69	41.7	18

NFC	No	Yards	Long	Avg	In 20
Sean Landeta, NY	75	3306	67	44.1	24
Mike Saxon, Dal	79	3413	62	43.2	20
Rich Camarillo, Pho	67	2865	63	42.8	16
Tommy Barnhardt, NO	70	2990	65	42.7	20
Harry Newsome, Min	78	3299	61	42.3	19

Punt Returns

AFC	No	Yds	Avg	Long	TD
Clarence Verdin, Ind	31	396	12.8	36	0
Rod Woodson, Pit	38	398	10.5	52-td	1
Chris Warren, Sea.	28	269	9.6	39	0
Tim Brown, LA.	34	295	8.7	39	0
Mitchell Price, Cin	29	251	8.7	66-td	1

NFC	No	Yds	Avg	Long	TD
Johnny Bailey, Chi.	36	399	11.1	95-td	1
Dave Meggett, NY.	43	467	10.9	68-td	1
Mel Gray, Det	34	361	10.6	39	0
Jeff Query, GB.	32	308	9.6	25	0
Deion Sanders, Atl	29	250	8.6	79-td	1

Kickoff Returns

AFC	No	Yds	Avg	Long	TD
Kevin Clark, Den.	20	505	25.3	75	0
Donnie Elder, SD.	24	571	23.8	90	0
Rod Woodson, Pit	35	764	21.8	49	0
Chris Warren, Sea.	23	478	20.8	71	0
Sammy Martin, NE	25	515	20.6	38	0

NFC	No	Yds	Avg	Long	TD
Dave Meggett, NY.	21	492	23.4	58	0
Mel Gray, Det	41	939	22.9	65	0
Charles Wilson, GB.	35	798	22.8	36	0
Gaston Green, LA.	25	560	22.4	99-td	1
Herschel Walker, Min	44	966	22.0	64	0

NFL Regular Season Team Leaders

Offense

AFC	Points For	Avg	Yardage Rush	Pass	Total	Avg
Houston	405	25.3	1417	4805	6222	388.9
Buffalo	428	26.8	2080	3196	5276	329.8
Kansas City	369	23.1	1948	3267	5215	325.9
Denver	331	20.7	1872	3341	5213	325.8
Cincinnati	360	22.5	2120	2943	5063	316.4
Miami	336	21.0	1535	3512	5047	315.4
San Diego	315	19.7	2257	2683	4940	308.8
New York	295	18.4	2127	2759	4886	305.4
Los Angeles	337	21.1	2028	2688	4716	294.8
Seattle	306	19.1	1749	2834	4583	286.4
Pittsburgh	292	18.3	1880	2645	4525	282.8
Cleveland	228	14.3	1220	3147	4367	272.9
New England	181	11.3	1398	2765	4163	260.2
Indianapolis	281	17.6	1282	2873	4155	259.7

Defense

AFC	Points Opp	Avg	Yardage Rush	Pass	Total	Avg
Pittsburgh	240	15.0	1615	2500	4115	257.2
Los Angeles	268	16.8	1716	2697	4413	275.8
San Diego	281	17.6	1515	2910	4425	276.6
Miami	242	15.1	1831	2716	4547	284.2
Buffalo	263	16.4	1808	2799	4607	287.9
Seattle	286	17.9	1605	3004	4609	288.1
Houston	307	19.2	1575	3060	4635	289.7
Kansas City	257	16.1	1640	3241	4881	305.1
Cleveland	462	28.9	2105	3085	5190	324.4
Denver	374	23.4	1963	3382	5345	334.1
New York	345	21.6	2018	3437	5455	340.9
Cincinnati	352	22.0	2085	3520	5605	350.3
Indianapolis	353	22.1	2212	3402	5614	350.9
New England	446	27.9	2676	3021	5697	356.1

NFC	Points For	Avg	Yardage Rush	Pass	Total	Avg
San Fran	353	22.1	1718	4177	5895	368.4
Philadelphia	396	24.8	2556	3144	5700	356.3
Washington	381	23.8	2083	3479	5562	347.6
Los Angeles	345	21.6	1951	3479	5430	339.4
Atlanta	348	21.8	1594	3461	5055	315.9
Minnesota	351	21.9	1867	3167	5034	314.6
Chicago	348	21.8	2436	2544	4980	311.3
Detroit	373	23.3	1927	3050	4977	311.1
New York	335	20.9	2049	2756	4805	300.3
Phoenix	268	16.8	1912	2833	4745	296.6
Green Bay	271	16.9	1369	3306	4675	292.2
New Orleans	274	17.1	1850	2626	4476	279.8
Tampa Bay	264	16.5	1626	2849	4475	279.7
Dallas	244	15.3	1500	2581	4081	255.1

NFC	Points Opp	Avg	Yardage Rush	Pass	Total	Avg
New York	211	13.2	1459	2747	4206	262.9
San Fran	239	14.9	1258	3015	4273	267.1
Chicago	280	17.5	1572	2920	4492	280.8
Dallas	308	19.3	1976	2639	4615	288.4
Philadelphia	299	18.7	1169	3491	4660	291.3
Minnesota	326	20.4	2074	2643	4717	294.8
Washington	301	18.8	1587	3143	4730	295.6
New Orleans	275	17.2	1559	3319	4878	304.9
Phoenix	396	24.8	2318	2898	5216	326.0
Atlanta	365	22.8	1357	3913	5270	329.4
Los Angeles	412	25.8	1649	3762	5411	338.2
Green Bay	347	21.7	2059	3383	5442	340.1
Tampa Bay	367	22.9	2223	3256	5479	342.4
Detroit	413	25.8	2388	3346	5734	358.4

Takeaways / Giveaways

AFC	Takeaways Int	Fum	Tot	Giveaways Int	Fum	Tot	Net Diff
Kansas City	20	25	45	5	14	19	+26
Buffalo	18	17	35	11	10	21	+14
Pittsburgh	24	18	42	15	17	32	+10
New York	18	11	29	11	13	24	+5
Miami	19	8	27	12	15	27	E
Los Angeles	13	9	22	10	14	24	-2
San Diego	19	11	30	19	13	32	-2
Houston	21	12	33	15	21	36	-3
Cincinnati	15	16	31	23	12	35	-4
New England	14	18	32	20	16	36	-4
Seattle	12	18	30	20	16	36	-6
Denver	10	15	25	18	14	32	-7
Indianapolis	9	15	24	21	10	31	-7
Cleveland	13	9	22	23	23	46	-24

NFC	Takeaways Int	Fum	Tot	Giveaways Int	Fum	Tot	Net Diff
New York	23	11	34	5	9	14	+20
Chicago	31	14	45	12	14	26	+19
Washington	21	12	33	22	6	28	+5
Philadelphia	19	11	30	13	15	28	+2
San Francisco	17	14	31	16	14	30	+1
Los Angeles	12	19	31	17	14	31	E
Detroit	17	18	35	20	16	36	-1
Tampa Bay	25	17	42	24	19	43	-1
Dallas	11	19	30	24	9	33	-3
Atlanta	17	18	35	18	21	39	-4
Minnesota	22	11	33	24	13	37	-4
Phoenix	16	11	27	18	14	32	-5
New Orleans	8	19	27	23	16	39	-12
Green Bay	16	14	30	21	22	43	-13

London Wins Inaugural WLAF Championship

On June 9, 1991, the London Monarchs shut out the Barcelona Dragons, 21-0, before 61,108 fans at Wembley Stadium in London to win the World League of American Football's first World Bowl championship game. The Monarchs were led by QB Stan Gelbaugh (191 yards and 2 TDs) on offense, while safety and game MVP Dan Crossman intercepted three passes on defense.

Established by the NFL as a spring development league and staffed with mostly American coaches and players, the 10-team WLAF began play on March 23, featuring three clubs in Europe and one in Canada.

Final Standings: EUROPEAN DIVISION—London Monarchs (9-1), Barcelona Dragons (8-2), Frankfort Galaxy (7-3); NORTH AMERICAN EAST—New York-New Jersey Knights (5-5), Orlando Thunder (5-5), Montreal Machine (4-6), Raleigh-Durham Skyhawks (0-10); NORTH AMERICAN WEST—Birmingham Fire (5-5), San Antonio Riders (4-6), Sacramento Surge (3-7).

Playoff Results: SEMIFINALS—Barcelona over Birmingham, 10-3 (at Birm.) and London over NY/NJ, 42-26 (at NY/NJ); CHAMPIONSHIP—London over Barcelona, 21-0 (at London).

AFC Team by Team Statistics

Players with more than one team during the regular season are listed with second club; (*) indicates rookies.

Buffalo Bills

QBs (5 Att)	Att	Cmp	Pct	Yds	TD	Rate
Jim Kelly	346	219	63.3	2829	24	101.2
Frank Reich	63	36	57.1	469	2	91.3
Gale Gilbert	15	8	53.3	106	2	76.0

Interceptions: Kelly 9, Gilbert 2.

Top 5 Receivers	No	Yds	Avg	Long	TD
Andre Reed	71	945	13.3	56-td	8
Thurman Thomas	49	532	10.9	63	2
James Lofton	35	712	20.3	71	4
Keith McKeller	34	464	13.6	43	5
Don Smith	21	225	10.7	39	0

Top 5 Rushers	Car	Yds	Avg	Long	TD
Thurman Thomas	271	1297	4.8	80-td	11
Kenneth Davis	64	302	4.7	47	4
Jamie Mueller	59	207	3.5	20	2
Don Smith	20	82	4.1	13	2
Jim Kelly	22	63	2.9	15	0

Top 5 Touchdowns	TD	Run	Rec	Ret	Pts
Thurman Thomas	13	11	2	0	78
Andre Reed	8	0	8	0	48
Kenneth Davis	5	4	1	0	30
Keith McKeller	5	0	5	0	30
James Lofton	4	0	4	0	24

Kicking	FG/Att	Lg	PAT/Att	Pts
Scott Norwood	20/29	48	50/52	110

Punts (10 or more)	No	Yds	Long	Avg	In 20
Rick Tuten*	53	2107	55	39.8	12

Most Interceptions
Kirby Jackson ... 3

Most Sacks
Bruce Smith ... 19

Cincinnati Bengals

QBs (5 Att)	Att	Cmp	Pct	Yds	TD	Rate
Erik Wilhelm	19	12	63.2	117	0	80.4
Boomer Esiason	402	224	55.7	3031	24	77.0

Interceptions: Esiason 22.
Also threw TD pass: Lee Johnson (1).

Top 5 Receivers	No	Yds	Avg	Long	TD
Eddie Brown	44	706	16.0	50-td	9
Tim McGee	43	737	17.1	52	1
Rodney Holman	40	596	14.9	53	5
James Brooks	26	269	10.3	35	4
Ickey Woods	20	162	8.1	22	0

Top 5 Rushers	Car	Yds	Avg	Long	TD
James Brooks	195	1004	5.1	56-td	5
Harold Green*	83	353	4.3	39	1
Ickey Woods	64	268	4.2	32	6
Craig Taylor	51	216	4.2	24	2
Boomer Esiason	50	157	3.1	21	0

Top 5 Touchdowns	TD	Run	Rec	Ret	Pts
James Brooks	9	5	4	0	54
Eddie Brown	9	0	9	0	54
Ickey Woods	6	6	0	0	36
Rodney Holman	5	0	5	0	30
Craig Taylor	3	2	1	0	18

Kicking	FG/Att	Lg	PAT/Att	Pts
Jim Breech	17/21	36	41/44	92

Punts (10 or more)	No	Yds	Long	Avg	In 20
Lee Johnson	64	2705	70	42.3	12

Most Interceptions
Barney Bussey ... 4
David Fulcher ... 4

Most Sacks
James Francis* ... 8

Cleveland Browns

QBs (5 Att)	Att	Cmp	Pct	Yds	TD	Rate
Bernie Kosar	423	230	54.4	2562	10	65.7
Mike Pagel	148	69	46.6	819	3	48.2

Interceptions: Kosar 15, Pagel 8.

Top 5 Receivers	No	Yds	Avg	Long	TD
Webster Slaughter	59	847	14.4	50	4
Eric Metcalf	57	452	7.9	35	1
Reggie Langhorne	45	585	13.0	39	2
Brian Brennan	45	568	12.6	28	2
Kevin Mack	42	360	8.6	30	2

Top 5 Rushers	Car	Yds	Avg	Long	TD
Kevin Mack	158	702	4.4	26	5
Eric Metcalf	80	248	3.1	17	1
Leroy Hoard*	58	149	2.6	42	3
Brent Fullwood	44	124	2.8	16	1
GB	44	124	2.8	16	1
CLE			—Kickoff returns only—		
Derrick Gainer	30	81	2.7	9	1

Acquired: RB Fullwood (Oct.9) from Green Bay.

Top 5 Touchdowns	TD	Run	Rec	Ret	Pts
Kevin Mack	7	5	2	0	42
Eric Metcalf	4	1	1	2	24
Webster Slaughter	4	0	4	0	24
Leroy Hoard*	3	3	0	0	18

Three tied with 2 each.

Kicking	FG/Att	Lg	PAT/Att	Pts
Jerry Kauric	14/20	47	24/27	66

Punts (10 or more)	No	Yds	Long	Avg	In 20
Bryan Wagner	74	2879	65	38.9	13

Most Interceptions
Felix Wright ... 3

Most Sacks
Michael Dean Perry ... 11½

Denver Broncos

QBs (5 Att)	Att	Cmp	Pct	Yds	TD	Rate
John Elway	502	294	58.6	3526	15	78.5
Gary Kubiak	22	11	50.0	145	0	31.6

Interceptions: Elway 14, Kubiak 4.

Top 5 Receivers	No	Yds	Avg	Long	TD
Mark Jackson	57	926	16.2	66	4
Vance Johnson	54	747	13.8	49	3
Clarence Kay	29	282	9.7	22	0
Melvin Bratton	29	276	9.5	63	1
Michael Young	28	385	13.8	42	4

Top 5 Rushers	Car	Yds	Avg	Long	TD
Bobby Humphrey	288	1202	4.2	37-td	7
John Elway	50	258	5.2	21	3
Sammy Winder	42	120	2.9	19	2
Melvin Bratton	27	82	3.0	10	3
Blake Ezor	23	81	3.5	15	0

Top 5 Touchdowns	TD	Run	Rec	Ret	Pts
Bobby Humphrey	7	7	0	0	42
Mark Jackson	5	1	4	0	30
Melvin Bratton	4	3	1	0	24
Michael Young	4	0	4	0	24

Three tied with 3 each.

Kicking	FG/Att	Lg	PAT/Att	Pts
David Treadwell	25/34	49	34/36	109

Punts (10 or more)	No	Yds	Long	Avg	In 20
Mike Horan	58	2575	67	44.4	14

Most Interceptions
Three tied with 2 each.

Most Sacks
Simon Fletcher ... 11

Houston Oilers

QBs (5 Att)	Att	Cmp	Pct	Yds	TD	Rate
Warren Moon	584	362	62.0	4689	33	96.8
Cody Carlson	55	37	67.3	383	4	96.3

Interceptions: Moon 13, Carlson 2.

Top 5 Receivers	No	Yds	Avg	Long	TD
Haywood Jeffires	74	1048	14.2	87-td	8
Drew Hill	74	1019	13.8	57	5
Ernest Givins	72	979	13.6	80-td	9
Curtis Duncan	66	785	11.9	37-td	1
Lorenzo White	39	368	9.4	29	4

Top 5 Rushers	Car	Yds	Avg	Long	TD
Lorenzo White	168	702	4.2	22	8
Allen Pinkett	66	268	4.1	19	0
Warren Moon	55	215	3.9	17	2
Victor Jones	14	75	5.4	14	0
Ernest Givins	3	65	21.7	31	0

Signed: RB Jones (Oct.2) as free agent.

Top 5 Touchdowns	TD	Run	Rec	Ret	Pts
Lorenzo White	12	8	4	0	72
Ernest Givins	9	0	9	0	54
Haywood Jeffires	8	0	8	0	48
Tony Jones	6	0	6	0	36
Drew Hill	5	0	5	0	30

Kicking	FG/Att	Lg	PAT/Att	Pts
Teddy Garcia	14/20	49	26/28	68
Tony Zendejas	7/12	45	20/21	41

Signed: PK Garcia (Oct.24) as free agent after Zendejas broke left leg vs New Orleans (Oct.21).

Punts (10 or more)	No	Yds	Long	Avg	In 20
Greg Montgomery	34	1530	60	45.0	7

Most Interceptions		Most Sacks	
Richard Johnson	8	Sean Jones	12½

Kansas City Chiefs

QBs (5 Att)	Att	Cmp	Pct	Yds	TD	Rate
Steve DeBerg	444	258	58.1	3444	23	96.3
Steve Pelluer	5	2	40.0	14	0	8.3

Interceptions: DeBerg 4, Pelluer 1.

Top 5 Receivers	No	Yds	Avg	Long	TD
Stephone Paige	65	1021	15.7	86-td	5
Robb Thomas	41	545	13.3	47-td	4
Emile Harry	41	519	12.7	60	2
Todd McNair	40	507	12.7	65	2
Bill Jones	19	137	7.2	19	5

Top 5 Rushers	Car	Yds	Avg	Long	TD
Barry Word	204	1015	5.0	53-td	4
Christian Okoye	245	805	3.3	32	7
Todd McNair	14	61	4.4	13	0
Bill Jones	10	47	4.7	14	0
James Saxon	3	15	5.0	8	0

Top 5 Touchdowns	TD	Run	Rec	Ret	Pts
Christian Okoye	7	7	0	0	42
Bill Jones	5	0	5	0	30
Stephone Paige	5	0	5	0	30
Robb Thomas	4	0	4	0	24
Barry Word	4	4	0	0	24

Kicking	FG/Att	Lg	PAT/Att	Pts
Nick Lowery	34/37	48	37/38	139

Punts (10 or more)	No	Yds	Long	Avg	In 20
Bryan Barker	64	2479	56	38.7	16

Most Interceptions		Most Sacks	
Kevin Ross	5	Derrick Thomas	20

Indianapolis Colts

QBs (5 Att)	Att	Cmp	Pct	Yds	TD	Rate
Jack Trudeau	144	84	58.3	1078	6	78.4
Jeff George*	334	181	54.2	2152	16	73.8
Joe Ferguson	8	2	25.0	21	0	0.0

Interceptions: George 13, Trudeau 6, Ferguson 2.

Top 5 Receivers	No	Yds	Avg	Long	TD
Albert Bentley	71	664	9.4	73	2
Bill Brooks	62	823	13.3	75	5
Jessie Hester	54	924	17.1	64-td	6
Stanley Morgan	23	364	15.8	42-td	5
Eric Dickerson	18	92	5.1	17	0

Top 5 Rushers	Car	Yds	Avg	Long	TD
Eric Dickerson	166	677	4.1	43	4
Albert Bentley	137	556	4.1	26-td	4
Jack Trudeau	10	28	2.8	9	0
Ken Clark*	7	10	1.4	11	0
Jessie Hester	4	9	2.3	10	0

Top 5 Touchdowns	TD	Run	Rec	Ret	Pts
Albert Bentley	6	4	2	0	36
Jessie Hester	6	0	6	0	36
Bill Brooks	5	0	5	0	30
Stanley Morgan	5	0	5	0	30
Eric Dickerson	4	4	0	0	24

Kicking	FG/Att	Lg	PAT/Att	Pts
Dean Biasucci	17/24	55	32/33	83

Punts (10 or more)	No	Yds	Long	Avg	In 20
Rohn Stark	71	3084	61	43.4	24

Most Interceptions		Most Sacks	
Mike Prior	3	Sam Clancy	7½

Los Angeles Raiders

QBs (5 Att)	Att	Cmp	Pct	Yds	TD	Rate
Jay Schroeder	334	182	54.5	2849	19	90.8

Interceptions: Schroeder 9.

Top 5 Receivers	No	Yds	Avg	Long	TD
Mervyn Fernandez	52	839	16.1	66-td	5
Willie Gault	50	985	19.7	68-td	3
Ethan Horton	33	404	12.2	36	3
Tim Brown	18	265	14.7	51	3
Marcus Allen	15	189	12.6	30	1

Top 5 Rushers	Car	Yds	Avg	Long	TD
Bo Jackson	125	698	5.6	88	5
Marcus Allen	179	682	3.8	28	12
Steve Smith	81	327	4.0	17	2
Greg Bell	47	164	3.5	21	1
Jay Schroeder	37	81	2.2	17	0

Top 5 Touchdowns	TD	Run	Rec	Ret	Pts
Marcus Allen	13	12	1	0	78
Mervyn Fernandez	5	0	5	0	30
Bo Jackson	5	5	0	0	30
Steve Smith	5	2	3	0	30
Tim Brown	3	0	3	0	18
Willie Gault	3	0	3	0	18
Ethan Horton	3	0	3	0	18

Kicking	FG/Att	Lg	PAT/Att	Pts
Jeff Jaeger	15/20	50	40/42	85

Punts (10 or more)	No	Yds	Long	Avg	In 20
Jeff Gossett	60	2315	57	38.6	18

Most Interceptions		Most Sacks	
Three tied with 3 each.		Greg Townsend	12½

Miami Dolphins

QBs (5 Att)	Att	Cmp	Pct	Yds	TD	Rate
Dan Marino	531	306	57.6	3563	21	82.6
Scott Secules	7	3	42.9	17	0	10.7

Interceptions: Marino 11, Secules 1.

Top 5 Receivers	No	Yds	Avg	Long	TD
Mark Duper	52	810	15.6	69-td	5
Jim Jensen	44	365	8.3	18	1
Tony Paige	35	247	7.1	17-td	4
Mark Clayton	32	406	12.7	43	3
Ferrell Edmunds	31	446	14.4	35	1

Top 5 Rushers	Car	Yds	Avg	Long	TD
Sammie Smith	226	831	3.7	33	8
Marc Logan	79	317	4.0	17	2
Troy Stradford	37	138	3.7	15	1
Tony Paige	32	95	3.0	11	2
Dan Marino	16	29	1.8	15	0

Top 5 Touchdowns	TD	Run	Rec	Ret	Pts
Sammie Smith	9	8	1	0	54
Tony Paige	6	2	4	0	36
Mark Duper	5	0	5	0	30
Mark Clayton	3	0	3	0	18
James Pruitt	3	0	3	0	18

Signed: WR Pruitt (Nov.16) as free agent.

Kicking	FG/Att	Lg	PAT/Att	Pts
Pete Stoyanovich	21/25	53	37/37	100

Punts (10 or more)	No	Yds	Long	Avg	In 20
Reggie Roby	72	3022	62	42.0	20

Most Interceptions
Louis Oliver 5
Jarvis Williams 5

Most Sacks
Jeff Cross 11

New York Jets

QBs (5 Att)	Att	Cmp	Pct	Yds	TD	Rate
Troy Taylor*	10	7	70.0	49	1	114.2
Ken O'Brien	411	226	55.0	2855	13	77.3
Tony Eason	28	13	46.4	155	0	49.0

Interceptions: O'Brien 10, Eason 1

Top 5 Receivers	No	Yds	Avg	Long	TD
Al Toon	57	757	13.3	46-td	6
Rob Moore*	44	692	15.7	69-td	6
Mark Boyer	40	334	8.4	25	1
Blair Thomas*	20	204	10.2	55	1
Terance Mathis*	19	245	12.9	23	0

Top 5 Rushers	Car	Yds	Avg	Long	TD
Blair Thomas*	123	620	5.0	41	1
Brad Baxter	124	539	4.3	28-td	6
Freeman McNeil	99	458	4.6	29	6
Johnny Hector	91	377	4.1	22	2
Ken O'Brien	21	72	3.4	15	0

Top 5 Touchdowns	TD	Run	Rec	Ret	Pts
Brad Baxter*	6	6	0	0	36
Freeman McNeil	6	6	0	0	36
James Moore*	6	0	6	0	36
Al Toon	6	0	6	0	36
Johnny Hector	2	2	0	0	12
Blair Thomas*	2	1	1	0	12

Kicking	FG/Att	Lg	PAT/Att	Pts
Pat Leahy	23/26	47	32/32	101

Punts (10 or more)	No	Yds	Long	Avg	In 20
Joe Prokop	59	2363	58	40.1	18

Most Interceptions
Erik McMillan 5

Most Sacks
Dennis Byrd 13

New England Patriots

QBs (5 Att)	Att	Cmp	Pct	Yds	TD	Rate
Steve Grogan	92	50	54.3	615	4	76.1
Tommy Hodson*	156	85	54.5	968	4	68.5
Marc Wilson	265	139	52.5	1625	6	61.6

Interceptions: Wilson 11, Hodson 5, Grogan 3.

Top 5 Receivers	No	Yds	Avg	Long	TD
Irving Fryar	54	856	15.9	56	4
Marv Cook	51	455	8.9	35-td	5
Hart Lee Dykes	34	549	16.1	35-td	2
John Stephens	28	196	7.0	43	1
Greg McMurtry*	22	240	10.9	26	0

Top 5 Rushers	Car	Yds	Avg	Long	TD
John Stephens	212	808	3.8	26	2
Marvin Allen	63	237	3.8	29	1
George Adams	28	111	4.0	13	0
Tommy Hodson*	12	79	6.6	23	0
Mosi Tatupu	16	56	3.5	15	0

Top 5 Touchdowns	TD	Run	Rec	Ret	Pts
Marv Cook	5	0	5	0	30
Irving Fryar	4	0	4	0	24
John Stephens	3	2	1	0	18
Hart Lee Dykes	2	0	2	0	12

Five tied with 1 each.

Kicking	FG/Att	Lg	PAT/Att	Pts
Jason Staurovsky	16/22	53	19/19	67

Punts (10 or more)	No	Yds	Long	Avg	In 20
Brian Hansen	90	3752	69	41.7	18

Most Interceptions
Three tied with 4 each.

Most Sacks
Brent Williams 6

Pittsburgh Steelers

QBs (5 Att)	Att	Cmp	Pct	Yds	TD	Rate
Bubby Brister	387	223	57.6	2725	20	81.6
Rick Strom	21	14	66.7	162	0	69.9

Interceptions: Brister 14, Strom 1.

Top 5 Receivers	No	Yds	Avg	Long	TD
Louis Lipps	50	682	13.6	37	3
Merril Hoge	40	342	8.6	27	3
Eric Green*	34	387	11.4	46	7
Mike Mularkey	32	365	11.4	28	3
Derek Hill	25	391	15.6	66	0

Top 5 Rushers	Car	Yds	Avg	Long	TD
Merril Hoge	203	772	3.8	41-td	7
Tim Worley	109	418	3.8	38	0
Warren Williams	68	389	5.7	70-td	3
Barry Foster*	36	203	5.6	38	1
Bubby Brister	25	64	2.6	11	0

Top 5 Touchdowns	TD	Run	Rec	Ret	Pts
Merril Hoge	10	7	3	0	60
Eric Green*	7	0	7	0	42
Warren Williams	4	3	1	0	24
Louis Lipps	3	0	3	0	18
Mike Mularkey	3	0	3	0	18

Kicking	FG/Att	Lg	PAT/Att	Pts
Gary Anderson	20/25	48	32/32	92

Punts (10 or more)	No	Yds	Long	Avg	In 20
Dan Stryzinski	65	2454	51	37.8	18

Most Interceptions
Rod Woodson 5

Most Sacks
Gerald Williams 6

San Diego Chargers

QBs (5 Att)	Att	Cmp	Pct	Yds	TD	Rate
B.J.Tolliver	410	216	52.7	2574	16	68.9
John Friesz*	22	11	50.0	98	1	58.5
Mark Vlasic	40	19	47.5	168	1	46.7

Interceptions: Tolliver 16, Vlasic 2, Friesz 1.

Top 5 Receivers	No	Yds	Avg	Long	TD
Anthony Miller	63	933	14.8	31-td	7
Ronnie Harmon	46	511	11.1	36-td	2
Craig McEwen	29	325	11.2	32	3
Wayne Walker	23	240	10.4	23	1
Marion Butts	16	117	7.3	26	0

Top 5 Rushers	Car	Yds	Avg	Long	TD
Marion Butts	265	1225	4.6	52	8
Rod Bernstine	124	589	4.8	40-td	4
Ronnie Harmon	66	363	5.5	41	0
Nate Lewis*	4	25	6.3	10-td	1
Billie Joe Tolliver	14	22	1.6	14	0

Top 5 Touchdowns	TD	Run	Rec	Ret	Pts
Marion Butts	8	8	0	0	48
Anthony Miller	7	0	7	0	42
Rod Bernstine	4	4	0	0	24
Nate Lewis*	3	1	1	1	18
Craig McEwen	3	0	3	0	18

Kicking	FG/Att	Lg	PAT/Att	Pts
John Carney	19/21	43	27/28	84

Punts (10 or more)	No	Yds	Long	Avg	In 20
John Kidd	61	2442	59	40.0	14

Most Interceptions
Gill Byrd 7

Most Sacks
Leslie O'Neal 13½

Seattle Seahawks

QBs (5 Att)	Att	Cmp	Pct	Yds	TD	Rate
Dave Krieg	448	265	59.2	3194	15	73.6

Interceptions: Krieg 20.

Top 5 Receivers	No	Yds	Avg	Long	TD
John L.Williams	73	699	9.6	60	0
Tommy Kane	52	776	14.9	63-td	4
Brian Blades	49	525	10.7	24	3
Jeff Chadwick	27	478	17.7	54-td	4
Paul Skansi	22	257	11.7	25-td	2

Top 5 Rushers	Car	Yds	Avg	Long	TD
Derrick Fenner	215	859	4.0	36	14
John L.Williams	187	714	3.8	25	3
Dave Krieg	32	115	3.6	25	0
James Jones	5	20	4.0	5	0
Brian Blades	3	19	6.3	12	0

Top 5 Touchdowns	TD	Run	Rec	Ret	Pts
Derrick Fenner	15	14	1	0	90
Jeff Chadwick	4	0	4	0	24
Tommy Kane	4	0	4	0	24
Brian Blades	3	0	3	0	18
John L.Williams	3	3	0	0	18

Kicking	FG/Att	Lg	PAT/Att	Pts
Norm Johnson	23/32	51	33/34	102

Punts (10 or more)	No	Yds	Long	Avg	In 20
Rick Donnelly	67	2722	54	40.6	18

Most Interceptions
Dwayne Harper 3
Eugene Robinson 3

Most Sacks
Jacob Green 12½

NFC Team by Team Statistics

Players with more than one team during the regular season are listed with second club; (*) indicates rookies.

Atlanta Falcons

QBs (5 Att)	Att	Cmp	Pct	Yds	TD	Rate
Hugh Millen	63	34	54.0	427	1	80.6
Chris Miller	388	222	57.2	2735	17	78.7
Scott Campbell	76	36	47.4	527	3	61.7

Interceptions: Miller 14, Campbell 4.

Top 5 Receivers	No	Yds	Avg	Long	TD
Andre Rison	82	1208	14.7	75-td	10
Floyd Dixon	38	399	10.5	34	4
Shawn Collins	34	503	14.8	61	2
Michael Haynes	31	445	14.4	60	0
Steve Broussard*	24	160	6.7	18	0

Top 4 Rushers	Car	Yds	Avg	Long	TD
Mike Rozier	163	717	4.4	67	3
HOU	10	42	4.2	11	0
ATL	153	675	4.4	67	3
Steve Broussard*	126	454	3.6	50-td	4
Keith Jones	49	185	3.8	22	0
Tracy Johnson	30	106	3.5	12	3

Signed: RB Rozier (Oct.3) after release by Houston (Oct.2).

Top 5 Touchdowns	TD	Run	Rec	Ret	Pts
Andre Rison	10	0	10	0	60
Steve Broussard*	4	4	0	0	24
Floyd Dixon	4	0	4	0	24
Tracy Johnson	4	3	1	0	24

Two tied with 3 each.

Kicking	FG/Att	Lg	PAT/Att	Pts
Greg Davis	22/33	53	40/40	106

Punts (10 or more)	No	Yds	Long	Avg	In 20
Scott Fulhage	70	2913	59	41.6	15

Most Interceptions
Five tied with 3.

Most Sacks
Tim Green 6

Chicago Bears

QBs (5 Att)	Att	Cmp	Pct	Yds	TD	Rate
Peter Tom Willis*	13	9	69.2	106	1	87.3
Jim Harbaugh	312	180	57.7	2178	10	81.9
Mike Tomczak	104	39	37.5	521	3	43.8

Interceptions: Harbaugh 6, Tomczak 5, Willis 1.

Top 5 Receivers	No	Yds	Avg	Long	TD
Brad Muster	47	452	9.6	48	0
Neal Anderson	42	484	11.5	50-td	3
Wendell Davis	39	572	14.7	51	3
Ron Morris	31	437	14.1	67-td	3
Dennis Gentry	23	320	13.9	80-td	2

Top 5 Rushers	Car	Yds	Avg	Long	TD
Neal Anderson	260	1078	4.1	52	10
Brad Muster	141	664	4.7	28	6
Jim Harbaugh	51	321	6.3	17	4
Mark Green	27	126	4.7	14	0
Johnny Bailey*	26	86	3.3	9	0

Top 5 Touchdowns	TD	Run	Rec	Ret	Pts
Neal Anderson	13	10	3	0	78
Brad Muster	6	6	0	0	36
Jim Harbaugh	4	4	0	0	24
Wendell Davis	3	0	3	0	18
Ron Morris	3	0	3	0	18

Kicking	FG/Att	Lg	PAT/Att	Pts
Kevin Butler	26/37	52	36/37	114

Punts (10 or more)	No	Yds	Long	Avg	In 20
Maury Buford	76	3073	59	40.4	22

Most Interceptions
Mark Carrier* 10

Most Sacks
Richard Dent 12

Dallas Cowboys

QBs (5 Att)	Att	Cmp	Pct	Yds	TD	Rate
Troy Aikman	399	226	56.6	2579	11	66.6
Babe Laufenberg	67	24	35.8	279	1	16.9

Interceptions: Aikman 18, Laufenberg 6.

Top 5 Receivers	No	Yds	Avg	Long	TD
Kelvin Martin	64	732	11.4	45	0
Jay Novacek	59	657	11.1	41	4
Tommie Agee	30	272	9.1	30	1
Emmitt Smith	24	228	9.5	57	0
Michael Irvin	20	413	20.7	61-td	5

Top 5 Rushers	Car	Yds	Avg	Long	TD
Emmitt Smith	241	937	3.9	48-td	11
Tommie Agee	53	213	4.0	28	0
Troy Aikman	40	172	4.3	20	1
Robert Perryman	32	97	3.0	13	1
NE.	32	97	3.0	13	1
DAL			—Did not play—		
James Dixon	26	86	3.3	9	0

Signed: RB Perryman (Nov.9) after release by New England (Nov.7).

Top 5 Touchdowns	TD	Run	Rec	Ret	Pts
Emmitt Smith	11	11	0	0	66
Michael Irvin	5	0	5	0	30
Jay Novacek	4	0	4	0	24
Daryl Johnston	2	1	1	0	12

Six tied with 1 each.

Kicking	FG/Att	Lg	PAT/Att	Pts
Ken Willis*	18/25	49	26/26	80

Punts (10 or more)	No	Yds	Long	Avg	In 20
Mike Saxon	79	3413	62	43.2	20

Most Interceptions
Issiac Holt 3
James Washington 3

Most Sacks
Jimmie Jones* 7½
Daniel Stubbs 7½

Detroit Lions

QBs (5 Att)	Att	Cmp	Pct	Yds	TD	Rate
Rodney Peete	271	142	52.4	1974	13	79.8
Bob Gagliano	159	87	54.7	1190	10	73.6
Andre Ware	30	13	43.3	164	1	44.3

Interceptions: Gagliano 10, Peete 8, Ware 2.

Top 5 Receivers	No	Yds	Avg	Long	TD
Richard Johnson	64	727	11.4	44-td	6
Robert Clark	52	914	17.6	57	8
Barry Sanders	36	480	13.3	47-td	3
Aubrey Matthews	30	349	11.6	52	1
Terry Greer	20	332	16.6	68-td	3

Top 4 Rushers	Car	Yds	Avg	Long	TD
Barry Sanders	255	1304	5.1	45-td	13
Rodney Peete	47	363	7.7	37	6
Bob Gagliano	46	145	3.2	22	0
Andre Ware	7	64	9.1	30	0

Top 5 Touchdowns	TD	Run	Rec	Ret	Pts
Barry Sanders	16	13	3	0	96
Robert Clark	8	0	8	0	48
Richard Johnson	6	0	6	0	36
Rodney Peete	6	6	0	0	36
Terry Greer	3	0	3	0	18

Kicking	FG/Att	Lg	PAT/Att	Pts
Eddie Murray	13/19	47	34/34	73
Rich Karlis	4/7	39	12/12	24

Signed: PK Karlis (Oct.10) as free agent.
Released: Karlis (Nov.26).

Punts (10 or more)	No	Yds	Long	Avg	In 20
Jim Arnold	63	2560	59	40.6	10

Most Interceptions
William White 5

Most Sacks
Michael Cofer 10

Green Bay Packers

QBs (5 Att)	Att	Cmp	Pct	Yds	TD	Rate
Blair Kiel	85	51	60.0	504	2	74.8
Don Majkowski	264	150	56.8	1925	10	73.5
Anthony Dilweg	192	101	52.6	1267	8	72.1

Interceptions: Majkowski 12, Dilweg 7, Kiel 2.

Top 5 Receivers	No	Yds	Avg	Long	TD
Sterling Sharpe	67	1105	16.5	76-td	6
Perry Kemp	44	527	12.0	29	2
Jeff Query	34	458	13.5	47-td	2
Clarence Weathers	33	390	11.8	29	1
Herman Fontenot	31	293	9.5	59	1

Top 5 Rushers	Car	Yds	Avg	Long	TD
Michael Haddix	98	311	3.2	13	0
Darrell Thompson*	76	264	3.5	37	1
Don Majkowski	29	186	6.4	24	1
Keith Woodside	46	182	4.0	21	1
Anthony Dilweg	21	114	5.4	22	0

Top 5 Touchdowns	TD	Run	Rec	Ret	Pts
Sterling Sharpe	6	0	6	0	36
Ed West	5	0	5	0	30
Jeff Query	3	0	2	1	18
Michael Haddix	2	0	2	0	12
Perry Kemp	2	0	2	0	12
Darrell Thompson*	2	1	0	1	12

Kicking	FG/Att	Lg	PAT/Att	Pts
Chris Jacke	23/30	53	28/29	97

Punts (10 or more)	No	Yds	Long	Avg	In 20
Don Bracken	64	2431	59	38.0	17

Most Interceptions
Three tied with 3.

Most Sacks
Tim Harris 7

Los Angeles Rams

QBs (5 Att)	Att	Cmp	Pct	Yds	TD	Rate
Jim Everett	554	307	55.4	3989	23	79.3
Chuck Long	5	1	20.0	4	0	39.6

Interceptions: Everett 17.
Also threw TD pass: Buford McGee (1).

Top 5 Receivers	No	Yds	Avg	Long	TD
Henry Ellard	76	1294	17.0	50-td	4
Willie Anderson	51	1097	21.5	55-td	4
Pete Holohan	49	475	9.7	28	2
Buford McGee	47	388	8.3	25	4
Cleveland Gary	30	150	5.0	22-td	1

Top 5 Rushers	Car	Yds	Avg	Long	TD
Cleveland Gary	204	808	4.0	48	14
Gaston Green	68	261	3.8	31	0
Buford McGee	44	234	5.3	19	1
Curt Warner	49	139	2.8	9	1
Marcus Dupree*	19	72	3.8	13	0

Top 5 Touchdowns	TD	Run	Rec	Ret	Pts
Cleveland Gary	15	14	1	0	90
Buford McGee	5	1	4	0	30
Willie Anderson	4	0	4	0	24
Robert Delpino	4	0	4	0	24
Henry Ellard	4	0	4	0	24

Kicking	FG/Att	Lg	PAT/Att	Pts
Mike Lansford	15/24	46	42/43	87

Punts (10 or more)	No	Yds	Long	Avg	In 20
Keith English	68	2663	58	39.2	8

Most Interceptions
Bobby Humphrey 4
Vince Newsome 4

Most Sacks
Kevin Greene 13

Minnesota Vikings

QBs (5 Att)	Att	Cmp	Pct	Yds	TD	Rate
Wade Wilson	146	82	56.2	1155	9	79.6
Rich Gannon	349	182	52.1	2278	16	68.9

Interceptions: Gannon 16, Wilson 8.

Top 5 Receivers	No	Yds	Avg	Long	TD
Anthony Carter	70	1008	14.4	56-td	8
Hassan Jones	51	810	15.9	75-td	7
Steve Jordan	45	636	14.1	38	3
Herschel Walker	35	315	9.0	32	4
Cris Carter	27	413	15.3	78-td	3

Top 5 Rushers	Car	Yds	Avg	Long	TD
Herschel Walker	184	770	4.2	58-td	5
Rick Fenney	87	376	4.3	27	2
Rich Gannon	52	268	5.2	27	1
Alfred Anderson	59	207	3.5	14	2
Alan Rice	15	74	4.9	13	0

Top 5 Touchdowns	TD	Run	Rec	Ret	Pts
Herschel Walker	9	5	4	0	54
Anthony Carter	8	0	8	0	48
Hassan Jones	7	0	7	0	42
Cris Carter	3	0	3	0	18
Steve Jordan	3	0	3	0	18

Kicking	FG/Att	Lg	PAT/Att	Pts
Fuad Reveiz	13/19	45	26/27	65
SD	2/7	42	7/8	13
MIN	11/12	45	19/19	52
Donald Igwebuike	14/16	48	19/19	61

Signed: PK Reveiz (Nov.3) after release by San Diego (Oct.2).
Roster Exemption: Igwebuike (Nov.9).

Punts (10 or more)	No	Yds	Long	Avg	In 20
Harry Newsome	78	3299	61	42.3	19

Most Interceptions	Most Sacks
Joey Browner ... 7	Chris Doleman ... 11

New Orleans Saints

QBs (5 Att)	Att	Cmp	Pct	Yds	TD	Rate
Steve Walsh	336	179	53.3	2010	12	67.2
DAL	9	4	44.4	40	0	67.2
NO	327	175	53.5	1970	12	67.2
John Fourcade	116	50	43.1	785	3	46.1

Interceptions: Walsh 13, Fourcade 8.
Acquired: QB Walsh (Sep.25) from Dallas.

Top 5 Receivers	No	Yds	Avg	Long	TD
Eric Martin	63	912	14.5	58	5
Brett Perriman	36	382	10.6	29	2
Floyd Turner	21	396	18.9	68-td	4
Gill Fenerty	18	209	11.6	28	0
Craig Heyward	18	121	6.7	12	0

Top 5 Rushers	Car	Yds	Avg	Long	TD
Craig Heyward	129	599	4.6	47-td	4
Rueben Mayes	138	510	3.7	18	7
Gill Fenerty	73	355	4.9	60-td	2
Dalton Hilliard	90	284	3.2	17	0
John Fourcade	15	77	5.1	12	1

Top 5 Touchdowns	TD	Run	Rec	Ret	Pts
Rueben Mayes	7	7	0	0	42
Eric Martin	5	0	5	0	30
Craig Heyward	4	4	0	0	24
Floyd Turner	4	0	4	0	24
Three tied with 2 each.					

Kicking	FG/Att	Lg	PAT/Att	Pts
Morten Andersen	21/27	52	29/29	92

Punts (10 or more)	No	Yds	Long	Avg	In 20
Tommy Barnhardt	70	2990	65	42.7	20

Most Interceptions	Most Sacks
Four tied with 2.	Pat Swilling ... 11

New York Giants

QBs (5 Att)	Att	Cmp	Pct	Yds	TD	Rate
Phil Simms	311	184	59.2	2284	15	92.7
Jeff Hostetler	87	47	54.0	614	3	83.2

Interceptions: Simms 4, Hostetler 1.

Top 5 Receivers	No	Yds	Avg	Long	TD
Dave Meggett	39	410	10.5	38	1
Mark Bavaro	33	393	11.9	61	5
Rodney Hampton*	32	274	8.6	27-td	2
Stephen Baker	26	541	20.8	80-td	4
Mark Ingram	26	499	19.2	57-td	5

Top 5 Rushers	Car	Yds	Avg	Long	TD
Ottis Anderson	225	784	5.5	28	11
Rodney Hampton*	109	455	4.2	41	2
Lewis Tillman	84	231	2.8	17	1
Jeff Hostetler	39	190	4.9	30	2
Dave Meggett	22	164	7.5	51	0

Top 5 Touchdowns	TD	Run	Rec	Ret	Pts
Ottis Anderson	11	11	0	0	66
Mark Bavaro	5	0	5	0	30
Mark Ingram	5	0	5	0	30
Stephen Baker	4	0	4	0	24
Rodney Hampton*	4	2	2	0	24

Kicking	FG/Att	Lg	PAT/Att	Pts
Matt Bahr	17/23	49	29/30	80
Raul Allegre	4/5	46	9/9	21

Signed: PK Bahr (Sep.28) as free agent after Allegre placed on injured reserve list (Sep.28).

Punts (10 or more)	No	Yds	Long	Avg	In 20
Sean Landeta	75	3306	67	44.1	24

Most Interceptions	Most Sacks
Everson Walls ... 6	Lawrence Taylor ... 10½

Philadelphia Eagles

QBs (5 Att)	Att	Cmp	Pct	Yds	TD	Rate
R.Cunningham	465	271	58.3	3466	30	91.6
Jim McMahon	9	6	66.7	63	0	86.8

Interceptions: Cunningham 13.
Also threw TD passes: Keith Byars (4).

Top 5 Receivers	No	Yds	Avg	Long	TD
Keith Byars	81	819	10.1	54	3
Keith Jackson	50	670	13.4	37-td	6
Calvin Williams*	37	602	16.3	45-td	9
Fred Barnett*	36	721	20.0	95-td	8
Heath Sherman	23	167	7.3	26	3

Top 5 Rushers	Car	Yds	Avg	Long	TD
Randall Cunningham	118	942	8.0	52-td	5
Heath Sherman	164	685	4.2	36	1
Anthony Toney	132	452	3.4	20	1
Thomas Sanders	56	208	3.7	39	1
Keith Byars	37	141	3.8	23	0

Signed: RB Sanders (Oct.25) as free agent.

Top 5 Touchdowns	TD	Run	Rec	Ret	Pts
Calvin Williams*	9	0	9	0	54
Fred Barnett*	8	0	8	0	48
Keith Jackson	6	0	6	0	36
Randall Cunningham	5	5	0	0	30
Heath Sherman	4	1	3	0	24
Anthony Toney	4	1	3	0	24

Kicking	FG/Att	Lg	PAT/Att	Pts
Roger Ruzek	21/29	53	45/48	108

Punts (10 or more)	No	Yds	Long	Avg	In 20
Jeff Feagles	72	3026	60	42.0	4

Most Interceptions	Most Sacks
Wes Hopkins ... 5	Reggie White ... 15

Phoenix Cardinals

QBs (5 Att)	Att	Cmp	Pct	Yds	TD	Rate
Timm Rosenbach	437	237	54.2	3098	16	72.8

Interceptions: Rosenbach 17.

Top 5 Receivers	No	Yds	Avg	Long	TD
Ricky Proehl*	56	802	14.3	45-td	4
Roy Green	53	797	15.0	54	4
Ernie Jones	43	724	16.8	68-td	4
Johnny Johnson*	25	241	9.6	35	0
J.T. Smith	18	225	12.5	45-td	2
Walter Reeves	18	126	7.0	16	0

Top 5 Rushers	Car	Yds	Avg	Long	TD
Johnny Johnson*	234	926	4.0	41	5
Timm Rosenbach	85	473	5.6	25	3
Anthony Thompson*	106	390	3.7	40	4
Terrence Flagler	13	85	6.5	29-td	1
Ernie Jones	4	33	8.3	15	0

Signed: RB Flagler (Sep.27) as free agent.

Top 5 Touchdowns	TD	Run	Rec	Ret	Pts
Johnny Johnson*	5	5	0	0	30
Roy Green	4	0	4	0	24
Ernie Jones	4	0	4	0	24
Ricky Proehl*	4	0	4	0	24
Anthony Thompson*	4	4	0	0	24

Kicking	FG/Att	Lg	PAT/Att	Pts
Al Del Greco	17/27	50	31/31	82

Punts (10 or more)	No	Yds	Long	Avg	In 20
Rich Camarillo	67	2865	63	42.8	16

Most Interceptions	Most Sacks
Tim McDonald 4	Ken Harvey 10

Tampa Bay Buccaneers

QBs (5 Att)	Att	Cmp	Pct	Yds	TD	Rate
Vinny Testaverde	365	203	55.6	2818	17	75.6
Chris Chandler	83	42	50.6	464	1	41.4

Interceptions: Testaverde 18, Chandler 6.

Top 5 Receivers	No	Yds	Avg	Long	TD
Mark Carrier	49	813	16.6	68-td	4
Bruce Hill	42	641	15.3	48-td	5
Reggie Cobb*	39	299	7.7	17	0
Gary Anderson	38	464	12.2	74	2
Ron Hall	31	464	15.0	54-td	2

Top 5 Rushers	Car	Yds	Avg	Long	TD
Gary Anderson	166	646	3.9	22	3
Reggie Cobb*	151	480	3.2	17	2
Vinny Testaverde	38	280	7.4	48-td	1
John Harvey	27	113	4.2	14	0
Chris Chandler	13	71	5.5	18	1

Top 5 Touchdowns	TD	Run	Rec	Ret	Pts
Gary Anderson	5	3	2	0	30
Bruce Hill	5	0	5	0	30
Mark Carrier	4	0	4	0	24
Wayne Haddix	3	0	0	3	18
Reggie Cobb*	2	2	0	0	12
Ron Hall	2	0	2	0	12
Bruce Perkins*	2	0	2	0	12

Kicking	FG/Att	Lg	PAT/Att	Pts
Steve Christie*	23/27	54	27/27	96

Punts (10 or more)	No	Yds	Long	Avg	In 20
Mark Royals	72	2902	62	40.3	8

Most Interceptions	Most Sacks
Wayne Haddix 7	Broderick Thomas 7½

San Francisco 49ers

QBs (5 Att)	Att	Cmp	Pct	Yds	TD	Rate
Steve Young	62	38	61.3	427	2	92.6
Joe Montana	520	321	61.7	3944	26	89.0

Interceptions: Montana 16.

Top 5 Receivers	No	Yds	Avg	Long	TD
Jerry Rice	100	1502	15.0	64-td	13
Brent Jones	56	747	13.3	67-td	5
John Taylor	49	748	15.3	78-td	7
Tom Rathman	48	327	6.8	28	0
Dexter Carter*	25	217	8.7	26	0
Roger Craig	25	201	8.0	31	0

Top 5 Rushers	Car	Yds	Avg	Long	TD
Dexter Carter*	114	460	4.0	74-td	1
Roger Craig	141	439	3.1	26	1
Tom Rathman	101	318	3.1	22	7
Harry Sydney	35	166	4.7	19	2
Joe Montana	40	162	4.1	20	1

Top 5 Touchdowns	TD	Run	Rec	Ret	Pts
Jerry Rice	13	0	13	0	78
Tom Rathman	7	7	0	0	42
John Taylor	7	0	7	0	42
Brent Jones	5	0	5	0	30
Harry Sydney	3	2	1	0	18

Kicking	FG/Att	Lg	PAT/Att	Pts
Mike Cofer	24/36	56	39/39	111

Punts (10 or more)	No	Yds	Long	Avg	In 20
Barry Helton	69	2537	56	36.8	15

Most Interceptions	Most Sacks
Dave Waymer 7	Charles Haley 16

Washington Redskins

QBs (5 Att)	Att	Cmp	Pct	Yds	TD	Rate
Mark Rypien	304	166	54.6	2070	16	78.4
Stan Humphries	156	91	58.3	1015	3	57.5
Jeff Rutledge	68	40	58.8	455	2	82.7
Brian Mitchell*	6	3	50.0	40	0	71.5

Interceptions: Rypien 11, Humphries 10, Rutledge 1.
Also threw TD pass: Earnest Byner (1).

Top 5 Receivers	No	Yds	Avg	Long	TD
Gary Clark	75	1112	14.8	53-td	8
Art Monk	68	770	11.3	44	5
Ricky Sanders	56	727	13.0	38	3
Earnest Byner	31	279	9.0	19	1
Kelvin Bryant	26	248	9.5	37	1

Top 5 Rushers	Car	Yds	Avg	Long	TD
Earnest Byner	297	1219	4.1	22	6
Gerald Riggs	123	475	3.9	20	6
Stan Humphries	23	106	4.6	17	2
Reggie Dupard	19	85	4.5	11	0
Brian Mitchell*	15	81	5.4	21	1

Top 5 Touchdowns	TD	Run	Rec	Ret	Pts
Gary Clark	8	0	8	0	48
Earnest Byner	7	6	1	0	42
Gerald Riggs	6	6	0	0	36
Art Monk	5	0	5	0	30
Ricky Sanders	3	0	3	0	18

Kicking	FG/Att	Lg	PAT/Att	Pts
Chip Lohmiller	30/40	56	41/41	131

Punts (10 or more)	No	Yds	Long	Avg	In 20
Ralf Mojsiejenko	43	1687	53	39.2	17

Most Interceptions	Most Sacks
Martin Mayhew 7	Fred Stokes............ 7½

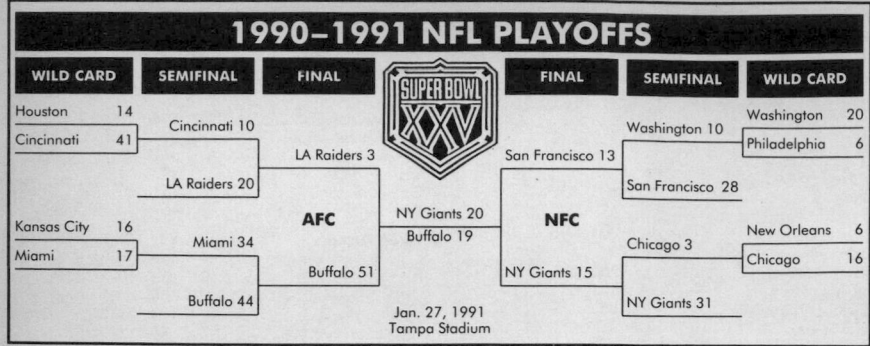

1990-1991 NFL PLAYOFFS

WILD CARD	SEMIFINAL	FINAL	SUPER BOWL XXV	FINAL	SEMIFINAL	WILD CARD
Houston 14						Washington 20
Cincinnati 41	Cincinnati 10				Washington 10	Philadelphia 6
		LA Raiders 3		San Francisco 13	San Francisco 28	
	LA Raiders 20					
		AFC	NY Giants 20	**NFC**		New Orleans 6
Kansas City 16			Buffalo 19		Chicago 3	Chicago 16
Miami 17	Miami 34			NY Giants 15		
		Buffalo 51			NY Giants 31	
	Buffalo 44					

Jan. 27, 1991
Tampa Stadium

Game Summaries

Team records listed in parentheses indicate records before game. Attendance numbers listed in parentheses indicate "No shows."

AFC

First Round

Kansas City (11-5)	3	7	6	0—**16**
Miami (12-4)	0	3	0	14—**17**

Touchdowns: MIA (2)—Tony Paige 1-yd run; Mark Clayton 12-yd pass from Marino. **KC** (1)— Stephone Paige 26-yd pass from Steve DeBerg.
  Field Goals: KC (3)—Nick Lowery (27,25,38 yds). **MIA** (1)—Pete Stoyanovich (58 yds).
  Date—Jan.5. **Att**—67,276 (5,791). **Time**—2:59.

Houston (9-7)	0	0	7	7—**14**
Cincinnati (9-7)	10	10	14	7—**41**

Touchdowns: CIN (5)—Ickey Woods 1-yd run; Harold Green 2-yd pass from Boomer Esiason; Eric Ball 3-yd run; Esiason 10-yd run; Eric Kattus 9-yd pass from Esiason. **HOU** (2)—Ernest Givins 16-yd pass from Cody Carlson; Givins 5-yd pass from Carlson.
  Field Goals: CIN (2)—Jim Breech (27,30 yds).
  Date—Jan.6. **Att**—60,012. **Time**—3:05.

Semifinals

Miami (13-4)	3	14	3	14—**34**
Buffalo (13-3)	13	14	3	14—**44**

Touchdowns: BUF (5)—Andre Reed 40-yd pass from Jim Kelly; Thurman Thomas 5-yd run; James Lofton 13-yd pass from Kelly; Thomas 5-yd run; Reed 26-yd pass from Kelly. **MIA** (4)—Mark Duper 64-yd pass from Dan Marino; Marino 2-yd run; Roy Foster 2-yd pass from Marino; Tony Martin 8-yd pass from Marino.
  Field Goals: BUF (2)—Scott Norwood (24,22,28 yds). **MIA** (2)—Pete Stoyanovich (49,22 yds).
  Date—Jan.12. **Att**—77,087 (3,165). **Time**—3:23.

Cincinnati (10-7)	0	3	0	7—**10**
LA Raiders (12-4)	0	7	3	10—**20**

Touchdowns: LA (2)—Mervyn Fernandez 13-yd pass from Jay Schroeder; Ethan Horton 41-yd pass from Schroeder. **CIN**—Stanford Jennings 8-yd pass from Boomer Esiason.
  Field Goals: LA (2)—Jeff Jaeger (49,25 yds). **CIN**— Jim Breech (27 yds).
  Date—Jan.13. **Att**—92,045 (443). **Time**—2:35.

NFC

First Round

Washington (10-6)	0	10	10	0—**20**
Philadelphia (10-6)	3	3	0	0— **6**

Touchdowns: WASH (2)—Art Monk 16-yd pass from Mark Rypien; Gary Clark 3-yd pass from Rypien.
  Field Goals: WASH (2)—Chip Lohmiller (20,19 yds). **PHI** (2)—Roger Ruzek (37,28 yds).
  Date—Jan.5. **Att**—65,287 (987). **Time**—2:55.

New Orleans (8-8)	0	3	0	3— **6**
Chicago (11-5)	3	7	3	3—**16**

Touchdown: CHI—James Thornton 18-yd pass from Mike Tomczak.
  Field Goals: CHI (3)—Kevin Butler (19,22,21 yds). **NO** (2)—Morten Andersen (47,38 yds).
  Date—Jan.6. **Att**—60,767 (6179). **Time**—3:14.

Semifinals

Washington (11-6)	10	0	0	0—**10**
San Francisco (14-2)	7	14	0	7—**28**

Touchdowns: SF (4)—Tom Rathman 1-yd run; Jerry Rice 10-yd pass from Joe Montana; Mike Sherrard 8-yd pass from Montana; Michael Carter 61-yd interception return. **WASH**—Art Monk 31-yd pass from Mark Rypien.
  Field Goal: WASH—Chip Lohmiller (44 yds).
  Date—Jan.12. **Att**—65,292 (1,001). **Time**—2:57.

Chicago (12-5)	0	3	0	0— **3**
NY Giants (13-3)	10	7	7	7—**31**

Touchdowns: NY (4)—Stephen Baker 21-yd pass from Jeff Hostetler; Howard Cross 5-yd pass from Hostetler; Hostetler 3-yd run; Maurice Carthon 1-yd run.
  Field Goal: NY—Matt Bahr (46 yds). **CHI**—Kevin Butler (33 yds).
  Date—Jan.13. **Att**—77,025 (228). **Time**—2:52.

AFC Championship

LA Raiders (13-4)	3	0	0	0—	3
Buffalo (14-3)	21	20	0	10—	51

Touchdowns: BUF (7)—James Lofton 13-yd pass from Jim Kelly; Thurman Thomas 12-yd run; Darryl Talley 27-yd interception return; Kenneth Davis 1-yd run; K.Davis 3-yd run; Lofton 8-yd pass from Kelly; K.Davis 1-yd run.
Field Goals: LA—Jeff Jaeger (41 yds); **BUF**— Scott Norwood (39 yds).
Date—Jan.20. **Att**—80,324 (38). **Time**—3:17.

NFC Championship

NY Giants (14-3)	3	3	3	6—	15
San Francisco (15-2)	3	3	7	0—	13

Touchdowns: SF—John Taylor 61-yd pass from Joe Montana.
Field Goals: NY (5)—Matt Bahr (28,42,46,38,42 yds); **SF** (2)—Mike Cofer (47,35 yds).
Date—Jan.20. **Att**—65,750 (584). **Time**—3:07.

Super Bowl XXV

Buffalo (15-3)	3	9	0	7—	19
NY Giants (15-3)	3	7	7	3—	20

1st Quarter
NY—Matt Bahr 28-yd FG, 7:14; BUF—Scott Norwood 23-yd FG, 9:09.

2nd Quarter
BUF—Don Smith 1-yd run (Norwood kick), 2:30; BUF—safety (QB Jeff Hostetler of NY tackled in end zone), 6:33; NY—Stephen Baker 14-yd pass from Hostetler (Bahr kick), 14:35.

3rd Quarter
NY—Ottis Anderson 1-yd run (Bahr kick), 9:29.

4th Quarter
BUF—Thurman Thomas 31-yd run (Norwood kick), 0:08; NY—Bahr 21-yd FG, 7:40.

Date: Jan. 27
Site: Tampa
Weather: Overcast
Attendance: 73,813
Time: 3:19
Favorite: Bills by 7
Surface: Grass
TV Rating: 41.8 (ABC)
Shares: Winners—$36,000
Losers: —$18,000

Team Statistics

	Bills	Giants
First downs	18	24
Rushing	8	10
Passing	9	13
Penalties	1	1
3rd down efficiency	1/8	9/16
4th down efficiency	0/0	0/1
Time of possession	19:27	40:33
Total offense (net yards)	371	386
Plays	56	73
Average gain	6.6	5.3
Rushes/yards	25/166	39/172
Passing yards	205	214
Completions/attempts	18/30	20/32
Times intercepted	0	0
Times sacked-yards lost	1/7	2/8
Fumbles-lost	1/0	0/0
Penalties-yards	6/35	5/31
Punts-Average	6/38.8	4/43.8
Punts blocked	0	0

Individual Statistics

Buffalo Bills

Passing

	Att	Cmp	Pct	Yds	TD	Int
Jim Kelly	30	18	60.0	212	0	0

Receiving

	No	Yds	Avg	Lg	TD
Andre Reed	8	62	7.8	20	0
Thurman Thomas	5	55	11.0	15	0
Kenneth Davis	2	23	11.5	19	0
Keith McKeller	2	11	5.5	6	0
James Lofton	1	61	61.0	61-td	0
TOTAL	18	212	11.8	61	0

Rushing

	Car	Yds	Avg	Long	TD
Thurman Thomas	15	135	9.0	31-td	1
Jim Kelly	6	23	3.8	9	0
Kenneth Davis	2	4	2.0	3	0
Jamie Mueller	1	3	3.0	3	0
Don Smith	1	1	1.0	1	1
TOTAL	25	166	6.6	31	2

Field Goals

	20-29	30-39	40-49	Total
Scott Norwood	1-1	0-0	0-1	1-2

Punting

	No	Yds	Long	Avg	In 20
Rick Tuten	6	233	47	38.8	2

Punt Returns

	FC	Ret	Yds	Long	Avg	TD
Al Edwards	3	0	0	0	0.0	0

Kickoff Returns

	No	Yds	Long	Avg	TD
Don Smith	4	66	24	16.5	0
Al Edwards	2	48	33	24.0	0

Sacks

	No
Bruce Smith	1
Jeff Wright	1

New York Giants

Passing

	Att	Cmp	Pct	Yds	TD	Int
Jeff Hostetler	32	20	62.5	222	1	0

Receiving

	No	Yds	Avg	Lg	TD
Mark Ingram	5	74	14.8	22	0
Mark Bavaro	5	50	10.0	19	0
Howard Cross	4	39	9.8	13	0
Stephen Baker	2	31	15.5	17	1
Dave Meggett	2	18	9.0	11	0
Ottis Anderson	1	7	7.0	7	0
Maurice Carthon	1	3	3.0	3	0
TOTAL	20	222	11.1	22	1

Rushing

	Car	Yds	Avg	Long	TD
Ottis Anderson	21	102	4.9	24	1
Dave Meggett	9	48	5.3	17	0
Maurice Carthon	3	12	4.0	5	0
Jeff Hostetler	6	10	1.7	5	0
TOTAL	39	172	4.4	24	1

Field Goals

	20-29	30-39	40-49	Total
Matt Bahr	2-2	0-0	0-0	2-2

Punting

	No	Yds	Long	Avg	In 20
Sean Landeta	4	175	54	43.8	2

Punt Returns

	FC	Ret	Yds	Long	Avg	TD
Dave Meggett	3	2	37	20	18.5	0

Kickoff Returns

	No	Yds	Long	Avg	TD
Dave Duerson	1	22	22	22.0	0
Dave Meggett	2	26	16	13.0	0

Sacks

	No
Leonard Marshall	1

Overall Playoff Statistics

New York Giants (3-0)

Passing	Att	Cmp	Pct	Yds	TD	Rate
Jeff Hostetler	76	45	59.2	510	3	92.5
Matt Cavanaugh	1	0	0.0	0	0	0.0
Dave Meggett	1	0	0.0	0	0	0.0

Interceptions: None.

Receiving	No	Yds	Avg	Long	TD
Mark Bavaro	13	129	9.9	19	0
Mark Ingram	11	168	15.3	22	0
Stephen Baker	7	111	15.9	25	2
Howard Cross	5	44	8.8	13	1
Dave Meggett	4	33	8.3	15	0
Ottis Anderson	3	16	5.3	7	0
Robert Mrosko	1	6	6.0	6	0
Maurice Carthon	1	3	3.0	3	0
TOTAL	45	510	11.3	25	3

Rushing	Car	Yds	Avg	Long	TD
Ottis Anderson	62	249	4.0	27	1
Dave Meggett	21	102	4.9	17	0
Jeff Hostetler	15	64	4.3	11	1
Maurice Carthon	13	39	3.0	6	1
Lewis Tillman	9	31	3.4	6	0
Gary Reasons	1	30	30.0	30	0
Rodney Hampton	2	3	1.5	3	0
TOTAL	123	518	4.2	30	3

Touchdowns	TD	Run	Rec	Ret	Pts
Stephen Baker	2	0	2	0	12
Ottis Anderson	1	1	0	0	6
Maurice Carthon	1	1	0	0	6
Howard Cross	1	0	1	0	6
Jeff Hostetler	1	1	0	0	6
TOTAL	6	3	3	0	36

Kicking	FG/Att	Lg	PAT/Att	Pts
Matt Bahr	8/9	46	6/6	30

Punting	No	Yds	Long	Avg	In 20
Sean Landeta	10	421	55	42.1	3

Interceptions		Sacks	
Mark Collins	1	Leonard Marshall	3
Everson Walls	1	Erik Howard	½
TOTAL	2	Lawrence Taylor	½
		TOTAL	4

Fumbles Recovered
Lawrence Taylor 1

Buffalo Bills (2-1)

Passing	Att	Cmp	Pct	Yds	TD	Rate
Jim Kelly	82	54	65.9	851	5	110.4

Interceptions: Kelly (2).

Receiving	No	Yds	Avg	Long	TD
Andre Reed	14	213	15.2	43	2
James Lofton	13	323	24.8	61	3
Thurman Thomas	13	154	11.8	20	0
Keith McKeller	8	70	8.8	23	0
Kenneth Davis	3	26	8.7	19	0
Steve Tasker	2	53	26.5	44	0
Al Edwards	1	12	12.0	12	0
TOTAL	54	851	15.8	61	5

Rushing	Car	Yds	Avg	Long	TD
Thurman Thomas	72	390	5.4	31-td	4
Jim Kelly	13	72	5.5	16	0
Kenneth Davis	12	25	2.1	6	3
Jamie Mueller	4	9	2.3	6	0
Don Smith	4	4	1.0	4	1
Carwell Gardner	1	23	23.0	23	0
Frank Reich	2	−1	−0.5	−1	0
TOTAL	108	522	4.8	31-td	8

Touchdowns	TD	Run	Rec	Ret	Pts
Thurman Thomas	4	4	0	0	24
Kenneth Davis	3	3	0	0	18
James Lofton	3	0	3	0	18
Andre Reed	2	0	2	0	12
Don Smith	1	1	0	0	6
Darryl Talley	1	0	0	1*	6
TOTAL	14	8	5	1	84

*27-yard interception return.

Kicking	FG/Att	Lg	PAT/Att	Pts
Scott Norwood	5/6	39	13/14	28

Punting	No	Yds	Long	Avg	In 20
Rick Tuten	9	355	47	39.4	4

Interceptions		Sacks	
Mark Kelso	2	Kirby Jackson	1
Darryl Talley	2	Bruce Smith	1
Ray Bentley	1	Jeff Wright	1
Nate Odomes	1	TOTAL	3
Leonard Smith	1		
TOTAL	7		

Annual Awards

The NFL does not sanction any postseason awards for player or coaches, but many are given out. Among the presenters for the 1990 regular season were AP, UPI, The Sporting News and the Pro Football Writers of America. MVP awards are also given out by the Maxwell Club of Philadelphia (Bert Bell Award) and the NFL Players Assn.(Jim Thorpe Trophy).

Most Valuable Player — Selectors
Randall Cunningham, Phila., QB .... Bell,PFWA
Warren Moon, Houston, QB. .... Thorpe
Joe Montana, San Francisco, QB. .... AP
Jerry Rice, San Francisco, WR .... TSN

Offensive Players of the Year
NFL — Warren Moon, Houston, QB .... AP
AFC — Warren Moon, Houston, QB .... UPI
NFC — Randall Cunningham, Philadelphia, QB .... UPI

Defensive Players of the Year
NFL — Bruce Smith, Buffalo, DE .... AP
AFC — Bruce Smith, Buffalo, DE .... UPI
NFC — Charles Haley, San Francisco, LB .... UPI

Rookies of the Year — Selectors
NFL — Mark Carrier, Chicago, S .... PFWA
NFL — Richmond Webb, Miami, OT .... TSN
AFC — Richmond Webb, Miami, OT .... UPI
NFC — Mark Carrier, Chicago, S .... UPI
Offense — Emmitt Smith, Dallas, RB .... AP
Defense — Mark Carrier, Chicago, S .... AP

Coaches of the Year
NFL — Jimmy Johnson, Dallas .... AP
George Seifert, San Francisco .... TSN
Art Shell, LA Raiders .... PFWA
AFC — Art Shell, LA Raiders .... UPI
NFC — Jimmy Johnson, Dallas .... UPI

All-NFL Team

The 1990 All-NFL team combining the All-Pro selections of the Associated Press and the Pro Football Writers of America (PFWA). Holdovers from the 1989 All-NFL team in **bold** type.

Offense

Pos		Selectors
WR	**Jerry Rice**, San Francisco	AP,PFWA
WR	Andre Rison, Atlanta	AP,PFWA
TE	**Keith Jackson**, Philadelphia	AP,PFWA
T	**Anthony Munoz**, Cincinnati	AP,PFWA
T	**Jim Lachey**, Washington	AP,PFWA
G	**Bruce Matthews**, Houston	AP,PFWA
G	Randall McDaniel, Minnesota	AP
G	Steve Wisniewski, LA Raiders	PFWA
C	Kent Hull, Buffalo	AP,PFWA
QB	**Joe Montana**, San Francisco	AP
QB	Randall Cunningham, Philadelphia	PFWA
RB	Thurman Thomas, Buffalo	AP,PFWA
RB	**Barry Sanders**, Detroit	AP,PFWA

Defense

Pos		Selectors
DE	**Reggie White**, Philadelphia	AP,PFWA
DE	Bruce Smith, Buffalo	AP,PFWA
DT	**Michael Dean Perry**, Cleveland	AP,PFWA
DT	Jerome Brown, Philadelphia	AP
DT	Ray Childress, Houston	PFWA
OLB	Derrick Thomas, Kansas City	AP,PFW
OLB	Charles Haley, San Francisco	AP,PFWA
ILB	Pepper Johnson, NY Giants	AP,PFWA
ILB	John Offerdahl, Miami	AP,PFWA
CD	Rod Woodson, Pittsburgh	AP,PFWA
CD	**Albert Lewis**, Kansas City	AP,PFWA
S	**Ronnie Lott**, San Francisco	AP,PFWA
S	Joey Browner, Minnesota	AP,PFWA

Specialists

K	Nick Lowery, Kansas City	AP,PFWA	KR	Mel Gray, Detroit	AP,PFWA
P	**Sean Landeta**, NY Giants	AP,PFWA	PR	**Dave Meggett**, NY Giants	PFWA

Pro Bowl Game

41st NFL Pro Bowl Game and 21st AFC-NFC contest (NFC leads series, 12-9). **Date:** Feb.3 at Aloha Stadium in Honolulu; **Coaches:** Art Shell, LA Raiders (AFC) and George Seifert, San Francisco (NFC); **MVP:** quarterback Jim Kelly, Buffalo (AFC), 13 of 19 for 210 yards and two TDs.

American	3	0	3	17	23
National	0	7	7	7	21

1st Quarter
AFC—Nick Lowery 26-yd FG, 4:08.

2nd Quarter
NFC—Johnny Johnson 1-yd run (Morten Andersen kick), 14:13.

3rd Quarter
AFC—Lowery 43-yd FG, 8:34; **NFC**—J.Johnson 9-yd run (Andersen kick), 13:56. kick), 14:41.

4th Quarter
AFC—Andre Reed 20-yd pass from Jim Kelly (Lowery kick), 3:07; **NFC**—Barry Sanders 22-yd run (Andersen kick), 9:49; **AFC**—Lowery 34-yd FG, 12:02; **AFC**—Ernest Givins 13-yd pass from Kelly (Lowery kick), 13:11. **Att**—50,345; **Time**—3:06.

STARTING LINEUPS

American Conference

Offense		Defense	
WR	Andre Reed, Buf.	E	Greg Townsend, LA
T	Richmond Webb, Mia.	NT	M.D.Perry, Cle.
G	Mike Munchak, Hou.	E	Bruce Smith, Buf.
C	Kent Hull, Buf.	OLB	Leslie O'Neal, SD
G	Bruce Matthews, Hou.	ILB	David Little, Pit.
T	Bruce Armstrong, NE	ILB	Shane Conlan, Buf.
TE	Rodney Holman, Cin.	OLB	Derrick Thomas, KC
WR	Anthony Miller, SD	CB	Albert Lewis, KC
QB	Warren Moon, Hou.	CB	Rod Woodson, Pit.
RB	Thurman Thomas, Buf.	S	David Fulcher, Cin.
RB	Bobby Humphrey, Den.	S	Steve Atwater, Den.
K	Nick Lowery, KC	P	Rohn Stark, Ind.

Bench
Offense: WR—Ernest Givins, Hou. and Drew Hill, Hou.; **TE**—Ferrell Edmunds, Mia; **T**—Will Wolford, Buf.; **G**—Steve Wisniewski, LA; **C**—Don Mosebar, LA; **QB**—Jim Kelly, Buf.; **RB**—James Brooks, Cin. and John L.Williams, Sea.
Defense: E—Jeff Cross, Mia.; **NT**—Ray Childress, Hou.; **LB**—Cornelius Bennett, Buf. and Mike Johnson, Cle.; **CB**—Kevin Ross, KC; **S**—Dennis Smith, Den.
Specialists: KR—Clarence Verdin, Ind.; **Sp. Teams**—Steve Tasker, Buf.
Replacements: RB Brooks and Williams for Marion Butts, SD and Bo Jackson, LA; OT Wolford for Anthony Munoz, Cin.; and LB Johnson for John Offerdahl, Mia.
Rookie: Webb.

National Conference

Offense		Defense	
WR	Jerry Rice, SF	E	Reggie White, Phi.
T	Jim Lachey, Wash.	NT	Jerry Ball, Det.
G	Randall McDaniel, Min.	E	Chris Doleman, Min.
C	Jay Hilgenberg, Chi.	OLB	Charles Haley, SF
G	Mark Bortz, Chi.	ILB	Pepper Johnson, NY
T	Jackie Slater, LA	ILB	Mike Singletary, Chi.
TE	Keith Jackson, Phi.	OLB	Lawrence Taylor, NY
WR	Andre Rison, Atl.	CB	Darrell Green, Wash.
QB	Randall Cunningham, Phi.	CB	Carl Lee, Min.
RB	Barry Sanders, Det.	S	Joey Browner, Min.
RB	Earnest Byner, Wash.	S	Ronnie Lott, SF
K	Morten Andersen, NO	P	Sean Landeta, NY

Bench
Offense: WR—Gary Clark, Wash., and Sterling Sharpe, GB; **TE**—Steve Jordan, Min.; **T**—Lomas Brown, Det.; **G**—Guy McIntyre, SF; **C**—Bart Oates, NY; **QB**—Jim Everett, LA; **RB**—Johnny Johnson, Pho. and Emmitt Smith, Dal.
Defense: E—Richard Dent, Chi.; **NT**—Erik Howard, NY; **LB**—Vaughn Johnson, NO and Pat Swilling, NO; **CB**—Wayne Haddix, TB; **S**—Mark Carrier, Chi.
Specialists: KR—Mel Gray, Det.; **Sp. Teams**—Reyna Thompson, NY
Replacements: QB Everett for Joe Montana, SF; RB Smith for Neal Anderson, Chi.; NT Howard for Jerome Brown, Phi.
Rookies: Carrier, J.Johnson and E.Smith.

NFL College Draft

First and second round selections at the 60th annual NFL College Draft held April 21-22, 1991, in New York City. Six underclassmen were among the first 55 players chosen and are listed in CAPITAL letters.

First Round

No		Pos
1	a-Dallas . . . . Russell Maryland, Miami-FL	DT
2	Cleveland . . . . Eric Turner, UCLA	S
3	Atlanta . . . . Bruce Pickens, Nebraska	CB
4	Denver . . . . Mike Croel, Nebraska	LB
5	LA Rams . . . . Todd Lyght, Notre Dame	CB
6	Phoenix . . . . ERIC SWANN, No college	DE
7	Tampa Bay . . . . Charles McRae, Tennessee	OT
8	b-Philadelphia . . . . Antone Davis, Tennessee	OT
9	San Diego . . . . Stanley Richard, Texas	S
10	Detroit . . . . HERMAN MOORE, Virginia	WR
11	c-New England . . . . . Pat Harlow, USC	OT
12	Dallas . . . . Alvin Harper, Tennessee	WR
13	d-Atlanta . . . . Mike Pritchard, Colorado	WR
14	e-New England . . . . . LEONARD RUSSELL, Ariz.St.	RB
15	Pittsburgh . . . . Huey Richardson, Florida	LB
16	Seattle . . . . Dan McGwire, S.Diego St.	QB
17	f-Washington . . . . Bobby Wilson, Mich.St.	DT
18	Cincinnati . . . . Alfred Williams, Colorado	LB
19	g-Green Bay . . . . Vinnie Clark, Ohio St.	CB
20	h-Detroit . . . . Kelvin Pritchett, Ole Miss	DT
21	Kansas City . . . . Harvey Williams, LSU	RB
22	Chicago . . . . Stan Thomas, Texas	OT
23	Miami . . . . Randal Hill, Miami-FL	WR
24	LA Raiders . . . . TODD MARINOVICH, USC	QB
25	San Francisco . . . . . . Ted Washington, Louisville	DT
26	Buffalo . . . . Henry Jones, Illinois	CB
27	NY Giants . . . . Jarrod Bunch, Michigan	FB

Acquired Picks : a—from New England; **b**—from Green Bay; **c**—from Minnesota through Dallas; **d**—from Indianapolis; **e**—from New Orleans through Dallas; **f**—from Houston through New England and Dallas; **g**—from Philadelphia; **h**—from Washington through Dallas.

Second Round

No		Pos
28	i-Houston . . . . Mike Dumas, Indiana	S
29	Cleveland . . . . ED KING, Auburn	G
30	Denver . . . . Reggie Johnson, Fla.St.	TE
31	LA Rams . . . . Roman Phifer, UCLA	LB
32	Phoenix . . . . Mike Jones, N.C.State	DE
33	Atlanta . . . . Brett Favre, So.Miss	QB
34	NY Jets . . . . Browning Nagle, Louisville	QB
35	Green Bay . . . . Esera Tuaolo, Oregon St.	DT
36	San Diego . . . . George Thornton, Alabama	DT
37	j-Dallas . . . . Dixon Edwards, Mich.St.	LB
38	k-Houston . . . . Darryl Lewis, Arizona	CB
39	l-San Diego . . . . Eric Bieniemy, Colorado	RB
40	Indianapolis . . . . Shane Curry, Miami-FL	DE
41	m-New England . . . . . Jerome Henderson, Clemson	DB
42	New Orleans . . . . Wesley Carroll, Miami-FL	WR
43	n-LA Raiders . . . . Nick Bell, Iowa	RB
44	Houston . . . . John Flannery, Syracuse	C
45	o-San Francisco . . . . . Ricky Watters, Notre Dame	RB
46	Pittsburgh . . . . Jeff Graham, Ohio St.	WR
47	p-San Diego . . . . Eric Moten, Mich.St.	G
48	Philadelphia . . . . JESSE CAMPBELL, N.C.State	DB
49	Chicago . . . . Chris Zorich, Notre Dame	DT
50	Kansas City . . . . Joe Valerio, Penn	OT
51	Seattle . . . . Doug Thomas, Clemson	WR
52	q-Cincinnati . . . . Lamar Rogers, Auburn	DT
53	San Francisco . . . . . . John Johnson, Clemson	LB
54	Buffalo . . . . Phil Hansen, N.Dakota St.	DE
55	NY Giants . . . . Kanavis McGhee, Colorado	LB

Acquired Picks: i—from New England; **j**—from Detroit; **k**—from Minnesota through Dallas; **l**—from Tampa Bay; **m**—from Dallas; **n**—from Seattle; **o**—from Cincinnati; **p**—from Washington; **q**—from Miami through San Francisco.

Notes: The NY Jets forfeited their 1991 first round pick (No.8 overall) by selecting WR Rob Moore of Syracuse in the 1990 Supplemental Draft. Also, Notre Dame junior RB Raghib (Rocket) Ismail, the odds-on overall Number One pick, bypassed the NFL on Draft Day to sign with Toronto of the Canadian Football League. Ismail was chosen by the LA Raiders in the 4th round (No.100 overall).

Canadian Football League

Final 1990 Standings

Division champions (*) and other playoff qualifiers (†) are noted.

Eastern Division

	W	L	T	Pts	PF	PA	vs Div
*Winnipeg	12	6	0	24	472	398	7-3-0
†Toronto	10	8	0	20	689	538	6-4-0
†Ottawa	7	11	0	14	540	602	3-7-0
Hamilton	6	12	0	12	476	628	4-6-0

Head Coaches: Win—Mike Riley (4th season); **Tor**—Don Matthews (1st); **Ott**—Steve Goldman (2nd); **Ham**—replaced Al Bruno (8th, 4-8) with David Beckman (2-4) on Sept.24.

Western Division

	W	L	T	Pts	PF	PA	vs Div
*Calgary	11	6	1	23	588	566	5-4-1
†Edmonton	10	8	0	20	612	510	6-4-0
†Saskatchewan	9	9	0	18	557	592	4-6-0
British Columbia	6	11	1	13	520	620	4-5-1

Head Coaches: Calg—Wally Buono (1st season); **Edm**—Joe Faragalli (4th); **Sask**—John Gregory (4th); **BC**—replaced Larry Kuharich (1st, 2-7-1) with interim coach Jim Young (0-1) on Sept.10, then with Bob O'Billovich (4-3) on Sept.14.

1990 Playoffs

Division Semifinals (Nov.11)
Eastern: at Toronto 34 . . . . Ottawa 25
Western: at Edmonton 43 . . . . Saskatchewan 27

Division Championships (Nov.18)
Eastern: at Winnipeg 20 . . . . Toronto 17
Western: Edmonton 43 . . . . at Calgary 23

78th Grey Cup

Nov. 25, 1990 at B.C.Place, Vancouver
Attendance: 46,968

Edmonton (12-8)	0	4	0	7	**11**
Winnipeg (13-6)	10	0	28	12	**50**

Players of the Game
Offense: Tom Burgess, Winnipeg, QB
(18-of-31, 286 yards, 3 TDs)
Defense: Greg Battle, Winnipeg, LB
(2 INTs, 1 TD, 4 tackles)
Canadian: Warren Hudson, Winnipeg, FB
(4 catches, 2 TDs)

Regular Season Award Winners

Player . . . . Mike Clemons, Toronto, RB
Canadian . . . . Ray Elgaard, Saskatchewan, Slot
Off.Lineman . . . . Jim Mills, Brit.Columbia, OT
Def.Player . . . . Greg Battle, Winnipeg, LB
Rookie . . . . Reggie Barnes, Ottawa, RB
Coach . . . . Mike Riley, Winnipeg

THE 1992 INFORMATION PLEASE SPORTS ALMANAC

PRO FOOTBALL
S T A T I S T I C S

THROUGH THE YEARS
1920-1991

SUPERBOWLS • NFL LEADERS

SEC
B

PAGE
199

The Super Bowl

The first AFL-NFL World Championship Game, as it was originally called, was played seven months after the two leagues agreed to merge in June of 1966. It became the Super Bowl (complete with roman numerals) by the third game in 1969. The Super Bowl winner has been presented the Vince Lombardi Trophy since 1971. Lombardi, whose Green Bay teams won the first two title games, died in 1970.

NFL champions (1966-69) and NFC champions (since 1970) are listed in CAPITAL letters.

Multiple winners: Pittsburgh and San Francisco (4); Oakland-LA Raiders (3); Dallas, Green Bay, Miami, NY Giants and Washington (2).

Season	Bowl	Winner	Head Coach	Score	Loser	Head Coach	Site
1966	I	GREEN BAY	Vince Lombardi	35-21	Kansas City	Hank Stram	Los Angeles
1967	II	GREEN BAY	Vince Lombardi	33-14	Oakland	John Rauch	Miami
1968	III	NY Jets	Weeb Ewbank	16- 7	BALTIMORE	Don Shula	Miami
1969	IV	Kansas City	Hank Stram	23- 7	MINNESOTA	Bud Grant	New Orleans
1970	V	Baltimore	Don McCafferty	16-13	DALLAS	Tom Landry	Miami
1971	VI	DALLAS	Tom Landry	24- 3	Miami	Don Shula	New Orleans
1972	VII	Miami	Don Shula	14- 7	WASHINGTON	George Allen	Los Angeles
1973	VIII	Miami	Don Shula	24- 7	MINNESOTA	Bud Grant	Houston
1974	IX	Pittsburgh	Chuck Noll	16- 6	MINNESOTA	Bud Grant	New Orleans
1975	X	Pittsburgh	Chuck Noll	21-17	DALLAS	Tom Landry	Miami
1976	XI	Oakland	John Madden	32-14	MINNESOTA	Bud Grant	Pasadena
1977	XII	DALLAS	Tom Landry	27-10	Denver	Red Miller	New Orleans
1978	XIII	Pittsburgh	Chuck Noll	35-31	DALLAS	Tom Landry	Miami
1979	XIV	Pittsburgh	Chuck Noll	31-19	LA RAMS	Ray Malavasi	Pasadena
1980	XV	Oakland	Tom Flores	27-10	PHILADELPHIA	Dick Vermeil	New Orleans
1981	XVI	SAN FRANCISCO	Bill Walsh	26-21	Cincinnati	Forrest Gregg	Pontiac, MI
1982	XVII	WASHINGTON	Joe Gibbs	27-17	Miami	Don Shula	Pasadena
1983	XVIII	LA Raiders	Tom Flores	38- 9	WASHINGTON	Joe Gibbs	Tampa
1984	XIX	SAN FRANCISCO	Bill Walsh	38-16	Miami	Don Shula	Stanford
1985	XX	CHICAGO	Mike Ditka	46-10	New England	Raymond Berry	New Orleans
1986	XXI	NY GIANTS	Bill Parcells	39-20	Denver	Dan Reeves	Pasadena
1987	XXII	WASHINGTON	Joe Gibbs	42-10	Denver	Dan Reeves	San Diego
1988	XXIII	SAN FRANCISCO	Bill Walsh	20-16	Cincinnati	Sam Wyche	Miami
1989	XXIV	SAN FRANCISCO	George Seifert	55-10	Denver	Dan Reeves	New Orleans
1990	XXV	NY GIANTS	Bill Parcells	20-19	Buffalo	Marv Levy	Tampa

Most Valuable Players

Currently selected by an 11-member panel made up of national pro football writers and broadcasters chosen by the NFL. Presented by *Sport* magazine from 1967-89 and by the NFL since 1990. Winners who did not play for Super Bowl champions are in **bold** type.

Multiple winners: Joe Montana (3); Terry Bradshaw and Bart Starr (2).

Bowl	Date	Pos		Bowl	Date	Pos	
I	1/15/67	QB	Bart Starr, Green Bay	XIII	1/21/79	QB	Terry Bradshaw, Pittsburgh
II	1/14/68	QB	Bart Starr, Green Bay	XIV	1/20/80	QB	Terry Bradshaw, Pittsburgh
III	1/12/69	QB	Joe Namath, NY Jets	XV	1/25/81	QB	Jim Plunkett, Oakland
IV	1/11/70	QB	Len Dawson, Kansas City	XVI	1/24/82	QB	Joe Montana, San Francisco
V	1/17/71	LB	**Chuck Howley**, Dallas	XVII	1/30/83	RB	John Riggins, Washington
VI	1/16/72	QB	Roger Staubach, Dallas	XVIII	1/22/84	RB	Marcus Allen, LA Raiders
VII	1/14/73	S	Jake Scott, Miami	XIX	1/20/85	QB	Joe Montana, San Francisco
VIII	1/13/74	RB	Larry Csonka, Miami	XX	1/26/86	DE	Richard Dent, Chicago
IX	1/12/75	RB	Franco Harris, Pittsburgh				
X	1/18/76	WR	Lynn Swann, Pittsburgh	XXI	1/25/87	QB	Phil Simms, NY Giants
				XXII	1/31/88	QB	Doug Williams, Washington
XI	1/ 9/77	WR	Fred Biletnikoff, Oakland	XXIII	1/22/89	WR	Jerry Rice, San Francisco
XII	1/15/78	DE	Harvey Martin, Dallas and	XXIV	1/28/90	QB	Joe Montana, San Francisco
		DT	Randy White, Dallas	XXV	1/27/91	RB	Ottis Anderson, NY Giants

All-Time Super Bowl Leaders
Through Super Bowl XXV, Jan. 27, 1991.

CAREER

Passing

Yards Gained	Gm	Att	Cmp	Pct	Yds
Joe Montana, SF	4	122	83	68.0	1142
Terry Bradshaw, Pit	4	84	49	58.3	932
Roger Staubach, Dal	4	98	61	62.2	734
John Elway, Den	3	101	46	45.5	669
Fran Tarkenton, Min	3	89	46	51.7	489
Bart Starr, GB	2	47	29	61.7	452
Jim Plunkett, Raiders	2	46	29	63.0	433
Joe Theismann, Wash	2	58	31	53.4	386
Len Dawson, KC	2	44	28	63.6	353
Doug Williams, Wash	1	29	18	62.1	340

Touchdown Passes	Gm	TD	Int
Joe Montana, San Francisco	4	11	0
Terry Bradshaw, Pittsburgh	4	9	4
Roger Staubach, Dallas	4	8	4
Jim Plunkett, Oak-LA Raiders	2	4	0
Doug Williams, Washington	1	4	1
Phil Simms, NY Giants	1	3	0
Bart Starr, Green Bay	2	3	1
Daryle Lamonica, Oak.Raiders	1	2	1
Ken Anderson, Cincinnati	1	2	2
Len Dawson, Kansas City	2	2	2
Joe Theismann, Washington	2	2	4
John Elway, Denver	3	2	6

Receiving

Catches	Gm	No	Yds	Avg	TD
Roger Craig, SF	3	20	212	10.6	3
Jerry Rice, SF	2	18	363	20.2	4
Lynn Swann, Pit	4	16	364	22.8	3
Chuck Foreman, Min	3	15	139	9.3	0
Cliff Branch, Raiders	3	14	181	12.9	3
Preston Pearson, Bal-Pit-Dal	5	12	105	8.8	0
John Stallworth, Pit	4	11	268	24.4	3
Dan Ross, Cin	1	11	104	9.5	2
Three tied with 10 each.					

Super Bowl Appearances
Through Super Bowl XXV (1991), nine NFL teams have yet to play for the Vince Lombardi Trophy. In alphabetical order: Atlanta, Cleveland, Detroit, Houston, New Orleans, Phoenix, San Diego, Seattle and Tampa Bay. Of the 19 teams that have made the trip, Dallas and Miami have the most appearances (5) while Pittsburgh and San Francisco have the most titles (4).

App		W	L	Pct	PF	PA
5	Dallas	2	3	.400	112	85
5	Miami	2	3	.400	74	103
4	Pittsburgh	4	0	1.000	103	73
4	San Francisco	4	0	1.000	139	63
4	Oakland-LA Raiders	3	1	.750	111	66
4	Washington	2	2	.500	85	79
4	Minnesota	0	4	.000	34	95
3	Denver	0	3	.000	50	163
2	Green Bay	2	0	1.000	68	24
2	NY Giants	2	0	1.000	59	39
2	Baltimore Colts	1	1	.500	23	29
2	Kansas City	1	1	.500	33	42
2	Cincinnati	0	2	.000	37	46
1	Chicago	1	0	1.000	46	10
1	NY Jets	1	0	1.000	16	7
1	Buffalo	0	1	.000	19	20
1	LA Rams	0	1	.000	19	31
1	New England	0	1	.000	10	46
1	Philadelphia	0	1	.000	10	27

Rushing

Yards Gained	Gm	Car	Yds	Avg	TD
Franco Harris, Pit	4	101	354	3.5	4
Larry Csonka, Mia	3	57	297	5.2	2
John Riggins, Wash	2	64	230	3.6	2
Timmy Smith, Wash	1	22	204	9.3	2
Roger Craig, SF	3	52	201	3.9	2
Marcus Allen, Raiders	1	20	191	9.5	2
Tony Dorsett, Dal	2	31	162	5.2	1
Mark van Eeghen, Raiders	2	37	153	4.1	0
Rocky Bleier, Pit	4	44	144	3.3	0
Walt Garrison, Dal	2	26	139	5.3	0

All-Purpose Running

Yards Gained	Gm	Run	Rec	Ret	Total
Franco Harris, Pit	4	354	114	0	468
Roger Craig, SF	3	201	212	0	413
Lynn Swann, Pit	4	-7	364	34	391
Jerry Rice, SF	2	5	363	0	368
Larry Csonka, Mia	3	297	17	0	314
Fulton Walker, Mia	2	0	0	298	298
Preston Pearson, Balt-Pit-Dal	5	31	105	122	258
John Riggins, Wash	2	230	16	0	246
Ricky Sanders, Wash	1	-4	193	46	235
Chuck Foreman, Min	3	80	139	0	219
Tony Dorsett, Dal	2	162	55	0	217
Wendall Tyler, Rams-SF	2	125	90	0	215
Timmy Smith, Wash	1	204	9	0	213
Marcus Allen, Raiders	1	191	18	0	209

Scoring

Points	Gm	TD	FG	PAT	Pts
Roger Craig, SF	3	4	0	0	24
Franco Harris, Pit	4	4	0	0	24
Jerry Rice, SF	2	4	0	0	24
Ray Wersching, SF	2	0	5	7	22
Don Chandler, GB	2	0	4	8	20
Cliff Branch, Raiders	3	3	0	0	18
John Stallworth, Pit	4	3	0	0	18
Lynn Swann, Pit	4	3	0	0	18
Chris Bahr, Raiders	2	0	3	8	17
Mike Cofer, SF	2	0	2	9	15
Uwe von Schamann, Mia	2	0	4	3	15

Touchdowns	Gm	TD	Run	Rec	Ret
Roger Craig, SF	3	4	2	2	0
Franco Harris, Pit	4	4	4	0	0
Jerry Rice, SF	2	4	0	4	0
Cliff Branch, Raiders	3	3	0	3	0
John Stallworth, Pit	4	3	0	3	0
Lynn Swann, Pit	4	3	0	3	0
Eighteen tied with 2 each.					

Miscellaneous
Interceptions

	Gm	No	Yds	TD
Chuck Howley, Dallas	2	3	63	0
Rod Martin, Oakland-LA Raiders	2	3	44	0
Six tied with 2 each.				

Punting Average
(Minimum 10 punts)

	Gm	No	Yds	Avg
Jerrel Wilson, KC	2	11	511	46.5
Ray Guy, Raiders	3	14	587	41.9
Larry Seiple, Mia	3	15	620	41.3

SINGLE GAME

Passing

Yards Gained	Year	Att/Cmp	Yds
Joe Montana, SF vs Cin	1989	36/23	357
Doug Williams, Wash vs Den	1988	29/18	340
Joe Montana, SF vs Mia	1985	35/24	331
Terry Bradshaw, Pit vs Dal	1979	30/17	318
Dan Marino, Mia vs SF	1985	50/29	318
Terry Bradshaw, Pit vs Rams	1980	21/14	309
John Elway, Den vs NYG	1987	37/22	304
Ken Anderson, Cin vs SF	1982	34/25	300
Joe Montana, SF vs Den	1990	29/22	297
Ron Jaworski, Phi vs Raid	1981	38/18	291

Touchdown Passes	Year	TD	Int
Joe Montana, SF vs Den	1990	5	0
Terry Bradshaw, Pit vs Dal	1979	4	1
Doug Williams, Wash vs Den	1988	4	1
Roger Staubach, Dal vs Pit	1979	3	1
Jim Plunkett, Raiders vs Phi	1981	3	0
Joe Montana, SF vs Mia	1985	3	0
Phil Simms, NYG vs Den	1987	3	0

Note: QBs have thrown two TD passes in a game nine times.

Scoring

Points	Year	TD	FG	PAT	Pts
Roger Craig, SF vs Mia.	1985	3	0	0	18
Jerry Rice, SF vs Den.	1990	3	0	0	18
Don Chandler, GB vs Raid	1968	0	4	3	15
Ray Wersching, SF vs Cin.	1982	0	4	2	14
Kevin Butler, Chi vs NE.	1986	0	3	5	14

Fourteen tied with 12 points each (2 TDs).

Touchdowns	Year	TD	Run	Rec
Roger Craig, SF vs Mia.	1985	3	1	2
Jerry Rice, SF vs Den.	1990	3	0	3
Max McGee, GB vs KC	1967	2	0	2
Bill Miller, Raid vs GB	1968	2	0	2
Larry Csonka, Mia vs Min	1974	2	2	0
Pete Banaszak, Raid vs Min	1977	2	2	0
John Stallworth, Pit vs Dal	1979	2	0	2
Franco Harris, Pit vs Rams	1980	2	2	0
Cliff Branch, Raid vs Phi	1981	2	0	2
Dan Ross, Cin vs SF	1982	2	0	2
Marcus Allen, Raid vs Wash.	1984	2	2	0
Jim McMahon, Chi vs NE.	1986	2	2	0
Ricky Sanders, Wash vs Den	1988	2	0	2
Timmy Smith, Wash vs Den	1988	2	2	0
Tom Rathman, SF vs Den.	1990	2	2	0

Receiving

Catches	Year	No	Yds	TD
Dan Ross, Cin vs SF	1982	11	104	2
Jerry Rice, SF vs Cin	1989	11	215	1
Ricky Sanders, Wash vs Den	1988	9	193	2
George Sauer, NYJ vs Bal	1969	8	133	0
Roger Craig, SF vs Cin	1989	8	101	0
Andre Reed, Buf vs NYG	1991	8	62	0
Max McGee, GB vs KC	1967	7	138	2
John Henderson, Min vs KC	1970	7	111	0
Lynn Swann, Pit vs Dal	1979	7	124	1
Stanley Morgan, NE vs Chi	1986	7	70	0
Jerry Rice, SF vs Den.	1990	7	148	3

Rushing

Yards Gained	Year	Car	Yds	TD
Timmy Smith, Wash vs Den	1988	22	204	2
Marcus Allen, Raid vs Wash.	1984	20	191	2
John Riggins, Wash vs Mia	1983	38	166	1
Franco Harris, Pit vs Min	1975	34	158	1
Larry Csonka, Mia vs Min	1974	33	145	2
Clarence Davis, Raid vs Min	1977	16	137	0
Thurman Thomas, Buf vs NYG	1991	15	135	1
Matt Snell, NYJ vs Bal.	1969	30	121	1
Tom Matte, Bal vs NYJ.	1969	11	116	0
Larry Csonka, Mia vs Wash.	1973	15	112	1

All-Purpose Running

Yards Gained	Year	Yds
Ricky Sanders, Wash vs Den	1988	235
Jerry Rice, SF vs Cin	1989	220
Marcus Allen, Raiders vs Wash	1984	209
Stephen Starring, NE vs Chi.	1986	192
Fulton Walker, Mia vs Wash	1983	190
Thurman Thomas, Buf vs NYG	1991	190

Interceptions

	Year	No	Yds	TD
Rod Martin, Oak vs Phi	1981	3	44	0
Chuck Howley, Dal vs Bal	1971	2	22	0
Randy Beverly, NYJ vs Bal	1969	2	0	0
Jake Scott, Mia vs Wash.	1973	2	63	0
Barry Wilburn, Wash vs Den	1988	2	11	0

Super Bowl Playoffs

The Super Bowl created pro football's first guaranteed multiple-game playoff format. Only four teams qualified for the playoffs in 1966, but by the time the 10 AFL teams joined the NFL in 1970, the field had doubled. Since 1978, 10 teams (out of 28) have made the postseason cut.

In the strike year of 1982, when the regular season was shortened to just nine games, playoff berths were extended to 16 teams and a 15-game tournament was played.

Throughout the following year-by-year playoff summary, home teams are listed in CAPITAL letters and records of the finalists include all games leading up to the Super Bowl; (*) indicates Wild Card teams.

1966 Season

AFL Playoffs
Championship .... Kansas City 31, BUFFALO 7

NFL Playoffs
Championship .... Green Bay 34, DALLAS 27

Super Bowl I
Memorial Coliseum, Los Angeles
(Favorite: Packers by 14)

Kansas City (12-2-1)	0	10	0	0—**10**
Green Bay (13-2)	7	7	14	7—**35**

MVP: Green Bay QB Bart Starr (16 for 23, 250 yds, 2 TD, 1 Int)

1967 Season

AFL Playoffs
Championship .... OAKLAND 40, Houston 7

NFL Playoffs
Eastern Conf .... DALLAS 52, Cleveland 14
Western Conf .... GREEN BAY 28, LA Rams 7
Championship .... GREEN BAY 21, Dallas 17

Super Bowl II
Orange Bowl, Miami
(Favorite: Packers by 13½)

Green Bay (11-4-1)	3	13	10	7—**33**
Oakland (14-1)	0	7	0	07—**14**

MVP: Green Bay QB Bart Starr (13 for 24, 202 yds, 1 TD)

Super Bowl Playoffs (Cont.)

1968 Season
AFL Playoffs
Western Div.Playoff .... OAKLAND 41, Kan.City 6
AFL Championship .... NY JETS 27, Oakland 23
NFL Playoffs
Eastern Conf .... CLEVELAND 31, Dallas 20
Western Conf .... BALTIMORE 24, Minnesota 14
NFL Championship ..... Baltimore 34, CLEVELAND 0
Super Bowl III
Orange Bowl, Miami
(Favorite: Colts by 18)

NY Jets (12-3) 0	7	6	3	**—16**
Baltimore (15-1) 0	0	0	7	**— 7**

MVP: NY Jets QB Joe Namath (17 for 28, 206 yds)

1969 Season
AFL Playoffs
Inter-Division .... Kansas City 13, NY JETS 6
.... OAKLAND 56, Houston 7
AFL Championship .... Kansas City 17, OAKLAND 7
NFL Playoffs
Eastern Conf .... Cleveland 38, DALLAS 14
Western Conf .... MINNESOTA 23, LA Rams 20
NFL Championship .... MINNESOTA 27, Cleveland 7
Super Bowl IV
Tulane Stadium, New Orleans
(Favorite: Vikings by 12)

Minnesota (14-2) 0	0	7	0	**— 7**
Kansas City (13-3) 3	13	7	0	**—23**

MVP: Kansas City QB Len Dawson (12 for 17, 142 yds, 1 TD, 1 Int)

1970 Season
AFC Playoffs
First Round .... BALTIMORE 17, Cincinnati 0
.... OAKLAND 21, Miami* 14
Championship .... BALTIMORE 27, Oakland 17
NFC Playoffs
First Round .... DALLAS 5, Detroit* 0
.... San Francisco 17, MINNESOTA 14
Championship ...... Dallas 17, SAN FRANCISCO 10
Super Bowl V
Orange Bowl, Miami
(Favorite: Cowboys by 2½)

Baltimore (13-2-1) 0	6	0	10	**—16**
Dallas (12-4) 3	10	0	0	**—13**

MVP: Dallas LB Chuck Howley (2 Interceptions for 22 yds)

1971 Season
AFC Playoffs
First Round .... Miami 27, KANSAS CITY 24 (OT)
.... Baltimore* 20, CLEVELAND 3
Championship .... MIAMI 21, Baltimore 0
NFC Playoffs
First Round .... Dallas 20, MINNESOTA 12
... SAN FRANCISCO 24, Washington* 20
Championship .... DALLAS 14, San Francisco 3
Super Bowl VI
Tulane Stadium, New Orleans
(Favorite: Cowboys by 6)

Dallas (13-3) 3	7	7	7	**—24**
Miami (12-3-1) 0	3	0	0	**— 3**

MVP: Dallas QB Roger Staubach (12 for 19, 119 yds, 2 TD)

1972 Season
AFC Playoffs
First Round .... PITTSBURGH 13, Oakland 7
.... MIAMI 20, Cleveland* 14
Championship .... Miami 21, PITTSBURGH 17
NFC Playoffs
First Round .... Dallas* 30, SAN FRANCISCO 28
.... WASHINGTON 16, Green Bay 3
Championship .... WASHINGTON 26, Dallas 3
Super Bowl VII
Memorial Coliseum, Los Angeles
(Favorite: Redskins by 1½)

Miami (16-0) 7	7	0	0	**—14**
Washington (13-3) 0	0	0	7	**— 7**

MVP: Miami safety Jake Scott (2 Interceptions for 63 yds)

1973 Season
AFC Playoffs
First Round .... OAKLAND 33, Pittsburgh* 14
.... MIAMI 34, Cincinnati 16
Championship .... MIAMI 27, Oakland 10
NFC Playoffs
First Round .... MINNESOTA 27, Washington* 20
.... DALLAS 27, LA Rams 16
Championship .... Minnesota 27, DALLAS 10
Super Bowl VIII
Rice Stadium, Houston
(Favorite: Dolphins by 6½)

Minnesota (14-2) 0	0	0	7	**— 7**
Miami (12-4) 14	3	7	0	**—24**

MVP: Miami FB Larry Csonka (33 carries, 145 yds, 2 TD)

1974 Season
AFC Playoffs
First Round .... OAKLAND 28, Miami 26
.... PITTSBURGH 32, Buffalo* 14
Championship .... Pittsburgh 24, OAKLAND 13

NFC Playoffs
First Round .... MINNESOTA 30, St.Louis 14
.... LA RAMS 19, Washington* 10
Championship .... MINNESOTA 14, LA Rams 10

Super Bowl IX
Tulane Stadium, New Orleans
(Favorite: Steelers by 3)

Pittsburgh (12-3-1) 0   2   7   7—**16**
Minnesota (12-4) 0   0   0   6— **6**
MVP: Pittsburgh RB Franco Harris (34 carries, 158 yds, 1 TD)

1975 Season
AFC Playoffs
First Round .... PITTSBURGH 28, Baltimore 10
.... OAKLAND 31, Cincinnati* 28
Championship .... PITTSBURGH 16, Oakland 10

NFC Playoffs
First Round .... LA RAMS 35, St.Louis 23
.... Dallas 17, MINNESOTA 14
Championship .... Dallas 37, LA RAMS 7

Super Bowl X
Orange Bowl, Miami
(Favorite: Steelers by 6½)

Dallas (12-4) 7   3   0   7—**17**
Pittsburgh (14-2) 7   0   0   14—**21**
MVP: Pittsburgh WR Lynn Swan (4 catches, 161 yds, 1 TD)

1976 Season
AFC Playoffs
First Round .... OAKLAND 24, New England* 21
.... Pittsburgh 40, BALTIMORE 14
Championship .... OAKLAND 24, Pittsburgh 7

NFC Playoffs
First Round .... MINNESOTA 35, Washington* 20
.... LA Rams 14, DALLAS 12
Championship .... MINNESOTA 24, LA Rams 13

Super Bowl XI
Rose Bowl, Pasadena
(Favorite: Raiders by 4½)

Oakland (15-1) 0   16   3   13—**32**
Minnesota (13-2-1) 0   0   7   7—**14**
MVP: Oakland WR Fred Biletnikoff (4 catches, 79 yds)

1977 Season
AFC Playoffs
First Round .... DENVER 34, Pittsburgh 21
..... Oakland* 37, BALTIMORE 31 (OT)
Championship .... DENVER 20, Oakland 17

NFC Playoffs
First Round .... DALLAS 37, Chicago* 7
.... Minnesota 14, LA RAMS 7
Championship .... DALLAS 23, Minnesota 6

Super Bowl XII
Louisiana Superdome, New Orleans
(Favorite: Cowboys by 6)

Dallas (14-2) 10   3   7   7—**27**
Denver (14-2) 0   0   10   0—**10**
MVPs: Dallas DE Harvey Martin and DT Randy White
(Cowboys' defense forced 8 turnovers)

1978 Season
AFC Playoffs
Wild Cards .... Houston 17, MIAMI 9
Second Round ..... Houston 31, NEW ENGLAND 14
.... PITTSBURGH 33, Denver 10
Championship .... PITTSBURGH 34, Houston 5

NFC Playoffs
Wild Cards .... ATLANTA 14, Philadelphia 13
Second Round .... DALLAS 27, Atlanta 20
.... LA RAMS 34, Minnesota 10
Championship .... Dallas 28, LA RAMS 0

Super Bowl XIII
Orange Bowl, Miami
(Favorite: Steelers by 3½)

Pittsburgh (16-2) 7   14   0   14—**35**
Dallas (14-4) 7   7   3   14—**31**
MVP: Pittsburgh QB Terry Bradshaw (17 for 30, 318 yds, 4 TD, 1 Int)

1979 Season
AFC Playoffs
Wild Cards .... HOUSTON 13, Denver 7
Second Round .... Houston 17, SAN DIEGO 14
.... PITTSBURGH 34, Miami 14
Championship .... PITTSBURGH 27, Houston 13

NFC Playoffs
Wild Cards: PHILADELPHIA 27, Chicago 17
Second Round ...... TAMPA BAY 24, Philadelphia 17
.... LA Rams 21, DALLAS 19
Championship .... LA Rams 9, TAMPA BAY 0

Super Bowl XIV
Rose Bowl, Pasadena
(Favorite: Steelers by 10½)

LA Rams (11-7) 7   6   6   0—**19**
Pittsburgh (14-4) 3   7   7   14—**31**
MVP: Pittsburgh QB Terry Bradshaw (14 for 21, 309 yds, 2 TD, 3 Int)

Super Bowl Playoffs (Cont.)

1980 Season

AFC Playoffs

Wild Cards .... OAKLAND 27, Houston 7
Second Round .... SAN DIEGO 20, Buffalo 14
.... Oakland 14, CLEVELAND 12
Championship .... Oakland 34, SAN DIEGO 27

NFC Playoffs

Wild Cards .... DALLAS 34, LA Rams 13
Second Round ...... PHILADELPHIA 31, Minnesota 16
.... Dallas 30, ATLANTA 27
Championship: .... PHILADELPHIA 20, Dallas 7

Super Bowl XV
Louisiana Superdome, New Orleans
(Favorite: Eagles by 3)

Oakland (14-5) 14   0   10   3—**27**
Philadelphia (14-4) 0   3   0   7—**10**
MVP: Oakland QB Jim Plunket (13 for 21, 261 yds, 3 TD)

1981 Season

AFC Playoffs

Wild Cards .... Buffalo 31, NY JETS 27
Second Round .... San Diego 41, MIAMI 38 (OT)
.... CINCINNATI 28, Buffalo 21
Championship .... CINCINNATI 27, San Diego 7

NFC Playoffs

Wild Cards .... NY Giants 27, PHILADELPHIA 21
Second Round .... DALLAS 38, Tampa Bay 0
... SAN FRANCISCO 38, NY Giants 24
Championship ...... SAN FRANCISCO 28, Dallas 27

Super Bowl XVI
Pontiac Silverdome, Pontiac,MI
(Favorite: Pick'em)

San Francisco (15-3) 7   13   0   6—**26**
Cincinnati (14-4) 0   0   7   14—**21**
MVP: San Francisco QB Joe Montana (14 for 22, 157 yds, 1 TD; 6 carries, 18 yds, 1 TD)

1982 Season

A 57-day players' strike shortened the regular season from 16 games to nine. The playoff format was changed to a 16-team tournament open to the top eight teams in each conference.

AFC Playoffs

First Round .... LA RAIDERS 27, Cleveland 10
.... MIAMI 28, New England 3
.... NY Jets 44, CINCINNATI 17
.... San Diego 31, PITTSBURGH 28
Second Round .... NY Jets 17, LA RAIDERS 14,
.... MIAMI 34, San Diego 13,
Championship .... MIAMI 14, NY Jets 0

NFC Playoffs

First Round .... WASHINGTON 31, Detroit 7
.... DALLAS 30, Tampa Bay 17
.... GREEN BAY 41, St.Louis 16
.... MINNESOTA 30, Atlanta 24
Second Round ...... WASHINGTON 21, Minnesota 7
.... DALLAS 37, Green Bay 26
Championship .... WASHINGTON 31, Dallas 17

Super Bowl XVII
Rose Bowl, Pasadena
(Favorite: Dolphins by 3)

Miami (10-2) 7   10   0   0—**17**
Washington (11-1) 0   10   3   14—**27**
MVP: Washington RB John Riggins (38 carries, 166 yds, 1 TD; 1 catch, 15 yds)

1983 Season

AFC Playoffs

Wild Cards .... SEATTLE 31, Denver 7
Second Round .... Seattle 27, MIAMI 20
.... LA RAIDERS 38, Pittsburgh 10
Championship .... RAIDERS 30, Seattle 14

NFC Playoffs

Wild Cards .... LA Rams 24, DALLAS 17
Second Round ...... SAN FRANCISCO 24, Detroit 23
.... WASHINGTON 51, LA Rams 7
Championship . WASHINGTON 24, San Francisco 21

Super Bowl XVIII
Tampa Stadium, Tampa
(Favorite: Redskins by 3)

Washington (16-2) 0   3   6   0— **9**
LA Raiders (14-4) 7   14   14   3—**38**
MVP: LA Raiders RB Marcus Allen (20 carries, 191 yds, 2 TD; 2 catches, 18 yds)

1984 Season

AFC Playoffs

Wild Cards .... SEATTLE 13, LA Raiders 7
Second Round .... MIAMI 31, Seattle 10
.... Pittsburgh 24, DENVER 17
Championship .... MIAMI 45, Pittsburgh 28

NFC Playoffs

Wild Cards .... NY Giants 16, LA RAMS 13
Second Round ... SAN FRANCISCO 21, NY Giants 10
.... Chicago 23, WASHINGTON 19
Championship ..... SAN FRANCISCO 23, Chicago 0

Super Bowl XIX
Stanford Stadium, Stanford,CA
(Favorite: 49ers by 3)

Miami (16-2) 10   6   0   0—**16**
San Francisco (17-1) 7   21   10   0—**38**
MVP: San Francisco QB Joe Montana (24 for 35, 331 yds, 2 TD; 5 carries, 59 yards, 1 TD)

1985 Season
AFC Playoffs
Wild Cards .... New England 26, NY JETS 14
Second Round .... MIAMI 24, Cleveland 21
..... New England 27, LA RAIDERS 20
Championship .... New England 31, MIAMI 14

NFC Playoffs
Wild Cards .... NY GIANTS 17, San Francisco 3
Second Round .... LA RAMS 20, Dallas 0
.... CHICAGO 21, NY Giants 0
Championship .... CHICAGO 24, LA Rams 0

Super Bowl XX
Louisiana Superdome, New Orleans
(Favorite: Bears by 10)

Chicago Bears (17-1) .... 13 10 21 2—**46**
New England (14-5) .... 3 0 0 7—**10**
MVP: Chicago DE Richard Dent (Bears defense: 7 sacks, 6 turnovers, 1 safety and gave up just 123 total yards)

1986 Season
AFC Playoffs
Wild Cards .... NY JETS 35, Kansas City 15
Second Round ...... CLEVELAND 23, NY Jets 20 (OT)
.... DENVER 22, New England 17
Championship ..... Denver 23, CLEVELAND 20 (OT)

NFC Playoffs
Wild Cards .... WASHINGTON 19, LA Rams 7
Second Round .... Washington 27, CHICAGO 13
...... NY GIANTS 49, San Francisco 3
Championship .... NY GIANTS 17, Washington 0

Super Bowl XXI
Rose Bowl, Pasadena
(Favorite: Giants by 9½)

Denver (13-5) .... 10 0 0 10—**20**
NY Giants (16-2) .... 7 2 17 13—**39**
MVP: NY Giants QB Phil Simms (22 for 25, 268 yds, 3 TD; 3 carries, 25 yds)

1987 Season
A 24-day players' strike shortened the regular season from 16 games to 15 with replacement teams playing for three weeks. The playoffs proceeded as usual.
AFC Playoffs
Wild Cards .... HOUSTON 23, Seattle 20 (OT)
Second Round ...... CLEVELAND 38, Indianapolis 21
.... DENVER 34, Houston 10
Championship .... DENVER 38, Cleveland 33

NFC Playoffs
Wild Cards .... Minnesota 44, NEW ORLEANS 10
Second Round ... Minnesota 36, SAN FRANCISCO 24
.... Washington 21, CHICAGO 17
Championship .... WASHINGTON 17, Minnesota 10

Super Bowl XXII
San Diego Jack Murphy Stadium
(Favorite: Broncos by 3½)

Washington (13-4) .... 0 35 0 7—**42**
Denver (12-4-1) .... 10 0 0 0—**10**
MVP: Washington QB Doug Williams (18 for 29, 340 yds, 4 TD, 1Int)

1988 Season
AFC Playoffs
Wild Cards .... Houston 24, CLEVELAND 23
Second Round .... BUFFALO 17, Houston 10
.... CINCINNATI 21, Seattle 13
Championship .... CINCINNATI 21, Buffalo 10

NFC Playoffs
Wild Cards .... MINNESOTA 28, LA Rams 17
Second Round .... SAN FRANCISCO 34, Minnesota 9
.... CHICAGO 20, Philadelphia 12
Championship .... San Francisco 28, CHICAGO 3

Super Bowl XXIII
Joe Robbie Stadium, Miami
(Favorite: 49ers by 7)

Cincinnati (17-1) .... 0 3 10 3—**16**
San Francisco (14-5) .... 3 0 3 14—**20**
MVP: San Francisco WR Jerry Rice (11 catches, 215 yds, 1 TD; 1 carry, 5 yds)

1989 Season
AFC Playoffs
Wild Cards .... Pittsburgh 26, HOUSTON 23
Second Round .... CLEVELAND 34, Buffalo 30
.... DENVER 24, Pittsburgh 23
Championship: .... DENVER 37, Cleveland 21

NFC Playoffs
Wild Cards .... LA Rams 21, PHILADELPHIA 7
Second Round ..... LA Rams 19, NY GIANTS 13 (OT)
... SAN FRANCISCO 41, Minnesota 13
Championship ..... SAN FRANCISCO 30, LA Rams 3

Super Bowl XXIV
Louisiana Superdome, New Orleans
(Favorite: 49ers by 12½)

San Francisco (17-2) .... 13 14 14 14—**55**
Denver (13-6) .... 3 0 7 0—**10**
MVP: San Francisco QB Joe Montana (22 for 29, 297 yds, 5 TD, 0 Int)

1990 Season
AFC Playoffs
First Round .... MIAMI* 17, Kansas City* 16
.... CINCINNATI 41, Houston* 14
Second Round .... BUFFALO 44, Miami 34
.... LA RAIDERS 20, Cincinnati 10
Championship .... BUFFALO 51, LA Raiders 3

NFC Playoffs
First Round ...... Washington* 20, PHILADELPHIA* 6
.... CHICAGO 16, New Orleans* 6
Second Round . SAN FRANCISCO 28, Washington 10
.... NY GIANTS 31, Chicago 3
Championship .. NY Giants 15, SAN FRANCISCO 13

Super Bowl XXV
Tampa Stadium, Tampa
(Favorite: Bills by 7)

Buffalo (15-4) .... 3 9 0 7—**19**
NY Giants (16-3) .... 3 7 7 3—**20**
MVP: NY Giants RB Ottis Anderson (21 carries, 102 yds, 1 TD; 1 catch, 7 yds)

Before the Super Bowl

Time did not begin with the Super Bowl, it only seems that way. The first NFL champion was the Akron Pros in 1920, when the league was called the American Professional Football Association (APFA) and the title went to the team with the best regular season record.

The first playoff game with the championship at stake came in 1932, when the Chicago Bears beat the Portsmouth, Ohio, Spartans, 9-0. Due to a snowstorm and bitter cold weather, the game was moved from Wrigley Field to an improvised 80-yard dirt field at Chicago Stadium, making it the first indoor title game as well.

The NFL Championship Game decided the league title until the NFL merged with the AFL and the first Super Bowl was played following the 1966 season.

NFL Champions, 1920-31

Multiple winners: Green Bay (3); Canton (2).

Year	Champion	Head Coach
1920	Akron Pros	Fritz Pollard, HB & Elgie Tobin, QB
1921	Chicago Staleys (Renamed Bears in 1922)	George Halas, E
1922	Canton Bulldogs	Guy Chamberlin, E
1923	Canton Bulldogs	Guy Chamberlin, E
1924	Cleveland Bulldogs	Guy Chamberlin, E
1925	Chicago Cardinals	Norm Barry
1926	Frankford Yellow Jackets	Guy Chamberlin, E
1927	New York Giants	Earl Potteiger, QB
1928	Providence Steam Roller	Jimmy Conzelman, HB
1929	Green Bay Packers	Curly Lambeau, QB
1930	Green Bay Packers	Curly Lambeau
1931	Green Bay Packers	Curly Lambeau
1932	Chicago Bears (beat Portsmouth-OH in playoff, 9-0)	Ralph Jones

NFL-NFC Championship Game

NFL Championship games from 1933-69 and NFC Championship games since the completion of the NFL-AFL merger by the 1970 season.

Multiple winners: Green Bay (8); Chicago Bears (7); Washington (6); Dallas and NY Giants (5); Cleveland Browns, Detroit, Minnesota, Philadelphia and San Francisco (4); Baltimore and Los Angeles Rams (2).

Season	Winner	Head Coach	Score	Loser	Head Coach	Site
1933	Chicago Bears	George Halas	23-21	New York	Steve Owen	Chicago
1934	New York	Steve Owen	30-13	Chicago Bears	George Halas	New York
1935	Detroit	Potsy Clark	26-7	New York	Steve Owen	Detroit
1936	Green Bay	Curly Lambeau	21-6	Boston Redskins	Ray Flaherty	New York
1937	Washington Redskins	Ray Flaherty	28-21	Chicago Bears	George Halas	Chicago
1938	New York	Steve Owen	23-17	Green Bay	Curly Lambeau	New York
1939	Green Bay	Curly Lambeau	27-0	New York	Steve Owen	Milwaukee
1940	Chicago Bears	George Halas	73-0	Washington	Ray Flaherty	Washington
1941	Chicago Bears	George Halas	37-9	New York	Steve Owen	Chicago
1942	Washington	Ray Flaherty	14-6	Chicago Bears	Hunk Anderson & Luke Johnsos	Washington
1943	Chicago Bears	Hunk Anderson & Luke Johnsos	41-21	Washington	Arthur Bergman	Chicago
1944	Green Bay	Curly Lambeau	14-7	New York	Steve Owen	New York
1945	Cleveland Rams	Adam Walsh	15-14	Washington	Dudley DeGroot	Cleveland
1946	Chicago Bears	George Halas	24-14	New York	Steve Owen	New York
1947	Chicago Cards	Jimmy Conzelman	28-21	Philadelphia	Greasy Neale	Chicago
1948	Philadelphia	Greasy Neale	7-0	Chicago Cards	Jimmy Conzelman	Philadelphia
1949	Philadelphia	Greasy Neale	14-0	LA Rams	Clark Shaughnessy	Los Angeles
1950	Cleveland Browns	Paul Brown	30-28	Los Angeles	Joe Stydahar	Cleveland
1951	Los Angeles	Joe Stydahar	24-17	Cleveland	Paul Brown	Los Angeles
1952	Detroit	Buddy Parker	17-7	Cleveland	Paul Brown	Cleveland
1953	Detroit	Buddy Parker	17-16	Cleveland	Paul Brown	Detroit
1954	Cleveland	Paul Brown	56-10	Detroit	Buddy Parker	Cleveland
1955	Cleveland	Paul Brown	38-14	Los Angeles	Sid Gillman	Los Angeles
1956	New York	Jim Lee Howell	47-7	Chicago Bears	Paddy Driscoll	New York
1957	Detroit	George Wilson	59-14	Cleveland	Paul Brown	Detroit
1958	Baltimore	Weeb Ewbank	23-17*	New York	Jim Lee Howell	New York
1959	Baltimore	Weeb Ewbank	31-16	New York	Jim Lee Howell	Baltimore
1960	Philadelphia	Buck Shaw	17-13	Green Bay	Vince Lombardi	Philadelphia
1961	Green Bay	Vince Lombardi	37-0	New York	Allie Sherman	Green Bay
1962	Green Bay	Vince Lombardi	16-7	New York	Allie Sherman	New York
1963	Chicago	George Halas	14-10	New York	Allie Sherman	Chicago
1964	Cleveland	Blanton Collier	27-0	Baltimore	Don Shula	Cleveland
1965	Green Bay	Vince Lombardi	23-12	Cleveland	Blanton Collier	Green Bay
1966	Green Bay	Vince Lombardi	34-27	Dallas	Tom Landry	Dallas
1967	Green Bay	Vince Lombardi	21-17	Dallas	Tom Landry	Green Bay
1968	Baltimore	Don Shula	34-0	Cleveland	Blanton Collier	Cleveland
1969	Minnesota	Bud Grant	27-7	Cleveland	Blanton Collier	Minnesota
1970	Dallas	Tom Landry	17-10	San Francisco	Dick Nolan	San Francisco
1971	Dallas	Tom Landry	14-3	San Francisco	Dick Nolan	Dallas
1972	Washington	George Allen	26-3	Dallas	Tom Landry	Washington

*Sudden death overtime

Season	Winner	Head Coach	Score	Loser	Head Coach	Site
1973	Minnesota	Bud Grant	27-10	Dallas	Tom Landry	Dallas
1974	Minnesota	Bud Grant	14-10	Los Angeles	Chuck Knox	Minnesota
1975	Dallas	Tom Landry	37-7	Los Angeles	Chuck Knox	Los Angeles
1976	Minnesota	Bud Grant	24-13	Los Angeles	Chuck Knox	Minnesota
1977	Dallas	Tom Landry	23-6	Minnesota	Bud Grant	Dallas
1978	Dallas	Tom Landry	28-0	Los Angeles	Ray Malavasi	Los Angeles
1979	Los Angeles	Ray Malavasi	9-0	Tampa Bay	John McKay	Tampa Bay
1980	Philadelphia	Dick Vermeil	20-7	Dallas	Tom Landry	Philadelphia
1981	San Francisco	Bill Walsh	28-27	Dallas	Tom Landry	San Francisco
1982	Washington	Joe Gibbs	31-17	Dallas	Tom Landry	Washington
1983	Washington	Joe Gibbs	24-21	San Francisco	Bill Walsh	Washington
1984	San Francisco	Bill Walsh	23-0	Chicago	Mike Ditka	San Francisco
1985	Chicago	Mike Ditka	24-0	Los Angeles	John Robinson	Chicago
1986	New York	Bill Parcells	17-0	Washington	Joe Gibbs	New York
1987	Washington	Joe Gibbs	17-10	Minnesota	Jerry Burns	Washington
1988	San Francisco	Bill Walsh	28-3	Chicago	Mike Ditka	Chicago
1989	San Francisco	George Seifert	30-3	Los Angeles	John Robinson	San Francisco
1990	New York	Bill Parcells	15-13	San Francisco	George Seifert	San Francisco

NFL-NFC Championship Game Appearances

App		W	L	Pct	PF	PA	App		W	L	Pct	PF	PA
16	NY Giants	5	11	.313	240	322	8	San Francisco	4	4	.500	156	103
13	Chicago Bears	7	6	.538	286	245	6	Minnesota	4	2	.667	108	80
12	Dallas Cowboys	5	7	.417	227	213	5	Detroit	4	1	.800	129	100
12	Cleveland-LA Rams	3	9	.250	123	270	5	Philadelphia	4	1	.800	79	48
11	Boston-Wash.Redskins	6	5	.545	181	245	4	Baltimore Colts	3	1	.750	88	60
11	Cleveland Browns	4	7	.364	224	253	2	Chicago Cardinals	1	1	.500	28	28
10	Green Bay	8	2	.800	223	116	1	Tampa Bay	0	1	.000	0	9

AFL-AFC Championship Game

AFL Championship games from 1960-69 and AFC Championship games since the completion of the NFL-AFL merger by the 1970 season.

Multiple winners: Miami (5), Denver, Oakland-LA Raiders and Pittsburgh (4); Buffalo and Dallas Texans-KC Chiefs (3); Cincinnati and Houston (2).

Season	Winner	Head Coach	Score	Loser	Head Coach	Site
1960	Houston	Lou Rymkus	24-16	LA Chargers	Sid Gillman	Houston
1961	Houston	Wally Lemm	10-3	SD Chargers	Sid Gillman	San Diego
1962	Dallas	Hank Stram	20-17*	Houston	Pop Ivy	Houston
1963	San Diego	Sid Gillman	51-10	Boston Patriots	Mike Holovak	San Diego
1964	Buffalo	Lou Saban	20-7	San Diego	Sid Gillman	Buffalo
1965	Buffalo	Lou Saban	23-0	San Diego	Sid Gillman	San Diego
1966	Kansas City	Hank Stram	31-7	Buffalo	Joel Collier	Buffalo
1967	Oakland	John Rauch	40-7	Houston	Wally Lemm	Oakland
1968	NY Jets	Webb Ewbank	27-23	Oakland	John Rauch	New York
1969	Kansas City	Hank Stram	17-7	Oakland	John Madden	Oakland
1970	Baltimore	Don McCafferty	27-17	Oakland	John Madden	Baltimore
1971	Miami	Don Shula	21-0	Baltimore	Don McCafferty	Miami
1972	Miami	Don Shula	21-17	Pittsburgh	Chuck Noll	Pittsburgh
1973	Miami	Don Shula	27-10	Oakland	John Madden	Miami
1974	Pittsburgh	Chuck Noll	24-13	Oakland	John Madden	Oakland
1975	Pittsburgh	Chuck Noll	16-10	Oakland	John Madden	Pittsburgh
1976	Oakland	John Madden	24-7	Pittsburgh	Chuck Noll	Oakland
1977	Denver	Red Miller	20-17	Oakland	John Madden	Denver
1978	Pittsburgh	Chuck Noll	34-5	Houston	Bum Phillips	Pittsburgh
1979	Pittsburgh	Chuck Noll	27-13	Houston	Bum Phillips	Pittsburgh
1980	Oakland	Tom Flores	34-27	San Diego	Don Coryell	San Diego
1981	Cincinnati	Forrest Gregg	27-7	San Diego	Don Coryell	Cincinnati
1982	Miami	Don Shula	14-0	NY Jets	Walt Michaels	Miami
1983	LA Raiders	Tom Flores	30-14	Seattle	Chuck Knox	Los Angeles
1984	Miami	Don Shula	45-28	Pittsburgh	Chuck Noll	Miami
1985	NE Patriots	Raymond Berry	31-14	Miami	Don Shula	Miami
1986	Denver	Dan Reeves	23-20*	Cleveland	Marty Schottenheimer	Cleveland
1987	Denver	Dan Reeves	38-33	Cleveland	Marty Schottenheimer	Denver
1988	Cincinnati	Sam Wyche	21-10	Buffalo	Marv Levy	Cincinnati
1989	Denver	Dan Reeves	37-21	Cleveland	Bud Carson	Denver
1990	Buffalo	Marv Levy	51-3	LA Raiders	Art Shell	Buffalo

*Sudden death overtime

AFL-AFC Championship Game Appearances

App		W	L	Pct	PF	PA	App		W	L	Pct	PF	PA
12	Oakland-LA Raiders	4	8	.333	228	264	3	Dallas Texans/ KC Chiefs	3	0	1.000	68	31
7	Pittsburgh	4	3	.571	153	131	3	Cleveland	0	3	.000	74	98
7	LA-San Diego Chargers	1	6	.143	111	148	2	Cincinnati	2	0	1.000	48	17
6	Miami	5	1	.833	142	86	2	Baltimore Colts	1	1	.500	27	38
6	Houston	2	4	.333	76	140	2	Boston-NE Patriots	1	1	.500	41	65
5	Buffalo	3	2	.600	111	62	2	NY Jets	1	1	.500	27	37
4	Denver	4	0	1.000	118	91	1	Seattle	0	1	.000	14	30

NFL Playoff Bowl

The NFL staged a postseason exhibition game between its Eastern and Western Conference runners-up from the 1960 season through 1969. Called the Bert Bell Benefit Bowl (Bell was league commissioner from 1946 until his death in 1959) and referred to as the Playoff Bowl, it gave the winner little more than bragging rights to third place in the NFL. All 10 Playoff Bowls were played in Miami and game statistics do not count in career player and coaching records. Western Division teams won eight of the 10 games, losing only to St.Louis in 1965 and Dallas in 1969.
Multiple winners: Detroit (3); Baltimore (2); LA Rams (2).

Season	Winner	Head Coach	Score	Loser	Head Coach	Site
1960	Detroit	George Wilson	17-16	Cleveland	Paul Brown	Miami
1961	Detroit	George Wilson	38-10	Philadelphia	Nick Skorich	Miami
1962	Detroit	George Wilson	17-10	Pittsburgh	Buddy Parker	Miami
1963	Green Bay	Vince Lombardi	40-23	Cleveland	Blanton Collier	Miami
1964	St.Louis	Wally Lemm	24-17	Green Bay	Vince Lombardi	Miami
1965	Baltimore	Don Shula	35-3	Dallas	Tom Landry	Miami
1966	Baltimore	Don Shula	20-14	Philadelphia	Joe Kuharich	Miami
1967	LA Rams	George Allen	30-6	Cleveland	Blanton Collier	Miami
1968	Dallas	Tom Landry	17-13	Minnesota	Bud Grant	Miami
1969	LA Rams	George Allen	31-0	Dallas	Tom Landry	Miami

Champions Of Leagues That Didn't Make It

No professional league in American sports has had to contend with more pretenders to the throne than the NFL. Seven times in as many decades a rival league has risen up to challenge the NFL and six of them went under in less than five seasons. Only the fourth American Football League (1960-69) succeeded, forcing the older league to sue for peace and a full partnership in 1966.

Of the six leagues that didn't make it, only the All-America Football Conference (1946-49) lives on—the Cleveland Browns and San Francisco 49ers joined the NFL after the AAFC folded in 1949.

The champions of leagues past are listed below. Home teams in championship games are noted in CAPITAL letters.

American Football League I

Year	Champion	Head Coach
1926	Philadelphia Quakers	Bob Folwell

American Football League II

Year	Champion	Head Coach
1936	Boston Shamrocks	George Kenneally
1937	Los Angeles Bulldogs	Gus Henderson

American Football League III

Year	Champion	Head Coach
1940	Columbus Bullies	Phil Bucklew
1941	Columbus Bullies	Phil Bucklew

All-America Football Conference

Year	Championship Game	Head Coach
1946	CLEVE.BROWNS 14, NY Yankees 9	Paul Brown
1947	Cleve.Browns 14, NY YANKEES 3	Paul Brown
1948	CLEVE.BROWNS 49, Buffalo 7	Paul Brown
1949	CLEVE.BROWNS 21, S.F.49ers 7	Paul Brown

World Football League

Year	World Bowl	Head Coach
1974	BIRMINGHAM 22, Florida 21	Jack Gotta
1975	Folded mid-season	—

United States Football League

Year	Championship Game	Head Coach
1983	Michigan 24, Phila.Stars 22	Jim Stanley
1984	Phila.Stars 23, Arizona 3	Jim Mora
1985	Balt.Stars 28, Oakland 24	Jim Mora

USFL Championship Game sites: Denver (1983), Tampa (1984), East Rutherford, N.J. (1985).

NFL Franchise Origins

Here is what the current 28 teams in the National Football League have to show for the years they have put in as members of the American Professional Football Association (APFA), the NFL, the All-America Football Conference (AAFC) and the American Football League (AFL).

American Football Conference

	First Season		League Titles	Franchise Stops
Buffalo Bills	1960	(AFL)	2 AFL (1964-65)	Buffalo (1960-72)
				Orchard Park, NY (1973—)
Cincinnati Bengals	1968	(AFL)	None	Cincinnati (1968—)
Cleveland Browns	1946	(AAFC)	4 AAFC (1946-49)	Cleveland (1946—)
			4 NFL (1950,54-55,64)	
Denver Broncos	1960	(AFL)	None	Denver (1960—)
Houston Oilers	1960	(AFL)	2 AFL (1960-61)	Houston (1960—)
Indianapolis Colts	1953	(NFL)	3 NFL (1958-59,68)	Baltimore (1953-83)
			1 Super Bowl (1970)	Indianapolis (1984—)
Kansas City Chiefs	1960	(AFL)	3 AFL (1962,66,69)	Dallas (1960-62)
			1 Super Bowl (1969)	Kansas City (1963—)
Los Angeles Raiders	1960	(AFL)	1 AFL (1967)	Oakland (1960-81)
			3 Super Bowls (1976,80,83)	Los Angeles (1982—)
Miami Dolphins	1966	(AFL)	2 Super Bowls (1972-73)	Miami (1966—)
New England Patriots	1960	(AFL)	None	Boston (1960-70)
				Foxboro, MA (1971—)
New York Jets	1960	(AFL)	1 AFL (1968)	New York (1960-83)
			1 Super Bowl (1968)	E.Rutherford, NJ (1984—)
Pittsburgh Steelers	1933	(NFL)	4 Super Bowls (1974-75,78-79)	Pittsburgh (1933—)
San Diego Chargers	1960	(AFL)	1 AFL (1963)	Los Angeles (1960)
				San Diego (1961—)
Seattle Seahawks	1976	(NFL)	None	Seattle (1976—)

National Football Conference

	First Season		League Titles	Franchise Stops
Atlanta Falcons	1966	(NFL)	None	Atlanta (1966—)
Chicago Bears	1920	(APFA)	7 NFL (1932-33,40-41,43,46,63)	Decatur,IL (1920)
			1 Super Bowl (1985)	Chicago (1921—)
Dallas Cowboys	1960	(NFL)	2 Super Bowls (1971,77)	Dallas (1960-70)
				Irving,TX (1971—)
Detroit Lions	1930	(NFL)	4 NFL (1935,52-53,57)	Portsmouth,OH (1930-33)
				Detroit (1934-74)
				Pontiac,MI (1975—)
Green Bay Packers	1921	(APFA)	8 NFL (1936,39,44,61-62,65-67)	Green Bay (1921—)
			2 Super Bowls (1966-67)	
Los Angeles Rams	1937	(NFL)	2 NFL (1945,51)	Cleveland (1937-45)
				Los Angeles (1946-79)
				Anaheim (1980—)
Minnesota Vikings	1961	(NFL)	1 NFL (1969)	Bloomington, MN (1961-81)
				Minneapolis,MN (1982—)
New Orleans Saints	1967	(NFL)	None	New Orleans (1967—)
New York Giants	1925	(NFL)	3 NFL (1934,38,56)	New York (1925-73,75)
			2 Super Bowls (1986,90)	New Haven,CT (1973-74)
				E.Rutherford,NJ (1976—)
Philadelphia Eagles	1933	(NFL)	3 NFL (1948-49,60)	Philadelphia (1933—)
Phoenix Cardinals	1920	(APFA)	1 NFL (1947)	Chicago (1920-59)
				St.Louis (1960-87)
				Phoenix (1988—)
San Francisco 49ers	1946	(AAFC)	4 Super Bowls (1981,84,88-89)	San Francisco (1946—)
Tampa Bay Buccaneers	1976	(NFL)	None	Tampa,FL (1976—)
Washington Redskins	1932	(NFL)	2 NFL (1937,42)	Boston (1932-36)
			2 Super Bowls (1982,87)	Washington,DC (1937—)

Annual NFL Leaders

Individual NFL leaders (1932-69) and NFC leaders (since 1970). Individual AFL leaders (1960-69) and AFC leaders (since 1970).

Rushing
NFL-NFC

Multiple winners: Jim Brown (8); Walter Payton (5); Steve Van Buren (4); Eric Dickerson (3); Cliff Battles, John Brockington, Larry Brown, Bill Dudley, Leroy Kelly, Bill Paschal, Joe Perry, Barry Sanders, Gale Sayers and Whizzer White (2).

Year		Att	Yds	Avg	Year		Att	Yds	Avg
1932	Cliff Battles, Bos	148	576	3.9	1963	Jim Brown, Cle	291	1863	6.4
1933	Jim Musick, Bos	173	809	4.7	1964	Jim Brown, Cle	280	1446	5.1
1934	Beattie Feathers, Chi. Bears	101	1004	9.9	1965	Jim Brown, Cle	289	1544	5.3
1935	Doug Russell, Chi. Cards	140	499	3.6	1966	Gale Sayers, Chi	229	1231	5.4
1936	Tuffy Leemans, NY	206	830	4.0	1967	Leroy Kelly, Cle	235	1205	5.1
1937	Cliff Battles, Wash	216	874	4.0	1968	Leroy Kelly, Cle	248	1239	5.0
1938	Byron (Whizzer) White, Pit.	152	567	3.7	1969	Gale Sayers, Chi	236	1032	4.4
1939	Bill Osmanski, Chi. Bears	121	699	5.9					
1940	Byron (Whizzer) White, Det.	146	514	3.5	1970	Larry Brown, Wash	237	1125	4.7
1941	Pug Manders, Bklyn	111	486	4.4	1971	John Brockington, GB.	216	1105	5.1
1942	Bill Dudley, Pit	162	697	4.3	1972	Larry Brown, Wash	285	1216	4.3
1943	Bill Paschal, NY	147	572	3.9	1973	John Brockington, GB.	265	1144	4.3
1944	Bill Paschal, NY	196	737	3.8	1974	Lawrence McCutcheon, LA.	236	1109	4.7
1945	Steve Van Buren, Phi.	143	832	5.8	1975	Jim Otis, St.L	269	1076	4.0
1946	Bill Dudley, Pit	146	604	4.1	1976	Walter Payton, Chi	311	1390	4.5
1947	Steve Van Buren, Phi.	217	1008	4.6	1977	Walter Payton, Chi	339	1852	5.5
1948	Steve Van Buren, Phi.	201	945	4.7	1978	Walter Payton, Chi	333	1395	4.2
1949	Steve Van Buren, Phi.	263	1146	4.4	1979	Walter Payton, Chi	369	1610	4.4
1950	Marion Motley, Cle	140	810	5.8	1980	Walter Payton, Chi	317	1460	4.6
1951	Eddie Price, NY Giants	271	971	3.6	1981	George Rogers, NO	378	1674	4.4
1952	Dan Towler, LA	156	894	5.7	1982	Tony Dorsett, Dal	177	745	4.2
1953	Joe Perry, SF	192	1018	5.3	1983	Eric Dickerson, LA	390	1808	4.6
1954	Joe Perry, SF	173	1049	6.1	1984	Eric Dickerson, LA	379	2105	5.6
1955	Alan Ameche, Bal	213	961	4.5	1985	Gerald Riggs, Atl.	397	1719	4.3
1956	Rick Casares, Chi. Bears	234	1126	4.8	1986	Eric Dickerson, LA	404	1821	4.5
1957	Jim Brown, Cle	202	942	4.7	1987	Charles White, LA	324	1374	4.2
1958	Jim Brown, Cle	257	1527	5.9	1988	Herschel Walker, Dal	361	1514	4.2
1959	Jim Brown, Cle	290	1329	4.6	1989	Barry Sanders, Det	280	1470	5.3
1960	Jim Brown, Cle	215	1257	5.8	1990	Barry Sanders, Det	255	1304	5.1
1961	Jim Brown, Cle	305	1408	4.6					
1962	Jim Taylor, GB.	272	1474	5.4					

Note: Jim Brown led the NFL in rushing eight of his nine years in the league. The one season he didn't win (1962) he finished fourth (996 yds) behind Taylor, John Henry Johnson of Pittsburgh (1141 yds) and Dick Bass of the LA Rams (1033 yds).

AFL-AFC

Multiple winners: Earl Campbell and O.J. Simpson (4); Cookie Gilchrist, Eric Dickerson, Floyd Little, Jim Nance and Curt Warner (2).

Year		Att	Yds	Avg	Year		Att	Yds	Avg
1960	Abner Haynes, Dal.	157	875	5.6	1976	O.J.Simpson, Buf	290	1503	5.2
1961	Billy Cannon, Hou.	200	948	4.7	1977	Mark van Eeghen, Oak	324	1273	3.9
1962	Cookie Gilchrist, Buf.	214	1096	5.1	1978	Earl Campbell, Hou	302	1450	4.8
1963	Clem Daniels, Oak.	215	1099	5.1	1979	Earl Campbell, Hou	368	1697	4.6
1964	Cookie Gilchrist, Buf.	230	981	4.3	1980	Earl Campbell, Hou	373	1934	5.2
1965	Paul Lowe, SD	222	1121	5.0	1981	Earl Campbell, Hou	361	1376	3.9
1966	Jim Nance, Bos	299	1458	4.9	1982	Freeman McNeil, NY	151	786	5.2
1967	Jim Nance, Bos	269	1216	4.5	1983	Curt Warner, Sea	335	1449	4.3
1968	Paul Robinson, Cin	238	1023	4.3	1984	Earnest Jackson, SD	296	1179	4.0
1969	Dickie Post, SD	182	873	4.8	1985	Marcus Allen, LA	380	1759	4.6
1970	Floyd Little, Den.	209	901	4.3	1986	Curt Warner, Sea	319	1481	4.6
1971	Floyd Little, Den.	284	1133	4.0	1987	Eric Dickerson, LA Rams-Ind	283	1288	4.6
1972	O.J.Simpson, Buf	292	1251	4.3	1988	Eric Dickerson, Ind	388	1659	4.3
1973	O.J.Simpson, Buf	332	2003	6.0	1989	Christian Okoye, KC.	370	1480	4.0
1974	Otis Armstrong, Den.	263	1407	5.4	1990	Thurman Thomas, Buf	271	1297	4.8
1975	O.J.Simpson, Buf	329	1817	5.5					

Passing
NFL-NFC

Since 1932, the NFL has used several formulas to determine passing leadership, from Total Yards alone (1932-37), to the current rating system—adopted in 1973—that takes Completions, Completion Pct, Yards Gained, TD Passes, Interceptions, Interception Pct and other factors into account. The quarterbacks listed below all led the league according to the system in use at the time.

Multiple winners: Sammy Baugh (6); Joe Montana and Roger Staubach (5); Arnie Herber, Sonny Jurgensen, Bart Starr and Norm Van Brocklin (3); Otto Graham, Cecil Isbell, Milt Plum and Bob Waterfield (2).

Year		Att	Cmp	Yds	TD	Year		Att	Cmp	Yds	TD
1932	Arnie Herber, GB	101	37	639	9	1963	Y.A.Tittle, NY	367	221	3145	36
1933	Harry Newman, NY	136	53	973	11	1964	Bart Starr, GB	272	163	2144	15
1934	Arnie Herber, GB	115	42	799	8	1965	Rudy Bukich, Chi.	312	176	2641	20
1935	Ed Danowski, NY	113	57	794	10	1966	Bart Starr, GB	251	156	2257	14
1936	Arnie Herber, GB	173	77	1239	11	1967	Sonny Jergensen, Wash.	508	288	3747	31
1937	Sammy Baugh, Wash.	171	81	1127	8	1968	Earl Morrall, Bal	317	182	2909	26
1938	Ed Danowski, NY	129	70	848	7	1969	Sonny Jurgensen, Wash.	442	274	3102	22
1939	Parker Hall, Cle.Rams	208	106	1227	9						
1940	Sammy Baugh, Wash.	177	111	1367	12	1970	John Brodie, SF	378	223	2941	24
1941	Cecil Isbell, GB	206	117	1479	15	1971	Roger Staubach, Dal.	211	126	1882	15
1942	Cecil Isbell, GB	268	146	2021	24	1972	Norm Snead, NY	325	196	2307	17
1943	Sammy Baugh, Wash.	239	133	1754	23	1973	Roger Staubach, Dal.	286	179	2428	23
1944	Frank Filchock, Wash.	147	84	1139	13	1974	Sonny Jurgensen, Wash.	167	107	1185	11
1945	Sammy Baugh, Wash.	182	128	1669	11	1975	Fran Tarkenton, Min.	425	273	2994	25
	& Sid Luckman, Chi. Bears.	217	117	1725	14	1976	James Harris, LA.	158	91	1460	8
1946	Bob Waterfield, LA	251	127	1747	18	1977	Roger Staubach, Dal.	361	210	2620	18
1947	Sammy Baugh, Wash.	354	210	2938	25	1978	Roger Staubach, Dal.	413	231	3190	25
1948	Tommy Thompson, Phi.	246	141	1965	25	1979	Roger Staubach, Dal.	461	267	3586	27
1949	Sammy Baugh, Wash.	255	145	1903	18	1980	Ron Jaworski, Phi	451	257	3529	27
1950	N.Van Brocklin, LA	233	127	2061	18	1981	Joe Montana, SF	488	311	3565	19
1951	Bob Waterfield, LA	176	88	1566	13	1982	Joe Theismann, Wash	252	161	2033	13
1952	N.Van Brocklin, LA	205	113	1736	14	1983	Steve Bartkowski, Atl.	432	274	3167	22
1953	Otto Graham, Cle	258	167	2722	11	1984	Joe Montana, SF	432	279	3630	28
1954	N.Van Brocklin, LA	260	139	2637	13	1985	Joe Montana, SF	494	303	3653	27
1955	Otto Graham, Cle	185	98	1721	15	1986	Tommy Kramer, Min.	372	208	3000	24
1956	Ed Brown, Chi. Bears	168	96	1667	11	1987	Joe Montana, SF	398	266	3054	31
1957	Tommy O'Connell, Cle	110	63	1229	9	1988	Wade Wilson, Min	332	204	2746	15
1958	Eddie LeBaron, Wash.	145	79	1365	11	1989	Don Majkowski, GB	599	353	4318	27
1959	Charlie Conerly, NY	194	113	1706	14	1990	Joe Montana, SF	520	321	3944	26
1960	Milt Plum, Cle	250	151	2297	21						
1961	Milt Plum, Cle	302	177	2416	16						
1962	Bart Starr, GB	285	178	2438	12						

Note: In 1945, Baugh and Luckman tied with 8 points on an inverse rating system.

AFL-AFC

Multiple winners: Ken Anderson, Len Dawson, Dan Marino (4); Bob Griese, Daryle Lamonica and Ken Stabler (2).

Year		Att	Cmp	Yds	TD	Year		Att	Cmp	Yds	TD
1960	Jack Kemp, LA.	406	211	3018	20	1976	Ken Stabler, Oak	291	194	2737	27
1961	George Blanda, Hou	362	187	3330	36	1977	Bob Griese, Mia	307	180	2252	22
1962	Len Dawson, Dal	310	189	2759	29	1978	Terry Bradshaw, Pit	368	207	2915	28
1963	Tobin Rote, SD	286	170	2510	20	1979	Dan Fouts, SD	530	332	4082	24
1964	Len Dawson, KC	354	199	2879	30	1980	Brian Sipe, Cle	554	337	4132	30
1965	John Hadl, SD	348	174	2798	20	1981	Ken Anderson, Cin	479	300	3753	29
1966	Len Dawson, KC	284	159	2527	26	1982	Ken Anderson, Cin	309	218	2495	12
1967	Daryle Lamonica, Oak.	425	220	3228	30	1983	Dan Marino, Mia	296	173	2210	20
1968	Len Dawson, KC	224	131	2109	17	1984	Dan Marino, Mia	564	362	5084	48
1969	Greg Cook, Cin	197	106	1854	15	1985	Ken O'Brien, NY	488	297	3888	25
1970	Daryle Lamonica, Oak.	356	179	2516	22	1986	Dan Marino, Mia	623	378	4746	44
1971	Bob Griese, Mia	263	145	2089	19	1987	Bernie Kosar, Cle	389	241	3033	22
1972	Earl Morrall, Mia.	150	83	1360	11	1988	Boomer Esiason, Cin	388	223	3572	28
1973	Ken Stabler, Oak	260	163	1997	14	1989	Dan Marino, Mia	550	308	3997	24
1974	Ken Anderson, Cin	328	213	2667	18	1990	Warren Moon, Hou	584	362	4689	33
1975	Ken Anderson, Cin	377	228	3169	21						

Annual NFL Leaders (Cont.)
Receiving
NFL-NFC

Multiple winners: Don Hutson (8); Raymond Berry, Tom Fears, Pete Pihos and Billy Wilson (3); Dwight Clark, Ahmad Rashad, Jerry Rice and Charley Taylor (2).

Year		No	Yds	Avg	TD	Year		No	Yds	Avg	TD
1932	Ray Flaherty, NY	21	350	16.7	3	1963	Bobby Joe Conrad, St.L	73	967	13.2	10
1933	Shipwreck Kelly, Bklyn	22	246	11.2	3	1964	Johnny Morris, Chi. Bears	93	1200	12.9	10
1934	Joe Carter, Phi	16	238	14.9	4	1965	Dave Parks, SF	80	1344	16.8	12
	& Red Badgro, NY	16	206	12.9	1	1966	Charley Taylor, Wash	72	1119	15.5	12
1935	Tod Goodwin, NY	26	432	16.6	4	1967	Charley Taylor, Wash	70	990	14.1	9
1936	Don Hutson, GB	34	536	15.8	8	1968	Clifton McNeil, SF	71	994	14.0	7
1937	Don Hutson, GB	41	552	13.5	7	1969	Dan Abramowicz, NO	73	1015	13.9	7
1938	Gaynell Tinsley, Chi. Cards	41	516	12.6	1						
1939	Don Hutson, GB	34	846	24.9	6	1970	Dick Gordon, Chi	71	1026	14.5	13
						1971	Bob Tucker, NY	59	791	13.4	4
1940	Don Looney, Phi	58	707	12.2	4	1972	Harold Jackson, Phi	62	1048	16.9	4
1941	Don Hutson, GB	58	739	12.7	10	1973	Harold Carmichael, Phi	67	1116	16.7	9
1942	Don Hutson, GB	74	1211	16.4	17	1974	Charle Young, Phi.	63	696	11.0	3
1943	Don Hutson, GB	47	776	16.5	11	1975	Chuck Foreman, Min	73	691	9.5	9
1944	Don Hutson, GB	58	866	14.9	9	1976	Drew Pearson, Dal	58	806	13.9	6
1945	Don Hutson, GB	47	834	17.7	9	1977	Ahmad Rashad, Min	51	681	13.4	2
1946	Jim Benton, LA	63	981	15.6	6	1978	Rickey Young, Min	88	704	8.0	5
1947	Jim Keane, Chi. Bears	64	910	14.2	10	1979	Ahmad Rashad, Min	80	1156	14.5	9
1948	Tom Fears, LA	51	698	13.7	4						
1949	Tom Fears, LA	77	1013	13.2	9	1980	Earl Cooper, SF	83	567	6.8	4
						1981	Dwight Clark, SF	85	1105	13.0	4
1950	Tom Fears, LA	84	1116	13.3	7	1982	Dwight Clark, SF	60	913	12.2	5
1951	Elroy Hirsch, LA	66	1495	22.7	17	1983	Roy Green, St.L	78	1227	15.7	14
1952	Mac Speedie, Cle	62	911	14.7	5		Charlie Brown, Wash	78	1225	15.7	8
1953	Pete Pihos, Phi	63	1049	16.7	10		& Earnest Gray, NY	78	1139	14.6	5
1954	Pete Pihos, Phi	60	872	14.5	10	1984	Art Monk, Wash	106	1372	12.9	7
	& Billy Wilson, SF	60	830	13.8	5	1985	Roger Craig, SF	92	1016	11.0	6
1955	Pete Pihos, Phi	62	864	13.9	7	1986	Jerry Rice, SF	86	1570	18.3	15
1956	Billy Wilson, SF	60	889	14.8	5	1987	J.T.Smith, St.L	91	1117	12.3	8
1957	Billy Wilson, SF	52	757	14.6	6	1988	Henry Ellard, LA	86	1414	16.4	10
1958	Raymond Berry, Bal	56	794	14.2	9	1989	Sterling Sharpe, GB	90	1423	15.8	12
	& Pete Retzlaff, Phi	56	766	13.7	2						
1959	Raymond Berry, Bal	66	959	14.5	14	1990	Jerry Rice, SF	100	1502	15.0	13
1960	Raymond Berry, Bal	74	1298	17.5	10						
1961	Red Phillips, LA	78	1092	14.0	5						
1962	Bobby Mitchell, Wash	72	1384	19.2	11						

AFL-AFC

Multiple winners: Lionel Taylor (5); Lance Alworth and Kellen Winslow (3); Fred Biletnikoff, Todd Christensen, Lydell Mitchell and Al Toon (2).

Year		No	Yds	Avg	TD	Year		No	Yds	Avg	TD
1960	Lionel Taylor, Den	92	1235	13.4	12	1976	MacArthur Lane, KC	66	686	10.4	1
1961	Lionel Taylor, Den	100	1176	11.8	4	1977	Lydell Mitchell, Bal	71	620	8.7	4
1962	Lionel Taylor, Den	77	908	11.8	4	1978	Steve Largent, Sea	71	1168	16.5	8
1963	Lionel Taylor, Den	78	1101	14.1	10	1979	Joe Washington, Bal	82	750	9.1	3
1964	Charley Hennigan, Hou	101	1546	15.3	8						
1965	Lionel Taylor, Den	85	1131	13.3	6	1980	Kellen Winslow, S.D	89	1290	14.5	9
1966	Lance Alworth, SD	73	1383	18.9	13	1981	Kellen Winslow, S.D	88	1075	12.2	10
1967	George Sauer, NY	75	1189	15.9	6	1982	Kellen Winslow, S.D	54	721	13.4	6
1968	Lance Alworth, SD	68	1312	19.3	10	1983	Todd Christensen, LA	92	1247	13.6	12
1969	Lance Alworth, SD	64	1003	15.7	4	1984	Ozzie Newsome, Cle	89	1001	11.2	5
						1985	Lionel James, SD	86	1027	11.9	6
1970	Marlin Briscoe, Buf	57	1036	18.2	8	1986	Todd Christensen, LA	95	1153	12.1	8
1971	Fred Biletnikoff, Oak	61	929	15.2	9	1987	Al Toon, NY	68	976	14.4	5
1972	Fred Biletnikoff, Oak	58	802	13.8	7	1988	Al Toon, NY	93	1067	11.5	5
1973	Fred Willis, Hou	57	371	6.5	1	1989	Andre Reed, Buf	88	1312	14.9	9
1974	Lydell Mitchell, Bal	72	544	7.6	2						
1975	Reggie Rucker, Cle	60	770	12.8	3	1990	Haywood Jeffires, Hou	74	1048	14.2	8

Scoring

NFL-NFC

Multiple winners: Don Hutson (5); Dutch Clark, Pat Harder, Paul Hornung and Mark Moseley (3); Kevin Butler, Mike Cofer, Fred Cox, Jack Manders, Chester Marcol, Eddie Murray, Gordy Soltau and Doak Walker (2)

Year		TD	FG	PAT	Pts	Year		TD	FG	PAT	Pts
1932	Dutch Clark, Portsmouth	6	3	10	55	1963	Don Chandler, NY	0	18	52	106
1933	Glenn Presnell, Portsmouth	6	6	10	64	1964	Lenny Moore, Bal	20	0	0	120
	& Ken Strong, NY	6	5	13	64	1965	Gale Sayers, Chi	22	0	0	132
1934	Jack Manders, Chi. Bears	3	10	31	79	1966	Bruce Gossett, LA	0	28	29	113
1935	Dutch Clark, Det	6	1	16	55	1967	Jim Bakken, St.L	0	27	36	117
1936	Dutch Clark, Det	7	4	19	73	1968	Leroy Kelly, Cle	20	0	0	120
1937	Jack Manders, Chi. Bears	5	8	15	69	1969	Fred Cox, Min	0	26	43	121
1938	Clarke Hinkle, GB	7	3	7	58	1970	Fred Cox, Min	0	30	35	125
1939	Andy Farkas, Wash	11	0	2	68	1971	Curt Knight, Wash	0	29	27	114
1940	Don Hutson, GB	7	0	15	57	1972	Chester Marcol, GB	0	33	29	128
1941	Don Hutson, GB	12	1	20	95	1973	David Ray, LA	0	30	40	130
1942	Don Hutson, GB	17	1	33	138	1974	Chester Marcol, GB	0	25	19	94
1943	Don Hutson, GB	12	3	26	117	1975	Chuck Foreman, Min	22	0	0	132
1944	Don Hutson, GB	9	0	31	85	1976	Mark Moseley, Wash	0	22	31	97
1945	Steve Van Buren, Phi	18	0	2	110	1977	Walter Payton, Chi	16	0	0	96
1946	Ted Fritsch, GB	10	9	13	100	1978	Frank Corral, LA	0	29	31	118
1947	Pat Harder, Chi. Cards	7	7	39	102	1979	Mark Moseley, Wash	0	25	39	114
1948	Pat Harder, Chi. Cards	6	7	53	110	1980	Eddie Murray, Det	0	27	35	116
1949	Gene Roberts, NY Giants	17	0	0	102	1981	Rafael Septien, Dal	0	27	40	121
	& Pat Harder, Chi. Cards	8	3	45	102		& Eddie Murray, Det	0	25	46	121
1950	Doak Walker, Det	11	8	38	128	1982	Wendell Tyler, LA	13	0	0	78
1951	Elroy Hirsch, LA	17	0	0	102	1983	Mark Moseley, Wash	0	33	62	161
1952	Gordy Soltau, SF	7	6	34	94	1984	Ray Wersching, SF	0	25	56	131
1953	Gordy Soltau, SF	6	10	48	114	1985	Kevin Butler, Chi	0	31	51	144
1954	Bobby Walston, Phi	11	4	36	114	1986	Kevin Butler, Chi	0	28	36	120
1955	Doak Walker, Det	7	9	27	96	1987	Jerry Rice, SF	23	0	0	138
1956	Bobby Layne, Det	5	12	33	99	1988	Mike Cofer, SF	0	27	40	121
1957	Sam Baker, Wash	1	14	29	77	1989	Mike Cofer, SF	0	29	49	136
	& Lou Groza, Cle	0	15	32	77	1990	Chip Lohmiller, Wash	0	30	41	131
1958	Jim Brown, Cle	18	0	0	108						
1959	Paul Hornung, GB	7	7	31	94						
1960	Paul Hornung, GB	15	15	41	176						
1961	Paul Hornung, GB	10	15	41	146						
1962	Jim Taylor, GB	19	0	0	114						

AFL-AFC

Multiple winners: Gino Cappelletti (5); Gary Anderson (3); Jim Breech, Roy Gerela, Gene Mingo, Nick Lowery, John Smith and Jim Turner (2).

Year		TD	FG	PAT	Pts	Year		TD	FG	PAT	Pts
1960	Gene Mingo, Den	6	18	33	123	1976	Toni Linhart, Bal	0	20	49	109
1961	Gino Cappelletti, Bos	8	17	48	147	1977	Errol Mann, Oak	0	20	39	99
1962	Gene Mingo, Den	4	27	32	137	1978	Pat Leahy, NY	0	22	41	107
1963	Gino Cappelletti, Bos	2	22	35	113	1979	John Smith, NE	0	23	46	115
1964	Gino Cappelletti, Bos	7	25	36	155	1980	John Smith, NE	0	26	51	129
1965	Gino Cappelletti, Bos	9	17	27	132	1981	Nick Lowery, KC	0	26	37	115
1966	Gino Cappelletti, Bos	6	16	35	119		& Jim Breech, Cin	0	22	49	115
1967	George Blanda, Oak	0	20	56	116	1982	Marcus Allen, LA	14	0	0	84
1968	Jim Turner, NY	0	34	43	145	1983	Gary Anderson, Pit	0	27	38	119
1969	Jim Turner, NY	0	32	33	129	1984	Gary Anderson, Pit	0	24	45	117
1970	Jan Stenerud, KC	0	30	26	116	1985	Gary Anderson, Pit	0	33	40	139
1971	Garo Yepremian, Mia	0	28	33	117	1986	Tony Franklin, NE	0	32	44	140
1972	Bobby Howfield, NY	0	27	40	121	1987	Jim Breech, Cin	0	24	25	97
1973	Roy Gerela, Pit	0	29	36	123	1988	Scott Norwood, Buf	0	32	33	129
1974	Roy Gerela, Pit	0	20	33	93	1989	David Treadwell, Den	0	27	39	120
1975	O.J. Simpson, Buf	23	0	0	138	1990	Nick Lowery, KC	0	34	37	139

All-Time NFL Leaders

Through 1990 regular season.

CAREER

Players active in 1990 in **bold** type.

Quarterback Ratings

Ratings based on performance standards established by the NFL for completion percentage, average gain, touchdown percentage, and interception percentage. Quarterbacks are allocated points according to how their statistics measure up to those standards. Minimum 1500 passing attempts.

	Yrs	Att	Comp	Comp%	Yards	Gain	TD	TD%	Int	Int%	Rating
Joe Montana	12	4579	2914	63.6	34,998	7.64	242	5.3	123	2.7	93.4
Dan Marino	8	4181	2480	59.3	31,416	7.51	241	5.8	136	3.3	88.5
Jim Kelly	5	2088	1251	59.9	15,730	7.53	105	5.0	72	3.4	85.8
Boomer Esiason	7	2687	1520	56.6	21,381	7.96	150	5.6	98	3.6	85.8
Roger Staubach	11	2958	1685	57.0	22,700	7.67	153	5.2	109	3.7	83.4
Neil Lomax	8	3153	1817	57.6	22,771	7.22	136	4.3	90	2.9	82.7
Sonny Jurgensen	18	4262	2433	57.1	32,224	7.56	255	6.0	189	4.4	82.6
Len Dawson	19	3741	2136	57.1	28,711	7.67	239	6.4	183	4.9	82.6
Dave Krieg	11	3291	1909	58.0	24,052	7.31	184	5.6	136	4.1	82.3
Jim Everett	5	2038	1154	56.6	15,345	7.53	101	5.0	73	3.6	82.2
Ken O'Brien	7	2878	1697	59.0	20,444	7.10	109	3.8	78	2.7	82.2
Ken Anderson	16	4475	2654	59.3	32,838	7.34	197	4.4	160	3.6	81.9
Danny White	13	2950	1761	59.7	21,959	7.44	155	5.3	132	4.5	81.7
Bart Starr	16	3149	1808	57.4	24,718	7.85	152	4.8	138	4.4	80.5
Fran Tarkenton	18	6467	3686	57.0	47,003	7.27	342	5.3	266	4.1	80.4
Bernie Kosar	6	2363	1364	57.7	16,450	6.96	85	3.6	62	2.6	80.3
Dan Fouts	15	5604	3297	58.8	43,040	7.68	254	4.5	242	4.3	80.2
Warren Moon	7	3025	1701	56.2	22,989	7.60	134	4.4	112	3.7	79.9
Tony Eason	8	1564	911	58.2	11,142	7.12	61	3.9	51	3.3	79.7
Jim McMahon	9	1840	1056	57.4	13,398	7.28	77	4.2	66	3.6	79.3
Randall Cunningham	6	2253	1230	54.6	15,399	6.83	107	4.7	71	3.2	78.8
Bert Jones	10	2551	1430	56.1	18,190	7.13	124	4.9	101	4.0	78.2
Johnny Unitas	18	5186	2830	54.6	40,239	7.76	290	5.6	253	4.9	78.2
Otto Graham	6	1565	872	55.7	13,499	8.63	88	5.6	94	6.0	78.2
Frank Ryan	13	2133	1090	51.1	16,042	7.52	149	7.0	111	5.2	77.6

Note: The NFL does not recognize records from the All-American Football Conference (1946-49). If it did, **Otto Graham** would rank 3rd (after Marino) with the following stats: 10 Yrs; 2,626 Att; 1,464 Comp; 55.8 Comp Pct; 23,584 Yards; 8.98 Avg Gain; 174 TD; 6.6 TD Pct; 135 Int; 5.1 Int Pct; and 86.6 Rating Pts.

Passing Yardage

	Yrs	Att	Comp	Pct	Yards
Fran Tarkenton	18	6467	3686	57.0	47,003
Dan Fouts	15	5604	3297	58.8	43,040
Johnny Unitas	18	5186	2830	54.6	40,239
Joe Montana	12	4579	2914	63.6	34,998
Jim Hart	19	5076	2593	51.1	34,665
John Hadl	16	4687	2363	50.4	33,513
Ken Anderson	16	4475	2654	59.3	32,838
Sonny Jurgensen	18	4262	2433	57.1	32,224
John Brodie	17	4491	2469	55.0	31,548
Dan Marino	8	4181	2480	59.3	31,416
Norm Snead	15	4353	2276	52.3	30,797
Joe Ferguson	18	4519	2369	52.4	29,817
Roman Gabriel	16	4498	2366	52.6	29,444
Len Dawson	19	3741	2136	57.1	28,711
Phil Simms	11	3969	2164	54.5	28,519
Steve DeBerg	14	4179	2376	56.9	28,490
Y.A.Tittle	15	3817	2118	55.5	28,339
Ron Jaworski	16	4117	2187	53.1	28,190
Terry Bradshaw	14	3901	2025	51.9	27,989
Ken Stabler	15	3793	2270	59.8	27,938
Craig Morton	18	3786	2053	54.2	27,908
Joe Namath	13	3762	1886	50.1	27,663
George Blanda	26	4007	1911	47.7	26,920
Steve Grogan	16	3593	1879	52.3	26,886
Bobby Layne	15	3700	1814	49.0	26,768

Note: The NFL does not recognize records from the All-American Football Conference (1946-49). If it did, **Y.A.Tittle** would rank 7th (after Hadl) with the following stats: 17 Yrs; 4,395 Att; 2,427 Comp; 55.2 Pct; and 33,070 Yards.

Touchdown Passes

	Yrs	TD	Int
Fran Tarkenton	18	342	266
Johnny Unitas	18	290	253
Sonny Jurgensen	18	255	189
Dan Fouts	15	254	242
John Hadl	16	244	268
Joe Montana	12	242	123
Dan Marino	8	241	136
Len Dawson	19	239	183
George Blanda	26	236	277
John Brodie	17	214	224
Terry Bradshaw	14	212	210
Y.A.Tittle	15	212	221
Jim Hart	19	209	247
Roman Gabriel	15	201	149
Ken Anderson	16	197	160
Norm Snead	15	196	253
Joe Ferguson	18	196	209
Bobby Layne	15	196	243
Ken Stabler	15	194	222
Bob Griese	14	192	172
Sammy Baugh	16	187	203
Dave Krieg	11	184	136
Craig Morton	18	183	187
Steve Grogan	16	182	208
Ron Jaworski	16	179	164

Note: The NFL does not recognize records from the All-American Football Conference (1946-49). If it did, **Y.A.Tittle** would rank 6th (tied with Montana) with the following stats: 17 Yrs; 242 TD; and 248 Int. Also, **Otto Graham** would rank 26th (after Jaworski) with the following stats: 10 Yrs; 174 TD; 135 Int.

Receiving

	Yrs	No	Yards	Avg	TD		Yrs	No	Yards	Avg	TD
Steve Largent	14	819	13,089	16.0	100	Harold Jackson	16	579	10,372	17.9	76
Charlie Joiner	18	750	12,146	16.2	65	Lionel Taylor	10	567	7,195	12.7	45
Art Monk	11	730	9,935	13.6	52	Wes Chandler	11	559	8,966	16.0	56
Ozzie Newsome	13	662	7,980	12.1	47	**Stanley Morgan**	14	557	10,716	19.2	72
Charley Taylor	13	649	9,110	14.0	79	**J.T.Smith**	13	544	6,974	12.8	35
James Lofton	13	642	11,963	18.6	61	Lance Alworth	11	542	10,266	18.9	85
Don Maynard	15	633	11,834	18.7	88	Kellen Winslow	10	541	6,741	12.5	45
Raymond Berry	13	631	9,275	14.7	68	John Stallworth	14	537	8,723	16.2	63
Harold Carmichael	14	590	8,985	15.2	79	**Roy Green**	12	522	8,496	16.3	66
Fred Biletnikoff	14	589	8,974	15.2	76	Bobby Mitchell	11	521	7,954	15.3	65

Rushing Yardage

	Yrs	Car	Yards	Avg	TD
Walter Payton	13	3838	16,726	4.4	110
Tony Dorsett	12	2936	12,739	4.3	77
Jim Brown	9	2359	12,312	5.2	106
Franco Harris	13	2949	12,120	4.1	91
Eric Dickerson	8	2616	11,903	4.6	86
John Riggins	14	2916	11,352	3.9	104
O.J.Simpson	11	2404	11,236	4.7	61
Ottis Anderson	12	2499	10,101	4.0	80
Earl Campbell	8	2187	9,407	4.3	74
Jim Taylor	10	1941	8,597	4.4	83
Joe Perry	14	1737	8,378	4.8	53
Larry Csonka	11	1891	8,081	4.3	64
Marcus Allen	9	1960	7,957	4.1	75
Gerald Riggs	9	1911	7,940	4.2	58
Freeman McNeil	10	1704	7,604	4.5	36
Mike Pruitt	11	1844	7,378	4.0	51
James Brooks	10	1515	7,347	4.8	47
Leroy Kelly	10	1727	7,274	4.2	74
George Rogers	7	1692	7,176	4.2	54
Roger Craig	8	1686	7,064	4.2	50

Note: The NFL does not recognize records from the All-American Football Conference (1946-49). If it did, **Joe Perry** would rank 9th (after Anderson) with the following stats: 16 Yrs; 1,929 Car; 9,723 Yards; 5.0 Avg; and 71 TD.

All-Purpose Running

	Yrs	Rush	Rec	Ret	Total
Walter Payton	13	16,726	4,538	539	21,803
Tony Dorsett	12	12,739	3,554	33	16,326
Jim Brown	9	12,312	2,499	648	15,459
Franco Harris	13	12,120	2,287	215	14,622
O.J.Simpson	11	11,236	2,142	990	14,368
Bobby Mitchell	11	2,735	7,954	3,389	14,078
James Brooks	10	7,347	3,274	3,088	13,709
Eric Dickerson	8	11,903	1,725	15	13,643
John Riggins	14	11,352	2,090	−7	13,435
Steve Largent	14	83	13,089	224	13,396
Greg Pruitt	12	5,672	3,069	4,521	13,262
Ottis Anderson	12	10,101	3,021	29	13,151
Ollie Matson	14	5,173	3,285	4,426	12,884
Timmy Brown	10	3,862	3,399	5,423	12,684
Lenny Moore	12	5,174	6,039	1,238	12,451
Don Maynard	15	70	11,834	475	12,379
Charlie Joiner	18	22	12,146	199	12,367
Leroy Kelly	10	7,274	2,281	2,775	12,330
Floyd Little	9	6,323	2,418	3,432	12,173
Abner Haynes	8	4,630	3,535	3,900	12,065

Scoring

Points

	Yrs	TD	FG	PAT	Total
George Blanda	26	9	335	943	2002
Jan Stenerud	19	0	373	580	1699
Jim Turner	16	1	304	521	1439
Mark Moseley	16	0	300	482	1382
Jim Bakken	17	0	282	534	1380
Fred Cox	15	0	282	519	1365
Pat Leahy	17	0	278	528	1362
Lou Groza	17	1	234	641	1349
Chris Bahr	14	0	241	490	1213
Nick Lowery	12	0	259	375	1152
Gino Cappelletti	11	42	176	350	1130†
Ray Wersching	15	0	222	456	1122
Don Cockroft	13	0	216	432	1080
Garo Yepremian	14	0	210	444	1074
Jim Breech	13	0	201	459	1062
Bruce Gossett	11	0	219	374	1031
Eddie Murray	11	0	225	341	1016
Sam Baker	15	2	179	428	977
Matt Bahr	12	0	199	378	975
Rafael Septien	10	0	180	420	960
Lou Michaels	13	1	187	386	955†
Gary Anderson	9	0	206	292	910
Roy Gerela	11	0	184	351	903
Bobby Walston	12	46	80	365	881
Tony Franklin	10	0	177	341	872

†Cappelletti's total includes four 2-point conversions, and Michaels' total includes one safety.

Note: The NFL does not recognize records from the All-American Football Conference (1946-49). If it did, **Lou Groza** would rank 3rd (after Stenerud) with the following stats: 21 Yrs; 1 TD; 264 FG; 810 PAT; 1608 Pts.

Touchdowns

	Yrs	Rush	Rec	Ret	Total
Jim Brown	9	106	20	0	126
Walter Payton	13	110	15	0	125
John Riggins	14	104	12	0	116
Lenny Moore	12	63	48	2	113
Don Hutson	11	3	99	3	105
Steve Largent	14	1	100	0	101
Franco Harris	13	91	9	0	100
Marcus Allen	9	75	17	1	93
Jim Taylor	10	83	10	0	93
Tony Dorsett	12	77	13	1	91
Bobby Mitchell	11	18	65	8	91
Eric Dickerson	8	86	4	0	90
Leroy Kelly	10	74	13	3	90
Charley Taylor	13	11	79	0	90
Don Maynard	15	0	88	0	88
Lance Alworth	11	2	85	0	87
Paul Warfield	13	1	85	0	86
Ottis Anderson	12	80	5	0	85
Tommy McDonald	12	0	84	1	85
Jerry Rice	6	4	79	0	83
Pete Johnson	8	76	6	0	82
Art Powell	10	0	81	1	82
Harold Carmichael	14	0	79	0	79
Frank Gifford	12	34	43	1	78
Fred Biletnikoff	14	0	76	1	77
Steve Van Buren	8	69	3	5	77

Note: The NFL does not recognize records from the All-American Football Conference (1946-49). If it did, **Joe Perry** would rank 20th (after McDonald) with the following stats: 16 Yrs; 71 Rush; 12 Rec; 1 Ret; 84 TDs.

All-Time NFL Leaders (Cont.)
Miscellaneous

Interceptions

	Yrs	No	Yards	TD
Paul Krause	16	81	1185	3
Emlen Tunnell	14	79	1282	4
Dick "Night Train" Lane	14	68	1207	5
Ken Riley	15	65	596	5
Dick LeBeau	13	62	762	3
Dave Brown	15	62	698	5

Punting Average
Minimum 300 punts.

	Yrs	No	Yards	Avg
Sammy Baugh	16	338	15,245	45.1
Tommy Davis	11	511	22,833	44.7
Yale Lary	11	503	22,279	44.3
Rohn Stark	9	664	29,267	44.1
Horace Gillom	7	385	16,872	43.8
Jerry Norton	11	358	15,671	43.8

Kickoff Return Average
Minimum 75 returns.

	Yrs	No	Yards	Avg	TD
Gale Sayers	7	91	2781	30.6	6
Lynn Chandnois	7	92	2720	29.6	3
Abe Woodson	9	193	5538	28.7	5
Buddy Young	6	90	2514	27.9	2
Travis Williams	5	102	2801	27.5	6

Punt Return Average
Minimum 75 returns.

	Yrs	No	Yards	Avg	TD
George McAfee	8	112	1431	12.8	2
Jack Christiansen	8	85	1084	12.8	8
Claude Gibson	5	110	1381	12.6	3
Clarence Verdin	5	76	931	12.3	2
Bill Dudley	9	124	1515	12.2	3

Safeties

	Yrs	No
Ted Hendricks	15	4
Doug English	10	4

Eleven players tied with three.

SINGLE SEASON
Scoring

Points

	Year	TD	PAT	FG	Pts
Paul Hornung, GB	1960	15	41	15	176
Mark Moseley, Wash	1983	0	62	33	161
Gino Cappelletti, Bos	1964	7	38	25	155
Gino Cappelletti, Bos	1961	8	48	17	147
Paul Hornung, GB	1961	10	41	15	146
Jim Turner, NY Jets	1968	0	43	34	145
John Riggins, Wash	1983	24	0	0	144
Kevin Butler, Chi	1985	0	51	31	144
Tony Franklin, NE	1986	0	44	32	140
Gary Anderson, Pit	1985	0	40	33	139
Nick Lowery, KC	1990	0	37	34	139

Note: The NFL regular season schedule grew from 12 games (1947-60) to 14 (1961-77) to 16 (1978-present). The AFL regular season schedule was always 14 games (1960-69).

Field Goals

	Year	Att	No
Ali Haji-Sheikh, NY Giants	1983	42	35
Nick Lowery, Kansas City	1990	37	34
Jim Turner, NY Jets*	1968	46	34
Gary Anderson, Pittsburgh	1985	42	33
Mark Moseley, Washington*	1983	47	33
Chester Marcol, Green Bay	1972	48	33
Scott Norwood, Buffalo	1988	37	32
Tony Franklin, New England	1986	41	32
Jim Turner, NY Jets*	1969	47	32
Morten Andersen, New Orleans	1985	35	31
Kevin Butler, Chicago	1985	37	31
Rich Karlis, Minnesota	1989	39	31

*Old-style, straight ahead kicker

Touchdowns

	Year	Rush	Rec	Ret	Total
John Riggins, Wash	1983	24	0	0	24
O.J.Simpson, Buf	1975	16	7	0	23
Jerry Rice, SF	1987	1	22	0	23
Gale Sayers, Chi.	1966	14	6	2	22
Chuck Foreman, Min	1975	13	9	0	22
Jim Brown, Cle	1965	17	4	0	21
Joe Morris, NY Giants	1985	21	0	0	21
Lenny Moore, Bal	1964	16	3	1	20
Leroy Kelly, Cle	1968	16	4	0	20
Eric Dickerson, LA Rams	1983	18	2	0	20

Touchdowns Passing

	Year	No
Dan Marino, Miami	1984	48
Dan Marino, Miami	1986	44
George Blanda, Houston	1961	36
Y.A.Tittle, NY Giants	1963	36
Y.A.Tittle, NY Giants	1962	33
Dan Fouts, San Diego	1981	33
Warren Moon, Houston	1990	33
Johnny Unitas, Baltimore	1959	32
Sonny Jurgensen, Philadelphia	1961	32
Lynn Dickey, Green Bay	1983	32
Dave Krieg, Seattle	1984	32

Touchdowns Rushing

	Year	No
John Riggins, Washington	1983	24
Joe Morris, NY Giants	1985	21
Jim Taylor, Green Bay	1962	19
Earl Campbell, Houston	1979	19
Chuck Muncie, San Diego	1981	19
Eric Dickerson, LA Rams	1983	18
George Rogers, Washington	1986	18
Jim Brown, Cleveland	1958	17
Jim Brown, Cleveland	1965	17

Touchdowns Receiving

	Year	No
Jerry Rice, San Francisco	1987	22
Mark Clayton, Miami	1984	18
Don Hutson, Green Bay	1942	17
Elroy "Crazylegs" Hirsch, LA Rams	1951	17
Bill Groman, Houston	1961	17
Jerry Rice, San Francisco	1989	17
Art Powell, Oakland	1963	16
Jerry Rice, San Francisco	1986	15

Passing

Yards Gained	Year	Att	Cmp	Pct	Yds
Dan Marino, Mia	1984	564	362	64.2	5084
Dan Fouts, SD	1981	609	360	59.1	4802
Dan Marino, Mia	1986	623	378	60.7	4746
Dan Fouts, SD	1980	589	348	59.1	4715
Warren Moon, Hou	1990	584	362	62.0	4689
Neil Lomax, St.L	1984	560	345	61.6	4614
Lynn Dickey, GB	1983	484	289	59.7	4458
Dan Marino, Mia	1988	606	354	58.4	4434
Bill Kenney, KC	1983	603	346	57.4	4348
Don Majkowski, GB	1989	599	353	58.9	4318

Rushing

Yards Gained	Year	Att	Yds	Avg
Eric Dickerson, Rams	1984	379	2105	5.6
O.J.Simpson, Buf	1973	332	2003	6.0
Earl Campbell, Hou	1980	373	1934	5.2
Jim Brown, Cle	1963	291	1863	6.4
Walter Payton, Chi	1977	339	1852	5.5
Eric Dickerson, Rams	1986	404	1821	4.5
O.J.Simpson, Buf	1975	329	1817	5.5
Eric Dickerson, Rams	1983	390	1808	4.6
Marcus Allen, Raiders	1985	390	1759	4.6
Gerald Riggs, Atl	1985	397	1719	4.3

Receiving

Catches	Year	No	Yds
Art Monk, Wash	1984	106	1372
Charley Hennigan, Hou	1964	101	1546
Jerry Rice, SF	1990	100	1502
Lionel Taylor, Den	1961	100	1176
Todd Christensen, Raiders	1986	95	1153
Johnny Morris, Chi	1964	93	1200
Al Toon, Jets	1988	93	1067
Todd Christensen, Raiders	1983	92	1247
Lionel Taylor, Den	1960	92	1235
Roger Craig, SF	1985	92	1016

All-Purpose Running

	Year	Run	Rec	Ret	Total
Lionel James, SD	1985	516	1027	992	2535
Terry Metcalf, StL	1975	816	378	1268	2462
Mack Herron, NE	1974	824	474	1146	2444
Gale Sayers, Chi	1966	1231	447	762	2440
Timmy Brown, Phi	1963	841	487	1100	2428
Tim Brown, Raid	1988	50	725	1542	2317
Marcus Allen, Rad	1985	1759	555	−6	2308
Timmy Brown, Phi	1962	545	849	912	2306
Gale Sayers, Chi	1965	867	507	898	2272
E.Dickerson, Rams	1984	2105	139	15	2259
O.J.Simpson, Buf	1975	1817	426	0	2243

Miscellaneous

Interceptions

Qualifiers	Year	No
Dick "Night Train" Lane, Detroit	1952	14
Dan Sandifer, Washington	1948	13
Spec Sanders, NY Yanks	1950	13
Lester Hayes, Oakland	1980	13

Punt Return Average

Qualifiers	Year	Avg
Herb Rich, Baltimore	1950	23.0
Jack Christiansen, Detroit	1952	21.5
Dick Christy, NY Titans	1961	21.3
Bob Hayes, Dallas	1968	20.8

Kickoff Return Average

Qualifiers	Year	Avg
Travis Williams, Green Bay	1967	41.1
Gale Sayers, Chicago	1967	37.7
Ollie Matson, Chicago Cards	1958	35.5
Jim Duncan, Baltimore	1970	35.4
Lynn Chandnois, Pittsburgh	1952	35.2

Punting Average

Qualifiers	Year	Avg
Sammy Baugh, Washington	1940	51.4
Yale Lary, Detroit	1963	48.9
Sammy Baugh, Washington	1941	48.7
Yale Lary, Detroit	1961	48.4
Sammy Baugh, Washington	1942	48.2

SINGLE GAME
Scoring

Points

	Date	Pts
Ernie Nevers, Chi. Cards vs Chi. Bears	11/28/29	40
Dub Jones, Cle vs Chi. Bears	11/25/51	36
Gale Sayers, Chi vs SF	12/12/65	36
Paul Hornung, GB vs Bal	10/8/61	33
Bob Shaw, Cle. Cards vs Bal	10/2/50	30
Jim Brown, Cle vs Bal	11/1/59	30
Abner Haynes, Dal.Texans vs Oak	11/26/61	30
Billy Cannon, Hou vs NY Titans	12/10/61	30
Cookie Gilchrist, Buf vs NY Jets	12/8/63	30
Kellen Winslow, SD vs Oak	11/22/81	30
Jerry Rice, SF at Atl	10/14/90	30

Note: Nevers celebrated Thanksgiving, 1929, by scoring all the Chicago Cardinals' points on six rushing TDs and four PATs. The Cards beat Red Grange and the Chicago Bears, 40-6.

Touchdowns Rushing

	Date	No
Ernie Nevers, Chi. Cards vs Chi. Bears	11/28/29	6
Dub Jones, Cle vs Chi. Bears	11/25/51	6
Gale Sayers, Chi vs SF	12/12/65	6

Eight players tied with five TDs.

Touchdowns Passing

	Date	No
Sid Luckman, Chi Bears vs NYG	11/14/43	7
Adrian Burk, Phi vs Wash	10/17/54	7
George Blanda, Hou vs NY Titans	11/19/61	7
Y.A.Tittle, NYG vs Wash	10/28/62	7
Joe Kapp, Min vs Bal	9/28/69	7

Touchdowns Receiving

	Date	No
Bob Shaw, Chi. Cards vs Bal	10/2/50	5
Kellen Winslow, SD vs Oak	11/22/81	5
Jerry Rice, SF at Atl	10/14/90	5

Field Goals

	Date	No
Jim Bakken, St.L vs Pit	9/24/67	7
Rich Karlis, Min vs Rams	11/5/89	7

Eight players tied with 6 FGs.
Note: Bakken was 7-for-9, Karlis 7-for-7.

Extra Point Kicks

	Date	No
Pat Harder, Cards vs NYG	10/17/48	9
Bob Waterfield, LA vs Bal	10/22/50	9
Charlie Gogolak, Wash vs NYG	11/27/66	9

All-Time NFL Leaders (Cont.)
SINGLE GAME

Passing

Yards Gained	Date	Yds
Norm Van Brocklin, LA vs NY Yanks	9/28/51	554
Warren Moon, Hou at KC	12/16/90	527
Dan Marino, Mia vs NYJ	10/23/88	521
Phil Simms, NYG vs Cin	10/13/85	513
Vince Ferragamo, Rams vs Chi	12/26/82	509

Completions	Date	No
Richard Todd, NYJ vs SF	9/21/80	42
Ken Anderson, Cin vs SD	12/20/82	40
Phil Simms, NYG vs Cin	10/13/85	40
Dan Marino, Mia vs Buf	11/16/86	39
Tommy Kramer, Min vs Cle	12/14/80	38
Joe Ferguson, Buf vs Mia (OT)	10/9/83	38

Rushing

Yards Gained	Date	Yds
Walter Payton, Chi vs Min	11/20/77	275
O.J.Simpson, Buf vs Det	11/25/76	273
O.J.Simpson, Buf vs NE	9/16/73	250
Willie Ellison, LA Rams vs NO	12/5/71	247
Cookie Gilchrist, Buf vs NYJ	12/8/63	243

Receiving

Catches	Date	No
Tom Fears, LA vs GB	12/3/50	18
Clark Gaines, NYJ vs SF	9/21/80	17
Sonny Randle, St.L vs NYG	11/4/62	16
Five tied with 15 each.		

Yards Gained	Date	Yds
Flipper Anderson, LA Rams vs NO	11/26/89	336
Stephone Paige, KC vs SD	12/22/85	309
Jim Benton, Cle vs Det	11/22/45	303
Cloyce Box, Det vs Bal	12/3/50	302
John Taylor, SF vs LA Rams	12/11/89	286

All-Purpose Running

	Date	Yds
Billy Cannon, Hou vs NY Titans	12/10/61	373
Lionel James, SD vs Raiders	11/10/85	345
Timmy Brown, Phi vs St.L	12/16/62	341
Gale Sayers, Chi vs Min	12/18/66	339
Gale Sayers, Chi vs SF	12/12/65	336

LONGEST PLAYS

Passing (all for TDs)	Date	Yds
Frank Filchock		
to Andy Farkas, Wash vs Pit	10/15/39	99
George Izo		
to Bobby Mitchell, Wash vs Cle	9/15/63	99
Karl Sweetan		
to Pat Studstill, Det vs Bal	10/16/66	99
Sonny Jurgensen		
to Gerry Allen, Wash vs Chi	9/15/68	99
Jim Plunkett		
to Cliff Branch, LA Raiders vs Wash	10/2/83	99
Ron Jaworski		
to Mike Quick, Phi vs Atl	11/10/85	99

Runs from Scrimmage (all for TDs)	Date	Yds
Tony Dorsett, Dal vs Min	1/3/83	99
Andy Uram, GB vs Chi. Cards	10/8/39	97
Bob Gage, Pit vs Bears	12/4/49	97

Field Goals	Date	Yds
Tom Dempsey, NO vs Det	11/8/70	63
Steve Cox, Cle vs Cin	10/21/84	60
Tony Franklin, Phi vs Dal	11/12/79	59

Punts	Date	Yds
Steve O'Neal, NYJ vs Den	9/21/69	98
Joe Lintzenich, Chi. Bears vs NYG	10/16/31	94
Randall Cunningham, Phi vs NYG	12/3/89	91
Don Chandler, GB vs SF	10/10/65	90

Punt Returns (all for TDs)	Date	Yds
Gil LeFebvre, Cin vs Bklyn	12/3/33	98
Charlie West, Min vs Wash	11/3/68	98
Dennis Morgan, Dal vs St.L	10/13/74	98

Kickoff Returns (all for TDs)	Date	Yds
Al Carmichael, GB vs Chi. Bears	10/7/56	106
Noland Smith, KC vs Den	12/17/67	106
Roy Green, St.L vs Dal	10/21/79	106
Seven players tied with 105-yd returns.		

Interception Returns (for TD)	Date	Yds
Vencie Glenn, SD vs Den	11/29/87	103
Four players tied with 102-yd returns.		

NFL Pro Bowl

A postseason All-Star game between the new league champion and a team of professional all-stars was added to the NFL schedule in 1939. In the first game at Wrigley Field in Los Angeles, the NY Giants beat a team made up of players from NFL teams and two independent clubs in L.A. (the LA Bulldogs and Hollywood Stars). An all-NFL All-Star team provided the opposition over the next four seasons, but the game was cancelled in 1943.

The Pro Bowl was revived in 1951 as a contest between conference all-star teams: American vs National (1951-53), Eastern vs Western (1954-70), and AFC vs NFC (1971-present). The NFC leads the current series with the AFC, 12-9.

Date	Winner	Score	Loser	Site
1/15/39	NY Giants	13-10	All-Stars	Los Ang.
1/14/40	Green Bay	16-7	All-Stars	Los Ang.
12/29/40	Chi.Bears	28-14	All-Stars	Los Ang.
1/4/42	Chi.Bears	35-24	All-Stars	New York
12/27/42	All-Stars	17-14	Washington	Phila.
1943-50	No game			

Year	Winner	MVP
1951	Amer., 28-27	Otto Graham, Cle., QB
1952	Natl., 30-13	Dan Towler, LA, HB
1953	Natl., 27-7	Don Doll, Det., DB

Year	Winner	MVP
1954	East, 20-9	Chuck Bednarik, Phi., LB
1955	West, 26-19	Billy Wilson, SF, E
1956	East, 31-30	Ollie Matson, Cards, HB
1957	West, 19-10	Back—Bert Rechicahr, Bal.
		Line—Ernie Stautner, Pit.
1958	West, 26-7	Back—Hugh McElhenny, SF
		Line—Gene Brito, Wash.
1959	East, 28-21	Back—Frank Gifford, NY
		Line—Doug Atkins, Chi

Year	Winner	MVP
1960	West, 38-21	Back—Johnny Unitas, Bal.
		Line—Big Daddy Lipscomb, Pit.
1961	West, 35-31	Back—Johnny Unitas, Bal.
		Line—Sam Huff, NY
1962	West, 31-30	Back—Jim Brown, Cle.
		Line—Henry Jordan, GB
1963	East, 30-20	Back—Jim Brown, Cle.
		Line—Big Daddy Lipscomb, Pit.
1964	West, 31-17	Back—Johnny Unitas, Bal.
		Line—Gino Marchetti, Bal
1965	West, 34-14	Back—Fran Tarkenton, Min
		Line—Terry Barr, Det.
1966	East, 36-7	Back—Jim Brown, Cle.
		Line—Dale Meinhart, St.L.
1967	East, 20-10	Back—Gale Sayers, Chi.
		Line—Floyd Peters, Phi.
1968	West, 38-20	Back—Gale Sayers, Chi.
		Line—Dave Robinson, GB
1969	West, 10-7	Back—Roman Gabriel, LA
		Line—Merlin Olsen, LA
1970	West, 16-13	Back—Gale Sayers, Chi.
		Line—George Andrie, Dal.
1971	NFC, 27-6	Back—Mel Renfro, Dal.
		Line—Fred Carr, GB

Year	Winner	MVP
1972	AFC, 26-13	Off—Jan Stenerud, KC
		Def—Willie Lanier, KC
1973	AFC, 33-28	O.J.Simpson, Buf., RB
1974	AFC, 15-13	Garo Yepremian, Mia, PK
1975	NFC, 17-10	James Harris, LA Rams, QB
1976	NFC, 23-20	Billy Johnson, Hou., KR
1977	AFC, 24-14	Mel Blount, Pit., CB
1978	NFC, 14-13	Walter Payton, Chi., RB
1979	NFC, 13-7	Ahmad Rashad, Min., WR
1980	NFC, 37-27	Chuck Muncie, NO, RB
1981	NFC, 21-7	Eddie Murray, Det., PK
1982	AFC, 16-13	Kellen Winslow, SD, WR
		& Lee Roy Selmon, TB, DE
1983	NFC, 20-19	Dan Fouts, SD, QB
		& John Jefferson, GB, WR
1984	NFC, 45-3	Joe Theismann, Wash., QB
1985	AFC, 22-14	Mark Gastineau, NYJ, DE
1986	NFC, 28-24	Phil Simms, NYG, QB
1987	AFC, 10-6	Reggie White, Phi., DE
1988	AFC, 15-6	Bruce Smith, Buf., DE
1989	NFC, 34-3	Randall Cunningham, Phi., QB
1990	NFC, 27-21	Jerry Gray, LA Rams, CB
1991	AFC, 23-21	Jim Kelly, Buf., QB

Playing sites (since 1951)**:** Memorial Coliseum in Los Angeles (1951-72 and 1979); Texas Stadium in Irving,TX (1973); Arrowhead Stadium in Kansas City (1974); Orange Bowl in Miami (1975); Superdome in New Orleans (1976); Kingdome in Seattle (1977); Tampa Stadium in Tampa (1978) and Aloha Stadium in Honolulu (since 1980).

AFL All-Star Game

The AFL did not play an All-Star game after its first season in 1960 but did stage All-Star games from 1962-70. All-Star teams from the Eastern and Western divisions played each other every year except 1966 with the West winning the series, 6-2. In 1966, the league champion Buffalo Bills met an elite squad made up of the best players from the league's other eight clubs and lost, 30-19.

Year	Winner	MVP
1962	West, 47-27	Cotton Davidson, Oak., QB
1963	West, 21-14	Off—Curtis McClinton, Dal.
		Def—Earl Faison, SD
1964	West, 27-24	Off—Keith Lincoln, SD
		Def—Archie Matsos, Oak.
1965	West, 38-14	Off—Keith Lincoln, SD
		Def—Willie Brown, Den.
1966	All-Stars 30	Off—Joe Namath, NY
	Buffalo Bills 19	Def—Frank Buncom, SD

Year	Winner	MVP
1967	East, 30-23	Off—Babe Parilli, Bos.
		Def—Verlon Biggs, NY
1968	East, 25-24	Off—Joe Namath, NY
		& Don Maynard, NY
		Def—Speedy Duncan, SD
1969	West, 38-25	Off—Len Dawson, KC
		Def—George Webster, Hou.
1970	West, 26-3	John Hadl, SD, QB

Playing sites: Balboa Stadium in San Diego (1962-64); Jeppesen Stadium in Houston (1965); Rice Stadium in Houston (1966); Oakland Coliseum (1967); Gator Bowl in Jacksonville (1968-69) and Astrodome in Houston (1970).

Chicago College All-Star Game

On Aug.31, 1934, a year after sponsoring Major League Baseball's first All-Star Game, the Chicago Tribune and sports editor Arch Ward presented the first Chicago College All-Star Game at Soldier Field. A crowd of 79,432 turned out to see an all-star team of graduated college seniors battle the 1933 NFL champion Chicago Bears to a scoreless tie. The preseason game was played annually at Soldier Field until it was cancelled in 1977.

Year		Year		Year	
1934	Chi.Bears 0, All-Stars 0	1950	All-Stars 17, Philadelphia 7	1964	Chi.Bears 28, All-Stars 17
1935	Chi.Bears 5, All-Stars 0	1951	Cleveland 33, All-Stars 0	1965	Cleveland 24, All-Stars 16
1936	Detroit 7, All-Stars 0	1952	LA Rams 10, All-Stars 7	1966	Green Bay 38, All-Stars 0
1937	All-Stars 6, Green Bay 0	1953	Detroit 24, All-Stars 10	1967	Green Bay 27, All-Stars 0
1938	All-Stars 28, Washington 16	1954	Detroit 31, All-Stars 6	1968	Green Bay 34, All-Stars 17
1939	NY Giants 9, All-Stars 0	1955	All-Stars 30, Cleveland 27	1969	NY Jets 26, All-Stars 24
		1956	Cleveland 26, All-Stars 0		
1940	Green Bay 45, All-Stars 28	1957	NY Giants 22, All-Stars 12	1970	Kansas City 24, All-Stars 3
1941	Chi.Bears 37, All-Stars 13	1958	All-Stars 35, Detroit 19	1971	Baltimore 24, All-Stars 17
1942	Chi.Bears 21, All-Stars 0	1959	Baltimore 29, All-Stars 0	1972	Dallas 20, All-Stars 7
1943	All-Stars 27, Washington 7			1973	Miami 14, All-Stars 3
1944	Chi.Bears 24, All-Stars 21	1960	Baltimore 32, All-Stars 7	1974	No Game (NFLPA Strike)
1945	Green Bay 19, All-Stars 7	1961	Philadelphia 28, All-Stars 14	1975	Pittsburgh 21, All-Stars 14
1946	All-Stars 16, LA Rams 0	1962	Green Bay 42, All-Stars 20	1976	Pittsburgh 24, All-Stars 0*
1947	All-Stars 16, Chi.Bears 0	1963	All-Stars 20, Green Bay 17		
1948	Chi.Cards 28, All-Stars 0			*Downpour flooded field, game called with
1949	Philadelphia 38, All-Stars 0			1:22 left in 3rd quarter.

All-Time Winningest NFL Coaches

Top 20 NFL career victories through the 1990 season. Career, regular season and playoff records are noted along with NFL, AFL and Super Bowl titles won. Active coaches in **bold** type.

	Yrs	Career				Regular Season				Playoffs			League Titles
		W	L	T	Pct	W	L	T	Pct	W	L	Pct	
George Halas	40	325	151	31	.672	319	148	31	.692	6	3	.667	5 NFL
Don Shula	28	298	137	6	.683	281	123	6	.693	17	14	.548	2 Super Bowls and 1 NFL
Tom Landry	29	270	178	6	.601	250	162	6	.605	20	16	.556	2 Super Bowls
Curly Lambeau	33	229	134	22	.623	226	132	22	.624	3	2	.600	6 NFL
Chuck Noll	22	202	147	1	.579	186	139	1	.572	16	8	.667	4 Super Bowls
Chuck Knox	18	171	116	1	.595	164	105	1	.609	7	11	.389	—None—
Paul Brown	21	170	108	6	.609	166	100	6	.621	4	8	.333	3 NFL
Bud Grant	18	168	108	5	.607	158	96	5	.620	10	12	.455	1 NFL
Steve Owen	23	153	108	17	.581	151	100	17	.595	2	8	.200	2 NFL
Hank Stram	17	136	100	10	.573	131	97	10	.571	5	3	.625	1 Super Bowl, and 3 AFL
Webb Ewbank	20	134	130	7	.507	130	129	7	.502	4	1	.800	1 Super Bowl, 2 NFL & 1 AFL
Sid Gillman	18	123	104	7	.541	122	99	7	.550	1	5	.167	1 AFL
George Allen	12	118	54	5	.681	116	47	5	.705	2	7	.222	—None—
Don Coryell	14	114	89	1	.561	111	83	1	.572	3	6	.333	—None—
Joe Gibbs	10	113	55	0	.673	101	51	0	.664	12	4	.750	2 Super Bowls
John Madden	10	112	39	7	.731	103	32	7	.750	9	7	.563	1 Super Bowl
Buddy Parker	15	107	76	9	.581	104	75	9	.577	3	1	.750	2 NFL
Vince Lombardi	10	105	35	6	.740	96	34	6	.728	9	1	.900	2 Super Bowls & 5 NFL
Bill Walsh	10	102	63	1	.617	92	59	1	.609	10	4	.714	3 Super Bowls
Lou Saban	16	97	101	7	.490	95	100	7	.488	2	1	.667	2 AFL

Notes: The NFL does not recognize records from the All-American Football Conference (1946-49). If it did, Paul Brown (52-4-3 in four AAFC seasons) would move up to 5th on the all-time list with the following career stats—25 Yrs; 222 Wins; 112 Losses; 9 Ties; .660 Pct; 9-8 playoff record; and 4 AAFC titles.

Where They Coached

Allen—LA Rams (1966-70), Washington (1971-77); **Brown**—Cleveland (1950-62), Cincinnati (1968-75); **Coryell**—St.Louis (1973-77), San Diego (1978-86); **Ewbank**—Baltimore (1954-62), NY Jets (1963-73); **Gibbs**—Washington (1981—); **Gillman**—LA Rams (1955-59), LA-San Diego Chargers (1960-69), Houston (1973-74); **Grant**—Minnesota (1967-83,1985); **Halas**—Chicago Bears (1920-29,33-42,46-55,58-67); **Knox**—LA Rams (1973-77), Buffalo (1978-82), Seattle (1983—); **Lambeau**—Green Bay (1921-49), Chicago Cards (1950-51), Washington (1952-53); **Landry**—Dallas (1960-88); **Lombardi**—Green Bay (1959-67), Washington (1969); **Madden**—Oakland (1969-78); **Noll**—Pittsburgh (1969—); **Owen**—NY Giants (1931-53); **Parker**—Chicago Cards (1949), Detroit (1951-56), Pittsburgh (1957-64); **Saban**—Boston Patriots (1960-61), Buffalo (1962-65,72-76), Denver (1967-71); **Shula**—Baltimore (1963-69), Miami (1970—); **Stram**—Dallas-Kansas City (1960-74), New Orleans (1976-77); **Walsh**—San Francisco (1979-88).

Top Winning Percentages

Minimum 85 NFL wins, including playoffs.

	Yrs	W	L	T	Pct
Vince Lombardi	10	105	35	6	.740
John Madden	10	112	39	7	.731
Don Shula	28	298	137	6	.683
George Allen	12	118	54	5	.681
Joe Gibbs	10	113	55	0	.673
George Halas	40	325	151	31	.672
Mike Ditka	9	96	51	0	.653
Curly Lambeau	33	229	134	22	.623
Bill Parcells	8	85	52	1	.620
Tom Flores	9	91	56	0	.619
Bill Walsh	10	102	63	1	.617
Paul Brown	21	170	108	6	.609
Bud Grant	18	168	108	5	.607
Tom Landry	29	270	178	6	.601
Chuck Knox	18	171	116	1	.595
Dan Reeves	10	96	66	1	.592
Steve Owen	23	153	108	17	.581
Buddy Parker	15	107	76	9	.581
Chuck Noll	22	202	147	1	.579
Hank Stram	17	136	100	10	.573
Jimmy Conzelman	15	88	64	18	.571
Don Coryell	14	114	89	1	.561
Sid Gillman	18	123	104	7	.541
Bum Phillips	11	86	80	0	.518
Weeb Ewbank	20	134	130	7	.507
Lou Saban	16	97	101	7	.490

Note: If AAFC records are included, Paul Brown moves to 7th with a percentage of .660 (25 yrs, 222-112-9), and Buck Shaw ties for 10th at .619 (8 yrs, 91-55-5).

Active Coaches' Victories

Through 1990 season, including playoffs.

	Yrs	W	L	T	Pct
Don Shula, Miami	28	298	137	6	.683
Chuck Noll, Pittsburgh	22	202	147	1	.579
Chuck Knox, Seattle	18	171	116	1	.595
Joe Gibbs, Washington	10	113	55	0	.673
Mike Ditka, Chicago	9	96	51	0	.653
Dan Reeves, Denver	10	96	66	1	.592
Marv Levy, Buffalo	10	77	72	0	.517
John Robinson, LA Rams	8	76	61	0	.555
Marty Schottenheimer, KC	7	65	44	1	.595
Sam Wyche, Cincinnati	7	61	55	0	.526
Ron Meyer, Indianapolis	8	54	47	0	.535
Jack Pardee, Houston	7	53	54	0	.495
Jerry Burns, Minnesota	5	47	38	0	.553
Jim Mora, New Orleans	5	46	35	0	.568
Jerry Glanville, Atlanta	6	40	46	0	.465
Dan Henning, San Diego	6	34	61	1	.359
George Seifert, San Francisco	2	32	5	0	.865
Art Shell, LA Raiders	2	20	10	0	.667
Lindy Infante, Green Bay	3	20	28	0	.417
Wayne Fontes, Detroit	3	15	22	0	.405
Jimmy Johnson, Dallas	2	8	24	0	.250
Bruce Coslet, NY Jets	1	6	10	0	.375
Joe Bugel, Phoenix	1	5	11	0	.313
Richard Williamson, T.Bay	1	1	2	0	.333
Bill Belichick, Cleveland	0	0	0	0	.000
Ray Handley, NY Giants	0	0	0	0	.000
Rich Kotite, Philadelphia	0	0	0	0	.000
Dick MacPherson, N.Eng	0	0	0	0	.000

Annual Awards
NFL Player of the Year

Unlike the other major pro team sports, the NFL no longer sanctions a Most Valuable Player award. The league gave out the Joe F.Carr Trophy (Carr was NFL president from 1921-39) for nine years but discontinued it in 1947. Since then, four principal MVP awards have been given out: UPI (1953-69), AP (since 1957), the Maxwell Club of Philadelphia's Bert Bell Trophy (since 1959) and the Pro Football Writers Assn.(since 1976). UPI switched to AFC and NFC Player of the Year awards in 1970.

Multiple winners (named in more than one season): Jim Brown (4); Johnny Unitas and Y.A.Tittle (3); Earl Campbell, Randall Cunningham, Otto Graham, Don Hutson, Joe Montana, Walter Payton and Joe Theismann (2).

Year		Awards
1938	Mel Hein, NY Giants, C	Carr
1939	Parker Hall, Cleveland Rams, HB	Carr
1940	Ace Parker, Brooklyn, HB	Carr
1941	Don Hutson, Green Bay, E.	Carr
1942	Don Hutson, Green Bay, E.	Carr
1943	Sid Luckman, Chicago Bears, QB	Carr
1944	Frank Sinkwich, Detroit, HB	Carr
1945	Bob Waterfield, Cleveland Rams, QB	Carr
1946	Bill Dudley, Pittsburgh, HB	Carr
1947-49	No award	
1950-52	No award	
1953	Otto Graham, Cleveland Browns, QB	UPI
1954	Joe Perry, San Francisco, FB	UPI
1955	Otto Graham, Cleveland, QB	UPI
1956	Frank Gifford, NY Giants, HB	UPI
1957	Y.A.Tittle, San Francisco, QB	UPI
	& Jim Brown, Cleveland, FB	AP
1958	Jim Brown, Cleveland, FB	UPI
	& Gino Marchetti, Baltimore, DE	AP
1959	Johnny Unitas, Baltimore, QB	UPI-Bell
	& Charley Conerly, NY Giants, QB	AP
1960	Norm Van Brocklin, Phi., QB	UPI-AP(tie)-Bell
	& Joe Schmidt, Detroit, LB	AP (tie)
1961	Paul Hornung, Green Bay, HB	UPI-AP-Bell
1962	Y.A.Tittle, NY Giants, QB	UPI
	Jim Taylor, Green Bay, FB	AP
	& Andy Robustelli, NY Giants, DE	Bell
1963	Jim Brown, Cleveland, FB	UPI-Bell
	& Y.A.Tittle, NY Giants, QB	AP
1964	Johnny Unitas, Baltimore, QB	UPI-AP-Bell
1965	Jim Brown, Cleveland, FB	UPI-AP
	& Pete Retzlaff, Philadelphia, TE	Bell
1966	Bart Starr, Green Bay, QB	UPI-AP
	& Don Meredith, Dallas, QB	Bell
1967	Johnny Unitas, Baltimore, QB	UPI-AP-Bell
1968	Earl Morrall, Baltimore, QB	UPI-AP
	& Leroy Kelly, Cleveland, RB	Bell

Year		Awards
1969	Roman Gabriel, LA Rams, QB	UPI-AP-Bell
1970	John Brodie, San Francisco, QB	AP
	& George Blanda, Oakland, QB-PK	Bell
1971	Alan Page, Minnesota, DT	AP
	& Roger Staubach, Dallas, QB	Bell
1972	Larry Brown, Washington, RB	AP-Bell
1973	O.J.Simpson, Buffalo, RB	AP-Bell
1974	Ken Stabler, Oakland, QB	AP
	& Merlin Olsen, LA Rams, DT	Bell
1975	Fran Tarkenton, Minnesota, QB	AP-Bell
1976	Bert Jones, Baltimore, QB	AP-PFWA
	& Ken Stabler, Oakland, QB	Bell
1977	Walter Payton, Chicago, RB	AP-PFWA
	& Bob Griese, Miami, QB	Bell
1978	Terry Bradshaw, Pittsburgh, QB	AP-Bell
	& Earl Campbell, Houston, RB	PFWA
1979	Earl Campbell, Houston, RB	AP-Bell-PFWA
1980	Brian Sipe, Cleveland, QB	AP-PFWA
	& Ron Jaworski, Philadelphia, QB	Bell
1981	Ken Anderson, Cincinnati, QB	AP-Bell-PFWA
1982	Mark Moseley, Washington, PK	AP
	Joe Theismann, Washington, QB	Bell
	& Dan Fouts, San Diego, QB	PFWA
1983	Joe Theismann, Washington, QB	AP-PFWA
	& John Riggins, Washington, RB	Bell
1984	Dan Marino, Miami, QB	AP-Bell-PFWA
1985	Marcus Allen, LA Raiders, RB	AP-PFWA
	& Walter Payton, Chicago, RB	Bell
1986	Lawrence Taylor, NY Giants, LB	AP-Bell-PFWA
1987	Jerry Rice, San Francisco, WR	Bell-PFWA
	& John Elway, Denver, QB	AP
1988	Boomer Esiason, Cincinnati, QB	AP-PFWA
	& Randall Cunningham, Phila, QB	Bell
1989	Joe Montana, San Francisco, QB	AP-Bell-PFWA
1990	Randall Cunningham, Phila., QB	Bell-PFWA
	& Joe Montana, San Francisco, QB	AP

NFC Player of the Year

Given out by UPI since 1970. Offensive and defensive players have been honored since 1983. Rookie winners are in **bold** type.

Multiple winners: Eric Dickerson and Mike Singletary (3); Walter Payton and Lawrence Taylor (2).

Year		Pos
1970	John Brodie, San Francisco	QB
1971	Alan Page, Minnesota	DT
1972	Larry Brown, Washington	RB
1973	John Hadl, Los Angeles	QB
1974	Jim Hart, St.Louis	QB
1975	Fran Tarkenton, Minnesota	QB
1976	Chuck Foreman, Minnesota	RB
1977	Walter Payton, Chicago	RB
1978	Archie Manning, New Orleans	QB
1979	**Ottis Anderson**, St.Louis	RB
1980	Ron Jaworski, Philadelphia	QB
1981	Tony Dorsett, Dallas	RB
1982	Mark Moseley, Washington	PK
1983	Off—**Eric Dickerson**, Los Angeles	RB
	Def—Lawrence Taylor, New York	LB

Year		Pos
1984	Off—Eric Dickerson, Los Angeles	RB
	Def—Mike Singletary, Chicago	LB
1985	Off—Walter Payton, Chicago	RB
	Def—Mike Singletary, Chicago	LB
1986	Off—Eric Dickerson, Los Angeles	RB
	Def—Lawrence Taylor, New York	LB
1987	Off—Jerry Rice, San Francisco	WR
	Def—Reggie White, Philadelphia	DE
1988	Off—Roger Craig, San Francisco	RB
	Def—Mike Singletary, Chicago	LB
1989	Off—Joe Montana, San Francisco	QB
	Def—Keith Millard, Minnesota	DT
1990	Off—Randall Cunningham, Philadelphia	QB
	Def—Charles Haley, San Francisco	LB

AFL-AFC Player of the Year

Presented by UPI to the top player in the AFL (1960-69) and AFC (since 1970). Offensive and defensive players have been honored since 1983. Rookie winners are noted in **bold** type.

Multiple winners: O.J.Simpson and Bruce Smith (3); George Blanda, Dan Fouts, Daryle Lamonica and Curt Warner (2).

Year		Pos	Year		Pos
1960	**Abner Haynes**, Dallas Texans	HB	1980	Brian Sipe, Cleveland	QB
1961	George Blanda, Houston	QB	1981	Ken Anderson, Cincinnati	QB
1962	Cookie Gilchrist, Buffalo	FB	1982	Dan Fouts, San Diego	QB
1963	Lance Alworth, San Diego	FL	1983	Off—**Curt Warner**, Seattle	RB
1964	Gino Cappelletti, Boston	FL-PK		Def—Rod Martin, Los Angeles	LB
1965	Paul Lowe, San Diego	HB	1984	Off—Dan Marino, Miami	QB
1966	Jim Nance, Boston	FB		Def—Mark Gastineau, New York	DE
1967	Daryle Lamonica, Oakland	QB	1985	Off—Marcus Allen, Los Angeles	RB
1968	Joe Namath, New York	QB		Def—Andre Tippett, New England	LB
1969	Daryle Lamonica, Oakland	QB	1986	Off—Curt Warner, Seattle	RB
1970	George Blanda, Oakland	QB-PK		Def—Rulon Jones, Denver	DE
1971	Otis Taylor, Kansas City	WR	1987	Off—John Elway, Denver	QB
1972	O.J.Simpson, Buffalo	RB		Def—Bruce Smith, Buffalo	DE
1973	O.J.Simpson, Buffalo	RB	1988	Off—Boomer Esiason, Cincinnati	QB
1974	Ken Stabler, Oakland	QB		Def—Bruce Smith, Buffalo	DE
1975	O.J.Simpson, Buffalo	RB		& Cornelius Bennett, Buffalo	LB
1976	Bert Jones, Baltimore	QB	1989	Off—Christian Okoye, Kansas City	RB
1977	Craig Morton, Denver	QB		Def—Michael Dean Perry, Cleveland	NT
1978	**Earl Campbell**, Houston	RB	1990	Off—Warren Moon, Houston	QB
1979	Dan Fouts, San Diego	QB		Def—Bruce Smith, Buffalo	DE

NFL-NFC Rookie of the Year

Presented by UPI to the top rookie in the NFL (1955-69) and NFC (since 1970).

Year		Pos	Year		Pos	Year		Pos
1955	Alan Ameche, Bal	FB	1968	Earl McCullough, Det	FL	1980	Billy Sims, Det.	RB
1956	Lenny Moore, Bal	HB	1969	Calvin Hill, Dal.	RB	1981	George Rogers, NO	RB
1957	Jim Brown, Cle.	FB	1970	Bruce Taylor, SF	DB	1982	Jim McMahon, Chi.	QB
1958	Jimmy Orr, Bal.	FL	1971	John Brockington, GB	RB	1983	Eric Dickerson, LA	RB
1959	Boyd Dowler, GB	FL	1972	Chester Marcol, GB	PK	1984	Paul McFadden, Phi.	PK
1960	Gail Cogdill, Det	FL	1973	Charle Young, Phi	TE	1985	Jerry Rice, SF.	WR
1961	Mike Ditka, Chi	TE	1974	John Hicks, NY	G	1986	Reuben Mayes, NO.	RB
1962	Ronnie Bull, Chi	FB	1975	Mike Thomas, Wash	RB	1987	Robert Awalt, St.L.	TE
1963	Paul Flatley, Min.	FL	1976	Sammy White, Min.	WR	1988	Keith Jackson, Phi	TE
1964	Charley Taylor, Wash.	HB	1977	Tony Dorsett, Dal.	RB	1989	Barry Sanders, Det.	RB
1965	Gale Sayers, Chi.	HB	1978	Bubba Baker, Det	DE	1990	Mark Carrier, Chi	S
1966	Johnny Roland, St.L	HB	1979	Ottis Anderson, St.L.	RB			
1967	Mel Farr, Det	RB						

AFL-AFC Rookie of the Year

Presented by UPI to the top rookie in the AFL (1960-69) and AFC (since 1970).

Year		Pos	Year		Pos	Year		Pos
1960	Abner Haynes, Dal	HB	1971	Jim Plunkett, NE	QB	1980	Joe Cribbs, Buf	RB
1961	Earl Faison, SD	DE	1972	Franco Harris, Pit	RB	1981	Joe Delaney, KC	RB
1962	Curtis McClinton, Dal	FB	1973	Boobie Clark, Cin	RB	1982	Marcus Allen, LA	RB
1963	Billy Joe, Den	FB	1974	Don Woods, SD	RB	1983	Curt Warner, Sea.	RB
1964	Matt Snell, NY	FB	1975	Robert Brazile, Hou	LB	1984	Louis Lipps, Pit	WR
1965	Joe Namath, NY	QB	1976	Mike Haynes, NE	DB	1985	Kevin Mack, Cle.	RB
1966	Bobby Burnett, Buf	HB	1977	A.J.Duhe, Mia	DE	1986	Leslie O'Neal, SD	DE
1967	George Webster, Hou	LB	1978	Earl Campbell, Hou	RB	1987	Shane Conlan, Buf.	LB
1968	Paul Robinson, Cin	RB	1979	Jerry Butler, Buf	WR	1988	John Stephens, NE.	RB
1969	Greg Cook, Cin	QB				1989	Derrick Thomas, KC	LB
1970	Dennis Shaw, Buf	QB				1990	Richmond Webb, Mia	OT

NFL-NFC Coach of the Year

Presented by UPI to the top coach in the NFL (1955-69) and NFC (since 1970). Records indicate how much coach's team improved over one season.

Multiple winners: George Allen, Leeman Bennett, Mike Ditka, George Halas, Tom Landry, Jack Pardee, Allie Sherman, Don Shula and Bill Walsh (2).

Year		Improvement	Year		Improvement
1955	Joe Kuharich, Washington	3-9 to 8-4	1958	Weeb Ewbank, Baltimore	7-5 to 9-3
1956	Buddy Parker, Detroit	3-9 to 9-3	1959	Vince Lombardi, Green Bay	1-10-1 to 7-5
1957	Paul Brown, Cleveland	5-7 to 9-2-1			

Year		Improvement	Year		Improvement
1960	Buck Shaw, Philadelphia	7-5 to 10-2	1976	Jack Pardee, Chicago	4-10 to 7-7
1961	Allie Sherman, New York	6-4-2 to 10-3-1	1977	Leeman Bennett, Atlanta	4-10 to 7-7
1962	Allie Sherman, New York	10-3-1 to 12-2	1978	Dick Vermeil, Philadelphia	5-9 to 9-7
1963	George Halas, Chicago	9-5 to 11-1-2	1979	Jack Pardee, Washington	8-8 to 10-6
1964	Don Shula, Baltimore	8-6 to 12-2			
1965	George Halas, Chicago	5-9 to 9-5	1980	Leeman Bennett, Atlanta	6-10 to 12-4
1966	Tom Landry, Dallas	7-7 to 10-3-1	1981	Bill Walsh, San Francisco	6-10 to 13-3
1967	George Allen, Los Angeles	8-6 to 11-1-2	1982	Joe Gibbs, Washington	8-8 to 8-1
1968	Don Shula, Baltimore	11-1-2 to 13-1	1983	John Robinson, Los Angeles	2-7 to 9-7
1969	Bud Grant, Minnesota	8-6 to 12-2	1984	Bill Walsh, San Francisco	10-6 to 15-1
			1985	Mike Ditka, Chicago	10-6 to 15-1
1970	Alex Webster, New York	6-8 to 9-5	1986	Bill Parcells, New York	10-6 to 14-2
1971	George Allen, Washington	6-8 to 9-4-1	1987	Jim Mora, New Orleans	7-9 to 12-3
1972	Dan Devine, Green Bay	4-8-2 to 10-4	1988	Mike Ditka, Chicago	11-4 to 12-4
1973	Chuck Knox, Los Angeles	6-7-1 to 12-2	1989	Lindy Infante, Green Bay	4-12 to 10-6
1974	Don Coryell, St.Louis	4-9-1 to 10-4	1990	Jimmy Johnson, Dallas	1-15 to 7-9
1975	Tom Landry, Dallas	8-6 to 10-4			

AFL-AFC Coach of the Year

Presented by UPI to the top coach in the AFL (1960-69) and AFC (since 1970). Records indicate how much coach's team improved over one season. The AFC began play in 1960.
Multiple winners: Chuck Knox, Sam Rutigliano, Lou Saban and Don Shula (2)

Year		Improvement	Year		Improvement
1960	Lou Rymkus, Houston	10-4	1976	Chuck Fairbanks, New England	3-11 to 11-3
1961	Wally Lemm, Houston	10-4 to 10-3-1	1977	Red Miller, Denver	9-5 to 12-2
1962	Jack Faulkner, Denver	3-11 to 7-7	1978	Walt Michaels, New York	3-11 to 8-8
1963	Al Davis, Oakland	1-13 to 10-4	1979	Sam Rutigliano, Cleveland	8-8 to 9-7
1964	Lou Saban, Buffalo	7-6-1 to 12-2			
1965	Lou Saban, Buffalo	12-2 to 10-3-1	1980	Sam Rutigliano, Cleveland	9-7 to 11-5
1966	Mike Holovak, Boston	4-8-2 to 8-4-2	1981	Forrest Gregg, Cincinnati	6-10 to 12-4
1967	John Rauch, Oakland	8-5-1 to 13-1	1982	Tom Flores, Los Angeles	7-9 to 8-1
1968	Hank Stram, Kansas City	9-5 to 12-2	1983	Chuck Knox, Seattle	4-5 to 9-7
1969	Paul Brown, Cincinnati	3-11 to 4-9-1	1984	Chuck Knox, Seattle	9-7 to 12-4
			1985	Raymond Berry, New England	9-7 to 11-5
1970	Don Shula, Miami	3-10-1 to 10-4	1986	Marty Schottenheimer, Cleveland	8-8 to 12-4
1971	Don Shula, Miami	10-4 to 10-3-1	1987	Ron Meyer, Indianapolis	3-13 to 9-6
1972	Chuck Noll, Pittsburgh	6-8 to 11-3	1988	Marv Levy, Buffalo	7-8 to 12-4
1973	John Ralston, Denver	5-9 to 7-5-2	1989	Dan Reeves, Denver	8-8 to 11-5
1974	Sid Gillman, Houston	1-13 to 7-7	1990	Art Shell, Los Angeles	8-8 to 12-4
1975	Ted Marchibroda, Baltimore	2-12 to 10-4			

Number One Draft Choices

In an effort to blunt the dominance of the Chicago Bears and New York Giants in the 1930s and distribute talent more evenly throughout the league, the NFL established the college draft in 1936.

The first player chosen in the first draft was Jay Berwanger, who was also college football's Heisman Trophy winner. In all, 16 Heisman winners have also been the NFL's No.1 draft choice. They are noted in **bold** type.

The American Football League (formed in 1960) held its own draft for six years before agreeing to merge with the NFL and select players in a common draft starting in 1967.

Year	Team		Year	Team	
1936	Philadelphia	**Jay Berwanger**, HB, Chicago	1954	Cleveland	Bobby Garrett, QB, Stanford
1937	Philadelphia	Sam Francis, FB, Nebraska	1955	Baltimore	George Shaw, QB, Oregon
1938	Cleve.Rams	Corbett Davis, FB, Indiana	1956	Pittsburgh	Gary Glick, DB, Colo.A&M
1939	Chicago Cards	Ki Aldrich, C, TCU	1957	Green Bay	**Paul Hornung**, QB, N.Dame
			1958	Chicago Cards	King Hill, QB, Rice
1940	Chicago Cards	George Cafego, HB, Tennessee	1959	Green Bay	Randy Duncan, QB, Iowa
1941	Chicago Bears	**Tom Harmon**, HB, Michigan	1960	NFL—LA Rams	**Billy Cannon**, HB, LSU
1942	Pittsburgh	Bill Dudley, HB, Viginia		AFL—No choice	
1943	Detroit	**Frank Sinkwich**, HB, Georgia	1961	NFL—Minnesota	Tommy Mason, HB, Tulane
1944	Boston Yanks	**Angelo Bertelli**, QB, N.Dame		AFL—Buffalo	Ken Rice, G, Auburn
1945	Chicago Cards	Charley Trippi, HB, Georgia	1962	NFL—Washington	**Ernie Davis**, HB, Syracuse
1946	Boston Yanks	Frank Dancewicz, QB, N.Dame		AFL—Oakland	Roman Gabriel, QB, N.C.State
1947	Chicago Bears	Bob Fenimore, HB, Okla.A&M	1963	NFL—LA Rams	**Terry Baker**, QB, Oregon St.
1948	Washington	Harry Gilmer, QB, Alabama		AFL—Kan.City	Buck Buchanan, DT, Grambling
1949	Philadelphia	Chuck Bednarik, C, Penn	1964	NFL—San Fran	Dave Parks, E, Texas Tech
				AFL—Boston	Jack Concannon, QB, Boston Col.
1950	Detroit	**Leon Hart**, E, Notre Dame	1965	NFL—NY Giants	Tucker Frederickson, HB, Auburn
1951	NY Giants	Kyle Rote, HB, SMU		AFL—Houston	Lawrence Elkins, E, Baylor
1952	LA Rams	Bill Wade, QB, Vanderbilt			
1953	San Francisco	Harry Babcock, E, Georgia			

Number One Draft Choices (Cont.)

Year	Team	
1966	NFL—Atlanta	Tommy Nobis, LB, Texas
	AFL—Miami	Jim Grabowski, FB, Illinois
1967	Baltimore	Bubba Smith, DT, Michigan St.
1968	Minnesota	Ron Yary, T, USC
1969	Buffalo	**O.J.Simpson**, RB, USC
1970	Pittsburgh	Terry Bradshaw, QB, La.Tech
1971	New England	**Jim Plunkett**, QB, Stanford
1972	Buffalo	Walt Patulski, DE, Notre Dame
1973	Houston	John Matuszak, DE, Tampa
1974	Dallas	Ed "Too Tall" Jones, Tenn.St.
1975	Atlanta	Steve Bartkowski, QB, Calif.
1976	Tampa Bay	Lee Roy Selmon, DE, Oklahoma
1977	Tampa Bay	Ricky Bell, RB, USC
1978	Houston	**Earl Campbell**, RB, Texas
1979	Buffalo	Tom Cousineau, LB, Ohio St.

Year	Team	
1980	Detroit	**Billy Sims**, RB, Oklahoma
1981	New Orleans	**George Rogers**, RB, S.Carolina
1982	New England	Kenneth Sims, DT, Texas
1983	Baltimore	John Elway, QB, Stanford
1984	New England	Irving Fryar, WR, Nebraska
1985	Buffalo	Bruce Smith, DE, Va.Tech
1986	Tampa Bay	**Bo Jackson**, RB, Auburn
1987	Tampa Bay	**V. Testaverde**, QB, Miami-FL
1988	Atlanta	Aundray Bruce, LB, Auburn
1989	Dallas	Troy Aikman, QB, UCLA
1990	Indianapolis	Jeff George, QB, Illinois
1991	Dallas	Russell Maryland, DL, Miami-FL

Canadian Football League
CFL Grey Cup Champions

Earl Grey, the Governor-General of Canada (1904-11) donated a trophy in 1909 for the Rugby Football Championship of Canada. The trophy, which later became known as the Grey Cup, was originally open to competition for teams registered with the Canada Rugby Union. Since 1954, the Cup has gone to the champion of the Canadian Football League (CFL).

Multiple winners (since 1954): Edmonton (10); Winnipeg (7); Hamilton (6); Ottawa (5); Montreal (3); BC Lions and Saskatchewan (2).

Year	Grey Cup Final	Winning Coach
1954	Edmonton 26, Montreal 25	Pop Ivy
1955	Edmonton 34, Montreal 19	Pop Ivy
1956	Edmonton 50, Montreal 27	Pop Ivy
1957	Hamilton 32, Winnipeg 7	Jim Trimble
1958	Winnipeg 35, Hamilton 28	Bud Grant
1959	Winnipeg 21, Hamilton 7	Bud Grant
1960	Ottawa 16, Edmonton 6	Frank Clair
1961	Winnipeg 21, Hamilton 14 (OT)	Bud Grant
1962	Winnipeg 28, Hamilton 27	Bud Grant
1963	Hamilton 21, BC Lions 10	Ralph Sazio
1964	BC Lions 34, Hamilton 24	Dave Skrien
1965	Hamilton 22, Winnipeg 16	Ralph Sazio
1966	Saskatchewan 29, Ottawa 14	Eagle Keys
1967	Hamilton 24, Saskatchewan1	Ralph Sazio
1968	Ottawa 24, Calgary 21	Frank Clair
1969	Ottawa 29, Saskatchewan 11	Frank Clair
1970	Montreal 23, Calgary 10	Sam Etcheverry
1971	Calgary 14, Toronto 11	Jim Duncan
1972	Hamilton 13, Saskatchewan10	Jerry Williams

Year	Grey Cup Final	Winning Coach
1973	Ottawa 22, Edmonton 18	Jack Gotta
1974	Montreal 20, Edmonton 7	Marv Levy
1975	Edmonton 9, Montreal 8	Ray Jauch
1976	Ottawa 23, Saskatchewan 20	George Brancato
1977	Montreal 41, Edmonton 6	Marv Levy
1978	Edmonton 20, Montreal 13	Hugh Campbell
1979	Edmonton 17, Montreal 9	Hugh Campbell
1980	Edmonton 48, Hamilton 10	Hugh Campbell
1981	Edmonton 26, Ottawa 23	Hugh Campbell
1982	Edmonton 32, Toronto 16	Hugh Campbell
1983	Toronto 18, BC Lions 17	Bob O'Billovich
1984	Winnipeg 47, Hamilton 17	Cal Murphy
1985	BC Lions 37, Hamilton 24	Don Matthews
1986	Hamilton 39, Edmonton 15	Al Bruno
1987	Edmonton 38, Toronto 36	Joe Faragalli
1988	Winnipeg 22, BC Lions 21	Mike Riley
1989	Saskatchewan 43, Hamilton 40	John Gregory
1990	Winnipeg 50, Edmonton 11	Mike Riley

CFL Player of the Year

CFL regular season Most Outstanding Player from 1953-90.
Multiple winners: Russ Jackson and Jackie Parker (3); Dieter Brock and Ron Lancaster (2).

Year			Year			Year		
1953	Billy Vessels, Edm., RB		1966	Russ Jackson, Ott., QB		1980	Dieter Brock, Win., QB	
1954	Sam Etcheverry, Mon., QB		1967	Peter Liske, Calg., QB		1981	Dieter Brock, Win., QB	
1955	Pat Abbruzzi, Mon., RB		1968	Bill Symons, Tor., RB		1982	Condredge Holloway, Tor., QB	
1956	Hal Patterson, Mon., E-DB		1969	Russ Jackson, Ott., QB		1983	Warren Moon, Edm., QB	
1957	Jackie Parker, Edm., RB					1984	Willard Reaves, Win., RB	
1958	Jackie Parker, Edm., QB		1970	Ron Lancaster, Sask., QB		1985	Merv Fernandez, BC, WR	
1959	Johnny Bright, Edm., RB		1971	Don Jonas, Win., QB		1986	James Murphy, Win., WR	
1960	Jackie Parker, Edm., QB		1973	Geo. McGowan, Edm., WR		1987	Tom Clements, Win., QB	
1961	Bernie Faloney, Ham., QB		1974	Tom Wilkinson, Edm., QB		1988	David Williams, BC WR	
1962	George Dixon, Mon., RB		1975	Willie Burden, Calg., RB		1989	Tracy Ham, Edm., QB	
1963	Russ Jackson, Ott., QB		1976	Ron Lancaster, Sask., QB		1990	Mike Clemons, Tor., RB	
1964	Lovell Coleman, Calg., RB		1977	Jimmy Edwards, Ham., RB				
1965	George Reed, Sask., RB		1978	Tony Gabriel, Ott., TE				
			1979	David Green, Mon., RB				

Duke center **Christian Laettner**, the Most Outstanding Player of the NCAA tournament, stands tall against Kansas in the championship game.

COLLEGE BASKETBALL

King Duke

Coach K and the Blue Devils finally wear the crown after four consecutive trips to the NCAA Final Four.

April's fool no more, Mike Krzyzewski finally delivered Duke the national championship it craved and, in the process, presented followers of the 1990-91 season the upset they never expected.

After eight consecutive NCAA tournament invitations, four straight Final Four appearances and back-to-back title game showdowns, Krzyzewski at last walked off the court with something to show for his troubles other than a headache and a heartache. This time he had two victories for the ages: a win against Kansas in the final and a stunning upset against previously unbeaten and top-ranked UNLV in the semifinal.

Fair or not, Krzyzewski's tournament legacy had become one of near misses. Every March, especially in recent years, his Blue Devils would skip happily through the early round tournament pairings, make their way to the Sweet 16, then to the Great Eight, then to the Final Four. . . only to lose when it mattered most. Entering the season finale against Kansas, Krzyzewski owned an impressive 26-4 record in March Madness, but was a dismal 0-for-3 when the calendar struck April. It was obvious Krzyzewski was an excellent coach, but could he lead Duke to a national championship?

Gene Wojciechowski has been the national college basketball writer for the *Los Angeles Times* since the 1989–90 season.

The Blue Devils addressed that particular question with a convincing 72-65 victory against Kansas on *April* 1st, in front of 47,185 fans at the Hoosier Dome in Indianapolis. The final score didn't do the win justice. The Jayhawks never owned a lead and with just 6:10 remaining in the game, trailed by as many as 14 points.

Blue Devil center Christian Laettner, named the Final Four's Most Outstanding Player, point guard Bobby Hurley, forward Grant Hill and reserve guard Bill McCaffrey all provided performances suitable for framing. Laettner was only three-of-eight from the field, but he sank all 12 of his free throw attempts and added 10 rebounds to a solid night's work. Hurley, who may have been the MVP of the entire tournament, scored 12 points, but more importantly, ran the Duke offense to near perfection while playing his usual brand of annoying defense. Hill, only a freshman, had 10 points, eight rebounds, three assists, two blocks and two steals. Pity the Atlantic Coast Conference opponents assigned to handle him during the next three seasons. As for McCaffrey, he came off the bench to score 16 points, six of which came from three-point range.

Kansas did what it could, but it was hardly enough. The Jayhawks, who were nowhere to be found in the Associated Press Top 25 poll at the beginning of the season, surprised everyone, including

Ben Weaver/The National

Consensus Player of the Year **Larry Johnson** of UNLV (right) beats Arkansas center **Oliver Miller** to a loose ball in the second half of the Rebels' 112-105 win over the Razorbacks Feb. 10 in Fayetteville.

themselves at times, by earning a place in the Final Four. To get there, KU, coached brilliantly by Roy Williams, had to beat New Orleans, Pittsburgh, Indiana and Arkansas. And to reach the championship game, Williams had to figure out a way to slip past North Carolina and his former Tar Heel boss, the venerable Dean Smith. Sure enough, the Jayhawks beat UNC, 79-73, in a game marred by referee Pete Pavia's questionable ejection of Smith with just 35 seconds left.

In the final, Williams was unable to solve the Blue Devil attack. Despite KU's best efforts, Duke controlled the game's pace, shot 56 percent from the field (compared to Kansas' 41.5%) and converted 20 of 28 free throws (compared to just four of eight for the Jayhawks). Afterward, a gracious Williams congratulated Krzyzewski. "I know they're feeling extremely well right now," he said. "Mike and his staff got something off their backs that never should have been there in the first place—I mean winning tonight after not winning the so-called 'big game' before."

As satisfying as Duke's victory was against Kansas, nothing could compare to the energized state of the Hoosier Dome when the Blue Devils met mighty Vegas in the semifinals. A season earlier, UNLV had crushed Duke by 30 points. This time, Krzyzewski's team was given a better chance to keep the game close, but little else. What with consensus All-America forwards Larry Johnson and Stacey Augmon, guards Greg Anthony and Anderson Hunt and center George Ackles, UNLV was considered a lock to become, a) the first team since Indiana in 1976 to finish as unbeaten national champions, and b) the first team since UCLA ended its seven-year run of titles in 1973 to repeat as NCAA champions.

The Runnin' Rebels had enhanced their reputation during the regular season when, on Feb. 10, they ran up a 23-point second half lead against No. 2 Arkansas in Fayetteville before coasting to a 112-105 win. Despite such notions of invincibility, Vegas coach Jerry Tarkanian insisted that the Rebels were indeed beatable and complained about his team's lack of defensive intensity—a must in the UNLV system. Media, fans, even Krzyzewski were not swayed by Tarkanian's reservations.

But the UNLV coach was right. The Rebels appeared sluggish, almost confused at times as Duke scored 15 of the game's first 21 points. UNLV recovered and led, 43-41, at halftime, but unlike last season's championship game Vegas was unable to distance itself from the much improved and more athletic Blue Devils when the second half began. Unaccustomed to close scores, the Rebels were in serious trouble, especially when Anthony fouled out with 3:51 remaining and Vegas up, 74-71. Without Anthony to guide the offense, UNLV scored just one more field goal and a single foul shot and eventually lost, 79-77. In an ironic twist of fate, Hunt, the tournament's Most Outstanding Player a year ago, missed the potential game-winning shot moments before the buzzer sounded. He finished with 29 points, the exact number he scored against Duke in the 1990 title game.

For Tarkanian, the loss was a bitter experience, made even harder to take when ESPN later reported that David Berst, chief of enforcement for the NCAA and Tark's archenemy, was allegedly heard to say, "Drinks are on me," following the Vegas defeat. Tarkanian and the NCAA have been feuding for years, but the relationship, if you can call it that, reached new and interesting highs and lows during the 1990-91 season.

It began Nov. 29, when the NCAA, in an unprecedented move, overturned an earlier decision by the Committee on Infractions and allowed the Rebels to defend their national title. The committee had ruled in July that Vegas be prohibited from 1990-91 postseason competition. The sanction was considered the most severe of the penalties stemming from an infractions case that caused Tarkanian to challenge the NCAA in court 14 years ago.

However, fearing a threatened lawsuit by UNLV players, the NCAA presented Vegas with a pair of compromise proposals, including the one the Rebels accepted: Remain eligible to defend in 1991, but forfeit live regular season television appearances and postseason play for the 1991-92 season. The other proposal would have required Tarkanian to

be suspended during postseason play in 1991 and UNLV to be ineligible for postseason competition in 1992.

Not everyone found the compromise so reasonable. Kansas, for instance. KU, which was prevented from defending its 1988 NCAA championship because of probation, felt betrayed because it wasn't given the same opportunity to negotiate. Jayhawks' coach Williams put it this way: "I sure wish they'd given us a multiple-choice penalty."

Of course, the deal didn't stop Tarkanian from publicly voicing his displeasure with the NCAA, nor did it stop Berst & Co. from pursuing UNLV on other investigative matters, most notably the recruiting of New York high school legend Lloyd Daniels. Talk all you like about the great rivalries in college sports, but none of them are more intense and meanspirited than Tarkanian vs. the NCAA (see "College Sports").

Vegas wasn't the only school to earn the attention of the NCAA enforcement division. A detailed series of articles by the Syracuse *Post-Standard* revealed numerous alleged violations in Jim Boeheim's Orangemen program, which, in turn, prompted an in-house investigation by SU. An NCAA probe was expected to follow.

Notre Dame coach Digger Phelps, whose program never aroused the suspicion of NCAA investigators, decided in April to step down after 20 years in South Bend (see box).

Colleagues Dean Smith (30 years at UNC) and Bob Knight (20 years at Indiana) continued on the fast track, however. Smith passed 700 career wins (he now has 717) and Knight accepted both nomination and election to the Basketball Hall of Fame.

Coaching longevity was not in the cards for Texas A&M's Kermit Davis, who was sacked after only one season. Davis was accused, among other things, of using a New York City talent broker to send him players. It didn't help that the Aggies went 8-21 and finished last in the SWC. In all, over 30 coaches were replaced during the offseason, down from over 50 a year ago.

The consensus Coach of the Year was Ohio State's Randy Ayers, who, in his second year, directed the Buckeyes to a 25-3 regular season record, a No. 5 ranking; and a share of the Big Ten title (with Indiana).

New Hampshire coach Jim Boylam had exactly the opposite record (3-25), but his Wildcats did finally manage to break a three-year, 32-game home losing streak. UNH beat Holy Cross, 72-56, on Feb. 11.

Rick Pitino's Kentucky program continued to come back from a devastating two-year NCAA probation and a legal pad's worth of sanctions. The Wildcats captured the Southeastern Conference regular season championship and finished the year with a 22-6 record and a No. 9 ranking. UK will be eligible for both the SEC and NCAA tournaments in 1992.

Three survivors of Kentucky's recent shady past resurfaced with championship teams in Oklahoma in 1990-91. Eddie and Sean Sutton, the former father and son, coach and point guard combination at UK, regrouped at Eddie's alma mater, Oklahoma State, and led the Cowboys to a share of the Big Eight regular season title. Meanwhile, forward Eric Manuel, who was banned for life by the NCAA in 1989 for allegedly cheating on a UK entrance exam, led Oklahoma City to a 77-74 win over Central Arkansas in the NAIA championship game.

Then there was the saga of Kevin Bradshaw, the 26-year-old U.S. International guard who was also a Navy veteran and divorced father. USIU went bankrupt and filed for Chapter 11 in 1991, leaving the basketball program to fend for itself, but Bradshaw didn't let that stop him from leading the nation in scoring with nearly 38 points a game. He also set an NCAA record for points against a Division I opponent with 72—including 21 on three-point shots—against Loyola Marymount on Jan. 5. The old record of 69 had been set by LSU's Pete Maravich against Alabama in 1970. By the way, USIU lost to Loyola, 186-140, and the Gulls ended up with a 2-26 record.

UNLV's Johnson was the consensus Player of the Year, averaging 22 points and 11 rebounds a game. Unselfish to a fault, the 6-7, 250-pound Johnson dominated inside and could have easily upped his scoring average.

Moments after being presented the John Wooden Award in Los Angeles, Johnson acknowledged the presence of runner-up Shaquille O'Neal and said, "I'm overwhelmed. I just can't wait to get home

Ben Weaver/The National

LSU sophomore sensation **Shaquille O'Neal** won two Player of the Year awards, but elected to return to Baton Rouge for his junior year.

and tell my mom, 'I beat out Shaquille.' She's a bigger fan of Shaquille than she is of me."

O'Neal, LSU's gifted 7-1, 295-pound center, won the two wire service Player of the Year awards that escaped Johnson. As a sophomore, he averaged 27.7 points a game (seventh best in the country), five blocks (third best), 14.6 rebounds (first), made 63.4% of his shots from the field (13th best) and played on a fractured left leg in the NCAA tournament, where the Tigers lost in the first round to Connecticut. Realizing he still has some lessons to learn before moving up to the NBA, the "Real Deal" announced his intention to return for his junior year.

While O'Neal dominated the SEC and encountered few non-conference opponents who could handle him, he was clearly outplayed by Duke's Laettner in a Feb. 10 road game. Much to the delight of the Cameron Indoor Stadium crazies who serenaded O'Neal with chants of "Overrated, Overrated" and "One, two, three, four, Shaquille can't play no more," Laettner, a 6-11, 235-pound junior, scored 24 points and grabbed 11 rebounds while holding O'Neal to just nine shots, 15 points and 10 boards.

Twelve underclassmen announced their intentions to forego their remaining eligibility and pursue an NBA career. Sophomore Kenny Anderson of Georgia Tech and juniors Hunt of UNLV, Billy Owens of Syracuse, and Terrell Brandon of Oregon were the biggest names to do so. Also, as expected, Brigham Young's 7-6 freshman center Shawn Bradley decided to embark on a two-year Mormon mission to Australia.

Of course, BYU wasn't the best college team in the state. The University of Utah was. With the exception of Kansas, the Runnin' Utes confounded preseason prognosticators more than any other program. Rick Majerus did wonders with his club, which finished the regular season 28-3 and ranked 10th before reaching the tournament Sweet 16.

Elsewhere in the NCAAs, Eastern Michigan scored two tournament victories and Mark Macon led the Temple Owls all the way to the East Regional final before losing to North Carolina. Arizona State's Bill Frieder did an admirable job with the Sun Devils, while Colorado, Seton Hall, Penn State, and Creighton recorded seasons to cherish.

Penn State won the Atlantic 10 tournament for the first time in 15 years then left the conference for one year of independent play before joining Big 10 competition in 1992-93. Florida State and South Carolina also moved on, leaving the Metro for the ACC and SEC, respectively (see "College Sports").

Tennessee beat Virginia, 70-67, in overtime to win the NCAA women's championship, and by doing so presented Coach Pat Summitt with her third title in five seasons. Indiana's Knight is the only other active coach—man or woman—to have won three NCAA championships.

Ironically, it was Virginia that ended Tennessee's dream of back-to-back titles in 1990. This time, the Lady Vols got superb performances from 6-3, All-America center Daedra Charles (19 points, 12 rebounds) and senior guard Dena Head

Digger Says 20 Years Is Long Enough

In 1965, an earnest Digger Phelps wrote a heartfelt letter to then-Notre Dame football coach Ara Parseghian and proclaimed his desire to one day be part of the Irish legacy.

On April 15, Phelps, his place in Irish history secure, reached for pen and paper again, this time to inform Notre Dame athletic director Dick Rosenthal of his decision to resign as the school's basketball coach—or, as Phelps insisted, to retire and enjoy a "moment of celebration."

Thus ended a 20-season reign that produced a 393-197 record, 14 NCAA tournament invitations, one Final Four appearance (in 1978), a pristine player graduation mark, and mixed feelings about an outspoken and occasionally arrogant coach. There was also the great come-from-behind, 71-70 victory over Bill Walton and UCLA on Jan. 19, 1974, which snapped the Bruins' all-time college winning streak at 88.

Phelps' departure also raised questions about Notre Dame's role in the matter and set into motion a sometimes embarrassing nationwide search that saw at least three candidates—Xavier's Pete Gillen, Georgia Tech's Bobby Cremins and Duke's Mike Krzyzewski—withdraw from consideration. The Irish finally found their man in the NBA, anointing John MacLeod on May 4, two days after he had quit as coach of the New York Knicks.

At his farewell press conference, which was attended by neither Rosenthal nor Notre Dame executive vice president Rev. E. William Beauchamp, Phelps said his decision to retire was based on a personal timetable established long ago.

"I've put my life into time blocks," he said. "There is only so much time in the game of life. Between the ages of 50 and 60 one better attempt the other challenges, because things change between 60 and 70. I want to live the other life after basketball at Notre Dame.

"This was my decision," he said. "I have great love for this place and I'm not cutting ties with Notre Dame. Whatever comes up, our home will still be South Bend."

Digger Phelps had 17 winning seasons, 14 NCAA tournament appearances and a trip to the Final Four during his career at Notre Dame—and his players graduated. Yet, many feel he was forced out.

Of course, Phelps' reasons for stepping down differed from those who said his days were numbered as head coach. The program was in free-fall, his detractors pointed out—declining from a 21-9 mark in 1988-89, to 16-13 the following year, to 12-20 last season. Sure, it was only the third time in 20 years that the Irish had suffered through a losing season, but attendance was down and the students were getting restless. Phelps was also criticized for a perceived lack of interest in the recruiting process and an inability to lead his NCAA tournament teams past the first or second rounds of play (the Irish were 15-16 in their 14 NCAA appearances during the Phelps era).

In fairness, Phelps was hardly to blame for Notre Dame's most recent problems. His 1990-91 team was gutted by injuries and could ill afford the loss of starting forward LaPhonso Ellis to academic ineligibility. The Irish also were victims of their well-known independent status, which helps in football but hurts in basketball where league membership eases recruiting and scheduling problems. During one stretch in the second semester, Notre Dame had to play four games in eight days.

As expected, Phelps' retirement, rumored for weeks following the dismal Irish season, was met with mixed emotions.

"Digger always said he didn't want to coach after age 50 (Phelps turned 50 on July 4), so I was not totally surprised," said associate athletic director Roger Valdiserri to the South Bend Tribune. "I think he felt the time was right in his life to do other things, and you've got to respect his decision."

Added Notre Dame football coach Lou Holtz: "He told me on several occasions that I was foolish to continue to coach after we won the national championship. He said, 'Man, you ought to retire and get on to other things.' I think there are a lot of things Digger wanted to do with his life."

Now he gets his chance. A career in broadcasting remains a possibility, as does a novel or screenplay about college sports. Phelps also said he might one day entertain offers to return to the sidelines, but likely in a less stressful environment.

Whatever his choice, Phelps' stay at Notre Dame won't soon be forgotten. His record both on and off the court will see to that.

"There have been times when we've loved him and times when we've hated him," guard Elmer Bennett told the South Bend Tribune. "I have a lot of respect for him. We have a bad taste in our mouths from last season and we're really looking forward to starting over."

So is Phelps.

(28 points, 9 rebounds) and were able to withstand the Cavaliers' remarkable 5-6 guard Dawn Staley. Staley, the tournament's Most Outstanding Player and the country's consensus Player of the Year, scored 28 points and added 11 rebounds. She was also the first player from the losing side to be named MOP in the 10 years since the NCAA started the women's tournament.

Played in New Orleans in front of 7,865 fans at Lakefront Arena, the championship game marked the 10th year the NCAA has overseen the women's Final Four. It was also the first time the semifinal games—Tennessee vs. Stanford and Virginia vs. Connecticut—were shown on network television.

Stanford won the National Invitation Tournament by beating Oklahoma, 78-72, in the championship game. While noteworthy, the NIT was hardly a match for the mighty NCAA tournament, which included its usual collection of first-round upsets. The major surprise came in the Eastern Regional where second-seeded Syracuse lost to Richmond in the first round—the first time in tournament history that a 15th-seeded team had knocked off such a high seed. Elsewhere, Penn State shocked UCLA, Xavier beat Nebraska and Eastern Michigan defeated Mississippi State. Also, Pete Carril's Princeton team, which can't seem to get a pairings break, lost once more in the first round, this time to an equally patient squad from Villanova.

For the most part, the tournament selection committee did a creditable job issuing invitations. Conspicuous by their absence, however, were the aforementioned Oklahoma and Louisville, who suffered through dreadful regular seasons, and Providence, which was probably penalized because its conference—the Big East—already had seven teams going to the dance.

Too bad, since the Friars featured one of the country's best guards in Eric Murdock. Murdock became the all-time NCAA leader in steals with 376 and also averaged 25.6 points a game. Only a year earlier, doctors detected a "skip beat" in Murdock's regular heart rhythm. Tests were conducted and Murdock later received clearance to return to the court. Two other guards who finished their careers with all-time NCAA records were

David Greene

Women's Player of the Year **Dawn Staley**, a 5-6 guard from Virginia, was also named the Most Outstanding Player of the NCAA tournament.

N.C.State's Chris Corchiani with 1,038 assists and East Tennessee State's 5-7 Keith Jennings with a 49.3 three-point field goal percentage.

When the season finally ended in Indianapolis, no one could question Duke's claim as the nation's best team. Nor could anyone argue with those who suggested that the Blue Devils could challenge for a second consecutive NCAA championship in 1992.

When the team returned to Durham April 2 for a rally at Cameron, Krzyzewski looked up at the rafters and asked the crowd, "Well, where do you think we should hang it?"

The foot-stomping roar he got in return said, "Anywhere you want, Coach K!"

Krzyzewski laughed. "We don't want to take up too much space," he said. "Maybe we won't take 53 years to get another one." □

COLLEGE BASKETBALL
S T A T I S T I C S

THE SEASON IN REVIEW
1990-1991
TOP 25 • NCAA'S • STANDINGS

SEC
A

PAGE
233

Final AP Top 25 Poll
Taken before start of NCAA tournament.

The sportswriters & broadcasters poll: first place votes in parentheses; records through March 10; total points (based on 25 for 1st, 24 for 2nd, etc.); record in NCAA tourney and team lost to; head coach (career years and record, including NCAA tourney), and preseason ranking. Teams in **bold** type went on to reach NCAA Final Four.

		Mar.10 Record	Points	NCAA Recap	Head Coach	Preseason Rank
1	**UNLV** (64)	30-0	1600	4-1 (Duke)	Jerry Tarkanian (23rd:599-120)	1
2	Arkansas	31-3	1490	3-1 (Kansas)	Nolan Richardson (11th: 260-92)	2
3	Indiana	27-4	1446	2-1 (Kansas)	Bob Knight (26th: 561-203)	8
4	**North Carolina**	25-5	1398	4-1 (Kansas)	Dean Smith (30th: 717-209)	5
5	Ohio St.	25-3	1360	2-1 (St.John's)	Randy Ayers (2nd: 44-17)	10
6	**Duke**	26-7	1234	6-0	Mike Krzyzewski (16th: 336-174)	6
7	Syracuse	26-5	1232	0-1 (Richmond)	Jim Boeheim (15th: 369-114)	13
8	Arizona	26-6	1203	2-1 (Seton Hall)	Lute Olson (18th: 381-162)	3
9	Kentucky	22-6	952	On probation	Rick Pitino (9th: 169-94)	34
10	Utah	28-3	923	2-1 (UNLV)	Rick Majerus (7th: 133-58)	55
11	Nebraska	26-7	878	0-1 (Xavier)	Danny Nee (11th: 194-139)	NR
12	**Kansas**	22-7	796	5-1 (Duke)	Roy Williams (3rd: 76-25)	26
13	Seton Hall	22-8	785	3-1 (UNLV)	P.J.Carlesimo (16th: 223-242)	52
14	Oklahoma St	22-7	691	2-1 (Temple)	Eddie Sutton (21st: 454-172)	37
15	New Mexico St	23-5	687	0-1 (Creighton)	Neil McCarthy (16th: 319-163)	38
16	UCLA	23-8	609	0-1 (Penn St.)	Jim Harrick (12th: 233-127)	11
17	East Tennessee St.	28-4	589	0-1 (Iowa)	Alan LaForce (10th: 158-95)	30
18	Princeton	24-2	517	0-1 (Villanova)	Pete Carril (25th: 432-231)	57
19	Alabama	21-9	469	2-1 (Arkansas)	Wimp Sanderson (11th: 239-109)	7
20	St.John's	20-8	364	3-1 (Duke)	Lou Carnesecca (23rd: 507-189)	25
21	Mississippi St	20-8	319	0-1 (E.Mich.)	Richard Williams (5th: 70-74)	71
22	LSU	20-9	290	0-1 (UConn)	Dale Brown (19th: 360-212)	14
23	Texas	22-8	234	1-1 (St.John's)	Tom Penders (20th: 342-236)	22
24	DePaul	20-8	164	0-1 (Ga.Tech)	Joey Meyer (7th: 148-70)	32
25	Southern Miss.	21-7	154	0-1 (N.C.State)	M.K.Turk (15th: 233-191)	24

Others receiving votes: 26. Missouri (20-10, 136 pts); **27.** N.C.State (19-10, 42); **28.** Wake Forest (18-10, 29); **29.** Iowa (20-10, 27); **30.** Florida St.(20-10, 22); **31.** Georgetown (18-12, 21); **32.** BYU (20-12, 20); **33.** Virginia (21-11, 17); **34.** Connecticut (18-10, 16) and Michigan (14-14, 16); **36.** Pittsburgh (20-11, 13); **37.** Illinois (21-10, 10); **38.** Eastern Michigan (24-6, 9); **39.** Creighton (23-7, 7); **40.** New Orleans (23-7, 6); **41.** St.Peter's (24-6, 5); **42.** Pepperdine (22-8, 3); **43.** Arizona St.(19-9, 2), Louisiana Tech (21-9, 2), Northern Illinois (25-5, 2); New Mexico (20-9, 2) and Oklahoma (16-14, 2); **48.** Georgia Tech (16-12, 1); Houston (18-10, 1), St.Francis-PA (24-7, 1), South Alabama (22-8, 1), Temple (21-9, 1), WI-Green Bay (24-6, 1) and Xavier-OH (21-9, 1).

NCAA Division I Tournament Seeds

	EAST		SOUTHEAST		MIDWEST		WEST
1	**N.Carolina** (25-5)	1	Arkansas (31-3)	1	Ohio St. (25-3)	1	**UNLV** (30-0)
2	Syracuse (26-5)	2	Indiana (27-4)	2	**Duke** (26-7)	2	Arizona (26-6)
3	Oklahoma St.(22-7)	3	**Kansas** (22-7)	3	Nebraska (26-7)	3	Seton Hall (22-8)
4	UCLA (23-8)	4	Alabama (21-9)	4	St.John's (20-8)	4	Utah (28-3)
5	Mississippi St.(20-8)	5	Wake Forest (18-10)	5	Texas (22-8)	5	Michigan St.(18-10)
6	N.C.State (19-10)	6	Pittsburgh (20-11)	6	LSU (20-9)	6	N.Mexico St.(23-5)
7	Purdue (17-11)	7	Florida St.(20-10)	7	Iowa (20-10)	7	Virginia (21-11)
8	Princeton (24-2)	8	Arizona St.(19-9)	8	Georgia Tech (16-12)	8	Georgetown (18-12)
9	Villanova (16-14)	9	Rutgers (19-9)	9	DePaul (20-8)	9	Vanderbilt (17-12)
10	Temple (21-9)	10	USC (19-9)	10	East Tenn.St.(28-4)	10	BYU (20-12)
11	Southern Miss.(21-7)	11	Georgia (17-12)	11	Connecticut (18-10)	11	Creighton (23-7)
12	Eastern Mich.(24-6)	12	La.Tech (21-9)	12	St.Peter's (24-6)	12	WI-Green Bay (24-6)
13	Penn St. (20-10)	13	Murray St.(24-8)	13	Northern Ill.(25-5)	13	S.Alabama (22-8)
14	New Mexico (20-9)	14	New Orleans (23-7)	14	Xavier-OH (21-9)	14	Pepperdine (22-8)
15	Richmond (21-9)	15	C.Carolina (24-7)	15	NE Louisiana (25-7)	15	St.Francis-PA (24-7)
16	Northeastern (22-10)	16	Georgia St.(16-14)	16	Towson St.(19-10)	16	Montana (23-7)

1991 NCAA BASKETBALL MEN'S DIVISION I

1991 FINAL FOUR — INDIANAPOLIS

EAST

1st ROUND (March 14–15)

Seed	Team	Score
1	N. Carolina	101
16	Northeastern	66
8	Princeton	48
9	Villanova	50
5	Mississippi St.	56
12	Eastern Mich.	76
4	UCLA	69
13	Penn State	74
6	N.C. State	114
11	Southern Miss.	85
3	Oklahoma St.	67
14	New Mexico	54
7	Purdue	63
10	Temple	80
2	Syracuse	69
15	Richmond	73

2nd ROUND (March 16–17)
- N. Carolina 84
- Villanova 69
- Eastern Mich. 71 (OT)
- Penn State 68
- N.C. State 64
- Oklahoma St. 73
- Temple 77
- Richmond 64

REGIONALS (March 21–24) — E. RUTHERFORD, NJ
- N. Carolina 93
- Eastern Mich. 67
- Oklahoma St. 63 (OT)
- Temple 72
- N. Carolina 75
- Temple 72
- **N. Carolina 73**

SOUTHEAST

1st ROUND (March 14–15)

Seed	Team	Score
1	Arkansas	117
16	Georgia St.	76
8	Arizona St.	79
9	Rutgers	76
5	Wake Forest	71
12	La. Tech	65
4	Alabama	89
13	Murray St.	79
6	Pittsburgh	76 (OT)
11	Georgia	68
3	Kansas	55
14	New Orleans	49
7	Florida St.	75
10	USC	72
2	Indiana	79
15	Coastal Carolina	69

2nd ROUND (March 16–17)
- Arkansas 97
- Arizona St. 90
- Wake Forest 88
- Alabama 96
- Pittsburgh 66
- Kansas 77
- Florida St. 60
- Indiana 82

REGIONALS (March 21–24) — CHARLOTTE, NC
- Arkansas 93
- Alabama 70
- Kansas 83
- Indiana 65
- Arkansas 81
- Kansas 93
- **Kansas 79**

WEST

1st ROUND (March 14–15)

Seed	Team	Score
1	UNLV	99
16	Montana	65
8	Georgetown	70
9	Vanderbilt	60
5	Michigan St.	60
12	Wi-Green Bay	58
4	Utah	82
13	S. Alabama	72
6	New Mexico St.	56
11	Creighton	64
3	Seton Hall	71
14	Pepperdine	51
7	Virginia	48
10	BYU	61
2	Arizona	93
15	St. Francis-PA	80

2nd ROUND (March 16–17)
- UNLV 62
- Georgetown 54
- Michigan St. 84 (2OT)
- Utah 85
- Creighton 69
- Seton Hall 81
- BYU 61
- Arizona 76

REGIONALS (March 21–24) — SEATTLE
- UNLV 83
- Utah 66
- Seton Hall 81
- Arizona 77
- UNLV 77
- Seton Hall 65
- **UNLV 77**

MIDWEST

1st ROUND (March 14–15)

Seed	Team	Score
1	Ohio State	97
16	Towson St.	86
8	Georgia Tech	87
9	DePaul	70
5	Texas	73
12	St. Peter's	65
4	St. John's	75
13	No. Illinois	68
6	LSU	62
11	Connecticut	79
3	Nebraska	84
14	Xavier-OH	89
7	Iowa	76
10	East Tenn. St.	73
2	Duke	102
15	NE Louisiana	73

2nd ROUND (March 16–17)
- Ohio State 65
- Georgia Tech 61
- Texas 76
- St. John's 84
- Connecticut 66
- Xavier-OH 50
- Iowa 70
- Duke 85

REGIONALS (March 21–24) — PONTIAC, MI
- Ohio State 74
- St. John's 91
- Connecticut 67
- Duke 81
- St. John's 61
- Duke 78
- **Duke 79**

NATIONAL CHAMPIONSHIP
- Duke 72
- Kansas 65

FINAL FOUR
at Hoosier Dome

***

Semifinals: March 30
Final: April 1

Tournament Finalists' Box Scores

Championship Game

Kansas 65

	Min	FG M-A	FT M-A	Pts	Rb	A	F
Alonzo Jamison	25	1-10	0-0	2	4	5	4
Mike Maddox	19	2-4	0-0	4	3	4	3
Mark Randall	33	7-9	3-6	18	10	2	4
Terry Brown	31	6-15	0-0	16	4	1	1
Adonis Jordan	34	4-6	1-2	11	0	3	0
Steve Woodberry	18	1-4	0-0	2	4	0	4
Richard Scott	15	3-9	0-0	6	2	0	1
Sean Tunstall	15	1-5	0-0	2	1	0	3
Kirk Wagner	3	1-1	0-0	2	1	0	0
David Johanning	3	1-1	0-0	2	2	1	1
Patrick Richey	4	0-1	0-0	0	1	0	0
TOTALS	200	27-65	4-8	65	32	16	21

Three-point FG: 7-18 (Brown 4-11, Jordan 2-2, Randall 1-1, Richey 0-1, Tunstall 0-1, Jamison 0-2); **Team Rebounds:** none; **Blocked Shots:** 2 (Maddox, Tunstall); **Turnovers:** 14 (Jordan 3, Randall 3, Brown 2, Maddox 2, Jamison, Scott, Tunstall, Woodberry); **Steals:** 10 (Jamison 4, Brown 3, Jordan, Randall, Woodberry). **Percentages:** 2-Pt FG (.426), 3-Pt FG (.389), Total FG (.415), Free Throws (.500).

Duke 72

	Min	FG M-A	FT M-A	Pts	Rb	A	F
Greg Koubek	17	2-4	0-0	5	4	0	1
Grant Hill	28	4-6	2-8	10	8	3	1
Christian Laettner	32	3-8	12-12	18	10	0	3
Bobby Hurley	40	3-5	4-4	12	1	9	1
Thomas Hill	23	1-5	0-0	3	4	1	2
Brian Davis	24	4-5	0-2	8	2	1	4
Crawford Palmer	9	0-0	0-0	0	0	0	0
Tony Lang	1	0-0	0-0	0	0	0	0
Bill McCaffrey	26	6-8	2-2	16	1	0	1
TOTALS	200	23-41	20-28	72	30	14	13

Three-point FG: 6-10 (Hurley 2-4, McCaffrey 2-3, T.Hill 1-1, Koubek 1-2); **Team Rebounds:** 1 (not listed above); **Blocked Shots:** 2 (G.Hill 2); **Turnovers:** 18 (Laettner 4, McCaffrey 4, Hurley 3, G.Hill 2, Koubek 2, Davis, Lang, Palmer); **Steals:** 6 (G.Hill 2, Hurley 2, Laettner, Koubek). **Percentages:** 2-Pt FG (.549), 3-Pt FG (.600), Total FG (.561), Free Throws (.714).

Kansas (Big 8)	34	31—65
Duke (ACC)	42	30—72

Technical Fouls: none. **Officials:** Mickey Crowley, Charles Range, James Burr. **Attendance:** 47,100. **TV Rating:** 19.4/30 share (CBS).

Six-Game Composite

Duke (6-0)

	GM	FG%	TPts	—Per Game— Pts	Reb	Ast
Christian Laettner	6	.617	125	20.8	5.7	1.8
Bobby Hurley	6	.475	65	10.8	2.7	7.2
Thomas Hill	6	.500	61	10.2	2.7	1.5
Bill McCaffrey	6	.556	61	10.2	1.8	1.2
Grant Hill	6	.550	59	9.8	5.7	3.0
Brian Davis	6	.541	55	9.2	4.7	1.3
Greg Koubek	6	.421	41	6.8	2.8	1.3
Crawford Palmer	6	1.000	12	2.0	0.5	0.0
Tony Lang	6	.800	9	1.5	1.0	0.3
Marty Clark	4	.667	5	1.3	0.5	0.5
Christian Ast	3	1.000	2	0.7	0.0	0.0
Clay Buckley	4	1.000	2	0.5	1.0	0.0
DUKE	6	.547	497	82.8	30.5	18.0
OPPONENTS	6	.445	413	68.8	32.3	13.5

Three-pointers: Hurley (12 for 28), Koubek (6-18), T.Hill (4-6), McCaffrey (3-4), Laettner (2-4), Clark (0-1).

Kansas (5-1)

	GM	FG%	TPts	—Per Game— Prs	Reb	Ast
Adonis Jordan	6	.434	80	13.3	3.2	3.5
Terry Brown	6	.347	77	12.8	3.7	0.8
Alonzo Jamison	6	.574	69	11.5	7.5	3.3
Mark Randall	6	.528	68	11.3	7.3	3.5
Mike Maddox	6	.538	46	7.7	3.5	3.0
Sean Tunstall	6	.406	43	7.2	2.5	0.5
Richard Scott	6	.447	39	6.5	3.0	0.0
Steve Woodberry	6	.286	15	2.5	3.2	0.7
Kirk Wagner	6	.400	10	1.7	0.7	0.0
Patrick Richey	5	.400	6	1.2	0.6	0.0
David Johanning	4	.500	2	0.5	1.0	0.3
Macolm Nash	1	1.000	0	0.0	0.0	0.0
Doug Elstun	1	.000	0	0.0	0.0	0.0
KANSAS	6	.454	455	75.8	39.2	15.5
OPPONENTS	6	.429	406	67.7	34.4	13.3

Three-pointers: Jordan (14 for 29), Brown (14-45), Tunstall (6-14), Randall (1-1), Jamison (1-3), Maddox (0-1), Woodberry (0-1), Richey (0-2).

> **Most Outstanding Player:** Christian Laettner, Duke center. Semifinal—40 minutes, 28 points (9-11 from foul line), 7 rebounds. Final—32 minutes, 18 points (12-for-12 from foul line), 10 rebounds.
>
> **All-Tournament Team:** Laettner, Bobby Hurley and Bill McCaffrey of Duke; Mark Randall of Kansas; and Anderson Hunt of UNLV.

National Invitational Tournament

The 54th annual National Invitational Tournament had a 32-team field. First three rounds played on home courts of higher seeded teams. Semifinal, Third Place and Championship games played March 25 and 27 at Madison Square Garden in New York.

First Round—Arkansas St. 78, Rice 71; Cincinnati 82, Ball St. 55; Colorado 71, Michigan 64; Fordham 76, South Florida 68; Massachusetts 93, La Salle 90; Memphis St. 82, Ala-Birmingham 76; Oklahoma 111, Tulsa 86; Providence 98, James Madison 93 (2 OT); Siena 90, Fairleigh Dickinson 85; South Carolina 69, George Washington 63; Southern Ill. 75, Boise St. 74; SW Missouri St. 57, Coppin St. 47; Stanford 93, Houston 86; Wisconsin 87, Bowling Green 79 (OT); West Virginia 86, Furman 67; Wyoming 63, Butler 61.

Second Round—Arkansas St. 58, Memphis St. 57; Colorado 83, Wyoming 75; Massacusetts 78, Fordham 74; Oklahoma 89, Cincinnati 81 (OT); Providence 85, West Virginia 79; Siena 63, South Carolina 58; Southern Ill. 72, SW Missouri St. 69; Stanford 80, Wisconsin 72. **Quarterfinals**—Colorado 81, Arkansas St. 75; Massachusetts 82, Siena 80 (OT); Oklahoma 83, Providence 74; Stanford 78, Southern Ill. 68. **Semifinals**—Oklahoma 88, Colorado 78; Stanford 73, Massachusetts 71. **Championship**—Stanford 78, Oklahoma 72. **MVP**—Adam Keefe, Stanford center.

NCAA Men's Division I Leaders

Includes games through NCAA and NIT tournaments.

INDIVIDUAL

Scoring

	Cl	Gm	Pts	Avg
Kevin Bradshaw, U.S.Int'l.	Sr	28	1054	37.6
Alphonso Ford, Miss.Valley.	So	28	915	32.7
Von McDade, WI-Milwaukee.	Sr	28	830	29.6
Steve Rogers, Alabama St	Jr	29	852	29.4
Terrell Lowery, Loyola-CA	Jr	31	884	28.5
Bobby Phills, Southern-BR	Sr	28	795	28.4
Shaquille O'Neal, LSU	So	28	774	27.6
John Taft, Marshall.	Sr	28	764	27.3
Rodney Monroe, N.C.State	Sr	31	836	27.0
Terrell Brandon, Oregon	Jr	28	745	26.6
Kenny Anderson, Ga.Tech	So	30	776	25.9
Eric Murdock, Providence.	Sr	32	818	25.6
Keith Gailes, Loyola-IL.	Sr	26	657	25.3
Curtis Stuckey, Bradley.	Sr	28	702	25.1
Steve Smith, Michigan St	Sr	30	752	25.1
Rod Parker, Chicago St	Sr	25	621	24.8
Tom Davis, Delaware St.	Sr	30	740	24.7
Michael Ervin, Prairie View.	Sr	25	612	24.5
R.Youngblood, Southern-BR	Sr	28	679	24.3
Mike Iuzzolino, St.Fran-PA	Sr	32	772	24.1

Rebounds

	Cl	Gm	No	Avg
Shaquille O'Neal, LSU	So	28	411	14.7
Popeye Jones, Murray St	Jr	33	469	14.2
Larry Stewart, Coppin St	Sr	30	403	13.4
Tim Burroughs, Jacksonville.	Jr	27	350	13.0
Warren Kidd, Mid.Tenn.St.	So	30	370	12.3
Clarence Weatherspoon, S.Miss	Jr	29	355	12.2
Ervin Johnson, New Orleans	So	30	367	12.2
Tom Davis, Delaware St.	Sr	30	366	12.2
Dikembe Mutombo, Geo'town	Sr	32	389	12.2
Dale Davis, Clemson	Sr	28	340	12.1

Blocked Shots

	Cl	Gm	No	Avg
Shawn Bradley, BYU.	Fr	34	177	5.2
Cedric Lewis, Maryland	Sr	28	143	5.1
Shaquille O'Neal, LSU	So	28	140	5.0
Dikembe Mutombo, Georgetown.	Sr	32	151	4.7
Kevin Roberson, Vermont.	Jr	28	104	3.7
Lorenzo Williams, Stetson	Sr	31	113	3.6
Acie Earl, Iowa.	So	32	106	3.3
Jim McIlvaine, Marquette.	Fr	28	92	3.3
Luc Longley, New Mexico	Sr	30	95	3.2
Damon Lopez, Fordham	Sr	33	100	3.0

Assists

	Cl	Gm	No	Avg
Chris Corchiani, N.C.State	Sr	31	299	9.6
Danny Tirado, Jacksonville.	Jr	28	259	9.3
Terrell Lowery, Loyola-CA	Jr	31	283	9.1
Keith Jennings, E.Tenn.St.	Sr	33	301	9.1
Greg Anthony, UNLV.	Sr	35	310	8.9
Van Usher, Tennessee Tech	Jr	28	233	8.3
Orlando Smart, San Fran	Fr	29	237	8.2
Ray Johnson, Sam Houston St	Jr	24	193	8.0
Glover Cody, TX-Arlington.	Jr	29	229	7.9
Arnold Bernard, SW Mo.St.	Sr	34	257	7.6

Steals

	Cl	Gm	No	Avg
Van Usher, Tenn.Tech	Jr	28	104	3.7
Scott Burrell, UConn	So	31	112	3.6
Eric Murdock, Providence.	Sr	32	111	3.5
Von McDade, WI-Milwaukee.	Sr	28	97	3.5
Lynn Smith, St.Francis-NY	Jr	29	100	3.4
Emanual Davis, Delaware St	Sr	25	84	3.4

Field Goal Percentage

Minimum 5 Field Goals made per game.

	Cl	Gm	FG	FGA	Pct
Oliver Miller, Ark.	Jr	38	254	361	.704
Warren Kidd, M.Tenn.St	So	30	173	247	.700
Pete Freeman, Akron	Sr	28	175	250	.700
Lester James, St.Fran-NY	Jr	29	149	215	.693
Marcus Kennedy, E.Mich	Sr	33	240	352	.682

Free Throw Percentage

Minimum 2.5 Free Throws made per game.

	Cl	Gm	FG	FGA	Pct
Darin Archbold, Butler	Jr	29	187	205	.912
William Lewis, Monmouth	Jr	28	91	101	.901
D.Alexander, Okla.St	Jr	32	96	107	.897
K.Jennings, E.Tenn.St.	Sr	33	136	152	.895
Rodney Monroe, N.C.State	Sr	31	162	183	.885
M.Iuzzolino, St.Fran-PA	Sr	32	215	243	.885

3-Pt Field Goal Percentage

Minimum 1.5 Three-Point FG made per game.

	Cl	Gm	FG	FGA	Pct
K.Jennings, E.Tenn.St.	Sr	33	84	142	.593
Tony Bennett, WI-G.Bay	Jr	31	80	150	.533
M.Iuzzolino, St.Fran-PA	Sr	32	103	195	.528
R.Richardson, Loyola-CA	Fr	25	61	116	.526
David Mitchell, Samford	So	26	41	78	.526

3-Pt Field Goals Per Game

	Cl	Gm	FG	Avg
Bobby Phills, Southern-BR	Sr	28	123	4.4
Ronnie Schmitz, MO-Kan.City	So	29	116	4.0
Jeff Herdman, UC-Irvine	Sr	30	112	3.7
Doug Day, Radford.	So	29	106	3.7

Three tied with 3.5 each.

TEAM

Scoring Offense

	Gm	W-L	Pts	Avg
Southern-BR.	28	19-9	2924	104.4
Loyola,CA	31	16-15	3211	103.6
Arkansas	38	34-4	3783	99.6
UNLV	35	34-1	3420	97.7
Oklahoma	35	20-15	3363	96.1
Texas-Arlington	29	20-9	2743	94.6
East Tennessee St	33	28-5	3103	94.0
Southern Utah St	28	16-12	2604	93.0
Wright St	28	19-9	2594	92.6
UCLA	32	23-9	2954	92.3

Scoring Defense

	Gm	W-L	Pts	Avg
Princeton	27	24-3	1320	48.9
Northern Illinois	31	25-6	1781	57.5
Yale	26	15-11	1508	58.0
Wisconsin-Green Bay	31	24-7	1893	61.1
Georgetown	32	19-13	1964	61.4
Colorado St	29	15-14	1783	61.5
St.Peter's	31	24-7	1954	63.0
Monmouth	29	19-10	1838	63.4
Temple	34	24-10	2177	64.0
Utah	34	30-4	2184	64.2

Scoring Margin

	Off	Def	Margin
UNLV	97.7	71.0	26.7
Arkansas.	99.6	80.4	19.2
East Tennessee St.	94.0	76.8	17.3
Ohio St.	84.6	68.5	16.2
North Carolina.	87.6	71.6	16.0

Final NCAA Men's Division I Standings

Conference records include regular season games only. Overall records include all postseason tournament games.

American South Conference

	Conference			Overall		
	W	L	Pct	W	L	Pct
*New Orleans	9	3	.750	23	8	.742
†Arkansas St	9	3	.750	23	9	.719
*Louisiana Tech	8	4	.667	21	10	.677
SW Louisiana	6	6	.500	21	10	.677
Lamar	4	8	.333	15	13	.536
Central Florida	3	9	.250	10	17	.370
Texas-Pan American	3	9	.250	7	21	.250

Note: New Orleans seeded 1st in conference tourney.
Conf.Tournament Final: La.Tech 61, New Orleans 56.
***NCAA Tournament (0-2):** New Orleans (0-1); La.Tech (0-1).
†NIT Tournament (2-1): Arkansas St.(2-1).

Atlantic Coast Conference

	Conference			Overall		
	W	L	Pct	W	L	Pct
*Duke.....................	11	3	.786	32	7	.821
*North Carolina	10	4	.714	29	6	.829
*N.C.State	8	6	.571	20	11	.645
*Wake Forest	8	6	.571	19	11	.633
*Virginia	6	8	.429	21	12	.636
*Georgia Tech	6	8	.429	17	13	.567
Maryland	5	9	.357	16	12	.571
Clemson...................	2	12	.143	11	17	.393

Note: Maryland on probation, ineligible for ACC and NCAA tournaments.
Conf.Tournament Final: N.Carolina 96, Duke 74.
***NCAA Tournament (13-5):** Duke (6-0); N.Carolina (4-1); N.C. State (1-1); W.Forest (1-1); Ga.Tech (1-0); Virginia (0-1).

Atlantic 10 Conference

	Conference			Overall		
	W	L	Pct	W	L	Pct
*Rutgers	14	4	.778	19	10	.655
*Temple	13	5	.722	24	10	.706
*Penn St..................	10	8	.556	21	11	.656
†George Washington	10	8	.556	19	12	.613
†Massachusetts	10	8	.556	20	13	.606
†West Virginia	10	8	.556	17	14	.548
Duquesne	10	8	.556	13	15	.464
St.Joseph's	7	11	.389	13	17	.433
Rhode Island	6	12	.333	11	17	.393
St.Bonaventure.............	0	18	.000	5	23	.179

Conf.Tournament Final: Penn St.81, G.Washington 75.
***NCAA Tournament (4-3):** Temple (3-1); Penn St. (1-1); Rutgers (0-1).
†NIT Tournament (4-4): UMass (3-2); West Va. (1-1); G.Washington (0-1).

Big East Conference

	Conference			Overall		
	W	L	Pct	W	L	Pct
*Syracuse.................	12	4	.750	26	6	.813
*St.John's.................	10	6	.625	23	9	.719
*Seton Hall	9	7	.563	25	9	.735
*Pittsburgh...............	9	7	.563	21	12	.636
*Connecticut.............	9	7	.563	20	11	.645
*Georgetown.............	8	8	.500	19	13	.594
†Providence	7	9	.438	19	13	.594
*Villanova................	7	9	.438	17	15	.531
Boston College	1	15	.063	11	19	.367

Conf.Tournament Final: Seton Hall 74, Georgetown 62
***NCAA Tournament (11-7):** St.John's (3-1); Seton Hall (3-1); UConn (2-1); Pitt (1-1); Georgetown (1-1); Villanova (1-1); Syracuse (0-1).
†NIT Tournament (2-1): Providence (2-1).

Big Eight Conference

	Conference			Overall		
	W	L	Pct	W	L	Pct
*Oklahoma St..............	10	4	.714	24	8	.750
*Kansas	10	4	.714	27	8	.771
*Nebraska	9	5	.643	26	8	.765
Missouri	8	6	.571	20	10	.667
Iowa St	6	8	.429	12	19	.387
†Colorado.................	5	9	.357	19	14	.576
†Oklahoma	5	9	.357	20	15	.571
Kansas St	3	11	.214	13	15	.464

Note: Missouri on probation, eligible for Big 8 tournament but not NCAAs.
Conf.Tournament Final: Missouri 90, Nebraska 82.
***NCAA Tournament (7-3):** Kansas (5-1); Okla.St.(2-1); Nebraska (0-1).
†NIT Tournament (8-2): Oklahoma (4-1); Colorado (4-1).

Big Sky Conference

	Conference			Overall		
	W	L	Pct	W	L	Pct
*Montana..................	13	3	.813	23	8	.742
Nevada	12	4	.750	17	14	.548
Idaho	11	5	.688	19	11	.633
†Boise St..................	10	6	.625	18	11	.621
Idaho St	7	9	.438	11	18	.379
Weber St	7	9	.438	12	16	.429
Montana St...............	6	10	.375	12	16	.429
Eastern Washington	5	11	.313	11	16	.407
Northern Arizona...........	1	15	.063	4	23	.148

Conf.Tournament Final: Montana 76, Idaho 68. I
***NCAA Tournament (0-1):** Montana (0-1).
†NIT Tournament (0-1): Boise St.(0-1).

Big South Conference

	Conference			Overall		
	W	L	Pct	W	L	Pct
*Coastal Carolina..........	13	1	.929	24	8	.750
Radford..................	12	2	.857	22	7	.759
Augusta..................	9	5	.643	14	16	.467
Davidson.................	6	8	.429	10	19	.345
Winthrop.................	5	9	.357	8	20	.286
NC-Asheville..............	4	10	.357	8	20	.286
Charleston Southern	4	10	.286	9	20	.310
Campbell	3	11	.214	9	19	.321

Note: Davidson joined conference in 1990; Baptist College changed name to Charleston Southern in 1991.
Conf.Tournament Final: Coastal 89, Augusta 54.
NCAA Play-in: Coastal beat SWAC champ Jackson St., 78-59.
***NCAA Tournament (0-1):** Coastal (0-1).

Big Ten Conference

	Conference			Overall		
	W	L	Pct	W	L	Pct
*Ohio St.	15	3	.833	27	4	.871
*Indiana..................	15	3	.833	29	5	.853
Illinois	11	7	.611	21	10	.677
*Michigan St	11	7	.611	19	11	.633
*Iowa	9	9	.500	21	11	.656
*Purdue	9	9	.500	17	12	.586
†Wisconsin	8	10	.444	15	15	.500
†Michigan	7	11	.389	14	15	.483
Minnesota	5	13	.278	12	16	.429
Northwestern	0	18	.000	5	23	.179

Notes: Ohio St. beat Indiana twice during regular season; Illinois on probation, ineligible for NCAA tournament.
Conf.Tournament Final: Big Ten has no tournament.
***NCAA Tournament (6-5):** Ohio St. (2-1); Indiana (2-1); Mich.St.(1-1); Iowa (1-1); Purdue (0-1).
†NIT Tournament (1-2): Wisconsin (1-1); Michigan (0-1).

Final NCAA Men's Division I Standings (Cont.)

Big West Conference

	Conference			Overall		
	W	L	Pct	W	L	Pct
*UNLV	18	0	1.000	34	1	.971
*New Mexico St	15	3	.833	23	6	.793
Pacific	9	9	.500	14	15	.483
UC-Santa Barbara	8	10	.444	14	15	.483
Utah St	8	10	.444	11	17	.393
CS-Fullerton	7	11	.389	14	14	.500
Fresno St	7	11	.389	14	16	.467
Long Beach St	7	11	.389	11	17	.393
UC-Irvine	6	12	.333	11	19	.367
San Jose St	5	13	.278	7	20	.259

Conf.Tournament Final: UNLV 98, Fresno St.74.
*NCAA Tournament (4-2): UNLV (4-1); N.Mexico St.(0-1).

Colonial Athletic Association

	Conference			Overall		
	W	L	Pct	W	L	Pct
†James Madison	12	2	.857	19	10	.655
*Richmond	10	4	.714	22	10	.688
American	8	6	.571	15	14	.517
George Mason	8	6	.571	14	16	.467
William & Mary	6	8	.429	13	15	.464
NC-Wilmington	6	8	.429	11	17	.393
East Carolina	4	10	.286	12	16	.429
Navy	2	12	.143	8	21	.276

Conf.Tournament Final: Richmond 81, George Mason 78.
*NCAA Tournament (1-1): Richmond (1-1).
†NIT Tournament (0-1): James Madison (0-1).

East Coast Conference

	Conference			Overall		
	W	L	Pct	W	L	Pct
*Towson St	10	2	.833	19	11	.633
Delaware	8	4	.667	16	13	.552
Hofstra	7	5	.583	14	14	.500
Drexel	7	5	.583	12	16	.429
Rider	4	8	.333	14	16	.467
MD-Baltimore County	4	8	.333	7	22	.241
Central Conn.St	2	10	.167	4	24	.143

Note: Cent.Conn.St. and MD-Balt.County joined ECC in 1990
after Bucknell, Lafayette and Lehigh moved to new Patriot League.
Conf.Tournament Final: Towson St.69, Rider 63.
*NCAA Tournament (0-1): Towson St.(0-1).

Ivy League

	Conference			Overall		
	W	L	Pct	W	L	Pct
*Princeton	14	0	1.000	24	3	.889
Yale	9	5	.643	15	11	.577
Cornell	6	8	.429	13	13	.500
Brown	6	8	.429	11	15	.423
Harvard	6	8	.429	9	17	.346
Penn	6	8	.429	9	17	.346
Columbia	5	9	.357	7	19	.269
Dartmouth	4	10	.286	8	17	.320

Conf.Tournament Final: Ivy League has no tournament.
*NCAA Tournament (0-1): Princeton (0-1).

Metro Conference

	Conference			Overall		
	W	L	Pct	W	L	Pct
*Southern Miss.	10	4	.714	21	8	.724
*Florida St.	9	5	.643	21	11	.656
†Cincinnati	8	6	.571	18	12	.600
Tulane	7	7	.500	15	13	.536
†Memphis St	7	7	.500	17	15	.531
Virginia Tech	6	8	.429	13	16	.448
†South Carolina	5	9	.357	20	13	.606
Louisville	4	10	.286	14	16	.467

Conf.Tournament Final: Florida St.76, Louisville 69.
*NCAA Tournament (1-2): Florida St.(1-1); So.Miss.(0-1).
†NIT Tournament (3-3): Cincinnati (1-1); Memphis St.(1-1);
S.Carolina (1-1).

Metro Atlantic Conference

	Conference			Overall		
	W	L	Pct	W	L	Pct
†Siena	12	4	.750	25	10	.714
†La Salle	12	4	.750	19	10	.655
*St.Peter's	11	5	.688	24	7	.774
Iona	11	5	.688	17	13	.567
Manhattan	8	8	.500	13	15	.464
Niagara	6	10	.375	8	20	.286
Loyola-MD	5	11	.313	12	16	.429
Fairfield	4	12	.250	8	20	.286
Canisius	3	13	.188	10	19	.345

Conf.Tournament Final: St.Peter's 64, Iona 58.
*NCAA Tournament (0-1): St.Peter's (0-1).
†NIT Tournament (2-2): Siena (2-1); La Salle (0-1).

Mid-American Conference

	Conference			Overall		
	W	L	Pct	W	L	Pct
*Eastern Michigan	13	3	.813	26	7	.788
†Ball State	10	6	.625	21	10	.677
Miami-OH	10	6	.625	16	12	.571
†Bowling Green	9	7	.563	17	13	.567
Ohio Univ.	9	7	.563	16	12	.571
Central Michigan	8	8	.500	14	14	.500
Toledo	7	9	.438	17	16	.515
Kent	4	12	.250	10	18	.357
Western Michigan	2	14	.125	5	22	.185

Conf.Tournament Final: Eastern Mich.67, Toledo 66.
*NCAA Tournament (2-1): Eastern Mich.(2-1).
†NIT Tournament (0-2): Ball St.(0-1); Bowling Green (0-1).

Mid-Continent Conference

	Conference			Overall		
	W	L	Pct	W	L	Pct
*Northern Illinois	14	2	.875	25	6	.806
*Wisc-Green Bay	13	3	.813	24	7	.774
Eastern Illinois	10	6	.625	17	12	.586
Cleveland St	8	8	.500	12	16	.429
Northern Iowa	8	8	.500	13	19	.406
Akron	6	10	.375	15	13	.536
Western Illinois	6	10	.375	13	15	.464
IL-Chicago	5	11	.313	15	15	.500
Valparaiso	2	14	.125	5	22	.185

Conf.Tournament Final: Green Bay 56, Northern Ill.39.
*NCAA Tournament (0-2): Northern Ill.(0-1); Green Bay (0-1).

Mid-Eastern Athletic Conference

	Conference			Overall		
	W	L	Pct	W	L	Pct
†Coppin St.	14	2	.875	19	11	.633
Delaware St.	10	6	.625	19	11	.633
North Carolina A&T	10	6	.625	17	10	.630
South Carolina St.	10	6	.625	13	15	.464
Florida A&M	9	7	.563	17	14	.548
Howard	7	9	.438	8	20	.286
Morgan St.	6	10	.375	7	22	.241
MD-Eastern Shore	3	13	.188	5	23	.179
Bethune-Cookman	3	13	.188	5	24	.172

Conf.Tournament Final: Fla.A&M 84, Delaware St.80 (OT)
NCAA Play-in: Fla.A&M lost to Southland champ NE La., 87-63.
†NIT Tournament (0-1): Coppin St.(0-1).

Midwestern Collegiate Conference

	Conference			Overall		
	W	L	Pct	W	L	Pct
*Xavier-OH	11	3	.786	22	10	.688
†Butler	10	4	.714	18	11	.621
St.Louis	8	6	.571	19	14	.576
Dayton	8	6	.571	14	15	.483
Evansville	7	7	.500	14	14	.500
Marquette	7	7	.500	11	18	.379
Loyola-IL	3	11	.214	10	19	.345
Detroit	2	12	.143	9	19	.321

Conf.Tournament Final: Xavier 81, St.Louis 68.
*NCAA Tournament (1-1): Xavier (1-1).
†NIT Tournament (0-1): Butler (0-1).

Missouri Valley Conference

	Conference			Overall		
	W	L	Pct	W	L	Pct
*Creighton	12	4	.750	24	8	.750
†SW Missouri St.	11	5	.688	22	12	.647
†Tulsa	10	6	.625	18	12	.600
†Southern Illinois	9	7	.563	18	14	.563
Indiana St.	9	7	.563	14	14	.500
Wichita St.	7	9	.438	14	17	.452
Bradley	6	10	.375	8	20	.286
Drake	4	12	.250	8	21	.276
Illinois St.	4	12	.250	5	23	.179

Note: SW Missouri St. left Mid-Continent to join Mo.Valley in 1990.
Conf.Tournament Final: Creighton 68, SW Missouri St.52.
*NCAA Tournament (1-1): Creighton (1-1).
†NIT Tournament (3-3): Southern Ill.(2-1); SW Missouri St.(1-1); Tulsa (0-1).

North Atlantic Conference

	Conference			Overall		
	W	L	Pct	W	L	Pct
*Northeastern	8	2	.800	22	11	.667
Maine	7	3	.700	13	16	.448
Vermont	5	5	.500	15	13	.536
Hartford	5	5	.500	13	16	.448
Boston University	5	5	.500	11	18	.379
New Hampshire	0	10	.000	3	25	.107

Note: Colgate left N.Atlantic for new Patriot League in 1990.
Conf.Tournament Final: Northeastern 57, Maine 46.
*NCAA Tournament (0-1): Northeastern (0-1).

Northeast Conference

	Conference			Overall		
	W	L	Pct	W	L	Pct
*St.Francis-PA	13	3	.813	24	8	.750
†Fairleigh Dickinson	13	3	.813	22	9	.710
Robert Morris	12	4	.750	17	11	.607
Monmouth	10	6	.625	19	10	.655
St.Francis-NY	8	8	.500	15	14	.517
Mount St.Mary's	6	10	.375	8	19	.296
Long Island	4	12	.250	10	18	.357
Marist	4	12	.250	6	22	.214
Wagner	2	14	.125	4	26	.133

Note: Robt.Morris on probation, ineligible for NEC and NCAA tournaments.
Conf.Tournament Final: St.Francis-PA 97, F-Dickinson 82.
NCAA Play-in: St.Francis-PA beat Patriot champ Fordham, 70-64.
*NCAA Tournament (0-1): St.Francis-PA (0-1).
†NIT Tournament (0-1): F-Dickinson (0-1).

Ohio Valley Conference

	Conference			Overall		
	W	L	Pct	W	L	Pct
*Murray St.	10	2	.833	24	9	.727
Eastern Kentucky	9	3	.750	19	10	.655
Middle Tenn.St.	6	6	.500	21	9	.700
Austin Peay	6	6	.500	15	14	.517
Tennessee Tech	6	6	.500	12	16	.429
Morehead St.	4	8	.333	16	13	.552
Tennessee St.	1	11	.083	5	23	.179

Conf.Tournament Final: Murray St.79, Mid.Tenn.St.67
*NCAA Tournament (0-1): Murray St.(0-1).

Pacific-10 Conference

	Conference			Overall		
	W	L	Pct	W	L	Pct
*Arizona	14	4	.778	28	7	.800
*UCLA	11	7	.611	23	9	.719
*Arizona St.	10	8	.556	20	10	.667
*USC	10	8	.556	19	10	.655
†Stanford	8	10	.444	20	13	.606
Washington St.	8	10	.444	16	12	.571
Oregon St.	8	10	.444	14	14	.500
Oregon	8	10	.444	13	15	.464
California	8	10	.444	13	15	.464
Washington	5	13	.278	14	14	.500

Conf.Tournament Final: Pac-10 discontinued tournament in 1991 after four years.
*NCAA Tournament (3-4): Arizona (2-1); Ariz.St.(1-1); UCLA (0-1); USC (0-1).
†NIT Tournament (5-0): Stanford (5-0).

Patriot League

	Conference			Overall		
	W	L	Pct	W	L	Pct
†Fordham	11	1	.917	25	8	.758
Lehigh	10	2	.750	19	10	.655
Holy Cross	8	4	.500	18	12	.600
Bucknell	7	5	.500	18	13	.581
Army	3	9	.500	6	22	.214
Colgate	2	10	.333	5	23	.179
Lafayette	1	11	.083	7	21	.250

Note: New conference for 1990-91 season. Bucknell, Lafayette and Lehigh moved from East Coast; Army, Fordham and Holy Cross from Metro Atlantic; Colgate from North Atlantic.
Conf.Tournament Final: Fordham 84, Holy Cross 81 (OT).
NCAA Play-in: Fordham lost to Northeast champ St.Francis-PA, 70-64.
†NIT Tournament (1-1): Fordham (1-1).

Final NCAA Men's Division I Standings (Cont.)

Southeastern Conference

	Conference			Overall		
	W	L	Pct	W	L	Pct
Kentucky	14	4	.778	22	6	.786
*Mississippi St	13	5	.722	20	9	.690
*LSU	13	5	.722	20	10	.667
*Alabama	12	6	.667	23	10	.697
*Vanderbilt	11	7	.611	17	13	.567
*Georgia	9	9	.500	17	13	.567
Florida	7	11	.389	11	17	.393
Auburn	5	13	.278	13	16	.448
Tennessee	3	15	.167	12	22	.353
Mississippi	3	15	.167	9	19	.321

Note: Kentucky on probation, ineligible for SEC and NCAA tournaments.
Conf.Tournament Final: Alabama 88, Tennessee 69
*NCAA Tournament (2-5): Alabama (2-1); Miss.St.(0-1); LSU (0-1); Vanderbilt (0-1); Georgia (0-1).

Southern Conference

	Conference			Overall		
	W	L	Pct	W	L	Pct
†Furman	11	3	.786	20	9	.690
* East Tennessee St	11	3	.786	28	5	.848
Tenn-Chattanooga	11	3	.786	19	10	.655
Appalachian St	7	7	.500	16	14	.533
Marshall	7	7	.500	14	14	.500
VMI	5	9	.357	10	18	.357
Western Carolina	3	11	.214	11	17	.393
Citadel	1	13	.071	6	22	.214

Note: Marshall on probation, ineligible for Southern or NCAA tournaments.
Conf.Tournament Final: E.Tenn.St.101, Appalach.St.82.
*NCAA Tournament (0-1): E.Tenn.St.(0-1).
†NIT Tournament (0-1): Furman (0-1).

Southland Conference

	Conference			Overall		
	W	L	Pct	W	L	Pct
*NE Louisiana	13	1	.929	25	8	.758
Texas-Arlington	11	3	.786	20	9	.690
North Texas	11	3	.786	17	13	.567
Stephen F.Austin	6	8	.429	11	17	.393
Sam Houston St	5	9	.357	7	20	.259
SW Texas St	4	10	.286	10	17	.370
McNeese St	4	10	.286	8	19	.296
Northwestern LA	2	12	.143	6	22	.214

Note: N'western LA on probation, ineligible for Southland and NCAA tournaments.
Conf.Tournament Final: NE Louisiana 87, TX-Arlington 60.
NCAA Play-in: NE Louisiana. beat Mid-Eastern champ Florida A&M, 87-63.
*NCAA Tournament (0-1): NE Louisiana.(0-1).

Southwest Conference

	Conference			Overall		
	W	L	Pct	W	L	Pct
*Arkansas	15	1	.938	34	4	.895
*Texas	13	3	.813	23	9	.719
†Houston	10	6	.625	18	11	.621
TCU	9	7	.563	18	10	.643
†Rice	9	7	.563	16	14	.533
SMU	6	10	.375	12	17	.414
Baylor	4	12	.250	12	15	.444
Texas Tech	4	12	.250	8	23	.258
Texas A&M	2	14	.125	8	21	.276

Conf.Tournament Final: Arkansas 120, Texas 89.
*NCAA Tournament (4-2): Arkansas (3-1); Texas (1-1).
†NIT Tournament (0-2): Houston (0-1); Rice (0-1).

Southwestern Athletic Conference

	Conference			Overall		
	W	L	Pct	W	L	Pct
Jackson St	10	2	.833	17	13	.567
Southern Univ	8	4	.667	19	9	.679
Alabama St	7	5	.583	18	11	.621
Texas Southern	7	5	.583	13	17	.433
Miss.Valley St	4	8	.333	9	19	.321
Alcorn St	3	9	.250	8	21	.276
Grambling	3	9	.250	6	22	.214
Prairie View A&M	0	0	.000	4	21	.160

Note: Prairie View on probation, ineligible for SWAC regular season, SWAC tournament and NCAA tournament.
Conf.Tournament Final: Jackson St.70, TX-Southern 66.
NCAA Play-in: Jackson St. lost to Big South champ Coastal Carolina, 78-59.

Sun Belt Conference

	Conference			Overall		
	W	L	Pct	W	L	Pct
*South Alabama	11	3	.786	22	9	.710
†Ala-Birmingham	9	5	.643	18	13	.581
†South Florida	8	6	.571	19	11	.633
Western Kentucky	8	6	.571	14	14	.500
VCU	7	7	.500	14	17	.452
NC-Charlotte	6	8	.429	14	14	.500
Old Dominion	5	9	.357	14	18	.438
Jacksonville	2	12	.143	6	22	.214

Conf.Tournament Final: S.Alabama 86, Old Dominion 81.
*NCAA Tournament (0-1): S.Alabama (0-1).
†NIT Tournament (0-2): Ala-Birm.(0-1); S.Florida (0-1).

Trans America Athletic Conference

	Conference			Overall		
	W	L	Pct	W	L	Pct
Texas-San Antonio	12	2	.857	21	8	.724
Centenary	10	4	.714	17	12	.586
Georgia Southern	9	5	.643	14	13	.519
Stetson	9	5	.643	15	16	.484
*Georgia St	7	7	.500	16	15	.516
Ark-Little Rock	8	6	.429	10	20	.333
Stamford	2	12	.143	6	22	.214
Mercer	1	13	.071	2	25	.074

Conf.Tournament Final: Georgia St. 80, Ark-LR 60.
*NCAA Tournament (0-1): Georgia St.(0-1).

West Coast Athletic Conference

	Conference			Overall		
	W	L	Pct	W	L	Pct
*Pepperdine	13	1	.929	22	9	.710
Loyola Marymount	9	5	.643	16	15	.516
San Diego	8	6	.571	17	12	.586
Santa Clara	7	7	.500	16	13	.552
St.Mary's	7	7	.500	13	17	.433
Gonzaga	5	9	.357	13	14	.481
San Francisco	4	10	.286	12	17	.414
Portland	3	11	.214	5	23	.179

Conf.Tournament Final: Pepperdine 71, St.Mary's 68 (OT)
*NCAA Tournament (0-1): Pepperdine (0-1).

Western Athletic Conference

	Conference			Overall		
	W	L	Pct	W	L	Pct
*Utah	15	1	.938	30	4	.882
*BYU	11	5	.688	21	13	.618
*New Mexico	10	6	.625	20	10	.667
†Wyoming	8	8	.500	20	12	.625
Hawaii	7	9	.438	16	13	.552
UTEP	7	9	.438	15	13	.536
San Diego St	6	10	.375	13	16	.448
Colorado St	6	10	.375	15	14	.517
Air Force	2	14	.125	9	20	.310

Conf.Tournament Final: BYU 51, Utah 49 (OT)
***NCAA Tournament (3-3):** Utah (2-1); BYU (1-1); N.Mexico (0-1).
†NIT Tournament (1-1): Wyoming (1-1).

Division I Independents

	Overall		
	W	L	Pct
*DePaul	20	9	.690
Wright St	19	9	.679
Wisconsin-Milwaukee	18	10	.643
Southern Utah	16	12	.571
Missouri-Kansas City	15	14	.517
Youngstown St	12	16	.429
Brooklyn	11	16	.407
Notre Dame	12	20	.375
Miami-FL	9	19	.321
Southeastern Louisiana	9	19	.321
CS-Northridge	8	20	.286
Florida International	6	22	.214
Liberty	5	23	.179
Chicago St	4	24	.143
Nicholls St	3	25	.107
Northeastern Illinois	2	25	.074
US International	2	26	.071

Note: Akron, Central Conn.St., Davidson, MD-Balt.County and No.Illinois joined conferences in 1990; WI-Milwaukee, CS-Northridge, NE Illinois moved up from Division II.
***NCAA Tournament (0-1):** DePaul (0-1).

Conference Moves

Nearly 30 Division I schools will begin the 1991-92 season as members of conferences different from the ones they played in during 1990-91.

The 1991-92 season will gain one new conference (Great Midwest) and lose one (American South).

See "College Sports" for further details.

NAIA Tournament

The quarterfinalists, in alphabetical order, after two rounds of the 32-team NAIA tournament: Athens St.,AL (24-9); Central Arkansas (27-4); David Lipscomb,TN (35-3); Oklahoma City (31-3); Pfeiffer,NC (28-3); St.Mary's,MI (26-11); Taylor,IN (33-3); Wisconsin-Eau Claire (29-2).

All tournament games played, March 12-18, at Kemper Arena in Kansas City. There was no Third Place game.

Quarterfinals

Central Arkansas 95	Athens St. 64
Oklahoma City 112	St.Mary's 94
Pfeiffer 105	David Lipscomb 95
Taylor 64	WI-Eau Claire 57

Semifinals

Central Arkansas 66	Taylor 60
Oklahoma City 100	Pfeiffer 83

Championship

Oklahoma City 77	Central Arkansas 74

Annual Awards
Players of the Year

Larry Johnson, UNLV	NABC,Naismith USBWA,Wooden
Shaquille O'Neal, LSU	AP,UPI

Coaches of the Year

Randy Ayers, Ohio St	AP,Naismith,USBWA
Rick Majerus, Utah	UPI
Mike Krzyzewski, Duke	NABC

Consensus All-America

The NCAA Division I players cited most frequently by the following All-America selectors: AP, US Basketball Writers, National Assn. of Basketball Coaches, and UPI.

First Team

	Class	Hgt	Pos
Kenny Anderson, Ga.Tech	So.	6-2	G
Jimmy Jackson, Ohio St	So.	6-6	F/G
Larry Johnson, UNLV	Sr.	6-7	F
Shaquille O'Neal, LSU	So.	7-1	C
Billy Owens, Syracuse	Jr.	6-9	F

Second Team

	Class	Hgt	Pos
Stacey Augmon, UNLV	Sr.	6-8	F
Keith Jennings, E.Tenn.St	Sr.	5-7	G
Christian Laettner, Duke	Jr.	6-11	F/C
Eric Murdock, Providence	Sr.	6-2	G
Steve Smith, Mich.St	Sr.	6-6	G

Other NCAA Tournaments
Division II

The eight regional winners of the 32-team Division II tournament: NEW ENGLAND—Bridgeport,CT (24-7); EAST—Philadelphia Textile (24-7); SOUTH ATLANTIC—Virginia Union (26-4); SOUTH—North Alabama (26-4); SOUTH CENTRAL—SW Baptist,MO (29-2); GREAT LAKES—Ashland,OH (26-4); NORTH CENTRAL—North Dakota (29-3); WEST—CS-Bakersfield (24-7).

The Elite Eight played for the Division II championship, March 21-23, in Springfield, MA. There was no Third Place game.

Quarterfinals

Bridgeport 69	Phila.Textile 62
CS-Bakersfield 55	SW Baptist 52
North Alabama 92	Ashland 84
Virginia Union 64	North Dakota 63

Semifinals

Bridgeport 73	OT	CS-Bakersfield 66
North Alabama 97		Virginia Union 76

Championship

North Alabama 79	Bridgeport 72

Division III

The four sectional winners of the 40-team Division II tournament: ATLANTIC/NORTHEAST—Ramapo,NJ (24-6); EAST/MID-ATLANTIC—Franklin & Marshall,PA (27-2); SOUTH/MIDWEST—Wisconsin-Platteville (26-3); WEST/GREAT LAKES—Otterbein,OH (29-2).

The Final Four played for the Division III championship, March 15-16, in Springfield, OH.

Semifinals

Franklin & Marshall 108	Ramapo 56
WI-Platteville 96	Otterbein 94

Third Place

Otterbein 113	Ramapo 84

Championship

WI-Platteville 81	Franklin & Marshall 74

Final Women's Top 25 Poll

Taken before start of NCAA tournament.

The *Philadelphia Inquirer* coaches' poll, compiled by Mel Greenberg: first place votes in parentheses; records through March 10; total points (based on 25 for 1st, 24 for 2nd, etc.); record in NCAA tourney and team lost to; head coach (career years and record, including NCAA tourney), and preseason ranking. Teams in **bold** type went on to reach NCAA Final Four.

		Mar.10 Record	Points	NCAA Recap	Head Coach	Preseason Rank
1	Penn St. (49)	29-1	1528	0-1 (J.Madison)	Rene Portland (15th: 338-119)	18
2	**Virginia** (9)	27-2	1486	4-1 (Tennessee)	Debbie Ryan (14th: 301-122)	1
3	Georgia (2)	26-3	1395	2-1 (Stanford)	Andy Landers (12th: 304-79)	4
4	**Tennessee** (1)	25-5	1343	5-0	Pat Summitt (17th: 442-118)	6
5	Purdue	26-2	1308	0-1 (Vanderbilt)	Lin Dunn (20th: 335-215)	9
6	Auburn	24-5	1254	2-1 (Tennessee)	Joe Ciampi (14th: 347-85)	3
7	N.C.State	25-5	1195	1-1 (UConn)	Kay Yow (20th: 423-143)	8
8	LSU	24-6	1109	0-1 (Lamar)	Sue Gunter (27th: 458-162)	19
9	Arkansas	27-3	1093	1-1 (Lamar)	John Sutherland (7th: 150-60)	10
10	Western Ky.	28-2	951	1-1 (Tennessee)	Paul Sanderford (9th: 221-69)	28
11	**Stanford**	23-5	912	3-1 (Tennessee)	Tara VanDerveer (13th: 292-95)	2
12	Washington	23-4	862	1-1 (Stanford)	Chris Gobrecht (12th: 231-128)	14
13	**Connecticut**	26-4	796	3-1 (Virginia)	Geno Auriemma (6th: 121-56)	24
14	S.F.Austin	25-4	640	1-1 (Virginia)	Gary Blair (6th: 154-35)	26
15	Providence	25-5	573	1-1 (Clemson)	Bob Foley (6th: 135-52)	30
16	Texas	21-8	549	0-1 (Lamar)	Jody Conradt (22nd: 577-135)	7
17	UNLV	24-6	476	1-1 (Georgia)	Jim Bolla (9th: 222-60)	17
18	Long Beach St	23-7	467	1-1 (Georgia)	Joan Bonvicini (12th: 325-71)	12
19	Mississippi	20-8	448	0-1 (S.F.Austin)	Van Chancellor (13th: 312-102)	16
20	Rutgers	23-6	307	0-1 (Toledo)	Theresa Grentz (17th: 379-114)	23
21	Clemson	20-10	298	2-1 (UConn)	Jim Davis (5th: 104-49)	21
22	Northwestern	20-8	258	1-1 (Arkansas)	Don Perrelli (15th: 297-149)	15
23	Iowa	20-8	240	1-1 (Washington)	Vivian Stringer (19th: 436-103)	11
24	Lamar	26-3	114	3-1 (Virginia)	Al Barbre (5th: 82-62)	NR
25	Oklahorna St.	25-5	90	2-1 (Virginia)	Dick Halterman (8th: 148-92)	31

Others receiving votes: 26. Michigan St.(21-7, 85 pts); **27.** Texas Tech (23-7, 51); **28.** Florida St.(24-6, 42); **29.** George Washington (22-6, 38); **30.** Holy Cross (24-5, 31); **31.** CS-Fullerton (24-7, 28) and Notre Dame (23-6, 28); **33.** Montana (26-3, 27); **34.** Maryland (17-12, 23); **35.** Fairfield (25-5, 14); **36.** Kentucky (20-8, 13) and Richmond (26-4, 13); **38.** DePaul (19-11, 12) and Santa Clara (25-3, 12); **40.** Toledo (23-6, 8); **41.** Louisiana Tech (18-11, 7) and USC (17-11, 7); **43.** SW Missouri St.(25-4, 6); **44.** St.Joseph;s-PA (18-12, 5); **45.** Northern Ill.(23-8, 3); **46.** James Madison (24-4, 2) and Utah (20-9, 2); **48.** Tennessee Tech (22-7, 1).

NCAA Women's Division I

Individual Leaders

Includes games through NCAA Tournament

Scoring

	Cl	Gm	Pts	Avg
Jan Jensen, Drake	Sr	30	888	29.6
Genia Miller, CS-Fullerton	Sr	33	969	29.4
Lisa McMullen, Alabama St	Jr	28	815	29.1
Tari Phillips, Central Fla	Sr	21	532	25.3
Rehema Stephens, UCLA	Jr	28	709	25.3
Sheila Ethridge, La.Tech	Sr	30	756	25.2
Torcha Hollis, Grambling	Sr	29	729	25.1
Andrea Congreaves, Mercer	So	27	662	24.5
Lisa Foss, Northern Ill.	Sr	35	853	24.4
Kirsten Brendel, Penn	Sr	26	631	24.3

Rebounds

	Cl	GGm	No	Avg
Tarcha Hollis, Grambling	Sr	29	443	15.3
Sirena Autman, S.Houston St	Sr	27	356	13.2
Latrice Robinson, Chicago St	So	28	358	12.8
Natalie Cleckley, Furman	Sr	28	356	12.7
Leslie Schlegel, Hofstra	Sr	30	373	12.4
Tari Phillips, Central Fla	Sr	21	261	12.4

Assists

	Cl	GGm	Ast	Avg
Michelle Burden, Kent	Fr	29	294	10.1
Shanya Evans, Providence	Sr	32	312	9.8
Anja Bordt, St.Mary's-CA	Sr	28	270	9.6
Mariann Murtaugh, Loyola-IL	Jr	28	251	9.0
Margaret McKeon, St.John's	Sr	27	237	8.8

Tournament Seeds

EAST		MIDEAST
1 Penn St. (29-1)		1 **Tennessee** (25-5)
2 N.C.State (26-5)		2 Purdue (26-2)
3 **Connecticut** (26-4)		3 Auburn (24-5)
4 Clemson (20-10)		4 Western Ky.(28-2)
5 Providence (25-5)		5 Florida St.(24-6)
6 Rutgers (23-6)		6 Maryland (17-12)
7 Richmond (26-4)		7 S.Carolina (22-8)
8 J.Madison (24-4)		8 SW Mo.St.(25-4)
9 Kentucky (24-4)		9 Tenn.Tech (22-7)
10 G.Washington (22-6)		10 Vanderbilt (17-11)
11 Toledo (23-6)		11 Holy Cross (24-5)
12 Fairfield (25-5)		12 Appalach.St.(19-13)

MIDWEST		WEST
1 **Virginia** (27-2)		1 Georgia (26-3)
2 LSU (24-6)		2 **Stanford** (23-5)
3 Arkansas (27-3)		3 Washington (23-4)
4 Michigan St.(21-7)		4 L.Beach St.(23-7)
5 Oklahoma St.(25-5)		5 USC (17-11)
6 Northwestern (20-8)		6 Iowa (20-8)
7 Texas (21-8)		7 CS-Fullerton (24-7)
8 S.F.Austin (25-4)		8 UNLV (24-6)
9 Mississippi (20-8)		9 Texas State (23-7)
10 Lamar (26-3)		10 La.Tech (18-11)
11 Wash.St.(18-10)		11 Montana (26-3)
12 DePaul (19-11)		12 Utah (20-9)

1991 NCAA BASKETBALL WOMEN'S DIVISION I

FINAL FOUR
at Lakefront Arena
* * * *
Semifinals: March 30
Final: March 31

EAST

1st ROUND — March 13
- 8 J. Madison 70
- 9 Kentucky 62
- 5 Providence 88
- 12 Fairfield 87
- 6 Rutgers 65
- 11 Toledo 83
- 7 Richmond 62
- 10 Geo. Wash. 73
- 8 S.F. Austin 73
- 9 Mississippi 62
- 5 Oklahoma St. 81
- 12 DePaul 80
- 6 Northwestern 82
- 11 Washington St. 62
- 7 Texas 63
- 10 Lamar 77

2nd ROUND — March 16-17
- J. Madison 73 / 1 Penn State 71
- Providence 91 / 4 Clemson 103
- Toledo 80 / 3 Connecticut 81
- Geo. Wash. 83 / 2 N.C. State 94
- S.F. Austin 72 / 1 Virginia 74
- Okla. St. 96 (3OT) / 4 Mich. St. 94
- Northwestern 68 / 3 Arkansas 105
- Lamar 93 / 2 LSU 73

REGIONALS — March 21 & 23 (PHILADELPHIA / AUSTIN, TX)
- J. Madison 55 / Clemson 57
- Connecticut 82 / N.C. State 71
- Virginia 76 / Oklahoma St. 61
- Arkansas 75 / Lamar 91

- Clemson 57
- Connecticut 60
- Virginia 85
- Lamar 70

- Connecticut 55
- Virginia 61 (MIDWEST)

WEST / MIDEAST

1st ROUND — March 13
- 8 UNLV 70
- 9 Texas Tech 65
- 5 USC 63
- 12 Utah 52
- 6 Iowa 64
- 11 Montana 53
- 7 CS-Fullerton 84
- 10 La. Tech 80
- 8 SW Mo. St. 94
- 9 Tenn. Tech 64
- 5 Florida St. 96
- 12 Appalach. St. 57
- 6 Maryland 74
- 11 Holy Cross 81
- 7 S. Carolina 64
- 10 Vanderbilt 73

2nd ROUND — March 16-17
- UNLV 62 / 1 Georgia 86
- USC 58 / 4 L. Beach St. 83
- Iowa 53 / 3 Washington 70
- CS-Fullerton 67 / 2 Stanford 91
- SW Mo. St. 47 / 1 Tennessee 55
- Florida St. 69 / 4 Western Ky. 72
- Holy Cross 58 / 3 Auburn 84
- Vanderbilt 69 / 2 Purdue 63

REGIONALS — March 21 & 23 (LAS VEGAS / KNOXVILLE, TN)
- Georgia 87 / L. Beach St. 77
- Washington 47 / Stanford 73
- Tennessee 68 / Western Ky. 61
- Auburn 58 / Vanderbilt 45

- Georgia 67 (WEST)
- Stanford 75
- Tennessee 69 (MIDEAST)
- Auburn 65

- Stanford 60
- Tennessee 68

NATIONAL CHAMPIONSHIP

- Tennessee 70
- Virginia 67 (OT)

NCAA Women's Division I (Cont.)

Championship Game

Virginia 67

	Min	FG M-A	FT M-A	Pts	Rb	A	F
Dena Evans	10	0-0	0-0	0	0	0	1
Tekshia Ward	7	0-0	1-2	1	1	0	0
Melanee Wagener	27	1-1	0-1	2	6	0	3
Tonya Cardoza	43	4-11	2-2	11	1	1	5
Dawn Staley	41	11-26	3-4	28	11	6	5
Heather Burge	31	5-11	0-3	10	11	0	4
Tammi Reiss	40	3-12	1-4	7	1	4	2
Heidi Burge	15	4-5	0-1	8	6	0	5
Audra Smith	11	0-0	0-2	0	5	0	2
TOTALS	225	28-66	7-19	67	42	11	27

Three-point FG: 4-8 (Staley 3-5, Cardoza 1-2, Reiss 0-1); **Team Rebounds:** 3 (not included above); **Blocked Shots:** 3 (Hea. Burge, Hei.Burge, Wagener); **Turnovers:** 20 (Staley 8, Hea. Burge 3, Hei.Burge 3, Reiss 3, Cardoza, Evans, Smith); **Steals:** 9 (Staley 3, Hei.Burge 2, Cardoza 2, Hea.Burge, Smith). **Percentages:** 2-Pt FG (.414); 3-Pt FG (.500); Total FG (.424); Free Throws (.368).

Tennessee 70

	Min	FG M-A	FT M-A	Pts	Rb	A	F
Jody Adams	37	0-7	2-4	2	2	1	3
Regina Clark	3	0-1	0-0	0	0	0	0
Dena Head	41	9-17	10-14	28	9	3	3
Peggy Evans	20	3-5	1-3	7	2	0	5
Lisa Harrison	36	3-10	2-3	8	13	0	3
Daedra Charles	40	7-13	5-7	19	12	0	5
Nikki Caldwell	19	1-1	0-1	2	3	3	2
Kelli Casteel	29	1-7	2-3	4	5	1	2
TOTALS	225	24-61	22-35	70	46	8	23

Three-point FG: 0-3 (Adams 0-3); **Team Rebounds:** 3 (not included above); **Blocked Shots:** 5 (Charles 3, Evans, Harrison); **Turnovers:** 23 (Head 8, Charles 3, Evans 3, Adams 2, Caldwell 2, Casteel 2, Harrison 2, Clark); **Steals:** 7 (Head 3, Charles 2, Caldwell, Harrison). **Percentages:** 2-Pt FG (.414); 3-Pt FG (.000); Total FG (.393); Free Throws (.629).

Virginia (ACC)	26	34	(7)—67	
Tennessee (SEC)	27	33	(10)—70	

Technical Fouls: none. **Officials:** Patty Broderick and Lou Pitt. **Attendance:** 7,865. **TV Rating:** 5.2/16 share (CBS).

THE FINAL FOUR
Lakefront Arena, New Orleans

Semifinals
Virginia 61 .... Connecticut 55
Tennessee 68 .... Stanford 60

Championship
Tennessee 70 .... OT .... Virginia 67

Final records: Tennessee (30-5), Virginia (31-3), Connecticut (29-5), Stanford (26-6).

Most Outstanding Player: Dawn Staley, Virginia guard. Semifinal—34 minutes, 11 points, 8 rebounds, 5 assists. Final—41 minutes, 28 points, 11 rebounds, 6 assists.

All-Tournament Team: Staley and Tonya Cardoza, Virginia; Daedra Charles and Dena Head Tennessee; Sonja Henning, Stanford.

Annual Awards
Players of the Year
Dawn Staley, Virginia .... Naismith,WBCA,USBWA
Daedra Charles, Tennessee .... Wade
Note: The Wade Trophy is awarded for academics and community service as well as player performance.

Coaches of the Year
Rene Portland, Penn St .... USBWA,WBCA
Debbie Ryan, Virginia .... Naismith

Consensus All-America
The NCAA Division I players cited by both the US Basketball Writers Assn. and the Women's Basketball Coaches Assn.

First Team

	Class	Hgt	Pos
Dana Chatman, LSU	Sr.	5-5	G
Delmonica DeHorney, Arkansas	Sr.	6-4	C
Genia Miller, CS-Fullerton	Sr.	6-3	C
Dawn Staley, Virginia	Jr.	5-5	G
Andrea Stinson, NC State	Sr.	5-10	G/F

Other Women's Tournaments

NCAA Division II
The eight regional winners of the 32-team Division II tournament: NEW ENGLAND—Bentley,MA (31-2); EAST—Clarion,PA (24-7); SOUTH ATLANTIC—Norfolk St.,VA (32-0); SOUTH—Jacksonville St.,AL (26-3); SOUTH CENTRAL—SE Missouri St.(29-3); GREAT LAKES—Bellarmine,KY (26-4); NORTH CENTRAL—North Dakota St.(28-2); WEST—Cal Poly-Pomona (22-8).

Quarterfinal games played at campus sites. The Final Four played March 22-23, in Cape Girardeau, MO.
Quarterfinals—Bentley 97, Jacksonville St. 92; Norfolk St. 91, Clarion 69; North Dakota St. 87, Bellarmine 64; SE Missouri St. 82, Cal Poly-Pomona 52.
Semifinals—North Dakota St. 83, Bentley 76; SE Missouri St. 85, Norfolk St. 52. **Third Place**—Bentley 60, Norfolk St. 58. **Championship**—North Dakota St. 81, SE Missouri St. 74.

NCAA Division III
The four regional winners of the 32-team Division II tournament: ATLANTIC—Muskingum,OH (27-4); NORTHEAST—Eastern Conn.St.(21-5); SOUTH—Washington,MO (24-5); WEST—St.Thomas,MN (27-2).

The Final Four played March 15-16, in St.Paul, MN.
Semifinals—Muskingum 85, Washington-MO 60; St.Thomas-MN 91, Eastern Conn.St. 55. **Third Place**—Eastern Conn.St. 83, Washington-MO 74. **Championship**—Muskingum 73, St.Thomas-MN 55.

NAIA Tournament
The quarterfinalists, in alphabetical order, after two rounds of the 32-team NAIA tournament: Belmont,TN (32-4); Claflin,SC (30-1); Fort Hays St.,KS (31-2); IU-PU-Indianapolis (19-11); St.Edward's,TX (31-1); SW Oklahoma (28-3); Wayland Baptist,TX (28-6); Wingate, NC (28-2).

All tournament games played, March 6-12, at Oman Arena, Jackson, TN. There was no Third Place game.
Quarterfinals—Claflin 67, St.Edward's 66. Fort Hays St. 78, Wayland Baptist 65. IU-PU-Indianapolis 99, Wingate 96. SW Oklahoma 70, Belmont 65 (OT).
Semifinals—Fort Hays St. 75, Claflin 63. SW Oklahoma 69, IU-PU-Indianapolis 49. **Championship**—Fort Hayes St. 57, SW Oklahoma 53.

COLLEGE BASKETBALL

S T A T I S T I C S

THROUGH THE YEARS

1901-1991

NCAA'S • ALL-TIME LEADERS

THE 1992

SEC B

PAGE 245

National Champions

The Helms Foundation of Los Angeles, under the direction of founder Bill Schroeder, selected national college basketball champions from 1942-82 and researched retroactive picks from 1901-41. The first NIT tournament and then the NCAA tournament have settled the national championship since 1938, but there are four years (1939,'40,'44 and '54) where the Helms selections differ.

Multiple champions (1901-37): Chicago, Columbia and Wisconsin (3); Kansas, Minnesota, Notre Dame, Penn, Pittsburgh, Syracuse and Yale (2).

Multiple champions (since 1938): UCLA (10); Kentucky (6); Indiana (5); Cincinnati, Kansas, Louisville, North Carolina, N.C.State, Oklahoma A&M and San Francisco (2).

Year	Champion	Record	Head Coach	Outstanding Player
1901	Yale	10-4	No coach	G.M.Clark, F
1902	Minnesota	11-0	Louis Cooke	W.C.Deering, F
1903	Yale	15-1	W.H.Murphy	R.B.Hyatt, F
1904	Columbia	17-1	No coach	Harry Fisher, F
1905	Columbia	19-1	No coach	Harry Fisher, F
1906	Dartmouth	16-2	No coach	George Grebenstein, F
1907	Chicago	22-2	Joseph Raycroft	John Schommer, C
1908	Chicago	21-2	Joseph Raycroft	John Schommer, C
1909	Chicago	12-0	Joseph Raycroft	John Schommer, C
1910	Columbia	11-1	Harry Fisher	Ted Kiendl, F
1911	St.John's-NY	14-0	Claude Allen	John Keenan, F/C
1912	Wisconsin	15-0	Doc Meanwell	Otto Stangel, F
1913	Navy	9-0	Louis Wenzell	Laurence Wild, F
1914	Wisconsin	15-0	Doc Meanwell	Gene Van Gent, C
1915	Illinois	16-0	Ralph Jones	Ray Woods, G
1916	Wisconsin	20-1	Doc Meanwell	George Levis, F
1917	Washington St	25-1	Doc Bohler	Roy Bohler, G
1918	Syracuse	16-1	Edmund Dollard	Joe Schwarzer, G
1919	Minnesota	13-0	Louis Cooke	Arnold Oss, F
1920	Pennsylvania	22-1	Lon Jourdet	George Sweeney, F
1921	Pennsylvania	21-2	Edward McNichol	Danny McNichol, G
1922	Kansas	16-2	Phog Allen	Paul Endacott, G
1923	Kansas	17-1	Phog Allen	Paul Endacott, G
1924	North Carolina	25-0	Bo Shepard	Jack Cobb, F
1925	Princeton	21-2	Al Wittmer	Art Loeb, G
1926	Syracuse	19-1	Lew Andreas	Vic Hanson, F
1927	Notre Dame	19-1	George Keogan	John Nyikos, C
1928	Pittsburgh	21-0	Doc Carlson	Chuck Hyatt, F
1929	Montana St.	36-2	Schubert Dyche	John (Cat) Thompson, F
1930	Pittsburgh	23-2	Doc Carlson	Chuck Hyatt, F
1931	Northwestern	16-1	Dutch Lonborg	Joe Reiff, C
1932	Purdue	17-1	Piggy Lambert	John Wooden, G
1933	Kentucky	20-3	Adolph Rupp	Forest Sale, F
1934	Wyoming	26-3	Willard Witte	Les Witte, G
1935	NYU	19-1	Howard Cann	Sid Gross, F
1936	Notre Dame	22-2-1	George Keogan	John Moir, F
1937	Stanford	25-2	John Bunn	Hank Luisetti, F

Year	Champion	Record	Winner	Head Coach	Outstanding Player
1938	Temple	23-2	NIT	James Usilton	Meyer Bloom, G
1939	Oregon	29-5	NCAA	Howard Hobson	Slim Wintermute, C
	LIU (Helms)	24-0	NIT	Clair Bee	Irv Torgoff, F
1940	Indiana	20-3	NCAA	Branch McCracken	Marv Huffman, G
	USC (Helms)	20-3	*	Sam Barry	Ralph Vaughn, F

National Champions (Cont.)

Year	Champion	Record	Winner	Head Coach	Outstanding Player
1941	Wisconsin	20-3	NCAA	Bud Foster	Gene Englund, F
1942	Stanford	27-4	NCAA	Everett Dean	Jim Pollard, F
1943	Wyoming	31-2	NCAA	Everett Shelton	Kenny Sailors, G
1944	Utah	21-4	NCAA	Vadal Peterson	Arnie Ferrin, F
	Army (Helms)	15-0	**	Ed Kelleher	Dale Hall, F
1945	Oklahoma A&M	27-4	NCAA	Hank Iba	Bob Kurland, C
1946	Oklahoma A&M	31-2	NCAA	Hank Iba	Bob Kurland, C
1947	Holy Cross	27-3	NCAA	Doggie Julian	George Kaftan, F
1948	Kentucky	36-3	NCAA	Adolph Rupp	Ralph Beard, G
1949	Kentucky	32-2	NCAA	Adolph Rupp	Alex Groza, C
1950	CCNY	24-5	NCAA/NIT	Nat Holman	Irwin Dambrot, G
1951	Kentucky	32-2	NCAA	Adolph Rupp	Bill Spivey, C
1952	Kansas	28-3	NCAA	Phog Allen	Clyde Lovellette, C
1953	Indiana	23-3	NCAA	Branch McCracken	Don Schlundt, C
1954	La Salle	26-4	NCAA	Ken Loeffler	Tom Gola, F
	Kentucky (Helms)	25-0	***	Adolph Rupp	Cliff Hagan, G
1955	San Francisco	28-1	NCAA	Phil Woolpert	Bill Russell, C
1956	San Francisco	29-0	NCAA	Phil Woolpert	Bill Russell, C
1957	North Carolina	32-0	NCAA	Frank McGuire	Lennie Rosenbluth, F
1958	Kentucky	23-6	NCAA	Adolph Rupp	Vern Hatton, G
1959	California	24-4	NCAA	Pete Newell	Darrall Imhoff, C
1960	Ohio St	25-3	NCAA	Fred Taylor	Jerry Lucas, C
1961	Cincinnati	27-3	NCAA	Ed Jucker	Bob Wiesenhahn, F
1962	Cincinnati	29-2	NCAA	Ed Jucker	Paul Hogue, C
1963	Loyola-IL	29-2	NCAA	George Ireland	Jerry Harkness, F
1964	UCLA	30-0	NCAA	John Wooden	Walt Hazzard, G
1965	UCLA	28-2	NCAA	John Wooden	Gail Goodrich, G
1966	Texas Western	28-1	NCAA	Don Haskins	Bobby Joe Hill, G
1967	UCLA	30-0	NCAA	John Wooden	Lew Alcindor, C
1968	UCLA	29-1	NCAA	John Wooden	Lew Alcindor, C
1969	UCLA	29-1	NCAA	John Wooden	Lew Alcindor, C
1970	UCLA	28-2	NCAA	John Wooden	Sidney Wicks, F
1971	UCLA	29-1	NCAA	John Wooden	Sidney Wicks, F
1972	UCLA	30-0	NCAA	John Wooden	Bill Walton, C
1973	UCLA	30-0	NCAA	John Wooden	Bill Walton, C
1974	N.C.State	30-1	NCAA	Norm Sloan	David Thompson, F
1975	UCLA	28-3	NCAA	John Wooden	Dave Meyers, F
1976	Indiana	32-0	NCAA	Bobby Knight	Scott May, F
1977	Marquette	25-7	NCAA	Al McGuire	Butch Lee, G
1978	Kentucky	30-2	NCAA	Joe B.Hall	Jack Givens, F
1979	Michigan St	26-6	NCAA	Jud Heathcote	Magic Johnson, G
1980	Louisville	33-3	NCAA	Denny Crum	Darrell Griffith, G
1981	Indiana	26-9	NCAA	Bob Knight	Isiah Thomas, G
1982	North Carolina	32-2	NCAA	Dean Smith	James Worthy, F
1983	N.C.State	28-8	NCAA	Jim Valvano	Sidney Lowe, G
1984	Georgetown	34-3	NCAA	John Thompson	Patrick Ewing, C
1985	Villanova	25-10	NCAA	Rollie Massimino	Ed Pinckney, C
1986	Louisville	32-7	NCAA	Denny Crum	Pervis Ellison, C
1987	Indiana	30-4	NCAA	Bob Knight	Steve Alford, G
1988	Kansas	27-11	NCAA	Larry Brown	Danny Manning, C
1989	Michigan	30-7	NCAA	Steve Fisher	Glen Rice, F
1990	UNLV	35-5	NCAA	Jerry Tarkanian	Larry Johnson, F
1991	Duke	32-7	NCAA	Mike Krzyzewski	Christian Laettner, F/C

*USC was beaten by Kansas in the West regional of the NCAA tournament.

**Army did not lift its policy against postseason play until accepting a bid to the 1961 NIT.

***Unbeaten Kentucky turned down a bid to the NCAA tournament after the NCAA declared seniors Cliff Hagan, Frank Ramsey and Lou Tsioropoulos ineligible for postseason play.

The Red Cross Benefit Games, 1943-45

For three seasons during World War II, the NCAA and NIT champions met in a benefit game at Madison Square Garden in New York to raise money for the Red Cross. The NCAA champs won all three games.

Year	Winner	Score	Loser
1943	Wyoming (NCAA)	52-47	St.John's (NIT)
1944	Utah (NCAA)	43-36	St.John's (NIT)
1945	Oklahoma A&M (NCAA)	52-44	DePaul (NIT)

NCAA Final Four

The NCAA basketball tournament began in 1939 under the sponsorship of the National Association of Basketball Coaches, but was taken over by the NCAA in 1940.

From 1939-51, the winners of the Eastern and Western Regionals played for the national championship, while regional runners-up shared third place. The concept of a Final Four originated in 1952 when four teams qualified for the first national semifinals. Consolation games to determine overall third place were held between regional finalists from 1946-51 and then national semifinalists from 1952-81. Consolation games were discontinued in 1982.

Multiple winners: UCLA (10); Indiana and Kentucky (5); Cincinnati, Kansas, Louisville, North Carolina, N.C. State, Oklahoma A&M (now Okla.St.) and San Francisco (2).

Year	Champion	Runner-up	Score	Final Two		Third Place
1939	Oregon	Ohio St.	46-33	@ Evanston,IL	Oklahoma	Villanova
1940	Indiana	Kansas	60-42	@ Kansas City	Duquesne	USC
1941	Wisconsin	Washington St.	39-34	@ Kansas City	Arkansas	Pittsburgh
1942	Stanford	Dartmouth	53-38	@ Kansas City	Colorado	Kentucky
1943	Wyoming	Georgetown	46-34	@ New York	DePaul	Texas
1944	Utah	Dartmouth	42-40	@ New York	Iowa St.	Ohio St.
1945	Oklahoma A&M	NYU	49-45	@ New York	Arkansas	Ohio St.

Year	Champion	Runner-up	Score	Final Two	Third Place	Fourth Place
1946	Oklahoma A&M	North Carolina	43-40 (OT)	@ New York	Ohio St.	California
1947	Holy Cross	Oklahoma	58-47	@ New York	Texas	CCNY
1948	Kentucky	Baylor	58-42	@ New York	Holy Cross	Kansas St.
1949	Kentucky	Oklahoma A&M	46-36	@ Seattle	Illinois	Oregon St.
1950	CCNY	Bradley	71-68	@ New York	N.C.State	Baylor
1951	Kentucky	Kansas St.	68-58	@ Minneapolis	Illinois	Oklahoma A&M

Year	Champion	Runner-up	Score	Third Place	Fourth Place	Final Four
1952	Kansas	St.John's	80-63	Illinois	Santa Clara	@ Seattle
1953	Indiana	Kansas	69-68	Washington	LSU	@ Kansas City
1954	La Salle	Bradley	92-76	Penn St.	USC	@ Kansas City
1955	San Francisco	La Salle	77-63	Colorado	Iowa	@ Kansas City
1956	San Francisco	Iowa	83-71	Temple	SMU	@ Evanston,IL
1957	North Carolina	Kansas	54-53 (3OT)	San Francisco	Michigan St.	@ Kansas City
1958	Kentucky	Seattle	84-72	Temple	Kansas St.	@ Louisville
1959	California	West Virginia	71-70	Cincinnati	Louisville	@ Louisville
1960	Ohio St.	California	75-55	Cincinnati	NYU	@ San Francisco
1961	Cincinnati	Ohio St.	70-65 (OT)	St.Joseph's-PA	Utah	@ Kansas City
1962	Cincinnati	Ohio St.	71-59	Wake Forest	UCLA	@ Louisville
1963	Loyola-IL	Cincinnati	60-58 (OT)	Duke	Oregon St.	@ Louisville
1964	UCLA	Duke	98-83	Michigan	Kansas St.	@ Kansas City
1965	UCLA	Michigan	91-80	Princeton	Wichita St.	@ Portland,OR
1966	Texas Western	Kentucky	72-65	Duke	Utah	@ College Park,MD
1967	UCLA	Dayton	79-64	Houston	North Carolina	@ Louisville
1968	UCLA	North Carolina	78-55	Ohio St.	Houston	@ Los Angeles
1969	UCLA	Purdue	92-72	Drake	North Carolina	@ Louisville
1970	UCLA	Jacksonville	80-69	New Mexico St.	St.Bonaventure	@ College Park,MD
1971	UCLA	Villanova	68-62	Western Ky.	Kansas	@ Houston
1972	UCLA	Florida St.	81-76	North Carolina	Louisville	@ Los Angeles
1973	UCLA	Memphis St.	87-66	Indiana	Providence	@ St.Louis
1974	N.C.State	Marquette	76-64	UCLA	Kansas	@ Greensboro,NC
1975	UCLA	Kentucky	92-85	Louisville	Syracuse	@ San Diego
1976	Indiana	Michigan	86-68	UCLA	Rutgers	@ Philadelphia
1977	Marquette	North Carolina	67-59	UNLV	NC-Charlotte	@ Atlanta
1978	Kentucky	Duke	94-88	Arkansas	Notre Dame	@ St.Louis
1979	Michigan St.	Indiana St.	75-64	DePaul	Penn	@ Salt Lake City
1980	Louisville	UCLA	59-54	Purdue	Iowa	@ Indianapolis
1981	Indiana	North Carolina	63-50	Virginia	LSU	@ Philadelphia

Year	Champion	Runner-up	Score	Third Place		Final Four
1982	North Carolina	Georgetown	63-62	Houston	Louisville	@ New Orleans
1983	N.C.State	Houston	54-52	Georgia	Louisville	@ Albuquerque
1984	Georgetown	Houston	84-75	Kentucky	Virginia	@ Seattle
1985	Villanova	Georgetown	66-64	Memphis St.	St.John's	@ Lexington
1986	Louisville	Duke	72-69	Kansas	LSU	@ Dallas
1987	Indiana	Syracuse	74-73	Providence	UNLV	@ New Orleans
1988	Kansas	Oklahoma	83-79	Arizona	Duke	@ Kansas City
1989	Michigan	Seton Hall	80-79 (OT)	Duke	Illinois	@ Seattle
1990	UNLV	Duke	103-73	Arkansas	Georgia Tech	@ Denver
1991	Duke	Kansas	72-65	Arkansas	North Carolina	@ Indianapolis

Note: Five teams have had their standing in the Final Four vacated for using ineligible players: **1961**—St.Joseph's-PA (3rd place); **1971**—Villanova (Runner-up) and Western Kentucky (3rd place); **1980**—UCLA (Runner-up); **1985**—Memphis St.(3rd place).

Most Outstanding Player

A Most Outstanding Player has been selected every year of the NCAA tournament. Winners who did not play for the tournament champion are listed in **bold** type. The 1939 and 1951 winners are unofficial and not recognized by the NCAA.

Multiple winners: Lew Alcindor (3); Alex Groza, Bob Kurland, Jerry Lucas and Bill Walton (2).

Year		Year		Year	
1939	**Jimmy Hull**, Ohio St.	1957	**Wilt Chamberlain**, Kansas	1975	Richard Washington, UCLA
1940	Marv Huffman, Indiana	1958	**Elgin Baylor**, Seattle	1976	Kent Benson, Indiana
1941	John Kotz, Wisconsin	1959	**Jerry West**, West Virginia	1977	Butch Lee, Marquette
1942	Howie Dallmar, Stanford			1978	Jack Givens, Kentucky
1943	Kenny Sailors, Wyoming	1960	Jerry Lucas, Ohio St.	1979	Magic Johnson, Michigan St.
1944	Arnie Ferrin, Utah	1961	**Jerry Lucas**, Ohio St.		
1945	Bob Kurland, Okla.A&M	1962	Paul Hogue, Cincinnati	1980	Darrell Griffith, Louisville
1946	Bob Kurland, Okla.A&M	1963	**Art Heyman**, Duke	1981	Isiah Thomas, Indiana
1947	George Kaftan, Holy Cross	1964	Walt Hazzard, UCLA	1982	James Worthy, N.Carolina
1948	Alex Groza, Kentucky	1965	**Bill Bradley**, Princeton	1983	**Akeem Olajuwon**, Houston
1949	Alex Groza, Kentucky	1966	**Jerry Chambers**, Utah	1984	Patrick Ewing, Georgetown
1950	Irwin Dambrot, CCNY	1967	Lew Alcindor, UCLA	1985	Ed Pinckney, Villanova
1951	Bill Spivey, Kentucky	1968	Lew Alcindor, UCLA	1986	Pervis Ellison, Louisville
1952	Clyde Lovellette, Kansas	1969	Lew Alcindor, UCLA	1987	Keith Smart, Indiana
1953	**B.H.Born**, Kansas			1988	Danny Manning, Kansas
1954	Tom Gola, La Salle	1970	Sidney Wicks, UCLA	1989	Glen Rice, Michigan
1955	Bill Russell, San Francisco	1971	**Howard Porter**, Villanova		
1956	**Hal Lear**, Temple	1972	Bill Walton, UCLA	1990	Anderson Hunt, UNLV
		1973	Bill Walton, UCLA	1991	Christian Laettner, Duke
		1974	David Thompson, N.C.State		

Note: Howard Porter (1971) was declared ineligible by the NCAA after the tournament and his award was vacated.

All-Time NCAA Division I Tournament Leaders
CAREER

Scoring

Points	Years	Gm	Pts
Elvin Hayes, Houston	1966-68	13	358
Danny Manning, Kansas	1985-88	16	328
Oscar Robertson, Cincinnati	1958-60	10	324
Glen Rice, Michigan	1986-89	13	308
Lew Alcindor, UCLA	1967-69	12	304

Average	Years	Pts	Avg
Austin Carr, Notre Dame	1969-71	289	41.3
Bill Bradley, Princeton	1963-65	303	33.7
Oscar Robertson, Cincinnati	1958-60	324	32.4
Jerry West, W.Virginia	1958-60	275	30.6
Bob Pettit, LSU	1953-54	183	30.5

Rebounds

Total	Years	Gm	No
Elvin Hayes, Houston	1966-68	13	222
Lew Alcindor, UCLA	1967-69	12	201
Jerry Lucas, Ohio St	1960-62	12	197
Paul Hogue, Cincinnati	1960-62	12	160
Bill Walton, UCLA	1972-74	12	159

Average	Years	Reb	Avg
Johnny Green, Mich.St.	1957-59	118	19.7
Artis Gilmore, Jacksonville	1970-71	115	19.2
Paul Silas, Creighton	1962-64	111	18.5
Len Chappell, Wake Forest	1961-62	137	17.1
Elvin Hayes, Houston	1966-68	222	17.1

SINGLE TOURNAMENT
Scoring

Points	Year	Gm	Pts
Glen Rice, Michigan	1989	6	184
Bill Bradley, Princeton	1965	5	177
Elvin Hayes, Houston	1968	5	167
Danny Manning, Kansas	1988	6	163
Hal Lear, Temple	1956	5	160
Jerry West, W.Virginia	1959	5	160

Average	Year	Gm	Pts	Avg
Austin Carr, Notre Dame	1970	3	158	52.7
Austin Carr, Notre Dame	1971	3	125	41.7
Jerry Chambers, Utah	1966	4	143	35.8
Bo Kimble, Loyola-CA	1990	4	143	35.8
Bill Bradley, Princeton	1965	5	177	35.4
Clyde Lovellette, Kansas	1952	4	141	35.3
Gail Goodrich, UCLA	1965	4	140	35.0

SINGLE GAME
Scoring

Points	Year	Pts
Austin Carr, N.Dame vs Ohio U	1970	61
Bill Bradley, Princeton vs Wich.St	1965	58
Oscar Robertson, Cinn.vs Arkansas	1958	56
Austin Carr, N.Dame vs Kentucky	1970	52
Austin Carr, N.Dame vs TCU	1971	52
David Robinson, Navy vs Michigan	1987	50
Elvin Hayes, Houston vs Loyola-IL	1968	49
Hal Lear, Temple vs SMU	1956	48
Austin Carr, N.Dame vs Houston	1971	47
Dave Corzine, DePaul vs Louisville	1978	46
Bob Houbregs, Wash.vs Seattle	1956	45
Austin Carr, N.Dame vs Iowa	1970	45
Bo Kimble, Loyola-CA vs N.Mex.St	1990	45

Rebounds

Total	Year	Gm	No	Avg
Elvin Hayes, Houston	1968	5	97	19.4
Artis Gilmore, Jacksonville	1970	5	93	18.6
Elgin Baylor, Seattle	1958	5	91	18.2
Sam Lacey, New Mexico St.	1970	5	90	18.0
Clarence Glover, Western Ky	1971	5	89	17.8

Rebounds

Total	Year	No
Fred Cohen, Temple vs UConn	1956	34
Nate Thurmond, B.Green vs Miss.St	1963	31
Jerry Lucas, Ohio St.vs Kentucky	1961	30
Toby Kimball, UConn vs St.Joe's-PA	1965	29
Elvin Hayes, Houston vs Pacific	1966	28

Final Four All-Decade Teams

To celebrate the 50th anniversary of the NCAA tournament in 1989, five All-Decade teams were selected by a blue ribbon panel of coaches and administrators. An All-Time Final Four team was also chosen.

Selection panel: Vic Bubas, Denny Crum, Wayne Duke, Dave Gavitt, Joe B. Hall, Jud Heathcote, Hank Iba, Pete Newell, Dean Smith, John Thompson and John Wooden.

All-Time Team

	Years
Lew Alcindor, UCLA	1967–69
Larry Bird, Indiana St.	1979
Wilt Chamberlain, Kansas	1957
Magic Johnson, Michigan St.	1979
Michael Jordan, North Carolina	1982

All-1960s

	Years
Lew Alcindor, UCLA	1967–69
Bill Bradley, Princeton	1965
Gail Goodrich, UCLA	1964–65
John Havlicek, Ohio St	1961–62
Elvin Hayes, Houston	1967
Walt Hazzard, UCLA	1964
Jerry Lucas, Ohio St.	1960–61
Jeff Mullins, Duke	1964
Cazzie Russell, Michigan	1965
Charlie Scott, North Carolina	1968–69

All-1940s

	Years
Ralph Beard, Kentucky	1948–49
Howie Dallmar, Stanford	1942
Dwight Eddleman, Illinois	1949
Arnie Ferrin, Utah	1944
Alex Groza, Kentucky	1948–49
George Kaftan, Holy Cross	1947
Blb Kurland, Oklahoma A&M	1945–46
Jim Pollard, Stanford	1942
Kenny Sailors, Wyoming	1943
Gerry Tucker, Oklahoma	1947

All-1970s

	Years
Kent Benson, Indiana	1976
Larry Bird, Indiana St	1979
Jack Givens, Kentucky	1978
Magic Johnson, Michigan St	1979
Marques Johnson, UCLA	1975–76
Scott May, Indiana	1976
David Thompson, N.C. State	1974
Bill Walton, UCLA	1972–74
Sidney Wicks, UCLA	1969–71
Keith Wilkes, UCLA	1972–74

All-1950s

	Years
Elgin Baylor, Seattle	1958
Wilt Chamberlain, Kansas	1957
Tom Gola, La Salle	1954
K.C. Jones, San Francisco	1955
Clyde Lovellette, Kansas	1952
Oscar Robertson, Cincinnati	1959–60
Guy Rodgers, Temple	1958
Lennie Rosenbluth, North Carolina	1957
Bill Russell, San Francisco	1955–56
Jerry West, West Virginia	1959

All-1980s

	Years
Steve Alford, Indiana	1987
Johnny Dawkins, Duke	1986
Patrick Ewing, Georgetown	1982–84
Darrell Griffith, Louisville	1980
Michael Jordan, North Carolina	1982
Rodney McCray, Louisville	1980
Akeem Olajuwon, Houston	1983–84
Ed Pinckney, Villanova	1985
Isiah Thomas, Indiana	1981
James Worthy, North Carolina	1982

Note: Lew Alcindor later changed his name to Kareem Abdul-Jabbar; and Keith Wilkes later changed his first name to Jamaal.

NCAA Tournament Appearances

Through 1991; listed are schools with most appearances, overall tournament record, times reaching Final Four, and number of NCAA championships.

App		W-L	F4	Championships	App		W-L	F4	Championships
33	Kentucky	55-30	9	5 (1948-49, 51,58,78)	17	N.C.State	27-16	3	2 (1974-83)
27	UCLA	64-21	14	10 (1964-65, 67-73,75)	17	Ohio St	28-16	8	1 (1960)
25	N.Carolina	54-26	10	2 (1957,82)	17	Marquette	25-18	2	1 (1977)
24	Notre Dame	25-28	1	None	17	Houston	26-22	5	None
21	Louisville	38-23	7	2 (1980,86)	17	Arkansas	21-18	5	None
21	Villanova	35-21	3	1 (1985)	17	Princeton	11-21	1	None
21	St.John's	22-23	2	None	16	Duke	44-15	9	1 (1991)
20	Indiana	41-15	6	5 (1940,53, 76,81,87)	16	Georgetown	29-15	4	1 (1984)
20	Kansas	42-20	9	2 (1952,88)	16	West Va.	11-16	1	None
20	Kansas St	27-24	4	None	16	Oregon St.	12-19	2	None
19	Syracuse	26-20	2	None					
19	DePaul	20-22	2	None					

Collegiate Commissioners Association Tournament

The Collegiate Commissioners Association staged an eight team-tournament for teams that didn't make the NCAA tournament in 1974 and '75. The tourney was played at St. Louis Arena the first year and Freedom Hall in Louisville the second.

Most Valuable Players: 1974—Kent Benson, Indiana: 1975—Bob Elliot, Arizona.

Year	Winner	Score	Loser	Site	Year	Winner	Score	Loser	Site
1974	Indiana	85-60	USC	St.Louis	1975	Drake	83-76	Arizona	Louisville

NIT Championship

The National Invitation Tournament began under the sponsorship of the Metropolitan New York Basketball Writers Association in 1938. The NIT is now administered by the Metropolitan Intercollegiate Basketball Association. All championship games have been played at Madison Square Garden; (*) indicates overtime.

Multiple winners: St.John's (5); Bradley (4); BYU, Dayton, Kentucky, LIU, Providence and Temple (2).

Year	Winner	Score	Loser
1938	Temple	60-36	Colorado
1939	Long Island U.	44-32	Loyola-IL
1940	Colorado	51-40	Duquesne
1941	Long Island U.	56-42	Ohio Univ.
1942	West Virginia	47-45	Western Ky.
1943	St.John's	48-27	Toledo
1944	St.John's	47-39	DePaul
1945	DePaul	71-54	Bowling Green
1946	Kentucky	46-45	Rhode Island
1947	Utah	49-45	Kentucky
1948	St.Louis	65-52	NYU
1949	San Francisco	48-47	Loyola-IL
1950	CCNY	69-61	Bradley
1951	BYU	62-43	Dayton
1952	La Salle	75-64	Dayton
1953	Seton Hall	58-46	St.John's
1954	Holy Cross	71-62	Duquesne
1955	Duquesne	70-58	Dayton
1956	Louisville	93-80	Dayton
1957	Bradley	84-83	Memphis St.
1958	Xavier-OH	78-74*	Dayton
1959	St.John's	76-71*	Bradley
1960	Bradley	88-72	Providence
1961	Providence	62-59	St.Louis
1962	Dayton	73-67	St.John's
1963	Providence	81-66	Canisius
1964	Bradley	86-54	New Mexico
1965	St.John's	55-51	Villanova
1966	BYU	97-84	NYU
1967	So.Illinois	71-56	Marquette
1968	Dayton	61-48	Kansas
1969	Temple	89-76	Boston College
1970	Marquette	65-53	St.John's
1971	North Carolina	84-66	Georgia Tech
1972	Maryland	100-69	Niagara
1973	Virginia Tech	92-91*	Notre Dame

Year	Winner	Score	Loser
1974	Purdue	97-81	Utah
1975	Princeton	80-69	Providence
1976	Kentucky	71-67	NC-Charlotte
1977	St.Bonaventure	94-91	Houston
1978	Texas	101-93	N.C.State
1979	Indiana	53-52	Purdue
1980	Virginia	58-55	Minnesota
1981	Tulsa	86-84*	Syracuse
1982	Bradley	67-58	Purdue
1983	Fresno St.	69-60	DePaul
1984	Michigan	83-63	Notre Dame
1985	UCLA	65-62	Indiana
1986	Ohio St.	73-63	Wyoming
1987	Southern Miss.	84-80	La Salle
1988	Connecticut	72-67	Ohio St.
1989	St.John's	73-65	St.Louis
1990	Vanderbilt	74-72	St.Louis
1991	Stanford	78-72	Oklahoma

Teams in both NCAA and NIT

Year		NIT	NCAA
1940	Colorado	**Won Final**	Lost 1st Rd
	Duquesne	Lost Final	Lost 2nd Rd
1944	Utah	Lost 1st Rd	**Won Final**
1949	Kentucky	Lost 2nd Rd	**Won Final**
1950	CCNY	**Won Final**	**Won Final**
	Bradley	Lost Final	Lost Final
1951	BYU	**Won Final**	Lost 2nd Rd
	St.John's	Lost 3rd Rd	Lost 2nd Rd
	N.C.State	Lost 2nd Rd	Lost 2nd Rd
	Arizona	Lost 2nd Rd	Lost 1st Rd
1952	St.John's	Lost Final	Lost 2nd Rd
	Dayton	Lost 1st Rd	Lost Final
	Duquesne	Lost 2nd Rd	Lost 2nd Rd
	St.Louis	Lost 2nd Rd	Lost 2nd Rd

Most Valuable Player

A Most Valuable Player has been selected every year of the NIT tournament. Winners who did not play for the tournament champion are listed in **bold** type.

Multiple winners: None. However, Tom Gola is the only player to be named MVP in both the NIT (1952) and NCAA (1954) tournaments.

Year			
1938	Don Shields, Temple		
1939	**Bill Lloyd**, St.John's		
1940	Bob Doll, Colorado		
1941	**Frank Baumholtz**, Ohio U.		
1942	Rudy Baric, West Virginia		
1943	Harry Boykoff, St.John's		
1944	Bill Kotsores, St.John's		
1945	George Mikan, DePaul		
1946	**Ernie Calverley**, Rhode Is.		
1947	Vern Gardner, Utah		
1948	Ed Macauley, St.Louis		
1949	Don Lofgran, San Francisco		
1950	Ed Warner, CCNY		
1951	Roland Minson, BYU		
1952	Tom Gola and Norm Grekin, La Salle		
1953	Walter Dukes, Seton Hall		
1954	Togo Palazzi, Holy Cross		
1955	**Maurice Stokes**, St.Francis-PA		

Year	
1956	Charlie Tyra, Louisville
1957	**Win Wilfong**, Memphis St.
1958	Hank Stein, Xavier-OH
1959	Tony Jackson, St.John's
1960	**Len Wilkens**, Providence
1961	Vin Ernst, Providence
1962	Bill Chmielewski, Dayton
1963	Ray Flynn, Providence
1964	Lavern Tart, Bradley
1965	Ken McIntyre, St.John's
1966	**Bill Melchionni**, Villanova
1967	Walt Frazier, So.Illinois
1968	Don May, Dayton
1969	**Terry Driscoll**, Boston Col.
1970	Dean Meminger, Marquette
1971	Bill Chamberlain, N.Carolina
1972	Tom McMillen, Maryland
1983	**John Shumate**, Notre Dame
1974	**Mike Sojourner**, Utah

Year	
1975	**Ron Lee**, Oregon
1976	**Cedric Maxwell**, NC-Charlotte
1977	Greg Sanders, St. Bonaventure
1978	Ron Baxter and Jim Krivacs, Texas
1979	Clarence Carter and Ray Tolbert, Indiana
1980	Ralph Sampson, Virginia
1981	Greg Stewart, Tulsa
1982	Mitchell Anderson, Bradley
1983	Ron Anderson, Fresno St.
1984	Tim McCormick, Michigan
1985	Reggie Miller, UCLA
1986	Brad Sellers, Ohio St.
1987	Randolph Keys, So.Miss.
1988	Phil Gamble, Connecticut
1989	Jayson Williams, St.John's
1990	Scott Draud, Vanderbilt
1991	Adam Keefe, Stanford

Associated Press Final Polls

The Associated Press introduced its weekly college basketball poll of sportswriters (later, sportswriters and broadcasters) during the 1948-49 season.

Since the NCAA Division I tournament has determined the national champion since 1939, the final AP poll ranks the nation's best teams through the regular season and conference tournaments.

The final AP poll has always been released prior to the NCAA and NIT tournaments and has gone from a Top 10 (1949 and 1963-67) to a Top 20 (1950-62 and 1968-89) to a Top 25 (since 1990). Tournament champions are in **bold** type.

1949

		Before Tourns	Head Coach	Final Record
1	**Kentucky**	29-1	Adolph Rupp	32-2
2	Oklahoma A&M	21-4	Hank Iba	23-5
3	St.Louis	22-3	Eddie Hickey	22-4
4	Illinois	19-3	Harry Combes	21-4
5	Western Ky.	25-3	Ed Diddle	25-4
6	Minnesota	18-3	Ozzie Cowles	same
7	Bradley	25-6	Forddy Anderson	27-8
8	**San Francisco**	21-5	Pete Newell	25-5
9	Tulane	24-4	Cliff Wells	same
10	Bowling Green	21-6	Harold Anderson	24-7

NCAA Final Four (at Edmundson Pavilion, Seattle): **Third Place**—Illinois 57, Oregon St.53. **Championship**—Kentucky 46, Oklahoma A&M 36.
NIT Final Four (at Madison Sq.Garden): **Semifinals**—San Francisco 49, Bowling Green 39; Loyola-IL 55, Bradley 50. **Third Place**—Bowling Green 82, Bradley 77. **Championship**—San Francisco 48, Loyola-IL 47.

1950

		Before Tourns	Head Coach	Final Record
1	Bradley	28-3	Forddy Anderson	32-5
2	Ohio St.	21-3	Tippy Dye	22-4
3	Kentucky	25-4	Adolph Rupp	25-5
4	Holy Cross	27-2	Buster Sheary	27-4
5	N.C.State	25-5	Everett Case	27-6
6	Duquesne	22-5	Dudey Moore	23-6
7	UCLA	24-5	John Wooden	24-7
8	Western Ky.	24-5	Ed Diddle	25-6
9	St.John's	23-4	Frank McGuire	24-5
10	La Salle	20-3	Ken Loeffler	21-4
11	Villanova	25-4	Al Severance	same
12	San Francisco	19-6	Pete Newell	19-7
13	LIU	20-4	Clair Bee	20-5
14	Kansas St.	17-7	Jack Gardner	same
15	Arizona	26-4	Fred Enke	26-5
16	Wisconsin	17-5	Bud Foster	same
17	San Jose St.	21-7	Walter McPherson	same
18	Washington St.	19-13	Jack Friel	same
19	Kansas	14-11	Phog Allen	same
20	Indiana	17-5	Branch McCracken	same

Note: Unranked CCNY, coached by Nat Holman, won both the NCAAs and NIT. The Beavers entered the postseason at 17-5 and had a final record of 24-5.

NCAA Final Four (at Madison Square Garden): **Third Place**—N.Carolina St.53, Baylor 41. **Championship**—CCNY 71, Bradley 68.
NIT Final Four (at Madison Sq.Garden): **Semifinals**—Bradley 83, St.John's 72; CCNY 62, Duquesne 52. **Third Place**—St.John's 69, Duquesne 67 (OT). **Championship**—CCNY 69, Bradley 61.

1951

		Before Tourns	Head Coach	Final Record
1	**Kentucky**	28-2	Adolph Rupp	32-2
2	Oklahoma A&M	27-4	Hank Iba	29-6
3	Columbia	22-0	Lou Rossini	22-1
4	Kansas St.	22-3	Jack Gardner	25-4
5	Illinois	19-4	Harry Combes	22-5
6	Bradley	32-6	Forddy Anderson	same
7	Indiana	19-3	Branch McCracken	same
8	N.C.State	29-4	Everett Case	30-7
9	St.John's	22-3	Frank McGuire	26-5
10	St.Louis	21-7	Eddie Hickey	22-8
11	**BYU**	22-8	Stan Watts	26-10
12	Arizona	24-4	Fred Enke	24-6
13	Dayton	24-4	Tom Blackburn	27-5
14	Toldeo	23-8	Jerry Bush	same
15	Washington	22-5	Tippy Dye	24-6
16	Murray St.	21-6	Harlan Hodges	same
17	Cincinnati	18-3	John Wiethe	18-4
18	Siena	19-8	Dan Cunha	same
19	USC	21-6	Forrest Twogood	same
20	Villanova	25-6	Al Severance	25-7

NCAA Final Four (at Williams Arena, Minneapolis): **Third Place**—Illinois 61, Oklahoma St.46. **Championship**—Kentucky 68, Kansas St.58.
NIT Final Four (at Madison Sq.Garden): **Semifinals**—Dayton 69, St.John's 62 (OT); BYU 69, Seton Hall 59. **Third Place**—St.John's 70, Seton Hall 68 (2 OT). **Championship**—BYU 62, Dayton 43.

1952

		Before Tourns	Head Coach	Final Record
1	Kentucky	28-2	Adolph Rupp	29-3
2	Illinois	19-3	Harry Combes	22-4
3	Kansas St.	19-5	Jack Gardner	same
4	Duquesne	21-1	Dudey Moore	23-4
5	St.Louis	22-6	Eddie Hickey	23-8
6	Washington	25-6	Tippy Dye	same
7	Iowa	19-3	Bucky O'Connor	same
8	**Kansas**	24-3	Phog Allen	28-3
9	West Virginia	23-4	Red Brown	same
10	St.John's	22-3	Frank McGuire	25-5
11	Dayton	24-3	Tom Blackburn	28-5
12	Duke	24-6	Harold Bradley	same
13	Holy Cross	23-3	Buster Sheary	24-4
14	Seton Hall	25-2	Honey Russell	25-3
15	St.Bonaventure	19-5	Ed Melvin	21-6
16	Wyoming	27-6	Everett Shelton	28-7
17	Louisville	20-5	Peck Hickman	20-6
18	Seattle	29-7	Al Brightman	29-8
19	UCLA	19-10	John Wooden	19-12
20	SW Texas St.	30-1	Milton Jowers	same

Note: Unranked La Salle, coached by Ken Loefler, won the NIT. The Explorers entered the postseason at 21-7 and had a final record of 25-7.

NCAA Final Four (at U.of Wash.Pavillion, Seattle): **Semifinals**—St.John's 61, Illinois 59; Kansas 74, Santa Clara 59. **Third Place**—Illinois 67, Santa Clara 64. **Championship**—Kansas 80, St.John's 63.
NIT Final Four (at Madison Sq.Garden): **Semifinals**—La Salle 59, Duquesne 46; Dayton 69, St.Bonaventure 62. **Third Place**—St.Bonaventure 48, Duquesne 34. **Championship**—La Salle 75, Dayton 64.

Associated Press Final Polls (Cont.)

Taken before NCAA and NIT tournaments

1953

		Before Tourns	Head Coach	Final Record
1	**Indiana**	19-3	Branch McCracken	23-3
2	**Seton Hall**	28-2	Honey Russell	31-2
3	Kansas	16-5	Phog Allen	19-6
4	Washington	27-2	Tippy Dye	30-3
5	LSU	22-1	Harry Rabenhorst	24-3
6	La Salle	25-2	Ken Loeffler	25-3
7	St.John's	14-5	Al DeStefano	17-6
8	Oklahoma A&M	22-6	Hank Iba	23-7
9	Duquesne	18-7	Dudey Moore	21-8
10	Notre Dame	17-4	John Jordan	19-5
11	Illinois	18-4	Harry Combes	same
12	Kansas St.	17-4	Jack Gardner	same
13	Holy Cross	18-5	Buster Sheary	20-6
14	Seattle	27-3	Al Brightman	29-4
15	Wake Forest	21-6	Murray Greason	22-7
16	Santa Clara	18-6	Bob Feerick	20-7
17	Western Ky.	25-5	Ed Diddle	25-6
18	N.C.State	26-6	Everett Case	same
19	DePaul	18-7	Ray Meyer	19-9
20	SW Missouri St.	19-4	Bob Vanatta	24-4

NCAA Final Four (at Municipal Auditorium, Kansas City): **Semifinals**—Indiana 80, LSU 67; Kansas 79, Washington 53. **Third Place**—Washington 88, LSU 69. **Championship**—Indiana 69, Kansas 68.

NIT Final Four (at Madison Sq.Garden): **Semifinals**—Seton Hall 74, Manhattan 56; St.John's 64, Duquesne 55. **Third Place**—Duquesne 81, Manhattan 67. **Championship**—Seton Hall 58, St.John's 46.

1955

		Before Tourns	Head Coach	Final Record
1	**San Francisco**	23-1	Phil Woolpert	28-1
2	Kentucky	22-2	Adolph Rupp	23-3
3	La Salle	22-4	Ken Loeffler	26-5
4	N.C.State	28-4	Everett Case	same
5	Iowa	17-5	Bucky O'Connor	19-7
6	**Duquesne**	19-4	Dudey Moore	22-4
7	Utah	23-3	Jack Gardner	24-4
8	Marquette	22-2	Jack Nagle	24-3
9	Dayton	23-3	Tom Blackburn	25-4
10	Oregon St.	21-7	Slats Gill	22-8
11	Minnesota	15-7	Ozzie Cowles	same
12	Alabama	19-5	Johnny Dee	same
13	UCLA	21-5	John Wooden	same
14	G. Washington	24-6	Bill Reinhart	same
15	Colorado	16-5	Bebe Lee	19-6
16	Tulsa	20-6	Clarence Iba	21-7
17	Vanderbilt	16-6	Bob Polk	same
18	Illinois	17-5	Harry Combes	same
19	West Virginia	19-10	Fred Schaus	19-11
20	St.Louis	19-7	Eddie Hickey	20-8

NCAA Final Four (at Municipal Auditorium, Kansas City): **Semifinals**—La Salle 76, Iowa 73; San Francisco 62, Colorado 50. **Third Place**—Colorado 75, Iowa 74. **Championship**—San Francisco 77, La Salle 63.

NIT Final Four (at Madison Sq.Garden): **Semifinals**—Dayton 79, St.Francis-PA 73 (OT); Duquesne 65, Cincinnati 51. **Third Place**—Cincinnati 96, St.Francis-PA 91 (OT). **Championship**—Duquesne 70, Dayton 58.

1954

		Before Tourns	Head Coach	Final Record
1	Kentucky	25-0	Adolph Rupp	same
2	**La Salle**	21-4	Ken Loeffler	26-4
3	**Holy Cross**	23-2	Buster Sheary	26-2
4	Indiana	19-3	Branch McCracken	20-4
5	Duquesne	24-2	Dudey Moore	26-3
6	Notre Dame	20-2	John Jordan	22-3
7	Bradley	15-12	Forddy Anderson	19-13
8	Western Ky.	28-1	Ed Diddle	29-3
9	Penn St.	14-5	Elmer Gross	18-6
10	Oklahoma A&M	23-4	Hank Iba	24-5
11	USC	17-12	Forrest Twogood	19-14
12	G. Washington	23-2	Bill Reinhart	23-3
13	Iowa	17-5	Bucky O'Connor	same
14	LSU	21-3	Harry Rabenhorst	21-5
15	Duke	22-6	Harold Bradley	same
16	Niagara	22-5	Taps Gallagher	24-6
17	Seattle	26-1	Al Brightman	26-2
18	Kansas	16-5	Phog Allen	same
19	Illinois	17-5	Harry Combes	17-5
20	Maryland	23-7	Bud Millikan	same

NCAA Final Four (at Municipal Auditorium, Kansas City): **Semifinals**—La Salle 69, Penn St. 54; Bradley 74, USC 72. **Third Place**—Penn St. 70, USC 61. **Championship**—La Salle 92, Bradley 76.

NIT Final Four (at Madison Sq.Garden): **Semifinals**—Duquesne 66, Niagara 51; Holy Cross 75, Western Ky. 69. **Third Place**—Niagara 71, Western Ky. 65. **Championship**—Holy Cross 71, Duquesne 62.

1956

		Before Tourns	Head Coach	Final Record
1	**San Francisco**	25-0	Phil Woolpert	29-0
2	N.C.State	24-3	Everett Case	24-4
3	Dayton	23-3	Tom Blackburn	25-4
4	Iowa	17-5	Bucky O'Connor	20-6
5	Alabama	21-3	Johnny Dee	same
6	**Louisville**	23-3	Peck Hickman	26-3
7	SMU	22-2	Doc Hayes	25-4
8	UCLA	21-5	John Wooden	22-6
9	Kentucky	19-5	Adolph Rupp	20-6
10	Illinois	18-4	Harry Combes	same
11	Oklahoma City	18-6	Abe Lemons	20-7
12	Vanderbilt	19-4	Bob Polk	same
13	North Carolina	18-5	Frank McGuire	same
14	Holy Cross	22-4	Roy Leenig	22-5
15	Temple	23-3	Harry Litwack	27-4
16	Wake Forest	19-9	Murray Greason	same
17	Duke	19-7	Harold Bradley	same
18	Utah	21-5	Jack Gardner	22-6
19	Oklahoma A&M	18-8	Hank Iba	18-9
20	West Virginia	21-8	Fred Schaus	21-9

NCAA Final Four (at McGaw Hall, Evanston,IL): **Semifinals**—Iowa 83, Temple 76; San Francisco 76, SMU 68. **Third Place**—Temple 90, SMU 81. **Championship**—San Francisco 83, Iowa 71.

NIT Final Four (at Madison Sq.Garden): **Semifinals**—Dayton 89, St.Francis-NY 58; Louisville 89, St.Joseph's-PA 79. **Third Place**—St.Joseph's-PA 93, St.Francis-NY 82. **Championship**—Louisville 93, Dayton 80.

1957

	Before Tourns	Head Coach	Final Record
1 North Carolina	27-0	Frank McGuire	32-0
2 Kansas	21-2	Dick Harp	24-3
3 Kentucky	22-4	Adolph Rupp	23-5
4 SMU	21-3	Doc Hayes	22-4
5 Seattle	24-2	John Castellani	24-3
6 Louisville	21-5	Peck Hickman	same
7 West Va.	25-4	Fred Schaus	25-5
8 Vanderbilt	17-5	Bob Polk	same
9 Oklahoma City	17-8	Abe Lemons	19-9
10 St. Louis	19-7	Eddie Hickey	19-9
11 Michigan St.	14-8	Forddy Anderson	16-10
12 Memphis St.	21-5	Bob Vanatta	24-6
13 California	20-4	Pete Newell	21-5
14 UCLA	22-4	John Wooden	same
15 Mississippi St.	17-8	Babe McCarthy	same
16 Idaho St.	24-2	John Grayson	25-4
17 Notre Dame	18-7	John Jordan	20-8
18 Wake Forest	19-9	Murray Greason	same
19 Canisius	20-5	Joe Curran	22-6
20 Oklahoma A&M	17-9	Hank Iba	same

Note: Unranked Bradley, coached by Chuck Orsborn, won the NIT. The Braves entered the tourney at 19-7 and had a final record of 22-7.

NCAA Final Four (at Municipal Auditorium, Kansas City): **Semifinals**—North Carolina 74, Michigan St. 70 (3 OT); Kansas 80, San Francisco 56. **Third Place**—San Francisco 67, Michigan St. 60. **Championship**—North Carolina 54, Kansas 53 (3 OT).

NIT Final Four (at Madison Sq.Garden): **Semifinals**—Memphis St. 80, St.Bonaventure 78; Bradley 78, Temple 66. **Third Place**—Temple 67, St.Bonaventure 50. **Championship**—Bradley 84, Memphis St. 83.

1958

	Before Tourns	Head Coach	Final Record
1 West Virginia	26-1	Fred Schaus	26-2
2 Cincinnati	24-2	George Smith	25-3
3 Kansas St.	20-3	Tex Winter	22-5
4 San Francisco	24-1	Phil Woolpert	25-2
5 Temple	24-2	Harry Litwack	27-3
6 Maryland	20-6	Bud Millikan	22-7
7 Kansas	18-5	Dick Harp	same
8 Notre Dame	22-4	John Jordan	24-5
9 Kentucky	19-6	Adolph Rupp	23-6
10 Duke	18-7	Harold Bradley	same
11 Dayton	23-3	Tom Blackburn	25-4
12 Indiana	12-10	Branch McCracken	13-11
13 North Carolina	19-7	Frank McGuire	same
14 Bradley	20-6	Chuck Orsborn	20-7
15 Mississippi St.	20-5	Babe McCarthy	same
16 Auburn	16-6	Joel Eaves	same
17 Michigan St.	16-6	Forddy Anderson	same
18 Seattle	20-6	John Castellani	24-7
19 Oklahoma St.	19-7	Hank Iba	21-8
20 N.C.State	18-6	Everett Case	same

Note: Unranked Xavier-OH, coached by Jim McCafferty, won the NIT. The Musketeers entered the tourney at 15-11 and had a final record of 19-11.

NCAA Final Four (at Freedom Hall, Louisville): **Semifinals**—Kentucky 61, Temple 60; Seattle 73, Kansas St. 51. **Third Place**—Temple 67, Kansas St. 57. **Championship**—Kentucky 84, Seattle 72.

NIT Final Four (at Madison Sq.Garden): **Semifinals**—Dayton 80, St.John's 56; Xavier-OH 72, St.Bonaventure 53. **Third Place**—St.Bonaventure 84, St.John's 69. **Championship**—Xavier-OH 78, Dayton 74 (OT).

1959

	Before Tourns	Head Coach	Final Record
1 Kansas St.	24-1	Tex Winter	25-2
2 Kentucky	23-2	Adolph Rupp	24-3
3 Mississippi St.	24-1	Babe McCarthy	same*
4 Bradley	23-3	Chuck Orsborn	25-4
5 Cincinnati	23-3	George Smith	26-4
6 N.C.State	22-4	Everett Case	same
7 Michigan St.	18-3	Forddy Anderson	19-4
8 Auburn	20-2	Joel Eaves	same
9 North Carolina	20-4	Frank McGuire	20-5
10 West Virginia	25-4	Fred Schaus	29-5
11 California	20-4	Pete Newell	24-4
12 St. Louis	20-5	John Benington	20-6
13 Seattle	22-4	Vince Cazzetta	same
14 St.Joseph's-PA	22-3	Jack Ramsay	22-5
15 St.Mary's-CA	18-5	Jim Weaver	19-6
16 TCU	18-3	Buster Brannon	same
17 Oklahoma City	20-6	Abe Lemons	20-7
18 Utah	21-5	Jack Gardner	21-7
19 St.Bonaventure	20-2	Eddie Donovan	20-3
20 Marquette	22-4	Eddie Hickey	23-6

Note: Unranked St.John's, coached by Joe Lapchick, won the NIT. The Redmen entered the tourney at 16-6 and had a final record of 20-6.

NCAA Final Four (at Freedom Hall, Louisville): **Semifinals**—West Virginia 94, Louisville 79; California 64, Cincinnati 58. **Third Place**—Cincinnati 98, Louisville 85. **Championship**—California 71, West Virginia 70.

NIT Final Four (at Madison Sq.Garden): **Semifinals**—Bradley 59, NYU 57; St.John's 76, Providence 55. **Third Place**—NYU 71, Providence 57. **Championship**—St.John's 76, Bradley 71 (OT).

1960

	Before Tourns	Head Coach	Final Record
1 Cincinnati	25-1	George Smith	28-2
2 California	24-1	Pete Newell	28-2
3 Ohio St.	21-3	Fred Taylor	25-3
4 Bradley	24-2	Chuck Orsborn	27-2
5 West Virginia	24-4	Fred Schaus	26-5
6 Utah	24-2	Jack Gardner	26-3
7 Indiana	20-4	Branch McCracken	same
8 Utah St.	22-4	Cecil Baker	24-5
9 St.Bonaventure	19-3	Eddie Donovan	21-5
10 Miami-FL	23-3	Bruce Hale	23-4
11 Auburn	19-3	Joel Eaves	same
12 NYU	19-4	Lou Rossini	22-5
13 Georgia Tech	21-5	Whack Hyder	22-6
14 Providence	21-4	Joe Mullaney	24-5
15 St.Louis	19-7	John Benington	19-8
16 Holy Cross	20-5	Roy Leenig	20-6
17 Villanova	19-5	Al Severance	20-6
18 Duke	15-10	Vic Bubas	17-11
19 Wake Forest	21-7	Bones McKinney	same
20 St.John's	17-7	Joe Lapchick	17-8

NCAA Final Four (at the Cow Palace, San Fran.): **Semifinals**—Ohio St.76, NYU 54; California 77, Cincinnati 69. **Third Place**—Cincinnati 95, NYU 71. **Championship**—Ohio St.75, California 55.

NIT Final Four (at Madison Sq.Garden): **Semifinals**—Bradley 82, St.Bonaventure 71; Providence 68, Utah St.62. **Third Place**—Utah St.99, St.Bonaventure 93. **Championship**—Bradley 88, Providence 72.

Associated Press Final Polls (Cont.)

Taken before NCAA and NIT tournaments

1961

		Before Tourns	Head Coach	Final Record
1	Ohio St.	24-0	Fred Taylor	27-1
2	**Cincinnati**	23-3	Ed Jucker	27-3
3	St.Bonaventure	22-3	Eddie Donovan	24-4
4	Kansas St.	22-3	Tex Winter	23-4
5	North Carolina	19-4	Frank McGuire	same
6	Bradley	21-5	Chuck Orsborn	same
7	USC	20-6	Forrest Twogood	21-8
8	Iowa	18-6	S. Scheuerman	same
9	West Virginia	23-4	George King	same
10	Duke	22-6	Vic Bubas	same
11	Utah	21-6	Jack Gardner	23-8
12	Texas Tech	14-9	Polk Robison	15-10
13	Niagara	16-4	Taps Gallagher	16-5
14	Memphis St.	20-2	Bob Vanatta	20-3
15	Wake Forest	17-10	Bones McKinney	19-11
16	St.John's	20-4	Joe Lapchick	20-5
17	St.Joseph's-PA	22-4	Jack Ramsay	25-5
18	Drake	19-7	Maury John	same
19	Holy Cross	19-4	Roy Leenig	22-5
20	Kentucky	18-8	Adolph Rupp	19-9

Note: Unranked Providence, coached by Joe Mullaney, won the NIT. The Friars entered the tourney at 20-5 and had a final record of 24-5.

NCAA Final Four (at Municipal Auditorium, Kansas City): **Semifinals**—Ohio St. 95, St. Joseph's- PA 69; Cincinnati 82, Utah 67. **Third Place**—St. Joseph's-PA 127, Utah 120 (4 OT). **Championship**—Cincinnati 70, Ohio St. 65 (OT).
NIT Final Four (at Madison Sq.Garden) **Semifinals**—St.Louis 67, Dayton 60; Providence 90, Holy Cross 83 (OT). **Third Place**—Holy Cross 85, Dayton 67. **Championship**—Providence 62, St.Louis 59.

1962

		Before Tourns	Head Coach	Final Record
1	Ohio St.	23-1	Fred Taylor	26-2
2	**Cincinnati**	25-2	Ed Jucker	29-2
3	Kentucky	22-2	Adolph Rupp	23-3
4	Mississippi St.	19-6	Babe McCarthy	same
5	Bradley	21-6	Chuck Orsborn	21-7
6	Kansas St.	22-3	Tex Winter	same
7	Utah	23-3	Jack Gardner	same
8	Bowling Green	21-3	Harold Anderson	same
9	Colorado	18-6	Sox Walseth	19-7
10	Duke	20-5	Vic Bubas	same
11	Loyola-IL	21-3	George Ireland	23-4
12	St.John's	19-4	Joe Lapchick	21-5
13	Wake Forest	18-8	Bones McKinney	22-9
14	Oregon St.	22-4	Slats Gill	24-5
15	West Virginia	24-5	George King	24-6
16	Arizona St.	23-3	Ned Wulk	23-4
17	Duquesne	20-5	Red Manning	22-7
18	Utah St.	21-5	Ladell Andersen	22-7
19	UCLA	16-9	John Wooden	18-11
20	Villanova	19-6	Jack Kraft	21-7

Note: Unranked Dayton, coached by Tom Blackburn, won the NIT. The Flyers entered the tourney at 20-6 and had a final record of 24-6.

NCAA Final Four (at Freedom Hall, Louisville): **Semifinals**—Ohio St. 84, Wake Forest 68; Cincinnati 72, UCLA 70. **Third Place**—Wake Forest 82, UCLA 80. **Championship**—Cincinnati 71, Ohio St. 59.
NIT Final Four (at Madison Sq.Garden): **Semifinals**—Dayton 98, Loyola-IL 82; St.John's 76, Duquesne 65. **Third Place**—Loyola-IL 95, Duquesne 84. **Championship**—Dayton 73, St.John's 67.

1963

AP ranked only 10 teams from the 1962-63 season through 1967-68.

		Before Tourns	Head Coach	Final Record
1	Cincinnati	23-1	Ed Jucker	26-2
2	Duke	24-2	Vic Bubas	27-3
3	**Loyola-IL**	24-2	George Ireland	29-2
4	Arizona St.	24-2	Ned Wulk	26-3
5	Wichita	19-7	Ralph Miller	19-8
6	Mississippi St.	21-5	Babe McCarthy	22-6
7	Ohio St.	20-4	Fred Taylor	same
8	Illinois	19-5	Harry Combes	20-6
9	NYU	17-3	Lou Rossini	18-5
10	Colorado	18-6	Sox Walseth	19-7

Note: Unranked Providence, coached by Joe Mullaney, won the NIT. The Friars entered the tourney at 21-4 and had a final record of 24-4.

NCAA Final Four (at Freedom Hall, Louisville): **Semifinals**—Loyola-IL 94, Duke 75; Cincinnati 80, Oregon St. 46. **Third Place**—Duke 85, Oregon St. 63. **Championship**—Loyola-IL 60, Cincinnati 58 (OT).
NIT Final Four (at Madison Sq.Garden): **Semifinals**—Providence 70, Marquette 64; Canisius 61, Villanova 46. **Third Place**—Marquette 66, Villanova 58. **Championship**—Providence 81, Canisius 66.

Undefeated National Champions

The 1964 UCLA team is one of only seven NCAA champions to win the title with an undefeated record.

Year		W-L	Year		W-L
1956	San Francisco	29-0	1972	UCLA	30-0
1957	North Carolina	32-0	1973	UCLA	30-0
1964	UCLA	30 0	1976	Indiana	32-0
1967	UCLA	30-0			

1964

AP ranked only 10 teams from the 1962-63 season through 1967-68.

		Before Tourns	Head Coach	Final Record
1	**UCLA**	26-0	John Wooden	30-0
2	Michigan	20-4	Dave Strack	23-5
3	Duke	23-4	Vic Bubas	26-5
4	Kentucky	21-4	Adolph Rupp	21-6
5	Wichita St.	22-5	Ralph Miller	23-6
6	Oregon St.	25-3	Slats Gill	25-4
7	Villanova	22-3	Jack Kraft	24-4
8	Loyola-IL	20-5	George Ireland	22-6
9	DePaul	21-3	Ray Meyer	21-4
10	Davidson	22-4	Lefty Driesell	same

Note: Unranked Bradley, coached by Chuck Orsborn, won the NIT. The Braves entered the tourney at 20-6 and finished with a record of 23-6.

NCAA Final Four (at Municipal Auditorium, Kansas City): **Semifinals**—Duke 91, Michigan 80; UCLA 90, Kansas St. 84. **Third Place**—Michigan 100, Kansas St. 90. **Championship**—UCLA 98, Duke 83.
NIT Final Four (12 at Madison Sq.Garden): **Semifinals**—New Mexico 72, NYU 65; Bradley 67, Army 52. **Third Place**—Army 60, NYU 59. **Championship**—Bradley 86, New Mexico 54.

1965

AP ranked only 10 teams from the 1962-63 season through 1967-68.

		Before Tourns	Head Coach	Final Record
1	Michigan	21-3	Dave Strack	24-4
2	UCLA	24-2	John Wooden	28-2
3	St.Joseph's-PA	25-1	Jack Ramsay	26-3
4	Providence	22-1	Joe Mullaney	24-2
5	Vanderbilt	23-3	Roy Skinner	24-4
6	Davidson	24-2	Lefty Driesell	same
7	Minnesota	19-5	John Kundla	same
8	Villanova	21-4	Jack Kraft	23-5
9	BYU	21-5	Stan Watts	21-7
10	Duke	20-5	Vic Bubas	same

Note: Unranked St.John's, coached by Joe Lapchick, won the NIT. The Redmen entered the tourney at 17-8 and finished with a record of 21-8).

NCAA Final Four (at Memorial Coliseum, Portland,OR): **Semifinals**—Michigan 93, Princeton 76; UCLA 108, Wichita St. 89. **Third Place**—Princeton 118, Wichita St. 82. **Championship**—UCLA 91, Michigan 80.

NIT Final Four (at Madison Sq.Garden): **Semifinals**—Villanova 91, NYU 69; St.John's 67, Army 60. **Third Place**—Army 75, NYU 74. **Championship**—St.John's 55, Villanova 51.

1966

AP ranked only 10 teams from the 1962-63 season through 1967-68.

		Before Tourns	Head Coach	Final Record
1	Kentucky	24-1	Adolph Rupp	27-2
2	Duke	23-3	Vic Bubas	26-4
3	**Texas Western**	23-1	Don Haskins	28-1
4	Kansas	22-3	Ted Owens	23-4
5	St.Joseph's-PA	22-4	Jack Ramsay	24-5
6	Loyola-IL	22-2	George Ireland	22-3
7	Cincinnati	21-5	Tay Baker	21-7
8	Vanderbilt	22-4	Roy Skinner	same
9	Michigan	17-7	Dave Strack	18-8
10	Western Ky.	23-2	Johnny Oldham	25-3

Note: Unranked BYU, coached by Stan Watts, won the NIT. The Cougars entered the tourney at 17-5 and had a final record of 20-5.

NCAA Final Four (at Cole Fieldhouse, College Park,MD): **Semifinals**—Kentucky 83, Duke 79; Texas Western 85, Utah 78. **Third Place**—Duke 79, Utah 77. **Championship**—Texas Western 72, Kentucky 65.

NIT Final Four (at Madison Sq.Garden): **Semifinals**—BYU 66, Army 60; NYU 69, Villanova 63. **Third Place**—Villanova 76, Army 65. **Championship**—BYU 97, NYU 84.

1967

AP ranked only 10 teams from the 1962-63 season through 1967-68.

		Before Tourns	Head Coach	Final Record
1	UCLA	26-0	John Wooden	30-0
2	Louisville	23-3	Peck Hickman	23-5
3	Kansas	22-3	Ted Owens	23-4
4	North Carolina	24-4	Dean Smith	26-6
5	Princeton	23-2	B.vanBreda Kolff	25-3
6	Western Ky.	23-2	Johnny Oldham	23-3
7	Houston	23-3	Guy Lewis	27-4
8	Tennessee	21-5	Ray Mears	21-7
9	Boston College	19-2	Bob Cousy	21-3
10	Texas Western	20-5	Don Haskins	22-6

Note: Unranked Southern Illinois, coached by Jack Hartman, won the NIT. The Salukis entered the tourney at 20-2 and had a final record of 24-2.

NCAA Final Four (at Freedom Hall, Louisville): **Semifinals**—Dayton 76, N.Carolina 62; UCLA 73, Houston 58. **Third Place**—Houston 84, N.Carolina 62. **Championship**—UCLA 79, Dayton 64.

NIT Final Four (at Madison Sq.Garden): **Semifinals**—Marquette 83, Marshall 78; Southern Ill.79, Rutgers 70. **Third Place**—Rutgers 93, Marshall 76. **Championship**—Southern Ill.71, Marquette 56.

1968

AP ranked only 10 teams from the 1962-63 season through 1967-68.

		Before Tourns	Head Coach	Final Record
1	Houston	28-0	Guy Lewis	31-2
2	UCLA	25-1	John Wooden	29-1
3	St.Bonaventure	22-0	Larry Weise	23-2
4	North Carolina	25-3	Dean Smith	28-4
5	Kentucky	21-4	Adolph Rupp	22-5
6	New Mexico	23-3	Bob King	23-5
7	Columbia	21-4	Jack Rohan	23-5
8	Davidson	22-4	Lefty Driesell	24-5
9	Louisville	20-6	John Dromo	21-7
10	Duke	21-5	Vic Bubas	22-6

Note: Unranked Dayton, coached by Don Donoher, won the NIT. The Flyers entered the tourney at 17-9 and had a final record of 21-9.

NCAA Final Four (at the Sports Arena, Los Angeles): **Semifinals**—N.Carolina 80, Ohio St. 66; UCLA 101, Houston 69. **Third Place**—Ohio St. 89, Houston 85. **Championship**—UCLA 78, N.Carolina 55.

NIT Final Four (at Madison Sq.Garden): **Semifinals**—Dayton 76, Notre Dame 74 (OT); Kansas 58, St.Peter's 46. **Third Place**—Notre Dame 81, St.Peter's 78. **Championship**—Dayton 61, Kansas 48.

Highest-Rated College Games on TV

The dozen highest-rated college basketball games seen on U.S. television have been NCAA tournament championship games, led by the 1979 Michigan State-Indiana State final that featured Magic Johnson and Larry Bird. The upset wins by Villanova in 1985 and N.C. State in 1983 round out the Top 3.

Listed below are the finalists (winning team first), date of game, TV network, and TV rating and audience share (according to Nielson Media Research).

	Date	Net	Rtg/Sh			Date	Net	Rtg/Sh
1 Michigan St.-Indiana St.	3/26/79	NBC	24.1/38		7 Louisville Duke	3/32/86	CBS	20.7/31
2 Georgetown-Villanova	4/1/85	CBS	23.3/33		8 Indiana-N.Carolina	3/30/81	NBC	20.7/29
3 N.C.State-Houston	4/4/83	CBS	22.3/32		9 UCLA-Memphis St.	3/26/73	NBC	20.5/32
4 N.Carolina-Georgetown	3/29/82	CBS	21.6/31		10 Indiana Michigan	3/29/76	NBC	20.4/31
5 UCLA-Kentucky	3/31/75	NBC	21.3/33		11 UNLV-Duke	4/2/90	CBS	20.0/31
6 Michigan-Seton Hall	4/3/89	CBS	21.3/33		12 Kentucky-Duke	3/27/78	NBC	19.9/31

Associated Press Final Polls (Cont.)

Taken before NCAA, NIT and Collegiate Commissioner's Assn. (1974-75) tournaments; (*) indicates on probation.

1969

	Before Tourns	Head Coach	Final Record
1 UCLA	25-1	John Wooden	29-1
2 La Salle	23-1	Tom Gola	same*
3 Santa Clara	26-1	Dick Garibaldi	27-2
4 North Carolina	25-3	Dean Smith	27-5
5 Davidson	24-2	Lefty Driesell	26-3
6 Purdue	20-4	George King	23-5
7 Kentucky	22-4	Adolph Rupp	23-5
8 St.John's	22-4	Lou Carnesecca	23-6
9 Duquesne	19-4	Red Manning	21-5
10 Villanova	21-4	Jack Kraft	21-5
11 Drake	23-4	Maury John	26-5
12 New Mexico St.	23-3	Lou Henson	24-5
13 South Carolina	20-6	Frank McGuire	21-7
14 Marquette	22-4	Al McGuire	24-5
15 Louisville	20-5	John Dromo	21-6
16 Boston College	21-3	Bob Cousy	24-4
17 Notre Dame	20-6	Johnny Dee	20-7
18 Colorado	20-6	Sox Walseth	21-7
19 Kansas	20-6	Ted Owens	20-7
20 Illinois	19-5	Harvey Schmidt	same

Note: NIT champ Temple, coached by Harry Litwak, entered the tourney unranked at 18-8 and had a final record of 22-8.

NCAA Final Four (at Freedom Hall, Louisville): **Semifinals**—Purdue 92, N.Carolina 65; UCLA 85, Drake 82. **Third Place**—Drake 104, N.Carolina 84. **Championship**—UCLA 92, Purdue 72. †

NIT Final Four (at Madison Sq.Garden): **Semifinals**—Temple 63, Tennessee 58; Boston College 73, Army 61. **Third Place**—Tennessee 64, Army 52. **Championship**—Temple 89, Boston College 76.

1971

	Before Tourns	Head Coach	Final Record
1 UCLA	25-1	John Wooden	29-1
2 Marquette	26-0	Al McGuire	28-1
3 Penn	26-0	Dick Harter	28-1
4 Kansas	25-1	Ted Owens	27-3
5 USC	24-2	Bob Boyd	24-2
6 South Carolina	23-4	Frank McGuire	23-6
7 Western Ky.	20-5	John Oldham	24-6
8 Kentucky	22-4	Adolph Rupp	22-6
9 Fordham	25-1	Digger Phelps	26-3
10 Ohio St.	19-5	Fred Taylor	20-6
11 Jacksonville	22-3	Tom Wasdin	22-4
12 Notre Dame	19-7	Johnny Dee	20-9
13 North Carolina	22-6	Dean Smith	26-6
14 Houston	20-6	Guy Lewis	22-7
15 Duquesne	21-3	Red Manning	21-4
16 Long Beach St.	21-4	Jerry Tarkanian	23-5
17 Tennessee	20-6	Ray Mears	21-7
18 Villanova	19-5	Jack Kraft	23-6
19 Drake	20-7	Maury John	21-8
20 BYU	18-9	Stan Watts	18-11

NCAA Final Four (at The Astrodome, Houston): **Semifinals**—Villanova 92, Western Ky.89 (2 OT); UCLA 68, Kansas 60. **Third Place**—Western Ky.77, Kansas 75. **Championship**—UCLA 68, Villanova 62.

NIT Final Four (at Madison Sq.Garden): **Semifinals**—N.Carolina 73, Duke 69; Ga.Tech 76, St.Bonaventure 71 (2 OT). **Third Place**—St.Bonaventure 92, Duke 88 (OT). **Championship**—N.Carolina 84, Ga.Tech 66.

1970

	Before Tourns	Head Coach	Final Record
1 Kentucky	25-1	Adolph Rupp	26-2
2 UCLA	24-2	John Wooden	28-2
3 St.Bonaventure	22-1	Larry Weise	25-3
4 Jacksonville	23-1	Joe Williams	27-2
5 New Mexico.St.	23-2	Lou Henson	27-3
6 South Carolina	25-3	Frank McGuire	25-3
7 Iowa	19-4	Ralph Miller	20-5
8 Marquette	22-3	Al McGuire	26-3
9 Notre Dame	20-6	Johnny Dee	21-8
10 N.C.State	22-6	Norm Sloan	23-7
11 Florida St.	22-3	Hugh Durham	23-3
12 Houston	24-3	Guy Lewis	25-5
13 Penn	25-1	Dick Harter	25-2
14 Drake	21-6	Maury John	22-7
15 Davidson	22-4	Terry Holland	22-5
16 Utah St.	20-6	Ladell Andersen	22-7
17 Niagara	21-5	Frank Layden	22-7
18 Western Ky.	22-2	John Oldham	22-3
19 Long Beach St.	23-3	Jerry Tarkanian	24-5
20 USC	18-8	Bob Boyd	18-8

NCAA Final Four (at Cole Fieldhouse, College Park,MD): **Semifinals**—Jacksonville 91, St.Bonaventure 83; UCLA 93, New Mexico St.77. **Third Place**—N.Mexico St.79, St.Bonaventure 73. **Championship**—UCLA 80, Jacksonville 69.

NIT Final Four (at Madison Sq.Garden): **Semifinals**—St.John's 60, Army 59; Marquette 101, LSU 79. **Third Place**—Army 75, LSU 68. **Championship**—Marquette 65, St.John's 53.

1972

	Before Tourns	Head Coach	Final Record
1 UCLA	26-0	John Wooden	30-0
2 North Carolina	23-4	Dean Smith	26-5
3 Penn	23-2	Chuck Daly	25-3
4 Louisville	23-4	Denny Crum	26-5
5 Long Beach St.	23-3	Jerry Tarkanian	25-4
6 South Carolina	22-4	Frank McGuire	24-5
7 Marquette	24-2	Al McGuire	25-4
8 SW Louisiana	23-3	Beryl Shipley	25-4
9 BYU	21-4	Stan Watts	21-5
10 Florida St.	23-5	Hugh Durham	27-6
11 Minnesota	17-6	Bill Musselman	18-7
12 Marshall	22-3	Carl Tacy	23-4
13 Memphis St.	21-6	Gene Bartow	21-7
14 Maryland	23-5	Lefty Driesell	27-5
15 Villanova	19-6	Jack Kraft	20-8
16 Oral Roberts	25-1	Ken Trickey	26-2
17 Indiana	17-7	Bobby Knight	17-8
18 Kentucky	20-6	Adolph Rupp	21-7
19 Ohio St.	18-6	Fred Taylor	same
20 Virginia	21-6	Bill Gibson	21-7

NCAA Final Four (at the Sports Arena, Los Angeles): **Semifinals**—Florida St.79, N.Carolina 75; UCLA 96, Louisville 77. **Third Place**—N.Carolina 105, Louisville 91. **Championship**—UCLA 81, Florida St.76.

NIT Final Four (at Madison Sq.Garden): **Semifinals**—Maryland 91, Jacksonville 77; Niagara 69, St.John's 67. **Third Place**—Jacksonville 83, St.John's 80. **Championship**—Maryland 100, Niagara 69.

1973

		Before Tourns	Head Coach	Final Record
1	UCLA	26-0	John Wooden	30-0
2	N.C.State	27-0	Norm Sloan	same*
3	Long Beach St.	24-2	Jerry Tarkanian	26-3
4	Providence	24-2	Dave Gavitt	27-4
5	Marquette	23-3	Al McGuire	25-4
6	Indiana	19-5	Bobby Knight	22-6
7	SW Louisiana	23-2	Beryl Shipley	24-5
8	Maryland	22-6	Lefty Driesell	23-7
9	Kansas St.	22-4	Jack Hartman	23-5
10	Minnesota	20-4	Bill Musselman	21-5
11	North Carolina	22-7	Dean Smith	25-8
12	Memphis St.	21-5	Gene Bartow	24-6
13	Houston	23-3	Guy Lewis	23-4
14	Syracuse	22-4	Roy Danforth	24-5
15	Missouri	21-5	Norm Stewart	21-6
16	Arizona St.	18-7	Ned Wulk	19-9
17	Kentucky	19-7	Joe B.Hall	20-8
18	Penn	20-5	Chuck Daly	21-7
19	Austin Peay	21-5	Lake Kelly	22-7
20	San Francisco	22-4	Bob Gaillard	23-5

Note:.NIT champ Va.Tech, coached by Don DeVoe, entered the tourney unranked at 18-5 and had a final record of 22-5.

NCAA Final Four (at The Arena, St.Louis): **Semifinals**—Memphis St.98, Providence 85; UCLA 70, Indiana 59. **Third Place**—Indiana 97, Providence 79. **Championship**—UCLA 87, Memphis St. 66.
NIT Final Four (at Madison Sq.Garden): **Semifinals**—Va.Tech 74, Alabama 73; Notre Dame 78, N.Carolina 71. **Third Place**—N.Carolina 88, Alabama 69. **Championship**—Va.Tech 92, Notre Dame 91 (OT).

1974

		Before Tourns	Head Coach	Final Record
1	N.C.State	26-1	Norm Sloan	30-1
2	UCLA	24-2	John Wooden	27-3
3	Marquette	22-4	Al McGuire	26-5
4	Maryland	23-5	Lefty Driesell	same
5	Notre Dame	24-2	Digger Phelps	26-3
6	Michigan	21-4	Johnny Orr	22-5
7	Kansas	21-5	Ted Owens	23-7
8	Providence	26-3	Dave Gavitt	28-4
9	Indiana	20-5	Bobby Knight	23-5
10	Long Beach St.	24-2	Lute Olson	same
11	Purdue	18-8	Fred Schaus	22-8
12	North Carolina	22-5	Dean Smith	22-6
13	Vanderbilt	23-3	Roy Skinner	23-5
14	Alabama	22-4	C.M.Newton	same
15	Utah	19-7	Bill Foster	22-8
16	Pittsburgh	23-3	Buzz Ridl	25-4
17	USC	22-4	Bob Boyd	24-5
18	Oral Roberts	21-5	Ken Trickey	23-6
19	South Carolina	22-4	Frank McGuire	22-5
20	Dayton	19-7	Don Donoher	20-9

NCAA Final Four (at Greensboro,NC Coliseum): **Semifinals**—N.C.State 80, UCLA 77 (2 OT); Marquette 64, Kansas 51. **Third Place**—UCLA 78, Kansas 61. **Championship**—N.C.State 76, Marquette 64.
NIT Final Four (at Madison Sq.Garden): **Semifinals**—Purdue 78, Jacksonville 63; Utah 117, Boston Col.93. **Third Place**—Boston Col.87, Jacksonville 77. **Championship**—Purdue 87, Utah 81.
CCA Final Four (at The Arena, St.Louis): **Semifinals**—Indiana 73, Toledo 72; USC 74, Bradley 73. **Championship**—Indiana 85, USC 60.

1975

		Before Tourns	Head Coach	Final Record
1	UCLA	23-3	John Wooden	28-3
2	Kentucky	22-4	Joe B.Hall	26-5
3	Indiana	29-0	Bobby Knight	31-1
4	Louisville	24-2	Denny Crum	28-3
5	Maryland	22-4	Lefty Driesell	24-5
6	Syracuse	20-7	Roy Danforth	23-9
7	N.C.State	22-6	Norm Sloan	22-6
8	Arizona St.	23-3	Ned Wulk	25-4
9	North Carolina	21-7	Dean Smith	23-8
10	Alabama	22-4	C.M.Newton	22-5
11	Marquette	23-3	Al McGuire	23-4
12	**Princeton**	18-8	Pete Carril	22-8
13	Cincinnati	21-5	Gale Catlett	23-6
14	Notre Dame	18-8	Digger Phelps	19-10
15	Kansas St.	18-8	Jack Hartman	20-9
16	**Drake**	16-10	Bob Ortegel	19-10
17	UNLV	22-4	Jerry Tarkanian	24-5
18	Oregon St.	18-10	Ralph Miller	19-12
19	Michigan	19-7	Johnny Orr	19-8
20	Penn	23-4	Chuck Daly	23-5

NCAA Final Four (at San Diego Sports Arena): **Semifinals**—Kentucky 95, Syracuse 79; UCLA 75, Louisville 74 (OT). **Third Place**—Louisville 96, Syracuse 88 (OT). **Championship**—UCLA 92, Kentucky 85.
NIT Championship (at Madison Sq.Garden): Princeton 80, Providence 69. No.12 Princeton was only Top 20 team in NIT.
CCA Final Four (at Freedom Hall, Louisville): **Semifinals**—Arizona 102, Purdue 96; Drake 78, Bowling Green 65. **Championship**—Drake 83, Arizona 76. No. 16 Drake was only Top 20 team in CCA.

1976

		Before Tourns	Head Coach	Final Record
1	**Indiana**	27-0	Bobby Knight	32-0
2	Marquette	25-1	Al McGuire	27-2
3	UNLV	28-1	Jerry Tarkanian	29-2
4	Rutgers	28-0	Tom Young	31-2
5	UCLA	24-3	Gene Bartow	28-4
6	Alabama	22-4	C.M.Newton	23-5
7	Notre Dame	22-5	Digger Phelps	23-6
8	North Carolina	25-3	Dean Smith	25-4
9	Michigan	21-6	Johnny Orr	25-7
10	Western Mich.	24-2	Eldon Miller	25-3
11	Maryland	22-6	Lefty Driesell	same
12	Cincinnati	25-5	Gale Catlett	25-6
13	Tennessee	21-5	Ray Mears	21-6
14	Missouri	24-4	Norm Stewart	26-5
15	Arizona	22-8	Fred Snowden	24-9
16	Texas Tech	24-5	Gerald Myers	25-6
17	DePaul	19-8	Ray Meyer	20-9
18	Virginia	18-11	Terry Holland	18-12
19	Centenary	22-5	Larry Little	same
20	Pepperdine	21-5	Gary Colson	22-6

NCAA Final Four (at The Spectrum, Phila.); **Semifinals**—Michigan 86, Rutgers 70; Indiana 65, UCLA 51. **Third Place**—UCLA 106, Rutgers 92. **Championship**—Indiana 86, Michigan 68.
NIT Championship (at Madison Sq.Garden): Kentucky 71, NC-Charlotte 67. No Top 20 teams played in NIT.

Associated Press Final Polls (Cont.)

Taken before NCAA and NIT Tournaments; (*) indicates on probation.

1977

		Before Tourns	Head Coach	Final Record
1	Michigan	24-3	Johnny Orr	26-4
2	UCLA	24-3	Gene Bartow	25-4
3	Kentucky	24-3	Joe B.Hall	26-4
4	UNLV	25-2	Jerry Tarkanian	29-3
5	North Carolina	24-4	Dean Smith	28-5
6	Syracuse	25-3	Jim Boeheim	26-4
7	**Marquette**	20-7	Al McGuire	25-7
8	San Francisco	29-1	Bob Gaillard	29-2
9	Wake Forest	20-7	Carl Tacy	22-8
10	Notre Dame	21-6	Digger Phelps	22-7
11	Alabama	23-4	C.M.Newton	25-6
12	Detroit	24-3	Dick Vitale	25-4
13	Minnesota	24-3	Jim Dutcher	same*
14	Utah	22-6	Jerry Pimm	23-7
15	Tennessee	22-5	Ray Mears	22-6
16	Kansas St.	23-6	Jack Hartman	24-7
17	NC-Charlotte	25-3	Lee Rose	28-5
18	Arkansas	26-1	Eddie Sutton	26-2
19	Louisville	21-6	Denny Crum	21-7
20	VMI	25-3	Charlie Schmaus	26-4

NCAA Final Four (at The Omni, Atlanta): **Semifinals**—Marquette 51, NC-Charlotte, 49; N.Carolina 84, UNLV 83. **Third Place**—UNLV 106, NC-Charlotte 94. **Championship**—Marquette 67, N.Carolina 59.

NIT Championship (at Madison Square Garden): St.Bonaventure 94, Houston 91. No.11 Alabama was only Top 20 team in NIT.

1978

		Before Tourns	Head Coach	Final Record
1	**Kentucky**	25-2	Joe B.Hall	30-2
2	UCLA	24-2	Gary Cunningham	25-3
3	DePaul	25-2	Ray Meyer	27-3
4	Michigan St.	23-4	Jud Heathcote	25-5
5	Arkansas	28-3	Eddie Sutton	32-3
6	Notre Dame	20-6	Digger Phelps	23-8
7	Duke	23-6	Bill Foster	27-7
8	Marquette	24-3	Hank Raymonds	24-4
9	Louisville	22-6	Denny Crum	23-7
10	Kansas	24-4	Ted Owens	24-5
11	San Francisco	22-5	Bob Gaillard	23-6
12	New Mexico	24-3	Norm Ellenberger	24-4
13	Indiana	20-7	Bobby Knight	21-8
14	Utah	22-5	Jerry Pimm	23-6
15	Florida St.	23-5	Hugh Durham	23-6
16	North Carolina	23-7	Dean Smith	23-8
17	**Texas**	22-5	Abe Lemons	26-5
18	Detroit	24-3	Dave Gaines	25-4
19	Miami-OH	18-8	Darrell Hedric	19-9
20	Penn	19-7	Bob Weinhauer	20-8

NCAA Final Four (at The Checkerdome, St.Louis): **Semifinals**—Kentucky 64, Arkansas 59; Duke 90, Notre Dame 86. **Third Place**—Arkansas 71, Notre Dame 69. **Championship**—Kentucky 94, Duke 88.

NIT Championship (at Madison Square Garden): Texas 101, N.C.State 93. No.17 Texas and No.18 Detroit were only Top 20 teams in NIT.

1979

		Before Tourns	Head Coach	Final Record
1	Indiana St.	29-0	Bill Hodges	33-1
2	UCLA	23-4	Gary Cunningham	25-5
3	**Michigan St.**	21-6	Jud Heathcote	26-6
4	Notre Dame	22-5	Digger Phelps	24-6
5	Arkansas	23-4	Eddie Sutton	25-5
6	DePaul	22-5	Ray Meyer	26-6
7	LSU	22-5	Dale Brown	23-6
8	Syracuse	25-3	Jim Boeheim	26-4
9	North Carolina	23-5	Dean Smith	23-6
10	Marquette	21-6	Hank Raymonds	22-7
11	Duke	22-7	Bill Foster	22-8
12	San Francisco	21-6	Dan Belluomini	22-7
13	Louisville	23-7	Denny Crum	24-8
14	Penn	21-5	Bob Weinhauer	25-7
15	Purdue	23-7	Lee Rose	27-8
16	Oklahoma	20-9	Dave Bliss	21-10
17	St.John's	18-10	Lou Carnesecca	21-11
18	Rutgers	21-8	Tom Young	22-9
19	Toledo	21-6	Bob Nichols	22-7
20	Iowa	20-7	Lute Olson	20-8

NCAA Final Four (at Special Events Center, Salt Lake City): **Semifinals**—Michigan St. 101, Penn 67; Indiana St.76, DePaul 74. **Third Place**—DePaul 96, Penn 93. **Championship**—Michigan St.75, Indiana St.64.

NIT Championship (at Madison Square Garden): Indiana 53, Purdue 52. No.15 Purdue was only Top 20 team in NIT.

1980

		Before Tourns	Head Coach	Final Record
1	DePaul	26-1	Ray Meyer	26-2
2	**Louisville**	28-3	Denny Crum	33-3
3	LSU	24-5	Dale Brown	26-6
4	Kentucky	28-5	Joe B.Hall	29-6
5	Oregon St.	26-3	Ralph Miller	26-4
6	Syracuse	25-3	Jim Boeheim	26-4
7	Indiana	20-7	Bob Knight	21-8
8	Maryland	23-6	Lefty Driesell	24-7
9	Notre Dame	20-7	Digger Phelps	20-8
10	Ohio St.	24-5	Eldon Miller	21-8
11	Georgetown	24-5	John Thompson	26-6
12	BYU	24-4	Frank Arnold	24-5
13	St.John's	24-4	Lou Carnesecca	24-5
14	Duke	22-8	Bill Foster	24-9
15	North Carolina	21-7	Dean Smith	21-8
16	Missouri	23-5	Norm Stewart	25-6
17	Weber St.	26-2	Neil McCarthy	26-3
18	Arizona St.	21-6	Ned Wulk	22-7
19	Iona	28-4	Jim Valvano	29-5
20	Purdue	19-9	Lee Rose	23-10

NCAA Final Four (at Market Sq.Arena, Indianapolis): **Semifinals**—Louisville 80, Iowa 72; UCLA 67, Purdue 62; **Championship**—Louisville 59, UCLA 54.

NIT Championship (at Madison Sq.Garden): Virginia 58, Minnesota 55. No Top 20 teams played in NIT.

1981

		Before Tourns	Head Coach	Final Record
1	DePaul	27-1	Ray Meyer	27-2
2	Oregon St.	26-1	Ralph Miller	26-2
3	Arizona St.	24-3	Ned Wulk	24-4
4	LSU	28-3	Dale Brown	31-5
5	Virginia	25-3	Terry Holland	29-4
6	North Carolina	25-7	Dean Smith	29-8
7	Notre Dame	22-5	Digger Phelps	23-6
8	Kentucky	22-5	Joe B.Hall	22-6
9	**Indiana**	21-9	Bob Knight	26-9
10	UCLA	20-6	Larry Brown	20-7
11	Wake Forest	22-6	Carl Tacy	22-7
12	Louisville	21-8	Denny Crum	21-9
13	Iowa	21-6	Lute Olson	21-7
14	Utah	24-4	Jerry Pimm	25-5
15	Tennessee	20-7	Don DeVoe	21-8
16	BYU	22-6	Frank Arnold	25-7
17	Wyoming	23-5	Jim Brandenburg	24-6
18	Maryland	20-9	Lefty Driesell	21-10
19	Illinois	20-7	Lou Henson	21-8
20	Arkansas	22-7	Eddie Sutton	24-8

NCAA Final Four (at The Spectrum, Phila.): **Semifinals**—N.Carolina 78, Virginia 65; Indiana 67, LSU 49. **Third Place**—Virginia 78, LSU 74. **Championship**—Indiana 63, N.Carolina 50.
NIT Championship (at Madison Sq.Garden): Tulsa 86, Syracuse 84. No Top 20 teams played in NIT.

1983

		Before Tourns	Head Coach	Final Record
1	Houston	27-2	Guy Lewis	31-3
2	Louisville	29-3	Denny Crum	32-4
3	St.John's	27-4	Lou Carnesecca	28-5
4	Virginia	27-4	Terry Holland	29-5
5	Indiana	23-5	Bob Knight	24-6
6	UNLV	28-2	Jerry Tarkanian	28-3
7	UCLA	23-5	Larry Farmer	23-6
8	North Carolina	26-7	Dean Smith	28-8
9	Arkansas	25-3	Eddie Sutton	26-4
10	Missouri	26-7	Norm Stewart	26-8
11	Boston Col.	24-6	Gary Williams	25-7
12	Kentucky	22-7	Joe B.Hall	23-8
13	Villanova	22-7	Rollie Massimino	24-8
14	Wichita St.	25-3	Gene Smithson	same*
15	Tenn-Chatt.	26-3	Murray Arnold	26-4
16	**N.C.State**	20-10	Jim Valvano	26-10
17	Memphis St.	22-7	Dana Kirk	23-8
18	Georgia	21-9	Hugh Durham	24-10
19	Okla.State	24-6	Paul Hansen	24-7
20	Georgetown	21-9	John Thompson	22-10

NCAA Final Four (at The Pit, Albuquerque,NM): **Semifinals**—N.C.State 67, Georgia 60; Houston 94, Louisville 81. **Championship**—N.C.State 54, Houston 52.
NIT Championship (at Madison Sq.Garden): Fresno St.69, DePaul 60. No Top 20 teams played in NIT.

1982

		Before Tourns	Head Coach	Final Record
1	**North Carolina**	27-2	Dean Smith	32-2
2	DePaul	26-1	Ray Meyer	26-2
3	Virginia	29-3	Terry Holland	30-4
4	Oregon St.	23-4	Ralph Miller	25-5
5	Missouri	26-3	Norm Stewart	27-4
6	Georgetown	26-6	John Thompson	30-7
7	Minnesota	22-5	Jim Dutcher	23-6
8	Idaho	26-2	Don Monson	27-3
9	Memphis St.	23-4	Dana Kirk	24-5
10	Tulsa	24-5	Nolan Richardson	24-6
11	Fresno St.	26-2	Boyd Grant	27-3
12	Arkansas	23-5	Eddie Sutton	23-6
13	Alabama	23-6	Wimp Sanderson	24-7
14	West Virginia	26-3	Gale Catlett	27-4
15	Kentucky	22-7	Joe B.Hall	22-8
16	Iowa	20-7	Lute Olson	21-8
17	Alabama-Birm.	23-5	Gene Bartow	25-6
18	Wake Forest	20-8	Carl Tacy	21-9
19	UCLA	21-6	Larry Farmer	21-6
20	Louisville	20-9	Denny Crum	23-10

NCAA Final Four (at The Superdome, New Orleans): **Semifinals**—N.Carolina 68, Houston 63; Georgetown 50, Louisville 46. **Championship**—N.Carolina 63, Georgetown 62.
NIT Championship (at Madison Sq.Garden): Bradley 67, Purdue 58. No Top 20 teams played in NIT.

1984

		Before Tourns	Head Coach	Final Record
1	North Carolina	27-2	Dean Smith	28-3
2	**Georgetown**	29-3	John Thompson	34-3
3	Kentucky	26-4	Joe B.Hall	29-5
4	DePaul	26-2	Ray Meyer	27-3
5	Houston	28-4	Guy Lewis	32-5
6	Illinois	24-4	Lou Henson	26-5
7	Oklahoma	29-4	Billy Tubbs	29-5
8	Arkansas	25-6	Eddie Sutton	25-7
9	UTEP	27-3	Don Haskins	27-4
10	Purdue	22-6	Gene Keady	22-7
11	Maryland	23-7	Lefty Driesell	24-8
12	Tulsa	27-3	Nolan Richardson	27-4
13	UNLV	27-5	Jerry Tarkanian	29-6
14	Duke	24-9	Mike Krzyzewski	24-10
15	Washington	22-6	Marv Harshman	24-7
16	Memphis St.	24-6	Dana Kirk	26-7
17	Oregon St.	22-6	Ralph Miller	22-7
18	Syracuse	22-8	Jim Boeheim	23-9
19	Wake Forest	21-8	Carl Tacy	23-9
20	Temple	25-4	John Chaney	26-5

NCAA Final Four (at The Kingdome, Seattle): **Semifinals**—Houston 49, Virginia 47 (OT); Georgetown 53, Kentucky 40. **Championship**—Georgetown 84, Houston 75.
NIT Championship (at Madison Sq.Garden): Michigan 83, Notre Dame 63. No Top 20 teams played in NIT.

Associated Press Final Polls (Cont.)

Taken before NCAA and NIT Tournaments; (*) indicates on probation.

1985

		Before Tourns	Head Coach	Final Record
1	Georgetown	30-2	John Thompson	35-3
2	Michigan	25-3	Bill Frieder	26-4
3	St.John's	27-3	Lou Carnesecca	31-4
4	Oklahoma	28-5	Billy Tubbs	31-6
5	Memphis St.	27-3	Dana Kirk	31-4
6	Georgia Tech	24-7	Bobby Cremins	27-8
7	North Carolina	24-8	Dean Smith	27-9
8	Louisiana Tech	27-2	Andy Russo	29-3
9	UNLV	27-3	Jerry Tarkanian	28-4
10	Duke	22-7	Mike Krzyzewski	23-8
11	VCU	25-5	J.D.Barnett	26-6
12	Illinois	24-8	Lou Henson	26-9
13	Kansas	25-7	Larry Brown	26-8
14	Loyola-IL	25-5	Gene Sullivan	27-6
15	Syracuse	21-8	Jim Boeheim	22-9
16	N.C.State	20-9	Jim Valvano	23-10
17	Texas Tech	23-7	Gerald Myers	23-8
18	Tulsa	23-7	Nolan Richardson	23-8
19	Georgia	21-8	Hugh Durham	22-9
20	LSU	19-9	Dale Brown	19-10

Note: Unranked Villanova, coached by Rollie Massimino, won the NCAAs. The Wildcats entered the tourney at 19-10 and had a final record of 25-10.

NCAA Final Four (at Rupp Arena, Lexington, KY): **Semifinals**— Georgetown 77, St.John's 59; Villanova 52, Memphis St.45. **Championship**—Villanova 66, Georgetown 64.

NIT Championship (at Madison Sq.Garden): UCLA 65, Indiana 62. No Top 20 teams played in NIT.

1986

		Before Tourns	Head Coach	Final Record
1	Duke	32-2	Mike Krzyzewski	37-3
2	Kansas	31-3	Larry Brown	35-4
3	Kentucky	29-3	Eddie Sutton	32-4
4	St.John's	30-4	Lou Carnesecca	31-5
5	Michigan	27-4	Bill Frieder	28-5
6	Georgia Tech	25-6	Bobby Cremins	27-7
7	**Louisville**	26-7	Denny Crum	32-7
8	North Carolina	26-5	Dean Smith	28-6
9	Syracuse	25-5	Jim Boeheim	26-6
10	Notre Dame	23-5	Digger Phelps	23-6
11	UNLV	31-4	Jerry Tarkanian	33-5
12	Memphis St.	27-5	Dana Kirk	28-6
13	Georgetown	23-7	John Thompson	24-8
14	Bradley	31-2	Dick Versace	32-3
15	Oklahoma	25-8	Billy Tubbs	26-9
16	Indiana	21-7	Bob Knight	21-8
17	Navy	27-4	Paul Evans	30-5
18	Michigan St.	21-7	Jud Heathcote	23-8
19	Illinois	21-9	Lou Henson	22-10
20	UTEP	27-5	Don Haskins	27-6

NCAA Final Four (at Reunion Arena, Dallas): **Semifinals**—Duke 71, Kansas 67; Louisville 88, LSU 77. **Championship**—Louisville 72, Duke 69.

NIT Championship (at Madison Sq.Garden): Ohio St.73, Wyoming 63. No Top 20 teams played in NIT.

1987

		Before Tourns	Head Coach	Final Record
1	UNLV	33-1	Jerry Tarkanian	37-2
2	North Carolina	29-3	Dean Smith	32-4
3	**Indiana**	24-4	Bob Knight	30-4
4	Georgetown	26-4	John Thompson	29-5
5	DePaul	26-2	Joey Meyer	28-3
6	Iowa	27-4	Tom Davis	30-5
7	Purdue	24-4	Gene Keady	25-5
8	Temple	31-3	John Chaney	32-4
9	Alabama	26-4	Wimp Sanderson	28-5
10	Syracuse	26-6	Jim Boeheim	31-7
11	Illinois	23-7	Lou Henson	23-8
12	Pittsburgh	24-7	Paul Evans	25-8
13	Clemson	25-5	Cliff Ellis	25-6
14	Missouri	24-9	Norm Stewart	24-10
15	UCLA	24-6	Walt Hazzard	25-7
16	New Orleans	25-3	Benny Dees	26-4
17	Duke	22-8	Mike Krzyzewski	24-9
18	Notre Dame	22-7	Digger Phelps	24-8
19	TCU	23-6	Jim Killingsworth	24-7
20	Kansas	23-10	Larry Brown	25-11

NCAA Final Four (at The Superdome, New Orleans): **Semifinals**—Syracuse 77, Providence 63; Indiana 97, UNLV 93. **Championship**—Indiana 74, Syracuse 73.

NIT Championship (at Madison Sq. Garden): Southern Miss 84, La Salle 80. No Top 20 teams played in NIT.

1988

		Before Tourns	Head Coach	Final Record
1	Temple	29-1	John Chaney	32-2
2	Arizona	31-2	Lute Olson	35-3
3	Purdue	27-3	Gene Keady	29-4
4	Oklahoma	30-3	Billy Tubbs	35-4
5	Duke	24-6	Mike Krzyzewski	28-7
6	Kentucky	25-5	Eddie Sutton	27-6
7	North Carolina	24-6	Dean Smith	27-7
8	Pittsburgh	23-6	Paul Evans	24-7
9	Syracuse	25-8	Jim Boeheim	26-9
10	Michigan	24-7	Bill Frieder	26-8
11	Bradley	26-4	Stan Albeck	26-5
12	UNLV	27-5	Jerry Tarkanian	28-6
13	Wyoming	26-5	Benny Dees	26-6
14	N.C.State	24-7	Jim Valvano	24-8
15	Loyola-CA	27-3	Paul Westhead	28-4
16	Illinois	22-9	Lou Henson	23-10
17	Iowa	22-9	Tom Davis	24-10
18	Xavier-OH	26-3	Pete Gillen	26-4
19	BYU	25-5	Ladell Andersen	26-6
20	Kansas St.	22-8	Lon Kruger	25-9

Note: Unranked Kansas, coached by Larry Brown, won the NCAAs. The Jayhawks entered the tourney at 21-11 and had a final record of 27-11.

NCAA Final Four (at Kemper Arena, Kansas City): **Semifinals**—Kansas 66, Duke 59; Oklahoma 86, Arizona 78. **Championship**—Kansas 83, Oklahoma 79.

NIT Championship (at Madison Sq. Garden): Connecticut 72, Ohio St.67. No Top 20 team played in NIT.

1989

		Before Tourns	Head Coach	Final Record
1	Arizona	27-3	Lute Olson	29-4
2	Georgetown	26-4	John Thompson	29-5
3	Illinois	27-4	Lou Henson	31-5
4	Oklahoma	28-5	Billy Tubbs	30-6
5	North Carolina	27-7	Dean Smith	29-8
6	Missouri	27-7	Norm Stewart & Rich Daly	29-8
7	Syracuse	27-7	Jim Boeheim	30-8
8	Indiana	25-7	Bob Knight	27-8
9	Duke	24-7	Mike Krzyzewski	28-8
10	**Michigan**	24-7	Bill Frieder & Steve Fisher	30-7
11	Seton Hall	26-6	P.J.Carlesimo	31-7
12	Louisville	22-8	Denny Crum	24-9
13	Stanford	26-6	Mike Montgomery	26-7
14	Iowa	22-9	Tom Davis	23-10
15	UNLV	26-7	Jerry Tarkanian	29-8
16	Florida St.	22-7	Pat Kennedy	22-8
17	West Virginia	25-4	Gale Catlett	26-5
18	Ball State	28-2	Rick Majerus	29-3
19	N.C.State	20-8	Jim Valvano	22-9
20	Alabama	23-7	Wimp Sanderson	23-8

NCAA Final Four (at The Kingdome, Seattle): **Semifinals**—Seton Hall 95, Duke 78; Michigan 83, Illinois 81. **Championship**—Michigan 80, Seton Hall 79 (OT).
NIT Championship (at Madison Sq. Garden): St.John's 73, St.Louis 65. No Top 20 teams played in NIT.

1991

		Before Tourns	Head Coach	Final Record
1	UNLV	30-0	Jerry Tarkanian	34-1
2	Arkansas	31-3	Nolan Richardson	34-4
3	Indiana	27-4	Bob Knight	29-5
4	North Carolina	25-5	Dean Smith	29-6
5	Ohio St.	25-3	Randy Ayers	27-4
6	**Duke**	26-7	Mike Krzyzewski	32-7
7	Syracuse	26-5	Jim Boeheim	26-6
8	Arizona	26-6	Lute Olson	28-7
9	Kentucky	22-6	Rick Pitino	same*
10	Utah	28-3	Rick Majerus	30-4
11	Nebraska	26-7	Danny Nee	26-8
12	Kansas	22-7	Roy Williams	27-8
13	Seton Hall	22-8	P.J.Carlesimo	25-9
14	Oklahoma St.	22-7	Eddie Sutton	24-8
15	New Mexico St.	23-5	Neil McCarthy	23-6
16	UCLA	23-8	Jim Harrick	23-9
17	E.Tennessee St.	28-4	Alan LaForce	28-5
18	Princeton	24-2	Pete Carril	24-3
19	Alabama	21-9	Wimp Sanderson	23-10
20	St.John's	20-8	Lou Carnesecca	23-9
21	Mississippi St.	20-8	Richard Williams	20-9
22	LSU	20-9	Dale Brown	20-10
23	Texas	22-8	Tom Penders	23-9
24	DePaul	20-8	Joey Meyer	20-9
25	So.Mississippi	21-7	M.K.Turk	21-8

NCAA Final Four (at the Hoosier Dome, Indianapolis): **Semifinals**—Kansas 79, North Carolina 73; Duke 79, UNLV 77. **Championship**—Duke 72, Kansas 65.
NIT Championship (at Madison Sq.Garden): Stanford 78, Oklahoma 72. No Top 20 teams played in NIT.

1990

		Before Tourns	Head Coach	Final Record
1	Oklahoma	26-4	Billy Tubbs	27-5
2	**UNLV**	29-5	Jerry Tarkanian	35-5
3	Connecticut	28-5	Jim Calhoun	31-6
4	Michigan St.	26-5	Jud Heathcote	28-6
5	Kansas	29-4	Roy Williams	30-5
6	Syracuse	24-6	Jim Boeheim	26-7
7	Arkansas	26-4	Nolan Richardson	30-5
8	Georgetown	23-6	John Thompson	24-7
9	Georgia Tech	24-6	Bobby Cremins	28-7
10	Purdue	21-7	Gene Keady	22-8
11	Missouri	26-5	Norm Stewart	26-6
12	La Salle	29-1	Speedy Morris	30-2
13	Michigan	22-7	Steve Fisher	23-8
14	Arizona	24-6	Lute Olson	25-7
15	Duke	24-8	Mike Krzyzewski	29-9
16	Louisville	26-7	Denny Crum	27-8
17	Clemson	24-8	Cliff Ellis	26-9
18	Illinois	21-7	Lou Henson	21-8
19	LSU	22-8	Dale Brown	23-9
20	Minnesota	20-8	Clem Haskins	23-9
21	Loyola-CA	23-5	Paul Westhead	26-6
22	Oregon St.	22-6	Jim Anderson	22-7
23	Alabama	24-8	Wimp Sanderson	26-9
24	New Mexico St.	26-4	Neil McCarthy	26-5
25	Xavier-OH	26-4	Pete Gillen	28-5

NCAA Final Four (at McNichols Sports Arena, Denver): **Semifinals**—Duke 97, Arkansas 83; UNLV 90, Georgia Tech 81. **Championship**—UNLV 103, Duke 73.
NIT Championship (at Madison Sq.Garden): Vanderbilt 74, St.Louis 72. No Top 20 teams played in NIT.

All-Time AP Top 20

The composite AP Top 20 from the 1948-49 season through 1990-91 is based on the final rankings of each year. The final AP poll has been taken before the NCAA and NIT tournaments since 1949 and does not determine the national champion. Team point totals are based on 20 points for all 1st place finishes, 19 for each 2nd, etc.). Also listed are the number of times ranked No.1 by AP going into the tournaments, and times ranked in the pre-tournament Top 10 and Top 20.

		AP Pts	No.1	Top10	Top 20
1	Kentucky	469	7	26	31
2	North Carolina	386	3	21	28
3	UCLA	373	7	19	26
4	Duke	255	1	14	23
5	Indiana	248	2	14	19
6	Louisville	203	0	10	18
7	Kansas	201	0	11	17
8	Notre Dame	188	0	11	17
9	Marquette	168	0	10	13
10	N.C. St.	167	1	9	15
11	Michigan	165	2	10	12
12	UNLV	158	2	7	12
13	Illinois	156	0	7	17
14	Bradley	152	1	8	11
	Syracuse	152	0	10	13
16	Cincinnati	148	2	7	10
17	Kansas St.	145	1	7	12
18	DePaul	143	2	8	10
	St. John's	143	0	8	14
20	Ohio St.	131	2	8	9

All-Time Winningest Division I Teams

Division I schools with best winning percentages through 1990-91 season (including tournament games). Years in Division I only; minimum 25 years. **NCAA Tourney** columns indicate years in tournament, record and number of championships.

Top 20 Winning Percentage

		First Year	Yrs	Gm	W	L	T	Pct	NCAA Tourney Yrs	W-L	Titles
1	UNLV	1961	31	917	700	217	0	.763	12	30-11	1
2	Kentucky	1903	88	1997	1501	495	1	.752	33	55-30	5
3	North Carolina	1911	81	2058	1508	550	0	.733	25	54-26	2
4	St.John's	1908	84	2057	1444	613	0	.702	21	22-23	0
5	UCLA	1920	72	1805	1244	561	0	.689	27	64-21	10
6	Kansas	1899	93	2136	1459	677	0	.683	20	42-20	2
7	Syracuse	1901	90	1943	1318	625	0	.678	19	26-20	0
8	Western Kentucky	1915	72	1825	1237	588	0	.678	13	12-14	0
9	DePaul	1924	68	1631	1098	533	0	.673	19	20-22	0
10	Notre Dame	1898	86	2004	1335	668	1	.666	24	25-28	0
11	Duke	1906	86	2070	1377	693	0	.665	16	44-15	1
12	La Salle	1931	61	1543	1009	534	0	.654	10	11-9	1
13	Louisville	1912	77	1822	1188	634	0	.652	21	38-23	2
14	North Carolina St	1913	79	1897	1234	663	0	.651	17	27-16	2
15	Temple	1895	95	2091	1356	735	0	.648	15	18-15	0
16	Weber St	1963	29	816	528	288	0	.647	10	4-11	0
17	Illinois	1906	86	1875	1213	662	0	.647	14	20-15	0
18	Houston	1946	46	1273	821	452	0	.645	17	26-22	0
19	Indiana	1901	91	1971	1271	700	0	.645	20	41-15	5
20	Arkansas	1924	68	1699	1093	606	0	.643	17	21-18	0

Top 35 Victories

Division I schools with most victories through 1990-91 (including postseason tournaments)
Totals reflect games won in Division I only.

		Wins			Wins			Wins
1	North Carolina	1508	13	UCLA	1244	25	Texas	1180
2	Kentucky	1501	14	Fordham	1242	26	Montana St	1169
3	Kansas	1459		Princeton	1242	27	St.Joseph's-PA	1139
4	St.John's	1444	16	Western Ky	1237	28	Villanova	1139
5	Oregon St	1387	17	N.C.State	1234	29	DePaul	1098
6	Duke	1377	18	West Virginia	1225	30	Arkansas	1093
7	Temple	1356	19	Purdue	1221	31	Virginia	1072
8	Notre Dame	1335	20	Bradley	1218	32	Duquesne	1062
9	Penn	1324	21	Illinois	1213	33	Wake Forest	1028
10	Syracuse	1318	22	Utah	1200	34	Navy	1013
11	Washington	1293	23	Washington St	1195	35	La Salle	1009
12	Indiana	1271	24	Louisville	1188			

Winning Streaks

	Full Season (Including tournaments)					Regular Season (Not including tournaments)			
No		Seasons	Broken by	Score	No		Seasons	Broken by	Score
88	UCLA	1971-74	Notre Dame	71-70	76	UCLA	1971-74	Notre Dame	71-70
60	San Francisco	1955-57	Illinois	62-33	57	Indiana	1975-77	Toledo	59-57
47	UCLA	1966-68	Houston	71-69	56	Marquette	1970-72	Detroit	70-49
45	UNLV	1990-91	Duke	79-77	54	Kentucky	1952-55	Georgia Tech	59-58
44	Texas	1913-17	Rice	24-18	51	San Francisco	1955-57	Illinois	62-33
43	Seton Hall	1939-41	LIU-Bklyn	49-26	48	Penn	1970-72	Temple	57-52
43	LIU-Bklyn	1935-37	Stanford	45-31	47	Ohio St	1960-62	Wisconsin	86-67
41	UCLA	1968-69	USC	46-44	44	Texas	1913-17	Rice	24-18
39	Marquette	1970-71	Ohio St.	60-59	43	UCLA	1966-68	Houston	71-69
37	Cincinnati	1962-63	Wichita St.	65-64	43	LIU-Bklyn	1935-37	Stanford	45-31
37	North Carolina	1957-58	West Virginia	75-64	42	Seton Hall	1939-41	LIU-Bklyn	49-26
36	N.C.State	1974-75	Wake Forest	83-78					
35	Arkansas	1927-29	Texas	26-25					

Annual NCAA Division I Leaders
Scoring

The NCAA did not begin keeping individual scoring records until the 1947-48 season. All averages include postseason games where applicable.

Multiple winners: Pete Maravich, Oscar Robertson (3); Darrell Floyd, Harry Kelly, Frank Selvy and Freeman Williams (2).

Year		Gm	Pts	Avg	Year		Gm	Pts	Avg
1948	Murray Wier, Iowa	19	399	21.0	1970	Pete Maravich, LSU	31	1381	44.5
1949	Tony Lavelli, Yale	30	671	22.4	1971	Johnny Neumann, Ole Miss	23	923	40.1
					1972	Dwight Lamar, SW La	29	1054	36.3
1950	Paul Arizin, Villanova	29	735	25.3	1973	William Averitt, Pepperdine	25	848	33.9
1951	Bill Mlkvy, Temple	25	731	29.2	1974	Larry Fogle, Canisius	25	835	33.4
1952	Clyde Lovellette, Kansas	28	795	28.4	1975	Bob McCurdy, Richmond	26	855	32.9
1953	Frank Selvy, Furman	25	738	29.5	1976	Marshall Rodgers, Pan Am	25	919	36.8
1954	Frank Selvy, Furman	29	1209	41.7	1977	Freeman Williams, Portland St.	26	1010	38.8
1955	Darrell Floyd, Furman	25	897	35.9	1978	Freeman Williams, Portland St.	27	969	35.9
1956	Darrell Floyd, Furman	28	946	33.8	1979	Lawrence Butler, Idaho St	27	812	30.1
1957	Grady Wallace, S.Carolina	29	906	31.2					
1958	Oscar Robertson, Cinncinati	28	984	35.1	1980	Tony Murphy, Southern-BR	29	932	32.1
1959	Oscar Robertson, Cinncinati	30	978	32.6	1981	Zam Fredrick, S.Carolina	27	781	28.9
					1982	Harry Kelly, TX-Southern	29	862	29.7
1960	Oscar Robertson, Cincinnati	30	1011	33.7	1983	Harry Kelly, TX-Southern	29	835	28.8
1961	Frank Burgess, Gonzaga	26	842	32.4	1984	Joe Jakubick, Akron	27	814	30.1
1962	Billy McGill, Utah	26	1009	38.8	1985	Xavier McDaniel, Wichita St.	31	844	27.2
1963	Nick Werkman, Seton Hall	22	650	29.5	1986	Terrance Bailey, Wagner	29	854	29.4
1964	Howie Komives, Bowl.Green	23	844	36.7	1987	Kevin Houston, Army	29	953	32.9
1965	Rick Barry, Miami-FL	26	973	37.4	1988	Hersey Hawkins, Bradley	31	1125	36.3
1966	Dave Schellhase, Purdue	24	781	32.5	1989	Hank Gathers, Loyola-CA	31	1015	32.7
1967	Jimmy Walker, Providence	28	851	30.4					
1968	Pete Maravich, LSU	26	1138	43.8	1990	Bo Kimble, Loyola-CA	32	1131	35.3
1969	Pete Maravich, LSU	26	1148	44.2	1991	Kevin Bradshaw, US Int'l	28	1054	37.6

Note: Fourteen underclassmen have won the title: **Sophomores** (4)—Robertson (1958), Maravich (1968), Neumann (1971), Fogle (1974); **Juniors** (10)—Selvy (1953), Floyd (1955), Robertson (1959), Werkman (1963), Maravich (1969), Lamar (1972), Williams (1977), Kelly (1982), Bailey (1986), Gathers (1989).

Rebounds

The NCAA did not begin keeping individual rebounding records until the 1950-51 season. From 1956-62, the championship was decided on highest percentage of recoveries out of all rebounds made by both teams in all games. All averages include postseason games where applicable; (*) indicates also led nation in scoring.

Multiple winners: Artis Gilmore, Jerry Lucas, Xavier McDaniel, Kermit Washington and Leroy Wright (2).

Year		Gm	Reb	Avg	Year		Gm	Reb	Avg
1951	Ernie Beck, Penn	27	556	20.6	1974	Marvin Barnes, Providence	32	597	18.7
1952	Bill Hannon, Army	17	355	20.9	1975	John Irving, Hofstra	21	323	15.4
1953	Ed Conlin, Fordham	26	612	23.5	1976	Sam Pellom, Buffalo	26	420	16.2
1954	Art Quimby, Connecticut	26	588	22.6	1977	Glenn Moseley, Seton Hall	29	473	16.3
1955	Charlie Slack, Marshall	21	538	25.6	1978	Ken Williams, N. Texas	28	411	14.7
1956	Joe Holup, G. Washington	26	604	.256	1979	Monti Davis, Tennessee State	26	421	16.2
1957	Elgin Baylor, Seattle	25	508	.235					
1958	Alex Ellis, Niagara	25	536	.262	1980	Larry Smith, Alcorn State	26	392	15.1
1959	Leroy Wright, Pacific	26	652	.238	1981	Darryl Watson, Mississippi Valley	27	379	14.0
					1982	LaSalle Thompson, Texas	27	365	13.5
1960	Leroy Wright, Pacific	17	380	.234	1983	Xavier McDaniel, Wichita State	28	403	14.4
1961	Jerry Lucas, Ohio State	27	470	.198	1984	Akeem Olajuwon, Houston	37	500	13.5
1962	Jerry Lucas, Ohio State	28	499	.211	1985	Xavier McDaniel, Wichita State*	31	460	14.8
1963	Paul Silas, Creighton	27	557	20.6	1986	David Robinson, Navy	35	455	13.0
1964	Bob Pelkington, Xavier-Ohio	26	567	21.8	1987	Jerome Lane, Pittsburgh	33	444	13.5
1965	Toby Kimball, Connecticut	23	483	21.0	1988	Kenny Miller, Loyola-IL	29	395	13.6
1966	Jim Ware, Oklahoma City	29	607	20.9	1989	Hank Gathers, Loyola-CA*	31	426	13.7
1967	Dick Cunningham, Murray State	22	479	21.8					
1968	Neal Walk, Florida	25	494	19.8	1990	Anthony Bonner, St. Louis	33	456	13.8
1969	Spencer Haywood, Detroit	22	472	21.5	1991	Shaquille O'Neal, LSU	28	411	14.7
1970	Artis Gilmore, Jacksonville	28	621	22.2					
1971	Artis Gilmore, Jacksonville	26	603	23.2					
1972	Kermit Washington, American	23	455	19.8					
1973	Kermit Washington, American	22	439	20.0					

All-Time NCAA Division I Individual Leaders

Through 1990-91; includes regular season and tournament games.

CAREER

Scoring

Points	Years	Gm	Pts	Average	Years	No	Avg
Pete Maravich, LSU................	1968-70	83	3667	Pete Maravich, LSU................	1968-70	3667	44.2
Freeman Williams, Portland St	1975-78	106	3249	Austin Carr, Notre Dame..........	1969-71	2560	34.6
Lionel Simmons, La Salle...........	1987-90	131	3217	Oscar Robertson, Cincinnati	1958-60	2973	33.8
Harry Kelly, Tex-Southern..........	1980-83	110	3066	Calvin Murphy, Niagara	1968-70	2548	33.1
Hersey Hawkins, Bradley	1985-88	125	3008	Dwight Lamar, SW La	1972-73	1862	32.7
Oscar Robertson, Cincinnati	1968-60	88	2973	Frank Selvy, Furman...............	1952-54	2538	32.5
Danny Manning, Kansas	1985-88	147	2951	Rick Mount, Purdue...............	1968-70	2323	32.3
Alfredrick Hughes, Loyola-IL	1982-85	120	2914	Darrell Floyd, Furman	1954-56	2281	32.1
Elvin Hayes, Houston	1966-68	93	2884	Nick Werkman, Seton Hall	1962-64	2273	32.0
Larry Bird, Indiana St	1977-79	94	2850	Willie Humes, Idaho St.............	1970-71	1510	31.5

Field Goal Pct.	Years	FG	FGA	Pct	Free Throw Pct.	Years	FT	FTA	Pct
Stephen Scheffler, Purdue	1987-90	408	596	68.5	Greg Starrick, Ky/So.Ill.......	1969-72	341	375	90.9
Steve Johnson, Ore.St	1978-81	828	1222	67.8	Jack Moore, Nebraska.......	1979-82	446	495	90.1
Murray Brown, Fla.St	1977-80	566	847	66.8	Steve Henson, Kansas St	1986-90	361	401	90.0
Lee Campbell, SW Mo.St.......	1987-90	411	618	66.5	Steve Alford, Indiana	1984-87	535	596	89.8
Joe Senser, W.Chester	1976-79	476	719	66.2	Bob Lloyd, Rutgers	1965-67	543	605	89.8
Note: Minimum 400 FGs scored.					**Note:** Minimum 250 FTs scored.				

Rebounds

Total (before 1973)	Years	Gm	No	Total (since 1973)	Years	Gm	No
Tom Gola, La Salle................	1952-55	118	2201	Derrick Coleman, Syracuse	1987-90	143	1537
Joe Holup, G.Washington	1953-56	104	2030	Ralph Sampson, Virginia	1980-83	132	1511
Charlie Slack, Marshall	1953-56	88	1916	Pete Padgett, NV-Reno.............	1973-76	104	1464
Ed Conlin, Fordham...............	1951-55	102	1884	Lionel Simmons, La Salle	1987-90	131	1429
Dickie Hemric, W.Forest............	1952-55	104	1802	Anthony Bonner, St.Louis...........	1987-90	133	1424
Note: Minimum 650 rebounds.							

2000 Points/1000 Rebounds

For a combined total of 4000 or more.

	Gm	Pts	Reb	Total		Gm	Pts	Reb	Total
Tom Gola, La Salle............	118	2462	2201	4663	Harry Kelly, TX-Southern	110	3066	1085	4151
Lionel Simmons, La Salle	131	3217	1429	4646	Danny Manning, Kansas	147	2951	1187	4138
Elvin Hayes, Houston	93	2884	1602	4486	Larry Bird, Indiana St	94	2850	1247	4097
Dickie Hemric, W.Forest........	104	2587	1802	4389	Elgin Baylor, Col. Idaho/Seattle..	80	2500	1559	4059
Oscar Robertson, Cinn..........	88	2973	1338	4311	Michael Brooks, La Salle	114	2628	1372	4000
Joe Holup, Geo.Wash	104	2226	2030	4256					

Years Played—Baylor (1956-58); **Bird** (1977-79); **Brooks** (1977-80); **Gola** (1952-55); **Hayes** (1966-68); **Hemric** (1952-55); **Holup** (1953-56); **Kelly** (1980-83); **Manning** (1985-88); **Robertson** (1958-60); **Simmons** (1987-90).

Assists

Total	Years	Gm	No	Average	Years	No	Avg
Chris Corchiani, N.C.State	1988-91	124	1038	Avery Johnson, Cameron/South.-BR. .	1986-88	838	8.91
Keith Jennings, E.Tennessee St	1988-91	127	983	Mark Wade, Okla/UNLV...........	1985-87	693	8.77
Sherman Douglas, Syracuse	1986-89	138	960	Chris Corchiani, N.C.State	1988-91	1038	8.37
Gary Payton, Oregon St............	1987-90	120	938	Taurence Chisholm, Delaware	1985-88	877	7.97
Andre LaFleur, N'eastern............	1984-87	128	894	Anthony Manuel, Bradley...........	1986-89	855	7.92
				Note: Minimum 550 assists.			

SINGLE SEASON

Scoring

Points	Year	Gm	Pts	Average	Year	Pts	Avg
Pete Maravich, LSU.................	1970	31	1381	Pete Maravich, LSU.................	1970	1381	44.5
Elvin Hayes, Houston	1968	33	1214	Pete Maravich, LSU.................	1969	1148	44.2
Frank Selvy, Furman.................	1954	29	1209	Pete Maravich, LSU.................	1968	1138	43.8
Pete Maravich, LSU.................	1969	26	1148	Frank Selvy, Furman................	1954	1209	41.7
Pete Maravich, LSU.................	1968	26	1138	Johnny Neumann, Ole Miss	1971	923	40.1
Bo Kimble, Loyola-CA	1990	32	1131	Freeman Williams, Port.St	1977	1010	38.8
Hersey Hawkins, Bradley	1988	31	1125	Billy McGill, Utah	1962	1009	38.8
Austin Carr, Notre Dame.............	1970	29	1106	Calvin Murphy, Niagara	1968	916	38.2
Austin Carr, Notre Dame.............	1971	29	1101	Austin Carr, Notre Dame.............	1970	1106	38.1
Otis Birdsong, Houston	1977	36	1090	Austin Carr, Notre Dame.............	1971	1101	38.0

Field Goal Pct.

	Year	FG	FGA	Pct
Steve Johnson, Oregon St.	1981	235	315	74.6
Dwayne Davis, Florida	1989	179	248	72.2
Keith Walker, Utica	1985	154	216	71.3
Steve Johnson, Oregon St.	1980	211	297	71.0
Oliver Miller, Arkansas	1991	254	361	70.4

Free Throw Pct.

	Year	FG	FGA	Pct
Craig Collins, Penn St	1985	94	98	95.9
Rod Foster, UCLA	1982	95	100	95.0
Carlos Gibson, Marshall	1978	84	89	94.4
Jim Barton, Dartmouth	1986	65	69	94.2
Jack Moore, Nebraska	1982	123	131	93.9

3-Pt Field Goal Pct.

	Year	FG	FGA	Pct
Glenn Tropf, Holy Cross	1988	52	82	63.4
Keith Jennings, E.TennesseeSt	1991	84	142	59.2
Dave Calloway, Monmouth	1989	48	82	58.5
Steve Kerr, Arizona	1988	114	199	57.3
Reginald Jones, Prairie	1987	64	112	57.1

Assists

Average	Year	Gm	No	Avg
Avery Johnson, Southern-BR	1988	30	399	13.3
Anthony Manuel, Bradley	1988	31	373	12.0
Avery Johnson, Southern-BR	1987	31	333	10.7
Mark Wade, UNLV	1987	38	406	10.7
Glenn Williams, Holy Cross	1989	28	278	9.9

Steals

Average	Year	Gm	No	Avg
Darron Bittman, Chicago St.	1986	28	139	4.96
Aldwin Ware, Fla.A&M	1988	29	142	4.90
Ronn McMahon, E.Wash	1990	29	130	4.48
Jim Paguaga, St.Fran-NY	1986	28	120	4.29
Marty Johnson, Towson St	1988	30	124	4.13

Rebounds

Total	Year	Gm	No
Walter Dukes, Seton Hall	1953	33	734
Leroy Wright, Pacific	1959	26	652
Tom Gola, La Salle	1954	30	652
Charlie Tyra, Louisville	1956	29	645
Paul Silas, Creighton	1964	29	631

Average (before 1973)	Year	No	Avg
Charlie Slack, Marshall	1955	538	25.6
Leroy Wright, Pacific	1959	652	25.1
Art Quimby, Connecticut	1955	611	24.4
Charlie Slack, Marshall	1956	520	23.6
Ed Conlin, Fordham	1953	612	23.5

Average (since 1973)	Year	No	Avg
Kermit Washington, American	1973	439	20.0
Marvin Barnes, Providence	1973	571	19.0
Marvin Barnes, Providence	1974	597	18.7
Pete Padgett, NV-Reno	1973	462	17.8
Jim Bradley, Northern.Ill	1973	426	17.8

Blocked Shots

Average	Year	Gm	No	Avg
David Robinson, Navy	1986	35	207	5.91
Shawn Bradley, BYU	1991	34	177	5.21
Cedric Lewis, Maryland	1991	28	143	5.11
Shaquille O'Neal, LSU	1991	28	140	5.00
Alonzo Mourning, G'town	1989	34	169	4.97

SINGLE GAME

Scoring

Points vs Div.I Team	Year	Pts
Kevin Bradshaw, US Int'l vs Loyola-CA	1991	72
Pete Maravich, LSU vs Alabama	1970	69
Calvin Murphy, Niagara vs Syracuse	1969	68
Jay Handlan, Wash.& Lee vs Furman	1951	66
Pete Maravich, LSU vs Tulane	1969	66
Anthony Roberts, O.Roberts vs N.C.A&T	1977	66
Scott Haffner, Evansville vs Dayton	1989	65
Anthony Roberts, O.Roberts vs Oregon	1977	65
Pete Maravich, LSU vs Kentucky	1970	64
Hersey Hawkins, Bradley vs Detroit	1988	63
Johnny Neumann, Ole Miss vs LSU	1971	63

Points vs Non-Div.I Team	Year	Pts
Frank Selvy, Furman vs Newberry	1954	100
Paul Arizin, Villanova vs Phi.NAMC	1949	85
Freeman Williams, Portland St.vs Rocky Mt	1978	81
Bill Mlkvy, Temple vs Wilkes	1951	73
Freeman Williams, Portland St.vs So.Ore	1977	71

Rebounds

Total (before 1973)	Year	No
Bill Chambers, Wm.& Mary vs Virginia	1953	51
Charlie Slack, Marshall vs M.Harvey	1954	43
Tom Heinsohn, Holy Cross vs BC	1955	42
Art Quimby, UConn vs BU	1955	40
Maurice Stokes, St.Fran-PA vs J.Carroll	1955	39
Dave DeBusschere, Detroit vs C.Michigan	1960	39
Keith Swagerty, Pacific vs UCSB	1965	39

Total (since 1973)	Year	No
David Vaughn, O.Roberts vs Brandeis	1973	34
Robert Parish, Centenary vs So.Miss	1973	33
Jim Bradley, No.III vs WI-Milwaukee	1973	31
Calvin Natt, NE La. vs Ga.Southern	1976	31
Eddie Woods, O.Roberts vs Lamar	1972	30
Eddie Woods, O.Roberts vs La.Tech	1972	30
Brad Robinson, Kent St.vs C.Michigan	1974	30

All-Time NCAA Division I Team Leaders

SINGLE SEASON
Scoring

	Year	Gm	Pts	Avg
Loyola-CA	1990	32	3918	122.4
Loyola-CA	1989	31	3486	112.5
UNLV	1976	31	3426	110.5
Loyola-CA	1988	32	3528	110.3
UNLV	1977	32	3426	107.1
Oral Roberts	1972	28	2943	105.1
Southern-BR	1991	28	2924	104.4
Loyola-CA	1991	31	3211	103.6
Oklahoma	1988	39	4012	102.9
Oklahoma	1989	36	3680	102.2

SINGLE GAME
Scoring

	Score	Opponent	Date
Loyola-CA	186-140	US Int'l	1/5/91
Loyola-CA	181-150	US Int'l	1/31/89
Oklahoma	173-101	US Int'l	11/29/89
Arkansas	166-101	US Int'l	12/9/89
UNLV	164-111	Hawaii-Hilo	2/19/76
Loyola-CA	164-138	Azusa-Pacific	11/28/88
Loyola-CA	162-144	US Int'l	1/7/89
Loyola-CA	157-115	US Int'l	2/5/90
Oral Roberts	155-113	Union-TN	2/24/72

Four tied at 152 points.

All-Time Winningest Division I Coaches

Minimum of 10 seasons as Division I head coach; regular season and tournament games included; coaches active during 1990-91 in **bold** type.

Top 25 Winning Percentage

	Yrs	Won	Lost	Pct
Jerry Tarkanian	23	599	120	**.833**
Clair Bee	21	410	86	**.827**
Adolph Rupp	41	875	190	**.822**
John Wooden	29	664	162	**.804**
Dean Smith	30	717	209	**.774**
John Chaney	19	441	130	**.772**
George Keogan	24	385	117	**.767**
Jack Ramsay	11	231	71	**.765**
Frank Keaney	28	403	124	**.765**
Jim Boeheim	15	369	114	**.764**
Vic Bubas	10	213	67	**.761**
Chick Davies	21	314	106	**.748**
Ray Mears	21	399	135	**.747**
John Thompson	19	442	155	**.740**
Al McGuire	20	405	143	**.739**
Everett Case	18	376	133	**.739**
Nolan Richardson	11	260	92	**.739**
Phog Allen	48	746	264	**.739**
Denny Crum	20	477	172	**.735**
Bob Knight	26	561	203	**.734**
Lou Carnesecca	23	507	189	**.728**
Lew Andreas	25	355	134	**.726**
Eddie Sutton	21	454	172	**.725**
Fred Schaus	12	251	96	**.723**
Joe Lapchick	20	335	130	**.720**

Top 25 Victories

	Yrs	Won	Lost	Pct
Adolph Rupp	41	**875**	190	.822
Hank Iba	41	**767**	338	.694
Ed Diddle	42	**759**	302	.715
Phog Allen	48	**746**	264	.739
Ray Meyer	42	**724**	354	.672
Dean Smith	30	**717**	209	.774
John Wooden	29	**664**	162	.804
Ralph Miller	38	**657**	382	.632
Marv Harshman	40	**642**	448	.589
Norm Sloan	37	**627**	395	.614
Cam Henderson	36	**611**	245	.714
Jerry Tarkanian	23	**599**	120	.833
Slats Gill	36	**599**	392	.604
Abe Lemons	34	**597**	343	.636
Guy Lewis	30	**592**	279	.680
Lefty Driesell	29	**579**	259	.691
Don Haskins	30	**578**	256	.693
Lou Henson	29	**577**	267	.684
Norm Stewart	30	**572**	283	.669
Bob Knight	26	**561**	203	.734
Tony Hinkle	41	**560**	392	.588
Gene Bartow	29	**554**	292	.655
Frank McGuire	30	**550**	235	.701
Harry Miller	34	**534**	374	.588
Glenn Wilkes	34	**527**	405	.565

Note: Clarence "Bighouse" Gaines of Division II Winston-Salem St.(since 1947) is No.2 on the all-time NCAA list of all coaches regardless of division. His record is 816–410 .666 over 45 seasons.

Where They Coached

Allen—Baker (1906-08), Haskell (1909), Central Mo.St.(1913-19), Kansas (1908-09, 20-56); **Andreas**—Syracuse (1925-43; 45-50); **Bee**—Rider (1929-31), LIU-Brooklyn (1932-45, 46-51); **Boeheim**—Syracuse (1977—); **Bubas**—Duke (1960-69); **Carnesecca**—St.John's (1966-70, 74—); **Case**—N.C.State (1947-64); **Crum**—Louisville (1972—); **Davies**—Duquesne (1925-43, 47-48); **Diddle**—Western Ky.(1923-64); **Driesell**—Davidson (1961-69), Maryland (1970-86), J.Madison (1989—). **Gill**—Oregon St.(1929-64); **Harshman**—Pacific Lutheran (1946-58), Wash.St.(1959-71), Washington (1972-85); **Haskins**—UTEP (1962—); **Henderson**—Muskingum (1920-22), Davis & Elkins (1923-35), Marshall (1936-55); **Henson**—Hardin-Simmons (1963-66), New Mexico St.(1967-75), Illinois (1976—); **Hinkle**—Butler (1927-42, 46-70); **Iba**—NW Missouri St.(1930-33), Colorado (1934), Oklahoma St.(1935-70). **Keaney**—Rhode Island (1921-48); **Knight**—Army (1966-71), Indiana (1972—); **Koegan**—St.Louis (1916), Allegheny (1919), Valparaiso (1920-21), Notre Dame (1924-43); **Lemons**—Okla.City (1956-73), Pan American (1974-76), Texas (1977-82), Okla.City (1984-90); **Lewis**—Houston (1957-86); **A.McGuire**—Belmont Abbey (1958-64), Marquette (1965-77); **F.McGuire**—St.John's (1948-52), North Carolina (1953-61), South Carolina (1965-80); **Mears**—Wittenberg (1957-62), Tennessee (1963-77); **Miller**—Wichita St.(1952-64), Iowa (1965-70), Oregon St.(1971-89). **Ramsay**—St.Joseph's-PA (1956-66); **Rupp**—Kentucky (1931-72); **Sloan**—Presbyterian (1952-55), Citadel (1957-60), Florida (1961-66), N.C.State (1967-80), Florida (1981-89); **Smith**—North Carolina (1962—); **Tarkanian**—Long Beach St.(1969-73), UNLV (1974—); **Thompson**—Georgetown (1973—); **Wooden**—Indiana St.(1947-48), UCLA (1949-75).

Most NCAA Tournaments

Through 1991; listed are number of appearances, overall tournament record, times reaching Final Four, and number of NCAA championships.

App		W-L	F4	Championships
21	**Dean Smith**	47-22	8	1 (1982)
20	Adolph Rupp	30-18	6	4 (1948-49,51,58)
17	**Lou Carnesecca**	17-19	1	None
16	John Wooden	47-10	12	10 (1964-65, 67-73,75)
16	**Jerry Tarkanian**	37-16	4	1 (1990)
15	**Bob Knight**	31-12	4	3 (1976,81,87)
15	**Denny Crum**	32-15	6	2 (1980,86)
15	**John Thompson**	27-14	3	1 (1984)
15	**Lou Henson**	18-16	2	None
15	**Digger Phelps**	17-17	1	None
14	Guy Lewis	26-18	5	None
14	**Eddie Sutton**	19-14	1	None

Active Coaches' Victories

Minimum five seasons in Division I.

	Yrs	W	L	Pct
Dean Smith, North Carolina	30	**717**	209	.774
Jerry Tarkanian, UNLV	23	**599**	120	.833
Lefty Driesell, J.Madison	29	**579**	259	.691
Don Haskins, UTEP	30	**578**	256	.693
Lou Henson, Illinois	29	**577**	267	.684
Norm Stewart, Missouri	30	**572**	283	.669
Bob Knight, Indiana	26	**561**	203	.734
Gene Bartow, UAB	29	**554**	292	.655
Glenn Wilkes, Stetson	34	**527**	405	.565
Lou Carnesecca, St.John's	23	**507**	189	.728
Gary Colson, Fresno St.	30	**501**	328	.604
Eldon Miller, No.Iowa	29	**482**	311	.608
Denny Crum, Louisville	20	**477**	172	.735
Hugh Durham, Georgia	25	**465**	256	.645
Eddie Sutton, Okla.St	21	**454**	172	.725

Annual Player Awards

UPI picked the first national Division I Player of the Year in 1955. Since then, The U.S.Basketball Writers Assn.(1959), the Commonwealth Athletic Club of Kentucky's Adolph Rupp Trophy (1961), the Atlanta Tip-Off Club (1969), the National Assn. of Basketball Coaches (1975), and the LA Athletic Club's John Wooden Award (1977) have joined in.

Since 1977, the first year all six awards were given out, the same player has won all of them in the same season seven times: Marques Johnson in 1977, Larry Bird in 1979, Ralph Sampson in both 1982 and '83, Michael Jordan in 1984, David Robinson in 1987 and Lionel Simmons in 1990.

United Press International

Voted on by a panel of UPI college basketball writers and first presented in 1955.
Multiple winners: Oscar Robertson, Ralph Sampson and Bill Walton (3); Lew Alcindor and Jerry Lucas (2).

Year		Year		Year	
1955	Tom Gola, La Salle	1968	Elvin Hayes, Houston	1980	Mark Aguirre, DePaul
1956	Bill Russell, San Francisco	1969	Lew Alcindor, UCLA	1981	Ralph Sampson, Virginia
1957	Chet Forte, Columbia			1982	Ralph Sampson, Virginia
1958	Oscar Robertson, Cincinnati	1970	Pete Maravich, LSU	1983	Ralph Sampson, Virginia
1959	Oscar Robertson, Cincinnati	1971	Austin Carr, Notre Dame	1984	Michael Jordan, N.Carolina
		1972	Bill Walton, UCLA	1985	Chris Mullin, St.John's
1960	Oscar Robertson, Cincinnati	1973	Bill Walton, UCLA	1986	Walter Berry St.John's
1961	Jerry Lucas, Ohio St.	1974	Bill Walton, UCLA	1987	David Robinson, Navy
1962	Jerry Lucas, Ohio St.	1975	David Thompson, N.C.State	1988	Hersey Hawkins, Bradley
1963	Art Heyman, Duke	1976	Scott May, Indiana	1989	Danny Ferry, Duke
1964	Gary Bradds, Ohio St.	1977	Marques Johnson, UCLA		
1965	Bill Bradley, Princeton	1978	Butch Lee, Marquette	1990	Lionel Simmons, La Salle
1966	Cazzie Russell, Michigan	1979	Larry Bird, Indiana St.	1991	Shaquille O'Neal, LSU
1967	Lew Alcindor, UCLA				

U.S. Basketball Writers Association

Voted on by the USBWA and first presented in 1959.
Multiple winners: Ralph Sampson and Bill Walton (3); Lew Alcindor, Jerry Lucas, Oscar Robertson (2).

Year		Year		Year	
1959	Oscar Robertson, Cincinnati	1972	Bill Walton, UCLA	1984	Michael Jordan, N.Carolina
		1973	Bill Walton, UCLA	1985	Chris Mullin, St.John's
1960	Oscar Robertson, Cincinnati	1974	Bill Walton, UCLA	1986	Walter Berry St.John's
1961	Jerry Lucas, Ohio St.	1975	David Thompson, N.C.State	1987	David Robinson, Navy
1962	Jerry Lucas, Ohio St.	1976	Adrian Dantley, Notre Dame	1988	Hersey Hawkins, Bradley
1963	Art Heyman, Duke	1977	Marques Johnson, UCLA	1989	Danny Ferry, Duke
1964	Walt Hazzard, UCLA	1978	Phil Ford, North Carolina		
1965	Bill Bradley, Princeton	1979	Larry Bird, Indiana St.	1990	Lionel Simmons, La Salle
1966	Cazzie Russell, Michigan			1991	Larry Johnson, UNLV
1967	Lew Alcindor, UCLA	1980	Mark Aguirre, DePaul		
1968	Elvin Hayes, Houston	1981	Ralph Sampson, Virginia		
1969	Lew Alcindor, UCLA	1982	Ralph Sampson, Virginia		
		1983	Ralph Sampson, Virginia		
1970	Pete Maravich, LSU				
1971	Sidney Wicks, UCLA				

Rupp Trophy

Voted on by AP sportswriters and broadcasters and first presented in 1961 by the Commonwealth Athletic Club of Kentucky in the name of former Univ.of Kentucky coach Adolph Rupp.
Multiple winners: Ralph Sampson (3); Lew Alcindor, Jerry Lucas, David Thompson and Bill Walton (2).

Year		Year		Year	
1961	Jerry Lucas, Ohio St.	1972	Bill Walton, UCLA	1983	Ralph Sampson, Virginia
1962	Jerry Lucas, Ohio St.	1973	Bill Walton, UCLA	1984	Michael Jordan, N.Carolina
1963	Art Heyman, Duke	1974	David Thompson, N.C.State	1985	Patrick Ewing, Georgetown
1964	Gary Bradds, Ohio St.	1975	David Thompson, N.C.St.	1986	Walter Berry, St.John's
1965	Bill Bradl ey, Princeton	1976	Scott May, Indiana	1987	David Robinson, Navy
1966	Cazzie Russell, Michigan	1977	Marques Johnson, UCLA	1988	Hersey Hawkins, Bradley
1967	Lew Alcindor, UCLA	1978	Butch Lee, Marquette	1989	Sean Elliott, Arizona
1968	Elvin Hayes, Houston	1979	Larry Bird, Indiana St.		
1969	Lew Alcindor, UCLA			1990	Lionel Simmons, La Salle
		1980	Mark Aguirre, DePaul	1991	Shaquille O'Neal, LSU
1970	Pete Maravich, LSU	1981	Ralph Sampson, Virginia		
1971	Austin Carr, Notre Dame	1982	Ralph Sampson, Virginia		

Annual Player Awards (Cont.)

Naismith Award

Voted on by a panel of coaches, sportswriters and broadcasters and first presented in 1969 by the Atlanta Tip-Off Club in 1969 in the name of the inventor of basketball, Dr. James Naismith.

Multiple winners: Ralph Sampson and Bill Walton (3).

Year		Year		Year	
1969	Lew Alcindor, UCLA	1977	Marques Johnson, UCLA	1985	Patrick Ewing, Georgetown
1970	Pete Maravich, LSU	1978	Butch Lee, Marquette	1986	Johnny Dawkins, Duke
1971	Austin Carr, Notre Dame	1979	Larry Bird, Indiana St.	1987	David Robinson, Navy
1972	Bill Walton, UCLA	1980	Mark Aguirre, DePaul	1988	Danny Manning, Kansas
1973	Bill Walton, UCLA	1981	Ralph Sampson, Virginia	1989	Danny Ferry, Duke
1974	Bill Walton, UCLA	1982	Ralph Sampson, Virginia		
1975	David Thompson, N.C.State	1983	Ralph Sampson, Virginia	1990	Lionel Simmons, La Salle
1976	Scott May, Indiana	1984	Michael Jordan, North Carolina	1991	Larry Johnson, UNLV

Eastman Award

Voted on by the National Assn. of Basketball Coaches and first presented by the Eastman Kodak Co. in 1975.

Multiple winner: Ralph Sampson (2).

Year		Year		Year	
1975	David Thompson, N.C.State	1981	Danny Ainge, BYU	1987	David Robinson, Navy
1976	Scott May, Indiana	1982	Ralph Sampson, Virginia	1988	Danny Manning, Kansas
1977	Marques Johnson, UCLA	1983	Ralph Sampson, Virginia	1989	Sean Elliott, Arizona
1978	Phil Ford, North Carolina	1984	Michael Jordan, North Carolina		
1979	Larry Bird, Indiana St.	1985	Patrick Ewing, Georgetown	1990	Lionel Simmons, La Salle
1980	Michael Brooks, La Salle	1986	Walter Berry St.John's	1991	Larry Johnson, UNLV

Wooden Award

Voted on by a panel of coaches, sportswriters and broadcasters and first presented in 1977 by the Los Angeles Athletic Club in the name of former Purdue All-America and UCLA coach John Wooden. Unlike the other five Player of the Year awards, candidates for the Wooden must have a minimum grade point average of 2.00 (out of 4.00).

Multiple winner: Ralph Sampson (2).

Year		Year		Year	
1977	Marques Johnson, UCLA	1982	Ralph Sampson, Virginia	1988	Danny Manning, Kansas
1978	Phil Ford, North Carolina	1983	Ralph Sampson, Virginia	1989	Sean Elliott, Arizona
1979	Larry Bird, Indiana St.	1984	Michael Jordan, North Carolina		
1980	Darrell Griffith, Louisville	1985	Chris Mullin, St.John's	1990	Lionel Simmons, La Salle
1981	Danny Ainge, BYU	1986	Walter Berry St.John's	1991	Larry Johnson, UNLV
		1987	David Robinson, Navy		

Iba Defensive Player Award

Officially, the Henry Iba Corinthian Award and given to the outstanding defensive player in the nation. Voted on by the National Association of Basketball Coaches and first presented in 1987 by the Rotary Club of River Oakes in Houston in the name of former Oklahoma State and US Olympic coach Hank Iba.

Multiple winner: Stacey Augmon (3).

Year		Year		Year	
1987	Tommy Amaker, Duke	1989	Stacey Augmon, UNLV	1991	Stacey Augmon, UNLV
1988	Billy King, Duke	1990	Stacey Augmon, UNLV		

Annual Coaching Awards

UPI picked the first national Division I Coach of the Year in 1955. Since then, The U.S.Basketball Writers Assn. (1959), AP (1967), the National Assn. of Basketball Coaches (1969), and the Atlanta Tip-Off Club (1987) have joined in. Since 1987, the first year all five awards were given out, no coach has won all of them in the same season.

United Press International

Voted on by a panel of UPI college basketball writers and first presented in 1955.

Multiple winners: John Wooden (6); Bob Knight, Ray Meyer, Adolph Rupp, Fred Taylor and Phil Woopert (2).

Year		Year		Year	
1955	Phil Woolpert, San Francisco	1958	Tex Winter, Kansas St.	1961	Fred Taylor, Ohio St.
1956	Phil Woolpert, San Francisco	1959	Adolph Rupp, Kentucky	1962	Fred Taylor, Ohio St.
1957	Frank McGuire, North Carolina	1960	Pete Newell, California	1963	Ed Jucker, Cincinnati

Year		Year		Year	
1964	John Wooden, UCLA	1974	Digger Phelps, Notre Dame	1983	Jerry Tarkanian, UNLV
1965	Dave Strack, Michigan	1975	Bobby Knight, Indiana	1984	Ray Meyer, DePaul
1966	Adolph Rupp, Kentucky	1976	Tom Young, Rutgers	1985	Lou Carnesecca, St.John's
1967	John Wooden, UCLA	1977	Bob Gaillard, San Francisco	1986	Mike Krzyzewski, Duke
1968	Guy Lewis, Houston	1978	Eddie Sutton, Arkansas	1987	John Thompson, Georgetown
1969	John Wooden, UCLA	1979	Bill Hodges, Indiana St.	1988	John Chaney, Temple
1970	John Wooden, UCLA			1989	Bob Knight, Indiana
1971	Al McGuire, Marquette	1980	Ray Meyer, DePaul		
1972	John Wooden, UCLA	1981	Ralph Miller, Oregon St.	1990	Jim Calhoun, Connecticut
1973	John Wooden, UCLA	1982	Norm Stewart, Missouri	1991	Rick Majerus, Utah

U.S. Basketball Writers Association

Voted on by the USBWA and first presented in 1959.
Multiple winners: John Wooden (5); Bob Knight (3); Lou Carnesecca, John Chaney and Ray Meyer (2).

Year		Year		Year	
1959	Eddie Hickey, Marquette	1970	John Wooden, UCLA	1981	Ralph Miller, Oregon St.
		1971	Al McGuire, Marquette	1982	John Thompson, Georgetown
1960	Pete Newell, California	1972	John Wooden, UCLA	1983	Lou Carnesecca, St. John's
1961	Fred Taylor, Ohio St.	1973	John Wooden, UCLA	1984	Gene Keady, Purdue
1962	Fred Taylor, Ohio St.	1974	Norm Sloan, N.C.State	1985	Lou Carnesecca, St. John's
1963	Ed Jucker, Cincinnati	1975	Bobby Knight, Indiana	1986	Dick Versace, Bradley
1964	John Wooden, UCLA	1976	Bobby Knight, Indiana	1987	John Chaney, Temple
1965	B.van Breda Kolff, Princeton	1977	Eddie Sutton, Arkansas	1988	John Chaney, Temple
1966	Adolph Rupp, Kentucky	1978	Ray Meyer, DePaul	1989	Bob Knight, Indiana
1967	John Wooden, UCLA	1979	Dean Smith, North Carolina		
1968	Guy Lewis, Houston			1990	Roy Williams, Kansas
1969	Maury John, Drake	1980	Ray Meyer, DePaul	1991	Randy Ayers, Ohio St.

Associated Press

Voted on by AP sportswriters and broadcasters and first presented in 1967.
Multiple winners: John Wooden (5); Bob Knight (3); Guy Lewis, Ray Meyer, Ralph Miller and Eddie Sutton (2).

Year		Year		Year	
1967	John Wooden, UCLA	1976	Bobby Knight, Indiana	1984	Ray Meyer, DePaul
1968	Guy Lewis, Houston	1977	Bob Gailliard, San Francisco	1985	Bill Frieder, Michigan
1969	John Wooden, UCLA	1978	Eddie Sutton, Arkansas	1986	Eddie Sutton, Kentucky
		1979	Bill Hodges, Indiana St.	1987	Tom Davis, Iowa
1970	John Wooden, UCLA			1988	John Chaney, Temple
1971	Al McGuire, Marquette	1980	Ray Meyer, DePaul	1989	Bob Knight, Indiana
1972	John Wooden, UCLA	1981	Ralph Miller, Oregon St.		
1973	John Wooden, UCLA	1982	Ralph Miller, Oregon St.	1990	Jim Calhoun, Connecticut
1974	Norm Sloan, N.C.State	1983	Guy Lewis, Houston	1991	Randy Ayers, Ohio St.
1975	Bobby Knight, Indiana				

National Association of Basketball Coaches

Voted on by NABC and first presented in 1969.
Multiple winner: John Wooden (3).

Year		Year		Year	
1969	John Wooden, UCLA	1978	Bill Foster, Duke & Abe Lemons, Texas	1984	Marv Harshman, Washington
1970	John Wooden, UCLA	1979	Ray Meyer, DePaul	1985	John Thompson, Georgetown
1971	Jack Kraft, Villanova			1986	Eddie Sutton, Kentucky
1972	John Wooden, UCLA	1980	Lute Olson, Iowa	1987	Rick Pitino, Providence
1973	Gene Bartow, Memphis St.	1981	Ralph Miller, Oregon St. & Jack Hartman, Kansas St.	1988	John Chaney, Temple
1974	Al McGuire, Marquette			1989	P.J.Carlesimo, Seton Hall
1975	Bobby Knight, Indiana	1982	Don Monson, Idaho		
1976	Johnny Orr, Michigan	1983	Lou Carnesecca, St.John's	1990	Jud Heathcote, Michigan St.
1977	Dean Smith, North Carolina			1991	Mike Krzyzewski, Duke

Naismith Award

Voted on by a panel of coaches, sportswriters and broadcasters and first presented in 1969 by the Atlanta Tip-Off Club in 1969 in the name of the inventor of basketball, Dr.James Naismith.
Multiple winners: Ralph Sampson and Bill Walton (2).

Year		Year		Year	
1987	Bob Knight, Indiana	1989	Mike Krzyzewski, Duke	1990	Bobby Cremins, Georgia Tech.
1988	Larry Brown, Kansas			1991	Randy Ayers, Ohio St.

Other Men's Champions

NCAA Div. II Finals

Year	Winner	Score	Loser
1957	Wheaton,IL	89-65	Ky.Wesleyan
1958	South Dakota	75-53	St.Michaels,VT
1959	Evansville,IN	83-67	SW Missouri St.
1960	Evansville,IN	90-69	Chapman,CA
1961	Wittenberg,OH	42-38	SE Missouri St.
1962	Mt.St.Mary's, MD	58-57*	CS-Sacramento
1963	South Dakota St.	42-40	Wittenberg,OH
1964	Evansville,IN	72-59	Akron,OH
1965	Evansville,IN	85-82*	Southern Illinois
1966	Ky.Wesleyan	54-51	Southern Illinois
1967	Winston-Salem,NC	77-74	SW Missouri St.
1968	Ky.Wesleyan	63-52	Indiana St.
1969	Ky.Wesleyan	75-71	SW Missouri St.
1970	Phila.Textile	76-65	Tennessee St.
1971	Evansville,IN	97-82	Old Dominion,VA
1972	Roanoke,VA	84-72	Akron,OH
1973	Ky.Wesleyan	78-76*	Tennessee St.
1974	Morgan St.,MD	67-52	SW Missouri St.
1975	Old Dominion,VA	76-74	New Orleans,LA
1976	Puget Sound, WA	83-74	Tennessee-Chatt.
1977	Tennessee-Chatt.	71-62	Randolph-Macon
1978	Cheyney,PA	47-40	WI-Green Bay
1979	North Alabama	64-50	WI-Green Bay
1980	Virginia Union	80-74	New York Tech
1981	Florida Southern	73-68	Mt.St.Mary's,MD
1982	Dist.of Columbia	73-63	Florida Southern
1983	Wright St.,OH	92-73	Dist.of Columbia
1984	Central Mo.St.	81-77	St.Augustine's,NC
1985	Jacksonville St.	74-73	South Dakota St.
1986	Sacred Heart,CT	93-87	SE Missouri St.
1987	Ky.Wesleyan	92-74	Gannon,PA
1988	Lowell,MA	75-72	AK-Anchorage
1989	N.C.Central	73-46	SE Missouri St.
1990	Ky.Wesleyan	93-79	CS-Bakersfield
1991	North Alabama	79-72	Bridgeport, CT

*Overtime

NCAA Div. III Finals

Year	Winner	Score	Loser
1975	LeMoyne-Owen,TN	57-54	Glassboro St.,NJ
1976	Scranton,PA	60-57	Wittenberg,OH
1977	Wittenberg,OH	79-66	Oneonta St.,NY
1978	North Park,IL	69-57	Widener,PA
1979	North Park,IL	66-62	Potsdam St.,NY
1980	North Park,IL	83-76	Upsala,NJ
1981	Potsdam St.,NY	67-65*	Augustana,IL
1982	Wabash,IN	83-62	Potsdam St.,NY
1983	Scranton,PA	64-63	Wittenberg,OH
1984	WI-Whitewater	103-86	Clark,MA
1985	North Park,IL	72-71	Potsdam St.,NY
1986	Potsdam St.,NY	76-73	LeMoyne-Owen,TN
1987	North Park,IL	106-100	Clark,MA
1988	Ohio Wesleyan	92-70	Scranton,PA
1989	WI-Whitewater	94-86	Trenton St.,NJ
1990	Rochester, NY	43-42	DePauw, IN
1991	WI-Platteville	81-74	Franklin Marshall

*Overtime

NAIA Finals

NAIA tournament held in Kansas City at Municipal Auditorium (1937-74) and Kemper Arena (since 1975).

Year	Winner	Score	Loser
1937	Central Missouri	35-24	Morningside,IA
1938	Central Missouri	45-30	Roanoke,VA
1939	Southwestern,KS	32-31	San Diego St.
1940	Tarkio,MO	52-31	San Diego St.
1941	San Diego St.	36-32	Murray St.,KY
1942	Hamline,MN	33-31	S'eastern Okla.
1943	SE Missouri St.	34-32	NW Missouri St.
1944	Not held		
1945	Loyola-LA	49-36	Pepperdine,CA
1946	Southern Illinois	49-40	Indiana St.
1947	Marshall,WV	73-59	Mankato St.,MN
1948	Louisville,KY	82-70	Indiana St.
1949	Hamline,MN	57-46	Regis,CO
1950	Indiana St.	61-47	East Central,OK
1951	Hamline,MN	69-61	Millikin,IL
1952	SW Missouri St.	73-64	Murray St.,KY
1953	SW Missouri St.	79-71	Hamline,MN
1954	St.Benedict's,KS	62-56	Western Illinois
1955	East Texas St.	71-54	S'eastern Okla.
1956	McNeese St.,LA	60-55	Texas Southern
1957	Tennessee St.	92-73	S'eastern Okla.
1958	Tennessee St.	85-73	Western Illinois
1959	Tennessee St.	97-87	Pacific-Luth., WA
1960	SW Texas St.	66-44	Westminster,PA
1961	Grambling,LA	95-75	Georgetown,KY
1962	Prairie View,TX	62-53	Westminster,PA
1963	Pan American,TX	73-62	Western Carolina
1964	Rockhurst,MO	66-56	Pan American,TX
1965	Central St.,OH	85-51	Oklahoma Baptist
1966	Oklahoma Baptist	88-59	Georgia Southern
1967	St.Benedict's,KS	71-65	Oklahoma Baptist
1968	Central St.,OH	51-48	Fairmont St.,WV
1969	Eastern New Mexico	99-76	MD-Eastern Shore
1970	Kentucky St.	79-71	Central Wash.
1971	Kentucky St.	102-82	Eastern Michigan
1972	Kentucky St.	71-62	WI-Eau Claire
1973	Guilford,NC	99-96	MD-Eastern Shore
1974	West Georgia	97-79	Alcorn St.,MS
1975	Grand Canyon,AZ	65-54	M'western St.,TX
1976	Coppin St.,MD	96-91	Henderson St.,AR
1977	Texas Southern	71-44	Campbell,NC
1978	Grand Canyon,AZ	79-75	Kearney St.,NE
1979	Drury,MO	60-54	Henderson St.,AR
1980	Cameron,OK	84-77	Alabama St.
1981	Beth.Nazarene,OK	86-85*	AL-Huntsville
1982	SC-Spartanburg	51-38	Biola,CA
1983	Charleston,SC	57-53	WV-Wesleyan
1984	Fort Hays St.,KS	48-46*	WI-Stevens Pt.
1985	Fort Hays St.,KS	82-80*	Wayland Bapt.,TX
1986	David Lipscomb,TN	67-54	AR-Monticello
1987	Washburn,KS	79-77	West Virginia St.
1988	Grand Canyon,AZ	88-86*	Auburn-Montg,AL
1989	St.Mary's,TX	61-58	East Central,OK
1990	Birm-Southern,AL	88-80	WI-Eau Claire
1991	Oklahoma City	77-74	Central Ark.

*Overtime

NCAA Women's Final Four

Replaced the Association of Intercollegiate Athletics for Women (AIAW) tournament in 1982 as the official playoff for the national championship; (*) indicates overtime.

Multiple winners: Tennessee (3); Louisiana Tech and USC (2)

Year	Champion	Head Coach	Score	Runner-up	Third Place	
1982	Louisiana Tech	Sonya Hogg	76-62	Cheyney	Maryland	Tennessee
1983	USC	Linda Sharp	69-67	Louisiana Tech	Georgia	Old Dominion
1984	USC	Linda Sharp	72-61	Tennessee	Cheyney	Louisiana Tech
1985	Old Dominion	Marianne Stanley	70-65	Georgia	NE Louisiana	Western Ky.
1986	Texas	Jody Conradt	97-81	USC	Tennessee	Western Ky.
1987	Tennessee	Pat Summitt	67-44	Louisiana Tech	Long Beach St.	Texas
1988	Louisiana Tech	Leon Barmore	56-54	Auburn	Long Beach St.	Tennessee
1989	Tennessee	Pat Summitt	76-60	Auburn	Louisiana Tech	Maryland
1990	Stanford	Tara VanDerveer	88-81	Auburn	Louisiana Tech	Virginia
1991	Tennessee	Pat Summitt	70-67*	Virginia	Connecticut	Stanford

Most Outstanding Player

A Most Outstanding Player has been selected every year of the NCAA tournament. Winners who did not play for the tournament champion are listed in **bold** type.

Multiple winner: Cheryl Miller (2).

Year		Year		Year	
1982	Janice Lawrence, La.Tech	1986	Clarissa Davis, Texas	1990	Jennifer Azzi, Stanford
1983	Cheryl Miller, USC	1987	Tonya Edwards, Tennessee	1991	**Dawn Staley**, Virginia
1984	Cheryl Miller, USC	1988	Erica Westbrooks, La.Tech		
1985	Tracy Claxton, Old Dominion	1989	Bridgette Gordon, Tennessee		

All-Time Winningest Division I Teams

Top 10 Winning Percentage

		Yrs	W	L	T	Pct
1	Louisiana Tech	17	478	82	0	.854
2	Texas	17	498	90	0	.847
3	Tennessee	17	442	118	0	.789
4	Long Beach St	29	534	144	0	.788
5	N.C.State	17	378	128	0	.747
	Rutgers	17	363	123	0	.747
7	Auburn	20	401	142	0	.738
8	Mississippi	17	390	141	0	.734
9	Tennessee Tech	21	476	176	0	.730
	S.F. Austin St	19	438	162	0	.730

Top 10 Victories

		Yrs	W	L	T	Pct
1	Long Beach St	29	534	144	0	.788
2	James Madison	69	506	268	5	.653
3	Texas	17	498	90	0	.847
4	Louisiana Tech	17	478	82	0	.854
5	Tennessee Tech	21	476	176	0	.730
6	Kansas St	23	447	220	0	.670
7	Tennessee	17	442	118	0	.789
8	S.F.Austin St	19	438	162	0	.730
9	Ohio St	26	436	163	0	.728
	Old Dominion	22	436	174	0	.715

Annual Awards

The Broderick Award was first given out to the Women's Division I or Large School Player of the Year in 1977. Since then, the National Assn. for Girls and Women in Sports (1978), the Women's Basketball Coaches Assn. (1983) and the Atlanta Tip-Off Club (1983) have joined in.

Since 1983, the first year all four awards were given out, the same player has won all of them in the same season once: Cheryl Miller of USC in 1985.

Broderick Award

Voted on by a national panel of women's collegiate athletic directors and first presented by the late Thomas Broderick, an athletic outfitter, in 1976. Honda has presented the award since 1987. Basketball Player of the Year is one of 10 nominated for Collegiate Woman Athlete of the Year; (*) indicates player also won Athlete of the Year.

Multiple winners: Nancy Lieberman and Cheryl Miller (2).

Year		Year		Year	
1977	Lucy Harris, Delta St.*	1982	Pam Kelly, La.Tech.	1988	Teresa Weatherspoon, La.Tech*
1978	Anne Meyers, UCLA*	1983	Anne Donovan, Old Dominion	1989	Bridgette Gordon, Tennessee
1979	Nancy Lieberman, Old Dominion*	1984	Cheryl Miller, USC*	1990	Jennifer Azzi, Stanford
1980	Nancy Lieberman, Old Dominion*	1985	Cheryl Miller, USC	1991	TBA in Fall
1981	Lynette Woodward, Kansas	1986	Kamie Ethridge, Texas*		
		1987	Katrina McClain, Georgia		

Wade Trophy

Voted on by the National Assn. for Girls and Women in Sports (NAGWS) and first presented in 1978 in the name of former Delta St. coach Margaret Wade.

Multiple winner: Nancy Lieberman (2).

Year		Year		Year	
1978	Carol Blazejowski, Montclair St.	1983	LaTaunya Pollard, L.Beach St.	1988	Teresa Weatherspoon, La.Tech.
1979	Nancy Lieberman, Old Dominion	1984	Janice Lawrence, La.Tech.	1989	Clarissa Davis, Texas
1980	Nancy Lieberman, Old Dominion	1985	Cheryl Miller, USC	1990	Jennifer Azzi, Stanford
1981	Lynette Woodward, Kansas	1986	Kamie Ethridge, Texas	1991	Daedra Charles, Tennessee
1982	Pam Kelly, La.Tech.	1987	Shelly Pennefather, Villanova		

Naismith Trophy

Voted on by a panel of coaches, sportwriters and broadcasters and first presented in 1983 by the Atlanta Tip-Off Club in the name of the inventor of basketball, Dr. James Naismith.

Multiple winners: Cheryl Miller (3); Clarissa Davis (2).

Year		Year		Year	
1983	Anne Donovan, Old Dominion	1986	Cheryl Miller, USC	1989	Clarissa Davis, Texas
1984	Cheryl Miller, USC	1987	Clarissa Davis, Texas	1990	Jennifer Azzi, Stanford
1985	Cheryl Miller, USC	1988	Sue Wicks, Rutgers	1991	Dawn Staley, Virginia

Women's Basketball Coaches Association

Voted on by the WBCA and first presented by Champion athletic outfitters in 1983.

Multiple winner: Cheryl Miller (2).

Year		Year		Year	
1983	Anne Donovan, Old Dominion	1986	Cheryl Miller, USC	1989	Clarissa Davis, Texas
1984	Janice Lawrence, La.Tech.	1987	Katrina McClain, Georgia	1990	Venus Lacey, La.Tech
1985	Cheryl Miller, USC	1988	Michelle Edwards, Iowa	1991	Dawn Staley, Virgina

Coach of the Year Award

Voted on by the Women's Basketball Coaches Assn. and first presented by Converse athletic outfitters in 1983.

Multiple winner: Jody Conradt (2).

Year		Year		Year	
1983	Pat Summitt, Tennessee	1986	Jody Conradt, Texas	1989	Tara VanDerveer, Stanford
1984	Jody Conradt, Texas	1987	Theresa Grentz, Rutgers	1990	Kay Yow, N.C.State
1985	Jim Foster, St. Joseph's-PA	1988	Vivian Stringer, Iowa	1991	Rene Portland, Penn St.

Other Women's Champions

AIAW Finals

The Association of Intercollegiate Athletics for Women Large College tournament determined the women's national champion for 10 years until supplanted by the NCAA. In 1982, most Division I teams entered the first NCAA tournament rather than the last one staged by the AIAW.

Year	Winner	Score	Loser
1972	Immaculata,PA	52-48	West Chester,PA
1973	Immaculata,PA	59-52	Queens College,NY
1974	Immaculata,PA	68-53	Mississippi College
1975	Delta St.,MS	90-81	Immaculata,PA
1976	Delta St.,MS	69-64	Immaculata,PA
1977	Delta St.,MS	68-55	LSU
1978	UCLA	90-74	Maryland
1979	Old Dominion	75-65	Louisiana Tech
1980	Old Dominion	68-53	Tennessee
1981	Louisiana Tech	79-59	Tennessee
1982	Rutgers	83-77	Texas

NCAA Div. III Finals

Division III Finals held in Elizabethtown,PA (1982); Worcester,MA (1983); Scranton,PA (1984,87); De-Pere,WI (1985); Salem,MA (1986); Moorhead,MN (1988); Danville,KY (1989); Holland,MI (1990); St. Paul, MN (1991).

Year	Winner	Score	Loser
1982	Elizabethtown,PA	67-66*	NC-Greensboro
1983	North Central,IL	83-71	Elizabethtown,PA
1984	Rust College,MS	51-49	Elizabethtown,PA
1985	Scranton,PA	68-59	New Rochelle,NY
1986	Salem St.,MA	89-85	Bishop,TX
1987	WI-Stevens Pt.	81-74	Concordia,MN
1988	Concordia,MN	65-57	St.John Fisher,NY
1989	Elizabethtown,PA	66-65	CS-Stanislaus
1990	Hope	65-63	St. John Fisher
1991	Muskingum, OH	73-55	St. Thomas, MN

*Overtime

Note: Concordia,MN is Concordia College in Moorhead,MN, not Concordia College in St.Paul,MN.

NCAA Div. II Finals

Division II Finals held in Springfield,MA (1982-87); Fargo,ND (1988); Cleveland,MS (1989); Pomona,CA (1990); Cape Girardeau, MO (1991).

Year	Winner	Score	Loser
1982	Cal Poly Pomona	93-74	Tuskegee,AL
1983	Virginia Union	73-60	Cal Poly Pomona
1984	Central Mo.St.	80-73	Virginia Union
1985	Cal Poly Pomona	80-69	Central Mo.St.
1986	Cal Poly Pomona	70-63	North Dakota St.
1987	New Haven,CT	77-75	Cal Poly Pomona
1988	Hampton,VA	65-48	West Texas St.
1989	Delta St.,MS	88-58	Cal Poly Pomona
1990	Delta St.,MS	77-43	Bentley,MA
1991	North Dakota St.	81-74	SE Missouri St.

NAIA Finals

NAIA tournament held in Kansas City,MO (1981- 83, and since 1987); and Cedar Rapids,IA (1984-86).

Year	Winner	Score	Loser
1981	Kentucky St.	73-67	Texas Southern
1982	S'western Okla.	80-45	Mo.Southern
1983	S'western Okla.	80-68	AL-Huntsville
1984	NC-Asheville	72-70*	Portland,OR
1985	S'western Okla.	55-54	Saginaw Val.,MI
1986	Francis Marion,SC	75-65	Wayland Bapt.,TX
1987	S'western Okla.	60-58	North Georgia
1988	Oklahoma City	113-95	Claflin,SC
1989	So.Nazarene	98-96	Claflin,SC
1990	SW Oklahoma	82-75	AR-Monticello
1991	Ft. Hays St., KS	57-53	SW Oklahoma

*Overtime

An emotional **Michael Jordan** clutches the NBA championship trophy after leading Chicago to a 5-game win over the L.A. Lakers in the Finals.

PRO BASKETBALL

Raging Bulls

No longer a one-man cattle drive, Chicago stampedes NBA playoffs and Michael Jordan proves a point.

Now that Michael Jordan has finally earned an NBA championship ring, here's a number to ponder: 55. That's the number of teammates he's had during his glittering career with the Chicago Bulls.

As great a talent as Michael is, he could not bring a title to Chicago without help. Any championship team in any sport involves a delicate balance of ability, personality, work habits and maybe even a little luck here and there.

The reason Chicago won the NBA title—and eliminated any possibility that Jordan would be remembered as the Ernie Banks of basketball—was that general manager Jerry Krause found, after six seasons on the job, the proper blend of players (not to mention the appropriate coach) to play with, off and around the most gifted individual ever to put on a basketball uniform.

Krause had to sift through the talent pile to find the right teammates for his virtuoso superstar. This is not as easy as you might think.

"We are," contends Krause, "the first NBA championship team ever built around a '2 guard.'" (In NBA parlance, a 2 guard is the shooting guard, or off guard, as opposed to the point guard, lead guard or 1 guard.)

The Bulls won a franchise record 61 games during the regular season. "We're just trying to mosey along," said Jordan as the playoffs approached. "From here on, we control our own destiny. I feel real good going toward the playoffs."

More prophetic words were never spoken. The Bulls swept the Knicks in three; took out the 76ers in five; embarrassed the two-time champion Pistons in four; and then won the NBA Finals by swatting the Lakers in five—winning four straight after losing the opener at home. That adds up to a 15-2 record, and that represents one of the great playoff blitzes of all time.

Jordan, of course, was the Finals' Most Valuable Player, averaging 31.2 points and 11.4 assists a game against L.A. For the 17 games of the playoffs, he averaged 31.1 points and 6.4 assists, while shooting .524 from the floor. He also won his second MVP award for his regular season exploits, which included leading the league in scoring for the fifth season in a row. His mantelpiece will soon be sagging under the weight of the accumulated hardware that dates back to his Rookie of the Year award in 1984-85.

But the trophies weren't as important to Jordan as shaking the label of a one-man show who couldn't win it all. "Now they

---

Bob Ryan is a columnist for *The Boston Globe* and has covered the NBA for 17 years. He is also a regular on ESPN's "Sports Reporters."

Andrew D. Bernstein/NBA Photos

Magic Johnson (left), who had squared off against Julius Erving, Larry Bird and Isiah Thomas in previous championship rounds, added **Michael Jordan** to his all-Final dance card in June.

can't say I'm not a winner," he proclaimed.

The Lakers' Magic Johnson, who has played on five NBA championship teams and shared marquee billing in the Finals with Julius Erving, Larry Bird, Isiah Thomas and Jordan, agreed.

"When I went to congratulate him after the game I could see tears in his eyes," said Magic. "You heard so much talk about Michael as an individual player, but he's proven everyone wrong. It's gonna taste sweet for him for a long time."

There isn't much more you can say about Jordan, except that now he joins Quinn Buckner, K.C. Jones, Clyde Lovellette, Jerry Lucas and Bill Russell as the only players to win NCAA, Olympic and NBA championships.

But NBA insiders realize that what made Chicago special as a team was its defense. The Bulls, after all, held their playoff foes under 100 points 14 times. Whereas Detroit favored a World War I in-the-trenches style of defense, Bulls' coach Phil Jackson advocated an attacking mode, featuring Jordan and the destructive Scotty Pippen, a 6-7 forward whose long arms and great foot speed enable him to cover an extraordinary amount of ground.

The Lakers, who blew through Houston (3-0), Golden State (4-1) and Portland (4-2) in the first three rounds, were handicapped by an injured James Worthy (sprained ankle) and an unproductive bench in the Finals. Still, by any measure, they enjoyed a surprisingly pleasant season under first-year coach Mike Dunleavy. A 1-4 start had their antsy fans concerned that their heroes had gotten old overnight, but with Magic enjoying another great season—he averaged 12.5 assists a game and, on Apr. 15, passed Oscar Robertson as the NBA's all-time assist leader with No. 9,888—L.A. won 58 games. It was a record-breaking 12th consecutive season of 50 wins or more and marked the Lakers' 15th straight year in the playoffs.

While L.A. did not disappoint, Portland did. The Trail Blazers won a league-high 63 games and ended the Lakers' nine-year reign in the Pacific Division, but were unable to return to the Finals.

Portland stormed to a 12-1 record in November, emerged from January with a 37-8 log, then finished the season by winning 16 of their last 17 games. Beaten by Detroit in the 1990 Finals, the Blazers appeared to have patched their only hole by adding veteran Danny Ainge as a sixth man. A deep bench and exceptional team balance carried coach Rick Adelman's club in the playoffs, but in the opening round they got into immediate trouble when eighth-seeded Seattle extended them to five games.

Portland needed only five games to dispose of Utah in the best-of-seven second round, but the wheels fell off in the opening game of the Western Conference finals when they blew a 12-point third period lead and lost to the Lakers at home. The Blazers came back to win Game 2, but L.A. won three of the next four to take the series in six.

"I like this team," said Adelman. "And I want to see if we can improve it. We can be better next season just by playing together another year." Perhaps. But the faithful Portland fans had been led to believe *this* was going to be their year, and they may judge this team a bit more harshly in 1991-92.

The same might be said about the Phoenix Suns, who showed such promise knocking the Lakers out of the 1990 playoffs. A year later, they won 55 games and were eliminated by Utah in the opening round. The Suns made a major trade on Dec. 7, sending veteran swingman Eddie Johnson to Seattle for forward Xavier McDaniel. By season's end the word was out: you can have the X-man for the right deal. But he wasn't the only problem. Spectacular point guard Kevin Johnson started off the season hurt and All-Star forward Tom Chambers was severely hampered by back problems.

The Golden State Warriors stayed in character as the league's most intriguing team. Coach Don Nelson's offense consisted of three men: forward Chris Mullin and guards Mitch Richmond and Tim Hardaway (see box). So prolific was this trio—they averaged 76.5 points a game between them in February and 71.1 for the season—that the San Francisco Examiner held a contest to give them a nickname. The winner was "Run TMC." Among the more printable losers was

Guards Are New Centers Of NBA Attention

For years and years, NBA conventional wisdom clasped one inviolable tenet to its breast: in order to prevail in this greatest of all basketball leagues, you must have a great center.

It didn't matter if it was Mikan or Russell or Chamberlain or Abdul-Jabbar, you had to be strong in the middle.

Not any more. Now the thinking is that you can work around the problem. If you don't have a great center, it doesn't matter, not as long as you have a great point guard.

Point guard. Lead guard. One guard. Those are the new kingmakers in the NBA.

Consider that in the 1991 Finals all the marquee centers were home watching on TV. David Robinson, Hakeem Olajuwon, Patrick Ewing, Robert Parish, Brad Daugherty and Kevin Duckworth weren't playing, and neither were Bill Laimbeer, Moses Malone, Jack Sikma or assorted other Blasts From the Recent Past. There, in front of 40 million people, were Bill Cartwright and Vlade Divac.

The Bulls were able to win their first championship because Michael Jordan is a combination guard, forward and all-purpose Mr. Fixit who defies categorization. The Lakers got to the Finals because, among other reasons, Magic Johnson is the league's quintessential floor leader. Neither team got there because of phenomenal pivot play.

In fact, the 6-foot-9 Johnson may have started this whole movement away from the pivot in the 1980 Finals when he filled in at center for an injured Abdul-Jabbar in Game 6 and got 42 points, 15 rebounds and seven assists against Philadelphia to clinch the title and the MVP award.

Now, point guards are the rage. Aside from Jordan, the most electrifying player in the entire playoffs was 5-11 Tim Hardaway of Golden State. This kid went wherever he wanted to on the floor and no one could stop him. As a result, teams are scouring the land for more Hardaways, just as they were searching a few years ago for more Isiah Thomases, John Stocktons and Kevin Johnsons.

Point guards can control a game. They can determine whether the ball will be pushed

Andrew D. Bernstein/NBA Photos

Quick, savvy point guards, like Golden State's **Tim Hardaway**, are now the dominant players in the NBA.

quickly up the floor for what coaches like to call "early offense" or walked up court to milk the 24-second clock. Once in the half-court, a savvy point guard can break down the defense by advancing into the lane and forcing defensive players to make decisions.

The great Bob Cousy, who led the NBA in assists eight seasons with the Boston Celtics and is considered by basketball historians to be the preeminent playmaker of his time, has his own definition of what makes a true point guard.

"If," says the Cooz, "the guy comes across halfcourt and thinks about passing first and shooting second, then he's a real point guard. If he thinks about shooting first and passing second, he isn't."

Magic Johnson, who passed Oscar Robertson in 1991 to become the NBA's all-time career assist leader with 9,921, fulfills Cousy's vision of a point guard more than anyone. He has always understood that his first duty on offense is to involve as many teammates as he can in the action.

It has never been his quest to score 50 points in a game or average 30 over a season. He seldom scores 40 (his all-time game high is 46) and it's a big night when he hits 25. But if the situation calls for it, he can score. In 1989-90, the first year of the Lakers' post-Kareem era, the team circumstance was such that it was imperative Johnson take on more of the scoring load. So he increased his average to a career-high 22.5 points a game and walked off with another Most Valuable Player award. In this, as in most point guard matters, Magic remains the model for all to follow.

Many coaches ask their point guards to be their direct personal representative on the floor. When Maurice Cheeks was in his heyday as a 76er playing for Billy Cunningham, he was regarded by insiders as the perfect floor leader. "Maurice," marveled then Laker assistant Dave Wohl, "is plugged into Billy's neurons." Such a close relationship can get pretty testy as a player feels enormous pressure to please the boss.

If a point guard's personality is strong enough, the team almost automatically becomes his. Golden State's Chris Mullin, for example, says this of Hardaway: "When he's on the floor, we never feel like we're down. We never feel like we're out of it."

After seeing Hardaway play as a rookie in 1989-90, Golden State coach Don Nelson declared, "I've never had a point guard like this before, and I don't want to be without one ever again." This year, Nelson added, "There isn't anything I don't like about Tim. You sell your soul to get a player like him."

Or you do the next best thing and find your own. Minnesota has high praise for Pooh Richardson. Miami likes Sherman Douglas. Boston is ecstatic about Dee Brown. Indiana couldn't be happier with Michael Williams. The league is well-stocked with exciting young point guards who can run, shoot and pass. No team wants to be caught without one.

It's no longer a matter of throwing the ball into the pivot and cutting off him. Offenses rely more on two-man games and passing offenses that showcase the talent and judgment of clever guards. A great center isn't exactly a hindrance, but he's no longer a necessity.

"The Bloodthirsty Gymrats from Hell."

With Nelson frequently employing a lineup with no one over 6-feet-6, the Warriors jolted favored San Antonio in the first round of the playoffs, before running afoul of the Lakers.

San Antonio (55-27) and Utah (54-28) battled down to the final game of the season for the Midwest Division pennant. The Spurs were led by the magnificent David Robinson, who sailed through his second season scoring 25 points a game, leading the league in rebounding and blocking 320 shots. He was also the runaway choice as the center on the All-NBA team. Once again, the Jazz went as far as Karl Malone and John Stockton could carry them. Stockton set a new single season assist record (1,164) on the way to leading the league for the third straight year, while Malone was runner-up to Jordan in scoring for the third year in a row.

The most interesting stories in the Midwest Division, however, were in Houston and Denver.

In Houston, the Rockets lost the services of All-Star center Hakeem Olajuwon for two months on Jan.3, when a stray elbow belonging to Chicago's Bill Cartwright caught Olajuwon in the face and fractured his right eye socket. Don Chaney subsequently earned Coach of the Year honors by adjusting his lineup and coaxing superior efforts from forward Otis Thorpe (the NBA's current consecutive game leader with 460), guard Kenny Smith and rebounder *extraordinaire* Larry Smith. The Rockets went 15-10 in Olajuwon's absence and finished the season at 52-30. By the way, Olajuwon, who had answered to "Akeem" since arriving in the U.S. from Nigeria 10 years ago, added the "H" in March. Hakeem means wise man and doctor in Arabic.

In Denver, nobody seemed to know what new coach Paul Westhead meant by installing his revolutionary hurry-up offense. Nuggets' fans could only look on in horror as their once-proud heroes fell into complete disarray and ended the season with a league-low 20 wins. How bad did it go? In one exhibition game the Atlanta Hawks scored 194 points, prompting Dominique Wilkins to say, "I ran out of dunks by halftime." Once the season started, Phoenix ran up a 107-67 halftime lead in one game and Orlando guard Scott Skiles set a single game assist record of 30 in another.

Westhead, the former Mad Professor of Loyola-Marymount, had to flunk himself on defense as Denver gave up an NBA-record 130.8 points per game. But the Nuggets appeared to have learned their lesson by the NBA Draft. They traded high scorer Michael Adams to Washington for the No.8 pick, then, combining that with their No.4 selection, chose two defensive specialists—Georgetown center Dikembe Mutombo and Temple guard Mark Macon.

The top pick of the June draft was forward and college Player of the Year Larry Johnson of UNLV, who went to lottery winner Charlotte. Since the Hornets led the NBA in attendance with 23,906 a game, Johnson doesn't have to worry about saving the franchise—just getting it out of the cellar. Since joining the league three years ago, Charlotte has finished last in three different divisions—the Atlantic in 1989, the Midwest in '90 and the Central in '91.

Last year's No. 1 pick, Derrick Coleman of New Jersey, was named Rookie of the Year, averaging 18.4 points and 10.3 rebounds for the Nets. He is only the fourth top pick since 1966 to gain top rookie honors the following season.

The Boston Celtics got off to a sensational 29-5 start for rookie coach Chris Ford by blending experience up front—Larry Bird, Kevin McHale and Robert Parish—with young legs in the backcourt—Brian Shaw, Reggie Lewis, rookie Dee Brown and swingman Kevin Gamble. Then recurring back pain brought down Bird, who wound up missing 22 games, and Boston was never the same.

Bird underwent back surgery in June, while the local debate raged over whether or not the Celtics should continue to build around its veteran front line (37 years of NBA experience) or back up the truck. The five-year hiatus since its last championship in 1986 ties the longest such Celtic drought since Bill Russell showed up 35 years ago.

Boston had no trouble winning another Atlantic Division title, although Philadelphia, led by the irrepressible Charles Barkley, gave a good showing after losing point guard Johnny Dawkins to a knee injury in the fourth game of the season. Barkley

Wide World Photos

Boston's aging front line of **Larry Bird, Kevin McHale** and **Robert Parish** were instrumental in winning the Atlantic Division, but the Celtics were eliminated by Detroit in the second round of the playoffs.

had his usual solid regular season—averaging 27.6 points and 10.1 rebounds a game—and was named MVP at the All-Star game when he paced the East to a 116-114 win with 17 points and 22 boards.

Ironically, Barkley had been a reluctant participant in Charlotte, agreeing to play only when league higher-ups refused to let him beg off with a minor injury. Other than that, he didn't back down much and easily led the league in fines again. "Before it's over, I'll get the credit I deserve," he said defiantly. "Right now, people say my name, and it's 'controversy' first and 'player' second."

The Sixers were the overtime champs of the NBA in 1990-91, going into OT 14 times and winning eight. Unfortunately, none of their playoff games with Chicago went past regulation and they were gone in six.

The New York Knicks had the revolving door working overtime in 1990-91. To wit: John MacLeod replaced Stu Jackson as coach on Dec. 1; Dave Checketts replaced Al Bianchi as general manager on Mar. 1; MacLeod quit on May 2 to take the coaching job at Notre Dame; Pat Riley left NBC Sports on May 31 to take MacLeod's place; and center Patrick Ewing filed for arbitration on July 2, rejecting a team contract offer that would have made him the highest paid player in team sports (see "Updates").

Surprisingly, there were only three other coaching changes made—in Indiana early in the season and in Minnesota and Miami afterward. Minnesota fired Bill Musselman and named Jimmy Rodgers, while Ron Rothstein resigned the Miami job and was replaced by Kevin Loughery, who has now coached in four of the Atlantic Division's six cities.

Indiana cashiered Dick Versace on Dec. 20, and promoted assistant Bob Hill. The 9-16 Pacers responded to Hill's up-tempo style and finished the year at 41-41, then pushed Boston to a fifth game in the first round of the playoffs. Led by forward Chuck Person, point guard Michael Williams and Sixth Man Award winner Detlef Schrempf, Indiana is a team to watch.

Seattle, the league's other .500 team, made the year's most radical roster moves, trading away the aforementioned

McDaniel, center Olden Polynice and guard Dale Ellis in exchange for Eddie Johnson, center Benoit Benjamin of the L.A. Clippers and guard Ricky Pierce of the Milwaukee Bucks. The Sonics also got great mileage from second-year forward Sean Kemp, who one evening terrorized the Lakers with 10 blocked shots.

A contract hassle forced Milwaukee to deal Pierce, but losing their leading scorer and sixth man didn't keep the Bucks from finishing a respectable 48-34 and making the playoffs for the 19th time in 23 years.

The singular comeback story of the year was Bernard King's resurrection in Washington. The wondrous forward had a stated goal of becoming "the first player ever to make the All-Star Game without an anterior cruciate ligament." And he did, too, taking his reconstructed knee to Charlotte after leading the league in scoring for the first two months of the season. His knee never gave out, but his back did and when that happened the Bullets likewise crumbled.

Hard luck team of the year? How about Cleveland. First, forward John "Hot Rod" Williams, offseason recipient of the league's first $4 million contract, missed 37 games with a leg injury. Then, by the time he got back, guard Mark Price was out for the year after tearing up his left knee on Nov. 30.

Defending NBA champion Detroit got off to a best-ever, 13-2 start that had Motown thinking "three-peat," but injuries soon reduced the expectation level. The key blow was the loss of All-Star guard Isiah Thomas to wrist surgery in late January. The Pistons even started losing at home, as all personnel solutions brought only temporary relief. They did win two playoff series, but after expending a great deal of energy to get by Boston they were running on empty when they met Chicago and got run over.

Unfortunately, the Pistons reacted poorly to getting swept at home and exited the playoffs in disgrace. After trying to intimidate the Bulls throughout Game 4, they upstaged them by walking off the floor before the game was over and in the locker room afterward said everything but "Congratulations."

Even GM John McCloskey, a basically honorable man, hissed on network radio,

Porter Binks/USA Today

Bernard King provided the year's top comeback story, returning from knee surgery to play in the NBA All-Star Game.

"They have two guys who are great athletes—Jordan and Pippen. That's all they've got. We just happened to play awful."

Only coach Chuck Daly conceded that the Bulls were the better team, but then he was the only Piston who had to be diplomatic. In February, Daly was named coach of the 1992 U.S. Olympic team, which will include NBA players for the first time.

But leave it to the renowned Prince of Pessimism to point out that the honor isn't everything it's cracked up to be. "Did you know that the coach doesn't get a gold medal?" he inquired. "Only the players." At the season's end he quelled persistent departure rumors by agreeing to coach the team for one more year. □

THE 1992 SPORTS ALMANAC — INFORMATION PLEASE

PRO BASKETBALL
STATISTICS

THE SEASON IN REVIEW
1990-1991

STANDINGS • PLAYOFFS • DRAFT

SEC A

PAGE 281

Final NBA Standings

Division champions (*) and playoff qualifiers (+) are noted. Number of seasons listed after each head coach refers to current tenure with club through 1990-91 season.

Western Conference

Midwest Division

	W	L	Pct	GB	—Per Game—For	Opp
*San Antonio	55	27	.671	—	107.1	102.6
†Utah	54	28	.659	1	104.0	100.7
†Houston	52	30	.634	3	106.7	103.2
Orlando	31	51	.378	24	105.9	109.9
Minnesota	29	53	.354	26	99.6	103.5
Dallas	28	54	.341	27	99.9	104.5
Denver	20	62	.244	35	119.9	130.8

Head Coaches: SA—Larry Brown (3rd season); **Utah**—Jerry Sloan (3rd); **Hou**—Don Chaney (3rd); **Orl**—Matt Guokas (2nd); **Min**—Bill Musselman (2nd); **Dal**—Richie Adubato (2nd); **Den**—Paul Westhead (1st).

1989-90 Standings: 1.San Antonio (56-26); 2.Utah (55-27); 3.Dallas (47-35); 4.Denver (43-39); 5.Houston (41-41); 6.Minnesota (22-60); 7.Charlotte (19-63).

Pacific Division

	W	L	Pct	GB	—Per Game—For	Opp
*Portland	63	19	.768	—	114.7	106.0
†LA Lakers	58	24	.707	5	106.9	99.6
†Phoenix	55	27	.671	8	114.0	107.5
†Golden St.	44	38	.537	19	116.6	115.0
†Seattle	41	41	.500	22	106.6	105.4
LA Clippers	31	51	.378	32	103.5	107.0
Sacramento	25	57	.305	38	96.7	103.5

Head Coaches: Por—Rick Adelman (3rd season); **LAL**—Mike Dunleavy (1st); **Pho**—Cotton Fitzsimmons (3rd); **GS**—Don Nelson (3rd); **Sea**—K.C.Jones (1st); **LAC**—Mike Schuler (1st); **Sac**—Dick Motta (2nd).

1989-90 Standings: 1.Lakers (63-19); 2.Portland (59-23); 3.Phoenix (54-28); 4.Seattle (41-41); 5.Golden St.(37-45); 6.Clippers (30-52); 7.Sacramento (23-59).

Eastern Conference

Atlantic Division

	W	L	Pct	GB	—Per Game—For	Opp
*Boston	56	26	.683	—	111.5	105.7
†Philadelphia	44	38	.537	12	105.4	105.6
†New York	39	43	.476	17	103.1	103.3
Washington	30	52	.366	26	101.4	106.4
New Jersey	26	56	.317	30	102.9	107.5
Miami	24	58	.293	32	101.8	107.8

Head Coaches: Bos—Chris Ford (1st season); **Phi**—Jim Lynam (4th); **NY**—replaced Stu Jackson (2nd, 7-8) with John MacLeod (32-35) on Dec.3; **Wash**—Wes Unseld (4th); **NJ**—Bill Fitch (2nd); **Mia**—Ron Rothstein (3rd).

1989-90 Standings: 1.Philadelphia (53-29); 2. Boston (52-30); 3. New York (45-37); 4.Washington (31-51); 5.Miami (18-64); 6.New Jersey (17-65).

Central Division

	W	L	Pct	GB	—Per Game—For	Opp
*Chicago	61	21	.744	—	110.0	101.0
†Detroit	50	32	.610	11	100.1	96.8
†Milwaukee	48	34	.585	13	106.4	104.0
†Atlanta	43	39	.524	18	109.8	109.0
†Indiana	41	41	.500	20	111.7	112.1
Cleveland	33	49	.402	28	101.7	104.2
Charlotte	26	56	.317	35	102.8	108.0

Head Coaches: Chi—Phil Jackson (2nd season); **Det**—Chuck Daly (8th); **Mil**—Del Harris (4rd); **Atl**—Bob Weiss (1st); **Ind**—replaced Dick Versace (3rd, 9-16) with Bob Hill (32-25) on Dec.20; **Cle**—Lenny Wilkens (5th); **Char**—Gene Littles (2nd).

1989-90 Standings: 1.Detroit (59-23); 2.Chicago (55-27); 3. Milwaukee (44-38); 4.Cleveland (42-40); 5.Indiana (42-40); 6.Atlanta (41-41); 7.Orlando (18-64).

Overall Conference Standings

Sixteen teams—eight from each conference—qualify for the NBA Playoffs; (*) denotes division champions.

Western Conference

	W	L	Home	Away	Conf
1 Portland*	63	19	36-5	27-14	42-14
2 San Antonio*	55	27	33-8	22-19	36-19
3 LA Lakers	58	24	33-8	25-16	40-16
4 Phoenix	55	27	32-9	23-18	35-21
5 Utah	54	28	36-5	18-23	37-18
6 Houston	52	30	31-10	21-20	33-23
7 Golden St.	44	38	30-11	14-27	28-28
8 Seattle	41	41	28-13	13-28	27-29
LA Clippers	31	51	23-18	8-33	26-30
Orlando	31	51	24-17	7-34	23-34
Minnesota	29	53	21-20	8-33	17-39
Dallas	28	54	20-21	8-33	17-39
Sacramento	25	57	24-17	1-40	18-37
Denver	20	62	17-24	3-38	12-45

Eastern Conference

	W	L	Home	Away	Conf
1 Chicago*	61	21	35-6	26-15	42-12
2 Boston*	56	26	35-6	21-20	35-19
3 Detroit	50	32	32-9	18-23	33-21
4 Milwaukee	48	34	33-8	15-26	33-21
5 Philadelphia	44	38	29-12	15-26	32-22
6 Atlanta	43	39	29-12	14-27	26-28
7 Indiana	41	41	29-12	12-29	27-27
8 New York	39	43	21-20	18-23	28-26
Cleveland	33	49	23-18	10-31	23-31
Washington	30	52	21-20	9-32	22-33
New Jersey	26	56	20-21	6-35	18-36
Charlotte	26	56	17-24	9-32	17-37
Miami	24	58	18-23	6-35	15-39

NBA Regular Season Leaders
Scoring
(Minimum 70 games or 1400 points)

	Gm	FG	FT	Pts	Avg
Michael Jordan, Chi	82	990	571	2580	31.5
Karl Malone, Utah	82	847	684	2382	29.0
Bernard King, Wash	64	713	383	1817	28.4
Charles Barkley, Phi	67	665	475	1849	27.6
Patrick Ewing, NY	81	845	464	2154	26.6
Michael Adams, Den	66	560	465	1752	26.5
Dominique Wilkins, Atl	81	770	476	2101	25.9
Chris Mullin, GS	82	777	513	2107	25.7
David Robinson, SA	82	754	592	2101	25.6
Mitch Richmond, GS	77	703	394	1840	23.9
Tim Hardaway, GS	82	739	306	1881	22.9
Reggie Miller, Ind	82	596	551	1855	22.6
Kevin Johnson, Pho	77	591	519	1710	22.2
Hersey Hawkins, Phi	80	590	479	1767	22.1
Tony Campbell, Min	77	652	358	1678	21.8
Brad Daugherty, Cle	76	605	435	1645	21.6
Clyde Drexler, Por	82	645	416	1767	21.5
James Worthy, LAL	78	716	212	1670	21.4
Ricky Pierce, Mil-Sea	78	561	430	1598	20.5
Joe Dumars, Det	80	622	371	1629	20.4

Rebounds

	Avg
Robinson, SA	13.0
Rodman, Det	12.5
Oakley, NY	12.1
K.Malone, Utah	11.8
Ewing, NY	11.2

Assists

	Avg
Stockton, Utah	14.2
Johnson, LAL	12.5
Adams, Den	10.5
Johnson, Pho	10.1
Hardaway, GS	9.7

Note: Olajuwon of Houston averaged 13.8 rebounds a game, but missed the 800-rebound minimum by 30.

Field Goals

	Pct
Williams, Port	.602
Parish, Bos	.598
Gamble, Bos	.587
Barkley, Phi	.570
Divac, LAL	.565

Free Throws

	Pct
Miller, Ind	.918
J.Malone, Utah	.917
Pierce, Mil-Sea	.913
Tripucka, Char	.910
Johnson, LAL	.906

Blocked Shots

	Avg
Olajuwon, Hou	3.95
Robinson, SA	3.90
Ewing, NY	3.19
Bol, Phi	3.01
Dudley, NJ	2.51
Nance, Cle	2.50

Steals

	Avg
Robertson, Mil	3.04
Stockton, Utah	2.85
Jordan, Chi	2.72
Hardaway, GS	2.61
Pippen, Chi	2.35
Blaylock, NJ	2.35

3-Pt Field Goals

	Pct
Les, Sac	.461
Tucker, NY	.418
Hornacek, Pho	.418
Porter, Port	.415
Skiles, Orl	.408

Triple Doubles

	Pct
Johnson, LAL	13
Drexler, Port	4
Walker, Wash	4

Four tied with 3 each.

Game High Points
Pts
54 Adams, Den (vs Mil)
52 King, Wash (vs Den)
52 Smith, LAC (at Den)
51 Maxwell, Hou (vs Cle)
50 Ewing, NY (vs Char)
50 King, Wash (vs Utah)
49 King, Wash (at NY)
47 King, Wash (vs NJ)
46 Jordan, Chi (vs Mil)
46 King, Wash (at Cle)
46 King, Wash (vs Char)

Personal Fouls
Mitchell, Min 338
Spencer, Min 337
Kemp, Sea 319
Carr, Sac 315
White, Dal 308

Disqualifications
Rasmussen, Den 15
Carr, Sac 14
Spencer, Min 14
Mitchell, Min 13
Kemp, Sea 11

NBA All-Star Game
East 116, West 114

41st NBA All-Star Game. **Date:** Feb.10, at Charlotte Coliseum; **Coaches:** Chris Ford, Boston (East) and Rick Adelman, Portland (West); **MVP:** Charles Barkley, Philadelphia (East)—17 points, 22 rebounds.

Western Conference

Pos	Starters	Min	FG M-A	Pts	Rb	A
F	Karl Malone, Utah	31	6-11	16	11	4
C	David Robinson, SA	18	6-13	16	6	0
G	Magic Johnson, LAL	28	7-16	16	4	3
F	Chris Mullin, GS	24	4-8	13	2	2
G	Kevin Johnson, Pho	23	2-5	5	2	7
	Bench					
G	Clyde Drexler, Port	19	4-9	12	4	2
F	James Worthy, LAL	21	3-11	9	2	0
F	Tom Chambers, Pho	18	4-11	8	4	1
C	Kevin Duckworth, Port	19	2-3	6	4	0
G	Tim Hardaway, GS	12	2-7	5	3	4
G	Terry Porter, Port	15	2-6	4	3	4
G	John Stockton, Utah	12	1-6	4	1	2
	TOTALS	240	43-106	114	46	29

All starters able to play.

Three-Point FG: 4-12 (M.Johnson 2-5, Mullin 1-1, Hardaway 1-2, Chambers 0-1, Stockton 0-1, Porter 0-2); **Free Throws:** 24-31 (Drexler 4-4, Mullin 4-4, Robinson 4-5, Malone 4-6, Worthy 3-4, Duckworth 2-2, K.Johnson 1-2, Stockton 2-4); **Percentages:** Two-Pt FG (39-94/.415), Three-Pt FG (4-12/.333), Combined FG (43-106/406), Free Throws (24-31/.774); **Turnovers:** 22 (Chambers 4, K.Johnson 3, M.Johnson 3, Malone 3, Porter 3, Duckworth 2, Mullin 2, Robinson 2); **Steals:** 17 (K.Johnson 3, Hardaway 3, Mullin 2, Porter 2, Robinson 2, Worthy 2, Chambers, Drexler, Duckworth, Malone); **Blocked Shots:** 8 (Robinson 3, Drexler, K.Johnson, Malone, Porter, Worthy); **Fouls:** 27 (Robinson 5, Chambers 3, Drexler 3, Duckworth 3, K.Johnson 3, Mullin 2, Porter 2, Stockton 2, Worthy 2, Hardaway, M.Johnson, Malone).

Eastern Conference

Pos	Starters	Min	FG M-A	Pts	Rb	A
G	Michael Jordan, Chi	36	10-25	26	5	5
C	Patrick Ewing, NY	30	8-10	18	10	0
F	Charles Barkley, Phi	35	7-15	17	22	4
F	Bernard King, Wash	26	2-8	8	3	3
G	Joe Dumars, Det	15	1-4	2	2	1
	Bench					
F	Dominique Wilkins, Atl	22	3-11	12	3	4
G	Ricky Pierce, Mil	19	4-8	9	2	2
C	Brad Daugherty, Cle	12	3-7	8	5	1
C	Alvin Robertson, Mil	12	2-4	6	2	0
G	Hersey Hawkins, Phi	14	3-5	6	0	1
F	Kevin McHale, Bos	14	0-3	2	3	2
C	Robert Parish, Bos	5	1-2	2	4	0
	TOTALS	240	44-102	116	61	23

Two starters unable to play due to injuries: Boston's Larry Bird (back) and Detroit's Isiah Thomas (right wrist).

Three-Point FG: 0-7 (Jordan 0-2, Wilkins 0-2, Dumars 0-1, Hawkins 0-1, McHale 0-1); **Free Throws:** 28-35 (Jordan 6-7, Wilkins 6-8, King 4-4, Barkley 3-6, Ewing 2-2, McHale 2-2, Robertson 2-2, Daugherty 2-3, Pierce 1-1); **Percentages:** Two-Pt FG (44-95/.463), Three-Pt FG (0-7/.000), Combined FG (44-102/.431), Free Throws (28-35/.800); **Turnovers:** 29 (Jordan 10, Dumars 4, Barkley 3, Robertson 3, Ewing 2, Pierce 2, Wilkins 2, Hawkins, King, Parish); **Steals:** 6 (Jordan 2, Barkley, Ewing, McHale, Wilkins); **Blocked Shots:** 7 (Ewing 4, Barkley, King, Wilkins); **Fouls:** 26 (Barkley 5, Ewing 5, Daugherty 3, Jordan 2, McHale 2, Parish 2, Pierce 2, Wilkins 2, Dumars, Hawkins, King).

	1	2	3	4		Final
West	23	35	34	22	—	**114**
East	22	45	27	22	—	**116**

Halftime—East, 67-58; **Third Quarter**—East, 94-92; **Technical Fouls**—None; **Officials**—Ed T.Rush, Mike Mathis, Lee Jones; **Attendance**—23,530; **Time**—2:25; **TV Rating**—7.8/21 share (NBC).

Team by Team Statistics

At least 25 games played. Players who competed for more than one team during the regular season are listed with their final club; (*) denotes rookies.

Atlanta Hawks

	Gm	FG%	TPts	Pts	Reb	Ast
Dominique Wilkins	81	.470	2101	25.9	9.0	3.3
Doc Rivers	79	.435	1197	15.2	3.2	4.3
John Battle	79	.461	1078	13.6	2.0	2.7
Spud Webb	75	.447	1003	13.4	2.3	5.6
Kevin Willis	80	.504	1051	13.1	8.8	1.2
Moses Malone	82	.468	869	10.6	8.1	0.8
Duane Ferrell	78	.489	475	6.1	2.3	0.7
Rumeal Robinson*	47	.446	265	5.6	1.5	2.8
Sidney Moncrief	72	.488	337	4.7	1.8	1.4
Tim McCormick	56	.497	252	4.5	2.9	0.6
Jon Koncak	77	.436	313	4.1	4.9	1.6
Trevor Wilson*	25	.300	55	2.2	1.6	0.4

Triple Doubles: None.
Signed: Ferrell as free agent (Nov.3).

Boston Celtics

	Gm	FG%	TPts	Pts	Reb	Ast
Larry Bird	60	.454	1164	19.4	8.5	7.2
Reggie Lewis	79	.491	1478	18.7	5.2	2.5
Kevin McHale	68	.553	1251	18.4	7.1	1.9
Kevin Gamble	82	.587	1281	15.6	3.3	3.1
Robert Parish	81	.598	1207	14.9	10.6	0.8
Brian Shaw	79	.469	1091	13.8	4.7	7.6
Dee Brown*	82	.464	712	8.7	2.2	4.2
Ed Pinckney	70	.539	366	5.2	4.9	0.6
Michael Smith	47	.475	218	4.6	1.2	0.9
Joe Kleine	72	.468	258	3.6	3.4	0.3
Stojko Vrankovic*	31	.462	58	1.9	1.6	0.1

Triple Doubles: Bird (3).

Charlotte Hornets

	Gm	FG%	TPts	Pts	Reb	Ast
Johnny Newman	81	.470	1371	16.9	3.1	2.3
Rex Chapman	70	.445	1102	15.7	2.7	3.6
J.R.Reid	80	.466	902	11.3	6.3	1.1
Kendall Gill*	82	.450	906	11.0	3.2	3.7
Dell Curry	76	.471	802	10.6	2.6	2.2
Mike Gminski	80	.442	844	10.6	7.3	1.2
PHI	30	.384	272	9.1	6.7	1.1
CHAR	50	.473	572	11.4	7.6	1.2
Kenny Gattison	72	.532	650	9.0	5.3	0.6
Kelly Tripucka	77	.454	541	7.0	2.3	2.1
Muggsy Bogues	81	.460	568	7.0	2.7	8.3
Eric Leckner	72	.446	324	4.5	4.1	0.5
SAC	32	.406	94	2.9	2.7	0.6
CHAR	40	.465	230	5.8	5.2	0.5
Randolph Keys	44	.407	140	3.2	2.3	0.4
Steve Scheffler*	39	.513	59	1.5	1.2	0.2

Triple Doubles: None.
Acquired: Gminski from Phi.(Jan.4); Leckner from Sac.(Jan.29).

Chicago Bulls

	Gm	FG%	TPts	Pts	Reb	Ast
Michael Jordan	82	.539	2580	31.5	6.0	5.5
Scottie Pippen	82	.520	1461	17.8	7.3	6.2
Horace Grant	78	.547	1000	12.8	8.4	2.3
Bill Cartwright	79	.490	760	9.6	6.2	1.6
B.J.Armstrong	82	.481	720	8.8	1.8	3.7
John Paxson	82	.548	710	8.7	1.1	3.6
Stacey King	76	.467	419	5.5	2.7	0.9
Craig Hodges	73	.424	362	5.0	0.6	1.3
Dennis Hopson	61	.426	264	4.3	1.8	1.1
Will Perdue	74	.494	307	4.1	4.5	0.6
Cliff Levingston	78	.450	314	4.0	2.9	0.7
Scott Williams*	51	.510	127	2.5	1.9	0.3

Triple Doubles: Pippen (3).

Cleveland Cavaliers

	Gm	FG%	TPts	Pts	Reb	Ast
Brad Daugherty	76	.524	1645	21.6	10.9	3.3
Larry Nance	80	.524	1537	19.2	8.6	3.0
John Williams	43	.463	505	11.7	6.7	2.3
Craig Ehlo	82	.445	832	10.1	4.7	4.6
Darnell Valentine	65	.464	609	9.4	2.6	5.4
Danny Ferry*	81	.428	697	8.6	3.5	1.8
Chucky Brown	74	.524	627	8.5	2.9	1.1
Henry James	37	.441	300	8.1	2.1	0.9
Gerald Paddio*	70	.419	504	7.2	1.7	1.3
John Morton	66	.438	357	5.4	1.6	3.7
Steve Kerr	57	.444	271	4.8	0.6	2.3
Winston Bennett	27	.374	115	4.3	2.4	1.0

Triple Doubles: None.
Signed: Valentine as free agent (Dec.3); James as free agent (Dec.31).

Dallas Mavericks

	Gm	FG%	TPts	Pts	Reb	Ast
Rolando Blackman	80	.482	1590	19.9	3.2	3.8
Derek Harper	77	.467	1519	19.7	3.0	7.1
Herb Williams	60	.507	747	12.5	6.0	1.6
Rodney McCray	74	.495	844	11.4	7.6	3.5
James Donaldson	82	.532	819	10.0	8.9	0.8
Alex English	79	.439	763	9.7	3.2	1.3
Randy White	79	.398	695	8.8	6.4	0.8
Kelvin Upshaw	48	.450	270	5.6	1.1	1.8
Brad Davis	80	.426	151	5.4	1.5	2.9
Steve Alford	34	.504	54	4.4	0.7	0.6
Jim Grandholm	26	.517	79	3.0	1.9	0.3
John Shasky	57	.440	150	2.6	2.4	0.2

Triple Doubles: None.
Signed: Grandholm as free agent (Nov.11); Upshaw as free agent (Nov.13).

Team by Team Statistics (Cont.)

Denver Nuggets

	Gm	FG%	TPts	Pts	Reb	Ast
Michael Adams	66	.394	1752	26.5	3.9	10.5
Orlando Woolridge	53	.498	1330	25.1	6.8	2.2
Chris Jackson*	67	.413	942	14.1	1.8	3.1
Todd Lichti	29	.439	405	14.0	3.9	2.5
Reggie Williams	73	.449	991	13.6	4.2	1.8
SA	22	.480	171	7.8	2.7	2.1
DEN	51	.444	820	16.1	4.8	1.7
Blair Rasmussen	70	.458	875	12.5	9.7	1.0
Jim Farmer	27	.453	255	9.4	2.5	1.4
PHI	2	.286	6	3.0	2.5	0.0
DEN	25	.458	249	10.0	2.5	1.5
Jerome Lane	62	.438	463	7.5	9.3	2.0
Joe Wolf	74	.451	539	7.3	5.4	1.4
Marcus Liberty*	76	.421	507	6.7	2.9	0.8
Kenny Battle	56	.472	339	6.1	3.1	1.1
PHO	16	.442	96	6.0	3.3	0.9
DEN	40	.485	243	6.1	3.1	1.2
Anthony Cook*	58	.417	307	5.3	5.6	0.4
Gregg Anderson	68	.430	292	4.3	4.7	0.2
MIL	26	.370	70	2.7	2.9	0.1
NJ	1	1.000	8	8.0	6.0	1.0
DEN	41	.440	214	5.2	5.8	0.3

Triple Double: Adams (1).
Acquired: Anderson from NJ (Jan.23).
Signed: Williams as free agent (Jan.6); Battle as free agent (Jan.25); Farmer as free agent (Mar.7).

Houston Rockets

	Gm	FG%	TPts	Pts	Reb	Ast
Hakeem Olajuwon	56	.508	1187	21.2	13.8	2.3
Kenny Smith	78	.520	1380	17.7	2.1	7.1
Otis Thorpe	82	.556	1435	17.5	10.3	2.4
Vernon Maxwell	82	.404	1397	17.0	2.9	3.7
Buck Johnson	73	.477	991	13.6	4.5	1.9
Eric Floyd	82	.411	1005	12.3	1.9	3.9
David Wood	82	.424	432	5.3	3.0	1.1
Kennard Winchester*	64	.400	239	3.7	1.0	0.4
Larry Smith	81	.487	268	3.3	8.8	1.1
Dave Jamerson*	37	.381	113	3.1	0.8	0.7
Dave Feitl	52	.371	137	2.6	1.9	0.2
Adrian Caldwell	42	.422	77	1.8	2.4	0.2

Triple Double: Olajuwon (1).

Detroit Pistons

	Gm	FG%	TPts	Pts	Reb	Ast
Joe Dumars	80	.481	1629	20.4	2.3	5.5
Isiah Thomas	48	.435	776	16.2	3.3	9.3
Mark Aguirre	78	.462	1104	14.2	4.8	1.8
James Edwards	72	.484	982	13.6	3.8	0.9
Vinnie Johnson	82	.434	958	11.7	3.4	3.3
Bill Laimbeer	82	.478	904	11.0	9.0	1.9
Dennis Rodman	82	.493	669	8.2	12.5	1.0
John Salley	74	.475	544	7.4	4.4	0.9
William Bedford	60	.438	272	4.5	2.2	0.5
John Long	25	.412	96	3.8	1.3	0.7
Scott Hastings	27	.571	48	1.8	1.0	0.3
Lance Blanks*	38	.426	64	1.7	0.5	0.7
Tree Rollins	37	.424	36	1.0	1.1	0.1

Triple Doubles: None.
Signed: Long as free agent (Jan.25).

Indiana Pacers

	Gm	FG%	TPts	Pts	Reb	Ast
Reggie Miller	82	.512	1855	22.6	3.4	4.0
Chuck Person	80	.504	1474	18.4	5.2	3.0
Detlef Schrempf	82	.520	1320	16.1	8.0	3.7
Vern Fleming	69	.531	877	12.7	3.1	5.3
Michael Williams	73	.499	813	11.1	2.4	4.8
Rik Smits	76	.485	828	10.9	4.7	1.1
LaSalle Thompson	82	.488	625	7.6	6.9	1.8
Mike Sanders	80	.417	463	5.8	2.3	1.3
George McCloud	74	.373	343	4.6	1.6	2.0
Greg Dreiling	73	.505	259	3.5	3.5	0.7
Ken Williams*	75	.520	220	2.9	1.7	0.4
Randy Wittman	41	.443	74	1.8	0.8	0.6

Triple Doubles: Miller (1); Schrempf (1).

Golden State Warriors

	Gm	FG%	TPts	Pts	Reb	Ast
Chris Mullin	82	.536	2107	25.7	5.4	4.0
Mitch Richmond	77	.494	1840	23.9	5.9	3.1
Tim Hardaway	82	.476	1881	22.9	4.0	9.7
S.Marciulionis	50	.501	545	10.9	2.4	1.7
Rod Higgins	82	.463	776	9.5	4.3	1.4
Tom Tolbert	62	.423	500	8.1	4.4	1.2
Mario Elie	33	.497	237	7.2	3.3	1.4
PHI	3	.286	6	2.0	0.3	0.3
GS	30	.507	231	7.7	3.6	1.5
Alton Lister	77	.478	491	6.4	6.3	1.2
Tyrone Hill*	74	.492	390	5.3	5.2	0.3
Jim Petersen	62	.483	279	4.5	3.2	0.4
Kevin Pritchard*	62	.384	243	3.9	1.0	1.3
Larry Robinson*	36	.413	139	3.9	1.4	1.0
WASH	12	.418	83	6.9	2.3	2.0
GS	24	.407	56	2.3	1.0	0.5
Paul Mokeski	36	.356	57	1.6	1.9	0.3

Triple Doubles: None.
Signed: Robinson as free agent (Jan.7); Mokeski as free agent (Jan.12); Elie as free agent (Feb.23).

Los Angeles Clippers

	Gm	FG%	TPts	Pts	Reb	Ast
Charles Smith	74	.469	1480	20.0	8.2	1.8
Ron Harper	39	.391	763	19.6	4.8	5.4
Ken Norman	70	.501	1219	17.4	7.1	2.3
Danny Manning	73	.519	1159	15.9	5.8	2.7
Olden Polynice	79	.560	778	9.8	7.0	0.5
SEA	48	.545	397	8.3	5.6	0.3
LAC	31	.579	381	12.3	9.1	0.8
Gary Grant	68	.451	590	8.7	3.1	8.6
Winston Garland	69	.426	564	8.2	2.9	4.6
Jeff Martin	74	.422	523	7.1	1.8	0.9
Bo Kimble*	62	.380	429	6.9	1.9	1.2
Loy Vaught*	73	.487	399	5.5	4.8	0.5
Tom Garrick	67	.424	260	3.9	1.9	3.3
Ken Bannister	47	.531	111	2.4	2.0	0.2

Triple Doubles: None.
Acquired: Polynice from Sea.(Feb.20).

Los Angeles Lakers

	Gm	FG%	TPts	—Per Game—		
				Pts	Reb	Ast
James Worthy	78	.492	1670	21.4	4.6	3.5
Magic Johnson	79	.477	1531	19.4	7.0	12.5
Byron Scott	82	.477	1191	14.5	3.0	2.2
Sam Perkins	73	.495	983	13.5	7.4	1.5
Vlade Divac	82	.565	921	11.2	8.1	1.1
Terry Teagle	82	.443	815	9.9	2.2	1.0
A.C.Green	82	.476	750	9.1	6.3	0.9
Mychal Thompson	72	.496	288	4.0	3.2	0.3
Tony Smith*	64	.441	234	3.7	1.1	2.1
Larry Drew	48	.432	139	2.9	0.7	2.5
Elden Campbell*	52	.455	144	2.8	1.8	0.2
Irving Thomas*	26	.340	46	1.8	1.2	0.4

Triple Doubles: Johnson (13).

Miami Heat

	Gm	FG%	TPts	—Per Game—		
				Pts	Reb	Ast
Sherman Douglas	73	.504	1352	18.5	2.9	8.5
Glen Rice	77	.461	1342	17.4	4.9	2.5
Rony Seikaly	64	.481	1050	16.4	11.1	1.5
Kevin Edwards	79	.410	955	12.1	2.6	3.0
Willie Burton*	76	.441	915	12.0	3.4	1.4
Grant Long	80	.492	734	9.2	7.1	2.2
Billy Thompson	73	.499	499	6.8	4.3	1.5
Alec Kessler*	78	.425	486	6.2	4.3	0.4
Terry Davis	55	.487	300	5.5	4.8	0.7
Vernell Coles*	82	.412	401	4.9	1.9	2.8
Keith Askins*	39	.420	86	2.2	1.7	0.5
Alan Ogg*	31	.436	54	1.7	1.6	0.1

Triple Doubles: None.

Milwaukee Bucks

	Gm	FG%	TPts	—Per Game—		
				Pts	Reb	Ast
Dale Ellis	51	.474	857	16.8	3.4	1.9
SEA	30	.463	451	15.0	3.1	2.1
MIL	21	.486	406	19.3	3.9	1.5
Jay Humphries	80	.502	1215	15.2	2.8	6.7
Alvin Robertson	81	.485	1098	13.6	5.7	5.5
Frank Brickowski	75	.527	942	12.6	5.7	1.7
Fred Roberts	82	.533	888	10.8	3.4	1.6
Dan Schayes	82	.499	870	10.6	6.5	1.2
Jack Sikma	77	.427	802	10.4	5.7	1.9
Jeff Grayer	82	.433	521	6.4	3.0	1.5
Brad Lohaus	81	.431	428	5.3	2.7	0.9
Lester Conner	74	.464	260	3.5	1.5	2.2
NJ	35	.523	145	4.1	1.6	1.7
MIL	39	.396	115	2.9	1.4	2.7
Steve Henson*	68	.418	214	3.1	0.8	1.9
Frank Kornet	32	.371	58	1.8	0.8	0.3

Triple Doubles: Robertson (3).
Acquired: Conner from NJ (Jan.16); Ellis from Sea.(Feb.15).

Minnesota Timberwolves

	Gm	FG%	TPts	—Per Game—		
				Pts	Reb	Ast
Tony Campbell	77	.434	1678	21.8	4.5	2.8
Tyrone Corbin	82	.448	1472	18.0	7.2	4.2
Jerome Richardson	82	.470	1401	17.1	3.5	9.0
Sam Mitchell	82	.441	1197	14.6	6.3	1.6
Felton Spencer*	81	.512	572	7.1	7.9	0.3
Gerald Glass*	51	.438	352	6.9	2.0	0.8
Randy Breuer	73	.453	429	5.9	4.7	1.0
Scott Brooks	80	.430	424	5.3	0.9	2.6
Tod Murphy	52	.396	251	4.8	4.9	1.2
Doug West	75	.480	294	3.9	1.8	0.6
Richard Coffey*	52	.373	68	1.3	1.5	0.1

Triple Double: Corbin (1).

New Jersey Nets

	Gm	FG%	TPts	—Per Game—		
				Pts	Reb	Ast
Reggie Theus	81	.468	1510	18.6	2.8	4.7
Derrick Coleman*	74	.467	1364	18.4	10.3	2.2
Mookie Blaylock	72	.416	1017	14.1	3.5	6.1
Chris Morris	79	.425	1042	13.2	6.6	2.8
Sam Bowie	62	.434	801	12.9	7.7	2.4
Drazen Petrovic	61	.493	623	10.2	1.8	1.4
PORT	18	.451	80	4.4	1.0	1.1
NJ	43	.500	543	12.6	2.1	1.5
Derrick Gervin	56	.416	425	7.6	2.0	0.5
Chris Dudley	61	.408	434	7.1	8.4	0.6
Terry Mills	55	.465	315	5.7	4.2	0.6
DEN	17	.467	128	7.5	5.2	0.9
NJ	38	.464	187	4.9	3.7	0.4
Jack Haley	78	.469	434	5.6	4.6	0.4
Tate George*	56	.415	192	3.4	0.8	1.9
Jud Buechler*	74	.416	232	3.1	1.9	0.7
Kurk Lee*	48	.268	66	1.4	0.6	0.7

Triple Double: Morris (1).
Acquired: Petrovic from Port.(Jan.23); Mills fron Den.(Jan.23).

New York Knicks

	Gm	FG%	TPts	—Per Game—		
				Pts	Reb	Ast
Patrick Ewing	81	.514	2154	26.6	11.2	3.0
Kiki Vandeweghe	75	.494	1226	16.3	2.4	1.5
Gerald Wilkins	68	.473	938	13.8	3.0	4.0
Charles Oakley	76	.516	853	11.2	12.1	2.7
Mark Jackson	72	.492	630	8.8	2.7	6.3
Maurice Cheeks	76	.499	592	7.8	2.3	5.7
John Starks	61	.439	466	7.6	2.1	3.3
Trent Tucker	65	.440	463	7.1	1.6	1.7
Brian Quinnett	68	.459	319	4.7	2.1	0.8
Jerrod Mustaf*	62	.465	268	4.3	2.7	0.6
Kenny Walker	54	.435	230	4.3	2.9	0.2
Eddie Lee Wilkins	68	.447	279	4.1	2.6	0.2

Triple Double: Jackson (1).

Orlando Magic

	Gm	FG%	TPts	—Per Game—		
				Pts	Reb	Ast
Scott Skiles	79	.445	1357	17.2	3.4	8.4
Dennis Scott*	82	.425	1284	15.7	2.9	1.6
Terry Catledge	51	.462	745	14.6	7.0	1.1
Nick Anderson	70	.467	990	14.1	5.5	1.5
Otis Smith	75	.451	1044	13.9	5.2	2.3
Jerry Reynolds	80	.434	1034	12.9	3.7	2.5
Jeff Turner	71	.487	609	8.6	5.1	1.4
Sam Vincent	49	.431	406	8.3	2.2	4.0
Michael Ansley	67	.548	379	5.7	3.8	0.4
Greg Kite	82	.491	395	4.8	7.2	0.7
Mark Acres	68	.509	285	4.2	5.3	0.4
Morlon Wiley	34	.417	113	3.3	0.5	2.1

Triple Doubles: None.

Team by Team Statistics (Cont.)

Philadelphia 76ers

	Gm	FG%	TPts	—Per Game— Pts	Reb	Ast
Charles Barkley	67	.570	1849	27.6	10.1	4.2
Hersey Hawkins	80	.472	1767	22.1	3.9	3.7
Armon Gilliam	75	.487	1242	16.6	8.0	1.4
CHAR	25	.513	494	19.8	9.4	1.1
PHI	50	.470	748	15.0	7.3	1.6
Ron Anderson	82	.485	1198	14.6	4.5	1.4
Rickey Green	79	.463	793	10.0	1.7	5.2
Rick Mahorn	80	.467	711	8.9	7.8	1.5
Andre Turner	70	.439	412	5.9	2.2	4.4
Brian Oliver*	73	.408	279	3.8	1.1	1.2
Kenny Payne	47	.360	166	3.5	1.4	0.3
Jayson Williams*	52	.447	182	3.5	2.1	0.3
Dave Hoppen	30	.463	64	2.1	1.3	0.1
CHAR	19	.563	44	2.3	1.6	0.2
PHI	11	.500	20	1.8	0.8	0.0
Manute Bol	82	.396	155	1.9	4.3	0.2

Triple Doubles: None.
Acquired: Gilliam and Hoppen from Char.(Jan.4).
Signed: Turner as free agent (Nov.20).

Sacramento Kings

	Gm	FG%	TPts	—Per Game— Pts	Reb	Ast
Antoine Carr	77	.511	1551	20.1	5.5	2.5
Wayman Tisdale	33	.483	660	20.0	7.7	2.0
Lionel Simmons*	79	.422	1421	18.0	8.8	4.0
Travis Mays*	64	.406	915	14.3	2.8	4.0
Rory Sparrow	80	.491	831	10.4	2.3	4.5
Anthony Bonner*	34	.448	250	7.4	4.7	1.4
Jim Les	55	.444	395	7.2	2.0	5.4
Duane Causwell*	76	.508	525	6.9	5.1	0.9
Bobby Hansen*	36	.375	229	6.4	2.7	2.5
Bill Wennington	77	.436	437	5.7	4.4	0.9
Anthony Frederick	35	.399	177	5.1	2.4	1.3
Rick Calloway*	64	.391	205	3.2	1.2	1.0
Ralph Sampson	25	.366	74	3.0	4.4	0.7

Triple Doubles: None.
Signed: Les as free agent (Dec.31); Frederick as free agent (Jan.14).

Phoenix Suns

	Gm	FG%	TPts	—Per Game— Pts	Reb	Ast
Kevin Johnson	77	.516	1710	22.2	3.5	10.1
Tom Chambers	76	.437	1511	19.9	6.4	2.6
Xavier McDaniel	81	.497	1373	17.0	6.9	2.3
SEA	15	.479	327	21.8	5.4	2.5
PHO	66	.503	1046	15.8	7.2	2.3
Jeff Hornacek	80	.518	1350	16.9	4.0	5.1
Dan Majerle	77	.484	1051	13.6	5.4	2.8
Cedric Ceballos*	63	.487	519	8.2	2.4	0.6
Mark West	82	.647	629	7.7	6.9	0.5
Negele Knight*	64	.425	339	5.3	1.1	3.0
Andrew Lang	63	.577	311	4.9	4.8	0.4
Tim Perry	46	.521	193	4.2	2.7	0.6
Kurt Rambis	62	.497	226	3.6	4.3	1.0
Ed Nealy	55	.464	123	2.2	2.7	0.7

Triple Doubles: None.
Acquired: McDaniel from Sea.(Dec.7).

San Antonio Spurs

	Gm	FG%	TPts	—Per Game— Pts	Reb	Ast
David Robinson	82	.552	2101	25.6	13.0	2.5
Terry Cummings	67	.484	1177	17.6	7.8	2.3
Sean Elliott	82	.490	1301	15.9	5.6	2.9
Willie Anderson	75	.457	1083	14.4	4.7	4.8
Rod Strickland	58	.482	800	13.8	3.8	8.0
Paul Pressey	70	.472	528	7.5	2.5	3.9
Sidney Green	66	.461	443	6.7	4.7	0.8
David Wingate	25	.384	136	5.4	3.0	1.8
Avery Johnson	68	.469	320	4.7	1.1	3.4
DEN	21	.426	79	3.8	1.0	3.7
SA	47	.483	241	5.1	1.2	3.3
Sean Higgins*	50	.458	225	4.5	1.3	0.7
David Greenwood	63	.503	239	3.8	3.5	0.8
Dwayne Schintzius*	42	.439	158	3.8	2.9	0.4
Tony Massenburg*	35	.450	82	2.3	1.7	0.1

Triple Doubles: Robinson (3).
Signed: Johnson as free agent (Jan.17).

Portland Trail Blazers

	Gm	FG%	TPts	—Per Game— Pts	Reb	Ast
Clyde Drexler	82	.482	1767	21.5	6.7	6.0
Terry Porter	81	.515	1381	17.0	3.5	8.0
Kevin Duckworth	81	.481	1282	15.8	6.6	1.1
Jerome Kersey	73	.478	1084	14.8	6.6	3.1
Walter Davis	71	.468	924	13.0	2.5	1.8
DEN	39	.474	728	18.7	3.2	2.2
PORT	32	.446	196	6.1	1.8	1.3
Cliff Robinson	82	.463	957	11.7	4.3	1.8
Buck Williams	80	.602	933	11.7	9.4	1.2
Danny Ainge	80	.472	890	11.1	2.6	3.6
Mark Bryant	53	.488	272	5.1	3.6	0.5
Danny Young	75	.380	283	3.8	1.0	1.9
Alaa Abdelnaby*	43	.474	135	3.1	2.1	0.3
Wayne Cooper	67	.393	147	2.2	2.8	0.3

Triple Doubles: Drexler (4).
Acquired: Davis from Den.(Jan.23).

Seattle Supersonics

	Gm	FG%	TPts	—Per Game— Pts	Reb	Ast
Ricky Pierce	78	.485	1598	20.5	2.4	2.2
MIL	46	.499	1037	22.5	2.5	2.1
SEA	32	.463	561	17.5	2.3	2.3
Eddie Johnson	81	.484	1354	16.7	3.3	1.4
PHO	15	.473	203	13.5	3.1	1.1
SEA	66	.486	1151	17.4	3.4	1.4
Derrick McKey	73	.517	1115	15.3	5.8	2.3
Shawn Kemp	81	.508	1214	15.0	8.4	1.8
Benoit Benjamin	70	.496	982	14.0	10.3	1.7
LAC	39	.492	581	14.9	12.0	1.9
SEA	31	.502	401	12.9	8.2	1.5
Sedale Threatt	80	.519	1013	12.7	1.2	3.4
Gary Payton*	82	.450	397	7.2	3.0	6.4
Michael Cage	82	.508	588	6.4	6.8	1.1
Dana Barros	66	.495	418	6.3	1.1	1.7
Quintin Dailey	30	.471	184	6.1	1.1	0.5
Nate McMillan	78	.433	338	4.3	3.2	4.8
Dave Corzine	28	.447	47	1.7	1.2	0.1

Triple Doubles: Payton (1).
Acquired: Johnson from Pho.(Dec.7); Pierce from Mil.(Feb.15); Benjamin from LAC (Feb.20).

Utah Jazz

	Gm	FG%	TPts	—Per Game— Pts	Reb	Ast
Karl Malone	82	.527	2382	29.0	11.8	3.3
Jeff Malone	69	.508	1282	18.6	3.0	2.1
John Stockton	82	.507	1413	17.2	2.9	14.2
Thurl Bailey	82	.458	1017	12.4	5.0	1.5
Blue Edwards	62	.526	576	9.3	3.2	1.7
Darrell Griffith	75	.391	430	5.7	1.2	0.5
Mark Eaton	80	.579	409	5.1	8.3	0.6
Mike Brown	82	.454	390	4.8	4.1	0.6
Delaney Rudd	82	.435	324	4.0	0.8	2.6
Andy Toolson*	47	.403	137	2.9	1.4	0.7
Tony Brown	30	.375	83	2.8	1.4	0.5
LAL	7	.667	5	0.7	0.6	0.4
UTAH	23	.364	78	3.4	1.7	0.6
Walter Palmer*	28	.333	40	1.4	0.8	0.2

Triple Doubles: None.
Signed: T.Brown as free agent (Feb.28).

Washington Bullets

	Gm	FG%	TPts	—Per Game— Pts	Reb	Ast
Bernard King	64	.472	1817	28.4	5.0	4.6
Harvey Grant	77	.498	1405	18.2	7.2	2.6
Ledell Eackles	67	.453	868	13.0	1.9	2.0
John Williams	33	.417	411	12.5	5.4	4.0
Pervis Ellison	76	.513	791	10.4	7.7	1.3
A.J.English*	70	.439	616	8.8	2.1	2.5
Haywoode Workman	73	.454	581	8.0	3.3	4.8
Darrell Walker	71	.430	553	7.8	7.0	6.5
Mark Alarie	42	.440	244	5.8	2.8	1.1
Tom Hammonds	70	.461	367	5.2	2.9	0.6
Byron Irvin	33	.465	171	5.2	1.4	0.7
Greg Foster*	54	.460	236	4.4	2.8	0.7
Charles Jones	62	.540	163	2.6	5.8	0.8

Triple Doubles: Walker (4); Williams (1).
Signed: Eackles as free agent (Nov.12).

Annual Awards

Podoloff Trophy

For Most Valuable Player, voting by 96-member panel of local and national pro basketball writers and broadcasters. Each ballot has five entries; points awarded on 10-7-5-3-1 basis.

	1st	2nd	3rd	4th	5th	Pts
Michael Jordan, Chi	77	15	2	2	0	891
Magic Johnson, LAL	10	31	27	13	6	497
David Robinson, SA	6	31	29	16	6	476*
Charles Barkley, Phi	2	8	16	15	21	222
Karl Malone, Utah	0	4	8	18	20	142
Clyde Drexler, Port	1	4	4	3	8	75
Kevin Johnson, Pho	0	1	2	2	9	32
Dominique Wilkins, Atl	0	1	2	3	3	29
Terry Porter, Port	0	1	2	2	2	25
Larry Bird, Bos	0	0	1	5	5	25

Gottlieb Trophy

For Rookie of the Year, voting by 96-member panel of local and national pro basketball writers and broadcasters. Each ballot has one entry.

	Pos	Votes
Derrick Coleman, New Jersey	F	69
Lionel Simmons, Sacramento	F	22
Dennis Scott, Orlando	G	3
Dee Brown, Boston	G	2

Auerbach Trophy

For Coach of the Year, voting by 96-member panel of local and national pro basketball writers and broadcasters. Each ballot has one entry. Vote totals followed by 1990-91 record and division standing.

	Votes	Record	Div
Don Chaney, Houston	69	52-30	3rd
Rick Adelman, Portland	11	63-19	1st
Chris Ford, Boston	7	56-26	1st
Phil Jackson, Chicago	4	61-21	1st
Larry Brown, San Antonio	2	55-27	1st
Del Harris, Milwaukee	2	48-34	3rd
Chuck Daly, Detroit	1	50-32	2nd

Other Awards

Defensive Player of the Year—Dennis Rodman, Detroit; **Most Improved Player**—Scott Skiles, Orlando; **Sixth Man Award**—Detlef Schrempf, Indiana; **Schick Award** (for contributing most to team's success)—David Robinson, San Antonio; **Kennedy Citizenship Award**—Kevin Johnson, Phoenix; **Executive of the Year**—Bucky Buckwalter, Portland.

All-NBA Teams

Voting by a 96-member panel of local and national pro basketball writers and broadcasters. Repeaters from 1989-90 first team are in **bold** type.

Pos	First Team	1st	Pts
G	**Michael Jordan**, Chicago	94	476
G	**Magic Johnson**, LA Lakers	93	472
C	David Robinson, San Antonio	87	458
F	**Karl Malone**, Utah	88	464
F	**Charles Barkley**, Philadelphia	82	452

Pos	Second Team	1st	Pts
G	Kevin Johnson, Phoenix	3	212
G	Clyde Drexler, Portland	2	202
C	Patrick Ewing, New York	7	240
F	Dominique Wilkins, Atlanta	11	224
F	Chris Mullin, Golden St.	1	141

Pos	Third Team	1st	Pts
G	John Stockton, Utah	0	160
G	Joe Dumars, Detroit	0	61
C	Hakeem Olajuwon, Houston	2	100
F	James Worthy, LA Lakers	2	117
F	Bernard King, Washington	3	111

All-Defensive Teams

Voting by NBA head coaches. Repeaters from 1989-90 first team are in **bold** type.

Pos	First Team	1st	Pts
F	**Dennis Rodman**, Detroit	25	51
F	**Buck Williams**, Portland	14	32
C	David Robinson, San Antonio	16	40
G	**Michael Jordan**, Chicago	14	37
G	Alvin Robertson, Milwaukee	13	37

Pos	Second Team	1st	Pts
F	Scottie Pippen, Chicago	3	14
F	Dan Majerle, Phoenix	3	12
C	Hakeem Olajuwon, Houston	9	25
G	Joe Dumars, Detroit	15	36
G	John Stockton, Utah	3	13

All-Rookie Team

Voting by NBA head coaches.

First Team	College	Pts
Derrick Coleman, New Jersey	Syracuse	52
Lionel Simmons, Sacramento	La Salle	52
Dee Brown, Boston	Jacksonville	49
Kendall Gill, Charlotte	Illinois	44
Dennis Scott, Orlando	Ga.Tech	42

1991 NBA PLAYOFFS

FIRST ROUND	SEMI-FINAL	FINAL		FINAL	SEMI-FINAL	FIRST ROUND

Portland 3
Seattle 2 — Portland 4
Phoenix 1
Utah 3 — Utah 1
— Portland 2
San Antonio 1
Golden St. 3 — Golden St. 1
LA Lakers 3
Houston 0 — LA Lakers 4
— LA Lakers 4

WESTERN CONFERENCE — Chicago 4 / LA Lakers 1 — **EASTERN CONFERENCE**

Chicago 3
New York 0 — Chicago 4
Milwaukee 0
Philadelphia 3 — Philadelphia 1
— Chicago 4
Boston 3
Indiana 2 — Boston 2
Detroit 3
Atlanta 2 — Detroit 4
— Detroit 0

Series Summaries

Western Conference

FIRST ROUND (Best of 5)

	W	L	Avg	Leading Scorers
Portland	3	2	106.4	Drexler (25.0)
Seattle	2	3	103.6	E.Johnson (24.0)

Date	Winner	Home Court
Apr.26	Blazers, 110-102	at Portland
Apr.28	Blazers, 115-106	at Portland
Apr.30	Sonics, 102-99	at Seattle
May 2	Sonics, 101-89	at Seattle
May 4	Blazers, 119-107	at Portland

	W	L	Avg	Leading Scorers
Golden St.	3	1	112.8	Mullin (25.3)
San Antonio	1	3	107.8	Robinson (25.8)

Date	Winner	Home Court
Apr.25	Spurs, 130-121	at San Antonio
Apr.27	Warriors, 111-98	at San Antonio
May 1	Warriors, 109-106	at Golden St.
May 3	Warriors, 110-97	at Golden St.

	W	L	Avg	Leading Scorers
Utah	3	1	107.3	K.Malone (29.8)
Phoenix	1	3	95.8	Hornacek (18.3)

Date	Winner	Home Court
Apr.25	Jazz, 129-90	at Phoenix
Apr.27	Suns, 102-92	at Phoenix
Apr.30	Jazz, 107-98	at Utah
May 2	Jazz, 101-93	at Utah

	W	L	Avg	Leading Scorers
LA Lakers	3	0	99.0	M.Johnson (22.7)
Houston	0	3	93.3	Olajuwon (22.0)

Date	Winner	Home Court
Apr.25	Lakers, 94-92	at Los Angeles
Apr.27	Lakers, 109-98	at Los Angeles
Apr.30	Lakers, 94-90	at Houston

SEMIFINALS (Best of 7)

	W	L	Avg	Leading Scorers
Portland	4	1	108.6	Porter (22.2)
Utah	1	4	103.4	K.Malone (29.6)

Date	Winner	Home Court
May 7	Blazers, 117-97	at Portland
May 9	Blazers, 118-116	at Portland
May 12	Blazers, 104-101	at Utah
May 14	Blazers, 103-96	at Utah

	W	L	Avg	Leading Scorers
LA Lakers	4	1	122.4	M.Johnson (25.8)
Golden St.	1	4	115.8	Hardaway (26.8)

Date	Winner	Home Court
May 5	Lakers, 126-116	at Los Angeles
May 8	Warriors, 125-124	at Los Angeles
May 10	Lakers, 115-112	at Golden St.
May 12	Lakers, 123-107	at Golden St.
May 14	Lakers, 124-119 (OT)	at Los Angeles

CHAMPIONSHIP (Best of 7)

	W	L	Avg	Leading Scorers
LA Lakers	4	2	101.0	M. Johnson (20.7)
Portland	2	4	97.8	Drexler (20.5)

Date	Winner	Home Court
May 18	Lakers, 111-106	at Portland
May 21	Blazers, 109-98	at Portland
May 24	Lakers, 106-92	at Los Angeles

Date	Winner	Home Court
May 26	Lakers, 116-95	at Los Angeles
May 28	Blazers, 95-84	at Portland
May 30	Lakers, 91-90	at Los Angeles

Eastern Conference

FIRST ROUND (Best of 5)

	W	L	Avg	Leading Scorers
Chicago	3	0	106.0	Jordan (29.0)
New York	0	3	86.0	Vandeweghe (17.0)

Date	Winner	Home Court
Apr.25	Bulls, 126-85	at Chicago
Apr.28	Bulls, 89-79	at Chicago
Apr.30	Bulls, 103-94	at New York

	W	L	Avg	Leading Scorers
Boston	3	2	118.8	Lewis (21.8)
Indiana	2	3	118.4	Person (26.0)

Date	Winner	Home Court
Apr.26	Celtics, 127-120	at Boston
Apr.28	Pacers, 130-118	at Boston
May 1	Celtics, 112-105	at Indiana
May 3	Pacers, 116-113	at Indiana
May 5	Celtics, 124-121	at Boston

Triple double: Apr.26—Bird (21p,11r,12a).

	W	L	Avg	Leading Scorers
Philadelphia	3	0	112.0	Barkley (23.7)
Milwaukee	0	3	100.7	Robertson (23.7)

Date	Winner	Home Court
Apr.25	Sixers, 99-90	at Milwaukee
Apr.25	Sixers, 116-112 (OT)	at Milwaukee
Apr.30	Sixers, 121-100	at Philadelphia

	W	L	Avg	Leading Scorers
Detroit	3	2	105.2	Dumars (23.8)
Atlanta	2	3	97.2	Wilkins (20.8)

Date	Winner	Home Court
Apr.26	Hawks, 103-98	at Detroit
Apr.28	Pistons, 101-88	at Detroit
Apr.30	Pistons, 103-91	at Atlanta
May 2	Hawks, 123-111	at Atlanta
May 5	Pistons, 113-81	at Detroit

SEMIFINALS (Best of 7)

	W	L	Avg	Leading Scorers
Chicago	4	1	103.0	Jordan (33.4)
Philadelphia	1	4	94.2	Barkley (25.6)

Date	Winner	Home Court
May 4	Bulls, 105-92	at Chicago
May 6	Bulls, 112-100	at Chicago
May 10	Sixers, 99-97	at Philadelphia
May 12	Bulls, 101-85	at Philadelphia
May 14	Bulls, 100-95	at Chicago

	W	L	Avg	Leading Scorers
Detroit	4	2	101.5	Dumars (23.3)
Boston	2	4	103.3	Lewis (22.8)

Date	Winner	Home Court
May 7	Pistons, 86-75	at Boston
May 9	Celtics, 109-103	at Boston
May 11	Celtics, 115-83	at Detroit
May 13	Pistons, 104-97	at Detroit
May 15	Pistons, 116-111	at Boston
May 17	Pistons, 117-113 (OT)	at Detroit

CHAMPIONSHIP (Best of 7)

	W	L	Avg	Leading Scorers
Chicago	4	0	106.8	Jordan (29.8)
Detroit	0	4	95.3	V.Johnson (21.0)

Date	Winner	Home Court
May 19	Bulls, 94-83	at Chicago
May 21	Bulls, 105-97	at Chicago
May 25	Bulls, 113-107	at Detroit
May 27	Bulls, 115-94	at Detroit

NBA FINALS
(Best of 7)

	W	L	Avg	Leading Scorers
Chicago	4	1	101.4	Jordan (31.2)
L.A.Lakers	1	4	91.6	Worthy (19.3)

Date	Winner	Home Court
Jun. 2	Lakers, 93-91	at Chicago
Jun. 5	Bulls, 107-86	at Chicago
Jun. 7	Bulls, 104-96 (OT)	at Los Angeles
Jun. 9	Bulls, 97-82	at Los Angeles
Jun.12	Bulls, 108-101	at Los Angeles

Most Valuable Player
Michael Jordan, Chicago

Leading Scorers
At least three games played.

	Gm	FG	FT	Pts	Avg
Michael Jordan, Chi	17	197	125	529	31.1
Karl Malone, Utah	9	95	77	267	29.7
Chuck Person, Ind	5	48	17	130	26.0
David Robinson, SA	4	35	33	103	25.8
Tim Hardaway, GS	9	90	30	227	25.2
Charles Barkley, Phi	8	74	49	199	24.9
Eddie Johnson, Sea	5	46	24	120	24.0
Chris Mullin, GS	8	69	43	190	23.8
Alvin Robertson, Mil	3	29	10	71	23.7
Reggie Lewis, Bos	11	95	56	246	22.4
Mitch Richmond, GS	9	85	23	201	22.3
Hakeem Olajuwon, Hou	3	26	14	66	22.0
Magic Johnson, LAL	19	118	157	414	21.8
Clyde Drexler, Port	16	128	76	347	21.7
Scottie Pippen, Chi	17	142	80	368	21.6
Reggie Miller, Ind	5	34	32	108	21.6
James Worthy, LAL	18	161	53	379	21.1
Hersey Hawkins, Phi	8	47	59	167	20.9
Dominique Wilkins, Atl	5	35	32	104	20.8
Kevin McHale, Bos	11	78	66	228	20.7

Final Standings

	Gm	W	L	Pct	—Per Game— For	Opp
Chicago	17	15	2	.882	103.9	92.2
LA Lakers	19	12	7	.632	103.8	102.8
Portland	16	9	7	.563	103.9	102.6
Detroit	15	7	8	.467	101.1	102.2
Boston	11	5	6	.455	110.4	109.2
Philadelphia	8	4	4	.500	100.9	102.1
Utah	9	4	5	.444	105.1	102.9
Golden St	9	4	5	.444	114.4	115.9
Indiana	5	2	3	.400	118.4	118.8
Seattle	5	2	3	.400	103.6	106.4
Atlanta	5	2	3	.400	97.2	105.2
San Antonio	4	1	3	.250	107.8	112.8
Phoenix	4	1	3	.250	95.8	107.3
Houston	3	0	3	.000	93.3	99.0
Milwaukee	3	0	3	.000	100.7	112.0
New York	3	0	3	.000	86.0	106.0

NBA Finalists' Composite Box Score

Chicago Bulls (15-2)

	Gm	FG%	TPts	Per Game Pts	Reb	Ast
Michael Jordan	17	.524	529	31.1	6.4	8.4
Scottie Pippen	17	.504	368	21.6	8.9	5.8
Horace Grant	17	.583	226	13.3	8.1	2.2
Bill Cartwright	17	.519	162	9.5	4.7	1.9
John Paxson.......	17	.530	140	8.2	1.4	3.1
B.J.Armstrong	17	.500	93	5.5	1.6	2.5
Craig Hodges	17	.423	80	4.7	0.2	0.6
Will Perdue........	17	.547	70	4.1	3.8	0.2
Cliff Levingston	17	.512	45	2.6	2.4	0.4
Stacy King	11	.296	23	2.1	2.0	0.2
Scott Williams	12	.462	23	1.9	1.7	0.3
Dennis Hopson	5	.333	8	1.6	0.8	0.2
BULLS.............	17	.514	1767	103.9	40.2	25.5
OPPONENTS......	17	.450	1568	92.2	35.9	19.2

Three-point FG: Hodges (11 for 28), Jordan (10-26), Pippen (4-17), Armstrong (3-5), Paxson (2-14), King (0-1), Williams (0-1); TEAM (30 for 92 = .326 pct.).

Los Angeles Lakers (12-7)

	Gm	FG%	TPts	Per Game Pts	Reb	Ast
Magic Johnson	19	.440	414	21.8	8.1	12.6
James Worthy	18	.465	379	21.1	4.1	3.9
Sam Perkins.......	19	.548	336	17.7	8.3	1.7
Vlade Divac	19	.564	252	13.3	6.7	1.1
Byron Scott	18	.511	237	13.2	3.2	1.6
Terry Teagle.......	18	.376	119	6.6	1.6	0.6
A.C.Green.........	19	.423	124	6.5	5.4	0.5
Elden Campbell....	14	.658	57	4.1	2.1	0.2
Tony Smith........	7	.462	14	2.0	0.4	0.3
Larry Drew........	18	.424	35	1.9	0.4	1.2
Irving Thomas	3	1.000	2	0.7	0.0	0.0
Mychal Thompson...	8	.286	4	0.5	1.1	0.0
LAKERS...........	19	.483	1973	103.8	39.3	23.1
OPPONENTS......	19	.487	1953	102.8	40.1	24.8

Three-point FG: Johnson (21 for 71), Scott (20-38), Perkins (11-30), Green (4-8), Worthy (4-24), Drew (3-11), Divac (1-6); TEAM (64 for 188 = .340 pct.).

NBA Draft

First and second round picks at the 45th annual NBA College Draft held June 26, 1991 in New York City. The order of the first 11 positions determined by a Draft Lottery held May 19. Positions 12-27 reflect regular season records in reverse order. Underclassmen selected are noted in CAPITAL letters.

First Round

	Team	Player	Pos
1	Charlotte..................	Larry Johnson, UNLV	F
2	New Jersey	KENNY ANDERSON, Ga.Tech	G
3	Sacramento...........	BILLY OWENS, Syracuse	F
4	Denver..............	Dikembe Mutombo, G'town	C
5	Miami	Steve Smith, Michigan St.	G
6	Dallas	Doug Smith, Missouri	F
7	Minnesota	Luc Longley, New Mexico	C
8	Washington	Mark Macon, Temple	G
9	a-Atlanta	Stacey Augmon, UNLV	F
10	Orlando	BRIAN WILLIAMS, Arizona	F
11	Cleveland	TERRELL BRANDON, Oregon	G
12	New York	Greg Anthony, UNLV	G
13	Indiana	Dale Davis, Clemson	F
14	Seattle..................	Rich King, Nebraska	C
15	Atlanta................	Anthony Avent, Seton Hall	F
16	b-Golden St	Chris Gatling, Old Dom.	F
17	Golden St.............	Victor Alexander, Iowa St.	F
18	Milwaukee................	Kevin Brooks, SW La.	G
19	c-Washington	LaBradford Smith, Louisville	G
20	Houston	John Turner, Phillips-OK	F
21	Utah	Eric Murdock, Providence	G
22	d-LA Clippers	LeRon Ellis, Syracuse	F
23	e-Orlando	Stanley Roberts, Spain	C
24	Boston	Rick Fox, N.Carolina	F
25	f-Golden St	Shaun Vandiver, Colorado	F
26	Chicago	Mark Randall, Kansas	F
27	g-Sacramento	Pete Chilcutt, N.Carolina	F

Second Round

	Team	Player	Pos
28	h-Charlotte	Kevin Lynch, Minnesota	G
29	Miami	George Ackles, UNLV	C
30	i-Atlanta..............	Rodney Monroe, N.C.State	G
31	j-Sacramento	Randy Brown, N.Mexico St.	G
32	k-Phoenix..............	Chad Gallagher, Creighton	F
33	Dallas	DONALD HODGE, Temple	C
34	Minnesota	Myron Brown, Slippery Rock	G
35	l-Dallas	Mike Iuzzolino, St.Fran-PA	G
36	Orlando	Chris Corchiani, N.C.State	G
37	LA Clippers	Elliot Perry, Memphis St.	G
38	m-LA Clippers	Joe Wylie, Miami-FL	F
39	n-Cleveland	Jimmy Oliver, Purdue	G
40	o-Detroit	Doug Overton, La Salle	G
41	Indiana	Sean Green, Iona	G
42	p-Sacramento	Steve Hood, J.Madison	G
43	Golden St...........	Lamont Strothers, C.Newport	G
44	Philadelphia	Alvaro Teheran, Houston	C
45	Milwaukee................	Bobby Phills, Southern	G
46	q-Phoenix	Richard Dumas, Okla.St.	G
47	Houston	Keith Hughes, Rutgers	F
48	Utah	Issac Austin, Ariz.St.	F
49	San Antonio	Greg Sutton, O.Roberts	G
50	Phoenix	Joey Wright, Texas	G
51	r-Houston	ZAN TABAK, Yugoslavia	C
52	LA Lakers..............	Anthony Jones, O.Roberts	G
53	s-New Jersey	Von McDade, WI-Milwaukee	G
54	Portland	Marcus Kennedy, E.Michigan	F

Acquired Picks

First Round: a- from LA Clippers; b- from Philadelphia; c- from Denver via Detroit and Dallas; d- from Phoenix via Seattle; e- from San Antonio; f- from LA Lakers; g- from Portland.

Second Round: h- from Denver; i- from Sacramento; j- from New Jersey; k- from Charlotte; l- from Washington; m- from Cleveland; n- from New York via Charlotte; o- from Seattle; p- from Atlanta; q- from Detroit; r- from Boston via New Jersey and Cleveland; s- from Chicago.

Underclassmen Not Drafted

Juniors (5): Tony Farmer, Nebraska; Jerome Harmon, Louisville; Anderson Hunt, UNLV; Raoul Hutchens, Whittier; Chancellor Nichols, James Madison. **Sophomores (1):** Ty Moseler, WI-Waukesha.

PRO BASKETBALL
STATISTICS

THROUGH THE YEARS
1947-1991
CHAMPIONS • NBA LEADERS

SEC
B

PAGE
291

THE 1992 INFORMATION PLEASE SPORTS ALMANAC

The NBA Finals

Although the National Basketball Association traces its first championship back to the 1946-47 season, the league was then called the Basketball Association of America (BAA). It did not become the NBA until after the 1948-49 season when the BAA and the National Basketball League (NBL) agreed to merge.

In the chart below, the Eastern finalists (representing the NBA Eastern Division from 1947-70, and the NBA Eastern Conference since 1971) are listed in CAPITAL letters. Also, each NBA champion's wins and losses are noted in parentheses after the series score.

Year	Winner	Head Coach	Series	Loser	Head Coach
1947	PHILADELPHIA WARRIORS	Eddie Gottlieb	4-1 (WWWLW)	Chicago Stags	Harold Olsen
1948	Baltimore Bullets	Buddy Jeannette	4-2 (LWWWLW)	PHILA.WARRIORS	Eddie Gottlieb
1949	Minnesota Lakers	John Kundla	4-2 (WWWLLW)	WASH.CAPITOLS	Red Auerbach
1950	Minnesota Lakers	John Kundla	4-2 (WLWWLW)	SYRACUSE	Al Cervi
1951	Rochester	Les Harrison	4-3 (WWWLLLW)	NEW YORK	Joe Lapchick
1952	Minnesota Lakers	John Kundla	4-3 (WLWWLLW)	NEW YORK	Joe Lapchick
1953	Minnesota Lakers	John Kundla	4-1 (LWWWW)	NEW YORK	Joe Lapchick
1954	Minnesota Lakers	John Kundla	4-3 (WLWWLWW)	SYRACUSE	Al Cervi
1955	SYRACUSE	Al Cervi	4-3 (WWLLLWW)	Ft.Wayne Pistons	Charles Eckman
1956	PHILADELPHIA WARRIORS	George Senesky	4-1 (WLWWW)	Ft.Wayne Pistons	Charles Eckman
1957	BOSTON	Red Auerbach	4-3 (LWLWWLW)	St.Louis Hawks	Alex Hannum
1958	St.Louis Hawks	Alex Hannum	4-2 (WLWLWW)	BOSTON	Red Auerbach
1959	BOSTON	Red Auerbach	4-0	Minn.Lakers	John Kundla
1960	BOSTON	Red Auerbach	4-3 (WLWLWLW)	St.Louis Hawks	Ed Macauley
1961	BOSTON	Red Auerbach	4-1 (WLWWW)	St.Louis Hawks	Paul Seymour
1962	BOSTON	Red Auerbach	4-3 (WLLWLWW)	LA Lakers	Fred Schaus
1963	BOSTON	Red Auerbach	4-2 (WWLWLW)	LA Lakers	Fred Schaus
1964	BOSTON	Red Auerbach	4-1 (WLWWW)	SF Warriors	Alex Hannum
1965	BOSTON	Red Auerbach	4-1 (WWLWW)	LA Lakers	Fred Schaus
1966	BOSTON	Red Auerbach	4-3 (LWWWLLW)	LA Lakers	Fred Schaus
1967	PHILADELPHIA 76ERS	Alex Hannum	4-2 (WLWWLW)	SF Warriors	Bill Sharman
1968	BOSTON	Bill Russell	4-2 (WLWLWW)	LA Lakers	B.van Breda Kolff
1969	BOSTON	Bill Russell	4-3 (LLWWLWW)	LA Lakers	B.van Breda Kolff
1970	NEW YORK	Red Holzman	4-3 (WLWLWLW)	LA Lakers	Joe Mullaney
1971	Milwaukee	Larry Costello	4-0	BALT.BULLETS	Gene Shue
1972	LA Lakers	Bill Sharman	4-1 (LWWWW)	NEW YORK	Red Holzman
1973	NEW YORK	Red Holzman	4-1 (LWWWW)	LA Lakers	Bill Sharman
1974	BOSTON	Tommy Heinsohn	4-3 (WLWLWLW)	Milwaukee	Larry Costello
1975	Golden St.Warriors	Al Attles	4-0	WASH.BULLETS	K.C. Jones
1976	BOSTON	Tommy Heinsohn	4-2 (WWLLWW)	Phoenix	John MacLeod
1977	Portland	Jack Ramsay	4-2 (LLWWWW)	PHILA.76ERS	Gene Shue
1978	WASHINGTON BULLETS	Dick Motta	4-3 (LWLWLWW)	Seattle	Lenny Wilkens
1979	Seattle	Lenny Wilkens	4-1 (LWWWW)	WASH.BULLETS	Dick Motta
1980	LA Lakers	Paul Westhead	4-2 (WLWLWW)	PHILA.76ERS	Billy Cunningham
1981	BOSTON	Bill Fitch	4-2 (WLWLWW)	Houston	Del Harris
1982	LA Lakers	Pat Riley	4-2 (WLWLWW)	PHILA 76ERS	Billy Cunningham
1983	PHILADELPHIA 76ERS	Billy Cunningham	4-0	LA Lakers	Pat Riley
1984	BOSTON	K.C. Jones	4-3 (LWLWLWW)	LA Lakers	Pat Riley
1985	LA Lakers	Pat Riley	4-2 (LWWLWW)	BOSTON	K.C. Jones
1986	BOSTON	K.C. Jones	4-2 (WWLWLW)	Houston	Bill Fitch
1987	LA Lakers	Pat Riley	4-2 (WWLWLW)	BOSTON	K.C. Jones
1988	LA Lakers	Pat Riley	4-3 (LWWLLWW)	DETROIT PISTONS	Chuck Daly
1989	DETROIT PISTONS	Chuck Daly	4-0	LA Lakers	Pat Riley
1990	DETROIT	Chuck Daly	4-1 (WLWWW)	Portland	Rick Adelman
1991	CHICAGO	Phil Jackson	4-1 (LWWWW)	LA Lakers	Mike Dunleavy

Note: Four Finalists were led by player-coaches: **1948**—Buddy Jeannette (guard) of Baltimore; **1950**—Al Cervi (guard) of Syracuse; **1968**—Bill Russell (center) of Boston; **1969**—Bill Russell (center) of Boston.

Most Valuable Players

Selected by an 11-member media panel. Winners who did not play for the NBA champion are in **bold** type.
Multiple winners: Magic Johnson (3); Kareem Abdul-Jabbar and Larry Bird (2).

Year		Year		Year	
1969	**Jerry West**, LA Lakers, G	1977	Bill Walton, Portland, C	1985	K. Abdul-Jabbar, LA Lakers, C
1970	Willis Reed, New York, C	1978	Wes Unseld, Washington, C	1986	Larry Bird, Boston, F
1971	Lew Alcindor, Milwaukee, C	1979	Dennis Johnson, Seattle, G	1987	Magic Johnson, LA Lakers, G
1972	Wilt Chamberlain, LA Lakers, C	1980	Magic Johnson, LA Lakers, G/C	1988	James Worthy, LA Lakers, F
1973	Willis Reed, New York, C	1981	Cedric Maxwell, Boston, F	1989	Joe Dumars, Detroit, G
1974	John Havlicek, Boston, F	1982	Magic Johnson, LA Lakers, G		
1975	Rick Barry, Golden State, F	1983	Moses Malone, Philadelphia, C	1990	Isiah Thomas, Detroit, G
1976	Jo Jo White, Boston, G	1984	Larry Bird, Boston, F	1991	Michael Jordan, Chicago, G

Note: Alcindor changed his name to Kareem Abdul-Jabbar after the 1970-71 season.

All-Time NBA Playoff Leaders

Through 1991 playoffs.

CAREER

Years listed indicate number of playoff appearances. Players active in 1991 playoffs in **bold** type.

Points

	Yrs	Gm	Pts	Avg
Kareem Abdul-Jabbar	18	237	5762	24.3
Jerry West	13	153	4457	29.1
Larry Bird	11	160	3852	24.1
John Havlicek	13	172	3776	22.0
Magic Johnson	12	186	3640	19.6
Elgin Baylor	12	134	3623	27.0
Wilt Chamberlain	13	160	3607	22.5
Dennis Johnson	13	180	3116	17.3
Julius Erving	11	141	3088	21.9
James Worthy	8	138	2953	21.4
Kevin McHale	11	155	2941	19.0
Sam Jones	12	154	2909	18.9
Bill Russell	13	165	2673	16.2
Robert Parish	12	164	2616	16.0
Michael Jordan	7	70	2425	34.6
Bob Pettit	9	88	2240	25.5
Elvin Hayes	10	96	2194	22.9
Isiah Thomas	8	106	2191	20.7
George Mikan	9	91	2141	23.5
Moses Malone	12	94	2077	22.1

Scoring Average

Minimum of 25 games or 700 points.

	Yrs	Gm	Pts	Avg
Michael Jordan	7	70	2425	34.6
Jerry West	13	153	4457	29.1
Bernard King	4	25	679	27.2
Elgin Baylor	12	134	3623	27.0
Karl Malone	6	37	999	27.0
George Gervin	9	59	1592	27.0
Hakeem Olajuwon	7	50	1326	26.5
Dominique Wilkins	7	48	1255	26.1
Bob Pettit	9	88	2240	25.5
Rick Barry	7	74	1833	24.8
Alex English	10	68	1661	24.4
Kareem Abdul-Jabbar	18	237	5762	24.3
Paul Arizin	8	49	1186	24.2
Larry Bird	11	160	3852	24.1
George Mikan	9	91	2141	23.5
Patrick Ewing	4	26	598	23.0
Elvin Hayes	10	96	2194	22.9
Bob Love	6	47	1076	22.9
Wilt Chamberlain	13	160	3607	22.5
Tom Chambers	6	56	1254	22.4

Field Goals

	Yrs	FGA	FGM	Pct
Kareem Abdul-Jabbar	18	4422	2356	.533
Jerry West	13	3460	1622	.469
John Havlicek	13	3329	1451	.436
Larry Bird	11	3048	1437	.471
Wilt Chamberlain	13	2728	1425	.522
Elgin Baylor	12	3161	1388	.439

Free Throws

	Yrs	FTA	FTM	Pct
Jerry West	13	1507	1213	.805
Kareem Abdul-Jabbar	18	1419	1050	.740
Magic Johnson	12	1241	1040	.838
Larry Bird	11	1008	898	.891
John Havlicek	13	1046	874	.836
Elgin Baylor	12	1101	847	.769

Assists

	Yrs	Gm	Ast	Avg
Magic Johnson	12	186	2320	12.5
Larry Bird	11	160	1041	6:5
Dennis Johnson	13	180	1006	5.6
Jerry West	13	153	970	6.3
Isiah Thomas	8	106	950	9.0
Bob Cousy	13	109	937	8.6

Rebounds

	Yrs	Gm	Reb	Avg
Bill Russell	13	165	4104	24.9
Wilt Chamberlain	13	160	3913	24.5
Kareem Abdul-Jabbar	18	237	2481	10.5
Wes Unseld	12	119	1777	14.9
Elgin Baylor	12	134	1725	12.9

Personal Fouls

	Yrs	Gm	Fouls	DQ
Kareem Abdul-Jabbar	18	237	797	7
Robert Parish	12	164	577	16
Dennis Johnson	13	180	575	8
Bill Russell	13	165	546	8
Kevin McHale	11	155	531	8
Magic Johnson	12	186	521	3
Tom Sanders	11	130	508	26

Appearances

	No		No
K.Abdul-Jabbar	18	John Havlicek	13
Dolph Schayes	15	Dennis Johnson	13
Paul Silas	14	Bill Russell	13
Wilt Chamberlain	13	Chet Walker	13
Bob Cousy	13	Jerry West	13
Hal Greer	13		

Games Played

	No		No
K. Abdul-Jabbar	237	Bill Russell	165
Magic Johnson	186	**Robert Parish**	164
Dennis Johnson	180	Paul Silas	163
John Havlicek	172	**Larry Bird**	160
Michael Cooper	168	Wilt Chamberlain	160

SINGLE GAME

Points

	Date	FG-FT—Pts
Michael Jordan, Chi.at Bos.*	4/20/86	22-19—63
Elgin Baylor, LA at Bos	4/14/62	22-17—61
Wilt Chamberlain, Phi.vs Syr	3/22/62	22-12—56
Rick Barry, SF vs Phi	4/18/67	22-11—55
Michael Jordan, Chi.vs Cle.	5/1/88	24- 7—55

*Double overtime.

Field Golds

	Date	FGA	FGM
Wilt Chamberlain, Phi.vs Syr	3/14/60	42	24
John Havlicek, Bos.vs Atl.	4/1/73	36	24
Michael Jordan, Chi.vs Cle.	5/1/88	45	24

Seven players tied with 22 each.

Free Throws

	Date	FTA	FTM
Bob Cousy, Bos.vs Syr.*	3/21/53	32	30
Michael Jordan, Chi.vs NY.	5/14/89	28	23
Michael Jordan, Chi.vs Cle.	5/5/89	27	22
Oscar Robertson, Cin.at Bos	4/10/63	22	21

Four players tied with 20 each.

*Four overtimes.

3-Pt Field Goals

	Date	No
Michael Cooper, LA Lakers vs Bos	6/4/87	6
Michael Adams, Den.vs Pho	4/30/89	6
Eddie Johnson, Pho.vs Utah	5/4/90	6
Bill Laimbeer, Det.vs Port.*	6/7/90	6

Five players tied with 5 each.

*One overtime.

Assists

	Date	No
Magic Johnson, LA vs Pho	5/15/84	24
John Stockton, Utah at LA Lakers	5/17/88	24
Magic Johnson, LA Lakers at Port.	5/3/85	23
Doc Rivers, Atl.vs Bos.	5/16/88	22
Magic Johnson, LA vs Bos.	6/3/84	21
Magic Johnson, LA Lakers vs Hou	4/27/91	21
Magic Johnson, LA Lakers at Port.	5/18/91	21

Rebounds

	Date	No
Wilt Chamberlain, Phi.vs Bos	4/5/67	41
Bill Russell, Bos.vs Phi	3/23/58	40
Bill Russell, Bos.vs St.L	3/29/60	40
Bill Russell, Bos.vs LA*	4/18/62	40

Three players tied with 39 each.

*One overtime.

Blocked Shots

	Date	No
Mark Eaton, Utah vs Hou	4/26/85	10
Akeem Olajuwon, Hou.at LA Lakers	4/29/90	10
Kareem Abdul-Jabbar, LA vs GS	4/22/77	9
Manute Bol, Wash.at Phi	4//18/86	9

Thirteen players tied with 8 each.

Steals

	Date	No
Rick Barry, GS vs Sea.	4/14/75	8
Lionel Hollins, Port.at LA	5/8/77	8
Maurice Cheeks, Phi.vs NJ	4/11/79	8
Craig Hodges, Mil.at Phi	5/9/86	8

Nine players tied with 7 each.

Appearances in NBA Finals

Standings of all teams that have reached the NBA Finals since 1947.

App		Titles	Last Won
24	Minneapolis-LA Lakers	11	1988
19	Boston Celtics	16	1986
8	Syracuse Nats-Phila.76ers	3	1983
6	Phila-SF-Golden St.Warriors	3	1975
6	New York Knicks	2	1973
4	Ft.Wayne-Detroit Pistons	2	1990
4	St.Louis-Atlanta Hawks	1	1958
4	Baltimore-Washington Bullets	1	1978
2	Milwaukee Bucks	1	1971
2	Portland Trail Blazers	1	1977
2	Seattle SuperSonics	1	1979
2	San Diego-Houston Rockets	0	—
1	Baltimore Bullets	1	1948
1	Rochester-Cincinnati-KC/Omaha-Sacramento Royals/Kings	1	1951
1	Chicago Bulls	1	1991
1	Chicago Stags	0	—
1	Washington Capitols	0	—

Teams now defunct: (3): Chicago Stags (1946-50), Washington Capitols (1946-51) and Baltimore Bullets (1947-55).

SINGLE NBA FINALS

Points

Series		Year	Pts
4-Gm	Rick Barry, GS vs Wash	1975	118
5-Gm	Jerry West, LA vs Bos	1965	169
6-Gm	Rick Barry, SF vs Phi	1967	245
7-Gm	Elgin Baylor, LA vs Bos	1962	284

Field Goals

Series		Year	No
4-Gm	K.Abdul-Jabbar, Mil.vs Bal.	1971	46
5-Gm	Michael Jordan, Chi.vs LAL	1991	63
6-Gm	Rick Barry, SF vs Phi	1967	94
7-Gm	Elgin Baylor, LA vs Bos	1962	101

Assists

Series		Year	No
4-Gm	Bob Cousy, Bos.vs Mpls	1959	51
5-Gm	Magic Johnson, LAL vs Chi	1991	62
6-Gm	Magic Johnson, LAL vs Bos	1985	84
7-Gm	Magic Johnson, LA vs Bos	1984	95

Rebounds

Series		Year	No
4-Gm	Bill Russell, Bos.vs Mpls	1959	118
5-Gm	Bill Russell, Bos.vs St.L	1961	144
6-Gm	Wilt Chamberlain, Phi.vs SF	1967	171
7-Gm	Bill Russell, Bos.vs LA	1962	189

NBA Franchise Origins

Here is what the current 27 teams in the National Basketball Association have to show for the years they have put in as members of the National Basketball League (NBL), Basketball Association of America (BAA), the NBA, and the American Basketball Association (ABA). League titles are noted by year won.

Western Conference

	First Season		League Titles	Franchise Stops
Dallas Mavericks	1980-81	(NBA)	None	Dallas (1980—)
Denver Nuggets	1967-68	(ABA)	None	Denver (1967—)
Golden St. Warriors	1946-47	(BAA)	1 BAA (1947)	Philadelphia (1946-62)
			2 NBA (1956,75)	San Francisco (1962-71)
				Oakland (1971—)
Houston Rockets	1967-68	(NBA)	None	San Diego (1967-71)
				Houston (1971—)
LA Clippers	1970-71	(NBA)	None	Buffalo (1970-78)
				San Diego (1978-84)
				Los Angeles (1984—)
LA Lakers	1947-48	(NBL)	1 NBL (1947)	Minneapolis (1947-60)
			1 BAA (1949)	Los Angeles (1960-67)
			10 NBA (1950,52-54,72,	Inglewood,CA (1967—)
			80,82,85,87-88)	
Minn. Timberwolves	1989-90	(NBA)	None	Minneapolis (1989—)
Phoenix Suns	1968-69	(NBA)	None	Phoenix (1968—)
Portland Trail Blazers	1970-71	(NBA)	1 NBA (1977)	Portland (1970—)
Sacramento Kings	1945-46	(NBL)	1 NBL (1946)	Rochester,NY (1945-58)
			1 NBA (1951)	Cincinnati (1958-72)
				KC-Omaha (1972-75)
				Kansas City (1975-85)
				Sacramento (1985—)
San Antonio Spurs	1967-68	(ABA)	None	Dallas (1967-73)
				San Antonio (1973—)
Seattle SuperSonics	1967-68	(NBA)	1 NBA (1979)	Seattle (1967—)
Utah Jazz	1974-75	(NBA)	None	New Orleans (1974-79)
				Salt Lake City (1979—)

Eastern Conference

	First Season		League Titles	Franchise Stops
Atlanta Hawks	1946-47	(NBL)	1 NBA (1958)	Tri-Cities (1946-51)
				Milwaukee (1951-55)
				St.Louis (1955-68)
				Atlanta (1968—)
Boston Celtics	1946-47	(BAA)	16 NBA (1957,59-66,68-69	Boston (1946—)
			74,76,81,84,86)	
Charlotte Hornets	1988-89	(NBA)	None	Charlotte (1988—)
Chicago Bulls	1966-67	(NBA)	1 NBA (1991)	Chicago (1966—)
Cleveland Cavaliers	1970-71	(NBA)	None	Cleveland (1970-74)
				Richfield, OH (1974—)
Detroit Pistons	1941-42	(NBL)	2 NBL (1944-45)	Ft.Wayne,IN (1941-57)
			2 NBA (1989-90)	Detroit (1957-78)
				Pontiac,MI (1978-88)
				Auburn Hills,MI (1988—)
Indiana Pacers	1967-68	(ABA)	3 ABA (1970,72-73)	Indianapolis (1967—)
Miami Heat	1988-89	(NBA)	None	Miami (1988—)
Milwaukee Bucks	1968-69	(NBA)	1 NBA (1971)	Milwaukee (1968—)
New Jersey Nets	1967-68	(ABA)	2 ABA (1974,76)	Paramus,NJ (1967-68)
				Commack,NY (1968-69)
				W.Hempstead,NY (1969-71)
				Uniondale,NY (1971-77)
				Piscataway,NJ (1977-81)
				E.Rutherford,NJ (1981—)
New York Knicks	1946-47	(BAA)	2 NBA (1970,73)	New York (1946—)
Orlando Magic	1989-90	(NBA)	None	Orlando,FL (1989—)
Philadelphia 76ers	1949-50	(NBA)	3 NBA (1955,67,83)	Syracus,NY (1949-63)
				Philadelphia (1963—)
Washington Bullets	1961-62	(NBA)	1 NBA (1978)	Chicago (1961-63)
				Baltimore (1963-73)
				Landover,MD (1973—)

Note: The Tri-Cities Blackhawks represented Moline and Rock Island, Ill., and Davenport, Iowa.

Annual NBA Leaders
Scoring

Championship decided by total points from 1947-69, and per game average since 1970.

Multiple winners: Wilt Chamberlain (7); Michael Jordan (5); George Gervin (4); Neil Johnston, Bob McAdoo and George Mikan (3); Kareem Abdul-Jabbar, Paul Arizin, Adrian Dantley and Bob Pettit (2).

Year		Gm	Pts	Avg	Year		Gm	Pts	Avg
1947	Joe Fulks, Phi	60	1389	23.2	1970	Jerry West, LA	74	2309	31.2
1948	Max Zaslofsky, Chi	48	1007	21.0	1971	Lew Alcindor, Mil	82	2596	31.7
1949	George Mikan, Mpls	60	1698	28.3	1972	Kareem Abdul-Jabbar, Mil	81	2822	34.8
					1973	Nate Archibald, KC-Oma	80	2719	34.0
1950	George Mikan, Mpls	68	1865	27.4	1974	Bob McAdoo, Buf	74	2261	30.6
1951	George Mikan, Mpls	68	1932	28.4	1975	Bob McAdoo, Buf	82	2831	34.5
1952	Paul Arizin, Phi	66	1674	25.4	1976	Bob McAdoo, Buf	78	2427	31.1
1953	Neil Johnston, Phi	70	1564	22.3	1977	Pete Maravich, NO	73	2273	31.1
1954	Neil Johnston, Phi	72	1759	24.4	1978	George Gervin, SA	82	2232	27.2
1955	Neil Johnston, Phi	72	1631	22.7	1979	George Gervin, SA	80	2365	29.6
1956	Bob Pettit, St.L	72	1849	25.7					
1957	Paul Arizin, Phi	71	1817	25.6	1980	George Gervin, SA	78	2585	33.1
1958	George Yardley, Det	72	2001	27.8	1981	Adrian Dantley, Utah	80	2452	30.7
1959	Bob Pettit, St.L	72	2105	29.2	1982	George Gervin, SA	79	2551	32.3
					1983	Alex English, Den	82	2326	28.4
1960	Wilt Chamberlain, Phi	72	2707	37.6	1984	Adrian Dantley, Utah	79	2418	30.6
1961	Wilt Chamberlain, Phi	79	3033	38.4	1985	Bernard King, NY	55	1809	32.9
1962	Wilt Chamberlain, Phi	80	4029	50.4	1986	Dominique Wilkins, Atl	78	2366	30.3
1963	Wilt Chamberlain, SF	80	3586	44.8	1987	Michael Jordan, Chi	82	3041	37.1
1964	Wilt Chamberlain, SF	80	2948	36.9	1988	Michael Jordan, Chi	82	2868	35.0
1965	Wilt Chamberlain, SF-Phi	73	2534	34.7	1989	Michael Jordan, Chi	81	2633	32.5
1966	Wilt Chamberlain, Phi	79	2649	33.5					
1967	Rick Barry, SF	78	2775	35.6	1990	Michael Jordan, Chi	82	2753	33.6
1968	Dave Bing, Det	79	2142	27.1	1991	Michael Jordan, Chi	82	2580	31.5
1969	Elvin Hayes, SD	82	2327	28.4					

Note: Alcindor changed his name to Kareem Abdul-Jabbar after the 1970-71 season.

Assists

NBA assist championship was decided by Total Assists from 1952-69 and Per Game Average since 1970.

Multiple winners: Bob Cousy (8); Oscar Robertson (6); Magic Johnson, Kevin Porter and John Stockton (4); Andy Phillip and Guy Rodgers (2).

Year		Gm	Ast	Avg	Year		Gm	Ast	Avg
1947	Ernie Calverley, Prov	59	202	3.4	1970	Lenny Wilkens, Sea	75	683	9.1
1948	Howie Dallmar, Phi	48	120	2.5	1971	Norm Van Lier, Chi	82	832	10.1
1949	Bob Davies, Roch	60	321	5.4	1972	Jerry West, LA	77	747	9.7
					1973	Nate Archibald, KC-Oma	80	910	11.4
1950	Dick McGuire, NY	68	386	5.7	1974	Ernie DiGregorio, Buf	81	663	8.2
1951	Andy Phillip, Phi	66	414	6.3	1975	Kevin Porter, Wash	81	650	8.0
1952	Andy Phillip, Phi	66	539	8.2	1976	Slick Watts, Sea	82	661	8.1
1953	Bob Cousy, Bos	71	547	7.7	1977	Don Buse, Ind	81	685	8.5
1954	Bob Cousy, Bos	72	518	7.2	1978	Kevin Porter, Det-NJ	82	837	10.2
1955	Bob Cousy, Bos	71	557	7.8	1979	Kevin Porter, Det	82	1099	13.4
1956	Bob Cousy, Bos	72	642	8.9					
1957	Bob Cousy, Bos	64	478	7.5	1980	Michael Ray Richardson, NY	82	832	10.1
1958	Bob Cousy, Bos	65	463	7.1	1981	Kevin Porter, Wash	81	734	9.1
1959	Bob Cousy, Bos	65	557	8.6	1982	Johnny Moore, SA	79	762	9.6
					1983	Magic Johnson, LA	79	829	10.5
1960	Bob Cousy, Bos	75	715	9.5	1984	Magic Johnson, LA	67	875	13.1
1961	Oscar Robertson, Cin	71	690	9.7	1985	Isiah Thomas, Det	81	1123	13.9
1962	Oscar Robertson, Cin	79	899	11.4	1986	Magic Johnson, LA Lakers	72	907	12.6
1963	Guy Rodgers, SF	79	825	10.4	1987	Magic Johnson, LA Lakers	80	977	12.2
1964	Oscar Robertson, Cin	79	868	11.0	1988	John Stockton, Utah	82	1128	13.8
1965	Oscar Robertson, Cin	75	861	11.5	1989	John Stockton, Utah	82	1118	13.6
1966	Oscar Robertson, Cin	76	847	11.1					
1967	Guy Rodgers, Chi	81	908	11.2	1990	John Stockton, Utah	78	1134	14.5
1968	Wilt Chamberlain, Phi	82	702	8.6	1991	John Stockton, Utah	82	1164	14.2
1969	Oscar Robertson, Cin	79	772	9.8					

All-Time NBA Leaders

Through the 1990-91 regular season.

CAREER

Players active in 1990-91 in **bold** type.

Points

	Yrs	Gm	Pts	Avg
Kareem Abdul-Jabbar	20	1560	38,387	24.6
Wilt Chamberlain	14	1045	31,419	30.1
Elvin Hayes	16	1303	27,313	21.0
Oscar Robertson	14	1040	26,710	25.7
John Havlicek	16	1270	26,395	20.8
Moses Malone	15	1164	25,737	22.1
Alex English	15	1193	25,613	21.5
Jerry West	14	932	25,192	27.0
Adrian Dantley	15	955	23,177	24.3
Elgin Baylor	14	846	23,149	27.4
Hal Greer	15	1122	21,586	19.2
Walt Bellamy	14	1043	20,941	20.1
Larry Bird	12	852	20,883	24.5
Bob Pettit	11	792	20,880	26.4
George Gervin	10	791	20,708	26.2
Robert Parish	15	1181	19,519	16.5
Bernard King	13	842	19,432	23.1
Dolph Schayes	16	1059	19,249	18.2
Bob Lanier	14	959	19,248	20.1
Gail Goodrich	14	1031	19,181	18.6
Walter Davis	14	987	19,064	19.3
Reggie Theus	13	1026	19,015	18.5
Chet Walker	13	1032	18,831	18.2
Dominique Wilkins	9	720	18,796	26.1
Bob McAdoo	14	852	18,787	22.1

Scoring Average

Minimum of 400 games or 10,000 points.

	Yrs	Gm	Pts	Avg
Michael Jordan	7	509	16,596	32.6
Wilt Chamberlain	14	1045	31,419	30.1
Elgin Baylor	14	846	23,149	27.4
Jerry West	14	932	25,192	27.0
Bob Pettit	11	792	20,880	26.4
George Gervin	10	791	20,708	26.2
Dominique Wilkins	9	720	18,796	26.1
Oscar Robertson	14	1040	26,710	25.7
Karl Malone	6	489	12,498	25.6
Kareem Abdul-Jabbar	20	1560	38,387	24.6
Larry Bird	12	852	20,883	24.5
Adrian Dantley	15	955	23,177	24.3
Pete Maravich	10	658	15,948	24.2
Patrick Ewing	6	438	10,323	23.6
Charles Barkley	7	535	12,454	23.3
Rick Barry	10	794	18,395	23.2
Bernard King	13	842	19,432	23.1
Hakeem Olajuwon	7	524	12,065	23.0
Paul Arizin	10	713	16,266	22.8
George Mikan	9	520	11,764	22.6
David Thompson	8	509	11,264	22.1
Moses Malone	15	1164	25,737	22.1
Bob McAdoo	14	852	18,787	22.1
Julius Erving	11	836	18,364	22.0
Mark Aguirre	10	758	16,691	22.0
Kiki Vandeweghe	11	702	15,259	21.7
Terry Cummings	9	698	15,154	21.7
Chris Mullin	6	439	9,462	21.6
Alex English	15	1193	25,613	21.5

Combined NBA-ABA Top 25 Points

NBA players with ABA experience are listed in CAPITAL letters. Players active during 1990-91 are in **bold** type.

	Yrs	Gm	Pts	Avg
Kareem Abdul-Jabbar	20	1560	38,387	24.6
Wilt Chamberlain	14	1045	31,419	30.1
JULIUS ERVING	16	1243	30,026	24.2
MOSES MALONE	17	1290	27,908	21.6
DAN ISSEL	15	1218	27,482	22.6
Elvin Hayes	16	1303	27,313	21.0
Oscar Robertson	14	1040	26,710	25.7
GEORGE GERVIN	14	1060	26,595	25.1
John Havlicek	16	1270	26,395	20.8
Alex English	15	1193	25,613	21.5
RICK BARRY	14	1020	25,279	24.8
Jerry West	14	932	25,192	27.0
ARTIS GILMORE	17	1329	24,941	18.8
Adrian Dantley	15	955	23,177	24.3
Elgin Baylor	14	846	23,149	27.4
Hal Greer	15	1122	21,586	19.2
Walt Bellamy	14	1043	20,941	20.1
Larry Bird	12	852	20,883	24.5
Bob Pettit	11	792	20,880	26.4
Robert Parish	15	1181	19,519	16.5
Bernard King	13	842	19,432	23.1
Dolph Schayes	16	1059	19,249	18.2
Bob Lanier	14	959	19,248	20.1
Gail Goodrich	14	1031	19,181	18.6
Walter Davis	14	987	19,064	19.3

ABA Totals: BARRY (4 yrs, 226 gm, 6884 pts, 30.5 avg); ERVING (5 yrs, 407 gm, 11,662 pts, 28.7 avg); GERVIN (4 yrs, 269 gm, 5887 pts, 21.9 avg); GILMORE (5 yrs, 420 gm, 9362 pts, 22.3 avg); ISSEL (6 yrs, 500 gm, 12,823 pts, 25.6 avg); MALONE (2 yrs, 126 gm, 2171 pts, 17.2 avg).

Field Goals

	Yrs	FGA	FGM	Pct
Kareem Abdul-Jabbar	20	28,307	15,837	.559
Wilt Chamberlain	14	23,497	12,681	.540
Elvin Hayes	16	24,272	10,976	.452
John Havlicek	16	23,900	10,513	.440
Alex English	15	21,036	10,659	.507
Oscar Robertson	14	19,620	9,508	.485
Jerry West	14	19,032	9,016	.474
Moses Malone	15	17,987	8,867	.493
Elgin Baylor	14	20,171	8,693	.431
Hal Greer	15	18,811	8,504	.452

Note: If field goals made in the ABA are included, consider these NBA-ABA totals: Julius Erving (11,818), Dan Issel (10,431), George Gervin (10,368), Moses Malone (9,709), Rick Barry (9,695) and Artis Gilmore (9,403).

Free Throws

	Yrs	FTA	FTM	Pct
Moses Malone	15	10,406	7999	.769
Oscar Robertson	14	9,185	7694	.838
Jerry West	14	8,801	7160	.814
Dolph Schayes	16	8,273	6979	.844
Adrian Dantley	15	8,351	6832	.818
Kareem Abdul-Jabbar	20	9,304	6712	.721
Bob Pettit	11	8,119	6182	.761
Wilt Chamberlain	14	11,862	6057	.511
Elgin Baylor	14	7,391	5763	.780
Lenny Wilkins	14	6,973	5394	.774

Note: If free throws made in the ABA are included, consider these totals: Moses Malone (8,486), Dan Issel (6,591), Julius Erving (6,256), and Artis Gilmore (6,132).

Assists

	Yrs	Gm	Ast	Avg
Magic Johnson	12	874	9921	11.4
Oscar Robertson	14	1040	9887	9.5
Isiah Thomas	10	764	7431	9.7
Lenny Wilkens	15	1077	7211	6.7
Maurice Cheeks	13	1010	7100	7.0
Bob Cousy	14	924	6955	7.5
Guy Rodgers	12	892	6917	7.8
Nate Archibald	13	876	6476	7.4
John Lucas	14	928	6454	7.0
Reggie Theus	13	1026	6453	6.3

Rebounds

	Yrs	Gm	Reb	Avg
Wilt Chamberlain	14	1045	23,924	22.9
Bill Russell	13	963	21,620	22.5
Kareem Abdul-Jabbar	20	1560	17,440	11.2
Elvin Hayes	16	1303	16,279	12.5
Moses Malone	15	1164	15,150	13.0
Nate Thurmond	14	964	14,464	15.0
Walt Bellamy	14	1043	14,241	13.7
Wes Unseld	13	984	13,769	14.0
Jerry Lucas	11	829	12,942	15.6
Bob Petit	11	792	12,849	16.2

Note: If rebounds pulled down in the ABA are included, consider the following totals: Artis Gilmore (16,330), Moses Malone (15,960).

Personal Fouls

	Yrs	Gm	Fouls	DQ
Kareem Abdul-Jabbar	20	1560	4657	48
Elvin Hayes	16	1303	4193	53
Jack Sikma	14	1107	3879	80
Hal Greer	15	1122	3855	72
Dolph Schayes	16	1059	3664	90

Note: If ABA records are included, consider the following personal foul totals: Artis Gilmore (4,529), Caldwell Jones (4,436), and Dan Issel (3,504).

Disqualifications

	Yrs	Gm	No
Vern Mikkelsen	10	699	127
Walter Dukes	8	553	121
Charlie Share	8	555	105
Paul Arizin	10	713	101
Darryl Dawkins	14	726	100

Years Played

	Yrs	Career	Gm
Kareem Abdul-Jabbar	20	1970-89	1560
Elvin Hayes	16	1969-84	1303
John Havlicek	16	1963-78	1270
Paul Silas	16	1965-80	1254
Dolph Schayes	16	1949-64	1059
Alex English	15	1977—	1193
Robert Parish	15	1977—	1181
Moses Malone	15	1977—	1164
Hal Greer	15	1959-73	1122
Lenny Wilkens	15	1961-75	1077
Adrian Dantley	15	1977—	955

Note: If ABA records are included, consider the following year totals: Artis Gilmore (17, 1972-88); Caldwell Jones (17, 1974-90); Moses Malone (17, 1975—); Julius Erving (16, 1972-87); Dan Issel (15, 1971-85).

Games Played

	Yrs	Career	No
Kareem Abdul-Jabbar	20	1970-89	1560
Elvin Hayes	16	1969-84	1303
John Havlicek	16	1963-78	1270
Paul Silas	16	1965-80	1254
Alex English	15	1977—	1193
Robert Parish	15	1977—	1181
Moses Malone	15	1977—	1164

Note: If ABA records are included, consider the following game totals: Artis Gilmore (1,329); Caldwell Jones (1,299); Moses Malone (1,290); Julius Erving (1,243); Dan Issel (1,218); Billy Paultz (1,124).

SINGLE SEASON

Scoring

	Season	Avg
Wilt Chamberlain, Phi	1961-62	50.4
Wilt Chamberlain, SF	1962-63	44.8
Wilt Chamberlain, Phi	1960-61	38.4
Elgin Baylor, LA	1961-62	38.3
Wilt Chamberlain, Phi	1959-60	37.6
Michael Jordan, Chi	1986-87	37.1
Wilt Chamberlain, SF	1963-64	36.9
Rick Barry, SF	1966-67	35.6
Michael Jordan, Chi	1987-88	35.0
Elgin Baylor, LA	1960-61	34.8
Kareem Abdul-Jabbar, Mil	1971-72	34.8
Wilt Chamberlain, SF-Phi	1964-65	34.7

Field Goals

	Season	Pct
Wilt Chamberlain, LA	1972-73	.727
Wilt Chamberlain, SF	1966-67	.683
Artis Gilmore, Chi	1980-81	.670
Artis Gilmore, Chi	1981-82	.652
Wilt Chamberlain, LA	1971-72	.649

Free Throws

	Season	Pct
Calvin Murphy, Hou	1980-81	.958
Rick Barry, Hou	1978-79	.947
Ernie DiGregorio, Buf	1976-77	.945
Ricky Sobers, Chi	1980-81	.935
Rick Barry, Hou	1979-80	.935

3-Pt Field Goals

	Season	Pct
Jon Sundvold, Mia	1988-89	.522
Steve Kerr, Cle	1989-90	.507
Craig Hodges, Mil-Pho	1987-88	.491
Mark Price, Cle	1987-88	.486
Kiki Vandeweghe, Port	1986-87	.481
Craig Hodges, Chi	1989-90	.481

Assists

	Season	Avg
John Stockton, Utah	1989-90	14.5
John Stockton, Utah	1990-91	14.2
Isiah Thomas, Det	1984-85	13.9
John Stockton, Utah	1987-88	13.8
John Stockton, Utah	1988-89	13.6
Kevin Porter, Det	1978-79	13.4
Magic Johnson, LA	1983-84	13.1
Magic Johnson, LA Lakers	1988-89	12.8

Rebounds

	Season	Avg
Wilt Chamberlain, Phi	1960-61	27.2
Wilt Chamberlain, Phi	1959-60	27.0
Wilt Chamberlain, Phi	1961-62	25.7
Bill Russell, Bos	1963-64	24.7
Wilt Chamberlain, Phi	1965-66	24.6
Wilt Chamberlain, SF	1962-63	24.2
Wilt Chamberlain, Phi	1966-67	24.2
Bill Russell, Bos	1964-65	24.1

All-Time NBA Leaders (Cont.)

Blocked Shots

	Season	Avg
Mark Eaton, Utah	1984-85	5.56
Manute Bol, Wash	1985-86	4.96
Elmore Smith, LA	1973-74	4.85
Mark Eaton, Utah	1985-86	4.61
Akeem Olajuwon, Hou	1989-90	4.59

Steals

	Season	Avg
Alvin Robertson, SA	1985-86	3.67
Don Buse, Ind	1976-77	3.47
Magic Johnson, LA	1980-81	3.43
Michael Ray Richardson, NY	1979-80	3.23
Alvin Robertson, SA	1986-87	3.21

SINGLE GAME

Points

	Date	Pts
Wilt Chamberlain, Phi.vs NY	3/2/62	100
Wilt Chamberlain, Phi.vs LA*	12/8/61	78
Wilt Chamberlain, Phi.vs Chi	1/13/62	73
Wilt Chamberlain, SF at NY	11/16/62	73
David Thompson, Den.at Det	4/9/78	73
Wilt Chamberlain, SF at LA	11/3/62	72
Elgin Baylor, LA at NY	11/15/60	71
Wilt Chamberlain, SF at Syr	3/10/63	70

*Triple overtime.
Note: Chamberlain's 100-point game vs New York was played at Hershey, PA.

Field Goals

	Date	FGA	FGM
Wilt Chamberlain, Phi.vs NY	3/2/62	63	36
Wilt Chamberlain, Phi.vs LA*	12/8/61	62	31
Wilt Chamberlain, Phi.at Chi	12/16/67	40	30
Rick Barry, GS vs Port	2/26/74	45	30
Four players tied with 29 each.			

*Triple overtime.

Free Throws

	Date	FGA	FGM
Wilt Chamberlain, Phi.vs NY	3/2/62	32	28
Adrian Dantley, Utah vs Hou	1/4/84	29	28
Adrian Dantley, Utah vs Den	11/25/83	31	27
Adrian Dantley, Utah vs Dal	10/21/80	29	26
Michael Jordan, Chi.vs NJ	2/26/87	27	26

3-Pt Field Goals

	Date	No
Dale Ellis, Sea.vs LA Clippers	4/20/90	9
Michael Adams, Den.at LA Clippers	4/12/91	9
Three tied with 8 each.		

Assists

	Date	No
Scott Skiles, Orl.vs Den	12/30/90	30
Kevin Porter, NJ vs Hou	2/24/78	29
Bob Cousy, Bos.vs Mnpls	2/27/59	28
Guy Rodgers, SF vs St.L	3/14/63	28
Geoff Huston, Cle.vs GS	1/27/82	27
John Stockton, Utah at NY	12/19/89	27

Rebounds

	Date	No
Wilt Chamberlain, Phi.vs Bos	11/24/60	55
Bill Russell, Bos.vs Syr	2/5/60	51
Bill Russell, Bos.vs Phi	11/16/57	49
Bill Russell, Bos.vs Det	3/11/65	49
Wilt Chamberlain, Phi.vs Syr	22/6/60	45
Wilt Chamberlain, Phi.vs LA.	1/21/61	45

Blocked Shots

	Date	No
Elmore Smith, LA vs Port	10/28/73	17
Manute Bol, Wash.vs Atl	1/25/86	15
Manute Bol, Wash.vs Ind	2/26/87	15
Four tied with 14 each.		

Steals

	Date	No
Larry Kenon, San Antonio vs KC	2/9/80	11

10 players tied with 10 steals in one game, including Alvin Robertson (4 times).

NBA All-Star Game

The NBA staged its first All-Star Game before 10,094 at Boston Garden on March 2, 1951. From that year on, the All-Star game has matched the best players in the East against the best in the West. Winning coaches are listed first.

Series: East leads, 27-14.

Multiple MVP winners: Bob Pettit (4); Oscar Roberston (3); Bob Cousy, Julius Erving and Isiah Thomas (2).

Year		Host	Coaches	Most Valuable Player
1951	East 111, West 94	Boston	Joe Lapchick, John Kundla	Ed Macauley, Boston
1952	East 108, West 91	Boston	Al Cervi, John Kundla	Paul Arizin, Phila.
1953	West 79, East 75	Ft.Wayne	John Kundla, Joe Lapchick	George Mikan, Minn.
1954	East 98, West 93 (OT)	New York	Joe Lapchick, John Kundla	Bob Cousy, Boston
1955	East 100, West 91	New York	Al Cervi, Charley Eckman	Bill Sharman, Boston
1956	West 108, East 94	Rochester	Charley Eckman, George Senesky	Bob Pettit, St.Louis
1957	East 109, West 97	Boston	Red Auerbach, Bobby Wanzer	Bob Cousy, Boston
1958	East 130, West 118	St.Louis	Red Auerbach, Alex Hannum	Bob Pettit, St.Louis
1959	West 124, East 108	Detroit	Ed Macauley, Red Auerbach	Bob Pettit, St.Louis & Elgin Baylor, Minn.
1960	East 125, West 115	Philadelphia	Red Auerbach, Ed Macauley	Wilt Chamberlain, Phila.
1961	West 153, East 131	Syracuse	Paul Seymour, Red Auerbach	Oscar Robertson, Cinn.
1962	West 150, East 130	St.Louis	Fred Schaus, Red Auerbach	Bob Pettit, St.Louis
1963	East 115, West 108	Los Angeles	Red Auerbach, Fred Schaus	Bill Russell, Boston
1964	East 111, West 107	Boston	Red Auerbach, Fred Schaus	Oscar Robertson, Cinn.
1965	East 124, West 123	St.Louis	Red Auerbach, Alex Hannum	Jerry Lucas, Cinn.
1966	East 137, West 94	Cincinnati	Red Auerbach, Fred Schaus	Adrian Smith, Cinn.

Year		Host	Coaches	Most Valuable Player
1967	West 135, East 120	San Francisco	Fred Schaus, Red Auerbach	Rick Barry, San Fran.
1968	East 144, West 124	New York	Alex Hannum, Bill Sharman	Hal Greer, Phila.
1969	East 123, West 112	Baltimore	Gene Shue, Richie Guerin	Oscar Robertson, Cinn.
1970	East 142, West 135	Philadelphia	Red Holzman, Richie Guerin	Willis Reed, New York
1971	West 108, East 107	San Diego	Larry Costello, Red Holzman	Lenny Wilkens, Seattle
1972	West 112, East 110	Los Angeles	Bill Sharman, Tom Heinsohn	Jerry West, Los Ang.
1973	East 104, West 84	Chicago	Tom Heinsohn, Bill Sharman	Dave Cowens, Boston
1974	West 134, East 123	Seattle	Larry Costello, Tom Heinsohn	Bob Lanier, Detroit
1975	East 108, West 102	Phoenix	K.C.Jones, Al Attles	Walt Frazier, New York
1976	East 123, West 109	Philadelphia	Tom Heinsohn, Al Attles	Dave Bing, Washington
1977	West 125, East 124	Milwaukee	Larry Brown, Gene Shue	Julius Erving, Phila.
1978	East 133, West 125	Atlanta	Billy Cunningham, Jack Ramsay	Randy Smith, Buffalo
1979	West 134, East 129	Detroit	Lenny Wilkens, Dick Motta	David Thompson, Denver
1980	East 144, West 135 (OT)	Washington	Billy Cunningham, Len Wilkens	George Gervin, San Ant.
1981	East 123, West 120	Cleveland	Billy Cunningham, John MacLeod	Nate Archibald, Boston
1982	East 120, West 118	New Jersey	Bill Fitch, Pat Riley	Larry Bird, Boston
1983	East 132, West 123	Los Angeles	Billy Cunningham, Pat Riley	Julius Erving, Phila.
1984	East 154, West 145 (OT)	Denver	K.C.Jones, Frank Layden	Isiah Thomas, Detroit
1985	West 140, East 129	Indiana	Pat Riley, K.C.Jones	Ralph Sampson, Houston
1986	East 139, West 132	Dallas	K.C.Jones, Pat Riley	Isiah Thomas, Detroit
1987	West 154, East 149 (OT)	Seattle	Pat Riley, K.C.Jones	Tom Chambers, Seattle
1988	East 138, West 133	Chicago	Mike Fratello, Pat Riley	Michael Jordan, Chicago
1989	West 143, East 134	Houston	Pat Riley, Lenny Wilkens	Karl Malone, Utah
1990	West 130, West 113	Miami	Chuck Daly, Pat Riley	Magic Johnson, LA Lakers
1991	East 116, West 114	Charlotte	Chris Ford, Rick Adelman	Charles Barkley, Phila.

Annual Awards

Podoloff Trophy

Awarded to the Most Valuable player for the regular season and named after the first commissioner of the NBA. Winners first selected by the NBA players (1956-80) then a national panel of pro basketball writers and broadcasters (since 1981). Winners' scoring averages are provided; (*) indicates led league.

Multiple winners: Kareem Abdul-Jabbar (6); Bill Russell (5); Wilt Chamberlain (4); Larry Bird, Magic Johnson and Moses Malone (3); Michael Jordan and Bob Pettit (2).

Year		Pts	Year		Pts
1956	Bob Pettit, St. Louis, F	25.7*	1974	Kareem Abdul-Jabbar, LA, C	27.0
1957	Bob Cousy, Boston, G	20.6	1975	Bob McAdoo, Buffalo, F	34.5*
1958	Bill Russell, Boston, C	16.6	1976	Kareem Abdul-Jabbar, LA, C	27.7
1959	Bob Pettit, St. Louis, F	29.2*	1977	Kareem Abdul-Jabbar, LA, C	26.2
			1978	Bill Walton, Portland, C	18.9
1960	Wilt Chamberlain, Philadelphia, C	37.6*	1979	Moses Malone, Houston, C	24.8
1961	Bill Russell, Boston, C	16.9			
1962	Bill Russell, Boston, C	18.9	1980	Kareem Abdul-Jabbar, LA, C	24.8
1963	Bill Russell, Boston, C	16.8	1981	Julius Erving, Philadelphia, F	24.6
1964	Oscar Robertson, Cincinnati, G	31.4	1982	Moses Malone, Houston, C	31.1
1965	Bill Russell, Boston, C	14.1	1983	Moses Malone, Philadelphia, C	24.5
1966	Wilt Chamberlain, Philadelphia, C	33.5*	1984	Larry Bird, Boston, F	24.2
1967	Wilt Chamberlain, Philadelphia, C	24.1	1985	Larry Bird, Boston, F	28.7
1968	Wilt Chamberlain, Philadelphia, C	24.3	1986	Larry Bird, Boston, F	25.8
1969	Wes Unseld, Baltimore, C	13.8	1987	Magic Johnson, LA Lakers, G	23.9
			1988	Michael Jordan, Chicago, G	35.0*
1970	Willis Reed, New York, C	21.7	1989	Magic Johnson, LA Lakers, G	22.5
1971	Lew Alcindor, Milwaukee, C	31.7*			
1972	Kareem Abdul-Jabbar, Milwaukee, C	34.8*	1990	Magic Johnson, LA Lakers, G	22.3
1973	Dave Cowens, Boston, C	20.5	1991	Michael Jordan, Chicago, G	31.5*

Note: Alcindor changed his name to Kareem Abdul-Jabbar after the 1970-71 season.

Gottlieb Trophy

Awarded to the Outstanding Rookie of the regular season and named after the pro basketball pioneer and owner-coach of the first NBA champion Philadelphia Warriors. Winners selected by a national panel of pro basketball writers and broadcasters. Winners' scoring averages provided; (*) indicates led league; winners who were also named MVP are in **bold** type.

Year		Pts	Year		Pts
1953	Don Meineke, Ft.Wayne, F	10.8	1957	Tommy Heinsohn, Boston, F	16.2
1954	Ray Felix, Baltimore, C	17.6	1958	Woody Sauldsberry, Philadelphia, F/C	12.8
1955	Bob Pettit, Mil. Hawks, F	20.4	1959	Elgin Baylor, Minneapolis, F	24.9
1956	Maurice Stokes, Rochester., F/C	16.8			

Annual Awards (Cont.)
Gottlieb Trophy

Year		Pts	Year		Pts
1960	**Wilt Chamberlain**, Philadelphia	37.6*	1976	Alvan Adams, Phoenix, C	19.0
1961	Oscar Robertson, Cincinnati, G	30.5	1977	Adrian Dantley, Buffalo, F	20.3
1962	Walt Bellamy, Chi. Packers, C	31.6	1978	Walter Davis, Phoenix, G	24.2
1963	Terry Dischinger, Chi. Zephyrs, F	25.5	1979	Phil Ford, Kansas City, G	15.9
1964	Jerry Lucas, Cincinnati, F/C	17.7			
1965	Willis Reed, New York, C	19.5	1980	Larry Bird, Boston, F	21.3
1966	Rick Barry, San Francisco, F	25.7	1981	Darrell Griffith, Utah, G	20.6
1967	Dave Bing, Detroit, G	20.0	1982	Buck Williams, New Jersey, F	15.5
1968	Earl Monroe, Baltimore, G	24.3	1983	Terry Cummings, San Diego, F	23.7
1969	**Wes Unseld**, Baltimore, C	13.8	1984	Ralph Sampson, Houston, C	21.0
			1985	Michael Jordan, Chicago, G	28.2
1970	Lew Alcindor, Mil. Bucks, C	28.8	1986	Patrick Ewing, New York, C	20.0
1971	Dave Cowens, Boston, C	17.0	1987	Chuck Person, Indiana, F	18.8
	& Geoff Petrie, Portland, F	24.8	1988	Mark Jackson, New York, G	13.6
1972	Sidney Wicks, Portland, F	24.5	1989	Mitch Richmond, Golden St., G	22.0
1973	Bob McAdoo, Buffalo, C/F	18.0			
1974	Ernie DiGregorio, Buffalo, G	15.2	1990	David Robinson, San Antonio, C	24.3
1975	Keith Wilkes, Golden St., F	14.2	1991	Derrick Coleman, New Jersey	18.4

Note: Alcindor changed his name to Kareem Abdul-Jabbar after the 1970-71 season.

Auerbach Trophy

Awarded to the outstanding coach of the year and renamed in 1967 for the former Boston coach who led the Celtics to nine NBA titles. Winners selected by a national panel of pro basketball writers and broadcasters. Previous season and winning season records are provided; (*) indicates division title.
   Multiple winners: Bill Fitch, Cotton Fitzsimmons, Don Nelson and Gene Shue (2).

Year		Improvement		Year		Improvement	
1963	Harry Gallatin, St.L	29-51	to 48-32	1980	Bill Fitch, Bos	29-53	to 61-21 *
1964	Alex Hannum, SF	31-49	to 48-32*	1981	Jack McKinney, Ind	37-45	to 44-38
1965	Red Auerbach, Bos	59-21*	to 61-18*	1982	Gene Shue, Wash	39-43	to 43-39
1966	Dolph Schayes, Phi	40-40	to 55-25*	1983	Don Nelson, Mil.	55-27*	to 51-31 *
1967	Johnny Kerr, Chi	Expan.	to 33-48	1984	Frank Layden, Utah	30-52	to 45-37 *
1968	Richie Guerin, St.L	39-42	to 56-26*	1985	Don Nelson, Milw	50-32*	to 59-23 *
1969	Gene Shue, Balt.	36-46	to 57-25*	1986	Mike Fratello, Atl	34-48	to 50-32
1970	Red Holzman, NY	54-28	to 60-22*	1987	Mike Schuler, Port	40-42	to 49-33
1971	Dick Motta, Chi	39-43	to 51-31	1988	Doug Moe, Den	37-45	to 54-28 *
1972	Bill Sharman, LA	48-34*	to 69-13*	1989	Cotton Fitzsimmons, Pho	28-54	to 55-27
1973	Tommy Heinsohn, Bos	56-26*	to 68-14*				
1974	Ray Scott, Det	40-42	to 52-30	1990	Pat Riley, LA Lakers	57-25*	to 63-19 *
1975	Phil Joh	33-49	to 44-38	1991	Don Chaney, Hou	41-41	to 52-30
1976	Bill Fitch, Cle.	40-42	to 49-33*				
1977	Tom Nissalke, Hou	40-42	to 49-33*				
1978	Hubie Brown, Atl	31-51	to 41-41				
1979	Cotton Fitzsimmons, KC	31-51	to 48-34*				

Number One Draft Choices

Overall first choices in the NBA Draft since the abolition of the Territorial Draft in 1966. Players who became Rookie of the Year are in **bold** type.

Year	Team	Overall 1st Pick	Year	Team	Overall 1st Pick
1966	New York	Cazzie Russell, Michigan	1980	Golden St.	Joe Barry Carroll, Purdue
1967	Detroit	Jimmy Walker, Providence	1981	Dallas	Mark Aguirre, DePaul
1968	Houston	Elvin Hayes, Houston	1982	LA Lakers	James Worthy, N.Carolina
1969	Milwaukee	**Lew Alcindor,** UCLA	1983	Houston	**Ralph Sampson,** Virginia
			1984	Houston	Akeem Olajuwon, Houston
1970	Detroit	Bob Lanier, St.Bonaventure	1985	New York	Patrick Ewing, Georgetown
1971	Cleveland	Austin Carr, Notre Dame	1986	Cleveland	Brad Daugherty, N.Carolina
1972	Portland	LaRue Martin, Loyola-Chicago	1987	San Antonio	**David Robinson,** Navy
1973	Philadelphia	Doug Collins, Illinois St.	1988	LA Clippers	Danny Manning, Kansas
1974	Portland	Bill Walton, UCLA	1989	Sacramento	Pervis Ellison, Louisville
1975	Atlanta	David Thompson, N.C.State			
		(signed with Denver of ABA)	1990	New Jersey	**Derrick Coleman,** Syracuse
1976	Houston	John Lucas, Maryland	1991	Charlotte	Larry Johnson, UNLV
1977	Milwaukee	Kent Benson, Indiana			
1978	Portland	Mychal Thompson, Minnesota			
1979	LA Lakers	Magic Johnson, Michigan St.			

Notes: Alcindor changed his name to Kareem Abdul-Jabbar after the 1970-71 season and Robinson joined NBA for 1989-90 season after fulfilling military obligation.

All-Time Winningest NBA Coaches

Top 20 NBA career victories through the 1990-91 season. Career, regular season and playoff records are noted along with NBA titles won. Coaches active during 1990-91 season in **bold** type.

	Yrs	Career W	L	Pct	Regular Season W	L	Pct	Playoffs W	L	Pct	NBA Titles
Red Auerbach	20	**1037**	548	.654	938	479	.662	99	69	.589	9 (1957,59-66)
Jack Ramsay	21	**908**	841	.519	864	783	.525	44	58	.431	1 (1977)
Dick Motta	21	**905**	915	.497	849	845	.501	56	70	.444	1 (1978)
Bill Fitch	20	**859**	883	.493	805	835	.491	54	48	.529	1 (1981)
Gene Shue	22	**814**	908	.473	784	861	.477	30	47	.390	—None—
Lenny Wilkens	18	**801**	737	.521	758	696	.521	43	41	.512	1 (1979)
Cotton Fitzsimmons	18	**782**	758	.508	752	716	.512	30	42	.417	—None—
Red Holzman	18	**754**	651	.537	696	604	.535	58	47	.552	2 (1970,73)
John MacLeod	18	**754**	711	.515	707	657	.518	47	54	.465	—None—
Don Nelson	14	**714**	521	.578	664	466	.588	50	55	.476	—None—
Doug Moe	14	**642**	542	.542	609	492	.549	33	50	.398	—None—
Pat Riley	9	**635**	241	.725	533	194	.733	102	47	.685	4 (1982,85,87-88)
Al Attles	14	**588**	548	.518	557	518	.518	31	30	.508	1 (1975)
K.C.Jones	9	**585**	291	.668	504	234	.683	81	57	.587	2 (1984,86)
Billy Cunningham	8	**520**	235	.689	454	196	.698	66	39	.629	1 (1983)
Alex Hannum	12	**516**	446	.536	471	412	.533	45	34	.570	2 (1958,67)
Chuck Daly	9	**497**	308	.617	428	269	.614	69	39	.639	2 (1989-90)
John Kundla	11	**483**	337	.589	423	302	.583	60	35	.632	5 (1949-50,52-54)
Tommy Heinsohn	9	**474**	296	.616	427	263	.619	47	33	.588	2 (1974,76)
Larry Costello	10	**467**	323	.591	430	300	.589	37	23	.617	1 (1971)

Note: The NBA does not recognize records from the National Basketball League (1937-49) or the American Basketball Assn.(1968-76), so the following NBL—**Kundla** (51-19 and a title in 1 year) and ABA—**Hannum** (194-164 and one title in 4 yrs), **Jones** (30-58 in 1 yr).

Where They Coached

Attles—Golden St.(1970-80,80-83); **Auerbach**—Washington (1946-49); Tri-Cities (1949-50); Boston (1950-66); **Costello**—Milwaukee (1968-76), Chicago (1978-79); **Cunningham**—Philadelphia (1977-85); **Daly**—Cleveland (1981-82), Detroit (1983—); **Fitch**—Cleveland (1970-79), Boston (1979-83), Houston (1983-88), New Jersey (1989—); **Fitzsimmons**—Phoenix (1970-72), Atlanta (1972-76), Buffalo (1977-78), Kansas City (1978-84), San Antonio (1984-86), Phoenix (1988—); **Hannum**—St.Louis (1957-58), Syracuse (1960-63), San Francisco (1963-66), Phila.76ers (1966-68), Houston (1970-71); **Heinsohn**—Boston (1969-77); **Holzman**—Milwaukee-St.Louis Hawks (1954-57), NY Knicks (1968-77,78-82).

Jones—Washington (1973-76), Boston (1983-88), Seattle (1990—); **Kundla**—Minneapolis (1948-57,58-59); **MacLeod**—Phoenix (1973-87), Dallas (1987-89), NY Knicks (1990-91); **Moe**—San Antonio (1976-80), Denver (1981-90); **Motta**—Chicago (1968-76), Washington (1976-80), Dallas (1980-87), Sacramento (1990—); **Nelson**—Milwaukee (1976-87), Golden St.(1988—); **Ramsay**—Philadelphia (1968-72), Buffalo (1972-76), Portland (1976-86), Indiana (1986-89); **Riley**—LA Lakers (1981-90); **Shue**—Baltimore (1967-73), Philadelphia (1973-77), San Diego Clippers (1978-80), Washington (1980-86), LA Clippers (1987-89); **Wilkens**—Seattle (1969-72), Portland (1974-76), Seattle (1977-85), Cleveland (1986—).

Top Winning Percentages

Minimum of 355 victories.

	Yrs	W	L	Pct
Pat Riley	9	635	241	**.725**
Billy Cunningham	8	520	235	**.689**
K.C.Jones	9	585	291	**.668**
Red Auerbach	20	1037	548	**.654**
Chuck Daly	9	497	308	**.617**
Tommy Heinsohn	9	474	296	**.616**
Larry Costello	10	467	323	**.591**
John Kundla	11	483	337	**.589**
Bill Sharman	7	368	267	**.580**
Don Nelson	14	714	521	**.578**
Al Cervi	9	359	267	**.573**
Larry Brown	8	364	292	**.555**
Joe Lapchick	9	356	277	**.562**
Doug Moe	14	642	542	**.542**
Bill Russell	8	375	317	**.542**
Red Holzman	18	754	651	**.537**
Alex Hannum	12	516	446	**.536**
Lenny Wilkens	18	801	737	**.521**
Jack Ramsay	21	908	841	**.519**
Al Attles	14	588	548	**.518**
John MacLeod	18	754	711	**.515**
Cotton Fitzsimmons	18	782	758	**.508**
Dick Motta	21	905	915	**.497**
Bill Fitch	20	859	883	**.493**
Gene Shue	22	814	908	**.473**

Active Coaches' Victories

Through 1990-91 season, including playoffs.

	Yrs	W	L	Pct
Dick Motta, Sacramento	21	**905**	915	.497
Bill Fitch, New Jersey	20	**859**	883	.493
Lenny Wilkens, Cleveland	18	**801**	737	.521
Cotton Fitzsimmons, Phoenix	18	**782**	758	.508
Don Nelson, Golden St	14	**714**	521	.578
Pat Riley, New York	9	**635**	241	.725
K.C.Jones, Seattle	9	**585**	291	.668
Chuck Daly, Detroit	9	**497**	308	.617
Larry Brown, San Antonio	8	**364**	292	.555
Del Harris, Milwaukee	8	**345**	363	.487
Kevin Loughery, Miami	13	**345**	518	.400
Jerry Sloan, Utah	6	**251**	216	.537
Jim Lynam, Philadelphia	6	**219**	230	.488
Don Chaney, Houston	6	**193**	249	.437
Matt Guokas, Orlando	5	**176**	212	.454
Paul Westhead, Denver	5	**172**	172	.500
Mike Schuler, LA Clippers	4	**160**	141	.532
Rick Adelman, Portland	3	**157**	82	.657
Phil Jackson, Chicago	2	**141**	56	.716
Wes Unseld, Washington	4	**133**	173	.435
Bob Weiss, Atlanta	3	**104**	150	.409
Jimmy Rodgers, Minnesota	2	**96**	76	.558
Richie Adubato, Dallas	3	**82**	144	.363
Mike Dunleavy, LA Lakers	1	**70**	31	.693
Chris Ford, Boston	1	**61**	32	.656
Bob Hill, Indiana	2	**54**	74	.422
Allan Brislow, Charlotte	0	**0**	0	.000

American Basketball Association
ABA Finals

The American Basketball Assn. began play in 1967-68 as a 10-team rival of the 21 year-old NBA. The ABA, which introduced the three-point basket, a multi-colored ball and the All-Star Game Slam Dunk Contest, lasted nine seasons before folding following the 1975-76 season. Four ABA teams—Denver, Indiana, New York and San Antonio—survived to enter the NBA in 1976-77. The NBA also adopted the 3-pt basket (in 1979-80) and the All-Star Game Slam Dunk Contest. The older league, however, refused to take in the ABA ball.

In the chart below, each ABA champion's wins and losses are noted in parentheses after the series score.

Year	Winner	Head Coach	Series	Loser	Head Coach
1968	Pittsburgh Pipers	Vince Cazetta	4-2 (WLLWLWW)	New Orleans Bucs	Babe McCarthy
1969	Oakland Oaks	Alex Hannum	4-1 (WLWWW)	Indiana Pacers	Bob Leonard
1970	Indiana Pacers	Bob Leonard	4-2 (WWLWLW)	Los Angeles Stars	Bill Sharman
1971	Utah Stars	Bill Sharman	4-3 (WWLLWLW)	Kentucky Colonels	Frank Ramsey
1972	Indiana Pacers	Bob Leonard	4-2 (WLWLWW)	New York Nets	Lou Carnesecca
1973	Indiana Pacers	Bob Leonard	4-3 (WLLWWLW)	Kentucky Colonels	Joe Mullaney
1974	New York Nets	Kevin Loughery	4-1 (WWWLW)	Utah Stars	Joe Mullaney
1975	Kentucky Colonels	Hubie Brown	4-1 (WWWLW)	Indiana Pacers	Bob Leonard
1976	New York Nets	Kevin Loughery	4-2 (WLWWLW)	Denver Nuggets	Larry Brown

Most Valuable Player

Winners' scoring averages provided; (*) indicates led league.

Multiple winners: Julius Erving (3); Mel Daniels (2).

Year		Pts
1968	Connie Hawkins, Pittsburgh, C	26.8*
1969	Mel Daniels, Indiana, C	24.0
1970	Spencer Haywood, Denver, C	30.0*
1971	Mel Daniels, Indiana, C	21.0
1972	Artis Gilmore, Kentucky, C	23.8
1973	Billy Cunningham, Carolina, F	24.1
1974	Julius Erving, New York, F	27.4*
1975	(Tie) George McGinnis, Indiana, F	29.8*
	Julius Erving, New York, F	27.9
1976	Julius Erving, New York, F	29.3*

Rookie of the Year

Winners' scoring averages provided; (*) indicates led league. Rookies who were also named Most Valuable Player are in **bold** type.

Year		Pts
1968	Mel Daniels, Minnesota, C	22.2
1969	Warren Armstrong†, Oakland, G	21.5
1970	**Spencer Haywood**, Denver, C	30.0*
1971	(Tie) Dan Issel, Kentucky, C	29.8*
	Charlie Scott, Virginia, G	27.1
1972	**Artis Gilmore**, Kentucky, C	23.8
1973	Brian Taylor, New York, G	15.3
1974	Swen Nater, Virginia-SA, C	14.1
1975	Marvin Barnes, St. Louis, C	24.0
1976	David Thompson, Denver, F	26.0

†Armstrong changed his name to Warren Jabali after the 1970-71 season.

Coach of the Year

Previous season and winning season records are provided; (*) indicates division title.

Multiple winners: Larry Brown (3).

Year		Improvement
1968	Vince Cazetta, Pit	54-24*
1969	Alex Hannum, Oak	22-56 to 60-18*
1970	Joe Belmont, Den	44-34 to 51-33*
	& Bill Sharman, LA	33-45 to 43-41
1971	Al Bianchi, Vir	44-40 to 55-29*
1972	Tom Nissalke, Dal	30-54 to 42-42
1973	Larry Brown, Caro	35-49 to 57-27*
1974	Babe McCarthy, Ky	56-28 to 53-31
	& Joe Mullaney, Utah	55-29* to 51-33*
1975	Larry Brown, Den	37-47 to 65-19*
1976	Larry Brown, Den	65-19* to 60-24*

Scoring Leaders

Scoring championship decided by per game point average.

Multiple winners: Julius Erving (3).

Year		Gm	Avg	Pts
1968	Connie Hawkins, Pit	70	1875	26.8
1969	Rick Barry, Oak	35	1190	34.0
1970	Spencer Haywood, Den	84	2519	30.0
1971	Dan Issel, Ky	83	2480	29.8
1972	Charlie Scott, Vir	73	2524	34.6
1973	Julius Erving, Vir	71	2268	31.9
1974	Julius Erving, NY	84	2299	27.4
1975	George McGinnis, Ind	79	2353	29.8
1976	Julius Erving, NY	84	2462	29.3

ABA All-Star Game

The ABA All-Star Game was an Eastern Division vs Western Division contest from 1968-75. League membership had dropped to seven teams by 1976, the ABA's last season, so the team in first place at the break (Denver) played an All-Star team made up from the other six clubs.

Series: East won 5, West 3 and Denver 1.

Year	Result	Host	Coaches	Most Valuable Player
1968	East 126, West 120	Indiana	Jim Pollard, Babe McCarthy	Larry Brown, NO
1969	West 133, East 127	Louisville	Alex Hannum, Gene Rhodes	John Beasley, Dal.
1970	West 128, East 98	Indiana	Babe McCarthy, Bob Leonard	Spencer Haywood, Den.
1971	East 126, West 122	Carolina	Al Bianchi, Bob Leonard	Mel Daniels, Ind.
1972	East 142, West 115	Louisville	Joe Mullaney, Ladell Andersen	Dan Issel, Ky.
1973	West 123, East 111	Utah	Ladell Andersen, Larry Brown	Warren Jabali, Den.
1974	East 128, West 112	Virginia	Babe McCarthy, Joe Mullaney	Artis Gilmore, Ky.
1975	East 151, West 124	San Antonio	Kevin Loughery, Larry Brown	Freddie Lewis, St.L.
1976	Denver 144, ABA 138	Denver	Larry Brown, Kevin Loughery	David Thompson, Den.

Pittsburgh's **Mario Lemieux** missed the first 50 games of the season, but he was the Most Valuable Player of the Stanley Cup playoffs.

HOCKEY

Super Mario

Lemieux overcomes back injury to lead rebuilt Penguins to Stanley Cup and take his place among NHL's best.

It took Mario Lemieux seven years to live up to the promise of his surname. *Le mieux.* In French, the best.

And for a lot of that time, he was pretty close to being the best, too. Twice the National Hockey League's scoring champion. Once its Most Valuable Player. Lemieux graduated from the Quebec major junior league in 1984 and saved the faltering Pittsburgh Penguins' franchise by turning a frigid public on to an unfamiliar game.

In team sports, however, greatness demands that individual achievements be linked to team accomplishments. In hockey, that means winning the Stanley Cup, and through the years the game's greatest players, from Morenz to Richard to Howe to Gretzky, have all done it. So, no matter how much Lemieux did individually, his critics were quick to point out that the Penguins had failed to make the playoffs in five of his first six seasons. Mario, they said, you're not there yet.

He arrived on May 25. That night in Bloomington, Minn., the Penguins shut out the Minnesota North Stars, 8-0, to win the Cup in six games. And Lemieux, the playoffs' Most Valuable Player with 16 goals and 44 points, capped an amazing

personal comeback by accepting the Cup from NHL president John Ziegler.

"This is nice," said Lemieux afterward, touching the Conn Smythe Trophy he won as MVP. Then he kissed the Stanley Cup and added, "But this is nicer."

After the first three games of the final, it looked like all those nice things were going to happen to the North Stars, who held a 2-1 series lead.

The unsung Stars had entered the playoffs with fewer regular season wins (27) than any other qualifier, yet went on to reach the championship round by upsetting the two teams with the most wins— Chicago (49) and St.Louis (47)—and then disposing of defending Cup champion Edmonton.

But the Minnesota miracle fell two victories short. Pittsburgh came back to sweep the last three games—outscoring the Stars, 19-7—and the year's surprise team could only watch as Lemieux and the Pens skated off with the Cup.

Paradoxically, Lemieux earned almost as much notoriety during the 1990-91 season for not playing hockey as he did for playing. In July of '90, he underwent surgery to remove a herniated disc from his back. By September, he was taking the first tentative steps in his comeback attempt when an infection delayed his recovery. Lemieux spent most of the next two months following doctors' orders to do nothing. In December, he received

---

Eric Duhatschek has covered the NHL for the *Calgary Herald* since 1980. He is also a columnist for *The Hockey News.*

UPI/Bettmann

Minnesota pushed everybody around in the first three rounds of the playoffs, including regular season MVP **Brett Hull** (left) of St. Louis. Hull is seen here taking a hit from North Stars' forward **Stewart Gavin**.

permission to begin light workouts and found that close to 10 months of complete inactivity had left him in miserable physical condition.

When he finally returned to the lineup on Jan. 26, after missing the first 50 games of the season, his role was visibly diminished. He couldn't do it all himself, but the Pens didn't expect him to. In his absence they had managed to hold their own, going 26-21-3, and the experience proved to be invaluable for a team that used to rely on Lemieux for everything.

The rebirth of the Penguins can be traced back to Dec. 5, 1989, the day owner Edward DeBartolo Sr. hired Craig Patrick as general manager. Patrick, who represents the third generation of pro hockey's most legendary family—both his grandfather Lester and father Lynn are in the Hall of Fame—quickly made himself at home in (where else?) the Patrick Division.

After coaching the team himself for the rest of the 1989-90 season, Patrick hired 59-year-old Bob Johnson, who stepped down as executive director of USA Hockey to accept the job. Experienced on the college, international and NHL levels, Johnson had won three NCAA championships at the University of Wisconsin, coached the 1976 US Olympic team and guided the Calgary Flames to the Stanley Cup final in 1986. Next, Patrick convinced Scotty Bowman, who had coached Montreal to five Stanley Cups in the 1970s, to quit his budding broadcasting career and sign on as the Pens' player development director.

In Patrick, Johnson and Bowman—the Three Wise Men—the Penguins' front office achieved a kind of order and competency never before seen in the club's 24-year history.

They knew that with two of the six top talents in the game—Lemieux and defenseman Paul Coffey—the hard part of building a winning team was done. So Patrick went out and found some older players with previous championship experience—forwards Bryan Trottier of the New York Islanders and Joey Mullen of Calgary—to go with youngsters like forwards Kevin Stevens, Mark Recchi and

305

Jaromir Jagr. He then swung a bold late-season trade on Mar. 4 that brought center Ron Francis and defenseman Ulf Samuelsson over from Hartford in exchange for the Pens' leading scorer John Cullen (31-63—94), and defenseman Zarley Zalapski.

Pittsburgh had lost seven games in a row leading up to the trade and as Johnson put it, "We knew we weren't going anywhere." But as April came on so did the Penguins, posting a 9-2-1 record over their last 12 games to pass the slumping New York Rangers and win their first division title ever.

In the playoffs, the Penguins began slowly and needed seven games to get past the New Jersey Devils in the first round. But gradually as Mario got healthier, the pieces started falling into place. As other teams ran out of gas or succumbed to injuries during the two-month playoff grind, the Penguins survived injuries to goaltender Tom Barrasso, Coffey and even Lemieux, who missed the third game of the Cup finals when his back spasms flared up as he bent over to lace up his skates.

Between Games 3 and 4, Lemieux slept with a sheet of plywood under his mattress to provide his back with more support. The Penguins had lost the night Lemieux came up lame—falling behind the North Stars two games to one—but two nights later, Mario was back and they never trailed the rest of the way.

"This means everything," said Lemieux. "To be part of a championship team after the back problems and the surgery and the infection. This is the ultimate dream."

Not quite. The ultimate dream would have been Minnesota winning the Cup after all it went through.

Only one year before, because of mounting losses and poor box office support, owners George and Gordon Gund threatened to move the team out of the Twin Cities. After lengthy and complicated negotiations, the Gunds reached a compromise with the NHL, agreeing to sell the club in exchange for an expansion team in San Jose, Calif.

They sold the North Stars to a trio of investors headed by Norm Green, a part-owner of the Calgary Flames, who then turned around and bought out his part-

Gretzky Stars, Lindros A Hit In Canada Cup

The 1991 Canada Cup—or Wayne and Eric's Excellent Adventure—proved many things about the state of hockey: here and abroad:

► Wayne Gretzky is still the Great One; the best player on the planet, the man who makes all things happen. Maybe the finish wasn't as dramatic as in 1987, but he led the tournament in scoring (4-8—12) and you'd be hard-pressed to argue that this wasn't his best Canada Cup.

► American hockey continues to make great strides and even if the U.S. didn't win this time around—losing two straight to Canada in the best-of-three-game final—it will contend from now on.

► For the moment, the chaos in Eastern Europe can be plainly seen in the hockey programs of its national teams. Neither the USSR nor Czechoslovakia qualified for the tournament semifinals.

► Look out for Eric Lindros. If there was an enduring memory of the '91 Canada Cup, it was his smashing debut on the world stage.

At 18-years-old and 230 pounds, Lindros was the youngest and heaviest player in the tournament. And despite the fact that he had never played a game in the NHL, he turned out to be the most dominant physical player as well.

Sweden's Ulf Samuelsson learned that lesson the hard way. So did Czechoslovakia's Martin Rucinsky. Lindros knocked both of them out of the Canada Cup with crushing, legal hits. In the finals against Team USA, Lindros ran roughshod over the American players. On one memorable shift, he staggered two of the biggest U.S. players, Kevin Hatcher and Joel Otto, and then bulldogged Joey Mullen to the ice like a steer wrestler at a rodeo.

Lindros did not show exceptional scoring ability—he had three goals and two assists—but then Canadian coach Mike Keenan didn't put him in many offensive situations either, using him mainly as a checker.

One of the more memorable sideshows of the tournament came in Quebec City, site of the Canada-USSR game. Lindros, chosen by Quebec as the first overall pick in the

1991 draft, had refused to report to the Nordiques, citing tax and language reasons. He was booed sporadically at the Colisee that night, but the reception, as he was to say later, "wasn't as bad as I thought."

So would he change his mind and join the Nordiques? "No," replied Lindros, bluntly. In September, Lindros and the Nords were involved in a high-stakes game of chicken, with neither side showing any willingness to back down. "They say the kid is stubborn," said Nordiques' GM Pierre Page. "Well, I'm stubborn too."

Tactically, the '91 Canada Cup differed from previous editions of the tournament because of the dominance of the two North American teams. Canada (6-0-2) was unbeaten and the U.S.(5-3-0) lost only to the Canadians.

After Olympic gold medals in 1960 and 1980, qualifying for the finals was arguably the most important moment in U.S. hockey history. That the Americans got as far as they did was even more significant considering they lost their coach, Bob Johnson, only days before the tournament opened.

Johnson underwent surgery to remove a cancerous brain tumor on Aug.30. Even so, he communicated with his coaching staff by sending them notes.

On the day they defeated Finland in the semifinals, Johnson wrote an impassioned letter to his team, saying in part: "Gretzky is the hero to all kids playing hockey. I want American kids to look up to (Jeremy) Roenick and (Mike) Modano in the same way."

Gretzky missed the final game of the tournament because of back spasms, brought on by an injury suffered in the first game of the final. On the play, U.S. defenseman Gary Suter bodychecked Gretzky into the boards, causing a storm of controversy in Canada about the legality of the hit.

One day later, Gretzky absolved Suter of all blame, but not before a sellout crowd in Hamilton, Ont., made life miserable for the U.S. defender in the deciding game. As fate would have it, Suter turned the puck over to Canada's Steve Larmer for the winning goal in a 4-2 victory.

The Canadians won the tournament despite the absence of half-a-dozen of their top players, including Mario Lemieux, who scored the winning goal in the '87 tournament. Lemieux begged off to rest his injured back. Others, like Ray Bourque and Stephane Richer, had more feeble excuses.

Canapress

Team Canada captains **Wayne Gretzky** (left) and **Mark Messier** celebrate two-game sweep of Team USA in 1991 Canada Cup final.

Then coach Mike Keenan took a calculated risk with his player selection by dropping such NHL luminaries as Steve Yzerman and Joe Sakic. Anticipating a Canada-USA final, Keenan built his team to strict NHL specifications: A handful of scorers surrounded by a larger group of grinders.

"We felt very strongly about the players we selected," said Keenan. "We were supportive of them and they never let us down."

The prototypical Keenan player may be Lindros, known as The Next One. But in the end, the Canada Cup belonged to The Great One. Maybe the finish wasn't as dramatic as in 1987—in which he set up Lemieux for the game winner in the second to last minute of the deciding game—but you'd be hard-pressed to argue that this wasn't Gretzky's best Canada Cup.

After watching the final game from a private box in Copps Coliseum, Gretzky said he may play again in 1995. Which may be the best news Canada received all tournament long.

ners, Howard Baldwin and Morris Belzberg.

Green tried to overcome the negative feeling the Gunds had left behind by hiring two former Stanley Cup-winning captains to run the team—Bob Clarke of Philadelphia as general manager and Bob Gainey as coach. Clarke had just been fired as GM of the Flyers and Gainey's previous coaching experience had been the year before as coach of the Epinal Squirrels, a second-division team in the mediocre French league.

At the All-Star break, the "No Stars" were squirrelled away near the bottom of the NHL standings with a 13-28-8 record and average home game "crowds" of less than 6,500.

But Gainey wouldn't let his players quit. And in the second half of the season they began to respond to his call for smart defensive play. Led by Jon Casey in goal and experienced free agents Bobby Smith and Brian Propp up front, Minnesota went 12-5-6 after the break only to stumble in the last two weeks of the season, losing six of eight.

The magic returned in the playoffs, however, as the Stars stunned Chicago and St. Louis in six games and Edmonton in five to win the Campbell Conference title with an overall 12-5 mark. Along the way, the fans returned to the Met Center in droves, stuffing the old arena to the rafters throughout the playoffs.

"My only thoughts are good thoughts about all we've accomplished," said owner Green after losing to Pittsburgh in the final. "We had an empty building and we filled it. We had a losing team and they became champions."

Before running into Minnesota in the playoffs, Chicago was the league's regular-season champion, finishing with 106 points. Part of Mike Keenan's coaching ethic involves intimidation, but the NHL's referees refused to let his team get away with it in the North Stars series. The Hawks took 54 penalties in six games, allowed a record 15 power-play goals and bowed out, if not meekly, then at least decisively.

Chicago's playoff failure overshadowed a strong regular season run that saw the emergence of 25-year-old rookie goaltender Ed Belfour. Belfour posted a league-high 43 wins and a league-low

Tim Parker/The Sporting News

Rookie of the Year **Ed Belfour** of Chicago won 43 games for the Blackhawks and was named the league's best goaltender.

2.47 goals-against average—a performance that earned him the Vezina (top goalie) and Calder (top rookie) trophies as well as a first team All-Star berth at season's end.

Chicago's defense was further strengthened by the presence of Chris Chelios, who returned to his hometown in a blockbuster offseason trade that sent Denis Savard to Montreal. Savard had become expendable the year before with the development of rookie center Jeremy Roenick. In 1990-91, Roenick and linemate Steve Larmer teamed for 85 goals to become one of the more potent one-two punches in the league.

However, the most potent NHL duo was unquestionably the St. Louis Blues' Brett Hull and Adam Oates. Hull and Oates finished second and third behind Wayne Gretzky in the scoring race with 131 and 115 points, respectively. Hull led the league in goals with 86, becoming the fifth player to score 50 times in 50 games and only the second (after

Gretzky) to net 80 in a season. He was also named the winner of the Hart Trophy as league MVP, an honor his father Bobby won twice in the mid-1960s. Oates, meanwhile, missed 19 games and still topped 100 points for the second straight year.

The Blues entered the season having spent lavishly (many said irresponsibly) to sign Hull to a four-year contract worth just over $7.1 million. They shelled out another $5 million to sign free agent defenseman Scott Stevens away from the Washington Capitals, a deal that also cost them five first round draft picks in compensation. But Stevens was worth it, steadying the Blues' young defense and becoming captain of the team within a month of his arrival. As a result, the Blues went from an 83-point team to a 105-point team, and earned Coach of the Year honors for Brian Sutter.

The summer of 1990 gave the NHL its first taste of the million-dollar salaries that have become routine in other sports. As many as 10 players signed deals that average out to $1 million a season over the length of the contracts. Oddly enough, every one of the new millionaires returned dividends on their investment, an extraordinary turn of events in these money-for-nothing times. The closest anyone came to flopping was Savard who, restricted by Montreal's defensive style, produced only 59 points in 70 games.

The league's charter millionaire, Wayne Gretzky, makes it a habit to give service for the buck. After becoming the first player to reach the 2,000-point mark early in the season, Gretzky became the fourth to score 700 goals. More importantly, he gave the L.A. Kings a fighting chance for respectability. With the Great One scoring 163 points to win his ninth scoring title, the Kings rose from a fourth place finish in the Smythe Division in 1989-90 to win their first division title in 24 seasons.

That the Kings fizzled out in the playoffs can be attributed to a pair of developments: injuries to Gretzky and his right-hand man Tomas Sandstrom, plus the Edmonton Oilers' brief—but illusory—discovery of the fountain of youth. The Oilers, defending champions and winners of five of the last seven Stanley Cups,

struggled to a .500 record in the regular season and a disappointing 12th place overall. Their captain, Mark Messier, played most of the season with a nagging knee injury, and their top goalie, Grant Fuhr, spent the first 40 games on suspension for cocaine use.

Then for one magical month, they played like the Oilers of old. Fuhr came back in February and sent a signal to the rest of the league that his layoff hadn't set him back at all. In his return, Fuhr did not allow a goal in a 4-0 win over New Jersey. Messier made only a modest contribution in the playoffs, but the combination of Esa Tikkanen's timely scoring and Fuhr's exceptional goaltending carried Edmonton through two rounds against a pair of heavy favorites, Calgary and Los Angeles.

Reality set in, however, when they met Minnesota. As well as the North Stars played, they were the beneficiaries of timing more than anything else. Collectively, the Oilers' battered, thirtysomething lineup could not muster the same high level of hockey in the third round as they had in the first two and fell in five games.

Boston's peerless defenseman Ray Bourque turned 30 in December and celebrated by winning his fourth Norris Trophy in the last five seasons. In the playoffs, however, the Bruins lost to Pittsburgh in a six-game Wales Conference final.

After the playoffs, coaches Mike Milbury of Boston and John Muckler of Edmonton, opponents in the 1990 Stanley Cup final, both stepped down to accept assistant GM jobs—Milbury in Boston and Muckler in Buffalo.

The biggest front office move, however, came in Toronto where the once dominant Maple Leafs signed Cliff Fletcher as president and GM for a staggering $4 million over five years. Fletcher quit the same job in Calgary in May after 19 years with the Flames.

Expansion was the talk of the NHL in December and again in May as the league moved to add three new teams over the next two seasons.

On Dec. 6, expansion franchises were awarded to Ottawa and Tampa Bay, which will begin play in 1992-93. Ottawa's admission brought the Canadian capital city back into the NHL after the original Senators moved to St. Louis in

Wide World Photos

Eric Lindros waves to his family after being selected first in the 1991 NHL entry draft, June 22 in Buffalo. Quebec general manager **Pierre Page** is no doubt thinking what it's going to cost to sign Lindros.

1934 (and folded in 1935). Ottawa won the Stanley Cup four times in the 1920s. Tampa Bay constitutes new territory, but the NHL's second foray into the South— the Flames played in Atlanta from 1972-80 before moving to Calgary. Both groups were obliged to pay $50 million to join the league, a steep fee that led Ottawa to enlist singer and native son Paul Anka as a co-owner and sent Tampa Bay Lightning president and GM Phil Esposito to Japan to recruit foreign investors.

On May 30, the San Jose Sharks, who join the Smythe Division in 1991-92, stocked their roster in the NHL's first expansion draft since 1974. Actually they shared the draft with Minnesota. When the Gund brothers agreed to sell the North Stars in 1990, they asked for and received the right to claim 24 players from the Stars' roster and farm system. In exchange, Minnesota participated as an equal partner in the draft, collecting 10 players from other NHL teams.

Overseas, the 1991 World Championship may have signalled the beginning of the end of the Eastern Bloc's domination of international competition. With a number of the top Soviets, young and old, now playing in the NHL and virtually half the Czech national team scattered around Europe, the tournament was a wide-open competition that saw Sweden emerge with the gold medal.

Quebec, the worst team in the NHL, struck gold in June's entry draft when it selected 17-year-old Eric Lindros from the Oshawa Generals. Lindros, the most highly regarded junior player since Lemieux, showed his appreciation by declining to pull on a Nordique sweater for photographers.

While Lindros will be a hard sell, Quebec knows that he resembles Lemieux in many ways—size, reach, an exceptionally high skill level for a big man, plus great natural scoring ability.

Lindros may indeed be the heir apparent, but in 1991, the story was Lemieux, the player of great promise who finally delivered on all those expectations. *Merveilleux.* □

HOCKEY STATISTICS

SEC A

THE 1992 INFORMATION PLEASE SPORTS ALMANAC

THE SEASON IN REVIEW
1990-1991

NHL • WORLD • U.S. COLLEGES

PAGE 311

Final NHL Standings

Division champions (*) and playoff qualifiers (†) are noted. Number of seasons listed after each head coach refers to current tenure with club through 1990-91 season.

Campbell Conference

Norris Division

	W	L	T	Pts	Goals For	Goals Opp	+/−
*Chicago	49	23	8	106	284	211	+73
†St.Louis	47	22	11	105	310	250	+60
†Detroit	34	38	8	76	273	298	−25
†Minnesota	27	39	14	68	256	266	−10
Toronto	23	46	11	57	241	318	−77

Head Coaches: Chi—Mike Keenan (3rd season); **StL**—Brian Sutter (3rd); **Det**—Bryan Murray (1st); **Min**—Bob Gainey (1st); **Tor**—replaced Doug Carpenter (2nd, 1-9-1) with assistant Tom Watt, Oct.26.

1989-90 Standings: 1.Chicago (41-33-6, 88 points); 2.St-.Louis (37-34-9, 83 pts); 3.Toronto (38-38-4, 80 pts); 4.Minnesota (36-40-4, 76 pts); 5.Detroit (28-38-14, 70 pts).

Smythe Division

	W	L	T	Pts	Goals For	Goals Opp	+/−
*Los Angeles	46	24	10	102	340	254	+86
†Calgary	46	26	8	100	344	263	+81
†Edmonton	37	37	6	80	272	272	E
†Vancouver	28	43	9	65	243	315	−72
Winnipeg	26	43	11	63	260	288	−28

Head Coaches: LA—Tom Webster (2nd Season); **Calg**—Doug Risebrough (1st); **Edm**—John Muckler (2nd); **Van**—replaced Bob McCammon (4th, 19-30-5) with GM Pat Quinn, Jan.31; **Win**—Bob Murdoch (2nd).

1989-90 Standings: 1.Calgary (42-23-15, 99 points); 2.Edmonton (38-28-14, 90 pts); 3.Winnipeg (37-32-11, 85 pts); 4.Los Angeles (34-39-7, 75 pts); 5.Vancouver (25-41-14, 64 pts).

Wales Conference

Adams Division

	W	L	T	Pts	Goals For	Goals Opp	+/−
*Boston	44	24	12	100	299	264	+35
†Montreal	39	30	11	89	273	249	+24
†Buffalo	31	30	19	81	292	278	+14
†Hartford	31	38	11	73	238	276	−38
Quebec	16	50	14	46	236	354	−118

Head Coaches: Bos—Mike Milbury (2nd season); **Mon**—Pat Burns (3rd); **Buf**—Rick Dudley (2nd); **Hart**—Rick Ley (2nd); **Que**—Dave Chambers (1st).

1989-90 Standings: 1.Boston (46-25-9, 101 points); 2.Buffalo (45-27-8, 98 pts); 3.Montreal (41-28-11, 93 pts); 4.Hartford (38-33-9, 85 pts); 5.Quebec (12-61-7, 31 pts).

Patrick Division

	W	L	T	Pts	Goals For	Goals Opp	+/−
*Pittsburgh	41	33	6	88	342	305	+37
†NY Rangers	36	31	13	85	297	265	+32
†Washington	37	36	7	81	258	258	E
†New Jersey	32	33	15	79	272	264	+8
Philadelphia	33	37	10	76	252	267	−15
NY Islanders	25	45	10	60	223	290	−67

Head Coaches: Pit—Bob Johnson (1st season); **NYR**—Roger Neilson (2nd); **Wash**—Terry Murray (2nd); **NJ**—replaced John Cunniff (2nd, 28-28-11) with interim coach Tom McVie on Mar.4; **Phi**—Paul Holmgren (3rd); **NYI**—Al Arbour (3rd).

1989-90 Standings: 1.NY Rangers (36-31-13, 85 points); 2.New Jersey (37-34-9, 83 pts); 3.Washington (36-38-6, 78 pts); 4.NY Islanders (31-38-11, 73 pts); 5.Pittsburgh (32-40-8, 72 pts); 6. Philadelphia (30-39-11, 71 pts).

Home & Away, Division Records

Team-by-team records (wins-losses-ties) for games at home, away and within the division. Teams are ranked by overall points.

Campbell Conference

	Pts	Home	Away	Div
Chicago	106	28- 8-4	21-15-4	20-8-4
St.Louis	105	24- 9-7	23-13-4	18-11-3
Los Angeles	102	26- 9-5	20-15-5	19-9-4
Calgary	100	29- 8-3	17-18-5	18-10-4
Edmonton	80	22-15-3	15-22-3	13-16-3
Detroit	76	26-14-0	8-24-8	13-16-3
Minnesota	68	19-15-6	8-24-8	10-17-5
Vancouver	65	18-17-5	10-26-4	11-20-1
Winnipeg	63	17-18-5	9-25-6	10-16-6
Toronto	57	15-21-4	8-25-7	10-19-3

Wales Conference

	Pts	Home	Away	Div
Boston	100	26-9- 5	18-15-7	19-8-5
Montreal	89	23-12- 5	16-18-6	15-13-4
Pittsburgh	88	25-12- 3	16-21-3	19-14-2
NY Rangers	85	22-11- 7	14-20-6	15-14-6
Washington	81	21-14- 5	16-22-2	20-12-3
Buffalo	81	15-13-12	16-17-7	11-12-9
New Jersey	79	23-10- 7	9-23-8	13-16-6
Philadelphia	76	18-16- 6	15-21-4	12-16-7
Hartford	73	18-16- 6	13-22-5	9-16-7
NY Islanders	60	15-19- 6	10-26-4	12-19-4
Quebec	46	9-23- 8	7-27-6	9-14-9

NHL Regular Season Leaders

(*)indicates rookies.

Scoring

	Pos	Gm	G	A	Pts	PM
Wayne Gretzky, LA	C	78	41	122	163	16
Brett Hull, St.L	R	78	86	45	131	22
Adam Oates, St.L	C	61	25	90	115	29
Mark Recchi, Pit	R	78	40	73	113	48
John Cullen, Pit-Hart	C	78	39	71	110	101
Joe Sakic, Que	C	80	48	61	109	24
Steve Yzerman, Det	C	80	51	57	108	34
Theo Fleury, Calg	R	79	51	53	104	136
Al MacInnis, Calg	D	78	28	75	103	90
Steve Larmer, Chi	R	80	44	57	101	79
Jeremy Roenick, Chi	C	79	41	53	94	80
Ray Bourque, Bos	D	76	21	73	94	75
Paul Coffey, Pit	D	76	24	69	93	128
Craig Janney, Bos	C	77	26	66	92	8
Cam Neely, Bos	R	69	51	40	91	98
Luc Robitaille, LA	L	76	45	46	91	68

Goals

Hull, StL	86
Fleury, Calg	51
Neely, Bos	51
Yzerman, Det	51
Gartner, NYR	49
Sakic, Que	48
Four tied with 45 each.	

Assists

Gretzky, LA	122
Oates, StL	90
MacInnis, Calg	75
Bourque, Bos	73
Recchi, Pit	73
Leetch, NYR	72
Cullen, Pit-Hart	71

Power Play Goals

Hull, St.L	29
Gartner, NYR	22
Nieuwendyk, Calg	22
Gagner, Min	20
MacLean, NJ	19

Short-Handed Goals

Reid, Tor	8
Fleury, Calg	7
Graham, Chi	6
MacTavish, Edm	6
Yzerman, Det	6

Plus/Minus

Fleury, Calg	+48
McSorley, LA	+48
MacInnis, Calg	+42
Roenick, Chi	+38
Larmer, Chi	+37

Penalty Minutes

Ray, Buf	348
Peluso, Chi*	320
Probert, Det	315
Odjick, Van*	296
Berube, Phi	293

Goaltending

(Minimum 25 games)

	Gm	Min	GA	SO	Avg
Ed Belfour, Chi*	74	4127	170	4	2.47
Don Beaupre, Wash	45	2572	113	5	2.64
Patrick Roy, Mon	48	2835	128	1	2.71
Andy Moog, Bos	51	2844	136	4	2.87
Pete Peeters, Phi	26	1270	61	1	2.88
Kelly Hrudey, LA	47	2730	132	3	2.90
Chris Terreri, NJ	53	2970	144	1	2.91
Jon Casey, Min	55	3185	158	3	2.98
Vincent Riendeau, StL	44	2671	134	3	3.01
Rick Wamsley, Calg	29	1670	85	0	3.05

Wins

	W- L -T
Belfour, Chi*	43-19-7
Vernon, Calg	31-19-3
Cheveldae, Det	30-26-5
Riendeau, StL	29- 9-6
Barrasso, Pit	27-16-3
Ranford, Edm	27-27-3

Shutouts

Beaupre, Wash	5
Belfour, Chi*	4
Essensa, Win	4
Moog, Bos	4
Four tied with 3.	

Save Pct.

Belfour, Chi*	.910
Roy, Mon	.906
Richter, NYR	.903
Peeters, Phi	.902
Hrudey, LA	.900

Losses

	W- L- T
Tugnutt, Que	12-29-10
Ing, Tor	16-29- 8
Ranford, Edm	27-27- 3
Cheveldae, Det	30-26- 5
Essensa, Win	19-24- 6
Healy, NYI	18-24- 9

NHL All-Star Game
Campbell 11, Wales 5

Date: Jan.19, at Chicago Stadium; **Coaches:** John Muckler (Campbell) and Mike Milbury (Wales); **MVP:** Vincent Damphousse (Campbell).

Wales Conference

Starters	Pos	G	A	Pts	PM
Rick Tocchet, Philadelphia	LW	1	1	2	0
Ray Bourque, Boston	D	0	1	1	0
Joe Sakic, Quebec	C	0	1	1	0
Cam Neely, Boston	RW	0	0	0	0
Paul Coffey, Pittsburgh	D	0	0	0	0
Patrick Roy, Montreal	G	0	0	0	0
Bench					
Pat LaFontaine, NY Islanders	C	2	0	2	0
John MacLean, New Jersey	RW	1	0	1	0
Kevin Stevens, Pittsburgh	LW	1	0	1	0
John Cullen, Pittsburgh	C	0	1	1	0
Kevin Hatcher, Washington	D	0	1	1	0
Darren Turcotte, NY Rangers	C	0	1	1	0
Pat Verbeek, Hartford	RW	0	1	1	0
Denis Savard, Montreal	C	0	0	0	0
Dave Christian, Boston	LW	0	0	0	0
Mark Recchi, Pittsburgh	RW	0	0	0	0
Guy Lafleur, Quebec	RW	0	0	0	0
Garry Galley, Boston	D	0	0	0	0
Brian Leetch, NY Rangers	D	0	0	0	0
Uwe Krupp, Buffalo	D	0	0	0	0
TOTALS		5	7	12	0

Replacements: Christian for Boston defenseman Chris Nilan (sprained ankle); Savard for Montreal center Brian Skrudland (fractured foot).

Goaltenders	Mins	Shots	Saves	GA
Patrick Roy, Mon	30:12	26	21	5
Andy Moog, Bos. (L)	29:48	15	9	6

Campbell Conference

Starters	Pos	G	A	Pts	PM
Chris Chelios, Chicago	D	1	1	2	0
Wayne Gretzky, Los Angeles	C	1	0	1	0
Tomas Sandstrom, Los Ang.	RW	0	1	1	0
Luc Robitaille, Los Angeles	LW	0	0	0	0
Al MacInnis, Calgary	D	0	0	0	0
Mike Vernon, Calgary	G	0	0	0	0
Bench					
Adam Oates, St.Louis	C	1	4	5	0
Vincent Damphousse, Toronto	LW	4	0	4	0
Jeremy Roenick, Chicago	C	1	2	3	0
Phil Housley, Winnipeg	D	0	2	2	4
Steve Larmer, Chicago	RW	0	2	2	0
Steve Smith, Edmonton	D	0	2	2	0
Theo Fleury, Calgary	C	1	0	1	0
Dave Gagner, Minnesota	C	1	0	1	0
Gary Suter, Calgary	D	1	0	1	0
Mark Messier, Edmonton	C	0	1	1	0
Steve Yzerman, Detroit	C	0	1	1	0
Trevor Linden, Vancouver	RW	0	0	0	0
Bobby Smith, Minnesota	C	0	0	0	0
Scott Stevens, St.Louis	D	0	0	0	0
TOTALS		11	16	27	4

Replacements: Oates for St.Louis RW Brett Hull (sprained ankle).

Goaltenders	Mins	Shots	Saves	GA
Mike Vernon, Calg	30:12	15	13	2
Bill Ranford, Edm. (W)	29:48	26	23	3

Score by Periods

	1	2	3	Final
Wales (East)	1	2	2	— 5
Campbell (West)	2	5	4	— 11

Power plays—Wales (2 for 2), Campbell (0 for 0); **Officials**—Terry Gregson (Referee), Dan Schachte and Jerry Pateman (Linesmen). **Attendance**—18,472.

Team by Team Statistics

At least 15 points scored for skaters and five games played for goaltenders. Players with more than one team during the regular season are listed with final club; (*) indicates rookies.

Boston Bruins

Top Scorers	Pos	Gm	G	A	Pts	+/-	PM
Ray Bourque	D	76	21	73	94	+33	75
Craig Janney	C	77	26	66	92	+15	8
Cam Neely	R	69	51	40	91	+26	98
Ken Hodge*	C	70	30	29	59	+11	20
Dave Christian	L	78	32	21	53	+8	41
Bob Sweeney	C	80	15	33	48	+12	115
Glen Wesley	D	80	11	32	43	E	78
Randy Burridge	L	62	15	13	28	+17	40
Petri Skriko	R	48	9	18	27	-5	17
VAN.		20	4	4	8	-9	8
BOS.		28	5	14	19	+4	9
Garry Galley	D	70	6	21	27	E	84
Jim Wiemer	D	61	4	19	23	+3	62
Don Sweeney	D	77	8	13	21	+2	67
Dave Poulin	C	31	8	12	20	+5	25
Jeff Lazaro*	L	49	5	13	18	+7	67
Bob Carpenter	L	29	8	8	16	+2	22
Vladimir Ruzicka	C	29	8	8	16	+1	19
Wes Walz*	C	56	8	8	16	-14	32
Chris Nilan	R	41	6	9	15	+4	277

Acquired: Skriko from Van. (Jan.16).

Goaltending	GP	Min	Avg	SO	Record
Andy Moog	51	2844	2.87	4	25-13-9
Reggie Lemelin	33	1829	3.64	1	17-10-3
Others	4	194	4.38	0	2-1-0
BOSTON	80	4872	3.25	5	44-24-12

Assists: Moog (2). **PM:** Moog (20), Lemelin (10).

Calgary Flames

Top Scorers	Pos	Gm	G	A	Pts	+/-	PM
Theo Fleury	R	79	51	53	104	+48	136
Al Macinnis	D	78	28	75	103	+42	90
Joe Nieuwendyk	C	79	45	40	85	+19	36
Doug Gilmour	C	78	20	61	81	+27	144
Sergei Makarov	R	78	30	49	79	+15	44
Gary Suter	D	79	12	58	70	+26	102
Gary Roberts	L	80	22	31	53	+15	252
Robert Reichel*	C	66	19	22	41	+17	22
Joel Otto	C	76	19	20	39	-4	183
Paul Fenton	L	78	14	21	35	-5	28
WIN.		17	4	4	8	-4	18
TOR.		30	5	10	15	-3	0
CALG		31	5	7	12	+2	10
Stephane Matteau*	L	78	15	19	34	+17	93
Paul Ranheim	L	39	14	16	30	+20	4
Carey Wilson	C	57	11	18	29	-13	18
HART.		45	8	15	23	-14	16
CALG		12	3	3	6	+1	2
Brian MacLellan	L	57	13	14	27	+15	55
Frantisek Musil	D	75	7	16	23	+12	183
MIN.		8	0	2	2	E	23
CALG		67	7	14	21	+12	160
Jamie Macoun	D	79	7	15	22	+29	84
Ric Nattress	D	58	5	13	18	-1	63
Roger Johansson	D	38	4	13	17	+9	47
Tim Sweeney*	L	42	7	9	16	+1	4

Acquired: Musil from Min. Oct.26); Fenton from Tor. by way of Wash. (Jan.24); Wilson from Hart. (Mar.5).

Goaltending	Gm	Min	Avg	SO	Record
Rick Wamsley	29	1670	3.05	0	14-7-5
Mike Vernon	54	3121	3.31	1	31-19-3
Others	1	60	4.00	0	1-0-0
CALGARY	80	4859	3.25	1	46-26-8

Assists: Vernon (4), Wamsley (1). **PM:** Vernon (8).

Buffalo Sabres

Top Scorers	Pos	Gm	G	A	Pts	+/-	PM
Dale Hawerchuk	C	80	31	58	89	+2	32
Pierre Turgeon	C	78	32	47	79	+14	26
Dave Andreychuk	L	80	36	33	69	+11	32
Alexander Mogilny	L	62	30	34	64	+14	16
Rick Vaive	R	71	25	27	52	+11	74
Christian Ruuttu	C	77	16	34	50	-6	96
Benoit Hogue	C	76	19	28	47	-8	76
Uwe Krupp	D	74	12	32	44	+14	66
Grant Ledyard	D	60	8	23	31	+13	46
Doug Bodger	D	58	5	23	28	-8	54
Tony Tanti	R	56	7	19	26	+3	50
PIT.		46	6	12	18	+1	44
BUF.		10	1	7	8	+2	6
Dave Snuggerud	L	80	9	15	24	-13	32
Mikko Makela	L	60	15	7	22	-2	25
Greg Paslawski	R	55	11	11	22	-6	14
WIN.		43	9	10	19	-6	10
BUF.		12	2	1	3	E	4
Mike Ramsey	D	71	6	14	20	+14	46
Rob Ray	R	66	8	8	16	-11	50

Acquired: Paslawski from Win. (Feb.4); Tanti from Pit. (Mar.5).

Goaltending	Gm	Min	Avg	SO	Record
Darcy Wakaluk*	16	630	3.33	0	4-5-3
Clint Malarchuk	37	2131	3.35	1	12-14-10
Daren Puppa	38	2092	3.38	2	15-11-6
Others	1	36	5.00	0	0-0-0
BUFFALO	80	4902	3.40	3	31-30-19

Assists: Malarchuk and Puppa (4). **PM:** Malarchuk (19), Puppa (6), Wakaluk (2).

Chicago Blackhawks

Top Scorers	Pos	Gm	G	A	Pts	+/-	PM
Steve Larmer	R	80	44	57	101	+37	79
Jeremy Roenick	C	79	41	53	94	+38	80
Michel Goulet	R	74	27	38	65	+27	65
Chris Chelios	D	77	12	52	64	+23	192
Steve Thomas	L	69	19	35	54	+8	129
Adam Creighton	C	72	22	29	51	E	135
Dirk Graham	R	80	24	21	45	+12	86
Doug Wilson	D	51	11	29	40	+25	32
Troy Murray	C	75	14	23	37	+13	74
Tony McKegney	L	59	17	17	34	-27	48
QUE.		50	17	16	33	-25	44
CHI.		9	0	1	1	-2	4
Wayne Presley	R	71	15	19	34	+11	122
Dave Manson	D	75	14	15	29	+20	191
Greg Gilbert	L	72	10	15	25	+6	58
Mike Hudson	C	55	7	9	16	+5	62
Trent Yawney	D	61	3	13	16	+6	77
Paul Gillis	C	62	3	13	16	-18	144
QUE.		49	3	8	11	-19	91
CHI.		13	0	5	5	+1	53
Frantisek Kucera*	D	40	2	12	16	+3	32

Acquired: McKegney from Que. (Jan.29); Gillis from Que. (Mar.5).

Goaltending	Gm	Min	Avg	SO	Record
Dominic Hasek	5	195	2.46	0	3-0-1
Ed Belfour*	74	4127	2.47	4	43-19-7
Others*	14	521	3.46	0	3-4-0
CHICAGO	80	4846	2.61	4	49-23-8

Assists: Belfour (3). **PM:** Belfour (34).

Team by Team Statistics (Cont.)

Detroit Red Wings

Top Scorers	Pos	Gm	G	A	Pts	+/-	PM
Steve Yzerman	C	80	51	57	108	-2	34
Sergei Fedorov*	C	77	31	48	79	+11	66
Kevin Miller	C	74	22	28	50	-3	67
NYR		63	17	27	44	+1	63
DET		11	5	1	6	-4	4
Shawn Burr	L	80	20	30	50	+14	112
Yves Racine	D	62	7	40	47	+1	33
Jimmy Carson	C	64	21	25	46	+3	28
Paul Ysebaert*	L	62	19	21	40	-7	22
NJ		11	4	3	7	+1	6
DET		51	15	18	33	-8	16
Dave Barr	R	70	18	22	40	+19	55
Johan Garpenlov*	L	71	18	21	39	-4	18
Bob Probert	R	55	16	23	39	-3	315
Doug Crossman	D	74	8	29	37	-23	48
NYI		16	1	6	7	-4	12
HART		41	4	19	23	-13	19
DET		17	3	4	7	-6	17
Brent Fedyk	R	67	16	19	35	+21	38
Gerard Gallant	L	45	10	16	26	+6	111
Rick Zombo	D	77	4	19	23	-2	57
Steve Chiasson	D	42	3	17	20	E	80
Mark Habscheid	C	46	9	8	17	-10	22
Rick Green	D	65	2	14	16	+10	24
Keith Primeau*	C	58	3	12	15	-12	106

Acquired: Ysebaert from NJ (Nov.27); Crossman from Hart. (Feb.20); Miller from NYR (Mar.5).

Goaltending	Gm	Min	Avg	SO	Record
Glen Hanlon	19	862	3.20	0	4-6-3
Tim Cheveldae	65	3615	3.55	2	30-26-5
Allan Bester	9	425	4.38	0	0-7-0
TOR	6	247	4.37	0	0-4-0
DET	3	178	4.38	0	0-3-0
Others	6	188	6.07	0	0-3-0
DETROIT	80	4485	3.68	2	34-38-8

Assists: Cheveldae (5); PM: Cheveldae (2); Hanlon (4).
Acquired: Bester from Tor. (Mar.5).

Edmonton Oilers

Top Scorers	Pos	Gm	G	A	Pts	+/-	PM
Esa Tikkanen	L	79	27	42	69	+22	85
Petr Klima	L	70	40	28	68	+24	113
Mark Messier	C	53	12	51	63	+15	34
Joe Murphy	R	80	27	35	62	+2	35
Craig Simpson	L	75	30	27	57	-8	66
Glenn Anderson	R	74	24	31	55	-7	59
Steve Smith	D	77	13	41	54	+14	193
Martin Gelinas	L	73	20	20	40	-7	34
Ken Linseman	C	56	7	29	36	+15	94
Craig MacTavish	C	80	17	15	32	-1	76
Anatoli Semenov	L	57	15	16	31	+17	26
Charlie Huddy	D	53	5	22	27	+4	32
Adam Graves	R	76	7	18	25	-21	127
Chris Joseph	D	49	5	17	22	+3	59
Kevin Lowe	D	73	3	13	16	-9	113

Goaltending	Gm	Min	Avg	SO	Record
Grant Fuhr	13	778	3.01	0	6-4-3
Bill Ranford	60	3415	3.20	0	27-27-3
Kari Takko	13	648	4.54	0	4-6-0
MIN	2	119	6.05	0	0-2-0
EDM	11	529	4.20	0	4-4-0
Others	2	120	4.50	0	0-2-0
EDMONTON	80	4850	3.36	1	37-37-6

Assists: Ranford (4), Takko (1); PM: Ranford (6).
Acquired: Takko from Min. (Nov.22).

Hartford Whalers

Top Scorers	Pos	Gm	G	A	Pts	+/-	PM
John Cullen	C	78	39	71	110	-6	101
PIT		65	31	63	94	E	83
HART		13	8	8	16	-6	18
Pat Verbeek	R	80	43	39	82	E	246
Rob Brown	R	69	24	34	58	-7	132
PIT		25	6	10	16	E	31
HART		44	18	24	42	-7	101
Zarley Zalapski	D	77	15	39	54	+8	65
PIT		66	12	36	48	+15	59
HART		11	3	3	6	-7	6
Kevin Dineen	R	61	17	30	47	-15	104
Bobby Holik*	L	78	21	22	43	-3	113
Mark Hunter	R	68	14	18	32	+2	165
CALG		57	10	15	25	-1	125
HART		11	4	3	7	-3	40
Brad Shaw	D	72	4	28	32	-10	29
Todd Krygier	L	72	13	17	30	+1	95
Dean Evason	C	75	6	23	29	-6	170
Paul Cyr	L	70	12	13	25	-8	107
Sylvain Cote	D	73	7	12	19	-17	17
Mike Tomlak	L	64	8	8	16	-9	55

Acquired: Brown from Pit. (Dec.21); Cullen and Zalapski from Pit. (Mar.4); Hunter from Calg. (Mar.5).

Goaltending	Gm	Min	Avg	SO	Record
Daryl Reaugh*	20	1010	3.15	1	7-7-1
Peter Sidorkiewicz	52	2953	3.33	1	21-22-7
Kay Whitmore*	18	850	3.67	0	3-9-3
Others	1	35	5.14	0	0-0-0
HARTFORD	80	4867	3.40	2	31-38-11

Assists: Sidorkiewicz (4), Whitmore (1); PM: Sidorkiewicz (6), Reaugh and Whitmore (4).

Los Angeles Kings

Top Scorers	Pos	Gm	G	A	Pts	+/-	PM
Wayne Gretzky	C	78	41	122	163	+30	16
Luc Robitaille	L	76	45	46	91	+28	68
Tomas Sandstrom	R	68	45	44	89	+27	106
Tony Granato	L	68	30	34	64	+22	156
Steve Duchesne	D	78	21	41	62	+19	66
Todd Elik	C	74	21	37	58	+20	58
Dave Taylor	R	73	23	30	53	+27	148
Rob Blake*	D	75	12	34	46	+3	125
Marty McSorley	D	61	7	32	39	+48	221
Robert Kudelski	R	72	23	13	36	+9	46
Brian Benning	D	61	7	24	31	+12	123
John Tonelli	L	71	14	16	30	+3	49
Steve Kasper	C	67	9	19	28	+3	33
Larry Robinson	D	62	1	22	23	+22	16
Brad Jones	L	53	9	11	20	+11	57
Jay Miller	L	66	8	12	20	+9	259
Ilkka Sinisalo	R	53	5	12	17	-6	26
MIN		46	5	12	17	-10	24
LA		7	0	0	0	+4	2
John McIntyre	C	69	8	8	16	+6	140
TOR		13	0	3	3	E	25
LA		56	8	5	13	+6	115

Acquired: McIntyre from Tor. (Nov.9); Sinisalo from Min. (Mar.5).

Goaltending	Gm	Min	Avg	SO	Record
Kelly Hrudey	47	2730	2.90	3	26-13-6
Daniel Berthiaume	37	2119	3.31	1	20-11-4
LOS ANGELES	80	4863	3.13	4	46-24-10

Assists: None; PM: Hrudey (14), Berthiaume (10).

Minnesota North Stars

Top Scorers	Pos	Gm	G	A	Pts	+/-	PM
Dave Gagner	C	73	40	42	82	+9	114
Brian Bellows	L	80	35	40	75	-13	43
Brian Propp	L	79	26	47	73	+7	58
Neal Broten	C	79	13	56	69	-3	26
Mike Modano	R	79	28	36	64	+2	65
Bobby Smith	C	73	15	31	46	-9	60
Ulf Dahlen	R	66	21	18	39	+7	6
Mark Tinordi	D	69	5	27	32	+1	191
Doug Smail	L	72	8	15	23	-8	48
WIN.		15	1	2	3	-6	10
MIN.		57	7	13	20	-2	38
Brian Glynn	D	66	8	11	19	-5	83
Gaetan Duchesne	L	68	9	9	18	+4	18
Perry Berezan	C	52	11	6	17	-2	26
Jim Johnson	D	68	1	14	15	+6	123
PIT.		24	0	5	5	-3	23
MIN.		44	1	9	10	+9	100

Acquired: Smail from Win. (Nov.7); Johnson from Pit. (Dec.11).

Goaltending	Gm	Min	Avg	SO	Record
Jon Casey	47	2730	2.90	3	21-20-11
Brian Hayward	26	1473	3.14	2	6-15-3
MON			Did not play		
MIN	26	1473	3.14	2	6-15-3
Others	4	197	6.10	0	0-4-0
MINNESOTA	80	4876	3.27	5	27-39-14

Assists: Casey (2); **PM:** Casey (22); Hayward and Jarmo Myllys (2).
Acquired: Hayward from Mon. (Nov.7).

Montreal Canadiens

Top Scorers	Pos	Gm	G	A	Pts	+/-	PM
Russ Courtnall	R	79	26	50	76	+5	29
Stephane Richer	R	75	31	30	61	E	53
Denis Savard	C	70	28	31	59	-1	52
Stephan Lebeau	C	73	22	31	53	+4	24
Shayne Corson	L	71	23	24	47	+9	138
Guy Carbonneau	C	78	20	24	44	-1	63
Mike McPhee	L	64	22	21	43	+6	56
Mike Keane	R	73	13	23	36	+6	50
Brian Skrudland	C	57	15	19	34	+12	85
Matt Schneider	D	69	10	20	30	+7	63
Peter Svoboda	D	60	4	22	26	+5	52
Eric Desjardins	D	62	7	18	25	+7	27
Andrew Casseold*	C	54	6	19	25	+2	20
Sylvain Lefebvre	D	63	5	18	23	-11	30
Tom Chorske*	L	57	9	11	20	-8	32
J.J.Daigneault	D	51	3	16	19	-2	31
Brent Gilchrist	C	51	6	9	15	-3	10
Donald Dufresne	D	53	2	13	15	+5	55

Goaltending	Gm	Min	Avg	SO	Record
Patrick Roy	48	2835	2.71	1	25-15-6
Andre Racicot*	21	975	3.20	1	7-9-2
J.C.Bergeron*	18	941	3.76	0	7-6-2
Others	3	108	3.33	0	0-0-1
MONTREAL	80	4869	3.07	2	39-30-11

Assists: Roy (2), Bergeron (1), Racicot (1); **PM:** Roy (6).

New Jersey Devils

Top Scorers	Pos	Gm	G	A	Pts	+/-	PM
John MacLean	R	78	45	33	78	+8	150
Kirk Muller	L	80	19	51	70	+1	76
Brendan Shanahan	R	75	29	37	66	+4	141
Peter Stastny	C	77	18	42	60	E	53
Claude Lemieux	R	78	30	17	47	-8	105
Patrik Sundstrom	C	71	15	31	46	+7	48
Bruce Driver	D	73	9	36	45	+11	62
Alexi Kasatonov	D	78	10	31	41	+23	76
Eric Weinrich*	D	76	4	34	38	+10	48
Doug Brown	R	58	14	16	30	+18	4
Jon Morris*	C	53	9	19	28	+9	27
Zdeno Ciger*	L	45	8	17	25	+3	8
David Maley	L	64	8	14	22	+9	151
Laurie Boschman	C	78	11	9	20	-1	79
Ken Daneyko	D	80	4	16	20	-10	249
Viacheslav Fetisov	D	67	3	16	19	+5	62
Pat Conacher	L	49	5	11	16	+9	27
Lee Norwood	D	49	6	9	15	+5	137
DET		21	3	7	10	+6	50
NJ		28	3	2	5	-1	87

Acquired: Norwood from Det. (Nov.27).

Goaltending	Gm	Min	Avg	SO	Record
Chris Terreri	53	2970	2.91	1	24-21-7
Sean Burke	35	1870	3.59	0	8-12-8
Others	1	20	6.00	0	0-0-0
NEW JERSEY	80	4876	3.25	1	32-33-15

Assists: Terreri (3); **PM:** Burke (18), Terreri (2).

New York Islanders

Top Scorers	Pos	Gm	G	A	Pts	+/-	PM
Pat LaFontaine	C	75	41	44	85	-6	42
Dave Volek	L	77	22	34	56	-10	57
Brent Sutter	C	75	21	32	53	-8	49
Patrick Flatley	R	56	20	25	45	-2	74
Derek King	L	66	19	26	45	+1	44
Randy Wood	L	76	24	18	42	-12	45
Ray Ferraro	C	76	21	21	42	-12	70
HART.		15	2	5	7	-1	18
NYI		61	19	16	35	-11	52
Jeff Norton	D	44	3	25	28	-13	16
Bill Berg*	L	78	9	14	23	-3	67
Gary Nylund	D	72	2	21	23	-8	105
Wayne McBean	D	52	5	14	19	-21	47
Joe Reekie	D	66	3	16	19	+17	96
Brad Dalgarno	R	41	3	12	15	-10	24

Acquired: Ferraro from Hart. (Nov.13).

Goaltending	Gm	Min	Avg	SO	Record
Glenn Healy	53	2999	3.32	0	18-24-9
Jeff Hackett	30	1508	3.62	0	5-18-1
Others	8	340	4.59	0	2-3-0
NY ISLANDERS	80	4867	3.58	0	25-45-10

Assists: Healy (2); **PM:** Healy (14), Hackett (4), George Maneluk (2).

Team by Team Statistics (Cont.)

New York Rangers

Top Scorers	Pos	Gm	G	A	Pts	+/−	PM
Brian Leetch	D	80	16	72	88	+2	42
Bernie Nicholls	C	71	25	48	73	+5	96
Mike Gartner	R	79	49	20	69	−9	53
Darren Turcotte	C	74	26	41	67	−5	37
Brian Mullen	R	79	19	43	62	+12	44
James Patrick	D	74	10	49	59	−5	58
John Ogrodnick	L	79	31	23	54	+15	10
Ray Sheppard	R	59	24	23	47	+8	21
Kelly Kisio	C	51	15	20	35	+3	58
Kris King	L	72	11	14	25	−1	156
Jan Erixon	L	53	7	18	25	+13	8
Randy Moller	D	61	4	19	23	+13	161
Troy Mallette	L	71	12	10	22	−8	252
Mark Janssens	C	67	9	7	16	−1	172

Goaltending	Gm	Min	Avg	SO	Record
Mike Richter*	45	2596	3.12	0	21-13-7
John Vanbiesbrouck	40	2257	3.35	3	15-18-6
NY RANGERS	80	4872	3.26	3	36-31-13

Assists: Vanbiesbrouck (3), Richter (1); **PM:** Vanbiesbrouck (18), Richter (4).

Philadelphia Flyers

Top Scorers	Pos	Gm	G	A	Pts	+/−	PM
Rick Tocchet	R	70	40	31	71	+2	150
Pelle Eklund	C	73	19	50	69	−2	14
Murray Craven	L	77	19	47	66	−2	53
Ron Sutter	C	80	17	28	45	+2	92
Gord Murphy	D	80	11	31	42	−7	58
Mike Ricci*	C	68	21	20	41	−8	64
Scott Mellanby	R	74	20	21	41	+8	155
Keith Acton	C	76	14	23	37	−9	131
Terry Carkner	D	79	7	25	32	−15	204
Normand Lacombe	R	74	11	20	31	−1	27
Kjell Samuelsson	D	78	9	19	28	+4	82
Mark Pederson*	L	59	10	16	26	−5	23
MON.		47	8	15	23	+3	18
PHI.		12	2	1	3	−8	5
Jiri Latal	D	50	5	21	26	−19	14
Tim Kerr	R	27	10	14	24	−8	8
Derrick Smith	L	72	11	10	21	E	37
Dale Kushner*	L	63	7	11	18	−4	195
Craig Berube	L	74	8	9	17	−6	293
Murray Baron*	F	67	8	8	16	−3	74

Acquired: Pederson from Mon. (Mar.5).

Goaltending	Gm	Min	Avg	SO	Record
Pete Peeters	26	1270	2.88	1	9-7-1
Ron Hextall	36	2035	3.13	0	13-16-5
Ken Wregget	30	1484	3.56	0	10-14-3
Others	2	39	4.62	0	1-0-1
PHILADELPHIA	80	4853	3.30	1	33-37-10

Assists: Hextall (1), Peeters (1); **PM:** Peeters (14), Hextall (10), Wregget (6).

Pittsburgh Penguins

Top Scorers	Pos	Gm	G	A	Pts	+/−	PM
Mark Recchi	R	78	40	73	113	E	48
Paul Coffey	D	76	24	69	93	−18	128
Ron Francis	C	81	23	64	87	−2	72
HART.		67	21	55	76	−2	51
PIT.		14	2	19	11	E	21
Kevin Stevens	L	80	40	46	86	−1	133
Jaromir Jagr*	R	80	27	30	57	−4	42
Mario Lemieux	C	26	19	26	45	+8	30
Larry Murphy	D	75	9	34	43	−6	68
MIN.		31	4	11	15	−8	38
PIT.		44	5	23	28	+2	30
Bob Errey	L	79	20	22	42	+11	115
Scott Young	R	77	17	25	42	−6	41
HART.		34	6	9	15	−9	8
PIT.		43	11	16	27	+3	33
Joe Mullen	R	47	17	22	39	+9	6
Phil Bourque	L	78	20	14	34	+7	106
Bryan Trottier	C	52	9	19	28	+5	24
Ulf Samuelsson	D	76	4	22	26	+17	211
HART.		62	3	18	21	+13	174
PIT.		14	1	4	5	+4	37
Randy Gilhen	C	72	15	10	25	+3	51
Jiri Hrdina	C	51	6	17	23	−6	17
CALG		14	0	3	3	−4	4
PIT.		37	6	14	20	−2	13
Paul Stanton*	D	75	5	18	23	+11	40
Troy Loney	L	44	9	16	9	+10	85
Gordie Roberts	D	64	3	13	16	+17	78
STL.		3	0	1	1	−8	8
PIT.		61	3	12	15	+18	70

Acquired: Roberts from St.L (Oct.27); Murphy from Min. (Dec.11); Hrdina from Calg. (Dec.13); Young from Hart. (Dec.21); Francis and Samuelsson from Hart. (Mar.4).

Goaltending	Gm	Min	Avg	SO	Record
Tom Barrasso	48	2754	3.59	1	27-16-3
Frank Pietrangelo	25	1311	3.94	0	10-11-1
Wendell Young	18	773	4.04	0	4-6-2
PITTSBURGH	80	4843	3.78	1	41-33-6

Assists: Barrasso (5), Pietrangelo (1), Young (1); **PM:** Barrasso (40), Pietrangelo (24).

Quebec Nordiques

Top Scorers	Pos	Gm	G	A	Pts	+/−	PM
Joe Sakic	C	80	48	61	109	−26	24
Mats Sundin*	R	80	23	36	59	−24	58
Tony Hrkac	C	70	16	32	48	−22	16
Stephane Morin*	C	48	13	27	40	+6	28
Mike Hough	R	63	13	20	33	−7	111
Bryan Fogarty	D	45	9	22	31	−11	24
Guy Lafleur	R	59	12	16	28	−10	2
Steve Finn	D	71	6	13	19	−26	228
Craig Wolanin	D	80	5	13	18	−13	89
Scott Pearson	L	47	11	4	15	−9	106
TOR.		12	0	0	0	−5	20
QUE.		35	11	4	15	−4	86

Acquired: Pearson from Tor. (Nov.17).

Goaltending	Gm	Min	Avg	SO	Record
Ron Tugnutt	56	3145	4.04	0	12-29-10
John Tanner*	6	228	4.21	0	1-3-1
Jacques Cloutier	25	1231	4.14	0	5-11-2
CHI.	10	403	3.57	0	2-3-0
QUE.	15	828	4.42	0	3-8-2
Scott Gordon*	13	484	5.95	0	0-8-0
Others	3	186	3.87	0	0-2-1
QUEBEC	80	4883	4.35	0	16-50-14

Assists: None; **PM:** Cloutier (6), Tanner (2).
Acquired: Cloutier from Chi. (Jan.29).

St. Louis Blues

Top Scorers	Pos	Gm	G	A	Pts	+/-	PM
Bret Hull	R	78	86	45	131	+23	22
Adam Oates	C	61	25	90	115	+15	29
Dan Quinn	C	78	22	38	60	-33	66
VAN.		64	18	31	49	-28	46
STL.		14	4	7	11	-5	20
Jeff Brown	D	67	12	47	59	+4	39
Rod Brind'Amour	C	78	17	32	49	+2	93
Scott Stevens	D	78	5	44	49	+23	150
Dave Lowry	L	79	19	21	40	+19	168
Ron Wilson	C	73	10	27	37	-1	54
Paul Cavallini	D	67	10	25	35	+19	89
Gino Cavallini	L	78	8	27	35	+4	81
Bob Bassen	C	79	16	18	34	+17	183
Rich Sutter	R	77	16	11	27	+6	122
Garth Butcher	D	82	6	16	22	-14	289
VAN.		69	6	12	18	-18	257
STL.		13	0	4	4	+4	32
Glen Featherstone	D	68	5	15	20	+19	204
Paul MacLean	R	37	6	11	17	-2	24
Mario Marois	D	64	2	14	16	+17	81

Acquired: Quinn and Butcher from Van. (Mar.5).

Goaltending	Gm	Min	Avg	SO	Record
Vincent Riendeau	44	2671	3.01	3	29-9-6
Pat Jablonski*	8	492	3.05	0	2-3-3
Curtis Joseph*	30	1710	3.12	0	16-10-2
ST.LOUIS	80	4877	3.08	3	47-22-11

Assists: Riendeau (2), Jablonski (1), Joseph (1); **PM:** None.

Vancouver Canucks

Top Scorers	Pos	Gm	G	A	Pts	+/-	PM
Trevor Linden	R	80	33	36	69	-25	65
Geoff Courtnall	L	77	33	32	65	+16	64
STL.		66	27	30	57	+19	56
VAN.		11	6	2	8	-3	8
Greg Adams	L	55	21	24	45	-5	10
Cliff Ronning	C	59	20	24	44	E	10
STL.		48	14	18	32	+2	10
VAN.		11	6	6	12	-2	0
Dave Capuano	L	61	13	31	44	+1	42
Doug Lidster	D	78	6	32	38	-6	77
Sergio Momesso	L	70	16	20	36	+13	174
STL.		59	10	18	28	+12	131
VAN.		11	6	2	8	+1	43
Igor Larionov	C	64	13	21	34	-3	14
Steve Bozek	L	62	15	17	32	-6	22
Robert Kron*	L	76	12	20	32	-11	21
Jyrki Lumme	D	80	5	27	32	-15	59
Tom Kurvers	D	51	4	26	30	-25	28
TOR.		19	0	3	3	-12	8
VAN.		32	4	23	27	-13	20
Garry Valk*	R	59	10	11	21	-23	67
Jay Mazur*	R	36	11	7	18	+3	14
Petr Nedved*	C	61	10	6	16	-21	20

Acquired: Kurvers from Tor. (Jan. 12); Courtnall, Momesso and Ronning from St.L (Mar. 5).

Goaltending	Gm	Min	Avg	SO	Record
Troy Gamble*	47	2433	3.45	1	16-16-6
Kirk McLean	41	1969	3.99	0	10-22-3
Bob Mason	6	353	4.93	0	2-4-0
Others	2	79	6.06	0	0-1-0
ST.LOUIS	80	4856	3.89	1	28-43-9

Assists: None; **PM:** McLean (4).

Toronto Maple Leafs

Top Scorers	Pos	Gm	G	A	Pts	+/-	PM
Vincent Damphousse	L	79	26	47	73	-31	65
Dave Ellett	D	77	12	37	49	-8	75
WIN.		17	4	7	11	-4	6
TOR.		60	8	30	38	-4	69
Mike Krushelnyski	C	74	18	27	45	+1	58
LA.		15	1	5	6	+7	10
TOR.		59	17	22	39	-6	48
Brian Bradley	C	70	11	31	42	-9	62
VAN.		44	11	20	31	-2	42
TOR.		26	0	11	11	-7	20
Peter Zezel	C	52	21	19	40	-20	14
WASH.		20	7	5	12	-13	10
TOR.		32	14	14	28	-7	4
Michel Petit	D	73	13	26	39	-34	179
QUE.		19	4	7	11	-15	47
TOR.		54	9	19	28	-19	132
Wendel Clark	L	63	18	16	34	-5	152
Dave Hannan	C	74	11	23	34	-9	82
Rob Ramage	D	80	10	24	34	+2	173
Dan Marois	C	78	21	9	30	-16	112
Gary Leeman	R	52	17	12	29	-25	39
Dave Reid	L	69	15	13	28	-10	18
Lucien DeBlois	C	52	12	14	26	-3	43
QUE.		14	2	2	4	+1	13
TOR.		38	10	12	22	-4	30

Top Scorers	Pos	Gm	G	A	Pts	+/-	PM
Bob Rouse	D	60	7	19	26	-18	75
WASH.		47	5	15	20	-7	65
TOR.		13	2	4	6	-11	10
Mike Foligno	R	68	12	12	24	+1	107
BUF.		31	4	5	9	+4	42
TOR.		37	8	7	15	-3	65
Todd Gill	D	72	2	21	23	-4	113
Aaron Broten	C	47	11	8	19	+9	38
QUE.		20	5	4	9	-3	6
TOR.		27	6	4	10	+12	32
Doug Shedden	C	23	8	10	18	+2	10
Claude Loiselle	C	66	6	11	17	-20	86
QUE.		59	5	10	15	-20	86
TOR.		7	1	1	2	E	2

Acquired: Krushelnyski from LA (Nov.9); Ellett from Win. (Nov.10); Broten, DeBlois and Petit from Que. (Nov.17); Foligno from Buf. (Dec.17); Bradley from Van. (Jan.12); Rouse and Zezel from Wash. (Jan.16); Loiselle from Que. by way of Calg. (Mar.5).

Goaltending	Gm	Min	Avg	SO	Record
Peter Ing*	56	3126	3.84	1	16-29-8
Jeff Reese	30	1430	3.86	1	6-13-3
Others	7	307	3.68	0	1-4-0
TORONTO	80	4874	3.91	2	23-46-11

Assists: Reese (1); **PM:** Ing (6).

Washington Capitals

Top Scorers	Pos	Gm	G	A	Pts	+/−	PM
Kevin Hatcher	D	79	24	50	74	−10	69
Mike Ridley	C	79	23	48	71	+9	26
Michal Pivonka	C	79	20	49	69	+3	34
John Druce	R	80	22	36	58	+4	46
Calle Johansson	D	80	11	41	52	−2	23
Kelly Miller	L	80	24	26	50	+10	29
Dale Hunter	C	76	16	30	46	−22	234
Dino Ciccarelli	R	54	21	18	39	−17	66
Al Iafrate	D	72	9	23	32	−16	237
TOR.		42	3	15	18	−15	113
WASH.		30	6	8	14	−1	124
Stephen Leach	R	68	11	19	30	−9	99
Peter Bondra*	R	54	12	16	28	−10	47
Dimitri Khristich*	L	40	13	14	27	−1	21
Mikhail Tatarinov*	D	65	8	15	23	−4	82
Nick Kypreos	L	79	9	9	18	−4	196
Dave Tippett	C	61	6	9	15	−13	24

Acquired: Iafrate from Tor.(Jan.16).

Goaltending	Gm	Min	Avg	SO	Record
Don Beaupre	45	2572	2.64	5	20-18-3
Jim Hrivnak*	9	432	3.61	0	4-2-1
Mike Liut	35	1834	3.73	0	13-16-3
WASHINGTON	80	4850	3.19	5	37-36-7

Assists: None; **PM:** Beaupre (18).

Winnipeg Jets

Top Scorers	Pos	Gm	G	A	Pts	+/−	PM
Phil Housley	D	78	23	53	76	−13	24
Ed Olczyk	C	79	30	41	71	−27	82
TOR.		18	4	10	14	−7	13
WIN.		61	26	31	57	−20	69
Thomas Steen	C	58	19	48	67	−3	49
Pat Elynuik	R	80	31	34	65	−13	73
Fredrik Olausson	D	71	12	29	41	−22	24
Paul MacDermid	R	69	15	21	36	−6	128
Brent Ashton	L	61	12	24	36	−10	58
Doug Evans	L	70	7	27	34	−1	108
Teppo Numminen	D	80	8	25	33	−15	28
Randy Carlyle	D	52	9	19	28	+6	44
Dave McIlwain	R	60	14	11	25	−13	46
Danton Cole*	C	66	13	11	24	−14	24
Moe Mantha	D	57	9	15	24	−20	33
Phil Sykes	L	70	12	10	22	−9	59
Mark Osborne	L	55	11	11	22	−11	63
TOR.		18	3	3	6	−10	4
WPG.		37	8	8	16	−1	59
Scott Arniel	C	75	5	17	22	−12	87

Acquired: Olczyk and Osborne from Tor.(Nov.10).

Goaltending	Gm	Min	Avg	SO	Record
Bob Essensa	55	2916	3.15	4	19-24-6
Rick Tabaracci*	24	1093	3.90	1	4-9-4
Steph.Beauregard*	16	836	3.95	0	3-10-1
WINNIPEG	80	4860	3.56	5	26-43-11

Assists: Essensa (3), Beauregard (1), Tabaracci (1); **PM:** Tabaracci (8), Essensa (6), Beauregard (2).

Annual Awards

Field of candidates for each award narrowed to three before final vote. Except for Vezina Trophy and Adams Award, voting done by 66 members of the Pro Hockey Writers Assn. The Vezina Trophy is voted on by the NHL's 21 general managers and the Adams Award is decided by NHL broadcasters. Points awarded on 5-3-1 basis.

Hart Trophy

For Most Valuable Player.

	1st	2nd	3rd	Pts
Brett Hull, St.Louis	44	18	3 —	227
Wayne Gretzky, Los Angeles	20	37	9 —	220
Ed Belfour, Chicago	2	7	32 —	63

Calder Trophy

For Rookie of the Year.

	1st	2nd	3rd	Pts
Ed Belfour, Chicago	59	6	0 —	313
Sergei Fedorov, Detroit	6	55	5 —	200
Ken Hodge, Boston	0	2	18 —	24

Norris Trophy

For Best Defenseman.

	1st	2nd	3rd	Pts
Ray Bourque, Boston	35	27	1 —	257
Al MacInnis, Calgary	27	28	9 —	228
Chris Chelios, Chicago	2	9	19 —	56

Vezina Trophy

For Outstanding Goaltender.

	1st	2nd	3rd	Pts
Ed Belfour, Chicago	19	2	0 —	101
Patrick Roy, Montreal	1	12	3 —	44
Mike Richter, NY Rangers	1	1	4 —	12

Adams Award

For Coach of the Year.

	1st	2nd	3rd	Pts
Brian Sutter, St.Louis	15	14	10 —	127
Tom Webster, Los Angeles	14	9	9 —	106
Mike Keenan, Chicago	8	8	4 —	68

Other Awards

Lady Byng Trophy (gentlemanly play and ability)— Wayne Gretzky, Los Angeles; **Lester Pearson Award** (NHL Players Assn.MVP)—Brett Hull, St.Louis; **Selke Trophy** (best defensive forward)—Dirk Graham, Chicago; **Jennings Trophy** (fewest team goals against)—Ed Belfour and 4 other goalies, Chicago; **Masterton Trophy** (for perserverence and dedication to hockey)—Dave Taylor, Los Angeles; **King Clancy Trophy** (for humanitarian contribution)—Dave Taylor, Los Angeles.

All-NHL Teams

Voting by Pro Hockey Writers' Association (PHWA). Holdovers from 1989-90 first team in **bold** type.

	First Team	1st	2nd	3rd	Pts
G	Ed Belfour, Chicago	65	1	0 —	328
D	**Ray Bourque**, Boston	63	1	2 —	320
D	**Al MacInnis**, Calgary	54	12	0 —	306
C	Wayne Gretzky, Los Angeles	65	1	0 —	328
R	**Brett Hull**, St.Louis	63	1	0 —	318
L	**Luc Robitaille**, Los Angeles	49	11	6 —	284

	Second Team	1st	2nd	3rd	Pts
G	Patrick Roy, Montreal	1	43	17 —	144
D	Chris Chelios, Chicago	10	33	16 —	165
D	Brian Leetch, NY Rangers	4	33	31 —	150
C	Adam Oates, St.Louis	1	36	19 —	132
R	Cam Neely, Boston	2	24	12 —	94
L	Kevin Stevens, Pittsburgh	10	31	16 —	159

All-Rookie Team

Voting by PHWA. Vote totals not released.

G	Ed Belfour, Chicago	F	Sergei Fedorov, Detroit
D	Rob Blake, Los Angeles	F	Ken Hodge, Boston
D	Eric Weinrich, New Jersey	F	Jaromir Jagr, Pittsburgh

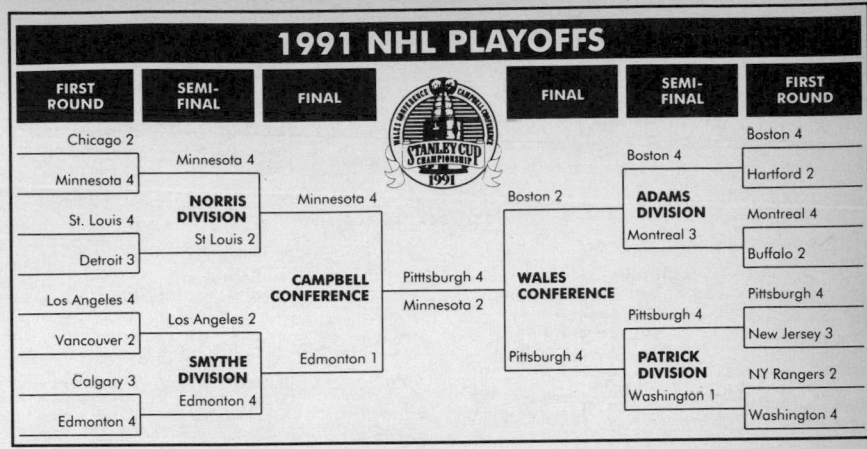

1991 NHL PLAYOFFS

FIRST ROUND	SEMI-FINAL	FINAL		FINAL	SEMI-FINAL	FIRST ROUND
Chicago 2					Boston 4	Boston 4
Minnesota 4	Minnesota 4					Hartford 2
St. Louis 4	**NORRIS DIVISION**	Minnesota 4		Boston 2	**ADAMS DIVISION**	Montreal 4
Detroit 3	St Louis 2				Montreal 3	Buffalo 2
Los Angeles 4	**CAMPBELL CONFERENCE**	Pittsburgh 4	**WALES CONFERENCE**		Pittsburgh 4
Vancouver 2	Los Angeles 2	Minnesota 2				New Jersey 3
Calgary 3	**SMYTHE DIVISION**	Edmonton 1		Pittsburgh 4	**PATRICK DIVISION**	NY Rangers 2
Edmonton 4	Edmonton 4				Washington 1	Washington 4

Series Summaries
All series Best-of-7 games.
Campbell Conference

NORRIS DIVISION
Semifinals

	W-L	GF	Leading Scorers
Minnesota	4-2	23	Bellows (4-8—12)
Chicago	2-4	16	Roenick (3-5—8)
			& Chelios (1-7—8)

Date	Winner	Home Ice
Apr. 4	North Stars, 4-3 (OT)	at Chicago
Apr. 6	Blackhawks, 5-2	at Chicago
Apr. 8	Blackhawks, 6-5	at Minnesota
Apr.10	North Stars, 3-1	at Minnesota
Apr.12	North Stars, 6-0	at Chicago
Apr.14	North Stars, 3-1	at Minnesota

Shutout: Apr.12—Casey (25 saves).

	W-L	GF	Leading Scorers
St.Louis	4-3	24	Hull (8-5—13)
			& Oates (4-9—13)
Detroit	3-4	20	Yzerman (3-3—6)
			& Fedorov (1-5—6)

Date	Winner	Home Ice
Apr. 4	Red Wings, 6-3	at St.Louis
Apr. 6	Blues, 4-2	at St.Louis
Apr. 8	Red Wings, 5-2	at Detroit
Apr.10	Red Wings, 4-3	at Detroit
Apr.12	Blues, 6-1	at St.Louis
Apr.14	Blues, 3-0	at Detroit
Apr.16	Blues, 3-2	at St.Louis

Shutout: Apr.14—Riendeau (23 saves).

Final

	W-L	GF	Leading Scorers
Minnesota	4-2	22	Modano (3-4—7)
			& Smith (2-5—7)
St.Louis	2-4	17	Oates (3-4—7)

Date	Winner	Home Ice
Apr.18	North Stars, 2-1	at St.Louis
Apr.20	Blues, 5-2	at St.Louis
Apr.22	North Stars, 5-1	at Minnesota
Apr.24	North Stars, 8-4	at Minnesota
Apr.26	Blues, 4-2	at St.Louis
Apr.28	North Stars, 3-2	at Minnesota

SMYTHE DIVISION
Semifinals

	W-L	GF	Leading Scorers
Los Angeles	4-2	26	Gretzky (4-6—10)
Vancouver	2-4	16	Ronning (6-3—9)

Date	Winner	Home Ice
Apr. 4	Canucks, 6-5	at Los Angeles
Apr. 6	Kings, 3-2 (OT)	at Los Angeles
Apr. 8	Canucks, 2-1 (OT)	at Vancouver
Apr.10	Kings, 6-1	at Vancouver
Apr.12	Kings, 7-4	at Los Angeles
Apr.14	Kings, 4-1	at Vancouver

	W-L	GF	Leading Scorers
Edmonton	4-3	22	Tikkanen (7-3—10)
Calgary	3-4	20	Fleury (2-5—7)
			& Suter (1-6—7)

Date	Winner	Home Ice
Apr. 4	Oilers, 3-1	at Calgary
Apr. 6	Flames, 3-1	at Calgary
Apr. 8	Oilers, 4-3	at Edmonton
Apr.10	Oilers, 5-2	at Edmonton
Apr.12	Flames, 5-3	at Calgary
Apr.14	Flames, 2-1 (OT)	at Edmonton
Apr.16	Oilers, 5-4 (OT)	at Calgary

Final

	W-L	GF	Leading Scorers
Edmonton	4-2	21	Tikkanen (4-2—6),
			Gelinas (3-3—6)
			& Semenov (3-3—6)
Los Angeles	2-4	20	Robitaille (8-2—10)

Date	Winner	Home Ice
Apr.18	Kings, 4-3 (OT)	at Los Angeles
Apr.20	Oilers, 4-3 (2OT)	at Los Angeles
Apr.22	Oilers, 4-3 (2OT)	at Edmonton
Apr.24	Oilers, 4-2	at Edmonton
Apr.26	Kings, 5-2	at Los Angeles
Apr.28	Oilers, 4-3 (OT)	at Edmonton

Stanley Cup Playoffs (Cont.)
CAMPBELL CONFERENCE FINAL

	W-L	GF	Leading Scorers
Minnesota	4-1	20	Bellows (2-7—9)
Edmonton	1-4	14	Klima (3-2—5),
			Simpson (2-3—5)
			& Messier (1-4—5)

Date	Winner	Home Ice
May 2	North Stars, 3-1	at Edmonton
May 4	Oilers, 7-2	at Edmonton
May 6	North Stars, 7-3	at Minnesota
May 8	North Stars, 5-1	at Minnesota
May 10	North Stars, 3-2	at Edmonton

Wales Conference

ADAMS DIVISION
Semifinals

	W-L	GF	Leading Scorers
Boston	4-2	24	Neely (5-3—8),
			Bourque (2-6—8)
			& Janney (1-7—8)
Hartford	2-4	17	Cullen (2-7—9)

Date	Winner	Home Ice
Apr. 3	Whalers, 5-2	at Boston
Apr. 5	Bruins, 4-3	at Boston
Apr. 7	Bruins, 6-3	at Hartford
Apr. 9	Whalers, 4-3	at Hartford
Apr. 11	Bruins, 6-1	at Boston
Apr. 13	Bruins, 3-1	at Hartford

	W-L	GF	Leading Scorers
Montreal	4-2	29	Savard (2-8—10)
Buffalo	2-4	24	Ledyard (3-3—6),
			Hawerchuk (2-4—6)
			& Mogilny (0-6—6)

Date	Winner	Home Ice
Apr. 3	Canadiens, 7-5	at Montreal
Apr. 5	Canadiens, 5-4	at Montreal
Apr. 7	Sabres, 5-4	at Buffalo
Apr. 9	Sabres, 6-4	at Buffalo
Apr. 11	Canadiens, 4-3 (OT)	at Montreal
Apr. 13	Canadiens, 5-1	at Buffalo

Final

	W-L	GF	Leading Scorers
Boston	4-3	18	Bourque (2-6—8)
Montreal	3-4	18	Corson (5-4—9)

Date	Winner	Home Ice
Apr. 17	Bruins, 2-1	at Boston
Apr. 19	Canadiens, 4-3 (OT)	at Boston
Apr. 21	Bruins, 3-2	at Montreal
Apr. 23	Canadiens, 6-2	at Montreal
Apr. 25	Bruins, 4-1	at Boston
Apr. 27	Canadiens, 3-2 (OT)	at Montreal
Apr. 29	Bruins, 2-1	at Boston

PATRICK DIVISION
Semifinals

	W-L	GF	Leading Scorers
Pittsburgh	4-3	21	Recchi (2-9—11)
New Jersey	3-4	21	MacLean (5-3—8)
			& Shanahan (3-5—8)

Date	Winner	Home Ice
Apr. 3	Devils, 3-1	at Pittsburgh
Apr. 5	Penguins, 5-4 (OT)	at Pittsburgh
Apr. 7	Penguins, 4-3	at New Jersey
Apr. 9	Devils, 4-1	at New Jersey
Apr. 11	Devils, 4-2	at Pittsburgh
Apr. 13	Penguins, 4-3	at New Jersey
Apr. 15	Penguins, 4-0	at Pittsburgh

Shutout: Apr. 15—Pietrangelo (27 saves).

	W-L	GF	Leading Scorers
Washington	4-2	16	Hunter (0-6—6)
NY Rangers	2-4	16	Nicholls (4-3—7)

Date	Winner	Home Ice
Apr. 3	Rangers, 2-1	at New York
Apr. 5	Capitals, 3-0	at New York
Apr. 7	Rangers, 6-0	at Washington
Apr. 9	Capitals, 3-2	at Washington
Apr. 11	Capitals, 5-4 (OT)	at New York
Apr. 13	Capitals, 4-2	at Washington

Shutouts: Apr. 5—Beaupre (35 saves); Apr. 7—Richter (37 saves).

Final

	W-L	GF	Leading Scorers
Pittsburgh	4-1	19	Recchi (4-6—10)
Washington	1-4	13	Johansson (2-5—7)

Date	Winner	Home Ice
Apr. 17	Capitals, 4-2	at Pittsburgh
Apr. 19	Penguins, 7-6 (OT)	at Pittsburgh
Apr. 21	Penguins, 3-1	at Washington
Apr. 23	Penguins, 3-1	at Washington
Apr. 25	Penguins, 4-1	at Pittsburgh

WALES CONFERENCE FINAL

	W-L	GF	Leading Scorers
Pittsburgh	4-2	27	Lemieux (6-9—15)
Boston	2-4	18	Bourque (3-6—9)

Date	Winner	Home Ice
May 1	Bruins, 6-3	at Boston
May 3	Bruins, 5-4 (OT)	at Boston
May 5	Penguins, 4-1	at Pittsburgh
May 7	Penguins, 4-1	at Pittsburgh
May 9	Penguins, 7-2	at Boston
May 11	Penguins, 5-3	at Pittsburgh

STANLEY CUP CHAMPIONSHIP

	W-L	GF	Leading Scorers
Pittsburgh	4-2	28	Lemieux (5-7—12)
Minnesota	2-4	16	Gagner (4-2—6)

Date	Winner	Home Ice
May 15	North Stars, 5-4	at Pittsburgh
May 17	Penguins, 4-1	at Pittsburgh
May 19	North Stars, 3-1	at Minnesota
May 21	Penguins, 5-3	at Minnesota
May 23	Penguins, 6-4	at Pittsburgh
May 25	Penguins, 8-0	at Minnesota

Shutout: May 25—Barrasso (39 saves).

Conn Smythe Trophy (MVP)
Mario Lemieux, Pittsburgh

Stanley Cup Individual Leaders

Scoring

	Pos	Gm	G	A	Pts	+/-	PM
Mario Lemieux, Pit.	C	23	16	28	44	+14	16
Mark Recchi, Pit	R	24	10	24	34	+6	33
Kevin Stevens, Pit	L	24	17	16	33	+14	53
Brian Bellows, Min	L	23	10	19	29	-6	30
Dave Gagner, Min	C	23	12	15	27	-4	28
Ray Bourque, Bos	D	19	7	18	25	-4	12
Brian Propp, Min	L	23	8	15	23	-4	28
Larry Murphy, Pit	D	23	5	18	23	+17	44
Neal Broten, Min.	C	23	9	13	22	+2	6
Craig Janney, Bos.	C	18	4	18	22	-4	11
Cam Neely, Bos.	R	19	16	4	20	-4	36
Esa Tikkanen, Edm.	L	18	12	8	20	+3	24
Mike Modano, Min.	R	23	8	12	20	-3	16
Adam Oates, St.L	C	13	7	13	20	+7	10
Brett Hull, St.L.	R	13	11	8	19	+5	4

Goals

Stevens, Pit	17
Neely, Bos	16
Lemieux, Pit	16
Robitaille, LA	12
Tikkanen, Edm.	12
Gagner, Min	12

Assists

Lemieux, Pit	28
Recchi, Pit	24
Bellows, Min.	19
Janney, Bos	18
Bourque, Bos	18
Murphy, Pit.	18

Power Play Goals

Neely, Bos	9
Propp, Min	8
Stevens, Pit	7
Three tied with 6 each.	

Short-Handed Goals

Courtnall, Mon	2
Lemieux, Pit	2
Ten tied with 1 each.	

Plus/Minus

Mullen, Pit	+17
Murphy, Pit.	+17
Lemieux, Pit	+14
Stevens, Pit	+14
Francis, Pit	+13
Roberts, Pit	+13

Penalty Minutes

McRae, Min	94
Churla, Min	90
Tinordi, Min	78
Roberts, Pit	63
Nilan, Bos	62

Goaltending

(Minimum 10 games)

	Gm	Min	GA	SO	Avg
Tom Barrasso, Pit	20	1175	51	1	2.60
Kelly Hrudey, LA	12	798	37	0	2.78
Don Beaupre, Wash	11	624	29	1	2.79
Grant Fuhr, Edm	17	1019	51	0	3.00
Patrick Roy, Mon	13	785	40	0	3.06
Jon Casey, Min	23	1205	61	1	3.04
Vincent Riendeau, St.L.	13	687	35	1	3.06
Andy Moog, Bos	19	1133	60	0	3.18

Wins

	W-L
Casey, Min	14-7
Barrasso, Pit	12-7
Moog, Bos	10-9
Fuhr, Edm	8-7
Roy, Mon	7-5

Save Pct.

Barrasso, Pit	.919
Hrudey, LA	.903
Terreri, NJ	.903
Beaupre, Wash	.901
Roy, Mon	.898

Final Standings

	Gm	W	L	Pts	Goals For	Goals Opp	Goals Dif
Pittsburgh	24	16	8	32	95	68	+27
Minnesota	23	14	9	28	81	75	+6
Boston	19	10	9	20	60	62	-2
Edmonton	18	9	9	18	57	60	-3
Montreal	13	7	6	14	47	42	+5
Los Angeles	12	6	6	12	46	37	+9
St.Louis	13	6	7	12	41	42	-1
Washington	11	5	6	10	29	35	-6
New Jersey	7	3	4	6	21	21	E
Calgary	7	3	4	6	20	22	-2
Detroit	7	3	4	6	20	24	-4
NY Rangers	6	2	4	4	16	16	E
Buffalo	6	2	4	4	24	29	-5
Hartford	6	2	4	4	17	24	-7
Chicago	6	2	4	4	16	23	-7
Vancouver	6	2	4	4	16	26	-10

Finalists' Composite Box Scores

Pittsburgh Penguins (16-8)

Scoring	Pos	Gm	G	A	Pts	+/-	PM
Mario Lemieux	C	23	16	28	44	+14	16
Mark Recchi	R	24	10	24	34	+6	33
Kevin Stevens	L	24	17	16	33	+14	53
Larry Murphy	D	23	5	18	23	+17	44
Joe Mullen	R	22	8	9	17	+17	4
Ron Francis	C	24	7	10	17	+13	24
Phil Bourque	L	24	6	7	13	+6	16
Jaromir Jagr*	R	24	3	10	13	+2	6
Paul Coffey	D	12	2	9	11	-1	6
Bob Errey	L	24	5	2	7	+5	29
Bryan Trottier	C	3	3	4	7	-1	49
Scott Young	R	7	1	6	7	+1	2
Ulf Samuelsson	D	0	3	2	5	+7	34
Jiri Hrdina	C	4	2	2	4	+1	6
Troy Loney*	L	4	2	2	4	-3	41
Paul Stanton*	D	2	1	2	3	+6	24
Gordie Roberts	D	4	1	2	3	+13	63
Peter Taglianetti	D	9	0	3	3	+7	49
Grant Jennings	D	3	1	1	2	+3	16
Jim Paek*	D	8	1	0	1	+2	2
Randy Gilhen	C	6	1	0	1	-4	14
Randy Hillier	D	8	1	0	0	+1	24

Goaltending	Gm	Min	GA	Avg	SO	Record
Tom Barrasso	20	1175	51	2.60	1	12-7
Frank Pietrangelo	5	288	15	3.13	1	4-1
PITTSBURGH	24	1465	68	2.78	2	16-8

Empty Net Goals: 2.
Assists: Barrasso (1), Pietrangelo (1). **PM:** Barrasso (2), Pietrangelo (2).

Minnesota North Stars (14-9)

Scoring	Pos	Gm	G	A	Pts	+/-	PM
Brian Bellows	L	23	10	19	29	-6	30
Dave Gagner	C	23	12	15	27	-4	28
Brian Propp	L	23	8	15	23	-4	28
Neal Broten	C	23	9	13	22	+2	6
Mike Modano	R	23	8	12	20	-3	16
Bobby Smith	C	23	8	8	16	-5	56
Stewart Gavin	L	21	3	10	13	+9	20
Mark Tinordi	D	23	5	6	11	-1	78
Ulf Dahlen	R	15	2	6	8	-4	4
Brian Glynn	D	23	2	6	8	-8	18
Chris Dahlquist	D	23	1	6	7	+4	20
Shawn Chambers	D	23	0	7	7	-7	16
Neil Wilkinson	D	22	3	3	6	+1	12
*Marc Bureau	C	23	3	2	5	-4	20
Gaetan Duchesne	L	23	2	3	5	E	34
Shane Churla	R	22	2	1	3	-2	90
*Mike Craig	R	10	1	1	2	-2	20
Basil McRae	L	22	1	1	2	-3	94
Curt Giles	D	10	1	0	1	-4	16
Jim Johnson	D	14	0	1	1	+8	52

Goaltending	Gm	Min	GA	Avg	SO	Record
Jon Casey	23	1205	61	3.04	1	14-7
Brian Hayward	6	171	11	3.86	0	0-2
MINNESOTA	23	1384	75	3.25	1	14-9

Empty net goals: 3.
Assists: Casey (1); **PM:** Casey (12).

NHL Drafts

Dispersal Draft

On May 30, 1991, the expansion San Jose Sharks acquired 34 players in the controversial "cross-pollination" dispersal draft. In 1990, George and Gordon Gund agreed to sell the Minnesota franchise to owners who would keep the North Stars in Minnesota. In return, the Gunds were granted an expansion team and the right to pick 24 players from the Minnesota system.

FORWARDS—Shane Churla, Ed Courtenay, Kevin Evans, Murray Garbutt, Robert Gaudreau, Peter Lappin, Mike McHugh, J.F.Quintin, John Weisbrod. DEFENSEMEN—Link Gaetz, Shaun Kane, Dan Keczmer, Dean Kolstad, Pat MacLeod, Larry Olimb, Tom Pederson, Neil Wilkinson, Rob Zettler, Doug Zmolek. GOALTENDERS—Scott Cashman, Brian Hayward, Artur Irbe, Jarmo Myllys, Bryan Schoen.

Expansion Draft

Both San Jose and Minnesota participated in an Expansion Draft, picking 10 players each from a pool of unprotected players provided by the NHL's other 20 teams. Only one player per club could be chosen.

San Jose	Pos	Minnesota	Pos
Jeff Hackett, NYI	G	Rob Ramage, Tor	D
Jayson More, Mon	D	Dave Babych, Hart	D
Rick Lessard, Calg	D	Allen Pedersen, Bos	D
Bob McGill, Chi	D	Charlie Huddy, Edm	D
Tim Kerr, Phi	F	Kelly Kisio, NYR	F
Jeff Madill, NJ	F	Randy Gilhen, Pit	F
David Bruce, St.L	F	Rob Murray, Wash	F
Greg Paslawski, Buf	F	Tyler Larter, Win	F
Bengt Gustafsson, Det	F	Jim Thomson, LA	F
Craig Coxe, Van	F	Guy Lafleur, Que	F

Entry Draft

NHL Draft held June 22, 1991, in Buffalo.

First Round

	Team	Player	Pos
1	Quebec	Eric Lindros, Oshawa	C
2	San Jose	Pat Falloon, Spokane	C-R
3	a-N.Jersey	Scott Niedermeyer, Kamloops	D
4	NY Isles	Scott Lachance, Boston U.	D
5	Winnipeg	Aaron Ward, Michigan	D
6	Phila	Peter Forsberg, MoDo	C
7	Vancouver	Alex Stojanov, Hamilton	L
8	Minnesota	Rich. Matvichuk, Saskatoon	D
9	Hartford	Patrick Poulin, St.Hyacinthe	L
10	Detroit	Martin Lapointe, Laval	R
11	N.Jersey	Brian Ralston, Detroit-NAJHL	C
12	Edmonton	Tyler Wright, Swift Current	C
13	Buffalo	Philippe Boucher, Granby	D
14	Washington	Patrick Peake, Detroit-OHL	C
15	NY Rangers	Alexei Kovalev, Moscow Dynamo	C
16	Pittsburgh	Markus Naslund, MoDo	R
17	Montreal	Brent Bilodeau, Seattle	D
18	Boston	Glenn Murray, Sudbury	R
19	Calgary	Niklas Sunblad, AIK	L-R
20	b-Edmonton	Martin Rucinsky, Litvinov	C-L
21	c-Wash	Trevor Halverson, North Bay	L
22	Chicago	Dean McAmmond, Prin.Albert	C

Acquired picks: a—from Toronto; **b**—from Los Angeles; **c**—from St.Louis.

Affiliations: OHL (Ontario Hockey League) Detroit, Hamilton, North Bay, Oshawa, Sudbury; **WHL** (Western Hockey League)—Kamloops, Prince Albert, Saskatoon, Seattle, Spokane, Swift Current; **QMJHL** (Quebec Major Jr.Hockey League), Granby, Laval, St-Hyacinthe, **Junior B**—Springfield (MA); **NAJHL** (No.America Jr.Hockey League)—Detroit; **US Colleges**—Boston Univ.(Hockey East), Michigan (CCHA); **Foreign Teams**—Litvinov, (CZE); AIK and MoDo (SWE); Moscow Dynamo (USSR).

World Hockey Championship

The 44th World Hockey Championships, held in Turku, Finland, Apr.19-May 4, 1991. Eight teams participate in preliminary round-robin with top four teams advancing to the medal round and the bottom four teams playing a consolation. Rosters for Canada and USA were limited to players not participating in Stanley Cup playoffs.

Final Standings

MEDAL GROUP

Top four teams after preliminary round-robin. Only Medal Round games count in standings, overall tournament record in parentheses.

	W	L	T	Pts	GF	GA
Sweden (5-0-5)	2	0	1	5	13	8
Canada (5-2-3)	1	0	2	4	15	10
USSR (7-1-2)	1	1	1	3	10	9
USA (3-5-2)	0	3	0	0	12	23

Round One—Sweden 3, Canada 3; USSR 6, USA 4. **Round Two**—Canada 3, USSR 3; Sweden 8, USA 4. **Round Three**—Canada 9, USA 4; Sweden 2, USSR 1.

CONSOLATION GROUP

Bottom four teams after preliminary round-robin. All tournament games count in standings, Consolation Group record in parentheses.

	W	L	T	Pts	GF	GA
Finland (3-0-0)	6	3	1	13	35	21
Czechoslovakia (1-2-0)	4	6	0	8	28	27
Switzerland (1-1-1)	2	7	1	5	22	38
Germany (0-2-1)	0	8	2	2	19	51

Round One—Finland 4, Germany 2; Switzerland 4, Czechoslovakia 3. **Round Two**—Czechoslovakia 4, Germany 1; Finland 6, Switzerland 2. **Round Three**—Finland 3, Czechoslovakia 2; Switzerland 3, Germany 3.

Leading Scorers

	Gm	G	A	Pts
Mats Sundin, Sweden	10	7	5	12
Jari Kurri, Finland	10	6	6	12
Valery Kamensky, USSR	10	6	5	11
Joe Sakic, Canada	10	6	5	11
Teemu Selanne, Finland	10	6	5	11
Jeremy Roenick, USA	10	5	6	11
Teppo Nieminen, Finland	10	5	6	11
Pavel Bure, USSR	10	3	8	11
Christian Ruuttu, Finland	10	7	3	10
Danton Cole, USA	10	6	4	10
Thomas Rundqvist, Sweden	10	6	4	10
Theo Fleury, Canada	10	5	5	10
Sergei Makarov, USSR	10	3	7	10

All-Tournament

First Team

Goal—Sean Burke, Canada. **Defense**—Alexei Kasatanov, USSR; Viacheslav Fetisov, USSR. **Forwards**—Thomas Rundqvist, Sweden; Jari Kurri, Finland; Valery Kamensky, USSR.

Second Team

Goal—Markus Ketterer, Finland. **Defense**—Jamie Macoun, Canada; Dimitry Mironov, USSR. **Forwards**—Theo Fleury, Canada; Pavel Bure, USSR; Mats Sundin, Sweden.

U.S. College Hockey
NCAA Division I

Regular season standings; overall records, including league tournament and NCAA tournament games, in parentheses.

Central Collegiate Hockey Assn. (CCHA)

	W	L	T	Pts	GF	GA
*Lake Superior St.(36-5-4)	26	2	4	56	181	77
*Michigan (34-10-3)	24	5	3	51	178	107
Ferris St.(23-14-5)	15	12	5	35	122	111
W.Michigan (22-17-3)	16	14	2	34	121	115
Michigan St.(17-18-5)	14	13	5	33	130	101
Bowling Green (15-23-2)	13	17	2	28	123	144
Ohio St.(11-25-4)	9	19	4	22	99	158
IL-Chicago (13-23-2)	9	21	2	20	112	150
Miami-OH (5-29-3)	3	26	3	9	78	181

Conf.Tourney Final: Lake Superior St. 6, Michigan 5 (OT).
NCAA Tournament: Michigan (2-3); Lake Superior St.(1-2).

Western Collegiate Hockey Assn. (WCHA)

	W	L	T	Pts	GF	GA
*No.Michigan (38-5-4)	25	3	4	54	185	89
*Minnesota (30-10-5)	22	5	5	49	151	97
*Wisconsin (26-15-3)	19	11	2	40	132	108
North Dakota (24-17-2)	18	12	2	38	148	127
St. Cloud St.(18-19-4)	12	16	4	28	124	152
Minn-Duluth (14-19-7)	11	15	6	28	114	133
Michigan Tech (13-25-3)	9	21	2	20	105	134
Colorado Col.(13-26-1)	9	22	1	19	106	139
Denver (6-30-2)	5	25	2	12	95	182

Conf.Tourney Final: Northern Michigan 4, Minnesota 2.
NCAA Tournament: Northern Michigan (4-0); Minnesota (2-3); Wisconsin (0-2).

Eastern Collegiate Athletic Assn. (ECAC)

	W	L	T	Pts	GF	GA
*Clarkson (29-9-2)	15	5	2	32	113	77
*Cornell (18-11-3)	14	5	3	31	93	69
St.Lawrence (22-13-1)	15	6	1	31	101	79
Harvard (14-12-3)	13	7	2	28	130	74
RPI (19-12-1)	14	8	0	28	118	93
Vermont (17-14-2)	12	8	2	26	89	83
Colgate (15-12-4)	9	9	4	22	93	81
Yale (10-16-2)	9	11	2	20	80	89
Brown (9-14-3)	9	11	2	20	78	99
Princeton (8-17-1)	7	14	1	15	84	106
Army (8-18-3)	3	17	2	8	56	106
Dartmouth (1-24-3)	0	19	3	3	52	131

Conf.Tourney Final: Clarkson 5, St.Lawrence 4.
NCAA Tournament: Clarkson (4-2); Cornell (1-2).

Hockey East

	W	L	T	Pts	GF	GA
*Boston Col.(27-12-0)	16	5	0	32	106	77
*Maine (32-9-2)	15	5	1	31	110	73
*Boston Univ.(28-11-2)	13	6	2	28	104	69
*Providence (22-12-2)	10	9	2	22	94	84
New Hampshire (22-11-2)	10	9	2	22	79	78
Merrimack (13-19-1)	7	14	0	14	71	103
Lowell (10-23-1)	5	15	1	11	69	108
Northeastern (8-25-2)	3	16	2	8	86	127

Conf.Tourney Final: Boston University 4, Maine 3 (OT).
NCAA Tournament: Boston Univ.(3-1); Maine (2-1); Providence (1- 2); Boston College (0-2).

NCAA Top 15
Final Regular Season Poll

Final regular season poll taken Feb. 25, 1991. Records do not include postseason games.

			W	L	T	Pts
1	Lake Superior St	CCHA	31	3	4	60
2	No.Michigan	WCHA	30	5	4	54
3	Boston College	H.East	27	9	0	53
4	Maine	H.East	28	7	2	49
5	Michigan	CCHA	29	6	3	44
6	Boston University	H.East	22	10	2	38
	Minnesota	WCHA	25	6	5	38
8	Clarkson	ECAC	21	7	2	32
9	Wisconsin	WCHA	24	11	3	28
10	Cornell	ECAC	15	8	3	20
11	Providence	H.East	20	9	2	19
12	New Hampshire	H.East	22	10	2	18
13	North Dakota	WCHA	21	15	2	13
14	St.Lawrence	ECAC	19	11	1	6
15	Ferris St	CCHA	21	12	5	4

Leading Scorers

Including all postseason games; (*) indicates defenseman.

West	Cl	Gm	G	A	Pts
Scott Beattie, No.Mich	So	46	48	41	89
Greg Johnson, N.Dakota	So	38	18	61	79
Jim Dowd, L.Superior	Sr	44	24	54	78
Denny Felsner, Michigan	Jr	46	40	35	75
Doug Weight, L.Superior	So	42	29	46	75
David Roberts, Michigan	So	43	26	45	71
Dixon Ward, N.Dakota	Jr	43	34	35	69
Russ Romaniuk, N.Dakota	Fr	38	40	28	68
Brad Werenka, No.Mich.*	Sr	47	20	43	63
John dePourco, Ferris St.	Sr	42	15	48	63

East	Cl	Gm	G	A	Pts
Jean-Yves Roy, Maine	So	43	37	45	82
Shawn McEachern, BU	Jr	41	34	48	82
David Emma, BC	Sr	39	35	46	81
Jim Montgomery, Maine	So	43	24	57	81
Hugo Belanger, Clark	So	40	32	43	75
Dave Trombley, Clark	Sr	36	31	38	69
Mike Lappin, St.Law	Jr	35	27	42	69
Tony Amonte, BU	So	38	31	37	68
Doug Derraugh, Cornell	Sr	32	30	36	66
Andy Pritchard, St.Law	Sr	35	29	35	64

Leading Goaltenders

Including all postseason games; minimum 10 games.

West	Cl	Record	GA	Avg
Darrin Madeley, L.Super	So	29- 3-3	93	2.61
Mike Gilmore, Mich.St	Jr	9- 8-3	54	2.66
Jeff Stolp, Minn	Jr	18- 8-3	82	2.79
Bill Pye, No.Mich	Sr	32- 3-4	109	2.84
Pat Mazzoli, Ferris St.	Fr	13- 8-1	66	3.13

East	Cl	Record	GA	Avg
Garth Snow, Maine	Jr	18- 4-0	64	2.98
Mike Dunham, Maine	Fr	14- 5-2	64	3.01
Brad Mullahy, Prov	So	14- 5-1	65	3.10
Jeff Levy, N.Hamp	Fr	15- 7-2	80	3.22
Les Kuntar, SLU	Sr	19-11-1	97	3.24

U.S. College Hockey (Cont.)
Annual Awards

Hobey Baker Award

For College Player of the Year. National coaches' vote determines 10 finalists. Winner then selected by 16-member panel of writers, broadcasters, coaches and pro scouts. First presented in 1981 by the Decathlon Athletic Club of Bloomington,MN, in the name of the late Princeton collegiate hockey and football star.

Top Vote Getters

Vote totals not released.

Winner: David Emma, Boston College, Sr., C.

Runner-up: Brad Werenka, No.Michigan, Sr., D.

Other finalists (8): Scott Beattie, No.Mich., Soph., C; Peter Ciavaglia, Harvard, Sr., F; Jim Dowd, L.Superior St., Sr., C; Denny Felsner, Michigan, Jr., RW; Greg Johnson, N.Dakota, Soph., C; Joe Juneau, RPI, Sr., C; Shawn McEachern, Boston Univ., Jr., F; Jean-Yves Roy, Maine, Soph., RW.

Division I All-America

Regional First Team selections as chosen by the American Hockey Coaches Association. Holdovers from 1989-90 All-America first teams are in **bold** type.

West Team

Pos		Yr	Hgt	Wgt
G	Darrin Madeley, Lake Superior	So	5-11	165
D	Brad Werenka, No.Michigan	Sr	6- 2	204
D	Jason Wooley, Michigan St	Jr	6- 0	195
F	Jim Dowd, Lake Superior	Sr	6- 2	185
F	Scott Beattie, No.Michigan	So	5- 7	158
F	Greg Johnson, N.Dakota	So	5-10	180

East Team

Pos		Yr	Hgt	Wgt
G	Les Kuntar, St.Lawrence	Sr	6- 2	195
D	Keith Carney, Maine	Jr	6- 2	205
D	Dan Ratushny, Cornell	Jr	6- 1	202
F	**Dave Emma**, Boston College	Sr	5- 9	175
F	Shawn McEachern, Boston Univ	Jr	6- 0	190
F	Jean-Yves Roy, Maine	So	5-10	175

NCAA Division I Tournament

Tournament Seeds

East	West
1 Maine (30-8-2)	1 Lake Superior (35-3-4)
2 **Boston Univ.** (25-10-2)	2 **No.Michigan** (32-5-4)
3 Boston Col.(27-10)	3 Michigan (32-7-3)
4 Clarkson (24-7-2)	4 Minnesota (28-6-5)
5 Providence (20-10-2)	5 Wisconsin (26-12-3)
6 Cornell (17-9-3)	6 AK-Anchorage (15-15-4)

First Round (Best of 3)

ALASKA-ANCHORAGE over Boston College, 2 games to none (3-2,3-1); CLARKSON over Wisconsin, 2 games to none (8-3,5-4); MINNESOTA over Providence, 2 games to none 1 (3-4,8-4,8-3); MICHIGAN over Cornell 2 games to 1 (4-5 OT,6-4,9-3).

Quarterfinals (Best of 3)

MAINE over Minnesota, 2 games to none (4-0,5-3); NO.MICHIGAN over Alaska-Anchorage, 2 games to none (8-5,5-3); BOSTON UNIV.over Michigan, 2 games to none (4-1,8-1); CLARKSON over Lake Superior St., 2 games to 1 (7-3,2-6,4-3).

Final Four (single games)

at St.Paul (MN) Civic Center

Semifinals: NO.MICHIGAN 5, Maine 3; BOSTON UNIV. 7, Clarkson 3. **Championship:** NO.MICHIGAN 8, Boston Univ.7 (3 OT).

Championship Game

No. Michigan 8, Boston Univ. 7 (3 OT)

Saturday, March 30, 1991
at St.Paul (MN) Civic Center (12,564)

	1	2	3	OT	OT	OT	F
Boston Univ. (28-11-2)	3	0	4	0	0	0	7
No. Michigan (38-5-4)	0	5	2	0	0	1	8

Scoring

1st Period: BU—Ed Ronan (David Tomlinson, Peter Ahola), 1:00; BU—David Sacco (Chris McCann, Mike Bavis), 8:24; BU—Ronan 2 (Scott Lachance, Tomlinson), 9:26.

2nd Period: NM—Dean Antos (Brad Werenka, Scott Beattie), power play, 1:33; NM—Mark Beaufait (Lou Melone, Phil Soukoroff), 5:24; NM—Beattie (Melone, Kevin Scott), 14:45; NM—Darryl Plandowski (Joe Frederick, Antos), 15:39; NM—Beattie 2 (unassisted), 17:18.

3rd Period: NM—Beattie 3 (unassisted), 3:08; BU—Tomlinson (unassisted), 5:59; NM—Plandowski 2 (Soukoroff, Melone), power play, 8:24; BU—Tony Amonte (Shawn McEachern, Keith Tkachuk), 12:24; BU—McEachern (Amonte), 14:59; BU—Sacco 2 (Lachance, McEachern), 19:21.

3rd Overtime: NM—Plankowski 3 (Beaufait, Antos), 1:57.

Goaltenders

Saves: NM—Bill Pye (33); BU—John Bradley (18), Scott Cashman (21).

Outstanding Player: Scott Beattie, F, No.Michigan (Semifinal—2 assists; Final—3 goals, 1 assist). **All-Tournament Team:** F—Beattie of No.Michigan, Tony Amonte of BU and Jean-Yves Roy of Maine; D—Brad Werenka and Lou Melone of No.Michigan; G—Bill Pye of No. Michigan.

NCAA Division III Tournament

All rounds decided in two games with mini-game (one 20-minute period), if necessary; winning teams in CAPITAL letters. There is no Division II tournament.

First Round

ELMIRA over Mercyhurst in 3 games (4-5,7-6,2-1); BABSON over Oswego St. in 2 games (4-1,10-4); WISCONSIN-STEVENS POINT over Lake Forest in 2 games (9-1,6-3); MANKATO ST. over Gustavus Adolphus in 2 games (4-4,7-2).

Final Four

(March 15-16 at Elmira, NY)

Semifinals—WI-STEVENS PT. 5, Babson 2; MANKATO ST. 7, Elmira 3. **Consolation**—Babson 3, Elmira 2. **Championship**—WI-STEVENS PT. 6, Mankato St. 2.

Most Outstanding Player—Paul Caufield, WI-Stevens Pt., F. **Final records:** WI-Stevens Pt.(27-9),Mankato St.(23-7-6), Babson (20-8), Elmira (28-6).

HOCKEY STATISTICS
THROUGH THE YEARS
1893-1991

STANLEY CUP • NHL LEADERS

THE 1992 INFORMATION PLEASE SPORTS ALMANAC

SEC B

PAGE 325

The Stanley Cup

The Stanley Cup was originally donated to the Canadian Amateur Hockey Assn. by Sir Frederick Arthur Stanley, Lord Stanley of Preston and 16th Earl of Derby, who had become interested in the sport while Governor General of Canada from 1888 to 1893. Stanley wanted the trophy to be a challenge cup, contested for each year by the best amateur hockey teams in Canada.

In 1893, the Cup was presented without a challenge to the AHA champion Montreal Amateur Athletic Assn. team. Every year since, however, there has been a playoff. In 1914, Cup trustees limited the field challenging for the trophy to the champion of the eastern professional National Hockey Assn.(NHA, organized in 1910) and the western professional Pacific Coast Hockey Assn.(PCHA, organized in 1912).

The NHA became the National Hockey League (NHL) in November, 1917. From 1918 to 1926, the NHL and PCHL champions played for the Cup with the Western Canada Hockey League (WCHL) champion joining in a three-way challenge in 1923 and '24. The PCHA disbanded after the 1925-26 season and the NHL playoffs have decided the winner of the Stanley Cup ever since.

Stanley Cup Champions, 1893-1917

Year	Champion	Year	Champion	Year	Champion
1893	Montreal A.A.A.	1901	Winnipeg Victorias	1909	Ottawa Senators
1894	Montreal A.A.A.	1902	Montreal A.A.A.	1910	Montreal Wanderers
1895	Montreal Victorias	1903	Ottawa Silver Seven	1911	Ottawa Senators
1896	(Feb.) Winnipeg Victorias	1904	Ottawa Silver Seven	1912	Quebec Bulldogs
	(Dec.) Montreal Victorias	1905	Ottawa Silver Seven	1913	Quebec Bulldogs
1897	Montreal Victorias	1906	Montreal Wanderers	1914	Toronto Blueshirts (NHA)
1898	Montreal Victorias	1907	(Jan.) Kenora Thistles	1915	Vancouver Millionaires (PCHA)
1899	Montreal Shamrocks		(Mar.) Mon.Wanderers	1916	Montreal Canadiens (NHA)
1900	Montreal Shamrocks	1908	Montreal Wanderers	1917	Seattle Metropolitans (PCHA)

Stanley Cup Champions since 1918

Year	Winner	Head Coach	Series	Loser	Head Coach
1918	Toronto Arenas	Dick Carroll	3-2 (WLWLW)	Vancouver (PCHA)	Frank Patrick
1919	No Decision: (see below).				
1920	Ottawa	Pete Green	3-2 (WWLLW)	Seattle (PCHA)	Pete Muldoon
1921	Ottawa	Pete Green	3-2 (LWWLW)	Vancouver (PCHA)	Frank Patrick
1922	Toronto St.Pats	Eddie Powers	3-2 (LWLWW)	Vancouver (PCHA)	Frank Patrick
1923	Ottawa	Pete Green	3-1 (WLWW)	Vancouver (PCHA)	Frank Patrick
			2-0	Edmonton (WCHL)	K.C.McKenzie
1924	Montreal	Leo Dandurand	2-0	Vancouver (PCHA)	Frank Patrick
			2-0	Calgary (WCHL)	Eddie Oatman
1925	Victoria (PCHA)	Lester Patrick	3-1 (WWLW)	Montreal	Leo Dandurand
1926	Montreal Maroons	Eddie Gerard	3-1 (WWLW)	Victoria (PCHA)	Lester Patrick
1927	Ottawa	Dave Gil	2-0 (TWTW)	Boston	Art Ross
1928	NY Rangers	Lester Patrick	3-2 (LWLWW)	Montreal	Cecil Hart
1929	Boston	Art Ross	2-0	NY Rangers	Lester Patrick
1930	Montreal	Cecil Hart	2-0	Boston	Art Ross
1931	Montreal	Cecil Hart	3-2 (WLLWW)	Chicago	Art Duncan
1932	Toronto	Dick Irvin	3-0	NY Rangers	Lester Patrick
1933	NY Rangers	Lester Patrick	3-1 (WWLW)	Toronto	Dick Irvin
1934	Chicago	Tommy Gorman	3-1 (WWLW)	Detroit	Jack Adams
1935	Montreal Maroons	Lionel Conacher	3-0	Toronto	Dick Irvin
1936	Detroit	Jack Adams	3-1 (WWLW)	Toronto	Dick Irvin
1937	Detroit	Jack Adams	3-2 (LWLWW)	NY Rangers	Lester Patrick
1938	Chicago	Bill Stewart	3-1 (WLWW)	Toronto	Dick Irvin
1939	Boston	Art Ross	4-1 (WLWWW)	Toronto	Dick Irvin
1940	NY Rangers	Frank Boucher	4-2 (WWLLWW)	Toronto	Dick Irvin
1941	Boston	Cooney Weiland	4-0	Detroit	Jack Adams
1942	Toronto	Hap Day	4-3 (LLLWWWW)	Detroit	Jack Adams

Note: The 1919 Finals were cancelled after five games due to an influenza epidemic with Montreal and Seattle tied at 2-2-1.

Stanley Cup Champions since 1918 (Cont.)

Year	Winner	Head Coach	Series	Loser	Head Coach
1943	Detroit	Jack Adams	4-0	Boston	Art Ross
1944	Montreal	Dick Irvin	4-0	Chicago	Paul Thompson
1945	Toronto	Hap Day	4-3 (WWWLLLW)	Detroit	Jack Adams
1946	Montreal	Dick Irvin	4-1 (WWWLW)	Boston	Dit Clapper
1947	Toronto	Hap Day	4-2 (LWWWLW)	Montreal	Dick Irvin
1948	Toronto	Hap Day	4-0	Detroit	Tommy Ivan
1949	Toronto	Hap Day	4-0	Detroit	Tommy Ivan
1950	Detroit	Tommy Ivan	4-3 (WLWLLWW)	NY Rangers	Lynn Patrick
1951	Toronto	Joe Primeau	4-1 (WLWWW)	Montreal	Dick Irvin
1952	Detroit	Tommy Ivan	4-0	Montreal	Dick Irvin
1953	Montreal	Dick Irvin	4-1 (WLWWW)	Boston	Lynn Patrick
1954	Detroit	Tommy Ivan	4-3 (WLWWLLW)	Montreal	Dick Irvin
1955	Detroit	Jimmy Skinner	4-3 (WWLLWLW)	Montreal	Dick Irvin
1956	Montreal	Toe Blake	4-1 (WWLWW)	Detroit	Jimmy Skinner
1957	Montreal	Toe Blake	4-1 (WWLWW)	Boston	Milt Schmidt
1958	Montreal	Toe Blake	4-2 (WLWLWW)	Boston	Milt Schmidt
1959	Montreal	Toe Blake	4-1 (WWLWW)	Toronto	Punch Imlach
1960	Montreal	Toe Blake	4-0	Toronto	Punch Imlach
1961	Chicago	Rudy Pilous	4-2 (WLWLWW)	Detroit	Sid Abel
1962	Toronto	Punch Imlach	4-2 (WWLLWW)	Chicago	Rudy Pilous
1963	Toronto	Punch Imlach	4-1 (WWLWW)	Detroit	Sid Abel
1964	Toronto	Punch Imlach	4-3 (WLLWLWW)	Detroit	Sid Abel
1965	Montreal	Toe Blake	4-3 (WWLWLLW)	Chicago	Billy Reay
1966	Montreal	Toe Blake	4-2 (LLWWWW)	Detroit	Sid Abel
1967	Toronto	Punch Imlach	4-2 (LWWLWW)	Montreal	Toe Blake
1968	Montreal	Toe Blake	4-0	St. Louis	Scotty Bowman
1969	Montreal	Claude Ruel	4-0	St. Louis	Scotty Bowman
1970	Boston	Harry Sinden	4-0	St. Louis	Scotty Bowman
1971	Montreal	Al MacNeil	4-3 (LLWWLWW)	Chicago	Billy Reay
1972	Boston	Tom Johnson	4-2 (WWLWLW)	NY Rangers	Emile Francis
1973	Montreal	Scotty Bowman	4-2 (WWLWLW)	Chicago	Billy Reay
1974	Philadelphia	Fred Shero	4-2 (LWWWLW)	Boston	Bep Guidolin
1975	Philadelphia	Fred Shero	4-2 (WWLLWW)	Buffalo	Floyd Smith
1976	Montreal	Scotty Bowman	4-0	Philadelphia	Fred Shero
1977	Montreal	Scotty Bowman	4-0	Boston	Don Cherry
1978	Montreal	Scotty Bowman	4-2 (WWLLWW)	Boston	Don Cherry
1979	Montreal	Scotty Bowman	4-1 (LWWWW)	NY Rangers	Fred Shero
1980	NY Islanders	Al Arbour	4-2 (WLWLWW)	Philadelphia	Pat Quinn
1981	NY Islanders	Al Arbour	4-1 (WWWLW)	Minnesota	Glen Sonmor
1982	NY Islanders	Al Arbour	4-0	Vancouver	Roger Neilson
1983	NY Islanders	Al Arbour	4-0	Edmonton	Glen Sather
1984	Edmonton	Glen Sather	4-1 (WLWWW)	NY Islanders	Al Arbour
1985	Edmonton	Glen Sather	4-1 (LWWWW)	Philadelphia	Mike Keenan
1986	Montreal	Jean Perron	4-1 (LWWWW)	Calgary	Bob Johnson
1987	Edmonton	Glen Sather	4-3 (WWLWLLW)	Philadelphia	Mike Keenan
1988	Edmonton	Glen Sather	4-0	Boston	Terry O'Reilly
1989	Calgary	Terry Crisp	4-2 (WLLWWW)	Montreal	Pat Burns
1990	Edmonton	John Muckler	4-1 (WWWLW)	Boston	Mike Milbury
1991	Pittsburgh	Bob Johnson	4-2 (LWLWWW)	Minnesota	Bob Gainey

Conn Smythe Trophy

The Most Valuable Player of the Stanley Cup Playoffs, as selected by the Pro Hockey Writers Assn. Presented since 1965 by Maple Leaf Gardens Limited in the name of the former Toronto coach, GM and owner, Conn Smythe. Winners who did not play for the Cup champion are in **bold** type.

Multiple winners: Wayne Gretzky, Bobby Orr, Bernie Parent (2).

Year		Year		Year	
1965	Jean Beliveau, Mon., C	1974	Bernie Parent, Phil., G	1983	Billy Smith, NY Isles, G
1966	**Roger Crozier,** Det., G	1975	Bernie Parent, Phil., G	1984	Mark Messier, Edm., LW
1967	Dave Keon, Tor., C	1976	**Reggie Leach,** Phil., RW	1985	Wayne Gretzky, Edm., C
1968	**Glenn Hall,** St.L., G	1977	Guy Lafleur, Mon., RW	1986	Patrick Roy, Mon., G
1969	Serge Savard, Mon., D	1978	Larry Robinson, Mon., D	1987	**Ron Hextall,** Phil., G
1970	Bobby Orr, Bos., D	1979	Bob Gainey, Mon., LW	1988	Wayne Gretzky, Edm., C
1971	Ken Dryden, Mon., G	1980	Bryan Trottier, NY Isles, C	1989	Al MacInnis, Cal., D
1972	Bobby Orr, Bos., D	1981	Butch Goring, NY Isles, C	1990	Bill Ranford, Edm., G
1973	Yvan Cournoyer, Mon., RW	1982	Mike Bossy, NY Isles, RW	1991	Mario Lemieux, Pit., C

Note: Ken Dryden (1971) and Patrick Roy (1986) are the only players to win the Smythe Trophy as rookies.

All-Time Stanley Cup Playoff Leaders

Stanley Cup Playoff leaders through 1991.

CAREER

Years listed indicate number of playoff appearances. Players active in 1991 playoffs in **bold** type.

Scoring

Points

	Yrs	Gm	G	A	Pts
Wayne Gretzky	12	150	93	206	299
Mark Messier	12	166	80	135	215
Jari Kurri	10	146	92	110	202
Glenn Anderson	11	164	81	102	183
Bryan Trottier	15	198	67	110	177
Jean Beliveau	17	162	79	97	176
Denis Potvin	14	185	56	108	164
Mike Bossy	10	129	85	75	160
Gordie Howe	20	157	68	92	160
Bobby Smith	12	177	63	92	155
Stan Mikita	18	155	59	91	150
Brian Propp	13	159	64	84	148
Larry Robinson	19	225	28	116	144
Jacques Lemaire	11	145	61	78	139
Phil Esposito	15	130	61	76	137
Denis Savard	11	112	55	80	135
Guy Lafleur	14	128	58	76	134
Bobby Hull	14	119	62	67	129
Henri Richard	18	180	49	80	129
Paul Coffey	9	117	40	89	129

Goals

	Yrs	Gm	No
Wayne Gretzky	12	150	93
Jari Kurri	10	146	92
Mike Bossy	10	129	85
Maurice Richard	17	133	82
Glenn Anderson	11	164	81
Mark Messier	12	166	80
Jean Beliveau	17	162	79
Gordie Howe	20	157	68
Bryan Trottier	15	198	67
Yvon Cornoyer	12	147	64
Brian Propp	13	159	64

Assists

	Yrs	Gm	No
Wayne Gretzky	12	150	206
Mark Messier	12	166	135
Larry Robinson	19	225	116
Jari Kurri	10	146	110
Bryan Trottier	15	198	110
Denis Potvin	13	185	108
Glenn Anderson	11	164	102
Jean Beliveau	17	162	97
Gordie Howe	20	157	92
Bobby Smith	12	177	92
Stan Mikita	18	155	91

Appearances in Cup Final

Standings of all teams that have reached the Stanley Cup championship round, since 1918.

App		Cups	Last Won
30	Montreal Canadiens	22*	1986
21	Toronto Maple Leafs	13†	1967
18	Detroit Red Wings	7	1955
17	Boston Bruins	5	1972
9	Chicago Blackhawks	3	1961
9	New York Rangers	3	1940
6	Edmonton Oilers	5	1990
6	Philadelphia Flyers	2	1975
5	New York Islanders	4	1983
5	Vancouver Millionaires (PCHA)	0	—
4	Ottawa Senators	4	1927
3	Montreal Maroons	2	1935
3	St.Louis Blues	0	—
2	Calgary Flames	1	1989
2	Minnesota North Stars	0	—
1	Victoria Cougars (PCHA)	1	1925
1	Pittsburgh Penguins	1	1991
1	Buffalo Sabres	0	—
1	Calgary Tigers (WCHL)	0	—
1	Edmonton Eskimos (WCHL)	0	—
1	Seattle Metropolitans (PCHA)	0	—
1	Vancouver Canucks	0	—

*Montreal Canadiens also won the Cup in 1916 for a total of 23. Also, their final with Seattle in 1919 was cancelled due to an influenza epidemic that claimed the life of the Habs' Joe Hall.

†Toronto won the Cup under three nicknames—Arenas (1918), St.Pats (1922) and Maple Leafs (1932,42,45,47-49,51,62-64,67).

Teams now defunct (6): Calgary Tigers, Edmonton Eskimos, Montreal Maroons, Ottawa, Seattle, Vancouver Millionaires and Victoria. Edmonton (1923) and Calgary (1924) represented the Western Canada Hockey League, while Vancouver (1918,1921-24) and Seattle (1919-20) played out of the Pacific Coast Hockey Assn.

Goaltending

Wins

	Gm	Mins	W-L	ShO	Avg
Billy Smith	132	7645	88-36	5	2.73
Ken Dryden	112	6841	80-32	10	2.40
Grant Fuhr	111	6528	74-32	2	3.03
Jacques Plante	112	6651	71-37	15	2.17
Turk Broda	102	6406	58-42	13	1.99
Terry Sawchuk	106	6291	54-48	12	2.64
Andy Moog	89	4979	51-31	2	2.94
Glenn Hall	115	6899	49-65	6	2.79
Gerry Cheevers	88	5396	47-35	8	3.30
Gump Worsley	70	4080	41-25	5	2.82
Bernie Parent	71	4302	38-33	6	2.43

Shutouts

	Gm	No
Clint Benedict	48	15
Jacques Plante	112	15
Turk Broda	102	13
Terry Sawchuk	106	12
Ken Dryden	112	10

Goals Against Average

Minimum of 50 games played.

	Gm	Mins	GA	Avg
George Hainsworth	52	3486	112	1.93
Turk Broda	101	6348	211	1.98
Jacques Plante	112	6651	241	2.17
Ken Dryden	112	6841	274	2.40
Bernie Parent	71	4302	174	2.43

Note: Clint Benedict had an average of 1.88 but played in only 48 games.

All-Time Stanley Cup Playoff Leaders (Cont.)
Miscellaneous

Playoff Appearances

	App	Gm
Gordie Howe, Detroit-Hartford	20	157
Larry Robinson, Montreal-LA	19	225
Red Kelly, Detroit-Toronto	19	164
Henri Richard, Montreal	18	180
Stan Mikita, Chicago	18	155

Championships

	Yrs	Cups
Henri Richard, Montreal	18	11
Yvan Cournoyer, Montreal	15	10
Jean Beliveau, Montreal	17	10
Claude Provost, Montreal	14	9
Jacques Lemaire, Montreal	11	8
Maurice Richard, Montreal	17	8
Red Kelly, Detroit-Toronto	19	8

Games Played

	Yrs	Gm
Larry Robinson, Montreal	19	225
Bryan Trottier, NY Islanders	15	198
Denis Potvin, NY Islanders	15	185
Bob Gainey, Montreal	16	182
Henri Richard, Montreal	18	180

Most Penalty Minutes

	Yrs	Gm	PMin
Dale Hunter, Que-Wash	11	113	548
Chris Nilan, Mon-NYR-Bos	11	104	526
Willi Plett, Atl-Calg-Min-Bos	10	83	466
Dave Williams, Tor-Van-LA	12	83	455
Dave Schultz, Phi-LA-Buf	6	73	412

Games Played in Goal

	Yrs	Gm
Billy Smith, NY Islanders	13	132
Glenn Hall, Det-Chi-StL	17	115
Jacques Plante, Mon-StL-Tor-Bos	16	112
Ken Dryden, Montreal	8	112
Grant Fuhr, Edmonton	9	111
Terry Sawchuk, Det-Tor-LA-NYR	15	106

SINGLE SEASON
Scoring
Points

	Year	Gm	G	A	Pts
Wayne Gretzky, Edm	1985	18	17	30	47
Mario Lemieux, Pit	1991	23	16	28	44
Wayne Gretzky, Edm	1988	19	12	31	43
Wayne Gretzky, Edm	1983	16	12	26	38
Paul Coffey, Edm	1985	18	12	25	37
Mike Bossy, NYI	1981	18	17	18	35
Wayne Gretzky, Edm	1984	19	13	22	35
Mark Messier, Edm	1988	19	11	23	35
Mark Recchi, Pit	1991	24	10	24	34
Wayne Gretzky, Edm	1987	21	5	29	34

Goaltending
Wins

	Year	Gm	Mins	W-L
Grant Fuhr, Edm	1988	19	1136	16- 2
Mike Vernon, Calg	1989	22	1381	16- 5
Bill Ranford, Edm	1990	22	1401	16- 6
Billy Smith, NYI	1982	18	1120	15- 3
Grant Fuhr, Edm	1985	18	1064	15- 3
Billy Smith, NYI	1980	20	1198	15- 4
Patrick Roy, Mon	1986	20	1218	15- 5
Ron Hextall, Phi	1987	26	1540	15-11
Billy Smith, NYI	1981	17	994	14- 3
Grant Fuhr, Edm	1987	19	1148	14- 5
Jon Casey, Min	1991	23	1205	14- 7

Goals

	Year	Gm	No
Reggie Leach, Phi	1976	16	19
Jari Kurri, Edm	1985	18	19
Mike Bossy, NYI	1981	18	17
Wayne Gretzky, Edm	1985	18	17
Steve Payne, Minn	1981	19	17
Mike Bossy, NYI	1982	19	17
Mike Bossy, NYI	1983	19	17
Kevin Stevens, Pit	1991	24	17

Shutouts

	Year	Gm	ShO
Terry Sawchuck, Det	1952	8	4
Clint Benedict, Mon.Maroons	1928	9	4
Dave Kerr, NY Rangers	1937	9	4
Frank McCool, Tor	1945	13	4
Ken Dryden, Mon	1977	14	4
Bernie Parent, Phi	1975	17	4

Assists

	Year	Gm	No
Wayne Gretzky, Edm	1988	19	31
Wayne Gretzky, Edm	1985	18	30
Wayne Gretzky, Edm	1987	21	29
Mario Lemieux, Pit	1991	23	28
Wayne Gretzky, Edm	1983	16	26
Paul Coffey, Edm	1985	18	25

Goals Against Average
Minimum of eight games played.

	Year	Gm	Min	GA	Avg
Terry Sawchuk, Det	1952	8	480	5	0.63
Turk Broda, Tor	1951	9	509	9	1.06
Dave Kerr, NYR	1937	9	553	10	1.08
Jacques Plante, Mon	1960	8	488	11	1.35
Jacques Plante, StL	1969	10	589	14	1.43

SINGLE GAME
Scoring
Points

	Date	G	A	Pts
Patrik Sundstrom, NJ vs Wash	4/22/88	3	5	8
Mario Lemieux, Pit.vs Phi	4/25/89	5	3	8
Wayne Gretzky, Edm.at Calg	4/17/83	4	3	7
Wayne Gretzky, Edm.at Win	4/25/85	3	4	7
Wayne Gretzky, Edm.vs LA	4/9/87	1	6	7

Goals

	Date	No
Maurice Richard, Mon.vs Tor	3/23/44	5
Darryl Sittler, Tor.vs Phi	4/22/76	5
Reggie Leach, Phi.vs Bos	5/6/76	5
Mario Lemieux, Pit.vs Phi	4/25/89	5

NHL Franchise Origins

Here is what the current 22 teams in the National Hockey League have to show for the years they have put in as members of the NHL and World Hockey Association (WHA). League titles are noted by year won. Conferences named after Clarence Campbell, the NHL's third president (1946-77); and Edward VIII, who, while Prince of Wales, donated a trophy to the league in 1924. Edward became king of England in 1936 and abdicated the same year.

Clarence Campbell Conference

	First Season	League Titles	Franchise Stops
Calgary Flames	1972-73 (NHL)	1 NHL (1989)	Atlanta (1972-80)
			Calgary (1980—)
Chicago Blackhawks	1926-27 (NHL)	3 NHL (1934,38,61)	Chicago (1926—)
Detroit Red Wings	1926-27 (NHL)	7 NHL (1936-37,43,50, 52,54-55)	Detroit (1926—)
Edmonton Oilers	1973-74 (WHA)	5 NHL (1984-85,87-88, 90)	Edmonton (1972—)
Los Angeles Kings	1967-68 (NHL)	None	Los Angeles (1967—)
Minn.North Stars	1967-68 (NHL)	None	Bloomington,MN (1967—)
St.Louis Blues	1967-68 (NHL)	None	St.Louis (1967—)
San Jose Sharks	1991-92 (NHL)	None	San Jose, CA (1991—)
Toronto Maple Leafs	1917-18 (NHL)	13 NHL (1918,22,32,42,45 47-49,51,62-64,67)	Toronto (1917—)
Vancouver Canucks	1970-71 (NHL)	None	Vancouver (1970—)
Winnipeg Jets	1972-73 (WHA)	3 WHA (1976,78-79)	Winnipeg (1972—)

Prince of Wales Conference

	First Season	League Titles	Franchise Stops
Boston Bruins	1924-25 (NHL)	5 NHL (1929,39,41,70,72)	Boston (1924—)
Buffalo Sabres	1970-71 (NHL)	None	Buffalo (1970—)
Hartford Whalers	1972-73 (WHA)	1 WHA (1973)	Boston (1972-74)
			W.Springfield,MA (1974-75)
			Hartford,CT (1975-78)
			Springfield,MA (1978-80)
			Hartford (1980—)
Montreal Canadiens	1917-18 (NHL)	22 NHL (1924,30-31,44,46,53, 56-60,65-66,68-69, 71,73,76-79,86)	Montreal (1917—)
New Jersey Devils	1974-75 (NHL)	None	Kansas City (1974-76)
			Denver (1976-82)
			E.Rutherford,NJ (1982—)
New York Islanders	1972-73 (NHL)	4 NHL (1980-83)	Uniondale,NY (1972—)
New York Rangers	1926-27 (NHL)	3 NHL (1928,33,40)	New York (1926—)
Philadelphia Flyers	1967-68 (NHL)	2 NHL (1974-75)	Philadelphia (1967—)
Pittsburgh Penguins	1967-68 (NHL)	1 NHL (1991)	Pittsburgh (1967—)
Quebec Nordiques	1972-73 (WHA)	1 WHA (1977)	Quebec City (1972—)
Washington Capitals	1974-75 (NHL)	None	Landover,MD (1974—)

Note: The Hartford Civic Center roof caved in Jan,1978, forcing the Whalers to move home games to the Springfield,MA Civic Center for two years.

Expansion Will Give NHL 24 Teams By 1992-93

The expansion San Jose Sharks became the newest active member of the 22-team National Hockey League in October, opening the league's 75th season in the Norris Division. The Sharks are the first team to join the NHL since Edmonton, Hartford, Quebec and Winnipeg were added in 1979 following the demise of the World Hockey Association.

Two more expansion teams, the Ottawa Senators and Tampa Bay Lightning, were awarded franchises in 1991 and will suit up in time for the 1992-93 season. Ottawa was a charter member of the NHL in1917 and the original Senators won four Stanley Cups (1920-21, 1923 and 1927) before moving to St. Louis in 1934 and folding a year later. Tampa's arrival marks a return to the South by the NHL for the first time since the Atlanta Flames moved to Calgary in 1980.

The NHL was a six team league—Boston, Chicago, Detroit, Montreal, NY Rangers and Toronto—from the middle of World War II through the 1966-67 season. The league then doubled in size, adding Los Angeles, Minnesota, Philadelphia, Pittsburgh, Oakland and St. Louis. Six more teams were added the next seven years: Buffalo and Vancouver in 1970, Atlanta and NY Islanders in 1972, and Kansas City and Washington in 1974.

The Oakland Seals moved to Cleveland and became the Barons in 1976, then merged with Minnesota in 1978. The Kansas City Scouts moved to Denver in '76, becoming the Colorado Rockies, then moved to New Jersey in 1982 and became the Devils.

All-Time NHL Leaders

Through the 1990-91 regular season.

CAREER

Players active during 1990-91 in **bold** type.

Scoring

Points

	Yrs	Gm	G	A	Pts
Wayne Gretzky	12	925	718	1424	2142
Gordie Howe	26	1767	801	1049	1850
Marcel Dionne	18	1348	731	1040	1771
Phil Esposito	18	1282	717	873	1590
Stan Mikita	22	1394	541	926	1467
Bryan Trottier	16	1175	509	872	1381
John Bucyk	23	1540	556	813	1369
Guy Lafleur	17	1126	560	793	1353
Gilbert Perreault	17	1191	512	814	1326
Alex Delvecchio	24	1549	456	825	1281
Jean Ratelle	21	1281	491	776	1267
Norm Ullman	20	1410	490	739	1229
Jean Beliveau	20	1125	507	712	1219
Bobby Clarke	15	1144	358	852	1210
Bobby Hull	16	1063	610	560	1170
Bernie Federko	14	1000	369	761	1130
Mike Bossy	10	752	573	553	1126
Darryl Sittler	15	1096	484	637	1121
Peter Stastny	11	826	403	716	1119
Frank Mahovlich	18	1181	533	570	1103
Denis Savard	11	806	379	693	1072
Denis Potvin	15	1060	310	742	1052
Henri Richard	20	1256	358	688	1046
Paul Coffey	11	809	307	738	1045
Jari Kurri	10	754	474	569	1043
Mark Messier	12	851	392	641	1033
Rod Gilbert	18	1065	406	615	1021
Dave Taylor	14	953	411	607	1018
Dale Hawerchuk	10	793	410	608	1018
Michel Goulet	12	895	487	528	1015

Goals

	Yrs	Gm	No
Gordie Howe	26	1767	801
Marcel Dionne	18	1348	731
Wayne Gretzky	12	925	718
Phil Esposito	18	1282	717
Bobby Hull	16	1063	610
Mike Bossy	10	752	573
Guy Lafleur	17	1126	560
John Bucyk	23	1540	556
Maurice Richard	18	978	544
Stan Mikita	22	1394	541
Frank Mahovlich	18	1181	533
Gilbert Perreault	17	1191	512
Bryan Trottier	16	1175	509
Jean Beliveau	18	1125	507
Lanny McDonald	16	1111	500
Mike Gartner	12	929	498
Jean Ratelle	21	1281	491
Norm Ullman	20	1410	490
Michel Goulet	12	895	487
Darryl Sittler	15	1096	484
Jari Kurri	10	754	474
Alex Delvecchio	24	1549	456
Rick Middleton	14	1005	448
Rick Vaive	12	856	440
Yvan Cournoyer	16	968	428
Steve Shutt	13	930	424
Bill Barber	12	903	420
Glenn Anderson	11	828	413
Garry Unger	16	1105	413
Dave Taylor	14	953	411

Assists

	Yrs	Gm	No
Wayne Gretzky	12	925	1424
Gordie Howe	26	1767	1049
Marcel Dionne	18	1348	1040
Stan Mikita	22	1394	926
Phil Esposito	18	1281	873
Bryan Trottier	16	1175	872
Bobby Clarke	15	1144	852
Alex Delvecchio	24	1549	825
Gilbert Perreault	17	1191	814
John Bucyk	23	1540	813
Guy Lafleur	17	1126	793
Jean Ratelle	21	1281	776
Bernie Federko	14	1000	761
Denis Potvin	15	1060	742
Larry Robinson	19	1328	740

Penalty Minutes

	Yrs	Gm	PMin
Dave Williams	13	962	3966
Willi Plett	12	834	2572
Chris Nilan	12	632	2783
Dale Hunter	10	838	2471
Dave Schultz	9	535	2294
Tim Hunter	9	515	2237
Bryan Watson	16	878	2212
Terry O'Reilly	14	891	2095
Al Secord	11	766	2093
Laurie Boschman	12	864	2043
Phil Russell	15	1016	2038
Harold Snepsts	17	1033	2009
Rob Ramage	12	915	1995
Andre Dupont	13	810	1986
Garry Howatt	12	720	1836

NHL-WHA Top 15

NHL players with WHA experience are listed in CAPITAL letters. Players active during 1990-91 are in **bold** type.

Points

	Yrs	Gm	G	A	Pts
GORDIE HOWE	32	2186	975	1383	2358
WAYNE GRETZKY	13	985	764	1488	2252
BOBBY HULL	23	1474	913	895	1808
Marcel Dionne	18	1348	731	1040	1771
Phil Esposito	18	1282	717	873	1590
Stan Mikita	22	1394	541	926	1467
Bryan Trottier	16	1175	509	872	1381
John Bucyk	23	1540	556	813	1369
NORM ULLMAN	22	1554	537	822	1359
Guy Lafleur	17	1126	560	793	1353
FRANK MAHOVLICH	22	1418	622	713	1335
Gilbert Perreault	17	1191	512	814	1326
Alex Delvecchio	24	1549	456	825	1281
DAVE KEON	22	1597	498	779	1277
Jean Ratelle	21	1281	491	776	1267

WHA Totals: GRETZKY (1 yr, 60 gm, 46-64–110); HOWE (6 yrs, 419 gm, 174-334–508); HULL (7 yrs, 411 gm, 303-335–638); KEON (4 yrs, 301 gm, 102-189–291); MAHOVLICH (4 yrs, 237 gm, 89-143–232); ULLMAN (2 yrs, 144 gm, 47-83–130).

Years Played

	Yrs	Career	Gm
Gordie Howe	26	1946–71, 79–80	1767
Alex Delvecchio	24	1950–74	1549
Tim Horton	24	1949–50, 51–74	1446
John Bucyk	23	1955–75	1540
Stan Mikita	22	1958–80	1394
Doug Mohns	22	1953–75	1390
Dean Prentice	22	1952–74	1378
Harry Howell	21	1952–73	1411
Ron Stewart	21	1952–73	1353
Jean Ratelle	21	1960–81	1281
Allan Stanley	21	1948–69	1244
Eric Nesterenko	21	1951–72	1219
Terry Sawchuk	21	1949–70	971
Gump Worsley	21	1952–53, 54–74	862

Eight tied with 20 each.

Note: Combined NHL-WHA years played: Howe (32); Howell (24); Bobby Hull (23), Norm Ullman, Eric Nesterenko, Frank Mahovlich and Dave Keon (22).

Games Played

	Yrs	Career	No
Gordie Howe	26	1946–71, 79–80	1767
Alex Delvecchio	24	1950–74	1549
John Bucyk	23	1955–75	1540
Tim Horton	24	1949–50, 51–74	1446
Harry Howell	21	1952–73	1411
Norm Ullman	20	1955–75	1410
Stan Mikita	22	1958–80	1394
Doug Mohns	22	1953–75	1390
Dean Prentice	22	1952–74	1378
Ron Stewart	21	1952–73	1353
Marcel Dionne	18	1971–89	1348
Larry Robinson	19	1972––	1328
Red Kelly	20	1947–67	1316
Dave Keon	18	1960–75, 79–82	1296
Phil Esposito	18	1963–81	1282

Note: Combined NHL-WHA games played: Howe (2,186), Keon (1,597), Howell (1,581), Ullman (1,554), Bobby Hull (1,474), and Frank Mahovlich (1,418).

Goaltending

Wins

	Yrs	Gm	W	L	T	Pct
Terry Sawchuk	21	971	435	337	188	.551
Jacques Plante	18	837	434	246	137	.615
Tony Esposito	16	886	423	307	151	.566
Glenn Hall	18	906	407	327	165	.544
Rogie Vachon	16	795	355	291	115	.542
Gump Worsley	21	862	335	353	150	.489
Harry Lumley	16	804	332	324	143	.505
Billy Smith	18	680	305	233	105	.556
Turk Broda	12	629	302	224	101	.562
Ed Giacomin	13	610	289	206	97	.570
Dan Bouchard	14	655	286	232	113	.543
Tiny Thompson	12	553	284	194	75	.581
Mike Liut	12	642	283	264	72	.515
Bernie Parent	13	608	270	197	121	.562
Gilles Meloche	18	761	270	342	126	.446
Ken Dryden	8	397	258	57	74	.758
Frank Brimsek	10	514	252	182	80	.568
Johnny Bower	15	549	251	196	90	.551
George Hainsworth	11	465	247	146	74	.608
Pete Peeters	12	489	246	155	51	.600

Shutouts

	Yrs	Gm	No
Terry Sawchuk	21	971	103
George Hainsworth	11	465	94
Glenn Hall	18	906	84
Jacques Plante	18	837	82
Tiny Thompson	12	552	81
Alex Connell	12	416	80
Tony Esposito	16	886	76
Lorne Chabot	11	412	73
Harry Lumley	16	803	71
Roy Worters	12	488	66
Turk Broda	12	628	62
Clint Benedict	13	360	58
John Roach	14	492	58
Bernie Parent	13	608	55
Ed Giacomin	13	610	54
Dave Kerr	11	427	51
Rogie Vachon	16	795	51
Ken Dryden	8	397	46
Gump Worsley	21	860	43
Chuck Gardiner	7	316	42

Goals Against Average

Minimum of 300 games played.

Before 1950

	Gm	Mins	GA	Avg
George Hainsworth	465	29,415	937	1.91
Alex Connell	416	26,030	837	2.01
Chuck Gardiner	316	19,687	664	2.02
Lorne Chabot	412	25,309	861	2.04
Tiny Thompson	552	34,174	1183	2.08
Dave Kerr	426	26,519	960	2.17
Roy Worters	484	30,175	1143	2.27
Clint Benedict	362	22,321	863	2.32
Bill Durnan	383	22,945	901	2.36
John Roach	491	30,423	1246	2.46

After 1950

	Gm	Mins	GA	Avg
Ken Dryden	397	23,352	870	2.24
Jacques Plante	837	49,633	1965	2.38
Glenn Hall	906	53,484	2239	2.51
Terry Sawchuk	971	57,205	2401	2.52
Johnny Bower	552	32,077	1347	2.52
Bernie Parent	608	35,136	1493	2.55
Turk Broda	628	37,680	1605	2.56
Frank Brimsek	515	31,210	1404	2.70
Charlie Hodge	358	20,593	927	2.70
Harry Lumley	803	48,107	2210	2.76

NHL-WHA Top 15

NHL goaltenders with WHA experience are listed in CAPITAL letters. Players active during 1990-91 are in **bold** type.

Wins

	Yrs	Gm	W	L	T	Pct
JACQUES PLANTE	19	868	449	260	138	.612
Terry Sawchuk	21	971	435	337	188	.551
Tony Esposito	16	886	423	307	151	.566
Glenn Hall	18	906	407	327	165	.544
Rogie Vachon	16	795	355	291	115	.542
Gump Worsley	21	862	335	353	150	.489
Harry Lumley	16	804	332	324	143	.505
GERRY CHEEVERS	16	609	329	172	83	.634
MIKE LIUT	14	688	314	303	76	.508
Billy Smith	18	680	305	233	105	.556
BERNIE PARENT	14	671	303	225	121	.560
Turk Broda	12	629	302	224	101	.562
Ed Giacomin	13	610	289	206	97	.570
Dan Bouchard	14	655	286	232	113	.543
Tiny Thompson	12	553	284	194	75	.581

WHA Totals: CHEEVERS (4 yrs, 191 gm, 99-78-9); LIUT (2 yrs, 81 gm, 31-39-4); PARENT (1 yr, 63 gm, 33-28-0); PLANTE (1 yr, 31 gm, 15-14-1).

All-Time NHL Leaders (Cont.)
SINGLE SEASON

Scoring
Points

	Season	G	A	Pts
Wayne Gretzky, Edm	1985-86	52	163	215
Wayne Gretzky, Edm	1981-82	92	120	212
Wayne Gretzky, Edm	1984-85	73	135	208
Wayne Gretzky, Edm	1983-84	87	118	205
Mario Lemieux, Pit	1988-89	85	114	199
Wayne Gretzky, Edm	1982-83	71	125	196
Wayne Gretzky, Edm	1986-87	62	121	183
Mario Lemieux, Pit	1987-88	70	98	168
Wayne Gretzky, LA	1988-89	54	114	168
Wayne Gretzky, Edm	1980-81	55	109	164
Wayne Gretzky, LA	1990-91	41	122	163
Steve Yzerman, Det	1988-89	65	90	155
Phil Esposito, Bos	1970-71	76	76	152
Bernie Nicholls, LA	1988-89	70	80	150
Phil Esposito, Bos	1973-74	68	77	145

WHA 150 points or more: 154—Marc Tardif, Que. (1977-78).

Goals

	Season	Gm	No
Wayne Gretzky, Edm	1981-82	80	92
Wayne Gretzky, Edm	1983-84	74	87
Brett Hull, St.L	1990-91	78	86
Mario Lemieux, Pit	1988-89	76	85
Phil Esposito, Bos	1970-71	78	76
Wayne Gretzky, Edm	1984-85	80	73
Brett Hull, St.L	1989-90	80	72
Jari Kurri, Edm	1984-85	73	71
Wayne Gretzky, Edm	1982-83	80	71
Mario Lemieux, Pit	1987-88	77	70
Bernie Nicholls, LA	1988-89	79	70
Mike Bossy, NYI	1978-79	80	69
Phil Esposito, Bos	1973-74	78	68
Jari Kurri, Edm	1985-86	78	68
Mike Bossy, NYI	1980-81	79	68
Phil Esposito, Bos	1971-72	76	66
Lanny McDonald, Calg	1982-83	80	66
Steve Yzerman, Det	1988-89	80	65

WHA 65 goals or more: 77—Bobby Hull, Win. (1974-75); **75**—Real Cloutier, Que. (1978-79); **71**—Marc Tardif, Que. (1975-76); **70**—Anders Hedberg, Win. (1976-77); **66**—Real Cloutier, Que. (1976-77); **65**—Marc Tardif, Que. (1977-78) and Morris Lukowich, Win. (1978-79).

Assists

	Season	Gm	No
Wayne Gretzky, Edm	1985-86	80	163
Wayne Gretzky, Edm	1984-85	80	135
Wayne Gretzky, Edm	1982-83	80	125
Wayne Gretzky, LA	1990-91	78	122
Wayne Gretzky, Edm	1986-87	79	121
Wayne Gretzky, Edm	1981-82	80	120
Wayne Gretzky, Edm	1983-84	74	118
Mario Lemieux, Pit	1988-89	76	114
Wayne Gretzky, LA	1988-89	78	114
Wayne Gretzky, Edm	1987-88	64	109
Wayne Gretzky, Edm	1980-81	80	109
Wayne Gretzky, LA	1989-90	73	102
Bobby Orr, Bos	1970-71	78	102
Mario Lemieux, Pit	1987-88	77	98
Mario Lemieux, Pit	1985-86	79	93
Peter Stastny, Que	1981-82	80	93
Adam Oates, St.L	1990-91	61	90
Bobby Orr, Bos	1973-74	74	90
Paul Coffey, Edm	1985-86	79	90
Steve Yzerman, Det	1988-89	80	90

WHA 90 assists or more: 106—Andre Lacroix, S.Diego (1974-75); **94**—Ulf Nilsson, Win. (1974-75).

Goaltending
Wins

	Season	Record
Bernie Parent, Phi	1973-74	47-13-12
Bernie Parent, Phi	1974-75	44-14- 9
Terry Sawchuk, Det	1950-51	44-13-13
Terry Sawchuk, Det	1951-52	44-14-12
Ed Belfour, Chi	1990-91	43-19- 7
Jacques Plante, Mon	1955-56	42-12-10
Jacques Plante, Mon	1961-62	42-14-14
Ken Dryden, Mon	1975-76	42-10- 8

WHA 40 wins or more: 44—Richard Brodeur, Que.(1975-76); **41**—Joe Daley, Win.(1975-76) and Dave Dryden, Edm.(1978-79).

Losses

	Season	Record
Gary Smith, Cal	1970-71	19-48- 4
Al Rollins, Chi	1953-54	12-47- 7
Harry Lumley, Chi.	1951-52	17-44- 9
Harry Lumley, Chi.	1950-51	12-41-10
Eddie Johnston, Bos	1963-64	18-40-12

Most WHA losses in one season: 36—Don McLeod, Van.(1974-75) and Andy Brown, Ind.(1974-75).

Shutouts

	Season	Gm	ShO
George Hainsworth, Mon	1928-29	44	22
Alex Connell, Ottawa	1925-26	36	15
Alex Connell, Ottawa	1927-28	44	15
Hal Winkler, Bos.	1927-28	44	15
Tony Esposito, Chi	1969-70	63	15
George Hainsworth, Mon	1926-27	44	14

Most WHA shutouts in one season: 5—Gerry Cheevers, Cle.(1972-73) and Joe Daly, Win.(1975-76).

Goals Against Average
Before 1950

	Season	Gm	Avg
George Hainsworth, Mon	1928-29	44	0.98
George Hainsworth, Mon	1927-28	44	1.09
Alex Connell, Ottawa	1925-26	36	1.17
Tiny Thompson, Bos	1928-29	44	1.18
Roy Worters, NY Amer.	1928-29	38	1.21

Since 1950

	Season	Gm	Avg
Tony Esposito, Chi	1971-72	48	1.77
Al Rollins, Tor	1950-51	40	1.77
Harry Lumley, Tor.	1953-54	69	1.86
Jacques Plante, Mon.	1955-56	64	1.86
Jacques Plante, Tor.	1970-71	40	1.88

Penalty Minutes

	Season	PMin
Dave Schultz, Phi	1974-75	472
Paul Baxter, Pit	1981-82	409
Dave Schultz, LA	1977-78	405
Basil McRae, Min	1987-88	382
Tim Hunter, Calg	1988-89	375
Steve Durbano, Pit-KC	1975-76	370
Basil McRae, Min	1988-89	365
Tim Hunter, Calg	1986-87	361
Tiger Williams, LA	1986-87	358
Tiger Williams, Tor	1977-78	351
Basil McRae, Min	1989-90	351

WHA 350 minutes or more: 365—Curt Brackenbury, Min-Que.(1975-76); **351**—Kim Clackson, Ind.(1975-76)

SINGLE GAME
Scoring
Points

	Date	G	A	Pts		Date	G	A	Pts
Darryl Sittler, Tor.vs Bos	2/7/76	6	4	10	Wayne Gretzky, Edm. vs NJ.	11/19/83	3	5	8
Maurice Richard, Mon.vs Det.	12/28/44	5	3	8	Wayne Gretzky, Edm.vs Min.	1/4/84	4	4	8
Bert Olmstead, Mon.vs Chi	1/9/54	4	4	8	Paul Coffey, Edm.vs Det	3/14/86	2	6	8
Tom Bladon, Phi.vs Cle	12/11/77	4	4	8	Mario Lemieux, Pit.vs StL	10/15/88	2	6	8
Bryan Trottier, NYI vs NYR	12/23/78	5	3	8	Bernie Nicholls, LA vs Tor	12/1/88	2	6	8
Peter Stastny, Que.at Wash	2/22/81	4	4	8	Mario Lemieux, Pit.vs NJ	12/31/88	5	3	8
Anton Stastny, Que.at Wash	2/22/81	3	5	8					

NHL All-Star Game

The NHL All-Star Game began at the start of the 1947-48 season as an exhibition contest between the defending league champion and a squad of star players from the other five teams. Two All-Star teams played each other in 1951 and '52, but 1953 saw a return to the original format. The game moved to mid-season in 1967, became an East Division vs West Division contest in 1969, and finally a Wales Conference vs Campbell Conference contest in 1975. Winning coaches are listed first.

Campbell-Wales series: Wales (East), 11-4.
Multiple MVP winners: Mario Lemieux (3); Wayne Gretzky, Bobby Hull and Frank Mahovlich (2).

Year		Host	Coaches	Most Valuable Player
1947	All-Stars 4, Toronto 3	Toronto	Dick Irvin, Hap Day	No award
1948	All-Stars 3, Toronto 1	Chicago	Tommy Ivan, Hap Day	No award
1949	All-Stars 3, Toronto 1	Toronto	Tommy Ivan, Hap Day	No award
1950	Detroit 7, All-Stars 1	Detroit	Tommy Ivan, Lynn Patrick	No award
1951	1st Team 2, 2nd Team 2	Toronto	Joe Primeau, Hap Day	No award
1952	1st Team 1, 2nd Team 1	Detroit	Tommy Ivan, Dick Irvin	No award
1953	All-Stars 3, Montreal 1	Montreal	Lynn Patrick, Dick Irvin	No award
1954	All-Stars 2, Detroit 2	Detroit	King Clancy, Jim Skinner	No award
1955	Detroit 3, All-Stars 1	Detroit	Jim Skinner, Dick Irvin	No award
1956	All-Stars 1, Montreal 1	Montreal	Jim Skinner, Toe Blake	No award
1957	All-Stars 5, Montreal 3	Montreal	Milt Schmidt, Toe Blake	No award
1958	Montreal 6, All-Stars 3	Montreal	Toe Blake, Milt Schmidt	No award
1959	Montreal 6, All-Stars 1	Montreal	Toe Blake, Punch Imlach	No award
1960	All-Stars 2, Montreal 1	Montreal	Punch Imlach, Toe Blake	No award
1961	All-Stars 3, Chicago 1	Chicago	Sid Abel, Rudy Pilous	No award
1962	Toronto 4, All-Stars 1	Toronto	Punch Imlach, Rudy Pilous	Eddie Shack, Toronto
1963	All-Stars 3, Toronto 3	Toronto	Sid Abel, Punch Imlach	Frank Mahovlich, Tor.
1964	All-Stars 3, Toronto 2	Toronto	Sid Abel, Punch Imlach	Jean Beliveau, Mont.
1965	All-Stars 5, Montreal 2	Montreal	Billy Reay, Toe Blake	Gordie Howe, Detroit
1966	No Game (see below)			
1967	Montreal 3, All-Stars 0	Montreal	Toe Blake, Sid Abel	Henri Richard, Mont.
1968	Toronto 4, All-Stars 3	Toronto	Punch Imlach, Toe Blake	Bruce Gamble, Tor.
1969	West 3, East 3	Montreal	Scotty Bowman, Toe Blake	Frank Mahovlich, Det.
1970	East 4, West 1	St.Louis	Claude Ruel, Scotty Bowman	Bobby Hull, Chicago
1971	West 2, East 1	Boston	Scotty Bowman, Harry Sinden	Bobby Hull, Chicago
1972	East 3, West 2	Minnesota	Al MacNeil, Billy Reay	Bobby Orr, Boston
1973	East 5, West 4	NY Rangers	Tom Johnson, Billy Reay	Greg Polis, Pit.
1974	West 6, East 4	Chicago	Billy Reay, Scotty Bowman	Garry Unger, St.L.
1975	Wales 7, Campbell 1	Montreal	Bep Guidolin, Fred Shero	Syl Apps,Jr.,Pit.
1976	Wales 7, Campbell 5	Philadelphia	Floyd Smith, Fred Shero	Peter Mahovlich, Mont.
1977	Wales 4, Campbell 3	Vancouver	Scotty Bowman, Fred Shero	Rick Martin, Buffalo
1978	Wales 3, Campbell 2 (OT)	Buffalo	Scotty Bowman, Fred Shero	Billy Smith, NYI
1979	No Game (see below)			
1980	Wales 6, Campbell 3	Detroit	Scotty Bowman, Al Arbour	Reggie Leach, Phila.
1981	Campbell 4, Wales 1	Los Angeles	Pat Quinn, Scotty Bowman	Mike Liut, St.Louis
1982	Wales 4, Campbell 2	Washington	Al Arbour, Glen Sonmor	Mike Bossy, NYI
1983	Campbell 9, Wales 3	NY Islanders	Roger Neilson, Al Arbour	Wayne Gretzky, Edm.
1984	Wales 7, Campbell 6	New Jersey	Al Arbour, Glen Sather	Don Maloney, NYR
1985	Wales 6, Campbell 4	Calgary	Al Arbour, Glen Sather	Mario Lemieux, Pit.
1986	Wales 4, Campbell 3 (OT)	Hartford	Mike Keenan, Glen Sather	Grant Fuhr, Edm.
1987	No Game (see below)			
1988	Wales 6, Campbell 5 (OT)	St.Louis	Mike Keenan, Glen Sather	Mario Lemieux, Pit.
1989	Campbell 9, Wales 5	Edmonton	Glen Sather, Terry O'Reilly	Wayne Gretzky, LA
1990	Wales 12, Campbell 7	Pittsburgh	Pat Burns, Terry Crisp	Mario Lemieux, Pit.
1991	Campbell 11, Wales 5	Chicago	John Muckler, Mike Milbury	Vincent Damphousse, Tor.

No All-Star Game: in 1966 (moved from start of season to mid-season); in 1979 (replaced by Challenge Cup series with USSR); in 1987 (replaced by Rendez-Vous'87 series with USSR). See "International Series" (p.340).

All-Time Winningest NHL Coaches

Top 20 NHL career victories through the 1990-91 season. Career, regular season and playoff records are noted along with NHL titles won. Coaches active during 1990-91 season in **bold** type.

		Career				Regular Season					Playoffs		
	Yrs	W	L	T	Pct	W	L	T	Pct	W	L	T	Pct Stanley Cups
Scotty Bowman	17	853	399	210	.655	739	327	210	.661	114	72	0	.612 5 (1973,76-79)
Dick Irvin	26	790	609	228	.556	690	521	226	.559	100	88	2	.532 4 (1932,44,46,53)
Al Arbour	19	785	542	218	.579	671	469	218	.574	114	73	0	.610 4 (1980-83)
Billy Reay	16	599	445	175	.563	542	385	175	.571	57	60	0	.487 —None—
Toe Blake	13	582	292	159	.640	500	255	159	.634	82	37	0	.689 8 (1956-60, 65-66,68)
Glen Sather	10	531	278	99	.639	442	241	99	.629	89	37	0	.706 4 (1984-85,87-88)
Jack Adams	21	475	449	163	.512	423	397	162	.513	52	52	1	.500 3 (1936-37,43)
Punch Imlach	15	467	421	163	.522	423	373	163	.526	44	48	0	.478 4 (1962-64,67)
Fred Shero	10	451	272	120	.606	390	225	120	.612	61	47	0	.565 2 (1974-75)
Emile Francis	13	433	326	112	.561	393	273	112	.556	40	53	0	.430 —None—
Sid Abel	16	414	470	155	.473	382	426	155	.477	32	44	0	.421 —None—
Bryan Murray	10	404	317	91	.554	377	284	91	.562	27	33	0	.450 —None—
Art Ross	18	395	333	95	.538	368	300	90	.545	27	33	5	.454 1 (1939)
Michel Bergeron ...	10	369	387	104	.490	338	350	104	.492	31	37	0	.456 —None—
Bob Pulford	11	364	348	130	.510	336	305	130	.520	28	43	0	.394 —None—
Mike Keenan	7	360	245	54	.587	307	199	54	.596	53	46	0	.535 —None—
Tommy Ivan	9	324	205	111	.593	288	174	111	.599	36	31	0	.537 3 (1950,52,54)
Bob Berry	9	315	306	100	.506	311	292	100	.514	4	14	0	.222 —None—
Lester Patrick	13	312	242	115	.552	281	216	107	.554	31	26	8	.538 2 (1928,33)
Hap Day	10	308	237	81	.557	259	206	81	.549	49	31	0	.613 5 (1942,45,47-49)

Note: The NHL does not recognize records from the Pacific Coast Hockey Assn.(1912-25), the Western Canada Hockey League (1922-26), or the World Hockey Assn.(1972-79), so the following PCHA, WCHL and WHA overall coaching records are not included above: PCHA & WCHL—**Patrick** (15-year record unavailable, but won 1925 Stanley Cup); WHA—**Sather** (103-97-1 in 3 yrs).

Where They Coached

Abel—Chicago (1952-54), Detroit (1957-68,69-70), St.Louis (1971-72), Kansas City (1975-76); **Adams**—Toronto (1922-23), Detroit (1927-47); **Arbour**—St.Louis (1970-73), NY Islanders (1973-86,88—); **Bergeron**—Quebec (1980-87), NY Rangers (1987-89), Quebec (1989-90); **Berry**—Los Angeles (1978-81), Montreal (1981-84), Pittsburgh (1984-87); **Blake**—Montreal (1955-68); **Bowman**—St.Louis (1967-71), Montreal (1971-79), Buffalo (1979-87); **Day**—Toronto (1940-50); **Francis**—NY Rangers (1965-75), St.Louis (1976-77,81-83). **Imlach**—Toronto (1958-69), Buffalo (1970-72), Toronto (1979-81); **Irvin**—Chicago (1930-31), Toronto (1931-40), Montreal (1940-55); **Ivan**—Detroit (1947-54), Chicago (1956-58); **Keenan**—Philadelphia (1984-88), Chicago (1988—); **Murray**—Washington (1982-90), Detroit (1990—); **Patrick**—NY Rangers (1926-39); **Pulford**—Los Angeles (1972-77), Chicago (1977-79,81-82,85-87); **Reay**—Toronto (1957-59), Chicago (1963-77); **Ross**—Mont.Wanderers (1917-18), Hamilton (1922-23), Boston (1924-28,29-34,36-39,41-45); **Sather**—Edmonton (1979-89); **Shero**—Philadelphia (1971-78), NY Rangers (1978-81).

Top Winning Percentages

Minimum 275 victories, including playoffs.

	Yrs	W	L	T	Pct
Scotty Bowman	17	853	399	210	**.655**
Toe Blake	13	582	292	159	**.640**
Glen Sather	10	531	278	99	**.639**
Fred Shero	10	451	272	120	**.606**
Don Cherry	6	281	177	77	**.597**
Tommy Ivan	9	324	205	111	**.593**
Mike Keenan	7	360	245	54	**.587**
Al Arbour	19	785	542	218	**.579**
Billy Reay	16	599	445	175	**.563**
Emile Francis	13	433	326	112	**.561**
Hap Day	10	308	237	81	**.557**
Dick Irvin	26	790	609	228	**.556**
Bryan Murray	10	404	317	91	**.554**
Lester Patrick	13	312	242	115	**.552**
Bob Johnson	6	276	224	58	**.547**
Art Ross	18	395	333	95	**.538**
Punch Imlach	15	467	421	163	**.522**
Roger Neilson	9	290	261	100	**.522**
Jack Adams	17	465	442	164	**.512**
Bob Pulford	14	364	348	130	**.510**

Active Coaches' Victories

Through 1990-91 season, including playoffs.

	Yrs	W	L	T	Pct
Al Arbour, NYI..............	19	**785**	542	218	.579
Bryan Murray, Det..........	10	**404**	317	91	.554
Mike Keenan, Chi..........	7	**360**	245	54	.587
Roger Neilson, NYR........	9	**290**	261	100	.522
Bob Johnson, Pit	6	**276**	224	58	.547
Pat Quinn, Van	8	**249**	211	75	.536
Pat Burns, Mon	3	**159**	95	31	.612
Tom Watt, Tor	6	**147**	218	55	.415
Brian Sutter, St.L...........	3	**135**	108	32	.549
Paul Holmgren, Phi.........	3	**109**	121	29	.477
Tom McVie, NJ	7	**100**	227	65	.338
Tom Webster, LA	3	**95**	82	19	.533
Rick Dudley, Buf...........	2	**80**	65	27	.544
Terry Murray, Wash.........	2	**68**	63	9	.518
Doug Risebrough, Calg	1	**49**	30	8	.609
Bob Gainey, Min	1	**41**	48	14	.466
Jim Roberts, Hart	1	**21**	15	9	.567
Dave Chambers, Que........	1	**16**	50	14	.288
Rick Bowness, Bos	1	**8**	17	3	.339
Ted Green, Edm	0	**0**	0	0	.000
George Kingston, SJ	0	**0**	0	0	.000
John Paddock, Win	0	**0**	0	0	.000

Annual Awards
Hart Trophy

Awarded to the player "adjudged to be the most valuable to his team" and named after Cecil Hart, the former manager-coach of the Montreal Canadiens. Winners selected by Pro Hockey Writers Assn. (PHWA). Winners' scoring statistics or goaltender W-L records and goals against average are provided; (*) indicates led league in scoring.

Multiple winners: Wayne Gretzky (9); Gordie Howe (6); Eddie Shore (4); Bobby Clarke, Howie Morenz and Bobby Orr (3); Jean Beliveau, Bill Cowley, Phil Esposito, Bobby Hull, Guy Lafleur, Stan Mikita, and Nels Stewart (2).

Year		G	A	Pts	Year		G	A	Pts
1924	Frank Nighbor, Ottawa., C	10	3	13	1960	Gordie Howe, Det., RW	28	45	73
1925	Billy Burch, Hamilton, C	20	4	24	1961	Bernie Geoffrion, Mon., RW	50	45	95*
1926	Nels Stewart, Maroons, C	34	8	42*	1962	Jacques Plante, Mon., G	42-14-14;		2.37*
1927	Herb Gardiner, Mon., D	6	6	12	1963	Gordie Howe, Det., RW	38	48	86*
1928	Howie Morenz, Mon, C	33	18	51*	1964	Jean Beliveau, Mon., C	28	50	78
1929	Roy Worters, NYA, G	16-13-9;		1.21	1965	Bobby Hull, Chi., LW	39	32	71
					1966	Bobby Hull, Chi., LW	54	43	97*
1930	Nels Stewart, Maroons, C	39	16	55	1967	Stan Mikita, Chi., C	35	62	97*
1931	Howie Morenz, Mon., C	28	23	51*	1968	Stan Mikita, Chi., C	40	47	87*
1932	Howie Morenz, Mon., C	24	25	49	1969	Phil Esposito, Bos., C	49	77	126*
1933	Eddie Shore, Bos, D	8	27	35					
1934	Aurel Joliat, Mon., LW	22	15	37	1970	Bobby Orr, Bos., D	33	87	120*
1935	Eddie Shore, Bos., D	7	26	33	1971	Bobby Orr, Bos., D	37	102	139
1936	Eddie Shore, Bos., D	3	16	19	1972	Bobby Orr, Bos., D	37	80	117
1937	Babe Siebert, Mon., D	8	20	28	1973	Bobby Clarke, Phi., C	37	67	104
1938	Eddie Shore, Bos., D	3	14	17	1974	Phil Esposito, Bos., C	68	77	145*
1939	Toe Blake, Mon., LW	24	23	47*	1975	Bobby Clarke, Phi., C	27	89	116
					1976	Bobby Clarke, Phi., C	30	89	119
1940	Ebbie Goodfellow, Det.,D	11	17	28	1977	Guy Lafleur, Mon., RW	56	80	136*
1941	Bill Cowley, Bos., C	17	45	62*	1978	Guy Lafleur, Mon., RW	60	72	132*
1942	Tommy Anderson, NYA, D	12	29	41	1979	Bryan Trottier, NYI., C	47	87	134*
1943	Bill Cowley, Bos, C	27	45	72					
1944	Babe Pratt, Tor., D	17	40	57	1980	Wayne Gretzky, Edm., C	51	86	137
1945	Elmer Lach, Mon., C	26	54	80*	1981	Wayne Gretzky, Edm., C	55	109	164*
1946	Max Bentley, Chi., C	31	30	61*	1982	Wayne Gretzky, Edm., C	92	120	212*
1947	Maurice Richard, Mon., RW	45	26	71	1983	Wayne Gretzky, Edm., C	71	125	196*
1948	Buddy O'Connor, NYR, C	24	36	60	1984	Wayne Gretzky, Edm., C	87	118	205*
1949	Sid Abel, Det., C	28	26	54	1985	Wayne Gretzky, Edm., C	73	135	208*
					1986	Wayne Gretzky, Edm., C	52	163	215*
1950	Chuck Rayner, NYR, G	28-30-11;		2.62	1987	Wayne Gretzky, Edm., C	62	121	183*
1951	Milt Schmidt, Bos., C	22	39	61	1988	Mario Lemieux, Pit., C	70	98	168*
1952	Gordie Howe, Det., RW	47	39	86*	1989	Wayne Gretzky, LA, C	54	114	168
1953	Gordie Howe, Det., RW	49	46	95*					
1954	Al Rollins, Chi., G	12-47-7;		3.23	1990	Mark Messier, Edm., C	45	84	129
1955	Ted Kennedy, Tor., C	10	42	52	1991	Brett Hull, St. L., RW	86	45	131
1956	Jean Beliveau, Mon., C	47	41	88*					
1957	Gordie Howe, Det., RW	44	45	89*					
1958	Gordie Howe, Det., RW	33	44	77					
1959	Andy Bathgate, NRY, RW	40	48	88					

Art Ross Trophy

Given to the player who leads the league in points scored and named after the former Boston Bruins general manager-coach. First presented in 1947, names of prior leading scorers have been added retroactively. A tie for the scoring championship is broken three ways: 1. total goals; 2. fewest games played; 3. first goal scored.

Multiple winners: Wayne Gretzky (9); Gordie Howe (6); Phil Esposito (5); Stan Mikita (4); Guy Lafleur (3); Max Bentley, Charlie Conacher, Bill Cook, Babe Dye, Bernie Geoffrion, Bobby Hull, Elmer Lach, Newsy Lalonde, Mario Lemieux, Joe Malone, Dickie Moore, Howie Morenz, Bobby Orr and Sweeney Schriner (2).

Year		Gm	G	A	Pts	Year		Gm	G	A	Pts
1918	Joe Malone, Mon	20	44	n.a.	44	1934	Charlie Conacher, Tor	42	32	20	52
1919	Newsy Lalonde, Mon	17	23	9	32	1935	Charlie Conacher, Tor	47	36	21	57
						1936	Sweeney Schriner, NYA	48	19	26	45
1920	Joe Malone, Que	24	39	6	45	1937	Sweeney Schriner, NYA	48	21	25	46
1921	Newsy Lalonde, Mon	24	33	8	41	1938	Gordie Drillon, Tor	48	26	26	52
1922	Punch Broadbent, Ott	24	32	14	46	1939	Toe Blake, Mon	48	24	23	47
1923	Babe Dye, Tor	22	26	11	37						
1924	Cy Denneny, Ott	21	22	1	23	1940	Milt Schmidt, Bos	48	22	30	52
1925	Babe Dye, Tor	29	38	6	44	1941	Bill Cowley, Bos	46	17	45	62
1926	Nels Stewart, Maroons	36	34	8	42	1942	Bryan Hextall, NYR	48	24	32	56
1927	Bill Cook, NYR	44	33	4	37	1943	Doug Bentley, Chi	50	33	40	73
1928	Howie Morenz, Mon	43	33	18	51	1944	Herbie Cain, Bos	48	36	46	82
1929	Ace Bailey, Tor	44	22	10	32	1945	Elmer Lach, Mon	50	26	54	80
						1946	Max Bentley, Chi	47	31	30	61
1930	Cooney Weiland, Bos	44	43	30	73	1947	Max Bentley, Chi	60	29	43	72
1931	Howie Morenz, Mon	39	28	23	51	1948	Elmer Lach, Mon	60	30	31	61
1932	Busher Jackson, Tor	48	28	25	53	1949	Roy Conacher, Chi	60	26	42	68
1933	Bill Cook, NYR	48	28	22	50						

Annual Awards (Cont.)
Art Ross Trophy

Year		Gm	G	A	Pts	Year		Gm	G	A	Pts
1950	Ted Lindsay, Det	69	23	55	78	1971	Phil Esposito, Bos	78	76	76	152
1951	Gordie Howe, Det	70	43	43	86	1972	Phil Esposito, Bos	76	66	67	133
1952	Gordie Howe, Det	70	47	39	86	1973	Phil Esposito, Bos	78	55	75	130
1953	Gordie Howe, Det	70	49	46	95	1974	Phil Esposito, Bos	78	68	77	145
1954	Gordie Howe, Det	70	33	48	81	1975	Bobby Orr, Bos	80	46	89	135
1955	Bernie Geoffrion, Mon	70	38	37	75	1976	Guy Lafleur, Mon	80	56	69	125
1956	Jean Beliveau, Mon	70	47	41	88	1977	Guy Lafleur, Mon	80	56	80	136
1957	Gordie Howe, Det	70	44	45	89	1978	Guy Lafleur, Mon	79	60	72	132
1958	Dickie Moore, Mon	70	36	48	84	1979	Bryan Trottier, NYI	76	47	87	134
1959	Dickie Moore, Mon	70	41	55	96						
						1980	Marcel Dionne, LA*	80	53	84	137
1960	Bobby Hull, Chi	70	39	42	81	1981	Wayne Gretzky, Edm	80	55	109	164
1961	Bernie Geoffrion, Mon	64	50	45	95	1982	Wayne Gretzky, Edm	80	92	120	212
1962	Bobby Hull, Chi.*	70	50	34	84	1983	Wayne Gretzky, Edm	80	71	125	196
1963	Gordie Howe, Det	70	38	48	86	1984	Wayne Gretzky, Edm	74	87	118	205
1964	Stan Mikita, Chi	70	39	50	89	1985	Wayne Gretzky, Edm	80	73	135	208
1965	Stan Mikita, Chi	70	28	59	87	1986	Wayne Gretzky, Edm	80	52	163	215
1966	Bobby Hull, Chi	65	54	43	97	1987	Wayne Gretzky, Edm	79	62	121	183
1967	Stan Mikita, Chi	70	35	62	97	1988	Mario Lemieux, Pit	77	70	98	168
1968	Stan Mikita, Chi	72	40	47	87	1989	Mario Lemieux, Pit	76	85	114	199
1969	Phil Esposito, Bos	74	49	77	126						
1970	Bobby Orr, Bos	76	33	87	120	1990	Wayne Gretzky, LA	73	40	102	142
						1991	Wayne Gretzky, LA	78	41	122	163

*Note: The two times players have tied for total points in one season the player with more goals has won the trophy. In 1961-62, Hull outscored Andy Bathgate of NY Rangers, 50 goals to 28. In 1979-80, Dionne outscored Wayne Gretzky of Edmonton, 53-51.

Vezina Trophy

From 1926-80, given to the principal goaltender(s) on the team allowing the fewest goals during the regular season and named after 1920's goalie Georges Vezina of the Montreal Canadiens, who died of tuberculosis in 1926.

Since the 1980-81 season, the trophy has been awarded to the most outstanding goaltender of the year as selected by the league's general managers.

Multiple winners: Jacques Plante (7, one of them shared); Bill Durnan (6); Ken Dryden (5, three shared); Bunny Larocque (4, all shared); Tiny Thompson (4); Terry Sawchuk (4, one shared); Tony Esposito (3, one shared); George Hainsworth (3); Glenn Hall (3, two shared); Frank Brimsek (2); Turk Broda (2); Johnny Bower (2, one shared); Chuck Gardiner (2); Charlie Hodge (2, one shared); Bernie Parent (2); Patrick Roy (2); Gump Worsley (2, both shared).

Year		Record	Avg	Year		Record	Avg
1927	George Hainsworth, Mon	28-14-2	1.52	1957	Jacques Plante, Mon	31-18-12	2.02
1928	George Hainsworth, Mon	26-11-7	1.09	1958	Jacques Plante, Mon	34-14-8	2.11
1929	George Hainsworth, Mon	22-7-15	0.98	1959	Jacques Plante, Mon	38-16-13	2.18
1930	Tiny Thompson, Bos	38-5-1	2.23	1960	Jacques Plante, Mon	40-17-12	2.54
1931	Roy Worters, NYA	18-16-10	1.68	1961	Johnny Bower, Tor	33-15-10	2.50
1932	Chuck Gardiner, Chi	18-19-11	2.10	1962	Jacques Plante, Mon	42-14-14	2.37
1933	Tiny Thompson, Bos	25-15-8	1.83	1963	Glenn Hall, Chi	30-20-16	2.51
1934	Chuck Gardiner, Chi	20-17-11	1.73	1964	Charlie Hodge, Mon	33-18-11	2.26
1935	Lorne Chabot, Chi	26-17-5	1.83	1965	Johnny Bower, Tor	13-13-8	2.38
1936	Tiny Thompson, Bos	22-20-6	1.73		& Terry Sawchuk, Tor	17-13-6	2.56
1937	Norm Smith, Det	25-14-9	2.13	1966	Gump Worsley, Mon	29-14-6	2.36
1938	Tiny Thompson, Bos	30-11-7	1.85		& Charlie Hodge, Mon	12-7-2	2.58
1939	Frank Brimsek, Bos	33-9-1	1.59	1967	Glenn Hall, Chi	19-5-5	2.38
					& Denis Dejordy, Chi	22-12-7	2.46
1940	Dave Kerr, NYR	27-11-10	1.60	1968	Gump Worsley, Mon	19-9-8	1.98
1941	Turk Broda, Tor	28-14-6	2.06		& Rogie Vachon, Mon	23-13-2	2.48
1942	Frank Brimsek, Bos	24-17-6	2.44	1969	Jacques Plante, St.L	18-12-6	1.96
1943	Johnny Mowers, Det	25-14-11	2.48		& Glenn Hall, St.L	19-12-8	2.17
1944	Bill Durnan, Mon	38-5-7	2.18				
1945	Bill Durnan, Mon	38-8-4	2.42	1970	Tony Esposito, Chi	38-17-8	2.17
1946	Bill Durnan, Mon	24-11-5	2.60	1971	Ed Giacomin, NYR	27-10-7	2.16
1947	Bill Durnan, Mon	34-16-10	2.30		& Gilles Villemure, NYR	22-8-4	2.30
1948	Turk Broda, Tor	32-15-13	2.38	1972	Tony Esposito, Chi	31-10-6	1.77
1949	Bill Durnan, Mon	28-23-9	2.10		& Gary Smith, Chi	14-5-6	2.42
				1973	Ken Dryden, Mon	33-7-13	2.26
1950	Bill Durnan, Mon	26-21-17	2.20	1974	(Tie) Bernie Parent, Phi	47-13-12	1.89
1951	Al Rollins, Tor	27-5-8	1.75		Tony Esposito, Chi	34-14-21	2.04
1952	Terry Sawchuk, Det	44-14-12	1.90	1975	Bernie Parent, Phi	44-14-10	2.03
1953	Terry Sawchuk, Det	32-15-16	1.90	1976	Ken Dryden, Mon	42-10-8	2.03
1954	Harry Lumley, Tor	32-24-13	1.85	1977	Ken Dryden, Mon	41-6-8	2.14
1955	Terry Sawchuk, Det	40-17-11	1.94		& Bunny Larocque, Mon	19-2-4	2.09
1956	Jacques Plante, Mon	42-12-10	1.86				

Year	Record	Avg	Year	Record	Avg
1978 Ken Dryden, Mon.	37-7-7	2.05	1983 Pete Peeters, Bos	40-11-9	2.36
& Bunny Larocque	22-3-4	2.67	1984 Tom Barrasso, Buf.	26-12-3	2.84
1979 Ken Dryden, Mon	30-10-7	2.30	1985 Pelle Lindbergh, Phi.	40-17-7	3.02
& Bunny Larocque	22-7-4	2.84	1986 John Vanbiesbrouck, NYR.	31-21-5	3.32
1980 Bob Sauve, Buf.	20-8-4	2.36	1987 Ron Hextall, Phi	37-21-6	3.00
& Don Edwards	27-9-12	2.57	1988 Grant Fuhr, Edm	40-24-9	3.43
1981 Richard Sevigny, Mon	20-4-3	2.40	1989 Patrick Roy, Mon	33-5-6	2.47
Denis Herron, Mon	6-9-6	3.50			
& Bunny Larocque	16-9-3	3.03	1990 Patrick Roy, Mon	31-16-5	2.53
1982 Billy Smith, NYI.	32-9-4	2.97	1991 Ed Belfour, Chi.	43-19-7	2.47

Norris Memorial Trophy

Awarded to the most outstanding defenseman of the year and named after James Norris, the late Detroit Red Wings owner-president. Winners selected by PHWA.

Multiple winners: Bobby Orr (8); Doug Harvey (7); Ray Bourque (4); Pierre Pilote and Denis Potvin (3); Paul Coffey, Rod Langway and Larry Robinson (2).

Year		Year		Year	
1954	Red Kelly, Detroit	1967	Harry Howell, NY Rangers	1980	Larry Robinson, Montreal
1955	Doug Harvey, Montreal	1968	Bobby Orr, Boston	1981	Randy Carlyle, Pittsburgh
1956	Doug Harvey, Montreal	1969	Bobby Orr, Boston	1982	Doug Wilson, Chicago
1957	Doug Harvey, Montreal	1970	Bobby Orr, Boston	1983	Rod Langway, Washington
1958	Doug Harvey, Montreal	1971	Bobby Orr, Boston	1984	Rod Langway, Washington
1959	Tom Johnson, Montreal	1972	Bobby Orr, Boston	1985	Paul Coffey, Edmonton
1960	Doug Harvey, Montreal	1973	Bobby Orr, Boston	1986	Paul Coffey, Edmonton
1961	Doug Harvey, Montreal	1974	Bobby Orr, Boston	1987	Ray Bourque, Boston
1962	Doug Harvey, NY Rangers	1975	Bobby Orr, Boston	1988	Ray Bourque, Boston
1963	Pierre Pilote, Chicago	1976	Denis Potvin, NY Islanders	1989	Chris Chelios, Montreal
1964	Pierre Pilote, Chicago	1977	Larry Robinson, Montreal		
1965	Pierre Pilote, Chicago	1978	Denis Potvin, NY Islanders	1990	Ray Bourque, Boston
1966	Jacques Laperriere, Mon.	1979	Denis Potvin, NY Islanders	1991	Ray Bourque, Boston

Calder Memorial Trophy

Awarded to the most outstanding rookie of the year and named after Frank Calder, the late NHL president (1917-43). Winners selected by PHWA. Winners' scoring statistics or goaltender W-L record & goals against average are provided.

Year		G	A	Pts	Year		G	A	Pts
1933	Carl Voss, NYR-Det., C	8	15	23	1963	Kent Douglas, Tor., D	7	15	22
1934	Russ Blinco, M.Maroons, C	14	9	23	1964	Jacques Laperriere, Mon., D	2	28	30
1935	Sweeney Schriner, NYA., LW	18	22	40	1965	Roger Crozier, Det., G	40-23-7;		2.42
1936	Mike Karakas, Chi., G	21-19-8;		1.92	1966	Brit Selby, Tor., LW	14	13	27
1937	Syl Apps, Tor., C	16	29	45	1967	Bobby Orr, Bos., D	13	28	41
1938	Cully Dahlstrom, Chi., C	10	9	19	1968	Derek Sanderson, Bos., C	24	25	49
1939	Frank Brimsek, Bos, G	33-9-1;		1.58	1969	Danny Grant, Min., LW	34	31	65
1940	Kilby MacDonald, NYR, LW	15	13	28	1970	Tony Esposito, Chi., G	38-17-8;		2.17
1941	John Quilty, Mon., C	18	16	34	1971	Gilbert Perreault, Buf., C	38	34	72
1942	Knobby Warwick, NYR, RW	16	17	33	1972	Ken Dryden, Mon., G	39-8-15;		2.24
1943	Gaye Stewart, Tor., LW	24	23	47	1973	Steve Vickers, NYR, LW	30	23	53
1944	Gus Bodnar, Tor., C	22	40	62	1974	Denis Potvin, NYI, D	17	37	54
1945	Frank McCool, Tor., G	24-22-2;		3.22	1975	Eric Vail, Atl., LW	39	21	60
1946	Edgar Laprade, NYR, C	15	19	34	1976	Bryan Trottier, NYI, C	32	63	95
1947	Howie Meeker, Tor., RW	27	18	45	1977	Willi Plett, Atl., RW	33	23	56
1948	Jim McFadden, Det., C	24	24	48	1978	Mike Bossy, NYI, RW	53	38	91
1949	Penny Lund, NYR, RW	14	16	30	1979	Bobby Smith, Min., C	30	44	74
1950	Jack Gelineau, Bos., G	22-30-15;		3.28	1980	Ray Bourque, Bos., D	17	48	65
1951	Terry Sawchuck, Det., G	44-13-13;		1.99	1981	Peter Stastny, Que., C	39	70	109
1952	Bernie Geoffrion, Mon., RW	30	24	54	1982	Dale Hawerchuk, Win., C	45	58	103
1953	Gump Worsley, NYR, G	13-29-13;		3.06	1983	Steve Larmer, Chi., RW	43	47	90
1954	Camille Henry, NYR, LW	24	15	39	1984	Tom Barrasso, Buf., G	26-12-3;		2.84
1955	Ed Litzenberger, Mon-Chi., RW	24	40	64	1985	Mario Lemieux, Pit., C	43	57	100
1956	Glenn Hall, Det., G	30-24-16;		2.11	1986	Gary Suter, Calg., D	18	50	68
1957	Larry Regan, Bos., RW	14	19	33	1987	Luc Robitaille, LA, LW	45	39	84
1958	Frank Mahovlich, Tor., LW	20	16	36	1988	Joe Nieuwendyk, Calg., C	51	41	92
1959	Ralph Backstrom, Mon., C	18	22	40	1989	Brian Leetch, NYR, D	23	48	71
1960	Billy Hay, Chi., C	18	37	55	1990	Sergei Makarov, Calg., RW	24	62	86
1961	Dave Keon, Tor., C	20	25	45	1991	Ed Belfour, Chi., G	43-19-7;		2.47
1962	Bobby Rousseau, Mon., RW	21	24	45					

Annual Awards (Cont.)
Lady Byng Memorial Trophy

Awarded to the player "adjudged to have exhibited the best type of sportsmanship and gentlemanly conduct combined with a high standard of playing ability" and named after the wife of former Canadian Governor General (1921-26) Baron Byng of Vinny. Winners selected by PHWA.

Multiple winners: Frank Boucher (7); Red Kelly (4); Bobby Bauer, Mike Bossy and Alex Delvecchio (3); Johnny Bucyk, Marcel Dionne, Wayne Gretzky, Dave Keon, Stan Mikita, Joey Mullen, Frank Nighbor, Jean Ratelle, Clint Smith and Sid Smith (2).

Year		Year		Year	
1925	Frank Nighbor, Ott., C	1948	Buddy O'Connor, NYR, C	1970	Phil Goyette, St.L., C
1926	Frank Nighbor, Ott., C	1949	Bill Quackenbush, Det., D	1971	Johnny Bucyk, Bos., LW
1927	Billy Burch, NYA, C			1972	Jean Ratelle, NYR, C
1928	Frank Boucher, NYR, C	1950	Edgar Laprade, NYR,	1973	Gilbert Perreault, Buf., C
1929	Frank Boucher, NYR, C	1951	Red Kelly, Det., D	1974	Johnny Bucyk, Bos., LW
		1952	Sid Smith, Tor., LW	1975	Marcel Dionne, Det., C
1930	Frank Boucher, NYR, C	1953	Red Kelly, Det., D	1976	Jean Ratelle, NY-Bos., C
1931	Frank Boucher, NYR, C	1954	Red Kelly, Det., D	1977	Marcel Dionne, LA, C
1932	Joe Primeau, Tor., C	1955	Sid Smith, Tor., LW	1978	Butch Goring, LA, C
1933	Frank Boucher, NYR, C	1956	Earl Reibel, Det., C	1979	Bob MacMillan, Atl., RW
1934	Frank Boucher, NYR, C	1957	Andy Hebenton, NYR, RW		
1935	Frank Boucher, NYR, C	1958	Camille Henry, NYR, LW	1980	Wayne Gretzky, Edm., C
1936	Doc Romnes, Chi., F	1959	Alex Delvecchio, Det., LW	1981	Rick Kehoe, Pit., RW
1937	Marty Barry, Det., C			1982	Rick Middleton, Bos., RW
1938	Gordie Drillon, Tor., RW	1960	Don McKenney, Bos., C	1983	Mike Bossy, NYI, RW
1939	Clint Smith, NYR, C	1961	Red Kelly, Tor., D	1984	Mike Bossy, NYI, RW
		1962	Dave Keon, Tor., C	1985	Jari Kurri, Edm., RW
1940	Bobby Bauer, Bos., RW	1963	Dave Keon, Tor., C	1986	Mike Bossy, NYI, RW
1941	Bobby Bauer, Bos., RW	1964	Ken Wharram, Chi., RW	1987	Joey Mullen, Calg., C
1942	Syl Apps, Tor., C	1965	Bobby Hull, Chi., LW	1988	Mats Naslund, Mon., LW
1943	Max Bentley, Chi., C	1966	Alex Delvecchio, Det., LW	1989	Joey Mullen, Calg., RW
1944	Clint Smith, Chi., C	1967	Stan Mikita, Chi., C		
1945	Bill Mosienko, Chi., RW	1968	Stan Mikita, Chi., C	1990	Brett Hull, St.L., RW
1946	Toe Blake, Mon., LW	1969	Alex Delvecchio, Det., LW	1991	Wayne Gretzky, LA, C
1947	Bobby Bauer, Bos., RW				

Note: Quackenbush and Kelly are the only defensemen to win the Lady Byng.

Lester Pearson Award

Awarded to the season's most outstanding player and named after the former diplomat, Nobel Peace Prize winner and Canadian prime minister. Winners selected by the NHL Players Assn.

Multiple winners: Wayne Gretzky (5); Guy Lafleur (3); Marcel Dionne, Phil Esposito and Mario Lemieux (2).

Year		Year		Year	
1971	Phil Esposito, Bos., C	1979	Marcel Dionne, LA, C	1986	Mario Lemieux, Pit., C
1972	Jean Ratelle, NY R, C			1987	Wayne Gretzky, Edm., C
1973	Phil Esposito, Bos., C	1980	Marcel Dionne, LA, C	1988	Mario Lemieux, Pit., C
1974	Bobby Clarke, Phila., C	1981	Mike Liut, St. L., G	1989	Steve Yzerman, Det., C
1975	Bobby Orr, Bos., D	1982	Wayne Gretzky, Edm., C		
1976	Guy Lafleur, Mon., RW	1983	Wayne Gretzky, Edm., C	1990	Mark Messier, Edm., C
1977	Guy Lafleur, Mon., RW	1984	Wayne Gretzky, Edm., C	1991	Brett Hull, St. L., RW
1978	Guy Lafleur, Mon., RW	1985	Wayne Gretzky, Edm., C		

Jack Adams Award

Awarded to the coach "adjudged to have contributed the most to his team's success" and named after the late Detroit Red Wings coach and general manager. Winners selected by NHL Broadcasters' Assn.; (*) indicates division champion.

Multiple winner: Jacques Demers (2).

Year		Improvement			Year		Improvement		
1974	Fred Shero, Phi	37-30-11	to	50-16-12*	1983	Orval Tessier, Chi	30-38-12	to	47-23-10*
1975	Bob Pulford, Chi	41-14-23	to	37-35- 8	1984	Bryan Murray, Wash	39-25-16	to	48-27- 5
1976	Don Cherry, Bos	40-26-14	to	48-15-17*	1985	Mike Keenan, Phi	44-26-10	to	53-20- 7*
1977	Scotty Bowman, Mon	58-11-11*	to	60- 8-12*	1986	Glen Sather, Edm	49-20-11*	to	56-17- 7*
1978	Bobby Kromm, Det	16-55- 9	to	32-34-14	1987	Jacques Demers, Det	17-57- 6	to	34-36-10
1979	Al Arbour, NYI	48-17-15*	to	51-15-14*	1988	Jacques Demers, Det	34-36-10	to	41-28-11*
					1989	Pat Burns, Mon	45-22-13	to	53-18- 9*
1980	Pat Quinn, Phi	40-25-15	to	48-12-20*	1990	Bob Murdoch, Win	26-42-12	to	37-32-11
1981	Red Berenson, StL	34-34-12	to	45-18-17*	1991	Brian Sutter, St. L	37-34-9	to	47-22-11
1982	Tom Watt, Win	9-57-14	to	33-33-14					

World Hockey Association, 1973–79
WHA Finals

The World Hockey Association began play in 1972-73 as a 12-team rival of the 56-year-old NHL. The WHA played for the Avco World Trophy in its seven playoff finals (Avco Financial Services underwrote the playoffs).

Year	Winner	Head Coach	Series	Loser	Head Coach
1973	NE Whalers	Jack Kelley	4-1 (WWLWW)	Winnipeg Jets	Bobby Hull
1974	Houston Aeros	Bill Dineen	4-0	Chicago Cougars	Pat Stapleton
1975	Houston Aeros	Bill Dineen	4-0	Que.Nordiques	Jean-Guy Gendron
1976	Winnipeg Jets	Bobby Kromm	4-0	Houston Aeros	Bill Dineen
1977	Quebec Nordiques	Marc Boileau	4-3 (LWLWWLW)	Winnipeg Jets	Bobby Kromm
1978	Winnipeg Jets	Larry Hillman	4-0	NE Whalers	Harry Neale
1979	Winnipeg Jets	Larry Hillman	4-2 (WWLWLW)	Edmonton Oilers	Glen Sather

Playoff MVPs, 1973–79

1973—No award; **1974**—No award; **1975**—Ron Grahame, Houston, G; **1976**—Ulf Nilsson, Winnipeg, C; **1977**—Serg Bernier, Quebec, C; **1978**—Bobby Guindon, Winnipeg, C; **1979**—Rich Preston, Winnipeg, RW.

Annual Awards

Most Valuable Player
(Gordie Howe Trophy, 1976-79)

Year		G	A	Pts
1973	Bobby Hull, Win., LW	51	52	103
1974	Gordie Howe, Hou., RW	31	69	100
1975	Bobby Hull, Win., LW	77	65	142
1976	Marc Tardif, Que., LW	71	77	148
1977	Robbie Ftorek, Pho., C	46	71	117
1978	Marc Tardif, Que., LW	65	89	154
1979	Dave Dryden, Edm., G	41-17-2;		2.89

Scoring Leaders

Year		Gm	G	A	Pts
1973	Andre Lacroix, Phi	78	50	74	124
1974	Mike Walton, Min	78	57	60	117
1975	Andre Lacroix, S.Diego	78	41	106	147
1976	Marc Tardif, Que.	81	71	77	148
1977	Real Cloutier, Que.	76	66	75	141
1978	Marc Tardif, Que.	78	65	89	154
1979	Real Cloutier, Que.	77	75	54	129

Note: In 1979, 18 year-old Rookie of the Year Wayne Gretzky finished third in scoring (46-64—110).

Rookie of the Year

Year		G	A	Pts
1973	Terry Caffery, N.Eng., C	39	41	100
1974	Mark Howe, Hou., LW	38	41	79
1975	Anders Hedberg, Win., RW	53	47	100
1976	Mark Napier, Tor., RW	43	50	93
1977	George Lyle, N.Eng., LW	39	33	72
1978	Kent Nilsson, Win., C	42	65	107
1979	Wayne Gretzky, Edm., C	46	64	110

Best Goaltender

Year		Record	Avg
1973	Gerry Cheevers, Cle	32-20-0	2.84
1974	Don MacLeod, Hou	33-13-3	2.56
1975	Ron Grahame, Hou.	33-10-0	3.03
1976	Michel Dion, Indy.	14-15-1	2.74
1977	Ron Grahame, Hou.	27-10-2	2.74
1978	Al Smith, N.Eng	30-20-3	3.22
1979	Dave Dryden, Edm	41-17-2	2.89

Best Defenseman

Year	
1973	J.C.Tremblay, Quebec
1974	Pat Stapleton, Chicago
1975	J.C.Tremblay, Quebec
1976	Paul Shmyr, Cleveland
1977	Ron Plumb, Cincinnati
1978	Lars-Erik Sjoberg, Winnipeg
1979	Rick Ley, New England

Coach of the Year

Year		Improvement	
1973	Jack Kelley, N.Eng		46-30-2*
1974	Billy Harris, Tor.	35-39-4 to	41-33-4
1975	Sandy Hucul, Pho	Expan. to	39-31-8
1976	Bobby Kromm, Win	38-35-5 to	52-27-2*
1977	Bill Dineen, Hou.	53-27-0* to	50-24-6*
1978	Bill Dineen, Hou.	50-24-6* to	42-34-4
1979	John Brophy, Birm	36-41-3 to	32-42-6

*Won Division.

WHA All-Star Game

The WHA All-Star Game was an Eastern Division vs Western Division contest from 1973-75. In 1976, the league's five Canadian-based teams played the nine teams in the US. Over the final three seasons—East played West in 1977; AVCO Cup champion Quebec played a WHA All-Star team in 1978; and in 1979, a full WHA All-Star team played a three-game series with Moscow Dynamo of the Soviet Union.

Year	Result	Host	Coaches	Most Valuable Player
1973	East 6, West 2	Quebec	Jack Kelley, Bobby Hull	Wayne Carleton, Ottawa
1974	East 8, West 4	St.Paul,MN	Jack Kelley, Bobby Hull	Mike Walton, Minnesota
1975	West 6, East 4	Edmonton	Bill Dineen, Ron Ryan	Rejean Houle, Quebec
1976	Canada 6, USA 1	Cleveland	Jean-Guy Gendron, Bill Dineen	Can—Real Cloutier, Que. USA—Paul Shmyr, Cleve.
1977	East 4, West 2	Hartford	Jacques Demers, Bobby Kromm	East—L.Levasseur, Min. West—W.Lindstrom, Win.
1978	Quebec 5, WHA 4	Quebec	Marc Boileau, Bill Dineen	Quebec—Marc Tardif WHA—Mark Howe, NE
1979	WHA 4, Moscow Dynamo 2	Edmonton	Larry Hillman, P.Iburtovich	No awards
	WHA 4, Moscow Dynamo 2	Edmonton		
	WHA 4, Moscow Dynamo 3	Edmonton		

International Hockey
World Championships

The World Hockey Championship tournament has been held during non-Olympic years since 1930. The International Ice Hockey Federation, which governs both the Olympic and World tourneys, considers Olympic champions from 1920-68 to be world champions as well. The IIHF sanctioned separate world championships in 1972 and 1976, but has not arranged one since. The IIHF does not recognize Olympic champions since 1980 as world champions.

Multiple winners: Soviet Union (22), Canada (19), Czechoslovakia (6), Sweden (5), USA (2). There were no tournaments during World War II (1940-45) and 1946.

Year	Winner	Year	Winner	Year	Winner	Year	Winner
1920	Canada	1948	Canada				
1924	Canada	1949	Czechoslovakia	1962	Sweden	1977	Czechoslovakia
1928	Canada			1963	Soviet Union	1978	Soviet Union
		1950	Canada	1964	Soviet Union	1979	Soviet Union
1930	Canada	1951	Canada	1965	Soviet Union		
1931	Canada	1952	Canada	1966	Soviet Union	1980	Not held
1932	Canada	1953	Sweden	1967	Soviet Union	1981	Soviet Union
1933	United States	1954	Soviet Union	1968	Soviet Union	1982	Soviet Union
1934	Canada	1955	Canada	1969	Soviet Union	1983	Soviet Union
1935	Canada	1956	Soviet Union			1984	Not held
1936	Great Britain	1957	Sweden	1970	Soviet Union	1985	Czechoslovakia
1937	Canada	1958	Canada	1971	Soviet Union	1986	Soviet Union
1938	Canada	1959	Canada	1972	Czechoslovakia	1987	Sweden
1939	Canada			1973	Soviet Union	1988	Not held
		1960	United States	1974	Soviet Union	1989	Soviet Union
1940-46	Not held	1961	Canada	1975	Soviet Union		
1947	Czechoslovakia			1976	Czechoslovakia	1990	Soviet Union
						1991	Sweden

Canada vs USSR Summits

The first competition between the Soviet National Team and the NHL took place Sept.2-28, 1972. A team of NHL All-Stars emerged as the winner of the heralded 8-game series, but just barely—winning with a record of 4-3-1 after trailing 1-3-1.

Two years later a WHA All-Star team played the Soviet Nationals and could win only one game and tie three others in eight contests. Two other Canada vs USSR series took place during NHL All-Star breaks: the three-game Challenge Cup at New York in 1979, and the two-game Rendez-Vous '87 in Quebec City in 1987.

The NHL All-Stars played the USSR in a three-game Challenge Cup series in 1979.

1972 Team Canada vs USSR
NHL All-Stars vs Soviet National Team.

Date	City	Result	Goaltenders
9/2	Montreal	USSR, 7-3	Tretiak/Dryden
9/4	Toronto	Canada, 4-1	Esposito/Tretiak
9/6	Winnipeg	Tie, 4-4	Tretiak/Esposito
9/8	Vancouver	USSR, 5-4	Tretiak/Dryden
9/22	Moscow	USSR, 5-4	Tretiak/Esposito
9/24	Moscow	Canada, 3-2	Dryden/Tretiak
9/26	Moscow	Canada, 4-3	Esposito/Tretiak
9/28	Moscow	Canada, 6-5	Dryden/Tretiak

Standings

	W	L	T	Pts	GF	GA
Team Canada (NHL)	4	3	1	9	32	32
Soviet Union	3	4	1	7	32	32

Leading Scorers
1. Phil Esposito, Canada, (7-6—13); **2.** Aleksandr Yakushev, USSR (7-4—11); **3.** Paul Henderson, Canada (7-2—9); **4.** Boris Shadrin, USSR (3-5—8); **5.** Valeri Kharlamov, USSR (3-4—7) and Vladimir Petrov, USSR (3-4—7); **7.** Bobby Clarke, Canada (2-4—6).

1974 Team Canada vs USSR
WHA All-Stars vs Soviet National Team.

Date	City	Result	Goaltenders
9/17	Quebec	Tie, 3-3	Tretiak/Cheevers
9/19	Toronto	Canada, 4-1	Cheevers/Tretiak
9/21	Winnipeg	USSR, 8-5	Tretiak/McLeod
9/23	Vancouver	Tie, 5-5	Tretiak/Cheevers
10/1	Moscow	USSR, 3-2	Tretiak/Cheevers
10/3	Moscow	USSR, 5-2	Tretiak/Cheevers
10/5	Moscow	Tie, 4-4	Cheevers/Tretiak
10/6	Moscow	USSR, 3-2	Sdn'kov/Cheevers

Standings

	W	L	T	Pts	GF	GA
Soviet Union	4	1	3	11	32	27
Team Canada (WHA)	1	4	3	5	27	32

Leading Scorers
1. Bobby Hull, Canada (7-2—9); **2.** Aleksandr Yakushev, USSR (6-2—8), Ralph Backstrom, Canada (4-4—8) and Valeri Kharlamov, USSR (2-6—8); **5.** Gordie Howe, Canada (3-4—7), Andre Lacroix, Canada (1-6—7) and Vladimir Petrov, USSR (1-6—7).

1979 Challenge Cup Series
NHL All-Stars vs Soviet National Team

Date	City	Result	Goaltenders
2/8	New York	NHL, 4-2	K.Dryden/Tretiak
2/10	New York	USSR, 5-4	Tretiak/K.Dryden
2/11	New York	USSR, 6-0	Myshkin/Cheevers

Rendez-Vous '87
NHL All-Stars vs Soviet National Team

Date	City	Result	Goaltenders
2/11	Quebec	NHL, 4-3	Fuhr/Belosheykhin
2/13	Quebec	USSR, 5-3	Belosheykhin/Fuhr

The Canada Cup

After organizing the historic 8-game Team Canada-Soviet Union series of 1972, NHL Players Association executive director Alan Eagleson and the NHL created the Canada Cup in 1976. For the first time, the best players from the world's six major hockey powers—Canada, Czechoslovakia, Finland, Russia, Sweden and the USA competed together in one tournament.

1976

Round Robin Standings

	W	L	T	Pts	GF	GA
Canada	4	1	0	8	22	6
Czechoslovakia	3	1	1	7	19	9
Soviet Union	2	2	1	5	23	14
Sweden	2	2	1	5	16	18
United States	1	3	1	3	14	21
Finland	1	4	0	2	16	42

Finals (Best of 3 Games)

Date	City	Score
9/13	Toronto	Canada 6, Czechoslovakia 0
9/15	Montreal	Canada 5, Czechoslovakia 4 (OT)

Note: Darryl Sittler scored the winning goal for Canada at 11:33 in overtime to clinch the Cup, 2 games to none.

Team MVPs

Canada—Rogie Vachon
Czech.—Milan Novy
USSR—Alexandr Maltsev
Sweden—Borje Salming
USA—Robbie Ftorek
Finland—Matti Hagman

Tournament MVP—Bobby Orr, Canada

1981

Round Robin Standings

	W	L	T	Pts	GF	GA
Canada	4	0	1	9	32	13
Soviet Union	3	1	1	7	20	13
Czechoslovakia	2	1	2	6	21	13
United States	2	2	1	5	17	19
Sweden	1	4	0	2	13	20
Finland	0	4	1	1	6	31

Semifinals

Date	City	Score
9/11	Ottawa	USSR 4, Czechoslovakia 1
9/15	Montreal	Canada 4, United States 1

Finals

Date	City	Score
9/13	Montreal	USSR 8, Canada 1

Leading Scorers

1. Wayne Gretzky, Canada (5-7—12); 2. Mike Bossy, Canada (8-3—11), Bryan Trottier, Canada (3-8--11), Guy Lafleur, Canada (2-9—11), Alexei Kasatonov, USSR (1-10—11).

All-Star Team

Goal—Vladislav Tretiak, USSR; **Defense**—Arnold Kadlec, Czech. and Alexei Kasatonov, USSR; **Forwards**—Mike Bossy, Canada, Gil Perreault, Canada, and Sergei Shepelev, USSR. **Tournament MVP**—Tretiak.

1984

Round Robin Standings

	W	L	T	Pts	GF	GA
Soviet Union	5	0	0	10	22	7
United States	3	1	1	7	21	13
Sweden	3	2	0	6	15	16
Canada	2	2	1	5	23	18
West Germany	0	4	1	1	13	29
Czechoslovakia	0	4	1	1	10	21

Semifinals

Date	City	Score
9/12	Edmonton	Sweden 9, United States 2
9/15	Montreal	Canada 3, USSR 2 (OT)

Note: Mike Bossy scored the winning goal for Canada at 12:29 in overtime.

Finals (Best of 3 Games)

Date	City	Score
9/16	Calgary	Canada 5, Sweden 2
9/18	Edmonton	Canada 6, Sweden 5

Leading Scorers

1. Wayne Gretzky, Canada (5-7—12); 2. Michel Goulet, Canada (5-6—11), Kent Nilsson, Sweden (3-8—11), Paul Coffey, Canada (3-8—11); 5. Hakan Loob, Sweden (6-4—10).

All-Star Team

Goal—Vladimir Myshkin, USSR; **Defense**—Paul Coffey, Canada and Rod Langway, USA; **Forwards**—Wayne Gretzky, Canada, John Tonelli, Canada, and Sergei Makarov, USSR. **Tournament MVP**—Tonelli.

1987

Round Robin Standings

	W	L	T	Pts	GF	GA
Canada	3	0	2	8	19	13
Soviet Union	3	1	1	7	22	13
Sweden	3	2	0	6	17	14
Czechoslovakia	2	2	1	5	12	15
United States	2	3	0	4	13	14
Finland	0	5	0	0	9	23

Semifinals

Date	City	Score
9/8	Hamilton	USSR 4, Sweden 2
9/9	Montreal	Canada 5, Czechoslovakia 3

Finals (Best of 3 Games)

Date	City	Score
9/11	Montreal	USSR 6, Canada 5 (OT)
9/13	Hamilton	Canada 6, USSR 5 (2 OT)
9/15	Hamilton	Canada 6, USSR 5

Note: In Game 1, Alexander Semak of USSR scored at 5:33 in overtime. In Game 2, Mario Lemieux of Canada scored at 10:07 in the second overtime period. Lemieux also won Game 3 on a goal with 1:26 left in regulation time.

Leading Scorers

1. Wayne Gretzky, Canada (3-18—21); 2. Mario Lemieux, Canada (11-7—18); 3. Sergei Makarov, USSR (7-8—15); 4. Vladimir Krutov, USSR (7-7—14); 5. Viacheslav Bykov, USSR (2-7—9); 6. Ray Bourque, Canada (2-6—8).

All-Star Team

Goal—Grant Fuhr, Canada; **Defense**—Ray Bourque, Canada and Viacheslav Fetisov, USSR; **Forwards**—Wayne Gretzky, Canada, Mario Lemieux, Canada, and Vladimir Krutov, USSR. **Tournament MVP**—Gretzky.

U.S. College Hockey
NCAA Division I Championship

Multiple winners: Michigan (7); Denver, North Dakota and Wisconsin (5); Boston Univ., Michigan Tech and Minnesota (3); Colorado Col., Cornell, Michigan St. and RPI (2).

Year	Winner	Score	Loser	Year	Winner	Score	Loser
1948	Michigan	8-4	Dartmouth	1970	Cornell	6-4	Clarkson
1949	Boston College	4-3	Dartmouth	1971	Boston University	4-2	Minnesota
1950	Colorado College	13-4	Boston University	1972	Boston University	4-0	Cornell
1951	Michigan	7-1	Brown	1973	Wisconsin	4-2	Denver
1952	Michigan	4-1	Colorado College	1974	Minnesota	4-2	Michigan Tech
1953	Michigan	7-3	Minnesota	1975	Michigan Tech	6-1	Minnesota
1954	RPI	5-4 OT	Minnesota	1976	Minnesota	6-4	Michigan Tech
1955	Michigan	5-3	Colorado College	1977	Wisconsin	6-5 OT	Michigan
1956	Michigan	7-5	Michigan Tech	1978	Boston University	5-3	Boston College
1957	Colorado College	13-6	Michigan	1979	Minnesota	4-3	North Dakota
1958	Denver	6-2	North Dakota	1980	North Dakota	5-2	No. Michigan
1959	North Dakota	4-3 OT	Michigan St.	1981	Wisconsin	6-3	Minnesota
1960	Denver	5-3	Michigan Tech	1982	North Dakota	5-2	Wisconsin
1961	Denver	12-2	St.Lawrence	1983	Wisconsin	6-2	Harvard
1962	Michigan Tech	7-1	Clarkson	1984	Bowling Green	5-4 OT	Minn.-Duluth
1963	North Dakota	6-5	Denver	1985	RPI	2-1	Providence
1964	Michigan	6-3	Denver	1986	Michigan St.	6-5	Harvard
1965	Michigan Tech	8-2	Boston College	1987	North Dakota	5-3	Michigan St.
1966	Michigan St.	6-1	Clarkson	1988	Lake Superior St.	4-3 OT	St.Lawrence
1967	Cornell	4-1	Boston University	1989	Harvard	4-3 OT	Minnesota
1968	Denver	4-0	North Dakota	1990	Wisconsin	7-3	Colgate
1969	Denver	4-3	Cornell	1991	No. Michigan	8-7 OT	Boston University

Overtime Goals: 1954—1:54; **1959**—4:22; **1977**—0:23; **1984**—7:11 in 4th OT; **1988**—4:46; **1989**—4:16; **1991**—1:57 in 3rd OT.

Most Outstanding Player

The Most Outstanding Players of each NCAA Div.I tournament since 1948. Winners of the award who did not play for the tournament champion are in **bold** type. In 1960, three players, none on the winning team, shared the award.
   Multiple winners: Lou Angotti and Marc Behrend (2).

Year		Year		Year	
1948	**Joe Riley,** Dartmouth, F	1962	Lou Angotti, Mich. Tech,	1978	Jack O'Callahan, Boston U., D
1949	**Dick Desmond,** Dart., G	1963	Al McLean, N.Dakota, F	1979	Steve Janaszak, Minn., G
1950	**Ralph Bevins,** Boston U., G	1964	Bob Gray, Michigan, G	1980	Doug Smail, N.Dakota, F
1951	**Ed Whiston,** Brown, G	1965	Gary Milroy, Mich. Tech, F	1981	Marc Behrend, Wisc., G
1952	**Ken Kinsley,** Colo. Col., F	1966	Gaye Cooley, Mich. St., G	1982	Phil Sykes, N.Dakota, F
1953	John Matchefts, Mich., F	1967	Walt Stanowski, Cornell, D	1983	Marc Behrend, Wisc., G
1954	Abbie Moore, RPI, F	1968	Gerry Powers, Denver, G	1984	Gary Kruzich, Bowl.Green, G
1955	**Phil Hilton,** Colo. Col., D	1969	Keith Magnuson, Denver, D	1985	**Chris Terreri,** Prov., G
1956	Lorne Howes, Mich., G	1970	Dan Lodboa, Cornell, D	1986	Mike Donnelly, Mich.St., F
1957	Bob McCusker, Colo.Col., F	1971	Dan Brady, Boston U., G	1987	Tony Hrkac, N.Dakota, F
1958	Murray Massier, Denver, F	1972	Tim Regan, Boston, U., G	1988	Bruce Hoffort, Lk.Superior, G
1959	Reg Morelli, N.Dakota, F	1973	Dean Talafous, Wisc., F	1989	Ted Donato, Harvard, F
1960	**Lou Angotti,**Mich.Tech, F;	1974	Brad Shelstad, Minn., G	1990	Chris Tancill, Wisconsin, F
	Bob Marquis, Boston U., F;	1975	Jim Warden, Mich. Tech, G	1991	Scott Beattie, No. Mich., F
	& **Barry Urbanski,** Bos.U., G	1976	Tom Vanelli, Minn., F		
1961	Bill Masterton, Denver, F	1977	Julian Baretta, Wisc., G		

Hobey Baker Award

College hockey's Player of the Year award; voted on by a national panel of sportswriters, broadcasters, college coaches and pro scouts. First presented in 1981 by the Decathlon Athletic Club of Bloomington,MN, in the name of the Princeton collegiate hockey and football star who was killed in World War I.

Year		Class	Year		Class
1981	Neal Broten, Minnesota, F	So.	1987	Tony Hrkac, North Dakota, F	So.
1982	George McPhee, Bowling Green, F	Sr.	1988	Robb Stauber, Minnesota, G	So.
1983	Mark Fusco, Harvard, D	Sr.	1989	Lane MacDonald, Harvard, F	Sr.
1984	Tom Kurvers, Minnesota-Duluth, D	Sr.	1990	Kip Miller, Michigan St., F	Sr.
1985	Bill Watson, Minnesota-Duluth, F	Jr.	1991	Dave Emma, Boston College, F	Sr.
1986	Scott Fusco, Harvard, F	Sr.			

Executive Director **Dick Schultz** addressing January's NCAA Convention where delegates voted for an array of reform and cost-cutting measures.

COLLEGE SPORTS

Crunch Time

NCAA struggles to broaden reforms and tighten its belt as legislatures and economy mount a full-court press.

What college athletics will look like in 10 years—or five, or even as few as two or three—is anybody's guess.

Such is the wave of change sweeping across the nation's playing fields. New-look conferences. New, academics-first rules. A new blueprint for the future, drawn up in March by the high-powered Knight Commission.

All of which mean new challenges. And new threats to *Life As We Know It*.

The NCAA, orchestrating its own reform movement with one hand last year, was using the other to hold off Congress and a horde of unhappy, impatient state legislatures. Among them: Nevada's, pouting over the treatment of Jerry Tarkanian and the scandal-struck basketball program at UNLV.

Football bowls, despite drawing up a clever new wrinkle in the formula for choosing a national champion, faced a variety of financial hurdles.

And everywhere, wary eyes were being cast at the bottom line. Money was tight, tighter, and tightest, and NCAA executive director Dick Schultz estimated that 70 percent of the athletic programs in big-time Division I-A were operating at deficits.

"Without a doubt," Schultz said, "the 90s are going to be a decade of change in intercollegiate athletics.. Everybody is going to have to pull their belts up a notch or two and realize that there are going to be some tough times ahead if we are not prepared to deal with them."

Fallout from the financial crunch was very apparent in 1990-91. William & Mary felt the wrath of women's sports advocates when it announced on Feb. 12 that it was eliminating women's basketball, men's wrestling and men's and women's swimming to save an estimated $300,000. UCLA, facing an accumulated budget deficit of $3 million, announced that it was dropping men's water polo and men's and women's crew. And Wisconsin cut shockingly deep on March 22, saying goodbye to men's and women's gymnastics, men's and women's fencing and its 116-year-old baseball program.

The 70-percent-in-the-red figure, the NCAA's Schultz suggested, would grow if the nationwide recession continued, the cost of running athletic programs climbed, and alumni donations and other revenue sources started leveling off or shrinking.

The first pre-emptive steps were taken in January, when NCAA convention delegates in Nashville voted for an array of cost-saving measures: cutting coaching staffs in most Division I sports by at least

---

Steve Wieberg has covered college sports for *USA Today* since the national newspaper first appeared in 1982.

The 44-member Presidents Commission seized even firmer control of the NCAA in 1991. Among the members attending the group's summer meetings in Kansas City were (from left to right): **Stephen Trachtenberg**, president of George Washington University; **Olin Sansbury, Jr.,** chancellor of South Carolina-Spartanburg; **Rev. Albert DiUbio**, president of Marquette; and **Curtis McCray**, president of Long Beach State.

one position by August 1992 (from an average of 16 in I-A football to a maximum of 13), reducing scholarships by 10 percent by August 1993 (from 95 to 85 in I-A football), and scaling back travel and recruiting.

Approved, too, were landmark proposals to phase out athletic dorms and restrict athletes to one training-table meal a day by August, 1996, and, with an eye to "mainstreaming" athletes into everyday campus life, limit their playing and mandatory practice time to four hours a day and 20 hours a week.

The measures were considered a significant victory for reform-minded college presidents, represented by the NCAA's 44-member Presidents Commission, which railroaded them through the voting process. But they brought cries of protest from coaches and athletic directors, who vowed to push for revisions at the NCAA's January 1992 convention in Anaheim, California.

"Many presidents have neglected their duty over the last 10 or 15 years," said Georgia athletic director Vince Dooley. "Now, they're overreacting to their duty."

The presidents, however, showed no inclination to retreat, and spent the summer of 1991 plotting their next offensive—in the area of academics. In June, they approved a proposal to strengthen the requirements of already-controversial Proposition 48 by raising both the number of college preparatory courses athletes must complete and the grade-point average they must attain to receive athletic scholarships as freshmen. A related proposal would mandate strict, year-by-year progress toward a degree.

While skeptics worried that blacks and other minorities, already disproportionately affected by Prop 48, would find their shots at both a college education and big-time college athletics even harder to come by, Schultz heralded it as legislation "that will come as close to guaranteeing graduation as you can."

Indeed, athletes' graduation rates became nearly as notable a statistic in 1990-91 as points per game or yards per carry. In July, surveys by the Chronicle of Higher Education, then USA Today, revealed what the NCAA's own research confirmed: that too many athletes who walked onto the nation's campuses were walking away without their degrees.

Predictably, the numbers were lower in the high-stakes, high-pressure sports of football and basketball (a 42.1 percent graduation rate, compared to 45.7 percent for all athletes in the NCAA study). And they were alarmingly low for blacks (26.6 percent, compared to 52.3 percent for whites).

The shortcomings caught the attention of Congress, where Sen. Bill Bradley (D-N.J.) and Rep. Tom McMillen (D-Md.) successfully co-sponsored the federal Student Right to Know Act—mandating the compilation and public release of school-by-school graduation rates. That prodded the NCAA into adopting a similar measure and its first report was due in December 1991.

"What it will do," said McMillen, the former University of Maryland basketball star, "is put more pressure on schools that are doing a lousy job of graduating their student-athletes. Schools that are doing a good job will continue to do a good job. Schools that are not will be forced into a different way of doing business."

As far as Schultz and the NCAA are concerned, McMillen and other lawmakers could stop there. But they didn't.

At least four more bills were introduced in the House in 1991—including McMillen's Collegiate Athletic Reform Act, which would reorganize the NCAA into a Department of Education-approved entity run by a new Board of Presidents. It would also require a plan to divide TV and postseason revenue on some basis other than won-lost records.

All that doesn't include 10 other bills—calling for constitutional due process in NCAA infractions investigations—passed or pending in state legislatures.

"They (the NCAA) feel they can get their house in order," McMillen said. "But this problem is very deeply rooted. It's rooted in money. It's rooted in the fact there's tremendous incentive to not educate, to not pay attention to schoolwork. That's going to take some restructuring."

And the pressure wasn't coming just from McMillen.

► The Federal Trade Commission subpoenaed a decade's worth of records from the 106 major football-playing schools in the NCAA's Division I-A, hoping to prove that the sport has "commercial, not educational, objectives." That would have allowed the commission to challenge the College Football Association's five-year, $300-million TV contract with ABC as a violation of antitrust laws; however, the FTC's hopes rested on its appeal of a judge's Aug. 6 ruling that it lacks jurisdiction over non-profit organizations.

► The Internal Revenue Service, as of late summer, was expected to rule that money from corporate sponsors was not merely a donation, but payment for advertising and thus fully taxable. This sent shudders through the already problem-plagued bowls, who wondered how many of those sponsors would continue to open up their checkbooks.

► The Knight Commission on Intercollegiate Athletics, ending an 18-month study, concluded in its March 19 report that "on too many campuses, big-time revenue sports are out of control," and called for university presidents to take greater charge. Run athletics like any other department at the school, it said. Remove alumni and booster clubs from the process of hiring and firing coaches. Take control of the coaches' contracts with broadcasters, shoe companies and other outside revenue sources. Require annual "certification." Or face heavier-handed government regulation.

The timing of the report was ironic. Tarkanian and UNLV, symbolic to many of everything wrong with intercollegiate athletics, were three days away from playing in the NCAA basketball tournament's Sweet 16. The unbeaten, No. 1-ranked Rebels were steamrolling toward a second consecutive berth in the Final Four and heavily favored to repeat as national champions.

Did someone say, "Crime doesn't pay"?

"It goes back to the time of Leo Durocher," said Frank Remington, a Wisconsin law professor and immediate past chairman of one of Tarkanian's chief

ORANGE BOWL

NEW BOWL ALLIANCE
- BIG EIGHT CONFERENCE
- SOUTHWEST CONFERENCE
- SOUTHEASTERN CONFERENCE
- ATLANTIC COAST CONFERENCE
- BIG EAST CONFERENCE
- NOTRE DAME

FIESTA BOWL PHOENIX, ARIZONA

COTTON BOWL DALLAS, TEXAS

SUGAR BOWL NEW ORLEANS LOUISIANA

ORANGE BOWL MIAMI, FLORIDA

ORANGE BOWL STADIUM

Orange Bowl Committee president **W.Harper Davidson**, Jr., at July 10 press briefing in Miami, discussing plans for the college football bowl alliance that will involve four major bowls, five conferences and Notre Dame.

antagonists, the NCAA Committee on Infractions. "Nice guys finish last."

The fact that UNLV was eligible for the title at all was hard for like-minded officials to digest. Thirteen years after it tried to suspend Tarkanian, but was rebuffed by a Nevada court injunction, the NCAA had returned in July 1990 with a stiff substitute penalty: no postseason tournament appearance for the Rebels in '91. But the school reacted bitterly, players threatened legal action, and the infractions committee—now chaired by Virginia history professor D. Alan Williams—came back in December with yet another variation: UNLV could play in the 1991 tournament, but had to sit out in '92.

UNLV also had to choose between suspending Tarkanian from the 1991 tournament or staying off TV during the '92 season, and chose the latter.

Two other high-profile basketball programs were hit with NCAA probation within a week of each other in November 1990. Missouri and Illinois were placed on two and three years probation, re-

spectively, ordered to sit out the 1991 postseason and saddled with recruiting and scholarship limitations. But the Tigers' Norm Stewart and Illinois' Lou Henson remained at the controls.

The jury was still out in late summer on Syracuse's Jim Boeheim, whose Orangemen were broadsided in December 1990 by a series of Syracuse *Post-Standard* stories charging that players might have violated NCAA rules by receiving merchandise, heavily discounted use of cars and even cash from boosters.

Minnesota felt both edges of the NCAA ax in March, when its football program was ordered to sit out the following postseason and basketball was stripped of scholarships. Tentacles from that case reached all the way to South Bend and another big name: Notre Dame's Lou Holtz, who had coached the Gophers' football team in 1984 and 1985 and admitted giving $250 to a former player to help pay for a correspondence course and $20 to a recruit whose wallet had been lost or stolen during a visit.

Holtz escaped untouched by both the NCAA and a Notre Dame administration that concluded "the matters in question were not deliberate."

Still sizzling in the NCAA frying pan was Miami of Florida, where an internal investigation revealed in June that athletes and other students—mostly football players—had filed false applications for need-based Pell Grants with the U.S. Department of Education. Federal authorities launched an investigation and the NCAA said it would stay abreast.

Meanwhile, NCAA investigators found themselves being investigated. First, by the growing group of state legislators drawing up due-process bills. And, then, by the NCAA itself, which formed a committee chaired by former U.S. Supreme Court Chief Justice Warren Burger to review and, if needed, revamp the entire process.

It was a year for self-inspection. College football's bowls, beset by public criticism of their messy and increasingly early selection process, voted to adhere to a mid-November team pick'em date and fine violators up to $250,000. That, it was hoped, would prevent deserving, fast-closing teams from being shut out and, in an upset-filled season like 1990, make efforts to match the nation's top two teams less of a late-October guessing game.

To further enhance the chances of a No. 1 vs. No. 2 matchup, four top bowls—the Orange, Sugar, Cotton and Fiesta—formed a new alliance with the new-to-football Big East Conference, the Atlantic Coast Conference and Notre Dame. Starting in January 1993, the bowl with the highest-ranked conference champion will pick from the highest-ranked team among the Big East and ACC champions and the Fighting Irish.

"If this helps eliminate or reduce further discussion of national championship (playoff) games," said the Rev. William Beauchamp, executive vice-president of Notre Dame, "I'm for it."

Still, the bowls had problems—particularly the middle and lower-class members of the bowl family.

In addition to the IRS threat, the NCAA-enforced minimum payout from sponsors jumped from $500,000 to $600,000 per team in 1990, and will rise to $750,000

Tarkanian Era Ends In Hot Tub

In 18 turbulent seasons at Nevada-Las Vegas, Jerry Tarkanian thought he had seen—and survived—it all. Complaints of academic short-changing. Player arrests. War with the NCAA.

But his dark, deep-set Armenian eyes blinked in disbelief the morning of May 26, when he picked up the Las Vegas Review-Journal and saw the front-page smiles of three of his former players, Moses Scurry, Anderson Hunt and David Butler. They were lounging in a hot tub, one holding a beer, with convicted sports "fixer" Richard Perry.

Another photo showed the foursome playing basketball at Perry's house. The accompanying story pointed out the obvious: players and known gamblers aren't supposed to mix, and the association with Perry posed "grave problems" for the Rebels' program.

Less than two weeks later, on June 7, Tarkanian blinked again, this time into the glare of a half-dozen television lights and announced he would resign at the end of the 1991-92 season. "I love this university and do not want to cause it any harm," he said. "In addition, although I have been toughened over the years by the pressures of these battles, the pain I now see in my children's eyes makes me realize none of this is fun for anyone."

So ended not one, but two eras.

Nobody has fought the NCAA and its rules enforcers like Tarkanian. A 1977 case, in which the NCAA ordered his suspension for two years, went all the way to the U.S. Supreme Court. In June, at a Congressional hearing in Washington D.C., he complained bitterly of the association's "reign of terror" and called for federal intervention. In September, he and other UNLV officials were to head to Boston for yet another hearing on another set of allegations of rules violations.

At the same time, Tarkanian was transforming the game of basketball on the court. His teams ran and played relentless pressure defense before running and defense were fashionable. He built a struggling, little known program into a national powerhouse—averaging almost 27 wins a season—and he led the Rebels to four NCAA tournament Final Fours and one championship in 1990.

"He brought a national spotlight to (Las Vegas') Maryland Parkway, to a little campus that was not mature enough to have a spotlight on it," said UNLV President Robert Maxson. ". . . There is no question Jerry Tarkanian is a legend."

Nor is there much question that Maxson, despite his fond farewell, wanted Tarkanian gone.

He had expressed frustration often in the previous months over the failure of the basketball program to shed its outlaw image at a time when the rest of the university—the No. 1 "up and comer" in the West, according to *U.S. News and World Report* magazine—was making significant strides. When the photos of Perry, who pleaded guilty to sports bribery in the 1984 Boston College point-shaving scandal, and the three UNLV players were published, Maxson boiled.

"It diminishes everyone," he said. "It diminishes the program. It diminishes the university. I'm not just concerned about it; I'm angry."

UNLV already had been barred from television and postseason appearances during the 1991-92 season, closing the books on the 1977 case. And the school was complet-

LAS VEGAS REVIEW-JOURNAL   LAS VEGAS ⦿ SUN
SUNDAY
Las Vegas, Nevada

Three UNLV basketball players in 1989 enjoy the hospitality of Richie "The Fixer" Perry, who was once convicted in a basketball point-shaving scandal. From left are Moses Scurry, Perry, Anderson Hunt and David Butler.

Photos tie Rebels to 'The Fixer'

☐ Photographs show three players partying in 1989 with gambler Richie Perry, a convicted sports fixer.

By A.D. Hopkins
Review-Journal

Richie "The Fixer" Perry entertained at his home three key players on UNLV's 1990 national championship basketball team.

Photographs obtained by the Review-Journal confirm the convicted sports-event fixer, associated with players near the start of the 1989-90 season.

Perry is under consideration by state gaming investigators for inclusion in Nevada's so-called Black Book, the list of people banned by law from Nevada casinos. Perry also figures in the National Collegiate Athletic Association's current inquiry into the UNLV basketball program.

The players in the photographs are David Butler, Anderson Hunt and Moses Scurry. Hunt and Butler were starters on the 1989-90 team, and Scurry was the No. 1 substitute. One photo shows the players in a hot tub with Perry, Hunt and Scurry holding a beer. In another, they are playing basketball with Perry on his distinctive backyard basketball court, which has "Perry's Court" painted on the backboard.

The players' association with Perry may pose grave problems for the Rebel basketball program with the NCAA.

NCAA bylaws prohibit any involvement in gambling activities or any

Three Rebels try out the home court — the home in question being the residence of Richie "The Fixer" Perry, twice convicted of fixing sporting events to win bets. From left are Perry, Anderson Hunt, Moses Scurry and David Butler. The backboard confirms the location.

Las Vegas Review-Journal

The May 26 front page that convinced UNLV basketball coach Jerry Tarkanian that the time had come to step down.

ing its response to 29 new charges of alleged violations, most related to the Rebels' recruitment of former New York City prep star Lloyd Daniels. Those charges revolved around the appointment of a former UNLV assistant coach as Daniels' guardian in 1986 and whether the program allowed him to provide Daniels with otherwise-prohibited extra benefits.

Tarkanian vehemently denied any serious violations in the Daniels case or any connection between his program and Perry.

"We didn't do anything wrong," Tark said. But UNLV athletic director Dennis Finfrock suggested overall control of the program "is always a consideration."

Tarkanian met once with the UNLV board of regents, twice with Maxson, and agreed that the time finally had come to step aside. His destination after a final season with the Rebels is expected to be the NBA.

UNLV planned to start a formal search for his replacement by early November, but Finfrock didn't expect to hire a new coach until after the '91-92 season. One thing is for sure: anyone with a hint of scandal in his resume need not apply.

"We will not intentionally start out by creating problems for ourselves," Maxson said. "That's one spotlight we need to get this university out of."

by 1993. As the economy struggled, worries about losing formerly deep-pocketed sponsors grew after Sunkist pulled out of the Fiesta Bowl.

One bowl, the All American, died. More are expected to follow in the coming years.

In Birmingham, however, they wept not for the departed All American. Instead, they went out and picked a bigger plum: the Southeastern Conference playoff, which debuts when the expanding league admits Arkansas and South Carolina and splits into two six-team divisions in 1992.

The ACC also made its 1992 addition of perennial football power Florida State pay off, securing a place in the bowl alliance. The built-for-basketball Big East was welcomed after adding Miami of Florida, then Rutgers, Temple, Virginia Tech and West Virginia and going into the football business.

Most moves in this spate of conference restructuring led to countermoves (see pages 357 and 362 for complete list).

The Southwest Athletic Conference considered adding Tulane, opted in June not to expand, but continued talking with the Big Eight about a package of weekly interconference football games and other joint ventures. That, while wondering how much longer league cornerstones Texas and Texas A&M would stay put.

The two Texas schools talked to the Pacific 10 before that league announced it wasn't interested in expansion, and subsequently said they weren't interested in moving. But neither decision carried a stamp of permanence.

"Our conference (the Pac-10) is not in a strong position. That's why I think we need to look at expansion," said Arizona athletic director Cedric Dempsey. "The only reason to consider expansion is economics. The only schools that make sense, then, are the Texas schools."

Eyes also were on the Big Ten, in spite of its vow to stand pat for four years after adding Penn State. No one expected the league to stick with an unwieldy 11 teams and there were murmurs it was looking unofficially at Big Eight member Missouri and—drumroll please—fiercely independent Notre Dame.

In the midst of all this attention to the big-time, big-money sports at big-time, big-money schools, another issue

UC-San Diego

Judy Sweet, the athletic director at UC-San Diego, was named the NCAA's first woman president in January.

loomed on the horizon. Almost 20 years after the passage of Title IX, Donna Lopiano and other leading spokespersons complained that women still were getting the short end of the athletic stick.

In January, after the NCAA's 20-percent cut in scholarships, they pointed out that female athletes receive only 33 percent of all scholarships and charged that cutting men and women equally was discriminatory. In June, an NCAA-commissioned study found 85 percent of the respondents agreeing that discrimination exists in athletic administration and 93 percent at least partly blamed the colleges' "old-boy network."

The calls don't figure to fall on deaf ears. The NCAA elected its first female president, Cal-San Diego athletic director Judy Sweet, in January 1991. That, a few months before Washington made Barbara Hedges only the second woman ever to run a combined men's and women's athletic department at a major football playing school.

"I hope women are realistic enough to know I'm not going to be a savior," Sweet said. "But I know I'm in a position to have my voice heard. People will listen.

"I am the first. I want to make sure I'm not the last." □

USA Today Division I All-Sports Rankings

Unofficial national rankings, compiled by Steve Williams of USA Today and released June 24, 1991. Division I athletic programs ranked according to NCAA's Top 10 participated-in sports for men and women; points based on 20 for a national championship, 19 for runner-up, etc. Where Top 20 finishers in any sport were unavailable (football, basketball, tennis, etc.) USA Today poll and other final polls were used.

MEN

	Conf.	Cross-country	Soccer	Football	Wrestling	Swimming	Basketball	Tennis	Outdoor Track	Golf	Baseball	TOTAL
1 Texas	SWC	17	0	11	0	20	0	0	16	11	10	85
2 Tennessee	SEC	14	0	14	0	16	0	11	20	0	0	75
3 Florida	SEC	15	0	8	0	18	0	12	0½	1	17½	72
4 Arkansas	SWC	20	0	0	0	0	14½	0	14	11	0	59½
5 Oklahoma St.	Big 8	0	0	0	19	0	8	0	0	20	12	59
USC	Pac-10	0	0	0	0	17	0	20	0	14	8	59
7 Clemson	ACC	0	16	12	0	0	0	0	7½	8	13½	57
LSU	SEC	0	0	0	0	7	0	15	15	0	20	57
9 Arizona St.	Pac-10	0	0	0	8	12	0	13	0	18	0	51
10 UCLA	Pac-10	0	20	0	0	11	0	16	3½	0	0	50½

Others in Top 30 standings: 11. Michigan (45); **12.** Stanford (44½); **13.** Oregon (41); **14.** North Carolina (40½); **15. (tie)** Miami-FL and Notre Dame (36); **17.** Iowa St.(35½); **18. (tie)** BYU and Georgia Tech (34); **20.** Iowa (32); **21.** Ohio St.(31); **22. (tie)** Florida St. and UNLV (30½); **24.** Georgia (30); **25.** Indiana (29½); **26. (tie)** N.C.State and Penn St.(28); **28. (tie)** Arizona and California (26½); **30.** Fresno St.(25½).

WOMEN

	Conf.	Field Hockey	Soccer	Cross-country	Volleyball	Swimming	Basketball	Tennis	Golf	Softball	Outdoor Track	TOTAL
1 UCLA	Pac-10	0	0	0	20	16	0	19	20	19	17	111
2 Stanford	Pac-10	0	13	0	16	19	17½	20	15	0	8½	109
3 Texas	SWC	0	0	0	15	20	0	15	14	0	19	83
4 Georgia	SEC	0	0	12	0	13	14½	17½	16	0	0	73
5 Arizona	Pac-10	0	0	0	0	14	0	12½	18	20	0	64½
6 Florida	SEC	0	0	0	0	18	0	17½	6	0	15	56½
7 Tennessee	SEC	0	0	9	0	4	20	6	0	0	16	55
8 LSU	SEC	0	0	0	17½	7	3	2½	3	0	20	53
9 BYU	WAC	0	0	13	8½	10	0	8	0	0	13	52½
10 North Carolina	ACC	19	20	0	0	1	0	0	0	0	10½	50½

Others in Top 30 standings: 11. Connecticut (44½); **12.** California (41½); **13. (tie)** Clemson and Penn St.(41); **15. (tie)** Providence and Virginia (36); **17.** Nebraska (35½); **18.** Duke (35); **19. (tie)** Arkansas and Florida St.(34½); **21. (tie)** Iowa, SMU and Villanova (34); **24.** San Jose St.(33½); **25. (tie)** Arizona St. and N.C.State (33⅕); **27.** Long Beach St.(32); **28.** Lamar (27½); **29.** UC-Santa Barbara (27); **30.** Massachusetts (23).

1990-91 NCAA Team Champions

LSU and **UCLA** each won three Division I national championships over the 1990-91 season, the only schools to claim that many in any of the NCAA's three divisions. The Tigers, as usual, were strong in women's track—winning their third indoor and fifth outdoor titles—but also won their first College World Series in baseball. The Bruins won for the second time in Men's Soccer and Women's Volleyball and for the first time in Women's Golf. Thirteen other schools won two national titles.

Note that numbers in parentheses indicate overall championships won in that sport.

FALL
Cross-country

Men's Division I	Arkansas (4)
Division II	Edinboro, PA (4)
Division III	Wisconsin-Oshkosh (3)
Women's Division I	Villanova (2)
Division II	Cal Poly-SLO (9)
Division III	Cortland St., NY (2)

1990-91 NCAA Team Champions (Cont.)

Field Hockey

Women's Division I .... Old Dominion (5)
Division III .... Trenton St., NJ (5)

Football

Men's Division I-A .... AP: Colorado (1)
UPI: Georgia Tech (1)
Division I-AA............. Georgia Southern (4)
Division II................ North Dakota St. (5)
Division III .... Allegheny College, PA (1)
Note: There is no official NCAA Div.I-A playoff.

Soccer

Men's Division I.......................... UCLA (2)
Division II .... So.Connecticut St. (2)
Division III .... Glassboro St., NJ (2)

Women's Division I .... North Carolina (8)
Division II .... Sonoma St., CA (1)
Division III.......... Ithaca College, NY (1)

Volleyball

Women's Division I .... UCLA (2)
Division II................. West Texas St. (1)
Division III .... UC-San Diego (6)

Water Polo

Men's Champion .... California (9)

WINTER

Basketball

Men's Division I .... Duke (1)
Division II.................. North Alabama (2)
Division III .... Wisconsin-Platteville (1)

Women's Division I .... Tennessee (3)
Division II .... North Dakota St. (1)
Division III .... St.Thomas, MN (1)

Fencing

Men/Women Combined .... Penn St. (2)

Gymnastics

Men's Champion .... Oklahoma (3)
Women's Champion.................... Alabama (2)

Ice Hockey

Men's Division I .... Northern Michigan (1)
Division III .... Wisconsin-Stevens Pt. (3)

Rifle

Men/Women Combined............ West Virginia (7)

Skiing

Men/Women Combined.............. Colorado (12)

Swimming & Diving

Men's Division I............................ Texas (5)
Division II.................... CS-Bakersfield (6)
Division III .... Kenyon, OH (12)

Women's Division I........................... Texas (7)
Division II .... Oakland, MI (2)
Division III .... Kenyon, OH (8)

Indoor Track

Men's Division I .... Arkansas (8)
Division II .... St.Augustine's Col., NC (5)
Division III .... Wisconsin-La Crosse (3)

Women's Division I .... LSU (3)
Division II.......... Abilene Christian, TX (4)
Division III .... Cortland St., NY (1)

Wrestling

Men's Division I .... Iowa (12)
Division II .... Nebraska-Omaha (1)
Division III .... Augsburg College, MN (1)

SPRING

Baseball

Men's Division I .... LSU (1)
Division II............... Jacksonville St., AL (2)
Division III .... Southern Maine (1)

Golf

Men's Division I .... Oklahoma St. (7)
Division II................. Florida Southern (6)
Division III .... Methodist College, NC (2)

Women's Champion....................... UCLA (1)

Lacrosse

Men's Division I .... North Carolina (4)
Division II .... Hobart, NY (12)

Women's Division I .... Virginia (1)
Division III .... Trenton St., NJ (4)

Softball

Women's Division I....................... Arizona (1)
Division II .... Augustana College, SD (1)
Division III .... Central College, IA (2)

Tennis

Men's Division I............................ USC (13)
Division II .... Rollins College, FL (3)
Division III......... Kalamazoo College, MI (5)

Women's Division I..................... Stanford (8)
Division II .... Cal Poly-Pomona (1)
Division III.... Mary Washington Col., VA (2)

Outdoor Track

Men's Division I .... Tennessee (2)
Division II .... St.Augustine's Col., NC (3)
Division III .... Wisconsin-La Crosse (3)

Women's Division I .... LSU (5)
Division II.................. Cal Poly-SLO (6)
Division III .... Wisconsin-Oshkosh (2)

Volleyball

Men's Champion.................. Long Beach St. (1)

NCAA Schools on Probation

As of Sept. 1, 1991, there were 30 member institutions serving NCAA probations.

School (Division)	Sport	Yrs	Penalty To End	School (Division)	Sport	Yrs	Penalty To End
Pan American (I)	W Basketball	1	9/1/91	Oklahoma St.(I-A)	Football	4	1/9/93
Kansas (I)	Basketball	3	11/1/91		& Wrestling	4	1/9/93
Cincinnati (I)	Football	3	11/3/91	Miami-OH (I)	Basketball	2	1/17/93
	& Basketball	3	11/3/91	Hampton (II)	Football	2	2/1/93
Oklahoma (I-A)	Football	3	12/27/91	Lowell (II)	Ice Hockey	2	3/21/93
Houston (I-A)	Football	3	12/31/91	Michigan (I)	Baseball	2	3/26/93
W.Texas St.(II)	Basketball	3	1/1/92	Minnesota (I)	Basketball	2	3/29/93
N.C.State (I)	Basketball	2	1/2/92		Football	2	3/29/93
Marshall (I)	Basketball	2	3/11/92		& Wrestling	2	3/29/93
Plattsburgh St.(III)	Ice Hockey	2	4/13/92	Houston Bapt.(I)	M/W Gymnastics	3	4/2/93
Kentucky (I)	Basketball	3	5/19/92	Pacific (I)	Basketball	2	4/3/93
Robert Morris (I)	Basketball	2	5/31/92	Maryland (I)	Basketball	3	8/3/93
Florida A&M (I)	W Tennis	2	6/14/92	Tulane (I)	Tennis	2	8/23/93
Adelphi (II)	Basketball	3	7/7/92	SE Louisiana (I)	Basketball	5	10/2/94
Memphis St.(I-A)	Football	3	8/3/92	Northwestern St.(I)	Basketball	3	10/5/93
Florida (I)	Football	2	9/24/92	Illinois (I)	Basketball	3	11/12/93
	& Basketball	2	9/24/92	Upsala (III)	Basketball	5	9/7/95
Missouri (I)	Basketball	2	11/7/92				

Also: Brooklyn College banned from 1991 and '92 NCAA Division I Soccer Tournament for "unsportsmanlike conduct" towards officials in first round defeat (0-1, to Adelphi) in 1990 tournament.

Violations & Sanctions

Adelphi—VIOLATIONS: improper financial aid and transportation; improper recruiting entertainment, inducements, lodging and transportation; eligibility; unethical conduct; institution control; certification of compliance. SANCTIONS: 3-year probation; no 1990 postseason; no initial grants for 1990-91 except to those already committed; recertification; annual compliance reports; forfeited all contests and deleted team records for 1986-87; show cause why disciplinary action should not be taken if any member institution hires former head coach during next 5 years.

Cincinnati—VIOLATIONS: im0proper financial aid; extra benefits; out-of-season practice; improper recruiting inducements, lodging and transportation; eligibility; institutional control. SANCTIONS: 3-year probation for both programs; no 1988-89 postseason for either program; maximum 11 basketball grants for 1989-90 and 12 for 1990-91; maximum 12 initial football grants for 1989-90, 21 for 1990-91 and 22 for 1991-92; recertification; annual compliance reports.

Florida—VIOLATIONS: improper transportation; extra benefits; improper recruiting transportation; eligibility; unethical conduct; certification of compliance. SANCTIONS: 2-year probation for both programs; no 1990-91 postseason for football; maximum 13 grants for 1991-92 and 14 grants for 1992-93 in basketball; returned revenue from 1988 basketball championship; deleted team and individual records for 1987 and '88 basketball championships; recertification; annual compliance reports; show cause why disciplinary action should not be taken if any member institution hires former head football and basketball coaches during next 5 years.

Florida A&M—VIOLATIONS: improper entertainment, financial aid, lodging and transportation; improper recruiting entertainment; tryouts; unethical conduct. SANCTIONS: 2-year probation; no 1990-91 postseason; no initial grants until Aug.1, 1992; recertification; disassociated one representative; show cause why more penalties should not be imposed if institution does not disassociate former head coach; show cause why disciplinary action should not be taken if any member institution hires former head coach during next 5 years.

Hampton—VIOLATIONS: eligibility; institutional control. SANCTIONS: 2-year probation; no 1991 postseason; forfeited all victories for 1986 and '87; recertification.

Houston—VIOLATIONS: improper employment, financial aid, lodging and transportation; extra benefits; improper recruiting contacts, entertainment, inducements and transportation; unethical conduct; institutional control; certification of compliance. SANCTIONS: 3-year probation, no 1989-90 and 1990-91 postseason; no 1989-90 TV games; maximum 15 initial grants for 1989-90; annual compliance reports; show cause why more penalties should not be imposed if institution does not restrict head coach's contact with prospective and enrolled student-athletes; show cause why disciplinary action should not be taken if any member institution hires 5 former assistant coaches during next 5 years.

Houston Baptist—VIOLATIONS: improper transportation; improper recruiting entertainment and lodging; tryouts; unethical conduct; institutional control. SANCTIONS: 3-year probation for both men's and women's teams; no 1989-90 and 1990-91 postseason for men; no initial grants for 1990-91 and 1991-92 and no increase in percentage of aid for 1990-91 and 1991-92 for men; deleted team and individual records for 1987,'88,'89 men's championships; annual audits; no participation in or support for participation in outside club competition for 1990-91 and 1991-92 for men; show cause why more penalties should not be imposed if institution does not prohibit head coach from all coaching and athletically related responsibilities until July 1, 1991 and off-campus recruiting until Dec. 15, 1991.

NCAA Schools on Probation (Cont.)

Illinois—VIOLATIONS: improper financial aid; extra benefits; complimentary tickets; improper recruiting contacts, inducements and lodging; institutional control. SANCTIONS: 3-year probation; no 1990-91 postseason; maximum 2 initial grants for 1991-92 and 1992-93; no off-campus recruiting for 1991, and only head coach and one assistant coach may recruit for 1992; no official visits for 1991; recertification; annual compliance reports; show cause why more penalties should not be imposed if institution does not disassociate one representative; head coach and 2 assistant coaches salaries frozen until May 1, 1991, and they may not receive bonuses; placed one assistant coach on probation for 2 years; one assistant coach prohibited from recruiting for 2 years.

Kansas—VIOLATIONS: improper lodging; improper recruiting contacts, entertainment, inducements and transportation; institutional control; certification of compliance. SANCTIONS: 3-year probation; no 1989 postseason; reduced grants by one for 1989-90; no official visits for 1989; recertification; annual compliance reports; show cause why disciplinary action should not be taken if institution does not disassociate 3 representatives.

Kentucky—VIOLATIONS: improper financial aid and lodging; improper recruiting contact, entertainment, inducements, lodging and transportation; eligibility; academic fraud; unethical conduct; institutional control. SANCTIONS: 3-year probation; no 1989-90 and 1990-91 postseason; no 1989-90 TV games; maximum 3 initial grants for 1989-90 and 1990-91; returned revenue from 1988 championship; annual compliance reports; disassociated one representative; show cause why disciplinary action should not be taken if any member institution hires one ex-assistant coach during next 5 years.

Lowell—VIOLATIONS: improper financial aid and lodging; extra benefits; improper recruiting contact, entertainment, inducements, lodging and transportation; unethical conduct; institutional control. SANCTIONS: 2-year probation; no 1991-92 postseason; recertification; annual compliance reports; required self-study; show cause why disciplinary action should not be taken if any member institution hires former head coach during next 5 years.

Marshall—VIOLATIONS: improper financial aid, lodging and transportation; extra benefits; improper recruiting contacts, inducements, lodging and transportation; unethical conduct; institutional control. SANCTIONS: 2-year probation; no 1990-91 postseason; one grant cut for 1990-91 and 2 cut for 1991-92; 3 official visits cut for 1989-90 and 1990-91; deleted team and individual records for 1987 championship; returned revenue from '87 championship; student-athletes with grants must live in university housing; annual compliance reports; show cause why more penalties should not be imposed if institution does not disassociate 3 representatives; show cause why disciplinary action should not be taken if any member institution hires former head coach during next 5 years.

Maryland—VIOLATIONS: improper transportation; extra benefits; complimentary tickets; improper recruiting contacts, inducements and transportation; unethical conduct; institutional control. SANCTIONS: 3-year probation; no 1990-91 and 1991-92 postseason; no 1990-91 TV games; maximum 13 grants for 1990-91 and 1991-92; returned revenue from 1988 champion-

ship; deleted team and individual records from '88 championship; recertification; annual compliance reports; show cause why more penalties should not be imposed if institution does not disassociate 2 representatives; show cause why disciplinary action should not be taken if any member institution hires former head coach, graduate assistant and part-time assistant coaches and administrative assistant during next 5 years.

Memphis St.—VIOLATIONS: improper recruiting employment; unethical conduct. SANCTIONS: 3-year probation; no 1989-90 postseason; no 1989-90 TV games; maximum 21 initial grants for 1990-91; maximum 55 official visits for 1989-90; recertification; annual compliance reports; disassociated one representative; show cause why disciplinary action should not be taken if any member institution hires former head coach during next 5 years.

Miami-OH—VIOLATIONS: academic fraud; eligibility; unethical conduct. SANCTIONS: 2-year probation; deleted team and individual records and forfeited all contests in which ineligible student-athlete participated; recertification; annual compliance reports; show cause why disciplinary action should not be taken if any member institution hires former head coach during next 3 years.

Michigan—VIOLATIONS: improper employment; entertainment, financial aid and transportation; extra benefits; improper recruiting contact, entertainment, inducements, lodging and transportation; tryouts; excessive number of official visits; unethical conduct; institutional control. SANCTIONS: 2-year probation; no 1990-91 and 1991-92 postseason; no 1990-91 and 1991-92 TV games; no initial grants for 1990-91; maximum 10 total grants for 1991-92 and 11 for 1992-93; no off-campus recruiting through Aug.31, 1990; no expense-paid visits for 1989-90; eliminated one coaching position; returned revenue from 6 championships (1984-89); deleted team and individual records for those championships; recertification; show cause why disciplinary action should not be taken if any member institution hires former head coach during next 5 years.

Minnesota—VIOLATIONS: improper employment, entertainment, financial aid and transportation; extra benefits; improper recruiting contacts, employment, lodging and inducements; tryouts; eligibility; institutional control. SANCTIONS: 2-year probation for all 3 programs; no 1991-92 postseason for football; maximum 14 grants for 1991-92 basketball; no initial grants for 1990-91 wrestling; no off-campus recruiting by head basketball coach during January, 1991, evaluation period; no off-campus recruiting in wrestling until after 1990-91 championship; head basketball and wrestling coaches placed on probation through 1990-91; head wrestling coach's salary frozen for 1990-91; recertification; annual compliance reports; wrestling team shall operate separately from outside wrestling club involved in case.

Missouri—VIOLATIONS: improper entertainment, lodging and transportation; extra benefits; improper recruiting contacts, employment, entertainment, inducements, lodging and transportation; eligibility; unethical conduct; institutional control. SANCTIONS: 2-year probation; no 1990-91 postseason; maximum one initial grant for 1991-92 and 2 for 1992-93; maximum one coach may recruit off campus in 1991; no official visits in 1991; annual compliance reports.

N.C. State—VIOLATIONS: improper entertainment, lodging and transportation; extra benefits; complimentary tickets; institutional control. SANCTIONS: 2-year probation; no 1989-90 postseason; maximum 12 grants for 1990-91 and 1991-92; no off-campus recruiting for 1989-90; no official visits for 1989-90; coaching staff limited to head, 2 assistants and either one volunteer or one part-time coach; annual compliance reports.

Northwestern St.—VIOLATIONS: improper employment, financial aid and transportation; extra benefits; improper recruiting contacts, entertainment, inducements and transportation; tryouts; academic fraud; eligibility; unethical conduct; institutional control; certification of compliance. SANCTIONS: 3-year probation; no 1990-91 and 1991-92 postseason; no 1990-91 TV games; maximum 13 grants for 1990-91; maximum 2 initial grants for 1991-92 and 3 for 1992-93; maximum 8 official visits for 1990-91 and 12 for 1991-92; limit coaching staff to head coach, one assistant coach and one graduate assistant coach for probationary period; recertification; annual compliance reports; show cause why disciplinary action should not be taken if any member institution hires former head coach during next 15 years, former volunteer coach during next 7 years and 2 former assistant coaches during next 5 years.

Oklahoma—VIOLATIONS: improper transportation; extra benefits; complimentary tickets; improper recruiting contacts, employment, entertainment, inducements and transportation; unethical conduct; outside fund; institutional control; certification of compliance. SANCTIONS: 3-year probation; no 1989-90 and 1990-91 postseason; no 1989-90 TV games; maximum 18 initial grants for 1989-90 and 1990-91; maximum 8 coaches may recruit off campus for 1989-90; maximum 50 official visits for 1988-89 and 1989-90; annual compliance reports; show cause why more penalties should not be imposed if Sooners do not remove 2 assistant coaches and recruiting coordinator and disassociate one representative.

Oklahoma St.—VIOLATIONS: improper financial aid and transportation; extra benefits; improper recruiting contacts, employment, entertainment, inducements, lodging and transportation; eligibility; improper administration of financial aid; unethical conduct; institutional control; certification of compliance. SANCTIONS: 4-year probation; no 1989-90, 1990-91 and 1991-92 postseason; no 1989-90 and 1990-91 TV games; maximum 20 initial grants for 1989-90, 1990-91 and 1991-92; maximum 50 official visits for 1989-90 and 1990-91; recertification; annual compliance reports; show cause why more penalties should not be imposed if institution does not disassociate 14 representatives; show cause why disciplinary action should not be taken if any member institution hires one former assistant coach during next 12 years.

Pacific—VIOLATIONS: improper transportation; extra benefits; improper recruiting transportation; unethical conduct. SANCTIONS: 2-year probation; maximum 14 total grants for 1991-92 and 13 for 1992-93; recertification; show cause why disciplinary action should not be taken if any member institution hires former assistant coach, former director of athletics or former business manager during next 5 years.

Pan American—VIOLATIONS: improper transportation; extra benefits; out-of-season practice; improper

recruiting contact, entertainment, inducements, publicity and transportation; tryouts; institutional control; certification of compliance. SANCTIONS: 1-year probation; no 1990-91 postseason; no 1990-91 TV games; no off-campus recruiting for 1990-91; maximum 10 official visits for 1990-91; head coach prohibited from use of complimentary auto and participation in any basketball camp for 1990-91; recertification; annual compliance reports.

Pittsburgh St.—VIOLATIONS: improper entertainment, lodging and transportation; extra benefits; institutional control; certification of compliance. SANCTIONS: 2-year probation; no 1990-91 postseason; no official visits by representatives; recertification; annual compliance reports; deleted team and individual records for 1986,'87 and '88 championships; self-imposed restrictions regarding off-campus housing; show cause why more penalties should not be imposed if institution does not disassociate 8 representatives.

Robert Morris—VIOLATIONS: improper financial aid; extra benefits; eligibility; institutional control. SANCTIONS: 2-year probation; no 1990-91 postseason; no 1990-91 TV games; maximum 2 initial grants for 1991-92; deleted team and individual records from 1989 and '90 championships; returned revenue from '89 championship; recertification; annual compliance reports.

SE Louisiana—VIOLATIONS: improper employment; extra benefits; improper recruiting entertainment, inducements and transportation; tryouts; unethical conduct; institutional control; certification of compliance. SANCTIONS: 5-year probation; accepted action to suspend program until at least 1990-91; annual compliance reports; required self-study; show cause why disciplinary action should not be taken if any member institution hires one former assistant coach during next 5 years.

Tulane—VIOLATIONS: improper employment and financial aide; improper fund; unethical conduct. SANCTIONS: 2-year probation; recertification; annual compliance reports; show cause why disciplinary action should not be taken if any member institution hires former head coach during next five years.

Upsala—VIOLATIONS: improper employment, entertainment and financial aid; extra benefits; out-of-season practice; improper recruiting inducements; institutional control; certification of compliance. SANCTIONS: 5-year probation; no 1990-91, 1991-92 and 1992-93 postseasons; maximum 22 contests for 1990-91; no representative may recruit; deleted team and individual records for 1986 championship; annual compliance reports; disassociated one representative; show cause why more penalties should not be imposed if institution does not disassociate another representative.

West Texas St.—VIOLATIONS: improper financial aid and transportation; extra benefits; improper recruiting, entertainment, inducements and transportation; unethical conduct; institutional control; certification of compliance. SANCTIONS: 3-year probation; no 1988-89 postseason; maximum 10 grants for 1989-90 and 1990-91; no official visits for 1989-90; annual compliance reports; show cause why disciplinary action should not be taken if any member institution hires one former assistant coach during next 5 years or ex-head coach during next 3 years.

Major NCAA Coaching Changes

New head coaches were named at 39 Division I basketball schools after the 1990-91 season and at 16 Division I football schools following the 1990 season. Coaching changes listed below are as of Sept. 1, 1991.

Division I Basketball

School	Old Head Coach	New Head Coach
Bradley	Stan Albeck	Jim Molinari
Brown	Mike Cingiser	Frank Dobbs
Central Conn.	Mike Brown	Mark Adams
Central Mich	Charlie Coles	Keith Dambrot
Colorado St	Boyd Grant	Stew Morrill
Cornell	Mike Dement	Jan van Breda Kolff
Creighton	Tony Barone	Rick Johnson
Dartmouth	Paul Cormier	Dave Faucher
Drexel	Eddie Burke	Bill Herrion
East Carolina	Mike Steele	Eddie Payne
Fairfield	Mitch Buonaguro	Paul Cormier
Harvard	Peter Roby	Frank Sullivan
Iona	Gary Brokaw	Jerry Welsh
Jacksonville	Rich Haddad	Matt Kilcullen
Mercer	Brad Siegfried	Bill Hodges
Middle Tenn.St.	Bruce Stewart	Dave Farrar
Montana	Stew Morrill	Blaine Taylor
Morehead St	Tommy Gaither	Dick Fick
Murray St	Steve Newton	Scott Edgar
NC-Greensboro	Bob McEvoy	Mike Dement
Northern Ill	Jim Molinari	Brian Hammel
Notre Dame	Digger Phelps	John MacLeod
Old Dominion	Tom Young	Oliver Purnell
Radford	Oliver Purnell	Ron Bradley
St.Francis-NY	Rich Zvosec	Ron Ganulin
St.Mary's-CA	Paul Landreaux & Dave Fehte*	Ernie Kent
Sam Houston St.	Larry Brown	Jerry Hopkins

*Interim coach in 1990-91.

School	Old Head Coach	New Head Coach
Samford	Ed McLean	John Brady
South Carolina	George Felton	Steve Newton
SW Texas St	Harry Larrabee	Jim Wooldridge
Tennessee St	Ron Abernathy	Frankie Allen
Texas A&M	Kermit Davis Jr.	Tony Barone
Texas Tech	Gerald Myers	James Dickey
Toledo	Jay Eck	Larry Gipson
Tulsa	J.D.Barnett	Tubby Smith
UC-Irvine	Bill Mulligan	Rod Baker
Virginia Tech	Frankie Allen	Bill Foster
Weber St	Denny Huston	Ron Abegglen

Division I-A Football

School	Old Head Coach	New Head Coach
Army	Jim Young	Bob Sutton
Boston Collage	Jack Bicknell	Tom Coughlin
Bowling Green	Moe Ankney	Gary Blackney
Kent	Dick Crum	Pete Cordelli
Long Beach St	George Allen	Willie Brown
LSU	Mike Archer	Curley Hallman
Mississippi St	Rockey Felker	Jackie Sherrill
Northern Ill	Jerry Pettibone	Charlie Sadler
Oregon St	Dave Kragthorpe	Jerry Pettibone
Purdue	Fred Akers	Jim Colletto
SMU	Forrest Gregg	Tom Rossley
Southern Miss	Curley Hallman	Jeff Bower
Syracuse	Dick MacPherson	Paul Pasqualoni
Toledo	Nick Saban	Gary Pinkel
Vanderbilt	Watson Brown	Gerry DiNardo
Wyoming	Paul Roach	Joe Tiller

1990-91 NAIA Team Champions

Lubbock Christian of Texas and **Central State** of Ohio each won two of the NAIA's 21 team championships during the 1990-91 school year. They were the only member schools to win more than once. Lubbock won titles in Men's Cross-country and Men's Indoor Track & Field, while Central had winners in Division I Football and Women's Outdoor Track & Field.

Note that numbers in parentheses indicate overall championships won in that sport.

FALL

Cross-country
Men's . . . . Lubbock Christian, TX (1)
Women's . . . . Western St., CO (1)

Football
Men's Division I . . . . Central St., OH (1)
Division II . . . . Peru St., NE (1)

Soccer
Men's . . . . West Virginia Weslayan (4)
Women's . . . . Berry College, GA (2)

Volleyball
Women's . . . . Hawaii Pacific (1)

WINTER

Basketball
Men's . . . . Oklahoma City (1)
Women's . . . . Ft.Hayes State, KS (1)

Swimming & Diving
Men's . . . . Drury College, MO (7)
Women's . . . . Simon Fraser, BC (4)

Indoor Track
Men's . . . . Lubbock Christian, TX (1)
Women's . . . . Prairie View A&M, TX (3)

Wrestling
Men's . . . . Northern Montana (1)

SPRING

Baseball
Men's . . . . Lewis-Clark St., ID (7)

Golf
Men's . . . . North Florida (1)

Softball
Women's . . . . Hawaii Loa (1)

Tennis
Men's . . . . Lander College, SC (3)
Women's . . . . Flagler College, FL (5)

Outdoor Track
Men's . . . . Azusa Pacific, CA (8)
Women's . . . . Central St., OH (1)

NCAA Division I Basketball Schools
(Conferences and coaches as of Aug. 1, 1991.)

New conference: Great Midwest (Ala-Birmingham, DePaul, Cincinnati, Marquette, Memphis St. and St.Louis).

Conference merger: American South and Sun Belt, becoming new Sun Belt (Arkansas St., Ark-Little Rock, Central Fla., Jacksonville, Lamar, La.Tech, New Orleans, South Alabama, Southwestern La., Pan American and Western Ky.).

Switching conferences (26): Ala-Birmingham from Sun Belt to Great Midwest; Arkansas from SWC to SEC; Ark-Little Rock from Trans America to Sun Belt; Arkansas St. from American South to Sun Belt; Central Florida from American South to Sun Belt; Cincinnati from Metro to Great Midwest; Delaware from East Coast to North Atlantic; Drexel from East Coast to North Atlantic; Florida St. from Metro to ACC; Lamar from American South to Sun Belt; La.Tech from American South to Sun Belt; Marquette from Midwestern to Great Midwest; Memphis St. from Metro to Great Midwest; Navy from Colonial to Patriot; New Orleans from American South to Sun Belt; NC-Charlotte from Sun Belt to Metro; Old Dominion from Sun Belt to Colonial; Pan American from American South to Sun Belt; Penn St. from Atlantic 10 to Big 10; St.Louis from Midwestern to Great Midwest; South Carolina from Metro to SEC; South Florida from Sun Belt to Metro; SW Louisiana from American South to Sun Belt; Texas-San Antonio from Trans America to Southland; VCU from Sun Belt to Metro.

Leaving conference and Division I: Augusta from Big South to Division II.

Independents joining conferences (11): Brooklyn to East Coast; Buffalo (up from Div.II) to East Coast; DePaul to Great Midwest; Florida International to Trans America; Liberty to Big South; Miami-FL to Big East; Nicholls St. to Southland; SE Louisiana to Trans America; SE Missouri St. (up from Div.II) to Ohio Valley; Wright St. to Mid-Continent; Youngstown St. to Mid Continent.

Independent gone out of business: U.S.International.

New Independents (3): Cal.St-Sacramento, Charleston-SC and NC-Greensboro (all moved up from Division II).

School name change: Baptist College of the Big South becomes Charleston Baptist.

School nickname change: Eastern Michigan from Hurons to Eagles.

Switching conferences in 1992-93 (5): Fresno St. from Big West to WAC; Davidson from Big South to Southern; Georgia Southern from Trans America to Southern; Nevada from Big Sky to Big West; Rider from East Coast to Northeast.

Independent joining conference in 1992-93: Charleston-SC to Trans America.

	Nickname	Conference	Head Coach	Location	Colors
Air Force	Falcons	WAC	Reggie Minton	Colo.Springs,CO	Blue/Silver
Akron	Zips	Mid-Cont.	Coleman Crawford	Akron,OH	Blue/Gold
Alabama	Crimson Tide	SEC-West	Wimp Sanderson	Tuscaloosa,AL	Crimson/White
Alabama St	Hornets	S'western	James Oliver	Montgomery,AL	Black/Gold
Alabama-Birm	Blazers	Gt.Midwest	Gene Bartow	Birmingham,AL	Green/Gold
Alcorn St	Braves	S'western	Lonnie Walker	Lorman,MS	Purple/Gold
American	Eagles	Colonial	Chris Knoche	Washington,DC	Red/White/Blue
Appalachian St	Mountaineers	Southern	Tom Apke	Boone,NC	Black/Gold
Arizona	Wildcats	Pac-10	Lute Olson	Tucson,AZ	Cardinal/Navy
Arizona St	Sun Devils	Pac-10	Bill Frieder	Tempe,AZ	Maroon/Gold
Arkansas	Razorbacks	SEC-West	Nolan Richardson	Fayetville,AR	Cardinal/White
Arkansas St	Indians	Sun Belt	Nelson Catalina	Jonesboro,AR	Scarlet/Black
Ark-Little Rock	Trojans	Sun Belt	Jim Platt	Little Rock,AR	Maroon/White
Army	Cadets	Patriot	Tom Miller	West Point,NY	Black/Gold/Gray
Auburn	Tigers	SEC-West	Tommy Joe Eagles	Auburn,AL	Orange/Blue
Austin Peay	Governors	Ohio Valley	Dave Loos	Clarksville,TN	Red/White
Ball St	Cardinals	MAC	Dick Hunsaker	Muncie,IN	Cardinal/White
Baylor	Bears	SWC	Gene Iba	Waco,TX	Green/Gold
Bethune-Cookman	Wildcats	Mid-Eastern	Jack McLairen	Daytona Beach,FL	Maroon/Gold
Boise St	Broncos	Big Sky	Bobby Dye	Boise,ID	Orange/Blue
Boston College	Eagles	Big East	Jim O'Brien	Chestnut Hill,MA	Maroon/Gold
Boston Univ	Terriers	North Atl.	Bob Brown	Boston,MA	Scarlet/White
Bowling Green	Falcons	MAC	Jim Larranaga	Bowling Green,OH	Orange/Brown
Bradley	Braves	Mo.Valley	Jim Molinari	Peoria,IL	Red/White
BYU	Cougars	WAC	Roger Reid	Provo,UT	Blue/White
Brooklyn	Kingsmen	East Coast	Ron Kestenbaum	Brooklyn,NY	Maroon/Gold
Brown	Bruins	Ivy	Frank Dobbs	Providence,RI	Brown/Red/White
Bucknell	Bison	Patriot	Charlie Woollum	Lewisburg,PA	Orange/Blue
Buffalo	Bulls	East Coast	Dan Bazzani	Buffalo,NY	Blue/Red/White
Butler	Bulldogs	Midwestern	Barry Collier	Indianapolis,IN	Blue/White
California	Golden Bears	Pac-10	Lou Campanelli	Berkeley,CA	Blue/Gold
CS-Fullerton	Titans	Big West	John Sneed	Fullerton,CA	Orange/Blue/White
CS-Northridge	Matadors	Indep.	Pete Cassidy	Northridge,CA	Red/White
CS-Sacramento	Hornets	Indep.	Joe Anders	Sacramento,CA	Green/Gold
Campbell	Fighting Camels	Big South	Billy Lee	Buies Creek,NC	Orange/Black
Canisius	Golden Griffins	Metro Atl.	Marty Marbach	Buffalo,NY	Blue/Gold
Centenary	Gentlemen	Trans Am.	Tom Canterbury	Shreveport,LA	Maroon/White
Central Conn	Blue Devils	East Coast	Mark Adams	New Britain,CT	Blue/White
Central Fla	Knights	Sun Belt	Joe Dean Jr.	Orlando,FL	Black/Gold
Central Mich	Chippewas	MAC	Keith Dambrot	Mt.Pleasant,MI	Maroon/Gold

NCAA Division I Basketball Schools (Cont.)

	Nickname	Conference	Head Coach	Location	Colors
Charleston-SC	Cougars	Indep.	John Kresse	Charleston,SC	Maroon/White
Charl.Southern	Buccaneers	Big South	Gary Edwards	Charleston,SC	Blue/Gold
Chicago St	Cougars	Indep.	Tommy Suitts	Chicago,IL	Green/White
Cincinnati	Bearcats	Gt.Midwest	Bob Huggins	Cincinnati,OH	Red/Black
The Citadel	Bulldogs	Southern	Randy Nesbit	Charleston,SC	Blue/White
Clemson	Tigers	ACC	Cliff Ellis	Clemson,SC	Purple/Orange
Cleveland St	Vikings	Mid-Cont.	Mike Boyd	Cleveland,OH	Green/White
Coastal Carolina	Chanticleers	Big South	Russ Bergman	Conway,SC	Red/White/Black
Colgate	Red Raiders	Patriot	Jack Bruen	Hamilton,NY	Maroon/White
Colorado	Buffaloes	Big 8	Joe Harrington	Boulder,CO	Silver/Gold/Black
Colorado St	Rams	WAC	Stew Morrill	Ft.Collins,CO	Green/Gold
Columbia	Lions	Ivy	Jack Rohan	New York,NY	Lt.Blue/White
Connecticut	Huskies	Big East	Jim Calhoun	Storrs,CT	Blue/White
Coppin St	Eagles	Mid-Eastern	Ron Mitchell	Baltimore,MD	Blue/Gold
Cornell	Big Red	Ivy	Jan van Breda Kolff	Ithaca,NY	Red/White
Creighton	Bluejays	Mo.Valley	Rick Johnson	Omaha,NE	Blue/White
Dartmouth	Big Green	Ivy	Dave Faucher	Hanover,NH	Green/White
Davidson	Wildcats	Big South	Bob McKillop	Davidson,NC	Red/Black
Dayton	Flyers	Midwestern	Jim O'Brien	Dayton,OH	Red/Blue
DePaul	Blue Demons	Gt.Midwest	Joey Meyer	Chicago,IL	Scarlet/Blue
Delaware	Blue Hens	North Atl.	Steve Steinwedel	Newark,DE	Blue/Gold
Delaware St	Hornets	Mid-Eastern	Jeff Jones	Dover,DE	Red/Blue
Detroit	Titans	Midwestern	Ricky Byrdsong	Detroit,MI	Cardinal/White
Drake	Bulldogs	Mo.Valley	Rudy Washington	Des Moines,IA	Blue/White
Drexel	Dragons	North Atl.	Bill Herrion	Philadelphia,PA	Navy/Gold
Duke	Blue Devils	ACC	Mike Krzyzewski	Durham,NC	Royal Blue/White
Duquesne	Dukes	Atlantic 10	John Carroll	Pittsburgh,PA	Red/Blue
East Carolina	Pirates	Colonial	Eddie Payne	Greenville,NC	Purple/Gold
East Tenn.St	Buccaneers	Southern	Alan LeForce	Johnson City,TN	Blue/Gold
Eastern Ill	Panthers	Mid-Cont.	Rick Samuels	Charleston,IL	Blue/Gray
Eastern Ky	Colonels	Ohio Valley	Mike Pollio	Richmond,KY	Maroon/White
Eastern Mich	Eagles	MAC	Ben Braun	Ypsilanti,MI	Green/White
Eastern Wash	Eagles	Big Sky	John H.Wade II	Cheney,WA	Red/White
Evansville	Purple Aces	Midwestern	Jim Crews	Evansville,IN	Purple/White
Fairfield	Stags	Metro Atl.	Paul Cormier	Fairfield,CT	Cardinal
FDU-Teaneck	Knights	Northeast	Tom Green	Teaneck,NJ	Maroon/White/Blue
Florida	Gators	SEC-East	Lon Kruger	Gainesville,FL	Orange/Blue
Florida A&M	Rattlers	Mid-Eastern	Willie Booker	Tallahassee,FL	Orange/Green
Florida Int'l	Golden Panthers	Trans Am.	Bob Weltlich	Miami,FL	Blue/Gold
Florida St	Seminoles	ACC	Pat Kennedy	Tallahassee,FL	Garnet/Gold
Fordham	Rams	Patriot	Nick Macarchuk	Bronx,NY	Maroon/White
Fresno St	Bulldogs	Big West	Gary Colson	Fresno,CA	Cardinal/Blue
Furman	Paladins	Southern	Butch Estes	Greenville,SC	Purple/White
George Mason	Patriots	Colonial	Ernie Nestor	Fairfax,VA	Green/Gold
Geo.Washington	Colonials	Atlantic 10	Mike Jarvis	Washington,DC	Buff/Blue
Georgetown	Hoyas	Big East	John Thompson	Washington,DC	Blue/Gray
Georgia	Bulldogs,'Dawgs	SEC-East	Hugh Durham	Athens,GA	Red/Black
Ga.Southern	Eagles	Trans Am.	Frank Kerns	Statesboro,GA	Blue/White
Georgia St	Crimson Panthers	Trans Am.	Bob Reinhart	Atlanta,GA	Royal Blue/Crimson
Georgia Tech	Yellow Jackets	ACC	Bobby Cremins	Atlanta,GA	Old Gold/White
Gonzaga	Bulldogs,Zags	West Coast	Dan Fitzgerald	Spokane,WA	Blue/White/Red
Grambling	Tigers	S'western	Robert Hopkins	Grambling,LA	Black/Gold
Hartford	Hawks	North Atl.	Jack Phelan	W.Hartford,CT	Scarlet/White
Harvard	Crimson	Ivy	Frank Sullivan	Cambridge,MA	Crimson/Black/White
Hawaii	Rainbows	WAC	Riley Wallace	Honolulu,HI	Green/White
Hofstra	Flying Dutchmen	East Coast	Bill van Breda Kolff	Hempstead,NY	Blue/White/Gold
Holy Cross	Crusaders	Patriot	George Blaney	Worcester,MA	Royal Purple
Houston	Cougars	SWC	Pat Foster	Houston,TX	Cougar Red/White
Howard	Bison	Mid-Eastern	Butch Beard	Washington,DC	Blue/White
Idaho	Vandals	Big Sky	Larry Eustachy	Moscow,ID	Silver/Gold
Idaho St	Bengals	Big Sky	Herb Williams	Pocatello,ID	Orange/Black
Illinois	Fighting Illini	Big 10	Lou Henson	Champaign,IL	Orange/Blue
Ill-Chicago	Flames	Mid-Cont.	Bob Hallberg	Chicago,IL	Indigo/Flame
Illinois St	Redbirds	Mo.Valley	Bob Bender	Normal,IL	Red/White

	Nickname	Conference	Head Coach	Location	Colors
Indiana	Hoosiers	Big 10	Bob Knight	Bloomington,IN	Cream/Crimson
Indiana St	Sycamores	Mo.Valley	Tates Locke	Terre Haute,IN	Blue/White
Iona	Gaels	Metro Atl.	Jerry Welsh	New Rochelle,NY	Maroon/Gold
Iowa	Hawkeyes	Big 10	Tom Davis	Iowa City,IA	Old Gold/Black
Iowa St	Cyclones	Big 8	Johnny Orr	Ames,IA	Cardinal/Gold
Jackson St	Tigers	S'western	John Prince	Jackson,MS	Blue/White
Jacksonville	Dolphins	Sun Belt	Matt Kilcullen	Jacksonville,FL	Green/Gold
James Madison	Dukes	Colonial	Lefty Driesell	Harrisonburg,VA	Purple/Gold
Kansas	Jayhawks	Big 8	Roy Williams	Lawrence,KS	Crimson/Blue
Kansas St	Wildcats	Big 8	Dana Altman	Manhattan,KS	Purple/White
Kent	Golden Flashes	MAC	Jim McDonald	Kent,OH	Navy Blue/Gold
Kentucky	Wildcats	SEC-East	Rick Pitino	Lexington,KY	Blue/White
La Salle	Explorers	Metro Atl.	Bill Morris	Philadelphia,PA	Blue/Gold
Lafayette	Leopards	Patriot	John Leone	Easton,PA	Maroon/White
Lamar	Cardinals	Sun Belt	Mike Newell	Beaumont,TX	Red/White
Lehigh	Engineers	Patriot	Dave Duke	Bethlehem,PA	Brown/White
Liberty	Flames	Big South	Jeff Meyer	Lynchburg,VA	Red/White/Blue
Long Beach St	49ers	Big West	Seth Greenberg	Long Beach,CA	Brown/Gold
LIU-Brooklyn	Blackbirds	Northeast	Paul Lizzo	Brooklyn,NY	Blue/White
LSU	Fighting Tigers	SEC-West	Dale Brown	Baton Rouge,LA	Purple/Gold
Louisiana Tech	Bulldogs	Sun Belt	Jerry Loyd	Ruston,LA	Red/Blue
Louisville	Cardinals	Metro	Denny Crum	Louisville,KY	Red/Black/White
Loyola-CA	Lions	West Coast	Jay Hillock	Los Angeles,CA	Crimson/Gray/Lt.Blue
Loyola-IL	Ramblers	Midwestern	Will Rey	Chicago,IL	Maroon/Gold
Loyola-MD	Greyhounds	Metro Atl.	Tom Schneider	Baltimore,MD	Green/Gray
Maine	Black Bears	North Atl.	Rudy Keeling	Orono,ME	Blue/White
Manhattan	Jaspers	Metro Atl.	Steve Lappas	Riverdale,NY	Green/White
Marist	Red Foxes	Northeast	Dave Magarity	Poughkeepsie,NY	Red/White
Marquette	Warriors	Gt.Midwest	Kevin O'Neill	Milwaukee,WI	Blue/Gold
Marshall	Thundering Herd	Southern	Dwight Freeman	Huntington,WV	Green/White
Maryland	Terrapins	ACC	Gary Williams	College Park,MD	Red/White/Black/Gold
Md-Balt.County	Retrievers	East Coast	Earl Hawkins	Baltimore,MD	Black/Old Gold
Md-E.Shore	Hawks	Mid-Eastern	Robert Hopkins	Princess Anne,MD	Maroon/Gray
Massachusetts	Minutemen	Atlantic 10	John Calipari	Amherst,MA	Maroon/White
McNeese St	Cowboys	Southland	Steve Welch	Lake Charles,LA	Blue/Gold
Memphis St	Tigers	Gt.Midwest	Larry Finch	Memphis,TN	Blue/Gray
Mercer	Bears	Trans Am.	Bill Hodges	Macon,GA	Orange/Black
Miami-FL	Hurricanes	Big East	Leonard Hamilton	Miami,FL	Orange/Green/White
Miami-OH	Redskins	MAC	Joby Wright	Oxford,OH	Red/White
Michigan	Wolverines	Big 10	Steve Fisher	Ann Arbor,MI	Maize/Blue
Michigan St	Spartans	Big 10	Jud Heathcote	East Lansing,MI	Green/White
Mid.Tenn.St	Blue Raiders	Ohio Valley	Dave Farrar	Murfreesboro,TN	Blue/White
Minnesota	Golden Gophers	Big 10	Clem Haskins	Minneapolis,MN	Maroon/White
Mississippi	Rebels,Ole Miss	SEC-West	Ed Murphy	Oxford,MS	Red/Blue
Mississippi St	Bulldogs	SEC-West	Richard Williams	Starkville,MS	Maroon/White
Miss.Valley	Delta Devils	S'western	Lafayette Stribling	Itta Bena,MS	Green/White
Missouri	Tigers	Big 8	Norm Stewart	Columbia,MO	Old Gold/Black
Missouri-KC	Kangaroos	Indep.	Lee Hunt	Kansas City,MO	Blue/Gold
Monmouth	Hawks	Northeast	Wayne Szoke	W.Long Branch,NJ	Royal Blue/White
Montana	Grizzlies	Big Sky	Blaine Taylor	Missoula,MT	Copper/Silver/Gold
Montana St	Bobcats	Big Sky	Mick Durham	Bozeman,MT	Blue/Gold
Morehead St	Eagles	Ohio Valley	Dick Fick	Morehead,KY	Blue/Gold
Morgan St	Bears	Mid-Eastern	Michael Holmes	Baltimore,MD	Blue/Orange
Mt.St.Mary's	Mountaineers	Northeast	Joe McGuinness	Emmitsburg,MD	Navy Blue/Old Gold
Murray St	Racers	Ohio Valley	Scott Edgar	Murray,KY	Blue/Gold
Navy	Midshipmen	Patriot	Pete Herrmann	Annapolis,MD	Navy Blue/Gold
Nebraska	Cornhuskers	Big 8	Danny Nee	Lincoln,ME	Scarlet/Cream
Nevada	Wolf Pack	Big Sky	Len Stevens	Reno,NV	Silver/Blue
New Hampshire	Wildcats	North Atl.	Jim Boylan	Durham,NH	Blue/White
New Mexico	Lobos	WAC	Dave Bliss	Albuquerque,NM	Cherry/Silver
New Mexico St	Aggies	Big West	Neil McCarthy	Las Cruces,NM	Crimson/White
New Orleans	Privateers	Sun Belt	Tim Floyd	New Orleans,LA	Royal Blue/Silver
Niagara	Purple Eagles	Metro Atl.	Jack Armstrong	Niagara,NY	Purple/White/Gold
Nicholls St	Colonels	Southland	Rickey Broussard	Thibodaux,LA	Red/Gray
N.Carolina	Tar Heels	ACC	Dean Smith	Chapel Hill,NC	Carolina Blue/White
N.CarolA&T	Aggies	Mid-Eastern	Don Corbett	Greensboro,NC	Blue/Gold
N.C.State	Wolfpack	ACC	Les Robinson	Raleigh,NC	Red/White

NCAA Division I Basketball Schools (Cont.)

	Nickname	Conference	Head Coach	Location	Colors
NC-Asheville	Bulldogs	Big South	Don Doucette	Asheville,NC	Royal Blue/White
NC-Charlotte	49ers	Metro	Jeff Mullins	Charlotte,NC	Green/White
NC-Greensboro	Spartans	Indep.	Mike Dement	Greensboro,NC	Gold/White/Navy
NC-Wilmington	Seahawks	Colonial	Kevin Eastman	Wilmington,NC	Green/Gold
North Texas	Mean Green	Southland	Jimmy Gales	Denton,TX	Green/White
NE Illinois	Golden Eagles	Indep.	Rees Johnson	Chicago,IL	Royal Blue/Gold
NE Louisiana	Indians	Southland	Mike Vining	Monroe,LA	Maroon/Gold
Northeastern	Huskies	North Atl.	Karl Fogel	Boston,MA	Red/Black
Northern Ariz	Lumberjacks	Big Sky	Harold Merritt	Flagstaff,AZ	Blue/Gold
Northern Ill	Huskies	Mid-Cont.	Brian Hammel	De Kalb,IL	Cardinal/Black
Northern Iowa	Panthers	Mo.Valley	Eldon Miller	Cedar Falls,IA	Purple/Old Gold
Northwestern	Wildcats	Big 10	Bill Foster	Evanston,IL	Purple/White
Northwestern-LA	Demons	Southland	Dan Bell	Natchitoches,LA	Burnt Orange/Purple
Notre Dame	Fighting Irish	Indep.	John MacLeod	South Bend,IN	Gold/Blue
Ohio Univ	Bobcats	MAC	Larry Hunter	Athens,OH	Kelly Green/White
Ohio St	Buckeyes	Big 10	Randy Ayers	Columbus,OH	Scarlet/Gray
Oklahoma	Sooners	Big 8	Billy Tubbs	Norman,OK	Crimson/Cream
Oklahoma St	Cowboys	Big 8	Eddie Sutton	Stillwater,OK	Orange/Black
Old Dominion	Monarchs	Colonial	Oliver Purnell	Norfolk,VA	Slate Blue/Silver
Oregon	Ducks	Pac-10	Don Monson	Eugene,OR	Green/Yellow
Oregon St	Beavers	Pac-10	Jim Anderson	Corvallis,OR	Orange/Black
Pacific	Tigers	Big West	Bob Thomason	Stockton,CA	Orange/Black
Pan American	Broncs	Sun Belt	Kevin Wall	Edinburg,TX	Green/White
Penn St	Nittany Lions	Big 10	Bruce Parkhill	Univ.Park,PA	Blue/White
Penn	Quakers	Ivy	Fran Dunphy	Philadelphia,PA	Red/Blue
Pepperdine	Waves	West Coast	Tom Asbury	Malibu,CA	Blue/Orange
Pittsburgh	Panthers	Big East	Paul Evans	Pittsburgh,PA	Gold/Blue
Portland	Pilots	West Coast	Larry Steele	Portland,OR	Purple/White
Prairie View	Panthers	S'western	Jim Duplantier	Prairie View,TX	Purple/Gold
Princeton	Tigers	Ivy	Pete Carril	Princeton,NJ	Orange/Black
Providence	Friars	Big East	Rick Barnes	Providence,RI	Black/White
Purdue	Boilermakers	Big 10	Gene Keady	W.Lafayette,IN	Old Gold/Black
Radford	Highlanders	Big South	Ron Bradley	Radford,VA	Blue/Red/Green
Rhode Island	Rams	Atlantic 10	Al Skinner	Kingston,RI	Blue/White
Rice	Owls	SWC	Scott Thompson	Houston,TX	Blue/Gray
Richmond	Spiders	Colonial	Dick Tarrant	Richmond,VA	Red/Blue
Rider	Broncs	East Coast	Kevin Bannon	Lawrenceville,NJ	Purple/Gold
Robert Morris	Colonials	Northeast	Jarrett Durham	Coraopolis,PA	Blue/White
Rutgers	Scarlet Knights	Atlantic 10	Bob Wenzel	New Brunswick,NJ	Scarlet
St.Bonaventure	Bonnies	Atlantic 10	Tom Chapman	St.Bonaventure,NY	Brown/White
St.Francis-NY	Terriers	Northeast	Ron Ganulin	Brooklyn,NY	Red/Blue
St.Francis-PA	Red Flash	Northeast	Jim Baron	Loretto,PA	Red/White
St.John's	Redmen	Big East	Lou Carnesecca	Jamaica,NY	Red/White
St.Joseph's-PA	Hawks	Atlantic 10	John Griffin	Philadelphia,PA	Crimson/Gray
St.Louis	Billikens	Midwestern	Rich Grawer	St. Louis,MO	Blue/White
St.Mary's-CA	Gaels	West Coast	Ernie Kent	Moraga,CA	Red/Blue
St.Peter's	Peacocks	Metro Atl.	Ted Fiore	Jersey City,NJ	Blue/White
Sam Houston St	Bearkats	Southland	Jerry Hopkins	Huntsville,TX	Orange/White
Samford	Bulldogs	Trans-Am.	John Brady	Birmingham,AL	Crimson/Blue
San Diego	Toreros	West Coast	Hank Egan	San Diego,CA	Lt.Blue/Navy/White
San Diego St	Aztecs	WAC	Jim Brandenburg	San Diego, CA	Scarlet/Black
San Francisco	Dons	West Coast	Jim Brovelli	San Francisco,CA	Green/Gold
San Jose St	Spartans	Big West	Stan Morrison	San Jose,CA	Gold/White/Blue
Santa Clara	Broncos	West Coast	Carroll Williams	Santa Clara,CA	Bronco Red/White
Seton Hall	Pirates	Big East	P.J.Carlesimo	South Orange,NJ	Blue/White
Siena	Saints	Metro Atl.	Mike Deane	Loudonville,NY	Green/Gold
S.Alabama	Jaguars	Sun Belt	Ronnie Arrow	Mobile,AL	Red/White/Blue
S.Carolina	Gamecocks	SEC-East	Steve Newton	Columbia,SC	Garnet/Black
S.Carolina St	Bulldogs	Mid-Eastern	Cy Alexander	Orangeburg,SC	Garnet/Black
S.Florida	Bulls	Metro	Bobby Paschal	Tampa,FL	Green/Gold
SE Louisiana	Lions	Trans Am.	Don Wilson	Hammond,LA	Green/Gold
SE Missouri St	Indians	Ohio Valley	Ron Shumate	Cape Girardeau,MO	Red/Black

	Nickname	Conference	Head Coach	Location	Colors
Southern Ill	Salukis	Mo.Valley	Rich Herrin	Carbondale,IL	Maroon/White
SMU	Mustangs	Southwest	John Shumate	Dallas,TX	Red/Blue
Southern Miss	Golden Eagles	Metro	M.K.Turk	Hattiesburg,MS	Black/Gold
So.Utah St	Thunderbirds	Indep.	Neil Roberts	Cedar City,UT	Scarlet/Royal Blue
Southern-BR	Jaguars	S'western	Ben Jobe	Baton Rouge,LA	Blue/Gold
SW Missouri St	Bears	Mo.Valley	Charlie Spoonhour	Springfield,MO	Maroon/White
SW Texas St	Bobcats	Southland	Jim Wooldridge	San Marcos,TX	Maroon/Gold
SW Louisiana	Ragin' Cajuns	Sun Belt	Marty Fletcher	Lafayette,LA	Vermilion/White
Stanford	Cardinal	Pac 10	Mike Montgomery	Stanford,CA	Cardinal/White
S.F.Austin St	Lumberjacks	Southland	Ned Fowler	Nacogdoches,TX	Purple/White
Stetson	Hatters	Trans Am.	Glenn Wilkes	DeLand,FL	Green/White
Syracuse	Orangemen	Big East	Jim Boeheim	Syracuse,NY	Orange
Temple	Owls	Atlantic 10	John Chaney	Philadelphia,PA	Cherry/White
Tennessee	Volunteers	SEC-East	Wade Houston	Knoxville,TN	Orange/White
Tennessee-Chatt.	Moccasins	Southern	Mack McCarthy	Nashville,TN	Blue/White
Tennessee St	Tigers	Ohio Valley	Frankie Allen	Cookeville,TN	Purple/Gold
Tenn Tech	Golden Eagles	Ohio Valley	Tom Deaton	Chattanooga,TN	Navy Blue/Gold
Texas	Longhorns	SWC	Tom Penders	Austin,TX	Burnt Orange/White
Texas A&M	Aggies	SWC	Tony Barone	College Station,TX	Maroon/White
TCU	Horned Frogs	SWC	Moe Iba	Ft. Worth,TX	Purple/White
Texas Southern	Tigers	S'western	Robert Moreland	Houston,TX	Maroon/Gray
Texas Tech	Red Raiders	SWC	James Dickey	Lubbock,TX	Scarlet/Black
TX-Arlington	Mavericks	Southland	Mark Nixon	Arlington,TX	Royal Blue/White
TX-S.Antonio	Roadrunners	Southland	Stu Starner	San Antonio,TX	Orange/Navy Blue
Toledo	Rockets	MAC	Larry Gipson	Toledo,OH	Blue/Gold
Towson St	Tigers	East Coast	Terry Truax	Towson,MD	Gold/White/Black
Tulane	Green Wave	Metro	Perry Clark	New Orleans,LA	Olive Green/Sky Blue
Tulsa	Golden Hurricane	Mo.Valley	Tubby Smith	Tulsa,OK	Blue/Red/Gold
UC-Irvine	Anteaters	Big West	Rod Baker	Irvine,CA	Blue/Gold
UCLA	Bruins	Pac-10	Jim Harrick	Los Angeles,CA	Blue/Gold
UC-S.Barbara	Gauchos	Big West	Jerry Pimm	Santa Barbara,CA	Blue/Gold
UNLV	Runnin' Rebels	Big West	Jerry Tarkanian	Las Vegas,NV	Scarlet/Gray
USC	Trojans	Pac-10	George Raveling	Los Angeles,CA	Cardinal/Gold
Utah	Utes	WAC	Rick Majerus	Salt Lake City,UT	Crimson/White
Utah St	Aggies	Big West	Kohn Smith	Logan,UT	Navy Blue/White
UTEP	Miners	WAC	Don Haskins	El Paso,TX	Orange/White/Blue
Valparaiso	Crusaders	Mid-Cont.	Homer Drew	Valparaiso,IN	Brown/Gold
Vanderbilt	Commodores	SEC-East	Eddie Fogler	Nashville,TN	Black/Gold
Vermont	Catamounts	North Atl.	Tom Brennan	Burlington,VT	Green/Gold
Villanova	Wildcats	Big East	Rollie Massimino	Villanova,PA	Blue/White
Virginia	Cavaliers	ACC	Jeff Jones	Charlottesville,VA	Orange/Blue
VCU	Rams	Metro	Sonny Smith	Richmond,VA	Black/Gold
VMI	Keydets	Southern	Joe Cantafio	Lexington,VA	Red/White/Yellow
Virginia Tech	Hokies,Gobblers	Metro	Bill Foster	Blacksburg,VA	Orange/Maroon
Wagner	Seahawks	Northeast	Tim Capstraw	Staten Island,NY	Green/White
Wake Forest	Demon Deacons	ACC	Dave Odom	Winston-Salem,NC	Old Gold/Black
Washington	Huskies	Pac-10	Lynn Nance	Seattle,WA	Purple/Gold
Washington St	Cougars	Pac-10	Kelvin Sampson	Pullman,WA	Crimson/Gray
Weber St	Wildcats	Big Sky	Ron Abegglen	Ogden,UT	Royal Purple/White
West Virginia	Mountaineers	Atlantic 10	Gale Catlett	Morgantown,WV	Old Gold/Blue
Western Caro	Catamounts	Southern	Greg Blatt	Cullowhee,NC	Purple/Gold
Western Ill	Leathernecks	Mid-Cont.	Jack Margenthaler	Macomb,IL	Purple/Gold
Western Ky	Hilltoppers	Sun Belt	Ralph Willard	Bowling Green,KY	Red/White
Western Mich	Broncos	MAC	Bob Donewald	Kalamazoo,MI	Brown/Gold
Wichita St	Shockers	Mo.Valley	Mike Cohen	Wichita,KS	Yellow/Black
William & Mary	Indians	Colonial	Chuck Swenson	Williamsburg,VA	Green/Gold/Silver
Winthrop	Eagles	Big South	Steve Vacendak	Rock Hill,SC	Garnet/Gold
Wisconsin	Badgers	Big 10	Steve Yoder	Madison,WI	Cardinal/White
WI-Green Bay	Phoenix	Mid-Cont.	Dick Bennett	Green Bay,WI	Cardinal/Green
Wright St	Raiders	Mid-Cont.	Ralph Underhill	Dayton,OH	Green/Gold
Wyoming	Cowboys	WAC	Benny Dees	Laramie,WY	Brown/Yellow
Xavier	Musketeers	Midwestern	Pete Gillen	Cincinnati,OH	Blue/White
Yale	Bulldogs,Elis	Ivy	Dick Kuchen	New Haven,CT	Yale Blue/White
Youngstown St	Penguins	Mid-Cont.	Jim Cleamons	Youngstown,OH	Scarlet/White

NCAA Division I-A Football Schools

New conference in 1991: Big East (Boston College, Miami-FL, Pittsburgh, Rutgers, Syracuse, Temple, Virginia Tech and West Virginia).

Switching conferences in 1992 (3): Arkansas from SWC to SEC; Fresno St. from Big West to WAC; Nevada from Big Sky (Div.I-AA) to Big West.

Independents joining conferences in 1991 (8): Boston College to Big East; Miami-FL to Big East; Pittsburgh to Big East; Rutgers to Big East; Syracuse to Big East; Temple to Big East; Virginia Tech to Big East; West Virginia to Big East.

Independents joining conferences in 1992 (2): Florida St. to ACC; South Carolina to SEC.

Independent joining conference in 1993: Penn St. to Big 10.

School nickname change: Eastern Michigan from Hurons to Eagles.

	Nickname	Conference	Head Coach	Location	Colors
Air Force	Falcons	WAC	Fisher DeBerry	Colo.Springs,CO	Blue/Silver
Akron	Zips	Indep.	Gerry Faust	Akron,OH	Blue/Gold
Alabama	Crimson Tide	SEC	Gene Stallings	Tuscaloosa,AL	Crimson/White
Arizona	Wildcats	Pac-10	Dick Tomey	Tucson,AZ	Cardinal/Navy
Arizona St	Sun Devils	Pac-10	Larry Marmie	Tempe,AZ	Maroon/Gold
Arkansas	Razorbacks	SEC ('92)	Jack Crowe	Fayetteville,AR	Cardinal/White
Army	Cadets	Indep.	Bob Sutton	West Point,NY	Black/Gold/Gray
Auburn	Tigers	SEC	Pat Dye	Auburn,AL	Orange/Blue
Ball St	Cardinals	MAC	Paul Schudel	Muncie,IN	Cardinal/White
Baylor	Bears	SWC	Grant Teaff	Waco,TX	Green/Gold
Boston College	Eagles	Big East	Tom Coughlin	Chestnut Hill,MA	Maroon/Gold
Bowling Green	Falcons	MAC	Gary Blackney	Bowling Green,OH	Orange/Brown
BYU	Cougars	WAC	LaVell Edwards	Provo,UT	Blue/White
California	Golden Bears	Pac-10	Bruce Snyder	Berkeley,CA	Blue/Gold
CS-Fullerton	Titans	Big West	Gene Murphy	Fullerton,CA	Orange/Blue/White
Central Mich	Chippewas	MAC	Herb Deromedi	Mt.Pleasant,MI	Maroon/Gold
Cincinnati	Bearcats	Metro	Tim Murphy	Cincinnato,OH	Red/Black
Clemson	Tigers	ACC	Ken Hatfield	Clemson,SC	Purple/Orange
Colorado	Buffaloes	Big 8	Bill McCartney	Boulder,CO	Silver/Gold/Black
Colorado St	Rams	WAC	Earle Bruce	Ft.Collins,CO	Green/Gold
Duke	Blue Devils	ACC	Barry Wilson	Durham,NC	Royal Blue/White
East Carolina	Pirates	Indep.	Bill Lewis	Greenville,NC	Purple/Gold
Eastern Mich	Eagles	MAC	Jim Harkema	Ypsilanti,MI	Green/White
Florida	Gators	SEC	Steve Spurrier	Gainesville,FL	Orange/Blue
Florida St.	Seminoles	ACC ('92)	Bobby Bowden	Tallahassee,FL	Garnet/Gold
Fresno St	Bulldogs	WAC ('92)	Jim Sweeney	Fresno,CA	Cardinal/Blue
Georgia	Bulldogs,'Dawgs	SEC	Ray Goff	Athens,GA	Red/Black
Georgia Tech	Yellow Jackets	ACC	Bobby Ross	Atlanta,GA	Old Gold/White
Hawaii	Rainbows	WAC	Bob Wagner	Honolulu,HI	Green/White
Houston	Cougars	SWC	John Jenkins	Houston,TX	Cougar Red/White
Illinois	Fighting Illini	Big 10	John Mackovic	Champaign,IL	Orange/Blue
Indiana	Hoosiers	Big 10	Bill Mallory	Bloomington,IN	Cream/Crimson
Iowa	Hawkeyes	Big 10	Hayden Fry	Iowa City,IA	Old Gold/Black
Iowa St	Cyclones	Big 8	Jim Walden	Ames,IA	Cardinal/Gold
Kansas	Jayhawks	Big 8	Glen Mason	Lawrence,KS	Crimson/Blue
Kansas St	Wildcats	Big 8	Bill Snyder	Manhattan,KS	Purple/White
Kent	Golden Flashes	MAC	Pete Cordelli	Kent,OH	Navy Blue/Gold
Kentucky	Wildcats	SEC	Bill Curry	Lexington,KY	Blue/White
Long Beach St	49ers	Big West	Willie Brown	Long Beach,CA	Brown/Gold
LSU	Fighting Tigers	SEC	Curley Hallman	Baton Rouge,LA	Purple/Gold
Louisiana Tech	Bulldogs	Indep.	Joe Raymond Peace	Ruston,LA	Red/Blue
Louisville	Cardinals	Indep.	H.Schnellenberger	Louisville,KY	Red/Black/White
Maryland	Terrapins,Terps	ACC	Joe Krivak	College Park,MD	Red/White/Black/Gold
Memphis St	Tigers	Indep.	Chuck Stobart	Memphis,TN	Blue/Gray
Miami-FL	Hurricanes	Big East	Dennis Erickson	Miami,FL	Orange/Green/White
Miami-OH	Redskins	MAC	Randy Walker	Oxford,OH	Red/White

	Nickname	Conference	Head Coach	Location	Colors
Michigan	Wolverines	Big 10	Gary Moeller	Ann Arbor,MI	Maize/Blue
Michigan St.	Spartans	Big 10	George Perles	E.Lansing,MI	Green/White
Minnesota	Golden Gophers	Big 10	John Gutekunst	Minneapolis,MN	Maroon/Gold
Mississippi	Rebels,Ole Miss	SEC	Billy Brewer	Oxford,MS	Cardinal/Navy Blue
Mississippi St	Bulldogs	SEC	Jackie Sherrill	Starkville,MS	Maroon/White
Missouri	Tigers	Big 8	Bob Stull	Columbia,MO	Old Gold/Black
Navy	Midshipmen	Indep.	George Chaump	Annapolis,MD	Navy Blue/Gold
Nebraska	Cornhuskers	Big 8	Tom Osborne	Lincoln,NE	Scarlet/Cream
New Mexico	Lobos	WAC	Mike Sheppard	Albuquerque,NM	Cherry/Silver
New Mexico St	Aggies	Big West	Jim Hess	Las Cruces,NM	Crimson/White
North Carolina	Tar Heels	ACC	Mack Brown	Chapel Hill,NC	Carolina Blue/White
N.C.State	Wolfpack	ACC	Dick Sheridan	Raleigh,NC	Red/White
Northern III.	Huskies	Indep.	Charlie Sadler	De Kalb,IL	Cardinal/Black
Northwestern	Wildcats	Big 10	Francis Peay	Evanston,IL	Purple/White
Notre Dame	Fighting Irish	Indep.	Lou Holtz	South Bend,IN	Gold/Blue
Ohio Univ	Bobcats	MAC	Tom Lichtenberg	Athens,OH	Kelly Green/White
Ohio St.	Buckeyes	Big 10	John Cooper	Columbus,OH	Scarlet/Gray
Oklahoma	Sooners	Big 8	Gary Gibbs	Norman,OK	Crimson/Cream
Oklahoma St	Cowboys	Big 8	Pat Jones	Stillwater,OK	Orange/Black
Oregon	Ducks	Pac-10	Rich Brooks	Eugene,OR	Green/Yellow
Oregon St	Beavers	Pac-10	Jerry Pettibone	Corvallis,OR	Orange/Black
Pacific	Tigers	Big West	Walt Harris	Stockton,CA	Orange/Black
Penn St	Nittany Lions	Big 10 ('93)	Joe Paterno	Univ.Park,PA	Blue/White
Pittsburgh	Panthers	Big East	Paul Hackett	Pittsburgh,PA	Blue/Gold
Purdue	Boilermakers	Big 10	Jim Colletto	W.Lafayette,IN	Old Gold/Black
Rice	Owls	SWC	Fred Goldsmith	Houston,TX	Blue/Gray
Rutgers	Scarlet Knights	Big East	Doug Graber	New Brunswick,NJ	Scarlet
San Diego St	Aztecs	WAC	Al Luginbill	San Diego, CA	Scarlet/Black
San Jose St	Spartans	Big West	Terry Shea	San Jose, CA	Gold/White/Blue
South Carolina	Gamecocks	SEC ('92)	Sparky Woods	Columbia, SC	Garnet/Black
SMU	Mustangs	SWC	Tom Rossley	Dallas, TX	Red/Blue
Southern Miss	Golden Eagles	Indep.	Jeff Bower	Hattiesburg, MS	Black/Gold
SW Louisiana	Ragin' Cajuns	Indep.	Nelson Stokley	Lafayette, LA	Vermilion/White
Stanford	Cardinal	Pac-10	Dennis Green	Stanford, CA	Cardinal/White
Syracuse	Orangemen	Big East	Paul Pasqualoni	Syracuse, NY	Orange
Temple	Owls	Big East	Jerry Berndt	Philadelphia,PA	Cherry/White
Tennessee	Volunteers	SEC	Johnny Majors	Knoxville,TN	Orange/White
Texas	Longhorns	SWC	David McWilliams	Austin,TX	Burnt Orange/White
Texas A&M	Aggies	SWC	R.C.Slocum	College Station,TX	Maroon/White
TCU	Horned Frogs	SWC	Jim Wacker	Ft.Worth,TX	Purple/White
Texas Tech	Red Raiders	SWC	Spike Dykes	Lubbock,TX	Scarlet/Black
Toledo	Rockets	MAC	Gary Pinkel	Toledo,OH	Blue/Gold
Tulane	Green Wave	Indep.	Greg Davis	New Orleans,LA	Olive Green/Sky Blue
Tulsa	Golden Hurricane	Indep.	Dave Rader	Tulsa,OK	Blue/Gold
UCLA	Bruins	Pac-10	Terry Donahue	Los Angeles,CA	Blue/Gold
UNLV	Runnin' Rebels	Big West	Jim Strong	Las Vegas,NV	Scarlet/Gray
USC	Trojans	Pac-10	Larry Smith	Los Angeles, CA	Cardinal/Gold
Utah	Utes	WAC	Ron McBride	Salt Lake City,UT	Crimson/White
Utah St	Aggies	Big West	Chuck Shelton	Logan,UT	Navy Blue/White
UTEP	Miners	WAC	David Lee	El Paso,TX	Orange/White/Blue
Vanderbilt	Commodores	SEC	Gerry DiNardo	Nashville,TN	Black/Gold
Virginia	Cavaliers	ACC	George Welsh	Charlottesville,VA	Orange/Blue
Virginia Tech	Hokies,Gobblers	Big East	Frank Beamer	Blacksburg,VA	Orange/Maroon
Wake Forest	Demon Deacons	ACC	Bill Dooley	Winston-Salem,NC	Old Gold/Black
Washington	Huskies	Pac-10	Don James	Seattle,WA	Purple/Gold
Washington St	Cougars	Pac-10	Mike Price	Pullman,WA	Crimson/Gray
West Virginia	Mountaineers	Big East	Don Nehlen	Morgantown,WV	Old Gold/Blue
Western Mich.	Broncos	MAC	Al Molde	Kalamazoo,MI	Brown/Gold
Wisconsin	Badgers	Big 10	Barry Alvarez	Madison,WI	Cardinal/White
Wyoming	Cowboys	WAC	Joe Tiller	Laramie,WY	Brown/Yellow

NCAA Division I-AA Football Schools

Independent joining conference in 1992: *Western Ky. to Gateway.*

Independents joining conferences in 1993 (3): *James Madison to Yankee; Northeastern to Yankee; William & Mary to Yankee.*

Switching conferences in 1992: *Nevada from Big Sky to Big West (Div.I-A).*

	Nickname	Conference	Head Coach	Location	Colors
Alabama St	Hornets	S'western	Houston Markham	Montgomery,AL	Black/Gold
Alcorn St	Braves	S'western	Cardell Jones	Lorman,MS	Purple/Gold
Appalachian St	Mountaineers	Southern	Jerry Moore	Boone,NC	Black/Gold
Arkansas St	Indians	Indep.	Al Kincaid	State Univ.,AR	Scarlet/Black
Austin Peay	Governors	Ohio Valley	Roy Gregory	Clarksville,TN	Red/White
Bethune-Cookman	Wildcats	Mid-Eastern	Larry Little	Daytona Beach,FL	Maroon/Gold
Boise St	Broncos	Big Sky	Skip Hall	Boise,ID	Orange/Blue
Boston Univ.	Terriers	Yankee	Dan Allen	Boston,MA	Scarlet/White
Brown	Bruins	Ivy	Mickey Kwiatkowski	Providence,RI	Brown/Red/White
Bucknell	Bison	Patriot	Lou Maranzana	Lewisburg,PA	Orange/Blue
Central Fla.	Knights	Indep.	Gene McDowell	Orlando,FL	Black/Gold
The Citadel	Bulldogs	Southern	Charlie Taaffe	Charleston SC	Blue/White
Colgate	Red Raiders	Patriot	Mike Foley	Hamilton,NY	Maroon/White
Columbia	Lions	Ivy	Ray Tellier	New York,NY	Lt.Blue/White
Connecticut	Huskies	Yankee	Tom Jackson	Storrs,CT	Blue/White
Cornell	Big Red	Ivy	Jim Hofher	Ithaca,NY	Red/White
Dartmouth	Big Green	Ivy	Buddy Teevens	Hanover,NH	Green/White
Delaware	Blue Hens	Yankee	Tubby Raymond	Newark,DE	Blue/Gold
Delaware St	Hornets	Mid-Eastern	Bill Collick	Dover,DE	Red/Blue
East Tenn.St	Buccaneers	Southern	Don Riley	Johnson City,TN	Blue/Gold
Eastern Ill	Panthers	Gateway	Bob Spoo	Charleston,IL	Blue/Gold
Eastern Ky.	Colonels	Ohio Valley	Roy Kidd	Richmond,KY	Maroon/White
Eastern Wash.	Eagles	Big Sky	Dick Zornes	Cheney,WA	Red/White
Florida A&M	Rattlers	Mid-Eastern	Ken Riley	Tallasassee,FL	Orange/Green
Fordham	Rams	Patriot	Larry Glueck	New York,NY	Maroon/White
Furman	Paladins	Southern	Jim Satterfield	Greenville,SC	Purple/White
Ga.Southern	Eagles	Indep.	Tim Stowers	Statesboro,GA	Blue/White
Grambling	Tigers	S'western	Eddie Robinson	Grambling,LA	Black/Gold
Harvard	Crimson	Ivy	Joe Restic	Cambridge,MA	Crimson/Black/White
Holy Cross	Crusaders	Patriot	Mark Duffner	Worcester,MA	Royal Purple
Howard	Bison	Mid-Eastern	Steve Wilson	Washington,DC	Blue/White
Idaho	Vandals	Big Sky	John L.Smith	Moscow,ID	Silver/Gold
Idaho St.	Bengals	Big Sky	Garth Hall	Pocatello,ID	Orange/Black
Illinois St	Redbirds	Gateway	Jim Heacock	Normal,IL	Red/White
Indiana St	Sycamores	Gateway	Dennis Raetz	Terre Haute,IN	Blue/White
Jackson St	Tigers	S'western	W.C.Gorden	Jackson,MS	Blue/White
J.Madison	Dukes	Indep.	Rip Scherer	Harrisonburg,VA	Purple/Gold
Lafayette	Leopards	Patriot	Bill Russo	Easton,PA	Maroon/White
Lehigh	Engineers	Patriot	Hank Small	Bethlehem,PA	Brown/White
Liberty	Flames	Indep.	Sam Rutigliano	Lynchburg,VA	Red/White/Blue
Maine	Black Bears	Yankee	Kirk Ferentz	Orono,ME	Blue/White
Marshall	Thundering Herd	Southern	Jim Donnan	Huntington,WV	Green/White
Massachusetts	Minutemen	Yankee	Jim Reid	Amherst,MA	Maroon/White
McNeese St	Cowboys	Southland	Bobby Keasler	Lake Charles,LA	Blue/Gold
Mid.Tenn.St.	Blue Raiders	Ohio Valley	Boots Donnelly	Murfreesboro,TN	Blue/White
Miss.Valley	Delta Devils	S'western	Larry Dorsey	Itta Bena,MS	Green/White
Montana	Grizzlies	Big Sky	Don Read	Missoula,MT	Copper/Silver/Gold
Montana St.	Bobcats	Big Sky	Earle Solomonson	Bozeman,MT	Blue/Gold
Morehead St	Eagles	Ohio Valley	Cole Proctor	Morehead,KY	Blue/Gold
Morgan St	Bears	Mid-Eastern	Ricky Diggs	Baltimore,MD	Blue/Orange
Murray St	Racers	Ohio Valley	Mike Mahoney	Murray,KY	Blue/Gold
Nevada	Wolf Pack	Big West ('92)	Chris Ault	Reno,NV	Silver/Blue
New Hampshire	Wildcats	Yankee	Bill Bowes	Durham,NH	Blue/White
Nicholls St	Colonels	Indep.	Phil Greco	Thibodaux,LA	Red/Gray
N.Carolina A&T	Aggies	Mid-Eastern	Bill Hayes	Greensboro,NC	Blue/Gold
North Texas	Mean Green	Southland	Dennis Parker	Denton,TX	Green/White
NE Louisiana	Indians	Southland	Dave Roberts	Monroe,LA	Maroon/Gold
Northeastern	Huskies	Indep.	Barry Gallup	Boston,MA	Red/Black
Northern Ariz	Lumberjacks	Big Sky	Steve Axman	Flagstaff,AZ	Blue/Gold

Nickname		Conference	Head Coach	Location	Colors
Northern Iowa	Panthers	Gateway	Terry Allen	Cedar Falls,IA	Purple/Old Gold
Northwestern St	Demons	Southland	Sam Goodwin	Natchitoches,LA	Purple/White
Penn	Quakers	Ivy	Gary Steele	Philadelphia,PA	Red/Blue
Prairie View	Panthers	S'western	Ronald Beard	Prairie View,TX	Purple/Gold
Princeton	Tigers	Ivy	Steve Tosches	Princeton,NJ	Orange/Black
Rhode Island	Rams	Yankee	Bob Griffin	Kingston,RI	Blue/White
Richmond	Spiders	Yankee	Jim Marshall	Richmond,VA	Red/Blue
Sam Houston St	Bearkats	Southland	Ron Randleman	Huntsville, TX	Orange/White/Blue
Samford	Bulldogs	Indep.	Terry Bowden	Birmingham,AL	Crimson/Blue
S.Carolina St	Bulldogs	Mid Eastern	Willie Jeffries	Orangeburg,SC	Garnet/Blue
SE Missouri St	Indians	Ohio Valley	John Mumford	Cape Girardeau,MO	Red/Black
Southern Ill	Salukis	Gateway	Bob Smith	Carbondale,IL	Maroon/White
Southern-BR	Jaguars	S'western	Gerald Kimble	Baton Rouge,LA	Blue/Gold
SW Missouri St	Bears	Gateway	Jesse Branch	Springfield,MO	Maroon/White
SW Texas St	Bobcats	Southland	Dennis Franchione	San Marcos,TX	Maroon/Gold
S.F.Austin St	Lumberjacks	Southland	Lynn Graves	Nacogdoches,TX	Purple/White
Tenn-Chatt	Moccasins	Southern	Buddy Nix	Chattanooga,TN	Navy Blue/Gold
Tennessee St	Tigers	Ohio Valley	Joe Gilliam,Sr.	Nashville,TN	Blue/White
Tenn.Tech	Golden Eagles	Ohio Valley	Jim Ragland	Cookeville,TN	Purple/Gold
TX Southern	Tigers	S'western	Walter Highsmith	Houston,TX	Maroon/Gray
Towson St	Tigers	Indep.	Phil Albert	Towson,MD	Gold/White
Villanova	Wildcats	Yankee	Andy Talley	Villanova,PA	Blue/White
VMI	Keydets	Southern	Jim Shuck	Richmond,VA	Black/Gold
Weber St	Wildcats	Big Sky	Dave Arslanian	Ogden,UT	Purple/White
W.Carolina	Catamounts	Southern	Steve Hodgin	Cullowhee,NC	Purple/Gold
Western Ill	Leathernecks	Gateway	Randy Ball	Macomb,IL	Purple/Gold
Western Ky	Hilltoppers	Gateway ('92)	Jack Harbaugh	Bowling Green,KY	Red/White
William & Mary	Indians	Indep.	Jimmye Laycock	Williamsburg,VA	Green/Gold
Yale	Bulldogs,Elis	Ivy	Carmen Cozza	New Haven,CT	Yale Blue/White
Youngstown St	Penguins	Indep.	Jim Tressel	Youngstown,OH	Scarlet/White

Annual NCAA Division I Team Champions

Men's and Women's NCAA Division I team champions from Cross-country to Wrestling. Rowing is included, although the NCAA does not sanction championships in the sport. Team champions in baseball, basketball, football, golf, ice hockey, soccer and tennis can be found in appropriate chapters throughout the almanac.

CROSS-COUNTRY

Men

Multiple winners: Michigan St. (8); UTEP (7); Oregon and Villanova (4); Arkansas, Drake, Indiana, Penn St. and Wisconsin (3); San Jose St. and Western Mich. (2).

Year		Year		Year		Year		Year	
1938	Indiana	1948	Michigan St.	1959	Michigan St.	1970	Villanova	1981	UTEP
1939	Michigan St.	1949	Michigan St.	1960	Houston	1971	Oregon	1982	Wisconsin
1940	Indiana	1950	Penn St.	1961	Oregon St.	1972	Tennessee	1983	Vacated
1941	Rhode Island	1951	Syracuse	1962	San Jose St.	1973	Oregon	1984	Arkansas
1942	Indiana	1952	Michigan St.	1963	San Jose St.	1974	Oregon	1985	Wisconsin
	& Penn St.	1953	Kansas	1964	Western Mich.	1975	UTEP	1986	Arkansas
1943	Not held	1954	Oklahoma St.	1965	Western Mich.	1976	UTEP	1987	Arkansas
1944	Drake	1955	Michigan St.	1966	Villanova	1977	Oregon	1988	Wisconsin
1945	Drake	1956	Michigan St.	1967	Villanova	1978	UTEP	1989	Iowa St.
1946	Drake	1957	Notre Dame	1968	Villanova	1979	UTEP	1990	Arkansas
1947	Penn St.	1958	Michigan St.	1969	UTEP	1980	UTEP		

Women

Multiple winners: Oregon, Villanova, Virginia and Wisconsin (2).

Year		Year		Year		Year		Year	
1981	Virginia	1983	Oregon	1985	Wisconsin	1987	Oregon	1989	Villanova
1982	Virginia	1984	Wisconsin	1986	Texas	1988	Kentucky	1990	Villanova

FENCING

Men (1941-89)

Multiple winners: NYU (12); Columbia (11); Wayne St.(7); Navy, Notre Dame and Penn (3); Illinois (2).

Year		Year		Year		Year		Year	
1941	Northwestern	1953	Penn	1962	Navy	1971	Columbia	1980	Wayne St-MI
1942	Ohio St.	1954	Columbia	1963	Columbia		& NYU	1981	Penn
	1943-46 Not held		& NYU	1964	Princeton	1972	Detroit	1982	Wayne St-MI
1947	NYU	1955	Columbia	1965	Columbia	1973	NYU	1983	Wayne St-MI
1948	CCNY	1956	Illinois	1966	NYU	1974	NYU	1984	Wayne St-MI
1949	Army	1957	NYU	1967	NYU	1975	Wayne St-MI	1985	Wayne St-MI
	& Rutgers	1958	Illinois	1968	Columbia	1976	NYU	1986	Notre Dame
1950	Navy	1959	Navy	1969	Penn	1977	Notre Dame	1987	Columbia
1951	Columbia	1960	NYU	1970	NYU	1978	Notre Dame	1988	Columbia
1952	Columbia	1961	NYU			1979	Wayne St-MI	1989	Columbia

Women (1982-89)

Multiple winners: Wayne St.(3); Yale (2).

Year		Year		Year	
1982	Wayne St-MI	1985	Yale	1988	Wayne St-MI
1983	Penn St.	1986	Penn	1989	Wayne St-MI
1984	Yale	1987	Notre Dame		

Men & Women

Multiple winner: Penn St.(2)

Year		Year	
1990	Penn St.	1991	Penn St.

FIELD HOCKEY

Women

Multiple winners: Old Dominion (5); Connecticut (2).

Year		Year		Year		Year		Year	
1981	Connecticut	1983	Old Dominion	1985	Connecticut	1987	Maryland	1989	North Carolina
1982	Old Dominion	1984	Old Dominion	1986	Iowa	1988	Old Dominion	1990	Old Dominion

GYMNASTICS

Men

Multiple winners: Illinois and Penn St.(9); Nebraska (7); So.Illinois (4); Iowa St. and Oklahoma (3); California, Florida St., Michigan and UCLA (2).

Year		Year		Year		Year		Year	
1938	Chicago	1953	Penn St.	1963	Michigan	1972	So.Illinois	1982	Nebraska
1939	Illinois	1954	Penn St.	1964	So.Illinois	1973	Iowa St.	1983	Nebraska
1940	Illinois	1955	Illinois	1965	Penn St.	1974	Iowa St.	1984	UCLA
1941	Illinois	1956	Illinois	1966	So.Illinois	1975	California	1985	Ohio St.
1942	Illinois	1957	NYU	1967	So.Illinois	1976	Penn St.	1986	Arizona St.
	1943-47 Not held	1958	Michigan St. &	1968	California	1977	Indiana St.	1987	UCLA
1948	Penn St.		Illinois	1969	Iowa &		& Oklahoma	1988	Nebrasksa
1949	Temple	1959	Penn St.		Michigan (T)	1978	Oklahoma	1989	Illinois
1950	Illinois	1960	Penn St.	1970	Michigan	1979	Nebraska	1990	Nebraska
1951	Florida St.	1961	Penn St.		& Michigan (T)	1980	Nebraska	1991	Oklahoma
1952	Florida St.	1962	USC	1971	Iowa St.	1981	Nebraska		

(T) indicates won trampoline competition (1969 and '70).

Women

Multiple winners: Utah (6); Georgia and Alabama (2).

Year		Year		Year		Year		Year	
1982	Utah	1984	Utah	1986	Utah	1988	Alabama	1990	Utah
1983	Utah	1985	Utah	1987	Georgia	1989	Georgia	1991	Alabama

INDOOR TRACK

Men

Multiple winners: Arkansas (8); UTEP (7); Kansas and Villanova (3); USC (2).

Year		Year		Year		Year		Year	
1965	Missouri	1971	Villanova	1977	Washington St.	1982	UTEP	1988	Arkansas
1966	Kansas	1972	USC	1978	UTEP	1983	SMU	1989	Arkansas
1967	USC	1973	Manhattan	1979	Villanova	1984	Arkansas	1990	Arkansas
1968	Villanova	1974	UTEP	1980	UTEP	1985	Arkansas	1991	Arkansas
1969	Kansas	1975	UTEP	1981	UTEP	1986	Arkansas		
1970	Kansas	1976	UTEP			1987	Arkansas		

Women

Multiple winners: LSU and Texas (3); Nebraska (2).

Year		Year		Year		Year		Year	
1983	Nebraska	1985	Florida St.	1987	LSU	1989	LSU	1991	LSU
1984	Nebraska	1986	Texas	1988	Texas	1990	Texas		

LACROSSE

Men

Multiple winners: Johns Hopkins (7); North Carolina and Syracuse (4); Cornell (3); Maryland (2).

Year		Year		Year		Year		Year	
1971	Cornell	1976	Cornell	1980	Johns Hopkins	1985	Johns Hopkins	1990	Syracuse
1972	Virginia	1977	Cornell	1981	North Carolina	1986	North Carolina	1991	North Carolina
1973	Maryland	1978	Johns Hopkins	1982	North Carolina	1987	Johns Hopkins		
1974	Johns Hopkins	1979	Johns Hopkins	1983	Syracuse	1988	Syracuse		
1975	Maryland			1984	Johns Hopkins	1989	Syracuse		

Women

Multiple winners: Penn St. and Temple (2).

Year		Year		Year		Year		Year	
1982	Massachusetts	1984	Temple	1986	Maryland	1988	Alabama	1990	Harvard
1983	Deleware	1995	New Hampshire	1987	Penn St.	1989	Georgia	1991	Virginia

RIFLE

Men & Women

Multiple winners: West Virginia (7); Tennessee Tech (3); Murray St.(2).

Year		Year		Year		Year		Year	
1980	Tenn. Tech	1983	West Virginia	1986	West Virginia	1988	West Virginia	1990	West Virginia
1981	Tenn. Tech	1984	West Virginia	1987	Murray St.	1989	West Virginia	1991	West Virginia
1982	Tenn. Tech	1985	Murray St.						

SKIING

Men & Women

Multiple winners: Denver (14); Colorado (12); Utah (6); Vermont (3); Dartmouth and Wyoming (2).

Year		Year		Year		Year		Year	
1954	Denver	1963	Denver	1971	Denver	1978	Colorado	1986	Utah
1955	Denver	1964	Denver	1972	Colorado	1979	Colorado	1987	Utah
1956	Denver	1965	Denver	1973	Colorado	1980	Vermont	1988	Utah
1957	Denver	1966	Denver	1974	Colorado	1981	Utah	1989	Vermont
1958	Dartmouth	1967	Denver	1975	Colorado	1982	Colorado	1990	Vermont
1959	Colorado	1968	Wyoming	1976	Colorado & Dartmouth	1983	Utah	1991	Colorado
1960	Colorado	1969	Denver	1977	Colorado	1984	Utah		
1961	Denver	1970	Denver			1985	Wyoming		
1962	Denver								

SOFTBALL

Women

Multiple winners: UCLA (6); Texas A&M (2).

Year		Year		Year		Year		Year	
1982	UCLA	1984	UCLA	1986	CS-Fullerton	1988	UCLA	1990	UCLA
1983	Texas A&M	1985	UCLA	1987	Texas A&M	1989	UCLA	1991	Arizona

SWIMMING & DIVING

Men

Multiple winners: Ohio St.(11); Michigan (10); USC (9); Indiana (6); Texas (5); Stanford and Yale (4); California and Florida (2).

Year		Year		Year		Year		Year	
1937	Michigan	1949	Ohio St.	1960	USC	1971	Indiana	1982	UCLA
1938	Michigan	1950	Ohio St.	1961	Michigan	1972	Indiana	1983	Florida
1939	Michigan	1951	Yale	1962	Ohio St.	1973	Indiana	1984	Florida
1940	Michigan	1952	Ohio St.	1963	USC	1974	USC	1985	Stanford
1941	Michigan	1953	Yale	1964	USC	1975	USC	1986	Stanford
1942	Yale	1954	Ohio St.	1965	USC	1976	USC	1987	Stanford
1943	Ohio St.	1955	Ohio St.	1966	USC	1977	USC	1988	Texas
1944	Yale	1956	Ohio St.	1967	Stanford	1978	Tennessee	1989	Texas
1945	Ohio St.	1957	Michigan	1968	Indiana	1979	California	1990	Texas
1946	Ohio St.	1958	Michigan	1969	Indiana	1980	California	1991	Texas
1947	Ohio St.	1959	Michigan	1970	Indiana	1981	Texas		
1948	Michigan								

Women

Multiple winners: Texas (7); Stanford (2).

Year		Year		Year		Year		Year	
1982	Florida	1984	Texas	1986	Texas	1988	Texas	1990	Texas
1983	Stanford	1985	Texas	1987	Texas	1989	Stanford	1991	Texas

OUTDOOR TRACK & FIELD

Men

Multiple winners: USC (26); UCLA (8); UTEP (6); Illinois and Oregon (5); Kansas, LSU and Stanford (3), SMU and Tennessee (2).

Year		Year		Year		Year		Year	
1921	Illinois	1937	USC	1952	USC	1967	USC	1980	UTEP
1922	California	1938	USC	1953	USC	1968	USC	1981	UTEP
1923	Michigan	1939	USC	1954	USC	1969	San Jose St.	1982	UTEP
1924	Not held	1940	USC	1955	USC	1970	BYU, Kansas & Oregon	1983	SMU
1925	Stanford*	1941	USC	1956	UCLA			1984	Oregon
1926	USC*	1942	USC	1957	Villanova	1971	UCLA	1985	Arkansas
1927	Illinois*	1943	USC	1958	USC	1972	UCLA	1986	SMU
1928	Stanford	1944	Illinois	1959	Kansas	1973	UCLA	1987	UCLA
1929	Ohio St.	1945	Navy	1960	Kansas	1974	Tennessee	1988	UCLA
1930	USC	1946	Illinois	1961	USC	1975	UTEP	1989	LSU
1931	USC	1947	Illinois	1962	Oregon	1976	USC	1990	LSU
1932	Indiana	1948	Minnesota	1963	USC	1977	Arizona St.	1991	Tennessee
1933	LSU	1949	USC	1964	Oregon	1978	UCLA & UTEP		
1934	Stanford	1950	USC	1965	Oregon & USC	1979	UTEP		
1935	USC	1951	USC	1966	UCLA				
1936	USC								

(*) indicates unofficial championship.

Women

Multiple winners: LSU (5); UCLA (2).

Year		Year		Year		Year		Year	
1982	UCLA	1984	Florida St.	1986	Texas	1988	LSU	1990	LSU
1983	UCLA	1985	Oregon	1987	LSU	1989	LSU	1991	LSU

VOLLEYBALL

Men

Multiple winners: UCLA (13); USC (4); Pepperdine (3).

Year		Year		Year		Year		Year	
1970	UCLA	1975	UCLA	1980	USC	1985	Pepperdine	1990	USC
1971	UCLA	1976	UCLA	1981	UCLA	1986	Pepperdine	1991	L. Beach St.
1972	UCLA	1977	USC	1982	UCLA	1987	UCLA		
1973	San Diego St.	1978	Pepperdine	1983	UCLA	1988	USC		
1974	UCLA	1979	UCLA	1984	UCLA	1989	UCLA		

Women

Multiple winners: Hawaii (3); Pacific and UCLA (2).

Year		Year		Year		Year		Year	
1981	USC	1983	Hawaii	1985	Pacific	1987	Hawaii	1989	Long Beach St.
1982	Hawaii	1984	UCLA	1986	Pacific	1988	Texas	1990	UCLA

WATER POLO

Multiple winners: California (9); Stanford (6); UC-Irvine and UCLA (3).

Year		Year		Year		Year		Year	
1969	UCLA	1974	California	1979	UC-S.Barbara	1984	California	1988	California
1970	UC-Irvine	1975	California	1980	Stanford	1985	Stanford	1989	UC-Irvine
1971	UCLA	1976	Stanford	1981	Stanford	1986	Stanford	1990	California
1972	UCLA	1977	California	1982	UC-Irvine	1987	California		
1973	California	1978	Stanford	1983	California				

WRESTLING

Multiple winners: Okla.St.(29); (Iowa 12); Iowa St.(8); Oklahoma (7).

Year		Year		Year		Year		Year	
1928	Okla.A&M*	1940	Okla.A&M	1955	Okla.A&M	1968	Okla.St.	1980	Iowa
1929	Okla.A&M	1941	Okla.A&M	1956	Okla.A&M	1969	Iowa St.	1981	Iowa
1930	Okla.A&M*	1942	Okla.A&M	1957	Oklahoma	1970	Iowa St.	1982	Iowa
1931	Okla.A&M*	1943-45	Not held	1958	Okla.St.	1971	Okla.St.	1983	Iowa
1932	Indiana*	1946	Okla.A&M	1959	Okla.St.	1972	Iowa St.	1984	Iowa
1933	Okla.A&M* & Iowa St.*	1947	Cornell Col.	1960	Oklahoma	1973	Iowa St.	1985	Iowa
1934	Okla.A&M	1948	Okla.A&M	1961	Okla.St.	1974	Oklahoma	1986	Iowa
1935	Okla.A&M	1949	Okla.A&M	1962	Okla.St.	1975	Iowa	1987	Iowa St.
1936	Oklahoma	1950	Northern Iowa	1963	Oklahoma	1976	Iowa	1988	Arizona St.
1937	Okla.A&M	1951	Oklahoma	1964	Okla.St.	1977	Iowa St.	1989	Okla.St.
1938	Okla.A&M	1952	Oklahoma	1965	Iowa St.	1978	Iowa	1990	Okla.St.
1939	Okla.A&M	1953	Penn St.	1966	Okla.St.	1979	Iowa	1991	Iowa
		1954	Okla.A&M	1967	Michigan St.				

(*) indicates unofficial champions.
Note: Oklahoma A&M became Oklahoma St. in 1958.

OTHER

Intercollegiate Rowing Association Regatta

VARSITY EIGHTS

The Intercollegiate Rowing Association (IRA) was formed in 1895 by several northeastern schools, shortly after Harvard and Yale quit the Rowing Association (established in 1871) to stage an annual race of their own. Since then the IRA Regatta has been contested over courses of varying lengths in Poughkeepsie, N.Y., Marietta, Ohio,and Onondaga Lake in Syracuse, N.Y. The race has been over a 2000-meter course in Syracuse since 1968.
    Distances: 4 miles (1895-97,1899-1916,1925-41); 3 miles (1898,1921-24,1947-49,1952-63,1965-67); 2 miles (1920,1950-51); 2000 meters (1964,since 1968).
    Multiple winners: Cornell (24); Navy (12); California and Washington (10); Penn (8); Wisconsin (7); Syracuse (6); Brown and Columbia (4); Northwestern (2).

Year		Year		Year		Year		Year	
1895	Columbia	1897	Cornell	1899	Penn	1901	Cornell	1903	Cornell
1896	Cornell	1898	Penn	1900	Penn	1902	Cornell	1904	Syracuse

Intercollegiate Rowing (Cont.)

Year		Year		Year		Year		Year	
1905	Cornell	1924	Washington	1942	Not held	1960	California	1977	Cornell
1906	Cornell	1925	Navy	1943	Not held	1961	California	1978	Syracuse
1907	Cornell	1926	Washington	1944	Not held	1962	Cornell	1979	Brown
1908	Syracuse	1927	Columbia	1945	Not held	1963	Cornell		
1909	Cornell	1928	California	1946	Not held	1964	California	1980	Navy
1910	Cornell	1929	Columbia	1947	Navy	1965	Navy	1981	Cornell
1911	Cornell			1948	Washington	1966	Wisconsin	1982	Cornell
1912	Cornell	1930	Cornell	1949	California	1967	Penn	1983	Brown
1913	Syracuse	1931	Navy			1968	Penn	1984	Navy
1914	Columbia	1932	California	1950	Washington	1969	Penn	1985	Princeton
1915	Cornell	1933	Not held	1951	Wisconsin			1986	Brown
1916	Syracuse	1934	California	1952	Navy	1970	Washington	1987	Brown
1917	Not held	1935	California	1953	Navy	1971	Cornell	1988	Northeastern
1918	Not held	1936	Washington	1954	Navy*	1972	Penn	1989	Penn
1919	Not held	1937	Washington	1955	Cornell	1973	Wisconsin		
		1938	Navy	1956	Cornell	1974	Wisconsin	1990	Wisconsin
1920	Syracuse	1939	California	1957	Cornell	1975	Wisconsin	1991	Northeastern
1921	Navy			1958	Cornell	1976	California		
1922	Navy	1940	Washington	1959	Wisconsin				
1923	Washington	1941	Washington						

*In 1954, Navy was disqualified because of an ineligble coxwain; no trophies were given.

National Collegiate Championships

VARSITY EIGHTS

The University of Pennsylvania men and Boston University women won the 1991 National Collegiate Rowing Championships' Varsity Eights titles, June 8, at Harsha Lake in Bantam, Ohio. Penn won the Herschede Cup with a time of 5:58.21 over the 2,000-meter course, beating IRA champion Northeastern by less than a second. BU won the Ferguson Bowl with a time of 7:03.2 over 2,000 meters, beating Cornell by three seconds.

Men

National championship determined at Cincinnati Regatta over a 2000-meter course on Harsha Lake since 1982. Winner receives Herschede Cup.

Multiple winners: Harvard (5); Wisconsin (2).

Year	Champion	Time	Runner-up	Time
1982	Yale	5:50.8	Cornell	5:54.15
1983	Harvard	5:59.6	Washington	6:00.0
1984	Washington	5:51.1	Yale	5:55.6
1985	Harvard	5:44.4	Princeton	5:44.87
1986	Wisconsin	5:57.8	Brown	5:59.9
1987	Harvard	5:35.17	Brown	5:35.63
1988	Harvard	5:35.98	Northeastern	5:37.07
1989	Harvard	5:36.6	Washington	5:38.93
1990	Wisconsin	5:52.5	Harvard	5:56.84
1991	Penn	5:58.21	Northeastern	5:58.48

Women

National championship held over various distances at 10 different venues since 1979. Distances—1000 meters (1979-81); 1500 meters (1982-83); 1000 meters (1984); 1750 meters (1985); 2000 meters (1986-88, since 1991); 1852 meters (1989-90). Winner receives Ferguson Bowl.

Multiple winners: Washington (7).

Year	Champion	Time	Runner-up	Time
1979	Yale	3:06	California	3:08.6
1980	California	3:05.4	Oregon St.	3:05.8
1981	Washington	3:20.6	Yale	3:22.9
1982	Washington	4:56.4	Wisconsin	4:59.83
1983	Washington	4:57.5	Dartmouth	5:03.02
1984	Washington	3:29.48	Radcliffe	3:31.08
1985	Washington	5:28.4	Wisconsin	5:32.0
1986	Wisconsin	6:53.28	Radcliffe	6:53.34
1987	Washington	6:33.8	Yale	6:37.4
1988	Washington	6:41.0	Yale	6:42.37
1989	Cornell	5:34.9	Wisconsin	5:37.5
1990	Princeton	5:52.2	Radcliffe	5:54.2
1991	Boston Univ.	7:03.2	Cornell	7:06.21

The Harvard-Yale Regatta

Harvard won the 126th Harvard-Yale Regatta for varsity eights for the seventh year in a row, June 1, covering the 4-mile course in 21 minutes, 18.5 seconds. The Harvard-Yale Regatta is the country's oldest intercollegiate event and Harvard holds a 75-51 edge.

Les Leverett/The NCAA News

Tennis Hall-of-Famer **Althea Gibson** holds up the Theodore Roosevelt Award after becoming the first woman to win the NCAA's highest honor in January. See page 402.

HALLS OF FAME & AWARDS

AUTO RACING

Indianapolis Motor Speedway Hall of Fame

Originally the Auto Racing Hall of Fame. Established by the American Automobile Association Contest Board in 1952, disbanded in 1955, and revived by the Indianapolis Speedway Foundation in 1962. **Address:** 4790 West 16th Street, Indianapolis, IN 46222. **Telephone:** (317) 248-6747.

Eligibility: Candidates cannot be nominated until at least 20 years after the date of first active participation in auto racing. Voting done by 100-member panel made up of racing officials, Hall of Fame members and media representatives.

Class of 1991 (2)**:** Driver—**Lloyd Ruby**. Contributor—**Darrell Drake**.

Members are listed with year of induction; (+) indicates deceased members.

Drivers

+Aitken, Johnny. 1981
+Anderson, Gil 1983
Andretti, Mario 1986
+Baker, Cannonball 1981
Banks, Henry. 1985
+Bergere, Cliff. 1976
+Bettenhausen, Tony 1968
+Boyer, Joe 1985
+Bruce-Brown, David 1980
+Burman, Bob. 1953-54
+Bryan, Jimmy 1973
+Chevrolet, Gaston 1964
+Chevrolet, Louis 1952
+Clark, Jimmy. 1988
+Cooper, Earl 1953-54
+Cummings, Bill 1970
+Dawson, Joe 1976
+DePalma, Ralph 1953-54
+DePaolo, Peter 1963
+Durant, Cliff 1983

+Agajanian, J.C.. 1990
+Allison, James A 1964
Bignotti, George 1975
+Brawner, Clint. 1984
+Christie, Walter 1980
+Cloutier, Joe 1989
+Dingley, Bert 1952
+Drake, Darrell 1991
+Duesenberg, Augie. 1963
+Duesenberg, Fred. 1962
+Edenburn, Eddie. 1986

+Fengler, Harlan. 1983
Foyt, A.J. 1978
+Frame, Fred 1984
+Goux, Jules 1989
+Grant, Harry 1982
Gurney, Dan 1988
+Hanks, Sam. 1981
+Harroun, Ray. 1952
+Hartz, Harry 1963
+Hearne, Eddie. 1964
+Hepburn, Ralph 1970
+Horn, Ted 1964
Jones, Parnelli 1985
+Keech, Ray. 1984
+Lockhart, Frank. 1965
+Mays, Rex 1963
+McGrath, Jack. 1987
Meyer, Louis 1963
+Milton, Tommy 1953-54
+Moore, Lou 1969

+Mulford, Ralph 1953-54
+Murphy, Jimmy. 1964
Nalon, Dennis (Duke) 1983
+Oldfield, Barney 1952
+Parsons, Johnnie. 1986
+Resta, Dario 1953-54
+Rickenbacker, Eddie. 1954
+Roberts, Floyd 1985
+Rose, Mauri. 1967
Ruby, Lloyd 1991
Rutherford, Johnny 1987
+Shaw, Wilbur. 1963
+Snyder, Jimmy. 1981
+Stevens, Myron 1983
+Strang, Lewis 1982
Unser, Al 1986
Unser, Bobby 1990
+Vukovich, Bill. 1972
Ward, Roger 1981
+Wilcox, Howard 1963

Contributors

+Firestone, Harvey, Sr 1952
+Fisher, Carl 1952
+Ford, Henry. 1952
+Gilmore, Earl 1987
+Goossen, Leo 1978
+Henning, Harry (Cotton) 1969
+Hulman, Tony. 1967
+Kurtis, Frank 1983
+Marcenac, Jean 1968
+Miller, Harry 1963
+Myers, T.E.(Pop) 1952

+Offenhauser, Fred 1982
+Pillsbury, Art 1981
+Ricker, Chester 1989
+Robertson, George 1980
+Sparks, Art. 1987
+Stutz, Henry 1963
+Vanderbilt, William K 1952
+Wagner, Fred 1952
Watson, A.J.. 1981
+Welch, Lew 1986
+Winfield, Ed. 1983

Motorsports Hall of Fame of America

Established in 1989. **Address:** P.O.Box 194, Novi, MI 48050. **Telephone:** (313) 349-7223.

Eligibility: nominees must be retired at least three years or engaged in their area of motor sports for at least 20 years. Areas include: open wheel, stock car, dragster, sports car, motorcycle, power boat and air racing.

Class of 1991 (9)**:** Auto drivers—**Dan Gurney, Junior Johnson, Joe Leonard, Wilbur Shaw, Roscoe Turner** and **Al Unser**. Land speed record holder—**Art Arfons**; Drag racer **Don Prudhomme**. Contributor— late Indianapolis Speedway owner **Tony Hulman**.

Members are listed with year of induction; (+) indicates deceased members.

Drivers

Andretti, Mario 1990
Arfons, Art. 1991
+Baker, Cannonball 1989
+Chenoweth, Dean 1991
+Clark, Jim 1990
+Curtiss, Glenn 1990
+Donahue, Mark 1990
Doolittle, Jimmy 1989
Foyt, A.J. 1989
Garlits, Don. 1989

Gurney, Dan. 1991
Hill, Phil 1989
Johnson, Junior. 1991
Leonard, Joe. 1991
Muldowney, Shirley. 1990
+Muncy, Bill. 1989
+Oldfield, Barney 1989
Petty, Richard. 1989
Prudhomme, Don. 1991
Roberts, Kenny 1990

+Shaw, Wilbur. 1991
+Thompson, Mickey. 1990
+Turner, Roscoe 1991
+Wood, Gar 1990

Contributors

France, Bill Sr 1990
+Hulman, Tony. 1991

International Motorsports Hall of Fame

Established in 1990 by the International Motor Sports Hall of Fame Commission. **Address:** P.O.Box 1018, Talladega, AL, 35160. **Telephone:** (205) 362-5002.

Eligibility: Nominees must be retired from their specialty in motor sports for five years. Voting done by 150-member panel made up of the world-wide auto racing media.

Class of 1991 (10): Indy car drivers **Tony Bettenhausen, Ralph DePalma, Wilbur Shaw** and **Bill Vukovich**; stock car drivers **Tim Flock, Ned Jarrett** and **Fred Lorenzen**; international racing drivers **Phil Hill** and **Bruce McLaren**; driver-builder **Carroll Shelby**.

Members are listed with year of induction; (+) indicates deceased members.

Indy Car Drivers
+Bettenhausen, Tony 1991
+DePalma, Ralph 1991
+Donahue, Mark 1990
  Gurney, Dan 1990
  Jones, Parnelli 1990
+Oldfield, Barney 1990
+Shaw, Wilbur 1991
  Unser, Bobby 1990
+Vukovich, Bill 1991

World Record Holder
+Campbell, Sir Malcolm 1990

Stock Car Drivers
Baker, Buck 1990
Flock, Tim 1991
Jarrett, Ned 1991
Johnson, Junior 1990
Lorenzen, Fred 1991
Petty, Lee 1990
Roberts, Fireball 1990

Driver-Builders
Shelby, Carroll 1991
+Thompson, Mickey 1990
Yunick, Smokey 1990

International Drivers
Brabham, Jack 1990
+Clark, Jim 1990
+Juan Manuel Fangio 1990
+Hill, Graham 1990
Hill, Phil 1991
+McLaren, Bruce 1991
Moss, Stirling 1990
Stewart, Jackie 1990

Contributors
France, Bill, Sr 1990
+Hulman, Tony 1990

BASEBALL

National Baseball Hall of Fame

Established in 1935 by Major League Baseball to celebrate the game's 100th anniversary. **Address:** P.O.Box 590, Cooperstown, NY 13326. **Telephone:** (607) 547-9988.

Eligibility: Nominated players must have played at least part of 10 seasons in the Major Leagues and be retired for five years. Voting done by Baseball Writers Association of America. Any nominated player not elected after 15 years on the writers' ballot becomes eligible for consideration by the Veterans' Committee after a three-year wait. The Hall of Fame board of directors voted unanimously on Feb. 4, 1991, to exclude players on baseball's permanently ineligible list (Pete Rose is the only living member on that list) from consideration.

Class of 1991 (5): Players—1st and 2nd baseman **Rod Carew**, Minnesota (1967-78), California (1979-85); pitcher **Gaylord Perry**, San Francisco (1962-71), Cleveland (1972-75), Texas (1975-77,80), San Diego (1978-79), NY Yankees (1980), Atlanta (1981), Seattle (1982-83); pitcher **Ferguson Jenkins**, Philadelphia (1965-66), Chicago Cubs (1966-73,82-83), Texas (1974-75,78-81), Boston (1976-77). Veterans Committee—second baseman **Tony Lazzeri**, NY Yankees (1926-37), Chicago Cubs (1938), Brooklyn (1939), NY Giants (1939); owner **Bill Veeck**, Cleveland (1946-49), St.Louis Browns (1951-53), Chicago White Sox (1959-61,76-80).

Top 10 vote-getters (333 votes to elect): Carew (401); Perry (342); Jenkins (334); Rollie Fingers (291); Jim Bunning (282), Orlando Cepeda (192); Tony Oliva (160); Bill Mazeroski (142), Ron Santo (116); Harvey Kuenn (100). Last year of eligibility on writers' ballot for Bunning and Mazeroski.

Elected first year on ballot (22): Hank Aaron, Ernie Banks, Johnny Bench, Lou Brock, **Rod Carew**, Bob Feller, Bob Gibson, Al Kaline, Sandy Koufax, Mickey Mantle, Willie Mays, Willie McCovey, Joe Morgan, Stan Musial, Jim Palmer, Brooks Robinson, Frank Robinson, Jackie Robinson, Warren Spahn, Willie Stargell, Ted Williams and Carl Yastrzemski.

Members are listed with years of induction; (+) indicates deceased members.

1st Basemen
+Anson, Cap 1939
+Beckley, Jake 1971
+Bottomley, Jim 1974
+Brouthers, Dan 1945
  Carew, Rod 1991
+Chance, Frank 1946

+Connor, Roger 1976
+Foxx, Jimmie 1951
+Gehrig, Lou 1939
+Greenberg, Hank 1956
+Kelly, George 1973
  Killebrew, Harmon 1984

McCovey, Willie 1986
Mize, Johnny 1981
+Sisler, George 1939
Stargell, Willie 1988
+Terry, Bill 1954

2nd Basemen
+Collins, Eddie 1939
  Doerr, Bobby 1986
+Evers, Johnny 1946
+Frisch, Frankie 1947

Gehringer, Charlie 1949
  Herman, Billy 1975
+Hornsby, Rogers 1942
+Lajoie, Nap 1937

+Lazzeri, Tony 1991
  Morgan, Joe 1990
+Robinson, Jackie 1962
  Schoendienst, Red 1989

  Aparicio, Luis 1984
+Appling, Luke 1964
+Bancroft, Dave 1971
  Banks, Ernie 1977
  Boudreau, Lou 1970
+Cronin, Joe 1956

Shortstops
+Jackson, Travis 1982
+Jennings, Hugh 1945
+Maranville, Rabbit 1954
  Reese, Pee Wee 1984
+Sewell, Joe 1977

+Tinker, Joe 1946
+Vaughan, Arky 1985
+Wagner, Honus 1936
+Wallace, Bobby 1953
+Ward, Monte 1964

National Baseball Hall of Fame (Cont.)

3rd Basemen

+Baker, Frank 1955
+Collins, Jimmy. 1945
 Kell, George 1983

+Lindstrom, Fred. 1976
 Mathews, Eddie. 1978

 Robinson, Brooks 1983
+Traynor, Pie. 1948

Left Fielders

 Brock, Lou 1985
+Burkett, Jesse. 1946
+Clarke, Fred 1945
+Delahanty, Ed 1945
+Goslin, Goose. 1968
+Hafey, Chick 1971

+Kelley, Joe 1971
 Kiner, Ralph. 1975
+Manush, Heinie. 1964
+Medwick, Joe 1968
 Musial, Stan 1969
+O'Rourke, Jim. 1945

+Simmons, Al 1953
+Wheat, Zack 1959
 Williams, Billy 1987
 Williams, Ted 1966
 Yastrzemski, Carl 1989

Center Fielders

+Averill, Earl 1975
+Carey, Max 1961
+Cobb, Ty 1936
+Combs, Earle 1970
 DiMaggio, Joe 1955

+Duffy, Hugh. 1945
+Hamilton, Billy. 1961
 Mantle, Mickey 1974
 Mays, Willie. 1979
+Roush, Edd 1962

 Snider, Duke 1980
+Speaker, Tris 1937
+Waner, Lloyd. 1967
+Wilson, Hack. 1979

Right Fielders

 Aaron, Hank 1982
+Clemente, Roberto 1973
+Crawford, Sam 1957
+Cuyler, Kiki 1968
+Flick, Elmer 1963
+Heilmann, Harry. 1952
+Hooper, Harry. 1971

 Kaline, Al 1980
+Keeler, Willie. 1939
+Kelly, King 1945
+Klein, Chuck 1980
+McCarthy, Tommy 1946
+Ott, Mel 1951
+Rice, Sam. 1963

 Robinson, Frank 1982
+Ruth, Babe. 1936
 Slaughter, Enos. 1985
+Thompson, Sam 1974
+Waner, Paul 1952
+Youngs, Ross. 1972

Catchers

 Bench, Johnny. 1989
 Berra, Yogi 1972
+Bresnahan, Roger. 1945
 Campanella, Roy 1969

+Cochrane, Mickey. 1947
 Dickey, Bill. 1954
+Ewing, Buck. 1939
 Ferrell, Rick 1984

+Hartnett, Gabby 1955
+Lombardi, Ernie 1986
+Schalk, Ray 1955

Pitchers

+Alexander, Grover 1938
+Bender, Chief 1953
+Brown, Mordecai 1949
+Chesbro, Jack 1946
+Clarkson, John 1963
+Coveleski, Stan 1969
+Dean, Dizzy. 1953
 Drysdale, Don 1984
+Faber, Red. 1964
 Feller, Bob. 1962
 Ford, Whitey 1974
+Galvin, Pud 1965
 Gibson, Bob 1981
+Gomez, Lefty. 1972
+Grimes, Burleigh. 1964
+Grove, Lefty. 1947
+Haines, Jess. 1970

+Hoyt, Waite 1969
+Hubbell, Carl 1947
 Hunter, Catfish 1987
 Jenkins, Ferguson. 1991
+Johnson, Walter 1936
+Joss, Addie 1978
+Keefe, Tim. 1964
 Koufax, Sandy. 1972
 Lemon, Bob. 1976
+Lyons, Ted 1955
 Marichal, Juan 1983
+Marquard, Rube 1971
+Mathewson, Christy 1936
+McGinnity, Joe 1946
+Nichols, Kid. 1949
 Palmer, Jim. 1990

+Pennock, Herb 1948
 Perry, Gaylord. 1991
+Plank, Eddie 1946
+Radbourne, Old Hoss 1939
+Rixey, Eppa 1963
 Roberts, Robin. 1976
+Ruffing, Red. 1967
+Rusie, Amos. 1977
 Spahn, Warren 1973
+Vance, Dazzy 1955
+Waddell, Rube 1946
+Walsh, Ed 1946
+Welch, Mickey. 1973
 Wilhelm, Hoyt 1985
 Wynn, Early. 1972
+Young, Cy. 1937

From Negro Leagues

+Bell, Cool Papa (OF) 1974
+Charleston, Oscar (1B-OF) 1976
 Dandridge, Ray (3B). 1987
+Dihigo, Martin (P-OF). 1977

+Foster, Rube (P-Mgr). 1981
+Gibson, Josh (C). 1972
 Irvin, Monte (OF) 1973
+Johnson, Judy (3B). 1975

 Leonard, Buck (1B) 1972
+Lloyd, Pop (SS) 1977
+Paige, Satchel (P) 1971

Managers

+Alston, Walter 1983
+Harris, Bucky. 1975
+Huggins, Miller 1964
 Lopez, Al 1977

+Mack, Connie 1937
+McCarthy, Joe. 1957
+McGraw, John 1937

+McKechnie, Bill 1962
+Robinson, Wilbert 1945
+Stengel, Casey 1966

Umpires

 Barlick, Al 1989
+Conlan, Jocko. 1974

+Connolly, Tom 1953
+Evans, Billy. 1973

+Hubbard, Cal 1976
+Klem, Bill 1953

Veeck—As In Cooperstown
by Ed Linn

Bill Veeck, in the Hall of Fame. Who'da thunk it.

This is the man, for the luv of God, who had earned the emnity of the baseball establishment by sending a midget up to bat; who was so insensitive to basic human rights that he put the names of his players on the backs of their uniforms; who invented the exploding scoreboard.

The man, afterall, who had conceived a long list of innovations and promotions to make the game more fun for the fans—most of which have been copied by the same people who had castigated him at the time for "making a travesty of the game."

Veeck delighted in being baseball's bad boy. He loved to pull at the wig of the rich and powerful and to prick—as in Frick—the bubble of their pomposity. "If baseball owners were running Congress," he said, "Kansas and Nebraska would still be trying to get into the union."

All he was really trying to do was to drag baseball into the 20th Century. This is the man who, in 1947, signed the first black to play in the American League, Larry Doby; who put ageless Satchel Paige into a Cleveland uniform a year later; and who testified for Curt Flood in his anti-trust suit against baseball in 1970.

Veeck, who died at age 71 in 1986, was around baseball all his life. His father, William Sr., was a sportswriter who became president of the Chicago Cubs in 1918 when Bill was four. By the time he was 28, he had taken over the bankrupt Milwaukee Brewers of the American Association, and promptly won a pennant while setting all kinds of minor league attendance records.

Over a period of years that stretched from 1946 to 1980 he owned four major league ballclubs, with frequent hiatuses—not always voluntary—in between. He won a World Series in Cleveland in 1948 and a pennant in Chicago in 1959 and set attendance records in both cities. Yet he failed miserably with the Browns and left St. Louis virtually bankrupt in 1953.

"I've had the biggest of winners and the most abject of losers," he would say, "and I can tell you that the next best thing to

Wide World Photos

Bill Veeck with the keys to Chicago's old Comiskey Park in 1975.

operating a winning ballclub is operating a losing one."

Hank Greenberg, his friend and partner over 40 years, would tell him that if he could forget about baseball and put his remarkable talents to work making money he'd become an instant multimillionaire. "You don't understand, Henry," Bill would say. "I don't want to be a multimillionaire."

Operating a baseball team, that's all he wanted to do. "The most beautiful sight in the world," he said, "is a baseball stadium filled with people having fun."

Bill Veeck's natural habitat was the bleachers and the barroom. His greatest pleasure was drinking beer with a bunch of fans and talking baseball. "My guys are the guys in the lumbermen's jackets," he once said. "The working stiffs."

And they knew it. And they loved him. To walk through the streets of Chicago with Bill Veeck was to encounter a never-ending stream of faces lighting up at the sight of him. Calling out to him. Stopping to talk to him. Wanting to touch him.

Walking alongside him I would think: *This has to be the richest man in the world.*

Ed Linn co-wrote three books with Bill Veeck: *Veeck—As in Wreck, The Hustler's Handbook,* and *Thirty Tons a Day.*

National Baseball Hall of Fame (Cont.)

Pioneers and Executives

+Barrow, Ed. 1953
+Bulkeley, Morgan 1937
+Cartwright, Alexander 1938
+Chadwick, Henry 1938
+Chandler, Happy 1982
+Comiskey, Charles 1939
+Cummings, Candy 1939

+Frick, Ford 1970
+Giles, Warren 1979
+Griffith, Clark 1946
+Harridge, Will 1972
+Johnson, Ban 1937
+Landis, Kenesaw 1944
+MacPhail, Larry 1978

+Rickey, Branch 1967
+Spalding, Al. 1939
+Veeck, Bill 1991
+Weiss, George 1971
+Wright, George 1937
+Wright, Harry 1953
+Yawkey, Tom 1980

J.G. Taylor Spink Award

First presented in 1962 by the Baseball Writers Association of America for meritorious contributions by members of the BBWAA. Named in honor of the late publisher of *The Sporting News*, the Spink Award does not constitute induction into the Hall of Fame. Winners are honored in the year following their selection.

Year		Year		Year	
1962	J.G. Taylor Spink	1973	Warren Brown,	1979	Bob Broeg & Tommy Holmes
1963	Ring Lardner		John Drebinger		
1964	Hugh Fullerton		& John Kieran	1980	Joe Reichler & Milt Richman
1965	Charley Dryden	1974	John Carmichael	1981	Bob Addie & Allen Lewis
1966	Grantland Rice		& James Isaminger	1982	Si Burick
1967	Damon Runyon	1975	Tom Meaney	1983	Ken Smith
1968	H.G. Salsinger		& Shirley Povich	1984	Joe McGuff
1969	Sid Mercer	1976	Harold Kaese	1985	Earl Lawson
			& Red Smith	1986	Jack Lang
1970	Heywood Broun	1977	Gordon Cobbledick	1987	Jim Murray
1971	Frank Graham		& Edgar Munzel	1988	Bob Hunter & Ray Kelly
1972	Dan Daniel, Fred Lieb	1978	Tim Murnane	1989	Jerome Holtzman
	& J. Roy Stockton		& Dick Young	1990	Phil Collier

Ford Frick Award

First presented in 1978 by Hall of Fame for meritorious contributions by baseball broadcasters. Named in honor of the late broadcaster, National League president and commissioner, the Frick Award does not constitute induction into the Hall of Fame.

Year		Year		Year	
1978	Mel Allen & Red Barber	1983	Jack Brickhouse	1988	Lindsey Nelson
1979	Bob Elson	1984	Curt Gowdy	1989	Harry Caray
		1985	Buck Canel		
1980	Russ Hodges	1986	Bob Prince	1990	Byrum Saam
1981	Ernie Harwell	1987	Jack Buck	1991	Joe Garagiola
1982	Vin Scully				

▋ BASKETBALL ▋

Naismith Memorial Basketball Hall of Fame

Established in 1949 by the National Association of Basketball Coaches in memory of the sport's inventor, Dr. James Naismith. Original Hall opened in 1968 and current Hall in 1985. **Address:** 1150 West Columbus Avenue, Springfield, MA 01105. **Telephone:** (413) 781-6500.

Eligibility: Nominated players and referees must be retired for five years, coaches must have coached 25 years or be retired for five, and contributors must have already completed their noteworthy service to the game. Voting done by 24-member committee made up of media representatives, Hall of Fame members and trustees. Any nominee not elected after five years becomes eligible for consideration by the Veterans' Committee after a five-year wait.

Class of 1991 (7): Players—guard **Nate (Tiny) Archibald**, college (Ariz.Western-UTEP, 1966-69), NBA (Cin.Royals/KC Kings-NY Nets-Buf-Bos-Mil, 1970-84); center **Dave Cowens**, college (Fla.St.,1966-70), NBA (Bos-Mil, 1970-80,82-83); Coach—**Bob Knight**, Army (1966-71), Indiana (1972—), US Olympic Team (1984); Contributors—**Larry Fleisher**, founder-director of NBA Players Assn. (1962-88); **Larry O'Brien**, NBA commissioner (1975-84); **Boris Stankovic**, secretary-general of FIBA (1976—). Veterans Committee—forward **Harry Gallatin**, NY Knicks (1948-57), Detroit (1957-58).

Members are listed with years of induction; (+) indicates deceased members.

Players

Archibald, Nate 1991
Arizin, Paul 1977
+Barlow, Thomas (Babe) 1980
Barry, Rick 1987
Baylor, Elgin 1976
+Beckman, John 1972
Bing, Dave 1990

+Borgmann, Benny 1961
Bradley, Bill 1982
+Brennan, Joe 1974
Cervi, Al. 1984
Chamberlain, Wilt 1978
+Cooper, Charles (Tarzan) 1976
Cousy, Bob 1970

Cowens, Dave. 1991
Cunningham, Billy 1986
Davies, Bob 1969
+DeBernardi, Forrest 1961
DeBusschere, Dave. 1982
+Dehnert, Dutch 1968
Endacott, Paul 1971

Foster, Bud 1964	Jones, Sam 1983	Reed, Willis 1981
Frazier, Walt 1987	Krause, Edward (Moose) 1975	Robertson, Oscar 1979
+Friedman, Marty 1971	Kurland, Bob 1961	+Roosma, John 1961
+Fulks, Joe. 1977	+Lapchick, Joe 1966	+Russell, John (Honey) 1964
Gale, Laddie 1976	Lovellette, Clyde 1988	Russell, Bill. 1974
Gallatin, Harry 1991	Lucas, Jerry 1979	Schayes, Dolph 1972
Gates, William (Pop) 1989	Luisetti, Hank 1959	+Schmidt, Ernest J. 1973
Gola, Tom. 1975	Macauley, Ed 1960	+Schommer, John. 1959
Greer, Hal 1981	+Maravich, Pete 1987	+Sedran, Barney 1962
+Gruenig, Robert 1963	Martin, Slater. 1981	Sharman, Bill. 1975
Hagan, Cliff 1977	+McCracken, Branch 1960	+Steinmetz, Christian 1961
+Hanson, Victor 1960	+McCracken, Jack 1962	+Thompson, John (Cat) 1962
Havlicek, John. 1983	McDermott, Bobby 1988	Thurmond, Nate 1984
Hayes, Elvin. 1990	Mikan, George 1959	Twyman, Jack 1982
Heinsohn, Tom 1986	Monroe, Earl. 1990	Unseld, Wes 1988
Holman, Nat. 1964	Murphy, Charles (Stretch). 1960	+Vandivier, Robert (Fuzzy) 1974
Houbregs, Bob 1987	+Page, Harlan (Pat) 1962	+Wachter, Ed. 1961
+Hyatt, Chuck 1959	Pettit, Bob 1970	Wanzer, Bobby 1987
+Johnson, Bill (Skinny) 1976	Phillip, Andy 1961	West, Jerry 1979
+Johnston, Neil. 1990	Pollard, Jim. 1977	Wilkens, Lenny 1989
Jones, K. C 1989	Ramsey, Frank 1981	Wooden, John 1960

Coaches

+Anderson, Harold (Andy) 1984	Harshman, Marv 1984	McCutchan, Arad 1980
Auerbach, Red 1968	+Hickey, Eddie 1978	McGuire, Frank. 1976
+Barry, Sam 1978	+Hobson, Howard (Hobby) 1965	+Meanwell, Walter (Doc) 1959
+Blood, Ernest (Prof) 1960	Holzman, Red 1986	Meyer, Ray 1978
Cann, Howard 1967	Iba, Hank 1968	Miller, Ralph 1988
+Carlson, Henry (Doc) 1959	+Julian, Alvin (Doggie) 1967	+Rupp, Adolph 1968
Carnevale, Ben 1969	+Keaney, Frank. 1960	+Sachs, Leonard 1961
+Case, Everett 1981	+Keogan, George. 1961	+Shelton, Everett 1979
Dean, Everett. 1966	Knight, Bob 1991	Smith, Dean 1982
+Diddle, Ed 1971	+Lambert, Ward (Piggy) 1960	Taylor, Fred. 1985
Drake, Bruce. 1972	Litwack, Harry 1975	Wade, Margaret. 1984
Gaines, Clarence 1981	+Leoffler, Ken 1964	Watts, Stan 1985
Gardner, Jack. 1983	+Lonborg, Dutch 1972	Wooden, John 1972
+Gill, Amory (Slats). 1967		

Teams

Buffalo Germans 1961	New York Renaissance 1963	Original Celtics 1959
First Team 1959		

Referees

+Enright, Jim. 1978	+Leith, Lloyd 1982	Shirley, J. Dallas 1979
+Hepbron, George. 1960	Mihalik, Red 1986	Tobey, Dave 1961
+Hoyt, George 1961	Nucatola, John 1977	+Walsh, David. 1961
+Kennedy, Pat. 1959	+Quigley, Ernest (Quig) 1961	

Contributors

+Abbott, Senda Berenson 1984	Hinkle, Tony 1965	+Porter, Henry (H.V.) 1960
+Allen, Forrest (Phog) 1959	+Irish, Ned. 1964	+Reid, William A 1963
Bee, Clair 1967	+Jones, R. William 1964	+Ripley, Elmer 1972
+Brown, Walter A 1965	+Kennedy, Walter 1980	+St. John, Lynn W 1962
+Bunn, John 1964	+Liston, Emil (Liz) 1974	+Saperstein, Abe. 1970
+Douglas, Bob 1971	McLendon, John 1978	+Schabinger, Arthur 1961
+Duer, Al. 1981	+Mokray, Bill 1965	+Stagg, Amos Alonzo. 1959
Fagen, Clifford B 1983	+Morgan, Ralph 1959	Stankovic, Boris. 1991
+Fisher, Harry 1973	+Morgenweck, Frank (Pop) 1962	+Steitz, Ed 1983
+Fleisher, Larry 1991	Naismith, James 1959	+Taylor, Chuck 1968
+Gottlieb, Eddie 1971	Newell, Pete 1978	+Teague, Bertha 1984
+Gulick, Luther 1959	+O'Brien, John J. (Jack) 1961	+Tower, Oswald 1959
Harrison, Les. 1979	+O'Brien, Larry 1991	+Trester, Ather (A.L.). 1961
+Hepp, Ferenc 1980	+Olsen, Harold G. 1959	+Wells, Cliff 1971
+Hickox, Ed 1959	+Podoloff, Maurice 1973	+Wilke, Lou 1982

Curt Gowdy Award

First presented in 1990 by the Hall of Fame Board of Trustees for meritorious contributions by the media. Named in honor of the NBC sportscaster, the Gowdy Award does not constitute induction into the Hall of Fame.

Year	**Year**
1990 Curt Gowdy and Dick Herbert	1991 Dave Dorr and Marty Glickman

BOWLING

National Hall of Fame

The National Bowling Hall is one museum with separate wings for honorees of the American Bowling Congress (ABC), Professional Bowlers' Association (PBA) and Women's International Bowling Congress (WIBC). **Address:** 111 Stadium Plaza, St.Louis, MO 63102. **Telephone:** (314) 231-6340.

American Bowling Congress

Established in 1941 and open to professional and amateur bowlers. **Eligibility:** Nominated bowlers must have competed in at least 20 years of ABC tournaments. Voting done by 150-member panel made up of ABC officials, Hall of Fame members and media representatives.

Class of 1991 (5): Performance—**Bill Beach, Les Schissler, Teata Semiz, Bud Stoudt** and **Rod Toft**. Members are listed with years of induction; (+) indicates deceased members.

Performance

Allison, Glenn 1979	Golembiewski, Billy 1979	+Patterson, Pat 1974
Anthony, Earl. 1986	Guenther, Johnny. 1988	Ritger, Dick 1984
+Asplund, Harold 1978	Hardwick, Billy 1985	Salvino, Carmen. 1979
Baer, Gordy 1987	Hennessey, Tom 1976	Schissler, Les 1991
Beach, Bill 1991	Hoover, Dick. 1974	Schroeder, Jim 1990
Benkovic, Frank 1958	Howard, George 1986	+Schwoegler, Connie 1968
Billick, George 1982	Jackson, Eddie 1988	Semiz, Teata 1991
+Blouin, Jimmy 1953	Johnson, Don 1982	+Sielaff, Lou 1968
Bluth, Ray 1973	Johnson,Earl. 1987	+Sinke, Joe 1977
+Bodis, Joe 1941	+Joseph, Joe 1969	+Sixty, Billy 1961
+Bomar, Buddy. 1966	+Jouglard, Lee 1979	Smith, Harry 1978
+Brandt, Allie. 1960	+Kartheiser, Frank 1967	+Smith, Jimmy. 1941
+Brosius, Eddie 1976	+Kawolics, Ed 1968	Soutar, Dave. 1985
+Bujack, Fred 1967	+Kissoff, Joe 1976	+Sparando, Tony 1968
Bunetta, Bill 1968	Klares, John 1982	Spinella, Barney 1968
Burton, Nelson, Sr 1964	+Knox, Billy 1954	+Steers, Harry 1941
Burton, Nelson, Jr. 1981	+Koster, John 1941	Stefanich, Jim 1983
+Campi, Lou 1968	+Krems, Eddie. 1973	+Stein, Otto, Jr 1971
+Carlson, Adolph 1941	Kristof, Joe. 1968	Stoudt, Bud 1991
Carter, Don. 1970	+Krumske, Paul. 1968	Strampe, Bob 1977
+Caruana, Frank 1977	+Lange, Herb 1941	+Thoma, Sykes 1971
+Cassio, Marty 1972	Lauman, Hank 1976	Toft, Rod 1991
+Castellano, Graz 1976	Lillard, Bill 1972	Tountas, Pete. 1989
+Clause, Frank 1980	Lindenmann, Tony 1979	Tucker, Bill. 1988
Cohn, Alfred 1985	+Lindsey, Mort. 1941	+Varipapa, Andy. 1957
Crimmins, John 1962	Lippe, Harry 1989	+Ward, Walter 1959
Davis, Dave. 1990	Lubanski, Ed 1971	Weber, Dick 1970
+Daw, Charlie. 1941	Lucci, Vince, Sr 1978	+Welu, Billy 1975
+Day, Ned. 1952	+Marino, Hank 1941	+Wilman, Joe 1951
+Easter, Sarge. 1963	+Martino, John 1969	+Wolf, Phil. 1961
Ellis, Don 1981	+McMahon, Junie. 1967	Wonders, Rich. 1990
+Falcaro, Joe. 1968	+Mercurio, Skang 1967	+Young, George. 1959
Faragalli, Lindy. 1968	+Meyers, Norm 1984	Zahn, Wayne 1980
Fazio, Buzz 1963	+Nagy, Steve. 1963	Zikes, Les. 1983
+Gersonde, Russ. 1968	Norris, Joe. 1954	+Zunker, Gil 1941
+Gibson, Therm 1965	O'Donnell, Chuck 1968	
Godman, Jim 1987	Pappas, George 1989	

Meritorious Service

+Allen, Harold. 1966	+Hagerty, Jack 1963	+Petersen, Louie 1963
Baker, Frank 1975	+Hattstrom, H.A.(Doc) 1980	Pezzano, Chuck 1982
+Baumgarten, Elmer 1963	+Hermann, Cone 1968	Pluckhahn, Bruce 1989
+Bellisimo, Lou 1986	+Howley, Pete. 1941	Raymer, Milt 1972
Bensinger, Bob 1969	+Kennedy, Bob 1981	+Reed, Elmer. 1978
+Chase, LeRoy 1972	+Langtry, Abe 1963	Rudo, Milt 1984
+Coker, John 1980	+Levine, Sam. 1971	Schenkel, Chris 1988
+Collier, Chuck 1963	+Luby, David. 1969	+Sweeney, Dennis. 1974
+Cruchon, Steve 1983	Luby, Mort, Jr. 1988	+Thum, Joe 1980
+Ditzen, Walt. 1973	+Luby, Mort, Sr. 1974	Weinstein, Sam 1970
+Doehrman, Bill 1968	+McCullough, Howard. 1971	+Whitney, Eli 1975
Elias, Eddie 1985	+Patterson, Morehead 1985	Wolf, Fred 1976

Professional Bowlers Association

Established in 1975. **Eligibility:** Nominees must be PBA members and at least 35 years-old. Voting done by 50-member panel that includes writers who have covered bowling for at least 12 years.

Class of 1991 (3): Performance—**Paul Colwell**; Veterans—**Don McCune**; Meritorious Service—**Al Thompson**. Members are listed with years of induction; (+) indicates deceased members.

Performance

Allen, Bill	1983	Fazio, Buzz	1976	Roth, Mark	1987
Anthony, Earl	1986	Godman, Jim	1987	Salvino, Carmen	1975
Berardi, Joe	1990	Hardwick, Billy	1977	Smith, Harry	1975
Bluth, Ray	1975	Holman, Marshall	1990	Soutar, Dave	1979
Burton, Nelson, Jr.	1979	Hudson, Tommy	1989	Stefanich, Jim	1980
Carter, Don	1975	Johnson, Don	1977	Weber, Dick	1975
Colwell, Paul	1991	Laub, Larry	1985	+Welu, Billy	1975
Davis, Dave	1978	Pappas, George	1986	Zahn, Wayne	1981
Dickinson, Gary	1988	Petraglia, John	1982		
Durbin, Mike	1984	Ritger, Dick	1978		

Veterans

Allison, Glenn	1984	+Joseph, Joe	1985	McGrath, Mike	1988
Asher, Barry	1988	Marzich, Andy	1990	+St.John, Jim	1989
Guenther, Johnny	1986	McCune, Don	1991	Strampe, Bob	1987

Meritorious Service

Archibald, John	1989	Frantz, Lou	1978	Pezzano, Chuck	1975
Elias, Eddie	1976	Golden, Harry	1983	+Richards, Joe	1976
Esposito, Frank	1975	Hoffman, Ted, Jr.	1985	Schenkel, Chris	1976
Evans, Dick	1986	Jowdy, John	1988	Stitzlein, Lorraine	1980
Firestone, Raymond	1987	Kelley, Joe	1989	Thompson, Al	1991
Fisher, E.A.(Bud)	1984	+Nagy, Steve	1977		

Women's International Bowling Congress

Established in 1953. **Eligibility:** Performance nominees must have won at least one WIBC Championship Tournament title, a WIBC Queens tournament title or an international competition title and have bowled in at least 15 national WIBC Championship Tournaments (unless injury or illness cut career short).

Class of 1991 (3): Performance—**Vesma Grinselds** and **Betty Mivelaz**. Meritorious Service—**Anne Simone**. Members are listed with years of induction; (+) indicates deceased members.

Performance

Abel, Joy	1984	+Hartrick, Stella	1972	Norton, Virginia	1988
Bolt, Mae	1978	+Hatch, Grayce	1953	Notaro, Phyllis	1979
Bouvia, Gloria	1987	Havlish, Jean	1987	Ortner, Bev	1972
Boxberger, L oa	1984	Hoffman, Martha	1979	Powers, Connie	1973
Buckner, Pam	1990	Holm, Joan	1974	+Robinson, Leona	1969
Burling, Catherine	1958	+Humphreys, Birdie	1979	+Rump, Anita	1962
Burns, Nina	1977	Jacobson, D.D	1981	+Ruschmeyer, Addie	1961
Cantaline, Anita	1979	+Jaeger, Emma	1953	+Ryan, Esther	1963
Carter, LaVerne	1977	Kelly, Annesse	1985	+Sablatnik, Ethel	1979
Coburn, Doris	1976	+Knechtges, Doris	1983	+Schulte, Myrtle	1965
Costello, Pat	1986	Kuczynski, Betty	1981	+Shablis, Helen	1977
Costello, Patty	1989	Ladewig, Marion	1964	+Simon, Violet (Billy)	1960
Dryer, Pat	1978	Martin, Sylvia Wene	1966	+Small, Tess	1971
Duval, Helen	1970	Martorella, Millie	1975	+Smith, Grace	1968
Fellmeth, Catherine	1970	+Matthews, Merle	1974	Soutar, Judy	1976
Fothergill, Dotty	1980	+McCutcheon, Floretta	1956	+Stockdale, Louise	1953
+Fritz, Deane	1966	Merrick, Marge	1980	Toepfer, Elvira	1976
Garms, Shirley	1971	+Mikiel, Val	1979	+Twyford, Sally	1964
Gloor, Olga	1976	+Miller, Dorothy	1954	+Warmbier, Marie	1953
Graham, Mary Lou	1989	Mivelaz, Betty	1991	Wilkinson, Dorothy	1990
+Greenwald, Goldie	1953	Morris, Betty	1983	+Winandy, Cecelia	1975
Grinfelds, Vesma	1991	Nichols, Lorrie	1989	Zimmerman, Donna	1982
+Harman, Janet	1985				

Women's International Bowling Congress (Cont.)
Meritorious Service

Baetz, Helen 1977	+Haas, Dorothy............... 1977	+Phaler, Emma 1965
Baker, Helen 1989	+Higley, Margaret............ 1969	Porter, Cora 1986
Berger, Winifred 1976	+Hochstadter, Bee 1967	+Quinn, Zoe 1979
+Bohlen, Philena 1955	+Kay, Nora 1964	+Rishling, Gertrude........... 1972
Borschuk, Lo 1988	+Kelly, Ellen.................. 1979	Simone, Anne 1991
Botkin, Freda............... 1986	Kelone, Theresa 1978	Sloan, Catherine............ 1985
+Chapman, Emily............ 1957	+Knepprath, Jeannette 1963	+Speck, Berdie 1966
+Crowe, Alberta 1982	+Lasher, Iolia................. 1967	†Spring, Alma 1979
+Dornblaser, Gertrude........ 1979	Marrs, Mabel 1979	+Switzer, Pearl.............. 1973
Duffy, Agnes 1987	+McBride, Bertha 1968	+Veatch, Georgia 1974
Finke, Gertrude............. 1990	+Menne, Catherine........... 1979	+White, Mildred 1975
+Fisk, Rae 1983	+Mraz, Jo................... 1959	+Wood, Ann 1970

BOXING

International Boxing Hall of Fame

Established in 1989 and opened in 1990. **Address:** 1 Hall of Fame Drive, Canastota, NY 13032. **Telephone:** (315) 697-7095.

Eligibility: all nominees must be retired for five years. Voting done by 115-member panel made up of Boxing Writers' Association members and world-wide boxing historians.

Class of 1991: 26 second-year members (see below).

Members are listed with year of induction; (+) indicates deceased members.

Modern Era

Ali, Muhammad 1990	Griffith, Emile 1990	Ortiz, Carlos 1991
+Armstrong, Henry........... 1990	Jack, Beau.................. 1991	Patterson, Floyd 1991
Basilio, Carmen 1990	LaMotta, Jake 1990	Pep, Willie 1990
+Cerdan, Marcel............. 1991	+Liston, Sonny............... 1991	+Robinson, Sugar Ray 1990
+Charles, Ezzard............. 1990	+Louis, Joe 1990	Saddler, Sandy 1990
Conn, Billy.................. 1990	+Marciano, Rocky 1990	+Sanchez, Salvadore 1991
Foster, Bob 1990	Monzon, Carlos 1990	+Tiger, Dick 1991
Frazier, Joe 1990	Moore, Archie.............. 1990	Walcott, Jersey Joe 1990
Fullmer, Gene............... 1991	Napoles, Jose 1990	Williams, Ike 1990
Gavilan, Kid 1990	Olivares, Ruben 1991	Zale, Tony 1991
+Graziano, Rocky 1991		

Old-Timers

+Attell, Abe 1990	+Fitzsimmons, Bob 1990	+Loughran, Tommy 1991
+Britton, Jack................ 1990	+Gans, Joe 1990	+McCoy, Charles (Kid) 1991
+Canzoneri, Tony............. 1990	+Greb, Harry................ 1990	+McGovern, Terry............ 1990
+Carpentier, Georges 1991	+Griffo, Young 1991	McLarnin, Jimmy............ 1991
+Chocolate, Kid 1991	+Jackson, Peter 1990	+Ross, Barney 1990
+Corbett, James J 1990	+Jeffries, James J 1990	+Ryan, Tommy 1991
+Dempsey, Jack 1990	+Johnson, Jack 1990	+Tunney, Gene 1990
+Dixon, George 1990	+Ketchel, Stanley 1990	+Walker, Mickey 1990
+Driscoll, Jim................ 1990	+Langford, Sam 1990	+Walcott, Joe............... 1991
+Dundee, Johnny 1991	+Leonard, Benny............. 1990	+Wilde, Jimmy 1990

Pioneers

+Broughton, Jack 1990	+Mendoza, Daniel 1990	+Sullivan, John L............. 1990
+Cribb, Tom 1991	+Sayers, Tom 1990	+Thompson, William 1991
+Mace, Jem................. 1990		

Non-Participants

Arcel, Ray 1991	+Fleischer, Nat 1990	+Parnassus, George.......... 1991
+Chambers, John Graham 1990	+Jacobs, Mike............... 1990	+Queensberry, Marquis of...... 1990
+Coffroth, James W 1991	+Kearns, Jack (Doc) 1990	+Rickard, Tex................ 1990
+Egan, Pierce 1991	+Lonsdale, Lord 1990	

FOOTBALL

College Football Hall of Fame

Established in 1955 by the National Football Foundation. **Address:** 5440 Kings Island Drive, Kings Island, OH 45034 (move to Memphis, TN, called off in 1991). **Telephone:** (513) 398-5410.

Eligibility: Nominated players must be out of college 10 years and a first team All-America pick by a major selector during career; coaches must be retired three years. Voting done by 12-member panel of athletic directors, conference and bowl officials and media representatives.

Class of 1991 (15)**:** Players—E **Hub Bechtol**, Texas (1944-46); T **Bobby Bell**, Minnesota (1960-62); WR **Fred Biletnikoff**, Florida St.(1962-64); S **Kenny Easley**, UCLA (1977-80); HB **Parker Hall**, Ole Miss (1936-38); T **Alex Karras**, Iowa (1955-57); RB **Ed Marinaro**, Cornell (1969-71); MG **Wayne Meylan**, Nebraska (1965-67); RB **Steve Owens**, Oklahoma (1967-69); T **George Savitsky**, Penn (1944-47); MG **Jim Stillwagon**, Ohio St.(1968-70); QB **Pat Sullivan**, Auburn (1969-71). Coaches—**Allyn McKeen**, Memphis St.(1937-38), Miss.St.(1939-45); **Dave Maurer**, Wittenberg (1969-83); **Tommy Prothro**, Oregon St.(1955-64), UCLA (1965-70).

Players are listed with final year they played in college and coaches are listed with year of induction; (+) indicates deceased members.

Players

+Abell, Earl–Colgate 1915	Bomar, Lynn–Vanderbilt 1924	Connor, George–HC/ND 1947
Agase, Alex–Purdue/Ill. 1946	+Bomeisler, Bo–Yale 1913	+Corbin, William–Yale.......... 1888
+Agganis, Harry–Boston U 1952	+Booth, Albie–Yale 1931	Corbus, William–Stanford 1933
Albert, Frank–Stanford 1941	+Borries, Fred–Navy........... 1934	+Cowan, Hector–Princeton 1889
+Aldrich, Ki–TCU 1938	Bosely, Bruce–West Va. 1955	+Coy, Edward (Tad)–Yale 1909
+Aldrich, Malcolm–Yale....... 1921	Bosseler, Don–Miami,FL 1956	+Crawford, Fred–Duke 1933
+Alexander, Joe–Syracuse 1920	Bottari, Vic–California 1938	Crow, John David–Tex.A&M ... 1957
Alworth, Lance–Arkansas..... 1961	+Boynton, Ben–Williams 1920	+Crowley, Jim–Notre Dame 1924
+Ames, Knowlton–Princeton 1889	+Brewer, Charles–Harvard 1895	Csonka, Larry–Syracuse....... 1967
+Ameche, Alan–Wisconsin 1954	+Bright, Johnny–Drake......... 1951	Cutter, Slade–Navy 1934
Amling, Warren–Ohio St 1946	Brodie, John–Stanford 1956	+Czarobski, Ziggie–N.Dame.... 1947
Anderson, Donny–Tex.Tech.... 1966	+Brooke, George–Penn 1895	
+Anderson, Hunk–N.Dame...... 1921	Brown, Geo–Navy/S.Diego St.. 1947	Dale, Carroll–Va.Tech 1959
Atkins, Doug–Tennessee 1952	+Brown, Gordon–Yale 1900	+Dalrymple, Gerald–Tulane ... 1931
	+Brown, John, Jr.–Navy........ 1913	Daniell, Averell–Pitt........... 1936
Bacon, Everett–Wesleyan...... 1912	+Brown, Johnny Mack–Ala 1925	+Daniell, James–Ohio St 1941
Bagnell, Reds–Penn 1950	Brown, Tay–USC 1932	Dalton, John–Navy............ 1911
+Baker, Hobey–Princeton....... 1913	+Bunker, Paul–Army........... 1902	Daly, Chas.–Harvard/Army.... 1902
+Baker, John–USC 1931	Burton, Ron–N'western 1959	+Davies, Tom–Pittsburgh 1921
+Baker, Moon–N'western 1926	Butkus, Dick–Illinois 1964	+Davis, Ernie–Syracuse 1961
Baker, Terry–Oregon St....... 1962	+Butler, Robert–Wisconsin 1912	Davis, Glenn–Army 1946
+Ballin, Harold–Princeton 1914		Davis, Robert–Ga.Tech 1947
+Banker, Bill–Tulane........... 1929	Cafego, George–Tenn......... 1939	Dawkins, Pete–Army.......... 1958
Banonis, Vince–Detroit........ 1941	+Cagle, Red–SWLa/Army 1929	DeRogatis, Al–Duke........... 1948
+Barnes, Stan–California....... 1921	+Cain, John–Alabama.......... 1932	+DesJardien, Paul–Chicago 1914
+Barrett, Charles–Cornell 1915	Cameron, Ed–Wash.& Lee 1924	+Devine, Aubrey–Iowa......... 1921
+Baston, Bert–Minnesota 1916	+Campbell, David–Harvard 1901	+DeWitt, John–Princeton 1903
+Battles, Cliff–WV Wesleyan ... 1931	Campbell, Earl–Texas 1977	Ditka, Mike–Pittsburgh 1960
Baugh, Sammy–TCU 1936	+Cannon, Jack–N.Dame........ 1929	Dobbs, Glenn–Tulsa 1942
Baughan, Maxie–Ga.Tech..... 1959	Carideo, Frank–N.Dame....... 1930	+Dodd, Bobby–Tennessee...... 1930
+Bausch, James–Kansas 1930	Caroline, J.C.–Illinois......... 1954	Donan, Holland–Princeton 1950
Beagle, Ron–Navy 1955	+Carney, Charles–Illinois....... 1921	+Donchess, Joseph–Pitt 1929
Beban, Gary–UCLA 1967	Carpenter, Bill–Army 1959	+Dougherty, Nathan–Tenn 1909
Bechtol, Hub–Texas.......... 1946	+Carpenter, Hunter–Va.Tech.... 1905	Drahos, Nick–Cornell 1940
+Beckett, John–Oregon........ 1916	Carroll, Chas.–Washington 1928	+Driscoll, Paddy–N'western..... 1917
Bednarik, Chuck–Penn........ 1948	+Casey, Edward–Harvard 1919	+Drury, Morley–USC 1927
Behm, Forrest–Nebraska...... 1940	Cassady, Howard–Ohio St 1955	Dudley, Bill–Virginia.......... 1941
Bell, Bobby–Minnesota........ 1962	+Chamberlin, Guy–Neb......... 1915	
Bellino, Joe–Navy............ 1960	Chapman, Sam–California.... 1938	Easley, Kenny–UCLA 1980
Below, Marty–Wisconsin 1923	Chappuis, Bob–Michigan 1947	+Eckersall, Walter–Chicago..... 1906
+Benbrook, Al–Michigan 1910	+Christman, Paul–Missouri 1940	+Edwards, Turk–Wash.St 1931
Bertelli, Angelo–N.Dame...... 1943	+Clark, Dutch–Colo. Col. 1929	Edwards, Wm.–Princeton...... 1899
+Berry, Charlie–Lafayette....... 1924	Cleary, Paul–USC............ 1947	+Eichenlaub, Ray–N.Dame...... 1914
Berwanger, Jay–Chicago....... 1935	+Clevenger, Zora–Indiana...... 1903	Elliott, Bump–Mich/Purdue ... 1947
+Bettencourt, L.–St.Mary's 1927	Cloud, Jack–Wm&Mary....... 1948	Evans, Ray–Kansas........... 1947
Biletnikoff, Fred–Fla.St. 1964	+Cochran, Gary–Princeton 1897	+Exendine, Albert–Carlisle...... 1907
Blanchard, Doc–Army 1946	+Cody, Josh–Vanderbilt........ 1919	
+Blozis, Al–Georgetown........ 1942	Coleman, Don–Mich.St 1951	Falaschi, Nello–S.Clara 1936
Bock, Ed–Iowa St 1938	Conerly, Charlie–Miss 1947	Fears, Tom–S.Clara/UCLA 1947
		+Feathers, Beattie–Tenn........ 1933

College Football Hall of Fame (Cont.)

Fenimore, Bob–Okla.St 1946
+Fenton, Doc–LSU 1909
Ferraro, John–USC 1944
Fesler, Wes–Ohio St. 1930
+Fincher, Bill–Ga.Tech 1920
Fischer, Bill–Notre Dame 1948
+Fish, Hamilton–Harvard. 1909
+Fisher, Robert–Harvard 1911
+Flowers, Allen–Ga.Tech 1920
Fortmann Danny–Colgate 1935
Francis, Sam–Nebraska 1936
Franco, Ed–Fordham 1937
Frank, Clint–Yale 1937
Franz, Rodney–California 1949
+Friedman, Benny–Michigan. . . . 1926

Gabriel, Roman–N.C.State 1961
Gain, Bob–Kentucky. 1950
+Galiffa, Arnold–Army. 1949
Gallarneau, Hugh–Stanford 1940
+Garbisch, Edgar–W.& J./Army . 1924
Garrett, Mike–USC 1965
+Gelbert, Charles–Penn. 1896
+Geyer, Forest–Oklahoma 1915
Giel, Paul–Minnesota. 1953
Gifford, Frank–USC. 1951
+Gilbert, Walter–Auburn 1936
+Gipp, George–N.Dame 1920
+Gladchuk, Chet–Boston Col . . . 1940
Glass, Bill–Baylor 1956
Goldberg, Marshall–Pitt. 1938
Goodreault, Gene–BC. 1940
+Gordon, Walter–Calif 1918
+Governali, Paul–Columbia 1942
Graham, Otto–N'western 1943
+Grange, Red–Illinois. 1925
+Grayson, Bobby–Stanford 1935
+Green, Jack–Tulane/Army. 1945
+Green, Joe–N.Texas St. 1968
Griese, Bob–Purdue. 1966
Griffin, Archie–Ohio St. 1975
+Gulick, Merle–Toledo/Hobart . . 1929
+Guyon, Joe–Ga.Tech. 1918

+Hale, Edwin–Miss.College 1921
Hall, Parker–Miss 1938
Ham, Jack–Penn.St 1970
Hamilton, Bob–Stanford 1935
Hamilton, Tom–Navy. 1926
+Hanson, Vic–Syracuse 1926
+Hardwick, Tack–Harvard. 1914
+Hare, T.Truxton–Penn 1900
+Harley, Chick–Ohio St. 1919
+Harmon, Tom–Michigan 1940
+Harpster, Howard–Carnegie. . . 1928
+Hart, Edward–Princeton 1911
Hart, Leon–Notre Dame 1949
Hartman, Bill–Georgia. 1937
+Hazel, Homer–Rutgers. 1924
+Hazeltine, Matt–Calif 1954
+Healey, Ed.–Dartmouth 1916
+Heffelfinger, Pudge–Yale. 1891
Hein, Mel–Washington St 1930
Heinrich, Don–Washington 1952
Hendricks, Ted–Miami,FL 1968
+Henry, Wilbur–Wash&Jeff 1919
Herschberger, C.–Chicago 1898
Herwig, Robert–Calif 1937
+Heston, Willie–Michigan 1904
+Hickman, Herman–Tenn. 1931
+Hickok, William–Yale. 1894

Hill, Dan–Duke. 1938
+Hillebrand, Art–Princeton. 1899
+Hinkey, Frank–Yale 1894
Hinkle, Carl–Vanderbilt 1937
Hinkle, Clarke–Bucknell. 1931
Hirsch, Elroy–Wisc./Mich 1943
+Hitchcock, James–Auburn 1932
Hoffmann, Frank–N.Dame 1931
+Hogan, James J.–Yale 1904
+Holland, Brud–Cornell. 1938
Holleder, Don–Army 1955
+Hollenback, Bill–Penn 1908
Holovak, Mike–Boston Col 1942
Holub, E.J.–Texas Tech 1960
Hornung, Paul–N.Dame 1956
Horrell, Edwin–California 1924
Horvath, Les–Ohio St. 1944
+Howe, Arthur–Yale. 1911
+Howell, Dixie–Alabama 1934
+Hubbard, Cal–Centenary 1926
+Hubbard, John–Amherst 1906
+Hubert, Pooley–Ala. 1925
Huff, Sam–West Virginia 1955
Humble, Weldon–Rice 1946
+Hunt, Joe–Texas A&M 1927
Huntington, Ellery–Colgate 1914
Hutson, Don–Alabama 1934

+Ingram, Jonas–Navy 1906
+Isbell, Cecil–Purdue 1937

+Jablonsky, J.–Army/Wash 1933
Janowicz, Vic–Ohio St 1951
+Jenkins, Darold–Missouri. 1941
+Jensen, Jackie–California 1948
+Joesting, Herbert–Minn 1927
Johnson, Bob–Tennessee. 1967
+Johnson, Jimmie–Carlisle/
N'western . . . 1903
+Jones, Calvin–Iowa 1955
+Jones, Gomer–Ohio St 1935
Jordan, Lee Roy–Alabama 1962
+Juhan, Frank–U.of South. 1910
Justice, Charlie–N.Car. 1949

Kaer, Mort–USC 1926
Karras, Alex–Iowa 1957
Kavanaugh, Ken–LSU 1939
+Kaw, Edgar–Cornell. 1922
Kazmaier, Dick–Princeton 1951
+Keck, James–Princeton. 1921
Kelley, Larry–Yale 1936
+Kelly, Wild Bill–Montana 1926
Kenna, Doug–Army 1944
+Kerr, George–Boston Col 1941
+Ketcham, Henry–Yale 1913
Keyes, Leroy–Purdue 1968
+Killinger, Glenn–Penn St 1921
+Kilpatrick, John–Yale 1910
Kimbrough, John–TexA&M 1940
+Kinard, Frank–Mississippi 1937
+King, Phillip–Princeton 1893
+Kinnick, Nile–Iowa 1939
+Kipke, Harry–Michigan 1923
+Kirkpatrick, John–Yale. 1910
+Kitzmiller, John–Oregon 1930
+Koch, Barton–Baylor. 1931
+Koppisch, Walt–Columbia. . . . 1924
Kramer, Ron–Michigan 1956
Krueger, Charlie–Tex.A&M 1957
Kutner, Malcolm–Texas 1941
Kwalick, Ted–Penn St 1968

+Lach, Steve–Duke. 1941
+Lane, Myles–Dartmouth. 1927
Lattner, Johnny–N.Dame. 1953
Lauricella, Hank–Tenn. 1952
+Lautenschlaeger–Tulane 1925
+Layden, Elmer–N.Dame 1924
Layne, Bobby–Texas. 1947
+Lea, Langdon–Princeton 1895
LeBaron, Eddie–Pacific. 1949
+Leech, James–VMI 1920
Lester, Darrell–TCU 1935
Lilly, Bob–TCU 1960
Little, Floyd–Syracuse 1966
+Lio, Augie–Georgetown 1940
+Locke, Gordon–Iowa 1922
+Lourie, Don–Princeton 1921
Lucas, Richie–Penn St. 1959
Luckman, Sid–Columbia 1938
Lujack, Johnny–N.Dame 1947
Lund, Pug–Minnesota 1934

+Macomber, Bart–Illinois 1915
MacLeod, Robert–Dart. 1938
Maegle, Dick–Rice 1954
+Mahan, Eddie–Harvard 1915
Majors, John–Tennessee 1956
+Mallory, William–Yale 1923
Mancha, Vaughn–Ala 1947
+Mann, Gerald–SMU 1927
Manning, Archie–Miss 1970
Manske, Edgar–N'western 1933
Marinaro, Ed–Cornell 1971
Markov, Vic–Washington 1937
+Marshall, Bobby–Minn 1906
Matson, Ollie–San Fran. 1952
Matthews, Ray–TCU 1927
+Maulbetsch, John–Mich 1914
+Mauthe, Pete–Penn St. 1912
+Maxwell, Robert–Chicago/
Swarthmore . . 1906
McAfee, George–Duke 1939
+McClung, Thomas–Yale. 1891
McColl, Bill–Stanford 1951
+McCormick, Jim–Princeton 1907
McDonald, Tommy–Okla 1956
+McDowall, Jack–N.C.State 1927
McElhenny, Hugh–Wash 1951
+McEver, Gene–Tennessee 1931
+McEwan, John–Army 1916
McFadden, Banks–Clemson . . . 1939
McFadin, Bud–Texas 1950
McGee, Mike–Duke. 1959
+McGinley, Edward–Penn 1924
+McGovern, John–Minn 1910
McGraw, Thurman–Colo.St. . . . 1949
+McKeever, Mike–USC 1960
+McLaren, George–Pitt 1918
+McMillan, Dan–USC/Calif. . . . 1922
+McMillin, Bo–Centre. 1921
+McWhorter, Bob–Georgia 1913
+Mercer, LeRoy–Penn. 1912
Meredith, Don–SMU 1959
+Metzger, Bert–N.Dame 1930
+Meylan, Wayne–Nebraska 1967
Mickal, Abe–LSU 1935
Miller, Creighton–N.Dame 1943
+Miller, Don–Notre Dame 1924
Miller, Rip–Notre Dame. 1924
+Miller, Eugene–Penn St 1913
+Miller, Fred–Notre Dame. 1928

College Football Hall of Fame (Cont.)

+Yarr, Tommy–N.Dame 1931
  Yary, Ron–USC............. 1967
+Yoder, Lloyd–Carnegie 1926

+Young, Buddy–Illinois......... 1946
+Young, Harry–Wash.& Lee 1916

+Young, Waddy–Okla 1938
  Zarnas, Gust–Ohio State...... 1937

Coaches

+Aillet, Joe.................. 1989
+Alexander, Bill............. 1951
+Anderson, Ed 1971
+Armstrong, Ike 1957
+Bachman, Charlie........... 1978
+Baujan, Harry 1990
+Bell, Matty 1955
+Bezdek, Hugo 1954
+Bible, Dana X 1951
+Bierman, Bernie 1955
  Blackman, Bob 1987
+Blaik, Earl (Red)............ 1965
  Broyles, Frank 1983
+Bryant, Paul (Bear) 1986
+Caldwell, Charlie 1961
+Camp, Walter.............. 1951
  Casanova, Len 1977
+Cavanaugh, Frank.......... 1954
+Colman, Dick 1990
+Crisler, Fritz 1954
+Daugherty, Duffy 1984
  Devaney, Bob 1981
  Devine, Dan 1985
+Dobie, Gil 1951
+Donohue, Michael 1951
+Dorais, Gus................. 1954
+Edwards, Bill 1986
+Engle, Rip 1973
  Faurot, Don................ 1961
  Gaither, Jake 1973
  Gillman, Sid 1989
+Godfrey, Ernest 1972
  Graves, Ray................ 1990
+Gustafson, Andy 1985
+Hall, Edward 1951
+Harding, Jack 1980
+Harlow, Richard 1954
+Harman, Harvey........... 1981

+Harper, Jesse 1971
+Haughton, Percy............ 1951
+Hayes, Woody............. 1983
+Heisman, John W 1954
+Higgins, Robert............ 1954
+Hollingberry, Babe 1979
  Howard, Frank 1989
+Ingram, Bill 1973
+Jennings, Morley........... 1973
+Jones, Howard 1951
+Jones, Biff 1954
+Jones, Tad 1958
+Jordan, Lloyd 1978
+Jordan, Ralph (Shug) 1982
+Kerr, Andy 1951
+Leahy, Frank 1970
+Little, George 1955
+Little, Lou................. 1960
+Madigan, Slip 1974
  Maurer, Dave 1991
  McClendon, Charley 1986
  McCracken, Herb 1973
+McGugin, Dan 1951
  McKay, John 1988
+McKeen, Allyn 1991
+McLaughry, Tuss 1962
+Meyer, Dutch 1956
+Mollenkopf, Jack........... 1988
+Moore, Bernie 1954
+Moore, Scrappy 1980
+Morrison, Ray 1954
+Munger, George........... 1976
+Munn, Clarence (Biggie) 1959
+Murray, Bill 1974
+Murray, Frank 1983
+Mylin, Ed (Hooks) 1974
+Neale, Earle (Greasy)........ 1967
+Neely, Jess................. 1971

  Nelson, David.............. 1987
+Neyland, Robert 1956
+Norton, Homer............. 1971
+O'Neill, Frank (Buck) 1951
+Owen, Bennie 1951
  Parseghian, Ara 1980
  Perry, Doyt................. 1988
+Phelan, Jimmy............. 1973
  Prothro, Tommy 1991
+Robinson, E.N.............. 1955
+Rockne, Knute............. 1951
+Romney, Dick 1954
+Roper, Bill 1951
  Royal, Darrell 1983
+Sanford, George............ 1971
+Schmidt, Francis 1971
  Schwartzwalder, Ben 1982
+Shaughnessy, Clark 1968
+Shaw, Buck 1972
+Smith, Andy............... 1951
+Snavely, Carl.............. 1965
+Stagg, Amos Alonzo........ 1951
+Sutherland, Jock 1951
+Tatum, Jim 1984
+Thomas, Frank 1951
+Vann, Thad 1987
  Vaught, Johnny............. 1979
+Wade, Wallace 1955
+Waldorf, Lynn (Pappy) 1966
+Warner, Glenn (Pop)......... 1951
+Wieman, E.E.(Tad) 1956
  Wilce, John 1954
  Wilkinson, Bud 1969
+Williams, Henry............. 1951
+Woodruff, George 1963
  Woodson, Warren 1989
+Yost, Fielding (Hurry Up) 1951
+Zuppke, Bob 1951

Pro Football Hall of Fame

Established in 1963 by National Football League to commemorate the sport's professional origins. **Address:** 2121 George Halas Drive NW, Canton, OH 44708. **Telephone:** (216) 456-8207.

Eligibility: nominated players must be retired five years, coaches must be retired, and contributors can still be active. Voting done by 31-member panel made up of media representatives from all 28 NFL cities, one PFWA representative and two selectors-at-large.

Class of 1991 (5): Players—RB **Earl Campbell**, Houston (1978-84), New Orleans (1984-85); guard **John Hannah**, New England (1973-85); lineman **Stan Jones**, Chicago Bears (1954-65), Washington (1966); PK **Jan Stenerud**, Kansas City (1967-79), Green Bay (1980-83), Minnesota (1984-85). Contributor—**Tex Schramm**, Dallas GM (1960-88).

1991 Finalists (nominated, but not elected): Players—Lem Barney, Bob Brown, Carl Eller, L.C.Greenwood, John Mackey, John Riggins, Ken Stabler, Lynn Swann, Jack Youngblood. Contributor—Al Davis.

Members are listed with year of induction; (+) indicates deceased members.

Quarterbacks

  Baugh, Sammy.............. 1963
  Blanda, George (also PK) 1981
  Bradshaw, Terry 1989
+Clark, Dutch 1963
  Conzelman, Jimmy........... 1964
  Dawson, Len 1987
+Driscoll, Paddy 1965
  Graham, Otto............... 1965

  Griese, Bob 1990
+Herber, Arnie 1966
  Jurgensen, Sonny 1983
+Layne, Bobby 1967
  Luckman, Sid 1965
  Namath, Joe 1985
  Parker, Clarence (Ace) 1972

  Starr, Bart 1977
  Staubach, Roger 1985
  Tarkenton, Fran 1986
  Tittle, Y.A................. 1971
  Unitas, Johnny 1979
+Van Brocklin, Norm 1971
+Waterfield, Paul 1965

Running Backs

+Battles, Cliff	1968	Hornung, Paul	1986
Brown, Jim	1971	Johnson, John Henry	1987
Campbell, Earl	1991	+Leemans, Tuffy	1978
Canadeo, Tony	1974	Matson, Ollie	1972
Csonka, Larry	1987	McAfee, George	1966
Dudley, Bill	1966	McElhenny, Hugh	1970
Gifford, Frank	1977	+McNally, Johnny (Blood)	1963
+Grange, Red	1963	Moore, Lenny	1975
+Guyon, Joe	1966	Motley, Marion	1968
Harris, Franco	1990	+Nagurski, Bronko	1963
+Hinkle, Clarke	1964		

+Nevers, Ernie	1963
Perry, Joe	1969
Sayers, Gale	1977
Simpson, O.J	1985
+Strong, Ken	1967
Taylor, Jim	1976
Thorpe, Jim	1963
Trippi, Charley	1968
Van Buren, Steve	1965
Walker, Doak	1986

Ends & Wide Receivers

Alworth, Lance	1978	+Hewitt, Bill	1971
Badgro, Red	1981	Hirsch, Elroy (Crazylegs)	1968
Berry, Raymond	1973	Hutson, Don	1963
Biletnikoff, Fred	1988	Lavelli, Dante	1975
Ditka, Mike	1988	Maynard, Don	1987
Fears, Tom	1970		

+Millner, Wayne	1968
Mitchell, Bobby	1983
Pihos, Pete	1970
Taylor, Charley	1984
Warfield, Paul	1983

Linemen (pre-World War II)

+Edwards, Turk (T)	1969	+Hubbard, Cal (T)	1963
Fortmann, Dan (G)	1985	Kiesling, Walt (G)	1966
+Healey, Ed (T)	1964	+Kinard, Bruiser (T)	1971
Hein, Mel (C)	1963	Lyman, Link (T)	1964
+Henry, Pete (T)	1963	+Michalske, Mike (G)	1964

Musso, George (T-G)	1982
+Stydahar, Joe (T)	1967
Trafton, George (C)	1964
Turner, Bulldog (C)	1966
Wojciechowicz, Alex (C)	1968

Offensive Linemen

Bednarik, Chuck (C-LB)	1967	Jones, Stan (T-G-DT)	1991
Brown, Roosevelt (T)	1975	Langer, Jim (C)	1987
Gatski, Frank (C)	1985	McCormack, Mike (T)	1984
Gregg, Forrest (T-G)	1977	Mix, Ron (T-G)	1979
Groza, Lou (T-PK)	1974	Otto, Jim (C)	1980
Hannah, John (G)	1991		

Parker, Jim (G)	1973
Ringo, Jim (C)	1981
St.Clair, Bob (T)	1990
Shell, Art	1989
Upshaw, Gene	1987

Defensive Linemen

Atkins, Doug	1982	Jones, Deacon	1980
Buchanan, Buck	1990	Lilly, Bob	1980
Davis, Willie	1981	Marchetti, Gino	1972
Donovan, Art	1968	Nomellini, Leo	1969
+Ford, Len	1976	Olsen, Merlin	1982
Greene, Joe	1987		

Page, Alan	1988
Robustelli, Andy	1971
Stautner, Ernie	1969
Weinmeister, Arnie	1984
Willis, Bill	1977

Linebackers

Bell, Bobby	1983	Ham, Jack	1988
Butkus, Dick	1979	Hendricks, Ted	1990
Connor, George (DT-OT)	1975	Huff, Sam	1982
+George, Bill	1974	Lambert, Jack	1990

Lanier, Willie	1986
Nitschke, Ray	1978
Schmidt, Joe	1973

Defensive Backs

Adderley, Herb	1980	Houston, Ken	1986
Blount, Mel	1989	Lane, Dick (Night Train)	1974
Brown, Willie	1984	Lary, Yale	1979
+Christiansen, Jack	1970		

+Tunnell, Emlen	1967
Wilson, Larry	1978
Wood, Willie	1989

Placekicker

Stenerud, Jan	1991

Player/Coach

+Chamberlin, Guy	1965	Flaherty, Ray	1976
+Conzelman, Jimmy	1964	+Hallas, George	1963

+Lambeau, Curly	1963
+Owen, Steve	1966

Coaches

+Brown, Paul	1967	Gillman, Sid	1983
Ewbank, Weeb	1978	Landry, Tom	1990

+Lombardi, Vince	1971
+Neale, Earle (Greasy)	1969

Contributors

+Bell, Bert	1963	+Lambeau, Curly	1963
+Bidwill, Charles	1967	+Mara, Tim	1963
+Carr, Joe	1963	+Marshall, George	1963
+Hallas, George	1963	+Ray, Hugh (Shorty)	1966
Hunt, Lamar	1972		

+Reeves, Dan	1967
+Rooney, Art	1964
Rozelle, Pete	1985
Schramm, Tex	1991

Canadian Football Hall of Fame

Established in 1963. Current Hall opened in 1972. **Address:** 58 Jackson Street West, Hamilton, Ontario, L8P 1L4. **Telephone:** (416) 528-7566.

Eligibility: Nominated players must be retired three years and coaches must be retired. Voting done by 14-member panel of Canadian pro and amateur football officials.

Class of 1991 (4): Players—guard **Tom Hinton**, B.C.Lions (1958-66); WR **Brian Kelly**, Edmonton (1979-87); RB-WR **Jim Young**, B.C.Lions (1967-79). Builders—administrator **Norm Kimball**, Edmonton (1964-86), Montreal (1986-87).

Members are listed with year of induction; (+) indicates deceased members.

Players

Atchison, Ron 1978	Helton, John 1986	Patterson, Hal 1971
Bailey, Byron 1975	Henley, Garney. 1979	Perry, Gordon 1970
Barrow, John. 1976	Hinton, Tom 1991	+Perry, Norm. 1963
+Batstone, Harry 1963	+Huffman, Dick. 1987	Ploen, Ken 1975
+Beach, Ormond 1963	+Isbister, Bob Sr 1965	+Quilty, S.P.(Silver) 1966
Box, Ab 1965	Jackson, Russ 1973	Rebholz, Russ 1963
+Breen, Joseph 1963	+Jacobs, Jack 1963	Reed, George 1979
+Bright, Johnny 1970	+James, Eddie. 1963	+Reeve, Ted. 1963
Brown, Tom. 1984	James, Gerry 1981	Rigney, Frank 1985
Casey, Tom. 1964	+Kabat, Greg 1966	+Rodden, Michael. 1964
Coffey, Tommy Joe 1977	Kapp, Joe 1984	+Rowe, Paul. 1964
+Conacher, Lionel 1963	Keeling, Jerry 1989	Ruby, Martin 1974
Copeland, Royal. 1988	Kelly, Brian 1991	+Russel, Jeff. 1963
Corrigall, Jim 1990	Krol, Joe 1963	Scott, Vince 1982
+Cox, Ernest 1963	Kwong, Normie 1969	Shatto, Dick. 1975
+Craig, Ross 1964	Lancaster, Ron 1982	+Simpson, Ben 1963
+Cronin, Carl 1967	+Lawson, Smirle 1963	Simpson, Bob 1976
+Cutler, Wes 1968	+Leadlay, Frank 1963	+Sprague, David. 1963
+Dixon, George 1974	+Lear, Les 1974	Stevenson, Art. 1969
+Eliowitz, Abe 1969	Lewis, Leo 1973	Stewart, Ron 1977
+Emerson, Eddie. 1963	Lunsford, Earl 1983	Stirling, Hugh (Bummer) 1966
Etcheverry, Sam 1969	Luster, Marv 1990	Thelen, Dave 1989
Evanshen, Terry. 1984	Luzzi, Don 1986	+Timmis, Brian 1963
Faloney, Bernie 1974	+McCance, Ches 1976	Tinsley, Bud. 1982
+Fear, A.H. (Cap). 1967	+McGill, Frank 1965	+Tommy, Andy 1989
Fennell, Dave 1990	McQuarters, Ed. 1988	+Trawick, Herb 1975
+Ferraro, John 1966	Miles, Rollie 1980	+Tubman, Joe. 1968
Fieldgate, Norm 1979	+Molson, Percy 1963	Urness, Ted. 1989
Fleming, Willie 1982	Morris, Frank. 1983	Vaughan, Kaye 1978
Gabriel, Tony 1985	+Morris, Teddy 1964	Wagner, Virgil 1980
+Gall, Hugh 1963	Mosca, Angelo 1987	+Welch, Hawley (Huck) 1964
Golab, Tony 1964	Nelson, Roger 1986	Wilkinson, Tom. 1987
Gray, Herbert 1983	Neumann, Peter 1979	Wylie, Harvey 1980
Griffing, Dean. 1965	O'Quinn, John Red 1981	Young, Jim 1991
Hanson, Fritz. 1963	Pajaczkowski, Tony. 1988	+Zock, William 1985
Harris, Wayne 1976	Parker, Jackie 1971	

Builders

+Back, Leonard. 1971	+Grey, Lord Earl 1963	+Newton, Jack 1964
+Bailey, Harold 1965	+Griffith, Harry 1963	Preston, Ken 1990
+Ballard, Harold 1987	+Halter, Sydney. 1966	+Ritchie, Alvin 1963
+Brook, Tom 1975	+Hannibal, Frank 1963	+Ryan, Joe B.. 1968
+Brown, D.Wes 1963	+Hayman, Lew 1975	Sazio, Ralph 1988
Chipman, Arthur. 1969	+Hughes, W.P.(Billy) 1974	+Shaughnessy, Frank (Shag) 1963
Clair, Frank. 1981	Keys, Eagle 1990	+Shouldice, W.T.(Hap) 1977
+Crighton, Hec 1986	Kimball, Norman 1991	+Simpson, Jimmie 1986
+Currie, Andrew 1974	Kramer, R.A. (Bob) 1987	+Slocomb, Karl 1989
+Davies, Dr. Andrew 1969	+Lieberman, M.I.(Moe). 1973	+Spring, Harry. 1976
+DeGruchy, John 1963	+McBrien, Harry 1978	Stukus, Annis 1974
Dojack, Paul 1978	+McCaffrey, Jimmy 1967	+Taylor, N.J.(Piffles) 1963
+Duggan, Eric. 1981	+McCann, Dave 1966	Tindall, Frank 1985
+DuMoulin, Seppi 1963	+McPherson, Don 1983	+Warner, Clair J. 1965
+Foulds, Willliam 1963	+Metras, Johnny 1980	+Warwick, Bert 1964
Gaudaur, J.G.(Jake). 1984	+Montgomery, Ken. 1970	+Wilson, Seymour. 1984
Grant, Bud 1983		

GOLF

There are two principal golf halls of fame: the PGA/World Golf Hall of Fame in Pinehurst, NC, and the LPGA Hall of Fame in Daytona Beach, FL. A third museum, the old PGA Hall, was abandoned in 1983 when the PGA took over the running of the World Golf Hall of Fame. Plans call for all members of the old PGA Hall to be included in a separate wing of the PGA/World Hall.

PGA/World Golf Hall of Fame

Established in 1974 and taken over by PGA of America in 1983. **Address:** PGA Boulevard, P.O.Box 1908, Pinehurst, NC 28374. **Telephone:** (919) 295-6651.
   Eligibility: nominees can still be active. Voting done by Golf Writers Association of America.
   Class of 1991: None. Members are listed with year of induction; (+) indicates deceased members.

Men

+Anderson, Willie ... 1975	+Hagen, Walter ... 1974	Palmer, Arnold ... 1974
+Armour, Tommy ... 1976	+Hilton, Harold ... 1978	Player, Gary ... 1974
+Ball, John, Jr ... 1977	Hogan, Ben ... 1974	Runyan, Paul ... 1990
+Barnes, Jim ... 1989	+Jones, Bobby ... 1974	Sarazen, Gene ... 1974
Boros, Julius ... 1982	+Little, Lawson ... 1980	+Smith, Horton ... 1990
+Braid, James ... 1976	Littler, Gene ... 1990	Snead, Sam ... 1974
Casper, Billy ... 1978	+Locke, Bobby ... 1977	+Taylor, John H. ... 1975
+Cotton, Thomas ... 1980	Middlecoff, Cary ... 1986	Thomson, Peter ... 1988
+Demaret, Jimmy ... 1983	+Morris, Tom, Sr ... 1976	+Travers, Jerry ... 1976
DeVicenzo, Roberto ... 1989	+Morris, Tom, Jr ... 1975	+Travis, Walter ... 1979
+Evans, Chick ... 1975	Nelson, Byron ... 1974	Trevino, Lee ... 1981
Floyd, Ray ... 1989	Nicklaus, Jack ... 1974	+Vardon, Harry ... 1974
+Guldahl, Ralph ... 1981	+Ouimet, Francis ... 1974	Watson, Tom ... 1988

Women

Berg, Patty ... 1974	Rawls, Betsy ... 1987	Whitworth, Kathy ... 1982
+Howe, Dorothy C.H ... 1978	Suggs, Louise ... 1979	Wright, Mickey ... 1976
Carner, JoAnne ... 1985	+Vare, Glenna Collett ... 1975	+Zaharias, Babe Didrikson ... 1974
Lopez, Nancy ... 1989	+Wethered, Joyce ... 1975	

Contributors

Campbell, William ... 1990	+Graffis, Herb ... 1977	Jones, Robert Trent ... 1987
+Corcoran, Fred ... 1975	+Harlow, Robert ... 1988	+Roberts, Clifford ... 1978
+Crosby, Bing ... 1978	Hope, Bob ... 1983	+Ross, Donald ... 1977
+Dey, Joe ... 1975		

Old PGA Hall Members Not in PGA/World Hall

The original PGA Hall of Fame was established in 1940 by the PGA of America, but abandoned after the 1982 inductions in favor of the PGA/World Hall of Fame. Twenty-six members of the old PGA Hall have since been elected to the PGA/World Hall of Fame. Players yet to make the cut are listed below with year of induction into old PGA Hall.

+Brady, Mike ... 1960	+Farrell, Johnny ... 1961	+Mangrum, Lloyd ... 1964
+Burke, Billy ... 1966	Ford, Doug ... 1975	+McLeod, Fred ... 1960
Burke, Jack, Jr ... 1975	+Ghezzi, Vic ... 1965	+Picard, Henry ... 1961
Cooper, Harry ... 1959	Harbert, Chick ... 1968	+Revolta, Johnny ... 1963
+Cruickshank, Bobby ... 1967	Harper, Chandler ... 1969	+Shute, Denny ... 1957
+Diegel, Leo ... 1955	+Harrison, Dutch ... 1962	+Smith, Alex ... 1940
+Dudley, Ed ... 1964	+Hutchison, Jock, Sr ... 1959	+Smith, Macdonald ... 1954
+Dutra, Olin ... 1962	+McDermott, John ... 1940	+Wood, Craig ... 1956

LPGA Hall of Fame

Established in 1967 by the LPGA to replace the old Women's Golf Hall of Fame (founded in 1950). Originally located in Augusta, GA (1967-77), the Hall has been moved to Pinehurst, NC (1977-83), Sugar Land, TX (1983-89) and Daytona Beach, FL (since 1990). There is currently no museum to visit, but a new building is scheduled to open in October of 1992. **Address:** LPGA Headquarters, 2570 Volusia Ave., Suite B, Daytona Beach, FL, 32114. **Telephone:** (904) 254-8800.
   Eligibility: players must have played 10 years and won 30 official events, including two major championships; or 35 official events and one major; or 40 official events and no majors.
   Last inductee: Nancy Lopez in 1987 (10 years, 35 wins, one major).
   Leading candidates (through Aug. 15, 1991): Amy Alcott (29 wins, 4 majors), Pat Bradley (27 wins, 6 majors) and Beth Daniel (27 wins, 1 major). Members are listed with year of induction; (+) indicates deceased members.

Berg, Patty ... 1951	Lopez, Nancy ... 1987	Whitworth, Kathy ... 1975
Carner, JoAnne ... 1982	Mann, Carol ... 1977	Wright, Mickey ... 1964
Haynie, Sandra ... 1977	Rawls, Betsy ... 1960	+Zaharias, Babe Didrikson ... 1951
Jameson, Betty ... 1951	Suggs, Louise ... 1951	

HOCKEY

Hockey Hall of Fame

Established in 1945 by the National Hockey League and opened in 1961. **Current Address:** Exhibition Place, Toronto, Ontario, M6K 3C3. **New Address:** BCE Place in downtown Toronto by October, 1992. **Current Telephone:** (416) 595-1345.

Eligibility: Nominated players and referees must be retired three years. Voting done by 12-member panel made up of NHL personalities and media representatives.

Class of 1991 (5): Players—right wing **Mike Bossy**, NY Islanders (1977-87); defenseman **Denis Potvin**, NY Islanders (1973-88); left wing **Bob Pulford**, Toronto (1956-70), Los Angeles (1970-72). Veteran—center **Clint Smith**, NY Rangers (1936-43), Chicago (1943-47). Builder—**Scotty Bowman**, coach St.Louis (1967-70,71), Montreal (1971-79), Buffalo (1979-80,81-85,86).

Members are listed with year of induction; (+) indicates deceased members.

Forwards

Abel, Sid	1969	+Frederickson, Frank	1958
+Adams, Jack	1959	+Gardner, Jimmy	1962
Apps, Syl	1961	Geoffrion, Bernie	1972
Armstrong, George	1975	+Gerard, Eddie	1945
Bailey, Ace	1975	Gilbert, Rod	1982
+Bain, Dan	1945	+Gilmour, Billy	1962
Baker, Hobey	1945	+Griffis, Si	1950
Barber, Bill	1990	+Hay, George	1958
+Barry, Marty	1965	+Hextall, Bryan	1969
Bathgate, Andy	1978	+Hooper, Tom	1962
Beliveau, Jean	1972	Howe, Gordie	1972
+Bentley, Doug	1964	+Howe, Syd	1965
+Bentley, Max	1966	Hull, Bobby	1983
Blake, Toe	1966	+Hyland, Harry	1962
Bossy, Mike	1991	+Irvin, Dick	1958
+Boucher, Frank	1958	+Jackson, Busher	1971
+Bowie, Dubbie	1945	+Joliat, Aurel	1947
+Broadbent, Punch	1962	+Keats, Duke	1958
Bucyk, John (Chief)	1981	Kennedy, Ted (Teeder)	1966
Burch, Billy	1974	Keon, Dave	1986
Clarke, Bobby	1987	Lach, Elmer	1966
Colville, Neil	1967	Lafleur, Guy	1988
Conacher, Charlie	1961	+Lalonde, Newsy	1950
+Cook, Bill	1952	Lemaire, Jacques	1984
Cournoyer, Yvan	1982	+Lewis, Herbie	1989
Cowley, Bill	1968	Lindsay, Ted	1966
+Crawford, Rusty	1962	+MacKay, Mickey	1952
+Darragh, Jack	1962	Mahovlich, Frank	1981
+Davidson, Scotty	1950	+Malone, Joe	1950
Day, Hap	1961	+Marshall, Jack	1965
Delvecchio, Alex	1977	+Maxwell, Fred	1962
+Denneny, Cy	1959	+McGee, Frank	1945
+Drillon, Gordie	1975	+McGimsie, Billy	1962
+Drinkwater, Graham	1950	Mikita, Stan	1983
+Dunderdale, Tommy	1974	Moore, Dickie	1974
+Dye, Babe	1970	+Morenz, Howie	1945
Esposito, Phil	1984	+Mosienko, Bill	1965
+Farrell, Arthur	1965	+Nighbor, Frank	1947
+Foyston, Frank	1958	+Noble, Reg	1962

+O'Connor, Buddy	1988
+Oliver, Harry	1967
Olmstead, Bert	1985
+Patrick, Lynn	1980
Perreault, Gilbert	1990
+Phillips, Tom	1945
+Primeau, Joe	1963
Pulford, Bob	1991
+Rankin, Frank	1961
Ratelle, Jean	1985
Richard, Henri	1979
Richard, Maurice (Rocket)	1961
+Richardson, George	1950
+Roberts, Gordie	1971
+Russel, Blair	1965
+Russell, Ernie	1965
+Ruttan, Jack	1962
+Scanlan, Fred	1965
Schmidt, Milt	1961
+Schriner, Sweeney	1962
+Seibert, Oliver	1961
+Siebert, Babe	1964
Sittler, Darryl	1989
+Smith, Alf	1962
Smith, Clint	1991
+Smith, Hooley	1972
+Smith, Tommy	1973
+Stanley, Barney	1962
+Stewart, Nels	1962
+Stuart, Bruce	1961
+Taylor, Fred (Cyclone)	1947
+Trihey, Harry	1950
Ullman, Norm.	1982
+Walker, Jack	1960
+Walsh, Marty	1962
+Watson, Harry (Moose)	1962
+Weiland, Cooney	1971
+Westwick, Harry (Rat)	1962
+Whitcroft, Fred	1962

Defensemen

Boivin, Leo	1986	+Dutton, Red	1958
+Boon, Dickie	1952	Flaman, Fernie	1990
Bouchard, Butch	1966	Gadsby, Bill	1970
+Boucher, George	1960	+Gardiner, Herb	1958
+Cameron, Harry	1962	+Goheen, F.X.(Moose)	1952
+Clancy, King	1958	+Goodfellow, Ebbie	1963
+Clapper, Dit	1947	+Grant, Mike	1950
+Cleghorn, Sprague	1958	+Green, Wilf (Shorty)	1962
Coulter, Art	1974	Hall, Joe	1961

Harvey, Doug	1973
Horner, Red	1965
+Horton, Tim	1977
Howell, Harry	1979
+Johnson, Ching	1958
+Johnson, Ernie	1952
Johnson, Tom	1970
Kelly, Red	1969

+Laviolette, Jack 1962
Leperrier, Jacques........... 1987
+Mantha, Sylvio 1960
+McNamara, George 1958
Orr, Bobby 1979
Park, Brad 1988
+Patrick, Lester 1947
Pilote, Pierre 1975

+Benedict, Clint.............. 1965
Bower, Johnny.............. 1976
Brimsek, Frank 1966
+Broda, Turk 1967
Cheevers, Gerry 1985
+Connell, Alex............... 1958
Dryden, Ken 1983
+Durnan, Bill............... 1964
Esposito, Tony............. 1988
+Gardiner, Chuck............ 1945

Armstrong, Neil 1991
Ashley, John 1981
Chadwick, Bill.............. 1964
+Elliott, Chaucer 1961

+Adams, Charles 1960
+Adams, Weston W.,Sr 1972
+Ahearn, Frank.............. 1962
+Ahearn, J.F.(Bunny) 1977
+Allan, Sir Montagu 1945
+Ballard, Harold............. 1977
+Bauer, Fr. David 1989
+Bickell, J.P 1978
+Brown, George 1961
+Brown, Walter 1962
+Buckland, Frank 1975
Butterfield, Jack............. 1980
+Calder, Frank 1945
+Campbell, Angus 1964
+Campbell, Clarence 1966
+Cattarinich, Joseph......... 1977
+Dandurand, Leo 1963
Dilio, Frank 1964
+Dudley, George 1958
+Dunn, James............... 1968
Eagleson, Alan 1989
Francis, Emile 1982
+Gibson, Jack 1976
+Gorman, Tommy 1963
+Hanley, Bill 1986

+Pitre, Didier 1962
Potvin, Denis 1991
+Pratt, Babe................. 1966
Pronovost, Marcel 1978
+Pulford, Harvey............. 1945
Quackenbush, Bill 1976
Reardon, Kenny 1966
+Ross, Art................... 1945

Goaltenders

Giacomin, Eddie............. 1987
+Hainsworth, George......... 1961
Hall, Glenn 1975
+Hern, Riley................. 1962
+Holmes, Hap............... 1972
+Hutton, J.B.(Bouse)......... 1962
+Lehman, Hughie............ 1958
+LeSueur, Percy............. 1961
Lumley, Harry 1980
+Moran, Paddy.............. 1958

Referees & Linesmen

+Hayes, George 1988
+Hewitson, Bobby........... 1963
+Ion, Mickey 1961
Pavelich, Matt 1987

Builders

+Hay, Charles................ 1984
+Hendy, Jim................. 1968
+Hewitt, Foster 1965
+Hewitt, W.A................ 1945
+Hume, Fred................. 1962
+Imlach, Punch.............. 1984
Ivan, Tommy............... 1964
+Jennings, William 1975
Juckes, Gordon............. 1979
+Kilpatrick, John 1960
+Leader, Al 1969
LeBel, Bob................. 1970
+Lockhart, Thomas........... 1965
+Loicq, Paul................. 1961
+Mariucci, John.............. 1985
+McLaughlin, Frederic 1963
+Milford, Jake............... 1984
Molson, Hartland 1973
+Nelson, Francis............. 1945
+Norris, Bruce............... 1969
+Norris, James D 1962
+Norris, James, Sr 1958
+Northey, William............ 1945
+O'Brien, J.A................ 1962
+Patrick, Frank 1958

Savard, Serge 1986
Seibert, Earl................. 1963
+Shore, Eddie 1947
+Simpson, Joe............... 1962
Stanley, Allan 1981
+Stewart, Jack 1964
+Stuart, Hod 1945
+Wilson, Gordon (Phat) 1962

Parent, Bernie 1984
+Plante, Jacques 1978
Rayner, Chuck.............. 1973
+Sawchuk, Terry 1971
+Thompson, Tiny 1959
Tretiak, Vladislav........... 1989
+Vezina, Georges 1945
Worsley, Gump.............. 1980
Worters, Roy 1969

Rodden, Mike 1962
+Smeaton, J. Cooper 1961
Storey, Red 1967
Udvari, Frank 1973

+Pickard, Allan 1958
Pilous, Rudy................ 1985
Poile, Bud 1990
Pollock, Sam 1978
+Raymond, Donat 1958
+Robertson, John Ross 1945
+Robinson, Claude........... 1945
+Ross, Philip 1976
+Selke, Frank 1960
Sinden, Harry 1983
+Smith, Frank 1962
+Smythe, Conn 1958
Snider, Ed 1988
+Stanley, Lord of Preston 1945
+Sutherland, James 1945
Tarasov, Anatoli 1974
+Turner, Lloyd 1958
+Tutt, William Thayer 1978
Voss, Carl 1974
+Waghorne, Fred 1961
+Wirtz, Arthur 1971
Wirtz, Bill 1976
Ziegler, John............... 1987

Elmer Ferguson Award

First presented in 1984 by the Professional Hockey Writers Association for meritorious contributions by members of the PHWA. Named in honor of the late Montreal newspaper reporter, the Ferguson Award does not constitute induction into the Hall of Fame.

1984—Jacques Beauchamp, Jim Burchard, Red Burnett, Dink Carroll, Jim Coleman, Ted Damata, Marcel Desjardins, Jack Dulmage, Milt Dunnell, Elmer Ferguson, Tom Fitzgerald, Trent Frayne, Al Laney, Joe Nichols, Basil O'Meara, Jim Vipond and Lewis Walter

1985—Charlie Barton, Red Fisher, George Gross, Zotique L'Esperance, Charles Mayer and Andy O'Brien

1986—Dick Johnston, Leo Monahan and Tim Moriarty

1987—Bill Brennan, Rex MacLeod, Ben Olan and Fran Rosa

1988—Jim Proudfoot and Scott Young

1989—Claude Larochelle and Frank Orr

1990—Bertrand Raymond

1991—Hugh Delano

Hockey Hall of Fame (Cont.)
Foster Hewitt Award

First presented in 1984 by the NHL Broadcasters Association for meritorious contributions by members of the NHLBA. Named in honor of Canada's legendary "Voice of Hockey," the Hewitt Award does not constitute induction into the Hall of Fame.

1984—Fred Cusick, Danny Gallivan, Foster Hewitt & Rene Lecavelier
1985—Budd Lynch & Doug Smith

1986—Wes McKnight & Lloyd Petit
1987—Bob Wilson
1988—Dick Irvin

1989—Dan Kelly
1990—Jiggs McDonald
1991—Bruce Martyn

U.S. Hockey Hall of Fame

Established in 1968 by the Eveleth (Minn.) Civic Association Project H Committee and opened in 1973. **Address:** 801 Hat Trick Ave., Eveleth, MN 55734. **Telephone:** (218) 744-5167.

Eligibility: nominated players and referees must be American-born and retired five years; coaches must be American-born and must have coached predominantly American teams. Voting done by 12-member panel made up of Hall of Famer members and U.S. hockey officials.

Class of 1991 (3): Players—**Robbie Ftorek** and **John Matchefts.** Coach—**Bob Johnson.** Members are listed with year of induction; (+) indicates deceased members.

Players

+Abel, Clarence (Taffy)	1973	
+Baker, Hobey	1973	
Bartholome, Earl	1977	
Bessone, Peter	1978	
Blake, Bob	1985	
Brimsek, Frank	1973	
+Chaisson, Ray	1974	
Chase, John	1973	
Christian, Bill	1984	
Christian, Roger	1989	
Cleary, Bob	1981	
Cleary, Bill	1976	
+Conroy, Tony	1975	
Dahlstrom, Carl (Cully)	1973	
DesJardins, Vic	1974	
Desmond, Richard	1988	
+Dill, Bob	1979	

Everett, Doug 1974
Ftorek, Robbie............. 1991
+Garrison, John 1974
Garrity, Jack 1986
+Goheen, Frank (Moose)....... 1973
Harding, Austie........... 1975
Iglehart, Stewart 1975
Ikola, Willard............. 1990
Johnson, Virgil 1974
Karakas, Mike 1973
Kirrane, Jack 1987
Lane, Myles 1973
+Linder, Joe.............. 1975
+LoPresti, Sam............ 1973
+Mariucci, John........... 1973
Matchefts, John........... 1991
Mayasich, John........... 1976

McCartan, Jack............. 1983
Moe, Bill 1974
Moseley, Fred 1975
+Murray, Hugh (Muzz) Sr. 1987
+Nelson, Hub 1978
Olson, Eddie............... 1977
+Owen, George 1973
+Palmer, Winthrop 1973
Paradise, Bob 1989
Purpur, Clifford (Fido) ... 1974
Riley, Bill 1977
+Romnes, Elwin (Doc)........ 1973
Rondeau, Dick 1985
Williams, Tommy 1981
+Winters, Frank (Coddy) 1973
+Yackel, Ken 1986

Coaches

+Almquist, Oscar 1983
Brooks, Herb 1990
+Gordon, Malcolm........... 1973
Heyliger, Vic 1974
Ikola, Willard............. 1990

+Jeremiah, Eddie 1973
Johnson, Bob 1991
+Kelley, John (Snooks) 1974
Pleban, Connie 1990
Riley, Jack 1979

Ross, Larry................. 1988
+Thompson, Cliff 1973
+Stewart, Bill 1982
+Winsor, Ralph 1973

Referee

Chadwick, Bill.............. 1974

Administrators

+Brown, George 1973
+Brown, Walter.............. 1973
Bush, Walter 1980
Clark, Don 1978
+Gibson, J.C. (Doc) 1973

+Jennings, William 1981
+Kahler, Nick 1980
+Lackhart, Tom.............. 1973
Marvin, Cal 1982
Ridder, Bob 1976

Trumble, Hal............... 1970
+Tutt, Thayer 1973
Wirtz, William 1967
+Wright, Lyle................. 1973

HORSE RACING

National Horse Racing Hall of Fame

Established in 1950 by the Saratoga Springs Racing Association and opened in 1955. **Address:** National Museum of Racing and Hall of Fame, Union Ave., Saratoga Springs, NY 12866. **Telephone:** (518) 584-0400.

Eligibility: nominated horses must be retired five years; jockeys must be active at least 15 years; trainers must be active at least 25 years. Voting done by 100-member panel of horse racing media.

Class of 1991 (5): Jockey—**Pat Day**. Trainer—**Mesh Tenney**. Horses—**Black Helen**, **Hill Prince** and **Princess Rooney**.

Members are listed with year of induction; (+) indicates deceased members.

Exemplars of Racing

+Hanes, John W 1982
+Jeffords, Walter M 1973
Mellon, Paul 1989
+Widener, George D 1971

Jockeys

+Adams, Frank (Dooley)*....... 1970
+Adams, John................ 1965
+Aitcheson, Joe Jr.*.......... 1978
Arcaro, Eddie 1958
Atkinson, Ted 1957
Baeza, Braulio.............. 1976
+Bassett, Carroll*............ 1972
+Blum, Walter............... 1987
+Bostwick, George H.*........ 1968
+Boulmetis, Sam............. 1973
+Brooks, Steve.............. 1963
+Burns, Tommy.............. 1983
+Butwell, Jimmy 1984
Day, Pat................... 1991
+Coltiletti, Frank 1970
Cordero, Angel Jr........... 1988
+Crawford, Robert (Specs)* 1973
+Fator, Laverne.............. 1955
+Ensor, Lavelle (Buddy) 1962
+Garner, Andrew (Mack)....... 1969
+Garrison, Snapper 1955
+Griffin, Henry 1956
*Steeplechase jockey

Guerin, Eric................. 1972
Hartack, Bill................ 1959
+Johnson, Albert............. 1971
+Knapp, Willie.,............. 1969
+Kummer, Clarence........... 1972
+Kurtsinger, Charles.......... 1967
+Loftus, John................ 1959
Longden, Johnny 1958
+Maher, Danny.............. 1955
+McAtee, Linus 1956
McCarron, Chris............ 1989
+McCreary, Conn............. 1974
+McKinney, Rigan............ 1968
+McLaughlin, James.......... 1955
+Miller, Walter............... 1955
+Murphy, Isaac.............. 1955
+Neves, Ralph............... 1960
+Notter, Joe................. 1963
+Odom, George.............. 1955
+O'Connor, Winnie 1956
+O'Neill, Frank.............. 1956
+Parke, Ivan 1978

+Patrick, Gil................. 1970
Pincay, Laffit Jr 1975
+Purdy, Sam 1970
+Reiff, John 1956
+Robertson, Alfred 1971
Rotz, John L................ 1983
+Sande, Earl 1955
+Schilling, Carroll............ 1970
Shoemaker, Bill............. 1958
+Simms, Willie............... 1977
+Sloan, Todhunter 1955
+Smithwick, A. Patrick*........ 1973
+Stout, James 1968
+Taral, Fred................. 1955
+Tuckman, Bayard Jr.*........ 1973
Turcotte, Ron................ 1979
+Turner, Nash............... 1955
Ussery, Robert............... 1980
Velasquez, Jorge.............. 1990
+Woolfe, George 1955
+Workman, Raymond 1956
Ycaza, Manuel 1977

Trainers

+Barrera, Laz................. 1979
+Bedwell, H.Guy.............. 1971
+Brown, Edward D 1984
Burch, Elliot 1980
+Burch, Preston M............ 1963
+Burch, W.P................. 1955
+Burlew, Fred 1973
+Byers, J.D. (Dilly)............ 1967
+Childs, Frank E 1968
Cocks, W. Burling............ 1985
+Duke, William 1956
+Feustel, Louis................ 1964
+Fitzsimmons, J.(Sunny Jim)..... 1958
+Gaver, John M 1966
+Healey, Thomas 1955
+Hildreth, Samuel............. 1955
+Hirsch, Max 1959
+Hirsch, W.J.(Buddy) 1982
+Hitchcock, Thomas Sr......... 1973
+Hughes, Hollie 1973

+Hyland, John................ 1956
+Jacobs, Hirsch.............. 1958
Jerkens, H. Allen............. 1975
+Johnson, William R........... 1986
+Jolley, LeRoy 1987
+Jones, Ben A 1958
Jones, H.A.(Jimmy)........... 1959
+Joyner, Andrew.............. 1955
Laurin, Lucien 1977
+Lewis, J. Howard............. 1969
Luro, Horatio................ 1980
+Madden, John............... 1983
+Maloney, Jim................ 1989
Martin, Frank (Pancho)........ 1981
McAnally, Ron............... 1990
+McDaniel, Henry............. 1956
+Miller, MacKenzie 1987
+Molter, William, Jr 1960
+Mulholland, Winbert.......... 1967
+Neloy, Eddie 1983

Nerud, John 1972
+Parke, Burley............... 1986
Penna, Angel Sr 1988
+Pincus, Jacob............... 1988
+Rogers, John 1955
+Rowe, James Sr............. 1955
Sheppard, Jonathan........... 1990
+Smith, Robert A............. 1976
+Smithwick, Mike 1976
Stephens, Woody 1976
+Thompson, H.J.............. 1969
+Trotsek, Harry 1984
Van Berg, Jack 1985
+Van Berg, Marion 1970
+Veitch, Sylvester............. 1977
+Walden, Robert.............. 1970
+Ward, Sherrill 1978
Whiteley, Frank Jr............. 1978
Whittingham, Charlie......... 1974
Winfrey, W.C. (Bill) 1971

Horses
Year foaled in parentheses.

+Ack Ack (1966).............. 1986
Affectionately (1960) 1989
Affirmed (1975) 1980
All-Along (1979)............. 1990
+Alsab (1939)................ 1976
+Alydar (1975) 1989
+American Eclipse (1814) 1970
+Armed (1941)............... 1963
+Artful (1902) 1956
+Assault (1943)............... 1964
+Battleship (1927) 1969
+Bed O'Roses (1947).......... 1976
+Beldame (1901) 1956
+Ben Brush (1893) 1955
+Bewitch (1945) 1977
+Bimelech (1937)............. 1990
+Black Gold (1919) 1989
+Black Helen (1935)........... 1939
+Blue Larkspur (1926) 1957
+Bold Ruler (1954)............ 1973
+Bon Nouvel (1960).......... 1976
+Boston (1833)............... 1955
+Broomstick (1901) 1956

+Buckpasser (1963) 1970
+Busher (1942)............... 1964
+Bushranger (1930)........... 1967
+Cafe Prince (1970) 1985
+Carry Back (1958) 1975
+Challendon (1936).......... 1977
+Chris Evert (1988)........... 1971
+Cicada (1959) 1967
+Citation (1945) 1959
+Coaltown (1945) 1983
+Colin (1905)................ 1956
+Commando (1898) 1956
+Count Fleet (1940).......... 1961
+Dahlia (1971)............... 1981
+Damascus (1964)............ 1974
+Dark Mirage (1965).......... 1974
+Davona Dale (1976) 1985
+Desert Vixen (1970)......... 1979
+Devil Diver (1939) 1980
+Discovery (1931)............ 1969
+Domino (1891).............. 1955
+Dr. Fager (1964) 1971

+Elkridge (1938).............. 1966
+Emperor of Norfolk (1885) 1988
+Equipoise (1928) 1957
+Exterminator (1915)......... 1957
+Fairmount (1921)........... 1985
+Fair Play (1905) 1956
+Firenze (1885)............... 1981
+Forego (1970)............... 1979
+Gallant Bloom (1966) 1977
+Gallant Fox (1927)........... 1957
+Gallant Man (1954).......... 1987
+Gallorette (1942) 1962
+Gamely (1964).............. 1980
Genuine Risk (1977) 1986
+Good and Plenty (1900) 1956
+Grey Lag (1918).............. 1957
+Hamburg (1895)............. 1986
+Hanover (1884)............. 1955
+Henry of Navarre (1891)...... 1985
+Hill Prince 1947
+Hindoo (1878)............... 1955

National Horse Racing Hall of Fame (Cont.)

+Imp (1894) 1965	+Oedipus (1941) 1978	+Shuvee (1966) 1975
+Jay Trump (1957) 1971	+Old Rosebud (1911) 1968	+Silver Spoon (1956) 1978
John Henry (1975) 1990	+Omaha (1932) 1965	+Sir Archy (1805) 1955
+Jolly Roger (1922) 1965	+Pan Zareta (1910) 1972	+Sir Barton (1916) 1957
+Kingston (1884) 1955	+Parole (1873) 1984	+Stymie (1941) 1975
+Kelso (1957) 1967	+Peter Pan (1904) 1956	+Susan's Girl (1969) 1976
+Kentucky (1861) 1983	Princess Rooney 1980	+Swaps (1952) 1966
+L'Escargot (1963) 1977	+Real Delight (1949) 1987	+Sword Dancer (1956) 1977
+Lexington (1850) 1955	+Regret (1912) 1957	+Sysonby (1902) 1956
+Longfellow (1867) 1971	+Reigh Count (1925) 1978	+Tim Tam (1955) 1985
+Luke Blackburn (1877) 1956	+Roamer (1911) 1981	+Tom Fool (1949) 1960
+Majestic Prince (1966) . . . . 1988?	+Roseben (1901) 1956	+Top Flight (1929) 1966
+Man O'War (1917) 1957	+Round Table (1954) 1972	+Tosmah (1961) 1984
+Miss Woodford (1880) 1967	+Ruffian (1972) 1976	+Twenty Grand (1928) 1957
+Myrtlewood (1933) 1979	+Ruthless (1864) 1975	+Twilight Tear (1941) 1963
+Nashua (1952) 1965	+Salvator (1886) 1955	+War Admiral (1934) 1958
+Native Dancer (1950) 1963	+Sarazen (1921) 1957	+Whirlaway (1938) 1959
+Native Diver (1959) 1978	+Seabiscuit (1933) 1958	+Whisk Broom II (1907) 1979
+Northern Dancer (1961) 1976	+Searching (1952) 1978	Zaccio (1976) 1990
+Neji (1950) 1966	Seattle Slew (1974) 1981	+Zev (1920) 1983
	+Secretariat (1970) 1974	

OLYMPICS

U.S. Olympic Hall of Fame

Established in 1983 by the United States Olympic Committee. **Current Address:** U.S. Olympic Committee, 1750 East Boulder Street, Colorado Springs, CO 80909. A permanent museum site is in the planning stages. **Telephone:** (719) 578-4529.

Eligibility: nominated athletes must be five years removed from active competition. Voting done by National Sportscasters and Sportswriters Association, Hall of Fame members and the USOC board of directors.

Class of 1991: To be announced (see "Updates").

Members are listed with year of induction; (+) indicates deceased members.

Bobsled
+Eagan, Eddie (see Boxing) 1983

Boxing
Clay, Cassius* 1983
+Eagan, Eddie (see Bobsled) 1983
Foreman, George 1990
Frazier, Joe 1989
Leonard, Sugar Ray 1985
Patterson, Floyd 1987
*Clay changed name to Muhammad Ali in 1964.

Figure Skating
Albright, Tenley 1988
Button, Dick 1983
Fleming, Peggy 1983
Hamilton, Scott 1990

Gymnastics
Retton, Mary Lou 1985

Rowing
+Kelly, Jack, Sr. 1990

Speed Skating
Heiden, Eric 1983

Swimming & Diving
Babashoff, Shirley 1987
Caulkins, Tracy 1990

+Daniels, Charles 1988
de Varona, Donna 1987
+Kahanamoku, Duke 1984
Lee, Sammy 1990
Louganis, Greg 1985
McCormick, Pat 1985
Meyer, Debbie 1986
Naber, John 1984
Schollander, Don 1983
Spitz, Mark 1983
+Weissmuller, Johnny 1983

Track & Field
Beamon, Bob 1983
Boston, Ralph 1985
Davis, Glenn 1986
+Didrikson, Babe 1983
Dillard, Harrison 1983
Evans, Lee 1989
+Ewry, Ray 1983
Jenner, Bruce 1986
Johnson, Rafer 1983
+Kraenzlein, Alvin 1985
Lewis, Carl 1985
Mathias, Bob 1983
Mills, Billy 1984
Morrow, Bobby 1989
Moses, Edwin 1985

O'Brien, Parry 1984
Oerter, Al 1983
+Owens, Jesse 1983
Richards, Bob 1983
Rudolph, Wilma 1983
+Sheppard, Mel 1989
Shorter, Frank 1984
+Thorpe, Jim 1983
Toomey, Bill 1984
Tyus, Wyomia 1985
Whitfield, Mal 1988
+Wykoff, Frank 1984

Weight Lifting
+Davis, John 1989
Kono, Tommy 1990

Wrestling
Gable, Dan 1985

Contributors
Arledge, Roone 1989
+Brundage, Avery 1983
+Bushnell, Asa 1990
Iba, Henry 1985
Kane, Robert 1986
McKay, Jim 1988
Miller, Don 1984
Walker, Leroy 1987

Teams

1956 Basketball—Dick Boushka, Carl Cain, Chuck Darling, Bill Evans, Gib Ford, Burdy Haldorson, Bill Hougland, Bob Jeangerard, K.C.Jones, Bill Russell, Ron Tomsic, +Jim Walsh and coach +Gerald Tucker.

1960 Basketball—Jay Arnette, Walt Bellamy, Bob Boozer, Terry Dischinger, Burdy Haldorson, Darrall Imhoff, Allen Kelley, +Lester Lane, Jerry Lucas, Oscar Robertson, Adrian Smith, Jerry West and coach Pete Newell.

1964 Basketball—Jim Barnes, Bill Bradley, Larry Brown, Joe Caldwell, Mel Counts, Richard Davies, Walt Hazzard, Luke Jackson, John McCaffrey, Jeff Mullins, Jerry Shipp, George Wilson and coach Hank Iba.

1960 Ice Hockey—Billy Christian, Roger Christian, Billy Cleary, Bob Cleary, Gene Grazia, Paul Johnson, Jack Kirrane, John Mayasich, Jack McCartan, Bob McKay, Dick Meredith, Weldon Olson, Ed Owen, Rod Paavola, Larry Palmer, Dick Rodenheiser, Tom Williams and coach Jack Riley.

1980 Ice Hockey—Bill Baker, Neal Broten, Dave Christian, Steve Christoff, Jim Craig, Mike Eruzione, John Harrington, Steve Janaszak, Mark Johnson, Ken Morrow, Rob McClanahan, Jack O'Callahan, Mark Pavelich, Mike Ramsey, Buzz Schneider, Dave Silk, Eric Strobel, Bob Suter, Phil Verchota, Mark Wells and coach Herb Brooks.

MEDIA

National Sportscasters and Sportswriters Hall of Fame

Established in 1959 by the National Sportscasters and Sportswriters Association. **Temporary Address:** 322 East Innes Street, Salisbury, NC 28144. A permanent museum is scheduled to open in April of 1992. **Telephone:** (704) 633-4275.

Eligibility: nominees must be active for at least 25 years. Voting done by NSSA membership and other media representatives.

Class of 1991 (2): Sportscaster—**Vin Scully**, KABC and KTTV in Los Angeles. Sportswriter—**Blackie Sherrod**, Dallas Morning News.

Members are listed with year of induction; (+) indicates deceased members.

Sportscasters

Allen, Mel ... 1972	Gowdy, Curt ... 1981	Nelson, Lindsey ... 1979
Barber, Walter (Red) ... 1973	Harwell, Ernie ... 1989	+Prince, Bob ... 1986
Brickhouse, Jack ... 1983	+Hodges, Russ ... 1975	Schenkel, Chris ... 1981
Buck, Jack ... 1990	+Husing, Ted ... 1963	Scott, Ray ... 1982
Caray, Harry ... 1989	+McCarthy, Clem ... 1970	Scully, Vin ... 1991
+Dean, Dizzy ... 1976	McKay, Jim ... 1987	+Stern, Bill ... 1974
Dunphy, Don ... 1986	+McNamee, Graham ... 1964	

Sportswriters

Anderson, Dave ... 1990	+Kieran, John ... 1971	+Runyon, Damon ... 1964
Bisher, Furman ... 1989	+Lardner, Ring ... 1967	Russell, Fred ... 1988
Burick, Si ... 1985	+Murphy, Jack ... 1988	Sherrod, Blackie ... 1991
+Cannon, Jimmy ... 1986	Murray, Jim ... 1978	+Smith, Walter (Red) ... 1977
+Considine, Bob ... 1980	+Parker, Dan ... 1975	+Spink, J.G.Taylor ... 1969
+Daley, Arthur ... 1976	Povich, Shirley ... 1984	+Ward, Arch ... 1973
Gould, Alan ... 1990	+Rice, Grantland ... 1962	+Woodward, Stanley ... 1974
+Grimsley, Will ... 1987		

Contributors

Ronald Reagan ... 1989	+John Wayne ... 1979

American Sportscasters Hall of Fame

Established in 1984 by the American Sportscasters Association. **Address:** 5 Beekman Street, New York, NY 10038. A permanent museum site is planned for late 1992. **Telephone:** (212) 227-8080.

Eligibility: Nominations made by 12-member selection committee, voting by ASA membership.

Class of 1991 (1): **Ernie Harwell.** Members are listed with year of induction; (+) indicates deceased members.

Allen, Mel ... 1985	Dunphy, Don ... 1984	McKay, Jim ... 1987
Barber, Walter (Red) ... 1984	Gowdy, Curt ... 1985	+McNamee, Graham ... 1984
Brickhouse, Jack ... 1985	Harwell, Ernie ... 1991	Nelson, Lindsey ... 1986
Buck, Jack ... 1990	+Husing, Ted ... 1984	+Stern, Bill ... 1984
Caray, Harry ... 1989	+McCarthy, Clem ... 1987	

TENNIS

International Tennis Hall of Fame

Originally the National Tennis Hall of Fame. Established in 1953 by James Van Alen and sanctioned by the U.S. Tennis Association in 1954. Renamed the International Tennis Hall of Fame in 1976. **Address:** 194 Bellevue Ave., Newport, RI 02840. **Telephone:** (401) 849-4567.

Eligibility: nominated players must be five years removed from being a "significant factor" in competitive tennis. Voting done by members of the international tennis media.

Class of 1991 (3): Players—**Ashley Cooper**, Australia; **Ilie Nastase**, Romania; and **Guillermo Vilas**, Argentina.

Members are listed with year of induction; (+) indicates deceased members.

Men

+Adee, George	1964	+Hackett, Harold ... 1961
+Alexander, Fred	1961	Hoad, Lew ... 1980
+Allison, Wilmer	1963	+Hovey, Fred ... 1974
+Alonso, Manuel	1977	+Hunt, Joe ... 1966
Ashe, Arthur	1985	+Hunter, Frank ... 1961

+Adee, George 1964
+Alexander, Fred 1961
+Allison, Wilmer 1963
+Alonso, Manuel. 1977
Ashe, Arthur 1985
+Behr, Karl 1969
Borg, Bjorn 1987
Borotra, Jean 1976
Bromwich, John 1984
+Brookes, Norman 1977
+Brugnon, Jacques. 1976
Budge, Don 1964
+Campbell, Oliver 1955
+Chace, Malcolm 1961
+Clark, Clarence 1983
+Clark, Joseph 1955
+Clothier, William 1956
+Cochet, Henri 1976
Cooper, Ashley 1991
Crawford, Jack 1979
+Doeg, John 1962
+Doherty, Lawrence 1980
+Doherty, Reginald. 1980
Drobny, Jaroslav. 1983
+Dwight, James 1955
Emerson, Roy 1982
+Etchebaster, Pierre 1978
Falkenburg, Bob. 1974
Fraser, Neale 1984
+Garland, Chuck 1969
Gonzales, Pancho 1968
+Grant, Bryan (Bitsy). 1972
+Griffin, Clarence. 1970

+Hackett, Harold 1961
Hoad, Lew. 1980
+Hovey, Fred. 1974
+Hunt, Joe 1966
+Hunter, Frank 1961
+Johnston, Bill 1958
+Jones, Perry 1970
Kodes, Jan. 1990
Kramer, Jack. 1968
Lacoste, Rene 1976
+Larned, William 1956
Larsen, Art. 1969
Laver, Rod. 1981
Lott, George 1964
Mako, Gene 1973
+McKinley, Chuck 1986
+McLoughlin, Maurice 1957
McNeill, Don. 1965
Mulloy, Gardnar. 1972
+Murray, Lindley 1958
+Myrick, Julian 1963
Nastase, Ilie 1991
Newcombe, John 1986
+Nielsen, Arthur 1971
Olmedo, Alex 1987
+Osuna, Rafael. 1979
Parker, Frank 1966
+Patterson, Gerald 1989
Patty, Budge 1977
Perry, Fred. 1975
+Pettitt, Tom. 1982
Peitrangeli, Nicola 1986
Quist, Adrian. 1984

Ralston, Dennis 1987
+Renshaw, Ernest 1983
+Renshaw, William 1983
+Richards, Vincent. 1961
Riggs, Bobby. 1967
Roche, Tony. 1986
Rosewall, Ken 1980
Santana, Manuel 1984
Savitt, Dick. 1976
Schroeder, Ted 1966
+Sears, Richard. 1955
Sedgman, Frank. 1979
Segura, Pancho 1984
Seixas, Vic 1971
+Shields, Frank 1964
+Slocum, Henry 1955
Smith, Stan 1987
Stolle, Fred 1985
Talbert, Bill 1967
+Tilden, Bill 1959
Trabert, Tony. 1970
Van Ryn, John. 1963
Vilas, Guillermo 1991
Vines, Ellsworth 1962
+von Cramm, Gottfried 1977
+Ward, Holcombe 1956
+Washburn, Watson. 1965
+Whitman, Malcolm 1955
+Wilding, Anthony 1978
+Williams, Richard 2nd 1957
Wood, Sidney 1964
+Wrenn, Robert. 1955
+Wright, Beals. 1956

Women

+Atkinson, Juliette. 1974
+Barger-Wallach, Maud. 1958
Betz Addie, Pauline. 1965
Brough Clapp, Louise 1967
+Browne, Mary 1957
Bueno, Maria 1978
+Bjurstedt Mallory, Molla 1958
+Cahill, Mabel 1976
+Connolly Brinker, Maureen 1968
+Dod, Charlotte (Lottie) 1983
+Douglass Chambers, Dorothy. . 1981
Fry Irvin, Shirley. 1970
Gibson, Althea 1971

+Hansell, Ellen 1965
Hard, Darlene. 1973
Hart, Doris. 1969
Hayden Jones, Ann 1985
Heldman, Gladys 1979
+Hotchkiss Wightman, Hazel. . . . 1957
Jacobs, Helen Hull 1962
King, Billie Jean. 1987
+Lenglen, Suzanne 1978
+Marble, Alice. 1964
McKane Godfree, Kathleen. . . . 1978
+Moore, Elisabeth. 1971
+Nuthall Shoemaker, Betty 1977

Osborne duPont, Margaret 1967
Palfrey Danzig, Sarah. 1963
+Roosevelt, Ellen. 1975
+Round Little, Dorothy 1986
+Ryan, Elizabeth 1972
+Sears, Eleanora. 1968
Smith Court, Margaret. 1979
+Sutton Bundy, May 1956
+Townsend Toulmin, Bertha 1974
Wade, Virginia 1989
+Wagner, Marie 1969
Wills Moody Roark, Helen 1959

Contributors

+Baker, Lawrence, Sr 1975
Cullman, Joseph F.3rd. 1990
+Danzig, Allison 1968
+Davis, Dwight 1956
+Gray, David 1985
+Gustaf, V (King of Sweden) 1980

Hester, W.E.(Slew). 1981
+Hopman, Harry 1978
+Laney, Al 1979
Martin, Alastair. 1973
Martin, William McC 1982

+Outerbridge, Mary. 1981
+Pell, Theodore. 1966
+Tingay, Lance 1982
+Tinling, Ted 1986
+Van Alen, James. 1965

TRACK & FIELD

National Track & Field Hall of Fame

Established in 1974 by the The Athletics Congress. Originally located in Charleston, WV, the Hall moved to Indianapolis in 1983 and reopened at the Hoosier Dome in 1986. **Address:** One Hoosier Dome, Indianapolis, IN 46225. **Telephone:** (317) 261-0483.

Eligibility: nominated athletes must be retired three years and coaches must have coached at least 20 years, if retired, or 35 years, if still coaching. Voting done by 800-member panel made up of Hall of Fame and TAC officials, Hall of Famer members, current U.S. champions and members of the Track & Field Writers of America.

Class of 1991 (4): Men—high jumper and long jumper **Ellery Clark**, distance runner **Bob Schul**. Women—women's and age group pioneer **Roxanne Andersen**. Contributor—journalist **Bert Nelson**, co-founder and editor of *Track & Field News.*

Men

Albritton, Dave	1980	Held, Bud	1987	Richards, Bob	1975
Ashenfelter, Horace	1975	Hines, Jim	1979	+Rose, Ralph	1976
+Bausch, James	1979	Houser, Bud	1979	Ryun, Jim	1980
Beamon, Bob	1977	+Hubbard, DeHart	1979	+Scholz, Jackson	1977
Beatty, Jim	1990	Jenner, Bruce	1980	Schul, Bob	1991
Bell, Greg	1988	Johnson, Rafer	1974	Seagren, Bob	1986
+Boeckmann, Dee	1976	Jones, Hayes	1976	+Sheppard, Mel	1976
Boston, Ralph	1974	Kelley, John	1980	+Sheridan, Martin	1988
+Calhoun, Lee	1974	Kiviat, Abel	1985	Shorter, Frank	1989
Campbell, Milt	1989	+Kraenzlein, Alvin	1974	Sime, Dave	1981
+Clark, Ellery	1991	Laird, Ron	1986	+Simpson, Robert	1974
Connolly, Harold	1984	Mathias, Bob	1974	Smith, Tommie	1978
Courtney, Tom	1978	Matson, Randy	1984	+Stanfield, Andy	1977
+Cunningham, Glenn	1974	+Meredith, Ted	1982	Steers, Les	1974
+Curtis, William	1979	+Metcalfe, Ralph	1975	Thomas, John	1985
Davenport, Willie	1982	Mills, Billy	1976	+Thomson, Earl	1977
Davis, Glenn	1974	Moore, Tom	1988	+Thorpe, Jim	1975
Davis, Harold	1974	Morrow, Bobby	1975	+Tolan, Eddie	1982
Dillard, Harrison	1974	+Myers, Lawrence	1974	Toomey, Bill	1975
Dumas, Charley	1990	O'Brien, Parry	1974	+Towns, Forrest (Spec)	1976
Evans, Lee	1983	Oerter, Al	1974	Warmerdam, Cornelius	1974
Ewell, Barney	1986	+Osborn, Harold	1974	White, Willye	1981
+Ewry, Ray	1974	+Owens, Jesse	1974	Whitfield, Mal	1974
+Flanagan, John	1975	+Paddock, Charley	1976	Wohlhuter, Rick	1990
Fosbury, Dick	1981	Patton, Mel	1985	Woodruff, John	1978
+Gordien, Fortune	1979	Peacock, Eulace	1987	Wottle, Dave	1982
+Hahn, Archie	1983	+Prefontaine, Steve	1976	+Wykoff, Frank	1977
+Hardin, Glenn	1978	+Ray, Joie	1976	Young, George	1981
Hayes, Bob	1976	+Rice, Greg	1977		

Women

Coachman, Alice	1975	+Jackson, Nell	1989	Rudolph, Wilma	1974
+Didrikson, Babe	1974	Manning, Madeline	1984	Stephens, Helen	1975
Faggs, Mae	1976	McDaniel, Mildred	1983	Tyus, Wyomia	1980
Ferrell, Barbara	1988	McGuire, Edith	1979	+Walsh, Stella	1975
Hall, Evelyne	1988	Robinson, Betty	1977	Watson, Martha	1987
Heritage, Doris Brown	1990		

Coaches

Baskin, Weems	1982	+Hamilton, Brutus	1974	+Littlefield, Clyde	1981
Beard, Percy	1981	+Haydon, Ted	1975	+Moakley, Jack	1988
Botts, Tom	1983	+Hayes, Billy	1976	+Murphy, Michael	1974
Bowerman, Bill	1981	Haylett, Ward	1979	+Snyder, Larry	1978
Bush, Jim	1987	Higgins, Ralph	1982	Temple, Ed	1989
+Cromwell, Dean	1974	+Hillman, Harry	1976	+Templeton, Dink	1976
Doherty, Ken	1976	+Hurt, Edward	1975	Walker, LeRoy	1983
Easton, Bill	1975	+Hutsell, Wilbur	1977	Wilt, Fred	1981
+Elliott, Jumbo	1981	+Jones, Thomas	1977	+Winter, Bud	1985
+Giegengack, Bob	1978	Jordan, Payton	1982	+Yancy, Joseph	1984

Contributors

+Abramson, Jesse	1981	+Brundage, Avery	1974	Nelson, Cordner	1988
Andersen, Roxanne	1991	+Ferris, Dan	1974	Nelson, Bert	1991
+Bakjian, Andy	1986	+Griffith, John	1979	+Sullivan, James	1977

OTHER

B'nai B'rith Sports Hall of Fame

Established in 1991 by B'nai B'rith to recognize the achievements and contributions of Jewish athletes and sportsmen in America. **Address:** 1640 Rhode Island Ave.NW, Washington, DC 20036. A permanent museum site is scheduled to open in October, 1992. **Telephone:** (202) 857-6580.

Eligibility: Nominees must be prominent Jewish athletes, coaches, administrators or media figures. Voting done by 7-member panel of B'nai B'rith lay persons.

Class of 1990: 13 charter members (see below).

Members are listed with year of induction; (+) indicates deceased members.

Allen, Mel 1991	+Leonard, Benny 1991	Rosen, Al 1991
Auerbach, Red 1991	Luckman, Sid 1991	Savitt, Dick 1991
+Gottlieb, Eddie 1991	Pollin, Abe 1991	Schayes, Dolph 1991
+Greenberg, Hank 1991	Povich, Shirley 1991	Spitz, Mark 1991
Koufax, Sandy 1991		

International Women's Sports Hall of Fame

Established in 1980 by the Women's Sports Foundation. **Current Address:** Women's Sports Foundation, 342 Madison Avenue, Suite 728, New York, NY 10173. A permanent museum site is in the planning stages. **Telephone:** (212) 972-9170.

Eligibility: Nominees' achievements and commitment to the development of women's sports must be internationally recognized. Athletes are elected in two categories—Pioneer (before 1960) and Contemporary (since 1960). Members are divided below by sport for the sake of easy reference; (*) indicates member inducted in Pioneer category. Coaching nominees must have coached at least 10 years.

Class of 1991 (6): Pioneers—**Christl Cranz,** skier; **Alice Coachman Davis,** track & field. Contemporary—**Vera Caslavska,** gymnastics; **Cheryl Miller,** basketball. Coaches—**Constance Applebee,** field hockey; **Muriel Grossfeld,** gymnastics.

Members are listed with year of induction; (+) indicates deceased members.

Alpine Skiing
Cranz, Christl* 1991
Lawrence, Andrea Mead* 1983
Moser-Proell, Annemarie 1982

Auto Racing
Guthrie, Janet 1980

Aviation
+Earhart, Amelia* 1980
+Marvingt, Marie* 1987

Basketball
Meyers, Ann 1985
Miller, Cheryl 1991

Bowling
Ladewig, Marion* 1984

Cycling
Carpenter Phinney, Connie 1990

Fencing
Schacherer-Elek, Ilona* 1989

Figure Skating
Albright, Tenley* 1983
+Blanchard, Theresa Weld* 1989
Fleming, Peggy 1981
+Henie, Sonja* 1982
Rodnina, Irena 1988

Golf
Berg, Patty* 1980
Carner, JoAnne 1987
Mann, Carol 1982
Rawls, Betsy* 1986

Suggs, Louise* 1987
+Vare, Glenna Collett* 1981
Whitworth, Kathy 1984
Wright, Mickey 1981

Golf/Track & Field
+Zaharias, Babe Didrikson* 1980

Gymnastics
Caslavska, Vera 1991
Comaneci, Nadia 1990
Korbut, Olga 1982
Latynina, Larissa* 1985
Tourischeva, Lyudmila 1987

Shooting
Murdock, Margaret 1988

Softball
Joyce, Joan 1989

Speed Skating
Young, Sheila 1981

Swimming & Diving
Caulkins, Tracy 1986
Curtis Cuneo, Ann* 1985
de Varona, Donna 1983
Ederle, Gertrude* 1980
Fraser, Dawn 1985
Holm, Eleanor* 1980
King Hogue, Micki 1983
Meyer-Reyes, Debbie 1987
McCormick, Pat* 1984
Riggin, Aileen* 1988

Tennis
+Connelly, Maureen* 1987
+Dod, Charlotte (Lottie)* 1986
Evert, Chris 1981
Gibson, Althea* 1980
Goolagong Cawley, Evonne . . . 1989
+Hotchkiss Wightman, Hazel* . . . 1986
King, Billie Jean 1980
+Lenglen, Suzanne* 1984
Navratilova, Martina 1984
+Sears, Eleanora* 1984
Smith Court, Margaret 1986

Track & Field
Blankers-Koen, Fanny* 1982
Coachman Davis, Alice* 1991
Manning Mims, Madeline 1987
Rudolph, Wilma 1980
Stephens, Helen* 1983
Tyus, Wyomia 1981
White, Willye 1988

Volleyball
+Hyman, Flo 1986

Water Skiing
McGuire, Willa Worthington* . . 1990

Coaches
Applebee, Constance 1991
Grossfeld, Muriel 1991
+Jackson, Nell 1990
Summit, Pat Head 1990

RETIRED NUMBERS

Major League Baseball

The New York Yankees have retired the most uniform numbers (12) in the Major Leagues; followed by Pittsburgh and the Brooklyn-Los Angeles Dodgers (8), the Chicago White Sox (7), the New York-San Francisco Giants (6) and the St.Louis Cardinals (5). Three players and a manager have had their numbers retired by two teams: **Hank Aaron**—#44 by the Boston-Milwaukee-Atlanta Braves and the Milwaukee Brewers; **Rod Carew**—#29 by Minnesota and California; **Frank Robinson**—#20 by Cincinnati and Baltimore; and **Casey Stengel**—#37 by the New York Yankees and New York Mets.

Numbers retired in 1991 (2): Minnesota #6, worn by **Tony Oliva** (1962-76); Oakland #27, worn by **Catfish Hunter** (1965-74).

American League

Three AL teams—the Seattle Mariners, Texas Rangers and Toronto Blue Jays—have not retired any numbers.

Baltimore
4 Earl Weaver
5 Brooks Robinson
20 Frank Robinson
22 Jim Palmer
33 Eddie Murray

Boston Red Sox
1 Bobby Doerr
4 Joe Cronin
8 Carl Yastrzemski
9 Ted Williams

California Angels
26 Gene Autry
29 Rod Carew

Chicago White Sox
2 Nellie Fox
3 Harold Baines
4 Luke Appling
11 Minnie Minoso
16 Luis Aparicio
16 Ted Lyons
19 Billy Pierce

Cleveland Indians
3 Earl Averill
5 Lou Boudreau
18 Mel Harder
19 Bob Feller

Detroit Tigers
2 Charlie Gehringer
5 Hank Greenberg
6 Al Kaline

Kansas City Royals
10 Dick Howser

Milwaukee Brewers
44 Hank Aaron

Minnesota Twins
3 Harmon Killebrew
6 Tony Oliva
29 Rod Carew

New York Yankees
1 Billy Martin
3 Babe Ruth
4 Lou Gehrig
5 Joe DiMaggio
7 Mickey Mantle
8 Yogi Berra & Bill Dickey
9 Roger Maris
10 Phil Rizzuto
15 Thurman Munson
16 Whitey Ford
32 Elston Howard
37 Casey Stengel

Oakland Athletics
27 Catfish Hunter

National League

One NL team—the Montreal Expos—has not retired a number. Also, San Francisco has honored former N.Y.Giants Christy Mathewson and John McGraw even though they played before numbers were worn.

Atlanta Braves
21 Warren Spahn
35 Phil Niekro
41 Eddie Mathews
44 Hank Aaron

Chicago Cubs
14 Ernie Banks
26 Billy Williams

Cincinnati Reds
1 Fred Hutchinson
5 Johnny Bench

Houston Astros
32 Jim Umbricht
40 Don Wilson

Los Angeles Dodgers
1 Pee Wee Reese
4 Duke Snider
19 Jim Gilliam
24 Walter Alston
32 Sandy Koufax
39 Roy Campanella
42 Jackie Robinson
53 Don Drysdale

New York Mets
14 Gil Hodges
37 Casey Stengel
41 Tom Seaver

Philadelphia Phillies
1 Richie Ashburn
20 Mike Schmidt
32 Steve Carlton
36 Robin Roberts

Pittsburgh Pirates
1 Billy Meyer
4 Ralph Kiner
8 Willie Stargell
9 Bill Mazeroski
20 Pie Traynor
21 Roberto Clemente
33 Honus Wagner
40 Danny Murtaugh

St.Louis Cardinals
6 Stan Musial
14 Ken Boyer
17 Dizzy Dean
20 Lou Brock
45 Bob Gibson

San Diego Padres
6 Steve Garvey

San Francisco Giants
3 Bill Terry
4 Mel Ott
11 Carl Hubbell
24 Willie Mays
27 Juan Marichal
44 Willie McCovey

National Basketball Association

Boston has retired the most numbers (15) in the NBA; followed by the New York Knicks (7); Milwaukee, Portland and the Rochester-Cincinnati Royals/Kansas City-Omaha-Sacramento Kings (6); and the Syracuse Nats/Philadelphia 76ers (5). Four players have had their numbers retired by two teams: **Wilt Chamberlain**—#13 by the Los Angeles Lakers and Philadelphia; **Julius Erving**—#6 by Philadelphia and #32 by New Jersey; **Oscar Robertson**—#1 by Milwaukee and #14 by Sacramento; and **Nate Thurmond**—#42 by Cleveland and Golden State.

Numbers retired in 1991 (4): New Jersey #23 worn by **John Williamson** (1973-80); Philadelphia #13 worn by **Wilt Chamberlain** (Warriors, 1959-62, and 76ers, 1965-68); Portland #32 worn by **Bill Walton** (1974-78); and Boston retired a microphone for radio announcer **Johnny Most** (1953-90).

Western Conference

Three Western teams—the Dallas Mavericks, Los Angeles Clippers and Minnesota Timberwolves—have not retired any numbers.

Denver Nuggets
40 Byron Beck
44 Dan Issel

Golden St.Warriors
14 Tom Meschery
16 Al Attles
24 Rick Barry
42 Nate Thurmond

Houston Rockets
23 Calvin Murphy
45 Rudy Tomjanovich

Los Angeles Lakers
13 Wilt Chamberlain
22 Elgin Baylor
33 Kareem Abdul-Jabbar
44 Jerry West

National Basketball Association (Cont.)

Phoenix Suns
5 Dick Van Arsdale
33 Alvan Adams
42 Connie Hawkins
44 Paul Westphal

Portland Trail Blazers
13 Dave Twardzik
15 Larry Steele
20 Maurice Lucas
32 Bill Walton
36 Lloyd Neal
45 Geoff Petrie

Sacramento Kings
6 Fans ("Sixth Man")
11 Bob Davies
12 Maurice Stokes
14 Oscar Robertson
27 Jack Twyman
44 Sam Lacey

San Antonio Spurs
13 James Silas
44 George Gervin

Seattle SuperSonics
19 Lenny Wilkens
32 Fred Brown

Utah Jazz
1 Frank Layden
7 Pete Maravich

Eastern Conference

Three Eastern teams—the Charlotte Hornets, Miami Heat, and Orlando Magic—have not retired any numbers.

Atlanta Hawks
9 Bob Pettit
23 Lou Hudson

Boston Celtics
1 Walter A. Brown
2 Red Auerbach
6 Bill Russell
10 Jo Jo White
14 Bob Cousy
15 Tom Heinsohn
16 Tom (Satch) Sanders
17 John Havlicek
18 Dave Cowens
19 Don Nelson
21 Bill Sharman
22 Ed Macauley
23 Frank Ramsey
24 Sam Jones
25 K.C. Jones
Loscy Jim Loscutoff
Radio mike Johnny Most

Chicago Bulls
4 Jerry Sloan

Cleveland Cavaliers
7 Bingo Smith
34 Austin Carr
42 Nate Thurmond

Detroit Pistons
21 Dave Bing

Indiana Pacers
30 George McGinnis
34 Mel Daniels
35 Roger Brown

Milwaukee Bucks
1 Oscar Robertson
2 Junior Bridgeman
4 Sidney Moncrief
14 Jon McGlocklin
16 Bob Lanier
32 Brian Winters

New York Knicks
10 Walt Frazier
12 Dick Barnett
15 Earl Monroe
19 Willis Reed
22 Dave DeBusschere
24 Bill Bradley
613 Red Holzman

New Jersey Nets
4 Wendell Ladner
23 John Williamson
25 Bill Melchionni
32 Julius Erving

Philadelphia 76ers
6 Julius Erving
13 Wilt Chamberlain
15 Hal Greer
24 Bobby Jones
32 Billy Cunningham
P.A. mike Dave Zinkoff

Washington Bullets
11 Elvin Hayes
25 Gus Johnson
41 Wes Unseld

National Football League

The Chicago Bears have retired the most uniform numbers (10) in the NFL; followed by the Baltimore-Indianapolis Colts, New York Giants and San Francisco (7); Detroit (6); and the Boston-New England Patriots, Cleveland, the Dallas Texans/Kansas City Chiefs and Philadelphia (5). No player has ever had his number retired by more than one NFL team.

Numbers retired in 1990 (1): New England #73 worn by **John Hannah** (1973-85).

AFC

Three AFC teams—the Buffalo Bills, Los Angeles Raiders and Pittsburgh Steelers—have not retired any numbers.

Cincinnati Bengals
54 Bob Johnson

Cleveland Browns
14 Otto Graham
32 Jim Brown
45 Ernie Davis
46 Don Fleming
76 Lou Groza

Denver Broncos
18 Frank Tripucka
44 Floyd Little

Houston Oilers
34 Earl Campbell
43 Jim Norton
65 Elvin Bethea

Indianapolis Colts
19 Johnny Unitas
22 Buddy Young
24 Lenny Moore
70 Art Donovan
77 Jim Parker
82 Raymond Berry
89 Gino Marchetti

Kansas City Chiefs
16 Len Dawson
28 Abner Haynes
33 Stone Johnson
36 Mack Lee Hill
78 Bobby Bell

Miami Dolphins
12 Bob Griese

New England Patriots
20 Gino Cappelletti
57 Steve Nelson
73 John Hannah
79 Jim Hunt
89 Bob Dee

New York Jets
12 Joe Namath
13 Don Maynard

San Diego Chargers
14 Dan Fouts

Seattle Seahawks
12 Fans ("12th Man")

NFC

Dallas is the only NFC team that hasn't retired a number. Instead, the Cowboys have a "Ring of Honor" at Texas Stadium that includes seven players—Chuck Howley, Lee Roy Jordan, Bob Lilly, Don Meredith, Don Perkins, Mel Renfro and Roger Staubach.

Atlanta Falcons
31 William Andrews
57 Jeff Van Note
60 Tommy Nobis

Chicago Bears
3 Bronko Nagurski
5 George McAfee
28 Willie Galimore
34 Walter Payton
41 Brian Piccolo
42 Sid Luckman
56 Bill Hewitt
61 Bill George
66 Bulldog Turner
77 Red Grange
GSH George Halas

Detroit Lions
7 Dutch Clark
22 Bobby Layne
37 Doak Walker
56 Joe Schmidt
85 Chuck Hughes
88 Charlie Sanders

Green Bay Packers
3 Tony Canadeo
14 Don Hutson
15 Bart Starr
66 Ray Nitschke

Los Angeles Rams
7 Bob Waterfield
74 Merlin Olsen

Minnesota Vikings
10 Fran Tarkenton
88 Alan Page

New Orleans Saints
31 Jim Taylor
81 Doug Atkins

New York Giants
1 Ray Flaherty
7 Mel Hein
14 Y.A.Tittle
32 Al Blozis
40 Joe Morrison
42 Charlie Conerly
50 Ken Strong

Philadelphia Eagles
15 Steve Van Buren
40 Tom Brookshier
44 Pete Retzlaff
60 Chuck Bednarik
70 Al Wistert

Phoenix Cardinals
8 Larry Wilson
77 Stan Mauldin
88 J.V.Cain
99 Marshall Goldberg

San Francisco 49ers
12 John Brodie
34 Joe Perry
37 Jimmy Johnson
39 Hugh McElhenny
70 Charlie Krueger
73 Lou Nomellini
87 Dwight Clark

Tampa Bay Bucs
63 Lee Roy Selmon

Wash. Redskins
33 Sammy Baugh

National Hockey League

The Boston Bruins have retired the most uniform numbers (7) in the NHL; followed by Montreal (6); Chicago, St.Louis and Philadelphia (4); and the Boston-New England-Hartford Whalers (3). Two players have had their numbers retired by two teams: **Gordie Howe**—#9 by Detroit and Hartford; and **Bobby Hull**—#9 by Chicago and Winnipeg.

Numbers retired in 1991 (4): Buffalo #11 worn by **Gilbert Perreault** (1970-87); Los Angeles #16 worn by **Marcel Dionne** (1975-87); Philadelphia #7 worn by **Bill Barber** (1972-85); St.Louis #24 worn by **Bernie Federko** (1977-89).

Campbell Conference

The expansion San Jose Sharks are the only Campbell team that has not retired a number.

Calgary Flames
9 Lanny McDonald

Chicago Blackhawks
1 Glenn Hall
9 Bobby Hull
21 Stan Mikita
35 Tony Esposito

Detroit Red Wings
6 Larry Aurie
9 Gordie Howe

Edmonton Oilers
3 Al Hamilton

Los Angeles Kings
16 Marcel Dionne
30 Rogie Vachon

Minnesota North Stars
19 Bill Masterton

St.Louis Blues
3 Bob Gassoff
8 Barclay Plager
11 Brian Sutter
24 Bernie Federko

Toronto Maple Leafs
5 Bill Barilko
6 Ace Bailey

Vancouver Canucks
11 Wayne Maki

Winnipeg Jets
9 Bobby Hull

Wales Conference

Two Wales teams—the New Jersey Devils and New York Islanders—have not retired any numbers. Also, two numbers listed as retired in last year's book—Buffalo #2 (Tim Horton) and NY Islanders #5 (Denis Potvin)—have not been worn by another player, but are not officially retired.

Boston Bruins
2 Eddie Shore
3 Lionel Hitchman
4 Bobby Orr
5 Dit Clapper
7 Phil Esposito
9 Johnny Bucyk
15 Milt Schmidt

Buffalo Sabres
11 Gilbert Perreault

Hartford Whalers
2 Rick Ley
9 Gordie Howe
19 John McKenzie

Montreal Canadiens
2 Doug Harvey
4 Jean Beliveau
& Aurele Joliat
7 Howie Morenz
9 Maurice Richard
10 Guy Lafleur
16 Henri Richard
& Elmer Lach

New York Rangers
1 Eddie Giacomin
7 Rod Gilbert

Philadelphia Flyers
1 Bernie Parent
4 Barry Ashbee
7 Bill Barber
16 Bobby Clarke

Pittsburgh Penguins
21 Michel Briere

Quebec Nordiques
3 J.C.Tremblay
8 Marc Tardif

Washington Capitals
7 Yvon Labre

AWARDS

Associated Press Athletes of the Year

Selected annually by AP newspaper sports editors since 1931.

Male

Multiple winners: Don Budge, Sandy Koufax, Carl Lewis, Joe Montana and Byron Nelson (2).

Year			
1931 **Pepper Martin**, baseball	1952 **Bob Mathias**, track	1972 **Mark Spitz**, swimming
1932 **Gene Sarazen**, golf	1953 **Ben Hogan**, golf	1973 **O.J.Simpson**, pro football
1933 **Carl Hubbell**, baseball	1954 **Willie Mays**, baseball	1974 **Muhammad Ali**, boxing
1934 **Dizzy Dean**, baseball	1955 **Hopalong Cassady**, football	1975 **Fred Lynn**, baseball
1935 **Joe Louis**, boxing	1956 **Mickey Mantle**, baseball	1976 **Bruce Jenner**, track
1936 **Jesse Owens**, track & field	1957 **Ted Williams**, baseball	1977 **Steve Cauthen**, horse racing
1937 **Don Budge**, tennis	1958 **Herb Elliot**, track	1978 **Ron Guidry**, baseball
1938 **Don Budge**, tennis	1959 **Ingemar Johansson**, boxing	1979 **Willie Stargell**, baseball
1939 **Nile Kinnick**, football		
	1960 **Rafer Johnson**, track	1980 **US Olympic hockey team**
1940 **Tom Harmon**, football	1961 **Roger Maris**, baseball	1981 **John McEnroe**, tennis
1941 **Joe DiMaggio**, baseball	1962 **Maury Wills**, baseball	1982 **Wayne Gretzky**, hockey
1942 **Frank Sinkwich**, football	1963 **Sandy Koufax**, baseball	1983 **Carl Lewis**, track
1943 **Gunder Haegg**, track	1964 **Don Schollander**, swimming	1984 **Carl Lewis**, track
1944 **Byron Nelson**, golf	1965 **Sandy Koufax**, baseball	1985 **Dwight Gooden**, baseball
1945 **Byron Nelson**, golf	1966 **Frank Robinson**, baseball	1986 **Larry Bird**, pro basketball
1946 **Glenn Davis**, football	1967 **Carl Yastrzemski**, baseball	1987 **Ben Johnson**, track
1947 **Johnny Lujack**, football	1968 **Denny McLain**, baseball	1988 **Orel Hershiser**, baseball
1948 **Lou Boudreau**, baseball	1969 **Tom Seaver**, baseball	1989 **Joe Montana**, football
1949 **Leon Hart**, football		
	1970 **George Blanda**, pro football	1990 **Joe Montanta**, football
1950 **Jim Konstanty**, baseball	1971 **Lee Trevino**, golf	
1951 **Dick Kazmaier**, football		

Female

Multiple winners: Babe Didrikson Zaharias (6); Chris Evert (4); Patty Berg and Maureen Connolly (3); Tracy Austin, Althea Gibson, Billie Jean King, Nancy Lopez, Alice Marble, Martina Navratilova, Wilma Rudolph, Kathy Whitworth and Mickey Wright (2).

Year			
1931 **Helene Madison**, swimming	1952 **Maureen Connolly**, tennis	1972 **Olga Korbut**, gymnastics
1932 **Babe Didrikson**, track	1953 **Maureen Connolly**, tennis	1973 **Billie Jean King**, tennis
1933 **Helen Jacobs**, tennis	1954 **Babe Didrikson Zaharias**, golf	1974 **Chris Evert**, tennis
1934 **Virginia Van Wie**, golf	1955 **Patty Berg**, golf	1975 **Chris Evert**, tennis
1935 **Helen Wills Moody**, tennis	1956 **Pat McCormick**, diving	1976 **Nadia Comaneci**, gymnastics
1936 **Helen Stephens**, track	1957 **Althea Gibson**, tennis	1977 **Chris Evert**, tennis
1937 **Katherine Rawls**, swimming	1958 **Althea Gibson**, tennis	1978 **Nancy Lopez**, golf
1938 **Patty Berg**, golf	1959 **Maria Bueno**, tennis	1979 **Tracy Austin**, tennis
1939 **Alice Marble**, tennis		
	1960 **Wilma Rudolph**, track	1980 **Chris Evert Lloyd**, tennis
1940 **Alice Marble**, tennis	1961 **Wilma Rudolph**, track	1981 **Tracy Austin**, tennis
1941 **Betty Hicks Newell**, golf	1962 **Dawn Fraser**, swimming	1982 **Mary Decker Tabb**, track
1942 **Gloria Callen**, swimming	1963 **Mickey Wright**, golf	1983 **Martina Navratilova**, tennis
1943 **Patty Berg**, golf	1964 **Mickey Wright**, golf	1984 **Mary Lou Retton**, gymnastics
1944 **Ann Curtis**, swimming	1965 **Kathy Whitworth**, golf	1985 **Nancy Lopez**, golf
1945 **Babe Didrikson Zaharias**, golf	1966 **Kathy Whitworth**, golf	1986 **Martina Navratilova**, tennis
1946 **Babe Didrikson Zaharias**, golf	1967 **Billie Jean King**, tennis	1987 **Jackie Joyner-Kersee**, track
1947 **Babe Didrikson Zaharias**, golf	1968 **Peggy Fleming**, skating	1988 **Florence Griffith Joyner**, track
1948 **Fanny Blankers-Koen**, track	1969 **Debbie Meyer**, swimming	1989 **Steffi Graf**, tennis
1949 **Marlene Bauer**, golf		
	1970 **Chi Cheng**, track	1990 **Beth Daniel**, golf
1950 **Babe Didrikson Zaharias**, golf	1971 **Evonne Goolagong**, tennis	
1951 **Maureen Connolly**, tennis		

UPI International Athlete of the Year

Selected annually by United Press International's European newspaper sports editors since 1974.

Male

Multiple winners: Sebastian Coe, Alberto Juantorena and Carl Lewis (2).

Year			
1974 **Muhammad Ali,** boxing	1980 **Eric Heiden**, speed skating	1986 **Diego Maradona**, soccer
1975 **Joao Oliveira**, track	1981 **Sebastian Coe**, track	1987 **Ben Johnson**, track
1976 **Alberto Juantorena**, track	1982 **Daley Thompson**, track	1988 **Matt Biondi**, swimming
1977 **Alberto Juantorena**, track	1983 **Carl Lewis**, track	1989 **Boris Becker**, tennis
1978 **Henry Rono**, track	1984 **Carl Lewis**, track	
1979 **Sebastian Coe**, track	1985 **Steve Cram**, track	1990 **Stefan Edberg**, tennis

Female

Multiple winners: Nadia Comaneci, Steffi Graf and Marita Koch (2).

Year	Year	Year
1974 **Irena Szewinska,** track	1980 **Hanni Wenzel,** alpine skiing	1986 **Heike Drechsler,** track
1975 **Nadia Comaneci,** gymnastics	1981 **Chris Evert Lloyd,** tennis	1987 **Steffi Graf,** tennis
1976 **Nadia Comaneci,** gymnastics	1982 **Marita Koch,** track	1988 **Florence Griffith Joyner,** track
1977 **Rosie Ackermann,** track	1983 **Jarmila Kratochvilova,** track	1989 **Steffi Graf,** tennis
1978 **Track Caulkins,** swimming	1984 **Martina Navratilova,** tennis	1990 **Merlene Ottey,** track
1979 **Marita Koch,** track	1985 **Mary Decker Slaney,** track	

Jesse Owens International Trophy

Presented annually by the International Amateur Athletic Association since 1981 and selected by a worldwide panel of electors. The Jesse Owens International Trophy is named after the late American Olympic champion, who won four gold medals at the 1936 Summer Games in Berlin.

Year	Year	Year
1981 **Eric Heiden,** speed skating	1985 **Carl Lewis,** track	1989 **Florence Griffith Joyner,** track
1982 **Sebastian Coe,** track	1986 **Said Aouita,** track	1990 **Roger Kingdom,** track
1983 **Mary Decker,** track	1987 **Greg Louganis,** diving	1991 **Greg LeMond,** cycling
1984 **Edwin Moses,** track	1988 **Ben Johnson,** track	

James E. Sullivan Award

Presented annually by The Amateur Athletic Union since 1930. The James E. Sullivan Memorial Award is named after the former AAU president and given to the athlete who ''by his or her performance, example and influence as an amateur, has done the most during the year to advance the cause of sportsmanship.''
   An athlete cannot win the award twice.

Year	Year	Year
1930 **Bobby Jones,** golf	1950 **Fred Wilt,** track	1970 **John Kinsella,** swimming
1931 **Barney Berlinger,** track	1951 **Bob Richards,** track	1971 **Mark Spitz,** swimming
1932 **Jim Bausch,** track	1952 **Horace Ashenfelter,** track	1972 **Frank Shorter,** track
1933 **Glenn Cunningham,** track	1953 **Sammy Lee,** diving	1973 **Bill Walton,** basketball
1934 **Bill Bonthron,** track	1954 **Mal Whitfield,** track	1974 **Rich Wohlhuter,** track
1935 **Lawson Little,** golf	1955 **Harrison Dillard,** track	1975 **Tim Shaw,** swimming
1936 **Glenn Morris,** track	1956 **Pat McCormick,** diving	1976 **Bruce Jenner,** track
1937 **Don Budge,** tennis	1957 **Bobby Morrow,** track	1977 **John Naber,** swimming
1938 **Don Lash,** track	1958 **Glenn Davis,** track	1978 **Tracy Caulkins,** swimming
1939 **Joe Burk,** rowing	1959 **Parry O'Brien,** track	1979 **Kurt Thomas,** gymnastics
1940 **Greg Rice,** track	1960 **Rafer Johnson,** track	1980 **Eric Heiden,** speed skating
1941 **Leslie MacMitchell,** track	1961 **Wilma Rudolph,** track	1982 **Mary Decker,** track
1942 **Cornelius Warmerdam,** track	1963 **John Pennel,** track	1983 **Edwin Moses,** track
1943 **Gilbert Dodds,** track	1964 **Don Schollander,** swimming	1984 **Greg Louganis,** diving
1944 **Ann Curtis,** swimming	1965 **Bill Bradley,** basketball	1985 **Joan B. Samuelson,** track
1945 **Doc Blanchard,** football	1966 **Jim Ryun,** track	1986 **Jackie Joyner-Kersee,** track
1946 **Arnold Tucker,** football	1967 **Randy Matson,** track	1987 **Jim Abbott,** baseball
1947 **John B. Kelly, Jr.,** rowing	1968 **Debbie Meyer,** swimming	1988 **Florence Griffith Joyner,** track
1948 **Bob Mathias,** track	1969 **Bill Toomey,** track	1989 **Janet Evans,** swimming
1949 **Dick Button,** skating		1990 **John Smith,** wrestling

Sports Illustrated Sportsman of the Year

Selected annually by *Sports Illustrated* magazine since 1954.

Year	Year	Year
1954 **Roger Bannister,** track	1970 **Bobby Orr,** hockey	1984 **Mary Lou Retton,** gymnastics
1955 **Johnny Podres,** baseball	1971 **Lee Trevino,** golf	& **Edwin Moses,** track
1956 **Bobby Morrow,** track	1972 **Billie Jean King,** tennis	1985 **K.Abdul-Jabbar,** basketball
1957 **Stan Musial,** baseball	& **John Wooden,** basketball	1986 **Joe Paterno,** football
1958 **Rafer Johnson,** track	1973 **Jackie Stewart,** auto racing	1987 **"8 Athletes Who Care"**
1959 **Ingemar Johansson,** boxing	1974 **Muhammad Ali,** boxing	**Bob Bourne,** hockey
	1975 **Pete Rose,** baseball	**Kip Keino,** track
1960 **Arnold Palmer,** golf	1976 **Chris Evert,** tennis	**Judi Brown King,** track
1961 **Jerry Lucas,** basketball	1977 **Steve Cauthen,** horse racing	**Dale Murphy,** baseball
1962 **Terry Baker,** football	1978 **Jack Nicklaus,** golf	**Chip Rives,** football
1963 **Pete Rozelle,** pro football	1979 **Terry Bradshaw,** football	**Patty Sheehan,** golf
1964 **Ken Venturi,** golf	& **Willie Stargell,** baseball	**Rory Sparrow,** basketball
1965 **Sandy Koufax,** baseball		**Reggie Williams,** football
1966 **Jim Ryun,** track	1980 **US Olympic hockey team**	1988 **Orel Hershiser,** baseball
1967 **Carl Yastrzemski,** baseball	1981 **Sugar Ray Leonard,** boxing	1989 **Greg LeMond,** cycling
1968 **Bill Russell,** basketball	1982 **Wayne Gretzky,** hockey	1990 **Joe Montana,** football
1969 **Tom Seaver,** baseball	1983 **Mary Decker,** track	

The Sporting News Man of the Year

Selected annually by *The Sporting News* since 1968.

Year		Year		Year	
1968	**Denny McLain**, baseball	1976	**Larry O'Brien**, basketball	1984	**Peter Ueberroth**, LA Olympics
1969	**Tom Seaver**, baseball	1977	**Steve Cauthen**, horse racing	1985	**Pete Rose**, baseball
		1978	**Ron Guidry**, baseball	1986	**Larry Bird**, pro basketball
1970	**John Wooden**, basketball	1979	**Willie Stargell**, baseball	1987	No award
1971	**Lee Trevino**, golf			1988	**Jackie Joyner-Kersee**, track
1972	**Charles O.Finley**, baseball	1980	**George Brett**, baseball	1989	**Joe Montana**, football
1973	**O.J.Simpson**, pro football	1981	**Wayne Gretzky**, hockey		
1974	**Lou Brock**, baseball	1982	**Whitey Herzog**, baseball	1990	**Nolan Ryan**, baseball
1975	**Archie Griffin**, football	1983	**Bowie Kuhn**, baseball		

Honda Broderick Cup

To the outstanding collegiate woman athlete of the year in NCAA competition. Winner is chosen from nominees in each of the NCAA's 10 competitive sports. Final voting is done by member athletic directors. Award is named after founder and sportswear manufacturer Thomas Broderick.
Multiple winner: Tracy Caulkins (2).

Year		Year	
1977	**Lucy Harris**, Delta St .... basketball	1984	**Tracy Caulkins**, Florida .... swimming
1978	**Ann Meyers**, UCLA .... basketball		**& Cheryl Miller**, USC .... basketball
1979	**Nancy Lieberman**, Old Dominion .... basketball	1985	**Jackie Joyner**, UCLA................. track & field
1980	**Julie Shea**, N.C.State .... track & field	1986	**Kamie Ethridge**, Texas. .... basketball
1981	**Jill Sterkel**, Texas. .... swimming	1988	**Teresa Weatherspoon**, La.Tech......... basketball
1982	**Tracy Caulkins**, Florida .... swimming	1989	**Vicki Huber**, Villanova...................... track
1983	**Deitre Collins**, Hawaii .... volleyball	1990	**Suzy Favor**, Wisconsin .... track

Flo Hyman Award

Presented annually since 1987 by the Women's Sports Foundation for "exemplifying dignity, spirit and commitment to excellence" and named in honor of the late captain of the 1984 U.S. Women's Volleyball team. Voting is done by WSF members.

Year		Year		Year	
1987	**Martina Navratilova**, tennis	1989	**Evelyn Ashford**, track	1991	**Diana Golden,** skiing
1988	**Jackie Joyner-Kersee**, track	1990	**Chris Evert**, tennis		

Theodore Roosevelt Award

First presented in 1967 by the NCAA, "to honor a distinguished citizen of national reputation and outstanding accomplishment who earned a varsity athletic award in college and has demonstrated a continuing interest in physical fitness and intercollegiate sports." The Teddy Award is the highest honor the NCAA confers on an individual and is named after the 26th President of the United States, who boxed at Harvard (Class of 1880) and played an instrumental role in the formation of the NCAA in 1906.

Year		College Class	Year		College Class
1967	**Gen.Dwight Eisenhower**	Army, 1915	1980	**Dr.Denton Cooley**	Texas, 1941
1968	**Leverett Saltonstall**	Harvard, 1914	1981	**Art Linkletter**	San Diego St., 1934
1969	**Byron (Whizzer) White**	Colorado, 1938	1982	**Bill Cosby**	Temple, 1977
1970	**Frederick Hovde**	Minnesota, 1929	1983	**Arnold Palmer**	Wake Forest, 1951
1971	**Christopher Kraft**	VPI, 1944	1984	**Vice Adm.William Lawrence**	Navy, 1951
1972	**Jerome Holland**	Cornell, 1939	1985	**Robben Fleming**	Beloit, 1938
1973	**Gen.Omar Bradley**...............	Army, 1915	1986	**George Bush**	Yale, 1948
1974	**Jesse Owens**	Ohio St., 1937	1987	**Walter Zable**	Wm.& Mary, 1937
1975	**Gerald Ford**	Michigan, 1935	1988	No award	
1976	**Adm.Tom Hamilton**	Navy, 1927	1989	**Dr.Paul Ebert**....................	Ohio St., 1954
1977	**Tom Bradley**	UCLA, 1941			
1978	**Gerald Zornow**	Rochester, 1937	1990	**Ronald Reagan**...................	Eureka, 1932
1979	**Otis Chandler**	Stanford, 1950	1991	**Althea Gibson**	Florida A&M, 1953

Note: No Teddy Award was given in 1988, so that the NCAA could recognize retiring Executive Director Walter Byers with a special award after 37 years of leadership.

Hockey legend **Gordie Howe** (left) highsticks an 11-year-old phenom named **Wayne Gretzky** at a 1972 banquet in Toronto. Twenty years later, Gretzky is just 83 goals shy of Howe's all-time NHL record of 801.

WHO'S WHO

Sports Personalities

Six hundred and twenty-nine noteworthy names dating back to the turn of the century.

Hank Aaron (b.1934): Baseball OF; led NL in HRs and RBI 4 times each and batting twice; MVP in 1957; played in 24 All-Star Games, all-time leader in HRs (755) and RBI (2,297), 3rd in hits (3,771).

Kareem Abdul-Jabbar (b.Lew Alcindor,1947): Basketball C; led UCLA to 3 NCAA titles (1967-69); tourney MVP 3 times; Player of Year twice; led Milwaukee (1) and LA Lakers (5) to 6 NBA titles; playoff MVP twice (1971,85), reg.season MVP 6 times (1971-72, 74,76-77, 80); retired after 20 seasons as all-time leader in over 20 categories.

Tenley Albright (b.1935): Figure skater; 2-time world champion (1953,55), won Olympic silver (1952) and gold (1956) medals.

Grover Cleveland Alexander (1887-1950): Baseball RHP; won 20 or more games 9 times; 373 career wins and 90 shutouts.

Vasily Alexeyev (b.1942): Soviet weightlifter; 8-time world champion; 2-time Olympic super-heavyweight champ (1972,76); set 80 world records between 1970-77.

Muhammad Ali (b.Cassius Clay,1942): Boxer; 1960 Olympic light-heavyweight champion; 3-time world heavyweight champion (1964-67,74-78,78-79); pro record 56-5 with 37 KOs; 19 successful title defenses.

Forrest (Phog) Allen (1885-74): Basketball; college coach 48 years; directed Kansas to NCAA title (1952), 746 career wins.

Bobby Allison (b.1937): Auto racer; 3-time winner of Daytona 500 (1978,82,88); NASCAR national champ in 1983; father of Davey.

Walter Alston (1911-84): Baseball; managed Brooklyn-LA Dodgers 23 years, won 7 pennants and 4 World Series (1955,59,63,65).

Sparky Anderson (b.1934): Baseball; only manager to win World Series in each league—Cincinnati in NL (1975-76) and Detroit in AL (1984).

Mario Andretti (b.1940): Auto racer; only driver to win Daytona 500 (1967), Indy 500 (1969) and Formula One world championship (1978); 4-time USAC/CART national champ (1965-66,69,84); father of Michael.

Earl Anthony (b.1938): Bowler; 6-time PBA Bowler of Year; 41 career titles; first to earn $100,000 in 1 season (1975); first to earn $1 million in career.

Said Aouita (b.1960): Moroccan runner; world record holder in 5 events—1500m, 2000m, 3000m, 2-mile, 5000m—entering 1991.

Luis Aparicio (b.1934), Baseball SS; all-time leader in most games, assists, chances and double plays by shortstop; led AL in stolen bases 9 times (1956-64); 506 career steals.

Al Arbour (b.1932): Hockey; coached NY Islanders to 4 straight Stanley Cup titles (1980-83); 3rd on all-time career list with 785 wins.

Eddie Arcaro (b.1916): Jockey; 2-time Triple Crown winner (Whirlaway in 1941, Citation in '48); won Kentucky Derby 5 times, Preakness and Belmont 6 times each.

Roone Arledge (b.1931): Sports TV innovator of live events, anthology shows, Olympic coverage and "Monday Night Football;" ran ABC Sports from 1968-86; has run ABC News since 1977.

Henry Armstrong (1912-88): Boxer; held feather-, light- and welterweight titles simultaneously in 1938; pro record 145-20-9 with 98 KOs.

Arthur Ashe (b.1943): Tennis; first black man to win U.S. Championship (1968) and Wimbledon (1975); 1st U.S. player to earn $100,000 in 1 year (1970); won Davis Cup as player (1968-70) and captain (1981-82); wrote black sports history *Hard Road to Glory* (1988).

Red Auerbach (b.1917): Basketball; winningest coach in NBA history; won 1,037 times (including playoffs) in 20 years; as coach-GM, led Boston to 9 NBA titles, including 8 in a row (1959-66); also coached defunct Wash. Capitols (1946-49); NBA Coach of the Year award named after him; retired as Celtics' coach in 1966 and as GM in '84; club president since 1970.

Hobey Baker (1892-1918): Football and hockey star at Princeton (1911-14); member of college football and pro hockey halls of fame; college hockey Player of the Year award named after him; killed in WWI plane crash.

Seve Ballesteros (b.1957): Spanish golfer; has won British Open 3 times (1979,84,88) and Masters twice (1980,83).

Ernie Banks (b.1931): Baseball SS-1B; led NL in home runs and RBI twice each; 2-time MVP (1958-59) with Chicago Cubs; 512 career HRs.

Roger Bannister (b.1929): British runner; first to run mile in less than 4 minutes (3:59.4 on May 6, 1954).

Walter (Red) Barber (b.1908): Radio-TV; renowned baseball play-by-play broadcaster for Cincinnati, Brooklyn and N.Y. Yankees from 1937-64; won Peabody Award for commentary in 1991.

Rick Barry (b.1944): Basketball F; only player to lead both NBA and ABA in scoring; 5-time All-NBA 1st team; playoff MVP with Golden St. in 1975.

Sammy Baugh (b.1914): Football QB; led Washington to NFL titles in 1937 (his rookie year) and '42; led league in passing 6 times, punting 4 times and interceptions once.

Elgin Baylor (b.1934): Basketball F; MVP of NCAA tournament in 1958; led Minn.-LA Lakers to 8 NBA Finals; 10-time All-NBA 1st team (1959-65,67-69).

Bob Beamon (b.1946): Track & Field; won 1968 Olympic gold medal in long jump with world record (29-ft, 2½ in.) that shattered old mark by nearly 2 feet; record finally broken by 2 inches in 1991 by Mike Powell.

Franz Beckenbauer (b.1945): Soccer; captain of West German World Cup champions in 1974 then coached West Germany to World Cup title in 1990; invented sweeper position; played in U.S. for NY Cosmos (1977-80,83).

Boris Becker (b.1967): German tennis player; 3-time Wimbledon champ (1985-86,89); youngest male (17) to win Wimbledon; led country to 1st Davis Cup win in 1988; won Australian Open in1991.

Jean Beliveau (b.1931): Hockey C; led Montreal to 10 Stanley Cups in 17 playoffs; playoff MVP (1965); 2-time regular season MVP (1956,64).

Bert Bell (1895-1959): Football; team owner and 2nd NFL commissioner (1946-59); proposed college draft in 1935 and instituted TV blackout rule.

Deane Beman (b.1938): Golf; PGA commissioner since 1974; introduced "stadium golf"; as player, won U.S. Amateur twice and British Amateur once.

Johnny Bench (b.1947): Baseball C; led NL in HRs twice and RBI 3 times; 2-time regular season MVP (1970,72) with Cincinnati, World Series MVP in 1976; 389 career HRs.

Patty Berg (b.1918): Golfer; 57 career pro wins including 15 Majors; 3-time AP Female Athlete of Year (1938,43,55).

Yogi Berra (b.1925): Baseball C; played on 10 World Series winners with NY Yankees; 3-time AL MVP (1951,54-55); managed both Yankees (1964) and NY Mets (1973) to pennants.

Jay Berwanger (b.1915): Football HB; U.of Chicago star; won 1st Heisman Trophy in 1935.

Abebe Bikila (1932-1973): Ethiopian runner; 1st to win consecutive Olympic marathons (1960,64).

Matt Biondi (b.1965): Swimmer; won 5 gold medals (2 individual), 1 silver and 1 bronze in 1988 Olympics.

Larry Bird (b.1956): Basketball F; college Player of Year (1979); 9-time All-NBA 1st team; 3-time regular season MVP (1984-86); led Boston to 3 NBA titles; playoff MVP (1984,86).

The Black Sox—Eight Chicago White Sox players who were banned from baseball for life in 1921 for allegedly throwing the 1919 World Series: RHP **Eddie Cicotte** (1884-1969), OF **Happy Felsch** (1891-1964), 1B **Chick Gandil** (1887-1970), OF **Shoeless Joe Jackson** (1887-1951), INF **Fred McMullan** (1891-1952), SS **Swede Risberg** (1894-1975), 3B-SS **Buck Weaver** (1890-1956), and LHP **Lefty Williams** (1893-1959).

Earl (Red) Blaik (1897-89): Football; coached Army to consecutive national titles in 1944-45; 166 career wins and 3 Heisman Trophy winners (Blanchard, Davis, Dawkins).

Bonnie Blair (b.1964): Speedskater; won 500m gold medal at 1988 Winter Olympics; World Sprint champion in 1989.

Toe Blake (b.1912): Hockey LW; led Montreal to 2 Stanley Cups as a player and 8 more as coach; regular season MVP in 1939.

Felix (Doc) Blanchard (b.1924): Football FB; 3-time All-America; led Army to national titles in 1944-45; Glenn Davis' running mate; won Heisman Trophy and Sullivan Award in 1945.

George Blanda (b.1927): Football QB-PK; NFL's all-time leading scorer (2,002 points); led Houston to 2 AFL titles (1960-61); played 26 pro seasons; retired at 48.

Fanny Blankers-Koen (b.1918): Dutch sprinter; 30 year-old mother of two, who won 4 gold medals (100m, 200m,800m hurdles and 4x100m relay) at 1948 Olympics.

Wade Boggs (b.1958): Baseball 3B; entered 1991 season with 5 AL batting titles (1983,85-88) at Boston and .346 career average.

Michael Bonallack (b.1934): Golf; secretary of Royal & Ancient Golf Club of St.Andrews; 5-time winner of British Amateur (1961,65,68-70).

Bjorn Borg (b.1956): Swedish tennis player; 2-time Player of Year (1979-80); won 6 French Opens and 5 straight Wimbledons (1976-80); led Sweden to 1st Davis Cup win in 1975; unsuccessful comeback attempt in 1991.

Mike Bossy (b.1957): Hockey RW; led NY Islanders to 4 Stanley Cups; playoff MVP in 1982; scored 50 goals or more 9 straight years; 573 career goals.

Ralph Boston (b.1939): Track & Field; medaled in 3 consecutive Olympic long jumps—gold (1960), silver (1964), bronze (1968).

Ray Bourque (b.1960): Hockey D; 8-time All-NHL 1st team, has won Norris Trophy 4 times (1987-88,1990-91) with Boston.

Bobby Bowden (b.1929): Football; entered 1991 regular season with 205 career wins in 25 years as coach at Samford, West Va. and Florida St.

Scotty Bowman (b.1933): Hockey; all-time winningest NHL coach with 853 career wins in 17 years; led Montreal to 5 Stanley Cups (1973,76-79); also coached St.Louis and Buffalo.

Jack Brabham (b.1926): Australian auto racer; 3-time Formula One champion (1959-60,66); 14 career wins.

Bill Bradley (b.1943): Basketball F; 3-time All-America at Princeton, Player of Year and NCAA tourney MVP in 1965; led NY Knicks to 2 NBA titles (1970,73); U.S. Senator (D,NJ) since 1979.

Terry Bradshaw (b.1948): Football QB; led Pittsburgh to 4 Super Bowl titles (1975-76,79-80); 2-time Super Bowl MVP (1979-80).

George Brett (b.1953): Baseball 3B-1B; has led AL in batting 3 times (1976,80,90); MVP in 1980; led KC to World Series title in 1985.

Lou Brock (b.1939): Baseball OF; former all-time stolen base leader (938); led NL in steals 8 times; led St.Louis to 2 World Series titles (1964,67); had 3,023 career hits.

Herb Brooks (b.1937): Hockey; former U.S. Olympic player (1964,68) who coached 1980 team to gold medal; coached Minnesota to 3 NCAA titles (1974,76,78); also coached NY Rangers and Minnesota in NHL.

Jim Brown (b.1936): Football FB; led NFL in rushing 8 times; 8-time All-Pro (1957-61,63-65); 3-time MVP (1958,63,65) with Cleveland; ran for 12,312 yards and scored 756 points in just 9 seasons.

Paul Brown (1908-91): Football innovator; coached Ohio St. to national title in 1942; in pros, directed Cleveland Browns to 4 straight AAFC titles (1946-49) and 3 NFL titles (1950,54-55); formed Cincinnati Bengals in 1968 (reached playoffs in '70).

Walter A. Brown (1905-64): member of both basketball and hockey halls of fame; succeeded father George as GM of Boston Garden in 1937; later became president of Garden and co-owner of both Bruins and Celtics.

Valery Brumel (b.1942): Soviet high jumper; dominated event from 1961-64; broke world record 5 times; won silver medal in 1960 Olympics and gold in 1964; highest jump 7-5¾.

Avery Brundage (1887-1975): Amateur sports czar for over 40 years as president of AAU (1928-35), U.S. Olympic Committee (1929-53) and Int'l Olympic Committee (1952-72).

Paul (Bear) Bryant (1913-1983): Football; coached at 4 colleges over 38 years; directed Alabama to 5 national titles (1961,64-65,78-79); 323 career wins; 15 bowl wins including 8 Sugar Bowls.

Sergei Bubka (b.1963): 1st man to clear 20 feet both indoors and out; holder of indoor (20-1) and outdoor (20-0¼) world records as of Sept. 1, 1991; 3-time world champion (1983, 87, 91); won gold medal at 1988 Olympics.

Don Budge (b.1915): Tennis; in 1938 became 1st player to win the Grand Slam—the French, Wimbledon, U.S. and Australian titles in 1 year; led U.S. to 2 Davis Cups (1937-38); turned pro in late '38.

Maria Bueno (b.1939): Brazilian tennis player; won 4 U.S. Championships (1959,63-64,66) and 3 Wimbledons (1959-60,64).

George Bush (b.1924): 41st President of U.S. (1989-) and avid sportsman; played 1B on 1947 and '48 Yale baseball teams that placed 2nd in College World Series; captain of 1948 team.

Susan Butcher (b.1956): Sled Dog racer; 4-time winner of Iditarod Trail race (1986-88,90).

Dick Butkus (b.1942): Football LB; 2-time All-America at Illinois (1963-64); All-Pro 7 of 9 NFL seasons with Chicago.

Dick Button (b.1929): Figure skater; 5-time world champion (1948-52); 2-time Olympic champ (1948,52).

Walter Byers (b.1923): College athletics; 1st executive director of NCAA, serving from 1951-88.

Frank Calder (1877-1943): Hockey; 1st NHL president (1917-43); guided league through its formative years; NHL's rookie of the year award named after him.

Lee Calhoun (1933-89): Track & Field: won consecutive Olympic gold medals in the 110m hurdles (1956,60).

Walter Camp (1859-1925): Football coach and innovator; established scrimmage line, center snap, downs, 11 players per side; named 1st All-America team (1889).

Roy Campanella (b.1921): Baseball C; 3-time NL MVP (1951,53,55); led Brooklyn to 5 pennants and 1st World Series title (1955).

Clarence Campbell (1905-84): Hockey; 3rd NHL president (1946-77), league tripled in size from 6 to 18 teams during his tenure; NHL's western conference named after him.

Earl Campbell (b.1955): Football RB; won Heisman Trophy in 1977; led NFL in rushing 3 times; 3-time All-Pro; 2-time MVP (1978-80) at Houston.

Milt Campbell (b.1933): Track & field; won silver medal in 1952 Olympic decathlon and gold medal in '56.

Tony Canzoneri (1908-59): Boxer; 2-time world lightweight champion (1930-33,35-36); pro record 141-24-10 with 44 KOs.

Jennifer Capriati (b.1976): Tennis; youngest Grand Slam semifinalist ever (age 14 at 1990 French Open); also youngest ever to win a match at Wimbledon (1990).

Harry Caray (b.1920): Radio-TV; baseball play-by-play broadcaster for St.Louis Cardinals, Oakland, Chicago White Sox and Cubs since 1945; father of sportscaster Skip and grandfather of sportscaster Chip.

Rod Carew (b.1945): Baseball 2B-1B; led AL in batting 7 times (1969,72-75,77-78) with Minnesota; MVP in 1977; had 3,053 career hits.

Steve Carlton (b.1944): Baseball LHP; won 20 or more games 6 times; 4-time Cy Young winner (1972,77,80,82) with Philadelphia; 329 career wins.

JoAnn Carner (b.1939): Golfer; 5-time U.S. Amateur champion; 2-time U.S. Open champ; 3-time LPGA Player of Year (1974,81-82).

Don Carter (b.1926): Bowler; 6-time Bowler of Year (1953-54,57-58,60-61); voted Greatest of All-Time in 1970.

Billy Casper (b.1931): Golfer; 2-time PGA Player of Year (1966,70); has won U.S. Open (1959,66), Masters (1970), U.S. Sr.Open (1983).

Tracy Caulkins (b.1963): Swimmer; won 3 gold medals (2 individual) at 1984 Olympics; set 5 world records and won 48 U.S. national titles from 1978-84.

Evonne Goolagong Cawley (b.1951): Australian tennis player; won Australian Open 4 times, Wimbledon twice (1971-79), French once.

Florence Chadwick (b.1918): Dominant distance swimmer of 1950s; set English Channel records from France to England (1950) and England to France (1951 and '55).

Wilt Chamberlain (b.1936): Basketball C; led NBA in scoring 7 times and rebounding 11 times; 7-time All-NBA first team; 4-time MVP (1960,66-68) in Philadelphia; scored 100 pts vs. NY Knicks in Hershey, Pa., Mar. 2, 1962; led Phila. 76ers (1967) and LA Lakers (1972) to NBA titles; playoff MVP in 1972.

A.B.(Happy) Chandler (1898-1991): Baseball; former Kentucky governor and U.S. Senator who became commissioner when Judge Landis died in 1945; backed Branch Rickey's move in 1947 to make Jackie Robinson 1st black player in major leagues; deemed pro-player and ousted by owners in 1951.

Julio Cesar Chavez (b.1962): Boxing; world junior welterweight champion; entered 1991 undefeated in 73 fights with 60 KOs.

Waldemar Cierpinski (b.1950): East German runner; won consecutive Olympic marathons (1976,80).

Jim Clark (1936-68): Scottish auto racer; 2-time Formula One world champion (1963,65); won Indy 500 in 1965; killed in car crash.

Bobby Clarke (b.1949): Hockey C; led Philadelphia to consecutive Stanley Cups in 1974-75; 3-time regular season MVP (1973,75-76).

Ron Clarke (b.1937): Australian runner; from 1963-70 set 17 world records in races from 2 miles to 20,000 meters; never won Olympic gold medal.

Roger Clemens (b.1962): Baseball RHP; fanned record 20 batters in 9-inning game (1986); 2 Cy Young Awards (1986-87) with Boston; AL MVP in 1986.

Roberto Clemente (1934-72): Baseball OF; hit .300 or better 13 times with Pittsburgh; led NL in batting 4 times; World Series MVP in 1971; regular season MVP in 1966; had 3,000 career hits; killed in plane crash.

Ty Cobb (1886-1961): Baseball OF; all-time highest career batting average (.367); hit .400 or better 3 times; led AL in batting 12 times and stolen bases 6 times with Detroit; MVP in 1911; had 4,191 career hits and 892 steals.

Mickey Cochrane (1903-62): Baseball C; led Phila.A's (1929-30) and Detroit (1935) to 3 World Series titles; 2-time AL MVP (1928,34).

Sebastian Coe (b.1956): British runner; won consecutive gold medals in 1,500m and silver medals in 800m at 1980 and '84 Olympics; held world records in 1,500m, mile and 800m in 1979.

Eddie Collins (1887-1951): Baseball 2B; led Phila.A's (1910-11) and Chicago White Sox (1917) to 3 World Series titles; AL MVP in 1914; had 3,311 career hits and 743 stolen bases.

Nadia Comaneci (b.1961): Romanian gymnast; 1st to record perfect 10 in Olympics; won 3 individual gold medals at 1976 Olympics and 2 more in '80.

Lionel Conacher (1902-54): Canada's greatest all-around athlete; NHL hockey (2 Stanley Cups), CFL football (1 Grey Cup), minor league baseball, soccer, lacrosse, track, amateur boxing champion; also member of Parliament (1949-54).

Billy Conn (b.1917): Boxer; world light heavyweight champion (1939-41); pro record 63-11-1 with 14 KOs.

Dennis Connor (b.1942): Sailing; 2-time America's Cup-winning skipper (1980,87), but 1st American to lose Cup (1983).

Maureen Connolly (1934-69): Tennis; in 1953 1st woman to win Grand Slam (at age 19); riding accident ended her career in '54; won both Wimbledon and U.S. titles 3 times (1951-53); 3-time AP Female Athlete of Year (1951-53).

Jimmy Connors (b.1952): Tennis; No.1 player in world 5 times (1974-78); has won 5 U.S. Opens, 2 Wimbledons and 1 Australian.

Jack Kent Cooke (b.1912): Football; sole owner of NFL Washington Redskins since 1985; also owned NBA Lakers and NHL Kings in LA; built LA Forum for $12 million in 1967.

Angel Cordero,Jr. (b.1942): Jockey; winner of more than 6,800 races; has won Kentucky Derby 3 times, Preakness twice and Belmont once; 2-time Eclipse winner (1982-83).

Howard Cosell (b.1920): Radio-TV; former ABC commentator on "Monday Night Football" and "Wide World of Sports," who energized TV sports journalism with "Tell it like it is" style.

James (Doc) Counsilman (b. 1920): coached Indiana men's swim team to 6 NCAA championships (1968-73); coached the 1964 and '76 U.S. Men's Olympic teams that won a combined 21 of 24 gold medals (the Hoosiers' Mark Spitz won 7 in 1976); in 1979 became oldest person (59) to swim English Channel; retired in 1990 with dual meet record of 287-36-1.

Margaret Smith Court (b.1942): Australian tennis player; won Grand Slam in both singles (1970) and mixed doubles (1963 with Ken Fletcher); 26 Grand Slam singles titles—11 Australian, 7 U.S., 5 French and 3 Wimbledon.

Bob Cousy (b.1928): Basketball G; led NBA in assists 8 times; 10-time All-NBA 1st team (1952-61); MVP in 1957; led Boston to 6 NBA titles (1957,59-63).

Joe Cronin (1906-84): Baseball SS; hit over .300 and drove in over 100 runs 8 times each, MVP in 1930; player-manager in Washington and Boston (1933-47); AL president (1959-73).

Glenn Cunningham (1910-88): Track & Field; dominant U.S. miler of 1930s; ran sub-4:10 mile 12 times; lost Olympic 1,500m to Jack Lovelock in 1936.

Ann Curtis (b.1926): Swimming; won 2 gold medals and 1 silver in 1948 Olympics; set 4 world and 18 U.S. records during career; 1st woman and swimmer to win Sullivan Award (1944).

Chuck Daly (b.1930): Basketball; has coached Detroit Pistons to two NBA titles (1989-90); entered 1991-92 with 497 wins in 9 years; 1st NBA coach to lead U.S. Olympic team (1992).

Stanley Dancer (b.1927): Harness racing; winner of 4 Hambletonians; trainer-driver of 2 Trotting Triple Crown winners (1968,72); one Pacing Triple Crown winner (1970).

Gary Davidson (b.1934): Entrepreneur; fueled boom in new sports leagues from 1967-75; 1st president of ABA, WHA and WFL.

Al Davis (b.1929): Football; GM-coach of Oakland 1963-66; helped force AFL-NFL merger as AFL commissioner (April-July,1966); returned to Oakland as managing general partner and directed club to 3 Super Bowl wins (1977,81,84); moved Raiders to LA in 1982.

Dwight Davis (1879-1945): Tennis; donor of Davis Cup; played for winning U.S. team in 1st two Cup finals (1900,02); won U.S. and Wimbledon doubles titles in 1901; Secretary of War (1925-29) in Coolidge administration.

Glenn Davis (b.1924): Football HB; 3-time All-America; led Army to national titles in 1944-45; Doc Blanchard's running mate; won Heisman Trophy in 1946.

John Davis (1921-84): Weightlifting; 6-time world champion; 2-time Olympic super-heavyweight champ (1948,52), undefeated 1938-53.

Pierre de Coubertin (1862-1940): French educator; father of the Modern Olympic Games; IOC president from 1896-1925.

Dizzy Dean (1911-74): Baseball RHP; led NL in strikeouts and complete games 4 times; last NL pitcher to win 30 games (30-7 in 1934); MVP in 1934 with St. Louis; 150 career wins.

Dave DeBusschere (b.1940): Basketball F; 3-time All-America at Detroit; youngest coach in NBA history (24 in 1964); player-coach of Detroit Pistons (1964-67); played in 8 All-Star games; won 2 NBA titles as player with NY Knicks; ABA commissioner (1975-76); also pitched 2 seasons for Chicago White Sox (1962-63) with 3-4 record.

Frank Deford (b.1938): 6-time Sportswriter of the Year during 27 years at Sports Illustrated; left SI in 1989 to launch The National as editor in chief; National folded June 13, 1991.

Anita DeFrantz (b.1952): one of two American delegates to International Olympic Committee; member of bronze medal-winning U.S. women's eight-oared shell at Montreal in 1976.

Clarence DeMar (1888-58): Track & Field; only 7-time winner of Boston Marathon (1911,22-24,27-28, 30); Olympic bronze in 1924.

Jack Dempsey (1895-1983): Boxer; world heavyweight champion from 1919-26; lost title and rematch to Gene Tunney; pro record 62-6-10 with 49 KOs.

Klaus Dibiasi (b.1947): Italian diver; won 3 consecutive Olympic gold medals in Platform Diving (1968,72,76).

Eric Dickerson (b.1960): Football RB; has led NFL in rushing 4 times (1983-84,86,88); All-Pro 5 times, traded from LA Rams to Indianapolis (Oct.31,1987).

Harrison Dillard (b.1923): Track & Field; only man to win Olympic gold medals in both sprints (100m in 1948) and hurdles (110m in 1952).

Joe DiMaggio (b.1914): Baseball OF; hit safely in 56 straight games (1941), led AL in batting, HRs and RBI twice each; 3-time MVP (1939,41,47); led NY Yankees to 10 World Series titles in 13 seasons.

Marcel Dionne (b.1951): Hockey C; scored 50 or more goals 6 times; led NHL in scoring in 1980, 2nd in all-time goals (731); 3rd in assists (1,348) and 3rd in points (1,771).

James (Buster) Douglas (b. 1960): Boxing; 50-1 shot who knocked out undefeated Mike Tyson in 10th round on Feb.10, 1990 to win heavyweight title in Tokyo; 10 months later, lost 1st title defense to Evander Holyfield by KO in 3rd round.

Ken Dryden (b.1947): Hockey G; led Montreal to 6 Stanley Cup titles; playoff MVP as rookie in 1971; won or shared 5 Vezina Trophies.

Charley Dumas (b.1937): U.S. high jumper; first man to clear 7 feet (7-0½) on June 29, 1956; won gold medal at 1956 Olympics.

Margaret Osborne du Pont (b.1918): Tennis; won 5 French, 7 Wimbledon and an unprecedented 24 U.S. national titles in singles, doubles and mixed doubles from 1941-62.

Roberto Duran (b.1951): Panamanian boxer; world lightweight champion (1972-79); world welterweight champ (1980); entered 1991 with pro record of 86-8-0 and 60 KOs.

Leo Durocher (b.1905): Baseball; managed in NL 24 years; won 2,010 games; 3 pennants with Brooklyn (1941) and NY Giants (1951,54); won World Series in 1954.

Eddie Eagan (1898-1967): Only U.S. athlete to win gold medals in Summer and Winter Olympics (Boxing in 1920, Bobsled in 1932).

Alan Eagleson (b.1933): Hockey; executive director of NHL players union 1967-90; arranged Team Canada vs Soviet Union (1972) and Canada Cup.

Dale Earnhardt (b.1952): Auto racer; 4-time NASCAR national champion (1980,86-87,90); yet to win Daytona 500.

Stefan Edberg (b.1966): Swedish tennis player; 2-time winner of both Wimbledon (1988,90) and Australian Open (1985,87); won U.S. Open in 1991; No. 1 player in 1990.

Gertrude Ederle (b.1906): Swimmer; 1st woman to swim English Channel, breaking men's record by 2 hours in 1926; won 3 medals in 1924 Olympics.

Bill Elliott (b.1955): Auto racer; 2-time winner of Daytona 500 (1985,87); NASCAR national champ in 1988; won 11 races in '85.

Herb Elliott (b.1938): Australian runner; undefeated from 1958-60; ran 17 sub-4:00 miles; 3 world records; won gold medal in 1,500m of 1960 Olympics; retired at 22.

Roy Emerson (b.1936): Australian tennis player; won 12 Majors in singles—6 Australian, 2 French, 2 Wimbledon and 2 U.S. from 1961-67.

Kornelia Ender (b.1958): East German swimmer; 1st woman to win 4 gold medals at one Olympics (1976), all in world record time.

Julius Erving (b.1950): Basketball F; in ABA (1972-76)—3-time MVP, 2-time playoff MVP, led NY Nets to 2 titles (1974-76); in NBA (1977-87)—5-time All-NBA 1st team, MVP in 1981, led Phila.76ers to title in 1983.

Phil Esposito (b.1942): Hockey C; 1st NHL player to score 100 points in a season (126 in 1969); 6-time All-NHL 1st team with Boston; 2-time MVP (1969,74); 5-time scoring champ; star of 1972 Canada-Soviet series; president-GM of new Tampa Bay entry in NHL.

Janet Evans (b.1971): Swimmer; won 3 individual gold medals (400m & 800m freestyle,400m IM) at 1988 Olympics; 1989 Sullivan Award winner, entered 1991 with 3 world records.

Lee Evans (b.1947): Track & Field; dominant quarter-miler in world from 1966-72; world record in 400m at 1968 Olympics stood 20 years.

Chris Evert (b.1954): Tennis; No.1 player in world 5 times (1975-77,80-81); won at least 1 Grand Slam singles title every year from 1974-86; 18 Majors in all—7 French, 6 U.S., 3 Wimbledon and 2 Australian.

Weeb Ewbank (b.1907): Football; only coach to win league championships in both NFL and AFL; led Baltimore to 2 NFL titles (1958-59) and NY Jets to victory in Super Bowl III.

Patrick Ewing (b.1962): Basketball C; 3-time All-America; led Georgetown to 3 NCAA Finals; tourney MVP in 1984; NBA Rookie of Year with New York in 1986.

Ray Ewry (1873-1937): Track & Field; won 10 gold medals over 4 consecutive Olympics (1900,04,06,08); all events he won (Standing HJ,LJ and TJ) were discontinued in 1912.

Nick Faldo (b.1957): British golfer; 2-time winner of both Masters (1989-90) and British Open (1987,90).

Juan Manuel Fangio (b.1911): Argentine auto racer; 5-time Formula One world champion (1951,54-57); 24 career wins, retired in 1958.

Donald Fehr (b.1928): Baseball; executive director and general counsel of Major League Players Assn. since 1983.

Bob Feller (b.1918): Baseball RHP; led AL in strikeouts 7 times and wins 6 times with Cleveland; threw 3 no-hitters and 12 one-hitters; 266 career wins.

Tom Ferguson (b.1950): Rodeo; 6-time All-Around champion (1974-79); 1st cowboy to win $100,000 in one season (1978); 1st to win $1 million in career (1986).

Herve Filion (b.1940): Harness racing; 10-time Driver of the Year; entered 1991 season as all-time leader in races won with 12,667 in 30 years.

Rollie Fingers (b.1946): Baseball RHP; all-time save leader with 341; won AL MVP and Cy Young awards in 1981 with Milwaukee; World Series MVP in 1974 with Oakland.

Charles O.Finley (b.1918): Baseball owner; moved KC A's to Oakland in 1968; won 3 straight World Series from 1972-74; also owned teams in NHL and ABA.

Bobby Fischer (b.1943): Chess; only American to hold world championship (1972-75); resigned title in 1975.

Emerson Fittipaldi (b.1946): Brazilian auto racer; 2-time Formula One world champion (1972,74); won Indy 500 and overall CART title in 1989.

Bob Fitzsimmons (1863-1917): British boxer; held three world titles—middleweight (1981-97), heavyweight (1897-99) and light heavyweight (1903-05); pro record 40-11 with 32 KOs.

James (Sunny Jim) Fitzsimmons (1873-1966): Horse racing; trained horses that won over 2,275 races, including 2 Triple Crown winners—Gallant Fox in 1930 and Omaha in '35.

Larry Fleisher (1930-89): Basketball; led NBA players union from 1961-89; in that time, increased average yearly salary from $9,400 in 1967 to $600,000 without a strike.

Peggy Fleming (b.1948): Figure skating; 3-time world champion (1966-68); won Olympic gold medal in 1968.

Curt Flood (b.1938): Baseball OF; played 15 years (1956-71); lost challenge to MLB's reserve clause in Supreme Court in 1972 (see Peter Seitz).

Gerald Ford (b.1913): 38th President of the U.S.; lettered as center on undefeated Michigan football teams in 1932 and '33, team MVP of 1934 squad.

Whitey Ford (b.1928): Baseball LHP; all-time leader in World Series wins (10); led AL in wins 3 times; won both Cy Young and World Series MVP in 1961 with NY Yankees.

George Foreman (b.1948): Boxer; 1968 Olympic heavyweight champion; world heavyweight champ (1973-74); returned to ring after 10-year hiatus in 1987; entered 1991 with pro record of 69-2-0 and 65 KOs; weighed 257 lbs in Apr. 19, 1991 bid to regain title, but lost decision to Evander Holyfield.

Dick Fosbury (b.1947): Track & Field; revolutionized high jump with back-first "Fosbury Flop;" won gold medal at 1968 Olympics.

Bob Foster (b.1938): Boxer; world light-heavyweight champion (1968-74); pro record 56-8-1 with 46 KOs.

The Four Horsemen—Senior backfield that led Notre Dame to national collegiate football championship in 1924: HB **Jim Crowley** (1902-86), FB **Elmer Layden** (1903-73), HB **Don Miller** (1902-79) and QB **Harry Stuhldreher** (1901-65).

The Four Musketeers—French quartet that dominated men's world tennis in 1920s and '30s, winning 8 straight French singles titles (1925-32), 6 Wimbledons in a row (1924-29) and 6 consecutive Davis Cups (1927-32): **Jean Borotra** (b.1898), **Jacques Brugnon** (1895-1978), **Henri Cochet** (1901-1987), **Rene Lacoste** (b.1904).

Jimmie Foxx (1907-67): Baseball 1B; led AL in HRs 4 times and batting twice; won Triple Crown in 1933; 3-time MVP (1932-33,38) with Phila. and Boston; hit 30 HRs or more 12 years in a row; 534 career HRs.

A.J.Foyt (b.1935): Auto racer; 4-time Indy 500 winner (1961,64,67,77); 7-time USAC/CART national champ; only driver to win Indy 500, Daytona 500 (1972) and 24 Hours of LeMans (1967 with Dan Gurney).

Bill France, Sr. (b.1909): stock car pioneer and promoter; founded NASCAR in 1948; guided race circuit through formative years; built both Daytona (Fla.) International Speedway and Talladega (Ala.) Super- speedway.

Dawn Fraser (b.1937): Australian swimmer; won gold medals in 100m freestyle at 3 consecutive Olympics (1956,60,64).

Joe Frazier (b.1944): Boxer; 1964 Olympic heavyweight champion; world heavyweight champ (1970-73); fought Muhammad Ali 3 times; pro record 32-4-1 with 27 KOs.

Ford Frick (1894-78): Baseball; sportswriter and radio announcer who served as NL president (1934-51) and commissioner (1951-65); put asterisk next to Roger Maris' 61 homers in 162 games in 1961; major leagues moved to west coast and expanded from 16 to 20 teams during his tenure.

Frankie Frisch (1898-1973): Baseball 2B; played on 8 NL pennant winners in 19 years with NY and St.Louis; hit .300 or better 11 years in a row (1921-31); MVP in 1931; player-manager from 1933-37.

Dan Gable (b.1948): Wrestling; 2-time NCAA champ at Iowa St.; tourney MVP in 1969 (137 lbs.); won gold medal (149 lbs) at 1972 Olympics; coached Iowa to 9 straight NCAA titles (1978-86).

Eddie Gaedel (1925-61): Baseball PH; St.Louis Browns' midget whose career lasted one at bat (he walked) on Aug.19,1951 (see Bill Veeck).

Clarence (Bighouse) Gaines (b.1924): Basketball; entered 1991-92 season ranked 2nd on all-time college wins list with 816; trails Adolph Rupp by 59; has coached at Div.II Winston-Salem since 1947.

Lou Gehrig (1903-41): Baseball 1B; played in 2,130 consecutive games from 1923-39; led AL in RBI 5 times and HRs 3 times; drove in 100 runs or more 13 years in a row; 2-time MVP (1927,36); led NY Yankees to 7 World Series titles.

Charlie Gehringer (b.1903): Baseball 2B; hit .300 or better 13 times; AL batting champion and MVP with Detroit in 1937.

Al Geiberger (b.1937): Golf; shot PGA-record 59 (June 10, 1977) in the 2nd round of Danny Thomas-Memphis Classic at 7249-yard Colonial CC; won 11 PGA events, including PGA Championship in 1966; entered 1991 with 5 wins on Seniors tour.

A.Bartlett Giamatti (1938-89): Scholar and 7th commissioner of baseball; banned Pete Rose for life for betting on Major League games and associating with known gamblers and drug dealers; also served as president of Yale (1978-86) and National League (1986-89).

Althea Gibson (b. 1927): Tennis; won both Wimbledon and U.S. championships in 1957 and '58; 1st black to play in either tourney and 1st to win each title.

Bob Gibson (b. 1935): Baseball RHP; won 20 or more games 5 times; won 2 NL Cy Young Awards (1968,70); MVP in 1968; led St. Louis to 2 World Series titles; Series MVP twice (1964,67); 251 career wins.

Josh Gibson (1911-47): Baseball C; the "Babe Ruth of the Negro Leagues;" Satchel Paige's battery mate with Pittsburgh Crawfords.

Kirk Gibson (b.1957): All-America flanker at Mich.St. in 1978; chose baseball career and was AL playoff MVP with Detroit in 1984 and NL regular season MVP with Los Angeles in 1988.

Frank Gifford (b. 1930): Football HB; 4-time All-Pro (1955-57,59); MVP in 1956; led NY Giants to 3 NFL title games; TV sportscaster since 1958 (while still player).

Sid Gillman (b.1911): Football innovator; coached LA Rams (1955-59) in NFL, then led LA-SD Chargers of AFL to 5 Western titles and 1 championship in the league's 1st six years.

George Gipp (1895-1920): Football FB; died of throat infection (Dec.14) 2 weeks before he made All-America (Notre Dame's 1st); rushed for 2,341 yards, scored 156 points and averaged 38 yards a punt in 4 years (1917-20).

Tom Gola (b.1933): Basketball F; 4-time All-America and 1955 Player of the Year at La Salle; MVP in 1952 NIT and '54 NCAA tournaments, leading Pioneers to both titles; won NBA title as rookie with Phila.Warriors in 1956; 4-time NBA All-Star.

Pancho Gonzalez (b.1928): Tennis; won consecutive U.S. Championships in 1947-48 before turning pro at 21; dominated pro tour from 1950-61; in 1969 at age 41, played longest Wimbledon match ever (5:12) beating Charlie Pasarell 22-24,1-6,16-14,6-3,11-9.

Shane Gould (b.1956): Australian swimmer; set world records in 5 different freestyle events between July,1971 and Jan,1972; won 3 gold medals, a silver and bronze in 1972 Olympics then retired at age 16.

Steffi Graf (b.1969): German tennis player; won Grand Slam in 1989 at age 19; 3-time winner at Wimbledon and Australia; No.1 player in world four times (1987-90).

Gillis Grafstrom (1894-1938): Swedish figure skater; 3-time world champ; won 3 straight gold medals then a silver in 4 Olympics (1920,24,28,32).

Otto Graham (b.1921): Football QB and basketball All-America at Northwestern; in pro ball, led Cleve. Browns to 7 league titles in 10 years, winning 4 AAFC championships (1946-50) and 3 NFL (1950,54-55); 5-time All-Pro; 2-time NFL MVP (1953,55).

Red Grange (1903-91): Football HB; 3-time All-America at Illinois who brought 1st huge crowds to pro football when he signed with Chicago in 1925; formed 1st AFL with manager C.C.Pyle in 1926, but league folded and he returned to NFL.

Hank Greenberg (1911-86): Baseball 1B; led AL in HRs and RBI 4 times each; 2-time MVP (1935,40) with Detroit; 331 career HRs.

Joe Greene (b.1946): Football DT; 5-time All-Pro (1972-74,77,79); led Pittsburgh to 4 Super Bowl titles.

Wayne Gretzky (b.1961): Hockey C; 9-time regular season MVP (1979-87,89); 9-time scoring champ; has scored 200 points or more in a season 4 times; led Edmonton to 4 Stanley Cups (1984-85,87-88); 2-time playoff MVP (1985,88); traded to LA Kings (Aug.9, 1988); all-time NHL leader in points (2,142) and assists (1,424); trails all-time goals leader Gordie Howe by 83 (801 to 718).

Bob Griese (b.1945): Football QB; 2-time All-Pro (1971,77); led Miami to undefeated season (17-0) in 1972 and consecutive Super Bowl titles (1973-74).

Archie Griffin (b.1954): Football RB; only college player to win two Heisman Trophies (1974-75); rushed for 5,177 yards in career at Ohio St.

Emile Griffith (b.1938): Boxer; world welterweight champion (1961,62-63,63-65); world middlweight champ (1966-67,67-68); pro record 85-24-2 with 23 KOs.

Florence Griffith Joyner (b.1959): Track & Field; set world records in 100 and 200 meters in 1988; won 3 gold medals at '88 Olympics (100m,200m,4x100 relay).

Dick Groat (b.1930): Two-time basketball All-America at Duke and college Player of the Year in 1951; chose baseball career and won NL MVP award as shortstop with Pittsburgh in 1960; won World Series with Pirates (1960) and St.Louis (1964).

Lefty Grove (1900-75): Baseball LHP; won 20 or more games 8 times; led AL in ERA 9 times and strikeouts 7 times; 31-4 record and MVP in 1931 with Phila.; 300 career wins.

Lou Groza (b.1924): Football T-PK; 6-time All-Pro; played in 13 championship games for Cleveland from 1946-67; kicked winning field goal in 1950 NFL title game; 1,608 career points (1,349 in NFL).

Janet Guthrie (b.1938): Auto racer; in 1977, became 1st woman to race in Indianapolis 500; placed 9th at Indy in 1978.

Tony Gwynn (b.1960): Baseball OF; entered 1990 season with 4 NL batting titles (1984,87-89) at San Diego and .332 career average.

Harvey Haddix (b.1925): Baseball LHP; pitched 12 perfect innings for Pittsburgh, but lost to Milwaukee in the 13th, 1-0 (May 26,1959).

Walter Hagen (1892-1969): Pro golf pioneer; won 2 U.S. Opens (1914,19), 4 British Opens (1922,24,28-29), 5 PGA Championships (1921,24-27) and 5 Western Opens; U.S. Ryder Cup captain 6 times.

Marvin Hagler (b.1954): Boxer; world middleweight champion 1980-87; pro record 62-3-2 with 52 KOs.

George Halas (1895-1983): Football pioneer; MVP in 1919 Rose Bowl; player-coach-owner of Chicago Bears from 1920-83; signed Red Grange in 1925; coached Bears for 40 seasons and won 7 NFL titles (1932-33,40- 41,43,46,63); all-time leader in career wins (325).

Dorothy Hamill (b.1956): Figure skater; won Olympic gold medal and world championship in 1976.

Scott Hamilton (b.1958): Figure skater; 4-time world champion (1981-84); won gold medal at 1984 Olympics.

Franco Harris (b.1950): Football RB; ran for over 1,000 yards a season 8 times; rushed for 12,120 yards in 13 years; led Pittsburgh to 4 Super Bowl titles.

Bill Hartack (b.1932): Jockey; won Kentucky Derby 5 times (1957,60,62,64,69), Preakness 3 times (1956,64,69), but the Belmont only once (1960).

Doug Harvey (1924-90): Hockey D; 10-time All-NHL 1st team; won Norris Trophy 7 times (1955-58,60-62); led Montreal to 6 Stanley Cups.

Billy Haughton (1923-86): Harness racing; 4-time winner of Hambletonian; trainer-driver of one Pacing Triple Crown winner (1968); winner of 4,910 races in career.

John Havlicek (b.1940): Basketball; played in 3 NCAA finals at Ohio St.(1960-62); led Boston to 8 NBA titles (1963-66,68-69,74,76); playoff MVP in 1974; 4-time All-NBA 1st team.

Bob Hayes (b.1942): Track & Field/Football; won gold medal in 100m at 1964 Olympics; All-Pro SE for Dallas in 1966; convicted of drug trafficking in 1979 and served 18 months of a 5-year sentence.

Woody Hayes (1913-87): Football; coached Ohio St. to 3 national titles (1954,57,68) and 4 Rose Bowl victories; 238 career wins.

Thomas Hearns (b.1958): Boxer; claimed 5th different world title in June, 1991, winning WBA light heavyweight crown at age 32; raised pro record to 50-3-1 with 40 KOs.

Eric Heiden (b.1958): Speed skater; 3-time overall world champion (1977-79), won all 5 men's gold medals at 1980 Olympics setting new records in each.

Mel Hein (b.1909): Football C; NFL All-Pro 8 straight years (1933-40); MVP in 1938 with NY Giants; didn't miss a game in 15 seasons.

John W.Heisman (1869-1936): Football; coached at 9 colleges from 1892-1927; won 185 games; Dir.of Athletics at Downtown Athletic Club in NYC (1928-36); DAC named Heisman Trophy after him.

Carol Heiss (b.1940): Figure skater; 5-time world champion (1956-60); won Olympic silver medal in 1956 and gold in '60; married 1956 men's gold medalist Hayes Jenkins.

Robert Helmick (b.1937): president of U.S. Olympic Committee since 1984; one of two American delegates to IOC.

Rickey Henderson (b.1958): Baseball OF; set single season base stealing record of 130 in 1982; has led AL in steals 9 times; broke Lou Brock's all-time record of 938 on May 1, 1991.

Sonja Henie (1912-69): Norwegian figure skater; 10-time world champion (1927-36); won 3 consecutive Olympic gold medals (1928,32,36); became movie star.

Graham Hill (1929-75): British auto racer; 2-time Formula One world champion (1962,68); won Indy 500 in 1966; killed in plane crash.

Phil Hill (b.1927): Auto racer; first U.S. driver to win Formula One championship (1961); 3 career wins (1958-64).

Max Hirsch (1880-1969): Horse racing; trained 1,933 winners from 1908-68; won Triple Crown with Assault in 1946.

Tommy Hitchcock (1900-44): Polo; world class player at 20; achieved 10-goal rating 18 times from 1922-40.

Ben Hogan (b.1912): Golfer; 4-time PGA Player of Year; won 4 U.S. Opens, 2 Masters, 2 PGA and 1 British Open between 1946-53; won 3 of 4 Majors (Masters, U.S. Open, British Open) in 1953; 62 career wins.

Eleanor Holm (b.1912): Swimmer; won gold medal in 100m backstroke at 1932 Olympics; thrown off '36 U.S. team for drinking champagne in public and shooting craps on boat to Germany.

Nat Holman (b.1896): Basketball pioneer; played pro with Original Celtics (1920-28); coached CCNY to both NCAA and NIT titles in 1950 (a year later, several of his players were caught up in a point-shaving scandal); 423 career wins.

Larry Holmes (b.1949): Boxer; heavyweight champion (WBC or IBF) from 1978-85; defended title 21 times; pro record 48-3 with 34 KOs; launched comeback attempt in 1991.

Evander Holyfield (1962): Boxer; knocked out Buster Douglas to become world heavyweight champion in 1990; lost shot at Olympic gold medal in 1984 when he lost controversial light heavy semifinal after knocking his opponent out (referee ruled it was a late hit).

Rogers Hornsby (1896-1963): Baseball 2B; hit .400 three times, including .424 in 1924; led NL in batting 7 times; 2-time MVP (1925,29) with St. Louis; career average of .358 over 23 years is all-time highest.

Paul Hornung (b.1935): Football HB-PK; only Heisman Trophy winner to play for losing team (2-8 Notre Dame in 1956); 3-time NFL scoring leader (1959-61) at Green Bay; 176 points in 1960 all-time record; MVP in 1961.

Gordie Howe (b.1928): Hockey RW; played 32 seasons in NHL and WHA from 1946-80; led NHL in scoring 6 times; All-NHL 1st team 12 times; MVP 6 times in NHL (1952-53,57-58,60,63) with Detroit and once in WHA (1974) with Houston; all-time NHL leader in goals (801) and in points (1,850) to Wayne Gretzky.

Cal Hubbard (1900-77): Member of college football, pro football and baseball halls of fame; 9 years in NFL; 4-time All-Pro at end and tackle; AL umpire for 15 years (1936-51).

Carl Hubbell (1903-88): Baseball LHP; led NL in wins and ERA 3 times each; 2-time MVP (1933,36) with NY Giants; fanned Ruth, Gehrig, Foxx, Simmons and Cronin in succession in 1934 All-Star Game; 253 career wins.

Miller Huggins (1880-1929): Baseball; managed NY Yankees to 6 pennants and 3 World Series titles from 1921-27.

Bobby Hull (b.1939): Hockey LW; led NHL in scoring 3 times; 2-time MVP (1965-66) with Chicago; All-NHL first team 10 times; jumped to WHA in 1972, 2-time MVP there (1973,75) with Winnipeg; scored 913 goals in both leagues; father of Brett.

Brett Hull (b.1964): Hockey RW; named NHL MVP in 1991 with St.Louis; holds RW scoring record with 86 goals; he and father Bobby have both won Hart (MVP) and Lady Byng (sportsmanship) trophies.

Jim (Catfish) Hunter (b.1946): Baseball RHP; won 20 games or more 5 times (1971-75); played on 5 World Series winners with Oakland, NY Yankees; threw perfect game in 1968; won Cy Young Award in '74.

Don Hutson (b.1913): Football E-PK; led NFL in receptions 8 times and interceptions once; 9-time All-Pro (1936, 38-45) for Green Bay.

Flo Hyman (1954-86): Volleyball; 3-time All-America spiker at Houston and captain of 1984 U.S. Women's Olympic team; died of heart attack caused by Marfan Syndrome during a match in Japan in 1986; Women's Sports Foundation's Hyman Award for excellence and dedication named after her.

Hank Iba (b.1904): Basketball; coached Oklahoma A&M to 2 straight NCAA titles (1945-46); 767 career wins in 41 years; coached U.S. Olympic team to 2 gold medals (1964,68), but lost to Soviets in controversial '72 final.

Punch Imlach (1918-1987): Hockey; directed Toronto to 4 Stanley Cups (1962-64,67) in 11 seasons as GM-coach.

Hale Irwin (b.1945): Golf; oldest player ever to win U.S. Open (45 in 1990); entered 1991 with 19 PGA victories, including 3 U.S. Opens.

Bo Jackson (b.1962): Baseball OF and Football RB; won Heisman Trophy in 1985 and MVP of baseball All-Star Game in 1989; starter for both baseball's KC Royals and NFL's LA Raiders in 1988 and '89; severely injured left hip Jan. 13, 1991, in NFL playoffs; waived by Royals in March, but signed by Chi. White Sox on Apr. 4 and returned to line-up on Sept. 2.

WHO'S WHO

WHO'S WHO **411**

Joe Jackson (1887-1951): Baseball OF; hit .300 or better 11 times; career average of .356 (see Black Sox).

Reggie Jackson (b.1946): Baseball OF; led AL in HRs 4 times; MVP in 1973; played on 5 World Series winners with Oakland, NY Yankees; 1977 Series MVP with 5 HRs; 563 career HRs; all-time strikeout leader (2,597).

Helen Jacobs (b.1908): Tennis; 4-time winner of U.S. Championship (1932-35); Wimbledon winner in 1936; lost 4 Wimbledon finals to arch-rival Helen Wills Moody.

Jim Jacobs (1930-88): Handball/Boxing; won 12 U.S. Handball titles (6 singles and 6 doubles) from 1955-68; also managed 4 world champion boxers, including Mike Tyson (from 1985-88).

James J.Jeffries (1875-1953): Boxer; world heavyweight champion (1899-1905); retired undefeated but came back to fight Jack Johnson in 1910 and lost (KO,15th).

David Jenkins (b.1936): Figure skater; brother of Hayes; 3-time world champion (1957-59); won gold medal at 1960 Olympics.

Hayes Jenkins (b.1933): Figure skater; 4-time world champion (1953-56), won gold medal at 1956 Olympics; married 1960 women's gold medalist Carol Heiss.

Bruce Jenner (b.1949): Track & Field; won gold medal in 1976 Olympic decathlon.

Ben Johnson (b.1961): Canadian sprinter; set 100m world record (9.83) at 1987 World Championships; won 100m at 1988 Olympics, but flunked drug test and forfeited gold medal; 1987 world record revoked in '89 for admitted steroid use; returned drug-free in 1991, but performed poorly.

Bob Johnson (b.1931): Hockey; coached Pittsburgh to 1st Stanley Cup title in 1991; led Wisconsin to 3 NCAA titles (1973,77,81) in 15 years; also coached 1976 U.S. Olympic team and NHL Calgary (1982-87).

Earvin (Magic) Johnson (b.1959): Basketball G; led Mich.St. to NCAA title in 1979 and was tourney MVP; All-NBA 1st team 9 times; all-time NBA assist leader with 9,921; 3-time MVP (1987,89-90); has led LA Lakers to 5 NBA titles; 3-time playoff MVP (1980,82,87).

Jack Johnson (1878-1946): Boxer; 1st black world heavyweight champion (1908-15); pro record 78-8-12 with 45 KOs.

Rafer Johnson (b.1935): Track & Field; won silver medal in 1956 Olympic decathlon and gold medal in 1960.

Walter Johnson (1887-1946): Baseball RHP; won 20 games or more 10 straight years; led AL in ERA 5 times, wins 6 times and strikeouts 12 times; twice MVP (1913, 24) with Washington; all-time leader in shutouts (113) and 2nd in wins (416).

Ben A. Jones (1882-1961): Horse racing; Calumet Farm trainer (1939-47); saddled 6 Kentucky Derby champions and 2 Triple Crown winners—Whirlaway in 1941 and Citation in '48.

Bobby Jones (1902-71): Won U.S. and British Opens plus U.S. and British Amateurs in 1930 to become golf's only Grand Slam winner ever; from 1922-30, won 4 U.S. Opens, 5 U.S. Amateurs, 3 British Opens, and played in 6 Walker Cups; founded Masters tournament in 1934.

Deacon Jones (b. 1938): Football DE; 5-time All-Pro (1965-69) with LA Rams.

Michael Jordan (b. 1963): Basketball G; College Player of Year in 1984; has led NBA in scoring 5 years in a row (1987-91); 5-time All-NBA 1st team; regular season MVP in 1988 and '91; led Chicago to NBA title in 1991 and was playoff MVP.

Jackie Joyner-Kersee (b. 1962): Track & Field; entered 1991 as world record holder in heptathlon (7,291 pts); won gold medals in heptathlon and long jump at 1988 Olympics.

Alberto Juantorena (b. 1951): Cuban runner; won both 400m and 800m gold medals at 1976 Olympics.

Sonny Jurgensen (b.1934): Football QB; played 18 seasons with Phila. and Wash.; led NFL in passing twice (1967,69); All-Pro in 1961; 255 career TD passes.

Duke Kahanamoku (1890-1968): Swimmer; won 3 gold medals and 2 silver over 3 Olympics (1912,20,24); also surfing pioneer.

Al Kaline (b.1934): Baseball; youngest player (20) to win batting title (led AL with .340 in 1955); had 3,007 hits, 399 HRs in 22 years with Detroit.

Anatoly Karpov (b.1951): Chess; Soviet world champion, 1975-85. **Gary Kasparov** (b.1963): Chess; Soviet world champion since 1985; defeated Karpov for title.

Kip Keino (b.1940): Kenyan runner; won one gold medal in 1,500m at 1968 Olympics and another in steeplechase at 1972 Games.

Walter Kennedy (1912-77): Basketball; 2nd NBA commissioner (1963-75), league doubled in size to 18 teams during his term of office.

Stanley Ketchel (1886-1910): Boxer; claimed 3 world titles—welterweight (1908,08-10), middleweight (1908-10) and light heavyweight (1909-10); murdered at age 24; pro record 53-4-5 with 50 KOs.

Harmon Killebrew (b.1936): Baseball 3B-1B; led AL in HRs 6 times and RBI 4 times; MVP in 1969 with Minnesota; 573 career HRs.

Jean Claude Killy (b.1943): French alpine skier; 2-time World Cup champion (1967-68); won 3 gold medals 1968 Olympics; co-president of 1992 Winter Games in Albertville.

Ralph Kiner (b.1922): Baseball OF; led NL in home runs 7 straight years (1946-52) with Pittsburgh; 369 career HRs.

Billie Jean King (b.1943): Tennis; Wimbledon singles champ 6 times; U.S. champ 4 times; first woman athlete to earn $100,000 in one year (1971); beat 55-year-old Bobby Riggs 6-4, 6-3, 6-3, to win $100,000 in 1973.

Don King (b.1933): Boxing promoter; controlled heavyweight title from 1978-90 while Larry Holmes and Mike Tyson were champions; 1st major bout Muhammad Ali's comeback fight in 1970; former numbers operator who served 4 years for manslaughter (1967-70); acquitted of tax evasion and fraud in 1984.

Gene Klein (1921-1990): Horseman; won 3 Eclipse awards as top owner (1985-87); filly Winning Colors won 1988 Kentucky Derby; also owned San Diego Chargers football team (1966-84).

Bob Knight (b.1940): Basketball; has coached Indiana to 3 NCAA titles (1976,81,87); 561 career wins; coached 1984 U.S. Olympic team to gold.

Olga Korbut (b.1955): Soviet gymnast; 3 gold medals 1972 Olympics; first to perform back somersault on balance beam.

Sandy Koufax (b.1935): Baseball LHP; led NL in strikeouts 4 times and ERA 5 straight years; won 3 Cy Young Awards (1963,65,66) with LA Dodgers; MVP in 1963; 2-time World Series MVP (1963,65); pitched 1 perfect game and 3 other no-hitters.

Alvin Kraenzlein (1876-1928): Track & Field; won 4 individual gold medals in 1900 Olympics (60m,long jump, and 110m & 200m hurdles).

Jack Kramer (b.1921): Tennis; Wimbledon singles champ 1947; U.S. champ 1946-47; promoter and Open pioneer.

Ingrid Kristiansen (b.1956): Norwegian runner; 2-time Boston Marathon winner (1986,89); world record holder in 5,000m, 10,000m and marathon.

Bob Kurland (b.1924): Basketball C; 3-time All-America (1944-46); led Okla.A&M to 2 NCAA titles (1945-46) and U.S. to 2 Olympic gold medals (1948,52); did not turn pro.

Marion Ladewig (b.1914): named Woman Bowler of the Year 9 times, (1950-54,57-59,63).

Guy Lafleur (b.1951): Hockey RW; has led NHL in scoring 3 times (1975-78); 2-time MVP (1977-78), played for 5 Stanley Cup winners in Montreal; playoff MVP in 1977; returned to NHL as player in 1988 after election to Hall of Fame; retired again in 1991.

Napoleon Lajoie (1875-1959): Baseball 2B; led AL in batting 4 times (1901-04); hit .422 in 1901; had 3,251 career hits.

Jack Lambert (b.1952): Football LB; 6-time All-Pro (1975-76,79-82); led Pittsburgh to 4 Super Bowl titles.

Kenesaw Mountain Landis (1866-1944): Baseball's first commissioner (1920-44); banned Black Sox for life.

Tom Landry (b.1924): Football; coached Dallas for 29 years (1960-88); won 2 Super Bowls (1972,78); 271 career wins.

Steve Largent (b.1954): Football WR; retired in 1989 after 14 years with Seattle as all-time NFL leader in passes caught (819) and TD passes caught (100).

Don Larsen (b.1929): Baseball RHP; pitched only perfect game in World Series history—NY Yankees 2, Brooklyn 0 (Oct.8,1956); Series MVP that year.

Larissa Latynina (b.1934): Soviet gymnast; won total of 18 medals, (9 gold) in 3 Olympics (1956,60,64).

Nikki Lauda (b.1949): Austrian auto racer; 3-time world Formula One champion (1975,77,84), 25 career wins from 1971-85.

Rod Laver (b.1938): Australian tennis player; only player to win Grand Slam twice (1962,69); Wimbledon champion 4 times; 1st to earn $1 million in prize money.

Andrea Mead Lawrence (b.1932): Alpine skier; won 2 gold medals at 1952 Olympics.

Bobby Layne (1926-86): Football QB; college star at Texas; led Detroit to 2 straight NFL titles (1952-53).

Frank Leahy (1908-73): Football; coached Notre Dame to four national titles (1943,46-47,49); career record of 107-13-9.

Greg LeMond (b.1962): Cyclist; 3-time Tour de France winner (1986,89-90); only American to win event.

Mario Lemieux (b.1965): Hockey C; has led NHL in scoring twice (1988-89); 2-time All-NHL 1st team; regular season MVP in 1988; 3-time All-Star Game MVP; led Pittsburgh to Stanley Cup title in 1991 and was playoff MVP.

Ivan Lendl (b.1960): Tennis; No.1 player in the world 4 times (1985-87,89); has won both French and U.S. Opens 3 times.

Suzanne Lenglen (1899-1938): French tennis player; dominated women's tennis from 1919-26; won both Wimbledon and French singles titles 6 times.

Sugar Ray Leonard (b.1956): Boxer; light welterweight Olympic champ (1976); won world welterweight title 1979 and four more titles; retired after losing to Terry Norris on Feb. 9, 1991, with record of 36-2-1 and 25 KOs.

Carl Lewis (b.1961): Track & Field; won 4 gold medals in· 1984 Olympics (100m,200m,400m relay and long jump); 2 more (100m, long jump) in 1988; set world record of 9.86 in 100 meters on Aug. 25, 1991.

Sonny Liston (1932-70): Boxer; heavyweight champ (1962-64); lost title to Muhammad Ali (then Cassius Clay) in 1964; pro record 50-4 with 39 KOs.

Vince Lombardi (1913-70): Football; coached Green Bay to 5 NFL titles; won first 2 Super Bowls (1967-68).

Johnny Longden (b.1907): Jockey; first to win 6,000 races; rode Count Fleet to Triple Crown in 1943.

Nancy Lopez (b.1957): Golfer; 4-time LPGA Player of the Year (1978-79,85,88); reached Hall of Fame by age 30.

Greg Louganis (b.1960): U.S. diver; won platform and springboard gold medals at both 1984 and '88 Olympics.

Joe Louis (1914-81): Boxer; world heavyweight champion (1937-49); reign of 11 years, 8 months longest in division history; pro record 63-3 with 49 KOs.

Sid Luckman (b.1916): Football QB; 6-time All-Pro; led Chicago Bears to 4 NFL titles (1940-41,43,46); MVP in 1943.

Hank Luisetti (b. 1916): Basketball F; 3-time All-America at Stanford (1935-38); revolutionized game with one-handed shot.

Johnny Lujack (b.1925): Football QB; led Notre Dame to three national titles (1943,46-47); won Heisman Trophy in 1947.

Gen.Douglas MacArthur (1880-1964): Leading U.S. general in World War II and Korea; president of U.S. Olympic Committee (1927-28); college football devotee; National Football Foundation MacArthur Bowl (for No.1 team) named after him.

Larry MacPhail (1890-1975): Baseball executive and innovator; introduced major leagues to night games at Cincinnati (May 24, 1935); won pennant in Brooklyn (1948) and World Series with NY Yankees (1947); father of Lee.

Lee MacPhail (b.1917): Baseball; AL president (1974-83); president of owners' Player Relations Committee (1984-85); also GM of Baltimore (1959-65) and NY Yankees (1967-74); father of Andy, current Minnesota GM.

Connie Mack (1862-1956): Baseball owner; managed Phila.A's until he was 87 (1901-50); won 9 AL pennants and 5 World Series (1910-11,13,29-30); also finished last 18 times.

John Madden (b.1936): Football; won 112 games and a Super Bowl as coach of the Oakland Raiders; has won 8 Emmy Awards as television analyst with CBS.

Larry Mahan (b.1943): Rodeo; 6-time All-Around Cowboy (1966-70,73).

Phil Mahre (b.1957): Alpine skier; 3-time World Cup overall champ (1981-83); finished 1-2 with twin brother Steve in 1984 Olympic slalom.

Moses Malone (b.1955): Basketball C; signed with Utah of ABA at age 19; has led NBA in rebounding 6 times; 4-time All-NBA 1st team; 3-time NBA MVP (1979,82-83); playoff MVP with Philadelphia in 1983.

Mickey Mantle (b.1931): Baseball OF; led AL in home runs 4 times; won Triple Crown in 1956; 3-time MVP (1956-57,62); 536 career HRs; played on 7 World Series winners with NY Yankees.

Pete Maravich (1948-88): Basketball; NCAA scoring leader 3 times (1968-70); averaged 44.2 points a game over career; Player of Year in 1970; NBA scoring champ in 1977.

Alice Marble (1913-90): Tennis; 4-time U.S. champion (1936,38-40); won Wimbledon in 1939; swept U.S. singles, doubles and mixed doubles from 1938-40.

Gino Marchetti (b.1927): Football DE; 8-time NFL All-Pro (1957-64) with Baltimore Colts.

Rocky Marciano (1923-69): Boxer; heavyweight champion (1952-56); retired undefeated; pro record of 49-0 with 43 KOs; killed in plane crash.

Juan Marichal (b.1937): Baseball RHP; won 21 or more games 6 times with S.F. Giants; 243 career wins.

Dan Marino (b.1961): Football QB; set NFL single-season records for TD passes (48) and passing yards (5,084) with Miami in 1984.

Roger Maris (1934-85): Baseball OF; broke Babe Ruth's single season HR record with 61 in 1961; 2-time AL MVP (1960-61) with NY Yankees.

Billy Martin (1928-1989): Baseball; 5-time manager of NY Yankees; won 2 pennants and 1 World Series (1977); also managed Minnesota, Detroit, Texas and Oakland; played 2B on 4 Yankee world champions in 1950s.

Eddie Mathews (b.1931): Baseball 3B; led NL in HRs twice (1953,59); hit 30 or more home runs 9 straight years; 512 career HRs.

Christy Mathewson (1880-1925): Baseball RHP; won 22 or more games 12 straight years (1903-14); 373 career wins; pitched 3 shutouts in 1905 World Series.

Bob Mathias (b.1930): Track & Field; first 2-time Olympic decathlon champion (1948,52).

Willie Mays (b.1931): Baseball OF; led NL in HRs and stolen bases 4 times each; 2-time MVP (1954,65) with NY-SF Giants; played in 24 All-Star Games; 660 HRs and 3,283 hits in career.

Joe McCarthy (1887-1978): Baseball; managed NY Yankees to 8 pennants and 7 World Series titles (1931-46).

Mark McCormack (b.1930): founder and CEO of International Management Group, the sports management conglomerate.

Pat McCormick (b.1930): U.S. diver; won women's platform and springboard gold medals in both 1952 and '56 Olympics.

Willie McCovey (b.1938): Baseball 1B; led NL in HRs 3 times and RBI twice; MVP in 1969 with SF; 521 career HRs.

John McEnroe (b.1959): Tennis; No.1 player in the world from 1981-84; 4-time U.S. Open singles champ (1979-81,84); 3-time Wimbledon champ (1981,83-84); played on 5 Davis Cup winners (1978-79,81-82).

John McGraw (1873-1934): Baseball; managed NY Giants to 10 NL pennants and 3 World Series titles in 30 years; 4,879 career wins.

Jim McKay (b.1921): Radio-TV; host and commentator of ABC's Olympic coverage and "Wide World of Sports" show since 1961; 12-time Emmy winner; also given Peabody Award in 1988 and Life Achievement Emmy in 1990.

John McKay (b.1923): Football; coached USC to 3 national titles (1962,67,72); won Rose Bowl 5 times; reached NFL playoffs 3 times with Tampa Bay.

Tamara McKinney (b.1962): Alpine skier; only American woman to win World Cup overall title (1983).

Denny McLain (b.1944): Baseball RHP; last pitcher to win 30 games (1968); 2-time Cy Young winner (1968-69) with Detroit; convicted of racketeering, extortion and drug possession in 1985, served 29 months of 25-year jail term, sentence overturned when court ruled he had not received a fair trial.

Bruce McNall (b.1950): Owner; bought NHL LA Kings in 1988; sent 5 players and $15 million to Edmonton for Wayne Gretzky (Aug.8,1988); bought CFL Toronto Argonauts in 1990; signed Notre Dame's Rocket Ismail for $18.2 million (Apr.21,1991).

Rick Mears (b.1951): Auto racer; 4-time winner of Indianapolis 500 (1979,84,88,91); 3-time CART national champ (1979,81-82).

Debbie Meyer (b.1952): Swimmer; 1st swimmer to win 3 individual gold medals at one Olympics (1968).

George Mikan (b.1924): Basketball C; 3-time All-America (1944-46); led DePaul to NIT title (1945); led Minneapolis Lakers to 5 NBA titles in 6 years (1949-54); Commissioner of ABA (1967-69).

Stan Mikita (b.1940): Hockey C; led NHL in scoring 4 times; won both MVP and Lady Byng awards in 1967 and '68 with Chicago.

Cheryl Miller (b.1964): Basketball; 3-time college Player of Year (1984-86); led USC to NCAA title and U.S. to Olympic gold medal in 1984.

Del Miller (b.1913): Harness racing; driver, trainer, owner, breeder, seller and track owner; has driven over 2,400 winners since 1939.

Marvin Miller (b.1917): Baseball; executive director of Players' Assn. from 1966-82; increased average salary from $19,000 to over $240,000; led 13-day strike in 1972 and 50-day walkout in '81.

Billy Mills (b.1938): Track & Field; upset winner of 10,000m gold medal at 1964 Olympics.

Joe Montana (b.1956): Football QB; led Notre Dame to national title in 1977; has since led San Francisco to 4 Super Bowls (1982,85,89-90); 2-time NFL MVP (1989-90); only 3-time Super Bowl MVP.

Helen Wills Moody (b.1905): Tennis; won 8 Wimbledon singles titles, 7 U.S. and 4 French from 1923-38.

Archie Moore (b.1913): Boxer; world light-heavyweight champion (1952-60); pro record 199-26-8 with 145 KOs.

Howie Morenz (1902-37): Hockey C; 3-time NHL MVP (1928,31-32); led Montreal Canadiens to 3 Stanley Cups; voted Outstanding Player of the Half-Century in 1950.

Joe Morgan (b.1943): Baseball 2B; led NL in walks 4 times; regular season MVP both years he led Cincinnati to World Series titles (1975-76).

Bobby Morrow (b.1935): Track & Field; won 3 gold medals at 1956 Olympics (100m,200m and 4x400m relay).

Willie Mosconi (b.1913), Pocket Billiards; 14-time world champion from 1941-57.

Edwin Moses (b.1955): Track & Field; won 400m hurdles at 1976 and '84 Olympics, bronze medal in '88; also winner of 122 consecutive races from 1977-87.

Stirling Moss (b.1929): Auto racer; won 194 of 466 career races and 16 Formula One events, but was never world champion.

Marion Motley (b.1920): Football FB; all-time leading AAFC rusher; rushed for over 4,700 yards and 31 TDs for Cleveland Browns (1946-53).

Dale Murphy (b.1956): Baseball OF; led NL in HRs and RBI twice each; 2-time MVP (1982-83) with Atlanta.

Jim Murray (b.1919): sports columnist for LA Times since 1961; 14-time Sportswriter of the Year; won Pulitzer Prize for commentary in 1990.

Stan Musial (b.1920): Baseball OF-1B; led NL in batting 7 times; 3-time MVP (1943,46,48) with St. Louis; played in 24 All-Star Games; had 3,630 career hits and .331 average.

John Naber (b.1956): Swimmer; won 4 gold medals and a silver in 1976 Olympics.

Bronko Nagurski (1908-90): Football FB-T; All-America at Minnesota (1929); All-Pro with Chicago Bears (1932-34); charter member of both college and pro halls of fame.

James Naismith (1861-1939): Canadian physical education instructor who invented basketball in 1891 at the YMCA Training School (now Springfield College) in Springfield, Mass.

Joe Namath (b.1943): Football QB; signed for unheard of $400,000 as rookie with AFL's NY Jets in 1965; 2-time All-AFL (1968-69) and All-NFL (1972); led Jets to Super Bowl title as MVP in '69.

Ilie Nastase (b.1946): Rumanian tennis player; No.1 in the world twice (1972-73); won U.S. (1972) and French (1973) Opens.

Martina Navratilova (b.1956): Tennis; all-time money winner; No.1 player in the world 7 times (1978-79,82-86); won her record 9th Wimbledon singles title in 1990; has also won 4 U.S., 3 Australian and 2 French.

Byron Nelson (b.1912): Golfer; won Masters and PGA twice, U.S. Open once; also won 11 consecutive tournaments (19 overall) in 1945.

Lindsey Nelson (b.1919): Radio-TV; all-purpose play-by-play broadcaster for CBS, NBC and others; 4-time Sportscaster of the Year (1959-62); voice of Cotton Bowl for 25 years and NY Mets from 1962-78; given Life Achievement Emmy Award in 1991.

Ernie Nevers (1903-76): Football FB; earned 11 letters in four sports at Stanford; played pro football, baseball and basketball; scored 40 points for Chicago Cardinals in one NFL game (1929).

John Newcombe (b.1943): Australian tennis player; No.1 player in world 3 times (1967,70-71); won Wimbledon 3 times, U.S. twice.

Bob Neyland (1892-1962): Football; 3-time coach at Tennessee; had 173-31-12 record in 21 years; won national title in 1951; Vols' stadium named for him; also Army general who won Distinguished Service Cross as supply officer in World War II.

Jack Nicklaus (b.1940): Golfer; winner of 20 major tournaments, including 6 Masters, 5 PGAs, 4 U.S. Opens and 3 British Opens; PGA Player of the Year 5 times (1967,72-73,75-76); named Golfer of Century by PGA in 1988.

Chuck Noll (b.1931): Football; coached Pittsburgh to 4 Super Bowl titles (1975-76,79-80); entered 1991 regular season with 202 wins (including playoffs).

Leo Nomellini (b.1924): Football DT; played in 174 consecutive regular season games over 14 seasons with San Francisco (1950-63).

James D. Norris (1906-66): boxing promoter and NHL owner; president of International Boxing Club from 1949 until US Supreme Court ordered its break-up (for anti-trust violations) in 1958; only NHL owner to win Stanley Cups in two cities—Detroit (1936-37,43) and Chicago (1961).

Paavo Nurmi (1897-1973): Finnish runner; won 9 gold medals (6 individual) in 1920,'24 and'28 Olympics; from 1921-31 broke 23 world outdoor records in events ranging from 1,500 to 20,000 meters.

Larry O'Brien (1917-90): Basketball; former U.S. Postmaster General and 3rd NBA commissioner (1975-84); league absorbed 4 ABA teams and created salary cap during his term in office.

Parry O'Brien (b.1932): Track & field; in 4 consecutive Olympics, won two gold medals, a silver and placed 4th in the shot put (1952-64).

Al Oerter (b.1936): Track & Field; won 4 consecutive Olympic gold medals in discus (1956-68).

Sadaharu Oh (b.1940): Baseball 1B; led Japan League in HRs 15 times; 9-time MVP for Tokyo Giants; hit 868 HRs in 22 years.

Barney Oldfield (1878-1946): Auto racing pioneer; drove cars built by Henry Ford; first man to drive car a mile per minute (1903).

Walter O'Malley (1903-79): Baseball owner; moved Brooklyn Dodgers to Los Angeles after 1957 season; won 4 World Series (1955,59,63,65).

Bobby Orr (b.1948) Hockey D; 8-time Norris Trophy winner as best defenseman; led NHL in scoring twice and assists 5 times; All-NHL 1st team 8 times; regular season MVP 3 times (1970-72); playoff MVP twice (1970,72) with Boston.

Mel Ott (1909-58): Baseball OF; joined NY Giants at age 17; led NL in HRs 6 times; had 511 HRs and 1,860 RBI in 22 years.

Kristin Otto (b.1966): East German swimmer; 1st woman to win 6 gold medals (4 individual) at one Olympics (1988).

Francis Ouimet (1893-1967): Golfer; won 1913 U.S. Open as 20-year-old amateur playing on Brookline, Mass. course where he used to caddie; won U.S. Amateur twice; 8-time Walker Cup player.

Jesse Owens (1913-80): Track & Field; broke 5 world records at Big 10 Championships (May 25, 1935); a year later, won 4 gold medals (100m, 200m, 4 × 100 relay and long jump) at Berlin Olympics.

Satchel Paige (1906-82): Baseball RHP; pitched 55 career no-hitters in Negro Leagues, entered Major Leagues in 1948 at age 42.

Arnold Palmer (b.1929): Golfer; winner of 4 Masters, 2 British Opens and 1 U.S. Open; PGA Player of the Year twice (1960,62); first player to earn over $1 million in career (1968).

Jim Palmer (b.1945): Baseball RHP; 3-time Cy Young Award winner (1973,75-76); won 20 or more games 8 times with Baltimore; 1991 comeback attempt at age 45 scrubbed in spring training.

Bernie Parent (b.1945): Hockey G; led Philadelphia Flyers to 2 Stanley Cups as playoff MVP (1974,75); 2-time Vezina Trophy winner.

Joe Paterno (b.1926): Football; has coached Penn State to 2 national titles (1982,85) in 25 years; entered 1991 regular season with 229 career wins.

Lester Patrick (1883-1960): Pro hockey pioneer as player, coach and manager for 4 decades; managed NY Rangers to their only Stanley Cups (1928,33,40).

Floyd Patterson (b.1935): Boxer; Olympic middleweight champ in 1952; world heavyweight champion (1956-59,60-62); 1st to regain heavyweight crown; pro record 55-8-1 with 40 KOs.

Walter Payton (b.1954): Football RB; NFL's all-time leading rusher with 16,726 yards; scored 109 TDs; All-Pro 7 times with Chicago; MVP in 1977.

Pelé (b.1940) Brazilian soccer F; given name—Edson Arantes do Nascimento; led Brazil to 3 World Cup titles (1958,62,70); came to U.S. in 1975 to play for NY Cosmos in NASL; scored 1,281 goals in 22 years.

Roger Penske (b.1937): Auto racing; national sports car driving champion (1964); established racing team in 1961; his cars have won record 8 Indianapolis 500s (including 1991) and record 7 Indy Car points championships.

Willie Pep (b.1922): Boxer; 2-time world featherweight champion (1942-48,49-50); pro record 230-11-1 with 65 KOs.

Fred Perry (b.1909): British tennis player; 3-time Wimbledon champ (1934-36), last native to win All-England men's title.

Gaylord Perry (b.1938): Baseball RHP; won Cy Young Awards in each league; 314 wins and 3,534 strikeouts in 22 years.

Bob Pettit (b.1932): Basketball F; All-NBA 1st team 10 times (1955-64); 2-time MVP (1956,59) with St. Louis Hawks; first player to score 20,000 points.

Richard Petty (b.1937): Auto racer; 7-time champion of Daytona 500; 7-time NASCAR national champ (1964, 67,71-72,74-75,79); first stock car driver to win $1 million in career.

Laffit Pincay, Jr. (b.1946): Jockey; 5-time Eclipse award winner (1971,73-74,79,85); trails only Bill Shoemaker in career wins; winner of 3 Belmonts and 1 Kentucky Derby (aboard Swale in 1984).

Nelson Piquet (b.1952): Brazilian auto racer; 3-time Formula One world champion (1981,83,87); entered 1990 win 20 career wins.

Jacques Plante (1929-86): Hockey G; led Montreal to 6 Stanley Cups (1953,56-60); won 7 Vezina Trophies; MVP in 1962; first goalie to regularly wear a mask.

Gary Player (b.1936): South African golfer; 3-time winner of Masters and British Open; also won 2 PGAs, a U.S. Open and 2 U.S. Senior Opens.

Jim Plunkett (b.1947): Football QB; Heisman Trophy winner in 1970; led Oakland-LA Raiders to Super Bowl wins in 1981 and '84; MVP in '81.

Maurice Podoloff (1890-85): Basketball; engineered merger of Basketball Assn. of America and National Basketball League into NBA in 1949; NBA commissioner (1949-63); league MVP trophy named after him.

Sam Pollack (b.1925): Hockey GM; managed NHL Montreal Canadiens to 9 Stanley Cups in 14 years (1965-78).

Fritz Pollard (1894-1986): Football; 1st black All-America RB (1916 at Brown); 1st black to play in Rose Bowl; 7-year NFL pro (1920-26); 1st black NFL coach, at Milwaukee and Hammond, Ind.

Denis Potvin (b.1953): Hockey D; won Norris Trophy 3 times (1976,78-79); 5-time All-NHL 1st-team; led NY Islanders to 4 Stanley Cups.

Mike Powell (b.1963): Track and Field; broke Bob Beamon's "unbreakable" 23-year-old long jump world record by 2 inches with leap of 29-ft., 4½ in., on Aug. 30, 1991, in Tokyo.

Annemarie Moser Proell (b.1953): Austrian alpine skier; won World Cup overall title 6 times (1971-75,79); won Downhill in 1980 Olympics.

Alain Prost (b.1955): French auto racer; 3-time Formula One world champion (1985-86,89), entered 1991 with 44 career wins.

C.C.Pyle (1884-1939): Promotor; known as "Cash and Carry"; hyped Red Grange's pro football debut by arranging 1925 barnstorming tour with Chicago Bears; had Grange bolt NFL for new AFL in 1926 (AFL folded in '27); also staged 2 Transcontinental Races (1928-29), known as "Bunion Derbies."

Willis Reed (b.1942): Basketball C; led NY Knicks to NBA titles in 1970 and '73, playoff MVP both years; regular season MVP 1970.

Mary Lou Retton (b.1968): Gymnast; won gold medal in women's All-Around at the 1984 Olympics, also won a silver and 2 bronzes.

Willy T.Ribbs (b.1956): Auto racer; successful IMSA driver; 1st black to race in Indianapolis 500 (1991).

Grantland Rice (1880-54): first celebrated American sportswriter; chronicled the Golden Age of Sport in 1920s; immortalized Notre Dame's "Four Horsemen."

Jerry Rice (b.1962): Football WR; 4-time All-Pro, regular season MVP in 1987 and Super Bowl MVP in 1989 with San Francisco.

Maurice Richard (b.1921): Hockey RW; 8-time NHL 1st team All-Star; MVP in 1947; 1st to score 50 goals in one season (1945); 544 career goals; played on 8 Stanley Cup winners in Montreal.

Bob Richards (b.1926): Track & Field; only 2-time Olympic gold medalist in pole vault (1952,56).

Tex Rickard (1870-1929): Promoter who handled boxing's first $1 million gate (Dempsey vs Carpentier in 1921); built Madison Square Garden in 1925.

Branch Rickey (1881-1965): In baseball 59 years as player, manager and GM; made Jackie Robinson 1st black player in Major Leagues (1947).

Bobby Riggs (b.1918): Tennis; won Wimbledon once (1939) and U.S. title twice (1939,41) before turning pro in 1941; beat Margaret Court Smith but lost to Billie Jean King in 1973 exhibition matches.

Pat Riley (b.1945): Basketball; coached LA Lakers to 4 of their 5 NBA titles in 1980s (1982,85,87-88); all-time leader in playoff wins with 102; quit in 1990; returned to coach NY Knicks in 1991.

Cal Ripken, Jr. (b.1961): Baseball SS; AL MVP in 1983; consecutive game playing streak passed 1,500 on July 20 (began May 30, 1982); 2nd only to Gehrig's 2,130 in a row.

Joe Robbie (1916-90): Football; original owner of Miami Dolphins (1965-90); won 2 Super Bowls (1972-73); built $115 Robbie Stadium with private funds in 1987.

Oscar Robertson (b.1938): Basketball G; 3-time college Player of Year (1958-60); 9-time All-NBA first team; MVP in 1964 with Cinn. Royals; 2nd in career assists with 9,887.

Paul Robeson (1898-1976): Black 4-sport star and 2-time football All-America (1917-18) at Rutgers; 3-year NFL pro; also scholar, lawyer, singer, actor and political activist.

Brooks Robinson (b.1937): Baseball 3B; led AL in fielding 12 times from 1960-72 with Baltimore; regular season MVP in 1964; World Series MVP in 1970.

Eddie Robinson (b.1919): Football; coaching at Grambling for over 45 years; winningest coach in college history; entered 1991 regular season with 366 career wins.

Frank Robinson (b.1935): Baseball OF; won MVP in NL (1961) and AL (1966); Triple Crown winner and World Series MVP in 1966 with Baltimore; 1st black manager in Major Leagues with Cleveland in 1975; also managed in SF and Baltimore.

Jackie Robinson (1919-72): Baseball 2B; 4-sport athlete at UCLA; 1st black player in Majors with Brooklyn in 1947; Rookie of the Year in 1947; NL MVP in 1949.

Sugar Ray Robinson (1920-89): Boxer; world welterweight champion (1946-51); 5-time middleweight champ; retired at age 45 after 25 years in the ring; pro record 174-19-6 with 109 KOs.

Knute Rockne (1888-1931): Football; coached Notre Dame to 3 consensus national titles (1924,29,30), career record of 105-12-5 in 13 years; killed in plane crash.

Bill Rodgers (b.1947): Track & Field; won Boston and New York City marathons 4 times each from 1975-80.

Irina Rodnina (b.1953): Soviet figure skater; won 10 world championships and 3 Olympic gold medals in pairs competiton from 1971-80.

Art Rooney (1901-1988): Sportsman and pro football pioneer, owned Pittsburgh Steelers for 55 years.

Theodore Roosevelt (1838-1919): 26th President of the U.S.; physical fitness buff who boxed as undergraduate at Harvard; credited with presidential assist in forming of Intercollegiate Athletic Assn. (now NCAA) in 1905-06.

Mauri Rose (1906-81): Auto racer; 3-time winner of Indy 500 (1941,47-48).

Murray Rose (b.1939): Australian swimmer; won 3 gold medals at 1956 Olympics; added a gold, silver and bronze in 1960.

Pete Rose (b.1941): Baseball OF-Inf.; all-time hits leader with 4,256; led NL in batting 3 times; regular season MVP in 1973; World Series MVP in 1975; had 44-game hitting streak in '78; managed Cincinnati (1984-89); banned for life in '89 for betting on baseball and associating with known gamblers and drug dealers; convicted of tax evasion in 1990 and sentenced to 5 months in prison; released Jan. 7, 1991.

Ken Rosewall (b.1934): Tennis; won French singles title at age 17 and Australian at 18; U.S. champ twice, but never won Wimbledon.

Mark Roth (b.1951): Bowler; 4-time PBA Player of the Year (1977-79,84); entered 1991 season with 33 tournament wins, including 1984 U.S. Open.

Pete Rozelle (b.1926): Football; NFL Commissioner from 1960-89; presided over growth of league from 12 to 28 teams, merger with AFL, creation of Super Bowl and advent of huge TV rights fees.

Wilma Rudolph (b.1940): Track & Field; won 3 gold medals (100m,200m and 4x400m relay) at 1960 Olympics.

Adolph Rupp (1901-77) Basketball; all-time college wins leader with 875; coached Kentucky to 4 NCAA titles (1948-49,51,58).

Bill Russell (b.1934): Basketball C; won titles in college, Olympics and pros; 5-time NBA MVP; led Boston to 11 titles, also became first big league black head coach in 1966.

Babe Ruth (1895-1948): Baseball LHP-OF; 2-time 20-game winner with Boston Red Sox; sold to NY Yankees in 1920; led AL in HRs 12 times and RBI 6 times; hit 60 HRs in 1927; ended career in 1935 with 714 HRs, 2,211 RBI and batting average of .342.

Johnny Rutherford (b.1938): Auto racer; 3-time winner of Indy 500 (1974,76,80); CART national champion in 1980.

Nolan Ryan (b.1947): Baseball RHP; pitched 7th no-hitter against Toronto May 1, 1991, at age 44; entered 1991 season with 302 wins and all-time record 5,308 strikeouts.

Juan Antonio Samaranch (b.1920): of Spain, President of International Olympic Committee since 1980.

Joan Benoit Samuelson (b.1957): Track & Field; has won Boston marathon twice (1979,83); winner of first women's Olympic marathon in 1984.

Earl Sande (1889-1968): Jockey; rode Gallant Fox to Triple Crown in 1930; won 5 Belmonts and 3 Kentucky Derbys.

Abe Saperstein (1902-66): Basketball; founded all-black, Harlem Globetrotters barnstorming team in 1927; coached sharpshooting comedians to 1940 world pro title in Chicago and established troop as game's foremost goodwill ambassadors; also served as 1st commissioner of American Basketball League (1961-62).

Gene Sarazen (b.1901): Golfer; won Masters, British Open, 2 U.S. Opens and 3 PGA titles between 1922-35; invented sand wedge in 1930.

Glen Sather (b.1943): Hockey; GM-coach of 4 Stanley Cup winners in Edmonton (1984-85,87-88) and GM-only for another in 1990.

Terry Sawchuk (1929-1970): Hockey G; recorded 103 shutouts in 21 NHL seasons; 4-time Vezina Trophy winner; played on 4 Stanley Cup winners at Detroit and Toronto.

Gale Sayers (b.1943): Football HB; 5-time All-Pro with Chicago; scored then-record 22 TDs in rookie year (1965).

Bo Schembechler (b.1929): Football; retired in 1989 as 5th winningest Div.I college coach ever; 234-65-8 record in 27 years; coached Michigan from 1969-89; 12 Rose Bowls but only 2 wins; president of Detroit Tigers since 1990.

Mike Schmidt (b.1949): Baseball 3B; led NL in HRs 8 times; 3-time MVP (1980,81,86) with Phila.; 548 career HRs; 10 gold gloves.

Don Schollander (b.1946): Swimming; won 4 gold medals at 1964 Olympics, plus one gold and one silver in 1968.

Dick Schultz (b.1929): executive director of NCAA since 1988; head coach of baseball (1964-70) and basketball (1970-74) at Iowa; athletic director at Cornell (1976-81) and Virginia (1981-87).

Bob Seagren (b.1946): Track & Field; won gold medal in pole vault at 1968 Olympics; broke world outdoor record 5 times.

Tom Seaver (b.1944): Baseball RHP; won 3 Cy Young Awards (1969,73,75); had 311 wins and 3,640 strikeouts over 20 years.

Peter Seitz (b.1905): Baseball arbitrator; ruled in 1975 (Dec.23) that players who perform for one season without a signed contract can become free agents; decision ushered in big money era for players.

Monica Seles (b.1973): Yugoslavian tennis player; youngest to win Grand Slam title this century when she won 1990 French Open at 16; winner of 1991 Australian, French and U.S. Opens.

Frank Selke (1893-1985): Hockey; GM of 6 Stanley Cup champions in Montreal (1953,56-60).

Wilbur Shaw (1902-54): Auto racer; 3-time winner and 3-time runner-up of Indy 500 from 1933-1940.

Bill Shoemaker (b.1931): Jockey; all-time career wins leader with 8,833; won Belmont 5 times, Kentucky Derby 4 times and Preakness twice; retired in 1990 to become trainer; paralyzed in auto accident on Apr. 8, 1991.

Eddie Shore (1902-85): Hockey D; only NHL defenseman (including Bobby Orr) to win MVP trophy 4 times (1933,35- 36,38), all with Boston.

Frank Shorter (b.1947): Track & Field; won gold medal in marathon at 1972 Olympics, 1st U.S. marathoner to win in 64 years.

Don Shula (b.1930): Football; has taken 6 teams to Super Bowls; won twice with Miami (1973-74); entered 1991 regular season with 298 career wins (including playoffs), second only to George Halas.

Al Simmons (1902-56): Baseball OF; led AL in batting twice (1930-31) and knocked in 100 runs or more 11 straight years (1924-34).

O.J.Simpson (b.1947): Football RB; won Heisman Trophy in 1966 at USC; ran for 2,003 yards in NFL in 1973; All-Pro 5 times; MVP in 1973; rushed for 11,236 career yards.

Harry Sinden (b.1932): Hockey; in 1970, coached Boston to 1st Stanley Cup title since 1941; came out of retirement in 1972 to coach victorious Team Canada in landmark, 8-game summit with USSR; Boston GM since 1972.

George Sisler (1893-73): Baseball 1B; hit over .400 twice (1920,22); 257 hits in 1920 still a major league record.

Mary Decker Slaney (b.1958): US middle distance runner; has held 7 separate American track & field records from the 800 to 10,000 meters; won both 1,500 and 3,000 meters at 1983 World Championships in Helsinki, but no Olympic medals.

Billy Smith (b.1950): Hockey G; led NY Islanders to 4 consecutive Stanley Cups (1979-83); won Vezina Trophy in 1982 and was Stanley Cup MVP in 1983.

Dean Smith (b.1931): Basketball; has coached North Carolina to 21 NCAA tournaments in 30 years; won title in 1982; coached U.S. Olympic team to gold medal in 1976; entered 1991-92 season with more wins (717) than any other active Division I coach.

John Smith (b.1966): Wrestler; winner of 1988 Olympic gold medal at 134 lbs; 3-time world champion; won 1990 Sullivan Award as top U.S. amateur athlete; 1st wrestler to win honor.

Ozzie Smith (b.1954): Baseball SS; entered 1991 with 11 straight gold gloves; 8-time starter for NL in All-Star Game.

Walter (Red) Smith (1905-82): Sportswriter for newspapers in Philadelphia and New York from 1936-82; won Pulitzer Prize for commentary in 1976.

Conn Smythe (1895-80): Hockey pioneer; built Maple Leaf Gardens in 1931; managed Toronto to 7 Stanley Cups before retiring in 1961.

Sam Snead (b.1912): Golfer; won both Masters and PGA 3 times, British Open once; runner-up in U.S. Open 4 times but never won; PGA Player of Year in 1949; PGA career victory leader with 84.

Peter Snell (b.1939): New Zealander who won gold medal in 800m at 1960 Olympics, then won both the 800m and 1,500m at 1964 Games.

Javier Sotomayor (b.1967): Cuban high jumper; first man to clear 8 feet (8-0) on July 29, 1989.

Warren Spahn (b.1921): Baseball LHP; led NL in wins 8 times; won 20 or more games 13 times; Cy Young winner in 1957; most career wins (363) by a left-hander.

Tris Speaker (1888-1958): Baseball OF; all-time leader in outfield assists (449) and doubles (793); had .344 career batting average and 3,515 hits.

J.G. Taylor Spink (1888-1962): Publisher of The Sporting News from 1914-62; Baseball Writers' Assn. annual meritorious service award named after him.

Mark Spitz (b.1950): Swimmer; set 23 world and 35 U.S. records; won record 7 gold medals (4 individual, 3 relay) at 1972 Olympics; comeback attempt at age 41 foundered in 1991.

Amos Alonzo Stagg (1862-1965): Football innovator; coached at U.of Chicago for 41 seasons and College of the Pacific for 14 more; won 314 games; elected to both college football and basketball halls of fame.

Willie Stargell (b.1941): Baseball OF-1B; led NL in home runs twice (1971,73); 475 career HRs; regular season and World Series MVP in 1979.

Bart Starr (b.1934): Football QB; led Green Bay to 5 NFL titles and 2 Super Bowl wins from 1961-67; reg-.season MVP in 1966; 2-time Super Bowl MVP (1967,68).

Roger Staubach (b.1942): Football QB; Heisman Trophy winner as Navy junior in 1963; led NFL in passing 4 times, led Dallas to 2 Super Bowl titles (1972,78); Super Bowl MVP in 1972.

George Steinbrenner (b.1930): principal owner of NY Yankees from 1973-90; teams won 2 World Series (1977-78); changed managers 19 times in 17 years; ordered by baseball commissioner Fay Vincent on July 30, 1990, to surrender control of club for dealings with small-time gambler Howard Spira.

Casey Stengel (1890-1975): Baseball; player for 14 years and manager for 25; guided NY Yankees to 10 pennants and 7 World Series titles from 1949-60.

Ingemar Stenmark (b.1956): Swedish alpine skier; 3-time World Cup overall champ (1976-78); 86 World Cup wins in 16 years; won 2 gold medals at 1980 Olympics.

David Stern (b.1942): Basketball; marketing expert and NBA commissioner since 1984, has presided over growth of league from 23 to 27 teams; received unprecedented 5-year, $27.5 million contract extension in 1990.

Teofilo Stevenson (b.1951): Cuban boxer; won 3 consecutive gold medals as Olympic heavyweight (1972,76,80); did not turn pro.

Jackie Stewart (b.1939): Auto racer; won 27 Formula One races and 3 world driving titles from 1965-73.

Curtis Strange (b.1955): Golfer, won consecutive U.S. Open titles (1988-89); first PGA player to win $1 million in one year (1988).

Louise Suggs (b.1923): Golfer; won 11 Majors and 50 LPGA events overall from 1949-62.

John L.Sullivan (1858-1918): Boxer; world heavyweight champion (1882-92); last of bare-knuckle champions.

Barry Switzer (b.1937): Football; coached Oklahoma to 3 national titles (1974-75,85); 157 career wins in 16 years.

Paul Tagliabue (b.1940): Football; NFL attorney who was elected league's 4th commissioner in 1989.

Anatoli Tarasov (b.1918): Hockey; coached USSR to 9 straight world championships and 3 Olympic gold medals (1964,68,72).

Jerry Tarkanian (b.1930): Basketball; UNLV coach who entered 1991-92 season with 599 career wins in 23 seasons; led Rebels to NCAA title in 1990; has fought running battle with NCAA since 1977 over purity of program.

Fran Tarkenton (b.1940): Football QB; 2-time All-Pro (1973,75); threw for 47,003 yards and 342 TDs (both NFL records) in 18 seasons.

Gustave Thoeni (b.1951): Italian alpine skier; 4-time World Cup overall champion (1971-73,75); won Giant Slalom at 1972 Olympics.

Daley Thompson (b.1958): British track & field; won consecutive gold medals in decathlon at 1980 and '84 Olympics.

Jim Thorpe (1888-1953): 2-time All-America in football; won both pentathlon and decathlon at 1912 Olympics; played major league baseball (1913-19) and pro football (1920- 26,28); chosen "Athlete of the Half Century" by AP in 1950.

Bill Tilden (1893-1953): Tennis; won 7 U.S. and 3 Wimbledon titles in 1920s; led U.S. to 7 straight Davis Cup victories (1920-26).

Tinker to Evers to Chance—Chicago Cubs double play combination from 1903-08; immortalized in poem by New York sportswriter Franklin P. Adams: SS **Joe Tinker** (1880-1948), 2B **Johnny Evers** (1883-1947) and 1B **Frank Chance** (1877-1924); all 3 managed the Cubs and made the Hall of Fame.

Y.A.Tittle (b.1926): Football QB; played 17 years in AFC and NFL; All-Pro 4 times; league MVP with San Francisco (1957) and NY Giants (1962); passed for 28,339 career yards.

Bill Toomey (b.1939): Track & Field; won decathlon gold medal at 1968 Olympics.

Pie Traynor (1899-1972): Baseball 3B; hit .300 or better 10 times; led Pittsburgh to World Series title in 1925.

Vladislav Tretiak (b.1952): Hockey G; led USSR to Olympic gold medals in 1972 and '76; starred for Soviets against Team Canada in 1972, and again in 2 Canada Cups (1976,81).

Lee Trevino (b.1939): Golfer; 2-time winner of 3 Majors—U.S. Open (1968,71), British Open (1971-72) and PGA (1974,84); joined Seniors Tour in 1990 winning 7 titles, including U.S. Senior Open, and over $1 million.

Bryan Trottier (b.1956): Hockey C; led NY Islanders to 4 straight Stanley Cups (1980-83); regular season MVP in 1979, playoff MVP in 1980; added 5th Cup with Pittsburgh in 1991.

Gene Tunney (b.1897-78): Boxer; world heavyweight champion (1926-28); defeated Jack Dempsey twice on points; pro record 65-2-1 with 43 KOs.

Ted Turner (b.1938): Sportsman, skippered *Courageous* to America's Cup win in 1977; owner of both Atlanta Braves and Hawks; cable TV pioneer; founder of Goodwill Games.

Mike Tyson (b.1965): Boxer; youngest (age 19) to win heavyweight title (WBC, 1986); undisputed champ from 1987 until upset loss to Buster Douglas on Feb. 10, 1990; entered 1991 with pro record of 39-1 with 35 KOs.

Wyomia Tyus (b.1945): Track & Field; 1st woman to win consecutive Olympic gold medals in 100m (1964-68).

Peter Ueberroth (b.1937): Organizer of financially successful 1984 Summer Olympics in LA; 1984 *Time* Man of the Year; baseball commissioner from 1984-89.

Johnny Unitas (b.1933): Football QB; led Baltimore Colts to 2 NFL titles (1958-59) and a Super Bowl win (1971); All-Pro; 3-time MVP (1959,64,67); passed for 40,239 career yards and 290 TDs.

Al Unser,Sr. (b.1939): Auto racer; brother of Bobby; 4-time winner of Indy 500 (1970-71,78,87); 3-time USAC/CART national champ.

Al Unser, Jr. (b.1962): Auto racer; won unprecedented four straight races and CART title in 1990.

Bobby Unser (b.1934): Auto racer; brother of Al; 3-time winner of Indy 500 (1968,75,81); 2-time USAC-CART national champ.

Norm Van Brocklin (1926-83): Football QB; led NFL in passing 3 times and punting twice; led LA Rams (1951) and Philadelphia (1960) to NFL titles; MVP in 1960.

Steve Van Buren (b.1920): Football HB; led Philadelphia to 2 NFL titles (1948-49); league's top rusher 4 times.

Johnny Vander Meer (b.1914): Baseball LHP; only major leaguer to pitch consecutive no-hitters (June 11 & 15, 1938).

Harold S. Vanderbilt (1884-70): Sportsman; successfully defended America's Cup 3 times (1930, 34,37); also invented contract bridge in 1926.

Glenna Collett Vare (1904-89): Golfer; won record 6 U.S. Women's Amateur titles from 1922-35.

Andy Varipapa (1891-1984): Bowler; trick-shot artist; won consecutive All-Star match game titles (1947-48) at age 53.

Bill Veeck (1914-86): Maverick baseball executive; owned American League teams in Cleveland, St.Louis and Chicago from 1946-80; introduced ballpark giveaways, exploding scoreboards, and midget Eddie Gaedel; won World Series with Indians (1948) and pennant with White Sox (1959).

Fay Vincent (b.1938): Baseball; became 8th commissioner after death of A.Bartlett Giamatti in 1989; presided over World Series earthquake, owners' lockout and banishment of NY Yankees owner George Steinbrenner in his first year on the job.

Lasse Viren (b.1949): Finnish runner; won gold medals in 5,000m and 10,000m at both the 1972 and '76 Olympics.

Honus Wagner (1874-1955): Baseball SS; hit .300 for 17 consecutive seasons (1897-1913) with Pittsburgh; led NL in batting 8 times; had 3,430 career hits.

Grete Waitz (b.1953): Norwegian runner; 9-time winner of New York City Marathon from 1978-88.

Doak Walker (b.1927): Football HB; won Heisman Trophy as SMU junior in 1948; led Detroit to 2 NFL titles (1952-53); All-Pro 4 times in 6 years.

Herschel Walker (b.1962): Football RB; led Georgia to national title as freshman in 1980, won Heisman as junior in 1982, jumped to USFL in '83; traded by Dallas of NFL to Minnesota in 1989 for 5 players and 6 draft picks.

Bill Walsh (b.1931): Football; coached San Francisco to 3 Super Bowl titles (1982,85,89).

Bill Walton (b.1950): Basketball C; 3-time college Player of Year (1972-74); led UCLA to 2 national titles (1972-73); led Portland to NBA title as MVP in 1977, regular season MVP in 1978.

Darrell Waltrip (b.1947): Auto racer; 3-time NASCAR national champion (1981-82,85); won 1989 Daytona 500.

Paul Waner (1903-65): Baseball OF; led NL in batting 3 times; MVP in 1927 with Pittsburgh; had 3,152 hits and .333 career average; brother of Lloyd.

Arch Ward (1896-55): Promoter and sports editor of Chicago Tribune from 1930-55; founder of baseball All-Star Game (1933), Chicago College All-Star Football Game (1934) and the All-America Football Conference (1946-49).

Cornelius (Dutch) Warmerdam (b.1915): Track & Field; 1st pole vaulter to clear 15 feet (1940).

Glenn (Pop) Warner (1872-54): Football innovator; coached at 7 colleges over 49 years; 313 career wins; produced 47 All-Americas, including Jim Thorpe and Ernie Nevers.

Tom Watson (b.1949): Golfer; 6-time PGA player of the Year (1977-80,82,84); has won 5 British Opens, 2 Masters and 1 U.S. Open.

Dick Weber (b.1929): Bowler; 3-time PBA Bowler of the Year (1961,63,65); won 30 PBA titles in 4 decades.

Johnny Weismuller (1904-84): Swimmer; won 3 gold medals at 1924 Olympics and 2 more at 1928 Games; became Hollywood's most famous Tarzan.

Jerry West (b.1938): Basketball G; 2-time All-America at W.Va.; 10-time All-NBA first-team; led LA Lakers to NBA title once as player (1972) and 5 times as GM.

Bill White (1934): Baseball; NL president since 1989; highest ranking black executive in sports; as 1st baseman, won 7 gold gloves and hit .286 with 202 HRs.

Byron (Whizzer) White (b.1918): Football; All-America HB at Colorado (1935-37); signed with Pittsburgh in 1938 for the then largest contract in pro history ($15,800); took Rhodes scholarship in 1939; returned to NFL in 1940 to lead league in rushing and retired in 1941; named to US Supreme Court in 1962.

Kathy Whitworth (b.1939): Golf; 7-time LPGA Player of the Year (1966-69,71-73); won 6 Majors; 88 tour wins most on LPGA or PGA tour.

Hazel Hotchkiss Wightman (1886-1974): Tennis; won 16 U.S. national titles; 4-time U.S. Women's champion (1909-11,19); donor of Wightman Cup.

Mats Wilander (b.1964): Swedish tennis player; 1988 Player of the Year; has won Australian and French Opens 3 times each and U.S. Open in 1988.

Bud Wilkinson (b.1916): Football; coached Oklahoma to 3 national titles (1950,55,56); 145 career wins in 17 years.

Ted Williams (b.1919): Baseball OF; led AL in batting 6 times; won Triple Crown twice (1942,47); MVP twice (1946,49); last player to hit .400 (1941); hit .344 with 521 HRs in 19 years.

Katarina Witt (b.1965): East German figure skater; 4-time world champion (1984-85,87-88); won consecutive Olympic gold medals (1984,88).

John Wooden (b.1910): Basketball; college Player of Year at Purdue in 1932; coached UCLA to 10 national titles (1964-65,67-73,75); only member of Basketball Hall of Fame inducted as player and coach.

Mickey Wright (b.1935): Golfer; won 3 of 4 Majors (LPGA, U.S. Open, Titleholders) in 1961; 4-time winner of both U.S. Open and LPGA titles; 82 career wins including 13 Majors.

Early Wynn (b.1920): Baseball RHP; won 20 games 5 times; Cy Young winner in 1959; 300 career wins in 23 years.

Cale Yarborough (b.1939): Auto racer; 4-time winner of Daytona 500 (1968,77,83-84); NASCAR national champ 3 times (1976-78).

Carl Yastrzemski (b.1939): Baseball OF; led AL in batting 3 times; won Triple Crown and MVP in 1967; had 3,419 hits and 452 HRs in 23 years with Boston.

Cy Young (1867-1955): Baseball RHP; won 20 games or more 16 times; holds record for career wins (511) and innings pitched (7,377).

Sheila Young (b.1950): Speed skater-cyclist; 1st U.S. athlete to win 3 medals at Winter Olympics (1976); won speed skating overall and sprint cycling world titles in 1976.

Robin Yount (b.1955): Baseball SS-OF; 2-time AL MVP (1982,89) for Milwaukee; entered 1991 season with 2,747 hits at age 35.

Mario Zagalo (b.1931): Soccer; Brazilian forward who is one of only two men (Franz Beckenbauer is the other) to serve as both captain (1962) and coach (1970) of World Cup champion.

Babe Didrikson Zaharias (1914-56): won 2 gold medals and a silver at 1932 Olympics; took up golf in 1935; won 55 pro & amateur events; helped found LPGA in 1949; won 10 Majors including 3 U.S. Opens (1948,50,54); chosen female "Athlete of the Half Century" by AP in 1950.

Tony Zale (b.1913): Boxer; world middleweight champion (1941-47,48); pro record 67-18-2 with 44 KOs.

Frank Zamboni (1901-88): mechanic, ice salesman and skating rink owner in Paramount, Calif.; invented 1st ice-resurfacing machine in 1949; 4,000 sold in over 33 countries since then.

Emile Zatopek (b.1922): Czech runner; won total of 4 Olympic gold medals, including unprecedented triple (5,000m, 10,000m and marathon), in 1952.

John Ziegler (b.1934): Hockey; NHL president since 1977; negotiated settlement with rival WHA in 1979 that led to inviting four WHA teams (Edmonton, Hartford, Quebec and Winnipeg) to join NHL.

Pirmin Zurbriggen (b.1963): Swiss alpine skier; 4-time World Cup overall champ (1984,87,88,90) and 3-time runner-up; 40 World Cup wins in 10 years; won gold and bronze medals at 1988 Olympics.

Frank Deford, editor in chief of *The National*, holds a proof of the final edition the night before the newspaper folded on June 13.

BUSINESS & MEDIA

Tapped Out

*The sports industry's spending spree appears to be over,
yet leagues expand and player salaries continue to climb.*

In the burgeoning business administration lexicon of sport, it's called a massive correction. But in sports terms, 1990-91 will most likely go down as the year the $70 billion American sports industry hit the wall.

Blame it on the recession, bad timing or just plain mismanagement—but everywhere you looked it seemed as if someone was losing his shirt.

► CBS lost $154 million in the first year of its four-year, $1.06 billion baseball contract.

► The country's only daily sports newspaper, *The National*, ceased publication after losing $100 million in its first 18 months.

► Calumet Farm, one of horse racing's oldest and most successful stables, filed for bankruptcy with debts of over $70 million.

► The owners of the NBA's Seattle SuperSonics called off plans to build a new $100 million arena because the financing couldn't be arranged.

► Even yachting shipped red ink, as the America's Cup Organizing Committee in San Diego announced it was reducing its overall two-year Cup Defense budget from $31 million to $20 million.

What happened?

John McManus covers the sports media as an editor and reporter at *Media Week* magazine.

In television, it was overspending.

Annual sports rights fees for the Big Three networks, plus ESPN and Turner Network Television (TNT) jumped 87%, from $908 million in 1989-90 to $1.7 billion for 1990-91. The aggregate cost of TV rights for the NFL, NBA, major league baseball, college football and the NCAA basketball tournament exploded 131%, from $3.2 billion under the previous series of contracts to $7.4 billion under the present deals.

Nearly half of that amount will come from CBS, which, in addition to baseball, is committed to the NFL for $1.06 billion over four years, the NCAA basketball tournament for $1 billion over seven, and the 1992 and '94 Winter Olympic Games for a combined $543 million.

Too much.

On May 8, CBS Inc. chairman Laurence Tisch was obliged to humble himself before his company's shareholders in Los Angeles when he said the network expected to lose another $115 million on baseball before the contract runs out in 1993.

"Was it a mistake? Certainly. Would we do it again at this level? Absolutely not," said Tisch, an otherwise highly-regarded financial wizard who in five years of ownership has yet to prove to the broadcasting industry that his interests in CBS are more than as an investment.

Robert Tisch, the billionaire president of Loews Corporation, showed little of his

Wide World Photos

Two years after signing a four-year, $1.06 billion TV deal with major league baseball, CBS Inc. chairman **Laurence Tisch** (left) admitted that the contract worked out with then commissioner **Peter Ueberroth** was a big mistake.

brother's newfound restraint on Feb. 20, when he shelled out a reported $75 million for 50 percent of the New York Giants—less than a month after the Giants won the Super Bowl.

In 1925, the year before Tisch was born, co-owner Wellington Mara's father, Tim Mara, bought the franchise for $500.

In this tale of two Tisches, TV executives agreed with Laurence that their spending spree was ill-advised. Robert Wright, the head of NBC, said as much about his network's four-year, $852-million deal with the NFL. The agreement, which includes the 1993 Super Bowl, can only make money if the ad marketplace comes back strong.

ABC Sports president Dennis Swanson, who saw lean times coming sooner than most and started reining in his division's budget shortly after succeeding the free-spending Roone Arledge in 1986, doesn't see things getting better anytime soon.

"I'm not optimistic for the short range at all," said Swanson. "Things will be worse in 1991 than last year. And 1992 will be even worse, with the two Olympic events coming up (NBC has the Summer Games). That's a lot of inventory to sell in the middle of an economic downturn."

Advertisers are not buying commercial time the way they used to. Where annual double-digit increases were the norm a decade ago, ad spending has flattened out, and a five percent increase is all that's expected in 1991.

Economic hard times and a lack of advertising also combined to strike out *The National* on June 13.

Launched into the teeth of the recession on Jan. 31, 1990, *The National* was the country's first sports daily and fielded a veritable all-star team of editors, reporters and high profile columnists like Dave Kindred, Mike Lupica and Scott Ostler. More importantly, it had former *Sports Illustrated* star feature writer Frank Deford as editor in chief and the financial backing of Mexican media mogul Emilio Azcarraga.

But on the day Azcarraga decided to pull the plug, the 44-page *National* carried only four pages of advertising, had serious distribution problems, and at 75 cents a copy was overpriced in a very competitive business. Circulation was estimated to be less than 200,000.

"With pay-per-view and additional sports channels on all cable systems, not to mention new publications, this is an oversaturated market," media ad director Bob Zach of Chiat/Day/Mojo told *The Wall Street Journal*. "There are too few bodies for viewing and reading all this stuff."

Two months before *The National* went under, *The Racing Times* and *USA Today's Baseball Weekly* debuted to make the newsstands even more crowded. *The Racing Times*, edited by former *New York Times* turf writer Steve Crist and bankrolled by British communications magnate Robert Maxwell, challenged the entrenched *Daily Racing Form* (owned until recently by Maxwell rival Rupert Murdoch), while *Baseball Weekly* sought to carve out a niche between *The Sporting News* (the former "Bible of Baseball") and minor leagues-oriented *Baseball America*. As of mid-August, both papers were doing as well as or better than expected, with circulation at 16,000 a day for the $2.50 *Racing Times* and 250,000 a week for the $1 *Baseball Weekly*.

Racing's saddest story of the year was the demise of Calumet Farm (see "Horse Racing"), the old Kentucky home of eight Derby winners and Triple Crown champions Whirlaway (1941) and Citation (1948). Mismanagement, lawsuits and the unexpected death of the stable's renowned sire Alydar in November combined to force the Wright family to file for reorganization.

Bruce McNall, the owner of the NHL's Los Angeles Kings, and his star player Wayne Gretzky co-own several horses, including 1990 Arlington Million winner Golden Pheasant. In 1991, they bought a 1910 Honus Wagner baseball card for $451,000 and scooped up the Toronto Argonauts of the Canadian Football League with a third investor—actor John Candy—for $5 million.

In April, McNall, who owns 60 percent of the Argos, stunned the pro football world by signing the NFL's designated No. 1 draft pick, Notre Dame kick return specialist Raghib (Rocket) Ismail, to a guaranteed, four-year contract worth $18.2 million and a piece of the team.

It was the same sort of blockbuster deal McNall swung in 1988 to pry Gretzky loose from the Edmonton Oilers and turn the Kings around. By early September, it looked as though the gamble to land Rocket was also paying off. Nine games into the CFL season, Ismail was second in overall yardage but more importantly, attendance at Argos games was up by almost 10,000 at home and way up on the road (near-sellouts in Vancouver and Saskatchewan) and viewership of Toronto games on Canadian TV had doubled to 850,000.

Ismail's salary, which came to $4.5 million in 1991, placed him 27th on *Forbes* magazine's list of the Top 40 Highest Paid Athletes of 1990-91 (see page 427). Gretzky, who pockets a mere $3 million a year playing hockey but picks up $4 million more in off-ice income, was tied for 19th.

Four heavyweight boxers—world champion Evander Holyfield and challengers Mike Tyson, George Foreman and Razor Ruddock—held down four of the first seven spots, with Holyfield and Tyson ranked 1-2 at $60.5 million and $31.5 million apiece. With their eagerly-awaited title showdown scheduled for Nov. 8 in Las Vegas and on pay-per-view TV (see box), they figure to remain on top for 1991-92.

Basketball's Michael Jordan (3rd); Formula One auto racers Ayrton Senna (5th), Alain Prost (6th) and Nigel Mansell (9th); and golfing institutions Arnold Palmer (8th) and Jack Nicklaus (10th) round out the Top 10.

The *Forbes* list also included two teen-age women's tennis stars—17-year-old Monica Seles (12th) and 15-year-old Jennifer Capriati (26th).

Jordan, who led the Chicago Bulls to their first NBA championship ever in 1991, pulled down a staggering $13.2 million for pitching as many as 15 products. That amount figures to increase with the Aug. 8 announcement that he had left Coca-Cola for an estimated $18 million deal to gulp Gatorade for the next 10 years.

San Francisco 49ers quarterback Joe Montana was the only full-time NFL player in the Top 40, ranking No. 13 in

Owner-collector **Bruce McNall** (left) stunned the pro football world on April 21 when he signed Notre Dame's **Rocket Ismail** to a four-year contract with the CFL's Toronto Argonauts for $18.2 million.

on- and off-field income. He was replaced as the highest-paid player in the league, however, on Aug. 20 when the Miami Dolphins signed QB Dan Marino to a five-year contract extension worth $4.5 million a year.

There were only five baseball players in the Top 40 and they all ranked in the 30s—two-sport star Bo Jackson of the Chicago White Sox (the Kansas City Royals released him after he injured his hip in the NFL playoffs), Darryl Strawberry of Los Angeles, Will Clark and Kevin Mitchell of San Francisco, and Joe Carter of Toronto.

Pitchers Roger Clemens of Boston and Dwight Gooden of the New York Mets signed contracts in 1991 that would put Clemens at $5.4 million for four years and Gooden at $5.2 million for three, beginning in 1992.

Salaries soared throughout baseball, where 39 players made at least $3 million a year, 123 players made $2 million or more, and 226 had reached the once-unimagined $1 million-per-season level.

Despite the clear evidence that CBS and ESPN grossly overspent on their current contracts and that the next TV deals will be for much less, baseball owners continued to hand out pay raises that bore little relation to team income.

"Baseball seems to be ignoring the situation," said Jon Miller, NBC Sports' vice president of program planning and development. "TV is not the gravy train any more. They [baseball] are headed for some real problems, especially in the smaller markets."

One additional source of revenue that kept owners' heads in the clouds in 1991 came in June, when Denver and Miami were invited to join the National League (starting in 1993) and paid $95 million each for the privilege. Blockbuster Video chairman Wayne Huizenga wrote the check for the Florida Marlins, while a partnership headed by beer and wine wholesaler John Antonucci and backed by the Coors Brewing Co. paid up for the Colorado Rockies.

The combined $190 million entry fee was a $12.3 million windfall for each of the 12 current NL owners. The 14 American League teams, on the other hand, had to settle for $3 million apiece—but only after agreeing to supply three players each in the 1992 expansion draft. When the AL expanded to Seattle and Toronto in 1977, the combined entry fee was less than $14 million.

The NHL, which opened the 1991-92 season with the brand new San Jose

Sharks skating in the Smythe Division, announced the addition of two more expansion teams on Dec. 6, 1990. The Ottawa Senators and Tampa Bay Lightning agreed to pay $50 million apiece to begin play in 1992-93, but both franchises had to scramble in 1991 to meet payment deadlines.

Ottawa, which had a team in the NHL from 1917-34, was nevertheless a long shot for selection. Tampa's bid was considered dead in the water on Oct. 18, 1990, when the Pritzer family (Hyatt Hotels) withdrew as the Lightning's principal owner. But team president and general manager Phil Esposito revived the effort by flying to Japan at the 11th hour and lining up 50 percent backing from four Japanese companies—including the Nippon Meat Packers, Inc., owner of the Nippon Ham Fighters baseball team of Japan's Pacific League.

Espo wasn't the only one in the NHL looking for a financial helping hand. As of early September, the league still didn't have a national cable TV contract to replace the three-year, $51 million deal with SportsChannel America that expired in June.

For the first time in three years, the NBA did not expand in 1990-91. The league had grown to 27 teams over the previous two seasons with Charlotte and Miami joining in 1988-89, followed by Minnesota and Orlando for 1989-90. All four paid an expansion fee of $32.5 million.

The NFL, which hasn't added any teams since Seattle and Tampa Bay came aboard in 1976, announced plans in 1991 to become a 30-team league and set a Sept. 16 deadline for all interested cities to apply. Two of the most interested were Baltimore and St. Louis, who lost the Colts and Cardinals to other cities in the 1980s. The NFL is expected to name its two newest members by October of 1992 and have them on the field by 1994. Entry fee estimates range from $125 to $150 million per team.

The NFL gave birth to the moderately successful World League of American Football in 1991. While an unqualified success in its three European outposts—Barcelona, Frankfurt and London—the WLAF was little more than a springtime diversion in the U.S., where TV ratings on ABC and USA network were dismal.

PPV Packs A Wallop, Sometimes
by Jack Craig

Pay-per-view television coverage is the recurring dream of most sports entrepreneurs, and it is a really big dream. Obtain TV rights to a truly compelling event, persuade only a tiny share of tens of millions of sports fans to pay to watch, and get rich.

Mike Tyson turns the PPV dream into reality every time he steps into the ring. Close to a million households punched up his fight with Razor Ruddock in March and that audience increased to 1.3 million when Tyson-Ruddock II took place in June after a disputed decision in the first fight. At somewhere around $40 a pop, the two bouts averaged about $43 million—45 percent of which went to cable operators, with the remainder split among the fighters and their dreamers-promoters.

There is even evidence that when PPV is in play, clever marketing can substitute for legitimate fighters. George Foreman, a middle-aged man with nary a chance against Evander Holyfield, promoted himself as a good guy representing every overweight male in America. Presto, he and Holyfield pulled down a PPV-record $48.9 million gross in their April 19 heavyweight championship fight. And Foreman even went the distance.

Boxing, in fact, has generated the six biggest PPV gates, including entertainment programs. (Wrestlemania VII and VI rank seventh and eighth.) But the sport's latest PPV experiment, TVKO's monthly bouts that began in April, has been disappointing, with audiences ranging around one half of one percent among 18 million potential subscribers. "If we can get up to one percent we'll be fine," says Ross Levinsohn of TVKO, a Time-Warner creation. So much money from such a miniscule percentile is proof of PPV's financial sizzle.

NBC and Cablevision will jointly offer three simultaneous PPV channels during the 1992 Summer Olympics. From July 25 through Aug. 9, they will pump out 12 hours daily (5 A.M.-5 P.M. EDT) of live coverage

Jack Craig has been the TV sports critic for *The Boston Globe* since 1969.

Wide World Photos

Heavyweight title fights are what pay-per-view TV is all about. April's bout between 42-year-old **George Foreman** (left, with drumstick) and champion **Evander Holyfield** made a record $55 million.

and rerun it all for the next 12 hours. For $170, a viewer can watch it all while receiving gift packets of Olympic goodies. For $125, he/she can watch it all without perks. For $95, the three channels will open for the first seven days or for all three weekends.

Ellen Cooper, publicist for Olympic PPV, dares to project 10-percent of up to 40 million potential subscribers will pay to watch. Using the middle buy price of $125 as the average, gross revenue would approach $500 million.

But are the Olympics not one of a kind? Even if Cooper's optimism proves warranted, can an event held every four years blaze a trail for PPV? Yes, Cooper claims.

"We're creating PPV infrastructure. We're going to make the entire country aware of pay-per-view," she says, and cites futuristic TV likely to be initiated on PPV. (Never mind the future. Imagine the joy of watching the Olympics on PPV without the commercial interruptions of the past.)

But the future of PPV does not rest with boxing and the Olympics. It is linked to the National Football League. The most common of several PPV concepts would make one or all of the Sunday games not on the networks available for a price. How much?

Pick a number. How many junkies and wagerers are out there? No one has a clue; there is no available data.

The NFL's dream about PPV is edging toward reality from fear that its current $3.6 billion TV contract with the three networks, ESPN and TNT faces a drastic cut when the deals expire after the 1993 season. Where else to turn to retrieve the really big bucks?

If the NFL experiments with PPV in 1994, reducing free TV coverage, it will face a war of the roses with Congress. But if it eventually is allowed to plunge ahead, other leagues will try to make their dreams come true, despite the handicap of playing so many games that none may seem important enough to lure fans to pay a special price.

"For PPV, you could use high definition TV and interactive TV (the viewer selects the cameras)," says John Mansell of Paul Kagan Associates, the cable industry firm. Mansell even envisions such technology enabling the NFL to put the Super Bowl on PPV as merely an alternative and thereby maintain commissioner Paul Tagliabue's pledge to Congress to keep the big game on free TV through 1999.

With PPV offering such a huge prize, there will be no shortage of ideas.

The value of major league franchises made headlines in June when *Financial World* magazine came out with a highly-speculative survey on the worth of all 102 teams in major league baseball, the NFL, NBA and NHL.

Based on earnings posted through 1990, the New York Yankees were listed as the most valuable team in sports, with an estimated worth of $225 million. Although the Yankees were only ninth in gate receipts and 14th in stadium revenue in 1990, they benefited from lucrative local broadcast and cable TV packages.

The Miami Dolphins were second at $205 million, followed by five teams with a value of $200 each—the New York Mets, Los Angeles Dodgers, Los Angeles Lakers and surprisingly, the Baltimore Orioles and Green Bay Packers.

Only one NFL team, the New England Patriots, was valued at less than $100 million, though at $99.8 million the Pats were close. The NHL had the two lowest-ranked franchises—the Minnesota North Stars and the Winnipeg Jets—both valued at $30 million. In fact, 15 of the NHL's 21 teams were valued at less than the $50 million expansion fee charged to Ottawa and Tampa.

One other ownership note: Bertram Lee, who was NBA commissioner David Stern's choice in 1989 to become the first black owner of a major league team, was ousted as co-owner of the Denver Nuggets in April when he failed to meet his share of a $5 million capital call. Peter Bynoe, who is also black, remains managing general partner.

The NBA opened the 1991-92 season with a new arena in Salt Lake City, where the Utah Jazz left the 12,616-seat Salt Palace for the wide open spaces of the 19,500-seat Delta Center. Delta Airlines paid an undisclosed amount to be the corporate sponsor for the $66 million building.

The Phoenix Suns are scheduled to move into a new 19,000-seat arena of their own in 1992-93. Originally named the America West Arena, the $89 million facility has been without a name since corporate sponsor America West Airlines filed for bankruptcy in July.

Suns' owner Jerry Colangelo said that the deal with American West was strictly an advertising agreement and would not affect the construction of the arena.

Wide World Photos

Michael Jordan, everybody's Most Valuable Pitchman, earned $13.2 million off the court in 1990-91.

Meanwhile in Seattle, the Ackerley family, which owns the SuperSonics, announced it was abandoning plans to build a new $100 million arena for a variety of reasons, including the sluggish economy and a number of local challenges to fight their bid for a building permit.

Speaking of the high cost of playing facilities, NFL commissioner Paul Tagliabue told Will McDonough of *The Boston Globe* in July that the league was thinking about getting into the construction game.

"I think the time is here for the league to get into the stadium-building business," said Tagliabue. "States and cities no longer can afford to finance and build stadiums. The money just isn't there. Times are tough."

The NFL's first construction project may be to replace 20-year-old Foxboro Stadium in New England. Patriots' owner Victor Kiam has threatened to move the team to Jacksonville, Fla., if the Pats can't get a new stadium deal that includes the luxury boxes and preferred seating needed to generate the money it takes to compete these days.

"Tell the governor I'll be calling him shortly," Tagliabue told McDonough. "We have to get something done up there." □

The Forbes' Top 40

The 40 highest-paid athletes of 1990-91 (including salary, winnings, endorsements, etc.) according to the Aug.19, 1991 issue of *Forbes* Magazine. Nationality, birthdate and each athlete's 1990 rank are also listed. Age refers to athlete's age as of Aug.1, 1991.

		Sport	Salary/ Winnings	Other Income	Total	Nat	Birthdate (Age)	1990 Rank
1	Evander Holyfield	Boxing	$60.0	$0.5	$60.5	USA	Oct.19, 1962 (28)	10
2	Mike Tyson	Boxing	30.0	1.5	31.5	USA	Jan.30, 1966 (25)	1
3	Michael Jordan	Basketball	2.8	13.2	16.0	USA	Feb.17, 1963 (28)	8
4	George Foreman	Boxing	14.0	0.5	14.5	USA	Jan.10, 1949 (42)	—
5	Ayrton Senna	Auto Racing	12.0	1.0	13.0	BRA	Mar.21, 1960 (31)	4
6	Alain Prost	Auto Racing	10.0	1.0	11.0	FRA	Feb.24, 1955 (26)	5
7	Razor Ruddock	Boxing	10.0	0.2	10.2	USA	Dec.21, 1963 (27)	—
8	Arnold Palmer	Golf	0.3	9.0	9.3	USA	Sep.10, 1929 (61)	9
9	Nigel Mansell	Auto Racing	8.0	1.0	9.0	GBR	Aug. 8, 1953 (37)	12
10	Jack Nicklaus	Golf	0.5	8.0	8.5	USA	Jan.21, 1940 (51)	6
11	Larry Bird	Basketball	7.4	0.5	7.9	USA	Dec. 7, 1956 (34)	—
12	Monica Seles	Tennis	1.6	6.0	7.6	YUG	Dec. 2, 1973 (17)	—
13	Joe Montana	Football	3.5	4.0	7.5	USA	Jun.11, 1956 (35)	25
14	Stefan Edberg	Tennis	1.4	6.0	7.4	SWE	Jan.19, 1966 (25)	17
	Greg Norman	Golf	0.4	7.0	7.4	AUS	Feb.10, 1955 (36)	7
16	Steffi Graf	Tennis	1.3	6.0	7.3	GER	Jun.14, 1969 (22)	13
	Andre Agassi	Tennis	0.8	6.5	7.3	USA	Apr.29, 1970 (21)	16
18	Boris Becker	Tennis	1.2	6.0	7.2	GER	Nov.22, 1967 (23)	11
19	Gerhard Berger	Auto Racing	6.0	1.0	7.0	AUT	Aug.27, 1959 (31)	28
	Wayne Gretzky	Hockey	3.0	4.0	7.0	CAN	Jan.26, 1961 (30)	15
21	Jean Alesi	Auto Racing	6.0	0.5	6.5	FRA	Jun.11, 1964 (27)	—
22	Gabriela Sabatini	Tennis	1.3	5.0	6.3	ARG	May 16, 1970 (21)	22
23	Magic Johnson	Basketball	2.5	3.0	5.5	USA	Aug.14, 1959 (31)	23
24	David Robinson	Basketball	2.4	3.0	5.4	USA	Aug. 6, 1965 (25)	—
	Nick Faldo	Golf	0.4	5.0	5.4	GBR	Jul.18, 1957 (34)	—
26	Jennifer Capriati	Tennis	0.6	4.5	5.1	USA	Mar.29, 1976 (15)	—
27	Rocket Ismail	Football	4.5	0.5	5.0	USA	Nov.18, 1969 (21)	—
	Patrick Ewing	Basketball	4.0	1.0	5.0	USA	Aug. 5, 1962 (28)	26
29	Hot Rod Williams	Basketball	4.8	0.1	4.9	USA	Aug. 9, 1961 (29)	—
30	Ivan Lendl	Tennis	0.8	4.0	4.8	CZE	Mar. 7, 1960 (31)	18
31	Bo Jackson	Baseball & Football	2.0	2.5	4.5	USA	Nov.30, 1962 (28)	21
32	Pete Sampras	Tennis	0.4	4.0	4.4	USA	Aug.12, 1971 (19)	—
33	Hakeem Olajuwon	Basketball	3.8	0.5	4.3	NGR	Jan.21, 1963 (28)	—
	Darryl Strawberry	Baseball	3.8	0.5	4.3	USA	Mar.12, 1962 (29)	—
	Greg LeMond	Cycling	1.8	2.5	4.3	USA	Jun.26, 1961 (30)	27
36	Will Clark	Baseball	3.8	0.4	4.2	USA	Mar.13, 1964 (27)	30
	Nelson Piquet	Auto Racing	4.0	0.2	4.2	BRA	Aug.17, 1952 (38)	—
38	Kevin Mitchell	Baseball	3.8	0.3	4.1	USA	Jan.13, 1962 (29)	—
39	Curtis Strange	Golf	0.5	3.5	4.0	USA	Jan.30, 1955 (36)	29
40	Joe Carter	Baseball	3.7	0.2	3.9	USA	Mar. 7, 1960 (31)	—

1990-91 Top 25 Prime Time TV Series

Final 1990-91 prime time network television ratings, according to Nielsen Media Research. Covers period from Sept.17, 1990 through April 14, 1991, and includes all series of 12 episodes or more. Events are listed with ratings points and audience share; each ratings point represents 931,000 households and shares indicate percentage of TV sets in use.

	Series	Net	Rating	Share		Series	Net	Rating	Share
1	Cheers	NBC	21.6	34	14	Unsolved Mysteries	NBC	16.2	26
2	60 Minutes	CBS	20.5	34	15	Full House	ABC	16.0	28
3	Roseanne	ABC	18.2	28	16	Family Matters	ABC	15.8	27
4	A Different World	NBC	17.9	29	17	**Coach**	ABC	15.5	24
5	The Cosby Show	NBC	17.4	28		Matlock	NBC	15.5	24
6	**Monday Night Football**	ABC	17.2	30	19	In the Heat of the Night	NBC	15.2	24
7	Funniest Home Videos	ABC	17.0	26	20	Major Dad	CBS	14.9	23
8	Murphy Brown	CBS	16.9	26	21	L.A. Law	NBC	14.8	26
9	Empty Nest	NBC	16.7	30		CBS Sunday Movie	CBS	14.8	24
	Designing Women	CBS	16.7	26		Who's the Boss?	ABC	14.8	24
	Funniest People	ABC	16.7	25		Doogie Howser, M.D.	ABC	14.8	23
12	Golden Girls	NBC	16.6	29	25	Grand	NBC	14.6	24
13	Murder, She Wrote	CBS	16.4	25					

1990-91 Top 50 TV Sports Events

Final 1990-91 network television ratings for sports events, according to Nielsen Media Research. Covers period from Sept.17, 1990 through Aug.1, 1991. Events are listed with ratings points and audience share; each ratings point represents 931,000 households and shares indicate percentage of TV sets in use.

		Date	Net	Rtg/Sh				Date	Net	Rtg/Sh
1	**Super Bowl XXV** (Bills vs Giants)	1/27	ABC	41.9/63		27	**NFL Thanksgiving** (Redskins at Cowboys)	11/22	CBS	14.7/42
2	**NFC Championship** (Giants at 49ers)	1/20	CBS	28.5/49		28	**NFL Reg.Season Early Game** (Various teams)	Season	CBS	14.6/37
3	**AFC Semifinal** (Bengals at Raiders)	1/13	NBC	24.7/47		29	**Baseball NLCS Game 5** (Reds at Pirates)	10/10	CBS	14.5/24
4	**NFC First Round** (Saints at Bears)	1/6	CBS	24.2/46		30	**Baseball ALCS Game 2** (A's at Red Sox)	10/7	CBS	14.2/24
5	**NFC Semifinal** (Bears at Giants)	1/13	CBS	22.6/52		31	**Monday Night Football** (Rams at Saints)	12/31	ABC	13.9/27
6	**AFC Championship** (Raiders at Bills)	12/31	NBC	22.0/46		32	**NFL Single Saturday** (Various teams)	*	NBC	13.3/34
7	**World Series Game 2** (A's at Reds)	10/17	CBS	21.8/37		33	**NFL Reg.Season Late Game** (Various teams)	Season	CBS	12.9/27
8	**World Series Game 4** (Reds at A's)	10/20	CBS	21.4/38			**Baseball NLCS Game 4** (Reds at Pirates)	10/9	CBS	12.9/21
9	**NFC Semifinal** (Redskins at 49ers)	1/12	CBS	21.2/41		35	**NCAA Final Four Semifinal** (Kansas vs.N.Carolina)	3/30	CBS	12.7/28
10	**World Series Game 1** (A's at Reds)	10/16	CBS	20.2/32		36	**NBA Finals Game 1** (Lakers at Bulls)	6/2	NBC	12.6/35
11	**AFC First Round** (Chiefs at Dolphins)	1/6	ABC	19.9/41			**NCAA Tournament Sunday** (Various teams)	**	CBS	12.6/26
12	**NBA Finals Game 5** (Bulls at Lakers)	6/12	NBC	19.7/36		38	**Baseball ALCS Game 1** (A's at Red Sox)	10/6	CBS	12.3/24
13	**World Series Game 3** (Reds at A's)	10/19	CBS	19.4/35		39	**NFL Reg.Season Late Game** (Various teams)	Season	NBC	12.2/26
	NCAA Championship (Duke vs Kansas)	4/1	ABC	19.4/30			**Baseball NLCS Game 1** (Pirates at Reds)	10/4	CBS	12.2/21
15	**AFC First Round** (Oilers at Bengals)	1/6	NBC	18.5/44		41	**Rose Bowl** (Washington vs.Iowa)	1/1	ABC	11.9/21
16	**AFC Semifinal** (Dolphins at Bills)	1/12	NBC	18.3/42		42	**NBA Western Final Game 6** (Blazers at Lakers)	5/30	NBC	11.8/22
	Orange Bowl (Colo.vs N.Dame)	1/1	NBC	18.3/30		43	**NFL Regular Season** (Chiefs at Bears)	12/29	NBC	11.7/32
18	**Baseball All-Star Game** (at Toronto)	7/9	CBS	17.4/32		44	**NFL Regular Season** (Eagles at Cardinals)	12/29	CBS	11.3/26
19	**NFC First Round** (Redskins at Eagles)	1/5	ABC	17.2/42			**Saturday Night Football** (Redskins at Colts)	12/22	ABC	11.3/21
	Monday Night Football (Various teams)	Season	ABC	17.2/30		46	**NFL Single Sunday** (Various teams)	***	NBC	10.9/28
21	**NBA Finals Game 2** (Lakers at Bulls)	6/5	NBC	16.1/29		47	**NFL Regular Season** (Lions at Packers)	12/22	CBS	10.6/31
22	**NBA Finals Game 3** (Bulls at Lakers)	6/7	NBC	15.7/31		48	**College Football** (Notre Dame at USC)	11/24	ABC	10.1/19
	NCAA Semifinal (Duke vs UNLV)	3/30	CBS	15.7/29			**NBA Western Finals Game 5** (Lakers at Portland)	5/28	NBC	10.1/18
24	**NFL Thanksgiving** (Broncos at Lions)	11/22	NBC	15.5/44		50	**Florida Citrus Bowl** (Ga.Tech vs Nebraska)	1/1	ABC	9.7/21
25	**NBA Finals Game 4** (Bulls at Lakers)	6/9	NBC	15.2/30			**World Figure Skating** (at Munich)	3/17	NBC	9.7/16
	Baseball NLCS Game 6 (Pirates at Reds)	10/12	CBS	15.2/27						

*__NFL Single Saturday__ refers to the combined rating of the Dec.15, 22 and 29 regular season telecasts on NBC.
**__NCAA Tournament Sunday__ refers to the combined rating of the March 17 and 24 telecasts on CBS.
***__NFL Single Sunday__ refers to the combined rating of all regular season non-doubleheader Sundays on NBC.

1990-91 Top 5 Cable TV Sports Events

Final 1990-91 cable television ratings for sports events, according to ESPN and Turner Sports research. Covers period from Sept. 1, 1990 through Aug. 31, 1991.

NFL Telecasts

		Date	Net	Rtg
1	Pittsburgh at Houston	12/30	ESPN	13.8
2	San Francisco at Dallas	11/11	ESPN	13.1
3	Philadelphia at Miami	12/9	ESPN	12.5
4	Green Bay at Minnesota	12/2	ESPN	11.1
5	Chicago at Detroit	12/16	ESPN	10.6

Non-NFL Telecasts

		Date	Net	Rtg
1	NBA: Detroit-Chicago	5/21	TNT	6.5
	CFA: Notre Dame-Pitt.	10/27	ESPN	6.5
	CFA: Penn St-Notre Dame	11/17	ESPN	6.5
4	CFA: Miami-BYU	9/8	ESPN	5.9
5	Bowl: Ohio St-Air Force	12/27	ESPN	5.4

All-Time Top-Rated TV Programs

NFL Football dominates television's All-Time Top-Rated 50 Programs with 18 Super Bowls and the 1981 NFC Championship Game making the list. Rankings based on surveys taken from July, 1960 through Jan.31, 1991; include only sponsored programs seen on individual networks; and programs under 30 minutes scheduled duration are excluded. Programs are listed with ratings points, audience share and number of households watching, according to Nielsen Media Research.

Multiple entries: The Super Bowl (18); "The Beverly Hillbillies" and "Roots" (7); "The Thorn Birds" (3); "The Bob Hope Christmas Show," "The Ed Sullivan Show" and "Gone With the Wind" (2).

	Program	Episode/Game	Net	Date	Rating	Share	Households
1	M*A*S*H (series)	Final episode	CBS	2/28/83	60.2	77	50,150,000
2	Dallas (series)	"Who Shot J.R.?"	CBS	11/21/80	53.3	76	41,470,000
3	Roots (mini-series)	Part 8	ABC	1/30/77	51.1	71	36,380,000
4	Super Bowl XVI	49ers 26, Bengals 21	CBS	1/24/82	49.1	73	40,020,000
5	Super Bowl XVII	Redskins 27, Dolphins 17	NBC	1/30/83	48.6	69	40,480,000
6	Super Bowl XX	Bears 46, Patriots 10	NBC	1/26/86	48.3	70	41,490,000
7	Gone With the Wind (movie)	Part 1	NBC	11/7/76	47.7	65	33,960,000
8	Gone with the Wind (movie)	Part 2	NBC	11/8/76	47.4	64	33,750,000
9	Super Bowl XII	Cowboys 27, Broncos 10	CBS	1/15/78	47.2	67	34,410,000
10	Super Bowl XIII	Steelers 35, Cowboys 31	NBC	1/21/79	47.1	74	35,090,000
11	Bob Hope Special	Christmas Show	NBC	1/15/70	46.6	64	27,260,000
12	Super Bowl XVIII	Raiders 38, Redskins 9	CBS	1/22/84	46.4	71	38,800,000
	Super Bowl XIX	49ers 38, Dolphins 16	ABC	1/20/85	46.4	63	39,390,000
14	Super Bowl XIV	Steelers 31, Rams 19	CBS	1/20/80	46.3	67	35,330,000
15	ABC Theater (special)	"The Day After"	ABC	11/20/83	46.0	62	38,550,000
16	Roots (mini-series)	Part 6	ABC	1/28/77	45.9	66	32,680,000
	The Fugitive (series)	Final episode	ABC	8/29/67	45.9	72	25,700,000
18	Super Bowl XXI	Giants 39, Broncos 20	CBS	1/25/87	45.8	66	40,030,000
19	Roots (mini-series)	Part 5	ABC	1/27/77	45.7	71	32,540,000
20	The Ed Sullivan Show	Beatles' 1st appearance	CBS	2/9/64	45.3	60	23,240,000
21	Bob Hope Special	Christmas Show	NBC	1/14/71	45.0	61	27,050,000
22	Roots (mini-series)	Part 3	ABC	1/25/77	44.8	68	31,900,000
23	Super Bowl XI	Raiders 32, Vikings 14	NBC	1/9/77	44.4	73	31,610,000
	Super Bowl XV	Raiders 27, Eagles 10	NBC	1/25/81	44.4	63	34,540,000
25	Super Bowl VI	Cowboys 24, Dolphins 3	CBS	1/16/72	44.2	74	27,450,000
26	Roots (mini-series)	Part 2	ABC	1/24/77	44.1	62	31,400,000
27	The Beverly Hillbillies	Regular episode	CBS	1/8/64	44.0	65	22,570,000
28	Roots (mini-series)	Part 4	ABC	1/26/77	43.8	66	31,190,000
	The Ed Sullivan Show	Beatles' 2nd appearance	CBS	2/16/64	43.8	60	22,445,000
30	Super Bowl XXIII	49ers 20, Bengals 16	NBC	1/22/89	43.5	68	39,320,000
31	The Academy Awards	John Wayne wins Oscar	ABC	4/7/70	43.4	78	25,390,000
32	Thorn Birds (mini-series)	Part 3	ABC	3/29/83	43.2	62	35,990,000
33	Thorn Birds (mini-series)	Part 4	ABC	3/30/83	43.1	62	35,900,000
34	NFC Championship Game	49ers 28, Cowboys 27	CBS	1/10/82	42.9	62	34,940,000
35	The Beverly Hillbillies	Regular episode	CBS	1/15/64	42.8	62	21,960,000
36	Super Bowl VII	Dolphins 14, Redskins 7	NBC	1/14/73	42.7	72	27,670,000
37	Thorn Birds (mini-series)	Part 2	ABC	3/28/83	42.5	59	35,400,000
38	Super Bowl IX	Steelers 16, Vikings 6	NBC	1/12/75	42.4	72	29,040,000
	The Beverly Hillbillies	Regular episode	CBS	2/26/64	42.4	60	21,750,000
40	Super Bowl X	Steelers 21, Cowboys 17	CBS	1/18/76	42.3	78	29,440,000
	ABC Sunday Night Movie	"Airport"	ABC	11/11/73	42.3	63	28,000,000
	ABC Sunday Night Movie	"Love Story"	ABC	10/1/72	42.3	62	27,410,000
	Cinderella	Musical special	CBS	2/22/65	42.3	59	22,250,000
	Roots (mini-series)	Part 7	ABC	1/29/77	42.3	65	30,120,000
45	The Beverly Hillbillies	Regular episode	CBS	3/25/64	42.2	59	21,650,000
46	The Beverly Hillbillies	Regular episode	CBS	2/6/64	42.0	61	21,550,000
47	Super Bowl XXV	Giants 20, Bills 19	ABC	1/27/91	41.9	63	39,010,000
	The Beverly Hillbillies	Regular episode	CBS	1/29/64	41.9	62	21,490,000
	Super Bowl XXII	Redskins 42, Broncos 10	ABC	1/31/88	41.9	62	37,120,000
50	Miss America Pageant	Miss Michigan wins	CBS	9/9/61	41.8	75	19,600,000
	The Beverly Hillbillies	Regular episode	CBS	1/1/64	41.8	59	21,440,000

All-Time Top 5 Cable TV Sports Events

All-time cable television ratings for sports events, according to ESPN and Turner Sports research. Covers period from Sept. 1, 1980 through Aug. 31, 1991.

NFL Telecasts

		Date	Net	Rtg
1	Chicago at Minnesota	12/6/87	ESPN	17.6
2	Chicago at Minnesota	12/3/89	ESPN	14.7
3	Cleveland at San Fran	11/29/87	ESPN	14.2
4	Pittsburgh at Houston	12/30/90	ESPN	13.8
5	Three games tied		ESPN	13.1

Non-NFL Telecasts

		Date	Net	Rtg
1	NBA: Detroit-Boston	6/1/88	TBS	8.8
2	NBA: Chicago-Detroit	5/31/89	TBS	8.2
3	NBA: Detroit-Boston	5/26/88	TBS	8.1
4	NCAA: G'town-St.John's	2/27/85	ESPN	8.0
5	MLB: SF-Atlanta	9/27/83	TBS	7.7

Who Has What in 1991-92

The network-by-network roster of TV rights as of Sept.1, 1991.

ABC

Auto Racing—Indianapolis 500.
Bowling—PBA Winter and Spring Tours.
NCAA Basketball—Regular season.
Cycling—Tour de France (probable).
NFL Football—Monday Night Football; 1st Round of NFL Playoffs; WLAF Spring Football.
College Football—Big 10/Pac-10 regular season; CFA (except Notre Dame home games); Rose Bowl; Sugar Bowl.
Golf—U.S. Open; British Open; U.S. Senior Open; U.S. Women's Open; PGA Skins; Seniors Skins; LPGA Skins.
Horse Racing—Kentucky Derby; Preakness; Belmont Stakes.
Yachting—1992 America's Cup (1st race of Final).

CBS

Auto Racing—Daytona 500.
Major League Baseball—Regular season; All-Star Game; AL and NL Playoffs; World Series.
NCAA Basketball—Regular season; NCAA Tournament.
NFL Football—NFC regular season; NFC Playoffs; 1992 Super Bowl.
College Football—Army-Navy Game; Blockbuster Bowl; Cotton Bowl.
Golf—PGA Tour; Masters; PGA Championship.
Olympics—1992 (Albertville) and 1994 (Lillehammer) Winter Games.
Tennis—US Open.

NBC

NBA Basketball—Regular season; All-Star Game; playoffs; NBA Finals.
NCAA Basketball—Regular season.
Bowling—PBA Fall Tour.
Figure Skating—European Championships; World Championships.
NFL Football—AFC regular season; AFC playoffs; 1993 Super Bowl.
College Football—Notre Dame home games, Heisman Trophy Show; Fiesta Bowl; Orange Bowl.
Golf—Ryder Cup; Players Championship; PGA, Seniors Championship; LPGA Championship.
Horse Racing—Breeders' Cup.
Olympics—1992 Summer Games (Barcelona); all 1992 U.S. Olympic trials; Tournament of the Americas basketball qualifiers.
Tennis—French Open; Wimbledon.
Volleyball—AVP Pro Beach Tour.

ESPN

Alpine Skiing—World Cup.
Auto Racing—CART; NASCAR; Formula One.
Major League Baseball—Regular season.
College Basketball—Regular season.
Bowling—PBA and LPBT tours.
Boxing—Top Rank series.
NFL Football—Sunday Night Football (2nd half of season); Pro Bowl.
College Football—Regular season CFA, Big 10 and Pac-10; 4 bowl games.
Golf—U.S. Open and British Open (early rounds); PGA, Senior and LPGA tours.
Tennis—Australian Open and French Open (early rounds); Davis Cup; Grand Slam Cup.
Yachting—1992 America's Cup (Challenger and Defender races and Cup Final).

Turner

Auto Racing—NASCAR on TBS.
Major League Baseball—Atlanta Braves on TBS.
NBA Basketball—Regular season on TNT; Playoffs on TNT; Atlanta Hawks on TBS.
NFL Football—Sunday Night Football (1st half of season) on TNT.
College Football—SEC regular season on TBS.
Golf—PGA early rounds on TBS.
Goodwill Games—1994 (USSR) on TBS.
Olympics—cable coverage of 1992 (Albertville) and 1994 (Lillehammer) Winter Games on TNT.

HBO

Boxing—Championship Fights.
NFL Football—"Inside the NFL" (series)
Tennis—Wimbledon (early rounds).

USA Network

Boxing—Tuesday Night Fights.
NFL Football—WLAF Spring Football.
Golf—Ryder Cup (early rounds); Masters (early rounds).
Tennis—U.S. Open (early rounds).

Prime Network

NCAA Basketball—Regular season; conference tournaments.
NCAA Football—Big 8, Pac-10 and SWC regular season.
Golf—European PGA Tour.
Tennis—ATP and Virginia Slims tours.
Volleyball—AVP Pro Beach Tour.

Olympic Games TV Rights

The reported cost of securing exclusive U.S. television rights for the Olympic Games has skyrocketed over the last 30 years. In 1960, CBS paid $50,000 for the Winter Olympics. In 1989, CBS agreed to pay $300 million for the 1994 Winter Games—an increase of 6,000 percent. In the same time, the cost of the Summer Games has gone from just under $400,000 to just over $400 million.

Year	Games	Location	Rights Fee	Net	Year	Games	Location	Rights Fee	Net
1960	Winter	Squaw Valley	$ 50,000	CBS	1984	Winter	Sarajevo	$ 91,500,000	ABC
	Summer	Rome	394,000	CBS		Summer	Los Angeles	$225,000,000	ABC
1964	Winter	Innsbruck	$ 597,000	ABC	1988	Winter	Calgary	$309,000,000	ABC
	Summer	Tokyo	1,500,000	NBC		Summer	Seoul	$300,000,000	NBC
1968	Winter	Grenoble	$2,500,000	ABC	1992	Winter	Albertville	$243,000,000	CBS
	Summer	Mexico City	4,500,000	ABC		Summer	Barcelona	$401,000,000	NBC
1972	Winter	Sapporo	$6,400,000	NBC	1994	Winter	Lillehammer	$300,000,000	CBS
	Summer	Munich	7,500,000	ABC	1996	Summer	Atlanta	To be determined	
1976	Winter	Innsbruck	$10,000,000	ABC	1998	Winter	Nagano	To be determined	
	Summer	Montreal	25,000,000	ABC					
1980	Winter	Lake Placid	$15,500,000	ABC					
	Summer	Moscow	85,000,000	NBC					

Note: Since the U.S. boycotted the 1980 Summer Olympics, NBC did not cover the Games and did not pay the rights fee.

AWARDS

The Peabody Award

Presented annually since 1940 for outstanding achievement in radio and television broadcasting. Only 11 Peabodys have been given for sports programming.

Named after Georgia banker and philanthropist George Foster Peabody, the awards are administered by the Henry W.Grady College of Journalism and Mass Communication at the University of Georgia.

Television

Year
1960 **CBS** for coverage of 1960 Winter and Summer Olympic Games (for Outstanding Contribution to International Understanding).
1966 ABC's **"Wide World of Sports"** (for Outstanding Achievement in Promotion of International Understanding).
1968 **ABC Sports** coverage of both the 1968 Winter and Summer Olympic Games.
1972 **ABC Sports** coverage of the 1972 Summer Olympics in Munich.
1973 **Joe Garagiola** of NBC Sports (for "The Baseball World of Joe Garagiola").
1976 **ABC Sports** coverage of both the 1976 Winter and Summer Olympic Games.
1984 **Roone Arledge**, president of ABC News & Sports (for significant contributions to television news and sports programming.
1986 **WFAA-TV,** Dallas for its investigation of the Southern Methodist University football program.
1988 **Jim McKay** of ABC Sports (for pioneering efforts and career accomplishments in the world of TV sports).

Radio

Year
1974 **WSB** radio in Atlanta for "Henry Aaron: A Man with a Mission."
1991 **Red Barber** of National Public Radio (for his six decades as a broadcaster and his 10 years as a commentator on NPR's "Morning Edition").

National Emmy Awards
Sports Programs

Presented by the Academy of Television Arts and Sciences since 1948. Eligibility period covered the calendar year from 1948-57 and since 1988.

Multiple Major Award Winners: ABC "Wide World of Sports" (18); ABC Olympic Coverage (9); CBS NFL Coverage (7); NFL Films Football Coverage (5); ABC "Monday Night Football" (4); ABC "The American Sportsman," ABC Indianapolis 500 Coverage, and CBS NCAA Basketball Coverage (3); ABC Kentucky Derby Coverage, and NBC World Series Coverage (2).

1949
Coverage—"Wrestling"(KTLA, Los Angeles)

1950
Program—"Rams Football" (KNBH-TV, Los Angeles)

1954
Program—"Gillette Cavalcade of Sports" (NBC)

1965-66
Programs—"Wide World of Sports" (ABC), "Shell's Wonderful World of Golf" (NBC) and "CBS Golf Classic" (CBS)

1966-67
Program—"Wide World of Sports" (ABC)

1967-68
Program—"Wide World of Sports" (ABC)

1968-69
Program—"1968 Summer Olympics" (ABC)

1969-70
Programs—"NFL Football" (CBS) and "Wide World of Sports" (ABC)

1970-71
Program—"Wide World of Sports" (ABC)

1971-72
Program—"Wide World of Sports" (ABC)

1972-73
News Special—"Coverage of Munich Olympic Tragedy" (ABC)
Sports Programs—"1972 Summer Olympics" (ABC) and "Wide World of Sports" (ABC)

1973-74
Program—"Wide World of Sports" (ABC)

1974-75
Non-Edited—"Jimmy Connors vs. Rod Laver Tennis Challenge" (CBS)
Edited—"Wide World of Sports" (ABC)

1975-76
Live Special—"1975 World Series" (NBC)
Live Series—"NFL Monday Night Football" (ABC)
Edited Specials—"1976 Winter Olympics" (ABC) and "Triumph and Tragedy: The Olympic Experience" (ABC)
Edited Series—"Wide World of Sports" (ABC)

1976-77
Live Special—"1976 Summer Olympics" (ABC)
Live Series—"The NFL Today/NFL Football" (CBS)
Edited Special—"1976 Summer Olympics Preview" (ABC)
Edited Series—"The Olympiad" (PBS)

1977-78
Live Special—"Muhammad Ali vs. Leon Spinks Heavyweight Championship Fight (CBS)
Live Series—"The NFL Today/NFL Football" (CBS)
Edited Special—"The Impossible Dream: Ballooning Across the Atlantic" (CBS)
Edited Series—"The Way It Was" (PBS)

1978-79
Live Special—"Super Bowl XIII—Pittsburgh vs Dallas" (NBC)
Live Series—"NFL Monday Night Football" (ABC)
Edited Special—"Spirit of '78: The Flight of Double Eagle II" (ABC)
Edited Series—"The American Sportsman" (ABC)

A Peabody In The Peapatch

by Curt Smith

Walter Lanier (Red) Barber won a Peabody Award in March for his commentary on the National Public Radio Network. The honor delighted, but did not surprise, anyone familiar with the Ol' Redhead. The reason: for nearly 60 years, Red Barber has made listening to sports an almost existential pleasure.

Barber started his broadcasting career in 1934 at Cincinnati—via the hypnotic fabric of Western Union, re-creating Reds' road games with poetry and charm. From the start, he was different—"a class act, no-nonsense," said Ernie Harwell. "What impressed me was his absolute bid for perfection."

Born in Mississippi in 1908 and educated in Florida, Barber attracted listeners with soft, rhythmic accents and a steadfast contempt for provincialism.

He moved to Ebbets Field in 1939 and Yankee Stadium in 1954, called five All-Star Games and 13 World Series, and taught several generations of fans the language of baseball. In 1978, he became the first of two broadcasters—his frequent partner Mel Allen was the other—to be honored by the Hall of Fame.

Barber is often compared to Allen, but the links are tenuous at best. Mel was peanuts, popcorn, and the United States Marine Band. Red was pure honey and bluegrass music. Allen filibustered, brilliantly, for hours. Barber sat back on the small of his chair, a three-minute egg timer at his elbow (a constant reminder to give the score), and chatted, as around a pot-bellied stove, soft-voiced and evocative.

In Cincinnati, Barber covered baseball's first night game on May 24, 1935. Four years later, he became the voice of the Dodgers when Brooklyn president Larry MacPhail brought everyday baseball to New York City radios—ending a five-year ban on regular season broadcasts. With play-by-play blanketing the borough, Barber stirred a kinship and zealotry—a sense that baseball belonged to the fans—that was new to the game.

In Brooklyn, Barber described Jackie Robinson's historic rookie year in 1947 and talked from his catbird seat of *the peapatch, rhubarbs,* and *bases FOB* (full of Brooklyns).

Beverly Frick

Now 83, **Red Barber** has been a regular commentator on National Public Radio's "Morning Edition" since 1981.

He also aired surpassing moments in baseball history, like Cookie Lavagetto's hit to wreck Bill Beven's no-hitter in Game 4 of the 1947 World Series, and Al Gionfriddo's robbery of Joe DiMaggio ("Oh-ho, Doctor!") in Game 6 of the same Series.

But baseball wasn't all Barber did. He also covered college and pro football and was hired by none other than Edward R. Murrow in 1946 to replace Ted Husing as sports director at CBS Radio.

Twenty years later, he was working for CBS again following the network's decision to buy the Yankees in 1965. By 1966, however, the team had fallen on hard times and Barber was fired after reporting to both his TV and radio audiences that the "crowd" at the final home game of the season was only 413—the smallest ever at Yankee Stadium.

"The Yankees presented me with the greatest gift I could think of," Barber said later. "They gave me back my life."

Since then, he has written hundreds of newspaper columns, authored seven books, and in 1981, became a Friday morning fixture on NPR's popular "Morning Edition."

At eighty-three, Red Barber is still a household word. And his voice the voice of a friend.

Curt Smith is a speechwriter for President Bush and the author of the definitive book on baseball broadcasting, *Voices of The Game.*

National Emmy Awards (Cont.)

1979-80

Live Special—"1980 Winter Olympics" (ABC)
Live Series—"NCAA College Football" (ABC)
Edited Special—"Gossamer Albatross: Flight of Imagination" (CBS)
Edited Series—"NFL Game of the Week" (NFL Films)

1980-81

Live Special—"1981 Kentucky Derby" (ABC)
Live Series—"PGA Golf Tour" (CBS)
Edited Special—"Wide World of Sports 20th Anniversary Show" (ABC)
Edited Series—"The American Sportsman" (ABC)

1981-82

Live Special—"1982 NCAA Basketball Final: North Carolina vs Georgetown" (CBS)
Live Series—"NFL Football" (CBS)
Edited Special—"1982 Indianapolis 500" (ABC)
Edited Series—"Wide World of Sports" (ABC)

1982-83

Live Special—"1982 World Series" (NBC)
Live Series—"NFL Football" (CBS)
Edited Special—"Wimbledon '83" (NBC)
Edited Series—"Wide World of Sports" (ABC)

1983-84

No awards given

1984-85

Live Special—"1984 Summer Olympics" (ABC)
Live Series—No award given
Edited Special—"Road to the Super Bowl '85" (NFL Films)
Edited Series—"The American Sportsman" (ABC)

1985-86

No awards given

1986-87

Live Special—"1987 Daytona 500" (CBS)
Live Series—"NFL Football" (CBS)
Edited Special—"Wide World of Sports 25th Anniversary Special (ABC)
Edited Series—"Wide World of Sports" (ABC)

1987-88

Live Special—"1987 Kentucky Derby" (ABC)
Live Series—"NFL Monday Night Football" (ABC)
Edited Special—"Paris Roubaix Bike Race" (CBS)
Edited Series—"Wide World of Sports" (ABC)

1988

LIve Special— "1988 Summer Olympics" (NBC)
Live Series—"1988 NCAA Basketball" (CBS)
Edited Special—"Road to the Super Bowl '88" (NFL Films)
Edited Series—"Wide World of Sports" (ABC)
Studio Show—"NFL GameDay" (ESPN)

1989

Live Special—"1989 Indianapolis 500" (ABC)
Live Series—"NFL Monday Night Football" (ABC)
Edited Special—"Trans-Antarctica! The International Expedition" (ABC)
Edited Series—"This is the NFL" (NFL Films)
Studio Show—"NFL Today" (CBS)

1990

Live Special—"1990 Indianapolis 500" (ABC)
Live Series—"1990 NCAA Basketball Tournament" (CBS)
Edited Special—"Road to Super Bowl XXIV" (NFL Films)
Edited Series—"Wide World of Sports" (ABC)
Studio Show—"SportsCenter" (ESPN)

Sportscasters

First presented as Outstanding Host/Commentator award for the 1967-68 TV season and given annually since 1972-73 (except in 1983-84 and 1985-86). Split into Host and Analyst awards for the 1980-81 season. Eligibility period has covered calendar year since 1988.
Multiple winners: Jim McKay (10); John Madden (8); Dick Enberg (3); Bob Costas and Al Michaels (2).

Season	Host/Commentator	Season	Host	Season	Analyst
1967-68	Jim McKay, ABC	1980-81	Dick Enberg, NBC	1980-81	Dick Button, ABC
1968-69	No award	1981-82	Jim McKay, ABC	1981-82	John Madden, CBS
		1982-83	Dick Enberg, NBC	1982-83	John Madden, CBS
1969-70	No award	1983-84	No award	1983-84	No award
1970-71	Jim McKay, ABC	1984-85	George Michael, NBC	1984-85	John Madden, CBS
	& Don Meredith, ABC	1985-86	No award	1985-86	No award
1971-72	No award	1986-87	Al Michaels, ABC	1986-87	John Madden, CBS
1972-73	Jim McKay, ABC	1987-88	Bob Costas, NBC	1987-88	John Madden, CBS
1973-74	Jim McKay, ABC	1988	Bob Costas, NBC	1988	John Madden, CBS
1974-75	Jim McKay, ABC	1989	Al Michaels, ABC	1989	John Madden, CBS
1975-76	Jim McKay, ABC	1990	Dick Enberg, NBC	1990	John Madden, CBS
1976-77	Frank Gifford, ABC				
1977-78	Jack Whitaker, CBS				
1978-79	Jim McKay, ABC				
1979-80	Jim McKay, ABC				

Life Achievement Award

For outstanding work as an exemplary sportscaster over many years.

Season		Season	
1989	Jim McKay	1990	Lindsay Nelson

News Commentary

Presented on special occasions to a sportscaster who distinguishes himself reporting a sports event that becomes a breaking news story.

Season	
1972-73	Jim McKay, ABC (Munich Olympics)

Note: Jim McKay has won a total of 13 Emmy awards: 10 for Host/Commentator, two for Sports Writing, and one for News Commentary.

Sportscaster of the Year
NSSA Award

Presented annually since 1959 by the National Sportscasters and Sportswriters Association, based in Salisbury, N.C. Voting is done by NSSA members and selected national media.

Multiple winners: Keith Jackson (5); Lindsey Nelson and Chris Schenkel (4); Bob Costas, Dick Enberg, Al Michaels and Vin Scully (3); Chris Berman, Curt Gowdy and Ray Scott (2).

Year		Year		Year	
1959	Lindsey Nelson, NBC	1972	Keith Jackson, ABC	1981	Dick Enberg, NBC
1960	Lindsey Nelson, NBC	1973	Keith Jackson, ABC	1982	Vin Scully, LA Dodgers/NBC
1961	Lindsey Nelson, NBC	1974	Keith Jackson, ABC	1983	Al Michaels, ABC
1963	Chris Schenkel, CBS	1975	Keith Jackson, ABC	1984	John Madden, CBS
1964	Chris Schenkel, ABC	1976	Keith Jackson, ABC	1985	Bob Costas, NBC
1965	Vin Scully, LA Dodgers	1977	Pat Summerall, CBS	1986	Al Michaels, ABC
1967	Chris Schenkel, ABC	1978	Vin Scully, LA Dodgers/CBS	1987	Bob Costas, NBC
1968	Ray Scott, CBS	1979	Dick Enberg, NBC	1988	Bob Costas, NBC
1969	Curt Gowdy, NBC			1989	Chris Berman, ESPN
1970	Chris Schenkel, ABC	1980	Dick Enberg, NBC	1990	Chris Berman, ESPN
1971	Ray Scott, CBS		& Al Michaels, ABC		

ASA Award

Presented annually since 1984 by the American Sportscasters Association, based in New York. Voting is done by ASA members and officials.

Multiple winners: Dick Enberg (4); Bob Costas (2).

Year		Year		Year	
1984	Dick Enberg, NBC	1987	Dick Enberg, NBC	1990	Dick Enberg, NBC
1985	Vin Scully, NBC & LA Dodgers	1988	No award	1991	Bob Costas, NBC
1986	Dick Enberg, NBC	1989	Bob Costas, NBC		

Best Newspaper Sports Sections of 1990

Winners of the annual Associated Press Sports Editors' contest for best daily and Sunday sports sections in newspapers of 175,000 circulation or more. Selections made by a national committee of APSE members and released on Mar.1, 1991.

Top 10 Dailies

Atlanta Journal-Constitution
Boston Globe
Dallas Morning News
Detroit Free Press
Ft.Lauderdale Sun Sentinel

Los Angeles Times
Miami Herald
Newsday
Orange County Register
USA Today

Honorable mention: Chicago Tribune; Dallas Times Herald; Detroit News; Houston Chronicle; Minneapolis Star-Tribune; Orlando Sentinel; Philadelphia Daily News; St.Petersburg Times; Seattle Times and Washington Post.

Top 10 Sunday

Atlanta Journal-Constitution
Baltimore Sun
Boston Globe
Dallas Morning News
Detroit News

Los Angeles Times
Louisville Courier-Journal
Miami Herald
Newsday
Washington Post

Honorable mention: Chicago Tribune; Ft.Lauderdale Sun-Sentinel; Ft.Worth Star-Telegram; Hartford Courant; Houston Chronicle; New York Times; Orange County Register; Orlando Sentinel; Palm Beach Post and Philadelphia Inquirer.

The Pulitzer Prize

The Pulitzer Prizes for journalism, letters and music have been presented annually since 1917 in the name of Joseph Pulitzer (1847-1911), the publisher of the New York World. Prizes are awarded by the president of Columbia University on the recommendation of a board of review.

Since 1917, eight Pulitzers have been awarded for newspaper sportswriting or reporting on sports-related general news.

Commentary
1976 **Red Smith,** NY Times, for his 1975 columns.
1981 **Dave Anderson,** NY Times, for his 1980 columns.
1990 **Jim Murray,** LA Times, for his 1989 columns.

General Reporting
1956 **Arthur Daley,** NY Times, for his 1955 "Sports of the Times" columns.

Investigative Reporting
1986 **Jeffrey Marx & Michael York,** Lexington (Ky.) Herald-Leader, for their 1985 investigation of the basketball program at the University of Kentucky and other major colleges.

News Coverage
1935 **Bill Taylor,** NY Herald Tribune, for reporting on the 1934 America's Cup yacht races.

Special Citation
1952 **Max Kase,** NY Journal-American, for his reporting on the 1951 college basketball point-shaving scandal.

Specialized Reporting
1985 **Randall Savage & Jackie Crosby,** Macon (Ga.) Telegraph and News, for their 1984 investigation of athletics and academics at the University of Georgia and Georgia Tech.

King Features Syndicate

Jim Borgman of the *Cincinnati Enquirer* won the 1991 Pulitzer Prize for editorial cartooning. Borgman's 10 winning cartoons included the one above, which makes fun of the difficulties the NFL and Cincinnati Bengals had with women sportswriters in the locker room in 1990.

Sportswriter of the Year
NSSA Award

Presented annually since 1959 by the National Sportscasters and Sportswriters Association, based in Salisbury, N.C. Voting is done by NSSA members and selected national media.

Multiple winners: Jim Murray (14); Frank Deford (6); Red Smith (5); Will Grimsley (4); Peter Gammons (2).

Year	Year	Year
1959 Red Smith, NY Herald-Tribune	1970 Jim Murray, LA Times	1980 Will Grimsley, AP
1960 Red Smith, NY Herald-Tribune	1971 Jim Murray, LA Times	1981 Will Grimsley, AP
1961 Red Smith, NY Herald-Tribune	1972 Jim Murray, LA Times	1982 Frank Deford, Sports Ill.
1962 Red Smith, NY Herald-Tribune	1973 Jim Murray, LA Times	1983 Will Grimsley, AP
1963 Arthur Daley, NY Times	1974 Jim Murray, LA Times	1984 Frank Deford, Sports Ill.
1964 Jim Murray, LA Times	1975 Jim Murray, LA Times	1985 Frank Deford, Sports Ill.
1965 Red Smith, NY Herald-Tribune	1976 Jim Murray, LA Times	1986 Frank Deford, Sports Ill.
1966 Jim Murray, LA Times	1977 Jim Murray, LA Times	1987 Frank Deford, Sports Ill.
1967 Jim Murray, LA Times	1978 Will Grimsley, AP	1988 Frank Deford, Sports Ill.
1968 Jim Murray, LA Times	1979 Jim Murray, LA Times	1989 Peter Gammons, Sports Ill.
1969 Jim Murray, LA Times		1990 Peter Gammons, Boston Globe

Red Smith Award

Presented annually since 1981 by the Associated Press Sports Editors for "extended meritorious labor in the art of sports writing" and named in honor of the late newspaper columnist for the *New York Herald-Tribune* and *New York Times*. Voting is done by AP sports editors across the country.

Year	Year
1981 Red Smith, New York Times	1987 Will Grimsley, Associated Press
1982 Jim Murray, Los Angeles Times	1988 Furman Bisher, Atlanta Journal
1983 Shirley Povich, Washington Post	1989 Edwin Pope, Miami Herald
1984 Fred Russell, Nashville Banner	1990 Dave Smith, Dallas Morning News
1985 Blackie Sherrod, Dallas Morning News	1991 Dave Kindred, The National
1986 Si Burdick, Dayton Daily News	

Sports Directory

Listing of organizations, teams and media addresses and officials as of Sept. 20, 1991

AUTO RACING

CART (Championship Auto Racing Teams)
390 Enterprise Court, Bloomfield Hills, MI 48302
(313) 334-8500
President .... John Capels
Director of Public Relations................ Mel Poole

Formula One
(Federation Internationale de Sport Automobile)
8 Plade de la Concorde, 75008 Paris, France
TEL : 011-33-1-42659951
President .... Jean Marie Balestre
Director of Public Relations .... Martin Whiticker

NASCAR
(National Assn. of Stock Car Auto Racing)
P.O. Box 2875, Daytona Beach, FL 32120
(904) 253-0611
President .... Bill France, Jr.
Director of Public Relations .... Bill Seaborn, Jr.

MAJOR LEAGUE BASEBALL

Office of the Commissioner
350 Park Ave., New York, NY 10022
(212) 339-7800
Commissioner......................... Fay Vincent
Deputy Commissioner .... Steve Greenberg
Director of Public Relations................ Rich Levin

MLB Players Association
805 Third Ave., New York, NY 10022
(212) 826-0808
Exec. Director .... Donald Fehr
Special Assistant...................... Mark Belanger

AL

American League Office
350 Park Ave., New York, NY 10022
(212) 339-7600
President .... Bobby Brown
Director of Public Relations........... Phyllis Merhige

Baltimore Orioles
401 West Camden St, Baltimore, MD 21202
(301) 243-9800
Owners .... Eli Jacobs and Sargent Shriver
General Manager................... Roland Hemond
Director of Public Relations .... Rick Vaughn

Boston Red Sox
Fenway Park, 4 Yawkey Way, Boston, MA 02215
(617) 267-9440
General Partners..... Jean Yawkey, Haywood Sullivan
and John Harrington
General Manager .... Lou Gorman
Director of Public Relations............ Dick Bresciani

California Angels
P.O. Box 2000, Anaheim, CA 92803
(714) 937-7200 or (213) 625-1123
Owner................................. Gene Autry
President .... Richard Brown
General Manager .... Whitey Herzog
Director of Public Relations .... Tim Mead

Chicago White Sox
Comiskey Park, 333 W. 35th St., Chicago, IL 60616
(312) 924-1000
Owners............ Jerry Reinsdorf and Eddie Einhorn
General Manager...................... Ron Schueler
Director of Public Relations............. Chuck Adams

Cleveland Indians
Cleveland Stadium, Cleveland, OH 44114
(216) 861-1200
Owners .... Richard and David Jacobs
General Manager .... Hank Peters
Director of Public Relations.............. Bob DiBiasio

Detroit Tigers
Tiger Stadium, Detroit, MI 48216
(313) 962-4000
Owner.............................. Tom Monaghan
President .... Bo Schembechler
Senior V.P.-Acting GM .... Joe McDonald
Director of Public Relations................ Dan Ewald

Kansas City Royals
P.O. Box 419969, Kansas City, MO 64141
(816) 921-2200
Owner .... Ewing Kauffman
General Manager .... Herk Robinson
Director of Public Relations........... Dean Vogelaar

Milwaukee Brewers
County Stadium, 201 S. 46th St., Milwaukee, WI 53214
(414) 933-4114
Owner.................................... Bud Selig
General Manager .... Harry Dalton
Director of Public Relations.............. Tom Skibosh

Minnesota Twins
Hubert H. Humphrey Metrodome
501 Chicago Ave. So., Minneapolis, MN 55415
(612) 375-1366
Owner .... Carl Pohlad
General Manager .... Andy MacPhail
Director of Public Relations .... Tom Mee

New York Yankees
Yankee Stadium, Bronx, NY 10451
(212) 293-4300
Principal Owner .... George Steinbrenner
Managing General Partner .... Robert Nederlander
General Manager .... Gene Michael
Director of Public Relations .... Jeff Idelson

Oakland Athletics
Oakland Alameda County Coliseum
Oakland, CA 94621
(415) 638-4900
Owner .... Walter Haas, Jr.
General Manager .... Sandy Alderson
Director of Public Relations .... Kathy Jacobson

Seattle Mariners
P.O. Box 4100, Seattle, WA 98104
(206) 628-3555
Owner.................................. Jeff Smulyan
General Manager .... Woody Woodward
Director of Public Relations .... Dave Aust

Texas Rangers
P.O. Box 90111, Arlington, TX 76004
(817) 273-5222
Owners.............. Geo. W. Bush and Edward Rose
General Manager .... Tom Grieve
Director of Public Relations................ John Blake

Toronto Blue Jays
Sky Dome, 300 Bremner Blvd., Suite 3200
Toronto, Ontario M5V 3B3
(416) 341-1000
Owner .... N.E. Hardy
General Manager........................ Pat Gillick
Director of Public Relations .... Howie Starkman

NL

National League Office
350 Park Ave., New York, NY 10022
(212) 339-7700
President .... Bill White
Director of Public Relations .... Katy Feeney

Atlanta Braves
P.O. Box 4064, Atlanta, GA 30302
(404) 522-7630
Owner .... Ted Turner
General Manager .... John Schuerholz
Director of Public Relations .... Jim Schultz

Chicago Cubs
1060 West Addison St., Chicago, IL 60613
(312) 404-2827
Owner .... The Tribune Company
President .... Don Grenesko
General Manager .... Jim Frey
Director of Public Relations .... Sharon Pannozzo

Cincinnati Reds
100 Riverfront Stadium, Cincinnati, OH 45202
(513) 421-4510
Owner .... Marge Schott
General Manager .... Bob Quinn
Director of Public Relations .... Jon Braude

Houston Astros
P.O. Box 288, Houston, TX 77001
(713) 799-9500
Owner .... John McMullen
General Manager .... Bill Wood
Director of Public Relations .... Rob Matwick

Los Angeles Dodgers
1000 Elysian Park Ave., Los Angeles, CA 90012
(213) 224-1500
Owner .... Peter O'Malley
General Manager .... Fred Claire
Director of Public Relations .... Jay Lucas

Montreal Expos
P.O. Box 500, Station M, Montreal, Quebec H1V 3P2
(514) 253-3434
General Partner .... Claude Brochu
General Manager .... Dan Duquette
Director of Public Relations .... Pierre Vidal

New York Mets
Shea Stadium, Flushing, NY 11368
(718) 507-6387
Owners .... Nelson Doubleday and Fred Wilpon
Executive V.P.-GM .... Frank Cashen
Director of Public Relations .... Jay Horwitz

Philadelphia Phillies
P.O. Box 7575, Philadelphia, PA 19101
(215) 463-6000
Managing General Partner .... Bill Giles
General Manager .... Lee Thomas
Director of Public Relations .... Larry Shenk

Pittsburgh Pirates
P.O. Box 7000, Pittsburgh, PA 15212
(412) 323-5000
Owner .... Douglas Danforth
General Manager .... Larry Doughty
Director of Public Relations .... Rick Cerrone

St. Louis Cardinals
250 Stadium Plaza, St. Louis, MO 63102
(314) 421-3060
Owner .... Anheuser Busch Company
President .... Fred Kuhlmann
General Manager .... Dal Maxvill
Director of Public Relations .... Jeff Wehling

San Diego Padres
P.O. Box 2000, San Diego, CA 92112
(619) 283-7294
Owner .... Tom Werner
General Manager .... Joe McIlvaine
Director of Public Relations .... Andy Strasberg

San Francisco Giants
Candlestick Park, San Francisco, CA 94124
(415) 468-3700
Owner .... Bob Lurie
General Manager .... Al Rosen
Director of Public Relations .... Duffy Jennings

1993 Expansion Teams

Colorado Rockies
1700 Lincoln St., Suite 3710, Denver, CO 80203
(303) 866-0428
Owner-Chairman .... John Antonucci
Owner-President .... Steve Ehrhart
General Manager .... Bob Gebhard
Director of Public Relations .... TBA

Florida Marlins
Owner .... Wayne Huizenga
President .... Carl Barger
General Manager .... Dave Dombrowski
Director of Public Relations .... TBA

PRO BASKETBALL

NBA

League Office
Olympic Tower, 645 Fifth Ave., New York, NY 10022
(212) 826-7000
Commissioner .... David Stern
Deputy Commissioner .... Russell Granik
Director of Public Relations .... Brian McIntyre

NBA Players Association
1775 Broadway, Suite 2401, New York, NY 10019
(212) 333-7510
Executive Director .... Charles Grantham

Atlanta Hawks
One CNN Center, South Tower, Suite 405
Atlanta, GA 30303
(404) 827-3800
Owner .... Ted Turner
General Manager .... Pete Babcock
Director of Public Relations .... Arthur Triche

Boston Celtics
151 Merrimac St., 5th Floor, Boston, MA 02114
(617) 523-6050
Owners .... Don Gaston, Paul Dupee
                              and Alan Cohen
President .... Red Auerbach
Sr. Vice Pesident .... Dave Gavitt
General Manager .... Jan Volk
Director of Public Relations .... Jeff Twiss

Charlotte Hornets
One Hive Drive
Charlotte, NC 28217
(704) 357-0252
Owner .... George Shinn
General Manager .... Dave Twardzik
Director of Public Relations .... Harold Kaufman

Chicago Bulls
One Magnificent Mile, 960 N. Michigan Ave.
Suite 1600, Chicago, IL 60611
(312) 943-5800
Owner .... Jerry Reinsdorf
General Manager .... Jerry Krause
Director of Public Relations .... Tim Hallam

Cleveland Cavaliers
2923 Streetsboro Rd., Richfield, OH 44286
(216) 659-9100
Owner .... Gordon Gund
General Manager .... Wayne Embry
Director of Public Relations .... Bob Price

Dallas Mavericks
Reunion Arena, 777 Sports St., Dallas, TX 75207
(214) 988-0117
Owner .... Donald Carter
General Manager....................... Norm Sonju
Director of Public Relations .... Kevin Sullivan

Denver Nuggets
1635 Clay St., Denver, CO 80204
(303) 893-6700
Owners.............. Robert Wussler and Peter Bynoe
General Manager .... Bernie Bickerstaff
Director of Public Relations .... Jay Clark

Detroit Pistons
The Palace of Auburn Hills
Two Championship Dr., Auburn Hills, MI 48057
(313) 377-0100
Owner .... Bill Davidson
General Manager .... Jack McCloskey
Director of Public Relations............... Matt Dobek

Golden State Warriors
Oakland Coliseum Arena, Oakland, CA 94621
(415) 638-6300
Owner .... James Fitzgerald
General Manager-Head Coach .... Don Nelson
Director of Public Relations....... Julie Gumlia-Marvel

Houston Rockets
The Summit, 10 Greenway Plaza East
Houston, TX 77277
(713) 627-0600
Owner............................... Charlie Thomas
General Manager .... Steve Patterson
Director of Public Relations .... Jay Goldberg

Indiana Pacers
300 East Market St., Indianapolis, IN 46204
(317) 263-2100
Owner .... Herbert Simon
General Manager .... Donnie Walsh
Director of Public Relations .... Dale Ratermann

Los Angeles Clippers
L.A. Sports Arena
3939 S. Figueroa St., Los Angeles, CA 90037
(213) 748-8000
Owner............................... Donald Sterling
General Manager .... Elgin Baylor
Director of Public Relations............. Mike Williams

Los Angeles Lakers
Great Western Forum
3900 W.Manchester Blvd., Inglewood, CA 90306
(213) 419-3100
Owner .... Jerry Buss
General Manager......................... Jerry West
Director of Public Relations................ John Black

Miami Heat
Miami Arena, Miami, FL 33136
(305) 577-4328
Owner.................................... Ted Arison
General Manager .... Lewis Schaffel
Director of Public Relations .... Mark Pray

Milwaukee Bucks
Bradley Center
1001 N. Fourth St., Milwaukee, WI 53203
(414) 227-0500
President .... Herb Kohl
General Manager .... John Steinmiller
Director of Public Relations .... Bill King II

Minnesota Timberwolves
Target Center, 600 First Ave. North
Minneapolis, MN 55403
(612) 673-1600
Owners .... Marv Wolfenson and Harvey Ratner
General Manager .... Bob Stein
Director of Public Relations .... Bill Robertson

New Jersey Nets
Meadowlands Arena, East Rutherford, NJ 07073
(201) 935-8888
Owners .... Alan Aufzien, Bernard Mann
                                    and David Gerstein
General Manager .... Willis Reed
Director of Public Relations................ John Mertz

New York Knickerbockers
Madison Square Garden
4 Pennsylvania Plaza, New York, NY 10001
(212) 465-6000
Owner................... Paramount Communications
President-General Manager .... Dave Checketts
Director of Public Relations .... John Cirillo

Orlando Magic
Orlando Arena, 1 Magic Place, Orlando, FL 32801
(407) 649-3200
Owner .... Rick DeVos
General Manager....................... Pat Williams
Director of Public Relations .... Alex Martins

Philadelphia 76ers
Veterans Stadium
Broad St. and Pattison Ave., Philadelphia, PA 19147
(215) 339-7600
Owner.................................. Harold Katz
General Manager......................... Gene Shue
Director of Public Relations.................. Zack Hill

Phoenix Suns
2910 N. Central Ave., Phoenix, AZ 85012
(602) 266-5753
Owner-General Manager .... Jerry Colangelo
Director of Public Relations............... Barry Ringel

Portland Trail Blazers
Suite 950 Lloyd Building
700 N.E. Multnomah St., Portland, OR 97232
(503) 234-9291
Owner .... Paul Allen
General Manager .... Geoff Petrie
Director of Public Relations............. John Lashway

Sacramento Kings
One Sports Parkway, Sacramento, CA 95834
(916) 928-0000
Owner............................... Gregg Lukenbill
General Manager .... Rick Benner
Director of Public Relations .... Julie Fie

San Antonio Spurs
600 East Market St., Suite 102, San Antonio, TX 78205
(512) 554-7787
Owner .... Red McCombs
General Manager......................... Bob Bass
Director of Public Relations .... Wayne Witt

Seattle Supersonics
190 Queene Anne Ave. North, Suite 200
Seattle WA 98109
(206) 281-5800
Owner .... Barry Ackerley
General Manager .... Bob Whitsitt
Director of Public Relations .... Jim Rupp

Utah Jazz
5 Triad Center, 5th Floor, Salt Lake City, UT 84180
(801) 575-7800
Owner .... Larry Miller
President............................... Frank Layden
General Manager....................... Tim Howells
Director of Public Relations .... Kim Turner

Washington Bullets
One Harry S Truman Dr., Landover, MD 20785
(301) 773-2255
Owner .... Abe Pollin
General Manager .... John Nash
Director of Public Relations .... Rick Moreland

CBA

Continental Basketball Association
425 S. Cherry Street, Suite 230
Denver, CO 80222
(303) 331-0404
Commissioner .... Terdema Ussery
Director of Public Relations .... Greg Anderson

BOWLING

BPAA (Bowling Proprietors' Assn. of America)
P.O. Box 5802, Arlington, TX 76011
(817) 649-5105
President .... Walter Hall
Director of Public Relations.............. Rosie Crews

LPBT (Ladies Professional Bowlers Tour)
7171 Cherryvale Blvd., Rockford, IL 61112
(815) 332-5756
President .... John Falzone
Director of Public Relations .... Jeff Allen

PBA (Professional Bowlers Association)
1720 Merriman Road, P.O. Box 5118
Akron, OH 44334
(216) 836-5568
Commissioner .... Mike Connor
Director of Public Relations............. Kevin Shippy

BOXING

IBF (International Boxing Federation)
134 Evergreen Place, 9th Floor
East Orange, NJ 07018
(201) 414-0300
President .... Bob Lee
Director of Public Relations .... Cy Roseman

WBA (World Boxing Association)
President........................ Gilberto Mendoza
General Counsel
& U.S. Spokesman..................... Jimmy Binns
300 Walnut Street
Philadelphia, PA 19106
(215) 922-4000

WBC (World Boxing Council)
President .... Jose Sulaiman
Treasurer
& U.S. Contact....................... Haig Kelegian
850 W. Washington Blvd.
Los Angeles, CA 90015
(213) 742-0255

COLLEGE SPORTS

NAIA
(National Assn. of Intercollegiate Athletics)
1221 Baltimore Ave., Kansas City, MO 64105
(816) 842-5050
President-CEO...................... James Chasteen
Director of Communications .... John Mulbihill

NCAA
(National Collegiate Athletic Assn.)
6201 College Blvd., Overland Park, KS 66211
(913) 339-1906
Executive Director .... Dick Schultz
Director of Enforcement .... David Berst
Director of Communications.......... Jim Marchiony

Major NCAA Conferences
Division I in basketball and football.

Atlantic Coast Conference
P.O.Drawer ACC
Greensboro, NC 27419
(919) 854-8787
Commissioner .... Gene Corrigan
Director of Information................... Tom Mickle

Atlantic 10 Conference
10 Woodbridge Center Drive
Woodbridge, NJ 07095
(908) 634-6900
Commissioner........................ Ron Bertovich
Director of Information.................... Ray Cella

Big East Conference
56 Exchange Terrace
Providence, RI 02903
(401) 272-9108
Commissioner....................... Mike Tranghese
Director of Information .... Mark Rudner

Big Eight Conference
104 West 9th Street, Suite 408
Kansas City, MO 64105-1755
(816) 471-5088
Commissioner........................... Carl James
Director of Information .... Jeff Bollig

Big Sky Conference
P.O. Box 1736
Boise, ID 83701
(208) 345-0281
Commissioner .... Ron Stephenson
Director of Information .... Arnie Sgalio

Big South Conference
1551 21st Avenue North, Suite 11
Myrtle Beach, SC 29577
(803) 448-9998
Commissioner .... Buddy Sasser
Director of Information .... Karen Clark

Big 10 Conference
1500 West Higgins Road
Park Ridge, IL 60068-6300
(708) 696-1010
Commissioner .... Jim Delany
Director of Information .... Mark Rudner

Big West Conference
1700 East Dyer Road, Suite 140
Santa Ana, CA 92705
(714) 261-2525
Commissioner........................... Jim Haney
Director of Information .... Andy Geerken

Colonial Athletic Association
2550 Professional Road, Suite 16
Richmond, VA 23235
(804) 272-1616
Commissioner . . . . Tom Yeager
Director of Information . . . . Tripp Sheppard

East Coast Conference
946 Farnsworth Avenue
Bordentown, NJ 08505
(609) 298-5308
Commissioner . . . . John Carpenter
Director of Information . . . . Marie Wozniak

Gateway Conference
7750 Clayton Road, Suite 204
St. Louis, MO 63117
(314) 645-8760
Commissioner . . . . Patty Viverito
Director of Information . . . . Mike Kern

Great Midwest Conference
3600 Three First National Plaza
Chicago, IL 60602
(312) 977-4389
Commissioner . . . . Mike Slive
Director of Information . . . . Tim Stephens

Ivy League
120 Alexander Street
Princeton, NJ 08544
(609) 258-6426
Executive Director . . . . Jeffrey Orleans
Director of Information . . . . Chuck Yrigoyen

Metro Conference
Two Ravinia Drive, Suite 210
Atlanta, GA 30346
(404) 395-6444
Commissioner . . . . Ralph McFillen
Director of Information . . . . Jamie Kimbrough

Metro Atlantic Athletic Conference
1099 Wall Street West, Suite 242
Lyndhurst, NJ 07071-3617
(201) 896-8443
Commissioner . . . . Richard Ensor
Director of Information . . . . Carolanne McAuliffe

Mid-American Conference
Four SeaGate, Suite 102
Toledo, OH 43604
(419) 249-7177
Executive Director . . . . Karl Benson
Director of Information . . . . Sue Brague

Mid-Continent Conference
310 South Peoria, Suite 210
Chicago, IL 60607
(312) 829-9122
Commissioner . . . . Jerry Ippoliti
Director of Information . . . . Tom Lessig

Mid-Eastern Athletic Conference
P.O.Box 21205
Greensboro, NC 27420-1205
(919) 275-9961
Commissioner . . . . Ken Free
Director of Information . . . . Larry Barber

Midwestern Collegiate Conference
Pan American Plaza
201 South Capitol Ave., Suite 500
Indianapolis, IN 46225
(317) 237-5622
Commissioner . . . . Tucker DiEdwardo
Director of Information . . . . Mike Hermann

Missouri Valley Conference
100 North Broadway, Suite 1135
St.Louis, MO 63102
(314) 421-0339
Commissioner . . . . Doug Elgin
Director of Information . . . . Ron English

North Atlantic Conference
P.O.Box 69, 28 Main Street
Orono, ME 04473
(207) 866-2383
Commissioner . . . . Stuart Haskell
Director of Information . . . . Len Harlow

Northeast Conference
900 Route 9, Suite 120
Woodbridge, NJ 07095
(908) 636-9119
Commissioner . . . . Chris Monasch
Director of Information . . . . Dave Siroty

Ohio Valley Conference
278 Franklin Road, Suite 103
Brentwood, TN 37027
(615) 371-1698
Commissioner . . . . Dan Beebe
Director of Information . . . . Angela Hazel

Pacific-10 Conference
800 South Broadway, Suite 400
Walnut Creek, CA 94596
(510) 932-4411
Commissioner . . . . Thomas Hansen
Director of Information . . . . Jim Muldoon

Patriot League
3897 Adler Place, Bethlehem Office Commons
Building C, Suite 310, Bethlehem, PA 18017
(215) 691-2414
Executive Director . . . . Carl Ullrich
Director of Information . . . . Todd Newcomb

Southeastern Conference
2201 Civic Center Boulevard
Birmingham, AL 35203
(205) 458-3000
Commissioner . . . . Roy Kramer
Director of Information . . . . Mark Whitworth

Southern Conference
1 West Pack Square, Suite 1508
Asheville, NC 28801
(704) 255-7872
Commissioner . . . . Wright Waters
Director of Information . . . . Geoff Cabe

Southland Conference
1309 West 15th Street, Suite 303
Plano, TX 75075
(214) 424-4833
Executive Director . . . . Bill Belknap
Director of Information . . . . Pam Rapkin

Southwest Athletic Conference
P.O.Box 569420
Dallas, TX 75356-9420
(214) 634-7353
Commissioner . . . . Fred Jacoby
Director of Information . . . . Bo Carter

Southwestern Athletic Conference
Louisiana Superdome
1500 Sugar Bowl Drive
New Orleans, LA 70112
(504) 523-7573
Commissioner . . . . James Frank
Director of Information . . . . Lonza Hardy, Jr.

Sun Belt Conference
One Galleria Boulevard, Suite 2115
Metairie, LA 70001
(504) 834-6600
Commissioner...................... Craig Thompson
Director of Information................ Tom Burnett, Jr.

Trans America Conference
337 South Milledge Avenue, Suite 200
Athens, GA 30605-1061
(404) 548-3369
Acting Commissioner................ Lou McCullough
Acting Director of Information........... Chris Phillips

West Coast Conference
400 Oyster Point Blvd., Suite 221
South San Francisco, CA 94080
(415) 873-8622
Commissioner...................... Michael Gilleran
Director of Information..................... Don Ott

Western Athletic Conference
14 West Dry Creek Circle
Littleton, CO 80120
(303) 795-1962
Commissioner......................... Joe Kearney
Director of Information.................... Jeff Hurd

Yankee Conference
c/o Delaware Field House
University of Delaware
Newark, DE 19716
(302) 451-2186
Commissioner........................ David Nelson
Director of Information................ Ernie Larossa

PRO FOOTBALL

National Football League

League Office
410 Park Ave., New York, NY 10022
(212) 758-1500
Commissioner .... Paul Tagliabue
President .... Neil Austrian
Director of Information .... Pete Abitante

NFL Players Association
2021 L. Street NW, Washington, DC 20036
(202) 463-2200
Executive Director .... Gene Upshaw
Assistant Director .... Doug Allen
Director of Public Relations........... Frank Woschitz

AFC

Buffalo Bills
One Bills Drive, Orchard Park, NY 14127
(716) 648-1800
Owner................................. Ralph Wilson,Jr.
General Manager .... Bill Polian
Director of Public Relations............. Denny Lynch

Cincinnati Bengals
200 Riverfront Stadium, Cincinnati, OH 45202
(513) 621-3550
Owner................................. John Sawyer
General Manager .... Mike Brown
Director of Public Relations .... Al Heim

Cleveland Browns
Tower B, Cleveland Stadium, Cleveland, OH 44114
(216) 696-5555
Owner.................................. Art Modell
General Manager .... Ernie Accorsi
Director of Public Relations .... Kevin Byrne

Denver Broncos
13655 East Dove Valley Parkway,
Englewood, CO 80112
(303) 649-9000
Owner.................................. Pat Bowlen
V.P.-Head Coach...................... Dan Reeves
General Manager .... John Beake
Director of Public Relations .... Jim Saccomano

Houston Oilers
6910 Fannin St., Houston, TX 77030
(713) 797-9111
Owner.................................. Bud Adams
General Manager .... Mike Holovak
Director of Public Relations .... Chip Namias

Indianapolis Colts
P.O. Box 535000, Indianapolis, IN 46253
(317) 297-2658
Owner.................................. Robert Irsay
General Manager .... Jim Irsay
Director of Public Relations .... Craig Kelley

Kansas City Chiefs
One Arrowhead Drive, Kansas City, MO 64129
(816) 924-9300
Owner.................................. Lamar Hunt
President-GM........................... Carl Peterson
Director of Public Relations .... Bob Moore

Los Angeles Raiders
332 Center St., El Segundo, CA 90245
(213) 322-3451
Managing General Partner .... Al Davis
Executive Assistant....................... Al LoCasale

Miami Dolphins
Joe Robbie Stadium
2269 NW 199th Street, Miami, FL 33056
(305) 620-5000
Owner .... Tim Robbie
General Manager .... Eddie Jones
Director of Public Relations........... Harvey Greene

New England Patriots
Foxboro Stadium, Route 1, Foxboro, MA 02035
(508) 543-8200
Owner................................. Victor Kiam
General Manager .... Sam Jankovich
Director of Public Relations .... Pat Hanlon

New York Jets
1000 Fulton Ave., Hempstead, NY 11550
(516) 538-6600
Owner .... Leon Hess
General Manager..................... Dick Steinberg
Director of Public Relations.............. Frank Ramos

Pittsburgh Steelers
Three Rivers Stadium
300 Stadium Circle, Pittsburgh, PA 15212
(412) 323-1200
Owner-General Manager .... Dan Rooney
Director of Public Relations .... Dan Edwards

San Diego Chargers
San Diego/Jack Murphy Stadium
Box 609609, San Diego, CA 92160
(619) 280-2111
Owner .... Alex Spanos
General Manager .... Bobby Beathard
Director of Public Relations .... Bill Johnston

Seattle Seahawks
11220 NE 53rd Street, Kirkland, WA 98033
(206) 827-9777
Owner .... Ken Behring
General Manager....................... Tom Flores
Director of Public Relations .... Gary Wright

NFC

Atlanta Falcons
Suwanee Road at I-85, Suwanee, GA 30174
(404) 945-1111
Owner............................. Rankin Smith, Sr.
President................................ Taylor Smith
Director of Public Relations............. Charlie Taylor

Chicago Bears
Halas Hall, 250 N. Washington, Lake Forest, IL 60045
(708) 295-6600
Owner .... Edward McCaskey
President............................. Mike McCaskey
Director of Public Relations .... Bryan Harlan

Dallas Cowboys
Cowboys Center
One Cowboys Parkway, Irving, TX 75063
(214) 556-9900
Owner-General Manager................. Jerry Jones
Director of Public Relations............ Rich Dalrymple

Detroit Lions
Pontiac Silverdome
1200 Featherstone Road, Pontiac, MI 48057
(313) 335-4131
Owner........................... William Clay Ford
General Manager .... Chuck Schmidt
Director of Public Relations .... Mike Murray

Green Bay Packers
1265 Lombardi Ave., Green Bay, WI 54304
(414) 496-5700
Owner........................... Community owned
President............................... Bob Harlan
General Manager .... Tom Braatz
Director of Public Relations .... Lee Remmel

Los Angeles Rams
2327 West Lincoln Ave., Anaheim, CA 92801
(714) 535-7267
Owner........................... Georgia Frontiere
General Manager .... Jack Faulkner
Director of Public Relations.............. John Oswald

Minnesota Vikings
9520 Viking Drive, Eden Prairie, MN 55344
(612) 828-6500
Chairman........................... John Skoglund
President .... Roger Headrick
Director of Public Relations .... Merrill Swanson

New Orleans Saints
1500 Poydras St., New Orleans, LA 70003
(504) 733-0255
Owner................................ Tom Benson
General Manager......................... Jim Finks
Director of Public Relations .... Rusty Kasmiersky

New York Giants
Giants Stadium, East Rutherford, NJ 07073
(201) 935-8111
Owners............ Wellington Mara and Robert Tisch
General Manager .... George Young
Director of Public Relations .... Ed Croke

Philadelphia Eagles
Veterans Stadium, Broad St. & Pattison Ave.
Philadelphia, PA 19148
(215) 463-2500
Owner............................. Norman Braman
General Manager...................... Harry Gamble
Director of Public Relations .... Ron Howard

Phoenix Cardinals
P.O. Box 888, Phoenix, AZ 85001
(602) 379-0101
Owner .... Bill Bidwill
General Manager....................... Larry Wilson
Director of Public Relations .... Paul Jensen

San Francisco 49ers
4949 Centennial Blvd., Santa Clara, CA 95054
(408) 562-4949
Owner....................... Edward DeBartolo, Jr.
General Manager....................... John McVay
Director of Public Relations .... Jerry Walker

Tampa Bay Buccaneers
One Buccaneer Place, Tampa, FL 33607
(813) 870-2700
Owner .... Hugh Culverhouse
General Manager....................... Phil Krueger
Director of Public Relations.............. Rick Odioso

Washington Redskins
Redskin Park, P.O. Box 17247, Dulles Int'l Airport,
Washington, DC 20041
(703) 471-9100
Owner............................. Jack Kent Cooke
General Manager................... Charlie Casserly
Director of Public Relations .... Mike McCall

World League of American Football

540 Madison Ave., New York, NY 10022
(212) 838-9400
President .... TBA
Director of Public Relations .... Bob Rose

Canadian Football League

League Office
CFL Building
110 Eglinton Ave., 5th Floor
Toronto, Ontario M4R 1A3
(416) 322-9650
Commissioner .... Donald Crump
Directors of Public Relations ..... Diane Côté-Milhalek
                                      and Norm Miller

B.C. Lions
10605 135th St., Surrey, B.C. V3T 4C8
(604) 585-3323
Owner.............................. Murray Pezim
GM-Head Coach .... Bob O'Billovich
Director of Public Relations .... Roger Kelly

Calgary Stampeders
McMahon Stadium, 1817 Crowchild Tr. NW
Calgary, Alberta T2M 4R6
(403) 289-0205
Owner.............................. Larry Ryckman
General Manager .... Norman Kwong
Director of Public Relations .... Kevin Gallant

Edmonton Eskimos
9023 — 111 Ave., Edmonton, Alberta T5B 0C3
(403) 448-1525
Owner........................... Community owned
President .... Gary Campbell
General Manager .... Hugh Campbell
Director of Public Relations .... Allan Watt

Hamilton Tiger-Cats
14 Hughson St. S., Hamilton, Ontario L8N 4H3
(416) 547-2418
Owner................................. David Braley
General Manager........................ Joe Zuger
Director of Public Relations .... Chris Dowhun

Ottawa Rough Riders
Coliseum Building, Lansdowne Park
Ottawa, Ontario K1S 3W7
(613) 563-4551
Owner..................... Taken over by CFL in Aug.
General Manager...................... Jo-Anne Polak
Director of Public Relations.............. Sal De Meo

Saskatchewan Roughriders
2940 — 10th Ave., P.O.Box 1277
Regina, Saskatchewan S4P 3B8
(306) 569-2323
Owner.......................... Community owned
President............................... Phil Kershaw
General Manager........................ Alan Ford
Director of Public Relations............. Barry Taman

Toronto Argos
Exhibition Place, Toronto, Ontario M6K 3C3
(416) 595-9600
Owners................ Bruce McNall, Wayne Gretzky
and John Candy
General Manager..................... Mike McCarthy
Director of Public Relations .... David Watkins

Winnipeg Blue Bombers
1465 Maroons Road, Winnipeg, Manitoba R3G 0L6
(204) 784-2583
Owner........................... Community owned
President............................... Ted Bartman
General Manager .... Cal Murphy
Director of Public Relations .... Kevin O'Donovan

GOLF

LPGA Tour
(Ladies Professional Golf Association)
2570 Volusia Ave., Daytona Beach, FL 32114
(904) 254-8800
Commissioner...................... Charles Mechem
Director of Public Relations........... Beth McCombs

PGA Tour
(Professional Golfer's Association)
Sawgrass, Ponte Vedra, FL 32082
(904) 285-3700
Commissioner .... Deane Beman
Director of Information................... Tom Place

USGA
(United States Golf Association)
P.O. Box 708, Liberty Corner Road, Far Hills, NJ 07931
(908) 234-2300
President .... Grant Spaeth
Executive Director .... David Fay
Director of Communications .... Bob Sommers

PGA of America
100 Avenue of the Champions
Palm Beach Gardens, FL 33418
(407) 624-8400
President.............................. Dick Smith
Executive Director .... Jim Awtrey
Director of Public Relations.......... Terry McSweeney

PGA European Tour
Wentworth Club, Wentworth Drive
Virginia Water, Surrey, England GU25 4LS
TEL: 011-44-344-842881
Executive Director...................... Ken Schofield
Director of Communications......... Scott MacCallum

Royal & Ancient Golf Club of St. Andrews
St. Andrews, Fife, Scotland KY16 9JD
TEL: 011-44-334-72112
Secretary .... Michael Bonallack

PRO HOCKEY
NHL
President .... John Ziegler
Executive Vice President................ Brian O'Neill
Dir. of Public Relations (Toronto)....... Gary Meagher

League Offices
Montreal Office: 1155 Metcalfe St., Suite 960
Montreal, Quebec H3B 2W2
(514) 871-9220

New York Office: 650 Fifth Ave., 33rd Floor
New York, NY 10019
(212) 398-1100

Toronto Office: 75 International Blvd., Suite 300
Rexdale, Ontario M9W 6L9
(416) 798-0820

NHL Players' Association
37 Maitland St., Toronto, Ontario M4Y 1C8
(416) 924-7800
Executive Director.................... Bob Goodenow
Director of Operations................ Sam Simpson

Boston Bruins
Boston Garden, 150 Causeway St., Boston, MA 02114
(617) 227-3206
Owner .... Jeremy Jacobs
President-GM .... Harry Sinden
Director of Public Relations.............. Heidi Holland

Buffalo Sabres
Memorial Auditorium, 140 Main St.,
Buffalo, NY 14202
(716) 856-7300
Owner .... Seymour Knox, III
General Manager .... Gerry Meehan
Director of Public Relations .... John Gurtler

Calgary Flames
Olympic Saddledome, P.O. Box 1540 Station M,
Calgary, Alberta T2P 3B9
(403) 261-0475
Owners............ Harley Hotchkiss, Norman Kwong
Sonia Scarfield, Byron and Daryl Seamen
General Manager-Head Coach ..... Doug Risebrough
Director of Public Relations............... Rick Skaggs

Chicago Blackhawks
Chicago Stadium, 1800 West Madison St.,
Chicago, IL 60612
(312) 733-5300
Owner .... William Wirtz
General Manager-Head Coach .... Mike Keenan
Director of Public Relations.............. Jim DeMaria

Detroit Red Wings
Joe Louis Sports Arena
600 Civic Center Drive, Detroit, MI 48226
(313) 567-7333
Owner .... Mike Ilitch
General Manager-Head Coach......... Bryan Murray
Director of Public Relations.............. Bill Jamieson

Edmonton Oilers
Northlands Coliseum, Edmonton, Alberta T5B 4M9
(403) 474-8561
Owner............................ Peter Pocklington
President-GM .... Glen Sather
Director of Public Relations .... Bill Tuele

Hartford Whalers
Hartford Civic Center Coliseum
One Civic Center Plaza, Hartford, CT 06103
(203) 728-3366
Managing General Partner.......... Richard Gordon
General Manager...................... Ed Johnston
Director of Public Relations............. John Forslund

Los Angeles Kings
Great Western Forum, 3900 West Manchester Blvd.
Inglewood, CA 90306
(213) 419-3160
Owner............................... Bruce NcNall
General Manager .... Rogie Vachon
Director of Public Relations .... Sue Carpenter

Minnesota North Stars
Metropolitan Sports Center
7901 Cedar Ave. South, Bloomington, MN 55425
(612) 853-9333
Owners.......... Norman Green and Morris Belzberg
General Manager...................... Bob Clarke
Director of Public Relations........... Elaine Woddell

Montreal Canadiens
Montreal Forum, 2313 St. Catherine Street West,
Montreal, Quebec H3H 1N2
(514) 932-2582
Owner................... Molson Companies Limited
President.............................. Ronald Corey
General Manager...................... Serge Savard
Director of Public Relations.......... Michele Lapointe

New Jersey Devils
Meadowlands Arena
P.O. Box 504, East Rutherford, NJ 07073
(201) 935-6050
Owner............................... John McMullen
General Manager .... Lou Lamoriello
Director of Public Relations .... Dave Freed

New York Islanders
Nassau Veterans' Memorial Coliseum
Uniondale, NY 11553
(516) 794-4100
Owner............................. John Pickett, Jr.
General Manager........................ Bill Torrey
Director of Public Relations.............. Greg Bouris

New York Rangers
Madison Square Garden, 14th Floor
4 Pennsylvania Plaza, New York, NY 10001
(212) 465-6000
Owner.................. Paramount Communications
President.. TBA
General Manager .... Neil Smith
Director of Public Relations............. Barry Watkins

Philadelphia Flyers
The Spectrum, Pattison Place, Philadelphia, PA 19148
(215) 465-4500
Owner.................................... Ed Snider
General Manager...................... Russ Farwell
Director of Public Relations.......... Rodger Gottlieb

Pittsburgh Penguins
Civic Arena, Pittsburgh, PA 15219
(412) 642-1800
Owner........................ Edward DeBartolo, Sr.
General Manager .... Craig Patrick
Director of Press Relations.............. Cindy Himes

Quebec Nordiques
Colisée de Québec, 2205 Ave. du Colisée
Quebec City, Quebec G1L 4W7
(418) 529-8441
Owner................................. Marcel Aubut
General Manager....................... Pierre Page
Director of Public Relations .... Nicole Bouchard

St. Louis Blues
St. Louis Arena
5700 Oakland Ave., St. Louis, MO 63110
(314) 781-5300
Owner........................... Michael Shanahan
General Manager....................... Ron Caron
Director of Public Relations............. Susie Mathieu

San Jose Sharks
10 Almaden Blvd., Suite 600, San Jose, CA
(451)-00-0000
Owners .... George and Gordon Gund
General Manager .... Jack Ferreira
Dir. of Public Relations.................... Tim Bryant

Toronto Maple Leafs
Maple Leaf Gardens
60 Carlton St., Toronto, Ontario M5B 1L1
(416) 977-1641
Managing Director..................... Donald Giffen
Presiden-GM .... Cliff Fletcher
Director of Public Relations .... Bob Stellick

Vancouver Canucks
Pacific Coliseum, 100 North Renfrew St.,
Vancouver, British Columbia V5K 3N7
(604) 254-5141
President-GM-Head Coach .... Frank Griffiths
General Manager........................ Pat Quinn
Director of Public Relations.......... Steve Tambellini

Washington Capitals
Capital Centre, Landover, MD 20785
(301) 350-3400
Owner.................................... Abe Pollin
General Manager .... Dave Poile
Director of Public Relations .... Lou Corletto

Winnipeg Jets
Winnipeg Arena, 15-1430 Maroons Road,
Winnipeg, Manitoba R3G 0L5
(204) 783-5387
Owner............................. Barry Shenkarow
General Manager....................... Mike Smith
Director of Public Relations .... Mike O'Hearn

1992-93 Expansion Teams
Ottawa Senators
301 Moodie Dr., Nepean, Ontario K2H 9C4
(613) 721-0115
Owner .... Terrace Investments, Ltd.
President .... Jim Durrell
General Manager...................... Mel Bridgman
Dir. of Public Relations .... Randy Burgess

Tampa Bay Lightning
501 East Kennedy Blvd., Suite 175, Tampa, FL 33602
(813) 229-2658
Owners .... TBA
President-GM........................... Phil Esposito
Director of Public Relations............. Gerry Helper

HORSE RACING

TRA
(Thoroughbred Racing Associations)
420 Fair Hill Dr., Suite 1, Elkton, MD 21921
(301) 392-9200
President............................ Thomas Meeker
Director of Public Relations............. Kennith Knelly

USTA
(United States Trotting Association)
750 Michigan Ave., Columbus, OH 43215
(614) 224-2291
Exec. Vice President .... Francis X. Ready
Director of Public Relations .... John Pawlak

MEDIA

DAILY NEWSPAPER

USA Today
1000 Wilson Blvd. Arlington, VA 22229
(703) 276-3400
Owner .... Gannett Company
Publisher .... Thomas Curley
Managing Editor/Sports .... Gene Policinski

WEEKLY MAGAZINES

Sports Illustrated
Time&Life Bldg., Rockefeller Ctr.,
New York, NY 10020
(212) 586-1212
Publisher .... Mark Mulvoy
Managing Editor .... John Papanek

The Sporting News
1212 N.Lindbergh Blvd., St. Louis, MO 63132
(314) 997-7111
Publisher .... Thomas Osenton
Editor .... John Rawlings

TELEVISION

ABC Sports
47 West 66th St., 13th Floor, New York, NY 10023
(212) 887-4867
President .... Dennis Swanson
Senior V.P., Production .... Dennis Lewin
Executive Producer..................... Jack O'Hara
Director of Public Relations .... Mark Mandel

CBS Sports
51 West 52nd St., 30th Floor, New York, NY 10019
(212) 975-5230
President .... Neal Pilson
Executive Producer .... Ted Shaker
V.P., Programming .... Jay Rosenstein
Director of Information .... Susan Kerr

ESPN
ESPN Plaza, Bristol, CT 06010
(203) 585-2000
President .... Steve Bornstein
Exec. V.P., Operations.................... Jim Allegro
Executive Editor .... John Walsh
Managing Editor .... Steve Anderson
Director of Communications............ Chris LaPlaca

HBO Sports
1100 Ave. of the Americas, New York, NY 10036
(212) 512-1000
President .... Seth Abraham
V.P., Executive Producer.............. Ross Greenburg
V.P., Programming .... Bob Greenway

NBC Sports
30 Rockefeller Plaza, New York, NY 10112
(212) 664-4444
President .... Dick Ebersol
Executive Vice President .... Ken Schanzer
Executive Producer..................... Terry O'Neil
Director of Public Relations................ Ed Markey

Prime Network
5251 Gulfton St., Houston, TX 77081
(713) 661-0078
President-CEO.......................... Ed Frazier
Executive V.P. .... Mott Tinley
Director of Media Relations .... Bob Wheeler

SportsChannel America
3 Crossways Park West, Woodbury, NY 11797
(516) 921-3764
President .... Jeff Ruhe
V.P., Programming..................... Mike Lardner
Director of Information................ Dan Martinsen

Turner Sports
One CNN Center, Suite 1300, Atlanta, GA 30303
(404) 827-1735
President .... Terry McGuirk
Sr. V.P., Executive Producer............. Don McGuire
Sr. V.P., Programming................ Kevin O'Malley
Director of Public Relations............ Mark Parkman

USA Network
1230 Ave. of the Americas, New York, NY 10020
(212) 408-8895
Executive Producer .... Gordon Beck
Director of Public Relations .... Leslie Anne Wade

OLYMPICS

IOC
(International Olympic Committee)
Chateau de Vidy, CH-1007 Lausanne, Switzerland
TEL: 011-41-21-253-271
President.................. Juan Antonio Samaranch
Director General .... Francois Carrard
Director of Information.............. Michele Verdier

1992 GAMES
Albertville Olympic Organizing Committee
11 rue Pargoux, 73200 Albertville, France
TEL: 011-33-79-45-1992
Co-Presidents........................ Michel Barnier
                          and Jean-Claude Killy

Barcelona Olympic Organizing Committee
Edificio Hellos, C/Mejia Lequerica, S/N 08028
Barcelona, Spain
TEL: 011-34-3-411-1992
Chairman and President .... M. Pasqual Maragall

1994 WINTER GAMES
Lillehammer Olympic Organizing Committee
Storgatan 95, P.O. Box 106
N-2601, Lillehammer, Norway
TEL: 011-47-62-57455
President .... Gerhard Heiberg

1996 SUMMER GAMES
Atlanta Committee for the Olympic Games
250 Williams St., Suite 6000, Atlanta, GA 30303
(404) 224-1996
President............................... Billy Payne
Sr. Executive V.P. .... A.D. Frazier, Jr.
Director of Public Relations............. Bob Brennan

USOC
(United States Olympic Committee)
1750 East Boulder St., Colorado Springs, CO 80909
(719) 578-4529
Interim President . . . . William Hybl
IOC Members (2) . . . Robert Helmick & Anita DeFrantz
Director of Information . . . . Mike Moran

U.S. Olympic Festival
(1993 Organizing Committee)
P.O. Box 830386, San Antonio, TX 78283
(512) 246-1993
President. . . . . Robert Morbot, Jr.

COA
(Canadian Olympic Association)
1600 James Naismith Dr., Ottawa, Ontario K1B 5N4
(613) 748-5647
President . . . . Carl Anne Letheren
IOC Members (2) . . . . Richard Pound
& Carol Anne Letheren
Director of Communications . . . . Frank Ratcliffe

SOCCER

FIFA
(Federation Internationale de Football Assn.)
11 Hitzigweg, 8032 Zurich, Switzerland
TEL: 011-41-1-384-9595
President . . . . Joao Havelange (Brazil)
General Secretary . . . . Joseph Blatter (Switz.)
Director of Public Relations. . . . . Guido Tognoni

USS
(United States Soccer)
1750 East Boulder St., Colorado Springs, CO 80909
(719) 578-4678
President. . . . . Alan Rothenberg
Director of Public Relations. . . . . John Polis

World Cup USA 1994
(U.S. World Cup Organizing Committee)
Suite 400, 2029 Century
(213)552-1994
President. . . . . Chuck Cale
Director of Public Relations . . . . Jim Trecker
1270 Ave. of the Americas
Suite 220, New York, NY 10020
(212) 332-1994

American Professional Soccer League
10620 Guilford Rd., Suite 204, Jessup, MD 20794
(301)498-4990
Co-Chairmen . . . . Clive Toye
and Bill Sage
Operations Director . . . . Diane Fritschner
Director of Public Relations . . . . Donn Risolo
P.O. Box 92861
Pasadena, CA 91109
(818) 791-3076

Major Soccer League
4500 College Blvd., Suite 308,
Overland Park, KS 66211
(913) 339-6475
Commissioner. . . . . Earl Foreman
Director of Public Relations. . . . . John Griffin

MSL Players Association
2021 L Street NW, 6th Floor, Washington 20036
(202) 463-2246
Executive Director. . . . . John Kerr
Special Assistant . . . . Will Bray

TENNIS

ATP
(Association of Tennis Professionals)
200 ATP Tour Blvd., Ponte Vedra Beach, FL 32082
(904) 285-8000
Chief Executive Officer. . . . . Mark Miles
Director of Communications . . . . Jay Beck

ITF
(International Tennis Federation)
Pallisert Road, Barons Court
London, England W14 9EN
TEL: 011-44-71- 3818060
President. . . . . Brian Tobin
Director of Public Relations . . . . Ians Barnes

USTA
(United States Tennis Association)
1212 Ave. of the Americas, 12th Floor
New York, NY 10036
(212) 302-3322
Executive Director. . . . . Marshall Happer
Director of Communications . . . . Edwin Fabricius

WTA
(Women's Tennis Association)
133 First Street NE, St. Petersburg, FL 33701
(813) 895-5000
Executive Director. Gerard Smith
Director of Public Relations. . . . . Ana Leaird

TRACK & FIELD

AAU
(Amateur Athletic Union)
3400 W.86th St., Indianapolis, IN 46268
(317) 872-2900
President. . . . . Gussie Crawford
Executive Director . . . . Stan Hooley
Director of Communications. . . . . David Morton

IAAF
(International Amateur Athletics Federation)
3 Hans Crescent, Knightsbridge
London, England SWIX 0LN
TEL: 011-44-71- 581-8771
President. . . . . Primo Nebiolo
General Secretary . . . . John Holt
Director of Information . . . . Jayne Pearce

TAC
(The Athletics Congress)
One Hoosier Dome, Suite 140
Indianapolis, IN 46225
(317) 261-0500
Executive Director. . . . . Ollan Cassell
Director of Information . . . . Pete Cava

YACHTING

1992 America's Cup

America's Cup Organizing Committee
1660 Hotel Circle North, Suite 710
San Diego, CA 92108
(619) 296-9224
President . . . . Malin Burnham
Exec. V.P.-General Manager . . . . Tom Ehman, Jr.
Director of Information . . . . Jane Eagleson

The National Trust for Historic Preservation placed eighty-year-old
Tiger Stadium on its Most Endangered List in 1991. The Detroit
Tigers are planning to build a new ball park.

ARENAS & BALLPARKS

Where They Play

The home fields, home courts and home ice of the AL, NL, NBA, NFL, CFL, NHL, NCAA Division I-A college football and Division I basketball. Also, selected Auto Racing and Horse Racing tracks and Grand Slam Tennis center courts. Attendance figures for the 1990 NFL regular season and the 1990-91 NBA and NHL regular seasons are provided. See Baseball chapter for 1991 AL and NL attendance figures.

MAJOR LEAGUE BASEBALL

American League

				Outfield Fences					
		Built	Capacity	LF	LCF	CF	RCF	RF	Field
Baltimore Orioles	Camden Yards	1992	47,000	334	410	400	380	319	Grass
Boston Red Sox	Fenway Park	1912	34,142	315	379	390	380	302	Grass
California Angels	Anaheim Stadium	1966	64,593	333	386	404	386	333	Grass
Chicago White Sox	Comiskey Park	1991	44,702	347	382	400	382	347	Grass
Cleveland Indians	Cleveland Stadium	1932	74,483	320	400	415	400	320	Grass
Detroit Tigers	Tiger Stadium	1912	52,416	340	365	440	375	325	Grass
Kansas City Royals	Royals Stadium	1973	40,625	330	385	410	385	330	Turf
Milwaukee Brewers	County Stadium	1953	53,192	315	392	402	392	315	Grass
Minnesota Twins	Hubert H. Humphrey Metrodome	1982	55,883	343	385	408	367	327	Turf
New York Yankees	Yankee Stadium	1923	57,545	318	399	408	385	314	Grass
Oakland Athletics	Oakland-Alameda County Coliseum	1968	47,313	330	375	400	375	330	Grass
Seattle Mariners	The Kingdome	1976	57,748	331	372	405	349	312	Turf
Texas Rangers	Arlington Stadium	1965	43,521	330	380	400	380	330	Grass
Toronto Blue Jays	SkyDome	1989	50,516	328	375	400	375	328	Turf

Note: St. Louis will move in and lower outfield fences in 1992. New dimensions at Busch Stadium will be 402 ft. to CF and 375 ft. in power alleys; both foul lines, however, will remain at 330 ft.

National League

				Outfield Fences					
		Built	Capacity	LF	LCF	CF	RCF	RF	Field
Atlanta Braves	Atlanta-Fulton County Stadium	1966	52,007	330	385	402	385	330	Grass
Chicago Cubs	Wrigley Field	1914	38,710	355	368	400	368	353	Grass
Cincinnati Reds	Riverfront Stadium	1970	52,952	330	375	404	375	330	Turf
Houston Astros	The Astrodome	1965	54,816	330	380	400	380	330	Turf
Los Angeles Dodgers	Dodger Stadium	1962	56,000	330	385	395	385	330	Grass
Montreal Expos	Olympic Stadium	1976	43,739	325	375	404	375	325	Turf
New York Mets	Shea Stadium	1964	55,601	338	371	410	371	338	Grass
Philadelphia Phillies	Veterans Stadium	1971	62,382	330	371	408	371	330	Turf
Pittsburgh Pirates	Three Rivers Stadium	1970	58,729	335	375	400	375	335	Turf
St. Louis Cardinals	Busch Stadium	1966	56,227	330	383	414	383	330	Turf
San Diego Padres	San Diego/ Jack Murphy Stadium	1967	59,022	327	370	405	370	327	Grass
San Francisco Giants	Candlestick Park	1960	58,000	335	365	400	365	335	Grass

Rank by Capacity

AL		NL	
Cleveland	74,483	Veterans	62,382
Anaheim	64,593	SD/Murphy	59,022
Kingdome	57,748	Three Rivers	58,729
Yankee	57,545	Candlestick	58,000
HHH Metrodome	55,883	Busch	56,227
County	53,192	Dodger	56,000
Tiger	52,416	Shea	55,601
SkyDome	50,516	Astrodome	54,816
Oakland	47,313	Riverfront	52,952
Camden Yards	47,000	Atlanta	52,007
Comiskey	44,702	Olympic	43,739
Arlington	43,521	Wrigley	38,710
Royals	40,625		
Fenway	34,142		

Rank by Age

AL		NL	
Fenway	1912	Wrigley	1914
Tiger	1912	Candlestick	1960
Yankee	1923	Dodger	1962
Cleveland	1932	Shea	1964
County	1953	Astrodome	1965
Arlington	1965	Atlanta	1965
Anaheim	1966	Busch	1966
Oakland	1966	SD/Murphy	1967
Royals	1973	Riverfront	1970
Kingdome	1977	Three Rivers	1970
HHH Metrodome	1982	Veterans	1971
SkyDome	1989	Olympic	1976
Comiskey	1991		
Camden Yards	1992		

Note: Yankee Stadium was rebuilt in 1976.

1991 AL and NL Attendance

See "Baseball."

Home Fields

Listed below are the principal home fields used through the years by current American and National League teams. The NL became a major league in 1876, the AL in 1901.

The capacity figures in the right hand column indicate the largest seating capacity of the ballpark while the club played there. Capacity figures before 1915 (and the introduction of concrete grandstands) are sketchy at best and have been left blank.

American League

Baltimore Orioles

1901	Lloyd Street Grounds (Milwaukee)	—
1902-53	Sportsman's Park II (St.Louis)	30,500
1954-91	Memorial Stadium (Baltimore)	53,371
1992-	Camden Yards	47,000

Boston Red Sox

1901-11	Huntington Ave.Grounds	—
1912-	Fenway Park	34,142
	(1934 capacity—27,000)	

California Angels

1961	Wrigley Field (Los Angeles)	20,457
1962-65	Dodger Stadium	56,000
1966-	Anaheim Stadium	64,593
	(1966 capacity—43,250)	

Chicago White Sox

1901-10	Southside Park	—
1910-90	Comiskey Park I	43,931
1991-	Comiskey Park II	44,702

Cleveland Indians

1901-09	League Park I	—
1910-46	League Park II	21,414
1932-	Cleveland Stadium	74,483
	(1932 capacity—77,797)	

Detroit Tigers

1901-11	Bennett Park	—
1912-	Tiger Stadium	52,416
	(1912 capacity—23,000)	

Kansas City Royals

1969-72	Municipal Stadium	35,020
1973-	Royals Stadium	40,625
	(1973 capacity—40,762)	

Milwaukee Brewers

1969	Sick's Stadium (Seattle)	25,420
1970-	County Stadium (Milwaukee)	53,192
	(1970 capacity—46,625)	

Minnesota Twins

1901-02	American League Park (Wash.,DC)	—
1903-60	Griffith Stadium	27,410
1960-81	Metropolitan Stadium (Bloomington,MN)	45,919
1982-	HHH Metrodome (Minneapolis)	55,883
	(1982 capacity—54,000)	

New York Yankees

1901-02	Oriole Park (Baltimore)	—
1903-12	Hilltop Park (New York)	—
1913-22	Polo Grounds II	38,000
1923-73	Yankee Stadium I	67,224
1974-75	Shea Stadium	55,101
1976-	Yankee Stadium II	57,545
	(1976 capacity—57,145)	

Oakland Athletics

1901-08	Columbia Park (Philadelphia)	—
1909-54	Shibe Park	33,608
1955-67	Municipal Stadium (Kansas City)	35,020
1968-	Oakland Alameda County Coliseum	47,313
	(1968 capacity—48,621)	

Seattle Mariners

1977-	The Kingdome	57,748
	(1977 capacity—59,438)	

Texas Rangers

1961	Griffith Stadium (Wash.,DC)	27,410
1962-71	RFK Stadium	45,016
1972-	Arlington Stadium (Texas)	43,521
	(1972 capacity—35,698)	

Toronto Blue Jays

1977-89	Exhibition Stadium	43,737
1989-	SkyDome	50,516
	(1989 capacity—49,500)	

Ballpark Name Changes: CHICAGO—**Comiskey Park I** originally White Sox Park (1910-12), then Comiskey Park in 1913, then White Sox Park again in 1962, then Comiskey Park again in 1976; CLEVELAND—**League Park** renamed Dunn Field in 1920, then League Park again in 1928; **Cleveland Stadium** originally Municipal Stadium (1932-74); DETROIT—**Tiger Stadium** originally Navin Field (1912-37), then Briggs Stadium (1938-60); LOS ANGELES—**Dodger Stadium** referred to as Chavez Ravine by AL while Angels played there (1962-65); PHILADELPHIA—**Shibe Park** renamed Connie Mack Stadium in 1953; ST.LOUIS—**Sportsman's Park** renamed Busch Stadium in 1953; WASHINGTON—**Griffith Stadium** originally National Park (1892-20), **RFK Stadium** originally D.C. Stadium (1961-68).

National League

Atlanta Braves

1876-94	South End Grounds I (Boston)	—
1894-1914	South End Grounds II	—
1915-52	Braves Field	40,000
1953-65	County Stadium (Milwaukee)	43,394
1966-	Atlanta-Fulton County Stadium	52,007
	(1966 capacity—50,000)	

Chicago Cubs

1876-77	State Street Grounds	—
1878-84	Lakefront Park	—
1885-91	West Side Park	—
1891-93	Brotherhood Park	—
1893-1915	West Side Grounds	—
1916-	Wrigley Field	38,710
	(1916 capacity—16,000)	

Major League Baseball (Cont.)

Cincinnati Reds

1876-79	Avenue Grounds	—
1880	Bank Street Grounds	—
1890-1901	Redland Field I	—
1902-11	Palace of the Fans	—
1912-70	Crosley Field	29,603
1970–	Riverfront Stadium	52,952
	(1970 capacity—52,000)	

Houston Astros

1962-64	Colt Stadium	32,601
1965–	The Astrodome	54,816
	(1965 capacity—45,011)	

Los Angeles Dodgers

1890	Washington Park I (Brooklyn)	—
1891-97	Eastern Park	—
1898-1912	Washington Park II	—
1913-56	Ebbets Field	31,497
1957	Ebbets Field	31,497
	& Roosevelt Stadium	24,167
	(Jersey City)	
1958-61	Memorial Coliseum (Los Angeles)	93,600
1962–	Dodger Stadium	56,000

Montreal Expos

1969-76	Jarry Park	28,000
1977–	Olympic Stadium	43,739
	(1977 capacity—58,500)	

New York Mets

1962-63	Polo Grounds	55,987
1964–	Shea Stadium	55,601
	(1964 capacity—55,101)	

Philadelphia Phillies

1883-86	Recreation Park	—
1887-94	Huntingdon Ave.Grounds	—
1895-1938	Baker Bowl	18,800
1938-70	Shibe Park	33,608
1971–	Veterans Stadium	62,382
	(1971 capacity—56,371)	

Pittsburgh Pirates

1887-90	Recreation Park	—
1891-1909	Exposition Park	—
1909-70	Forbes Field	35,000
1970–	Three Rivers Stadium	58,729
	(1970 capacity—50,235)	

St.Louis Cardinals

1876-77	Sportsman's Park I	—
1885-86	Vandeventer Lot	—
1892-1920	Robison Field	18,000
1920-66	Sportsman's Park II	30,500
1966–	Busch Stadium	56,227
	(1966 capacity—50,126)	

San Diego Padres

1969–	San Diego/Jack Murphy Stadium	59,022
	(1969 capacity—47,634)	

San Francisco Giants

1876	Union Grounds (Brooklyn)	—
1883-88	Polo Grounds I (New York)	—
1889-90	Manhattan Field	—
1891-1957	Polo Grounds II	55,987
1958-59	Seals Stadium (San Francisco)	22,900
1960–	Candlestick Park	58,000
	(1960 capacity—42,553)	

Ballpark Name Changes: ATLANTA—**Atlanta-Fulton County Stadium** originally Atlanta Stadium (1966-1974); CHICAGO— **Wrigley Field** originally Weeghman Park (1914-17), then Cubs Park (1918-25); CINCINNATI—**Redland Field** originally League Park (1890-93) and **Crosley Field** originally Redland Field II (1912-33); HOUSTON—**Astrodome** originally Harris County Domed Stadium before it opened in 1965; PHILADELPHIA—**Shibe Park** renamed Connie Mack Stadium in 1953; ST.LOUIS—**Robison Field** originally Vandeventer Lot, then League Park, then Cardinal Park all before becoming Robison Field in 1901, **Sportsman's Park** renamed Busch Stadium in 1953, and **Busch Stadium** originally Busch Memorial Stadium (1966-82); SAN DIEGO—**San Diego/Jack Murphy Stadium** originally San Diego Stadium (1967-81).

NATIONAL BASKETBALL ASSOCIATION

Western Conference

		Location	Built	Capacity
Dallas Mavericks	**Reunion Arena**	Dallas, TX	1980	**17,007**
Denver Nuggets	**McNichols Arena**	Denver, CO	1975	**17,022**
Golden State Warriors	**Oakland Coliseum Arena**	Oakland, CA	1966	**15,025**
Houston Rockets	**The Summit**	Houston, TX	1975	**16,279**
Los Angeles Clippers	**Los Angeles Sports Arena**	Los Angeles, CA	1959	**15,350**
Los Angeles Lakers	**Great Western Forum**	Inglewood, CA	1967	**17,505**
Minnesota Timberwolves	**Target Center** .	Minneapolis, MN	1990	**18,500**
Phoenix Suns	**Arizona Veterans Coliseum**	Phoenix, AZ	1965	**14,487**
Portland Trail Blazers	**Memorial Coliseum**	Portland, OR	1960	**12,884**
Sacramento Kings	**ARCO Arena**	Sacramento, CA	1988	**17,014**
San Antonio Spurs	**HemisFair Arena**	San Antonio, TX	1968	**15,908**
Seattle SuperSonics	**The Coliseum**	Seattle, WA	1962	**14,132**
	& The Kingdome	Seattle, WA	1976	**38,808**
Utah Jazz	**Delta Center**	Salt Lake City, UT	1991	**19,500**

Note: Seattle is scheduled to play four of 41 regular season games at the Kingdome in 1991-92.

Eastern Conference

		Location	Built	Capacity
Atlanta Hawks	**The Omni**	Atlanta, GA	1972	**16,371**
Boston Celtics	**Boston Garden**	Boston, MA	1928	**14,890**
	& Hartford Civic Center	Hartford, CT	1975	**16,371**
Charlotte Hornets	**Charlotte Coliseum**	Charlotte, NC	1988	**23,906**
Chicago Bulls	**Chicago Stadium**	Chicago, IL	1929	**17,339**
Cleveland Cavaliers	**The Coliseum**	Richfield, OH	1974	**20,723**
Detroit Pistons	**The Palace of Auburn Hills**	Auburn Hills, MI	1988	**21,454**
Indiana Pacers	**Market Square Arena**	Indianapolis, IN	1974	**16,530**
Miami Heat	**Miami Arena**	Miami, FL	1988	**15,008**
Milwaukee Bucks	**Bradley Center**	Milwaukee, WI	1988	**18,633**
New Jersey Nets	**Meadowlands Arena**	E.Rutherford, NJ	1981	**20,039**
New York Knicks	**Madison Square Garden**	New York, NY	1968	**19,081**
Orlando Magic	**Orlando Arena**	Orlando, FL	1989	**15,077**
Philadelphia 76ers	**The Spectrum**	Philadelphia	1967	**18,168**
Washington Bullets	**Capital Centre**	Landover, MD	1973	**18,756**
	& Baltimore Arena	Baltimore, MD	1962	**12,654**

Note: Boston is scheduled to play three of 41 regular season games at Hartford Civic Center and Washington is scheduled to play four of 41 regular season games in Baltimore Arena in 1991-92.

Rank by Capacity

Western		Eastern	
Delta Center	19,500	Charlotte	23,906
Target Center	18,500	Palace	21,454
GW Forum	17,505	Cleveland	20,723
Reunion	17,007	Meadowlands	20,039
McNichols	17,022	Mad.Sq.Garden	19,081
ARCO	17,014	Capital Centre	18,756
Summit	16,279	Bradley Center	18,633
HemisFair	15,908	Spectrum	18,168
LA Sports	15,350	Chicago Stadium	17,339
Oakland	15,025	Market Square	16,530
Ariz.Vets	14,487	Omni	16,371
Seattle	14,132	Orlando	15,077
Portland	12,884	Miami	15,008
		Boston Garden	14,890

Note: Figures do not include Standing Room.

Rank by Age

Western		Eastern	
LA Sports	1959	Boston Garden	1928
Portland	1960	Chicago Stadium	1929
Seattle	1962	Spectrum	1967
Ariz.Vets	1965	Mad.Sq.Garden	1968
Oakland	1966	Omni	1972
GW Forum	1967	Capital Centre	1973
HemisFair	1968	Cleveland	1974
McNichols	1975	Market Square	1974
Summit	1975	Meadowlands	1981
Reunion	1980	Charlotte	1988
ARCO	1988	Palace	1988
Target Center	1990	Miami	1988
Delta Center	1991	Bradley Center	1988
		Orlando	1989

1990-91 NBA Attendance

Overall attendance in the NBA was 16,876,125 in 1107 games for an average per game crowd of 15,245. Teams in each conference are ranked by attendance over 41 home games; **S/O** heading indicates number of sellouts. Figures provided by NBA league office. Numbers in parentheses indicate rank in 1989-90.

Western Conference

Orlando, seventh in attendance in the East in 1989-90, moved to the Western Conference in 1990-91.

		Attendance	S/O	Average
1	Minnesota (1)	779,470	41	19,011
2	Sacramento (4)	697,574	41	17,014
3	LA Lakers (3)	697,203	18	17,005
4	Dallas (5)	683,927	25	16,681
5	San Antonio (8)	651,965	40	15,902
6	Orlando	617,668	40	15,065
7	Golden St.(7)	616,025	41	15,025
8	Houston (6)	613,230	13	14,957
9	Phoenix (9)	589,591	41	14,380
10	Portland (10)	528,244	41	12,884
11	LA Clippers (14)	522,104	5	12,734
12	Utah (12)	514,751	41	12,555
13	Seattle (13)	510,166	6	12,443
14	Denver (11)	438,103	2	10,685
	TOTAL	8,460,021	395	14,739

Note: Seattle played 38 games at Seattle Coliseum (6 sellouts, 12,451 avg.) and three at Tacomadome (no sellouts, 12,340 avg.); Phoenix and Utah opened the regular season with one "home game" each in a 2-game series at sold out Tokyo Metropolitan Gymnasium (10,111); Utah played its other 40 home games (40 sellouts, 12,616 average) at the Salt Palace.

Eastern Conference

Charlotte, second in attendance in the West in 1989-90, moved to the Eastern Conference in 1990-91.

		Attendance	S/O	Average
1	Charlotte	980,141	41	23,906
2	Detroit (1)	879,614	41	21,454
3	Chicago (3)	757,745	41	18,482
4	Milwaukee (5)	676,687	10	16,505
5	New York (2)	654,962	8	15,975
6	Philadelphia (9)	634,210	10	15,469
7	Cleveland (4)	623,906	3	15,217
8	Miami (6)	615,328	41	15,008
9	Boston (8)	611,537	41	14,916
10	Atlanta (10)	529,671	5	12,919
11	New Jersey (12)	489,915	2	11,949
12	Washington (13)	487,097	10	11,880
13	Indiana (11)	475,291	6	11,592
	TOTAL	8,416,104	257	15,790

Note: Boston played 38 games at Boston Garden (38 sellouts, 14,890 avg.) and three at Hartford Civic Center (3 sellouts, 15,239 avg.); Washington played 37 games at Capital Centre (10 sellouts, 11,875 avg.) and four at Baltimore Arena (no sellouts, 11,924 avg.).

National Basketball Association (Cont.)
Home Courts

Listed below are the principal home courts used through the years by current NBA teams. The largest capacity of each arena is noted in the right hand column. ABA arenas (1972-76) are included for Denver, Indiana, New Jersey and San Antonio.

Western Conference

Dallas Mavericks

1980–	Reunion Arena	17,007
	(1980 capacity—17,828)	

Denver Nuggets

1967-75	Auditorium Arena	6,841
1975–	McNichols Sports Arena	17,022
	(1975 capacity—16,700)	

Golden State Warriors

1946-52	Philadelphia Arena	7,777
1952-62	Convention Hall (Philadelphia)	9,200
	& Philadelphia Arena	7,777
1962-64	Cow Palace (San Francisco)	13,862
1964-66	Civic Auditorium	7,500
	& (USF Memorial Gym)	6,000
1966-67	Cow Palace, Civic Auditorium	
	& Oakland Coliseum Arena	15,000
1967-71	Cow Palace	14,500
1971–	Oakland Coliseum Arena	15,025
	(1971 capacity—12,905)	

Houston Rockets

1967-71	San Diego Sports Arena	14,000
1971-72	Hofheinz Pavilion (Houston)	10,218
	& six other sites	
1972-73	Hofheinz Pavilion	10,218
	& HemisFair Arena (San Antonio)	10,446
1973-75	Hofheinz Pavilion	10,218
1975–	The Summit	16,279
	(1975 capacity—15,600)	

Note: During the 1971-72 season, the Rockets played 21 games at Hofheinz, 8 at Astrohall and 6 at the Astrodome in Houston, as well as 3 games in San Antonio, 2 in Waco and 1 in El Paso. In 1972-73, they played 28 games at Hofheinz and 13 at the HemisFair in San Antonio.

Los Angeles Clippers

1970-78	Memorial Auditorium (Buffalo)	17,300
1978-84	San Diego Sports Arena	12,167
1985–	Los Angeles Sports Arena	15,350
	(1985 capacity—15,300)	

Los Angeles Lakers

1948-60	Minneapolis Auditorium	10,000
1960-67	Los Angeles Sports Arena	14,781
1967–	Great Western Forum (Inglewood,CA)	17,505
	(1967 capacity—17,086)	

Minnesota Timberwolves

1989-90	Hubert H.Humphrey Metrodome	23,000
1990–	Target Center	18,500

Phoenix Suns

1968–	Ariz.Veteran's Memorial Coliseum	14,487
	(1968 capacity—12,200)	

Portland Trail Blazers

1970–	Memorial Coliseum	12,884
	(1970 capacity—12,366)	

Sacramento Kings

1948-55	Edgarton Park Arena	
	(Rochester,NY)	5,000
1955-58	Rochester War Memorial	10,000
1958-72	Cincinnati Gardens	11,438
1972-74	Municipal Auditorium (Kansas City)	9,929
	& Omaha,Neb. Civic Auditorium	9,136
1974-78	Kemper Arena (Kansas City)	16,785
	& Omaha Civic Auditorium	9,136
1978-85	Kemper Arena	16,785
1985-88	ARCO Arena I	10,333
1988–	ARCO Arena II	17,014
	(1988 capacity—16,517)	

San Antonio Spurs

1967-70	Memorial Auditorium (Dallas)	8,088
	& Moody Coliseum (Dallas)	8,500
1970-71	Three courts—Moody Coliseum	8,500
	Tarrant Conven.Center(Ft.Worth)	13,500
	& Municipal Coliseum (Lubbock)	10,400
1971-73	Two courts—Moody Coliseum	9,500
	& Memorial Auditorium	8,088
1973–	HemisFair Arena (San Antonio)	15,908
	(1973 capacity—10,446)	

Seattle Supersonics

1967-78	Seattle Center Coliseum	14,098
1978-85	Kingdome	40,192
1985–	The Coliseum	14,132
	(1985 capacity—14,000)	

Utah Jazz

1974-75	Municipal Auditorium	7,853
	& Louisiana Superdome	47,284
1975-79	Superdome	47,284
1979-83	Salt Palace (Salt Lake City)	12,519
1983-84	Salt Palace	12,519
	& Thomas-Mack Center (Las Vegas)	18,500
1985-91	Salt Palace	12,616
1991–	Delta Center	19,500

Eastern Conference

Atlanta Hawks

1949-51	Wheaton Field House (Moline,IL)	6,000
1951-55	Milwaukee Arena	11,000
1955-68	Kiel Auditorium (St.Louis)	10,000
1968-72	Alexander Mem. Coliseum (Atlanta)	7,166
1972–	The Omni	16,371
	(1972 capacity—16,818)	

Boston Celtics

1946–	Boston Garden	14,890
	(1946 capacity—13,909)	

Note: Since 1975-76, the Celtics have played some regular season games at the Hartford Civic Center (16,344).

Charlotte Hornets

1988–	Charlotte Coliseum	23,906
	(1988 capacity—23,500)	

Chicago Bulls

1966-67	Chicago Amphitheater	11,002
1967–	Chicago Stadium	17,339
	(1967 capacity—17,374)	

Cleveland Cavaliers

1970-74	Cleveland Arena	11,000
1974–	The Coliseum (Richfield,OH)	20,723
	(1974 capacity—19,500)	

Detroit Pistons

1948-52	North Side H.S.Gym (Ft.Wayne,IN)	3,800
1952-57	Memorial Coliseum (Ft.Wayne)	9,306
1957-61	Olympia Stadium (Detroit)	14,000
1961-78	Cobo Arena	11,147
1978-88	Silverdome (Pontiac,MI)	22,366
1988–	The Palace (Auburn Hills, MI)	21,454

Indiana Pacers

1967-74	State Fairgrounds (Indianapolis)	9,479
1974–	Market Square Arena	16,530
	(1974 capacity—17,287)	

Miami Heat

1988–	Miami Arena	15,008
	(1988 capacity—15,362)	

Milwaukee Bucks

1968-88	Milwaukee Arena (The Mecca)	11,052
1988–	Bradley Center	18,633

New Jersey Nets

1967-68	Teaneck,NJ Armory	3,500
1968-69	Long Island Arena (Commack,NY)	6,500
1969-71	Island Garden (W.Hempstead,NY)	5,200
1971-77	Nassau Coliseum (Uniondale,NY)	15,500
1977-81	Rutgers Ath.Center (Piscataway,NJ)	9,050
1981–	Meadowlands Arena (E.Ruth.,NJ)	20,039

New York Knicks

1946-68	Madison Sq. Garden III (50th St)	18,496
1968–	Madison Sq. Garden IV (33rd St.)	19,081
	(1968 capacity—19,694)	

Orlando Magic

1989–	Orlando Arena	15,077

Philadelphia 76ers

1949-51	State Fair Coliseum (Syracuse,NY)	7,500
1951-63	Onondaga County (NY)	
	War Memorial	8,000
1963-67	Convention Hall (Philadelphia)	12,000
1949-51	State Fair Coliseum (Syracuse,NY)	7,500
	& Philadelphia Arena	7,777
1967–	The Spectrum	18,168
	(1967 capacity—15,205)	

Washington Bullets

1961-62	Chicago Amphitheater	11,000
1962-63	Chicago Coliseum	7,100
1963-73	Baltimore Civic Center	12,289
1973–	Capital Centre (Landover,MD)	18,756
	(1973 capacity—17,500)	

Note: Since 1988-89, the Bullets have played four regular season games at Baltimore Arena.

NATIONAL FOOTBALL LEAGUE

American Conference

		Location	Built	Capacity	Field
Buffalo Bills	Rich Stadium	Orchard Park, NY	1973	**80,290**	Turf
Cincinnati Bengals	Riverfront Stadium	Cincinnati, OH	1970	**59,755**	Turf
Cleveland Browns	Cleveland Stadium	Cleveland, OH	1932	**80,098**	Grass
Denver Broncos	Mile High Stadium	Denver, CO	1948	**76,273**	Grass
Houston Oilers	The Astrodome	Houston, TX	1965	**60,502**	Turf
Indianapolis Colts	The Hoosier Dome	Indianapolis, IN	1984	**60,127**	Turf
Kansas City Chiefs	Arrowhead Stadium	Kansas City, MO	1972	**78,067**	Turf
Los Angeles Raiders	LA Memorial Coliseum	Los Angeles, CA	1923	**92,488**	Grass
Miami Dolphins	Joe Robbie Stadium	Miami, FL	1987	**73,000**	Grass
New England Patriots	Foxboro Stadium	Foxboro, MA	1971	**60,794**	Grass
New York Jets	Giants Stadium	E.Rutherford, NJ	1976	**76,891**	Turf
Pittsburgh Steelers	Three Rivers Stadium	Pittsburgh, PA	1970	**59,030**	Turf
San Diego Chargers	San Diego/Jack Murphy Stadium	San Diego, CA	1967	**60,750**	Grass
Seattle Seahawks	The Kingdome	Seattle, WA	1976	**64,984**	Turf

National Conference

		Location	Built	Capacity	Field
Atlanta Falcons	Atlanta-Fulton County Stadium	Atlanta, GA	1965	**59,643**	Grass
Chicago Bears	Soldier Field	Chicago, IL	1924	**66,946**	Grass
Dallas Cowboys	Texas Stadium	Irving, TX	1971	**65,024**	Turf
Detroit Lions	Pontiac Silverdome	Pontiac, MI	1975	**80,494**	Turf
Green Bay Packers	Lambeau Field	Green Bay, WI	1957	**59,543**	Grass
	& County Stadium	Milwaukee, WI	1953	**56,051**	Grass
Los Angeles Rams	Anaheim Stadium	Anaheim, CA	1966	**69,008**	Grass
Minnesota Vikings	Hubert H.Humphrey Metrodome	Minneapolis, MN	1982	**63,000**	Turf
New Orleans Saints	Louisiana Superdome	New Orleans, LA	1975	**69,065**	Turf
New York Giants	Giants Stadium	E.Rutherford, NJ	1976	**77,152**	Turf
Philadelphia Eagles	Veterans Stadium	Philadelphia, PA	1971	**65,356**	Turf
Phoenix Cardinals	Sun Devil Stadium	Tempe, AZ	1958	**72,000**	Grass
San Francisco 49ers	Candlestick Park	San Francisco, CA	1960	**65,729**	Grass
Tampa Bay Buccaneers	Tampa Stadium	Tampa, FL	1967	**74,315**	Grass
Washington Redskins	Robert F.Kennedy Stadium	Washington, DC	1961	**55,672**	Grass

Note: Green Bay is scheduled to play three of five home games in Milwaukee in 1991.

National Football League (Cont.)

Rank by Capacity

AFC		NFC	
LA Coliseum	92,488	Silverdome	80,494
Rich	80,290	Giants	77,152
Cleveland	80,098	Tampa	74,315
Arrowhead	78,067	Sun Devil	72,000
Giants	76,891	Superdome	69,065
Mile High	76,273	Anaheim	69,008
Joe Robbie	73,000	Soldier Field	66,946
Kingdome	64,984	Candlestick	65,729
Foxboro	60,794	Veterans	65,356
SD/Murphy	60,750	Texas	65,024
Astrodome	60,502	HHH Metrodome	63,000
Hoosier Dome	60,127	Atlanta	59,643
Riverfront	59,755	Lambeau Field	59,543
Three Rivers	59,030	RFK	55,672

Rank by Age

AFC		NFC	
LA Coliseum	1923	Soldier Field	1924
Cleveland	1931	Lambeau Field	1957
Mile High	1948	Sun Devil	1958
Astrodome	1965	Candlestick	1960
SD/Murphy	1967	RFK	1961
Riverfront	1970	Atlanta	1965
Three Rivers	1970	Anaheim	1966
Foxboro	1971	Tampa	1967
Arrowhead	1972	Texas	1971
Rich	1973	Veterans	1971
Giants	1976	Silverdome	1975
Kingdome	1976	Superdome	1975
Hoosier Dome	1984	Giants	1976
Joe Robbie	1987	HHH Metrodome	1982

1990 NFL Attendance

The official overall attendance figure released by the NFL for the 224-game 1990 regular season was 13,959,896. The official average per game crowd was 62,321. Since the NFL does not release team-by-team attendance figures, the totals below were compiled from published newspaper game summaries. Those figures show overall attendance was 13,377,259 with an average per game crowd of 59,720. Teams in each conference are ranked by attendance over 8 home games; numbers in parentheses indicate rank in 1990 (based on published attendance figures).

	AFC	Attendance	Gm	Average
1	Buffalo (1)	621,549	8	77,694
2	Cleveland (2)	568,093	8	71,012
3	Denver (3)	560,703	8	70,088
4	Kansas City (4)	560,193	8	70,024
5	Miami (7)	510,707	8	63,838
6	Cincinnati (9)	483,288	8	60,411
7	LA Raiders (11)	468,393	8	58,549
8	NY Jets (10)	466,519	8	58,315
9	Seattle (5)	465,881	8	58,235
10	Houston (8)	449,275	8	56,159
11	Indianapolis (6)	440,681	8	55,085
12	Pittsburgh (12)	434,769	8	54,346
13	San Diego (13)	393,747	8	49,218
14	New England (14)	311,623	8	38,953
	TOTAL	6,735,421	112	60,138

	NFC	Attendance	Gm	Average
1	NY Giants (1)	599,570	8	74,946
2	New Orleans (5)	536,038	8	67,005
3	Philadelphia (3)	520,358	8	65,045
4	Detroit (12)	519,633	8	64,954
5	San Francisco (2)	506,397	8	63,300
6	Chicago (4)	485,651	8	60,706
7	LA Rams (6)	479,356	8	59,920
8	Dallas (11)	475,432	8	59,429
9	Tampa Bay (9)	455,796	8	56,975
10	Minnesota (7)	452,064	8	56,508
11	Green Bay (8)	441,792	8	55,224
12	Washington (10)	427,246	8	53,406
13	Atlanta (14)	394,853	8	49,357
14	Phoenix (13)	347,652	8	43,457
	TOTAL	6,641,838	112	59,302

Note: Green Bay played 5 games at Lambeau Field (56,195 avg.) and 3 at County Stadium (53,606 avg.).

Home Fields

Listed below are the principal home fields used through the years by current NFL teams. The largest capacity of each stadium is noted in the right hand column. All-America Football Conference stadiums (1946-49) are included for Cleveland and San Francisco; and American Football League stadiums (1960-69) are included for Buffalo, Cincinnati, Denver, Houston, Kansas City, LA (Oakland) Raiders, Miami, New England (Boston), NY Jets and San Diego.

AFC

Buffalo Bills

1960-72	War Memorial Stadium	45,748
1973–	Rich Stadium (Orchard Park,NY)	80,290
	(1973 capacity—80,020)	

Cincinnati Bengals

1968-69	Nippert Stadium (U.of Cincinnati)	26,500
1970–	Riverfront Stadium	59,755
	(1970 capacity—56,200)	

Cleveland Browns

1946–	Cleveland Stadium	80,098
	(1946 capacity—85,703)	

Denver Broncos

1960–	Mile High Stadium	76,273
	(1960 capacity—34,000)	

Houston Oilers

1960-64	Jeppesen Stadium	23,500
1965-67	Rice Stadium (Rice Univ.)	70,000
1968–	Astrodome	60,502
	(1968 capacity—52,000)	

Indianapolis Colts

1953-83	Memorial Stadium (Baltimore)	60,020
1984–	Hoosier Dome (Indianapolis)	60,127
	(1984 capacity—60,127)	

Kansas City Chiefs

1960-62	Cotton Bowl (Dallas)	72,000
1963-71	Municipal Stadium (Kansas City)	47,000
1972–	Arrowhead Stadium	78,067
	(1972 capacity—78,097)	

Los Angeles Raiders

1960	Kesar Stadium (San Francisco)	59,636
1961	Candlestick Park	42,500
1962-65	Frank Youell Field (Oakland)	20,000
1666-81	Oakland-Alameda County Coliseum	54,587
1982–	Memorial Coliseum (Los Angeles)	92,488
	(1982 capacity—92,604)	

Miami Dolphins

1966-86	Orange Bowl	75,206
1987–	Joe Robbie Stadium	73,000
	(1987 capacity—75,500)	

New England Patriots

1960-62	Nickerson Field (Boston Univ.)	17,369
1963-68	Fenway Park	33,379
1969	Alumni Stadium (Boston College)	26,000
1970	Harvard Stadium	37,300
1971–	Foxboro Stadium	60,794
	(1971 capacity—61,114)	

New York Jets

1960-63	Polo Grounds	55,987
1964-83	Shea Stadium	60,372
1984–	Giants Stadium (E.Rutherford,NJ)	76,891

Pittsburgh Steelers

1933-57	Forbes Field	35,000
1958-63	Forbes Field	35,000
	& Pitt Stadium	54,500
1964-69	Pitt Stadium	54,500
1970–	Three Rivers Stadium	59,030
	(1970 capacity—49,000)	

San Diego Chargers

1960	Memorial Coliseum (Los Angeles)	92,604
1961-66	Balboa Stadium (San Diego)	34,000
1967–	San Diego/Jack Murphy Stadium	60,750
	(1967 capacity—54,000)	

Seattle Seahawks

1976–	Kingdome	64,984
	(1976 capacity—65,000)	

Ballpark Nam Changes: CLEVELAND—**Cleveland Stadium** originally Municipal Stadium (1932-74); DENVER —**Mile High Stadium** originally Bears Stadium (1948-66); NEW ENGLAND—**Foxboro Stadium** originally Schaefer Stadium (1971-82), then Sullivan Stadium (1983-89); SAN DIEGO—**San Diego/Jack Murphy Stadium** originally San Diego Stadium (1967-81).

NFC

Atlanta Falcons

1966–	Atlanta-Fulton County Stadium	59,643
	(1966 capacity—58,850)	

Chicago Bears

1920	Staley Field (Decatur,IL)	—
1921-70	Wrigley Field (Chicago)	37,741
1971–	Soldier Field	66,946
	(1971 capacity—55,049)	

Dallas Cowboys

1960-70	Cotton Bowl	72,132
1971–	Texas Stadium (Irving,TX)	65,024
	(1971 capacity—65,101)	

Detroit Lions

1930-33	Spartan Stadium (Portsmouth,OH)	8,200
1934-37	Univ.of Detroit Stadium	25,000
1938-74	Tiger Stadium	54,468
1975–	Pontiac Silverdome	80,494
	(1975 capacity—80,638)	

Green Bay Packers

1921-22	Hagemeister Brewery Park	—
1923-24	Bellevue Park	—
1925-56	City Stadium I	24,800
1957–	Lambeau Field	59,543
	(1957 capacity—32,150)	

Note: The Packers have played some games in Milwaukee each season since 1933: at Borchert Field, State Fair Park and Marquette Stadium (1933-52), and County Stadium (56,051) since 1953.

Los Angeles Rams

1937-42	Municipal Stadium (Cleveland)	85,703
1945	Suspended operations for one year	
1944-45	Municipal Stadium	85,703
1946-79	Memorial Coliseum (Los Angeles)	92,604
1980–	Anaheim Stadium	69,008

Minnesota Vikings

1961-81	Metropolitan Stadium (Bloomington)	48,446
1982–	HHH Metrodome (Minneapolis)	63,000
	(1982 capacity—62,220)	

New Orleans Saints

1967-74	Tulane Stadium	80,997
1975–	Louisiana Superdome	69,065
	(1975 capacity—74,472)	

New York Giants

1925-55	Polo Grounds II	55,200
1956-73	Yankee Stadium I	63,800
1973-74	Yale Bowl (New Haven,CT)	70,896
1975	Shea Stadium	60,372
1976–	Giants Stadium (E.Rutherford,NJ)	77,152
	(1976 capacity—76,800)	

Philadelphia Eagles

1933-35	Baker Bowl	18,800
1936-39	Municipal Stadium	73,702
1940	Shibe Park	33,608
1941	Municipal Stadium	73,702
1942	Shibe Park	33,608
1943	Forbes Field (Pittsburgh)	34,528
1944-57	Shibe Park	33,608
1958-70	Franklin Field (Univ.of Penn.)	60,546
1971–	Veterans Stadium	65,356
	(1971 capacity—65,000)	

Phoenix Cardinals

1920-21	Normal Field (Chicago)	7,500
1922-25	Comiskey Park	28,000
1926-28	Normal Field	7,500
1929-59	Comiskey Park	52,000
1960-65	Busch Stadium (St.Louis)	34,000
1966-87	Busch Memorial Stadium	54,392
1988–	Sun Devil Stadium (Tempe,AZ)	72,000

National Football League (Cont.)

San Francisco 49ers

1946-70	Kezar Stadium	59,636
1971-	Candlestick Park	65,729
	(1971 capacity—61,246)	

Tampa Bay Buccaneers

1976-	Tampa Stadium	74,315
	(1976 capacity—71,951)	

Washington Redskins

1932	Braves Field (Boston)	40,000
1933-36	Fenway Park	27,000
1937-60	Griffith Stadium (Wash.,DC)	35,000
1961-	RFK Stadium	55,672
	(1961 capacity—55,004)	

Ballpark Name Changes: ATLANTA—**Atlanta-Fulton County Stadium** originally Atlanta Stadium (1966-74); CHICAGO—**Wrigley Field** originally Cubs Park (1916-25), also, **Comiskey Park** originally White Sox Park (1910-12); DETROIT— **Tiger Stadium** originally Navin Field (1912-37), then Briggs Stadium (1938-60), also, **Pontiac Silverdome** originally Pontiac Metropolitan Stadium (1975); GREEN BAY—**Lambeau Field** originally City Stadium II (1957-64); PHILADELPHIA—**Shibe Park** renamed Connie Mack Stadium in 1953; ST. LOUIS—**Busch Memorial Stadium** renamed Busch Stadium in 1983; WASHINGTON—**RFK Stadium** originally D.C.Stadium (1961-68).

NATIONAL HOCKEY LEAGUE

Campbell Conference

		Location	Built	Capacity
Calgary Flames	**Olympic Saddledome**	Calgary, Alb.	1983	**20,132**
Chicago Blackhawks	**Chicago Stadium**	Chicago, IL	1929	**17,317**
Detroit Red Wings	**Joe Louis Sports Arena**	Detroit, MI	1979	**19,875**
Edmonton Oilers	**Northlands Coliseum**	Edmonton, Alb.	1974	**17,503**
Los Angeles Kings	**Great Western Forum**	Inglewood, CA	1967	**16,005**
Minnesota North Stars	**Met Center**	Bloomington, MN	1967	**15,093**
St.Louis Blues	**St.Louis Arena**	St.Louis, MO	1929	**17,188**
San Jose Sharks	**Cow Palace**	San Francisco, CA	1941	**10,800**
Toronto Maple Leafs	**Maple Leaf Gardens**	Toronto, Ont.	1931	**16,382**
Vancouver Canucks	**Pacific Coliseum**	Vancouver, B.C.	1968	**16,123**
Winnipeg Jets	**Winnipeg Arena**	Winnipeg, Man.	1954	**15,569**

Wales Conference

		Location	Built	Capacity
Boston Bruins	**Boston Garden**	Boston, MA	1928	**14,448**
Buffalo Sabres	**Memorial Auditorium**	Buffalo, NY	1940	**16,325**
Hartford Whalers	**Civic Center Coliseum**	Hartford, CT	1975	**15,635**
Montreal Canadiens	**Montreal Forum**	Montreal, Que	1924	**16,197**
New Jersey Devils	**Meadowlands Arena**	E.Rutherford, NJ	1981	**19,040**
New York Islanders	**Veterans' Coliseum**	Uniondale, NY	1971	**16,297**
New York Rangers	**Madison Sqare Garden**	New York, NY	1968	**16,792**
Philadelphia Flyers	**The Spectrum**	Philadelphia, PA	1967	**17,382**
Pittsburgh Penguins	**Civic Arena**	Pittsburgh, PA	1961	**16,164**
Quebec Nordiques	**Colisee de Quebec**	Quebec City, Que	1951	**15,399**
Washington Capitals	**Capital Centre**	Landover, MD	1973	**18,130**

Rank by Capacity

Campbell		Wales	
Saddledome	20,132	Meadowlands	19,040
Joe Louis	19,875	Capital Centre	18,130
Northlands	17,503	Spectrum	17,382
Chicago Stadium	17,317	Mad.Sq.Garden	16,792
St.Louis	17,188	Buffalo Aud	16,325
M.Leaf Gardens	16,382	Nassau Col	16,297
Pacific	16,123	Montreal Forum	16,197
GW Forum	16,005	Pittsburgh	16,164
Winnipeg	15,569	Hartford	15,635
Met Center	15,093	Le Colisee	15,399
Cow Palace	10,800	Boston Garden	14,448

Note: Figures do not include Standing Room.

Rank by Age

Campbell		Wales	
Chicago Stadium	1929	Montreal Forum	1924
St.Louis	1929	Boston Garden	1928
M.Leaf Gardens	1931	Buffalo Aud.	1940
Cow Palace	1941	Le Colisee	1951
Winnipeg	1954	Pittsburgh	1961
Met Center	1967	Spectrum	1967
GW Forum	1967	Mad.Sq.Garden	1968
Pacific	1968	Nassau Col.	1971
Northlands	1974	Capital Centre	1973
Joe Louis	1979	Hartford	1975
Saddledome	1983	Meadowlands	1981

Note: Montreal Forum was rebuilt in 1968; Hartford Civic Center was rebuilt in 1980.

1990-91 NHL Attendance

The official overall attendance figure released by the NHL for the 840-game 1990-91 regular season was 12,343,897. The official average per game crowd was 14,695. Since the NHL does not release team-by-team attendance figures, the totals below were compiled from published newspaper game summaries. Those figures show overall attendance was 12,961,373 with an average per game crowd of 15,430. Teams in each conference are ranked by attendance over 40 home games; **S/O** heading indicates number of sellouts; numbers in parentheses indicate rank in 1989-90 (based on published attendance figures).

Campbell Conference

		Attendance	S/O	Average
1	Calgary (1)	799,614	25	19,990
2	Detroit (2)	785,966	17	19,649
3	Chicago (3)	716,824	40	17,921
4	St.Louis (8)	686,338	24	17,158
5	Edmonton (4)	673,749	15	16,844
6	Toronto (5)	650,172	26	16,254
7	Los Angeles (6)	626,957	34	15,674
8	Vancouver (7)	606,036	9	15,151
9	Winnipeg (9)	517,276	2	12,932
10	Minnesota (10)	316,522	0	7,913
	TOTAL	6,379,454	192	15,949

Wales Conference

		Attendance	S/O	Average
1	Philadelphia (1)	693,674	27	17,342
2	Montreal (3)	680,011	40	17,000
3	Washington (2)	664,653	9	16,616
4	Pittsburgh (5)	637,072	28	15,927
5	NY Rangers (4)	635,579	8	15,889
6	Buffalo (6)	626,171	12	15,654
7	Boston (9)	573,607	29	14,340
8	Quebec (7)	567,540	4	14,189
9	New Jersey (8)	525,934	6	13,148
10	Hartford (10)	496,170	3	12,404
11	NY Islanders (11)	481,508	3	12,038
	TOTAL	6,581,919	169	14,959

Home Ice

Listed below are the principal home buildings used through the years by current NHL teams. The largest capacity of each arena is noted in the right hand column. World Hockey Association arenas (1972-76) are included for Edmonton, Hartford, Quebec and Winnipeg.

Campbell Conference

Calgary Flames
1972-80	The Omni (Atlanta)	15,278
1980-83	Calgary Corral	7,424
1983–	Olympic Saddledome	20,132
	(1983 capacity—16,674)	

Chicago Stadium
1926-29	Chicago Coliseum	5,000
1929–	Chicago Stadium	17,317
	(1929 capacity—16,500)	

Detroit Red Wings
1926-27	Border Cities Arena (Windsor,Ont.)	3,200
1927-79	Olympia Stadium (Detroit)	16,700
1979–	Joe Louis Arena	19,875
	(1979 capacity—19,275)	

Edmonton Oilers
1972-74	Edmonton Gardens	7,200
1974–	Northlands Coliseum	17,503
	(1974 capacity—15,513)	

Los Angeles Kings
1967–	Great Western Forum	16,005
	(1967 capacity—15,651)	

Note: The Kings played 17 games at Long Beach Sports Arena and LA Sports Arena at the start of the 1967-68 season.

Minnesota North Stars
1967–	Met Center	15,093
	(1967 capacity—14,400)	

St.Louis Blues
1967–	St.Louis Arena	17,188
	(1967 capacity—14,200)	

San Jose Sharks
1991–	Cow Palace	10,800

Toronto Maple Leafs
1917-31	Mutual Street Arena	8,000
1931–	Maple Leaf Gardens	16,382
	(1931 capacity—13,542)	

Vancouver Canucks
1970–	Pacific Coliseum	16,123
	(1970 capacity—15,760)	

Winnipeg Jets
1972–	Winnipeg Arena	15,569
	(1972 capacity—10,177)	

Building Name Changes: LOS ANGELES—**Great Western Forum** originally The Forum (1967-88); MINNESOTA—**Met Center** originally Metropolitan Sports Center (1967-82); ST.LOUIS—**St.Louis Arena** renamed The Checkerdome in 1977, then St.Louis Arena again in 1982.

Wales Conference

Boston Bruins
1924-28	Boston Arena	6,200
1928–	Boston Garden	14,448
	(1928 capacity—14,500)	

Buffalo Sabres
1970–	Memorial Auditorium	16,325
	(1970 capacity—10,429)	

National Hockey League (Cont.)

Hartford Whalers

1972-73	Boston Garden	14,442
1973-74	Boston Garden (regular season)	14,442
	W.Springfield,MA Big E (playoffs)	5,513
1974-75	West Springfield Big E	5,513
	& Hartford (CT) Civic Center	10,507
1975-77	Hartford Civic Center	10,507
1977-78	Hartford Civic Center	10,507
	& Springfield (MA) Civic Center	7,725
1978-79	Springfield Civic Center	7,725
1979-80	Springfield Civic Center	7,725
	& Hartford Civic Center II	14,250
1980–	Hartford Civic Center II	15,635
	(1980 capacity—14,460)	

Note: The Hartford Civic Center roof caved in Jan, 1978, forcing the Whalers to move their home games to Springfield,MA, for two years.

Montreal Canadiens

1910-20	Jubilee Arena	3,200
1913-18	Montreal Arena (Westmount)	6,000
1918-26	Mount Royal Arena	6,750
1926-68	Montreal Forum I	15,500
1968–	Montreal Forum II	16,197
	(1968 capacity—16,074)	

Note: The Forum (original capacity: 9,200) was built in 1924 for Montreal's other NHL team, the Maroons, who were its only tenant from 1924-26. The Maroons, who folded after the 1937-38 season, shared the Forum with the Canadiens from 1924-38.

New Jersey Devils

1974-76	Kemper Arena (Kansas City)	16,300
1976-82	McNichols Arena (Denver)	15,900
1982–	Meadowlands Arena	
	(E.Rutherford,NJ)	19,040
	(1982 capacity—19,023)	

New York Islanders

1972–	Nassau Veterans' Mem.Coliseum	16,297
	(1972 capacity—14,500)	

New York Rangers

1925-68	Madison Square Garden III	15,925
1968–	Madison Square Garden IV	16,792
	(1968 capacity—17,250)	

Philadelphia Flyers

1967–	The Spectrum	17,382
	(1967 capacity—14,558)	

Note: A section of Spectrum roof blew off in March,1968, forcing the Flyers to play their last seven regular season home games at Madison Sq.Garden (1 game), Maple Leaf Gardens (1) and Le Colisqee in Quebec (5). The roof was fixed by the playoffs.

Pittsburgh Penguins

1967–	Civic Arena	16,164
	(1967 capacity—12,508)	

Quebec Nordiques

1972–	Le Colisée de Québec	15,399
	(1972 capacity—10,004)	

Washington Capitals

1974–	Capital Centre (Landover,MD)	18,130

COLLEGE BASKETBALL

The 41 Largest Arenas

The 41 largest arenas in Division I college basketball. Note that (*) indicates part-time home court.

Arena	Seats	Home Team	Arena	Seats	Home Team
Carrier Dome	32,683	Syracuse	Hartford Civic Center	16,016	UConn*
Thompson-Boling Center	24,535	Tennessee	Kibbie-Asui Dome	16,000	Idaho
Charlotte Coliseum	23,906	NC-Charlotte	Allen Field House	15,800	Kansas
Rupp Arena	23,000	Kentucky	Memorial Auditorium	15,564	Canisius*
Marriott Center	22,700	BYU	Carver-Hawkeye	15,550	Iowa
Dean Smith Center	21,444	N.Carolina	LA Sports Arena	15,509	USC
Meadowlands Arena	20,039	Seton Hall* & St.Peter's*	Knickerbocker Arena	15,500	Siena*
			Memorial Gymnasium	15,387	Vanderbilt
Madison Square Garden	19,081	St.John's*	Breslin Student Events Center	15,100	Michigan St.
Freedom Hall	18,865	Louisville	Coleman Coliseum	15,043	Alabama
Capital Centre	18,756	Georgetown	Arena-Auditorium	15,028	Wyoming
Bradley Center	18,633	Marquette	Miami Arena	15,008	Miami-FL
Thomas & Mack Center	18,500	UNLV	Huntsman Center	15,000	Utah
The Spectrum	18,168	Villanova*	Cole Fieldhouse	14,500	Maryland
Rosemont Horizon	17,500	DePaul & Loyola-IL	Joel Coliseum	14,500	Wake Forest
			Devaney Sports Center	14,478	Nebraska
Assembly Hall	17,357	Indiana	University Center	14,287	Arizona St.
The Pit	17,126	New Mexico	Maravich Center	14,164	LSU
Pittsburgh Civic Arena	16,798	Pittsburgh*	Mackey Arena	14,123	Purdue
Williams Arena	16,434	Minnesota	Hilton Coliseum	14,020	Iowa St.
Erwin Special Events Center	16,231	Texas	WVU Coliseum	14,000	West Va.
Assembly Hall	16,153	Illinois			

Future NCAA Final Four Sites

Year	Arena	Seats	Location	Year	Arena	Seats	Location
1992	HHH Metrodome	23,000	Minneapolis	1995	Kingdome	38,808	Seattle
1993	Superdome	65,000	New Orleans	1996	Meadowlands	20,039	E.Rutherford
1994	Charlotte Coliseum	23,906	Charlotte	1997	Hoosier Dome	38,000	Indianapolis

Conference Home Courts

Arenas played in by NCAA Men's Division I basketball teams. Teams with home games in more than one arena are noted.

Atlantic Coast

Home Floor		Seats
Clemson	Littlejohn Coliseum	11,020
Duke	Cameron Indoor Stadium	9,314
Florida St	Leon County Civic Center	12,500
Georgia Tech	Alexander Memorial Coliseum	9,800
Maryland	Cole Field House	14,500
North Carolina	Dean E.Smith Center	21,572
N.C.State	Reynolds Coliseum	12,400
Virginia	University Hall	8,864
Wake Forest	Lawrence Joel Coliseum	14,407

Atlantic 10

Home Floor		Seats
Duquesne	A.J.Palumbo Center	6,200
G.Washington	Charles E.Smith Center	5,000
Massachusetts	Curry Hicks Cage	4,024
	& Springfield Civic Center	8,200
Rhode Island	Keaney Gymnasium	5,000
	& Providence Civic Center	13,410
Rutgers	Louis Brown Athletic Center	9,000
St.Bonaventure	Reilly Center	6,000
St.Joseph's-PA	Alumni Memorial Fieldhouse	3,200
Temple	McGonigle Hall	3,900
West Virginia	WVU Coliseum	14,000

Big East

Home Floor		Seats
Boston College	Conte Forum	8,624
Connecticut	Gampel Pavilion	8,028
	& Hartford Civic Center	16,016
Georgetown	Capital Centre	18,756
Miami-FL	Miami Arena	15,008
Pittsburgh	Fitzgerald Field House	6,798
	& Pittsburgh Civic Arena	16,798
Providence	Providence Civic Center	13,410
St.John's	Alumni Hall	6,008
	& Madison Square Garden	19,081
Seton Hall	Walsh Gymnasium	3,200
	& Meadowlands Arena	20,039
Syracuse	Carrier Dome	32,683
Villanova	duPont Pavilion	6,500
	& The Spectrum	18,168

Big Eight

Home Floor		Seats
Colorado	Coors Events Center	11,199
Iowa St	Hilton Coliseum	14,020
Kansas	Allen Fieldhouse	15,800
Kansas St	Bramlage Coliseum	13,500
Missouri	Hearnes Center	13,143
Nebraska	Devaney Sports Center	14,302
Oklahoma	Lloyd Noble Center	10,861
Okla.St	Gallagher-Iba Arena	6,381

Big Sky

Home Floor		Seats
Boise St	BSU Pavilion	12,200
Eastern Wash	Reese Court	5,000
Idaho	Kibbie-Asui Dome	9,000
Idaho St	Holt Arena	7,938
Montana	Dahlberg Arena	9,059
Montana St	Brick Breeden Fieldhouse	7,848
Nevada	Lawlor Event Center	11,200
Northern Ariz	Walkup Skydome	7,500
Weber St	Dee Events Center	12,000

Note: Nevada will leave Big Sky to join Big West in 1992-93.

Big South

Home Floor		Seats
Campbell	Carter Gym	1,500
	& Cumberland Civic Center	5,500
Charleston	Charleston Southern Fieldhouse	2,500
Coastal Caro	Kimbel Gym	1,800
Davidson	John M.Belk Arena	6,000
Liberty	Vines Center	9,000
NC-Asheville	Justice Center	2,500
	& Asheville Civic Center	6,800
Radford	Dedmon Center	5,000
Winthrop	Winthrop Coliseum	6,100

Note: Davidson will leave Big South to join Southern in 1992-93.

Big Ten

Home Floor		Seats
Illinois	Assembly Hall	16,153
Indiana	Assembly Hall	17,357
Iowa	Carver-Hawkeye Arena	15,500
Michigan	Crisler Arena	13,609
Michigan St	Breslin Events Center	15,138
Minnesota	Williams Arena	16,434
Northwestern	Welsh-Ryan Arena	8,117
Ohio St	St.John Arena	13,276
Penn St	Rec Hall	6,846
Purdue	Mackey Arena	14,123
Wisconsin	Wisconsin Field House	11,886

Note: Penn St. will not compete for conference title until 1992-93.

Big West

Home Floor		Seats
CS-Fullerton	Titan Gym	4,000
Fresno St	Selland Arena	10,159
Long Beach St	University Gym	2,200
	& Long Beach Arena	12,000
New Mexico St	Pan American Center	13,222
Pacific	Alex G.Spanos Center	6,000
San Jose St	Recreation & Events Center	4,800
UC-Irvine	Donald Bren Events Center	5,000
UC-Santa Barbara	Campus Events Center	6,000
UNLV	Thomas & Mack Center	18,500
Utah St	The Spectrum	10,270

Note: Fresno St. will leave Big West to join WAC in 1992-93, while Nevada will leave Big Sky to join Big West.

Colonial

Home Floor		Seats
American	Bender Arena	5,000
East Carolina	Minges Coliseum	6,500
George Mason	Patriot Center	10,000
James Madison	JMU Convocation Center	7,612
NC-Wilmington	Trask Coliseum	6,100
Old Dominion	Norfolk Scope	10,253
Richmond	Robbins Center	9,171
Wm.& Mary	William & Mary Hall	10,000

East Coast

Home Floor		Seats
Brooklyn	Roosevelt Gym	1,500
Buffalo	Alumni Arena	10,000
Cent.Conn.St	Detrick Gymnasium	4,000
Hofstra	Physical Fitness Center	3,500
MD-Balt.County	UMBC Fieldhouse	4,024
Rider	Alumni Gymnasium	2,000
Towson St	Towson Center	5,000

College Basketball (Cont.)

Great Midwest

Home Floor		Seats
Ala-Birmingham....	UAB Arena	8,500
	& Birmingham Civic Center	17,500
Cincinnati.........	Myrl Shoemaker Center	13,176
DePaul...........	Rosemont Horizon	17,500
	& Alumni Hall	5,229
Marquette........	Bradley Center	18,633
Memphis St.......	Great American Pyramid	20,000
St.Louis..........	The Arena	11,200

Ivy League

Home Floor		Seats
Brown...........	Pizzitola Sports Center	2,500
Columbia........	Levien Gymnasium	3,200
Cornell..........	Alberding Field House	4,473
Dartmouth.......	Leede Arena	2,100
Harvard.........	Briggs Athletic Center	3,000
Penn............	The Palestra	8,722
Princeton........	Jadwin Gymnasium	7,442
Yale............	Payne Whitney Gymnasium	3,000

Metro

Home Floor		Seats
Louisville........	Freedom Hall	18,865
NC-Charlotte.....	Charlotte Coliseum	23,901
South Florida.....	Sun Dome	10,347
Southern Miss.....	Reed Green Coliseum	8,095
Tulane..........	Fogelman Arena	3,600
VCU............	Richmond Coliseum	10,716
Virginia Tech.....	Cassell Coliseum	9,971

Metro Atlantic

Home Floor		Seats
Canisius.........	Memorial Auditorium	15,564
	& Koessler Athletic Center	1,800
Fairfield.........	Alumni Hall	3,022
Iona............	Mulcahy Campus Center	3,200
La Salle.........	Philadelphia Civic Center	10,000
Loyola-MD.......	Reitz Arena	3,000
Manhattan.......	Draddy Gymnasium	3,000
Niagara.........	Niagara Falls Conv.Center	6,000
	& Gallagher Center	3,200
St.Peter's........	Yanitelli Center	3,200
	& Meadowlands	19,761
Siena...........	Alumni Recreation Center	4,000
	& Knickerbocker Arena	15,500

Mid-American

Home Floor		Seats
Ball St..........	Activities Complex	12,000
Bowling Green.....	Anderson Arena	5,000
Central Mich......	Rose Arena	6,000
Eastern Mich......	Bowen Field House	5,600
Kent............	Memorial Gym	6,034
Miami-OH........	Millett Hall	9,200
Ohio Univ........	Convocation Center	13,080
Toledo..........	John F.Savage Hall	9,000
Western Mich.....	Read Fieldhouse	8,250

Mid-Continent

Home Floor		Seats
Akron...........	Rhodes Arena	5,500
Cleveland St......	Convocation Center	13,500
Eastern Ill.......	Lantz Gym	6,500
IL-Chicago.......	UIC Pavillion	10,000
Northern Ill......	Evans Field House	6,076
Valparaiso.......	Athletics Rec.Center	4,500
Western Ill.......	Western Hall	5,139
WI-Green Bay.....	Brown County Arena	5,600
Wright St........	Ervin Nutter Center	10,632
Youngstown St.....	Beeghly Center	7,500

Note: Youngstown St. will not compete for conference championship until 1992-93.

Mid-Eastern

Home Floor		Seats
Bethune-Cookman.........	Moore Gym	2,000
Coppin St.........	Pullen Gym	3,000
Delaware St.......	Memorial Hall	4,000
Florida A&M.......	Gaither Gym	6,000
Howard..........	Burr Gym	3,900
MD-East.Shore....	Tawes Gym	3,500
Morgan St........	T.L.Hill Field House	7,500
N.Carolina A&T....	Corbett Sports Center	7,500
S.Carolina St......	Smith-Hammond-Middleton	3,200

Midwestern

Home Floor		Seats
Butler...........	Hinkle Fieldhouse	10,800
Dayton.........	Univ.of Dayton Arena	13,455
Detroit..........	Cobo Arena	11,143
Evansville........	Roberts Stadium	12,300
Loyola-IL........	Rosemont Horizon	17,500
Xavier-OH........	Cincinnati Gardens	10,400

Missouri Valley

Home Floor		Seats
Bradley..........	Carver Arena	10,401
Creighton........	Omaha Civic Auditorium	9,800
Drake...........	Veterans Mem.Auditorium	9,564
Illinois St........	Redbird Arena	10,500
Indiana St........	Hulman Center	10,200
Northern Iowa.....	UNI-Dome	10,000
Southern Ill.......	SIU Arena	10,014
SW Missouri St.....	Hammons Student Center	8,858
Tulsa...........	Maxwell Convention Center	9,200
Wichita St........	Levitt Arena	10,656

North Atlantic

Home Floor		Seats
Boston Univ.......	Walter Brown Arena	4,200
Delaware.........	Delaware Field House	3,000
Drexel..........	Phys.Ed.Athletic Center	2,500
Hartford.........	Sports Center	4,500
Maine..........	Alfond Arena	6,000
New Hampshire....	Lundholm Gym	3,500
Northeastern.....	Matthews Arena	6,500
Vermont.........	Patrick Gym	3,200

Northeast

Home Floor		Seats
FDU-Teaneck......	Rothman Center	5,000
LIU-Bklyn.........	Schwartz Athletic Center	2,000
Marist..........	McCann Center	3,944
Monmouth........	Alumni Memorial Gym	2,800
Mt.St.Mary's......	Knot Arena	3,500
Robert Morris.....	Charles Sewall Center	3,056
St.Francis-NY......	Physical Ed Center	1,400
St.Francis-PA......	Maurice Stokes Center	4,000
Wagner..........	Sutter Gym	1,650

Ohio Valley

Home Floor		Seats
Austin Peay........	Dunn Center	9,000
Eastern Ky........	Alumni Coliseum	6,500
Middle Tenn.St.....	Murphy Athletic Center	11,520
Morehead St.......	Academic-Athletic Center	6,500
Murray St........	Racer Arena	5,550
SE Missouri St......	Show Me Center	7,000
Tennessee St.......	Gentry Center	10,500
Tennessee Tech....	Eblen Center	10,150

Pacific-10

Home Floor		Seats
Arizona	McKale Center	13,477
Arizona St	University Activity Center	14,287
California	Harmon Arena	6,578
Oregon	McArthur Court	10,063
Oregon St	Gill Coliseum	10,400
Stanford	Maples Pavilion	7,500
UCLA	Pauley Pavilion	12,543
USC	LA Sports Arena	15,509
Washington	Hec Edmundson Pavilion	8,000
Wash.St.	Friel Court	12,058

Patriot League

Home Floor		Seats
Army	Cristl Arena	5,043
Bucknell	Davis Gym	2,100
Colgate	Cotterell Court	3,000
Fordham	Rose Hill Gymnaslum	3,470
Holy Cross	Hart Center	4,000
Lafayette	Kirby Fieldhouse	3,500
Lehigh	Stabler Center	5,800
Navy	Halsey Field House	5,000

Southeastern

EASTERN	Home Floor	Seats
Florida	O'Connell Center	12,000
Georgia	Georgia Coliseum	11,200
Kentucky	Rupp Arena	23,000
South Carolina	Carolina Coliseum	12,401
Tennessee	Thompson-Boling Arena	24,535
Vanderbilt	Memorial Gymnasium	15,399

WESTERN	Home Floor	Seats
Alabama	Coleman Coliseum	15,043
Arkansas	Barnhill Arena	9,000
Auburn	Eaves-Memorial Coliseum	12,500
LSU	Maravich Assembly Center	14,236
Mississippi	Tad Smith Coliseum	8,135
Mississippi St.	Humphrey Coliseum	10,000

Southern

Home Floor		Seats
Appalachian St.	Varsity Gymnasium	8,000
The Citadel	McAlister Field House	6,200
E.Tenn.St.	Memorial Center	12,000
Furman	Greenville Memorial Aud.	6,000
Marshall	Henderson Center	10,250
Tenn-Chatt	UTC Arena	11,218
VMI	Cameron Hall	5,029
W.Carolina	Ramsey Center	7,826

Southland

Home Floor		Seats
McNeese St.	Burton Coliseum	8,000
Nicholls St.	Stopher Gym	3,800
North Texas	UNT Super Pit	10,000
NE Louisiana	Ewing Coliseum	8,000
N'western St	Prather Coliseum	3,900
Sam Houston St	Johnson Coliseum	6,172
SW Texas St	Strahan Coliseum	7,200
S.F.Austin	SFA Coliseum	7,050
TX-Arlington	Texas Hall	4,200
TX-San Antonio	Convocation Center	5,100

Southwest

Home Floor		Seats
Baylor	Ferrell Center	10,084
Houston	Hofheinz Pavilion	10,060
Rice	Autry Court	5,400
SMU	Moody Coliseum	9,007
Texas	Erwin Center	16,231
Texas A&M	G.Rollie White Coliseum	7,500
TCU	Daniel-Meyer Coliseum	7,166
Texas Tech	Lubbock Municipal Coliseum	8,174

Southwestern

Home Floor		Seats
Alabama St.	C.J.Dunn Arena	3,200
Alcorn St	Scalpin' Grounds Arena	7,000
Grambling	Memorial Gym	5,000
Jackson St.	Williams Ath. & Assembly	8,000
Miss.Valley	Henderson Ath.Complex	6,000
Prairie View	Little Dome	6,000
Southern-BR	F.G.Clark Activity Center	7,500
TX Southern	Health & Phys.Ed.Arena	7,500

Sun Belt

Home Floor		Seats
Ark-Little Rock	Barton Coliseum	8,303
Arkansas St.	Convocation Center	10,563
Central Fla	UCF Arena	5,100
Jacksonville	Jacksonville Coliseum	10,000
Lamar	Montagne Center	10,080
Louisiana Tech	Thomas Assembly Center	8,000
New Orleans	Kiefer Lakefront Arena	10,000
Pan American	UT-Pan Am Field House	5,000
South Alabama	Mobile Civic Center	10,000
SW Louisiana	Cajundome	12,000
Western Ky	E.A.Diddle Arena	12,370

Trans America

Home Floor		Seats
Centenary	Gold Dome	4,002
Florida Int'l	Golden Panther Arena	4,661
Ga.Southern	Hanner Fieldhouse	5,500
Georgia St	GSU Sports Arena	5,500
Mercer	Macon Coliseum	9,000
Samford	Seibert Gym	4,000
SE Louisiana	University Center	7,500
Stetson	Edmunds Center	5,000

West Coast Athletic

Home Floor		Seats
Gonzaga	Charlotte Martin Centre	4,000
Loyola-CA	Gersten Pavilion	4,500
Pepperdine	Firestone Fieldhouse	3,104
Portland	Earle Chiles Center	5,000
St.Mary's-CA	McKeon Pavilion	3,500
San Diego	USD Sports Center	2,500
San Francisco	Memorial Gymnasium	5,300
Santa Clara	Toso Pavilion	5,000

Western Athletic

Home Floor		Seats
Air Force	Cadet Fieldhouse	6,007
BYU	Marriott Center	22,700
Colorado St	Moby Arena	9,001
Hawaii	Blaisdell Center	7,575
New Mexico	The Pit	17,126
San Diego St	San Diego Sports Arena	13,741
UTEP	Special Events Center	12,200
Utah	Jon Huntsman Center	15,000
Wyoming	Arena-Auditorium	15,028

Note: Fresno St. will join WAC for 1992-93 season.

Independents

Home Floor		Seats
CS-Northridge	Matador Gymnasium	3,000
CS-Sacramento	Hornet Gym	1,800
Charleston-SC	F.Mitchell Johnson Center	3,052
Chicago St	Phys.Ed.& Athletics Building	2,500
Missouri-KC	Municipal Auditorium	10,000
NC-Greensboro	Spectator Gymnasium	2,500
NE Illinois	Chick Evans Field House	6,076
Notre Dame	Joyce Center	11,418
So.Utah St.	The Centrum	5,300
WI-Milwaukee	Klotsche Center	4,000
	& The Mecca	11,052

COLLEGE FOOTBALL

UPI/Bettmann

The **Rose Bowl** is the country's largest football stadium, seating 104,091 for UCLA home games and the annual New Year's Day battle between the champions of the Pacific-10 and Big 10.

The 30 Largest Stadiums

The 30 largest stadiums in Division I college football. Note that (*) indicates part-time home field.

		Location	Seats	Home Team	Conference	Built	Field
1	Rose Bowl	Pasadena, CA	104,091	UCLA	Pac-10	1922	Grass
2	Michigan Stadium	Ann Arbor, MI	101,701	Michigan	Big Ten	1927	Grass
3	Beaver Stadium	University Park, PA	93,000	Penn St.	Big Ten/'93	1960	Grass
4	Memorial Coliseum	Los Angeles, CA	92,516	USC	Pac-10	1923	Grass
5	Neyland Stadium	Knoxville, TN	91,902	Tennessee	SEC	1921	Turf
6	Ohio Stadium	Columbus, OH	86,071	Ohio St.	Big Ten	1922	Grass
7	Stanford Stadium	Palo Alto, CA	86,019	Stanford	Pac-10	1921	Grass
8	Sanford Stadium	Athens, GA	85,432	Georgia	SEC	1929	Grass
9	Jordan-Hare Stadium	Auburn, AL	85,214	Auburn	SEC	1939	Grass
10	Legion Field	Birmingham, AL	84,000	Alabama*	SEC	1927	Turf
11	Florida Field	Gainesville, FL	83,000	Florida	SEC	1929	Grass
12	Tiger Stadium	Baton Rouge, LA	80,140	LSU	SEC	1924	Grass
13	Memorial Stadium	Clemson, SC	79,854	Clemson	ACC	1942	Grass
14	Memorial Stadium	Austin, TX	77,809	Texas	SWC	1924	Turf
15	Camp Randall Stadium	Madison, WI	77,745	Wisconsin	Big Ten	1917	Turf
16	Giants Stadium	E.Rutherford, NJ	76,000	Rutgers*	Big East	1976	Turf
17	Spartan Stadium	East Lansing, MI	76,000	Michigan St.	Big Ten	1957	Turf
18	Memorial Stadium	Berkeley, CA	75,662	California	Pac-10	1923	Turf
19	Orange Bowl	Miami, FL	75,500	Miami-FL	Big East	1935	Grass
20	Owen Field	Norman, OK	75,004	Oklahoma	Big Eight	1923	Turf
21	Sun Devil Stadium	Tempe, AZ	74,865	Arizona St.	Pac-10	1958	Grass
22	Memorial Stadium	Lincoln, NE	73,650	Nebraska	Big Eight	1923	Turf
23	Husky Stadium	Seattle, WA	72,500	Washington	Pac-10	1920	Turf
24	Williams-Brice Stadium	Columbia, SC	72,400	S.Carolina	SEC	1934	Grass
25	Kyle Field	College Station, TX	72,387	Texas A&M	SWC	1925	Turf
26	Cotton Bowl	Dallas, TX	72,032	SMU*	SWC	1932	Turf
27	Yale Bowl	New Haven, CT	70,896	Yale	Ivy League	1914	Grass
28	Kinnick Stadium	Iowa City, IA	70,311	Iowa	Big Ten	1929	Grass
29	Bryant-Denny Stadium	Tuscaloosa, AL	70,123	Alabama	SEC	1929	Grass
30	Rice Stadium	Houston, TX	70,000	Rice	SWC	1950	Turf

Conference Home Fields

Conference by conference listing for the 1992 regular season, including the Big East and the Southeastern Conference's move to two divisions. Note that Penn St. is listed with the Big Ten, although it will not officially compete for the conference title until 1993.

ACC

	Stadium	Built	Seats	Field
Clemson	Memorial	1942	79,854	Grass
Duke	Wallace Wade	1929	33,941	Grass
Florida St	Doak Campbell	1950	60,519	Grass
Ga.Tech	Dodd	1914	46,000	Turf
Maryland	Byrd	1950	45,000	Grass
N.Carolina	Kenan	1927	52,000	Grass
N.C.State	Carter-Finley	1966	53,500	Grass
Virginia	Scott	1931	42,000	Turf
Wake Forest	Groves	1968	31,500	Grass

Note: Florida St. joins ACC for 1992 season.

Big East

	Stadium	Built	Seats	Field
Boston Col	Alumni	1957	32,000	Turf
Miami-FL	Orange Bowl	1935	75,500	Grass
Pittsburgh	Pitt	1925	56,500	Turf
Rutgers	Rutgers	1938	25,000	Grass
	& Giants	1976	76,000	Turf
Syracuse	Carrier Dome	1980	50,000	Turf
Temple	Veterans	1971	66,592	Turf
Va.Tech	Lane	1965	51,000	Grass
West Va.	Mountaineer Fld	1980	63,500	Grass

Big Eight

	Stadium	Built	Seats	Field
Colorado	Folsom Field	1924	51,941	Turf
Iowa St	Trice Field	1975	50,000	Turf
Kansas	Memorial	1927	51,250	Turf
Kansas St	KSU	1968	42,000	Turf
Missouri	Faurot Field	1926	62,000	Turf
Nebraska	Memorial	1923	73,650	Turf
Oklahoma	Owen Field	1923	75,004	Turf
Oklahoma St	Lewis Field	1920	50,440	Turf

Big Ten

	Stadium	Built	Seats	Field
Illinois	Memorial	1923	69,359	Turf
Indiana	Memorial	1960	52,354	Turf
Iowa	Kinnick	1929	70,311	Grass
Michigan	Michigan	1927	101,701	Grass
Michigan St.	Spartan	1957	76,000	Turf
Minnesota	HHH Metrodome	1982	63,699	Turf
Northwestern	Dyche	1926	49,256	Turf
Ohio St	Ohio	1922	86,071	Grass
Penn St	Beaver	1960	93,000	Grass
Purdue	Ross-Ade	1924	67,861	Grass
Wisconsin	Camp Randall	1917	77,745	Turf

Note: Penn St. will not compete for Big Ten title until 1993.

Big West

	Stadium	Built	Seats	Field
CS-Fullerton	Santa Ana	1963	12,000	Grass
L.Beach St.	Veterans	1966	12,500	Grass
Nevada	Mackay	1965	26,000	Grass
N.Mexico St	Aggie Memorial	1978	30,343	Grass
Pacific	Stagg Memorial	1950	30,153	Grass
San Jose St	Spartan	1932	31,218	Grass
UNLV	Silver Bowl	1971	32,000	Turf
Utah St	Romney	1968	30,257	Grass

Note: Fresno St. left after 1991 season to join WAC. Nevada moves up from the Div.I-AA Big Sky to join Big West in 1992 (stadium seats will increase to 30,000).

Mid-American

	Stadium	Built	Seats	Field
Ball St	Ball State	1967	16,319	Grass
Bowl.Green	Perry Field	1966	30,599	Grass
Cent.Mich	Kelly/Shorts	1972	20,086	Turf
East.Mich	Rynearson	1969	19,800	Grass
Kent	Dix	1969	30,520	Grass
Miami-OH	Yager	1983	25,183	Grass
Ohio Univ.	Peden	1929	20,000	Grass
Toledo	Glass Bowl	1937	26,248	Turf
West.Mich	Waldo	1939	30,000	Turf

Pacific-10

	Stadium	Built	Seats	Field
Arizona	Arizona	1928	56,167	Grass
Arizona St	Sun Devil	1958	74,865	Grass
California	Memorial	1923	75,662	Turf
Oregon	Autzen	1967	41,698	Turf
Oregon St.	Parker	1953	35,362	Turf
Stanford	Stanford	1921	86,019	Grass
UCLA	Rose Bowl	1922	104,091	Grass
USC	LA Coliseum	1923	92,516	Grass
Washington	Husky	1920	72,500	Turf
Washington.St	Martin	1972	40,000	Turf

Southeastern

Divisional play begins with 1992 season.

EASTERN	Stadium	Built	Seats	Field
Florida	Florida Field	1929	83,000	Grass
Georgia	Sanford	1929	85,434	Grass
Kentucky	Commonwealth	1973	57,800	Grass
S.Carolina	Williams-Brice	1934	72,400	Grass
Tennessee	Neyland	1921	91,902	Turf
Vanderbilt	Vanderbilt	1981	41,000	Turf

WESTERN	Stadium	Built	Seats	Field
Alabama	Bryant-Denny	1929	70,123	Grass
	& Legion Field	1927	84,000	Turf
Arkansas	Razorback	1938	52,968	Turf
	& War Memorial	1948	53,645	Turf
Auburn	Jordan-Hare	1939	85,214	Grass
LSU	Tiger	1924	80,140	Grass
Mississippi	Vaught-Hem'way	1941	42,577	Grass
	& Memorial	1953	60,549	Grass
Miss.St.	Scott Field	1935	41,200	Grass

Note: At **Alabama**, Bryant-Denny Stadium is in Tuscaloosa and Legion Field is in Birmingham; at **Mississippi**, Vaught-Hemingway Stadium is in Oxford and Memorial Stadium is in Jackson.

Southwest

	Stadium	Built	Seats	Field
Baylor	Casey	1950	48,500	Turf
Houston	Astrodome	1965	60,502	Turf
Rice	Rice	1950	70,000	Turf
SMU	Ownby	1926	23,783	Turf
	& Cotton Bowl	1932	72,032	Turf
Texas	Memorial	1924	77,809	Turf
Texas A&M	Kyle Field	1925	72,387	Turf
TCU	Carter	1929	46,000	Turf
Texas Tech	Jones	1947	50,500	Turf

Note: Arkansas left after 1991 season to join SEC.

College Football (Cont.)

WAC

Stadium		Built	Seats	Field
Air Force	Falcon	1962	52,123	Grass
BYU	Cougar	1964	65,000	Grass
Colorado St	Hughes	1968	30,000	Grass
Fresno St.	Bulldog	1980	40,541	Grass
Hawaii	Aloha	1975	50,000	Turf
New Mexico	University	1960	30,646	Grass
S.Diego St.	SD/Murphy	1967	60,409	Grass
Utah	Rice	1927	35,000	Turf
UTEP	Sun Bowl	1963	52,000	Turf
Wyoming	War Memorial	1950	33,500	Grass

Note: Fresno joins WAC for 1992 season.

I-A Independents

Stadium		Built	Seats	Field
Akron	Rubber Bowl	1940	35,482	Turf
Army	Michie	1924	39,929	Turf
Cincinnati	Nippert	1924	34,500	Turf
E.Carolina	Ficklin	1963	35,000	Grass
La.Tech	Aillet	1968	30,600	Grass
Louisville	Cardinal	1956	35,500	Turf
Memphis St.	Liberty Bowl	1965	63,244	Grass
Navy	Navy-Marine Corps Memorial	1959	30,000	Grass
Northern Ill.	Huskie	1965	30,998	Turf
Notre Dame	Notre Dame	1930	59,075	Grass
Penn St.	Beaver	1960	93,000	Grass
SW La	Cajun Field	1970	31,000	Grass
So.Miss	Roberts	1976	33,000	Grass
Tulane	La.Superdome	1975	69,065	Turf
Tulsa	Skelly	1930	40,385	Turf

Notes: Cincinnati's Nippert Stadium will seat 34,500 for the 1992 season; Penn St. will compete as an independent in 1992, then join Big Ten in 1993.

Bowl Games

Stadium		Built	Seats	Field
Aloha	Aloha	1975	50,000	Turf
Blockbuster	Joe Robbie	1986	73,000	Grass
Calif. Raisin	Bulldog	1980	40,541	Grass
Copper	Arizona	1928	57,000	Grass
Cotton	Cotton Bowl	1932	72,032	Turf
Fiesta	Sun Devil	1958	74,865	Grass
Fla.Citrus	Fla.Citrus Bowl-Orlando	1936	60,000	Grass
Freedom	Anaheim	1966	69,008	Grass
Gator	Gator Bowl	1949	82,000	Grass
Hall of Fame	Tampa	1967	74,314	Grass
Holiday	Jack Murphy	1967	60,750	Grass
John Hancock	Sun Bowl	1963	52,000	Turf
Independence	Independence	1936	50,560	Grass
Liberty	Liberty Bowl	1965	63,244	Grass
Orange	Orange Bowl	1935	75,500	Grass
Peach	Atlanta	1965	59,643	Grass
Rose	Rose Bowl	1922	104,091	Grass
Sugar	Superdome	1975	69,065	Turf

Bowl Game Sites

Aloha—Honolulu; **Blockbuster**—Miami; **Calif. Raisin**—Fresno; **Copper**—Tucson,AZ; **Cotton**—Dallas; **Fiesta**—Tempe,AZ; **Florida Citrus**—Orlando; **Freedom**—Anaheim,CA; **Gator**—Jacksonville,FL; **Hall of Fame**—Tampa, FL; **Holiday**—San Diego; **John Hancock**—El Paso,TX; **Independence**—Shreveport,LA; **Liberty**—Memphis,TN; **Orange**—Miami; **Peach**—Atlanta; **Rose**—Pasadena,CA; **Sugar**—New Orleans.

CANADIAN FOOTBALL LEAGUE

Western Division

	Stadium	Location	Built	Capacity	Field
British Columbia Lions	B.C.Place	Vancouver, BC	1983	59,478	Turf
Calgary Stampeders	McMahon Stadium	Calgary, ALB.	1960	38,200	Turf
Edmonton Eskimos	Commonwealth Stadium	Edmonton, ALB.	1978	60,081	Grass
Saskatchewan Roughriders	Taylor Field	Regina, SASK.	1948	27,637	Turf

Eastern Division

	Stadium	Location	Built	Capacity	Field
Hamilton Tiger-Cats	Ivor Wynne Stadium	Hamilton, ONT.	1932	29,183	Turf
Ottawa Rough Riders	Lansdowne Stadium	Ottawa, ONT.	1967	30,927	Turf
Toronto Argos	SkyDome	Toronto, ONT.	1989	53,595	Turf
Winnipeg Blue Bombers	Winnipeg Stadium	Winnipeg, MAN.	1953	32,648	Turf

MISCELLANEOUS

Auto Racing's two biggest 500-mile races—the Daytona 500 and Indianapolis 500; the Tennis Grand Slam—Wimbledon and the Australian, French and U.S. Opens; Horse Racing's Triple Crown—the Kentucky Derby, Preakness Stakes and Belmont Stakes; are all held annually at the same sites. Note that seating does not include standing room, and infield capacity for auto and horse racing is estimated.

Auto Racing

Oval	Seats	Infield
Daytona International Speedway	94,500	55,000
Indianapolis Motor Speedway	265,000	135,000

Tennis

Event	Main Stadium	Seats
Australian Open	National Tennis Centre	15,000
French Open	Stade Roland Garros	16,500
Wimbledon	Centre Court	13,107
U.S.Open	Louis Armstrong Stadium	20,000

Horse Racing

Race	Racetrack	Seats	Infield
Kentucky Derby	Churchill Downs	51,500	100,000
Preakness	Pimlico Race Course	40,000	50,000
Belmont Stakes	Belmont Park	32,491	50,000

Record crowds: Kentucky Derby—163,628 (1974, 100th running, won by Cannonade); Preakness—90,14 (1989, 114th running, won by Sunday Silence); Belmont Stakes—82,694 (1971, 103rd running, Canonero II loses bid to win Triple Crown).

Cynthia Greer

American **John Harkes** (left), of English First Division team Sheffield Wednesday, and former high school teammate **Tony Meola** of the U.S. National team, with the Philadelphia Cup trophy after the USA beat Sheffield, 1-0, on Aug. 2.

SOCCER

All Tied Up

Penalty kick shoot-outs and lack of offense still plague international game; but things are looking up in the U.S.

Call 1991 a transition year. Certainly, the first requirement for a transition was there: dissatisfaction with the *status quo*. The 1990 World Cup left too many people unhappy with the quality of the soccer for that to be in doubt.

There was, too, an air of change about the sport. FIFA, the governing body of international soccer, introduced a number of rule changes, including several designed to promote attacking soccer. For example, tougher penalties were introduced for defensive fouls that thwarted goal-scoring opportunities, while the offside rule was modified in favor of players on offense. And in an attempt to cut down on time wasting, goalkeepers were banned from handling the ball twice on the same play. FIFA also cast a critical eye over increasingly way-out uniform styles, commenting that players should not be permitted "to dress like clowns."

One proposal that did not go over well was the perennial suggestion that goal-scoring be increased by enlarging the goals. Opponents protested that it would make scoring too easy and thus distort the sport. It would also involve far too much upheaval and expense to alter the

goals and the field markings on hundreds of thousands of fields throughout the world. ("We cannot afford bigger goals, would it be all right if we use smaller goalkeepers?" as the old joke has it.) There were hints that the idea was really designed "to satisfy the Americans," who were seen as wanting to give the fans more scoring during the 1994 World Cup.

This knee-jerk opposition to any change in the rules—not uncommon in soccer's conservative leaders—made it difficult to predict where soccer's transition would end up. But the guardians of the *status quo* were dealt a wicked blow by the Yugoslav team Red Star and its coach Ljupko Petrovic. Against Marseille of France in the 1991 European Cup Final—the climax of the European season—Red Star played nothing but turgid defense. Throughout the 90-minute game, and on into 30 minutes of overtime, Red Star took no risks at all—and only *three* shots at the Marseille goal (all of them off target)! As Marseille's technical director, Franz Beckenbauer, put it: "Red Star refused to play."

Nevertheless, Red Star took the trophy by winning the penalty kick shoot-out. Coach Petrovic defiantly admitted the ugly truth: his team had deliberately stalled for two hours because they didn't think they could beat Marseille by playing soccer, but they felt confident of winning the shoot-out.

Paul Gardner has been a columnist for *Soccer America* since 1982. He has covered international soccer as a writer and broadcaster in Europe and the United States since 1964 and has written three books on the sport.

David Jacobs/Action Images

Olympique Marseille's **Bernard Casoni** (right) ignores the outstretched hand of Red Star Belgrade midfielder **Robert Prosinecki** after Red Star deliberately played for a penalty kick shootout victory in the European Cup final in May.

Petrovic was not apologetic for spoiling the occasion: "We did not invent the present rules, and the rules include penalties and invite the use of tactics to reach the penalty shoot-out stage."

In the 1990 World Cup final, Argentina had been heavily criticized for the same tactics. But Argentina had an excuse: injuries and suspensions had greatly weakened its team. Red Star had its full team available—a team that, on the very day of the game, the European press had hailed for its exciting, attacking style.

But Petrovic and his players had performed a service, by showing so starkly that the penalty-kick tie-breaker, far from encouraging teams to play riskily to avoid a tie, was just as likely to *cause* a dull, defensive performance.

Unfortunately, FIFA was reluctant to alter the system. One month after the Red Star-Marseille travesty, Portugal and Brazil played to a 0-0 tie in the final of the World Championship for U-20 players (players under 20 years-old). Portugal took the title on penalty kicks. For good measure, the Soviet Union won the third place game over Australia, also on PKs.

A ray of hope came from the United States Organizing Committee for the 1994 World Cup. It requested that the 1994 final—should it end in a tie—be replayed rather than going to penalty kicks. FIFA is debating the matter. Another FIFA move was to appoint a "Football 2000" task force to report on the state of the game. After its first meeting in March, the committee announced that the game "lacks appeal, but is not in crisis." In August, the group chairman, Lennart Johansson, admitted that 80 percent of the letters it had received were hostile to the penalty kick tie-breaker, and "the same opinion has been expressed at all our meetings."

In the South American championship—the Copa America—they got around the problem by playing the tournament as a round-robin, which allowed games to be tied. The Copa produced a healthy goals-per-game average of 2.8 and was won by Argentina, under new coach Alfio Basile.

But penalty kicks proved the downfall

467

of the United States team during the Under-17 World Cup in Italy. After a splendid first round in which the Americans won all three of their games, beating China and—for the first time ever, at any level of soccer—both Italy and Argentina, the U.S. bowed to Qatar in the shootout.

The same fate befell the U.S. in the 1991 World University Games in Sheffield, England. First round wins over Ireland, England and Iran took the American team to the quarterfinals, where it tied Uruguay, 1-1, and lost on penalty kicks.

For the United States senior team, work resumed under new coach Bora Milutinovic whose mission was clear: to produce a team that would be competitive in the 1994 World Cup.

Bora proved a winner on two fronts— both on the field (see box), and in the PR department, where his willngness, nay eagerness, to talk to everyone (in somewhat fractured English) quickly made him a lot of friends.

Chuck Cale, CEO of World Cup USA 1994, had more good news in May when he announced that 26 cities had filed bids to host games in '94. "This is an historic occasion for us and for the World Cup," said Cale. "Never have so many sites bid to participate in a World Cup."

The news was particularly significant because the cities had to come with real, live cash with their bids. Over $3.7 million in deposit checks flowed into the World Cup coffers. The total included $265,000 from a decidedly optimistic New York City—which frankly admitted that while it didn't have a suitable stadium, it was thinking of converting Aqueduct Race Track to soccer purposes. Such was the desire of FIFA and the U.S. Organizing Committee to stage some World Cup games in New York, that the suggestion was taken seriously.

The first major soccer event of World Cup 1994 was scheduled for December 1991 in New York, where the draw to decide which country plays which in the world-wide qualifying rounds will be announced. Sadly, the weekend chosen (by FIFA, apparently) conflicted with the NCAA Division I Final Four, one of the few national soccer events in the U.S.

Not that the college tournament had exactly distinguished itself in 1990, when

Bora Turns U.S. National Team Around

Taking over as coach of the United States national team in March, Bora Milutinovic was thrown right into the deep end. He inherited a squad of unfamiliar players, and a schedule of tough games against world class opponents.

Two key players were unavailable because of their success with European clubs. Tab Ramos was playing with Spanish 2nd division club Figueras, while John Harkes was helping another 2nd division team, England's Sheffield Wednesday, gain promotion to the 1st division. (In the process, Harkes became the first American ever to play in a major Cup final at Wembley, where Sheffield won the League Cup before 80,000 fans.)

Despite the obstacles, four months after his appointment the ever-smiling Bora could beam down on a 6-1-3 record that included a win over Uruguay and a triumph in the Gold Cup—the championship of the Caribbean, North and Central American region. The Gold Cup victory was particularly satisfying, as it included a solid 2-0 semifinal win over eternal rival Mexico—a win that may well mark the end of Mexico's almost unchallenged dominance of the region.

Said Bora: "I'm really very surprised at the quality of my players. What they have done in the games since I've been the coach is extraordinary—only great athletes could have done it. We've been playing very well, but we still have a lot of work to do. You don't measure soccer in terms of one week . . ."

Bora's influence is measured in that ever-present smile. His easygoing attitude was a sharp contrast to that of his predecessor, Bob Gansler, and the players responded with a more flowing, less uptight performance on the field. "He gives you an open end on flexibility, as long as you benefit the team," said team captain Peter Vermes. "That's what's good about him and different from before. He gets the best of each player, but it's for the whole team."

Looking for the essential ingredient of any team with ambitions—an experienced midfield playmaker—Bora brought back 27-year-old Hugo Perez, who had been

Cynthia Greer

U.S. National team coach **Bora Milutinovic** (right) discusses strategy with American captain **Peter Vermes** before playing Ireland to a 1-1 draw on June 1, before a crowd of 51,273 in Foxboro, Mass.

dropped by Gansler. Perez responded with a series of skillful performances, and an optimistic view of the team: "I'm very hopeful. The situation is different now . . . Bora allows me the maximum freedom to express myself on the field."

Keeping pace with the team's lengthening strides was the marketing side of things. Niftily dubbed "The World Series of Soccer," the USA's 12-match series was scheduled in cities seeking to operate as playing sites during the 1994 World Cup. Local promotion proved a winner, with crowds of 35,772 in Denver (USA 1, Uruguay 0); 31,761 in Stanford, Calif. (Argentina 1, USA 0); 51,273 in Foxboro, Mass. (USA 1, Ireland 1). In Philadelphia, 44,261 were present to see the U.S. score a 2-0 win over John Harkes and Sheffield Wednesday.

Bora then took the team on a European tour that opened with a 2-1 loss to the Soviet Olympic team on Aug. 17. Having avoided one nasty shock by departing Moscow the day before the abortive coup, the Americans then ran into another when they were walloped 4-0 in Austria by club team FC Tirol. But Bora's Boys bounced back to defeat Romania 2-0 in Bucharest and tie Turkey 1-1 in Istanbul.

Meanwhile, in Cuba, the U.S. Olympic team, under coach Lothar Osiander, won the gold medal at the Pan American Games with a 2-1 overtime win against Mexico.

"It's like we're on a never-ending roll," said USSF president Alan Rothenberg, whose first year in office was taken up with turning the federation into a modern, professionally-run sports body. The announcement that the USSF would move its offices from remote Colorado Springs to Chicago was proof of the intention.

When the USSF held its 1991 Annual General Meeting in Detroit in August, general secretary Hank Steinbrecher told the applauding delegates: "Our time has come." Yet, just as the USSF and the national team seemed to be taking off, American professional soccer was taking a nose dive.

The Major Soccer League will enter the 1991-92 season with fewer than eight teams for the first time since 1978-79. And the American Professional Soccer League, which had operated with 22 teams in 1990, was reduced to a mere eight in 1991.

The APSL insisted that the disappearance or merger of 14 clubs was the result of the league's increasingly stringent standards: "We are now a smaller but stronger league," said APSL co-chairman, Clive Toye.

Certainly smaller, anyway.

UCLA took the NCAA Division I title in Tampa without scoring a goal in its final two games. Once again, the penalty-kick tie-breaker was the culprit. The Bruins played 0-0 ties against North Carolina State in the semifinals and Rutgers in the championship game—and won both on PKs.

Said a disgruntled Rutgers goalkeeper Bill Andracki, afterward: "Penalty kicks don't end the game. They kill the game."

Indoors, the Major Soccer League celebrated the end of its season in the now traditional way: by crowning the San Diego Sockers as champions (for the sixth time in the last seven years), and by immediately going into crisis as clubs threatened to withdraw. By late summer the eight-team league that began the 1990-91 season had been reduced to seven with the folding of the Kansas City Comets and an unsuccessful attempt to bring back a team in Pittsburgh.

The U.S. women's national team provided a sparkling bright spot in its quest to qualify for the first-ever women's World Cup, scheduled for China in November 1991. It ran away with the trophy in the regional qualifying tournament, winning all five of its games and outscoring its opponents by a combined 49-0.

In Europe, West German captain Lothar Matthaeus was voted the 1990 Player of the Year, then led his club, Inter of Milan, to the 1991 UEFA Cup championship. That was it for Italian teams, which failed to repeat their 1990 sweep of the three club trophies. Red Star of Yugoslavia, of course, stalled its way to victory in the European Cup, while Manchester United's win in the Cup Winners' Cup marked the successful return of the English clubs. The remaining restraint on English participation in the club competitions was later lifted when Liverpool was allowed to enter the 1991-92 UEFA Cup.

Liverpool, which lost out to Arsenal in the English championship, provided one sensation when its manager, Kenny Dalglish, abruptly quit in mid-season. At a tearful press conference, he cited the pressures and stresses of the game.

There were other, rather more devious, coaching changes. Ron Atkinson denied that he was joining Aston Villa, declaring that his post with Sheffield Wednesday was "the best job in the world." A week later, he resigned . . . and signed for Aston Villa. Red Star coach Petrovic, after the exertions of the European Cup final, announced that he was stepping down because he "needed a rest from the pressures of the game." He denied that he was taking another job. But a few weeks later, he turned up in Barcelona, where he signed as coach for the Spanish first division team Espanol.

The pressures of the game also weighed heavily on some of its top players. On Italy's Toto Schillaci, for instance: the top-scorer in the 1990 World Cup with six goals, and then . . . the abyss. Between November 1990 and May 1991, Schillaci—starting regularly for Juventus—did not find the net once. Six months without a goal. And the strain began to show, when Toto was reported to the Italian league authorities for having told an opponent that he would "have him shot."

Toto was not the only one in trouble. All in all, 1991 was not a good year to be a soccer star. Tony Adams, captain of the English champions, Arsenal, was sent to jail for four months for drunken driving and was fined $1,600 for an obscene gesture he made to opposing fans during a game.

Problems, too, for the man acclaimed as the sport's rising star: Paul (Gazza) Gascoigne, of the London club Tottenham Hotspur. He had impressed during World Cup 1990, and at one point had been mentioned as a possible successor to Diego Maradona at Napoli. But Napoli GM Luciano Moggi squelched that, saying: "We're not interested in British players. They generally find it very difficult to adapt to both our football and our way of life."

There was more than a grain of truth in that, but it didn't stop another Italian club, Lazio of Rome, from offering a staggering $12 million for Gazza. Many in England scoffed at the idea, portraying Gazza as a highly skilled but very immature and reckless youngster who wouldn't last five minutes in the cynical, knowing world of Italian pro soccer.

It was an assessment that received spectacular confirmation in the English Cup Final. Gazza—evidently determined to impress in what looked like his last game for Tottenham—charged onto the

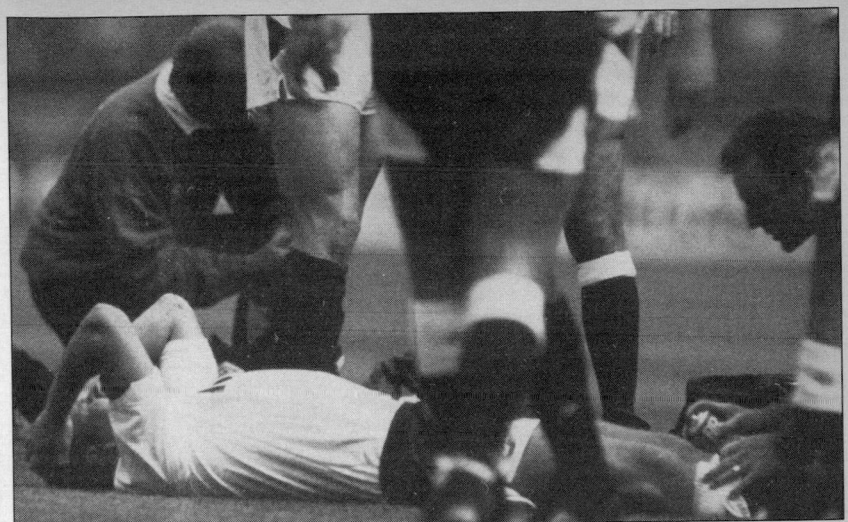

David Jacobs/Action Images

Tottenham Hotspur star **Paul Gascoigne** is administered to on the pitch at Wembly after tearing knee ligaments in the English Cup final. The injury is expected to keep him out of action until early 1992.

famous Wembley Stadium turf, committed one dreadful foul almost immediately, and followed it 15 minutes later with another one that resulted in disastrous consequences for himself. He tore his knee ligaments, was stretchered off and taken straight to the hospital. There he learned that he would be out of action for at least eight months. He also learned that Tottenham had won the Cup without his help. After his release, Gazza emphasized his wild-boy reputation by attacking an over-attentive photographer with his crutches. Lazio hesitated for a while, but decided it would buy Gascoigne anyway.

Elsewhere, things turned sour very quickly for promising 19-year-old Argentine Juan Esnaider. Signed to a five-year contract by Real Madrid after he had been the top scorer in the South American youth championship, the unknown Esnaider was hastily presented to the Spanish press—as the successor to their fabled Mexican goal-scorer Hugo Sanchez. That sort of pressure on a young player did not bode well. Esnaider played a few games for Real, without distinction; then, at the end of the season, turned out for Argentina in the U-20 World Cup. Disaster. During an opening round 3-0 loss to Portugal, Esnaider was ejected from the game for trying to head-butt the referee. He was later suspended from all international games for one year.

But it was, inevitably, that other Argentine—Diego Maradona—who made most of the headlines. Things started well enough. He turned up on time in Naples for pre-season training, and swore that he was "ready to take the field in a wheelchair," if that would help his club Napoli win the European Cup. But his behavior became increasingly erratic as the season wore on. Maradona blithely announced that he wouldn't travel with the team to Moscow for a crucial European Cup tie. He then changed his mind, arrived a day late by private jet, and was kept on the bench for the first half. He played in the second half, but could do nothing to prevent Napoli's elimination (on PKs, of course). On another occasion, when Napoli called to find out why he was not at practice, they were told by his personal manager that "Maradona is still sleeping, and has given instructions not to be disturbed."

Now there was no more talk of wheelchairs. Maradona said he would play only when fully fit, and frequently indicated that, after six years, he wanted to leave Napoli and Italy, and that he was thinking of quitting the game.

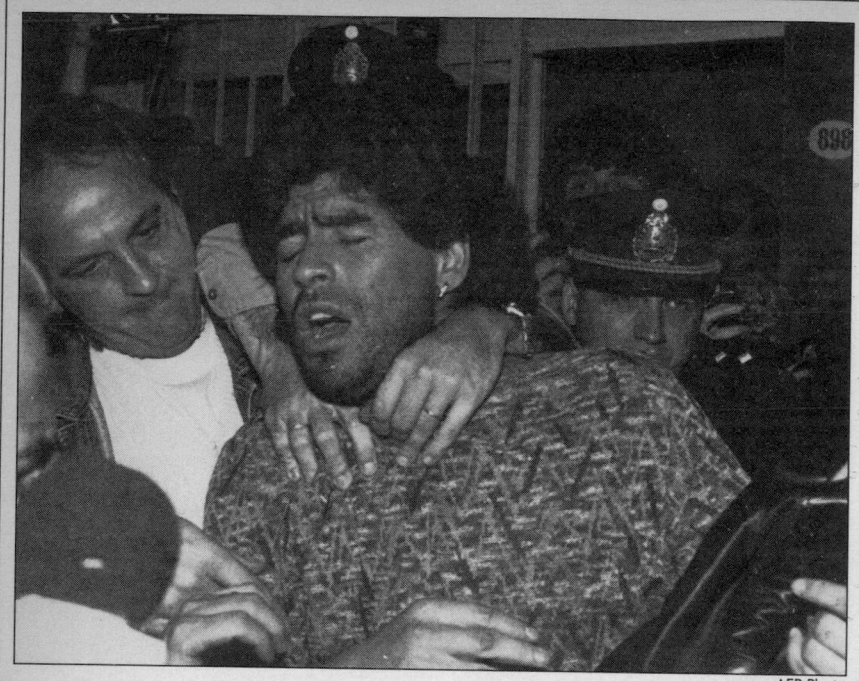

AFP Photo

Argentine star **Diego Maradona** is removed by policemen from a Buenos Aires apartment on Apr. 26, after being arrested for cocaine possession. His arrest followed suspensions by both the Italian soccer league and FIFA for drug use.

A scandal began to unfold in February, when Maradona's name was linked to dealings with known drug-suppliers in Naples. Maradona denied any involvement, but the roof fell in a month later when the Italian soccer league suspended him because he had failed a drug test—traces of cocaine had been found in his blood. FIFA followed by banning him from all soccer, worldwide, for 15 months.

Within four days, Maradona had fled to Buenos Aires, taking his family with him. But the troubled star was to find no peace there, either. In a television interview, he declared that he was finished with soccer: "I don't want any more training camps. I want to start living."

A week later, the soccer world was shocked at the pictures of an unshaven Maradona being arrested by police officers after a drug raid on a Buenos Aires apartment.

Charged with cocaine possession and use, Maradona plea-bargained to avoid a jail sentence, and entered a treatment program. His former colleagues rallied to his support, while Argentine President Carlos Menem described him as "a sick young man who needs help."

They remembered him back in Naples, too—remembered that it was Maradona who had inspired Napoli to its first ever victory in the national championship. The huge banners at Napoli's home games said, simply, "Thank You, Diego."

The final word on the tribulations of being a soccer star belongs with Adriano Samaniego of the Paraguayan club, Olimpia. Samaniego entered a bar in Asuncion and demanded free beer in the name of Olimpia. He was refused. He then drew a gun, and he got his beer. But on the way back to his car, he dropped the gun and it went off . . . shooting him in the foot! □

SOCCER STATISTICS

THE SEASON IN REVIEW
1990-1991
WORLD • EUROPE • AMERICA

THE 1992 INFORMATION PLEASE SPORTS ALMANAC

SEC A

PAGE 473

International Champions
NATIONAL TEAM COMPETITION
WORLDWIDE
1991 U-20 Championship: Portugal 0, Brazil 0 (Portugal wins on penalty kicks, 4-2)

1991 U-17 Championship: Ghana 1, Spain 0

1991 Women's Championship: in China (Nov.16-30)

SOUTH AMERICA
1991 Copa America

The South American Championship; held July 6-21 in Chile. The 10-team field divided into two groups with each group playing a four-game round-robin. The top two teams in each group advance to the round-robin final where the team with the most points wins the title. Copa America has been contested irregularly since 1916.

First Round

GROUP A	W	L	T	Pts	GF	GA
*Argentina	4	0	0	8	11	3
*Chile	3	1	0	6	10	3
Paraguay	2	2	0	4	7	8
Peru	1	3	0	2	9	9
Venezuela	0	4	0	0	1	15

Results
July 6—Chile 2, Venezuela 0; Paraguay 1, Peru 0. **July 8**—Argentina 3, Venezuela 0; Chile 4, Peru 2. **July 10**—Argentina 1, Chile 0; Paraguay 5, Venezuela 0. **July 12**—Argentina 4, Paraguay 1; Peru 5, Venezuela 1. **July 14**—Argentina 3, Peru 2; Chile 4, Paraguay 0.

GROUP B	W	L	T	Pts	GF	GA
*Colombia	2	1	1	5	4	2
*Brazil	2	1	1	5	6	5
Uruguay	1	0	3	5	4	3
Ecuador	1	2	1	3	6	5
Bolivia	0	2	2	2	3	8

Results
July 7—Colombia 1, Ecuador 0; Uruguay 1, Bolivia 1. **July 9**—Brazil 2, Bolivia 1; Uruguay 1, Ecuador 1. **July 11**—Brazil 1, Uruguay 1; Colombia 1, Bolivia 1. **July 13**—Colombia 2, Brazil 0; Ecuador 4, Bolivia 0. **July 15**—Brazil 3, Ecuador 1; Uruguay 1, Colombia 0.

Final Round Robin
(Overall tournament records in parentheses)

	W	L	T	Pts	GF	GA
Argentina (6-0-1)	2	0	1	5	5	3
Brazil (4-2-1)	2	1	0	4	6	3
Chile (3-2-2)	0	1	2	2	1	3
Colombia (2-3-2)	0	2	1	1	2	5

Results
July 17—Argentina 3, Brazil 2; Chile 1, Colombia 1. **July 19**—Argentina 0, Chile 0; Brazil 2, Colombia 0. **July 21**—Argentina 2, Colombia 1; Brazil 2, Chile 0.

CONCACAF
1991 Gold Cup

The Confederation of North, Central American and Caribbean Football Championship; held June 28-July 7 in Los Angeles. The 8-team field divided into two groups with each group playing a three-game round-robin. The top two teams in each group advance to the semifinal round; the two winners meet for the title and the two losers play for third place.

First Round

GROUP A	W	L	T	Pts	GF	GA
*Honduras	2	0	1	5	10	3
*Mexico	2	0	1	5	8	3
Canada	1	2	0	2	6	9
Jamaica	0	3	0	0	3	12

Results
June 28—Honduras 4, Canada 2; Mexico 4, Jamaica 1. **June 30**—Honduras 5, Jamaica 0; Mexico 3, Canada 1. **July 3**—Honduras 2, Mexico 1; Canada 3, Jamaica 2.

GROUP B	W	L	T	Pts	GF	GA
*United States	3	0	0	6	8	3
*Costa Rica	1	2	0	2	5	5
Trinidad/Tobago	1	2	0	2	3	4
Guatemala	1	2	0	2	1	5

Results
June 29—USA 2, Trinidad/Tobago 1; Costa Rica 2, Guatemala 0. **July 1**—USA 3, Guatemala 0; Trinidad/Tobago 2, Costa Rica 1. **July 3**—USA 3, Costa Rica 2; Guatemala 1, Triniidad/Tobago 0.

Semifinals
Honduras 2 .... Costa Rica 0
United States 2 .... Mexico 0

Third Place
Mexico 2 .... Costa Rica 0

Championship
United States 0 .... Honduras 0
(USA wins on penalty kicks, 4-3)

Most Valuable Player: Tony Meola, G, USA.
Leading Scorer: Benjamin Galindo, MF, Mexico (4 goals).

CLUB TEAM COMPETITION
WORLDWIDE
1990 Toyota Cup Final: AC Milan 3, Olimpia 0

EUROPE

European Champions Cup

Contested by league champions of countries belonging to the Union of European Football Associations (UEFA). Semifinals use two-game/total goals format. The final is one game.

Semifinals
Red Star Belgrade vs. **Bayern Munich**

Red Star 2............................... at Bayern 1
at Red Star 2............................... Bayern 2
(Red Star wins, 4-3)

Olympique Marseille vs. **Spartak Moscow**

Marseille 3............................... at Spartak 1
at Marseille 2............................... Spartak 1
(Marseille wins, 5-2)

Final
(May 29 at Bari, Italy)

Red Star 0............................... Marseille 0
(Red Star wins on penalty kicks, 5-3)

European Cup Winners Cup

Contested by cup winners of countries belonging to the Union of European Football Associations (UEFA). Semifinals use two-game/total goals format. The final is one game.

Semifinals
Manchester United vs. **Legia Warsaw**

Manchester United 3....................... at Legia 1
at Manchester United 1..................... Legia 1
(Manchester wins, 4-2)

Barcelona vs. **Juventus**

at Barcelona 3............................ Juventus 1
at Juventus 1............................. Barcelona 0
(Barcelona wins, 3-2)

Final
(May 15 at Rotterdam, Holland)

Manchester United 2....................... Barcelona 1

UEFA Cup

Contested by teams other than league champions and cup winners and selected by UEFA based on each country's previous performance in the tournament. Semifinals and final use two-game/total goals format.

Semifinals
AS Roma vs. **Broendby**

AS Roma 0............................... at Broendby 0
at AS Roma 2............................... Broendby 1
(AS Roma wins, 2-1)

Inter Milan vs. **Sporting Lisbon**

Inter Milan 0............................... at Sporting 0
at Inter Milan 2............................... Sporting 0
(Inter Milan wins, 2-0)

Final
(May 8 at Milan; May 22 at Rome)

Inter Milan vs. **AS Roma**

at Inter Milan 2............................... AS Roma 0
at AS Roma 1............................... Inter Milan 0
(Inter Milan wins, 2-1)

National Champions

Country	League Champion	Cup Winner
Austria	Austria Vienna	Stockerau
Belgium	Anderlecht	Brugge
Czechoslovakia	Sparta Prague	Banik Ostrava
England	Arsenal	Tottenham
France	Marseille	Monaco
Holland	PSV Eindhoven	Feyenoord
Hungary	Honved	Ferencvaros
Italy	Sampdoria	AS Roma
Poland	Zagelbie Lubin	GKS Katowice
Portugal	Benfica	FC Porto
Romania	U.Craiova	U.Craiova
Scotland	Glasgow Rangers	Motherwell
Spain	Barcelona	Atletico Madrid
USSR	(In progress)	CSKA Moscow
W.Germany	Kaiserslautern	Bremen
Yugoslavia	Red Star	Hajduk Split

SOUTH AMERICA
Copa Liberatodores

Contested by the league champions of South America's football union. Semifinals and final use two-game/total goals format.

Semifinals
Colo Colo vs. **Boca Juniors**

at Boca Juniors 1.......................... Colo Colo 0
at Colo Colo 3............................. Boca Juniors 1
(Colo Colo wins, 3-2)

Olimpia vs. **Atletico Nacional**

Olimpia 0.......................... at Atletico Nacional 0
at Olimpia 1.......................... Atletico Nacional 0
(Olimpia wins, 1-0)

Final
Colo Colo vs. **Olimpia**
(May 29 at Asuncion; June 6 at Santiago)

Colo Colo 0............................. at Olimpia 0
at Colo Colo 3............................. Olimpia 0
(Colo Colo wins, 3-0)

U.S. National Team

International Schedule

(Through Sept. 14, 1991)

Date		Score	Site	Crowd
2/1	Switzerland-a	L, 0-1	Miami	10,323
2/3	Bayern Munich-a	L, 0-4	Miami	5,107
2/21	Bermuda	L, 0-1	Hamilton	12,000
3/9	Olimpia (PAR)	W, 2-0	Tampa	11,256
3/12	Mexico-b	T, 2-2	Los Angeles	6,261
3/16	Canada-b	W, 2-0	Torrance	2,705
4/5	Korean Olympic	L, 1-2	Pusan	4,500
4/7	South Korea	L, 0-2	Pohang	8,500
5/5	Uruguay	W, 1-0	Denver	35,772
5/19	Argentina	L, 0-1	Stanford	31,761
6/1	Ireland	T, 1-1	Foxboro	51,273
6/9	Juventus	T, 0-0	New Haven	33,547
6/16	AC Milan	T, 1-1	Chicago	41,572
6/29	Trin/Tobago-c	W, 2-1	Los Angeles	18,435
7/1	Guatemala-c	W, 3-0	Pasadena	6,344
7/3	Costa Rica-c	W, 3-2	Los Angeles	36,703
7/5	Mexico-c	W, 2-0	Los Angeles	41,103
7/7	Honduras-c	W, 0-0	Los Angeles	39,873
	(USA wins on PKs)			
8/2	Sheffield Wed.	W, 2-0	Philadelphia	44,261
8/17	Soviet Olympic	L, 1-2	Moscow	22,000
8/21	FC Tirol	L, 0-4	Innsbruck	1,620
8/28	Romania	W, 2-0	Bucharest	7,500
9/4	Turkey	T, 1-1	Istanbul	17,500
9/14	Jamaica	W, 1-0	N.Carolina	9,128

Record: 11-8-5 (.563); 27 goals for; 25 against.
Cup Tournaments: (a) Miami Cup; (b) North American Nations' Cup; (c) Concacaf Gold Cup.

Team Roster

The United States national team that toured Europe for four games from Aug. 17 to Sept. 4, 1991.

Goalkeepers	Age	Club
Mark Dodd	25	Colorado Foxes
Tony Meola	22	Ft.Laud.Strikers
Defenders	**Age**	**Club**
Jeff Agoos	23	Maryland Bays
Desmond Armstrong	26	Maryland Bays
Marcelo Balboa	24	SF Bay Blackhawks
Fernando Clavijo	34	St.Louis Storm
John Doyle	25	Orgryte IS
Bruce Savage	30	Baltimore Blast
Troy Snyder	25	Dallas Sidekicks
Steve Trittscuh	24	Tampa Bay Rowdies
Midfielders	**Age**	**Club**
Paul Caligiuri	27	Hansa Rostock
Chris Henderson	20	UCLA
Dominic Kinnear	24	SF Bay Blackhawks
Janusz Michallik	25	Granio Luitano
Brian Quinn	31	S.D.Sockers
Forwards	**Age**	**Club**
Ted Eck	24	KC Comets
Bruce Murray	25	Maryland Bays
Hugo Perez	27	Orgryte IS
Peter Vermes	24	Figueras (Spain)
Eric Wynalda	22	SF Bay Blackhawks

Head Coach: Bora Milutinovic
Assistant Coach: John Kowalski, Ralph Perez
Captain: Peter Vermes

Goals Scored

Bruce Murray	6	Brian Quinn	2	John Doyle	1
Peter Vermes	5	Dante Washington	2	Sadri Gjonbalaj	1
Hugo Perez	4	Eric Wynalda	2	Frank Klopas	1
Marcelo Balboa	3				

U.S. Olympic Team

International Schedule

(Through Aug. 25, 1991)

Toulon Festival

Date		Score	Site	Crowd
5/28	France	L,1-3	LaCiotat	5,000
5/30	Poland	T,1-1	SixFours	1,000
6/1	Scotland	L,2-3	Saint-Cyr	1,600

Olympic Qualifying

Date		Score	Site	Crowd
6/23	Haiti	W, 8-0	Colo.Sprgs	2,198
7/14	Panama	T, 1-1	Panama	12,000
7/20	Panama	W, 7-1	Dublin,OH	10,256
8/25	Haiti	W, 2-0	Haiti	30,000

Pan American Games

Date		Score	Site	Crowd
8/5	Suriname	W,1-0	Santiago	1,800
8/7	Canada	W,3-1	Santiago	1,800
8/9	Honduras	W,2-1	Santiago	1,800
8/11	Cuba (semifinal)	W,2-1	Havana	4,500
8/13	Mexico (final)	W,2-1*	Havana	6,000

* Overtime
Record: 8-2-2 (.750); 32 goals for, 13 against.

Team Roster

The United States Olympic Team (U-23) roster for the Pan American Games tournament in Havana, Aug. 5-13.

Goalkeepers	Age	Club
Brad Friedel	20	UCLA
Kasey Keller	21	U.of Portland
Defenders	**Age**	**Club**
Michael Burns	20	Hartwick
Rhett Harty	21	Stanford
Alexi Lalas	21	Rutgers
Mike Lapper	20	UCLA
Curt Onalfo	21	Virginia
Cam Rast	21	Santa Clara
Midfielders	**Age**	**Club**
Yari Allnutt	21	U.of Portland
Dario Brose	21	N.C.State
Erik Imler	20	Virginia
Manny Lagos	20	Wi-Milwaukee
Joe-Max Moore	20	UCLA
Claudio Reyna	17	Virginia
Eloy Salgado	21	Dallas Sidekicks
Forwards	**Age**	**Club**
Cobi Jones	21	UCLA
Steve Snow	20	Tilleur
Dante Washington	20	Radford

Head Coach: Lother Osiander
Assistant Coach: Collin Lindores
Captain: Cam Rast

U.S. Pro Leagues

MSL (Indoor)
Final 1990-91 Standings
Eastern Division

	W	L	Pct	GB	GF	GA
*Cleveland	29	23	.558	—	322	280
+Kansas City	26	26	.500	3	263	283
+Wichita	21	31	.404	8	257	308
Baltimore	21	31	.404	8	298	315

Note: Wichita gains final playoff berth based on 5-3 head-to-head record against Baltimore.

Western Division

	W	L	Pct	GB	GF	GA
*San Diego	34	18	.654	—	302	250
+St.Louis	32	20	.615	2	320	288
+Tacoma	25	27	.481	9	254	259
Dallas	20	32	.385	14	257	294

Playoffs

Division Semifinals (best of 3): WEST—Tacoma def. St.Louis (2-1); EAST—Kansas City def. Wichita (2-0). **Division Finals** (best of 7): WEST—San Diego def. St.Louis (4-1); EAST—Cleveland def. Kansas City (4-3). **MSL Championship** (best of 7): San Diego def. Cleveland (4-2).

APSL (Outdoor)
Final 1991 Standings
American Division

	W	L	Pct	Pts	GF	GA
*Ft.Lauderdale	15	6	.714	117	43	23
+Albany	10	11	.476	92	27	32
Tampa Bay	8	13	.381	69	26	27
Penn-Jersey	6	15	.286	61	27	52
Miami	6	15	.286	52	20	53

Western Division

	W	L	Pct	Pts	GF	GA
*Maryland	19	2	.905	158	55	23
+S.F. Bay	17	4	.810	126	37	17
Colorado	13	8	.619	111	37	28

Note: Salt Lake folded on July 5.
Points: Teams earn six points for a win and one point per goal up to a maximum of three per game. No points given for goals scored in overtime. In penalty-kick tiebreakers, the winning team earns four points and the loser gets two.

Playoffs

Semifinals (best of 2, with mini-game): Albany def. Maryland (in mini-game on PKs); S.F.Bay def. Ft.Lauderdale (2-0). **APSL Championship** (best of 2, with mini-game): S.F. def. Albany (in mini-game on PKs).

Colleges

Soccer America Top 20
Final 1990 Regular Season

Final 1990 poll conducted by the national weekly Soccer America, with records through conference playoffs. also included are records in NCAA tournament and team lost to. Teams in **bold** type went on to reach NCAA Final Four.

		W	L	T	NCAA Recap
1	**Evansville**	22	0	2	2-1 (Rutgers)
2	**N.C.State**	16	4	0	2-1 (UCLA)
3	**Rutgers**	17	2	2	3-1 (UCLA)
4	Clemson	16	3	1	0-1 (S.Carolina)
5	**UCLA**	15	1	4	4-0
6	Santa Clara	13	3	3	0-1 (Fresno St.)
7	Indiana	14	3	2	2-1 (Evansville)
8	Virginia	10	5	6	2-1 (N.C. State)
9	South Carolina	13	4	2	1-1 (N.C. State
10	SMU	16	3	1	2-1 (UCLA)
11	Fresno St.	17	3	2	1-1 (SMU)
12	St. Louis	17	4	2	1-1 (Indiana)
13	North Carolina	12	6	0	1-1 (Virginia)
14	Duke	12	6	1	Did not play
15	Wake Forest	10	6	4	0-1 (N. Carolina)
16	Dartmouth	12	1	2	2-1 (Rutgers)
17	WI-Milwaukee	16	3	2	0-1 (Indiana)
18	Boston Univ	13	2	6	1-1 (Evansville)
19	U. of San Diego	15	2	5	1-1 (UCLA)
20	Portland	12	5	1	0-1 (San Diego)

1990 Division I All-America

Selected by National Soccer Coaches Assn.

First Team	Pos	Second Team
Kasey Keller, Portland	G	Trey Harrington, E'ville
Scott Cannon, Evansville	B	Pete DiMaggio, Columbia
Jeff Agoos, Virginia	B	Trong Nguyen, S.D.St.
Tom Loeber, S.Carolina	B	George Dunn, Duke
Mark Santel, St.Louis	M	G.Paulo Pedroso, SMU
Dario Brose, N.C.St.	M	Chris Verhaegen, BU
Chad Deering, Indiana	M	Nick Stavrou, Cle.St.
Bill Thompson, UCLA	F	Henry Gutierrez, N.C.St.
David Weir, Evansville	F	Robert Ukrop, Davidson
Ken Snow, Indiana	F	James Glenn, Clemson
Steve Rammel, Rutgers	F	Manuel Logos, WI-Milw.

NCAA Division I Tournament
First Round

Adelphi 1		Brooklyn 0
Columbia 2		Seton Hall 0
Dartmouth 1	(2 OT)	Vermont 1
	(Dartmouth wins in PKs, 4-1)	
Boston Univ. 3		Boston College 2
Indiana 5		WI-Milwaukee 0
St.Louis 3		George Mason 0
South Carolina 3		Clemson 0
North Carolina 2		Wake Forest 1
Virginia 1		Richmond 0
San Diego 4		Portland (OR) 2
Fresno St. 3	(2 OT)	Santa Clara 2
SMU 2		Illinois St. 1

Second Round

Rutgers 2	(2 OT)	Adelphi 2
	(Rutgers wins in PKs, 3-2)	
Dartmouth 2		Columbia 1
Evansville 1	(2 OT)	Boston Univ. 0
Indiana 2		St.Louis 1
N.C.State 3		South Carolina 1
Virginia 3		North Carolina 1
UCLA 2	(2 OT)	San Diego 1
SMU 2		Fresno St. 1

Quarterfinals

Rutgers 1		Dartmouth 0
Evansville 1		Indiana 0
N.C.State 1	(2 OT)	Virginia 1
	(N.C.State wins on PKs, 7-6)	
UCLA 2		SMU 0

FINAL FOUR
(at Tampa, Dec.1-2)

Semifinals

UCLA 0		N.C.State 1
	(UCLA wins on PKs, 5-3)	
Rutgers 1		Evansville 0

Championship

UCLA 0	(2 OT)	Rutgers 0
	(UCLA wins on PKs, 4-3)	

THE 1992 INFORMATION PLEASE SPORTS ALMANAC

SOCCER STATISTICS

THROUGH THE YEARS
1916-1991
WORLD CUP • INT'L CHAMPS

SEC B

PAGE 477

The World Cup

The Federation Internationale de Football Association (FIFA) began the World Cup championship tournament in 1930 with a 13-team field in Uruguay. Sixty years later, the 1990 World Cup in Italy marked the eighth time the competition has been held in Europe. Countries in South and Central America have hosted the Cup six times and the United States will host the tournament for the first time in 1994.

Brazil retired the first World Cup (called the Jules Rimet Trophy for FIFA's first president) in 1970 after winning it for the third time. Since 1974, the award has been known as simply the World Cup.

The 1942 and '46 World Cup tournaments were cancelled because of World War II. European finalists are in CAPITAL letters; (*) indicates score after extra time.

Multiple winners: Brazil, Italy and West Germany (3); Argentina and Uruguay (2).

Year	Champion	Manager	Score	Runner-up	Host Country	Third Place
1930	Uruguay	Alberto Supicci	4-2	Argentina	Uruguay	No game
1934	ITALY	Vittorio Pozzo	2-1*	CZECHOSLOVAKIA	Italy	Germany 3, Austria 2
1938	ITALY	Vittorio Pozzo	4-2	HUNGARY	France	Brazil 4, Sweden 2
1942–46	Not held					
1950	Uruguay	Juan Lopez	2-1	Brazil	Brazil	No game
1954	W.GERMANY	Sepp Herberger	3-2	HUNGARY	Switzerland	Austria 3, Uruguay 1
1958	Brazil	Vicente Feola	5-2	SWEDEN	Sweden	France 6, W.Germany 3
1962	Brazil	Aymore Moreira	3-1	CZECHOSLOVAKIA	Chile	Chile 1, Yugoslavia 0
1966	ENGLAND	Alf Ramsey	4-2*	W.GERMANY	England	Portugal 2, USSR 1
1970	Brazil	Mario Zagalo	4-1	ITALY	Mexico	W.Ger. 1, Uruguay 0
1974	W.GERMANY	Helmut Schoen	2-1	HOLLAND	W.Germany	Poland 1, Brazil 0
1978	Argentina	Cesar Menotti	3-1*	HOLLAND	Argentina	Brazil 2, Italy 1
1982	ITALY	Enzo Bearzot	3-1	W.GERMANY	Spain	Poland 3, France 2
1986	Argentina	Carlos Bilardo	3-2	W.GERMANY	Mexico	France 4, Belgium 2*
1990	W.GERMANY	Franz Beckenbauer	1-0	Argentina	Italy	Italy 2, England 1

The United States in the World Cup

While the United States has fielded a national team every year of the World Cup, only four of those teams have been able to make it past the preliminary competition and qualify for the final World Cup tournament. The U.S. played in three of the first four World Cups (1930,'34 and '50) then not again until 1990.

The U.S. has won only three World Cup tournament matches—two opening round games in 1930 (which enabled the Americans to reach the semifinals) and a stunning first round, 1-0, upset of England in 1950. Center forward Joe Gaetjens scored the goal and goalkeeper Frank Borghi had the shutout against the English.

1930
1st Round Matches
United States 3 .... Belgium 0
United States 3 .... Paraguay 0
Semifinals
Argentina 6 .... United States 1
US Scoring—Bert Patenaude (3), Bart McGhee (2), James Brown, Ed Florie.

1934
1st Round Match
Italy 7 .... United States 1
US Scoring—Buff Donelli (who later became a noted college and NFL football coach).

1950
1st Round Matches
Spain 3 .... United States 1
United States 1 .... England 0
Chile 5 .... United States 2
US Scoring—John Souza (2), Joe Gaetjens, Gino Pariani.

1990
1st Round Matches
Czechoslovakia 5 .... United States 1
Italy 1 .... United States 0
Austria 2 .... United States 1
US Scoring—Paul Caligiuri, Bruce Murray.

All-Time World Cup Leaders

Career Goals

World Cup scoring leaders through 1990. Years listed are years played in World Cup.

	No
Gerd Mueller, West Germany (1970,74)	14
Just Fontaine, France (1958)	13
Pele, Brazil (1958,70)	12
Sandor Kocsis, Hungary (1954)	11
Teofilo Cubillas, Peru (1970, 78)	10
Gregorz Lato, Poland (1974, 78, 82)	10
Gary Lineker, England (1986,90)	10
Helmut Rahn, West Germany (1954,58)	10

Most Valuable Player

Officially, the Golden Ball Award, the Most Valuable Player of the World Cup tournament has been selected since 1982 by a panel of international soccer journalists.

Year		Year	
1982	Paolo Rossi, Italy	1990	Toto Schillaci, Italy
1986	Diego Maradona, Arg.		

Single Tournament Goals

World Cup tournament scoring leaders through 1990.

Year		Gm	No
1930	Guillermo Stabile, Argentina	4	8
1934	Angelo Schiavio, Italy	3	4
	Oldrich Nejedly, Czechoslovakia	4	4
	& Edmund Conen, Germany	4	4
1938	Leonidas, Brazil	3	8
1950	Ademir, Brazil	6	7
1954	Sandor Kocsis, Hungary	5	11
1958	Just Fontaine, France	6	13
1962	Drazen Jerkovic, Yugoslavia	6	5
1966	Eusebio, Portugal	6	9
1970	Gerd Mueller, West Germany	6	10
1974	Grzegorz Lato, Poland	7	7
1978	Mario Kempes, Argentina	7	6
1982	Paolo Rossi, Italy	7	6
1986	Gary Lineker, England	5	6
1990	Toto Schillaci, Italy	7	6

World Cup Appearances

The World Cup tournament field has grown from 13 (1930) to 16 (1934-78) to 24 (since 1982). Brazil is the only team to have played in every World Cup tournament, but eight other countries have qualified teams at least nine times.

The following FIFA Table ranks all national teams by total points earned in World Cup play through 1990. Note that West Germany's appearances include two by Germany in 1934 and 1938.

		App	Gm	W	L	T	Pts
1	Brazil	14	66	44	11	11	99
2	West Germany	12	68	39	14	15	93
3	Italy	12	54	31	11	12	74
4	Argentina	10	48	24	15	9	57
5	England	9	41	18	11	12	48
6	Uruguay	9	37	15	14	8	38
7	Soviet Union	7	31	15	10	6	36
8	France	9	34	15	14	5	35
	Yugoslavia	8	33	14	12	7	35
10	Hungary	9	32	15	14	3	33
	Spain	8	32	13	12	7	33
12	Poland	5	25	13	7	5	31
13	Sweden	8	31	11	14	6	28
14	Czechoslovakia	8	30	11	14	5	27
15	Austria	6	26	12	12	2	26
16	Holland	5	20	8	6	6	22
17	Belgium	8	25	7	14	4	18
	Mexico	9	29	6	17	6	18
19	Chile	6	21	7	11	3	17
20	Scotland	7	20	4	10	6	14
21	Portugal	2	9	6	3	0	12
	Switzerland	6	18	5	11	2	12
24	Peru	4	15	4	8	3	11
	Northern Ireland	3	13	3	5	5	11
25	Paraguay	4	11	3	4	4	10
26	Cameroon	2	8	3	2	3	9
	Romania	5	12	3	6	3	9
28	Denmark	1	4	3	1	0	6
	United States	4	10	3	7	0	6
	East Germany	1	6	2	2	2	6

World Cup Finals

West Germany has appeared in the most World Cup championship games (6), winning three. Brazil (3-1), Italy (3-1) and Argentina (2-2) have each appeared in four finals. A four-team round robin decided the 1950 World Cup—fortunately, the deciding game turned out to be the last one of the tournament between Uruguay and Brazil.

1930

Uruguay 4, Argentina 2
(at Montevideo, Uruguay)

	1	2—T
July 30 Uruguay (4-0)	1	3—4
Argentina (4-1)	2	0—2

Goals: Uruguay—Pablo Dorado (12th minute), Pedro Cea (54th), Santos Iriarte (68th), Castro (89th); Argentina—Carlos Peucelle (20th), Guillermo Stabile (37th).

Uruguay—Ballestrero, Nasazzi, Mascheroni, Andrade, Fernandez, Gestido, Dorado, Scarone, Castro, Cea, Iriarte.

Argentina—Botasso, Della Torre, Paternoster, J.Evaristo, Monti, Suarez, Peucelle, Varallo, Stabile, M.Ferreyra, M.Evaristo.

Attendance: 90,000. **Referee:** Langenus (Belgium).

1934

Italy 2, Czechoslovakia 1 (OT)
(at Rome)

	1	2	OT—T
June 10 Italy (4-0-1)	1	2	1—2
Czechoslovakia (3-1)	1	2	0—1

Goals: Italy—Raimondo Orsi (80th minute), Angelo Schiavio (95th); Czechoslovakia—Puc (70th).

Italy—Combi, Monzeglio, Allemandi, Ferraris IV, Monti, Bertolini, Guaita, Meazza, Schiavio, Ferrari, Orsi.

Czechoslovakia—Planicka, Zenisek, Ctyroky, Kostalek, Cambal, Krcil, Junek, Svoboda, Sobotka, Nejedly, Puc.

Attendance: 55,000. **Referee:** Eklind (Sweden).

1938

Italy 4, Hungary 2
(at Paris)

	1	2—T
June 19 Italy (4-0)	3	1—4
Hungary (3-1)	1	1—2

Goals: Italy—Gino Colaussi (5th minute), Silvio Piola (16th), Colassi (35th), Piola (82nd); Hungary—Titkos (7th), Georges Sarosi (70th).

Italy—Olivieri, Foni, Rava, Serantoni, Andreolo, Locatelli, Biavati, Meazza, Piola, Ferrari, Colaussi.

Hungary—Szabo, Polgar, Biro, Szalay, Szucs, Lazar, Sas, Vincze, G.Sarosi, Szengeller, Titkos.

Attendance: 65,000. **Referee:** Capdeville (France)

1950

Uruguay 2, Brazil 1
(at Rio de Janeiro)

	1	2—T
July 16 Uruguay (3-0-1)	0	2—2
Brazil (4-1-1)	0	1—1

Goals: Uruguay—Juan Schiaffino (66th minute), Chico Ghiggia (79th); Brazil—Friaca (47th).

Uruguay—Maspoli, M.Gonzales, Tejera, Gambetta, Varela, Andrade, Ghiggia, Perez, Miguez, Schiaffino, Moran.

Brazil—Barbosa, Augusto, Juvenal, Bauer, Danilo, Bigode, Friaca, Zizinho, Ademir, Jair, Chico.

Attendance: 199,854. **Referee:** Reader (England)

1954

West Germany 3, Hungary 2
(at Berne, Switzerland)

	1	2—T
July 4 West Germany (5-1)	2	1—3
Hungary (4-1)	2	0—2

Goals: West Germany—Max Morlock (10th minute), Helmut Rahn (18th), Rahn (84th); Hungary—Ferenc Puskas (4th), Zoltan Czibor (9th).

West Germany—Turek, Posipal, Liebrich, Kohlmeyer, Eckel, Mai, Rahn, Morlock, O.Walter, F.Walter, Schaeffer.

Hungary—Grosics, Buzansky, Lorant, Lantos, Bozsik, Zakarias, Csibor, Kocsis, Higegkuti, Puskas, J.Toth.

Attendance: 60,000. **Referee:** Ling (England).

1958

Brazil 5, Sweden 2
(at Stockholm)

	1	2—T
June 29 Brazil (5-0-1)	2	3—5
Sweden (4-1-1)	1	1—2

Goals: Brazil—Vava (9th minute), Vava (32nd), Pele (55th), Mario Zagalo (68th), Pele (90th); Sweden—Nils Liedholm (3rd), Agne Simonsson (80th).

Brazil—Gilmar, D.Santos, N.Santos, Zito, Bellini, Orlando, Garrincha, Didi, Vava, Pele, Zagalo.

Sweden—Svensson, Bergmark, Axbom, Boerjesson, Gustavsson, Parling, Hamrin, Gren, Simonsson, Liedholm, Skoglund.

Attendance: 49,737. **Referee:** Guigue (France).

1962

Brazil 3, Czechoslovakia 1
(at Santiago, Chile)

	1	2—T
June 17 Brazil (5-0-1)	1	2—3
Czechoslovakia (3-2-1)	1	0—1

Goals: Brazil—Amarildo (17th minute), Zito (68th), Vava (77th); Czechoslovakia—Josef Masopust (15th).

Brazil—Gilmar, D.Santos, N.Santos, Zito, Mauro, Zozimo, Garrincha, Didi, Vava, Amarildo, Zagalo.

Czechoslovakia—Schroiff, Tichy, Novak, Pluskal, Popluhar, Masopust, Pospichal, Scherer, Kvasniak, Kadraba, Jelinek.

Attendance: 68,679. **Referee:** Latishev (USSR).

1966

England 4, West Germany 2 (OT)
(at London)

	1	2	OT—T
July 30 England (5-0-1)	1	1	2—4
West Germany (4-1-1)	1	1	0—2

Goals: England—Geoff Hurst (18th minute), Martin Peters (78th), Hurst (101st), Hurst (120th); West Germany—Helmut Haller (12th), Wolfgang Weber (90th).

England—Banks, Cohen, Wilson, Stiles, J.Charlton, Moore, Ball, Hurst, B.Charlton, Hunt, Peters.

West Germany—Tilkowski, Hottges, Schnellinger, Beckenbauer, Schulz, Weber, Haller, Seeler, Held, Overath, Emmerich.

Attendance: 93,802. **Referee:** Dienst (Switzerland).

1970

Brazil 4, Italy 1
(at Mexico City)

	1	2—T
June 20 Brazil (6-0)	1	3—4
Italy (3-1-2)	1	0—1

Goals: Brazil—Pele (18th minute), Gerson (65th), Jairzinho (70th), Carlos Alberto (86th); Italy—Roberto Boninsegna (37th).

Brazil—Felix, C.Alberto, Everaldo, Clodoaldo, Brito, Piazza, Jairzinho, Gerson, Tostao, Pele, Rivelino.

Italy—Albertosi, Burgnich, Facchetti, Bertini (Juliano, 73rd), Rosato, Cera, Domenghini, Mazzola, Boninsegna (Rivera, 84th), De Sisti, Riva.

Attendance: 107,412. **Referee:** Gloeckner (E. Germany).

1974

West Germany 2, Holland 1
(at Munich)

	1	2—T
July 7 West Germany (6-1)	2	0—2
Holland (5-1-1)	1	0—1

Goals: West Germany—Paul Breitner (25th minute, penalty kick), Gerd Mueller (43rd); Holland—Johan Neeskens (1st, penalty kick).

West Germany—Maier, Beckenbauer, Vogts, Breitner, Schwarzenbeck, Overath, Bonhof, Hoeness, Grabowski, Mueller, Holzenbein.

Holland—Jongbloed, Suurbier, Rijsbergen (De Jong, 58th), Krol, Haan, Jansen, Van Hanegem, Neeskens, Rep, Cruyff, Rensenbrink (R.Van de Kerkhof, 46th).

Attendance: 77,833. **Referee:** Taylor (England).

World Cup Finals (Cont.)

1978
Argentina 3, Holland 1 (OT)
(at Buenos Aires)

	1	2	OT—T
June 25 Argentina (5-1-1)	1	0	2—3
Holland (3-2-2)	0	1	1—1

Goals: Argentina—Mario Kempes (37th minute), Kempes (104th), Daniel Bertoni (114th); Holland—Dirk Nanninga (81st).

Argentina—Fillol, Olguin, L.Galvan, Passarella, Tarantini, Ardiles (Larrosa, 65th), Gallego, Kempes, Luque, Bertoni, Ortiz (Houseman, 77th).

Holland—Jongbloed, Jansen (Suurbier, 72nd), Brandts, Krol, Poortvliet, Haan, Neeskens, W.Van de Kerkhof, R.Van de Kerkhof, Rep (Nanninga, 58th), Rensenbrink.

Attendance: 77,000. **Referee:** Gonella (Italy).

1982
Italy 3, West Germany 1
(at Madrid)

	1	2—T
July 11 Italy (4-0-3)	0	3—3
West Germany (4-2-1)	0	1—1

Goals: Italy—Paolo Rossi (57th minute), Marco Tardelli (68th), Alessandro Altobelli (81st); West Germany—Paul Breitner (83rd).

Italy—Zoff, Scirea, Gentile, Cabrini, Collovati, Bergomi, Tardelli, Oriali, Conti, Rossi, Graziani (Altobelli, 8th, and Causio, 89th).

West Germany—Schumacher, Stielike, Kaltz, Briegel, K.H.Foerster, B.Foerster, Breitner, Dremmler (Hrubesch, 61st), Littbarski, Fischer, Rummenigge (Mueller, 69th).

Attendance: 90,080. **Referee:** Coelho (Brazil).

1986
Argentina 3, West Germany 2
(at Mexico City)

	1	2—T
June 29 Argentina (6-0-1)	1	2—3
West Germany (4-2-1)	0	2—2

Goals: Argentina—Jose Brown (22nd minute), Jorge Valdano (55th), Jorge Burruchaga (83rd); West Germany—Karl-Heinz Rummenigge (73rd), Rudi Voeller (81st).

Argentina—Pumpido, Cuciuffo, Olarticoechea, Ruggeri, Brown, Batista, Burruchaga (Trobbiani, 89th), Giusti, Enrique, Maradona, Valdano.

West Germany—Schumacher, Jakobs, K.H.Foerster, Berthold, Briegel, Eder, Brehme, Matthaeus, Rummenigge, Magath (Hoeness, 61st), Allofs (Voeller, 46th).

Attendance: 114,580. **Referee:** Filho (Brazil).

1990
West Germany 1, Argentina 0
(at Rome)

	1	2—T
July 8 West Germany (6-0-1)	0	1—1
Argentina (4-2-1)	0	0—0

Goals: West Germany—Andreas Brehme (85th minute, penalty kick).

West Germany—Illgner, Berthold (Reuter, 75th), Kohler, Augenthaler, Buchwald, Brehme, Haessler, Matthaeus, Littbarski, Klinsmann, Voeller.

Argentina: Goycoechea, Ruggeri (Monzon, 46th), Simon, Serrizuela, Lorenzo, Basualdo, Troglio, Burruchaga (Calderon, 53rd), Sensini, Dezotti, Maradona.

Attendance: 73,603. **Referee:** Codesal (Mexico).

Other Worldwide Competition
The Olympic Games

Held every four years since 1896, except during World War I (1916) and World War II (1940-44). Soccer was not a medal sport in 1896 at Athens or in 1932 at Los Angeles. By agreement between FIFA and the IOC, Olympic soccer competition is currently limited to players under the age of 24.

Multiple winners: England and Hungary (3); USSR and Uruguay (2).

Year		Year		Year		Year	
1896	Not held	1920	Belgium	1944	Not held	1968	Hungary
1900	England	1924	Uruguay	1948	Sweden	1972	Poland
1904	Canada	1928	Uruguay	1952	Hungary	1976	East Germany
1906	Denmark	1932	Not held	1956	Soviet Union	1980	Czechoslovakia
1908	England	1936	Italy	1960	Yugoslavia	1984	France
1912	England	1940	Not held	1964	Hungary	1988	Soviet Union
1916	Not held						

The Under-20 World Cup

Held every two years since 1977. Officially called The World Youth Championship for the FIFA/Coca-Cola Cup.

Multiple winners: Brazil and Portugal (2).

Year		Year	
1977	Soviet Union	1985	Brazil
1979	Argentina	1987	Yugoslavia
1981	West Germany	1989	Portugal
1983	Brazil	1991	Portugal

Women's World Championship

The first FIFA world championship tournament for women is scheduled for Nov. 16-30, 1991, in China.

The Under-17 World Cup

Held every two years since 1985. Officially called The FIFA U-17 World Tournament for the JVC Cup.

Year		Year	
1985	Nigeria	1989	Saudi Arabia
1987	Soviet Union	1991	Ghana

Five-a-Side Championship

First held in 1989. FIFA's only indoor tournament.

Year		Year	
1989	Brazil	1992	at Hong Kong

Continental Competition
European Championship

Held every four years since 1960. Officially called the European Football Championship.
Multiple winner: West Germany (2).

Year		Year		Year		Year	
1960	Soviet Union	1968	Italy	1976	Czechoslovakia	1984	France
1964	Spain	1972	West Germany	1980	West Germany	1988	Holland

South American Championship

Held irregularly since 1916. Officially called the Copa America.
Multiple winners: Argentina and Uruguay (13), Brazil (4), Paraguay and Peru (2).

Year		Year		Year		Year	
1916	Uruguay	1926	Uruguay	1946	Argentina	1963	Bolivia
1917	Uruguay	1927	Argentina	1947	Argentina	1967	Uruguay
1919	Brazil	1929	Argentina	1949	Brazil	1975	Peru
1920	Uruguay	1935	Uruguay	1953	Paraguay	1979	Paraguay
1921	Argentina	1937	Argentina	1955	Argentina	1983	Uruguay
1922	Brazil	1939	Peru	1956	Uruguay	1987	Uruguay
1923	Uruguay	1941	Argentina	1957	Argentina	1989	Brazil
1924	Uruguay	1942	Uruguay	1958	Argentina	1991	Argentina
1925	Argentina	1945	Argentina	1959	Uruguay		

CONCACAF Gold Cup

The Confederation of North, Central American and Caribbean Football (CONCACAF) Championship. First held in Los Angeles in 1991 and won by the United States.

Club Competition
Toyota Cup

Contested annually in December between the winners of the previous year's European Cup and Libertadores Copa (see below). On four occasions, the European Cup winner has refused to participate. In each case, the European Cup runner-up went instead—Panathinaikos (Greece) in 1971, Juventus (Italy) in 1973, Atletico Madrid (Spain) in 1974, and Malmo (Sweden) in 1979.

Originally the **Intercontinental Cup** (1960-79). Best-of-three game format until 1968, then two-game/total-goal format was used. Toyota became sponsor in 1980, changed the format to one-game championship and moved it to Tokyo.
Multiple winners: AC Milan, Nacional and Penarol (3); Independiente, Inter Milan and Santos (2).

Year		Year		Year	
1960	Real Madrid (Spain)	1972	Ajax Amsterdam (Holland)	1982	Penarol (Uruguay)
1961	Penarol (Uruguay)	1973	Independiente (Argentina)	1983	Gremio (Brazil)
1962	Santos (Brazil)	1974	Atletico Madrid (Spain)	1984	Independiente (Argentina)
1963	Santos (Brazil)	1975	Not held	1985	Juventus (Italy)
1964	Inter Milan (Italy)	1976	Bayern Munich (W.Germany)	1986	River Plate (Argentina)
1965	Inter Milan (Italy)	1977	Boca Juniors (Argentina)	1987	FC Porto (Portugal)
1966	Penarol (Uruguay)	1978	Not held	1988	Nacional (Uruguay)
1967	Racing Club (Argentina)	1979	Olimpia (Paraguay)	1989	AC Milan (Italy)
1968	Estudiantes (Argentina)			1990	AC Milan (Italy)
1969	AC Milan (Italy)	1980	Nacional (Uruguay)		
		1981	Flamengo (Brazil)		
1970	Feyenoord (Holland)				
1971	Nacional (Uruguay)				

Copa Libertadores

Contested annually since the 1955-56 season by the league champions of South America's football union.
Multiple winners: Independiente (7); Penarol (5); Estudiantes and Nacional-Uruguay (3); Boca Juniors, Olimpia and Santos (2).

Year		Year		Year	
1960	Penarol (Uruguay)	1972	Independiente (Argentina)	1982	Penarol (Uruguay)
1961	Penarol (Uruguay)	1973	Independiente (Argentina)	1983	Gremio (Brazil)
1962	Santos (Brazil)	1974	Independiente (Argentina)	1984	Independiente (Argentina)
1963	Santos (Brazil)	1975	Independiente (Argentina)	1985	Argentinos Jrs.(Argentina)
1964	Independiente (Argentina)	1976	Cruzeiro (Brazil)	1986	River Plate (Argentina)
1965	Independiente (Argentina)	1977	Boca Juniors (Argentina)	1987	Penarol (Uruguay)
1966	Penarol (Uruguay)	1978	Boca Juniors (Argentina)	1988	Nacional (Uruguay)
1967	Racing Club (Argentina)	1979	Olimpia (Paraguay)	1989	Nacional Medellin (Colombia)
1968	Estudiantes (Argentina)			1990	Olimpia (Paraguay)
1969	Estudiantes (Argentina)	1980	Nacional (Uruguay)	1991	Colo Colo (Chile)
		1981	Flamengo (Brazil)		
1970	Estudiantes (Argentina)				
1971	Nacional (Uruguay)				

Club Competition (Cont.)
European Cup

Contested annually since the 1955-56 season by the league champions of the member countries of the Union of European Football Associations (UEFA).

Multiple winners: Real Madrid (6); AC Milan and Liverpool (4); Ajax Amsterdam and Bayern Munich (3); Benfica, Inter Milan and Nottingham Forest (2).

Year		Year		Year	
1956	Real Madrid (Spain)	1968	Manchester United (England)	1980	Nottingham Forest (England)
1957	Real Madrid (Spain)	1969	AC Milan (Italy)	1981	Liverpool (England)
1958	Real Madrid (Spain)			1982	Aston Villa (England)
1959	Real Madrid (Spain)	1970	Feyenoord (Holland)	1983	SV Hamburg (W.Germany)
		1971	Ajax Amsterdam (Holland)	1984	Liverpool (England)
1960	Real Madrid (Spain)	1972	Ajax Amsterdam (Holland)	1985	Juventus (Italy)
1961	Benfica (Portugal)	1973	Ajax Amsterdam (Holland)	1986	Steaua Bucharest (Romania)
1962	Benfica (Portugal)	1974	Bayern Munich (W.Germany)	1987	FC Porto (Portugal)
1963	AC Milan (Italy)	1975	Bayern Munich (W.Germany)	1988	PSV Eindhoven (Holland)
1964	Inter Milan (Italy)	1976	Bayern Munich (W.Germany)	1989	AC Milan (Italy)
1965	Inter Milan (Italy)	1977	Liverpool (England)		
1966	Real Madrid (Spain)	1978	Liverpool (England)	1990	AC Milan (Italy)
1967	Glasgow Celtic (Scotland)	1979	Nottingham Forest (England)	1991	Red Star (Yugoslavia)

European Cup Winners' Cup

Contested annually since the 1960-61 season by the cup winners of the member countries of the Union of European Football Associations (UEFA).

Multiple winners: Barcelona (3); AC Milan, Anderlecht and Dynamo Kiev (2).

Year		Year		Year	
1961	Fiorentina (Italy)	1972	Glasgow Rangers (Scotland)	1983	Aberdeen (Scotland)
1962	Atletico Madrid (Spain)	1973	AC Milan (Italy)	1984	Juventus (Italy)
1963	Tottenham Hotspur (England)	1974	FC Magdeburg (E.Germany)	1985	Everton (England)
1964	Sporting Lisbon (Portugal)	1975	Dynamo Kiev (USSR)	1986	Dynamo Kiev (USSR)
1965	West Ham United (England)	1976	Anderlecht (Belgium)	1987	Ajax Amsterdam (Holland)
1966	Borussia Dortmund (W.Germany)	1977	SV Hamburg (W.Germany)	1988	Mechelen (Belgium)
1967	Bayern Munich (W.Germany)	1978	Anderlecht (Belgium)	1989	Barcelona (Spain)
1968	AC Milan (Italy)	1979	Barcelona (Spain)		
1969	Slovan Bratislava (Czech.)			1990	Sampdoria (Italy)
		1980	Valencia (Spain)	1991	Manchester United (England)
1970	Manchester City (England)	1981	Dynamo Tbilisi (USSR)		
1971	Chelsea (England)	1982	Barcelona (Spain)		

UEFA Cup

Contested annually since the 1957-58 season by teams other than league champions and cup winners of the Union of European Football Associations (UEFA). Teams selected by UEFA based on each country's previous performance in the tournament. Teams from England were banned from UEFA Cup play from 1985-90 for the criminal behavior of their supporters.

Multiple winners: Barcelona (3); Borussia Moenchengladbach, IFL Gothenburg, Juventus, Leeds United, Liverpool, Real Madrid, Tottenham Hotspur and Valencia (2).

Year		Year		Year	
1958	Barcelona (Spain)	1970	Arsenal (England)	1980	Eintracht Frankfurt (W.Germany)
1959	Not held	1971	Leeds United (England)	1981	Ipswich Town (England)
		1972	Tottenham Horspur (England)	1982	IFK Gothenburg (Sweden)
1960	Barcelona (Spain)	1973	Liverpool (England)	1983	Anderlecht (Belgium)
1961	AS Roma (Italy)	1974	Feyenoord (Holland)	1984	Tottenham Hotspur (England)
1962	Valencia (Spain)	1975	Borussia Moenchen- gladbach (W.Germany)	1985	Real Madrid (Spain)
1963	Valencia (Spain)			1986	Real Madrid (Spain)
1964	Real Zaragoza (Spain)	1976	Liverpool (England)	1987	IFK Gothenburg (Sweden)
1965	Ferencvaros (Hungary)	1977	Juventus (Italy)	1988	Bayer Leverksen (W.Germany)
1966	Barcelona (Spain)	1978	PSV Eindhoven (Holland)	1989	Napoli (Italy)
1967	Dynamo Zagreb (Yugoslavia)	1979	Borussia Moenchen- gladbach (W.Germany)		
1968	Leeds United (England)			1990	Juventus (Italy)
1969	Newcastle United (England)			1991	Inter Milan (Italy)

Annual Awards
European Player of the Year

Officially, the "Ballon d'Or" and presented by France Football magazine since 1956. Candidates are limited to European players in European leagues and winners are selected by a panel of 27 European soccer journalists.

Multiple winners: Johan Cruyff and Michel Platini (3); Franz Beckenbauer, Alfredo di Stefano, Kevin Keegan, Karl-Heinz Rummenigge and Marco Van Basten (2).

Year		Nat'l Team	Year		Nat'l Team
1956	Stanley Matthews, Blackpool	England	1974	Johan Cruyff, Barcelona	Holland
1957	Alfredo di Stefano, Real Madrid	Arg./Spain	1975	Oleg Blokhin, Dynamo Kiev	Soviet Union
1958	Raymond Kopa, Real Madrid	France	1976	Franz Beckenbauer, Bayern Munich	W.Ger.
1959	Alfredo di Stefano, Real Madrid	Arg./Spain	1977	Allan Simonsen, B.M'chengladbach	Denmark
			1978	Kevin Keegan, SV Hamburg	England
1960	Luis Suarez, Barcelona	Spain	1979	Kevin Keegan, SV Hamburg	England
1961	Enrique Sivori, Juventus	Arg./Italy			
1962	Josef Masopust, Dukla Prague	Czech.	1980	K.H.Rummenigge, Bayern Munich	W.Ger.
1963	Lev Yachin, Dynamo Moscow	Soviet Union	1981	K.H.Rummenigge, Bayern Munich	W.Ger.
1964	Denis Law, Manchester United	Scotland	1982	Paolo Rossi, Juventus	Italy
1965	Eusebio, Benfica	Portugal	1983	Michel Platini, Juventus	France
1966	Bobby Charlton, Manchester United	England	1984	Michel Platini, Juventus	France
1967	Florian Albert, Ferencvaros	Hungary	1985	Michel Platini, Juventus	France
1968	George Best, Manchester United	N.Ireland	1986	Igor Belanov, Dynamo Kiev	Soviet Union
1969	Gianni Rivera, AC Milan	Italy	1987	Ruud Gullit, AC Milan	Holland
			1988	Marco Van Basten, AC Milan	Holland
1970	Gerd Mueller, Bayern Munich	W.Ger.	1989	Marco Van Basten, AC Milan	Holland
1971	Johan Cruyff, Ajax	Holland			
1972	Franz Beckenbauer, Bayern Munich	W.Ger.	1990	Lothar Matthaeus, Inter Milan	W. Ger.
1973	Johan Cruyff, Barcelona	Holland			

South American Player of the Year

Presented by El Pais of Uruguay since 1971. Candidates are limited to South American players in South American leagues and winners are selected by a panel of 67 Latin American sports editors.

Multiple winners: Elias Figueroa and Zico (3); Diego Maradona (2).

Year		Nat'l Team	Year		Nat'l Team
1971	Tostao, Cruzeiro	Brazil	1982	Zico, Flamengo	Brazil
1972	Teofilo Cubillas, Alianza Lima	Peru	1983	Socrates, Corinthians	Brazil
1973	Pele, Santos	Brazil	1984	Enzo Francescoli, River Plate	Uruguay
1974	Elias Figueroa, Internacional	Chile	1985	Julio Cesar Romero, Fluminense	Paraguay
1975	Elias Figueroa, Internacional	Chile	1986	Antonio Alzamendi, River Plate	Uruguay
1976	Elias Figueroa, Internacional	Chile	1987	Carlos Valderrama, Deportivo Cali	Colombia
1977	Zico, Flamengo	Brazil	1988	Ruben Paz, Racing Buenos Aires	Uruguay
1978	Mario Kempes, Valencia	Argentina	1989	Bebeto, Vasco da Gama	Brazil
1979	Diego Maradona, Argentinos Juniors	Argentina			
			1990	Raul Amarilla, Olimpia	Paraguay
1980	Diego Maradona, Boca Juniors	Argentina			
1981	Zico, Flamengo	Brazil			

All-Time International Matches Played

The all-time list of players with 100 or more international matches played through 1990 according to FIFA News. Caps are given for each international match.

	Pos	Caps		Pos	Caps
Peter Shilton, England	G	125	Grzegorz Lato, Poland	F	104
Pat Jennings, No.Ireland	G	119	Torbjorn Svenssen, Norway	G	104
Bjorn Nordqvist, Sweden	D	115	Franz Beckenbauer, West Germany	D	103
Dino Zoff, Italy	G	112	Soon-Ho Choi, South Korea	F	102
Oleg Blochin, USSR	F	109	Kenny Dalglish, Scotland	F	102
Ladislau Boloni, Romania	M	108	Kazimierz Deyna, Poland	M	102
Bobby Moore, England	D	108	Morten Olsen, Denmark	D	102
Bobby Charlton, England	M	106	Joachim Streich, East Germany	F	102
Heinz Hermann, Switzerland	M	105	Joszef Bozsik, Hungary	F	100
Billy Wright, England	M	105	Djalma Santos, Brazil	D	100
Hector Chumpitaz, Peru	D	104	Hans-Jurgen Dorner, East Germany	D	100

U.S. Pro Leagues
OUTDOOR
National Professional Soccer League (1967)

Not sanctioned by FIFA, the international soccer federation. The NPSL recruited individual players to fill the rosters of its 10 teams. The league lasted only one season.

Year	Winner	Playoff Final Score(s)	Loser	Regular Season Leading Scorer	G	A	Pts
1967	Oakland Clippers	0-1,4-1	Baltimore Bays	Yanko Daucik, Toronto	208		48

United Soccer Association (1967)

Sanctioned by FIFA. Originally called the North American Soccer League, it became the USA to avoid being confused with the National Professional Soccer League (see below). Instead of recruiting individual players, the USA imported 12 entire teams from Europe to represent its 12 franchises. It, too, only lasted a season. The league champion Los Angeles Wolves were actually Wolverhampton of England and the runner-up Washington Whips were Aberdeen of Scotland.

Year	Winner	Playoff Final Score	Loser	Regular Season Leading Scorer	G	A	Pts
1967	Los Angeles Wolves	6-5 (OT)	Washington Whips	Roberto Boninsegna, Chicago	10	1	21

North American Soccer League (1968-84)

The NPSL and USA merged to form the NASL in 1968 and the new league lasted until 1985. The NASL championship was known as the Soccer Bowl from 1975-84. One game decided the NASL title every year but five. There were no playoffs in 1969; a two-game/aggregate goals format was used in 1968 and '70; and a best-of-three games format was used in 1971 and '84; (*) indicates overtime and (†) indicates tie-breaker.

Multiple winners: NY Cosmos (5); Chicago (2).

Year	Winner	Playoff Final Score(s)	Loser	Regular Season Leading Scorer	G	A	Pts
1968	Atlanta Chiefs	0-0,3-0	San Diego Toros	John Kowalik, Chicago	30	9	69
1969	Kansas City Spurs	No game	Atlanta Chiefs	Kaiser Motaung, Atlanta	16	4	36
1970	Rochester Lancers	3-0,1-3	Washington Darts	Kirk Apostolidis, Dallas	16	3	35
1971	Dallas Tornado	1-2*,4-1,2-0	Atlanta Chiefs	Carlos Metidieri, Rochester	19	8	46
1972	New York Cosmos	2-1	St.Louis Stars	Randy Horton, New York	9	4	22
1973	Philadelphia Atoms	2-0	Dallas Tornado	Kyle Rote, Jr., Dallas	10	10	30
1974	Los Angeles Aztecs	4-3†	Miami Toros	Paul Child, San Jose	15	6	36
1975	Tampa Bay Rowdies	2-0	Portland Timbers	Steve David, Miami	23	6	52
1976	Toronto Metros	3-0	Minnesota Kicks	Giorgio Chinaglia, New York	19	11	49
1977	New York Cosmos	2-1	Seattle Sounders	Steve David, Los Angeles	26	6	58
1978	New York Cosmos	3-1	Tampa Bay Rowdies	Giorgio Chinaglia, New York	34	11	79
1979	Vancouver Whitecaps	2-1	Tampa Bay Rowdies	Oscar Fabbiani, Tampa Bay	25	8	58
1980	New York Cosmos	3-0	Ft.Laud.Strikers	Giorgio Chinaglia, New York	32	13	77
1981	Chicago Sting	1-0†	New York Cosmos	Giorgio Chinaglia, New York	29	16	74
1982	New York Cosmos	1-0	Seattle Sounders	Giorgio Chinaglia, New York	20	15	55
1983	Tulsa Roughnecks	2-0	Toronto Blizzard	Roberto Cabanas, New York	25	16	66
1984	Chicago Sting	2-1,3-2	Toronto Blizzard	Steve Zungul, Golden Bay	20	10	50

Regular Season MVP
Regular season Most Valuable Player as designated by the NASL.

Multiple winner: Carlos Metidieri (2).

Year		Year		Year	
1967	Rueben Navarro, Phila (NPSL)	1973	Warren Archibald, Miami	1979	Johan Cruyff, LA
1968	John Kowalik, Chicago	1974	Peter Silvester, Baltimore	1980	Roger Davis, Seattle
1969	Cirilio Fernandez, KC	1975	Steve David, Miami	1981	Giorgio Chinaglia, NY
1970	Carlos Metidieri, Rochester	1976	Pele, New York	1982	Peter Ward, Seattle
1971	Carlos Metidieri, Rochester	1977	Franz Beckenbauer, NY	1983	Roberto Cabanas, NY
1972	Randy Horton, New York	1978	Mike Flanagan, N.Eng.	1984	Steve Zungul, San Jose

American Professional Soccer League

Formed in 1990 after the merger of the Western Soccer League (WSL) and New American Soccer League (NASL). The APSL will be officially sanctioned as an outdoor professional league in 1992.

Year		Year	
1990	Maryland Bays	1991	SF Bay Blackhawks

INDOOR
Major Soccer League

Originally the Major Indoor Soccer League from 1979-90. The MISL championship was decided by one game in 1980 and 1981; a best-of-three games series in 1979, best-of-five games in 1982 and 1983; and best-of-seven games since 1984.

Multiple winners: San Diego (7); New York (4).

Playoff Final / Regular Season

Year	Winner	Series	Loser	Leading Scorer	G	A	Pts
1979	New York Arrows	2-0 (WW)	Phila.Fever	Fred Grgurev, Philadelphia	46	28	74
1980	New York Arrows	7-4 (1 game)	Hou.Summit	Steve Zungul, New York	90	46	136
1981	New York Arrows	6-5 (1 game)	St.L.Steamers	Steve Zungul, New York	108	44	152
1982	New York Arrows	3-2 (LWWLW)	St.L.Steamers	Steve Zungul, New York	103	60	163
1983	San Diego Sockers	3-2 (WWLLW)	Balt.Blast	Steve Zungul, NY/Golden Bay	75	47	122
1984	Baltimore Blast	4-1 (LWWWW)	St.L.Steamers	Stan Stamenkovic, Baltimore	34	63	97
1985	San Diego Sockers	4-1 (WWLWW)	Balt.Blast	Steve Zungul, San Diego	68	68	136
1986	San Diego Sockers	4-3 (WLLLWWW)	Minn.Strikers	Steve Zungul, Tacoma	55	60	115
1987	Dallas Sidekicks	4-3 (LLWWLWW)	Tacoma Stars	Tatu, Dallas	73	38	111
1988	San Diego Sockers	4-0	Cleve.Force	Eric Rasmussen, Wichita	55	57	112
1989	San Diego Sockers	4-3 (LWWWLLW)	Balt.Blast	Preki, Tacoma	51	53	104
1990	San Diego Sockers	4-2 (LWWWLW)	Balt.Blast	Tatu, Dallas	64	49	113
1991	San Diego Sockers	4-2 (WLWLWW)	Cleve.Crunch	Tatu, Dallas	78	66	144

MSL Playoff MVPs

MSL playoff Most Valuable Players, selected by a panel of soccer media covering the playoffs.

Multiple winners: Steve Zungul (4); Brian Quinn (2).

Year		Year	
1979	Shep Messing, NY	1986	Brian Quinn, SD
1980	Steve Zungul, NY	1987	Tatu, Dallas
1981	Steve Zungul, NY	1988	Hugo Perez, SD
1982	Steve Zungul, NY	1989	Victor Nogueira, SD
1983	Juli Veee, SD	1990	Brian Quinn, SD
1984	Scott Manning, Bal.	1991	Ben Collins, SD
1985	Steve Zungul, SD		

MSL Regular Season MVPs

MSL regular season Most Valuable Players, selected by a panel of soccer media from every city in the MISL.

Multiple winner: Steve Zungul (6).

Year		Year	
1979	Steve Zungul, NY	1985	Steve Zungul, SD
1980	Steve Zungul, NY	1986	Steve Zungul, SD/Tac.
1981	Steve Zungul, NY	1987	Tatu, Dallas
1982	Steve Zungul, NY & Stan Terlecki, Pit.	1988	Erik Rasmussen, Wich.
		1989	Preki, Tacoma
1983	Alan Mayer, G, SD	1990	Tatu, Dallas
1984	Stan Stamenkovic, Bal.	1991	Victor Nogueira, SD

NASL Indoor Champions (1979-83)

The North American Soccer League had both outdoor and indoor schedules from 1979-83. The indoor version of the NASL folded midway through the 1982-83 season, while the outdoor closed down after the 1984 season (see above).

Year		Year		Year		Year	
1980	Tampa Bay	1981	Edmonton	1982	San Diego	1983	Season cancelled

American Soccer League (1934-80)

The American Soccer League was the first professional soccer league in the U.S. The ASL lasted until 1980, but was primarily a semi-pro circuit after World War II.

Year	Champion	Year	Champion	Year	Champion
1934	Kearny Irish	1950	Phila.Nationals	1966	Roma SC
1935	Phila.Germans	1951	Phila.Nationals	1967	Balt.St.Gerard's
1936	NY Americans	1952	Phila.Americans	1968	Ukranian Nationals & Washington Darts
1937	Kearny Scots	1953	Phila.Nationals		
1938	Kearny Scots	1954	NY Americans	1969	Washington Darts
1939	Kearny Scots	1955	Uhrik Truckers		
		Year	Champion	1970	Phila.Ukranians
1940	Kearny Scots	1956	Uhrik Truckers	1971	NY Greeks
1941	Kearny Scots	1957	NY Hakoah	1972	Cincinnati Comets
1942	Phila.Americans	1958	NY Hakoah	1973	NY Apollo
1943	B'klyn Hispanos	1959	NY Hakoah	1974	Rhode Is.Oceaneers
1944	Phila.Americans			1975	Boston Astros-NY Apollo
1945	NY Brookhattan	1960	Columbo	1976	LA Skyhawks
1946	Balt.Americans	1961	Ukranian Nationals	1977	NJ Americans
1947	Phila.Americans	1962	Ukranian Nationals	1978	NY Apollo
1948	Phila.Americans	1963	Ukranian Nationals	1979	Sacramento Gold
1949	Phila.Nationals	1964	Ukranian Nationals	1980	Pennsylvania Stoners
		1965	Hartford SC		

Colleges
NCAA Division I Champions

NCAA Division I champions since the first title was contested in 1959. The championship game has ended in a tie three times—in 1967, 1968 and 1989.

Multiple winners: St.Louis (10); San Francisco (5); Indiana (3); Clemson, Howard and Michigan St.(2).

Year	Champion	Score	Runner-up	Year	Champion	Score	Runner-up
1959	St.Louis	5-2	Bridgeport	1975	San Francisco	4-0	SIU-Edwardsville
1960	St.Louis	3-2	Maryland	1976	San Francisco	1-0	Indiana
1961	West Chester-PA	2-0	St.Louis	1977	Hartwick	2-1	San Francisco
1962	St.Louis	4-3	Maryland	1978	San Francisco†	2-0	Indiana
1963	St.Louis	3-0	Navy	1979	SIU-Edwardsville	3-2	Clemson
1964	Navy	1-0	Michigan St.	1980	San Francisco	4-3*	Indiana
1965	St.Louis	1-0	Michigan St.	1981	Connecticut	2-1*	Alabama A&M
1966	San Francisco	5-2	LIU	1982	Indiana	2-1*	Duke
1967	Michigan St. & St.Louis	0-0	—tie—	1983	Indiana	1-0*	Columbia
				1984	Clemson	2-1	Indiana
1968	Michigan St. & Maryland	2-2*	—tie—	1985	UCLA	1-0*	American
				1986	Duke	1-0	Akron
1969	St.Louis	4-0	San Francisco	1987	Clemson	2-0	San Diego St.
1970	St.Louis	1-0	UCLA	1988	Indiana	1-0	Howard
1971	Howard†	3-2	St.Louis	1989	Santa Clara & Virginia	1-1	—tie—
1972	St.Louis	4-2	UCLA				
1973	St.Louis	2-1*	UCLA	1990	UCLA	1-0*	Rutgers
1974	Howard	2-1*	St.Louis				

*Overtime games: 1968—two OT (game called a draw); 1973—one OT; 1974—four OT; 1980—one OT; 1981—one OT; 1982—eight OT; 1983—two OT; 1985—eight OT; 1989—two OT (game called a draw); 1990—four OT, then decided on penalty kicks (4-3).
†Vacated titles: 1971—Howard; 1978—San Francisco.

Women's NCAA Division I Champions

NCAA Division I women's champions since the first title was contested in 1982.
Multiple winner: North Carolina (8).

Year	Champion	Score	Runner-up	Year	Champion	Score	Runner-up
1982	North Carolina	2-0	Central Florida	1987	North Carolina	1-0	Massachusetts
1983	North Carolina	4-0	George Mason	1988	North Carolina	4-1	N.C.State
1984	North Carolina	2-0	Connecticut	1989	North Carolina	2-0	Colorado College
1985	George Mason	2-0	North Carolina	1990	North Carolina	6-0	Connecticut
1986	North Carolina	2-0	Colorado College				

Annual Awards

The Hermann Trophy was was first given to the Division I Player of the Year in 1967. The Missouri Athletic Club Player of the Year Award has been presented since 1986. A second Hermann Trophy has been presented to the Division I Women's Player of the Year since 1988.

Hermann Trophy

Voted on by Division I college coaches and selected sportswriters and first presented in 1967 in the name of Robert Hermann, one of the founders of the North American Soccer League.
Multiple winners: Mike Seerey, Ken Snow and Al Trost (2).

Year		Year		Year	
1967	Dov Markus, LIU	1975	Steve Ralbovsky, Brown	1983	Mike Jeffries, Duke
1968	Manuel Hernandez, S.Jose St.	1976	Glenn Myernick, Hartwick	1984	Amr Aly, Columbia
1969	Al Trost, St.Louis	1977	Billy Gazonas, Hartwick	1985	Tom Kain, Duke
		1978	Angelo DiBernardo, Indiana	1986	John Kerr, Duke
1970	Al Trost, St.Louis	Year		1987	Bruce Murray, Clemson
1971	Mike Seerey, St.Louis	1979	Jim Stamatis, Penn St.	1988	Ken Snow, Indiana
1972	Mike Seerey, St.Louis			1989	Tony Meola, Virginia
1973	Dan Counce, St.Louis	1980	Joe Morrone, Jr., UConn	1990	Ken Snow, Indiana
1974	Farrukh Quraishi, Oneonta	1981	Armando Betancourt, Ind.		
		1982	Joe Ulrich, Duke		

Missouri Athletic Club Award

Voted on by 1,100 college and junior college coaches. First presented to the U.S. College Player of the Year in 1986 by the Missouri Athletic Club of St.Louis.
Multiple winner: Ken Snow (2).

Year		Year		Year	
1986	John Kerr, Duke	1988	Ken Snow, Indiana	1990	Ken Snow, Indiana
1987	John Harkes, Virginia	1989	Tony Meola, Virginia		

Reuters/Bettmann

Mike Powell on his way to shattering Bob Beamon's world long jump record, Aug. 30, at the World Track and Field Championships in Tokyo.

INTERNATIONAL SPORTS

INTERNATIONAL SPORTS

By Phil Hersh

9.86 and 29-4½!

*In a year when Germany reunites and the USSR falls apart,
Carl Lewis and Mike Powell produce some amazing numbers.*

Every so often it is healthy to see sport in its purest terms, unfiltered by all the political, psychological and financial prisms through which our view is constantly altered. Then it is sport as the fulfillment of competitive urges and the desire to push the limits of man's physical ability—the simple acts of doing and excelling.

And what could be simpler than running and jumping? Or more purely beautiful, too, especially the way Carl Lewis and Mike Powell of the United States ran and jumped in the third World Championships of Track and Field at Japan's National Stadium in late summer?

There was Lewis, arms slashing like knives through the air, coming from behind to break the world record in the 100 meters, the race no more complicated than who is the fastest from here to there. And here came Powell, the man who leaped into outer space, beyond even the limits Bob Beamon had reached in 1968 with his long jump over the moon.

Lewis, 9.86 seconds—faster than the world record of 9.90. Powell, 29 feet, 4½ inches—longer than the world record of 29-2½. Those numbers can serve not only as exemplars of the achievements during the past year in Olympic-related

sports, but as touchstones for the years and generations to come.

And, truth be told, the future has precious few reference points once one looks beyond the simplicity of running and jumping. What possible measure is there for a sports world changing at a pace Lewis would be hard-pressed to match, one that requires Powellian leaps even to imagine?

This world seemed so much easier to contemplate only three years ago, after the 1988 Olympic Games in Seoul, the first since 1972 free of boycott by significant members of the Olympic movement. Reunification was the word of the hour, although no one knew then it would apply to East and West Germany.

Ironically, Germany's reunification —as discordant as it remains—became the exception in 1991, when the Soviet Union's name became an oxymoron, Yugoslavia lingered on the brink of civil war, Czechs picked at Slovaks and South Africa's readmission to the Olympic movement was rendered almost meaningless by continued factionalism.

While it was nearly impossible to predict what impact all this would have on the 1992 Olympics, it was clear that for the second straight year a sporting era had ended.

In 1990, only a year after the Berlin Wall had fallen, it was the end of East Germany, the country of less than 17 million that

---

Phil Hersh covers international sports for the *Chicago Tribune* and has been the *Tribune's* full-time Olympics writer since 1986.

Newly-crowned world long jump champion **Mike Powell** (center) shares the victory platform in Tokyo with teammates **Larry Myricks** (left), who won the bronze medal, and defending champion **Carl Lewis**, who won the silver.

had come to rival the United States and Soviet Union as a sporting superpower. The merger with West Germany proved to be subtraction by addition, its results in nearly every sport less than what East Germany's ruthlessly efficient system (and chemical additives?) had produced.

In 1991, it would be, astonishingly, the apparent end of the Soviet Union, which has dominated the Olympics almost since its first appearance in 1952. As International Olympic Committee President Juan Antonio Samaranch put it during the World Track Championships, when the Soviet team led the total medal count, "I think we are seeing the red flag for the last time."

The splintering Soviet Union could produce 15 new Olympic member countries, although not immediately. But at least three former Soviet republics—the Baltic states of Estonia, Latvia, and Lithuania—will likely fly their own flags by the 1992 Summer Games that begin July 25 in Barcelona. Since the three were individual IOC members between the World Wars, it will constitute only readmission for them to have what Samaranch calls a "symbolic representation" in Spain.

That absence of the Baltic athletes from the Soviet team will have a tremendous impact in several sports, notably basketball, where Lithuanian players had starring roles on the Soviets' 1988 Olympic champions.

In Yugoslavia, where long-standing republican frictions have degenerated into warfare, the powerful basketball team and much of the Winter Olympic team—nearly all from Slovenia—could also be victims of partisan strife. Until the political situation is sorted out, the IOC will not recognize any of the six republics as independent members. The IOC has also asked that these republics not use athletes as hostages to gain leverage—that is, not prevent them from representing Yugoslavia if there is as yet no alternative.

On July 9, the IOC voted to readmit South Africa, excluded as a member since 1970 and from the Olympics since 1960 because of its racial discrimination laws. The road from there to Olympic participation will not prove smooth, as merging the various racially-designated federations that each control a piece of South African sport is a process complicated by individual agendas. Some feel that the

(Continued on p. 492)

Carl Lewis raises his arms in triumph after setting a world record of 9.86 seconds in the 100 meters. Former holder **Leroy Burrell** (far right) was second, **Denis Mitchell** (far left) third, and **Linford Christie** fourth.

Reuters/Bettmann

Lewis and Powell Dominate World Meet

If there was any doubt about his stature as the greatest performer in the sport's history, Carl Lewis put it to rest at the third World Track and Field Championships, which ran from Aug. 24 to Sept. 1 in Tokyo.

Lewis set a world record (9.86 seconds) to win the greatest 100-meter race in history; ran anchor on the 4 x 100-meter relay team that lowered the world record by .17 seconds to 37.50; and had the four longest long jumps of his career, three of them 29 feet or better.

Yet even though he was the main attraction in Japan, the 30-year-old Lewis did not provide the most enduring moment of the championships.

That individual highlight belonged to Mike Powell, 27, a Philadelphian who has lived half his life in Los Angeles. He broke Bob Beamon's 23-year-old world record and ended Lewis' 10-year, 65-meet win streak in the long jump with a single bound of 29 feet, 4½ inches. That was two inches more than the mark Beamon had set in the thin (7,400 feet) air of Mexico City at the 1968 Olympics.

That Lewis did not win with jumps of 28-11¾ (wind-aided), 29-2¾ (wind-aided), 29-1¼, and 29-0 was incredible, especially to him. "He had one jump, and I had the greatest series of all time, but he just did it," lamented Lewis.

Lewis now has seven gold and two silver medals in three world meets. The second place in the long jump prevented him from joining pole vaulter Sergei Bubka of the Soviet Union and 110-meter hurdler Greg Foster of the U.S. as three-time champions in a single event.

Bubka, bothered by recurring pain in his heel, was one miss from finishing sixth when he cleared the winning height of 19 feet, 6¼ inches. Foster won in a photo finish over teammate Jack Pierce, with both timed in 13.06 seconds.

But Powell and Lewis were the dominant figures in a meet that may be remembered more for illustrating how the world of track and field has changed since the previous championships four years ago.

This was the first major track meet in 27 years with a unified German team and prob-

Steven E. Sutton

German sprinter **Katrin Krabbe**
was both the only double winner in Tokyo
and the only ex-East German athlete to
win a gold medal.

ably the last with the Soviet Union. It was also the first after three years of widespread random testing to stop the use of performance-enhancing drugs—the legacy of Canadian sprinter Ben Johnson's steroid bust after the 100 meters at the 1988 Olympics.

Measuring those issues says as much about track and field in 1991 as did the results of the world meet:

Doping control obviously has had an effect, especially among the women. In only five of the 19 women's events was the winning result better than that at the previous World Championships in 1987. The same drop-off occurred in six of the seven men's and women's throwing events.

Johnson, whose comeback after a two-year suspension produced great fanfare at his first race in January and little else thereafter, was no longer good enough even to qualify for the 100 meters (he finished fourth in the Canadian championships). He wound up running a leg on the relay team that finished last in the final.

East Germany's women alone won more gold (6) and total medals (23) in 1987 than the combined German men's and women's teams won (5 gold, 17 total) in Tokyo. Glamor girl Katrin Krabbe was both the only individual event double winner (100 and 200 meters) and the only ex-East German woman to win a gold medal. Four of the five individual German gold medals and 12 of the 15 total individual medals were won by former Easties.

The Soviet Union claimed many of the medals won previously by the East Germans and were able to beat the United States in the total medal count, 28-26. The Soviets' eight individual medalists included two Ukrainians (Bubka and Tatiana Dorovskikh); two Russians (Natalya Lisovskaya and Lyudmila Narozhilenko) and a Byelorussian (Aleksandr Potashov). All may soon be competing for their individual republics, which lack the organization and funding of the centralized Soviet system.

Meanwhile, African men won five of the six golds, five of the six silvers and 13 of the 18 total medals from 800 meters to the marathon. In the first World Championships at Helsinki in 1983, the Africans had just one silver and one bronze medal in those events.

African women made an impact for the first time as well. Five days after Susan Sirma of Kenya (3,000 meters) became Africa's first female medalist in the World Championships, Hassiba Boulmerka of Algeria (1,500) became the first gold medalist.

When Noureddine Morceli won the men's 1,500, it made Algeria the first country ever to have both metric mile champions in an Olympics or World Championships.

The 100 meters, as usual, lived up to its billing, with Lewis and Leroy Burrell (9.88) both breaking the world record of 9.90 that Burrell had set two months earlier in the U.S. Nationals. Dennis Mitchell of the U.S. was third at 9.91, and six runners broke 10 seconds. Never before had more than three entrants broken 10 seconds in the same race.

The 100 sweep was one of two (the long jump was the other) for the U.S., which was the only country to take all the medals in an event. The Americans had a meet-leading 10 gold medals and would have had another had Jackie Joyner-Kersee not pulled a hamstring midway through the heptathlon, forcing her to withdraw. A day before, Joyner-Kersee had successfully defended her title in the long jump.

(Continued from p. 489)
readmission, granted after repeal of the apartheid laws, should wait until greater real equality between the races is achieved.

World records—even as amazing as those of Lewis and Powell—are more easily attained and understood.

Summer Sports

Archery. Simon Fairweather of Australia, who was 20th in 1989, scored a major upset to win the men's title at the biennial World Championships in Cracow, Poland. Vadim Shikarev of the Soviet Union was second, with Chang Hoon Yang of South Korea third. Ed Eliason, 53, was the top U.S. finisher at seventh. South Korea won the men's team title, with Finland second, Australia third, and the U.S. fourth.

In the women's event, Kim Soo Nyung of South Korea successfully defended her world title, with teammate Li Eun Kyung second. Denise Parker of the U.S., who had been third in 1989, dropped to sixth, but the U.S. women managed a third in the team event, behind Korea and the Soviets.

Baseball. A funny thing happened on the way to an expected dramatic confrontation between the United States and Cuba in the Pan Am Games finals. . .The U.S. was routed by Puerto Rico 7-1 in the semifinals. Cuba went on to crush the Puerto Ricans 18-3 in the final, giving it a sixth straight Pan Am gold and 10-0 record for the tournament. The veteran Cuban team did that without two of its best pitchers—Rene Arocha, who defected to the U.S. in July, and Lazaro Valle, who was sidelined with a blood clot in the arm. Not that they needed much pitching: the Cubans batted .399 as a team, hit 38 home runs and outscored opponents 145-27. Their only close game had been with the U.S. in the preliminary round. Then it took a brilliant diving stop by shortstop German Mesa on Charles Johnson's eighth-inning, bases-loaded grounder to save a 3-2 Cuban win before 55,000 at Latin American Stadium. The U.S. wound up with the bronze medal.

Basketball. The Pan Am Games turned into an utter debacle for both the U.S. men and women.

The women saw a 42-game, eight-year winning streak end with an 87-84

Wide World Photos

Brazilian defenders **Maria Da Silva** (left) and **Nadia Bento** surround America's **Andrea Lloyd** during the first half of the Brazil-USA women's basketball contest at the Pan Am Games. Brazil upset the U.S., 87-84, on its way to the gold medal.

loss to Brazil in the preliminary round and then were knocked out of contention for the gold by Cuba (86-81) in the semifinals. Led by star guards Hortencia Marcari (who became famous for posing topless in the Brazilian edition of Playboy after the 1987 Pan Am Games) and Maria da Silva, Brazil crushed Cuba 97-76 in the final for its first women's hoop gold since 1971. The U.S. took the bronze with a 92-61 rout of Canada.

The men's team infuriated some of the poorer Pan Am countries by twice jetting off to Florida for better accommodations during breaks in the tournament. Said USA Basketball executive director Bill Wall: "If we're spoiled and arrogant, so be it."

Puerto Rico got revenge for the rest of the hemisphere with a 73-68 semifinal win over the Americans, whose star guard, Jimmy Jackson of Ohio state, was sidelined by a foot stress fracture. Puerto Rico beat Mexico 77-65 for the Pan Am title. The U.S. went on to defeat Cuba for

Twelve-year-old **Fu Mingxia** of China after winning the women's platform diving title at the World Swimming Championships at Perth in January.

the bronze medal, but this will be remembered as the fifth straight major international event (two Pan Am Games, one Olympics, one World Championships and the Goodwill Games) in which the U.S. team did not win the gold.

That streak is certain to end next year at the Olympics, when NBA players will be able to represent the U.S. for the first time. And their travails in the Pan Am Games should be lessened, if, as expected, a rules change to limit that competition to players 22 & under is passed.

Boxing. USA Boxing's decision to send a "B" team to the Pan American Games, apparently based on a desire not to have its best fighters humiliated in Cuba before the November World Championships, took a lot of fun out of the competition in Havana. Cuba won 11 of the 12 boxing golds while the U.S. collected just one gold, three silvers and a bronze. Steve Johnston won the gold at 139 pounds, the only weight class where the Cubans did not make the final.

Late in 1990, Eric Griffin was the only U.S. boxer (at 106) to win at the World Championships Challenge in Berlin, where Cuba had five golds and one silver medal in the 12 weight classes.

Canoe/Kayak. At the World Championships in Paris, double Olympic gold medalist Greg Barton of the U.S., returning to kayak competition after a year off, won the 10,000 (a non-Olympic event) and a bronze in the 1,000 meters. That was the only U.S. medal in Olympic events.

Cycling. Throughout the spring, even though his results were characteristically poor, Greg LeMond was uncharacteristically healthy. That seemed to augur well for his chances to win a third straight title in the Tour de France, but this time it was in the race itself that LeMond's body betrayed him.

Spain's Miguel Indurain won the 78th Tour, with LeMond seventh, a whopping 13 minutes and 13 seconds behind after 21 stages and 2,500 miles of riding. Yet he was applauded by the French simply for finishing after two disastrous stages midway through the Tour in the Pyrenees, which he had entered wearing the leader's yellow jersey for four straight days. Worn down by an infection and sore feet, Lemond lost nearly seven minutes in two days.

From then on the race belonged to Indurain, 27, who had spent several years as a domestique, or helper, for 1988 Tour champion Pedro Delgado. A pair of Italians, Gianni Bugno and Claudio Chiappucci, were 2-3. For the 30-year-old LeMond, it was the first time out of the top three in six Tours de France. His season ended a total loss when he dropped out of the World Championship road race after 12 of 16 laps. That race was won by Bugno.

Germany dominated the World Championships, with twice as many gold (6) and total (12) medals as runner-up Holland.

For the U.S., Janie Eickhoff, 21, won silver (individual pursuit) and bronze (points race) medals, while Inga Thompson (road race) and four-time world champion Connie Paraskevin Young (bronze) were the other medalists.

Diving. China's Fu Mingxia, 12, became the youngest world champion in the history of any sport when she won the women's platform title at Perth. That record will not be broken, because the International Swimming Federation has passed a rule allowing only athletes who are at least 14 during the calendar year to participate in a World Championships or Olympics. The Chinese women swept the world diving titles, with Gao Min winning both springboard events, and also were 1-2 in the men's platform. Edwin Jongejans of Holland (1-meter) and Kent Ferguson of the U.S. (3-meter) took the only crowns that eluded the Chinese.

Drugs. The fates of two U.S. world record-holders suspended for steroid use in 1990 diverged on different legal courses. Shot-putter Randy Barnes lost an appeal to The Athletics Congress/USA, tried pro football and was quickly cut by the San Francisco 49ers. Quarter-miler Butch Reynolds delayed his TAC appeal to try the federal courts, then won an arbitrator's injunction to compete in the U.S. nationals, where he finished a badly-beaten seventh of eight in a first-round heat.

The International Amateur Athletic Federation voted to increase its penalty for use of performance-enhancing drugs from two to four years. Delisa Floyd, U.S. champion in the 800 meters, became the first to earn the longer suspension when she tested positive for an amphetamine after finishing last in a semifinal heat at the World Championships.

Two Australian medalists in the professional match sprint at the World Cycling Championships—Carey Hall (gold) and Stephen Pate (bronze)—lost those medals for steroid use. Their suspension, though, was only a three-month slap-on-the-wrist from the professional cycling federation (UCI), which continues to lag behind amateur cycling in the fight against doping.

Fencing. Cuba's first-ever World Championship gold—in the team event—was the highlight of the 1991 worlds in Budapest. Cubans had not won any major men's fencing titles since the 1904 Olympics in St. Louis. The Soviet Union, (3), Hungary (3) and Italy (2) won 8 of the 10 golds. For the third straight World Championships since the last Olympics, none of the defending champions kept a title, although 1989 sabre champion Grigori Kirienko won again.

Gymnastics. "This is the end of an era of Soviet domination," proclaimed Bela Karolyi, the Romanian emigre who has come to be the godfather of U.S. gymnastics.

Karolyi's vision of a new world order was fashioned in the euphoria over what

Wide World Photos

U.S. gymnast **Kim Zmeskal** waves her bouquet after winning the world All-Around title in Indianapolis

one of his pupils, Kim Zmeskal, had done at the World Gymnastics Championships in Indianapolis on Sept. 13. Zmeskal, 15, of Houston, won the all-around, an event in which no U.S. woman has previously finished higher than seventh. Two other U.S. gymnasts, Betty Okino, 16, of Elmhurst, Ill., and Shannon Miller, 14, of Edmond, Okla., were fourth and sixth.

Two days before that, a six-woman U.S. team (four of whom train at Karolyi's Houston gym) finished second to the Soviet Union in the team competition, earning the first medal ever in that event for the United States. Miller (silver, uneven bars), Zmeskal (bronze, floor exercise), and Okino (bronze, balance beam) went on to win individual apparatus medals. The five-medal total was three more than U.S. women had ever won in a single world meet.

Yet the Soviets still won the men's and women's team titles, swept the men's all-around medals (gold to Grigori Misutin), had a second in women's all-around, (defending champion Svetlana Boguinskaia) and won half of both the men's and women's apparatus finals. And many felt the U.S. results were inflated by judges reacting to widly partisan home crowds at

Neal Hamberg

Poland's **Wanda Panfil** was 1991's top female marathon runner, winning in Boston and at the World Track and Field Championships in Tokyo.

only the second world championships held in the U.S., although even the home-gym advantage could not bring the U.S. men a medal.

At the June national championships in Cincinnati, Zmeskal became the first woman to win successive U.S. titles in the all-around since Tracee Talavera in 1981-82. Chris Waller of Arlington Heights, Ill., won the men's all-around title.

Marathons. Poland's Wanda Panfil emerged as the world's leading female marathoner when she added the World Championships marathon title to her wins at Boston in 1991 (her time of 2:24:18, second-best ever by a woman at Boston) and New York in 1990. Rosa Mota, who has dominated women's marathoning since 1986, won London but had to drop out of the World Championships race after 16 miles with abdominal cramps.

Two Kenyans, Douglas Wakiihuri and Ibrahim Hussein, won New York (1990) and Boston (1991), respectively, but both scratched from the worlds. On a steamy Tokyo morning, that race was won by Japan's Hirom Taniguchi in 2:14:57, the slowest time for a world or Olympic champion since 1960. Steve Spence of Chambersburg, Pa., was a surprise third in that race—beating the likes of 1988 Olympic champion Gelindo Bordin of Italy, who was eighth—to win the first U.S. medal in an international championship since Frank Shorter's Olympic silver in 1976.

Olympics. Robert Helmick resigned Sept. 18 as president of the United States Olympic Committee in the wake of revelations that he had represented a variety of clients who do business with the Olympic movement. Helmick, 54, an attorney from Des Moines, Iowa, had served as president since March, 1985, when he replaced John B. Kelly, who had died of a heart attack. Helmick was then elected to a four-year term in February, 1989. The USOC's executive committee was empowered to find a replacement for Helmick until the next election in late fall, 1992.

Helmick admitted only to "errors of judgment concerning appearance of conflict of interest" and tried to stay in the job, but mounting pressure led him to resign 13 days after *USA Today* disclosed his business relationships. Helmick's status as one of the two U.S. members to the International Olympics Committee and a member of the IOC executive board was also jeopardized by his domestic problems. The day after he resigned, the IOC's executive board announced a three-man committee to investigate Helmick's potential conflicts of interest.

The USOC named Colorado Springs businessman William Hybl to replace Helmick as interim president.

On Sept. 18, the IOC reinstated the three former Baltic republics of the Soviet Union—Latvia, Lithuania and Estonia—as individual member nations. The three countries had competed under their own flags between the World Wars, after which they were absorbed into the Soviet Union. All three expected to send between two and three dozen athletes to both 1992 Olympic Games. The return of the Baltics raised the number of national Olympic committees within the IOC to 170. Some 20 others have asked for admission, but those decisions will not be taken until after the 1992 Olympics.

Nagano, Japan, was selected host city for the 1998 Winter Olympics, defeating Salt Lake City 46-42 on the final ballot in a controversial vote at the International Olympic Committee's annual meeting in Birmingham, England. Salt Lake City,

Wide World Photos

Cuban president **Fidel Castro** salutes the American flag at the Pan American Games in Havana following the U.S. victory in the women's quadruple sculls rowing race. To the left of Castro are **Michelle Knox-Zaldon** and **Susan Teifen**, while **Karen Carpenter** and **Betsy Kimmel** are to the right.

one of five candidates, was nearly eliminated in the first round of balloting. Nagano, 110 miles northwest of Tokyo, is the second Asian city chosen as a winter host, after Sapporo, Japan in 1972.

In July, the IOC reinstated South Africa, which lost its membership in 1970 (and has been out of the Olympics since 1960) because of its racial discrimination policies.

Pan American Games. The country's economy is a shambles, with bread rationing and oxen replacing tractors to save fuel, but Cuban President Fidel Castro's circus provided two weeks of diversion for his sports-mad people.

And Castro, as expected, was ringmaster—joining in the wave at a women's basketball game, presenting medals to friend and foe alike, appearing in so many places during a day it seemed there were Castro clones. And his athletes showed high fidelity to the tenets of the Cuban revolution, by praising the workers whose virtual forced labor had miraculously gotten all the facilities finished on time. Cuban athletes did very well, topping the gold medal count of the 39 participating nations with 140. The United States won only 130 golds, marking the first time in 11 Pan American Games that the hemisphere's rich Uncle Sam has not won the most gold.

The U.S. did lead in total medals, however, 322-265. That total was second highest ever for the U.S., behind only the 369 at Indianapolis four years ago.

The relatively weak U.S. performance was due to the decision by many U.S. athletes, especially in track and field, to shun what they felt would be a boot camp in the Pan Am sites of Havana and Santiago. Several U.S. sports federations also chose to send second or third teams to Cuba, although the policy of keeping first-stringers out of the Pan Ams was not new for sports like swimming.

The Cuban crowds didn't care. Given free admission, they packed arenas and stadiums and cheered wildly for the home team, which became a problem only when they jeered opposing divers about to risk life and limb on the 10-meter platform.

From the minute the aptly-named Alberto Cuba won the men's marathon (the Games' first event) the Cuban athletes responded. They won 29 of 30 golds in weightlifting, 11 of 12 in boxing, an astounding 10 of 12 in canoe/kayak, a sixth straight title in baseball, a first-ever gold medal in swimming, and an upset of the U.S. in the water polo gold-medal game.

The U.S. also came away with one unexpected triumph—a first gold in soccer, although that tournament was weakened by the absence of traditional South American powers Argentina, Brazil and Uruguay, who refused to play a qualifying round. Team USA beat Mexico 2-1 in overtime in a scintillating gold-medal game.

Rowing. Germany, led by former East Germans, dominated the World Championships in Vienna, with seven golds and 10 total medals. This was one of the few sports where a combined German team bettered what the East Germans alone had done in the previous world meet. Italy's Abbagnale brothers, Giuseppe and Claudio, won their seventh world title in the pair with coxswain.

Swimming. Nowhere was the decline of the former East German sports empire clearer than in swimming. At the World Championships and European Championships, unified German teams won fewer gold medals combined than the East German women alone had won in a single meet at the 1988 Olympics. The numbers:
- ▶ 1986 Worlds: 14 East German golds, 13 (in 16 events) by the women.
- ▶ 1988 Olympics: 11 East German golds, 10 by the women.
- ▶ 1989 Europeans: 15 East German golds, 14 by the women.
- ▶ 1991 Worlds: 4 German golds, 1 by the women.
- ▶ 1991 Europeans: 4 German golds, 2 by the women.

The downfall is attributed to two major reasons: lack of government funding for the unified team after years of total support from the East German government; and strict doping controls after years in which East German swimmers were suspected of taking performance-enhancing drugs.

Hungary and the Soviet Union capitalized on the Germans' weakness to become the leading teams at the European Championships in Athens. The Soviets won a meet-leading nine gold medals, while Hungary's four golds included three world records—by Kristina Egerszegi in both backstrokes and Norbert Rosza in the 100 breaststroke. Egerszegi, the 1988 Olympic champion who is still only 17, also won the 400 individual medley.

Of the 13 world records set in 1991, six were by Hungarians and four by the U.S.

Six of those records came at January's World Championships in Perth, Australia,

Wide World Photos

America's **Janet Evans** waves to friends after winning one of her two individual freestyle gold medals at the World Swimming Championships at Perth.

where Hungary's Tamas Darnyi was the big star with golds and world records in both individual medleys. Former East German Joerg Hoffmann (400 and 1,500 freestyles, the latter in a world record) was the only other man to win two individual events.

Egerszegi, China's Li Lin and the United States' Janet Evans (a triple Olympic gold medalist in 1988) each won two women's events. China's women won four golds, their first ever in a world meet, and are considered potential successors to the East Germans. For the first time in six World Championships, no world records were set by women, a dropoff that likely can be related to increased doping controls.

Elsewhere in a busy swimming year, the U.S. dominated the Pan Pacific Games in Edmonton, winning 26 gold medals in 36 events. But Australia's Kieren Perkins was the swimmer of the meet, winning three golds and setting a world record for 800 meters freestyle en route to a triumph in the 1,500.

Track & Field. The most noteworthy event of the outdoor season leading up to the World Championships was Leroy Burrell's 100-meter world record of 9.90 at

AFP Photo

Soviet pole vaulter **Sergei Bubka** became the first man to vault 20 feet when he cleared the height both indoors and outdoors in 1991. In all, Bubka reset his indoor and outdoor world records four times each.

the U.S. Championships in June. Finland's Seppo Raty improved the world record in the javelin to 318 feet, 1 inch, but the continuing controversy about the technical characteristics of the spear has made all new records questionable.

And throughout it all there was Sergei Bubka, the Czar of the Pole Vault. Before the worlds began Bubka had improved his own world records eight times in 1991—four indoors and four outdoors. In both venues, he became the first over 20 feet—doing it inside on Mar. 15 at San Sebastian, Spain; then reaching the same height outside on Aug. 5 at Malmo, Sweden. He pushed the indoor record up to 20-1 before that season ended.

The third World Indoor Championships at Seville, Spain, produced six world records, all but one—Merlene Ottey equalled her own mark of 22.24 in the 200 meters—of lesser importance. Ben Johnson capped his indoor season with his most respectable performance of 1991, a fourth in the 60 meters. Algeria's Morceli produced the major world record

of the indoor season with a 3:34.16 in the 1,500 meters on the same Seville track two weeks before the world meet—lopping .05 off the mark set by Peter Elliott of Great Britain in 1990.

As winter ended, Khalid Skah of Morocco and Lynn Jennings of the U.S. successfully defended their titles in the World Cross-Country Championships at Antwerp, Belgium. The East African distance-running dominance was never clearer than at Antwerp, as Kenya and Ethiopia took first and second in team scoring in each of the four races (senior and junior men and women). After Skah in the senior men's race, the next six places went to Kenyans, and East Africans (Kenya, Ethiopia, Tanzania) won the first 13 places in the junior men's race. Lydia Cheromei of Kenya, the junior women's champion, became at age 13 by far the youngest person ever to win an athletics world title in any event.

Weightlifting. Cuba's results in the Pan Am Games, after a year of virtual isolation from international competition, led

Austria's **Rudolf Nierlich**, seen here at the World Cup stop in Aspen in March, won the Giant Slalom at the World Alpine Championships in January. He was killed in a May auto accident.

to strong feelings the Cubans had beaten the new anti-doping measures put into the sport after the 1988 Olympics. While weight totals have been down in every other major competition since then, the Cubans set 21 Pan Am records (out of a possible 30) and won 29 of 30 gold medals.

The Soviets won four overall (total weight) gold medals and the team title in the 1990 World Championships, where the weight totals lifted were lower than 1989 in nine of the 10 weight classes.

Naim (Pocket Hercules) Suleymanoglu of Turkey, hero of the 1988 Olympics, came out of brief retirement to start training for the 1992 Olympics. He won three gold medals at the Mediterranean Games in the 132-pound class.

Wrestling. John Smith of Stillwater, Okla., became the first wrestler to win the Sullivan Award after taking a third world title (136.5 pounds) in September, 1990.

Smith was among seven U.S. wrestlers to win gold medals at the Pan American Games. Brad Penrith of Phoenix scored the biggest upset, beating Cuban world champion Alejandro Puerto on his home mat.

Winter Sports
Persian Gulf War. The outbreak of hostilities in the Persian Gulf in January

led officials of two U.S. federations—skiing and speed skating—to bring their athletes home from Europe out of fears of potential terrorism.

For the skiers, the middle-of-the-night evacuation occurred only five days before the World Alpine Championships began in Saalbach, Austria. The U.S. team eventually arrived in Saalbach after missing the first two events. The speed skaters also returned to Europe in time for their World Championships.

Alpine Skiing. It was a season of gloom. Austrian skier Gernot Reinstadler, 20, died in a Jan. 18 qualifying run crash prior to the famed downhill at Wengen, Switzerland, which was cancelled after the tragedy. The World Championships in Saalbach, Jan. 22-Feb. 3, were overshadowed by the outbreak of war in the Persian Gulf a week earlier. And in late May, Austrian star Rudolf Nierlich was killed in an automobile accident.

Nierlich, 25, who had won the giant slalom at the 1991 Worlds and both the slalom and giant slalom at the 1989 Worlds, figured to be one of the leading medal contenders at the 1992 Winter Olympics. He died when his car skidded off a wet road and crashed into a guardrail near his hometown of Bad Ischl.

The 1991 World Championships began under heavy security after the opening ceremonies were cancelled. Once the skiing began, the home team put some good cheer into the situation.

Nierlich's gold medal in the giant slalom on the final day of the meet completed Austria's return to world ski leadership after a decade of Swiss dominance. The Austrians won five of the 10 events and 11 total medals, while the Swiss took three golds and six total medals.

Austria's Stefan Eberharter was the only double champion, with victories in the super giant and combined. Luxembourg's Marc Girardelli, who went on to a record-tying fourth World Cup overall title, won his third gold medal in three World Championships, this one in slalom.

The U.S. team needn't have bothered to return to the World Championships. Its best finish was a fifth by Eva Twardokens in giant slalom, marking the first time in six world meets since 1974 that the U.S. has not won a medal.

For the umpteenth year in a row, U.S. ski hopes in both the World Championships and World Cup were dashed by injuries to top skiers. Diann Roffe and Kristi Terzian were the victims in 1990-91.

One bright spot: on the final weekend of the World Cup season, Julie Parisien won the giant slalom at Waterville Valley, N.H., giving the U.S. its first World Cup victory since 1987—ending the longest drought in U.S. history.

On the World Cup circuit, Austria's Petra Kronberger got off to a phenomenal start—four firsts and two seconds in the first six races—and was able to survive a knee injury to win her second straight overall title as well as the slalom crown. Kronberger opened the World Championships with a win in the downhill and was a lock to win the combined when she was hurt in the slalom section of the event.

Girardelli's overall title capped his comeback from an injury-ruined 1990 and tied the record of four shared by Italy's Gustavo Thoeni and Switzerland's Pirmin Zurbriggen. Girardelli also won World Cup titles in slalom and combined.

Biathlon. The combined German team dominated the 1991 World Championships, winning half the eight events. Former East German Mark Kirchner was the big winner, taking both individual

events (10- and 20-kilometers) and a relay gold. Women will make their Olympic biathlon debut in 1992.

Bobsled. U.S. sledding got an unusual amount of publicity for a non-Olympic year, and not all of it was favorable.

The media was first attracted by the presence of Olympic hurdles gold medalist Edwin Moses and two football stars, Willie Gault and Herschel Walker, among the sled pushers on the U.S. team.

That attention led indirectly to revelations of mismanagement and the unexplained loss of between $200,000 and $400,000 within the U.S. Bobsled and Skeleton Federation, which was forced to reorganize by the U.S. Olympic committee.

And then there was further controversy at the sled pusher trials at Lake Placid in July, when Moses walked out in what was considered a personality clash with the other athletes, some of whom resented the high profile of the more famous newcomers.

After Moses, Gault and tight end Greg Harrell were narrowly beaten in the team push trials, none competed in the side-push event. Gault and Harrell had to report to the Raiders' training camp. Moses, however, just left.

Walker earned an Olympic alternate berth in brakeman trials and was to get a chance to win a regular spot before the Games in February.

The U.S. Olympic team drivers were picked in March—Brian Shimer and Brian Richardson in two-man, Chuck Leonowicz and Randy Will in four-man. Moses had ridden with Shimer in both two- and four-man sleds at the World Championships, earning the top U.S. finishes of seventh in both events. Their four-man sled also included Gault and Harrell. It won the 4-man World Push Championships, proving the addition of athletes like Moses and Gault did have the desired effect. In 1990, the top U.S. sleds had been only 12th (two man) and 13th (four-man) at the worlds.

German sleds upset Swiss defending champion Gustav Weder in both World Championship events. It was a triumph of the merged Germanies—former West Germans won the two-man and ex-East Germans took the four-man.

Cross-country Skiing. Gunde (The Great) Svan of Sweden was as stunning

Bobsled hopefuls **Greg Harrell** (left), **Edwin Moses** (center) and **Willie Gault** prepare for a run at the U.S. National Push Championships at Lake Placid in July. They placed second.

off the snow as he was on it at the World Championships in Val di Fiemme, Italy. Svan, 29, won a gold and three silvers and then announced he intended to skip the Olympic season to make his Svan song at the 1993 Worlds in Sweden. Svan has won four Olympic titles and six World Championship titles. Norway (5 gold, 10 overall medals) and the Soviet Union (4 gold, 8 overall) were the big winners at the worlds. The Soviets' Elena Vialbe established herself as the leading woman, taking gold at 10 and 15 kilometers, silver at 30 kilometers and gold in the relay.

Freestyle Skiing. The moguls event has been given medal status for the 1992 Olympics, and that gives the U.S. perhaps its surest bet for a gold medal in the entire Games. The favorite is Donna Weinbrecht of West Milford, N.J., world champion in 1991 and overwhelming World Cup winner in 1990 and 1991.

Hockey. For the second time in the last four World Championships, Sweden upset the Soviet Union for the title. The United States made the medal round for the first time since 1985 and finished fourth. The Soviets were 1-1-1 in the medal round, tying Canada and losing 2-1 to Sweden.

In a new Olympic tournament format, the teams will play round-robin only in the preliminary round of two six-team groups. The top four in each group then advance into a single-elimination bracket, meaning the final game will now absolutely determine the gold and silver medals.

Luge. Unrest in the Soviet republic of Latvia forced a move of the World Championships to Winterberg, Germany, where the home team dominated the event.

In the women's race, former East Germans Susi Erdman and Gabi Kohlisch finished 1-2, with ex-West German Jana Bode third. It was also 1-2 for former East Germans in doubles with Stephan Krausse and Jan Behrendt winning the gold. Arnold Huber of Italy upset Germany's George Hackl, the 1989-90 winner, for the men's title.

The U.S. performance was off in women's where Cammy Myler and Bonny

Warner slipped to 9th and 10th (from 6-7 a year ago), but improved in men's and doubles. The seventh-place finishes by Duncan Kennedy and the doubles teams of Wendel Suckow-Bill Tavares and Mark Grimmette-Jon Edwards (they tied for 7th) were the best in U.S. history.

Ski Jumping. With 1988 Olympic star Matti Nykaenen of Finland once again tormented by personal problems, two young skiers took advantage of his absence at the 1991 World Championships in Val di Fiemme, Italy. Franci Petek of Yugoslavia and Heinz Kuttin of Austria, both 20, won the large and normal hill events, respectively. Top U.S. finisher in either event was Jim Holland, 29th in the normal hill.

Speed Skating. Desultory results during the 1990-91 season led to a coaching shakeup in the U.S. long-track (400-meter oval) program, with Peter Mueller and Polish emigre Stanislaw Klotkowski replacing Mike Crowe as head coach. Mueller, 1976 Olympic gold medalist in the 1,000 meters, had spent the past three seasons as coach of the West German (now German) team.

Olympic champion Bonnie Blair, slowed by a lingering virus, failed to win a medal at the World Sprint Championships for the first time since 1985. Blair, the 1989 sprint champion and 1990 runner-up, was a badly-beaten fifth to Monique Garbrecht of Germany (ex-East). Defending champion Angela Hauck of Germany (ex-East) had to withdraw with an ankle injury after two of the four races in the championships at Inzell, Germany.

On the men's side, Igor Zhelezovski of the Soviet Union regained the title he had won in 1989 (defending champion Ki Tae Bae of South Korea retired after last season). Meanwhile, Dan Jansen was the top American finisher—a frustrating fourth for the third straight year.

In the men's World All-Around meet at Heerenveen, Holland, Norway's Johann Olav Koss was totally dominant—winning three of four races, breaking two world records (10,000 meters and total points) and winning his second straight title by a whopping margin. Former East German Gunda Kleeman also won three of the four races en route to the women's all-around title at Hamar, Norway. □

U.S. Women Prove Mettle In Munich

When the moment came, no one was prepared for it.

That was to be expected, since history is often made without warning.

Never before in the 73-year history of women's competition at the World Figure Skating Championships had one country swept all the medals.

That explains why officials of the International Skating Union sent aides scurrying around the Munich Olympic complex late in the afternoon of March 16. They were desperately seeking the third American flag necessary for the medal ceremony after Kristi Yamaguchi, Tonya Harding and Nancy Kerrigan, all of the United States, finished 1-2-3 in women's singles at the 1991 World Championships. U.S. men have swept the worlds three times—in 1952, '55 and '56.

Their unprecedented achievement capped the best performance by a U.S. team at the figure skating worlds since 1959. It also included surprising bronzes by two-time national champion Todd Eldredge in men's singles and by the May-September pair of Natasha Kuchiki, 14, and Todd Sand, 27.

"We'll be seeing this more and more because it's all freestyle now, and the U.S. is always strong in freestyle," Yamaguchi said.

She was referring to the absence of compulsory figures in singles skating, a change that went into effect for the 1990-91 season. Ironically, one of the reasons for that change had been to encourage skaters in smaller countries where ice time is limited, because practicing compulsories was so expensive and time consuming.

Yamaguchi, who has yet to win a United States title, became the world champion in the absence of defender Jill Trenary of the U.S. (sidelined by ankle problems) and after the literal downfall of 1989 champion Midori Ito of Japan. Ito crashed into the boards surrounding the rink during the short program and fell in the long program. She had also undergone surgery for a glandular infection in late January.

Meanwhile, Kurt Browning, the Canadian jumping machine, won a third straight men's title over a dismayed Viktor Petrenko

Tom Treick/The Oregonian

World champion **Kristi Yamaguchi** (center) with fellow medalists **Tonya Harding** (left) and **Nancy Kerrigan** after the three U.S. women swept the World Figure Skating Championships in March.

of the Soviet Union, in a clear call for the athlete over the artist. And the French revolutionaries of ice dancing, Isabelle and Paul Duchesnay, finally toppled the Soviets from power. The USSR's lone title came in pairs, where Natalia Mishkuteniok and Artur Dmitriev were technically brilliant, balletically exquisite and creatively breathtaking.

There was also some history made in February at the U.S. Nationals in Minneapolis. The unlikely protagonist was Harding, a 20-year-old ice princess from Portland, Ore., who is more Madonna than Cinderella.

Harding, who had finished only seventh in the 1990 Nationals, not only upset Yamaguchi for the title but became the first U.S. woman to land a triple axel jump in competition. The triple axel, in which the skater spins 3½ times in the air, had previously been executed successfully only by Japan's Ito.

Both Yamaguchi and Kerrigan are expected to add a triple axel to their programs as they prepare for the Winter Olympics in February.

"There's really no reason I can't land it," Yamaguchi told reporters. "It's just mental."

The United States has not captured the

Olympic gold medal in women's figure skating since Dorothy Hamill won it in 1976.

Eldredge left no doubt about his stature as the country's best male skater with a second straight title. In 1990, his victory seemed tainted because defending champion Christopher Bowman dropped out midway through the competition with a bad back. This time, the flamboyant Bowman was suffering only from a lack of self-confidence as he attempted to resurrect his flagging career. His skating, however, simply was not the equal of Eldredge's.

The Nationals were a dream come true for Calla Urbanski, then 30, of Skokie, Ill. After nine years of pairs competition with five partners, the resolute Urbanski—and partner Rocky Marval—finished second to qualify for the World Championships for the first time. Urbanski, who works as a bartender and waitress to pay skating expenses, had been the oldest woman competitor in Nationals the past four years and was the oldest of 161 skaters at the world meet.

That she and Marval finished ninth in Munich seemed inconsequential. "I liked my name up there on the scoreboard where it said, 'World Championships,'" she said.

INT'L SPORTS
S T A T I S T I C S

THE SEASON IN REVIEW
1990-1991
CHAMPIONS • RECORDS

THE 1992 SPORTS ALMANAC — INFORMATION PLEASE

SEC
A

PAGE
504

Track & Field
World Championships
at Tokyo (Aug.24-Sept.1)

MEN

Event		Time
100m	Carl Lewis, USA	9.86 **WR**
200m	Michael Johnson, USA	20.01
400m	Antonio Pettigrew, USA	44.57
800m	Billy Konchellah, KEN	1:43.99
1500m	Noureddine Morceli, ALG	3:32.84
5000m	Yobes Ondieki, KEN	13:14.45
10,000m	Moses Tanui, KEN	27:38.74
Marathon	Hiromi Taniguchi, JPN	2:14:57.00
110m H	Greg Foster, USA	13.06
400m H	Samuel Matete, ZAM	47.64
3000m stple	Moses Kiptanui, KEN	8:12.59
20-km walk	Maurizio Damilano, ITA	1:19:37.00
50-km walk	Aleksandr Potashov, USSR	3:53:09.00
4 × 100m relay	USA (Andre Cason, Leroy Burrell, Dennis Mitchell, Carl Lewis)	37.50 **WR**
4 × 400m relay	Great Britain	2:57.53

Event		Mark
High Jump	Charles Austin, USA	7- 9¾
Pole Vault	Sergei Bubka, USSR	19- 6¼
Long Jump	Mike Powell, USA	29- 4½ **WR**
Triple Jump	Kenny Harrison, USA	58- 4
Shot Put	Werner Gunthor, SWI	71-11¼
Discus	Lars Riedel, GER	217- 2
Hammer	Yuri Sedykh, USSR	260- 0
Javelin	Kimmo Kinnunen, FIN	297-11
Decathlon	Dan O'Brien, USA	8812 pts

WOMEN

Event		Time
100m	Katrin Krabbe, GER	10.99
200m	Katrin Krabbe, GER	22.09
400m	Marie-Josee Perec, FRA	49.13
800m	Lilia Nurutdinova, USSR	1:57.50
1500m	Hassiba Boulmerka, ALG	4:02.21
3000m	Tatiana Dorovskikh, USSR	8:35.82
10,000m	Liz McColgan, GBR	31:14.31
Marathon	Wanda Panfil, POL	2:29:53.00
100m H	Lyudmila Narozhilenko, USSR	12.59
400m H	Tatiana Ledovskaya, USSR	53.11
10-km walk	Alina Ivanova, USSR	42:57.00
4 × 100m relay	Jamaica	41.94
4 × 400m relay	USSR	3:18.43

Event		Mark
High Jump	Heike Henkel, GER	6- 8¾
Long Jump	Jackie Joyner-Kersee, USA	24- 0¼
Shot Put	Zhihong Huang, CHN	68- 4¼
Discus	Tsvetanka Khristova, BUL	233- 0
Javelin	Demei Xu, CHN	225- 8
Heptathlon	Sabine Braun, GER	6672 pts

World Indoor Championships
at Seville, Spain (Mar.8-10)

MEN

Event		Time
60m	Andre Cason, USA	6.54
200m	Nikolai Antonov, BUL	20.67
400m	Devon Moris, JAM	46.17
800m	Paul Ereng, KEN	1:47.08
1500m	Noureddine Morceli, ALG	3:41.57
3000m	Frank O'Mara, IRE	7:41.14
60m H	Greg Foster, USA	7.45
5-km walk	Mikhail Shchennikov, USSR	18:23.55 **WR**
4 × 400m relay	Germany	3:03.05 **WR**

Event		Mark
High Jump	Hollis Conway, USA	7-10½
Pole Vault	Sergei Bubka, USSR	19- 8¼
Long Jump	Dietmar Haaf, GER	26- 9
Triple Jump	Igor Lapshin, USSR	56- 9½
Shot Put	Werner Gunthor, SWI	69- 5½

WOMEN

Event		Time
60m	Irina Sergeyeva, USSR	7.02
200m	Merlene Ottey, JAM	22.24 **WR**
400m	Diane Dixon, USA	50.64
800m	Christine Wachtel, GER	2:01.51
1500m	Lyudmila Rogachova, USSR	4:05.09
3000m	Marie-Pierre Duros, FRA	8:50.69
60m H	Lyudmila Narozhilenko, USSR	7.88
3-km walk	Beate Anders, GER	11:50.90 **WR**
4 × 400m relay	Germany	3:27.22 **WR**

Event		Mark
High Jump	Heike Henkel, GER	6- 6¾
Long Jump	Larisa Berezhnaya, USSR	22- 5¼
Shot Put	Xinmei Sui, CHN	67- 4¾

WORLD OUTDOOR RECORDS

As of Oct. 1, 1991.
World outdoor records officially recognized by the International Amateur Athletics Federation (IAAF).

MEN

Running

Event	Time		Date Set	Location
100 meters	9.86	**Carl Lewis,** USA	Aug. 25, 1991	Tokyo
200 meters	19.72	**Pietro Mennea,** Italy	Sept. 17, 1979	Mexico City
400 meters	43.29	**Butch Reynolds,** USA	Aug. 16, 1988	Zurich, Switzerland
800 meters	1:41.73	**Sebastian Coe,** Britain	June 10, 1981	Florence, Italy
1000 meters	2:12.18	**Sebastian Coe,** Britain	July 11, 1981	Oslo, Norway
1500 meters	3:29.46	**Said Aouita,** Morocco	Aug. 23, 1985	West Berlin
Mile	3:46.32	**Steve Cram,** Britain	July 27, 1985	Oslo, Norway
2000 meters	4:50.81	**Said Aouita,** Morocco	July 16, 1987	Paris
3000 meters	7:29.45	**Said Aouita,** Morocco	Aug. 20, 1989	Cologne, W.Ger.
5000 meters	12:58.39	**Said Aouita,** Morocco	July 22, 1987	Rome
10,000 meters	27:08.23	**Arturo Barrios,** Mexico	Aug. 18, 1989	West Berlin
20,000 meters	56:55.60	**Arturo Barrios,** Mexico	Mar. 30, 1991	La Fleche, France
25,000 meters	1:13:55.80	**Toshihiko Seko,** Japan	Mar. 22, 1981	Christchurch, N.Zea.
30,000 meters	1:29:18.80	**Toshihiko Seko,** Japan	Mar. 22, 1981	Christchurch, N.Zea.
Marathon	2:06:50.00	**Belayneh Densimo,** Ethiopia	Apr. 17, 1988	Rotterdam, Holland

Note: The **Mile** run is 1,609.344 meters and the **Marathon** is 42,194.988 meters (26 miles, 385 yards).

Hurdles

Event	Time		Date Set	Location
110-meter High	12.92	**Roger Kingdom,** USA	Aug. 16, 1989	Zurich, Switzerland
400-meter Low	47.02	**Edwin Moses,** USA	Aug. 31, 1983	Koblenz, W. Ger.

Note: The hurdles at 110 meters are 3 feet 6 inches high and the hurdles at 400 meters are 3 feet. There are 10 hurdles in each race.

Steeplechase

Event	Time		Date Set	Location
3000m Steeplechase	8:05.35	**Peter Koech,** Kenya	July 3, 1989	Stockholm

Note: The steeplechase course consists of 28 hurdles (3 feet high) and seven water jumps (12 feet long).

Walking

Event	Time		Date Set	Location
20 kilometers	1:18:40.0	**Ernesto Canto,** Mexico	May 5, 1984	Bergen, Norway
30 kilometers	2:03:56.5	**Thierry Toutain,** Spain	Mar. 24, 1991	Hericourt, France
50 kilometers	3:41:38.4	**Raul Gonzalez,** Mexico	May 25, 1979	Bergen, Norway

Relays

Event	Time		Date Set	Location
4 × 100-meter	37.50	**USA** (Andre Cason, Leroy Burrell, Dennis Mitchell, Carl Lewis)	Sept. 1, 1991	Tokyo
4 × 200-meter	1:19.38	**USA** (Danny Everett, Leroy Burrell, Floyd Heard, Carl Lewis)	Aug. 23, 1989	Koblenz, W. Ger.
4 × 400-meter	2:56.16	**USA** (Vince Matthews, Ron Freeman, Larry James, Lee Evans)	Oct. 20, 1968	Mexico City
		USA (Danny Everett, Steve Lewis, Kevin Robinzine, Butch Reynolds)	Oct. 1, 1988	Seoul
4 × 800-meter	7:03.89	**Britain** (Peter Elliott, Garry Cook, Steve Cram, Sebastian Coe)	Aug. 30, 1982	London
4 × 1500-meter	14:38.8	**West Germany**	Aug. 14, 1977	Cologne, W. Ger.
4 × Mile	15:49.08	**Ireland**	Aug. 17, 1985	Dublin

Decathlon

Event	Points		Date Set	Location
Decathlon	8847	**Daley Thompson,** Britain	Aug. 8-9, 1984	Los Angeles

Note: the Decathlon consists of 10 events—**100m** (10.44) **LJ** (26-3½) **SP** (51-7), **HJ** (6-8), **400m** (46.97), **100m H** (14.33), **Discus** (152-9), **PV** (16-4¾), **Javelin** (214-0), **1500m** (4:35.00).

Field Events

Event	Mark		Date Set	Location
High Jump	8-0	**Javier Sotomayor,** Cuba	July 29, 1989	San Juan, P.R.
Pole Vault	20-0	**Sergei Bubka,** USSR	Aug. 5, 1991	Malmo, Sweden
Long Jump	29-4½	**Mike Powell,** USA	Aug. 30, 1991	Tokyo
Triple Jump	58-11½	**Willie Banks,** USA	June 16, 1985	Indianapolis
Shot Put	75-10¼	**Randy Barnes,** USA	May 20, 1990	Los Angeles
Discus	243-0	**Jurgen Schult,** E.Germany	June 6, 1986	Neubrandenburg, EG
Javelin	318-1	**Seppo Raty,** Finland	Jun. 2, 1991	Punkalaidun, Finland
Hammer	284-7	**Yuri Sedykh,** USSR	Aug. 30, 1986	Stuttgart, W. Ger.

Note: The international weights for men—**Shot** (16 lb), **Discus** (4 lb/6.55 oz), **Hammer** (16 lb), new **Javelin** (minimum 1 lb/12¼ oz).

Track & Field (Cont.)

World Outdoor Records Set in 1991

MEN

Event		Record	Old Mark	Former Holder
100 meters	Carl Lewis, USA	9.86	9.90	Leroy Burrell, USA (1991)
100 meters	Leroy Burrell, USA	9.90	9.92	Carl Lewis, USA (1988)
20,000 meters	Arturo Barrios, MEX	56:55.60	57:18.40	Dionisio Castro, POR (1990)
30-km walk	Thierry Toutain, SPA	2:03:56.50	2:07:59.80	Jose Marin, SPA (1979)
4 × 100 relay	USA (Andre Cason, Leroy Burrell, Dennis Mitchell, Carl Lewis)	37.50	37.67	Santa Monica Track Club (1991)
4 × 100m relay	Santa Monica Track Club (Mike Marsh, Burrell, Mitchell, Lewis)	37.67	37.79	FRA (Max Morniere, Daniel Sangouma, J.C. Trouabel, Bruno Marie-Rose), 1990
Pole Vault	Sergei Bubka, USSR	20- 0	19-11¾	Bubka, USSR (1991)
Pole Vault	Sergei Bubka, USSR	19-11¾	19-11¼	Bubka, USSR (1991)
Pole Vault	Sergei Bubka, USSR	19-11¼	19-11	Bubka, USSR (1991)
Pole Vault	Sergei Bubka, USSR	19-11	19-10½	Bubka, USSR (1988)
Long Jump	Mike Powell, USA	29- 4½	29- 2½	Bob Beamon, USA (1968)
Javelin	Seppo Raty, FIN	318- 1	301- 9	Seppo Raty, FIN (1991)
Javelin	Seppo Raty, FIN	301- 9	298- 6	Steve Backley, GBR (1990)

WOMEN

Event		Record	Old Mark	Former Holder
Triple Jump	Inessa Kravets, USSR	49- 0¾	47- 8½	Li Huirong, CHN (1990)

WOMEN

Running

Event	Time		Date Set	Location
100 meters	10.49	Florence Griffith Joyner, USA	July 16, 1988	Indianapolis
200 meters	21.34	Florence Griffith Joyner, USA	Sept. 29, 1988	Seoul
400 meters	47.60	Marita Koch, E.Germany	Oct. 6, 1985	Canberra, Australia
800 meters	1:53.28	Jarmila Kratochvilova, Czech.	July 26, 1983	Munich
1000 meters	2:30.60	Tatyana Providokhina, USSR	Aug. 20, 1978	Podolsk, USSR
1500 meters	3:52.47	Tatyana Providokhina, USSR	Aug. 13, 1980	Zurich
Mile	4:15.61	Paula Ivan, Romania	July 10, 1989	Nice, France
2000 meters	5:28.69	Maricica Puica, Romania	July 11, 1986	London
3000 meters	8:22.62	Tatyana Providokhina, USSR	Aug. 26, 1984	Leningrad, USSR
5000 meters	14:37.33	Ingrid Kristiansen, Norway	Aug. 5, 1986	Stockholm
10,000 meters	30:13.74	Ingrid Kristiansen, Norway	July 5, 1986	Oslo, Norway
Marathon	2:21:06	Ingrid Kristiansen, Norway	Apr. 21, 1985	London

Note: The **Mile** run is 1,609.344 meters; and the **Marathon** is 42,194.988 meters (26 miles, 385 yards).

Hurdles

Event	Time		Date Set	Location
100-meter High	12.21	Yordanka Donkova, Bulgaria	Aug. 21, 1988	Stara Zagora, Bulg.
400-meter Low	52.94	Marina Stepanova, USSR	Sept. 17, 1986	Tashkent, USSR

Note: The hurdles at 100 meters are 2 feet 9 inches high and the hurdles at 400 meters are 2 feet 6 inches. There are 10 hurdles in each race.

Walking

Event	Time		Date Set	Location
5 kilometers	20:07.52	Beate Anders, E.Germany	June 23, 1990	Rostock, E. Ger.
10 kilometers	41:46.21	Nadezhda Ryashkina, USSR	July 24, 1990	Seattle

Relays

Event	Time		Date Set	Location
4 × 100-meter	41.37	East Germany	Oct. 6, 1985	Canberra, Aus.
4 × 200-meter	1:28.15	East Germany	Aug. 9, 1980	Jena, E. Germany
4 × 400-meter	3:15.18	USSR	Oct. 1, 1988	Seoul
4 × 800-meter	7:50.17	USSR	Aug. 5, 1984	Moscow

Field Events

Event	Mark		Date Set	Location
High Jump	6-10¼	Stefka Kostadinova, Bulgaria	Aug. 30, 1987	Rome
Long Jump	24- 8¼	Galina Chistyakova, USSR	June 11, 1988	Leningrad, USSR
Triple Jump	49- 0¾	Inessa Kravets, USSR	June 10, 1991	Moscow
Shot Put	74- 3	Natalya Lisovskaya, USSR	June 7, 1987	Moscow
Discus	252- 0	Gabriele Reinsch, E.Germany	July 9, 1988	Neubrandenburg, EG
Javelin	262- 5	Petra Felke, E.Germany	Sept. 9, 1988	West Berlin

Note: The international weights for women—**Shot** (8 lb/13 oz), **Discus** (2 lb/3.27 oz), **Javelin** (minimum 1 lb/5.16 oz).

Heptathlon

Event	Points		Date Set	Location
Heptathlon	7291	**Jackie Joyner-Kersee**, USA	Sept. 23, 1988	Seoul

Note: Joyner-Kersee's record-setting times, distances and heights in the 7 heptathlon events, chronologically over 2 days—100m H (12.69), HJ (6-1¼), SP (51-10), 200m (22.56), LJ (23-10)¼), Javelin (149-10), 800m (2:08.51).

AMERICAN OUTDOOR RECORDS

American outdoor records officially recognized by The Athletics Congress (TAC) through Oct. 1, 1991. Note that (*) indicates a world record.

MEN

Running

Event	Time	Record Holder
100 m	9.86*	**Carl Lewis** (1991)
200 m	19.75	**Carl Lewis** (1983) & **Joe DeLoach** (1988)
400 m	43.29*	**Butch Reynolds** (1988)
800 m	1:42.60	**Johnny Gray** (1985)
1000 m	2:13.90	**Rick Wohlhuter** (1974)
1500 m	3:29.77	**Sydney Maree** (1985)
Mile	3:47.69	**Steve Scott** (1982)
2000 m	4:52.44	**Jim Spivey** (1987)
3000 m	7:35.84	**Doug Padilla** (1983)
5000 m	13:01.15	**Sydney Maree** (1985)
10,000 m	27:20.56	**Mark Nenow** (1986)
20,000 m	58:25.00	**Bill Rodgers** (1977)
25,000 m	1:14:11.80	**Bill Rodgers** (1979)
30,000 m	1:31:49	**Bill Rodgers** (1979)
Marathon	2:08:52	**Alberto Salazar** (1982)

Hurdles

Event	Time	Record Holder
110-m High	12.92*	**Roger Kingdom** (1989)
400-m Low	47.02*	**Edwin Moses** (1983)

Steeplechase

Event	Time	Record Holder
3000 m	8:09.17	**Henry Marsh** (1985)

Walking

Event	Time	Record Holder
20 km	1:24:50	**Tim Lewis** (1988)
30 km	2:23:14	**Goetz Klopfer** (1970)
50 km	3:56:55	**Marco Evoniuk** (1988)

Relays

Event	Time	Record Holder
4 × 100 m	37.50*	**National team** (1991)
4 × 200 m	1:19.38*	**Santa Monica Track Club** (1989)
4 × 400 m	2:56.16*	**Olympic Team** (1968) & **Olympic Team** (1988)
4 × 800 m	7:06.50	**Santa Monica Track Club** (1988)
4 × 1500 m	14:46.30	**National Team** (1979)

Decathlon

Event	Points	Record Holder
Decathlon	8812	**Dan O'Brien** (1991)

Field Events

Event	Mark	Record Holder
High Jump	7-10½	**Charles Austin** (1991)
Pole Vault	19- 6½	**Joe Dial** (1987)
Long Jump	29- 4½*	**Mike Powell** (1991)
Triple Jump	58-11½*	**Willie Banks** (1985)
Shot Put	75-10¼	**Randy Barnes** (1990)
Discus	237- 4	**Ben Plucknett** (1981)
Javelin	280- 1	**Tom Petranoff** (1986)
Hammer	268- 8	**Jud Logan** (1988)

Note: Tom Petranoff was suspended by TAC in early 1989 (for competing in a banned country), so even though he bettered his U.S. javelin record twice in 1990 (283-2 and 283-8), neither throw was recognized.

WOMEN

Running

Event	Time	Record Holder
100 m	10.49*	**F.Griffith Joyner** (1988)
200 m	21.34*	**F.Griffith Joyner** (1988)
400 m	48.83	**Valerie Brisco** (1984)
800 m	1:56.90	**Mary Slaney** (1985)
1000 m	2:34.65	**Mary Slaney** (1988)
1500 m	3:57.12	**Mary Slaney** (1983)
Mile	4:16.71	**Mary Slaney** (1985)
2000 m	5:32.70	**Mary Slaney** (1984)
3000 m	8:25.83	**Mary Slaney** (1985)
5000 m	14:59.99	**PattiSue Pulmer** (1989)
10,000 m	31:28.92	**Francie Larrieu-Smith** (1991)
Marathon	2:21:21	**Joan Benoit Samuelson** (1985)

Hurdles

Event	Time	Record Holder
100-m High	12.61	**Gail Devers** (1988) & **Jackie Joyner-Kersee** (1988)
400-m Low	53.37	**Sandra Farmer-Patrick** (1989)

Walking

Event	Time	Record Holder
5 km	22:38.0	**Teresa Vaill** (1989)
10 km	45:28.4	**Debbie Lawrence** (1991)

Relays

Event	Time	Record Holder
4 × 100 m	41.55	**National team** (1987)
4 × 200 m	1:32.57	**Louisiana St.** (1989)
4 × 400 m	3:15.51	**Olympic Team** (1988)
4 × 800 m	8:17.09	**Athletics West** (1983)

Heptathlon

Event	Points	Record Holder
Heptathlon	7291*	**J.Joyner-Kersee** (1988)

Field Events

Event	Mark	Record Holder
High Jump	6-8 (twice)	**Louise Ritter** (1988)
Long Jump	24- 5½	**J.Joyner-Kersee** (1987)
Triple Jump	46- 0¼	**Sheila Hudson** (1990)
Shot Put	66- 2½	**Ramona Pagel** (1988)
Discus	216-10	**Carol Cady** (1986)
Javelin	227- 5	**Kate Schmidt** (1977)

Track & Field (Cont.)

WORLD INDOOR RECORDS

As of Oct. 1, 1991.
World indoor records officially recognized by the International Amateur Athletics Federation (IAAF).

MEN
Running

Event	Time		Date Set	Location
50 meters	5.61	**Manfred Kokot,** E.Germany	Feb. 4, 1973	East Berlin
	5.61	**James Sanford,** USA	Feb. 20, 1981	San Diego
60 meters	6.48	**Leroy Burrell,** USA	Feb. 12, 1991	Madrid
200 meters	20.36	**Bruno Marie-Rose,** France	Feb. 22, 1987	Lievin, France
400 meters	45.04	**Danny Everett,** USA	Feb. 4, 1990	Stuttgart, W. Ger
800 meters	1:44.84	**Paul Ereng,** Kenya	Mar. 4, 1989	Budapest, Hungary
1000 meters	2:16.40	**Rob Druppers,** Holland	Feb. 20, 1988	The Hague, Holland
1500 meters	3:34.16	**Noureddine Morceli,** Algeria	Feb. 28, 1991	Seville, Spain
Mile	3:49.78	**Eammon Coghlan,** Ireland	Feb. 27, 1983	E. Rutherford, NJ
3000 meters	7:39.20	**Emiel Puttemans,** Belgium	Feb. 18, 1973	West Berlin
5000 meters	13:20.40	**Suleiman Nyambui,** Tanzania	Feb. 6, 1981	New York City

Note: The Mile run is 1,609.344 meters.

Hurdles

Event	Time		Date Set	Location
50 meters	6.25	**Mark McKoy,** Canada	Jan. 27, 1985	Rosemont, IL
60 meters	7.36	**Greg Foster,** USA	Jan. 31, 1987	Ottawa, Ontario
			Jan. 16, 1987	Los Angeles

Note: The hurdles for both distances are 3 feet 6 inches high. There are four hurdles in the 50 and five in the 60.

Walking

Event	Time		Date Set	Location
5000 meters	18:23.55	**Mikhail Shchennikov,** USSR	Mar. 10, 1991	Seville, Spain

Relays

Event	Time		Date Set	Location
4 × 200-meter	1:22.11	**Britain** (Linford Christie, Darren Braithwaite, Ade Mafe, John Regis)	Mar. 3, 1991	Glasgow
4 × 400-meter	3:03.05	**Germany** (Rico Lieder, Jens Carlowitz, Karsten Just, Thomas Schoenlebe)	Mar. 10, 1991	Seville, Spain

Field Events

Event	Mark		Date Set	Location
High Jump	7-11½	**Javier Sotomayor,** Cuba	Mar. 4, 1989	Budapest, Hungary
Pole Vault	20- 1	**Sergei Bubka,** USSR	Mar. 23, 1991	Grenoble
Long Jump	28-10¼	**Carl Lewis,** USA	Jan. 27, 1984	New York City
Triple Jump	58- 3¼	**Mike Conley,** USA	Feb. 27, 1987	New York City
Shot Put	74- 4¼	**Randy Barnes,** USA	Jan. 20, 1989	Los Angeles

Note: The international weights for men—Shot (16 lbs).

WOMEN
Running

Event	Time		Date Set	Location
50 meters	6.06	**Angella Issajenko,** Canada	Feb. 2, 1980	Grenoble, France
60 meters	7.00	**Nelli Cooman,** Holland	Feb. 23, 1986	Madrid, Spain
200 meters	22.24	**Merlene Ottey,** JAM	Mar. 10, 1991	Seville, Spain
400 meters	49.59	**Jarmila Kratochvilova,** Czech.	Mar. 7, 1982	Milan, Italy
800 meters	1:56.40	**Christine Wachtel,** E.Germany	Feb. 14, 1988	Vienna, Austria
1000 meters	2:34.80	**Brigitte Kraus,** W.Germany	Feb. 19, 1978	Dortmund, W. Ger.
1500 meters	4:00.27	**Doina Melinte,** Romania	Feb. 9, 1990	E. Rutherford, NJ
Mile	4:17.13	**Doina Melinte,** Romania	Feb. 9, 1990	E. Rutherford, NJ
3000 meters	8:33.82	**Elly van Hulst,** Holland	Feb. 8, 1986	Cosford, England
5000 meters	15:13.72	**Uta Pippig,** GER	Feb. 10, 1991	Stuttgart

Note: The Mile run is 1,609.344 meters.

Hurdles

Event	Time		Date Set	Location
50-meter	6.58	**Cornelia Oschkenat,** E.Germany	Feb. 20, 1988	East Berlin
60-meter	7.69	**Lyudmila Narozhilenko,** USSR	Feb. 4, 1990	Chelyabinsk, USSR

Note: The hurdles for both distances are 2 feet 9 inches high. There are four hurdles in the 50 and five in the 60.

Walking

Event	Time		Date Set	Location
3000 meters	11:50.90	**Beate Anders,** GER	Mar. 9, 1991	Seville, Spain

Relays

Event	Time		Date Set	Location
4 × 200-meters	1:32.55	**W.Germany**	Feb. 20, 1988	Dortmund, W.Ger.
4 × 400-meters	3:27.22	**Germany** (Sandra Seuser, Katrin Schreiter, Annett Hesselbarth, Grit Breuer)	Mar. 10, 1991	Seville, Spain

Field Events

Event	Mark		Date Set	Location
High Jump	6- 9	**Stefka Kostadinova,** Bulgaria	Feb. 20, 1988	Athens, Greece
Long Jump	24- 2¼	**Heike Drechsler,** E.Germany	Feb. 14, 1988	Vienna, Austria
Triple Jump	47- 4½	**Inessa Kravets,** USSR	Mar. 9, 1991	Seville, Spain
Shot Put	73-10	**Helena Fibingerova,** Czech.	Feb. 19, 1977	Jablonec, Czech.

Note: The international weights for women—Shot (8 lb/13 oz).

AMERICAN INDOOR RECORDS

American indoor records officially recognized by The Athletics Congress (TAC) through Oct. 1, 1991. Note that (*) indicates a world record.

MEN

Running

Event	Time	
50 meters	5.61*	**James Sanford** (1981)
60 meters	6.48	**Leroy Burrell** (1991)
200 meters	20.55	**Michael Johnson** (1991)
400 meters	45.04	**Danny Everett** (1990)
800 meters	1:45.64	**Johnny Gray** (1990)
1000 meters	2:18.19	**Ocky Clark** (1989)
1500 meters	3:36.00	**Steve Scott** (1981)
Mile	3:51.80	**Steve Scott** (1981)
3000 meters	7:39.94	**Steve Scott** (1989)
5000 meters	13:20.55	**Doug Padilla** (1982)

Note: The Mile run is 1,609.344 meters.

Hurdles

Event	Time	
50 meters	6.35*	**Greg Foster** (1985)
	6:35*	**Greg Foster** (1987)
60 meters	7.36*	**Greg Foster** (1987)

Note: The hurdles for both distances are 3 feet 6 inches high. There are four hurdles in the 50 and five in the 60.

Walking

Event	Time	
5000 meters	19:18.40	**Tim Lewis** (1987)

Relays

Event	Time	
4 × 200-meters	1:22.71	**National Team** (1991)
4 × 400-meters	3:03.24	**National Team** (1991)
4 × 800-meters	7:19.86	**Georgetown** (1991)

Field Events

Event	Mark	
High Jump	7-10½	**Hollis Conway** (1991)
Pole Vault	19- 5½	**Billy Olson** (1986)
Long Jump	28-10¼*	**Carl Lewis** (1984)
Triple Jump	58- 3¼*	**Mike Conley** (1987)
Shot Put	74- 4¼*	**Randy Barnes** (1989)
Weight Throw	78- 0¼	**Lance Deal** (1990)

Note: The international weights for men—**Shot** (16 lbs); **Weight Throw** (35 lbs).

WOMEN

Running

Event	Time	
50 meters	6.13	**Jeanette Bolden** (1981)
60 meters	7.07	**Gwen Torrence** (1989)
200 meters	22.87	**Dawn Sowell** (1989)
400 meters	50.64	**Diane Dixon** (1991)
800 meters	1:58.90	**Mary Slaney** (1980)
1000 meters	2:37.60	**Mary Slaney** (1989)
1500 meters	4:00.80	**Mary Slaney** (1980)
Mile	4:20.50	**Mary Slaney** (1982)
3000 meters	8:40.45	**Lynn Jennings** (1990)
5000 meters	15:22.64	**Lynn Jennings** (1990)

Note: The Mile run is 1,609.344 meters.

Hurdles

Event	Time	
50 meters	6.84	**Kim McKenzie** (1989)
60 meters	7.81	**J.Joyner-Kersee** (1989)

Note: The hurdles for all three distances are 2 feet 9 inches high. There are four hurdles in the 50 and five in the 60.

Walking

Event	Time	
3000 meters	12:45.38	**Maryanne Torrellas** (1988)

Relays

Event	Time	
4 × 200-meters	1:36.8	**Morgan St.**(1981)
4 × 400-meters	3:29.00	**National Team** (1991)
4 × 800-meters	8:25.50*	**Villanova**(1987)

Field Events

Event	Mark	
High Jump	6-6¾	**Coleen Sommer** (1982)
Long Jump	23-0½	**J.Joyner-Kersee** (1988)
Triple Jump	45-3	**Yvette Bates** (1987)
Shot Put	65-0¾	**Romona Pagel** (1987)

Note: The international weights for women—**Shot** (8 lb/13 oz).

Swimming
Long Course World Championships
at Perth, Australia (Jan.3-13)

MEN

Event		Time
50m free	Tom Jager, USA	22.16
100m free	Matt Biondi, USA	49.18
200m free	Giorgio Lamberti, ITA	1:47.27
400m free	Joerg Hoffmann, GER	3:48.04
800m free		
1500m free	Joerg Hoffmann, GER	14:50.36 WR
100m back	Jeff Rouse, USA	55.23
200m back	Martin Zubero, SPA	1:59.52
100m breast	Norbert Rozsa, HUN	1:01.45
200m breast	Mike Barrowman, USA	2:11.23 WR
100m fly	Anthony Nesty, SUR	53.29
200m fly	Melvin Stewart, USA	1:55.69 WR
200m IM	Tamas Darnyi, HUN	1:59.36 WR
400m IM	Tamas Darnyi, HUN	4:12.36 WR
25 kilometers	Chad Hundeby, USA	5:01:45.78
4 × 100m free	USA (Tom Jager, Brent Lang, Doug Gjertsen, Matt Biondi)	3:17.15
4 × 200m free	Germany	7:13.50
4 × 100m medley	USA (Jeff Rouse, Eric Wunderlich, Mark Henderson, Matt Biondi)	3:39.66

WOMEN

Event		Time
50m free	Zhuang Yong, CHN	25.47
100m free	Nicole Haislett, USA	55.17
200m free	Hayley Lewis, AUS	2:00.48
400m free	Janet Evans, USA	4:08.63
800m free	Janet Evans, USA	8:24.05
1500m free		
100m back	Krisztina Egerszegi, HUN	1:01.78
200m back	Krisztina Egerszegi, HUN	2:09.15
100m breast	Linley Frame, AUS	1:08.81
200m breast	Elena Volkova, USSR	2:29.53
100m fly	Qian Hong, CHN	59.68
200m fly	Summer Sanders, USA	2:09.24
200m IM	Lin Li, CHN	2:13.40
400m IM	Lin Li, CHN	4:41.45
25 kilometers	Shelley Taylor-Smith, AUS	5:21:05.53
4 × 100m free	USA (Nicole Haislett, Julie Cooper, Whitney Hedgepeth, Jenny Thompson)	3:43.36
4 × 200m free	Germany	8:02.56
4 × 100m medley	USA (Janie Wagstaff, Tracey McFarlane, Crissy Ahmann-Leighton, Nicole Haislett)	406.51

Diving

		Points
10m platform	Sun Shuwei, CHN	626.79
1m springboard	Edwin Jongejans, HOL	588.51
3m springboard	Kent Ferguson, USA	650.25

Water Polo

		Result
Final		Yugoslavia 8, Spain 7

Diving

		Points
10m platform	Fu Mingxia, CHN	426.51
1m springboard	Gao Min, CHN	
3m springboard	Gao Min, CHN	539.01

Synchronized

Duet	Karen & Sarah Josephson, USA	199.762

WORLD & AMERICAN RECORDS
Through Oct. 1, 1991

MEN
Freestyle

Distance	Record	Time		Date Set	Location
50 meters	World	21.18	Tom Jager, USA	Mar. 24, 1990	Nashville
	American	same			
100 meters	World	48.42	Matt Biondi, USA	Aug. 10, 1988	Austin, Texas
	American	same			
200 meters	World	1:46.69	Giorgio Lamberti, Italy	Aug. 15, 1989	Bonn, W. Ger.
	American	1:47.72p	Matt Biondi	Aug. 8, 1988	Austin, Texas
400 meters	World	3:46.95	Uwe Dassler, E.Germany	Sept. 23, 1988	Seoul
	American	3:48.06	Matt Cetlinski	Aug. 11, 1988	Austin, Texas
800 meters	World	7:47.85s	Kieren Perkins, Australia	Aug. 25, 1991	Edmonton
	American	7:52.45	Sean Killion	July 27, 1987	Clovis, Calif.
1500 meters	World	14:50.36	Joerg Hoffmann, Germany	Jan. 13, 1991	Perth
	American	15:01.51	George DiCarlo	June 30, 1984	Indianapolis

Backstroke

Distance	Record	Time		Date Set	Location
100 meters	World	53.93r	Jeff Rouse, USA	Aug. 25, 1991	Edmonton
	American	same			
200 meters	World	1:57.30p	Martin Zubero, Spain	Aug. 13, 1991	Ft. Lauderdale
	American	1:58.86	Rick Carey	June 27, 1984	Indianapolis

Breaststroke

Distance	Record	Time		Date Set	Location
100 meters	World	1:01.29p	Norbert Rosza, Hungary	Aug. 20, 1991	Athens
	American	1:01.65	Steve Lundquist	July 29, 1984	Los Angeles
200 meters	World	2:10.90	Mike Barrowman, USA	Aug. 13, 1991	Ft. Lauderdale
	American	same			

Butterfly

Distance	Record	Time		Date Set	Location
100 meters	World	52.84	**Pablo Morales,** USA	June 23, 1986	Orlando, Fla.
	American	same			
200 meters	World	1:55.69	**Melvin Stewart,** USA	Jan. 12, 1991	Perth
	American	same			

Individual Medley

Distance	Record	Time		Date Set	Location
200 meters	World	1:59.36	**Tamas Darnyi,** Hungary	Jan. 13, 1991	Perth
	American	2:00.11	**David Wharton**	Aug. 20, 1989	Tokyo
400 meters	World	4:12.36	**Tamas Darnyi,** Hungary	Jan. 8, 1991	Perth
	American	4:15.21	**Eric Namesnik**	Jan. 8, 1991	Perth

Relays

Distance	Record	Time		Date Set	Location
400-m free	World	3:16.53	**USA** (Chris Jacobs, Troy Dalbey, Tom Jager, Matt Biondi)	Sept. 23, 1988	Seoul
	American	same			
800-m free	World	7:12.511	**USA** (Troy Dalbey, Matt Cetlinski, Doug Gjartsen, Matt Biondi)	Sept. 21, 1988	Seoul
	American	same			
400-m medley	World	3:36.93	**USA** (David Berkoff, Rich Schroeder, Matt Biondi, Chris Jacobs)	Sept. 25, 1988	Seoul
	American	same			

Note: (r) indicates relay lead-off split; (p) preliminary heat swim; and (s) split time.

World Records Set in 1991

Men

Event	Record	Old Mark	Former Holder
800m free .... Kieren Perkins, AUS	7:47.85	7:50.64	Vladimir Salnikov, USSR (1983)
1500m free .... Joerg Hoffmann, GER	14:50.36	14:54.76	Vladimir Salnikov, USSR (1983)
100m back .... Jeff Rouse, USA	53.93	54.51	David Berkoff, USA (1988)
200m back .... Martin Zubero, SPA	1:57.30	1:58.14	Igor Poliansky, USSR (1985)
100m breast .... Norbert Rosza, HUN	1:01.45	1:01.49	Adrian Moorhouse, GBR (1990)
100m breast .... Norbert Rosza, HUN	1:01.29	1:01.45	Norbert Rosza, HUN (1991)
200m breast .... Mike Barrowman, USA	2:11.23	2:11.53	Mike Barrowman, USA (1990)
200m breast .... Mike Barrowman, USA	2:10.90	2:11.23	Mike Barrowman, USA (1991)
200m fly .... Melvin Stewart, USA	1:55.69	1:56.24	Michael Gross, W.Ger. (1986)
200m IM .... Tamas Darnyi, HUN	1:59.36	2:00.11	Dave Wharton, USA (1989)
400m IM .... Tamas Darnyi, HUN	4:12.36	4:14.75	Tamas Darnyi, HUN (1988)

Women

Event	Record	Old Mark	Former Holder
100m back .... Kristina Egerszegi, HUN	1:00.31	1:00.59	Ina Kleber, E.Ger. (1984)
200m back .... Kristina Egerszegi, HUN	2:06.62	2:08.60	Betsy Mitchell, USA (1986)

WOMEN

Freestyle

Distance	Record	Time		Date Set	Location
50 meters	World	24.98	**Yang Wenyi,** China	Mar. 24, 1990	Nashville
	American	25.50	**Leigh Ann Fetter**	Aug. 13, 1988	Austin, Texas
		25.50	**Leigh Ann Fetter**	Jan. 23, 1991	Perth
100 meters	World	54.73r	**Kristin Otto,** E.Germany	Aug. 19, 1986	Madrid, Spain
	American	55.14p	**Angel Martino**	Aug. 23, 1991	Edmonton
200 meters	World	1:57.55	**Heike Friedrich,** E.Germany	June 18, 1986	Berlin
	American	1:58.23	**Cynthia Woodhead**	Sept. 3, 1979	Tokyo
400 meters	World	4:03.85	**Janet Evans,** USA	Sept. 22, 1988	Seoul
	American	same			
800 meters	World	8:16.22	**Janet Evans,** USA	Aug. 20, 1989	Tokyo
	American	same			
1500 meters	World	15:52.10	**Janet Evans,** USA	Mar. 26, 1988	Orlando, Fla.
	American	same			

*Set on first leg of relay race.

Backstroke

Distance	Record	Time		Date Set	Location
100 meters	World	1:00.31p	**Kristina Egerszegi,** Hungary	Aug. 20, 1991	Athens
	American	1:01.00	**Janie Wagstaff**	Aug. 22, 1991	Edmonton
200 meters	World	2:06.62	**Kristina Egerszegi,** Hungary	Aug. 26, 1991	Athens
	American	2:08.60	**Betsy Mitchell,** USA	June 27, 1986	Orlando

*Set on first leg of relay race.

Breaststroke

Distance	Record	Time		Date Set	Location
100 meters	World	1:07.91	**Silke Hoerner,** E.Germany	Aug. 21, 1987	Strasbourg, FRA
	American	1:08.91	**Tracey McFarlane**	Aug. 11, 1988	Austin, Texas
200 meters	World	2:26.71	**Silke Hoerner,** E.Germany	Sept. 21, 1988	Seoul
	American	2:07.08	**Anita Nall**	Apr. 4, 1991	Federal Way, Wash.

Swimming (Cont.)
WOMEN
Butterfly

Distance	Record	Time		Date Set	Location
100 meters	World	57.93	**Mary T.Meagher,** USA	Aug. 16, 1981	Brown Deer, WI
	American	same			
200 meters	World	2:05.96	**Mary T.Meagher,** USA	Aug. 13, 1981	Brown Deer, WI
	American	same			

Individual Medley

Distance	Record	Time		Date Set	Location
200 meters	World	2:11.73	**Uta Geweniger,** E.Germany	July 4, 1981	Berlin
	American	2:12.64	**Tracy Caulkins**	Aug. 3, 1984	Los Angeles
400 meters	World	4:36.10	**Petra Schneider,** E.Germany	Aug. 1, 1982	Guayaquil, EQU
	American	4:37.76	**Janet Evans**	Sept. 19, 1988	Seoul

Relays

Distance	Record	Time		Date Set	Location
4 × 100m free	World	3:40.57	**E. Ger.** (Kristin Otto, Manuella Stellmach, Sabine Schulze, Heike Friedrich)	Aug. 19, 1986	Madrid, Spain
	American	3:43.26	**USA** (Nicole Haislett, Julie Cooper, Whitney Hedgepeth, Jenny Thompson)	Jan. 9, 1991	Perth
4 × 200m free	World	7:55.47	**E.Ger.** (Manuella Stellmach, Astrid Strauss, Anke Mohring, Heike Friedrich)	Aug. 18, 1987	Strasbourg, FRA
	American	8:02.12	**USA** (Betsy Mitchell, Mary T. Meagher, Kim Brown, Mary Wayte)	Aug. 17, 1986	Madrid, Spain
4 × 100m medley	World	4:03.69	**E.Ger.** (Ina Kleber, Sylvia Gerasch, Ines Geissler, Birgit Meineke)	Aug. 24, 1984	Moscow
	American	4:05.98	**USA** (Janie Wagstaff, Keli King, Crissy Ahmann-Leighton, Nicole Haislett)	Aug. 25, 1991	Edmonton

Note: (r) indicates relay lead-off split; (p) preliminary heat swim; and (s) split time.

Other 1991 Champions
WINTER SPORTS

Alpine Skiing

World Cup Champions
MEN

Overall .... Marc Girardelli, LUX
Downhill .... Franz Heinzer, SWI
Slalom .... Marc Girardelli, LUX
Giant Slalom .... Alberto Tomba, ITA
Super Giant Slalom .... Franz Heinzer, SWI
Nation's Cup .... Austria

WOMEN

Overall .... Petra Kronberger, AUT
Downhill .... Chantal Bournissen, SWI
Slalom......................... Petra Kronberger, AUT
Giant Slalom....................... Vreni Schneider, SWI
Super Giant Slalom.................. Carole Merle, FRA
Nation's Cup .... Austria

World Championships
at Saalbach, Austria
MEN

Combined .... Stefen Eberharter, AUT
Downhill .... Franz Heinzer, SWI
Slalom .... Marc Girardelli, LUX
Giant Slalom .... Rudolf Nierlich, AUT
Super Giant Slalom................ Stefan Eberharter, AUT

WOMEN

Combined..................... Chantal Bournissen, SWI
Downhill .... Petra Kronberger, AUT
Slalom .... Vreni Schneider, SWI
Giant Slalom........................ Pernilla Wiberg, SWE
Super Giant Slalom................... Ulrike Maier, AUT

U.S.Championships
(Open to foreign competitors)

MEN

Combined............... Joe Levins, White Bear Lake, MN
Downhill............................A.J.Kitt, Rochester, NY
Slalom .... Joe Levins
Giant Slalom......................... Alain Feutrier, FRA
Super Giant Slalom .... A.J.Kitt

WOMEN

Combined............... Wendy Fisher, Incline Village, NV
Downhill .... Megan Gerety, Sun Valley, ID
Slalom................. Eva Twardokens, Santa Cruz, CA
Giant Slalom.......................... Eva Twardokens
Super Giant Slalom .... Julie Parisien, Auburn, ME

Biathlon

World Championships
at Lahti, Finland

MEN
10 kilometers .... Mark Kirchner, GER
20 kilometers .... Mark Kirchner, GER
20-km Relay .... Italy
4 × 7.5-km Relay .... Germany

WOMEN
7.5 kilometers .... Grete Ingeborg, NOR
15 kilometers .... Petra Schaaf, GER
15-km Relay .... Soviet Union
3x7.5-km Relay........................... Soviet Union

U.S. Championships

MEN
10 kilometers................... Curt Schreiner, Day, NY
20 kilometers.......................... Curt Schreiner

WOMEN
7.5 kilometers .... Patrice Anderson, Eden, UT
15 kilometers .... Anna Sonnerup, Hanover, NH

Bobsled

World Championships
at Altenburgh, Germany

TWO-MAN
Germany II............ Rudi Lochner, Markus Zimmermann

FOUR-MAN
Germany II... Wolfgang Hoppe, Bogdan Musio, Axel Kuehn, Christoph Langen

U.S. Olympic Trials
Two-Man .... Brian Shimer & Edwin Moses

Four-Man............... Chuck Leonowicz, Todd Snavely, Bryan Leturgez & Jeff Woodard

Figure Skating

World Championships
at Munich, Germany
Men's .... Kurt Browning, CAN
Women's......................... Kristi Yamaguchi, USA
Pairs .... Natalia Mishkuteniok & Artur Dmitriev, USSR
Ice Dancing .... Isabelle & Paul Duchesnay, FRA

U.S. Championships
Men's................ Todd Eldredge, South Chatham, MA
Women's.................... Tonya Harding, Portland, OR
Pairs....................... Natasha Kuchiki, Los Angeles
& Todd Sand, Costa Mesa, CA
Ice Dance .... Elizabeth Punsalan, Sheffield Lake, OH
& Jerod Swallow, Northville, MI

Luge

World Championships
Winterberg, Germany

MEN
Singles .... Arnold Huber, ITA
Doubles .... Stefan Krauss, Jan Behrendt, GER

WOMEN
Singles .... Susi Erdman, GER

U.S. Champions

MEN
Singles................. Duncan Kennedy, Lake Placid, NY
Doubles.................... Chris Thorpe, Marquette, MI
& Gordy Sheer, Croton, NY

WOMEN
Singles .... Cammy Myler, Lake Placid, NY

Nordic Skiing

World Championships
Val di Fiemme, Italy

Cross-country

MEN
10-km classic......................... Terje Langli, NOR
15-km freestyle.................... Bjorn Daehlie, NOR
30-km classic........................ Gunde Svan, SWE
50-km freestyle.................... Torgny Mogren, SWE
4 × 10-km relay .... Norway

WOMEN
5-km classic.................... Trude Dybendahl, NOR
10-km freestyle .... Elena Vialbe, USSR
15-km classic..................... Elena Vialbe, USSR
30-km freestyle .... Lyubov Egorova, USSR
4 × 5-km relay............................. Soviet Union

Ski Jumping
Normal hill (70 meters) .... Heinz Kuttin, AUT
Large hill (90 meters) .... Franci Petek, YUG
Team large hill .... Austria

Nordic Combined
Individual .... Fred-Boerre Lundberg, NOR
Team... Austria

U.S. Championships

Cross-country

MEN
10-km classic .... John Farra, Saratoga, NY
15-km freestyle .... John Bauer, Champlin, MN
30-km classic .... Todd Boonstra, Norwich, VT
30-km freestyle............... John Aalberg, Salt Lake City

WOMEN
5-km classic .... Nancy Fiddler, Crowley Lake, CA
10-km freestyle .... Leslie Thompson, Stowe, VT
15-km classic .... Nancy Fiddler
30-km freestyle .... Nancy Fiddler

Ski Jumping
70-meter hill .... Jim Holland, Norwich, VT
90 meter hill .... Ryan Heckman, Winter Park, CO

Nordic Combined
Individual..................... John Holland, Norwich, VT

Speed Skating

World All-Around Championships

MEN
at Heerenveen, Holland

500 meters .... Peter Adeberg, GER
1,500 meters .... Johann Olav Koss, NOR
5,000 meters .... Johann Olav Koss, NOR
10,000 meters .... Johann Olav Koss, NOR
Overall......................... Johann Olav Koss, NOR

WOMEN
at Hamar, Norway

500 meters .... Qiaobo Ye, CHN
1,500 meters .... Gunda Kleeman, GER
3,000 meters .... Gunda Kleeman, GER
5,000 meters .... Gunda Kleeman, GER
Overall .... Gunda Kleeman, GER

World Sprint Championships
at Inzell Germany

MEN
Combined .... Igor Zhelezovski, USSR

WOMEN
Combined .... Monique Garbrecht, GER

Other 1991 Champions (Cont.)
SUMMER SPORTS

Championships held in 1991 unless otherwise indicated.

Basketball
Worldwide Champions

CBA .... Wichita Falls Texans
WBL .... Dayton Wings
European .... POP 84 Split
French League .... Antibes
Italian League .... Phonola Caserta
Spanish (ACB) League .... Joventut
1990 McDonald's Open .... NY Knicks (NBA)

Pan American Games

Men .... Puerto Rico
Women .... Brazil

Boxing
World Championships
(Nov. 13-25 in Sydney, Australia)
U.S. Championships

Weight
106 lbs .... Eric Griffin, Houston
112 .... Timmy Austin, Cincinnati
119 .... Sergio Reyes, U.S.Marines
125 .... Ivan Robinson, Philadelphia
132 .... Oscar De la Hoya, Los Angeles
139 .... Vernon Forrest, Marquette, MI
147 .... Pepe Reilly, Glendale, CA
156 .... Raul Marquez, Houston
165 .... Chris Byrd, Flint, MI
178 .... Terry McGroom, Chicago
Heavyweight .... John Bray, Van Nuys, CA
Super Heavyweight .... Larry Donald, Cincinnati

Cycling
Tour de France
79th Tour de France (July 6–28); 22 stages covering 2,445 miles from Lyon to Paris; 158 out of 198 riders finished race.
Winning time: 101 hours, 1 minute, 20 seconds.

		Behind
1	Miguel Indurain, Spain	–
2	Gianni Bugno, Italy	3:36
3	Claudio Chiappucci, Italy	5:56
4	Charly Mottet, France	7:37
5	Luc Leblanc, France	10:10
6	Laurent Fignon, France	11:27
7	Greg LeMond, USA	13:13
8	Andy Hampsten, USA	13:40
9	Pedro Delgado, Spain	20:10
10	Gerard Rue, France	20:13

Worldwide Champions
MEN

Tour de France .... Miguel Indurain, SPA
Giro d'Italia (Italy) .... Franco Chioccioli, ITA
Vuelta de Espana (Spain) .... Melchor Mauri, SPA
Tour du Pont (USA) .... Erik Breukink, HOL
World Pro Road Race .... Gianni Bugno, ITA
World Amateur Road Race .... Victor Riaksinski, USSR

WOMEN

Ore-ida Challenge (USA) .... Jeannie Longo, FRA
World Road Race .... Leontien Van Moorsel, HOL

Cross-country
1991 World Championships

Men .... Khalid Skah, MOR
Women .... Lynn Jennings, USA

1991 U.S. Champions

Men .... Bob Kempainen, Minnetonka, MN
Women .... Lynn Jennings, Newmarket, NH

Gymnastics
World Championships
(Indianapolis)

Men's All-Around .... Grigori Misutin, USSR
Team .... Soviet Union
Women's All-Around .... Kim Zmeskal, USA
Team .... Soviet Union

U.S. Championships

Men's All-Around .... Chris Waller, Los Angeles
Women's All-Around .... Kim Zmeskal, Houston

Marathons
World Championships
(Tokyo)

Men .... Hiromi Taniguchi, JPN
Women .... Wanda Panfil, POL

Other Winners

Boston: Men .... Ibrahim Hussein, KEN
        Women .... Wanda Panfil, POL
London/World Cup: Men .... Yakov Tolstikov, USSR
              Women .... Rosa Mota, POR
Osaka (Women only) .... Katrin Dorre, GER
Rotterdam: Men .... Rob de Castella, AUS
           Women .... Joke Kleiweg, HOL

Late 1990 Winners

Chicago: Men .... Martin Pitayo, MEX
         Women .... Aurora Cunha, POR
Fukuoka (Men only) .... Belayneh Densimo, ETH
New York City: Men .... Douglas Wakiihuri, KEN
               Women .... Wanda Panfil, POL

Rowing
World Championships
(Vienna)
MEN

Single sculls .... Thomas Lange, GER
Lightweight Eights .... Italy
Eights .... Germany

WOMEN

Single sculls .... Silken Laumann, CAN
Eights .... Canada

U.S. Nationals
MEN

Single sculls .... John Riley, Phila.
Lightweight Eights .... Harvard
Eights .... Pre-Elite Camp

WOMEN

Single sculls .... Angie Herron, Phila.
Eights .... Boston Rowing Center

THE 1992 INFORMATION PLEASE **SPORTS ALMANAC**

INT'L SPORTS
STATISTICS

THROUGH THE YEARS
1896-1991
WINNERS • RECORDS

SEC **B**

PAGE **515**

Track & Field
World Championships

While the Summer Olympic Games have usually served as the world outdoor championships for track and field throughout the century, a separate World Championship Meet for track and field was started in 1983 by the International Amateur Athletic Federation (IAAF). Quadrennial meets have been held in Helsinki in 1983 and Rome in 1987, and Tokyo in 1991 (see page 504).

MEN

Helsinki, 1983

Running

Event		Time
100m	Carl Lewis, USA	10.07
200m	Calvin Smith, USA	20.14
400m	Bert Cameron, Jamaica	45.05
800m	Willi Wulbeck, W.Germany	1:43.65
1500m	Steve Cram, Britain	3:41.59
5000m	Eamonn Coghlan, Ireland	13:28.53
10,000m	Alberto Cova, Italy	28:01.04
Marathon	Rob de Castella, Australia	2:10:03.00

Hurdles

Event		Time
110m	Greg Foster, USA	13.42
400m	Edwin Moses, USA	47.50

Steeplechase

Event		Time
3000m	Patriz Ilg, W.Germany	8:15.06

Walking

Event		Time
20 km	Ernesto Canto, Mexico	1:20:49
50 km	Ronald Weigel, E.Germany	3:43:08

Relays

Event		Time
4 × 100m	United States	37.86
4 × 400m	United States	3:00.79

Field Events

Event		Mark
High Jump	Gennadiy Avdeyenko, USSR	7-7¼
Pole Vault	Sergei Bubka, USSR	18-8¼
Long Jump	Carl Lewis, USA	28-0¾
Triple Jump	Zdzislaw Hoffmann, Poland	57-2
Shot Put	Edward Sarul, Poland	70-2¼
Discus	Imrich Bugar, Czech.	222-2
Hammer	Sergey Litvinov, USSR	271-3
Javelin	Detlef Michel, E. Germany	293-7

Decathlon

		Points
	Daley Thompson, Britain	8714

Rome, 1987

Running

Event		Time
100m	Ben Johnson, Canada	9.83
200m	Calvin Smith, USA	20.16
400m	Thomas Schonlebe, E.Germany	44.33
800m	Billy Konchellah, Kenya	1:43.06
1500m	Abdi Bile, Somalia	3:36.80
5000m	Said Aouita, Morocco	13:26.44
10,000m	Paul Kipkoech, Kenya	27:38.63
Marathon	Douglas Wakiihuri, Kenya	2:11:48.00

Hurdles

Event		Time
110m	Greg Foster, USA	13.21
400m	Edwin Moses, USA	47.46

Steeplechase

Event		Time
3,000m	Francesco Panetta, Italy	8:08.57

Walking

Event		Time
20 km	Maurizio Damilano, Italy	1:20:45
50 km	Hartwig Gauder, E.Germany	3:40:53

Relays

Event		Time
4 × 100m	United States	37.90
4 × 400m	United States	2:57.29

Field Events

Event		Mark
High Jump	Patrik Sjoberg, Sweden	7- 9¾
Pole Vault	Sergei Bubka, USSR	19- 2¼
Long Jump	Carl Lewis, USA	28- 5¼
Triple Jump	Khristo Markov, Bulgaria	58- 9½
Shot Put	Werner Gunthor, Switzerland	72-11¼
Discus	Juergen Schult, E.Germany	225- 6
Hammer	Sergei Litvinov, USSR	272- 6
Javelin	Seppo Raty, Finland	274- 1

Decathlon

		Points
	Torsten Voss, E.Germany	8680

Track & Field (Cont.)
WOMEN

Helsinki, 1983
Running

Event		Time
100m	Marlies Gohr, E.Germany	10.97
200m	Marita Koch, E.Germany	22.13
400m	Jarmila Kratochvilova, Czech.	47.99
800m	Jarmila Kratochvilova, Czech.	1:54.68
1500m	Mary Decker, USA	4:00.90
3000m	Mary Decker, USA	8:34.62
10,000m	Not held	
Marathon	Grete Waitz, Norway	2:28:09

Hurdles

Event		Time
100m	Bettina Jahn, E.Germany	12.35
400m	Yekaterina Fesenko, USSR	54.14

Relays

Event		Time
4 × 100m	East Germany	41.76
4 × 400m	East Germany	3:19.73

Field Events

Event		Mark
High Jump	Tamara Bykova, USSR	6- 7
Long Jump	Heike Daute, E.Germany	23-10¼
Shot Put	Helena Fibingerova, Czech.	69- 0¾
Discus	Martina Opitz, E.Germany	226- 2
Javelin	Tiina Lillak, Finland	232- 4

Heptathlon

	Points
Ramona Neubert, E.Germany	6770

Rome, 1987
Running

Event		Time
100m	Silke Gladisch, E.Germany	10.90
200m	Silke Gladisch, E.Germany	21.74
400m	Olga Bryzgina, USSR	49.38
800m	Sigrun Wodars, E.Germany	1:55.26
1500m	Tatyana Samolenko, USSR	3:58.56
3000m	Tatyana Samolenko, USSR	8:38.73
10,000m	Ingrid Kristiansen, Norway	31:05.85
Marathon	Rosa Mota, Portugal	2:25.17

Hurdles

Event		Time
100m	Ginka Zagorcheva, Bulgaria	12.34
400m	Sabine Busch, E.Germany	53.62

Relays

Event		Time
4 × 100m	United States	41.58
4 × 400m	East Germany	3:18.63

Field Events

Event		Mark
High Jump	Stefka Kostadinova, Bulgaria	6-10¼
Long Jump	Jackie Joyner-Kersee, USA	24- 1¾
Shot Put	Natalya Lisovskaya, USSR	69- 8¼
Discus	Martina O.Hellman, E.Germany	235- 0
Javelin	Fatima Whitbread, Britain	251- 5

Heptathlon

	Points
Jackie Joyner-Kersee, USA	7128

Boston Marathon

America's oldest regularly contested foot race, the Boston Marathon is held on Patriots' Day every April. It has been run at four different distances: 24 miles, 1232 yards (1897-1923); 26 miles, 209 yards (1924-26); 26 miles, 385 yards (1927-52); 25 miles, 958 yards (1953-56); and 26 miles, 385 yards (since 1957).

Multiple winners: MEN: Clarence DeMar (7); Gerard Cote and Bill Rodgers (4); Tarzan Brown, Jim Caffery, John A. Kelley, John Miles, Eino Oksanen, Leslie Pawson, Geoff Smith and Aurele Vandendriessche (2). WOMEN: Rosa Mota (3); Joan Benoit, Miki Gorman and Ingrid Kristiansen (2).

MEN

Year		Time	Year		Time
1897	John McDermott, New York	2:55:10	1920	Peter Trivoulidas, New York	2:29:31
1898	Ronald McDonald, Massachusetts	2:42:00	1921	Frank Zuna, New Jersey	2:18:57
1899	Lawrence Brignolia, Massachusetts	2:54:38	1922	Clarence DeMar, Massachusetts	2:18:10
			1923	Clarence DeMar, Massachusetts	2:23:37
1900	Jim Caffrey, Canada	2:39:44	1924	Clarence DeMar, Massachusetts	2:29:40
1901	Jim Caffrey, Canada	2:29:23	1925	Charles Mellor, Illinois	2:33:00
1902	Sam Mellor, New York	2:43:12	1926	John Miles, Nova Scotia	2:25:40
1903	J.C. Lorden, Massachusetts	2:41:29	1927	Clarence DeMar, Massachusetts	2:40:22
1904	Mike Spring, New York	2:38:04	1928	Clarence DeMar, Massachusetts	2:37:07
1905	Fred Lorz, New York	2:38:25	1929	John Miles, Nova Scotia	2:33:08
1906	Tim Ford, Massachusetts	2:45:45			
1907	Tom Longboat, Canada	2:24:24	1930	Clarence DeMar, Massachusetts	2:34:48
1908	Tom Morrissey, New York	2:25:43	1931	James Henigan, Massachusetts	2:46:45
1909	Henri Renaud, New Hampshire	2:53:36	1932	Paul deBruyn, Germany	2:33:36
			1933	Leslie Pawson, Rhode Island	2:31:01
1910	Fred Cameron, Nova Scotia	2:28:52	1934	Dave Komonen, Canada	2:32:53
1911	Clarence DeMar, Massachusetts	2:21:39	1935	John A. Kelley, Massachusetts	2:32:07
1912	Mike Ryan, Illinois	2:21:18	1936	Ellison Brown, Rhode Island	2:33:40
1913	Fritz Carlson, Minnesota	2:25:14	1937	Walter Young, Canada	2:33:20
1914	James Duffy, Canada	2:25:01	1938	Leslie Pawson, Rhode Island	2:35:34
1915	Edouard Fabre, Canada	2:31:41	1939	Ellison (Tarzan) Brown, Rhode Is	2:28:51
1916	Arthur Roth, Massachusetts	2:27:16			
1917	Bill Kennedy, New York	2:28:37	1940	Gerard Cote, Canada	2:28:28
1918	World War relay race		1941	Leslie Pawson, Rhode Island	2:30:38
1919	Carl Linder, Massachusetts	2:29:13	1942	Joe Smith, Massachusetts	2:26:51

Year		Time	Year		Time
1943	Gerard Cote, Canada	2:28:25	1968	Amby Burfoot, Connecticut	2:22:17
1944	Gerard Cote, Canada	2:31:50	1969	Yoshiaki Unetani, Japan	2:13:49
1945	John A.Kelley, Massachusetts	2:30:40			
1946	Stylianos Kyriakides, Greece	2:29:27	1970	Ron Hill, England	2:10:30
1947	Yun Bok Suh, Korea	2:25:39	1971	Alvaro Mejia, Colombia	2:18:45
1948	Gerard Cote, Canada	2:31:02	1972	Olavi Suomalainen, Finland	2:15:39
1949	Karle Leandersson, Sweden	2:31:50	1973	Jon Anderson, Oregon	2:16:03
			1974	Neil Cusack, Ireland	2:13:39
1950	Kee Yonh Ham, Korea	2:32:39	1975	Bill Rodgers, Massacusetts	2:09:55
1951	Shigeki Tanaka, Japan	2:27:45	1976	Jack Fultz, Pennsylvania	2:20:19
1952	Doroteo Flores, Guatemala	2:31:53	1977	Jerome Drayton, Canada	2:14:46
1953	Keizo Yamada, Japan	2:18:51	1978	Bill Rodgers, Massachusetts	2:10:13
1954	Veiko Karvonen, Finland	2:20:39	1979	Bill Rodgers, Massachusetts	2:09:27
1955	Hideo Hamamura, Japan	2:18:22			
1956	Antti Viskari, Finland	2:14:14	1980	Bill Rodgers, Massachusetts	2:12:11
1957	John J.Kelley, Connecticut	2:20:05	1981	Toshihiko Seko, Japan	2:09:26
1958	Franjo Mihalic, Yugoslavia	2:25:54	1982	Alberto Salazar, Massachusetts	2:08:52
1959	Eino Oksanen, Finland	2:22:42	1983	Greg Meyer, New Jersey	2:09:00
			1984	Geoff Smith, England	2:10:34
1960	Paavo Kotila, Finland	2:20:54	1985	Geoff Smith, England	2:14:05
1961	Eino Oksanen, Finland	2:23:39	1986	Rob de Castella, Australia	2:07:51*
1962	Eino Oksanen, Finland	2:23:48	1987	Toshihiko Seko, Japan	2:11:50
1963	Aurele Vandendriessche, Belgium	2:18:58	1988	Ibrahim Hussein, Kenya	2:08:43
1964	Aurele Vandendriessche, Belgium	2:19:59	1989	Abebe Mekonnen, Ethiopia	2:09:06
1965	Morio Shigematsu, Japan	2:16:33			
1966	Kenji Kimihara, Japan	2:17:11	1990	Gelindo Bordin, Italy	2:08:19
1967	David McKenzie, New Zealand	2:15:45	1991	Ibraham Hussein, Kenya	2:11:06

*Record for distance.

WOMEN

Year		Time	Year		Time
1972	Nina Kuscsik, New York	3:08:58	1982	Charlotte Teske, West Germany	2:29:33
1973	Jacqueline Hansen, California	3:05:59	1983	Joan Benoit, Maine	2:22:43*
1974	Miki Gorman, California	2:47:11	1984	Lorraine Moller, New Zealand	2:29:28
1975	Liane Winter, West Germany	2:42:24	1985	Lisa Larsen Weidenbach, Mass	2:34:06
1976	Kim Merritt, Wisconsin	2:47:10	1986	Ingrid Kristiansen, Norway	2:24:55
1977	Miki Gorman, California	2:48:33	1987	Rosa Mota, Portugal	2:25:21
1978	Gayle Barron, Georgia	2:44:52	1988	Rosa Mota, Portugal	2:24:30
1979	Joan Benoit, Maine	2:35:15	1989	Ingrid Kristiansen, Norway	2:24:33
1980	Jacqueline Gareau, Canada	2:34:28	1990	Rosa Mota, Portugal	2:25:23
1981	Allison Roe, New Zealand	2:26:46	1991	Wanda Panfil, Poland	2:24:18

*Record for distance.

New York City Marathon

Started in 1970, the New York City Marathon is run in the fall, through all of the city's five boroughs and finishes in Central Park.

Multiple winners: MEN—Bill Rodgers (4); Alberto Salazar (3); Tom Fleming and Orlando Pizzolato (2). WOMEN: Greta Waitz (9); Miki Gorman and Nina Kuscsik (2).

	MEN			WOMEN	
Year		Time	Year		Time
1970	Gary Muhrcke, USA	2:31:38	1970	No Finisher	
1971	Norman Higgins, USA	2:22:54	1971	Beth Bonner, USA	2:55:22
1972	Sheldon Karlin, USA	2:27:52	1972	Nina Kuscsik, USA	3:08:41
1973	Tom Fleming, USA	2:21:54	1973	Nina Kuscsik, USA	2:57:07
1974	Norbert Sander, USA	2:26:30	1974	Katherine Switzer, USA	3:07:29
1975	Tom Fleming, USA	2:19:27	1975	Kim Merritt, USA	2:46:14
1976	Bill Rodgers, USA	2:10:09	1976	Miki Gorman, USA	2:39:11
1977	Bill Rodgers, USA	2:11:28	1977	Miki Gorman, USA	2:43:10
1978	Bill Rodgers, USA	2:12:12	1978	Greta Waitz, Norway	2:32:30
1979	Bill Rodgers, USA	2:11:42	1979	Greta Waitz, Norway	2:27:33
1980	Alberto Salazar, USA	2:09:41	1980	Greta Waitz, Norway	2:25:41
1981	Alberto Salazar, USA	2:08:13	1981	Allison Roe, New Zealand	2:25:29
1982	Alberto Salazar, USA	2:09:29	1982	Greta Waitz, Norway	2:27:14
1983	Rod Dixon, New Zealand	2:08:59	1983	Greta Waitz, Norway	2:27:00
1984	Orlando Pizzolato, Italy	2:14:53	1984	Greta Waitz, Norway	2:29:30
1985	Orlando Pizzolato, Italy	2:11:34	1985	Greta Waitz, Norway	2:28:34
1986	Gianni Poli, Italy	2:11:06	1986	Greta Waitz, Norway	2:28:06
1987	Ibrahim Hussein, Kenya	2:11:01	1987	Priscilla Welch, Britain	2:30:17
1988	Steve Jones, Wales	2:08:20	1988	Greta Waitz, Norway	2:28:07
1989	Juma Ikangaa, Tanzania	2:08:01	1989	Ingrid Kristiansen, Norway	2:25:30
1990	Douglas Wakiihuri, Kenya	2:12:39	1990	Wanda Panfil, Poland	2:30:45

Cycling
Tour de France

The world's premier cycling event, the Tour de France is staged throughout the country (sometimes passing through neighboring countries) over four weeks. The 1946 Tour, however, the first after World War II, was only a five-day race.

Multiple winners: Jacques Anquetil, Bernard Hinault and Eddy Merckx (5); Louison Bobet, Gred LeMond and Philippe Thys (3); Gino Bertali, Ottavio Bottecchia, Gausto Coppi, Laurent Fignon, Nicholas Frantz, Firmin Lambot, Andred Leducq, Sylvere Maes, Antonin Magne, Lucien Petit-Breton (2).

Year		Year		Year	
1903	Maurice Garin, France	1934	Antonin Magne, France	1967	Roger Pingeon, France
1904	Henri Cornet, France	1935	Romain Maes, Belgium	1968	Jan Janssen, Holland
1905	Louis Trousselier, France	1936	Sylvere Maes, Belgium	1969	Eddy Merckx, Belgium
1906	Rene Pottier, France	1937	Roger Lapebie, France		
1907	Lucien Petit-Breton, France	1938	Gino Bartali, Italy	1970	Eddy Merckx, Belgium
1908	Lucien Petit-Breton, France	1939	Sylvere Maes, Belgium	1971	Eddy Merckx, Belgium
1909	Francois Faber, Luxembourg			1972	Eddy Merckx, Belgium
		1940–45	Not held	1973	Luis Ocana, Spain
1910	Octave Lapize, France	1946	Jean Lazarides, France	1974	Eddy Merckx, Belgium
1911	Gustave Garrigou, France	1947	Jean Robic, France	1975	Bernard Thevenet, France
1912	Odile Defraye, Belgium	1948	Gino Bartali, Italy	1976	Lucien van Impe, Belgium
1913	Philippe Thys, Belgium	1949	Fausto Coppi, Italy	1977	Bernard Thevenet, France
1914	Philippe Thys, Belgium			1978	Bernard Hinault, France
1915–18	Not held	1950	Ferdinand Kubler, Switzerland	1979	Bernard Hinault, France
1919	Firmin Lambot, Belgium	1951	Hugo Koblet, Switzerland		
		1952	Fausto Coppi, Italy	1980	Joop Zoetemilk, Holland
1920	Philippe Thys, Belgium	1953	Louison Bobet, France	1981	Bernard Hinault, France
1921	Leon Scieur, Belgium	1954	Louison Bobet, France	1982	Bernard Hinault, France
1922	Firmin Lambot, Belgium	1955	Louison Bobet, France	1983	Laurent Fignon, France
1923	Henri Pelissier, France	1956	Roger Walkowiak, France	1984	Laurent Fignon, France
1924	Ottavio Bottecchia, Italy	1957	Jacques Anquetil, France	1985	Bernard Hinault, France
1925	Ottavio Bottecchia, Italy	1958	Charly Gaul, Luxembourg	1986	Greg LeMond, USA
1926	Lucien Buysse, Belgium	1959	Federico Bahamontes, Spain	1987	Stephen Roche, Ireland
1927	Nicholas Frantz, Luxembourg			1988	Pedro Delgado, Spain
1928	Nicholas Frantz, Luxembourg	1960	Gastone Nencini, Italy	1989	Greg LeMond, USA
1929	Maurice Dewaele, Belgium	1961	Jacques Anquetil, France		
		1962	Jacques Anquetil, France	1990	Greg LeMond, USA
1930	Andre Leducq, France	1963	Jacques Anquetil, France	1991	Miguel Indurain, Spain
1931	Antonin Magne, France	1964	Jacques Anquetil, France		
1932	Andre Leducq, France	1965	Felice Gimondi, Italy		
1933	Georges Speicher, France	1966	Lucien Aimar, France		

Alpine Skiing
World Cup Overall Champions

World Cup Overall Champions (downhill and slalom events combined) since the tour was organized in 1967.

Multiple winners: MEN—Gustavo Thoeni, Pirmin Zurbriggen and Marc Girardelli (4); Phil Mahre and Ingemar Stenmark (3); Jean Claude Killy and Karl Schranz (2). WOMEN—Annemarie Moser-Proell (6); Michela Figini, Nancy Greene, Erica Hess, Petra Kronberger, Maria Walliser and Hanni Wenzel (2).

MEN

Year		Year		Year	
1967	Jean-Claude Killy, France	1976	Ingemar Stenmark, Sweden	1984	Pirmin Zurbriggen, Switzerland
1968	Jean Claude Killy, France	1977	Ingemar Stenmark, Sweden	1985	Marc Girardelli, Luxembourg
1969	Karl Schranz, Austria	1978	Ingemar Stenmark, Sweden	1986	Marc Girardelli, Luxembourg
		1979	Peter Luescher, Switzerland	1987	Pirmin Zurbriggen, Switzerland
1970	Karl Schranz, Austria			1988	Pirmin Zurbriggen, Switzerland
1971	Gustavo Thoeni, Italy	1980	Andreas Wenzel, Lichtenstein	1989	Marc Girardelli, Luxembourg
1972	Gustavo Thoeni, Italy	1981	Phil Mahre, USA		
1973	Gustavo Thoeni, Italy	1982	Phil Mahre, USA	1990	Pirmin Zurbriggen, Switzerland
1974	Piero Gros, Italy	1983	Phil Mahre, USA	1991	Marc Girardelli, Luxembourg
1975	Gustavo Thoeni, Italy				

WOMEN

Year		Year		Year	
1967	Nancy Greene, Canada	1976	Rosi Mittermaier, W.Germany	1984	Erika Hess, Switzerland
1968	Nancy Greene, Canada	1977	Lise-Marie Morerod, Switzerland	1985	Michela Figini, Switzerland
1969	Gertrud Gabi, Austria	1978	Hanni Wenzel, Lichtenstein	1986	Maria Walliser, Switzerland
		1979	Annemarie Moser-Proell, Austria	1987	Maria Walliser, Switzerland
1970	Michele Jacot, France			1988	Michela Figini, Switzerland
1971	Annemarie Proell, Austria	1980	Hanni Wenzel, Lichtenstein	1989	Vreni Schneider, Switzerland
1972	Annemarie Proell, Austria	1981	Marie-Theres Nadig, Switzerland		
1973	Annemarie Proell, Austria	1982	Erika Hess, Switzerland	1990	Petra Kronberger, Austria
1974	Annemarie Proell, Austria	1983	Tamara McKinney, USA	1991	Petra Kronberger, Austria
1975	Annemarie Moser-Proell, Austria				

Figure Skating
World Champions
MEN

Skaters who won world and Olympic championships in the same year are listed in **bold** type.
Multiple winners: Ulrich Salchow (10); Karl Schafer (7); Dick Button (5); Willy Bockl, Scott Hamilton and Hayes Jenkins (4); Kurt Browning, Emmerich Danzor, Gillis Grafstrom, Gustav Hugel, David Jenkins, Fritz Kachler and Ondrej Nepela (3); Brian Boitano, Gilbert Fuchs, Jan Hoffmann, Felix Kaspar, Vladimir Kovalev and Tim Wood (2).

Year	Year	Year
1896 Gilbert Fuchs, Germany	1932 **Karl Schafer**, Austria	1965 Alain Calmat, France
1897 Gustav Hugel, Austria	1933 Karl Schafer, Austria	1966 Emmerich Danzer, Austria
1898 Henning Grenander, Sweden	1934 Karl Schafer, Austria	1967 Emmerich Danzer, Austria
1899 Gustav Hugel, Austria	1935 Karl Schafer, Austria	1968 Emmerich Danzer, Austria
	1936 **Karl Schafer**, Austria	1969 Tim Wood, USA
1900 Gustav Hugel, Austria	1937 Felix Kaspar, Austria	
1901 Ulrich Salchow, Sweden	1938 Felix Kaspar, Austria	1970 Tim Wood, USA
1902 Ulrich Salchow, Sweden	1939 Graham Sharp, Britain	1971 Ondrej Nepela, Czechoslovakia
1903 Ulrich Salchow, Sweden		1972 **Ondrej Nepela**, Czechoslovakia
1904 Ulrich Salchow, Sweden	1940-46 Not held	1973 Ondrej Nepela, Czechoslovakia
1905 Ulrich Salchow, Sweden	1947 Hans Gerschwiler, Switzerland	1974 Jan Hoffmann, E.Germany
1906 Gilbert Fuchs, Germany	1948 **Dick Button**, USA	1975 Sergie Volkov, USSR
1907 Ulrich Salchow, Sweden	1949 Dick Button, USA	1976 **John Curry**, Britain
1908 **Ulrich Salchow**, Sweden		1977 Vladimir Kovalev, USSR
1909 Ulrich Salchow, Sweden	1950 Dick Button, USA	1978 Charles Tickner, USA
	1951 Dick Button, USA	1979 Vladimir Kovalev, USSR
1910 Ulrich Salchow, Sweden	1952 **Dick Button**, USA	
1911 Ulrich Salchow, Sweden	1953 Hayes Jenkins, USA	1980 Jan Hoffmann, E.Germany
1912 Fritz Kachler, Austria	1954 Hayes Jenkins, USA	1981 Scott Hamilton, USA
1913 Fritz Kachler, Austria	1955 Hayes Jenkins, USA	1982 Scott Hamilton, USA
1914 Gosta Sandhal, Sweden	1956 **Hayes Jenkins**, USA	1983 Scott Hamilton, USA
1915-21 Not held	1957 David Jenkins, USA	1984 **Scott Hamilton**, USA
	1958 David Jenkins, USA	1985 Alexander Fadeev, USSR
1922 Gillis Grafstrom, Sweden	1959 David Jenkins, USA	1986 Brian Boitano, USA
1923 Fritz Kachler, Austria		1987 Brian Orser, Canada
1924 **Gillis Grafstrom**, Sweden	1960 Alan Giletti, France	1988 **Brian Boitano**, USA
1925 Willy Bockl, Austria	1961 Not held	1989 Kurt Browning, Canada
1926 Willy Bockl, Austria	1962 Donald Jackson, Canada	
1927 Willy Bockl, Austria	1963 Donald McPherson, Canada	1990 Kurt Browning, Canada
1928 Willy Bockl, Austria	1964 **Manfred Schneldorfer**, W.Ger	1991 Kurt Browning, Canada
1929 Gillis Grafstrom, Sweden		
1930 Karl Schafer, Austria		
1931 Karl Schafer, Austria		

WOMEN

Skaters who won World and Olympic championships in the same year are listed in **bold** type.
Multiple winners: Sonja Henie (10); Carol Heiss and Herma Planck Szabo (5); Lily Kronberger and Katarina Witt (4); Sjoukje Dijkstra, Peggy Fleming, Meray Horvath (3); Tenley Albright, Linda Fratianne, Anett Poetzsch, Beatrix Schuba, Barbara Ann Scott, Gabriele Seyfert, Megan Taylor and Alena Vrzanova (2).

Year	Year	Year
1906 Madge Syers, Britain	1932 **Sonja Henie**, Norway	1958 Carol Heiss, USA
1907 Madge Syers, Britian	1933 Sonja Henie, Norway	1959 Carol Heiss, USA
1908 Lily Kronberger, Hungary	1934 Sonja Henie, Norway	
1909 Lily Kronberger, Hungary	1935 Sonja Henie, Norway	1960 **Carol Heiss**, USA
	1936 **Sonja Henie**, Norway	1961 Not held
1910 Lily Kronberger, Hungary	1937 Cecilia Colledge, Britain	1962 Sjoukje Dijkstra, Holland
1911 Lily Kronberger, Hungary	1938 Megan Taylor, Britain	1963 Sjoukje Dijkstra, Holland
1912 Meray Horvath, Hungary	1939 Megan Taylor, Britain	1964 **Sjoukje Dijkstra**, Holland
1913 Meray Horvath, Hungary		1965 Petra Burka, Canada
1914 Meray Horvath, Hungary	1940–46 Not held	1966 Peggy Fleming, USA
1915-21 Not held	1947 Barbara Ann Scott, Canada	1967 Peggy Fleming, USA
	1948 **Barbara Ann Scott**, Canada	1968 **Peggy Fleming**, USA
1922 Herma Planck-Szabo, Austria	1949 Alena Vrzanova, Czechoslovakia	1969 Gabriele Seyfert, E.Germany
1923 Herma Planck-Szabo, Austria		
1924 **Herma Planck-Szabo**, Austria	1950 Alena Vrzanova, Czechoslovakia	1970 Gabriele Seyfert, E.Germany
1925 Herma Planck-Szabo, Austria	1951 Jeannette Altwegg, Britain	1971 Beatrix Schuba, Austria
1926 Herma Planck-Szabo, Austria	1952 Jacqueline Du Bief, France	1972 **Beatrix Schuba**, Austria
1927 Sonja Henie, Norway	1953 Tenley Albright, USA	1973 Karen Magnussen, Canada
1928 **Sonja Henie**, Norway	1954 Gundi Busch, W.Germany	1974 Christine Errath, E.Germany
1929 Sonja Henie, Norway	1955 Tenley Albright, USA	1975 Dianne DeLeeuw, Holland
	1956 Carol Heiss, USA	1976 **Dorothy Hamill**, USA
1930 Sonja Henie, Norway	1957 Carol Heiss, USA	1977 Linda Fratianne, USA
1931 Sonja Henie, Norway		

Figure Skating (Cont.)

Year		Year		Year	
1978	Anett Poetzsch, E.Germany	1983	Rosalyn Sumners, USA	1988	**Katarina Witt**, E.Germany
1979	Linda Fratianne, USA	1984	**Katarina Witt**, E.Germany	1989	Midori Ito, Japan
1980	**Anett Poetzsch**, E.Germany	1985	Katarina Witt, E.Germany	1990	Jill Trenary, USA
1981	Denise Biellmann, Switzerland	1986	Debi Thomas, USA	1991	Kristi Yamaguchi, USA
1982	Elaine Zayak, USA	1987	Katarina Witt, E.Germany		

U.S. Champions
MEN

Skaters who won U.S., world and Olympic championships in same year are in **bold** type.

Multiple winners: Dick Button and Roger Turner (7); Sherwin Badger, Robin Lee (5); Brian Boitano, Scott Hamilton, David Jenkins, Hayes Jenkins and Charles Tickner (4); Gordon McKellen, Nathaniel Niles and Tim Wood (3); Scott Allen, Todd Eldredge, Eugene Turner and Gary Visconti (2).

Year		Year		Year		Year	
1914	Norman Scott	1934	Roger Turner	1954	Hayes Jenkins	1974	Gordon McKellen
1915	Not held	1935	Robin Lee	1955	Hayes Jenkins	1975	Gordon McKellen
1916	Not held	1936	Robin Lee	1956	**Hayes Jenkins**	1976	Terry Kubicka
1917	Not held	1937	Robin Lee	1957	David Jenkins	1977	Charles Tickner
1918	Nathaniel Niles	1938	Robin Lee	1958	David Jenkins	1978	Charles Tickner
1919	Not held	1939	Robin Lee	1959	David Jenkins	1979	Charles Tickner
1920	Sherwin Badger	1940	Eugene Turner	1960	David Jenkins	1980	Charles Tickner
1921	Sherwin Badger	1941	Eugene Turner	1961	Bradley Lord	1981	Scott Hamilton
1922	Sherwin Badger	1942	Robert Specht	1962	Monty Hoyt	1982	Scott Hamilton
1923	Sherwin Badger	1943	Arthur Vaughn	1963	Thomas Litz	1983	Scott Hamilton
1924	Sherwin Badger	1944	Not held	1964	Scott Allen	1984	**Scott Hamilton**
1925	Nathaniel Niles	1945	Not held	1965	Gary Visconti	1985	Brian Boitano
1926	Chris Christenson	1946	Dick Button	1966	Scott Allen	1986	Brian Boitano
1927	Nathaniel Niles	1947	Dick Button	1967	Gary Visconti	1987	Brian Boitano
1928	Roger Turner	1948	**Dick Button**	1968	Tim Wood	1988	**Brian Boitano**
1929	Roger Turner	1949	Dick Button	1969	Tim Wood	1989	Christopher Bowman
1930	Roger Turner	1950	Dick Button	1970	Tim Wood	1990	Todd Eldredge
1931	Roger Turner	1951	Dick Button	1971	John (Misha) Petkevich	1991	Todd Eldredge
1932	Roger Turner	1952	**Dick Button**	1972	Ken Shelley		
1933	Roger Turner	1953	Hayes Jenkins	1973	Gordon McKellen		

WOMEN

Skaters who won U.S. world and Olympic championships in same year are in **bold** type.

Multiple winners: Maribel Vinson (9); Theresa Weld Blanchard and Gretchen Merrill (6); Tenley Albright, Peggy Fleming, and Janet Lynn (5); Linda Fratianne and Carol Heiss (4); Dorothy Hamill, Beatrix Loughran, Rosalyn Summers, Joan Tozzer and Jill Trenary (3); Yvonne Sherman and Debi Thomas (2).

Year		Year		Year		Year	
1914	Theresa Weld	1936	Maribel Vinson	1956	Tenley Albright	1976	**Dorothy Hamill**
1915–17	Not held	1937	Maribel Vinson	1957	Carol Heiss	1977	Linda Fratianne
1918	Rosemary Beresford	1938	Joan Tozzer	1958	Carol Heiss	1978	Linda Fratianne
1919	Not held	1939	Joan Tozzer	1959	Carol Heiss	1979	Linda Fratianne
1920	Theresa Weld	1940	Joan Tozzer	1960	**Carol Heiss**	1980	Linda Fratianne
1921	Theresa Blanchard	1941	Jane Vaughn	1961	Laurence Owen	1981	Elaine Zayak
1922	Theresa Blanchard	1942	Jane Sullivan	1962	Barbara Pursley	1982	Rosalyn Sumners
1923	Theresa Blanchard	1943	Gretchen Merrill	1963	Lorraine Hanlon	1983	Rosalyn Sumners
1924	Theresa Blanchard	1944	Gretchen Merrill	1964	Peggy Fleming	1984	Rosalyn Sumners
1925	Beatrix Loughran	1945	Gretchen Merrill	1965	Peggy Fleming	1985	Tiffany Chin
1926	Beatrix Loughran	1946	Gretchen Merrill	1966	Peggy Fleming	1986	Debi Thomas
1927	Beatrix Loughran	1947	Gretchen Merrill	1967	Peggy Fleming	1987	Jill Trenary
1928	Maribel Vinson	1948	Gretchen Merrill	1968	**Peggy Fleming**	1988	Debi Thomas
1929	Maribel Vinson	1949	Yvonne Sherman	1969	Janet Lynn	1989	Jill Trenary
1930	Maribel Vinson	1950	Yvonne Sherman	1970	Janet Lynn	1990	Jill Trenary
1931	Maribel Vinson	1951	Sonya Klopfer	1971	Janet Lynn	1991	Tanya Harding
1932	Maribel Vinson	1952	Tenley Albright	1972	Janet Lynn		
1933	Maribel Vinson	1953	Tenley Albright	1973	Janet Lynn		
1934	Suzanne Davis	1954	Tenley Albright	1974	Dorothy Hamill		
1935	Maribel Vinson	1955	Tenley Albright	1975	Dorothy Hamill		

A German worker chisels the name of Jesse Owens into the wall of the Olympic Stadium in 1936 after Owens won four gold medals at the Berlin Summer Games.

OLYMPICS
1896-1988

Modern Olympic Games

The Winter and Summer Olympic Games will be held in the same year for the last time in 1992. This special 80-page section reviews all Summer Games since 1896 and Winter Games since 1924.

Summer Games

Year	No	Location	Dates	Nations	Most Medals	USA Medals
1896	I	Athens, GRE	Apr 6-15	13	Greece (10-19-18—47)	11- 6- 2—19 (2nd)
1900	II	Paris, FRA	May 20-Oct 28	22	France (29-41-32—102)	20-14-19—53 (2nd)
1904	III	St.Louis, USA	July 1-Nov 23	12	USA (80-86-72—238)	80-86-72—238 (1st)
1906-a	—	Athens, GRE	Apr 22-May 2	20	France (15-9-16—40)	12- 6- 5—23 (4th)
1908	IV	London, GBR	Apr 27-Oct 31	23	Britain (56-50-39—145)	23-12-12—47 (2nd)
1912	V	Stockholm, SWE	May 5-July 22	28	Sweden (24-24-17—65)	23-19-19—61 (2nd)
1916	VI	Berlin, GER	Cancelled (WWI)			
1920	VII	Antwerp, BEL	Apr 20-Sept 12	29	USA (41-27-28—96)	41-27-28—96 (1st)
1924	VIII	Paris, FRA	May 4-July 27	44	USA (45-27-27—99)	45-27-27—99 (1st)
1928	IX	Amsterdam, HOL	May 17-Aug 12	46	USA (22-18-16—56)	22-18-16—56 (1st)
1932	X	Los Angeles, USA	July 30-Aug 14	37	USA (41-32-31—104)	41-32-31—104 (1st)
1936	XI	Berlin, GER	Aug 1-16	49	Germany (33-26-30-89)	24-20-12—56 (2nd)
1940	XII	Tokyo, JPN	Cancelled (WWII)			
1944	XIII	London, GBR	Cancelled (WWII)			
1948	XIV	London, GBR	July 29-Aug 14	59	USA (38-27-19—84)	38-27-19—84 (1st)
1952	XV	Helsinki, FIN	July 19-Aug 3	69	USA (40-19-17—76)	40-19-17—76 (1st)
1956-b	XVI	Melbourne, AUS	Nov 22-Dec 8	67	USSR (37-29-32—98)	32-25-17—74 (2nd)
1960	XVII	Rome, ITA	Aug 25-Sept 11	83	USSR (43-29-31—103)	34-21-16—71 (2nd)
1964	XVIII	Tokyo, JPN	Oct 10-24	93	USA (36-26-28—90)	36-26-28—90 (1st)
1968	XIX	Mexico City, MEX	Oct 12-27	112	USA (45-28-34—107)	45-28-34—107 (1st)
1972	XX	Munich, W.GER	Aug 26-Sept 10	122	USSR (50-27-22-99)	33-31-30—94 (2nd)
1976-c	XXI	Montreal, CAN	July 17-Aug 1	92	USSR (49-41-35—125)	34-35-25—94 (3rd)
1980-d	XXII	Moscow, USSR	July 19-Aug 3	81	USSR (80-69-46—195)	Boycotted Games
1984-e	XXIII	Los Angeles, USA	July 28-Aug 12	144	USA (83-61-30—174)	83-61-30—174 (1st)
1988	XXIV	Seoul, S.KOR	Sept 17-Oct 2	159	USSR (55-31-46—132)	36-31-27—94 (3rd)
1992	XXV	Barcelona, SPA	July 25-Aug 9			
1996	XXVI	Atlanta, GA	July 20-Aug 4			

a—The 1906 Intercalated Games in Athens are considered unofficial by the IOC because they did not take place in the four-year cycle established in 1896. However, most record books include these interim games with the others.
b—Due to Australian quarantine laws, the equestrian events for the 1956 Games were held in Stockholm, June 10-17.
c—The 1976 Games were boycotted by 32 nations, most of them from black Africa, because the IOC would not ban New Zealand. A rugby team from New Zealand had toured racially-segregated South Africa in the Spring.
d—The 1980 Games were boycotted by 64 nations, led by the USA, to protest the Russian invasion of Afghanistan on Dec.27, 1979.
e—The 1984 Games were boycotted by 14 Eastern Bloc nations, led by the USSR, to protest America's overcommercialization of the Games, inadequate security and an anti-Soviet attitude by the U.S. government. Most believed, however, the communist walkout was simply revenge for 1980.

Winter Games

Year	No	Location	Dates	Nations	Most medals	USA Medals
1924	I	Chamonix, FRA	Jan 25-Feb 4	16	Norway (4-7-6—17)	1-2-1—4 (4th)
1928	II	St.Moritz, SWI	Feb 11-19	25	Norway (6-4-5—15)	2-2-2—6 (2nd)
1932	III	Lake Placid, NY	Feb 4-15	17	USA (6-4-2—12)	6-4-2—12 (1st)
1936	IV	Garmisch-Partenkirchen, GER	Feb 6-16	28	Norway (7-5-3—15)	1-0-3—4 (T-5th)
1940-a	—	Sapporo, JPN	Cancelled (WWII)			
1944	—	Cortina d'Ampezzo, ITA	Cancelled (WWII)			
1948	V	St.Moritz, SWI	Jan 30-Feb 8	28	Norway (4-3-3—10), Sweden (4-3-3—10) & Switz.(3-4-3—10)	3-4-2—9 (4th)
1952	VI	Oslo, NOR	Feb 14-25	30	Norway (7-3-6—16)	4-6-1—11 (2nd)
1956	VII	Cortina d'Ampezzo, ITA	Jan 26-Feb 5	32	USSR (7-3-6—16)	2-3-2—7 (T-4th)
1960	VIII	Squaw Valley, CA	Feb 18-28	30	USSR (7-5-9—21)	3-4-3—10 (2nd)
1964	IX	Innsbruck, AUT	Jan 29-Feb 9	36	USSR (11-8-6—25)	1-2-3—6 (7th)
1968	X	Grenoble, FRA	Feb 6-18	37	Norway (6-6-2—14)	1-5-1—7 (T-7th)
1972	XI	Sapporo, JPN	Feb 3-13	35	USSR (8-5-3—16)	3-2-3—8 (6th)
1976-b	XII	Innsbruck, AUT	Feb 4-15	37	USSR (13-6-8—27)	3-3-4—10 (T-3rd)
1980	XIII	Lake Placid, NY	Feb 14-23	37	E.Ger.(9-7-7—23)	6-4-2—12 (3rd)
1984	XIV	Sarajevo, YUG	Feb 7-19	49	USSR (6-10-9—25)	4-4-0—8 (T-5th)
1988	XV	Calgary, CAN	Feb 13-28	57	USSR (11-9-9—29)	2-1-3—6 (8th)
1992	XVI	Albertville, FRA	Feb 8-23			
1994-c	XVII	Lillehammer, NOR	Feb 12-27			
1998	XVIII	Nagano, JPN	TBA			

a—The 1940 Winter Games were originally scheduled for Sapporo, but Japan resigned as host in 1937 when the Sino-Japanese war broke out. St.Moritz was the next choice, but the Swiss felt that ski instructors should not be considered professionals and the IOC withdrew its offer. Finally, Garmisch-Partenkirchen was asked to serve again as host, but the Germans invaded Poland in 1939.
b—The IOC originally granted the 1976 Winter Games to Denver, but in 1972 Colorado voters rejected a $5 million bond issue to finance the undertaking. Denver immediately withdrew as host and the IOC designated Innsbruck, the site of the 1964 Games.
c—Starting in 1994, the Winter Games will no longer be held in the same year as the Summer Games, but rather two years *before*.

THE 1992 INFORMATION PLEASE SPORTS ALMANAC

O L Y M P I C S
S T A T I S T I C S
THROUGH THE YEARS
1896-1988
SUMMER GAMES

SEC A

PAGE 523

1896

Athens

The ruins of ancient Olympia were excavated by the German archaeologist Ernst Curtius from 1875-81.

Among the remains uncovered was the ancient stadium where the original Olympic Games were celebrated as a religious festival from 776 B.C. to 393 A.D., when Roman emperor Theodosius I banned all pagan festivals (the Olympics celebrated the Greek god Zeus). There is evidence to suggest that the Games continued until the site was physically demolished in 426 A.D. by a Roman army sent by Theodosius II.

On June 23, 1894, French educator Baron Pierre de Coubertin, speaking at the Sorbonne in Paris to a gathering of international sports leaders from nine nations—including the United States and Russia—proposed that the ancient games be revived on an international scale. The idea was enthusiastically received and the Modern Olympics, as we know them, were born.

The first Olympics were held two years later in Athens, where 311 athletes from 13 nations competed in the ancient Panathenaic stadium to large and enthusiastic crowds.

Americans swept the track and field events, but Greece won the most medals with 47. The highlight was the victory by native peasant Spiridon Loues in the first marathon race, which was run over the same course covered by the Greek hero Pheidippides after the battle of Marathon in 490 B.C.

Top 10 Standings

National medal standings are not recognized by the IOC. The unofficial point totals are based on 3 points for a gold medal, 2 for a silver and 1 for a bronze. Total medals are in parentheses.

		Gold	Silver	Bronze	Pts
1	Greece (47)	10	19	18	86
2	USA (19)	11	6	2	47
3	Germany (15)	7	5	3	34
4	France (11)	5	4	2	25
5	Great Britain (7)	3	3	1	16

		Gold	Silver	Bronze	Pts
6	Hungary (6)	2	1	3	11
	Denmark (7)	1	2	4	11
8	Austria (5)	2	0	3	9
9	Switzerland (3)	1	2	0	7
10	Australia (2)	2	0	0	6

Leading Medal Winners

Number of individual medals won on the left; gold, silver and bronze breakdown to the right.

No		Sport	G-S-B
6	Hermann Weingärtner, GER	Gymnastics	3-2-1
4	Karl Schuman, GER	Gynamastics & Wrestling	4-0-0
4	Alfred Flatow, GER	Gymnastics	3-1-0
4	Bob Garrett, USA	Track/Field	2-1-1
4	Viggo Jensen, DEN	Shooting & Weightlifting	1-2-1
3	Paul Masson, FRA	Cycling	3-0-0
3	Jules Zutter, SWI	Gymnastics	1-2-0
3	James Connolly, USA	Track/Field	1-1-1
3	Leon Flameng, FRA	Cycling	1-1-1
3	Adolf Schmal, AUT	Cycling	1-0-2
3	Efstathios Choraphas, GRE	Swimming	0-1-2
3	Holger Nielsen, DEN	Shooting	0-1-2

Track & Field

Event		Time
100m	Tom Burke, USA	12.0
400m	Tom Burke, USA	54.2
800m	Teddy Flack, AUS	2:11.0
1500m	Teddy Flack, AUS	4:33.2
Marathon	Spiridon Louis, GRE	2:58:50
110m H	Tom Curtis, USA	17.6

Event		Mark
High Jump	Ellery Clark, USA	5-11¼
Pole Vault	William Hoyt, USA	10-10
Long Jump	Ellery Clark, USA	20-10
Triple Jump	James Connolly, USA	44-11¾
Shot Put	Bob Garrett, USA	36- 9¾
Discus	Bob Garrett, USA	95- 7½

Swimming

Event		Time	
100m Free	Alfréd Hajós, HUN	1:22.2	OR
500m Free	Paul Neumann, AUT	8:12.6	
1200m Free	Alfréd Hajós, HUN	18:22.2	OR

Other		Time	
Sailors' 100m Free	Ioannis Malokinis, GRE	2:20.4	

Team Sports

None

Also Contested

Cycling, Fencing, Gymnastics, Shooting, Tennis, Weight-lifting and Greco-Roman Wrestling.

1900

Paris

The success of the re-vived Olympics moved Greece to declare itself the rightful host of all fu-ture Games, but de Coubertin and the Inter-national Olympic Com-mittee were determined to move the athletic feast around. In France, however, the Games were overshadowed by the brand new Eiffel Tower and all but ignored by the organizers of the 1900 Paris Exposition.

Despite their sideshow status, the Games at-tracted 1,330 athletes from 22 nations and en-joyed more publicity, if not bigger crowds, than in Athens.

University of Pennsylvania roommates Alvin Kraenzlein, Irving Baxter and John Tewksbury and Purdue grad Ray Ewry dominated the 23 track and field events, winning 11 and taking five seconds and a third. Kraenzlein remains the only track and fielder to win four individual titles in one year. Women were invited to compete for the first time and Britain's Charlotte Cooper winning singles and mixed doubles in tennis.

No gold medals were given out in Paris. Win-ners received silver medals with bronze for sec-ond place.

Top 10 Standings

National team medal standings are not recognized by the IOC. The unofficial point totals are based on 3 points for a gold medal, 2 for a silver and 1 for a bronze. Total medals are in parentheses.

	Gold	Silver	Bronze	Pts
1 France (102)	29	41	32	201
2 USA (53)	20	14	19	107
3 Great Britain (35)	17	8	10	77
4 Belgium (20)	8	7	5	43
5 Switzerland (9)	6	2	1	23
6 Australia (8)	4	0	4	16
7 Germany (7)	3	2	2	15
8 Denmark (7)	2	3	2	14
9 Hungary (6)	1	3	2	11
10 Italy (4)	2	2	0	10

Leading Medal Winners

Number of individual medals won on the left; gold, silver and bronze breakdown to the right.

MEN

No		Sport	G-S-B
5	Irving Baxter, USA	Track/Field	2-3-0
5	John W.Tewksbury, USA	Track/Field	2-2-1
4	Alvin Kraenzlein, USA	Track/Field	4-0-0
4	Konrad Stäheli, SWI	Shooting	3-0-1
4	Achille Paroche, FRA	Shooting	1-2-1
4	Stan Rowley, AUS	Track/Field	1-0-3
4	Ole Östmo, NOR	Shooting	0-2-2
3	Ray Ewry, USA	Track/Field	3-0-0
3	Charles Bennett, AUS	Track/Field	2-1-0
3	Emil Kellenberger, SWI	Shooting	2-1-0
3	Hubert van Innis, BEL	Archery	2-1-0
3	Laurie Doherty, GBR	Tennis	2-0-1
3	Reggie Doherty, GBR	Tennis	2-0-1
3	E.Michelet, FRA	Yachting	1-0-2
3	F. Michelet, FRA	Yachting	1-0-2
3	Anders Nielsen, DEN	Shooting	0-3-0
3	Zoltán Halmay, HUN	Swimming	0-2-1
3	Léon Moreaux, FRA	Shooting	0-2-1

WOMEN

No		Sport	G-S-B
2	Charlotte Cooper, GBR	Tennis	2-0-0
2	Marion Jones, USA	Tennis	0-0-2

Track & Field

Event		Time	
60m	Alvin Kraenzlein, USA	7.0	WR
100m	Frank Jarvis, USA	11.0	
200m	John W.Tewksbury, USA.	22.2	
400m	Maxey Long, USA	49.4	OR
800m	Alfred Tysoe, GBR	2:01.2	
1500m	Charles Bennett, GBR	4:06.2	WR
Marathon	Michel Théato, FRA	2:59:45	
110m H	Alvin Kraenzlein, USA	15.4	OR
200m H	Alvin Kraenzlein, USA	25.4	
400m H	John W.Tewksbury, USA.	57.6	
3000m Steeple	George Orton, CAN	7:34.4	
4000m Steeple	John Rimmer, GBR	12:58.4	
5000m Team	GBR (Chas.Bennett, John Rimmer, Sidney Robinson, Alfred Tysoe, Stanley Rowley)	26 pts	

Event		Mark	
High Jump	Irving Baxter, USA	6- 2¾	OR
Pole Vault	Irving Baxter, USA	10-10	
Long Jump	Alvin Kraenzlein, USA	23- 6¾	OR
Triple Jump	Meyer Prinstein, USA	47- 5¾	OR
Shot Put	Richard Sheldon, USA	46- 3¼	OR
Discus	Rudolf Bauer, HUN	118- 3	OR
Hammer	John Flanagan, USA	163- 1	

Standing		Mark	
High Jump	Ray Ewry, USA	5- 5	WR
Long Jump	Ray Ewry, USA	10- 6¼	
Triple Jump	Ray Ewry, USA	34- 8½	

Swimming

Event		Time	
220yd Free	Frederick Lane, AUS	2:25.2	OR
1000m Free	John Jarvis, GBR	13:40.2	
4000m Free	John Jarvis, GBR	58:24.0	
200m Back	Ernst Hoppenberg, GER	2:47.0	
200m Team	GER (Ernst Hoppenberg, Max Hainle, Max Schone, Julius Frey, Herbert von Petersdorff)	32 pts	

Team Sports

Sport	Champion
Cricket	Great Britain
Polo	Great Britain/USA
Rugby	France
Soccer	Great Britain
Tug-of-War	Sweden/Norway
Water Polo	Great Britain

Note: In Polo, Foxhunters Hurlingham defeated Club Rugby in a contest of teams made up of British and American players. A combined 6-man team of Swedes and Norwegians won the Tug-of-War.

Also Contested

Archery, Croquet, Cycling, Equestrian, Fencing, Golf, Gymnastics, Rowing, Shooting, Tennis and Yachting.

1904

St.Louis

Originally scheduled for Chicago, the Games were moved to St.Louis and held in conjunction with the centennial celebration of the Louisiana Purchase.

The program included more sports than in Paris, but with only 11 nations sending athletes, the first Olympics to be staged in the United States had a decidedly All-American flavor—over 500 of the 681 competitors were Americans. Little wonder the home team won 80 percent of the medals.

The rout was nearly total in track and field where the U.S.—led by triple-winners Ray Ewry, Archie Hahn, Jim Lightbody and Harry Hillman—took 23 of 25 gold medals and swept 20 events.

The marathon, which was run over dusty roads in brutally hot weather, was the most bizarre event of the Games. Thomas Hicks of the U.S. won, but only after his handlers fed him painkillers during the race. And an imposter nearly stole the victory when Fred Lorz, who dropped out after nine miles, was seen trotting back to the finish line to retrieve his clothes. Amused that officials thought he had won the race, Lorz played along until he was found out shortly after the medal ceremony. Banned for life by the AAU, Lorz was reinstated a year later and won the 1905 Boston Marathon.

Top 10 Standings

National medal standings are not recognized by the IOC. The unofficial point totals are based on 3 points for a gold medal, 2 for a silver and 1 for a bronze. Total medals are in parentheses.

		Gold	Silver	Bronze	Pts
1	USA (238)	80	86	72	484
2	Germany (15)	5	4	6	29
3	Cuba (11)	5	3	3	24
4	Canada (6)	4	1	1	15
5	Hungary (4)	2	1	1	9
6	Austria (3)	1	1	1	6
7	Greece (2)	1	0	1	4
	Switzerland (2)	1	0	1	4
9	Ireland (1)	1	0	0	3
	Great Britain (2)	0	1	1	3

Leading Medal Winners

Number of individual medals won on the left; gold, silver and bronze breakdown to the right.

MEN

No		Sport	G-S-B
6	Anton Heida, USA	Gymnastics	5-1-0
6	Burton Downing, USA	Cycling	2-3-1
5	Marcus Hurley, USA	Cycling	4-0-1
5	George Eyser, USA	Gymnastics	2-2-1
5	Charles Daniels, USA	Swimming	3-1-1
5	Albertson Van Zo Post, USA	Fencing	2-1-2
4	Jim Lightbody, USA	Track/Field	3-1-0
4	Francis Gailey, USA	Swimming	0-3-1
4	Teddy Billington, USA	Cycling	0-1-3
4	Frank Kungler, USA	Weightlifting, Wrestling & Tug of War	0-1-3
4	William Merz, USA	Gymnastics	0-1-3
3	Ray Ewry, USA	Track/Field	3-0-0
3	Ramón Fonst, CUB	Fencing	3-0-0
3	Archie Hahn, USA	Track/Field	3-0-0
3	Harry Hillman, USA	Track/Field	3-0-0
3	Julius Lenhart, AUT	Gymnastics	2-1-0
3	George Bryant, USA	Archery	2-0-1
3	Emil Rausch, GER	Swimming	2-0-1
3	Robert Williams, USA	Archery	1-2-0
3	Ralph Rose, USA	Track/Field	1-1-1
3	William Thompson, USA	Archery	1-0-2
3	Charles Tatham, USA	Fencing	0-2-1
3	William Hogenson, USA	Track/Field	0-1-2
3	Emil Voigt, USA	Gymnastics	0-1-2

WOMEN

No		Sport	G-S-B
3	Lida Howell, USA	Archery	3-0-0
2	Emma Cooke, USA	Archery	0-2-0
2	Jessie Pollack, USA	Archery	0-0-2

Track & Field

Event		Time	
60m	Archie Hahn, USA	7.0	=WR
100m	Archie Hahn, USA	11.0	
200m	Archie Hahn, USA	21.6	OR
400m	Harry Hillman, USA	49.2	OR
800m	Jim Lightbody, USA	1:56.0	OR
1500m	Jim Lightbody, USA	4:05.4	WR
Marathon	Thomas Hicks, USA	3:28:53	
110m H	Frederick Schule, USA	16.0	
200m H	Harry Hillman, USA	24.6	OR
400m H	Harry Hillman, USA	53.0	
3000m Steeple	Jim Lightbody, USA	7:39.6	
4-mile Team	New York AC (Arthur Newton, George Underwood, Paul Pilgrim, Howard Valentine, David Munson)	27 pts	

Event		Mark	
High Jump	Sam Jones, USA	5-11	
Pole Vault	Charles Dvorak, USA	11- 5¾	
Long Jump	Meyer Prinstein, USA	24- 1	OR
Triple Jump	Meyer Prinstein, USA	47- 1	
Shot Put	Ralph Rose, USA	48- 7	WR
56-lb Throw	Étienne Desmarteau, CAN	34- 4	
Discus	Martin Sheridan, USA	128-10½	OR
Hammer	John Flanagan, USA	168- 1	OR
Triathlon	Max Emmerich, USA	35.7 pts	
Decathlon	Tom Kiely, IRL	6036 pts	

Note: Sheridan won Discus throw-off after tying with Rose for 1st.

Standing		Mark	
High Jump	Ray Ewry, USA	5- 3	
Long Jump	Ray Ewry, USA	11- 4⅞	WR
Triple Jump	Ray Ewry, USA	34- 7¼	

1904 (Cont.)
Swimming

Event		Time
50yd Free	Zoltán Halmay, HUN	28.0
100yd Free	Zoltán Halmay, HUN	1:02.8
220yd Free	Charles Daniels, USA	2:44.2
440yd Free	Charles Daniels, USA	6:16.2
880yd Free	Emil Rausch, GER	13:11.4
Mile Free	Emil Rausch, GER	27:18.2
100yd Back	Walter Brack, GER	1:16.8
400yd Brst	Georg Zacharias, GER	7:23.6
4x50yd Free	USA (Joe Ruddy, Leo Goodwin,	
	Louis Handle, Charles Daniels)	2:04.6

Note: Halmay won 50-Free in swim-off with Scott Leary of U.S.

Diving

		Points
Platform	George Sheldon, USA	12.66
Plunge		**Mark**
for Distance	William Daley, USA	62-6

Team Sports

Sport	Champion
Lacrosse	Canada (Shamrock-Winnipeg)
Soccer	Canada (Galt Football Club)
Tug-of-War	USA (Milwaukee AC)
Water Polo	USA (New York AC)

Also Contested
Archery, Boxing, Cycling, Fencing, Golf, Gymnastics, Roque (Croquet), Rowing, Tennis, Weightlifting and Freestyle Wrestling.

ΟΛΥΜΠΙΑΚΟΙ
ΑΓΩΝΕΣ
Les Jeux Olympiques
ΑΘΗΝΑΙ
Athènes
776 - 1896 - 1906

1906
Athens

After disappointing receptions in Paris and St Louis, the Olympic movement returned to Athens for the Intercalated Games of 1906. The mutual desire of Greece and Baron de Coubertin to recapture the spirit of the 1896 Games led to an understanding that the Greeks would host an interim games every four years between Olympics.

Nearly 900 athletes from 20 countries came to Athens, including, for the first time, an official American team picked by the USOC.

As usual, the U.S. dominated track and field, taking 11 of 21 events, including double wins by Martin Sheridan (shot put and freestyle discus), Ray Ewry (standing high and long jumps) and Paul Pilgrim (400 and 800 meters). The previously unknown Pilgrim had been an 11th-hour addition to the team.

Verner Jarvinen, the first Finn to compete in the Olympics, won the Greek-style discus throw and placed second in the freestyle discus. He returned home a national hero and inspired Finland to become a future Olympic power.

The Intercalated Games were cancelled due to political unrest in 1910 and never reappeared. Medals won are considered unofficial by the IOC.

Top 10 Standings

National medal standings are not recognized by the IOC. The unofficial point totals are based on 3 points for a gold medal, 2 for a silver and 1 for a bronze. Total medals are in parentheses.

	Gold	Silver	Bronze	Pts
1 France (40)	15	9	16	79
2 Greece (34)	8	13	13	63
3 USA (23)	12	6	5	53
4 Great Britain (25)	8	11	6	52
5 Italy (16)	7	6	3	36
6 Germany (14)	4	6	4	28
7 Switzerland (11)	5	4	2	25
8 Sweden (14)	2	5	7	23
9 Hungary (10)	2	5	3	19
10 Austria (8)	3	3	2	17

Leading Medal Winners

Number of individual medals won on the left; gold, silver and bronze breakdown to the right.

MEN

No		Sport	G-S-B
5	Martin Sheridan, USA	Track/Field	2-3-0
5	Léon Moreaux, FRA	Shooting	2-1-2
4	Louis Richardet, SWI	Shooting	4-0-0
4	Gustav Casmir, GER	Fencing	2-2-0
4	Jean Reich, SWI	Shooting	1-1-2
3	Francesco Verri, ITA	Cycling	3-0-0
3	Enrico Bruna, ITA	Rowing	3-0-0
3	Georgio Cesana, ITA	Rowing	3-0-0
3	Max Decugis, FRA	Tennis	3-0-0
3	Emilio Fontanella, ITA	Rowing	3-0-0
3	Georges Dillon-Cavanaugh, FRA	Fencing	2-1-0
3	Konrad Stäheli, SWI	Shooting	1-2-0
3	Henry Taylor, GBR	Swimming	1-1-1
3	Eric Lemming, SWE	Track/Field	1-0-2
3	Fernand Vast, FRA	Cycling	1-0-2
3	Raoul de Boigne, FRA	Shooting	0-2-1
3	John Jarvis, GBR	Swimming	0-1-2

WOMEN

No		Sport	G-S-B
2	Sophia Marinou, USA	Tennis	0-2-0

Track & Field

Event		Time
100m	Archie Hahn, USA	11.2
400m	Paul Pilgrim, USA	53.2
800m	Paul Pilgrim, USA	2:01.5
1500m	Jim Lightbody, USA	4:12.0
5 Miles	Henry Hawtrey, GBR	26:11.8
Marathon	Billy Sherring, CAN	2:51:23.6
110m H	Robert Leavitt, USA	16.2
1500m Walk	George Bonhag, USA	7:12.6
3000m Walk	György Sztantics, HUN	15:13.2

Event		Mark
High Jump	Con Leahy, GBR/IRL	5- 10
Pole Vault	Fernand Gonder, FRA	11- 5¾
Long Jump	Meyer Prinstein, USA	23- 7½
Triple Jump	Peter O'Connor, GBR/IRL	46- 2¼
Shot Put	Martin Sheridan, USA	40- 5¼
Stone Throw	Nicolaos Georgantas, GRE	65- 4½
Discus	Martin Sheridan, USA	136- 0
Greek Disc	Verner Järvinen, FIN	115- 4½
Freestyle Javelin	Eric Lemming, SWE	176-10 **WR**
Pentathlon	Hjalmar Mellander, SWE	24 pts

Notes: Weight in Stone Throw was 14.08 lbs; spinning not allowed in Greek-style Discus.

Standing		Mark
High Jump	Ray Ewry, USA	5- 1¼
Long Jump	Ray Ewry, USA	10-10

Swimming

Event		Time
100m Free	Charles Daniels, USA	1:13.4
400m Free	Otto Scheff, AUT	6:23.8
Mile Free	Henry Taylor, GBR	28:28.0
4x250m Free	HUN (József Ónody, Henrik Hajós, Geza Kiss, Zoltán Halmay)	16:52.4
Diving		Points
Platform	Gottlob Walz, GER	156.0

Team Sports

Sport	Champion
Soccer	Denmark
Tug-of-War	Germany

Also Contested

Canoeing, Cycling, Fencing, Gymnastics, Rowing, Shooting, Tennis, Weightlifting and Greco-Roman Wrestling.

1908

London

The fourth Olympic Games were certainly the wettest and probably the most contentious in history.

Held at a new 68,000-seat stadium in the Shepherds Bush section of London, the 1908 Games were played out under continually rainy skies and suffered from endless arguments between British officials and many of the other countries involved—especially the United States.

"The Battle of Shepherds Bush" began almost immediately, when the U.S. delegation noticed that there was no American flag among the national flags decorating the stadium for the opening ceremonies. U.S. flag bearer and discus champion Martin Sheridan responded by refusing to dip the Stars and Stripes when he passed King Edward VII's box in the parade of athletes. "This flag dips to no earthly king," Sheridan said. And it hasn't since.

The Americans, at least, got to march with their flag. Finland, then ruled by Russia, could not. Informed they would have to use a Russian flag, the furious Finns elected to march with no flag at all.

Once again the marathon proved to be the Games' most memorable event. Laid out over a 26-mile, 365-yard course that stretched from Windsor Castle to the royal box at Shepherds Bush, the race ended in controversy when leader Dorando Pietri of Italy staggered into the packed stadium, took a wrong turn, collapsed, was helped up by doctors, wobbled and fell three more times before being half-carried across the finish line by race officials. Caught up in the drama of Pietri's agony, the cheering crowd hardly noticed that he was declared the winner just as second place runner, Johnny Hayes of the U.S., entered the stadium.

Pietri was later disqualified in favor of Hayes, but only after British and U.S. officials argued for an hour and fights had broken out in the stands.

Top 10 Standings

National medal standings are not recognized by the IOC. The unofficial point totals are based on 3 points for a gold medal, 2 for a silver and 1 for a bronze. Total medals are in parentheses.

		Gold	Silver	Bronze	Pts
1	Great Britain (145)	56	50	39	307
2	USA (47)	23	12	12	105
3	Sweden (25)	8	6	11	47
4	France (19)	5	5	9	34
5	Canada (16)	3	3	10	25
6	Germany (13)	3	5	5	24
7	Hungary (9)	3	4	2	19
8	Norway (8)	2	3	3	15
	Belgium (8)	1	5	2	15
10	Italy (4)	2	2	0	10

Leading Medal Winners

Number of individual medals won on the left; gold, silver and bronze breakdown to the right.

MEN

No		Sport	G-S-B
3	Mel Sheppard, USA	Track/Field	3-0-0
3	Henry Taylor, GBR	Swimming	3-0-0
3	Benjamin Jones, GBR	Cycling	2-1-0
3	Martin Sheridan, USA	Track/Field	2-0-1
3	Oscar Swahn, SWE	Shooting	2-0-1
3	Josiah Ritchie, GBR	Tennis	1-1-1
3	Ted Ranken, GBR	Shooting	0-3-0

WOMEN

No		Sport	G-S-B
2	Madge Syers, GBR	Figure Skating	1-0-1

Track & Field

Event		Time	
100m	Reggie Walker, SAF	10.8	=OR
200m	Bobby Kerr, CAN	22.6	
400m	Wyndham Halswelle, GBR	50.0	
800m	Mel Sheppard, USA	1:52.8	WR
1500m	Mel Sheppard, USA	4:03.4	OR
5 Miles	Emil Voigt, GBR	25:11.2	
Marathon	Johnny Hayes, USA	2:55:18.4	OR
110m H	Forrest Smithson, USA	15.0	WR
400m H	Charley Bacon, USA	55.0	WR
3200m Steeple	Arthur Russell, GBR	10:47.8	
3500m Walk	George Larner, GBR	14:55.0	
10-mi Walk	George Larner, GBR	1:15:57.4	
Medley Relay	USA (William Hamilton, Nathaniel Cartmell, John Taylor, Mel Sheppard)	3:29.4	
3-mile Relay	GBR (Joseph Deakin, Archie Robertson, Wilfred Coales)	6 pts	

Note: Medley Relay made up of two 200m runs, a 400m and an 800m.

1908 (Cont.)

Event		Mark	
High Jump	Harry Porter, USA	6-3	OR
Pole Vault	Edward Cooke, USA	12-2	OR
Long Jump	Frank Irons, USA	24-6½	OR
Triple Jump	Timothy Ahearne, GBR/IRL	48-11¼	OR
Shot Put	Ralph Rose, USA	46-7½	
Discus	Martin Sheridan, USA	134-2	OR
Greek Disc	Martin Sheridan, USA	128-4	OR
Hammer	John Flanagan, USA	170-4	OR
Javelin	Eric Lemming, SWE	179-10	WR
Freestyle Javelin	Eric Lemming, SWE	178-7½	

Note: Spinning not allowed in Greek-style Discus.

Standing		Mark
High Jump	Ray Ewry, USA	5-2
Long Jump	Ray Ewry, USA	10-11¼

Swimming
MEN

Event		Time	
100m Free	Charles Daniels, USA	1:05.6	WR
400m Free	Henry Taylor, GBR	5:36.8	
1500m Free	Henry Taylor, GBR	22:48.4	WR
100m Back	Arno Bieberstein, GER	1:24.6	WR
200m Brst	Frederick Holman, GBR	3:09.2	WR
4x200m Free	GBR (John Derbyshire, Paul Radmilovic, William Foster, Henry Taylor)	10:55.6	WR

Diving		Points
Platform	Hjalmar Johansson, SWE	83.75
Spring	Albert Zürner, GER	85.5

Team Sports

Sport	Champion
Field Hockey	Great Britain (England)
Lacrosse	Canada
Polo	Great Britain (Roehampton)
Rugby	Australia
Soccer	Great Britain
Tug-of-War	Great Britain (City Police)
Water Polo	Great Britain

Also Contested

Archery, Boxing, Cycling, Fencing, Figure Skating, Gymnastics, Jeu de Paume (court tennis), Racquets, Rowing, Shooting, Tennis, Freestyle Wrestling, Greco-Roman Wrestling and Yachting.

1912
Stockholm

The belligerence of 1908 was replaced with benevolence four years later, as Sweden provided a well-organized and pleasant haven for the troubled Games.

And then there were Jim Thorpe and Hannes Kolemainen.

Thorpe, a 24-year-old American Indian who was a two-time consensus All-America football player at Carlisle (Pa.) Institute, won the two most demanding events in track and field—the pen-tathlon and decathlon. And he did it with ease. "You sir," said the Swedes' King Gustav V at the medal ceremony, "are the greatest athlete in the world." To which Thorpe is said to have replied, "Thanks, King."

Kolehmainen, a 22-year-old Finnish vegetarian, ran away with three distance events being run for the first time—the 5,000- and 10,000-meter races and the 12,000-meter cross-country run. He also picked up a silver medal in the 12,000-meter team race.

Ralph Craig of the U.S. was the only other winner of two individual track gold medals, taking both the 100 and 200-meter runs. The 100 final had seven false starts, one with Craig sprinting the entire distance before being called back.

Although Thorpe returned to the U.S. a hero, a year later it was learned that he had played semi-pro baseball for $25 a week in 1910. The IOC, with the full support of the American Olympic Committee, stripped him of his medals and erased his records.

The medals and records were returned in 1982—30 years after Thorpe's death.

Top 10 Standings

National medal standings are not recognized by the IOC. The unofficial point totals are based on 3 points for a gold medal, 2 for a silver and 1 for a bronze. Total medals are in parentheses.

		Gold	Silver	Bronze	Pts
1	Sweden (65)	24	24	17	137
2	USA (61)	23	19	19	126
3	Great Britain (41)	10	15	16	76
4	Finland (26)	9	8	9	52
5	Germany (25)	5	13	7	48
6	France (14)	7	4	3	32
7	Denmark (12)	1	6	5	20
8	Norway (10)	4	1	5	19
9	South Africa (6)	4	2	0	16
	Canada (8)	3	2	3	16
	Hungary (8)	3	2	3	16

Leading Medal Winners

Number of individual medals won on the left; gold, silver and bronze breakdown to the right.

MEN

No		Sport	G-S-B
4	Wilhelm Carlberg, SWE	Shooting	3-1-0
4	Hannes Kolehmainen, FIN	Track/Field	3-1-0
4	Carl Osburn, USA	Shooting	1-2-1
3	Alfred Lane, USA	Shooting	3-0-0
3	Eric Carlberg, SWE	Shooting	2-1-0
3	Åke Lundeberg, SWE	Shooting	2-1-0
3	Frederick Hird, USA	Shooting	2-0-1
3	Jean Cariou, FRA	Equestrian	1-1-1
3	Charles Dixon, GBR	Tennis	1-1-1
3	Johan von Holst, SWE	Shooting	1-1-1
3	Harold Hardwick, AUS	Swimming	1-0-2
3	Jack Hatfield, GBR	Swimming	0-2-1
3	Charles Stewart, GBR	Shooting	0-0-3

WOMEN

No		Sport	G-S-B
2	Edith Hannam, GBR	Tennis	2-0-0
2	Jennie Fletcher, GBR	Swimming	1-0-1
2	Sigrid Fick, SWE	Tennis	0-1-1

Track & Field

Event		Time	
100m	Ralph Craig, USA	10.8	
200m	Ralph Craig, USA	21.7	
400m	Charlie Reidpath, USA	48.2	**OR**
800m	Ted Meredith, USA	1:51.9	**WR**
1500m	Arnold Jackson, GBR	3:56.8	**OR**
5000m	Hannes Kolehmainen, FIN	14:36.6	**WR**
10,000m	Hannes Kolehmainen, FIN	31:20.8	
X-country (12,000m)	Hannes Kolehmainen, FIN	45:11.6	
Marathon	Kenneth McArthur, SAF	2:36:54.8	
110m H	Frederick Kelly, USA	15.1	
10k Walk	George Goulding, CAN	46:28.4	
4x100m	GBR (David Jacobs, Harold Macintosh, Victor d'Arcy, William Applegate)	42.4	**OR**
4x400m	USA (Mel Sheppard, Edward Lindberg, Ted Meredith, Charlie Reidpath)	3:16.6	**WR**
3000m Team	USA (Tel Berna, Norman Taber, George Bonhag)	9 pts	
X-country (12,000m)	SWE (Hjalmar Andersson, John Eke, Josef Ternström)	10 pts	

Event		Mark	
High Jump	Alma Richards, USA	6- 4	**OR**
Pole Vault	Harry Babcock, USA	12-11½	**OR**
Long Jump	Albert Gutterson, USA	24-11¼	**OR**
Triple Jump	Gustaf Lindblom, SWE	48- 5¼	
Shot Put	Babe McDonald, USA	50- 4	**OR**
Discus	Armas Taipale, FIN	148- 3	**OR**
Hammer	Matt McGrath, USA	179- 7	**OR**
Javelin	Eric Lemming, SWE	198-11	**WR**
Pentathlon	Jim Thorpe, USA	7 pts	
Decathlon	Jim Thorpe, USA	8412 pts	**WR**

Standing		Mark
High Jump	Platt Adams, USA	5- 4¼
Long Jump	Constantin Tsiklitiras, GRE	11- 0¾

Both Hands		Mark
Shot Put	Ralph Rose, USA	90-10½
Discus	Armas Taipale, FIN	271-10
Javelin	Juho Saaristo, FIN	359- 0

Swimming

MEN

Event		Time	
100m Free	Duke Kahanamoku, USA	1:03.4	
400m Free	George Hodgson, CAN	5:24.4	
1500m Free	George Hodgson, CAN	22:00.0	**WR**
100m Back	Harry Hebner, USA	1:21.2	
200m Brst	Walter Bathe, GER	3:01.8	**OR**
400m Brst	Walter Bathe, GER	6:29.6	**OR**
4x200m Free	AUS (Cecil Healy, Malcolm Champion, Leslie Boardman, Harold Hardwick)	10:11.6	**WR**

Diving		Points
Spring	Paul Günther, GER	79.23
Platform	Erik Adlerz, SWE	73.94
Plain High	Erik Adlerz, SWE	40.0

WOMEN

Event		Time	
100m Free	Fanny Durack, AUS	1:22.2	
4x100m Free	GBR (Bella Moore, Jennie Fletcher, Annie Speirs, Irene Steer)	5:52.8	**WR**

Diving		Points
Platform	Greta Johansson, SWE	39.9

Team Sports

Sport	Champion
Soccer	Great Britain
Tug-of-War	Sweden
Water Polo	Great Britain

Also Contested

Cycling, Equestrian, Fencing, Gymnastics, Modern Pentathlon, Rowing, Shooting, Tennis, Greco-Roman Wrestling and Yachting.

1920

Antwerp

The Olympic quadrennial, scheduled for Berlin in 1916, was interrupted by World War I—the so-called "War to End All Wars," which had involved 28 countries and killed nearly 10 million troops in four years.

The four-year cycle of Olympiads—Berlin would have been the sixth—is still counted, however, even though the Games were not played.

Less than two years after the armistice, the Olympics resumed in Belgium, a symbolic and austere choice considering it had been occupied for four years by enemy forces. Still, 29 countries (one more than participated in the war) sent a record 2,600 athletes to the Games. Germany and Austria, the defeated enemy of Belgium and the Allies, were not invited.

The United States turned in the best overall team performance, winning 41 gold medals, but the talk of the Games was 23-year-old distance runner Paavo Nurmi of Finland. Nurmi won the 10,000-meter run and 8,000-meter cross-country, took a third gold in the team cross-country and silver in the 5,000-meter run. In all, Finland won nine track and field gold medals to break the U.S. dominance in the sport.

Elsewhere, Albert Hill of Britain made his Olympic debut at age 36 and won both the 800- and 1,500-meter runs. World record holder Charley Paddock of the U.S. won the 100 meters, but was upset in the 200 by teammate Allan Woodring, who was a last-minute addition to the team.

And in swimming, the U.S. won 11 of 15 events, led by triple gold medalists Norman Ross and Ethelda Bleibtrey, defending men's 100-meter freestyle champion Duke Kahanamoku and 14-year-old springboard diving champion Aileen Riggin.

The Antwerp Games were also noteworthy for the introduction of the Olympic oath—uttered for the first time by Belgium fencer Victor Bion—and the Olympic flag, with its five multicolored, intersecting rings.

1920 (Cont.)
Top 10 Standings

National medal standings are not recognized by the IOC. The unofficial point totals are based on 3 points for a gold medal, 2 for a silver and 1 for a bronze. Total medals are in parentheses.

		Gold	Silver	Bronze	Pts
1	USA (96)	41	27	28	205
2	Sweden (63)	19	20	24	121
3	Great Britain (43)	15	15	13	88
4	France (41)	9	19	13	78
5	Finland (34)	15	10	9	74
	Belgium (35)	14	11	10	74
7	Norway (28)	13	7	8	61
8	Italy (23)	13	5	5	54
9	Denmark (13)	3	9	1	28
10	Holland (11)	4	2	5	21

Leading Medal Winners

Number of individual medals won on the left; gold, silver and bronze breakdown to the right.

MEN

No		Sport	G-S-B
7	Willis Lee, USA	Shooting	5-1-1
7	Lloyd Spooner, USA	Shooting	4-1-2
6	Hubert van Innis, BEL	Archery	4-2-0
6	Carl Osburn, USA	Shooting	4-1-1
5	Nedo Nadi, ITA	Fencing	5-0-0
5	Larry Nuesslein, USA	Shooting	2-1-2
5	Julien Brulé, FRA	Archery	1-3-1
4	Dennis Fenton, USA	Shooting	3-1-0
4	Aldo Nadi, ITA	Fencing	3-1-0
4	Paavo Nurmi, FIN	Track/Field	3-1-0
4	Otto Olsen, NOR	Shooting	2-2-0
4	Harold Natvig, NOR	Shooting	2-1-1
4	Östen Östensen, NOR	Shooting	0-2-2
4	Erik Backman, SWE	Track/Field	0-1-3
4	Fritz Kuchen, SWI	Shooting	0-0-4
3	Norman Ross, USA	Swimming	3-0-0
3	Albert Hill, GBR	Track/Field	2-1-0
3	Morris Kirksey, USA	Track/Field & Rugby	2-1-0
3	Charley Paddock, USA	Track/Field	2-1-0
3	Bevil Rudd, SAF	Track/Field	1-0-2
3	Ettore Caffaratti, ITA	Equestrian	0-1-2

Fourteen shooters tied with 3 each.

WOMEN

No		Sport	G-S-B
3	Ethelda Bleibtrey, USA	Swimming	3-0-0
3	Suzanne Lenglen, FRA	Tennis	2-0-1
3	Frances Schroth, USA	Swimming	1-0-2
2	Irene Guest, USA	Swimming	1-1-0
2	Margaret Woodbridge, USA	Swimming	1-1-0
2	Kitty McKane, GBR	Tennis	1-0-1
2	Dorothy Holman, GBR	Tennis	0-2-0

Track & Field

Event		Time
100m	Charley Paddock, USA	10.8
200m	Allen Woodring, USA	22.0
400m	Bevil Rudd, SAF	49.6
800m	Albert Hill, GBR	1:53.4
1500m	Albert Hill, GBR	4:01.8
5000m	Joseph Guillemot, FRA	14:55.6
10,000m	Paavo Nurmi, FIN	31:45.8
X-country (8000m)	Paavo Nurmi, FIN	27:15.0
Marathon	Hannes Kolehmainen, FIN	2:32:35.8

Event		Time	
110m H	Earl Thomson, CAN	14.8	WR
400m H	Frank Loomis, USA	54.0	WR
3000m Steeple	Percy Hodge, GBR	10:00.4	OR
3k Walk	Ugo Frigerio, ITA	13:14.2	OR
10k Walk	Ugo Frigerio, ITA	48:06.2	
4x100m	USA (Charley Paddock, Jackson Scholz, Loren Murchison, Morris Kirksey)	42.2	WR
4x400m	GBR (Cecil Griffiths, Robert Lindsay, John Ainsworth-Davis, Guy Butler)	3:22.2	
3000m Team	USA (Horace Brown, Arlie Schardt, Ivan Dresser)	10 pts	
X-country (8000m)	FIN (Paavo Nurmi, Heikki Liimatainen, Teudor Koskenniemi)	10 pts	

Event		Mark	
High Jump	Richmond Landon, USA	6-4	=OR
Pole Vault	Frank Foss, USA	13-5	WR
Long Jump	William Petersson, SWE	23-5½	
Triple Jump	Vilho Tuulos, FIN	47-7	
Shot Put	Ville Pörhölä, FIN	48-7¼	
56-lb Throw	Babe McDonald, USA	36-11½	
Discus	Elmer Niklander, FIN	146-7	
Hammer	Pat Ryan, USA	173-5	
Javelin	Jonni Myyrä, FIN	215-10	OR
Pentathlon	Eero Lehtonen, FIN	14 pts	
Decathlon	Helge Lövland, NOR	6803 pts	

Swimming
MEN

Event		Time	
100m Free	Duke Kahanamoku, USA	1:01.4	
400m Free	Norman Ross, USA	5:26.8	
1500m Free	Norman Ross, USA	22:23.2	
100m Back	Warren Kealoha, USA	1:15.2	
200m Brst	Håkan Malmroth, SWE	3:04.4	
400m Brst	Håkan Malmroth, SWE	6:31.8	
4x200m Free	USA (Perry McGillivray, Pua Kealoha, Norman Ross, Duke Kahanamoku)	10:04.4	WR

Diving		Points
Plain High	Arvid Wallman, SWE	183.5
Platform	Clarence Pinkston, USA	100.67
Spring	Louis Kuehn, USA	675.4

WOMEN

Event		Time	
100m Free	Ethelda Bleibtrey, USA	1:13.6	WR
400m Free	Ethelda Bleibtrey, USA	4:34.0	WR
4x100m Free	USA (Margaret Woodbridge, Frances Schroth, Irene Guest, Ethelda Bleibtrey)	5:11.6	WR

Diving		Points
Platform	Stefani Fryland-Clausen, DEN	34.6
Spring	Aileen Riggin, USA	539.9

Team Sports

Sport	Champion
Field Hockey	Great Britain
Ice Hockey	Canada
Polo	Great Britain
Soccer	Belgium
Rugby	United States
Tug-of-War	Great Britain
Water Polo	Great Britain/Ireland

Also Contested

Archery, Boxing, Cycling, Equestrian, Fencing, Figure Skating, Gymnastics, Modern Pentathlon, Rowing, Shooting, Tennis, Weightlifting, Freestyle Wrestling, Greco-Roman Wrestling and Yachting.

1924

Paris

Paavo Nurmi may have been the talk of Antwerp in 1920, but he was the sensation of Paris four years later.

It wasn't just that the "Flying Finn" won five gold medals, it was the way he did it. Running with a stopwatch on his wrist, Peerless Paavo captured the 1,500 and 5,000-meter finals within an hour of each other and set Olympic records in both. Two days later, he blew away the field in the 10,000-meter cross-country run where the heat and an unusually difficult course combined to knock out 23 of 38 starters (Finland also won the team gold in the event). And finally, the next day he led the Finns to victory in the 3,000-meter team race. His performance overshadowed the four gold medals of teammate Ville Ritola.

The gold medals won by British runners Harold Abrahams in the 100 meters and Eric Liddell in the 400 were chronicled in the 1981 Academy Award-winning film *Chariots of Fire*. The movie, however, was not based on fact. Liddell, a devout Christian, knew months in advance that the preliminary for the 100 (his best event) was on a Sunday, so he had plenty of time to change plans and train for the 400. Also, he and Abrahams never competed against each other in real life.

Speaking of the movies, Johnny Weissmuller of the U.S. won three swimming gold medals in the 100- and 400-meter freestyles and water polo. He would later become Hollywood's most famous Tarzan.

Top 10 Standings

National medal standings are not recognized by the IOC. The unofficial point totals are based on 3 points for a gold medal, 2 for a silver and 1 for a bronze. Total medals are in parentheses.

	Gold	Silver	Bronze	Pts
1 USA (99)	45	27	27	216
2 France (38)	13	15	10	79
3 Finland (37)	14	13	10	78
4 Great Britain (34)	9	13	12	65
5 Sweden (29)	4	13	12	50
6 Switzerland (25)	7	8	10	47
7 Italy (17)	9	3	5	38
8 Norway (10)	5	2	3	22
9 Holland (10)	4	1	5	19
10 Denmark (9)	2	5	2	18

Leading Medal Winners

Number of individual medals won on the left; gold, silver and bronze breakdown to the right.

MEN
No		Sport	G-S-B
6	Ville Ritola, FIN	Track/Field	4-2-0
5	Paavo Nurmi, FIN	Track/Field	5-0-0

No		Sport	G-S-B
4	Roger Ducret, FRA	Fencing	3-1-0
4	Johnny Weissmuller, USA	Swimming & Water Polo	3-0-1
3	Ole Lilloe-Olsen, NOR	Shooting	2-1-0
3	Vincent Richards, USA	Tennis	2-1-0
3	Albert Séquin, FRA	Gymnastics	1-2-0
3	Boy Carlton, AUS	Swimming	1-1-1
3	August Güttinger, SWI	Gymnastics	1-0-2
3	Robert Präzak, CZE	Gymnastics	0-3-0
3	Arne Borg, SWE	Swimming	0-2-1
3	Jean Gutweniger, SWI	Gymnastics	0-2-1
3	Henri Hoevenaers, BEL	Cycling	0-2-1

WOMEN
No		Sport	G-S-B
3	Gertrude Ederle, USA	Swimming	1-0-2
2	Ethel Lackie, USA	Swimming	2-0-0
2	Hazel Wightman, USA	Tennis	2-0-0
2	Helen Wills, USA	Tennis	2-0-0
2	Betty Becker, USA	Diving	1-1-0
2	Mariechen Wehselau, USA	Swimming	1-1-0
2	Kitty McKane, GBR	Tennis	0-1-1
2	Aileen Riggin, USA	Swim.& Diving	0-1-1

Track & Field

Event		Time	
100m	Harold Abrahams, GBR	10.6	=OR
200m	Jackson Scholz, USA	21.6	
400m	Eric Liddell, GBR	47.6	OR
800m	Douglas Lowe, GBR	1:52.4	
1500m	Paavo Nurmi, FIN	3:53.6	OR
5000m	Paavo Nurmi, FIN	14:31.2	OR
10,000m	Ville Ritola, FIN	30:23.2	WR
X-country (10,000m)	Paavo Nurmi, FIN	32:54.8	
Marathon	Albin Stenroos, FIN	2:41:22.6	
110m H	Daniel Kinsey, USA	15.0	
400m H	Morgan Taylor, USA	52.6	
3000m Steeple	Ville Ritola, FIN	9:33.6	OR
10k Walk	Ugo Frigerio, ITA	47:49.0	
4x100m	USA (Francis Hussey, Louis Clarke, Loren Murchison, Alfred Leconey)	41.0	=WR
4x400m	USA (C.S.Cochrane, Alan Helffrich, J.O.MacDonald, William Stevenson)	3:16.0	WR
3000m Team	FIN (Paavo Nurmi, Ville Ritola, Elias Katz)	8 pts	
X-country (10,000m)	FIN (Paavo Nurmi, Ville Ritola, Hekki Liimatainen)	11 pts	

Event		Mark	
High Jump	Harold Osborn, USA	6-6	OR
Pole Vault	Lee Barnes, USA	12-11½	
Long Jump	De Hart Hubbard, USA	24-5	
Triple Jump	Nick Winter, AUS	50-11¼	WR
Shot Put	Bud Houser, USA	49-2¼	
Discus	Bud Houser, USA	151-4	OR
Hammer	Fred Tootell, USA	174-10	
Javelin	Jonni Myyrä, FIN	206-7	
Pentathlon	Eero Lahtonen, FIN	14 pts	
Decathlon	Harold Osborn, USA	7711 pts	WR

Swimming
MEN
Event		Time	
100m Free	Johnny Weissmuller, USA	59.0	OR
400m Free	Johnny Weissmuller, USA	5:04.2	OR
1500m Free	Boy Charlton, AUS	20:06.6	WR
100m Back	Warren Kealoha, USA	1:13.2	OR
200m Brst	Robert Skelton, USA	2:56.6	

1924 (Cont.)

Event		Time
4x200m Free	USA (Wallace O'Connor, Harry Glancy, Ralph Breyer, Johnny Weissmuller)	9:53.4 **WR**

Diving		Points
Plain High	Richmond Eve, AUS.	160.0
Platform	Albert White, USA.	97.46
Spring	Albert White, USA.	696.4

WOMEN

Event		Time
100m Free	Ethel Lackie, USA	1:12.4
400m Free	Martha Norelius, USA	6:02.2 **OR**
100m Back	Sybil Bauer, USA.	1:23.2 **OR**
200m Brst	Lucy Morton, GBR	3:33.2 **OR**
4x100m Free	USA (Gertrude Ederle, Euphrasia Donnelly, Ethel Lackie, Mariechen Wehselau)	4:58.8 **WR**

Diving		Points
Platform	Caroline Smith, USA	33.2
Spring	Elizabeth Becker, USA.	474.5

Team Sports

Sport	Champion
Polo.	Argentina
Rugby	United States
Soccer.	Uruguay
Water Polo	France

Also Contested

Boxing, Cycling, Equestrian, Fencing, Gymnastics, Modern Pentathlon, Rowing, Shooting, Tennis, Weightlifting, Freestyle Wrestling, Greco-Roman Wrestling and Yachting.

1928

Amsterdam

"We are here to represent the greatest country on earth. We did not come here to lose gracefully. We came here to win—and win decisively."

So ordered American Olympic Committee president Gen. Douglas MacArthur before the start of the 1928 Games and his athletes delivered, easily winning the unofficial national standings for the third Olympiad in a row.

The U.S. men won eight gold medals in track and field, but were victorious in only one individual running race (Ray Barbuti in the 400 meters). In the sprints, Canada's Percy Williams became the first non-American to win both the 100 and 200. Finland claimed four running titles, including Paavo Nurmi's win in the 10,000 meters—his ninth overall gold medal in three Olympic Games. Teammate and arch-rival Villa Ritola placed second in the 10,000 and outran Nurmi in the 5,000.

These Games also marked the return of Germany to the Olympic fold, the arrival of women's

track and field and double gold medal performances by U.S. swimmers Martha Norelius, Albina Osipowich and Johnny Weissmuller, and diver Peter DesJardins.

Top 10 Standings

National medal standings are not recognized by the IOC. The unofficial point totals are based on 3 points for a gold medal, 2 for a silver and 1 for a bronze. Total medals are in parentheses.

	Gold	Silver	Bronze	Pts
1 USA (56)	22	18	16	118
2 Germany (31)	10	7	14	58
3 Finland (25)	8	8	9	49
4 Sweden (25)	7	6	12	45
5 France (21)	6	10	5	43
6 Holland (19)	6	9	4	40
7 Italy (19)	7	5	7	38
8 Great Britain (20)	3	10	7	36
9 Switzerland (15)	7	4	4	33
10 Canada (15)	4	4	7	27

Leading Medal Winners

Number of individual medals won on the left; gold, silver and bronze breakdown to the right.

MEN

No		Sport	G-S-B
4	Georges Miez, SWI.	Gymnastics	3-1-0
4	Hermann Hänggi, SWI.	Gymnastics	2-1-1
4	Lucien Gaudin, FRA	Fencing	2-2-0
3	Eugen Mack, SWI.	Gymnastics	2-0-1
3	Paavo Nurmi, FIN.	Track/Field	1-2-0
3	Ladislav Vácha, CZE.	Gymnastics	1-2-0
3	Leon Štukelj, YUG.	Gymnastics	1-0-2
3	Emanuel Löffler, CZE.	Gymnastics	0-2-1

WOMEN

No		Sport	G-S-B
3	Joyce Cooper, GBR	Swimming	0-1-2
2	Martha Norelius, USA	Swimming	2-0-0
2	Albina Osipowich, USA	Swimming	2-0-0
2	Maria Braun, HOL	Swimming	1-1-0
2	Eleanor Garatti, USA	Swimming	1-1-0
2	Betty Robinson, USA	Track/Field	1-1-0
2	Fanny Rosenfeld, CAN	Track/Field	1-1-0
2	Ethel Smith, CAN.	Track/Field	1-0-1
2	Ellen King, GBR	Swimming	0-2-0
2	Georgia Coleman, USA.	Diving	0-1-1

Track & Field
MEN

Event		Time
100m	Percy Williams, CAN	10.8
200m	Percy Williams, CAN	21.8
400m	Ray Barbuti, USA	47.8
800m	Douglas Lowe, GBR.	1:51.8 **OR**
1500m	Harri Larva, FIN	3:53.2 **OR**
5000m	Ville Ritola, FIN.	14:38.0
10,000m	Paavo Nurmi, FIN	30:18.8 **OR**
Marathon	Mohamed El Ouafi, FRA	2:32:57.0
110m H	Syd Atkinson, SAF	14.8
400m H	David Burghley, GBR.	53.4 **OR**
3000m Steeple	Toivo Loukola, FIN.	9:21.8 **WR**
4x100m	USA (Frank Wykoff, Jimmy Quinn, Charley Borah, Hank Russell)	41.0 **=WR**
4x400m	USA (George Baird, Bud Spencer, Fred Alderman, Ray Barbuti)	3:14.2 **WR**

Event		Mark
High Jump	Bob King, USA	6- 4½
Pole Vault	Sabin Carr, USA	13- 9¼ OR
Long Jump	Ed Hamm, USA	25- 4½ OR
Triple Jump	Mikio Oda, JPN	49-11
Shot Put	Johnny Kuck, USA	52- 0¾ WR
Discus	Bud Houser, USA	155- 3 OR
Hammer	Pat O'Callaghan, IRL	168- 7
Javelin	Erik Lundkvist, SWE	218- 6 OR
Decathlon	Paavo Yrjölä, FIN	8053 pts WR

WOMEN

Event		Time
100m	Betty Robinson, USA	12.2 =WR
800m	Lina Radke, GER	2:16.8 WR
4x100m	CAN (Fanny Rosenfeld, Ethel Smith, Florence Bell, Myrtle Cook)	48.4 WR
High Jump	Ethel Catherwood, CAN	5- 2½
Discus	Halina Konopacka, POL	129-11¾ WR

Swimming

MEN

Event		Time
100m Free	Johnny Weissmuller, USA	58.6 OR
400m Free	Alberto Zorilla, ARG	5:01.6 OR
1500m Free	Arne Borg, SWE	19:51.8 OR
100m Back	George Kojac, USA	1:08.2 WR
200m Brst	Yoshiyuki Tsuruta, JPN	2:48.8 OR

Event		Time
4x200m Free	USA (Austin Clapp, Walter Laufer, George Kojac Johnny Weissmuller)	9:36.2 WR

Diving		Points
Platform	Pete DesJardins, USA	98.74
Spring	Pete DesJardins, USA	185.04

WOMEN

Event		Time
100m Free	Albina Osipowich, USA	1:11.0 OR
400m Free	Martha Norelius, USA	5:42.8 WR
100m Back	Maria Braun, HOL	1:22.0
200m Brst	Hilde Schrader, GER	3:12.6
4x100m Free	USA (Adelaide Lambert, Eleanor Garatti, Albina Osipowich, Martha Norelius)	4:47.6 WR

Diving		Points
Platform	Elizabeth Becker Pinkston, USA	31.6
Spring	Helen Meany, USA	78.62

Team Sports

Sport	Champion
Field Hockey	India
Soccer.	Uruguay
Water Polo	Germany

Also Contested

Boxing, Cycling, Equestrian, Fencing, Gymnastics, Modern Pentathlon, Rowing, Weightlifting, Freestyle Wrestling, Greco-Roman Wrestling and Yachting.

1932

Los Angeles

Despite a world-wide economic depression and predictions that the 1932 Summer Olympics were doomed to failure, 37 countries sent over 1,300 athletes to southern California and the Games were a huge success.

Energized by perfect weather and the buoyant atmosphere of the first Olympic Village, the competition was fierce. Sixteen world and Olympic records fell in men's track and field alone.

In women's track, 18-year-old Babe Didrikson, who had set world records in the 80-meter hurdles, javelin and high jump at the AAU Olympic Trials three weeks before, came to L.A. and announced, "I am out to beat everybody in sight." She almost did, too—winning the hurdles and javelin, but taking second in the high jump (despite tying teammate Jean Shiley for first) when her jumping style was ruled illegal.

Didrikson's heroics, along with American Eddie Tolan's double in the 100 and 200 meters and Italian Luigi Beccali's upset victory in the 1,500, were among the Games' highlights, but they didn't quite make up for the absence of Finland's famed distance runner Paavo Nurmi.

Just before the Games, the IOC said that Nurmi would not be allowed to participate in his fourth Olympics because he had received excessive expense money on a trip to Germany in 1929. The ruling came as no surprise in the track world where it was said, "Nurmi has the lowest heartbeat and the highest asking price of any athlete in the world."

Top 10 Standings

National medal standings are not recognized by the IOC. The unofficial point totals are based on 3 points for a gold medal, 2 for a silver and 1 for a bronze. Total medals are in parentheses.

	Gold	Silver	Bronze	Pts
1 USA (104)	41	32	31	218
2 Italy (36)	12	12	12	72
3 Sweden (23)	9	5	9	46
4 France (19)	10	5	4	44
5 Finland (25)	5	8	12	43
6 Germany (21)	4	12	5	41
7 Japan (18)	7	7	4	39
8 Hungary (15)	6	4	5	31
Great Britain (16)	4	7	5	31
10 Canada (15)	2	5	8	24

Leading Medal Winners

Number of individual medals won on the left; gold, silver and bronze breakdown to the right.

MEN

No		Sport	G-S-B
4	István Pelle, HUN	Gymnastics	2-2-0
4	Giulio Gaudini, ITA.	Fencing	0-3-1
4	Heikki Savolainen, FIN.	Gymnastics	0-1-3
3	Romeo Neri, ITA.	Gymnastics	3-0-0
3	Alex Wilson, CAN	Track/Field	0-1-2
3	Philip Edwards, CAN.	Track/Field	0-0-3

1932 (Cont.)
WOMEN

No		Sport	G-S-B
3	Helene Madison, USA .... Swimming		3-0-0
3	Babe Didrikson, USA .... Track/Field		2-1-0
2	Georgia Coleman, USA .... Diving		1-1-0
2	Eleanor Garatti, USA .... Swimming		1-0-1
2	Willy den Ouden, HOL .... Swimming		0-2-0
2	Valerie Davies, GBR.............. Swimming		0-0-2

Track & Field
MEN

Event		Time	
100m	Eddie Tolan, USA..................	10.3	OR
200m	Eddie Tolan, USA.................	21.2	OR
400m	Bill Carr, USA....................	46.2	WR
800m	Tommy Hampson, GBR.........	1:49.7	WR
1500m	Luigi Beccali, ITA................	3:51.2	OR
5000m	Lauri Lehtinen, FIN.............	14:30.0	OR
10,000m	Janusz Kusociński, POL........	30:11.4	OR
Marathon	Juan Carlos Zabala, ARG	2:31:36.0	OR
110m H	George Saling, USA	14.6	
400m H	Bob Tisdall, IRL..................	51.7	
3000m Steeple	Volmari Iso-Hollo, FIN.........	10:33.4	
50k Walk	Thomas Green, GBR	4:50:10	

Note: Due to a lap count error, the 3000-meter Steeplechase actually went 3460 meters, or one lap too many.

Event		Mark	
4x100m	USA (Bob Kiesel, Emmett Toppino, Hector Dyer, Frank Wykoff)	40.0	WR
4x400m	USA (Ivan Fuqua, Edgar Ablowich, Karl Warner, Bill Carr)	3:08.2	WR
High Jump	Duncan McNaughton, CAN	6- 5½	
Pole Vault	Bill Miller, USA	14- 1¾	OR
Long Jump	Edward Gordon, USA	25- 0¾	
Triple Jump	Chuhei Nambu, JPN.........	51- 7	WR
Shot Put	Leo Sexton, USA	52- 6	OR
Discus	John Anderson, USA........	162- 4	OR
Hammer	Pat O'Callaghan, IRL	176-11	
Javelin	Matti Järvinen, FIN	238- 6	OR
Decathlon	Jim Bausch, USA..........	8462 pts	WR

WOMEN

Event		Time	
100m	Stella Walsh, POL	11.9	=WR
80m H	Babe Didrikson, USA............	11.7	WR
4x100m	USA (Mary Carew, Evelyn Furtsch, Annette Rogers, Wilhelmina Von Bremen)	46.9	WR

Event		Mark	
High Jump	Jean Shiley, USA	5- 5¼	WR
Discus	Lillian Copeland, USA	133- 2	OR
Javelin	Babe Didrikson, USA	143- 4	OR

Swimming
MEN

Event		Time	
100m Free	Yasuji Miyazaki, JPN	58.2	
400m Free	Buster Crabbe, USA............	4:48.4	OR
1500m Free	Kusuo Kitamura, JPN.........	19:12.4	OR
100m Back	Masaji Kiyokawa, JPN	1:08.6	
200m Brst	Yoshiyuki Tsuruta, JPN.........	2:45.4	
4x200m Free	JPN (Yasuji Miyazaki, Masonori Yusa, Takashi Yokoyama, Hisakichi Toyoda)...........	8:58.4	WR

Diving		Points
Platform	Harold Smith, USA	124.80
Spring	Michael Galitzen, USA	161.38

WOMEN

Event		Time	
100m Free	Helene Madison, USA	1:06.8	OR
400m Free	Helene Madison, USA	5:28.5	WR
100m Back	Eleanor Holm, USA	1:19.4	
200m Brst	Clare Dennis, AUS............	3:06.3	OR
4x100m Free	USA (Josephine McKim, Helen Johns, Eleanor Saville-Garatti, Helene Madison)	4:38.0	WR

Diving		Points
Platform	Dorothy Poynton, USA................	40.26
Spring	Georgia Coleman, USA	87.52

Team Sports

Sport	Champion
Field Hockey	India
Water Polo...................................	Hungary

Also Contested
Boxing, Cycling, Equestrian, Fencing, Gymnastics, Modern Pentathlon, Rowing, Shooting, Weightlifting, Freestyle Wrestling, Greco-Roman Wrestling and Yachting.

1936
Berlin

At the Big Ten track and field championships of 1935, Ohio State's Jesse Owens equaled or set world records in four events: the 100- and 220-yard dashes, 200-yard low hurdles and the long jump. He was also credited with world marks in the 200-meter run and 200-meter hurdles. That's six world records in one afternoon, and he did it all in 45 minutes!

The following year, he swept the 100 and 200 meters and long jump at the Olympic Trials and headed for Germany favored to win all three.

In Berlin, dictator Adolf Hitler and his Nazi followers felt sure that the Olympics would be the ideal venue to demonstrate Germany's oft-stated racial superiority. He directed that $25 million be spent on the finest facilities, the cleanest streets and the temporary withdrawal of all outward signs of the state-run anti-Jewish campaign. By the time over 4,000 athletes from 49 countries arrived for the Games, the stage was set.

Then Jesse Owens, a black sharecropper's son from Alabama, stole the show—winning his three individual events and adding a fourth gold medal in the 400-meter relay. The fact that four other American blacks also won did little to please Herr Hitler, but the applause from the German crowds, especially for Owens, was thunderous. As it was for New Zealander Jack Lovelock's thrilling win over Glenn Cunningham and defending champ Luigi Beccali in the 1,500 meters.

Germany won only five combined gold medals in men's and women's track and field, but saved face for the "master race" in the overall medal count with an 89-56 margin over the United States.

Elsewhere, Dutch swimmer Rie Mastenbroek won three gold medals and American sprinter Helen Stephens won two to pace the women, and the U.S. men won the first basketball gold medal, beating Canada, 19-8, outdoors in the rain.

Top 10 Standings

National medal standings are not recognized by the IOC. The unofficial point totals are based on 3 points for a gold medal, 2 for a silver and 1 for a bronze. Total medals are in parentheses.

	Gold	Silver	Bronze	Pts
1 Germany (89)	33	26	30	181
2 USA (56)	24	20	12	124
3 Italy (22)	8	9	5	47
4 Finland (19)	7	6	6	39
France (19)	7	6	6	39
6 Hungary (16)	10	1	5	37
Sweden (20)	6	5	9	37
8 Japan (18)	6	4	8	34
9 Holland (17)	6	4	7	33
10 Great Britain (14)	4	7	3	29

Leading Medal Winners

Number of individual medals won on the left; gold, silver and bronze breakdown to the right.

MEN

No		Sport	G-S-B
6	Konrad Frey, GER	Gymnastics	3-1-2
5	Alfred Schwarzmann, GER	Gymnastics	3-0-2
5	Eugen Mack, SWI	Gymnastics	0-4-1
4	Jesse Owens, USA	Track/Field	4-0-0
3	Robert Charpentier, FRA	Cycling	3-0-0
3	Guy Lapébie, FRA	Cycling	2-1-0
3	Jack Medica, USA	Swimming	1-2-0
3	Matthias Volz, GER	Gymnastics	1-0-2

WOMEN

No		Sport	G-S-B
4	Rie Mastenbroek, HOL	Swimming	3-1-0
2	Helen Stephens, USA	Track/Field	2-0-0
2	Dorothy Poynton Hill, USA	Diving	1-0-1
2	Gisela Arendt, GER	Swimming	0-1-1

Track & Field
MEN

Event		Time	
100m	Jesse Owens, USA	10.3	
200m	Jesse Owens, USA	20.7	OR
400m	Archie Williams, USA	46.5	
800m	John Woodruff, USA	1:52.9	
1500m	Jack Lovelock, NZE	3:47.8	WR
5000m	Gunnar Höckert, FIN	14:22.2	OR
10,000m	Ilmari Salminen, FIN	30:15.4	
Marathon	Kee-Chung Sohn, JPN	2:29:19.2	OR
110m H	Forrest Towns, USA	14.2	
400m H	Glenn Hardin, USA	52.4	
3000m Steeple	Volmari Iso-Hollo, FIN	9:03.8	WR
50k walk	Harold Whitlock, GBR	4:30:41.4	OR

Note: Marathon winner Sohn was a Korean but was forced to run for Japan, which occupied his country.

4x100m	USA (Jesse Owens, Ralph Metcalfe, Foy Draper, Frank Wykoff)	39.8	WR
4x400m	GBR (Frederick Wolff, Godfrey Rampling, William Roberts, A.G.Brown)	3:09.0	

Event		Mark	
High Jump	Cornelius Johnson, USA	6-8	OR
Pole Vault	Earle Meadows, USA	14- 3¼	OR
Long Jump	Jesse Owens, USA	26- 5½	OR
Triple Jump	Naoto Tajima, JPN	52- 6	WR
Shot Put	Hans Woelke, GER	53- 1¾	OR
Discus	Ken Carpenter, USA	165- 7	OR
Hammer	Karl Hein, GER	185- 4	OR
Javelin	Gerhard Stöck, GER	235- 8	
Decathlon	Glenn Morris, USA	7900 pts	WR

WOMEN

Event		Time	
100m	Helen Stephens, USA	11.5	w
80m H	Trebisonda Valla, ITA	11.7	
4x100m	USA (Harriet Bland, Annette Rogers, Betty Robinson, Helen Stephens)	46.9	

W indicates wind-aided.

Event		Mark	
High Jump	Ibolya Csák, HUN	5- 3	
Discus	Gisela Mauermayer, GER	156- 3	OR
Javelin	Tilly Fleischer, GER	148- 3	OR

Swimming
MEN

Event		Time	
100m Free	Ferenc Csík, HUN	57.6	
400m Free	Jack Medica, USA	4:44.5	OR
1500m Free	Noboru Terada, JPN	19:13.7	
100m Back	Adolf Kiefer, USA	1:05.9	OR
200m Brst	Tetsuo Hamuro, JPN	2:41.5	OR
4x200m Free	JPN (Masanori Yusa, Shigeo Sugiura, Masaharu Taguchi, Shigeo Arai)	8:51.5	WR

Diving		Points
Platform	Marshall Wayne, USA	113.58
Spring	Richard Degener, USA	163.57

WOMEN

Event		Time	
100m Free	Rie Mastenbroek, HOL	1:05.9	OR
400m Free	Rie Mastenbroek, HOL	5:26.4	OR
100m Back	Nida Senff, HOL	1:18.9	
200m Brst	Hideko Maehata, JPN	3:03.6	
4x100m Free	HOL (Johanna Selback, Catherina Wagner, Willemijntje den Ouden, Rie Mastenbroek)	4:36.0	OR

Diving		Points
Platform	Dorothy Poynton Hill, USA	33.93
Spring	Marjorie Gestring, USA	89.27

Team Sports

Sport	Champion
Basketball	United States
Field Hockey	India
Handball	Germany
Polo	Argentina
Soccer	Italy
Water Polo	Hungary

Note: In Water Polo, both Hungary and Germany finished with records of 8-0-1. The Hungarians were awarded the gold medal on total goals (57-56).

Also Contested

Boxing, Canoeing, Cycling, Equestrian, Fencing, Gymnastics, Modern Pentathlon, Rowing, Shooting, Weightlifting, Freestyle Wrestling, Greco-Roman Wrestling and Yachting.

OLYMPIC GAMES

29 JULY 1948 14 AUGUST
LONDON

1948

London

The Summer Olympics were scheduled for Tokyo in 1940, but by mid-1938, Japan was at war with China and withdrew as host. The IOC immediately transferred the Games to Helsinki and the Finns eagerly began preparations only to be invaded by Russia in 1939.

By then, of course, Germany had marched into Poland and World War II was on. The Japanese attacked Pearl Harbor two years later, and the bombs didn't stop falling until 1945. Against this backdrop of global conflict, the Olympic Games were cancelled again in 1940 and '44. Many of the participants in the 1936 Games died in the war.

Eager to come back after two dormant Olympiads, the IOC offered the 1948 Games to London. Much of the British capital had been reduced to rubble in the blitz, but the offer was accepted and the Games went on—successfully, without frills, and without invitations extended to Germany and Japan. The Soviet Union was invited, but chose not to show.

The United States reclaimed its place at the top of the overall medal standings, but the primary individual stars were a 30-year-old Dutch mother of two and a 17-year-old kid from California.

Fanny Blankers-Koen duplicated Jesse Owens' track and field grand slam of 12 years before by winning the 100-meter run and 200-meter run, the 80-meter hurdles, and anchoring the women's 400-meter relay.

And Bob Mathias, just two months after graduating from Tulare High School, won the gold medal in the decathlon, an event he had taken up for the first time during the summer.

Top 10 Standings

National medal standings are not recognized by the IOC. The unofficial point totals are based on 3 points for a gold medal, 2 for a silver and 1 for a bronze. Total medals are in parentheses.

	Gold	Silver	Bronze	Pts
1 USA (84)	38	27	19	187
2 Sweden (44)	16	11	17	87
3 Italy (29)	8	12	9	57
4 France (29)	10	6	13	55
5 Hungary (27)	10	5	12	52
6 Finland (20)	8	7	5	43
Great Britain (23)	3	14	6	43
8 Switzerland (20)	5	10	5	40
9 Denmark (20)	5	7	8	37
10 Turkey (12)	6	4	2	28
Holland (16)	5	2	9	28

Leading Medal Winners

Number of individual medals won on the left; gold, silver and bronze breakdown to the right.

MEN

No		Sport	G-S-B
5	Veikko Huhtanen, FIN	Gymnastics	3-1-1
4	Paavo Aaltonen, FIN	Gymnastics	3-0-1
3	Jimmy McLane, USA	Swimming	2-1-0
3	Humberto Mariles, MEX	Equestrian	2-0-1
3	Mal Whitfield, USA	Track/Field	2-0-1
3	Barney Ewell, USA	Track/Field	1-2-0
3	Michael Reusch, SWI	Gymnastics	1-2-0
3	Josef Stalder, SWI	Gymnastics	1-1-1
3	Ferenc Pataki, HUN	Gymnastics	1-0-2
3	Walter Lehmann, SWI	Gymnastics	0-3-0
3	Edoardo Mangiarotti, ITA	Fencing	0-2-1
3	Thomas Godwin, GBR	Cycling	0-1-2
3	János Mogyorósi, HUN	Gymnastics	0-1-2

WOMEN

No		Sport	G-S-B
4	Fanny Blankers-Koen, HOL	Track/Field	4-0-0
3	Ann Curtis, USA	Swimming	2-1-0
3	Micheline Ostermeyer, FRA	Track/Field	2-0-1
3	Karen-Margrete Harup, DEN	Swimming	1-2-0
3	Shirley Strickland, AUS	Track/Field	0-1-2

Track & Field

MEN

Event		Time	
100m	Harrison Dillard, USA	10.3	=OR
200m	Mel Patton, USA	21.1	
400m	Arthur Wint, JAM	46.2	
800m	Mal Whitfield, USA	1:49.2	OR
1500m	Henri Eriksson, SWE	3:49.8	
5000m	Gaston Reiff, BEL	14:17.6	OR
10,000m	Emil Zátopek, CZE	29:59.6	OR
Marathon	Delfo Cabrera, ARG	2:34:51.6	
110m H	Bill Porter, USA	13.9	OR
400m H	Roy Cochran, USA	51.1	OR
3000 Steeple	Thore Sjöstrand, SWE	9:04.6	
10k Walk	John Mikaelsson, SWE	45:13.2	
50k Walk	John Ljunggren, SWE	4:41:52	
4x100m	USA (Barney Ewell, Lorenzo Wright, Harrison Dillard, Mel Patton)	40.6	
4x400m	USA (Art Harnden, Cliff Bourland, Roy Cochran, Mal Whitfield)	3:10.4	

Event		Mark	
High Jump	John Winter, AUS	6- 6	
Pole Vault	Guinn Smith, USA	14- 1¼	
Long Jump	Willie Steele, USA	25- 8	
Triple Jump	Arne Åhman, SWE	50- 6¼	
Shot Put	Wilbur Thompson, USA	56- 2	OR
Discus	Adolfo Consolini, ITA	173- 2	OR
Hammer	Imre Németh, HUN	183-11	
Javelin	Tapio Rautavaara, FIN	228-10	
Decathlon	Bob Mathias, USA	7139 pts	

WOMEN

Event		Time	
100m	Fanny Blankers-Koen, HOL	11.9	
200m	Fanny Blankers-Koen, HOL	24.4	
80m H	Fanny Blankers-Koen, HOL	11.2	OR
4x100m	HOL (Xenia Stad-de Jong, Jeanette Witziers-Timmer, Gerda van der Kade-Koudijs, Fanny Blankers-Koen)	47.5	

Event		Mark
High Jump	Alice Coachman, USA	5- 6 **OR**
Long Jump	Olga Gyarmati, HUN	18- 8¼
Shot Put	Micheline Ostermeyer, FRA	45- 1½
Discus	Micheline Ostermeyer, FRA	137- 6
Javelin	Herma Bauma, AUT	149- 6

Note: Coachman and Dorothy Odam of Britain tied for 1st place, but Coachman was awarded gold medal for making height on first try.

Swimming

MEN

Event		Time
100m Free	Wally Ris, USA	57.3 **OR**
400m Free	Bill Smith, USA	4:41.0 **OR**
1500m Free	Jimmy McLane, USA	19:18.5
100m Back	Allen Stack, USA	1:06.4
200m Brst	Joe Verdeur, USA	2:39.3 **OR**
4x200m Free	USA (Wally Ris, Jimmy McLane, Wally Wolf, Bill Smith)	8:46.0 **WR**
Diving		Points
Platform	Sammy Lee, USA	130.05
Spring	Bruce Harlan, USA	163.64

WOMEN

Event		Time
100m Free	Greta Andersen, DEN	1:06.3
400m Free	Ann Curtis, USA	5:17.8 **OR**
100m Back	Karen M.Harup, DEN	1:14.4 **OR**
200m Brst	Nel van Vliet, HOL	2:57.2
4x100m Free	USA (Marie Corridon, Thelma Kalama, Brenda Helser, Ann Curtis)	4:29.2 **OR**
Diving		Points
Platform	Vicki Draves, USA	68.87
Spring	Vicki Draves, USA	108.74

Team Sports

Sport	Champion
Basketball	United States
Field Hockey	India
Soccer	Sweden
Water Polo	Italy

Also Contested

Boxing, Canoeing, Cycling, Equestrian, Fencing, Gymnastics, Modern Pentathlon, Rowing, Shooting, Weightlifting, Freestyle Wrestling, Greco-Roman Wrestling and Yachting.

1952

Helsinki

The Soviet Union returned to the Olympic fold in 1952 after a 40-year absence, a period of time that included a revolution and two world wars. Ironically, the Soviets chose to make their comeback in Finland, a country they had invaded twice during World War II.

This time it was the United States that was surprised by the Russians, and the USA had to scramble on the last day of competition to hold off the USSR's assault on first place in the overall

standings. It was the beginning of an all-consuming 36-year Cold War rivalry.

Despite the Soviets' impressive debut, it was a Communist from another Iron Curtain country who turned in the most memorable individual performance of the Games. Emil Zátopek of Czechoslovakia, the 10,000-meter champion in London, not only repeated at 10,000 meters, but also won at 5,000 and in the marathon—an event he had never run before. He also set Olympic records in each race and topped it off by watching his wife Dana Zátopková win the women's javelin.

Zátopek's unique triple was wildly applauded by the distance-minded Finns, but their greatest outburst came in the opening ceremonies when legendary countryman Paavo Nurmi, now 56, ran into the stadium with the Olympic torch and handed it off to another native legend Hannes Kolehmainen, now 62, who lit the flame to start the Games.

Also, Harrison Dillard of the U.S. won the 110-meter hurdles. In 1948, Dillard, the world's best hurdler, failed to qualify for the hurdles and won the 100-meter dash instead.

Top 10 Standings

National medal standings are not recognized by the IOC. The unofficial point totals are based on 3 points for a gold medal, 2 for a silver and 1 for a bronze. Total medals are in parentheses.

		Gold	Silver	Bronze	Pts
1	USA (76)	40	19	17	175
2	USSR (71)	22	30	19	145
3	Hungary (42)	16	10	16	84
4	Sweden (35)	12	13	10	72
5	Italy (21)	8	9	4	46
6	Finland (22)	6	3	13	37
7	France (18)	6	6	6	36
8	Germany (24)	0	7	17	31
9	Czechoslovakia (13)	7	3	3	30
10	Australia (11)	6	2	3	25

Leading Medal Winners

Number of individual medals won on the left; gold, silver and bronze breakdown to the right.

MEN

No		Sport	G-S-B
6	Viktor Chukarin, USSR	Gymnastics	4-2-0
4	Edoardo Mangiarotti, ITA	Fencing	2-2-0
4	Grant Shaginyan, USSR	Gymnastics	2-2-0
4	Josef Stalder, SWI	Gymnastics	0-2-2
3	Emil Zátopek, CZE	Track/Field	3-0-0
3	Ford Konno, USA	Swimming	2-1-0
3	Herb McKenley, JAM	Track/Field	1-2-0
3	Hans Eugster, SWI	Gymnastics	1-1-1

WOMEN

No		Sport	G-S-B
7	Maria Gorokhovskaya, USSR	Gymnastics	2-5-0
4	Margit Korondi, HUN	Gymnastics	1-1-3
4	Nina Bocharova, USSR	Gymnastics	2-2-0
4	Ágnes Keleti, HUN	Gymnastics	1-1-2
3	Yekaterina Kalinchuk, USSR	Gymnastics	1-1-1
3	Éva Novák, HUN	Swimming	1-2-0
3	Galina Minaicheva, USSR	Gymnastics	1-1-1
3	Aleksandra Chudina, USSR	Track/Field	0-2-1

1952 (Cont.)
Track & Field
MEN

Event		Time	
100m	Lindy Remigino, USA	10.4	
200m	Andy Stanfield, USA	20.7	
400m	George Rhoden, JAM	45.9	OR
800m	Mal Whitfield, USA	1:49.2	=OR
1500m	Josy Barthel, LUX	3:45.1	OR
5000m	Emil Zátopek, CZE	14:06.6	OR
10,000m	Emil Zátopek, CZE	29:17.0	OR
Marathon	Emil Zátopek, CZE	2:23:03.2	OR
110m H	Harrison Dillard, USA	13.7	OR
400m H	Charley Moore, USA	50.8	OR
3000m Steeple	Horace Ashenfelter, USA	8:45.4	WR
10k Walk	John Mikaelsson, SWE	45:02.8	OR
50k Walk	Giuseppe Dordoni, ITA	4:28:07.8	OR
4x100m	USA (Dean Smith, Harrison Dillard, Lindy Remigino, Andy Stanfield)	40.1	
4x400m	JAM (Arthur Wint, Leslie Laing, Herb McKenley, George Rhoden)	3:03.9	WR

Event		Mark	
High Jump	Walt Davis, USA	6- 8½	OR
Pole Vault	Bob Richards, USA	14-11	OR
Long Jump	Jerome Biffle, USA	24-10	
Triple Jump	Adhemar da Silva, BRA	53- 2¾	WR
Shot Put	Parry O'Brien, USA	57- 1½	OR
Discus	Sim Iness, USA	180- 6	OR
Hammer	József Csérmák, HUN	197-11	WR
Javelin	Cy Young, USA	242- 1	OR
Decathlon	Bob Mathias, USA	7887 pts	WR

WOMEN

Event		Time	
100m	Marjorie Jackson, AUS	11.5	=WR
200m	Marjorie Jackson, AUS	23.7	
80m H	Shirley Strickland, AUS	10.9	WR
4x100m	USA (Mae Faggs, Barbara Jones, Janet Moreau, Catherine Hardy)	45.9	WR

Event		Mark	
High Jump	Esther Brand, SAF	5- 5¾	
Long Jump	Yvette Williams, NZE	20- 5¾	OR
Shot Put	Galina Zybina, USSR	50- 1¾	WR
Discus	Nina Romaschkova, USSR	168- 8	OR
Javelin	Dana Zátopková, CZE	165- 7	

Swimming
MEN

Event		Time	
100m Free	Clarke Scholes, USA	57.4	
400m Free	Jean Boiteux, FRA	4:30.7	OR
1500m Free	Ford Konno, USA	18:30.3	OR
100m Back	Yoshi Oyakawa, USA	1:05.4	OR
200m Brst	John Davies, AUS	2:34.4	OR
4x200m Free	USA (Wayne Moore, Bill Woosley, Ford Konno, Jimmy McLane)	8:31.1	OR

Diving		Points
Platform	Sammy Lee, USA	156.28
Spring	Skippy Browning, USA	205.29

WOMEN

Event		Time	
100m Free	Katalin Szöke, HUN	1:06.8	
400m Free	Valéria Gyenge, HUN	5:12.1	OR
100m Back	Joan Harrison, SAF	1:14.3	
200m Brst	Éva Székely, HUN	2:51.7	OR
4x100m Free	HUN (Ilona Novák, Judit Temes, Éva Novák, Katalin Szöke)	4:24.4	WR

Diving		Points
Platform	Pat McCormick, USA	79.37
Spring	Pat McCormick, USA	147.30

Team Sports

Sport	Champion
Basketball	United States
Field Hockey	India
Soccer	Hungary
Water Polo	Hungary

Also Contested

Boxing, Canoeing, Cycling, Equestrian, Fencing, Gymnastics, Modern Pentathlon, Rowing, Shooting, Weightlifting, Freestyle Wrestling, Greco-Roman Wrestling and Yachting.

1956
Melbourne

Armed conflicts in Egypt and Hungary threatened to disrupt the 1956 Games, which were scheduled to begin on Nov. 22 (during the summer Down Under).

In July, Egypt seized the Suez Canal from British and French control. In October, Britain and France invaded Egypt in an attempt to retake the canal. Then in November, Russian tanks rolled into Hungary to crush an anti-Communist revolt.

The only direct bearing these events had in Melbourne came when the Soviet water polo team met the Hungarians in the semifinals. Hungary won 4-0, but the match turned ugly after a Hungarian player was pulled bleeding from the pool with a deep gash over his eye from a Russian head butt. A brawl quickly ensued involving both players and spectators and the police had to step in to prevent a riot.

Otherwise, the Soviets outmedaled the U.S. for the first time, cleaning up in gymnastics and winning their first track and field titles when Vladimir Kuts won the 5,000 and 10,000 meters.

The American men won 15 track and field titles, including three golds for sprinter Bobby Morrow.

Harold Connolly of the U.S. won the hammer throw and the heart of the women's javelin champion, Olga Fikotova of Czechoslovakia. Their romance captured the imagination of the world and three months after the Games they were married.

Emil Zátopek, the Czech hero of Helsinki, returned to defend his marathon title and came in sixth. Winner Alain Mimoun, of France, had finished second to Zátopek three times in previous Olympics.

Top 10 Standings

National medal standings are not recognized by the IOC. The unofficial point totals are based on 3 points for a gold medal, 2 for a silver and 1 for a bronze. Total medals are in parentheses.

		Gold	Silver	Bronze	Pts
1	USSR (98)	37	29	32	201
2	USA (74)	32	25	17	163
3	Australia (35)	13	8	14	69
4	Hungary (26)	9	10	7	54
5	Germany (27)	6	13	8	52
6	Italy (25)	8	8	9	49
7	Great Britain (24)	6	7	11	43
8	Sweden (19)	8	5	6	40
9	Japan (19)	4	10	5	37
10	Romania (13)	5	3	5	26
	France (14)	4	4	6	26

Leading Medal Winners

Number of individual medals won on the left; gold, silver and bronze breakdown to the right.

MEN

No		Sport	G-S-B
5	Viktor Chukarin, USSR	Gymnastics	3-1-1
5	Takashi Ono, JPN	Gymnastics	1-3-1
4	Valentin Muratov, USSR	Gymnastics	3-1-0
4	Yuriy Titov, USSR	Gymnastics	1-1-2
4	Masao Takemoto, JPN	Gymnastics	0-1-3
3	Bobby Morrow, USA	Track/Field	3-0-0
3	Murray Rose, AUS	Swimming	3-0-0
3	Edoardo Mangiarotti, ITA	Fencing	2-0-1
3	Thane Baker, USA	Track/Field	1-1-1
3	Masami Kubota, JPN	Gymnastics	0-2-1
3	George Breen, USA	Swimming	0-1-2

WOMEN

No		Sport	G-S-B
6	Ágnes Keleti, HUN	Gymnastics	4-2-0
6	Larissa Latynina, USSR	Gymnastics	4-1-1
4	Tamara Manina, USSR	Gymnastics	1-2-1
4	Sofiya Muratova, USSR	Gymnastics	1-0-3
3	Betty Cuthbert, AUS	Track/Field	3-0-0
3	Lorraine Crapp, AUS	Swimming	2-1-0
3	Dawn Fraser, AUS	Swimming	2-1-0
3	Olga Tass, HUN	Gymnastics	1-1-1

Track & Field

MEN

Event		Time	
100m	Bobby Morrow, USA	10.5	
200m	Bobby Morrow, USA	20.6	OR
400m	Charley Jenkins, USA	46.7	
800m	Tom Courtney, USA	1:47.7	OR
1500m	Ron Delany, IRL	3:41.2	OR
5000m	Vladimir Kuts, USSR	13:39.6	OR
10,000m	Vladimir Kuts, USSR	28:45.6	OR
Marathon	Alain Mimoun, FRA	2:25:00.0	
110m H	Lee Calhoun, USA	13.5	OR
400m H	Glenn Davis, USA	50.1	=OR
3000m Steeple	Chris Brasher, GBR	8:41.2	OR
20k Walk	Leonid Spirin, USSR	1:31:27.4	
50k Walk	Norman Read, NZE	4:30:42.8	
4x100m	USA (Ira Murchison, Leamon King, Thane Baker, Bobby Morrow)	39.5	WR
4x400m	USA (Lou Jones, Jesse Mashburn, Charlie Jenkins, Tom Courtney)	3:04.8	

Event		Mark	
High Jump	Charley Dumas, USA	6-11½	OR
Pole Vault	Bob Richards, USA	14-11½	OR
Long Jump	Greg Bell, USA	25- 8¼	
Triple Jump	Adhemar da Silva, BRA	53- 7¾	OR
Shot Put	Parry O'Brien, USA	60-11¼	OR
Discus	Al Oerter, USA	184-11	OR
Hammer	Harold Connolly, USA	207- 3	OR
Javelin	Egil Danielson, NOR	281- 2	WR
Decathlon	Milt Campbell, USA	7937 pts	OR

WOMEN

Event		Time	
100m	Betty Cuthbert, AUS	11.5	
200m	Betty Cuthbert, AUS	23.4	=OR
80m H	Shirley Strickland, AUS	10.7	OR
4x100m	AUS (Shirley Strickland, Norma Croker, Fleur Mellor, Betty Cuthbert)	44.5	WR

Event		Mark	
High Jump	Mildred McDaniel, USA	5- 9¼	WR
Long Jump	Elzbieta Krzesińska, POL	20-10	=WR
Shot Put	Tamara Tyshkevich, USSR	54- 5	OR
Discus	Olga Fikotová, CZE	176- 1	OR
Javelin	Inese Jaunzeme, USSR	176- 8	

Swimming

MEN

Event		Time	
100m Free	Jon Henricks, AUS	55.4	OR
400m Free	Murray Rose, AUS	4:27.3	OR
1500m Free	Murray Rose, AUS	17:58.9	
100m Back	David Theile, AUS	1:02.2	OR
200m Brst	Masaru Furukawa, JPN	2:34.7	OR
200m Fly	Bill Yorzyk, USA	2:19.3	OR
4x200m Free	AUS (Kevin O'Halloran, John Devitt, Murray Rose, Jon Henricks)	8:23.6	WR

Diving		Points	
Platform	Joaquin Capilla, MEX	152.44	
Spring	Bob Clotworthy, USA	159.56	

WOMEN

Event		Time	
100m Free	Dawn Fraser, AUS	1:02.0	WR
400m Free	Lorraine Crapp, AUS	4:54.6	OR
100m Back	Judy Grinham, GBR	1:12.9	OR
200m Brst	Ursula Happe, GER	2:53.1	OR
100m Fly	Shelly Mann, USA	1:11.0	OR
4x100m Free	AUS (Dawn Fraser, Faith Leech, Sandra Morgan, Lorraine Crapp)	4:17.1	WR

Diving		Points	
Platform	Pat McCormick, USA	84.85	
Spring	Pat McCormick, USA	142.36	

Team Sports

Sport	Champion
Basketball	United States
Field Hockey	India
Soccer	Soviet Union
Water Polo	Hungary

Also Contested

Canoeing, Cycling, Equestrian, Fencing, Gymnastics, Modern Pentathlon, Rowing, Shooting, Weightlifting, Freestyle Wrestling, Greco-Roman Wrestling and Yachting.

Note: Equestrian events were held in Stockholm, Sweden, June 10-17, due to Australian quarantine laws.

JEUX DE LA XVII OLYMPIADE
ROMA   ⊙⊙⊙⊙⊙   25.VIII-11.IX

1960
Rome

Free of political entanglements, save the ruling that Nationalist China had to compete as Formosa, the 1960 Games attracted a record 5,348 athletes from 83 countries. More importantly, it was the first Summer Games covered by U.S. television. CBS bought the rights for $394,000.

Rome was a coming-out party for 18-year-old Louisville boxer Cassius Clay. The brash but engaging Clay, who would later change his name to Muhammad Ali and hold the world heavyweight title three times, won the Olympic light heavyweight crown, pummeling Polish opponent Zbigniew Pietryskowsky in the final. Clay was so proud of his gold medal he didn't take it off for two days.

Sprinter Wilma Rudolph and swimmer Chris von Saltza each won three gold medals for the U.S. Rudolph, who was one of 19 children and who couldn't walk without braces until she was 11, struck gold at 100 and 200 meters and anchored the winning 400-meter relay team. Von Saltza won the 400-meter freestyle, placed second in the 100-free and anchored the winning 400-free and medley relays.

The U.S. men won nine track and field titles, including repeat gold medals for Lee Calhoun, Glenn Davis and Al Oerter. Rafer Johnson and C.K. Yang of Formosa, college teammates at UCLA, finished 1-2 in the decathlon.

Among the other stars in Rome were barefoot Ethiopian marathoner Abebe Bikila, Australia's Herb Elliott in the 1,500 meters, Russian gymnasts Boris Shakhlin and Larissa Latynina, and the gold medal U.S. basketball team—led by Oscar Robertson, Jerry Lucas and Jerry West.

Top 10 Standings

National medal standings are not recognized by the IOC. The unofficial point totals are based on 3 points for a gold medal, 2 for a silver and 1 for a bronze. Total medals are in parentheses.

		Gold	Silver	Bronze	Pts
1	USSR (103)	43	29	31	218
2	USA (71)	34	21	16	160
3	Germany (45)	13	19	13	90
4	Italy (36)	13	10	13	72
5	Australia (22)	8	8	6	46
6	Hungary (21)	6	8	7	41
7	Poland (21)	4	6	11	35
8	Japan (18)	4	7	7	33
9	Great Britain (20)	2	6	12	30
10	Turkey (9)	7	2	0	25

Leading Medal Winners

Number of individual medals won on the left; gold, silver and bronze breakdown to the right.

MEN

No		Sport	G-S-B
7	Boris Shakhlin, USSR	Gymnastics	4-2-1
6	Takashi Ono, JPN	Gymnastics	3-1-2
3	Murray Rose AUS	Swimming	1-1-1
3	John Konrads, AUS.	Swimming	1-0-2
3	Yuri Titov, USSR	Gymnastics	0-2-1

WOMEN

No		Sport	G-S-B
6	Larissa Latynina, USSR	Gymnastics	3-2-1
4	Christine von Saltza, USA	Swimming	3-1-0
4	Polina Astakhova, USSR	Gymnastics	2-1-1
4	Sofia Muratova, USSR.	Gymnastics	1-2-1
3	Wilma Rudolph, USA.	Track/Field	3-0-0
3	Dawn Fraser, AUS.	Swimming	1-2-0
3	Tamara Lyukhina, USSR	Track/Field	1-0-2

Track & Field
MEN

Event		Time	
100m	Armin Hary, GER	10.2	OR
200m	Livio Berruti, ITA	20.5	=WR
400m	Otis Davis, USA	44.9	WR
800m	Peter Snell, NZE	1:46.3	OR
1500m	Herb Elliott, AUS.	3:35.6	WR
5000m	Murray Halberg, NZE	13:43.4	
10,000m	Pyotr Bolotnikov, USSR.	28:32.2	OR
Marathon	Abebe Bikila, ETH.	2:15:16.2	WB
110m H	Lee Calhoun, USA.	13.8	OR
400m H	Glenn Davis, USA	49.3	=OR
3000m Steeple	Zdzislaw Krzyszkowiak, POL	8:34.2	OR
20k Walk	Vladimir Golubnichiy, USSR	1:34:07.2	
50k Walk	Don Thompson, GBR.	4:25:30.0	OR
4x100m	GER (Bernd Cullmann, Armin Hary, Walter Mahlendorf, Martin Lauer)	39.5	=WR
4x400m	USA (Jack Yerman, Earl Young, Glenn Davis, Otis Davis)	3:02.2	WR

Event		Mark	
High Jump	Robert Shavlakadze, USSR.	7- 1	OR
Pole Vault	Don Bragg, USA.	15- 5	OR
Long Jump	Ralph Boston, USA.	26- 7¾	OR
Triple Jump	Józef Schmidt, POL.	55- 2	
Shot Put	Bill Nieder, USA.	64- 6¾	OR
Discus	Al Oerter, USA	194- 2	OR
Hammer	Vasily Rudenkov, USSR	220- 2	OR
Javelin	Viktor Tsibulenko, USSR.	277- 8	
Decathlon	Rafer Johnson, USA	8392 pts	OR

WOMEN

Event		Time	
100m	Wilma Rudolph, USA.	11.0 w	
200m	Wilma Rudolph, USA.	24.0	
800m	Lyudmila Shevtsova, USSR.	2:04.3	=WR
80m H	Irina Press, USSR	10.8	
4x100m	USA (Martha Hudson, Lucinda Williams, Barbara Jones, Wilma Rudolph)	44.5	

ᵂ indicates wind-aided.

Event		Mark	
High Jump	Iolanda Balaş, ROM	6- 0¾	OR
Long Jump	Vyera Krepkina, USSR.	20-10¾	OR
Shot Put	Tamara Press, USSR	56-10	OR
Discus	Nina R.Ponomaryeva, USSR.	180- 9	OR
Javelin	Elvira Ozolina, USSR.	183- 8	OR

Boxing

Weight Class	Champion
Flyweight (112 lbs)	Gyula Török, HUN
Bantamweight (119)	Oleg Grigoryev, USSR
Featherweight (125)	Francesco Musso, ITA
Lightweight (132)	Kazimierz Pazdzio, POL
Lt.Welterweight (139)	Bohumil Nemecek, CZE
Welterweight (148)	Nino Benvenuti, ITA
Lt.Middleweight (156)	Skeeter McClure, USA
Middleweight (165)	Eddie Crook, USA
Lt.Heavyweight (178)	Cassius Clay, USA
Heavyweight (178+)	Franco De Piccoli, ITA

Gymnastics

MEN

Individual		Points
All-Around	Boris Shakhlin, USSR	115.95
Floor	Nobuyuki Aihara, JPN	19.45
Horiz.Bar	Takashi Ono, JPN	19.60
Paral.Bars	Boris Shakhlin, USSR	19.40
Rings	Albert Azaryan, USSR	19.725

Individual		Points
Side Horse	Boris Shakhlin, USSR & Eugen Ekman, FIN	19.375
Vault	Boris Shakhlin, USSR & Takashi Ono, JPN	19.35

Team		Points
All-Around	JPN (Ono, Tsurumi, Aihara, Endo, Takemoto, Mitsukuri)	575.20

WOMEN

Individual		Points
All-Around	Larissa Latynina, USSR	77.031
Bal.Beam	Eva Bosáková, CZE	19.283
Floor	Larissa Latynina, USSR	19.583
Uneven Bars	Polina Astakhova, USSR	19.616
Vault	Margarita Nikolayeva, USSR	19.316

Team		Points
All-Around	USSR (Latynina, Muratova, Astakhova, Nikolayeva, Ivanova, Lyukhina)	382.320

Swimming

MEN

Event		Time	
100m Free	John Devitt, AUS	55.2	OR
400m Free	Murray Rose, AUS	4:18.3	OR
1500m Free	John Konrads, AUS	17:19.6	OR
100m Back	David Theile, AUS	1:09.9	OR
200m Brst	Bill Mulliken, USA	2:37.4	
200m Fly	Mike Troy, USA	2:12.8	WR
4x200m Free	USA (George Harrison, Dick Blick, Mike Troy, Jeff Farrell)	8:10.2	WR
4x100m Mdly	USA (Frank McKinney, Paul Hait, Lance Larson, Jeff Farrell)	4:05.4	WR

Diving		Points
Platform	Bob Webster, USA	165.56
Spring	Gary Tobian, USA	170.00

WOMEN

Event		Time	
100m Free	Dawn Fraser, AUS	1:01.2	OR
400m Free	Chris von Saltza, USA	4:50.6	OR
100m Back	Lynn Burke, USA	1:09.3	OR
200m Brst	Anita Lonsbrough, GBR	2:49.5	WR
100m Fly	Carolyn Schuler, USA	1:09.5	OR
4x100m Free	USA (Joan Spillane, Shirley Stobs, Carolyn Wood, Chris von Saltza)	4:08.9	WR
4x100m Mdly	USA (Lynn Burke, Patty Kempner, Carolyn Schuler, Chris von Saltza)	4:41.1	WR

Diving		Points
Platform	Ingrid Krämer, GER	91.28
Spring	Ingrid Krämer, GER	155.81

Team Sports

Men	Champion
Basketball	United States
Field Hockey	Pakistan
Soccer	Yugoslavia
Water Polo	Italy

Also Contested

Canoeing, Cycling, Equestrian, Fencing, Modern Pentathlon, Rowing, Shooting, Weightlifting, Freestyle Wrestling, Greco-Roman Wrestling and Yachting.

1964

Tokyo

Twenty-six years after Japan's wartime government forced the Japanese Olympic Committee to resign as hosts of the 1940 Summer Games, Tokyo welcomed the world to the first Asian Olympics. The new Japan spared no expense—a staggering $3 billion was spent to rebuild the city—and was rewarded with a record-breaking fortnight.

Twelve world and six Olympic records fell in swimming, with Americans accounting for 13. Eighteen-year-old Don Schollander led the way, winning two individual and two relay gold medals to become the first swimmer to win four events in one Games. Sharon Stouder collected three golds and a silver for the U.S. women, but the most remarkable performance of all belonged to Australian Dawn Fraser, who won the 100-meter freestyle for the third straight Olympics.

In track and field, Al Oerter of the U.S. won the discus for the third straight time. His record toss was one of 25 world and Olympic marks broken. Another fell when Billy Mills of the U.S. electrified the Games by coming from behind for an upset win in the 10,000 meters. New Zealander Peter Snell, the defending 800-meter champion, won both the 800 and 1,500 (last done in 1920).

Sprinter Bob Hayes of the U.S. equaled the world record of 10 seconds flat in the 100 meters, but stunned the crowd with a sub-9 second, come-from-behind anchor leg to lead the U.S. to a new world record in the 4 x 100 meters.

Abebe Bikila of Ethiopia became the first runner to win consecutive marathons. The remarkable Betty Cuthbert of Australia, who won three sprint gold medals in Melbourne, came back eight years later at age 26 to win the 400. And Russian gymnast Larissa Latynina won six medals for the second Olympics in a row.

1964 (Cont.)
Top 10 Standings

National medal standings are not recognized by the IOC. The unofficial point totals are based on 3 points for a gold medal, 2 for a silver and 1 for a bronze. Total medals are in parentheses.

		Gold	Silver	Bronze	Pts
1	USA (90)	36	26	28	188
2	USSR (96)	30	31	35	187
3	Germany (54)	10	25	19	99
4	Japan (29)	16	5	8	66
5	Italy (27)	10	10	7	57
6	Hungary (22)	10	7	5	49
7	Poland (23)	7	6	10	43
8	Great Britain (18)	4	12	2	38
9	Australia (18)	6	2	10	32
10	Czechoslovakia (14)	5	6	3	30

Leading Medal Winners

Number of individual medals won on the left; gold, silver and bronze breakdown to the right.

MEN

No		Sport	G-S-B
4	Don Schollander, USA	Swimming	4-0-0
4	Yukio Endo, JPN	Gymnastics	3-1-0
4	Shuji Tsurumi, JPN	Gymnastics	1-3-0
4	Boris Shakhlin, USSR	Gymnastics	1-2-1
4	Viktor Lisitsky, USSR	Gymnastics	0-4-0
4	Hans-Joachim Klein, GER	Swimming	0-3-1
3	Steve Clark, USA	Swimming	3-0-0
3	Gary Ilman, USA	Swimming	2-0-1
3	Franco Menichelli, ITA	Gymnastics	1-1-1
3	Frank Wiegard, GER	Swimming	0-3-0

WOMEN

No		Sport	G-S-B
6	Larissa Latynina, USSR	Gymnastics	2-2-2
4	Vera Cáslavská, CZE	Gymnastics	3-1-0
4	Polina Astakhova, USSR	Gymnastics	2-1-1
4	Sharon Stouder, USA	Swimming	3-1-0
4	Kathy Ellis, USA	Swimming	2-0-2
3	Irena Klobukowska, POL	Track/Field	1-2-0
3	Ada Kok, HOL	Swimming	1-2-0
3	Edith Maguire, USA	Track/Field	1-2-0
3	Mary Rand, GBR	Track/Field	1-1-1

Track & Field
MEN

Event		Time	
100m	Bob Hayes, USA	10.0	=WR
200m	Henry Carr, USA	20.3	OR
400m	Mike Larrabee, USA	45.1	
800m	Peter Snell, NZE	1:45.1	OR
1500m	Peter Snell, NZE	3:38.1	
5000m	Bob Schul, USA	13:48.8	
10,000m	Billy Mills, USA	28:24.4	OR
Marathon	Abebe Bikila, ETH	2:12:11.2	WB
110m H	Hayes Jones, USA	13.6	
400m H	Rex Cawley, USA	49.6	
3000m Steeple	Gaston Roelants, BEL	8:30.8	OR
20k Walk	Ken Matthews, GBR	1:29:34.0	OR
50k Walk	Abdon Pamich, ITA	4:11:12.4	OR
4x100m	USA (Paul Drayton, Gerald Ashworth, Richard Stebbins, Bob Hayes)	39.0	WR
4x400m	USA (Ollan Cassell, Mike Larrabee, Ulis Williams, Henry Carr)	3:00.7	WR

Event		Mark	
High Jump	Valery Brumel	7- 1¾	OR
Pole Vault	Fred Hansen, USA	16- 8¾	OR
Long Jump	Lynn Davies, GBR	26- 5¾	
Triple Jump	Józef Schmidt, POL	55- 3½	OR
Shot Put	Dallas Long, USA	66- 8½	OR
Discus	Al Oerter, USA	200- 1	OR
Hammer	Romuald Klim, USSR	228-10	OR
Javelin	Pauli Nevala, FIN	271- 2	
Decathlon	Willi Holdorf, GER	7887 pts	

WOMEN

Event		Time	
100m	Wyomia Tyus, USA	11.4	
200m	Edith McGuire, USA	23.0	OR
400m	Betty Cuthbert, AUS	52.0	OR
800m	Ann Packer, GBR	2:01.1	OR
80m H	Karin Balzer, GER	10.5ʷ	
4x100m	POL (Teresa Ciepla, Irena Kirszenstein, Halina Górecka, Ewa Klobukowska)	43.6	

ʷ indicates wind-aided.

Event		Mark	
High Jump	Iolanda Balaş, ROM	6- 2¾	OR
Long Jump	Mary Rand GBR	22- 2¼	WR
Shot Put	Tamara Press, USSR	59- 6¼	OR
Discus	Tamara Press, USSR	187-10	OR
Javelin	Mihaela Peneş, ROM	198- 7	
Pentathlon	Irina Press, USSR	5246 pts	WR

Boxing

Weight Class	Champion
Flyweight (112 lbs)	Fernando Atzori, ITA
Bantamweight (119)	Takao Sakurai, JPN
Featherweight (125)	Stanislav Stepashkin, USSR
Lightweight (132)	Józef Grudzien, POL
Lt.Welterweight (139)	Jerzy Kulej, POL
Welterweight (148)	Marian Kasprzyk, POL
Lt.Middleweight (156)	Boris Lagutin, USSR
Middleweight (165)	Valery Popenchenko, USSR
Lt.Heavyweight (178)	Cosimo Pinto, ITA
Heavyweight (178+)	Joe Frazier, USA

Gymnastics
MEN

Individual		Points
All-Around	Yukio Endo, JPN	115.95
Floor	Franco Menichelli, ITA	19.45
Horiz.Bar	Boris Shakhlin, USSR	19.625
Paral.Bars	Yukio Endo, JPN	19.675
Rings	Takuji Haytta, JPN	19.475
Side Horse	Miroslav Cerar, YUG	19.525
Vault	Haruhiro Yamashita, JPN	19.60

Team		Points
All-Around	JPN (Endo, Tsurumi, Yamashita, Hayata, Mitsukuri, Ono)	577.95

WOMEN

Individual		Points
All-Around	Vera Cáslavská, CZE	77.564
Bal.Beam	Vera Cáslavská, CZE	19.449
Floor	Larissa Latynina, USSR	19.599
Uneven Bars	Polina Astakhova, USSR	19.332
Vault	Vera Cáslavská, CZE	19.483

Team		Points
All-Around	USSR (Latynina, Astakhova, Volchetskaya, Zamotailova, Manina, Gromova)	280.890

Swimming
MEN

Event		Time	
100m Free	Don Schollander, USA	53.4	OR
400m Free	Don Schollander, USA	4:12.2	WR
1500m Free	Robert Windle, AUS	17:01.7	OR
200m Back	Jed Graef, USA	2:10.3	WR
200m Brst	Ian O'Brien, AUS	2:27.8	WR
200m Fly	Kevin Berry, AUS	2:06.6	WR
400m I.M.	Dick Roth, USA	4:45.4	WR
4x100m Free	USA (Steve Clark, Mike Austin, Gary Ilman, Don Schollander)	3:32.3	WR
4x200m Free	USA (Steve Clark, Roy Saari, Gary Ilman, Don Schollander)	7:52.1	WR
4x100m Mdly	USA (Thompson Mann, Bill Craig, Fred Schmidt, Steve Clark)	3:58.4	WR

Diving		Points
Platform	Bob Webster, USA	148.58
Spring	Ken Sitzberger, USA	159.90

WOMEN

Event		Time	
100m Free	Dawn Fraser, AUS	59.5	OR
400m Free	Ginny Duenkel, USA	4:43.3	OR
100m Back	Cathy Ferguson, USA	1:07.7	WR
200m Brst	G. Prozumenshikova, USSR	2:46.4	OR
100m Fly	Sharon Stouder, USA	1:04.7	WR

Event		Time	
400m Mdly	Donna de Varona, USA	5:18.7	OR
4x100m Free	USA (Sharon Stouder, Donna de Varona, Pokey Watson, Kathy Ellis)	4:03.8	WR
4x100m Mdly	USA (Cathy Ferguson, Cynthia Goyette, Sharon Stouder, Kathy Ellis)	4:33.9	WR

Diving		Points
Platform	Lesley Bush, USA	99.80
Spring	Ingrid Engel-Krämer, GER	145.00

Team Sports

Men	Champion
Basketball	United States
Field Hockey	India
Soccer	Hungary
Volleyball	Soviet Union
Water Polo	Hungary

Women	Champion
Volleyball	Japan

Also Contested

Canoeing, Cycling, Equestrian, Fencing, Judo, Modern Pentathlon, Rowing, Shooting, Weightlifting, Freestyle Wrestling, Greco-Roman Wrestling and Yachting.

1968

Mexico City

The Games of the Nineteenth Olympiad were the highest and most controversial ever held.

Staged at 7,349 feet above sea level where the thin air was a major concern to many competing countries, the Mexico City Olympics were another chapter in a year buffeted by the Vietnam War, the assasinations of Martin Luther King and Robert Kennedy, the Democratic Convention in Chicago, and the Russian invasion of Czechoslovakia.

Ten days before the Olympics were scheduled to open on Oct. 12, over 30 Mexico City university students were killed by army troops when a campus protest turned into a riot. Still, the Games began on time and were free of discord until black Americans Tommy Smith and John Carlos, who finished 1-3 in the 200-meter run, bowed their heads and gave the Black Power salute during the national anthem as a protest against racism in the U.S.

They were immediately thrown off the team by the USOC.

The thin air helped shatter records in every men's and women's race up to 1,500 meters and played a role in U.S. long jumper Bob Beamon's incredible gold medal leap of 29-feet, 2½ inches—beating the existing world mark by nearly two feet.

Other outstanding American performances included Al Oerter's record fourth consecutive discus title, Debbie Meyer's three individual swimming gold medals, the innovative Dick Fosbury winning the high jump with his backwards "flop," and Wyomia Tyus becoming the first woman to win back-to-back golds in the 100 meters.

Top 10 Standings

National medal standings are not recognized by the IOC. The unofficial point totals are based on 3 points for a gold medal, 2 for a silver and 1 for a bronze. Total medals are in parentheses.

		Gold	Silver	Bronze	Pts
1	USA (107)	45	28	34	225
2	USSR (91)	29	32	30	181
3	Hungary (32)	10	10	12	62
4	Japan (25)	11	7	7	54
5	E.Germany (25)	9	9	7	52
6	W.Germany (26)	5	11	10	47
7	Australia (17)	5	7	5	34
8	France (15)	7	3	5	32
9	Poland (18)	5	2	11	30
10	Czechoslovakia (13)	7	2	4	29
	Romania (15)	4	6	5	29

Leading Medal Winners

Number of individual medals won on the left; gold, silver and bronze breakdown to the right.

MEN

No		Sport	G-S-B
7	Mikhail Voronin, USSR	Gymnastics	2-4-1
6	Akinori Nakayama, JPN	Gymnastics	4-1-1
4	Charles Hickcox, USA	Swimming	3-1-0
4	Sawao Kato, JPN	Gymnastics	3-0-1
4	Mark Spitz, USA	Swimming	2-1-1
4	Mike Wenden, AUS	Swimming	2-1-1
3	Roland Matthes, E.Ger.	Swimming	2-1-0
3	Ken Walsh, USA	Swimming	2-1-0
3	Pierre Trentin, FRA	Cycling	2-0-1
3	Vladimir Kosinski, USSR	Swimming	0-2-1
3	Leonid Ilyichev, USSR	Swimming	0-1-2

1968 (Cont.)

WOMEN

No		Sport	G-S-B
6	Vera Čáslavská, CZE	Gymnastics	4-2-0
4	Sue Pedersen, USA	Swimming	2-2-0
4	Natalya Kuchinskaya, USSR	Gymnastics	2-0-2
4	Jan Henne, USA	Swimming	2-1-1
4	Zinaida Voronina, USSR	Gymnastics	1-1-2
3	Debbie Meyer, USA	Swimming	3-0-0
3	Kaye Hall, USA	Swimming	2-0-1
3	Larissa Petrik, USSR	Gymnastics	2-0-1
3	Ellie Daniel, USA	Swimming	1-1-1
3	Linda Gustavson, USA	Swimming	1-1-1
3	Elaine Tanner, CAN	Swimming	0-2-1

Track & Field

MEN

Event		Time	
100m	Jim Hines, USA	9.95	WR
200m	Tommie Smith, USA	19.83	WR
400m	Lee Evans, USA	43.86	WR
800m	Ralph Doubell, AUS	1:44.3	=WR
1500m	Kip Keino, KEN	3:34.9	OR
5000m	Mohamed Gammoudi, TUN	14:05.0	
10,000m	Naftali Temu, KEN	29:27.4	
Marathon	Mamo Wolde, ETH	2:20:26.4	
110m H	Willie Davenport, USA	13.3	OR
400m H	David Hemery, GBR	48.12	WR
3000m Steeple	Amos Biwott, KEN	8:51.0	
20k Walk	Vladimir Golubnichiy, USSR	1:33:58.4	
50k Walk	Christoph Höhne, E.Ger	4:20:13.6	
4x100m	USA (Charlie Greene, Mel Pender, Ronnie Ray Smith, Jim Hines)	38.2	WR
4x400m	USA (Vince Matthews, Ron Freeman, Larry James, Lee Evans)	2:56.16	WR

Event		Mark	
High Jump	Dick Fosbury, USA	7- 4¼	OR
Pole Vault	Bob Seagren, USA	17- 8½	OR
Long Jump	Bob Beamon, USA	29- 2½	WR
Triple Jump	Viktor Saneyev, USSR	57- 0¾	WR
Shot Put	Randy Matson, USA	67- 4¾	
Discus	Al Oerter, USA	212- 6	OR
Hammer	Gyula Zsivóyzky, HUN	240- 8	OR
Javelin	Jānis Lūsis, USSR	295- 7	OR
Decathlon	Bill Toomey, USA	8193 pts	OR

WOMEN

Event		Time	
100m	Wyomia Tyus, USA	11.0	WR
200m	Irena K. Szewińska, POL	22.5	WR
400m	Colette Besson, FRA	52.0	=OR
800m	Madeline Manning, USA	2:00.9	OR
80m H	Maureen Caird, AUS	10.3	OR
4x100m	USA (Barbara Ferrell, Margaret Bailes, Mildrette Netter, Wyomia Tyus)	42.8	WR

Event		Mark	
High Jump	Miloslava Režková, CZE	5-11½	
Long Jump	Viorica Viscopoleanu, ROM	22- 4½	WR
Shot Put	Margitta Gummel, E.Ger	64- 4	WR
Discus	Lia Manoliu, ROM	191- 2	OR
Javelin	Angèla Németh, HUN	198- 0	
Pentathlon	Ingrid Becker, GER	5098 pts	

Boxing

Weight Class	Champion
Lt. Flyweight (106 lbs)	Francisco Rodriquez, VEN
Flyweight (112)	Ricardo Delgado, MEX
Bantamweight (119)	Valery Sokolov, USSR
Featherweight (125)	Antonio Roldan, MEX
Lightweight (132)	Ron Harris, USA

Weight Class	Champion
Lt.Welterweight (139)	Jerzy Kulej, POL
Welterweight (148)	Manfred Wolke, E.Ger
Lt.Middleweight (156)	Boris Lagutin, USSR
Middleweight (165)	Chris Finnegan, GBR
Lt.Heavyweight (178)	Dan Poznyak, USSR
Heavyweight (178+)	George Foreman, USA

Gymnastics

MEN

Individual		Points
All-Around	Sawao Kato, JPN	115.9
Floor	Sawao Kato, JPN	19.475
Horiz.Bar	Akinori Nakayama, JPN & Mikhail Voronin, USSR	19.55

Individual		Points
Paral.Bars	Akinori Nakayama, JPN	19.475
Rings	Akinori Nakayama, JPN	19.45
Side Horse	Miroslav Cerar, YUG	19.325
Vault	Mikhail Voronin, USSR	19.00

Team		Points
All-Around	JPN (Kato, Nakayama, Kenmotsu, Kato, Endo, Tsukahara)	575.90

WOMEN

Individual		Points
All-Around	Vera Čáslavská CZE	78.25
Bal.Beam	Natayla Kuchinskaya, USSR	19.65
Floor	Vera Càslavská, CZE & Larissa Petrik, USSR	19.675
Uneven Bars	Vera Čáslavská, CZE	19.65
Vault	Vera Čáslavská, CZE	19.775

Team		Points
All-Around	USSR (Voronina, Kuchinskaya, Petrik, Karasseva, Tourischeva, Burda)	382.85

Swimming

MEN

Event		Time	
100m Free	Mike Wenden, AUS	52.2	WR
200m Free	Mike Wenden, AUS	1:55.2	OR
400m Free	Mike Burton, USA	4:09.0	OR
1500m Free	Mike Burton, USA	16:38.9	OR
100m Back	Roland Matthes, E.Ger	58.7	WR
200m Back	Roland Matthes, E.Ger	2:09.6	OR
100m Brst	Don McKenzie, USA	1:07.7	OR
200m Brst	Felipe Muñoz, MEX	2:28.7	
100m Fly	Doug Russell, USA	55.9	OR
200m Fly	Carl Robie, USA	2:08.7	
200m I.M.	Charles Hickcox, USA	2:12.0	OR
400m I.M.	Charles Hickcox, USA	4:48.4	
4x100m Free	USA (Zack Zorn, Steve Rerych, Mark Spitz, Ken Walsh)	3:31.7	WR
4x200m Free	USA (John Nelson, Steve Rerych, Mark Spitz, Don Schollander)	7:52.33	
4x100m Mdly	USA (Charles Hickcox, Don McKenzie, Doug Russell, Ken Walsh)	3:54.9	WR

Diving		Points
Platform	Klaus Dibiasi, ITA	164.18
Spring	Bernie Wrightson, USA	170.15

WOMEN

Event		Time	
100m Free	Jan Henne, USA	1:00.0	
200m Free	Debbie Meyer, USA	2:10.5	OR
400m Free	Debbie Meyer, USA	4:31.8	OR
800m Free	Debbie Meyer, USA	9:24.0	OR
100m Back	Kaye Hall, USA	1:06.2	WR
200m Back	Pokey Watson, USA	2:24.8	OR
100m Brst	Djurdjica Bjedov, YUG	1:15.8	OR
200m Brst	Sharon Wichman, USA	2:44.4	OR

Event		Time
100m Fly	Lyn McClements, AUS	1:05.5
200m Fly	Ada Kok, HOL	2:24.7 **OR**
200m I.M.	Claudia Kolb, USA	2:24.7 **OR**
400m I.M.	Claudia Kolb, USA	5:08.5 **OR**
4x100m Free	USA (Jane Barkman, Linda Gustavson, Sue Pedersen, Jan Henne)	4:02.5 **OR**
4x100m Mdly	USA (Kaye Hall, Catie Ball, Ellie Daniel, Sue Pedersen)	4:28.3 **OR**
Diving		**Points**
Platform	Milena Duchková, CZE	109.59
Spring	Sue Gossick, USA	150.77

Team Sports

Men	Champion
Basketball	United States
Field Hockey	Pakistan
Soccer	Hungary
Volleyball	Soviet Union
Water Polo	Yugoslavia
Women	**Champion**
Volleyball	Soviet Union

Also Contested

Canoeing, Cycling, Equestrian, Fencing, Modern Pentathlon, Rowing, Shooting, Weightlifting, Freestyle Wrestling, Greco-Roman Wrestling and Yachting.

1972

Munich

On Sept. 5, with six days left in the Games, Arab terrorists slipped into the Olympic Village, killed two Israeli team members and seized nine others as hostages. Later that night, all nine were killed in a shootout between the terrorists and West German police at a military airport.

The tragedy stunned the world and stopped the XXth Olympiad in its tracks. But after suspending competition for 24 hours and holding a memorial service attended by 80,000, 84-year-old outgoing IOC president Avery Brundage and his committee ordered the Games to continue.

They went on without one of its heroes—swimmer Mark Spitz, who had set an Olympic gold medal record by winning four individual and three relay events, all in world record times. Spitz, an American Jew, was an inviting target for further terrorism and agreed with West German officials when they advised him to leave the country.

The pall that fell over Munich quieted an otherwise boisterous Games that saw American swimmer Rick DeMont stripped of a gold medal for taking asthma medication, track medalists Vince Matthews and Wayne Collett of the U.S. banned for life for fooling around on the victory stand during the American national anthem, and the USA lose an Olympic basketball game for the

first time ever (they were 62-0) when the Russians were given three chances to convert a last-second inbound pass and finally won, 51-50.

Munich was also where 17-year-old Soviet gymnast Olga Korbut and 16-year-old swimmer Shane Gould of Australia won three gold medals each and Britain's 33-year-old Mary Peters won the pentathlon.

Top 10 Standings

National medal standings are not recognized by the IOC. The unofficial point totals are based on 3 points for a gold medal, 2 for a silver and 1 for a bronze. Total medals are in parentheses.

		Gold	Silver	Bronze	Pts
1	USSR (99)	50	27	22	226
2	USA (94)	33	31	30	191
3	E.Germany (66)	20	23	23	129
4	W.Germany (40)	13	11	16	77
5	Japan (29)	13	8	8	63
6	Hungary (35)	6	13	16	60
7	Bulgaria (21)	6	10	5	43
8	Australia (17)	8	7	2	40
	Poland (21)	7	5	9	40
10	Italy (18)	5	3	10	31
	Great Britain (18)	4	5	9	31

Leading Medal Winners

Number of individual medals won on the left; gold, silver and bronze breakdown to the right.

MEN

No		Sport	G-S-B
7	Mark Spitz, USA	Swimming	7-0-0
5	Sawao Kato, JPN	Gymnastics	3-2-0
4	Jerry Heidenreich, USA	Swimming	2-1-1
4	Roland Matthes, E.Ger	Swimming	2-1-1
4	Akinori Nakayama, JPN	Gymnastics	2-1-1
4	Shigeru Kasamatsu, JPN	Gymnastics	1-1-2
4	Eizo Kenmotsu, JPN	Gymnastics	1-1-2
3	Valery Borsov, USSR	Track/Field	2-1-0
3	Mitsuo Tsukahara, JPN	Gymnastics	2-0-1
3	Steve Genter, USA	Swimming	1-2-0
3	Viktor Klimenko, USSR	Gymnastics	1-2-0
3	Mike Stamm, USA	Swimming	1-2-0
3	Vladimir Bure, USSR	Swimming	0-1-2

WOMEN

No		Sport	G-S-B
5	Shane Gould, AUS	Swimming	3-1-1
5	Karin Janz, E.Ger	Gymnastics	2-2-1
4	Olga Korbut, USSR	Gymnastics	3-1-0
4	Lyudmila Tourischeva, USSR	Gymnastics	2-1-1
4	Tamara Lazakovitch, USSR	Gymnastics	1-1-2

Track & Field
MEN

Event		Time	
100m	Valery Borzov, USSR	10.14	
200m	Valery Borzov, USSR	20.00	
400m	Vince Matthews, USA	44.66	
800m	Dave Wottle, USA	1:45.9	
1500m	Pekka Vasala, FIN	3:36.3	
5000m	Lasse Viren, FIN	13:26.4	**OR**
10,000m	Lasse Viren, FIN	27:38.4	**WR**
Marathon	Frank Shorter, USA	2:12:19.8	
110m H	Rod Milburn, USA	13.24	**=WR**
400m H	John Akii-Bua, UGA	47.82	**WR**
3000m Steeple	Kip Keino, KEN	8:23.6	**OR**

1972 (Cont.)

Event		Time	
20k Walk	Peter Frenkel, E.Ger	1:26:42.4	OR
50k Walk	Bernd Kannenberg, W.Ger . . .	3:56:11.6	OR
4x100m	USA (Larry Black, Robert Taylor, Gerald Tinker, Eddie Hart)	38.19	=WR
4x400m	KEN (Charles Asati, Hezaklah Nyamau, Robert Ouko, Julius Sang)	2:59.8	

Event		Mark	
High Jump	Yuri Tarmak, USSR	7- 3¾	
Pole Vault	Wolfgang Nordwig, E.Ger.	18- 0½	OR
Long Jump	Randy Williams, USA	27- 0½	
Triple Jump	Viktor Saneyev, USSR	56-11¼	
Shot Put	Wladyslaw Komar, POL	69- 6	OR
Discus	Ludvik Daněk, CZE	211- 3	
Hammer	Anatoly Bondarchuk, USSR . . .	247- 8	OR
Javelin	Klaus Wolfermann, W.Ger . . .	296-10	OR
Decathlon	Nikolai Avilov, USSR	8454 pts	WR

WOMEN

Event		Time	
100m	Renate Stecher, E.Ger	11.07	
200m	Renate Stecher, E.Ger	22.40	=WR
400m	Monika Zehrt, E.Ger	51.08	OR
800m	Hildegard Falck, W.Ger	1:58.55	OR
1500m	Lyudmila Bragina, USSR	4:01.4	WR
100m H	Annelie Ehrhardt, E.Ger	12.59	WR
4x100m	W.Ger.(Christiane Krause, Ingrid Mickler, Annegret Richter, Heidemarie Rosendahl)	42.81	=WR
4x400m	E.Ger.(Dägmar Käsling, Rita Kühne, Helga Seidler, Monika Zehrt) . .	3:23.0	WR

Event		Mark	
High Jump	Ulrike Meyfarth, W.Ger	6- 3½	=WR
Long Jump	Heidemarie Rosendahl, W.Ger . .	22- 3	
Shot Put	Nadezhda Chizhova, USSR	69- 0	WR
Discus	Faina Melnik, USSR	218- 7	OR
Javelin	Ruth Fuchs, E.Ger	209- 7	OR
Pentathlon	Mary Peters, GBR	4801 pts	WR

Boxing

Weight Class	Champion
Lt.Flyweight (106 lbs)	György Gedö, HUN
Flyweight (112)	Georgi Kostadinov, BUL
Bantamweight (119)	Orlando Martinez, CUB
Featherweight (125)	Boris Kousnetsov, USSR
Lightweight (132)	Jan Szczepanski, POL
Lt.Welterweight (139)	Sugar Ray Seales, USA
Welterweight (148)	Emilio Correa, CUB
Lt.Middleweight (156)	Dieter Kottysch, W.Ger
Middleweight (165)	Vyacheslav Lemechev, USSR
Lt.Heavyweight (178)	Mate Parlov, YUG
Heavyweight (178+)	Teófilo Stevenson, CUB

Gymnastics

MEN

Individual		Points
All-Around	Sawao Kato, JPN	114.650
Floor	Nikolai Andrianov, USSR	19.175
Horiz.Bar	Mitsuo Tsukahara, JPN	19.725
Paral.Bars	Sawao Kato, JPN	19.475
Rings	Akinori Nakayama, JPN	19.35
Side Horse	Viktor Klimenko, USSR	19.125
Vault	Klaus Köste, E.Ger	18.85

Team		Points
All-Around	JPN (Kato, Kenmotsu, Kasamatsu, Nakayama, Tsukahara, Okamura)	571.25

WOMEN

Individual		Points
All-Around	Lyudmila Tourischeva, USSR	77.025
Bal.Beam	Olga Korbut, USSR	19.40

WOMEN

Individual		Points
Floor	Olga Korbut, USSR	19.575
Uneven Bars	Karin Janz, E.Ger	19.675
Vault	Karin Janz, E.Ger	19.525

Team		Points
All-Around	USSR (Tourischeva, Korbut, Lazakovitch, Burda, Saadi, Koshel)	380.50

Swimming

MEN

Event		Time	
100m Free	Mark Spitz, USA	51.22	WR
200m Free	Mark Spitz, USA	1:52.78	WR
400m Free	Brad Cooper, USA	4:00.27	OR
1500m Free	Mike Burton, USA	15:52.58	WR
100m Back	Roland Matthes, E.Ger	56.58	OR
200m Back	Roland Matthes, E.Ger	2:02.82	= WR
100m Brst	Nobutaka Taguchi, JPN . . .	1:04.94	WR
200m Brst	John Hencken, USA	2:21.55	WR
100m Fly	Mark Spitz, USA	54.27	WR
200m Fly	Mark Spitz, USA	2:00.70	WR
200m I.M.	Gunnar Larsson, SWE	2:07.17	WR
400m I.M.	Gunnar Larsson, SWE	4:31.98	OR
4x100m Free	USA (Dave Edgar, John Murphy, Jerry Heidenreich, Mark Spitz)	3:26.42	WR
4x200m Free	USA (John Kinsella, Fred Tyler, Steve Genter, Mark Spitz)	7:35.78	WR
4x100m Mdly	USA (Mike Stamm, Tom Bruce, Mark Spitz, Jerry Heidenreich)	3:48.16	WR

Diving		Points
Platform	Klaus Dibiasi, ITA	504.12
Spring	Vladimir Vasin, USSR	594.09

WOMEN

Event		Time	
100m Free	Sandra Neilson, USA	58.59	WR
200m Free	Shane Gould, AUS	2:03.56	WR
400m Free	Shane Gould, AUS	4:19.44	WR
800m Free	Keena Rothhammer, USA . . .	8:53.68	WR
100m Back	Melissa Belote, USA	1:05.78	OR
200m Back	Melissa Belote, USA	2:19.19	WR
100m Brst	Cathy Carr, USA	1:13.58	WR
200m Brst	Beverly Whitfield, AUS	2:41.71	OR
100m Fly	Mayumi Aoki, JPN	1:03.34	WR
200m Fly	Karen Moe, USA	2:15.57	WR
200m I.M.	Shane Gould, AUS	2:23.07	WR
400m I.M.	Gail Neall, AUS	5:02.97	WR
4x100m Free	USA (Sandra Neilson, Jennifer Kemp, Jane Barkman, Shirley Babashoff)	3:55.19	WR
4x100m Mdly	USA (Melissa Belote, Cathy Carr, Deena Deardurff, Sandra Neilson)	4:20.75	WR

Diving		Points
Platform	Ulrika Knape, SWE	390.00
Spring	Micki King, USA	450.03

Team Sports

Men	Champion
Basketball	Soviet Union
Field Hockey	West Germany
Handball	Yugoslavia
Soccer	Poland
Volleyball	Japan
Water Polo	Soviet Union

Women	Champion
Volleyball	Soviet Union

Also Contested

Archery, Canoeing, Cycling, Equestrian, Fencing, Judo, Modern Pentathlon, Rowing, Shooting, Weightlifting, Free-style Wrestling, Greco-Roman Wrestling and Yachting.

1976

CANADA
1976

Montreal

In 1970, when Montreal was named to host the Summer Olympics '76, organizers estimated it would cost $310 million to stage the Games. However, due to political corruption, mismanagement, labor disputes, inflation and a $100 million outlay for security to prevent another Munich, the final bill came to more than $1.5 billion.

Then, right before the Games were scheduled to open in July, 32 nations, most of them from black Africa, walked out when the IOC refused to ban New Zealand because its national rugby team was touring racially-segregated South Africa. Taiwan also withdrew when Communist China pressured trading partner Canada to deny the Taiwanese the right to compete as the Republic of China.

When the Games finally got started they were quickly stolen by 14-year-old Romanian gymnast Nadia Comaneci, who scored seven perfect 10s on her way to three gold medals.

East Germany's Kornelia Ender did Comaneci one better, winning four times as the GDR captured 11 of 13 events in women's swimming. John Naber (4 gold) and the U.S. men did the East German women one better when they won 12 of 13 in swimming.

In track and field, Cuba's Alberto Juantorena won the 400- and 800-meter runs, and Finland's Lasse Viren took the 5,000 and 10,000. Viren missed a third gold when he placed fifth in the marathon.

Four Americans who became household names during the Games were decathlon winner Bruce Jenner and three future world boxing champions—Ray Leonard and the Spinks brothers, Michael and Leon.

Top 10 Standings

National medal standings are not recognized by the IOC. The unofficial point totals are based on 3 points for a gold medal, 2 for a silver and 1 for a bronze. Total medals are in parentheses.

	Gold	Silver	Bronze	Pts
1 USSR (125)	49	41	35	264
2 USA (94)	34	35	25	197
3 E.Germany (90)	40	25	25	195
4 W.Germany (39)	10	12	17	71
5 Japan (25)	9	6	10	49
6 Poland (26)	7	6	13	46
7 Romania (27)	4	9	14	44
8 Bulgaria (22)	6	9	7	43
9 Cuba (13)	6	4	3	29
10 Hungary (22)	4	5	13	35

Leading Medal Winners

Number of individual medals won on the left; gold, silver and bronze breakdown to the right.

MEN

No		Sport	G-S-B
7	Nikolai Andrianov, USSR	Gymnastics	4-2-1
5	John Naber, USA	Swimming	4-1-0
5	Mitsuo Tsukahara, JPN	Gymnastics	2-1-2
4	Jim Montgomery, USA	Swimming	3-0-1
3	John Hencken, USA	Swimming	2-1-0
3	Sawao Kato, JPN	Gymnastics	2-1-0
3	Eizo Kenmotsu, JPN	Gymnastics	1-2-0
3	Rüdiger Helm, E.Ger.	Canoeing	1-0-2

WOMEN

No		Sport	G-S-B
5	Kornelia Ender, E.Ger	Swimming	4-1-0
5	Nadia Comaneci, ROM.	Gymnastics	3-1-1
5	Shirley Babashoff, USA	Swimming	1-4-0
4	Nelli Kim, USSR	Gymnastics	3-1-0
4	Andrea Pollack, E.Ger	Swimming	2-2-0
4	Lyudmila Touristcheva, USSR	Gymnastics	1-2-1
3	Ulrike Richter, E.Ger.	Swimming	3-0-0
3	Annagret Richter, W.Ger	Track/Field	1-2-0
3	Renate Stecher, E.Ger.	Track/Field	1-1-1
3	Teodora Ungureanu, USSR	Gymnastics	0-2-1

Track & Field

MEN

Event		Time	
100m	Hasely Crawford, TRI	10.06	
200m	Donald Quarrie, JAM	20.23	
400m	Alberto Juantorena, CUB	44.26	
800m	Alberto Juantorena, CUB	1:43.50	WR
1500m	John Walker, NZE	3:39.17	
5000m	Lasse Viren, FIN	13:24.76	
10,000m	Lasse Viren, FIN	27:40.38	
Marathon	Waldemar Cierpinski, E. Ger	2:09:55.0	OR
110m H	Guy Drut,FRA	13.30	
400m H	Edwin Moses, USA	47.64	WR
3000m Steeple	Anders Gärdeud, SWE	8:08.2	WR
20k Walk	Daniel Bautista, MEX	1:24:40.6	OR
4x100m	USA (Harvey Glance, Johnny Jones, Millard Hampton, Steve Riddick)	38.33	
4x400m	USA (Herman Frazier, Benjamin Brown, Fred Newhouse, Maxie Parks)	2:58.65	

Event		Mark	
High Jump	Jacek Wszola, POL	7- 4½	OR
Pole Vault	Tadeusz Ślusarski, POL	18- 0½	=OR
Long Jump	Arnie Robinson, USA	27- 4¾	
Triple Jump	Viktor Saneyev, USSR	56- 8¾	
Shot Put	Udo Beyer, E.Ger.	69- 0¾	
Discus	Mac Wilkins, USA	221- 5	
Hammer	Yuri Sedykh, USSR	254- 4	OR
Javelin	Miklos Németh, HUN	310- 4	WR
Decathlon	Bruce Jenner, USA	8617 pts	WR

WOMEN

Event		Time	
100m	Annegret Richter, W.Ger	11.08	
200m	Bärbel Eckert, E.Ger	22.37	OR
400m	Irena K.Szewińska, POL	49.29	WR
800m	Tatyana Kazankina, USSR	1:54.94	WR
1500m	Tatyana Kazankina, USSR	4:05.48	
100m H	Johanna Schaller, E.Ger	12.77	

1976 (Cont.)

Event		Time
4x100m	E.Ger.(Marlies Oelsner, Renate Stecher, Carla Bodendorf, Bärbel Eckert)	42.55 OR
4x400m	E.Ger.(Doris Maletzki, Brigitte Rohde, Ellen Streidt, Christina Brehmer)	3:19.23 WR

Event		Mark
High Jump	Rosemarie Ackermann, E.Ger	6- 4 OR
Long Jump	Angela Voigt, E.Ger	22- 0¾
Shot Put	Ivanka Hristova, BUL	69- 5¼ OR
Discus	Evelin Schlaak, E.Ger	226- 4 OR
Javelin	Ruth Fuchs, E.Ger	216- 4 OR
Pentathlon	Siegrun Siegl, E.Ger	4745 pts

Boxing

Weight Class	Champion
Lt.Flyweight (106 lbs)	Jorge Hernandez, CUB
Flyweight (112)	Leo Randolph, USA
Bantamweight (119)	Yong-Jo Gu, N.Kor
Featherweight (125)	Angel Herrera, CUB
Lightweight (132)	Howard Davis, USA
Lt.Welterweight (139)	Sugar Ray Leonard, USA
Welterweight (148)	Jochen Bachfeld, E.Ger
Lt.Middleweight (156)	Jerzy Rybicki, POL
Middleweight (165)	Michael Spinks, USA
Lt.Heavyweight (178)	Leon Spinks, USA
Heavyweight (178+)	Teófilo Stevenson, CUB

Gymnastics

MEN

Individual		Points
All-Around	Nikolai Andrianov, USSR	116.65
Floor	Nikolai Andrianov, USSR	19.45
Horiz.Bar	Mitsuo Tsukahara, JPN	19.675
Paral.Bars	Sawao Kato, JPN	19.675
Rings	Nikolai Andrianov, USSR	19.65
Side Horse	Zoltàn Magyar, HUN	19.70
Vault	Nikolai Andrianov, USSR	19.45

Team		Points
All-Around	JPN (Kato, Tsukahara, Kajiyama, Kenmotsu, Igarashi, Fujimoto)	576.85

WOMEN

Individual		Points
All-Around	Nadia Comaneci, ROM	79.275
Bal.Beam	Nadia Comaneci, ROM	19.95
Floor	Nelli Kim, USSR	19.85
Uneven Bars	Nadia Comaneci, ROM	20.00
Vault	Nelli Kim, USSR	19.80

Team		Points
All-Around	USSR (Kim, Tourischeva, Korbut, Saadi, Filatova, Grozdova)	466.00

Swimming

MEN

Event		Time
100m Free	Jim Montgomery, USA	49.99 WR
200m Free	Bruce Furniss, USA	1:50.29 WR
400m Free	Brian Goodell, USA	3:51.93 WR
1500m Free	Brian Goodell, USA	15:02.40 WR
100m Back	John Naber, USA	55.49 WR
200m Back	John Naber, USA	1:59.19 WR
100m Brst	John Hencken, USA	1:03.11 WR
200m Brst	David Wilkie, GBR	2:15.11 WR
100m Fly	Matt Vogel, USA	54.35
200m Fly	Mike Bruner, USA	1:59.23 WR
400m I.M.	Rod Strachan, USA	4:23.68 WR
4x200m Free	USA (Mike Bruner, Bruce Furniss, John Naber, Jim Montgomery)	7:23.22 WR

Event		Time
4x100m Mdly	USA (John Naber, John Hencken, Matt Vogel, Jim Montgomery)	3:42.22 WR

Diving		Points
Platform	Klaus Dibiasi, ITA	600.51
Spring	Phil Boggs, USA	619.05

WOMEN

Event		Time	
100m Free	Kornelia Ender, E.Ger	55.65	WR
200m Free	Kornelia Ender, E.Ger	1:59.26	WR
400m Free	Petra Thümer, E.Ger	4:09.89	WR
800m Free	Petra Thümer, E.Ger	8:37.14	WR
100m Back	Ulrike Richter, E.Ger	1:01.83	OR
200m Back	Ulrike Richter, E.Ger	2:13.43	OR
100m Brst	Hannelore Anke, E.Ger	1:11.16	
200m Brst	Marina Koshevaia, USSR	2:33.35	WR
100m Fly	Kornelia Ender, E.Ger	1:00.13	=WR
200m Fly	Andrea Pollack, E.Ger	2:11.41	OR
400m I.M.	Ulrike Tauber, E.Ger	4:42.77	WR
4x100m Free	USA (Kim Peyton, Wendy Boglioli, Jill Sterkel, Shirley Babashoff)	3:44.82	WR
4x100m Mdly	GDR (Ulrike Richter, Hannelore Anke, Andrea Pollack, Kornelia Ender)	4:07.95	WR

Diving		Points
Platform	Elena Vaytsekhosvkaya, USSR	406.59
Spring	Jennifer Chandler, USA	506.19

Team Sports

Men	Champion
Basketball	United States
Field Hockey	New Zealand
Handball	Soviet Union
Soccer	East Germany
Volleyball	Poland
Water Polo	Hungary

Women	Champion
Basketball	Soviet Union
Handball	Soviet Union
Volleyball	Japan

Also Contested

Archery, Canoeing, Cycling, Equestrian, Fencing, Judo, Modern Pentathlon, Rowing, Shooting, Weightlifting, Freestyle Wrestling, Greco-Roman Wrestling and Yachting.

OLYMPIAD 80
MOSCOW MOCKBA MOCKBA

1980

Moscow

Four years after 32 nations walked out of the Montreal Games, twice that many chose to stay away from Moscow—many in support of an American-led boycott to protest the December, 1979, Russian invasion of Afghanistan.

Unable to persuade the IOC to cancel or move the Summer Games, U.S. President Jimmy Carter pressured the USOC to officially withdraw in April. Many western governments, like West Germany and Japan, followed suit and withheld their athletes. But others, like Britain and France, while supporting the boycott, allowed their Olympic committees to participate if they wished.

The first Games to be held in a Communist country opened in July with 81 nations in attendance and were dominated by the USSR and East Germany. They were also plagued by charges of rigged judging and poor sportsmanship by Moscow fans who, without the Americans around, booed the Poles and East Germans unmercifully.

Otherwise, Soviet gymnast Aleksandr Dityatin became the first athlete to win eight medals in one year; the belle of Montreal, Nadia Comaneci of Romania, returned to win two more gold medals; Cuban heavyweight Teofilo Stevenson became the first boxer to win three golds in the same weight division; and Britons Sebastian Coe and Steve Ovett split the 800 and 1,500 meters.

Top 10 Standings

National medal standings are not recognized by the IOC. The unofficial point totals are based on 3 points for a gold medal, 2 for a silver and 1 for a bronze. Total medals are in parentheses.

	Gold	Silver	Bronze	Pts
1 USSR (195)...........	80	69	46	424
2 E.Germany (126).......	47	37	42	257
3 Bulgaria (41)...........	8	16	17	73
4 Hungary (32)...........	7	10	15	56
5 Poland (32)............	3	14	15	52
6 Cuba (20).............	8	7	5	43
Romania (25).........	6	6	13	43
8 Great Britain (21)......	5	7	9	38
9 Italy (15).............	8	3	4	34
10 France (14)..........	6	5	3	31

Leading Medal Winners

Number of individual medals won on the left; gold, silver and bronze breakdown to the right.

MEN

No		Sport	G-S-B
8	Aleksandr Dityatin, USSR........	Gymnastics	3-4-1
5	Nikolai Andrianov, USSR........	Gymnastics	2-2-1
4	Roland Brückner, E.Ger........	Gymnastics	1-1-2
3	Vladimir Parfenovich, USSR.......	Canoeing	3-0-0
3	Vladimir Salnikov, USSR........	Swimming	3-0-0
3	Sergei Kopliakov, USSR.........	Swimming	2-1-0
3	Aleksandr Tkachyov, USSR......	Gymnastics	2-1-0
3	Andrei Krylov, USSR...........	Swimming	1-2-0
3	Arsen Miskarov, USSR..........	Swimming	0-2-1

WOMEN

No		Sport	G-S-B
5	Ines Diers, E.Ger.............	Swimming	2-2-1
4	Caren Metschuck, E.Ger........	Swimming	3-1-0
4	Nadia Comaneci, ROM........	Gymnastics	2-2-0
4	Natalya Shaposhnikova, USSR....	Gymnastics	2-0-2
4	Maxi Gnauck, E.Ger...........	Gymnastics	1-1-2
3	Barbara Krause, E.Ger.........	Swimming	3-0-0
3	Rica Reinisch, E.Ger...........	Swimming	3-0-0
3	Yelena Davydova, USSR........	Gymnastics	2-1-0
3	Steffi Kraker, E.Ger...........	Gymnastics	0-1-2
3	Melita Ruhn, ROM............	Gymnastics	0-1-2

Track & Field

MEN

Event		Time
100m	Allan Wells, GBR...............	10.25
200m	Pietro Mennea, ITA..............	20.19
400m	Viktor Markin, USSR.............	44.60
800m	Steve Ovett, GBR..............	1:45.4
1500m	Sebastian Coe, GBR..........	3:38.4
5000m	Miruts Yifter, ETH.............	13:21.0
10,000m	Miruts Yifter, ETH.............	27:42.7
Marathon	Waldemar Cierpinski, E.Ger .	2:11:03.0
110m H	Thomas Munkelt, E.Ger..........	13.39
400m H	Volker Beck, E.Ger..............	48.70
3000m Steeple	Bronislaw Malinowski, POL......	8:09.7
20k Walk	Maurizio Damilano, ITA......	1:23:35.5 OR
50k Walk	Hartwig Gauder, E.Ger......	3:49:24.0
4x100m	USSR (Vladimir Muravyov, Nikolai Sidorov, Aleksandr Aksinin, Andrei Prokofiev)............	38.26
4x400m	USSR (Remigius Valiulis, Mikhail Linge, Nikolai Chernetsky, Viktor Markin)................	3:01.1

Event		Mark	
High Jump	Gerd Wessig, E.Ger...........	7- 8¾	WR
Pole Vault	Wladyslaw Kozakiewicz, POL ..	18-11½	WR
Long Jump	Lutz Dombrowski, E.Ger......	28- 0¼	
Triple Jump	Jaak Uudmäe, USSR........	56-11¼	
Shot Put	Vladimir Kiselyov, USSR.......	70- 0½	OR
Discus	Viktor Rashchupkin, USSR ...	218- 8	
Hammer	Yuri Sedykh, USSR..........	268- 4	WR
Javelin	Dainis Kula, USSR.........	299- 2	
Decathlon	Daley Thompson, GBR.....	8495 pts	

WOMEN

Event		Time	
100m	Lyudmila Kondratyeva, USSR......	11.06	
200m	Bärbel E.Wöckel, E.Ger...........	22.03	OR
400m	Marita Koch, E.Ger.............	48.88	OR
800m	Nadezhda Olizarenko, USSR....	1:53.42	WR
1500m	Tatyana Kazankina, USSR.......	3:56.6	OR
100m H	Vera Komisova, USSR............	12.56	OR
4x100m	E.Ger.(Romy Müller, Bärbel E. Wöckel, Ingrid Auerswald, Marlies O.Göhr)................	41.60	WR
4x400m	USSR (Tatyana Prororchenko, Tatyana Goistchik, Nina Zyuskova, Irina Nazarova)...............	3:20.2	

Event		Mark	
High Jump	Sara Simeoni, ITA..............	6- 5½	OR
Long Jump	Tatiana Kolpakova, USSR.....	23- 2	OR
Shot Put	Ilona Slupianke, E.Ger........	73- 6¼	
Discus	Evelin S.Jahl, E.Ger..........	229- 6	OR
Javelin	Maria Colon, CUB..........	224- 5	OR
Pentathlon	Nadezhda Tkachenko, USSR .	5083 pts	WR

Boxing

Weight Class	Champion
Lt.Flyweight (106 lbs)...............	Shamil Sabyrov, USSR
Flyweight (112).........................	Peter Lessov, BUL
Bantamweight (119)...............	Juan Hernandez, CUB
Featherweight (125).................	Rudi Fink, E.Ger
Lightweight (132).................	Angel Herrera, CUB
Lt.Welterweight (139)..................	Patrizio Oliva, ITA
Welterweight (148)	Andrés Aldama, CUB
Lt.Middleweight (156)......	Armando Martinez, CUB
Middleweight (165).................	José Gomez, CUB
Lt.Heavyweight (178)......	Slobodan Kacar, YUG
Heavyweight (178+)	Teófilo Stevenson, CUB

1980 (Cont.)
Gymnastics
MEN

Individual		Points
All-Around	Aleksandr Dityatin, USSR	118.65
Floor	Roland Brückner, E.Ger.	19.75
Horiz.Bar	Stoyan Deltchev, BUL.	19.825
Paral.Bars	Aleksandr Tkachyov, USSR	19.775
Rings	Aleksandr Dityatin, USSR.	19.875
Side Horse	Zoltán Magyar, HUN.	19.925
Vault	Nikolai Andrianov, USSR.	19.825

Team		Points
All-Around	USSR (Dityatin, Andrianov, Azaryan, Tkachyov, Makuts, Markelov)	598.60

WOMEN

Individual		Points
All-Around	Yelena Davydova, USSR	79.15
Bal.Beam	Nadia Comaneci, ROM	19.80
Floor	Nadia Comaneci, ROM & Nelli Kim, USSR	19.875
Uneven Bars	Maxi Gnauk, E.Ger	19.875
Vault	Natalya Shaposhnikova, USSR	19.725

Team		Points
All-Around	USSR (Shaposhnikova, Davydova, Kim, Filatova, Zakharova, Naimuschina)	394.90

Swimming
MEN

Event		Time	
100m Free	Jörg Woithe, E.Ger	50.40	
200m Free	Sergei Kopliakov, USSR	1:49.91	OR
400m Free	Vladimir Salnikov, USSR	3:51.31	OR
1500m Free	Vladimir Salnikov, USSR	14:58.27	WR
100m Back	Bengt Baron, SWE	56.33	
200m Back	Sándor Wladár, HUN	2:01.93	
100m Brst	Duncan Goodhew, GBR	1:03.44	
200m Brst	Robertas Zhulpa, USSR	2:15.85	
100m Fly	Pär Arvidsson, SWE	54.92	
200m Fly	Sergei Fesenko, USSR	1:59.76	
400m I.M.	Aleksandr Sidorenko, USSR	4:22.89	OR
4x200m Free	USSR (Sergei Kopliakov, Vladimir Salnikov, Ivar Stukolkin, Andrei Krylov)	7:23.50	
4x100m Mdly	AUS (Mark Kerry, Peter Evans, Mark Tonelli, Neil Brooks)	3:45.70	

Diving		Points
Platform	Falk Hoffmann, E.Ger	835.650
Spring	Aleksandr Portnov, USSR	905.025

WOMEN

Event		Time	
100m Free	Barbara Krause, E.Ger	54.79	WR
200m Free	Barbara Krause, E.Ger	1:58.33	OR
400m Free	Ines Diers, E.Ger	4:08.76	OR
800m Free	Michelle Ford, AUS	8:28.90	OR
100m Back	Rica Reinisch, E.Ger	1:00.86	WR
200m Back	Rica Reinisch, E.Ger	2:11.77	WR
100m Brst	Ute Geweniger, E.Ger	1:10.22	
200m Brst	Lina Kačiušytė, USSR	2:29.54	OR
100m Fly	Caren Metschuck, E.Ger	1:00.42	
200m Fly	Ines Geissler, E.Ger	2:10.44	OR
400m I.M.	Petra Schneider, E.Ger	4:36.29	WR
4x100m Free	E.Ger.(Barbara Krause, Caren Metschuck, Ines Diers, Sarina Hülsenbeck)	3:42.71	WR
4x100m Mdly	E.Ger.(Rica Reinisch, Ute Geweniger, Andrea Pollack, Caren Metschuck)	4:06.67	WR

Diving		Points
Platform	Martina Jäschke, E.Ger	596.250
Spring	Irina Kalinina, USSR	725.910

Team Sports

Men	Champion
Basketball	Yugoslavia
Field Hockey	India
Handball	East Germany
Soccer	Czechoslovakia
Volleyball	Soviet Union
Water Polo	Soviet Union

Women	Champion
Basketball	Soviet Union
Field Hockey	Zimbabwe
Handball	Soviet Union
Volleyball	Soviet Union

Also Contested
Archery, Canoeing, Cycling, Equestrian, Fencing, Judo, Modern Pentathlon, Rowing, Shooting, Weightlifting, Freestyle Wrestling, Greco-Roman Wrestling and Yachting.

1984
Los Angeles

For the third consecutive Olympiad, a boycott prevented all member nations from attending the Summer Games. This time, the Soviet Union and 13 Communist allies stayed home in an obvious payback for the West's snub of Moscow in 1980. Romania was the only Warsaw Pact country to come to L.A.

While a record 141 nations did show up, the level of competition was hardly what it might have been had the Soviets and East Germans made the trip. As a result, the United States won a record 83 gold medals in the most lopsided Summer Games since St. Louis 80 years before.

The American gold rush was led by 23-year-old Carl Lewis, who duplicated Jesse Owens' 1936 track and field grand slam by winning the 100 and 200 meters and the long jump, and anchoring the 400-meter relay. Teammate Valerie Brisco-Hooks won three times, taking the 200, 400 and 1,600 relay.

Sebastian Coe of Britain became the first repeat winner of the 1,500 meters since Jim Lightbody of the U.S. in 1906. Other repeaters were Briton Daley Thompson in the decathlon and U.S. hurdler Edwin Moses, who won in 1976 but was not allowed to defend his title in '80.

Romanian gymnast Ecaterina Szabó matched Lewis' four gold medals and added a silver, but the darling of the Games was little (4-foot-8¾), 16-year-old Mary Lou Retton, who won the women's All-Around with a pair of 10s in her last two events.

The L.A. Olympics were the first privately financed Games ever and made an unheard of profit of $215 million. *Time* magazine was so impressed it made Organizing president Peter Ueberroth its Man of the Year.

Top 10 Standings

National medal standings are not recognized by the IOC. The unofficial point totals are based on 3 points for a gold medal, 2 for a silver and 1 for a bronze. Total medals are in parentheses.

		Gold	Silver	Bronze	Pts
1	USA (174)	83	61	30	401
2	W.Germany (59)	17	19	23	112
3	Romania (53)	20	16	17	109
4	Canada (44)	10	18	16	82
5	China (32)	15	8	9	70
6	Italy (32)	14	6	12	66
7	Japan (32)	10	8	14	60
8	Great Britain (37)	5	10	22	57
9	France (27)	5	7	15	45
10	Australia (24)	5	2	6	40

Leading Medal Winners

Number of individual medals won on the left; gold, silver and bronze breakdown to the right.

MEN

No		Sport	G-S-B
6	Li Ning, CHN	Gymnastics	3-2-1
5	Koji Gushiken, JPN	Gymnastics	2-1-2
4	Carl Lewis, USA	Track/Field	4-0-0
4	Michael Gross, W.Ger	Swimming	2-2-0
4	Mitch Gaylord, USA	Gymnastics	1-1-2
3	Rick Carey, USA	Swimming	3-0-0
3	Ian Ferguson, NZE	Canoeing	3-0-0
3	Rowdy Gaines, USA	Swimming	3-0-0
3	Mike Heath, USA	Swimming	2-1-0
3	Peter Vidmar, USA	Gymnastics	2-1-0
3	Victor Davis, CAN	Swimming	1-2-0
3	Pablo Morales, USA	Swimming	1-2-0
3	Lou Yun, CHN	Gymnastics	1-2-0
3	Shinji Morisue, JPN	Gymnastics	1-1-1
3	Lars-Erik Moberg, SWE	Canoeing	0-3-0
3	Mark Stockwell, AUS	Swimming	0-2-1

WOMEN

No		Sport	G-S-B
5	Ecaterina Szabó, ROM	Gymnastics	4-1-0
5	Mary Lou Retton, USA	Gymnastics	1-2-2
4	Nancy Hogshead, USA	Swimming	3-1-0
3	Valerie Brisco-Hooks, USA	Track/Field	3-0-0
3	Tracy Caulkins, USA	Swimming	3-0-0
3	Mary T.Meagher, USA	Swimming	3-0-0
3	Agneta Andersson, SWE	Canoeing	2-1-0
3	Chandra Cheeseborough, USA	Track/Field	2-1-0
3	Simona Pauca, ROM	Gymnastics	2-0-1
3	Julie McNamara, USA	Gymnastics	1-2-0
3	Anne Ottenbrite, CAN	Swimming	1-1-1
3	Karin Seick, W.Ger	Swimming	0-1-2
3	Annemarie Verstappen, HOL	Swimming	0-1-2

Track & Field

MEN

Event		Time	
100m	Carl Lewis, USA	9.99	
200m	Carl Lewis, USA	19.80	OR
400m	Alonzo Babers, USA	44.27	
800m	Joaquim Cruz, BRA	1:43.00	OR
1500m	Sebastian Coe, GBR	3:32.53	OR
5000m	Said Aouita, MOR	13:05.59	OR
10,000m	Alberto Cova, ITA	27:47.54	
Marathon	Carlos Lopes, POR	2:09:21.0	OR
110m H	Roger Kingdom, USA	13.20	OR
400m H	Edwin Moses, USA	47.75	
3000m Steeple	Julius Korir, KEN	8:11.80	

Event		Time	
20k Walk	Ernesto Canto, MEX	1:23:13.0	OR
50k Walk	Raúl González, MEX	3:47:26.0	OR
4x100m	USA (Sam Graddy, Ron Brown, Calvin Smith, Carl Lewis)	37.83	WR
4x400m	USA (Sunder Nix, Ray Armstead, Alonzo Babers, Antonio McKay)	2:57.91	

Event		Mark	
High Jump	Dietmar Mögenburg, W.Ger	7- 8½	
Pole Vault	Pierre Quinon, FRA	18-10¼	
Long Jump	Carl Lewis, USA	28- 0¼	
Triple Jump	Al Joyner, USA	56- 7½	
Shot Put	Alessandro Andrei, ITA	69- 9	
Discus	Rolf Danneberg, W.Ger	218- 6	
Hammer	Juha Tiainen, FIN	256- 2	
Javelin	Arto Härkönen, FIN	284- 8	
Decathlon	Daley Thompson, GBR	8798 pts	=WR

WOMEN

Event		Time	
100m	Evelyn Ashford, USA	10.97	OR
200m	Valerie Brisco-Hooks, USA	21.81	OR
400m	Valerie Brisco-Hooks, USA	48.83	OR
800m	Doina Melinte, ROM	1:57.60	
1500m	Gabriella Dorio, ITA	4:03.25	
3000m	Maricica Puică, ROM	8:35.96	OR
Marathon	Joan Benoit, USA	2:24.52	
100m H	Benita Fitzgerald-Brown, USA	12.84	
400m H	Nawal El Moutawakel, MOR	54.61	OR
4x100m	USA (Alice Brown, Jeanette Bolden, Chandra Cheeseborough, Evelyn Ashford)	41.65	
4x400m	USA (Lillie Leatherwood, Sherri Howard, Valerie Brisco-Hooks, Chandra Cheeseborough)	3:18.29	OR

Event		Mark	
High Jump	Ulrike Meyfarth, W.Ger	6- 7½	OR
Long Jump	Anişoara Stanciu, ROM	22-10	
Shot Put	Claudia Losch, W.Ger	67- 2¼	
Discus	Ria Stalman, HOL	214- 5	
Javelin	Tessa Sanderson, GBR	228- 2	OR
Heptathlon	Glynis Nunn, AUS	6390 pts	OR

Boxing

Weight Class	Champion
Lt.Flyweight (106 lbs)	Paul Gonzales, USA
Flyweight (112)	Steve McCrory, USA
Bantamweight (119)	Maurizio Stecca, ITA
Featherweight (125)	Meldrick Taylor, USA
Lightweight (132)	Pernell Whitaker, USA
Lt.Welterweight (139)	Jerry Page, USA
Welterweight (148)	Mark Breland, USA
Lt.Middleweight (156)	Frank Tate, USA
Middleweight (165)	Joon-Sup Shin, S.Kor
Lt.Heavyweight (178)	Anton Josipovic, YUG
Heavyweight (200)	Henry Tillman, USA
Super Heavyweight (200+)	Tyrell Biggs, USA

Gymnastics

MEN

Individual		Points
All-Around	Koji Gushiken, JPN	118.7
Floor	Li Ning, CHN	19.925
Horiz.Bar	Shinji Morisue, JPN	20.00
Paral.Bars	Bart Conner, USA	19.95
Rings	Koji Gushiken, JPN & Li Ning, CHN	19.85
Side Horse	Li Ning, CHN	19.95
Vault	Lou Yun, CHN	19.95

Team		Points
All-Around	USA (Peter Vidmar, Bart Conner, Mitch Gaylord, Tim Daggett, James Hartung, Scott Johnson)	591.40

1984 (Cont.)
WOMEN

Individual

		Points
All-Around	Mary Lou Retton, USA	79.175
Bal.Beam	Simona Pauco, ROM & Ecaterina Szabó, ROM	19.80
Floor	Ecaterina Szabó, ROM	19.975
Uneven Bars	Julie McNamara, USA & Ma Yanhong, CHN	19.95
Vault	Ecaterina Szabó, ROM	19.875

Team

		Points
All-Around	ROM (Szabó, Cutina, Pauca, Grigoras, Stanulet, Agache)	392.02

Rhythmic

		Points
All-Around	Lori Fung, CAN	57.950

Swimming
MEN

Event		Time	
100m Free	Rowdy Gaines, USA	49.80	OR
200m Free	Michael Gross, W.Ger	1:47.44	WR
400m Free	George DiCarlo, USA	3:51.23	OR
1500m Free	Mike O'Brien, USA	15:05.20	
100m Back	Rick Carey, USA	55.79	
200m Back	Rick Carey, USA	2:00.23	
100m Brst	Steve Lundquist, USA	1:01.65	WR
200m Brst	Victor Davis, CAN	2:13.34	WR
100m Fly	Michael Gross, W.Ger	53.08	WR
200m Fly	Jon Sieben, AUS	1:57.04	WR
200m I.M.	Alex Baumann, CAN	2:01.42	WR
400m I.M.	Alex Baumann, CAN	4:17.41	WR
4x100m Free	USA (Chris Cavanaugh, Mike Heath, Matt Biondi, Rowdy Gaines)	3:19.03	WR
4x200m Free	USA (Mike Heath, David Larson, Jeff Float, Bruce Hayes)	7:15.69	WR
4x100m Mdly	USA (Rick Carey, Steve Lundquist, Pablo Morales, Rowdy Gaines)	3:39.30	WR

Diving

		Points
Platform	Greg Louganis, USA	710.91
Spring	Greg Louganis, USA	754.41

WOMEN

Event		Time	
100m Free	Nancy Hogshead, USA	55.92	
200m Free	Mary Wayte, USA	1:59.23	
400m Free	Tiffany Cohen, USA	4:07.10	OR
800m Free	Tiffany Cohen, USA	8:24.95	OR
100m Back	Theresa Andrews, USA	1:02.55	
200m Back	Jolanda de Rover, HOL	2:12.38	
100m Brst	Petra van Staveren, HOL	1:09.88	OR
200m Brst	Anne Ottenbrite, CAN	2:30.38	
100m Fly	Mary T.Meagher, USA	59.26	
200m Fly	Mary T.Meagher, USA	2:06.90	OR
200m I.M.	Tracy Caulkins, USA	2:12.64	OR
400m I.M.	Tracy Caulkins, USA	4:39.24	

Event		Time
4x100m Free	USA (Jenna Johnson, Carrie Steinseifer, Dara Torres, Nancy Hogshead)	3:43.43
4x100m Mdly	USA (Theresa Andrews, Tracy Caulkins, Mary T.Meagher, Nancy Hogshead)	4:08.34

Diving

		Points
Platform	Zhou Jihong, CHN	435.51
Spring	Sylvie Bernier, CAN	530.70

Team Sports

Men

	Champion
Basketball	United States
Field Hockey	Pakistan

Team Sports

Men

	Champion
Handball	Yugoslavia
Soccer	France
Volleyball	United States
Water Polo	Yugoslavia

Women

	Champion
Basketball	United States
Field Hockey	Holland
Handball	Yugoslavia
Volleyball	China

Also Contested

Archery, Canoeing, Cycling, Equestrian, Fencing, Judo, Modern Pentathlon, Rowing, Shooting, Synchronized Swimming, Weightlifting, Freestyle Wrestling, Greco-Roman Wrestling and Yachting.

SÉOUL 1988

1988

Seoul

For the first time since Munich in 1972, there was no organized boycott of the Summer Olympics. Cuba and Ethiopia stayed away in support of North Korea (the IOC turned down the North Koreans' demand to co-host the Games, so they refused to participate), but that was about it.

More countries (160) sent more athletes (9,627) to South Korea than to any previous Olympics. There were also more security personnel (100,000) than ever before given Seoul's proximity (30 miles) to the North and the possibility of student demonstrations for reunification.

Ten days into the Games, Canadian Ben Johnson beat defending champion Carl Lewis in the 100-meter dash with a world record time of 9.79. The next day, however, Johnson was stripped of his gold medal and sent packing by the IOC when his post-race drug test indicated steroid use.

Lewis, who finished second in the 100, was named the winner. He also repeated in the long jump, but was second in the 200 and did not run the 400 relay. Teammate Florence Griffith Joyner claimed four medals—gold in the 100, 200 and 400-meter relay, and silver in the 1,600 relay. Her sister-in-law Jackie Joyner-Kersee won the long jump and heptathlon.

The most gold medals were won by swimmers—Kristin Otto of East Germany (6) and American Matt Biondi (5). Otherwise, Steffi Graf added an Olympic gold medal to her Grand Slam sweep in tennis; Greg Louganis won both men's diving events for the second straight time, and the U.S. basketball team had to settle for third place after losing to the Soviets, 82-76, in the semifinals.

Top 10 Standings

National medal standings are not recognized by the IOC. The unofficial point totals are based on 3 points for a gold medal, 2 for a silver and 1 for a bronze. Total medals are in parentheses.

		Gold	Silver	Bronze	Pts
1	USSR (132)	55	31	46	273
2	E.Germany (102)	37	35	30	211
3	USA (94)	36	31	27	197
4	W.Germany (40)	11	14	15	76
5	Bulgaria (35)	10	12	13	67
	South Korea (33)	12	10	11	67
7	Hungary (23)	11	6	6	51
8	China (28)	5	11	12	49
	Romania (24)	7	11	6	49
10	Great Britain (24)	5	10	9	44

Leading Medal Winners

Number of individual medals won on the left; gold, silver and bronze breakdown to the right.

MEN

No		Sport	G-S-B
7	Matt Biondi, USA	Swimming	5-1-1
5	Vladimir Artemov, USSR	Gymnastics	4-1-0
4	Dmitri Bilozerchev, USSR	Gymnastics	3-0-1
4	Valeri Lyukin, USSR	Gymnastics	2-2-0
3	Chris Jacobs, USA	Swimming	2-1-0
3	Carl Lewis, USA	Track/Field	2-1-0
3	Holger Behrendt, E.Ger	Gymnastics	1-1-1
3	Uwe Dassler, E.Ger	Swimming	1-1-1
3	Paul McDonald, NZE	Canoeing	1-1-1
3	Igor Polianski, USSR	Swimming	1-0-2
3	Gennadi Prigoda, USSR	Swimming	0-1-2
3	Sven Tippelt, E.Ger	Gymnastics	0-1-2

WOMEN

No		Sport	G-S-B
6	Kristin Otto, E.Ger	Swimming	6-0-0
6	Daniela Silivaş, ROM	Gymnastics	3-2-1
4	Florence Griffith Joyner, USA	Track/Field	3-1-0
4	Svetlana Boguinskaya, USSR	Gymnastics	2-1-1
3	Elena Shushunova, USSR	Gymnastics	2-1-1
3	Janet Evans, USA	Swimming	3-0-0
3	Silke Hörner, E.Ger	Swimming	2-0-1
3	Daniela Hunger, E.Ger	Swimming	2-0-1
3	Katrin Meissner, E.Ger	Swimming	2-0-1
3	Birgit Schmidt, E.Ger	Canoeing	2-1-0
3	Birte Weigang, E.Ger	Swimming	1-2-0
3	Vania Guecheva, BUL	Canoeing	1-1-1
3	Gabriela Potorac, ROM	Gymnastics	0-2-1
3	Heike Drechsler, E.Ger	Track/Field	0-1-2

Track & Field

MEN

Event		Time	
100m	Carl Lewis, USA	9.92	OR
200m	Joe DeLoach, USA	19.75	OR
400m	Steve Lewis, USA	43.87	
800m	Paul Ereng, KEN	1:43.45	
1500m	Peter Rono, KEN	3:35.96	
5000m	John Ngugi, KEN	13:11.70	
10,000m	Brahim Boutaib, MOR	27:21.46	
Marathon	Gelindo Bordin, ITA	2:10:32	
110m H	Roger Kingdom, USA	12.98	OR
400m H	Andre Phillips, USA	47.19	OR
3000m			
Steeple	Julius Kariuki, KEN	8:05.51	OR
20k Walk	Jozef Pribilinec, CZE	1:19:57	OR
50k Walk	Viacheslav Ivanenko, USSR	3:38:29	OR

Event		Time	
4x100m	USSR (Victor Bryzgine, Vladimir Krylov, Vladimir Mouraviev, Vitali Savine)	38.19	
4x400m	USA (Danny Everett, Steve Lewis, Kevin Robinzine, Butch Reynolds)	2:56.16	=WR

Event		Mark	
High Jump	Guennadi Avdeenko, USSR	7- 9½	OR
Pole Vault	Sergei Bubka, USSR	19- 4¼	OR
Long Jump	Carl Lewis, USA	28- 7¼	
Triple Jump	Hristo Markov, BUL	57- 9¼	OR
Shot Put	Ulf Timmermann, E.Ger	73- 8¾	OR
Discus	Jürgen Schult, E.Ger	225- 9¼	OR
Hammer	Sergei Litvinov, USSR	278- 2½	OR
Javelin	Tapio Korjus, FIN	276- 6	
Decathlon	Christian Schenk, E.Ger	8488 pts	

WOMEN

Event		Time	
100m	Florence Griffith Joyner, USA	10.54	OR
200m	Florence Griffith Joyner, USA	21.34	WR
400m	Olga Bryzguina, USSR	48.65	OR
800m	Sigrun Wodars, E.Ger	1:56.10	
1500m	Paula Ivan, ROM	3:53.96	OR
3000m	Tatiana Samolenko, USSR	8:26.53	OR
10,000m	Olga Bondarenko, USSR	31:05.21	OR
Marathon	Rosa Mota, POR	2:25:40	
100m H	Jordanka Donkova, BUL	12.38	OR
400m H	Debra Flintoff-King, AUS	53.17	OR
4x100m	USA (Alice Brown, Sheila Echols, Florence Griffith Joyner, Evelyn Ashford)	41.98	
4x400m	USSR (Tatiana Ledovskaia, Olga Nazarova, Maria Piniguina, Olga Bryzgina)	3:15.18	WR

Event		Mark	
High Jump	Louise Ritter, USA	6- 8	OR
Long Jump	Jackie Joyner-Kersee, USA	24- 3½	OR
Shot Put	Natalya Lisovskaya, USSR	72-11½	OR
Discus	Martina Hellmann, E.Ger	237- 2	OR
Javelin	Petra Felke, E.Ger	245- 0	OR
Heptathlon	Jackie Joyner-Kersee, USA	7291 pts	WR

Boxing

Weight Class	Champion
Lt.Flyweight (106 lbs)	Ivailo Hristov, BUL
Flyweight (112)	Kwang-Sun Kim, S.Kor
Bantamweight (119)	Kennedy McKinney, USA
Featherweight (125)	Giovanni Parisi, ITA
Lightweight (132)	Andreas Zuelow, E.Ger
Lt.Welterweight (139)	Viatcheslav Yanovski, USSR
Welterweight (148)	Robert Wangila, KEN
Lt.Middleweight (156)	Si-Hun Park, S.Kor
Middleweight (165)	Henry Maske, E.Ger
Lt.Heavyweight (178)	Andrew Maynard, USA
Heavyweight (200)	Ray Mercer, USA
Super Heavyweight (200 +)	Lennox Lewis, CAN

Gymnastics

MEN

Individual		Points
All-Around	Vladimir Artemov, USSR	119.125
Floor	Sergei Kharikov, USSR	19.925
Horiz.Bar	Vladimir Artemov, USSR & Valeri Lyukin, USSR	19.900
Paral.Bars	Vladimir Artemov, USSR	19.925
Rings	Dmitri Bilozerchev, USSR & Hoger Behrendt, E.Ger	19.925

1988 (Cont.)
Gymnastics
MEN

Individual		Points
Side Horse	Dmitri Bilozerchev, USSR, Lyubomir Gueraskov, BUL & Zsolt Borkai, HUN	19.950
Vault	Lou Yun, CHN	19.875

Team		Points
All-Around	USSR (Artemov, Bilozerchev, Kharikov, Lyukin, Gogoladze, Nouvikov)	593.350

WOMEN

Individual		Points
All-Around	Elena Shushunova, USSR	79.662
Bal.Beam	Daniela Silivaş, ROM	19.924
Floor	Daniela Silivaş, ROM	19.937
Uneven Bars	Daniela Silivaş, ROM	20.000
Vault	Svetlana Boguinskaya, USSR	19.905

Team		Points
All-Around	USSR (Shushunova, Boguinskaya, Baitova, Chevtchenko, Strajeva, Lachtchenova)	395.475

Rhythmic		Points
All-Around	Marina Lobatch, USSR	60.0

Rowing
(All distances 2000 meters)
MEN

Event		Time
Sculls-1	Thomas Lange, E.Ger	6:49.86
Sculls-2	Holland	6:21.13
Sculls-4	Italy	5:53.37
Coxed-2	Italy	6:58.79
Coxless-2	Great Britain	6:36.84
Coxed-4	East Germany	6:10.74
Coxless-4	East Germany	6:03.11
Eights	West Germany	5:46.05

WOMEN

Event		Time
Sculls-1	Jutta Behrendt, E.Ger	7:47.19
Sculls-2	East Germany	7:00.48
Sculls-4	East Germany	6:21.06
Coxless-2	Romania	7:28.13
Coxed-4	East Germany	6:56.00
Eights	East Germany	6:15.17

Swimming
MEN

Event		Time	
50m Free	Matt Biondi, USA	22.14	WR
100m Free	Matt Biondi, USA	48.63	OR
200m Free	Duncan Armstrong, AUS	1:47.25	WR
400m Free	Uwe Dassler, E.Ger	3:46.95	WR
1500m Free	Vladimir Salnikov, USSR	15:00.04	
100m Back	Daichi Suzuki, JPN	55.05	
200m Back	Igor Polianski, USSR	1:59.37	
100m Brst	Adrian Moorhouse, GBR	1:02.04	
200m Brst	József Szabó, HUN	2:13.52	
100m Fly	Anthony Nesty, SUR	53.00	OR
200m Fly	Michael Gross, W.Ger	1:56.94	OR
200m I.M.	Tamás Darnyi, HUN	2:00.17	WR
400m I.M.	Tamás Darnyi, HUN	4:14.75	WR
4x100m Free	USA (Chris Jacobs, Troy Dalbey, Tom Jager, Matt Biondi)	3:16.53	WR
4x200m Free	USA (Troy Dalbey, Matt Cetlinski, Doug Gjertsen, Matt Biondi)	7:12.51	WR

Event		Time	
4x100m Med	USA (David Berkoff, Rich Schroeder, Matt Biondi, Chris Jacobs)	3:36.93	WR

Diving		Points
Platform	Greg Louganis, USA	638.61
Spring	Greg Louganis, USA	730.80

WOMEN

Event		Time	
50m Free	Kristin Otto, E.Ger	25.49	OR
100m Free	Kristin Otto, E.Ger	54.93	
200m Free	Heike Freidrich, E.Ger	1:57.65	OR
400m Free	Janet Evans, USA	4:03.85	WR
800m Free	Janet Evans, USA	8:20.20	OR
100m Back	Kristin Otto, E.Ger	1:00.89	
200m Back	Krisztina Egerszegi, HUN	2:09.29	OR
100m Brst	Tania Dangalakova, BUL	1:07.95	OR
200m Brst	Silke Hörner, E.Ger	2:26.71	WR

Event		Time	
100m Fly	Kristin Otto, E.Ger	59.00	OR
200m Fly	Kathleen Nord, E.Ger	2:09.51	
200m I.M.	Daniela Hunger, E.Ger	2:12.59	OR
400m I.M.	Janet Evans, USA	4:37.76	
4x100m Free	E.Ger (Kristin Otto, Katrin Meissner, Daniela Hunger, Manuela Stellmach)	3:40.63	OR
4x100m Med	E.Ger (Kristin Otto, Silke Hörner, Birte Weigang, Katrin Meissner)	4:03.74	OR

Diving		Points
Platform	Xu Yanmei, CHN	445.20
Spring	Gao Min, CHN	580.23

Tennis
MEN

Singles   Miloslav Mecir, CZE, def. Tim Mayotte, USA, 3-6,6-2,6-4,6-2.

Doubles   Ken Flach & Robert Seguso, USA, def. Emilio Sanchez & Sergio Casal, SPA, 6-3,6-4,6-7,6-7,9-7.

WOMEN

Singles   Steffi Graf, W.Ger, def. Gabriela Sabatini, ARG, 6-3,6-3.

Doubles   Pam Shriver and Zina Garrison, USA, def. Jana Novotna and Helena Sukova, CZE, 4-6,6-2,10-8.

Team Sports
Men

Men	Champion
Basketball	Soviet Union
Field Hockey	Great Britain
Handball	Soviet Union
Soccer	Soviet Union
Volleyball	United States
Water Polo	Yugoslavia

Women	Champion
Basketball	United States
Field Hockey	Australia
Handball	South Korea
Volleyball	Soviet Union

Also Contested
Archery, Cycling, Equestrian, Fencing, Judo, Modern Pentathlon, Rowing, Shooting, Synchronized Swimming, Table Tennis, Weightlifting, Freestyle Wrestling, Greco-Roman Wrestling and Yachting.

ALL-TIME LEADING MEDAL WINNERS

All Nations
Overall Medals

No		Sport	G-S-B
18	Larissa Latynina, USSR	Gymnastics	9-5-4
15	Nikolai Andrianov, USSR	Gymnastics	7-5-3
13	Boris Shakhlin, USSR	Gymnastics	7-4-2
13	Edoardo Mangiarotti, ITA	Fencing	6-5-2
13	Takashi Ono, JPN	Gymnastics	5-4-4
12	Paavo Nurmi, FIN	Track/Field	9-3-0
12	Sawao Kato, JPN	Gymnastics	8-3-1
11	Mark Spitz, USA	Swimming	9-1-1
11	Vera Čáslavská, CZH	Gymnastics	7-4-0
11	Viktor Chukarin, USSR	Gymnastics	7-3-1
11	Carl Osburn, USA	Shooting	5-4-2
10	Ray Ewry, USA	Track/Field	10-0-0
10	Aladar Gerevich, HUN	Fencing	7-1-2
10	Akinori Nakayama, JPN	Gymnastics	6-2-2
10	Ágnes Keleti, HUN	Gymnastics	5-3-2
10	Polina Astakhova, USSR	Gymnastics	5-2-3
10	Aleksandr Dityatin, USSR	Gymnastics	3-6-1

Games Participated In

Andrianov (1972,76,80); **Astakhova** (1956,60,64); **Čáslavská** (1960,64,68); **Chukarin** (1952,56); **Dityatin** (1976,80); **Ewry** (1900,04,06,08); **Gerevich** (1932,36,48,52, 56,60); **Kato** (1968,72,76); **Keleti** (1952,56); **Latynina** (1956,60,64); **Mangiarotti** (1936,48,52,56,60); **Nakayama** (1968,72); **Nurmi** (1920,24,28); **Ono** (1952,56,60,64); **Osburn** (1912, 20,24); **Shakhlin** (1956,60,64); **Spitz** (1968,72).

Gold Medals

No		Sport	G-S-B
10	Ray Ewry, USA	Track/Field	10-0-0
9	Larissa Latynina, USSR	Gymnastics	9-5-4
9	Paavo Nurmi, FIN	Track/Field	9-3-0
9	Mark Spitz, USA	Swimming	9-1-1
8	Sawao Kato, JPN	Gymnastics	8-3-1
7	Nikolai Andrianov, USSR	Gymnastics	7-5-3
7	Boris Shakhlin, USSR	Gymnastics	7-4-2
7	Vera Čáslavská, CZH	Gymnastics	7-4-0
7	Viktor Chukarin, USSR	Gymnastics	7-3-1
7	Aladar Gerevich, HUN	Fencing	7-1-2

Eleven athletes tied with six each.

Silver Medals

No		Sport	G-S-B
6	Alexandr Dityatin, USSR	Gymnastics	3-6-1
6	Mikhail Voronin, USSR	Gymnastics	2-6-1
6	Shirley Babashoff, USA	Swimming	2-6-0
5	Larissa Latynina, USSR	Gymnastics	9-5-4
5	Nikolai Andrianov, USSR	Gymnastics	7-5-3
5	Edoardo Mangiarotti, ITA	Fencing	6-5-2
5	Zoltan Halmay, HUN	Swimming	3-5-1
5	Philippe Cattiau, FRA	Fencing	3-5-0
5	Maria Gorokhovskaya, USSR	Gymnastics	2-5-0
5	Gustavo Marzi, ITA	Fencing	2-5-0
5	Yuri Titov, USSR	Gymnastics	1-5-3
5	Viktor Lisitsky, USSR	Gymnastics	0-5-0

Bronze Medals

No		Sport	G-S-B
6	Heikki Savolainen, FIN	Gymnastics	2-1-6
5	Daniel Revenu, FRA	Fencing	1-0-5
5	Philip Edwards, CAN	Track/Field	0-0-5
5	Adrianus Jong, HOL	Fencing	0-0-5

Eleven athletes tied with four each.

USA
Overall Medals

No		Sport	G-S-B
11	Mark Spitz	Swimming	9-1-1
11	Carl Osburn	Shooting	5-4-2
10	Ray Ewry	Track/Field	10-0-0
9	Martin Sheridan	Track/Field	5-3-1
8	Matt Biondi	Swimming	6-1-1
8	Charles Daniels	Swimming	5-1-2
8	Shirley Babashoff	Swimming	2-6-0
7	Carl Lewis	Track/Field	6-1-0
7	Willis Lee	Shooting	5-1-1
7	Lloyd Spooner	Shooting	4-1-2
6	Anton Heida	Gymnastics	5-1-0
6	Don Schollander	Swimming	5-1-0
6	Johnny Weissmuller	Swim/Water Polo	5-0-1
6	Alfred Lane	Shooting	5-0-1
6	Jim Lightbody	Track/Field	4-2-0
6	George Eyser	Gymnastics	3-2-1
6	Michael Plumb	Equestrian	2-4-0
6	Burton Downing	Cycling	2-3-1
6	Bob Garrett	Track/Field	2-2-2

Games Participated In

Babashoff (1972,76); **Biondi** (1984,88); **Daniels** (1904,06,08); **Downing** (1904); **Ewry** (1900,04, 06,08); **Eyser** (1904); **Garrett** (1896,1900); **Heida** (1904); **Lane** (1912-20); **Lee** (1920); **Lewis** (1984, 88); **Lightbody** (1904,06); **Osburn** (1912,20,24); **Plumb** (1960,64,68,72,76,84); **Schollander** (1964, 68); **Sheridan** (1904,06,08); **Spitz** (1968,72); **Spooner** (1920); **Weissmuller** (1924-28).

Gold Medals

No		Sport	G-S-B
10	Ray Ewry	Track/Field	10-0-0
9	Mark Spitz	Swimming	9-1-1
6	Matt Biondi	Swimming	6-1-1
6	Carl Lewis	Track/Field	6-1-0
5	Carl Osburn	Shooting	5-4-2
5	Martin Sheridan	Track/Field	5-3-1
5	Charles Daniels	Swimming	5-1-2
5	Willis Lee	Shooting	5-1-1
5	Anton Heida	Gymnastics	5-1-0
5	Don Schollander	Swimming	5-1-0
5	Johnny Weissmuller	Swim/Water Polo	5-0-1
5	Alfred Lane	Shooting	5-0-1
5	Morris Fisher	Shooting	5-0-0
4	Jim Lightbody	Track/Field	4-2-0
4	Lloyd Spooner	Shooting	4-1-2
4	Greg Louganis	Diving	4-1-0
4	John Naber	Swimming	4-1-0
4	Meyer Prinstein	Track/Field	4-1-0
4	Mel Sheppard	Track/Field	4-1-0
4	Marcus Hurley	Cycling	4-0-1
4	Archie Hahn	Track/Field	4-0-0
4	Alvin Kraenzlein	Track/Field	4-0-0
4	Pat McCormick	Diving	4-0-0
4	Al Oerter	Track/Field	4-0-0
4	Jesse Owens	Track/Field	4-0-0

Silver Medals

No		Sport	G-S-B
6	Shirley Babashoff	Swimming	2-6-0
4	Carl Osburn	Shooting	5-4-2
4	Michael Plumb	Equestrian	2-4-0
3	Martin Sheridan	Track/Field	5-3-1
3	Burton Downing	Cycling	2-3-1
3	Irving Baxter	Track/Field	2-3-0
3	Earl Thomson	Equestrian	2-3-0

Bronze Medals

No		Sport	G-S-B
4	William Merz	Gym/Track/Field	0-1-4

EVENT-BY-EVENT

Gold medal winners from 1896-1988 in the following events: basketball, boxing, diving, field hockey, gymnastics, soccer, swimming, tennis, track & field, volleyball, water polo, freestyle wrestling and yachting.

Basketball

MEN

Year		Year	
1936	**United States**, Canada, Mexico	1968	**United States**, Yugoslavia, Soviet Union
1948	**United States**, France, Brazil	1972	**Soviet Union**, United States, Cuba
1952	**United States**, Soviet Union, Uruguay	1976	**United States**, Yugoslavia, Soviet Union
1956	**United States**, Soviet Union, Uruguay	1980	**Yugoslavia**, Italy, Soviet Union
1960	**United States**, Soviet Union, Brazil	1984	**United States**, Spain, Yugoslavia
1964	**United States**, Soviet Union, Brazil	1988	**Soviet Union**, Yugoslavia, United States

WOMEN

Year		Year	
1976	**Soviet Union**, United States, Bulgaria	1984	**United States**, South Korea, China
1980	**Soviet Union**, Bulgaria, Yugoslavia	1988	**United States**, Yugoslavia, Soviet Union

Boxing

Light Flyweight (106 lbs)

Year		Final Match	Year		Final Match
1968	Francisco Rodriguez, VEN	Decision, 3-2	1980	Shamil Sabyrov, USSR	Decision, 3-2
1972	György Gedó, HUN	Decision, 5-0	1984	Paul Gonzales, USA	Default
1976	Jorge Hernandez, CUB	Decision, 4-1	1988	Ivailo Hristov, BUL	Decision, 5-0

Flyweight (112 lbs)

Year		Final Match	Year		Final Match
1904	George Finnegan, USA	Stopped, 1st	1960	Gyula Török, HUN	Decision, 3-2
1920	Frank DiGennara, USA	Decision	1964	Fernando Atzori, ITA	Decision, 4-1
1924	Fidel LaBarba, USA	Decision	1968	Ricardo Delgado, MEX	Decision, 5-0
1928	Antal Kocsis, HUN	Decision	1972	Georgi Kostadinov, BUL	Decision, 5-0
1932	István Énekes, HUN	Decision	1976	Leo Randolph, USA	Decision, 3-2
1936	Willi Kaiser, GER	Decision	1980	Peter Lessov, BUL	Stopped, 2nd
1948	Pascual Perez, ARG	Decision	1984	Steven McCrory, USA	Decision, 4-1
1952	Nathan Brooks, USA	Decision, 3-0	1988	Kim Swang-Sun, KOR	Decision, 4-1
1956	Terence Spinks, GBR	Decision			

Bantamweight (119 lbs)

Year		Final Match	Year		Final Match
1904	Oliver Kirk, USA	Stopped, 3rd	1956	Wolfgang Behrendt, GER	Decision
1908	A. Henry Thomas, GBR	Decision	1960	Oleg Grigoryev, USSR	Decision
1920	Clarence Walker, SAF	Decision	1964	Takao Sakurai, JPN	Stopped, 2nd
1924	William Smith, SAF	Decision	1968	Valery Sokolov, USSR	Stopped, 2nd
1928	Vittorio Tamagnini, ITA	Decision	1972	Orlando Martinez, CUB	Decision, 5-0
1932	Horace Gwynne, CAN	Decision	1976	Yong-Jo Gu, NKor	Decision, 5-0
1936	Ulderico Sergo, ITA	Decision	1980	Juan Hernandez, CUB	Decision, 5-0
1948	Tibor Csik, HUN	Decision	1984	Maurizio Stecca, ITA	Decision, 4-1
1952	Pentti Hämäläinen, FIN	Decision, 2-1	1988	Kennedy McKinney, USA	Decision, 5-0

Featherweight (125 lbs)

Year		Final Match	Year		Final Match
1904	Oliver Kirk, USA	Decision	1956	Vladimir Safronov, USSR	Decision
1908	Richard Gunn, GBR	Decision	1960	Francesco Musso, ITA	Decision, 4-1
1920	Paul Fritsch, FRA	Decision	1964	Stanislav Stepashkin, USSR	Decision, 3-2
1924	John Fields, USA	Decision	1968	Antonio Roldan, MEX	Won on Disq.
1928	Lambertus van Klaveren, HOL	Decision	1972	Boris Kousnetsov, USSR	Decision, 3-2
1932	Carmelo Robledo, ARG	Decision	1976	Angel Herrera, CUB	KO, 2nd
1936	Oscar Casanovas, ARG	Decision	1980	Rudi Fink, GER	Decision, 4-1
1948	Ernesto Formenti, ITA	Decision	1984	Meldrick Taylor, USA	Decision, 5-0
1952	Jan Zachara, CZE	Decision, 2-1	1988	Giovanni Parisi, ITA	Stopped, 1st

Lightweight (132 lbs)

Year		Final Match	Year		Final Match
1904	Harry Spanger, USA	Decision	1956	Richard McTaggart, GBR	Decision
1908	Frederick Grace, GBR	Decision	1960	Kazimierz Pazdzior, POL	Decision, 4-1
1920	Samuel Mosberg, USA	Decision	1964	Józef Grudzień, POL	Decision
1924	Hans Nielsen, DEN	Decision	1968	Ronnie Harris, USA	Decision, 5-0
1928	Carlo Orlandi, ITA	Decision	1972	Jan Szczepąnski, POL	Decision, 5-0
1932	Lawrence Stevens, SAF	Decision	1976	Howard Davis, USA	Decision, 5-0
1936	Imre Harangi, HUN	Decision	1980	Angel Herrera, CUB	Stopped, 3rd
1948	Gerald Dreyer, SAF	Decision	1984	Pernell Whitaker, USA	Foe quit, 2nd
1952	Aureliano Bolognesi, ITA	Decision, 2-1	1988	Andreas Zuelow, E.Ger.	Decision, 5-0

Light Welterweight (139 lbs)

Year		Final Match	Year		Final Match
1952	Charles Adkins, USA	Decision, 2-1	1972	Ray Seales, USA	Decision, 3-2
1956	Vladimir Yengibaryan, USSR	Decision	1976	Ray Leonard, USA	Decision, 5-0
1960	Bohumil Nemeček CZE	Decision, 5-0	1980	Patrizio Oliva, ITA	Decision, 4-1
1964	Jerzy Kulej, POL	Decision, 5-0	1984	Jerry Page, USA	Decision, 5-0
1968	Jerzy Kulej, POL	Decision, 3-2	1988	Viatcheslav Janovski, USSR	Decision, 5-0

Welterweight (148 lbs)

Year		Final Match	Year		Final Match
1904	Albert Young, USA	Decision	1960	Nino Benvenuti, ITA	Decision, 4-1
1920	Albert Schneider, CAN	Decision	1964	Marian Kasprzki, POL	Decision, 4-1
1924	Jean Delarge, BEL	Decision	1968	Manfred Wolke, E.Ger	Decision, 4-1
1928	Edward Morgan, NZE	Decision	1972	Emilio Correa, CUB	Decision, 5-0
1932	Edward Flynn, USA	Decision	1976	Jochen Bachfeld, E.Ger	Decision, 3-2
1936	Sten Suvio, FIN	Decision	1980	Andrés Aldama, CUB	Decision, 4-1
1948	Julius Torma, CZE	Decision	1984	Mark Breland, USA	Decision, 5-0
1952	Zygmunt Chychla, POL	Decision, 3-0	1988	Robert Wangila, KEN	Stopped, 2nd
1956	Nicolae Linca, ROM	Decision, 3-2			

Light Middleweight (156 lbs)

Year		Final Match	Year		Final Match
1952	László Papp, HUN	Decision, 3-0	1972	Dieter Kottysch, W.Ger	Decision, 3-2
1956	László Papp, HUN	Decision	1976	Jerzy Rybicki, POL	Decision, 5-0
1960	Skeeter McClure, USA	Decision, 4-1	1980	Armando Martinez, CUB	Decision, 4-1
1964	Boris Lagutin, USSR	Decision, 4-1	1984	Frank Tate, USA	Decision, 5-0
1968	Boris Lagutin, USSR	Decision, 5-0	1988	Si-Hun Park, SKor	Decision, 3-2

Middleweight (165 lbs)

Year		Final Match	Year		Final Match
1904	Charles Mayer, USA	Stopped, 3rd	1956	Gennady Schatkov, USSR	KO, 1st
1908	John Douglas, GBR	Decision	1960	Edward Crook, USA	Decision, 3-2
1920	Harry Mallin, GBR	Decision	1964	Valery Popenchenko, USSR	Stopped, 1st
1924	Harry Mallin, GBR	Decision	1968	Christopher Finnegan, GBR	Decision, 3-2
1928	Piero Toscani, ITA	Decision	1972	Vyacheslav Lemechev, USSR	KO, 1st
1932	Carmen Barth, USA	Decision	1976	Michael Spinks, USA	Stopped, 3rd
1936	Jean Despeaux, FRA	Decision	1980	José Gomez, CUB	Decision, 4-1
1948	László Papp, HUN	Decision	1984	Joon-Sup Shin, SKor	Decision, 3-2
1952	Floyd Patterson, USA	KO, 1st	1988	Henry Maske, E.Ger	Decision, 5-0

Light Heavyweight (178 lbs)

Year		Final Match	Year		Final Match
1920	Eddie Eagan, USA	Decision	1960	Cassius Clay, USA	Decision, 5-0
1924	Harry Mitchell, GBR	Decision	1964	Cosimo Pinto, ITA	Decision, 3-2
1928	Victor Avendatno, ARG	Decision	1968	Dan Poznyak, USSR	Default
1932	David Carstens, SAF	Decision	1972	Mate Parlov, YUG	Stopped, 2nd
1936	Roger Michelot, FRA	Decision	1976	Leon Spinks, USA	Stopped, 3rd
1948	George Hunter, SAF	Decision	1980	Slobodan Kacar, YUG	Decision, 4-1
1952	Norvel Lee, USA	Decision, 3-0	1984	Anton Josipović, YUG	Default
1956	James Boyd, USA	Decision	1988	Andrew Maynard, USA	Decision, 5-0

Heavyweight (200 lbs)

Year		Final Match	Year		Final Match
1984	Henry Tillman, USA	Decision, 5-0	1988	Ray Mercer, USA	Stopped, 1st

Super Heavyweight (Unlimited)

Year		Final Match	Year		Final Match
1904	Samuel Berger, USA	Decision	1956	Pete Rademacher, USA	Stopped, 1st
1908	Albert Oldham, GBR	KO, 1st	1960	Franco De Piccoli, ITA	KO, 1st
1920	Ronald Rawson, GBR	Decision	1964	Joe Frazier, USA	Decision, 3-2
1924	Otto von Porat, NOR	Decision	1968	George Foreman, USA	Stopped, 2nd
1928	Arturo Rodriguez Jurado, ARG	Stopped, 1st	1972	Teófilo Stevenson, CUB	Default
1932	Santiago Lovell, ARG	Decision	1976	Teófilo Stevenson, CUB	KO, 3rd
1936	Herbert Runge, GER	Decision	1980	Teófilo Stevenson, CUB	Decision, 4-1
1948	Rafael Iglesias, ARG	KO, 2nd	1984	Tyrell Biggs, USA	Decision, 4-1
1952	Ed Sanders, USA	Won on Disq.	1988	Lennox Lewis, CAN	Stopped, 2nd

Note: Heavyweight division until 1984.

Diving

MEN

Springboard

Year		Points	Year		Points
1908	Albert Zürner, GER	85.5	1956	Bob Clotworthy, USA	159.56
1912	Paul Günther, GER	79.23	1960	Gary Tobian, USA.	170.00
1920	Louis Kuehn, USA	675.4	1964	Ken Sitzberger, USA	159.90
1924	Albert White, USA	696.4	1968	Bernie Wrightson, USA.	170.15
1928	Pete DesJardins, USA	185.04	1972	Vladimir Vasin, USSR	594.09
1932	Michael Galitzen, USA	161.38	1976	Phil Boggs, USA	619.05
1936	Richard Degener, USA	163.57	1980	Aleksandr Portnov, USSR	905.025
1948	Bruce Harlan, USA	163.64	1984	Greg Louganis, USA.	754.41
1952	David Browning, USA	205.29	1988	Greg Louganis, USA.	730.80

Platform

Year		Points	Year		Points
1904	George Sheldon, USA.	12.66	1952	Sammy Lee, USA	156.28
1906	Gottlob Walz, GER	156.0	1956	Joaquin Capilla, MEX.	152.44
1908	Hjalmar Johansson, SWE	83.75	1960	Bob Webster, USA	165.56
1912	Erik Adlerz, SWE	73.94	1964	Bob Webster, USA	148.58
1920	Clarence Pinkston, USA	100.67	1968	Klaus Dibiasi, ITA	164.18
1924	Albert White, USA	97.46	1972	Klaus Dibiasi, ITA	504.12
1928	Pete DesJardins, USA	98.74	1976	Klaus Dibiasi, ITA	600.51
1932	Harold Smith, USA	124.80	1980	Falk Hoffmann, E.Ger	835.650
1936	Marshall Wayne, USA.	113.58	1984	Greg Louganis, USA.	710.91
1948	Sammy Lee, USA.	130.05	1988	Greg Louganis, USA.	638.61

WOMEN

Springboard

Year		Points	Year		Points
1920	Aileen Riggin, USA	539.9	1960	Ingrid Krämer, GER	155.81
1924	Elizabeth Becker, USA.	474.5	1964	Ingrid Engel-Krämer, GER	145.00
1928	Helen Meany, USA	78.62	1968	Sue Gossick, USA	150.77
1932	Georgia Coleman, USA	87.52	1972	Micki King, USA	450.03
1936	Marjorie Gestring, USA.	89.27	1976	Jennifer Chandler, USA	506.19
1948	Vicki Draves, USA	108.74	1980	Irina Kalinina, USSR	725.910
1952	Pat McCormick, USA.	147.30	1984	Sylvie Bernier, CAN.	530.70
1956	Pat McCormick, USA.	142.36	1988	Gao Min, CHN	580.23

Platform

Year		Points	Year		Points
1912	Greta Johansson, SWE	39.9	1960	Ingrid Krämer, GER.	91.28
1920	Stefani Fryland-Clausen, DEN	34.6	1964	Lesley Bush, USA.	99.80
1924	Caroline Smith, USA	33.2	1968	Melina Duchkova, CZE.	109.59
1928	Elizabeth Becker Pinkston, USA	31.6	1972	Ulrika Knape, SWE	390.00
1932	Dorothy Poynton, USA.	40.26	1976	Elena Vaytsekhovskaya, USSR	406.59
1936	Dorothy Poynton Hill, USA	33.93	1980	Martina Jäschke, E.Ger	596.250
1948	Vicki Draves, USA	68.87	1984	Zhou Jihong, CHN	435.51
1952	Pat McCormick, USA.	79.37	1988	Xu Yanmei, CHN	445.20
1956	Pat McCormick, USA.	84.85			

Field Hockey

MEN

Year		Year	
1908	**Great Britain**, Ireland, Scotland	1960	**Pakistan**, India, Spain
1920	**Great Britain**, Denmark, Belgium	1964	**India**, Pakistan, Australia
1928	**India**, Holland, Germany	1968	**Pakistan**, Australia, India
1932	**India**, Japan, United States	1972	**West Germany**, Pakistan, India
1936	**India**, Germany, Holland	1976	**New Zealand**, Australia, Pakistan
1948	**India**, Great Britain, Holland	1980	**India**, Spain, Soviet Union
1952	**India**, Holland, Great Britain	1984	**Pakistan**, West Germany, Great Britain
1956	**India**, Pakistan, Germany	1988	**Great Britain**, West Germany, Holland

WOMEN

Year		Year	
1980	**Zimbabwe**, Czechoslovakia, Soviet Union	1988	**Australia**, South Korea, Holland
1984	**Holland**, West Germany, United States		

Gymnastics
MEN
All-Around

Year		Points	Year		Points
1900	Gustave Sandras, FRA	302	1948	Veikko Huhtanen, FIN	229.7
1904	Julius Lenhart, AUT	69.80	1952	Viktor Chukarin, USSR	115.7
1906	Pierre Paysse, FRA	116	1956	Viktor Chukarin, USSR	114.25
1908	Alberto Braglia, ITA	317.0	1960	Boris Shakhlin, USSR	115.95
1912	Alberto Braglia, ITA	135.0	1964	Yukio Endo, JPN	115.95
1920	Giorgio Zampori, ITA	88.35	1968	Sawao Kato, JPN	115.9
1924	Leon Stukelj, YUG	110.340	1972	Sawao Kato, JPN	114.650
1928	Georges Miez, SWI	247.500	1976	Nikolai Andrianov, USSR	116.65
1932	Romeo Neri, ITA	140.625	1980	Aleksandr Dityatin, USSR	118.65
1936	Alfred Schwarzmann, GER	113.100	1984	Koji Gushiken, JPN	118.7
			1988	Vladimir Artemov, USSR	119.125

Horizontal Bar

Year		Points	Year		Points
1896	Hermann Weingartner, GER	—	1960	Takashi Ono, JPN	19.60
1904	Anton Heida, USA		1964	Boris Shakhlin, USSR	19.625
	& Edward Hennig, USA	40	1968	Akinori Nakayama, JPN	19.55
1924	Leon Stukelj, YUG	19.73	1972	Mitsuo Tsukahara, JPN	19.725
1928	Georges Miez, SWI	19.17	1976	Mitsuo Tsukahara, JPN	19.675
1932	Dallas Bixler, USA	18.33	1980	Stoyan Deltchev, BUL	19.825
1936	Aleksanteri Saarvala, FIN	19.367	1984	Shinji Morisue, JPN	20.00
1948	Josef Stalder, SWI	19.85	1988	Vladimir Artemov, USSR	
1952	Jack Günthard, SWI	19.55		& Valeri Lioukine, USSR	19.900
1956	Takashi Ono, JPN	19.60			

Parallel Bars

Year		Points	Year		Points
1896	Alfred Flatow, GER	—	1960	Boris Shakhlin, USSR	19.40
1904	George Eyser, USA	44	1964	Yukio Endo, JPN	19.675
1924	August Güttinger, SWI	21.63	1968	Akinori Nakayama, JPN	19.475
1928	Ladislav Vácha, CZE	18.83	1972	Sawao Kato, JPN	19.475
1932	Romeo Neri, ITA	18.97	1976	Sawao Kato, JPN	19.675
1936	Konrad Frey, GER	19.067	1980	Aleksandr Tkachyov, USSR	19.775
1948	Michael Reusch, SWI	19.75	1984	Bart Conner, USA	19.95
1952	Hans Eugster, SWI	19.65	1988	Vladimir Artemov, USSR	19.925
1956	Viktor Chukarin, USSR	19.20			

Vault

Year		Points	Year		Points
1896	Karl Schumann, GER	—	1956	Helmut Bantz, GER	18.85
1904	George Eyser, USA		1960	Takashi Ono, JPN	19.35
	& Anton Heida, USA	36	1964	Haruhiro Yamashita, JPN	19.60
1924	Frank Kriz, USA	9.98	1968	Makhail Voronin, USSR	19.00
1928	Eugen Mack, SWI	9.58	1972	Klaus Köste, E.Ger	18.85
1932	Savino Guglielmetti, ITA	18.03	1976	Nikolai Andrianov, USSR	19.45
1936	Alfred Schwarzmann, GER	19.20	1980	Nikolai Andrianov, USSR	19.825
1948	Paavo Aaltonen, FIN	19.55	1984	Lou Yun, CHN	19.95
1952	Viktor Chukarin, USSR	19.20	1988	Lou Yun, CHN	19.875

Pommel Horse

Year		Points	Year		Points
1896	Jules Zutter, SWI	—	1960	Eugen Ekman, FIN	19.375
1904	Anton Heida, USA	42	1964	Miroslav Cerar, YUG	19.525
1924	Josef Wilhelm, SWI	21.23	1968	Miroslav Cerar, YUG	19.325
1928	Hermann Hanggi, SWI	19.75	1972	Viktor Klimenko, SOV	19.125
1932	István Pelle, HUN	19.07	1976	Zoltán Magyar, HUN	19.70
1936	Konrad Frey, GER	19.333	1980	Zoltán Magyar, HUN	19.925
1948	Paavo Aaltonen, FIN	19.35	1984	Li Ning, CHN	19.95
1952	Viktor Chukarin, USSR	19.50	1988	Lyubomir Gueraskov, BUL	
1956	Boris Shakhlin, USSR	19.25		Dmitri Bilozertchev, USSR	
				& Zsolt Borkai, HUN	19.958

Gymnastics (Cont.)

Rings

Year		Points	Year		Points
1896	Ioannis Mitropoulos, GRE	—	1960	Albert Azaryan, USSR	19.725
1904	Hermann Glass, USA	45	1964	Takuji Haytta, JPN	19.475
1924	Francesco Martino, ITA	21.553	1968	Akinori Nakayama, JPN	19.45
1928	Leon Stukelj, YUG	19.25	1972	Akinori Nakayama, JPN	19.35
1932	George Gulack, USA	18.97	1976	Nikolai Andrianov, USSR	19.65
1936	Alois Hudec, CZE	19.433	1980	Aleksandr Dityatin, USSR	19.875
1948	Karl Frei, SWI	19.80	1984	Koji Gushiken, JPN	19.85
1952	Grant Shaginyan, USSR	19.75	1988	Holger Behrendt, E.Ger	
1956	Albert Azaryan, USSR	19.35		& Dmitri Bilozertchev, USSR	19.925

Floor Exercise

Year		Points	Year		Points
1932	István Pelle, HUN	9.60	1968	Sawao Kato, JPN	19.475
1936	Georges Miez, SWI	18.666	1972	Nikolai Andrianov, USSR	19.175
1948	Ferenc Pataki, HUN	19.35	1976	Nikolai Andrianov, USSR	19.45
1952	William Thoresson, SWE	19.25	1980	Rolant Brückner, E.Ger	19.75
1956	Valentin Muratov, USSR	19.20	1984	Li Ning, CHN	19.925
1960	Nobuyuki Aihara, JPN	19.45	1988	Sergei Kharikov, USSR	19.925
1964	Franco Menichelli, ITA	19.45			

Team Combined Exercises

Year		Points	Year		Points
1904	United States	374.43	1952	Soviet Union	574.40
1906	Norway	19.00	1956	Soviet Union	568.25
1908	Sweden	438	1960	Japan	575.20
1912	Italy	265.75	1964	Japan	577.95
1920	Italy	359.855	1968	Japan	575.90
1924	Italy	839.058	1972	Japan	571.25
1928	Switzerland	1718.625	1976	Japan	576.85
1932	Italy	541.850	1980	Soviet Union	598.60
1936	Germany	657.430	1984	United States	591.40
1948	Finland	1358.30	1988	Soviet Union	593.35

WOMEN

All-Around

Year		Points	Year		Points
1952	Maria Gorokhovskaya, USSR	76.78	1972	Lyudmila Tourischeva, USSR	77.025
1956	Larissa Latynina, USSR	74.933	1976	Nadia Comaneci, ROM	79.275
1960	Larissa Latynina, USSR	77.031	1980	Yelena Davydova, USSR	79.15
1964	Vera Cáslavská, CZE	77.564	1984	Mary Lou Retton, USA	79.175
1968	Vera Cáslavská, CZE	78.25	1988	Elena Shushunova, USSR	79.662

Vault

Year		Points	Year		Points
1952	Yekaterina Kalinchuk, USSR	19.20	1972	Karin Janz, E.Ger	19.525
1956	Larissa Latynina, USSR	18.833	1976	Nelli Kim, USSR	19.80
1960	Margarita Nikolayeva, USSR	19.316	1980	Natalya Shaposhnikova, USSR	19.725
1964	Vera Cáslavská, CZE	19.483	1984	Ecaterina Szabó, ROM	19.875
1968	Vera Cáslavská, CZE	19.775	1988	Svetlana Boguinskaya, USSR	19.905

Uneven Bars

Year		Points	Year		Points
1952	Margit Korondi, HUN	19.40	1972	Karin Janz, E.Ger	19.675
1956	Agnes Keleti, HUN	18.966	1976	Nadia Comaneci, ROM	20.00
1960	Polina Astakhova, USSR	19.616	1980	Maxi Gnauck, E.Ger	19.875
1964	Polina Astakhova, USSR	19.332	1984	Ma Yanhong, CHN	19.95
1968	Vera Cáslavská, CZE	19.65	1988	Daniela Silivas, ROM	20.00

Balance Beam

Year		Points	Year		Points
1952	Nina Bocharova, USSR	19.22	1972	Olga Korbut, USSR	19.40
1956	Agnes Keleti, HUN	18.80	1976	Nadia Comaneci, ROM	19.95
1960	Eva Bosáková, CZE	19.283	1980	Nadia Comaneci, ROM	19.80
1964	Vera Cástavská, CZE	19.449	1984	Simona Pauca, ROM	19.80
1968	Natalya Kuchinskaya, USSR	19.65	1988	Daniela Silivas, ROM	19.924

Floor Exercise

Year		Points	Year		Points
1952	Agnes Keleti, HUN	19.36	1972	Olga Korbut, USSR	19.575
1956	Agnes Keleti, HUN	18.733	1976	Nelli Kim, USSR	19.85
1960	Larissa Latynina, USSR	19.583	1980	Nadia Comaneci, ROM	19.875
1964	Larissa Latynina, USSR	19.599	1984	Ecaterina Szabó, ROM	19.975
1968	Vera Cáslavská, CZE	19.675	1988	Daniela Silivas, ROM	19.937

Team Combined Exercises

Year		Points	Year		Points
1928	Holland	316.75	1968	Soviet Union	382.85
1936	Germany	506.50	1972	Soviet Union	380.50
1948	Czechoslovakia	445.45	1976	Soviet Union	466.00
1952	Soviet Union	527.03	1980	Soviet Union	394.90
1956	Soviet Union	444.800	1984	Romania	392.02
1960	Soviet Union	382.320	1988	Soviet Union	395.475
1964	Soviet Union	280.890			

Rhythmic All-Around

Year		Points	Year		Points
1984	Lori Fung, CAN	57.950	1988	Marina Lobatch, USSR	60.00

Soccer

Year		Year	
1900	**Great Britain**, France, Belgium	1952	**Hungary**, Yugoslavia, Sweden
1904	**Canada**, USA I, USA II	1956	**Soviet Union**, Yugoslavia, Bulgaria
1906	**Denmark**, Smyrna (Int'l entry), Greece	1960	**Yugoslavia**, Denmark, Hungary
1908	**Great Britain**, Denmark, Holland	1964	**Hungary**, Czechoslovakia, Germany
1912	**Great Britain**, Denmark, Holland	1968	**Hungary**, Bulgaria, Japan
1920	**Belgium**, Spain, Holland	1972	**Poland**, Hungary, E. Germany
1924	**Uruguay**, Switzerland, Sweden	1976	**East Germany**, Poland, Soviet Union
1928	**Uruguay**, Argentina, Italy	1980	**Czechoslovakia**, E. Germany, Soviet Union
1936	**Italy**, Austria, Norway	1984	**France**, Brazil, Yugoslavia
1948	**Sweden**, Yugoslavia, Denmark	1988	**Soviet Union**, Brazil, W. Germany

Swimming
MEN

50-Meter Freestyle

Year		Time		Year		Time	
1904	Zoltán Halmay, HUN	28.0		1988	Matt Biondi, USA	22.14	WR

100-Meter Freestyle

Year		Time		Year		Time	
1896	Alfréd Hajós, HUN	1:22.2	OR	1952	Clarke Scholes, USA	57.4	
1904	Zoltán Halmay, HUN.	1:02.8		1956	Jon Henricks, AUS	55.4	OR
1906	Charles Daniels, USA.	1:13.4		1960	John Devitt, AUS	55.2	OR
1908	Charles Daniels, USA.	1:05.6	WR	1964	Don Schollander, USA	53.4	OR
1912	Duke Kahanamoku, USA	1:03.4		1968	Michael Wenden, AUS	52.2	OR
1920	Duke Kahanamoku, USA	1:00.4	WR	1972	Mark Spitz, USA	51.22	WR
1924	Johnny Weissmuller, USA	59.0	WR	1976	Jim Montgomery, USA	49.99	WR
1928	Johnny Weissmuller, USA	58.6	OR	1980	Jorg Woithe, E.Ger	50:40	
1932	Yasuji Miyazaki, JPN	58.2		1984	Rowdy Gaines, USA	49.80	OR
1936	Ferenc Csik, HUN	57.6		1988	Matt Biondi, USA	48.63	OR
1948	Wally Ris, USA	57.3	OR				

200-Meter Freestyle

Year		Time		Year		Time	
1900	Frederick Lane, AUS	2:25.2	OR	1976	Bruce Furniss, USA.	1:50.29	WR
1904	Charles Daniels, USA.	2:44.2		1980	Sergei Kopliakov, USSR.	1:49.81	OR
1968	Michael Wenden, AUS.	1:55.2	OR	1984	Michael Gross, W.Ger.	1:47.44	WR
1972	Mark Spitz, USA	1:52.78	WR	1988	Duncan Armstrong, AUS.	1:47.25	WR

400-Meter Freestyle

Year		Time		Year		Time	
1896	Paul Neumann, AUT	8:12.6		1952	Jean Boiteux, FRA.	4:30.7	OR
1904	Charles Daniels, USA.	6:16.2		1956	Murray Rose, AUS	4:27.3	OR
1906	Otto Scheff, AUT.	6:23.8		1960	Murray Rose, AUS	4:18.3	OR
1908	Henry Taylor, GBR	5:36.8		1964	Don Schollander, USA.	4:12.2	OR
1912	George Hodgson, CAN.	5:24.4		1968	Mike Burton, USA.	4:09.0	OR
1920	Norman Ross, USA	5:26.8		1972	Bradford Cooper, USA*	4:00.27	
1924	Johnny Weissmuller, USA	5:04.2	OR	1976	Brian Goodell, USA.	3:51.93	WR
1928	Alberto Zorilla, ARG.	5:01.6	OR	1980	Vladimir Salnikov, USSR	3:51.31	OR
1932	Buster Crabbe, USA.	4:48.4	OR	1984	George DiCarlo, USA	3:51.23	OR
1936	Jack Medica, USA.	4:44.5	OR	1988	Ewe Dassler, E.Ger	3:46.95	WR
1948	Bill Smith, USA	4:41.0	OR				

*Cooper finished second to Rick DeMont of the U.S. who was disqualified when he flunked the post-race drug test (his asthma medication was on the IOC's banned list).

Swimming (Cont.)
MEN
1500-Meter Freestyle

Year		Time		Year		Time	
1896	Alfréd Hajós, HUN.	18:22.2	OR	1948	James McLane, USA	19:18.5	
1900	John Arthur Jarvis, GBR.	13:40.2		1952	Ford Konno, USA.	18:30.3	OR
1904	Emil Rausch, GER.	27:18.2		1956	Murray Rose, AUS	17:58.9	
1906	Henry Taylor, GBR.	28:28.0		1960	John Konrads, AUS	17:19.6	OR
1908	Henry Taylor, GBR.	22:48.4	WR	1964	Robert Windle, AUS.	17:01.7	OR
1912	George Hodgson, CAN	22:00.0	WR	1968	Mike Burton, USA	16:38.9	OR
1920	Norman Ross, USA	22:23.2		1972	Mike Burton, USA	15:52.58	WR
1924	Boy Charlton, AUS.	20:06.6	WR	1976	Brian Goodell, USA.	15:02.40	WR
1928	Arne Borge, SWE	19:51.8	OR	1980	Vladimir Salnikov, USSR	14:58.27	WR
1932	Kusuo Kitamura, JPN.	19:12.4	OR	1984	Mike O'Brien, USA	15:05.20	
1936	Noboru Terada, JPN.	19:13.7		1988	Vladimir Salnikov, USSR	15:00.40	

100-Meter Backstroke

Year		Time		Year		Time	
1904	Walter Brack, GER	1:16.8		1952	Yoshinobu Oyakawa, USA	1:05.4	OR
1908	Arno Bieberstein, GER	1:24.6	WR	1956	David Theile, AUS	1:02.2	OR
1912	Harry Hebner, USA	1:21.2		1960	David Theile, AUS	1:01.9	OR
1920	Warren Kealoha, USA	1:15.2		1968	Roland Matthes, E.Ger	58.7	OR
1924	Warren Kealoha, USA	1:13.2	OR	1972	Roland Matthes, E.Ger	56.58	OR
1928	George Kojac, USA	1:08.2	WR	1976	John Naber, USA	55.49	WR
1932	Masaji Kiyokawa, JPN	1:08.6		1980	Bengt Baron, SWE	56.33	
1936	Adolf Kiefer, USA	1:05.9	OR	1984	Rick Carey, USA.	55.79	
1948	Allen Stack, USA.	1:06.4		1988	Daichi Suzuki, JPN.	55.05	

200-Meter Backstroke

Year		Time		Year		Time	
1900	Ernst Hoppenberg, GER	2:47.0		1976	John Naber, USA.	1:59.19	WR
1964	Jed Graef, USA	2:10.3	WR	1980	Sqandor Wladár, HUN	2:01.93	
1968	Roland Matthes, E.Ger.	2:09.6	OR	1984	Rick Carey, USA.	2:00.23	
1972	Roland Matthes, E.Ger.	2:02.82	=WR	1988	Igor Polianski, USSR.	1:59.37	

100-Meter Breaststroke

Year		Time		Year		Time	
1968	Don McKenzie, USA.	1:07.7	OR	1980	Duncan Goodhew, GBR	1:03.44	
1972	Nobutaka Taguchi, JPN	1:04.94	WR	1984	Steve Lundquist, USA.	1:01.65	WR
1976	John Hencken, USA.	1:03.11	WR	1988	Adrian Moorhouse, GBR.	1:02.04	

200-Meter Breaststroke

Year		Time		Year		Time	
1908	Frederick Holman, GBR.	3:09.2	WR	1956	Masaru Furukawa, JPN.	2:34.7	OR
1912	Walter Bathe, GER	3:01.8	OR	1960	Bill Mulliken, USA.	2:37.4	
1920	Hakan Malmroth, SWE	3:04.4		1964	Ian O'Brien, AUS.	2:27.8	WR
1924	Robert Skelton, USA.	2:56.6		1968	Felipe Munoz, MEX	2:28.7	
1928	Yoshiyuki Tsuruta, JPN.	2:48.8	OR	1972	John Hencken, USA.	2:21.55	WR
1932	Yoshiyuki Tsuruta, JPN.	2:45.4		1976	David Wilkie, GBR	2:15.11	WR
1936	Tetsuo Hamuro, JPN	2:41.5	OR	1980	Robertas Zhulpa, USSR	2:15.85	
1948	Joseph Verdeur, USA.	2:39.3	OR	1984	Victor Davis, CAN	2:13.34	WR
1952	John Davies, AUS.	2:34.4		1988	Jozsef Szabo, HUN	2:13.52	

100-Meter Butterfly

Year		Time		Year		Time	
1968	Doug Russell, USA.	55.9	OR	1980	Pär Arvidsson, SWE	54.92	
1972	Mark Spitz, USA.	54.27	WR	1984	Michael Gross, W.Ger	53.08	WR
1976	Matt Vogel, USA	54.35		1988	Anthony Nesty, SUR.	53.0	OR

200-Meter Butterfly

Year		Time		Year		Time	
1956	Bill Yorzyk, USA	2:19.3	OR	1976	Mike Bruner, USA.	1:59.23	WR
1960	Mike Troy, USA.	2:12.8	WR	1980	Sergei Fesenko, USSR	1:59.76	
1964	Kevin Berry, AUS	2:06.6	WR	1984	Jon Sieben, AUS.	1:57.04	WR
1968	Carl Robie, USA.	2:08.7		1988	Michael Gross, W.Ger.	1:56.94	OR
1972	Mark Spitz, USA.	2:00.70	WR				

200-Meter Individual Medley

Year		Time		Year		Time	
1968	Charles Hickcox, USA	2:12.0	OR	1984	Alex Baumann, CAN	2:01.42	WR
1972	Gunnar Larsson, SWE	2:07.17	WR	1988	Tamas Darnyi, HUN	2:00.17	WR

400-Meter Individual Medley

Year		Time		Year		Time	
1964	Richard Roth, USA	4:45.4	WR	1980	Aleksandr Sidorenko, USSR	4:22.89	OR
1968	Charles Hickcox, USA	4:48.4		1984	Alex Baumann, CAN	4:17.41	WR
1972	Gunnar Larsson, SWE	4:31.98	OR	1988	Tamas Darnyi, HUN	4:14.75	WR
1976	Rod Strachan, USA	4:23.68	WR				

4x100-Meter Freestyle Relay

Year		Time		Year		Time	
1964	United States	3:32.2	WR	1984	United States	3:19.03	WR
1968	United States	3:31.7	WR	1988	United States	3:16.53	WR
1972	United States	3:26.42	WR				

4x200-Meter Freestyle Relay

Year		Time		Year		Time	
1906	Hungary	16:52.4		1956	Australia	8:23.6	WR
1908	Great Britain	10:55.6	WR	1960	United States	8:10.2	WR
1912	Australia/New Zealand	10:11.6	WR	1964	United States	7:52.1	WR
1920	United States	10:04.4	WR	1968	United States	7:52.33	
1924	United States	9:53.4	WR	1972	United States	7:35.78	WR
1928	United States	9:36.2	WR	1976	United States	7:23.22	WR
1932	Japan	8:58.4	WR	1980	Soviet Union	7:23.50	
1936	Japan	8:51.5		1984	United States	7:15.69	WR
1948	United States	8:46.0	WR	1988	United States	7:12.51	WR
1952	United States	8:31.1	OR				

4x100-Meter Medley Relay

Year		Time		Year		Time	
1960	United States	4:05.4	WR	1976	United States	3:42.22	WR
1964	United States	3:58.4	WR	1980	Australia	3:45.70	
1968	United States	3:54.9	WR	1984	United States	3:39.30	WR
1972	United States	3:48.16	WR	1988	United States	3:36.93	WR

WOMEN

50-Meter Freestyle

Year		Time	
1988	Kristin Otto, E.Ger	25.49	OR

100-Meter Freestyle

Year		Time		Year		Time	
1912	Fanny Durack, AUS	1:22.2		1960	Dawn Fraser, AUS	1:01.2	OR
1920	Ethelda Bleibtrey, USA	1:13.6	WR	1964	Dawn Fraser, AUS	59.5	OR
1924	Ethel Lackie, USA	1:12.4		1968	Jan Henne, USA	1:00.0	
1928	Albina Osipowich, USA	1:11.0	OR	1972	Sandra Neilson, USA	58.59	OR
1932	Helene Madison, USA	1:06.8	OR	1976	Kornelia Ender, E.Ger	55.65	WR
1936	Rie Mastenbroek, HOL	1:05.9	WR	1980	Barbara Krause, E.Ger	54.79	WR
1948	Greta Andersen, DEN	1:06.3		1984	Nancy Hogshead, USA	55.92	
1952	Katalin Szöke, HUN	1:06.8			& Carrie Steinseifer, USA	55.92	
1956	Dawn Fraser, AUS	1:02.0	WR	1988	Kristin Otto, E.Ger	54.93	

200-Meter Freestyle

Year		Time		Year		Time	
1968	Debbie Meyer, USA	2:10.5	OR	1980	Barbara Krause, E.Ger	1:58.33	OR
1972	Shane Gould, AUS	2:03.56	WR	1984	Mary Wayte, USA	1:59.23	
1976	Kornelia Ender, E.Ger	1:59.26	WR	1988	Heike Friedrich, E.Ger	1:57.65	OR

400-Meter Freestyle

Year		Time		Year		Time	
1920	Ethelda Bleibtrey, USA	4:34.0	WR	1960	Chris Von Saltza, USA	4:50.6	OR
1924	Martha Norelius, USA	6:02.2	WR	1964	Ginny Duenkel, USA	4:43.3	OR
1928	Martha Norelius, USA	5:42.8	WR	1968	Debbie Meyer, USA	4:31.8	OR
1932	Helene Madison, USA	5:28.5	WR	1972	Shane Gould, AUS	4:19.44	WR
1936	Rie Mastenbroek, HOL	5:26.4	OR	1976	Petra Thümer, E.Ger	4:09.89	WR
1948	Ann Curtis, USA	5:17.8	OR	1980	Ines Diers, E.Ger	4:08.76	OR
1952	Valéria Gyenge, HUN	5:12.1	OR	1984	Tiffany Cohen, USA	4:07.10	OR
1956	Lorraine Crapp, AUS	4:54.6	OR	1988	Janet Evans, USA	4:03.85	WR

800-Meter Freestyle

Year		Time		Year		Time	
1968	Debbie Meyer, USA	9:24.0	OR	1980	Michelle Ford, AUS	8:28.90	OR
1972	Keena Rothhammer, USA	8:53.68	WR	1984	Tiffany Cohen, USA	8:24.95	OR
1976	Petra Thümer, E.Ger	8:37.14	WR	1988	Janet Evans, USA	8:20.20	OR

Swimming (Cont.)
WOMEN
100-Meter Backstroke

Year		Time		Year		Time	
1924	Sybil Bauer, USA	1:23.2	OR	1964	Cathy Ferguson, USA	1:07.7	WR
1928	Maria Braun, HOL	1:22.0		1968	Kaye Hall, USA	1:06.2	WR
1932	Eleanor Holm, USA	1:19.4		1972	Melissa Belote, USA	1:05.78	OR
1936	Nida Senff, HOL	1:18.9		1976	Ulrike Richter, E.Ger	1:01.83	OR
1948	Karen-Margrete Harup, DEN	1:14.4	OR	1980	Rica Reinisch, E.Ger	1:00.86	WR
1952	Joan Harrison, SAF	1:14.3		1984	Theresa Andrews, USA	1:02.55	
1956	Judith Grinham, GBR	1:12.9	OR	1988	Kristin Otto, E.Ger	1:00.89	
1960	Lynn Burke, USA	1:09.3	OR				

200-Meter Backstroke

Year		Time		Year		Time	
1968	Lillian Watson, USA	2:24.8	OR	1980	Rica Reinisch, E.Ger	2:11.77	WR
1972	Melissa Belote, USA	2:19.19	WR	1984	Jolanda de Rover, HOL	2:12.38	
1976	Ulrike Richter, E.Ger	2:13.43	OR	1988	Krisztina Egerszegi, HUN	2:09.29	OR

100-Meter Breaststroke

Year		Time		Year		Time	
1968	Djurdjica Bjedov, YUG	1:15.8	OR	1980	Ute Geweniger, E.Ger	1:10.22	
1972	Cathy Carr, USA	1:13.58	WR	1984	Petra van Staveren, HOL	1:09.88	OR
1976	Hannelore Anke, E.Ger	1:11.16		1988	Tania Dangalakova, BUL	1:07.95	OR

200-Meter Breaststroke

Year		Time		Year		Time	
1924	Lucy Morton, GBR	3:33.2	OR	1964	Galina Prozumenshikova, USSR	2:46.4	OR
1928	Hilde Schrader, GER	3:12.6		1968	Sharon Wichman, USA	2:44.4	OR
1932	Clare Dennis, AUS	3:06.3	OR	1972	Beverley Whitfield, AUS	2:41.71	OR
1936	Hideko Maehata, JPN	3:03.6		1976	Marina Koshevaia, USSR	2:33.35	WR
1948	Petronella van Vliet, HOL	2:57.2		1980	Lina Kaciusyte, USSR	2:29.54	OR
1952	Eva Szekely, HUN	2:51.7	OR	1984	Anne Ottenbrite, CAN	2:30.38	
1956	Ursula Happe, GER	2:53.1	OR	1988	Silke Hoerner, E.Ger	2:26.71	WR
1960	Anita Lonsbrough, GBR	2:49.5	WR				

100-Meter Butterfly

Year		Time		Year		Time	
1956	Shelly Mann, USA	1:11.0	OR	1976	Kornelia Ender, E.Ger	1:00.13=	WR
1960	Carolyn Schuler, USA	1:09.5	OR	1980	Caren Metschuck, E.Ger	1:00.42	
1964	Sharon Stouder, USA	1:04.7	WR	1984	Mary T. Meagher, USA	59.26	
1968	Lyn McClements, AUS	1:05.5		1988	Kristin Otto, E.Ger	59.00	OR
1972	Mayumi Aoki, JPN	1:03.34	WR				

200-Meter Butterfly

Year		Time		Year		Time	
1968	Ada Kok, HOL	2:24.7	OR	1980	Ines Geissler, E.Ger	2:10.44	OR
1972	Karen Moe, USA	2:15.57	WR	1984	Mary T. Meagher, USA	2:06.90	OR
1976	Andrea Pollack, E.Ger	2:11.41	OR	1988	Kathleen Nord, E.Ger	2:09.51	

200-Meter Individual Medley

Year		Time		Year		Time	
1968	Claudia Kolb, USA	2:24.7	OR	1984	Tracy Caulkins, USA	2:12.64	OR
1972	Shane Gould, AUS	2:23.07	WR	1988	Daniela Hunger, E.Ger	2:12.59	OR

400-Meter Individual Medley

Year		Time		Year		Time	
1968	Donna de Varona, USA	5:18.7	OR	1980	Petra Schneider, E.Ger	4:36.29	WR
1968	Claudia Kolb, USA	5:08.5	OR	1984	Tracy Caulkins, USA	4:39.24	
1972	Gail Neall, AUS	5:02.97	WR	1988	Janet Evans, USA	4:37.76	
1976	Ulrike Tauber, E.Ger	4:42.77	WR				

4x100-Meter Freestyle Relay

Year		Time		Year		Time	
1912	Great Britain	5:52.8	WR	1960	United States	4:08.9	WR
1920	United States	5:11.6	WR	1964	United States	4:03.8	WR
1924	United States	4:58.8	WR	1968	United States	4:02.5	OR
1928	United States	4:47.6	WR	1972	United States	3:55.19	WR
1932	United States	4:38.0	WR	1976	United States	3:44.82	WR
1936	Holland	4:36.0	OR	1980	East Germany	3:42.71	WR
1948	United States	4:29.2	OR	1984	United States	3:43.43	
1952	Hungary	4:24.4	WR	1988	East Germany	3:40.63	OR
1956	Australia	4:17.1	WR				

4x100-Meter Medley Relay

Year		Time		Year		Time	
1960	United States	4:41.1	WR	1976	East Germany	4:07.95	WR
1964	United States	4:33.9	WR	1980	East Germany	4:06.67	WR
1968	United States	4:28.3	OR	1984	United States	4:08.34	
1972	United States	4:20.75	WR	1988	East Germany	4:03.74	OR

Synchronized Swimming — Solo

Year		Points	Year		Points
1984	Tracie Ruiz, USA	198.467	1988	Carolyn Waldo, CAN	200.15

Synchronized Swimming — Duet

Year		Points	Year		Points
1984	Tracie Ruiz & Candy Costie, USA	195.584	1988	Carolyn Waldo & Michelle Cameron, CAN	197.717

Tennis
MEN
Singles

Year			Year		
1896	John Boland	Great Britain/Ireland	1912	Charles Winslow	South Africa
1900	Laurie Doherty	Great Britain		(Indoor) André Gobert	France
1904	Beals Wright	United States	1920	Louis Raymond	South Africa
1906	Max Decugis	France	1924	Vincent Richards	United States
1908	Josiah Ritchie	Great Britain	1988	Miloslav Mecir	Czechoslovakia
	(Indoor) Arthur Gore	Great Britain			

Doubles

Year		Year	
1896	John Boland, IRL & Fritz Traun, GER	1912	Charles Winslow & Harold Kitson, SAF
1900	Laurie and Reggie Doherty, GBR		(Indoor) André Gobert & Maurice Germot, FRA
1904	Edgar Leonard & Beals Wright, USA	1920	Noel Turnbull & Max Woosnam, GBR
1906	Max Decugis & Maurice Germot, FRA	1924	Vincent Richards & Frank Hunter, USA
1908	George Hillyard & Reggie Doherty, GRB	1988	Ken Flach & Robert Seguso, USA
	(Indoor) Arthur Gore & Herbert Barrett, GBR		

WOMEN
Singles

Year			Year		
1900	Charlotte Cooper	Great Britain	1912	Edith Hannam	Great Britain
1906	Esmee Simiriotu	Greece	1920	Suzanne Lenglen	France
1908	Dorothy Chambers	Great Britain	1924	Helen Wills	United States
1908	Gwendoline Eastlake-Smith	Great Britain	1988	Steffi Graf	West Germany
1912	Marguerite Broquedis	France			

Doubles

Year		Year	
1920	Winifred McNair & Kitty McKane, GBR	1988	Pam Shriver & Zina Garrison, USA
1924	Hazel Wightman & Helen Wills, USA		

Track & Field
MEN
100 Meters

Year		Time		Year		Time	
1896	Tom Burke, USA	12.0		1948	Harrison Dillard, USA	10.3	=OR
1900	Frank Jarvis, USA	11.0		1952	Lindy Remigino, USA	10.4	
1904	Archie Hahn, USA	11.0		1956	Bobby Morrow, USA	10.5	
1906	Archie Hahn, USA	11.2		1960	Armin Hary, GER	10.2	OR
1908	Reggie Walker, SAF	10.8	=OR	1964	Bob Hayes, USA	10.0	=WR
1912	Ralph Craig, USA	10.8		1968	Jim Hines, USA	9.95	WR
1920	Charley Paddock, USA	10.8		1972	Valery Borzov, USSR	10.14	
1924	Harold Abrahams, GBR	10.6	=OR	1976	Hasely Crawford, TRI	10.06	
1928	Percy Williams, CAN	10.8		1980	Allan Wells, GBR	10.25	
1932	Eddie Tolan, USA	10.3	OR	1984	Carl Lewis, USA	9.99	
1936	Jesse Owens, USA	10.3		1988	Carl Lewis, USA	9.92	WR

Track & Field (Cont.)

MEN

200 Meters

Year		Time		Year		Time	
1900	John Walter Tewksbury, USA	22.2		1952	Andy Stanfield, USA	20.7	
1904	Archie Hahn, USA	21.6	OR	1956	Bobby Morrow, USA	20.6	OR
1908	Bobby Kerr, CAN	22.6		1960	Livio Berruti, ITA	20.5	=WR
1912	Ralph Craig, USA	21.7		1964	Henry Carr, USA	20.3	OR
1920	Allen Woodring, USA	22.0		1968	Tommie Smith, USA	19.83	WR
1924	Jackson Scholz, USA	21.6		1972	Valery Borzov, USSR	20.00	
1928	Percy Williams, CAN	21.8		1976	Donald Quarrie, JAM	20.23	
1932	Eddie Tolan, USA	21.2	OR	1980	Pietro Mennea, ITA	20.19	
1936	Jesse Owens, USA	20.7	OR	1984	Carl Lewis, USA	19.80	OR
1948	Mel Patton, USA	21.1		1988	Joe DeLoach, USA	19.75	OR

400 Meters

Year		Time		Year		Time	
1896	Tom Burke, USA	54.2		1948	Arthur Wint, JAM	46.2	
1890	Maxey Long, USA	49.4	OR	1952	George Rhoden, JAM	45.9	
1904	Harry Hillman, USA	49.2	OR	1956	Charley Jenkins, USA	46.7	
1906	Paul Pilgrim, USA	53.2		1960	Otis Davis, USA	44.9	WR
1908	Wyndham Halswelle, GBR	50.0		1964	Mike Larrabee, USA	45.1	
1912	Charlie Reidpath, USA	48.2	OR	1968	Lee Evans, USA	43.86	WR
1920	Bevil Rudd, SAF	49.6		1972	Vince Matthews, USA	44.66	
1924	Eric Liddell, GBR	47.6	OR	1976	Alberto Juantorena, CUB	44.26	
1928	Ray Barbuti, USA	47.8		1980	Viktor Markin, USSR	44.60	
1932	Bill Carr, USA	46.2	WR	1984	Alonzo Babers, USA	44.27	
1936	Archie Williams, USA	46.5		1988	Steve Lewis, USA	43.87	

800 Meters

Year		Time		Year		Time	
1896	Teddy Flack, AUS	2:11.0		1948	Mal Whitfield, USA	1:49.2	OR
1900	Alfred Tysoe, GBR	2:01.2		1952	Mal Whitfield, USA	1:49.2	=OR
1904	Jim Lightbody, USA	1:56.0	OR	1956	Tom Courtney, USA	1:47.7	OR
1906	Paul Pilgrim, USA	2:01.5		1960	Peter Snell, NZE	1:46.3	OR
1908	Mel Sheppard, USA	1:52.8	WR	1964	Peter Snell, NZE	1:45.1	OR
1912	Ted Meredith, USA	1:51.9	WR	1968	Ralph Doubell, AUS	1:44.3	=WR
1920	Albert Hill, GBR	1:53.4		1972	Dave Wottle, USA	1:45.9	
1924	Douglas Lowe, GBR	1:52.4		1976	Alberto Juantorena, CUB	1:43.50	WR
1928	Douglas Lowe, GBR	1:51.8	OR	1980	Steve Ovett, GBR	1:45.4	
1932	Tommy Hampson, GBR	1:49.7	WR	1984	Joaquim Cruz, BRA	1:43.00	OR
1936	John Woodruff, USA	1:52.9		1988	Paul Ereng, KEN	1:43.45	

1500 Meters

Year		Time		Year		Time	
1896	Teddy Flack, AUS	4:33.2		1948	Henry Eriksson, SWE	3:49.8	
1900	Charles Bennett, GBR	4:06.2	WR	1952	Josy Barthel, LUX	3:45.1	OR
1904	Jim Lightbody, USA	4:05.4	WR	1956	Ron Delany, IRL	3:41.2	OR
1906	Jim Lightbody, USA	4:12.0		1960	Herb Elliott, AUS	3:35.6	WR
1908	Mel Sheppard, USA	4:03.4	OR	1964	Peter Snell, NZE	3:38.1	
1912	Arnold Jackson, GBR	3:56.8	OR	1968	Kip Keino, KEN	3:34.9	OR
1920	Albert Hill, GBR	4:01.8		1972	Pekkha Vasala, FIN	3:36.3	
1924	Paavo Nurmi, FIN	3:53.6	OR	1976	John Walker, NZE	3:39.17	
1928	Harry Larva, FIN	3:53.2	OR	1980	Sebastian Coe, GBR	3:38.4	
1932	Luigi Beccali, ITA	3:51.2	OR	1984	Sebastian Coe, GBR	3:32.53	OR
1936	John Lovelock, NZE	3:47.8	WR	1988	Peter Rono, KEN	3:35.96	

5000 Meters

Year		Time		Year		Time	
1912	Hannes Kolehmainen, FIN	14:36.6	WR	1960	Murray Halberg, NZE	13:43.4	
1920	Joseph Guillemot, FRA	14:55.6		1964	Bob Schul, USA	13:48.8	
1924	Paavo Nurmi, FIN	14:31.2	OR	1968	Mohamed Gammoudi, TUN	14:05.0	
1928	Ville Ritola, FIN	14:38.0		1972	Lasse Viren, FIN	13:26.4	OR
1932	Lauri Lehtinen, FIN	14:30.0	OR	1976	Lasse Viren, FIN	13:24.76	
1936	Gunnar Hrockert, FIN	14:22.2	OR	1980	Miruts Yifter, ETH	13:21.0	
1948	Gaston Reiff, BEL	14:17.6	OR	1984	Said Aouita, MOR	13:05.59	OR
1952	Emil Zátopek, CZE	14:06.6	OR	1988	John Ngugi, KEN	13:11.70	
1956	Vladimir Kuts, USSR	13:39.6	OR				

10,000 Meters

Year		Time	
1912	Hannes Kolehmainen, FIN	31:20.8	
1920	Paavo Nurmi, FIN	31:45.8	
1924	Ville Ritola, FIN	30:23.2	WR
1928	Paavo Nurmi, FIN	30:18.8	OR
1932	Janusz Kusocinski, POL	30:11.4	OR
1936	Ilmari Salminen, FIN	30:15.4	
1948	Emil Zátopek, CZE	29:59.6	OR
1952	Emil Zátopek, CZE	29:17.0	OR
1956	Vladimir Kuts, USSR	28:45.6	OR
1960	Pyotr Bolotnikov, USSR	28:32.2	OR
1964	Billy Mills, USA	28:24.4	OR
1968	Naftali Temu, KEN	29:27.4	
1972	Lasse Viren, FIN	27:38.4	WR
1976	Lasse Viren, FIN	27:40.38	
1980	Miruts Yifter, ETH	27:42.7	
1984	Alberto Cova, ITA	27:47.54	
1988	Brahim Boutaib, MOR	27:21.46	

Marathon

Year		Time	
1896	Spiridon Louis, GRE	2:58:50	
1900	Michel Thqeato, FRA	2:59:45	
1904	Thomas Hicks, USA	3:28:53	
1906	Billy Sherring, CAN	2:51:23.6	
1908	Johnny Hayes, USA*	2:55:18.4	
1912	Kenneth McArthur, SAF	2:36:54.8	
1920	Hannes Kolehmainen, FIN	2:32:35.8	WB
1924	Albin Stenroos, FIN	2:41:22.6	
1928	Boughêra El Ouafi, FRA	2:32:57.0	
1932	Juan Carlos Zabala, ARG	2:31:36.0	OR
1936	Kee-Chung Sohn, JPN†	2:29:19.2	OR
1948	Delfo Cabrera, ARG	2:34:51.6	
1952	Emil Zátopek, CZE	2:23:03.2	OR
1956	Alain Mimoun, FRA	2:25:00.0	
1960	Abebe Bikila, ETH	2:15:16.2	WB
1964	Abebe Bikila, ETH	2:12:11.2	WB
1968	Mamo Wolde, ETH	2:20:26.4	
1972	Frank Shorter, USA	2:12:19.8	
1976	Waldemar Cierpinski, E.Ger	2:09:55.0	OR
1980	Waldemar Cierpinski, E.Ger	2:11:03.0	
1984	Carlos Lopes, POR	2:09:21.0	OR
1988	Gelindo Bordin, ITA	2:10:32	

*Dorando Pietri of Italy placed first but was disqualified for being helped across the finish line.

†Sohn was a Korean, but forced to compete for Japan, which occupied Korea at the time.

Note: Marathon distances—40,000 meters (1896,1904); 40,260 meters (1900); 41,860 meters (1906); 42,195 meters (1908 and since 1924); 40,200 meters (1912); 42,750 meters (1920). Current distance of 42,195 meters measures 26 miles, 385 yards.

110-Meter Hurdles

Year		Time	
1896	Tom Curtis, USA	17.6	
1900	Alvin Kraenzlein, USA	15.4	OR
1904	Frederick Schule, USA	16.0	
1906	Robert Leavitt, USA	16.2	
1908	Forrest Smithson, USA	15.0	WR
1912	Frederick Kelly, USA	15.1	
1920	Earl Thomson, CAN	14.8	WR
1924	Daniel Kinsey, USA	15.0	
1928	Syd Atkinson, SAF	14.8	
1932	George Saling, USA	14.6	
1936	Forrest (Spec) Towns, USA	14.2	
1948	William Porter, USA	13.9	OR
1952	Harrison Dillard, USA	13.7	OR
1956	Lee Calhoun, USA	13.5	OR
1960	Lee Calhoun, USA	13.8	
1964	Hayes Jones, USA	13.6	
1968	Willie Davenport, USA	13.3	OR
1972	Rod Milburn, USA	13.24	=WR
1976	Guy Drut, FRA	13.30	
1980	Thomas Munkelt, E.Ger	13.39	
1984	Roger Kingdom, USA	13.20	OR
1988	Roger Kingdom, USA	12.98	OR

400-Meter Hurdles

Year		Time	
1900	John Walter Tewksbury, USA	57.6	
1904	Harry Hillman, USA	53.0	
1908	Charley Bacon, USA	55.0	WR
1920	Frank Loomis, USA	54.0	WR
1924	Morgan Taylor, USA	52.6	
1928	David Burghley, GBR	53.4	OR
1932	Bob Tisdall, IRL	51.7	
1936	Glenn Hardin, USA	52.4	
1948	Roy Cochran, USA	51.1	OR
1952	Charley Moore, USA	50.8	OR
1956	Glenn Davis, USA	50.1	=OR
1960	Glenn Davis, USA	49.3	=OR
1964	Rex Cawley, USA	49.6	
1968	David Hemery, GBR	48.12	WR
1972	John Akii-Bua, UGA	47.82	WR
1976	Edwin Moses, USA	47.64	WR
1980	Volker Beck, E.Ger	48.70	
1984	Edwin Moses, USA	47.75	
1988	Andre Phillips, USA	47.19	OR

3000-Meter Steeplechase

Year		Time	
1900	George Orton, CAN/USA	7:34.4	
1904	Jim Lightbody, USA	7:39.6	
1908	Arthur Russell, GBR	10:47.8	
1920	Percy Hodge, GBR	10:00.4	OR
1924	Ville Ritola, FIN	9:33.6	OR
1928	Toivo Loukola, FIN	9:21.8	WR
1932	Volmari Iso-Hollo, FIN*	10:33.4	
1936	Volmari Iso-Hollo, FIN	9:03.8	WR
1948	Thore Sjöstrand, SWE	9:04.6	
1952	Horace Ashenfelter, USA	8:45.4	WR
1956	Chris Brasher, GBR	8:41.2	OR
1960	Zdzislaw Krzyszkowiak, POL	8:34.2	OR
1964	Gaston Roelants, BEL	8:30.8	OR
1968	Amos Biwott, KEN	8:51.0	
1972	Kip Keino, KEN	8:23.6	
1976	Anders Gärderud, SWE	8:08.2	WR
1980	Bronislaw Malinowski, POL	8:09.7	
1984	Julius Korir, KEN	8:11.80	
1988	Julius Kariuki, KEN	8:05.51	OR

*Iso-Hollo ran one extra lap due to lap counter's mistake.

Track & Field (Cont.)
MEN
4x100-Meter Relay

Year		Time		Year		Time	
1912	Great Britain	42.4	OR	1960	Germany	39.5	=WR
1920	United States	42.2	WR	1964	United States	39.0	WR
1924	United States	41.0	=WR	1968	United States	38.2	WR
1928	United States	41.0	=WR	1972	United States	38.19	=WR
1932	United States	40.0	WR	1976	United States	38.33	
1936	United States	39.8	WR	1980	Soviet Union	38.26	
1948	United States	40.6		1984	United States	37.83	WR
1952	United States	40.1		1988	Soviet Union	38.19	
1956	United States	39.5	WR				

4x400-Meter Relay

Year		Time		Year		Time	
1908	United States	3:29.4		1956	United States	3:04.8	
1912	United States	3:16.6	WR	1960	United States	3:02.2	WR
1920	Great Britain	3:22.2		1964	United States	3:00.7	WR
1924	United States	3:16.0	WR	1968	United States	2:56.16	WR
1928	United States	3:14.2	WR	1972	Kenya	2:59.8	
1932	United States	3:08.2	WR	1976	United States	2:58.65	
1936	Great Britain	3:09.0		1980	Soviet Union	3:01.1	
1948	United States	3:10.4	WR	1984	United States	2:57.91	
1952	Jamaica	3:03.9	WR	1988	United States	2:56.16	=WR

20-Kilometer Walk

Year		Time		Year		Time	
1956	Leonid Spirin, USSR	1:31:27.4		1976	Daniel Bautista Rocha, MEX	1:24:40.6	OR
1960	Vladimir Golubnichiy, USSR	1:34:07.2		1980	Maurizio Damilano, ITA	1:23:35.5	OR
1964	Ken Matthews, GBR	1:29:34.0	OR	1984	Ernesto Canto, MEX	1:23:13.0	OR
1968	Vladimir Golubnichiy, USSR	1:33:58.4		1988	Josef Pribilinec, CZE	1:19:57.0	OR
1972	Peter Frenkel, E.Ger	1:26:42.4	OR				

50-Kilometer Walk

Year		Time		Year		Time	
1932	Thomas Green, GBR	4:50:10		1968	Christoph Höhne, E.Ger	4:20:13.6	
1936	Harold Whitlock, GBR	4:30:41.4	OR	1972	Bernd Kannenberg, W.Ger	3:56:11.6	OR
1948	John Ljunggren, SWE	4:41.52		1976	Not held		
1952	Giuseppe Dordoni, ITA	4:28:07.8	OR	1980	Hartwig Gauder, E.Ger	3:49:24.0	OR
1956	Norman Read, NZE	4:30:42.8		1984	Raúl González, MEX	3:47:26.0	OR
1960	Don Thompson, GBR	4:25:30.0	OR	1988	Vyacheslav Ivanenko, USSR	3:38:29.0	OR
1964	Abdon Pamich, ITA	4:11:12.4	OR				

High Jump

Year		Height		Year		Height	
1896	Ellery Clark, USA	5-11¼		1948	John Winter, AUS	6-6	
1900	Irving Baxter, USA	6-2¾	OR	1952	Walt Davis, USA	6-8½	OR
1904	Sam Jones, USA	5-11		1956	Charley Dumas, USA	6-11½	OR
1906	Cornelius Leahy, GBR/IRL	5-10		1960	Robert Shavlakadze, USSR	7-1	OR
1908	Harry Porter, USA	6-3	OR	1964	Valery Brumel, USSR	7-1¾	OR
1912	Alma Richards, USA	6-4	OR	1968	Dick Fosbury, USA	7-4¼	OR
1920	Richmond Landon, USA	6-4	=OR	1972	Yuri Tarmak, USSR	7-3¾	
1924	Harold Osborn, USA	6-6	OR	1976	Jacek Wszola, POL	7-4½	OR
1928	Bob King, USA	6-4½		1980	Gerd Wessig, E.Ger	7-8¾	WR
1932	Duncan McNaughton, CAN	6-5½		1984	Dietmar Mögenburg, W.Ger	7-8½	
1936	Cornelius Johnson, USA	6-8	OR	1988	Guennadi Avdeenko, USSR	7-9½	OR

Pole Vault

Year		Height		Year		Height	
1896	William Hoyt, USA	10-10		1948	Guinn Smith, USA	14-1¼	
1900	Irving Baxter, USA	10-10		1952	Bob Richards, USA	14-11	OR
1904	Charles Dvorak, USA	11-5¾		1956	Bob Richards, USA	14-11½	OR
1906	Fernand Gonder, FRA	11-5¾		1960	Don Bragg, USA	15-5	OR
1908	Edward Cooke, USA			1964	Fred Hansen, USA	16-8¾	OR
	& Alfred Gilbert, USA	12-2	OR	1968	Bob Seagren, USA	17-8½	OR
1912	Harry Babcock, USA	12-11½	OR	1972	Wolfgang Nordwig, E.Ger	18-0½	OR
1920	Frank Foss, USA	13-5	WR	1976	Tadeusz Slusarski, POL	18-0½	=OR
1924	Lee Barnes, USA	12-11½		1980	Wladyslaw Kozakiewicz, POL	18-11½	WR
1928	Sabin Carr, USA	13-9¼	OR	1984	Pierre Quinon, FRA	18-10¼	
1932	Bill Miller, USA	14-1¾	OR	1988	Sergei Bubka, USSR	19-9¼	OR
1936	Earle Meadows, USA	14-3¼	OR				

Long Jump

Year		Distance		Year		Distance	
1896	Ellery Clark, USA	20-10		1948	Willie Steele, USA	25-8	
1900	Alvin Kraenzlein, USA	23-6¼	OR	1952	Jerome Biffle, USA	24-10	
1904	Meyer Prinstein, USA	24-1	OR	1956	Greg Bell, USA	25-8¼	
1906	Meyer Prinstein, USA	23-7½		1960	Ralph Boston, USA	26-7¾	OR
1908	Frank Irons, USA	24-6½	OR	1964	Lynn Davies, GBR	26-5¾	
1912	Albert Gutterson, USA	24-11¼	OR	1968	Bob Beamon, USA	29-2½	WR
1920	William Petersson, SWE	23-5½		1972	Randy Williams, USA	27-0½	
1924	De Hart Hubbard, USA	24-5		1976	Arnie Robinson, USA	27-4¾	
1928	Ed Hamm, USA	25-4½	OR	1980	Lutz Dombrowski, E.Ger	28-0¼	
1932	Ed Gordon, USA	25-0¾		1984	Carl Lewis, USA	28-0¼	
1936	Jesse Owens, USA	26-5½	OR	1988	Carl Lewis, USA	28-7¼	

Triple Jump

Year		Distance		Year		Distance	
1896	James Connolly, USA	44-11¾		1948	Arne Ahman, SWE	50-6¼	
1900	Meyer Prinstein, USA	47-5¾	OR	1952	Adhemar da Silva, BRA	53-2¾	WR
1904	Meyer Prinstein, USA	47-1		1956	Adhemar da Silva, BRA	53-7¾	OR
1906	Peter O'Connor, GBR/IRL	46-2¼		1960	Józef Schmidt, POL	55-2	
1908	Timothy Ahearne, GBR/IRL	48-11¼	OR	1964	Józef Schmidt, POL	55-3½	OR
1912	Gustaf Lindblom, SWE	48-5¼		1968	Viktor Saneyev, USSR	57-0¾	WR
1920	Vilho Tuulos, FIN	47-7		1972	Viktor Saneyev, USSR	56-11¼	
1924	Nick Winter, AUS	50-11¼		1976	Viktor Saneyev, USSR	56-8¾	
1928	Mikio Oda, JPN	49-11		1980	Jaak Uudmräe, USSR	56-11¼	
1932	Chuhei Nambu, JPN	51-7	WR	1984	Al Joyner, USA	56-7½	
1936	Naoto Tajima, JPN	52-6	WR	1988	Hristo Markov, BUL	57-9¼	OR

Shot Put

Year		Distance		Year		Distance	
1896	Bob Garrett, USA	36-9¾		1948	Wilbur Thompson, USA	56-2	OR
1900	Richard Sheldon, USA	46-3¼	OR	1952	Parry O'Brien, USA	57-1½	OR
1904	Ralph Rose, USA	48-7	WR	1956	Parry O'Brien, USA	60-11¼	OR
1906	Martin Sheridan, USA	40-5¼		1960	Bill Nieder, USA	64-6¾	OR
1908	Ralph Rose, USA	46-7½		1964	Dallas Long, USA	66-8½	OR
1912	Patrick McDonald, USA	50-4		1968	Randy Matson, USA	67-4¾	OR
1920	Ville Pörhöla, FIN	48-7¼		1972	Wladyslaw Komar, POL	69-6	OR
1924	Bud Houser, USA	49-2¼		1976	Udo Beyer, E.Ger	69-0¾	
1928	John Kuck, USA	52-0¾	WR	1980	Vladimir Kiselyov, USSR	70-0½	OR
1932	Leo Sexton, USA	52-6	OR	1984	Alessandro Andrei, ITA	69-9	
1936	Hans Woellke, GER	53-1¾	OR	1988	Ulf Timmermann, E.Ger	73-8¾	OR

Discus Throw

Year		Distance		Year		Distance	
1896	Bob Garrett, USA	95-7½		1948	Adolfo Consolini, ITA	173-2	OR
1900	Rudolf Bauer, HUN	118-3		1952	Sim Iness, USA	180-6	OR
1904	Martin Sheridan, USA	128-10½	OR	1956	Al Oerter, USA	184-11	OR
1906	Martin Sheridan, USA	136-0		1960	Al Oerter, USA	194-2	OR
1908	Martin Sheridan, USA	134-2	OR	1964	Al Oerter, USA	200-1	OR
1912	Armas Taipale, FIN	148-3	OR	1968	Al Oerter, USA	212-6	OR
1920	Elmer Niklander, FIN	146-7		1972	Ludvik Daněk, CZE	211-3	
1924	Bud Houser, USA	151-4	OR	1976	Mac Wilkins, USA	221-5	
1928	Bud Houser, USA	155-3	OR	1980	Viktor Rashchupkin, USSR	218-8	
1932	John Anderson, USA	162-4	OR	1984	Rolf Danneberg, W.Ger	218-6	
1936	Ken Carpenter, USA	165-7	OR	1988	Jergen Schult, E.Ger	225-9¼	OR

Hammer Throw

Year		Distance		Year		Distance	
1900	John Flanagan, USA	163-1		1952	József Csérmák, HUN	197-11	WR
1904	John Flanagan, USA	168-1	OR	1956	Harold Connolly, USA	207-3	OR
1908	John Flanagan, USA	170-4	OR	1960	Vasily Rudenkov, USSR	220-2	OR
1912	Matt McGrath, USA	179-7	OR	1964	Romuald Klim, USSR	228-10	OR
1920	Pat Ryan, USA	173-5		1968	Gyula Zsivótzky, HUN	240-8	OR
1924	Fred Tootell, USA	174-10		1972	Anatoly Bondarchuk, USSR	247-8	OR
1928	Pat O'Callaghan, IRL	168-7		1976	Yuri Sedykh, USSR	254-4	OR
1932	Pat O'Callaghan, IRL	176-11		1980	Yuri Sedykh, USSR	268-4	WR
1936	Karl Hein, GER	185-4	OR	1984	Juha Tiainen, FIN	256-2	
1948	Imre Nqemeth, HUN	183-11		1988	Sergei Litinov, USSR	278-2½	OR

Track & Field (Cont.)

MEN

Javelin Throw

Year		Distance		Year		Distance	
1908	Eric Lemming, SWE	179-10	WR	1956	Egil Danielson, NOR	281-2	WR
1912	Eric Lemming, SWE	198-11	WR	1960	Viktor Tsibulenko, USSR	277-8	
1920	Jonni Myyrä, FIN	215-10	OR	1964	Pauli Nevala, FIN	271-2	
1924	Jonni Myyrä, FIN	206-7		1968	Jänis Lüsis, USSR	295-7	OR
1928	Erik Lundkvist, SWE	218-6	OR	1972	Klaus Wolfermann, W.Ger	296-10	OR
1932	Matti Järvinen, FIN	238-6	OR	1976	Miklos Németh, HUN.	310-4	WR
1936	Gerhard Stöck, GER.	235-8		1980	Dainis Kula, USSR.	299-2	
1948	Kai Tapio Rautavaara, FIN	228-10		1984	Arto Härkönen, FIN	284-8	
1952	Cy Young, USA.	242-1	OR	1988	Tapio Korjus, FIN	276-6	

Decathlon

Year		Points		Year		Points	
1904	Thomas Kiely, IRL	6036		1956	Milt Campbell, USA	7937	OR
1912	Jim Thrope, USA.	8412	WR	1960	Rafer Johnson, USA.	8392	OR
1920	Helge Lövland, NOR	6803		1964	Willi Holdorf, GER	7887	
1924	Harold Osborn, USA	7711	WR	1968	Bill Toomey, USA	8193	OR
1928	Paavo Yrjölä, FIN	8053	WR	1972	Nikolai Avilov, USSR.	8454	WR
1932	Jim Bausch, USA.	8462	WR	1976	Bruce Jenner, USA	8617	WR
1936	Glenn Morris, USA	7900	WR	1980	Daley Thompson, GBR.	8495	
1948	Bob Mathias, USA	7139		1984	Daley Thompson, GBR.	8798	=WR
1952	Bob Mathias, USA	7887	WR	1988	Christian Schenk, E.Ger	8488	

WOMEN

100 Meters

Year		Time		Year		Time	
1928	Betty Robinson, USA	12.2	=WR	1964	Wyomia Tyus, USA	11.4	
1932	Stella Walsh, POL*	11.9	=WR	1968	Wyomia Tyus, USA	11.0	WR
1936	Helen Stephens, USA.	11.5	ʷ	1972	Renate Stecher, E.Ger	11.07	
1948	Fanny Blankers-Koen, HOL	11.9		1976	Annegret Richter, W.Ger	11.08	
1952	Marjorie Jackson, AUS	11:5	=WR	1980	Lyudmila Kondratyeva, USSR	11.06	
1956	Betty Cuthbert, AUS	11.5		1984	Evelyn Ashford, USA	10.97	OR
1960	Wilma Rudolph, USA.	11.0	ʷ	1988	Florence Griffith Joyner, USA	10.54	OR

*An autopsy performed after Walsh's death in 1980 revealed that she was a man.
ʷ indicates wind-aided.

200 Meters

Year		Time		Year		Time	
1948	Fanny Blankers-Koen, HOL	24.4		1968	Irena Szewińska, POL	22.5	WR
1952	Marjorie Jackson, AUS	23.7		1972	Renate Stecher, E.Ger	22.40	=WR
1956	Betty Cuthbert, AUS.	23.4	=OR	1976	Brarbel Eckert, E.Ger.	22.37	OR
1960	Wilma Rudolph, USA	24.0		1980	Brarbel Eckert Wöckel, E.Ger	22.03	OR
1964	Edith McGuire, USA.	23.0	OR	1984	Valerie Brisco-Hooks, USA	21.81	OR
				1988	Florence Griffith Joyner, USA	21.34	WR

400 Meters

Year		Time		Year		Time	
1964	Betty Cuthbert, AUS.	52.0	OR	1980	Marita Koch, E.Ger	48.88	OR
1968	Colette Besson, FRA.	52.0	=OR	1984	Valerie Brisco-Hooks, USA	48.43	OR
1972	Monika Zehrt, E.Ger	51.08	OR	1988	Olga Bryzgina, USSR.	48.65	
1976	Irena Szewińska, POL	49.29	WR				

800 Meters

Year		Time		Year		Time	
1928	Lina Radke, GER	2:16.8	WR	1976	Tatyana Kazankina, USSR.	1:54.94	WR
1960	Lyudmila Shevtsova, USSR	2:04.3	=WR	1980	Nadezhda Olizarenko, USSR	1:53.42	WR
1964	Ann Packer, GBR	2:01.1	OR	1984	Doina Melinte, ROM	1:57.60	
1968	Madeline Manning, USA	2:00.9	OR	1988	Sigrun Wodars, E.Ger	1:56.10	
1972	Hildegard Falck, W.Ger	1:58.55	OR				

1500 Meters

Year		Time		Year		Time	
1972	Lyudmila Bragina, USSR	4:01.4	WR	1984	Gabriella Doria, ITA	4:03.25	
1976	Tatyana Kazankina, USSR.	4:05.48		1988	Paula Ivan, ROM	3:53.96	OR
1980	Tatyana Kazankina, USSR.	3:56.6	OR				

3000 Meters

Year		Time		Year		Time	
1984	Maricica Puică, ROM.	8:35.96	OR	1988	Tatyana Samolenko, USSR	8:26.53	OR

10,000 Meters

Year		Time
1988	Olga Boldarenko, USSR	31:44.69 **OR**

Marathon

Year	Time	Year	Time
1984	Joan Benoit, USA ... 2:24:52	1988	Rosa Mota, POR ... 2:25:39

100-Meter Hurdles

Year	Time		Year	Time	
1932	Babe Didrikson, USA ... 11.7	**WR**	1968	Maureen Caird, AUS ... 10.3	**OR**
1936	Trebisonda Valla, ITA ... 11.7		1972	Annelie Ehrhardt, E.Ger ... 12.59	**WR**
1948	Fanny Blankers-Koen, HOL ... 11.2	**OR**	1976	Johanna Schaller, E.Ger ... 12.77	
1952	Shirley Strickland, AUS ... 10.9	**WR**	1980	Vera Komisova, USSR ... 12.56	**OR**
1956	Shirley Strickland, AUS ... 10.7	**OR**	1984	Benita Fitzgerald-Brown, USA ... 12.84	
1960	Irina Press, USSR ... 10.8		1988	Jordanka Donkova, BUL ... 12.38	**OR**
1964	Karin Balzer, GER ... 10.5ʷ				

ʷ Wind-aided.
Note: Event held over 80 meters from 1932-68.

400-Meter Hurdles

Year	Time		Year	Time	
1984	Nawal El Moutawakel, MOR ... 54.61	**OR**	1988	Debra Flintoff-King, AUS ... 53.17	**OR**

4x100-Meter Relay

Year	Time		Year	Time	
1928	Canada ... 48.4	**WR**	1964	Poland ... 43.6	
1932	United States ... 46.9	**WR**	1968	United States ... 42.8	**WR**
1936	United States ... 46.9		1972	West Germany ... 42.81	=**WR**
1948	Holland ... 47.5		1976	East Germany ... 42.55	**WR**
1952	United States ... 45.9	**WR**	1980	East Germany ... 41.60	**WR**
1956	Australia ... 44.5	**WR**	1984	United States ... 41.65	
1960	United States ... 44.5		1988	United States ... 41.98	

4x400 Meter Relay

Year	Time		Year	Time	
1972	East Germany ... 3:23.0	**WR**	1984	United States ... 3:18.29	**OR**
1976	East Germany ... 3:19.23	**WR**	1988	Soviet Union ... 3:15.18	**WR**
1980	Soviet Union ... 3:20.2				

High Jump

Year	Height		Year	Height	
1928	Ethel Catherwood, CAN ... 5-2½		1964	Iolanda Balas, ROM ... 6-2¾	**OR**
1932	Jean Shiley, USA ... 5-5¼	**WR**	1968	Miloslava Režková, CZE ... 5-11½	
1936	Ibolya Csák, HUN ... 5-3		1972	Ulrike Meyfarth, W.Ger ... 6-3½	=**WR**
1948	Alice Coachman, USA ... 5-6	**OR**	1976	Rosemarie Ackermann, E.Ger ... 6-4	**OR**
1952	Esther Brand, SAF ... 5-5¾		1980	Sara Simeoni, ITA ... 6-5½	**OR**
1956	Mildred McDaniel, USA ... 5-9¼	**WR**	1984	Ulrike Meyfarth, W.Ger ... 6-7½	**OR**
1960	Iolanda Balas, ROM ... 6-0¾		1988	Louise Ritter, USA ... 6-8	**OR**

Long Jump

Year	Distance		Year	Distance	
1948	Olga Gyarmati, HUN ... 18-8¼		1972	Heidemarie Rosendahl, W.Ger ... 22-3	
1952	Yvette Williams, NZE ... 20-5¾	**OR**	1976	Angela Voigt, E.Ger ... 22-0¾	
1956	Elzbieta Krzesińska, POL ... 20-10	=**WR**	1980	Tatiana Kolpakova, USSR ... 23-2	**OR**
1960	Vyera Krepkina, USSR ... 20-10¾	**OR**	1984	Anisoara Cusmir-Stanciu, ROM ... 22-10	
1964	Mary Rand, GBR ... 22-2¼	**WR**	1988	Jackie Joyner-Kersee, USA ... 24-3½	**OR**
1968	Viorica Viscopoleanu, ROM ... 22-4½	**WR**			

Shot Put

Year	Distance		Year	Distance	
1948	Micheline Ostermeyer, FRA ... 45-1½		1972	Nadezhda Chizhova, USSR ... 69-0	**WR**
1952	Galina Zybina, USSR ... 50-1¾	**WR**	1976	Ivanka Hristova, BUL ... 69-5¼	**OR**
1956	Tamara Tyshkevich, USSR ... 54-5	**OR**	1980	Ilona Slupianek, E.Ger ... 73-6¼	**OR**
1960	Tamara Press, USSR ... 56-10	**OR**	1984	Claudia Losch, W.Ger ... 67-2¼	
1964	Tamara Press, USSR ... 59-6¼	**OR**	1988	Natalya Lisovskaya, USSR ... 72-11½	
1968	Margitta Gummel, E.Ger ... 64-4	**WR**			

Discus Throw

Year	Distance		Year	Distance	
1928	Halina Konopacka, POL ... 129-11¾	**WR**	1964	Tamara Press, USSR ... 187-10	**OR**
1932	Lillian Copeland, USA ... 133-2	**OR**	1968	Lia Manoliu, ROM ... 191-2	**OR**
1936	Gisela Mauermayer, GER ... 156-3		1972	Faina Meinik, USSR ... 218-7	**OR**
1948	Micheline Ostermeyer, FRA ... 137-6		1976	Evelin Schlaak, E.Ger ... 226-4	**OR**
1952	Nina Romaschkova, USSR ... 168-8	**OR**	1980	Evelin Schlaak Jahl, E.Ger ... 229-6	**OR**
1956	Olga Fikotová, CZE ... 176-1	**OR**	1984	Ria Stalman, HOL ... 214-5	
1960	Nina Ponomaryeva, USSR ... 180-9	**OR**	1988	Martina Hellmann, E.Ger ... 237-2¼	**OR**

Track & Field (Cont.)
WOMEN
Javelin Throw

Year		Distance		Year		Distance	
1932	Babe Didrikson, USA	143-4	OR	1968	Angéla Németh, HUN	198-0	
1936	Tilly Fleischer, GER	148-3	OR	1972	Ruth Fuchs, E.Ger.	209-7	
1948	Herma Bauma, AUT.	149-6		1976	Ruth Fuchs, E.Ger.	216-4	OR
1952	Dana Zqatopkovqa, CZE.	165-7		1980	Maria Colon Rueñes, CUB	224-5	OR
1956	Inese Jaunzeme, USSR.	176-8		1984	Tessa Sanderson, GBR.	228-2	OR
1960	Elvira Ozolina, USSR	183-8	OR	1988	Petra Felke, E.Ger.	245-0	OR
1964	Mihaela Penes, ROM	198-7					

Heptathlon

Year		Points		Year		Points	
1964	Irina Press, USSR.	5246	WR	1980	Nadezhda Tkachenko, USSR.	5083	WR
1968	Ingrid Becker, W.Ger	5098		1984	Glynis Nunn, AUS	6390	OR
1972	Mary Peters, GBR	4801	WR	1988	Jackie Joyner-Kersee, USA.	7215	WR
1976	Siegrun Siegl, E.Ger.	4745					

Note: Seven-event Heptathlon replaced five-event Pentathlon in 1984.

Volleyball
MEN

Year		Year	
1964	**Soviet Union**, Czechoslovakia, Japan	1980	**Soviet Union**, Bulgaria, Romania
1968	**Soviet Union**, Japan, Czechoslovakia	1984	**United States**, Brazil, Italy
1972	**Japan**, E. Germany, Soviet Union	1988	**United States**, Soviet Union, Argentina
1976	**Poland**, Soviet Union, Cuba		

WOMEN

Year		Year	
1964	**Japan**, Soviet Union, Poland	1980	**Soviet Union**, E. Germany, Bulgaria
1968	**Soviet Union**, Japan, Poland	1984	**China**, United States, Japan
1972	**Soviet Union**, Japan, N. Korea	1988	**Soviet Union**, Peru, China
1976	**Japan**, Soviet Union, S. Korea		

Water Polo

Year		Year	
1900	**Great Britain**, Belgium, France	1952	**Hungary**, Yugoslavia, Italy
1904	**USA (NY)**, USA (Chi.), USA (Mo.)	1956	**Hungary**, Yugoslavia, Soviet Union
1908	**Great Britain**, Belgium, Sweden	1960	**Italy**, Soviet Union, Hungary
1912	**Great Britain**, Sweden, Belgium	1964	**Hungary**, Yugoslavia, Soviet Union
1920	**Great Britain**, Belgium, Sweden	1968	**Yugoslavia**, Soviet Union, Hungary
1924	**France**, Belgium, United States	1972	**Soviet Union**, Hungary, United States
1928	**Germany**, Hungary, France	1976	**Hungary**, Italy, Holland
1932	**Hungary**, Germany, United States	1980	**Soviet Union**, Yugoslavia, Hungary
1936	**Hungary**, Germany, Belgium	1984	**Yugoslavia**, United States, W. Germany
1948	**Italy**, Hungary, Holland	1988	**Yugoslavia**, United States, Soviet Union

Freestyle Wrestling
Light Flyweight (106 lbs)

Year			Year		
1904	Robert Curry	United States	1980	Claudio Pollio	Italy
1972	Roman Dmitriev	Soviet Union	1984	Bobby Weaver	United States
1976	Hasan Isaev	Bulgaria	1988	Takashi Kobayashi	Japan

Flyweight (115 lbs)

Year			Year		
1904	George Mehnert	United States	1968	Shigeo Nakata	Japan
1948	Lennart Viitala	Finland	1972	Kiyoma Kato	Japan
1952	Hasan Gemici	Turkey	1976	Yuji Takada	Japan
1956	Mirian Tsalkalamanidze	Soviet Union	1980	Anatoly Beloglazov	Soviet Union
1960	Ahmet Bilek	Turkey	1984	Saban Trstena	Yugoslavia
1964	Yoshikatsu Yoshida	Japan	1988	Mitsuru Sato	Japan

Bantamweight (126 lbs)

Year			Year		
1904	Isidor Niflot	United States	1960	Terry McCann	United States
1908	George Mehnert	United States	1964	Yojiro Uetake	Japan
1924	Kustaa Pihlajamäki	Finland	1968	Yojiro Uetake	Japan
1928	Kaarlo Mäkinen	Finland	1972	Hideaki Yanagida	Japan
1932	Robert Pearce	United States	1976	Vladimir Umin	Soviet Union
1936	Ödön Zombori	Hungary	1980	Sergei Beloglazov	Soviet Union
1948	Nasuh Akar	Turkey	1984	Hideaki Tomiyama	Japan
1952	Shohachi Ishii	Japan	1988	Sergei Beloglazov	Soviet Union
1956	Mustafa Dagistanli	Turkey			

Featherweight (137 lbs)

Year			Year		
1904	Benjamin Bradshaw	United States	1956	Shozo Sasahara	Japan
1908	George Dole	United States	1960	Mustafa Dagistanli	Turkey
1920	Charles Ackerly	United States	1964	Osamu Watanabe	Japan
1924	Robin Reed	United States	1968	Masaaki Kaneko	Japan
1928	Allie Morrison	United States	1972	Zagalav Abdulbekov	Soviet Union
1932	Hermanni Pihlajamraki	Finland	1976	Jung-Mo Yang	South Korea
1936	Kustaa Pihlajamraki	Finland	1980	Magomedgasan Abushev	Soviet Union
1948	Gazanfer Bilge	Turkey	1984	Randy Lewis	United States
1952	Bayram Sit	Turkey	1988	John Smith	United States

Lightweight (150 lbs)

Year			Year		
1904	Otto Roehm	United States	1956	Emamali Habibi	Iran
1908	George de Relwyskow	Great Britain	1960	Shelby Wilson	United States
1920	Kalle Anttila	Finland	1964	Enyu Dimov	Bulgaria
1924	Russell Vis	United States	1968	Abdollah Movahhed	Iran
1928	Osvald Käpp	Estonia	1972	Dan Gable	United States
1932	Charles Pacôme	France	1976	Pavel Pinigin	Soviet Union
1936	Károly Kárpáti	Hungary	1980	Saipulla Absaidov	Soviet Union
1948	Celal Atik	Turkey	1984	In-Tak You	Korea
1952	Olle Anderberg	Sweden	1988	Arsen Fadzaev	Soviet Union

Welterweight (163 lbs)

Year			Year		
1904	Charles Erickson	United States	1960	Doug Blubaugh	United States
1924	Hermann Gehri	Switzerland	1964	Ismail Ogan	Turkey
1928	Arvo Haavisto	Finland	1968	Mahmut Atalay	Turkey
1932	Jack Van Bebber	United States	1972	Wayne Wells	United States
1936	Frank Lewis	United States	1976	Jiichiro Date	Japan
1948	Yasar Dogu	Turkey	1980	Valentin Angelov	Bulgaria
1952	Bill Smith	United States	1984	Dave Schultz	United States
1956	Mitsuo Ikeda	Japan	1988	Kenny Monday	United States

Middleweight (181 lbs)

Year			Year		
1908	Stanley Bacon	Great Britain	1960	Hasan Güngör	Turkey
1920	Eino Leino	Finland	1964	Prodan Gardzhev	Bulgaria
1924	Fritz Hagmann	Switzerland	1968	Boris Gurevitch	Soviet Union
1928	Ernst Kyburz	Switzerland	1972	Levan Tediashvili	Soviet Union
1932	Ivar Johansson	Sweden	1976	John Peterson	United States
1936	Emile Poilvé	France	1980	Ismail Abilov	Bulgaria
1948	Glen Brand	United States	1984	Mark Schultz	United States
1952	David Tsimakuridze	Soviet Union	1988	Han Myang-Woo	South Korea
1956	Nikola Stanchev	Bulgaria			

Light Heavyweight (198 lbs)

Year			Year		
1920	Anders Larsson	Sweden	1960	Ismet Atli	Turkey
1924	John Spellman	United States	1964	Aleksandr Medved	Soviet Union
1928	Thure Sjöstedt	Sweden	1968	Ahmet Ayik	Turkey
1932	Peter Mehringer	United States	1972	Ben Peterson	United States
1936	Knut Fridell	Sweden	1976	Levan Tediashvili	Soviet Union
1948	Henry Wittenberg	United States	1980	Sanasar Oganesyan	Soviet Union
1952	Wiking Palm	Sweden	1984	Ed Banach	United States
1956	Gholam Reza Takhti	Iran	1988	Makharbek Khadartsev	Soviet Union

Heavyweight (220 lbs)

Year			Year		
1972	Ivan Yarygin	Soviet Union	1984	Lou Banach	United States
1976	Ivan Yarygin	Soviet Union	1988	Vasile Puscasu	Romania
1980	Ilya Mate	Soviet Union			

Super Heavyweight (Unlimited)

Year			Year		
1904	Bernhuff Hansen	United States	1956	Hamit Kaplan	Turkey
1908	George Con O'Kelly	Great Britain/Ireland	1960	Wilfred Dietrich	Germany
1920	Robert Roth	Switzerland	1964	Aleksandr Ivanitsky	Soviet Union
1924	Harry Steel	United States	1968	Aleksandr Medved	Soviet Union
1928	Johan Richthoff	Sweden	1972	Aleksandr Medved	Soviet Union
1932	Johan Richthoff	Sweden	1976	Soslan Andiev	Soviet Union
1936	Kristjan Palusalu	Estonia	1980	Soslan Andiev	Soviet Union
1948	Gyula Bóbis	Hungary	1984	Bruce Baumgartner	United States
1952	Arsen Mekokishvili	Soviet Union	1988	David Gobedjichvili	Soviet Union

Yachting

MEN

470 Class

Year		Points	Year		Points
1976	Frank Hübner, Harro Bode, W.Ger	42.4	1984	Luis Doreste, Roberto Molina, SPA	33.7
1980	M.R.Soares, Eduardo Penido, BRA	36.4	1988	Thierry Peponnet, Luc Pillot, FRA	34.7

WOMEN

470 Class

Year		Points
1988	Allison Jolly, Lynne Jewell, USA	26.7

OPEN

Windglider

Year		Points	Year		Points
1984	Stephan van den Berg, HOL	27.7	1988	Bruce Kendall, NZE	35.4

Finn

Year		Points	Year		Points
1920	(12-ft) Johannes and Franciscus Hln, HOL	—	1960	Paul Elvström, DEN	8171
	(18-ft) Francis Richards & T.Hedberg, GBR	—	1964	Wilhelm Kuhweide, GER	7638
1924	Léon Huybrechts, BEL	—	1968	Valentin Mankin, USSR	11.7
1928	Sven Thorell, SWE	—	1972	Serge Maury, FRA	58.0
1932	Jacques Lebrun, FRA	87	1976	Jochen Schümann, E.Ger	35.4
1936	Daniel Kagchelland, HOL	163	1980	Esko Rechardt, FIN	36.7
1948	Paul Elvström, DEN	5543	1984	Russell Coutts, NZE	34.7
1952	Paul Elvström, DEN	8209	1988	Jose Luis Doreste, SPA	38.1
1956	Paul Elvström, DEN	7509			

Flying Dutchman

Year		Points	Year		Points
1960	Peder Lunde, Björn Bervall, NOR	6774	1976	Jörg and Eckart Diesch, W.Ger	34.7
1964	Helmer Pedersen, Earle Wells, NZE	6255	1980	Alesandro Abascal, M.Noguer, SPA	19.0
1968	Rod Pattison, I.Macd-Smith, GBR	3.0	1984	Jonathon McKee, W.C.Buchan, USA	19.7
1972	Rod Pattison, Chris Davies, GBR	22.7	1988	J.Bojsen-Mroller, C.Grronberg, DEN	31.4

Star

Year		Points	Year		Points
1932	Gilbert Gray, Andrew Libano, USA	46	1964	Durward Knowles, Cecil Cooke, BAH	5664
1936	Peter Bischoff, Hans Weise, GER	80	1968	Lowell North, Peter Barrett, USA	14.4
1948	Hilary and Paul Smart, USA	5828	1972	David Forbes, John Anderson, AUS	28.1
1952	Agost.Straulio, Nicolo Rode, ITA	7635	1980	Valentin Mankin, A.Muzychenko, USSR	24.7
1956	Herb Williams, Lawrence Low, USA	5876	1984	Wm.Buchan, Steve Erickson, USA	29.7
1960	Timir Pinegin, Fyodor Shutkov, USSR	7619	1988	Michael McIntyre, P.B.Vaile, GBR	45.7

Tornado

Year		Points	Year		Points
1976	Reg White, John Osborn, GBR	18.0	1984	Rex Sellers, Chris Timms, NZE	14.7
1980	Alex Welter, Lars Björkström, BRA	21.4	1988	J.Y.Le Deroff, Nicolas Henard, FRA	16.0

Soling

Year		Points	Year		Points
1972	United States	8.7	1984	United States	33.7
1976	Denmark	46.7	1988	East Germany	11.7
1980	Denmark	23.0			

Note: Current events not included in this summary: archery, canoeing, cycling, equestrian, fencing, team handball, judo, modern pentathlon, rowing, shooting, table tennis, weightlifting, and Greco-Roman wrestling.

THE 1992 INFORMATION PLEASE SPORTS ALMANAC

OLYMPICS
STATISTICS

THROUGH THE YEARS
1924-1988
WINTER GAMES

SEC B

PAGE 575

Winter Olympics

The move toward a winter version of the Olympics began in 1908 when figure skating made an appearance at the Summer Games in London.

Ten-time world champion Ulrich Salchow of Sweden, who originated the backwards, one revolution jump that bears his name, and Madge Syers of Britain were the first individual champions. Germans Anna Hubler and Heinrich Berger won the pairs competition.

Figure skating returned as a medal event in 1920 and was joined in Antwerp by ice hockey. Sweden's Gillis Grafstrom and Magda Julin took individual honors, while Ludovika and Walter Jakobsson were the top pair. In hockey, Canada won the gold medal with the United States second.

Although resisted at first by the Scandinavian countries,which had their own Nordic championships, the IOC inaugurated the Winter Games in 1924 at Chamonix, France, as a cold weather prelude to the Summer Games in Paris later that year.

1924

Chamonix

The first Winter Olympic Games were actually called "The International Winter Sports Week" and went on for 11 days in the French Alps, 60 miles northeast of Grenoble.

As expected, the Scandinavians dominated the 16-nation field. Norway and Finland won 27 of the 43 medals available, including all four Nordic events and four of the five speed skating races.

Speed skater Clas Thunberg of Finland and Norwegian Nordic skier and jumper Thorleif Haug each won three gold medals. Speed skater Charles Jewtraw of Lake Placid, N.Y., won the only American gold medal with a first in the 500 meters.

In its first four hockey games, Canada beat Switzerland 33-0, Czechoslovakia 30-0, Sweden 22-0 and Britain 19-2, before winning the tournament with a 6-1 victory over the U.S. in the final.

Top 5 Standings

National medal standings are not recognized by the IOC. The unofficial point totals are based on 3 points for a gold medal, 2 for a silver and 1 for a bronze. Total medals are in parentheses.

	Gold	Silver	Bronze	Pts
1 Norway (17).................	4	7	6	32
2 Finland (10).................	4	3	3	21
3 Austria (3)...................	2	1	0	8
USA (4)......................	1	2	1	8
5 Switzerland (2)...............	1	0	1	4
Great Britain (3)..............	0	1	2	4

Leading Medal Winners

Number of individual medals won on the left; gold, silver and bronze medal breakdown on the right.

No		Sport	G-S-B
5	Clas Thunberg, FIN..............	Sp.Skate	3-1-1
5	Roald Larsen, NOR..............	Sp.Skate	0-2-3
3	Thorleif Haug, NOR.............	X-country & Nordic Combined	3-0-0
3	Julius Skutnabb, FIN.............	Sp.Skate	1-1-1
3	Johan Gröttumsbråten, NOR......	X-country & Nordic Combined	0-1-2
2	Thoralf Strömstad, NOR.........	X-country & Nordic Combined	0-2-0

Bobsled

Event		Time
4-Man	SWI (Eduard Scherrer, Alfred Neveu, Alfred Schläppi, Heinrich Schläppi)	5:45.54

Figure Skating

Event		Points
Men	Gillis Grafström, SWE..................	367.89
Women	Herma Planck-Szabó, AUT...............	299.17
Pairs	Helene Engelmann & Alfred Berger, AUT....	10.64

Ice Hockey
Championship Round

Records include games played in two 4-team preliminary pools. Canada and Sweden qualified from one pool, the U.S. and Britain from the other.

	Gm	W-L-T	GF	GA
1 Canada	5	5-0-0	110	3
2 USA.............................	5	4-1-0	73	6
3 Great Britain	5	3-2-0	40	38
4 Sweden..........................	5	2-3-0	21	49

Semifinals: Canada over Britain, 19-2; USA over Sweden, 20-0.
Third Place: Britain over Sweden, 4-3 (also decided European title). **Final:** Canada over USA, 6-1.

1924 (Cont.)
Nordic Skiing
Cross-country

Event		Time
18km	Thorleif Haug, NOR	1:14:31
50km	Thorleif Haug, NOR	3:44:32

Ski Jumping

Event		Points
90m	Jacob Thams, NOR.	18.960

Nordic Combined

Event		Points
18km/Jump	Thorleif Haug, NOR	18.906

Speed Skating

Event		Time
500m	Charles Jewtraw, USA.	44.0
1500m	Clas Thunberg, FIN	2:20.8
5000m	Clas Thunberg, FIN	8:39.0
10,000m	Julius Skutnabb, FIN	18:04.8
Combined	Clas Thunberg, FIN	5.5 pts

1928

St.Moritz

Sonja Henie of Norway was only 11-years-old in 1924 when she participated in her first Olympics and finished last in women's figure skating. Three years later, she won the world championship at age 14 and the year after that was Olympic champion at 15.

Henie would go on to win two more gold medals, a record that men's champion Gillis Grafstrom of Sweden set in 1928 with his third straight victory in the Winter Games.

Otherwise, St. Moritz was plagued with warm weather that slowed bobsled and cross-country runs and cancelled the 10,000-meter speed skating race. Speed skater Bernt Evensen of Norway led the Games with three medals, sharing the 500-meter title with Finland's Clas Thunberg. Norway also got two gold medals from Johan Grottumsbraten in cross-country and the Nordic Combined and led the 25 nations competing with six gold and 15 overall medals. The U.S. edged Sweden for second place.

Top 5 Standings

National medal standings are not recognized by the IOC. The unofficial point totals are based on 3 points for a gold medal, 2 for a silver and 1 for a bronze. Total medals are in parentheses.

	Gold	Silver	Bronze	Pts
1 Norway (15)	6	4	5	31
2 USA (6)	2	2	2	12
3 Sweden (5)	2	2	1	11
4 Finland (4)	2	1	1	9
5 Austria (4)	0	3	1	7

Leading Medal Winners

Number of individual medals won on the left; gold, silver and bronze medal breakdown to the right.

No		Sport	G-S-B
3	Bernt Evensen, NOR	Sp.Skate	1-1-1
2	Johan Gröttumsbråten, NOR	X-country	2-0-0
2	Clas Thunberg, FIN	Sp.Skate	2-0-0
2	Jennison Heaton, USA	Bobsled & Cresta	1-1-0
2	Ivar Ballangrud, NOR	Sp.Skate	1-0-1

Note: Evensen also placed second in the 10,000-meter Speed Skating race that was later disallowed due to thawing ice conditions.

Bobsled

Event		Time
5-Man	USA (Billy Fiske, Nion Tucker, Geoff Mason, Clifford Gray, Richard Parke)	3:20.5

Cresta (Toboggan)

Event		Time
1-Man	Jennison Heaton, USA	3:01.8

Figure Skating

Event		Points
Men	Gillis Grafström, SWE	1630.75
Women	Sonja Henie, NOR	2452.25
Pairs	Andrée Joly & Pierre Brunet, FRA	100.50

Ice Hockey
Championship Round
(Overall record in parentheses)

		Gm	W-L-T	Pts	GF	GA
1	Canada (3-0-0)	3	3-0-0	6	38	0
2	Sweden (3-1-1)	3	2-1-0	4	7	12
3	Switzerland (2-2-1)	3	1-2-0	2	4	17
4	Britain (2-4-0)	3	0-3-0	0	1	21

Note: Canada received a bye to the 4-team championship round robin. The 10 other competing countries—not including the USA which did not send a team—were divided into three pools with the winners advancing to the final round. The Canadians routed Sweden, 11-0; Britain, 14-0 and the Swiss, 13-0.

Nordic Skiing
Cross-country

Event		Time
18km	Johan Gröttumsbråten, NOR	1:37:01
50km	Per Erik Hedlund, SWE	4:52.03

Ski Jumping

Event		Points
90m	Alf Andersen, NOR	19.208

Nordic Combined

Event		Points
18km/Jump	Johan Gröttumsbråten, NOR	17.833

Speed Skating

Event		Time
500m	Bernt Evensen, NOR & Clas Thunberg, FIN	43.4 **OR**
1500m	Clas Thunberg, FIN	2:21.1
5000m	Ivar Ballangrud, NOR	8:50.5
10,000m	No decision (thawing of ice)	

Note: Irving Jaffee of USA had the fastest time in the 10,000 meters (18:36.5) before the race was cancelled.

III Olympic Winter Games

Lake Placid, USA
February 4-13, 1932

1932

Lake Placid

Back in 1928, American Irving Jaffee had the fastest time in the 10,000-meter speed skating race at St. Moritz only to lose his gold medal when thawing ice made it necessary to call the event off with no official winner.

Four years later, Jaffee won the 10,000 and 5,000-meter races and local hero Jack Shea won at 500 and 1,500 meters as the U.S. swept all four speed skating events—which were run as actual races (not timed heats) for the only time in Olympic history.

Billy Fiske, who had driven the 5-man U.S. bobsled to a gold medal at St.Moritz when he was only 16, steered the 4-man sled to victory in 1932. On board was Eddie Eagan, the 1920 Olympic light heavyweight champion, who remains the only athlete ever to win gold medals in both the Winter and Summer Games.

Canada won its fourth consecutive hockey gold medal, but 38-year-old Gillis Grafstrom of Sweden missed in his bid for a fourth straight men's figure skating title, placing second to 22-year-old Austrian Karl Schafer.

Top 5 Standings

National medal standings are not recognized by the IOC. The unofficial point totals are based on 3 points for a gold medal, 2 for a silver and 1 for a bronze. Total medals are in parentheses.

	Gold	Silver	Bronze	Pts
1 USA (12)	6	4	2	28
2 Norway (10)	3	4	3	20
3 Canada (7)	1	1	5	10
4 Sweden (3)	1	2	0	7
5 Finland (3)	1	1	1	6

Leading Medal Winners

Number of individual medals won on the left; gold, silver and bronze medal breakdown on the right.

No		Sport	G-S-B
2	Irving Jaffee, USA	Sp.Skate	2-0-0
2	Jack Shea, USA	Sp.Skate	2-0-0
2	Veli Saarinen, FIN	X-country	1-0-1
2	Alex Hurd, CAN	Sp.Skate	0-1-1
2	William Logan, CAN	Sp.Skate	0-0-2

Bobsled

Event		Time
2-Man	USA (J.Hubert Stevens & Curtis Stevens)	8:14.74
4-Man	USA (Billy Fiske, Eddie Eagan, Clifford Gray, Jay O'Brien)	7:53.68

Figure Skating

Event		Points
Men	Karl Schäfer, AUT	2602.0
Women	Sonja Henie, NOR	2302.5
Pairs	Andrée Joly Brunet & Pierre Brunet, FRA	76.7

Ice Hockey

		Gm	W-L-T	Pts	GF	GA
1	Canada	6	5-0-1	11	32	4
2	USA	6	4-1-1	9	27	5
3	Germany	6	2-4-0	4	7	26
4	Poland	6	0-6-0	0	3	34

Note: Due to the worldwide Depression, only four teams completed. Each side played the other teams twice. Canada beat the U.S., 2-1, in their first game and tied the Americans, 2-2, in triple overtime in the second. A win by the U.S. in Game 2 would have resulted in a third contest to decide the gold medal.

Nordic Skiing

Cross-country

Event		Time
18km	Sven Utterström, SWE	1:23.07
50km	Veli Saarinen, FIN	4:28.00

Ski Jumping

Event		Points
90m	Birger Rudd, NOR	228.1

Nordic Combined

Event		Points
18km/Jump	Johan Gröttumsbråten, NOR	446.00

Speed Skating

Event		Time
500m	Jack Shea, USA	43.4 OR
1500m	Jack Shea, USA	2:57.5
5000m	Irving Jaffee, USA	9:40.8
10,000m	Irving Jaffee, USA	19:13.6

Note: For the only time in the history of the Winter Games, all events were staged as races rather than two-man heats against the clock.

IVes JEUX OLYMPIQUES D'HIVER
GARMISCH-PARTENKIRCHEN

1936

Garmisch-Partenkirchen

The fourth Winter Olympics were held in the neighboring villages of Garmisch and Partenkirchen in Germany's Bavarian Alps and included Alpine skiing for the first time. Also featured in these Games were Norwegians Ivar Ballangrud and Sonja Henie, and Rudi Ball—the Jewish star of the German hockey team.

Ballangrud won four individual gold medals and narrowly missed a fifth in speed skating, but his heroics paled compared to the attention lavished on Henie, who won her third straight gold medal. A week later, she won the world title for the 10th year in a row, then turned pro. Moving to the U.S., she toured in her own skating show, starred in nine Hollywood movies and was worth more than $45 million when she died in 1969 at age 57.

Ball, who had been the best player on Germany's bronze medal-winning hockey team in 1932, was invited back from voluntary exile in France to lead the 1936 German squad. He was the only Jew on the German Winter Olympic team and his presence was a token gesture by

1936 (Cont.)

the government of Adolf Hitler to mollify anxious IOC officials who objected to the Nazis' fervent anti-Semitism.

The story of the hockey tournament, however, wasn't one German Jew, but 11 British Canadians, who led Britain to the gold medal and stopped Canada's undefeated Olympic winning streak at 20. The best of the imported Brits was goaltender Jimmy Foster, who allowed just three goals in eight games.

After winning six gold medals in 1932, the U.S. had to settle for one this time, in the two-man bobsled.

Top 10 Standings

National medal standings are not recognized by the IOC. The unofficial point totals are based on 3 points for a gold medal, 2 for a silver and 1 for a bronze. Total medals are in parentheses.

	Gold	Silver	Bronze	Pts
1 Norway (15)	7	5	3	34
2 Germany (6)	3	3	0	15
3 Sweden (7)	2	2	3	13
4 Finland (6)	1	2	3	10
5 Switzerland (3)	1	2	0	7
6 Austria (4)	1	1	2	7
7 Great Britain (3)	1	1	1	6
8 USA (4)	1	0	3	6
9 Canada (1)	0	1	0	2
10 France (1)	0	0	1	1
Hungary (1)	0	0	1	1

Leading Medal Winners

Number of individual medals won on the left; gold, silver and bronze medal breakdown to the right.

No		Sport	G-S-B
4	Ivar Ballangrud, NOR	Sp.Skate	3-1-0
3	Oddbjörn Hagen, NOR	X-country & Nordic Combined	1-2-0
3	Birger Vasenius, FIN	Sp.Skate	0-2-1
2	Ernst Baier, GER	Fig.Skate	1-1-0
2	Joseph Beerli, SWI	Bobsled	1-1-0
2	Erik Larsson, SWE	X-country	1-0-1
2	Fritz Feierabend, SWI	Bobsled	0-2-0
2	Olaf Hoffsbakken, NOR	X-country	0-2-0
2	Sverre Brodahl, NOR	X-country	0-1-1

Alpine Skiing
MEN

Event		Pts
Combined	Franz Pfnür, GER	99.25

WOMEN

Event		Pts
Combined	Christl Cranz, GER	97.06

Bobsled

Event		Time
2-Man	USA (Ivan Brown, & Alan Washbond)	5:29.29
4-Man	SWI (Pierre Musy, Arnold Gartmann, Charles Bouvier, Joseph Beerli)	5:19.85

Figure Skating

Event		Points
Men	Karl Schäfer, AUT	2959.0
Women	Sonja Henie, NOR	425.5
Pairs	Maxi Herber & Ernst Baier, GER	11.5

Note: Ernst Baier also won silver medal in the Men's event.

Ice Hockey
Championship Round
(Overall records in parentheses).

		Gm	W-L-T	Pts	GF	GA
1	Britain (6-0-2)	3	2-0-1	5	7	1
2	Canada (7-2-0)	3	2-1-0	4	9	2
3	USA (6-2-1)	3	1-1-1	3	2	1
4	Czechoslovakia(5-4-0)	3	0-3-0	0	0	14

Scores: Britain beat Canada, 2-1; Czech.,5-0; and tied the U.S., 0-0 (OT). Canada beat Czech., 7-0, and the U.S., 1-0. The U.S. beat Czech., 2-0.

Nordic Skiing
Cross-country

Event		Time
18km	Erik-August Larsson, SWE	1:14:38
50km	Elis Wiklund, SWE	3:30:11
4x10km	FIN (Sulo Nurmela, Klaes Karppinen, Matti Lähde, Kalle Jalkanen)	2:41:33

Ski Jumping

Event		Points
90m	Birger Ruud, NOR	232.0

Nordic Combined

Event		Points
18km/Jump	Oddbjörn Hagen, NOR	430.3

Speed Skating

Event		Time	
500m	Ivar Ballangrud, NOR	43.4	=OR
1500m	Charles Mathisen, NOR	2:19.2	OR
5000m	Ivar Ballangrud, NOR	8:19.6	OR
10,000m	Ivar Ballangrud, NOR	17:24.3	OR

1948

St.Moritz

The Winter Games originally scheduled for Sapporo, Japan (1940) and Cortina d'Ampezzo, Italy (1944) were cancelled because of World War II. Untouched by the war, St.Moritz was picked to host the 1948 Games and 28 countries sent 706 athletes to compete.

The United States sent two hockey teams, one sanctioned by the American Olympic Committee and one by the American Hockey Association. The IOC ruled that the AOC team could march in the opening parade and the AHA team could play in the tournament, but neither would be eligible for a medal. Canada and Czechoslovakia each finished with 7-0-1 records, but the Canadians won the gold medal by goal differential, 64-62. Czech team member Jaroslav Drobny later distinguished himself as a tennis player, winning the men's singles title at Wimbledon in 1954.

Otherwise, Norway, Sweden and Switzerland each won 10 medals and the U.S. nine. Alpine skier Gretchen Fraser won a gold medal in the slalom and a silver in the combined for the Americans. French Alpine skier Henri Oreiller was the men's top individual performer with two golds and a bronze.

Top 10 Standings

National medal standings are not recognized by the IOC. The unofficial point totals are based on 3 points for a gold medal, 2 for a silver and 1 for a bronze. Total medals are in parentheses.

	Gold	Silver	Bronze	Pts
1 Norway (10)	4	3	3	21
Sweden (10)	4	3	3	21
3 Switzerland (10)	3	4	3	20
4 USA (9)	3	4	2	19
5 Austria (8)	1	3	4	13
6 Finland (6)	1	3	2	11
7 France (5)	2	1	2	10
8 Canada (3)	2	0	1	7
9 Belgium (2)	1	1	0	5
10 Italy (1)	1	0	0	3

Leading Medal Winners

Number of individual medals won on the left; gold, silver and bronze medal breakdown to the right.

MEN

No		Sport	G-S-B
3	Henri Oreiller, FRA	Alpine	2-0-1
2	Martin Lundström, SWE	X-country	2-0-0
2	Nils Östensson, SWE	X-country	1-1-0
2	Åke Seyffarth, SWE	Sp.Skate	1-1-0
2	Gunnar Eriksson, SWE	X-country	1-0-1
2	Karl Molitor, SWI	Alpine	1-0-1
2	James Couttet, FRA	Alpine	0-1-1
2	Odd Lundberg, NOR	Sp.Skate	0-1-1

WOMEN

No		Sport	G-S-B
2	Trude Beiser, AUT	Alpine	1-1-0
2	Gretchen Fraser, USA	Alpine	1-1-0
2	Erika Mahringer, AUT	Alpine	0-0-2

Alpine Skiing

MEN

Event		Time
Downhill	Henri Oreiller, FRA	2:55.0
Slalom	Edi Reinalter, SWI	2:10.3
Combined	Henri Oreiller, FRA	3.27 pts

WOMEN

Event		Time
Downhill	Hedy Schlunegger, SWI	2:28.3
Slalom	Gretchen Fraser, USA	1:57.2
Combined	Trude Beiser, AUT	6.58 pts

Bobsled

Event		Time
2-Man	SWI (Felix Endrich, & Friedrich Waller)	5:29.2
4-Man	USA (Francis Tyler, Patrick Martin, Edward Rimkus, William D'Amico)	5:20.1

Cresta (Toboggan)

Event		Time
1-Man	Nino Bibbia, ITA	5:23.2

Figure Skating

Event		Points
Men	Dick Button, USA	191.177
Women	Barbara Ann Scott, CAN	163.077
Pairs	Micheline Lannoy & Pierre Baugniet, BEL	11.227

Ice Hockey

		Gm	W-L-T	Pts	GF	GA
1	Canada	8	7-0-1	15	69	5
2	Czechoslovakia	8	7-0-1	15	80	18
3	Switzerland	8	6-2-0	12	67	21
4	USA (AHA)	8	5-3-0	10	86	33
5	Sweden	8	4-4-0	8	55	28
6	Great Britain	8	3-5-0	6	39	47
7	Poland	8	2-6-0	4	29	97
8	Austria	8	1-7-0	2	33	77
9	Italy	8	0-8-0	0	24	156

Note: Canada won championship on goal differential, 64-62.

Nordic Skiing

Cross-country

Event		Time
18km	Martin Lundström, SWE	1:13:50.0
50km	Nils Karlsson, SWE	3:47:48.0
4x10km	SWE (Nils Östensson, Nils Täpp, Gunnar Eriksson, Martin Lundström)	2:32:08.0

Ski Jumping

Event		Points
90m	Petter Hugsted, NOR	228.1

Nordic Combined

Event		Points
18km/Jump	Heikki Hasu, FIN	448.80

Speed Skating

Event		Time
500m	Finn Helgesen, NOR	43.1 OR
1500m	Sverre Farstad, NOR	2:17.6 OR
5000m	Reidar Liaklev, NOR	8:29.4
10,000m	Åke Seyffarth, SWE	17:26.3

1952

Oslo

Dick Button, who had revolutionized figure skating with his athletic jumps and spins at St. Moritz in 1948, repeated his gold medal performance in '52. The 22-year-old Harvard senior also won the world championship for the fifth straight year then turned pro.

Andrea Mead Lawrence, a 19-year-old whose parents built the Pico Peak ski resort in Vermont, became the first American skier to win two Olympic gold medals, taking both the slalom and giant slalom.

The star of the Games, however, was 28-year-old Norwegian truck driver Hjalmar Andersen who, urged on by his cheering countrymen, won three speed skating gold medals in three days and set Olympic records in two of the races.

The U.S. finished second to Norway in the overall medal count and was runner-up to Canada in hockey. The gold medal was the Canadians' seventh in eight Olympics and, as it turned out, their last.

1952 (Cont.)
Top 10 Standings

National medal standings are not recognized by the IOC. The unofficial point totals are based on 3 points for a gold medal, 2 for a silver and 1 for a bronze. Total medals are in parentheses.

	Gold	Silver	Bronze	Pts
1 Norway (16)	7	3	6	33
2 USA (11)	4	6	1	25
3 Finland (9)	3	4	2	19
4 Austria (8)	2	4	2	16
5 Germany (7)	3	2	2	15
6 Holland (3)	0	3	0	6
7 Canada (2)	1	0	1	4
Italy (2)	1	0	1	4
Sweden (4)	0	0	4	4
10 Great Britain (1)	1	0	0	3

Leading Medal Winners

Number of individual medals won on the left; gold, silver and bronze medal breakdown to the right.

MEN

No		Sport	G-S-B
3	Hjalmar Andersen, NOR	Sp.Skate	3-0-0
2	Andreas Ostler, GER	Bobsled	2-0-0
2	Lorenz Nieberl, GER	Bobsled	2-0-0
2	Hallgeir Brenden, NOR	X-country	1-1-0
2	Stein Eriksen, NOR	Alpine	1-1-0
2	Heikki Hasu, FIN	X-country & Nordic Combined	1-1-0
2	Tapio Mäkelä, FIN	X-country	1-1-0
2	Othmar Schneider, AUT	Alpine	1-1-0
2	Paavo Lonkila, FIN	X-country	1-0-1
2	Stan Benham, USA	Bobsled	0-2-0
2	Kees Broekman, HOL	Sp.Skate	0-2-0
2	Patrick Martin, USA	Bobsled	0-2-0
2	Magnar Estenstad, NOR	X-country	0-1-1
2	Christian Pravda, AUT	Alpine	0-1-1
2	Fritz Feierabend, SWI	Bobsled	0-0-2
2	Stephan Waser, SWI	Bobsled	0-0-2

WOMEN

No	WOMEN	Sport	G-S-B
3	Annemarie Buchner, GER	Alpine	0-1-2
2	Andrea Mead Lawrence, USA	Alpine	2-0-0

Alpine Skiing
MEN

Event		Time
Downhill	Zeno Colò, ITA	2:30.8
Slalom	Othmar Schneider, AUT	2:00.0
G.Slalom	Stein Eriksen, NOR	2:25.0

WOMEN

Event		Time
Downhill	Trude Jochum-Beiser, AUT	1:47.1
Slalom	Andrea Mead Lawrence, USA	2:10.6
G.Slalom	Andrea Mead Lawrence, USA	2:06.8

Bobsled

Event		Time
2-Man	GER (Andreas Ostler & Lorenz Nieberl)	5:24.54
4-Man	GER (Andreas Ostler, Friedrich Kuhn, Lorenz Nieberl, Franz Kemser)	5:07.84

Figure Skating

Event		Points
Men	Dick Button, USA	1730.3
Women	Jeanette Altwegg, GBR	1455.8
Pairs	Ria Falk & Paul Falk, GER	102.6

Ice Hockey

		Gm	W-L-T	Pts	GF	GA
1	Canada	8	7-0-1	15	71	14
2	USA	8	6-1-1	13	43	21
3	Sweden	8	6-2-0	12	48	19
4	Czechoslovakia	8	6-2-0	12	47	18
5	Switzerland	8	4-4-0	8	40	40
6	Poland	8	2-5-1	5	21	56
7	Finland	8	2-6-0	4	21	60
8	Germany	8	1-6-1	3	21	53
9	Norway	8	0-8-0	0	15	46

Note: Sweden defeated Czech. 5-3, in a ninth game to decide third place and the 1952 European championship.

Nordic Skiing
MEN
Cross-country

Event		Time
18km	Hallgeir Brenden, NOR	1:01:34.0
50km	Veikko Hakulinen, FIN	3:33:33.0
4x10km	FIN (Heikki, Hasu, Paavo Lonkila, Urpo Korhonen, Tapio Mäkelä)	2:20:16.0

Ski Jumping

Event		Points
90m	Arnfinn Bergman, NOR	226.0

Nordic Combined

Event		Points
18km/Jump	Simon Slåttvik, NOR	451.621

WOMEN
Cross-country

Event		Time
10km	Lydia Widerman, FIN	41:40.0

Speed Skating
MEN

Event		Time
500m	Ken Henry, USA	43.2
1500m	Hjalmar Andersen, NOR	2:20.4
5000m	Hjalmar Andersen, NOR	8:10.6 **OR**
10,000m	Hjalmar Andersen, NOR	16:45.8 **OR**

1956

Cortina d'Ampezzo

The Soviet Union emerged from the shadows of the Cold War in 1952 to make its Olympic debut at the Summer Games in Helsinki. Finishing a close second to the United States in overall medal count (74-71), the Russians served notice that they were an athletic superpower to be reckoned with.

In 1956, the USSR made its first appearance in the Winter Games and not only outmedaled the 32-nation field, but dethroned Canada as hockey champion. Four of the USSR's seven gold medals came in speed skating, where Yevgeny

Grishin led the way with gold medals in the 500 and 1,500 meters.

Despite a shortage of snow, the outstanding performance of the VIIth Winter Games belonged to a skier named Sailor. By winning the downhill, slalom and giant slalom, Toni Sailor of Austria became the first skier to sweep all three Alpine events and only the fifth winter athlete to win three goal medals at one Olympics.

Swedish cross-country skier Sixten Jernberg, who would eventually participate in three Winter Games and win a total of nine medals, led all contestants in Cortina with four, including a gold at 50 kilometers.

The women's and men's figure skating titles were won by Americans Tenley Albright and Hayes Jenkins, who were both reigning world champions.

Top 10 Standings

National medal standings are not recognized by the IOC. The unofficial point totals are based on 3 points for a gold medal, 2 for a silver and 1 for a bronze. Total medals are in parentheses.

	Gold	Silver	Bronze	Pts
1 USSR (16)	7	3	6	33
2 Austria (11)	4	3	4	22
3 Sweden (10)	2	4	4	18
4 Finland (7)	3	3	1	16
5 Switzerland (6)	3	2	1	14
USA (7)	2	3	2	14
7 Norway (4)	2	1	1	9
8 Italy (3)	1	2	0	7
9 Germany (2)	1	0	1	4
Canada (3)	0	1	2	4

Leading Medal Winners

Number of individual medals won on the left; gold, silver and bronze medal breakdown to the right.

MEN

No		Sport	G-S-B
4	Sixten Jernberg, SWE	X-country	1-2-1
3	Toni Sailer, AUT	Alpine	3-0-0
3	Veikko Hakulinen, FIN	X-country	1-2-0
3	Pavel Kolchin, USSR	X-country	1-0-2
2	Yevgeny Grishin, USSR	Sp.Skate	2-0-0
2	Sigvard Ericsson, SWE	Sp.Skate	1-1-0
2	Fedor Terentyev, USSR	X-country	1-0-1
2	Renzo Alvera, ITA	Bobsled	0-2-0
2	Eugenio Monti, ITA	Bobsled	0-2-0
2	Andreas Molterer, AUT	Alpine	0-1-1
2	Oleg Goncharenko, USSR	Sp.Skate	0-0-2

WOMEN

No		Sport	G-S-B
2	Lyubov Kozyreva, USSR	X-country	1-1-0
2	Radya Eroshina, USSR	X-country	0-2-0
2	Sonja Edstrom, SWE	X-country	0-0-2

Alpine Skiing
MEN

Event		Time
Downhill	Toni Sailer, AUT	2:52.2
Slalom	Toni Sailer, AUT	3:14.7
G.Slalom	Toni Sailer, AUT	3:00.1

WOMEN

Event		Time
Downhill	Madeleine Berthod, SWI	1:40.7
Slalom	Renee Colliard, SWI	1:52.3
G.Slalom	Ossi Reichert, GER	1:56.5

Bobsled

Event		Time
2-Man	ITA (Lamberto Dalla Costa & Giacomo Conti)	5:30.14
4-Man	SWI (Franz Kapus, Gottfried Diener, Robert Alt, Heinrich Angst)	5:10.44

Figure Skating

Event		Points
Men	Hayes Jenkins, USA	166.43
Women	Tenley Albright, USA	169.67
Pairs	Elisabeth Schwartz & Kurt Oppelt, AUT	11.31

Ice Hockey
Championship Round
(Overall records in parentheses)

	Gm	W-L-T	Pts	GF	GA
1 USSR (7-0-0)	5	5-0-0	10	25	5
2 USA (5-2-0)	5	4-1-0	8	26	12
3 Canada (6-2-0)	5	3-2-0	6	23	11
4 Sweden (2-4-1)	5	1-3-1	3	10	22
5 Czech.(3-4-0)	5	1-4-0	2	20	30
6 Germany (1-5-2)	5	0-4-1	1	6	35

Note: The USSR beat the U.S., 4-0, and Canada, 2-0. The U.S. beat Canada, 4-1.

Nordic Skiing
MEN
Cross-country

Event		Time
15km	Hallgeir Brenden, NOR	49:39.0
30km	Veikko Hakulinen, FIN	1:44:06.0
50km	Sixten Jernberg, SWE	2:50:27.0
4x10km	USSR (Fedor Terentyev, Pavel Kolchin, Nikolai Anikin, Vladimir Kuzin)	2:15:30.0

Ski Jumping

Event		Points
90m	Antti Hyvärinen, FIN	227.0

Nordic Combined

Event		Points
15km/Jump	Sverre Stenersen, NOR	455.000

WOMEN
Cross-country

Event		Time
10km	Lyubov Kosyreva, USSR	38:11.0
3x5km	FIN (Sirkka Polkunen, Mirja Hietamies, Siira Rantanen)	1:09:01.0

Speed Skating

Event		Time	
500m	Yevgeny Grishin, USSR	40.2	=WR
1500m	Yevgeny Grishin, USSR & Yuri Mikhailov, USSR	2:08.6	WR
5000m	Boris Shilkov, USSR	7:48.7	OR
10,000m	Sigvard Ericsson, SWE	16:35.9	OR

1960

Squaw Valley

The first Winter Olympics in the U.S. since 1932 was held at an obscure California ski resort near Lake Tahoe that had no bobsled run and in the days leading up to the opening ceremony, no snow. Luckily, an 11th hour drop in temperature changed a drenching rain into a much-needed blizzard and the Games got off to a wintry start.

The most exciting venue, however, was indoors at Blyth Arena where the underdog U.S. hockey team upset the Russians and Canadians to win the gold medal for the first time ever. Led by forwards Billy Cleary and Roger Christian and goaltender Jack McCarten, the Americans beat Canada 2-1, Russia 3-2, and the Czechs 9-4, in their last three games to clinch the title.

Blyth was also where Carol Heiss and David Jenkins won the women's and men's figure skating gold medals. Heiss had won a silver and Jenkins a bronze in 1956.

Outside, the best performances belonged to Russian speed skaters Yevgeny Grishin and Lydia Skoblikova, who each won two events; and 35-year-old cross-country skier Veikko Hakulinen of Finland, who won three medals (for a career total of seven) and came from 20 seconds back on the anchor leg to win the 40-kilometer relay.

Nineteen-year-old Alpine skier Penny Pitou was America's top medalist, placing second in both the downhill and slalom events. She was later married for a few years to 1964 men's downhill champion Egon Zimmermann of Austria.

Top 10 Standings

National medal standings are not recognized by the IOC. The unofficial point totals are based on 3 points for a gold medal, 2 for a silver and 1 for a bronze. Total medals are in parentheses.

	Gold	Silver	Bronze	Pts
1 USSR (21)	7	5	9	40
2 USA (10)	3	4	3	20
3 Germany (8)	4	3	1	19
4 Norway (6)	3	3	0	15
Sweden (7)	3	2	2	15
Finland (8)	2	3	3	15
7 Austria (6)	1	2	3	10
8 Canada (4)	2	1	1	9
9 Switzerland (2)	2	0	0	6
10 France (3)	1	0	2	5

Leading Medal Winners

Number of individual medals won on the left; gold, silver and bronze medal breakdown to the right.

MEN

No		Sport	G-S-B
3	Veikko Hakulinen, FIN	X-country	1-1-1
2	Yevgeny Grishin, USSR	Sp.Skate	2-0-0
2	Håkon Brusveen, NOR	X-country	1-1-0
2	Knut Johannesen, NOR	Sp.Skate	1-1-0
2	Sixten Jernberg, SWE	X-country	1-1-0
2	Viktor Kosichkin, USSR	Sp.Skate	1-1-0
2	Ernst Hinterseer, AUT	Alpine	1-0-1
2	Rolf Rämgård, SWE	X-country	0-1-1
2	Nikolai Anikin, USSR	X-country	0-0-2

WOMEN

No		Sport	G-S-B
2	Lydia Skoblikova, USSR	Sp.Skate	2-0-0
2	Maria Gusakova, USSR	X-country	1-1-0
2	Helga Haase, GER	Sp.Skate	1-1-0
2	Penny Pitou, USA	Alpine	0-2-0
2	Lyubov Baranova, USSR	X-country	0-2-0
2	Radya Eroshina, USSR	X-country	0-1-1

Alpine Skiing
MEN

Event		Time
Downhill	Jean Vuarnet, FRA	2:06.0
Slalom	Ernst Hinterseer, AUT	2:08.9
G.Slalom	Roger Staub, SWI	1:48.3

WOMEN

Event		Time
Downhill	Heidi Biebl, GER	1:37.6
Slalom	Anne Heggtveit, CAN	1:49.6
G.Slalom	Yvonne Rüegg, SWI	1:39.9

Biathlon

Event		MT	Adj.Time
20km	Klas Lestander, SWE	0	1:33:21.6

Bobsled

Not held—no facilities.

Figure Skating

Event		Points
Men	David Jenkins, USA	1440.2
Women	Carol Heiss, USA	1490.1
Pairs	Barbara Wagner & Robert Paul, CAN	80.4

Ice Hockey
Championship Round
(Overall records in parentheses)

	Gm	W-L-T	Pts	GF	GA
1 USA (7-0-0)	5	5-0-0	10	29	11
2 Canada (6-1-0)	5	4-1-0	8	31	12
3 USSR (4-2-1)	5	2-2-1	5	24	19
4 Czech.(3-4-0)	5	2-3-0	4	21	23
5 Sweden (2-4-1)	5	1-3-1	3	19	19
6 Germany (1-6-0)	5	0-5-0	0	5	45

Note: The U.S. beat Canada, 2-1, the USSR, 3-2, and Czech., 9-4, in its last three games. Canada beat the USSR, 8-5, and Sweden tied the Russians, 2-2.

Nordic Skiing
MEN
Cross-country

Event		Time
15km	Håkon Brusveen, NOR	51:55.5
30km	Sixten Jernberg, SWE	1:51:03.9
50km	Kalevi Hämäläinen, FIN	2:59:06.3

Event		Time
4x10km	FIN (Toimi Alatalo, Eero Mäntyranta, Väinö Huhtala, Veikko Hakulinen)	2:18:45.6

Ski Jumping

Event		Points
80m	Helmut Recknagel, GER	227.2

Nordic Combined

Event		Points
15km/Jump	Georg Thoma, GER	457.952

WOMEN
Cross-country

Event		Time
10km	Marija Gusakova, USSR	39:46.6
3x5km.	SWE (Irma Johansson, Britt Strandberg, Sonja Ruthström)	1:04:21.4

Speed Skating
MEN

Event		Time
500m	Yevgeny Grishin, USSR	40.2 =WR
1500m	Roald Aas, NOR & Yevgeny Grishin, USSR.	2:10.4
5000m	Viktor Kosichkin, USSR	7:51.3
10,000m	Knut Johannesen, NOR	15:46.6 WR

WOMEN

Event		Time
500m	Helga Haase, GER	45.9
1000m	Klara Guseva, USSR	1:34.1
1500m	Lydia Skoblikova, USSR	2:25.2 WR
3000m	Lydia Skoblikova, USSR	5:14.3

1964
Innsbruck

Death and unseasonably mild weather hung over the ninth Winter Games in the Tyrolean Alps.

Two athletes, 50-year-old British luger Kazimierz Kay-Skyszpeski and 19-year-old Australian downhill skier Ross Milne, were killed taking practice runs less than a week before the Games began. And three years before, on Feb. 15, 1961, a plane crash in Belgium had killed 18 members of the U.S. figure skating team—including America's top female skater, 16-year-old Laurence Owen.

Springlike temperatures plagued Innsbruck both before and during the Games, forcing the Austrian military to carry in over 50,000 cubic meters of snow from higher elevations.

The USSR won 11 gold medals—a combined seven by speed skater Lydia Skoblikova (4) and cross-country skier Claudia Boyarskikh (3). Other stars included the skiing Goitschel sisters, Christine and Marielle, of France; and cross-country skiers Eero Mantyranta of Finland and 34-year-old Sixten Jernberg of Sweden.

The lone U.S. gold medal was won by 23-year-old barber Terry McDermott in speed skating.

Top 10 Standings

National medal standings are not recognized by the IOC. The unofficial point totals are based on 3 points for a gold medal, 2 for a silver and 1 for a bronze. Total medals are in parentheses.

		Gold	Silver	Bronze	Pts
1	USSR (25)	11	8	6	55
2	Norway (15)	3	6	6	27
3	Austria (12)	4	5	3	25
4	Finland (10)	3	4	3	20
5	France (7)	3	4	0	17
6	Sweden (7)	3	3	1	16
	Germany (8)	3	2	3	16
8	USA (6)	1	2	3	10
9	Holland (2)	1	1	0	5
	Canada (3)	1	0	2	5
	Italy (4)	0	1	3	5

Leading Medal Winners

Number of individual medals won on the left; gold, silver and bronze medal breakdown to the right.

MEN

No		Sport	G-S-B
3	Eero Mäntyranta, FIN	X-country	2-1-0
3	Sixten Jernberg, SWE	X-country	2-0-1
2	Toralf Engan, NOR	Ski Jump	1-1-0
2	Veikko Kankkonen, FIN	Ski Jump	1-1-0
2	Assar Rönnlund, SWE	X-country	1-1-0
2	Knut Johannesen, NOR	Sp.Skate	1-0-1
2	Pepi Stiegler, AUT	Alpine	1-0-1
2	Harald Grönningen, NOR	X-country	0-2-0
2	Fred Maier, NOR.	Sp.Skate	0-1-1
2	Arto Tiainen, FIN	X-country	0-1-1
2	Torgeir Brandtzaeg, NOR	Ski Jump	0-0-2
2	Eugenio Monti, ITA	Bobsled	0-0-2
2	Sergio Siorpaes, ITA	Bobsled	0-0-2
2	Igor Voronchikin, USSR	X-country	0-0-2

WOMEN

No		Sport	G-S-B
4	Lydia Skoblikova, USSR	Sp.Skate	4-0-0
3	Claudia Boyarskikh, USSR	X-country	3-0-0
2	Christine Goitschel, FRA	Alpine	1-1-0
2	Marielle Goitschel, FRA	Alpine	1-1-0
2	Eudokia Mekshilo, USSR	X-country	1-1-0
2	Alevtina Kolchina, USSR	X-country	1-0-1
2	Mirja Lehtonen, FIN	X-country	0-1-1
2	Kaija Mustonen, FIN	Sp.Skate	0-1-1
2	Jean Saubert, USA	Alpine	0-1-1
2	Irina Yegorova, USSR	Sp.Skate	0-2-0

Alpine Skiing
MEN

Event		Time
Downhill	Egon Zimmermann, AUT	2:18.16
Slalom	Pepi Stiegler, AUT.	2:11.13
G.Slalom	Francois Bonlieu, FRA	1:46.71

Note: In the Slalom, Billy Kidd (2nd) and Jimmy Heuga (3rd) won first U.S. men's Alpine medals ever.

WOMEN

Event		Time
Downhill	Christl Haas, AUT	1:55.39
Slalom	Christine Goitschel, FRA	1:29.86
G.Slalom	Marielle Goitschel, FRA	1:52.24

Biathlon

Event		MT	Adj.Time
20km	Vladimir Melanin, USSR	0	1:20:26.8

Bobsled

Event		Time
2-Man	GBR (Tony Nash & Robin Dixon)	4:21.90
4-Man	CAN (Victor Emery, Peter Kirby, Doug Anakin, John Emery)	4:14.46

Figure Skating

Event		Points
Men	Manfred Schnelldorfer, GER.	1916.9
Women	Sjoukje Dijkstra, HOL	2018.5
Pairs	Lyudmila Belousova & Oleg Protopopov, USSR	104.4

Ice Hockey
Group A
(Overall records in parentheses)

		Gm	W-L-T	Pts	GF	GA
1	USSR (8-0-0)	7	7-0-0	14	54	10
2	Sweden (6-2-0)	7	5-2-0	10	47	16
3	Czechoslovakia (6-2-0)	7	5-2-0	10	38	19
4	Canada (6-2-0)	7	5-2-0	10	32	17
5	USA (3-5-0)	7	2-5-0	4	29	33
6	Finland (3-5-0)	7	2-5-0	4	10	31
7	Germany (3-5-0)	7	2-5-0	4	13	49
8	Switzerland (1-7-0)	7	0-7-0	0	9	57

Note: Pivotal game—USSR over Canada, 3-2, in final game for both teams. Places 2-4 and 5-7 decided by goal differential. Also, all eight teams had to win a one-game elimination round to qualify for Group A.

Luge
MEN

Event		Time
1-Seat	Thomas Köhler, GER	3:26.77
2-Seat	Josef Feistmantl & Manfred Stengl, AUT	1:41.62

WOMEN

Event		Time
1-Seat	Ortrun Enderlein, GER	3:24.67

Nordic Skiing
MEN
Cross-country

Event		Time
15km	Eero Mäntyranta, FIN	50:54.1
30km	Eero Mäntyranta, FIN	1:30:50.7
50km	Sixten Jernberg, SWE	2:43:52.6
4x10km	SWE (Karl-Åke Asph, Sixten Jernberg, Janne Stefansson, Assar Rönnlund)	2:18:34.6

Ski Jumping

Event		Points
70m	Veikko Kankkonen, FIN	229.9
80m	Toralf Engan, NOR	230.7

Nordic Combined

Event		Points
15km/Jump	Tormod Knutsen, NOR	469.28

WOMEN
Cross-country

Event		Time
5km	Claudia Boyarskikh, USSR	17:50.5
10km	Claudia Boyarskikh, USSR	40:24.3
3x5km	USSR (Alevtina Kolchina, Eudokia Mekshilo, Claudia Boyarskikh)	59:20.2

Speed Skating
MEN

Event		Time	
500m	Terry McDermott, USA	40.1	OR
1500m	Ants Antson, USSR	2:10.3	
5000m	Knut Johannesen, NOR	7:38.4	OR
10,000m	Jonny Nilsson, SWE	15:50.1	

WOMEN

Event		Time	
500m	Lydia Skoblikova, USSR	45.0	OR
1000m	Lydia Skoblikova, USSR	1:33.2	OR
1500m	Lydia Skoblikova, USSR	2:22.6	OR
3000m	Lydia Skoblikova, USSR	5:14.9	

1968
Grenoble

For the first time since they began attending the Winter Games in 1956, the Russians did not win the most medals—Norway did.

The host French team finished fourth in the overall standings—their best showing ever—thanks mainly to 24-year-old Val d'Isere native Jean-Claude Killy, who became the first skier to sweep all three Alpine events since Toni Sailor in 1956.

Killy was awarded his third gold medal in the slalom only after original winner Karl Schranz of Austria was disqualified for missing two gates on his second run in the two-heat race. Schranz had been allowed to retake his second heat run when a spectator interrupted his initial attempt, but officials ruled the missed gates came before the interruption.

Once again, the U.S. won only one gold medal—19-year-old Peggy Fleming in women's figure skating. Three of the five silver medals won by the U.S. came in one event—the women's 500-meter speed skating race, where Jenny Fish, Diane Holum and Mary Myers tied for second place with a time of 46.3 seconds.

Top 10 Standings

National medal standings are not recognized by the IOC. The unofficial point totals are based on 3 points for a gold medal, 2 for a silver and 1 for a bronze. Total medals are in parentheses.

		Gold	Silver	Bronze	Pts
1	Norway (14)	6	6	2	32
2	USSR (13)	5	5	3	28
3	Austria (11)	3	4	4	21
4	France (9)	4	3	2	20
5	Holland (9)	3	3	3	18
6	Sweden (8)	3	2	3	16
7	USA (7)	1	5	1	14
8	W.Germany (7)	2	2	3	13
9	Italy (4)	4	0	0	12
10	E.Germany (5)	1	2	2	9
	Finland (5)	1	2	2	9

Leading Medal Winners

Number of individual medals won on the left; gold, silver and bronze medal breakdown to the right.

MEN

No		Sport	G-S-B
3	Jean-Claude Killy, FRA	Alpine	3-0-0
3	Eero Mäntyranta, FIN	X-country	0-1-2
2	Eugenio Monti, ITA	Bobsled	2-0-0
2	Luciano De Paolis, ITA	Bobsled	2-0-0
2	Ole Ellefsaeter, NOR	X-country	2-0-0
2	Harald Grönningen, NOR	X-country	2-0-0
2	Thomas Köhler, E.Ger	Luge	1-1-0

No		Sport	G-S-B
2	Fred Maier, NOR	Sp.Skate	1-1-0
2	Odd Martinsen, NOR	X-country	1-1-0
2	Jiři Raška, CZE	Ski Jump	1-1-0
2	Manfred Schmid, AUT	Luge	1-1-0
2	Magnar Solberg, NOR	Biathlon	1-1-0
2	Aleksandr Tikhonov, USSR	Biathlon	1-1-0
2	Kees Verkerk, HOL	Sp.Skate	1-1-0
2	Klaus Bonsack, E.Ger	Luge	1-0-1
2	Vladimir Goundartsev, USSR	Biathlon	1-0-1
2	Gunnar Larsson, SWE	X-country	0-1-1

WOMEN

No		Sport	G-S-B
3	Toini Gustafsson, SWE	X-country	2-1-0
2	Carolina Geijssen, HOL	Sp.Skate	1-1-0
2	Nancy Greene, CAN	Alpine	1-1-0
2	Berit Mördre, NOR	X-country	1-1-0
2	Kaija Mustonen, FIN	Sp.Skate	1-1-0
2	Lyudmila Titova, USSR	Sp.Skate	1-1-0
2	Inger Aufles, NOR	X-country	1-0-1
2	Annie Famose, FRA	Alpine	0-1-1
2	Dianne Holum, USA	Sp.Skate	0-1-1
2	Galina Kulakova, USSR	X-country	0-1-1
2	Christina Kaiser, HOL	Sp.Skate	0-0-2
2	Alevtina Kolchina, USSR	X-country	0-0-2

Alpine Skiing

MEN

Event		Time
Downhill	Jean-Claude Killy, FRA	1:59.85
Slalom	Jean-Claude Killy, FRA	1:39.73
G.Slalom	Jean-Claude Killy, FRA	3:29.28

WOMEN

Event		Time
Downhill	Olga Pall, AUT	1:40.87
Slalom	Marielle Goitschel, FRA	1:25.86
G.Slalom	Nancy Greene, CAN	1:51.97

Biathlon

Event		MT	Adj.Time
20km	Magnar Solberg, NOR	0	1:13:45.9
4x7.5km	USSR (Tikonov, Pousanov, Mamatov, Goundartsev)	2	2:13:02.4

Bobsled

Event		Time
2-Man	ITA (Eugenio Monti & Luciano De Paolis)	4:41.54
4-Man	ITA (Monti, De Paolis, Zandonella, Armano)	2:17.39

Figure Skating

Event		Points
Men	Wolfgang Schwarz, AUT	1904.1
Women	Peggy Fleming, USA	1970.5
Pairs	Lyudmila Belousova & Oleg Protopopov, USSR	315.2

Ice Hockey

Group A

		Gm	W-L-T	Pts	GF	GA
1	USSR	7	6-1-0	12	48	10
2	Czechoslovakia	7	5-1-1	11	33	17
3	Canada	7	5-2-0	10	28	15
4	Sweden	7	4-2-1	9	23	18
5	Finland (4-3-1)	7	3-3-1	9	17	23
6	USA	7	2-4-1	5	23	28
7	West Germany (2-6-0)	7	1-6-0	2	13	39
8	East Germany (1-7-0)	7	0-7-0	0	13	48

Note: The Czechs beat the USSR, 5-4, and tied Sweden, 2-2. The U.S. squad included four future NHL coaches—Herb Brooks, John Cunniff, Lou Nanne and Larry Pleau. Also, Finland and the two Germanys had to win an elimination round game to qualify for Group A. Their overall records are in parentheses.

Luge

MEN

Event		Time
1-Seat	Manfred Schmid, AUT	2:52.48
2-Seat	Klaus Bonsack & Thomas Köhler, E.Ger	1:35.85

WOMEN

Event		Time
1-Seat	Erica Lechner, ITA	2:28.66

Note: Defending champion Ortrun Enderlein and teammate Anna-Maria Müller of East Germany finished 1-2, but were disqualified for heating the blades of their toboggans.

Nordic Skiing

MEN

Cross-country

Event		Time
15km	Harald Grönningen, NOR	47:54.2
30km	Franco Nones, ITA	1:35:39.2
50km	Ole Ellefsaeter, NOR	2:28:45.8
4x10km	NOR (Martinsen, Tyldum, Grönningen, Ellefsaeter)	2:08:33.5

Ski Jumping

Event		Points
70m	Jiři Raška, CZE	216.5
90m	Vladimir Beloussov, USSR	231.3

Nordic Combined

Event		Points
15km/Jump	Franz Keller, W.Ger	449.04

WOMEN

Cross-country

Event		Time
5km	Toini Gustafsson, SWE	16:45.2
10km	Toini Gustafsson, SWE	36:46.5
3x5km	NOR (Aufles, Damon-Enger, Mördre)	57:30.0

1968 (Cont.)
Speed Skating

MEN

Event		Time
500m	Erhard Keller, W.Ger	40.3
1500m	Kees Verkerk, HOL	2:03.4 **OR**
5000m	Fred Maier, NOR	7:22.4 **WR**
10,000m	Johnny Höglin, SWE	15:23.6 **OR**

WOMEN

Event		Time
500m	Lyudmila Titova, USSR.	46.1
1000m	Carolina Geijssen, HOL	1:32.6 **OR**
1500m	Kaija Mustonen, FIN	2:22.4 **OR**
3000m	Johanna Schut, HOL	4:56.2 **OR**

1972

Sapporo

The biggest controversy in the 48-year history of the Winter Games erupted just three days before the opening ceremonies were scheduled to get underway in northern Japan. That's when retiring IOC president Avery Brundage threatened to disqualify 40 Alpine skiers for professionalism.

At Grenoble in 1968, Brundage had demanded that all trademarks be removed from competitors' skis, but settled for having the offensive skis taken away from medal winners before they could be photographed. Now, the 84-year-old guardian of the Olympic flame wanted all the pros thrown out.

A compromise was reached when the IOC executive committee voted 28-14 to make an example of skiing's most commercialized star, 33-year-old Austrian World Cup champion Karl Schranz, who reportedly earned over $50,000 a year "testing" ski equipment. All other offenders were allowed to participate.

Said Schranz after being banished: "This thing of amateur purity is something that dates back to the 19th century when amateur sportsmen were regarded as gentlemen and everyone else was an outcast. The Olympics should be a competition of skill and strength and speed—and no more."

Top 10 Standings

National medal standings are not recognized by the IOC. The unofficial point totals are based on 3 points for a gold medal, 2 for a silver and 1 for a bronze. Total medals are in parentheses.

		Gold	Silver	Bronze	Pts
1	USSR (16)	8	5	3	37
2	E.Germany (14)	4	3	7	25
3	Switzerland (10)	4	3	3	21
	Norway (12)	2	5	5	21
5	Holland (9)	4	3	2	20
6	USA (8)	3	2	3	16
7	W.Germany (5)	3	1	1	12
8	Italy (5)	2	2	1	11
9	Austria (5)	1	2	2	9
	Finland (5)	0	4	1	9

Leading Medal Winners

Number of individual medals won on the left; gold, silver and bronze medal breakdown to the right.

MEN

No		Sport	G-S-B
3	Ard Schenk, HOL	Sp.Skate	3-0-0
3	Vyacheslav Vedenine, USSR	X-country	2-0-1
3	Pål Tyldum, NOR	X-country	1-2-0
2	Fedor Simashov, USSR	X-country	1-1-0
2	Gustav Thöni, ITA	Alpine	1-1-0
2	Wolfgang Zimmerer, W.Ger	Bobsled	1-0-1
2	Peter Utzschneider, W.Ger	Bobsled	1-0-1
2	Jean Wicki, SWI	Bobsled	1-0-1
2	Edy Hubacher, SWI.	Bobsled	1-0-1
2	Roar Grönvold, NOR	Sp.Skate	0-2-0
2	Ivar Formo, NOR	X-country	0-1-1
2	Johs Harviken, NOR	X-country	0-1-1
2	Hansjorg Knauthe, E.Ger	Biathlon	0-1-1
2	Wolfram Fiedler, E.Ger	Luge	0-0-2
2	Sten Stensen, NOR	Sp.Skate	0-0-2

WOMEN

No		Sport	G-S-B
3	Galina Kulakova, USSR	X-country	3-0-0
3	Marjatta Kajosmaa, FIN	X-country	0-2-1
2	Marie-Theres Nadig, SWI	Alpine	2-0-0
2	Dianne Holum, USA	Sp.Skate	1-1-0
2	Christina Baas-Kaiser, HOL	Sp.Skate	1-1-0
2	Alevtina Olunina, USSR	X-country	1-1-0
2	Anne Henning, USA	Sp.Skate	1-0-1
2	Annemarie Pröll, FRA	Alpine	0-2-0
2	Atje Keulen-Deelstra, HOL	Sp.Skate	0-1-1

Alpine Skiing
MEN

Event		Time
Downhill	Bernhard Russi, SWI.	1:51.43
Slalom	Francisco Ochoa, SPA	1:49.27
G.Slalom	Gustav Thöni, ITA.	3:09.62

WOMEN

Event		Time
Downhill	Marie-Theres Nadig, SWI	1:36.68
Slalom	Barbara Cochran, USA.	1:31.24
G.Slalom	Marie-Theres Nadig, SWI	1:29.90

Biathlon

Event		MT	Adj.Time
20km	Magnar Solberg, NOR	2	1:15:55.50
4x7.5km	USSR (Tikonov, Safine, Biakov, Mamatov).	3	1:51:44.92

Bobsled

Event		Time
2-Man	W.Ger.(Wolfgang Zimmerer & Peter Utzschneider)	4:57.07
4-Man	SWI (Wicki, Hubacher Leutenegger, Carmichel)	4:43.07

Figure Skating

Event		Points
Men	Ondrej Nepela, CZE	2739.1
Women	Trixi Schuba, AUT	2751.5
Pairs	Irina Rodnina & Aleksei Ulanov, USSR	420.4

Ice Hockey

Group A

(Overall records in parentheses)

	Gm	W-L-T	Pts	GF	GA
1 USSR(4-0-1)	5	4-0-1	9	33	13
2 USA (4-2-0)	5	3-2-0	6	18	15
3 Czechoslovakia (4-2-0)	5	3-2-0	6	26	13
4 Sweden (3-2-1)	5	2-2-1	5	17	13
5 Finland (3-3-0)	5	2-3-0	4	14	24
6 Poland (1-5-0)	5	0-5-0	0	9	39

Note: Pivotal game—USSR over Czech., 5-2, in final contest for both teams. The 5-1 U.S. victory over the Czechs gave the Americans second place. Canada did not send a team, having withdrawn from international amateur competition in 1969 to protest use of "professional amateurs" by Russia and other eastern bloc countries. Also, the USSR received a bye to Group A while the other seven teams had to win a one-game elimination round to qualify.

Luge

MEN

Event		Time
1-Seat	Wolfgang Scheidel, E.Ger	3:27.58
2-Seat	TIE—Horst Hörnlein	
	& Reinhard Bredow, E.Ger	1:28.35
	—Paul Hildgartner	
	& Walter Plaikner, ITA	1:28.35

WOMEN

Event		Time
1-Seat	Anna-Maria Müller, E.Ger	2:59.18

Nordic Skiing

MEN

Cross-country

Event		Time
15km	Sven-Ake Lundbäck, SWE	45:28:24
30km	Vyacheslav Vedenine, USSR	1:36:31.15
50km	Pål Tyldum, NOR	2:43:14.75
4x10km	USSR (Voronkov, Skobov, Simachev, Vedenine)	2:04:47.94

Ski Jumping

Event		Points
70m	Yukio Kasaya, JPN	244.2
90m	Wojciech Fortuna, POL	219.9

Nordic Combined

Event		Points
15km/Jump	Ulrich Wehling, E.Ger	413.340

WOMEN

Cross-country

Event		Time
5km	Galina Kulakova, USSR	17:00.50
10km	Galina Kulakova, USSR	34:17.82
3x5km	USSR (Moukhatcheva, Olunina, Kulakova)	48:46.15

Speed Skating

MEN

Event		Time	
500m	Erhard Keller, W.Ger	39.44	OR
1500m	Ard Schenk, HOL	2:02.96	OR
5000m	Ard Schenk, HOL	7:23.61	
10,000m	Ard Schenk, HOL	15:01.35	OR

WOMEN

Event		Time	
500m	Anne Henning, USA	43.33	OR
1000m	Monika Pflug, W.Ger	1:31.40	OR
1500m	Dianne Holum, USA	2:20.85	OR
3000m	Christina Baas-Kaiser, HOL	4:52.14	OR

1976

Innsbruck

The IOC originally gave the 1976 Winter Games to Denver, but in 1972 Colorado voters rejected a $5 million bond issue to finance the undertaking. Denver immediately withdrew as host and the IOC called on Innsbruck, site of the 1964 Games.

For the second straight Winter carnival the USSR and East Germany finished 1-2 in overall medals. In 1972, Dutch speed skater Ard Schenk and Soviet cross-country skier Galina Kulakova each won three gold medals. In '76, nobody won three, but 25-year-old West German skier Rosi Mittermaier almost did—winning two golds and a silver in the women's Alpine events.

The Russian hockey team, which had won the gold medal in 1972 and then battled the NHL's Team Canada to a virtual standoff six months later, returned with most of the same players and won its fourth straight Olympic title.

In figure skating, 19-year-old Dorothy Hamill of the U.S. and John Curry of Britain won gold medals. Both were coached by Carlo Fassi, who also coached Peggy Fleming in 1968.

Also, Bill Koch became the only U.S. skier to ever win an Olympic Nordic medal when he placed second in the 30-kilometers cross-country.

Top 10 Standings

National medal standings are not recognized by the IOC. The unofficial point totals are based on 3 points for a gold medal, 2 for a silver and 1 for a bronze. Total medals are in parentheses.

	Gold	Silver	Bronze	Pts
1 USSR (27)	13	6	8	59
2 E.Germany (19)	7	5	7	38
3 USA (10)	3	3	4	19
W.Germany (10)	2	5	3	19
5 Norway (7)	3	3	1	16
6 Finland (7)	2	4	1	15
7 Austria (6)	2	2	2	12
8 Switzerland (5)	1	3	1	10
Holland (6)	1	2	3	10
10 Italy (4)	1	2	1	8

1976 (Cont.)
Leading Medal Winners

Number of individual medals won on the left; gold, silver and bronze medal breakdown to the right.

MEN

No		Sport	G-S-B
3	Hans van Helden, HOL	Sp.Skate	0-0-3
2	Bernhard Germeshausen, E.Ger	Bobsled	2-0-0
2	Nikolai Kruglov, USSR	Biathlon	2-0-0
2	Meinhard Nehmer, E.Ger	Bobsled	2-0-0
2	Ivar Formo, NOR	X-country	1-1-0
2	Piet Kleine, HOL	Sp.Skate	1-1-0
2	Nikolai Bazhuko, USSR	X-country	1-0-1
2	Aleksandr Elizarov, USSR	Biathlon	1-0-1
2	Arto Koivisto, FIN	X-country	1-0-1
2	Hans Rinn, E.Ger	Luge	1-0-1
2	Sergei Saveliev, USSR	X-country	1-0-1
2	Karl Schnabl, AUT	Ski Jump	1-0-1
2	Sten Stensen, NOR	Sp.Skate	1-1-0
2	Neikki Ikola, FIN	Biathlon	0-2-0
2	Yevgeny Beliaev, USSR	X-country	0-1-1
2	Josef Benz, SWI	Bobsled	0-1-1
2	Valery Muratov, USSR	Sp.Skate	0-1-1
2	Erich Scharer, SWI	Bobsled	0-1-1
2	Manfred Schumann, W.Ger	Bobsled	0-1-1
2	Wolfgang Zimmerer, W.Ger	Bobsled	0-1-1
2	Ivan Garanin, USSR	X-country	0-0-2

WOMEN

No		Sport	G-S-B
4	Tatiana Averina, USSR	Sp.Skate	2-0-2
3	Rosi Mittermaier, W.Ger	Alpine	2-1-0
3	Raisa Smetanina, USSR	X-country	2-1-0
3	Helena Takalo, FIN	X-country	1-2-0
3	Sheila Young, USA	Sp.Skate	1-1-1
2	Galina Kulakova, USSR	X-country	1-0-1

Alpine Skiing
MEN

Event		Time
Downhill	Franz Klammer, AUT	1:45.73
Slalom	Piero Gros, ITA	2:03.29
G.Slalom	Heini Hemmi, SWI	3:26.97

WOMEN

Event		Time
Downhill	Rosi Mittermaier, W.Ger	1:46.16
Slalom	Rosi Mittermaier, W.Ger	1:30.54
G.Slalom	Kathy Kreiner, CAN	1:29.13

Note: Mittermaier finished second in the GS, missing the first women's alpine sweep by an eighth of a second.

Biathlon

Event		MT	Adj.Time
20km	Nikolai Kruglov, USSR	2	1:14:12.26
4x7.5km	USSR (Elizarov, Blakov, Kruglov, Tikonov)	0	1:57:55.64

Bobsled

Event		Time
2-Man	E.Ger.(Meinhard Nehmer & Bernhard Germeshausen)	3:44.42
4-Man	E.Ger.(Nehmer, Babock, Germeshausen, Lehmann)	3:40.43

Figure Skating

Event		Points
Men	John Curry, GBR	192.74
Women	Dorothy Hamill, USA	193.80
Pairs	Irina Rodnina & Aleksandr Zaitsev, USSR	140.54
Dance	Lyudmila Pakhomova & Aleksandr Gorshkov, USSR	209.92

Ice Hockey
Group A
(Overall records in parentheses)

	Gm	W-L-T	Pts	GF	GA
1 USSR (6-0-0)	5	5-0-0	10	40	11
2 Czechoslovakia (3-2-0)	4	2-2-0	6	17	10
3 West Germany (3-3-0)	5	2-3-0	4	21	24
4 Finland (3-3-0)	5	2-3-0	4	19	18
5 USA (3-3-0)	5	2-3-0	4	15	21
6 Poland (1-4-0)	5	0-4-0	0	9	37

Note: Czechoslovakia's 7-1 win over Poland was disallowed when a Czech player flunked a random post-game drug test. The Czechs were given a loss and their goals vs. Poland deleted from the records. The U.S. missed a bronze medal in its final game with a 4-1 loss to West Germany, which clinched third place by goal differential. Also, all eight teams had to win a one-game elimination round to qualify for Group A. Finally, Sweden did not send a team, admitting that its players were at least semi-professional.

Luge
MEN

Event		Time
1-Seat	Dettlef Günther, E.Ger	3:27.688
2-Seat	Hans Rinn & Norbert Hahn, E.Ger	1:25.604

WOMEN

Event		Time
1-Seat	Margit Schumann, E.Ger	2:50.621

Nordic Skiing
MEN
Cross-country

Event		Time
15km	Nikolai Bazhukov, USSR	43:58.47
30km	Sergei Saveliev, USSR	1:30:29.38
50km	Ivar Formo, NOR	2:37:30.05
4x10km	FIN (Pitkänen, Mieto, Teurajärvi, Koivisto)	2:07:59.72

Ski Jumping

Event		Points
70m	Hans-Goerg Aschenbach, E.Ger	252.0
90m	Karl Schnabl, AUT	234.8

Nordic Combined

Event		Points
15km/Jump	Ulrich Wehling, E.Ger	423.39

WOMEN
Cross-country

Event		Time
5km	Helena Takalo, FIN	15:48.69
10km	Raisa Smetanina, USSR	30:13.41
4x5km	USSR (Baldycheva, Amosova, Smetanina, Kulakova)	1:07:49.75

Speed Skating
MEN

Event		Time
500m	Yevgeny Kulikov, USSR	39.17 **OR**
1000m	Peter Mueller, USA	1:19.32
1500m	Jan Egil Storholt, NOR	1:59.38 **OR**
5000m	Sten Stensen, NOR	7:24.48
10,000m	Piet Kleine, HOL	14:50.59 **OR**

WOMEN

Event		Time
500m	Sheila Young, USA	42.76 **OR**
1000m	Tatiana Averina, USSR	1:28.43 **OR**
1500m	Galina Stepanskaya, USSR	2:16.58 **OR**
3000m	Tatiana Averina, USSR	4:45.19 **OR**

XIII OLYMPIC WINTER GAMES LAKE PLACID 1980

1980

Lake Placid

Eric and the Miracles. Over 1,100 athletes from 37 countries participated in the 1980 Winter Games, but the only ones most people will ever remember are 21-year-old American speed skater Eric Heiden, who won five individual gold medals, and the U.S. hockey team—a bunch of college kids (average age 22) who beat the unbeatable Russians.

No one before or since Heiden has won five individual gold medals in a single Olympic Games (three of swimmer Mark Spitz's seven gold medals in 1972 were for relay races). And Heiden's sweep of the men's speed skating events has never been duplicated.

The hockey team, on the other hand, was a decided underdog. Seeded seventh out of 12 teams in the first round, they had also been routed, 10-3, by the Soviet Union in an exhibition game only a week before the Olympics.

Nevertheless, the Americans reached the final round with a 4-0-1 record. Playing in front of a boisterous, flag-waving home crowd, the U.S. upset the Soviets, 4-3 (captain Mike Eruzione scored the winning goal midway through the third period and goalie Jim Craig made 39 saves), then beat Finland, 4-2, to win the gold medal.

"Do you believe in miracles?" asked ABC-TV announcer Al Michaels as the final seconds ticked off against the Russians. "Ye-s-s-s!"

That game was played on Feb. 22—five days short of exactly 20 years after the 1960 U.S. team beat the USSR, 3-2, on *their* way to the gold medal at Squaw Valley. Other links to the past included right wing Dave Christian, whose father Billy and uncle Roger were linemates on the 1960 team, and coach Herb Brooks, who had been the last player cut from the 1960 squad.

Top 10 Standings

National medal standings are not recognized by the IOC. The unofficial point totals are based on 3 points for a gold medal, 2 for a silver and 1 for a bronze. Total medals are in parentheses.

	Gold	Silver	Bronze	Pts
1 USSR (22)	10	6	6	48
E.Germany (23)	9	7	7	48
3 USA (12)	6	4	2	28
4 Finland (9)	1	5	3	16
5 Austria (7)	3	2	2	15
Norway (10)	1	3	6	15
7 Sweden (4)	3	0	1	10
Liechtenstein (4)	2	2	0	10
9 Holland (4)	1	2	1	8
Switzerland (5)	1	1	3	8

Leading Medal Winners

Number of individual medals won on the left; gold, silver and bronze medal breakdown to the right.

MEN

No		Sport	G-S-B
5	Eric Heiden, USA	Sp.Skating	5-0-0
3	Nikolai Zimatov, USSR.	X-country	3-0-0
3	Anatoly Alyabiev, USSR	Biathlon	2-0-1
3	Frank Ullrich, E.Ger.	Biathlon	1-2-0
3	Juha Mieto, FIN	X-country	0-2-1
2	Ingemar Stenmark, SWE.	Alpine	2-0-0
2	Vladimir Alikin, USSR.	Biathlon	1-1-0
2	Josef Benz, SWI.	Bobsled	1-1-0
2	Hans Jurgen Gerhardt, E.Ger.	Bobsled	1-1-0
2	Bernhard Germeshausen, E.Ger.	Bobsled	1-1-0
2	Vasili Rochev, USSR	X-country	1-1-0
2	Erich Schärer, SWI	Bobsled	1-1-0
2	Bogdan Musiol, E.Ger.	Bobsled	1-0-1
2	Meinhard Nehmer, E.Ger	Bobsled	1-0-1
2	Kai Arne Stenshjemmet, NOR	Sp.Skate	0-2-0
2	Ove Aunli, NOR.	X-country	0-1-1
2	Eberhard Rosch, E.Ger.	Biathlon	0-1-1
2	Tom Erik Oxholm, NOR	Sp.Skate	0-0-2

WOMEN

No		Sport	G-S-B
3	Hanni Wenzel, LIE.	Alpine	2-1-0
2	Barbara Petzold, E.Ger	X-country	2-0-0
2	Raisa Smetanina, USSR.	X-country	1-1-0
2	Natalia Petruseva, USSR.	Sp.Skate	1-0-1
2	Leah Mueller, USA	Sp.Skate	0-2-0
2	Hilkka Riihivuori, FIN.	X-country	0-2-0
2	Sabine Becker, E.Ger	Sp.Skate	0-1-1

Alpine Skiing

MEN

Event		Time
Downhill	Leonhard Stock, AUT	1:45.50
Slalom	Ingemar Stenmark, SWE.	1:44.26
G.Slalom	Ingemar Stenmark, SWE.	2:40.74

WOMEN

Event		Time
Downhill	Annemarie Moser-Pröll, AUT	1:37.52
Slalom	Hanni Wenzel, LIE.	1:25.09
G.Slalom	Hanni Wenzel, LIE.	2:41.66

Biathlon

Event		MT	Adj.Time
10km	Frank Ullrich, E.Ger.	2	32:10.69
20km	Anatoly Alyabiev, USSR	0	1:08:16.31
4x7.5km	USSR (Alikin, Tikonov, Barnashov, Alyabiev).	0	1:34:03.27

Bobsled

Event		Time
2-Man	SWI (Erich Schärer & Josef Benz)	4:09.36
4-Man	E.Ger.(Nehmer, Musiol Germeshausen, Gerhardt)	3:59.92

Figure Skating

Event		Points
Men	Robin Cousins, GBR	189.48
Women	Anett Pötzsch, E.Ger	189.00
Pairs	Irina Rodnina & Aleksandr Zaitsev, USSR	147.26
Dance	Natalia Linichuk & Gennady Karponosov, USSR	205.48

1980 (Cont.)

Ice Hockey
Medal Round
(Overall records in parentheses.)

	Gm	W-L-T	Pts	GF	GA
1 USA (6-0-1)	3	2-0-1	5	10	7
2 USSR (6-1-0)	3	2-1-0	4	16	8
3 Sweden (4-1-2)	3	0-1-2	2	7	14
4 Finland (3-3-1)	3	0-2-1	1	7	11

Note: Games against common opponents carried over from the preliminary round. FIRST ROUND—USA tied Sweden, 2-2, and USSR over Finland, 4-2. MEDAL ROUND—USA over USSR, 4-3, and Finland, 4-2; USSR over Sweden, 9-2; and Sweden tied Finland, 3-3.

Luge
MEN

Event		Time
1-Seat	Bernhard Glass, E.Ger	2:54.796
2-Seat	Hans Rinn & Norbert Hahn, E.Ger	1:19.331

WOMEN

Event		Time
1-Seat	Vera Zozulia, USSR	2:36.537

Nordic Skiing
MEN
Cross-country

Event		Time
15km	Thomas Wassberg, SWE	41:57.63
30km	Nikolai Zimyatov, USSR	1:27:02.80
50km	Nikolai Zimyatov, USSR	2:27:24.60
4x10km	USSR (Rochev, Bazhukov, Beliaev, Zimyatov)	1:57:03.46

Ski Jumping

Event		Points
70m	Anton Innauer, AUT	266.3
90m	Jouko Törmänen, FIN	271.0

Nordic Combined

Event		Points
15km/Jump	Ulrich Wehling, E.Ger	432.200

WOMEN
Cross-country

Event		Time
5km	Raisa Smetanina, USSR	15:06.92
10km	Barbara Petzold, E.Ger	30:31.54
4x5km	E.Ger.(Rostock, Anding, Hesse, Petzold)	1:02:11.10

Speed Skating
MEN

Event		Time	
500m	Eric Heiden, USA	38.03	OR
1000m	Eric Heiden, USA	1:15.18	OR
1500m	Eric Heiden, USA	1:55.44	OR
5000m	Eric Heiden, USA	7:02.29	OR
10,000m	Eric Heiden, USA	14:28.13	WR

WOMEN

Event		Time	
500m	Karin Enke, E.Ger	41.78	OR
1000m	Natalia Petruseva, USSR	1:24.10	OR
1500m	Annie Borckink, HOL	2:10.95	OR
3000m	Bjoerg Eva Jensen, NOR	4:32.13	OR

1984
Sarajevo

In 1980, the Soviet Union and East Germany finished the Winter Games in a virtual tie for the unofficial team championship. The USSR won more gold medals (10-9), but the GDR won more overall medals (23-22).

In 1984, the East Germans edged into the lead in the battle of state-controlled athletic programs, winning three more golds (9-6), while the Soviets won one more overall medal (25-24).

Karin Enke was the top East German performer, taking two gold medals and two silvers in the four women's speed skating events. Teammate Andrea Schone won a gold and two silvers.

Cross-country skier Marja-Liisa Hamalainen of Finland was the only athlete to win three events and one of only two—Swedish cross-country skier Gunde Svan was the other—to win four overall medals.

The U.S. hockey team failed to qualify for the medal round, but the men's Alpine ski team, which had never won an event before, won twice. Bill Johnson took the downhill and the Mahre brothers, Phil and Steve, finished 1-2 in the slalom.

Top 10 Standings

National medal standings are not recognized by the IOC. The unofficial point totals are based on 3 points for a gold medal, 2 for a silver and 1 for a bronze. Total medals are in parentheses.

	Gold	Silver	Bronze	Pts
1 E.Germany (24)	9	9	6	51
2 USSR (25)	6	10	9	47
3 Finland (13)	4	3	6	24
4 USA (8)	4	4	0	20
5 Sweden (8)	4	2	2	18
6 Norway (9)	3	2	4	17
7 Switzerland (5)	2	2	1	11
8 Canada (4)	2	1	1	9
W.Germany (4)	2	1	1	9
10 Czechoslovakia (6)	0	2	4	8

Leading Medal Winners

Number of individual medals won on the left; gold, silver and bronze medal breakdown to the right.

MEN

No		Sport	G-S-B
4	Gunde Svan, SWE	X-country	2-1-1
3	Gaétan Boucher, CAN	Sp.Skating	2-1-0
3	Peter Angerer, W.Ger	Biathlon	1-1-1
3	Eirik Kvalfoss, NOR	Biathlon	1-1-1
3	Aki Karvonen, FIN	X-country	0-1-2
2	Wolfgang Hoppe, E.Ger	Bobsled	2-0-0
2	Dietmar Schauerhammer, E.Ger	Bobsled	2-0-0
2	Thomas Wassberg, SWE	X-country	2-0-0

No		Sport	G-S-B
2	Tomas Gustafson, SWE	Sp.Skate	1-1-0
2	Igor Malkov, USSR.	Sp.Skate	1-1-0
2	Matti Nykänen, FIN	Ski Jump	1-1-0
2	Jens Weissflog, E.Ger.	Ski Jump	1-1-0
2	Nikolai Zimyatov, USSR.	X-country	1-1-0
2	Sergei Khlebnikov, USSR.	Sp.Skate	0-2-0
2	Bernhard Lehmann, E.Ger.	Bobsled	0-2-0
2	Bogdan Musiol, E.Ger.	Bobsled	0-2-0
2	Aleksandr Zavialov, USSR	X-country	0-2-0
2	Harri Kirvesniemi, FIN	X-country	0-0-2
2	Rene Schofisch, E.Ger.	Sp.Skate	0-0-2

WOMEN

No		Sport	G-S-B
4	Marja-Liisa Hämäläinen, FIN	X-country	3-0-1
4	Karin Enke, E.Ger.	Sp.Skating	2-2-0
3	Andrea Schöne, E.Ger.	Sp.Skating	1-2-0
2	Berit Aunli, NOR.	X-country	1-1-0
2	Anne Jahren, NOR.	X-country	1-0-1
2	Brit Pettersen, NOR	X-country	1-0-1
2	Kveta Jeriova, CZE	X-country	0-1-1
2	Perrine Pelen, FRA	Alpine	0-1-1
2	Natalia Petruseva, USSR	Sp.Skate	0-0-2

Alpine Skiing
MEN

Event		Time
Downhill	Bill Johnson, USA	1:45.59
Slalom	Phil Mahre, USA	1:39.41
G.Slalom	Max Julen, SWI	2:41.18

WOMEN

Event		Time
Downhill	Michela Figini, SWI	1:13.36
Slalom	Paoletta Magoni, ITA.	1:36.47
G.Slalom	Debbie Armstrong, USA	2:20.98

Biathlon

Event		MT	Adj.Time
10km	Erik Kvalfoss, NOR.	2	30:53.8
20km	Peter Angerer, W.Ger.	2	1:11:52.7
4x7.5km	USSR (Vasiliev, Kachkarov, Shalna, Bouliguin)	2	1:38:51.7

Bobsled

Event		Time
2-Man	E.Ger.(Wolfgang Hoppe & Dietmar Schauerhammer)	3:25.56
4-Man	E.Ger.(Hoppe, Wetzig, Schauerhammer, Kirchner)	3:20.22

Figure Skating

Event		Ordinals
Men	Scott Hamilton, USA.	3.4
Women	Katarina Witt, E.Ger.	3.2
Pairs	Elena Valova & Oleg Vasiliev, USSR.	1.4
Dance	Jayne Torvill & Christopher Dean, GBR	2.0

Ice Hockey
Medal Round
(Overall record in parentheses)

		Gm	W-L-T	Pts	GF	GA
1	USSR (7-0-0)	3	3-0-0	6	16	1
2	Czechoslovakia(6-1-0)	3	2-1-0	4	6	3
3	Sweden (5-2-0)	3	1-2-0	2	3	12
4	Canada (4-3-0)	3	0-3-0	0	0	10

Note: Games against common opponents carried over from the preliminary round. MEDAL ROUND—the USSR beat Sweden, 10-1; Canada, 4-0, and the Czechs, 2-0; the Czechs beat Canada, 4-0, and Sweden, 2-0; and Sweden beat Canada, 2-0.

Also: The U.S., featuring future NHL stars Chris Chelios and Pat LaFontaine, failed to qualify for the Medal Round, finishing 7th overall with a record of 2-2-2.

Luge
MEN

Event		Time
1-Seat	Paul Hildgartner, ITA.	3:04.258
2-Seat	Hans Stanggassinger & Franz Wembacher, W.Ger	1:23.620

WOMEN

Event		Time
1-Seat	Steffi Martin, E.Ger	2:46.570

Nordic Skiing
MEN
Cross-country

Event		Time
15km	Gunde Svan, SWE.	41:25.6
30km	Nikolai Zimyatov, USSR.	1:28:56.3
50km	Thomas Wassberg, SWE.	2:15:55.8
4x10km	SWE (Wassberg, Kohlberg, Ottoson, Svan).	1:55:06.3

Ski Jumping

Event		Points
70m	Jens Weissflog, E.Ger.	215.2
90m	Matti Nykänen, FIN.	231.2

Nordic Combined

Event		Points
15km/Jump	Tom Sandberg, NOR.	422.595

WOMEN
Cross-country

Event		Time
5km	Marja-Liisa Hämäläinen, FIN	17:04.0
10km	Marja-Liisa Hämäläinen, FIN	31:44.2
20km	Marja-Liisa Hämäläinen, FIN	1:01:45.0
4x5km	NOR (Nybråten, Jahren, Pettersen, Aunli)	1:06:49.7

Speed Skating
MEN

Event		Time
500m	Sergei Fokichev, USSR	38.19
1000m	Gaétan Boucher, CAN	1:15.80
1500m	Gaétan Boucher, CAN	1:58.36
5000m	Tomas Gustafson, SWE	7:12.28
10,000m	Igor Malkov, USSR	14:39.90

WOMEN

Event		Time
500m	Christa Rothenburger, E.Ger	41.02 OR
1000m	Karin Enke, E.Ger.	1:21.61 OR
1500m	Karin Enke, E.Ger.	2:03.42 WR
3000m	Andrea Schöne, E.Ger.	4:24.79 OR

CALGARY 1988

1988
Calgary

A record 1,750 athletes from 57 nations came to western Canada for the first Olympics north of the U.S. border. The Games featured an indoor speed skating oval and sporadic chinook winds that sent temperatures into the unwintry 70s.

Matti Nykänen of Finland became the first pure ski jumper to capture three titles, winning

1988 (Cont.)

gold medals at 70 and 90 meters and adding a third in the new team jumping competition.

Nykanen may have been the most decorated jumper in Calgary, but he wasn't the most celebrated. That honor belonged to Michael (Eddie the Eagle) Edwards, the accident-prone flying plasterer from Britain. Edwards finished 58th and last in the 70-meter jump and 55th and last in the 90-meter and was welcomed home after the Games by hundreds of fans at London's Heathrow Airport.

Back on the serious side, Dutch speed skater Yvonne van Gennip won three gold medals; East German figure skater Katarina Witt won her second straight women's title; and the USSR beat East Germany in both gold and overall medals in the last winterized confrontation of Communist super powers.

Top 10 Standings

National medal standings are not recognized by the IOC. The unofficial point totals are based on 3 points for a gold medal, 2 for a silver and 1 for a bronze. Total medals are in parentheses.

		Gold	Silver	Bronze	Pts
1	USSR (29)	11	9	9	60
2	E.Germany (25)	9	10	6	53
3	Switzerland (15)	5	5	5	30
4	Austria (10)	3	5	2	21
5	Finland (7)	4	1	2	16
	W.Germany (8)	2	4	2	16
7	Holland (7)	3	2	2	15
8	Sweden (6)	4	0	2	14
9	USA (6)	2	1	3	11
10	Italy (5)	2	1	2	10

Other countries with 5 medals (2): Norway (0-3-2) and Canada (0-2-3).

Leading Medal Winners

Number of individual medals won on the left; gold, silver and bronze medal breakdown to the right.

MEN

No		Sport	G-S-B
3	Matti Nykänen, FIN	Ski Jump	3-0-0
3	Valery Medvedtsev, USSR	Biathlon	1-2-0
3	Vladimir Smirnov, USSR	X-country	0-2-1
2	Alberto Tomba, ITA	Alpine	2-0-0
2	Frank-Peter Rötsch, E.Ger	Biathlon	2-0-0
2	Gunde Svan, SWE	X-country	2-0-0
2	Tomas Gustafson, SWE	Sp.Skate	2-0-0
2	Hubert Strolz, AUT	Alpine	1-1-0
2	Mikhail Deviatiarov, USSR	X-country	1-1-0
2	Hippolyt Kempf, SWI	Nordic Comb.	1-1-0
2	Jens-Uwe Mey, E.Ger	Sp.Skate	1-1-0
2	Alexei Prokurorov, USSR	X-country	1-1-0
2	Sergei Chepikov, USSR	Biathlon	1-0-1
2	Ianis Kipours, USSR	Bobsled	1-0-1
2	Vladimir Kozlov, USSR	Bobsled	1-0-1
2	Franck Piccard, FRA	Alpine	1-0-1
2	Pirmin Zurbriggen, SWI	Alpine	1-0-1
2	Wolfgang Hoppe, E.Ger	Bobsled	0-2-0
2	Bogdan Musiol, E.Ger	Bobsled	0-2-0
2	Matjaz, Debelak, YUG	Ski Jump	0-1-1
2	Michael Hadschieff, AUT	Sp.Skate	0-1-1
2	Erik Johnsen, NOR	Alpine	0-1-1
2	Klaus Sulzenbacher, AUT	Nordic Comb.	0-1-1
2	Leo Visser, HOL	Sp.Skate	0-1-1
2	Johann Passler, ITA	Biathlon	0-0-2

WOMEN

No		Sport	G-S-B
3	Yvonne van Gennip, HOL	Sp.Skating	3-0-0
3	Tamara Tikhonova, USSR	X-country	2-1-0
3	Marjo Matikänen, FIN	X-country	1-0-2
3	Andrea Ehrig, E.Ger	Sp.Skating	0-2-1
3	Karin Kania, E.Ger	Sp.Skating	0-2-1
2	Vreni Schneider, SWI	Alpine	2-0-0
2	Anfissa Reztsova, USSR	X-country	1-1-0
2	Christa Rothenburger, E.Ger	Sp.Skate	1-1-0
2	Bonnie Blair, USA	Sp.Skate	1-0-1
2	Vida Ventsene, USSR	X-country	1-0-1
2	Brigitte Oertli, SWI	Alpine	0-2-0
2	Christa Kinshofer, W.Ger	Alpine	0-1-1
2	Raisa Smetanina, USSR	X-country	0-1-1
2	Karen Percy, CAN	Alpine	0-0-2
2	Maria Walliser, SWI	Alpine	0-0-2
2	Gabi Zange, E.Ger	Sp.Skate	0-0-2

Alpine Skiing

MEN

Event		Time
Downhill	Pirmin Zurbriggen, SWI	1:59.63
Slalom	Alberto Tomba, ITA	1:39.47
G.Slalom	Alberto Tomba, ITA	2:06.37
Super GS	Franck Piccard, FRA	1:39.66
Combined	Hubert Strolz, AUT	36.55 pts

WOMEN

Event		Time
Downhill	Marina Kiehl, W.Ger	1:25.86
Slalom	Vreni Schneider, SWI	1:36.69
G.Slalom	Vreni Schneider, SWI	2:06.49
Super GS	Sigrid Wolf, AUT	1:19.03
Combined	Anita Wachter, AUT	29.25 pts

Biathlon

Event		Time
10km	Frank-Peter Rötsch, E.Ger	25:08.1
20km	Frank-Peter Rötsch, E.Ger	56:33.33
4x7.5km	USSR (Vasiliev, Chepikov, Popov, Medvedtsev)	1:22:30.0

Bobsled

Event		Time
2-Man	USSR (Ianis Kipours & Vladimir Kozlov)	3:53.48
4-Man	SWI (Fasser, Meier, Fässler, Stocker)	3:47.51

Figure Skating

Event		Ordinals
Men	Brian Boitano, USA	3.0
Women	Katarina Witt, E.Ger	4.2
Pairs	Ekaterina Gordeeva & Sergei Grinkov, USSR	1.4
Dance	Natalya Bestemianova & Andrei Bukin, USSR	2.0

Ice Hockey

Medal Round

(Overall records in parentheses.)

		Gm	W-L-T	Pts	GF	GA
1	USSR (7-1-0)	5	4-1-0	8	25	7
2	Finland (5-2-1)	5	3-1-1	7	18	10
3	Sweden (4-1-3)	5	2-1-2	6	15	16
4	Canada (5-2-1)	5	2-2-1	5	17	14
5	W.Germany (4-4-0)	5	1-4-0	2	8	26
6	Czechoslovakia(4-4-0)	5	1-4-0	2	12	22

Note: Games against common opponents carried over from preliminary round. The USSR lost its final game to Finland, 2-1, after clinching the gold medal. The U.S. finished 4th in its preliminary pool with a 2-3 record. The top three teams in each of two 6-team pools qualified for the medal round.

Luge
MEN

Event		Time
1-Seat	Jens Müller, E.Ger	3:05.548
2-Seat	Joerg Hoffmann & Jochen Pietzsch, E.Ger	1:31.940

WOMEN

Event		Time
1-Seat	Steffi Walter, E.Ger	3:03.973

Nordic Skiing
MEN
Cross-country

Event		Time
15km	Mikhail Deviatiarov, USSR	41:18.9
30km	Alexei Prokurorov, USSR	1:24:26.3
50km	Gunde Svan, SWE	2:04:30.9
4x10km	SWE (Ottosson, Wassberg, Svan, Mogren)	1:43:58.6

Ski Jumping

Event		Points
70m	Matti Nykänen, FIN	229.1
90m	Matti Nykänen, FIN	224.0
90m Team	FIN (Nikkola, Nykänen, Ylipulli, Puikkonen)	634.4

Nordic Combined

Event		Jump Pts	15 km
Individ.	Hippolyt Kempf, SWI	107.5	38:16.8
Team	W.Ger.(Pohl, Schwarz, Müller)	629.9	1:20:46.0

WOMEN
Cross-country

Event		Time
5km	Marjo Matikänen, FIN	15:04.0
10km	Vida Ventsene, USSR	30:08.3
20km	Tamara Tikhonova, USSR	55:53.6
4x5km	USSR (Nagueikina, Gavriliuk, Tikhonova, Reztsova)	59:51.1

Speed Skating
MEN

Event		Time	
500m	Jens-Uwe Mey, E.Ger	36.45	WR
1000m	Nikolai Gouliaev, USSR	1:13.03	OR
1500m	André Hoffmann, E.Ger	1:52.06	WR
5000m	Tomas Gustafson, SWE	6:44.63	WR
10,000m	Tomas Gustafson, SWE	13:48.20	WR

WOMEN

Event		Time	
500m	Bonnie Blair, USA	39.10	WR
1000m	Christa Rothenburger, E.Ger	1:17.65	WR
1500m	Yvonne van Gennip, HOL	2:00.68	OR
3000m	Yvonne van Gennip, HOL	4:11.94	WR
5000m	Yvonne van Gennip, HOL	7:14.13	WR

Editor's Note

Books used in researching this Olympic chapter included *The Complete Book of the Olympics* (1988) by David Wallechinsky; *Pursuit of Excellence, the Olympic Story* (1979) by the Associated Press; *An Illustrated History of the Olympics* (1975) by Dick Schaap; the official USOC Olympic Books from 1936-68.

All Olympic posters used in this section, with the exception of the 1906 Intercalated Games, are reprinted with the permission of the International Olympic Committee.

The poster used for the 1906 Games is original artwork by Olympic historian Harvey Abrams.

ALL-TIME MEDAL WINNERS

All Nations
Overall Medals

No		Sport	G-S-B
9	Sixten Jernberg, SWE	Cross-country	4-3-2
9	Raisa Smetanina, USSR	Cross-country	3-5-1
8	Galina Kulakova, USSR	Cross-country	4-2-2
7	Clas Thunberg, FIN	Speed Skating	5-1-1
7	Ivar Ballangrud, NOR	Speed Skating	4-2-1
7	Veikko Hakulinen, FIN	Cross-country	3-3-1
7	Eero Maentyranta, FIN	Cross-country	3-2-2
6	Lydia Skoblikova, USSR	Speed Skating	6-0-0
6	Johan Groettumsbraaten, NOR	Ski Jump & Cross-country	3-1-2
6	Eugenio Monti, ITA	Bobsled	2-2-2
6	Roald Larsen, NOR	Speed Skating	0-2-4

Gold Medals

No		Sport	G-S-B
6	Lydia Skoblikova, USSR	Speed Skating	6-0-0
5	Clas Thunberg, FIN	Speed Skating	5-1-1
5	Eric Heiden, USA	Speed Skating	5-0-0
4	Sixten Jernberg, SWE	Cross-country	4-3-2
4	Galina Kulakova, USSR	Cross-country	4-2-2
4	Ivar Ballangrud, NOR	Speed Skating	4-2-1
4	Yevgeny Grishin, USSR	Speed Skating	4-1-0
4	Nikolai Zimyatov, USSR	Cross-country	4-1-0
4	Aleksandr Tikonov, USSR	Biathlon	4-0-0
3	Raisa Smetanina, USSR	Cross-country	3-5-1
3	Veikko Hakulinen, FIN	Cross-country	3-3-1
3	Eero Maentyranta, FIN	Cross-country	3-2-2
3	Johan Groettumsbraaten, NOR	Ski Jump & Cross-country	3-1-2

USA
Overall Medals

No		Sport	G-S-B
5	Eric Heiden	Speed Skating	5-0-0
4	John Heaton	Bobsled/Cresta	0-3-1
4	Diane Holum	Speed Skating	1-2-1
3	Pat Martin	Bobsled	2-1-0
3	Sheila Young	Speed Skating	1-1-1
3	Leah Mueller	Speed Skating	0-3-0
3	Beatrix Loughran	Figure Skating	0-2-1

Gold Medals

No		Sport	G-S-B
5	Eric Heiden	Speed Skating	5-0-0
2	Pat Martin	Bobsled	2-1-0
2	Dick Button	Figure Skating	2-0-0
2	Billy Fiske	Bobsled	2-0-0
2	Cliff Gray	Bobsled	2-0-0
2	Irving Jaffee	Speed Skating	2-0-0
2	Jack Shea	Speed Skating	2-0-0

Note: Jaffee is often given credit for a third gold medal in the 10,000-meter race of 1928. He had the fastest time before the race was cancelled due to thawing ice. The IOC considers the race unofficial.

Silver Medals

No		Sport	G-S-B
3	John Heaton	Bobsled/Cresta	0-3-1
3	Leah Mueller	Speed Skating	0-3-1
2	Diane Holum	Speed Skating	1-2-1
2	Beatrix Loughran	Figure Skating	0-2-1
2	Stan Benham	Bobsled	0-2-0
2	Herb Drury	Ice Hockey	0-2-0
2	George Geran	Ice Hockey	0-2-0
2	Penny Pitou	Alpine Skiing	0-2-0

Bronze Medals

Fifty-eight athletes tied with one.

EVENT-BY-EVENT

Gold medal winners from 1924-88 in all of the current events: alpine skiing, biathlon, bobsled, figure skating, ice hockey, luge, nordic skiing, and speed skating.

Alpine Skiing
MEN
Downhill

Year		Time	Year		Time
1948	Henri Oreiller, FRA	2:55.0	1972	Bernhard Russi, SWI	1:51.43
1952	Zeno Colo, ITA	2:30.8	1976	Franz Klammer AUT	1:45.73
1956	Toni Sailer, AUT	2:52.2	1980	Leonhard Stock, AUS	1:45.50
1960	Jean Vuarnet, FRA	2:06.0	1984	Bill Johnson, USA	1:45.59
1964	Egon Zimmermann, AUT	2:18.16	1988	Pirmin Zurbriggen, SWI	1:59.63
1968	Jean-Claude Killy, FRA	1:59.85			

Slalom

Year		Time	Year		Time
1948	Edi Reinalter, SWI	2:10.3	1972	Francisco Ochoa, SPA	1:49.27
1952	Othmar Schneider, AUT	2:00.0	1976	Piero Gros, ITA	2:03.29
1956	Toni Sailer, AUT	3:14.7	1980	Ingemar Stenmark, SWE	1:44.26
1960	Ernst Hinterseer, AUT	2:08.9	1984	Phil Mahre, USA	1:39.41
1964	Pepi Stiegler, AUT	2:11.13	1988	Alberto Tomba, ITA	1:39.47
1968	Jean-Claude Killy, FRA	1:39.73			

Giant Slalom

Year		Time	Year		Time
1952	Stein Eriksen, NOR	2:25.0	1972	Gustav Thöni, ITA	3:09.62
1956	Toni Sailer, AUS	3:00.1	1976	Heini Hemmi, SWI	3:26.97
1960	Roger Staub, SWI	1:48.3	1980	Ingemar Stenmark, SWE	2:40.74
1964	Francois Bonlieu, FRA	1:46.71	1984	Max Julen, SWI	2:41.18
1968	Jean-Claude Killy, FRA	3:29.28	1988	Alberto Tomba, ITA	2:06.37

Super Giant Slalom

Year		Time
1988	Frank Piccard, FRA	1:39.66

Alpine Combined

Year		Points	Year		Points
1936	Franz Pfnür, GER	99.25	1988	Hubert Strolz, AUT	36.55
1948	Henri Oreiller, FRA	3.27			

WOMEN
Downhill

Year		Time	Year		Time
1948	Hedy Schlunegger, SWI	2:28.3	1972	Marie-Theres Nadig, SWI	1:36.68
1952	Trude Jochum-Beiser, AUT	1:47.1	1976	Rosi Mittermaier, W.Ger	1:46.16
1956	Madeleine Berthod, SWI	1:40.7	1980	Annemarie Moser-Pröll, AUT	1:37.52
1960	Heidi Biebl, GER	1:37.6	1984	Michela Figini, SWI	1:13.36
1964	Christl Haas, AUT	1:55.39	1988	Marina Kiehl, W.Ger	1:25.86
1968	Olga Pall, AUT	1:40.87			

Slalom

Year		Time	Year		Time
1948	Gretchen Fraser, USA	1:57.2	1972	Barbara Cochran, USA	1:31.24
1952	Andrea Mead Lawrence, USA	2:10.6	1976	Rosi Mittermaier, W.Ger	1:30.54
1956	Renée Colliard, SWI	1:52.3	1980	Hanni Wenzel, LIE	1:25.09
1960	Anne Heggtveit, CAN	1:49.6	1984	Paoletta Magoni, ITA	1:36.47
1964	Christine Goitschel, FRA	1:29.86	1988	Vreni Schneider, SWI	1:36.69
1968	Marielle Goitschel, FRA	1:25.86			

Giant Slalom

Year		Time	Year		Time
1952	Andrea Mead Lawrence, USA	2:06.8	1972	Marie-Theres Nadig, SWI	1:29.90
1956	Ossi Reichert, GER	1:56.5	1976	Kathy Kreiner, CAN	1:29.13
1960	Yvonne Rüegg, SWI	1:39.9	1980	Hanni Wenzel, LIE	2:41.66
1964	Marielle Goitschel, FRA	1:52.24	1984	Debbie Armstrong, USA	2:20.98
1968	Nancy Greene, CAN	1:51.97	1988	Vreni Schneider, SWI	2:06.49

Alpine Skiing (Cont.)
WOMEN
Super Giant Slalom

Year		Time
1988	Sigrid Wolf, AUT	1:19.03

Alpine Combined

Year	Points	Year	Points
1936	Christl Cranz, GER. 97.06	1988	Anita Wachter, AUT. 29.25
1948	Trude Beiser, AUT 6.58		

Biathlon
10 Kilometers

Year	Time	Year	Time
1980	Frank Ullrich, E.Ger....32:10.69	1988	Frank-Peter Roetsch, E.Ger 25:08.1
1984	Erik Kvalfoss, NOR....30:53.8		

20 Kilometers

Year	Time	Year	Time
1960	Klas Lestander, SWE....1:33:21.6	1976	Nikolai Kruglov, USSR....1:14:12.26
1964	Vladimir Melanin, USSR....1:20:26.8	1980	Anatoly Alyabiev, USSR....1:08:16.31
1968	Magnar Solberg, NOR....1:13:45.9	1984	Peter Angerer, W.Ger....1:11:52.7
1972	Magnar Solberg, NOR....1:15:55.50	1988	Frank-Peter Roetsch, E.Ger....56.33.33

4x7.5-Kilometer Relay

Year	Time	Year	Time
1968	Soviet Union....2:13:02.4	1980	Soviet Union....1:34:03.27
1972	Soviet Union....1:51:44.92	1984	Soviet Union....1:38:51.7
1976	Soviet Union....1:57:55.64	1988	Soviet Union....1:22:30.0

Bobsled

(Driver in parentheses)

Two-Man

Year	Time	Year	Time
1932	United States (Hubert Stevens)....8:14.74	1968	Italy (Eugenio Monti)....4:41.54
1936	United States (Ivan Brown)....5:29.29	1972	West Germany (Wolfgang Zimmerer)....4:57.07
1948	Switzerland (Felix Endrich)....5:29.2	1976	East Germany (Meinhard Nehmer)....3:44.42
1952	Germany (Andreas Ostler)....5:24.54	1980	Switzerland Erich Schärer)....4:09.36
1956	Italy (Lamberto Dalla Costa)....5:30.14	1984	East Germany (Wolfgang Hoppe)....3:25.56
1960	Not held	1988	Soviet Union (Janis Kipours)....3:54.19
1964	Great Britain (Anthony Nash)....4:21.90		

Four-Man

Year	Time	Year	Time
1924	Switzerland (Eduard Scherrer)....5:45.54	1964	Canada (Vic Emery)....4:14.46
1928	United States (Billy Fiske)....3:20.5	1968	Italy (Eugenio Monti)....2:17.39
1932	United States (Billy Fiske)....7:53.68	1972	Switzerland (Jean Wicki)....4:43.07
1936	Switzerland (Pierre Musy)....5:19.85	1976	East Germany (Meinhard Nehmer)....3:40.43
1948	United States (Francis Tyler)....5:20.1	1980	East Germany (Meinhard Nehmer)....3:59.92
1952	Germany (Andreas Ostler)....5:07.84	1984	East Germany (Wolfgang Hoppe)....3:20.22
1956	Switzerland (Franz Kapus)....5:10.44	1988	Switzerland (Ekkehard Fasser)....3:47.51
1960	Not held		

Figure Skating

Part of Summer Games in 1908 and 1920.

MEN

Year		Year	
1908	Ulrich Salchow ....Sweden	1960	David Jenkins....United States
1920	Gillis Grafström ....Sweden	1964	Manfred Schnelldorfer....Germany
1924	Gillis Grafström ....Sweden	1968	Wolfgang Schwarz....Austria
1928	Gillis Grafström ....Sweden	1972	Ondrej Nepela....Czechoslovakia
1932	Karl Schäfer ....Austria	1976	John Curry....Great Britain
1936	Karl Schäfer ....Austria	1980	Robin Cousins....Great Britain
1948	Dick Button....United States	1984	Scott Hamilton....United States
1952	Dick Button....United States	1988	Brian Boitano....United States
1956	Hayes Alan Jenkins ....United States		

WOMEN

Year			Year		
1908	Madge Syers	Great Britain	1960	Carol Heiss	United States
1920	Magda Julin	Sweden	1964	Sjoukje Dijkstra	Holland
1924	Herma Planck-Szabó	Austria	1968	Peggy Fleming	United States
1928	Sonja Henie	Norway	1972	Beatrix Schuba	Austria
1932	Sonja Henie	Norway	1976	Dorothy Hamill	United States
1936	Sonja Henie	Norway	1980	Anett Pötzsch	E.Germany
1948	Barbara Ann Scott	Canada	1984	Katarina Witt	E.Germany
1952	Jeanette Altwegg	Great Britain	1988	Katarina Witt	E.Germany
1956	Tenley Albright	United States			

PAIRS

Year		Years	
1908	Anna Hübler & Heinrich Burger, GER	1960	Barbara Wagner & Robert Paul, CAN
1920	Ludovika & Walter Jakobsson, FIN	1964	Lyudmila Belousova & Oleg Protopopov, USSR
1924	Helene Engelmann & Alfred Berger, AUT	1968	Lyudmila Belousova & Oleg Protopopov, USSR
1928	Andrée Joly & Pierre Brunet, FRA	1972	Irina Rodnina & Aleksei Ulanov, USSR
1932	Andrée & Pierre Brunet, FRA	1976	Irina Rodnina & Aleksandr Zaitsev, USSR
1936	Maxi Herber & Ernst Baier, GER	1980	Irina Rodnina & Aleksandr Zaitsev, USSR
1948	Micheline Lannoy & Pierre Baugniet, BEL	1984	Elena Valova & Oleg Vasiliev, USSR
1952	Ria & Paul Falk, GER	1988	Ekaterina Gordeeva & Sergei Grinkov, USSR
1956	Elisabeth Schwartz & Kurt Oppelt, AUT		

ICE DANCE

Year		Year	
1976	Lyudmila Pakhomova & Aleksandr Gorshkov, USSR	1984	Jayne Torvill & Christopher Dean, GBR
1980	Natalia Linichuk & Gennady Karponosov, USSR	1988	Natalia Bestemianova & Andrei Bukin, USSR

Ice Hockey

Part of Summer Games in 1920.

Year		Year	
1920	**Canada,** United States Czechoslovakia	1960	**United States**, Canada, Soviet Union
1924	**Canada**, United States, Great Britain	1964	**Soviet Union**, Sweden, Czechoslovakia
1928	**Canada**, Sweden, Switzerland	1968	**Soviet Union**, Czechoslovakia, Canada
1932	**Canada**, United States, Germany	1972	**Soviet Union**, United States, Czechoslovakia
1936	**Great Britain**, Canada, United States	1976	**Soviet Union**, Czechoslovakia, W.Germany
1948	**Canada**, Czechoslovakia, Switzerland	1980	**United States**, Soviet Union, Sweden
1952	**Canada**, United States, Sweden	1984	**Soviet Union**, Czechoslovakia, Sweden
1956	**Soviet Union**, United States, Canada	1988	**Soviet Union**, Finland, Sweden

Luge

MEN

Singles

Year		Time	Year		Time
1964	Thomas Köhler, GER	3:26.77	1980	Bernhard Glass, E.Ger	2:54.796
1968	Manfred Schmid, AUT	2:52.48	1984	Paul Hildgartner, ITA	3:04.258
1972	Wolfgang Scheidel, E.Ger	3:27.58	1988	Jens Mueller, E.Ger	3:05.548
1976	Dettlef Günther, E.Ger	3:27.688			

Doubles

Year		Time	Year		Time
1964	Austria	1:41.62	1980	East Germany	1:19.331
1968	East Germany	1:35.85	1984	West Germany	1:23.620
1972	East Germany & Italy	1:28.35	1988	East Germany	1:31.940
1976	East Germany	1:25.604			

WOMEN

Singles

Year		Time	Year		Time
1964	Ortrun Enderlein, GER	3:24.67	1980	Vera Zozulia, USSR	2:36.537
1968	Erica Lechner, ITA	2:28.66	1984	Steffi Martin, E.Ger	2:46.570
1972	Anna-Maria Müller, E.Ger	2:59.18	1988	Steffi Martin Walter, E.Ger	3:03.973
1976	Margit Schumann, E.Ger	2:50.621			

Nordic Skiing
CROSS-COUNTRY, MEN
15 Kilometers

Year		Time	Year		Time
1924	Thorleif Haug, NOR	1:14:31.0	1964	Eero Mäntyranta, FIN	50:54.1
1928	Johan Gröttumsbraten, NOR	1:37:01.0	1968	Harald Grönningen, NOR	47:54.2
1932	Sven Utterström, SWE	1:23:07.0	1972	Sven-Ake Lundbäck, SWE	45:28.24
1936	Erik-August Larsson, SWE	1:14:38.0	1976	Nikolai Bazhukov, USSR	43:58.47
1948	Martin Lundstrrom, SWE	1:13:50.0	1980	Thomas Wassberg, SWE	41:57.63
1952	Hallgeir Brenden, NOR	1:01:34.0	1984	Gunde Svan, SWE	41:25.6
1956	Hallgeir Brenden, NOR	49:39.0	1988	Mikhail Deviatiarov, USSR	41:18.9
1960	Hakon Brusveen NOR	51:55.5			

Note: Event was held over 18 kilometers from 1924-52.

30 Kilometers

Year		Time	Year		Time
1956	Veikko Hakulinen, FIN	1:44:06.0	1976	Sergei Saveliev, USSR	1:30:29.38
1960	Sixten Jernberg, SWE	1:51:03.9	1980	Nikolai Zimyatov, USSR	1:27:02.80
1964	Eero Mäntyranta, FIN	1:30:50.7	1984	Nikolai Zimyatov, USSR	1:28:56.3
1968	Franco Nones, ITA	1:35:39.2	1988	Alexi Prokourorov, USSR	1:24:26.3
1972	Vyacheslav Vedenine, USSR	1:36:31.15			

50 Kilometers

Year		Time	Year		Time
1924	Thorleif Haug, NOR	3:44:32.0	1964	Sixten Jernberg, SWE	2:43:52.6
1928	Per Erik Hedlund, SWE	4:52:03.0	1968	Ole Ellefsaeter, NOR	2:28:45.8
1932	Veli Saarinen, FIN	4:28:00.0	1972	Pal Tyldum, NOR	2:43:14.75
1936	Elis Wiklund, SWE	3:30:11.0	1976	Ivar Formo, NOR	2:37:30.05
1948	Nils Karlsson, SWE	3:47:48.0	1980	Nikolai Zimyatov, USSR	2:27:24.60
1952	Veikko Hakulinen, FIN	3:33:33.0	1984	Thomas Wassberg, SWE	2:15:55.8
1956	Sixten Jernberg, SWE	2:50:27.0	1988	Gunde Svan, SWE	2:04:30.9
1960	Kalevi Hämäläinen, FIN	2:59:06.3			

4x10-Kilometer Relay

Year		Time	Year		Time
1936	Finland	2:41:33.0	1968	Norway	2:08:33.5
1948	Sweden	2:32:08.0	1972	Soviet Union	2:04:47.94
1952	Finland	2:20:16.0	1976	Finland	2:07:59.72
1956	Soviet Union	2:15.30.0	1980	Soviet Union	1:57.03.46
1960	Finland	2:18.45.6	1984	Sweden	1:55:06.3
1964	Sweden	2:18:34.6	1988	Sweden	1:43:58.6

CROSS-COUNTRY, WOMEN
5 Kilometers

Year		Time	Year		Time
1964	Claudia Boyarskikh, USSR	17:50.5	1980	Raisa Smetanina, SOV	15:06.92
1968	Toini Gustafsson, SWE	16:45.2	1984	Marja-Liisa Hämäläinen, FIN	17:04.0
1972	Galina Kulakova, USSR	17:00.50	1988	Marjo Matikainen, FIN	15:04.0
1976	Helena Takalo, FIN	15:48.69			

10 Kilometers

Year		Time	Year		Time
1952	Lydia Wideman, FIN	41:40.0	1972	Galina Kulakova, USSR	34:17.82
1956	Lyubov Kosyreva, USSR	38:11.0	1976	Raisa Smetanina, USSR	30:13.41
1960	Maria Gusakova, USSR	39:46.6	1980	Barbara Petzold, E.Ger	30:31.54
1964	Claudia Boyarskikh, USSR	40:24.3	1984	Marja-Liisa Mämäläinen, FIN	31:44.2
1968	Toini Gustafsson, SWE	36:46.5	1988	Vida Ventsene, USSR	30:08.3

20 Kilometers

Year		Time	Year		Time
1984	Marja-Liisa Hämäläinen, FIN	1:01.45.0	1988	Tamara Tikhonova, USSR	55:53.6

4x5-Kilometer Relay

Year		Time	Year		Time
1956	Finland	1:09:01. 0	1976	Soviet Union	1:07:49.75
1960	Sweden	1:04:21. 4	1980	East Germany	1:02:11.10
1964	Soviet Union	59:20. 2	1984	Norway	1:06:49.7
1968	Norway	57:30. 0	1988	Soviet Union	59:51.1
1972	Soviet Union	48:46.15			

SKI JUMPING
Individual 70-Meter

Year	Points	Year	Points
1964 Veikko Kankkonen, FIN	229.9	1980 Anton Innauer, AUT	266.3
1968 Jiři Raška, CZE	216.5	1984 Jens Weissflog, E.Ger	215.2
1972 Yukio Kasaya, JPN	244.2	1988 Matti Nykänen, FIN	229.1
1976 Hans-Georg Aschenbach, E.Ger	252.0		

Individual 90-Meter

Year	Points	Year	Points
1924 Jacob Tullin Thams, NOR	18.960	1964 Toralf Engan, NOR	230.7
1928 Alf Andersen, NOR	19.208	1968 Vladimir Beloussov, USSR	231.3
1932 Birger Rudd, NOR	228.1	1972 Wojciech Fortuna, POL	219.9
1936 Birger Ruud, NOR	232.0	1976 Karl Schnabl, AUT	234.8
1948 Petter Hugsted, NOR	228.1	1980 Jouko Törmänen, FIN	271.0
1952 Arnfinn Bergmann, NOR	226.0	1984 Matti Nykänen, FIN	231.2
1956 Antti Hyvärinen, FIN	227.0	1988 Matti Nykranen, FIN	224.0
1960 Helmut Rechnagel, GER	227.2		

Team 90-Meter

Year	Points
1988 Finland	634.4

NORDIC COMBINED (Ski Jump and Cross-Country)
Individual

Year	Points	Year	Points
1924 Thorleif Haug, NOR	18.906	1964 Tormod Knutsen, NOR	469.28
1928 Johan Gröttumsbraten, NOR	17.833	1968 Franz Keller, W.Ger	449.04
1932 Johan Gröttumsbraten, NOR	446.00	1972 Ulrich Wehling, E.Ger	413.340
1936 Oddbjörn Hagen, NOR	430.3	1976 Ulrich Wehling, E.Ger	423.39
1948 Heikki Hasu, FIN	448.80	1980 Ulrich Wehling, E.Ger	432.200
1952 Simon Slattvik, NOR	451.621	1984 Tom Sandberg, NOR	422.595
1956 Sverre Stenersen, NOR	455.000	1988 Hippolyt Kempf, SWI	235.8
1960 Georg Thoma, GER	457.952		

Team

Year	Jump Pts	30-km Time
1988 West Germany	629.8	1:20:46

Speed Skating
MEN
500 Meters

Year	Time		Year	Time	
1924 Charles Jewtraw, USA	44.0		1960 Yevgeny Grishin, USSR	40.2	=WR
1928 Bernt Evensen, NOR	43.4	OR	1964 Terry McDermott, USA	40.1	OR
& Clas Thunberg, FIN	43.4	OR	1968 Erhard Keller, W.Ger	40.3	
1932 John Shea, USA	43.4	=OR	1972 Erhard Keller, W.Ger	39.44	OR
1936 Ivar Ballangrud, NOR	43.4	=OR	1976 Yevgeny Kulikov, USSR	39.17	OR
1948 Finn Helgesen, NOR	43.1	OR	1980 Eric Heiden, USA	38.03	OR
1952 Kenneth Henry, USA	43.2		1984 Sergei Fokichev, USSR	38.19	
1956 Yevgeny Grishin, USSR	40.2	=WR	1988 Jens-Uwe Mey, E.Ger	36.45	WR

1000 Meters

Year	Time		Year	Time	
1976 Peter Mueller, USA	1:19.32		1984 Gaétan Boucher, CAN	1:15.80	
1980 Eric Heiden, USA	1:15.18	OR	1988 Nikolai Guliaev, USSR	1:13.03	OR

1500 Meters

Year	Time		Year	Time	
1924 Clas Thunberg, FIN	2:20.8		1964 Ants Antson, USSR	2:10.3	
1928 Clas Thunberg, FIN	2:21.1		1968 Kees Verkerk, HOL	2:03.4	OR
1932 Jack Shea, USA	2:57.5		1972 Ard Schenk, HOL	2:02.96	OR
1936 Charles Mathisen, NOR	2:19.2	OR	1976 Jan Egil Storholt, NOR	1:59.38	OR
1948 Sverre Farstad, NOR	2:17.6	OR	1980 Eric Heiden, USA	1:55.44	OR
1952 Hjalmar Andersen, NOR	2:20.4		1984 Gaqetan Boucher, CAN	1:58.36	
1956 Yevgeny Grishin, USSR	2:08.6	WR	1988 Andre Hoffman, E.Ger	1:52.06	WR
1960 Roald Aas, NOR	2:10.4				

Speed Skating (Cont.)

5000 Meters

Year		Time		Year		Time	
1924	Clas Thunberg, FIN	8:39.0		1964	Knut Johannesen, NOR	7:38.4	OR
1928	Ivar Ballangrud, NOR	8:50.5		1968	Fred Anton Maier, NOR	7:22.4	WR
1932	Irving Jaffee, USA	9:40.8		1972	Ard Schenk, HOL	7:23.61	
1936	Ivar Ballangrud, NOR	8:19.6	OR	1976	Sten Stensen, NOR	7:24.48	
1948	Reidar Liaklev, NOR	8:29.4		1980	Eric Heiden, USA	7:02.29	OR
1952	Hjalmar Andersen, NOR	8:10.6	OR	1984	Tomas Gustafson, SWE	7:12.28	
1956	Boris Shilkov, USSR	7:48.7	OR	1988	Tomas Gustafson, SWE	6:44.63	WR
1960	Viktor Kosichkin, USSR	7:51.3					

10,000 Meters

Year		Time		Year		Time	
1924	Julius Skutnabb, FIN	18:04.8		1964	Jonny Nilsson, SWE	15:50.1	
1928	Irving Jaffee, USA*	18:36.5		1968	Johnny Höglin, SWE	15:23.6	OR
1932	Irving Jaffee, USA	19:13.6		1972	Ard Schenk, HOL	15:01.35	OR
1936	Ivar Ballangrud, NOR	17:24.3	OR	1976	Piet Kleine, HOL	14:50.59	OR
1948	Ake Seyffarth, SWE	17:26.3		1980	Eric Heiden, USA	14:28.13	WR
1952	Hjalmar Andersen, NOR	16:45.8	OR	1984	Igor Malkov, USSR	14:39.90	
1956	Sigvard Ericsson, SWE	16:35.9	OR	1988	Tomas Gustafson, SWE	13:48.20	WR
1960	Knut Johannesen, NOR	15:46.6	WR				

*Result is unofficial. Jaffee recorded the fastest time, but the event was called off in progress due to thawing ice.

WOMEN

500 Meters

Year		Time		Year		Time	
1960	Helga Haase, GER	45.9		1976	Sheila Young, USA	42.76	OR
1964	Lydia Skoblikova, USSR	45.0	OR	1980	Karin Enke, E.Ger	41.78	OR
1968	Lyudmila Titova, USSR	46.1		1984	Christa Rothenburger, E.Ger	41.02	OR
1972	Anne Henning, USA	43.33	OR	1988	Bonnie Blair, USA	39.10	WR

1000 Meters

Year		Time		Year		Time	
1960	Klara Guseva, USSR	1:34.1		1976	Tatiana Averina, USSR	1:28.43	OR
1964	Lydia Skoblikova, USSR	1:33.2	OR	1980	Natalia Petruseva, USSR	1:24.10	OR
1968	Carolina Geijssen, HOL	1:32.6	OR	1984	Karin Enke, E.Ger	1:21.61	OR
1972	Monika Pflug, W.Ger	1:31.40	OR	1988	Christa Rothenburger, E.Ger	1:17.65	WR

1500 Meters

Year		Time		Year		Time	
1960	Lydia Skoblikova, USSR	2:25.2	WR	1976	Galina Stepanskaya, USSR	2:16.58	OR
1964	Lydia Skoblikova, USSR	2:22.6	OR	1980	Annie Borckink, HOL	2:10.95	OR
1968	Kaija Mustonen, FIN	2:22.4	OR	1984	Karin Enke, E.Ger	2:03.42	WR
1972	Dianne Holum, USA	2:20.85	OR	1988	Yvonne Van Gennip, HOL	2:00.68	OR

3000 Meters

Year		Time		Year		Time	
1960	Lydia Skoblikova, USSR	5:14.3		1976	Tatiana Averina, USSR	4:45.19	OR
1964	Lydia Skoblikova, USSR	5:14.9		1980	Bjorg Eva Jensen, NOR	4:32.13	OR
1968	Johanna Schut, HOL	4:56.2	OR	1984	Andrea Schöne, E.Ger	4:24.79	OR
1972	Christina Baas-Kaiser, HOL	4:52.14	OR	1988	Yvonne Van Gennip, HOL	4:11.94	WR

5000 Meters

Year		Time	
1988	Yvonne Van Gennip, HOL	7:14.13	WR

The Olympic Truce: Myth And Reality

by Harvey Abrams

All wars were cancelled or postponed during the games.

Los Angeles Times
Oct. 18, 1983

Imagine that, the ancient Greeks stopped their wars in order to go to the Olympic Games. How wonderful the world would be if 20th century man (and woman) could be as bold and idealistic.

But, alas, another ideal bites the dust. It is a modern myth that wars came to an end during the ancient Games, a myth perpetuated by journalists, historians and even American presidents. It is an idealistic misunderstanding of the ancient Olympic Games and of the "sacred truce" or *ekecheiria*. A truce did in fact exist, but it certainly didn't stop wars.

In reality the ancient Greeks loved to fight. Their wars literally consumed them. The ancient victors killed all the men and then enslaved all the women and children. The cities were pillaged and destroyed. No truce for any sports event was about to interfere with this kind of conflict.

Our difficulties in studying the ancient Greeks are compounded because no record has ever been found with the rules of the truce. Only written references to its violations are recorded. It is known that the truce forbade the taking up of arms, the pursuit of legal disputes, and the use of the death penalty. But these rules cannot be interpreted to mean that all wars came to an end.

Three travelling heralds, called *spondophorol*, traveled from Elis to all regions of Greece and announced the beginning of the period of truce as well as the date of the Olympic festival. The Olympic Games were a religious festival in honor of the god Zeus, and the Greeks believed that Zeus protected them. A violation of the truce was sacrilegious.

What did the truce really mean? It meant that the travelers to the Olympic Games were safe. It meant that the city-state of Elis,

Olympian **Zeus** sitting on his throne, one of the seven ancient wonders of the world. Drawing by Adler, 1935. Abrams archives.

the host to the Games, was not to be warred against. It meant that once the athletes and pilgrims arrived, they wouldn't hurt each other, even if they were from opposite warring city-states.

The Eleans were the custodians of the sacred site of Olympia. They had adopted a policy of perpetual neutrality, a noble gesture that only lasted from 776 BC to 420 BC. They finally allied themselves against the Spartans who, outraged, threatened an invasion during the Games. A military force was needed to protect the festival from the invasion, which never came. The truce didn't stop the Eleans themselves in 364 BC, when they battled the Arcadians and Pisalans inside the sacred grove of Olympia during the Games. The truce didn't stop the Macedonians in 312 BC, when they plundered and looted the treasury buildings, and it didn't stop the Romans from pillaging and stealing under Sulla, Caligula and Nero.

Since the Modern Games were begun in 1896, we have cancelled three Olympic celebrations because of war—in 1916, 1940 and 1944. Yet the ancient Games lasted over 1,100 years without an interruption.

Given the global hostilities that have plagued the 20th century, the myth of an Olympic truce that outlawed warfare is very appealing. But such a truce never existed.

Harvey Abrams is an Olympic historian and antiquarian now completing his PH.D. at Penn State University.

World chess champion **Garry Kasparov** of the Soviet Union deep in thought during his 1990 title defense against former champion Anatoly Karpov in Lyons, France. Kasparov finally won the 24-game match, 12½ to 11½, on Dec. 31.

MISCELLANEOUS SPORTS

LITTLE LEAGUE BASEBALL

World Series

An Asian team won the Little League World Series for the 20th time in the last 25 years on Aug.24, when Taichung, Taiwan, routed San Ramon Valley, Calif., 11-0, in Williamsport, Pa. Pitcher Pan Chih-Chang struck out 14 and Lin Wei-Chu had a grand slam to lead the Taiwanese to their 15th LLWS title.

Multiple winners: Taiwan (15); Connecticut and Pennsylvania (4); California, Japan and New Jersey (3); Mexico, New York, South Korea and Texas (2).

Year	Winner	Score	Loser	Year	Winner	Score	Loser
1947	Williamsport, PA	16-7	Lock Haven, PA	1970	Wayne, NJ	2-0	Campbell, CA
1948	Lock Haven, PA	6-5	St. Petersburg, FL	1971	Tainan, Taiwan1	2-3	Gary, IN
1949	Hammonton, NJ	5-0	Pensacola, FL	1972	Taipei, Taiwan	6-0	Hammond, IN
1950	Houston, TX	2-1	Bridgeport, CT	1973	Tainan City, Taiwan	12-0	Tucson, AZ
1951	Stamford, CT	3-0	Austin, TX	1974	Kao Hsiung, Taiwan	7-2	El Cajun, CA
1952	Norwalk, CT	4-3	Monongahela, PA	1975	Lakewood, NJ	4-3*	Tampa, FL
1953	Birmingham, AL	1-0	Schenectady, NY	1976	Tokyo, Japan	10-3	Campbell, CA
1954	Schenectady, NY	7-5	Colton, CA	1977	Kao Hsiung, Taiwan	7-2	El Cajun, CA
1955	Morrisville, PA	4-3	Merchantville, NJ	1978	Pin-Tung, Taiwan	11-1	Danville, CA
1956	Roswell, NM	3-1	Merchantville, NJ	1979	Hsien, Taiwan	2-1	Campbell, CA
1957	Monterrey, Mex.	4-0	LaMesa, CA	1980	Hua Lian, Taiwan	4-3	Tampa, FL
1958	Monterrey, Mex.	10-1	Kankakee, IL	1981	Tai-Chung, Taiwan	4-2	Tampa, FL
1959	Hamtramck, MI	12-0	Auburn, CA	1982	Kirkland, WA	6-0	Hsien, Taiwan
1960	Levittown, PA	5-0	Ft. Worth, TX	1983	Marietta, GA	3-1	Barahona, D.Rep.
1961	El Cajon, CA	4-2	El Campo, TX	1984	Seoul, S.Korea	6-2	Altamonte Sgs, FL
1962	San Jose, CA	3-0	Kankakee, IL	1985	Seoul, S.Korea	7-1	Mexicali, Mex.
1963	Granada Hills, CA	2-1	Stratford, CT	1986	Tainan Park, Taiwan	12-0	Tucson, AZ
1964	Staten Island, NY	4-0	Monterrey, Mex.	1987	Hua Lian, Taiwan	21-1	Irvine, CA
1965	Windsor Locks, CT	3-1	Stoney Creek, Can.	1988	Tai-Chung, Taiwan	10-0	Pearl City, HI
1966	Houston, TX	8-2	W.New York, NJ	1989	Trumbull, CT	5-2	Kaohsiung, Taiwan
1967	West Tokyo, Japan	4-1	Chicago, IL	1990	Taipei, Taiwan	9-0	Shippensburg, PA
1968	Osaka, Japan	1-0	Richmond, VA	1991	Taichung, Taiwan	11-0	San Ramon Vly, CA
1969	Taipei, Taiwan	5-0	Santa Clara,CA				

*Foreign teams were banned from the tournament in 1975. The ban was lifted the next year.

CHESS

World Champions

Defending champion Garry Kasparov of the Soviet Union retained his world chess title on Dec. 31, 1990, by drawing the 24th and final game of his match with former champion and countryman Anatoly Karpov in Lyons, France. The match began in New York on Oct.8. Kasparov, 27, who won 12½ to 11½, pocketed $1.7 million for the victory, while Karpov took home $1.3 million.

Years		Years		Years	
1866-94	Wilhelm Steinitz, Austria	1937-46	Alexander Alekhine, France	1963-69	Tigran Petrosian, USSR
1894-		1948-57	Mikhail Botvinnik, USSR	1969-72	Boris Spassky, USSR
1921	Emanuel Lasker, Germany	1957-58	Vassily Smyslov, USSR	1972-75	Bobby Fischer, USA
1921-27	Jose Capablanca, Cuba	1958-59	Mikhail Botvinnik, USSR	1975-85	Anatoly Karpov, USSR
1927-35	Alexander Alekhine, France	1960-61	Mikhail Tal, USSR	1985-	Garry Kasparov, USSR
1935-37	Max Euwe, Holland	1961-63	Mikhail Botvinnik, USSR		

Note: Fischer defaulted Championship in 1975.

U.S. Champions (since 1900)

Gata Kamsky, a 17-year-old emigre from the Soviet Union, won the U.S.Invitational Chess Championship on Aug.9, 1991, by defeating 1987 co-champion Joel Benjamin, 2½ to 1½ in Los Angeles. Kamsky, who arrived in the U.S. in 1989, is the world's youngest grandmaster and the youngest to win the U.S. title since Bobby Fischer did so at age 14 in 1957.

Years		Years		Years	
1900-06	Harry Pillsbury	1969-72	Samuel Reshevsky	1983	Roman Dzindzichashvili,
1906-09	Vacant	1972-73	Robert Byrne		Larry Christiansen
1909-36	Frank Marshall	1973-74	Lubomir Kavalek		& Walter Browne
1936-44	Samuel Reshevsky		& John Grefe	1984-85	Lev Alburt
1944-46	Arnold Denker	1974-77	Walter Browne	1986	Yasser Seirawan
1946-48	Samuel Reshevsky	1978-80	Lubomir Kabalek	1987	Joel Benjamin
1948-51	Herman Steiner	1980-81	Larry Evans,		& Nick DeFirmian
1951-54	Larry Evans		Larry Christiansen,	1988	Michael Wilder
1954-57	Arthur Bisguier		& Walter Browne	1989	Roman Dzindzichashvili,
1957-61	Bobby Fischer	1981-83	Walter Browne		Stuart Rachels
1961-62	Larry Evans		& Yasser Seirawan		& Yasser Seirawan
1962-68	Bobby Fischer			1990	Lev Alburt
1968-69	Larry Evans			1991	Gata Kamsky

DOGS
Iditarod Sled Dog Race

Rick Swenson braved a howling blizzard on the last leg of the race to win the Iditarod Sled Dog Race for a record fifth time on Mar. 15, 1991. Swenson, who won $50,000 in prize money, finished 2 hours in front of runner-up Martin Buser and 5½ hours ahead of defending champion Susan Butcher, who finished third.

The annual 1,163-mile race stretches from Anchorage to Nome, Alaska. Begun in 1973, the course follows an old frozen river mail route and is named after a deserted mining town along the way. The Iditarod also commemorates a famous midwinter emergency mission to get medical supplies to Nome during a 1925 diptheria epidemic. Men and women mushers compete together.

Multiple winners: Rick Swenson (5); Susan Butcher (4); Rick Mackey (2).

Year		Elapsed Time	Year		Elapsed Time
1973	Dick Wilmarth	20 days, 00:49:41	1983	Rick Mackey	12 days, 14:10:44
1974	Carl Huntington	20 days, 15:02:07	1984	Dean Osmar	12 days, 15:07:33
1975	Emmitt Peters	14 days, 14:43:45	1984	Libby Riddles	18 days, 00:20:17
1976	Gerald Riley	18 days, 22:58:17	1986	Susan Butcher	11 days, 15:06:00
1977	Rick Swenson	16 days, 16:27:13	1987	Susan Butcher	11 days, 02:05:13
1978	Dick Mackey	14 days, 18:52:24	1988	Susan Butcher	11 days, 11:41:40
1979	Rick Swenson	15 days, 10:37:47	1989	Joe Runyan	11 days, 05:24:34
1980	Joe May	14 days, 07:11:51	1990	Susan Butcher	11 days, 01:53:23*
1981	Rick Swenson	12 days, 08:45:02	1991	Rick Swenson	12 days, 16:34:39
1982	Rick Swenson	16 days, 04:40:10	*Course record.		

Westminster Kennel Club
Best in Show

Champion Whisperwind on a Carousel, a 5-year-old poodle who is the top-winning male in breed history, was judged Best in Show, Feb.12, at the 115th Westminster Kennel Club show at Madison Square Garden in New York. The poodle, owned by Dr. Frederick Hartsock of Potomac, Md., was the first standard poodle to win since 1973.

The Westminster show is the most prestigious canine event in America. Held every year since 1877, it is one of the oldest annual sporting events in the country.

Multiple winners: Ch.Warren Remedy (3); Ch.Chinoe's Adamant James, Ch.Comejo Wycollar Boy, Ch.Flornell Spicy Piece of Halleston; Ch.Matford Vic, Ch.My Own Brucie, Ch.Pendley Calling of Blarney, Ch.Rancho Dobe's Storm (2).

Year		Breed	Year		Breed
1907	Warren Remedy	Fox Terrier	1940	My Own Brucie	Cocker Spaniel
1908	Warren Remedy	Fox Terrier	1941	My Own Brucie	Cocker Spaniel
1909	Warren Remedy	Fox Terrier	1942	Wolvey Pattern of Edgerstoune	W.Highland Terrier
1910	Sabine Rarebit	Fox Terrier	1943	Pitter Patter of Piperscroft	Miniature Poodle
1911	Tickle Em Jock	Scot.Terrier	1944	Flornell Rarebit of Twin Ponds	Welsh Terrier
1912	Kenmore Sorceress	Airedale	1945	Shieling's Signature	Scot.Terrier
1913	Strathway Prince Albert	Bulldog	1946	Hetherington Model Rhythm	Fox Terrier
1914	Brentwood Hero	Old Eng.Sheepdog	1947	Warlord of Mazelaine	Boxer
1915	Matford Vic	Old Eng.Sheepdog	1948	Rock Ridge Night Rocket	Bedling.Terrier
1916	Matford Vic	Old Eng.Sheepdog	1949	Mazelaine's Zazarac Brandy	Boxer
1917	Comejo Wycollar Boy	Fox Terrier	1950	Walsing Winning Trick of Edgerstoune	Scot.Terrier
1918	Haymarket Faultless	Bull Terrier	1951	Bang Away of Sirrah Crest	Boxer
1919	Briergate Bright Beauty	Airedale	1952	Rancho Dobe's Storm	Doberman
1920	Comejo Wycollar Boy	Fox Terrier	1953	Rancho Dobe's Storm	Doberman
1921	Midkiff Seductive	Cocker Spaniel	1954	Carmor's Rise and Shine	Cocker Spaniel
1922	Boxwood Barkentine	Airedale	1955	Kippax Fearnought	Bulldog
1923	No best-in-show award		1956	Wilber White Swan	Toy Poodle
1924	Barberryhill Bootlegger	Sealyham	1957	Shirkhan of Grandeur	Afghan Hound
1925	Governor Moscow	Pointer	1958	Puttencove Promise	Standard Poodle
1926	Signal Circuit	Fox Terrier	1959	Fontclair Festoon	Miniature Poodle
1927	Pinegrade Perfection	Sealyham	1960	Chick T'Sun of Caversham	Pekingese
1928	Talavera Margaret	Fox Terrier	1961	Cappoquin Little Sister	Toy Poodle
1929	Land Loyalty of Bellhaven	Collie	1962	Elfinbrook Simon	W.Highland Terrier
1930	Pendley Calling of Blarney	Fox Terrier	1963	Wakefield's Black Knight	English Springer Spaniel
1931	Pendley Calling of Blarney	Fox Terrier	1964	Courtenay Fleetfoot of Pennyworth	Whippet
1932	Nancolleth Markable	Pointer	1965	Carmichaels Fanfare	Scottish Terrier
1933	Warland Protector of Shelterock	Airedale	1966	Zeloy Mooremaides Magic	Fox Terrier
1934	Flornell Spicy Bit of Halleston	Fox Terrier	1967	Bardene Bingo	Scottish Terrier
1935	Nunsoe Duc de la Terrace of Blakeen	Standard Poodle	1968	Stingray of Derryabah	Lakeland Terrier
1936	St.Margaret Magnificent of Clairedale	Sealyham	1969	Glamoor Good News	Skye Terrier
1937	Flornell Spicy Bit of Halleston	Fox Terrier	1970	Arriba's Prima Donna	Boxer
1938	Daro of Maridor	English Setter	1971	Chinoe's Adamant James	E.S.Spaniel
1939	Ferry v.Rauhfelsen of Giralda	Doberman	1972	Chinoe's Adamant James	E.S.Spaniel

Dogs (Cont.)
West. K.C. Best in Show

Year		Breed	Year		Breed
1973	Acadia Command Performance	Stan.Poodle	1983	Kabik's The Challenger	Afghan Hound
1974	Gretchenhof Columbia River	German SH Pointer	1984	Seaward's Blackbeard	Newfoundland
1975	Sir Lancelot of Barvan	Old Eng.Sheepdog	1985	Braeburn's Close Encounter	Scot.Terrier
1976	Jo Ni's Red Baron of Crofton	Lakeland Terrier	1986	Marjetta National Acclaim	Pointer
1977	Dersade Bobby's Girl	Sealyham	1987	Covy Tucker Hill's Manhattan	Ger.Sheperd
1978	Cede Higgens	Yorkshire Terrier	1988	Great Elms Prince Charming II	Pomeranian
1979	Oak Tree's Irishtocrat	Irish Water Spaniel	1989	Royal Tudor's Wild As The Wind	Doberman
1980	Sierra Cinnar	Siberian Husky			
1981	Dhandy Favorite Woodchuck	Pug	1990	Wendessa Crown Prince	Pekingese
1982	St.Aubrey Dragonora of Elsdon	Pekingese	1991	Whisperwind on a Carousel	Stan. Poodle

FISHING
IGFA All-Tackle World Records

As of Sept. 5, 1991.

All-tackle records are maintained for the heaviest fish of any species caught on any line up to 130-lb (60 kg) class and certified by the International Game Fish Association. **Address:** 3000 East Las Olas Blvd., Ft.Lauderdale, FL, 33316. **Telephone:** 305-467-0161.

FRESHWATER FISH

Species	Lbs-Oz	Where Caught	Date	Angler
Barramundi	59-12	Pt.Stuart, Australia	Apr. 7,1983	Andrew Davern
Bass, largemouth	22- 4	Montgomery Lake, GA	Jun. 2,1932	George W.Perry
Bass, peacock	26- 8	Matevini River, Colombia	Jan.26,1982	Rod Neubert
Bass, redeye	8- 3	Flint River, GA	Oct.23,1977	David A.Hubbard
Bass, rock	3- 0	York River, Ontario	Aug. 1,1974	Peter Gulgin
Bass, smallmouth	11-15	Dale Hollow Lake, KY	Jul. 9,1955	David L.Hayes
Bass, spotted	9- 4	Parris Lake, CA	Jan.24,1987	Steven West
	9- 4	Lake Perris, CA	Apr. 1,1987	Gilbert Rowe
Bass, striped (landlocked)	66- 0	O'Neill Forebay, Los Banos, CA	Jun.29,1988	Ted Furnish
Bass, Suwannee	3-14	Suwannee River, FL	Mar. 2,1985	Ronnie Everett
Bass, white	6-13	Lake Orange, VA	Jul.31,1989	Ronald L.Sprouse
Bass, whiterock	24- 3	Leesville Lake, VA	May 12,1989	David N.Lambert
Bass, yellow	2- 4	Lake Monroe, IN	Mar.27,1977	Donald L.Stalker
Bluegill	4-12	Ketona Lake, AL	Apr. 9,1950	T.S.Hudson
Bowfin	21- 8	Florence, SC	Jan.29,1980	Robert L.Harmon
Buffalo, bigmouth	70- 5	Bussey Brake, Bastrop, LA	Apr.21,1980	Delbert Sisk
Buffalo, black	55- 8	Cherokee Lake, TN	May 3,1984	Edward H.McLain
Buffalo, smallmouth	68- 8	Lake Hamilton, AR	May 16,1984	Jerry L.Dolezal
Bullhead, black	8- 0	Lake Waccabuc, NY	Aug. 1,1951	Kani Evans
Bullhead, brown	5- 8	Veal Pond, GA	May 22,1975	Jimmy Andrews
Bullhead, yellow	4- 4	Mormon Lake, AZ	May 11,1984	Emily Williams
Burbot	18- 4	Pickford, MI	Jan.31,1980	Tom Courtemanche
Carp	75-11	Lac de St.Cassien, France	May 21,1987	Leo van der Gugten
Catfish, blue	109- 4	Cooper River, SC	Mar.14,1991	George Lijewski
Catfish, channel	58- 0	Santee-Cooper Res., SC	Jul. 7,1964	W.B. Whaley
Catfish, flathead	91- 4	Lake Lewisville, TX	Mar.28,1982	Mike Rogers
Catfish, white	17- 7	Success Lake, Tulare, CA	Nov.15,1981	Chuck Idell
Char, Arctic	32- 9	Tree River, Canada	Jul.30,1981	Jeffery Ward
Crappie, black	4- 8	Kerr Lake, VA	Mar. 1,1981	L.Carl Herring,Jr.
Crappie, white	5- 3	Enid Dam, MS	Jul.31,1957	Fred L.Bright
Dolly Varden	12- 5	Kenai River, AK	Sep.19,1990	Richard Seebold
Dorado	51- 5	Corrientes, Argentina	Sep.27,1984	Armando Giudice
Drum, freshwater	54- 8	Nickajack Lake, TN	Apr.20,1972	Benny E.Hull
Gar, alligator	279- 0	Rio Grande, TX	Dec. 2,1951	Bill Valverde
Gar, Florida	21- 3	Boca Raton, FL	June 3,1981	Jeff Sabol
Gar, longnose	50- 5	Trinity River, TX	Jul.30,1954	Townsend Miller
Gar, shortnose	5- 0	Sally Jones Lake, OK	Apr.26,1985	Buddy Croslin
Gar, spotted	8-12	Tennessee River, AL	Aug.26,1987	Winston H.Baker
Grayling, Arctic	5-15	Katseyedie River, N.W.T.	Aug.16,1967	Jeanne P.Branson
Goldfish	3- 0	Southland Pk., Livingston, TX	May 8,1988	Kenneth R.Kinsey
Inconnu	53- 0	Pah River, AK	Aug.20,1986	Lawrence E.Hudnall
Kokanee	9- 6	Okanagan Lake, Brit.Columbia	Jun.18,1988	Norm Kuhn
Muskellunge	69-15	St. Lawrence River, NY	Sep.22,1957	Arthur Lawton
Muskellunge, tiger	51- 3	Lac Vieux-Desert, WI-MI	Jul.16,1919	John A.Knobla

Species	Lbs-Oz	Where Caught	Date	Angler
Perch, Nile	155- 6	Nsese Islands, Uganda	Oct. 27,1990	Gunnar Thomsen
Perch, white	4-12	Messalonskee Lake, ME	Jun. 4,1949	Mrs.Earl Small
Perch, yellow	4- 3	Bordentown, NJ	May, 1865	Dr.C.C.Abbot
Pickerel, chain	9- 6	Homerville, GA	Feb.17,1961	Baxley McQuaig, Jr.
Pike, northern	55- 1	Lake of Grefeeřm, W.Germany	Oct.16,1986	Lothar Louis
Redhorse, greater	9- 3	Salmon River, Pulaski, NY	May 11,1985	Jason Wilson
Redhorse, river	5- 9	Mooresville, AL	Mar.27,1985	Don Hale
Redhorse, silver	11- 7	Plum Creek, WI	May 29,1985	Neal D.G.Long
Salmon, Atlantic	79- 2	Tana River, Norway	1928	Henrik Henriksen
Salmon, chinook	97- 4	Kenai River, AK	May 17,1985	Les Anderson
Salmon, chum	32- 0	Behm Canal, AK	Jun. 7,1985	Fredrick Thynes
Salmon, coho	33- 4	Salmon River, Pulaski, NY	Sep.27,1989	Jerry Lifton
Salmon, pink	12- 9	Morse & Kenai Rivers, AK	Aug.17,1974	Steven Alan Lee
Salmon, sockeye	15- 3	Kenai River, AK	Aug. 9,1987	Stan Roach
Sauger	8-12	Lake Sakakawea, ND	Oct. 6,1971	Mike Fischer
Shad, American	11- 4	Conn.River, S.Hadley, MA	May 19,1986	Bob Thibodo
Sturgeon, lake	92- 4	Kettle River, MN	Sep. 11,1986	James M.DeOtis
Sturgeon, white	468- 0	Benicia, CA	Jul. 9,1983	Joey Pallotta 3rd
Sunfish, green	2- 2	Stockton Lake, MO	Jun,18,1971	Paul M.Dilley
Sunfish, redbreast	1-12	Suwannee River, FL	May 29,1984	Alvin Buchanan
Sunfish, redear	4-13	Merritt's Pond, Mariana, FL	Mar.13,1986	Joey Floyd
Tigerfish	97- 0	Zaire River, Kinshasa, Zaire	Jul. 9,1988	Raymond Houtmans
Tilapia	6- 0	Lake Okeechobee, FL	Jun.24,1989	Joseph M.Tucker
Trout, Apache	4-15	Christmas Tree Lake, AZ	May 5,1990	Arthur L. Pearce II
Trout, brook	14- 8	Nipigon River, Ontario	July, 1916	Dr. W.J.Cook
Trout, brown	35-15	Nahuel Huapi, Argentina	Dec.16,1952	Eugenio Cavaglia
Trout, bull	32- 0	Lake Pond Orielle, ID	Oct.27,1949	N.L.Higgins
Trout, cutthroat	41- 0	Pyramid Lake, NV	Dec., 1925	John Skimmerhorn
Trout, golden	11- 0	Cooks Lake, WY	Aug. 5,1948	Charles S.Reed
Trout, lake	65- 0	Great Bear Lake, N.W.T.	Aug. 8,1970	Larry Daunis
Trout, rainbow	42- 2	Bell Island, AK	Jun.22,1970	David Robert White
Trout, tiger	20-13	Lake Michigan, WI	Aug.12,1978	Peter M.Friedland
Walleye	25- 0	Old Hickory Lake, TN	Apr. 1,1960	Mabry Harper
Warmouth	2- 7	Guess Lake, Holt, FL	Oct.19,1985	Tony D.Dempsey
Whitefish, lake	14- 6	Meaford, Ontario	May 21,1984	Dennis M.Laycock
Whitefish, mountain	5- 6	Rioh River, Saskatchewan	Jun.15,1988	John R.Bell
Whitefish, river	11- 2	Skrabean, Nymoua, Sweden	Dec. 9,1984	Jorgen Larsson
Whitefish, round	6- 0	Putahow River, Manitoba	Jun.14,1984	Allan J.Ristori
Zander	25- 2	Trosa, Sweden	Jun.12,1986	Harry Lee Tennison

SALTWATER FISH

Species	Lbs-Oz	Where Caught	Date	Angler
Albacore	88- 2	Gran Canaria, Canary Islands	Nov.19,1977	Siegfried Dickemann
Amberjack, greater	155-10	Challenger Bank, Bermuda	Jun.24,1981	Joseph Dawson
Amberjack, pacific	104- 0	Baja Calif., Mexico	Jul. 4,1984	Richard Cresswell
Barracuda, greater	83- 0	Lagos, Nigeria	Jan.13,1952	K.J.W.Hackett
Barracuda, Mexican	21- 0	Phantom Island, Costa Rica	Mar.27,1987	E.Greg Kent
Barracuda, slender	17- 4	Sitra Channel, Bahrain	Nov.21,1985	Roger Cranswick
Bass, barred sand	13- 3	Huntington Beach, CA	Aug.29,1988	Robert Halal
Bass, black sea	9- 8	Virginia Beach, VA	Jan. 9,1987	Joe Mizelle, Jr.
Bass, European	20-11	Stes Maries de la Mer, France	May. 6,1986	Jean Baptiste Bayle
Bass, giant sea	563- 8	Anacapa Island, CA	Aug.20,1968	J.D.McAdam, Jr.
Bass, striped	78- 8	Atlantic City, NJ	Sep.21,1982	Albert R.McReynolds
Bluefish	31-12	Hatteras, NC	Jan.30,1972	James M.Hussey
Bonefish	19- 0	Zululand, South Africa	May 26,1962	Brian W.Batchelor
Bonito, Atlantic	18- 4	Faial Island, Azores	Jul. 8,1953	D.Gama Higgs
Bonito, Pacific	23- 8	Victoria, Mahe, Seychelles	Feb.19,1975	Anne Cochain
Cabezon	23- 0	Juan de Fuca Strait, WA	Aug. 4,1990	Wesley Hunter
Cobia	135- 9	Shark Bay, W.Australia	Jul. 9,1985	Peter W.Goulding
Cod, Atlantic	98-12	Isle of Shoals, NH	Jun. 8,1969	Alphonse Bielevich
Cod, Pacific	30- 0	Andrew Bay, AK	Jul. 7,1984	Donald R.Vaughn
Conger	104- 8	Brixham, England	Jun. 5,1988	Philip John Greenway
Dolphin	87- 0	Papagallo Gulf, Costa Rica	Sep.25,1976	Manuel Salazar
Drum, black	113- 1	Lewes, DE	Sep.15,1975	Gerald M.Townsend
Drum, red	94- 2	Avon, NC	Nov. 7,1984	David G.Deuel
Eel, African mottled	36- 1	Durban, S. Africa	Jun.10,1984	Ferdie van Nooten
Eel, American	7- 7	Sandy Hook, NJ	Jun.20,1990	Robert Gray
Flounder, southern	20- 9	Nassau Sound, FL	Dec.23,1983	Larenza Mungin
Flounder, summer	22- 7	Montauk, NY	Sep.15,1975	Charles Nappi
Flounder, winter	7- 0	Fire Island, NY	May 8,1986	Einar F.Grell

Fishing (Cont.)
SALTWATER FISH

Species	Lbs-Oz	Where Caught	Date	Angler
Grouper, warsaw	436-12	Gulf of Mexico, Destin, FL	Dec.22,1985	Steve Haeusler
Haddock	9-15	Perkins Cove, Ogunquit, ME	May 24,1988	Jim Donohue
Halibut, Atlantic	255- 4	Gloucester, MA	Jul.28,1989	Sonny Manley
Halibut, California	53- 4	Santa Rosa Island, CA	Jul. 7,1988	Russell J.Harmon
Halibut, Pacific	356- 8	Castineau Channel, Juneau, AK	Nov. 6,1986	Gregory C.Olsen
Jack, crevalle	54- 7	Port Michel, Gabon	Jan.15,1982	Thomas F.Gibson, Jr.
Jack, horse-eye	24- 8	Miami, FL	Dec.20,1982	Tito Schnau
Jack, almaco (Pacific)	132- 0	La Paz, Baja Calif., Mexico	Jul.21,1964	Howard H.Hahn
Jewfish	680- 0	Fernandina Beach, FL	May 20,1961	Lynn Joyner
Kawakawa	29- 0	Clarion Island, Mexico	Dec.17,1986	Ronald Nakamura
Lingcod	66- 0	Granite Island, AK	Jul. 31,1990	James A. McKenzie
Mackerel, cero	17- 2	Islamorada, FL	Apr. 5,1986	G.Michael Mills
Mackerel, king	90- 0	Key West, FL	Feb.16,1976	Norton I.Thomton
Mackerel, Spanish	13- 0	Ocracoke Inlet, NC	Nov. 4,1987	Robert Cranton
Marlin, Atlantic blue	1282- 0	St.Thomas, Virgin Islands	Aug. 6,1977	Larry Martin
Marlin, Black	1560- 0	Cabo Blanco, Peru	Aug. 4,1953	A.C.Glassell, Jr.
Marlin, Pacific blue	1376- 0	Kaaiwi Point, Kona, HI	May 31,1982	Jay W.deBeaubien
Marlin, striped	494- 0	Tutakaka, New Zealand	Jan.16,1986	Bill Boniface
Marlin, white	181-14	Vitoria, Brazil	Dec. 8,1979	Evandro Luiz Coser
Permit	51- 8	Lake Worth, FL	Apr.28,1978	William M. Kenney
Pollack	27- 6	Salcombe, Devon, England	Jan.16,1986	Robert S. Milkins
Pollock	46-10	Perkins Cove, Ogunquit, ME	Oct.24,1990	Linda M. Paul
Pompano, African	50- 8	Daytona Beach, FL	Apr.21,1990	Tom Sargent
Roosterfish	114- 0	La Paz, Baja Calif., Mexico	Jun. 1,1960	Abe Sackheim
Runner, blue	8- 4	Bimini, Bahamas	Sep. 9,1990	Brent Rowland
Runner, rainbow	33-10	Clarion Island, Mexico	Mar.14,1976	Ralph A.Mikkelsen
Sailfish, Atlantic	128- 1	Luanda, Angola	Mar.27,1974	Harm Steyn
Sailfish, Pacific	221- 0	Santa Cruz Is., Ecuador	Feb.12,1947	C.W.Stewart
Seabass, white	83-12	San Felipe, Mexico	Mar.31,1953	L.C.Baumgardner
Seatrout, spotted	16- 0	Mason's Beach, VA	May 28,1977	William Katko
Shark, blue	437- 0	Catherine Bay, NSW, Australia	Oct. 2,1976	Peter Hyde
Shark, great white	2664- 0	Ceduna, S.Australia	Apr.21,1959	Alfred Dean
Shark, greenland	1708- 9	Trondheimsfjord, Norway	Oct.18,1987	Terje Nordtvedt
Shark, hammerhead	991- 0	Sarasota, FL	May 30,1982	Allen Ogle
Shark, mako	1115- 0	Black River, Mauritius	Nov.16,1988	Patrick Guillanton
Shark, porbeagle	465- 0	Padstow, Cornwall, England	Jul.23,1976	Jorge Potier
Shark, thresher	802- 0	Tutukaka, New Zealand	Feb. 8,1981	Dianne North
Shark, tiger	1780- 0	Cherry Grove, SC	Jun.14,1964	Walter Maxwell
Skipjack, black	20- 5	Alijos Rocks, Baja, Mexico	Oct.14,1983	Roger Torriero
Snapper, cubera	121- 8	Cameron, LA	Jul. 5,1982	Mike Hebert
Snapper, red	46- 8	Destin, FL	Oct. 1,1985	E.Lane Nichols, III
Snook	53-10	Parismina Ranch, Costa Rica	Oct.18,1978	Gilbert Ponzi
Spearfish	90-13	Madeira Island, Portugal	Jun. 2,1980	Joseph Larkin
Swordfish	1182- 0	Iquique, Chile	May 7,1953	L.Marron
Tanguigue	99- 0	Natal, S. Africa	Mar.14,1982	Michael Wilkinson
Tarpon	283- 0	Lake Maracaibo, Venezuela	Mar.19,1956	M.Salazar
Tautog	24- 0	Wachapreague, VA	Aug.25,1987	Gregory R.Bell
Toadfish, oyster	3-10	Ocracoke, NC	May 19,1990	Stuart C.Lee
Tuna, Atlantic bigeye	375- 8	Ocean City, MD	Aug.26,1977	Cecil Browne
Tuna, blackfin	42- 0	Bermuda	Jun.2,1978	Alan J. Card
	42- 0	Challenger Bank, Bermuda	Jul.18,1989	Gilbert C.Pearman
Tuna, bluefin	1496- 0	Aulds Cove, Nova Scotia	Oct.26,1979	Ken Fraser
Tuna, longtail	79- 2	Montague Is., NSW, Australia	Apr.12,1982	Tim Simpson
Tuna, Pacific bigeye	435- 0	Cabo Blanco, Peru	Apr.17,1957	Dr.Russell Lee
Tuna, skipjack	41-14	Pearl Beach, Mauritius	Nov.12,1985	Edmund Heinzen
Tuna, southern bluefin	348- 5	Whakatane, New Zealand	Jan.16,1981	Rex Wood
Tuna, yellowfin	388-12	San Benedicto Island, Mexico	Apr. 1,1977	Curt Wiesenhutter
Tunny, little	35- 2	Cape de Garde, Algeria	Dec.14,1988	Jean Yves Chatard
Wahoo	155- 8	San Salvador, Bahamas	Apr. 3,1990	William Bourne
Weakfish	19- 2	Jones Beach, Long Island, NY	Oct.11,1984	Dennis R.Rooney
Yellowtail, California	78- 0	Alijos Rocks, Baja, Mexico	Jun.27,1987	Richard W. Cresswell
Yellowtail, Southern	114-10	Tauranga, New Zealand	Feb. 5,1984	Mike Godfrey

POWER BOAT RACING
APBA Gold Cup

Mark Tate piloted the Winston Eagle to victory in the 1991 APBA Gold Cup finals, June 9, on the Detroit River. It was the first win in two years of hydroplane racing for Tate, whose average speed was 137.771 miles an hour. George Woods finished second for the third consecutive year.

The American Power Boat Association Gold Cup for unlimited hydroplane racing is the oldest active motor sports trophy in North America. The first Gold Cup was competed for on the Hudson River in New York in June and September of 1904. Since then several cities have hosted the race, led by Detroit (26 times, including 1990) and Seattle (14). Note that (*) indicates driver was also owner of the winning boat.

Drivers with multiple wins: Bill Muncey (8); Chip Hanauer (7); Gar Wood (5); Dean Chenoweth (4); Caleb Bragg, Tom D'Eath, Lou Fageol, Ron Musson, George Reis and Jonathon Wainwright (3); Danny Foster, George Henley, Vic Kliesrath, E.J.Schroeder, Bill Schumacher, Zalmon G.Simmons Jr., Joe Taggart and George Townsend (2).

Year	Boat	Driver	Avg. MPH	Year	Boat	Driver	Avg. MPH
1904	Standard (June)	*Carl Riotte	23.160	1948	Miss Great Lakes	Danny Foster	46.845
1904	Vingt-Et-Un II			1949	My Sweetie	Bill Cantrell	73.612
	(Sept.)	*W.Sharpe Kilmer	24.900	1950	Slo-Mo-Shun IV	Ted Jones	78.216
1905	Chip I	*J.Wainwright	15.000	1951	Slo-Mo-Shun V	Lou Fageol	90.871
1906	Chip II	*J.Wainwright	25.000	1952	Slo-Mo-Shun IV	Stan Dollar	79.923
1907	Chip II	*J.Wainwright	23.903	1953	Slo-Mo-Shun IV	Joe Taggart	99.108
1908	Dixie II	*E.J.Schroeder	29.938			& Lou Fageol	
1909	Dixie II	*E.J.Schroeder	29.590	1954	Slo-Mo-Shun IV	Joe Taggart	92.613
						& Lou Fageol	
1910	Dixie III	*F.K.Burnham	32.473	1955	Gale V	Lee Schoenith	99.552
1911	MIT II	*J.H.Hayden	37.000	1956	Miss Thriftaway	Bill Muncey	96.552
1912	P.D.Q. II	*A.G.Miles	39.462	1957	Miss Thriftaway	Bill Muncey	101.787
1913	Ankle Deep	*Cas Mankowski	42.779	1958	Hawaii Kai III	Jack Regas	103.000
1914	Baby Speed	Jim Blackton	48.458	1959	Maverick	Bill Stead	104.481
	Demon II	& Bob Edgren		1960	Not held		
1915	Miss Detroit	Johnny Milot	37.656	1961	Miss Century 21	Bill Muncey	99.678
		& Jack Beebe		1962	Miss Century 21	Bill Muncey	100.710
1916	Miss Minneapolis	Bernard Smith	48.860	1963	Miss Bardahl	Ron Musson	105.124
1917	Miss Detroit II	*Gar Wood	54.410	1964	Miss Bardahl	Ron Musson	103.433
1918	Miss Detroit II	Gar Wood	51.619	1965	Miss Bardahl	Ron Musson	103.132
1919	Miss Detroit III	*Gar Wood	42.748	1966	Tahoe Miss	Mira Slovak	93.019
1920	Miss America I	*Gar Wood	62.022	1967	Miss Bardahl	Bill Shumacher	101.484
1921	Miss America I	*Gar Wood	52.825	1968	Miss Bardahl	Bill Shumacher	108.173
1922	Packard Chriscraft	*J.G.Vincent	40.253	1969	Miss Budweiser	Bill Sterett	98.504
1923	Packard Chriscraft	Caleb Bragg	43.867	1970	Miss Budweiser	Dean Chenoweth	99.562
1924	Baby Bootlegger	*Caleb Bragg	45.302	1971	Miss Madison	Jim McCormick	98.043
1925	Baby Bootlegger	*Caleb Bragg	47.240	1972	Atlas Van Lines	Bill Muncey	104.277
1926	Greenwich Folly	*Geo.Townsend	47.984	1973	Miss Budweiser	Dean Chenoweth	99.043
1927	Greenwich Folly	*Geo.Townsend	47.662	1974	Pay 'n Pak	George Henley	104.428
1928	Not held			1975	Pay 'n Pak	George Henley	108.921
1929	Imp	*Richard Hoyt	48.662	1976	Miss U.S.	Tom D'Eath	100.412
1930	Hotsy Totsy	*Vic Kliesrath	52.673	1977	Atlas Van Lines	*Bill Muncey	111.822
1931	Hotsy Totsy	*Vic Kliesrath	53.602	1978	Atlas Van Lines	*Bill Muncey	111.412
1932	Delphine IV	Bill Horn	57.775	1979	Atlas Van Lines	*Bill Muncey	100.765
1933	El Lagarto	*George Reis	56.260	1980	Miss Budweiser	Dean Chenoweth	106.932
1934	El Lagarto	*George Reis	55.000	1981	Miss Budweiser	Dean Chenoweth	116.932
1935	El Lagarto	*George Reis	55.056	1982	Atlas Van Lines	Chip Hanauer	120.050
1936	Impshi	Kaye Don	45.735	1983	Atlas Van Lines	Chip Hanauer	118.507
1937	Notre Dame	Clell Perry	63.675	1984	Atlas Van Lines	Chip Hanauer	130.175
1938	Alagi	*Theo Rossi	64.340	1985	Miller American	Chip Hanauer	120.643
1939	My Sin	*Z.G.Simmons,Jr	66.133	1986	Miller American	Chip Hanauer	116.523
1940	Hotsy Totsy III	*Sidney Allen	48.295	1987	Miller American	Chip Hanauer	127.620
1941	My Sin	*Z.G.Simmons,Jr	52.509	1988	Miss Circus Circus	Chip Hanauer	123.756
1942	Not held					& Jim Prevost	
1943	Not held			1989	Miss Budweiser	Tom D'Eath	131.209
1944	Not held			1990	Miss Budweiser	Tom D'Eath	143.176
1945	Not held			1991	Winston Eagle	Mark Tate	137.771
1946	Tempo VI	*Guy Lombardo	68.132				
1947	Miss Peps V	Danny Foster	57.000				

PRO RODEO
All-Around Champion Cowboy

In 1990, Ty Murray of Stephenville, Texas, became the undisputed king of professional rodeo cowboys at age 21 by winning his second consecutive All-Around championship. Murray, who qualified for the December National Finals in three events—bareback riding, saddle bronc riding and bull riding—also set a single season earnings record with $213,772.

The Professional Rodeo Cowboys Association (PRCA) title of All-Around World Champion Cowboy goes to the rodeo athlete who wins the most prize money in a single year in two or more events. Only prize money earned in sanctioned PRCA rodeos is counted. From 1929-44, All-Around champions were named by the Rodeo Association of America (earnings for those years is not available).

Multiple winners: Tom Ferguson and Larry Mahan (6); Jim Shoulders (5); Lewis Feild and Dean Oliver (3); Everett Bowman, Lewis Brooks, Clay Carr, Bill Linderman, Phil Lyne, Ty Murray, Gerald Roberts, Casey Tibbs and Harry Tompkins (2).

Year		Year		Year		Year	
1929	Earl Thode	1934	Leonard Ward	1939	Paul Carney	1943	Louis Brooks
1930	Clay Carr	1935	Everett Bowman	1940	Fritz Truan	1944	Louis Brooks
1931	John Schneider	1936	John Bowman	1941	Homer Pettigrew	1945	No award
1932	Donald Nesbit	1937	Everett Bowman	1942	Gerald Roberts	1946	No award
1933	Clay Carr	1938	Burel Mulkey				

Year		Earnings	Year		Earnings	Year		Earnings
1947	Todd Whatley	$18,642	1962	Tom Nesmith	$32,611	1977	Tom Ferguson	$65,981
1948	Gerald Roberts	21,766	1963	Dean Oliver	31,329	1978	Tom Ferguson	83,734
1949	Jim Shoulders	21,495	1964	Dean Oliver	31,150	1979	Tom Ferguson	96,272
1950	Bill Linderman	30,715	1965	Dean Oliver	33,163	1980	Paul Tierney	105,568
1951	Casey Tibbs	29,104	1966	Larry Mahan	40,358	1981	Jimmie Cooper	105,861
1952	Harry Tompkins	30,934	1967	Larry Mahan	51,996	1982	Chris Lybbert	123,709
1953	Bill Linderman	33,674	1968	Larry Mahan	49,129	1983	Roy Cooper	153,391
1954	Buck Rutherford	40,404	1969	Larry Mahan	57,726	1984	Dee Picket	122,618
1955	Casey Tibbs	42,065	1970	Larry Mahan	41,493	1985	Lewis Feild	130,347
1956	Jim Shoulders	43,381	1971	Phil Lyne	49,245	1986	Lewis Feild	166,042
1957	Jim Shoulders	33,299	1972	Phil Lyne	60,852	1987	Lewis Feild	144,335
1958	Jim Shoulders	32,212	1973	Larry Mahan	64,447	1988	Dave Appleton	121,546
1959	Jim Shoulders	32,905	1974	Tom Ferguson	66,929	1989	Ty Murray	134,806
1960	Harry Tompkins	32,522	1975	Tom Ferguson	50,300	1990	Ty Murray	213,772
1961	Benny Reynolds	31,309	1976	Tom Ferguson	87,908			

SOAP BOX DERBY
All-American Soap Box Derby

Paul Greenwald of Saginaw, Mich., won the Kit Division and Danny Garland of San Diego, won the Masters Division of the 1991 All-American Soap Box Derby, held before a crowd of 17,500 on Aug. 10 in Akron, Ohio.

The All-American Soap Box Derby is a coasting race for small gravity-powered cars built by their drivers and assembled within strict guidelines on size, weight and cost. The Derby got its name in the 1930s when most cars were built from wooden soap boxes. Held every summer on the second Saturday of August at Derby Downs in Akron, the Soap Box Derby is open to all boys and girls from 9 to 16 years old who qualify.

There are two competitive divisions: Kit Cars (ages 9-16), made up of racers assembled from Derby-approved car kits, and Masters (ages 12-16), made up of racers designed by drivers but constructed with Derby-approved hardware. The racing ramp at Derby Downs is 953.75 feet with an 11 percent grade.

One champion was determined at the All-American Soap Box Derby each year from 1934-75, then Junior and Senior division champions from 1976-87, then Kit Car and Masters champions since 1988.

Year		Hometown	Age	Year		Hometown	Age
1934	Robert Turner	Muncie, IN	11	1953	Fred Mohler	Muncie, IN	14
1935	Maurice Bale, Jr.	Anderson, IN	13	1954	Richard Kemp	Los Angeles	14
1936	Herbert Muench, Jr.	St.Louis	14	1955	Richard Rohrer	Rochester, NY	14
1937	Robert Ballard	White Plains, NY	12	1956	Norman Westfall	Rochester, NY	14
1938	Robert Berger	Omaha, NE	14	1957	Terry Townsend	Anderson, IN	14
1939	Clifton Hardesty	White Plains, NY	11	1958	James Miley	Muncie, IN	15
1940	Thomas Fisher	Detroit	12	1959	Barney Townsend	Anderson, IN	13
1941	Claude Smith	Akron, OH	14	1960	Fredric Lake	South Bend, IN	11
1942-45	Not held			1961	Dick Dawson	Wichita, KS	13
1946	Gilbert Klecan	San Diego	14	1962	David Mann	Gary, IN	14
1947	Kenneth Holmboe	Charleston, WV	14	1963	Harold Conrad	Duluth, MN	12
1948	Donald Strub	Akron, OH	13	1964	Gregory Schumacher	Tacoma, WA	14
1949	Fred Derks	Akron, OH	15	1965	Robert Logan	Santa Ana, CA	12
1950	Harold Williamson	Charleston, WV	15	1966	David Krussow	Tacoma, WA	12
1951	Darwin Cooper	Williamsport, PA	15	1967	Kenneth Cline	Lincoln, NE	13
1952	Joe Lunn	Columbus, GA	11	1968	Branch Lew	Muncie, IN	11
				1969	Steve Souter	Midland, TX	12

Year		Hometown	Age	Year		Hometown	Age
1970	Samuel Gupton	Durham, NC	13	1983	JR: Tony Carlini	Del Mar, CA	10
1971	Larry Blair	Oroville, CA	13		SR: Mike Burdgick	Flint, MI	14
1972	Robert Lange, Jr.	Boulder, CO	14	1984	JR: Chris Hess	Hamilton, OH	11
1973	Bret Yarborough	Elk Grove, CA	11		SR: Anita Jackson	St.Louis	15
1974	Curt Yarborough	Elk Grove, CA	11	1985	JR: Michael Gallo	Danbury, CT	12
1975	Karren Stead	Lower Bucks, PA	11		SR: Matt Sheffer	York, PA	14
1976	JR: Phil Raber	Sugarcreek, OH	11	1986	JR: Marc Behan	Dover, NH	9
	SR: Joan Ferdinand	Canton, OH	14		SR: Tami Jo Sullivan	Lancaster, OH	13
1977	JR: Mark Ferdinand	Canton, OH	10	1987	JR: Matt Margules	Danbury, CT	11
	SR: Steve Washburn	Bristol, CT	15		SR: Brian Drinkwater	Bristol, CT	14
1978	JR: Darren Hart	Salem, OR	11	1988	KIT: Jason Lamb	Des Moines, IA	10
	SR: Greg Cardinal	Flint, MI	13		MAS: David Duffield	Kansas City	13
1979	JR: Russell Yurk	Flint, MI	10	1989	KIT: David Schiller	Dayton, OH	12
	SR: Craig Kitchen	Akron, OH	14		MAS: Faith Chavarria	Ventura, CA	12
1980	JR: Chris Fulton	Indianapolis	11	1990	KIT: Mark Mihal	Valparaiso, IN	12
	SR: Dan Porul	Sherman Oaks, CA	12		MAS: Sami Jones	Salem, OR	13
1981	JR: Howie Fraley	Portsmouth, OH	11	1991	KIT: Paul Greenwald	Saginaw, MI	13
	SR: Tonia Schlegel	Hamilton, OH	13		MAS: Danny Garland	San Diego, CA	14
1982	JR: Carol A.Sullivan	Rochester, NH	10				
	SR: Matt Wolfgang	Lehigh Val., PA	12				

SOFTBALL

Men's and women's national champions since 1933 in Major Fast Pitch, Major Slow Pitch and Super Slow Pitch (menonly). Sanctioned by the Amateur Softball Association of America.

MEN

Major Fast Pitch

Year		Year		Year	
1933	J.L.Gill Boosters, Chicago	1955	Raybestos Cardinals, Stratford, CT	1976	Raybestos Cardinals
1934	Ke-Nash-A, Kenosha, WI			1977	Billard Barbell, Reading, PA
1935	Crimson Coaches, Toledo, OH	1956	Clearwater Bombers	1978	Billard Barbell
1936	Kodak Park, Rochester, NY	1957	Clearwater Bombers	1979	McArdle Pontiac/Cadillac, Midland, MI
1937	Briggs Body Team, Detroit	1958	Raybestos Cardinals		
1938	The Pohlers, Cincinnati	1959	Sealmasters, Aurora, IL	1980	Peterbilt Western, Seattle
1939	Carr's Boosters, Covington, KY			1981	Archer Daniels Midland, Decatur, IL
1940	Kodak Park, Rochester, NY	1960	Clearwater Bombers		
1941	Bendix Brakes, South Bend, IN	1961	Sealmasters	1982	Peterbilt Western
1942	Deep Rock Oilers, Tulsa, OK	1962	Clearwater Bombers	1983	Franklin Cardinals, Stratford, CT
1943	Hammer Air Field, Fresno, CA	1963	Clearwater Bombers		
1944	Hammer Air Field	1964	Burch Tool, Detroit	1984	California Kings, Merced, CA
1945	Zollner Pistons, Ft.Wayne, IN	1965	Sealmasters	1985	Pay'n Pak, Seattle
1946	Zollner Pistons	1966	Clearwater Bombers	1986	Pay'n Pak
1947	Zollner Pistons	1967	Sealmasters	1987	Pay'n Pak
1948	Briggs Beautyware, Detroit	1968	Clearwater Bombers	1988	TransAire, Elkhart, IN
1949	Tip Top Tailors, Toronto	1969	Raybestos Cardinals	1989	Penn Corp, Sioux City, IA
1950	Clearwater (FL) Bombers	1970	Raybestos Cardinals	1990	Penn Corp
1951	Dow Chemical, Midland, MI	1971	Welty Way, Cedar Rapids, IA	1991	Guanella Bros., Rohnert Park, CA
1952	Briggs Beautyware	1972	Raybestos Cardinals		
1953	Briggs Beautyware	1973	Clearwater Bombers		
1954	Clearwater Bombers	1974	Gianella Bros, Santa Rosa, CA		
		1975	Rising Sun Hotel, Reading, PA		

Major Slow Pitch

Year		Year		Year	
1953	Shields Construction, Newport, KY	1965	Skip Hogan A.C.	1979	Nelco Mfg.Co., Okla.City
1954	Waldneck's Tavern, Cincinnati	1966	Michael's Lounge, Detroit	1980	Campbell Carpets
1955	Lang Pet Shop, Covington, KY	1967	Jim's Sport Shop, Pittsburgh	1981	Elite Coating, Gordon, CA
1956	Gatliff Auto Sales, Newport, KY	1968	County Sports, Levittown, NY	1982	Triangle Sports, Minneapolis
		1969	Copper Hearth, Milwaukee	1983	No.1 Electric & Heating, Gastonia, NC
1957	Gatliff Auto Sales	1970	Little Caesar's, Southgate, MI		
1958	East Side Sports, Detroit	1971	Pile Drivers, Va.Beach, VA	1984	Lilly Air Systems, Chicago
1959	Yorkshire Restaurant, Newport, KY	1972	Jiffy Club, Louisville, KY	1985	Blanton's Fayetteville, NC
		1973	Howard's Furniture, Denver, NC	1986	Non-Ferrous Metals, Cleveland
1960	Hamilton Tailoring, Cincinnati	1974	Howard's Furniture	1987	Stapath, Monticello, KY
1961	Hamilton Tailoring	1975	Pyramid Cafe, Lakewood, OH	1988	Bell Corp/FAF, Tampa, FL
1962	Skip Hogan A.C., Pittsburgh	1976	Warren Motors, J'ville, FL	1989	Ritch's Salvage, Harrisburg, NC
1963	Gatliff Auto Sales	1977	Nelson Painting, Okla.City	1990	New Construction, Shelbyville,IN
1964	Skip Hogan A.C.	1978	Campbell Carpets, Concord, CA	1991	Riverside Paving, Louisville

Softball (Cont.)
Super Slow Pitch

Year		Year		Year	
1981	Howard's/Western Steer, Denver, NC	1985	Steele's Sports, Grafton, OH	1989	Ritch's Salvage, Harrisburg, NC
1982	Jerry's Catering, Miami	1986	Steele's Sports		
1983	Howard's/Western Steer	1987	Steele's Sports	1990	Steele's Silver Bullets
1984	Howard's/Western Steer	1988	Starpath, Monticello, KY	1991	Sun Belt/Worth, Atlanta

WOMEN
Major Fast Pitch

Year		Year		Year	
1933	Great Northerns, Chicago	1954	Leach Motor Rockets, Fresno, CA	1973	Raybestos Brakettes
1934	Hart Motors, Chicago			1974	Raybestos Brakettes
1935	Bloomer Girls, Cleveland	1955	Orange Lionettes	1975	Raybestos Brakettes
1936	Nat'l Screw & Mfg., Cleveland	1956	Orange Lionettes	1976	Raybestos Brakettes
1937	Nat'l Screw & Mfg.	1957	Hacienda Rockets, Fresno, CA	1977	Raybestos Brakettes
1938	J.J.Krieg's, Alameda, CA	1958	Raybestos Brakettes, Stratford, CT	1978	Raybestos Brakettes
1939	J.J.Krieg's			1979	Sun City (AZ) Saints
		1959	Raybestos Brakettes		
1940	Arizona Ramblers, Phoenix			1980	Raybestos Brakettes
1941	Higgins Midgets, Tulsa, OK	1960	Raybestos Brakettes	1981	Orlando (FL) Rebels
1942	Jax Maids, New Orleans	1961	Gold Sox, Whittier, CA	1982	Raybestos Brakettes
1943	Jax Maids	1962	Orange Lionettes	1983	Raybestos Brakettes
1944	Lind & Pomeroy, Portland, OR	1963	Raybestos Brakettes	1984	Los Angeles Diamonds
1945	Jax Maids	1964	Erv Lind Florists, Portland, OR	1985	Hi-Ho Brakettes, Stratford, CT
1946	Jax Maids	1965	Orange Lionettes	1986	So.California Invasion, LA
1947	Jax Maids	1966	Raybestos Brakettes	1987	Orange County Majestics, Anaheim, CA
1948	Arizona Ramblers	1967	Raybestos Brakettes		
1949	Arizona Ramblers	1968	Raybestos Brakettes	1988	Hi-Ho Brakettes (CT)
		1969	Orange Lionettes	1989	Whittier (CA) Raiders
1950	Orange (CA) Lionettes				
1951	Orange Lionettes	1970	Orange Lionettes	1990	Raybestos Brakettes
1952	Orange Lionettes	1971	Raybestos Brakettes	1991	Raybestos Brakettes
1953	Betsy Ross Rockets, Fresno, CA	1972	Raybestos Brakettes		

TRIATHLON
Ironman Championship

Multiple winners: Dave Scott (6); Paula Newby-Fraser (3); Mark Allen, Erin Baker, Sylviane Puntous and Scott Tinley (2).

MEN

Year	Date	Winner	Time	Runner-up	Margin	Start	Finish	Location
I	2/18/78	Gordon Haller	11:46	John Dunbar	34:00	15	12	Waikiki Beach
II	1/14/79	Tom Warren	11:15:56	John Dunbar	48:00	15	12	Waikiki Beach
III	1/10/80	Dave Scott	9:24:33	Chuck Neumann	1:08	108	95	Ala Moana Park
IV	2/14/81	John Howard	9:38:29	Tom Warren	26:00	326	299	Kailua-Kona
V	2/6/82	Scott Tinley	9:19:41	Dave Scott	17:16	580	541	Kailua-Kona
VI	10/9/82	Dave Scott	9:08:23	Scott Tinley	20:05	850	775	Kailua-Kona
VII	10/22/83	Dave Scott	9:05:57	Scott Tinley	0:33	964	835	Kailua-Kona
VIII	10/6/84	Dave Scott	8:54:20	Scott Tinley	24:25	1036	903	Kailua-Kona
IX	10/25/85	Scott Tinley	8:50:54	Chris Hinshaw	25:46	1018	965	Kailua-Kona
X	10/18/86	Dave Scott	8:28:37	Mark Allen	9:47	1039	951	Kailua-Kona
XI	10/10/87	Dave Scott	8:34:13	Mark Allen	11:06	1380	1284	Kailua-Kona
XII	10/22/88	Scott Molina	8:31:00	Mike Pigg	2:11	1277	1189	Kailua-Kona
XIII	10/15/89	Mark Allen	8:09:15	Dave Scott	0:58	1285	1231	Kailua-Kona
XIV	10/6/90	Mark Allen	8:28:17	Scott Tinley	9:23	1386	1255	Kailua-Kona

WOMEN

Year	Winner	Time	Runner-up	Year	Winner	Time	Runner-up
1978	No finishers			1984	Sylviane Puntous	10:25:13	Patricia Puntous
1979	Lyn Lemaire	12:55.00	None	1985	Joanne Ernst	10:25:22	Liz Bulman
				1986	Paula Newby-Fraser	9:49:14	Sylviane Puntous
1980	Robin Beck	11:21:24	Eve Anderson				
1981	Linda Sweeney	12:00:32	Sally Edwards	1987	Erin Baker	9:35:25	Sylviane Puntous
1982	Kathleen McCartney	11:09:40	Julie Moss	1988	P.Newby-Fraser	9:01:01	Erin Baker
				1989	P.Newby-Fraser	9:00:56	Sylviane Puntous
1982	Julie Leach	10:54:08	Joann Dahlkoetter	1990	Erin Baker	9:13:42	P.Newby-Fraser
1983	Sylviane Puntous	10:43:36	Patricia Puntous				

YACHTING
The America's Cup

International yacht racing was launched in 1851 when England's Royal Yacht Squadron staged a 60-mile regatta around the Isle of Wight and offered a silver trophy to the winner. The 101-foot schooner **America**, sent over by the New York Yacht Club, won the race and the prize. Originally called the Hundred-Guinea Cup, the trophy was renamed The America's Cup after the winning boat's owners deeded it to the NYYC with instructions to defend it whenever challenged.

From 1870-1980, the NYYC successfully defended the Cup 25 straight times; first in large schooners and J-class boats that measured up to 140 feet in overall length, then in 12-meter boats.

A foreign yacht finally won the Cup in 1983 when **Australia II** beat defender **Liberty** in the seventh and deciding race off Newport, R.I. Four years later, the San Diego Yacht Club's **Stars & Stripes** won the Cup back, sweeping the four races of the final series off Fremantle, Australia.

Then in 1988, New Zealand's Mercury Bay Boating Club, unwilling to wait the usual three- to four-year period between Cup defenses, challenged the SDYC to a match race, citing the Cup's 102-year-old Deed of Gift, which clearly stated that every challenge had to be honored. Mercury Bay announced it would race a 133-foot monohull. San Diego countered with a 60-foot catamaran. The resulting best-of-three series (Sept.7-8) was a mismatch as the SDYC's catamaran **Stars & Stripes** won two straight by margins of better than 18 and 21 minutes.

Mercury Bay syndicate leader Michael Fay protested the outcome and took the SDYC to court in New York State (where the Deed of Gift was first filed) claiming San Diego had violated the spirit of the deed by racing a catamaran instead of a monohull. N.Y.State Supreme Court judge Carmen Ciparick agreed and on March 28, 1989, ordered the SDYC to hand the Cup over to Mercury Bay. The SDYC refused, but did consent to the court's appointment of the New York Yacht Club as custodian of the Cup until an appeal was ruled on.

On Sept.19, 1989, the Appellate Division of the N.Y.Supreme Court overturned Ciparick's decision and awarded the Cup back to the SDYC. An appeal by Mercury Bay was denied by the N.Y.Court of Appeals on Apr.26, 1990, ending three years of legal wrangling.

The America's Cup will be defended in May, 1992, off San Diego. To avoid the chaos of 1988-90, a new class of boat—75-foot monohulls with 110-foot masts—has been agreed to by all potential competitors.

Note that (*) indicates skipper was also owner of the boat.

Schooners and J-Class Boats

Year	Winner	Skipper	Series	Loser	Skipper
1851	America	Richard Brown	—	—	
1870	Magic	Andrew Comstock	1-0	Cambria, GBR	J.Tannock
1871	Columbia (2-1)	Nelson Comstock	4-0	Livonia, GBR	J.R.Woods
	& Sappho (2-0)	Sam Greenwood			
1876	Madeleine	Josephus Williams	2-0	Countess of Dufferin, CAN	J.E.Ellsworth
1881	Mischief	Nathanael Clock	2-0	Atalanta, CAN	Alexander Cuthbert*
1885	Puritan	Aubrey Crocker	2-0	Genesta, GBR	John Carter
1886	Mayflower	Martin Stone	2-0	Galatea, GBR	Dan Bradford
1887	Volunteer	Henry Haff	2-0	Thistle, GBR	John Barr
1893	Vigilant	William Hansen	3-0	Valkyrie II, GBR	Wm.Granfield
1895	Defender	Henry Haff	3-0	Valkyrie III, GBR	Wm.Granfield
1899	Columbia	Charles Barr	3-0	Shamrock I, GBR	Archie Hogarth
1901	Columbia	Charles Barr	3-0	Shamrock II, GBR	E.A.Sycamore
1903	Reliance	Charles Barr	3-0	Shamrock III, GBR	Bob Wringe
1920	Resolute	Charles F.Adams	3-2	Shamrock IV, GBR	William Burton
1930	Enterprise	Harold Vanderbilt*	4-0	Shamrock V, GBR	Ned Heard
1934	Rainbow	Harold Vanderbilt*	4-2	Endeavour, GBR	T.O.M.Sopwith
1937	Ranger	Harold Vanderbilt*	4-0	Endeavour II, GBR	T.O.M.Sopwith

12-Meter Boats

Year	Winner	Skipper	Series	Loser	Skipper
1958	Columbia	Briggs Cunningham	4-0	Sceptre, GBR	Graham Mann
1962	Weatherly	Bus Mosbacher	4-1	Gretel, AUS	Jock Sturrock
1964	Constellation	Bob Bavier & Eric Ridder	4-0	Sovereign, AUS	Peter Scott
1967	Intrepid	Bus Mosbacher	4-0	Dame Pattie, AUS	Jock Sturrock
1970	Intrepid	Bill Ficker	4-1	Gretel II, AUS	Jim Hardy
1974	Courageous	Ted Hood	4-0	Southern Cross, AUS	John Cuneo
1977	Courageous	Ted Turner	4-0	Australia	Noel Robins
1980	Freedom	Dennis Conner	4-1	Australia	Jim Hardy
1983	Australia II	John Bertrand	4-3	Liberty, USA	Dennis Conner
1987	Stars & Stripes	Dennis Conner	4-0	Kookaburra III, AUS	Iain Murray

60-ft Catamaran vs 133-ft Monohull

Year	Winner	Skipper	Series	Loser	Skipper
1988	Stars & Stripes	Dennis Conner	2-0	New Zealand, NZE	David Barnes

Other 1991 Championships

Championships held in 1991 unless otherwise indicated.

Arena Football

Arena Indoor League . . . . Tampa Bay Storm

Australian Rules Football
Victoria Football League

Grand Final . . . . Hawthorn Hawks

Billiards
World Championships

Men's Pro 9-ball . . . . Earl Strickland, USA
Women's Pro 9-ball . . . . Robin Bell, USA

U.S. Open Champions

Men's 9-ball . . . . Buddy Hall, Metropolis, IL
Women's 9-ball . . . . Ewa Mataya, Grand Ledge, MI

Cricket
England vs. Australia

The Ashes. . . . . Australia

West Indies vs. Australia

Sir Frank Worrell Trophy . . . . West Indies

Curling
World Champions

Men . . . . Scotland (skip: David Smith)
Women . . . . Norway (skip: Dordi Nordby)

U.S. Champions

Men . . . . Madison, WI (skip: Steve Brown)
Women . . . . Houston (skip: Maymar Gemmell)

Drag Racing
NHRA U.S. Nationals

Top Fuel . . . . Kenny Bernstein
Funny Car . . . . Jim White
Pro Stock . . . . Darrell Alderman

1990 NHRA Overall Champions

Top Fuel . . . . Joe Amato
Funny Car . . . . John Force
Pro Stock . . . . Darrell Alderman

Equestrian
Volvo World Cup

Show Jumping . . . . John Whitaker, GBR
Dressage . . . . Kyra Kyrklund, FIN

1991 U.S. Champions

Show Jumping . . . . Lisa Jacquin, Collegeville, PA
Dressage . . . . Carol Lavel, Fairfax, VT

Handball
World Championships
FOUR-WALL

Men . . . . Poncho Monreal, MEX
Women . . . . Anna Engele, USA
Open doubles . . . . Doug Glatt & Rod Prince, USA

U.S. Champions
FOUR-WALL

Men . . . . John Bike, Austin, TX
Women . . . . Anna Engele, St.Paul, MN

Horseshoe Pitching
1991 World Champions

Men . . . . Walter Ray Williams, Jr., Stockton, CA
Women . . . . Tari Powell, Rossville, IL

Indoor Lacrosse

Major Indoor League . . . . Detroit Turbos

Motorcycle Racing
ROAD RACING
Grand Prix Champions

125 cc . . . . Loris Capirossi, ITA
250 cc . . . . Luca Cadalora, ITA
500 cc . . . . Wayne Rainey, USA

MOTORCROSS
Motorcross des Nations

Team . . . . USA (Jeff Stanton, Mike Kiedrowski
& Damon Bradshaw)

Grand Prix Champions

125 cc . . . . Stefan Everts, BEL
250 cc . . . . Trampas Parker, USA
500 cc . . . . Georges Jobe, BEL

Racquetball
U.S. Amateur Champions

Men . . . . Tim Sweeney, Chicago
Women . . . . Michelle Gilman, Boise, ID

U.S. Pro Champions

Men . . . . Mike Ray, Atlanta
Women . . . . Michelle Gilman

Rugby
International Champions

World Cup . . . . Oct.2-Nov.3 (at N.Zealand)
Five Nations . . . . England

U.S. Champions

Club . . . . Old Mission Beach A.C. of San Diego
College . . . . California (Berkeley)

Volleyball
World Champions

1991: Men . . . . Nov. 22-30 (Japan)
 Women . . . . Nov. 8-16 (Japan)
1990: Men . . . . Italy
 Women . . . . USSR

U.S. Open Champions

Men's Gold Div . . . . Offshore, Woodland Hills, CA
Women's Gold Div . . . . Fitness, Champaign, IL

Pro Beach Tours
MEN (AVP)

Manhattan Beach Open . . . . Karch Kiraly & Kent Steffes
U.S.Championships . . . . Ricci Luyties & Adam Johnson
World Invitational . . . . Karch Kiraly & Kent Steffes

WOMEN (WPVA)

World Championships . . . . Linda Chisholm-Carrilo
& Liz Masakayan
U.S.Open . . . . Gail Castro & Lori Kostas

Water Skiing
World Champions

Overall: Men . . . . Patrice Martin, FRA
 Women . . . . Karen Neville, AUS

U.S. Open Champions

Overall: Men . . . . Sammy Duvall, USA
 Women . . . . Karen Neville, AUS

Skip Dickstein

Jockey **Jerry Bailey** exults after riding Hansel to victory in the Preakness.
They also won the Belmont for two-thirds of the 1991 Triple Crown.

HORSE RACING

HORSE RACING
by Sharon B. Smith

Ghosts

*Deaths of Northern Dancer and Alydar close tragic 1990;
ACRS debuts in 1991; Hansel wins Preakness and Belmont.*

Northern Dancer's death on Nov. 16, 1990, was neither surprising nor shocking. The most significant thoroughbred stallion of the century had been gone from the racetrack for 26 years and away from the breeding shed for nearly four. He was very old and very ill.

Turf writers and other admirers had planned to honor the 1964 Kentucky Derby and Preakness winner with respectful remembrances of his accomplishments. In other years, the only sadness would have been for the law of nature that makes a mere 29 years a very long life for a horse.

As it turned out, however, the Dancer's death was a jolting, final blow in what had to be the most agonizing three weeks in racing history. Less than 24 hours before the old stallion died, the breeding industry lost a horse who was much younger and nearly as important when Alydar was humanely destroyed following a stall accident that broke his rear right leg. Alydar was a very good racehorse—second to Affirmed in each of the Triple Crown races in 1978—but a great stallion. He was about half a length behind Affirmed on the racetrack and at least a furlong ahead in the breeding shed.

Sharon B. Smith is a contributing Editor of *Horse Illustrated* magazine and has been a reporter and commentator for ESPN and NBC Sports.

Within six months of Alydar's death, one son (Criminal Type) was to become Horse of the Year, another (Strike the Gold) won the Kentucky Derby, and Alydar himself was named posthumously as the world's leading stallion for 1990. Alydar's demise at the age of 15 was a disaster for his owners at troubled Calumet Farm (see box) and a tragedy for the entire sport. Furthermore, the sport had not yet recovered from still another tragedy less than three weeks earlier.

Indeed, it's hard to look at Breeders' Cup Day 1990 as anything but racing's blackest day. Certainly, Ruffian's destruction after the ill-conceived Match Race with Foolish Pleasure caused a pain that is still felt more than 16 years later. But the sheer impact of what happened on October 27 at New York's Belmont Park had never been felt before. The day started with disaster in the Breeders' Cup Sprint, when the popular older horse Mr. Nickerson died on the track from a pulmonary hemorrhage. A second horse, longshot Shaker Knit fell over him and suffered a fatal fracture. One race, two deaths. Nothing so bad had ever happened on racing's showcase day. But something much worse was yet to come.

The Distaff had been the most eagerly anticipated race of the day, featuring the two reigning champions among fillies and mares—three-year-old Go for Wand and five-year-old Bayakoa. Both were

Go For Wand and jockey Randy Romero hit the dirt during the final stretch of the 1990 Breeders' Cup Distaff at Belmont. Romero was not seriously hurt, but the 3-year-old filly snapped her right front ankle and had to be destroyed.

fast, consistent, and greatly admired. Go for Wand was particularly beloved by fans in New York for her grace and gritty determination. She wasn't quite Ruffian, but she wasn't far behind.

As the two thundered down the stretch head-to-head, far in front of the others, fans thought they were seeing the best that racing can offer. Instead, they saw the worst that racing can do. Go for Wand was leading by inches on the inside when she took a bad step. Her ankle splintered and she tumbled to the track. Go for Wand—healthy, sound, and never over-raced—had suffered an irreparable fracture and was put to death directly in front of the grandstand.

Bayakoa's trainer Ron McAnally accepted his winner's trophy with tears in his eyes. "They give their lives for our enjoyment," he told reporters. He knew his real victory was being able to take his mare home.

Unbridled's win in the $3 million Breeders' Cup Classic an hour later was overshadowed by the calamity, both on the day of the race and in the reports and discussions afterwards. But his impressive performance did much to restore equilib-rium in his sport, as did the fact that he returned to race at the age of four.

Unbridled was not the 1990 Horse of the Year—that honor went to Alydar's recently retired son Criminal Type—but he was three-year-old champion and went to the top of the list of good older horses set to compete in 1991.

The handicap horses had a lucrative new forum in which to display their talents. Ten important events for older horses—including most of the time-honored handicap races—were designated as the American Championship Racing Series. In addition to the substantial purses they could win in each race, the four horses with the highest point totals for placing in ACRS races would split a $1.5 million bonus at the completion of the series in September.

The objective was to create a season-long competition and test of mettle. Its organizers felt that a season's champion shouldn't be crowned at the one-day Breeders' Cup. As luck would have it, the inaugural ACRS season may have actually made Breeders' Cup Day 1991 even more important. Seven different horses won the 10 races. The winners included

5-year olds Festin and the late-blooming Black Tie Affair. Slightly more impressive were 4-year-olds In Excess, who ran the best race of the season in the Woodward Stakes on Sept. 15, and Farma Way, the Woodward runner-up who won the series' top bonus of $750,000. Other ACRS winners included 4-year-olds Jolie's Halo and Marquetry, and the 3-year-old Best Pal. Three-year-old? Don't they have their own series—a little something called the Triple Crown?

Indeed they do. Best Pal, who was not quite good enough in either the Kentucky Derby or the Preakness, tried an easier task in August. He dominated the million dollar Pacific Classic against almost all of the best ACRS horses. His easy win gave weight to what several trainers and riders had been saying for months—that the three-year-olds of 1991, although lacking a single standout, were something to savor.

The pre-Triple Crown season started on a high note, with 1990's two-year-old champion Fly So Free maintaining his lofty status with his winter performances in Florida. Dinard was equally impressive in California, and Unbridled's little brother Cahill Road thrilled the crowds in New York's Wood Memorial. The handsome Hansel dominated the Kentucky prep races. But by Derby Day on May 4, Dinard and Cahill Road were out with leg injuries, leaving Hansel as the Derby favorite.

In the meantime, the rapidly-improving Alydar colt Strike the Gold, a fast-closing second to Fly So Free in the Florida Derby, had turned the tables on the champion in the Blue Grass Stakes two weeks before the Kentucky Derby.

"You couldn't want a horse to come up to the Derby any better," said Strike the Gold's trainer Nick Zito. "He did everything right." Nor did he do anything wrong in the big race.

Strike the Gold, who went off third choice to Hansel and Fly So Free, broke 12th of 16, improved steadily for the first mile, then swept to the lead in the stretch, beating Best Pal to the wire by nearly two lengths. Fly So Free was a tired fifth and Hansel was 10th. Strike the Gold's win was impressive enough to make him a heavy favorite at Pimlico for the Preakness two weeks later. But he broke poorly, had to be rushed to remain in contention, and declined to run his race.

Bankruptcy Of Calumet Stuns Racing

It was the racing equivalent of the Fall of the Roman Empire or the stock market crash of '29.

It was epochal, shocking, and the result of outside forces, economic circumstance and the nature of the people involved.

It was the announcement on July 11, 1991, that historic Calumet Farm—breeders of Triple Crown winners Whirlaway and Citation and Triple Crown runner-up Alydar—had filed for bankruptcy. Calumet was $118 million in debt, while a partnership that owned many of the farm's broodmares was nearly $17 million in the red. The farm had been on the market for several months.

The filing came two months after Calumet-bred Strike the Gold won the Kentucky Derby and six months after Calumet-bred and co-owned Criminal Type was voted Horse of the Year for 1990. The farm had even received its first Eclipse Award as top breeder in North America in 1990.

Calumet was forced into bankruptcy court just nine years after a change of management put the farm under the control of J.T. Lundy, who had married into the family that created Calumet.

Lundy took over a breeding establishment that had sent some of the greatest names in American sporting history to the racetrack. Under the direction of Warren Wright Sr., Calumet horses won almost every major stake in North America. The two Triple Crown winners—Whirlaway and Citation—were nearly joined by a third when Tim Tam just missed in 1958. Among the victories: eight Kentucky Derbies, seven Peaknesses, six Arlington Classics, and five Kentucky Oaks. Calumet was the most successful Thoroughbred operation in the world. Although the big wins were not as frequent as they were thirty years before, the reputation remained virtually intact into the 1980's.

The farm was clear of debt when the management change occurred in 1982. It owned a collection of broodmares envied by breeders around the world. What's more, there were already indications that Alydar—whose first foals were handsome yearlings—might turn into a big red moneymaker.

Historic **Calumet Farm**, breeder of Triple Crown winners Whirlaway and Citation and Triple Crown runner-up Alydar, reported debts of $118 million in 1991.

Those indications were correct, and then some. Alydar became one of the world's leading sires, worth $15 to $20 million each year in income to Calumet. His destruction on Nov. 15, 1990, after a stall accident was a financial disaster for the farm, but not the death knell. That had been sounded months earlier.

So what went wrong? How do you go from being debt-free to as much as $134 million in the hole in less than 10 years—while succeeding in your industry at the same time? You do it by being a major player in the thoroughbred business during the latter half of the booming 1980s.

Calumet was not alone in its misfortune. Dozens of other racing operations, large and small, have self-destructed during the past decade. The causes have been many. The Tax Reform Act of 1986 hurt by eliminating capital gain protection and by restricting the tax benefits of passive partnerships, both of which were important in racing and breeding ownership. The overall recession in the U.S. economy hurt, too. But there was something else.

"Megalomania, I think," says bloodstock agent and consultant Arnold Kirkpatrick of Kentucky. Kirkpatrick watched a few years ago as his then-employer, Spendthrift Farm, suffered through a similar calamity. These farms and others, he says, began investing too heavily in unraced yearlings, in broodmares, in stud fees, and—worst of all—in unproven, multi-million dollar stallions.

Auctions and stallion syndications became feeding frenzies. Horsemen spent money that could not possibly be won back at the racetrack, even with good racing luck.

Kirkpatrick says of his industry, "For over a decade we lost sight of the fact that the basic foundation of the thoroughbred business is racing." Kirkpatrick believes the breeding industry is righting itself, but not soon enough to save the family farm for the people of Calumet. "The prices are getting more realistic," he says, "but I think we've got a little downward trend still ahead of us before we begin to recover."

Calumet will remain, in one form or another. It's too important to the sport and it's too beloved by the people of Kentucky to be turned into 880 acres of building lots. But whether another horse of the caliber of Citation or Alydar ever again gallops over those 880 acres remains to be seen.

Europe's best 3-year-old was **Generous**, seen here romping to victory in the Irish Derby in June. The direct descendant of Northern Dancer also won the English Derby and King George VI and Queen Elizabeth Diamond Stakes.

"That was the only way he was going to be discredited," trainer Zito said later. "He just doesn't want to be rushed. It was his only bad race this year."

Hansel, on the other hand, ran a perfect race—breaking sharply, stalking the leaders through the first half, then flying through the stretch to win by seven lengths. As jockey Jerry Bailey told the crowd afterwards, "He just ran out of his skin."

In spite of the contrasting performances, Strike the Gold was favored by the 51,000 fans at Belmont Park for the final leg of the Triple Crown on June 8. It was his home track, after all, and there

were questions about Hansel's ability to race without Lasix, the anti-bleeding drug.

After the race, there were no questions about the speed or heart of either horse. Each ran his race, with Hansel stalking the pacemakers to the stretch and Strike the Gold dropping well back. The Preakness winner had the lead by mid-stretch with the Derby winner flying on the outside. They went under the wire with Hansel inches in front of Strike the Gold in one of the fastest Belmonts ever at 2:28.

It's a good thing he has a long neck," Hansel's trainer Frank Brothers quipped to reporters after the race. Indeed, the finish was the closest since Strike the Gold's sire Alydar lost by a similar margin to Affirmed in 1978. Mane Minister was third, as he had been in the Derby and Preakness. No horse had ever done that before.

Hansel and Strike the Gold each rested, then came back later in the summer with third place finishes in 3-year-old stakes races. Fly So Free and Best Pal resurfaced with big wins and Lost Mountain developed into a championship contender.

All but Best Pal showed up for the Travers Stakes at Saratoga in August, but none was able to stake a claim as the division leader. Corporate Report, second in the Preakness but unplaced in the other two classics, led wire to wire. Hansel acquitted himself best of the rest, running a game second on what turned out to be an injured right foreleg. The colts entered the fall in a six-way race for divisional honors.

There was no such competition among 3-year-olds in Europe. One colt emerged as the best—so much so that he was spoken of as one of the best horses to appear on the British turf in years. The colt was Generous, who became only the sixth horse to win the three big races of the summer in the British Isles: the English and Irish Derbies, plus the richest race for handicappers, the King George VI and Queen Elizabeth Diamond Stakes. Generous, like the majority of the year's classic winners in Europe, is a direct descendant of Northern Dancer, whose influence will exceed his actual lifespan by a few centuries.

While the colts born in 1988 constitute an outstanding group, they may not be that much better than the fillies of the same crop. And the colts certainly fell

Corporate raider **Carl Icahn** (left) and master rapper **M.C. Hammer** (center, in shades) became friendly rivals during the summer when their fillies, Meadow Star and Lite Light, met twice and won one race each.

short of the fillies in the celebrity-ownership stakes. In one corner, there was Carl Icahn, the multi-millionaire corporate wheeler-dealer, whose filly Meadow Star was the returning champion of her division. In the other, the multi-millionaire Stanley Burrell—better known to rap music fans as M.C. Hammer—whose family's Lite Light developed during 1991 into a championship-level competitor. The Icahn-Hammer personal bets on meetings between the fillies ranged from $35,000 to $150,000, with the money going to favorite charities.

In Belmont's Mother Goose Stakes, Meadow Star prevailed by a nose. In the Coaching Club American Oaks a month later, Lite Light ran away by seven lengths. The scorecard was even, with more competition between them expected in the fall.

But other pretenders to the title emerged during the summer. A pretty daughter of Danzig named Versailles Treaty won the big filly race of the summer, the Alabama at Saratoga, and served notice that a multi-front war might be beginning rather than ending.

North of the border, another daughter of Danzig outdid them all when Dance Smartly became the first filly ever to win the Canadian Triple Crown—sweeping the Queen's Plate, the Prince of Wales Stakes, and the Breeders' Stakes to earn a million dollar bonus and acknowledgement as one of the finest horses ever to race in Canada. Jockey Pat Day rode her to victory in all three races.

In harness racing, a female horse also shone. Peace Corps, American-bred and Swedish-owned, tied a world record for trotters going a mile-and-a-half with her 12th straight win, a victory in the International Trot.

"She's the best horse in the world," owner Bjorn Petterson told reporters at Yonkers Raceway after the race. Few who saw her would disagree.

The three-year-old pacer Precious Bunny became the first harness horse to

Equi-photo

Jack Moiseyev won his first Hambletonian in 1991, driving Giant Victory to the win at the Meadowlands.

win two million-dollar races in one season with his victories in the North American Cup and the Meadowlands Pace. He then equalled a Yonkers track record with driver Jack Moiseyev in the Rooney Pace and tied a world record in the Adios in Pennsylvania.

The three-year-old trotter Giant Victory gave Moiseyev another big win at the Meadowlands on Aug.3, with a two-heat victory in the Hambletonian. Park Avenue Joe also won a Hambletonian in 1991, when a New Jersey appeals court finally laid to rest the controversy over the 1989 edition of the race. That year, Park Avenue Joe and Probe dead-heated in the raceoff, but Joe got the win based on a placing comparison. Nearly two years after Probe's owners challenged the decision of the Meadowlands stewards, Joe's owners were awarded the winner's purse for harness racing's most prestigious event.

The two most premier events in cross-country steeplechasing made big news in 1991 when a 22-year old rider became the first woman to win both in one year. Sanna Neilson rode Tom Bob to victory in the Maryland Hunt Cup, then came back a week later to win the Virginia Gold Cup aboard Joe's OK.

For another jockey, 1991 was the worst of years. In 1990, Bill Shoemaker, the most successful jockey in thoroughbred history, retired after four decades of riding. Within a year he was enjoying success in his new career as a trainer. But on Apr. 8, Shoemaker fractured his spine in a one-car accident near Los Angeles. As a rider, Shoemaker was able to walk away from countless racetrack spills and dozens of racing injuries. After his automobile accident, however, he faces life in a wheelchair.

Racing lost a legendary figure when 66-year-old Laz Barrera died in California on Apr. 25, a day after being hospitalized for pneumonia. Barrera learned the trainer's trade at Oriental Park near Havana, honed his talents in Mexico, then watched them flourish when he moved north of the border in the 1960's. In 1976, Barrera trained the sprinter Bold Forbes to last the 10 furlongs of the Kentucky Derby and the 12 furlongs of the Belmont Stakes. Three years later, he trained Triple Crown winner Affirmed to beat the handsomer and possibly faster Alydar almost every time they met. Barrera won four consecutive Eclipse Awards as trainer of the year from 1976-79 and was elected to the Horse Racing Hall of Fame in 1979.

As much as racing people like to look back and reminisce, they prefer to talk about the future and of Kentucky Derbies to come. The summer of 1991 saw the promising debuts of such two-year-olds as the Danzig colt Lure, who broke a Belmont Park track record the first time he set foot on a racetrack. There was Pine Bluff, another son of Danzig (and from the dam of the outstanding Demons Begone), who set a Saratoga crowd to buzzing one steamy August day. And how about Al Sabin, a product of Alydar and Sabin? Saratoga fans saw a performance worthy of his pedigree.

They also saw in Al Sabin the closing of a circle. Alydar is gone, and Sabin's grandsire Northern Dancer is gone. But the blood of thoroughbreds lives on, to the great joy of people who love to see them run. □

THE 1992 INFORMATION PLEASE SPORTS ALMANAC

HORSE RACING
STATISTICS
THE SEASON IN REVIEW
1990-1991
THOROUGHBRED • HARNESS

SEC A

PAGE 621

Thoroughbred Racing
Major Stakes Races
Winners of major stakes races from Sept. 9, 1990 through Sept. 15,1991; (F) indicates furlongs.

LATE 1990

Date	Race	Location	Miles	Winner	Jockey	Value to Winner
Sept. 9	Molson Export Million	Woodbine	1¼	Izvestia	D.J.Seymour	$600,000
Sept. 15	Woodward Stakes	Belmont	1⅛	Dispersal	Chris Antley	354,000
Sept. 23	Man o'War Stakes	Belmont	1⅜	Defensive Play	Pat Eddery	284,160
Sept. 23	Super Derby	La.Downs	1¼	Home At Last	Jerry Bailey	600,000
Oct. 6	Jockey Club Gold Cup	Belmont	1¼	Flying Continental	Corey Black	503,100
Oct. 6	Champagne Stakes	Belmont	1	Fly So Free	Jose Santos	381,600
Oct. 6	Oak Tree Invitational	Santa Anita	1½	Rail	Rafael Meza	300,000
Oct. 7	Arc de Triomphe	Longchamp	1½	Saumarez	Gerald Moss	853,500
Oct. 7	Turf Classic	Belmont	1½	Cacoethes	Ray Cochrane	360,000
Oct. 12	Meadowlands Cup	Meadowlands	1⅛	Great Normand	Carlos Lopez	300,000
Oct. 14	Rothmans International	Woodbine	1½	French Glory	Pat Eddery	619,650
Oct. 21	Budweiser International	Laurel	1¼	Fly Till Dawn	Laffit Pincay,Jr.	450,000
Oct. 22	Fla.Stallion Stakes	Calder	1¹/₁₆	Doradoradora	M.A.Gonzalez	276,000
Oct. 27	Breeders' Cup Classic	Belmont	1¼	Unbridled	Pat Day	1,350,000
Oct. 27	Breeders' Cup Turf	Belmont	1½	In the Wings	Gary Stevens	900,000
Oct. 27	Breeders' Cup Distaff	Belmont	1⅛	Bayakoa	Laffit Pincay.Jr.	450,000
Oct. 27	Breeders' Cup Mile	Belmont	1	Royal Academy	Lester Piggott	450,000
Oct. 27	Breeders' Cup Fillies	Belmont	1¹/₁₆	Meadow Star	Jose Santos	450,000
Oct. 27	Breeders' Cup Sprint	Belmont	6 F	Safely Kept	Craig Perret	450,000
Oct. 27	Breeders' Cup Juvenile	Belmont	1¹/₁₆	Fly So Free	Jose Santos	450,000
Nov. 3	NYRA Mile Handicap	Aqueduct	1	Quiet American	Chris McCarron	382,800
Nov. 24	Hawthorne Gold Cup	Hawthorne	1¼	Black Tie Affair	Jaime Diaz	307,800
Nov. 25	Hollywood Starlet Stakes	Hollywood	1	Cuddles	Gary Stevens	247,500
Dec. 9	Hollywood Futurity	Hollywood	1	Best Pal	Jose Santos	495,000
Dec. 16	Hollywood Turf Cup	Hollywood	1½	Itsallgreektome	Corey Nakatani	275,000

1991 (through Sept. 15)

Date	Race	Location	Miles	Winner	Jockey	Value to Winner
Feb. 9	Donn Handicap*	Gulfstream	1⅛	Jolie's Halo	Robin Platts	$300,000
Feb. 10	Charles H.Strub Stakes	Santa Anita	1¼	Defensive Play	Jose Santos	275,000
Mar. 9	Santa Anita Handicap*	Santa Anita	1¼	Farma Way	Gary Stevens	550,000
Mar. 16	Florida Derby	Gulfstream	1⅛	Fly So Free	Jose Santos	300,000
Mar. 30	Jim Beam Stakes	Turfway	1⅛	Hansel	Jerry Bailey	300,000
Apr. 6	Santa Anita Derby	Santa Anita	1⅛	Dinard	Chris McCarron	275,000
Apr. 13	Blue Grass Stakes	Keeneland	1⅛	Strike the Gold	Chris Antley	260,520
Apr. 13	California Derby	Golden Gate	1⅛	Green Alligator	Corey Nakatani	165,000
Apr. 13	Oaklawn Handicap*	Oaklawn	1⅛	Festin (ARG)	Eddie Delahoussaye	300,000
Apr. 20	Arkansas Derby	Oaklawn	1⅛	Olympio	Eddie Delahoussaye	300,000
Apr. 20	Wood Memorial	Aqueduct	1⅛	Cahill Road	Craig Perret	300,000
May 4	Kentucky Derby	Churchill Dns	1¼	Strike the Gold	Chris Antley	655,800
May 11	Pimlico Special*	Pimlico	1³/₁₆	Farma Way	Gary Stevens	450,000
May 18	Preakness Stakes	Pimlico	1³/₁₆	Hansel	Jerry Bailey	432,770
May 25	Acorn Stakes	Belmont	1	Meadow Star	Jerry Bailey	103,680
May 27	Metropolitan Handicap	Belmont	1	In Excess (IRE)	Pat Valenzuela	300,000
May 27	Hollywood Turf Handicap	Hollywood	1¼	Exbourne	Gary Stevens	275,000
May 27	Jersey Derby	Garden State	1¼	Greek Costume	Mike Smith	180,000

Major Stakes (Cont.)

Date	Race	Location	Miles	Winner	Jockey	Value to Winner
June 5	The English Derby	Epsom Downs	1½	Generous (IRE)	Alan Munro	$689,943
June 8	Belmont Stakes	Belmont	1½	Hansel	Jerry Bailey	1,417,480†
June 8	Nassau County Handicap*	Belmont	1⅛	Festin (ARG)	Eddie Delahoussaye	300,000
June 9	Mother Goose Stakes	Belmont	1⅛	Meadow Star	Jerry Bailey	120,000
June 29	Hollywood Gold Cup*	Hollywood	1¼	Marquetry	David Flores	550,000
June 30	The Irish Derby	Curragh	1½	Generous (IRE)	Alan Munro	654,936
July 4	Suburban Handicap	Belmont	1¼	In Excess (IRE)	Gary Stevens	300,000
July 7	Queen's Plate	Woodbine	1¼	Dance Smartly	Pat Day	234,840
July 20	New England Classic*	Rockingham	1⅛	Marquetry	David Flores	300,000
July 21	Caesar's International	Atlantic City	1 3/16	Exbourne	Chris McCarron	300,000
July 27	King George VI and Queen Elizabeth Diamond Stakes	Ascot	1½	Generous (IRE)	Alan Munro	537,339
July 27	Haskell Invitational	Monmouth	1⅛	Lost Mountain	Craig Perret	300,000
July 28	Prince of Wales Stakes	Fort Erie	1 3/16	Dance Smartly	Pat Day	111,640
Aug. 3	Whitney Handicap	Saratoga	1⅛	In Excess (IRE)	Gary Stevens	150,000
Aug. 10	Alabama Stakes	Saratoga	1¼	Versailles Treaty	Angel Cordero,Jr.	120,000
Aug. 10	Pacific Classic*	Del Mar	1¼	Best Pal	Pat Valenzuela	550,000
Aug. 17	Travers Stakes	Saratoga	1¼	Corporate Report	Chris McCarron	600,000
Aug. 18	Breeders' Stakes	Woodbine	1½	Dance Smartly	Pat Day	1,182,140†
Aug. 31	Beverly D.Stakes	Arlington	1 3/16	Fire the Groom	Gary Stevens	300,000
Sept. 1	Arlington Million	Arlington	1¼	Tight Spot	Laffit Pincay, Jr.	600,000
Sept. 1	Philip Iselin Handicap*	Monmouth	1⅛	Black Tie Affair	Pat Day	300,000
Sept. 15	Woodward Stakes*	Belmont	1⅛	In Excess	Gary Stevens	300,000

*One of 10 races in the inaugural American Championship Racing Series.
†Includes $1 million bonus

117th Kentucky Derby

Grade I for three-year-olds; 8th race at Churchill Downs in Louisville. **Date**—May 4, 1991; **Distance**—1¼ miles; **Stakes purse**—$905,800 ($655,800 to winner); **Track**—fast; **Off**—5:36 pm.

Winner—Strike the Gold; **Time**—2:03; **Won**—Driving; **Bloodlines**—Ch C, by Alydar-Majestic Gold, by Hatchet Man; **Breeder**—Calumet Farm (Ky.).

	PP	Finish	To $1	Jockey	Trainer	Owner
Strike the Gold	5	1—1¾	4.80	Chris Antley	Nick Zito	B.Giles Brophy
Best Pal	15	2—1¾	5.20	Gary Stevens	Ian Jory	Mr. & Mrs.John Mabee
Mane Minister	10	3—head	86.90	Alex Solis	Juan Gonzalez	John Toffan & Trudy McCaffery
Green Alligator	8	4—¾	16.30	Corey Nakatani	Murray Johnson	Anderson Fowler
Fly So Free	1	5—1¾	3.30	Jose Santos	Scotty Schulhofer	Verne Winchell
Quintana	16	6—½	28.50	Angel Cordero,Jr.	David Cross	Gary Garber
Paulrus	11	7—head	16.30	Shane Sellers	Steve Penrod	Warner Jones
Sea Cadet	4	8—2	15.90	Chris McCarron	Ron McAnally	Verne Winchell
Corporate Report	12	9—2	8.70	Pat Day	D.Wayne Lucas	Overbrook Farm
Hansel	6	10—head	2.50	Jerry Bailey	Frank Brothers	Lazy Lane Farm
Happy Jazz Band	14	11—½	107.80	Cash Asmussen	Phil Gleaves	Straus Medina Farm
Lost Mountain	9	12—8½	72.60	Herb McCauley	Tom Bohannan	Loblolly Stable
Another Review	13	13—neck	16.30	Art Madrid,Jr.	John Campo	Buckland Farm
Alydavid	2	14—1½	17.80	Corey Black	Phil Hauswald	David's Farm
Wilder Than Ever	3	15—16	16.30	Joe Deegan	John Churchman	Ray Cottrell
Forty Something	7	16	16.30	Andrea Seefeldt	Reggie Vardon	Sam Morrell

Times—0:23⅕; 0:46⅖; 1:11⅕; 1:37⅖; 2:03.
$2 Mutuel Prices—#4 Strike the Gold ($11.60, 6.20, 5.40); #10 Best Pal ($6.40, 5.40), #7 Mane Minister ($25.60).
Scratched—none; **Overweights**—none; **Attendance**—135,554; **TV Rating**—10.3/28 share (ABC).

116th Preakness Stakes

Grade I for three-year-olds; 10th race at Pimlico in Baltimore. **Date**—May 18, 1991; **Distance**—1 3/16 miles; **Stakes purse**—$665,800 ($432,770 to winner); **Track**—fast; **Off**—5:32 pm.

Winner—Hansel; **Time**—1:54; **Won**—Driving; **Bloodlines**—BC 3 by Woodman-Count on Bonnie, by Dancing Count; **Breeder**—Marvin Little, Jr.(Va.).

	PP	Finish	To $1	Jockey	Trainer	Owner
Hansel	4	1—7	9.10	Jerry Bailey	Frank Brothers	Lazy Lane Farm
Corporate Report	1	2—2¾	11.20	Pat Day	D.Wayne Lucas	Overbrook Farm
Mane Minister	2	3—½	18.90	Alex Solis	Juan Gonzalez	John Toffan & Trudy McCaffery
Olympio	7	4—1	2.40	Eddie Delahoussaye	Ron McAnally	Verne Mitchell
Best Pal	5	5—2½	2.70	Gary Stevens	Ian Jory	Mr. & Mrs.John Mabee
Strike the Gold	3	6—1½	1.80	Chris Antley	Nick Zito	B.Giles Brophy
Whadjathink	8	7—head	35.50	Jorge Velasquez	Mike Whittingham	Richard Duchossois
Honor Grades	6	8	24.20	Chris McCarron	Rodney Rash	Summa Stable

Times—0:23⅕; 0:46⅕; 1:10⅕; 1:35; 1:54.
$2 Mutuel Prices—#4 Hansel ($20.20, 10.80, 8.00); #1 Corporate Report ($11.00, 6.40), #2 Mane Minister ($5.80).
Scratched—none; **Overweights**—none; **Attendance**—96,695; **TV Rating**—5.9/16 share (ABC).

123rd Belmont Stakes

Grade I for three-year-olds; 8th race at Belmont Park in Elmont, NY. **Date**—June 8, 1991; **Distance**—1½ miles; **Stakes purse**—$1,695,800 ($1,417,480 to winner); **Track**—fast; **Off**—5:32 pm.

Winner—Hansel; **Time**—2:28; **Won**—Driving; **Bloodlines**—BC 3 by Woodman-Count on Bonnie, by Dancing Count; **Breeder**—Marvin Little, Jr.(Va.).

	PP	Finish	To $1	Jockey	Trainer	Owner
Hansel	5	1—head	4.10	Jerry Bailey	Frank Brothers	Lazy Lane Farm
Strike the Gold	11	2—3	2.20	Chris Antley	Nick Zito	B.Giles Brophy
Mane Minister	3	3—2½	17.90	Alex Solis	Juan Gonzalez	John Toffan & Trudy McCaffery
Corporate Report	6	4—2¼	8.20	Pat Day	D.Wayne Lucas	Overbrook Farm
Scan	2	5—10¾	10.30	Chris McCarron	Scotty Schulhofer	William H.Perry
Quintana	7	6—3½	26.00	Angel Cordero,Jr.	David Cross	Gary Garber
Lost Mountain	4	7—¾	19.10	Craig Perret	Tom Bohannan	Loblolly Stable
Smooth Performance	10	8—22½	7.00	Michael Kinane	Dermont Weld	William Haefner
Subordinated Debt	9	9—¾	21.70	Julie Krone	Dave Monaci	Leslie Grimm
Green Alligator	8	10	4.10	Corey Nakatani	Murray Johnson	Anderson Fowler
Another Review	1	11—Eased	99.20	Richard Migliore	John Campo	Buckland Farm

Times—0:23; 0:46⅗; 1:11⅗; 1:36⅗; 2:02; 2:28.
$2 Mutuel Prices—#5 Hansel ($10.20, 6.40, 5.00); #11 Strike the Gold ($5.00, 4.00); #3 Mane Minister ($4.00).
Scratched—none; **Overweights**—none; **Attendance**—51,766; **TV Rating**—5.5/18 share (ABC).

1991 Triple Crown Challenge

Thoroughbred racing's Triple Crown for 3-year-olds consists of the Kentucky Derby, Preakness Stakes and Belmont Stakes run over six weeks in May and June. Hansel won the 1991 Triple Crown Challenge as the best overall performer entered in all three races by winning the Preakness and Belmont after finishing 10th in the Derby. Derby winner Strike the Gold, who was sixth in the Preakness and second in the Belmont, finished second overall, while Mane Minister was third overall with three third place finishes. Statistics according to the *Daily Racing Form.*

1990-91 Money Leaders

Official Top 10 standings for 1990 and unofficial Top 10 standings for 1991, through the Woodward Stakes (Sept. 15), as compiled by the *Daily Racing Form.*

FINAL 1990 Horses	Age	Sts	1st	Earnings	1991 (through Sept.15) Horses	Age	Sts	1st	Earnings
Unbridled	3	11	4	$3,718,149	Farma Way	4	11	5	$2,598,350
Izvestia	3	11	8	2,486,667	Hansel	3	9	4	2,565,680
Criminal Type	5	11	4	2,270,290	Dance Smartly	3	7	7	2,356,821
In the Wings (GBR)	4	7	4	1,479,017	Festin (ARG)	5	9	2	1,493,250
Bayakoa (ARG)	6	10	7	1,234,406	In Excess (IRE)	4	7	5	1,328,800
Summer Squall	3	7	4	1,222,356	Strike the Gold	3	10	2	1,281,850
Ibn Bey (GBR)	6	8	2	1,132,414	Corporate Report	3	10	3	1,067,908
Flying Continental	4	7	3	1,096,700	Tight Spot	4	5	5	1,008,800
Ruhlmann	5	7	2	1,095,800	Marquetry	4	7	4	979,600
With Approval	4	11	5	1,043,840	Best Pal	3	7	2	967,500

Jockeys	Mts	1st	Earnings	Jockeys	Mts	1st	Earnings
Gary Stevens	1504	283	$13,881,198	Chris McCarron	1073	206	$10,524,998
*Jose Santos	1421	255	13,013,065	Gary Stevens	1169	191	10,124,835
Craig Perret	732	172	11,724,403	Pat Day	1071	326	10,028,591
*Pat Day	1426	364	10,431,194	Jerry Bailey	881	175	8,258,500
Angel Cordero, Jr	1371	263	9,777,937	Eddie Delahoussaye	989	151	7,640,995
*Jerry Bailey	1210	224	9,390,557	Mike Smith	1244	242	7,223,375
Mike Smith	1767	250	8,990,289	Cory Nakatani	1039	152	6,545,843
Chris McCarron	963	201	8,892,569	Julie Krone	1193	194	6,198,789
Alex Solis	1571	220	8,071,971	Laffit Pincay, Jr	1024	164	6,178,650
Eddie Delahoussaye	1348	183	8,049,758	Angel Cordero, Jr	944	165	6,103,488

*Includes foreign racing

Trainers	Sts	1st	Earnings	Trainers	Sts	1st	Earnings
D.Wayne Lucas	1396	267	$14,508,871	D.Wayne Lucas	1006	187	$10,711,003
Carl Nafzger	385	56	6,114,798	Ron McAnally	434	80	6,198,604
Charlie Whittingham	382	58	5,688,885	Bobby Frankel	219	51	4,484,932
Ron McAnally	498	81	5,435,327	Jim Day	187	53	4,306,503
Roger Attfield	272	67	5,053,580	Frank Brothers	174	32	3,261,337
Richard Mandella	430	100	3,778,362	Gary Jones	294	54	3,092,695
Shug McGaughey	175	53	3,758,712	Scotty Schulhofer	329	61	3,010,047
Jim Day	367	75	3,229,749	Bill Mott	304	63	2,998,714
Scotty Schulhofer	352	71	3,159,800	Charlie Whittingham	311	45	2,887,252
Gary Jones	358	58	3,151,402	Jack Van Berg	576	76	2,565,068

Harness Racing
Major 1990-91 Stakes Races

Winners of major stakes races from Sept. 8, 1990 through Sept. 2, 1991; all paces and trots cover one mile; (BC) indicates year-end Breeders' Crown series.

LATE 1990

Date	Race	Raceway	Winner	Driver	Value to Winner
Sept. 8	Messenger Stakes	Rosecroft	Jake and Elwood	John Cambell	$344,387
Sept. 21	Little Brown Jug	Delaware,OH	Beach Towel	Ray Remmen	149,955
Oct. 6	Kentucky Futurity	The Red Mile	Star Mystic	Jan Johnson	58,500
Nov. 2	BC 3-Yr-Old Colt/Geld.Pace	Pompano	Beach Towel	Ray Remmen	183,467
Nov. 2	BC 3-Yr-Old Colt/Geld.Trot	Pompano	Embassy Lobell	Michel Lachance	198,467
Nov. 2	BC 3-Yr-Old Filly Pace	Pompano	Town Pro	Doug Brown	152,467
Nov. 2	BC 3-Yr-Old Filly Trot	Pompano	Me Maggie	Berndt Lindstedt	189,467
Nov. 2	BC Aged Horse/Geld.Pace	Pompano	Bay's Fella	Paul MacDonell	136,729
Nov. 2	BC Aged Horse/Geld.Trot	Pompano	No Sex Please	Ron Waples	110,729
Nov. 2	BC Aged Mare Pace	Pompano	Caesars Jackpot	Bill Fahy	100,000
Nov. 2	BC Aged Mare Trot	Pompano	Peace Corps	Stig Johansson	101,729
Nov. 18	Governor's Cup	Garden St.	Artsplace	John Campbell	327,800
Nov. 30	BC 2-Yr-Old Colt/Geld.Pace	Pompano	Artsplace	John Campbell	302,935
Nov. 30	BC 2-Yr-Old Colt/Geld.Trot	Pompano	Crysta's Best	Dick Richardson	177,702
Nov. 30	BC 2-Yr-Old Filly Pace	Pompano	Miss Easy	John Campbell	257,435
Nov. 30	BC 2-Yr-Old Filly Trot	Pompano	Jean Bi	Jan Nordin	183,702

1991 (through Sept. 7)

Date	Race	Raceway	Winner	Driver	Value to Winner
May 26	Elitlopp (SWE)	Solvalla	Peace Corps	Stig Johansson	$140,625
June 22	North America Cup	Greenwood	Precious Bunny	John Campbell	500,000
July 12	Meadowlands Pace	Meadowlands	Precious Bunny	Jack Moiseyev	500,000
July 13	Yonkers Trot	Yonkers	Crown's Invitation	Michel Lachance	185,196
Aug. 3	Hambletonian	Meadowlands	Giant Victory	Jack Moiseyev	559,500
Aug. 16	Woodrow Wilson Pace	Meadowlands	Sportsmaster	Ron Waples	444,500
Aug. 16	Sweetheart Pace	Meadowlands	Summer Child	Richard Silverman	321,750
Aug. 24	Cane Pace	Yonkers	Silky Stallone	Jack Moiseyev	261,595

1990-91 Money Leaders

Official Top 10 standings for 1990 and unofficial Top 10 standings for 1991 through Sept.2, as compiled by the U.S.Trotting Association.

FINAL 1990

Horses	Age	Sts	1st	Earnings
Beach Towel	3/P	23	18	$2,091,860
Jake And Elwood	3/P	24	14	1,335,031
In the Pocket	3/P	21	10	745,051
Artsplace	2/P	15	11	1,180,271
Apaches Fame	3/P	26	20	1,157,732
Die Laughing	2/P	12	8	1,142,322
Miss Easy	2/P	17	15	1,128,956
Embassy Lobell	3/T	17	8	1,049,175
Harmonious	3/T	14	10	1,033,942
Dorunrun Bluegrass	A/P	31	17	851,755

Drivers	Sts	1st	Purses
John Campbell	2392	543	$11,620,878
Michel Lachance	2414	342	7,165,323
Doug Brown	1837	368	6,042,217
Cat Manzi	3750	641	5,511,211
Herve Filion	3727	660	4,309,598
Bill O'Donnell	1807	240	4,294,221
Bill Fahy	1638	187	4,034,219
Ron Waples	1206	190	3,683,735
Dave Magee	2522	396	3,455,951
Steve Condren	1690	240	3,243,361

1991 (through Sept.2)

Horses	Age	Sts	1st	Earnings
Precious Bunny	3/P	16	13	$1,599,057
Giant Victory	3/T	16	8	890,501
Artsplace	3/P	13	10	850,499
Die Laughing	3/P	10	6	742,620
Somatic	3/T	16	7	555,556
Crowns Invitation	3/T	18	12	543,346
Sportsmaster	2/P	10	7	538,205
Dontellmenomore	3/T	10	7	526,936
Jake and Elwood	A/P	19	8	442,950
Odds Against	A/P	15	8	439,480

Drivers	Sts	1st	Purses
John Campbell	1859	386	$7,160,596
Jack Moiseyev	2695	523	6,681,044
Michel Lachance	1809	242	4,480,139
Cat Manzi	2342	368	3,631,936
Herve Filion	2720	490	2,765,911
Ron Pierce	1440	195	2,556,225
Dave Magee	1720	334	2,381,920
Doug Brown	1180	249	2,362,208
Bill Fahey	963	103	2,211,906
Ron Waples	777	128	2,165,376

THE 1992 INFORMATION PLEASE SPORTS ALMANAC
HORSE RACING STATISTICS
THROUGH THE YEARS
1867-1991
THOROUGHBRED • HARNESS
SEC **B**
PAGE 625

Thoroughbred Racing
The Triple Crown

The term "Triple Crown" was coined by sportswriter Charles Hatton while covering the 1930 victories of Gallant Fox in the Kentucky Derby, Preakness Stakes and Belmont Stakes. Before then, only Sir Barton (1919) had won all three races in the same year. Since then, nine horses have won the Triple Crown. Two trainers, James (Sunny Jim) Fitzsimmons and Ben A.Jones, have saddled two Triple Crown champions, while Eddie Arcaro is the only jockey to ride two champions.

Year		Jockey	Trainer	Owner	Sire/Dam
1919	**Sir Barton**	Johnny Loftus	H.Guy Bedwell	J.K.L.Ross	Star Shoot/Lady Sterling
1930	**Gallant Fox**	Earle Sande	J.E. Fitzsimmons	Belair Stud	Sir Gallahad III/Marguerite
1935	**Omaha**	Willie Saunders	J.E. Fitzsimmons	Belair Stud	Gallant Fox/Flambino
1937	**War Admiral**	Chas.Kurtsinger	George Conway	Samuel Riddle	Man O'War/Brushup
1941	**Whirlaway**	Eddie Arcaro	Ben A.Jones	Calumet Farm	Blenheim II/Dustwhirl
1943	**Count Fleet**	Johnny Longden	Don Cameron	Mrs.J.D.Hertz	Reigh Count/Quickly
1946	**Assault**	Warren Mehrtens	Max Hirsch	King Ranch	Bold Venture/Igual
1948	**Citation**	Eddie Arcaro	Ben A.Jones	Calumet Farm	Bull Lea/Hydroplane II
1973	**Secretariat**	Ron Turcotte	Lucien Laurin	Meadow Stable	Bold Ruler/Somethingroyal
1977	**Seattle Slew**	Jean Cruguet	Billy Turner	Karen Taylor	Bold Reasoning/My Charmer
1978	**Affirmed**	Steve Cauthen	Laz Barrera	Harbor View Farm	Exclusive Native/Won't Tell You

Note: Gallant Fox (1930) is the only Triple Crown winner to sire another Triple Crown winner, Omaha (1935). Wm.Woodward Sr., owner of Belair Stud, was breeder-owner of both horses and both were trained by Sunny Jim Fitzsimmons.

Triple Crown Near Misses

Thirty-nine horses have won two legs of the Triple Crown. Of those, a dozen won the Kentucky Derby (KD) and Preakness Stakes (PS) only to be beaten in the Belmont Stakes (BS). Two others, Burgoo King (1932) and Bold Venture (1936), each won the Derby and Preakness but were forced out of the Belmont with the same injury—a bowed tendon—that effectively ended their racing careers. In 1978, Alydar finished second to Affirmed in all three races, the only time that has happened; (*) indicates won on disqualification.

Year		KD	PS	BS	Year		KD	PS	BS
1877	**Cloverbrook**	DNS	won	won	1958	**Tim Tam**	won	won	2nd
1878	**Duke of Magenta**	DNS	won	won	1961	**Carry Back**	won	won	7th
1880	**Grenada**	DNS	won	won	1963	**Chateaugay**	won	2nd	won
1881	**Saunterer**	DNS	won	won	1964	**Northern Dancer**	won	won	3rd
1895	**Belmar**	DNS	won	won	1966	**Kauai King**	won	won	4th
1920	**Man O'War**	DNS	won	won	1967	**Damascus**	3rd	won	won
1922	**Pillory**	DNS	won	won	1968	**Forward Pass**	won*	won	2nd
1923	**Zev**	won	12th	won	1969	**Majestic Prince**	won	won	2nd
1931	**Twenty Grand**	won	2nd	won	1971	**Canonero II**	won	won	4th
1932	**Burgoo King**	won	won	DNS	1972	**Riva Ridge**	won	4th	won
1936	**Bold Venture**	won	won	DNS	1974	**Little Current**	5th	won	won
1939	**Johnstown**	won	5th	won	1976	**Bold Forbes**	won	3rd	won
1940	**Bimelech**	2nd	won	won	1979	**Spectacular Bid**	won	won	3rd
1942	**Shut Out**	won	5th	won	1981	**Pleasant Colony**	won	won	3rd
1944	**Pensive**	won	won	2nd	1984	**Swale**	won	7th	won
1949	**Capot**	2nd	won	won	1987	**Alysheba**	won	won	4th
1950	**Middleground**	won	2nd	won	1988	**Risen Star**	3rd	won	won
1953	**Native Dancer**	2nd	won	won	1989	**Sunday Silence**	won	won	2nd
1955	**Nashua**	2nd	won	won	1991	**Hansel**	10th	won	won
1956	**Needles**	won	2nd	won					

The Triple Crown Challenge

Seeking to make the Triple Crown more than just a media event and to insure that owners would not be attracted to more lucrative races, officials at Churchill Downs, the Maryland Jockey Club and the New York Racing Association created Triple Crown Productions in 1985 and announced that a $1 million bonus would be given to the horse that performs best in the Kentucky Derby, Preakness Stakes and Belmont Stakes. Furthermore, a bonus of $5 million would be presented to any horse winning all three races. Chrysler Motors has been the sponsor since 1987.

Revised in 1991, the rules state that the winning horse must: 1. finish all three races; 2. earn points by finishing first, second, third or fourth in at least one of the three races; and 3. earn the highest number of points based on the following system—10 points to win, five to place, three to show and one to finish fourth. In the event of a tie, the $1 million is distributed equally among the top point-getters.

From 1987-90, the system was five points to win, three to place and one to show.

Year		KD	PS	BS	Pts	Year		KD	PS	BS	Pts
1987	1. **Bet Twice**	2nd	2nd	1st —	11	1990	1. **Unbridled**	1st	2nd	4th —	8
	2. Alysheba	1st	1st	4th —	10		2. Summer Squall	2nd	1st	DNR —	8
	3. Cryptoclearance	4th	3rd	2nd —	4		3. Go and Go	DNR	DNR	1st —	5
1988	1. **Risen Star**	3rd	1st	1st —	11		(Unbridled was only horse to run all 3 races.)				
	2. Winning Colors	1st	3rd	6th —	6	1991	1. **Hansel**	10th	1st	1st —	20
	3. Brian's Time	6th	2nd	3rd —	4		2. Strike the Gold	1st	6th	2nd —	15
1989	1. **Sunday Silence**	1st	1st	2nd —	13		3. Mane Minister	3rd	3rd	3rd —	9
	2. Easy Goer	2nd	2nd	1st —	11						
	3. Hawkster	5th	5th	5th —	0						

Kentucky Derby

For three-year-olds. Held the first Saturday in May at Churchill Downs in Louisville, Ky. Inaugurated in 1875.
   Originally run at 1½ miles (1875-95), shortened to present 1¼ miles in 1896.

   Trainers with most wins: Ben A. Jones (6); H.J.Thompson (4); Sunny Jim Fitzsimmons and Max Hirsch (3).

   Jockeys with most wins: Eddie Arcaro and Bill Hartack (5); Bill Shoemaker (4); Angel Cordero, Jr, Issac Murphy and Earl Sande (3).

   Winning fillies: Regret (1915), Genuine Risk (1980) and Winning Colors (1988).

Year		Time	Jockey	Trainer	2nd place	3rd place
1875	Aristides	2:37¾	Oliver Lewis	Andy Anderson	Volcano	Verdigris
1876	Vagrant	2:38¼	Bobby Swim	James Williams	Creedmoor	Harry Hill
1877	Baden-Baden	2:38	Billy Walker	Ed Brown	Leonard	King William
1878	Day Star	2:37¼	Jimmy Carter	Lee Paul	Himyar	Leveler
1879	Lord Murphy	2:37	Charlie Shauer	George Rice	Falsetto	Strathmore
1880	Fonso	2:37½	George Lewis	Tice Hutsell	Kimball	Bancroft
1881	Hindoo	2:40	Jim McLaughlin	James Rowe,Sr	Lelex	Alhambra
1882	Apollo	2:40¼	Babe Hurd	Green Morris	Runnymede	Bengal
1883	Leonatus	2:43	Billy Donohue	Raleigh Colston	Drake Carter	Lord Raglan
1884	Buchanan	2:40¼	Isaac Murphy	William Bird	Loftin	Audrain
1885	Joe Cotton	2:37¼	Babe Henderson	Alex Perry	Bersan	Ten Booker
1886	Ben Ali	2:36½	Paul Duffy	Jim Murphy	Blue Wing	Free Knight
1887	Montrose	2:39¼	Isaac Lewis	John McGinty	Jim Gore	Jackobin
1888	MacBeth II	2:38¼	Geo.Covington	John Campbell	Gallifet	White
1889	Spokane	2:34½	Thomas Kiley	John Rodegap	Proctor Knott	Once Again
1890	Riley	2:45	Isaac Murphy	Edward Corrigan	Bill Letcher	Robespierre
1891	Kingman	2:52¼	Isaac Murphy	Dud Allen	Balgowan	High Tariff
1892	Azra	2:41½	Lonnie Clayton	John Morris	Huron	Phil Dwyer
1893	Lookout	2:39¼	Eddie Kunze	Wm.McDaniel	Plutus	Boundless
1894	Chant	2:41	Frank Goodale	Eugene Leigh	Pearl Song	Sigurd
1895	Halma	2:37½	Soup Perkins	Byron McClelland	Basso	Laureate
1896	Ben Brush	2:07¼	Willie Simms	Hardy Campbell	Ben Eder	Semper Ego
1897	Typhoon II	2:12½	Buttons Garner	J.C.Cahn	Ornament	Dr. Catlett
1898	Plaudit	2:09	Willie Simms	John Madden	Lieber Karl	Isabey
1899	Manuel	2:12	Fred Taral	Robert Walden	Corsini	Mazo
1900	Lieut. Gibson	2:06¼	Jimmy Boland	Charles Hughes	Florizar	Thrive
1901	His Eminence	2:07¾	Jimmy Winkfield	F.B.VanMeter	Sannazarro	Driscoll
1902	Alan-a-Dale	2:08¾	Jimmy Winkfield	T.C.McDowell	Inventor	The Rival
1903	Judge Himes	2:09	Hal Booker	J.P.Mayberry	Early	Bourbon
1904	Elwood	2:08½	Shorty Prior	C.E.Durnell	Ed Tierney	Brancas
1905	Agile	2:10¾	Jack Martin	Robert Tucker	Ram's Horn	Layson
1906	Sir Huon	2:08⅕	Roscoe Troxler	Pete Coyne	Lady Navarre	James Reddick

Year		Time	Jockey	Trainer	2nd place	3rd place
1907	**Pink Star**	2:12⅗	Andy Minder	W.H.Fizer	Zal	Ovelando
1908	**Stone Street**	2:15⅕	Arthur Pickens	J.W.Hall	Sir Cleges	Dunvegan
1909	**Wintergreen**	2:08⅕	Vincent Power	Charles Mack	Miami	Dr. Barkley
1910	**Donau**	2:06⅖	Fred Herbert	George Ham	Joe Morris	Fighting Bob
1911	**Meridian**	2:05	Geo.Archibald	Albert Ewing	Governor Gray	Colston
1912	**Worth**	2:09⅖	C.H.Shilling	Frank Taylor	Duval	Flamma
1913	**Donerail**	2:04⅘	Roscoe Goose	Thomas Hayes	Ten Point	Gowell
1914	**Old Rosebud**	2:03⅖	John McCabe	F.D.Weir	Hodge	Bronzewing
1915	**Regret**	2:05⅖	Joe Notter	James Rowe,Sr	Pebbles	Sharpshooter
1916	**George Smith**	2:04	Johnny Loftus	Hollie Hughes	Star Hawk	Franklin
1917	**Omar Khayyam**	2:04⅗	Charles Borel	C.T.Patterson	Ticket	Midway
1918	**Exterminator**	2:10⅘	William Knapp	Henry McDaniel	Escoba	Viva America
1919	**SIR BARTON**	2:09⅘	Johnny Loftus	H.Guy Bedwell	Billy Kelly	Under Fire
1920	**Paul Jones**	2:09	Ted Rice	Billy Garth	Upset	On Watch
1921	**Behave Yourself**	2:04⅕	Chas.Thompson	H.J.Thompson	Black Servant	Prudery
1922	**Morvich**	2:04⅗	Albert Johnson	Fred Burlew	Bet Mosie	John Finn
1923	**Zev**	2:05⅖	Earl Sande	D.J.Leary	Martingale	Vigil
1924	**Black Gold**	2:05⅕	John Mooney	Hedley Webb	Chilhowee	Beau Butler
1925	**Flying Ebony**	2:07⅗	Earl Sande	William Duke	Captain Hal	Son of John
1926	**Bubbling Over**	2:03⅗	Albert Johnson	H.J.Thompson	Bagenbaggage	Rock Man
1927	**Whiskery**	2:06	Linus McAtee	Fred Hopkins	Osmond	Jock
1928	**Reigh Count**	2:10⅖	Chick Lang	Bert Michell	Misstep	Toro
1929	**Clyde Van Dusen**	2:10⅘	Linus McAtee	Clyde Van Dusen	Naishapur	Panchio
1930	**GALLANT FOX**	2:07⅗	Earl Sande	Jim Fitzsimmons	Gallant Knight	Ned O.
1931	**Twenty Grand**	2:01⅘	Chas.Kurtsinger	James Rowe,Jr	Sweep All	Mate
1932	**Burgoo King**	2:05⅕	Eugene James	H.J.Thompson	Economic	Stepenfetchit
1933	**Brokers Tip**	2:06⅘	Don Meade	H.J.Thompson	Head Play	Charley O.
1934	**Cavalcade**	2:04	Mack Garner	Bob Smith	Discovery	Agrarian
1935	**OMAHA**	2:05	Willie Saunders	Jim Fitzsimmons	Roman Soldier	Whiskolo
1936	**Bold Venture**	2:03⅗	Ira Hanford	Max Hirsch	Brevity	Indian Brown
1937	**WAR ADMIRAL**	2:03⅕	Chas.Kurtsinger	George Conway	Pompoon	Reaping Reward
1938	**Lawrin**	2:04⅘	Eddie Arcaro	Ben Jones	Dauber	Can't Wait
1939	**Johnstown**	2:03⅗	James Stout	Jim Fitzsimmons	Challedon	Heather Broom
1940	**Gallahadion**	2:05	Carroll Bierman	Roy Waldron	Bimelech	Dit
1941	**WHIRLAWAY**	2:01⅖	Eddie Arcaro	Ben Jones	Staretor	Market Wise
1942	**Shut Out**	2:04⅖	Wayne Wright	John Gaver	Alsab	Valdina Orphan
1943	**COUNT FLEET**	2:04	Johnny Longden	Don Cameron	Blue Swords	Slide Rule
1944	**Pensive**	2:04⅕	Conn McCreary	Ben Jones	Broadcloth	Stir Up
1945	**Hoop Jr**	2:07	Eddie Arcaro	Ivan Parke	Pot O'Luck	Darby Dieppe
1946	**ASSAULT**	2:06⅗	Warren Mehrtens	Max Hirsch	Spy Song	Hampden
1947	**Jet Pilot**	2:06⅘	Eric Guerin	Tom Smith	Phalanx	Faultless
1948	**CITATION**	2:05⅖	Eddie Arcaro	Ben Jones	Coaltown	My Request
1949	**Ponder**	2:04⅕	Steve Brooks	Ben Jones	Capot	Palestinian
1950	**Middleground**	2:01⅗	William Boland	Max Hirsch	Hill Prince	Mr. Trouble
1951	**Count Turf**	2:02⅗	Conn McCreary	Sol Rutchick	Royal Mustang	Ruhe
1952	**Hill Gail**	2:01⅗	Eddie Arcaro	Ben Jones	Sub Fleet	Blue Man
1953	**Dark Star**	2:02	Hank Moreno	Eddie Hayward	Native Dancer	Invigorator
1954	**Determine**	2:03	Raymond York	Willie Molter	Hasty Road	Hasseyampa
1955	**Swaps**	2:01⅘	Bill Shoemaker	Mesh Tenney	Nashua	Summer Tan
1956	**Needles**	2:03⅖	David Erb	Hugh Fontaine	Fabius	Come On Red
1957	**Iron Liege**	2:02⅕	Bill Hartack	Jimmy Jones	Gallant Man	Round Table
1958	**Tim Tam**	2:05	I.Valenzuela	Jimmy Jones	Lincoln Road	Noureddin
1959	**Tomy Lee**	2:02⅕	Bill Shoemaker	Frank Childs	Sword Dancer	First Landing
1960	**Venetian Way**	2:02⅖	Bill Hartack	Victor Sovinski	Bally Ache	Victoria Park
1961	**Carry Back**	2:04	John Sellers	Jack Price	Crozier	Bass Clef
1962	**Decidedly**	2:00⅖	Bill Hartack	Horatio Luro	Roman Line	Ridan
1963	**Chateaugay**	2:01⅘	Braulio Baeza	James Conway	Never Bend	Candy Spots
1964	**Northern Dancer**	2:00	Bill Hartack	Horatio Luro	Hill Rise	The Scoundrel
1965	**Lucky Debonair**	2:01⅕	Bill Shoemaker	Frank Catrone	Dapper Dan	Tom Rolfe

Kentucky Derby (Cont.)

Year		Time	Jockey	Trainer	2nd place	3rd place
1966	**Kauai King**	2:02	Don Brumfield	Henry Forrest	Advocator	Blue Skyer
1967	**Proud Clarion**	2:00⅗	Bobby Ussery	Loyd Gentry	Barbs Delight	Damascus
1968	**Forward Pass***	2:01⅕	I.Valenzuela	Henry Forrest	Francie's Hat	T.V. Commercial
1969	**Majestic Prince**	2:01⅘	Bill Hartack	Johnny Longden	Arts and Letters	Dike
1970	**Dust Commander**	2:03⅖	Mike Manganello	Don Combs	My Dad George	High Echelon
1971	**Canonero II**	2:03⅕	Gustavo Avila	Juan Arias	Jim French	Bold Reason
1972	**Riva Ridge**	2:01⅘	Ron Turcotte	Lucien Laurin	No Le Hace	Hold Your Peace
1973	**SECRETARIAT**	1:59⅖	Ron Turcotte	Lucien Laurin	Sham	Our Native
1974	**Cannonade**	2:04	Angel Cordero, Jr	Woody Stephens	Hudson County	Agitate
1975	**Foolish Pleasure**	2:02	Jacinto Vasquez	LeRoy Jolley	Avatar	Diabolo
1976	**Bold Forbes**	2:01⅗	Angel Cordero, Jr	Laz Barrera	Honest Pleasure	Elocutionist
1977	**SEATTLE SLEW**	2:02⅕	Jean Cruguet	Billy Turner	Run Dusty Run	Sanhedrin
1978	**AFFIRMED**	2:01⅕	Steve Cauthen	Laz Barrera	Alydar	Believe It
1979	**Spectacular Bid**	2:02⅖	Ron Franklin	Buddy Delp	General Assembly	Golden Act
1980	**Genuine Risk**	2:02	Jacinto Vasquez	LeRoy Jolley	Rumbo	Jaklin Klugman
1981	**Pleasant Colony**	2:02	Jorge Velasquez	John Campo	Woodchopper	Partez
1982	**Gato Del Sol**	2:02⅕	E.Delahoussaye	Eddie Gregson	Laser Light	Reinvested
1983	**Sunny's Halo**	2:02⅕	E.Delahoussaye	David Cross	Desert Wine	Caveat
1984	**Swale**	2:02⅖	Laffit Pincay,Jr	Woody Stephens	Coax Me Chad	At The Threshold
1985	**Spend A Buck**	2:00⅕	Angel Cordero, Jr	Cam Gambolati	Stephan's Odyssey	Chief's Crown
1986	**Ferdinand**	2:02⅘	Bill Shoemaker	Chas.Whittingham	Bold Arrangement	Broad Brush
1987	**Alysheba**	2:03⅖	Chris McCarron	Jack Van Berg	Bet Twice	Avies Copy
1988	**Winning Colors**	2:02⅕	Gary Stevens	D.Wayne Lukas	Forty Niner	Risen Star
1989	**Sunday Silence**	2:05	Pat Valenzuela	Chas.Whittingham	Easy Goer	Awe Inspiring
1990	**Unbridled**	2:02	Craig Perret	Carl Nafzger	Summer Squall	Pleasant Tap
1991	**Strike the Gold**	2:03	Chris Antley	Nick Zito	Best Pal	Mane Minister

*In 1968, Dancer's Image finished first but was disqualified after traces of prohibited medication were found in his system.

Preakness Stakes

For three-year-olds. Held two weeks after the Kentucky Derby at Pimlico Race Course in Baltimore, Md. Inaugurated 1873.

Originally run at 1½ miles (1873-88), then at 1¼ miles (1889), 1½ miles (1890), 1 1/16 miles (1894-1900), 1 mile & 70 yards (1901-07), 1 1/16 miles (1908), 1 mile (1909-10), 1⅛ miles (1911-24), and the present 1 3/16 miles since 1925.

Trainers with most wins: Robert W.Walden (7); T.J. Healey (5); Sunny Jim Fitzsimmons and Jimmy Jones (4); J. Whalen (3).

Jockeys with most wins: Eddie Arcaro (6); G. Barbee, Bill Hartack and Lloyd Hughes (3).

Winning fillies: Flocarline (1903), Whimsical (1906), Rhine Maiden (1915) and Nellie Morse (1924).

Year		Time	Jockey	Trainer	2nd place	3rd place
1873	**Survivor**	2:43	G.Barbee	A.D.Pryor	John Boulger	Artist
1874	**Culpepper**	2:56½	W.Donohue	H.Gaffney	King Amadeus	Scratch
1875	**Tom Ochiltre**	2:43½	L.Hughes	R.W.Walden	Viator	Bay Final
1876	**Shirley**	2:44¾	G.Barbee	W.Brown	Rappahannock	Algerine
1877	**Cloverbrook**	2:45½	C.Holloway	J.Walden	Bombast	Lucifer
1878	**Duke of Magenta**	2:41¾	C.Holloway	R.W.Walden	Bayard	Albert
1879	**Harold**	2:40½	L.Hughes	R.W.Walden	Jericho	Rochester
1880	**Grenada**	2:40½	L.Hughes	R.W.Walden	Oden	Emily F.
1881	**Saunterer**	2:40½	T.Costello	R.W.Walden	Compensation	Baltic
1882	**Vanguard**	2:44½	T.Costello	R.W.Walden	Heck	Col. Watson
1883	**Jacobus**	2:42½	G.Barbee	R.Dwyer	Parnell	—
1884	**Knight of Ellerslie**	2:39½	S.Fisher	T.B.Doswell	Welcher	—
1885	**Tecumseh**	2:49	Jim McLaughlin	C.Littlefield	Wickham	John C.
1886	**The Bard**	2:45	S.Fisher	J.Huggins	Eurus	Elkwood
1887	**Dunboyne**	2:39½	W.Donohue	W.Jennings	Mahoney	Raymond
1888	**Refund**	2:49	F.Littlefield	R.W.Walden	Judge Murray	Glendale
1889	**Buddhist**	2:17½	W.Anderson	J.Rogers	Japhet	—
1890	**Montague**	2:36¾	W.Martin	E.Feakes	Philosophy	Barrister
1891	Not held					
1892	Not held					
1893	Not held					
1894	**Assignee**	1:49¼	F.Taral	W.Lakeland	Potentate	Ed Kearney

Year		Time	Jockey	Trainer	2nd place	3rd place
1895	**Belmar**	1:50½	F.Taral	E.Feakes	April Fool	Sue Kittie
1896	**Margrave**	1:51	H.Griffin	Byron McClelland	Hamilton II	Intermission
1897	**Paul Kauvar**	1:51¼	T.Thorpe	T.P.Hayes	Elkins	On Deck
1898	**Sly Fox**	1:49⅗	W.Simms	H.Campbell	The Huguenot	Nuto
1899	**Half Time**	1:47	R.Clawson	F.McCabe	Filigrane	Lackland
1900	**Hindus**	1:48⅖	H.Spencer	J.H.Morris	Sarmation	Ten Candles
1901	**The Parader**	1:47⅕	F.Landry	T.J.Healey	Sadie S.	Dr. Barlow
1902	**Old England**	1:45⅘	L.Jackson	G.B.Morris	Maj.Daingerfield	Namtor
1903	**Flocarline**	1:44⅘	W.Gannon	H.C.Riddle	Mackey Dwyer	Rightful
1904	**Bryn Mawr**	1:44⅕	E.Hildebrand	W.F.Presgrave	Wotan	Dolly Spanker
1905	**Cairngorm**	1:45⅘	W.Davis	A.J.Joyner	Kiamesha	Coy Maid
1906	**Whimsical**	1:45	Walter Miller	T.J.Gaynor	Content	Larabie
1907	**Don Enrique**	1:45⅖	G.Mountain	J.Whalen	Ethon	Zambesi
1908	**Royal Tourist**	1:46⅖	Eddie Dugan	A.J.Joyner	Live Wire	Robert Cooper
1909	**Effendi**	1:39⅘	Willie Doyle	F.C.Frisbie	Fashion Plate	Hilltop
1910	**Layminister**	1:40⅗	R.Estep	J.S.Healy	Dalhousie	Sager
1911	**Watervale**	1:51	Eddie Dugan	J.Whalen	Zeus	The Nigger
1912	**Colonel Holloway**	1:56⅗	C.Turner	D.Woodford	Bwana Tumbo	Tipsand
1913	**Buskin**	1:53⅖	James Butwell	J.Whalen	Kleburne	Barnegat
1914	**Holiday**	1:53⅘	A.Schuttinger	J.S.Healy	Brave Cunarder	Defendum
1915	**Rhine Maiden**	1:58	Douglas Hoffman	F.Devers	Half Rock	Runes
1916	**Damrosch**	1:54⅘	Linus McAtee	A.G.Weston	Greenwood	Achievement
1917	**Kalitan**	1:54⅖	E.Haynes	Bill Hurley	Al M. Dick	Kentucky Boy
1918	**War Cloud**	1:53⅗	Johnny Loftus	W.B.Jennings	Sunny Slope	Lanius
1918	**Jack Hare Jr**	1:53⅖	Charles Peak	F.D.Weir	The Porter	Kate Bright
1919	**SIR BARTON**	1:53	Johnny Loftus	H.Guy Bedwell	Eternal	Sweep On
1920	**Man o'War**	1:51⅗	Clarence Kummer	L.Feustel	Upset	Wildair
1921	**Broomspun**	1:54⅕	F.Coltiletti	James Rowe,Sr	Polly Ann	Jeg
1922	**Pillory**	1:51⅗	L.Morris	Thomas Healey	Hea	June Grass
1923	**Vigil**	1:53⅗	B.Marinelli	Thomas Healey	General Thatcher	Rialto
1924	**Nellie Morse**	1:57⅕	John Merimee	A.B.Gordon	Transmute	Mad Play
1925	**Coventry**	1:59	Clarence Kummer	William Duke	Backbone	Almadel
1926	**Display**	1:59⅘	John Maiben	Thomas Healey	Blondin	Mars
1927	**Bostonian**	2:01⅗	Whitey Abel	Fred Hopkins	Sir Harry	Whiskery
1928	**Victorian**	2:00⅕	Sonny Workman	James Rowe,Jr.	Toro	Solace
1929	**Dr. Freeland**	2:01⅗	Louis Schaefer	Thomas Healey	Minotaur	African
1930	**GALLANT FOX**	2:00⅗	Earl Sande	Jim Fitzsimmons	Crack Brigade	Snowflake
1931	**Mate**	1:59	George Ellis	J.W.Healey	Twenty Grand	Ladder
1932	**Burgoo King**	1:59⅘	John Maiben	Thomas Healey	Tick On	Boatswain
1933	**Head Play**	2:02	Chas.Kurtsinger	Thomas Hayes	Ladysman	Utopian
1934	**High Quest**	1:58⅕	Robert Jones	Bob Smith	Cavalcade	Discovery
1935	**OMAHA**	1:58⅖	Willie Saunders	Jim Fitzsimmons	Firethorn	Psychic Bid
1936	**Bold Venture**	1:59	George Woolf	Max Hirsch	Granville	Jean Bart
1937	**WAR ADMIRAL**	1:58⅖	Chas.Kurtsinger	George Conway	Pompoon	Flying Scot
1938	**Dauber**	1:59⅘	Maurice Peters	Dick Handlen	Cravat	Menow
1939	**Challedon**	1:59⅘	George Seabo	Louis Schaefer	Gilded Knight	Volitant
1940	**Bimelech**	1:58⅗	F.A.Smith	Bill Hurley	Mioland	Gallahadion
1941	**WHIRLAWAY**	1:58⅘	Eddie Arcaro	Ben A. Jones	King Cole	Our Boots
1942	**Alsab**	1:57	Basil James	Sarge Swenke	Requested	Sun Again
1943	**COUNT FLEET**	1:57⅖	Johnny Longden	Don Cameron	Blue Swords	Vincentive
1944	**Pensive**	1:59⅕	Conn McCreary	Ben A. Jones	Platter	Stir Up
1945	**Polynesian**	1:58⅘	W.D.Wright	Morris Dixon	Hoop Jr.	Darby Dieppe
1946	**ASSAULT**	2:01⅖	Warren Mehrtens	Max Hirsch	Lord Boswell	Hampden
1947	**Faultless**	1:59	Doug Dobson	Jimmy Jones	On Trust	Phalanx
1948	**CITATION**	2:02⅖	Eddie Arcaro	Jimmy Jones	Vulcan's Forge	Boyard
1949	**Capot**	1:56	Ted Atkinson	J.M.Gaver	Palestinian	Noble Impulse
1950	**Hill Prince**	1:59⅕	Eddie Arcaro	Casey Hayes	Middleground	Dooley
1951	**Bold**	1:56⅖	Eddie Arcaro	Preston Burch	Counter Point	Alerted
1952	**Blue Man**	1:57⅖	Conn McCreary	Woody Stephens	Jampol	One Count
1953	**Native Dancer**	1:57⅘	Eric Guerin	Bill Winfrey	Jamie K.	Royal Bay Gem
1954	**Hasty Road**	1:57⅖	Johnny Adams	Harry Trotsek	Carrilation	Hasseyampa
1955	**Nashua**	1:54⅗	Eddie Arcaro	Jim Fitzsimmons	Saratoga	Traffic Judge

Preakness Stakes (Cont.)

Year		Time	Jockey	Trainer	2nd place	3rd place
1956	**Fabius**	1:58⅖	Bill Hartack	Jimmy Jones	Needles	No Regrets
1957	**Bold Ruler**	1:56⅕	Eddie Arcaro	Jim Fitzsimmons	Iron Liege	Inside Tract
1958	**Tim Tam**	1:57⅕	I.Valenzuela	Jimmy Jones	Lincoln Road	Gone Fishin'
1959	**Royal Orbit**	1:57	Wm.Harmatz	R. Cornell	Sword Dancer	Dunce
1960	**Bally Ache**	1:57⅗	Bobby Ussery	Jimmy Pitt	Victoria Park	Celtic Ash
1961	**Carry Back**	1:57⅗	Johnny Sellers	Jack Price	Globemaster	Crozier
1962	**Greek Money**	1:56⅕	John Rotz	V.W.Raines	Ridan	Roman Line
1963	**Candy Spots**	1:56⅕	Bill Shoemaker	Mesh Tenney	Chateaugay	Never Bend
1964	**Northern Dancer**	1:56⅘	Bill Hartack	Horatio Luro	The Scoundrel	Hill Rise
1965	**Tom Rolfe**	1:56⅕	Ron Turcotte	Frank Whiteley	Dapper Dan	Hail To All
1966	**Kauai King**	1:55⅖	Don Brumfield	H. Forrest	Stupendous	Amberoid
1967	**Damascus**	1:55⅕	Bill Shoemaker	Frank Whiteley	In Reality	Proud Clarion
1968	**Forward Pass**	1:56⅘	I.Valenzuela	Henry Forrest	Out Of the Way	Nodouble
1969	**Majestic Prince**	1:55⅗	Bill Hartack	Johnny Longden	Arts and Letters	Jay Ray
1970	**Personality**	1:56⅕	Eddie Belmonte	John Jacobs	My Dad George	Silent Screen
1971	**Canonero II**	1:54	Gustavo Avila	Juan Arias	Eastern Fleet	Jim French
1972	**Bee Bee Bee**	1:55⅗	Eldon Nelson	Red Carroll	No Le Hace	Key To The Mint
1973	**SECRETARIAT**	1:54⅖	Ron Turcotte	Lucien Laurin	Sham	Our Native
1974	**Little Current**	1:54⅗	Miguel Rivera	Lou Rondinello	Neapolitan Way	Cannonade
1975	**Master Derby**	1:56⅖	Darrel McHargue	Smiley Adams	Foolish Pleasure	Diabolo
1976	**Elocutionist**	1:55	John Lively	Paul Adwell	Play The Red	Bold Forbes
1977	**SEATTLE SLEW**	1:54⅖	Jean Cruguet	Billy Turner	Iron Constitution	Run Dusty Run
1978	**AFFIRMED**	1:54⅖	Steve Cauthen	Laz Barrera	Alydar	Believe It
1979	**Spectacular Bid**	1:54⅕	Ron Franklin	Buddy Delp	Golden Act	Screen King
1980	**Codex**	1:54⅕	Angel Cordero,Jr	D.Wayne Lukas	Genuine Risk	Colonel Moran
1981	**Pleasant Colony**	1:54⅗	Jorge Velasquez	John Campo	Bold Ego	Paristo
1982	**Aloma's Ruler**	1:55⅖	Jack Kaenel	John Lensini	Linkage	Cut Away
1983	**Deputed Testamony**	1:55⅖	Donald Miller	Bill Boniface	Desert Wine	High Honors
1984	**Gate Dancer**	1:53⅗	Angel Cordero,Jr	Jack Van Berg	Play On	Fight Over
1985	**Tank's Prospect**	1:53⅖	Pat Day	D.Wayne Lukas	Chief's Crown	Eternal Prince
1986	**Snow Chief**	1:54⅘	Alex Solis	Melvin Stute	Ferdinand	Broad Brush
1987	**Alysheba**	1:55⅘	Chris McCarron	Jack Van Berg	Bet Twice	Cryptoclearance
1988	**Risen Star**	1:56⅕	E.Delahoussaye	Louie Roussel	Brian's Time	Winning Colors
1989	**Sunday Silence**	1:53⅘	Pat Valenzuela	Chas.Whittingham	Easy Goer	Rock Point
1990	**Summer Squall**	1:53⅗	Pat Day	Neil Howard	Unbridled	Mister Frisky
1991	**Hansel**	1:54	Jerry Bailey	Frank Brothers	Corporate Report	Mane Minister

Belmont Stakes

For three-year-olds. Held three weeks after Preakness Stakes at Belmont Park in Elmont, N.Y. Inaugurated in 1867 at Jerome Park, moved to Morris Park in 1890 and Belmont Park in 1905.

Originally run at 1 mile and 5 furlongs (1867-89), then 1¼ miles (1890-1905), 1⅜ miles (1906-25), and the present 1½ miles since 1926.

Trainers with most wins: James Rowe, Sr.(8); Sam Hildreth (7); Sunny Jim Fitzsimmons (6); Woody Stephens (5); Max Hirsch and Robert W. Walden (4); Elliott Burch, Lucien Laurin, F. McCabe and D. McDaniel (3).

Jockeys with most wins: Eddie Arcaro and Jim McLaughlin (6); Earl Sande and Bill Shoemaker (5); Braulio Baeza, Laffit Pincay, Jr and James Stout (3).

Winning fillies: Ruthless (1867) and Tanya (1905).

Year		Time	Jockey	Trainer	2nd place	3rd place
1867	**Ruthless**	3:05	J.Gilpatrick	A.J.Minor	De Courcy	Rivoli
1868	**General Duke**	3:02	Bobby Swim	A.Thompson	Northumberland	Fannie Ludlow
1869	**Fenian**	3:04¼	C.Miller	J.Pincus	Glenelg	Invercauld
1870	**Kingfisher**	2:59½	W.Dick	R.Colston	Foster	Midday
1871	**Harry Bassett**	2:56	W.Miller	D.McDaniel	Stockwood	By-the-Sea
1872	**Joe Daniels**	2:58½	James Rowe	D.McDaniel	Meteor	Shylock
1873	**Springbok**	3:01¾	James Rowe	D.McDaniel	Count d'Orsay	Strachino
1874	**Saxon**	2:39½	G.Barbee	W.Pryor	Grinstead	Aaron Pennington
1875	**Calvin**	2:42¼	Bobby Swim	A.Williams	Aristides	Milner
1876	**Algerine**	2:40½	Billy Donohue	T.B.Doswell	Fiddlestick	Barricade
1877	**Cloverbrook**	2:46	C.Holloway	J.Walden	Loiterer	Baden-Baden
1878	**Duke of Magenta**	2:42¾	L.Hughes	R.W.Walden	Bramble	Sparta
1879	**Spendthrift**	2:42¾	George Evans	T.Puryear	Monitor	Jericho
1880	**Grenada**	2:47	L.Hughes	R.W.Walden	Ferncliffe	Turenne
1881	**Saunterer**	2:47	T.Costello	R.W.Walden	Eole	Baltic
1882	**Forester**	2:43	Jim McLaughlin	L.Stuart	Babcock	Wyoming
1883	**George Kinney**	2:42½	Jim McLaughlin	James Rowe,Sr	Trombone	Renegade
1884	**Panique**	2:42	Jim McLaughlin	James Rowe,Sr	Knight of Ellerslie	Himalaya

Year		Time	Jockey	Trainer	2nd place	3rd place
1885	**Tyrant**	2:43	Paul Duffy	C.Claypool	St.Augustine	Tecumseh
1886	**Inspector B**	2:41	Jim McLaughlin	F.McCabe	The Bard	Linden
1887	**Hanover**	2:43½	Jim McLaughlin	F.McCabe	Oneko	—
1888	**Sir Dixon**	2:40¼	Jim McLaughlin	F.McCabe	Prince Royal	—
1889	**Eric**	2:47	W.Hayward	J.Huggins	Diable	Zephyrus
1890	**Burlington**	2:07¾	Pike Barnes	A.Cooper	Devotee	Padishah
1891	**Foxford**	2:08¾	Ed Garrison	M.Donovan	Montana	Laurestan
1892	**Patron**	2:17	W.Hayward	L.Stuart	Shellbark	—
1893	**Comanche**	1:53¼	Willie Simms	G.Hannon	Dr.Rice	Rainbow
1894	**Henry of Navarre**	1:56½	Willie Simms	B.McClelland	Prig	Assignee
1895	**Belmar**	2:11½	Fred Taral	E.Feakes	Counter Tenor	Nanki Pooh
1896	**Hastings**	2:24½	H.Griffin	J.J.Hyland	Handspring	Hamilton II
1897	**Scottish Chieftain**	2:23½	J.Scherrer	M.Byrnes	On Deck	Octagon
1898	**Bowling Brook**	2:32	F.Littlefield	R.W.Walden	Previous	Hamburg
1899	**Jean Bereaud**	2:23	R.Clawson	Sam Hildreth	Half Time	Glengar
1900	**Ildrim**	2:21½	Nash Turner	H.E.Leigh	Petrucio	Missionary
1901	**Commando**	2:21	H.Spencer	James Rowe,Sr	The Parader	All Green
1902	**Masterman**	2:22½	John Bullman	J.J.Hyland	Ranald	King Hanover
1903	**Africander**	2:23⅕	John Bullman	R.Miller	Whorler	Red Knight
1904	**Delhi**	2:06⅖	George Odom	James Rowe,Sr	Graziallo	Rapid Water
1905	**Tanya**	2:08	E.Hildebrand	J.W.Rogers	Blandy	Hot Shot
1906	**Burgomaster**	2:20	Lucien Lyne	J.W.Rogers	The Quail	Accountant
1907	**Peter Pan**	N/A	G.Mountain	James Rowe,Sr	Superman	Frank Gill
1908	**Colin**	N/A	Joe Notter	James Rowe,Sr	Fair Play	King James
1909	**Joe Madden**	2:21⅗	E.Dugan	Sam Hildreth	Wise Mason	Donald MacDonald
1910	**Sweep**	2:22	James Butwell	James Rowe,Sr	Duke of Ormonde	—
1911	Not held					
1912	Not held					
1913	**Prince Eugene**	2:18	Roscoe Troxler	James Rowe,Sr	Rock View	Flying Fairy
1914	**Luke McLuke**	2:20	Merritt Buxton	J.F.Schorr	Gainer	Charlestonian
1915	**The Finn**	2:18⅖	George Byrne	E.W.Heffner	Half Rock	Pebbles
1916	**Friar Rock**	2:22	E.Haynes	Sam Hildreth	Spur	Churchill
1917	**Hourless**	2:17⅘	James Butwell	Sam Hildreth	Skeptic	Wonderful
1918	**Johren**	2:20⅖	Frank Robinson	A.Simons	War Cloud	Cum Sah
1919	**SIR BARTON**	2:17⅖	John Loftus	H.Guy Bedwell	Sweep On	Natural Bridge
1920	**Man o'War**	2:14⅕	Clarence Kummer	L.Feustel	Donnacona	—
1921	**Grey Lag**	2:16⅘	Earl Sande	Sam Hildreth	Sporting Blood	Leonardo II
1922	**Pillory**	2:18⅘	C.H.Miller	T.J.Healey	Snob II	Hea
1923	**Zev**	2:19	Earl Sande	Sam Hildreth	Chickvale	Rialto
1924	**Mad Play**	2:18⅘	Earl Sande	Sam Hildreth	Mr.Mutt	Modest
1925	**American Flag**	2:16⅘	Albert Johnson	G.R.Tompkins	Dangerous	Swope
1926	**Crusader**	2:32⅕	Albert Johnson	George Conway	Espino	Haste
1927	**Chance Shot**	2:32⅖	Earl Sande	Pete Coyne	Bois de Rose	Flambino
1928	**Vito**	2:33⅕	Clarence Kummer	Max Hirsch	Genie	Diavolo
1929	**Blue Larkspur**	2:32⅘	Mack Garner	C.Hastings	African	Jack High
1930	**GALLANT FOX**	2:31⅗	Earl Sande	Jim Fitzsimmons	Whichone	Questionnaire
1931	**Twenty Grand**	2:29⅗	Chas.Kurtsinger	James Rowe,Jr	Sun Meadow	Jamestown
1932	**Faireno**	2:32⅘	Tom Malley	Jim Fitzsimmons	Osculator	Flag Pole
1933	**Hurryoff**	2:32⅗	Mack Garner	H.McDaniel	Nimbus	Union
1934	**Peace Chance**	2:29⅕	W.D.Wright	Pete Coyne	High Quest	Good Goods
1935	**OMAHA**	2:30⅗	Willie Saunders	Jim Fitzsimmons	Firethorn	Rosemont
1936	**Granville**	2:30	James Stout	Jim Fitzsimmons	Mr.Bones	Hollyrood
1937	**WAR ADMIRAL**	2:28⅗	Chas.Kurtsinger	George Conway	Sceneshifter	Vamoose
1938	**Pasteurized**	2:29⅖	James Stout	George Odom	Dauber	Cravat
1939	**Johnstown**	2:29⅗	James Stout	Jim Fitzsimmons	Belay	Gilded Knight
1940	**Bimelech**	2:29⅗	Fred Smith	Bill Hurley	Your Chance	Andy K.
1941	**WHIRLAWAY**	2:31	Eddie Arcaro	Ben Jones	Robert Morris	Yankee Chance
1942	**Shut Out**	2:29⅕	Eddie Arcaro	John Gaver	Alsab	Lochinvar
1943	**COUNT FLEET**	2:28⅕	Johnny Longden	Don Cameron	Fairy Manhurst	Deseronto
1944	**Bounding Home**	2:32⅕	G.L.Smith	Matt Brady	Pensive	Bull Dandy
1945	**Pavot**	2:30⅕	Eddie Arcaro	Oscar White	Wildlife	Jeep
1946	**ASSAULT**	2:30⅘	Warren Mehrtens	Max Hirsch	Natchez	Cable
1947	**Phalanx**	2:29⅖	R.Donoso	Syl Veitch	Tide Rips	Tailspin
1948	**CITATION**	2:28⅕	Eddie Arcaro	Jimmy Jones	Better Self	Escadru
1949	**Capot**	2:30⅕	Ted Atkinson	John Gaver	Ponder	Palestinian

Belmont Stakes (Cont.)

Year		Time	Jockey	Trainer	2nd place	3rd place
1950	**Middleground**	2:28$\frac{3}{5}$	William Boland	Max Hirsch	Lights Up	Mr.Trouble
1951	**Counterpoint**	2:29	David Gorman	Syl Veitch	Battlefield	Battle Morn
1952	**One Count**	2:30$\frac{1}{5}$	Eddie Arcaro	Oscar White	Blue Man	Armageddon
1953	**Native Dancer**	2:28$\frac{3}{5}$	Eric Guerin	Bill Winfrey	Jamie K.	Royal Bay Gem
1954	**High Gun**	2:30$\frac{4}{5}$	Eric Guerin	Max Hirsch	Fisherman	Limelight
1955	**Nashua**	2:29	Eddie Arcaro	Jim Fitzsimmons	Blazing Count	Portersville
1956	**Needles**	2:29$\frac{3}{5}$	David Erb	Hugh Fontaine	Career Boy	Fabius
1957	**Gallant Man**	2:26$\frac{3}{5}$	Bill Shoemaker	John Nerud	Inside Tract	Bold Ruler
1958	**Cavan**	2:30$\frac{1}{5}$	Pete Anderson	Tom Barry	Tim Tam	Flamingo
1959	**Sword Dancer**	2:28$\frac{2}{5}$	Bill Shoemaker	Elliott Burch	Bagdad	Royal Orbit
1960	**Celtic Ash**	2:29$\frac{3}{5}$	Bill Hartack	Tom Barry	Venetian Way	Disperse
1961	**Sherluck**	2:29$\frac{1}{5}$	Braulio Baeza	Harold Young	Globemaster	Guadalcanal
1962	**Jaipur**	2:28$\frac{4}{5}$	Bill Shoemaker	B.Mulholland	Admiral's Voyage	Crimson Satan
1963	**Chateaugay**	2:30$\frac{1}{5}$	Braulio Baeza	James Conway	Candy Spots	Choker
1964	**Quadrangle**	2:28$\frac{2}{5}$	Manuel Ycaza	Elliott Burch	Roman Brother	Northern Dancer
1965	**Hail to All**	2:28$\frac{2}{5}$	John Sellers	Eddie Yowell	Tom Rolfe	First Family
1966	**Amberoid**	2:29$\frac{3}{5}$	William Boland	Lucien Laurin	Buffle	Advocator
1967	**Damascus**	2:28$\frac{4}{5}$	Bill Shoemaker	F.Y.Whiteley	Cool Reception	Gentleman James
1968	**Stage Door Johnny**	2:27$\frac{1}{5}$	Gus Gustines	John Gaver	Forward Pass	Call Me Prince
1969	**Arts and Letters**	2:28$\frac{4}{5}$	Braulio Baeza	Elliott Burch	Majestic Prince	Dike
1970	**High Echelon**	2:34	John Rotz	John Jacobs	Needles N Pins	Naskra
1971	**Pass Catcher**	2:30$\frac{2}{5}$	Walter Blum	Eddie Yowell	Jim French	Bold Reason
1972	**Riva Ridge**	2:28	Ron Turcotte	Lucien Laurin	Ruritania	Cloudy Dawn
1973	**SECRETARIAT**	2:24	Ron Turcotte	Lucien Laurin	Twice A Prince	My Gallant
1974	**Little Current**	2:29$\frac{1}{5}$	Miguel Rivera	Lou Rondinello	Jolly Johu	Cannonade
1975	**Avatar**	2:28$\frac{1}{5}$	Bill Shoemaker	Tommy Doyle	Foolish Pleasure	Master Derby
1976	**Bold Forbes**	2:29	Angel Cordero	Laz Barrera	McKenzie Bridge	Great Contractor
1977	**SEATTLE SLEW**	2:29$\frac{3}{5}$	Jean Cruguet	Billy Turner	Run Dusty Run	Sanhedrin
1978	**AFFIRMED**	2:26$\frac{4}{5}$	Steve Cauthen	Laz Barrera	Alydar	Darby Creek Road
1979	**Coastal**	2:28$\frac{3}{5}$	Ruben Hernandez	David Whiteley	Golden Act	Spectacular Bid
1980	**Temperence Hill**	2:29$\frac{4}{5}$	Eddie Maple	Joseph Cantey	Genuine Risk	Rockhill Native
1981	**Summing**	2:29	George Martens	Luis Barerra	Highland Blade	Pleasant Colony
1982	**Conquistador Cielo**	2:28$\frac{1}{5}$	Laffit Pincay,Jr	Woody Stephens	Gato Del Sol	Illuminate
1983	**Caveat**	2:27$\frac{4}{5}$	Laffit Pincay,Jr	Woody Stephens	Slew o'Gold	Barberstown
1984	**Swale**	2:27$\frac{1}{5}$	Laffit Pincay,Jr	Woody Stephens	Pine Circle	Morning Bob
1985	**Creme Fraiche**	2:27	Eddie Maple	Woody Stephens	Stephan's Odyssey	Chief's Crown
1986	**Danzig Connection**	2:29$\frac{4}{5}$	Chris McCarron	Woody Stephens	Johns Treasure	Ferdinand
1987	**Bet Twice**	2:28$\frac{1}{5}$	Craig Perret	Jimmy Croll	Cryptoclearance	Gulch
1988	**Risen Star**	2:26$\frac{2}{5}$	E.Delahoussaye	Louie Roussel	Kingpost	Brian's Time
1989	**Easy Goer**	2:26	Pat Day	Shug McGaughey	Sunday Silence	Le Voyageur
1990	**Go And Go**	2:27$\frac{1}{5}$	Michael Kinane	Dermot Weld	Thirty Six Red	Baron de Vaux
1991	**Hansel**	2:28	Jerry Bailey	Frank Brothers	Strike the Gold	Mane Minister

Breeders' Cup

Inaugurated on Nov. 10, 1984, the Breeders' Cup consists of seven races at one track on one day late in the year to determine thoroughbred racing's principal champions.

Breeders' Cup Day has been held at Hollywood Park (Calif.) in 1984, Aqueduct Racetrack (N.Y.) in 1985, Santa Anita Park (Calif.) in 1986, Hollywood Park in 1987, Churchill Downs (Ky.) in 1988 and Gulfstream Park (Fla.) in 1989. The 1990 running will be held at Belmont Park (N.Y.) on Oct. 27.

The steeplechase was added to the Breeders' Cup championship roster in 1986, but has been held each year at Fair Hill Race Course (Md.)

Trainers with most wins: D. Wayne Lukas (9); Neil Drysdale and Shug McCaughey (3); LeRoy Jolley, Ron McAnally and Scotty Schulhofer (2).

Jockeys with most wins: Laffit Pincay, Jr (6); Pat Day and Jose Santos (5); Angel Cordero, Jr (4); Chris McCarron, Craig Perret and Randy Romero (3).

Juvenile

Distances: one mile (1984-85, 87); 1$\frac{1}{16}$ miles (1986 and since 1988).

Year		Time	Jockey	Trainer	2nd place	3rd place
1984	**Chief's Crown**	1:36$\frac{1}{5}$	Don MacBeth	Roger Laurin	Tank's Prospect	Spend A Buck
1985	**Tasso**	1:36$\frac{1}{5}$	Laffit Pincay	Neil Drysdale	Storm Cat	Scat Dancer
1986	**Capote**	1:43$\frac{4}{5}$	Laffit Pincay	D.Wayne Lukas	Qualify	Alysheba
1987	**Success Express**	1:35$\frac{1}{5}$	Jose Santos	D.Wayne Lukas	Regal Classic	Tejano
1988	**Is It True**	1:46$\frac{3}{5}$	Laffit Pincay	D.Wayne Lukas	Easy Goer	Tagel
1989	**Rhythm**	1:43$\frac{3}{5}$	Craig Perret	Shug McGaughey	Grand Canyon	Slavic
1990	**Fly So Free**	1:43$\frac{2}{5}$	Jose Santos	Scotty Schulhofer	Take Me Out	Lost Mountain

Juvenile Fillies

Distances: one mile (1984-85, 87); 1¹⁄₁₆ miles (1986 and since 1988).

Year		Time	Jockey	Trainer	2nd place	3rd place
1984	**Outstandingly**	1:37⅘	Walter Guerra	Pancho Martin	Dusty Heart	Fine Spirit
1985	**Twilight Ridge**	1:35⅘	Jorge Velasquez	D.Wayne Lukas	Family Style	Steal A Kiss
1986	**Brave Raj**	1:43⅕	Pat Valenzuela	Melvin Stute	Tappiano	Saros Brig
1987	**Epitome**	1:36⅖	Pat Day	Phil Hauswald	Jeanne Jones	Dream Team
1988	**Open Mind**	1:46⅗	Angel Cordero,Jr	D.Wayne Lukas	Darby Shuffle	Lea Lucinda
1989	**Go for Wand**	1:44⅕	Randy Romero	William Badgett	Sweet Roberta	Stella Madrid
1990	**Meadow Star**	1:44	Jose Santos	LeRoy Jolley	Private Treasure	Dance Smartly

Note: in 1984, winner **Fran's Valentine** was disqualified for interference in the stretch and placed 10th.

Sprint

Distance: six furlongs (since 1984).

Year		Time	Jockey	Trainer	2nd place	3rd place
1984	**Eillo**	1:10⅕	Craig Perret	Budd Lepman	Commemorate	Fighting Fit
1985	**Precisionist**	1:08⅖	Chris McCarron	R.Fenstermaker	Smile	Mt.Livermore
1986	**Smile**	1:08⅖	Jacinto Vasquez	S.Schulhofer	Pine Tree Lane	Bedside Promise
1987	**Very Subtle**	1:08⅘	Pat Valenzuela	Melvin Stute	Groovy	Exclusive Enough
1988	**Gulch**	1:10⅖	Angel Cordero,Jr	D.Wayne Lukas	Play The King	Afleet
1989	**Dancing Spree**	1:09	Angel Cordero,Jr	Shug McGaughey	Safely Kept	Dispersal
1990	**Safely Kept**	1:09⅗	Craig Perret	Alan Goldberg	Dayjur	Black Tie Affair

Mile

Year		Time	Jockey	Trainer	2nd place	3rd place
1984	**Royal Heroine**	1:32⅗	Fernando Toro	John Gosden	Star Choice	Cozzene
1985	**Cozzene**	1:35	Walter Guerra	Jan Nerud	Al Mamoon	Shadeed
1986	**Last Tycoon**	1:35⅕	Yves St.-Martin	Robert Collet	Palace Music	Fred Astaire
1987	**Miesque**	1:32⅘	Freddie Head	Francois Boutin	Show Dancer	Sonic Lady
1988	**Miesque**	1:38⅗	Freddie Head	Francois Boutin	Steinlen	Simply Majestic
1989	**Steinlen**	1:37⅕	Jose Santos	D.Wayne Lukas	Sabona	Most Welcome
1990	**Royal Academy**	1:35⅕	Lester Piggott	M.V. O'Brien	Itsallgreektome	Priolo

Note: in 1985, 2nd place finisher **Palace Music** was disqualified for interference and placed 9th.

Distaff

Distances: 1¼ miles (1984-87); 1⅛ miles (since 1988).

Year		Time	Jockey	Trainer	2nd place	3rd place
1984	**Princess Rooney**	2:02⅖	E.Delahoussaye	Neil Drysdale	Life's Magic	Adored
1985	**Life's Magic**	2:02	Angel Cordero,Jr	D.Wayne Lukas	Lady's Secret	DontstopThemusic
1986	**Lady's Secret**	2:01⅕	Pat Day	D.Wayne Lukas	Fran's Valentine	Outstandingly
1987	**Sacahuista**	2:02⅘	Randy Romero	D.Wayne Lukas	Clabber Girl	Oueee Bebe
1988	**Personal Ensign**	1:52	Randy Romero	Shug McGaughey	Winning Colors	Goodbye Halo
1989	**Bayakoa**	1:47⅖	Laffit Pincay,Jr	Ron McAnally	Gorgeous	Open Mind
1990	**Bayakoa**	1:49⅕	Laffit Pincay, Jr.	Ron McAnally	Colonial Waters	Valay Maid

Turf

Distance: 1½ miles (since 1984).

Year		Time	Jockey	Trainer	2nd place	3rd place
1984	**Lashkari**	2:25⅕	Yves St-Martin	De Royer-Dupre	All Along	Raami
1985	**Pebbles**	2:27	Pat Eddery	Clive Brittain	Strawberry Rd.II	Mourjane
1986	**Manila**	2:25⅖	Jose Santos	Leroy Jolley	Theatrical	Estrapade
1987	**Theatrical**	2:24⅖	Pat Day	Bill Mott	Trempolino	Village Star II
1988	**Grt.Communicator**	2:35⅕	Ray Sibille	Thad Ackel	Sunshine Forever	Indian Skimmer
1989	**Prized**	2:28	E.Delahoussaye	Neil Drysdale	Sierra Roberta	Star Lift
1990	**In The Wings**	2:29⅗	Gary Stevens	Andre Fabre	With Approval	El Senor

Classic

Distance: 1¼ miles (since 1984).

Year		Time	Jockey	Trainer	2nd place	3rd place
1984	**Wild Again**	2:03⅖	Pat Day	V.Timphony	Slew O'Gold	Gate Dancer
1985	**Proud Truth**	2:00⅘	Jorge Velasquez	John Veitch	Gate Dancer	Turkoman
1986	**Skywalker**	2:00⅖	Laffit Pincay	M.Whittingham	Turkoman	Precisionist
1987	**Ferdinand**	2:01⅖	Bill Shoemaker	C.Whittingham	Alysheba	Judge Angelucci
1988	**Alysheba**	2:04⅘	Chris McCarron	Jack Van Berg	Seeking the Gold	Waquoit
1989	**Sunday Silence**	2:00⅕	Chris McCarron	C.Whittingham	Easy Goer	Blushing John
1990	**Unbridled**	2:02⅕	Pat Day	Carl Nofzger	Ibn Bey	Thirty-Six Red

Note: in 1984, 2nd place finisher **Gate Dancer** was disqualified for interference and placed 3rd.

Steeplechase

Distances: 2⅜ miles (1986); 2⅝ miles (since 1987).

Year		Time	Jockey	Trainer	2nd place	3rd place
1986	**Census**	4:27⅗	Jeff Teter	Janet Elliott	Kesslin	Pont du Loup
1987	**Gacko**	5:15⅕	Roger Duchene	Xavier Guigand	Inlander	Gateshead
1988	**Jimmy Lorenzo**	5:12⅖	Graham McCourt	J.E.Sheppard	Kalankoe	Polar Pleasure
1989	**Highland Bud**	4:58⅘	Rich. Dunwoody	J.E.Sheppard	Polar Pleasure	Victorian Hill
1990	**Morley Street**	4:53⅕	Jimmy Frost	Toby Balding	Summer Colony	Moonstruck

Annual Money Leaders

Horses

Annual money-leading horses since 1910, according to *The American Racing Manual*.
Multiple leaders: Round Table, Buckpasser and Alysheba (2).

Year		Age	Sts	1st	Purses	Year		Age	Sts	1st	Purses
1910	Novelty	2	16	11	$72,630	1951	Counterpoint	3	15	7	$250,525
1911	Worth	2	13	10	16,645	1952	Crafty Admiral	4	16	9	277,225
1912	Star Charter	4	17	6	14,655	1953	Native Dancer	3	10	9	513,425
1913	Old Rosebud	2	14	12	19,057	1954	Determine	3	15	10	328,700
1914	Roamer	3	16	12	29,105	1955	Nashua	3	12	10	752,550
1915	Borrow	7	9	4	20,195	1956	Needles	3	8	4	440,850
1916	Campfire	2	9	6	49,735	1957	Round Table	3	22	15	600,383
1917	Sun Briar	2	9	5	59,505	1958	Round Table	4	20	14	662,780
1918	External	2	8	6	56,173	1959	Sword Dancer	3	13	8	537,004
1919	Sir Barton	3	13	8	88,250						
1920	Man o'War	3	11	11	166,140	1960	Bally Ache	3	15	10	445,045
1921	Morvich	2	11	11	115,234	1961	Carry Back	3	16	9	565,349
1922	Pillory	3	7	4	95,654	1962	Never Bend	2	10	7	402,969
1923	Zev	3	14	12	272,008	1963	Candy Spots	3	12	7	604,481
1924	Sarazen	3	12	8	95,640	1964	Gun Bow	4	16	8	580,100
1925	Pompey	2	10	7	121,630	1965	Buckpasser	2	11	9	568,096
1926	Crusader	3	15	9	166,033	1966	Buckpasser	3	14	13	669,078
1927	Anita Peabody	2	7	6	111,905	1967	Damascus	3	16	12	817,941
1928	High Strung	2	6	5	153,590	1968	Forward Pass	3	13	7	546,674
1929	Blue Larkspur	3	6	4	153,450	1969	Arts and Letters	3	14	8	555,604
1930	Gallant Fox	3	10	9	308,275	1970	Personality	3	18	8	444,049
1931	Gallant Flight	2	7	7	219,000	1971	Riva Ridge	2	9	7	503,263
1932	Gusto	3	16	4	145,940	1972	Droll Role	4	19	7	471,633
1933	Singing Wood	2	9	3	88,050	1973	Secretariat	3	12	9	860,404
1934	Cavalcade	3	7	6	111,235	1974	Chris Evert	3	8	5	551,063
1935	Omaha	3	9	6	142,255	1975	Foolish Pleasure	3	11	5	716,278
1936	Granville	3	11	7	110,295	1976	Forego	6	8	6	401,701
1937	Seabiscuit	4	15	11	168,580	1977	Seattle Slew	3	7	6	641,370
1938	Stagehand	3	15	8	189,710	1978	Affirmed	3	11	8	901,541
1939	Challedon	3	15	9	184,535	1979	Spectacular Bid	3	12	10	1,279,334
1940	Bimelech	3	7	4	110,005	1980	Temperence Hill	3	17	8	1,130,452
1941	Whirlaway	3	20	13	272,386	1981	John Henry	6	10	8	1,798,030
1942	Shut Out	3	12	8	238,872	1982	Perrault (GB)	5	8	4	1,197,400
1943	Count Fleet	3	6	6	174,055	1983	All Along (FRA)	4	7	4	2,138,963
1944	Pavot	2	8	8	179,040	1984	Slew o'Gold	4	6	5	2,627,944
1945	Busher	3	13	10	273,735	1985	Spend A Buck	3	7	5	3,552,704
1946	Assault	3	15	8	424,195	1986	Snow Chief	3	9	6	1,875,200
1947	Armed	6	17	11	376,325	1987	Alysheba	3	10	3	2,511,156
1948	Citation	3	20	19	709,470	1988	Alysheba	4	9	7	3,808,600
1949	Ponder	3	21	9	321,825	1989	Sunday Silence	3	9	7	4,578,454
1950	Noor	5	12	7	346,940	1990	Unbridled	3	11	4	3,718,149

Jockeys

Annual money-leading jockeys since 1910, according to *The American Racing Manual*.
Multiple leaders: Bill Shoemaker (10); Laffit Pincay, Jr (7); Eddie Arcaro (6); Braulio Baeza (5); Jose Santos (4); Angel Cordero, Jr, Chris McCarron and Earl Sande (3); Ted Atkinson, Laverne Fator, Mack Garner, Bill Hartack, Charles Kurtsinger, Johnny Longden, Sonny Workman and Wayne Wright (2).

Year		Mts	Wins	Purses	Year		Mts	Wins	Purses
1910	Carroll Shilling	506	172	$176,030	1920	Clarence Kummer	353	87	$292,376
1911	Ted Koerner	813	162	88,308	1921	Earl Sande	340	112	263,043
1912	Jimmy Butwell	684	144	79,843	1922	Albert Johnson	297	43	345,054
1913	Merritt Buxton	887	146	82,552	1923	Earl Sande	430	122	569,394
1914	J.McCahey	824	155	121,845	1924	Ivan Parke	844	205	290,395
1915	Mack Garner	775	151	96,628	1925	Laverne Fator	315	81	305,775
1916	John McTaggart	832	150	155,055	1926	Laverne Fator	511	143	361,435
1917	Frank Robinson	731	147	148,057	1927	Earl Sande	179	49	277,877
1918	Lucien Lyke	756	178	201,864	1928	Linus McAtee	235	55	301,295
1919	John Loftus	177	65	252,707	1929	Mack Garner	274	57	314,975

Year		Mts	Wins	Purses	Year		Mts	Wins	Purses
1930	Sonny Workman	571	152	$420,438	1962	Bill Shoemaker	1126	311	$2,916,844
1931	Chas. Kurtsinger	519	93	392,095	1963	Bill Shoemaker	1203	271	2,526,925
1932	Sonny Workman	378	87	385,070	1964	Bill Shoemaker	1056	246	2,649,553
1933	Robert Jones	471	63	226,285	1965	Braulio Baeza	1245	270	2,582,702
1934	Wayne Wright	919	174	287,185	1966	Braulio Baeza	1341	298	2,951,022
1935	Silvio Coucci	749	141	319,760	1967	Braulio Baeza	1064	256	3,088,888
1936	Wayne Wright	670	100	264,000	1968	Braulio Baeza	1089	201	2,835,108
1937	Chas. Kurtsinger	765	120	384,202	1969	Jorge Velasquez	1442	258	2,542,315
1938	Nick Wall	658	97	385,161	1970	Laffit Pincay, Jr	1328	269	2,626,526
1939	Basil James	904	191	353,333	1971	Laffit Pincay, Jr	1627	380	3,784,377
1940	Eddie Arcaro	783	132	343,661	1972	Laffit Pincay, Jr	1388	289	3,225,827
1941	Don Meade	1164	210	398,627	1973	Laffit Pincay, Jr	1444	350	4,093,492
1942	Eddie Arcaro	687	123	481,949	1974	Laffit Pincay, Jr	1278	341	4,251,060
1943	Johnny Longden	871	173	573,276	1975	Braulio Baeza	1190	196	3,674,398
1944	Ted Atkinson	1539	287	899,101	1976	Angel Cordero, Jr	1534	274	4,709,500
1945	Johnny Longden	778	180	981,977	1977	Steve Cauthen	2075	487	6,151,750
1946	Ted Atkinson	1377	233	1,036,825	1978	Darrel McHargue	1762	375	6,188,353
1947	Douglas Dodson	646	141	1,429,949	1979	Laffit Pincay, Jr	1708	420	8,183,535
1948	Eddie Arcaro	726	188	1,686,230	1980	Chris McCarron	1964	405	7,666,100
1949	Steve Brooks	906	209	1,316,817	1981	Chris McCarron	1494	326	8,397,604
1950	Eddie Arcaro	888	195	1,410,160	1982	Angel Cordero, Jr	1838	397	9,702,520
1951	Bill Shoemaker	1161	257	1,329,890	1983	Angel Cordero, Jr	1792	362	10,116,807
1952	Eddie Arcaro	807	188	1,859,591	1984	Chris McCarron	1565	356	12,038,213
1953	Bill Shoemaker	1683	485	1,784,187	1985	Laffit Pincay, Jr	1409	289	13,415,049
1954	Bill Shoemaker	1251	380	1,876,760	1986	Jose Santos	1636	329	11,329,297
1955	Eddie Arcaro	820	158	1,864,796	1987	Jose Santos	1639	305	12,407,355
1956	Bill Hartack	1387	347	2,343,955	1988	Jose Santos	1867	370	14,877,298
1957	Bill Hartack	1238	341	3,060,501	1989	Jose Santos	1459	285	13,847,003
1958	Bill Shoemaker	1133	300	2,961,693	1990	Gary Stevens	1504	283	13,881,198
1959	Bill Shoemaker	1285	347	2,843,133					
1960	Bill Shoemaker	1227	274	2,123,961					
1961	Bill Shoemaker	1256	304	2,690,819					

All-Time Money Leaders

The all-time winning horses and jockeys of North America through 1990, according to *The American Racing Manual*. Records include all available information on races in foreign countries.

Top 20 Horses

Note that (*) indicates horse raced in 1990; (†) indicates foreign-bred; and (f) indicates female.

	Sts	1st	2nd	3rd	Purses
Alysheba	26	11	8	2	$6,679,242
John Henry	83	39	15	9	6,597,947
*Sunday Silence	14	9	5	0	4,968,554
*Easy Goer	20	14	5	1	4,873,770
Spend A Buck	15	10	3	2	4,220,689
Creme Fraiche	64	17	12	13	4,024,727
*Unbridled	17	6	5	4	3,892,695
Ferdinand	29	8	9	6	3,777,978
Slew o'Gold	21	12	5	1	3,533,534
Precisionist	46	20	10	4	3,485,393
Snow Chief	24	13	3	5	3,383,210
Cryptoclearence	44	12	10	7	3,376,327
Bet Twice	26	10	6	4	3,308,599
*†Steinlen	45	20	10	7	3,300,100
Gulch	32	13	8	4	3,095,521
Lady's Secret (f)	45	25	9	3	3,021,425
†All Along (f)	21	9	4	2	3,015,764
†Theatrical	22	10	4	2	2,943,627
*Gt.Communicator	56	14	10	7	2,922,615
Symboli Rudolf	16	13	1	1	2,909,593

Top 20 Jockeys

Note that (*) indicates jockey active in 1990.

	Yrs	Mts	Wins	Purses
Bill Shoemaker	42	40,350	8833	$123,375,524
*Laffit Pincay, Jr	25	34,739	7477	154,659,844
*Angel Cordero, Jr	29	37,270	6812	154,944,152
*Jorge Velasquez	28	36,748	6333	113,078,159
*Larry Snyder	31	33,342	6133	44,011,598
Johnny Longden	40	32,413	6032	24,665,800
*Sandy Hawley	23	27,125	5790	72,120,057
*David Gall	34	32,489	5712	16,120,904
*Carl Gambardella	35	35,325	5674	24,597,949
*Chris McCarron	16	24,541	5304	127,825,744
*Earlie Fires	26	34,182	5075	54,149,113
*Pat Day	18	23,779	5006	99,294,959
*Jacinto Vasquez	31	33,604	4787	71,824,307
Eddie Arcaro	31	24,092	4779	30,039,543
Don Brumfield	37	33,223	4573	43,567,861
*Eddie Delahoussaye	21	27,854	4506	94,768,041
Steve Brooks	34	30,330	4451	18,239,817
Walter Blum	22	28,673	4382	26,497,189
Bill Hartack	22	21,535	4272	26,466,758
Avelino Gomez	34	17,028	4081	11,777,297

Retired: Arcaro (1961); Blum (1975); Brooks (1975); Brumfield (1989); Gomez (1980); Hartack (1974); Longden (1966); Shoemaker (1990).

Horse of the Year (1936–70)

In 1971, the *Daily Racing Form*, the Thoroughbred Racing Associations, and the National Turf Writers Assn. joined forces to create the Eclipse Awards. Before then, however, the *Racing Form* (1936-70) and the TRA (1950-70) issued separate selections for Horse of the Year. Their picks differed only four times from 1950-70 and are so noted. Horses listed in CAPITAL letters are Triple Crown winners; (f) indicates female.

Multiple winners: Kelso (5); Challedon, Native Dancer and Whirlaway (2).

Year		Year		Year		Year	
1936	Granville	1946	ASSAULT	1955	Nashua	1964	Kelso
1937	WAR ADMIRAL	1947	Armed	1956	Swaps	1965	Roman Brother (DRF)
1938	Seabiscuit	1948	CITATION	1957	Bold Ruler (DRF)		Moccasin (TRA)
1939	Challedon	1949	Capot		Dedicate (TRA)	1966	Buckpasser
1940	Challedon	1950	Hill Prince	1958	Round Table	1967	Damascus
1941	WHIRLAWAY	1951	Counterpoint	1959	Sword Dancer	1968	Dr.Fager
1942	Whirlaway	1952	One Count (DRF)	1960	Kelso	1969	Arts and Letters
1943	COUNT FLEET		Native Dancer (TRA)	1961	Kelso	1970	Fort Marcy (DRF)
1944	Twilight Tear (f)	1953	Tom Fool	1962	Kelso		Personality (TRA)
1945	Busher (f)	1954	Native Dancer	1963	Kelso		

Eclipse Awards

The Eclipse Awards, honoring the Horse of the Year and other champions of the sport, are sponsored by the *Daily Racing Form*, the Thoroughbred Racing Associations and the National Turf Writers Assn.

The awards are named after the 18th century racehorse and sire, Eclipse, who began racing at age five and was unbeaten in 18 starts (eight wins were walkovers). As a stallion, Eclipse sired winners of 344 races, including three Epsom Derby champions.

Horses listed in CAPITAL letters won the Triple Crown that year. Age of horse in parentheses where necessary.

Multiple winners (horses)**:** Forego (8); John Henry (7); Affirmed and Secretariat (5); Flatterer, Seattle Slew and Spectacular Bid (4); Ack Ack, Susan's Girl and Zaccio (3); All Along, Alysheba, Bayakoa, Cafe Prince, Conquistador Cielo, Desert Vixen, Ferdinand, Go for Wand, Lady's Secret, Life's Magic, Miesque, Open Mind, Riva Ridge, Slew o'Gold and Spend A Buck (2).

Multiple winners (people)**:** Laffit Pincay, Jr.(5); Laz Barrera (4); Steve Cauthen, Pat Day, Harbor View Farm, Nelson Bunker Hunt, Mr.& Mrs. Gene Klein, Dan Lasater, D.Wayne Lucas, Ogden Phipps, Bill Shoemaker, Edward Taylor and Charlie Whittingham (3); Braulio Baeza, C.T.Chenery, Claiborne Farm, Angel Cordero, Jr., Kent Desormeaux, John Franks, John W.Galbreath, Fred Hooper, Chris McCarron and Paul Mellon.

Horse of the Year

Year		Year		Year		Year	
1971	Ack Ack (5)	1976	Forego (6)	1982	Conquistador Cielo (3)	1987	Ferdinand (4)
1972	Secretariat (2)	1977	SEATTLE SLEW (3)	1983	All Along (4)	1988	Alysheba (4)
1973	SECRETARIAT (3)	1978	AFFIRMED (3)	1984	John Henry (9)	1989	Sunday Silence (3)
1974	Forego (4)	1979	Affirmed (4)	1985	Spend A Buck (3)	1990	Criminal Type (5)
1975	Forego (5)	1980	Spectacular Bid (4)	1986	Lady's Secret (4)		
		1981	John Henry (6)				

Older Colt, Horse or Gelding

Year		Year		Year		Year	
1971	Ack Ack (5)	1977	Forego (7)	1982	Lemhi Gold (4)	1987	Ferdinand (4)
1972	Autobiography (4)	1978	Seattle Slew (4)	1983	Bates Motel (4)	1988	Alysheba (4)
1973	Riva Ridge (4)	1979	Affirmed (4)	1984	Slew o' Gold (4)	1989	Blushing John (4)
1974	Forego (4)	1980	Spectacular Bid (4)	1985	Vanlandingham (4)	1990	Criminal Type (5)
1975	Forego (5)	1981	John Henry (6)	1986	Turkoman (4)		
1976	Forego (6)						

Older Filly or Mare

Year		Year		Year		Year	
1971	Shuvee (5)	1977	Cascapedia (4)	1982	Track Robbery (6)	1987	North Sider (5)
1972	Typecast (6)	1978	Late Bloomer (4)	1983	Amb. of Luck (4)	1988	Personal Ensign (4)
1973	Susan's Girl (4)	1979	Waya (4)	1984	Princess Rooney (4)	1989	Bayakoa (5)
1974	Desert Vixen (4)	1980	Glorious Song (4)	1985	Life's Magic (4)	1990	Bayakoa (6)
1975	Susan's Girl (6)	1981	Relaxing (5)	1986	Lady's Secret (4)		
1976	Proud Delta (4)						

3-Year-Old Colt

Year		Year		Year		Year	
1971	Canonero II	1977	SEATTLE SLEW	1982	Conquistador Cielo	1987	Alysheba
1972	Key to the Mint	1978	AFFIRMED	1983	Slew o' Gold	1988	Risen Star
1973	SECRETARIAT	1979	Spectacular Bid	1984	Swale	1989	Sunday Silence
1974	Little Current	1980	Temperence Hill	1985	Spend A Buck	1990	Unbridled
1975	Wajima	1981	Pleasant Colony	1986	Snow Chief		
1976	Bold Forbes						

3-Year-Old Filly

Year		Year		Year		Year	
1971	Turkish Trousers	1977	Our Mims	1982	Christmas Past	1987	Sacahuista
1972	Susan's Girl	1978	Tempest Queen	1983	Heartlight No. One	1988	Winning Colors
1973	Desert Vixen	1979	Davona Dale	1984	Life's Magic	1989	Open Mind
1974	Chris Evert	1980	Genuine Risk	1985	Mom's Command	1990	Go for Wand
1975	Ruffian	1981	Wayward Lass	1986	Tiffany Lass		
1976	Revidere						

2-Year-Old Colt

Year		Year		Year		Year	
1971	Riva Ridge	1977	Affirmed	1982	Roving Boy	1987	Forty Niner
1972	Secretariat	1978	Spectacular Bid	1983	Devil's Bag	1988	Easy Goer
1973	Protagonist	1979	Rockhill Native	1984	Chief's Crown	1989	Rhythm
1974	Foolish Pleasure	1980	Lord Avie	1985	Tasso	1990	Fly So Free
1975	Honest Pleasure	1981	Deputy Minister	1986	Capote		
1976	Seattle Slew						

2-Year-Old Filly

Year		Year		Year		Year	
1971	Numbered Account	1977	Lakeville Miss	1982	Landaluce	1987	Epitome
1972	La Prevoyante	1978	Candy Eclair	1983	Althea	1988	Open Mind
1973	Talking Picture		& It's in the Air	1984	Outstandingly	1989	Go for Wand
1974	Ruffian	1979	Smart Angle	1985	Family Style	1990	Meadow Star
1975	Dearly Precious	1980	Heavenly Cause	1986	Brave Raj		
1976	Sensational	1981	Before Dawn				

Champion Turf Horse

Year		Year		Year		Year	
1971	Run the Gantlet (3)	1973	Secretariat (3)	1975	Snow Knight (4)	1977	Johnny D (3)
1972	Cougar II (6)	1974	Dahlia (4)	1976	Youth (3)	1978	Mac Diarmida (3)

Champion Male Turf Horse

Year		Year		Year		Year	
1979	Bowl Game (5)	1982	Perrault (5)	1985	Cozzene (4)	1988	Sunshine Forever (3)
1980	John Henry (5)	1983	John Henry (8)	1986	Manila (3)	1989	Steinlen (6)
1981	John Henry (6)	1984	John Henry (9)	1987	Theatrical (5)	1990	Itsallgreektome (3)

Champion Female Turf Horse

Year		Year		Year		Year	
1979	Trillion (5)	1982	April Run (4)	1985	Pebbles (4)	1988	Miesque (4)
1980	Just A Game II (4)	1983	All Along (4)	1986	Estrapade (6)	1989	Brown Bess (7)
1981	De La Rose (3)	1984	Royal Heroine (4)	1987	Miesque (3)	1990	Laugh and Be Merry (5)

Sprinter

Year		Year		Year		Year	
1971	Ack Ack (5)	1977	What a Summer (4)	1982	Gold Beauty (3)	1987	Groovy (4)
1972	Chou Croute (4)	1978	Dr.Patches (4)	1983	Chinook Pass (4)	1988	Gulch (4)
1973	Shecky Greene (3)		& J.O.Tobin (4)	1984	Eillo (4)	1989	Safely Kept (3)
1974	Forego (4)	1979	Star de Naskra (4)	1985	Precisionist (4)	1990	Housebuster (3)
1975	Gallant Bob (3)	1980	Plugged Nickle (3)	1986	Smile (4)		
1976	My Juliet (4)	1981	Guilty Conscience (5)				

Steeplechase or Hurdle Horse

Year		Year		Year		Year	
1971	Shadow Brook (7)	1976	Straight & True (6)	1981	Zaccio (5)	1986	Flatterer (7)
1972	Soothsayer (5)	1977	Cafe Prince (7)	1982	Zaccio (6)	1987	Inlander (6)
1973	Athenian Idol (5)	1978	Cafe Prince (8)	1983	Flatterer (4)	1988	Jimmy Lorenzo (6)
1974	Gran Kan (8)	1979	Martie's Anger (4)	1984	Flatterer (5)	1989	Highland Bud (4)
1975	Life's Illusion (4)	1980	Zaccio (4)	1985	Flatterer (6)	1990	Morley Street (7)

Outstanding Jockey

Year		Year		Year		Year	
1971	Laffit Pincay, Jr	1976	Sandy Hawley	1981	Bill Shoemaker	1986	Pat Day
1972	Braulio Baeza	1977	Steve Cauthen	1982	Angel Cordero, Jr	1987	Pat Day
1973	Laffit Pincay, Jr	1978	Darrel McHargue	1983	Angel Cordero, Jr	1988	Jose Santos
1974	Laffit Pincay, Jr	1979	Laffit Pincay, Jr	1984	Pat Day	1989	Kent Desormeaux
1975	Braulio Baeza	1980	Chris McCarron	1985	Laffit Pincay, Jr	1990	Craig Perret

Eclipse Awards (Cont.)

Outstanding Apprentice Jockey

Year		Year		Year		Year	
1971	Gene St. Leon	1976	George Martens	1981	Richard Migliore	1986	Allen Stacy
1972	Thomas Wallis	1977	Steve Cauthen	1982	Alberto Delgado	1987	Kent Desormeaux
1973	Steve Valdez	1978	Ron Franklin	1983	Declan Murphy	1988	Steve Capanas
1974	Chris McCarron	1979	Cash Asmussen	1984	Wesley Ward	1989	Michael Luzzi
1975	Jimmy Edwards	1980	Grank Lovato, Jr	1985	Art Madrid, Jr	1990	Mark Johnston

Outstanding Trainer

Year		Year		Year		Year	
1971	Charlie Whittingham	1976	Laz Barrera	1981	Ron McAnally	1986	D.Wayne Lukas
1972	Lucien Laurin	1977	Laz Barrera	1982	Charlie Whittingham	1987	D.Wayne Lukas
1973	H.Allen Jerkens	1978	Laz Barrera	1983	Woody Stephens	1988	Shug McGaughey
1974	Sherrill Ward	1979	Laz Barrera	1984	Jack Van Berg	1989	Charlie Whittingham
1975	Steve DiMauro	1980	Bud Delp	1985	D.Wayne Lukas	1990	Carl Nafzger

Outstanding Owner

Year		Year		Year		Year	
1971	Mr.& Mrs. E.E. Fogleson	1976	Dan Lasater	1981	Dotsam Stable	1986	Mr.& Mrs. Gene Klein
1972	No award	1977	Maxwell Gluck	1982	Viola Sommer	1987	Mr.& Mrs. Gene Klein
1973	No award	1978	Harbor View Farm	1983	John Franks	1988	Ogden Phipps
1974	Dan Lasater	1979	Harbor View Farm	1984	John Franks	1989	Ogden Phipps
1975	Dan Lasater	1980	Mr.& Mrs. Bertram Firestone	1985	Mr.& Mrs. Gene Klein	1990	Frances Genter

Outstanding Owner-Breeder

Year		Year		Year	
1971	Paul Mellon	1972	C. T. Chenery	1973	C. T. Chenery

Outstanding Breeder

Year		Year		Year		Year	
1974	John W.Galbreath	1979	Claiborne Farm	1983	Edward P.Taylor	1987	Nelson Bunker Hunt
1975	Fred W.Hooper	1980	Mrs. Henry Paxson	1984	Claiborne Farm	1988	Ogden Phipps
1976	Nelson Bunker Hunt	1981	Golden Chance Farm	1985	Nelson Bunker Hunt	1989	North Ridge Farm
1977	Edward P. Taylor	1982	Fred W.Hooper	1986	Paul Mellon	1990	Calumet Farm
1978	Harbor View Farm						

Man of the Year

Year		Year		Year		Year	
1972	John W.Galbreath	1973	Edward P. Taylor	1974	William L.McKnight	1975	John A. Morris

Outstanding Achievement

Year		Year	
1971*	Charles Engelhard	1972*	Arthur B.Hancock, Jr

*Awarded posthumously

Award of Merit

Year		Year		Year		Year	
1976	Jack J.Dreyfus	1979	Jimmy Kilroe	1984	John Gaines	1987	J.B.Faulconer
1977	Steve Cauthen	1980	John D.Schapiro	1985	Keene Daingerfield	1988	John Forsythe
1978	Dinny Phipps	1981	Bill Shoemaker	1986	Herman Cohen	1989	Michael Sandler

Special Award

Year		Year		Year		Year	
1971	Robert J.Kleberg	1980	John T.Landry & Pierre E. Bellocq	1985	Arlington Park	1988	Edward J. DeBartolo, Sr.
1974	Charles Hatton	1984	C.V.Whitney	1987	Anheuser-Busch		
1976	Bill Shoemaker					1989	Richard Duchossois

Harness Racing
Triple Crown Winners
TROTTERS

Six 3-year-olds have won the Yonkers Trot, Hambletonian and Kentucky Futurity in the same year since the Trotting Triple Crown was established in 1955. Stanley Dancer is the only driver/trainer to win it twice.

Year		Driver/Trainer	Owner
1955	**Scott Frost**	Joe O'Brien	S.A. Camp Farms
1963	**Speedy Scot**	Ralph Baldwin	Castleton Farms
1964	**Ayres**	John Simpson, Sr.	Charlotte Sheppard
1968	**Nevele Pride**	Stanley Dancer	Nevele Acres & Lou Resnick
1969	**Lindy's Pride**	Howard Beissinger	Lindy Farms
1972	**Super Bowl**	Stanley Dancer	Rachel Dancer & Rose Hild Breeding Farm

PACERS

Seven 3-year-olds have won the Cane Pace, Little Brown Jug and Messenger Stakes in the same year since the Pacing Triple Crown was established in 1956. No trainer or driver has won it more than once.

Year		Driver	Trainer	Owner
1959	**Adios Butler**	Clint Hodgins	Paige West	Paige West & Angelo Pellillo
1965	**Bret Hanover**	Frank Ervin	Frank Ervin	Richard Downing
1966	**Romeo Hanover**	Bill Myer & George Sholty*	Jerry Silverman	Lucky Star Stable & Morton Finder
1968	**Rum Customer**	Billy Haughton	Billy Haughton	Kennilworth Farms & L.C. Mancuso
1970	**Most Happy Fella**	Stanley Dancer	Stanley Dancer	Egyptian Acres Stable
1980	**Niatross**	Clint Galbraith	Clint Galbraith	Niagara Acres, Niatross Stables & Clint Galbraith
1983	**Ralph Hanover**	Ron Waples	Stan Firlotte	Waples Stable, Pointsetta Stable, Grant's Direct Stable & P.J. Baugh

*Myer drove Romeo Hanover in the Cane, Sholty in the other two races.

Triple Crown Near Misses

TROTTERS

Five horses have won the first two legs of the Triple Crown—the Yonkers Trot (YT) and the Hambletonian (Ham)—but not the third. The eventual winner of the Ky. Futurity (KF) is listed.

Year		YT	Ham	KF
1962	**AC's Viking**	won	won	Safe Mission
1976	**Steve Lobell**	won	won	Quick Pay
1977	**Green Speed**	won	won	Texas
1978	**Speedy Somolli**	won	won	Doublemint
1987	**Mack Lobell**	won	won	Napoletano

Note: Green Speed (1977) not eligible for Ky. Futurity.

PACERS

Five horses have won the first two legs of the Triple Crown, but not the third. The Cane Pace (CP), Little Brown Jug (LBJ), and Messenger Stakes (MS) have not always been run in the same order so numbers after races indicate sequence for that year.

Year	Horse	CP	LBJ	MS
1957	**Torpid**	won, 1	won, 2	DNF
1960	**Countess Adios**	won, 2	NE	won, 1
1971	**Albatross**	won, 2	2nd*	won, 1
1976	**Keystone Ore**	won, 1	won, 2	2nd*
1986	**Barberry Spur**	won, 1	won, 2	2nd*
1990	**Jake and Elwood**	won, 1	NE	won, 2

*****Winning horses:** Nansemond (1971), Windshield Wiper (1976), Amity Chef (1986).

Note: Torpid (1957) scratched before the final heat; Countess Adios (1960) not eligible for Messenger; Jake and Elwood (1990) not eligible for Little Brown Jug.

The Hambletonian

For three-year-old trotters. Inaugurated in 1926 and has been held in Syracuse, N.Y.; Lexington, Ky.; Goshen, N.Y, Yonkers, N.Y.; Du Quoin, Ill.; and, since 1981 at The Meadowlands in East Rutherford, N.J.

Run at one mile since 1947. Winning horse must win two heats.

Drivers with most wins: Ben White, Stanley Dancer and Bill Haughton (4); Howard Beissinger, Del Cameron, John Campbell and Henry Thomas (3).

Year		Driver	Fastest Heat	Year		Driver	Fastest Heat
1926	**Guy McKinney**	Nat Ray	2:04¾	1950	**Lusty Song**	Del Miller	2:02
1927	**Iosola's Worthy**	Marvin Childs	2:03¾	1951	**Mainliner**	Guy Crippen	2:02.3
1928	**Spencer**	W.H.Lessee	2:02½	1952	**Sharp Note**	Bion Shively	2:02.3
1929	**Walter Dear**	Walter Cox	2:02¾	1953	**Helicopter**	Harry Harvey	2:01.3
				1954	**Newport Dream**	Del Cameron	2:02.4
1930	**Hanover's Bertha**	Tom Berry	2:03	1955	**Scott Frost**	Joe O'Brien	2:00.3
1931	**Calumet Butler**	R.D.McMahon	2:03¼	1956	**The Intruder**	Ned Bower	2:01.2
1932	**The Marchioness**	Wm. Caton	2:01¼	1957	**Hickory Smoke**	John Simpson Sr.	2:00.1
1933	**Mary Reynolds**	Ben White	2:03¾	1958	**Emily's Pride**	Flave Nipe	1:59.4
1934	**Lord Jim**	Doc Parshall	2:02¾	1958	**Emily's Pride**	Flave Nipe	1:59.4
1935	**Greyhound**	Sep Palin	2:02¼	1959	**Diller Hanover**	Frank Ervin	2:01.1
1936	**Rosalind**	Ben White	2:01¾				
1937	**Shirley Hanover**	Henry Thomas	2:01½	1960	**Blaze Hanover**	Joe O'Brien	1:59.3
1938	**McLin Hanover**	Henry Tomas	2:02¼	1961	**Harlan Dean**	James Arthur	1:58.2
1939	**Peter Astra**	Doc Parshall	2:04¼	1962	**A.C.'s Viking**	Sanders Russell	1:59.3
				1963	**Speedy Scot**	Ralph Baldwin	1:57.3
1940	**Spencer Scott**	Fred Egan	2:02	1964	**Ayres**	John Simpson Sr.	1:56.4
1941	**Bill Gallon**	Lee Smith	2:05	1965	**Egyptian Candor**	Del Cameron	2:03.4
1942	**The Ambassador**	Ben White	2:04	1966	**Kerry Way**	Frank Ervin	1:58.4
1943	**Volo Song**	Ben White	2:02½	1967	**Speedy Streak**	Del Cameron	2:00
1944	**Yankee Maid**	Henry Thomas	2:04	1968	**Nevele Pride**	Stanley Dancer	1:59.2
1945	**Titan Hanover**	Harry Pownall,Sr.	2:04	1969	**Lindys Pride**	Howard Beissinger	1:57.3
1946	**Chestertown**	Thomas Berry	2:02½				
1947	**Hoot Mon**	Sep Palin	2:00	1970	**Timothy T.**	John Simpson, Jr.	1:58.2
1948	**Demon Hanover**	Harrison Hoyt	2:02	1971	**Speedy Crown**	Howard Beissinger	1:57.2
1949	**Miss Tilly**	Fred Egan	2:01.2	1972	**Super Bowl**	Stanley Dancer	1:56.2

The Hambletonian (Cont.)

Year		Driver	Fastest Heat	Year		Driver	Fastest Heat
1973	Flirth	Ralph Baldwin	1:57.1	1984	Historic Freight	Ben Webster	1:56.2
1974	Christopher T.	Bill Haughton	1:58.3	1985	Prakas	Bill O'Donnell	1:54.3
1975	Bonefish	Stanley Dancer	1:59	1986	Nuclear Kosmos	Ulf Thoresen	1:55.2
1976	Steve Lobell	Bill Haughton	1:56.2	1987	Mack Lobell	John Campbell	1:53.3
1977	Green Speed	Bill Haughton	1:55.3	1988	Armbro Goal	John Campbell	1:54.3
1978	Speedy Somolli	Howard Beissinger	1:55	1989	Park Avenue Joe	Ron Waples	1:54.3
1979	Legend Hanover	George Sholty	1:56.1		& Probe	Bill Fahy	
1980	Burgomeister	Bill Haughton	1:56.3	1990	Harmonious	John Campbell	1:54.1
1981	Shiaway St. Pat	Ray Remmen	2:01.1	1991	Giant Victory	Jack Moiseyev	1:55
1982	Speed Bowl	Tommy Haughton	1:56.4				
1983	Duenna	Stanley Dancer	1:57.2				

Note: In 1989, Park Avenue Joe and Probe finished in a dead heat in the race-off. They were later declared co-winners, but Park Avenue Joe was awarded 1st place money because his three-race summary (2-1-1) was better than Probe's (1-9-1).

All-Time Money Leaders

The all-time winning trotters, pacers and drivers through 1990, according to *The Trotting and Pacing Guide.* Purses for horses include races in foreign countries. Purses, starts and wins for drivers include only races held in North America.

Top 10 Horses

Note that (*) indicates horse raced in 1990.

	T/P	Sts	1st	Purses
*Ourasi (FRA)	T	N/A	32	$4,408,857
*Mack Lobell	T	86	65	3,907,454
Nihilator	P	38	35	3,225,653
Matt's Scooter	P	61	37	2,944,591
On the Road Again	P	61	44	2,819,102
Ideal du Gazeau (FRA)	T	N/A	21	2,744,777
Grades Singing	T	101	66	2,607,552
*Peace Corps	T	39	32	2,590,883
*Beach Towel	P	36	29	2,570,357
Napoletano	T	55	30	2,467,878

Top 10 Drivers

All drivers were active in 1990, except Billy Houghton.

	Yrs	Starts	Wins	Purses
John Campbell	19	26,715	5,136	$91,483,684
Bill O'Donnell	21	25,451	4,435	71,093,662
Herve Filion	30	63,391	12,667	71,005,819
Michel Lachance	23	31,900	5,904	53,730,189
Carmine Abbatiello	35	38,179	7,020	48,575,379
Ron Waples	25	27,069	5,084	43,797,245
Buddy Gilmour	36	32,770	5,352	43,474,617
Billy Houghton	37	22,885	4,910	40,160,336
Ben Webster	35	28,697	4,039	39,742,378
Doug Brown	24	24,719	4,301	32,931,160

Annual Awards
Horse of the Year

Selected since 1947 by U.S. Trotting Association and the U.S. Harness Writers Association; age of winning horse is noted; (t) indicates trotter and (p) indicates pacer. USTA added Trotter and Pacer of the Year awards in 1970.
    Multiple winners: Bret Hanover and Nevele Pride (3); Adios Butler, Albatross, Cam Fella, Good Time, Mack Lobell, Niatross and Scott Frost (2).

Year		Year		Year		Year	
1947	Victory Song (4t)	1959	Bye Bye Byrd (4p)	1970	Fresh Yankee (7t)	1981	Fan Hanover (3p)
1948	Rodney (4t)	1960	Adios Butler (4p)	1971	Albatross (3p)	1982	Cam Fella (3p)
1949	Good Time (3p)	1961	Adios Butler (5p)	1972	Albatross (4p)	1983	Cam Fella (4p)
1950	Proximity (8t)	1962	Su Mac Lad (8t)	1973	Sir Dalrai (4p)	1984	Fancy Crown (3t)
1951	Pronto Don (6t)	1963	Speedy Scot (3t)	1974	Delmonica Hanover (5t)	1985	Nihilator (3p)
1952	Good Time (6t)	1964	Bret Hanover (2p)	1975	Savoir (7t)	1986	Forrest Skipper (4p)
1953	Hi Lo's Forbes (5p)	1965	Bret Hanover (3p)	1976	Keystone Ore (3p)	1987	Mack Lobell (3t)
1954	Stenographer (3t)	1966	Bret Hanover (4p)	1977	Green Speed (3t)	1988	Mack Lobell (4t)
1955	Scott Frost (3t)	1967	Nevele Pride (2t)	1978	Abercrombie (3p)	1989	Matt's Scooter (4p)
1956	Scott Frost (4t)	1968	Nevele Pride (3t)	1979	Niatross (2p)	1990	Beach Towel (3p)
1957	Torpid (3p)	1969	Nevele Pride (4t)	1980	Niatross (3p)		
1958	Emily's Pride (3t)						

Driver of the Year

Determined by Universal Driving Rating System (UDR) and presented by the Harness Tracks of America since 1968. Eligible drivers must have at least 1000 starts for the season.
    Multiple winners: Herve Filion (10); John Campbell and Michel Lachance (3); Bill O'Donnell and Ron Waples (2).

Year		Year		Year		Year	
1968	Stanley Dancer	1975	Joe O'Brien	1980	Ron Waples	1986	Michel Lachance
1969	Herve Filion	1976	Herve Filion	1981	Herve Filion	1987	Michel Lachance
1970	Herve Filion	1977	Donald Dancer	1982	Bill O'Donnell	1988	John Campbell
1971	Herve Filion	1978	Carmine Abbatiello & Herve Filion	1983	John Campbell	1989	Herve Filion
1972	Herve Filion			1984	Bill O'Donnell	1990	John Campbell
1973	Herve Filion	1979	Ron Waples	1985	Michel Lachance		
1974	Herve Filion						

Mike Sinek

Former Firestone, U.S. Open and ABC Masters champion **Del Ballard, Jr.** recoils in disbelief after throwing a gutter ball in his final shot to lose the Fair Lanes Open in March.

BOWLING

Gutter Ball

Del Ballard Jr.'s well-publicized errant shot was only one of the bizarre happenings that tormented the PBA in 1991.

Pro bowling's "Shot Seen 'Round the World" was made on March 2—when, with one errant flip of his right wrist, Del Ballard, Jr. generated more publicity for the Professional Bowlers Association tour than anyone else in the PBA's 34-year history.

It tells you something about the kind of press the PBA normally gets that Ballard, who in the past few years has won three of bowling's four major titles, finally became famous for a gaffe that put him in the same company with Fred Merkle and Roy (Wrong Way) Riegels.

If you turned on ESPN, CNN or your local affiliate that night, there it was. The shot. On the final ball of the Fair Lanes Open in Randallstown, Md., Ballard, needing seven pins for a win, threw a gutter ball and lost the championship match to Pete Weber, 213-207.

A gutter ball with the title on the line. Talk about the "agony of defeat"!

Ballard's swim in the channel was just one of many bizarre and unusual happenings on the PBA's 1991 Winter and Spring Tours—all of which culminated with a bomb scare at the Firestone Tournament of Champions on April 27.

Dave Petruska of the Tucson (Ariz.) Citizen has written about professional and amateur bowling for 14 years and won several national awards. He also covers NFL football, PGA golf and college sports.

Mike Miller won the PBA National Championship without using his thumb. Weber, the beneficiary of Ballard's blunder, won the U.S. Open and two other tournaments while waging one of the longest appeals in sports history. He finally dropped the appeal following the Firestone and took his six-month suspension.

Oh, and Weber dropped something else, too—his U.S. Open trophy.

After winning the tournament for the second time in four years, he hoisted the prize for all to see, then lost his grip and watched in disbelief as the sculpted porcelain eagle on a walnut base hit the lanes and shattered into a hundred pieces.

Wait, there's more.

John Mazza picked up the difficult 7-10 split in the Bud Light Classic in Sunrise, Fla., and Jess Stayrook rolled another in the Tucson Open, but neither won the tournament.

There were two bomb threats before the scare at the Firestone. One, at the Quaker State Open in Grand Prairie, Texas, proved to be a false alarm, while the other, at the Tums Classic in Windsor Locks, Conn., was the real thing—fortunately, the bomb was safely removed without the bowlers or anyone in the crowd knowing about it.

Another tidbit that didn't make the news was the heist of the mobile pro shop. The tractor-trailer rig, owned by PBA Players Service Director Larry Lichstein, was

Earl Anthony, the winningest bowler in PBA history, looks on as his playing career comes to an end in June. Anthony announced his retirement at the start of the Flint Senior Open then reached the final before losing to Dick Beattie.

stolen from the parking lot of Carolier Lanes in North Brunswick, N.J., but was recovered later when the thieves tried to sell it to some undercover policemen.

Two of the PBA's more notable figures decided to step down in 1991: six-time Bowler of the Year Earl Anthony and PBA commissioner Joe Antenora.

The 61-year-old Anthony, who first retired from the PBA Tour in 1983, walked away from the Seniors Tour on June 20, after a second place finish in the Flint Senior Open. He had been bowling with the Seniors mainly at the request of an equipment firm he represents and announced that upon retirement he would spend most of his free time playing another sport: golf.

That did not endear him to a lot of PBA people. "How do you think Earl would feel if the bowlers at his lanes said they were sick of bowling and just wanted to golf?" said one miffed PBA official.

Antenora had been the PBA's commissioner since 1978, when he moved up

from executive director. He was replaced in late August by Mike Connor, a former executive with Firestone.

One of the new faces appearing in PBA tournaments in 1991 belonged to pro bowling's first two-sport star—San Francisco Giants righthanded pitcher John Burkett. Burkett, who was 14-7 with a 3.79 ERA with the Giants in 1990, competed in the ARC Pinole (Calif.) Open in January and proved he could throw strikes on the lanes, too—averaging 206.6 for 18 games and finishing 74th in the field of 160 bowlers.

Although there were nine multiple winners when the Summer Tour concluded in mid-August, people were still talking about Ballard's gutter ball when the Fall Tour started up on Sept. 30.

Let's set the scene. Ballard was in the 10th frame, trailing Weber by 26 pins. He needed two strikes and then seven pins on his last ball to win the tournament and the first prize of $30,000.

His first shot was a perfect strike. His

second shot was a perfect strike. His third shot was perfectly awful. It didn't hang on the edge and fall off at the last second. No such luck. It was in the gutter almost as soon as it left his hand.

"My adrenaline was pumping," he said. "I did everything I normally do, except I didn't take my time."

The crowd couldn't believe it and neither could Ballard. He covered his head with his arms and walked off the lanes in a daze, but returned to face the press 10 minutes later. He calmly told everyone that he hurried the shot and simply threw it in the gutter. The publicity he got for that momentary lapse in concentration, however, surprised him.

"I was simply thinking that I lost the tourney," Ballard said. "But the way I lost it was the thing. I guess the biggest part was how I looked when I got the double and then how I looked when I threw it in the gutter. I guess it made good TV."

Are you kidding? It made great TV! Let's go to the videotape.

Ballard bounced back two weeks later to win his sixth career title at the Leisure Long Island Open in Sayville, N.Y. Same scenario: he needed two strikes and seven pins to beat Jim Johnson, Jr. He rolled two strikes, then, refusing to play it safe, went out by the gutter and got a third strike for the 223-183 victory.

Vindication? Yes. National recognition? No way.

"I guess winning dramatically wasn't the same as losing that way," Ballard said. "There are a lot of people out there who probably have no idea that I bounced right back after the gutter ball to win a title."

Ballard didn't mind talking about the gutter ball. He would even joke about it with fans—to a point.

"I can tell in about 10 seconds what kind of comment I'm going to get from a person," he said. "Most people are great about it, very sympathetic. Others are just jerks and give me a lot of abuse. I just give it right back to them."

Despite the gutter ball, Ballard is in the middle of the hunt for the 1991 Player of the Year award, which has been won the past two years by Amleto Monacelli (see box). Ballard had three wins at the end of the Summer Tour, tying him with Weber, Mazza and David Ozio.

How Weber will do in the voting will be

Monacelli Has Come Long Way To Reach Top

Amleto Monacelli was born in Italy, raised in Venezuela and makes his living in the United States.

He has become proficient in three languages, as well as the universal language of bowling. He is a success on the PBA Tour, whether you say it in English, Italian (un successo) or Spanish (un exito).

PBA Hall of Famer Earl Anthony, the bowler of the decade for the 1970s, marvels at what Monacelli has achieved on the tour. He feels Monacelli could be the bowler of the 1990s, if he continues to bowl throughout the decade.

"When you consider what he has overcome to be where he is right now, I think he's just done fantastic," Anthony said. "I'm not just talking about his bowling, which he learned without any formal instruction. He had to overcome the language problem when he started and he bowled through some personal turmoil in 1990 and still managed to win Player of the Year. He's shown a strength of character not many people possess."

In May of 1990, Monacelli's younger sister, Andreina, died suddenly of leukemia. The illness struck so quickly that he was unable to get back to Venezuela to see her before she died. Monacelli skipped three weeks of competition because he was too distraught to bowl. He rejoined the tour in Portland, Ore., only to get food poisoning, which forced him to skip the Portland stop and three more tourneys.

But he pulled himself together after a trip to Italy with his wife, Teresa, and closed the year with three titles, $204,775 in prize money and his second straight PBA Player of the Year title. He also became the first player to have back-to-back years of earning more than $200,000 (he earned $231,815 in 1989).

At the end of the 1991 Summer Tour, Monacelli was in position to join Anthony and Mark Roth as the only bowlers to win three consecutive Player-of-the-Year awards. He was second on the money list behind David Ozio with $139,460, had two tournament victories and four other TV finals to his credit and was fifth in average at 215.80.

Two-time Player of the Year **Amleto Monacelli** (second from right) with his parents and his wife Teresa during a break at this year's Firestone Tournament of Champions in Akron.

This recent success is a far cry from Monacelli's rookie year in 1982 when he earned just $10,588 in 24 events. In fact, it wasn't until 1985 that he won more than $25,000 in a single season and 1987 that he won his first tournament (the Japan Cup).

"When I joined the tour, there was no doubt in my mind that I would become successful," Monacelli says. "I didn't put a time frame on how long I would try it here. I knew it would take me time to adjust to the tour—the bowling, the traveling and learning the language—but I had a lot of confidence in myself that I eventually would do well."

Monacelli's bowling style certainly shows a lack of formal training. He taught himself and has a unique style, to say the least. ESPN commentator Mike Durbin, a PBA Hall of Famer, says Monacelli's approach to the foul line "looks like someone trying to start a lawnmower."

Monacelli jokes that he is grateful his family didn't have a video camera when he was starting out.

"I didn't know how I looked bowling until I made the (televised) finals for the first time," he says. "I developed a style that felt right for me. I'm glad I didn't see myself because I might have changed my style and not done as well as I have."

But when Monacelli gets ready to release the ball, said noted bowling instructor John Jowdy, his style has substance.

"When Amleto gets to the line, his form is a good as you can want," Jowdy says. "Everything is in perfect order when he releases the ball."

Ozio, who beat Monacelli in the finals of the 1991 Firestone Tournament of Champions, says there is another facet of his game that is not noticed by the average fan.

"Amleto is one of the best I've ever seen at realizing how a ball is reacting to a lane condition and making the adjustment to that condition," says Ozio. "That's one of the reasons he is so good."

But whether Monacelli, who turned 30 in August, will be around at the end of the decade remains to be seen. Like many pros, he is frustrated by the limited earning potential on the tour.

"We don't get the same appreciation in terms of sponsorship that other sports do and that's hard for me to understand," he says. "Because of that, I'm just taking things day by day. It's hard to say how long I'll be out there. It could be for a long time or maybe just three of four more years."

interesting to watch. In just 15 tournaments entering the Fall Tour, he was third on the money list at $131,940, had cashed in all 15 tourneys, and made match play in 12 of them.

Weber drew his suspension for a lane misconduct violation during a tournament in November of 1990 in Milwaukee, Wis. Since he was on probation for past offenses, the suspension was automatic under PBA rules.

But Weber, who says he has kicked a drinking problem which has caused some of his past problems on the tour, appealed the suspension, first to a three-man appeals board and then to the executive board, as was his right. As things turned out, the appeals allowed Weber to compete on the entire 1991 Winter Tour, which is the more lucrative part of the PBA schedule.

"I feel if I come out in the fall, win a tourney or two and win a bunch of money that I deserve serious consideration," said Weber, who has yet to win Player of the Year. "If the guys don't vote for me, what am I going to do? That's their problem. I've proven that I can bowl well whether I'm drunk or sober."

Monacelli, who lost the title match at Firestone to Ozio, 236-203, entered the Fall with two titles and trailed Ozio on the money list by $28,255. Norm Duke of Albuquerque was also in the running for the title. Duke had won two titles, was fourth on the money list and had the top average score at 219.77.

But Ozio will be tough to beat. He opened the year with back-to-back titles, only the third time that had happened in PBA history (Dick Weber did it in 1962 and Don Johnson in 1972), then pulled out an emotional win over Monacelli to win the Firestone for his ninth career title, his first major and the winner's check of $50,000.

Ah, the Firestone. The PBA's diamond event was turned into cubic zirconium by a phoned-in bomb threat and a squeamish ABC Sports. The bomb threat came 12 minutes before air time and Riviera Lanes was quickly evacuated. Two of the finalists, Monacelli and Chris Warren, didn't even take the time to find their shoes—hightailing it to the parking lot in their socks.

"My momma didn't raise no fool," said Warren. "When they said bomb, I

was gone. I didn't want to get anything on my bowling shoes, so I just left them on the lanes. I didn't have the time to look for my street shoes."

After a 40-minute delay, the finals started and they were superb. Warren beat Scott Devers, 248-224, in the first match, but lost to Miller, 230-218, who then was ousted by Ozio, 240-227, setting up the Ozio-Monacelli title match.

Determined to help ABC make up for lost time, the bowlers quickened their pace and continued playing through the commercials, but when it came time for ABC to return the favor and go over its allotted 90-minute time period and show the final of the biggest tournament on the tour, the network bailed out.

In a moment of TV sports infamy reminiscent of NBC's Heidi-NFL fiasco of 1968, ABC told announcer Chris Schenkel to say goodbye and then switched to "Wide World of Sports."

And what was first up on "Wide World?" A taped gymnastics competition that was nearly a year old. To make things worse, ABC didn't update the PBA broadcast for the West Coast, where it is shown on a tape-delayed basis. Even though ABC taped the Ozio-Monacelli match, the West Coast saw the same show as the rest of the country.

Adding to the irony of the situation was that earlier in the day, Dennis Lewin, ABC's senior vice president for sports production, had gushed to a press conference how happy ABC was with its 30-year association with the PBA and the Winter Tour, which includes the PBA Championship and U.S. as well as the Firestone.

Despite ABC's decision to pull the plug on the biggest day of his professional life, Ozio was a trooper. It wasn't the first time he had been upstaged in 1991. His early season victory at the Showboat Invitational in Las Vegas had been bumped by a Persian Gulf War update.

"I don't mind getting preempted, if I keep coming up with these kinds of results," Ozio said afterward. "It's a little disappointing that it wasn't on, but there must be a reason for it. It's OK. I have the trophy. I have the money. I have the title. I'm the champions' champion. That's good enough. I'm not a glory seeker."

But glory seeks its own level and the winter, spring and summer of 1991 saw

David Ozio (left) won his first major at the Firestone in April, but a bomb scare held up the championship round and bumped the final round off national TV. The bomb threat emptied the Riviera Lanes so quickly that some finalists, like **Chris Warren**, made the trip to the parking lot in their socks.

Ozio rise to a new level. He is the James Brown of bowling—The Hardest Working Man on the PBA tour—and all that work has translated into success.

"You see Dave out there throwing practice game after practice game after practice game, trying this, trying that," says an admiring Monacelli. "I don't know how he does it. That would drive me nuts."

Ozio considered himself a solid touring pro entering the 1991 season. He was making a good living but had never topped $100,000 in a season until this year. With $167,715 in earnings after the Summer Tour, he was in position to become only the fourth bowler in PBA history to go over $200,000.

"I saw my name on the ballot for the PBA Hall of Fame this year and I just cringed because I didn't feel I belonged in that company," said the 37-year-old Ozio. "Now, with nine titles, including a Firestone, I feel a little bit different."

Miller's victory at the PBA National wasn't only his first major, but his first PBA win ever. And the $35,000 winner's check was more than he had earned in any single season since he turned pro in 1980.

Primarily a regional bowler until competing in 29 tourneys in 1990, Miller began experimenting with a style that enabled him to throw the ball without putting his thumb into the thumb hole. He is able to get much more hook and power

Only three bowlers have won the Firestone, U.S. Open and PBA Championship: Hall of Famers **Johnny Petraglia** (left) and **Billy Hardwick** (center), and **Pete Weber**, who won his second Open in 1991, then sat out a six-month suspension.

on the shot because he can cup the ball in his hand. He is able to use this style because he has great upper body strength and very large hands.

Another no-name pro, Doug Kent of Canandaigua, N.Y., won the American Bowling Congress Masters title, beating George Branham of Indianapolis in a two-frame rolloff after Kent struck out in the 10th frame to tie the match at 236-236.

On the Seniors Tour, John Handegard and Gene Stus ranked 1-2 going into the Fall. Each had won two tournaments, with Handegard leading in earnings with $45,170, and Stus leading in average with 220.66. On Aug. 24, Stus beat Handegard, 198-171, in the finals of the Seniors Championship at Battle Creek, Mich.

The Ladies Professional Bowlers Tour had two Players of the Year in 1990. Leanne Barrette, of Oklahoma City, was the choice of her peers in the LPBT, but Tish Johnson got the nod from the Bowling Writers after a strong finish in the autumn when she won three straight tournaments and tied the tour mark for con-

secutive wins held by Patty Costello, Mildred Ignizio and Lisa Wagner.

Barrette won three titles, earned $91,390 and was the runaway average leader at 211.53—more than two pins better per game then runner-up Nikki Gianulias. But Johnson, of Panorama, Calif., won four titles and led the money list with $94,420.

The 1991 season could be a repeat of the split vote pattern for Barrette, who throws one of the most powerful balls on the LPBA tour. At the end of August, she was first in earnings and average, and led the point standings by a comfortable margin. But she had only one win, despite making six TV finals. Gianulias, on the other hand, was the tour's only multiple winner with three victories and stood second in earnings.

Neither Barrette or Gianulias had won a major in '91. Barrette lost in the finals of the U.S. Open to Anne Marie Duggan, 196-185, while Dede Davidson won the WIBC Queens with a 231-159 victory over Jeanne Maiden. □

THE 1992 INFORMATION PLEASE SPORTS ALMANAC

BOWLING STATISTICS

THE SEASON IN REVIEW

1990-1991

PBA • SENIORS • LPBT

SEC A

PAGE 649

1990-91 Results

Winners of stepladder finals in all PBA, Seniors and LPBT tournaments from the Fall Tours of 1990 through the Summer Tours of 1991; (a) indicates amateur; major tournaments in **bold** type.

PBA

1990 Fall Tour

Final	Event	Winner	Earnings	Final	Runner-up
Oct. 14	Japan Cup Invitational	Chris Warren	$18,500	226-163	Dave Husted
Nov. 3	Chevy Truck Classic	Roger Bowker	27,000	235-192	Dave Husted
Nov. 10	Toyota Classic	Pete Weber	27,000	213-206	Doug Kent
Nov. 17	Brunswick World Open	Jimmy Johnson*	33,000	243-227	Robert Lawrence
Nov. 24	ABC Fall Classic	Parker Bohn III	27,000	213-200	Kelly Coffman
Dec. 1	Bud Touring Players Champs	Duane Fisher	27,000	248-244	Jess Stayrook
Dec. 10	Cambridge Pro Mixed Doubles	Amleto Monacelli/ Tish Johnson	40,000	+124 pins	Parker Bohn III/ Lisa Wagner

1991 Winter Tour

Final	Event	Winner	Earnings	Final	Runner-up
Jan. 12	AC-Delco Classic	David Ozio	$36,000	259-225	W.R.Williams, Jr.
Jan. 19	Showboat Invitational	David Ozio	34,000	279-224	Mike Miller
Jan. 26	ARC Pinole Open	Brian Voss	21,000	179-179*	Mark Thayer
Feb. 2	Quaker State Open	Amleto Monacelli	30,000	220-216	Mike Edwards
Feb. 9	Florida Open	John Mazza	20,000	238-211	Mike Edwards
Feb. 16	Bud Light Classic	Bob Benoit	30,000	204-183	Wayne Webb
Feb. 23	Flagship City Open	Jess Stayrook	20,000	256-207	W.R.Williams, Jr.
Mar. 2	Fair Lanes Open	Pete Weber	30,000	213-207	Del Ballard, Jr.
Mar. 9	Johnny Petraglia Open	Pete Weber	27,000	244-234	Bob Benoit
Mar. 16	Leisure Long Island Open	Del Ballard, Jr.	20,000	223-183	Jim Johnson, Jr.
Mar. 23	Bud Light Open	Norm Duke	30,000	221-185	Dave Husted
Mar. 30	**PBA National Championship**	Mike Miller	35,000	218-214	Norm Duke
Apr. 6	True Value Open	Amleto Monacelli	39,000	225-180	Kelly Coffman
Apr. 13	**BPAA U.S.Open**	Pete Weber	40,000	289-184	Mark Thayer
Apr. 20	Tums Hartford Classic	Billy Young	30,000	203-201	Dave D'Entremont
Apr. 27	**Firestone Tourn.of Champions**	David Ozio	50,000	236-203	Amleto Monacelli
May 4	**ABC Masters**	Doug Kent	43,500	236-236*	George Branham III

*Rolloffs (2): Pinole—Voss def. Thayer in 2 frames, 50-45; Masters—Kent def. Branham in 2 frames, 50-28.
Note: the American Bowling Congress Masters is not a PBA Tour event.

1991 Spring/Summer Tour

Final	Event	Winner	Earnings	Final	Runner-up
May 11	Fresno Open	John Mazza	$18,000	213-189	Mike Shady
May 18	Kessler Classic	Bryan Goebel	24,000	224-195	Mark Williams
May 25	Denver Open	John Mazza	18,000	269-190	Parker Bohn III
June 1	PBA Doubles Classic	Del Ballard/ Bob Benoit	28,000	243-200	Philip Ringener/ Steve Hoskins
June 15	Kessler Open	Del Ballard, Jr.	23,000	226-184	Mike Shady
June 22	Seattle Open	Danny Wiseman	18,000	203-174	Dave Ferraro
June 29	Oregon Open	Tony Westlake	18,000	235-225	Norm Duke
July 6	El Paso Open	Ray Edwards	20,000	216-180	Bob Benoit
July 13	Tucson Open	Norm Duke	18,000	215-173	John Mazza
July 20	Wichita Open	Chris Warren	20,000	238-210	Eric Forkel
July 27	Columbia 300 Open	Brian Voss	21,000	238-212	Scott Devers
Aug. 3	Summer Classic	Steve Jaros	38,000	202-189	Andy Neuer
Aug. 8	La Mode Classic	Tony Westlake	20,000	197-183	Marc McDowell
Aug. 15	Senior Touring Pro Doubles	Rick Steelsmith/ Teata Semiz	28,000	243-198	Steve Wunderlich/ John Handegard

1990-91 Results (Cont.)
SENIORS
1990 Fall Tour

Final	Event	Winner	Earnings	Final	Runner-up
Oct. 25	Treasure Coast Open	Jimmy Certain	$7,500	218-202	Bob Hart

1991 Tour

Final	Event	Winner	Earnings	Final	Runner-up
Mar. 14	AMF-HPL Open	Darrel Curtis	$ 8,500	244-244*	Earl Anthony
Mar. 21	Hammer Open	Paul Busch	7,500	225-214	Robert Gibbs
Mar. 28	Cal Bowl Open	Gene Stus	5,000	200-189	Robert Gibbs
June 8	Showboat Invitational	John Handegard	13,000	247-206	John Hricsina
June 20	Flint Open	Dick Beattie	5,000	245-236	Earl Anthony
June 27	Hammond Open	Mickey Spiezio	5,000	233-228	Robert Gibbs
July 11	St.Clair Open	Adam Toney	5,000	187-166	Mickey Spiezio
July 18	AMF Cobra Classic	John Handegard	7,500	248-237	Gene Stus
Aug. 15	Senior/Touring Pro Doubles	Teata Semiz/ Rick Steelsmith	28,000	243-198	John Handegard/ Steve Wunderlich
Aug. 24	Seniors Championship	Gene Stus	17,000	198-171	John Handegard

*Rolloff (1): AMF-HPL—Curtis def. Anthony in 2 frames, 50-40;

LPBT
1990 Fall Tour

Final	Event	Winner	Earnings	Final	Runner-up
Sept. 20	AMF Cobra Classic	Tish Johnson	$20,000	270-214	Aleta Sill
Sept. 27	Columbia 300 Del.Open	Tish Johnson	12,000	180-161	Sue Neidig
Oct. 4	Hammer Eastern Open	Tish Johnson	9,000	174-166	D. Miller-Mackie
Oct. 11	Brunswick Hammond Open	Leanne Barrette	9,000	247-235	Nikki Gianulas
Oct. 18	Hammer Midwest Open	Lorrie Nichols	9,000	214-184	Wendy Macpherson
Oct. 25	Lady Ebonite Open	Nikki Gianulas	8,000	191-169	Leanne Barrette
Nov. 1	Hammer Western Open	Leanne Barrette	7,000	259-169	Lisa Wagner
Nov. 8	Los Angeles Open	Nikki Gianulas	6,000	206-156	Robin Romeo
Nov. 11	**Sam's Town Invitational**	Wendy Macpherson	20,000	203-202	Jeanne Maiden
Dec. 10	Cambridge Pro Mixed Doubles	Tish Johnson/ Amleto Monacelli	40,000	+124 pins	Lisa Wagner/ Parker Bohn III

1991 Winter Tour

Final	Event	Winner	Earnings	Final	Runner-up
Feb. 6	Okeechobee Classic	Nikki Gianulias	$6,000	235-184	C.Coburn-Carroll
Feb. 14	Central Florida Classic	Tish Johnson	6,000	235-213	Wendy MacPherson
Feb. 21	Athens (Ga.) Open	Sandra Jo Shiery	6,000	221-204	Lorrie Nichols
Feb. 28	New Orleans Classic	Aleta Sill	6,000	227-180	Dede Davidson
Mar. 6	Garland Centennial Open	Nikki Gianulias	6,000	191-181	Kim Terrell

1991 Spring/Summer Tour

Final	Event	Winner	Earnings	Final	Runner-up
Apr. 11	Robby's Open	Donna Adamek	$ 7,000	203-188	Lorrie Nichols
Apr. 18	Lady Ebonite Classic	Leanne Barrette	7,000	286-244	Carol Gianotti
Apr. 25	Lady Fair Lanes Open	Dana Miller-Mackie	8,000	191-188	Aleta Sill
May 2	Ashland Blue Ribbon Classic	Rene Fleming	6,000	180-176	Leanne Barrette
May 9	Hoffman/Schaumberg Open	Karen Ellingsworth	6,000	244-197	Linda Kelly
May 16	**WIBC Queens Tournament**	Dede Davidson	13,245	231-159	Jeanne Maiden
May 23	Hammer Western Open	Nikki Gianulais	7,000	221-192	C.Coburn-Carroll
May 30	**BPAA US Open**	Anne Marie Duggan	16,000	196-185	Leanne Barrette
Aug. 17	Gold Rush Mixed Doubles	Sherrie Dodge/ Adam Apo	7,000	426-422	Tish Johnson/ Pete Weber
Aug. 21	National Doubles	Lisa Wagner/ Carolyn Dorin	14,000	217-211	Debbie McMullen/ Jan Schmidt

Note: the Women's International Bowling Congress Queens Tournament is not a LPBT Tour event.

1991 Fall Tour Schedules
PBA
Events (6)—Toyota Classic (Sept.30-Oct.5); Japan Cup '91 Invitational (Oct.6-16 in Tokyo); Brunswick World Open (Nov.10-16); Chevy Truck Classic (Nov.18-23); Touring Players Championship (Nov.25-30); Cambridge Mixed Doubles (Dec.5-8).

SENIORS
Events (2)—**Woodside Open** (Sept.28-Oct.3); **Villages Open** (Oct.5-10).

LPBT
Events (8)—Hammer Eastern Open (Oct.5-9); Columbia 300 Delaware Open (Oct.12-16); Brunswick Open (Oct.19-23); Hammer Midwest Open (Oct.26-30); Denver Open (Nov.2-6); Ebonite Fall Classic (Nov.9-13); **Sam's Town Invitational** (Nov.16-23); Cambridge Mixed Doubles (Dec.5-8).

Tour Leaders

Official Top 10 standings for 1990 and unofficial Top 10 standings (including summer tours) for 1991. PBA, Seniors and LPBT figures for 1991 reflect performances through Sept.1.

Final 1990

PBA

Top 10 Money Winners

		Tourn	Titles	Earnings
1	Amleto Monacelli	29	3	$204,775
2	Chris Warren	34	4	197,475
3	Parker Bohn, III	33	3	172,575
4	Ron Palombi, Jr	33	2	147,820
5	Brian Voss	30	1	143,370
6	Jim Pencak	29	3	138,770
7	Robert Lawrence	33	2	132,580
8	Dave Husted	33	1	128,840
9	Dave Ferraro	29	1	111,966
10	Tony Westlake	31	0	104,873

*Warren won three PBA titles and the ABC Masters, which is not a PBA event.

Top 5 Averages

		Gm	Pinfall	Avg
1	Amleto Monacelli	1024	223,394	218.16
2	Walter R.Williams Jr	970	210,331	216.84
3	Norm Duke	797	172,344	216.24
4	Parker Bohn, III	1009	217,800	215.86
5	Mike Edwards	1016	219,071	215.62

SENIORS

Top 10 Money Winners

		Tourn	Titles	Earnings
1	Earl Anthony	6	3	$41,130
2	John Hricsina	8	1	30,750
3	Jimmy Certain	8	1	30,070
4	Dave Soutar	7	1	28,360
5	John Handegard	8	2	24,700
6	Teata Semiz	8	0	23,250
7	Bob Hart	8	0	13,535
8	Bus Oswalt	7	0	12,980
9	Les Zikes	8	0	12,775
10	Dick Weber	8	0	12,363

Top 5 Averages

		Gm	Pinfall	Avg
1	Jimmy Certain	272	58,900	216.54
2	Richard Beattie	110	23,802	216.38
3	Dave Soutar	248	53,467	215.59
4	John Hricsina	280	60,300	215.36
5	John Handegard	285	61,092	214.36

LPBT

Top 10 Money Winners

		Tourn	Titles	Earnings
1	Tish Johnson	21	4	$94,420
2	Leanne Barrette	21	3	91,390
3	Lisa Wagner	21	2	58,055
4	Dana Miller-Mackie	18	2	57,805
5	Nikki Gianulias	21	2	57,088
6	Wendy Macpherson	21	1	54,245
7	Kim Terrell	21	2	50,028
8	Robin Romeo	21	0	45,645
9	Aleta Sill	21	0	44,868
10	Lorrie Nichols	18	1	38,373

Top 5 Averages

		Gm	Pinfall	Avg
1	Leanne Barrette	822	173,878	211.53
2	Nikki Gianulias	771	161,486	209.45
3	Robin Romeo	862	180,365	209.24
4	Lisa Wagner	818	170,847	208.86
5	Wendy Macpherson	737	153,259	207.95

1991 (through Sept.1)

PBA

Top 10 Money Winners

		Tourn	Titles	Earnings
1	David Ozio	26	3	$167,715
2	Amleto Monacelli	21	2	139,460
3	Pete Weber	15	3	131,940
4	Norm Duke	19	2	127,115
5	John Mazza	25	3	116,180
6	Del Ballard Jr	22	3	110,205
7	Bob Benoit	26	2	102,935
8	Mike Miller	17	1	97,273
9	Walter R.Williams Jr	26	0	88,600
10	Tony Westlake	28	2	78,525

Top 5 Averages

		Gm	Pinfall	Avg
1	Norm Duke	686	150,763	219.77
2	Pete Weber	606	132,450	218.56
3	Mike Miller	539	117,072	217.20
4	Walter R.Williams Jr	822	178,084	216.65
5	Amleto Monacelli	690	148,902	215.80

SENIORS

Top 10 Money Winners

		Tourn	Titles	Earnings
1	John Handegard	10	2	$45,170
2	Gene Stus	9	2	38,250
3	John Hricsina	10	0	23,880
4	Teata Semiz	9	1	22,650
5	Tommy Evans	10	0	19,653
6	Jimmy Certain	10	0	19,618
7	Mickey Spiezio	10	1	18,083
8	Don Johnson	10	0	16,840
9	Robert Gibbs	10	0	14,785
10	Dick Weber	10	0	14,410

Top 5 Averages

		Gm	Pinfall	Avg
1	Gene Stus	336	74,142	220.66
2	John Handegard	356	77,701	218.26
3	John Hricsina	336	72,490	215.74
4	Jimmy Certain	315	67,773	215.15
5	Robert Gibbs	277	59,593	215.14

LPBT

Top 10 Money Winners

		Tourn	Titles	Earnings
1	Leanne Barrette	13	1	$47,278
2	Nikki Gianulias	13	3	35,275
3	Donna Adamek	13	1	34,430
4	Dede Davidson	13	1	31,560
5	Sandra Jo Shiery	12	1	29,013
6	Anne Marie Duggan	13	1	27,360
7	Tish Johnson	12	1	26,990
8	Aleta Sill	12	1	24,120
9	Cindy Coburn-Carroll	12	0	23,600
10	Dana Miller-Mackie	10	1	23,260

Top 5 Averages

		Gm	Pinfall	Avg
1	Leanne Barrette	513	109,095	212.66
2	Donna Adamek	481	102,087	212.24
3	Sandra Jo Shiery	452	95,838	212.03
4	Wendy Macpherson	486	101,982	209.84
5	Cindy Coburn-Carroll	421	88,086	209.23

THE 1992 INFORMATION PLEASE SPORTS ALMANAC

BOWLING STATISTICS

THROUGH THE YEARS
1941-1991
CHAMPIONS • AWARDS

SEC B
PAGE 652

Major Championships
MEN
BPAA U.S. Open

Started in 1941 by the Bowling Proprietors' Association of America, 18 years before the founding of the Professional Bowlers Association. Originally the BPAA All-Star Tournament, it became the U.S. Open in 1971. There were two BPAA All-Star tournaments in 1955, in January and December.

Multiple winners: Don Carter and Dick Weber (4); Marshall Holman, Junie McMahon, Connie Schwoegler, Andy Varipapa and Pete Weber (2).

Year		Year		Year	
1941	John Crimmons	1958	Don Carter	1975	Steve Neff
1942	Connie Schwoegler	1959	Billy Welu	1976	Paul Moser
1943	Ned Day			1977	Johnny Petraglia
1944	Buddy Bomar	1960	Harry Smith	1978	Nelson Burton, Jr
1945	Joe Wilman	1961	Bill Tucker	1979	Joe Berardi
1946	Andy Varipapa	1962	Dick Weber		
1947	Andy Varipapa	1963	Dick Weber	1980	Steve Martin
1948	Connie Schwoegler	1964	Bob Strampe	1981	Marshall Holman
1949	Junie McMahon	1965	Dick Weber	1982	Dave Husted
		1966	Dick Weber	1983	Gary Dickinson
1950	Dick Hoover	1967	Les Schissler	1984	Mark Roth
1951	Junie McMahon	1968	Jim Stefanich	1985	Marshall Holman
1952	Don Carter	1969	Billy Hardwick	1986	Steve Cook
1953	Not held			1987	Del Ballard, Jr
1954	Don Carter	1970	Bobby Cooper	1988	Pete Weber
1955	Steve Nagy	1971	Mike Lemongello	1989	Mike Aulby
1955	Bill Lillard	1972	Don Johnson		
1956	Don Carter	1973	Mike McGrath	1990	Ron Palombi, Jr
1957	Not held	1974	Larry Laub	1991	Pete Weber

ABC Masters Tournament

Sponsored by the American Bowling Congress. The Masters is not a PBA event, but is considered one of the four major tournaments on the men's tour and is open to qualified pros and amateurs.

Multiple winners: Earl Anthony, Billy Golembiewski, Dick Hoover and Billy Welu (2).

Year		Year		Year	
1951	Lee Jouglard	1966	Bob Strampe	1980	Neil Burton
1952	Willard Taylor	1967	Lou Scalia	1981	Randy Lightfoot
1953	Rudy Habetler	1968	Pete Tountas	1982	Joe Berardi
1954	Red Elkins	1969	Jim Chestney	1983	Mike Lastowski
1955	Buzz Fazio			1984	Earl Anthony
1956	Dick Hoover	1970	Don Glover	1985	Steve Wunderlich
1957	Dick Hoover	1971	Jim Godman	1986	Mark Fahy
1958	Tom Hennessey	1972	Bill Beach	1987	Rick Steelsmith
1959	Ray Bluth	1973	Dave Soutar	1988	Del Ballard, Jr
		1974	Paul Colwell	1989	Mike Aulby
1960	Billy Golembiewski	1975	Eddie Ressler		
1961	Don Carter	1976	Nelson Burton, Jr	1990	Chris Warren
1962	Billy Golembiewski	1977	Earl Anthony	1991	Doug Kent
1963	Harry Smith	1978	Frank Ellenburg		
1964	Billy Welu	1979	Doug Myers		
1965	Billy Welu				

PBA National Championship

The Professional Bowlers Association was formed in 1958 and its first national championship tournament was held in Memphis in 1960. The tournament has been held in Toledo, Ohio, since 1981.

Multiple winners: Earl Anthony (6); Mike Aulby, Dave Davis, Mike McGrath and Wayne Zahn (2).

Year		Year		Year	
1960	Don Carter	1972	Johnny Guenther	1982	Earl Anthony
1961	Dave Soutar	1973	Earl Anthony	1983	Earl Anthony
1962	Carmen Salvino	1974	Earl Anthony	1984	Bob Chamberlain
1963	Billy Hardwick	1975	Earl Anthony	1985	Mike Aulby
1964	Bob Strampe	1976	Paul Colwell	1986	Tom Crites
1965	Dave Davis	1977	Tommy Hudson	1987	Randy Pedersen
1966	Wayne Zahn	1978	Warren Nelson	1988	Brian Voss
1967	Dave Davis	1979	Mike Aulby	1989	Pete Weber
1968	Wayne Zahn				
1969	Mike McGrath	1980	Johnny Petraglia	1990	Jim Pencak
		1981	Earl Anthony	1991	Mike Miller
1970	Mike McGrath				
1971	Mike Lemongello				

Firestone Tournament of Champions

The Tournament of Champions has been held in Akron, Ohio, since it began in 1965.

Multiple winners: Earl Anthony, Mike Durbin, Jim Godman, Marshall Holman and Mark Williams (2).

Year		Year		Year	
1965	Billy Hardwick	1974	Earl Anthony	1983	Joe Berardi
1966	Wayne Zahn	1975	Dave Davis	1984	Mike Durbin
1967	Jim Stefanich	1976	Marshall Holman	1985	Mark Williams
1968	Dave Davis	1977	Mike Berlin	1986	Marshall Holman
1969	Jim Godman	1978	Earl Anthony	1987	Pete Weber
		1979	George Pappas	1988	Mark Williams
1970	Don Johnson			1989	Del Ballard, Jr
1971	Johnny Petraglia	1980	Wayne Webb		
1972	Mike Durbin	1981	Steve Cook	1990	Dave Ferraro
1973	Jim Goodman	1982	Mike Durbin	1991	David Ozio

WOMEN
BPAA U.S.Open

Started by the Bowling Proprietors' Association of America in 1949, 11 years before the founding of the Professional Women's Bowling Association. Originally the BPAA Women's All-Star Tournament, it became the U.S. Open in 1971. There were two BPAA All-Star tournaments in 1955, in January and December. Note that (a) indicates amateur.

Multiple winners: Marion Ladewig (8); Donna Adamek, Paula Sperber Carter, Pat Costello, Dotty Fothergill, Dana Miller-Mackie and Sylvia Wene (2).

Year		Year		Year	
1949	Marion Ladewig	1963	Marion Ladewig	1978	Donna Adamek
		1964	LaVerne Carter	1979	Diana Silva
1950	Marion Ladewig	1965	Ann Slattery		
1951	Marion Ladewig	1966	Joy Abel	1980	Pat Costello
1952	Marion Ladewig	1967	Gloria Bouvia	1981	Donna Adamek
1953	Not held	1968	Dotty Fothergill	1982	Shinobu Saitoh
1954	Marion Ladewig	1969	Dotty Fothergill	1983	Dana Miller
1955	Sylvia Wene			1984	Karen Ellingsworth
1955	Anita Cantaline	1970	Mary Baker	1985	Pat Mercatanti
1956	Marion Ladewig	1971	a-Paula Sperber	1986	Wendy Macpherson
1957	Not held	1972	a-Lorrie Koch	1987	Carol Norman
1958	Merle Matthews	1973	Millie Martorella	1988	Lisa Wagner
1959	Marion Ladewig	1974	Pat Costello	1989	Robin Romeo
		1975	Paula Sperber Carter		
1960	Sylvia Wene	1976	Patty Costello	1990	Dana Miller-Mackie
1961	Phyllis Notaro	1977	Betty Morris	1991	Anne Marie Duggan
1962	Shirley Garms				

WIBC Queens

Sponsored by the Women's International Bowling Congress, the Queens is a double elimination, match play tournament. It is not an LPBT event, but is open to qualified pros and amateurs. Note that (a) indicates amateur.

Multiple winners: Mille Martorella (3); Donna Adamek, Dotty Fothergill, Aleta Sill and Katsuko Sugimoto (2).

Year		Year		Year	
1961	Janet Harman	1972	Dotty Fothergill	1982	Katsuko Sugimoto
1962	Dorothy Wilkinson	1973	Dotty Fothergill	1983	Aleta Sill
1963	Irene Monterosso	1974	Judy Soutar	1984	Kazue Inahashi
1964	D.D.Jacobsen	1975	Cindy Powell	1985	Aleta Sill
1965	Betty Kuczynski	1976	Pam Buckner	1986	Cora Fiebig
1966	Judy Lee	1977	Dana Stewart	1987	Cathy Almeida
1967	Millie Martorella	1978	Loa Boxberger	1988	Wendy Macpherson
1968	Phyllis Massey	1979	Donna Adamek	1989	Carol Gianotti
1969	Ann Feigel				
		1980	Donna Adamek	1990	a-Patty Ann
1970	Millie Martorella	1981	Katsuko Sugimoto	1991	Dede Davidson
1971	Millie Martorella				

Sam's Town Invitational

Originally held in Milwaukee as the Pabst Tournament of Champions, but discontinued after one year (1981). The event was revived in 1984, moved to Las Vegas and renamed Sam's Town Tournament of Champions. Since then it has been known as the LPBT Tournament of Champions (1985), the Sam's Town National Pro/Am (1986-88) and the Sam's Town Invitational (since 1989).

Multiple winner: Aleta Sill (2).

Year		Year		Year	
1981	Cindy Coburn	1985	Patty Costello	1988	Donna Adamek
1982-83	Not held	1986	Aleta Sill	1989	Tish Johnson
1984	Aleta Sill	1987	Debbie Bennett	1990	Wendy Macpherson

WPBA National Championship (1960-1980)

The Women's Professional Bowling Association National Championship tournament was discontinued when the WPBA broke up in 1981. The WPBA changed its name from the Professional Women Bowlers Association (PWBA) in 1978.

Multiple winners: Patty Costello (3); Dotty Fothergill (2).

Year		Year		Year	
1960	Marion Ladewig	1968	Dotty Fothergill	1975	Pam Buckner
1961	Shirley Garms	1969	Dotty Fothergill	1976	Patty Costello
1962	Stevie Balogh	1970	Bobbe North	1977	Vesma Grinfelds
1963	Janet Harman	1971	Patty Costello	1978	Toni Gillard
1964	Betty Kuczynski	1972	Patty Costello	1979	Cindy Coburn
1965	Helen Duval	1973	Betty Morris		
1966	Judy Lee	1974	Pat Costello	1980	Donna Adamek
1967	Betty Mivelas				

Annual Money Leaders
PBA Tour

Multiple winners: Earl Anthony (6); Dick Weber and Mark Roth (4); Mike Aulby and Don Carter (2).

Year		Earnings	Year		Earnings
1959	Dick Weber	$7,672	1975	Earl Anthony	$107,585
1960	Don Carter	22,525	1976	Earl Anthony	110,833
1961	Dick Weber	26,280	1977	Mark Roth	105,583
1962	Don Carter	49,972	1978	Mark Roth	134,500
1963	Dick Weber	46,333	1979	Mark Roth	124,517
1964	Bob Strampe	33,592	1980	Wayne Webb	116,700
1965	Dick Weber	47,675	1981	Earl Anthony	164,735
1966	Wayne Zahn	54,720	1982	Earl Anthony	134,760
1967	Dave Davis	54,165	1983	Earl Anthony	135,605
1968	Jim Stefanich	67,375	1984	Mark Roth	158,712
1969	Billy Hardwick	64,160	1985	Mike Aulby	201,200
1970	Mike McGrath	52,049	1988	Walter Ray Williams, Jr.	145,550
1971	Johnny Petraglia	85,065	1987	Peter Weber	179,516
1972	Don Johnson	56,648	1988	Brian Voss	225,485
1973	Don McCune	69,000	1989	Mike Aulby	298,237
1974	Earl Anthony	99,585	1990	Amleto Monacelli	204,775

WPBA and LPBT Tours

WPBA leaders through 1980; LPBT leaders since 1981.
Multiple winners: Aleta Sill (4); Donna Adamek, Patty Costello and Betty Morris (3); Dotty Fothergill and Nikki Gianulias (2).

Year		Earnings	Year		Earnings
1965	Betty Kuczynski	$3,792	1979	Donna Adamek	$26,280
1966	Joy Abel	5,795	1980	Donna Adamek	31,907
1967	Shirley Garms	4,920	1981	Nikki Gianulias	41,270
1968	Dotty Fothergill	16,170	1982	Nikki Gianulias	45,875
1969	Dotty Fothergill	9,220	1983	Aleta Sill	42,525
1970	Patty Costello	9,317	1984	Aleta Sill	81,452
1971	Vesma Grinfelds	4,925	1985	Aleta Sill	52,655
1972	Patty Costello	11,350	1988	Aleta Sill	36,212
1973	Judy Cook	11,200	1987	Betty Morris	55,095
1974	Betty Morris	30,037	1988	Lisa Wagner	105,500
1975	Judy Soutar	20,395	1989	Robin Romeo	113,750
1976	Patty Costello	39,585	1990	Tish Johnson	94,420
1977	Betty Morris	23,802			
1978	Donna Adamek	31,000			

All-Time Money Leaders

All-time leading money winners on the PBA and LPBT tours, through 1990. PBA figures date back to 1959, while LPBT figures include WPBA earnings through 1980.

Money Winners

	PBA Top 15	Titles	Earnings		WPBA-LPBT Top 15	Titles	Earnings
1	Marshall Holman	21	$1,496,201	1	Lisa Wagner	25	$436,969
2	Mark Roth	33	1,389,691	2	Aleta Sill	16	403,561
3	Earl Anthony	41	1,344,781	3	Lorrie Nichols	14	369,541
4	Pete Weber	15	1,174,197	4	Donna Adamek	17	363,664
5	Mike Aulby	19	1,148,145	5	Robin Romeo	12	358,960
6	Wayne Webb	17	935,936	6	Nikki Gianulias	13	344,902
7	Dave Husted	7	897,236	7	Betty Morris	17	315,935
8	Brian Voss	9	888,393	8	Tish Johnson	12	296,602
9	Dick Weber	26	825,861	9	Cindy Coburn-Carroll	13	275,929
10	Amleto Monacelli	9	818,551	10	Jeanne Maiden	8	247,736
11	Joe Berardi	10	811,374	11	Pat Costello	11	241,196
12	George Pappas	10	789,049	12	Patty Costello	25	240,705
13	Steve Cook	14	764,441	13	Cheryl Daniels	4	208,727
14	Gary Dickinson	8	741,320	14	Leanne Barrette	10	207,389
15	Mike Durbin	14	736,410	15	Judy Soutar	6	190,362

Annual Awards
MEN
BWAA Bowler of the Year

Winners selected by Bowling Writers Association of America.
Multiple winners: Earl Anthony and Don Carter (6); Mark Roth (4); Dick Weber (3); Mike Aulby, Buddy Bomar, Ned Day, Billy Hardwick, Don Johnson, Steve Nagy (2).

Year		Year		Year		Year	
1942	Johnny Crimmins	1955	Steve Nagy	1968	Jim Stefanich	1980	Wayne Webb
1943	Ned Day	1956	Bill Lillard	1969	Billy Hardwick	1981	Earl Anthony
1944	Ned Day	1957	Don Carter	1970	Nelson Burton Jr.	1982	Earl Anthony
1945	Buddy Bomar	1958	Don Carter	1971	Don Johnson	1983	Earl Anthony
1946	Joe Wilman	1959	Ed Lubanski	1972	Don Johnson	1984	Mark Roth
1947	Buddy Bomar	1960	Don Carter	1973	Don McCune	1985	Mike Aulby
1948	Andy Varipapa	1961	Dick Weber	1974	Earl Anthony	1986	Walter Ray Williams Jr.
1949	Connie Schwoegler	1962	Don Carter	1975	Earl Anthony	1987	Marshall Holman
1950	Junie McMahon	1963	Dick Weber	1976	Earl Anthony	1988	Brian Voss
1951	Lee Jouglard	1964	Billy Hardwick	1977	Mark Roth	1989	Mike Aulby
1952	Steve Nagy	1965	Dick Weber	1978	Mark Roth		
1953	Don Carter	1966	Wayne Zahn	1979	Mark Roth	1990	Amleto Monacelli
1954	Don Carter	1967	Dave Davis				

Annual Awards (Cont.)
PBA Player of the Year

Winners selected by members of Professional Bowlers Association. The PBA Player of the Year has differed from the BWAA Bowler of the Year three times—in 1963,'64 and '89.

Multiple winners: Earl Anthony (6); Mark Roth (4); Billy Hardwick, Don Johnson and Amleto Monacelli (2).

Year		Year		Year		Year	
1963	Billy Hardwick	1971	Don Johnson	1979	Mark Roth	1985	Mike Aulby
1964	Bob Strampe	1972	Don Johnson	1980	Wayne Webb	1986	Walter Ray Williams Jr
1965	Dick Weber	1973	Don McCune	1981	Earl Anthony	1987	Marshall Holman
1966	Wayne Zahn	1974	Earl Anthony	1982	Earl Anthony	1988	Brian Voss
1967	Dave Davis	1975	Earl Anthony	1983	Earl Anthony	1989	Amleto Monacelli
1968	Jim Stefanich	1976	Earl Anthony	1984	Mark Roth	1990	Amleto Monacelli
1969	Billy Hardwick	1977	Mark Roth				
1970	Nelson Burton, Jr	1978	Mark Roth				

PBA Rookie of the Year

Winners selected by members of Professional Bowlers Association.

Year		Year		Year		Year	
1964	Jerry McCoy	1972	Tommy Hudson	1980	Pete Weber	1986	Marc McDowell
1965	Jim Godman	1973	Steve Neff	1981	Mark Fahy	1987	Ryan Shafer
1966	Bobby Cooper	1974	Cliff McNealy	1982	Mike Steinbach	1988	Rick Steelsmith
1967	Mike Durbin	1975	Guy Rowbury	1983	Toby Contreras	1989	Steve Hoskins
1968	Bob McGregor	1976	Mike Berlin	1984	John Gant	1990	Brad Kiszewski
1969	Larry Lichstein	1977	Steve Martin	1985	Tom Crites		
1970	Denny Krick	1978	Joseph Groskind				
1971	Tye Critchlow	1979	Mike Aulby				

WOMEN
BWAA Bowler of the Year

Winners selected by Bowling Writers Association of America.

Multiple winners: Marion Ladewig (9); Donna Adamek (4); Betty Morris and Lisa Rathgeber Wagner (3); Patty Costello, Dotty Forthergill, Shirley Garms, Val Mikiel, Aleta Sill, Judy Soutar and Sylvia Wene (2).

Year		Year		Year		Year	
1948	Val Mikiel	1960	Sylvia Wene	1972	Patty Costello	1982	Nikki Gianulias
1949	Val Mikiel	1961	Shirley Garms	1973	Judy Soutar	1983	Lisa Rathgeber
1950	Marion Ladewig	1962	Shirley Garms	1974	Betty Morris	1984	Aleta Sill
1951	Marion Ladewig	1963	Marion Ladewig	1975	Judy Soutar	1985	Aleta Sill
1952	Marion Ladewig	1964	LaVerne Carter	1976	Patty Costello	1986	Lisa Wagner
1953	Marion Ladewig	1965	Betty Kuczynski	1977	Betty Morris	1987	Betty Morris
1954	Marion Ladewig	1966	Joy Abel	1978	Donna Adamek	1988	Lisa Wagner
1955	Sylvia Wene	1967	Millie Martorella	1979	Donna Adamek	1989	Robin Romeo
1956	Anita Cantaline	1968	Dotty Fothergill	1980	Donna Adamek	1990	Tish Johnson
1957	Marion Ladewig	1969	Dotty Fothergill	1981	Donna Adamek		
1958	Marion Ladewig	1970	Mary Baker				
1959	Marion Ladewig	1971	Paula Sperber				

LPBT Player of the Year

Winners selected by members of Ladies Professional Bowlers Tour. The LPBT Player of the Year has differed from the BWAA Bowler of the Year twice—in 1985 and '86.

Multiple winner: Lisa Rathgeber Wagner (2).

Year		Year		Year		Year	
1983	Lisa Rathgeber	1985	Patty Costello	1987	Betty Morris	1989	Robin Romeo
1984	Aleta Sill	1986	Jeanne Maiden	1988	Lisa Wagner	1990	Leanne Barrette

WPBA and LPBT Rookie of the Year

Winners selected by members of Women's Professional Bowlers Association (1978-80) and the Ladies Professional Bowlers Tour (since 1981).

Year		Year		Year		Year	
1978	Toni Gillard	1982	Carol Norman	1985	Dede Davidson	1988	Mary Martha Cerniglia
1979	Nikki Gianulias	1983	Anne Marie Pike	1986	Wendy Macpherson	1989	Kim Terrell
1980	Lisa Rathgeber	1984	Paula Vidad	1987	Paula Drake	1990	Debbie McMullen
1981	Cindy Mason						

Dave Joyner/BTSP

At 39, four-time champion **Jimmy Connors** conducted business at the U.S. Open like a drum major on Homecoming weekend, high-stepping it all the way to the semifinals.

TENNIS

He's Ba-a-c-k!

Hold that sunset; 39-year-old Jimmy Connors returns to steal U.S. Open from champions Stefan Edberg and Monica Seles.

In a year where the biggest stories at Wimbledon were Andre Agassi in white and Monica Seles in absentia, the most compelling figure in tennis was 39-year-old Jimmy Connors.

So what if he didn't win a tournament? Many thought Connors was through after an ankle injury late in 1989 and a wrist injury early in 1990 limited him to just three matches all that year. Yet there was Jimbo in 1991—thrilling crowds with the old bump and grind while reaching the third round of the French Open and Wimbledon and then marching to the semifinals at his old stomping grounds, the U.S. Open.

At the end of 1990, it looked like Connors was riding into the sunset of a brilliant 20-year career. Bothered by the left wrist injury, he had tumbled from 14th in the world to 936th. He underwent wrist surgery in October and laid off the game for five months.

The "Can Connors Come Back?" headlines that greeted his return were nothing new. The same question had been asked 10 years earlier, and Connors answered by winning his second Wimbledon in 1982 and his fourth and fifth U.S. Opens in 1982 and 1983.

Jim Martz is the Regional Sports Editor of the *Miami Herald* and has covered tennis for the paper since 1973.

In 1991, he answered by grunting, diving and throwing himself around the courts to surprise players half his age and set pulses racing from Paris to London to New York.

"It never occurred to me that I should retire," Connors said. "I'm not ready."

He meekly launched his comeback at Chicago in February by losing to Jaime Yzaga of Peru, 6-3, 6-0. A few weeks later at the Lipton International Players Championship in Key Biscayne, Fla., Connors found renewed vigor in his game as he defeated Udo Riglewski of Germany, 6-4, 6-4, for his first victory since October, 1989. A Caratti chop took the air out of his revival the next day as Italy's Cristiano Caratti beat him, 6-4, 6-4, but Connors left town smiling.

"It's a start," he said. "Maybe I came back too soon. But I'm having fun."

Over the next six months, Father Time in Sneakers created fun and frenzy wherever he went. As the French Open crowds chanted "Allez Jimbo," Connors split the first four sets in the third round against 19-year-old Michael Chang and won the first point of the fifth before running out of gas and defaulting.

"I could hardly stand," Connors said. "I played my butt off and that was it."

At Wimbledon, where he had enthralled spectators for years, the fans gave him something back. Matches had never been played on the middle Sunday

Carol L. Newsom

Wide World Photos

While Connors was the story of the 1991 U.S. Open, the champions were **Monica Seles** (left) and **Stefan Edberg**, both of whom won the tournament for the first time. They both ended the summer ranked No. 1 in the world as well.

at the All-England Lawn Tennis and Croquet Club. But when five days of rain backed up the schedule, tradition had to be broken. Wimbledon opened the gates to the first 25,000 to show up and they had a blast.

They hollered "Jim-mee, Jim-mee," they counted in unison as he hit in practice and, yes, they even did the wave at Centre Court. Never mind that Derrick Costagno won, 7-6, (7-2), 6-1, 6-4.

"To hear the crowd like it was at the French Open and then on middle Sunday," Connors said, "if you can't get pumped up by that, you must be dead. That's what I love about this game. The sound of that crowd."

The sounds grew to a crescendo in New York where Connors nearly turned the clock all the way back. There he kept fans up until 1:35 in the morning in the first round as he defeated 25-year-old Patrick McEnroe in five sets after losing the first two and trailing, 0-3, in the third. Three matches later, on his 39th birthday (Sept. 2), Connors clawed back again to beat Aaron Krickstein, 3-6, 7-6 (10-8), 1-6, 6-3, 7-6 (7-4). The 4,000 fans left

from the original 21,000 sang "Happy Birthday." Connors, now ranked 174th, had become the oldest Open quarterfinalist since 39-year-old Ken Rosewall in 1974. That year Rosewall reached the final where he was routed, 6-1, 6-0, 6-1, by 22-year-old Connors, who won his first Open.

In the quarters, before another revved-up, prime time crowd at the Stadium Court and a cable TV audience that set an all-time ratings record for USA Network, Connors dispatched Holland's Paul Haarhuis in four sets to become the first wild card in U.S. Open history to advance to the semifinals. It was his 14th semifinal appearance.

True, Connors had an easier path than most. He had played only one seeded player—No. 10 Karol Novacek—but he had also won five matches and only three other players could say that.

Finally, James Scott Connors lost in the semifinals to James Spencer Courier, the 21-year-old who established himself in 1991 as the top American player. Courier, blasting forehands to the corners, broke Connors early in each set and never let him in the match, winning 6-3, 6-3, 6-2. The crowd cheered more for the loser than the winner, and once again Connors exited smiling.

"This is where I wanted to play my best tennis," he said. "And for somebody who was never going to play again to be able to do this . . . I mean, like I've said every time, how can you not laugh? I'm doing what I've loved to do for the past 22 years."

And he is not finished. "I still have five more years in me," Connors said. That would take him to his 44th birthday in 1996, to the edge of Nolan Ryan territory.

Forgotten in the euphoria surrounding Connors' exploits was the sad comeback attempt of another blast from the past: 34-year-old Bjorn Borg.

Winner of 11 Grand Slam titles and holder of the No. 1 ranking for 104 weeks from 1978-80, Borg began training in the fall of 1990 and the following April played his first match in eight years. Jordi Arrese soundly defeated him, 6-2, 6-3, in the Monte Carlo Open as Borg played with one of his obsolete wooden racquets. He was scheduled to play in the Italian Open a few weeks later but never showed up and put the comeback on hold while continuing to sort out his personal and financial problems.

The 1991 headliner on the women's tour was Seles, the 17-year-old former Nick Bollettieri protege from Yugoslavia, who won three Grand Slam titles and missed a chance to win a fourth by sitting out Wimbledon.

She began her roll in November, 1990 by beating Gabriela Sabatini in an historic Virginia Slims Championships final at Madison Square Garden. Seles won, 6-4, 5-7, 3-6, 6-4, 6-2, in the first five-set women's match since 1901.

After winning the Australian Open in January, a newly-coiffed ("Just call me Madonna") Seles supplanted Steffi Graf as the No.1 player and captured her second French Open in May. She then stunned Wimbledon officials by withdrawing three days before the tournament because of injuries she sustained in a "minor" but unspecified accident. No further explanation was given for nearly three weeks, and she refused all inquiries from the Women's Tennis Association.

When she surfaced in July at an exhibition in Manwah, N.J., she expressed

Tour Teens Raking in Net Profits

When *Forbes* published its annual list of the 40 highest paid athletes in August, 1991, it wasn't boxers Evander Holyfield and Mike Tyson or basketball megastar Michael Jordan who graced the magazine's cover. Rather it was teen-age tennis whizzes Monica Seles and Jennifer Capriati.

Tennis players made up nearly 25 percent of the *Forbes* list of top-earning athletes. It was one of several indicators that there is renewed interest in tennis from both the marketing perspective and in terms of participation.

After losing virtually millions of players since the tennis boom of the 1970s, participation in the United States appeared to bottom out in the mid-1980s at 18 million players. There has been a gradual increase since then to more than 24 million players, according to the American Tennis Industry Federation.

There were 4 million racquets sold in the U.S. in 1990 compared with 3.6 million in 1989. Much of the increase could be attributed to junior racquet sales, which were up from 639,000 to 736,000, said the ATIF.

And the National Sporting Goods Association reported that nearly 1.5 million new players between the ages of 7 and 17 entered the game in 1990. In some cases, there were probably dollar signs in their—or, more to the point, their parents'—eyes. What they could see was that there is considerable money to be made in tennis by the top players, especially via endorsements.

Brad Patterson, executive director of the ATIF, attributed the increase to the popularity of young pros like Seles, Capriati, Andre Agassi and Pete Sampras.

Seventeen-year-old Seles ranked 12th on the *Forbes* list, one notch below Larry Bird of the Boston Celtics. She was expected to earn $1.6 million on the court and $6 million off it through appearance fees, exhibitions and million-dollar endorsement contracts with shoe, racquet and camera companies, a hair care concern and bottled water.

Capriati, who already had million-dollar deals when she turned pro at age 13 in 1990, made her debut on the *Forbes* list at

The world's 40 highest-paid athletes
Peter Drucker looks ahead
The media business: in adversity, opportunities

Forbes

August 19, 1991 · Four Dollars

**Jennifer Capriati
and Monica Seles**

Cover photo by Jonathan Levine

Teenage cover girls **Jennifer Capriati** (left) and **Monica Seles** were the youngest of seven tennis players listed in the 1991 *Forbes* magazine survey of the 40 highest-paid athletes in the world.

No. 26. She was expected to earn $600,000 in winnings and $4.5 million in endorsements. In other words, mamas let your daughters grow up to be tennis players.

"More and more people are getting their kids into tennis, whether looking for meal tickets or college scholarships," television commentator Bud Collins told *Forbes*. "You see the kids with the entourages: fathers, coaches, people training the kids to wipe their noses and clean their diapers."

In his 1991 book *Hard Courts*, author and tennis correspondent John Feinstein said recruiting of young tennis players by agents can be just as vicious as college basketball recruiting. But there is one difference: "In college basketball there are all sorts of rules that are always bent, frequently broken. In tennis, there are no rules. Anarchy reigns. That is why agents swarm junior tournaments, all of them carrying lists of names, buttonholing parents of players who may be as young as 10 years old."

Joining Seles and Capriati on the *Forbes* list were Stefan Edberg ($7.4 million in winnings and other income), Steffi Graf ($7.3 million), Andre Agassi ($7.3 million), Boris Becker ($7.2 million), Gabriela Sabatini ($6.3 million), Ivan Lendl ($4.8 million), and Pete Sampras ($4.4 million).

There were other indicators that tennis interest was increasing. Prize money on the women's tour surpassed $24 million, up from the $900,000 in 1973, the year of the ballyhooed Bobby Riggs-Billie Jean King Battle of the Sexes that helped kindle interest in tennis. ABC signed a two-year contract to televise the year-end Virginia Slims Championships. Eighteen months earlier when Women's Tennis Association executive director Gerry Smith went to ABC, he was told even if he had $500,000 the network might not sell him the air time.

Mark Miles, executive director of the Association of Tennis Professionals that oversees the men's tour, believes the improved image of the players compared to 15 years ago is a key factor to the growth in interest.

"Those were awful days in terms of the image of the game," Miles said. "Tennis players who project good citizenship and a professional image, are clean-cut and reliable, are on the rise. Guys like Stefan Edberg, Peter Sampras and Jim Courier."

661

surprise at rumors she had been hiding out at Donald Trump's Palm Beach, Fla., estate. She said emotional distress had kept her silent, and added the injury was a combination of shin splints and a stress fracture.

"I believe that if I played Wimbledon, I wouldn't have been able to play the U.S. Open," she said later. "My legs hurt too much to play Wimbledon. I couldn't run."

Seles accepted a six-figure guarantee to compete at Mahwah, and on the day the event began she withdrew from the 32-nation Federation Cup that would start two days later. She said she pulled out because of shin splints. The WTA fined Seles $6,000 for skipping Wimbledon and $20,000 for playing in the non-sanctioned exhibition. Then the International Tennis Federation banned her from the 1992 Summer Olympics, saying she didn't have a valid reason for skipping the Federation Cup.

"She looked OK to me," said Jennifer Capriati after defeating Seles, 6-3, 7-5, at Mahwah. The 15-year-old Capriati had distinguised herself at Wimbledon by defeating 34-year-old defending champion Martina Navratilova, 6-4, 7-5, in the quarterfinals. In August, she and Seles met in the semifinals of the U.S. Open and played what may have been the tournament's best match, with Seles winning, 6-3, 3-6, 7-6 (7-3).

Seles then beat Navratilova, 7-6 (7-1), 6-1 to win the U.S. title for the first time.

Afterward, Seles told *The New York Times*, "For me the biggest tournament now will be Wimbledon. Not playing this year, it will always be there, a little emptiness."

While Seles passed up Wimbledon, fans almost passed out at the sight of men's fashion plate Andre Agassi attired in a white shirt, white denim shorts, white Lycra tights, white socks and white shoes.

The first and last time Agassi had played there, in 1987, he stayed barely long enough for tea. Henri Leconte ousted him in the first round in straight sets. This time, he came within two points of reaching the semifinals. Playing with a thigh injury, he lost in five sets to David Wheaton, who in the third round had ended Ivan Lendl's hopes of finally winning Wimbledon.

The image-conscious Agassi had another stormy year. In November he beat Stefan Edberg in four sets to win the inaugural ATP Tour World Championship. Two weeks later he turned in a controversial performance at the 1990 Davis Cup final. In May, he reached the French Open final for the second year in a row and lost again. In August he was knocked out of the U.S. Open in the opening round by Aaron Krickstein. And in September he redeemed himself by leading the U.S. past Germany and into the 1991 Davis Cup final.

The 1990 USA-Australia Davis Cup final was played in a smoke-filled indoor baseball stadium and marked the 42nd time the two countries have met with the Cup on the line. The Americans chose to play on red clay to slow the serve-and-volley games of the Australians. It was the first time the U.S. played on clay at home since 1971.

The Aussies claimed the U.S. bent the rules by insisting on playing the opening match on a Friday at 5 p.m., which allowed little time for players to rest for the Saturday 12:30 p.m. doubles. The U.S. Tennis Association countered that the 5 p.m. start was needed to maximize the crowd and television audience.

Agassi, saying he felt the effects of the flu from the previous weekend, overcame the top Aussie clay court player, Richard Fromberg, 4-6, 6-2, 4-6, 6-4, to win the first match. Then Chang whipped Darren Cahill, 6-2, 7-6 (7-4), 6-0. The next afternoon, to the delight of beleaguered American coach Tom Gorman and a record U.S. Davis Cup crowd of 18,156, Rick Leach and Jim Pugh clinched the title with a 6-4, 6-3, 3-6, 7-6 victory over Pat Cash and John Fitzgerald.

That rendered meaningless the reverse singles matches on Sunday. But that didn't mean there wouldn't be fireworks. Agassi retired after splitting the first two sets with Cahill and went to a hospital for treatment of what was announced as a torn chest muscle. Fromberg beat Chang, 7-5, 2-6, 6-3.

Cynics wondered if Agassi was, indeed, hurt. Agassi had been accused before of tanking matches, and it was no secret he didn't want to play in the new $6 million Grand Slam Cup two weeks later in Munich, Germany.

That night, reporter Barry Lorge of the *San Diego Union*, accidentally overheard Agassi and his brother Philip in a restaurant knocking Gorman and saying they had to find a doctor who would certify that Agassi was too hurt to play in the Grand Slam Cup. Agassi said Lorge misunderstood the conversation, and three doctors later swore that Agassi was injured.

Prior to the Davis Cup final, Agassi had beaten Edberg, 5-7, 7-6, 7-5, 6-2, to win the first ATP Tour World title at Frankfurt, Germany. The event, featuring the eight top-ranked players and replacing the year-ending Masters tournament in New York, offered a purse of $2 million, including $600,000 to the winner. However, Agassi never did show up at the Grand Slam Cup. The ITF fined him a record $25,000, but did not suspend him from any majors.

Nine months later, playing for the first time since his early dismissal from the '91 U.S. Open, Agassi atoned for a disappointing year by beginning and ending the United States' 3-2 victory over Germany in the Davis Cup semifinals.

Playing on another indoor clay court in Kansas City, Agassi overwhelmed Wimbledon champ Michael Stich, 6-3, 6-1, 6-4, in the opening match. Then in the decisive final of the best-of-five series, he overcame the pressure instead of choking on it and trounced Carl-Uwe Steeb, 6-2, 6-2, 6-3. In between, Jim Courier split with Stich and Steeb, but Stich and Eric Jelen defeated the U.S. doubles team of Scott Davis and Dave Pate (a surprise choice by Gorman over the tested tandem of Rick Leach and Jim Pugh). The Americans thus advanced to the Nov.29-Dec. 1 final against France, a 5-0 victor over Yugoslavia.

The Germans played without Boris Becker, who had led them to back-to-back Davis Cup victories in 1988-89. Becker, who won the Australian Open for the first time in 1991, also reached the semifinals in the French (losing to Agassi) and the finals at Wimbledon (losing to Stich). He was a third round casualty at the U.S. Open, however, and after the loss announced that a nagging thigh injury would keep him out of the Davis Cup semis.

Becker's early exit from the U.S. Open enabled eventual Open champion Edberg to recapture the No.1 ranking he

Agence France Presse

Andre Agassi fell flat in Flushing, but rose to the occasion in Kansas City.

had relinquished to Becker at Wimbledon. Edberg, playing "the best match I've ever played," overwhelmed French Open champ Jim Courier in the final, 6-2, 6-4, 6-0. One year before, Edberg had come to New York as the ATP computer's newly-anointed No.1 player, only to be upset in straight sets in the opening round by Alexander Volkov.

Edberg reached the semifinals at the Australian Open and Wimbledon. In Melbourne, he lost to Lendl in five sets, while at Wimbledon he was beaten, 4-6, 7-6 (7-5), 7-6 (7-5), 7-6 (7-2) by Stich, although—incredibly— he never lost his serve.

Courier's victory in the French meant that for the second consecutive year, four different players—Becker, Courier, Stich and Edberg—won the major men's titles. It also meant that for only the second time since 1984, Ivan Lendl failed to win a major. He came close at the Australian— losing to Becker in the final, 1-6, 6-4, 6-4, 6-4— and again at the U.S. Open—bowing to Edberg in the semis, 6-3, 3-6, 4-6, 7-6 (7-5), 6-1.

Navratilova, who entered 1991 tied with Chris Evert at 18 major singles championships, didn't win any big ones, either, but it wasn't for lack of trying.

The McEnroe brothers, **Patrick** (left) and **John**, met for the first time in a championship final at the Chicago Volvo on March 3. Patrick won the first set, but John rallied to win the match.

Her bid for an unprecedented 10th Wimbledon title was derailed in the quarterfinals by Capriati, who became the youngest Wimbledon semifinalist in history at 15 years and 96 days. Navratilova, who had reached at least the semifinals every year since 1977, was weighed upon by the multimillion dollar lawsuit filed by her former companion Judy Nelson in May.

Yet Navratilova was able to put those difficulties behind her at the U.S. Open. Inspired by Connors' run for the ages, the 34-year-old became a sentimental favorite and stunned Wimbledon champ Graf in the semifinals, 7-6, 6-7, 6-4, before bowing to Seles in the final.

Navratilova and Connors gave Billie Jean King's Team Tennis League a boost in July by playing for the champion Atlanta Thunder and runner-up Los Angeles Strings, respectively. Connors also became the world's oldest Rookie of the Year.

Even more implausible was the March 3 meeting between 32-year-old John McEnroe and his 24-year-old brother Patrick in the final of the Volvo Tennis/Chicago tournament.

Six years earlier, John easily defeated Patrick, 6-2, 6-1, in a tournament at Stratton, Vt., but this time Patrick was in charge for a set until John called upon his experience and a variety of shots to win, 3-6, 6-2, 6-4. "Every emotion you can imagine was there," John said, "from worrying about how he's doing, to worrying that he might beat you."

In January, Mac the Younger had reached the semifinals of the Australian open before losing to Becker, 6-7 (2-7), 6-4, 6-1, 6-4.

In June, Mac the Elder returned from a self-imposed three-year Davis Cup exile to help the U.S. defeat Spain, 4-1, on grass at Newport, R.I.

A month later in Nottinhgam, England, Spain won the women's Federation Cup for the first time as Conchita Martinez and Arantxa Sanchez Vicario beat Gigi Fernandez and Zina Garrison of the U.S. in the decisive doubles match, 3-6, 6-1, 6-1. □

T E N N I S
S T A T I S T I C S

SEC A

THE 1992 INFORMATION PLEASE SPORTS ALMANAC

THE SEASON IN REVIEW

1990-1991

MEN • WOMEN • LEADERS

PAGE 665

Tournament Results

Winners of men's and women's pro singles championships from Nov.4, 1990 through Sept. 22, 1991.

Men's Tour

LATE 1990

Finals	Tournament	Winner	Earnings	Loser	Score
Nov. 4	Paris Open	Stefan Edberg	$270,000	B.Becker	3-3(wd)
Nov. 10	Citibank Open (Itaparica)	Mats Wilander	32,400	M.Filippini	61 62
Nov. 11	Diet Pepsi Indoor (London)	Jakob Hlasek	42,800	M.Chang	76 63
Nov. 11	Kremlin Cup (Moscow)	Andrei Cherkasov	42,800	T.Mayotte	62 61
Nov. 18	ATP World Championship (Frankfurt)	Andre Agassi	950,000	S.Edberg	57 76 75 62
Nov. 25	ATP Doubles Championship (Australia)	Guy Forget/ Jakob Hlasek	225,000	S.Casal/ E.Sanchez	64 76 57 64
Dec. 16	ITF Grand Slam Cup (Munich)	Pete Sampras	2,000,000	B.Gilbert	63 64 62

1991 (through Sept.22)

Finals	Tournament	Winner	Earnings	Loser	Score
Jan. 6	BP Nationals (Wellington)	Richard Fromberg	$21,600	L.Jonsson	61 64 64
Jan. 6	Australian Hardcourt (Adelaide)	Nicklas Kulti	21,600	M.Stich	63 16 62
Jan. 13	New South Wales Open (Sydney)	Guy Forget	32,400	M.Stich	63 64
Jan. 13	New Zealand Open (Auckland)	Karel Novacek	21,600	J.Fleurian	76 76
Jan. 27	**Australian Open** (Melbourne)	Boris Becker	266,778	I.Lendl	16 64 64 64
Feb. 10	Muratti Time Indoor (Milan)	Alexander Volkov	77,760	C.Caratti	61 75
Feb. 10	Volvo/San Francisco	Darren Cahill	32,400	B.Gilbert	62 36 64
Feb. 17	U.S. Pro Indoor (Philadelphia)	Ivan Lendl	135,000	P.Sampras	57 64 64 36 63
Feb. 17	Donnay Indoor (Brussels)	Guy Forget	77,500	A.Cherkasov	63 75 36 76
Feb. 24	Eurocard Classics (Stuttgart)	Stefan Edberg	137,500	J.Svensson	62 36 75 62
Feb. 24	Volvo Indoor (Memphis)	Ivan Lendl	99,000	M.Stich	75 63
Mar. 3	ABN Wereld Toernooi (Rotterdam)	Omar Camporese	65,000	I.Lendl	36 76 76
Mar. 3	Volvo/Chicago	John McEnroe	32,400	P.McEnroe	36 62 64
Mar. 10	Newsweek Champions Cup (Indian Wells)	Jim Courier	125,000	G.Forget	46 63 46 63 76
Mar. 24	Lipton International (Key Biscayne)	Jim Courier	179,000	D.Wheaton	46 63 64
Apr. 7	Estoril Open (Portugal)	Sergi Bruguera	48,600	K.Novacek	76 61
Apr. 7	Prudential-Bache Classic (Orlando)	Andre Agassi	32,400	D.Rostagno	62 16 63
Apr. 14	Trofeo Conde de Godo (Barcelona)	Emilio Sanchez	85,000	S.Bruguera	64 76 62
Apr. 14	Suntory Japan Open (Tokyo)	Stefan Edberg	137,500	I.Lendl	61 75 60
Apr. 21	Philips Open (Nice)	Martin Jaite	32,400	G.Prpic	36 76 63
Apr. 28	Volvo Monte Carlo Open	Sergi Bruguera	125,000	B.Becker	57 64 76 76
May 5	BMW Open (Munich)	Magnus Gustafsson	32,400	G.Perez-Roldan	36 63 43(ret)
May 5	USTA (Tampa)	Richey Reneberg	32,400	P.Korda	46 64 62
May 12	German Open (Hamburg)	Karel Novacek	125,000	M.Gustafsson	63 63 57 06 61
May 12	U.S. Clay Court (Charlotte)	Jaime Yzaga	30,960	J.Arias	63 75
May 19	Italian Open (Rome)	Emilio Sanchez	161,000	A.Mancini	63 61 30(ret)
May 19	Yugoslav Open (Umag)	Dimitri Poliakov	30,960	J.Sanchez	64 64
May 26	Internazionali di Tennis (Bologna)	Paolo Cane	32,400	J.Gunnarsson	57 63 75
June 9	**French Open** (Paris)	Jim Courier	436,909	A.Agassi	36 64 26 61 64
June 16	Stella Artois Grass Court (London)	Stefan Edberg	65,250	D.Wheaton	62 63
June 16	Continental Grass Court (Holland)	Christian Saceanu	32,400	M.Schapers	61 36 75
June 16	Torneo Internazionale (Florence)	Thomas Muster	32,400	H.Skoff	62 67 64
June 23	IP Cup (Genova)	Carl-Uwe Steeb	32,400	J.Arrese	63 64
June 23	Manchester Open	Goren Ivanisevic	32,400	P.Sampras	64 64
July 7	**Wimbledon** (London)	Michael Stich	445,008	B.Becker	64 76 64
July 14	Swiss Open (Gstaad)	Emilio Sanchez	39,600	S.Bruguera	61 64 64
July 14	Swedish Open (Bastad)	Magnus Gustafsson	32,400	A.Mancini	61 62

Tournament Results (Cont.)

Finals		Tournament	Winner	Earnings	Loser	Score
July	21	Mercedes Cup (Stuttgart)	Michael Stich	$135,000	A.Mancini	16 76 64 62
July	21	Sovran Bank Classic (Washington, DC)	Andre Agassi	77,700	P.Korda	63 64
July	28	Canadian Open (Toronto)	Andrei Chesnokov	155,000	P.Korda	36 64 63
July	28	Holland International (Hilversum)	Magnus Gustafsson	30,960	J.Arrese	57 76 26 61 60
Aug.	4	Austrian Open/Head Cup (Kitzbuhel)	Karel Novacek	48,000	M.Gustafsson	76 76 62
Aug.	4	San Marino Open	G.Perez-Roldan	32,400	F.Fontang	63 61
Aug.	4	Volvo/Los Angeles	Pete Sampras	32,400	B.Gilbert	62 67 63
Aug.	11	ATP Championship (Cincinnati)	Guy Forget	155,000	P.Sampras	26 76 64
Aug.	11	Czechoslovak Open (Prague)	Karel Novacek	43,920	M.Gustafsson	76 62
Aug.	18	U.S. Hardcourt (Indianapolis)	Pete Sampras	137,500	B.Becker	76 36 63
Aug.	18	Volvo International (New Haven)	Petr Korda	137,500	G.Ivanisevic	64 62
Aug.	25	Hamlet Challenge Cup (Long Island)	Ivan Lendl	32,400	S.Edberg	63 62
Aug.	25	OTB International (Schenectady)	Michael Stich	18,300	E.Sanchez	62 64
Sept.	8	**U.S. Open** (Flushing)	Stefan Edberg	400,000	J.Courier	62 64 60
Sept.	15	Grand Prix Passing Shot (Bordeaux)	Guy Forget	38,800	O.Delaitre	61 63
Sept.	15	Aberto da Republica (Brazilia)	Andres Gomez	32,400	J.Sanchez	64 36 63
Sept.	15	Barclay Open (Geneva)	Thomas Muster	32,400	H.Skoff	62 64

Women's Tour

LATE 1990

Finals		Tournament	Winner	Earnings	Loser	Score
Nov.	4	Va.Slims/California (Oakland)	Monica Seles	$70,000	M.Navratilova	63 76
Nov.	4	Va.Slims/Nashville	Natalia Medvedeva	27,000	S.Sloane	63 76
Nov.	11	Va.Slims/New England (Worcester)	Steffi Graf	70,000	G.Sabatini	76 63
Nov.	11	Jell-o Classic (Indianapolis)	Conchita Martinez	27,000	L.Meskhi	64 62
Nov.	18	Va.Slims Championships (New York)	Monica Seles	250,000	G.Sabatini	64 57 36 64 62

Note: Seles' Virginia Slims Championship prize money total does not include $400,000 bonus.

1991 (through Sept.22)

Finals		Tournament	Winner	Earnings	Loser	Score
Jan.	6	Danone Hardcourts (Brisbane)	Helena Sukova	$27,000	A.Kijimuta	64 63
Jan.	13	New South Wales Open (Sydney)	Jana Novotna	45,000	A.Vicario	64 62
Jan.	27	**Australian Open** (Melbourne)	Monica Seles	234,806	J.Novotna	57 63 61
Feb.	3	Pan Pacific Open (Toyko)	Gabriela Sabatini	70,000	M.Navratilova	26 62 64
Feb.	17	Va.Slims/Chicago	Martina Navratilova	70,000	Z.Garrison	61 62
Feb.	24	Va.Slims/Oklahoma (Okla.City)	Jana Novotna	27,000	A.Smith	36 63 62
Mar.	3	Va.Slims/Palm Springs	Martina Navratilova	70,000	M.Seles	62 76
Mar.	10	Va.Slims/Florida (Boca Raton)	Gabriela Sabatini	100,000	S.Graf	64 76
Mar.	24	Lipton International (Key Biscayne)	Monica Seles	112,500	G.Sabatini	63 75
Mar.	31	U.S.Hardcourts (San Antonio)	Steffi Graf	45,000	M.Seles	64 63
Apr.	7	Family Circle Cup (Hilton Head)	Gabriela Sabatini	100,000	L.Meskhi	61 61
Apr.	14	Bausch & Lomb Champs.(Amelia Is.)	Gabriela Sabatini	70,000	S.Graf	75 76
Apr.	14	Suntory Japan Open (Tokyo)	Lori McNeil	27,000	A.Appelmans	26 62 61
Apr.	21	Va.Slims/Houston	Monica Seles	70,000	M.J.Fernandez	64 63
Apr.	28	Intl.Champs of Spain (Barcelona)	Conchita Martinez	45,000	M.Fragniere	64 61
May	6	Citizen Cup (Hamburg)	Steffi Graf	70,000	M.Seles	75 67 63
May	12	Italian Open (Rome)	Gabriela Sabatini	100,000	M.Seles	63 62
May	20	Lufthansa Cup (Berlin)	Steffi Graf	100,000	A.Vicario	63 46 76
May	26	Geneva European Open	Manuela Fragniere	27,000	H.Kelesi	63 36 63
June	9	**French Open** (Paris)	Monica Seles	378,500	A.Vicario	63 64
June	16	Dow Classic (Birmingham)	Martina Navratilova	27,000	N.Zvereva	64 76
June	22	Pilkington Champs.(Eastbourne)	Martina Navratilova	70,000	A.Vicario	64 64
July	7	**Wimbledon** (London)	Steffi Graf	357,177	G.Sabatini	64 36 86
July	21	Austrian Open (Kitzbuhel)	Conchita Martinez	27,000	J.Wiesner	61 26 63
Aug.	4	Mazda Classic (San Diego)	Jennifer Capriati	45,000	M.Seles	46 61 76
Aug.	11	Canadian Open (Toronto)	Jennifer Capriati	100,000	K.Maleeva	62 63
Aug.	11	Va.Slims/Albuquerque	Gigi Fernandez	27,000	J.Halard	60 62
Aug.	18	Va.Slims/Los Angeles	Monica Seles	70,000	K.Date	63 61
Aug.	25	Va.Slims/Washington, DC	Arantxa Vicario	70,000	K.Maleeva	62 75
Aug.	25	OTB International (Schenectady)	Brenda Schultz	18,000	A.Dechaume	76 62
Sept.	8	**U.S. Open** (Flushing)	Monica Seles	400,000	M.Navratilova	76 61
Sept.	22	Nichirei International	Monica Seles	70,000	M.J.Fernandez	61 61
Sept.	22	Paris Open	Conchita Martinez	27,000	Gorrochategui	60 63

Grand Slam Champions

Australian Open

Men's Singles............................. Boris Becker
Men's Doubles................... Scott Davis/David Pate
Women's Singles........................ Monica Seles
Women's Doubles............ Patty Fendick/M.J.Fernandez
Mixed Doubles................... Jeremy Bates/Jo Durie

French Open

Men's Singles............................. Jim Courier
Men's Doubles............. John Fitzgerald/Anders Jarryd
Women's Singles........................ Monica Seles
Women's Doubles.......... Gigi Fernandez/Jana Novotna
Mixed Doubles................ Helena Sukova/Cyril Suk

Wimbledon

Men's Singles........................... Michael Stich
Men's Doubles............. John Fitzgerald/Anders Jarryd
Women's Singles............................ Steffi Graf
Women's Doubles.... Larisa Savchenko/Natalia Zvereva
Mixed Doubles................ Liz Smylie/John Fitzgerald

U.S. Open

Men's Singles........................... Stefan Edberg
Men's Doubles............. John Fitzgerald/Anders Jarryd
Women's Singles........................ Monica Seles
Women's Doubles........... Pam Shriver/Natalia Zvereva
Mixed Doubles............. Manon Bollegraf/Tom Nijssen

Singles Leaders

Official Top 15 computer rankings and money leaders of men's and women's tours for 1990 and unofficial rankings and money leaders for 1991 (through Sept.15), as compiled by ATP (Association of Tennis Professionals) and WTA (Women's Tennis Association). Note that money list includes doubles earnings.

Final 1990 Computer Rankings and Money Won

Listed are titles won (1st), record (W-L) and earnings for the year with rank on earnings list in parentheses.

MEN	1st	W-L	Earnings	(No)		WOMEN	1st	W-L	Earnings	(No)
1 Stefan Edberg	7	70-14	$1,995,901	(1)		1 Steffi Graf	10	72-5	$1,921,853	(1)
2 Boris Becker	5	71-15	1,587,502	(3)		2 Monica Seles	9	54-6	1,637,222	(2)
3 Ivan Lendl	5	53-11	1,145,742	(4)		3 Martina Navratilova	6	52-7	1,330,794	(3)
4 Andre Agassi	4	45-12	1,741,382	(2)		4 Mary Joe Fernandez	2	40-10	518,366	(8)
5 Pete Sampras	3*	47-17	900,057	(5)		5 Gabriela Sabatini	2	49-14	975,490	(4)
6 Andres Gomez	3	37-26	872,613	(6)		6 Katerina Maleeva	1	47-15	418,475	(11)
7 Thomas Muster	3	51-17	605,267	(11)		7 Arantxa Sanchez Vicario	2	41-15	517,662	(9)
8 Emilio Sanchez	2	50-25	734,286	(7)		8 Jennifer Capriati	1	42-11	283,597	(14)
9 Goran Ivanisevic	1	50-22	720,945	(8)		9 Manuela Fragniere	0	42-16	360,215	(12)
10 Brad Gilbert	3	47-22	555,733	(12)		10 Zina Garrison	1	51-20	602,203	(6)
11 Jonas Svensson	1	45-20	441,745	(13)		11 Conchita Martinez	3	42-10	248,184	(17)
12 Andrei Chesnokov	2	45-21	423,863	(15)		12 Natalia Zvereva	2	42-15	462,770	(10)
13 John McEnroe	1	33-15	372,505	(18)		13 Jana Novotna	1	43-16	645,500	(5)
14 Guillermo Perez-Roldan	1	41-21	317,538	(29)		14 Helena Sukova	0	41-17	562,715	(7)
15 Michael Chang	1	34-20	416,072	(17)		15 Barbara Paulus	1	35-15	184,164	(22)

*Does not include ITF Grand Slam Cup championship and winner's purse of $2 million.

1991 Computer Rankings (through Sept.22)

For Men's Tour, listed are tournaments played (TP), titles won (1st), record (W-L), and computer points earned (Pts). For Women's Tour, listed are tournaments played (TP), titles won (1st), record (W-L), and average computer points per game (Avg).

MEN

ATP/IBM singles rankings based on total computer points from each player's 14 best tournaments covering the calendar year Sept.15, 1990 through Sept.15, 1991. Tournaments, titles and match won-lost records, however, are for 1991 only.

	TP	1st	W-L	Pts
1 Stefan Edberg	16	4	61-15	3778
2 Boris Becker	11	1	40-10	3501
3 Jim Courier	15	3	50-14	2885
4 Ivan Lendl	16	3	45-13	2789
5 Michael Stich	19	3	63-18	2666
6 Guy Forget	18	4	47-15	1917
7 Pete Sampras	15	2	34-13	1650
8 Andre Agassi	15	2	30-13	1622
9 Karel Novacek	25	4	51-23	1523
10 Sergi Bruguera	19	2	40-17	1521
Magnus Gustafsson	20	3	52-16	1521
12 Emilio Sanchez	22	3	38-23	1396
13 David Wheaton	15	0	25-15	1392
14 Petr Korda	19	1	32-19	1250
15 Goran Ivanisevic	18	1	32-19	1198

Note: As of Sept. 15, John McEnroe was ranked 25th and Jimmy Connors 68th.

WOMEN

WTA/Va.Slims Slimstat rankings based on average computer points awarded for each tournament played during the calendar year Sept.22, 1990 through Sept.22, 1991. Tournaments, titles and match won-lost records, however, are for 1991 only.

	TP	1st	W-L	Avg
1 Monica Seles	12	7	59-5	263.9
2 Steffi Graf	11	4	50-7	232.9
3 Gabriela Sabatini	13	5	56-8	205.8
4 Martina Navratilova	10	4	39-6	165.2
5 Arantxa Vicario	13	1	56-12	149.0
6 Jennifer Capriati	11	2	38-10	130.0
7 Mary Joe Fernandez	14	0	44-15	129.8
8 Conchita Martinez	10	3	36-8	120.0
9 Jana Novotna	13	2	38-12	100.2
10 Manuela Fragniere	12	2	33-11	89.9
11 Katerina Maleeva	13	0	28-14	82.4
12 Zina Garrison	13	0	30-13	69.5
13 Leila Meskhi	12	1	24-11	66.4
14 Helena Sukova	14	1	25-13	59.2
15 Nathalie Tauziat	15	0	27-16	56.5

Singles Leaders (Cont.)
Money Won
Amounts include singles and doubles earnings.

MEN

	Earnings		Earnings		Earnings
1 Stefan Edberg	$1,367,840	6 Emilio Sanchez	$634,279	11 Andre Agassi	$490,366
2 Jim Courier	1,290,911	7 Guy Forget	629,532	12 Anders Jarryd	460,939
3 Michael Stich	1,101,936	8 Magnus Gustafsson	535,137	13 Goran Ivanisevic	430,005
4 Boris Becker	860,123	9 Karel Novacek	503,385	14 Petr Korda	426,810
5 Ivan Lendl	739,653	10 Pete Sampras	494,288	15 Sergi Bruguera	417,070

WOMEN

	Earnings		Earnings		Earnings
1 Monica Seles	$1,507,758	6 Jana Novotna	$557,619	11 Larisa Savchenko	$318,765
2 Gabriela Sabatini	914,571	7 Mary Joe Fernandez	534,260	12 Helena Sukova	271,899
3 Steffi Graf	907,336	8 Jennifer Capriati	464,917	13 Zina Garrison	270,734
4 Arantxa Sanchez	677,840	9 Natalia Zvereva	459,702	14 Conchita Martinez	221,265
5 Martina Navratilova	579,536	10 Gigi Fernandez	364,203	15 Katerina Maleeva	218,293

National Team Competition
Davis Cup

The United States won the 1990 Davis Cup at the Suncoast Dome in St.Petersburg, Fla., beating Australia, 3-2. The win marked the 29th time the U.S. has won the Cup and the 11th time it has beaten Australia in the final.

1990 Final
United States 3, Australia 2
(at St.Petersburg, Fla., Nov.30-Dec.2)

Day One—Andre Agassi (USA) def. Richard Fromberg (AUS), 4-6,6-2,4-6,6-2,6-4; Michael Chang (USA) def. Darren Cahill (AUS), 6-2,7-6(7-4), 6-0.
Day Two—Rick Leach & Jim Pugh (USA) def. Pat Cash & John Fitzgerald (AUS), 6-4,6-2,3-6,7-6(7-2). USA clinches final, 3-0.
Day Three—Fromberg (AUS) def. Chang (USA), 7-5,2-6,6-3; Cahill (AUS) def. Agassi (USA), 6-4,4-6,retired.

1991 Early Rounds
The United States will defend the Davis Cup on the road against France, Nov. 29-Dec.1, at Lyons. The French, who last won the Cup in 1932, lost to the U.S. by a 4-1 score in the final round at Grenoble in 1982.

1st ROUND
(Feb. 1-3)

Winner		Loser
Argentina 4	at New Zealand	1
at Australia 5	Belgium	0
at Czechoslovakia 4	Austria	1
at France 5*	Israel	0
at Germany 3	Italy	2
at Spain 4	Canada	1
United States 3*	at Mexico	2
at Yugoslavia 4	Sweden	1

*France-Israel and USA-Mexico matches were postponed until Mar.29-30, due to Persian Gulf War.

QUARTERFINALS
(Mar.28-30)

Winner		Loser
at France 3	Australia	2
at Germany 5	Argentina	0
at United States 4	Spain	1
Yugoslavia 4	at Czechoslovakia	1

France-Australia and USA-Spain matches postponed until June 14-16.

SEMIFINALS
United States 3, Germany 2
(Sept.20-22, at Kansas City)

Day One—Andre Agassi (USA) def. Michael Stich, (GER), 6-3,6-1,6-4; Jim Courier (USA) def. Carl-Uwe Steeb (GER), 4-6,6-1,6-3,6-4.
Day Two—Stich and Eric Jelen (GER) def. Scott Davis and David Pate (USA), 7-6(7-3), 6-4,6-4.
Day Three—Stich (GER) def. Courier (USA), 6-4,7-5,6-4; Agassi (USA) def. Steeb (GER), 6-2,6-2,6-3. USA wins, 3-2.
Note: Boris Becker declined to play for Germany because of a bad back.

France 5, Yugoslavia 0
(Sept.20-22, at Pau, France)

Day One—Guy Forget (FRA) def. Srdjan Muskatirovic (YUG), 6-2,6-1,6-4; Fabrice Santoro (FRA) def. Slobodan Zivojinovic (YUG), 4-6,7-5,7-6(7-0),3-6,6-3.
Day Two—Forget and Arnaud Boetsch (FRA) def. Muskatirovic and Zivojinovic (YUG), 6-4,6-3,6-2. France clinches semifinal, 3-0.
Day Three—Forget (FRA) def. Zivojinovic (YUG), 6-1,3-6,6-2; Santoro (FRA) def. Muskatirovic (YUG), 6-7(1-7),6-3,7-5.
Note: Top Yugoslav players Goran Ivanisevic and Goran Prpic quit the Davis Cup team because of fighting between their home republic of Croatia and the Serbian-dominated federal government.

FINAL
United States at France (Nov.29-Dec.1)

1991 Federation Cup

Spain beat the United States, 2-1, to win the women's Federation Cup for the first time. The week-long tournament featuring 32 international teams was held in Nottingham, England, July 22-28.

FINAL
Spain 2, United States 1

Singles—Jennifer Capriati (USA) def. Conchita Martinez (SPA), 4-6,7-6(7-3),6-1; Arantxa Sanchez Vicario (SPA) def. Mary Joe Fernandez (USA), 6-3,6-4.
Doubles—Martinez & Vicario (SPA) def. Zina Garrison & Gigi Fernandez (USA), 3-6,6-1,6-1. Spain clinches final, 2-1.

TENNIS STATISTICS

THROUGH THE YEARS
1877-1991

MAJOR TITLES • LEADERS

THE 1992 INFORMATION PLEASE SPORTS ALMANAC

SEC B

PAGE 669

Grand Slam Championships
Australian Open
MEN

Became an Open Championship in 1969. Two tournaments were held in 1977; the first in January, the second in December. Tournament moved back to January in 1987, so no championship was decided in 1986.

Surface: Synpave Rebound Ace (hardcourt surface composed of polyurethane and synthetic rubber).

Multiple winners: Roy Emerson (6); Jack Crawford, Ken Rosewall and Pat Wood (4); Rod Laver, Adrian Quist and Mats Wilander (3); James Anderson, John Bromwich, Ashley Cooper, Stefan Edberg, Rodney Heath, Johan Kriek, Ivan Lendl, John Newcombe, Frank Sedgman, Guillermo Vilas and Tony Wilding (2).

Year	Winner	Loser	Score
1905	Rodney Heath	A.Curtis	46 63 64 64
1906	Tony Wilding	H.Parker	60 64 64
1907	Horace Rice	H.Parker	63 64 64
1908	Fred Alexander	A.Dunlop	36 36 60 62 63
1909	Tony Wilding	E.Parker	61 75 62
1910	Rodney Heath	H.Rice	64 63 62
1911	Norman Brookes	H.Rice	61 62 63
1912	James Parke	A.Beamish	36 63 16 61 75
1913	Ernie Parker	H.Parker	26 61 62 63
1914	Pat Wood	G.Patterson	64 63 57 61
1915	Francis Lowe	H.Rice	46 61 61 64
1916-18	Not held		
1919	A.R.F.Kingscote	E.Pockley	64 60 63
1920	Pat Wood	R. Thomas	63 46 68 61 63
1921	Rhys Gemmell	A. Hedeman	75 61 64
1922	Pat Wood	G. Patterson	60 36 36 63 62
1923	Pat Wood	C.B. St. John	61 61 63
1924	James Anderson	R. Schlesinger	63 64 36 57 63
1925	James Anderson	G. Patterson	119 26 62 63
1926	John Hawkes	J. Willard	61 63 61
1927	Gerald Patterson	J. Hawkes	36 64 36 1816 63
1928	Jean Borotra	R.O. Cummings	64 61 46 57 63
1929	John Gregory	R. Schlesinger	62 62 57 75
1930	Gar Moon	H. Hopman	63 61 63
1931	Jack Crawford	H. Hopman	64 62 26 61
1932	Jack Crawford	H. Hopman	46 63 36 63 61
1933	Jack Crawford	K. Gledhill	26 75 63 62
1934	Fred Perry	J. Crawford	63 75 61
1935	Jack Crawford	F. Perry	26 64 64 64
1936	Adrian Quist	J. Crawford	62 63 46 36 97
1937	V.B. McGrath	J. Bromwich	63 16 60 26 61
1938	Don Budge	J. Bromwich	64 62 61
1939	John Bromwich	A. Quist	64 61 63
1940	Adrian Quist	J. Crawford	63 61 62
1941-45	Not held		
1946	John Bromwich	D. Pails	57 63 75 36 62
1947	Dinny Pails	J. Bromwich	46 64 36 75 86
1948	Adrian Quist	J. Bromwich	64 36 63 26 63
1949	Frank Sedgman	K. McGregor	63 63 62
1950	Frank Sedgman	K. McGregor	63 64 46 61
1951	Richard Savitt	K. McGregor	63 26 63 61
1952	Ken McGregor	F. Sedgman	75 1210 26 62
1953	Ken Rosewall	M. Rose	60 63 64
1954	Mervyn Rose	R. Hartwig	62 06 64 62
1955	Ken Rosewall	L. Hoad	97 64 64
1956	Lew Hoad	K. Rosewall	64 36 64 75
1957	Ashley Cooper	N. Fraser	63 911 64 62
1958	Ashley Cooper	M. Anderson	75 63 64
1959	Alex Olmedo	N. Fraser	61 62 36 63
1960	Rod Laver	N. Fraser	57 36 62 86 86
1961	Roy Emerson	R. Laver	16 63 75 64
1962	Rod Laver	R. Emerson	86 06 64 64
1963	Roy Emerson	K. Fletcher	63 63 61
1964	Roy Emerson	F. Stolle	63 64 62
1965	Roy Emerson	F. Stolle	79 26 64 75 61
1966	Roy Emerson	A. Ashe	64 68 62 63
1967	Roy Emerson	A. Ashe	64 61 61
1968	Bill Bowrey	J. Gisbert	75 26 97 64
1969	Rod Laver	A. Gimeno	63 64 75
1970	Arthur Ashe	D. Crealy	64 97 62
1971	Ken Rosewall	A. Ashe	61 75 63
1972	Ken Rosewall	M. Anderson	76 63 75
1973	John Newcombe	O. Parun	63 67 75 61
1974	Jimmy Connors	P. Dent	76 64 46 63
1975	John Newcombe	J. Connors	75 36 64 75
1976	Mark Edmonson	J. Newcombe	67 63 76 61
1977	Roscoe Tanner	G. Vilas	63 63 63
	Vitas Gerulaitis	J. Lloyd	63 76 57 36 62
1978	Guillermo Vilas	J. Marks	64 64 36 63
1979	Guillermo Vilas	J. Sadri	76 63 62
1980	Brian Teacher	K. Warwick	75 76 63
1981	Johan Kriek	S. Denton	62 76 67 64
1982	Johan Kriek	S. Denton	63 63 62
1983	Mats Wilander	I. Lendl	61 64 64
1984	Mats Wilander	K. Curran	67 64 76 62
1985	Stefan Edberg	M. Wilander	64 63 63
1986	Not held		
1987	Stefan Edberg	P. Cash	63 64 36 57 63
1988	Mats Wilander	P. Cash	63 67 36 61 86
1989	Ivan Lendl	M. Mecir	62 62 62
1990	Ivan Lendl	S. Edberg	46 76 52 (ret)
1991	Boris Becker	I. Lendl	16 64 64 64

Grand Slam Championships (Cont.)
Australian Open
WOMEN

Became an Open Championship in 1969. Two tournaments were held in 1977, the first in January, the second in December. Tournament moved back to January in 1987, so no championship was decided in 1986.

Multiple winners: Margaret Smith Court (11); Nancye Wynne Bolton (6); Daphne Akhurst (5); Evonne Goolagong Cawley (4); Steffi Graf, Jean Hartigan and Martina Navratilova (3); Coral Buttsworth, Chris Evert Lloyd, Thelma Long, Hana Mandlikova and Mall Molesworth (2).

Year	Winner	Loser	Score	Year	Winner	Loser	Score
1922	Mall Molesworth	E. Boyd	63 108	1960	Margaret Smith	J. Lehane	75 62
1923	Mall Molesworth	E. Boyd	61 75	1961	Margaret Smith	J. Lehane	61 64
1924	Sylvia Lance	E. Boyd	63 36 64	1962	Margaret Smith	J. Lehane	60 62
1925	Daphne Akhurst	E. Boyd	16 86 64	1963	Margaret Smith	J. Lehane	62 62
1926	Daphne Akhurst	E. Boyd	61 63	1964	Margaret Smith	L. Turner	63 62
1927	Esna Boyd	S. Harper	57 61 62	1965	Margaret Smith	M. Bueno	57 64 52 (ret)
1928	Daphne Akhurst	E. Boyd	75 62	1966	Margaret Smith	N. Richey	walkover
1929	Daphne Akhurst	L. Bickerton	61 57 62	1967	Nancy Richey	L. Turner	61 64
1930	Daphne Akhurst	S. Harper	108 26 75	1968	Billie Jean King	M. Smith	61 62
1931	Coral Buttsworth	M. Crawford	16 63 64	1969	Margaret Court	B. Jean King	64 61
1932	Coral Buttsworth	K. LeMessurier	97 64				
1933	Joan Hartigan	C. Buttsworth	64 63	1970	Margaret Court	K. Melville	63 61
1934	Joan Hartigan	M. Molesworth	61 64	1971	Margaret Court	E. Goolagong	26 76 75
1935	Dorothy Round	N. Bolton	16 61 63	1972	Virginia Wade	E. Goolagong	64 64
1936	Joan Hartigan	N. Bolton	64 64	1973	Margaret Court	E. Goolagong	64 75
1937	Nancye Wynne	E. Westacott	63 57 64	1974	Evonne Goolagong	C. Evert	76 46 60
1938	Dorothy Bundy	D. Stevenson	63 62	1975	Evonne Goolagong	M. Navratilova	63 62
1939	Emily Westacott	N. Hopman	61 62	1976	Evonne Cawley	R. Tomanova	62 62
1940	Nancye Wynne	T. Coyne	57 64 60	1977	Kerry Reid	D. Balestrat	75 62
1941-45	Not held				Evonne Cawley	H. Gourlay	63 60
1946	Nancye Bolton	J. Fitch	64 64	1978	Chris O'Neill	B. Nagelsen	63 76
1947	Nancye Bolton	N. Hopman	63 62	1979	Barbara Jordan	S. Walsh	63 63
1948	Nancye Bolton	M. Toomey	63 61				
1949	Doris Hart	N. Bolton	63 64	1980	Hana Mandlikova	W. Turnbull	60 75
1950	Louise Brough	D. Hart	64 36 64	1981	Martina Navratilova	C. Evert Lloyd	67 64 75
1951	Nancye Bolton	T. Long	61 75	1982	Chris Evert Lloyd	M. Navratilova	63 26 63
1952	Thelma Long	H. Angwin	62 63	1983	Martina Navratilova	K. Jordan	62 76
1953	Maureen Connelly	J. Sampson	63 62	1984	Chris Evert Lloyd	H. Sukova	67 61 63
1954	Thelma Long	J. Staley	63 64	1985	Martina Navratilova	C. Evert Lloyd	62 46 62
1955	Beryl Pemrose	T. Long	64 63	1986	Not held		
1956	Mary Carter	T. Long	36 62 97	1987	Hana Mandlikova	M. Navratilova	75 76
1957	Shirley Fry	A. Gibson	63 64	1988	Steffi Graf	C. Evert	61 76
1958	Angela Mortimer	L. Coghlan	63 64	1989	Steffi Graf	H. Sukova	64 64
1959	Mary Reitano	T. Schuman	62 63	1990	Steffi Graf	M.J. Fernandez	63 64
				1991	Monica Seles	J. Novotna	57 63 61

French Open
MEN

Prior to 1925, entry was restricted to members of French clubs. From 1941-45, tournament was closed to all foreigners. Became an Open Championship in 1968, but closed to contract pros in 1972.

Surface: Red clay.

First year: 1891. **Most wins:** Max Decugis (8).

Multiple winners (since 1925): Bjorn Borg (6); Henri Cochet (4); Rene Lacoste, Ivan Lendl, Yvon Petra and Mats Wilander (3); Bernard Destremau, Jaroslav Drobny, Roy Emerson, Jan Kodes, Rod Laver, Frank Parker, Nicola Pietrangeli, Ken Rosewall, Manuel Santana, Tony Trabert and Gottfried von Cramm (2).

Year	Winner	Loser	Score	Year	Winner	Loser	Score
1925	Rene Lacoste	J. Borotra	75 61 64	1936	Gottfried von Cramm	F. Perry	60 26 62 26 60
1926	Henri Cochet	R. Lacoste	62 64 63	1937	Henner Henkel	H. Austin	61 64 63
1927	Rene Lacoste	B. Tilden	64 46 57 63 119	1938	Don Budge	R. Menzel	63 62 64
1928	Henri Cochet	R. Lacoste	57 63 61 63	1939	Don McNeill	B. Riggs	75 60 63
1929	Rene Lacoste	J. Borotra	63 26 60 26 86	1940	Not held		
1930	Henri Cochet	B. Tilden	36 86 63 61	1941	Bernard Destremau		Not available
1931	Jean Borotra	C. Boussus	26 64 75 64	1942	Bernard Destremau		Not available
1932	Henri Cochet	G. de Stefani	60 64 46 63	1943	Yvon Petra		Not available
1933	Jack Crawford	H. Cochet	86 61 63	1944	Yvon Petra		Not available
1934	Gottfried von Cramm	J. Crawford	64 79 36 75 63	1945	Yvon Petra	B. Destremau	75 64 62
1935	Fred Perry	G. von Cramm	63 36 61 63	1946	Marcel Bernard	J. Drobny	36 26 61 64 63

Year	Winner	Loser	Score	Year	Winner	Loser	Score
1947	Joseph Asboth	E. Sturgess	86 75 64	1970	Jan Kodes	Z. Franulovic	62 64 60
1948	Frank Parker	J. Drobny	64 75 57 86	1971	Jan Kodes	I. Nastasi	86 62 26 75
1949	Frank Parker	Budge Patty	63 16 61 64	1972	Andres Gimeno	P. Proisy	46 63 61 61
				1973	Ilie Nastase	N. Pilic	63 63 60
1950	Budge Patty	J. Drobny	61 62 36 57 75	1974	Bjorn Borg	M. Orantes	67 60 61 61
1951	Jaroslav Drobny	E. Sturgess	63 63 63	1975	Bjorn Borg	G. Vilas	62 63 64
1952	Jaroslav Drobny	F. Sedgman	62 60 36 64	1976	Adriano Panatta	H. Solomon	61 64 46 76
1953	Ken Rosewall	V. Seixas	63 64 16 62	1977	Guillermo Vilas	B. Gottfried	60 63 60
1954	Tony Trabert	A. Larsen	64 75 61	1978	Bjorn Borg	G. Vilas	61 61 63
1955	Tony Trabert	S. Davidson	26 61 64 62	1979	Bjorn Borg	V. Pecci	63 61 67 64
1956	Lew Hoad	S. Davidson	64 86 63				
1957	Sven Davison	H. Flam	63 64 64	1980	Bjorn Borg	V. Gerulaitis	64 61 62
1958	Mervyn Rose	L. Ayala	63 64 64	1981	Bjorn Borg	I. Lendl	61 46 62 36 61
1959	Nicola Pietrangeli	I. Vermaak	36 63 64 61	1982	Mats Wilander	G. Vilas	16 76 60 64
				1983	Yannick Noah	M. Wilander	62 75 76
1960	Nicola Pietrangeli	L. Ayala	36 63 64 46 63	1984	Ivan Lendl	J. McEnroe	36 26 64 75 75
1961	Manuel Santana	N. Pietrangeli	46 61 36 60 62	1985	Mats Wilander	I. Lendl	36 64 62 62
1962	Rod Laver	R. Emerson	36 26 63 97 62	1986	Ivan Lendl	M. Pernfors	63 62 64
1963	Roy Emerson	P. Darmon	36 61 64 64	1987	Ivan Lendl	M. Wilander	75 62 36 76
1964	Manuel Santana	N. Pietrangeli	63 61 46 75	1988	Mats Wilander	H. Leconte	75 62 61
1965	Fred Stolle	T. Roche	36 60 62 63	1989	Michael Chang	S. Edberg	61 36 46 64 62
1966	Tony Roche	I. Gulyas	61 64 75				
1967	Roy Emerson	T. Roche	61 64 26 62	1990	Andres Gomez	A. Agassi	63 26 64 64
1968	Ken Rosewall	R. Laver	63 61 26 62	1991	Jim Courier	A. Agassi	36 64 26 61 64
1969	Rod Laver	K. Rosewall	64 63 64				

WOMEN

Prior to 1925, entry was restricted to members of French clubs. Became an Open Championship in 1968, but closed to contract pros in 1972.

First year: 1897. **Most wins:** Chris Evert Lloyd (7) and Suzanne Lenglen (6).

Multiple winners (since 1920): Chris Evert Lloyd (7); Margaret Smith Court (5); Helen Wills Moody (4); Hilde Sperling (3); Maureen Connolly, Steffi Graf, Margaret Osborne duPont, Doris Hart, Ann Haydon Jones, Suzanne Lenglen, Simone Mathieu, Margaret Scriven, Martina Navratilova, Monica Seles and Lesley Turner (2).

Year	Winner	Loser	Score	Year	Winner	Loser	Score
1925	Suzanne Lenglen	K. McKane	61 62	1961	Ann Haydon	Y. Ramirez	62 61
1926	Suzanne Lenglen	M. Browne	61 60	1962	Margaret Smith	L. Turner	63 36 75
1927	Kea Bouman	I. Peacock	62 64	1963	Lesley Turner	A. Jones	26 63 75
1928	Helen Wills	E. Bennett	61 62	1964	Margaret Smith	M. Bueno	57 61 62
1929	Helen Wills	S. Mathieu	63 64	1965	Lesley Turner	M. Smith	63 64
				1966	Ann Jones	N. Richey	63 61
1930	Helen Moody	H. Jacobs	62 61	1967	Francoise Durr	L. Turner	46 63 64
1931	Cilly Aussem	B. Nuthall	86 61	1968	Nancy Richey	A. Jones	57 64 61
1932	Helen Moody	S. Mathieu	75 61	1969	Margaret Court	A. Jones	61 46 63
1933	Margaret Scriven	S. Mathieu	62 46 64				
1934	Margaret Scriven	H. Jacobs	75 46 61	1970	Margaret Court	H. Niessen	62 64
1935	Hilde Sperling	S. Mathieu	62 61	1971	Evonne Goolagong	H. Gourlay	63 75
1936	Hilde Sperling	S. Mathieu	63 64	1972	Billie Jean King	E. Goolagong	63 63
1937	Hilde Sperling	S. Mathieu	62 64	1973	Margaret Court	C. Evert	67 76 64
1938	Simone Mathieu	N. Landry	60 63	1974	Chris Evert	O. Morozova	61 62
1939	Simone Mathieu	J. Jedrzejowska	63 86	1975	Chris Evert	M. Navratilova	26 62 61
				1976	Sue Barker	R. Tomanova	62 06 62
1940-45	Not held			1977	Mima Jausovec	F. Mihai	62 67 61
1946	Margaret Osborne	P. Betz	16 86 75	1978	Virginia Ruzici	M. Jausovec	62 62
1947	Patricia Todd	D. Hart	63 36 64	1979	Chris Evert Lloyd	W. Turnbull	62 60
1948	Nelly Landry	S. Fry	62 06 60				
1949	Margaret duPont	N. Adamson	75 62	1980	Chris Evert Lloyd	V. Ruzici	60 63
				1981	Hana Mandlikova	S. Hanika	62 64
1950	Doris Hart	P. Todd	64 46 62	1982	Martina Navratilova	A. Jaeger	76 61
1951	Shirley Fry	D. Hart	63 36 63	1983	Chris Evert Lloyd	M. Jausovec	61 62
1952	Doris Hart	S. Fry	64 64	1984	Martina Navratilova	C. Evert Lloyd	63 61
1953	Maureen Connolly	D. Hart	62 64	1985	Chris Evert Lloyd	M. Navratilova	63 67 75
1954	Maureen Connolly	G. Bucaille	64 61	1986	Chris Evert Lloyd	M. Navratilova	26 63 63
1955	Angela Mortimer	D. Knode	26 75 108	1987	Steffi Graf	M. Navratilova	64 46 86
1956	Althea Gibson	A. Mortimer	62 12 10	1988	Steffi Graf	N. Zvereva	60 60
1957	Shirley Bloomer	D. Knode	61 63	1989	Arantxa Sanchez	S. Graf	76 36 75
1958	Zsuzsi Kormoczy	S. Bloomer	64 16 62				
1959	Christine Truman	Z. Kormoczy	64 75	1990	Monica Seles	S. Graf	76 64
				1991	Monica Seles	A. Vicario	63 64
1960	Darlene Hard	Y. Ramirez	63 64				

Wimbledon

MEN

Officially called "The Lawn Tennis Championships" at the All-England Club, Wimbledon. Challenge round system (defending champion automatically qualifies for following year's final) used from 1877-1921. Became an Open Championship in 1968, but closed to contract pros in 1972.

Surface: Grass.

Multiple winners: William Renshaw (7); Bjorn Borg and Laurie Doherty (5); Reggie Doherty, Rod Laver and Tony Wilding (4); Wilfred Baddeley, Boris Becker, Arthur Gore, John McEnroe, Fred Perry and Bill Tilden (3); Jean Borotra, Norman Brookes, Don Budge, Henri Cochet, Jimmy Connors, Stefan Edberg, Roy Emerson, John Hartley, Lew Hoad, Rene Lacoste, Gerald Patterson and Joshua Pim (2).

Year	Winner	Loser	Score
1877	Spencer Gore	W.Marshall	61 62 64
1878	Frank Hadow	S.Gore	75 61 97
1879	John Hartley	V.St.L.Gould	62 64 62
1880	John Hartley	H.Lawford	60 62 26 63
1881	William Renshaw	J.Hartley	60 62 61
1882	William Renshaw	E.Renshaw	61 26 46 62 62
1883	William Renshaw	E.Renshaw	26 63 63 46 63
1884	William Renshaw	H.Lawford	60 64 97
1885	William Renshaw	H.Lawford	75 62 46 75
1886	William Renshaw	H.Lawford	60 57 63 64
1887	Herbert Lawford	E.Renshaw	16 63 36 64 64
1888	Ernest Renshaw	H.Lawford	63 75 60
1889	William Renshaw	E.Renshaw	64 61 36 60
1890	William Hamilton	W.Renshaw	68 62 36 61 61
1891	Wilfred Baddeley	J.Pim	64 16 75 60
1892	Wilfred Baddeley	J.Pim	46 63 63 62
1893	Joshua Pim	W.Baddeley	36 61 63 62
1894	Joshua Pim	W.Baddeley	108 62 86
1895	Wilfred Baddeley	W.Eaves	46 26 86 62 63
1896	Harold Mahoney	W.Baddeley	62 68 57 86 63
1897	Reggie Doherty	H.Mahoney	64 64 63
1898	Reggie Doherty	L.Doherty	63 63 26 57 61
1899	Reggie Doherty	A.Gore	16 46 62 63 63
1900	Reggie Doherty	S.Smith	68 63 61 62
1901	Arthur Gore	R.Doherty	46 75 64 64
1902	Laurie Doherty	A.Gore	64 63 36 60
1903	Laurie Doherty	F.Riseley	75 63 60
1904	Laurie Doherty	F.Riseley	61 75 86
1905	Laurie Doherty	N.Brookes	86 62 64
1906	Laurie Doherty	F.Riseley	64 46 62 63
1907	Norman Brookes	A.Gore	64 62 62
1908	Arthur Gore	R.Barrett	63 62 46 36 64
1909	Arthur Gore	M.Ritchie	68 16 62 62 62
1910	Tony Wilding	A.Gore	64 75 46 62
1911	Tony Wilding	R.Barrett	64 46 26 62 Ret
1912	Tony Wilding	A.Gore	64 64 46 64
1913	Tony Wilding	M.McLoughlin	86 63 108
1914	Norman Brookes	T.Wilding	64 64 75
1915-18	Not held		
1919	Gerald Patterson	N.Brookes	63 75 62
1920	Bill Tilden	G. Patterson	26 63 62 64
1921	Bill Tilden	B. Norton	46 26 61 60 75
1922	Gerald Patterson	R. Lycett	63 64 62
1923	Bill Johnston	F. Hunter	60 63 61
1924	Jean Borotra	R. Lacoste	61 36 61 36 64
1925	Rene Lacoste	J. Borotra	63 63 46 86
1926	Jean Borotra	H. Kinsey	86 61 63
1927	Henri Cochet	J. Borotra	46 46 63 64 75
1928	Rene Lacoste	H. Cochet	61 46 64 62
1929	Henri Cochet	J. Borotra	64 63 64
1930	Bill Tilden	W. Allison	63 97 64
1931	Sidney Wood	F. Shields	walkover
1932	Ellsworth Vines	H. Austin	64 62 60
1933	Jack Crawford	E. Vines	46 119 62 26 64
1934	Fred Perry	J. Crawford	63 60 75

Year	Winner	Loser	Score
1935	Fred Perry	G. von Cramm	62 64 64
1936	Fred Perry	G. von Cramm	61 61 60
1937	Don Budge	G. von Cramm	63 64 62
1938	Don Budge	H. Austin	61 60 63
1939	Bobby Riggs	E. Cooke	26 86 36 63 62
1940-45	Not held		
1946	Yvon Petra	G. Brown	62 64 79 57 64
1947	Jack Kramer	T. Brown	61 63 62
1948	Bob Falkenburg	J. Bromwich	75 06 62 36 75
1949	Ted Schroeder	J. Drobny	36 60 63 46 64
1950	Budge Patty	F. Sedgman	61 810 62 63
1951	Dick Savitt	K. McGregor	64 64 64
1952	Frank Sedgman	J. Drobny	46 63 62 63
1953	Vic Seixas	K. Nielsen	97 63 64
1954	Jaroslav Drobny	K. Rosewall	1311 46 62 97
1955	Tony Trabert	K. Nielsen	63 75 61
1956	Lew Hoad	K. Rosewall	62 47 75 64
1957	Lew Hoad	A. Cooper	62 62 62
1958	Ashley Cooper	N. Fraser	36 62 64 1311
1959	Alex Olmedo	R. Laver	64 63 64
1960	Neale Fraser	R. Laver	64 36 97 75
1961	Rod Laver	C. McKinley	63 61 64
1962	Rod Laver	M. Mulligan	62 62 61
1963	Chuck McKinley	F. Stolle	97 61 64
1964	Roy Emerson	F. Stolle	64 1210 46 63
1965	Roy Emerson	F. Stolle	62 64 64
1966	Manuel Santana	D. Rolston	64 119 64
1967	John Newcombe	W. Bungert	63 61 61
1968	Rod Laver	T. Roche	63 64 62
1969	Rod Laver	J. Newcombe	64 57 64 64
1970	John Newcombe	K. Rosewall	57 63 62 36 61
1971	John Newcombe	S. Smith	63 57 26 64 64
1972	Stan Smith	I. Nastase	46 63 63 46 75
1973	Jan Kodes	A. Metreveli	61 98 63
1974	Jimmy Connors	K. Rosewall	61 61 64
1975	Arthur Ashe	J. Connors	61 61 57 64
1976	Bjorn Borg	I. Nastase	64 62 97
1977	Bjorn Borg	J. Connors	36 62 61 57 64
1978	Bjorn Borg	J. Connors	62 62 63
1979	Bjorn Borg	R. Tanner	67 61 36 63 64
1980	Bjorn Borg	J. McEnroe	16 75 63 67 86
1981	John McEnroe	B. Borg	46 76 76 64
1982	Jimmy Connors	J. McEnroe	36 63 67 76 64
1983	John McEnroe	C. Lewis	62 62 62
1984	John McEnroe	J. Connors	61 61 62
1985	Boris Becker	K. Curran	63 67 76 64
1986	Boris Becker	I. Lendl	64 63 75
1987	Pat Cash	I. Lendl	76 62 75
1988	Stefan Edberg	B. Becker	46 76 64 62
1989	Boris Becker	S. Edberg	60 76 64
1990	Stefan Edberg	B. Becker	62 62 36 36 64
1991	Michael Stich	B. Becker	64 76 64

WOMEN

Officially called "The Lawn Tennis Championships" at the All-England Club, Wimbledon. Challenge round system (defending champion automatically qualifies for following year's final) used from 1886-1921. Became an Open Championship in 1968, but closed to contract pros in 1972.

Multiple winners: Martina Navratilova (9); Helen Wills Moody (8); Dorothea Douglass Chambers (7); Blanche Bingley Hillyard, Billie Jean King and Suzanne Lenglen (6); Lottie Dod and Charlotte Cooper Sterry (5); Louise Brough (4); Maria Bueno, Maureen Connolly, Margaret Smith Court, Steffi Graf and Chris Evert Lloyd (3); Evonne Goolagong Cawley, Althea Gibson, Dorothy Round, May Sutton and Maud Watson (2).

Year	Winner	Loser	Score	Year	Winner	Loser	Score
1884	Maud Watson	L.Watson	68 63 62	1938	Helen Moody	H. Jacobs	64 60
1885	Maud Watson	B.Bingley	61 75	1939	Alice Marble	K. Stammers	62 60
1886	Blanche Bingley	M.Watson	63 63				
1887	Lottie Dod	B.Bingley	62 60	1940-45	Not held		
1888	Lottie Dod	B.Hillyard	63 63	1946	Pauline Betz	L. Brough	62 64
1889	Blanche Hillyard	L.Rice	46 86 64	1947	Margaret Osborne	D. Hart	62 64
				1948	Louise Brough	D. Hart	63 86
1890	Lena Rice	L.Jacks	64 61	1949	Louise Brough	M. duPont	108 16 108
1891	Lottie Dod	B.Hillyard	62 61				
1892	Lottie Dod	B.Hillyard	61 61	1950	Louise Brough	M. duPont	61 36 61
1893	Lottie Dod	B.Hillyard	68 61 64	1951	Doris Hart	S. Fry	61 60
1894	Blanche Hillyard	L.Austin	61 61	1952	Maureen Connolly	L. Brough	64 63
1895	Charlotte Cooper	H.Jackson	75 86	1953	Maureen Connolly	D. Hart	86 75
1896	Charlotte Cooper	W.Pickering	62 63	1954	Maureen Connolly	L. Brough	62 75
1897	Blanche Hillyard	C.Cooper	57 75 62	1955	Louise Brough	B. Fleitz	75 86
1898	Charlotte Cooper	L.Martin	64 64	1956	Shirley Fry	A. Buxton	63 61
1899	Blanche Hillyard	C.Cooper	62 63	1957	Althea Gibson	D. Hard	63 62
				1958	Althea Gibson	A. Mortimer	86 62
1900	Blanche Hillyard	C.Cooper	46 64 64	1959	Maria Bueno	D. Hard	64 63
1901	Charlotte Sterry	B.Hillyard	62 62				
1902	Muriel Robb	C.Sterry	75 61	1960	Maria Bueno	S. Reynolds	86 60
1903	Dorothea Douglass	E.Thomson	46 64 62	1961	Angela Mortimer	C. Truman	46 64 75
1904	Dorothea Douglass	C.Sterry 60 63		1962	Karen Susman	V. Sukova	64 64
1905	May Sutton	D.Douglass	63 64	1963	Margaret Smith	B.J. Moffitt	63 64
1906	Dorothea Douglass	M.Sutton	63 97	1964	Maria Bueno	M. Smith	64 79 63
1907	May Sutton	D.Chambers	61 64	1965	Margaret Smith	M. Bueno	64 75
1908	Charlotte Sterry	A.Morton	64 64	1966	Billie Jean King	M. Bueno	63 36 61
1909	Dora Boothby	A.Morton	64 46 86	1967	Billie Jean King	A. Jones	63 64
				1968	Billie Jean King	J. Tegart	97 75
1910	Dorothea Chambers	D.Boothby	62 62	1969	Ann Jones	B.J. King	36 63 62
1911	Dorothea Chambers	D.Boothby	60 60				
1912	Ethel Larcombe	C.Sterry	63 61	1970	Margaret Court	B.J. King	1412 119
1913	Dorothea Chambers	R.McNair	60 64	1971	Evonne Goolagong	M. Court	64 61
1914	Dorothea Chambers	E.Larcombe	75 64	1972	Billie Jean King	E. Goolagong	63 63
1915-18	Not held			1973	Billie Jean King	C. Evert	60 75
1919	Suzanne Lenglen	D.Chambers	108 46 97	1974	Chris Evert	O. Morzova	60 64
				1975	Billie Jean King	E. Cawley	60 61
1920	Suzanne Lenglen	D. Chambers	63 60	1976	Chris Evert	E. Cawley	63 46 86
1921	Suzanne Lenglen	E. Ryan	62 60	1977	Virginia Wade	B. Stove	46 63 61
1922	Suzanne Lenglen	M. Mallory	62 60	1978	Martina Navratilova	C. Evert	26 64 75
1923	Suzanne Lenglen	K. McKane	62 62	1979	Martina Navratilova	C. Evert Lloyd	64 64
1924	Kathleen McKane	H. Wills	46 64 64				
1925	Suzanne Lenglen	J. Fry	62 60	1980	Evonne Cawley	C. Evert Lloyd	61 76
1926	Kathleen Godfree	L. de Alvarez	62 46 63	1981	Chris Evert Lloyd	H. Mandlikova	62 62
1927	Helen Wills	L. de Alvarez	62 64	1982	Martina Navratilova	C. Evert Lloyd	61 36 62
1928	Helen Wills	L. de Alvarez	62 63	1983	Martina Navratilova	A. Jaeger	60 63
1929	Helen Wills	H. Jacobs	61 62	1984	Martina Navratilova	C. Evert Lloyd	76 62
				1985	Martina Navratilova	C. Evert Lloyd	46 63 62
1930	Helen Moody	E. Ryan	62 62	1986	Martina Navratilova	H. Mandlikova	76 63
1931	Cilly Aussem	H. Kranwinkel	75 75	1987	Martina Navratilova	S. Graf	75 63
1932	Helen Moody	H. Jacobs	63 61	1988	Steffi Graf	M. Navratilova	57 62 61
1933	Helen Moody	D. Round	64 68 63	1989	Steffi Graf	M. Navratilova	62 67 61
1934	Dorothy Round	H. Jacobs	62 57 63				
1935	Helen Moody	H. Jacobs	63 36 75	1990	Martina Navratilova	Z. Garrison	64 61
1936	Helen Jacobs	H.K. Sperling	62 46 75	1991	Steffi Graf	G. Sabatini	64 36 86
1937	Dorothy Round	J. Jedrzejowska	62 26 75				

U.S. Open
MEN

Challenge round system (defending champion automatically qualifies for following year's final) used from 1884–1911. Amateur and Open Championships held in 1968 and '69. Became an exclusively Open Championship in 1970.

Surface: Decoturf II (acrylic cement). Known as Patriotic Tournament in 1917 during WWI.

Multiple winners: William Larned, Richard Sears and Bill Tilden (7); Jimmy Connors (5); John McEnroe and Robert Wrenn (4); Oliver Campbell, Ivan Lendl, Fred Perry and Malcolm Whitman (3); Wilmer Allison, Don Budge, Roy Emerson, Neale Fraser, Pancho Gonzalez, Bill Johnston, Jack Kramer, Rene Lacoste, Rod Laver, Maurice McLoughlin, R.L. Murray, John Newcombe, Frank Parker, Bobby Riggs, Ken Rosewall, Frank Sedgman, Henry Slocum, Tony Trabert, Ellsworth Vines and Richard Williams (2).

Year	Winner	Loser	Score	Year	Winner	Loser	Score
1881	Richard Sears	W.Glyn	60 63 62	1937	Don Budge	G. von Cramm	61 79 61 36 61
1882	Richard Sears	C.Clark	61 64 60	1938	Don Budge	G. Mako	63 68 62 61
1883	Richard Sears	J.Dwight	62 60 97	1939	Bobby Riggs	S. van Horn	64 62 64
1884	Richard Sears	H.Taylor	60 16 60 62	1940	Don McNeill	B. Riggs	46 68 63 63 75
1885	Richard Sears	G.Brinley	63 46 60 63	1941	Bobby Riggs	F. Kovacs	57 61 63 63
1886	Richard Sears	R.Beeckman	46 61 63 64	1942	Fred Schroeder	F. Parker	86 75 36 46 62
1887	Richard Sears	H.Slocum	61 63 62	1943	Joseph Hunt	J. Kramer	63 68 108 60
1888	Henry Slocum	H.Taylor	64 61 60	1944	Frank Parker	B. Talbert	64 36 63 63
1889	Henry Slocum	Q.Shaw	63 61 46 62	1945	Frank Parker	B. Talbert	1412 61 62
1890	Oliver Campbell	H.Slocum	62 46 63 61	1946	Jack Kramer	T. Brown, Jr.	97 63 60
1891	Oliver Campbell	C.Hobart	26 75 79 61 62	1947	Jack Kramer	F. Parker	46 26 61 60 63
1892	Oliver Campbell	F.Hovey	75 36 63 75	1948	Pancho Gonzalez	E. Sturgess	62 63 1412
1893	Robert Wrenn	F.Hovey	64 36 64 64	1949	Pancho Gonzalez	F. Schroeder	1618 26 61 62 64
1894	Robert Wrenn	M.Goodbody	68 61 64 64	1950	Arthur Larsen	H. Flam	63 46 57 64 63
1895	Fred Hovey	R.Wrenn	63 62 64	1951	Frank Sedgman	V. Seixas	64 61 61
1896	Robert Wrenn	F.Hovey	75 36 60 16 61	1952	Frank Sedgman	G. Mulloy	61 62 63
1897	Robert Wrenn	W.Eaves	46 86 63 26 62	1953	Tony Trabert	V. Seixas	63 62 63
1898	Malcolm Whitman	D.Davis	36 62 62 61	1954	Vic Seixas	R. Hartwig	36 62 64 64
1899	Malcolm Whitman	P.Paret	61 62 36 75	1955	Tony Trabert	K. Rosewall	97 63 63
1900	Malcolm Whitman	W.Larned	64 16 62 62	1956	Ken Rosewall	L. Hoad	46 62 63 63
1901	William Larned	B.Wright	62 68 64 64	1957	Mal Anderson	A. Cooper	108 75 64
1902	William Larned	R.Doherty	46 62 64 86	1958	Ashley Cooper	M. Anderson	62 36 46 108 86
1903	Laurie Doherty	W.Larned	60 63 108	1959	Neale Fraser	A. Olmedo	63 57 62 64
1904	Holcombe Ward	W.Clothier	108 64 97	1960	Neale Fraser	R. Laver	64 64 97
1905	Beals Wright	H.Ward	62 61 119	1961	Roy Emerson	R. Laver	75 63 62
1906	William Clothier	B.Wright	63 60 64	1962	Rod Laver	R. Emerson	62 64 57 64
1907	William Larned	R.LeRoy	62 62 64	1963	Rafael Osuna	F. Froehling	75 64 62
1908	William Larned	B.Wright	61 62 86	1964	Roy Emerson	F. Stolle	64 62 64
1909	William Larned	W.Clothier	61 62 57 16 61	1965	Manuel Santana	C. Drysdale	62 79 75 61
1910	William Larned	T.Bundy	61 57 60 68 61	1966	Fred Stolle	J. Newcombe	42 1210 63 64
1911	William Larned	M.McLoughlin	64 64 62	1967	John Newcombe	C. Graebner	64 64 86
1912	Maurice McLoughlin	W.F.Johnson	36 26 62 64 62	1968	Arthur Ashe	T. Okker	1412 57 63 36 63
1913	Maurice McLoughlin	R.Williams	64 57 63 61	1969	Rod Laver	T. Roche	79 61 63 62
1914	Richard Williams	M.McLoughlin	63 86 108	1970	Ken Rosewall	T. Roche	26 64 76 63
1915	Bill Johnston	M.McLoughlin	16 60 75 108	1971	Stan Smith	J. Kodes	36 63 62 76
1916	Richard Williams	B.Johnston	46 64 06 62 64	1972	Ilie Nastase	A. Ashe	36 63 67 64 63
1917	R.L.Murray	N.Niles	57 86 63 63	1973	John Newcombe	J. Kodes	64 16 46 62 63
1918	R.L.Murray	B.Tilden	63 61 75	1974	Jimmy Connors	K. Rosewall	61 60 61
1919	Bill Johnston	B.Tilden	64 64 63	1975	Manuel Orantes	J. Connors	64 63 63
1920	Bill Tilden	B. Johnston	61 16 75 57 63	1976	Jimmy Connors	B. Borg	64 36 76 64
1921	Bill Tilden	W. Johnston	61 63 61	1977	Guillermo Vilas	J. Connors	26 63 76 60
1922	Bill Tilden	B. Johnston	46 36 62 63 64	1978	Jimmy Connors	B. Borg	64 62 62
1923	Bill Tilden	B. Johnston	64 61 64	1979	John McEnroe	V. Gerulaitis	75 63 63
1924	Bill Tilden	B. Johnston	61 97 62	1980	John McEnroe	B. Borg	76 61 67 57 64
1925	Bill Tilden	B. Johnston	46 119 63 46 63	1981	John McEnroe	B. Borg	46 62 64 63
1926	Rene Lacoste	J. Borotra	64 60 64	1982	Jimmy Connors	I. Lendl	63 62 46 64
1927	Rene Lacoste	B. Tilton	110 63 119	1983	Jimmy Connors	I. Lendl	63 67 75 60
1928	Henri Cochet	F. Hunter	46 64 36 75 63	1984	John McEnroe	I. Lendl	63 64 61
1929	Bill Tilden	F. Hunter	36 63 46 62 64	1985	Ivan Lendl	J. McEnroe	76 63 64
1930	John Doeg	F. Shields	108 16 64 1614	1986	Ivan Lendl	M. Mecir	64 62 60
1931	Ellsworth Vines	G. Lott Jr.	79 63 97 75	1987	Ivan Lendl	M. Wilander	67 60 76 64
1932	Ellsworth Vines	H. Cochet	64 64 64	1988	Mats Wilander	I. Lendl	64 46 63 57 64
1933	Fred Perry	J. Crawford	63 1113 46 60 61	1989	Boris Becker	I. Lendl	76 16 63 76
1934	Fred Perry	W. Allison	64 63 16 86	1990	Pete Sampras	A. Agassi	64 63 62
1935	Wilmer Allison	S. Wood	62 62 63	1991	Stefan Edberg	J. Courier	62 64 60
1936	Fred Perry	D. Budge	26 62 86 16 108				

Note: In the last two U.S. championships open only to amateurs, Arthur Ashe def. Bob Lutz (4-6, 6-3, 8-10, 6-0, 6-4) in 1968; and Stan Smith def. Lutz (9-7, 6-3, 6-1) in 1969.

WOMEN

Amateur and Open Championships held in 1968 and '69. Became an exclusively Open Championship in 1970. Known as Patriotic Tournament in 1917 during WWI.

Multiple winners: Molla Mallory Bjurstedt (8); Helen Wills Moody (7); Chris Evert Lloyd (6); Margaret Smith Court (5); Pauline Betz, Mario Bueno, Helen Jacobs, Billie Jean King, Alice Marble, Elisabeth Moore, Martina Navratilova and Hazel Hotchkiss Wightman (4); Juliette Atkinson, Mary Browne, Maureen Connolly and Margaret Osborne duPont (3); Tracy Austin, Mabel Cahill, Sarah Palfrey Cooke, Darlene Hard, Doris Hart, Althea Gibson, Steffi Graf and Bertha Townsend (2).

Year	Winner	Loser	Score	Year	Winner	Loser	Score
1887	Ellen Hansell	L.Knight	61 60	1940	Alice Marble	H. Jacobs	62 63
1888	Bertha Townsend	E.Hansell	63 65	1941	Sarah Cooke	P. Betz	75 62
1889	Bertha Townsend	L.Voorhes	75 62	1942	Pauline Betz	L. Brough	46 61 64
1890	Ellen Roosevelt	B.Townsend	62 62	1943	Pauline Betz	L. Brough	63 57 63
1891	Mabel Cahill	E.Roosevelt	64 61 46 63	1944	Pauline Betz	M. Osborne	63 86
1892	Mabel Cahill	E.Moore	57 63 64 46 62	1945	Sarah Cooke	P. Betz	36 86 64
1893	Aline Terry	M.Cahill	default	1946	Pauline Betz	P. Canning	119 63
1894	Helen Hellwig	A.Terry	75 36 60 36 63	1947	Louise Brough	M. Osborne	86 46 61
1895	Juliette Atkinson	H.Hellwig	64 62 61	1948	Margaret duPont	L. Brough	46 64 1513
1896	Elisabeth Moore	J.Atkinson	64 46 62 62	1949	Margaret duPont	D. Hart	64 61
1897	Juliette Atkinson	E.Moore	63 63 46 36 63	1950	Margaret duPont	D. Hart	64 63
1898	Juliette Atkinson	M.Jones	63 57 64 26 75	1951	Maureen Connolly	S. Fry	63 16 64
1899	Marion Jones	J.Atkinson	default	1952	Maureen Connolly	D. Hart	63 75
1900	Myrtle McAteer	E.Parker	62 6260	1953	Maureen Connolly	D. Hart	62 64
1901	Elizabeth Moore	M.McAteer	64 36 75 26 62	1954	Doris Hart	L. Brough	68 61 86
1902	Marion Jones	E.Moore	61 10(ret)	1955	Doris Hart	P. Ward	64 62
1903	Elizabeth Moore	M.Jones	75 86	1956	Shirley Fry	A. Gibson	63 64
1904	May Sutton	E.Moore	61 62	1957	Althea Gibson	L. Brough	63 62
1905	Elizabeth Moore	M.Sutton	default	1958	Althea Gibson	D. Hard	36 61 62
1906	Helen Homans	E.Moore	default	1959	Maria Bueno	C. Truman	61 64
1907	Evelyn Sears	C.Neely	63 62	1960	Darlene Hard	M. Bueno	64 1012 64
1908	Maud B.Wallach	Ev.Sears	63 16 63	1961	Darlene Hard	A. Haydon	63 64
1909	Hazel Hotchkiss	M.Wallach	60 61	1962	Margaret Smith	D. Hard	97 64
1910	Hazel Hotchkiss	L.Hammond	64 62	1963	Maria Bueno	M. Smith	75 64
1911	Hazel Hotchkiss	F.Sutton	10 61 97	1964	Maria Bueno	C. Graebner	61 60
1912	Mary Browne	El.Sears	64 62	1965	Margaret Smith	B.J. Moffit	86 75
1913	Mary Browne	D.Green	62 75	1966	Maria Bueno	N. Richey	63 61
1914	Mary Browne	M.Wagner	62 16 61	1967	Billie Jean King	A. Haydon Jones	119 64
1915	Molla Bjurstedt	H.Wightman	46 62 60	1968	Virginia Wade	B. Jean King	64 62
1916	Molla Bjurstedt	L.Raymond	60 61	1969	Margaret Court	N. Richey	62 62
1917	Molla Bjurstedt	M.Vanderhoe	46 60 62	1970	Margaret Court	R. Casals	62 26 61
1918	Molla Bjurstedt	E.Gross	64 63	1971	Billie Jean King	R. Casals	64 76
1919	Hazel Wightman	M.Zinderstein	61 62	1972	Billie Jean King	K. Melville	63 75
1920	Molla Mallory	M. Zinderstein	63 61	1973	Margaret Court	E. Goolagong	76 57 62
1921	Molla Mallory	M. Browne	46 64 62	1974	Billie Jean King	E. Goolagong	36 63 75
1922	Molla Mallory	H. Wills	63 61	1975	Chris Evert	E. Cawley	57 64 62
1923	Helen Wills	M. Mallory	62 61	1976	Chris Evert	E. Cawley	63 60
1924	Helen Wills	M. Mallory	61 63	1977	Chris Evert	W. Turnbull	76 62
1925	Helen Wills	K. McKane	36 60 62	1978	Chris Evert	P. Shriver	76 64
1926	Molla Mallory	E. Ryan	46 64 97	1979	Tracy Austin	C. Evert Lloyd	64 63
1927	Helen Wills	B. Nuthall	61 64	1980	Chris Evert Lloyd	H. Mandlikova	57 61 61
1928	Helen Wills	H. Jacobs	62 61	1981	Tracy Austin	M. Navratilova	16 76 76
1929	Helen Wills	P. Watson	64 62	1982	Chris Evert Lloyd	H. Mandlikova	63 61
1930	Betty Nuthall	A. Harper	61 64	1983	Martina Navratilova	C. Evert Lloyd	61 63
1931	Helen Moody	E. Whitingstall	64 61	1984	Martina Navratilova	C. Evert Lloyd	46 64 64
1932	Helen Jacobs	C. Babcock	62 62	1985	Hana Mandlikova	M. Navratilova	76 16 76
1933	Helen Jacobs	H. Moody	86 36 30(ret)	1986	Martina Navratilova	H. Sukova	63 62
1934	Helen Jacobs	S. Palfrey	61 64	1987	Martina Navratilova	S. Graf	76 61
1935	Helen Jacobs	S. Fabyan	62 64	1988	Steffi Graf	G. Sabatini	63 36 61
1936	Alice Marble	H. Jacobs	46 63 62	1989	Steffi Graf	M. Navratilova	36 75 61
1937	Anita Lizana	J. Jedrzejowska	64 62	1990	Gabriela Sabatini	S. Graf	62 76
1938	Alice Marble	N. Wynne	60 63	1991	Monica Seles	M. Navratilova	76 61
1939	Alice Marble	H. Jacobs	60 810 64				

Note: In the last two U.S. championships open only to amateurs, Margaret Court def. Maria Bueno (6-2, 6-2) in 1968 and Virginia Wade (4-6, 6-3, 6-0) in 1969.

Grand Slam Summary

Men's and Women's singles winners of the four Grand Slam tournaments—Australian, French, Wimbledon and United States—since the French was opened to all comers in 1925. Note that there were two Australian Open championships in 1977 and none in 1986.

MEN

Only two men have won the Grand Slam—all four events in a single year: Don Budge in 1938 and Rod Laver in both 1962 and 1969.

Three wins in one year: Jack Crawford (1933); Fred Perry (1934); Tony Trabert (1955); Lew Hoad (1956); Ashley Cooper (1958); Roy Emerson (1964); Jimmy Connors (1974); Mats Wilander (1988).

Two wins in one year: Roy Emerson (4 times); Bjorn Borg (3 times); Rene Lacoste, Ivan Lendl, John Newcombe and Fred Perry (twice); Boris Becker, Don Budge, Henri Cochet, Jimmy Connors, Neale Fraser, Jack Kramer, John McEnroe, Alex Olmedo, Budge Patty, Bobby Riggs, Ken Rosewall, Dick Savitt, Frank Sedgman and Guillermo Vilas (once).

Year	Australia	French	Wimbledon	US
1925	Anderson	Lacoste	Lacoste	Tilden
1926	Hawkes	Cochet	Borotra	Lacoste
1927	Patterson	Lacoste	Cochet	Lacoste
1928	Borotra	Cochet	Lacoste	Cochet
1929	Gregory	Lacoste	Cochet	Tilde
1930	Moon	Cochet	Tilden	Doeg
1931	Crawford	Borotra	Wood	Vines
1932	Crawford	Cochet	Vines	Vines
1933	Crawford	Crawford	Crawford	Perry
1934	Perry	vonCramm	Perry	Perry
1935	Crawford	Perry	Perry	Allison
1936	Quist	vonCramm	Perry	Perry
1937	McGrath	Henkel	Budge	Budge
1938	**Budge**	**Budge**	**Budge**	**Budge**
1939	Bromwich	McNeill	Riggs	Riggs
1940	Quist	—	—	McNeill
1941	—	Destremau	—	Riggs
1942	—	Destremau	—	Schroeder
1943	—	Petra	—	Hunt
1944	—	Petra	—	Parker
1945	—	Petra	—	Parker
1946	Bromwich	Bernard	Petra	Kramer
1947	Pails	Asboth	Kramer	Kramer
1948	Quist	Parker	Falkenburg	Gonzalez
1949	Sedgman	Parker	Schroeder	Gonzalez
1950	Sedgman	Patty	Patty	Larse
1951	Savitt	Drobny	Savitt	Sedgman
1952	McGregor	Drobny	Sedgman	Sedgman
1953	Rosewall	Rosewall	Seixas	Trabert
1954	Rose	Trabert	Drobny	Seixas
1955	Rosewall	Trabert	Trabert	Trabert
1956	Hoad	Hoad	Hoad	Rosewall
1957	Cooper	Davidson	Hoad	Anderson
1958	Cooper	Rose	Cooper	Cooper
1959	Olmedo	Pietrangeli	Olmedo	Fraser
1960	Laver	Pietrangeli	Fraser	Fraser
1961	Emerson	Santana	Laver	Emerson
1962	**Laver**	**Laver**	**Laver**	**Laver**
1963	Emerson	Emerson	McKinley	Osuna
1964	Emerson	Santana	Emerson	Emerson
1965	Emerson	Stolle	Emerson	Santana
1966	Emerson	Roche	Santana	Stolle
1967	Emerson	Emerson	Newcombe	Newcombe
1968	Bowrey	Rosewall	Laver	Ashe
1969	**Laver**	**Laver**	**Laver**	**Laver**
1970	Ashe	Kodes	Newcombe	Rosewall
1971	Rosewall	Kodes	Newcombe	Smith
1972	Rosewall	Gimeno	Smith	Nastase
1973	Newcombe	Nastase	Kodes	Newcombe
1974	Connors	Borg	Connors	Connors
1975	Newcombe	Borg	Ashe	Orantes
1976	Edmondson	Panatta	Borg	Connors
1977	Tanner & Gerulaitis	Vilas	Borg	Vilas
1978	Vilas	Borg	Borg	Connors
1979	Vilas	Borg	Borg	McEnroe
1980	Teacher	Borg	Borg	McEnroe
1981	Kriek	Borg	McEnroe	McEnroe
1982	Kriek	Wilander	Connors	Connors
1983	Wilander	Noah	McEnroe	Connors
1984	Wilander	Lendl	McEnroe	McEnroe
1985	Edberg	Wilander	Becker	Lendl
1986	—	Lendl	Becker	Lendl
1987	Edberg	Lendl	Cash	Lendl
1988	Wilander	Wilander	Edberg	Wilander
1989	Lendl	Chang	Becker	Becker
1990	Lendl	Gomez	Edberg	Sampras
1991	Becker	Courier	Stich	Edberg

WOMEN

Only three women have won the Grand Slam—all four events in a single year: Maureen Connolly in 1953, Margaret Smith Court in 1970 and Steffi Graf in 1988.

Three in one year: Helen Wills Moody (1928 and 1929); Margaret Smith Court (1962,1965,1969 and 1973); Billie Jean King (1972); Martina Navratilova (1983 and 1984); Steffi Graf (1989); and Monica Seles (1991).

Two in one year: Chris Evert Lloyd (5 times); Helen Wills Moody and Martina Navratilova (3 times); Maria Bueno, Maureen Connolly, Margaret Smith Court, Althea Gibson, Billie Jean King (twice); Cilly Aussem, Pauline Betz, Louise Brough, Evonne Goolagong Cawley, Shirley Fry, Darlene Hard, Margaret Osborne duPont, Suzanne Lenglen and Alice Marble.

Year	Australia	French	Wimbledon	US
1925	Akhurst	Lenglen	Lenglen	Wills
1926	Akhurst	Lenglen	Godfree	Mallory
1927	Boyd	Bouman	Wills	Wills
1928	Akhurst	Wills	Wills	Wills
1929	Akhurst	Wills	Wills	Wills
1930	Akhurst	Moody	Moody	Nuthall
1931	Buttswrth	Aussem	Aussem	Moody
1932	Buttswrth	Moody	Moody	Jacobs
1933	Hartigan	Scriven	Moody	Jacobs
1934	Hartigan	Scriven	Round	Jacobs

Year	Australia	French	Wimbledon	US
1935	Round	Sperling	Moody	Jacobs
1936	Hartigan	Sperling	Jacobs	Marble
1937	Bolton	Sperling	Round	Lizana
1938	Bundy	Mathieu	Moody	Marble
1939	Westacott	Mathieu	Marble	Marble
1940	Bolton	—	—	Marble
1941	—	—	—	Cooke
1942	—	—	—	Betz
1943	—	—	—	Betz
1944	—	—	—	Betz
1945	—	—	—	Cooke
1946	Bolton	Osborne	Betz	Betz
1947	Bolton	Todd	Osborne	Brough
1948	Bolton	Landry	Brough	duPont
1949	Hart	duPont	Brough	duPont
1950	Brough	Hart	Brough	duPont
1951	Brough	Fry	Hart	Connolly
1952	Long	Hart	Connolly	Connolly
1953	Connolly	Connolly	Connolly	Connolly
1954	Long	Connolly	Connolly	Hart
1955	Penrose	Mortimer	Brough	Hart
1956	Carter	Gibson	Fry	Fry
1957	Fry	Bloomer	Gibson	Gibson
1958	Mortimer	Kormoczy	Gibson	Gibson
1959	Reitano	Truman	Bueno	Bueno
1960	Smith	Hard	Bueno	Hard
1961	Smith	Hayden	Mortimer	Hard
1962	Smith	Smith	Susman	Smith
1963	Smith	Turner	Smith	Bueno
1964	Smith	Smith	Bueno	Bueno

Year	Australia	French	Wimbledon	US
1965	Smith	Turner	Smith	Smith
1966	Smith	Jones	King	Bueno
1967	Richey	Durr	King	King
1968	King	Richey	King	Wade
1969	Court	Court	Jones	Court
1970	**Court**	**Court**	**Court**	**Court**
1971	Court	Goolagong	Goolagong	King
1972	Wade	King	King	King
1973	Court	Court	King	Court
1974	Goolagong	Evert	Evert	King
1975	Goolagong	Evert	King	Evert
1976	Cawley	Barker	Evert	Evert
1977	Reid & Cawley	Jausovec	Wade	Evert
1978	O'Neil	Ruzici	Navratilova	Evert
1979	Jordan	Lloyd	Navratilova	Austin
1980	Mandlikova	Lloyd	Cawley	Evert
1981	Navratilova	Mandlikova	Evert	Austin
1982	Lloyd	Navratilova	Navratilova	Evert
1983	Navratilova	Lloyd	Navratilova	Navratilova
1984	Lloyd	Navratilova	Navratilova	Navratilova
1985	Navratilova	Evert	Navratilova	Mandlikova
1986	—	Evert	Navratilova	Navratilova
1987	Mandlikova	Graf	Navratilova	Navratilova
1988	**Graf**	**Graf**	**Graf**	**Graf**
1989	Graf	Sanchez	Graf	Graf
1990	Graf	Seles	Navratilova	Sabatini
1991	Seles	Seles	Graf	Seles

All-Time Singles Wins

Men and Women with the most singles victories in the Australian, French, Wimbledon and U.S. championships, through 1991. Note that (*) indicates player did not play in that particular Grand Slam event; and players active in 1991 are in **bold** type.

Top 10 Men

	Aus	Fre	Wim	US	Total
Roy Emerson	6	2	2	2	— 12
Bjorn Borg	0	6	5	0	— 11
Rod Laver	3	2	4	2	— 11
Jimmy Connors	1	0	2	5	— 8
Ivan Lendl	2	3	0	3	— 8
Fred Perry	1	1	3	3	— 8
Ken Rosewall	4	2	0	2	— 8
Rene Lacoste	*	3	2	2	— 7
William Larned	*	*	*	7	— 7
John McEnroe	0	0	3	4	— 7
John Newcombe	2	0	3	2	— 7
William Renshaw	*	*	7	*	— 7
Richard Sears	*	*	*	7	— 7
Mats Wilander	3	3	0	1	— 7

Top 10 Women

	Aus	Fre	Wim	US	Total
Margaret Smith Court	11	5	3	5	— 24
Helen Wills Moody	*	4	8	7	— 19
Chris Evert Lloyd	2	7	3	6	— 18
Martina Navratilova	3	2	9	4	— 18
Billie Jean King	1	1	6	4	— 12
Steffi Graf	3	2	3	2	— 10
Maureen Connolly	1	2	3	3	— 9
Suzanne Lenglen	*	2	6	0	— 8
Molla Bjurstedt Malloy	*	*	0	8	— 8
Maria Bueno	0	0	3	4	— 7
Evonne Goolagong Cawley	4	1	2	0	— 7

Maiden & Married Names of Women Champions

Maiden Name	Married Name
Blanche Bingley	Blanche Hillyard
Molla Bjurstedt	Molla Mallory
Evonne Goolagong	Evonne Cawley
Charlotte Cooper	Charlotte Sterry
Dorothea Douglass	Dorothea Lambert Chambers
Chris Evert	Chris Evert Lloyd
Louise Hammond	Louise Raymond
Ann Haydon	Ann Jones
Hazel Hotchkiss	Hazel Wightman

Maiden Name	Married Name
Kerry Melville	Kerry Reid
Kathleen McKane	Kathleen Godfrey
Billie Jean Moffitt	Billie Jean King
Margaret Osborne	Margaret duPont
Sarah Palfrey	Sarah Fabyan Cooke
Arantxa Sanchez	Arantxa Vicario
Margaret Smith	Margaret Court
Helen Wills	Helen Moody
Nancye Wynne	Nancye Bolton

Year-end Tournaments
MEN
The Masters (1970-89)

The year-end championship of the men's tour from 1970-89. Contested by the year's top eight players. Originally a round-robin, the Masters was revised in 1972 to include a round-robin to decide the four semifinalists then a single elimination format after that. Held at Madison Square Garden in New York from 1978-89. Replaced by ATP Tour World Championship in 1990.

Multiple Winners: Ivan Lendl (5); Ilie Nastase (4); John McEnroe (3); Bjorn Borg (2).

Year	Winner		Runner-Up
1970	Stan Smith (4-1)		Rod Laver (4-1)
1971	Ilie Nastase (6-0)		Stan Smith (4-2)

Year	Winner	Loser	Score
1972	Ilie Nastase	S. Smith	63 62 36 26 63
1973	Ilie Nastase	T. Okker	63 75 46 63
1974	Guillermo Vilas	I. Nastase	76 62 36 36 64
1975	Ilie Nastase	B. Borg	62 62 61
1976	Manuel Orantes	W. Fibak	57 62 06 76 61
1978*	Jimmy Connors	B. Borg	64 16 64
1979	John McEnroe	A. Ashe	67 63 75

Year	Winner	Loser	Score
1980	Bjorn Borg	V. Gerulaitis	62 62
1981	Bjorn Borg	I. Lendl	64 62 62
1982	Ivan Lendl	V. Gerulaitis	67 26 76 62 64
1983	Ivan Lendl	J. McEnroe	64 64 62
1984	John McEnroe	I. Lendl	63 64 64
1985	John McEnroe	I. Lendl	75 60 64
1986	Ivan Lendl	B. Becker	62 76 63
1986*	Ivan Lendl	B. Becker	64 64 64
1987	Ivan Lendl	M. Wilander	62 62 63
1988	Boris Becker	I. Lendl	57 76 36 62 76
1989	Stefan Edberg	B. Becker	46 76 63 61

*Tournament switched from December to January in 1977-78, then back to December in 1986.
Note: In 1970, Smith was declared the winner because he beat Laver in their round-robin match (4-6, 6-3, 6-4).

ATP Tour World Championship

Replaced The Masters in 1990 as the year-end championship tournament for the Association of Tennis Professionals (ATP). Field made up of top eight players on ATP Tour (according to ATP computer rankings); round robin decides semifinalists. Held at the Festhalle in Frankfurt, Germany.

Year	Winner	Loser	Score
1990	Andre Agassi	S.Edberg	57 76 75 62

ITF Grand Slam Cup

Inaugurated in 1990 by the International Tennis Federation to compete directly with the ATP Tour Championship. The 1990 ITF Cup followed the ATP Championship by a month, was played in Munich, Germany, and more than doubled the prize money offered by the ATP. Field made up of top performers in year's Grand Slam events.

Year	Winner	Loser	Score
1990	Pete Sampras	B.Gilbert	63 64 62

WOMEN
Virginia Slims Championships

The year-end championship of the women's tour since 1977. Contested by the year's top 16 players. Since 1983, the tournament has featured the tour's only best-of-five set final.

Multiple winners: Martina Navratilova (6); Tracy Austin, Steffi Graf and Chris Evert Lloyd (2).

Year	Winner	Loser	Score
1977	Chris Evert	B.J. King	62 62
1978	Chris Evert	M. Navratilova	63 63
1979	M. Navratilova	T. Austin	62 61
1980	Tracy Austin	A. Jaeger	62 62
1981	Tracy Austin	M. Navratilova	26 64 62
1982	M. Navratilova	C. Evert Lloyd	46 61 62
1983	M. Navratilova	C. Evert Lloyd	63 75 64

Year	Winner	Loser	Score
1984	M. Navratilova	H. Sukova	63 75 64
1985	M. Navratilova	H. Mandlikova	62 60 36 61
1986	M. Navratilova	S. Graf	76 63 62
1987	Steffi Graf	G. Sabatini	46 64 60 64
1988	Gabriela Sabatini	P. Shriver	75 62 62
1989	Steffi Graf	M. Navratilova	64 75 26 62
1990	Monica Seles	G. Sabatini	64 57 36 64 62

Annual Number One Players

Unofficial world rankings for men and women determined by the London Daily Telegraph from 1914-72. Since then, official world rankings computed by men's and women's tours. Rankings included only amateur players from 1914 until the arrival of open (professional) tennis in 1968. No rankings were released during World Wars I and II.

MEN

Multiple winners: Bill Tilden (6); Jimmy Connors (5); Henri Cochet, Rod Laver, Ivan Lendl and John McEnroe (4); John Newcombe and Fred Perry (3); Bjorn Borg, Don Budge, Ashley Cooper, Roy Emerson, Neale Fraser, Jack Kramer, Rene Lacoste, Ilie Nastase, Frank Sedgman and Tony Trabert (2).

Year		Year		Year		Year	
1914	Maurice McLoughlin	1925	Bill Tilden	1933	Jack Crawford	1946	Jack Kramer
1915-18	No rankings	1926	Rene Lacoste	1934	Fred Perry	1947	Jack Kramer
1919	Gerald Patterson	1927	Rene Lacoste	1935	Fred Perry	1948	Frank Parker
1920	Bill Tilden	1928	Henri Cochet	1936	Fred Perry	1949	Pancho Gonzalez
1921	Bill Tilden	1929	Henri Cochet	1937	Don Budge	1950	Budge Patty
1922	Bill Tilden	1930	Henri Cochet	1938	Don Budge	1951	Frank Sedgman
1923	Bill Tilden	1931	Henri Cochet	1939	Bobby Riggs	1952	Frank Sedgman
1924	Bill Tilden	1932	Ellsworth Vines	1940-45	No rankings	1953	Tony Trabert

Year		Year		Year		Year	
1954	Jaroslav Drobny	1964	Roy Emerson	1973	Ilie Nastase	1982	John McEnroe
1955	Tony Trabert	1965	Roy Emerson	1974	Jimmy Connors	1983	John McEnroe
1956	Lew Hoad	1966	Manuel Santana	1975	Jimmy Connors	1984	John McEnroe
1957	Ashley Cooper	1967	John Newcombe	1976	Jimmy Connors	1985	Ivan Lendl
1958	Ashley Cooper	1968	Rod Laver	1977	Jimmy Connors	1986	Ivan Lendl
1959	Neale Fraser	1969	Rod Laver	1978	Jimmy Connors	1987	Ivan Lendl
				1979	Bjorn Borg	1988	Mats Wilander
1960	Neale Fraser	1970	John Newcombe			1989	Ivan Lendl
1961	Rod Laver	1971	John Newcombe	1980	Bjorn Borg		
1962	Rod Laver	1972	Ilie Nastase	1981	John McEnroe	1990	Stefan Edberg
1963	Rafael Osuna						

WOMEN

Multiple winners: Helen Wills Moody (9); Margaret Smith Court and Martina Navratilova (7); Chris Evert Lloyd (5); Margaret Osborne duPont, Steffi Graf and Billie Jean King (4); Maureen Connolly (3); Maria Bueno, Althea Gibson and Suzanne Lenglen (2).

Year		Year		Year		Year	
1925	Suzanne Lenglen	1946	Pauline Betz	1962	Margaret Smith	1977	Chris Evert
1926	Suzanne Lenglen	1947	Margaret Osborne	1963	Margaret Smith	1978	Martina Navratilova
1927	Helen Wills	1948	Margaret duPont	1964	Margaret Smith	1979	Martina Navratilova
1928	Helen Wills	1949	Margaret duPont	1965	Margaret Smith		
1929	Helen Wills			1966	Billie Jean King	1980	Chris Evert Lloyd
		1950	Margaret duPont	1967	Billie Jean King	1981	Chris Evert Lloyd
1930	Helen Wills Moody	1951	Doris Hart	1968	Billie Jean King	1982	Martina Navratilova
1931	Helen Wills Moody	1952	Maureen Connolly	1969	Margaret Court	1983	Martina Navratilova
1932	Helen Wills Moody	1953	Maureen Connolly			1984	Martina Navratilova
1933	Helen Wills Moody	1954	Maureen Connolly	1970	Margaret Court	1985	Martina Navratilova
1934	Dorothy Round	1955	Louise Brough	1971	Evonne Goolagong	1986	Martina Navratilova
1935	Helen Wills Moody	1956	Shirley Fry	1972	Billie Jean King	1987	Steffi Graf
1936	Helen Jacobs	1957	Althea Gibson	1973	Margaret Court	1988	Steffi Graf
1937	Anita Lizana	1958	Althea Gibson	1974	Billie Jean King	1989	Steffi Graf
1938	Helen Wills Moody	1959	Maria Bueno	1975	Chris Evert		
1939	Alice Marble			1976	Chris Evert	1990	Steffi Graf
		1960	Maria Bueno				
1940-45	No rankings	1961	Angela Mortimer				

All-Time Leaders
Overall Wins

All-time tournament wins for men and matches won for women, from the arrival of open tennis in 1968 through 1991. Totals include doubles earnings. Note that Billie Jean King and Margaret Smith Court started their careers before Open tennis, so their records are incomplete. Players active in 1990 in **bold** type.

MEN
Tournaments Won

1	**Jimmy Connors**	109
2	**Ivan Lendl**	88
3	**John McEnroe**	76
4	Bjorn Borg	65
5	Guillermo Vilas	61
6	Ilie Nastase	57
7	Rod Laver	47
8	Stan Smith	39
9	Arthur Ashe	33
	Mats Wilander	33
11	John Newcombe	32
	Manuel Orantes	32
	Ken Rosewall	32
14	Tom Okker	30
15	**Boris Becker**	29
16	**Stefan Edberg**	27
	Vitas Gerulaitis	27
18	Jose-Luis Clerc	25
	Brian Gottfried	25
20	**Yannick Noah**	23

WOMEN
Matches Won

		W	L	Pct
1	Chris Evert	1309	146	.903
2	**Martina Navratilova**	1268	173	.880
3	Virginia Wade	839	329	.718
4	Billie Jean King	695	155	.818
	Evonne Goolagong Cawley	695	158	.815
6	Wendy Turnbull	577	318	.644
7	Hana Mandlikova	567	195	.744
8	**Pam Shriver**	537	185	.743
9	Rosie Casals	528	308	.631
10	Virgina Ruzici	490	279	.637
11	Dianne Balestrat	468	271	.633
12	Margaret Smith Court	464	78	.906
13	**Steffi Graf**	449	61	.880
14	Helena Sukova	445	189	.701
15	**Sylvia Hanika**	423	243	.635
16	**Zina Garrison**	421	171	.711
17	**Claudia Kohde-Kilsch**	379	208	.645
18	Sue Barker	365	208	.637
19	Regina Marsikova	358	225	.614
20	**Gabriela Sabatini**	354	104	.772

Most tournaments won (since 1968): Chris Evert (157); Martina Navratilova (151); Margaret Smith Court (90); Evonne Goolagong Cawley (80); Billie Jean King (78); Steffi Graf (56); Virginia Wade (55).

All-Time Leaders (Cont.)
Money Won

Men's and women's all-time money winners, from the arrival of open tennis in 1968 through 1990. Totals include doubles earnings.

	MEN	Earnings		WOMEN	Earnings
1	Ivan Lendl	$16,772,078	1	Martina Navratilova	$16,674,607
2	John McEnroe	11,265,336	2	Chris Evert	8,896,195
3	Stefan Edberg	8,633,696	3	Steffi Graf	7,173,198
4	Boris Becker	8,160,207	4	Pam Shriver	4,323,497
5	Jimmy Connors	8,107,685	5	Gabriela Sabatini	3,656,136
6	Mats Wilander	7,310,656	6	Helena Sukova	3,473,097
7	Guillermo Vilas	4,897,967	7	Hana Mandlikova	3,340,959
8	Andres Gomez	3,958,682	8	Zina Garrison	2,783,770
9	Tomas Smid	3,665,330	9	Wendy Turnbull	2,769,024
10	Bjorn Borg	3,607,206	10	Claudia Kohde-Kilsch	2,034,541
11	Andre Agassi	3,342,838	11	Manuela Maleeva-Fragniere	1,966,679
12	Anders Jarryd	3,233,489	12	Billie Jean King	1,966,487
13	Yannick Noah	3,228,947	13	Tracy Austin	1,925,415
14	Brad Gilbert	3,217,946	14	Monica Seles	1,891,283
15	Brian Gottfried	2,782,514	15	Virginia Wade	1,542,278
16	Vitas Gerulaitis	2,778,748	16	Kathy Jordan	1,539,395
17	Wojtek Fibak	2,724,948	17	Evonne Goolagong Cawley	1,399,431
18	Miloslav Mecir	2,632,538	18	Lori McNeil	1,392,083
19	Kevin Curren	2,593,669	19	Andrea Jaeger	1,379,066
20	Emilio Sanchez	2,575,082	20	Barbara Potter	1,376,580

National Team Competition
Davis Cup

Established in 1900 as an annual international tournament by American player Dwight Davis. Originally called the International Lawn Tennis Challenge Trophy. Challenge round system until 1972. Since 1981, the top 16 nations in the world have played a straight knockout tournament over the course of a year. The format is a best-of-five match of two singles, one doubles and two singles over three days.

Multiple winners: USA (29); Australia (20); Australasia and France (6); British Isles (5); Britain and Sweden (4); West Germany (2).

Challenge Rounds

Year	Winner	Loser	Score	Site	Year	Winner	Loser	Score	Site
1900	USA	British Isles	3-0	Boston	1933	Britain	France	3-2	Paris
1901	Not held				1934	Britain	USA	4-1	Wimbledon
1902	USA	British Isles	3-2	New York	1935	Britain	USA	5-0	Wimbledon
1903	British Isles	USA	4-1	Boston	1936	Britain	Australia	3-2	Wimbledon
1904	British Isles	Belgium	5-0	Wimbledon	1937	USA	Britain	4-1	Wimbledon
1905	British Isles	USA	5-0	Wimbledon	1938	USA	Australia	302	Philadelphia
1906	British Isles	USA	5-0	Wimbledon	1939	Australia	USA	3-2	Philadelphia
1907	Australasia	British Isles	3-2	Wimbledon					
1908	Australasia	USA	5-0	Melbourne	1940-1945	Not held			
1909	Australasia	USA	5-0	Sydney	1946	USA	Australia	5-0	Melbourne
					1947	USA	Australia	4-1	New York
1910	Not held				1948	USA	Australia	5-0	New York
1911	Australasia	USA	5-0	N. Zealand	1949	USA	Australia	4-1	New York
1912	British Isles	Australasia	3-2	Melbourne					
1913	USA	British Isles	3-2	Wimbledon	1950	Australia	USA	4-1	New York
1914	Australasia	USA	3-2	New York	1951	Australia	USA	3-2	Sydney
1915-18	Not held				1952	Australia	USA	4-1	Adelaide
1919	Australasia	British Isles	4-1	Sydney	1953	Australia	USA	3-2	Melbourne
					1954	USA	Australia	3-2	Sydney
1920	USA	Australasia	5-0	N. Zealand	1955	Australia	USA	5-0	New York
1921	USA	Japan	5-0	New York	1956	Australia	USA	5-0	Adelaide
1922	USA	Australasia	4-1	New York	1957	Australia	USA	3-2	Melbourne
1923	USA	Australasia	4-1	New York	1958	USA	Australia	3-2	Brisbane
1924	USA	Australia	5-0	Philadelphia	1959	Australia	USA	3-2	New York
1925	USA	France	5-0	Philadelphia	1960	Australia	Italy	4-1	Sydney
1926	USA	France	4-1	Philadelphia	1961	Australia	Italy	5-0	Melbourne
1927	France	USA	3-2	Philadelphia	1962	Australia	Mexico	5-0	Brisbane
1928	France	USA	4-1	Paris	1963	USA	Australia	3-2	Adelaide
1929	France	USA	3-2	Paris	1964	Australia	USA	3-2	Cleveland
1930	France	USA	4-1	Paris	1965	Australia	Spain	4-1	Sydney
1931	France	Britain	3-2	Paris	1966	Australia	India	4-1	Melbourne
1932	France	USA	3.2	Paris	1967	Australia	Spain	4-1	Brisbane

Final Rounds

Year	Winner	Loser	Score	Site	Year	Winner	Loser	Score	Site
1968	USA	Australia	4-1	Adelaide	1980	Czech.	Italy	4-1	Prague
1969	USA	Romania	5-0	Cleveland	1981	USA	Argentina	3-1	Cincinnati
					1982	USA	France	4-1	Grenoble
1970	USA	W. Germany	5-0	Cleveland	1983	Australia	Sweden	3-2	Melbourne
1971	USA	Romania	3-2	Charlotte	1984	Sweden	USA	4-1	Gothenburg
1972	USA	Romania	3-2	Bucharest	1985	Sweden	W.Germany	3-2	Munich
1973	Australia	USA	5-0	Cleveland	1986	Australia	Sweden	3-2	Melbourne
1974	So. Africa	India	walkover	—	1987	Sweden	India	5-0	Gothenburg
1975	Sweden	Czech.	3-2	Stockholm	1988	W.Germany	Sweden	4-1	Gothenburg
1976	Italy	Chile	4-1	Santiago	1989	W.Germany	Sweden	3-2	Stuttgart
1977	Australia	Italy	3-1	Sydney					
1978	USA	Britain	4-1	Palm Springs	1990	USA	Australia	3-2	St. Petersburg
1979	USA	Italy	5-0	San Francisco					

Federation Cup

Started in 1963 by the International Lawn Tennis Federation as the Davis Cup of women's tennis. The major difference is that all competing countries gather at one site to decide the Cup winner in one week.

Multiple winners: USA (14); Australia (7); Czechoslovakia (5).

Year	Winner	Loser	Score	Site	Year	Winner	Loser	Score	Site
1963	USA	Australia	2-1	London	1978	USA	Australia	2-1	Melbourne
1964	Australia	USA	2-1	Philadelphia	1979	USA	Australia	3-0	Spain
1965	Australia	USA	2-1	Melbourne	1980	USA	Australia	3-0	W.Germany
1966	USA	Germany	3-0	Italy	1981	USA	Britain	3-0	Tokyo
1967	USA	Britain	2-0	W.Germany	1982	USA	W.Germany	3-0	Santa Clara
1968	Australia	Holland	3-0	Paris	1983	Czech.	W.Germany	2-1	Zurich
1969	USA	Australia	2-1	Athens	1984	Czech.	Australia	2-1	Brazil
1970	Australia	Britain	3-0	W.Germany	1985	Czech.	USA	2-1	Japan
1971	Australia	Britain	3-0	Perth	1986	USA	Czech.	3-0	Prague
1972	So. Africa	Britain	2-1	Africa	1987	W.Germany	USA	2-1	Vancouver
1973	Australia	So. Africa	3-0	W.Germany	1988	Czech.	USSR	2-1	Melbourne
1974	Australia	USA	2-1	Italy	1989	USA	Spain	3-0	Tokyo
1975	Czech.	Australia	3-0	France	1990	USA	USSR	2-1	Atlanta
1976	USA	Australia	2-1	Philadelphia	1991	Spain	USA	2-1	Nottingham
1977	USA	Australia	2-1	Eastbourne					

Colleges

The NCAA recognizes men's individual tennis champions since 1883, but team titles were not sanctioned until 1946. NCAA women's individual and team championships started in 1982.

Men's NCAA Individual Champions (1883-1945)

Multiple winners: Malcolm Chace and Pancho Segura (3); Edward Chandler, George Church, E.B.Dewhurst, Fred Hovey, Frank Guernsey, W.P.Knapp, Robert LeRoy, P.S.Sears, Cliff Sutter, Ernest Sutter and Richard Williams (2).

Year		Year		Year	
1883	J.Clark, Harvard (spring)	1904	Robert LeRoy, Columbia	1925	Edward Chandler, Calif.
	H.Taylor, Harvard (fall)	1905	E.B.Dewhurst, Penn	1926	Edward Chandler, Calif.
1884	W.P.Knapp, Yale	1906	Robert LeRoy, Columbia	1927	Wilmer Allison, Texas
1885	W.P.Knapp, Yale	1907	G.P.Gardner Jr, Harvard	1928	Julius Seligson, Lehigh
1886	G.M.Brinley, Trinity,CT	1908	Nat Niles, Harvard	1929	Berkeley Bell, Texas
1887	P.S.Sears, Harvard	1909	Wallace Johnson, Penn		
1888	P.S.Sears, Harvard	1910	R.A.Holden Jr, Yale	1930	Cliff Sutter, Tulane
1889	R.P.Huntington Jr, Yale	1911	E.H.Whitney, Harvard	1931	Keith Gledhill, Stanford
1890	Fred Hovey, Harvard	1912	Geo.Church, Princeton	1932	Cliff Sutter, Tulane
1891	Fred Hovey, Harvard	1913	Richard Williams, Harv.	1933	Jack Tidball, UCLA
1892	William Larned, Cornell	1914	Geo.Church, Princeton	1934	Gene Mako, USC
1893	Malcolm Chace, Brown	1915	Richard Williams, Harv.	1935	Wilbur Hess, Rice
1894	Malcolm Chace, Yale	1916	G.C.Caner, Harvard	1936	Ernest Sutter, Tulane
1895	Malcolm Chace, Yale	1917	Not held	1937	Ernest Sutter, Tulane
1896	Malcolm Whitman, Harvard	1918	Not held	1938	Frank Guernsey, Rice
1897	S.G.Thompson, Princeton	1919	Charles Garland, Yale	1939	Frank Guernsey, Rice
1898	Leo Ware, Harvard	1920	Lascelles Banks, Yale	1940	Don McNeill, Kenyon
1899	Dwight Davis, Harvard	1921	Philip Neer, Stanford	1941	Joseph Hunt, Navy
1900	Ray Little, Princeton	1922	Lucien Williams, Yale	1942	Fred Schroeder, Stanford
1901	Fred Alexander, Princeton	1923	Carl Fischer, Phi.Osteo.	1943	Pancho Segura, Miami-FL
1902	William Clothier, Harvard	1924	Wallace Scott, Wash.	1944	Pancho Segura, Miami-FL
1903	E.B.Dewhurst, Penn			1945	Pancho Segura, Miami-FL

Colleges (Cont.)

Men's NCAA Division I Champions

Multiple winners (teams): UCLA (15); USC (13); Stanford (11); Georgia and William & Mary (2). **Multiple winners** (players): Alex Olmedo, Mikael Pernfors, Dennis Ralston and Ham Richardson (2).

Year	Team winner	Individual Champion	Year	Team winner	Individual Champion
1946	USC	Bob Falkenburg, USC	1969	USC	Joaquin Loyo-Mayo, USC
1947	Wm.& Mary	Garner Larned, Wm.& Mary	1970	UCLA	Jeff Borowiak, UCLA
1948	Wm.& Mary	Harry Likas, San Francisco	1971	UCLA	Jimmy Connors, UCLA
1949	San Francisco	Jack Tuero, Tulane	1972	Trinity-TX	Dick Stockton, Trinity-TX
1950	UCLA	Herbert Flam, UCLA	1973	Stanford	Alex Mayer, Stanford
1951	USC	Tony Trabert, Cinncinati	1974	Stanford	John Whitlinger, Stanford
1952	UCLA	Hugh Stewart, USC	1975	UCLA	Bill Martin, UCLA
1953	UCLA	Ham Richardson, Tulane	1976	USC & UCLA	Bill Scanlon, Trinity-TX
1954	UCLA	Ham Richardson, Tulane	1977	Stanford	Matt Mitchell, Stanford
1955	USC	Jose Aguero, Tulane	1978	Stanford	John McEnroe, Stanford
1956	UCLA	Alex Olmedo, USC	1979	UCLA	Kevin Curren, Texas
1957	Michigan	Barry MacKay, Michigan	1980	Stanford	Robert Van't Hof, USC
1958	USC	Alex Olmedo, USC	1981	Stanford	Tim Mayotte, Stanford
1959	Tulane & Notre Dame	Whitney Reed, San Jose St.	1982	UCLA	Mike Leach, Michigan
			1983	Stanford	Greg Holmes, Utah
1960	UCLA	Larry Nagler, UCLA	1984	UCLA	Mikael Pernfors, Georgia
1961	UCLA	Allen Fox, UCLA	1985	Georgia	Mikael Pernfors, Georgia
1962	USC	Rafael Osuna, USC	1986	Stanford	Dan Goldie, Stanford
1963	USC	Dennis Ralston, USC	1987	Georgia	Andrew Burrow, Miami-FL
1964	USC	Dennis Ralston, USC	1988	Stanford	Robby Weiss, Pepperdine
1965	UCLA	Arthur Ashe, UCLA	1989	Stanford	Donni Leaycraft, LSU
1966	USC	Charlie Pasarell, UCLA	1990	Stanford	Steve Bryan, Texas
1967	USC	Bob Lutz, USC	1991	USC	Jared Palmer, Stanford
1968	USC	Stan Smith, USC			

Women's NCAA Champions

Multiple winners (teams): Stanford (8); USC (2). **Multiple winners** (players): Sandra Birch and Patty Fendick (2).

Year	Team winner	Individual Champion	Year	Team winner	Individual Champion
1982	Stanford	Alycia Moulton, Stanford	1987	Stanford	Patty Fendick, Stanford
1983	USC	Beth Herr, USC	1988	Stanford	Shaun Stafford, Florida
1984	Stanford	Lisa Spain, Georgia	1989	Stanford	Sandra Birch Stanford
1985	USC	Linda Gates, Stanford	1990	Stanford	Debbie Graham, Stanford
1986	Stanford	Patty Fendick, Stanford	1991	Stanford	Sandra Birch, Stanford

Unknown rookie **John Daly** got a last-minute invitation to the PGA Championship then blew away the competition to win the season's final major tournament by three strokes.

GOLF

by Marino Parascenzo

Long Shot

Big hitter John Daly made the PGA Championship field only after nine players cancelled, then he straightened out Crooked Stick.

The PGA Championship started in 1916 and they thought they had seen everything.

They'd seen Walter Hagen, the boulevardier with the slick hair and slick game; Ben Hogan, stalking the world in imperial silence, and Sam Snead, who made the golf swing look natural. They'd seen Jack Nicklaus, who won the tournament five times, and Arnold Palmer, who never won it. They'd seen Bob Tway beat Greg Norman out of the bunker on the final hole in 1986. But they'd never seen anything like John Daly—the gorilla who ate Crooked Stick.

The 25-year-old Daly took everybody by surprise. He isn't all that big, just 5-foot-10 and 185 pounds, but for sheer animal power and exuberance, he is huge—with a backswing that threatens to twist him off at the waist and a shot that would stagger a rhinoceros.

"I just came here to play golf and got lucky and won," he said. "Everybody knows I'm a Cinderella story."

Fairy tale or not, Daly was the story of 1991 in golf. Never mind that Welshman Ian Woosnam kept the Masters in British hands for the fourth straight year; that Payne Stewart survived the crumbling Scott Simpson in the U.S. Open; or that

Australian Ian Baker-Finch finally blossomed and won the British Open. In August, Daly beat the PGA into submission and stuffed it into his golf bag.

Daly's secret: "All four days, I didn't think. I just hit it." he said. "Squeaky (his caddie) just said 'Kill,' and I killed it." Daly is a self-taught golfer from the blue-collar ranks of Dardanelle, Ark. Before the PGA, he was known—if at all—as a sort of sideshow performer who hit the ball a ton, then couldn't find it. In 1990, he won once on the Ben Hogan Tour and twice in South Africa. He joined the PGA Tour in 1991 and by mid-August had missed the cut in 11 of 24 tournaments and stood 72nd on the money list with $166,590.

He hadn't even qualified for the PGA—in fact, he was a no-chance No. 9 on the list of alternates. It's rare that two or three players drop out of a major, so when PGA week began, Daly was sitting at home in Memphis, Tenn.

Then the miracle began. First, five openings appeared for one reason or another and were gobbled up in order. Then by Wednesday afternoon, the day before play was to start, three more qualifiers sent their regrets. That left Daly next up should another opening occur. And it did, when Nick Price withdrew to be with his wife for the arrival of their first child.

Daly was in. He drove 7½ hours to Carmel, Ind., arrived shortly after midnight and got some sleep. The next day,

Marino Parascenzo has been the *Pittsburgh Post-Gazette's* golf writer since 1975. He is also a contributing editor to *Golf Digest.*

Welshman **Ian Woosnam** punches in as he watches his eight-foot par putt drop to clinch the Masters on the final hole. His victory marked the sixth time in nine years that a European player has won at Augusta.

having never seen the Crooked Stick Golf Club course, he went out and shot a 69 in the first round. Nobody really noticed. Ken Knox and Ian Woosnam tied for the first-round lead at 5-under-par 67 and four other guys were at 68, so the big-jawed guy with the mane of blond hair down his neck was just another face in the crowd. Crooked Stick, a par 72 stretched over nearly 7,300 yards, was said to be the longest course ever used for a major. Daly reduced it to a pitch-and-putt exercise, crushing drives well over 300 yards, hitting 54 greens in regulation and shooting 69-67-69-71—276. At 12 under par, he beat runner-up Bruce Lietzke by three strokes.

"Do you realize," someone said," that you've become famous all over the world?"

Daly didn't even stop to mull it over.

"There's too much country in this boy," he said, "to worry about things like that."

Back in April, Woosnam won the Masters with a strong all-around game and plenty of spirit. They didn't call him the Welsh terrier for nothing. He used to box a little as a kid, and he was always the

smallest guy. He once was asked whether his size—5 foot 4½—was a disadvantage.

"If I got in the ring with a guy 6-feet tall," he said, "I'd bite him on the legs."

They say the Masters is won over the last nine holes. The '91 Masters came down to the very last hole.

There were some heroics before they got there, however. Steve Pate, who started the final day nine shots off the lead, went on a tear for a 65 that looked as though it might hold up. He eventually tied for third at 279. Tom Watson looked dead in the water when he dunked his tee shot and double-bogeyed the 12th, but he came back with a spectacular pair of eagles at the 13th, from 15 feet, and the 15th, from eight. Jose-Marie Olazabal, who had pulled even with Woosnam with a birdie at No. 7, was also in the hunt. Things would see-saw all day, but they approached No.18 in a three-way tie— Woosnam, Watson and Olazabal.

Olazabal, playing in the twosome ahead, was the first to bow out. He bunkered his drive, bunkered his approach, and bogeyed for a 2-under-par 70 and a 10-under 278. He would finish second by a shot. If any one hole had cost him the Masters, it was the par-3 sixth where he posted a record 7 in the second round.

Watson and Woosnam were the final twosome. Watson hit first and pushed his tee shot into the trees at the right of the dogleg right, uphill par-4. Woosnam took the fairway bunkers out of play by firing a big hook past them. Watson tried to slice a 3-iron out of the trees, but a bad lie kept him from getting enough club on the ball. He caught the front bunker. Woosnam hit a 140-yard 8-iron uphill, just off the left edge of the green, 40 feet from the pin.

Watson's blast from the bunker nearly holed out, but rolled 30 feet past the pin. Woosnam, using his putter from off the green, left the ball about eight feet to the right of the hole. Watson's long par putt from the back went six feet past. He would shoot 73-279 and tie for third.

Woosnam tapped that eight-footer, and as it neared the hole, he dropped into a crouch and fired a couple of belly shots into the air. The ball fell and he had his green jacket.

Woosnam takes a size 40 short. They found a member's jacket to put on him for the presentation ceremony. Someone wondered whose it was.

"I don't know," Woosnam said. "But it fits. It's mine now."

Woosnam's victory marked the sixth time in nine years that a European player had won at Augusta, dating back to Ballesteros in 1983 and followed by Germany's Bernhard Langer in 1985, England's Sandy Lyle in '88, and back-to-back wins by Nick Faldo in 1989-90. Faldo's attempt at an unprecedented three in a row never recovered from early rounds of 72-73 and he finished in a five-way tie for 12th place, five strokes back.

The U.S. Open in June—like the PGA two months later—began with tragedy. One spectator was killed and five others injured when lightning hit a tree they were huddled under during a storm. At the PGA, a man was hit on his way to his car in the parking lot.

The Open had returned to Hazeltine National Golf Club, near Minneapolis, probably the most ridiculed course in Open history. Back in 1970, Dave Hill earned a fine for suggesting that all Hazeltine

Emotional U.S. Squad Regains Ryder Cup

A lot of grown men were crying. And they weren't even playing for money. The Ryder Cup had come to mean that much.

Ever since British seed merchant Samuel Ryder put up the gold trophy in 1927, the American pros would politely go out every two years and put lumps all over their sad cousins from Great Britain-Ireland. That changed after 1979. Jack Nicklaus, noting a Spanish meteor named Seve Ballesteros, suggested that including all Europeans might relieve the boredom. There went the weekend.

And so after three wind-whipped September days on the new Ocean Course at Kiawah Island, S.C., the 1991 match came down to the last putt on the last hole of the last singles match—Germany's Bernhard Langer, before thousands of fans and millions watching on TV, facing a five-foot par putt to beat Hale Irwin.

If he makes it, Europe has a 14-14 tie and the cup to cuddle for two more years. But the putt wobbled past the hole, and the Americans took the cup by the narrowest of margins, 14½-13½.

The Americans hold an absurd edge, 22-5-2, but most of it's ancient history. They hadn't won since 1983. The Europeans won in '85 and '87, and tied in '89. Hence Lanny Wadkins, seven-time Ryder Cupper, sobbing into a towel and almost unable to talk after his singles win over Mark James gave the U.S. a 14-13 lead, clinching at least a tie. "That's the hardest I ever worked in my life," Wadkins finally managed to say.

The matches were wringing everything out of everybody, right to the end. Irwin, 46, in his fifth Ryder Cup, led 1-up with three holes to play, but let it get away. The yip-ridden Langer managed to drop a six-footer to halve the 16th in pars, then dropped another to win the 17th over Irwin's bogey and square the match.

Then it was Langer's to win. At the 18th, he was short in two, and putted about five feet past. Irwin hooked his drive, then missed the green. Then a poor chip left him a 20-footer for par. When he missed it, Langer turned to his winning five-footer. And missed. That was just the final drama. Among others:

AFP Photos

Kiawah Island, S.C., wasn't exactly the sands of Iwo Jima, but the American Ryder Cup squad was finally able to raise the flag in victory on Sept. 29, for the first time since 1983.

► Mark Calcavecchia suffered a gruesome collapse. He blew a lead of 4-up with four holes to play, making two bogeys and two triple bogeys. Scottish rookie Colin Montgomerie was also crumbling, thus had stumbled to a tie and salvaged a half-point. Calcavecchia went and found himself a lonely beach. "I just sat there in the sand and cried," he said.

► The Spanish juggernaut kept rolling. Seve Ballesteros, 34, and Jose Maria Olazabal, 25, went 3-0-1 in their four team matches, and now are 9-1-2 since being paired in 1987.

► Paul Azinger became a bone in the Spanish throat. He beat Ballesteros in singles in '89, then Olazabal this time in a fierce little war whose score changed 11 times.

► The Nick Faldo-Ian Woosnam powerhouse, 5-1-2 coming in, ran out of steam. They lost both team matches on opening day, and were split up. Faldo also lost with David Gilford as a partner.

► Fred Couples, the goat of '89 when he blew an easy shot to the final green and got beat, turned hero this time. He was 2-1-1 in team matches, then won in singles. He was 0-2 in '89, 3-1-1 this time. "The highlight of my career—just great," Couples said, choking up.

► Raymond Floyd, 49, captain in '89 and in his seventh playing appearance, may have been the key for the U.S. Non-playing captain Dave Stockton made him a wild-card pick, then paired him with ex-goat Couples, possibly as a steadying influence. They went 2-1 together.

Wide World Photos

British Open champion **Ian Baker-Finch** is upstaged by 2-year-old daughter **Haley** after posting a final round 66.

And the dream of the Grand Slam—winning all four majors in the same year—had long since died. Masters champ Ian Woosnam was a contender for the first two rounds, then shot 79 and 80 and finished in a tie for 55th place.

The next day, what was supposed to be a playoff battle turned into a death stagger. Last man standing wins. And that was Stewart. He made four bogeys and one birdie, and shot 3-over 75—the highest winning playoff score since 1927. Simpson made three birdies and eight bogeys and shot 77.

Five weeks later, the British Open was played at Royal Birkdale and it was liberation time for Ian Baker-Finch, who was known for the late fold. Baker-Finch, 30, began his career as a kid by burning rubbish on a golf course in Australia. This time he lit the golf course on fire.

Baker-Finch was tied for the lead going into the final round, then fired a 29 on the front nine. He led by four or five shots most of the way and finished with a 4-under-par 66. His 8-under 272 was good for a two-shot win over fellow-Aussie Mike Harwood.

Baker-Finch had surfaced in the 1984 British Open at St. Andrews, and almost sank there, too. He was tied for the lead going into the final round, watered his approach shot on the first hole, and blew up. After that, they called him Baker-Finch, a real nice guy who choked a lot. He said so himself.

"Every time I got on top," he said, "something seemed to knock me down." They couldn't lay a glove on him this time. He ran the table. He birdied the second, third and fourth holes from 12, 10 and 6 feet. Then he birdied the awful sixth, and the seventh as well. About this time, a dark memory crept into his head.

"When I got to four or five ahead," he said. "I thought, boy, you'd better not stuff up now or you'll really cop it."

Did he prove himself at last?

"Yeah," he said, and he started to mumble.

"It's hard to talk when you're crying," he finally said. "This erases all those memories."

On the Senior PGA Tour, if it weren't for Jack Nicklaus, Chi Chi Rodriguez might have owned the franchise. Rodriguez won four times before the 1991

needed was a herd of cows and some corn. But a renovated Hazeltine proved to be no joke this time.

This Open would go into the record books as the Open that was lost twice by the same guy—Scott Simpson.

"Well, here we are—another year, another playoff," Simpson said. Simpson, who won the 1987 Open outright, was referring to the two 18-hole playoffs in the previous three years: Curtis Strange winning in 1988 and Hale Irwin in '90.

This simply wasn't Simpson's week. In the third round, he bogeyed two of the last three holes and blew a two-shot lead. In the fourth round, he bogeyed two of the last three again, and blew not only another two-shot lead but the Open itself.

And in the 18-hole playoff against Payne Stewart on Monday, he bogeyed all three and lost the Open again—this time for good.

"It's disappointing," Simpson said, managing a smile, "to lose the U.S. Open two days in a row."

Stewart and Simpson shot par-72s in the final round and tied in regulation at 6-under 282. No one else was close. Larry Nelson (68) and Fred Couples (70) tied for third, three shots back at 285.

season was half over, and was still the leading money-winner by mid-September, although Mike Hill was closing in.

Nicklaus won three tournaments, including the two major stops on the tour—the PGA Seniors Championship and the U.S. Senior Open. He won the PGA Seniors in April by six strokes, then took the Senior Open in July, winning at tough Oakland Hills, near Detroit, in a playoff with Rodriguez.

It was this kind of Open: with just two holes to play, four guys were tied for the lead—Nicklaus, Rodriguez, Lee Trevino, and Al Geiberger. Nicklaus birdied the 17th and thought he had the lead at two over par.

But Rodriguez had made a miracle birdie at the 18th, hooking a downhill 6-iron that floated over the right bunker and ended up two feet from the pin.

Now Nicklaus had to par the tough 18th to catch him. He hit a big drive, landed a 155-yard 7-iron within 14 feet, and two-putted for the par. They both shot 71 and tied at 282.

The next day—the Senior Open also has an 18-hole playoff—Rodriguez shot a splendid 1-under 69. But Nicklaus shot a brilliant 5-under 65, for his third victory in five Senior events.

"This was one of the best rounds hitting the golf ball I've had in a long, long time," Nicklaus said. "That's the best I've seen him play in 15 years," said Rodriguez. "I thank him for not playing the Senior all the time."

On the LPGA Tour, a new kid barged onto the block, a freckled, easy-laughing 28-year-old named Meg Mallon. Mallon, winless in her first four years on the ladies' circuit, warmed up by taking the Oldsmobile Classic in February. Then she jolted the tour by winning its two biggest majors—the LPGA Championship at Bethesda (Md.) Country Club in late June, and the U.S. Women's Open two weeks later at Colonial C.C. in Forth Worth.

As far as the LPGA Championship is concerned, Mallon will always be known for "The Putt." The LPGA, played in steaming Maryland heat, was tied going into the final round. And it ended on the final green.

Pat Bradley's 20-footer stopped just short. Ayako Okamoto's 20-footer just grazed the hole and stayed out. Then it

Wide World Photos

Jack Nicklaus with U.S. Senior Open trophy after defeating Chi Chi Rodriguez 65-69 in a rainy 18-hole playoff.

was Mallon's turn. Faced with a downhill, left-to-right 15-footer, she made it look as though she'd been making that putt all her life. The ball crawled lazily down the slope and curved obediently into the hole.

"No big deal, right, Meg?" Beth Daniel said. "I mean, it was only for the LPGA Championship."

"It was something you dream about," Mallon said. "making a putt on the last green to win a major championship."

At the Open, it was a question of who would survive the 100-degree Texas heat. Mallon was trailing Bradley by three heading into the final turn. Then came the bump Mallon needed as Bradley bogeyed the ninth and 10th holes. Mallon then canned a 21-foot birdie at No. 11 and she was in a three-way tie for the lead with Bradley and Amy Alcott. But not for long.

Mallon got two quick birdies, an 18-footer at the 14th and a 25-footer at the 15th. She finished with a 4-under 67 for a 1-under 283 and beat Bradley by two, thus becoming the first player to win both the LPGA and the Women's Open in the same year since Sandra Haynie did it in 1974.

Alcott won the Nabisco Dinah Shore in March and Nancy Scranton won the du

Maurier Classic in September to account for the remaining majors. By mid-September, Mallon had won nearly $500,000 for the year, but trailed tour leader Bradley by over $125,000. Bradley, meanwhile, with two victories in 1991, was just two shy of the 30 career wins needed to qualify for the LPGA Hall of Fame.

Back on the PGA Tour, before Daly arrived on the scene in August, the rookie of the year was amateur Phil Mickelson. The left-handed Arizona State junior entered 1991 with two NCAA titles and the U.S. Amateur already in his bag. Then in January he entered the Northern Telecom (formerly Tuscon) Open and won it by a stroke. He rallied after a triple bogey on No. 14 to birdie the 18th and become only the second amateur in 37 years to win an official tour event. The first was Scott Verplank, who won the 1985 Western Open while a junior at Oklahoma State.

Asked if he was ready to turn pro yet, Mickelson said no, adding, "I'm just a 20-year-old kid trying to have a good time."

Mickelson was the low amateur at both the Masters and the U.S. Open, but failed to repeat as either NCAA or U.S. Amateur champion. He came back strong in the Walker Cup matches in September, however, helping the U.S. regain the Cup with a 14-10 victory over Britain and Ireland in Portmarnock. U.S. Amateur champion Mitch Voges, whose car vanity plates read "LIP OUT" was also instrumental in the victory.

On the European PGA Tour, Steven Richardson, a 24-year-old Englishman and tour sophomore, won two early events, the Girona Open and Portuguese Opens. In doing so, he stamped himself as the great new hope—a guy to step in when Faldo, Ballesteros and the others fade away.

While Faldo had won once and Woosnam twice, another hot European star wasn't even European. He was Craig Perry, part of the muscular new crop of golfers rising out of Australia. Perry won both the Italian and Scottish Opens.

Elsewhere, two of golf's most influential figures, Joe Dey and P.J.Boatwright, died. Dey, who helped shape the way the game is played today, died in March at age 83. A former executive director of the

Wide World Photos

Meg Mallon had plenty to laugh about in 1991, winning the U.S. Women's Open two weeks after her victory in the LPGA Championship.

U.S. Golf Association, he later became the first commissioner of the PGA Tour, holding the fledging organization together after its angry split with the PGA of America. Boatwright, a protege of Dey's, died in April, at 63. As executive director of rules and competitions for the USGA, he pretty much ran the U.S. Open.

And in an echo from the 1990 Shoal Creek discrimination case, Augusta National, the home of the Masters and the country's most prominent country club, admitted it first black member—Roy Townsend, a Washington, D.C. television executive. Among other clubs that changed their rules were two future U.S. Open sites, Baltusrol and Oakmont.

On the other hand, four clubs turned down lesser USGA events rather than change their policies. They were St. Louis Country Club, Chicago Golf Club, Annandale C.C., Pasadena, Calif., and Merion Golf Club, near Philadelphia. □

G O L F

S T A T I S T I C S

THE SEASON IN REVIEW
1990-1991
PGA • SENIORS • LPGA

SEC A
PAGE 691

Tournament Results

Winners of PGA, Seniors and LPGA tournaments from Nov.4, 1990 through Sept.22, 1991.

PGA Tour

LATE 1990

Last Rd	Tournament	Winner	Earnings	Runner-Up
Nov. 4	Asahi 4 Tours WCOG (Tokyo)	Australia/N.Z.(20 pts)%*	$480,000	USA (20)
Nov.10	Isuzu Kapalua International	David Peoples (264)	150,000	D.Love III (269)
Nov.18	RMCC Invitational	Fred Couples/	125,000	P.Jacobsen/
		Raymond Floyd (182)	125,000	A.Palmer (187)
Nov.25	Skins Game #8	Curtis Strange (9)*	220,000	G.Norman (5)
Nov.25	World Cup of Golf (Orlando)	GER—Bernhard Langer/	120,000	England
		Torsten Giedeon (556)	120,000	& Ireland (559)
Dec. 2	JCPenney Classic	Davis Love III/	100,000	J.Haas/
		Beth Daniel (266)	100,000	N.Lopez (271)
Dec. 9	Sazale Classic	Fred Couples/	90,000	C.Byrum/
		Mike Donald (254)	90,000	T.Byrum (258)

% Rain-shortened.
*Playoffs (2): **WCOG**—Australia/New Zealand declared winner on basis of lowest overall score; **Skins**—Strange def. Faldo for 3 skins in 4 extra holes.

1991 (through Sept.22)

Last Rd	Tournament	Winner	Earnings	Runner-Up
Jan. 6	Infiniti Tourn.of Champions	Tom Kite (272)	$144,000	L.Wadkins (273)
Jan.13	No.Telecom Open (Tucson)	a-Phil Mickelson (272)	—	T.Purtzer
				& B.Tway (273)
Jan.20	United Hawaiian Open	Lanny Wadkins (270)	198,000	J.Cook (274)
Jan.27	Phoenix Open	Nolan Henke (268)	180,000	3-way tie (269)
Feb. 3	AT&T Pebble Beach Nat'l Pro-Am	Paul Azinger (274)	198,000	B.Claar
				& C.Pavin (278)
Feb.10	Bob Hope Chrysler Classic	Corey Pavin (331)*	198,000	M.O'Meara (331)
Feb.17	Shearson Lehman Bros.Open	Jay Don Blake (268)	180,000	B.Sander (270)
Feb.24	Nissan Los Angeles Open	Ted Schulz (272)	180,000	J.Sluman (273)
Mar. 4	Doral Ryder Open	Rocco Mediate (276)*	252,000	C.Strange (276)
Mar.10	Honda Classic	Steve Pate (279)	180,000	D.Halldorson
				& P.Azinger (282)
Mar.17	Nestle Invitational	Andrew Magee (203)%	180,000	T.Sieckmann (205)
Mar.24	USF&G Classic	Ian Woosnam (275)*	180,000	J.Hallet (275)
Mar.31	The Players Championship	Steve Elkington (276)	288,000	F.Zoeller (277)
Apr. 7	Indep.Ins.Agent Open	Rained out#		
Apr.14	**The Masters** (Augusta, GA)	Ian Woosnam (277)	243,000	J.M.Olazabal (278)
Apr.14	Deposit Guaranty Classic	Larry Silveira (266)*	54,000	M.Nicolette
				& R.Cochrane (266)
Apr.21	MCI Heritage Classic	Davis Love III (271)	180,000	I.Baker-Finch(273)
Apr.28	K mart Greater Greensboro Open	Mark Brooks (275)*	225,000	G.Sauers (275)
May 5	GTE Byron Nelson Classic	Nick Price (270)	198,000	C.Stadler (271)
May 12	BellSouth Atlanta Classic	Corey Pavin (272)*	180,000	S.Pate (272)
May 19	Memorial Tournament	Kenny Perry (273)*	216,000	H.Irwin (273)
May 26	SW Bell Colonial	Tom Purtzer (267)	216,000	3-way tie (270)
June 2	Kemper Open	Billy Andrade (263)*	180,000	J.Sluman (263)
June 9	Buick Classic	Billy Andrade (273)	180,000	B.Bryant (275)
June 17	**U.S.Open** (Chaska, MN)	Payne Stewart (282)*	235,000	S.Simpson (282)
June 23	Anheuser-Busch Classic	Mike Hulbert (266)*	180,000	K.Knox (266)
June 30	Federal Express St.Jude Classic	Fred Couples (269)	180,000	R.Fehr (272)
July 7	Centel Western Open	Russ Cochran (275)	180,000	G.Norman (277)
July 14	New England Classic	Bruce Fleisher (268)*	180,000	I.Baker-Finch(268)
July 21	**British Open** (Royal Birkdale)	Ian Baker-Finch (272)	150,000	M.Harwood (274)
July 21	Chattanooga Classic	Dillard Pruitt (260)	126,000	L.Ten Broeck(262)

Tournament Results (Cont.)

Last Rd	Tournament	Winner	Earnings	Runner-Up
July 28	Canon Greater Hartford Open	Billy Ray Brown (271)*	$180,000	C.Pavin & R.Fehr (271)
Aug. 4	Buick Open	Brad Faxon (271)*	180,000	C.Beck (271)
Aug.11	PGA Championship (Carmel, IN)	John Daly (276)	230,000	B.Lietzke (279)
Aug.18	The International	Jose-Maria Olazabal (+10)	198,000	3-way tie (+7)
Aug.25	NEC World Series of Golf.....................	Tom Purtzer (279)*	216,000	J.Gallagher & D.Love (279)
Sept. 1	Greater Milwaukee Open....................	Mark Brooks (270)	180,000	R.Gamez (271)
Sept. 8	Canadian Open	Nick Price (273)	180,000	D.Edwards (274)
Sept.15	Hardee's Classic	D.A.Weibring (267)	180,000	P.Jacobsen & P.Azinger (268)
Sept.22	B.C.Open..................................	Fred Couples (269)	144,000	P.Jacobsen

%Rain-shortened;# Independent Insurance Agent Open rescheduled for Oct.23-26.

*Playoffs (14): Hope—Pavin won on 1st hole; Doral—Mediate won on 1st hole; USF&G—Woosnam won on 2nd hole; Deposit—Silveira won on 1st hole; Greensboro—Brooks won on 3rd hole; Atlanta—Pavin won on 2nd hole; Memorial—Perry won on 1st hole; Kemper—Andrade won on 1st hole; U.S.Open—Stewart def. S.Simpson, 75-77, in 18-hole playoff; Anheuser-Busch—Hulbert won on 1st hole; New England—Fleisher won on 7th hole; Hartford—Brown won on 1st hole; Buick—Faxon won on 1st hole; World Series—Purtzer won on 2nd hole.

Second place ties (3 players or more): 3-WAY—Phoenix (G.Morgan, C.Strange, T.Watson); Colonial (S.Hoch, D.Edwards, B.Lohr); International (I.Baker-Finch, S.Gump, B.Lohr).

Remaining events (12); Buick Southern Open (Sep.26-29); HEB Texas Open (Oct.3-6); Las Vegas Invitational (Oct.9-13); Walt Disney/Oldsmobile Classic (Oct.16-19); Independent Insurance Agent Open (Oct.23-26); PGA Tour Championship (Oct.31-Nov.3); Asahi Four Tours WCOG (Nov.7-10); Kapalua International (Nov.14-17); RMCC Invitational (Nov.21-24); Skins Game (Nov.30-Dec.1); JCPenny Classic (Dec.5-8) and Sazale Classic (Dec.12-15).

1991 Ryder Cup

The 29th Ryder Cup matches, Sept.27-29, at Ocean Course at Kiawah Island, S.C.

Rosters

United States: Paul Azinger, Chip Beck, Mark Calcavecchia, Fred Couples, Raymond Floyd, Hale Irwin, Wayne Levi, Mark O'Meara, Steve Pate, Corey Pavin, Payne Stewart, Lanny Wadkins, and captain Dave Stockton.

Europe: Seve Ballesteros, Paul Broadhurst, Nick Faldo, David Feherty, David Gilford, Mark James, Bernhard Langer, Colin Montgomerie, Jose-Marie Olazabal, Steve Richardson, Sam Torrance, Ian Woosnam and captain Bernard Gallacher.

First Day
MORNING ALTERNATE SHOTS

Winner	Score	Loser
Ballesteros/Olazabal	2&1	Azinger/Beck
Wadkins/Irwin	4&2	Gilford/Montgomerie
Floyd/Couples	2&1	Langer/James
Stewart/Calcavecchia	1-up	Faldo/Woosnam

USA wins, 3-1

Second Day
MORNING ALTERNATE SHOTS

Winner	Score	Loser
Azinger/O'Meara	7&6	Faldo/Gilford
Wadkins/Irwin	4&2	Feherty/Torrance
Calcavecchia/Stewart	1-up	James/Richardson
Ballesteros/Olazabal	3&2	Floyd/Couples

USA wins, 3-1
(USA leads, 7½-4½)

AFTERNOON BEST BALL

Winner	Score	Loser
Richardson/James	5&4	Calcavecchia/Pavin
O'Meara/Wadkins	tie	Torrance/Feherty
Floyd/Couples	5&3	Faldo/Woosnam
Ballesteros/Olazabal	2&1	Azinger/Beck

Europe wins, 2½-1½
(USA leads, 4½-3½)

AFTERNOON FOURBALL

Winner	Score	Loser
Woosnam/Broadhurst	2&1	Azinger/Irwin
Langer/Montgomerie	2&1	Pavin/Pate
James/Richardson	3&1	L.Wadkins/Levi
Ballesteros/Olazabal	tie	Stewart/Couples

Europe wins, 3½-½
(Match tied, 8-8)

Third Day
INDIVIDUAL MATCH PLAY

Matches Won

USA Winners	Score	Loser
Paul Azinger, USA	2-up	Jose-Marie Olazabal
Seve Ballesteros, EUR	3&2	Wayne Lev
Paul Broadhurst, USA	3&1	Mark O'Mearai
Chip Beck, EUR	3&1	Ian Woosnam
Fred Couples, USA	3&2	Sam Torrance
Nick Faldo, EUR	2-up	Raymond Floyd
David Feherty, EUR	2&1	Payne Stewart
Corey Pavin, USA	2&1	Steven Richardson
Lanny Wadkins, USA	3&2	Mark James

Matches Halved

USA	Score	Europe
Hale Irwin	tie	Bernhard Langer
Mark Calcavecchia	tie	Colin Montgomerie
Steve Pate	tie	David Gilford

Note: Pate/Gilford halved by agreement when injury forced Pate to withdraw.

USA wins day, 6½-5½
(USA wins Ryder Cup, 14½-13½)

Seniors Tour
LATE 1990

Last Rd	Tournament	Winner	Earnings	Runner-Up
Nov. 4	Security Pacific Classic	Mike Hill (201)	$75,000	G.Player (202)
Nov.11	DuPont Cup (USA at Japan)	USA (20 pts)	360,000	Japan (12)
Dec. 9	GTE Kaanapali Classic	Bob Charles (206)	67,500	L.Trevino & G.Archer (210)
Dec.16	New York Life Champions	Mike Hill (201)*	150,000	D.Douglass & L.Trevino (201)

*Playoff: NY Life—Hill won on 1st hole.

1991 (through Sept.15)

Last Rd	Tournament	Winner	Earnings	Runner-Up
Jan. 6	Infiniti Tourn.of Champions	Bruce Crampton (279)	$ 80,000	F.Beard (283)
Jan.27	Senior Skins Game #4	Jack Nicklaus (10)*	310,000	L.Trevino (7)
Feb. 3	Royal Caribbean Classic	Gary Player (200)	67,500	3-way tie (202)
Feb.10	GTE Suncoast Classic	Bob Charles (210)	67,500	G.Archer & L.Trevino (214)
Feb.17	Aetna Challenge	Lee Trevino (205)	67,500	D.Douglass (206)
Feb.24	Chrysler Cup	United States (58.5)	400,000	Int'l.team (41.5)
Mar. 3	GTE West Classic	Chi Chi Rodriguez (132)%	67,500	B.Crampton & G.Player (133)
Mar.17	Vantage at the Dominion	Lee Trevino (137)%	52,500	3-way tie (139)
Mar.24	Vintage ARCO Invitational	Chi Chi Rodriguez (206)	75,000	D.January & M.Hill (207)
Mar.31	Fuji Electric Grand Slam	Miller Barber (202)	77,000	L.Trevino (206)
Apr. 7	The Tradition	Jack Nicklaus (277)	120,000	3-way tie (278)
Apr.21	**PGA Seniors Championship**	Jack Nicklaus (271)	85,000	B.Crampton (277)
Apr.28	Doug Sanders Celebrity Classic	Mike Hill (203)	45,000	G.Archer (204)
May 5	Las Vegas Classic	Chi Chi Rodriguez (204)	67,500	W.Zembriski (207)
May 12	Murata Reunion Pro-Am	Chi Chi Rodriguez (208)*	60,000	J.Colbert (208)
May 19	Liberty Mutual Legends of Golf	Lee Trevino/ Mike Hill (252)	70,000 70,000	A.Geiberger/ H.Henning (254)
May 26	Bell Atlantic Classic	Jim Ferree (208)	82,500	J.Colbert & L.Trevino (210)
June 2	NYNEX Commemorative	Charles Coody (193)	60,000	D.Massengale (196)
June 9	Senior Players Championship	Jim Albus (279)	150,000	3-way tie (282)
June 16	MONY Syracuse Classic	Rocky Thompson (199)	60,000	J.Dent (200)
June 23	PaineWebber Invitational	Orville Moody (207)	67,500	D.Henrickson (208)
June 30	SW Bell Classic	Jim Colbert (201)	67,500	A.Geiberger & L.Laoretti (204)
July 7	Kroger Classic	Al Geiberger (203)	90,000	L.Laoretti (204)
July 14	Newport Cup	Larry Ziegler (199)	48,750	3-way tie (205)
July 21	Ameritech Open	Mike Hill (200)	75,000	B.Charles (202)
July 28	**U.S.Senior Open** (Detroit)	Jack Nicklaus (282)*	110,000	C.C.Rodriguez (282)
Aug. 4	Northville L.I. Classic	George Archer (204)	67,500	L.Laoretti & J.Colbert (206)
Aug.11	Showdown Classic	Dale Douglass (209)	52,500	G.Archer & D.Bies (210)
Aug.18	GTE Northwest Classic	Mike Hill (198)	60,000	C.C.Rodriguez (200)
Aug.25	Sunwest/Charley Pride Classic	Lee Trevino (200)	52,500	C.C.Rodriguez & J.O'Hearn (204)
Sept. 1	GTE North Classic	George Archer (199)	67,500	D.Douglass (200)
Sept. 8	First of America Classic	Harold Henning (202)*	52,500	G.Gilbert (202)
Sept.15	Digital Classic	Rocky Thompson (205)	60,000	B.Crampton (206)
Sept.22	Nationwide Championship	Mike Hill (212)	105,000	T.Shaw (213)

% Rain-shortened.
*Playoffs (4): **Sr.Skins**—Nicklaus def. G.Player for 9 skins in 3 extra hole; **Murata Reunion**—Rodriguez won on 4th hole; **U.S.Sr. Open**—Nicklaus def. Rodriguez, 65-69 in 18-hole playoff; **First of America**—Henning won on 1st hole.
Second place ties (3 players or more): 3-WAY—**Royal Caribbean** (B.Charles, C.C.Rodriguez, L.Trevino); **Vantage** (C.Coody, M.Hill, R.Thompson); **Tradition** (J.Colbert, J.Dent, P.Rodgers); **Players Championship** (B.Charles, C.Coody, D.Hill); **Newport** (G.Archer, J.Dent, T.Shaw).
Remaining events (8): Bank One Classic (Sep.27-29); Vantage Championship (Oct.4-6); Raley's Gold Rush (Oct.11-13); Trans-America Championship (Oct.18-20); Security Pacific Classic (Oct.25-27); DuPont Cup (Nov.15-17); Kaanapali Classic (Dec.6-8) and New York Life Champions (Dec.13-15).

Tournament Results (Cont.)
LPGA Tour
LATE 1990

Last Rd	Tournament	Winner	Earnings	Runner-Up
Nov. 4	Mazda Japan Classic	Debbie Massey (133)%	$82,500	D.Ammaccapane & C.Keggi (136)
Nov.18	Solheim Cup (Europe at USA)	USA (11 1/2 pts)	—	Europe (4½)
Dec. 2	JCPenney Classic	Beth Daniel/ Davis Love III (266)	100,000 100,000	N.Lopez/ J.Haas (271)
Dec. 9	Itoman World Match Play	Betsy King (2-up)	100,000	D.Richard

% Rain-shortened.

1991 (through Sept.22)

Last Rd	Tournament	Winner	Earnings	Runner-Up
Jan.20	Jamaica Classic	Jane Geddes (207)	$75,000	P.Sheehan (210)
Feb. 4	Oldsmobile Classic	Meg Mallon (276)	60,000	D.Lofland (278)
Feb.10	Phar-Mor at Inverrary	Beth Daniel (209)	75,000	N.Lopez (211)
Feb.24	Orix Hawaiian Ladies Open	Patty Sheehan (207)	52,500	B.Daniel (210)
Mar. 2	Women's Kemper Open	Deb Richard (275)*	75,000	C.Rarick (275)
Mar.10	Inamori Classic	Laura Davies (277)	60,000	J.Dickinson & L.Connelly (281)
Mar.17	Desert Inn International	Penny Hammel (211)	60,000	B.Daniel (212)
Mar.24	Standard Register Ping	D.Ammaccapane (283)	82,500	B.Bunkowsky & M.Mallon (285)
Mar.31	**Nabisco Dinah Shore**	Amy Alcott (273)	90,000	D.Mochrie (281)
Apr. 7	Ping/Welch's Championship	Chris Johnson (273)	52,500	K.Tschetter (277)
May 5	Sara Lee Classic	Nancy Lopez (206)	63,750	K.Monaghan (208)
May 12	Crestar-Farm Fresh Classic	Hollis Stacy (282)	60,000	3-way tie (283)
May 19	Centel Classic	Pat Bradley (278)	165,000	A.Okamoto (279)
May 19	Centel Senior Challenge	Sandra Palmer (143)	20,000	K.Whitworth (145)
May 26	Corning Classic	Betsy King (273)	60,000	D.Richard (279)
June 2	Rochester International	Rosie Jones (276)	60,000	D.Ammaccapane & B.Burton (278)
June 9	Atlantic City Classic	Jane Geddes (208)	45,000	C.Schreyer & A.Alcott (209)
June 1	Lady Keystone Open	Colleen Walker (207)	60,000	K.Tschetter & B.Daniel (209)
June 23	McDonald's Championship	Beth Daniel (273)	112,500	P.Bradley & S.Little (277)
June 30	**Mazda LPGA Championship**	Meg Mallon (274)	150,000	P.Bradley & A.Okamoto (275)
July 7	Jamie Farr Toledo Classic	Alice Miller (205)*	52,500	D.Richard (205)
July 14	**U.S.Women's Open** (Ft.Worth)	Meg Mallon (283)	110,000	P.Bradley (285)
July 21	JAL Big Apple Classic	Betsy King (279)	75,000	A.Okamoto (280)
July 28	Bay State Classic	Juli Inkster (275)	60,000	C.Keggi (276)
Aug. 4	Phar-Mor in Youngstown	Deb Richard (207)*	75,000	J.Geddes (207)
Aug.11	Stratton Mountain Classic	Melissa McNamara (278)	67,500	P.Sheehan (280)
Aug.18	Northgate Computer Classic	Cindy Rarick (211)*	60,000	J.Anschutz & B.Daniel (211)
Aug.25	Chicago Sun-Times Shoot-Out	Martha Nause (275)	63,750	K.Monaghan (276)
Sept. 3	Rail Charity Classic	Pat Bradley (197)	60,000	D.Ammaccapane (203)
Sept. 8	Ping-Cellular One Championship	Michelle Estill (208)	60,000	R.Jones (209)
Sept.15	**du Maurier Classic**	Nancy Scranton (279)	105,000	D.Massey (282)
Sept.22	Safeco Classic	Pat Bradley (280)*	60,000	R.Jones (280)

% Rain-shortened.

*Playoffs (5): **Kemper**—Richard won on 2nd hole; **Toledo**—Miller won on 3rd hole; **Youngstown**—Richard won on 1st hole; **Northgate**—Rarick won on 3rd hole; **Safeco**—Bradley won on 2nd hole.

Second place ties (3 players or more): 3-WAY—**Crestar** (E.Crosby, T.Green, P.Sheehan).

Remaining events (6): MBS Classic (Sep.26-29); Trophee Urban World Championship (Oct.10-13); Nichirei International (Nov.1-3); Mazda Japan Classic (Nov.8-10); JCPenny Classic (Dec.5-8) and Itoman Match Play Championship (Dec.12-15).

Money Leaders

Official Top 20 money leaders of men's, seniors and women's tours for 1990 and unofficial money leaders for 1991 (through Sept.22), as compiled by the PGA and LPGA.

PGA

FINAL 1990

Listed are tournaments played (TP), titles won (1st) and earnings for the year.

		TP	1st	Earnings
1	Greg Norman	17	2	$1,165,477
2	Wayne Levi	23	4	1,024,647
3	Payne Stewart	26	2	976,281
4	Paul Azinger	26	1	944,731
5	Jodie Mudd	23	2	911,746
6	Hale Irwin	17	2	838,249
7	Mark Calcavecchia	27	0	834,281
8	Tim Simpson	26	1	809,772
9	Fred Couples	22	1	757,999
10	Mark O'Meara	25	2	707,175
11	Gil Morgan	24	1	702,629
12	Billy Mayfair	32	0	693,658
13	Lanny Wadkins	23	1	673,433
14	Larry Mize	23	0	668,198
15	Tom Kite	22	1	658,202
16	Ian Baker-Finch	24	0	611,492
17	Chip Beck	25	0	571,816
18	Steve Elkington	26	1	548,564
19	Peter Jacobsen	22	1	547,279
20	Davis Love III	27	1	537,172

1991 (through Sept.22)

Listed are tournaments played (TP), titles won (1st) and earnings for the year.

		TP	1st	Earnings
1	Corey Pavin	21	2	$885,425
2	Fred Couples	20	2	750,683
3	Tom Purtzer	23	2	715,696
4	Steve Pate	24	1	694,597
5	Mark Brooks	25	2	620,027
6	Nick Price	20	2	617,889
7	Lanny Wadkins	20	1	615,495
8	Ian Baker-Finch	19	1	595,513
9	Davis Love III	24	1	583,691
10	Paul Azinger	18	1	570,203
11	Rocco Mediate	22	1	564,038
12	Billy Andrade	25	2	558,329
13	Jay Don Blake	23	1	486,364
14	Ian Woosnam	6	2	485,023
15	Jeff Sluman	26	0	442,097
16	Mike Hulbert	27	1	441,648
17	Andrew Magee	24	1	441,282
18	Craig Stadler	18	0	439,596
19	John Cook	21	0	434,859
20	Scott Hoch	26	0	434,851

SENIORS

FINAL 1990

Listed are tournaments played (TP), titles won (1st) and earnings for the year.

		TP	1st	Earnings
1	Lee Trevino	29	7	$1,190,518
2	Mike Hill	33	5	895,678
3	Charles Coody	33	1	762,901
4	George Archer	33	4	749,691
5	Chi Chi Rodriguez	32	3	729,788
6	Jim Dent	32	4	693,214
7	Bob Charles	28	2	584,318
8	Dale Douglass	32	1	568,198
9	Gary Player	23	1	507,268
10	Rives McBee	39	2	480,329
11	Bruce Crampton	26	2	464,569
12	Harold Henning	33	0	409,879
13	Al Geiberger	26	0	373,624
14	Dave Hill	28	0	354,046
15	Jack Nicklaus	4	2	340,000

1991 (through Sept.22)

Listed are tournaments played (TP), titles won (1st) and earnings for the year.

		TP	1st	Earnings
1	Mike Hill	25	4	$678,288
2	Chi Chi Rodriguez	25	4	629,783
3	Lee Trevino	22	3	545,954
4	George Archer	25	2	528,038
5	Bob Charles	22	1	458,027
6	Bruce Crampton	28	2	413,992
7	Dale Douglass	25	1	405,758
8	Charles Coody	25	1	379,922
9	Jim Colbert	16	1	379,631
10	Rocky Thompson	28	1	358,517
11	Jack Nicklaus	5	3	343,734
12	Jim Dent	25	0	341,867
13	Al Geiberger	19	1	338,784
14	Harold Henning	27	1	294,040
15	Gary Player	16	1	278,504

LPGA

FINAL 1990

Listed are tournaments played (TP), titles won (1st) and earnings for the year.

		TP	1st	Earnings
1	Beth Daniel	23	7	$863,578
2	Patty Sheehan	25	5	732,618
3	Betsy King	28	3	543,844
4	Cathy Gerring	30	3	487,326
5	Pat Bradley	28	3	480,018
6	Rosie Jones	25	0	353,832
7	Ayako Okamoto	21	1	302,885
8	Nancy Lopez	18	1	301,262
9	Danielle Ammaccapane	28	0	300,231
10	Cindy Rarick	30	1	259,163
11	Dawn Coe	25	0	240,478
12	Dottie Mochrie	28	1	231,410
13	Colleen Walker	28	1	225,518
14	Chris Johnson	25	1	187,486
15	Deb Richard	28	0	186,464

1991 (through Sept.22)

Listed are tournaments played (TP), titles won (1st) and earnings for the year.

		TP	1st	Earnings
1	Pat Bradley	24	3	$694,027
2	Meg Mallon	23	3	494,692
3	Beth Daniel	18	2	469,501
4	Deb Richard	24	2	366,110
5	Dottie Mochrie	25	0	357,838
6	Patty Sheehan	22	1	342,204
7	Ayako Okamoto	14	0	329,029
8	Betsy King	24	2	328,381
9	Danielle Ammaccapane	22	1	323,648
10	Jane Geddes	24	2	298,186
11	Colleen Walker	24	1	286,864
12	Rosie Jones	23	1	281,089
13	Amy Alcott	21	1	240,481
14	Judy Dickinson	26	0	225,479
15	Nancy Scranton	28	1	214,482

THE 1992 INFORMATION PLEASE SPORTS ALMANAC

GOLF STATISTICS

THROUGH THE YEARS 1860-1991

MAJOR TITLES • LEADERS

SEC B

PAGE 696

Major Championships
MEN
The Masters

The Masters has been played every year since 1934 at the Augusta National Golf Club in Augusta, GA. Both the course (6905 yards, par 72) and the tournament were created by Bobby Jones; (*) indicates playoff winner.

Multiple winners: Jack Nicklaus (6); Arnold Palmer (4); Jimmy Demaret, Gary Player and Sam Snead (3); Seve Ballesteros, Nick Faldo, Ben Hogan, Byron Nelson, Horton Smith and Tom Watson (2).

Year		Year		Year		Year	
1934	Horton Smith	1950	Jimmy Demaret	1964	Arnold Palmer	1978	Gary Player
1935	Gene Sarazen*	1951	Ben Hogan	1965	Jack Nicklaus	1979	Fuzzy Zoeller*
1936	Horton Smith	1952	Sam Snead	1966	Jack Nicklaus*		
1937	Byron Nelson	1953	Ben Hogan	1967	Gary Brewer	1980	Seve Ballesteros
1938	Henry Picard	1954	Sam Snead*	1968	Bob Goalby	1981	Tom Watson
1939	Ralph Guldahl	1955	Cary Middlecoff	1969	George Archer	1982	Craig Stadler*
		1956	Jack Burke, Jr.			1983	Seve Ballesteros
1940	Jimmy Demaret	1957	Doug Ford	1970	Billy Casper*	1984	Ben Crenshaw
1941	Craig Wood	1958	Arnold Palmer	1971	Charles Coody	1985	Bernhard Langer
1942	Byron Nelson*	1959	Art Wall, Jr.	1972	Jack Nicklaus	1986	Jack Nicklaus
1943–45	Not held			1973	Tommy Aaron	1987	Larry Mize*
1946	Herman Keiser	1960	Arnold Palmer	1974	Gary Player	1988	Sandy Lyle
1947	Jimmy Demaret	1961	Gary Player	1975	Jack Nicklaus	1989	Nick Faldo*
1948	Claude Harmon	1962	Arnold Palmer*	1976	Raymond Floyd	1990	Nick Faldo*
1949	Sam Snead	1963	Jack Nicklaus	1977	Tom Watson	1991	Ian Woosnam

*PLAYOFFS

1935: Sarazen (144) def. Craig Wood (149) in 36 holes. **1942:** Nelson (69) def. Ben Hogan (70) in 18 holes. **1954:** Snead (70) def. Ben Hogan (71) in 18 holes. **1962:** Palmer (68) def. Gary Player (71) and Dow Finsterwald (77) in 18 holes. **1966:** Nicklaus (70) def. Tommy Jacobs (72) and Gay Brewer (78) in 18 holes. **1970:** Casper (69) def. Gene Littler (74) in 18 holes. **1979:** Zoeller (4-3) def. Ed Sneed (4-4) and Tom Watson (4-4) on 2nd hole of sudden death. **1982:** Stadler (4) def. Dan Pohl (5) on 1st hole of sudden death. **1987:** Mize (4-3) def. Greg Norman (4-4) and Seve Ballesteros (5) on 2nd hole of sudden death. **1989:** Faldo (5-3) def. Scott Hoch (5-4) on 2nd hole of sudden death. **1990:** Faldo (4-4) def. Raymond Floyd (4-x) on second hole of sudden death.

U.S. Open

Played at a different course each year, the U.S. Open was launched by the new U.S. Golf Association in 1895. The Open switched from a 3-day, 36-hole Saturday finish to 4 days of play in 1965; (*) indicates playoff winner and (a) indicates amateur winner.

Multiple winners: Willie Anderson, Ben Hogan, Bobby Jones and Jack Nicklaus (4); Hale Irwin (3); Julius Boros, Billy Casper, Ralph Guldahl, Walter Hagen, John McDermott, Cary Middlecoff, Andy North, Gene Sarazen, Alex Smith, Curtis Strange and Lee Trevino (2).

Year		Year		Year		Year	
1895	Horace Rawlins	1908	Fred McLeod*	1922	Gene Sarazen	1935	Sam Parks, Jr.
1896	James Foulis	1909	George Sargent	1923	a-Bobby Jones*	1936	Tony Manero
1897	Joe Lloyd			1924	Cyril Walker	1937	Ralph Guldahl
1898	Fred Herd	1910	Alex Smith*	1925	Willie Macfarlane*	1938	Ralph Guldahl
1899	Willie Smith	1911	John McDermott*	1926	a-Bobby Jones	1939	Byron Nelson*
		1912	John McDermott	1927	Tommy Armour*		
1900	Harry Vardon	1913	a-Francis Ouimet*	1928	Johnny Farrell*	1940	Lawson Little*
1901	Willie Anderson*	1914	Walter Hagen	1929	a-Bobby Jones*	1941	Craig Wood
1902	Laurie Auchterlonie	1915	a-Jerry Travers			1942–45	Not held
1903	Willie Anderson*	1916	a-Chick Evans	1930	a-Bobby Jones	1946	Lloyd Mangrum*
1904	Willie Anderson	1917–18	Not held	1931	Billy Burke*	1947	Lew Worsham*
1905	Willie Anderson	1919	Walter Hagen*	1932	Gene Sarazen	1948	Ben Hogan
1906	Alex Smith			1933	a-John Goodman	1949	Cary Middlecoff
1907	Alex Ross	1920	Edward Ray	1934	Olin Dutra		
		1921	Jim Barnes				

Year		Year		Year		Year	
1950	Ben Hogan*	1961	Gene Littler	1972	Jack Nicklaus	1983	Larry Nelson
1951	Ben Hogan	1962	Jack Nicklaus*	1973	Johnny Miller	1984	Fuzzy Zoeller*
1952	Julius Boros	1963	Julius Boros*	1974	Hale Irwin	1985	Andy North
1953	Ben Hogan	1964	Ken Venturi	1975	Lou Graham*	1986	Raymond Floyd
1954	Ed Furgol	1965	Gary Player*	1976	Jerry Pate	1987	Scott Simpson
1955	Jack Fleck*	1966	Billy Casper*	1977	Hubert Green	1988	Curtis Strange*
1956	Cary Middlecoff	1967	Jack Nicklaus	1978	Andy North	1989	Curtis Strange
1957	Dick Mayer*	1968	Lee Trevino	1979	Hale Irwin		
1958	Tommy Bolt	1969	Orville Moody			1990	Hale Irwin*
1959	Billy Casper			1980	Jack Nicklaus	1991	Payne Stewart*
		1970	Tony Jacklin	1981	David Graham		
1960	Arnold Palmer	1971	Lee Trevino*	1982	Tom Watson		

*PLAYOFFS

1901: Anderson (85) def. Alex Smith (86) in 18 holes. **1903:** Anderson (82) def. David Brown (84) in 18 holes. **1908:** McLeod (77) def. Willie Smith (83) in 18 holes. **1910:** A.Smith (71) def. John McDermott (75) & Macdonald Smith (77) in 18 holes. **1911:** McDermott (80) def. Mike Brady (82) & George Simpson (85) in 18 holes. **1913:** Ouimet (72) def. Harry Vardon (77) & Edward Ray (78) in 18 holes. **1919:** Hagen (77) def. Mike Brady (78) in 18 holes. **1923:** Jones (76) def. Bobby Cruickshank (78) in 18 holes. **1925:** Macfarlane (75-72) def. Bobby Jones (75-73) in 36 holes. **1927:** Armour (76) def. Harry Cooper (79) in 18 holes. **1928:** Farrell (143) def. Bobby Jones (144) in 36 holes. **1929:** Jones (141) def. Al Espinosa (164) in 36 holes. **1931:** Burke (149-148) def. George Von Elm (149-149) in 72 holes. **1939:** B.Nelson (68-70) def. Craig Wood (68-73) in 36 holes. **1940:** Little (70) def. Gene Sarazen (73) in 18 holes. **1946:** Mangrum (72-72) def. Byron Nelson (72-73) and Vic Ghezzi (72-73) in 36 holes. **1947:** Worsham (69) def. Sam Snead (70) in 18 holes. **1950:** Hogan (69) def. Lloyd Mangrum (73) & George Fazio (75) in 18 holes. **1955:** Fleck (69) def. Ben Hogan (72) in 18 holes. **1957:** Mayer (72) def. Cary Middlecoff (79) in 18 holes. **1962:** Nicklaus (71) def. Arnold Palmer (74) in 18 holes. **1963:** Boros (70) def. Jacky Cupit (73) & Arnold Palmer (76) in 18 holes. **1965:** Player (71) def. Kel Nagle (74) in 18 holes. **1966:** Casper (69) def. Arnold Palmer (73) in 18 holes. **1971:** Trevino (68) def. Jack Nicklaus (71) in 18 holes. **1975:** L.Graham (71) def. John Mahaffey (73) in 18 holes. **1984:** Zoeller (67) def. Greg Norman (75) in 18 holes. **1988:** Strange (71) def. Nick Faldo (75) in 18 holes. **1990:** Irwin (74-3) def. Mike Donald (74-4) on 1st hole of sudden death after 18 holes. **1991:** Stewart (75) def. Scott Simpson (77) in 18 holes.

British Open

The oldest of the Majors, the British Open began in 1860 to determine "the champion golfer of the world." Conducted by the Royal and Ancient Golf Club of St.Andrews, The Open is rotated among select golf courses in England; (*) indicates playoff winner and (a) indicates amateur winner.

Multiple winners: Harry Vardon (6); James Braid, J.H.Taylor, Peter Thomson and Tom Watson (5); Walter Hagen, Bobby Locke, Tom Morris Sr, Tom Morris Jr, and Willie Park (4); Jamie Anderson, Seve Ballesteros, Henry Cotton, Robert Ferguson, Bobby Jones, Jack Nicklaus and Gary Player; Nick Faldo, Harold Hilton, Bob Martin, Arnold Palmer, Willie Park Jr, Lee Trevino (2).

Year		Year		Year		Year	
1860	Willie Park	1887	Willie Park, Jr.	1913	J.H.Taylor	1948	Henry Cotton
1861	Tom Morris, Sr.	1888	Jack Burns	1914	Harry Vardon	1949	Bobby Locke*
1862	Tom Morris, Sr.	1889	Willie Park, Jr.*	1915–19	Not held	1950	Bobby Locke
1863	Willie Park			1920	George Duncan	1951	Max Faulkner
1864	Tom Morris, Sr.	1890	a-John Ball	1921	Jock Hutchison*	1952	Bobby Locke
1865	Andrew Strath	1891	Hugh Kirkaldy	1922	Walter Hagen	1953	Ben Hogan
1866	Willie Park	1892	a-Harold Hilton	1923	Arthur Havers	1954	Peter Thomson
1867	Tom Morris, Sr.	1893	Wm.Auchterlinie	1924	Walter Hagen	1955	Peter Thomson
1868	Tom Morris, Jr.	1894	J.H.Taylor	1925	Jim Barnes	1956	Peter Thomson
1869	Tom Morris, Jr.	1895	J.H.Taylor	1926	a-Bobby Jones	1957	Bobby Locke
		1896	Harry Vardon*	1927	a-Bobby Jones	1958	Peter Thomson*
1870	Tom Morris, Jr.	1897	a-Harold Hilton	1928	Walter Hagen	1959	Gary Player
1871	Not held	1898	Harry Vardon	1929	Walter Hagen		
1872	Tom Morris, Jr.	1899	Harry Vardon			1960	Kel Nagle
1873	Tom Kidd			1930	a-Bobby Jones	1961	Arnold Palmer
1874	Mungo Park	1900	J.H.Taylor	1931	Tommy Armour	1962	Arnold Palmer
1875	Willie Park	1901	James Braid	1932	Gene Sarazen	1963	Bob Charles*
1876	Bob Martin*	1902	Sandy Herd	1933	Denny Shute*	1964	Tony Lema
1877	Jamie Anderson	1903	Harry Vardon	1934	Henry Cotton	1965	Peter Thomson
1878	Jamie Anderson	1904	Jack White	1935	Alf Perry	1966	Jack Nicklaus
1879	Jamie Anderson	1905	James Braid	1936	Alf Padgham	1967	Roberto de Vicenzo
1880	Bob Ferguson	1906	James Braid	1937	Henry Cotton	1968	Gary Player
1881	Bob Ferguson	1907	Arnaud Massy	1938	Reg Whitcombe	1969	Tony Jacklin
1882	Bob Ferguson	1908	James Braid	1939	Dick Burton		
1883	Willie Fernie*	1909	J.H.Taylor	1940–45	Not held	1970	Jack Nicklaus*
1884	Jack Simpson			1946	Sam Snead	1971	Lee Trevino
1885	Bob Martin	1910	James Braid	1947	Fred Daly	1972	Lee Trevino
1886	David Brown	1911	Harry Vardon*			1973	Tom Weiskopf
		1912	Ted Ray				

British Open (Cont.)

Year		Year		Year		Year	
1974	Gary Player*	1979	Seve Ballesteros	1984	Seve Ballesteros	1989	Mark Calcavecchia
1975	Tom Watson*	1980	Tom Watson	1985	Sandy Lyle	1990	Nick Faldo
1976	Johnny Miller	1981	Bill Rogers	1986	Greg Norman	1991	Ian Baker-Finch
1977	Tom Watson	1982	Tom Watson	1987	Nick Faldo		
1978	Jack Nicklaus	1983	Tom Watson	1988	Seve Ballesteros		

*PLAYOFFS

1876: Martin awarded title when David Strath refused playoff. **1883:** Fernie (158) def. Robert Ferguson (159) in 36 holes. **1889:** Park (158) def. Andrew Kirkaldy (163) in 36 holes. **1896:** Vardon (157) def. John H.Taylor (161) in 36 holes. **1911:** Vardon won when Arnaud Massy conceded at 35th hole. **1921:** Hutchison (150) def. Roger Wethered (159) in 36 holes. **1933:** Shute (149) def. Craig Wood (154) in 36 holes. **1949:** Locke (135) def. Harry Bradshaw (147) in 36 holes. **1958:** Thomson (139) def. Dave Thomas (143) in 36 holes. **1963:** Charles (140) def. Phil Rodgers (148) in 36 holes. **1970:** Nicklaus (72) def. Doug Sanders (73) in 18 holes. **1975:** Watson (71) def. Jack Newton (72) in 18 holes. **1989:** Calcavecchia (4-3-3—13) def. Wayne Grady (4-4-4-4—16) and Greg Norman (3-3-4-x) in 4 holes.

PGA Championship

The PGA Championship began in 1916 as a professional golfers match play tournament, but switched to stroke play in 1958. Conducted by the PGA of America, the tournament is played on a different course each year.

Multiple winners: Walter Hagen and Jack Nicklaus (5); Gene Sarazen and Sam Snead (3); Jim Barnes, Leo Diegel, Raymond Floyd, Ben Hogan, Byron Nelson, Larry Nelson, Gary Player, Paul Runyan, Denny Shute, Dave Stockton and Lee Trevino (2).

Year		Year		Year		Year	
1916	Jim Barnes	1936	Denny Shute	1955	Doug Ford	1974	Lee Trevino
1917–18	Not held	1937	Denny Shute	1956	Jack Burke, Jr.	1975	Jack Nicklaus
1919	Jim Barnes	1938	Paul Runyan	1957	Lionel Hebert	1976	Dave Stockton
1920	Jock Hutchison	1939	Henry Picard	1958	Dow Finsterwald	1977	Lanny Wadkins*
1921	Walter Hagen	1940	Byron Nelson	1959	Bob Rosburg	1978	John Mahaffey*
1922	Gene Sarazen	1941	Vic Ghezzi	1960	Jay Hebert	1979	David Graham*
1923	Gene Sarazen	1942	Sam Snead	1961	Jerry Barber*	1980	Jack Nicklaus
1924	Walter Hagen	1943	Not held	1962	Gary Player	1981	Larry Nelson
1925	Walter Hagen	1944	Bob Hamilton	1963	Jack Nicklaus	1982	Raymond Floyd
1926	Walter Hagen	1945	Byron Nelson	1964	Bobby Nichols	1983	Hal Sutton
1927	Walter Hagen	1946	Ben Hogan	1965	Dave Marr	1984	Lee Trevino
1928	Leo Diegel	1947	Jim Ferrier	1966	Al Geiberger	1985	Hubert Green
1929	Leo Diegel	1948	Ben Hogan	1967	Don January*	1986	Bob Tway
1930	Tommy Armour	1949	Sam Snead	1968	Julius Boros	1987	Larry Nelson*
1931	Tom Creavy	1950	Chandler Harper	1969	Raymond Floyd	1988	Jeff Sluman
1932	Olin Dutra	1951	Sam Snead	1970	Dave Stockton	1989	Payne Stewart
1933	Gene Sarazen	1952	Jim Turnesa	1971	Jack Nicklaus	1990	Wayne Grady
1934	Paul Runyan	1953	Walter Burkemo	1972	Gary Player	1991	John Daly
1935	Johnny Revolta	1954	Chick Harbert	1973	Jack Nicklaus		

*PLAYOFFS

1961: J.Barber (67) def. Don January (68) in 18 holes. **1967:** January (69) def. Don Massengale (71) in 18 holes. **1977:** L.Wadkins (4-4-4) def. Gene Littler (4-4-5) on 3rd hole of sudden death. **1978:** Mahaffey (4-3) def. Jerry Pate (4-4) and Tom Watson (4-5) on 2nd hole of sudden death. **1979:** D.Graham (4-4-2) def. Ben Crenshaw (4-4-4) on 3rd hole of sudden death. **1987:** Nelson (4) def. Lanny Wadkins (5) on 1st hole of sudden death.

U.S. Amateur

Match play from 1895-64, stroke play from 1965-72, match play since 1972.

Multiple winners: Bobby Jones (5); Jerry Travers (4); Walter Travis (3); Deane Beman, Charles Coe, Gary Cowan, H.Chandler Egan, Chick Evans, Lawson Little, Jack Nicklaus, Francis Ouimet, Jay Sigel, William Turnesa, Bud Ward, Harvie Ward and H.J.Whigham (2).

Year		Year		Year		Year	
1895	Charles Macdonald	1907	Jerry Travers	1920	Chick Evans	1932	Ross Somerville
1896	H.J.Whigham	1908	Jerry Travers	1921	Jesse Guilford	1933	George Dunlap
1897	H.J.Whigham	1909	Robert Gardner	1922	Jess Sweetser	1934	Lawson Little
1898	Findlay Douglas	1910	W.C.Fownes, Jr.	1923	Max Marston	1935	Lawson Little
1899	H.M.Harriman	1911	Harold Hilton	1924	Bobby Jones	1936	John Fischer
1900	Walter Travis	1912	Jerry Travers	1925	Bobby Jones	1937	John Goodman
1901	Walter Travis	1913	Jerry Travers	1926	George Von Elm	1938	William Turnesa
1902	Louis James	1914	Francis Ouimet	1927	Bobby Jones	1939	Bud Ward
1903	Walter Travis	1915	Robert Gardner	1928	Bobby Jones	1940	Richard Chapman
1904	H.Chandler Egan	1916	Chick Evans	1929	Harrison Johnston	1941	Bud Ward
1905	H.Chandler Egan	1917–18	Not held	1930	Bobby Jones	1942–45	Not held
1906	Eben Byers	1919	Davidson Herron	1931	Francis Ouimet	1946	Ted Bishop

Year		Year		Year		Year	
1947	Skee Riegel	1959	Jack Nicklaus	1970	Lanny Wadkins	1982	Jay Sigel
1948	William Turnesa			1971	Gary Cowan	1983	Jay Sigel
1949	Charles Coe	1960	Deane Beman	1972	Vinny Giles	1984	Scott Verplank
		1961	Jack Nicklaus	1973	Craig Stadler	1985	Sam Randolph
1950	Sam Urzetta	1962	Labron Harris	1974	Jerry Pate	1986	Buddy Alexander
1951	Billy Maxwell	1963	Deane Beman	1975	Fred Ridley	1987	Billy Mayfair
1952	Jack Westland	1964	Bill Campbell	1976	Bill Sander	1988	Eric Meeks
1953	Gene Littler	1965	Bob Murphy	1977	John Fought	1989	Chris Patton
1954	Arnold Palmer	1966	Gary Cowan	1978	John Cook		
1955	Harvie Ward	1967	Bob Dickson	1979	Mark O'Meara	1990	Phil Mickelson
1956	Harvie Ward	1968	Bruce Fleisher			1991	Mitch Voges
1957	Hillman Robbins	1969	Steve Melnyk	1980	Hal Sutton		
1958	Charles Coe			1981	Nathanial Crosby		

British Amateur

Match play since 1885.

Multiple winners: John Ball (8); Michael Bonallack (5); Harold Hilton (4); Joe Carr (3); Horace Hutchinson, Ernest Holderness, Trevor Homer, Johnny Laidley, Lawson Little, Peter McEvoy, Dick Siderowf, Frank Stranahan, Freddie Tait and Cyril Tolley (2).

Year		Year		Year		Year	
1885	Allen MacFie	1912	John Ball	1947	William Turnesa	1970	Michael Bonallack
1886	Horace Hutchinson	1913	Harold Hilton	1948	Frank Stranahan	1971	Steve Melnyk
1887	Horace Hutchinson	1914	J.L.C. Jenkins	1949	Samuel McCready	1972	Trevor Homer
1888	John Ball	1915–19	Not held			1973	Dick Siderowf
1889	Johnny Laidley			1950	Frank Stranahan	1974	Trevor Homer
		1920	Cyril Tolley	1951	Richard Chapman	1975	Vinny Giles
1890	John Ball	1921	William Hunter	1952	Harvie Ward	1976	Dick Siderowf
1891	Johnny Laidlay	1922	Ernest Holderness	1953	Joe Carr	1977	Peter McEvoy
1892	John Ball	1923	Roger Wethered	1954	Douglas Bachli	1978	Peter McEvoy
1893	Peter Anderson	1924	Ernest Holderness	1955	Joe Conrad	1979	Jay Sigel
1894	John Ball	1925	Robert Harris	1956	John Beharrell		
1895	Leslie Balfour	1926	Jesse Sweetser	1957	Reid Jack	1980	Duncan Evans
1896	Freddie Tait	1927	William Tweedell	1958	Joe Carr	1981	Phillipe Ploujoux
1897	Jack Allen	1928	Thomas Perkins	1959	Deane Beman	1982	Martin Thompson
1898	Freddie Tait	1929	Cyril Tolley			1983	Philip Parkin
1899	John Ball			1960	Joe Carr	1984	Jose-Maria Olazabal
		1930	Bobby Jones	1961	Michael Bonallack	1985	Garth McGimpsey
1900	Harold Hilton	1931	Eric Smith	1962	Richard Davies	1986	David Curry
1901	Harold Hilton	1932	John deForest	1963	Michael Lunt	1987	Paul Mayo
1902	Charles Hutchings	1933	Michael Scott	1964	Gordon Clark	1988	Christian Hardin
1903	Robert Maxwell	1934	Lawson Little	1965	Michael Bonallack	1989	Stephen Dodd
1904	Walter Travis	1935	Lawson Little	1966	Bobby Cole		
1905	Arthur Barry	1936	Hector Thomson	1967	Bob Dickson	1990	Rolf Muntz
1906	James Robb	1937	Robert Sweeny, Jr.	1968	Michael Bonallack	1991	Gary Wolstenholme
1907	John Ball	1938	Charles Yates	1969	Michael Bonallack		
1908	E.A.Lassen	1939	Alexander Kyle				
1909	Robert Maxwell						
		1940–45	Not held				
1910	John Ball	1946	James Bruen				
1911	Harold Hilton						

Major Championship Leaders

Through 1991; active players in **bold** type.

	US Open	British Open	PGA	Masters	US Am	British Am	Total
Jack Nicklaus	4	3	5	6	2	0	20
Bobby Jones	4	3	0	0	5	1	13
Walter Hagen	2	4	5	0	0	0	11
Ben Hogan	4	1	2	2	0	0	9
Gary Player	1	3	2	3	0	0	9
John Ball	0	1	0	0	0	8	9
Arnold Palmer	1	2	0	4	1	0	8
Tom Watson	1	5	0	2	0	0	8
Harold Hilton	0	2	0	0	1	4	7
Gene Sarazen	2	1	3	1	0	0	7
Sam Snead	0	1	3	3	0	0	7
Harry Vardon	1	6	0	0	0	0	7
Lee Trevino	2	2	2	0	0	0	6

Tournaments: U.S. Open, British Open, PGA Championship, Masters, U.S. Amateur, and British Amateur.

Grand Slam Summary

MEN

The only golfer ever to win a recognized Grand Slam—four major championships in a single season—was Bobby Jones in 1930. That year, Jones won the U.S. and British Opens as well as the U.S. and British Amateurs.

The men's professional Grand Slam—the Masters, U.S. Open, British Open and PGA Championship—did not gain acceptance until 30 years later when Arnold Palmer won the 1960 Masters and U.S. Open. The media wrote that the popular Palmer was chasing the "new" Grand Slam and would have to win the British Open and the PGA to claim it. He did not, but then nobody has before or since.

Three wins in one year (1): Ben Hogan (1953).

Two wins in one year (16): Jack Nicklaus (5 times); Ben Hogan, Arnold Palmer and Tom Watson (twice); Nick Faldo, Gary Player, Sam Snead, Lee Trevino and Craig Wood (once).

Year	Masters	US Open	Brit.Open	PGA	Year	Masters	US Open	Brit.Open	PGA
1934	H.Smith	Dutra	Cotton	Runyan	1963	Nicklaus	Boros	Charles	Nicklaus
1935	Sarazen	Parks	Perry	Revolta	1964	Palmer	Venturi	Lema	Nichols
1936	H.Smith	Manero	Padgham	Shute	1965	Nicklaus	Player	Thomson	Marr
1937	B.Nelson	Guldahl	Cotton	Shute	1966	Nicklaus	Casper	Nicklaus	Geiberger
1938	Picard	Guldahl	Whitcombe	Runyan	1967	Brewer	Nicklaus	DeVicenzo	January
1939	Guldahl	B.Nelson	Burton	Picard	1968	Goalby	Trevino	Player	Boros
					1969	Archer	Moody	Jacklin	Floyd
1940	Demaret	Little	—	B.Nelson					
1941	Wood	Wood	—	Ghezzi	1970	Casper	Jacklin	Nicklaus	Stockton
1942	B.Nelson	—	—	Snead	1971	Coody	Trevino	Trevino	Nicklaus
1943	—	—	—	—	1972	Nicklaus	Nicklaus	Trevino	Player
1944	—	—	—	Hamilton	1973	Aaron	J.Miller	Weiskopf	Nicklaus
1945	—	—	—	B.Nelson	1974	Player	Irwin	Player	Trevino
1946	Keiser	Mangrum	Snead	Hogan	1975	Nicklaus	L.Graham	T.Watson	Nicklaus
1947	Demaret	Worsham	F. Daly	Ferrier	1976	Floyd	J.Pate	Miller	Stockton
1948	Harmon	Hogan	Cotton	Hogan	1977	T.Watson	H.Green	T.Watson	L.Wadkins
1949	Snead	Middlecoff	Locke	Snead	1978	Player	North	Nicklaus	Mahaffey
1950	Demaret	Hogan	Locke	Harper	1979	Zoeller	Irwin	Ballesteros	D.Graham
1951	Hogan	Hogan	Faulkner	Snead	1980	Ballesteros	Nicklaus	T.Watson	Nicklaus
1952	Snead	Boros	Locke	Turnesa	1981	T.Watson	D.Graham	Rogers	L.Nelson
1953	**Hogan**	**Hogan**	**Hogan**	Burkemo	1982	Stadler	T.Watson	T.Watson	Floyd
1954	Snead	Furgol	Thomson	Harbert	1983	Ballesteros	L.Nelson	T.Watson	Sutton
1955	Middlecoff	Fleck	Thomson	Ford	1984	Crenshaw	Zoeller	Ballesteros	Trevino
1956	Burke	Middlecoff	Thomson	Burke	1985	Langer	North	Lyle	H.Green
1957	Ford	Mayer	Locke	L.Hebert	1986	Nicklaus	Floyd	Norman	Tway
1958	Palmer	Bolt	Thomson	Finsterwald	1987	Mize	S.Simpson	Faldo	L.Nelson
1959	Wall	Casper	Player	Rosburg	1988	Lyle	Strange	Ballesteros	Sluman
					1989	Faldo	Strange	Calcav'chia	Stewart
1960	Palmer	Palmer	Nagle	J.Hebert					
1961	Player	Littler	Palmer	J.Barber	1990	Faldo	Irwin	Faldo	Grady
1962	Palmer	Nicklaus	Palmer	Player	1991	Woosnam	Stewart	Baker-Finch	J. Daly

Major Championships

WOMEN

U.S. Women's Open

The U.S. Women's Open began under the direction of the defunct Women's Professional Golfers Assn. in 1946, passed to the LPGA in 1949 and to the U.S.GA in 1953. The tournament used a match play format its first year then switched to stroke play; (*) indicates playoff winner and (a) indicates amateur winner.

Multiple winners: Betsy Rawls and Mickey Wright (4); Susie M.Berning, Hollis Stacy and Babe Zaharias (3); JoAnne Carner, Donna Caponi, Betsy King and Louise Suggs (2).

Year		Year		Year		Year	
1946	Patty Berg	1958	Mickey Wright	1970	Donna Caponi	1981	Pat Bradley
1947	Betty Jameson	1959	Mickey Wright	1971	JoAnne Carner	1982	Janet Anderson
1948	Babe Zaharias			1972	Susie M.Berning	1983	Jan Stephenson
1949	Louise Suggs	1960	Betsy Rawls	1973	Susie M.Berning	1984	Hollis Stacy
		1961	Mickey Wright	1974	Sandra Haynie	1985	Kathy Baker
1950	Babe Zaharias	1962	Murle Lindstrom	1975	Sandra Palmer	1986	Jane Geddes*
1951	Betsy Rawls	1963	Mary Mills	1976	JoAnne Carner*	1987	Laura Davies*
1952	Louise Suggs	1964	Mickey Wright*	1977	Hollis Stacy	1988	Liselotte Neumann
1953	Betsy Rawls*	1965	Carol Mann	1978	Hollis Stacy	1989	Betsy King
1954	Babe Zaharias	1966	Sandra Spuzich	1979	Jerilyn Britz		
1955	Fay Crocker	1967	a-Catherine Lacoste	1980	Amy Alcott	1990	Betsy King
1956	Kathy Cornelius*	1968	Susie M.Berning			1991	Meg Mallon
1957	Betsy Rawls	1969	Donna Caponi				

*PLAYOFFS

1953: Rawls (71) def. Jackie Pung (77) in 18 holes. **1956:** Cornelius (75) def. Barbara McIntire (82) in 18 holes. **1964:** Wright (70) def. Ruth Jessen (72) in 18 holes. **1976:** Carner (76) def. Sandra Palmer (78) in 18 holes. **1986:** Geddes (71) def. Sally Little (73) in 18 holes. **1987:** Davies (71) def. Ayako Okamoto (73) and JoAnne Carner (74) in 18 holes.

LPGA Championship

Officially the Mazda LPGA Championship since 1987, the tournament began in 1955 and has had extended stays at the Stardust CC in Las Vegas (1961-66), Pleasant Valley CC in Sutton, MA (1967-68,70-74) and the Jack Nicklaus Sports Center at Kings Island, Ohio (1978-89); (*) indicates playoff winner.

Multiple winners: Mickey Wright (4); Nancy Lopez and Kathy Whitworth (3); Donna Caponi, Sandra Haynie, Mary Mills, Betsy Rawls and Patty Sheehan (2).

Year		Year		Year		Year	
1955	Beverly Hanson	1965	Sandra Haynie	1974	Sandra Haynie	1983	Patty Sheehan
1956	Marlene Hagge*	1966	Gloria Ehret	1975	Kathy Whitworth	1984	Patty Sheehan
1957	Louise Suggs	1967	Kathy Whitworth	1976	Betty Burfeindt	1985	Nancy Lopez
1958	Mickey Wright	1968	Sandra Post*	1977	Chako Higuchi	1986	Pat Bradley
1959	Betsy Rawls	1969	Betsy Rawls	1978	Nancy Lopez	1987	Jane Geddes
				1979	Donna Caponi	1988	Sherri Turner
1960	Mickey Wright	1970	Shirley Englehorn*			1989	Nancy Lopez
1961	Mickey Wright	1971	Kathy Whitworth	1980	Sally Little		
1962	Judy Kimball	1972	Kathy Ahern	1981	Donna Caponi	1990	Beth Daniel
1963	Mickey Wright	1973	Mary Mills	1982	Jan Stephenson	1991	Meg Mallon
1964	Mary Mills						

*PLAYOFFS

1956: Hagge def. Patti Berg in sudden death. **1968:** Post (68) def. Kathy Whitworth (75) in 18-holes. **1970:** Englehorn def. Kathy Whitworth in sudden death.

Nabisco Dinah Shore

Formerly known as the Colgate Dinah Shore from 1972-81, the tournament become the LPGA's fourth designated major championship in 1983. Named after the entertainer, this tourney has been played at Mission Hills CC in Rancho Mirage, CA since it began; (*) indicates playoff winner.

Multiple winners (as a major): Amy Alcott (3); Juli Inkster and Betsy King (2).

Year		Year		Year		Year	
1972	Jane Blalock	1977	Kathy Whitworth	1982	Sally Little	1987	Betsy King*
1973	Mickey Wright	1978	Sandra Post	1983	Amy Alcott	1988	Amy Alcott
1974	Jo Ann Prentice	1979	Sandra Post	1984	Juli Inkster*	1989	Juli Inkster
1975	Sandra Palmer	1980	Donna Caponi	1985	Alice Miller	1990	Betsy King
1976	Judy Rankin	1981	Nancy Lopez	1986	Pat Bradley	1991	Amy Alcott

*PLAYOFFS

1984: Inkster def. Pat Bradley in sudden death. **1987:** King def. Patty Sheehan in sudden death.

du Maurier Classic

Formerly known as La Canadienne in 1973 and the Peter Jackson Classic from 1974-83, this Canadian stop on the LPGA Tour became the third designated major championship in 1979; (*) indicates playoff winner.

Multiple winner (as a major): Pat Bradley (3).

Year		Year		Year		Year	
1973	Jocelyne Bourassa	1978	JoAnne Carner	1983	Hollis Stacy	1987	Jody Rosenthal
1974	Carole Jo Skala	1979	Amy Alcott	1984	Juli Inkster	1988	Sally Little
1975	JoAnne Carner	1980	Pat Bradley	1985	Pat Bradley	1989	Tammie Green
1976	Donna Caponi	1981	Jan Stephenson	1986	Pat Bradley*	1990	Cathy Johnston
1977	Judy Rankin	1982	Sandra Haynie			1991	Nancy Scranton

*PLAYOFF

1986: Bradley def. Ayako Okamoto in sudden death.

Titleholders Championship (1937–72)

The Titleholders was considered a major title on the women's tour until it was discontinued after the 1972 tournament.

Multiple winners: Patty Berg (7); Louise Suggs (4); Babe Zaharias (3); Dorothy Kirby, Marilynn Smith, Kathy Whitworth and Mickey Wright (2).

Year		Year		Year		Year	
1937	Patty Berg	1947	Babe Zaharias	1955	Patty Berg	1963	Marilynn Smith
1938	Patty Berg	1948	Patty Berg	1956	Louise Suggs	1964	Marilynn Smith
1939	Patty Berg	1949	Peggy Kirk	1957	Patty Berg	1965	Kathy Whitworth
				1958	Beverly Hanson	1966	Kathy Whitworth
1940	Betty Hicks	1950	Babe Zaharias	1959	Louise Suggs	1967-71	Not held
1941	Dorothy Kirby	1951	Pat O'Sullivan				
1942	Dorothy Kirby	1952	Babe Zaharias	1960	Fay Crocker	1972	Sandra Palmer
1943-45	Not held	1953	Patty Berg	1961	Mickey Wright		
1946	Louise Suggs	1954	Louise Suggs	1962	Mickey Wright		

Western Open (1937–67)

The Western Open was considered a major title on the women's tour until it was discontinued after the 1967 tournament.

Multiple winners: Patty Berg (7); Louise Suggs and Babe Zaharias (4); Mickey Wright (3); Betty Jameson and Betsy Rawls (2).

Year		Year		Year		Year	
1937	Betty Hicks	1945	Babe Zaharias	1953	Louise Suggs	1961	Mary Lena Faulk
1938	Bea Barrett	1946	Louise Suggs	1954	Betty Jameson	1962	Mickey Wright
1939	Helen Dettweiler	1947	Louise Suggs	1955	Patty Berg	1963	Mickey Wright
1940	Babe Zaharias	1948	Patty Berg	1956	Beverly Hanson	1964	Carol Mann
1941	Patty Berg	1949	Louise Suggs	1957	Patty Berg	1965	Susie Maxwell
1942	Betty Jameson	1950	Babe Zaharias	1958	Patty Berg	1966	Mickey Wright
1943	Patty Berg	1951	Patty Berg	1959	Betsy Rawls	1967	Kathy Whitworth
1944	Babe Zaharias	1952	Betsy Rawls	1960	Joyce Ziske		

U.S. Women's Amateur

Stroke play in 1895, match play since 1896.

Multiple winners: Glenna Collett Vare (6); JoAnne Gunderson Carner (5); Margaret Curtis, Beatrix Hoyt, Dorothy Campbell Hurd, Juli Inkster, Alexa Stirling, Virginia Van Wie, Anne Quast Decker Welts (3); Kay Cockerill, Beth Daniel, Katherine Harley, Genevieve Hecker, Betty Jameson and Barbara McIntire (2).

Year		Year		Year		Year	
1895	Mrs.Chas.S. Brown	1920	Alexa Stirling	1947	Louise Suggs	1970	Martha Wilkinson
1896	Beatrix Hoyt	1921	Marion Hollins	1948	Grace Lenczyk	1971	Laura Baugh
1897	Beatrix Hoyt	1922	Glenna Collett	1949	Dorothy Porter	1972	Mary Budke
1898	Beatrix Hoyt	1923	Edith Cummings			1973	Carol Semple
1899	Ruth Underhill	1924	Dorothy C. Hurd	1950	Beverly Hanson	1974	Cynthia Hill
		1925	Glenna Collett	1951	Dorothy Kirby	1975	Beth Daniel
1900	Frances Griscom	1926	Helen Stetson	1952	Jacqueline Pung	1976	Donna Horton
1901	Genevieve Hecker	1927	Miriam Burns Horn	1953	Mary Lena Faulk	1977	Beth Daniel
1902	Genevieve Hecker	1928	Glenna Collett	1954	Barbara Romack	1978	Cathy Sherk
1903	Bessie Anthony	1929	Glenna Collett	1955	Patricia Lesser	1979	Carolyn Hill
1904	Georgianna Bishop	1930	Glenna Collett	1956	Marlene Stewart		
1905	Pauline Mackay	1931	Helen Hicks	1957	JoAnne Gunderson	1980	Juli Inkster
1906	Harriot Curtis	1932	Virginia Van Wie	1958	Anne Quast	1981	Juli Inkster
1907	Margaret Curtis	1933	Virginia Van Wie	1959	Barbara McIntire	1982	Juli Inkster
1908	Katherine Harley	1934	Virginia Van Wie			1983	Joanne Pacillo
1909	Dorothy Campbell	1935	Glenna Collett Vare	1960	JoAnne Gunderson	1984	Deb Richard
		1936	Pamela Barton	1961	Anne Quast Decker	1985	Michiko Hattori
1910	Dorothy Campbell	1937	Estelle Lawson	1962	JoAnne Gunderson	1986	Kay Cockerill
1911	Margaret Curtis	1938	Patty Berg	1963	Anne Quast Welts	1987	Kay Cockerill
1912	Margaret Curtis	1939	Betty Jameson	1964	Barbara McIntire	1988	Pearl Sinn
1913	Gladys Ravenscroft			1965	Jean Ashley	1989	Vicki Goetze
1914	Katherine Harley	1940	Betty Jameson	1966	JoAnne G. Carner		
1915	Florence Vanderbeck	1941	Elizabeth Hicks	1967	Mary Lou Dill	1990	Pat Hurst
1916	Alexa Stirling	1942-45	Not held	1968	JoAnne G. Carner	1991	Amy Fruhwirth
1917	Not held	1946	Babe D. Zaharias	1969	Catherine Lacoste		
1918	Not held						
1919	Alexa Stirling						

Major Championship Leaders

Through 1991; active players in **bold** type.

	US Open	LPGA	duM	Dinah	Title-holders	Western	US Am	Brit Am	Total
Patty Berg	1	0	0	0	7	7	1	0	**16**
Mickey Wright	4	4	0	0	2	3	0	0	**13**
Louise Suggs	2	1	0	0	4	4	1	1	**13**
Babe Zaharias	3	0	0	0	3	4	1	1	**12**
Betsy Rawls	4	2	0	0	0	2	0	0	**8**
JoAnne Carner	2	0	0	0	0	0	5	0	**7**
Kathy Whitworth	0	3	0	0	2	1	0	0	**6**
Pat Bradley	1	1	3	1	0	0	0	0	**6**
Julie Inkster	0	0	1	2	0	0	3	0	**6**
Glenna C. Vare	0	0	0	0	0	0	6	0	**6**

Tournaments: U.S. Open, LPGA Championship, du Maurier Classic, Nabisco Dinah Shore, Titleholders (1937-72), Western Open (1937-67), U.S. Amateur, and British Amateur.

Grand Slam Summary
WOMEN

The women's Grand Slam has consisted of four tournaments only 19 years. From 1955-66, the U.S. Open, LPGA Championship, Western Open and Titleholders tournaments served as the major events. Since 1983, the U.S. Open, LPGA, du Maurier Classic in Canada and Nabisco Dinah Shore have been the major events. No one has won a four-event Grand Slam on the women's tour.

Three wins in one year (3): Babe Zaharias (1950), Mickey Wright (1961) and Pat Bradley (1986).

Two wins in one year (14): Patty Berg and Mickey Wright (3 times); Louise Suggs (twice); Sandra Haynie, Juli Inkster, Betsy King, Meg Mallon, Betsy Rawls and Kathy Whitworth (once).

Year	LPGA	US Open	T'holders	Western
1937	—	—	Berg	Hicks
1938	—	—	Berg	Barrett
1939	—	—	Berg	Dettweiler
1940	—	—	Hicks	Zaharias
1941	—	—	Kirby	Berg
1942	—	—	Kirby	Jameson
1943	—	—	—	Berg
1944	—	—	—	Zaharias
1945	—	—	—	Zaharias
1946	—	Berg	Suggs	Suggs
1947	—	Jameson	Zaharias	Suggs
1948	—	Zaharias	Berg	Berg
1949	—	Suggs	Kirk	Suggs
1950	—	**Zaharias**	**Zaharias**	**Zaharias**
1951	—	Rawls	O'Sullivan	Berg
1952	—	Suggs	Zaharias	Rawls
1953	—	Rawls	Berg	Suggs
1954	—	Zaharias	Suggs	Jameson
1955	Hanson	Crocker	Berg	Berg
1956	Hagge	Cornelius	Suggs	Hanson
1957	Suggs	Rawls	Berg	Berg
1958	Wright	Wright	Hanson	Berg
1959	Rawls	Wright	Suggs	Rawls
1960	Wright	Rawls	Crocker	Ziske
1961	**Wright**	**Wright**	**Wright**	Faulk
1962	Kimball	Breer	Wright	Wright
1963	Wright	Mills	M.Smith	Wright
1964	Mills	Wright	M.Smith	Mann
1965	Haynie	Mann	Whitworth	Berning

Year	LPGA	US Open	T'holders	Western
1966	Ehret	Spuzich	Whitworth	Wright
1967	Whitworth	a-LaCoste	—	Whitworth
1968	Post	Berning	—	—
1969	Rawls	Caponi	—	—
1970	Englehorn	Caponi	—	—
1971	Whitworth	Carner	—	—
1972	Ahern	Berning	Palmer	—
1973	Mills	Berning	—	—
1974	Haynie	Haynie	—	—
1975	Whitworth	Palmer	—	—
1976	Burfeindt	Carner	—	—
1977	Higuchi	Stacy	—	—
1978	Lopez	Stacy	—	—

Year	LPGA	US Open	duMaurier	D.Shore
1979	Caponi	Britz	Alcott	—
1980	Little	Alcott	Bradley	—
1981	Caponi	Bradley	Stephenson	—
1982	Stephenson	Anderson	Haynie	—
1983	Sheehan	Stephenson	Stacy	Alcott
1984	Sheehan	Stacy	Inkster	Inkster
1985	Lopez	Baker	Bradley	Miller
1986	**Bradley**	Geddes	**Bradley**	**Bradley**
1987	Geddes	Davies	Rosenthal	King
1988	Turner	Neumann	Little	Alcott
1989	Lopez	King	Green	Inkster
1990	Daniel	King	Johnston	King
1991	Mallon	Mallon	Scranton	Alcott

Major Championships
SENIORS
PGA Seniors Championship

First played in 1937. Two championships played in 1979 and 1984.

Multiple winners: Sam Snead (6); Gary Player and Eddie Williams (3); Julius Boros, Jock Hutchison, Don January, Arnold Palmer, Paul Runyan, Gene Sarazen and Al Watrous (2).

Year		Year		Year		Year	
1937	Jock Hutchison	1952	Ernest Newnham	1967	Sam Snead	1980	Arnold Palmer*
1938	Fred McLeod*	1953	Harry Schwab	1968	Chandler Harper	1981	Miller Barber
1939	Not held	1954	Gene Sarazen	1969	Tommy Bolt	1982	Don January
1940	Otto Hackbarth*	1955	Mortie Dutra			1983	Not Held
1941	Jack Burke	1956	Pete Burke	1970	Sam Snead	1984	Arnold Palmer
1942	Eddie Williams	1957	Al Watrous	1971	Julius Boros	1984	Peter Thomson
1943	Not held	1958	Gene Sarazen	1972	Sam Snead	1985	Not Held
1944	Not held	1959	Willie Goggin	1973	Sam Snead	1986	Gary Player
1945	Eddie Williams			1974	Robert de Vicenzo	1987	Chi Chi Rodriguez
1946	Eddie Williams*	1960	Dick Metz	1975	Charlie Sifford*	1988	Gary Player
1947	Jock Hutchison	1961	Paul Runyan	1976	Pete Cooper	1989	Larry Mowry
1948	Charles McKenna	1962	Paul Runyan	1977	Julius Boros		
1949	Marshall Crichton	1963	Herman Barron	1978	Joe Jiminez*	1990	Gary Player
		1964	Sam Snead	1979	Jack Fleck*	1991	Jack Nicklaus
1950	Al Watrous	1965	Sam Snead	1979	Don January		
1951	Al Watrous*	1966	Fred Haas				

*PLAYOFFS

1938: McLeod def. Otto Hackbarth in 18 holes. **1940:** Hackbarth def. Jock Hutchison in 36 holes. **1946:** Williams def. Jock Hutchison in 18 holes. **1951:** Watrous def. Jock Hutchison in 18 holes. **1975:** Sifford def. Fred Wampler on 1st extra hole. **1978:** Jiminez def. Joe Cheves and M.de la Torre on 1st extra hole. **1979:** Fleck def. Bill Johnston on 1st extra hole. **1980:** Palmer def. Paul Harney on 1st extra hole.

U.S. Senior Open

Established in 1980 for senior players 55 years-old and over, the minimum age was dropped to 50 (the PGA Seniors Tour entry age) in 1981. Arnold Palmer, Billy Casper, Orville Moody, Jack Nicklaus and Lee Trevino are the only golfers who have won both the U.S. Open and U.S. Senior Open.

Multiple winners: Miller Barber (3); Gary Player (2).

Year		Year		Year		Year	
1980	Roberto deVicenzo	1983	Bill Casper*	1986	Dale Douglass	1989	Orville Moody
1981	Arnold Palmer*	1984	Miller Barber	1987	Gary Player	1990	Lee Trevino
1982	Miller Barber	1985	Miller Barber	1988	Gary Player*	1991	Jack Nicklaus*

*PLAYOFFS

1981: Palmer (70) def. Bob Stone (74) and Billy Casper (77) in 18 holes. **1983:** Tied at 75 after 18-hole playoff, Casper def. Rod Funseth with a birdie on the 1st extra hole. **1988:** Player (68) def. Bob Charles (70) in 18 holes. **1991:** Nicklaus (65) def. Chi Chi Rodriguez (69) in 18 holes.

Annual Money Leaders

PGA

Multiple leaders: Jack Nicklaus (8); Ben Hogan and Tom Watson (5); Arnold Palmer (4); Sam Snead and Curtis Strange (3); Julius Boros, Billy Casper, Tom Kite and Byron Nelson (2).

Year	Earnings	Year	Earnings	Year	Earnings
1934	Paul Runyan $6,767	1953	Lew Worsham $34,002	1972	Jack Nicklaus $320,542
1935	Johnny Revolta 9,543	1954	Bob Toski 65,820	1973	Jack Nicklaus 308,362
1936	Horton Smith 7,682	1955	Julius Boros 63,122	1974	Johnny Miller 353,021
1937	Harry Cooper 14,139	1956	Ted Kroll 72,836	1975	Jack Nicklaus 298,149
1938	Sam Snead 19,534	1957	Dick Mayer 65,835	1976	Jack Nicklaus 266,438
1939	Henry Picard 10,303	1958	Arnold Palmer 42,608	1977	Tom Watson 310,653
		1959	Art Wall 53,168	1978	Tom Watson 362,429
1940	Ben Hogan 10,655			1979	Tom Watson 462,636
1941	Ben Hogan 18,358	1960	Arnold Palmer 75,263		
1942	Ben Hogan 13,143	1961	Gary Player 64,540	1980	Tom Watson 530,808
1943	No records kept	1962	Arnold Palmer 81,448	1981	Tom Kite 365,699
1944	Byron Nelson 37,968	1963	Arnold Palmer 128,230	1982	Craig Stadler 446,462
1945	Byron Nelson 63,336	1964	Jack Nicklaus 113,285	1983	Hal Sutton 426,668
1946	Ben Hogan 42,556	1965	Jack Nicklaus 140,752	1984	Tom Watson 476,260
1947	Jimmy Demaret 27,937	1966	Billy Casper 121,945	1985	Curtis Strange 542,321
1948	Ben Hogan 32,112	1967	Jack Nicklaus 188,998	1986	Greg Norman 653,296
1949	Sam Snead 31,594	1968	Billy Casper 205,169	1987	Curtis Strange 925,941
		1969	Frank Beard 164,707	1988	Curtis Strange ... 1,147,644
1950	Sam Snead 35,759			1989	Tom Kite 1,395,278
1951	Lloyd Mangrum 26,089	1970	Lee Trevino 157,037	1990	Greg Norman ... 1,165,477
1952	Julius Boros 37,033	1971	Jack Nicklaus 244,490		

Note: In 1944-45, Nelson's winnings were in War Bonds.

SENIORS

Multiple leaders: Don January (3); Miller Barber and Bob Charles (2).

Year	Earnings	Year	Earnings	Year	Earnings
1980	Don January $44,100	1984	Don January $328,597	1988	Bob Charles $533,929
1981	Miller Barber 83,136	1985	Peter Thomson 386,724	1989	Bob Charles 725,887
1982	Miller Barber 106,890	1986	Bruce Crampton 454,299	1990	Lee Trevino 1,190,518
1983	Don January 237,571	1987	Chi Chi Rodriguez 509,145		

LPGA

Multiple leaders: Kathy Whitworth (8); Mickey Wright (4); Patty Berg, JoAnne Carner and Nancy Lopez (3); Beth Daniel, Betsy King, Judy Rankin, Betsy Rawls, Louise Suggs and Babe Zaharis (2).

Year	Earnings	Year	Earnings	Year	Earnings
1950	Babe Zaharias $14,800	1964	Mickey Wright $29,800	1978	Nancy Lopez $189,814
1951	Babe Zaharias 15,087	1965	Kathy Whitworth 28,658	1979	Nancy Lopez 197,489
1952	Betsy Rawls 14,505	1966	Kathy Whitworth 33,517		
1953	Louise Suggs 19,816	1967	Kathy Whitworth 32,937	1980	Beth Daniel 231,000
1954	Patty Berg 16,011	1968	Kathy Whitworth 48,379	1981	Beth Daniel 206,978
1955	Patty Berg 16,497	1969	Carol Mann 49,152	1982	JoAnne Carner 310,399
1956	Marlene Hagge 20,235			1983	JoAnne Carner 291,404
1957	Patty Berg 16,272	1970	Kathy Whitworth 30,235	1984	Betsy King 266,771
1958	Beverly Hanson 12,639	1971	Kathy Whitworth 41,181	1985	Nancy Lopez 416,472
1959	Betsy Rawls 26,774	1972	Kathy Whitworth 65,063	1986	Pat Bradley 492,021
		1973	Kathy Whitworth 82,864	1987	Ayako Okamoto 466,034
1960	Louise Suggs 16,892	1974	JoAnne Carner 87,094	1988	Sherri Turner 350,851
1961	Mickey Wright 22,236	1975	Sandra Palmer 76,374	1989	Betsy King 654,132
1962	Mickey Wright 21,641	1976	Judy Rankin 150,734		
1963	Mickey Wright 31,269	1977	Judy Rankin 122,890	1990	Beth Daniel 863,578

All-Time Leaders

PGA, Seniors and LPGA leaders through 1990.

Tournaments Won

	PGA	No		SENIORS	No		LPGA	No
1	Sam Snead	81	1	Miller Barber	24	1	Kathy Whitworth	88
2	Jack Nicklaus	70	2	Don January	22	2	Mickey Wright	82
3	Ben Hogan	63	3	Bruce Crampton	17	3	Patty Berg	57
4	Arnold Palmer	60	4	Chi Chi Rodriguez	16	4	Betsy Rawls	55
5	Byron Nelson	52	5	Gary Player	15	5	Louise Suggs	50
6	Billy Casper	51		Bob Charles	15	6	Nancy Lopez	43
7	Walter Hagen	40	7	Peter Thomson	11	7	JoAnne Carner	42
	Cary Middlecoff	40	8	Arnold Palmer	10		Sandra Haynie	42
9	Gene Sarazen	38	9	Billy Casper	9	9	Carol Mann	38
10	Lloyd Mangrum	36		Orville Moody	9	10	Babe Zaharias	31
11	Horton Smith	32	11	Gene Littler	8	11	Jane Blaylock	29
	Tom Watson	32		Lee Elder	8	12	Amy Alcott	28
13	Harry Cooper	31	13	Lee Trevino	7	13	Pat Bradley	26
	Jimmy Demaret	31	14	Dale Douglass	6		Judy Rankin	26
15	Leo Diegel	30		Jim Dent	6	15	Beth Daniel	25
				Dave Hill	6		Marlene Hagge	25
							Patty Sheehan	25

Note: Patty Berg's victories include 13 official pro wins prior to formation of LPGA in 1950.

Money Won

	PGA	Earnings		SENIORS	Earnings		LPGA	Earnings
1	Tom Kite	$6,258,893	1	Bob Charles	$2,494,732	1	Pat Bradley	$3,364,047
2	Tom Watson	5,374,232	2	Miller Barber	2,488,787	2	Nancy Lopez	3,026,471
3	Curtis Strange	5,292,892	3	Chi Chi Rodriguez	2,235,159	3	Betsy King	3,013,538
4	Jack Nicklaus	5,170,465	4	Bruce Crampton	2,147,530	4	Beth Daniel	2,893,483
5	Lanny Wadkins	4,614,381	5	Orville Moody	2,136,180	5	Patty Sheehan	2,830,464
6	Payne Stewart	4,582,988	6	Gary Player	2,111,928	6	Amy Alcott	2,491,855
7	Ben Crenshaw	4,466,267	7	Don January	1,813,545	7	JoAnne Carner	2,386,888
8	Greg Norman	4,251,270	8	Dale Douglass	1,768,120	8	Ayako Okamoto	2,042,467
9	Hale Irwin	4,066,080	9	Harold Henning	1,758,416	9	Jan Stephenson	1,832,085
10	Ray Floyd	3,880,665	10	Gene Littler	1,540,366	10	Kathy Whitworth	1,719,804
11	Paul Azinger	3,687,384	11	Al Geiberger	1,514,190	11	Hollis Stacy	1,470,653
12	Lee Trevino	3,474,916	12	Dave Hill	1,490,370	12	Donna Caponi	1,387,920
13	Bruce Lietzke	3,442,624	13	Charles Coody	1,421,131	13	Sandra Palmer	1,291,039
14	Chip Beck	3,433,018	14	Billy Casper	1,363,694	14	Jane Blaylock	1,290,944
15	John Mahaffey	3,403,191	15	Mike Hill	1,307,782	15	Sally Little	1,277,179

Annual Awards
PGA of America Player of the Year

Awarded by the PGA of America; based on points scale that weighs performance in major tournaments, regular events, money earned and scoring average.

Multiple winners: Tom Watson (6); Jack Nicklaus (5); Ben Hogan (4); Julius Boros, Billy Casper and Arnold Palmer (2).

Year		Year		Year		Year	
1948	Ben Hogan	1960	Arnold Palmer	1971	Lee Trevino	1981	Bill Rogers
1949	Sam Snead	1961	Jerry Barber	1972	Jack Nicklaus	1982	Tom Watson
		1962	Arnold Palmer	1973	Jack Nicklaus	1983	Hal Sutton
1950	Ben Hogan	1963	Julius Boros	1974	Johnny Miller	1984	Tom Watson
1951	Ben Hogan	1964	Ken Venturi	1975	Jack Nicklaus	1985	Lanny Wadkins
1952	Julius Boros	1965	Dave Marr	1976	Jack Nicklaus	1986	Bob Tway
1953	Ben Hogan	1966	Billy Casper	1977	Tom Watson	1987	Paul Azinger
1954	Ed Furgol	1967	Jack Nicklaus	1978	Tom Watson	1988	Curtis Strange
1955	Doug Ford	1968	No award	1979	Tom Watson	1989	Tom Kite
1956	Jack Burke	1969	Orville Moody	1980	Tom Watson	1990	Nick Faldo
1957	Dick Mayer	1970	Billy Casper				
1958	Dow Finsterwald						
1959	Art Wall						

Annual Awards (Cont.)

PGA Tour Player of the Year

Awarded by the PGA Tour starting in 1990. Winner voted on by tour members from list of nominees.

Year
1990 Wayne Levi

PGA Senior Player of the Year

Awarded by the PGA Seniors Tour starting in 1990. Winner voted on by tour members from list of nominees.

Year
1990 Lee Trevino

LPGA Player of the Year

Awarded by the LPGA; based on performance points accumulated during the year.

Multiple winners: Kathy Whitworth (7); Nancy Lopez (4); JoAnne Carner (3); Beth Daniel, Betsy King and Judy Rankin (2).

Year		Year		Year		Year	
1966	Kathy Whitworth	1973	Kathy Whitworth	1980	Beth Daniel	1986	Pat Bradley
1967	Kathy Whitworth	1974	JoAnne Carner	1981	JoAnne Carner	1987	Ayako Okamoto
1968	Kathy Whitworth	1975	Sandra Palmer	1982	JoAnne Carner	1988	Nancy Lopez
1969	Kathy Whitworth	1976	Judy Rankin	1983	Patty Sheehan	1989	Betsy King
1970	Sandra Haynie	1977	Judy Rankin	1984	Betsy King	1990	Beth Daniel
1971	Kathy Whitworth	1978	Nancy Lopez	1985	Nancy Lopez		
1972	Kathy Whitworth	1979	Nancy Lopez				

The Skins Game

The Skins Game is a made-for-TV, $450,000 shootout between four premier golfers playing 18 holes over two days (nine each day). Each hole is counted as a skin with the first six skins worth $15,000 apiece, the second six worth $25,000, and the last six worth $35,000. If a hole is tied, the money is added to the worth of the next hole. The PGA Skins Game was started in 1983, followed by the Senior Skins in 1988 and the LPGA Skins in 1990. Due to scheduling conflicts, the LPGA Skins was not played in 1991, but will return in 1992.

PGA Skins

Played in late November.

Total Winnings (8 years, through 1990): Jack Nicklaus ($650,000); Fuzzy Zoeller ($625,000); Curtis Strange ($485,000); Lee Trevino ($435,000); Raymond Floyd ($350,000); Arnold Palmer ($245,000); Tom Watson ($230,000) and Gary Player ($170,000).

Year	Winner	Earnings	Outskinned	
1983	Gary Player	$170,000	Palmer	$140,000
			Nicklaus	40,000
			Watson	10,000
1984	Jack Nicklaus	$240,000	Watson	$120,000
			Palmer	0
			Player	0
1985	Fuzzy Zoeller	$225,000	Watson	$100,000
			Palmer	80,000
			Nicklaus	15,000
1986	Fuzzy Zoeller	$370,000	Trevino	$55,000
			Palmer	25,000
			Nicklaus	0
1987	Lee Trevino	$310,000	Nicklaus	$70,000
			Zoeller	70,000
			Palmer	0
1988	Ray Floyd	$290,000	Nicklaus	$125,000
			Trevino	35,000
			Strange	0
1989	Curtis Strange	$265,000	Nicklaus	$90,000
			Floyd	60,000
			Trevino	35,000
1990	Curtis Strange	$220,000	Norman	$90,000
			Faldo	70,000
			Nicklaus	70,000

Senior Skins

Played in early January.

Total Winnings (4 years, through 1991): Jack Nicklaus ($450,000); Chi Chi Rodriguez ($420,000); Arnold Palmer ($345,000); Lee Trevino ($195,000); Gary Player ($130,000); Billy Casper ($80,000); and Sam Snead (0).

Year	Winner	Earnings	Outskinned	
1988	C.C.Rodriguez	$300,000	Player	$40,000
			Palmer	20,000
			Snead	0
1989	C.C.Rodriguez	$120,000	Player	$90,000
			Casper	80,000
			Palmer	70,000
1990	Arnold Palmer	$240,000	Nicklaus	$140,000
			Trevino	70,000
			Player	0
1991	Jack Nicklaus	$310,000	Trevino	$125,000
			Palmer	15,000
			Player	0
			Rodriguez	0

LPGA Skins

Played in late May; the second LPGA Skins Game was postponed until 1992.

Total Winnings (1990): Jan Stephenson ($200,000); JoAnne Carner ($110,000); Nancy Lopez ($95,000) and Betsy King ($45,000).

Year	Winner	Earnings	Outskinned	
1990	Jan Stephenson	$200,000	Carner	$110,000
			Lopez	95,000
			King	45,000

National Team Competition
MEN
Ryder Cup

The Ryder Cup was presented by British businessman Samuel Ryder in 1927 for competition between professional golfers from Great Britain and the United States. Since 1979, the British have been joined by the rest of Europe in challenging the U.S. The U.S. leads the series with a 22-5-2 record after 29 matches.

Year		Year		Year	
1927	United States, 9½-2½	1953	United States, 6½-5½	1973	United States, 19-13
1929	Britain-Ireland, 7-5	1955	United States, 8-4	1975	United States, 21-11
1931	United States, 9-3	1957	Britain-Ireland, 7½-4½	1977	United States, 12½-7½
1933	Britain-Ireland, 6½-5½	1959	United States, 8½-3½	1979	United States, 17-11
1935	United States, 9-3	1961	United States, 14½-9½	1981	United States, 18½-9½
1937	United States, 8-4	1963	United States, 23-9	1983	United States, 14½-13½
1939-45	Not held	1965	United States, 19½-12½	1985	Europe, 16½-11½
1947	United States, 11-1	1967	United States, 23½-8½	1987	Europe, 15-13
1949	United States, 7-5	1969	Draw, 16-16	1989	Draw, 14-14
1951	United States, 9½-2½	1971	United States, 18½-13½	1991	United States, 14½-13½

Walker Cup

The Walker Cup was presented by American businessman George Herbert Walker in 1922 for competition between amateur golfers from Great Britain and the United States. The U.S. leads the series with a 29-3-1 record after 33 matches.

Year		Year		Year	
1922	United States, 8-4	1949	United States, 10-2	1971	Britain-Ireland, 13-11
1923	United States, 6-5	1951	United States, 7½-4½	1973	United States, 14-10
1924	United States, 9-3	1953	United States, 9-3	1975	United States, 15½-8½
1926	United States, 6½-5½	1955	United States, 10-2	1977	United States, 16-8
1928	United States, 11-1	1957	United States, 8½-3½	1979	United States, 15½-8½
1930	United States, 10-2	1959	United States, 9-	1981	United States, 15-9
1932	United States, 9½-2½	1961	United States, 11-1	1983	United States, 13½-10½
1934	United States, 9½-2½	1963	United States, 14-10	1985	United States, 13-11
1936	United States, 10½-1½	1965	Draw, 12-12	1987	United States, 16½-7½
1938	Britain-Ireland, 7½-4½	1967	United States, 15-9	1989	Britain-Ireland, 12½-11½
1940-46	Not held	1969	United States, 13-11	1991	United States, 14-10
1947	United States, 8-4				

WOMEN
Solheim Cup

The Solheim Cup was presented by the Karsten Manufacturing Co. in 1990 for competition between women professional golfers from Europe and the United States. The Cup was contested for the first time in 1990 in Orlando.

Year	
1990	United States, 11½-4½

Curtis Cup

Named after British golfing sisters Harriot and Margaret Curtis, the Curtis Cup was first contested in 1932 between teams of women amateurs from the United States and the British Isles.

Competed for every other year since 1932 (except during World War II). The U.S. leads the series with a 20-4-2 record after 26 matches.

Year		Year		Year	
1932	United States, 5½-3½	1952	British Isles, 5-4	1972	United States, 10-8
1934	United States, 6½-2½	1954	United States, 6-3	1974	United States, 13-5
1936	Draw, 4½-4½	1956	British Isles, 5-4	1976	United States, 11½-6½
1938	United States, 5½-3½	1958	Draw 4½-4½	1978	United States, 12-6
1940	Not held	1960	United States, 6½-2½	1980	United States, 13-5
1942	Not held	1962	United States, 8-1	1982	United States, 14½-3½
1944	Not held	1964	United States, 10½-7½	1984	United States, 9½-8½
1946	Not held	1966	United States, 13-5	1986	British Isles, 13-5
1948	United States, 6½-2½	1968	United States, 10½-7½	1988	British Isles, 11-7
1950	United States, 7½-1½	1970	United States, 11½-6½	1990	United States, 14-4

GOLF

Colleges
Men's NCAA Division I Champions

College championships decided by match play from 1897-1964, and stroke play since 1965.
Multiple winners (teams): Yale (21); Houston (16); Princeton (12); Oklahoma St.(7); Harvard and Stanford (6); LSU abd North Texas (4); Wake Forest (3); Florida, Michigan, Ohio St. and Texas (2).
Multiple winners (individuals): Ben Crenshaw (3); Dick Crawford, Dexter Cummings, G.T.Dunlop, Fred Lamprecht, Phil Mickelson and Scott Simpson (2).

Year	Team winner	Individual champion	Year	Team winner	Individual champion
1897	Yale	Louis Bayard, Princeton	1945	Ohio State	John Lorms, Ohio St.
1898	Harvard (spring)	John Reid, Yale	1946	Stanford	George Hamer, Georgia
1898	Yale (fall)	James Curtis, Harvard	1947	LSU	Dave Barclay, Michigan
1899	Harvard	Percy Pyne, Princeton	1948	San Jose St.	Bob Harris, San Jose St.
1900	Not held	—	1949	North Texas	Harvie Ward, N.Carolina
1901	Harvard	H.Lindsley, Harvard	1950	North Texas	Fred Wampler, Purdue
1902	Yale (spring)	Chas.Hitchcock, Jr., Yale	1951	North Texas	Tom Nieporte, Ohio St.
1902	Harvard (fall)	Chandler Egan, Harvard	1952	North Texas	Jim Vichers, Oklahoma
1903	Harvard	F.O.Reinhart, Princeton	1953	Stanford	Earl Moeller, Oklahoma St.
1904	Harvard	A.L.White, Harvard	1954	SMU	Hillman Robbins, Memphis St.
1905	Yale	Robert Abbott, Yale	1955	LSU	Joe Campbell, Purdue
1906	Yale	W.E.Clow Jr., Yale	1956	Houston	Rick Jones, Ohio St.
1907	Yale	Ellis Knowles, Yale	1957	Houston	Rex Baxter Jr., Houston
1908	Yale	H.H.Wilder, Harvard	1958	Houston	Phil Rodgers, Houston
1909	Yale	Albert Seckel, Princeton	1959	Houston	Dick Crawford, Houston
1910	Yale	Robert Hunter, Yale	1960	Houston	Dick Crawford, Houston
1911	Yale	George Stanley, Yale	1961	Purdue	Jack Nicklaus, Ohio St.
1912	Yale	F.C.Davison, Harvard	1962	Houston	Kermit Zarley, Houston
1913	Yale	Nathaniel Wheeler, Yale	1963	Oklahoma St.	R.H. Sikes, Arkansas
1914	Princeton	Edward Allis, Harvard	1964	Houston	Terry Small, San Jose St.
1915	Yale	Francis Blossom, Yale	1965	Houston	Marty Fleckman, Houston
1916	Princeton	J.W.Hubbell, Harvard	1966	Houston	Bob Murphy, Florida
1917-18	Not held	—	1967	Houston	Hale Irwin, Colorado
1919	Princeton	A.L.Walker, Jr., Columbia	1968	Florida	Grier Jones, Oklahoma St.
1920	Princeton	Jess Sweetster, Yale	1969	Houston	Bob Clark, Cal St.-LA
1921	Dartmouth	Simpson Dean, Princton	1970	Houston	John Mahaffey, Houston
1922	Princeton	Pollack Boyd, Dartmouth	1971	Texas	Ben Crenshaw, Texas
1923	Princeton	Dexter Cummings, Yale	1972	Texas	Ben Crenshaw, Texas
1924	Yale	Dexter Cummings, Yale			& Tom Kite, Texas
1925	Yale	Fred Lamprecht, Tulane	1973	Florida	Ben Crenshaw, Texas
1926	Yale	Fred Lamprecht, Tulane	1974	Wake Forest	Curtis Strange, W.Forest
1927	Princeton	Watts Gunn, Georgia Tech	1975	Wake Forest	Jay Haas, Wake Forest
1928	Princeton	Maurice McCarthy, G'town	1976	Oklahoma St.	Scott Simpson, U.S.C
1929	Princeton	Tom Aycock, Yale	1977	Houston	Scott Simpson, U.S.C
1930	Princeton	G.T.Dunlap Jr., Princeton	1978	Oklahoma St.	David Edwards, Okla.St.
1931	Yale	G.T.Dunlap Jr., Princeton	1979	Ohio St.	Gary Hallberg, Wake Forest
1932	Yale	J.W.Fischer, Michigan	1980	Oklahoma St.	Jay Don Blake, Utah St.
1933	Yale	Walter Emery, Oklahoma	1981	Brigham Young	Ron Commans, U.S.C
1934	Michigan	Charles Yates, Ga.Tech	1982	Houston	Billy Ray Brown, Houston
1935	Michigan	Ed White, Texas	1983	Oklahoma St.	Jim Carter, Arizona St.
1936	Yale	Charles Kocsis, Michigan	1984	Houston	John Inman, N.Carolina
1937	Princeton	Fred Haas, Jr., LSU	1985	Houston	Clark Burroughs, Ohio St.
1938	Stanford	John Burke, Georgetown	1986	Wake Forest	Scott Verplank, Okla.St.
1939	Stanford	Vincent D'Antoni, Tulane	1987	Oklahoma St.	Brian Watts, Oklahoma St.
1940	Princeton & LSU	Dixon Brooke, Virginia	1988	UCLA	E.J.Pfister, Oklahoma St.
1941	Stanford	Earl Stewart, LSU	1989	Oklahoma	Phil Mickelson, Ariz.St.
1942	LSU & Stanford	Frank Tatum Jr., Stanford	1990	Arizona St.	Phil Mickelson, Ariz.St.
1943	Yale	Wallace Ulrich, Carleton	1991	Oklahoma St.	Warren Schuette, UNLV
1944	Notre Dame	Louis Lick, Minnesota			

Women's NCAA Champions

College championships decided by stroke play since 1982.
Multiple winners (teams): Florida, San Jose St. and Tulsa (2).

Year	Team winner	Individual champion	Year	Team winner	Individual champion
1982	Tulsa	Kathy Baker, Tulsa	1987	San Jose St.	Caroline Keggi, N.Mexico
1983	TCU	Penny Hammel, Miami	1988	Tulsa	Melissa McNamara, Tulsa
1984	Miami-FL	Cindy Schreyer, Georgia	1989	San Jose St.	Pat Hurst, San Jose St.
1985	Florida	Danielle Ammaccapane, Ariz.St.	1990	Arizona St.	Susan Slaughter, Arizona
1986	Florida	Page Dunlap, Florida	1991	UCLA	Annika Sorenstam, Ariz.

Rick Mears celebrates his latest victory at the Indianapolis 500 after joining A.J. Foyt and Al Unser as the only four-time winners of the race.

AUTO RACING

Full Throttle

Rick Mears wins fourth Indy, but another longshot takes Daytona; parity opens up CART and NASCAR, and Mansell chases Senna in F-1.

It was perhaps the most competitive season ever in auto racing. Never before had so many won races.

In the first 10 NASCAR stock car races of the year, there were nine different winners. By midseason 12 drivers had won races.

The first six CART Indy-car events produced different winners, as did the first four ISMA GTP sports car races. "It's not so much parity among the teams, but the fact that the equipment is so good and the drivers are so good," said Darrell Waltrip, one of the NASCAR winners.

"It's really not unusual now to finish with a dozen cars on the lead lap in our races, and usually any one of 'em can win it right up to the last lap," Waltrip added.

Indy-car star Michael Andretti echoed Waltrip, saying, "Every race is like a trophy dash. You can't afford to play strategy games because if you hold back even a little for just a few laps, you're going to get left behind. There are just too many good cars and drivers out there now to do anything but go all out the whole race every race."

NASCAR's Winston Cup season began on Feb. 17 with a big surprise when Ernie

---

Mike Harris has been Motorsports Editor for the Associated Press since 1980. He has been covering the Indianapolis 500 since 1969 and covers more auto races during the year than any other writer in the country.

Irvan proved he could run with the big boys and won the Daytona 500. It was the second straight year that the Super Bowl of stock car racing had produced an unexpected winner (Derrike Cope took the checkered flag in 1990).

"That's just another example of the competitive level we race at now," said Waltrip, who needed 17 years before he won his first Daytona 500 in 1989. "Even our biggest race, where everybody is totally geared up, ready with new equipment, pointed for the race, we have guys winning who don't figure to do it. In the old days, it was always the established stars with the established teams that won the big races. But that just isn't true any more. We've probably got between 15 and 20 drivers who can win at any time, given the right circumstance."

Irvan, who earned $230,000 for the victory, led the final five laps and was seemingly assured of the victory when Dale Earnhardt and Davey Allison, battling for second, banged together and spun three laps from the end.

At that point, all Irvan had to do was finish under the caution flag for his biggest win ever. But, suddenly, his engine began to sputter.

"When I looked in my mirror and saw what was happening behind me, I thought, 'This can't be true.' Then I went into turn one behind the pace car and started to run out of gas. I thought this

Ernie Irvan (left) got the NASCAR season off to an unexpected start in February by taking the Daytona 500, but the biggest surprise of the year was 51-year-old **Harry Gant**, who came out of nowhere in September to win four straight races.

can't be happening to me.' So I went to the apron and just kept it running and, eventually, some of the gas must have sloshed up because we were able to get to the end.''

That was the best day of the season for Irvan, whose aggressive style of driving has earned him the nickname "Swervin' Irvan." After being criticized later in the season for allegedly causing several nasty crashes in which other drivers were injured, Irvan vowed at a pre-race drivers' meeting to mend his ways. But the jury remained out as the season neared its end with Irvan trying hard to catch leader Earnhardt and runner-up Ricky Rudd in the Winston Cup title chase.

Earnhardt, who earned his fourth series title in 1990—making him second in overall Winston Cup champions to seven-time winner Richard Petty—led the 1991 points race by a narrow margin over Rudd through most of the 29-race season. A year ago, Earnhardt, who earned a record $3 million in prize money, overtook and beat Mark Martin by just 26 points in the fifth closest NASCAR finish ever.

Check the Update chapter for late season results through October.

One thing that was decided early was the Winston Million. Nobody earned the $1 million bonus for winning at least three of NASCAR's Big Four events—the Daytona 500, Coca-Cola 600, Winston 500 and the Southern 500.

Irvan won at Daytona and Davey Allison won the Coca-Cola 600 at Charlotte Motor Speedway. The other two Crown Jewels were won by inspiring, 51-year-old Harry Gant, who took a $100,000 bonus for winning both the Winston 500 at Talladega Superspeedway and the Southern 500 at Darlington International Speedway.

Along the way, Gant kept upping his record for being the oldest winner in NASCAR's premier series and also became the biggest surprise of the racing season. Gant, who had never before won two races in a row in his 11 years on the circuit, won four straight in September—beginning at Darlington on Labor Day Weekend and continuing at Richmond, Va., and Dover, Del., and Martinsville, Va.

"Age don't have nothing to do with it,"

Gant said. "I stay in good shape, I race for a good team and I've got good equipment. There is no reason why I can't win some more.

"And a streak like that don't mean anything the next time out," he added. "Every race you got to try just the same to win. Sometimes you do and a lot of times you don't. That's the way this sport is."

Another veteran racer, 39-year-old Rick Mears, put on a pair of racing clinics in the two 500-mile Indy-car events of 1991, winning his fourth Indianapolis 500 as well as his first Marlboro 500 at boss Roger Penske's Michigan International Speedway.

Mears, who started from the pole at Indy for a record sixth time, joined A.J. Foyt and Al Unser as the only four-time winners of the world's richest and most prestigious race. For his efforts, he earned $1,219,704 from the record-breaking purse of $7,009,150.

To gain the big victory, Mears had to beat hungry 28-year-old Michael Andretti, whose father, Mario, won at Indy in 1969. Late in the race, with both drivers turning laps at speeds above 217 miles an hour, Andretti made a strong outside pass to take the lead from Mears only to see Mears, who previously won Indy in 1980, '84 and '88, make an even tougher outside pass a lap later.

The whole scenario was out of character, with the younger Andretti known as the charger and Mears as the laid back racer who takes advantage of what he is given and takes care of his equipment.

"It was the only choice I had," Mears said. "You've got to take the shot. After all, this is Indianapolis."

The 75th Indy 500 was significant for several other reasons.

Not only was it billed as the 34th (a record) and final appearance of 56-year-old A.J. Foyt (see box), but the Memorial Day Weekend classic was also the Indy debut of Willy T. Ribbs, the first known black driver to race at Indianapolis Motor Speedway.

Ironically, neither driver was around very long in the race. Foyt, who started from the front row despite the fact that he was coming back from serious foot and leg injuries, lasted just 25 laps, going out after running over debris from a crash by two other cars. Ribbs, who overcame severe

A.J. Foyt Can't Quite Walk Away

That tough old cowboy A.J. Foyt may finally be at the end of the trail—maybe.

At 56, you'd think the combative old boy from Houston would be ready to settle back into the role of team owner and leave the racing to younger, hungrier drivers.

But, even in the wake of the most serious accident in his long and illustrious career which left him with feet that "burn like hell" every time he pushes the accelerator, Foyt can't quite be sure he's ready to step out of the cockpit for the last time.

In September, 1990 it appeared that Foyt's career was over through no choice of his own.

Racing through a fast turn at the end of a 180-mph straightaway at Road American in Elkhart Lake, Wisc., the brakes of Foyt's Lola-Chevrolet failed.

He slid off the track at full speed, skidded over the berm, through a field and soared into a ditch, where the front of the car—and his feet and legs—were buried in a mound of dirt.

"When the rescue workers got to me, they weren't sure if I had any legs anymore," Foyt said. "I didn't know either."

It took more than an hour to get the badly-injured Foyt out of the mangled wreckage of his Indy car. But, despite the pain, shock and drugs that were administered, Foyt never lost consciousness.

"The pain was so bad I was begging someone to just take a hammer and knock me out," he said.

But weeks in hospitals and months of rehabilitation on his battered legs and crushed feet could not put out the competitive fire in the belly of the winningest driver in Indy-car history and the sport's first four-time Indianapolis 500 winner.

"I knew in my heart I was going to make it back," he said. "As soon as I saw that my feet were still attached to my legs and my legs were still attached to my body, I knew I was going to drive again."

Incredibly, he did.

The determined "Super Tex", owner of 67 Indy-car victories, announced he would be back by May for the Indianapolis 500 and that 1991 would be his last year as a driver.

Mario Andretti (left) administers an onsight gut check of **A.J. Foyt** after both old-timers qualified for the front row in this year's Indianapolis 500.

To make it happen, Foyt worked up to six or seven hours on rehabilitation almost every day and got back in an Indy-car for some testing at Indianapolis in February. Despite agonizing pain in his feet—compounded by the fact that doctors had pulled his remaining toenails the day before the tests to help promote healing—Foyt proved he could still drive a race car, turning several laps at more than 210 mph.

After deciding not to drive in an oval race at Phoenix in April in order to give the healing process more time, Foyt showed up at Indianapolis and wowed everyone, qualifying on the first day of time trials at 222.443 mph for four laps and earning a front row start with Rick Mears and Mario Andretti.

Beaming, an emotional Foyt told the big crowd, "It (Indy) has been a big part of my life. I love it."

Then came more disappointment. In the race, he fell from eighth to 11th during a long pit stop on lap 21. Then, on lap 25, he found himself in the wrong place at the wrong time and was victimized by a large piece of debris from an accident involving two other drivers.

He drove over the piece of broken suspension at more than 200 mph, damaging his car and forcing himself out of the race. Nev-

ertheless, Foyt was able to make a slow trip around the 2½-mile oval, waving to the throng of more than 450,000 spectators and absorbing their warm farewell.

After that, he continued racing, but it wasn't the same.

"My feet feel like they're on fire and they hurt like hell," Foyt said after a very bad showing at the New Jersey Meadowlands in July. "Right now, I'm in everybody else's way and I can't get out of my own way. That's not the way I race.

"I drove left-footed at the Meadowlands and I've never driven left-footed before. I know the car is capable of running up front, but right now, I'm not."

Foyt hired Mike Groff, the fastest rookie at Indianapolis in 1991, to drive for him the rest of the season and, probably, in 1992.

So, is Foyt through as a driver?

"Well, I don't know for sure," he said. "I guess I'm through with temporary circuits and probably road courses, but I'd still like to drive some ovals. And maybe Indy one more time.

"Really, though, I just don't know. It depends how I feel, what my sponsor says and if the fans want me back. We'll just have to wait and see, but I think I'm still capable of winning."

Wide World Photos

Michael Andretti drew a lot of attention on the CART circuit with a record seven victories and some spectacular driving.

engine problems to make the race, went out after just six laps with a broken engine.

The disappointed Foyt hinted to the partisan crowd that he might return for one more try in 1992, drawing a huge roar. Ribbs, who quickly became a crowd favorite with his tenacious effort and great style, also vowed to return.

The rest of the 17-race PPG Cup schedule was wide open, with two-time series champion Bobby Rahal out front most of the season on the basis of consistency. Rahal won just once in the first 15 events, but finished 12 of them, all in the top four positions.

Still, that wasn't good enough to hold the lead. After chasing Rahal for nine races from the beginning of June to the middle of September, Andretti caught and passed the man who beat him for series championships in 1986 and 1987.

Andretti, trying to win his first title, was easily the most spectacular performer of the season. Not only did he win a CART-record seven races during that period, Andretti did it with style. In a race in June at Portland, Ore., he dived between front-row starters Emerson Fittipaldi and

Mears at the start, made it cleanly to the lead and stayed ahead to the finish.

At Denver in August, Michael had an early tangle with Rahal but drove back through the field, made a spectacular tire-bumping, wall-scrubbing pass on Eddie Chever and managed to finish third.

A week later, at Vancouver, British Columbia, Andretti made three breathtaking passes, two of them on Rahal, to win again.

A week after that, the lead changed hands again at Lexington, Ohio, where Andretti won once more, this time controlling things from the front after winning his seventh pole of the season.

"You don't plan those passes," Andretti explained. "You just do them. You take what you're given to work with and do the best you can."

Rahal was impressed by Andretti's moves, particularly the final pass at Vancouver that gave Andretti a lead he never relinquished.

"That was some pass," Rahal said. "I'm still not sure how he did it. But I've enjoyed racing with Michael. That is fun."

Meanwhile, defending series champion Al Unser, Jr., who fended off Andretti for the title in 1990, and Mears continued working hard to overtake the leaders.

Going into the last two events of the season, Unser—who won six races in 1990—had two wins and was third in points. Mears also hung tough, but his chance for a fourth series title ended with a broken suspension three races from the finish.

"This gets harder every year," Mears said. 'Winning championships takes not only consistency but consistency at the front of the pack. You can't win a championship any more without running at or near the front virtually the whole year. A DNF (did not finish) or two can knock you right out of contention.

"That puts more pressure on the team to get the car right, it puts pressure on the pit crew to make every stop virtually perfect and it puts pressure on the driver to get the car up front and keep it there without doing anything stupid. But the fact that we have so many drivers racing for wins and for the championship shows just how good the teams and drivers in this series are."

British Grand Prix winner **Nigel Mansell** gives defending Formula One world champion **Ayrton Senna** a lift after the race in Silverstone. Senna ran out of gas on the last lap, but still led Mansell in the overall standings late in the season.

In 1990, Ayrton Senna of Brazil won the Formula One championship in a tense duel with longtime nemesis, former teammate and defending champion Alain Prost of France.

It looked for a while like Senna, considered by many racing experts the best driver in the world, would make a shambles of the 1991 title race. Driving again for McLaren-Honda, Senna won the first four events of the 16-race schedule and built a huge points lead.

Even when he stumbled with engine and gearshift problems in the next few events, it still appeared he would run away with his third Formula One championship. But a three-race winning streak by England's Nigel Mansell—who was trying to become the first British world champion since James Hunt in 1976—tightened things up considerably.

Senna then won two races in a row before Mansell, driving a Williams-Renault, won again at Monza, Italy in early September to keep it close.

"We have had problems this year with our new (V10) engines, the new transmission and fuel pickup, but when the car is able to finish the races, we have a very good chance to win," Senna said.

Before his winning streak, Mansell was reportedly considering a move to the Indy-car circuit before signing a new Formula One contract.

New horizons and all that," Mansell said. "I'd like to drive at Indianapolis one day. But that time has not yet come." On the Indy-car side, Michael Andretti, whose father was the 1978 Formula One champion, had a testing contract with McLaren and was hoping to get a competitive Formula One ride. But, when nothing materialized, he signed another one-year contract with Newman-Haas Racing and will again be teamed with his father in 1992.

Rahal, however, will leave Galles-Kraco Racing, where he is teamed with Unser Jr., to drive next season for Pat Patrick. Danny Sullivan took advantage of Rahal's leaving to bounce from Patrick Racing to Galles-Kraco.

The International Race of Champions series, a four-race set matching 12 all-star racers from NASCAR, CART and the world of road racing against one another in identically prepared Dodge Daytona cars, had a new winner in 1991—NASCAR's Rusty Wallace.

Wallace, the 1989 Winston Cup champion, won the final three events to become the first driver in IROC series history to win three races in a single season.

Scott Pruett, an Indy-car regular coming back from injuries that kept him out for the entire 1990 season, won the IROC opener at Daytona and wound up fourth in the final points, trailing Wallace and fellow stock car stars Bill Elliott and Mark Martin.

The IMSA Camel GT Prototype sports car series was looking like another relatively easy championship run for Australian-born Geoff Brabham, who has won the series title three straight times while driving Nissan prototypes.

Brabham finished fifth or better—with one victory and five second-place efforts—in 11 of the first 12 events. By that time, he had a seemingly solid lead over Nissan teammate Chip Robinson and Jaguar driver Davy Jones.

But a devastating crash at Road America in Elkhart Lake at the same place where Foyt was badly injured in 1990 in an Indy-car crash, put Brabham in the hospital with four broken ribs, two compressed fractures of the vertebrae and lots of scrapes, bruises and abrasions. The crash came during testing and was caused by a deflated tire.

When Brabham missed the ensuing race at Road America, Jones won and Robinson finished second, giving Robinson a lead of three points over Brabham and 10 over Jones with only one race remaining. Brabham, out of the hospital two weeks later, was determined to make it back in time for the finale on Oct. 13 at Del Mar, Calif., saying, "If those guys think I'm going to roll over and play dead because of this, they're out of their minds."

Ironically, the most prestigious event on the IMSA schedule—the season-opening 24 Hours of Daytona—was not won by any of the title combatants. That honor went to a Porsche GTP fivesome made up of Hurley Haywood, Frank Jelinsky, Bob Wollek, John Winter and Henri Fescarolo of Italy.

The victory made Haywood, the only American in the group, the all-time leader in sports car endurance victories with nine. The win at Daytona was his fifth first since 1979. To go along with those, he has two victories in the Sebring 12 Hours and two more in the LeMans 24 Hours.

At LeMans in June, the 24-hour race was won by the upstart Mazda team of Bertrand Gachot of Belgium, Volker Weidler of Germany and Johnny Herbert of England. The trio, driving a Mazda 787B with a four-rotor rotary engine, set a record by covering 3,059.9 miles in the twice-around-the-clock event.

It was the first time in the storied history of the world's oldest sports car endurance race that a car manufactured in Japan had come out on top. Many observers close to the scene credited the upset victory to new Mazda team manager Jackie Ickx of Belgium, who is the only six-time winner of LeMans.

Jaguars, which won the race in dominating fashion in 1990, came in second, third and fourth in 1991.

In the SCCA's Trans-Am series, 22-year-old Scott Sharp, a protege of part-time racer, Indy-car team owner and actor Paul Newman, won his first championship.

Sharp, with six wins, clinched his duel with Chevrolet teammate Jack Baldwin and Oldsmobile driver Darin Brassfield with a victory in the second to last race of the season at Elkart Lake.

The worst accident of a crash-filled year came in August at Watkins Glen N.Y., when longtime NASCAR racer J.D. McDuffie was killed instantly in a one-car accident. McDuffie, one of the last of the true independents—team owners who drive their own cars and make their living strictly from racing— had driven in 64 Winston Cup events without ever winning and had been racing on a limited schedule in recent years.

His accident came at the same spot where Trans-Am and IMSA star Tommy Kendall suffered a badly broken leg that ended his racing season in July. □

AUTO RACING STATISTICS

THE SEASON IN REVIEW
1990-1991
NASCAR • CART • FORMULA 1

SEC A

PAGE 717

NASCAR Results

Winners of NASCAR Winston Cup races from Sept.30, 1990 through Sept. 22, 1991.

LATE 1990

Date	Event	Winner (Pos.)	Avg.mph	Earnings	Pole	Qual.mph
Sept. 30	Holly Farms 400	Mark Martin (2)	93.818	$52,875	K.Petty	116.387
Oct. 7	Mello Yello 500	Davey Allison (5)	137.375	90,650	B.Bodine	174.385
Oct. 21	AC Delco 500	Alan Kulwicki (3)	125.378	53,300	K.Schrader	147.814
Nov. 4	Autoworks 500k	Dale Earnhardt (3)	96.786	72,100	R.Wallace	124.443
Nov. 18	Atlanta Journal 500	Morgan Shepherd (20)	140.911	62,250	R.Wallace	175.222

Winning Cars: Ford Thunderbird 4 (Allison, Kulwicki, Martin, Shepherd); Chevrolet Lumina (Earnhardt).

1991 (through Sept.22)

Date	Event	Winner (Pos.)	Avg.mph	Earnings	Pole	Qual.mph
Feb. 17	**Daytona 500**	Ernie Irvan (2)	148.128	$233,000	D.Allison	195.955
Feb. 24	Pontiac 400	Dale Earnhardt (19)	104.378	67,950	D.Allison	120.428
Mar. 3	Goodwrench 500	Kyle Petty (1)	124.083	131,450†	K.Petty	149.205
Mar. 17	Motorcraft 500	Ken Schrader (5)	140.470	69,259	A.Kulwicki	174.413
Apr. 7	TranSouth 500	Ricky Rudd (13)	135.594	62,185	G.Bodine	161.939
Apr. 14	Valleydale 500	Rusty Wallace (1)	67.673	74,100†	R.Wallace	118.051
Apr. 21	First Union 400	Darrell Waltrip (13)	79.603	53,800	B.Bodine	116.237
Apr. 28	Hanes 500	Dale Earnhardt (10)	75.139	63,600	M.Martin	91.949
May 5	**Winston 500**	Harry Gant (2)	165.620	81,950	E.Irvan	195.186
May 26	**Coca-Cola 600**	Davey Allison (10)	138.951	137,100	M.Martin	174.820
June 2	Budweiser 500	Ken Schrader (19)	120.192	64,800	M.Waltrip	143.392
June 9	Banquet Foods 300k	Davey Allison (13)*	72.970	61,950	R.Rudd	90.634
June 16	AC Spark Plug 500	Darrell Waltrip (13)	122.691	60,650	M.Martin	161.996
June 23	Miller Genuine 400	Davey Allison (4)	160.912	90,650	M.Waltrip	174.351
July 6	Pepsi 400	Bill Elliott (10)	159.116	75,000	S.Marlin	190.331
July 21	Miller Genuine 500	Rusty Wallace (10)	115.459	34,100	A.Kulwicki	161.473
July 28	DieHard 500	Dale Earnhardt (4)	147.383	88,670	S.Marlin	192.085
Aug. 11	Budweiser at the Glen	Ernie Irvan (3)	98.977	64,850	T.Labonte	121.652
Aug. 18	Champion Spark Plug 400	Dale Jarrett (11)	139.887	74,150	A.Kulwicki	173.431
Aug. 24	Bud 500	Alan Kulwicki (5)	82.628	61,400	B.Elliott	116.957
Sept. 1	**Heinz Southern 500**	Harry Gant (5)	133.508	179,450*	D.Allison	162.506
Sept. 8	Miller Genuine Draft 400	Harry Gant (13)	101.361	63,650	R.Wallace	120.590
Sept. 15	Peak Anti-Freeze 500	Harry Gant (10)	110.179	67,000	A.Kulwicki	146.825
Sept. 22	Goody's 500	Harry Gant (12)	74.535	64,000	M.Martin	93.171

*Rudd penalized five seconds for rough driving, moving him from 1st to 2nd place.
†Includes carryover Unocal 76 bonus for winning race from pole—K.Petty ($68,400); Wallace ($22,800).

Winning Cars: Chevy Lumina, 10 (Earnhardt 3, Irvan 2, Rudd, Schrader 2, D.Waltrip 2); Ford Thunderbird, 6 (Allison 3, Elliott, Jarrett, Kulwicki); Oldsmobile Cutlass, 5 (Gant 5); Pontiac Grand Prix, 3 (Wallace 2, Petty).

Remaining races (5): Tyson Holly Farms 400 (Sept.29); Mello-Yello 500 (Oct.6); AC Delco 500 (Oct.20); Checker 500 (Nov.3) and Atlanta Journal 500 (Nov.17).

1991 Race Locations

February—Daytona 500 at Daytona; Pontiac 400 at Richmond,VA. **March**—Goodwrench 500 at Rockingham, NC; Motorcraft 500 at Atlanta. **April**—TranSouth 500 at Darlington,SC; Valleydale 500 at Bristol,TN; First Union 400 at N.Wilkesboro,NC; Hanes 500 at Martinsville,VA. **May**—Winston 500 at Talladega,AL; Coca-Cola 600 at Charlotte, NC. **June**—Budweiser 500 at Dover,DE; Banquet 300km at Somona, CA; AC Spark Plug 500 at Pocono,PA; Miller Draft 400 at Brooklyn, MI.
July—Pepsi 400 at Daytona; Miller Draft 500 at Pocono,PA; DieHard 500 at Talladega,AL. **August**—Budweiser at the Glen at Watkins Glen,NY; Champion Spark Plug 400 at Brooklyn,MI; Bud 500 at Bristol,TN. **September**—Southern 500 at Darlington,SC; Miller Draft 400 at Richmond,VA; Peak Anti-Freeze 500 at Dover,DE; Goody's 500 at Martinsville,VA; Tyson Holly Farms 400 at North Wilkesboro,NC. **October**—Mello-Yello 500 at Charlotte,NC; AC Delco 500 at Rockingham,NC. **November**—Checker 500 at Phoenix; Atlanta Journal 500 at Atlanta.

NASCAR Results (Cont.)

1991 Daytona 500

Date—Sunday, Feb.17, 1991, at Daytona (Fla.) International Speedway. **Distance**—500 miles; **Course**—2.5 miles; **Field**—42 cars; **Average speed**—148.148 mph; **Margin of victory**—under caution; **Time of race**—3 hours, 22 minutes, 30 seconds; **Caution flags**—9 for 35 laps; **Lead changes**—21 among 9 drivers; **Attendance**—150,000 (estimated). **Defending champion**—Derrike Cope; **Pole sitter**—Davey Allison at 195.955 mph (45.929 seconds). Driver (start pos.)

Driver (start pos.)	Hometown	Car	Laps	Ended	Earnings
1 Ernie Irvan (2)	Rockwell, N.C.	Chevy Lumina	200	Running	$233,000
2 Sterling Marlin (12)	Columbia, Tenn.	Ford Thunderbird	200	Running	133,925
3 Joe Ruttman (14)	Franklin,Tenn.	Olds Cutlass	200	Running	111,450
4 Rick Mast (7)	Rockbridge Baths, Va.	Olds Cutlass	200	Running	100,900
5 Dale Earnhardt (4)	Doolie, N.C.	Chevy Lumina	200	Running	113,850
6 Dale Jarrett (17)	Conover, N.C.	Ford Thunderbird	199	Running	74,900
7 Bobby Hillin, Jr.(36)	Harrisburg, N.C.	Olds Cutlass	199	Running	50,925
8 Alan Kulwicki (27)	Charlotte	Ford Thunderbird	199	Running	52,450
9 Ricky Rudd (9)	Chesapeake, Va.	Chevy Lumina	199	Running	52,600
10 Bobby Hamilton (20)	Nashville	Olds Cutlass	199	Running	43,500
11 Dick Trickle (18)	Iron Station, N.C.	Pontiac G.Prix	199	Running	39,525
12 Eddie Bierschwale (40)	San Antonio	Olds Cutlass	199	Running	31,550
13 Terry Labonte (31)	Archdale, N.C.	Olds Cutlass	198	Running	34,455
14 Chad Little (30)	Charlotte, N.C.	Ford Thunderbird	198	Running	29,540
15 Davey Allison (1)	Hueytown, Ala.	Ford Thunderbird	197	Accident	77,350
16 Kyle Petty (6)	High Point, N.C.	Pontiac G.Prix	197	Accident	41,580
17 Mickey Gibbs (38)	Glencoe, Ala.	Pontiac G.Prix	197	Running	24,560
18 Robby Gordon (35)	Los Angeles	Ford Thunderbird	196	Running	23,740
19 Richard Petty (3)	Randleman, N.C.	Pontiac G.Prix	195	Running	43,120
20 Phil Barkdoll (29)	Phoenix	Olds Cutlass	194	Running	24,160
21 Mark Martin (18)	Jamestown, N.C.	Ford Thunderbird	193	Running	31,955
22 Brett Bodine (41)	Harrisburg, N.C.	Buick Regal	193	Running	23,400
23 Jim Sauter (21)	Necedah, Wisc.	Pontiac G.Prix	192	Running	21,845
24 Darrell Waltrip (10)	Franklin, Tenn.	Chevy Lumina	190	Running	25,440
25 Harry Gant (11)	Taylorsville, N.C.	Olds Cutlass	190	Accident	26,385
26 Derrike Cope (33)	Charlotte	Chevy Lumina	189	Accident	28,180
27 Rusty Wallace (8)	Concord, N.C.	Pontiac G.Prix	188	Accident	26,425
28 Bill Elliott (15)	Dawsonville, Ga.	Ford Thunderbird	188	Running	28,680
29 Hut Stricklin (5)	Calera, Ala.	Buick Regal	185	Accident	33,865
30 Ted Musgrave (37)	Franklin, Wis.	Pontiac G.Prix	180	Running	18,710
31 Ken Schrader (24)	Concord, N.C.	Chevy Lumina	176	Running	22,330
32 Geoff Bodine (19)	Julian, N.C.	Ford Thunderbird	150	Oil leak	28,150
33 Rick Wilson (26)	Cornelius, N.C.	Buick Regal	137	Running	21,545
34 Morgan Shepherd (34)	Conover, N.C.	Ford Thunderbird	70	Piston	23,490
35 Dave Marcis (42)	Avery's Creek, N.C.	Chevy Lumina	40	Valve	19,185
36 Jeff Purvis (22)	Clarksville, Tenn.	Olds Cutlass	37	Overheat	18,380
37 Buddy Baker (16)	Sherrill's Ford, N.C.	Pontiac G.Prix	35	Engine	18,800
38 Michael Waltrip (13)	Huntersville, N.C.	Pontiac G.Prix	35	Piston	21,520
39 Jimmy Means (39)	Forest City, N.C.	Pontiac G.Prix	29	Accident	27,660
40 Jimmy Spencer (23)	Mooresville, N.C.	Chevy Lumina	29	Accident	20,200
41 Sammy Swindell (32)	Bartlett, Tenn.	Olds Cutlass	28	Accident	16,500
42 Greg Sacks (25)	Maitland, Fla.	Chevy Lumina	20	Accident	17,450

NASCAR Point Standings

Official Top 10 NASCAR Winston Cup point leaders and Top 15 money leaders for 1999 and unofficial Top 10 point leaders and Top 15 money leaders for 1991 (through Sept.22). Points awarded for places 1 to 40 and lap leaders. Earnings include bonuses. Listed are starts (Sts), races won (1st), top five finishes (Top5), poles won (PW) and points (Pts).

FINAL 1990		Sts	1st	Top5	PW	Pts	1991 (thru Sept.22)		Sts	1st	Top5	PW	Pts
1	Dale Earnhardt	29	9	18	4	4430	1	Dale Earnhardt	24	3	12	0	3570
2	Mark Martin	29	3	16	3	4404	2	Ricky Rudd	24	1	9	1	3511
3	Geoff Bodine	29	3	11	2	4017	3	Ernie Irvan	24	2	10	1	3388
4	Bill Elliott	29	1	12	2	3999	4	Davey Allison	24	3	8	3	3271
5	Morgan Shepherd	29	1	7	0	3689	5	Mark Martin	24	0	11	4	3225
6	Rusty Wallace	29	2	9	2	3676	6	Harry Gant	24	5	11	0	3206
7	Ricky Rudd	29	1	8	2	3601	7	Ken Schrader	24	2	9	0	3175
8	Alan Kulwicki	29	1	5	1	3599	8	Sterling Marlin	24	0	5	2	3102
9	Ernie Irvan	29	1	6	3	3593	9	Darrell Waltrip	24	2	4	0	3089
10	Ken Schrader	29	0	7	3	3572	10	Rusty Wallace	24	2	8	2	3004

Money Leaders

FINAL 1990

	Earnings			Earnings			Earnings
1 Dale Earnhardt	$3,083,056	6 Ken Schrader	$769,934	11 Derrike Cope	$569,451
2 Mark Martin	1,302,958	7 Kyle Petty	746,326	12 Alan Kulwicki	550,936
3 Geoff Bodine	1,131,222	8 Morgan Shepherd	666,915	13 Ernie Irvan	535,280
4 Bill Elliott	1,090,730	9 Davey Allison	640,684	14 Darrell Waltrip	530,420
5 Rusty Wallace	954,129	10 Ricky Rudd	573,650	15 Harry Gant	522,519

1991 (through Sept.22)

	Earnings			Earnings			Earnings
1 Davey Allison	$1,105,945	6 Mark Martin	$633,425	11 Sterling Marlin	$437,485
2 Dale Earnhardt	952,980	7 Ricky Rudd	611,605	12 Geoff Bodine	415,470
3 Harry Gant	784,385	8 Bill Elliott	550,345	13 Rusty Wallace	394,605
4 Ernie Irvan	772,525	9 Darrell Waltrip	440,255	14 Morgan Shepherd	380,820
5 Kan Schrader	649,490	10 Alan Kulwicki	437,690	15 Dale Jarrett	369,190

CART Results

Winners of CART Indy car races from Oct.7, 1990 through Sept.22, 1991.

LATE 1990

Date	Event	Winner (Pos.)	Avg.mph	Earnings	Pole	Qual.mph
Oct. 7	Bosch Spark Plug GP	Emerson Fittipaldi (3)	112.170	$85,334	B.Rahal	175.936
Oct. 21	Champion S.P.300km.	Danny Sullivan (1)	103.556	86,908	D.Sullivan	110.113

Winning car: Penske 90-Chevrolet (Fittipaldi, Sullivan).

1991 (through Sept.22)

Date	Event	Winner (Pos.)	Avg.mph	Earnings	Pole	Qual.mph
Mar. 17	Surfers Paradise	John Andretti (9)	91.950	$118,625	Mi.Andretti	100.501
Apr. 14	Toyota GP of Long Beach	Al.Unser, Jr.(2)	81.195	133,134	Mi.Andretti	90.671
Apr. 21	Valvoline 200	Arie Luyendyk (9)	129.988	63,662	R.Mears	168.334
May 26	**Indianapolis 500**	Rick Mears (1)	176.457	1,219,704	R.Mears	224.113
June 2	Miller Genuine Draft 200	Michael Andretti (3)	134.557	63,476	R.Mears	162.267
June 16	Valvoline Detroit GP	Emerson Fittipaldi (2)	78.824	147,700	Mi.Andretti	88.721
June 23	Budweiser-G.I.Joe's 200	Michael Andretti (4)	115.208	79,398	E.Fittipaldi	122.470
July 7	Budweiser Cleveland GP	Michael Andretti (2)	117.763	78,922	E.Fittipaldi	140.842
July 14	Marlboro GP/Meadowlands	Bobby Rahal (4)	95.551	77,922	R.Mears	115.991
July 21	Molson Indy Toronto	Michael Andretti (1)	99.143	133,154	Mi.Andretti	108.469
Aug. 4	Marlboro 500	Rick Mears (1)	167.230	173,182	R.Mears	225.169
Aug. 25	Texaco/Havoline Denver GP	Al Unser, Jr.(3)	69.576	135,700	Mi.Andretti	79.631
Sept. 1	Molson Indy Vancouver	Michael Andretti (1)	93.888	138,920	Mi.Andretti	105.205
Sept. 15	Pioneer Electronics 200	Michael Andretti (1)	99.786	83,700	Mi.Andretti	116.589
Sept. 22	Texaco/Havoline 200	Michael Andretti (3)	126.205	78,700	B.Rahal	134.466

Winning cars: Lola-Chevrolet, 12 (Mi.Andretti 7, A.Unser,Jr. 2, J.Andretti, Luyendyk, Rahal); Penske-Chevrolet, 3 (Mears 2, Fittipaldi).
Remaining races (2): Bosch Spark Plug GP (Oct.6) and Toyota Monterey GP (Oct.20).

1991 Race Locations

March—Gold Coast Indy at Surfers Paradise, Australia. **April**—Toyota GP at Long Beach,CA; Valvoline 200 at Phoenix. **May**—Indianapolis 500 at Indianapolis Motor Speedway. **June**—Miller 200 at West Allis,WI; Detroit GP in downtown Detroit; Budweiser-G.I.Joe's 200 at Portland. **July**—Cleveland GP at Burke Lakefront Airport; Marlboro GP/Meadowlands at E.Rutherford, NJ; Molson Toronto at Exhibition Place.

August—Marlboro 500 at Brooklyn,MI; Havoline GP at Denver. **September**—Molson at Vancouver; Pioneer 200 at Lexington,OH; Texaco/Havoline 200 at Elkhart Lake,WI. **October**—Bosch GP at Nazareth,PA; Champion 300km at Monterey,CA.

CART Point Standings

Official Top 10 CART PPG Cup point leaders and Top 15 money leaders for 1990 and unofficial Top 10 point leaders and Top 15 money leaders for 1991 (through Sept.22). Points awarded for places 1 to 12, fastest qualifier and overall lap leader. Listed are starts (Sts), races won (1st), races running at finish (RAF), poles won (PW), and points.

FINAL 1990

	Sts	1st	RAF	PW	Pts
1 Al Unser, Jr	16	6	13	1	210
2 Michael Andretti	16	5	11	4	181
3 Rick Mears	16	1	14	3	168
4 Bobby Rahal	16	0	14	1	153
5 Emerson Fittipaldi	16	1	13	2	144
6 Danny Sullivan	16	2	10	4	139
7 Mario Andretti	16	0	11	0	136
8 Arie Luyendyk	16	1	11	0	90
9 Eddie Cheever	16	0	11	0	80
10 John Andretti	16	0	8	0	51

1991 (thru Sept.22)

	Sts	1st	RAF	PW	Pts
1 Michael Andretti	15	7	10	7	197
2 Bobby Rahal	15	1	12	1	184
3 Al Unser, Jr	15	2	12	0	169
4 Rick Mears	15	2	10	5	133
5 Emerson Fittipaldi	15	1	9	2	123
6 Arie Luyendyk	15	1	10	0	109
7 Mario Andretti	15	0	10	0	108
8 John Andretti	15	1	11	0	101
9 Eddie Cheever	15	0	9	0	75
10 Scott Pruett	15	0	6	0	61

CART Results (Cont.)

1991 Indianapolis 500

Date—Sunday, May 26, 1991, at Indianapolis Motor Speedway. **Distance**—500 miles; **Course**—2.5 mile oval; **Field**—33 cars; **Winner's average speed**—176.457 mph; **Margin of victory**—3.149 seconds; **Time of race**—2 hours, 50 minutes, 0.791 seconds; **Caution flags**—7 for 32 laps; **Lead changes**—19 by 6 drivers; **Attendance**—400,000 (estimated).

Defending champion—Arie Luyendyk; **Pole sitter**—Rick Mears at 224.113 mph.

Driver (start pos.)	Hometown	Car	Laps	Ended	Earnings
1 Rick Mears (1)	Bakersfield, Calif.	Penske-Chevrolet	200	Running	$1,219,704
2 Michael Andretti (5)	Nazareth, Pa.	Lola-Chevrolet	200	Running	607,753
3 Arie Luyendyk (14)	Scottsdale, Ariz.	Lola-Chevrolet	199	Running	317,053
4 Al Unser, Jr.(6)	Albuquerque, N.M.	Lola-Chevrolet	198	Running	223,916
5 John Andretti (7)	Indianapolis	Lola-Chevrolet	197	Running	205,153
6 Gordon Johncock (33)	Hastings, Mich.	'90 Lola-Cosworth	188	Running	275,690
7 Mario Andretti (3)	Nazareth, Pa.	Lola-Chevrolet	187	Engine	203,478
8 Stan Fox (17)	Janesville, Wis.	Lola-Buick	185	Running	201,090
9 Tony Bettenhausen (20)	Indianapolis	'90 Penske-Chevy	180	Running	170,016
10 Danny Sullivan (9)	Aspen, Colo.	Lola-Alfa Romeo	173	Engine	194,403
11 Emerson Fittipaldi (15)	Brazil	Penske-Chevrolet	171	Gearbox	183,728
12 Scott Pruett (27)	Dublin, Ohio	Truesports Judd	166	Engine	159,191
13 Dominci Dobson (30)	Fairfax, Calif.	'90 Lola-Judd	164	Running	159,190
14 Randy Lewis (32)	Hillsborough, Calif.	'90 Lola-Cosworth	159	Running	150,490
15 r-Jeff Andretti (11)	Nazareth, Pa.	Lola-Cosworth	150	Engine	167,490
16 r-Hiro Matsushita (24)	Japan	Lola-Buick	149	Running	154,891
17 Scott Brayton (19)	Coldwater, Mich.	Lola-Chevrolet	146	Engine	172,191
18 Bernard Jourdain (21)	Mexico	'90 Lola-Buick	141	Gearbox	140,190
19 Bobby Rahal (4)	Dublin, Ohio	Lola-Chevrolet	130	Engine	153,741
20 Geoff Brabham (22)	Australia	Truesports-Judd	109	Electrical	136,491
21 Pancho Carter (32)	Brownsburg, Ind.	'89 Lola-Buick	94	Engine	139,703
22 Gary Bettenhausen (13)	Monrovia, Ind.	Lola-Buick	89	Radiator	177,890
23 Tero Palmroth (26)	Finland	'90 Lola-Cosworth	77	Engine	131,990
24 r-Mike Groff (18)	Northridge, Calif.	Lola-Cosworth	68	Water leak	133,290
25 John Paul, Jr.(25)	W.Palm Beach, Fla.	'90 Lola-Buick	53	Oil leak	130,690
26 Jim Crawford (8)	Scotland	Lola-Buick	40	Engine	133,690
27 Scott Goodyear (12)	Toronto	Lola-Judd	38	Engine	127,791
28 A.J.Foyt (2)	Houston	Lola-Chevrolet	25	Suspension	153,591
29 Kevin Cogan (16)	Palos Verdes, Calif.	Lola-Buick	24	Crash	127,391
30 Roberto Guerrero (28)	Capistrano, Calif.	Lola-Alfa Romeo	23	Crash	125,203
31 Eddie Cheever (10)	Vail, Colo.	Lola-Chevrolet	17	Electrical	125,591
32 r-Willy T.Ribbs (29)	San Jose	'90 Lola-Buick	5	Engine	147,791
33 r-Buddy Lazier (23)	Vail, Colo.	'90 Lola-Cosworth	1	Hit wall	162,690

Note: (r) indicates rookie Indy 500 driver.

Money Leaders

FINAL 1990

	Earnings			Earnings				Earnings
1 Al Unser,Jr	$1,936,833		6 Michael Andretti	$1,303,526		11 Scott Brayton		$592,442
2 Arie Luyendyk	1,747,984		7 Mario Andretti	976,721		12 Raul Boesel		579,913
3 E.Fittipaldi	1,513,176		8 Danny Sullivan	965,161		13 A.J.Foyt		578,744
4 Bobby Rahal	1,462,458		9 Eddie Cheever	869,720		14 Roberto Guerrero		471,375
5 Rick Mears	1,414,744		10 Teo Fabi	614,335		15 John Andretti		456,594

1991 (through Sept.22)

	Earnings			Earnings				Earnings
1 Rick Mears	$1,957,113		6 E.Fittipaldi	$882,571		11 Scott Brayton		$634,132
2 Michael Andretti	1,532,582		7 Mario Andretti	797,515		12 Danny Sullivan		626,754
3 Bobby Rahal	1,092,971		8 John Andretti	722,619		13 Tony Bettenhausen		553,705
4 Al Unser,Jr	1,071,950		9 Scott Pruett	662,012		14 Jeff Andretti		552,633
5 Arie Luyendyk	909,412		10 Eddie Cheever	635,800		15 Scott Goodyear		544,228

Formula One Results

LATE 1990

Date	Grand Prix	Winner (Pos)	Time	Avg.MPH	Pole	Qual.mph
Sept. 30	Spain	Alain Prost (2)	1:48:01.461	106.270	A.Senna	120.369
Oct. 21	Japan	Nelson Piquet (6)	1:34:36.824	122.362	A.Senna	135.121
Nov. 4	Australia	Nelson Piquet (5)	1:49:44.570	104.017	A.Senna	111.742

Winning Constructors: Benetton-Ford 2 (Piquet 2); Ferrari (Prost).

1991 (through Sept.22)

Date	Grand Prix	Winner (Pos)	Time	Avg.MPH	Pole	Qual.mph
Mar. 10	United States	Ayrton Senna (1)	2:00:47.828	93.018	A.Senna	102.208
Mar. 24	Brazil	Ayrton Senna (1)	1:38:28.128	116.266	A.Senna	126.640
Apr. 27	San Marino	Ayrton Senna (1)	1:35:14.750	120.270	A.Senna	137.696
May 12	Monaco	Ayrton Senna (1)	1:53:02.334	85.615	A.Senna	92.660
June 2	Canada	Nelson Piquet (8)	1:38:51.490	115.022	R.Patrese	124.126
June 16	Mexico	Riccardo Patrese (1)	1:29:52.205	122.880	R.Patrese	128.947
July 7	France	Nigel Mansell (4)	1:38:00.056	117.001	R.Patrese	128.140
July 14	Britain	Nigel Mansell (1)	1:27:35.479	131.227	N.Mansell	144.420
July 28	Germany	Nigel Mansell (1)	1:19:29.661	143.554	N.Mansell	156.722
Aug. 11	Hungary	Ayrton Senna (1)	1:49:12.796	104.301	A.Senna	116.566
Aug. 25	Belgium	Ayrton Senna (1)	1:27:17.669	134.806	A.Senna	143.886
Sept. 8	Italy	Nigel Mansell (2)	1:17:54.319	147.109	A.Senna	159.951
Sept. 22	Portugal	Riccardo Patrese (1)	1:35:42.304	120.314	R.Patrese	133.295

Winning Constructors: McLaren-Honda 6 (Senna 6); Williams-Renault 6 (Mansell 4, Patrese 2); Benetton-Ford 1 (Piquet).
Remaining races (3): Spain (Sept.29); Japan (Oct.20); Australia (Nov.3).

1991 Race Locations

March—United States GP at Phoenix; Brazilian GP at Sao Paulo. **April**—San Marino GP at Imola, Italy; **May**—Monaco GP in downtown Monte Carlo. **June**—Canadian GP at Montreal; Mexican GP at Mexico City. **July**—French GP at Nevers; British GP at Silverstone in Towcester; German GP at Hockenheim. **August**—Hungarian GP at Hungaroring in Budapest; Belgian GP at Spa-Francorchamps. **September**—Italian GP at Monza in Milan; Portugese GP at Estoril; Spanish GP at Jerez. **October**—Japanese GP at Suzuka. **November**—Australian GP at Adelaide.

Formula One Point Standings

Official Top 10 Formula One World Championship point leaders and unofficial Top 10 point leaders for 1990 (through Sept.23). Points awarded for places 1 to 6. Listed are starts (Sts), races won (1st), top six finishes (T/6), poles won, and points. Only 11 best race results were counted.
Note: Formula One does not keep Money Leader standings.

FINAL 1990

		Sts	1st	T/6	PW	Pts
1	Ayrton Senna, BRA	16	6	11	10	78
2	Alain Prost, FRA	16	5	12	0	71
3	Nelson Piquet, BRA	16	2	12	0	43
	Gerhard Berger, AUT	16	0	11	2	43
5	Nigel Mansell, GBR	16	1	7	3	37
6	Thierry Boutsen, BEL	16	1	10	1	34
7	Riccardo Patrese, ITA	16	1	8	0	23
8	Alessandro Nannini, ITA	14	0	6	0	21
9	Jean Alesi, FRA	15	0	3	0	13
10	Roberto Moreno, BRA	14	0	1	0	6
	Ivan Capelli, ITA	14	0	1	0	6

Note: Overall, Prost earned 73 points and Piquet 44 in 16 races (only the best 11 results count).

1991 (thru Sept.22)

		Sts	1st	T/6	PW	Pts
1	Ayrton Senna, BRA	13	6	11	7	83
2	Nigel Mansell, GBR	13	4	8	2	59
3	Riccardo Patrese, ITA	13	2	8	4	44
4	Gerhard Berger, AUT	13	0	7	0	31
5	Nelson Piquet, BRA	13	1	7	0	25
	Alain Prost, FRA	13	0	6	0	25
7	Jean Alesi, FRA	13	0	6	0	18
8	Stefano Modena, ITA	13	0	2	0	9
	Andrea De Cesaris, ITA	12	0	4	0	9
10	Roberto Moreno, BRA	13	0	3	0	8

1991 Endurance Races

24 Hours at Daytona
Feb. 2-3 at Daytona Beach, FL

Officially the SunBank 24 Hours of Daytona and first held in 1962 (as a 3-hour race). An IMSA Camel GT race contested over a 3.56-mile road course at Daytona International Speedway. Listed are drivers, countries, car and laps completed. Starting positions in parentheses.

1 (7) Hurley Haywood (USA), Frank Jelinski (GER), Henri Pescarolo (FRA), John Winter (GER) and Bob Wollek (FRA); PORSCHE 962C; $71,500; 719 laps (2,559.64 miles) at 106.633. mph.
2 (4) Geoff Brabham (AUS), Derek Daley (IRL), Bob Earl (USA) and Chip Robinson (USA); NISSAN R90C; 701 laps.
3 (12) James Adams (USA), Chris Cord (USA), Rob Dyson (USA) and John Hotchkis (USA); PORSCHE 962; 692 laps.
4 (22) Wally Dallenbach (USA), Robby Gordon (USA) and Mark Martin (USA); FORD MUSTANG; 672 laps.
5 (6) Jeff Andretti (USA), Mario Andretti (USA) and Michael Andretti (USA); PORSCHE 962C; 663 laps.

Fastest lap: Julian Bailey (GBR), NISSAN R90-C; 128.461 mph (1:39.765).

24 Hours of Le Mans
June 22-23 at LeMans, France

Officially the Le Mans Grand Prix d'Endurance and first held in 1923. Contested over the 8.451-mile circuit in Le Mans, France. Listed are drivers, countries, car, and laps completed.

1 Johnny Herbert (GBR), Bertrand Gachot (BEL) and Volker Wiedler (GER); MAZDA 787-B; 362 laps; 3,059.262 miles at 127.589 mph.
2 Raul Boesel (BRA), Michel Ferte (FRA) and Davy Jones, (USA);JAGUAR XJR-12; 360 laps.
3 Kenny Acheson (GBR), Teo Fabi (ITA) and Bob Wollek (FRA); JAGUAR XJR-12; 358 laps.
4 John Nielsen (DEN), Andy Wallace (GBR) and Derek Warwick (GBR); JAGUAR XJR-12; 356 laps.
5 Fritz Freutzpointer (GER), Michael Schumacher (GER) and Karl Wendlinger (AUT); Mercedes C-11; 355.

Fastest lap: Schumacher (AUT), Mercedes C-11; 141.135 mph (3:35.564).

THE 1992 INFORMATION PLEASE SPORTS ALMANAC

AUTO RACING STATISTICS

THROUGH THE YEARS
1911-1991
MAJOR RACES • LEADERS

SEC B

PAGE 722

NASCAR Circuit
The Crown Jewels

The four biggest races on the NASCAR circuit are the Daytona 500, the Winston 500, the Coca-Cola 600 and the Heinz Southern 500. The Winston Cup Media Guide lists them as the richest (Daytona), the fastest (Winston), the longest (Coca-Cola) and the oldest (Southern). Winston has offered a $1 million bonus since 1985 to any driver who can win three of the four races. The only drivers to win three of the races in a single year are LeeRoy Yarbrough (1969), David Pearson (1976) and Bill Elliott (1985).

Daytona 500

Held early in the NASCAR season; 200 laps around a 2.5-mile high-banked oval at Daytona International Speedway in Daytona Beach, FL. First race in 1959, although stock car racing at Daytona dates back to 1936. Winning drivers who started from pole positions are in **bold** type.

Multiple winners: Richard Petty (7); Cale Yarborough (4); Bobby Allison (3); Bill Elliott (2). **Multiple poles:** Buddy Baker and Cale Yarborough (4); Bill Elliott, Fireball Roberts and Ken Schrader (3); Donnie Allison (2).

Year	Winner	Car	Owner	MPH	Pole Sitter	MPH
1959	Lee Petty	Oldsmobile	Petty Enterprises	135.521	Bob Welborn	140.121
1960	Junior Johnson	Chevrolet	Ray Fox	124.740	Cotton Owens	149.892
1961	Marvin Panch	Pontiac	Smokey Yunick	149.601	Fireball Roberts	155.709
1962	**Fireball Roberts**	Pontiac	Smokey Yunick	152.529	Fireball Roberts	156.999
1963	Tiny Lund	Ford	Wood Brothers	151.566	Fireball Roberts	160.943
1964	Richard Petty	Plymouth	Petty Enterprises	154.344	Paul Goldsmith	174.910
1965a	Fred Lorenzen	Ford	Holman-Moody	141.539	Darel Dieringer	171.151
1966b	**Richard Petty**	Plymouth	Petty Enterprises	160.627	Richard Petty	175.165
1967	Mario Andretti	Ford	Holman-Moody	149.926	Curtis Turner	180.831
1968	**Cale Yarborough**	Mercury	Wood Brothers	143.251	Cale Yarborough	189.222
1969	LeeRoy Yarbrough	Ford	Junior Johnson	157.950	Buddy Baker	188.901
1970	Pete Hamilton	Plymouth	Petty Enterprises	149.601	Cale Yarborough	194.015
1971	Richard Petty	Plymouth	Petty Enterprises	144.462	A.J.Foyt	182.744
1972	A.J.Foyt	Mercury	Wood Brothers	161.550	Bobby Issac	186.632
1973	Richard Petty	Dodge	Petty Enterprises	157.205	Buddy Baker	185.662
1974c	Richard Petty	Dodge	Petty Enterprises	140.894	David Pearson	185.017
1975	Benny Parsons	Chevrolet	L.G.DeWitt	153.649	Donnie Allison	185.827
1976	David Pearson	Mercury	Wood Brothers	152.181	Ramo Stott	183.456
1977	Cale Yarborough	Chevrolet	Junior Johnson	153.218	Donnie Allison	188.048
1978	Bobby Allison	Ford	Bud Moore	159.730	Cale Yarborough	187.536
1979	Richard Petty	Oldsmobile	Petty Enterprises	143.977	Buddy Baker	196.049
1980	**Buddy Baker**	Oldsmobile	Ranier Racing	177.602*	Buddy Baker	194.099
1981	Richard Petty	Buick	Petty Enterprises	169.651	Bobby Allison	194.624
1982	Bobby Allison	Buick	DiGard Racing	153.991	Benny Parsons	196.317
1983	Cale Yarborough	Pontiac	Ranier Racing	155.979	Ricky Rudd	198.864
1984	**Cale Yarborough**	Chevrolet	Ranier Racing	150.994	Cale Yarborough	201.848
1985	**Bill Elliott**	Ford	Melling Racing	172.265	Bill Elliott	205.114
1986	Geoff Bodine	Chevrolet	Hendrick Motorsports	148.124	Bill Elliott	205.039
1987	**Bill Elliott**	Ford	Melling Racing	176.263	Bill Elliott	210.364†
1988	Bobby Allison	Buick	Stavola Bros.Racing	137.531	Ken Schrader	193.823
1989	Darrell Waltrip	Chevrolet	Hendrick Motorsports	148.466	Ken Schrader	196.996
1990	Derrike Cope	Chevrolet	Whitcomb Racing	165.761	Ken Schrader	196.515
1991	Ernie Irvan	Chevrolet	Morgan McClure Racing	148.148	Davey Allison	195.955

*Track and race record for Winning Time.
†Track and race record for Qualifying Time.
Notes: a—rain shortened 1965 to 332+ miles; **b**—rain shortened 1966 race to 495 miles; **c**—in 1974, race shortened 50 miles due to energy crisis.
Also: Pole sitters determined by pole qualifying race (1959-65); by two-lap average (1966-68); by fastest single lap (since 1969).

Winston 500

Held at Talladega (Ala.) Superspeedway. **Multiple winners:** Bobby Allison, Buddy Baker and David Pearson (3); Davey Allison and Darrell Waltrip (2).

Year		Year		Year		Year	
1970	Pete Hamilton	1977	Darrell Waltrip	1983	Richard Petty	1988	Phil Parsons
1971	Donnie Allison	1978	Cale Yarborough	1984	Cale Yarborough	1989	Davey Allison
1972	David Pearson	1979	Bobby Allison	1985	Bill Elliott		
1973	David Pearson			1986	Bobby Allison	1990	Dale Earnhardt
1974	David Pearson	1980	Buddy Baker	1987	Davey Allison	1991	Harry Gant
1975	Buddy Baker	1981	Bobby Allison				
1976	Buddy Baker	1982	Darrell Waltrip				

Coca-Cola 600

Held at Charlotte (N.C.) Motor Speedway. **Multiple winners:** Darrell Waltrip (5); Buddy Baker, David Pearson (3); Bobby Allison, Neil Bonnett, Dale Earnhardt, Fred Lorenzen, Jim Paschal, Richard Petty (2).

Year		Year		Year		Year	
1960	Joe Lee Johnson	1969	Lee Roy Yarbrough	1977	Richard Petty	1985	Darrell Waltrip
1961	David Pearson	1970	Donnie Allison	1978	Darrell Waltrip	1986	Dale Earnhardt
1962	Nelson Stacy	1971	Bobby Allison	1979	Darrell Waltrip	1987	Kyle Petty
1963	Fred Lorenzen	1972	Buddy Baker			1988	Darrell Waltrip
1964	Jim Paschal	1973	Buddy Baker	1980	Benny Parsons	1989	Darrell Waltrip
1965	Fred Lorenzen	1974	David Pearson	1981	Bobby Allison		
1966	Marvin Panch	1975	Richard Petty	1982	Neil Bonnett	1990	Rusty Wallace
1967	Jim Paschal	1976	David Pearson	1983	Neil Bonnett	1991	Davey Allison
1968	Buddy Baker			1984	Bobby Allison		

Heinz Southern 500

Held at Darlington (S.C.) International Raceway. **Multiple winners:** Cale Yarborough (5); Bobby Allison (4); Buck Baker, Dale Earnhardt, David Pearson and Herb Thomas (3); Bill Elliott and Fireball Roberts (2).

Year		Year		Year		Year	
1950	Johnny Mantz	1962	Larry Frank	1973	Cale Yarborough	1983	Bobby Allison
1951	Herb Thomas	1963	Fireball Roberts	1974	Cale Yarborough	1984	Harry Gant
1952	Fonty Flock	1964	Buck Baker	1975	Bobby Allison	1985	Bill Elliott
1953	Buck Baker	1965	Ned Jarrett	1976	David Pearson	1986	Tim Richmond
1954	Herb Thomas	1966	Darel Dieringer	1977	David Pearson	1987	Dale Earnhardt
1955	Herb Thomas	1967	Richard Petty	1978	Cale Yarborough	1988	Bill Elliott
1956	Curtis Turner	1968	Cale Yarborough	1979	David Pearson	1989	Dale Earnhardt
1957	Speedy Thompson	1969	LeeRoy Yarbrough				
1958	Fireball Roberts	1970	Buddy Baker	1980	Terry Labonte	1990	Dale Earnhardt
1959	Jim Reed	1971	Bobby Allison	1981	Neil Bonnett	1991	Harry Gant
		1972	Bobby Allison	1982	Cale Yarborough		
1960	Buck Baker						
1961	Nelson Stacy						

All-Time Leaders

NASCAR's all-time Top 20 drivers in victories, pole positions and earnings, based on records through 1990. Drivers active in 1990 in **bold** type.

Victories

		No
1	**Richard Petty**	200
2	David Pearson	105
3	Bobby Allison	84
4	Cale Yarborough	83
5	**Darrell Waltrip**	79
6	Lee Petty	54
7	Ned Jarrett	50
	Junior Johnson	50
9	**Dale Earnhardt**	48
	Herb Thomas	48
11	Buck Baker	46
12	Tim Flock	40
13	Bobby Issac	37
14	Fireball Roberts	34
15	**Bill Elliott**	33
16	Rex White	28
17	Fred Lorenzen	26
18	Jim Paschal	25
19	Joe Weatherly	24
20	Benny Parsons	21
	Jack Smith	21

Pole Positions

		No
1	**Richard Petty**	127
2	David Pearson	113
3	Cale Yarborough	70
4	Bobby Allison	57
	Darrell Waltrip	57
6	Bobby Issac	51
7	Junior Johnson	47
8	Buck Baker	44
9	**Buddy Baker**	40
10	**Bill Elliott**	39
11	Herb Thomas	38
12	Tim Flock	37
	Fireball Roberts	37
14	Ned Jarrett	36
	Rex White	36
16	Fred Lorenzen	33
17	Fonty Flock	30
18	**Geoff Bodine**	27
	Marvin Panch	25
20	Jack Smith	24

Earnings

		Purses
1	**Dale Earnhardt**	$12,827,634
2	**Darrell Waltrip**	10,527,562
3	**Bill Elliott**	10,252,269
4	**Richard Petty**	7,140,959
5	Bobby Allison	7,102,233
6	**Rusty Wallace**	6,334,559
7	**Terry Labonte**	6,289,170
8	Cale Yarborough	5,003,716
9	**Ricky Rudd**	5,000,590
10	**Geoff Bodine**	4,999,971
11	**Harry Gant**	4,792,443
12	Benny Parsons	3,926,539
13	**Neil Bonnett**	3,847,146
14	**Buddy Baker**	3,526,435
15	**Dave Marcis**	3,375,669
16	**Ken Schrader**	3,280,689
17	**Kyle Petty**	3,246,735
18	**Mark Martin**	2,810,163
19	**Morgan Shepherd**	2,688,080
20	**Davey Allison**	2,522,037

NASCAR Circuit (Cont.)

Winston Cup Champions

Originally the Grand National Championship, 1949-70, and based on official NASCAR (National Association for Stock Car Auto Racing) records through the 1990 racing season.

Multiple winners: Richard Petty (7); Dale Earnhardt (4); David Pearson, Lee Petty, Darrell Waltrip and Cale Yarborough (3); Buck Baker, Tim Flock, Ned Jarrett, Herb Thomas and Joe Weatherly (2).

Year		Year		Year		Year	
1949	Red Byron	1960	Rex White	1971	Richard Petty	1982	Darrell Waltrip
1950	Bill Rexford	1961	Ned Jarrett	1972	Richard Petty	1983	Bobby Allison
1951	Herb Thomas	1962	Joe Weatherly	1973	Benny Parsons	1984	Terry Labonte
1952	Tim Flock	1963	Joe Weatherly	1974	Richard Petty	1985	Darrell Waltrip
1953	Herb Thomas	1964	Richard Petty	1975	Richard Petty	1986	Dale Earnhardt
1954	Lee Petty	1965	Ned Jarrett	1976	Cale Yarborough	1987	Dale Earnhardt
1955	Tim Flock	1966	David Pearson	1977	Cale Yarborough	1988	Bill Elliott
1956	Buck Baker	1967	Richard Petty	1978	Cale Yarborough	1989	Rusty Wallace
1957	Buck Baker	1968	David Pearson	1979	Richard Petty	1990	Dale Earnhardt
1958	Lee Petty	1969	David Pearson	1980	Dale Earnhardt		
1959	Lee Petty	1970	Bobby Issac	1981	Darrell Waltrip		

NASCAR Rookie of the Year

Award presented to rookie driver who accumulates the most Winston Cup points based on his best 15 finishes.

Year		Year		Year		Year	
1958	Shorty Rollins	1967	Donnie Allison	1976	Skip Manning	1984	Rusty Wallace
1959	Richard Petty	1968	Pete Hamilton	1977	Ricky Rudd	1985	Ken Schrader
1960	David Pearson	1969	Dick Brooks	1978	Ronnie Thomas	1986	Alan Kulwicki
1961	Woodie Wilson	1970	Bill Dennis	1979	Dale Earnhardt	1987	Davey Allison
1962	Tom Cox	1971	Walter Ballard	1980	Jody Ridley	1988	Ken Bouchard
1963	Billy Wade	1972	Larry Smith	1981	Ron Bouchard	1989	Dick Trickle
1964	Doug Cooper	1973	Lennie Pond	1982	Geoff Bodine	1990	Rob Moroso
1965	Sam McQuagg	1974	Earl Ross	1983	Sterling Marlin		
1966	James Hylton	1975	Bruce Hill				

CART Circuit

Indianapolis 500

Held every Memorial Day weekend; 200 laps around a 2.5-mile oval at Indianapolis Motor Speedway. First race was held in 1911. Winning drivers are listed with starting positions. Winners who started from pole position are in **bold** type.

Multiple wins: A.J.Foyt, Rick Mears and Al Unser (4); Louis Meyer, Mauri Rose, Johnny Rutherford, Wilbur Shaw and Bobby Unser (3); Gordon Johncock, Tommy Milton, Bill Vukovich and Rodger Ward (2).

Multiple poles: Rick Mears (6); Mario Andretti, A.J.Foyt and Tom Sneva (4); Rex Mays (3); Billy Arnold, Ralph DePalma, Walt Faulkner, Parnelli Jones, Jack McGrath, Jimmy Murphy, Duke Nalon, Johnny Rutherford and Jimmy Snyder (2).

Year	Winner (Pos.)	Car	MPH	Pole Sitter	MPH
1911	Ray Harroun (28)	Marmon Wasp	74.602	Lewis Strang	—
1912	Joe Dawson (7)	National	78.719	Gil Anderson	—
1913	Jules Goux (7)	Peugeot	75.933	Caleb Bragg	—
1914	Rene Thomas (15)	Delage	82.474	Jean Chassagne	—
1915	Ralph DePalma (2)	Mercedes	89.840	Howard Wilcox	98.90
1916a	Dario Resta (4)	Peugeot	84.001	John Aitken	96.69
1917-18	Not held				
1919	Howard Wilcox (2)	Peugeot	88.050	Rene Thomas	104.78
1920	Gaston Chevrolet (6)	Monroe	88.618	Ralph DePalma	99.15
1921	Tommy Milton (20)	Frontenac	89.621	Ralph DePalma	100.75
1922	**Jimmy Murphy** (1)	Murphy Special	94.484	Jimmy Murphy	100.50
1923	**Tommy Milton** (1)	H.C.S. Special	90.954	Tommy Milton	108.17
1924	L.L.Corum & Joe Boyer (21)	Duesenberg Special	98.234	Jimmy Murphy	108.037
1925	Peter DePaolo (2)	Duesenberg Special	101.127	Leon Duray	113.196
1926b	Frank Lockhart (20)	Miller Special	95.904	Earl Cooper	111.735
1927	George Souders (22)	Duesenberg	97.545	Frank Lockhart	120.100
1928	Louis Meyer (13)	Miller Special	99.482	Leon Duray	122.391
1929	Ray Keech (6)	Simplex Piston Ring Special	97.585	Cliff Woodbury	120.599
1930	**Billy Arnold** (1)	Miller-Hartz Special	100.448	Billy Arnold	113.268
1931	Louis Schneider (13)	Bowes Seal Fast Special	96.629	Russ Snowberger	112.796
1932	Fred Frame (27)	Miller-Hartz Special	104.144	Lou Moore	117.363

Year	Winner (Pos.)	Car	MPH	Pole Sitter	MPH
1933	Louis Meyer (6)	Tydol Special	104.162	Bill Cummings	118.530
1934	William Cummings (10)	Boyle Products Special	104.863	Kelly Petillo	119.329
1935	Kelly Petillo (22)	Gilmore Speedway Special	106.240	Rex Mays	120.736
1936	Louis Meyer (28)	Ring-Free Special	109.069	Rex Mays	119.644
1937	Wilbur Shaw (2)	Shaw-Gilmore Special	113.580	Bill Cummings	123.343
1938	**Floyd Roberts** (1)	Burd Piston Ring Special	117.200	Floyd Roberts	125.681
1939	Wilbur Shaw (3)	Boyle Special	115.035	Jimmy Snyder	130.138
1940	Wilbur Shaw (2)	Boyle Special	114.277	Rex Mays	127.850
1941	Floyd Davis & Mauri Rose(17)	Noc-Out Hose Clamp Special	115.117	Mauri Rose	128.691
1942-45	Not held				
1946	George Robson (15)	Thorne Engineering Special	114.820	Cliff Bergere	126.471
1947	Mauri Rose (3)	Blue Crown Spark Plug Spl.	116.338	Ted Horn	126.564
1948	Mauri Rose (3)	Blue Crown Spark Plug Spl.	119.814	Duke Nalon	131.603
1949	Bill Holland (4)	Blue Crown Spark Plug Spl.	121.327	Duke Nalon	132.939
1950c	Johnnie Parsons (5)	Wynn's Friction Proofing	124.002	Walt Faulkner	134.343
1951	Lee Wallard (2)	Belanger Special	126.244	Duke Nalon	136.498
1952	Troy Ruttman (7)	Agajanian Special	128.922	Fred Agabashian	138.010
1953	**Bill Vukovich** (1)	Fuel Injection Special	128.740	Bill Vukovich	138.392
1954	Bill Vukovich (19)	Fuel Injection Special	130.840	Jack McGrath	141.033
1955	Bob Sweikert (14)	John Zink Special	128.209	Jerry Hoyt	140.045
1956	**Pat Flaherty** (1)	John Zink Special	128.490	Pat Flaherty	145.596
1957	Sam Hanks (13)	Belond Exhaust Special	135.601	Pat O'Connor	143.948
1958	Jim Bryan (7)	Belond AP Parts Special	133.791	Dick Rathmann	145.974
1959	Rodger Ward (6)	Leader Card 500 Roadster	135.857	Johnny Thomson	145.908
1960	Jim Rathmann (2)	Ken-Paul Special	138.767	Eddie Sachs	146.592
1961	A.J.Foyt (7)	Bowes Seal-Fast Special	139.131	Eddie Sachs	147.481
1962	Rodger Ward (2)	Leader Card 500 Roadster	140.293	Parnelli Jones	150.370
1963	**Parnelli Jones** (1)	Agajanian-Willard Special	143.137	Parnelli Jones	151.153
1964	A.J.Foyt (5)	Sheraton-Thompson Special	147.350	Jim Clark	158.828
1965	Jim Clark (2)	Lotus Ford	150.686	A.J.Foyt	161.233
1966	Graham Hill (15)	American Red Ball Special	144.317	Mario Andretti	165.899
1967d	A.J.Foyt (4)	Sheraton-Thompson Special	151.207	Mario Andretti	168.982
1968	Bobby Unser (3)	Rislone Special	152.882	Joe Leonard	171.559
1969	Mario Andretti (2)	STP Oil Treatment Special	156.867	A.J.Foyt	170.568
1970	**Al Unser** (1)	Johnny Lightning 500 Spl.	155.749	Al Unser	170.221
1971	Al Unser (5)	Johnny Lightning Special	157.735	Peter Revson	178.696
1972	Mark Donohue (3)	Sunoco McLaren	162.962	Bobby Unser	195.940
1973e	Gordon Johncock (11)	STP Double Oil Filters	159.036	Johnny Rutherford	198.413
1974	Johnny Rutherford (25)	McLaren	158.589	A.J.Foyt	191.632
1975f	Bobby Unser (3)	Jorgensen Eagle	149.213	A.J.Foyt	193.976
1976g	**Johnny Rutherford** (1)	Hy-Gain McLaren/Goodyear	148.725	Johnny Rutherford	188.957
1977	A.J.Foyt (4)	Gilmore Racing Team	161.331	Tom Sneva	198.884
1978	Al Unser (5)	FNCTC Chaparral Lola	161.363	Tom Sneva	202.156
1979	**Rick Mears** (1)	The Gould Charge	158.899	Rick Mears	193.736
1980	**Johnny Rutherford** (1)	Pennzoil Chaparral	142.862	Johnny Rutherford	192.256
1981h	**Bobby Unser** (1)	Norton Spirit Penske PC-9B	139.084	Bobby Unser	200.546
1982	Gordon Johncock (5)	STP Oil Treatment	162.029	Rick Mears	207.004
1983	Tom Sneva (4)	Texaco Star	162.117	Teo Fabi	207.395
1984	Rick Mears (3)	Pennzoil Z-7	163.612	Tom Sneva	210.029
1985	Danny Sullivan (8)	Miller American Special	152.982	Pancho Carter	212.583
1986	Bobby Rahal (4)	Budweiser/Truesports/March	170.722	Rick Mears	216.828
1987	Al Unser (20)	Cummins Holset Turbo	162.175	Mario Andretti	215.390
1988	**Rick Mears** (1)	Penske-Chevrolet V-8	149.809	Rick Mears	219.198
1989	Emerson Fittipaldi (3)	Penske-Chevrolet PC-18	167.581	Rick Mears	223.885
1990	Arie Luyendyk (3)	Domino's Pizza Chevrolet	185.981*	Emerson Fittipaldi	225.301†
1991	**Rick Mears** (1)	Penske-Chevrolet	176.457	Rick Mears	224.113

*Track record for Winning Time
†Track record for Qualifying Time.

Notes: a—1916 race scheduled for 300 miles; **b**—rain shortened 1926 race to 400 miles; **c**—rain shortened 1950 race to 345 miles; **d**—1967 race postponed due to rain after 18 laps (May 30), resumed next day (May 31); **e**—rain shortened 1973 race to 332+ miles; **f**—rain shortened 1975 race to 435 miles; **g**—rain shortened 1976 race to 255 miles; **h**—in 1981, runner-up Mario Andretti was awarded 1st place when winner Bobby Unser was penalized a lap after the race was completed for passing cars illegally under the caution flag. Unser and car-owner Roger Penske appealed the race stewards' decision to the U.S.Auto Club. Four months later, USAC overturned the ruling, saying that the penalty was too harsh and Unser should be fined $40,000 rather than stripped of his championship.

CART Circuit (Cont.)

Indy 500 Rookie of the Year

Voted on by a panel of auto racing media. Award does not necessarily go to highest-finishing first year driver. Graham Hill won the race on this first try in 1966, but the rookie award went to Jackie Stewart.

Father and son winners: Mario and Michael Andretti (1965 and 1984); Bill and Billy Vukovich (1968 and 1988).

Year		Year		Year		Year	
1952	Art Cross	1962	Jimmy McElreath	1973	Graham McRae	1983	Teo Fabi
1953	Jimmy Daywalt	1963	Jim Clark	1974	Duane Carter, Jr	1984	Michael Andretti
1954	Larry Crockett	1964	Johnny White	1975	Bill Puterbaugh		& Robt. Guerrero
1955	Al Herman	1965	Mario Andretti	1976	Vern Schuppan	1985	Arie Luyendyk
1956	Bob Veith	1966	Jackie Stewart	1977	Jerry Sneva	1986	Randy Lanier
1957	Don Edmunds	1967	Denis Hulme	1978	Rick Mears	1987	Fabrizio Barbazza
1958	George Amick	1968	Bill Vukovich		& Larry Rice	1988	Billy Vukovich III
1959	Bobby Grim	1969	Mark Donohue	1979	Howdy Holmes	1989	Bernard Jourdain
							& Scott Pruett
1960	Jim Hurtubise	1970	Donnie Allison	1980	Tim Richmond		
1961	Parnelli Jones	1971	Denny Zimmerman	1981	Josele Garza	1990	Eddie Cheever
	& Bobby Marshman	1972	Mike Hiss	1982	Jim Hickman	1991	Jeff Andretti

All-Time Leaders

CART's all-time Top 20 drivers in victories, pole positions and earnings, based on records through 1990. Drivers active in 1990 in **bold** type.

Victories

		No
1	**A.J.Foyt**	67
2	**Mario Andretti**	51
3	**Al Unser**	39
4	Bobby Unser	35
5	**Rick Mears**	27
	Johnny Rutherford	27
7	Rodger Ward	26
8	**Gordon Johncock**	25
9	Ralph DePalma	24
10	Tommy Milton	23
11	Tony Bettenhausen	22*
12	Earl Cooper	21
13	Jimmy Bryan	19
	Jimmy Murphy	19
	Bobby Rahal	19
16	Ralph Mulford	17
17	**Danny Sullivan**	15
	Al Unser, Jr.	15
19	**Michael Andretti**	14
20	**Tom Sneva**	13

*Bettenhausen won one race (in Milwaukee on Aug.29, 1948) as Myron Fohr's relief driver.

Pole Positions

		No
1	**Mario Andretti**	64
2	**A.J.Foyt**	53
3	Bobby Unser	49
4	**Rick Mears**	34
5	**Al Unser**	27
6	Johnny Rutherford	23
7	**Gordon Johncock**	20
8	Rex Mays	19
	Danny Sullivan	19
10	Don Branson	15
11	Tony Bettenhausen	14
	Bobby Rahal	14
	Tom Sneva	14
	Michael Andretti	12
	Parnelli Jones	12
16	Danny Ongais	11
	Rodger Ward	11
18	Dan Gurney	10
	Johnny Thomson	10
20	Four drivers tied with 9 each.	

Earnings

		Purses
1	**Rick Mears**	$8,268,565
2	**Mario Andretti**	7,914,636
3	**Bobby Rahal**	7,416,807
4	**Al Unser, Jr.**	6,922,184
5	**Emerson Fittipaldi**	6,538,892
6	**Al Unser**	6,129,901
7	**Danny Sullivan**	6,010,839
8	**Michael Andretti**	5,832,197
9	**A.J.Foyt**	4,845,699
10	**Tom Sneva**	4,253,125
11	Johnny Rutherford	4,209,232
12	**Arie Luyendyk**	3,873,123
13	**Roberto Guerrero**	3,102,449
14	**Gordon Johncock**	3,009,721
15	**Kevin Cogan**	2,868,862
16	Bobby Unser	2,674,516
17	**Raul Boesel**	2,609,858
18	**Pancho Carter**	2,505,504
19	Teo Fabi	2,322,804
20	**Geoff Brabham**	2,256,632

PPG Cup Champions

Officially the PPG Indy Car World Series Championship since 1979 and based on official AAA (American Automobile Assn., 1909-55), USAC (U.S.Auto Club, 1956-79), and CART (Championship Auto Racing Teams, since 1979) records through the 1990 racing season.

Multiple titles: A.J.Foyt (7); Mario Andretti (4); Jimmy Bryan, Earl Cooper, Ted Horn, Rick Mears, Louis Meyer and Al Unser (3); Tony Bettenhausen, Ralph DePalma, Peter DePaolo, Joe Leonard, Rex Mays, Tommy Milton, Jimmy Murphy, Bobby Rahal, Wilbur Shaw, Tom Sneva, Bobby Unser and Rodger Ward (2).

AAA

Year		Year		Year		Year	
1909	George Robertson	1921	Tommy Milton	1932	Bob Carey	1946	Ted Horn
1910	Ray Harroun	1922	Jimmy Murphy	1933	Louis Meyer	1947	Ted Horn
1911	Ralph Mulford	1923	Eddie Hearne	1934	Bill Cummings	1948	Ted Horn
1912	Ralph DePalma	1924	Jimmy Murphy	1935	Kelly Petillo	1949	Johnnie Parsons
1913	Earl Cooper	1925	Peter DePaolo	1936	Mauri Rose		
1914	Ralph DePalma	1926	Harry Hartz	1937	Wilbur Shaw	1950	Henry Banks
1915	Earl Cooper	1927	Peter DePaolo	1938	Floyd Roberts	1951	Tony Bettenhausen
1916	Dario Resta	1928	Louis Meyer	1939	Wilbur Shaw	1952	Chuck Stevenson
1917	Earl Cooper	1929	Louis Meyer			1953	Sam Hanks
1918	Ralph Mulford	1930	Billy Arnold	1940	Rex Mays	1954	Jimmy Bryan
1919	Howard Wilcox	1931	Louis Schneider	1941	Rex Mays	1955	Bob Sweikert
				1942-45	No racing		
1920	Tommy Milton						

USAC

Year		Year		Year		Year	
1956	Jimmy Bryan	1962	Rodger Ward	1968	Bobby Unser	1974	Bobby Unser
1957	Jimmy Bryan	1963	A.J.Foyt	1969	Mario Andretti	1975	A.J.Foyt
1958	Tony Bettenhausen	1964	A.J.Foyt	1970	Al Unser	1976	Gordon Johncock
1959	Rodger Ward	1965	Mario Andretti	1971	Joe Leonard	1977	Tom Sneva
		1966	Mario Andretti	1972	Joe Leonard	1978	Tom Sneva
1960	A.J.Foyt	1967	A.J.Foyt	1973	Roger McCluskey	1979	A.J.Foyt
1961	A.J.Foyt						

CART

Year		Year		Year		Year	
1979	Rick Mears	1982	Rick Mears	1985	Al Unser	1988	Danny Sullivan
1980	Johnny Rutherford	1983	Al Unser	1986	Bobby Rahal	1989	Emerson Fittipaldi
1981	Rick Mears	1984	Mario Andretti	1987	Bobby Rahal	1990	Al Unser, Jr.

CART Rookie of the Year

Award presented to rookie who accumulates the most PPG Cup points among first year drivers.

Year		Year		Year		Year	
1979	Bill Alsup	1982	Bobby Rahal	1985	Arie Luyendyk	1988	John Jones
1980	Dennis Firestone	1983	Teo Fabi	1986	Dominic Dobson	1989	Bernard Jourdain
1981	Bob Lazier	1984	Roberto Guerrero	1987	Fabrizio Barbazza	1990	Eddie Cheever

Formula One Circuit

United States Grand Prix

There have been 54 official Formula One races held in the United States since 1950, including the Indianapolis 500 from 1950-60. FISA sanctioned two annual U.S. Grand Prix—USA/East and USA/West—from 1976-80 and 1983. Phoenix has been the site of the U.S. Grand Prix since 1989.

Indianapolis 500

Officially sanctioned as Grand Prix race from 1950-60 only. See CART Circuit for further details.

Year		Car	Year		Car
1950	Johnnie Parsons, USA	Wynn's Curtis	1956	Pat Flaberty, USA	Zink Special
1951	Lee Wallard, USA	Belanger Special	1957	Sam Hanks, USA	Belond Special
1952	Troy Ruttman, USA	Agajanian Special	1958	Jim Bryan, USA	Belond Special
1953	Bill Vukovich, USA	Fuel Injec.Special	1959	Rodger Ward, USA	Leader Roadster
1954	Bill Vukovich, USA	Fuel Injec.Special	1960	Jim Rathmann, USA	Ken-Paul Special
1955	Bob Sweikert, USA	Zink Special			

U.S. Grand Prix—East

Held from 1959-80 and 1981-88 at the following locations: Sebring, Fla. (1959); Riverside, Calif. (1960); Watkins Glen, N.Y. (1961-80); and Detroit (1982-88). There was no race in 1981.

Multiple winners: Jim Clark, Graham Hill and Ayrton Senna (3); James Hunt, Carlos Reutemann and Jackie Stewart (2).

Year		Car	Year		Car
1959	Bruce McLaren, NZE	Cooper Climax	1974	Carlos Reutemann, ARG	Brabham Ford
			1975	Niki Lauda, AUT	Ferrari
1960	Stirling Moss, GBR	Lotus Climax	1976	James Hunt, GBR	McLaren Ford
1961	Innes Ireland, GBR	Lotus Climax	1977	James Hunt, GBR	McLaren Ford
1962	Jim Clark, GBR	Lotus Climax	1978	Carlos Reutemann, ARG	Ferrari
1963	Graham Hill, GBR	BRM	1979	Gilles Villeneuve, CAN	Ferrari
1964	Graham Hill, GBR	BRM			
1965	Graham Hill, GBR	BRM	1980	Alan Jones, AUS	Williams Ford
1966	Jim Clark, GBR	Lotus BRM	1981	Not held	
1967	Jim Clark, GBR	Lotus Ford	1982	John Watson, GBR	McLaren Ford
1968	Jackie Stewart, GBR	Matra Ford	1983	Michele Alboreto, ITA	Tyrrell Ford
1969	Jochen Rindt, AUT	Lotus Ford	1984	Nelson Piquet, BRA	Brabham BMW Turbo
1970	Emerson Fittipaldi, BRA	Lotus Ford	1985	Keke Rosberg, FIN	Williams Honda Turbo
1971	Francois Cevert, FRA	Tyrrell Ford	1986	Ayrton Senna, BRA	Lotus Renault Turbo
1972	Jackie Stewart, GBR	Tyrrell Ford	1987	Ayrton Senna, BRA	Lotus Honda Turbo
1973	Ronnie Peterson, SWE	Lotus Ford	1988	Ayrton Senna, BRA	McLaren Honda Turbo

Formula One Circuit (Cont.)
U.S. Grand Prix—West

Held from 1976-83 at Long Beach, Calf. Races also held in Las Vegas (1981-82), Dallas (1984) and Phoenix (since 1989).

Multiple winners: Ayrton Senna (2) at Phoenix.

Long Beach

Year		Car
1976	Clay Regazzoni, SWI.	Ferrari
1977	Mario Andretti, USA.	Lotus Ford
1978	Carlos Reutemann, ARG	Ferrari
1979	Gilles Villeneuve, CAN	Ferrari
1980	Nelson Piquet, BRA	Brabham Ford
1981	Alan Jones, AUS.	Williams Ford
1982	Niki Lauda, AUT.	McLaren Ford
1983	John Watson, GBR	McLaren Ford

Las Vegas

Year		Car
1981	Alan Jones, AUS	Williams Ford
1982	Michele Alboreto, ITA	Tyrrell Ford

Dallas

Year		Car
1984	Keke Rosberg, FIN	Williams Honda Turbo

Phoenix

Year		Car
1989	Alain Prost, FRA	McLaren Honda
1990	Ayrton Senna, BRA	McLaren Honda
1991	Ayrton Senna, BRA	McLaren Honda

All-Time Leaders

The all-time Top 20 Grand Prix winning drivers, based on records through 1990. Listed are starts (Sts), poles won (Pole), wins (1st), second place finishes (2nd), and thirds (3rd). Drivers active in 1990 in **bold** type.

		Sts	Pole	1st	2nd	3rd
1	**Alain Prost**	169	20	44	29	16
2	Jackie Stewart	99	17	27	11	5
3	**Ayrton Senna**	110	52	26	17	11
4	Jim Clark	72	33	25	1	6
	Niki Lauda	171	24	25	20	9
6	Juan-Manuel Fangio	51	28	24	11	1
7	**Nelson Piquet**	188	24	22	20	15
8	**Nigel Mansell**	149	15	16	10	11
	Stirling Moss	66	16	16	5	3
10	Jack Brabham	126	13	14	10	8
	Emerson Fittipaldi	144	6	14	13	8

		Sts	Pole	1st	2nd	3rd
	Graham Hill	176	13	14	15	7
13	Alberto Ascari	32	14	13	4	0
14	Mario Andretti	128	18	12	2	5
	Alan Jones	116	6	12	8	5
	Carlos Reutemann	146	6	12	13	20
17	James Hunt	92	14	10	6	7
	Ronnie Peterson	123	14	10	10	6
	Jody Scheckter	112	3	10	14	9
20	Denis Hulme	112	1	8	9	16
	Jackie Ickx	116	13	8	7	10

Note #1: The following drivers either died or were killed in their final year of competition—**Clark** in a Formula Two race in W.Germany in 1968; **Hill** in a plane crash in 1975; **Ascari** in a private practice run in 1955; and **Peterson** following an accident in the 1978 Italian Grand Prix.

Note #2: Fittipaldi and Andretti are still active, but driving on the CART circuit.

World Champions

Officially called the World Championship of Drivers and based on Formula One (Grand Prix) records through the 1990 racing season.

Multiple winners: Juan-Manuel Fangio (5); Jack Brabham, Niki Lauda, Nelson Piquet, Alain Prost and Jackie Stewart (3); Alberto Ascari, Jim Clark, Emerson Fittipaldi, Graham Hill and Ayrton Senna (2).

Year		Car
1950	Guiseppe Farina, ITA.	Alfa Romeo
1951	Juan-Manuel Fangio, ARG	Alfa Romeo
1952	Alberto Ascari, ITA	Ferrari
1953	Alberto Ascari, ITA	Ferrari
1954	Juan-Manuel Fangio, ARG	Maserati/Mercedes
1955	Juan-Manuel Fangio, ARG	Mercedes
1956	Juan-Manuel Fangio, ARG.	Ferrari
1957	Juan-Manuel Fangio, ARG.	Maserati
1958	Mike Hawthorn, GBR	Ferrari
1959	Jack Brabham, AUS.	Cooper Climax
1960	Jack Brabham, AUS.	Cooper Climax
1961	Phil Hill, USA.	Ferrari
1962	Graham Hill, GBR	BRM
1963	Jim Clark, GBR.	Lotus Climax
1964	John Surtees, GBR.	Ferrari
1965	Jim Clark, GBR.	Lotus Climax
1966	Jack Brabham, AUS	Brabham Climax
1967	Denis Hulme, NZE	Brabham Repco
1968	Graham Hill, GBR	Lotus Ford
1969	Jackie Stewart,GBR	Matra Ford
1970	Jochen Rindt, AUT	Lotus Ford

Year		Car
1971	Jackie Stewart, GBR	Tyrrell Ford
1972	Emerson Fittipaldi, BRA	Lotus Ford
1973	Jackie Stewart, GBR	Tyrrell Ford
1974	Emerson Fittipaldi, BRA	McLaren Ford
1975	Niki Lauda, AUT.	Ferrari
1976	James Hunt, GBR	McLaren Ford
1977	Niki Lauda, AUT.	Ferrari
1978	Mario Andretti, USA.	Lotus Ford
1979	Jody Scheckter, SAF	Ferrari
1980	Alan Jones, AUS.	Williams Ford
1981	Nelson Piquet, BRA	Brabham Ford
1982	Keke Rosberg, FIN	Williams Ford
1983	Nelson Piquet, BRA	Brabham BMW Turbo
1984	Niki Lauda, AUT.	McL. TAG Porsche Turbo
1985	Alain Prost, FRA	McL. TAG Porsche Turbo
1986	Alain Prost, FRA	McL. TAG Porsche Turbo
1987	Nelson Piquet, BRA	Williams Honda Turbo
1988	Ayrton Senna, BRA.	McLaren-Honda Turbo
1989	Alain Prost, FRA	McLaren-Honda Turbo
1990	Ayrton Senna, BRA	McLaren-Honda

George Foreman (left) wasn't able to regain the heavyweight title on April 19, but he surprised the experts by going the distance against champion **Evander Holyfield**.

BOXING

Low Blows

Despite an abundance of riches at the top, boxing reels from network TV pullout, Tyson rape case and other woes.

Storm clouds again are blowing over boxing, perhaps the only sport with a perpetual public-relations problem. Those who have weathered previous squalls see the lightning and hear the thunder that made 1991 one of the more turbulent years in boxing history, but they figure these, too, will pass. What's a little more rain on the parade?

"Reports of boxing's death are premature," said Kevin Monaghan, former director of boxing for NBC, who has remained at the network in another capacity. "I think there's always going to be boxing and it's always going to be televised somewhere. No matter what, boxing seems to find a way to survive."

Mere survival wouldn't seem to be much of a problem for boxing, which, to outward appearances, is flourishing as never before. The April 19 heavyweight title bout between champion Evander Holyfield and challenger George Foreman generated tremendous interest in boxing, most of which, for a change, was positive.

The 42-year-old, 257-pound Foreman, aka "Captain Cheeseburger," made himself into a folk icon with his self-deprecating humor about being old

Bernard Fernandez joined the *Philadelphia Daily News* in 1984 and has been the paper's boxing writer since 1987. His father was a welterweight who fought on the undercard of several Archie Moore fights in the early 1940s.

and fat. "After a fight, I talk about hamburgers, about hot dogs, about what people want to hear," said the former champion. "How many people do you trust to come into your living room? I want to be someone they can trust."

America trusted and loved George Foreman, and cheered when he stunned the experts and went the distance against Holyfield. But he lost a relatively one-sided, unanimous decision and, temporarily at least, left center stage. Which meant that it fell to others to pick up the torch and carry it.

Financially, the transfer will be made without missing a beat. The purses commanded by premier attractions are staggering. Before his scheduled Nov. 8, 1991 defense against former champion Mike Tyson was postponed on Oct. 18 (see "Updates"), Holyfield was guaranteed a minimum of $20 million while Tyson was assured of no less than $15 million. Should the rescheduled fight gross a record $100 million, as many have predicted, Holyfield and Tyson could share an estimated $51 million when their percentages of the take are factored in.

While those numbers would have defied believability a few short years ago, they are emblematic of the skyrocketing riches to be had in the pay-per-view television market. Holyfield, who earned $8 million for winning the title from James "Buster" Douglas on Oct. 25, 1990,

Wide World Photos

Former heavyweight champion **Mike Tyson** (center) is escorted out of Marion County Criminal Court by sheriff's deputies after being arraigned on rape charges Sept. 11, in Indianapolis.

added almost $22 million for his first defense against Foreman. That's $30 million in six months. And if the Tyson fight is rescheduled for the first half of 1992, that would be $50 million in a year and a half.

No wonder Holyfield, who turned 29 on Oct. 19, hinted he might retire if he succeeded in beating Tyson.

"I'd have done everything I started out to do," Holyfield said. "After fighting Tyson, I'd have fought the best of my time. (Retirement) has been going through my mind since I beat Buster Douglas, because my goal was to become champion. Now it's time to retire undefeated, meaning I could quit at any time."

The chance that Holyfield, who would appear to be at the peak of his career, might retire prematurely is in contrast to the possibility of a forced departure from the scene by Tyson, 25, who has been the most compelling fixture in boxing for the past five years. A rape indictment, potentially the most catastrophic incident in a career marked by out-of-the-ring controversies, was handed down against Tyson on Sept. 9, by a special Marion County

(Ind.) grand jury after a contestant in the Miss Black America beauty pageant in Indianapolis accused the former champion of forcing himself on her in July.

Since Tyson's trial was not scheduled to begin until Jan. 27, 1992, he was allowed to proceed with preparations to fight Holyfield. Still his indictment caused a sensation.

"Holyfield was viewed as the good guy in the white hat anyway, so maybe even more people will want to see the bad guy, Tyson, get his butt kicked," said John Hand, Jr., the Philadelphia-area closed-circuit exhibitor. "And those people who don't believe Tyson is guilty are going to want to see him beat the rap and Holyfield, too."

Women's groups, however, were outraged that the fight would be allowed to go on as scheduled, and there were calls for it to be postponed until the charges against Tyson were resolved. Promoter Bob Arum even went so far as to say that if the fight went on as scheduled, it would mean "the end of boxing as we know it." But, as an archrival of Holyfield promoter Dan Duva and Tyson promoter Don King, it might be said that Arum had an axe to grind.

Nonetheless, Tyson's legal troubles constitute the darkest and more foreboding of the clouds now enshrouding boxing. But it hardly is the only one. For all the pay-per-view TV swag available to the superstars, boxing's visibility on network television, which long has been a major part of the sport's grass-roots appeal, diminished in 1991 to a point where it is almost nonexistent.

"Boxing is doing its best to kill the golden goose," says Bert Sugar, editor-publisher of Boxing Illustrated and one of the foremost historians of the sport. "Holyfield-Tyson is the Super Bowl, but what's happening to the regular season? It's down the toilet.

"At the top, boxing has never been healthier. At the bottom, it's never been sicker."

And how, Sugar was asked, should boxing go about healing itself?

"Put it on free TV, even if you have to give it away," Sugar said. "There is nothing to equal the exposure of network television. Pay-per-view is great, but if you don't have a showcase, you're in trouble. Who's going to buy you if they don't know you?

"Free TV made Tyson, who was on ABC about every 10 seconds at the outset of his career. It made Sugar Ray Leonard and a lot of other fighters you now have to pay to see. If the itch isn't created, no one is going to want to scratch."

The death of boxing on free TV—ESPN and USA continue to be the principal cable outlets with regular weekly telecasts—brings to mind the last major down cycle, in the early 1960s. NBC had canceled the "Gillette Cavalcade of Sports" in 1959 and, after the tragic death of Benny "Kid" Paret in 1962, TV more of less abandoned boxing for five years. The sweet science was able to rise above those doldrums in large part because of the personal charisma of Muhammad Ali.

"But the current situation is worse," Sugar said. "In the late '50s, there were a lot of old champions on the way out. Now, there are talented, young kids who aren't being properly exposed. Free TV creates superstars, and where is the next generation of superstars coming from?"

Maybe the 1992 Summer Olympics. Leonard and the Spinks brothers, Michael and Leon, became overnight sensations on ABC when they won gold medals at the 1976 Games in Montreal. Ironically, NBC will be handling the Olympics in Barcelona. A good showing by some talented American boxers and free TV might be back in business.

Mention of Benny Paret is noteworthy because the tragic implications of injuries suffered by a 22-year-old Nigerian immigrant named Kid Akeem Anifowoshe represent as much a threat to boxing as the Tyson rape indictment and vanishing number of air dates on network television.

In an ironic twist that illustrates all that is both good and bad in boxing, what may have been the most exciting fight of 1991 ended up furnishing the American Medical Association—which long has sought to have the sport banned—with ammunition for its cause. On June 15, following a bloody, 12-round slugfest with International Boxing Federation junior bantamweight champion Robert Quiroga of San Antonio, Anifowoshe lapsed into a coma. He eventually regained consciousness, but has been confined to a wheelchair ever since, his career over.

"By the time I got into the ring, Akeem was having convulsions," said Dr. Geraldo Zavala, a neurosurgeon who was one of the attending ringside physicians that night. "He was unconscious, having difficulty breathing and the pupil in his right eye was dilated. A dilated pupil means that the brain is trying to push through the hole that is in between the head and the spine in the neck. And that pressure inside the head was very high. It was like toothpaste being squeezed."

Post-fight reports said Anifowoshe had absorbed more than 400 blows to the head.

"A boxer's career is real short," said Quiroga, the man who threw those punches. "One day you're on top of the world, and one day you're out of it. You saw what happened to Akeem. That's why I'm planning on going back to school. I'm looking for a career that takes less blood."

The Anifowoshe furor scarcely had died down when, on the same weekend in September, two fighters suffered serious brain injuries in failed world title attempts. Michael Watson was put on a life support system following his 12th-round knockout loss to Chris Eubank for the vacant WBO super middleweight championship in London. Meanwhile, in Indio, Calif., bantamweight Fernie Morales underwent surgery to remove a blood clot from his brain after losing a 12-round decision to IBF champion Orlando Canizales.

In addition to the should-he-or-shouldn't-he matter of Tyson's challenge of Holyfield and the sad ending to the Quiroga-Kid Akeem fight, boxing was plagued by more standard woes.

As always, the scoring in a number of fights left something to be desired. Perhaps the most controversial finish came on June 28 in Las Vegas when World Boxing Council super featherweight champion Azumah Nelson retained his title with a draw with Australia's Jeff Fenech. Fenech, fighting for the first time in the United States, initiated the action throughout and seemingly was on the verge of a knockout victory in the 12th and final round when the bell sounded.

After watching a videotape of the fight back at his hotel, Fenech was even more convinced he had been robbed.

"What more do they want me to do?" he asked bitterly. "There obviously was some business being done."

Despite his displeasure, Fenech, a three-time former world champion, agreed to a December rematch with Nelson—in Sydney, Australia, where he presumably will find the judging more to his liking.

But, while boxing took shots from all sides in 1991, it still had its true believers. A group call The Boxing Centennial Group, Inc., is planning a year-long celebration in 1992 of the first 100 years of professional boxing in America. The group traces the origins of boxing in its modern, rules-governed, gloved form to the Sept. 7, 1892, heavyweight title fight in New Orleans between champion John L. Sullivan and challenger "Gentleman" Jim Corbett.

"Our goal is to recognize the history of the sport, and some of the great people and events that have helped make boxing one of the most universally popular sports," said Chuck Stogel, the BCG's executive vice president. It will be interesting to see how much recognition the troubled Mike Tyson gets.

Tyson, called "the only heavyweight that counts" in a pre-indictment article in KO Magazine, for years had been viewed

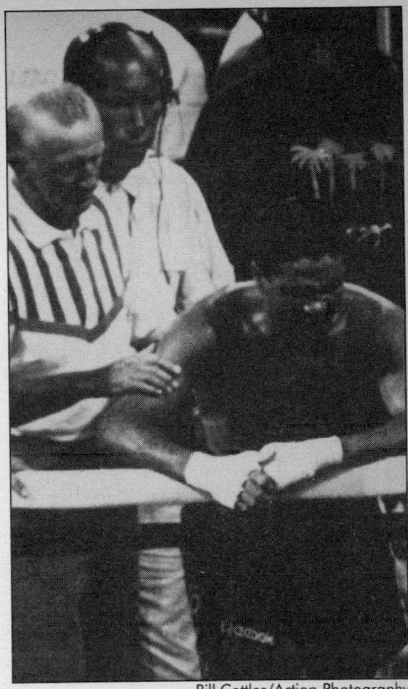

Bill Cottles/Action Photography

A stunned **Jeff Fenech** reacts to his controversial draw with WBC super featherweight champion Azumah Nelson in June.

as the man-beast who would carry on the tradition of the great champions. But, beginning with his shocking Feb. 10, 1990, knockout loss to the unheralded Douglas, Tyson has found himself in a state of almost constant turmoil both in and out of the ring.

From a pure boxing standpoint, a fighter who once had been viewed as invincible suddenly appeared ready for the taking. Onlookers decided his jab had all but disappeared and his defense had eroded. Those weaknesses, the theory went, could be exploited by a skilled opponent able to survive Tyson's early-round fury, as Douglas had.

Tyson fought and won three times from December 1990 until his date with Holyfield 11 months later. The first was a one round destruction of a scared-stiff Alex Stewart on Dec.8 in Atlantic City. Then two Las Vegas bouts with Donovan (Razor) Ruddock—a controversial seventh-round TKO (brought to a halt by referee

Richard Steele) on Mar. 18, followed by a unanimous 12-round decision on June 28 in which Ruddock suffered a broken jaw early. The two Ruddock fights seemed to confirm what many believed: Tyson was, indeed, slipping.

"Can you imagine the old Tyson not finishing a guy with a broken jaw?" said Tyson's former trainer, Kevin Rooney. "It's unthinkable." Even more disturbing were Tyson's volatile mood swings, which painted a picture of a man increasingly out of control.

"I think Mike Tyson belongs in a cage," Foreman said. "He needs to be sheltered like you would shelter a lion or a tiger. You lock him up, except when you want him to come out and jump through a few hoops. When that's over, you lock him up again."

Despite a growing perception that Tyson's once bright star was flaming out, the challenger opened as a 13-5 favorite in the Nevada sports books over Holyfield, whose serene nature had made him the straight man in every drama in which he was cast.

"He couldn't draw flies to a dump," Tyson's promoter, Don King, had said of Holyfield. But, for a guy widely thought of as colorless, Holyfield had had a dream year unmatched, at least in a financial sense, by any fighter ever.

Holyfield's unexpected emergence as the greatest moneymaking machine in boxing history began on Oct. 25, 1990, when, as the challenger, he was paid $8 million for a shot at Tyson's conqueror, Douglas. Douglas might have been a fat slob that night, showing up at blubbery 246 pounds—15 more than he weighed when he beat Tyson in Tokyo—but that hardly was Holyfield's fault. And when "The Real Deal" knocked Douglas back into obscurity with a single overhand right in the third round, boxing had a new king.

A $20 million-plus payday for his successful first defense, against 42-year-old George Foreman—who was even fatter (257 lbs.) than Douglas—solidified Holyfield's credentials as a heavyweight of substance and set the stage for the good-vs-evil megabucks confrontation with Tyson.

Lou Duva, Holyfield's co-manager, said the image of Holyfield as a hero was legitimate and that boxing "needed" him to cleanse the sport of Tyson, the ultimate villain.

Leonard Finds Out It's Time To Quit Ring

If the American public can't decide how much of a good thing is enough, especially when it comes to their aging sports heroes, why should Sugar Ray Leonard be expected to know?

Why should he have known enough to quit for good after what was arguably the greatest victory of his career—the April 6, 1987, shocker over undisputed middleweight champion Marvelous Marvin Hagler? How could the man not recognize a perfect ending when he saw it? For him to walk away then, beating the unbeatable foe to achieve the impossible dream after a three-year lay-off . . . well, it would have been glorious.

But then, if Leonard hadn't been so damn obstinate, he wouldn't have been able to win the last two of his five world titles in separate weight divisions by beating Donny Lalonde. He wouldn't have satisfied the public demand for a long-anticipated second fight with Thomas Hearns or a third fight with Roberto Duran. He wouldn't have become, in a fiscal sense, at least, the greatest box-office attraction in boxing history, with purses conservatively estimated at $90 million-plus.

As always, Leonard had his own reasons for pressing on. A self-described risk-taker, he couldn't bring himself to give up what he loved best until he had proved to himself that there were no more great achievements lurking around the next corner.

And so it came to be that 34-year-old Sugar Ray Leonard stepped into the ring at Madison Square Garden on Feb. 9, 1991, to face a 23-year-old mirror image of himself, World Boxing Council super welter-weight champion Terry Norris. It was the litmus test by which Leonard (36-2-1 with 25 knockouts), the premier fighter of the '80s, would prove to himself, if not the world, that he had enough tread on his tires to continue his journey of self-discovery into the '90s.

"I never think about losing. Never," Leonard had said at a press conference to announce the fight. "My motivation used to be a Hagler, a Hearns, a Duran. Now my motivation is not losing. I realize that, at this

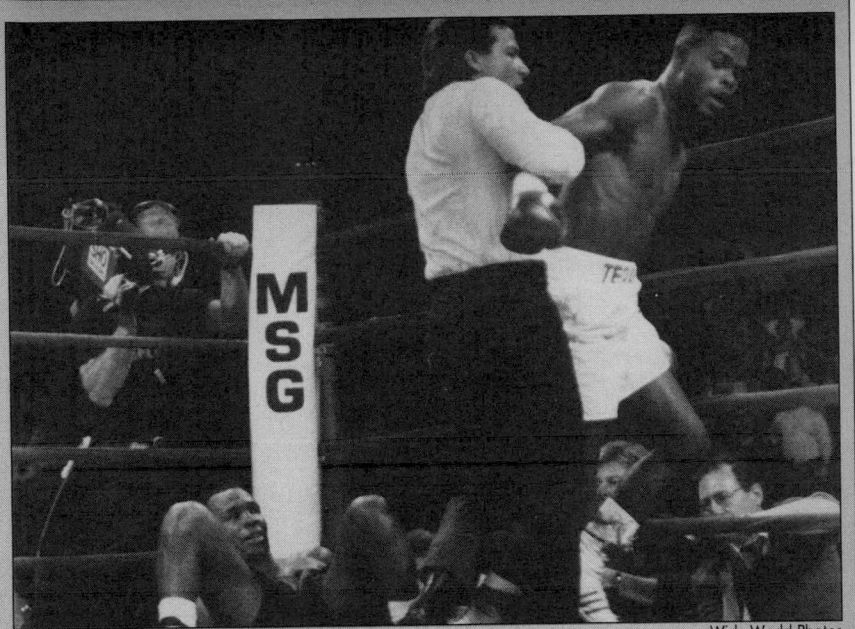

Wide World Photos

Five-time world champion **Sugar Ray Leonard** on his back after being knocked down in the second round by WBC super welterweight champion **Terry Norris**.

point of my career, every fight could be my last. But I have to find out for myself. When it's time to quit, I'll know.''

Presumably, that realization came early in his one-sided, unanimous decision loss to Norris. Leonard tried to land the trademark combinations of his youth, but Norris was not there to be hit, having landed a volley of his own punches before stepping away. The opponent Norris was routing that night was not so much the great Sugar Ray as it was the remnants of what used to be.

If Leonard was looking for a sign that he had gone as far as he could, the scorecards offered solid evidence that there would be no more last hurrahs. One judge had him trailing by a whopping 120-104, the other two by margins of 119-103 and 116-110. And if that weren't enough, well, one look in the mirror provided visual proof of the shellacking he had sustained.

''This is my last fight,'' Leonard told the Garden crowd. ''Thank you for coming out. God bless you.''

This time, the occasion of his fifth announced retirement, we finally believed him.

Two months later, those who wanted to dump on Leonard for staying too long, had a field day when the story broke that he had used cocaine from 1983 to '86, during which time he drank heavily and physically abused his ex-wife Juanita.

''I stand here ashamed, hurt,'' Leonard said in acknowledging the sordid aspects of that period of his life. ''I think about my parents, my ex-wife, my kids, people who care for me, my fans who made me what I am.''

And what is that, exactly? Is the real Ray Charles Leonard the smiling, unsullied hero of the 7-Up commercials? Or an overhyped impostor who was never the equal of his ring namesake, Sugar Ray Robinson?

The truth, of course, is neither. Leonard is an imperfect man,, subject to the same pitfalls that pose danger to those not in the spotlight. Perhaps his most unflattering characteristic is his arrogance, an absolute belief that he was impervious to any sort of misstep. But that arrogance also helped to make him a great fighter and, by any definition, one of the preeminent sports figures of his time.

"Evander carries himself like a true champion and a true gentleman," Duva said. "A lot of guys portray themselves that way, but it's an act. It's not act with Evander. I don't necessarily think kids should hold athletes up as role models, but if anyone qualified, it would be Evander. He's someone to be looked up to, like Rocky Marciano and Joe DiMaggio."

Elsewhere in boxing, the big news was the retirement of 34-year-old Sugar Ray Leonard after he lost a one-sided decision to WBC super welterweight champion Terry Norris (see box).

Somewhat less earthshaking were the goodbyes of two-time former welterweight champ Mark Breland and former welterweight and junior middleweight titlist Donald Curry. Once touted as the "next Sugar Ray Robinson," Breland never achieved the superstardom many predicted of him when he won a gold medal in the 1984 Olympics. He decided to hang up the gloves after being knocked out as a junior middleweight by Jorge Vaca on Sept. 13. The end for Curry, meanwhile, came in much the same way it had came for Leonard—a savage, eighth-round knockout loss to Norris on June 1.

While Leonard gave up the ghost, another aging warrior, 32-year-old Thomas Hearns, showed that he wasn't quite finished when he won the World Boxing Association light-heavyweight crown by outpointing Virgil Hill on June 3.

If you count the WBO super middleweight title—and not everyone does—Hearns has been a champion in five separate weight divisions. He apparently will try to add a sixth, most likely against WBA cruiserweight champ Bobby Czyz. And if he's successful? Well, 'The Hit Man' has hinted he'd like a go at Holyfield if he's still heavyweight champion.

"When you think about it, it's not the mismatch, size-wise, many people think it is," said Harold Smith, a Hearns adviser. "Tommy walks around at 185, 190 pounds. He really thinks he can beat Holyfield."

"Tommy must be dreaming," said former light-heavyweight champion Bob Foster, an all-time great at 175 pounds who never came close to beating a quality heavyweight.

You want dreamers whose dreams came true? How about James Toney, a

Wide World Photos

WBA light-heavyweight champion **Thomas Hearns** shows off his newly won title belt after beating Virgil Hill.

prohibitive underdog who won the IBF middleweight championship when he nailed previously unbeaten Michael Nunn with a crushing left hook in the 11th round on May 10. Or former lightweight champ Edwin Rosario, thought to be washed up at age 28, who won the WBA junior welterweight title with a dramatic, third-round KO of Loreto Garza.

Ex-IBF junior welterweight champion Meldrick Taylor still is waiting for a rematch of his controversial, final-round loss to Julio Cesar Chavez, but in the meantime, the fast-handed Philadelphian became king of the WBA welterweight hill in January by decisioning Aaron Davis.

And former WBA junior lightweight champ Brian Mitchell went into Sacramento and did something no one had done before, namely beat IBF junior lightweight titlist Tony "The Tiger" Lopez on his home turf. It was sweet revenge for Mitchell, who felt he deserved better than a draw in his controversial first meeting with Lopez. □

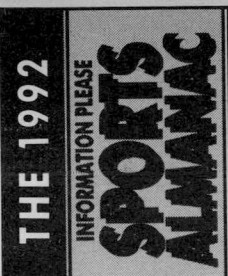

BOXING STATISTICS
THE SEASON IN REVIEW
1990-1991
CHAMPIONS • TITLE BOUTS

SEC A

PAGE 737

Current Champions
WBA, WBC and IBF Titleholders (through Oct.5, 1991)

The champions of professional boxing's 17 principal weight divisions, as recognized by the World Boxing Association (WBA), World Boxing Council (WBC) and International Boxing Federation (IBF). Heavyweight champion Evander Holyfield and lightweight champion Pernell (Sweet Pea) Whitaker are the only fighters currently holding all three titles.

	Weight Limit	WBA Champion	WBC Champion	IBF Champion
Heavyweight	—	Evander Holyfield 26-0-0, 21 KO	Evander Holyfield 26-0-0, 21 KO	Evander Holyfield 26-0-0, 21 KO
Jr.Heavyweight	190 lbs	Bobby Czyz 38-5-0, 26 KO	Anaclet Wamba 32-2-0, 12 KO	James Warring 12-1-0, 7 KO
Light Heavyweight	175 lbs	Thomas Hearns 50-3-2, 40 KO	Jeff Harding 21-1-0, 15 KO	Charles Williams 32-4-2, 22 KO
Super Middleweight	168 lbs	Victor Cordova 17-3-2, 13 KO	Mauro Galvano 17-1-2, 4 KO	Darrin Van Horn 46-2-0, 26 KO
Middleweight	160 lbs	Mike McCallum 40-1-0, 33 KO	Julian Jackson 41-1-0, 39 KO	James Toney 26-0-1, 19 KO
Jr.Middleweight	154 lbs	Vinny Pazienza 32-5-1, 24 KO	Terry Norris 28-3-0, 15 KO	Gianfranco Rosi 52-3-0, 16 KO
Welterweight	147 lbs	Meldrick Taylor 27-1-1, 14 KO	Simon Brown 34-1-0, 26 KO	Maurice Blocker 33-2-0, 19 KO
Jr.Welterweight	140 lbs	Edwin Rosario 37-4-0, 32 KO	Julio Cesar Chavez 75-0-0, 62 KO	Vacant*
Lightweight	135 lbs	Pernell Whitaker 27-1-0, 13 KO	Pernell Whitaker 27-1-0, 13 KO	Pernell Whitaker 27-1-0, 13 KO
Jr.Lightweight	130 lbs	Joey Gamache 25-0-0, 15 KO	Azumah Nelson 32-2-1, 24 KO	Brian Mitchell 43-1-2, 20 KO
Featherweight	126 lbs	Yung-Kyun Park 19-1-1, 11 KO	Marcos Villasana 45-7-3, 38 KO	Manuel Medina 35-3-0, 18 KO
Jr.Featherweight	122 lbs	Luis Mendoza 31-2-2, 18 KO	Daniel Zaragoza 45-2-1, 21 KO	Welcome Ncita 29-0-0, 14 KO
Bantamweight	118 lbs	Luisito Espinoza 26-5-0, 13 KO	Joichiro Tatsuyoshi 8-0-0, 6 KO	Orlando Canizales 28-1-1, 23 KO
Jr.Bantamweight	115 lbs	Khaosai Galaxy 48-1-0, 43 KO	Sung-Kil Moon 15-1-0, 12 KO	Robert Quiroga 18-0-0, 11 KO
Flyweight	112 lbs	Yong-Kang Kim 23-3-0, 10 KO	Muangchai Kittikasem 13-1-0, 9 KO	Dave McAuley 17-2-2, 7 KO
Jr.Flyweight	108 lbs	Myung-Woo Yuh 36-0-0, 14 KO	Humberto Gonzalez 30-1-0, 25 KO	Michael Carbajal 21-0-0, 13 KO
Strawweight	105 lbs	Hi-Yung Choi 10-0-0, 5 KO	Ricardo Lopez 27-0-0, 20 KO	Phalan Lukmingkwan 18-1-1, 7 KO

*Roger Mayweather and Rafael Pineda are scheduled to fight for vacant IBF title on Dec. 7, 1991.

Note: the following weight divisions are also known by these names—**Jr.Heavyweight** as Cruiserweight; **Jr.Middleweight** as Super Welterweight; **Jr.Welterweight** as Super Lightweight; **Jr.Lightweight** as Super Featherweight; **Jr.Featherweight** as Super Bantamweight; **Jr.Bantamweight** as Super Flyweight; **Jr.Flyweight** as Light Flyweight; and **Strawweight** as Minimum.

Evander Holyfield's Career Record

Undisputed heavyweight champion Evander Holyfield was 25-0 with 21 knockouts going into his Nov. 8, 1991 title bout with former champion Mike Tyson.

1984

Date	Opponent, location	Result
Nov. 15	Lionel Byarm, New York	W 6

1985

Date	Opponent, location	Result
Jan. 20	Eric Winbush, Atlantic City	W 6
Mar. 13	Freddie Brown, Norfolk	KO 1
Apr. 20	Mark Rivera, Corpus Christi	KO 2
July 20	Tyrone Booze, Norfolk	W 8
Aug. 29	Rick Myers, Atlanta	KO 1
Oct. 30	Jeff Meachem, Atlantic City	KO 5
Dec. 21	Anthony Davis, Virginia Beach	KO 4

1986

Date	Opponent, location	Result
Mar. 1	Chisanda Mutti, Lancaster, Pa	KO 3
Apr. 6	Jesse Shelby, Corpus Christi	KO 3
May 28	Terry Mims, Metairie, LA	KO 5
July 20	Dwight M.Qawi, Atlanta	W 15
	(Won WBA & IBF Jr. Heavyweight titles)	
Dec. 8	Mike Brothers, Paris	KO 3

1987

Date	Opponent, location	Result
Feb. 14	Henry Tillman, Reno	TKO 7
May 15	Rickey Parkey, Las Vegas	TKO 3
Aug. 15	Ossie Ocasio, St. Tropez, France	TKO 11
Dec. 4	Dwight M. Qawi, Atlantic City	TKO 4

1988

Date	Opponent, location	Result
Apr. 9	Carlos DeLeon, Las Vegas	KO 8
	(Won WBC Jr.Heavyweight title)	
July 16	James Tillis, Lake Tahoe	KO 5
Dec. 9	Pinklon Thomas, Atlantic City	TKO 7

1989

Date	Opponent, location	Result
Mar. 11	Michael Dokes, Las Vegas	TKO 10
July 15	Adilson Rodrigues, Lake Tahoe	KO 2
Nov. 4	Alex Stewart, Atlantic City	TKO 8

1990

Date	Opponent, location	Result
June 1	Seamus McDonagh, Atlantic City	TKO 4
Oct. 25	Buster Douglas, Las Vegas	KO 3
	(Won undisputed Heavyweight title)	

1991

Date	Opponent, location	Result
Apr. 19	George Foreman, Atlantic City	W 12
Nov. 8	vs. Mike Tyson at Las Vegas	

Major Bouts

Division by division, from Oct.10, 1990 through Oct.5, 1991.

Heavyweights

Evander Holyfield knocked out champion Buster Douglas in 3rd round to win WBA, WBC and IBF titles (Las Vegas, Oct.25, 1990).

Riddick Bowe knocked out Bert Cooper in 2nd round (Las Vegas, Oct.25, 1990).

Mike Tyson knocked out Alex Stewart in 1st round (Atlantic City, Dec.8, 1990).

Razor Ruddock knocked out Mike Rouse in 1st round (Atlantic City, Dec.8, 1990).

Riddick Bowe knocked out Tony Morrison in 1st round (Kansas City, Dec.14, 1990).

Riddick Bowe gained an 8th round TKO over Tyrell Biggs (Atlantic City, March 2).

Mike Tyson gained a 7th round TKO over Razor Ruddock (Las Vegas, March 18).

Evander Holyfield scored a unanimous 12-round decision over George Foreman to retain unified title (Atlantic City, April 19).

Riddick Bowe scored a unanimous 10-round decision over Tony Tubbs (Atlantic City, April 20).

Mike Tyson scored a unanimous 12-round decision over Razor Ruddock (Las Vegas, June 28).

Riddick Bowe gained a 3rd round TKO over Phil Brown (Atlantic City, July 23).

Michael Moorer knocked out Alex Stewart in 4th round (Norfolk, Va., July 27).

Riddick Bowe knocked out Bruce Seldon in 1st round (Atlantic City, Aug.9).

Junior Heavyweights

(Cruiserweights)

Robert Daniels fought a 12-round draw with Toufik Belbouli to retain WBA title (Madrid, Nov.22, 1990).

Massimiliano Duran declared winner of non-title bout in 12th round when Anaclet Wamba was disqualified for head butting (Ferrara, Italy, Dec.8, 1990).

Bobby Czyz scored a 12-round split decision over champion Robert Daniels to win WBA title (Atlantic City, March 8).

Anaclet Wamba gained an 11th round TKO over champion Massimiliano Duran to win WBC title (Palermo, Italy, July 20).

Bobby Czyz scored a unanimous 12-round decision over Bashiru Ali (Atlantic City, Aug.9).

James Warring knocked out James Pritchard in 1st round to win vacant IBF title (Salemi, Italy, Sept.7).

Light Heavyweights

Dennis Andries gained a 5th round TKO over Daniel Merani to retain WBC title (London, Oct.10, 1990). Michael Moorer gained an 8th round TKO over Danny Stonewalker to retain WBO title (Pittsburgh, Dec.15, 1990).

Virgil Hill scored a unanimous 12-round decision over Mike Peak to retain WBA title (Bismarck, Jan.6).

Charles Williams scored a unanimous 12-round decision over Mwehu Beya to retain IBF title (St.Vincent, Italy, Jan.12).

Dennis Andries scored a unanimous 12-round decision over Guy Waters to retain WBC title (Adelaide, Australia, Jan.19).

Charles Williams scored a 2nd round TKO over James Kinchen to retain IBF title (Atlantic City, April 20).

Thomas Hearns scored a unanimous 12-round decision over champion Virgil Hill to win WBA title (Las Vegas, June 3).

Charles Williams knocked out Vincent Boulware to retain IBF title (San Remo, Italy, July 11).

Jeff Harding scored a 12-round split decision over champion Dennis Andries to regain WBC title (London, Sept.11).

Super Middleweights

Christophe Tiozzo gained a 2nd round TKO over Danny Morgan to retain WBA title (Cergy-Pointoise, France, Nov.23, 1990).

Mauro Galvano scored a 12-round unanimous decision over Dario Matteoni to win vacant WBC title (Monte Carlo, Dec.15, 1990).

Lindell Holmes scored a 12-round unanimous decision over Thulani Malinga to retain IBF title (Marino, Italy, Dec.15, 1990).

Lindell Holmes scored a 12-round split decision over Antoine Byrd to retain IBF title (Madrid, March 7).

Victor Cordova gained a 9th round TKO over champion Christophe Tiozzo to win WBA title (Marseilles, France, April 5).

Darrin Van Horn knocked out champion Lindell Holmes in 11th round to win IBF title (Verbania, Italy, May 18).

Mauro Galvano scored a unanimous 12-round decision over Ron Essett to retain WBC title (Cannes, France, July 27).

Darrin Van Horn knocked out John Jarvis in 3rd round to retain IBF title (Irvine, Calif., Aug. 17).

Middleweights

Michael Nunn gained a 10th round TKO over Donald Curry to retain IBF title (Paris, Oct.18, 1990).

Julian Jackson knocked out Herol Graham in 4th round to win vacant WBC title (Benalmadena, Spain, Nov.24, 1990).

Mike McCallum scored a 12-round split decision over Sumbu Kalambay to retain WBA title (Monte Carlo, April 1).

James Toney knocked out champion Michael Nunn in 11th round to win IBF title (Davenport, Iowa, May 10).

James Toney scored a 12-round split decision over Reggie Johnson to retain IBF title (Las Vegas, June 29).

Julian Jackson knocked out Dennis Milton in 1st round to retain WBC title (Las Vegas, Sept.14).

Junior Middleweights
(Super Welterweights)

Gianfranco Rosi scored a unanimous 12-round decision over Rene Jacquot to retain IBF title (Marsala, Italy, Nov.30, 1990).

Terry Norris scored a unanimous 12-round decision over Sugar Ray Leonard to retain WBC title (New York, N.Y., Feb. 9).

Gilbert Dele gained a 7th round TKO over Carlos Elliot to win vacant WBA title (Guadeloupe, Feb.23).

Gianfranco Rosi scored a unanimous 12-round decision over Ron Amundsen to retain IBF title (St.Vincent, Italy, March 16).

Gilbert Dele scored a unanimous 12-round decision over Jun-Suk Hwang to retain WBA title (St.Maarten, May 4).

Terry Norris knocked out Donald Curry in 8th round to retain WBC title (Palm Springs, Calif., June 1).

Gianfranco Rosi scored a unanimous 12-round decision over Glenn Wolfe to retain IBF title (Avezzano, Italy, July 13).

Terry Norris knocked out Brett Lally in 1st round to retain WBC title (San Diego, Aug.17).

Vinny Pazienza gained a 12th round TKO over champion Gilbert Dele to win WBA title (Providence, R.I., Oct.1).

Welterweights

Simon Brown, the IBF champion, knocked out Ozzie O'Neal in 1st round of non-title bout (Atlantic City, Dec.8, 1990).

Meldrick Taylor scored a unanimous 12-round decision over champion Aaron Davis to win WBA title (Atlantic City, Jan.19).

Simon Brown, the IBF champion, gained a 10th round TKO over champion Maurice Blocker to win WBC title (Las Vegas, March 18). Brown renounced IBF title in April.

Meldrick Taylor scored a 12-round split decision over Luis Garcia to retain WBA title (Palm Springs, Calif., June 1).

Maurice Blocker scored a 12-round split decision over Glewood Brown to win vacant IBF title (Atlantic City, Oct.4).

Junior Welterweights
(Super Lightweights)

Loreto Garza declared winner in 11th round when Vinny Pazienza was disqualified for dirty fighting. Garza retained WBA title (Sacramento, Dec.1, 1990).

Julio Cesar Chavez gained a 3rd round TKO over Kyung-Duk Ahn to retain WBC and IBF titles (Atlantic City, Dec.8, 1990).

Julio Cesar Chavez gained a 4th round TKO over John Duplessis to retain WBC and IBF titles (Las Vegas, March 18).

Edwin Rosario gained a 3rd round TKO over champion Loreto Garza to win WBA title (Sacramento, June 14).

Julio Cesar Chavez scored a unanimous 12-round decision over Lonnie Smith to retain WBC title (Las Vegas, Sept.14). Chavez renounced IBF title in August.

Lightweights

Pernell Whitaker scored a unanimous 10-round decision over Benji Marquez in a non-title bout (Madrid, Nov.22, 1990).

Pernell Whitaker scored a 12-round decision over Poli Diaz to retain unified title (Norfolk, Va., July 27).

Pernell Whitaker scored a 12-round decision over Jorge Paez to retain unified title (Reno, Oct.5).

Junior Lightweights
(Super Featherweights)

Azumah Nelson scored a unanimous 12-round decision over Juan LaPorte to win vacant WBC title (Sydney, Oct.13, 1990).

Brian Mitchell, the WBA champion, and **Tony Lopez**, the IBF champion, fought to a 12-round draw; both fighters retained titles (Sacramento, March 15). Mitchell renounced WBA title in May.

Joey Gamache gained a 10th round TKO over Jerry N'Gobeni to win vacant WBA title (Lewiston, Me., June 28).

Azumah Nelson fought a 12-round draw with Jeff Fenech to retain WBC title (Las Vegas, June 28).

Tony Lopez gained a 6th round TKO over Lupe Gutierrez to retain IBF title (Stateline, Nev., July 12).

Brian Mitchell, who renounced WBA title in may, scored a unanimous 12-round decision over champion Tony Lopez to win IBF title (Sacramento, Sept.13).

Featherweights

Yung-Kyun Park scored a unanimous 12-round decision over champion Antonio Esparragoza to win WBA title (Kwangju, S.Korea, March 30).

Marcos Villasana gained a 6th round TKO over Rafael Zuniga to retain WBC title (Mexico City, April 11).

Troy Dorsey knocked out Alfred Rangel in 1st round to win vacant IBF title (Palm Springs, Calif., June 3).

Yung-Kyun Park gained a 6th round TKO over Masuaki Takeda to retain WBA title (Seoul, June 15).

Manuel Medina scored a unanimous 12-round decision over champion Troy Dorsey to win IBF title (Inglewood, Aug.12).

Marcos Villasana scored a unanimous 12-round decision over Ricardo Cepeda to retain WBC title (Marbella, Spain, Aug. 15).

Yung-Kyun Park scored a unanimous 12-round decision over Eloy Rojas to retain WBA title (Seoul, Sept.14).

Major Bouts (Cont.)

Junior Featherweights
(Super Bantamweights)

Luis Mendoza scored a 12-round split decision over Fabrice Benichou to retain WBA title (Paris, Oct.18, 1990).

Pedro Decima gained a 4th round TKO over champion Paul Banke to win WBC title (Inglewood, Nov.5, 1990).

Luis Mendoza gained an 8th round TKO over Noree Jockgym to retain WBA title (Bangkok, Jan.20).

Kiyoshi Hatanaka gained an 8th round TKO over champion Pedro Decima to win WBC title (Nagoya, Japan, Feb.3).

Welcome Ncita scored a 12-round split decision over Sugar Rojas to retain IBF title (St.Vincent, Italy, Feb.22).

Luis Mendoza knocked out Joao Cardoso in 7th round to retain WBA title (Madrid, May 30).

Daniel Zaragoza scored a 12-round split decision over champion Kiyoshi Hatanaka to regain WBC title (Nagoya, Japan, June 14).

Welcome Ncita scored a unanimous 12-round decision over Hurley Snead to retain IBF title (San Antonio, June 15).

Daniel Zaragoza scored a unanimous 12-round decision over Chun Huh to retain WBC title (Seoul, Aug. 24).

Bantamweights

Luisito Espinosa scored a 12-round unanimous decision over Thanomsak Sithboabey to retain WBA title (Bangkok, Nov.29, 1990).

Raul Perez knocked out Candelario Carmona in 8th round to retain WBC title (Tijuana, Dec.17, 1990).

Greg Richardson scored a unanimous 12-round decision over champion Raul Perez to win WBC title (Inglewood, Calif., Feb.25).

Orlando Canizalez knocked out Billy Hardy in 8th round to retain IBF title (Laredo, Texas, May 4).

Greg Richardson scored a 12-round split decision over Victor Rabanales to retain WBC title (Inglewood, Calif., May 20).

Joichiro Tatsuyoshi gained a 10th round TKO over champion Greg Richardson to win WBC title (Osaka, Japan, Sept.19).

Orlando Canizales scored a unanimous 12-round decision over Fernie Morales to retain IBF title (Indio, Calif., Sept.21).

Junior Bantamweights
(Super Flyweights)

Sung-Kil Moon scored a 12-round unanimous decision over Kenji Matsumura to retain WBC title (Seoul, Oct.20, 1990).

Khaosai Galaxy knocked out Ernesto Ford in 6th round to retain WBA title (Petchaboon, Thailand, Dec.9, 1990).

Sung-Kil Moon gained a 4th round TKO over Nana Yaw Konadu to retain WBC title (Zaragoza, Spain, March 16).

Khaosai Galaxy gained a 5th round TKO over Jae-Suk Park to retain WBA title (Samut-Sonkram, Thailand, April 7).

Robert Quiroga scored a unanimous 12-round decision over Akeem Anifowoshe to retain IBF title (San Antonio, June 15).

Khaosai Galaxy gained a 5th round TKO over David Griman to retain WBA title (Bangkok, July 20).

Sung-Kil Moon knocked out Ernesto Ford in 5th round to retain WBC title (Seoul, July 20).

Flyweights

Sot Chitalada scored a 12-round majority decision over Jung-Koo Chang to retain WBC title (Seoul, Nov.24, 1990).

Leopard Tamakuma fought a 12-round draw with Jesus Rojas to retain WBA title (Aomori, Japan, Dec.6, 1990).

Muangchai Kittikasem gained a 6th round TKO over champion Sot Chitalada to win WBC title (Ayuthaya, Thailand, Feb.15).

Elvis Alvarez scored a unanimous 12-round decision over champion Leopard Tamakuma to win WBA title (Tokyo, March 14).

Dave McAuley scored a unanimous 12-round decision over Pedro Feliciano to retain IBF title (Belfast, May 11).

Muangchai Kittikasem gained a 12th round TKO over Jung-Koo Chang to retain WBC title (Seoul, May 18).

Yong-Kang Kim scored a unanimous 12-round decision over champion Elvis Alvarez to win WBA title (Seoul, June 1).

Dave McAuley knocked out Jake Matlala in 10th round to retain IBF title (Belfast, Sept.7).

Junior Flyweights
(Light Flyweights)

Myung-Woo Yuh scored a 12-round unanimous decision over Leo Gamez to retain WBA title (Pohang, S.Korea, Nov.10, 1990).

Michael Carbajal knocked out Leon Salazar in 4th round to retain IBF title (Scottsdale, Dec.8, 1990).

Rolando Pascua knocked out champion Humberto Gonzalez to win WBC title (Inglewood, Dec.19, 1990).

Michael Carbajal knocked out Macario Santos in 2nd round to retain IBF title (Las Vegas, Feb.17).

Michael Carbajal scored a unanimous 12-round decision over Javier Varguez to retain IBF title (Las Vegas, March 17).

Melchor Cob Castro gained a 10th round TKO over champion Rolando Pascua to win WBC title (Inglewood, Calif., March 25).

Myung-Woo Yuh gained a 10th round TKO over Kajkong Danphoothai to retain WBA title (Masan, S.Korea, April 28).

Michael Carbajal scored a unanimous 12-round decision over Hector Patri to retain IBF title (Davenport, Iowa, May 10).

Humberto Gonzalez scored a unanimous 12-round decision over champion Melchor Cob Castro to regain WBC title (Palm Springs, June 3).

Strawweights
(Minimum)

Ricardo Lopez gained a 5th round TKO over champion Hideyuki Ohashi to win WBC title (Tokyo, Oct.25, 1990).

Bong-Jun Kim scored a 12-round split decision over Silverio Barcenas to retain WBA title (Seoul, Nov.3, 1990).

Phalan Lukmingkwan fought a 12-round draw with Domingo Lucas to retain IBF title (Bangkok, Dec.20, 1990).

Hi-Yong Choi scored a unanimous 12-round decision over champion Bong-Jun Kim to win WBA title (Seoul, Feb.2).

Ricardo Lopez gained an 8th round TKO over Kimio Hirano to retain WBC title (Shizuoka, Japan, May 19).

Hi-Yong Choi scored a unanimous 12-round decision over Sugar Rey Mike Bong-Jun Kim to win WBA title (Seoul, June 15).

Phalan Lukmingkwan scored a unanimous 12-round decision over Abdi Pohan to retain IBF title (Bangkok, July 2).

BOXING
STATISTICS

THROUGH THE YEARS
1884-1991
WORLD CHAMPIONS

THE 1992 INFORMATION PLEASE SPORTS ALMANAC

SEC B

PAGE 741

World Heavyweight Championship Fights

Widely accepted world champions in **bold** type. Note following result abbreviations: KO (knockout), TKO (technical knockout), Wu (unanimous decision), Wm (majority decision), Ws (split decision), Ref (referee's decision), ND (no decision), Disq (won on disqualification).

Year	Date	Winner	Age	Wt.	Loser	Wt.	Result	Location
1892	Sept. 7	James J.Corbett	26	178	**John L. Sullivan**	212	KO 21	New Orleans
1894	Jan. 25	**James J.Corbett**	27	184	Charley Mitchell	158	KO 3	Jacksonville, FL
1897	Mar. 17	Bob Fitzsimmons	34	167	**James J.Corbett**	183	KO 14	Carson City, NV
1899	June 9	James J. Jeffries	24	206	**Bob Fitzsimmons**	167	KO 11	Coney Island, NY
1899	Nov. 3	**James J. Jeffries**	24	215	Tom Sharkey	183	Ref 25	Coney Island, NY
1900	Apr. 6	**James J. Jeffries**	24	NA	Jack Finnegan	NA	KO 1	Detroit
1900	May 11	**James J. Jeffries**	25	218	James J.Corbett	188	KO 23	Coney Island, NY
1901	Nov. 15	**James J. Jeffries**	26	211	Gus Ruhlin	194	TKO 6	San Francisco
1902	July 25	**James J. Jeffries**	27	219	Bob Fitzsimmons	172	KO 8	San Francisco
1903	Aug. 14	**James J. Jeffries**	28	220	James J.Corbett	190	KO 10	San Francisco
1904	Aug. 25	**James J. Jeffries**	29	219	Jack Munroe	186	TKO 2	San Francisco
1905	July 3	Marvin Hart	28	190	Jack Root	171	KO 12	Reno, NV
1906	Feb. 23	Tommy Burns	24	180	**Marvin Hart**	188	Ref 20	Los Angeles
1906	Oct. 2	**Tommy Burns**	25	NA	Jim Flynn	NA	KO 15	Los Angeles
1906	Nov. 28	**Tommy Burns**	25	172	Phila.Jack O'Brien	163½	Draw 20	Los Angeles
1907	May 8	**Tommy Burns**	25	180	Phila.Jack O'Brien	167	Ref 20	Los Angeles
1907	July 4	**Tommy Burns**	26	181	Bill Squires	180	KO 1	Colma, Calif
1907	Dec. 2	**Tommy Burns**	26	177	Gunner Moir	204	KO 10	London
1908	Feb. 10	**Tommy Burns**	26	NA	Jack Palmer	NA	KO 4	London
1908	Mar. 17	**Tommy Burns**	26	NA	Jem Roche	NA	KO 1	Dublin
1908	Apr. 18	**Tommy Burns**	26	NA	Jewey Smith	NA	KO 5	Paris
1908	June 13	**Tommy Burns**	26	184	Bill Squires	183	KO 8	Paris
1908	Aug. 24	**Tommy Burns**	27	181	Bill Squires	184	KO 13	Sydney
1908	Sept. 2	**Tommy Burns**	27	183	Bill Lang	187	KO 6	Melbourne
1908	Dec. 26	Jack Johnson	30	192	**Tommy Burns**	168	TKO 14	Sydney
1909	Mar. 10	**Jack Johnson**	30	NA	Victor McLaglen	NA	ND 6	Vancouver
1909	May 19	**Jack Johnson**	31	205	Phila.Jack O'Brien	161	ND 6	Philadelphia
1909	June 30	**Jack Johnson**	31	207	Tony Ross	214	ND 6	Pittsburgh
1909	Sept. 9	**Jack Johnson**	31	209	Al Kaufman	191	ND 10	San Francisco
1909	Oct. 16	**Jack Johnson**	31	205½	Stanley Ketchel	170¼	KO 12	Colma, Calif.
1910	July 4	**Jack Johnson**	32	208	James J.Jeffries	227	KO 15	Reno, Nev.
1912	July 4	**Jack Johnson**	34	195½	Jim Flynn	175	TKO 9	Las Vegas, NM
1913	Dec. 19	**Jack Johnson**	35	NA	Jim Johnson	NA	Draw 10	Paris
1914	June 27	**Jack Johnson**	36	221	Frank Moran	203	Ref 20	Paris
1915	Apr. 5	Jess Willard	33	230	**Jack Johnson**	205½	KO 26	Havana
1916	Mar. 25	**Jess Willard**	34	225	Frank Moran	203	ND 10	NYC (Mad.Sq.Garden)
1919	July 4	Jack Dempsey	24	187	**Jess Willard**	245	TKO 4	Toledo, Ohio
1920	Sept. 6	**Jack Dempsey**	25	185	Billy Miske	187	KO 3	Benton Harbor, Mich.
1920	Dec. 14	**Jack Dempsey**	25	188¼	Bill Brennan	197	KO 12	NYC (Mad.Sq.Garden)
1921	July 2	**Jack Dempsey**	26	188	Georges Carpentier	172	KO 4	Jersey City, N.J.

World Heavyweight Championship Fights (Cont.)

Year	Date	Winner	Age	Wt.	Loser	Wt.	Result	Location
1923	July 4	**Jack Dempsey**	28	188	Tommy Givvons	175½	Ref 15	Shelby, Montana
1923	Sept. 14	**Jack Dempsey**	28	192½	Luis Firpo	216½	KO 2	NYC (Polo Grounds)
1926	Sept. 23	Gene Tunney	29	189½	**Jack Dempsey**	190	Wu 10	Philadelphia
1927	Sept. 22	**Gene Tunney**	30	189½	Jack Dempsey	192½	Wu 10	Chicago
1928	July 26	**Gene Tunney**	31	192	Tom Heeney	203½	TKO 11	NYC (Yankee Stadium)
1930	June 12	Max Schmeling	24	188	Jack Sharkey	197	Foul 4	NYC (Yankee Stadium)
1931	July 3	**Max Schmeling**	25	189	Young Stribling	186½	TKO 15	Cleveland
1932	June 21	Jack Sharkey	29	205	**Max Schmeling**	188	Ws 15	Long Island City, N.Y.
1933	June 29	Primo Carnera	26	260½	**Jack Sharkey**	201	KO 6	Long Island City, N.Y.
1933	Oct. 22	**Primo Carnera**	26	259½	Paulino Uzcudun	229¼	KO 15	Rome
1934	Mar. 1	**Primo Carnera**	27	270	Tommy Loughran	184	Wu 15	Miami
1934	June 14	Max Baer	25	209½	**Primo Carnera**	263¼	TKO 11	Long Island City, N.Y.
1935	June 13	James J.Braddock	29	193¾	**Max Baer**	209½	Wu 15	Long Island City, N.Y.
1937	June 22	**Joe Louis**	23	197¼	James J.Braddock	197	KO 8	Chicago
1937	Aug. 30	**Joe Louis**	23	197	Tommy Farr	204¼	Wu 15	NYC (Yankee Stadium)
1938	Feb. 23	**Joe Louis**	23	200	Nathan Mann	193½	KO 3	NYC (Mad.Sq.Garden)
1938	Apr. 1	**Joe Louis**	23	202½	Harry Thomas	196	KO 5	Chicago
1938	June 22	**Joe Louis**	24	198¼	Max Schmeling	193	KO 1	NYC (Yankee Stadium)
1939	Jan. 25	**Joe Louis**	24	200¼	John Henry Lewis	180¾	KO 1	NYC (Mad.Sq.Garden)
1939	Apr. 17	**Joe Louis**	24	201¼	Jack Roper	204¾	KO 1	Los Angeles
1939	June 28	**Joe Louis**	25	200¾	Tony Galento	233¾	TKO 4	NYC (Yankee Stadium)
1939	Sept. 20	**Joe Louis**	25	200	Bob Pastor	183	KO 11	Detroit
1940	Feb. 9	**Joe Louis**	25	203	Arturo Godoy	202	Ws 15	NYC (Mad.Sq.Garden)
1940	Mar. 29	**Joe Louis**	25	201½	Johnny Paychek	187½	KO 2	NYC (Mad.Sq.Garden)
1940	June 20	**Joe Louis**	26	199	Artoro Godoy	201¼	TKO 8	NYC (Yankee Stad.)
1940	Dec. 16	**Joe Louis**	26	202¼	Al McCoy	180¾	TKO 6	Boston
1941	Jan. 31	**Joe Louis**	26	202½	Red Burman	188	KO 5	NYC (Mad.Sq.Garden)
1941	Feb. 17	**Joe Louis**	26	203½	Gus Dorazio	193½	KO 2	Philadelphia
1941	Mar. 21	**Joe Louis**	26	202	Abe Simon	254½	TKO 13	Detroit
1941	Apr. 8	**Joe Louis**	26	203½	Tony Musto	199½	TKO 9	St. Louis
1941	May 23	**Joe Louis**	27	201½	Buddy Baer	237½	Disq 7	Washington, DC
1941	June 18	**Joe Louis**	27	199½	Billy Conn	174	KO 13	NYC (Polo Grounds)
1941	Sept. 29	**Joe Louis**	27	202¼	Lou Nova	202½	TKO 6	NYC (Polo Grounds)
1942	Jan. 9	**Joe Louis**	27	206¾	Buddy Baer	250	KO 1	NYC (Mad.Sq.Garden)
1942	Mar. 27	**Joe Louis**	27	207½	Abe Simon	255½	KO 6	NYC (Mad.Sq.Garden)
1942–45		World War II						
1946	June 9	**Joe Louis**	32	207	Billy Conn	187	KO 8	NYC (Yankee Stadium)
1946	Sept. 18	**Joe Louis**	32	211	Tami Mauriello	198½	KO 1	NYC (Yankee Stadium)
1947	Dec. 5	**Joe Louis**	33	211½	Jersey Joe Walcott	194½	Ws 15	NYC (Mad.Sq.Garden)
1948	June 25	**Joe Louis**	34	213½	Jersey Joe Walcott	194¾	KO 11	NYC (Yankee Stadium)
1949	June 22	Ezzard Charles	27	181¾	Jersey Joe Walcott	195½	Wu 15	Chicago
1949	Aug. 10	**Ezzard Charles**	28	180	Gus Lesnevich	182	TKO 8	NYC (Yankee Stadium)
1949	Oct. 14	**Ezzard Charles**	28	182	Pat Valentino	188½	KO 8	San Francisco
1950	Aug. 15	**Ezzard Charles**	29	183¼	Freddie Beshore	184½	TKO 14	Buffalo
1950	Sept. 27	**Ezzard Charles**	29	184½	Joe Louis	218	Wu 15	NYC (Yankee Stadium)
1950	Dec. 5	**Ezzard Charles**	29	185	Nick Barone	178½	KO 11	Cincinnati
1951	Jan. 12	**Ezzard Charles**	29	185	Lee Oma	193	TKO 10	NYC (Mad.Sq.Garden)
1951	Mar. 7	**Ezzard Charles**	29	186	Jersey Joe Walcott	193	Wu 15	Detroit
1951	May 30	**Ezzard Charles**	29	182	Joey Maxim	181½	Wu 15	Chicago
1951	July 18	Jersey Joe Walcott	37	194	**Ezzard Charles**	182	KO 7	Pittsburgh
1952	June 5	**Jersey Joe Walcott**	38	196	**Ezzard Charles**	191½	Wu 15	Philadelphia
1952	Sept. 23	Rocky Marciano	29	184	**Jersey Joe Walcott**	196	KO 13	Philadelphia
1953	May 15	**Rocky Marciano**	29	184½	Jersey Joe Walcott	197¾	KO 1	Chicago
1953	Sept. 24	**Rocky Marciano**	30	185	Roland LaStarza	184¾	TKO 11	NYC (Polo Grounds)
1954	June 17	**Rocky Marciano**	30	187½	Ezzard Charles	185½	Wu 15	NYC (Yankee Stadium)
1954	Sept. 17	**Rocky Marciano**	31	187	Ezzard Charles	192½	KO 8	NYC (Yankee Stadium)

Year	Date	Winner	Age	Wt.	Loser	Wt.	Result	Location
1955	May 16	**Rocky Marciano**	31	189	Don Cockell	205	TKO 9	San Francisco
1955	Sept. 21	**Rocky Marciano**	32	188¼	Archie Moore	188	KO 9	NYC (Yankee Stadium)
1956	Nov. 30	Floyd Patterson	21	182¼	Archie Moore	187¾	KO 5	Chicago
1957	July 29	**Floyd Patterson**	22	184	Tommy Jackson	192½	TKO 10	NYC (Polo Grounds)
1957	Aug. 22	**Floyd Patterson**	22	187¼	Pete Rademacher	202	KO 6	Seattle
1958	Aug. 18	**Floyd Patterson**	23	184½	Roy Harris	194	TKO 13	Los Angeles
1959	May 1	**Floyd Patterson**	24	182½	Brian London	206	KO 11	Indianapolis
1959	June 26	Ingemar Johansson	26	196	**Floyd Patterson**	182	TKO 3	NYC (Yankee Stadium)
1960	June 20	Floyd Patterson	25	190	**Ingemar Johansson**	194¾	KO 5	NYC (Polo Grounds)
1961	Mar. 13	**Floyd Patterson**	26	194¾	Ingemar Johansson	206½	KO 6	Miami Beach
1961	Dec. 4	**Floyd Patterson**	26	188½	Tom McNeeley	197	KO 4	Toronto
1962	Sept. 25	Sonny Liston	30	214	**Floyd Patterson**	189	KO 1	Chicago
1963	July 22	**Sonny Liston**	31	215	Floyd Patterson	194½	KO 1	Las Vegas
1964	Feb. 25	Cassius Clay*	22	210½	**Sonny Liston**	218	TKO 7	Miami Beach
1965	Mar. 5	Ernie Terrell WBA	25	199	Eddie Machen	192	Wu 15	Chicago
1965	May 25	**Muhammad Ali**	23	206	Sonny Liston	215¼	KO 1	Lewiston, Me.
1965	Nov. 1	Ernie Terrell WBA	26	206	George Chuvalo	209	Wu 15	Toronto
1965	Nov. 22	**Muhammad Ali**	23	210	Floyd Patterson	196¾	TKO 12	Las Vegas
1966	Mar. 29	**Muhammad Ali**	24	214½	George Chuvalo	216	Wu 15	Toronto
1966	May 21	**Muhammad Ali**	24	201½	Henry Cooper	188	TKO 6	London
1966	June 28	Ernie Terrell WBA	27	209½	Doug Jones	187½	Wu 15	Houston
1966	Aug. 6	**Muhammad Ali**	24	209½	Brian London	201½	KO 3	London
1966	Sept. 10	**Muhammad Ali**	24	203½	Karl Mildenberger	194¼	TKO 12	Frankfurt, W.Ger.
1966	Nov. 14	**Muhammad Ali**	24	212¾	Cleveland Williams	210½	TKO 3	Houston
1967	Feb. 6	**Muhammad Ali**	25	212¼	Ernie Terrell WBA	212½	Wu 15	Houston
1967	Mar. 22	**Muhammad Ali**	25	211½	Zora Folley	202½	KO 7	NYC (Mad.Sq.Garden)
1968	Mar. 4	Joe Frazier	24	204½	Buster Mathis	243½	TKO 11	NYC (Mad.Sq.Garden)
1968	Apr. 27	Jimmy Ellis	28	197	Jerry Quarry	195	Wm 15	Oakland
1968	June 24	Joe Frazier NY	24	203½	Manuel Ramos	208	TKO 2	NYC (Mad.Sq.Garden)
1968	Aug. 14	Jimmy Ellis WBA	28	198	Floyd Patterson	188	Ref 15	Stockholm
1968	Dec. 10	Joe Frazier NY	24	203	Oscar Bonavena	207	Wu 15	Philadelphia
1969	Apr. 22	Joe Frazier NY	25	204½	Dave Zyglewicz	190½	KO 1	Houston
1969	June 23	Joe Frazier NY	25	203½	Jerry Quarry	198½	TKO 8	NYC (Mad.Sq.Garden)
1970	Feb. 16	Joe Frazier NY	26	205	Jimmy Ellis WBA	201	TKO 5	NYC (Mad.Sq.Garden)
1970	Nov. 18	Joe Frazier	26	209	Bob Foster	188	KO 2	Detroit
1971	Mar. 8	Joe Frazier	27	205½	**Muhammad Ali**	215	Wu 15	NYC (Mad.Sq.Garden)
1972	Jan. 15	**Joe Frazier**	28	215½	Terry Daniels	195	TKO 4	New Orleans
1972	May 26	**Joe Frazier**	28	217½	Ron Stander	218	TKO 5	Omaha, Neb.
1973	Jan. 22	George Foreman	24	217½	**Joe Frazier**	214	TKO 2	Kingston, Jamaica
1973	Sept. 1	**George Foreman**	24	219½	Jose (King) Roman	196½	KO 1	Tokyo
1974	Mar. 26	**George Foreman**	25	224¼	Ken Norton	212¼	TKO 2	Caracas, Venezuela
1974	Oct. 30	Muhammad Ali	32	216½	**George Foreman**	220	KO 8	Kinshasa, Zaire
1975	Mar. 24	**Muhammad Ali**	33	223½	Chuck Wepner	225	TKO 15	Cleveland
1975	May 16	**Muhammad Ali**	33	224½	Ron Lyle	219	TKO 11	Las Vegas
1975	July 1	**Muhammad Ali**	33	224½	Joe Bugner	230	Wu 15	Kuala Lumpur, Malaysia
1975	Oct. 1	**Muhammad Ali**	33	224½	Joe Frazier	215	TKO 15	Manila, Philippines
1976	Feb. 20	**Muhammad Ali**	34	226	Jean Pierre Coopman	206	KO 5	San Juan, P.R.
1976	Apr. 30	**Muhammad Ali**	34	230	Jimmy Young	209	Wu 15	Landover, Md.
1976	May 24	**Muhammad Ali**	34	230	Richard Dunn	206½	TKO 5	Munich, W.Ger.
1976	Sept. 28	**Muhammad Ali**	34	221	Ken Norton	217½	Wu 15	NYC (Yankee Stadium)
1977	May 16	**Muhammad Ali**	35	221¼	Alfredo Evangelista	209¼	Wu 15	Landover, Md.
1977	Sept. 29	**Muhammad Ali**	35	225	Earnie Shavers	211¼	Wu 15	NYC (Mad.Sq.Garden)
1978	Feb. 15	Leon Spinks	24	197¼	**Muhammad Ali**	224¼	Ws 15	Las Vegas
1978	June 9	Larry Holmes	28	209	Ken Norton WBC†	220	Ws 15	Las Vegas
1978	Sept. 15	Muhammad Ali	36	221	**Leon Spinks**	201	Wu 15	New Orleans
1978	Nov. 10	Larry Holmes WBC	29	214	Alfredo Evangelista	208¼	KO 7	Las Vegas

*Muhammad Ali was known as Cassius Clay when he stopped Sonny Liston on Feb. 25, 1964.

World Heavyweight Championship Fights (Cont.)

Year	Date	Winner	Age	Wt.	Loser	Wt.	Result	Location
1979	Mar. 23	Larry Holmes WBC	929	214	Osvaldo Ocasio	207	TKO 7	Las Vegas
1979	June 22	Larry Holmes WBC	29	215	Mike Weaver	202	TKO 12	NYC (Mad.Sq.Garden)
1979	Sept. 28	Larry Holmes WBC	29	210	Earnie Shavers	211	TKO 11	Las Vegas
1979	Oct. 20	John Tate	24	240	Gerrie Coetzee	222	Wu 15	Pretoria, S.Africa
1980	Feb. 3	Larry Holmes WBC	30	213½	Lorenzo Zanon	215	TKO 6	Las Vegas
1980	Mar. 31	Mike Weaver	27	232	John Tate WBA	232	KO 15	Knoxville, Tenn.
1980	Mar. 31	Larry Holmes WBC	30	211	Leroy Jones	254½	TKO 8	Las Vegas
1980	July 7	Larry Holmes WBC	30	214¼	Scott LeDoux	226	TKO 7	Minneapolis
1980	Oct. 2	Larry Holmes WBC	30	211¼	Muhammad Ali	217½	TKO 11	Las Vegas
1980	Oct. 25	Mike Weaver WBA	28	210	Gerrie Coetzee	226½	KO 13	Sun City, Boph'swana
1981	Apr. 11	**Larry Holmes**	31	215	Trevor Berbick	215½	Wu 15	Las Vegas
1981	June 12	**Larry Holmes**	31	212¼	Leon Spinks	200¼	TKO 3	Detroit
1981	Oct. 3	Mike Weaver WBA	29	215	Quick Tillis	209	Wu 15	Rosemont, Ill.
1981	Nov. 6	**Larry Holmes**	32	213¼	Renaldo Snipes	215¾	TKO 11	Pittsburgh
1982	June 11	**Larry Holmes**	32	212½	Gerry Cooney	225½	TKO 13	Las Vegas
1982	Nov. 26	**Larry Holmes**	33	217½	Randall (Tex) Cobb	234¼	Wu 15	Houston
1982	Dec. 10	Michael Dokes	24	216	Mike Weaver WBA	209¾	TKO 1	Las Vegas
1983	Mar. 27	**Larry Holmes**	33	221	Lucien Rodriguez	209	Wu 12	Scranton, Pa.
1983	May 20	Michael Dokes WBA	24	223	Mike Weaver	218½	Draw 15	Las Vegas
1983	May 20	**Larry Holmes**	33	213	Tim Witherspoon	219½	Ws 12	Las Vegas
1983	Sept. 10	**Larry Holmes**	33	223	Scott Frank	211¼	TKO 5	Atlantic City
1983	Sept. 23	Gerrie Coetzee	28	215	Michael Dokes WBA	217	KO 10	Richfield, Ohio
1983	Nov. 25	**Larry Holmes**	34	219	Marvis Frazier	200	TKO 1	Las Vegas
1984	Mar. 9	Tim Witherspoon**	26	220¼	Greg Page	239½	Wm 12	Las Vegas
1984	Aug. 31	Pinklon Thomas	26	216	Tim Witherspoon WBC	217	Wm 12	Las Vegas
1984	Nov. 9	**Larry Holmes** IBF	35	221½	Bonecrusher Smith	227	TKO 12	Las Vegas
1984	Dec. 1	Greg Page	26	236½	Gerrie Coetzee WBA	218	KO 8	Sun City, Boph'swana
1985	Mar. 15	**Larry Holmes**	35	223½	David Bey	233¼	TKO 10	Las Vegas
1985	Apr. 29	Tony Tubbs	26	229	Greg Page WBA	239½	Wu 15	Buffalo
1985	May 20	**Larry Holmes**	35	222¼	Carl Williams	215	Wu 15	Las Vegas
1985	June 15	Pinklon Thomas	27	220¼	Mike Weaver	221¼	KO 8	Las Vegas
1985	Sept. 21	Michael Spinks	29	200	**Larry Holmes** IBF	221½	Wu 15	Las Vegas
1986	Jan. 17	Tim Witherspoon	28	227	Tony Tubbs WBA	229	Wm 15	Atlanta
1986	Mar. 22	Trevor Berbick	33	218½	Pinklon Thomas WBC	222¾	Wu 15	Las Vegas
1986	Apr. 19	**Michael Spinks**	29	205	Larry Holmes	223	Ws 15	Las Vegas
1986	July 19	Tim Witherspoon	28	234¾	Frank Bruno	228	TKO 11	Wembley, England
1986	Sept. 6	**Michael Spinks**	30	201	Steffen Tangstad	214¾	TKO 4	Las Vegas
1986	Nov. 22	Mike Tyson	20	221¼	Trevor Berbick WBC	218½	TKO 2	Las Vegas
1986	Dec. 12	Bonecrusher Smith	33	228½	Tim Witherspoon WBA	233½	TKO 1	NYC (Mad.Sq.Garden)
1987	Mar. 7	Mike Tyson WBC	20	219	James Smith WBA	233	Wu 12	Las Vegas
1987	May 30	Mike Tyson	20	218¾	Pinklon Thomas	217¾	TKO 6	Las Vegas
1987	May 30	Tony Tucker‡	28	222¼	Buster Douglas	227¼	TKO 10	Las Vegas
1987	June 15	**Michael Spinks**	30	208¾	Gerry Cooney	238	TKO 5	Atlantic City
1987	Aug. 1	Mike Tyson	21	221	Tony Tucker IBF	221	Wu 12	Las Vegas
1987	Oct. 16	Mike Tyson	21	216	Tyrell Biggs	228¾	TKO 7	Atlantic City
1988	Jan. 22	Mike Tyson	21	215¾	Larry Holmes	225¾	TKO 4	Atlantic City
1988	Mar. 20	Mike Tyson	21	216¼	Tony Tubbs	238¼	KO 2	Tokyo
1988	June 27	Mike Tyson	21	218¼	**Michael Spinks**	212¼	KO 1	Atlantic City
1989	Feb. 25	**Mike Tyson**	22	218	Frank Bruno	228	TKO 5	Las Vegas
1989	July 21	**Mike Tyson**	23	219¼	Carl Williams	218	TKO 1	Atlantic City
1990	Feb. 10	Buster Douglas	29	231½	**Mike Tyson**	220½	KO 10	Tokyo
1990	Oct. 25	Evander Holyfield	28	208	**Buster Douglas**	246	KO 3	Las Vegas
1991	Apr. 19	**Evander Holyfield**	28	208	George Foreman	257	Wu 12	Atlantic City

Notes

†WBC recognized Ken Norton as world champion when Leon Spinks refused to meet Norton before Spinks' rematch with Muhammad Ali. Norton had scored a 15-round split decision over Jimmy Young on Nov. 5, 1977 in Las Vegas.

**WBC recognized winner of Mar. 9, 1984 fight between Tim Witherspoon and Greg Page as world champion after Larry Holmes relinquished title in dispute. IBF then recognized Holmes.

‡IBF recognized winner of May 30, 1987 fight between Tony Tucker and James (Buster) Douglas as world champion after Michael Spinks relinquished title in dispute.

All-Time Heavyweight Upsets

Buster Douglas' Feb. 10, 1990, knockout of unbeaten heavyweight champion Mike Tyson ranks as the biggest upset in boxing history. It tops 11 other well-known upsets in the annals of the heavyweight division. All were fights for the world championship except the Max Schmeling-Joe Louis bout.

Note the following abbreviations: KO (knockout), Wu (unanimous decision), TKO (technical knockout, fight stopped), WS (split decision).

Date	Winner	Loser	Result	KO Time	Location
9/7/1892	James J.Corbett	John L.Sullivan	KO 21	1:30	Olympic Club, New Orleans
4/5/1915	Jess Willard	Jack Johnson	KO 26	1:26	Mariano Race Track, Havana
9/23/26	Gene Tunney	Jack Dempsey	Wu 10	—	Sesquicentennial Stadium, Phila.
6/13/35	James J.Braddock	Max Baer	Wu 15	—	Mad.Sq.Garden Bowl, L.I.City
6/19/36	Max Schmeling	Joe Louis	KO 12	2:29	Yankee Stadium, New York
7/18/51	Jersey Joe Walcott	Ezzard Charles	KO 7	0:55	Forbes Field, Pittsburgh
6/26/59	Ingemar Johansson	Floyd Patterson	TKO 3	2:03	Yankee Stadium, New York
2/25/64	Cassius Clay†	Sonny Liston	TKO 7	*	Convention Hall, Miami Beach
10/30/74	Muhammad Ali	George Foreman	KO 8	2:58	20th of May Stadium, Zaire
2/15/78	Leon Spinks	Muhammad Ali	Ws 15	—	Hilton Pavilion, Las Vegas
9/21/85	Michael Spinks	Larry Holmes	Wu 15	—	Riviera Hotel, Las Vegas
2/10/90	Buster Douglas	Mike Tyson	KO 10	1:23	Korakuen Stadium, Tokyo

*Liston failed to answer bell for Round 7.
†Cassius Clay changed his name to Muhammad Ali after winning title.

Major Titleholders

Note the following sanctioning body abbreviations: NBA (National Boxing Association), WBA (World Boxing Association), WBC (World Boxing Council), GBR (Great Britain), IBF (International Boxing Federation), plus other national and state commissions.

Fighters who retired as champion are indicated by (*) and champions who abandoned or relinquished their titles are indicated by (†).

Heavyweights

Widely accepted champions in CAPITAL letters. Current champions in **bold** type.

Champion	Held Title	Champion	Held Title
JOHN L.SULLIVAN	1885-92	Jimmy Ellis (WBA)	1968-70
JAMES J.CORBETT	1892-97	JOE FRAZIER	1970-73
BOB FITZSIMMONS	1897-99	GEORGE FOREMAN	1973-74
JAMES J.JEFFRIES	1899-1905*	MUHAMMAD ALI	1974-78*
MARVIN HART	1905-06	LEON SPINKS	1978
TOMMY BURNS	1906-08	Ken Norton (WBC)	1978
JACK JOHNSON	1908-15	Larry Holmes (WBC)	1978-80
JESS WILLARD	1915-19	MUHAMMAD ALI	1978-79
JACK DEMPSEY	1919-26	John Tate (WBA)	1979-80
GENE TUNNEY	1926-28*	Mike Weaver (WBA)	1980-82
MAX SCHMELING	1930-32	LARRY HOLMES	1980-85
JACK SHARKEY	1932-33	Michael Dokes (WBA)	1982-83
PRIMO CARNERA	1933-34	Gerrie Coetzee (WBA)	1983-84
MAX BAER	1934-35	Tim Witherspoon (WBC)	1984
JAMES J.BRADDOCK	1935-37	Pinklon Thomas (WBC)	1984-86
JOE LOUIS	1937-49*	Greg Page (WBA)	1984-85
EZZARD CHARLES	1949-51	MICHAEL SPINKS	1985-87
JERSEY JOE WALCOTT	1951-52	Tim Witherspoon (WBA)	1986
ROCKY MARCIANO	1952-56*	Trevor Berbick (WBC)	1986
FLOYD PATTERSON	1956-59	Mike Tyson (WBC)	1986-87
INGEMAR JOHANSSON	1959-60	James (Bonecrusher) Smith (WBA)	1986-87
FLOYD PATTERSON	1960-62	Tony Tucker (IBF)	1987
SONNY LISTON	1962-64	Mike Tyson (WBC,WBA,IBF)	1987-88
CASSIUS CLAY (MUHAMMAD ALI)	1964-70	MIKE TYSON	1988-90
Ernie Terrell (WBA)	1965-67	BUSTER DOUGLAS (WBC, WBA, IBF)	1990
Joe Frazier (NY)	1968-70	**EVANDER HOLYFIELD** (WBC, WBA, IBF)	1990-

Note: John L.Sullivan held the Bare Knuckle championship from 1882-85.

Light Heavyweights

Widely accepted champions in CAPITAL letters. Current champions in **bold** type.

Champion	Held Title	Champion	Held Title
JACK ROOT	1903	BATTLING SIKI	1922-23
GEORGE GARDNER	1903	MIKE McTIGUE	1923-25
BOB FITZSIMMONS	1903-05	PAUL BERLENBACH	1925-26
PHILADELPHIA JACK O'BRIEN	1905-12*	JACK DELANEY	1926-27†
JACK DILLON	1914-16	Jimmy Slattery (NBA)	1927
BATTLING LEVINSKY	1916-20	TOMMY LOUGHRAN	1927-29
GEORGES CARPENTIER	1920-22	JIMMY SLATTERY	1930

Light Heavyweights (Cont.)

Champion	Held Title
MAXIE ROSENBLOOM	1930-34
George Nichols (NBA)	1932
Bob Godwin (NBA)	1933
BOB OLIN	1934-35
JOHN HENRY LEWIS	1935-38
MELIO BETTINA (NY)	1939
Len Harvey (GBR)	1939-42
BILLY CONN	1939-40†
ANTON CHRISTOFORIDIS (NBA)	1941
GUS LESNEVICH	1941-48
Freddie Mills (GBR)	1942-46
FREDDIE MILLS	1948-50
JOEY MAXIM	1950-52
ARCHIE MOORE	1952-62
Harold Johnson (NBA)	1961
HAROLD JOHNSON	1962-63
WILLIE PASTRANO	1963-65
Eddie Cotton (Mich.)	1963-64
JOSE TORRES	1965-66
DICK TIGER	1966-68
BOB FOSTER	1968-74*
Vicente Rondon (WBA)	1971-72
John Conteh (WBC)	1974-77
Victor Galindez (WBA)	1974-78
Miguel A.Cuello (WBC)	1977-78

Champion	Held Title
Mate Parlov (WBC)	1978
Mike Rossman (WBA)	1978-79
Marvin Johnson (WBC)	1978-79
Matthew (Franklin) Saad Muhammad (WBC)	1979-81
Marvin Johnson (WBA)	1979-80
Eddie (Gregory) Mustapha Muhammad (WBA)	1980-81
Michael Spinks (WBA)	1981-83
Dwight (Braxton) Muhammad Qarvi (WBC)	1981-83
MICHAEL SPINKS	1983-85†
J.B.Williamson (WBC)	1985-86
Slobodan Kacar (IBF)	1985-86
Marvin Johnson (WBA)	1986-87
Dennis Andries (WBC)	1986-87
Bobby Czyz (IBF)	1986-87
Leslie Stewart (WBA)	1987
Virgil Hill (WBA)	1987-91
Prince Charles Williams (IBF)	1987-
Thomas Hearns (WBC)	1987
Donny Lalonde (WBC)	1987-88
Sugar Ray Leonard (WBC)	1988
Dennis Andries (WBC)	1989
Jeff Harding (WBC)	1989-90, 1991-
Dennis Andries (WBC)	1990-91
Thomas Hearns (WBA)	1991-

Middleweights

Widely accepted champions in CAPITAL letters. Current champions in **bold** type.

Champion	Held Title
JACK (NONPAREIL) DEMPSEY	1884-91
BOB FITZSIMMONS	1891-97
CHARLES (KID) McCOY	1897-98
TOMMY RYAN	1898-1907
STANLEY KETCHEL	1908
BILLY PAPKE	1908
STANLEY KETCHEL	1908-10
FRANK KLAUS	1913
GEORGE CHIP	1913-14
AL McCOY	1914-17
Jeff Smith (AUS)	1914
Mick King (AUS)	1914
Jeff Smith (AUS)	1914-15
Lee Darcy (AUS)	1915-17
MIKE O'DOWD	1917-20
JOHNNY WILSON	1920-23
Wm.Bryan Downey (Ohio)	1921-22
Dave Rosenberg (NY)	1922
Jock Malone (Ohio)	1922-23
Mike O'Dowd (NY)	1922
Lou Bogash (NY)	1923
HARRY GREB	1923-26
TIGER FLOWERS	1926
MICKEY WALKER	1926-31†
GORILLA JONES	1931-32
MARCEL THIL	1932-37
Ben Jeby (NY)	1932-33
Lou Brouillard (NBA,NY)	1933
Vince Dundee (NBA,NY)	1933-34
Teddy Yarosz (NBA,NY)	1934-35
Babe Risko (NBA,NY)	1935-36
Freddie Steele (NBA,NY)	1936-38
FRED APOSTOLI	1937-39
Al Hostak (NBA)	1938
Solly Krieger (NBA)	1938-39
Al Hostak (NBA)	1939-40
CEFERINO GARCIA	1939-40
KEN OVERLIN	1940-41

Champion	Held Title
Tony Zale (NBA)	1940-41
BILLY SOOSE	1941
TONY ZALE	1941-47
ROCKY GRAZIANO	1947-48
TONY ZALE	1948
MARCEL CERDAN	1948-49
JAKE LA MOTTA	1949-51
SUGAR RAY ROBINSON	1951
RANDY TURPIN	1951
SUGAR RAY ROBINSON	1951-52*
CARL (BOBO) OLSON	1953-55
SUGAR RAY ROBINSON	1955-57
GENE FULLMER	1957
SUGAR RAY ROBINSON	1957
CARMEN BASILIO	1957-58
SUGAR RAY ROBINSON	1958-60
Gene Fullmer (NBA)	1959-62
PAUL PENDER	1960-61
TERRY DOWNES	1961-62
PAUL PENDER	1962-63
Dick Tiger (WBA)	1962-63
DICK TIGER	1963
JOEY GIARDELLO	1963-65
DICK TIGER	1965-66
EMILE GRIFFITH	1966-67
NINO BENVENUTI	1967
EMILE GRIFFITH	1967-68
NINO BENVENUTI	1968-70
CARLOS MONZON	1970-77*
Rodrigo Valdez (WBC)	1974-76
RODRIGO VALDEZ	1977-78
HUGO CORRO	1978-79
VITO ANTUOFERMO	1979-80
ALAN MINTER	1980
MARVELOUS MARVIN HAGLER	1980-87
SUGAR RAY LEONARD	1987
Frank Tate (IBF)	1987-88
Sumbu Kalambay (WBA)	1987-89

Champion	Held Title	Champion	Held Title
Thomas Hearns (WBC)	1987-88	Mike McCallum (WBA)	1989-
Iran Barkley (WBC)	1988-89	Julian Jackson (WBC)	1990-
Michael Nunn (IBF)	1988-91	James Toney (IBF)	1991-
Roberto Duran (WBC)	1989-90*		

Welterweights

Widely accepted champions in CAPITAL letters. Current champions in **bold** type.

Champion	Held Title	Champion	Held Title
PADDY DUFFY	1888-90	KID GAVILAN	1951-54
MYSTERIOUS BILLY SMITH	1892-94	JOHNNY SAXTON	1954-55
TOMMY RYAN	1894-98	TONY DeMARCO	1955
MYSTERIOUS BILLY SMITH	1898-1900	CARMEN BASILIO	1955-56
MATTY MATTHEWS	1900	JOHNNY SAXTON	1956
EDDIE CONNOLLY	1900	CARMEN BASILIO	1956-57†
JAMES (RUBE) FERNS	1900	VIRGIL AKINS	1958
MATTY MATHEWS	1900-01	DON JORDAN	1958-60
JAMES (RUBE) FERNS	1901	BENNY (KID) PARET	1960-61
JOE WALCOTT	1901-04	EMILE GRIFFITH	1961
THE DIXIE KID	1904-05	BENNY (KID) PARET	1961-62
HONEY MELLODY	1906-07	EMILE GRIFFITH	1962-63
Mike (Twin) Sullivan	1907-08	LUIS RODRIGUEZ	1963
FRANK MANTELL	1907-08	EMILE GRIFFITH	1963-66†
HARRY LEWIS	1908-13	Charlie Shipes (Calif.)	1966-67
Jimmy Gardner	1908-09	CURTIS COKES	1966-69
Jimmy Clabby	1910-11	JOSE NAPOLES	1969-70
WALDEMAR HOLBERG	1914	BILLY BACKUS	1970-71
TOM McCORMICK	1914	JOSE NAPOLES	1971-75
MATT WELLS	1914-15	Hedgemon Lewis (NY)	1972-73
MIKE GLOVER	1915	Angel Espada (WBA)	1975-76
JACK BRITTON	1915	JOHN H. STRACEY	1975-76
TED (KID) LEWIS	1915-16	CARLOS PALOMINO	1976-79
JACK BRITTON	1916-17	Pipino Cuevas (WBA)	1976-80
TED (KID) LEWIS	1917-19	WILFREDO BENITEZ	1979
JACK BRITTON	1919-22	SUGAR RAY LEONARD	1979-80
MICKEY WALKER	1922-26	ROBERTO DURAN	1980
PETE LATZO	1926-27	Thomas Hearns (WBA)	1980-81
JOE DUNDEE	1927-29	SUGAR RAY LEONARD	1980-82
JACKIE FIELDS	1929-30	Donald Curry (WBA)	1983-85
YOUNG JACK THOMPSON	1930	Milton McCrory (WBC)	1983-85
TOMMY FREEMAN	1930-31	DONALD CURRY	1985-86
YOUNG JACK THOMPSON	1931	LLOYD HONEYGHAN	1986-87
LOU BROUILLARD	1931-32	JORGE VACA (WBC)	1987-88
JACKIE FIELDS	1932-33	LLOYD HONEYGHAN (WBC)	1988-89
YOUNG CORBETT III	1933	Mark Breland (WBA)	1987
JIMMY McLARNIN	1933-34	Marlon Starling (WBA)	1987-88
BARNEY ROSS	1934	Tomas Molinares (WBA)	1988-89
JIMMY McLARNIN	1934-35	Simon Brown (IBF)	1988-91
BARNEY ROSS	1935-38	Mark Breland (WBA)	1989-90
HENRY ARMSTRONG	1938-40	MARLON STARLING (WBC)	1989-90
FRITZIE ZIVIC	1940-41	Aaron Davis (WBA)	1990-91
Izzy Jannazzo (Md.)	1940-41	Maurice Blocker (WBC)	1990-91
Freddie (Red) Cochrane	1941-46	**Meldrick Taylor** (WBA)	1991-
MARTY SERVO	1946*	**Simon Brown** (WBC)	1991-
SUGAR RAY ROBINSON	1946-51†	**Maurice Blocker** (IBF)	1991-
JOHNNY BRATTON	1951		

Lightweights

Widely accepted champions in CAPITAL letters. Current champions in **bold** type.

Champion	Held Title	Champion	Held Title
JACK McAULIFFE	1886-94	FREDDIE WELSH	1915-17
GEORGE (KID) LAVIGNE	1896-99	BENNY LEONARD	1917-25*
FRANK ERNE	1899-02	JIMMY GOODRICH	1925
JOE GANS	1902-04	ROCKY KANSAS	1925-26
JIMMY BRITT	1904-05	SAMMY MANDELL	1926-30
BATTLING NELSON	1905-06	AL SINGER	1930
JOE GANS	1906-08	TONY CANZONERI	1930-33
BATTLING NELSON	1908-10	BARNEY ROSS	1933-35†
AD WOLGAST	1910-12	TONY CANZONERI	1935-36
WILLIE RITCHIE	1912-14	LOU AMBERS	1936-38

Lightweights (Cont.)

Champion	Held Title
HENRY ARMSTRONG	1938-39
LOU AMBERS	1939-40
Sammy Angott (NBA)	1940-41
LEW JENKINS	1940-41
SAMMY ANGOTT	1943-44
Beau Jack (NY)	1942-43
Slugger White (Md.)	1943
Bob Montgomery (NY)	1943
Sammy Angott (NBA)	1943-44
Beau Jack (NY)	1943-44
Bob Montgomery (NY)	1944-47
Juan Zurita (NBA)	1944-45
IKE WILLIAMS	1947-51
JAMES CARTER	1951-52
LAURO SALAS	1952
JAMES CARTER	1952-54
PADDY DeMARCO	1954
JAMES CARTER	1954-55
WALLACE (BUD) SMITH	1955-56
JOE BROWN	1956-62
CARLOS ORTIZ	1962-65
Kenny Lane (Mich.)	1963-64
ISMAEL LAGUNA	1965
CARLOS ORTIZ	1965-68
CARLOS TEO CRUZ	1968-69
MANDO RAMOS	1969-70
ISMAEL LAGUNA	1970
KEN BUCHANAN	1970-72
Pedro Carrasco (WBC)	1971-72
Mando Ramos (WBC)	1972
ROBERTO DURAN	1972-79†
Chango Carmona (WBC)	1972

Champion	Held Title
Rodolfo Gonzalez (WBC)	1972-74
Ishimatsu Suzuki (WBC)	1974-76
Esteban DeJesus (WBC)	1976-78
Jim Watt (WBC)	1979-81
Ernesto Espana (WBA)	1979-80
Hilmer Kenty (WBA)	1980-81
Sean O'Grady (WBA,WAA)	1981
Alexis Arguello (WBC)	1981-82
Claude Noel (WBA)	1981
Andrew Ganigan (WAA)	1981-82
Arturo Frias (WBA)	1981-82
Ray Mancini (WBA)	1982-84
ALEXIS ARGUELLO	1982-83
Edwin Rosario (WBC)	1983-84
Choo Choo Brown (IBF)	1984
Livingstone Bramble (WBA)	1984-86
Harry Arroyo (IBF)	1984-85
Jose Luis Ramirez (WBC)	1984-85
Jimmy Paul (IBF)	1985-86
Hector Camacho (WBC)	1985-86
Edwin Rosario (WBA)	1986-87
Greg Haugen (IBF)	1986-87
Julio Cesar Chavez (WBA)	1987-88
Jose Luis Ramirez (WBC)	1987-88
JULIO CESAR CHAVEZ (WBC,WBA)	1988-89
Vinny Pazienza (IBF)	1987-88
Greg Haugen (IBF)	1988-89
Pernell Whitaker (IBF,WBC)	1989-90
Edwin Rosario (WBA)	1989-90
Juan Nazario (WBA)	1990
PERNELL WHITAKER (IBF, WBC, WBA)	1990-

Featherweights

Widely accepted champions in CAPITAL letters. Current champions in **bold** type.

Champion	Held Title
TORPEDO BILLY MURPHY	1890
YOUNG GRIFFO	1890-92
GEORGE DIXON	1892-97
SOLLY SMITH	1897-98
Ben Jordan (GBR)	1898-99
Eddie Santry (GBR)	1899-1900
DAVE SULLIVAN	1898
GEORGE DIXON	1898-1900
TERRY McGOVERN	1900-01
YOUNG CORBETT II	1901-03
ABE ATTELL	1903-04
BROOKLYN TOMMY SULLIVAN	1904-05
ABE ATTELL	1906-12
JOHNNY KILBANE	1912-23
Jim Driscoll (GBR)	1912-13
EUGENE CRIQUI	1923
JOHNNY DUNDEE	1923-24†
LOUIS (KID) KAPLAN	1925-26†
Dick Finnegan (Mass.)	1926-27
BENNY BASS	1927-28
TONY CANZONERI	1928
ANDRE ROUTIS	1928-29
BATTLING BATTALINO	1929-32†
Tommy Paul (NBA)	1932-33
Kid Chocolate (NY)	1932-33
Freddie Miller (NBA)	1933-36
Baby Arizmendi (MEX)	1935-36
Mike Belloise (NY)	1936-37
Petey Sarron (NBA)	1936-37
HENRY ARMSTRONG	1937-38†
Joey Archibald (NY)	1938-39
Leo Rodak (NBA)	1938-39

Champion	Held Title
JOEY ARCHIBALD	1939-40
Petey Scalzo (NBA)	1940-41
Jimmy Perrin (La.)	1940-41
HARRY JEFFRA	1940-41
JOEY ARCHIBALD	1941
Richie Lemos (NBA)	1941
CHALKY WRIGHT	1941-42
Jackie Wilson (NBA)	1941-43
WILLIE PEP	1942-48
Jackie Callura (NBA)	1943
Phil Terranova (NBA)	1943-44
Sal Bartolo (NBA)	1944-46
SANDY SADDLER	1948-49
WILLIE PEP	1949-50
SANDY SADDLER	1950-57*
HOGAN (KID) BASSEY	1957-59
DAVEY MOORE	1959-63
ULTIMINIO (SUGAR) RAMOS	1963-64
VICENTE SALDIVAR	1964-67*
Howard Winstone (GBR)	1968
Raul Rojas (WBA)	1968
Jose Legra (WBC)	1968-69
Shozo Saijyo (WBA)	1968-71
JOHNNY FAMECHON (WBC)	1969-70
VICENTE SALDIVAR (WBC)	1970
KUNIAKI SHIBATA (WBC)	1970-72
Antonio Gomez (WBA)	1971-72
CLEMENTE SANCHEZ (WBC)	1972
Ernesto Marcel (WBA)	1972-74
JOSE LEGRA (WBC)	1972-73
EDER JOFRE (WBC)	1973-74
Ruben Olivares (WBA)	1974

Champion	Held Title	Champion	Held Title
Bobby Chacon (WBC)	1974-75	Barry McGuigan (WBA)	1985-86
ALEXIS ARGUELLO (WBA)	1974-76†	Ki-Young Chung (IBF)	1985-86
Ruben Olivares (WBC)	1975	Steve Cruz (WBA)	1986-87
David (Poison) Kotey (WBC)	1975-76	Antonio Rivera (IBF)	1986-88
DANNY (LITTLE RED) LOPEZ (WBC)	1976-80	Antonio Esparragoza (WBA)	1987-91
Rafael Ortega (WBA)	1977	Calvin Grove (IBF)	1988
Cecilio Lastra (WBA)	1977-78	Jorge Paez (IBF)	1988-91†
Eusebio Pedroza (WBA)	1978-85	Jeff Fenech (WBC)	1988-90†
SALVADOR SANCHEZ (WBC)	1980-82	**Marcos Villasana** (WBC)	1990-
Juan LaPorte (WBC)	1982-84	**Yung-Kyun Park** (WBA)	1991-
Wilfredo Gomez (WBC)	1984	Troy Dorsey	1991
Min-Keun Oh (IBF)	1984-85	**Manuel Medina** (IBF)	1991-
Azumah Nelson (WBC)	1984-88		

Bantamweights

Widely accepted champions in CAPITAL letters. Current champions in **bold** type.

Champion	Held Title	Champion	Held Title
HUGHEY BOYLE	1887-88	MANUEL ORTIZ	1947-50
CHAPPIE MORAN	1889-90	VIC TOWEEL	1950-52
TOMMY (SPIDER) KELLY	1890-92	JIMMY CARRUTHERS	1952-54*
BILLY PLIMMER	1892-95	ROBERT COHEN	1954-56
PEDLAR PALMER	1895-99	Raul Macias (NBA)	1955-57
TERRY McGOVERN	1899-1900	MARIO D'AGATA	1956-57
DANNY DOUGHERTY	1900-01	ALPHONSE HALIMI	1957-59
HARRY FORBES	1901-03	JOE BECERRA	1959-60*
FRANKIE NEIL	1903-04	Johnny Caldwell (EBU)	1961-62
JOE BOWKER	1904-05	EDER JOFRE	1961-65
JIMMY WALSH	1905-06†	MASAHIKO FIGHTING HARADA	1965-68
OWEN MORAN	1907-08	LIONEL ROSE	1968-69
MONTE ATTELL	1909-10	RUBEN OLIVARES	1969-70
FRANKIE CONLEY	1910-11	CHUCHO CASTILLO	1970-71
JOHNNY COULON	1911-14	RUBEN OLIVARES	1971-72
Digger Stanley (GBR)	1910-12	RAFAEL HERRERA	1972
Charles Ledoux (GBR)	1912-13	ENRIQUE PINDER	1972-73
Eddie Campi (GBR)	1913-14	ROMEO ANAYA	1973
KID WILLIAMS	1914-17	Rafael Herrera (WBC)	1973-74
Johnny Ertle	1915-18	ARNOLD TAYLOR	1973-74
PETE HERMAN	1917-20	SOO-HWAN HONG	1974-75
Memphis Pal Moore	1918-19	Rodolfo Martinez (WBC)	1974-76
JOE LYNCH	1920-21	ALFONSO ZAMORA	1975-77
PETE HERMAN	1921	Carlos Zarate (WBC)	1976-79
JOHNNY BUFF	1921-22	JORGE LUJAN	1977-80
JOE LYNCH	1922-24	Lupe Pintor (WBC)	1979-83
ABE GOLDSTEIN	1924	JULIAN SOLIS	1980
CANNONBALL EDDIE MARTIN	1924-25	JEFF CHANDLER	1980-84
PHIL ROSENBERG	1925-27	Albert Davila (WBC)	1983-85
Teddy Baldock (GBR)	1927	RICHARD SANDOVAL	1984-86
BUD TAYLOR (NBA)	1927-28†	Satoshi Shingaki (IBF)	1984-85
Willie Smith (GBR)	1927-28	Jeff Fenech (IBF)	1985
Bushy Graham (NY)	1928-29	Daniel Zaragoza (WBC)	1985
PANAMA AL BROWN	1929-35	Miguel (Happy) Lora (WBC)	1985-88
Sixto Escobar (NBA)	1934-35	GABY CANIZALES	1986
BALTAZAR SANGCHILLI	1935-36	BERNARDO PINANGO	1986-87
Lou Salica (NBA)	1935	Wilfredo Vasquez (WBA)	1987-88
Sixto Escobar (NBA)	1935-36	Kevin Seabrooks (IBF)	1987-88
TONY MARINO	1936	Kaokor Galaxy (WBA)	1988
SIXTO ESCOBAR	1936-37	Moon Sung-Kil (WBA)	1988-89
HARRY JEFFRA	1937-38	Kaokor Galaxy (WBA)	1989
SIXTO ESCOBAR	1938-39*	Raul Perez (WBC)	1988-91
Georgie Pace (NBA)	1939-40	**Orlando Canizales** (IBF)	1988-
LOU SALICA	1940-42	**Luisito Espinosa** (WBA)	1989-
MANUEL ORTIZ	1942-47	Greg Richardson	1991
HAROLD DADE	1947	**Joichiro Tatsuyoshi** (WBC)	1991-

Flyweights

Widely accepted champions in CAPITAL letters. Current champions in **bold** type.

Champion	Held Title	Champion	Held Title
SID SMITH	1913	JOE SYMONDS	1914-16
BILL LADBURY	1913-14	JIMMY WILDE	1916-23
PERCY JONES	1914	PANCHO VILLA	1923-25

Flyweights (Cont.)

Champion	Held Title	Champion	Held Title
FIDEL LaBARBA	1925-27*	Betulio Gonzalez (WBA)	1973-74
FRENCHY BELANGER (NBA,IBU)	1927-28	Shoji Oguma (WBC)	1974-75
Champion	Held Title	Susumu Hanagata (WBA)	1974-75
Izzy Schwartz (NY)	1927-29	Miguel Canto (WBC)	1975-79
Johnny McCoy (Calif.)	1927-28	Erbito Salavarria (WBA)	1975-76
Newsboy Brown (Calif.)	1928	Alfonso Lopez (WBA)	1976
FRANKIE GENARO (NBA,IBU)	1928-29	Guty Espadas (WBA)	1976-78
Johnny Hill (GBR)	1928-29	Betulio Gonzalez (WBA)	1978-79
SPIDER PLADNER (NBA,IBU)	1929	Chan-Hee Park (WBC)	1979-80
FRANKIE GENARO (NBA,IBU)	1929-31	Luis Ibarra (WBA)	1979-80
Willie LaMorte (NY)	1929-30	Tae-Shik Kim (WBA)	1980
Midget Wolgast (NY)	1930-35	Shoji Oguma (WBC)	1980-81
YOUNG PEREZ (NBA,IBU)	1931-32	Peter Mathebula (WBA)	1980-81
JACKIE BROWN (NBA,IBU)	1932-35	Santos Laciar (WBA)	1981
BENNY LYNCH	1935-38†	Antonio Avelar (WBC)	1981-82
Small Montana (NY,Calif.)	1935-37	Luis Ibarra (WBA)	1981
PETER KANE	1938-43	Juan Herrera (WBA)	1981-82
Little Dado (NBA,Calif.)	1938-40	Prudencio Cardona (WBC)	1982
JACKIE PATERSON	1943-48	Santos Laciar (WBA)	1982-85
RINTY MONAGHAN	1948-50*	Freddie Castillo (WBC)	1982
TERRY ALLEN	1950	Eleoncio Mercedes (WBC)	1982-83
SALVADOR (DADO) MARINO	1950-52	Charlie Magri (WBC)	1983
YOSHIO SHIRAI	1953-54	Frank Cedeno (WBC)	1983-84
PASCUAL PEREZ	1954-60	Soon-Chun Kwon (IBF)	1983-85
PONE KINGPETCH	1960-62	Koji Kobayashi (WBC)	1984
MASAHIKO (FIGHTING) HARADA	1962-63	Gabriel Bernal (WBC)	1984
PONE KINGPETCH	1963	Sot Chitalada (WBC)	1984-88
HIROYUKI EBIHARA	1963-64	Hilario Zapate (WBA)	1985-87
PONE KINGPETCH	1964-65	Chong-Kwan Chung (IBF)	1985-86
SALVATORE BURRINI	1965-66	Bi-Won Chung (IBF)	1986
Horacio Accavallo (WBA)	1966-68	Hi-Sup Shin (IBF)	1986-87
WALTER McGOWAN	1966	Dodie Penalosa (IBF)	1987
CHARTCHAI CHIONOI	1966-69	Fidel Bassa (WBA)	1987-89
EFREN TORRES	1969-70	Choi Chang-Ho (IBF)	1987-88
Hiroyuki Ebihara (WBA)	1969	Rolando Bohol (IBF)	1988
Bernabe Villacampo (WBA)	1969-70	Yong-Kang Kim (WBC)	1988-89
CHARTCHAI CHIONOI	1970	Duke McKenzie (IBF)	1988-89
Berkrerk Chartvanchai (WBA)	1970	**Dave McAuley** (IBF)	1989-
Masao Ohba (WBA)	1970-73	Sot Chitalada (WBC)	1989-91
ERBITO SALAVARRIA	1970-73	Jesus Rojas (WBA)	1989-90
Betulio Gonzalez (WBC)	1972	Yul-Woo Lee (WBA)	1990
Venice Borkorsor (WBC)	1972-73	Leopard Tamakuma (WBA)	1990-91
VENICE BORKORSOR	1973	**Muangchai Kittikasem** (WBC)	1991-
Chartchai Chionoi (WBA)	1973-74	**Yong-Kang Kim** (WBA)	1991-

Triple Champions

Fourteen fighters have won recognized world championships in three or more weight divisions. Sugar Ray Leonard has won the most divisions with five, while Roberto Duran and Thomas Hearns have four each. WBA, WBC and IBF titles are recognized, but WBO titles are not. Note that (*) indicates title claimant.

Sugar Ray Leonard (5)—WBC Welterweight (1979-80,80-82); WBA Jr.Middleweight (1981); WBC Middleweight (1987); WBC Super Middleweight (1988-90); WBC Light Heavyweight (1988).

Thomas Hearns (5)—WBA Welterweight (1980-81); WBC Jr.Middleweight (1982-84); WBC Light Heavyweight (1987); WBC Middleweight (1987-88); WBA Light Heavyweight (1991).

Roberto Duran (4)—Lightweight (1972-79); WBC Welterweight (1980); WBA Jr.Middleweight (1983); WBC Middleweight (1989-90).

Alexis Arguello (3)—WBA Featherweight (1974-77); WBC Jr.Lightweight (1978-80); WBC Lightweight (1981-82).

Henry Armstrong (3)—Featherweight (1937-38); Welterweight (1938-40); Lightweight (1938-39).

Wilfredo Benitez (3)—Jr.Welterweight (1976-79); Welterweight (1979); WBC Jr.Middleweight (1981-82).

Tony Canzoneri (3)—Featherweight (1928); Lightweight (1930-33); Jr.Welterweight (1931-32,33).

Julio Cesar Chavez (3)—WBC Jr.Lightweight (1984-87); WBA/WBC Lightweight (1987-89); WBC/IBF Jr.Welterweight (1989-91); WBC Jr.Welterweight (1991).

Jeff Fenech (3)—IBF Bantamweight (1985); WBC Jr.Featherweight (1986-88); WBC Featherweight (1988-90).

Bob Fitzsimmons (3)—Middleweight (1891-97); Light Heavyweight (1903-05); Heavyweight (1897-99).

Emile Griffith (3)—Welterweight (1961,62-63,63-66); Jr.Middleweight (1962-63); Middleweight (1966-67,67-68).

Stanley Ketchel (3)—Welterweight (1908,08-10); Middleweight (1908-10); Light Heavyweight (1909-10).

Terry McGovern (3)—Bantamweight (1899-1900); Featherweight (1900-01); Lightweight (1900-01).

Barney Ross (3)—Lightweight (1933-35); Jr.Welterweight (1933-35); Welterweight (1934-38).

Wide World Photos

Alydar (left), half of thoroughbred racing's keenest rivalry, died on Nov. 15, 1990, at age 15. In 1978, he placed second to **Affirmed** in all three Triple Crown races, losing the Belmont by a head. Affirmed's trainer, Laz Barrera, died on April 25.

DEATHS

(November, 1990 through October, 1991)

Wide World Photos   ESPN   Four Footed Fotos

Luke Appling   **Pete Axthelm**   **Laz Barrera**

George Allen, 72; led Los Angeles Rams (1966-70) and Washington Redskins (1971-77) to 118 NFL wins, ranking him fourth among NFL coaches in all-time winning percentage at .681 (118-54-5); noted for trading draft picks for proven players, saying "the future is now"; reached playoffs seven times but never won Super Bowl; later coached Chicago Blitz (1983) and Arizona Wranglers (1984) in USFL; came out of five-year retirement to coach Long Beach St. to 6-5 record in 1990; also served as chairman of the President's Council on Physical Fitness under President Reagan; of natural causes; in Rancho Palos Verdes, Calif., Dec. 31, 1990.

Alydar, 15; crowd-pleasing competitor who ran second to Affirmed in all three Triple Crown races in 1978; outstripped his rival and every other active stallion in a glittering career at stud for Calumet Farm; offspring included Kentucky Derby winners Alysheba (1987) and Strike the Gold (1990), 1989 Belmont winner Easy Goer, and 1990 Horse of the Year Criminal Type; put to death after breaking right hind leg in a stall accident; in Lexington, Ky., Nov. 15, 1990.

Luke Appling, 83; sure-hitting Hall of Fame shortstop for Chicago White Sox, who won AL batting titles in 1936 and '40; retired after 20 years in 1950 with .310 career average; noted hypochrondriac who was nicknamed "Old Aches and Pains"; stunned baseball world by hitting a home run in a 1982 old-timers' game at the age of 75; retired two days before his death as a minor league hitting instructor for the Atlanta Braves; during emergency surgery for abdominal aneurysism; in Cumming, Ga., Jan. 3.

Pete Axthelm, 47; noted newspaper and magazine columnist, who began as horse racing writer for New York Herald Tribune; was best known for the 20 years he spent editing and writing for Newsweek; later became sports commentator for NBC and ESPN; wrote classic The City Game, Basketball in New York; of complications caused by liver failure; in Pittsburgh, Feb. 3.

Mary Bacon, 43; one of horse racing's first female jockeys; won 286 races and purses totaling $997,117 between 1969 and 1990; did commercials for Revlon and appeared nude in Playboy; when forbidden by stewards in 1972 to race against then husband, jockey John Bacon, she responded by getting a divorce; later cancer made her too weak to ride; of an apparent self-inflicted gunshot wound; in Fort Worth, June 24.

Hope Barnes, 32; captain of the 1984 U.S. Women's Olympic rowing team; also a member of the 1980 Olympic rowing team; avid outdoorswoman; in rockclimbing accident in the Cascade Mountains of Washington state; Jan. 28.

Laz Barrera, 66; horse trainer who won the 1976 Kentucky Derby with Bold Forbes and the 1978 Triple Crown with Affirmed; over 50-year career that began in Cuba at age 16, he trained 128 different stakes winners; won four consecutive Eclipse Awards from 1976-79 as outstanding trainer; saddled 2,268 career winners and won $50 million in purses; after suffering a heart attack at Aqueduct Race Track in New York, April 25.

James (Cool Papa) Bell, 87; legendary star of Negro Leagues; widely regarded as the fastest man ever to play baseball; hit over .400 twice and had .338 career average in 24 seasons; named to Hall of Fame in 1974; retired year before Jackie Robinson broke the major league color barrier in 1947; after suffering a heart attack; in St.Louis, March 8.

Jack (Kid) Berg, 81; born Judah Bergman; whirlwind puncher who beat fellow Englishman Mushy Callahan for world junior welterweight title in 1930; lost title 14 months later when he was knocked out in third round by lightweight champion Tony Canzoneri; retired in 1945 with a record of 157 victories and 57 knockouts in 192 fights; after a long illness; in London, England, April 22.

Dan Birkholz, 35; Dr. Andrzej Komor, 39, and **Dr. Peter Van Handel, 45;** U.S. Olympic Committee employees who were among 20 passengers killed in a Colorado plane crash; Birkholz was a development coach, Komor a sports biomechanist, and Van Handel a sports physiologist; south of Colorado Springs, March 3.

P.J.Boatwright Jr., 63; world's foremost authority on the Rules of Golf; served as the United States Golf Association's executive director of rules and competitions since 1980; ran U.S. Open since 1984; as an amateur golfer, he won the Carolina Open in 1957 and 1959 and qualified for four U.S. Amateurs; of bone cancer; in Morristown, N.J., April 5.

Joe Bowman, 80; Philadelphia right-hander who was the losing pitcher in the major leagues' first night game on May 24, 1935 at Cincinnati's Crosley Field; gave up only four hits in seven innings, but lost to Paul Derringer and the Reds, 2-1; had 77-96 record over 11 seasons; lost 20 games with Phillies in 1936; won 10 games for Pittsburgh in 1939, but was also used frequently as a pinch hitter and batted .344; after a long illness; in Kansas City, Nov. 22, 1990.

Keith Brown, 76; college pole vault star at Yale, who set a 1935 world record of 14 feet 5⅛ inches using a bamboo pole in the intercollegiate IC4A championsips at Harvard Stadium; of emphysema; in Delmar, Calif., July 15.

Wide World Photos

Paul Brown

NYRA Photos

Fred Capossela

Wide World Photos

A.B. (Happy) Chandler

Paul Brown, 82; football innovator and founding father, who won championships with Ohio teams in high school, college and the pros; led Massillon High to five undefeated seasons in six years from 1935-40; became head coach at Ohio State in 1941 and won the national championship a year later with a 9-1 record; put together powerhouse team at Great Lakes Naval Training Center near Chicago during World War II; helped found All-American Football Conference in 1946 as part-owner, general manager and coach of Cleveland team that bore his name; led Browns to four straight AAFC titles before league folded; entered NFL in 1950 with team that included Otto Graham, Marion Motley, Mac Speedie and Lou Groza and won NFL title in first year; won two more NFL titles in 1954 and '55; first to establish year-round coaching staff, intelligence tests for players, face guards on helmets, and use of messenger guards to send in plays; fired by Browns' majority owner Art Modell in 1963; inducted into Pro Football Hall of Fame in 1967; resurfaced as part-owner and GM-coach of expansion Cincinnati Bengals in 1968; led Bengals to NFL playoff berth in third season; retired as coach after 11-3 season in 1975; posted record of 52-4-3 in four AAFC seasons and 170-108-6 record in 21 NFL seasons; named Coach of the Year in 1957 and 1969; five former players or assistants have gone on to win 11 Super Bowls—Chuck Noll (4), Bill Walsh (3), Don Shula (2), Weeb Ewbank and Don McCafferty; was GM of Bengals at the time of his death; of complications caused by pneumonia; in Cincinnati, Aug. 5.

Milt Bruhn, 78; head football coach at Wisconsin from 1956-66, where his teams went 52-46-6 and won Big Ten titles in 1959 and '62; in the 1963 Rose Bowl, the No.2 Badgers, quarterbacked by Ron VanderKelen, rallied from a 42-14 deficit in the fourth quarter, but lost to No.1 USC 42-37; of a heart attack; in Madison, Wis., May 14.

Pierre Brunet, 89; world and Olympic figure skating champion from France, who was also renowned as a skating teacher; won 10 consecutive French men's championships, and four pairs world titles with his wife, Andree Joly; won Olympic pairs gold medals with Joly in 1928 and '32; best known student was American star Carol Heiss, the five-time world champion and 1960 Olympic gold medalist; after a long battle with Parkinson's disease; in Boyne City, Mich., July 27.

Forrest (Smoky) Burgess, 64; catcher and pinch-hitting specialist, who retired in 1967 with a major league record 145 pinch hits; his record was broken by Manny Mota in 1979, but he still ranks second to Mota's 150; played with five teams from 1949-67, posting a .295 career batting average; hit .368 for Philadelphia in 1954, but didn't have enough at bats to qualify for batting title; hit .333 with Pittsburgh in 1960 World Series; named to NL All-Star five times; cause of death not disclosed; in Asheville, N.C., Sept. 15.

Robert Bushnel, 76; former president of FIBA, the International Basketball Federation from 1984-90; president of the French Basketball Federation from 1966-80; coached French team to silver medal at 1948 Olympics; killed in car accident outside Lyons, France, March 15.

William (Bill) Byrd, 83; outstanding Negro leagues pitcher, whose 115 victories rank him fourth in league history; pitched from 1932 to 1949 for the Columbus Blue Birds and the Elite Giants of Nashville, Washington and Baltimore; of cancer; in Philadelphia, Jan. 4.

Fred (Cappy) Capossela 88; perhaps the most famous of all horse race track announcers; former turf writer who worked New York thoroughbred tracks for 37 years until his retirement in 1971; renowned for accuracy, but celebrated for his distinctive nasal, high-pitched voice and coining phrases like: "And . . . they're off," "They're not going to catch him," and "It is now post time," which is one of the last things he said to his son before dying; of a stroke; in Upland, Calif., April 3.

Manley Lanier (Sonny) Carter, Jr., 43; former U.S. pro soccer player and shuttle astronaut; played with Atlanta Chiefs of NASL from 1970-73 before completing his medical studies at Emory University; took a soccer ball along for 79 orbits in 1989 mission; killed in same commuter airline crash that claimed former U.S. Senator John Tower; near Brunswick, Ga., April 5.

A.B. (Happy) Chandler, 92; former Governor of Kentucky and U.S. Senator, who was baseball's second commissioner and easily its most colorful; agreed to become commissioner in 1945, giving up Senate seat to succeed Judge Kenesaw Mountain Landis, who had died in 1944; supported efforts by Brooklyn president Branch Rickey to break color barrier in 1947 by putting Jackie Robinson in Dodgers' lineup; also suspended Brooklyn manager Leo Durocher the same season for associating with gamblers; forced out by owners in 1951, but elected to Hall of Fame in 1982; of a heart attack; in Versailles, Ky., June 15.

Wendell Cherry 55; vice chairman of Humana, Inc., operator of a nationwide chain of hospitals and health insurance; was the lawyer for a group of Louisville sportsmen who helped launch Cassius Clay's pro boxing career after Clay's return from the 1960 Olympics with the light heavyweight gold medal; four years later, Clay beat Sonny Liston for the world heavyweight championship and became Muhammad Ali; of lung cancer; in Louisville, July 16.

Wide World Photos   Wide World Photos   Wide World Photos

Walker Cooper   **Joseph C. Dey Jr.**   **Leo Durocher**

Harold Conrad, 80; former sportswriter-turned-boxing promoter, whose colorful personality inspired Humphrey Bogart's cynical fight press agent in the 1956 film "The Harder They Fall"; promoted 12 championship fights, including the Cassius Clay-Sonny Liston title bout in 1964; also promoted Evel Knievel's failed jump over Snake River Canyon in 1974; of a brain tumor; in La Gloria, Mexico, May 18.

Silvio O. Conte, 69; popular, 32-year U.S. Congressman from Pittsfield, Mass., known for his support of the poor, the environment, students and medical research; reveled in managing the GOP in the annual House Republicans vs. Democrats baseball game; holds the unique honor of having a medical research center named after him at Boston University and an athletic complex named after him at Boston College; of a cerebral hemorrhage; in Bethesda, Md., Feb. 8.

Jimmy (Scoops) Cooney, 96; Chicago Cubs shortstop who made National League's last unassisted triple play in 1927; play went this way—Paul Waner of Pittsburgh hit a line drive up the middle, Cooney caught the ball, touched second and tagged the runner coming from first for the third out; two years before, Cooney had been one of the runners tagged out when the Pirates' Glenn Wright pulled off the same play; of natural causes; in Warwick, R.I., Aug.7.

Walker Cooper, 76; catching half of brother battery combination that helped lead the St. Louis Cardinals to three straight NL pennants from 1942-44; brother Mort won 65 games in those three seasons and was the NL's MVP in '42; Walker hit .300 or better eight times in 18-year career; hit 35 homers and drove in 122 runs with New York Giants in 1947; retired in 1957 with .285 average, 173 home runs and 812 RBI; of respiratory failure; in Scottsdale, Ariz., April, 11.

Jack Crawford, 83; Australian tennis player who came within one match of winning the Grand Slam in 1933; won Australian, French and Wimbledon championships in '33, but lost the U.S. final to Fred Perry in five sets at Forest Hills 3-6, 13-11, 6-4, 0-6, 1-6; won Australian title four times and played on Australia's winning 1939 Davis Cup team; elected to Hall of Fame in 1979; after a long illness; in Sydney, Sept. 10.

Roy Cullenbine, 77; outfielder who batted .276 with six major league teams from 1939 to 1947; was among several players declared free agents in 1939 by Commissioner Kenesaw Mountain Landis and received $25,000 bonus when he signed with the Brooklyn Dodgers that year; of heart disease; in Mount Clemens, Mich., May 28.

William Davis, 68; founder and former editor of *Golf Digest* magazine, who retired as overseer of The New York Times magazine division in 1987; an avid golfer, he founded *Golf Digest* in 1950 and sold it to the Times in 1969; also wrote three books on golf; of heart failure; in Fairfield, Conn., Jan. 2.

Christian de Castries, 88; swashbuckling calvary officer who inspired French forces to an heroic, but doomed defense of the Vietnam fortress of Dien Bien Phu before surrendering to the Communists in 1953; 20 years earlier, de Castries, an accomplished horseman, guided his horse to a world record jump of 7 feet, 10 inches; no cause of death given; in Paris, July 30.

Helen Dettweiler, 75; one of LPGA's founders and charter members; competed on the LPGA Tour in the 50s and 60s and was the first LPGA Teacher of the Year Award winner in 1958; of natural causes; in Rancho Mirage, Calif., Nov. 12, 1990.

Joseph C. Dey Jr., 83; served as the executive director of the United States Golf Association from 1934 to 1969 and was generally regarded as the game's most influential administrator and rules expert; left the USGA at age 61 to become the first commissioner at the PGA Tour, a post he held for five years; dropped out of college at Penn in 1927 to become a sportswriter and covered Bobby Jones' 1930 Grand Slam for the *Philadelphia Bulletin*; member of golf's Hall of Fame and a Captain of the Royal and Ancient Golf Club of St. Andrews; of cancer; in Locust Valley, N.Y., March 4.

Bo Diaz, 37; former catcher, who played 13 seasons for four different clubs; hit .333 for Philadelphia in 1983 World Series; of injuries suffered in a freak TV satellite dish accident; in Venezuela, Nov. 23, 1990.

Bobby Dill, 71; journeyman American defenseman who played for two years in the NHL with the New York Rangers (1943-45); after retiring in 1950, became a scout for the Rangers, Chicago and Minnesota; elected to U.S. Hockey Hall of Fame in 1979; of liver cancer; in St.Paul, Minn., April 16.

Ed Dodd, 88; cartoonist who, in 1946, created the comic strip "Mark Trail," about the adventures of an outdoor writer and conservationist; illustrated the strip until failing eyesight made him turn it over to Jack Elrod in 1978; after a long illness; in Gainesville, Ga., May 27.

Jack Doland, 63; Louisiana state senator who was head football coach and then president of McNeese State University; led Cowboys to 64-32-3 record as coach, then served as president from 1979-87 before entering politics; of prostate cancer; in Lake Charles, La., April 25.

UPI/Bettmann

Ray Felix

Wide World Photos

Hamilton Fish

International Swimming Hall of Fame

Helen Meany Gravis

Leo Durocher, 86; fiery, dirt-kicking, win-at-all-costs former manager who led National League teams in Brooklyn, New York, Chicago and Houston from the late 1930s to early 1970s; originally reached major leagues as player with New York Yankees, but starred as sure-handed shortstop with St.Louis Cardinals' Gas House Gang in mid-1930s; hit .247 over 17 major league seasons; managed Brooklyn Dodgers to NL pennant in 1941 and New York Giants to NL flag 10 years later, beating Dodgers in three-game playoff that ended with Bobby Thomson's ninth inning home run off Ralph Branca; won only World Series in 1954 when Giants upset Cleveland in four straight; suspended for 1947 season by commissioner Happy Chandler for his association with gambling figures; gained entry into *Bartlett's Familiar Quotations* for his line: "Nice guys finish last"; wrote autobiography by same name in 1975; of natural causes; in Palm Springs, Calif., Oct. 7.

Walter (Hoot) Evers, 69; former outfielder and longtime executive with Detroit Tigers; played with four other clubs during a 12-year career over which he hit .278; served as Tigers' director of player development from 1971-78 then became special assignment scout; after short illness; in Houston, Jan. 25.

Ray Felix, 60; talented 6-foot-11 center who played for Hall of Fame coach Clair Bee at Long Island University and with the Baltimore Bullets; NBA Rookie of the Year in 1953-54, averaging 17.6 points a game; traded to the New York Knicks after the season for Al McGuire and Connie Simmons; ended his nine-year career with the Los Angeles Lakers; of a heart attack; in East Elmhurst, N.Y., July 28.

John Fetzer, 89; former owner of the Detroit Tigers and a broadcast pioneer; headed syndicate in 1956 that bought the Tigers from the Briggs family for $5.5 million; sold club to Domino's Pizza founder Tom Monaghan for $53 million in 1983; owned and operated radio and television stations in Michigan and Nebraska; cause of death not disclosed; in Honolulu, Feb. 21.

Hamilton Fish, 102; the last surviving member of Walter Camp's all-time All-America football team; a member of the College Football Hall of Fame, he was a star tackle at Harvard and captain of the 1909 team; elected to Congress in 1920 as a conservative Republican from upstate New York, he served for 24 years and gained prominence for both his opposition to the New Deal and his isolationist views prior to World War II; of heart failure after developing pneumonia; in Cold Spring, N.Y., Jan. 18.

Ralph Floyd, 65; athletic director at Indiana University since 1978; came to IU as assistant AD in 1976 after 19 years at South Carolina and two years as associate AD at Clemson; responsible for expanding and renovating athletic facilities in Bloomington, particularly the football, baseball and track stadiums; of cancer; in Indianapolis, Dec.15, 1990.

Vic Fusia, 77; head football coach at the University of Massachusetts from 1961-70; led Minutemen to record of 59-32-2; his 1964 team went to the Tangerine Bowl, but lost to East Carolina, 14-13; of a heart attack; in Amherst, Mass., Jan. 18.

Bob Goldham, 69; defenseman on five Stanley Cup championship teams, including two in Toronto and three in Detroit; as a 20-year-old, he helped Toronto win 1942 Cup after trailing Detroit three games to none; became a TV analyst on "Hockey Night in Canada" after his retirement in 1956; of a stroke; in Toronto, Sept. 6.

Charles Goren, 90; one of the most influential figures in the history of contract bridge; won the first of his major titles in 1933 and became bridge columnist for the *Chicago Tribune* and *New York Daily News*; became world champion in 1950 when he won the Bermuda Bowl; one of the few sportsmen to appear on the covers of both *Time* (1958) and *Sports Illustrated* (1957,'60 and '64); was S.I.'s bridge editor and wrote numerous best-selling books on bridge; of a heart attack; in Encino, Calif., April 3.

Red Grange, 87; the legendary "Galloping Ghost," whose exploits as a running back for Illinois and the Chicago Bears in the 1920s made him an idol in the Golden Age of Sport along with Babe Ruth, Jack Dempsey, Bobby Jones and Bill Tilden (see next page); due to complications from pneumonia; in Lake Wales, Fla., Jan. 28.

Helen Meany Gravis, 86; diver who won the gold medal in the women's 3-meter springboard at the 1928 Olympics; won her first national AAU diving championship as a 15-year-old in 1920; made 1920 and '24 Olympic teams, but did not medal; won 17 national championships from 1920 through 1928; of cancer; in Old Greenwich, Conn., July 21.

John H. Greene, 45; chief operating officer and executive vice president of Outward Bound U.S.A.; of a heart attack in Loch Eli, Scotland, while hiking with a group of magazine publishers, June 15.

Frankie Gustine, 71; infielder who played 10 of his 12 major league seasons with the Pittsburgh Pirates; named to NL All-Star team in 1946,'47 and '48; had a career batting average of .265; of a heart attack; in Davenport, Iowa, April 1.

Red Grange
1903–91
by Richard Whittingham

On an early autumn evening in 1925, 22-year-old Harold "Red" Grange stepped into the office of C.C. "Cash and Carry" Pyle at the Virginia Theater in Champaign, Illinois, and was greeted by the ebullient theater owner with: "Red, how would you like to make a hundred thousand dollars . . . maybe even a million?"

Pyle, a dandy with all the accoutrements from spats to his homburg hat, aspired to be an entrepreneur extraodinaire and saw enormous potential in the young halfback from the University of Illinois who was known as the "Galloping Ghost."

Red Grange, embarking on what would be his third consecutive season as a consensus All-America, was already as revered in sports as Babe Ruth and Jack Dempsey. The reason—he was simply the most dazzling running back the game of football had ever seen. The year before, in a game against Michigan, considered by many to be the top team in the country, the Ghost had streaked for five touchdowns, four in the first quarter alone, amassing a total of 402 yards rushing on 21 carries. It had been enough to move Grantland Rice to poetry:

A streak of fire, a breath of flame,
Eluding all who reach and clutch;
A gray ghost thrown into the game
That rival hands may never touch;
A rubber bounding, blasting soul
Whose destination is the goal—
Red Grange of Illinois!

What C.C. Pyle had in mind was for Red Grange to turn pro after his last game of the season, immediately join the Chicago Bears, and embark on a barnstorming tour around the country which Pyle would orchestrate. Grange labored over the decision—in those days playing pro football was generally frowned upon by college football coaches, most notably the legendary Amos Alonzo Stagg of Chicago and Bob Zuppke, Grange's coach at illinois. But he finally agreed, making a choice that would forever affect the destiny of professional football, popularizing it and giving it a respectability

Richard Whittingham is the author of several books, including *What a Game They Played* about the early days of pro football.

Richard Whittingham Collection

Red Grange (left) with manager **C.C. Pyle** on the Chicago Bears bench during Grange's pro debut on Thanksgiving Day, 1925.

it had not previously enjoyed.

Donning his famous number 77, Grange led the Bears on a grueling tour of exhibition games through the midwest and the east coast—*eight games in 12 days in eight different cities.* In New York, a crowd of more than 72,000 filled the Polo Grounds at a time when the first-year New York Giants were lucky to draw 10,000 fans. It saved their franchise.

Still, not everyone had heard of Grange. In Washington, he was introduced to President Calvin Coolidge thusly: "Mr. President, this is Red Grange, who plays with the Bears." To which Coolidge replied, "Nice to meet you young man, I've always liked animal acts."

Another nine-game tour took Grange and the Bears from Florida to California. When it was over, pro football had been put on the proverbial map. Grange and Pyle had pocketed about $250,000 and the Bears another $100,000, in an age when most football players earned about $200 a game.

The following year Grange and Pyle founded the American Football League, which failed, and Grange returned to the Bears to play another six seasons.

The Galloping Ghost, that streak of fire, that breath of flame, retired after the 1934 season. He was later inducted as a charter member of both the College and Pro Football halls of fame, where, upon his death in 1991, he leaves to us the enduring legends of his name, number and nickname.

Penn State
Dorothy Harris

Leonard L. Greif, Jr.
Howard Head

American Honda
Soichiro Honda

John Hannah, 88; president of Michigan State University from 1941-69; a passionate football fan, he led MSU into the Big Ten in 1949 and watched the Spartans win both the conference and the Rose Bowl in their first year of eligibility in 1953; also headed group of college presidents who investigated the recruiting and subsidization problems in college sports; served as chairman of U.S.Commission on Civil Rights from 1957-69, U.S. Agency for International Development from 1969-73, and as director of World Food Council from 1975-78; of cancer, in Kalamazoo, Mich., Feb. 23.

Dorothy Harris, 59; internationally recognized expert on sports psychology and one of the most influential pioneers in the American women's sports movement; a professor of exercise and sports psychology at Penn State since 1970; also board member of the Women's Sports Foundation; after a long bout with cancer; in State College, Pa., Jan. 4.

Howard Head, 76; aircraft engineer who invented the Head metal ski in the 1950s and the Prince tennis racket in the 1970s; much lighter than traditional wooden skis, the aluminum sandwich ski gained wide acceptance and won its first Olympic gold medal in 1964; the Prince racket, with its broader hitting surface, was even more popular; of complications after heart surgery; in Baltimore, March 3.

Howard (Hobby) Hobson, 87; coached the University of Oregon to the first NCAA basketball championship in 1939; nicknamed the "Tall Firs," his '39 squad went 29-5 and beat Ohio State, 46-33, for the title; was 212-124 in 10 years at Oregon before moving on to Yale in 1947; coached Yale through 1956 with a record of 121-118; elected to Hall of Fame in 1965; made first proposals for 3-point field goal, shot clock and wider free-throw lanes; of heart failure; in Portland, Ore., June 9.

Soichiro Honda, 84; Japanese auto mechanic and race car driver, who founded Honda Motor Co. in 1946; by 1964, Honda was the world's top motorcycle manufacturer; entered Formula One racing in 1964 and won its first Grand Prix race in Mexico in 1965, then withdrew from F-1 after 1969 season; returned to F-1 in 1983 and won four consecutive world championships with the McLaren and Tyrrell teams from 1987-90; defying a Japanese government order to keep making motorcycles and leave mass-production of cars to a handful of other firms, Honda began making cars in 1957; less than 20 years later, he introduced the Civic and Accord models in America; by 1991, Honda had replaced Chrysler as the third largest producer of passenger cars in the U.S.; inducted into Automobile Hall of Fame in 1989; of liver failure; in Tokyo, Aug.5.

Sheldon (Available) Jones, 69; pitcher with New York Giants from 1946-51, who went 16-8 in 1948; also played with Chicago and Boston in eight-year NL career; earned nickname by willingness to relieve between starts; 54-57 career record; of cancer; in Greenville, N.C., April 18.

John J. Jordan, 80; basketball coach who led Notre Dame to its first six NCAA tournament appearances; led Irish to 199-131 record from 1951-64; his 1954 team won 18 straight; cause of death not disclosed; in South Bend, Ind., June 13.

Edwin (Eddie) Kimball, 87; former head football and basketball coach and athletic director at Brigham Young University; a 1925 BYU grad, he returned to Provo as freshman football coach in 1935 and held varsity job from 1937-49; led Cougars to 34-32-8 record; coached basketball for four years and served as AD for 27; after a month-long illness; in Provo, Utah, Dec.26, 1990.

Abel Kiviat, 99; diminutive (5-foot-5, 110 pounds) former world record holder in the 1,500-meter run and a silver medalist in the 1912 Olympics; in the early 1900s, set three world records outdoors and six more indoors; lowered his 1,500 record to 3:55.8 in 1912; elected to National Track & Field Hall of Fame in 1985; participated in 1984 Olympic torch relay at age 92; of cancer; in Lakehurst, N.J., Aug. 24.

Robert Kullen, 41; former head hockey coach at the University of New Hampshire; named New England Division I Coach of the Year in 1989 one year after receiving a heart transplant; also coached varsity soccer and golf at UNH; of heart failure; in Dover, N.H., Nov. 2.

Fred Levy, Jr., 89; co-owner of NFL Cleveland Rams, along with Dan Reeves and comedian Bob Hope, when team was moved to Los Angeles in 1946; bought out by Reeves in 1962; also owned Riverside International Raceway (since closed); family owned Levy Brothers department store chain in Kentucky; cause of death not disclosed; in Palm Springs, Calif., April 21.

Herbie Lewis, 85; captain of the Detroit Red Wings hockey team that won back-to-back Stanley Cups in 1936-37; a left wing, he scored 148 goals in 11 seasons and was regarded as the fastest skater in the NHL during 1930s; elected to Hall of Fame in 1989; of heart failure; in Indianapolis, Jan. 20.

Robert Livermore, 81; member of the 1936 U.S. Olympic Alpine ski team, who was a founder and former chairman of the National Ski Patrol; also helped form 10th Mountain Infantry Division in World War II; member of Skiing Hall of Fame; cause of death not disclosed; in Lincoln, Mass., Feb. 13.

Alice Marble

John Mullen

Rudolf Nierlich

Dale Long, 64; former Pittsburgh first baseman who set a major league record in 1956 by hitting home runs in eight consecutive games (record was tied by Don Mattingly in 1987); spent 11 years in the majors, with Pirates, Chicago Cubs, Washington and New York Yankees; hit 27 homers in '56 and 132 in his career; of cancer; in Palm Coast, Fla., Jan. 27.

Hank Majeski, 74; former Philadelphia A's third baseman who set an AL fielding record in 1947 with a .989 fielding average and only five errors; hit .310 with 120 RBI for A's in 1948; played with World Series-winning Cleveland Indians in 1954; hit .279 over 13-year career with six clubs; of cancer; in Staten Island, N.Y., Aug. 9.

Alice Marble, 77; credited with introducing aggressive, athletic style to women's tennis in 1930s; No.1-ranked women's tennis player in the world in 1939 after sweeping singles, doubles and mixed doubles titles at both Wimbledon and the U.S. Championships; won four U.S. titles in singles, doubles and mixed doubles (12 titles in all) between 1936 and 1940; also a member of four winning Wightman Cup teams; elected to Hall of Fame in 1964; of pernicious anemia; in Palm Springs, Calif., Dec. 13, 1990.

T. Harvey Mathis, 58; real estate developer who was chosen to be chairman of Atlanta's 1996 Olympic Games Authority; died the day after his selection; of a heart attack; in Atlanta, June 7.

Ralph (Mac) McKinzie, 96; President Ronald Reagan's college football coach at Eureka (Ill.) College; coached 35 years at Eureka, Wartburg and Northern Illinois; also served as athletic director at Eureka from 1921-37; received Washington, D.C. Touchdown Club award from Reagan in 1977; a member of the NAIA Hall of Fame; of natural causes; in Eureka, Ill., Dec. 7, 1990.

Bill McPeak, 64; former three-time NFL Pro Bowl defensive end, who coached the Washington Redskins from 1961-65; compiled 21-46-3 record in five years with 'Skins; offensive coordinator with Detroit Lions from 1967-73; assistant coach with Miami Dolphins in 1974 when he suffered a stroke that left him with slurred speech and limited use of his left arm; rehabilitated himself over five years; named director of scouting for the New England Patriots in 1979; of a heart attack; in Foxboro, Mass., May 7.

Richard (Dick) Meyer, 74; former Anheuser-Busch executive, who became general manager of the St. Louis Cardinals when the brewery purchased the baseball team in 1953; returned to his duties at the brewery in 1957; named president of brewery in 1971, but quit three years later in a dispute with owner August Busch, Jr.; after a long illness; in suburban St.Louis, Dec. 10, 1990.

Edgar (Rip) Miller, 90; the last surviving member of the 1922-25 Notre Dame football teams that went 27-2-1 over four years and won the 1924 national championship for Knute Rockne; a right tackle, he was one of the "Seven Mules" who cleared the way for the "Four Horsemen"; assistant coach at Navy from 1926-30; Navy head coach from 1931-33 with a record of 12-15-2; responsible for starting Navy-Notre Dame Game which was played for the 65th consecutive time in 1991; assistant athletic director at Navy from 1948-74; member of College Football Hall of Fame; of Parkinson's Disease; in Annapolis, Md., Oct. 1.

Johnny Moore, 89; outfielder in National League for 10 seasons, who retired in 1945 with a career batting average of .307; best known as Chicago Cubs' centerfielder the day Babe Ruth allegedly pointed to the Wrigley Field fence in the 1932 World Series and homered over Moore's head; of natural causes; in Bradenton, Fla., April 4.

John Mullen, 66; Atlanta Braves vice president and special assistant to the general manager, who was one of the few remaining team officials to work for the club in Boston and Milwaukee; orchestrated signings of Hall of Famers Hank Aaron and Eddie Mathews in 1950s; general manager of 1982 team that won NL Western Division; 1991 team remembered him by wearing JWM initials on uniform sleeves; found dead in West Palm Beach, Fla., hotel room, April 3.

Chucky Mullins, 21; University of Mississippi defensive back, who was paralyzed from the neck down after making a tackle in a game against Vanderbilt on Oct.28, 1989; after the accident, he became an inspiration for the team and received financial support from around the country; of a blood clot in his lungs; in Memphis, May 6.

William Myer, 74; harness racing trainer and driver, who retired in 1980 after compiling 1,840 victories and $6.8 million in earnings over a 50-year career; one of nine brothers who were involved in harness racing; of heart failure; in Harrington, Del., Dec. 11.

Doyle Nave, 75; Southern Cal reserve quarterback who came off the bench in the fourth quarter to engineer a 7-3 upset of previously undefeated, untied and unscored-upon Duke in 1939 Rose Bowl; completed four straight passes in last two minutes, culminating in a 19-yard touchdown throw to reserve end Al Krueger; choosen by Detroit in the first round of the 1939 NFL draft, he decided to become a motion picture cameraman instead; cause of death not disclosed; in Burbank, Calif., Dec. 9, 1990.

Wide World Photos   NHRA Photo   Wide World Photos

King Olav   **Gary Ormsby**   **Bill Riordan**

Rudolf Nierlich, 25; Austrian Alpine skier and 1992 Winter Olympic hopeful; won gold medal in Giant Slalom at 1991 World Championships in Saalbach, Austria; killed in an auto accident near his home in St. Wolfgang, Austria, May 18.

Northern Dancer, 29; champion thoroughbred who won the Kentucky Derby and Preakness in 1964, but missed taking the Triple Crown with a third in the Belmont; racing career included 14 wins in 18 starts, 10 of them stakes victories; sired 635 foals, 467 of whom won at least one race and 123 of whom won stakes races and purses totaling more than $26 million; destroyed after developing sudden attack of colic, a painful gastrointestinal condition (his death came one day after his younger half-cousin Alydar was put down); in Chesapeake City, Md., Nov. 16, 1990.

Lou Nova, 76; former heavyweight boxing contender, who became better known as a character actor on the stage and in movies; fought Joe Louis for heavyweight title on Sept. 29, 1941 at the Polo Grounds in New York, losing by TKO in the sixth round; had career record of 53-9 with 33 knockouts; of cancer and heart failure; in Las Vegas, Sept. 29.

King Olav V, 87; king of Norway since 1957; as Crown Prince, he was a symbol of Norwegian resistance to Nazi occupation during World War II; an accomplished athlete, he was a member of Norway's gold medal-winning 6-meter yachting crew in the 1928 Amsterdam Olympics; also a skilled ski jumper and cross-country skier; of a heart attack; in Oslo, Jan. 17.

Gary Ormsby, 49; drag racer who was the National Hot Rod Association's Top Fuel champion in 1989; holds NHRA records for speed (296.05 mph), time (4.881 seconds) and the U.S. Nationals mark (287.72 mph), which he set in 1990; of cancer; in Clermont, Calif., Aug. 28.

Marv Owen, 85; third baseman for 1934-35 AL champion Detroit Tigers, who set World Series record that still stands: 31 trips to the plate without a hit; scuffle with Cardinals' Joe Medwick in Game 7 of 1934 Series resulted in ejection of Medwick when irate Detroit fans wouldn't let him take the field; Tigers won Series in 1935; had lifetime batting average of .275 in nine-year career; after suffering from Alzheimer's disease; in Mountain View, Calif., June 22.

Tommy Paul, 82; former 1927 National AAU bantamweight boxing champion, who won world featherweight title in 1932 with 15-round decision over Johnny Pena; lost title to Freddie Miller on a decision seven months later; retired from the ring in 1935 with a record of 77-27-8 with 25 knockouts; after a long illness; in Buffalo, April 28.

Marie Provaznik, 100; leader of the national Sokol gymnastics movement in Czechoslovakia, who defected to the United States after directing the Czech women's team at the 1948 Olympics in London; after suffering a stroke, in Schenectady, N.Y., Jan. 11.

Gernot Reinstadler, 20; Austrian Alpine skier in his first year on the World Cup circuit; of injuries suffered during a qualifying run for the Lauberhorn World Cup races (first World Cup fatality since 1970); in Wengen, Switz., Jan. 19.

Johnny Revolta, 79; self-taught golfer who won 1935 PGA Championship at age 23, beating Tommy Armour 5&4 at Twins Hills C.C. in Oklahoma City; led 1935 PGA Tour in wins with five and retired in 1952 with 18 career victories; elected to old PGA Hall of Fame in 1963; cause of death not disclosed; in Palm Springs, Calif., March 3.

Greg Rice, 75; diminutive (5-foot-4½) distance runner from Notre Dame who won 65 major indoor and outdoor races without a loss in just over three years (1940-43); set world indoor records in the three-mile run in 1942 and two-mile in 1943; finally lost to world record holder Gunder Haegg of Sweden in the 5,000-meter run at the National AAU championships in 1943; won 1940 Sullivan Award as country's top amateur athlete; after suffering a stroke; in Hackensack, N.J., May 19.

Bill Riordan, 71; freewheeling promoter who managed career of tennis star Jimmy Connors in the 1970s; after Connors won the 1974 U.S. Open, he concocted a series of lucrative, but improperly labeled, "winner-take-all" TV matches featuring Connors against Rod Laver, John Newcombe, Manuel Orantes and Ilie Nastase—all matches were in fact played for guaranteed money and all were won by Connors; from 1963-76, he promoted the U.S. National Indoor Championships in Salisbury, Md.; considered Muhammad Ali, Tex Rickard and Bill Veeck the greatest promoters ever; of heart failure, in Naples, Fla. Jan. 20.

Frank Rose, 70; president of the University of Alabama from 1958-69; presided over desegregation of university in 1963, acting as buffer between Gov. George Wallace and U.S. Justice Department; helped football coach Bear Bryant build the teams that won national championships in 1964-65; when accused of stressing sports over scholarship, he replied simply, "Character is not built by a losing team"; of cancer and pneumonia; in Washington, D.C., Feb. 1.

Sir Alec Rose, 82; English grocer who sailed alone around the world; spent 320 days at sea on his 28,500-mile voyage aboard his 36-foot ketch Lively Lady; returned to Portsmouth on July 4, 1968; after a long illness; in Cosham, Hampshire, outside London, Jan. 12.

NASCAR Photo

Detroit News

Wide World Photos

Wendell Scott   **Shelby Strother**   **Forrest (Spec) Towns**

Pete Runnels, 63; Boston Red Sox first baseman who won two American League batting titles, batting .320 in 1960 and .326 in 1962; hit over .300 six times in 14 major league seasons with Washington, Boston and Houston; retired in 1964 with a .291 lifetime average; following a stroke; Pasadena, Texas, May 20.

Schottzie, 9; beloved St. Bernard of Cincinnati Reds' owner Marge Schott; served as team mascot and public relations centerpiece for six and a half years, following Schott's purchase of the club in 1985; received new collar in the shape of a World Series ring after Reds beat Oakland in 1990; put to sleep and buried in Schott's backyard; in Cincinnati, Aug. 7.

Marchy Schwartz, 82; two-time All-America halfback at Notre Dame who rushed for 927 yards and scored 54 points as a junior on Knute Rockne's undefeated 1930 national championship team; named head coach at Stanford in 1942, went 6-4, then program was suspended for three seasons during WW II; of heart failure; in Danville, Calif., April 18.

Wendell Scott, 69; stock car race driver from 1949-73, who was the only black to gain prominence on NASCAR circuit; competed in more than 500 Grand National (now Winston Cup) races and finished in the top five 20 times; lone NASCAR win came in 1963 Jake 200 in Jacksonville, Fla.; won 128 races in lower Sportsmen division; portrayed by Richard Pryor in 1977 movie "Greased Lightning"; of cancer; in Danville, Va., Dec. 23, 1990.

William A. Shea, 84; politically powerful New York lawyer enlisted by Mayor Robert Wagner in 1957 to help return National League baseball to the city after the departure of the Brooklyn Dodgers and New York Giants to California; after threatening to start a third major league (headed by Branch Rickey), he succeeded in forcing the NL to announce in 1960 that it would add two new clubs in 1962 and that one of the expansion teams would play in New York (the other in Houston); when a new, 55,000-seat stadium was built for the New York Mets in 1964, it was named in Shea's honor; of complications following a 1989 stroke; in New York, Oct. 2.

Fred Shero, 65; innovative coach, free thinker, boxer and former New York Rangers defenseman (1947-50), who coached the Philadelphia Flyers to consecutive Stanley Cup titles in 1974 and 1975 and another Cup final in 1976; compiled 308-151-95 record in seven seasons with Flyers before becoming coach of the Rangers in 1978; led Rangers to Cup final in 1979; ranks fourth in winning percentage among all-time NHL coaches at .602 (451-272-120); NHL Coach of the Year in 1974; of cancer; in Camden, N.J., Nov. 24, 1990.

Chris Short, 53; left-handed pitcher who won 132 games with Philadelphia Phillies from 1959-72; went 20-10 in 1966 and was 17-9 on the ill-fated Phils squad of 1964 that blew a six-game lead with 10 games to go and lost the NL pennant; pitched for Milwaukee Brewers in 1973 then retired with 135-132 record over 15 seasons; of an aneurysm that left him in coma since October 1988; in Wilmington, Del., Aug. 1.

Kenneth Smith, 89; former New York City sportswriter who served as director of the Baseball Hall of Fame from 1963-79; covered Dodgers, Giants and Yankees for New York Graphic and then the Mirror for 38 years; secretary of Baseball Writers Association of America for 19 years; of natural causes; in Palatine Bridge, N.Y., March 1.

Shelby Strother, 44; award-winning sportswriter and columnist; wrote for the St. Petersburg Times, Denver Post, Cocoa Today and Detroit News; four-time Pulitzer Prize nominee who was known as a great story teller; covered fall of Berlin Wall for Detroit News in 1989; Detroit Pistons wore black patches on their uniforms in his memory; of cancer; in Detroit, March 3.

Cedric Tallis, 76; baseball executive for 43 years, who served as the Kansas City Royals' first general manager from 1968-75; named Sporting News Executive of the Year in 1971; supervised construction of Anaheim Stadium in California (opened 1966) and rebuilding of Yankee Stadium in New York (reopened 1976); served as Yankees GM from 1980-82; left New York in 1983 to head unsuccessful attempt to bring major league baseball franchise to Tampa Bay; after a heart attack; in Tampa, May 7.

Danny Thomas, 79; entertainer, philanthropist and onetime majority owner of the Miami Dolphins; best known as star of TV comedy show "Make Room for Daddy"; founder of St. Jude Children's Research Hospital in Memphis in 1962; recruited by friend Joe Robbie to bankroll Dolphins during their initial NFL season in 1966; their very first game saw running back Joe Auer return the opening kickoff 95 yards for a touchdown with an excited Thomas following him down the sideline and hugging him in the end zone; also sponsored the Danny Thomas Memphis Classic golf tournament on the PGA Tour from 1970-84; following a heart attack; in Los Angeles, Feb. 6.

Russ Thomas, 66; spent 42 years with the Detroit Lions as a player, assistant coach, scout, broadcaster, controller, personnel director and general manager; played tackle on offense and defense from 1946-49, until a knee injury ended his playing career; director of player personnel from 1964-67 and general manager from 1967-89; died in his sleep; in Naples, Fla., March 18.

International Tennis Hall of Fame

James Van Alen

Wide World Photos

Bucky Walters

NBC Sports

Arthur Watson

Earl Torgeson, 66; first baseman who played for five major league teams from 1947-61; batted .265 over 15 seasons with 149 home runs and 740 RBI; hit .389 for the Boston Braves in 1948 World Series; of leukemia; in Everett, Wash., Nov. 9, 1990.

Forrest (Spec) Towns, 77; world record holder in 110-meter hurdles, who won gold medal at 1936 Summer Olympics in Berlin; two weeks later, became first man to break 14 seconds in the event; given track scholarship to University of Georgia in 1933 although he had never run track in high school; won more than 60 consecutive races in mid-1930s; head track coach at Georgia from 1942-76, winning 21 outdoor and five indoor SEC titles; university track named in his honor; of a heart attack; in Athens, Ga., April 9.

Max Truex, 55; diminutive (5-foot-5) distance runner who won NCAA cross-country championship in 1957 while at USC; member of 1956 and 1960 U.S. Olympic teams; at Rome in 1960, became the first American to break 29:00 in the 10,000-meters when he ran a 28:50.2 to finish sixth in the event; after a long bout with Parkinson's disease; in Milton, Mass., March 24.

Frank Umont, 73; former pro football tackle with New York Giants (1943-45), who became an American League umpire in 1954 and officiated for 20 years; worked four World Series, four All-Star Games and a league championship series; of a heart attack; in Ft. Lauderdale, Fla., June 20.

James Van Alen, 88; innovative tennis contributor who founded the International Tennis Hall of Fame in Newport, R.I., in 1954, and invented the tie-breaker scoring system in 1958; proposed as a way to speed up long matches, the sudden death tie-breaker revolutionized tennis when it was finally adopted by the U.S.Open in 1970; from injuries suffered after falling off his terrace; in Newport, R.I., July 3.

Bill (Billy) Vukovich 3rd, 27; third-generation race car driver whose grandfather won back-to-back Indianapolis 500s in 1953-54, and whose father finished second in 1973 (grandfather was killed while leading the Indy 500 in 1955); finished 14th in the 1988 Indy 500 and was named Rookie of the Year; following a crash at Mesa Marin Speedway; in Bakersfield, Calif., Nov. 24, 1990.

Bucky Walters, 82; three-time 20-game winner for the Cincinnati Reds in late 1930s and 1940s; named NL MVP in 1939 with a record of 27-11 and a 2.29 ERA in 319 innnings; led Reds to NL pennant in 1939 and World Series title in 1940, beating Detroit twice after a 22-win regular season; named to NL All-Star team six times; had career record of 198-160 with four clubs from 1931-50; also managed Reds from 1948-49; cause of death not disclosed; in Abington, Pa., April 20.

Jimmy Ward, 84; right winger who played with Montreal Maroons and Canadiens from 1927-39; member of the 1934-35 Maroons teams that won Stanley Cup; scored 147 goals and 127 assists in 12 seasons; father of major league baseball player Pete Ward; of cancer; in Portland, Ore; Nov. 15, 1990.

Arthur Watson, 61; president of NBC Sports from 1979-89; shrewd bargainer who spent freely to win rights to Summer Olympics of 1988 ($300 million) and 1992 ($401 million), but balked at the high price of retaining major league baseball (nearly $1 billion), despite baseball's 40-year relationship with NBC; also responsible for acquiring the Breeders' Cup, Wimbledon tennis, the NBA and Notre Dame football home games; cause of death not disclosed; in Ridgewood, N.J., June 26.

Ed Weir, 88; former two-time consensus All-America tackle at Nebraska in 1924 and 1925; played in NFL with Frankford (Pa.) Yellow Jackets from 1926-28; track and field coach at Nebraska from 1939-55, winning 10 conference titles; member of College Football Hall of Fame; of natural causes; in Lincoln, Neb., May 15.

Alan Wiggins, 32; switch-hitting outfielder and second baseman with San Diego and Baltimore from 1981-87, whose drug problems undermined a promising career; had .259 lifetime batting average and 242 stolen bases; hit .364 for the Padres in 1984 World Series; of complications from AIDS; in Los Angeles, Jan. 6.

Travis Williams, 45; former kick return specialist for the Green Bay Packers, who ran back four kickoffs for touchdowns and averaged 41.1 yards per return (both NFL records) in 1967 as a rookie out of Arizona State; played on Packers team that won Super Bowl II in 1968; knee injury with Los Angeles Rams ended career in 1971; wrestled with alcohol, poverty and homelessness after retirement; of heart failure; in Martinez, Calif., Feb. 17.

Lee Wulff, 86; outdoorsman who was one of the world's best known and most respected sports fishermen; also wrote eight books and lectured widely; according to Newsweek magazine, he "did for American fly-fishing what Hemingway did for American prose: he saved it from British conventions and mannerisms"; died when his light plane crashed into a wooded hillside near Hancock, N.Y., April 28.

Joseph Yancey, 80; co-founder of the New York Pioneers track and field club, who became its first coach in 1936; head coach of the Jamaican Olympic track teams of 1948, 1952 and 1960; put together 1,600-meter relay team of Arthur Wint, Leslie Laing, Herb McKenley and George Rhoden that upset the U.S. in the 1952 Olympics with a world record of 3:03.9; elected to Hall of Fame in 1986; after a heart attack; in Teaneck, N.J., Feb. 22.

BIBLIOGRAPHY

Research Material

Many sources were used in the gathering of information for this almanac. Day-to-day material was almost always found in copies of USA TODAY, The National, The Boston Globe, and The New York Times.

Several weekly and biweekly periodicals were also used in the past year's pursuit of facts and figures, among them—Baseball America, Boxing Illustrated, FIFA (Soccer) News, Inside Women's Tennis, International Tennis Weekly, The Hockey News, The NCAA News, On Track, Soccer America, Sports Illustrated, The Sporting News, Track & Field News, and USA Today Baseball Weekly.

In addition, the following books provided background material for one or more chapters of the almanac.

Arenas & Ballparks

Ballparks of North America, by Michael Benson; McFarland & Company, Inc. (1989); Jefferson, N.C.

The Ballparks, by Bill Shannon and George Kalinsky; Hawthorn Books, Inc. (1975); New York.

Green Cathedrals, by Philip Lowry; Society for American Baseball Research (1986).

The NFL's Encyclopedic History of Professional Football, Macmillan Publishing Co. (1977); New York.

Take Me Out to the Ballpark, by Lowell Reidenbaugh; The Sporting News Publishing Co. (1983); St.Louis.

24 Seconds to Shoot (An Informal History of the NBA), by Leonard Koppett; Macmillan Publishing Co. (1968); New York. Plus many major league baseball, NBA, NFL, NHL league and team guides, and major college football and basketball guides.

Auto Racing

1991 CART Media Guide, edited by Mel Poole and Dave Elshoff; Championship Auto Racing Teams; Bloomfield Hills, Mich.

1991 Indianapolis 500 Media Fact Book, compiled Bob Laycock and Kurt Hunt; Indianapolis Motor Speedway; Indianapolis.

Marlboro Grand Prix Guide, 1950-90 (1991 Edition), compiled by Jacques Deschenaux; Charles Stewart & Company Ltd; Brentford, England.

1991 Winston Cup Media Guide, compiled and edited by Bob Kelly; NASCAR Winston Cup Series; Winston-Salem, N.C.

Baseball

The All-Star Game (A Pictorial History, 1933 to Present), by Donald Honig; The Sporting News Publishing Co. (1987); St. Louis.

The Baseball Encyclopedia (Eighth Edition), editorial director, Rick Wolff; Macmillan Publishing Co. (1989); New York.

The Complete 1991 Baseball Record Book, edited by Craig Carter; The Sporting News Publishing Co.; St. Louis.

1991 NCAA Baseball and Softball, compiled by John Painter, Sean Straziscar and James Wright; edited by Theodore Breidenthal; NCAA Books; Overland Park, Kan.

The Scrapbook History of Baseball by Jordan Deutsch, Richard Cohen, Roland Johnson and David Neft; Bobbs-Merrill Company, Inc. (1975); Indianapolis/New York.

1991 Sporting News Official Baseball Guide, edited by Dave Sloan; The Sporting News Publishing Co.; St. Louis.

1991 Sporting News Official Baseball Register, edited by Barry Siegel; The Sporting News Publishing Co.; St. Louis.

The Sports Encyclopedia Baseball (Sixth Edition), edited by David Neft and Richard Cohen; St. Martins's/Marek (1985); New York.

Total Baseball (Second Edition), edited by John Thorn and Pete Palmer; Warner Books (1991); New York.

College Basketball

All the Moves (A History of College Basketball), by Neil D. Issacs; J.B. Lippincott Company (1975); New York.

1990-91 Blue Ribbon College Basketball Yearbook, edited by Chris Wallace; Christopher Publishing (1990); Buckhannon, W.Va.

College Basketball, U.S.A. (Since 1892), by John D.-McCallum; Stein and Day (1978); New York.

Collegiate Basketball: Facts and Figures on the Cage Sport, by Edwin C. Caudle; The Paragon Press (1960); Montgomery, Ala.

The Final Four (Reliving America's Basketball Classic), compiled by Billy Reed; Host Communications, Inc. (1988); Lexington, Ky.

Final Four Records, 1939-90, compiled by Gary Johnson and James Van Valkenburg; edited by David Smale; NCAA Books; Overland Park, Kan.

The Modern Encyclopedia of Basketball (Second Revised Edition), edited by Zander Hollander; Dolphins Books (1979); Doubleday & Company, Inc.; Garden City, N.Y.

1991 NCAA Basketball, compiled by Gary Johnson, Richard Campbell, John Painter, Sean Straziscar, James Wright and James Van Valkenburg; edited by Michelle A. Pond; NCAA Books; Overland Park, Kan.

1991 NIT Tournament Guide, Madison Square Garden; New York. Plus many NCAA Division I conference guides from the American South to the WAC.

Pro Basketball

The Official NBA Basketball Encyclopedia, edited by Zander Hollander and Alex Sachere; Villard Books (1989); New York.

1990-91 Philadelphia 76ers Statistical Yearbook, edited by Harvey Pollack; Philadelphia 76ers; Philadelphia.

1990-91 Sporting News Official NBA Guide, edited by Alex Sachare and Dave Sloan; The Sporting News Publishing Co.; St. Louis.

1990-91 Sporting News Official NBA Register, edited by Alex Sachare and Dave Sloan; The Sporting News Publishing Co.; St. Louis.

Bowling

Bowlers Journal Annual, January, 1991; Chicago.

1991 LPBT Guide, Ladies Pro Bowlers Tour; Rockford, Ill.

1991 PBA Press-Radio-TV Guide; Professional Bowlers Association; Akron, Ohio.

Boxing

1991 Computer Boxing Update, compiled by Ralph Citro; Ralph Citro Inc.; Blackwood, N.J.

The Ring 1985 Record Book & Boxing Encyclopedia, edited by Herbert G. Goldman; The Ring Publishing Corp.; New York.

College Sports

1989-90 National Collegiate Championships, edited by Theodore Breidenthal; NCAA Books; Overland Park, Kan.

NCAA: The Voice of College Sports (A Diamond Anniversary History, 1906-81), by Jack Falla; NCAA Books; Overland Park, Kan.

NAIA Championship History and Records Book (1988-89), National Assn. of Intercollegiate Athletics; NAIA Books; Kansas City, Mo.

College Football

Football: A College History, by Tom Perrin; McFarland & Company, Inc. (1987); Jefferson, N.C.

Football: Facts & Figures, by Dr. L.H. Baker; Farrar & Rinehart, Inc. (1945); New York.

BIBLIOGRAPHY

Great College Football Coaches of the Twenties and Thirties, by Tim Cohane; Arlington House (1973); New Rochelle, N.Y.

1990 NCAA Football, compiled by Richard Campbell, John Painter, Sean Straziscar and James Van Valkenburg; edited by Michael Earle; NCAA Books; Overland Park, Kan.

Saturday Afternoon, by Richard Whittingham; Workman Publishing Co., Inc. (1985); New York.

Saturday's America, by Dan Jenkins; Sports Illustrated Books; Little, Brown & Company (1970); Boston.

Tournament of Roses, The First 100 Years, by Joe Hendrickson; Knapp Press (1989); Los Angeles. Plus numerous college football team and conference guides, especially the 1990 guides compiled by Notre Dame, the Atlantic Coast Conference, Southeastern Conference and Southwest Conference.

Pro Football

1990 Canadian Football League Guide, compiled by the CFL Communications Dept.; Toronto.

The Official NFL Encyclopedia, by Beau Riffenburgh; New American Library (1986); New York.

1990 Official 1990 NFL Record and Fact Book, edited by Leslie Hammond and Chuck Garrity, Jr.; produced by NFL Properties, Inc.; New York.

The Scrapbook History of Pro Football, by Richard Cohen, Jordan Deutsch, Roland Johnson and David Neft; Bobbs-Merrill Company, Inc. (1976); Indianapolis/New York.

1990 Sporting News Football Guide, edited by Dave Sloan; The Sporting News Publishing Co.; St. Louis.

1990 Sporting News Football Register, edited Howard Balzer and Barry Siegel; The Sporting News Publishing Co.; St. Louis.

1990 Sporting News Super Bowl Book, edited by Bob McCoy; The Sporting News Publishing Co.; St. Louis.

Golf

The Encyclopedia of Golf (Revised Edition), compiled by Nevin H. Gibson; A.S. Barnes and Company (1964); New York.

Guinness Golf Records: Facts and Champions, by Donald Steel; Guinness Superlatives Ltd. (1987); Middlesex, England.

The History of the PGA Tour, by Al Barkow; Doubleday (1989); New York.

1991 LPGA Player Guide, produced by LPGA Communications Dept.; Ladies Professional Golf Assn. Tour; Daytona Beach, Fla.

1991 Official PGA Tour Book, produced by PGA Tour Creative Services; Professional Golfers Assn. Tour; Ponte Vedra, Fla.

1991 Official Senior PGA Tour Book, produced by PGA Tour Creative Services; Professional Golfers Assn. Tour; Ponte Vedra, Fla.

USGA Record Books (1895-1959 and 1960-80); U.S. Golf Association; Far Hills, N.J.

Hockey

Canada Cup '87: The Official History, No.1 Publications Ltd.; Toronto.

Checking Back (A History of the National Hockey League), by Neil D. Isaacs; W.W.Norton & Company, Inc. (1977); New York.

1989-90 Division I College Hockey Record Manual, edited by Andrew K. Finnie; Andrew K. Finnie and Hockey East Association; Boston.

The Hockey Encyclopedia, by Stan Fischler and Shirley Walton Fischler; research editor, Bob Duff; Macmillan Publishing Co. (1983); New York.

Hockey Hall of Fame (The Official History of the Game and Its Greatest Stars), by Dan Diamond and Joseph

Romain; Doubleday (1988); New York.

The National Hockey League, by Edward F Dolan Jr.; W H Smith Publishers Inc. (1986); New York.

1990-91 Official NHL Guide & Record Book, compiled by the NHL Communications Dept.; New York/Montreal.

The Stanley Cup, by Joseph Romain and James Duplacey; Gallery Books (1989); New York.

The Trail of the Stanley Cup (Volumns I-III), by Charles L. Coleman; Progressive Publications Inc. (1969); Sherbrooke, Quebec.

Horse Racing

1991 American Racing Manual, compiled by the Daily Racing Form; Hightstown, N.J.

1990 Breeders' Cup Statistics; Breeders' Cup Limited; Lexington, Ky.

1991 Directory and Record Book, Thoroughbred Racing Associations of North America Inc.; Elkton, Md.

1991 Kentucky Derby Media Guide, compiled by Churchill Downs Public Relations Dept.; Louisville, Ky.

1991 NYRA Media Guide, The New York Racing Association Inc.; Jamaica, N.Y.

1991 Preakness Press Guide, compiled and edited by Joe Kelly; Maryland Jockey Club; Baltimore, Md.

1991 Trotting and Pacing Guide, compiled and edited by John Pawlak; United States Trotting Association; Columbus, Ohio.

International Sports

Athletics 1991 (The International Track and Field Annual), Association of Track & Field Statisticians; edited by Peter Matthews; Burlington Publishing Ltd.; Berkshire, England.

Track & Field News' Little Blue Book; Metric conversion tables; From the editors of Track & Field News (1989); Los Altos, Calif.

Miscellaneous

The Encyclopedia of Sports (Fifth Revised Edition), by Frank G. Menke; revisions by Suzanne Treat; A.S. Barnes and Co., Inc. (1975); Cranbury, N.J.

The Great American Sports Book, by George Gipe; Doubleday & Company, Inc. (1978); Garden City, N.Y.

1991 Official PRCA Media Guide, edited by Steve Fleming; Professional Rodeo Cowboys Association; Colorado Springs.

The Sail Magazine Book of Sailing, by Peter Johnson; Alfred A. Knopf (1989); New York.

The Sportspages Almanac 1990, edited by Matthew Engel and Ian Morrison; Simon and Schuster; London.

"Ten Years of the Ironman," Triathlete Magazine; October, 1988; Santa Monica, Calif.

Olympics

All That Glitters Is Not Gold (An Irreverent Look at the Olympic Games); by William O. Johnson, Jr.; G.P. Putnam's Sons (1972); New York.

An Approved History of the Olympic Games, by Bill Henry and Patricia Henry Yeomans; Alfred Publishing Co., Inc. (1984); Sherman Oaks, Calif.

An Illustrated History of the Olympics (Third Edition); by Dick Schaap; Alfred A. Knopf (1975); New York.

The Complete Book of the Olympics (Second Edition); by David Wallechinsky; Penguin Books (1988); New York.

The Games Must Go On (Avery Brundage and the Olympic Movement), by Allen Guttmann; Columbia University Press (1984); New York.

Hitler's Games (The 1936 Olympics), by Duff Hart-Davis; Harper & Row (1986); New York/London.

The Nazi Olympics, by Richard D. Mandell; Souvenir Press (1972); London.

The Official USOC Book of the 1984 Olympic Games, by Dick Schaap; Random House/ABC Sports; New York.

The Olympic Games Handbook, by David Chester;

Charles Scribner's Sons (1975); New York.

The Olympic Record Book, compiled by Bill Mallon; Garland Publishing Inc. (1988); New York & London.

Pursuit of Excellence (The Olympic Story), by The Associated Press and Grolier; Grolier Enterprises Inc. (1979); Danbury, Conn.

The Story of the Olympic Games (776 B.C. to 1948 A.D.), by John Kieran and Arthur Daley; J.B. Lippincott Company (1948); Philadelphia/New York.

United States Olympic Books (Seven Editions): 1936,48,52,56,60,61-65,68; U.S. Olympic Association; New York.

The USA and the Olympic Movement, produced by the USOC Information Dept.; edited by Gayle Plant; U.S. Olympic Committee (1988); Colorado Springs. Plus official IOC, COA and USOC records from the 1988 Winter Olympics in Calgary and 1988 Summer Olympics in Seoul.

Soccer

The American Encyclopedia of Soccer, edited by Zander Hollander; Everest House Publishers (1980); New York.

The Guinness Book of Soccer Facts & Feats, by Jack Rollin; Guinness Superlatives Ltd. (1978); Middlesex, England.

History of Soccer's World Cup, by Michael Archer; Chartwell Books, Inc. (1978); Secaucus, N.J.

The History of the World Cup, by Brian Glanville; Faber and Faber Limited (1984); London/Boston.

1990-91 MSL Official Guide, Major (Indoor) Soccer League; Overland Park, Kan.

The World Cup (The Players, Coaches, History and Excitement), by Filip Bondy; Mallard Press (1991); New York.

Tennis

The Illustrated Encyclopedia of World Tennis, by John Haylett and Richard Evans; Exeter Books (1989); New York.

Official Encyclopedia of Tennis, edited by the staff of the U.S. Lawn Tennis Assn.; Harper & Row (1972); New York.

1991 Official ATP Player Guide, edited by Michael Curet, Greg Sharko and Jay Beck; Association of Tennis Professionals; Ponte Vedra Beach, Fla.

1991 Official WITA Media Guide, compiled by WITA Public Relations staff; Women's International Tennis Association; St. Petersburg, Fla.

Who's Who

Facts & Dates of American Sports, by Gorton Carruth & Eugene Ehrlich; Harper & Row, Publishers, Inc. (1988); New York.

101 Greatest Athletes of the Century, by Will Grimsley and the Associated Press Sports Staff; Bonanza Books (1987); Crown Publishers, Inc.; New York.

Superstars, by Frank Litsky; Vineyard Books, Inc. (1975); Secaucus, N.J.

Other Reference Books

The New York Public Library Desk Reference, edited by Felice Levy and Lisa Wolff; Webster's New World (1989); Simon & Schuster; New York.

TV Facts, (Revised and Updated), by Cobbett Steinberg; Facts On File Publications (1985); New York.

The World Book Encyclopedia (1988 Edition); World Book, Inc.; Chicago.

The World Book Yearbook (Annual Supplements, 1954-91); World Book, Inc.; Chicago.

America's Most Popular Spectator Sports

According to a survey released November, 1989, by the Sports Marketing Group of Dallas:

1. NFL football
2. NCAA football
3. Winter Olympics
4. Summer Olympics
5. Major league baseball
6. High school baseball
7. NBA basketball
8. Ladies figure skating
9. Pairs figure skating
10. Pairs ice dancing
11. Men's figure skating
12. Boxing
13. Swimming
14. Men's college basketball
15. Olympic skiing
16. Thoroughbred racing
17. Women's gymnastics
18. College baseball
19. Minor league baseball
20. High school basketball
21. Men's gymnastics
22. Men's skiing
23. Women's skiing
24. Olympic basketball
25. NASCAR racing
26. CART racing
27. Billiards
28. NHRA racing
29. Amateur boxing
30. Pro wrestling
31. Tractor pulling
32. Rodeo
33. High school baseball
34. Olympic baseball
35. Bodybuilding
36. College gymnastics
37. Air shows
38. Formula I racing
39. Track and field
40. NHL hockey
41. Snowmobile racing
42. Olympic volleyball
43. PGA golf
44. Men's bowling
45. Harness racing
46. IMSA racing
47. Weightlifting
48. Women's pro basketball
49. Women's college basketball
50. Olympic hockey
51. Amateur softball
52. Water skiing
53. College wrestling
54. Pro volleyball
55. PGA Seniors golf
56. Ladies bowling
57. Speed skating
58. Roller derby
59. Minor league basketball
60. Springboard diving
61. Beach volleyball
62. Arena football
63. Platform diving
64. AHL hockey
65. America's Cup yachting
66. Australian Rules football
67. Motocross
68. Men's tennis
69. LPGA golf
70. Daredevil acts
71. Women's tennis
72. College hockey
73. Hydroplane
74. Karate
75. World Cup soccer
76. Arm wrestling
77. Running marathons
78. Power boating
79. Acrobatics
80. Luge-bobsled
81. Skeet shooting
82. Dog racing
83. Equestrian show jumping
84. Racquetball
85. Sailing
86. Equestrian, steeplechase
87. MSL soccer
88. Judo
89. Women's marathon
90. Men's marathon
91. Frisbee
92. Cliff diving
93. College tennis
94. Dog sledding
95. Triathlon
96. Mountain bike racing
97. Equestrian, dressage
98. Running, road races
99. Board sailing
100. Velodrome bicycling

The Year Boxing Put On Gloves

by Nathan Ward

One hundred years ago, in an historic upset on Sept. 7, 1892, James J. Corbett gave the champion, John L. Sullivan, a scientific beating for the heavyweight title in New Orleans.

Sullivan, the last of the bareknuckle champions, was powerful but slow following a long layoff touring the country in *Honest Hearts*. Corbett, while also hoping to take his own stage vehicle, *Gentleman Jim*, on the road once he was champion, was in prime shape and armed with a clever strategy. He would move in and out of range, taunting Sullivan into exhaustion as he swung more and more enraged. But the fight at the Olympia Club was noteworthy in the first place not for its action but simply because it was legal. By submitting to the use of gloves and the new Marquis of Queensbury rules, the bout's promoters could go public and the heavyweight championship was contested for the first time with the sanction of the police.

Corbett alternately ran or lay teasingly on the ropes the first few rounds, while the champion sputtered and fought below form. In the 17th round, after calling in vain to the nimble Corbett to stand and fight, Sullivan connected and sent him to the canvas. But four rounds later, Corbett finished off the exhausted John L., then helped carry him to his stool. "Gentlemen," Sullivan declared to his fans when he'd come to, "It's the old story. I fought once too often."

In another contrast to the heroic-drinking Sullivan, Gentleman Jim toasted his victory later that night with milk.

1942
Fifty years ago

This was the only year the Rose Bowl was not played in Pasadena. With the Dec. 7, 1941, attack on Pearl Harbor only a few days' old, Lt. Gen. John L. DeWitt of the U.S. Fourth Army decided that a parade drawing a million onlookers before a game attended by 90,000

Nathan Ward is an assistant editor of *American Heritage* magazine where he writes "The Time Machine" column each month.

Wide World Photos

James J. Corbett (left) tags champion **John L. Sullivan** in their historic title bout.

fans made too inviting a target for Japanese bombers. Even if no attack came, roads needed for regular American military transport would be unnecessarily tied up. On Dec. 13, Dewitt instructed California Gov. Culbert Olson to communicate his wishes to the tournament's board of directors.

Offers soon came in to move the Rose Bowl game to either Soldier Field in Chicago, under the auspices of the *Chicago Tribune,* or Duke Stadium in Durham, N.C., home of one of the game's two contestants, the Southern Conference champion Blue Devils of coach Wallace Wade. Duke beat out the Tribune for sponsorship despite its inadequate seating which, at best, equaled a little over half of the capacity in Pasadena.

On New Year's Day, Oregon State forced Duke into seven turnovers and won 20-16 on a 68-yard touchdown pass from Bob Dethman to Gene Grey. It was only the second time a team had scored as many as 20 points against the Blue Devils in 10 years.

But sadder than the Durham faithful sitting through their team's raw, wet loss to the Beavers was the Rose Parade contingent back in Pasadena. In order for the string of parades not to be broken, a caravan of five cars crawled along the route as usual, with tournament queen Dolores Brubach waving through the quiet streets. At halftime she was interviewed on the radio and joined others singing 'Auld Lang Syne' from the empty stadium.

1967
Twenty-Five Years Ago

In pro basketball, the Boston Celtics missed the NBA finals for the first time in eight years, falling to Wilt Chamberlain and the Philadelphia 76ers in five games in the Eastern Conference finals. The Sixers, who boasted the league's best-ever regular season record of 68-13, went on to win the title, beating the San Francisco Warriors, 4 games to 2.

Chamberlain was named the NBA's Most Valuable Player, but failed to lead the league in scoring for the first time in eight seasons.

On Feb. 2, a new pro league, the American Basketball Association, was formed with former NBA great George Mikan as its commissioner. Rick Barry, who had succeeded Chamberlain as NBA scoring champion in 1967, was one of the few star players lured away to the new league. The original 11-team league starting play in the fall included the Indiana Pacers, Kentucky Colonels, Minnesota Muskies, New Jersey Americans and Pittsburgh Pipers in the East, with the Anaheim Amigos, Dallas Chaparrals, Denver Rockets, Houston Mavericks, New Orleans Buccaneers and Oakland Oaks in the West.

The ABA, with its three-point basket and multicolored ball, survived until 1976.

* * *

A jury in Houston took 20 minutes to declare Muhammad Ali guilty of refusing induction into the armed forces. Judge Joe Ingraham then imposed the maximum sentence of $10,000 and five year's imprisonment. Ali, although still undefeated as a boxer, had already been stripped of his heavyweight title following his refusal in Houston in April to step forward and be inducted. He claimed exemption as a minister of Islam. New York suspended his license to box one hour after he refused induction; other states followed. In early June a group of 10 famous black athletes, including Jim Brown, Bill Russell, and Lew Alcindor (soon to become Kareem Abdul-Jabbar), met in Cleveland to support Ali in his decision, whichever way he chose. "I envy Muhammad Ali," Russell declared emerging from the meeting. "He has an absolute and sincere faith."

Refusing even a non-combat role in the war, Ali spent 3½ years lecturing around the country, unable to fight or travel abroad. The Supreme Court unanimously reversed his conviction in 1971. He regained his title in October, 1974.

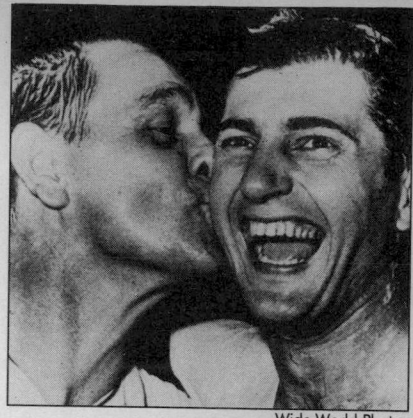

Wide World Photos

Carl Yastrzemski (right) gets a kiss from manager **Dick Williams** after Red Sox win '67 pennant.

It was the year of Carl Yastrzemski, and October saw the meeting of Boston's "Impossible Dream" team and the St. Louis Cardinals. The Red Sox had finished ninth the season before, but through Yastrzemski's heroics in left field and at the plate the team survived a four-way battle royal with Detroit, Minnesota and Chicago for the AL pennant that lasted into the final week.

The winter following the miserable 1966 season, Yastrzemski had undergone intensive weight training and the line-drive hitter began 1967 as a power to be reckoned with. Yaz batted .544 with five home runs over the final 12 games of the '67 season, going 7 for 8 with his 44th home run in a season-ending doubleheader against the Twins. He took batting's Triple Crown and remains the last player to do so in either league. Ted Williams, the man he had replaced in left in 1962, noted coyly that during that magnificent September, Carl Yastrzemski had been the greatest player who ever lived.

But it wasn't enough against the Cardinals in the World Series. Led by Lou Brock, who hit .414 and stole 12 bases, and Bob Gibson, who pitched three complete game victories, the Cards defeated Boston in seven games.

Yastrzemski batted .400 in the series and hit three homers. The baseball writers all but unanimously voted him 1967's Most Valuable Player except for a single bizarre vote for Cesar Tovar, a .267 hitter who had 6 home runs for Minnesota.

Other Milestones

1917

National Hockey League founded in Montreal (Nov. 26). New league will be comprised of four teams from disbanded National Hockey Association: Toronto Arenas, Ottawa Senators and Montreal's Canadiens and Wanderers.

1927

Heavyweight champion **Gene Tunney** scores unanimous 10-round decision over former champ Jack Dempsey in famous "Long Count" title fight in Chicago (Sept. 22).

Babe Ruth hits record 60th home run of season off Washington's Tom Zachary in New York (Sept. 30). Ruth's previous high had been 59 homers in 1921.

1937

First **Cotton Bowl** played at Fair Park Stadium in Dallas as TCU beats Marquette, 16-6, before 17,000 (Jan.1).

War Admiral, with jockey Charles Kurtsinger aboard, wins Belmont Stakes to become fourth horse to win Triple Crown (June 5).

Joe Louis knocks out champion James J.Braddock in 8th round to win heavyweight title in Chicago (June 22).

1942

The **Toronto Maple Leafs** lose first three games of Stanley Cup final to Detroit, then stage a miraculous rally—never duplicated before or since—to win four straight and take the Cup (April 18).

1947

Jackie Robinson becomes first black player to play in major leagues, going 0-for-3 and handling 11 chances at first base for the Brooklyn Dodgers (April 15).

Philadelphia Warriors beat Chicago Stags, 4 games to 1, to win first Basketball Association of America (later NBA) championship (April 22).

1952

Rocky Marciano knocks out champion Jersey Joe Walcott in 13th round to win heavyweight title in Philadelphia (Sept. 23).

1957

North Carolina beats Wilt Chamberlain and Kansas, 54-53, in triple overtime to win NCAA basketball championship at Municipal Auditorium in Kansas City (March 23).

Boston Celtics, led by rookie center Bill Russell, win their first NBA title, beating the St.Louis Hawks in Game 7, 125-123, in double overtime (April 13).

Althea Gibson sweeps women's titles at Wimbledon and Forest Hills, becoming first black player to win each championship.

1962

Wilt Chamberlain scores 100 points as Philadelphia beats New York, 169-147, in NBA game at Hershey, Pa. (March 2).

Houston Colt .45s and **New York Mets** join National League. Colts go 64-96, while Mets lose a major league record 120 games.

Jack Nicklaus wins first major tournament as pro, defeating Arnold Palmer by three strokes in 18-hole playoff for U.S. Open (June 17).

Australian **Rod Laver** completes first men's tennis Grand Slam sweep since Don Budge did it in 1938.

S.F. Giants beat L.A. Dodgers, 6-4, in Game 3 of best-of-three NL playoff and advance to World Series. (Oct. 3).

1967

The **Green Bay Packers** defeat the Kansas City Chiefs, 35-10, in Super Bowl I (officially: the AFL-NFL World Championship Game). A crowd of 61,946 looks on at L.A. Coliseum (Jan. 15).

Sophomore **Lew Alcindor** leads UCLA to 79-64 win over Dayton for Bruins' third straight NCAA basketball title. He also wins first of three consecutive Most Outstanding Player awards (March 25).

Two pro soccer leagues, the **United Soccer Association** and the **National Professional Soccer League** begin play. The USA imports whole teams from abroad, while the NPSL signs individual players. Both leagues fail, but merge to form the North American Soccer League in 1968.

National Hockey League doubles in size for 1967-68 season, adding six new teams: the Los Angeles Kings, Minnesota North Stars, Oakland Seals, Philadelphia Flyers, Pittsburgh Penguins and St.Louis Blues.

1972

NCAA allows freshmen to play varsity football and basketball.

Dispute with owners over health and pension benefits leads **Baseball players union** to walk out on strike April 1. Strike ends April 13 with season shortened by total of 86 games.

In 5-3 vote, Supreme Court rules in favor of Major League Baseball in 1970 **Curt Flood suit**, upholding legitimacy of reserve clause (June 18).

Arab terrorists kill 11 members of Israeli Olympic team at Summer Games in Munich (Sept. 5). Tragedy overshadows 7-gold medal performance of American swimmer Mark Spitz and Soviet Union's controversial basketball victory over U.S.

Twelve-team **World Hockey League** begins play for 1972-73 season; teams include the Cleveland Crusaders, New England Whalers, New York Raiders, Ottawa Nationals, Philadelphia Blazers and Quebec Nordiques in the East; and the Alberta (later Edmonton) Oilers, Chicago Cougars, Houston Aeros, Los Angeles Sharks, Minnesota Fighting Saints and Winnipeg Jets in the West. Jets are led by player-coach Bobby Hull, who jumped from Chicago of the NHL to the WHA for $1 million on June 27.

1977

A.J.Foyt wins Indianapolis 500 for record fourth time. Race also features first female driver, Janet Guthrie, who has to drop out after 27 laps (May 29).

Al Geiberger becomes first player to break 60 in an official PGA tour event, shooting a 59 in the second round of the Danny Thomas-Memphis Classic (June 10).

Seattle Slew, jockey Jean Cruguet up, wins Belmont Stakes to become 10th horse to win Triple Crown (June 11).

Reggie Jackson hits three home runs in Game 6 to clinch World Series as N.Y. Yankees beat L.A. Dodgers, 8-4 (Oct.18).

1982

North Carolina beats Georgetown, 63-62, at Superdome in New Orleans to win coach Dean Smith's first NCAA championship (March 29).

Federal District Court rules in favor of **Oakland Raiders** in antitrust suit against NFL, opening way to move to Los Angeles for '82 season (May 7).

NFL players strike over benefits and free agency two weeks into season (Sept. 20). Strike lasts 57 days and abbreviated season (9 games) resumes Nov. 21. Playoff field increased to 16 teams.

Olympics
Winter Games

Year	No.	Host city	Dates
1992	XVI	Albertville, France	Feb.8-23
1994	XVII	Lillehammer, Norway	Feb.12-27
1998	XVII	Nagano, Japan	TBA

Summer Games

Year	No.	Host city	Dates
1992	XXV	Barcelona, Spain	July 25-Aug.9
1996	XXVI	Atlanta, Georgia	July 20-Aug.4
2000	XXVII	TBA	

All-Star Games
Baseball

Year	Site	Date
1992	Jack Murphy Stadium, San Diego	July 14
1993	Camden Yards, Baltimore	TBA
1994	Three Rivers Stadium, Pittsburgh	TBA

NBA Basketball

Year	Site	Date
1992	Orlando Arena	Feb.9
1993	TBA	

NFL Pro Bowl

Year	Site	Date
1992	Aloha Stadium, Honolulu	Feb.2
1993	Aloha Stadium, Honolulu	Feb.7
1994	Aloha Stadium, Honolulu	Feb.6
1995	Aloha Stadium, Honolulu	Feb.5

NHL Hockey

Year	Site	Date
1992	The Spectrum, Philadelphia	Jan.18
1993	Montreal Forum	TBA
1994	TBA	

Auto Racing

The Daytona 500 stock car race is usually held on the third Sunday in February, while the Indianapolis 500 is usually held on the Sunday of Memorial Day weekend in May. Except for 1992, the following dates are tentative.

Year	Daytona 500	Indianapolis 500
1992	Feb.16	May 24
1993	Feb.21	May 30
1994	Feb.20	May 29
1995	Feb.19	May 28

NCAA Basketball
Men's Final Four

Year	Site	Dates
1992	HHH Metrodome, Minneapolis	April 4-6
1993	Superdome, New Orleans	April 3-5
1994	Charlotte (N.C.) Coliseum	April 2-4
1995	The Kingdome, Seattle	April 1-3
1996	Meadowlands (N.J.) Arena	Mar.30-Apr.1
1997	Hoosier Dome, Indianapolis	March 29-31

Women's Final Four

Year	Site	Dates
1992	L.A. Sports Arena	April 4-5
1993	The Omni, Atlanta	April 3-4
1994	Richmond (Va.) Coliseum	April 2-3
1995	Target Center, Minneapolis	April 1-2

NFL Football
Super Bowls

No.	Site	Date
XXVI	HHH Metrodome, Minneapolis	Jan.26,1992
XXVII	Rose Bowl, Pasadena	Jan.31,1993
XXVIII	Georgia Dome, Atlanta	Jan.30,1994
XXIX	Joe Robbie Stadium, Miami	Jan.29,1995
XXX	Sun Devil Stadium, Tempe	TBA

Golf
The Masters

Year	Site	Dates
1992	Augusta National, Ga.	April 9-12
1993	Augusta National, Ga.	April 8-11
1994	Augusta National, Ga.	April 7-10
1995	Augusta National, Ga.	April 6-9
1996	Augusta National, Ga.	April 11-14

U.S. Open

Year		Dates
1992	Pebble Beach (Calif) GL	Jun.18-21
1993	Baltusrol GC, Springfield, N.J	Jun.17-20
1995	Shinnecock Hills (N.Y.) GC	TBA
1996	Oakland Hills CC, Birmingham, Mich.	June 13-16

U.S.Women's Open

Year	Site	Dates
1992	Oakmont (Pa.) CC	July 23-26
1993	Crooked Stick GC, Carmel, Ind	July 22-25
1994	Indian Wood GC, Lake Orion, Mich.	July 21-24
1995	Broadmoor GC, Colorado Springs	July 13-16

U.S. Senior Open

Year	Site	Dates
1992	Saucon Valley CC, Bethlehem, Pa.	July 9-12
1993	Cherry Hills, CC, Engelwood, Colo.	July 8-11
1994	Pinehurst (N.C.) CC	Jun.30-Jul.3
1995	Congressional CC, Bethesda, Md	Jun.29-Jul.2

PGA Championship

Year	Site	Dates
1992	Bellerive CC, St.Louis	Aug.13-16
1993	Inverness Club, Toledo, Ohio	Aug.12-15
1994	Southern Hills CC, Tulsa, Okla.	Aug.11-14
1995	Riviera CC, Pacific Palisades, Cailf.	TBA

Horse Racing
The Triple Crown Races

The Kentucky Derby is always held at Churchill Downs in Louisville on the first Saturday in May, followed two weeks later by the Preakness Stakes at Pimlico Race Course in Baltimore and three weeks after that by the Belmont Stakes at Belmont Park in Elmont, NY.

Year	Ky Derby	Preakness	Belmont
1992	May 2	May 16	June 6
1993	May 1	May 15	June 5
1994	May 7	May 21	June 11
1995	May 6	May 20	June 10
1996	May 4	May 18	June 8

Tennis
U.S. Open

Usually held from the last Monday in August through the second Sunday in September, with Labor Day weekend the midway point in the tournament.

Year	Site	Dates
1992	US Tennis Center, NYC	Aug.31-Sept.13
1993	US Tennis Center, NYC	Aug.30-Sept.12
1994	US Tennis Center, NYC	Aug.29-Sept.11
1995	US Tennis Center, NYC	Aug.28-Sept.10

Yachting
America's Cup

All racing held off San Diego.

Year		Date
1992	Defender Selection Trials	Jan.14-May 1
	Challenger Selection Trials	Jan.25-Apr.29
	Final (Best-of-7)	starts May 9
	Races 1-4 scheduled for May 9-10-12-14	